EUROPEAN AUTHORS

1000-1900

THE AUTHORS SERIES

Edited by Stanley J. Kunitz and Howard Haycraft

AMERICAN AUTHORS: 1600-1900
BRITISH AUTHORS BEFORE 1800
BRITISH AUTHORS OF THE NINETEENTH CENTURY
THE JUNIOR BOOK OF AUTHORS
TWENTIETH CENTURY AUTHORS

Edited by Stanley J. Kunitz
TWENTIETH CENTURY AUTHORS: FIRST SUPPLEMENT

Edited by Muriel Fuller
MORE JUNIOR AUTHORS

Edited by Stanley J. Kunitz and Vineta Colby
EUROPEAN AUTHORS: 1000-1900

EUROPEAN AUTHORS
1000-1900

A Biographical Dictionary of European Literature

Edited by
STANLEY J. KUNITZ

and

VINETA COLBY

COMPLETE IN ONE VOLUME WITH
967 BIOGRAPHIES AND
309 PORTRAITS

NEW YORK
THE H. W. WILSON COMPANY
NINETEEN HUNDRED SIXTY-SEVEN

Preface

APPROXIMATELY half a century has passed since T. S. Eliot wrote, in "Tradition and the Individual Talent," in some respects the most influential of his essays, that "the historical sense involves a perception, not only of the pastness of the past, but of its presence; the historical sense compels a man to write not merely with his own generation in his bones, but with a feeling that the whole of the literature of Europe from Homer and within it the whole of the literature of his own country has a simultaneous existence and composes a simultaneous order."

In 1917 Eliot's point of view struck a generation as original and daring. Today, when Europe is only the next meal away by plane and instantaneously present, via communications satellite, on the television screen, the concept of a unified field of Western culture seems almost a commonplace. Our economics, our politics, and our wars confirm the extent of our interdependence. In our schools the dust has been swept out of the classrooms where foreign languages and literatures are studied. For the patron of the drugstore and the supermarket, the great foreign texts have been freshly, often brilliantly, translated and made accessible in cheap paperback editions. Many minor worthies are being translated for the first time; and scores of living European writers and artists are as well known in, say, Sioux City as they are at home. In 1917 this volume would have found neither publisher nor audience. Today the need for a compact but reasonably comprehensive biographical dictionary of European literature on the scale of the present work is so evident that the only wonder is that it has not been done before.

EUROPEAN AUTHORS covers almost a thousand years of the literary tradition of continental Europe, omitting ancient writers, on whom there is no dearth of information, and writers born or flourishing in this century (for whom see *Twentieth Century Authors*). The chronological rule of thumb for eligibility has been simple enough: born after the year 1000 A.D.; died before 1925. In the span of the work there is room at the entrance gate for Schoolmen and mystics, humanists and troubadours, and the precursors and inventors of the national tongues: writers as various as Michael Psellus (1018-1078), Byzantine historian; Ibn Gabirol (c. 1021-c. 1058), Hebrew poet of Spain; Peter Abelard (1079-1142), French theologian; Averroës (1126-1198), Spanish Moslem philosopher; Bertran de Born (1140?-1215), Provençal troubadour; Wolfram von Eschenbach (1165?-1220?), German poet; Snorri Sturluson (1179-1241), Icelandic poet and saga writer; Albrecht von Johannsdorf (fl. 1185-1209), Bavarian minnesinger; Albertus Magnus (1206?-1280), German humanist; Jacob van Maerlant (c. 1225-1291?), Dutch poet; Ramón Lull (1233-1315), Catalan poet; Guido Cavalcanti (c. 1255-1300), Dante's poet friend; and Saint Bridget (c. 1303-1373), Swedish visionary. At the terminus of the span we find, among others, Christian Morgenstern (1871-1914), German poet; Richard Dehmel (1863-1920), German poet; Solomon Rappoport (Sh. An-Ski, 1863-1920), Russian-Yiddish writer; Paul Jean Toulet (1867-1920), French poet and novelist; Nikolai Gumilëv (1886-1921), Russian poet; and Arne Garborg (1851-1924), Norwegian novelist and poet.

Nearly a thousand writers of thirty-one different literatures are included, representing the following main categories (national, regional, or linguistic): French, German, Italian, Spanish, Portuguese, Russian, East European (including Greek, Czech, Hungarian, Polish, Rumanian, Bulgarian, Slovene, etc.), Dutch, Scandinavian (including Norwegian, Swedish, Danish, and Icelandic), Hebrew, and Yiddish. Only a fraction of the writers have been translated into English; some are definitely secondary figures, not widely known even in their native tongues; but each occupies a place, however great or small, in the history of a literature and in the forging of the European tradition. As Eliot remarked, "the main current . . . does not at all flow invariably through the most distinguished reputations."

The proportionate length of the sketch usually offers a rough indication of the importance attached to the subject, but not infrequently the original assignment has been affected by peripheral considerations, such as the amount of available data, the familiarity of the material, the number of works published and translated, the variety of the life, and even the enthusiasm of the contributor. The sketches have been written and edited with the general reader, rather than the research student, in mind. This is particularly true of the bibliographical entries, including the listing and evaluation of translations, and the suggestion of biographical and critical sources for further study. Where name-forms in English are debatable, the editors have tended to follow popular usage. The birth- and death-dates of writers who flourished before the adoption of the Gregorian Calendar have been corrected to New Style.

EUROPEAN AUTHORS has been in progress for more than ten years. During that period the entries have been checked several times and brought up to date at every proofreading; but it would be foolhardy to suppose, in a work of this magnitude and of such polyglot background, that all the errors of omission and commission have been caught.

We are happy to acknowledge our indebtedness to Mr. Wilson G. Duprey for his painstaking work in tracing and establishing the portraits and to the staff and resources of the New York Public Library. In the long preparation of this work we have leaned heavily on the knowledge, patience, competence, and advice of the distinguished contributors listed below. Without the help and encouragement of these and numerous other scholars and literary specialists the task would have proved forbidding indeed.

S.J.K.
V.C.

June 1966

CONTRIBUTORS

A. A.	Artine Artinian, Professor Emeritus of French, Bard College
A. C. K.	Abraham C. Keller, Associate Professor of Romance Languages, University of Washington
A. J.	Assar Janzén, Professor of Scandinavian Languages, University of California, Berkeley
A. M.	Allen McCormick, Professor of German, Dartmouth College
A. M. H.	Anton M. Huffert, Associate Professor of German, Adelphi University
B. P. P.	Beatrice P. Patt, Associate Professor of Romance Languages, Queens College of the City University of New York
C. K. P.	Clarence K. Pott, Professor of German, University of Michigan
D. G. D.	Donald G. Daviau, Assistant Professor of German, University of California, Riverside

D. J. D.	Daniel J. Donno, Associate Professor of English, Queens College of the City University of New York
E. DA C.	Ernesto G. Da Cal, Professor of Romance Languages, Queens College of the City University of New York
E. DE P.	Elaine De Paul, New York City
E. F.	Eugenio Florit, Professor of Spanish, Barnard College
E. G.	Evelyn Geller, New York City
E. J. S.	Ernst J. Schlochauer, Assistant Professor of English, Queens College of the City University of New York
E. K. G.	Eugene K. Grotegut, Professor of German, University of Kansas
E. L. R.	Elias L. Rivers, Professor of Spanish, Johns Hopkins University
E. S. D.	Elizabeth Story Donno, Assistant Professor of English, Columbia University
E. V.	Elie Vidal, Assistant Professor of French, San Francisco State College
F. G.	Francis Golffing, Professor of English, Bennington College
F. G. R.	Frank G. Ryder, Professor of German, Indiana University
F. J. C.	Francis J. Carmody, Professor of French, University of California, Berkeley
F. R.	Frederick Ritter, Instructor in German, Illinois Institute of Technology
F. S. L.	Frank S. Lambasa, Associate Professor of German, Hofstra University
G. E.	Georgia Economou, New York City
G. M. M.	Gerald M. Moser, Professor of Romance Languages, Pennsylvania State University
H. B.	Hugo Bekker, Associate Professor of German, Ohio State University
H. C.	Herman Carmel, Associate Professor, Department of Germanic and Slavic Languages, Utica College
H. H.	Hanna Hafkesbrink, Professor of German, Connecticut College
H. K.	Henry Kučera, Associate Professor of Russian and Linguistics, Brown University
H. L.	Herbert Lindenberger, Professor of Comparative Literature and English, University of California, Riverside
H. W. D.	Horace W. Dewey, Professor of Slavic Languages and Literatures and Russian History, University of Michigan
H. Z.	Harry Zohn, Associate Professor of German, Brandeis University
I. R. T.	Irwin R. Titunik, Department of Slavic Languages and Literatures, University of California, Berkeley
J. K.	Janice Koch, New York City
J. M.	John Mersereau, Jr., Professor of Russian, University of Michigan
J. P. B.	Jean-Pierre Barricelli, Associate Professor of Foreign Languages, University of California, Riverside
L. B.	Loftur Bjarnason, Professor of Literature, U.S. Naval Postgraduate School, Monterey, California
L. P. G.	Lloyd P. Gartner, Assistant Professor of Jewish History, Jewish Theological Seminary of America
L. R. & H. H.	Leon Rutman and Harvey A. Harvey, New York City

KEY TO PRONUNCIATION

ā	āle	N	Not pronounced, but indicates the nasal tone of the preceding vowel, as in the French *bon* (bôN).	ū	cūbe
â	châotic			û	ûrn; French eu, as in *jeu* (zhû); German ö, oe, as in *schön* (shûn), *Goethe* (gû' tĕ)
â	câre				
ă	ădd				
ä	ärm				
à	àsk				
				ŭ	tŭb
ch	child			ü	Pronounced approximately as ē, with rounded lips: French u, as in *menu* (mē nü'); German ü, as in *grün*.
		ō	ōld		
ē	ēve	ô	ôrb		
ê	êvent	ŏ	ŏdd		
ĕ	ĕnd	ô	ôbey		
ẽ	makẽr	oi	oil		
		o͞o	o͞oze		
		o͝o	fo͝ot		
		ou	out	y	yet
ī	īce				
ĭ	ĭll				
ĸ	German ch as in *ich* (ĭĸ).	th	thin	zh	azure
		th	then	' =	main accent

x

European Authors

1000-1900

ABAILARD, PIERRE. See ABELARD,
PETER

*ABARBANEL, JUDAH (known also as
**LEO HEBRAEUS, LEO JUDAEUS,
LEONE EBREO, JUDAH LEON ME-
DIGO**) (c. 1460-c. 1535), Jewish philosopher and poet, was born in Lisbon, Portugal. His father, Isaac, was the leader of
the Portuguese and Spanish Jewish communities and an eminent scholar and philosopher. The family left Spain during the
expulsion of the Jews in 1492, although
one of Judah's sons was forcibly detained.

Settling in Naples and later Venice, Abarbanel gained prominence as a physician, but
his primary interests were in science, philosophy, and poetry. In 1503 he wrote an
elegiac poem in Hebrew lamenting the forced
conversion of his son and praying him "to
remain ever loyal to Judaism, to cultivate the
Hebrew language and literature, and to be
mindful of the sorrow of his father and the
grief of his mother."

It was during his sojourn in Italy that
Abarbanel came into contact with the thinkers of the Italian Renaissance, and, in particular, with the brilliant Pico della Mirandola. An astronomical work, *De Coeli Har-
monia* (Harmony of Heaven), written at the
request of Pico, is no longer extant.

The influence of Italian culture led Abarbanel to write his great work, the *Dialoghi
d'Amore* (Dialogues of Love; written 1502).
Cast in the form of three romantic dialogues
between Philo (the lover) and Sophia (wisdom), it is actually an exposition of Abarbanel's philosophic thought. The foundation
of the universe, for Abarbanel, is the principle of love, and he discusses this idea in
relation to all forms of existence, making use
of his scientific and classical learning. Per-
meating the entire world, he says, is the
Amor Dei, the love of God, and man's highest aim should be the union of lover with the
beloved, of himself with God. He proposes
this as an intellectual union of the human
and the divine intellect, and his emphasis is
on intellectual, rather than physical, love and
beauty.

* ä bär bä něl'

Abarbanel's book proved exceedingly popular in Italy. Its polished style and Neoplatonic, pantheistic thought were well received by educated Christian Europe. Besides
numerous Italian editions, the work was
translated into French, Spanish, Latin,
Hebrew, and English. However, despite
Abarbanel's repeated injection of Jewish
themes, it was never popular among Jews.
On the other hand, its fundamental idea,
the intellectual love of God, may very well
have been influential in the formation of
Spinoza's philosophical views on the same
subject.

The *Dialoghi d'Amore* was translated into English in 1937 by F. Friedeberg-Seeley and J. H.
Barnes as *The Philosophy of Love*, with an introduction by Cecil Roth. An Italian edition, edited by
C. Gebhardt, appeared in the *Bibliotheca Spinoziana*
in 1929.

ABOUT: Graetz, H. History of the Jews; Shorr,
P. "The Philosophy of Love," *in* Reflex, September
1927; Waxman, M. A History of Jewish Literature. [In German—see studies by C. Gebhardt,
H. Pflaum, B. Zimmels.]

M.R.

***ABELARD, PETER (PIERRE ABAI-
LARD, ABÉLARD, or ABAELARD)**
(1079-April 21, 1142), French scholastic
philosopher and theologian, considered to be
the first modern intellectual and teacher, was
born in Le Pallet, near Nantes in Brittany.
His father, Berenger, was a scholarly noble
and lord of the town. He helped the early
education of Peter who, as the eldest son of
the family, was to have a military career.
However, seized with a passion for study,
he left his inheritance to his younger brothers
and became a cleric, tonsured but not ordained. He soon went to the Cathedral
School of Notre Dame in Paris, whose master was William de Champeaux. The young
scholar, a brilliant polemicist, did not hesitate
to take issue with his master. William made
him leave but Abelard had become popular;
his students followed him to Melun and Cor-
beil, towns near Paris, where he continued to
teach successfully. He was then twenty-two.
Illness forced him to retire to Brittany, but
he returned to the capital, again to face his

* ăb' ĕ lärd

1

former master who, shaken, had to change his doctrine. But Abelard's criticisms went too far and again he had to withdraw. William's students had abandoned him, however, and the master ceased to teach. The young man came back to settle on the Montagne St. Geneviève, thus becoming the creator of the Latin Quarter in Paris. Interested in theology, he attended in Laon the famed lectures of the old master Anselm, but his dissatisfaction led him to give his own lectures, which again attracted crowds, largely because of his daring to apply logic to the sacrosanct subject of theology. He went back to Paris, followed by enthusiastic students from all parts of Europe. At the age of thirty-nine he knew fame.

At that time, 1118, Fulbert, Canon of Notre Dame Cathedral, had a very pretty niece, Heloise, already known for her wisdom and great culture. Flattered by Abelard's approaches, Fulbert made Heloise study with the master, who received room and board in the Canon's house. The relationship that swiftly developed between master and pupil has become one of the central episodes in the Western legend of tragic love. When the lovers were caught, Abelard had to leave the Canon's house. They met elsewhere, not even trying to hide, believing themselves above scandal. During an absence of Fulbert, Abelard sent Heloise to his sister in Brittany, where she gave birth to a male child, Astrolabius, who is said to have survived his father. Abelard could have married, but his brilliant career would have been compromised: scholars at the time were, for the most part, opposed to marriage. Heloise herself tried to discourage him from marrying her. An intellectual, she argued, should not mix philosophy and domesticity, meditation and the care of noisy infants. On Abelard's insistence a secret ceremony took place, in the presence of Fulbert. Abelard went back to his studies, but the Canon, still angry, wanted the union to be public knowledge. Abelard then persuaded Heloise to retire to a convent until all gossip had died down. Fulbert, furious and suspecting that the scholar would abandon his bride and force her to take the vows, sent hoodlums one night (1119) into Abelard's house to emasculate him. The unfortunate teacher fled to the Abbey of St. Denis to hide his shame and despair. Heloise became a nun. Once cured of his wounds, Abelard went back to work among ignorant and rough monks who resented the constant visits of his pupils. He wrote an introduction to theology, *Tractatus*

de Unitate et Trinitate Divinia. A synod at Soissons in 1121 condemned his rationalistic interpretation of the dogma of the Trinity. Abelard barely escaped lynching. His books were burned, and he was ordered to retire to a convent for the rest of his days. The Bishop of Troyes in Champagne gave him a plot of ground on which to build a small chapel. When his disciples discovered his retreat, a village of tents and huts arose on the place. The chapel was enlarged and dedicated to the Paraclete. After suffering more persecution, Abelard was elected abbot of a monastery in Brittany, whose monks were depraved and primitive to the extent that they wanted to poison him when he tried to educate them. Meanwhile, with his help, Heloise had become the head of a religious order at the Paraclete, and their immortal correspondence was going on. In 1136 he was again in the Latin Quarter in Paris, as popular as ever. About this time he wrote his *Historia Calamitatum*, an autobiographical work. He opposed Bernard de Clairvaux (St. Bernard), who preached the principle of unquestioning faith, while Abelard was bold in his rational method applied to theology. The two men faced each other in Sens (1141). Bernard had several bishops on his side and Abelard, accused of heresy, was excommunicated. In vain he appealed to the Pope and once more he fled, this time to the Abbey of Cluny. He was now a broken man. Finally, reconciled with Bernard and pardoned by Rome, he went to the convent of St. Marcel in Châlon-sur-Saône, where he died soon after.

As a logician, Abelard introduced a method for philosophers, *Logica Ingredientibus,* and in *Sic et Non* he showed that the fathers of the Church had never agreed on any question. Language must be not a tool obscuring reality, but an instrument to express it. As a moralist, in his ethical treatise *Scito Te Ipsum* (Know Thyself) he attacks the theory of the powerlessness of the sinner and claims that man has the power to accept or reject right conduct, that contrition eradicates sin. In his conviction that faith and reason should go hand in hand, Abelard can be considered an early humanist. He professes optimism in philosophy and, as a theologian, thinks that the love of God, excluding fear or self-interest, is the only source of religious morality. He also wrote *De Intellectibus*, a treatise on ideas, the *Dialectica*, a commentary on Aristotle, Porphyry, and Boethius, and a treatise, *De Generibus et Speciebus.*

Latin, although used exclusively for intellectual exchanges, was already a dead language in the twelfth century, and there was no great style in that period. As a stylist, however, Abelard shows at rare intervals some emotion and some cleverly contrived antitheses. If his style is labored, it remains clear and accurate.

The letters Abelard wrote to Heloise are the best known part of his writings. While Heloise's letters began with ardor and pathos, gradually subsiding into resignation, his were at first didactic, then pious and mystical.

Abelard also wrote poetry—poems about Heloise in the common language and an elegiac epistle to his son. His love songs, of which he wrote the words and composed the music, were extremely popular.

The first translation of the letters into English was made by the Reverend J. Berrington in 1787. With added poems by Pope and other poets, the letters reappeared in 1824. *Historia Calamitatum: The Story of My Misfortunes: an Autobiography by Peter Abelard* was translated into English by H. A. Bellows, St. Paul, Minn., 1922. C. K. Scott-Moncrieff translated *The Letters of Abelard and Heloise*, 1925. R. P. McKeon edited *Abailard, Pierre, Selections from Medieval Philosophers*, 1929. J. Ramsay McCallum translated *Abailard's Ethics* with an introduction, in 1935. J. T. Muckle's translation with an introduction of *Abelard's Letter of Consolation to a Friend* appeared in *Mediaeval Studies*, Toronto, 1950. Also, in *Mediaeval Studies*, he edited in 1953 *The Personal Letters of Abelard and Heloise*. In 1954 appeared his book *The Story of Abelard's Adversities*, a translation with notes of the *Historia Calamitatum*.

ABOUT: Compayré, G. Abelard and the Origin and Early History of Universities; Gilson, E. H. Héloïse and Abélard; Moore, G. E. Héloïse and Abélard (a novel); Poole, R. L. Illustrations of the History of Medieval Thought; Sikes, J. G. Peter Abailard; Waddell, H. J. Peter Abailard (a novel). [In French—see biography by C. de Rémusat and J. Le Goff's Les Intellectuals au Moyen Age.]

P. LA.

ABRAHAM, BEN MEIR ABEN EZRA.
See IBN EZRA, ABRAHAM

ABRAMOWITZ, SHALOM JACOB (known as *MENDELE MOCHER SEFORIM) (1836-1917), the father of modern Yiddish literature and an important Hebrew writer, was born in Kopyl, Lithuania. His father, Hayyim Moshe, was a rabbi and a leading citizen in the Jewish community. Mendele received not only the usual Talmudic education, but also a thorough training in Hebrew grammar and the Bible. Later, he studied at the Yeshivas in Slutzk and Vilna,

* mĕn' dŭ lŭ môĸ' ŭr sfô' rĭm

"MENDELE"

becoming known as a brilliant student. After his father's death and his mother's remarriage, he left his native town with a wandering band of beggars, traveling through White Russia, Volhynia, the Ukraine, and Podolia. These travels provided him with an excellent introduction to the life of the East European Jews. At the age of eighteen he settled in Kamenetz-Podolsk in Podolia. There, under the guidance of Abraham Gottlober, an eminent Hebrew writer, he studied secular subjects and obtained, in 1856, a position as teacher in the government-sponsored Jewish school. Here, also, he was married and divorced. In 1858 he moved to Berdichev, remarried, and entered upon the first phase of his literary career.

At this time Mendele wrote in Hebrew and was considered a promising younger member of the Russian Haskalah, the movement dedicated to the enlightenment of the Jews and the improvement of their economic and social position. In essays and books, such as *Mishpat Shalom* (Peaceful Judgment, 1860) and *En Mishpat* (Critical Eye, 1866), he preached his ideas on the reformation of East European Jewish life. To this period belongs also the beginning of a three volume adaptation of H. O. Lenz's *Naturgeschichte*, published as *Toldot ha-Teva* (Natural History, 1872).

Discouraged with the practical effects of his literary efforts in Hebrew, the language of the educated, he decided to turn to Yiddish, the language of the masses. His choice of the pseudonym Mendele Mocher Seforim,

3

or Mendele the Bookseller, illustrates his desire to influence the people, among whom the bookseller was a popular and respected figure. Not only did he change his name, but he also changed his style from that of the polemicist to that of the observant artist, presenting life and its defects without directly preaching about them.

The Yiddish works which followed this metamorphosis were to be the cornerstone of modern Yiddish literature. His first novel, *Der Kleine Menshele* (The Little Man, 1864), is a biting attack on the mismanagement of Jewish community leaders. The drama *Die Takse, oder die Bande Shtot Baale Tovot* (The Tax, or the Gang of Municipal Benefactors, 1868), deals with a similar theme. In *Fishke der Krumer* (Fishke the Lame, 1869) Mendele portrays, satirically yet sympathetically, the unfortunate life of the beggars. An allegorical work, *Die Kliatshe* (The Mare, 1873), uses the figure of an oppressed horse to symbolize the persecuted people of Israel. With bitter humor Mendele satirized the impractical naïveté and gullibility of some Jews in *Masa'ot Binyamin ha-Shelishi* (Travels of Benjamin the Third, 1878). This work, with its Quixotic hero, has led some to call Mendele the Jewish Cervantes. His *Vinshfingerl* (The Wishing Ring, 1879) deals with poverty in an East European Jewish town, but stresses the good which can come from suffering.

Moving to Odessa in 1881, where he became principal of the Hebrew school of the Jewish community, Mendele returned to writing in Hebrew. His short stories of this period reflect the decisive events of contemporary Russia, and pogroms and the new Jewish nationalism. Another major activity was the adaptation and translation of his Yiddish novels into Hebrew, in which process the works were transformed artistically into major factors in the revival of Hebrew literature. An autobiographical novel, *Ba-Yamin ha-Hem* (In Those Days), belongs to this last period.

Mendele's final years were marked by the acclaim of the whole Jewish world. His seventy-fifth birthday was the occasion for much celebration, and when he died in 1917, his passing was mourned by both the masses and the intellectuals.

Mendele's works illustrate his basic attitude toward the Jewish people. He had little faith in a national revival along the lines of Zionism, but felt that the real task was the patient, gradual eradication of the evils of ghetto life, and, ultimately, the political, economic, and cultural emancipation of the Jews within Western civilization. His fiction, strong in trenchant observation and deeply felt description, was satiric in form, but didactic in purpose. The typical Jewish small town of Eastern Europe found in Mendele its greatest critic. Yet, full of compassion, he could write, "The life of the Jews, although it seems externally ugly and of dark hue is inwardly beautiful; a mighty spirit animates it, the divine breath which flutters through it from time to time purifies it from all uncleanliness" (*Ba-Yamim ha-Hem*). Rich in local color, powerful in descriptions of both Jewish life and nature, permeated with a chastising love for the people, his work, more than that of any other, helped shape the course of Yiddish literature. Likewise, his enrichment of the modern Hebrew language and literature has been of primary importance.

Fishke the Lame was translated by A. S. Rappaport in 1929, and by Gerald Stillman in 1960. Moshe Spiegel translated *The Travels and Adventures of Benjamin the Third* in 1949 and *The Nag (Die Kliatshe)* in 1955. *Der Kleine Menshele* was translated by Gerald Stillman in 1956 as *The Parasite*. A number of other stories have been translated in anthologies such as Leo Schwarz's *The Jewish Caravan* and I. Howe & E. Greenberg, *A Treasury of Yiddish Stories*. Yiddish editions include *Ale Verk* (Cracow, 1911-12 and Warsaw, 1927); a Hebrew edition of his works is *Kol Kitve* (Tel Aviv, 1947).

ABOUT: Howe, I. & Greenberg, E. A Treasury of Yiddish Stories; Roback, A. The Story of Yiddish Literature; Slouschz, N. The Renascence of Hebrew Literature; Waxman, M. A History of Jewish Literature; Wiener, L. The History of Yiddish Literature in the Nineteenth Century; Commentary November 1948; Poet-Lore Summer 1922. [In Hebrew—see studies by Y. Frenkel, J. Klausner, A. Orinowsky. In Yiddish—see studies by U. Finkel, S. Gorelik, S. Niger, I. Serebryanny.]

M.R.

ABRAVANEL, JUDAH. See ABARBANEL, JUDAH

"ADAM." See LEBENSOHN, ABRAHAM DOB

*ADAM, PAUL AUGUSTE MARIE (December 7, 1862-January 2, 1920), French novelist, was born in Paris. A son and grandson of soldiers who had fought in Napoleon's armies, young Adam was imbued from childhood with the glories of the French empire. He intended to become a soldier but was deflected from that course into literature.

* à dän'

Interestingly enough, Adam was able to transfer to his literary career something of the vigor and energy he had hoped to bring to military life. Only once, in 1889 when he sought election as a Bonapartist on the side of the ill-fated General Boulanger, did Adam take any active part in politics. But in his massive "novels of action," as they have been termed, he rendered something at least of what Nitze and Dargan, in their *History of French Literature,* call "the intoxication of Napoleonic glory, the cult of energy and of appetites."

Adam's first novel, *Chair Molle* (1885), shows the influence of the naturalism that flourished with his contemporary Emile Zola. He soon came under the influence of the equally flourishing Symbolist movement, and, in collaboration with other writers, he founded several magazines—*Carcan* (with Jean Ajalbert), *Symboliste* (with Gustave Kahn and Jean Moréas), *Vogue* (with Kahn), and a second series of the *Revue Indépendante.* With Moréas he wrote two novels — *Le Thé chez Miranda* and *Les Demoiselles Joubert* (both published in 1886).

Ultimately Adam developed his own medium of expression — a socio-historical novel, sometimes called the *roman collectif,* which attempts to capture the whole spirit or psychology of an era. His novels are often turgid and overwritten, but they show a remarkable grasp of mass movements and mob psychology. M. E. Coindreau writes: "By his cosmic vision, by his ability to analyze the soul of collectivities, to animate crowds and groups of people, Paul Adam appears as a forerunner of what Jules Romains named unamism." A prolific writer, he produced whole series of novels. The best known of these is his tetralogy *Le Temps et la Vie,* which portrays the Napoleonic era of 1798 to 1830 and draws heavily upon Adam's own family history: *La Force* (1899), *L'Enfant d'Austerlitz* (1902), *La Ruse* (1903), *Au Soleil de Juillet* (1903). Another group, *L'Époque,* consists of twenty novels. Among all his works those that are probably of greatest interest to modern readers are *La Mystère des Foules* (1894), a political novel which predicted, with appalling correctness, a war between France and Germany; *Les Cœurs Nouveaux* (1896), a Utopian novel; and *Le Trust* (1910), a study of modern economic life that is set in America. He visited this country in 1904 and wrote a nonfiction account of it—*Vues d'Amérique* (1906). Among his other works of nonfiction (eighteen volumes in all) are *La Morale d'Education* (1908) and *La Morale de la France* (1908).

Adam was never elected to the French Academy, although many of his contemporaries considered him deserving of the honor. His personality, like his work, was vigorous and passionate. "Endowed with more genius than talent," W. H. Scheifley wrote in the *Sewanee Review,* "he was too often unable to hold his pen in check. His style was capricious and incoherent, but it conveyed the impression of palpitant life." Ugo Ojetti described him as "compact and squat, a helmet of shining, thick chestnut hair combed down over his forehead, the neckless head set on the square shoulders, the wide and round throat issuing from a black satin waistcoat . . . like a soldier in gala cuirass, legs and feet all attention. . . ."

Adam died in Paris at the age of fifty-seven. His wife, Marthe Meyer, became a Dominican nun after his death.

ABOUT: Columbia Dictionary of Modern European Literature; Gourmont, R. de, The Book of Masks; Nitze, W. A. & Dargan, E. P. A History of French Literature; Ojetti, U. As They Seemed to Me; Sewanee Review XXIX (1921). [In French —see studies by M. Batilliat and C. Mauclair.]

AENEAS SILVIUS. See PICCOLO-MINI, ENEA SILVIO

AGRIPPA D'AUBIGNÉ. See AUBIGNÉ, THÉODORE AGRIPPA D'

AGRICOLA, RUDOLF (August 23, 1443-October 23, 1485) is the Latinized name under which the Dutchman Roelof Huysman became known as an educator of European fame. He was an early (Biblical) humanist who had no difficulty whatsoever in combining his humanistic interests with a genuine concern for man's religious dimension. Not much is known of his early life. He was born in Baflo, The Netherlands, and received his first education at the St. Maartenschool in the nearby city of Groningen. This training was followed by studies at several universities. On May 1, 1456, he enrolled at the University of Erfurt, Germany, where he studied until 1462, the year in which he went to Cologne. He returned to his homeland when the first university in the Lowlands was opened in Louvain. This school granted him his master's degree *magna cum laude* in 1465. Four years later, following the example of so many of his contem-

5

poraries, he traveled to Italy. After a brief stay in his homeland in 1470 he returned to Pavia. Four years later Agricola was in Emmerik, Germany, where he encountered and befriended Alexander Hegius, the future rector of the Deventer school founded by the Brethren of the Common Life and directed in its mode of life by the views of the Devotio Moderna. Italy continued to fascinate Agricola; in 1475 he went to Ferrara where he followed the lectures of the Greek scholars Theodorus Gaza and Battista Guarino. While in Ferrara, he also studied music and was organist at the court. Returning to his homeland in 1479 he settled in Groningen where he joined the circle of educated men, including the famous humanist Wessel Gansfort, for whom the Aduard convent was the gathering place. After representing his city at the court of Maximilian of Burgundy, Agricola accepted the invitation of his friend Johann von Dalberg, bishop of Worms, to lecture at the University of Heidelberg (1482). Revealing his affiliation with the ideas of the Devotio Moderna, Agricola attached importance to the study of the Bible in the original form and advocated a return to the sources. With that in mind he began to study Hebrew and made plans for a new translation of the Old Testament. Interrupting his professorial activities in 1485, he made his last visit to Italy (Rome) and, following his return to Heidelberg, died at the age of forty-two.

More than through his writings—they are few in number—Agricola exerted great influence through his personality and his lectures. He zealously promoted the cause of good education as he conceived of it in the humanistic manner, and propagated the study of classical literature, thus contributing considerably to the purification of Latin, which had become polluted in course of time with medieval barbarisms. As a result of his attempt to serve his ideal of true learning and sound Christianity he became the opponent of scholastic, nominalistic philosophy as it was practiced in his day.

Agricola's main significance was as a philologist. It stands to reason that he could not summon popular appeal. But his learned contemporaries admired his *De Inventione Dialectica* in which he discussed the rhetorical method of the philosophers of antiquity, thus promoting the study of the classics. Alardus of Amsterdam published his work in two volumes, *De Inventione* and *Lucubrationes* (Cologne, 1539).

ABOUT: English Historical Review, XXI (1906). [In German—see studies by F. von Bezold, G. Ihm, W. Stammler, H. E. J. M. Van der Velden.]

H. B.

"AHLGREN, ERNST." See BENEDICTSSON, VICTORIA MARIA

*AIMERIC DE PEGUILHAN (c. 1175-1230), Provençal troubadour, was born in Toulouse of a family that had come originally from the village of Péguilhan, near Saint-Gaudens. His father was a cloth merchant. The scanty and unreliable details of his biography are contained in his brief Provençal *Vida* and in passing allusions to historical personages and events in his poems. As the story has it, Aimeric fell in love with a married woman in his native city and wrote many poems for her. Her husband discovered the affair; the two men quarreled, and in the course of a fight Aimeric wounded the husband and was then exiled from Toulouse.

Taking up the wandering life of a court poet, he went to Spain where he lived in Catalonia under the patronage of King Alfonso of Castile and Peter II of Aragon. Both these patrons are honored in his poems. The main bulk of his writing in Spain was love poetry, *cansos,* all addressed to ladies of the court. After several years in Spain, Aimeric moved on to Italy where he settled at the court of Montferrat. By 1212 he was at the court of Este and in 1220 he was living at the court of Malaspina. The poetry which Aimeric wrote in Italy includes not only conventional love songs, but also tributes to patrons and poems celebrating historical events — *tensons* and *partimens* (poetic debates), *sirventes* (occasional verse), and *planhs* (funeral songs).

Aimeric is reported to have accumulated a considerable fortune during his lifetime and to have died a wealthy man, but the circumstances and details of the last years of his life are not known. One of the last of the great Provençal poets, he stands close to Bernart de Ventadour in reputation. His work was graceful, tender, noble in thought. It was also lacking in brilliance and sometimes pedestrian in expression. "For the most part," F. M. Chambers writes, "he avoids the wilful obscurity that mars the work of some of the best troubadours; his poems are simple and clear, his expression direct, his images apt and unstrained."

* ĕ mē rēk′ dĕ pā gē län′

Aimeric's poems are available in an edition by W. P. Shepherd and F. M. Chambers (1950) which includes both the Provençal texts and English prose translations. The volume contains a biographical and critical introduction.

*AKSAKOV, SERGEI TIMOFEYE-VITCH (October 1, 1791-May 12, 1859),
Russian novelist, was born at Ufa. He was a scion of the ancient nobility. His early education was supervised by his mother, a woman of great culture by contemporary standards. Though his devotion to his studies was somewhat diluted by his eager pursuit of hobbies—hunting, fishing, butterfly collecting, and later the theatre—he was ready to enter the newly founded University of Kazan in 1805. He remained there until 1808.

His earliest writings (chiefly magazine articles) reveal the influence of Shishkov (1753-1841), a forerunner of the Slavophiles; the direct link between Shishkov and the later group is found in the works of Aksakov, according to Mirsky. Strongly influenced by French classicism, he settled in Moscow in 1812 and became active in theatre circles translating the plays of Molière and the work of Boileau.

After his marriage to Olga Semyonova Zaplatina, he left Moscow to live on his father's estate (Znamenskoye) where he remained until 1826. In that year he went back to Moscow to enter service in the Censorship Commission and other branches of the civil service where he remained until 1839.

On his father's death (1837) he came into a large fortune which enabled him to retire from the service and devote himself entirely to literature. Aksakov's literary life had begun early. While he was still in the university he and some young colleagues (Paneyev for one) published the *Journal of Our Studies*, a magazine to which he contributed his earliest writing. His style continued to develop along lines dictated by his devotion to his French models and the influence of Shishkov until, in the 1830's, he met Gogol and largely through his encouragement broke with the formal classicism of his youth.

His first attempt in the realistic style is "Buran" (Blizzard), a short story (1834) that enjoyed a considerable success. In 1847 there appeared his "Notes of an Angler," and in 1840 he began working on his most famous work, *A Family Chronicle,* which did not appear until 1856 although extracts were

* ŭ ksȧ′ kóf

AKSAKOV

published separately from time to time during the intervening years. *A Family Chronicle* is the story of Aksakov's parents and grandparents, and the entire period of the story takes place before the author's birth. Aksakov's grandfather was a pioneering colonist of the Bashkirian steppe in the time of Catherine the Great; and in the remote, sparsely populated area, he looms in the story like a patriarchal titan of the early American West. Because of the dispassionate objectivity of Aksakov's prose, *A Family Chronicle* was variously interpreted according to the point of view of the reader. The liberals saw in it an indictment of the despotic gentry while the conservatives found in it a defense of the *status quo.*

The Years of Childhood of Bagrov-Grandson, a sequel to *A Family Chronicle,* appeared in 1858. It is an uneventful record of Aksakov's own childhood experiences and education most notable for its descriptions of nature. Similarly of interest to lovers of nature and wild life are the sketches *Notes of a Hunter in the Province of Orenburg* (1852). Turgenev was particularly drawn to this work: "Everyone who loves nature in all its variety . . . everyone who is touched by the manifestations of universal life wherein man himself stands as a living link, superior to the others but closely connected with them, will not be able to forget Aksakov's work."

Other autobiographical writings include *Recollections,* which carries forward *Years of Childhood* to age sixteen but with real

7

names used, and *Literary and Theatrical Reminiscences,* dealing with the period 1810-30. Aksakov also did an admirable sketch of his early hero Shishkov and a sensitive memoir of Gogol. Aksakov, who felt he owed Gogol so much and who was that writer's long-time friend and admiring supporter, was bitterly disappointed at Gogol's *Selected Passages from a Correspondence with Friends* and wrote an indignant letter to Gogol denouncing the work. In his later memoir Aksakov was moved to delve more deeply into the psychology and motivation of Gogol than he had found necessary in any previous writing. He also left an unfinished novel, "Natasha."

In robust health during his early life, Aksakov was stricken with an eye ailment about 1845, and the effects of this illness caused him great suffering in his declining years. His two sons, Constantine (1817-61) and Ivan (1823-86), were both active in the literary world of Russia, the latter being a leading figure among the younger Slavophiles as a poet and political writer.

Aksakov stands out among his famous contemporaries, particularly Turgenev and Goncharov, as peculiarly devoted to objectivity in an age of the problem novel. It is conceded by most critics that his greatness lies in his objectivity and that he blossomed out only when he had freed himself of the classic models of form and the Slavophile influence of Shishkov.

A Family Chronicle was translated into English by J. D. Duff in 1917 as *A Russian Gentleman* and has gone through several editions. Another translation, *Chronicles of a Russian Family,* was made by M. C. Beverley (1924) and reprinted in a paperback edition in 1961. The sequels *Years of Childhood* and *A Russian Schoolboy,* in J. D. Duff's translation, were published in 1916 and 1917 respectively.

ABOUT: Matlaw, R. E. *Introduction to* A Family Chronicle (Dutton Paperback, 1961); Mirsky, D. History of Russian Literature; Times (London) Literary Supplement, September 18, October 9, 1959.

L. R. & H. H.

ALAIN. See ALANUS DE INSULIS

*ALAMANNI, LUIGI (October 28, 1495-April 18, 1556), Italian poet, was born in Florence of a noble family long associated with the Medicis. A friend of Machiavelli, he became deeply involved in the political intrigue of his time. In 1522 he took part in a conspiracy against Cardinal Giulio de' Medici (later Pope Clement VII) and was obliged to flee to France for safety. In 1527 he went back to Florence, but his long stay in France had made the Florentines suspicious of him and he left Italy again. He spent most of his life thereafter in exile in France. Like an earlier fellow-Florentine, Dante, Alamanni felt a bitter sense of loss and longing for his homeland. Unlike Dante, however, he returned to Florence on several occasions on diplomatic missions for his French patrons, Francis I and later Henry II. He died in France, at Avignon.

At the French court Alamanni was received with great honor. E. H. Wilkins writes: "He was the chief representative of Italian culture in France, so well contented as to be rather an expatriate than an exile, so prosperous as to be the patron of many less fortunate displaced Italians." He read Dante to Francis I and became that monarch's court poet. He served as major domo to Henry II's queen, Catherine de' Medici. He wrote satires in *terza rima* on court gossip, a conventional court tragedy, *Antigone,* and a comedy, *Flora.* He also wrote three long poems—the romances *Gyrone il Cortese, Avarchide,* and the didactic poem *Coltivazione.* In all his work Alamanni faithfully followed the literary forms and style of the classics, as interpreted by the Renaissance. *Gyrone* is a lengthy (28,000 lines) and elaborately told chivalric epic using Arthurian materials; *Avarchide* a retelling of the *Iliad* in an Arthurian setting. Only his *Coltivazione* (1546), a Virgilian imitation in blank verse on agriculture, survived as a work of any intrinsic merit. Rémy de Gourmont, who prepared his biographical sketch in *La Grande Encyclopédie,* summed up: "With all his faults and errors, thanks to the *Coltivazione,* Alamanni is one of the better poets of the second rank."

Some of Alamanni's court satires were freely translated into English by his contemporary, the English poet Sir Thomas Wyatt. A translation of his sonnet "To the River Seine," by T. G. Bergin, appears in L. R. Lind's *Lyric Poetry of the Italian Renaissance* (1954).

ABOUT: Wilkins, E. H. A History of Italian Literature. [In French—see study by H. Hauvette.]

ALAN OF LILLE. See ALANUS DE INSULIS

* ä lä män' ē

*ALANUS DE INSULIS (ALAIN, or ALAN OF LILLE) (d. 1202), French poet who shares with Albertus Magnus the title of *doctor universalis,* wrote in Latin two of the great allegorical poems of the Middle Ages, *De Planctu Naturae* and *Anticlaudianus.* Biographical information about him is almost completely lacking. He was born in the Flemish city of Lille during the first half of the twelfth century. It is possible that he studied at Chartres—his work, at least, shows the influence of the teachers of that school. He became a teacher himself in Paris and won fame for his prodigious learning. For some years he lived in the south of France at Montpellier, probably in Cistercian orders, where he taught and preached, and where he wrote his theological tract *Contra Haereticos.* He returned to Paris in 1194 and continued his teaching and writing. Ultimately he retired to the Cistercian abbey of Cîteaux, where he died.

Alanus composed his *De Planctu Naturae* between 1160 and 1170. An allegorical poem in the tradition of the *De Consolatione Philosophiae* of Boethius, *De Planctu* expresses Nature's complaint against man's abuse of her law. Nature is personified as a lady, wearing the starry firmament as a crown, a servant of God and a guide to mankind. Through Alanus—or his many imitators—this conception of nature dominated medieval poetry. It influenced a large part of the second half of the *Roman de la Rose.* It appears in Chaucer's *Parlement of Foules,* and its influence persisted into the Renaissance. Spenser mentions Alanus in the Mutability cantos of the *Faerie Queene,* and Giles Fletcher the younger was indebted to him in his poem *Christes Victorie, or Triumph in Heaven and Earth, Over and After Death.*

The *Anticlaudianus,* composed in 1182 or 1183 as an answer to the fifth century Claudian's attack on the depravity of man, has been described as "a *summa* of formal learning and Christian doctrine arranged in a clock-work of allegory." In this poem Nature resolves to fashion a man who will embody all her gifts, and she calls on personified Reason, Theology, the Virtues, and the Vices to assist her. A free adaptation of the poem was made in French in the thirteenth century by Ellebaut.

The complete works of Alanus in Latin are published in J. P. Migne's *Patrologia Latina,* vol. 210. *The Complaint of Nature* was translated into English by D. M. Moffat in 1908; an English translation of *Anticlaudianus* by W. H. Cornog was published in 1935.

ABOUT: Creighton, A. J. *Preface to* Ellebaut's Anticlaudian; Lewis, C. S. The Allegory of Love; Moffat, D. M. *Preface to* Complaint of Nature. [In French—see study by G. R. de Lage. In Italian —Archivio Muratoriano (1960).]

*ALARCÓN (or ALARCÓN Y ARIZA), PEDRO ANTONIO DE (March 10, 1833-July 20, 1891), Spanish novelist, statesman, and journalist, was born at Guadix in Granada, descendant of a distinguished family that had become impoverished by the War for Independence. He was educated at the seminary in Granada, receiving his baccalaureate at the age of fourteen. He had intended to prepare himself for the law, but economic and family difficulties forced his return to Guadix. For a time he planned to follow an ecclesiastical career, for opportunistic reasons, but seems to have regarded writing as his true vocation from his earliest years. His first literary opportunity came with the editorship of the periodical *El Eco de Occidente.* Ambition soon prompted him to run away from his parents' home to seek literary fame, first in Cadiz, then in Madrid. Temporarily discouraged, he returned to his native city where he formed part of a revolutionary faction known as the *Cuerda* (or Cordon) *Grenadina.* This marked his entry into active political life.

Shortly afterwards, Alarcón reestablished himself in Madrid, winning a reputation as the editor of *El Látigo* (The Whip), a satirical, anti-royal newspaper. To this period belongs also his first novel, *El Final de Norma* (1855). An important turning point in his career came in 1857, when his only play, *El Hijo Pródigo,* was hissed off the stage. This failure led him to enlist under Leopoldo O'Donnell as a volunteer in the Moroccan campaign. Out of this experience grew his engaging *Diario de un Testigo de la Guerra de Africa* (1859), an invaluable account of military life under primitive conditions that won him his first wide fame and financial success. The royalties enabled him to take a pleasure trip to Italy, bringing forth his travel diary, *De Madrid a Nápoles* (1861).

Upon his return from Morocco, Alarcón reentered political controversy, and during the second half of his life pursued a triple career as muck-raking journalist, government official, and fiction writer. For a time he edited the liberal paper *La Política.* In 1864, he was elected a member of the Cortés (par-

* à lã' nŭs dē in' sū lĭs

* ä lär kôn'

ALARCÓN

liament) from Cadiz. Later he was appointed minister to Norway and Sweden. However, Alarcón proved to be so chameleonlike in his political views that his influence seriously declined in his later years. As with many youthful radicals he ended his days as a staunch conservative. Gerald Brenan has characterized Alarcón as "the type of the unrooted man of his age, without fixed principles or beliefs, [moving] within a short space of time from the extreme Left to the extreme Right." In 1887, four years before his death, Alarcón retired from public life, becoming something of a recluse. His last years were harassed by attacks of hemiplegia, which eventually caused his death in Madrid. Artistically and politically he had been for most of his life an eclectic, but he remained firm in his religious beliefs, dying a devout Catholic.

It is not for his political essays, which were occasional and polemical, nor for his memoirs, which have never been translated, nor even for his novels that Alarcón survives, but for several gay, saucy, warm-hearted tales in which he has preserved for posterity the charming folk types and *costumbristas* of his age. The most famous of these is *El Sombrero de Tres Picos* (The Three-Cornered Hat), a novella which he refashioned in 1874 from an old romance. Moved up in time to the early nineteenth century, *El Sombrero* became in Alarcón's hands a sparkling, vivid *fabliau* of Andalusian village life during the Napoleonic era. The tale actually unravels a four-cornered in-

trigue, involving the clever, scheming miller Lucas, his too-beautiful young wife Frasquita, who attracts the roving eye of the Corregidor of the village (the gentleman of the three-cornered hat), and the Corregidor's wife, on whom Lucas almost wreaks revenge for Frasquita's suspected infidelity. That the latter manages to keep her marital vows, despite strong circumstantial evidence to the contrary, is a part of the delightful ingenuity of the story. The gracefulness of *El Sombrero* seems to call out for a musical setting, and it is in fact through Manuel de Falla's ballet suite that dance lovers the world over have become familiar with it. It has also been converted into an opera, *Der Corregidor*, by the German composer Hugo Wolf.

Generally it was in his shorter pieces that Alarcón achieved his greatest success. His long novels are marred by sensationalism, strident rhetoric, obvious didacticism, and needless complication of incident. His first novel, *El Final de Norma*, with its exotic setting and gaudy description is dismissed nowadays as "romantic trash." *El Escándalo* (1875), concerned with the spiritual redemption of a dissolute youth, and *La Pródiga* (1882), concerned with the conflict of love and politics, are now for the most part ignored. The novel of Alarcón's with the greatest staying power, to judge by recency of translation, is *El Niño de la Bola* (The Child with the Ball), written in 1880, in which is depicted the moral power of religious faith over unruly passion.

Alarcón's most charming tale next to *El Sombrero de Tres Picos* is *El Capitán Veneno* (Captain Venom) of 1882, the love story of a gruff soldier, which he may have drawn from his own earlier military experience. His collections of stories—*Cuentos Amatorios* (1881), *Historias Nacionales* (1881), and *Narraciones Inverosimiles* (1882)—are rich depositories of social history, and undoubtedly will continue as staples of introductory Spanish language courses.

There have been many translations of *El Sombrero de Tres Picos,* among them Mary Springer's *The Three-Cornered Hat* (1891), Lawrence M. Levin's *The Three-Cornered Hat* (1944), and Mary J. Serrano's *The Miller and the Mayor's Wife* (reprint, 1945). *El Capitán Veneno* has been translated by Gray Casement (1914). *El Niño de la Bola* was translated by the English poet Robert Graves (*The Infant with the Globe,* 1955). A selection of the shorter tales is available in *Moors and Christians, and Other Tales,* translated by Mary J. Serrano (1891). The best edition in Spanish is that of Martínez Kleiser (1943), a revision of the *Obras Completas* (19 vols., 1899).

ABOUT: Bourland, B. *Introduction to his edition of* El Sombrero de Tres Picos; Columbia Dictionary of Modern European Literature; Bulletin of Spanish Studies, 1933; Modern Language Notes, June 1938; Saturday Review, July 22, 1933. [In Spanish—see studies by Julio Romano and José F. Montesinos.]

R. A. C.

*ALAS Y UREÑA, LEOPOLDO ("CLARÍN")

(April 25, 1852- June 13, 1901), Spanish critic, polemist, satirist, novelist and short-story writer, better known by his pseudonym, was born in Zamora. His father, a landlord of modest means, became civil governor of several provinces, and at the age of six young Leopoldo entered the recently established Jesuit school at León. In 1859 his parents returned to their native Oviedo and four years later, at eleven, the boy entered the University of Oviedo for preparatory studies. Soon he had earned academic honors, and at the age of thirteen he wrote a serious play of which only the title remains: *El Sitio de Zamora.* From 1864 to 1869 he studied indefatigably and in May 1869 he received his bachelor of arts degree with honors. In 1871 he received the degree of *licenciado en derecho civil y canónico,* again with honors. For his doctorate he went to Madrid where he was influenced by the Krausist Camus and where he was the backbone of the *tertulia* of young Asturians at the Cervecería Inglesa on the Carrera de San Jerónimo.

To the *Revista de Asturias,* published in Oviedo, he contributed his first short stories. In 1877 he received the degree of Doctor of Civil and Canon Law and shortly after that took part in the *oposiciones* for the chair of Political Economy at the University of Salamanca. Although he was voted the best of the three candidates for the post, it was given to another by the Minister of Public Instruction, who had been irritated by some of Clarín's remarks. In 1880 he delivered a lecture at the University of Oviedo; one year later this lecture served as prologue to a translation of a work by Von Ihering, *La Lucha por el Derecho.*

In July 1882 he was appointed Professor of Political Economy and Statistics at the University of Zaragoza and in August of the same year he married Onofre García Argüelles. One year later he was transferred to the University of Oviedo as Professor of Roman Law. Now he could enjoy life in his beloved Oviedo, near friends and relatives. In the same year he began work on his great

* ä′ läs ē ōō rä′ nyä (klä rēn′)

novel *La Regenta* and completed the first volume in November 1884, the month his father died. Three months later he completed the work and wrote to a friend: "I have the satisfaction of having completed a work of art at the age of thirty-nine." This novel is considered by some to be the most naturalistic Spanish novel of the nineteenth century; the themes of tedium, religious rapture, and adultery in a provincial capital Vetusta, modeled after Oviedo, aroused such opposition in certain quarters that the Bishop of Oviedo warned the faithful that it was a dangerous book.

In 1886 Clarín prepared for publication his first collection of short stories, *Pipá,* which along with *Doña Berta* (1893) and *Cuentos Morales* (1896) established him as one of the great writers in this genre. In 1887 he almost fought a duel over what was considered a derisive remark made about the Spanish navy in one of his *Paliques,* the critical articles Clarín was writing in pithy, caustic language. His criticism of general incompetence of navy personnel made on the occasion of the sinking of the *Reina Regente* again got him into serious difficulties which only friends could resolve.

In 1890 he completed his second and last novel, *Su único Hijo,* outstanding for the surprising modernity of its theme and the psychological analysis of the characters. Hard work—he often wrote until dawn—was undermining Clarín's health. By 1891 his articles were so widely read and discussed that he won a supreme position in Spanish letters. In 1892 he fought a duel with Emilio Bobadilla, and on March 20, 1895, his play *Teresa* was badly received. The death of his mother, whom he visited every day after classes, was another shock to his delicate health. Soon it was found that he was suffering from advanced tuberculosis of the intestines, and he died in Oviedo at the age of forty-nine. Azorín has said of him: "Clarín is one of those writers . . . to whom the learned always turn."

There are a number of English translations of Clarín's stories. Among them are "Adiós Cordera!" in *Short Stories from the Spanish,* tr. by C. B. Mc-Michael (1920); "The Cock of Socrates" in *Spanish Stories and Tales,* ed. by H. DeOnis (1954); "Doña Berta" in *Great Spanish Short Stories,* ed. by Angel Flores (1956).

ABOUT: Brent, A. Leopoldo Alas and "La Regenta": A Study in Nineteenth Century Spanish Prose Fiction. [In Spanish—see studies by J. A. Cabezas, E. Clochiatti, A. Posada.]

M. N.

*ALBERTI, LEON BATTISTA (February 1404-1472), Italian scientist, artist, and writer, was born in Genoa, the natural son of Lorenzo Alberti, member of a patrician Florentine family that had made its money in the wool trade during the fourteenth century. The Albertis had been forced into exile from Florence by the persecution of the Albizzi factions. The child grew up mainly in Rome and Ferrara and was educated in Padua and in Bologna. He received every advantage that wealth and the devoted care of his father could give him. Truly an embodiment of the Renaissance ideal, he excelled in all things—scholarship, art, science, athletics. A brilliant student, he was able to pass off a Latin comedy which he wrote in school as an authentic classical work. In later life he was a painter, a sculptor, an architect, and an inventor. He was also a musician, a sportsman, and an engineer. And—not the least of his talents—he was a gifted writer in both Latin and Italian. Only Leonardo da Vinci and Michelangelo rival him in sheer versatility. Francesco De Sanctis wrote: "The people who measure genius by the quantity of output, or by the variety of cognitions, will think of Alberti as a person who was truly a miracle, as he was considered by his contemporaries. Certainly he was the man of greatest culture of his time, and the man who mirrored the century most completely in all its tendencies."

In 1426 the ban on the Alberti faction was lifted and they returned to Florence. Here young Leon Battista immediately joined the humanist circles, and in this stimulating atmosphere his talents flourished. In 1428 he entered the service of Cardinal Albergati. Three years later he became papal secretary to Eugenio IV and moved to Rome where he began to study art and classical architecture. He spent the last years of his life in Ferrara, Mantua, and Rome; he died in the latter city, at sixty-eight, departing, Vasari wrote, "content and tranquil, to a better life, leaving a most honorable name."

Alberti's achievements in science are known to us largely by hearsay. His biographers report that he experimented in optics, invented a camera obscura, devised various theories about elevation, engineering, and astronomy. The evidence of his achievement in architecture is more concrete and impressive. Strongly influenced by the principles of Roman design, he conceived the splendid church of St. Francis of Assisi in Rimini, sometimes called the "Malatesta Temple," a

* äl bĕr' tē

building which Aldous Huxley describes as "a hymn to intellectual beauty, an exaltation of reason as the only source of human greatness . . . a paean in praise of civilization couched in the language of Rome." He also designed the Rucellai palace in Florence and the church of Sant' Andrea in Mantua, now considered "one of the noblest churches of the Italian Renaissance."

Alberti wrote voluminously, but not all his works survive. Among his Latin writings the most interesting is a treatise on the aesthetics of architecture, De Re Aedificatoria. Among his other Latin writings are a collection of satirical dialogues — Intercoenales, "in the mood and manner of Lucian"—and essays on horsemanship and miscellaneous subjects. He was an ardent proponent of the use of the vernacular in literature and in 1441 sponsored a contest to award a silver crown for the best poem written in Italian. His own Italian writings include a long dialogue on Renaissance family life and education, Della Famiglia; the first Renaissance treatises on the arts of painting and sculpture; and De Iciarchia (On the Headship of a Family), which is chiefly concerned with the training of statesmen and rulers. This work, E. H. Wilkins points out, "anticipates ideas that were to be set forth by Castiglione a century later in his Book of the Courtier."

Alberti's complete works were published in five volumes in Italian under the editorship of A. Bonucci, 1843-49. English translations of excerpts from his writings on architecture and painting appear in E. B. G. Holt's Literary Sources of Art History (1947). Other brief selections are in The Portable Renaissance Reader, edited by J. B. Ross & M. M. McLaughlin (1953). His Ten Books on Architecture was translated by J. Leoni in 1955.

ABOUT: Clark, K. Leon Battista Alberti on Painting (British Academy Lectures 1944); Huxley, A. Essays New and Old; Papini, G. Four and Twenty Minds; Stokes, A. D. Art and Science; Vasari, G. Lives of the Painters; Wilkins, E. H. A History of Italian Literature; Burlington Magazine June 1954; Italian Studies, XII. [In Italian—see studies by M. Baussola Lemano, V. D. Alessandro, G. Santinello.]

ALBERTUS MAGNUS, Saint (1193?/1206?-November 15, 1280), German philosopher and theologian, was born in Lauingen, in Swabia, of a noble and pious family. The year of his birth is variously given as 1193 and 1206. In his youth he enjoyed hunting, falconry, and horsemanship, and he carried over into his adult life a love for and curiosity about all things in nature. He studied liberal arts in Venice and in Padua. In 1223 he entered the Dominican order. After his ordination he devoted himself to teaching and to study. In 1228 he became lector in theology at Cologne, the city which claims him, although he traveled and lived in many cities in Europe. In 1245 he received a mastership in theology and began teaching in Paris. For three years he had for a pupil Thomas Aquinas, who became his lifelong friend. An administrator as well as a teacher, Albert returned to Cologne in 1248 to organize the *studium generale.* In 1256 he was in Italy living at the court at Anagni. There, under orders of the Pope, he held a disputation against Averroism (that school of philosophy, denying personal immortality, which followed the commentaries on Aristotle written by the Moorish philosopher Averroës) and composed his *De Unitate Intellectus.* In 1260 he again left Cologne, this time to serve for two years as bishop of Ratisbon. He also traveled to Rome with Thomas Aquinas. In 1268 he retired to a convent in Cologne, but in 1277 he returned to public life when he went to Paris to defend Thomas, whose teachings had been condemned. He returned to Cologne where he died at an advanced age.

Albert the Great, as he became known after his death, has been called "the greatest German scholar of the Middle Ages," a *doctor universalis.* The epithet "great" was applied to his name probably to suggest his intellectual achievements. It was said that he was "great in his knowledge, small in his person." He was one of the first thinkers of his time to regard philosophy and science not merely as tools of theology but as "pure" fields of knowledge in their own right. He was also one of the first to draw upon the long neglected writings of the Arab philosophers and, primarily, upon the work of Aristotle. He devoted his life to the task of "christianizing Aristotle," rewriting the Greek philosopher in a form intelligible to his contemporaries, and probably his most significant achievement was his introducing of Aristotle to his illustrious pupil Thomas Aquinas. Along with his Aristotelianism, there was also in his work the elements of medieval Neoplatonism which, in their turn, had a strong influence upon the two Dominicans, the German mystics Dietrich of Freiburg and Meister Eckhart of Hochheim.

Albert's writings include philosophical works, consisting mainly of the commentaries on Aristotle; theological works, including sermons, Biblical commentaries, and an uncompleted *Summa*; and mystical works, mainly commentaries on the works of the pseudo-Dionysus. Further, he wrote a number of highly respected treatises on natural history, unusual for their time because they were based in part at least upon direct observation, experimentation, and induction rather than upon superstition and hearsay. Outstanding among these are *De Animalibus* and *De Vegetabilibus.* As a philosopher Albert lacked precision and a coherent system, but he utilized his erudition profitably as a teacher. Maurice de Wulf pointed out in his *History of Mediaeval Philosophy* that "Albert put into circulation material upon which others could work. His exceptional qualities as a scholar and a collector of information give him a unique place in the history of Scholasticism." He enjoyed widespread honor. His contemporaries ranked him alongside Aristotle, Avicenna, Averroës. In the *Divine Comedy* Dante placed him in the Heaven of the Sun at the right hand of Aquinas. He was canonized on December 16, 1931.

Elizabeth Stopp translated *Of Cleaving to God* in 1954. A few of the other writings attributed to Albertus are in English translation, but most of these date back to the sixteenth century, and they are of doubtful authenticity. William Copeland published *The Secretes of Nature* in London in 1549 and *The Boke of Secretes . . . of the Virtues of Herbes, Stones, and Certaine Beastes. Also a Boke . . . of the Maruaylous Thinges of the World* in 1565. In 1880 (?) there was a translation of his writings on *Egyptian Secrets; or White and Black Art for Man and Beast* published in New York.

ABOUT: Fremantle, A. The Age of Belief; Sister Mary Albert, Albert the Great; Raven, C. E. Natural Religion and Christian Theology; Schwertner, T. M. St. Albert the Great; Wilms, H. Albert the Great; Wulf M. de, History of Mediaeval Philosophy.

*ALBO, JOSEPH (c. 1380-c. 1444), the last great figure in medieval Jewish philosophy, was born in Monreal, Spain. Although little is known about the details of his life, Albo is considered to have been a disciple of the great Jewish philosopher Hasdai Crescas. He was well versed in both the Jewish learning and the science and philosophy of the day, and was proficient in Hebrew, Latin, and Spanish. It is believed that Albo earned his livelihood as a physician, but his philosophical writings indicate where his primary interest lay.

Albo did not hold any official rabbinic post, but was recognized as a leading scholar and preacher. As such, he participated (1413-14) in the great religious disputation of Tortosa, called by King Ferdinand of Aragon and Pope Benedict XIII. During this prolonged religious debate between Catholic and Jewish

* ăl' bō

representatives, Albo is said to have held firmly to his convictions. Angered at the inability of the Catholics to convince the Jews, Pope Benedict reacted harshly to the Jewish participants. Albo himself was forced to leave Monreal.

It was after settling at Soria that he wrote his famous *Sefer ha-'Ikkarim* (Book of Principles), a work which was intended to meet the two great needs of the time. First Albo aimed to clarify and fortify the doctrines of Judaism in an age of great persecution when there was imminent danger from the inroads of conversion. His second object was to demonstrate the compatibility and mutual reinforcement of the truths of Talmudic Judaism and speculative philosophy. He therefore attempted a definition of the creed of Judaism, a task which had led Maimonides to his thirteen articles of faith. Albo proclaimed but three basic dogmas: the existence of God, divine revelation, and reward and punishment after death. Derived from these fundamental principles are the subsidiary dogmas of God's unity, incorporeality, timelessness and perfection, and belief in prophecy, the uniqueness of Moses' prophecy, the binding force of the Torah, and bodily resurrection. In formulating these secondary dogmas, Albo analyzed the philosophical and theological problems involved and presented his solutions. His method demonstrated a rational approach to the whole question. While granting the need for absolute acceptance of the basic dogmas, he emphasized the need for justifying the secondary dogmas rationally. Thus he allowed the individual Jew freedom to speculate philosophically on matters of religion.

Albo's work is essentially apologetic in nature and his creative contribution to Jewish philosophy is not of prime significance. His importance lies in the fact that his clearly written statement of Jewish principles, combining philosophy and homiletics, became "one of the most popular philosophic works ever written by a Jewish scholar" (Waxman, *A History of Jewish Literature*).

The *Sefer ha-'Ikkarim* (Book of Principles) was translated and edited, with critical Hebrew text, in five volumes by Isaac Husik in 1929-30.

ABOUT: Graetz, H. History of the Jews; Husik, I. A History of Medieval Jewish Philosophy; Waxman, M. A History of Jewish Literature. [In German—see studies by S. Bäck, A. Tänzer.]

M. R.

*ALBRECHT VON JOHANNSDORF (fl. 1185-1209), Bavarian minnesinger, came of a family of landless noblemen (*ministeriales*) of Landau and is mentioned in documents between 1185 and 1209 as being in the service of the Bishop of Jassau. He certainly took part in a crusade, either that of 1190 or, more probably, that of 1197. Two of his sixteen poems are crusading songs. So far as is known, he wrote only lyric poetry. Sixteen poems (forty-two strophes) are extant (complete text in Lachmann/Kraus, *Des Minnesangs Frühling*; translation of selected songs by Margaret Richey in *Essays on the Medieval German Love Lyric*). Albrecht is mentioned with admiration by two later poets, Der Marner and Reinmar von Brennenberg. It is clear from his poetry that he knew the work of Walter von der Vogelweide. His work shows the formal Minnesang or love poetry in its most fully developed form. He is a complete master of meter and rhyme and of the expression of the idealized worship of the lady characteristic of the genre. The most personal of his poems are the crusading songs in which his sorrow at parting from the lady and his agony of mind when called upon to decide between his duty to God in going on the crusade and his duty to his lady seem to be quite genuine. He fears too that the parting may be fatal to his prospects of keeping her love. Although he lacks the brilliant verbal power of Heinrich von Morungen and the breadth of vision of Walther von der Vogelweide, Albrecht makes up for these deficiencies by a sincerity and naturalness rarely found in the *Minnesang*. Thus in some poems he appears to become exasperated with the artificiality of the love game and in others shows himself in direct conversation with his lady, attempting to persuade her to be merciful to him. In one of his poems we find direct imitation of a poem in Provençal, written by Albert Marques de Malaspina. Such direct imitation is relatively unusual.

Translations of Albrecht's poems are included in *Medieval German Lyrics*, translated by M. F. Richey (1958); *The Minnesingers*, translated by J. Bithell (1909); *Old German Love Songs*, translated by F. C. Nicholson (1907).

ABOUT: Richey, M. F. *in* Essays on the Medieval German Love Lyric. [In German—Stammler, W. Verfasserlexikon des Deutschen Mittelalters; de Boor, H. and Newald, R. Geschichte der Deutschen Literatur, Vol. II.]

W. T. H. J.

* äl' brĕkt fŏn jō häns' dôrf

*ALEARDI, ALEARDO (November 4, 1812-July 17, 1878), Italian poet and patriot, was born in Verona when that city was under Austrian rule, and he was therefore an Austrian subject. His first name was originally Gaetano. He was educated in Venice and at the University of Padua where (because it was his father's wish) he studied law. Returning then to Verona, Aleardi planned to practice law but was prevented from doing so by the Austrian government. His unemployment gave him the necessary leisure for writing poetry. Aleardi's principal subject was his country—his hatred of the foreign powers that dominated it, his desire for its independence and its development as a nation. He expressed these views not only in his poetry but also in a patriotic journal which he edited with Giovanni Prati, *Il Caffè Pedrocchi.*

Aleardi paid dearly for his outspoken views and was twice imprisoned by the Austrians, once in 1852 and again in 1859. In 1848 he represented the short-lived Venetian Republic in Paris, but when this new government was overthrown he returned to Italy to resume his fight for freedom. For a while he taught art history and aesthetics at the Institute of Fine Arts in Florence. As soon as the Austrians were driven out of Lombardy, he returned to his native city. Verona joined the kingdom of Italy in 1866, and Aleardi was elected as one of its representatives to the Italian parliament. In 1873 he became a senator. He served his native state in various official capacities until his death at the age of sixty-five.

Aleardi's poetic style was essentially delicate and restrained, but, fired with nationalistic fervor, he wrote stirring and effective patriotic verse. He published his first long poem, *Arnalda di Roca,* in 1844. His first literary success came two years later with a love poem, *Lettere a Maria.* In 1846 he began work on *Prime Storie,* a re-telling of the story of the Creation. In 1855 appeared his idyll *Raffaello e la Fornarina,* which was to become one of his most famous poems. A year later he published *Il Monte Circello* and *Le Città Italiane e Commercianti,* the latter being an attempt in poetry to show how Italy's greatness in the past derived from its sea-going commerce and shipping. He described the sources of his patriotic fervor in *Un' Ora della Mia Giovinezza* (1858), but his most moving and successful poem on this subject was *I Sette Soldati* (1861), a bitter attack on Austrian tyranny.

* ä lä är′ dē

Aleardi is a neglected figure in Italian literature. William Dean Howells considered him "one of the chief minor poets of the nineteenth century," but in recent years there has been little interest in his work. A collected edition of his poems appeared in 1864. Howells published translated selections from his poems in *Modern Italian Poets* (1887) and two of these are reprinted in the *Warner Library.*

ABOUT: [In Italian—see studies by G. Giuliano, V. Mazzini.]

*ALEMÁN, MATEO (September 1547-1614?), Spanish novelist, was born in Seville, where his father, Hernando, held the post of surgeon in the royal prison. He received his bachelor's degree from a local college in June 1564, and went on to study medicine at the national universities of Salamanca and Alcalá. His father's death in 1567 interrupted his studies briefly; he completed his fourth and final year of medicine in April 1568, but seems never to have taken a degree nor to have practiced medicine.

On his return to Seville a lifetime of financial hardships began for Mateo Alemán. After a scandalous affair with Doña Catalina de Espinosa, he was forced by her guardian to choose between prison and marriage; he finally consented to the marriage, but it soon ended in a legal separation. About 1572 he received an appointment in the royal bureaucracy of Seville, where he continued to live for at least ten more years, part of this time in prison as a debtor. He held a similar government post in Madrid between 1586 and 1599. It was during this period that he began to give public evidence of a literary career; he wrote a prologue for a friend's book (Alonso de Barros, *Proverbios Morales,* 1598) and a translation of two of Horace's odes. By 1597 he had finished the first part of a novel, *Guzmán de Alfarache,* which was to bring him, if not wealth, at least fame throughout Europe; it was published in 1599 and immediately achieved an unprecedented success. A spurious continuation was published in 1602 by Juan Martí, under the pseudonym of Mateo Luján de Sayavedra; the authentic second part was published by Alemán in 1604. (James Mabbe's translation, *The Rogue,* appeared in London in 1623; the translation of J. H. Brady, published in 1821, was based on the 1732 French version of Le Sage.)

Guzmán de Alfarache, Alemán's sole important work, is the picaresque novel *par excellence;* it brought to full maturity this Spanish genre, which had begun in 1554 with the anonymous *Lazarillo de Tormes.*

* ä lä män′

15

Within the autobiographical form, which focuses on society the satirical eyes of a servant lad, Alemán created a world which is not only anti-heroic and anti-idealistic, the antithesis of the chivalric and pastoral romances, but which implies an all-pervading pessimism based on a belief in mankind's essentially treacherous and evil nature. Despite moralizing digressions, which resemble the powerful sermons of a Stoic in the robes of a Dominican, this work, with its portrayal of grossly realistic situations and uniformly depraved characters in action, is of the greatest importance in the nascent tradition of the modern novel.

In 1601, still in debt, Alemán returned to Seville, where he lived for a while with Doña Francisca Calderón and was again imprisoned. In 1603 he published *San Antonio de Padua.* On June 12, 1608, he sailed for New Spain in the service of Fray García Guerra, archbishop first, and later viceroy, of Mexico. There he published his *Ortografía Castellana* (1609) and a biography of his master, *Sucesos de Don Fray García Guerra* (1613). The date and circumstances of his death are not known.

Alemán's obscure life, combining economic hardship, illicit love, humanistic learning, and literary imagination, resembles somewhat that of his precise contemporary Cervantes, and perhaps even more that of his picaresque hero Guzmán. His novel's influence in the seventeenth and eighteenth centuries was probably second only to that of *Don Quixote*; in moral tone, it might still appeal strongly to the reader of Mauriac and Graham Greene.

ABOUT: Brenan, G. Literature of the Spanish People; Chandler, F. W. The Literature of Roguery; Jones, C. E. ed. *Prefaces* to Three Eighteenth Century Novels; Ticknor, G. History of Spanish Literature. [In Spanish—see studies by E. Moreno Báez and F. Rodríguez Marín].

E. L. R.

*ALEMBERT, JEAN LEROND D' (November 16, 1717-October 29, 1783), French mathematician and encyclopedist, was born in Paris, the illegitimate son of the novelist Mme de Tencin and an army officer named Destouches. The infant was abandoned by his mother a few days after his birth and exposed on the steps of the chapel of St. Jean-Le-Rond, near the cathedral of Notre Dame, after which he took his name Lerond, later adding d'Alembert. He was adopted and raised, in humble circumstances but with love, by a Mme Rousseau, the wife of a

* á län bâr'

D'ALEMBERT

glazier. His father took some interest in the child and provided for his education, but his mother was completely indifferent to him. Years later, reputedly, when d'Alembert was an eminent figure, she sought to reclaim him, but her son turned away from her and reaffirmed his loyalty to his adopted mother.

D'Alembert was educated at the Collège Mazarin, a Jansenist school, and revealed such great precocity that his teachers called him a second Pascal and gave him mathematical training along with his theological studies. He also studied law and qualified as an advocate in 1738, but he never practiced. Instead he devoted himself to research in mathematics and science. His first published work, in 1739, was on integral calculus. In 1741 he was admitted to the Academy of Sciences. Two years later he published his *Traité de Dynamique* (1743), which outlined a mechanical principle known as d'Alembert's law. In 1754 he was elected to the French Academy and in 1772 he became its permanent secretary. In that capacity he wrote his graceful funeral orations on the deaths of Academy members. His reputation spread throughout Europe. Frederick the Great offered him the presidency of the Berlin Academy of Sciences; Catherine the Great invited him to Russia to be a tutor to her son; in Scotland the philosopher David Hume praised him highly.

The work for which d'Alembert is best remembered is his collaboration with Denis Diderot on the famous *La Grande Encyclo-*

pédie. As one of the Philosophes (along with Voltaire, Montesquieu, Rousseau, Buffon, and others), the skeptics and rationalists who conceived this vast project, d'Alembert made significant contributions. Voltaire described him and Diderot as the Atlas and the Hercules who carried the weight of this work. D'Alembert wrote the famous *Discours Préliminaire* (1751), the introduction to the work, which discusses the plan and the scope of the *Encyclopédie.* The *Discours* is a self-contained philosophical treatise, with a three-fold classification of knowledge according to human faculties—memory, reason, imagination (for this he acknowledges his indebtedness to Francis Bacon) and a historical sketch of the growth of knowledge. D'Alembert also contributed many articles, among them the highly controversial essay on Geneva which urged the citizens of that Calvinist city to free themselves of their prejudices and to establish a theatre. Rousseau attacked the article bitterly, and there was so much criticism from all sides that d'Alembert withdrew from the *Encyclopédie* in 1758. "I am worn out," he wrote to his friend Voltaire, "with the affronts and vexations of every kind that this work draws down upon us."

From that time until his death, d'Alembert lived quietly in Paris, though on one other occasion, in 1765, he got into difficulties with the church over his treatise *De la Suppression des Jésuites.* His other writings include *Eléments de Philosophie* (1759) and a treatise on music, which interested him as a science as well as an art, *Eléments de Musique Théorique et Pratique* (1779).

D'Alembert frequented the salons of Mme du Deffand and of Mlle de Lespinasse. He lived with the latter from 1765 until her death in 1776. During most of his life he suffered from ill health. He was slight in appearance, with a small face and a sharp, thin voice. John Morley described him as "restless, impatient, mobile, susceptible of irritation." He was also, however, friendly, generous, and staunchly independent in spirit. His scientific writings are little read today, but his *Discours* and his eulogies on departed members of the Academy are still admired for their fine lucid style. His correspondence with Voltaire, Morley wrote, "is the most instructive record that we possess of the many-sided doings of that busy time."

D'Alembert's *Discours Préliminaire* was published in English translation as *The Plan of the French Encyclopedia* in 1752. In 1963 a new translation by R. N. Schwab and W. E. Rex appeared.

An English translation of his *Miscellaneous Pieces in Literature, History, and Philosophy* appeared in 1764, his *An Account of the Destruction of the Jesuits* in 1766, and his *Select Eulogies of Members of the French Academy* (translated by J. Aiken) in 1799.

ABOUT: Morley, J. Diderot and the Encyclopedists; Pappas, J. N. Voltaire and D'Alembert; Tallentyre, S. G. The Friends of Voltaire; PMLA, LXXV (1960). [In French—see studies by J. Bertrand, M. Muller.]

*ALEXANDRI, VASILE (or ALEC-SANDRI, BASILE) (July 21, 1821-August 22, 1890), Rumanian poet and playwright, was born at Bacau, in Moldavia, the son of a wealthy landowner. He attended school at Jassy, in Rumania, until he was fourteen, when he was sent to Paris to study. He specialized for a time in law, then medicine, then mathematics, but soon found that he had no inclination for these subjects and that his talents and tastes were for literature. He returned to his native land in 1839 after a long tour of Italy during which he fell in love with that country. Back home he became interested in Rumanian folksongs and popular ballads. With a friend, Alecu Russo, he traveled through the land collecting these, and they published their first collection in 1852.

In 1844 Alexandri became a co-director of a Rumanian theatre group in Jassy and began to produce and write his own plays for them. In the course of his lifetime he wrote in a variety of dramatic forms some fifty plays in all—tragedies, comedies, farces, operettas. His serious plays—the best known of which are *Despot Voda* (1879) and *Ovidiu* (1885)—show considerable French influence, of the drama of Picard, Scribe, and Augier. They are well-plotted, slick, and full of action.

Throughout his life Alexandri was active in Rumanian politics. In 1844 he founded a literary and scientific review, *Progressul,* which was suppressed by the government after nine months. Self-exiled from his country, he traveled abroad in the Near East—visiting Constantinople, Athens, the Ionian isles—and in Italy. He was in Paris in 1848, deeply involved in revolutionary activity. In 1855, after his father's death, he returned to his native land to take over the family estate. He promptly freed all his serfs, setting an example which many other Rumanian landowners soon followed. That same year he founded another review, *Romania Literara,* which was also soon sup-

* ä lĕk sän′ drē

17

ALEXANDRI

pressed. In 1856 he wrote the words for the Rumanian national song "The Hour of Union."

In 1859, with the union of the separate Rumanian states, Alexandri became minister of foreign affairs. He later served as a deputy in the Rumanian parliament and, in 1885, as Rumanian ambassador to Paris. He was a literary adviser to Queen Elisabeth of Rumania, who wrote under the pen name Carmen Sylva (see sketch below).

Although intensely nationalistic and an ardent Rumanian patriot, Alexandri was essentially European in his cultural tastes, with close ties to France in particular. One of his poems, "Le Chant de la Race Latine," won the Félibrige silver cup at Montpellier for the best poem in any language of Latin origin. It was later translated into Provençal by Frédéric Mistral. Alexandri also published a Rumanian grammar in Paris in 1863 under the pen name "E. Mircescu."

Alexandri's collected works were published in Rumania in nine volumes from 1875 to 1880. His writings have been translated into French and German (Queen Elisabeth of Rumania translated some of his poems into German in 1898 but not into English).

ABOUT: [In French—see pamphlet by L. de Berluc-Perussis.]

*ALEXIS, WILLIBALD, pseudonym of WILHELM *HÄRING (June 29, 1798-December 16, 1871), German historical novelist, was born in Breslau. His father, the

* ä lĕk′ sĭs; hâ′ rĭng

descendant of a refugee French Huguenot family named Hareng, held an important position in the war ministry. His mother was related to the Berlin publishers Rellstab. After completing the Werder'sche *Gymnasium* in Berlin, Alexis entered the army in 1815 and participated in the battle of Ardennes. Subsequently, he studied law and history at the universities of Berlin and Breslau and for a time practiced law in Berlin. In 1828 he received the degree of Doctor of Philosophy from the University of Halle. From 1827 to 1830 Alexis directed the *Berliner Conversationsblatt*, a journal founded in collaboration with Friedrich Förster, and from 1830 to 1835 independently edited the periodical *Freimutiger*. Because his liberal policies drew a personal reprimand from Emperor Friedrich Wilhelm IV, Alexis forsook journalism for literature, until in 1849 he joined the editorial staff of the *Vossische Zeitung*. He retired in 1852 to Arnstadt in Thuringia, where he died after many years of broken health and bitter suffering.

Alexis began his literary career writing short stories (*Gesammelte Novellen*, 4 vols., 1830-31) in the manner of Ludwig Tieck. His interest in history led him to imitate the popular Waverley novels of Scott, and his first works, *Walladmor* (3 vols. 1824) and *Schloss Avalon* (1827), appeared as free translations from the English of Scott. With these books Alexis successfully introduced the historical novel into Germany. Since he applied Scott's method to his native Mark Brandenburg, Alexis has come to be known as "the Walter Scott of the Mark."

In a cycle of eight novels, beginning with *Cabanis* (1832), which is set in the time of Frederick the Great, Alexis treated all of the great historical periods of Brandenburg-Prussia. *Der Roland von Berlin* (1840) is set in the fifteenth century, and *Der Falsche Waldemar* (1842) in the Middle Ages, while the author's best individual work, *Die Hosen des Herrn von Bredow* (1846), with its sequel, *Der Werwolf* (1848), is set in the Reformation. *Die Ruhe Ist die Erste Bürgerpflicht* (1852) and its continuations, *Isegrimm* (1854) and *Dorothea* (1856), deal with the events of 1806. All these novels reflect Alexis' ability for masterful character portrayals and for blending the natural surroundings of his plots with the action of the story. Although his aim was to glorify his native province, the patriotism is kept within reasonable limits.

Alexis also wrote a number of travel books as well as a series of unsuccessful dramas. In collaboration with Julius Hitzig he published *Der Neue Pitaval* (1842), a collection of the most famous crimes and criminals of all times. His *Erinnerungen* were edited by M. Ewert in 1880.

The first English translation of *Walladmor* was made anonymously in 1825. W.A.G. translated *Der Roland von Berlin* in 1843 under the title *The Burgomaster of Berlin.* The short story *Hans Preller; a Legend of the Rhine Falls* appeared in 1889 in the translation of C. L. Lewes.

ABOUT: Modern Language Review, April 1950, April 1951, April 1954. [In German—see study by H. Palm.]

D. G. D.

*ALFIERI, VITTORIO, Count (January 17, 1749-October 8, 1803), Italian dramatist, was born of a wealthy patrician family at Asti in Piedmont, an area where the nobility, scorning Italian, spoke French. Alfieri's father, who was in his sixties, died shortly after his son's birth, whereupon his mother, Monica Maillard di Tournon, earlier the widow of the Marquis di Cacherano, married a third time, to enjoy, in the words of her son, "a very happy and exemplary union with the Cavaliere Giacinto Alfieri di Magliano."

In accord with the anti-intellectual attitude of the nobility, Alfieri's parents felt that a gentleman need not be learned and, accordingly, charged a good but ignorant priest with their son's early education. Delicate, introspective, and lonely, the boy Alfieri exhibited a marked tendency to melancholia and even attempted suicide before he was eight years old. In 1758 he was sent to the Royal Academy at Turin where neither his health nor his education improved. The laws of Piedmont, however, allowed him at the age of fourteen to enter into his vast inheritance; as a result, he joined a riding school which gave the impetus to his lifelong passion for horses and for equestrian feats. Alfieri describes this period of eight years at the Academy as one of "illness, idleness, and ignorance."

In 1766 he began the first of those travels which were to occupy most of the next six years: Italy; France, which he disliked; England, which he admired; and finally, Holland, where he fell fervidly in love with a married woman and attempted suicide after their separation. Returning to Italy, he set himself to a course of study and chanced upon a copy of Plutarch whose writings stirred

* äl fyä' rê

ALFIERI

in him bright ideals of liberty and independence. Six months later he restlessly took up traveling again—Germany, Denmark, and Sweden where the wildness of the countryside appealed to his romantic nature, then to Russia, and back to England. There an amorous involvement with a lady of rank terminated, following a duel with the lady's husband, in a grotesque fashion worthy of Ariosto's pen. Miserable and disillusioned, Alfieri continued his journeys through Holland, France, and Spain to Portugal where he formed a lasting friendship with Abbé di Caluso whom he styled "a living Montaigne."

In 1772 Alfieri's repatriation began. Purchasing a house in Turin, he settled down at the age of twenty-three to the idle life of a wealthy young aristocrat. Again he fell in love, but in 1775 he resolved to free himself from this third entanglement. Tied to a chair by his valet so that he could not escape, Alfieri found release in composition; the result was his first tragedy, *Cleopatra.* Followed by a short farce called *I Poeti,* it was produced in Turin in 1775 and well received.

Haunted now by the urge to become a great dramatic poet in Italian, Alfieri set himself rigorously to improving his knowledge of the language through study and travel in Tuscany. In order, furthermore, to lose his feudatory dependence, he "dispiedmontized" himself by transferring his property to his sister, the Countess Cumiana, reserving for himself an annuity. Idleness and dissipation gave way to a new sense of purpose. From 1777 when he was residing in Florence, Al-

19

fieri dated his fourth and final attachment—to the Countess of Albany, wife of Prince Charles Edward, Pretender to the English throne. Spurred to celebrate his lady as well as to dissipate his worries about her domestic problems, he began the writing of lyric poetry. The Countess moved to Rome where she succeeded in obtaining permission from the Pope to live apart from her husband; Alfieri discreetly followed her and continued to work feverishly at his writing.

His method of composition proceeded through three stages—"conceiving," which resulted in a précis; "setting out," which produced a prose version; and "versifying," which included not only the actual writing of the poetry but also the final polishing of the whole. By the age of thirty-two he had completed fourteen tragedies. In 1783 he arranged for the printing in Siena of the first volume, which included *Filippo, Polinice, Antigone,* and *Virginia.* This was followed by an additional pair of volumes (1783-85), containing the *Agamennone, Oreste, Rosmunda, Ottavia, Timoleone,* and *Merope,* which constituted his first publishing venture. He withheld four tragedies, largely through fear of a hostile reception. As the titles indicate, Alfieri did not rely on his immediate world but turned to legend and history for his tragic protagonists. His plays are short, involve few characters, and adhere strictly to the concept of the unities. The language is tense, nervous, abrupt. Benedetto Croce, in a severe judgment, styled it not poetry but passionate oratory.

Feeling at this time that a separation from his lady would be discreet, Alfieri traveled for sixteen months in Italy and England and then rejoined the Countess at Colmar in Alsace. Despite further uneasy separations and changes of residence, in 1787 he was able to arrange with Didot in Paris for a complete edition of his tragedies which now numbered nineteen and for the printing of his non-dramatic works at Kehl. In that year they also moved to Paris; in 1788 the Countess became a widow, and henceforth there was no need for separation. Fearful of the political turmoil, however, Alfieri arranged for their departure from Paris on August 17, 1792; vividly he recounts in his *Life* how they were stopped by an angry mob at the barrier and how he brandished his seven passports, shouting: "Alfieri is my name. I am Italian, not French; tall; thin; pallid face; red hair—that's my description."

With great relief Alfieri, together with the Countess, made his way back to Tuscany where he spent his last eleven years, studying Greek and trying to write the comedies for which his genius was ill-suited. Hatred of tyranny had been Alfieri's major passion and had motivated his hatred of the French and their "so-called republic." Ironically, he was to be revered by the Jacobins as the apostle of liberty.

In addition to his tragedies, Alfieri wrote many sonnets, epigrams, and a group of five grandiloquent odes entitled *America Libera;* additional works in prose and verse include the *Panegirico di Plinio a Traiano,* the *Satire,* two treatises *Della Tirannide* and *Del Principe e delle Lettere,* a satirical miscellany *Il Misogallo* (The Gallophobe) and the two parts of his *Vita* which, prompted by a realistic "self-love," detail his twenty-eight years of writing. Mme de Staël praised the patriotism and fervor of his writings; and shortly after his death the Countess of Albany arranged for a complete edition of his works (22 volumes) to be published in Pisa (1805-15).

The tragedies were translated by Charles Lloyd in 1815; the *Vita* in 1845 by C. Edwards Lester and by Sir Henry McAnally in 1953. In 1961 E. R. Vincent published a translation, *Memoirs.* A selection of his poetry is available in Lorna de' Lucchi's *Anthology of Italian Poems* (1924). The treatise *Of Tyranny* was translated by J. A. Molinaro and B. Corrigan (1961).

ABOUT: De Sanctis, F. The History of Italian Literature, II; Megaro, G. Vittorio Alfieri, Forerunner of Italian Nationalism; Miller, C. R. D. Alfieri: A Biography; Wilkins, E. H. History of Italian Literature; Modern Language Review, January 1946. [In Italian—see studies by V. Branca, M. Fubini, C. Jannaco, B. Maier.]

E. S. D.

*ALFONSO X, EL SABIO ("the Wise"), King of Castile and León (November 23, 1221-April 4, 1284), Spanish poet and royal patron of learning, was born in Toledo, the son of King Ferdinand the Saint and Beatrice of Suabia. By the age of sixteen he was taking active part in his father's wars against the Moors of southern Spain, the culmination of which was the conquest of Seville in 1248. After an affair with Doña Mayor Guillén de Guzmán, which produced a daughter who later married Alfonso III of Portugal, the prince in 1249 married Doña Violante of Aragon, daughter of James the Conqueror. Upon the death of his father in May 1252, Alfonso X began his politically indecisive but culturally brilliant reign.

Except for the kingdom of Granada, Spain was now wholly under Christian rule; hence

* äl fôn′ sō ĕl sä′ byō

relatively little of Alfonso's energies were devoted to continuing the Reconquest, or traditional war against the Moors. His main problems were to maintain royal authority against the now rebellious nobles of his realm and to establish the prestige of Castile throughout Western Christendom. His own brothers and sons led revolts against him; the question of succession, upon the death of his oldest son, himself the father of a son, was a serious cause of controversy. And this internal turbulence did not strengthen the hand of Alfonso in his ambitious foreign policy. Royal marriages confirmed alliances of Castile with Aragon, Portugal, and England. In the imperial elections of 1256 Alfonso was the leading contender for the title of Holy Roman Emperor, but Richard of Cornwall was proclaimed emperor and was so recognized by the Papacy; after twenty years, Alfonso succeeded in appealing personally to Gregory X, who persuaded him to abandon his imperial pretensions.

If Alfonso X was not a political success, he did win, deservedly, the title of "el Sabio" for his cultural enterprises. By giving substantial patronage and direction to the Archbishop of Toledo's school of translators, he was responsible for Castilian versions of important Arabic works on astronomy, astrology, chess, and magic. (*The Spanish Treatise on Chess Play,* translated by J. G. White, was published in two volumes in 1913.) Of more literary importance was *The Ladder of Mahomet,* the story of Mahomet's visions of Heaven and Hell under the guidance of the Angel Gabriel; this work, which may have contributed, directly or indirectly, to Dante's *Divine Comedy,* Alfonso X had translated first into Castilian and then, by Bonaventura of Siena, his notary, into French (*Livre de Leschiele Mahomet,* 1264). The king also commissioned the compiling of legal treatises, the most important of which is known as *Las Siete Partidas* (1256-65). These treatises were intended to supersede the traditional Germanic laws and customs of Spain, dating from Visigothic times; they are based upon Roman law (Justinian) and canon law (the Decretals) and have deeply influenced the laws of Spain and Spanish America (including Louisiana, where English translations were published in 1818). Finally, Alfonso's scholars produced two historical works: the *General Estoria,* a history of the world, completed as far as the birth of Christ, which was based on the Bible and on Latin and Arabic versions of the myths and histories of Egypt, Greece, and Rome; and the *Estoria de España* (or *Primera Crónica General*). a history of Spain

through the reign of Alfonso's father, Ferdinand III, which was based on the Latin chronicles of Lucas of Tuy and Rodrigo of Toledo and on Spanish epic poems, since lost.

How much of the above works was written by the king himself, it is impossible to say; he was certainly the general editor, supervising closely the work of his cosmopolitan team of scholars, Jews and Christians, Spaniards and Italians. He established the use of Castilian, instead of Latin, in Spanish science, law, history, and correspondence, even using it occasionally for diplomacy beyond the limits of the Iberian peninsula.

But for his most personal work of art, the *Cantigas de Santa María,* he used the Galician (Portuguese) dialect, already firmly established as the language of lyric poetry. This fascinating collection of 430 poems sings the praises of the Virgin and narrates her miracles, those known all over Europe as well as others of more local Spanish tradition, including a few recent ones involving the king himself. (English translations were published by Eleanor Hague, at Stanford University, in 1923 and 1929.) The four manuscripts in which these poems are preserved contain musical notation and beautiful miniatures representing the legends themselves, and the musicians, costumes, and customs of thirteenth century Spain.

Alfonso X died in the city of Seville; few monarchs have ever contributed so directly and substantially to letters, to the arts, and to the cultural establishment of a major modern language.

ABOUT: Ticknor, G. History of Spanish Literature; Procter, E. S. Alfonso X of Castile, Patron of Literature and Learning; Hispania, XLIV (1961). [In Spanish—see study by J. A. Sánchez Pérez.]

E. L. R.

*ALMEIDA GARRETT, JOÃO BAPTISTA DA SILVA LEITÃO DE (February 4, 1799-December 9, 1854), Portuguese poet, playwright, novelist, journalist, and orator, personified in his life as in his writings the passionately national and liberal phase of romanticism which Lord Byron inaugurated in England and Victor Hugo closed in France. Garrett represented all of liberal Portugal in his time: he lived in Oporto and Lisbon and on Terceira, the liberal stronghold in the Azores. Ties of family and friendship connected him with Brazil, whose intellectual independence he was the first Portuguese to welcome.

* äl mä′ ē thä går rĕt′

21

ALMEIDA GARRETT

ALMEIDA GARRETT

Garrett was born in Oporto, the second son of a customs inspector, António Bernardo da Silva, and Ana Augusta de Almeida Leitão, daughter of a "brasileiro," a Portuguese who had made a fortune in Brazil. The boy spent a happy childhood on the Quinta do Castelo near Oporto, among the ruins of a medieval castle. But when the French under Masséna invaded Portugal, the conservative family fled to Terceira, where they owned lands. Here Garrett received a classical training from his uncle, a bishop, who also steered the boy's early enthusiasm for poetry into calm neo-classical waters.

When he refused to become a priest, he was sent to Coimbra to study law (1816-21). At the university, he also discovered his two leading passions—politics and the stage. He combined both in support of the constitutionalist revolution of 1820. But he achieved real notoriety with a didactic poem on painting, the now forgotten *Retrato de Venus* of 1821. Tried for irreverence, he defended freedom of thought so well before a jury that he was acquitted and was publicly embraced by Correia da Serra, "the friend of Lafayette" (and of Jefferson). That same year he obtained a position in the Department of the Interior and married Luisa Midosi, a fifteen-year-old beauty.

When the reactionary Miguelistas triumphed in 1823 over the Constitutionalists, the young couple fled abroad. The Garretts found shelter with an English family in the Shakespeare country near Birmingham. The young poet's tastes underwent a radical change. He discovered the sources of romanticism in Shakespeare, the ballads, Scott, and Byron. He now wrote the works which introduced the romantic movement into Portugal, marked by enthusiasm for the common people and for the great medieval institutions, and dedicated to a genuinely national literature instead of pale imitations of antiquity. While extolling natural impulse, Garrett disliked extremes. "I am neither classic nor romantic," he declared in the 1825 preface to *Camões*, his first poem of national inspiration. "In my own behalf I say that I hold to no sect or party in poetry as in everything else; and so I let myself drift wherever my good or bad inspirations carry me. . . ." To this eclectic principle he adhered, undisturbed by its contradictions. In *Camões* he celebrated the man of genius fated to be exiled and abused by his countrymen and his prince—just like himself. Another theme from national history was treated lyrically in *Dona Branca* (1826), a kind of extended ballad about the conquest of southern Portugal from the Moors.

In 1826 the Garretts returned briefly to Portugal, where the poet became active as a journalist, was jailed, and once more, in 1828, fled to England and France. In jail he had completed *Adozinda* (1828), the first of many personal versions of old ballads. While the liberals were preparing an armed invasion from the Azores, the amazing Garrett found time to write simultaneously an epic, *O Magriço*, lost in a shipwreck, and the legislation destined to reshape Portuguese society. He and another young writer, his friend Alexandre Herculano, then participated in the siege of his home town Oporto (1832). During the siege he wrote a historical novel about an ostensibly medieval conflict between the city and its bishop, *O Arco de Santana* (revised and published in 2 volumes, 1845 and 1850). The victorious liberals sent him to Brussels as consul general (1834-36). After separation from Luisa, Garrett played the Don Juan. His later writings reflect the unconventional, cosmopolitan affairs with young Adelaide Deville, who died soon after she had borne him his only daughter, and with two mature, married women, the kindly Maria Krus and the capricious Andalusian Rosa Montufar, Viscountess Da Luz, his "cursed angel." The poems of the second part of *Flores sem Fruto* (completed 1843, published 1845) and in *Folhas Caídas* (written 1846-51, published 1853) confess these last passions with extraordinary frankness, while Adelaide lives on as the most appealing feminine figure in Portuguese literature, the dreamlike, green-eyed "girl of the nightingales" who appears in the whimsical, spontaneous *Viagens na minha Terra,* his best prose work (1846). The *Viagens* also contained his final political message of war on the robber barons, then headed by the finance minister Avila, who later aroused the hate of another great poet, Antero de Quental. This work crowned Garrett's most active years, between 1836 and 1846, when he shone as the best orator in parliament, organized a national theatre amid the worst political turmoil, and gave it a repertoire of four historical plays: *Un Auto de Gil Vicente* (1838), *O Alfageme de Santarém* (1842), *Dona Filipa de Vilhena* (1846), and *Frei Luís de Sousa* (1843), his one great tragedy, which combines the theme of the returning veteran who finds his wife remarried, with the national theme of independence from Spain and the personal theme of his daughter's illegitimacy.

When the "Regeneration" movement of Marshal Saldanha seized power, Garrett became Minister of Foreign Affairs for a few months in 1852. Then his health failed suddenly. Abandoned by all except his daughter and his faithful "Boswell," Gomes de Amorim, he died in Lisbon, aged fifty-five.

As a writer brilliantly combining action with reflection and politics with literature, Garrett had no rival save Francisco Manuel de Melo. His influence on Portuguese literature was incomparably greater than Melo's. It has lasted a century. He inspired the fluid, conversational prose of Camilo, Dinís, and Eça de Queiroz. The nationalistic *Neogarrettismo,* which poets promoted from 1890 on, led to António Nobre's and Teixeira de Pascoaes' cult of nostalgic *saudade* and to Fernando Pessoa's first poems in Portuguese in 1908.

In England Garrett's importance was recognized rather late. Although his hasty *Bosquejo da Poesia e Lingua Portuguesa* (1826) had been translated as early as 1829 by William M. Kinsey as a chapter of the latter's *Portugal Illustrated in a Series of Letters* (2d ed.), his great tragedy was rendered in English by Edgar Prestage only in 1909 as *Brother Luiz de Sousa.* Samples of Garrett's ballads were translated by John Adamson in vol. II of *Luisitania Illustrata* (1846), and of his other lyric poetry by A. F. G. Bell in *Studies in Portuguese Literature* (1914).

ABOUT: Bulletin of Hispanic Studies (1949); Lamb, N. J. The Romanticism of Almeida Garrett's "Viagens na minha Terra"; Prestage, E. J. B. Almeida Garrett, Brother Luiz de Sousa, a Study. [In Portuguese—See studies by T. Braga, C. Estorminho, F. de Figueiredo, F. Gomes de Amorim, J. O. de Oliveira, C. de A. Pereira. In French—Le Gentil, G. Almeida Garrett, un Grand Romantique Portugais. In German—Antscherl, O. J. B. de Almeida Garrett und seine Beziehungen zur Romantik.]

G. M. M.

*ALMQUIST, CARL JONAS LOVE

(November 28, 1793-September 26, 1866), Swedish novelist, short-story writer, poet, dramatist, was born and raised in Stockholm. His father was Carl Gustaf Almquist, farmer and quartermaster. His mother was Birgitta Louisa Gjörwell, daughter of Christoffer Gjörwell, a learned historian and librarian. The author claimed to have two souls, one "accountant soul" inherited from his father, and one "poetic soul," from his mother. He was a precocious youth and studied intensely. He also received indelible impressions from his father's farm north of Stockholm, which he later used in his stories. In 1815 he took his M.A. at the University of Uppsala and in 1822 he was appointed chancellery clerk in the Ministry of Church and Education. He was influenced by Rousseau's ideas and moved the next year to the province of Värmland to live an idealized peasant life. Here he married Anna Maria Andersdofter Lundström, earlier nursemaid at his father's farm. He returned to Stockholm where he served as teacher in secondary schools and published several textbooks on various subjects. After theological studies, he was ordained. He contributed to liberal newspapers, and during leave from his school work he visited Paris and London. His literary production was considered improper for a clergyman, and he was forced to resign from his position as a teacher. Now he led a peripatetic life, worried by matrimonial discords, financial anxieties, and an eye malady. Sued by a usurer for forgery and attempted poisoning, he fled in 1851 to America where he lived in various places under assumed names and where he seems to have married, although his first marriage had not been dissolved. In 1865 he returned to Europe and settled in Bremen, where he died.

During the earlier part of his literary career Almquist was an extreme romanticist, and most of his magnificent work *Törnrosens Bok* (The Book of the Wild Rose, 1825-35), on which he worked for more than a decade, is written in complete harmony with romantic principles. It consists of seven volumes including historical novels, *Hermitaget* (The Hermitage) and *Drottningens Juvelsmycke* (The Queen's Jewel), verse dramas such as *Ramido Marinesco* and *Signora Luna,* and the prose drama *Colombine.*

* ålm' kvĭst

ALMQUIST

After this literary feat, which made its author famous, Almquist left the romantic sphere of ideas and became a realist and social critic with liberal and radical tendencies. From 1838 to 1840 he added several new volumes to his principal work: the realistic novelettes *Kapellet* (The Chapel), *Skällnora Qvarn* (Skällnora Mill), and *Målaren* (The Painter), all describing the life of the common people, and the charming epistolary novel *Araminta May*. In 1840 he also published the first volume of a new series of *Törnrosens Bok*, in imperial octavo, which was continued in 1849-50. Included in this series are the witty satire on bureaucracy *Ormus och Ariman*, the epos *Arthurs Jagt* (Arthur's Hunting), and a collection of evocative lyrics with music, entitled *Songes*.

Almquist's classical story *Det Går An* (That's All Right), in which he advocates free union, caused heated debates in pamphlets and the press. In a series called "Folksrifter" (People's Books) are the optimistic novelettes *Grimstahamns Nybygge* (The Settlement at Grimstahamn) and *Ladugårdsarrendet* (The Cow-House Lease). The major part of Almquist's production during the 1840's consisted of novels, e.g., *Amalia Hillner* (1840) and *Tre Fruar i Småland* (Three Wives in Småland, 1842-43), which, however, are inferior in quality to his earlier prose stories.

In his treatise *Europeiska Missnöjets Grunder* (The Reasons for the European Dissatisfaction) he called for social reforms.

Almquist's novel *Gabrièle Mimanso* was published in 1846 in English translation by G. C. Hebbe,

and his stories—*Det Går An* as *Sara Videbeck* and *Kapellet* as *The Chapel*, 1919—by A. B. Benson. Two small poems in English translation are included in C. W. Stork's *Anthology of Swedish Lyrics*. A short extract from *Törnrosens Bok* and a poem are translated in Warner's *Library of the World's Best Literature*, I.

ABOUT: Howitt, W. and M. The Literature and Romance of Northern Europe, II. [In Swedish— see studies by K. W. Berg, R. G. Berg, O. Holmberg, A. T. Lysander, H. Olsson.]

A. J.

AMICIS. See DE AMICIS, EDMONDO

*AMIEL, HENRI FRÉDÉRIC (September 27, 1821-May 11, 1881), Swiss philosopher and diarist, was born in Geneva, of a prosperous French Protestant family which had fled to Switzerland for religious freedom in the seventeenth century. Both his father, a strong and domineering personality, and his mother died while Amiel was still a boy. He was separated from his two sisters, who were sent to a boarding school, and was raised by his uncle, Frédéric Amiel. The young orphan was given every advantage of education and travel. He studied at the Academy of Geneva under the German philologist Adolphe Piquet. He spent a year in Italy in 1841, and a long period in France in 1842. From 1844 to 1848 he studied at the University of Berlin. His education completed, he returned to Geneva and was promptly appointed professor of aesthetics at the Academy (later to become the University of Geneva). In 1854 he became professor of philosophy. All this was an auspicious beginning to a career which all of Amiel's friends expected would be a brilliant one. Instead, Amiel produced almost nothing—a few critical essays, a few volumes of undistinguished verse (*Grains de Mil*, 1854; *Poèmes*, 1863; *Jour à Jour*, 1880). He remained at his teaching post all his life, never married (although he had a love affair, as revealed in his *Journal Intime*, with a woman he calls Philine), died after a long period of ill health at fifty-nine, and was buried in the cemetery of Clarens, east of Lake Geneva. His friend the French journalist and critic Edmond Schérer expressed the disappointment of all who knew him: "He awakened in us but one regret; we could not understand how it was a man so richly gifted produced nothing, or only trivialities."

In 1882 Schérer and another friend of Amiel's, Fanny Mercier, published a selection of passages from the 173 notebooks (some 16,900 manuscript pages) of a journal which

* à myĕl'

Amiel had kept from 1847 to the time of his death. This book, *Fragments d'un Journal Intime,* was so successful that a second volume appeared in 1884. These volumes established Amiel's reputation as a writer of fine, sensitive prose, a penetrating analyst of the emotions, and a striking example of the "alienated" intellectual, the spectator who sits reflectively on the sidelines of life, observing but never acting. "Practical life makes me afraid," Amiel confessed in his *Journal.* "My privilege is to be the spectator of my own life drama." He wrote candidly of his "literary sterility"—"I am afraid of greatness. I am not afraid of ingenuity; all my published literary essays are little else than studies, games, exercises, for the purpose of testing myself. I play scales as it were. . . . But the work remains unachieved. I am always preparing and never accomplishing, and my energy is swallowed up in a kind of barren curiosity."

The *Journal,* for all its isolation from active life, immediately caught the sympathies of its late nineteenth century readers, for in his melancholy soul-searching, Amiel mirrored the spiritual fears and yearnings of his generation. Modern readers find the *Journal* exquisite in style but thin in intellectual content; but to Amiel's contemporaries he was—as John Middleton Murry remarks—"a microcosm of the moral effort and moral perturbation of a century in which moral effort and perturbation reached a climax." Some critics, Matthew Arnold in particular, found fault with it: "In reading it we are not so much pursuing a study of psychology as a study of mental pathology." Arnold nevertheless admired the *Journal* for Amiel's perceptive and original literary and social criticism—"in general well informed, just, and penetrating in an eminent degree." To most readers of its time, the *Journal* was a profoundly moving book. Mrs. Humphry Ward wrote: "His book is representative of human experience in its more intimate and personal forms to an extent hardly equaled since Rousseau."

The first English translation of Amiel's *Journal* was made by Mrs. Humphry Ward in 1885 and has gone into many editions; in 1935 Van Wyck and Charles Van Wyck Brooks published a new translation. In 1930 Van Wyck Brooks translated excerpts from the unpublished Journal under the title *Philine.* Brooks has also translated Amiel's essay on Rousseau (1922).

ABOUT: Arnold, M. Essays in Criticism: Second Series; Brooks, V. W. Malady of the Ideal; Collins, J. The Doctor Looks at Literature; Columbia Dictionary of Modern European Literature; Cournos, J. Modern Plutarch; De Casseres, B. Forty Immortals; Hutton, R. H. Brief Literary Criticisms; Murry, J. M. Countries of the Mind: First Series; Pater, W. Essays from "The Guar-

dian"; Ward, Mrs. H. *Introduction to* Amiel's Journal. [In French—see studies by L. Bopp, A. Thebaudet, P. Bourget.]

*AMYOT, JACQUES (October 29, 1513-February 7, 1593), French translator, was born in Melun, son of Nicolas Amyot, a tanner or a butcher, and his second wife, Marie Lamour. Although his parents were very poor, he received a good education. At fifteen he was sent to Paris to study at the *collège* of the Cardinal Lemoine. He learned Greek under the early humanists Pierre Danès and Jacques Toussaint. Coming under the patronage of Marguerite of Navarre, sister of Francis I, Amyot received a pension which enabled him to continue his studies. In about 1535 he was at the University of Bourges studying civil law. Soon after, he attained a chair at the university and taught Greek and Latin. In 1554, through the influence of his friends at court, he became tutor to the young sons of Henri II and Catherine de' Medici. These pupils later became the rulers of France, Charles IX and Henry III.

Amyot's major literary achievement was his translation from the Greek into French of Plutarch's *Parallel Lives.* This vast undertaking was commissioned by Francis I in 1542, and was published in Paris, after seventeen years of work by Amyot, in 1559. Its significance in literary history can scarcely be overestimated. To the classics-hungry readers of the French Renaissance, it opened a new world. Translated into English by Sir Thomas North in 1579, it became Shakespeare's primary source for his Greek and Roman plays. In itself Amyot's translation was an excellent one, thorough, scholarly, and a model of simplicity and purity of style. His slightly younger contemporary Michel de Montaigne considered it a masterpiece: "I find throughout his translation so beautiful, so well-connected and sustained a meaning, that certainly he has either fathomed the real thoughts of the author, or, having by such long intercourse with him, deeply implanted in his mind a general idea of Plutarch's mind, he has at least attributed to him nothing that belies or contradicts him."

Amyot also translated from the Greek the romances *Theagenes and Chariclea* of Meliodorus (1546) and the famous *Daphnis and Chloe* of Longus (1559). In 1572 he published a translation of Plutarch's *Morals.* In the course of his work as a translator, he spent four years in Italy searching for manu-

* à myō'

scripts. His discoveries there included manuscripts of the *Aethiopian History* of Heliodorus and the *Lives* of Diodorus Siculus (which he translated in part in 1554).

Amyot enjoyed many favors at court. He represented Henri II at the Council of Trent. In 1560 he became grand almoner of France, and in 1570 he was made bishop of Auxerre. His last years, however, were clouded by political persecution as a result of the religious wars of the period. He died, stripped of most of his honors and offices, in his eightieth year and was buried in the cathedral of Auxerre. A Christian, a humanist, a theologian, and a preacher, Amyot combined the finest qualities of the great age of the French Renaissance which his life spanned. In 1913 the town of Melun celebrated the 400th anniversary of his birth with ceremonies honoring his memory.

ABOUT: Wyndham, G. Essays in Romantic Literature; Renaissance News, X (1957). [In French —see studies by A. Cioranescu, R. Sturel.]

ANDERSEN

ANDERSEN, HANS CHRISTIAN

(April 2, 1805-August 4, 1875), fairy tale writer and novelist, was born in Odense, a small town on the island of Fyen (Funen), Denmark. All his life he retained some of the oversensitivity, emotionalism, vanity, and naïveté of his childhood.

His father was a frail young man, a bad cobbler with his head stuffed full of frustrated dreams; his mother hardworking, loving, but ignorant and superstitious. In later life, worn out, she became a drunkard and finally had to be institutionalized. His paternal grandfather was a harmless lunatic, a well known figure in the town. Both parents adored the child, spoiled him, played with him like children themselves. When he was eight his father died, leaving nothing.

The boy's great passion was the theatre; he wanted to be an actor, a dancer, a singer (he did have a clear sweet voice as a child) —failing that, a writer for the theatre. He loved to declaim, to recite, to anybody and everybody, but in the poor little schools to which he was sent he was the worst of scholars. Filled with a vague consciousness of genius, he felt the prosaic job of learning reading, writing, and arithmetic not worth his trouble. Then he left school altogether, built himself a little theatre, and set about writing grotesquely formless if highly imaginative "plays" for it.

His mother apprenticed him to a weaver, then to a tobacco factory; he fled from both places in horror of the rough jokes and teasing of the other workers. The mother had married another shoemaker, a lazy man who let her support the family by washing.

On his own at fourteen, practically penniless, dressed in shabby rags, Andersen set out for Copenhagen to conquer the world of the theatre. He was turned away at every door, laughed at, considered insane; he almost starved, but he would not give up. With his utter lack of self-consciousness he did manage to penetrate to the homes of the great; and finally his singing won him a patron, the director of the Theatre Music School, who took him as a pupil and gave him an allowance. But his voice failed. Then he was admitted to the Ballet School. Through his new friends a petition was sent to King Frederik VI for a grant, but the petition was denied.

He was saved by the interest of Jonas Collin, director of the Royal Theatre, who became a substitute father for him. But to his dismay Collin insisted that he must go back to school. So for five long years, from 1822 to 1827, Hans Christian Andersen sat with children on the benches of the grammar school at Slagelse. He was a backward pupil, and the school principal was jealous of his great connections in Copenhagen and made his life a torment.

He had already written two plays which were promptly returned to him. But before he went to school, at seventeen, he published (by subscription) his first story, "The Ghost at Palnatoke's Grave." It was not a fairy tale.

Back in Copenhagen at last, still under Collin's protection, a man of twenty-two but still a child who burst into tears at the slightest impetus and was subject to wild exhilaration and wilder despair, Andersen at last began to think of a professional writing career. His strange book of observations and reflections called "A Journey on Foot from Holmen's Canal to the East Point of Amager" (in other words, through the streets of Copenhagen) excited some comment but made no profit; neither did his first volume of poems. But in 1833, on a traveling stipend from the king, he set out on a sixteen-month journey to Germany, France, Switzerland, and Italy. During it he wrote a long poem, "Agnete and the Merman," and his first novel, "The Improvisatore," really autobiographical but transferred in setting and characters to Italy.

Back in Copenhagen in 1835, waiting for the novel to appear, Andersen wrote and published a catchpenny pamphlet to keep his rent paid. It contained four fairy tales for children.

It must be remembered that for most of his life Hans Christian Andersen thought of himself as a playwright and a novelist, and as a writer of travel books. Until the whole Western world hailed him as the greatest teller of fairy tales of all time, he refused to take these books seriously. "Really," he said, "I should drop these trifles and concentrate on my own work."

Neither was he the gentle sentimental child-lover of tradition. He preferred older children to young ones, and he would never have tolerated babies crawling on his knees as he read his stories—his readings were ordered rituals. He would rather have read his plays or poems in any event—and some at least of his poems are beautifully simple and heartfelt lyrics. Another thing that must be kept in mind is that the reputation of the fairy tales spread much faster outside than inside Denmark, and that in fact until past middle age Andersen was much more famous, courted, and honored abroad than at home. When at last he did win the adulation of his countrymen, however, it was forever. In 1867 the town of Odense turned itself inside out to do honor to the poor cobbler's son. By that time he was a State Councillor, the friend and guest of royalty and nobility, the holder of foreign honors—yet still at heart an overgrown, awkward boy who never quite understood the world, or the world him. One of the loveliest tributes paid him is the statue of the Little Mermaid who sits now in Copenhagen harbor surveying the busy scene with plaintive grace.

Through the years between 1835 and 1867 he had published other novels, travel books, poems, plays, an autobiography. But the celebration in Odense was in recognition of the writer of the fairy tales. Volume after volume of them poured out — 1836, 1837, 1838, 1845, 1847, 1848, until the last in 1872 —168 stories in all, and from the beginning they were translated immediately into every European language. In English, his first translator was Mary Howitt.

But Andersen has been unlucky in his translators—he had no distinguished ones in English until Jean Hersholt and particularly R. P. Keigwin, in our own time. The tales have been made syrupy, mawkish, whereas they were, as Rumer Godden says, characterized by "economy and strength, . . . witty, ironical. . . . [His style] can be intensely poignant and poetical, [but] it is always crisp." And the stories are not all sweet; some are painful and tragic, some cruel and horrible. They are in essence *real* fairy tales —that is to say, bits of the mythology of prehistoric man. (Or, as in "The Little Match Girl," realistic fantasies of the life of the poor from whom Andersen came.)

So far as Andersen's personal history goes, there is little to tell of him after he became a successful author. He lived in one house after another in Copenhagen, or made long visits in the mansions of the rich and great who became his friends. For decades he dined with a different friend regularly on each day of the week. He traveled a great deal, including two long trips to England and Scotland. He never married.

In 1872 he had a bad fall, and never was well again. He failed gradually, and finally died peacefully in the country home of friends.

All of Andersen's major works have been translated into English, the fairy tales many times over. Elias Bredsdorff has to devote an entire supplement to Andersen in his "Danish Literature in English Translation." Mary Howitt's first translations appeared in 1845. The best modern translations of the fairy tales are those of Jean Hersholt (whose great collection of Anderseniana was bequeathed to the Library of Congress)—the final edition in 1949 containing all the fairy tales, including some never before translated and some never published even in Danish—and of R. P. Keigwin, in 1950; Keigwin's translations have the flavor of Andersen's Danish, even to the use of colloquialisms and slang.

The earliest English translations of his novels and other writing for adults are *The Improvisatore* by Mary Howitt (1845); *Only a Fiddler* also by Mary Howitt (1845); *A Poet's Bazaar*, translator unnamed (1846); *The Two Baronesses* by Charles

B. Lohmeyer (1848); *To Be or Not to Be?* by Mrs. Bushby (1857); *Rambles in . . . the Hartz Mountains, Saxon Switzerland, etc.* by Charles Beckwith (1848); *Pictures of Sweden* by Charles B. Lohmeyer (1851); *In Spain* by Mrs. Bushby (1864); *The True Story of My Life* by Mary Howitt (1847); *Correspondence* edited by F. Crawford (1891); *The Andersen-Scudder Letters* edited by J. Hersholt and W. Waldemaar (1949). Ten volumes of *Collected Works* appeared in English in 1869-71.

ABOUT: Andersen, H. C. The Story of My Life; Bain, R. N. Hans Christian Andersen; Böök, F. H. C. Andersen, a Biography; Bredsdorff, E. Hans Andersen and Charles Dickens; Godden, R. Hans Christian Andersen; Lynd, R. Essays on Life and Literature; Manning-Sanders, R. Swan of Denmark; Meynell, E. H. M. The Story of Hans Andersen; Reumert, E. (trans. Bröchner, J.) Hans Andersen the Man; Toksvig, S. The Life of Hans Christian Andersen.

M. A. DE F.

*ANDRÉ LE CHAPELAIN (ANDREAS CAPELLANUS),

twelfth century author of the Latin tract *De Amore,* is known only by the survival of this remarkable document of medieval courtly love. Of his biography nothing is recorded except that he was at one time chaplain of Louis VII of France and that during the period 1170 to 1174 he was at the court of Louis' former wife Eleanor of Aquitaine at Poitiers and of their daughter Marie, Countess of Champagne. These royal ladies established around themselves a veritable academy of sophisticated courtiers — nobles, poets and troubadours, artists, ecclesiastics. Most probably at Marie's suggestion, André undertook to write a code of manners for this circle, one that would civilize and refine the essential crudities of feudal life.

Just how seriously his *De Amore* was meant to be taken is a matter of disagreement among scholars. André's model was the satirical *Ars Amatoria* of Ovid. Like its predecessor, André's book is "frankly erotic" and "a handbook of seduction." It is addressed to a young man named Walter, "a new recruit of Love," and discourses with precision and detail on matters pertaining to love and the behavior of lovers. The theory of courtly love which the book purports to treat is a glorification of woman—the object of the lover being an ideal constantly sought and reverenced but never attained. *De Amore,* on the other hand, treats of love in the most downright sensual sense. Scholars today argue that its loftier sentiments—where they appear—are meant ironically; or, if not, that they simply express the glaring inconsisten-

* än drä' lĕ shà plăn'

cies of the age in which ascetic Christianity existed side-by-side with feudal brutality. André, himself a clerk, boasts that the clergy make the best lovers. "The picture we get of Andreas," J. J. Parry writes, "is that of a man who is connected with the Church, but for whom spiritual affairs are not the first consideration."

De Amore begins with a general discussion of love, then proceeds to a series of illustrative dialogues between men and women of the different social orders. It includes a chapter on the love of the clergy and specific advice on behavior with women—with peasant women, André advises Walter, "do not hesitate to take what you seek"; but he cautions Walter to avoid prostitutes. The second book gives some case histories of love problems discussed in Eleanor's court, showing how the noble ladies passed judgment upon them. It also contains the celebrated thirty-one "Rules of Love"—among them "Marriage is no real excuse for not loving"; "None should be deprived of love without the very best of reasons"; and "Love is always a stranger in the heart of avarice." The third book of *De Amore* contains an extraordinary "about-face," a retraction in which André urges Walter to refrain from doing everything he has advised and speaks a passionate tirade against women.

The number of extant manuscripts of André's book indicates its great popularity. It was translated into French around 1290 and soon after into Italian, Spanish, and German. No English translation appeared, however, until J. J. Parry published one under the title *The Art of Courtly Love* in 1941.

ABOUT: Kelly, A. Eleanor of Aquitaine; Parry, J. J. Introduction to The Art of Courtly Love; Modern Philology, L (1953); Speculum, XVII (1942); Studies in Philology, LIX (1962); Valency, M. In Praise of Love.

*ANDREÄ, JOHANN VALENTIN

(August 17, 1586-June 27, 1654), German poet and theologian, was born in Herrenberg, grandson of the Lutheran theologian Jakob Andreä, and son of Johann Andreä, at one time abbot of Königsbrunn. His mother was Maria Moser, who moved to Tübingen with her six children after her husband died in 1601. Andreä was early interested in painting and music, and he was well versed in languages. In Tübingen, while studying mathematics and Latin history and literature, he helped his financially harassed mother by tutoring his schoolmates. In 1603 he received the baccalaureate and two years later his master's degree. As early as 1602, at the age

* än drä' â

of sixteen, Andreä wrote two comedies, *Esther* and *Hyazinth,* both modeled after English examples. Of the same time, but not published until 1616, was *Chymische Hochzeit Christiani Rosencreuz anno 1459,* an adventurous and fantastic piece. Andreä began his theological studies quite early but he left Tübingen in 1607, allegedly because of a venereal ailment, and traveled for some time. In 1610 he was in Geneva where he met and was impressed with Calvin; he also visited Lyon, Paris, Rome, and Venice. Returning to Tübingen and taking up his theological studies again, he became deacon in 1614, the year in which he also married. The period from 1614 until 1620 brought about a change in him; he turned more and more into a propagator of practically applied Christian love. His important works, of which the titles are often indicative of their content, were written in this period: *Summa Doctrinae Christianae, Collectanea Mathematica, Kämpfe des Christlichen Hercules, Christenburg* (a didactic poem presenting the history of the church and the Christian in the world as the history of a beleaguered city), *Turbo* (a comedy criticizing those who steep themselves in learning but have no eye for the needs of the time), *Menippus Inanitatum Nostratuum Speculum* (100 dialogues full of satire directed against learned activities) *Peregrini Errores* (depicting those who live only for this world), *Civis Christianus, Inmitatio Fraternitates Christi ad Sacri Amoris Candidatos, Christianopolis* (the idealization of Andreä's conception of a Christian model state, influenced by Thomas More's *Utopia;* it was translated into English by F. E. Held in 1916), *Christianae Societatis Idea,* and *Christiani Amoris Dextera Porrecta,* in which the reader is called upon to attempt living according to the ideals of Christianity.

In 1620 Andreä became superintendent in Calw. Between the years 1639 and 1650 he was court chaplain in Württemberg. Endeavoring to realize his ideal of neighborly love, he met with many disappointments in his career, even though he had the unabating support of the Duke of Brunswick. In 1641 he became doctor of theology, in 1650 abbot of Bebenhausen. Realizing that his many sermons did not bring him closer to the fulfillment of his ideals, he left the court at Stuttgart. Joining the Fruchtbringende Gesellschaft, he busied himself with the purification of the German language. He died in Stuttgart at sixty-seven.

ABOUT: [In German—see studies by W. Stammler, P. Wurm.]

H. B.

ANDREAS CAPELLANUS. See ANDRÉ LE CHAPELAIN

*ANGELUS SILESIUS (1624-1677) is the religious name of Johannes Scheffler, the son of a Polish nobleman, who was born in Breslau, the capital of Silesia. He studied medicine and philosophy at the universities of Strasbourg and Leiden. There he came under the influence of the great German mystics Meister Eckhart, Jacob Böhme, and Abraham von Franckenberg. To the surprise of his friends he gave up a position as a personal physician to the strictly Protestant Duke of Württemberg in order to join the Catholic Church in 1652. In baptism he adopted the name Angelus Silesius, under which he published his poetic and theological writings. After some years of service as physician to the Hapsburg emperor Ferdinand III, he was ordained a priest in 1661. From then on he was a fanatic propagandist of the Catholic counter-reformation and as such the target of the most vitriolic attacks from the Lutheran pamphleteers. He died, worn out by the violence of the religious controversy, at fifty-three.

The fame of Angelus Silesius as a poet rests chiefly on two works, which, though originating from approximately the same period of his life, have little in common. The *Heilige Seelenlust oder Geistliche Lieder der in ihren Jesus Verliebten Seele* is a collection of religious songs, to be used in community singing, published together with the music. It was an attempt to lead German Christendom out of the emotional wasteland into which the stiffening dogmatism of the Lutheran Church was forcing her followers. Against the exclusive Lutheran concept of justification through faith Angelus Silesius proclaimed justification through love as the first condition of redemption. The most striking feature of these hymns is the unrestrained use of baroque erotic language in the expression of religious feeling. The soul, in passionate love with her seducer Jesus, indulges in those very terms in which sensual passion voices its insatiable desire for ever repeated physical union. Though the orthodox Protestant Church looked with horror at the seeming sensuality of these hymns, many of them found their way into the hymnals of the Lutheran and other non-Catholic denominations and some of them are sung in their services up to this day.

Nowadays Angelus Silesius is chiefly remembered as the author of *Der Cherubinische*

* ăn' jĕ lŭs sĭ lē' shĭ ŭs

Wandersmann. Since this book in rhymed Alexandrine couplets was rediscovered by the German romanticists, it has influenced German literature to a degree unparalleled by any other work of religious character. The audacity of its views on the relationship between God and man is so much at variance with the content of Angelus Silesius' theological writings in defense of Catholic dogma that some scholars have doubted the identity of the poet Angelus Silesius and the theologian of the same name. In his identification of the created with the creator, Angelus Silesius goes even farther than philosophic pantheism, for he allows the soul, who experiences this identity in various degrees, to reach a state in which she feels God's complete dependence on her existence.

The originality of Angelus Silesius' pronouncements on the mystery of human existence has impressed and influenced such widely divergent poets as the devout Catholic Annette von Droste-Hülshoff and the confessed agnostic Gottfried Keller.

In 1909 there appeared a selective English translation of the *Cherubinischer Wandersmann* by Paul Carus under the title *A Selection from the Rhymes of a German Mystic.* Another volume of *Selections from the Cherubinic Wanderer,* translated by I. E. Crawford Flitch, was published in 1932. Julia Bilger offered still another selection, as *Alexandrines,* in 1944. Translations of several of Angelus Silesius' poems appear in George C. Schoolfield's *The German Baroque Lyric in English Translation* (1962).

From the *Heilige Seelenlust* the following hymns can be found in English translations in the hymnals of Protestant churches: "Thee Will I Love, My Strength, My Tower"; "O Love Who Formedst Me to Wear"; "Earth Hath Nothing Sweet or Fair."

ABOUT: Flitch, J. E. C. *Introduction to* Angelus Silesius; Goldecker, M. H. Angelus Silesius' Personality through His Ecclesiolagia. [In German— Ellinger, G. Angelus Silesius, Ein Lebensbild; Nigg, W. Angelus Silesius.]

F. R.

ANNA COMNENA. See COMNENA, ANNA

ANNENSKY, INNOKENTY FYODOROVICH (1856-1909), Russian poet, was born in Omsk, Siberia, the son of an important government official. He was educated in St. Petersburg, took a degree in classics, and planned to become a university professor. He gave up his advanced studies, however, to teach classical languages in a *Gymnasium.* A successful teacher and administrator, Annensky rose to be headmaster of the *Gymnasium* at Tsarskoye Selo and later a district director of the Russian secondary schools. Beginning in the 1880's he regularly contributed reviews and articles to the literary and scholarly journals. In the 1890's he began work on his translations and adaptations of the plays of Euripides. His versions of the tragedies were of only limited literary value, but they succeeded in their purpose of popularizing and modernizing the Greek tragedies.

Annensky is chiefly remembered for his small but interesting and significant collection of verse. In the course of his life he published only one volume—*Quiet Songs* (1904)—under the pseudonym of "Nik. T. O." standing for the Russian *nikto,* meaning "nobody." In 1910 *The Cypress Chest* was published posthumously. It was not until shortly before his death that Annensky received any recognition as a poet. He was then lionized in St. Petersburg literary circles, and his influence continued long after his death. The contemporary Russian poet and novelist Boris Pasternak was much in his debt.

Annensky was a symbolist. His masters were the French poets Baudelaire, Verlaine, Mallarmé, but he was not an imitator. His verse is compact, spare, difficult, but not obscure. "His poems are constructed with disconcerting and baffling subtleness and precision," D. S. Mirsky wrote. "Few readers . . . feel themselves capable of the creative effort required. But the work is worth the while."

Among Annensky's other literary works are two volumes of critical essays, some tragedies modeled upon the ancient Greek, and some translations from Horace. He died of heart failure in St. Petersburg at fifty-three. His writing is apparently regarded with favor in the Soviet Union and editions of his poems appeared in 1923, 1939, and 1959.

The Russian editions have not been translated into English, but selections from Annensky's work may be found in C. M. Bowra's *A Book of Russian Verse* (1943) and a *Second Book of Russian Verse* (1948).

ABOUT: Columbia Dictionary of Modern European Literature; Mirsky, D. S. A History of Russian Literature; Setchkarev, V. Studies in the Life and Work of Annenskij.

ANNUNZIO, GABRIELE D'. See "TWENTIETH CENTURY AUTHORS"

AN-SKI, SH. See RAPPOPORT, SOLOMON

ANTON ULRICH, DUKE OF BRUNS-WICK (October 4, 1633-March 27, 1714), German prince, poet, and novelist, was born at Hitzacker on the Elbe in Lower Saxony. In brilliance and range of activity he is exceptional, even for an age when versatility, or at least variety, was commonplace. This was partly a matter of inheritance—he was the scion of one of the more substantial ruling families of the Holy Roman Empire, the house of Braunschweig-Lüneburg-Wolfenbüttel. His elder brother Rudolf August appointed him his principal administrator in 1667 and made him co-regent in 1685. He remained co-regent until the Emperor himself deposed him, for an excess of military and political ambition, in 1702. In 1704, however, his brother died, and Anton Ulrich became sole ruler of the dukedom. In this eminence he could engage in the untrammeled exercise of his many talents—at least as far as his resources permitted.

Anton Ulrich did virtually everything on a large scale. In love of display he is often compared to his contemporary Louis XIV, who had more money but no more fertile imagination in disbursing it. The Duke of Brunswick is one of the prime creators of that paradox of the Baroque Age, artistic and architectural splendor rising almost without interruption or visible reason out of the wastes of the Thirty Years War. In 1659, as a member of the Fruchtbringende Gesellschaft (a literary-linguistic-pastoral society after the manner of the time), he already bore the name "Der Siegprangende" (he who is splendid in victory). Fortunately his love of display was not restricted to public monuments. He was an enthusiastic patron of the arts and sciences, the principal benefactor of the library at Wolfenbüttel (where Lessing later worked as librarian). He established what is said to be the first permanent theatre in Germany. He also sponsored the Shakespearean plays and other performances of the English Actors, one of the important "cultural exchange" phenomena of early modern times.

The Duke was not only a patron of the arts but an active contributor—in a style largely determined by contemporary fashion, but on a scale almost as generous as his public works. He wrote two immense novels, one of five volumes, the other of six. They were extremely popular, so much so that a condensation of the first one, still in three volumes, appeared a century later. In this story, *Die Durchleuchtige Syrerin Aramena*

(Aramena, the Illustrious Syrian Princess, 1669-1680), and in the other, *Die Römische Oktavia* (The Roman Octavia, 1677), the Duke allowed himself the greatest latitude in matters of structure. The novels move at a leisurely pace through labyrinthine plots. They are filled with allusions, now hopelessly obscure, to happenings in court society, but also with the Duke's reflections on politics, social problems, and nature.

In addition to these substantial prose works, Anton Ulrich wrote sixty-one religious poems, collected under the curious title of *Christ-Fürstliches Davids Harfenspiel* (Christian Prince David's Harp, 1667) and set to music by his stepmother, Sophia Elisabeth of Mecklenburg. Many have been anthologized. Earlier he was partial to the composing of operettas for performance at his elegant court.

Religious concerns occupied the Duke's mind extensively during his later years. In 1709 he turned Catholic. He had previously secured the conversion of his granddaughter and arranged her marriage to the Spanish Pretender, later Emperor Charles VI of the Holy Roman Empire. His own conversion he first kept secret. In 1710, however, he made a public avowal of faith and issued a justification called *Fifty Motives*. Liberal in every sense—and in this far ahead of his time—Anton Ulrich saw to the guarantee of strict religious freedom for his subjects. Earlier he had corresponded extensively with the philosopher Leibniz on the possibility of church union.

Selections from his poetry appear in English in *Hymns from the German* (London, 1864, 1890); *Lyra Germanica* (London, New York, 1855, etc.); A. Gilman, *Library of Religious Poetry* (London, 1881); and C. Winkworth, *Christian Singers of Germany* (London, 1869). A translation of one of Anton Ulrich's poems, "Sterblied" ("Dying Song") appears in George C. Schoolfield's *The German Baroque Lyric in English Translation* (1962).

ABOUT: Journal of English and Germanic Philology, LVII (1958). [In German—Sonnenburg, F. Herzog Anton Ulrich von Braunschweig als Dichter; Zeitschrift für Deutsche Philologie LXXVIII (1959).]

F. G. R.

*ANZENGRUBER, LUDWIG (November 29, 1839-December 10, 1889), Austrian dramatist, novelist, and short-story writer, was born in Vienna. His father, Johann Anzengruber, deriving from an Austrian peasant background, was an underpaid government clerk, who devoted his leisure time

* än' tsĕn grōō bĕr

ANZENGRUBER

through all of his works, often to their detriment. He called himself a servant of truth, and throughout life he combatted narrowmindedness, prejudice, and ignorance. Influenced by the philosopher Feuerbach, he believed that one should depict and draw one's conclusions from the world as it is, a belief which accounts for the strict verity of his work. He chose the form of the peasant play because this was the stratum of society he knew best and because he felt that for his tendentious purpose, the simpler life of the village afforded greater clarity of characterization and motivation. He does not sentimentalize or idealize his peasants as did his predecessor and model Berthold Auerbach, but depicts them with honest realism. His greatness lies in the accuracy and psychological depth of his ability to elevate the issues of country life to the artistic level of high comedy and tragedy.

Der Pfarrer von Kirchfeld was an attack on intolerance and narrow ecclesiasticism, and the play owed much of its initial popularity to the timeliness of its subject; for the *Kulturkampf* in Germany, the proclamation of the dogma of infallibility, and the repeal of the "Concordat" in Austria, separating church and state, had awakened widespread interest in questions of tolerance and religious doubts. Anzengruber here, as in later works, struck boldly at the heart of the matter, and for his portrayal of the martyrdom of an enlightened priest, he earned the lasting hostility of the church. The vigorous tone, the serious purpose, and the sure dramatic sense of this first successful play revealed Anzengruber as a vital and gifted dramatist. His great talent was confirmed by his next drama, *Der Meineidbauer* (1871), a masterpiece in both plot and character drawing. This tragedy of a peasant, who, after perjuring himself to gain wealth, attempts to circumvent his final religious confession by educating his son to the clergy, has found lasting popularity.

Anzengruber's gifts were equally great in a lighter vein as evidenced by *Die Kreuzelschreiber* (1872), *Der Gesissenswurm* (1874), and *Der Doppelselbstmord* (1876). Because they are written in dialect, these masterly comedies have never fully found the appreciation outside of Austria that they deserve. Only *Das Vierte Gebot* (1878), a somewhat gloomy tragedy of Viennese life, sermonizing that parents must prove themselves worthy of the respect of their children, gained favor in Berlin. In technique and theme this drama unintentionally antici-

to writing plays and poetry. After overwork had led to his father's early death in 1844, Anzengruber's mother, Marie, a resolute woman from the Viennese lower middle class, worked to put her son through school, but lack of funds when her health failed forced him at the age of sixteen to accept a position as book seller. In 1860 he became an actor in a traveling company, and for the next six years, accompanied by his mother, he toured the Austrian Empire, gaining a valuable first-hand knowledge of the stage and becoming acquainted with many of the types of character he later portrayed in his dramas. During these years he wrote folk dramas, for which he could not find a stage, and many short prose works which he sold for little compensation to newspapers and magazines. These were years of hardship and often dire poverty, until he accepted a clerkship at the Vienna police headquarters in 1866 in order to enjoy at least a modicum of security. The great success of *Der Pfarrer von Kirchfeld* (1870) enabled him to leave this position to devote himself entirely to writing. In the following nineteen years he produced twenty dramas, two novels, and a large number of short stories, tales, and sketches.

Anzengruber's art was motivated by the highest ethical aims. He believed that the issues of the day should be discussed from the stage, and since no one else was forthcoming, he undertook the responsibility himself. It was his ambition to be a true teacher of the people, and a strong didactic vein runs

pated the trend toward naturalism in the theatre, which became prevalent in Berlin in the 1890's. However, Anzengruber, the outstanding dramatist of his day, must be considered the culmination of the tradition of the Viennese folk drama rather than the beginning of the modern era.

After 1878, the year in which he was awarded the Schiller prize, Anzengruber turned increasingly to prose. He produced two novels of lasting value, *Der Schandfleck* (1876) and *Der Sternsteinhof* (1883-84), as well as a significant collection of short stories, *Wolken und Sonnenschein* (1888). His last years, which he spent writing calendar stories and editing the magazines *Die Heimat* (1882-85) and *Figaro* (1885-89), were clouded by unhappiness. His mother, in whom, as he said, he had found his allotted measure of love on earth, died in 1873, and his marriage the same year to Adelina Lipka proved so unfortunate that he finally felt it necessary to divorce her in 1889, the year of his death.

Das Vierte Gebot was translated into English as *The Fourth Commandment* by A. Sigmann in 1912, and *Der Meineidbauer* by A. Busse in 1914 with the title *The Farmer Forsworn.* B. Q. Morgan has translated *Die Kreuzelschreiber* as *The Cross Makers,* substituting an Irish for the original Bavarian setting, as well as selected chapters of *Der Schandfleck* under the title *The Blot of Shame.*

ABOUT: [In German—see studies by A. Bettelheim, A. Kleinberg, A. H. J. Knight *in* German Studies Presented to W. H. Bruford, P. Reimann *in* Weimarer Beiträge (1960).]

D. G. D.

AQUINAS, SAINT THOMAS. See THOMAS AQUINAS, Saint

*ARANY, JÁNOS (March 2, 1817-October 22, 1882), Hungarian poet, was born in Nagyszalonta, into a Calvinist family of noble origin but little money. He made a brilliant record as a student at the college of Debreczen, but spent his early adulthood in rather aimless drifting, holding a variety of jobs and offices—strolling actor, guardsman in the revolution of 1848, notary, tutor in a wealthy family. Such a background, however, prepared him well for his future career as a great national poet, giving him valuable knowledge of his country, its people, and their traditions.

In 1845 Arany made his literary debut with a satirical epic, *Az Elveszett Alkotmany* (The Lost Constitution), which received first

* ŏ′ rŏn y′

ARANY

prize in a competition sponsored by the Kisfaludy Society. He became acquainted with the prominent literary figures of the day— among them Sándor Petőfi (see sketch below), the leading national poet of Hungary.

Arany's reputation rests upon two epic poems, *Toldi* and *The Death of King Buda,* a number of fine ballads, and some excellent translations into Hungarian of Shakespeare (*Midsummer Night's Dream,* 1864, and *Hamlet* and *King John,* 1867) and Aristophanes. Combining sound classical scholarship with the ardent nationalistic and romantic fervor of the 1848 period, he produced verse of great simplicity and beauty and of real emotional depth. The materials on which he drew were traditional folk matter, the medieval chronicle legends of the Magyars. He also utilized English and Scottish ballads in his work, but drew as well on more sophisticated literary influences such as Virgil and Shakespeare.

Toldi is Arany's most celebrated poem. A folk epic telling (in rhymed hexameters) the exploits of a large and awkward youth, a "sort of male Cinderella," whose valorous deeds humble and put to shame an elder brother who had persecuted him, *Toldi* was published in 1847. It was so successful that Arany developed it into a trilogy—completing *The Eve of Toldi* in 1854 and *The Love of Toldi* in 1879. This revival of interest in the Hungarian past was further demonstrated in *Buda Halála* (1864)—an ambitious work of some 2,752 lines dealing with the fratricidal rivalry between the Hun Attila and his brother Buda. Arany planned this work also as a trilogy, but only part I and fragments of the other two parts were completed. Part II, "Ildikó," treated of Attila's campaigns in Europe, and part III, "Prince Csaba," was to cover Kriemhild's revenge and her murder of Attila. The work, a powerful poem revealing subtle psychological insights as well as much conventional epic pageantry and color, was of course related thematically to the German epic *Nibelungenlied,* as well as to the Icelandic *Eddas* and the *Volsungsaga.*

For *Buda* Arany was awarded the Nádasdy prize by the Hungarian academy, a group which he served for fifteen years as secretary. Except for one period, 1851 to 1860, when he taught in the *Gymnasium* at Nagy-Körös, Arany spent most of his professional career in Budapest as an editor of various literary periodicals, an influential and respected figure. He became a director of the Kisfaludy Society in 1860. He married Julianna Ercsei, daughter of a lawyer, in 1840. Their son László (1844-1898) was also a poet. Although his private life was a happy one, Arany suffered great grief and melancholy in his last years, depressed over the fate of the Hungarian people after their defeat in their struggle for independence. He died in Budapest. A statue of him was erected in the gardens of the National Museum of that city.

Toldi, Ballads and Selected Lyrics is available in an English translation by W. N. Loew (1914). *The Death of King Buda* was translated by W. Kirkconnell (1936), and the sixth canto was translated as *The Legend of the Wondrous Hunt* by E. D. Butler (1881). Selections from his poems also appear in *The Magyar Muse,* translated by W. Kirkconnell (1933).

ABOUT: Kirkconnell, W. *in* World Literature; Reich, E. Hungarian Literature; Columbia Dictionary of Modern European Literature; Slavonic Review, IX (1930-31).

ARASON, JÓN, Bishop (1474?/1484?-November 7, 1550), Icelandic poet, was born at Grýta, Eyjafjaðarsýsla, the son of Ari Sigurður and Elín Magnúsdóttir. Both parents were related to high church officials, but the family is not believed to have been wealthy. Little is known of Arason's early years except that he lost his father sometime around 1499 and that the boy was probably educated at the monastery of Múnkaþverá. Arason was ordained a priest in his early twenties and settled in Reykjadalur. He took for a common-law wife Helga Sigurðardóttir (Icelandic priests were forbidden to marry but concubinage was practiced widely) with whom he lived for the rest of his life. They had nine children, six of whom survived to adulthood.

Jón Arason rose rapidly in the ecclesiastical hierarchy and accumulated considerable wealth. His success was largely owing to the favor of the bishop of Hólar, to whose office Arason himself succeeded in 1520 after the bishop's death. For some time Arason's tenure of the office was in doubt. On August 18, 1522, he was elected bishop by the assembled clergy of the diocese, but it was not until 1524 that he was consecrated. The Roman Catholic Church of Iceland in the sixteenth century was torn with dissension. In part this was a result of the powerful pressures of the Reformation (Arason was the last Roman Catholic bishop of Iceland). In part though, too, it was the continuation of centuries of bitter strife among the bishops. They had their followers like feudal lords and led their parties in raids on neighboring enemies. They fought like soldiers and acted independently of any secular authority. (In Arason's day Iceland was under the rule of the Danish king, who was a Protestant.) Arason's own running quarrel with Bishop Ögmundur of Skalholt—once almost reaching the point of open war—reflects this tension and the rugged, militaristic character of the Icelandic Church. It was the Reformation, however, which destroyed Arason. He resisted the pressures as long as he could, but in 1550, while out on a raiding party on the property of a wealthy Protestant landowner, accompanied by two of his sons, he was captured by his Danish enemies and condemned to death. With his sons he was beheaded at Skalholt, dying bravely. His daughter instigated a raid against the Danes, and Arason's death was avenged with the killing of several of the enemy.

Although Arason died for a lost cause and Iceland became a Protestant country, his memory survived. He had died a martyr's death at the hands of foreign conquerors, the Danish, and he was therefore regarded as a patriotic hero. He was admired too for his vigor, his ambition, his generosity, and his friendliness. Physically he was tall "and of a commanding presence."

Arason was the leading poet of his age. The subject of his verse was his religion; his faith was sincere and warm, "rather easygoing," as W. P. Ker described it, thoroughly representative of the rapidly weakening power of the Catholic Church of Iceland. Arason's poetic masters were the Latin poets of the Middle Ages, but his poetry is purely Icelandic, showing characteristic Icelandic mastery of diction and intricate rhyming. He wrote five long religious poems—*Píslargrátur* (on the passion of Christ, a poem much influenced by Eysteinn Ásgrímsson's famous *Lilja*); *Ljomur* (a history of the world as it is recorded in the Bible); *Davíðsdiktur* (a commentary on the Fifty-first Psalm); *Niðurstigsvísur* (dealing with Christ's descent into Hell); and *Krossvísur* (on the Crucifixion and Resurrection). He also wrote some satirical and humorous verse.

Not the least of Arason's achievements was his introduction of the printing press into Iceland and his patronage of the first printer in that country, a Swede named Jón Matthiason.

Arason's poems appear in *Biskupa Sögur* (1878); an edition of the religious poems was published in 1918.
ABOUT: Ker, W. P. Collected Essays, II; Speculum April 1953, July 1954. [In Icelandic—see studies by P. E. Oleson and by G. Jonsson. Jonsson argues for 1474 as Arason's date of birth, but T. J. Oleson in *Speculum*, cited above, holds to the 1484 date.]

*ARETINO, PIETRO (April 20, 1492-October 21, 1556), Italian man of letters, self-designated "censor of the proud world," described by Ariosto as "the scourge of princes," and one of the most notorious libertines of his colorful age, was born in Arezzo, the natural son of an artist's model and prostitute named Tita and a father who, by Aretino's proud account, was a Venetian nobleman. Recent scholarship, however, indicates that he was the legitimate son of a poor shoemaker, giving his origins a respectability which Aretino himself scorned. He was raised in poverty and had little schooling— "I went to school just long enough to learn how to make the holy cross"—but he was later able to boast: "I wear my talent unmasked; I who do not know the beginnings of A, B, C am teaching persons who know it to X, Y, Z." At thirteen he got into trouble (some accounts say for robbing his mother, others for writing a satirical sonnet against indulgences) and ran away to Perugia, where he worked as an apprentice to a bookbinder for about six years. Then, ready for larger conquests, he went to Rome, where he became a domestic in the house of the banker and art collector Agosto Chigi. In Chigi's house he watched Raphael at work and rapidly developed his own exquisite taste in

* ä rä tē′ nō

ARETINO

art and, no doubt, his taste for the splendors and luxuries of Italian Renaissance life.

Aretino's extraordinary rise from obscurity to wealth and power is a spectacular success story. Of no particular talent himself, he capitalized on his one great asset, his genius for self-advertisement and self-aggrandizement. Unfettered by moral scruples, he moved swiftly and boldly. For a while, because it suited his ambitions, he was a Capuchin monk at Ravenna. But he soon threw off his clerical garb, returned to Rome, and won fame for his daring *pasquinate,* satirical, frequently libelous political broadsheets, written on behalf of his patron Cardinal Giulio de' Medici who was seeking the papacy. (He became Pope Clement VII in 1523.) He won additional notoriety—and expulsion from Rome—when in 1524 he published a group of obscene *Sonetti Lussuriosi* which served as a text for some equally questionable pieces of sculpture by the artist Giulio Romano. For a time he found favor in the court of Giovanni de' Medici in Milan, but his patron's death in 1527 left him unprotected and surrounded by his enemies (he was more than once stabbed by the angry victims of his libel and blackmail), so he fled to Venice, where he remained for the rest of his life.

Aretino arrived in Venice penniless but was soon established in a magnificent palace on the Grand Canal with a princely entourage, Venetian citizenship, and, for friends, the most brilliant and distinguished society of his day. His closest friends were the painter Titian and the architect Sansovino. He acted as

Titian's agent and sold many of his paintings —as well as those of other Italian artists of his acquaintance—to Francis I of France. This monarch rewarded him for his services in 1533 with a rich gold chain which Aretino wears in the splendid portrait by Titian which hangs in Pitti Palace in Florence. Aretino lived out his life with honors and dignities heaped on him. In 1530, after some maneuvering, to be sure, he received from Pope Clement VII a benediction and later a knighthood and a papal endorsement for his long epic poem on the Gonzaga family, *La Marfisa*. His name was known throughout Europe, and he did not exaggerate when he wrote in a letter: "Fame is working for me in every corner of the world." He maintained a veritable harem in his Venetian palace. The two women who figured most prominently in his life were Caterina Sandella, who bore him a daughter, Adria, and Pierina Riccia, whom he first met as the fourteen-year-old bride of one of his secretaries. He died suddenly, probably of apoplexy. Legend has it that he died "of a great fit of laughter," but the fact is that he was at peace with the church at his death and was buried in the Church of San Luca in Venice.

The secret of Aretino's success was relatively simple. He sought out noble patrons and wrote poems, plays, epics as they commanded. If they failed to reward him adequately, he wrote scurrilous satires libeling them, publishing far and wide their most intimate secrets (hence the epithet "scourge of princes"). On this kind of literary blackmail Aretino prospered. For centuries after his death he paid the price by carrying the reputation of a scoundrel. "His memory is infamous," the nineteenth century Italian critic Francesco De Sanctis wrote of him. "A decent man would never pronounce his name before a woman." Three years after his death, his works were put on the Index. Twentieth century scholars have looked upon him more generously, although, as J. B. Fletcher remarks, "All libels expunged, Aretino's career was scurvy enough." In his private life, in spite of its debauchery, they have found evidence of a generosity and kindness which the devotion of his friends and even the grudging respect of some of his enemies confirm. Perhaps because he epitomizes all the best and the worst of the Renaissance, he has survived in memory as a personality, though not as an author.

Aretino's canon includes some 3,000 letters, numerous pasquinades, lyrics, satires, epics, prose dialogues, religious tracts (which were so respectable that until the eighteenth century

they were widely used in convents in France and Italy), five prose comedies (*La Cortigiana,* 1525; *Il Marescalco,* 1526-27; *La Talanta,* 1541; *Lo Ipocrito,* 1542; *Il Filosofo,* 1544), and a tragedy—*Orazia,* 1546, which Ernest H. Wilkins calls "the best Italian tragedy of the sixteenth century." The only one of his books that is not forgotten today is the pornographic *I Ragionamenti* (published in 1600), dialogues in which Roman prostitutes quite frankly discuss their patrons, all easily identifiable among Aretino's contemporaries, and this book, described by Fletcher as "the nastiest book ever written," survives only as a collector's item. Even here, however, Aretino has his defenders. Edward Hutton, while acknowledging the obscenity of the *Ragionamenti,* wrote that "they have the vigor of life and are filled with action." Others have found in his work the glittering wit, though certainly on a smaller scale, of Rabelais and Molière. Guillaume Apollinaire, who wrote a monograph on him, called him "a satiric poet of the first rank."

A two-volume English translation of Aretino's writings was made by Samuel Putnam in 1926, and a brief selection from his works appears in *The Portable Renaissance Reader* (ed. J. B. Ross and M. M. McLaughlin, 1953). His sonnet to Ariosto, in Putnam's translation, appears in L. R. Lind's *Lyric Poetry of the Italian Renaissance* (1954). His collected letters (in Italian) were published in Milan in 1960.

ABOUT: Chubb, T. C. Aretino: Scourge of Princes; De Sanctis, F. History of Italian Literature; Fletcher, J. B. Literature of the Italian Renaissance; Hutton, E. Pietro Aretino, the Scourge of Princes; Rascoe, B. Prometheans; Roeder, R. The Man of the Renaissance; Wilkins, E. H. History of Italian Literature. [In French—see study by G. Apollinaire. In Italian—see studies in Belfagor, XII, XVII, also E. Camesasca, A. Foschini, G. Innamorati.]

ARI. See LURIA, ISAAC BEN SOLOMON

*ARI ÞORGILSSON, Fróði (1067/68-November 9, 1148), Icelandic historian, was born in the Breiðifjörðr district in northwestern Iceland. His father was Þorgils Gellisson, descended from one of Iceland's most prominent families of chieftains. His mother's name was Jóreiðr. Shortly after Ari's birth, his father drowned, and he went to the home of his grandfather Gellir Þorkilsson, who died on a pilgrimage to Rome. Ari was then seven years old and was sent to the learned octogenarian Hallr Þórarinsson at Haukadalr in the southwestern part of Ice-

* ä′ rĭ thôr′ gĭl sŏn frōō′ thĭ

land. Here Ari stayed till he was twenty-one. With Hallr lived also the erudite priest Teitr Ísleifsson, son of the first bishop in Iceland. Teitr educated Ari and told him about many old events which Ari later wrote down.

About the rest of Ari's life only little is known. He was ordained, but it is uncertain whether he ever served as a priest. It is also known that he was a chieftain of high repute. Most likely he lived on the peninsula Snæfellsnes, south of Breiðifjörðr, at Staðr, which was the home of his son Þorgils and grandson Ari the Strong.

Ari spent his youth among people who knew and taught him the history of the country. Thus, his interest in Icelandic history and his decision to record it probably grew out of the milieu in which he lived. There did exist manuscripts of law codes and genealogies in Icelandic when Ari in the 1120's wrote his famous *Íslendingabók* (Book of the Icelanders), but he was the first to write history in his native language. However, the first version of his book is lost. What has come down to us is a second abbreviated edition which is an extremely condensed account of Iceland's history from its colonization, c. 870, to 1120. Only the major events are recorded, and Ari gives them in chronological order, often with exact dates. The book is remarkable, since Ari's method was really scholarly, and every word in it is true. Ari is usually known as Ari Fróði (Ari the Wise, or Learned).

Íslendingabók was translated into English by H. Hermannson as *Book of the Icelanders* (1930). It also contains an introductory essay.

ABOUT: Craigie, W. A. A Father of History *in* The Scottish Review, XXXVI; Einarsson, S. A History of Icelandic Literature.

A. J.

ARIOSTO

*ARIOSTO, LUDOVICO (September 8, 1474-July 16, 1533), Italian poet, was the eldest of ten children of Niccolò Ariosto and his wife Daria Malaguzzi Valeri. He was born in Reggio Emilia, where his father—a professional military leader in the service of the house of Este—was captain of the town's citadel. In 1481-82 his father served as military governor of Rovigo, and in 1484 was made a ruling official of Ferrara.

When his father was sent on to Modena in 1489, Ludovico remained in Ferrara to study law. Literature interested him more than did law, however, and in 1494 he began instead to attend classes in Latin and Greek and to write poems in Latin. In 1500 Niccolò died,

* ä' rê ôs' tô

and Ludovico was left to support the family. The obvious course open to a young man of good birth but few means was, under the semi-feudal conditions of Renaissance Italy, to seek the favor of the ruling family. Ariosto accordingly attached himself to the house of Este. In 1502 he wrote a long Latin poem in honor of the marriage of Alfonso d'Este, son of the Duke of Ferrara, to Lucrezia Borgia, and he was shortly awarded a captaincy in the district of Reggio. The next year the duke's other son, the cardinal Ippolito d'Este, appointed Ariosto a gentleman of his household in Ferrara. Ippolito paid him an annual salary and later (although Ariosto never took holy orders) gave him several church livings.

About 1504 Ariosto began the composition of *Orlando Furioso*. The cardinal (stories to the contrary notwithstanding) took a strong interest in the poem and helped pay the costs of publishing the first edition in 1516. While in Ippolito's employ, Ariosto also wrote two comedies in Italian prose for presentation in Ferrara—*La Cassaria* (1508) and *I Suppositi* (1509).

In 1509 Ariosto had an illegitimate son, Virginio, by a woman named Orsolina Catinelli. Although he already had one or two other illegitimate children, Ariosto was especially fond of Virginio, whom he kept by him the rest of his life.

In 1513, while on a diplomatic mission to Florence, Ariosto formed a more romantic and lasting attachment to Alessandra Benucci, a married Florentine woman. His one famous lyric poem, "Non so s'io potrò ben chiudere in rima," celebrates his falling in love with her.

In 1517 Cardinal Ippolito decided to remove his court to his bishopric in Hungary. When Ariosto refused to accompany him, the cardinal angrily took away his annuity and some of his church benefices. The next year, however, Alfonso d'Este, now Duke of Ferrara, took Ariosto into his household. While on a ducal mission to Rome in 1520, Ariosto completed his verse comedy *Il Negromante* and supervised its performance. Alfonso appointed Ariosto governor of the territory of Garfagnana in 1522, and, although Ariosto disliked the post, he proved a capable administrator. About 1524 he was offered the ambassadorship to Rome, but declined it.

He returned to Ferrara in 1525, and in 1526 bought a cottage there. Sometime between 1526 and 1530 he secretly married Alessandra Benucci, now a widow. He spent the last years of his life revising *Orlando Furioso* and the comedies and writing a new verse comedy, *La Lena*. He also went on occasional missions for the duke, on the last of which—to Mantua, in 1532—he fell seriously ill. He died in Ferrara the next summer and was buried in the nearby church of San Benedetto; his remains were later moved to the Biblioteca Comunale of Ferrara. His son Virginio and his brother Gabriele served as his literary executors.

Ariosto described himself as tall, thin, slightly stooped, and prematurely bald. His health was always delicate, and he disliked the hardships imposed by long journeys. Although he was a likeable companion and an able diplomat, he preferred to live quietly and devote his time to writing.

His masterpiece, *Orlando Furioso*, is a continuation of the *Orlando Innamorato* of Boiardo (see sketch below). Boiardo had set out to describe the adventures (most of them of his own invention) that befell Charlemagne's knights during the war against the Saracens. His poem breaks off at the siege of Paris, and Ariosto's poem takes up the narrative at this point. *Orlando Furioso*, although a genuine continuation of *Orlando Innamorato*, is different in style and in emphasis. Boiardo had mingled serious knightly combats with bizarre magical happenings, but Ariosto did not take knightly doings as seriously as Boiardo had, and a tone of subdued mockery unifies all the events in the *Orlando Furioso*. Furthermore, in *Orlando Furioso* the main plot is no longer the love

of Orlando for Angelica, but the love of Bradamante and Ruggiero—whom Ariosto invented as the legendary ancestors of the house of Este. In *Orlando Innamorato*, Bradamante had been a male knight; Ariosto explains that she had disguised herself as a man in order to do battle for the Christian cause. Ruggiero, another minor character, becomes in *Orlando Furioso* a chief Saracen knight. Ariosto concludes the Orlando-Angelica story inherited from Boiardo by having Angelica marry a Saracen page. Orlando, hearing of her marriage, then goes out of his mind and engages in ridiculous adventures (hence the title *Orlando Furioso*—"Roland Mad"). His senses are returned to him (by the comic character Astolfo, who flies to the moon and finds Orlando's lost wits there) just in time to enable him to fight victoriously in the combat that ends the war against the Saracens. The poem does not stop with the end of the war but goes on to describe the further adventures and the final marriage of Bradamante and Ruggiero.

Orlando Furioso was one of the most popular works of its century; by 1600 it had been reprinted nearly two hundred times and had been translated into French, Spanish, and English. For Renaissance readers the appeal of the poem lay in its elegant style and its imaginative profusion of characters and adventures. Today the work is an accepted classic, but it understandably has fewer readers.

Ariosto's shorter poems include Latin compositions, Italian lyrics in the Petrarchan vein, *terza rima* poems, eclogues, and rejected fragments from *Orlando Furioso*. His Italian comedies—all of them patterned after Latin comedy—include, besides the four finished works, the incomplete *I Studenti*. His *Satires* comprise seven verse epistles, written between 1517 and 1525.

During the European Renaissance his shorter poems and his plays, as well as his *Orlando Furioso*, exercised enormous influence. His lyrics influenced the poetry of the French Pléiade, while his comedies were influential on the French seventeenth century theatre. In Spain *Orlando Furioso* served as a model for *Don Quixote*. In England *I Suppositi*, translated by Gascoigne as *The Supposes*, was one of the first classical comedies performed (1566). Shakespeare later adapted part of *The Supposes* for *The Taming of the Shrew*. The English writer to profit most from Ariosto was Spenser, whose *Faerie Queene* is largely modeled on *Orlando Furioso*. In the nineteenth century, when English poets again became interested in the Italian Renaissance, Ariosto again served as a source—for instance, for Keats' unfinished *Cap and Bells,* partly patterned on *Orlando Furioso.*

Ariosto's *Satires* were translated into English by R. Tofte (1608), and again by T. H. Croker (1759). Of the nine English translations or partial translations of *Orlando Furioso,* the most noteworthy are those by Sir John Harington (1591, in verse), by W. S. Rose (1823-31, in verse), and by A. Gilbert (1954, in prose; a scholarly edition with introduction and notes).

ABOUT: Croce, B. Ariosto, Shakespeare, and Corneille; Gardner, J. E. G. The King of Court Poets; Nicholson, J. S. Life and Genius of Ariosto. [In Italian—Toffanin, G. Ludovico Ariosto.]

J. K.

*ÁRNASON, JÓN (August 17, 1819-September 4, 1888), Icelandic folklorist, was born in Skagastrond, a fishing village in northern Iceland, son of Arm Illugason, a clergyman. He received an excellent education at the Bessastidir Latin School and began his career in 1848 as a teacher. Later that same year he was appointed librarian of the Stiftbokasfn (which later became the national library of Iceland). To supplement his meager salary, he took additional jobs. He was secretary to Helgi Þordersen, bishop of the Reykjavík Cathedral, librarian of the Reykjavík branch of the Icelandic Literary Society, a teacher and librarian at the Latin School, and a founder and custodian of an Icelandic antiquarian collection which ultimately became the nucleus of the Icelandic national museum. Árnason was married in 1866 to Katrin Þorvaldsdottir. He lived most of his life in Reykjavík and died there at sixty-seven.

Jón Árnason's major work was his large collection of Icelandic folk tales which was published in two volumes in 1862-1864 as *Íslenzkar Þjóðsögur og Aefintýri* (Icelandic Popular Legends and Tales). This project had been begun years earlier in 1845 at the Latin School by Árnason and a fellow student, Magnus Grimsson. In 1852 they published a small preliminary collection, *Íslenzk Aefintýri.* Encouraged by the friendly reception given the book, Árnason continued the search and worked at it for the rest of his life. He divided his material into ten classes: mythic stories, ghost stories, stories of witchcraft, stories of natural phenomena, legends, historical legends, stories of outlaws, fairy tales, comic stories, and superstitions. He also made a collection of riddles which was published posthumously in 1887.

* är' nä sŏn

Árnason's two-volume *Þjóðsögur* is considered one of the most important collections of folk literature ever assembled in any language. It has been compared to the collection of German folk tales (*Kinder- und Hausmärchen*) published by the Grimm brothers in 1812-1822. He tried to retain the local flavor and spirit of the tales, as well as to make his transcriptions as accurate as possible. The result is a product of scrupulous scholarship that is also lively and delightful to read. Many of the stories have been translated into other languages.

An English translation of Árnason's entire collection of tales, by G. E. J. Powell and E. Magnusson, was published in 1864.

ABOUT: Einarsson, S. History of Icelandic Prose Writers, 1800-1940; Powell, G. E. J. & Magnusson, E. *Preface to* Icelandic Legends Collected by Jón Árnason; Warner Library, II.

*ARNAUT DANIEL (fl. 12th century), Provençal poet, was one of a group of celebrated medieval troubadours, known for their technical ingenuity, who flourished in southern France in the latter part of the twelfth century. Of his life it is difficult to extract fact from legend. According to tradition, he was born in Ribéyrac in the Dordogne of a noble family. Apparently he preferred the adventurous life of the wandering jongleur to the more settled existence of the landed gentry, for he became associated with the court of King Richard the Lion-Hearted some time in the last decade of the twelfth century, as court entertainer, and apparently soon rose to the station of troubadour. Here he became the friend of the famed warrior-poet Bertran de Born. Little else is known about him. The coda of one of his poems indicates that he was present at the crowning of Philippe Augustus at Étampes (May 29, 1180). It is likely that he traveled to Spain, for several of his poems praise a beautiful Aragonese lady Laura, whose name he plays upon ("Laura l'aura"; "L'aura amara").

That Arnaut lives at all for us is owing to his brief emergence from the flames that envelop the carnal lovers in Dante's *Purgatorio* (Canto XXVI). Here he is introduced by a fellow poet, Guido Guinizelli, as one "who wrought better in the mother tongue than I" ("miglior fabbro del parlar materno"). There follows Arnaut's anguished lament for his sins, hope for salvation, and his poignant plea to Dante and Virgil to

* är nō' dà nyĕl'

39

remember him upon their return to earth ("Ara vos prec, per aquella valor. . . . Sovenga vos a temps de ma dolor"). These lines are noteworthy for being in Arnaut's own Provençal (the only verses in *The Divine Comedy* not in Italian) and closely imitative of his poetry. Dante paid Arnaut the further tribute of using passages from his songs as examples of perfect craftsmanship in his treatise *De Vulgari Eloquentia.* Two later Italian poets also extolled him, Petrarch, to whom he was "great master of love" ("Gran maestro d'amor"), and Tasso.

Modern critics have generally felt that Dante considerably overestimated Arnaut. His own countrymen have tended to dismiss him as obscure and overcomplicated. Some have even found his diction harsh and grating. Probably he would have remained unknown to English and American readers had not Ezra Pound written his master's thesis on him at the University of Pennsylvania, and passed on his enthusiasm to his disciple T. S. Eliot. In his famous essay on Arnaut, Pound characteristically lauds his "trying the speech in new fashions, and bringing new words into writing, and making new blendings of words." "The art of En Ar[naut] Daniel is not literature," he stresses, "but the art of fitting words well with music, well nigh a lost art." Pound brings out particularly Arnaut's skill at onomatopoeia, his ability to imitate bird-songs and other sounds from nature. Significantly, T. S. Eliot named one of his first volumes of poems *Ara Vos Prec,* dedicated *The Wasteland* to Ezra Pound as "il miglior fabbro," and incorporated a part of Arnaut's lament from the *Purgatorio* into the poem itself.

Dante has attributed several prose romances to Arnaut (the *Lancillotto* mentioned by Tasso and the *Rinaldo* several times cited by Luigi Pulci may be among them), but none has survived. Eighteen short lyrics (*canzos*) alone are extant. For the most part they celebrate various amorous intrigues, expressing the alternate moods of the intense lover—sensuous (at times sensual) joy, cynical disillusionment—with a remarkable intricacy of verse structure and rhyme scheme. According to Sir Maurice Bowra: "His complex emotions belong to a world of romantic Chivalry which is far indeed from modern experience; his boldness and his violence are more disturbing than attractive. But he wished to be not sweet but powerful, and that, with all his idiosyncrasies, he undoubtedly is."

Arnaut is said to have retired in his old age to a monastery, but this has never been confirmed.

The definitive edition of Arnaut Daniel's works remains that of Ugo A. Canello in Italian, published in 1883. R. Lavaud edited a bilingual text, Provençal and modern French, 1910-11. There is no complete text of his poems in English, but some of them are translated by Ezra Pound in his essay "Arnaut Daniel," which first appeared in *Instigations* (1920), and is reprinted in *Literary Essays of Ezra Pound,* edited by T. S. Eliot (1955). Passages are translated by Sir Maurice Bowra in his essay "Dante and Arnaut Daniel," *Inspiration and Poetry* (1955).

ABOUT: Bowra, M. Inspiration and Poetry; Cazamian, L. History of French Literature; Chaytor, H. The Troubadours of Dante; Ker, W. Form and Style in Poetry; Pound, E. Literary Essays; Valency, M. In Praise of Love.

R. A. C.

*ARNAUT DE MAREUIL (fl. 1170-1200), Provençal lyric poet, was born in Mareuil-sur-Belle, in the Dordogne district of France, of poor parents. Although he was trained as a scribe, he obviously preferred the uncertainties of the life of a professional poet and we find him at the court of Adelaide, daughter of Count Raymond of Toulouse and wife of Roger II, Viscount of Bezières. Thus far we have followed the account in the *vida,* or life, attached to his poetry in many manuscripts, but the statement in the *vida* that his first poems were anonymous hardly seems consistent with the necessity of any professional poet to gain recognition by his work. Nor can we trust the statement that after Roger's death, Adelaide's new suitor, Alphonso II of Aragon, was so jealous of Arnaut's intimacy with his lady that he expelled him from the court. This, like many other incidents in the *vidas,* seems to have been drawn from the poet's own work. Arnaut did leave the court in 1194 and spent the rest of his life at the court of William VIII, Count of Montpellier. More than twenty of his poems survive, most of them *canzos,* or formal love songs. Flattery of the lady, descriptions of her beauty and of the effects of that beauty upon the poet fill a large part of them. As usual, he alternates between hope and despair, is tortured by desire and inspired by love. No hints are given about the lady's identity but the wholesale panegyric makes it virtually certain that she was his patroness, Adelaide. Arnaut uses all the clichés of the troubadours, but he at least avoids obscurity both in language and verse forms. For this reason

* àr nō' dĕ mà rû' y'

he has often been compared with Bernart de Ventadorn, but the comparison is unjust to Bernart. Arnaut is completely lacking in freshness and sincerity. The best that can be said for him is that he has verbal felicity and charm. Arnaut also wrote the *ensenhamen*, a longer poem on morals and manners. Here again his conventionality is evident. He demands from all types and classes of society the same courtly virtues prescribed for the ladies and gentlemen to whom his songs were addressed.

There is no complete separate edition of Arnaut's work. The lyric poetry is to be found in R. C. Johnston, *Les Poésies Lyriques du Troubadour Arnaut de Mareuil* (Paris, 1935); complete works in the large collections, e.g., F. Diez, *Leben und Werke der Troubadours* (Leipzig, 1882). Arnaut's *Les Saluts d'Amour* was edited by P. Bec in 1961. Some translations are in anthologies: M. Chaytor, *The Troubadours* (1912); I. Farnell, *The Lives of the Troubadours* (1896).

ABOUT: Valency, M. In Praise of Love.

W. T. H. J.

*ARNDT, ERNEST MORITZ (December 26, 1769-January 29, 1860), German poet and historian, was born and raised at Schoritz on the Baltic island of Rügen, then under Swedish rule. His father, a former serf, taught him stern self-discipline, while his mother's guidance instilled in him the sincere religious feeling which dominated his life. He studied theology at the universities of Greifswald and Jena, but then gave up his intention of entering the ministry. Two years of travel through Austria, Hungary, Italy, France, and Belgium led to his first essay, *Germanien und Europa* (published 1803). In 1800 he became lecturer in history and philosophy at the University of Greifswald and in 1801 married Charlotte Quistorp, but his wife died the same year during childbirth.

In 1806 appeared the first volume of his essay *Geist der Zeit* (later volumes published up to 1818). With keen insight and uncompromising straightforwardness Arndt reminded his compatriots of past glories, took them to task for their indifference and dissension, and assailed the pseudo-culture of his day as "too wise for the earth, too cowardly for heaven." He attacked oppression from within and without, and his defiance of Napoleon forced him to flee to Sweden where he served in the government for three years. After a stay in Germany under an assumed name, he followed the call of Freiherr von Stein, himself an exile,

* ärnt

to St. Petersburg. While there, he wrote pamphlets stirring his countrymen to a reawakening of national conscience and a revolt against the foreign tyrant.

After Napoleon's defeat, Arndt returned to Prussia, worked in the government service for a while, and then settled in Bonn where he established a new home with his second wife, Nanna Schleiermacher. In 1818 he was appointed professor of history at the newly established Bonn University, where his fearless fight for social rights led to his suspension in 1820 for alleged revolutionary activity. Not until 1840 was he restored to his former post by the new king, Frederick William IV. In 1848 he was elected representative to the Frankfurt parliament, but, disappointed that his call for national unity remained unheeded, he returned to Bonn where he died soon after his ninetieth birthday.

Arndt is recognized as the foremost patriotic poet of the Prussian Wars of Liberation and as such ranks with Theodor Körner and Max von Schenkendorf. His lyrics are characterized by fervent patriotism, deep religious convictions, and a simple *Volkslied* style with almost Biblical language. In his collection *Lieder für Teutsche* (1813) he admonishes his countrymen to the realization that in throwing off the foreign yoke, they are performing a sacred duty. His battle hymn *Der Gott, der Eisen wachsen liess, der wollte keine Knechte* incites to a "holy" war. When peace came, he celebrated the heroes and the Leipzig battle, always with thanks to God whose will had been fulfilled. Many of Arndt's religious songs have become part of the Protestant hymnal. His *Bundeslied*, extolling God, fatherland, liberty, and steadfastness, became a popular student song. Through his post-war lyrics he exerted considerable influence on his nation in arousing the desire for German unification under the leadership of Prussia. His later writings include many autobiographical and travel accounts.

An English translation of parts of *Geist der Zeit* by P[eter] W[ill] appeared in 1808 under the title *Spirit of the Times*. Anna Dabis made an excellent translation of *Fairy Tales from the Isle of Rügen* in 1896. *Selections*, edited by H. Rosch & H. Meisner appeared in 7 vols. (1892-1903) and edited by H. Meisner & R. Geerds in 16 vols. (1908).

ABOUT: Pundt, A. G. Arndt and the Nationalist Awakening in Germany. [In German—see studies by G. Erdmann, H. Polag, E. Stapelfield.]

S. H. M.

*ARNIM, BETTINA (or ELISABETH) (BRENTANO) von (April 4, 1785-January 20, 1859), German memoirist, was born at Frankfurt am Main, the daughter of the wealthy Italian merchant Pietro Antonio Brentano and Maximiliane von LaRoche, whom Goethe had once greatly admired. Her grandmother was the novelist Sophie von LaRoche and her brother, Clemens von Brentano, was one of the leading writers of the Heidelberg romantic school. Bettina, whose mother died in 1793 and her father in 1797, was raised in a convent school in Fritzlar. From 1798 she lived alternately at Offenbach with her grandmother and at Frankfurt. Here she became acquainted with Goethe's mother, who told the young girl many anecdotes and tales about the early life of the great poet, whom Bettina worshipped. From 1803 to 1806 she lived at Marburg with her brother-in-law, the famous jurist Friedrich von Savigny. In 1811 Bettina married the well-known writer Achim von Arnim, the friend and collaborator of her brother. The two were extremely happy and raised a family of seven children. One daughter, Gisela von Arnim, later married the writer Hermann Grimm. After the death of her husband in 1831, Bettina became a leading figure in the intellectual life of Berlin, where she died in 1859.

Bettina was an enthusiastic, ingenuous person with a quixotic, fiery temperament. Her behavior was completely controlled by her senses and passions, and reflection was alien to her. She was endowed with great personal charm and warmth of character and possessed a genuine lyric gift. These qualities are apparent in her writings and constitute their main appeal.

Her first work, *Goethes Briefwechsel mit einem Kinde* (1835), consists of letters to Goethe and to Goethe's mother along with a tribute to Goethe and a personal diary. This volume is Bettina's monument to the idol of her youth, and although not a wholly genuine correspondence but rather a blend of fact and fiction, it is a unique and important document. This book was long popular in Germany and also enjoyed exceptional success in the United States in translation.

In 1840 Bettina wrote *Die Günderode*, a sympathetic biography of the unfortunate poetess Karoline von Günderode, who committed suicide in 1806. She similarly memorialized her brother in the volume *Clemens Brentanos Fruhlingskranz* (1844).

* är' nĭm

In Berlin Bettina came into contact with the liberal ideas of her time, as popularized by the Young Germany movement, and became increasingly interested in social and political issues. Her sympathies were particularly aroused by the plight of the Silesian weavers, and she wrote the volume *Dies Buch Gehört dem König* (1849) in the hope of stimulating King Frederick William IV to institute reforms. Among other things she requested relief for the oppressed working classes, the emancipation of the Jews, and the abolition of capital punishment.

Goethes Briefwechsel mit einem Kinde was translated in 1837-38 as *Goethe's Correspondence with a Child* by Bettina herself in conjunction with Mrs. Austin. The translation of *Die Günderode* was undertaken in 1842 by M. Fuller and was completed in 1861 by M. Wesselhoeft.

ABOUT: Helps, A. and Howard, E. J. Bettina. [In German—see studies by C. Alberti, B. Allason, G. Bäumer, K. H. Hahn, K. H. Storbl, M. Sussmann, and H. Wyss. In French—see A. Germain.]

D. G. D.

*ARNIM, LUDWIG ACHIM, Freiherr von (January 26, 1781-January 21, 1831), German novelist, was born in Berlin, the descendant of ancient Prussian nobility. His father, Baron Joachim Erdmann von Arnim, had served Frederick the Great as a diplomat and director of the royal opera. His mother, of middle-class ancestry, died two weeks after Achim's birth. The boy, together with an older brother, was raised by his maternal grandmother and saw little of his busy father throughout his childhood. After some years of private tutelage at home, he entered a Berlin secondary school in 1793. Five years later he entered the University of Halle, where his principal interests were mathematics and natural science. His first published writings were in the field of physics. In 1800 he entered the University of Göttingen and that summer he met Clemens Brentano, with whom he later collaborated on the influential collection of folk lyrics *Des Knaben Wunderhorn*. While at Göttingen he started his first novel, *Hollins Liebeleben*, modeled after Goethe's *Werther*.

Between 1801 and 1804 the two Arnim brothers undertook a "grand tour" of Italy, France, Holland, England, and the German-speaking countries. In 1802 he visited the Brentano family in Frankfort, met Clemens' sister Bettina (who was to become his wife in 1811), and with Clemens undertook a Rhine journey which helped sharpen his awareness of the national past.

* är'nĭm

ARNIM

In 1805-08, the years during which *Des Knaben Wunderhorn* appeared, Arnim lived in Heidelberg, where, with such figures as Brentano, Josef Görres, and the brothers Grimm, he became a leader of the younger romantics. In 1808 together with Görres, he edited a journal, *Zeitschrift für Einsiedler*, which, although it lasted for only five months, was influential in awakening interest in folk literature and in the German Middle Ages. Arnim's earlier essay "Von Volksliedern," attached to the *Wunderhorn*, was an enthusiastic idealization not only of folk songs, but of an older, nobler way of life whose spirit Arnim wished to restore within the weak, divided Germany of his time.

In 1809 Arnim returned to Prussia, spending the remainder of his life between his estate in Wiepersdorf and Berlin, which, as the site of a new university and as the center of resistance to Napoleon, was fast developing the liveliest intellectual atmosphere in Germany. During the war years Arnim played an active propaganda role and helped found the "Christian-German Table Society," which, with such members as the political theorist Adam Müller, Fichte, Kleist, and Clausewitz, was a rallying-point for Prussian conservatism and nationalism.

Arnim's mature creative work dates roughly from his return to Prussia. Although he produced a number of dramas and poems, his reputation rests largely on a few of his prose narratives. His uncompleted *Die Kronenwächter* (1817), a colorful pageant of German life during the declining Middle Ages, is

considered the first real historical novel in Germany. Of his numerous short novels, *Isabella von Egypten* (1812—translated in abridged form by C. F. Schreiber in the Pierce-Schreiber *Fiction and Fantasy of German Romance*, 1927), *Der Tolle Invalide* (1818), and *Die Majoratsherren* (1820), all characterized by Arnim's peculiar blend of grotesque fantasy and realistic detail, have contributed the most to his reputation. His position as a story-teller is today decidedly below that of his contemporaries Kleist and Hoffmann. His wife (see sketch above) created a solid literary reputation of her own during their marriage through her engaging collections of letters between herself, Goethe, and other friends. Both the Arnims are buried in Wiepersdorf.

The first volume of a collected edition, *Sämtliche Romane und Erzählungen* was published in 1961.

ABOUT: Liedke, H. R. Literary Criticism and Romantic Theory in the Work of Achim von Arnim; Tymms, R. German Romantic Literature; Wellek, R. History of Modern Criticism. [In German—see studies by F. Gundolf and I. Seidel. In French—by R. Guignard.]

H. L.

AROUET, F. M. See VOLTAIRE, FRANÇOIS MARIE AROUET DE

*ASBJØRNSEN, PETER CHRISTEN (January 15, 1812-January 1, 1885), Norwegian folklorist, was born in the Norwegian capital of Kristiania (now Oslo), where his father, Anders Asbjørnsen, of a Gudbrandsdal family, was a glazier. His mother was Thurine Elisabeth Bruun, daughter of a sheriff in the district of Sunnmøre in western Norway. The boy went to school in the capital, but he was rather lazy and much preferred to watch life in nature. His father wanted him to have a higher education, and in 1827 he was sent to a private school in Ringerike to study towards his matriculation examination. Here one of his schoolmates was Jørgen Moe (see sketch below). These two youngsters formed a friendship that lasted for life and resulted in a most valuable joint production. When Asbjørnsen took ill and returned home after a year, they carried on a lively correspondence. Asbjørnsen's studies were delayed by his father's bankruptcy and the ensuing miserable living conditions of the family. Not until 1833 did he pass his examination, after which he held positions as a private tutor in the province.

* ăs′ byûrn sĕn

43

ASBJØRNSEN

In 1837, Asbjørnsen was back in the capital and enrolled at the University where he studied mostly natural sciences. He earned a meager living by teaching, privately and in schools. Even before taking his matriculation examination, Asbjørnsen had begun to write down folk tales. This work he continued while tutoring out in the country. In 1837, Asbjørnsen and his friend Moe, who also was deeply interested in folklore, decided to devote their combined efforts to producing something similar to the Grimm brothers' *Kinder- und Haus-Märchen*. At the end of the year they published a little volume entitled *Nor,* to which Asbjørnsen contributed some folk tales and Moe only a poem. While studying zoology and practicing journalism, Asbjørnsen continued, in cooperation with his friend, to record folklore. In 1841 appeared the first volume of their *Norske Folkeeventyr* (Norwegian Folk Tales). A new volume was added each year through 1844, when the authors decided to stop their publication and rewrite their stories in a more uniform and systematic style.

Asbjørnsen traveled to all corners of the country on official business as a marine zoologist, forester, etc., and all the time he recorded folklore. In 1845-47 he published alone *Norske Huldreeventyr og Folkesagn* (Norwegian Fairy Tales and Folk Legends), constituting a combination of his own descriptions of nature and characters and a modified form of the dialectal speech. The new edition of *Norske Folkeeventyr* appeared at Christmas time in 1851. It contained all the tales that were included in the first edition in revised form and a few new ones. At the end of the book were added a large number of notes containing information about the places where the tales had been recorded, about variants of the stories found in Norway, and about related stories from other countries, thus establishing a sort of classification of the material. A scholarly introduction was written by Moe.

While Moe's folkloristic activity hibernated for two decades, partly because of a religious crisis, Asbjørnsen continued to collect stories which he published in small volumes. A larger collection appeared in 1871. From 1856 to 1858 he studied forestry in Germany and Austria. From 1860 to 1864 he served as chief forester in the Trondheim district, after which he was sent by the government to the continent to study peat-making. Upon his return he held a leading position in this field, from which he retired in 1876. Asbjørnsen published numerous scholarly papers and textbooks in natural sciences, forestry, peat-making, dietetics, etc.

A large number of Asbjørnsen and Moe's tales are included in G. W. Dasent's translations *Popular Tales from the Norse* (1858) and *Tales from the Fjeld* (1874). H. L. Brækstad translated several tales as *Round the Yule-Log* (1881) and *Fairy Tales from the Far North* (1897). A. Heywood published *Norwegian Fairy Tales* (1895). Later translations are H. and J. Gade, *Norwegian Fairy Tales* (1924), F. H. Martens, *The Norwegian Fairy Book* (1922), S. Undset, *True and Untrue* (1945).

ABOUT: Beyer, H. A History of Norwegian Literature; Grøndahl, I. and Raknes, O. Chapters in Norwegian Literature; Jorgenson, History of Norwegian Literature.

A. J.

ÁSGRÍMSSON, EYSTEINN. See EYSTEINN ÁSGRÍMSSON

*ATTERBOM, PER DANIEL AMADEUS (January 12, 1790-July 21, 1855), Swedish poet, critic, scholar, was born in Åsbo parish in the province of Östergötland. His father was Gabriel Atterbom, perpetuate curate, a practical, jovial man. His mother was the daughter of the dean of the parish, Hedvig Kristina Kernell, whose sentimentality and devotion influenced the young Atterbom strongly. During his adolescence he suffered from anguish, spleen, and satiety with life. In 1805 he matriculated at the University of Uppsala, where he attracted attention by his intellectual endowments and wide reading.

* ăt′ ĕr bōōm

His acquaintance with the philosophy of the Enlightenment caused a religious crisis from which he emerged a freethinker. He accepted with enthusiasm the mystic religion of the German masters, first and foremost Schelling, and he conceived poetry as a divine gift. In 1807, he and some fellow-believers founded a literary society, Musis Amici, next year changed to Auroraförbundet (The Aurora Union) with the hopeful expectation that it would bring the dawn of a new day in Sweden's literary and spiritual life. He decided to devote his life completely to the poetic calling.

Atterbom and the other young romanticists pursued a lively literary activity. They published their products in their society's monthly journal *Phosphoros* (1810-13), from which they got the name "phosphorists," in *Poetisk Kalender* (Poetic Calender, 1810-22), edited by Atterbom, and *Svensk Literaturtidning* (Swedish Literary Magazine, 1813-24). The contents of these publications inaugurated the neo-romantic era in Sweden. Atterbom advocated a Christian Platonic-romantic philosophy and emotional, euphonious poetry. Although his poetry from this period was partly immature and of fluctuating value, he did show an extraordinary talent. His verse was exquisitely melodious, imaginative, replete with feeling, full of new artistic ideas. Among the most prominent of his early poems are a cycle called *Blommorna* (The Flowers, 1811), to which he later added several new poems, and in which he used flowers as symbols of the human soul and life, and fragments of a poetic fairy play *Fågel Blå* (The Blue Bird), to which he later added new parts but which he never completed. He also published aesthetic treatises on Bellman, Thorild, and others.

During a long journey to Germany and Italy in 1817-18 he came into personal contact with some of the great contemporary spirits, such as Schelling, Schleiermacher, F. von Schlegel, Steffens, Tieck, Grillparzer. A new crisis changed his aesthetic pantheism into an altruistic ethical philosophy. In 1821 at the University of Uppsala he was appointed "docent" in Universal History; in 1828 he was promoted to professor of philosophy, later of aesthetics and modern literature. In 1826 he married a noble lady, Ebba Fredrika af Ekenstam, daughter of a colonel. Their marriage was extremely happy.

After his journey abroad Atterbom's zest for life increased, and he was able to come to terms with reality. In an article *Fridsrop* (Peace Cry, 1821) he called off the long literary feud and invited the poets to peaceful competition under the banner of concord. He completed his greatest poetic work, the fairy-tale play *Lycksalighetens Ö* (The Isle of Bliss), in two volumes (1824-27; revised edition 1854), one of the outstanding creations of Swedish romanticism. It was based on a well-known popular book, and in treating the material allegorically and symbolically Atterbom gave magnificent expression to the romantic longing for beauty and eternity, and also to his conviction that the value of life is not of aesthetic but religious nature.

Most important of Atterbom's scholarly publications is his work in literary history *Svenska Siare och Skalder* (Swedish Prophets and Poets), in six volumes, 1841-55, containing fine and affectionate analyses of some great poets.

A few of Atterbom's songs are available in English translation in H. W. Longfellow's collection *Poets and Poetry of Europe* (1845), in Warner's *Library of the World's Best Literature*, II, and in C. W. Stork's *Anthology of Swedish Lyrics* (1930).

ABOUT: Longfellow, H. W. Poets and Poetry of Europe; Warner's Library of the World's Best Literature, II. [In Swedish—see studies by G. Axberger, H. Frykenstedt, J. Kulling, A. Nilsson, C. Santesson, F. Vetterlund.]

A. J.

*AUBANEL, THÉODORE (March 26, 1829-October 31, 1886), Provençal poet and playwright, sometimes called "the French Petrarch," was born in Avignon, the youngest of four children of Laurent Aubanel, a stern and pious man, and his wife, whose maiden name was Seyssau. The Aubanel family had been in the printing business since the eighteenth century and carried the title "Printers to His Holiness." After completing his education under the Grey Friars at Aix, Théodore Aubanel planned to study medicine, but when his father died in 1854 he joined his brother Charles in the family business. He began his literary career as a poet writing in French, but he shifted to Provençal after 1854 when he came under the influence of Frédéric Mistral and Joseph Roumanille, founders of the Félibrige, a movement to restore the language and literature of Provence and the medieval troubadours. Provençal was not spoken in Aubanel's family, but he learned the dialect during long visits in the country with peasants who spoke it.

Aubanel's poetic output was small. Most of it was intensely personal love poetry lamenting his passion for young Jenny Manivet ("Zani"), who became a nun. He published a collection of his own poems in Provençal

* ō bȧ nĕl'

45

with parallel French translations, *La Mi-ougrano Entre-Duberto* (The Split Pome-granate) in 1860. The volume shocked many of its readers, but was praised by the critic Sainte-Beuve and generally hailed as an important contribution to the Félibrige movement. "It brought a new element to Provençal lyricism, that of pure passion," A. V. Roche wrote in the *Columbia Dictionary*. A quarter of a century later, in 1885, Aubanel published another collection of poems—*Li Fiho d'Avi-gnoun* (The Young Maidens of Avignon), described as "a confession of the author's mature age." Once again his frank expression of his passion outraged some readers. Although he was a devout Catholic, an eminently respectable member of his community, and a member of the Legion of Honor (1884), he was severely censured. The Church demanded that he suppress the book, and, according to his biographers, the furor raised by its publication brought on an apopletic stroke, in December 1885, which hastened his death. He was buried in Avignon, and his funeral oration was delivered by Mistral. Aubanel married Josephine Mazen in 1861. He was survived by a son, Jean Théodore, and had a grandson, Charles, who was killed in World War I at twenty-one. Aubanel's achievement was slight but not insignificant. With Mistral and Roumanille, he formed the triumvirate of the Félibrige. He was good-natured and had many devoted friends, among them Mallarmé and Alphonse Daudet. Nevertheless he was an unhappy man, carrying through his life the sorrow of a disappointed love which he sublimated in his poetry. He had for his motto the Provençal "Quan canto, soun mau en canto" ("Who sings enchants his unhappiness").

Aubanel also wrote some plays in Provençal. Most successful of these was *Lou Pan dòu Pecat* (The Bread of Sin), which was produced successfully in Montpellier in 1878. In 1871-72 he wrote part of a comic opera in French on a Provençal subject, but the manuscript is lost.

ABOUT: Columbia Dictionary of Modern European Literature. [In French—see studies by A. H. Chastain, L. Legré, C. Maurras, J. Vincent, and N. Welter. E. Ripert's La Renaissance Provençale gives an account of the Félibrige.]

---

*AUBIGNÉ, THÉODORE AGRIPPA D' (February 8, 1552-April 9, 1630), French poet, was born at the Hôtel Saint Maury, in Pons, the center of French Protestant activity in the sixteenth and seventeenth centuries.

* ō bē nyā'

His mother, Catherine de L'Estang, died in giving birth to him. His father, Jean d'Aubigné, a judge, had been converted to Protestantism by John Calvin and was a passionate fighter in the cause of French Protestantism. He early instilled that same ardor in his son who, at the age of eight, took an oath pledging his life to vengeance against the persecutors of his faith.

Much of the biographical material available on d'Aubigné comes from his memoirs, written as moral instruction for his children and not perhaps as objective as biographical data should be. According to *Sa Vie, à Ses Enfants* (published in 1729), he received an excellent classical education with a Parisian teacher who boasted that he could teach four languages at once. At six young d'Aubigné could read Greek, Latin, and Hebrew. He also mastered Italian and Spanish. At seven and a half, he says, he made a translation of Plato's *Crito*. At eight he was sent to school in Paris. After two years his schooling was interrupted by the outbreak of civil war and he fled to Orléans. On his way there he was arrested, and attempts were made to force the young Protestant to recant. He refused in the face of all threats, allegedly saying, "I am more afraid of the mass than of the stake." D'Aubigné finished his education at Orléans and at Geneva. In 1568, though only sixteen, he enlisted in the army and fought in the field for two years. In 1570 he retired to his small country estate, where he fell in love with Diane Salvati and was inspired to write *Le Printemps,* a collection of love poems in the style of Petrarch and Ronsard.

Though an avowed Protestant, d'Aubigné held a place in the French court for two years, serving under Prince Henry of Navarre (later to become King Henry IV). By nature pleasure-loving (as a boy he had chafed at the strict discipline of his Geneva schooling), he wrote masques, satires, and a verse drama, *Circé,* which won the approval of King Charles IX. Henry of Navarre meanwhile shuttled uneasily between Catholicism and Protestantism. In 1593 he became a Catholic. D'Aubigné nevertheless continued to serve under him as governor of Maillezais and vice admiral of Guyenne and Brittany. After Henry's death by assassination in 1610, d'Aubigné's position in France became increasingly hazardous. In 1620 he fled to Geneva where he was warmly welcomed and highly honored, and where he died in 1630. He was buried there in the cloister of St. Peter's. D'Aubigné married Suzanne de Lézay in 1583. They lived together very happily for thirteen years until her death and had five children, two of whom died early. His son Constant (whose daughter Françoise became Mme de Maintenon, the mistress and second wife of King Louis XIV) was a bitter disappointment to d'Aubigné; he lived riotously, got into serious trouble, and betrayed the Protestant cause at the battle of La Rochelle.

D'Aubigné's major literary achievement, one on which he worked for forty years, was his epic *Les Tragiques* (1616), which has been described as "the Jeremiad of the religious wars." A noble and lofty poem divided into seven books and written in alexandrines, it surveys the sufferings caused by the religious wars in France, attacks the follies and corruptions of the age, and ends with an eloquent statement of the poet's faith. The French scholar Gustave Lanson has written, "There is nothing greater in our language than the concluding pages of *Les Tragiques.*" Because it was the expression of a minority group in France, however, the poem never received widespread recognition. D'Aubigné also wrote a prose *Histoire Universelle* (1616-1620), and some satires—*Les Aventures du Baron de Fœneste* and *Confession Catholique du Sieur de Saucy.*

His complete works have not been translated into English. A selection from *Les Tragiques* is translated in H. Cairns *The Limits of Art* (1948). A collected French edition, edited by E. Réaume and F. de Caussade was published in six volumes, 1877-1892.

ABOUT: Buffum, I. Agrippa d'Aubigné's Les Tragiques; Macdowall, H. C. Henry of Guise and Other Portraits; Nitze, W. H. & Dargan, E. P. A History of French Literature; University of Toronto Quarterly, XXXIII (1964). [In French—see studies by A. Garnier, A. Jons, A. Lebois, J. Plattard, S. Rocheblave, M. Yourcenar *in* Nouvelle Revue Française, IX (1960).]

*AUERBACH, BERTHOLD (February 28, 1812-February 8, 1882), German novelist, was born at Nordstetten in the Württemberg Black Forest, the son of a merchant. Intending to follow in the footsteps of his ancestors, he first attended rabbinical school at Hechingen and then continued his education at Karlsruhe and Stuttgart. In 1832 he enrolled at the University of Tübingen. His participation in a radical students' organization there netted him two months' imprisonment. Under the influence of David Friedrich Strauss, Auerbach came to take a more liberal view of religion. His journalistic interests and travels in the Rhine and Neckar regions brought him

* ou' ĕr bäк

into contact with Freiligrath and Marx, and he took part in the 1848 revolution in Heidelberg and Vienna. The anti-Semitic riots that followed in its wake caused the death of his wife to whom he had been married for only a year. Auerbach subsequently married the sister of the writer Heinrich Landesmann (Hieronymus Lorm). From 1849 to 1859 he lived in Dresden, and his activities as an editor, critic, and publicist also took him to Weimar, Leipzig, Vienna, and Berlin. His last years were marred by illness and the rise of anti-Semitism, and his death occurred at Cannes, France, in 1882.

Auerbach's *magnum opus* and his chief claim to being regarded as one of the foremost story-tellers in German literature is the *Schwarzwälder Dorfgeschichten* (Village Tales from the Black Forest), some two dozen in all, which first appeared in four volumes between 1843 and 1854 and in an augmented eight-volume edition in 1871. Auerbach considered himself the originator of this *genre*. The stories, a masterful blend of realism, romanticism, and idealism, with a pronounced moralizing, didactic tendency, were translated into almost all European languages and made their author world-famous. Among the best-known are *Der Tolpatsch, Ivo der Hajrle, Diethelm von Buchenberg, Barfüssele,* and *Edelweiss. Die Frau Professorin* was dramatized by C. Birch-Pfeiffer as *Dorf und Stadt* and was a great success on the German stage, but Auerbach's own dramatic attempts were unsuccessful. Auerbach's later works of fiction, among them the philosophical novel *Auf der Höhe*, 1865, and the romance *Das Landhaus am Rhein*, 1869, found less favor than the *Dorfgeschichten.* In his last long novel, *Waldfried*, 1874, the disillusioned author suggested that on the centenary of the American Declaration of Independence a German university be established in America as an international academy of the spirit.

As a Jew who was deeply committed to German culture and also strove for the emancipation of the Jews, Auerbach was subject to the tragic dualism which has bedeviled so many German-Jewish writers. In 1837 he published a biographical novel, *Spinoza,* and four years later his five-volume translation of Spinoza's works appeared. In *Das Judentum und die Neueste Literatur* (1836), Auerbach tried to refute Wolfgang Menzel's charge that the "Young Germany" writers were mostly radical Jews. The novel *Dichter und Kaufmann,* 1840, presents a picture of the times of Moses Mendelssohn. In later life Auerbach tried to dissuade Moses Hess from publishing his study of the Jews as a distinct nationality and was increasingly saddened by the non-acceptance of his proffered assimilationism and by the anti-Semitism of men like Heinrich von Treitschke, Richard Wagner, and Theodore Billroth.

Auerbach was a short, stout, vigorous man with bright eyes and a full face framed with white hair. He has been described as a dynamic orator as well as a good listener and buoyant person generally.

The large number of translations of Auerbach's writings attests to his great popularity in the latter part of the nineteenth century. The *Village Tales from the Black Forest* were first translated by Meta Taylor in 1846-47. C. Goepp's translation appeared in 1869, and there were many other translations and reprints. *Barfüssele* appeared as *Little Barefoot* in the translation by H. W. Dulcken, 1873, which was abridged by P. B. Thomas for use in *The German Classics*, VIII. *Brigitta* was translated by C. Bell in 1880. *On the Heights* appeared 1867 (C. Bell, tr.) and *The Villa on the Rhine* in 1869 (James Davis, tr.). *Poet and Merchant* was translated by C. T. Brooks in 1877. Brooks published his translation of *Edelweiss* that same year. *The Professor's Lady* was first translated by M. Howitt in 1850. *Spinoza* was translated by E. Nicholson in 1882 and *Waldfried* by S. A. Stern in 1874.

ABOUT: Liptzin, S. Germany's Stepchildren. [In German—see studies by A. Bettelheim and M. G. Zwick.]

H. Z.

*AUGIER, (GUILLAUME VICTOR) ÉMILE** (September 17, 1820-October 25, 1889), French dramatist, was born in Valence, of a prosperous bourgeois family. His mother was the daughter of the well-known author Charles Pigault-Lebrun (who in 1831 dedicated his *Contes à Mon Petit Fils* to young Émile), and his father, Victor Augier, a lawyer, collaborated with his father-in-law on his last play. In 1828 the family moved to Paris where Victor Augier bought a notary's practice. Young Augier studied at the Collège Henri IV, received an excellent education, and, in 1839, entered the law offices of M. Masson to prepare for a career in law. His family did not oppose his decision, however, to switch from law to literature. In 1844 his play *La Ciguë* was produced in Paris with great success and from that time his career moved forward steadily.

Augier's life was generally a happy and uneventful one. Once, when asked to write an autobiography, he stated simply that he was born in 1820 and that nothing had ever happened to him since then. Actually very

* ō zhyā´

AUGIER

little did happen to him besides his very considerable success in the French theatre. He published a volume of verse, *Pariétaires*, in 1856; he wrote a libretto for Gounod's opera *Sappho*. He also flirted briefly with political life, but in 1855 he gave it up, saying: "I once put my foot on the threshold of public life to study the game of our institutions as a painter would visit a clinic to learn anatomy." He was elected to the Legion of Honor in 1850 and to the French Academy in 1858. In 1870 he retired from the theatre. Three years later, in Rome, he married a young actress, Laure Lambert, with whom he settled at Croissy. There he died at sixty-nine. He is buried near Paris in the cemetery of La Celle-Saint-Cloud, in a tomb with his grandfather Pigault-Lebrun, and his nephew Paul Déroulède, a poet, who died in 1914.

Augier's lifework consists of twenty-seven plays, written over a period of thirty-four years. The first nine of these were verse dramas, and although they were successful in their day, they are today considered his least distinguished work. Only one of this group, *Gabrielle* (1849), a domestic drama, foreshadows his major plays. These are solid, well-constructed dramas of bourgeois family life. They have been variously described as dramas of *bon sens* ("good sense"), thesis plays or plays of ideas, or *comédies de mœurs* (social comedies). Their purpose is generally the glorification of the home, the family, the substantial virtues of middle-class life. Augier, according to J. L.

Borgerhoff, "is a typical nineteenth century *honnête homme,* endowed with a good dose of common sense and of keen humor. Neither in his style . . . nor by his ideas is he a reformer. He aims rather at the ideals of the better bourgeoisie."

Outstanding among Augier's plays is *Le Gendre de M. Poirier* (M. Poirier's Son-in-Law, 1854), a dramatization of Jules Sandeau's novel *Sacs et Parchemins,* which has been called "the model comedy of the nineteenth century." His M. Poirier, a self-made man who has married off his daughter to a snobbish aristocrat, is richly conceived and characterized in the tradition of Molière's Georges Dandin and M. Jourdain. The play was popular throughout Europe and is still occasionally revived. In *Le Mariage d'Olympe* (1855) his bourgeois, anti-romantic sentiment came to full expression. Here, in a play which shows how a scheming courtesan wrecks the lives of the respectable family into which she marries, Augier wrote an indignant answer to the younger Alexandre Dumas' sympathetic portrait of the courtesan Marguerite Gautier in *La Dame aux Camélias.* He continued to expose what he considered the social evils of his day in *Les Lionnes Pauvres* (1858), a study of middle-class wives who are unfaithful to their husbands; *Le Fils de Giboyer* (1862), an attack on unscrupulous journalists and publicists; *Maître Guérin* (1864), a portrait of a shyster lawyer; *Madame Caverlet* (1876), the theme of which is divorce; and *Les Fourchambault* (1878), an ambitious study of a bourgeois family and its problems.

Augier's career spanned the period 1844 to 1878, forming a bridge as it were between the stylized, well-made but artificial drama of Scribe and the realistic, problem-grappling drama of Ibsen. Along with the younger Dumas, he was the most popular dramatist of his day. What he lacked essentially was inventiveness and originality. His characters, with the exception of Poirier and one or two others, are conventional; his stage tricks appear stereotyped; his plots are easily reduced to formula. Nevertheless he remains a solid and instructive dramatist of French bourgeois society.

English translations of Augier's major plays appear in many anthologies of European drama. Barrett H. Clark published translations of four of his plays—*Olympe's Marriage, M. Poirier's Son-in-Law, The House of Fourchambault,* and *The Post-Script*—in 1915. There have also been a number of "free adaptations" of the plays, including one based on *Les Lionnes Pauvres* called *A False Step,* by A. Matthison in 1878, and Thomas William Robertson's adaptation of his *L'Aventurière* as *Home* (c. 1890). Brief selections from several of the plays in English translation are in the Warner Library.

ABOUT: Borgerhoff, J. L. *Introduction to* Nineteenth Century French Plays; James, H. The Scenic Art; Lamm, M. Modern Drama; Smith, H. A. Main Currents of Modern French Drama; Warner Library, II; Waxman, S. M. Antoine and the Théâtre Libre; France Illustration November 12, 1949; PMLA March 1948. [In French—see studies by P. Morillot, H. Gaillard.]

*AVERROËS (KADHI ABOULWALID MOHAMMED IBN'AHMEN IBN-MOHAMMED IBN-ROSCHD)** (1126-December 10, 1198), Spanish-Moslem philosopher, was born in Cordova, of a prominent Andalusian family. For generations his family flourished in law and theology. Among his contemporaries, Averroës was known as "the grandson," so famous were his father and grandfather. He first studied theology and canon law and became known for his learning in medicine, mathematics, and astronomy, as well as in jurisprudence and philosophy; he later wrote in all these areas of study.

Averroës lived among the illustrious men of his century and was a favorite philosopher and aide in public affairs among the rulers and religious leaders of Spain and Morocco. Through Yusuf, a prince and patron of learning, he was appointed *kadhi,* or judge, of Seville in 1169, where he wrote part of the *History of Animals.* In 1171, he returned to Cordova, where he began his famous commentaries. Very active in public affairs, Averroës made frequent trips to Morocco and Seville. He wrote *De Substantia Orbis* while in Morocco in 1178; he composed one of his treatises on theology in Seville in 1179 and then returned to Africa in 1182 to become doctor to the king. Later, he returned to Cordova as *kadhi,* still complaining that his public duties required too much time from his studies.

The last years of his life were filled with misfortunes caused by intrigue in the court brought about by jealous enemies and by his heterodox philosophy. Branded with heresy during the rise of fanatic hatred towards freethinkers in Morocco, Averroës was persecuted with other rationalists and was exiled to Elisana. In 1198 Al-Mansûr, Yusuf's successor, recalled Averroës, who died a short time later in Morocco, leaving several sons, some of whom became *kadhis* and devoted themselves to theology and law.

* à věr' ō ēz

Averroës' biography is engulfed in fable; he is recorded as patient, generous, and forgiving, and capable of much intensive work and study. His life-span occupied almost the entire twelfth century and is linked with all the events of this decisive epoch in the history of Moslem civilization. He was the last representative of the efforts in the Orient and in Spain to create in Islam a rational and scientific development.

During the Middle Ages and the Renaissance, Averroës had much influence on and many disciples among Jews and Christians; however, except for a favorable reputation in Egypt, he had no renown among his fellow Moslems. Averroës left no school, but his philosophy is found in the school of Moses Maimonides and in the school of rationalism founded in Padua at the end of the thirteenth century. Moslem philosophers accused Maimonides of making atheists, or *moattil*, of Moslem worshippers. Among the Paduans, Averroïsm signified belief in the existence of a single active intellect, common to all men, which is immortal in itself but which does not confer personal immortality on the individual who has received his own intellect by a process of emanation from God.

Averroës was celebrated during the Renaissance as a doctor and as a commentator on Aristotle. By the end of the twelfth century, his most important works were translated into Latin and Hebrew. Among these are *De Substantia Orbis*, the *Colliget* (a summary of medicine), *Destructio Destructionis* (The Incoherence of the Incoherence), two treatises on the union of the intellect with man, and commentaries on Aristotle and Plato.

Considered the most scholarly and scrupulous commentaries on Aristotle, these analyses are of three types: the extensive ones in which Aristotle is quoted and discussed minutely; the middle commentaries, which are summaries; and the last, which are paraphrases.

Averroës' commentary on Plato's *Republic*, an integral part of his philosophical writings, together with his Commentary on Aristotle's *Nicomachean Ethics*, occupies an important place in Islamic political philosophy. Averroës interpreted the *Republic* in the light of Aristotle's *Ethics*, as well as the *Physica*, *De Anima*, and *Metaphysica;* moreover, he used the *Republic* as a manual for government and as a substitute for Aristotle's *Politics*, which was inaccessible at that time. His method was that of testing Plato's

thought by means of Aristotle's philosophy in order to gain a fuller insight into politics.

All of the commentaries are prolix but without dryness; the personality of the author reveals itself in knowing digressions and reflections. In general, polemics occupies a great place in his writings, giving them an interesting tone of vivacity. At times, his enthusiasm for science and his love of philosophy raise him to the point of a very eloquent morality. Many of his writings show an intention of oral exposition; it is probable that Averroës taught in mosques as did his grandfather. The crudeness of Averroës' language is not amazing when it is remembered that available works are very frequently translations of translations. Only recently have efforts been made to work with the rare Arabic manuscripts; the first Arab text was not published until 1859.

The translation from the Arabic of *Tahafut Al-Tahafut* (The Incoherence of the Incoherence) by Simon Van den Bergh (1954) and that of the *Commentary on Plato's Republic* by E. I. J. Rosenthal (1956), as well as the translation work done by H. A. Wolfsen, D. Baneth and F. H. Fobes on the *Corpus Commentariorum Averrois in Aristotelem* (1958), are all most noteworthy. Maurice Bouyges, the late French scholar, established important Arabic texts of the works of Averroës. Averroës himself burned his few poems during his old age.

ABOUT: DeBoer, T. J. History of Philosophy in Islam; Mohammed Jamil-ur-Rehman, The Philosophy and Theology of Averroës. [In French—see studies by L. Gauthier, E. Renan.]

R. P. C.

AVICEBRON. See IBN GABIROL

*AVVAKUM (PETROVICH), Prototype or Archpriest (December 5, 1620-April 24, 1682), Russian church reformer and writer, was born in Grigorovo, near Nizhny Novgorod. Little is known about his background other than his own statement that his father, a priest, was addicted to drink. He was orphaned young and at the age of seventeen married Anastasia Markovna, the daughter of a blacksmith. Contrary to regulations, he was initiated as deacon at the age of twenty and ordained priest at twenty-three.

From the very beginning of his career Avvakum displayed a relentless, uncompromising attitude towards drink and moral or ritual laxity. It was no doubt because of this that he was forcibly ejected from his first church. Arriving in Moscow, he was introduced to the circle of church dignitaries known as the "zealots of orthodoxy," who

* ŭv yă kōōm' pyĭ trô' vĭch

were intent on restoring the sermon and the complete rite, both of which were widely neglected at the time. Ordained Archpriest for the town of Yuryevets on the Volga, Avvakum adhered strictly to the tenets of the zealots, but was beaten repeatedly by mobs, often including women and priests, and was once left for dead in the street.

On fleeing to Moscow in 1652, he was soon involved in the dispute over bringing the Russian rite into accord with that of other orthodox countries. One of the chief points of contention was the position of the fingers when making the sign of the cross. Along with the other zealots, Avvakum violently resisted any alteration of the rite. This precipitated the Great Russian Schism or *raskol*, out of which grew the sects known as "Old Believers." Those who refused to accept the innovations were imprisoned or banished. Avvakum and his family were sent on a ten-year trek to Dauria (Transbaikalia) during which they suffered incredible hardships, including shipwreck, death of children from starvation, and imprisonment and torture at the hands of the leader of the expedition.

Permitted to return to Moscow in 1664, Avvakum maintained his intransigent attitude to the emendations of the liturgical books, asserting that the old rite must have been correct since "our fathers were saved by it." He was again banished, but was returned to Moscow for the great council of Patriarchs in 1666, at which he was defrocked, anathematized, and sentenced to lifelong imprisonment in a subterranean dungeon in Pustozersk on the Arctic Sea. Here Avvakum carried out the greater part of his literary work under the most difficult conditions imaginable. Here he no doubt acquired his legendary appearance: a tall, haggard, lean figure with a white beard and dressed in a single ragged robe. In 1682, for slander of the Orthodox Church and for defaming the memory of Czar Alexis, Avvakum and three other members of the Schism were burned at the stake.

There was widespread sympathy for the schismatics in the north of Russia, and Avvakum's religious writings had considerable, often drastic, influence. Distributed by sympathizing guards, they called on the faithful to resist the ultimate all attempts of the Patriarchate to introduce the reformed rite. Whole parishes of Old Believers barricaded themselves in their churches and committed mass suicide by fire. Avvakum is best known today, however, for his *Life* (translated in 1924 by Jane Harrison and Hope Mirrlees as *The Life of the Archpriest Avvakum by Himself*). This work is a remarkable document of seventeenth century Russia with humorous scenes of Avvakum driving bears and clowns from his parish; it also displays the most brilliant use up to that time of the native Russian idiom. With his very coarse realism, his indomitable spirit and his "Russianness," Avvakum was an early representative of the anti-Westernizing, native literary tradition and so a forerunner of such figures as Tolstoy, Dostoevsky, and Leskov. He was largely forgotten during the eighteenth century, but was rediscovered in the mid-nineteenth and has since been drawn from for stylistic devices (cf. passages in D. Merezhkovsky's *Peter and Alexis*).

ABOUT: Slonim, M. The Epic of Russian Literature. [In French—Pascal, P. Avvakum et les Débuts du Raskol.]

N. V.

*AYRER, JACOB (1543?-May 26, 1605), German dramatist, about whose birth and childhood nothing is known, received the freedom of the city of Nuremberg on October 13, 1593, and died in that city as a notary and proctor to the court. It is speculated that he went to Nuremberg as an indigent boy and eventually opened an ironmonger's shop. After the failure of the business, he is supposed to have gone to Bamberg where he became a clerk. Albert Cohn asserts that Catholic Bamberg did not suit Ayrer's Protestant temper and that he was thus prompted to return to Nuremberg.

In Nuremberg he wrote several important tragedies, comedies, and Shrovetide plays, which are the earliest of their kind in German literature. Cohn states that Ayrer "retained the old verse of Hans Sachs; but what constitutes his essential distinction from his Nuremberg predecessor, is the circumstance that he wrote all his pieces for the sole object of representation, and in many of his tragedies and comedies displays a degree of skill in theatrical arrangement and a knowledge of the requirements of the stage, which must place him far above Hans Sachs in this respect."

Ayrer's dramatic work, collected in 1618 in *Opus Theatricum*, contains thirty tragedies and thirty-six Shrovetide plays, but many more pieces are believed to have actually been written. Ayrer was a prolific writer. All plays, dated from his own manuscript, are supposed to have been written after 1593;

* ī′ rēr

51

sometimes two singing plays (Singspiele) were composed in one day.

Of special interest to students of English literature are the many references to the English actors who visited the continent and Ayrer's imitative creation of the character of the fool. The Shrovetide plays, although presumably original, share certain characteristics with the English jig. The *Comedy of the Beautiful Sidea* is generally assumed to have a common source with *The Tempest; The Comedy of the Beautiful Phoenicia* resembles *Much Ado About Nothing; Belimperia and Horatio* has been accepted by many scholars as fashioned after an early original of Thomas Kyd's *Spanish Tragedy.*

The *Comedy of the Beautiful Sidea* and *The Comedy of the Beautiful Phoenicia* have both been reprinted with an English translation in Albert Cohn, *Shakespeare in Germany in the Sixteenth and Seventeenth Centuries* (1865). F. S. Boas reprints *Belimperia and Horatio* in German, in *Works of Thomas Kyd,* 1901. The entire *Opus Theatricum* has been reprinted in five volumes in the *Bibliothek des Litterarischen Vereins in Stuttgart,* 1865, under the editorship of Adelbert von Keller. *Belimperia and Horatio* can also be found in J. L. Tieck's *Deutsches Theater,* I, Berlin, 1817.

ABOUT: Cohen, A. *in* Shakespeare in Germany in the Sixteenth and Seventeenth Centuries; Fouquet, K. Jakob Ayrers "Sidea." [In German—Shakespeares "Tempest" und das Märchen (Beiträge zur Deutschen Literaturwissenschaft, No. 32. Marburg, 1929); Wodick, W. Jakob Ayrers Dramen, in ihrem Verhältnis zur Einheimischen Literatur und zum Schauspiel der Englischen Komödianten.]

E. J. S.

*BACHOFEN, JOHANN JACOB (December 22, 1815-November 25, 1887), Swiss legal writer and cultural anthropologist, was born in Basel. His father, also named Johann Jacob, was a manufacturer of silk, operating a business that had been in the family for generations. Through his mother, Valerie Merian-Hoffmann before her marriage, he was related to Jacob Burckhardt, the historian of the Renaissance.

His father intended young Bachofen for a career in the family business, but the boy proved so outstanding in his academic studies that there seemed little question of what his future would be. He received his earliest education in schools in Basel. After completing his studies at the *Gymnasium* in that city he went on to the university, specializing in classics and philology. He also studied abroad—first in Berlin, where he came under the influence of the German jurist Friedrich von Savigny and as a result turned to the study of law, and later also in Göttingen,

* bȧк′ ō fĕn

in England, and in France. On returning to Basel in 1841 he joined the university faculty as professor of Roman law. In 1844, however, he resigned from his teaching post to devote himself to scholarship. The only other public office he held was that of judge in the criminal court in Basel, in which post he remained until 1877.

Bachofen's studies in ancient civilizations took him to Italy, Greece, and Spain. An indefatigable researcher, he was completely absorbed in and dedicated to his work. His major interest was Greek and Roman antiquity—the laws, customs, and rituals of ancient societies—and he did his most important work in the field we now call cultural anthropology. He was an imaginative and romantic thinker, not a mere digger-up of facts. His work had a strong element of the poetic and the mystic about it. One of his favorite sources of information was funeral urns, the iconography of which he interpreted with great skill and imagination but not always with the exactness that trained archeologists would demand. His erudition was enormous, and his influence on German thought, particularly on the works of Nietzsche, while not all-pervasive, was nevertheless significant. Unfortunately, although his prose was rich and expressive, his works were poorly constructed, formless, over-long and over-burdened with footnotes and learned citations. Sir James Frazer, who referred to him only in two footnotes in *The Golden Bough,* wrote: "To be frank, I have not had the patience to read through his long dissertation." The results of Bachofen's work have been superseded and in some cases completely rejected by modern studies. Nevertheless his contribution was original and it stimulated later students of primitive cultures into researches of more permanent value. Friedrich Engels paid tribute to Bachofen's pioneer work in his study *The Origin of the Family, Private Property and the State* (1884).

The work for which Bachofen is best known is his study of ancient matriarchies *Das Mutterecht: eine Untersuchung über die Gynaikokratie der Alten Welt nach ihrer Religiösen und Rechtlichen Natur* (1861). This is an amazingly erudite collection of evidence from ancient sources of the existence of matriarchies. Until Bachofen published his findings such manifestations had been regarded as mere cultural aberrations, but he demonstrated that the matriarchy existed among all primitive peoples. It was his conclusion that this phenomenon represented a phase of development during which each society went through a period of completely unregulated promiscuity. Since, as a result, it was difficult if not impossible to establish paternity, the line of descent was traced through the mother, and she therefore assumed a dominant role in society.

Other significant works of Bachofen are a study of the symbols on ancient burial urns—*Versuch über die Grabersymbolik der Alten* (1859); a study of the ancient Lycian people *Das Lykische Volk und seine Bedeutung für die Entwicklung des Altertums* (1862); and a study of the influence of orientalism in Rome *Die Sage von Tanaquil* (1870). He died very suddenly, in Basel, of a stroke, leaving incomplete a manuscript on Roman burial symbols. This work, *Römische Grablampen*, was published in 1890 by his wife (Luise Elisabeth Burckhardt-Wick, whom he had married in 1865) and his son Johann Jacob Bachofen. In more recent years K. Meuli has been publishing his *Kritische Gesamtausgabe* (1948-   ).

A passage from Bachofen's *Versuch über die Grabersymbolik* was translated by B. Q. Morgan under the title *Walls: Res Sanctae, Res Sacrae* (1962).

ABOUT: Mumford, L. Note *In* B. Q. Morgan's translation of Bachofen's Walls, cited above. [In German—Bernoulli, O. A. J. J. Bachofen und das Natursymbol; Burckhardt, M. J. J. Bachofen und die Politik; Kerenyi, K. Bachofen; Muschg, W. Bachofen als Schriftsteller. In French—Giraud-Teulon, A. *Foreword to* Bachofen's Römische Grablampen; Revue de l'Histoire des Religions (1926).]

*BAGGESEN, JENS (IMMANUEL)

(February 15, 1764-March 10, 1826), Danish poet, who wrote in both Danish and German, was born in Korsör. His parents were very poor, and the boy had an unhappy childhood; more than once during his early years he attempted suicide. Thanks to the assistance of friends, however, he was able to get a good education. In 1782 he enrolled at the University of Copenhagen.

Baggesen came into sudden fame at the age of twenty-one with the publication of a poetic work, *Comic Tales,* a product of his passionate admiration for the French, particularly Voltaire. In 1789 he left Denmark —partly because of the failure of his poem *Holge Danske* and partly as a result of a turbulent restlessness that kept him, for the remainder of his life, a wanderer throughout Europe. This same impetuous and vacillating spirit marked and probably marred his work.

* bàg′ ĕ sĕn

Always brilliant, facile, technically expert, he was not profound, and he never composed a masterpiece. His achievement was nevertheless significant. His poems show imagination and sensibility, grace and charm. His influence on Danish poetry was mainly stylistic. Giovanni Bach wrote: "Denmark owes to him the creation of a poetical style, elegant and pure, to which many poets of the youngest generation conformed. With his biting satire, he overturned many idols, freed Danish letters from French influence, and smoothed the way for the great poets of the romantic movement. . . ."

Baggesen's travels took him first to Germany, where he met the poets Klopstock and Schiller and became so fascinated by the works of Kant that he adopted the philosopher's first name, Immanuel, for his middle name. From Germany he moved to Switzerland, where he met the poet Lavater and announced his unconditional conversion to the *Sturm und Drang* movement. ("Oh, if I could tear Voltaire out of my consciousness I would give two years of my life!") In 1790 he returned to Denmark with his bride, Sophia von Haller, and in that year published a charming, impressionistic travel book *The Labyrinth*, that has often been compared to Laurence Sterne's *A Sentimental Journey*. He was soon traveling again— this time to Paris where he was an excited witness to the aftermath of the French Revolution. In 1796, back in Copenhagen, he translated Homer into Danish, and then was off again, this time to Germany, where his wife died. Two years later he married Fanny Reybaz, a Swiss.

By the close of the eighteenth century, Baggesen's poetic reputation was at its height, and he was hailed as Denmark's leading poet. He soon met serious competition, however, in the person of Adam Oehlenschläger, a greater and more enduring poet. At first the two men were friends, but they soon became involved in heated literary controversies, and it was Baggesen's reputation that suffered the decline. In 1822 he returned to Paris. There misfortunes piled up on him. His wife and his young son died; he was imprisoned for debt; he became ill and despondent; his melancholia advanced into madness. He died in Hamburg, on his way back to Copenhagen, and was buried in Kiel.

Of Baggesen's writings only a few pieces remain popular today. One is a simple poem on his childhood that is still loved in Denmark—"There was a time when I was very little." The other is *The Labyrinth*. None of his major poems has been translated into English, but the short poem "There was a time" was translated by Henry Wadsworth Longfellow and appears in Mark Van Doren's *Anthology of World Poetry* (1936). Two selections from *The Labyrinth* are translated in the Warner Library.

ABOUT: Bach, G. The History of the Scandinavian Literatures; Bredsdorff, E., Mortensen, B., & Popperwell, R. An Introduction to Scandinavian Literature; Warner Library, II.

*BAHYA BEN JOSEPH IBN PAKUDA

(fl. c. 1040-1110), a leading medieval Jewish writer on ethics and philosophy, lived in Spain, possibly in the city of Saragossa. The only fact known about his life was that he held the office of "dayan," or judge of the Jewish community.

The masterpiece for which Bahya is remembered is the *Hovot ha-Levavot* (Duties of the Heart), written originally in Arabic and later translated into Hebrew by Judah Ibn Tibben. In this work Bahya formulated the first extensive Jewish philosophical system of ethics. He says in the introduction, "The Torah is divided into two parts, one is the duties of the organs . . . and the other is the duties of the heart. . . . But while so many books were written on the first part, such as the codes, few have dealt with the other." He concerned himself, therefore, with questions of religious morality. As Isaac Husik points out in *A History of Medieval Jewish Philosophy*, Bahya's purpose "is not the rationalization of Jewish dogma . . . nor the reconciliation of religion and philosophy. It is the purification of religion itself."

After proving the existence of God and defining His attributes according to the principles of medieval philosophy, Bahya proceeds to his ethical system. For him, the foundation stone of ethics is a feeling of gratitude to God, and Bahya analyzes God's infinite wisdom and goodness and the worship due Him. The ethical implications of trust in God are examined, the thesis being that man must act solely to do the will of God and not for selfish reasons. Humility, penitence, and self-examination are discussed in detail. Preaching self-restraint rather than severe asceticism, he urges man to control his passions through the use of reason. The highest virtue for Bahya is the mystical, boundless love of God which is reached after passing through the prior ethical stages.

Another work, *Ma'ani al-Nafs* (Doctrine of the Soul), written in Arabic and translated into Hebrew as *Torat ha-Nefesh*, is a mystical treatment of the nature of the soul

* bă' ḵyă ĭb' 'n pă kōō' dă

and the creation of the world. Bahya was also a liturgical poet and his work in this field is marked by deep feeling and beauty.

Bahya's ethics emphasized his belief in the importance of the right attitude of heart and mind as the essence of the moral act. Although his ethical principles are Biblical and Talmudical, he stressed intention over mere external performance. On a deeper level, Bahya believed that the act itself is but a means of achieving communion with God and purification of the soul. His sharp insight, piety, and fervor made his work one of the most lastingly influential contributions to Jewish religious thought.

The *Duties of the Heart* was translated in five volumes by Moses Hyamson from 1925 to 1947. Excerpts from it appear in anthologies such as N. Glatzer's *In Time and Eternity*. The best Hebrew edition is that of Leipzig, 1846.

ABOUT: Graetz, H. History of the Jews; Hertz, J. H. "Bachya, the Jewish Thomas à Kempis," in Jewish Theological Seminary Sixth Biennial Report, 1898; Husik, I. A History of Medieval Jewish Philosophy; Waxman, M. A History of Jewish Literature.

M. R.

*BAÏF, JEAN ANTOINE DE (February

1532-September/October 1589), French poet, was born in Venice, the natural son of Lazare de Baïf and an Italian mother. His father, descendant of an old Anjou family, was a distinguished humanist and diplomat, at the time of his son's birth ambassador of Francis I to Venice, and later ambassador to the German court of Spire (Speyer). A scholar and translator of Euripides and Sophocles, he provided his young son with an excellent education in the best humanistic tradition, under such distinguished Renaissance scholars as Charles Estienne, Ange Vergèce, and Jean Dorat (or Daurat). While studying under Dorat at the Collège de Coqueret, Baïf met a fellow student, Pierre de Ronsard, who was to become the leading French poet of the period and chief of the Pléiade. Baïf is said to have learned French versification from Ronsard and in turn to have helped Ronsard in his study of Greek.

Lazare de Baïf died in 1547, leaving his son a comfortable income which permitted him to devote his energies to study and to writing. He became an active member of the Pléiade, a group which took its name from the cluster of seven stars in the firmament (although it had more than seven members) and its guiding principles from the poetic traditions of the ancient Greeks and

* bà ēf'

54

Romans. Baïf's contribution to the Pléiade was mainly in matters of reform in metrics and prosody. He wrote a great deal of poetry in his lifetime, but little of it is today considered of any intrinsic merit.

His first poems were published in 1551 in *Le Tombeau de Marguerite de Valois*. Soon after he produced a narrative poem adapted from the Greek pastoral poet Moschus called *Le Ravissement d'Europe*. From 1552 to 1555 he published a series of sonnet cycles, in close imitation of Italian sources, particularly Petrarch. These consisted of *Les Amours de Méline*, which celebrated an imaginary mistress; *Les Amours de Francine*, where the inspiration was apparently a real woman (possibly Francine de Gennes); and *Diverses Amours*. His most popular writings, in his own time, were his *Mimes, Enseignements, et Proverbes*, first published in 1576 and reprinted six times between that year and 1619. These witty and diverse poems range from satire and fable to allegory, epic, and ode, all written lightly and with grace. His other poetic work was a collection, *Les Passetemps* (1573), which contains perhaps his only poem well known today, *Du Printemps*, a poem often compared to the more famous *Avril* of Rémy Belleau. Baïf also wrote a verse comedy, *Le Brave* (1567), modeled after Plautus' *Miles Gloriosus*, and a tragedy, *Antigone*.

Baïf's talents were lively and inventive, but not essentially creative. He is best remembered as a scholar, a reformer of French verse, and ardent champion of classical meters and of a system of phonetic spelling. He was also deeply interested in music and in 1567, working with the musician Thibaut de Courville, he founded an Academy of Poetry and of Music, with the aim of fusing the two arts in the manner of the Grecian choral ode. The Academy had the support of King Charles IX but did not outlive its founder. Baïf also invented a verse form which attempted to adapt the quantitative meters of ancient poetry to French lyric verse—the *vers baïfin*.

Little is known of Baïf's personal life. He lost his money following the religious wars of 1568, appealed to Charles IX for assistance, and was appointed a royal secretary. He lived part of his life in Paris, part at Poitiers, where his father had left him a house. In 1558 he made a trip to Italy. He had a son, Guillaume de Baïf. He died at fifty-seven, shortly after the assassination of Henri III, which took place September 19, 1589.

Baïf's reputation suffered a sharp decline in the seventeenth century and he was almost completely forgotten. Sainte-Beuve, in the nineteenth century (in his *Tableau de la Poésie Française au 16ᵉ Siècle*), however, praised him and gave him his proper place in the Pléiade. Gustave Lanson, in his *Histoire de la Littérature Française*, considered him a curious figure, "animated by great ambition to which his talent was not equal." A. A. Tilley writes of him: "Nature had not endowed Baïf with more than a slender portion of poetic genius, and he did not sufficiently cultivate that portion. The faults more or less common to the whole school, the dependence on models, the pedantry, the artificiality, are more conspicuous in him than in any other member of it. But the classical Renaissance had no more enthusiastic or enterprising champion, not even in Ronsard himself."

English translations of selections from Baïf's poems appear in J. G. Legge's *Chanticleer: A Study of the French Muse* (1936) and in George Wyndham's *Ronsard and the Pléiade* (1906). His *Œuvres Complètes*, edited by C. Marty-Laveaux, was published in five volumes, 1881-90; his *Poésies Choisies*, edited by L. Becq de Fouquières, in 1874.

ABOUT: Legge, J. G. Chanticleer: A Study of the French Muse; Tilley, A. A. The Literature of the French Renaissance. [In French—Augé-Chiquet, M. Jean-Antoine de Baïf.]

*BAKUNIN, MIKAIL ALEKSANDROVICH (May 18, 1814-July 13, 1876), Russian anarchist, was born of an aristocratic family at Torjok in Tver province. He received a military education (artillery) but did not graduate. After he left school in 1833, he was commissioned an ensign in the artillery corps of the Imperial Guard and saw service in Poland, but resigned his commission two years later in disgust at the despotic methods employed against the Poles.

He returned to Moscow in 1836 where he soon gravitated to the "circle" led by Stankevitch and plunged into the study of Hegel in the company of Belinsky and others in the group. He joined with Belinsky in the ill-fated *Moscow Observer*, contributing articles on Hegelian philosophy.

In 1841 he moved to Berlin University (where Turgenev was just completing his studies) to continue his research on Hegel, shifting in the following year to Dresden, where he came under the influence of Arnold Rugge who edited a revolutionary-democratic periodical. Bakunin contributed articles under the pseudonym "Jules Elizard," and in one

* bŭ kōō′ nyĭn

55

The Bettmann Archive

BAKUNIN

of these appears the phrase "The passion for destruction is a creative passion" which indicates the early development of his anarchistic tendencies. This phrase eventually found its place in the history of art, for it was adopted as a slogan ("Destruction is also creation") by the post-World War I Dadaists.

In 1843 Bakunin shifted to Paris, joining the socialistic workers movement and meeting Proudhon. By 1844 the Russian government was becoming alarmed by his activities, particularly those in which he associated himself with Polish émigrés plotting a rising in Poland, and demanded that he return home at once. When Bakunin refused, his passport was revoked; his property was confiscated; he was stripped of his nobility and sentenced to exile in Siberia—a sentence which was to become effective later. He spent some time in Switzerland taking part in meetings of various socialist groups. His anti-Russian writings had made him unwelcome in Paris.

He took an active part both in the Slav Congress at Prague and in the popular uprisings of June 12-17, 1848, after the defeat of which he fled to Germany, remaining underground. In May 1849 Bakunin led an uprising in Dresden, the capital city of Saxony. He was arrested and sentenced to hang. The sentence was commuted to life imprisonment, and he was eventually handed over to the Austrian authorities who kept him in the fortresses of Prague and Olmutz for the next year and a half before turning him over to the Russians.

He was sent to the Peter and Paul Fortress where he wrote his famous "Confession"—allegedly addressed to Nicholas I—repenting of his activities. At any rate a letter in that spirit was written by him to Alexander II in 1857, in which year he was released from prison and exiled to eastern Siberia. Bakunin contrived to escape from his exile in 1861 and crossed the Pacific to San Francisco on an American freighter. He did not remain in the United States, but proceeded to London where he resumed his efforts on behalf of the Polish national liberation movement.

After the failure of the Polish uprising in 1863 Bakunin migrated to Italy where in 1865-66 he founded the underground "Alliance Internationale des Frères" with branches in Italy, Spain, and Switzerland. During the next several years he devoted himself to an unsuccessful attempt to win the international working class movement from the leadership of Marx and Engels. Although he never succeeded in gaining the leadership in the "International," his efforts did disrupt and confuse the various parties to it. His influence was greatest in the Italian and Spanish movements. In Spain, especially, anarchism continued to be a significant element in labor and peasant revolutionary thinking through the 1930's. He finally came into direct conflict with Marx at the congress of 1872 at The Hague where his ultra-revolutionary views were rejected by the majority in favor of Marx. Leaving the group, he reformed his own "International" in Italy and Spain. He retired to Lugano in 1873, and died at Bern three years later.

Bakunin's principal work, *God and the State*, was written between 1872 and 1874. In this and other works he developed his thesis that "the liberty of man consists solely in this, that he obeys the laws of nature, because he has himself recognized them as such, and not because they have been imposed upon him externally by any foreign will whatsoever, human or divine, collective or individual." He regarded all authority, religious or political, as belonging to the lower stages of the historical development of humanity, and now outmoded by the advances in man's understanding of himself and of nature. Contemporary Soviet opinion regards anarchism as "bourgeois individualism turned inside out" (Lenin), and Lenin remarked of Bakunin that his was the "philosophy of the petty bourgeois despairing of his salvation."

Many of Bakunin's writings were written in French and published in France. A collected edition of his works was published there in six volumes, 1895-1913. *God and the State* first appeared in English translation by B. R. Tucker in 1894. The first American edition was published in 1916. *Marxism, Freedom and the State* was translated by K. J. Kenafick in 1950.

ABOUT: Carr, E. H. Bakunin; Maximoff, G. P. Political Philosophy of Bakunin; Pyziur, E. Doctrine of Anarchism of Bakunin.

L. R. & H. H.

---

*BALMES, JAIME LUCIANO** (August 28, 1810-July 9, 1848), Spanish religious philosopher, was born in Vich, Barcelona. He studied at the seminary of his own birthplace, further pursuing theology and civil law at the University of Cervera. Like Juan Donoso Cortés in Spain and De Maistre and Chateaubriand in France, he was a champion of the nineteenth century Catholic reaction.

He is considered the most important thinker of his time, and in many ways far superior to his contemporary, Juan Donoso Cortés, with whom he is always intellectually associated. He was a priest and, as a Catholic journalist, waged various campaigns to reconcile the political and ideological bands that kept Spain divided. His most important work is of a religious and philosophical nature: *El Protestantismo Comparado con el Catolicismo en sus Relaciones con la Civilización Europea* (1844, Protestantism Compared with Catholicism in its Relations with European Civilization), an extensive literary essay notable for its interpretation of history. In a work intended as a philosophy of history, Balmes tried to point out the beneficent service of the Church in such areas as liberty, civilization, and social progress. Protestantism, according to the thesis he expounds, upset this pattern of progress.

In another outstanding work, *Filosofía Fundamental* based on the *Summa*, Balmes complements Thomistic Scholasticism with vigorous elements taken from the "modern philosophy" of his time.

El Criterio (1845), a study of logic and of the human mind, made a contribution to nineteenth century educational theory. In some articles, which he wrote for the magazines *La Civilización* and *La Sociedad*, he dealt with problems of public law and with social and political organization, judged by both a Spanish and a Catholic standard.

Among the thinkers and philosophers of the Catalonian "Renaixensa," the name of Balmes is perhaps foremost. However, it would be provincial, in a literary sense, to fail to recognize that while love for Barcelona

or Catalonia may have been the mainspring of his inspiration, the language and style in which he wrote, as well as the theories which he expounded, belong to the history of Spanish literature, rather than Catalonian literature.

Balmes is remembered primarily as an analytical thinker, methodical, clear, logical, and of strong traditional conviction. He not only argued well, but he also wrote well. He revived philosophical studies in Spain, deriving his system from that of St. Thomas Aquinas at a time when ideas of liberalism and democracy were flourishing in the most important countries of Europe, and when romanticism in literature was at high tide both abroad and in Spain. Balmes' traditional Catholic philosophy held sway until the latter part of the nineteenth century, when finally, in 1898, a dissatisfied and self-critical Spain developed a more liberal intellectual atmosphere.

Several of Balmes' works were translated into English and published in America in the mid-nineteenth century—*European Civilization*, by C. J. Hanford and R. Kershaw in 1850; *Fundamental Philosophy*, by H. F. Brownson in 1858; *Criterion, or How to Arrive at the Truth*, by "a Catholic Priest" in 1875.

The *Obras Completas*, edited by Casanovas, was published in Barcelona, 1925, in 33 vols.

ABOUT: [In Spanish—Roure, U. N. La Vida y las Obras de Balmes.]

L. S.

---

*BALZAC, HONORÉ DE** (May 20, 1799-August 18, 1850), French novelist, was born in Tours, the son of Bernard-François Balzac, a man of peasant stock who had become successful in the years following the French Revolution and had married, at fifty-one, a girl thirty-two years his junior, Anne Charlotte Laure Sallambier, the daughter of one of the chiefs at his bank. Honoré was the eldest of four children. He had a miserable childhood; his mother, according to Martin Turnell, described him as "the fruit of duty and chance," and displayed a stony indifference to his needs and promise. He was put out to nurse until he was four, then sent, several years later, to a gloomy ecclesiastical boarding school in Vendôme where he spent six dismal years as a sluggish, indifferent pupil, rarely visited by his parents. This period he later described in the semi-autobiographical *Louis Lambert*.

When his family moved to Paris at the end of 1814, Honoré went with them and completed his studies there. Following their

* bäl' mās

* bǎl zǎk'

BALZAC

wrote to his sister when he was twenty-two—to settle down with a rich widow who could at one stroke enable him to fulfill his "only two passionate desires—love and fame." At twenty-three, Honoré found at least the first —Mme Laure de Berny, who was forty-five at the time. Her rôle at first was that of a mother figure, one who gave the ugly, awkward youth his first encouragement, kind criticism, and lessons in tact. Their relationship, which soon blossomed into what turned out to be his most sustained and perhaps most sincere affair, eventually subsided into a warm friendship that lasted until her death in 1836. "There is nothing," he later wrote, "that can match the last love of a woman who is giving a man the fulfillment of his first love." Mme de Berny, who is known as "la Dilecta," became the prototype of the woman he would always seek—the older woman, disappointed and unhappy in her marriage and in life, who expected little and was flattered at being desired, who made few claims on his time and could offer solace (and, as it turned out, money to help him out of his constant financial embarrassments). Even the idealized portrait of Mme de Mortsauf in *Le Lys dans la Vallée* was, he claimed, only a pale reflection of Mme de Berny.

In 1825 Balzac interrupted his writing activities to undertake the first, longest, and most disastrous of his business enterprises when he entered into partnership with a bookseller and floundered in the fields of publishing, printing, and type-founding for three years. The business itself, which his mother and Mme de Berny had helped to finance, left Balzac crippled with debts that he would be repaying for the rest of his life. To escape his creditors, he moved to the rue Cassini under an assumed name, and hid out, on occasion, at the homes of several friends. In 1829 he stayed at the home of a Baron de Pommereul, where he gathered much material for his first successful book, *Les Chouans* (originally called *Le Dernier Chouan*), an historical novel influenced by Sir Walter Scott. Another retreat was with the Carraud family. Mme Zulma Carraud was a lifelong friend and correspondent of Balzac's, and their relationship was unusual in its complete sincerity, unselfishness, and purity.

Both *Les Chouans* and the very different, satiric *Physiologie du Mariage, par un Jeune Célibataire,* appeared in 1829. They launched him on a prolific literary career and on the long series of novels and stories that would eventually form the vast architectonics of the *Comédie Humaine.*

plans, he enrolled at the Sorbonne as a law student in November 1816 and worked after class in the offices of an advocate and a notary. In 1819, however, having obtained his *license,* the young man suddenly announced that he would become a writer. In a bare attic in Paris, he managed to live on the pittance that his parents had hoped would starve him into submission. Making merciless economies, he imposed upon himself the hermit-like existence, the austerity and self-discipline that always characterized his working habits. After an abortive attempt to write serious literature (a tragedy, *Cromwell,* was actually completed) he entered, in 1821, into collaboration with Auguste le Poitevin de l'Égreville, turning out blood-and-thunder stories of the *roman noir* type that Walpole and Mrs. Radcliffe had made famous. Until he was thirty he was engaged in a variety of hack jobs, writing novels (*Argow le Pirate* is perhaps the best-known of these anonymous works), stories, and pamphlets in an effort to achieve financial independence. The bad habits developed during those years—melodrama, sentimentality, hasty and slick writing—left a permanent mark on his work.

Though his parents began to look more kindly on his career as soon as it proved lucrative, Honoré's sister Laure was the only member of his family who sympathized with his ambitions, and she was the only intimate of his early years. His work and poverty left him little time for amusement or for female companionship, and even then he should have liked best—as he expressed it in a letter he

Almost from the beginning Balzac wrote in series. In 1830 he composed two volumes of stories called *Scènes de la Vie Privée,* then *La Peau de Chagrin,* which reappeared with *Le Chef d'Œuvre Inconnu* and other works in a three-volume collection. In 1832 he published *La Femme de Trente Ans* and *Louis Lambert,* as well as the Rabelaisian *Contes Drolatiques.* The next year he continued the *Contes* and started a new series of novels called *Études des Mœurs au XIXième Siècle,* whose *Scènes de la Vie de Province* contained the well-known *Eugénie Grandet.* In 1834, *Scènes de la Vie Parisienne* included *Le Recherche de l'Absolu,* and *La Duchesse de Langeais;* and in 1835 he started the *Études Philosophiques* which included *Le Père Goriot* and the rhapsodic novel *Séraphita.* In *Le Père Goriot* he reintroduced characters from earlier novels, beginning to elaborate the structure he had conceived for his works.

He outlined this scheme in October 1834. The total body of his work, he decided, would be divided into three parts: the Studies of Manners (Études des Mœurs), depicting "all the repercussions of social conditions"; the Philosophical Studies (Études Philosophiques)—motivational studies of the forces behind individual and social life; and the Analytical Studies (Études Analytiques; actually this included only a few conventional satires). The whole would culminate in an "Essay on the Forces by Which Man is Motivated," with the arabesque of the *Hundred Droll Stories* as a "childlike and humorous decoration."

In the Études Philosophiques he included *La Peau de Chagrin,* his first great work, in which the nemesis of accomplished desire was powerfully worked out; *La Recherche de l'Absolu,* the study of a scientist who destroys his family and himself through an obsessive search for the "simple substance"; *Le Chef d'Œuvre Inconnu,* a shorter work about a man who ruins himself in the quest for ideal beauty; and *Louis Lambert,* a semi-autobiographical account of a scholar whose reason is impaired as a result of his passion for knowledge. Balzac's aim was to paint the "ravages of thought" and emotion in these studies of monomaniacs whose obsessions disorganize their social functions and deflect their natural affections. The heroes burn themselves up in pursuit of whatever ideal they have chosen— in a manner not totally unlike that in which Balzac consumed himself completing this vast canvas.

The Studies of Manners, which were much more numerous, were divided into sections he had conceived of before—scenes of private life, provincial life, Parisian life, political and military life, country life. At the time he outlined his system they included *Le Médicin de Campagne, La Femme de Trente Ans, Eugénie Grandet, Le Père Goriot,* and *Les Chouans.* In later years he added to these *Le Lys dans la Vallée* (1835), *Illusions Perdues* (1837-43), *César Birotteau* (1837), *Une Passion dans le Désert* (1837), *Le Curé de Village* (1841), *Béatrix* (1839), *Ursule Mirouet* (1842), *Une Ténébreuse Affaire* (1843), and his final masterpieces, *Le Cousin Pons* (1846) and *La Cousine Bette* (1847).

The individuals in these novels were, in psychological conception, like those of the Études Philosophiques—"temperaments" or type characters who become identified with their ruling passion, e.g., Goriot for his daughters' well-being, Grandet for money. Balzac has been criticized for this kind of characterization which lacks, according to his critics, the characteristically French psychological subtlety and penetration. His gift, however, was rather for analyzing people in relation to their social environment. Moreover, he was concerned with society in an entirely new way; in contrast to the earlier studies of manners, he took a genuinely sociological approach. He was interested in the mechanism rather than the spectacle: the power struggle, the forces of the new commercialism, the machinations of the stock market, politics, and the press, the molding of public opinion, and especially that "great modern monster" Paris, where ambitions confronted each other in ferocious war. As his somber painting grew in dimension, he created an immense fresco of French society from Napoleonic times to the July Monarchy, peopled with the innumerable characters who appear and reappear in these works.

The theory of this structure was outlined in the famous preface to the *Comédie Humaine* in 1842. Balzac chose the title, while preparing the first edition of his collected works, as a contrast to Dante's *Divine Comedy,* emphasizing a sociological as opposed to theological structure. In the preface he expounded a system of human society which he compared with the systems of Geoffroy Saint-Hilaire and Buffon. He proclaimed his desire to describe social species as the naturalists had classified zoological species. As in nature various species of animals became more specialized according to their environment, so human beings developed under the influence of their social environment. If the artist chose a sampling of some three to four thousand characters, representing each stratum of society, each of its forms and passions, the result would depict an entire epoch—it would be a "natural history of society."

To complete this vast panorama was impossible, and Balzac's even partial success is astonishing. To achieve it he worked at a pace and with a furious energy that have become legendary. He would arise at midnight in order to avoid distraction and work until late in the afternoon, sometimes for sixteen hours at a stretch, drinking black coffee incessantly. He had little time for relaxation as he divided his hours between his new manuscripts and the galleys he was constantly revising.

His periods of respite, after weeks of monastic dedication, were extreme lapses in the opposite direction. From the beginning he had an absurd love of the aristocracy, and as soon as he became successful, after 1830, he equipped himself with valet, horses, and carriage, and went out in style with liveried footmen. With *La Peau de Chagrin* he added the aristocratic "de" to his name, furnished his apartment with opulent extravagance, and walked with a jewel-encrusted cane which he claimed held the nude likeness of an unknown mistress. He often cut a ridiculous figure in the literary salons, for he did not take easily to elegance. He was too short, stout, ugly, and sensual. He stuffed his knife into his mouth when he ate. The fat fingers that held his lorgnon had dirty nails; and his pomaded hair dripped grease on the frills of his collar. His shoelaces would come undone. Only his sparkling eyes, his wit, his enormous vitality, redeemed him socially.

Balzac's luxuries were bought on credit, for from the first he made new debts to pay his old ones. Though he was one of the most popular writers in Europe and made many contributions to periodicals, his standard of living and his costly working habits (he practically wrote his novels on galleys) ate up his earnings. Moreover, he squandered his money in abortive enterprises. In 1836 he was embroiled in a lawsuit over an unauthorized reprint of one of his works. The next year he made an unsuccessful attempt to run a magazine called the *Chronique de Paris*. In 1838 he went to Sardinia on a wild-goose chase, hoping to take possession of some silver mines. Another expensive enterprise, a country chalet built to his eccentric specifications, literally collapsed, largely because of the haste with which he had insisted it be built. In 1840 he again tried to run a maga-

zine, *La Revue Parisienne;* he gave it up after three months, but in that time contributed to it his famous essay on Stendhal's *La Chartreuse de Parme,* generously praising the unknown writer's genius. His attempts at playwriting, to which he turned after 1840 in order to make quick money, show similar blunders. *Vautrin,* for instance, opened to a half-empty house simply because he had spread the rumor that it was sold out.

Though Balzac was on good terms with most men of letters (Sainte-Beuve is a notable exception), he formed few real friendships with men, and his life is marked by his multifarious relationships with women. In his early works—the genre pictures of Parisian society, such as *Étude de Femme, La Femme de Trente Ans,* and *La Paix du Ménage*—Balzac had popularized a new type: the wife who pines away because of her husband's indifference. Through these treacly stories, and through his bold affirmation of the right to love of the woman who is past her first youth, he became the personal apologist for countless spinsters and disappointed wives throughout Europe, and soon letters came pouring in. The author was always ready to unveil his deepest feelings in response to fine stationery or an interesting line. From these admirers Balzac, who had not much spare time to court women or to seek a wife, was able to select his mistresses. A very incomplete catalog of his involvements, which are so central to his life and work, would include:

The Marquise de Castries, whom he pursued ardently in 1832—even to the point of writing pro-Royalist articles and running, unsuccessfully, for parliament as a Royalist candidate. Though she encouraged him for many months, the Marquise never capitulated, and Balzac's revenge was his portrait of her in *La Duchesse de Langeais.*

The Baroness Evelina Hanska, who introduced herself to him in 1832 through a letter signed "L'Étrangère." After an enthusiastic correspondence, he arranged to meet the Polish noblewoman in 1833 in Neuchâtel, where she was touring with her husband. They fell in love immediately, and she promised to marry him when her husband died. Since this did not occur for some years, they carried on a protracted and passionate epistolary romance, seeing each other only rarely. Even after her husband died in 1841, and they were able to spend more time together, she put him off for nine years before marrying him on March 14, 1850. Their honeymoon turned out to be appallingly brief: he died five months later. This seventeen-year courtship of Balzac's "Polar Star," as he liked to call her, is an extremely controversial one. It has been blown up to the dimension of a grand romance, or derided as a convenient relationship which neither permitted to interfere with personal interest.

The Contessa Visconti-Guidoboni *(née Sarah Lowell* in England), whose rôle and devotion have been highly underrated, according to Stefan Zweig, because she seems to have been more genuinely concerned with their emotional relationship than in her status as a famous writer's paramour. He met her at a reception in 1835, and their relationship lasted until 1839, during which time she apparently bore him, in May 1836, one of his illegitimate children. She showed an unusual concern for his welfare, arranging to have him take care of her husband's business affairs on two occasions (two trips to Italy to collect some debts for the Count). Later she paid several debts for him and even hid him at her home on the Champs-Élysées to keep his creditors away. Their affair ended when, after an unusually disastrous venture, one of Balzac's creditors sued the Count Visconti-Guidoboni himself.

In the last years of his life Balzac bought a house in Paris and furnished it with ornate rubbish, always with the illusion that he was buying priceless antiques. In an effort to attain status he tried twice, unsuccessfully, to secure election to the Académie Française. His output declined during these years, and in 1844 he began to complain of waning vigor. He was unable to finish the ambitious *Les Paysans* and devoted himself to lesser works, although the admirable *Le Cousin Pons* and *La Cousine Bette* date from these years. Weakened by heart trouble, lung inflammation, short-windedness, and impaired vision, he became seriously ill a few months after his marriage and died in Paris aged fifty-one. At his funeral on August 22 (at which Hugo, Dumas, Sainte-Beuve, and the Minister Baroche were pallbearers) Hugo in his eulogy economically summed up the character of his work as a blend of "observation and imagination."

It is the curious equilibrium of these two elements in his work that makes Balzac such a perplexing writer to categorize, and that underlies the debate between his realist and anti-realist interpreters. Baudelaire opened the issue when he affirmed that Balzac seemed to him not an observer but a "passionate visionary." The key seems to lie in Balzac's use of the formal devices of realism—documentation, detail, psychological and social determinism—in combination with a highly personal vision which is a projection of his imagination rather than a reflection of the outside world. As a realist he depicted social mores, personalities, physical detail, and atmosphere with a minute precision that was new in the history of the novel. Yet that studied observation was the result not of experience but of his cerebrations in the apartments where he spent so much of his working life. Similarly his characters, though carefully delineated, are so simplified in conception that they are a form of caricature (Balzac has been called "the French Dickens"). The net result is an "aura of otherworldliness," an occult atmosphere that heightens and distorts reality even while giving the impression of realism. Discussing one episode which could be "either a magnificent lurid document or the baseless fabric of a vision," Henry James commented, "We suffer at the hands of no other author this particular helplessness of immersion. It is *done*.... All we can do is to say that the truth itself can't be more than done and if the false in this way equals it we must give up looking for the difference. Alone among novelists Balzac has the secret of an insistence that somehow makes the difference nought. He warms his facts into life."

Balzac has had an immense influence on the course of the modern novel in France. Writing at the very beginning of the outburst of prose fiction that took place with the romantic movement, he was decisive in directing the French novel to an analytical rather than narrative emphasis, with a realism that leads logically through Champfleury and the Goncourts to the naturalism of Zola. With him the genre achieved new dimensions and a new dignity, penetrating into, and commenting on, every aspect of human life. His emphasis on detail, and especially on the influence of environment on character, later furnished the naturalists with a basis for their theory of art. His own genius, however, lies rather in his vitality, inexhaustible imagination, and the immense scope of the *Comédie Humaine*, before which, Henry James said, "criticism simply drops out."

The standard edition of Balzac's works is the *Œuvres Complètes*, ed. M. Bouteron and H. Longnon, 40 vols, Paris, 1910-40. The best-known English translation is the *Comédie Humaine*, ed. G. Saintsbury, 1899-1900. Translations of individual works have been made by Ellen Marriage, Clara Bell, G. Burnham Ives, Katherine Prescott Wormeley, and Jane M. Sedgwick. The Modern Library volume containing *Père Goriot* and *Eugénie Grandet* was translated by E. K. Brown, Dorothea Walter, and John Watkins. In 1955 a series of new translations of some of the less known works of the *Comédie Humaine* was launched with Frances Frenaye's translation of *César Birotteau*.

A Balzac Bibliography was compiled by W. H. Royce in 1929; in 1960 Albert Joseph George compiled *Books by Balzac,* a checklist compiled from the papers of W. H. Royce.

ABOUT: Benjamin, R. Balzac; Brunetière, F. Honoré de Balzac (the best critical work available in English translation); Dargan, E. P. Honoré de Balzac, a Force of Nature; Dargan, E. P. and Weinberg, B. Evolution of Balzac's Comédie Humaine; Hunt, H. J. Honoré de Balzac; James, H. French Poets and Novelists; James, H. Notes on Novelists; Levin, H. Contexts of Criticism; Proust, M. On Art and Literature, 1896-1919; Saintsbury, G. French Literature and Its Masters; Saintsbury, G. History of the French Novel; Sandars, M. F. Honoré de Balzac, Life and Writings; Symons, A. The Symbolist Movement in Literature; Turnell, M. The Novel in France; Yeats, W. B. Essays and Introductions; Zweig, S. Balzac. [In French— Bardeche, M. Balzac, Romancier; Bellessort, A. Balzac et Son Œuvre; Curtius, E. R. Balzac; LeBreton, A. Balzac, L'Homme et L'Œuvre; *see also* L'Année Balzacienne, 1960.]

E. G.

BANDELLO

*BANDELLO, MATTEO (1485-1561), Italian prose-writer and poet, was born in Castelnuovo Scrivia, then part of Lombardy, of a noble family. His education was supervised by his uncle, the Dominican teacher and theologian Vincenzio Bandello, prior of the convent of Santa Maria delle Grazie in Milan. Matteo entered the Dominican order early and accompanied his distinguished uncle on his travels in Italy, France, Spain, and Germany, visiting Dominican religious houses. The young monk, it is generally conceded, was more secular than spiritual in his inclinations, and on his travels gathered much experience in worldly matters, which he was later to draw upon in his *Novelle*.

After his uncle's death, Bandello returned to the convent in Milan, but he soon found the cloistered life unbearable and threw off his habit to become a soldier, a courtier, and a man of letters. From 1515 to 1521 he lived in Mantua as a tutor or court poet to the noblewoman Lucrezia Gonzaga. For his patroness he composed a tragedy—an adaptation of the *Hecuba* of Euripides—and the requisite number of conventional love poems. Also in Mantua he made the acquaintance of the humanist critic Julius Caesar Scaliger. Returning to Milan, Bandello became deeply involved in political intrigue, generally identifying himself with the French cause. In 1525 the defeat of the French at Pavia left Milan in the hands of the Spanish, and Bandello was forced to flee in disguise, leaving

* bän děl' lō

behind his books and his manuscripts, which were destroyed. In 1528 he became an adviser to Cesare Fregosa, general of the Venetian Republic. In 1542 he followed Fregosa into exile in France. After his patron's death, he was named Bishop of Agen by King Henry II of France in recognition of his services to that country. He held the post for five years, then retired and died at Bassens, in France, in his middle seventies.

Bandello's masterpiece is a collection of stories, *Le Novelle,* which he wrote over a period of almost half a century. It was not until he became Bishop of Agen that he had the leisure (having turned over his clerical duties to a colleague, the Bishop of Grasse) to collect the *Novelle* and publish them. The first three volumes, containing some 200 *novelle,* appeared in 1554; the fourth, with 30 *novelle,* was published posthumously in 1573. The stories—many of them coarse and downright licentious—are somewhat extraordinary productions for the Bishop of Agen, but they brilliantly reflect the vivacity and color of Bandello's secular life. "These novels of mine are not fables but true histories," he insisted. In point of fact, much of the material is legendary and romantic, though told in such a brisk journalistic style that it has the ring of actuality about it. Unlike Boccaccio, his predecessor in the *novella* form, Bandello does not try to unify his tales by grouping them within any kind of framework. Instead each story is dedicated separately to a contemporary, ranging from obscure friends to famous figures of the

Renaissance like Machiavelli, Trissino, Castiglione, and Berni.

The *Novelle* have little intrinsic literary merit. They are mainly memorable today for their widespread influence, particularly in England and France. In 1559 Pierre Boaistuau freely adapted six of them in *Histoires Tragiques Extraites des Œuvres Italiennes de Bandel.* In 1565 the more famous translations (actually adaptations) by Belleforest appeared in France. In England twenty-five of the *Novelle* appeared (adapted from the French rather than the Italian) in William Painter's *Palace of Pleasure* (1566) and thirteen in Geoffrey Fenton's *Tragicall Discourses* (1567). It was in Painter that Shakespeare found Bandello's story of *Giulietta e Romeo* which became his *Romeo and Juliet,* and it was also indirectly from Bandello that Shakespeare took material for *Much Ado About Nothing* (the story of Timbreo and Fenicia) and *Twelfth Night* (the story of Lattanzio and Nicuola). Other writers who drew upon Bandello were the English dramatists Webster, Massinger, and Beaumont and Fletcher, the Spanish dramatists Lope de Vega and Calderón de la Barca, and the poets Musset and Byron.

Many English translations of *Giulietta e Romeo* have been published over the years. A collection of *Twelve Stories* by Bandello in English was made by Percy Pinkerton in 1905. The complete works of Bandello in Italian were published in two volumes in 1934-35, edited by F. Flora.

ABOUT: Baldwin, C. S. Renaissance Literary Theory and Practice; Griffith, T. Bandello's Fiction: An Examination of the Novelle; Hartley, K. H. Bandello and the Heptameron; Pinkerton, P. Biographical Memoir *in* Twelve Stories of Bandello; Prevost, R. Matteo Bandello and Elizabethan Fiction; Wilkins, E. H. A History of Italian Literature. [In Italian—see study by G. Brognoligo.]

BANG, HERMAN. See "TWENTIETH CENTURY AUTHORS"

*BANVILLE, THÉODORE FAULLAIN DE (March 14, 1823-March 15, 1891), French poet and playwright, was born in Moulins, the son of Claude-Théodore de Banville, a naval officer, and Elisabeth Zélie Huet. He had an older sister, Zélie. A handsome, dreamy child, he adored his parents and had a happy childhood, first in the gardens of Font-Georges, near Moulins (he described himself as a child sitting under a mulberry tree and playing on a small red fiddle an accompaniment for the songs of

* bäN vēl'

BANVILLE

the birds), and then in Paris, where the family moved when he was seven. He was still a student, in law school, when his first volume of poetry, *Les Cariatides,* appeared in 1842, and he almost immediately won recognition. In general Banville's life was serene. He was admired and respected as a poet. He was influential in the leading literary movements of his day. He was named a Chevalier of the Legion of Honor in 1858, and he was socially popular. After a brief love affair with an actress, Marie Daubran, Banville married Mme Rochegrosse in 1866 and lived with her very happily. Perhaps his only disappointment was that he outlived his fame as a poet. He nevertheless had the consolation of seeing his plays in the repertory of the Comédie Française and of knowing that his work in reviving the poetry of the French Renaissance had influenced not only his own countrymen, but had spread to England as well.

Les Cariatides and *Les Stalactites* (1846), Banville's second book of verse, were products of nineteenth century romanticism, the work of an ardent disciple of Gautier, Musset, and Hugo. It was not until 1857, when he published his *Odes Funambulesques* under the pen-name "Bracquemond," that he struck out on his own in what has been called his "most original verse." These whimsical poetic satires were appropriately named for the *funambule* or rope-dancer, and, as Edmund Gosse remarked, "no versifier has ever lived who achieved more marvellous feats on the lyrical trapeze than he." The intellectual content of Banville's poems is slight. They celebrate joy, beauty, love. His favorite subject was Greek mythology—the mythology of Cupids, Venuses, and banqueting on Olympus.

Banville's skills were primarily technical. Ultimately he discovered his true poetic masters not in the romantics of his own century but in the strict formalists of the Renaissance—Ronsard in particular. He delighted in precise and virtuoso metrical and rhyming effects, and he found these in Ronsard and in his precessors—Charles d'Orléans, Villon, Marot. He revived the old forms—rondel, rondeau, ballade, triolet, villanelle, chant royal. Along with two much greater poets, Charles Baudelaire and Leconte de Lisle, he was a founder of the Parnassian movement, which sought to purify French poetry of the emotional excesses of romanticism and restore it to "Olympian calm" in attitude and technical precision in metrics. In 1872 he published an essay, *Petit Traité de Poésie Française,* which codified the Parnassian theories of poetry, laying emphasis upon rhyme and the poet's ingenuity in achieving it. The vogue of the Parnassians was short, but it spread widely. It became the basis of the English aesthetic movement of the nineteenth century, influencing the work of Swinburne, Morris, Rossetti, Andrew Lang, Austin Dobson, and others.

With the exception of *Gringoire, the Ballad Monger,* a one-act comedy, Banville's plays are little known today. Polished verse dramas, they lack dramatic power and to the modern reader appear artificial and over-refined. In his own day, however, Banville was a popular playwright. He was also a drama critic and for two years, 1850-1852, he edited the dramatic feuilleton *Pouvoir.* He wrote one short novel, *Marcelle Rabe* (1891), and published several collections of stories and journalistic essays in addition to many volumes of verse. In 1882 he published his memoirs (*Mes Souvenirs*).

Banville died in Paris on the day after his sixty-eighth birthday, neglected by the public but respected by many poets and men of letters. One of these, Anatole France, remembered him as "pale, clean-shaven, with black, nimble eyes, walking in the sunlight with short steps. . . . We shall never see him again, gliding along noiselessly, discreet and calm, yet enabling one to divine in his whole person an indefinable quality that was rare and exquisite and yet chimerical, which made this old gentleman a fantastic, dreamlike fig-

ure, escaped from a Venetian *festa* in the days of Tiepolo."

The *Ballades* of Banville were translated into English verse by A. T. Strong in 1913. Selections from his poems appear in the Warner Library and in many anthologies. There are several English translations of his play *Gringoire,* the first in 1888 (translator not named); other plays in English translation are *The Deputy of Bombignac* (1886); *Socrates and His Wife,* by C. Renauld (1889); and *Charming Léandre,* by B. H. Clark (1915).

ABOUT: Columbia Dictionary of Modern European Literature; France, A. Life and Letters: Fourth Series; Gosse, E. Silhouettes; Lang, A. Essays in Little; Whitridge, A. Critical Ventures in Modern French Literature; Philological Quarterly October 1925; PMLA September 1953. [In French —see biography by J. Carpentier.]

*BARATYNSKY (or BORATYNSKY), EVGENY ABRAMOVICH (1800-June 29, 1844), Russian poet, was born of an aristocratic family in St. Petersburg. At twelve he was sent to a fashionable military school which had connections with the royal court, but four years later he was expelled for theft. This disgrace may have been one of the factors that contributed to his lifelong pessimism and despondency. At nineteen Baratynsky became a private in the army and served first with the footguards in St. Petersburg and then for six years in Finland. During this period he began publishing his verse. In 1826, having received his discharge from the army, he settled in Moscow. He married and seems to have had a happy family life, but he suffered always from intense melancholia. He left Moscow in 1844 to travel in France and Italy and died suddenly in Naples at the early age of forty-four.

Baratynsky was a poet's poet rather than a widely popular writer. He was admired by Pushkin (who considered him one of the most original poets of the age) and his circle, but was otherwise scarcely noticed. His best-known work is narrative verse—in a simple, precise, and pure style showing the distinct influence of the eighteenth century classical revival—*Eda, The Ball, The Concubine* (sometimes called *The Gypsy Girl*). Equally interesting are his philosophical poems—*The Last Death, The Last Poem, Autumn, Death, On the Death of Goethe.* These, as their titles suggest, are profoundly melancholy, though not without considerable poetic grandeur. Baratynsky was an intellectual poet. D. S. Mirsky described him as "the one who made the best use of thought as material for poetry," and Marc Slonim calls him a "poet of philosophical analysis and intellectual quest."

* bŭ rŭ tĭn' skĭ

His verse is technically perfect, witty (though not humorous), and classical in both manner and spirit. Perhaps the closest parallel to it in English is the work of Alexander Pope.

Baratynsky wrote little prose, but, Mirsky remarked, "the little contains a quite disproportionate amount of the best things ever said in Russian on the subject of poetry." Two of his statements on poetry are worthy of special attention—his definition of lyric poetry as "the fullest awareness of a given moment"; and his comment that the two qualities which must be combined in a poet are "the fire of creative imagination and the coldness of controlling reason."

Brief selections from Baratynsky's poems appear in English translation in *A Treasury of Russian Verse,* edited by A. Yarmolinsky (1949), and in *A Second Book of Russian Verse,* edited by C. M. Bowra (1948).

ABOUT: Mirsky, D. S. A History of Russian Literature; Slonim, M. The Epic of Russian Literature; Yarmolinsky, A. A Treasury of Russian Verse. [In Russian—see study by N. P. Mazepa.]

*BARBEY D'AUREVILLY, JULES AMÉDÉE** (November 2, 1808-April 23, 1889), French novelist and critic, was born at Saint-Sauveur-le-Vicomte, near Coutances, into a proud and intensely conservative Norman family, son of Théophile Barbey and Ernestine Ango (who claimed Bourbon blood). He grew up imbued with pride in his ancestry and love for the rugged Norman region. He was educated at home by an abbé, then sent to Caen to study law. In Caen he met the famous English fop George (Beau) Brummel, who was later to inspire his essay on Dandyism. At seventeen Barbey broke with his family and became involved in democratic and liberal movements, but he ultimately returned to arch conservatism and strict Catholicism and was, indeed, for most of his life a bitter critic of change, progress, and reform. He lived in Paris but returned regularly to Normandy from which he drew constant inspiration for his novels. It was his wish to become "the Walter Scott of the Cotentin" (the northwestern peninsula of Normandy) and to capture in his work the cherished historical and legendary tradition, the rough scenery, and the sturdy individualistic types of the area.

Barbey had very little money. He lived in elegant poverty in an almost bare room, affected a costume of the romantic past and walked about Paris in frock coat, lace cuffs, and mousquetaire hat, and carried a jeweled

* bȧr bā' dôr vē yē'

BARBEY D'AUREVILLY

cane. Author of the famous essay "On Dandyism with Some Observations on Beau Brummel" (1845), he made Dandyism a way of life, not simply a fad of dress and behavior. "You can be a dandy in a ragged coat," he wrote. "It is not the coat which walks alone! It is a certain manner of wearing it which makes the dandy." He was aristocratic to his fingertips, and it was said of him that "he gave dignity to indigence." He believed, Charles Whibley wrote, "only in what was rare: great men, great wit, great character." He never traveled abroad because, he wrote, "There is something democratic in traveling, a secret love of majorities, which should be despised." He was arrogant, handsome, vain, and, according to his friends, charming. He never married, but lived for some years with Mlle Louise Read, who published his posthumous works.

An indefatigable writer, Barbey produced some fifty volumes, including about twenty-four volumes of criticism, many novels and collections of short stories, and several volumes of letters (among his correspondents were Léon Bloy and Eugénie de Guérin, sister of his friend the poet Maurice de Guérin). His criticism consisted mainly of articles contributed to periodicals—*Globe, Revue du Monde Catholique* (which he founded in 1846), *Journal des Débats, Revue Indépendante,* and others. It was strongly iconoclastic and opinionated; he denounced fads, popular successes, romanticism, anything that hinted of democracy or progress. Though a devout Catholic, he even from time to time

65

offended the clergy with his outspoken criticisms. There was a strong element of the devil's advocate in him, revealed best in his *romans de terroir*, novels of terror, of "satanic mysticism," weird, imaginative, "off-beat" stories which, one critic writes, "bear the imprint of a bold and original genius."

Barbey's reputation declined after his death and he was generally dismissed as an eccentric. George Saintsbury called him "that curious flawed genius . . . one of those who come short but a little of individual greatness." In recent years, however, there has been a revival of interest in his work. There is now a flourishing Société Barbey d'Aurevilly in Saint-Sauveur-le-Vicomte, where he was born and where he is buried.

The first of Barbey's books to appear in English was *Une Histoire sans Nom* (1882), translated by E. Saltus in 1891 as *The Story Without a Name*. *Les Diaboliques* (1874) was translated as *Weird Women* by C. Carrington in 1900 and as *The Diaboliques* by E. Boyd in 1925. *Ce Qui Ne Meurt Pas* (1883) was translated as *What Never Dies* by "Sebastian Melmoth" (Oscar Wilde?) in 1909; *L'Ensorcelée* (1854) as *Bewitched* by L. C. Willcox in 1928. Other important novels, as yet untranslated, are *Le Chevalier des Touches* (1864) and *Un Prêtre Marié* (1865). The essay *On Dandyism* was translated by D. Ainslie in 1897 and by D. B. Wyndham Lewis as *The Anatomy of Dandyism* in 1928.

ABOUT: Boyd, E. Introduction to Barbey's The Diaboliques; Columbia Dictionary of Modern European Literature; France, A. Life and Letters: Third Series; Gosse, E. French Profiles; Moers, E. The Dandy; Starkie, E. Petrus Borel; Whibley, C. The Pageantry of Life; Whitridge, A. Critical Ventures in Modern French Literature. [In French— see studies by R. Besus, J. Canu, G. Corbière-Gille, J. Gautier, J. Petit & P. J. Yarrow, J. P. Seguin.]

*BARBIER, (HENRI) AUGUSTE (April 29, 1805-February 13, 1882), French poet, was born in Paris, the son of a lawyer. He was educated at the Lycée Henri IV and went to law school to follow in his father's profession, but the outbreak of the July Revolution of 1830 inspired him to write the impassioned political poetry which made him, for a brief period, the most popular poet in France.

Barbier's only earlier literary attempt had been an undistinguished historical novel, *Les Mauvais Garçons,* which he wrote in collaboration with Alphonse Royer. In the summer of 1830 he rushed up to Paris from his country home at Seine-et-Marne to be an eyewitness to the brief and almost bloodless rebellion that led to the overthrow of Charles X. Inspired by these events, Barbier published a scathing political satire, "La Curée," in the *Revue de Paris* and he became an immediate sensation. Other timely poems followed —"L'Idole," "Popularité"— Edmund Gosse described them as "blasts on the trumpet of democracy." These were collected in the volume *Iambes et Poèmes* in 1831. Gosse wrote: "The ardent love of liberty and the impetuous virility of the style which animated these rhetorical lyrics concealed for the moment their defects, and from 1830 to 1835 Barbier lived in a blaze of glory." Lamartine compared him to the masters of classical satire Pindar and Juvenal. Balzac, in turn, compared him to Lamartine.

Barbier's fame was of short duration, however. His second volume, *Il Pianto* (1833), a satire on Italian politics, and the next, *Lazare* (1833), an attack on English industrialism, failed to excite the reading public. He was rapidly forgotten and his later works—*Chants Civils et Religieux* (1841); *Rimes Héroïques* (1843); *Silves* (1864); *Satires* (1865)— were completely negligible. He also produced some fiction, memoirs, travel writing, and a verse play which was turned by De Wailly into the libretto for Berlioz' opera *Benvenuto Cellini,* and he translated into French Shakespeare's *Julius Caesar,* Coleridge's *Rime of the Ancient Mariner,* and Boccaccio's *Decameron.* In 1869 Barbier was at last elected to the French Academy. The story is told that Montalembert, on hearing of his election, said: "Barbier? Mais il est mort!" He was awarded the Legion of Honor in 1878 and died at Nice, four years later, at the age of seventy-six. Perhaps the fairest summation of his career is Henri Van Laun's in his *History of French Literature:* "Some men make revolutions, but of Barbier it may be said that the Revolution made him."

ABOUT: Gosse, E. Inter Arma. [In French— Séché, L. Le Centenaire de Barbier; Revue Lyonnaise Jan.-June 1882.]

*BARETTI, GIUSEPPE MARC'ANTONIO (April 24, 1719-May 5, 1789), Italian prose writer, critic, and lexicographer, was born in Turin, the son of Luca Baretti, an architect and descendant of a noble family, and his wife, Caterina Tesio. The boy was at first intended for the priesthood, then for a career in architecture, but was obliged to give up the latter because of his poor eyesight. (Sir Joshua Reynolds' portrait of him, painted years later, shows him nearsightedly peering at a book.) In 1735 he went to work as a wine merchant's clerk. Two years later

* bàr byä'

* bä rāt' tē'

he moved to Venice, where he met the well-known essayist Count Gaspari Gozzi and embarked upon a literary career of his own. He lived in various cities—Venice, Milan, Turin—and held minor official positions. All this time he was contributing fairly regularly to periodicals and collections of verse. In 1750 he published his first small volume, *Piacevoli Poesie.*

A friendly, lively man of considerable personal charm, Baretti's success in society was nevertheless handicapped by his fiery temper and his extreme frankness. By 1750 he had become involved in so many bitter literary controversies that he was obliged to leave Italy. Early in 1751 he settled in London, where he rapidly mastered the English language and supported himself by giving Italian lessons and by miscellaneous writing, including an Italian grammar and *The Italian Library,* a biographical dictionary of leading Italian authors. Through a fortunate meeting with Dr. Samuel Johnson, he was introduced to the most distinguished literary society of the age. Dr. Johnson also encouraged him in his literary endeavors, and Baretti's major work, his often reprinted *Italian and English Dictionary* (1760), was published with a dedication by him.

Baretti returned to Italy in 1760 and settled in Venice where, using the pseudonym "Aristarco Scannabue," he began publication of a literary journal, *La Frusta Letteraria,* whose title ("The Literary Scourge") aptly describes the frank and furious way in which the journal attacked much contemporary Italian writing. In 1765, after twenty-five numbers, the journal was suppressed, and Baretti soon found it expedient to return to London. Here he won new popularity with a travel journal, *An Account of the Manners and Customs of Italy* (1768). His position in English society was by now so secure that in 1769 when he was arrested for killing a man in a street brawl he was able to produce for character witnesses as distinguished a group as Dr. Johnson, Edmund Burke, David Garrick, Sir Joshua Reynolds, and Oliver Goldsmith.

After his acquittal Baretti went back to work on new editions of his dictionary, on a translation (never completed) of *Don Quixote,* and on essays and prefaces to many English editions of Italian classics, among them Dante, Ariosto, and Machiavelli. In 1774 he was offered but declined a professorship of Italian at the University of Dublin. For several years he made his home with the wealthy Thrale family (Mrs. Thrale later became Mrs. Piozzi, best known today for her memoirs of Dr. Johnson and his circle) as Italian tutor to their eldest daughter. In 1775 he accompanied the Thrales and Dr. Johnson on their tour of France.

Once again, however, Baretti's celebrated temper got him into trouble. He quarreled bitterly with Mrs. Thrale (who later described him as "haughty and insolent and breathing defiance against all mankind") and with Dr. Johnson. In his last years he published a Spanish-English dictionary but produced little else of importance. He lived comfortably on an annual government pension and in addition received aid from a wealthy patron, Richard Barwell. He died in London at seventy and was buried at Marylebone.

Although his *Italian-English Dictionary* is worthy of a place beside Dr. Johnson's pioneer achievements in lexicography and his travel writings are fresh, original, and entertaining, Baretti is better remembered today as an influence than an author. He was the great popularizer of Italian literature in England in the eighteenth century, and he did much to promote understanding between the two nations. He modeled himself, probably quite consciously, upon Dr. Johnson in manner as well as in work, and would no doubt have valued Johnson's opinion of him, as reported by Boswell: "I know of no man who carries his head higher in conversation than Baretti. He has not, indeed, many hooks, but with what hooks he has he grapples very forcibly."

The standard edition of Baretti's works in Italian was edited by Piccioni in six volumes, 1911-1936. His principal works in English are: *A Dissertation Upon the Italian Poetry, in which are interspersed some remarks on Mr. Voltaire's "Essay on the Epic Poets,"* 1753; *The Italian Library,* 1757; *A Dictionary of the English and Italian Languages,* 1760; *A Grammar of the Italian Language,* 1762; *An Account of the Manners and Customs of Italy,* 1768; *A Journey from London to Genoa,* 1770; *Spanish and English Dictionary,* 1778.

ABOUT: Collison-Morley, L. Giuseppe Baretti; Dictionary of National Biography; Gallup, D. C. Baretti's Reputation in England *in* The Age of Johnson: Essays Presented to C. B. Tinker; Lubbers-van der Brugge, C. J. M. Johnson and Baretti.

BARTAS, GUILLAUME DE SALLUSTE, Seigneur du. See DU BARTAS, GUILLAUME DE SALLUSTE, Seigneur

BARTOLOMÉ DE LAS CASAS. See LAS CASAS, BARTOLOMÉ DE

*BASHKIRTSEFF (BASHKIRTSEVA), MARIA KONSTANTINOVNA (November 23, 1860-October 31, 1884), Russian memoirist who wrote in French, was born at Gavrontzi in the province of Poltava. Her parents were separated, and she lived abroad with her mother, having only occasional meetings with her father. Her childhood was spent mostly in various resorts in Germany and on the Riviera. She received an excellent education from private teachers and was taught not only several modern languages but also Latin and Greek. Her main ambition was to become a singer, but after some initial successful training her voice failed.

In 1877 Maria Bashkirtseff began the systematic study of painting at the Robert-Fleury studio in Paris and later at Julian's. She had some success as a painter. Several of her pictures were exhibited at the Salon in 1880; her self-portrait is in the museum at Nice; and a portrait of a woman (for which she won an honorable mention in 1884) is in the Luxembourg Gallery. The painter Bastien-Lepage, one of her teachers, became her devoted friend. She corresponded with various prominent persons; under an assumed name she started a correspondence with Guy de Maupassant, and a lively exchange of letters followed although they never met. The journal for which she is today remembered was begun by her at the age of twelve. She died of lung disease only three weeks before her twenty-fourth birthday.

Maria Bashkirtseff's memoirs are a frank and penetrating description of her artistic ambitions and her sentimental experiences. The earlier part is especially valuable as an authentic document of childhood, written day-by-day by an intelligent, introspective little girl. Although self-conscious, the memoirs have naturalness and charm; they reflect sensitivity and a valid imagination. She played with her dolls as ordinary children do, but her dreams of love were intermixed with a childish desire to shine, to wear the gown of Dante's Beatrice; her longing for unusual men did not prevent her from being happy whenever she was surrounded by a group of boys. When she grew up her observations became deeper and more acute, but her frankness did not diminish, making it possible for her to draw a convincing psychological self-portrait surpassing similar contemporary attempts. The text of the journal was first published, in French, in 1887, in an abbreviated version. It was received by the reading public with great interest and was soon translated into Russian, English, and German.

Mary J. Serrano's English translation of the *Journal* was published in 1889. Selections from the *Journal*, translated by A. D. Hall, appeared in 1890. Her letters, translated by Mary J. Serrano, were published in 1891. *Further Memoirs of Marie Bashkirtseff* and her correspondence with Guy de Maupassant were published in 1901.

ABOUT: Blind, M. Marie Bashkirtzev; Cahuet, A. Moussia: The Life and Death of Marie Bashkirtsev; Creston, D. Fountains of Youth.

M. G.

*BASILE, GIAMBATTISTA (1575-February 23, 1632), Italian poet and short-story writer, who published some work under the anagrammatic pseudonym of "Gian Alesio Abbattutis," was born in Naples. He served honorably as a soldier from about 1604 to 1607, then returned to Naples where he held various state offices. In 1612 he was received in Mantua at the court of Ferdinand Gonzaga, by whom he was named cavalier and County Palatine. In the latter part of his life he had the governorship of various small states, the last of which was Giugliano, where he died at about fifty-seven.

In a busy life devoted to practical duties, Basile nevertheless found time to devote to the study of the customs, traditions, and literature of his well-beloved native city of Naples. Nothing Neapolitan escaped his attention—its poetry, proverbs, popular sayings, music. With the aid of an old school friend, Giulio Cesare Cortese, he studied the native Neapolitan dialect, and began his collection of folktales which was not published until after his death in 1634. This was *Lo Cunto de li Cunti*, a group of fairy tales and folktales in the Neapolitan dialect. The framework for the collection is elaborate—a prince and his wife, a slave who has married him under false pretenses, are entertained on five days by ten women, each of whom tells one story a day. At the end, the rightful princess appears, tells her story, and unmasks the deceitful slave. The stories themselves include some of the most familiar tales in western European literature — Cinderella, Puss-in-Boots, Rapunzel, Snow White, Beauty and the Beast. They are full of Neapolitan detail, of course, but their substance is unchanged. As a story-teller Basile was forthright. "In narrative," Richard Garnett writes, "he is the breathless, loquacious, exuberant Neapolitan, too much in a hurry to trouble himself about style or art, but carrying all before him by his vigor and vehemence."

* būsh kyĕr' tsĕf

* bä sē' lĕ

BASILE

Basile also wrote some verse in Spanish and some in Italian. The best known of his poetic works is *Muse Napolitane*, nine dialogues in verse, of a moral-satirical nature, on Neapolitan life.

Lo Cunto de li Cunti is generally referred to as *Il Pentamerone*, a title given by its first editor on the analogy of Boccaccio's *Decameron*, which it resembles in form. The standard Italian translation was made by Benedetto Croce in 1925, and the best English translation was made from this edition by N. B. Penzer in 1932.

ABOUT: Garnett, R. History of Italian Literature; Wilkins, E. H. History of Italian Literature. [In Italian—Milano, P. Il Lettore di Professione.]

*BATAILLE, HENRY (April 4, 1872-March 2, 1922), French poet and dramatist, was born in Nîmes, of a magistrate and the daughter of a poet-farmer. He spent his youth in Bordeneuve, then, eager to make a career as a painter, studied in Paris at the École des Beaux Arts and the Académie Julian. He had composed poetry at the age of fifteen, and his hesitation between the two arts ended only in 1894, when he began editing the *Journal des Artistes* and gathered his first verse in *Têtes et Pensées*. His debut in the theatre, with *La Belle au Bois Dormant*, a musical fairy tale of 1894 in the veiled manner of Maeterlinck, was a disaster. Encouraged by Marcel Schwob, he turned again to poetry and published *La Chambre Blanche*.

* bà tä′ y′

Finally, by the chance request for two plays, *Ton Sang* and *La Lépreuse* (which he had held in reserve), for a charitable enterprise, he found the success he awaited and his vocation as a playwright.

Bataille's first plays are in the symbolist manner but show personal traits in a nervous poetic spirit, and emphasize sentiment and psychological analysis to the exclusion of satire and sensuousness. *La Lépreuse* (1897) is a lyrical dialogue in rhythmic prose, anticipating Claudel. *Ton Sang* (1896) represents Bataille's real début, showing a mastery of pathos that entranced the youth of the times. His adaptation of Tolstoy's *Resurrection*, in 1902, represents his turn to prose. A second period opens with Bataille's very successful *Maman Colibri* (1904), the story of an elderly woman who falls in love with her son's friend, proclaims her right to love, and returns after an amorous escapade; many critics were repelled by this indecorous subject, but the play exemplifies Bataille's more sensuous psychological portrayals of woman's sometimes tragic problem of love and deception. His masterpiece, *La Marche Nuptiale* (1905), tells the story of a girl who falls in love with her piano teacher, and poses the problem of the delicate soul crushed by the blind forces of reality, with a plea against the system of social castes. The dramatic force of *La Marche Nuptiale* rises from the inexorable way in which the tragedy emanates from the circumstances; Bataille leaves the conclusion in suspense, and makes no attempt to prove a point or a thesis. The play was immediately performed in many countries and is one of the monuments of the early twentieth century theatre.

Bataille's last plays are less effective. In *Le Phalène* (1913) the element of dissatisfaction becomes rather too acute, and the dramatist, abandoning the study of a truly spiritual conflict, concentrates on mere disorder, after the pattern of Flaubert's *Madame Bovary*, or of Ibsen. He seems to have lost his mastery of the genre, and to him the critics preferred, not unaptly, the younger Bernstein, and especially the latter's *Le Voleur* and *Le Secret*. One must note further *La Femme Nue* (1908), by some critics esteemed as one of his masterpieces.

Bataille's poetry is no less important than his theatre, though its fusion of romantic, pastoral, and cosmopolitan subjects sets it in no simple category or school. It reveals his private world of intimate musicality, in irregular verse close to rhythmic prose, and deals with such subjects as home, city, countryside, and passing time. *Le Beau Voyage* (1904) proposes a realistic and modernist image of man, and *La Quadrature de l'Amour* (1920) is reminiscent of Baudelaire. As a critic, Bataille composed *Écrits sur le Théâtre* (1917) and *Le Théâtre Après la Guerre* (1918). *L'Enfance Éternelle* (1931) is his autobiography. His *Théâtre Complet* appeared in twelve volumes from 1922 to 1929.

ABOUT: Clark, B. Contemporary French Dramatists. [In French—see studies by D. Amiel and M. Besançon.]

F. J. C.

*BATYUSHKOV, KONSTANTIN NI-KOLAEVICH (May 29, 1787-July 19, 1855), Russian poet, was born in Vologda of an ancient but impoverished noble family. His childhood was spent on his father's estate Danilovskoe (near Bezhetsk). He was still a child when his mother, *née* Alexandra Berdyaev, lost her mind and died. Batyushkov received his education in St. Petersburg, first in a French, then in an Italian, boarding school, where he began to write poetry. His uncle, a minor poet, introduced him to Horace and Tibullus, who, together with Tasso and Petrarch, remained his favorites.

A booklet with a French translation of an ecclesiastic oration was Batyushkov's first publication (1801). In 1802 he became a clerk at the Ministry of Education (a job he hated), met leading poets and began to write for literary reviews. Experiencing patriotic enthusiasm in 1807, he joined the militia, participated in battles against Napoleon, and was wounded at Heilsberg, Prussia; later he took part in the campaign against Sweden. During his stays in Russia, he became a member of the Olenin circle in St. Petersburg, where the cult of ancient Greece was combined with sentimentalism. His father's second marriage brought discord to the family, and Batyushkov with his sisters moved to his mother's estate Khantonovo, near Cherepovets. There he wrote "A Vision on the Shores of Lethe," a satire on conservative poets, which became famous in manuscript. He also lived in Moscow, writing poetry and prose, the former being influenced chiefly by Parny and combining neoclassical imagery with romantic treatment of words.

Batyushkov was appointed a curator at the Public Library at St. Petersburg (1812) when the war against Napoleon aroused his patriotism again. He joined the Army and entered Paris with the victorious allied

* bà′ tyŏŏsh kŏf

troops. Paris made a tremendous impression on him. The years 1815-16 were the climax of Batyushkov's literary career. His first collection of works, the two-volume *Essays in Verse and Prose* (1817), appeared. However, his personal life was far from happy (financial difficulties, unsuccessful marriage proposal) and in 1815 he went through a spiritual crisis, turning from the philosophy of the French Enlightenment to pessimism and faith in divine revelation.

Suffering from attacks of a congenital mental illness, he went in 1818 to Odessa for cure, then obtained a position at the Russian Embassy in Naples. After a recurrence of his illness, he went to Teplitz for treatment. There he wrote some of his greatest poems, full of "strange beauty" (Mirsky), then became insane and destroyed many manuscripts. Several years spent in mental hospitals in Russia and Germany could not bring any relief. Finally he was sent to his nephew in Vologda, where he had only brief periods of sanity and died of typhoid.

An important influence on Pushkin, Batyushkov was a creator of Russian elegy and nineteenth century poetical language (which he imagined as flexible, simple, clear, purged of Slavonisms, and close to Italian in sound). His idyllic and hedonistic poetry, small in output, began with themes of erotic love, friendship, solitude, then reflected his war experience, introduced melancholy motives, and ended with marvelous imitations of Greek poetry. It is uneven in quality but in its best examples is probably unmatched in Russian poetry. Pushkin called him "a sorcerer." After almost a century of eclipse, Batyushkov was discovered in our time by such various poets as Mandelshtam, Tsvetaeva, Tikhonov, and Bagritsky, who were probably drawn to him by the inimitable combination of virtuoso melodiousness on the one hand, and of inner discord on the other.

Translations from Batyushkov can be found in Leo Wiener's *Anthology of Russian Literature*, II. (1902-1903).

ABOUT: Mirsky, D. S. A History of Russian Literature. [In Russian—see study by L. Maykov.]

V. M.

*BAUDELAIRE, CHARLES PIERRE (April 9, 1821-August 31, 1867), French poet, translator, and critic, was born in Paris, the only child of Joseph François Baudelaire, a distinguished civil servant, and his wife Caroline Dufays. The boy's early years seem

* bō dlâr′

70

BAUDELAIRE

to have been happy. But after the sudden death of his father in 1827 and his mother's remarriage within a year to General Aupick, Baudelaire's disposition began to show signs of a marked change: he became sullen, utterly withdrawn, and he exhibited the first symptoms of that perversity which was later to discourage the advances of acquaintances and strangers alike. Towards his mother Charles continued ambivalent for decades to come; towards M. Aupick (who appears to have been strict but fundamentally fair-minded, a far cry from the domestic tyrant in whose colors the young poet liked to conceive him) he displayed the sharpest hostility, never lessened by his mother's anxious representations. The spark of rebelliousness which had been kindled in Baudelaire by his immediate family situation was soon fanned by his wide, if somewhat indiscriminate, readings. The authors he now turned to were mostly of the "oppositional" kind, distinguished for defying the moral or political code of their day. The revolt of 1848 found in Baudelaire an enthusiastic supporter, though he does not seem to have participated in the fighting; soon after he suffered a complete revulsion from his earlier democratic and libertarian leanings, and for the rest of his life professed an extreme conservatism in all matters except his personal style of living.

Baudelaire's earliest writings reflect both his temporary enthusiasm for the cause of freedom and brotherhood, and the profound disillusion that followed it. Disdaining a regular career because of the professionalism it implied, he had decided at the age of twenty to become a free lance, and from 1844 onwards his essays began to appear quite regularly in the leading weeklies and monthlies. Editors were quick to encourage Baudelaire's talent as a journalist and reviewer. He could write on a great variety of subjects, though his best efforts always went into his writings on the fine arts. His eloquent praises of such embattled figures as Wagner and Delacroix created considerable stir in contemporary artistic circles and won their author notoriety long before a single line of his equally bold yet infinitely more shocking poetry had appeared in print. (Baudelaire stood to Delacroix in much the same relation as Mallarmé, one generation later, was to stand to Degas. They both viewed their painter-friends as "doubles"—men who in the sister art tried to embody the selfsame ideals they were pursuing with such ardor. In music, Wagner and Debussy respectively took the place of Delacroix and Degas.) But the figure with whom Baudelaire identified himself most closely was Edgar Allan Poe, whom he spent many years translating and expounding (*Histoires Extraordinaires*, 5 vols., 1856-65) and for whose great popularity in France during the 1870's and 1880's he was almost alone responsible.

Baudelaire never married. In 1842 he met Jeanne Duval, an attractive but somewhat slovenly mulatto, and set up housekeeping with her. This liaison which was to last for fourteen years had the effect of exiling Baudelaire even more thoroughly from the social scene of Paris than he had previously been. He had few friends, and no close ones. Baudelaire never cared much for the literary confraternity; with the exception of Gautier, whom he warmly admired and whose luxuriant talent he envied, he considered all his contemporaries—even Victor Hugo—as second-raters. For weeks on end he would not leave his apartment, giving himself either to morose speculation, or to poetic and journalistic labor, or to experiments with drugs (described in *Les Paradis Artificiels,* Paris 1861). Before long this enigmatic poet—competing for no honors, rejecting the advances of his colleagues, cultivating in solitude a fastidious singularity—had become a legendary figure in Parisian artistic circles, especially after the infamous lawsuit which the State, in 1857, brought against the author of the *Fleurs du Mal,* charging him with gross immorality and forcing him to suppress six of his more daring pieces. Yet it is remarkable how little has come down to us in the way of gossip, malicious or otherwise; how little first-hand observation (Baudelaire had numerous contacts, after all, especially among painters and journalists); how threadbare our knowledge still is of the poet's day-to-day existence. He who exposed himself so largely, so shamelessly as it were, in his verse must have observed the most scrupulous reticence in his personal conduct.

At the time of his death Baudelaire was engaged in a bitter diatribe against the Belgians and Belgium, a country in which he had lectured shortly before without pleasure or success, and which represented to him everything he abominated: rampant mediocrity, liberalism gone to seed. Looking much older than his years, his health undermined by disease and nervous exhaustion, Baudelaire died in Paris at the age of forty-six, of a paralytic stroke aggravated by aphasia. He was buried on Montparnasse.

Baudelaire's posthumous fame is based largely, if not entirely, on his single collection of verse, *Les Fleurs du Mal* (Flowers of Evil, 1857, revised editions 1861, 1868; standard critical edition by Crépet & Blin, 1949). Seldom has a writer gained immortality on the strength of so small a body of literature. But it should be pointed out that he spent year after year upon improving his volume: now adding new poems, now deleting old ones; continuing all the while to file individual lines and stanzas within the main body. Nor was his literary output really as negligible as he himself would have it: the myth of the "sterile" Baudelaire was the neurasthenic poet's own invention and that invention has made for all kinds of distortions among later psychologists and critics. Baudelaire did produce, after all, a body of prose impressive in both size and quality—the latter fully recognized by himself as well as by his contemporaries. But his first and last love was verse. While his failure to get two volumes of his collected articles published during his lifetime hurt and depressed the poet, it would be rash to assume that any radical dismay resulted from this. Baudelaire knew that he would impose himself upon the imagination of posterity as a writer of poems, and that was enough.

Les Fleurs du Mal had been a *succès de scandale*, hardly more, when it was first published. Readers were both appalled and titillated by the lurid subjects of many of these poems, which stood in such strange contrast to the marmoreal coolness and perfection of their form. Others relished the ethics of

revolt so largely displayed in it, without probing more deeply into its complex origins. Even so acute a critic as Sainte-Beuve —who had the further advantage of knowing the poet quite intimately—failed to see the radical novelty of his departure. But during the eighties a dazzling rise in Baudelaire's prestige took place, aided in great part by the symbolists under the leadership of Stéphane Mallarmé who considered Baudelaire their "ancestor," a martyr in their own cause and a commanding stylistic as well as moral model. It was through them that Baudelaire entered the pantheon of great French poets—his apotheosis which even today has barely been challenged. Critics of every persuasion, both inside France and out, have over the past fifty years shown remarkable agreement in viewing Baudelaire both as an incomparable master of verse and as one of the most brilliant speculative minds France has yet produced (witness those original essays in intuitive psychology, "On the Essence of Laughter and the Comic Spirit" and "Ethics of the Toy"). And there can be no doubt of this poet's extreme distinction, a distinction based on profound originality as well as abundance of technical resource, on intellectual boldness as well as emotional resonance. His verse has aged much better than that of any other poet of his generation, including such extraordinary craftsmen as Gautier and Leconte de Lisle. While Baudelaire's once famous "Satanism" has perhaps begun to fade slightly, the discovery of the urban scene —both its beauty and its horror—is as exciting in his poems today as it was when they first appeared.

In recent years a slight shift in critical opinion has occurred, initiated by the Existentialist movement and well illustrated in Sartre's study *Situation de Baudelaire*. In this analysis, and in similar essays by members of the same group, Baudelaire's stature as one of the great martyrs of art is left untouched, if not added to. But the prestige of art itself has suffered deflation. Baudelaire, who was obsessed with art at the expense of all else, emerges as the classical victim of that grand existential adventure in which man must either absolutely engage or else risk radical failure. According to Sartre, Baudelaire failed radically yet magnificently.

Baudelaire's reputation as one of the great art critics of the Western world is of relatively recent date. His collected critical papers were not published until after his death (*L'Art Romantique*, 1868; *Curiosités Esthétiques*, 1868) and another sixty years had to elapse before they found translators and publishers in either England or America. His poignant journals *(Fusées, Mon Cœur Mis à Nu)*, though well known in France since 1920, have likewise found their way into English within the past two decades only.

By now all Baudelaire's major works are available in English, though the translations vary considerably in value, especially those of the *Fleurs du Mal*. These have been rendered in their entirety by Arthur Symons (1926), L. P. Shanks (1926), Edna Millay & George Dillon (1936), Geoffrey Wagner (1946), Beresford Egan & C. B. Alcock (1947), C. F. McIntyre (1947), Roy Campbell (1952), and by various hands (Jackson Mathews, ed.) in 1955. Baudelaire's prose poems were published by New Directions in 1947, under the title *Paris Spleen* (tr. Louise Varèse); an earlier version by Arthur Symons (1905) had reached a very limited audience only. The journals were translated by Christopher Isherwood in 1930 (published in England with a preface by T. S. Eliot); in 1947 they were republished in the U.S. with a preface by W. H. Auden. A large group of Baudelaire's essays was published in English by D. Parmée in 1949, under the title *Selected Critical Studies*. Baudelaire's *Letters to His Mother*, translated by A. Symons, was published in London in 1927. A selection from his letters, *Baudelaire: A Self-Portrait*, translated and edited by L. B. and F. E. Hyslop, was published in 1957. In 1956 Peter Quennell edited *The Essence of Laughter and Other Essays, Journals, and Letters* (translated by G. Hopkins, N. Cameron, and Quennell) for Meridian Books. Critical studies translated and edited by J. Mayne were published as *Mirror of Art* in 1955. A checklist, "Baudelaire in English," by W. T. Bandy appeared in *Bulletin of Bibliography*, XXIII (1961).

ABOUT: Good modern studies of Baudelaire available in English include: Porché, F. Charles Baudelaire; Quennell, P. Baudelaire and the Symbolists; Sartre, J.-P. Baudelaire; Starkie, E. Baudelaire; Turnell, M. Baudelaire. Margaret Gilman analyzes the poet's essays and critical writings in Baudelaire the Critic. An interesting study of the poet's personality from the psychoanalytical point of view is René Laforgue's The Defeat of Baudelaire. Marcel Raymond's From Baudelaire to Surrealism (tr. 1950) has a useful bibliography. See also Baudelaire: A Collection of Critical Essays, ed. H. Peyre (1961). [In French—see studies by L. J. Austin, J. Crépet, J. Prévost, H. Peyre, R. Vivier.]

F. G.

*BAYLE, PIERRE (November 18, 1647-December 28, 1706), French critic and philosopher, was born and raised in Carla, in what is now Ariège. His father was a Huguenot minister. As a Protestant in seventeenth century France, Bayle grew up in an atmosphere of religious dissent and controversy. He was taught Latin and Greek by his father, and he became a voracious reader. At twenty he was sent to a Jesuit college in Toulouse — a practice not unusual among Huguenots who admired Jesuit training

* bāl

BAYLE

though they did not share their faith. To his father's horror, Bayle was converted to Catholicism within one month. Within a year, however, he reverted to Protestantism and then, for safety, fled to Geneva where he continued his studies in theology and philosophy. Bayle supported himself by tutoring in private families, first in Geneva, then in Paris. In 1675 he received a professorship in philosophy at the Protestant University of Sedan where he remained until the university was closed in 1681 by order of Louis XIV. Through the aid of a former student, Bayle received an appointment as professor of philosophy at the École Illustre in Rotterdam. He left France and spent the rest of his life an emigré in Rotterdam, and he was buried in that city. Two centuries after his death, a statue in his honor was erected at his birthplace.

Two years before Bayle began his exile he wrote his first important philosophical work, his *Lettre sur les Comètes*, a treatise on the comet of 1680 which had inspired an outburst of superstition and interpretation as a "divine message." Bayle's work (published anonymously in 1682) was the first of his many attacks on superstition. Also in 1682 he published the first of his major theological writings, a critique of the Jesuit Father Maimbourg's history of Calvinism. This volume, though banned in France, became so popular that it went through three editions within two years of publication. The religious persecution of Bayle's family in France (his brother died in prison) led him to even more intense expressions of protest—a pamphlet, *La France Toute Catholique sous le Règne de Louis le Grand* (1685), attacking Louis' revocation of the Edict of Nantes, and the famous *Commentaire Philosophique* (1686), a general plea for tolerance, based on the interpretation of the words of Christ (Luke 14:23) "Compel them to come in."

Once settled in Rotterdam, Bayle took on an additional task — the editorship of the *Nouvelles de la République des Lettres.* From March 1684 to February 1687 when his health broke and he resigned the post, he edited this monthly journal, consisting mainly of book reviews and general items of literary and cultural interest. The journal established Bayle's fame throughout Europe (it even attracted the favorable notice of Queen Christina of Sweden). It did not, however, bring him any personal security. In 1690 an anonymous treatise, *Avis Important aux Réfugiés,* addressed to Protestants returning to France and attacking Protestantism in England and in France, was widely attributed to Bayle. He denied authorship, but in 1693 he was dismissed from his teaching post.

Bayle's dismissal in the long run proved a blessing, because it gave him the leisure he needed to work on his encyclopedic *Dictionnaire Historique et Critique,* his masterpiece and the book for which Voltaire hailed him as "one of the greatest men that France has produced" and "the father of the congregation of the wise men." It was also the work that inspired the great *Encyclopédie* of the *philosophes* a century later and in general laid the foundations of eighteenth century philosophical skepticism.

Bayle put more than four years of exacting labor into the two folio volumes of the dictionary published in 1697. It was a work of total dedication, of vast erudition, and of uncompromising independence of thought. In form it is a general biographical dictionary, but some articles on geography, mythology, and miscellaneous subjects are included so that it more resembles a modern encyclopedia. Inevitably, because this was a one-man project, the dictionary suffers from narrowness of view. While including obscure names, he left out major figures (Cicero and Horace, for example, are missing). The articles are brief and pithy, but appended to each is a frequently long and diffuse supplement in which Bayle roams freely, criticizing, expounding his own views, expressing his fundamental skepticism in all matters, his distrust of all authority.

The success of Bayle's *Dictionnaire* was immediate. It shocked many but it delighted more, and Bayle spent his remaining years defending it and collecting material for later editions. The second edition, in three volumes, appeared in 1702 and by 1820 it had gone through eleven editions. The *Dictionnaire* had many eminent detractors—among them the German philosopher Leibniz—and many equally enthusiastic admirers—among them the English philosopher Lord Shaftesbury, Edward Gibbon, and Frederick the Great of Prussia. But it was in France that the work had its greatest influence. Sainte-Beuve wrote that Bayle was "the great precursor of Voltaire." He was equally influential in the shaping of the *Encyclopédie.* In the Prospectus to that work Diderot cited him as a "pioneer" when "true philosophy was yet in the cradle," and he used his *Dictionnaire* as a source book for some of the articles in the *Encyclopédie.*

Bayle's reputation suffered a radical decline in the nineteenth century, and his work is mainly of antiquarian interest today. Partly this may be the result of Bayle's style which, though brisk, is careless and generally inartistic. George Saintsbury remarked in his *History of Criticism:* "Bayle perhaps needed nothing but better taste, greater freedom from prejudice, and a more exclusive bent towards purely literary criticism, to be one of the great literary critics of the world." A grave and sober man whose work was his life, he is better remembered for the questioning skeptical spirit he engendered than for the books he wrote. The judgment of the French critic Brunetière is probably the most fitting and most accurate summation of his achievement: "To forget Bayle or to suppress him is to mutilate and falsify the whole history of ideas in the eighteenth century."

The first English translation of the *Historical and Critical Dictionary* was made in 1709 by De la Roche, a French refugee in London. Another translation, with additions and corrections, appeared in 1710, still another in 1734. Other works of Bayle translated into English are his *A Philosophical Commentary* (1708) and *Miscellaneous Reflections Occasioned by the Comet* (1708).

ABOUT: L. P. Courtines' Bayle's Relations with England and the English contains an excellent bibliography of works about him in French and in English. See also—Essays in Intellectual History dedicated to J. H. Robinson; Moore, W. G., R. Sutherland, E. Starkie (eds.) The French Mind; Robinson, H. Bayle the Skeptic; French Studies 1954, 1963. [In French—Dibon, P., ed. Pierre Bayle, le Philosophe de Rotterdam.]

*BEAUMARCHAIS, PIERRE AUGUS-TIN CARON de (January 24, 1732-May 18, 1799), French playwright, was born in Paris, the son of a watchmaker, André Charles Caron. He acquired a somewhat rudimentary education at a school located in Alfort, then became a watchmaker in his turn. Before he was twenty-one, he had invented a watch escapement. Although a rival disputed his claims, Beaumarchais gained recognition for his invention from the Académie des Sciences, thus winning his spurs in what was to be a long career of legal battles and polemics. His court connections started with the office of royal watchmaker. He was later to turn his musical talents to advantage when he taught the harp to the ladies of the royal family. On November 22, 1756, young Caron married Marie-Madeleine Franquet, the widow of an old court official to whose office he had already succeeded during the husband's lifetime. At the time of the marriage he assumed the name of Beaumarchais, and four years later obtained a patent of nobility. His wife died within the year, but Beaumarchais married another wealthy widow, Genevieve Lévêque, in 1768. There was a third marriage in 1785(?) to Thérèse Willermawla.

During his years of tenure of various court offices, Beaumarchais began his literary career with two dramas after the fashion preached by Diderot. The first, *Eugénie* (1767), was based on an incident that had occurred in 1764 when the author took a journey to Spain. The mission was undertaken chiefly to seek out and chastise a young Spaniard, José Clavijo y Fajardo, who had twice promised to marry Beaumarchais' sister, but had failed to keep his word. The play was a failure, as was the next sentimental drama, *Les Deux Amis* (1769). When he returned to the drama, however, with *Le Barbier de Seville* (1775) and *Le Mariage de Figaro* (1784), his success was so overwhelming that he silenced his detractors forever.

Meanwhile, Beaumarchais had wrested a financial fortune in successful speculation with the court financier Pâris-Duverney. Some time before the latter's death in 1770 a duplicate settlement of the affairs between him and Beaumarchais had been drawn up in which the banker acknowledged himself debtor to Beaumarchais for 15,000 francs. Duverney's heir, M. La Blanche, denied the validity of the document, stopping just short

* bō mär shä′

BEAUMARCHAIS

of an accusation of forgery. While the case was before the courts, Beaumarchais was imprisoned as the result of a quarrel with the Duc de Chaulnes over Mlle Menard, an actress at the Comédie Italienne. His dealings with his lawyer, M. de Goëzman, involved bribes which again raised charges and counter-charges in a long series of legal battles. Beaumarchais extricated himself from all these entanglements with the utmost skill, and although he was at one time made to suffer "blâme," or loss of civil rights, all judgments against him were in time definitively reversed. The fact that Beaumarchais was able, almost overnight, to turn the most infamous notoriety into greatest popular success must be attributed to his masterly *Mémoires* (Pleadings) which excelled in eloquence, ingenuity of invective, and brilliant polemic style. Indeed, Beaumarchais has been called a French Junius, motivated by his personal interests.

The successful playwright now turned once more to financial operations, and again amassed millions by equipping a fleet that supplied arms to the fighting colonies of America. Beaumarchais also engaged in several delicate missions for the king, some so adventurous and fantastic that they might have provided the plots for his own intricate plays. Another successful law-suit was fought; then difficulties arose with the French government over arms contracts. The outbreak of the French Revolution forced Beaumarchais to seek refuge in England and Holland. On his return to France, he found himself impoverished. He died suddenly in Paris at the age of sixty-seven.

In assessing Beaumarchais' literary merits, one must take into account the fact that he has produced works in three different genres, achieving major and lasting success only in one. The bitingly clever eloquence of his *Mémoires* deserves admiration. His three "drames," *Eugénie, Les Deux Amis,* and *La Mère Coupable* (1792), are of interest mainly for forming a link between the classical tragedies of Corneille and Racine and the nineteenth century drama of Hugo and Sardou. In themselves they do not constitute much of an advance on the plays by Diderot. The two comedies, however, fashioned around the unique, novel, and immortal character of Figaro, will forever be outstanding theatre and have additional immortality in the operas of Mozart and Rossini. In them the author undoubtedly sketched his own versatile and adventurous life, framing it with brilliant dialogue and providing an ingeniously intricate plot. The two comedies, by exposing the privileged classes, the professions, the court, and the diplomatic service to universal ridicule were, perhaps in spite of their author, authentic harbingers of the French Revolution and of the social changes of centuries to come.

Among English translations of *The Barber of Seville* are those of Mrs. Elizabeth Griffith (1776), A. B. Myrick (1905), W. R. Taylor (1922), S. Robb (1939). *The Marriage of Figaro* was translated as *The Follies of a Day* by T. Holcroft (1785). A French edition of his *Théâtre Complet,* ed. P. Pia, was published in 1956.

ABOUT: Cox, C. The Real Figaro: The Extraordinary Career of Caron de Beaumarchais; Daheme, R. Beaumarchais, 1732-1799; de Loménie, L. Beaumarchais and his Times; Lemaître, G. Beaumarchais; Ratermanis, J. B. & Irwin, W. R. Comic Style of Beaumarchais. [In French—Pollitzer, M. Beaumarchais, le Père de Figaro; Scherer, J. La Dramaturgie de Beaumarchais; Van Tieghem, P. Beaumarchais par Lui-même.]

E. J. S.

*BECQUE, HENRI (or HENRY) FRANÇOIS (April 18, 1837-May 12, 1899),

French dramatist, was born in Paris, son of a government clerk and nephew of a minor dramatist, Martin Lubige. Becque was raised in an atmosphere of grinding poverty and bitterness, from which he never completely escaped. He was educated at the Lycée Bonaparte and went to work in 1853 as a clerk in a railroad office. For most of his life he drifted aimlessly from one poorly paid job to another. For a brief period he was a tutor

* běk

BECQUE

in literature. In 1860 he had a job with the Grand Chancellery, and in 1865 he was secretary to a Polish nobleman. Even after winning some recognition as a playwright, Becque was unable to support himself by literature, and he worked on the Bourse (stock exchange) and wrote hack journalism for a living. He served as a private in the Franco-Prussian war.

Becque's first literary endeavor was the libretto for an opera by Victorin de Joncières, *Sardanapole.* His first substantial work as a playwright was *L'Enfant Prodigue* (1868), a farce in which the bitter satiric humor (called the *comédie rosse*) which marked his later plays was already present. In 1870, unable to find a producer who would accept the play, Becque himself produced his *Michel Pauper,* a grim study of the struggle between capital and labor. A third play, *L'Enlèvement* (1871) was another failure, and for the next decade Becque remained in obscurity. In 1877 he began writing what was to be his masterpiece, the bitterly realistic drama *Les Corbeaux.* The play was produced at the Théâtre Français on September 14, 1882, and had only three performances, but these were enough to launch a raging controversy. *Les Corbeaux,* a study of a widow and her daughters victimized by her late husband's greedy creditors (the "crows" or "vultures" of the title), was a revolutionary departure in French drama. It marked a break from the smooth slickness and poetic language of the "well-made" play to the photographic reproduction of everyday reality and the pedestrian speech of commonplace life. Becque was not the first dramatist to bring realism and naturalism to the French stage—for this he shares honors with Émile Augier and the younger Alexandre Dumas—but he was beyond a doubt the most outspoken and uncompromising of the dramatists of this school. His view of life was completely pessimistic, and the public received his work coldly. "A dramatist may have two ends in view—" he wrote, "one to please the public, the other to satisfy only himself. I have chosen to satisfy myself."

Les Corbeaux might well have been forgotten had it not been for the efforts of André Antoine, founder of the Théâtre Antoine (1897-1906), who produced the play, as well as Becque's later work, and kept it alive long after his death. The play is today widely read and studied as a classic of its type. (John Gassner calls it a "Bible of Naturalism.") Almost matching it in sheer compelling power is *La Parisienne,* a study of a wife, her husband, and her lover. Its brutal frankness, particularly its unsentimental portrayal of a completely amoral heroine, shocked Parisian audiences, but brought Becque the admiration of a small but devoted literary circle. He was elected to the Legion of Honor in 1886 and was offered a government pension which he refused. He died, a lonely and embittered man, in a private sanatorium, at sixty-two, leaving unfinished a play, *Polichinelles,* on which he had worked for fifteen years. It was completed by Henri de Nausanne and published in 1910.

Writing of Becque in 1910, the English novelist Arnold Bennett observed that he was "one of the greatest dramatists of the nineteenth century and certainly the greatest realistic French dramatist." More recent criticism has tended to confirm this judgment. "The ghost of Becque," John Gassner writes, "hovers in the wings whenever a contemporary playwright addresses himself to the *laissez-faire* spirit in our civilization." Becque also published two volumes of his critical essays — *Querelles Littéraires* (1890) and *Souvenirs d'un Auteur Dramatique* (1895).

English translations of Becque's two most famous plays, *Les Corbeaux* (*The Vultures* or *The Crows*) and *La Parisienne* (*The Woman of Paris*) appear in many anthologies of European drama. Freeman Tilden translated these and *La Navette* (*The Merry-Go-Round*) as *Three Plays by Henry Becque* in 1913. A more recent translation of *La Parisienne* by Jacques Barzun appears in *The Modern Theatre,* I, ed. E. Bentley (1955).

ABOUT: Bennett, A. Books and Persons; Borgerhoff, J. L. *Introduction to* Nineteenth Century French Plays; Gassner, J. Theatre in Our Times; Huneker, J. Iconoclasts; Waxman, S. M. Antoine and the Théâtre Libre. [In French—see studies by A. Antoine, M. Descotes, L. Gouvet, E. Sée]

*BÉCQUER, GUSTAVO ADOLFO

(February 17, 1836-December 22, 1870), Spanish poet and romance-writer, was born at Seville, one of eight sons of Don José Dominguez Bécquer, well known genre painter of Seville, and Doña Joaquina Bostida de Vargas. The family was of distinguished Flemish ancestry. Before he was ten Gustavo Adolfo was orphaned; he was forced in his early years to depend on the generosity of a succession of relatives.

His education was a haphazard one, begun at the College of San Antonio Abad, continued at the College of San Telmo, a training school for navigators, set up by the government for orphans of noble extraction. At this school he first demonstrated literary precocity by beginning a novel and collaborating with a friend, Narciso Campillo, on the writing and presentation of a play, *Los Conjurados.* After this school was suppressed by royal orders, the young writer was received into the home of his godmother, Doña Manuela Monahay. Gustavo Adolfo immersed himself in this wealthy lady's private library—absorbing in particular the odes of Horace and the lyrics of the contemporary poet José Zorilla. Almost simultaneously his sensibilities were sharpened by the art training he undertook at the age of fourteen under the painter Don Antonio Cabral Bejarano.

Apparently Gustavo Adolfo could have inherited his godmother's fortune had he been willing to take up a mercantile career. But the business life was repugnant to his artistic conscience, and so, at the age of seventeen and a half, he uprooted himself and set off for Madrid to devote himself to the precarious life of literature. He arrived in the metropolis in the autumn of 1854 "with empty pockets," as his biographer Ramón Rodriguez Correa was to write, "but with a head full of treasures that were not, alas, to enrich him."

It was Correa, the most intimate friend of young Bécquer from the time of his arrival in Madrid, who persuaded him to publish his story *El Caudillo de las Manos Rojas* in the journal *La Crónica,* and thus his career was launched. Next, also at the behest of his friend, Bécquer entered the office of the Dirección de Bienes Nacionales as copyist, but was soon fired for drawing sketches of his fellow employees while on the job. Subse-

* bĕʹ kĕr

BÉCQUER

quently he earned a little money by assisting a painter.

In 1857 Bécquer was commissioned to edit a series on church buildings entitled *Los Templos de España.* Only one volume appeared, actually the only book by him that was published in his lifetime. *Los Templos* fuses his dual talents, since he both contributed to the text and helped illustrate it, and reveals that affinity for religious antiquities that was to manifest itself in his fiction.

At about this time Bécquer was drawn into a coterie of poets, artists, and musicians who gathered at the home of Don Joaquín Espín y Guillen, professor of music and organist of the Capilla Real. Here he read his first poems and fell deeply in love with Don Joaquín's daughter Julia, generally believed to be the inspiration for the idealized lady of the *Rimas.* However, Bécquer's devotion to the lady was unrequited; apparently she was repelled by his unkempt appearance and his Bohemianism.

About 1861 the poet married Casta Esteban y Navarro, daughter of a physician who attended him during one of his frequent sieges of illness. This union, like his romance, ended unhappily. However, Gustavo Adolfo was deeply devoted to the two sons born of the marriage and undertook their support after separation from his wife. For most of the rest of his life he lived with his brother Valeriano, an artist, who too had been through a brief and unsuccessful marriage.

Also in 1861 Bécquer secured, through the influence of Correa, a position on the newspaper *El Contemporaneo,* founded several years previously. This proved to be his principal literary outlet. Here were published most of his legends and tales as well as the beautiful series of letters that constitute his spiritual autobiography, *Desde Mi Celda* (From My Cell).

Some years later, Bécquer was fortunate to secure a Maecenas in the person of Luis González Brabo, prime minister of Queen Isobel II, who became interested in his poetry. In order to provide him with leisure Brabo gave Bécquer an official sinecure as censor of novels. Now the poet seemed on his way to realize his ambition of collecting his work into a volume. Luis González agreed to underwrite the expense of publication and to write a prologue to the book. But in 1868 came the revolution that dethroned Queen Isobel. Luis González was forced to flee to France, and somehow the manuscript was lost. Gustavo Adolfo was thus obliged to rewrite his entire *Rimas* from memory. Some were published in *El Museo Universal.* The whole series was eventually published in book form posthumously under the supervision of Correa.

With the loss of patronage, Bécquer was reduced during the last years of his life to supporting himself by various hack jobs like translating popular French novels and writing articles (such as the series called *Las Hojas Secas*). The year before his death he was the director of the periodical *La Ilustración de Madrid,* which his brother Valeriano illustrated.

The death of Valeriano, to whom he had always been devoted, in September 1870, profoundly shocked Gustavo Adolfo. His health, always frail, broke under the strain, and three months later he died of pneumonia and hepatitis, not yet having reached his thirty-fifth birthday.

Gustavo Adolfo Bécquer is remembered equally for his haunting tales and his poignant lyrics. His tales derive for the most part from legendary materials. The best of them are characterized by medieval settings, an aura of the mysterious and the supernatural, and an apocalyptic style. *Los Ojos Verdes* (The Green Eyes), the tale of a romantic young man lured to his doom by the spell of a wood-nymph, reveals his genius for evoking an eerie, fascinating atmosphere. One of his most popular stories, *Maese Pérez El Organista* (Master Perez the Organist), in which an organist continues to spellbind his congregation even after death, is emblematic of its author's own devotion to the spirit of art.

Bécquer's poetry, less gorgeously colored than his prose, is characterized by a tone of quiet resignation. The subtly assonanced *Rimas,* a sequence of seventy-six introspective short lyrics, relates the successive disillusionments of the poet seeking after an unobtainable ideal—first in art, then in love, eventually, after despairing of happiness in this world, finding consolation in the surcease that death offers. Of all the *Rimas* (influenced by Heine's *Intermezzo*), Poem X ("Los invisibles átomos del aire") describing the ineffable presence of love, and Poem LIII ("Volverán las oscuras golondrinas"), contrasting the permanence of nature's beauty with the transitoriness of human life and love, are the most famous.

Although Bécquer's genius was recognized by contemporaries, his greatest fame has been posthumous, with the more extensive publication of his works. In England the novelist Mrs. Humphry Ward, writing for *Macmillan's Magazine* in 1883, went so far as to declare him the only Spanish poet of the period worth translating. Among Hispanic writers Bécquer's influence has been pronounced on Rubén Darío, Miguel de Unamuno, and particularly on the imagist poet Juan Ramón Jiménez, who did much to revive his reputation. He remains, according to Everett Ward Olmstead, "one of the most original and charming authors of the Spanish Romantic school."

A selection of Bécquer's tales is available in English in *Romantic Legends and Tales of Spain,* edited by Cornelia Frances Bates and Katherine Lee Bates (1908). "Master Perez the Organist" is included in the anthology *Great Modern Spanish Stories,* ed. by Angel Flores (1956). The *Rimas* have been translated by Jules Renard (1908) and (as *The Infinite Passion*) by Young Allison (1924). The bilingual *Ten Centuries of Spanish Poetry* edited by Eleanor Turnbull (1955) includes a selection of Bécquer's poems. The best edition in Spanish is the *Obras Completas* (1942). English translations from *Rimas* appear in *An Anthology of Spanish Poetry,* edited by Angel Flores (Anchor Books, 1961).

ABOUT: Columbia Dictionary of Modern European Literature; King, E. Gustavo Adolfo Bécquer: From Painter to Poet; Olmstead, E. *Introduction to* Bécquer's Legends, Tales and Poems; Hispania March 1955; Macmillan's Magazine February 1883. [In Spanish—see studies by R. Brown, R. Correa, J. Guillen, B. Jarnés, J. López Jiménez, and M. León.]

R. A. C.

BEETS, NICOLAAS ("HILDE-BRAND") (September 13, 1814-March 13, 1903), Dutch writer and churchman, was born in Haarlem into a happy, modestly prosperous family. Solicitous parents provided sound educational and cultural opportunities with the result that both the boy and his older sister Dorothea (the "Serena" of his early poems) began literary composition at an early age. A young English friend, John Lockhart, turned Beets' attention and taste toward the English romantics—Sterne, Lamb, Scott, especially Byron.

In 1833 young Beets entered Leiden University to study theology; he remained there until 1839. The modest literary fame which had preceded him led to lasting friendships and associations with men destined to become significant as writers and critics. Theological study did not curtail literary activity: *José, een Spaansch-verhaal* (1834), *De Maskerade* and *Kuser* (both 1835), *Guy de Vlaming* (1837)—all these in the spirit of English romanticism. The melancholy of these pieces was, however, more a modish malaise than the expression of genuine personal sorrow; Beets was really a cheerful spirit.

After the successful conclusion on March 11, 1839, of his theological studies (with a dissertation on Pope Pius II (*De Aenea Sylvii*), Beets entered the ministry in 1840 in the small town of Heemstede. He now married Aleida van Foreest, a member of a patrician family. A warmhearted devotion to his calling earned him the lifelong esteem of his parishioners. In June 1854 he removed to Utrecht and in 1874 became professor of theology at the university. He died in Utrecht at the age of eighty-eight.

Already as a student at Leiden, Beets had been one of a movement of young men who in religious matters were repelled by the prevailing rationalistic deadness of the state church; socially the movement (Réveil) opposed the moral license engendered by the French Revolution. Placing "feeling above thought," these young enthusiasts stressed the ethical content of Christianity. In Beets this emphasis found expression in devotional literature and sermons which exercised a pronounced impact on church and society.

Beets' purely literary endeavors fall into several classifications: poetry, essays, and sketches. He contributed charming verse to such periodicals as the *Muzenalmanak* and *De Gids.* This poetry, later collected (*Korenbloemen,* 1853; *Volledige Dichtwerken,* 1873-1876), does not, it is true, strike profound

* bāts

79

universal chords, but it does admirably capture the unique folk qualities of the small people of the day. In the critical and general essay, too, Beets achieved significance; he does not command the erudition and stylistic excellence of distinguished contemporaries (Potgieter and Huet) but he proves himself to be a man of sensibility with a sure ear and heart for literary values.

But critics' censure cannot deprive Beets of the merits of his *Camera Obscura* (by "Hildebrand," 1839, last augmented edition 1854). It is a series of sketches of character types and situations taken from the comfortable middle-class life of nineteenth century Netherlands with meticulous realism and warm humor and written in a spirited natural prose. Granted its literalness, its too great sentimentality, *Camera Obscura* remains a matchless guide to the understanding of the mores and conventions of middle-class Dutch life. The work was translated into most of the European languages.

Selections from his work in English translation appear in *Fraser's Magazine* (1854), *Chambers' Journal* (1856, 1860), and James MacKinnon's *Leisure Hours in the Study*. Lockhart translated The *Leyden Eelbobber* in *The Country* (1877), and J. Ballingal translated *Tony* in *The Modern Church* (1892). J. P. Westervelt translated *The Life and Character of J. H. van der Palm* (1865).

ABOUT: [In Dutch—see study, 3 vols., by G. van Rijn & J. J. Deetman.]

C. K. P.

*BELINSKI, VISSARION GRIGORE-VICH (May 30, 1811-May 26, 1848), Russian critic, was born in Sveaborg, in what is now Finland, where his father, Gregor Belinski, was serving as a ship's doctor with the Russian navy. In 1816 the family moved to his father's native village of Chembar, in the province of Penza. The elder Belinski was a drunkard and an atheist, and the home in which Vissarion grew up was an unhappy one. He attended school in Chembar, then the *Gymnasium* at Penza, and in 1829 he entered Moscow University on a government grant. Belinski was an enthusiastic student, but he was impatient of the disciplines of formal academic study. In Moscow he found far greater stimulation in the heated discussions of "literary evenings" than in classroom lectures. He rapidly absorbed the romantic and radical ideas of his day. While still a student, in 1831, he wrote a play, *Dmitri Kalinin*, a stark tragedy, in which he condemned serfdom and expressed certain views

* byĭ lyēn′ skĭ

BELINSKI

interpreted by the university censors as atheistical. As a result the young student was expelled from the university.

Left penniless and with no prospect of attaining a university degree, Belinski supported himself by tutoring and by free lance journalism. In the course of his life he was literary critic for the four major "progressive" journals of his time—*The Telegraph* (1834-36) and *The Moscow Observer* (1838-39) in Moscow, and, after moving to St. Petersburg, *National Notes* (1839-1846) and *The Contemporary* (1846-47). His journalism never brought him an adequate income, and his life is a pathetic record of poverty, loneliness, and ill health (he had tuberculosis). In appearance he was slight and frail. He was nervous and irritable in temperament, but was a powerful and passionate speaker on subjects which interested him. He died in St. Petersburg a few days before his thirty-seventh birthday, leaving his wife and family penniless.

As a young man Belinski had become a member of the circle that surrounded the brilliant young Nicholas Stankevich, a student of German romanticism. Through Stankevich, Belinski became acquainted with the idealism of Schelling, Fichte, and Hegel. He also met Michael Bakunin, politically an anarchist and philosophically "the father of Russian idealism." Out of this ferment of thought, Belinski emerged, not surprisingly, as a passionate but widely vacillating intellectual. In the short span of his lifetime he moved from a romantic Hegelianism in which he justified the status quo as "inevitable links in the glorious chain of Divine Reason," to a kind of humanitarian socialism. Probably the most revealing and certainly the most moving statement of his intellectual position appeared in his "Letter to Gogol" published shortly before his death. The letter was written as a protest against what he viewed as Gogol's cynicism about Russia's future. In it he acknowledged the horror of serfdom but affirmed that "Russia sees its salvation not in mysticism, not in asceticism, not in pietism, but in the successes of civilization, of enlightenment, of humanity."

In 1834 Belinski published the first of the many studies which won him his reputation as the first major Russian literary critic— *Literary Reveries*, a diffuse but stimulating attempt to relate Russian literature to Russian cultural life. Most of Belinski's critical work appeared first in the various journals for which he wrote. Outstanding among these are essays on Gogol, Lermontov, and Pushkin. As H. E. Bowman points out, Russian critical thought before Belinski had moved between two extremes: "either toward an inadequate conception of the potentialities of Russian literature or toward a narrowly nationalistic conception of Russian life." Belinski brought Russian criticism into the mainstream of European literary thought. He believed, according to Marc Slonim, that the purpose of a critic "was to uncover the basic idea of each work of art, to establish its relationship with the environment in which it was conceived, and, finally, to examine how the main ideas had been expressed aesthetically." In writers whose grasp of society was surest and soundest—most especially in Gogol—Belinski found the highest fulfillment of literary art. He was also one of the first to recognize the genius of Dostoevsky and hailed his first book *Poor Folk* as a work of rare promise. (Dostoevsky was influenced by Belinski's social philosophy, as Philip Rahv points out in an article in *Partisan Review*, in the Grand Inquisitor section of *The Brothers Karamazov*.) In all his literary judgments, in spite of his impetuosity and his careless style, Belinski showed himself a sensitive and prophetic critic.

Belinski's rapid changes of thought and his lack of a coherent and fixed critical system expose him to multiple interpretations. In the Soviet Union he is today honored as the first Marxist critic (though his work was of course pre-Marxist), largely on the basis of his writings in the period 1842 to 1846 when he leaned toward atheism and utopian socialism. The one hundredth anniversary of his death was marked with much ceremony and there has been considerable Soviet scholarship on him.

Among the little of Belinski's work available in English translation is his *Selected Philosophical Works*, prepared and published in Moscow in the centennial year 1948. See also Ralph E. Matlaw, ed. *Belinsky, Chernyshevsky, and Dobrolyubov: Selected Criticism* (1962). The "Letter to Gogol" is translated in B. G. Guerney's *A Treasury of Russian Literature* (1943).

ABOUT: Bowman, H. E. Vissarion Belinski; Mathewson, R. W. The Positive Hero in Russian Literature; Mirsky, D. S. A History of Russian Literature; Slonim, M. R. The Epic of Russian Literature; American Slavic Review October 1948; Partisan Review May 1954; Russian Review January 1949. [In Russian—see studies by A. N. Pypin, P. Kogan, I. Kubikov, N. D. Mordovchenko, E. P. Subbotina. In German—see study by B. Schulze.]

BELLAY, JOACHIM DU. See DU BELLAY, JOACHIM

*BELLEAU, RÉMY (1528-March 6, 1577), French poet, was born at Nogent-le-Rotrou (near Chartres). Nothing is known about his origins except that his family was presumably of modest extraction since, at his death, his brother was still a locksmith at Nogent. His precocious talents were noticed by Abbé Chretophle de Choiseul, celebrated patron of the arts, who sent him to Paris to study under such distinguished humanists as Muret and Buchanan. He soon became acquainted with and took an active part in the new poetic movement of the time, acting, for example, in Jodelle's *Cléopâtre* (1553).

Belleau distinguished himself as a Hellenist and a poet and was formally named "seventh star" of the constellation of poets, the Pléiade, by its leader, Ronsard, upon publication in 1556 of a verse translation of Anacreon's *Odes*, to which were appended "some little hymns of the poet's invention." In these delicate poems, he sang of the Cherry, the Oyster, the Coral, the Turtle, the Hour, etc. He was influenced by Marot and Ronsard, but through use of rhythms and mythological narrative his pantheistic lyricism sought not a static representation of things, but a musical and dynamic cosmic order.

Belleau, eager for a title of nobility, served in the cavalry of the Marquis d'Elbeuf in the Naples expedition of 1557. Having returned to Paris, he wrote circumstantial poetry, became tutor of Charles of Lorraine, eleven-

* bě lō'

year-old son of the Marquis, and spent at the Château de Guise the most happy and studious years of his life (1563-66).

The Château, with its gracious ladies, was to become the setting for his new pastoral creation in prose and verse, the *Bergerie* (1565, 2nd edition 1572), in which he imitated Sannazaro's Arcadia and artificially juxtaposed minute genre paintings, bucolic scenes, and amorous poems. The unity of this composition rises from his art as a miniaturist, a master goldsmith, and a musician.

Belleau continued his services with the d'Elbeuf family as his former pupil's adviser and steward. He also became secretary to the King's Chambers. He often went to Paris where he was esteemed at the court and by the erudite and artistic world. He enjoyed the protection of Charles IX and of his successor, Henri III, to whom he dedicated the *Amours et Nouveaux Eschanges de Pierres Précieuses, Vertus et Proprietez d'Icelles* (1579). In this last important work, he utilized many Greco-Latin and medieval treatises on the properties of gems. This plastic poetry is charged with the same occult animism as were his earlier hymns.

A year later, while in Paris, Belleau died suddenly and his poet-friends, Ronsard, Baïf, Desportes, and Jamyn carried him on their shoulders to the convent of the Grands-Augustins where he had wished to lie. They manifested their profound respect for the "integrity of his life, matched only by his exceptional erudition," as a contemporary biographer put it, by publishing a "tombeau" of epitaphs, *Remigii Bellaquei Poetae Tumulus* (1577), and by editing his complete works (1578).

Some of his poems appear in English translation by W. Stirling in *Anthology of European Poetry, from Machant to Malherbe,* edited by M. Savill (1947).

ABOUT: PMLA, LXI (1946). [In French—see study by A. Eckhardt.]

M. B.

BELLI

BELLI, GIOACCHINO GIUSEPPE (September 10, 1791-December 21, 1863), Italian poet, was born in Rome, the son of Gaudenzio and Luigia (Mazio) Belli. His father, who had been in government service, died early, leaving his family penniless. His mother struggled to earn a living by needlework. She died when Belli was sixteen. The boy grew up in the seething and unsettled days of the Napoleonic occupation of Rome. What little formal education he received was

* bĕl' lē

under the Jesuits. Belli worked as a clerk in the households of various Roman noblemen and began writing verse as early as 1807. In 1816 he married Maria Conti, a well-to-do widow more than ten years his senior. They had one son, Ciro, born in 1824. The marriage appears to have been a fairly happy one—although Belli later formed a romantic attachment to a noblewoman, the Marchesa Roberti, to whom he dedicated many sonnets.

In the same year in which he married, Belli took a job at the Stamps and Registry Office which he held for ten years until he retired on a pension. His wife's death in 1837 left him in financial need and he returned to government service, this time to take a job with the corrupt papal bureaucracy that he himself had lampooned in many of his poems. With the years, however, Belli became increasingly conservative. Appalled by the violent revolutionary outbreaks of 1848, he stopped writing his satirical poetry and on his deathbed some years later he requested that his sonnets be burned. He died in Rome at seventy-two.

Belli began his career as a poet with conventional and quite undistinguished verse. It was not until he became acquainted with the work of Carlo Porta, the Milanese dialect poet, that he found the true medium for his expression—the crude and colorful dialect of the Roman people. In this language —making full use of its puns, obscenities, street-calls, tag-lines—Belli wrote some 2,279 sonnets, most of them during the period

1830-1840. His material was Rome and its people—the whole Roman society from Pope and clergy down to fishwife, beggar, and prostitute. "He gave the living city an immortality in art," Thomas G. Bergin remarks. The price that Belli paid for this specialization was complete neglect outside Rome. His work was never published during his lifetime and because of the difficulties of the dialect, it was not until almost a century after his death that his poems began appearing in English translation.

If Belli had a small public outside Rome, it was nevertheless an enthusiastic one. Among his admirers was the Russian novelist Gogol, who met him, heard him recite, and pronounced him one of the greatest poets of any age. The French critic Sainte-Beuve wrote: "He is original, witty in everything, but best of all in his artist's eye." James Joyce, not surprisingly, was delighted by the freedom and fertility of his language. More recently Eleanor Clark said of his work (in *Rome and a Villa*): "It is a record in sweep and intimacy comparable to the great European novels of the century. . . ." And Harold Nourse, his translator, observes that "Belli wrote with consummate mastery of form and verbal skills, and exhibits a novelist's range in his subjects, as well as in his mastery of the psychological and dramatic."

A savage satirist, outspoken in his attacks on all classes and institutions, Belli was nevertheless compassionate, deeply stirred by human suffering; and his sonnets, in spite of their coarseness of expression, reflect a hearty and healthy faith in his Church, his city, and her people. They in turn have paid him tributes—by naming a street after him and by erecting a monument to his memory in Trastevere with the inscription: "To their poet/ G. G. Belli/ The People of Rome."

Eleanor Clark translated some selections from Belli in *Rome and a Villa* (1952). A group of his sonnets in Harold Nourse's translation was published in *Hudson Review*, Spring 1956. The standard Italian editions were published in 6 vols., 1886-89 and in 1912. More recent editions include *Lo Zibaldone* (1960).

ABOUT: Clark, E. Rome and a Villa; Wilkins, E. H. A History of Italian Literature; Books Abroad Winter 1954; Hudson Review Spring 1956. [In Italian—see studies by E. Colombi, C. Muscetta, L. Silori, C. Zaccagnini and F. Clementi.]

BELLMAN, CARL MICHAEL (February 2, 1740-February 11, 1795), Swedish poet, was born in Stockholm. His father was Johan Arendt Bellman, of German descent,

BELLMAN

secretary at the Chancellery of the Royal Palace, later titular law-man. His mother was Catharina Hermonia, daughter of the parson Michel Hermonius. His pious parents gave him a good education. In 1759 he was employed at the Bank of Sweden, but a dissipated and prodigal life led to financial difficulties and unethical manipulations. In order to avoid debtors' prison he fled in 1763 to Norway. With the help of relatives he was able to settle his bankruptcy and pay his debts. After his return home he held poorly paid positions at various government offices. But bad luck pursued him. When he was employed at the Custom House this institution was reorganized, and Bellman lost his position, although he was allowed to retain his starvation salary. He was well known both for his poetic genius and his social and musical talents, and he was liked by King Gustaf III, who partly supported him and gave him the title Royal Secretary. In 1775 the King appointed him secretary of the government-operated lottery, a position with few or no duties and responsibilities. He hired a substitute on half salary and pocketed the other half himself. After his marriage in 1777 to Louisa Grönlund, daughter of a lower-grade public servant in Stockholm, the family grew rapidly, and so did his debts. In 1788 he was again declared bankrupt and was put in jail for a short time. He died consumptive and destitute, and his estate was put into liquidation.

Bellman holds a unique position in Swedish literature. He cannot be classified in any literary school. He was a child of genius of his time without any literary ambition. He simply wished to enjoy life and bring joy to others. In his teen-age years he wrote conventional religious songs and satirical poems, but after 1761 his production changed to convivial and drinking songs, patterned on French models. They were often exquisite parodies on Biblical themes, e.g., such extremely popular songs as *Gubben Noak* (Old Man Noah) and *Joachim uti Babylon* (Joachim in Babylon).

About 1765 Bellman's poetic talents blossomed to a dazzling brilliance. Now he created his famous poetic cycles, *Bacchi Orden* (The Order of Bacchus), later changed to *Bacchi Tempel, Fredmans Epistlar* (Fredman's Epistles), and *Fredmans Sånger* (Fredman's Songs). The first is a humorous travesty on the flourishing secret orders, describing all sorts of ceremonies in an imaginary order whose members are degenerated patrons of contemporary Stockholm taverns. *Fredmans Epistlar* is Bellman's greatest achievement, which contributed most to his immortality. The realistically drawn characters who pass in review are freely created but had real models, most of whom were poor, dissipated individuals. But Bellman's imagination elevated them into a fascinating world of rococo figures. The portrayal of the comic characters against a background of disease and death lends Bellman's humor a double aspect, which Esaias Tegnér ingeniously called "a sorrow in rosy red," and which is also reflected in abrupt changes in mood, from optimism to pessimism, from bacchantic revelry to melancholy pensiveness. The cycle *Fredmans Sånger*, published in 1791, contains a variety of earlier poems, some of which are masterpieces of lyrical beauty.

Bellman wrote his poems to music borrowed from contemporary plays, songs, dances, etc., and he revised them to fit his poetry. Words and music are so inseparably blended that the songs lose half their nature if one or the other is lacking. Accompanying himself with virtuosity on the zither, he displayed his remarkable gift for mimicry.

Five of Bellman's poems in English translation were published in Warner's *Library of the World's Best Literature*. Seven poems from *Fredmans Epistlar* and *Fredmans Sånger* are included in C. W. Stork's *Anthology of Swedish Lyrics* (1930), and scattered stanzas from the *Epistles* translated by Stork appear in his article on Fröding in *American-Scandinavian Review*, 1927. Several of his songs are also translated into English in *The Last of the Troubadours* by H. W. Van Loon & G. Castagnetta (1939).

ABOUT: Harrison, J. A. A Group of Poets and Their Haunts; Howitt, W. & M. The Literature and Romance of Northern Europe, II; Stork, C. W. Bellman the Incomparable (*in* American-Scandinavian Review, 1927); Van Loon, H. W. & Castagnetta, G. The Last of the Troubadours; Warner Library, IV; Winkel Horn, F. History of the Literature of the Scandinavian North.

A. J.

*BEMBO, PIETRO (May 20, 1470-January 18, 1547), Italian humanist and man of letters, was born in Venice, son of a senator, Bernardo Bembo, and member of a noble family. Young Pietro grew up in the various Italian courts to which his father went as Venetian envoy. In 1474 he was taken to Florence where he received the finest education available. He was fluent in Latin and studied Greek with the humanist Constantine Lascaris, and philosophy with Pietro Pomponazzi. As a young man he wrote the conventional Petrarchan love poems produced by all noble young gentlemen, but his first important work was in prose, not verse. This was *Gli Asolani*, written during the period 1498 to 1500 when Bembo accompanied his father to Ferrara. The book was finished in 1502 and published in 1505, dedicated to Lucrezia Borgia.

Gli Asolani rapidly became one of the most popular and influential books of the Renaissance. Described (by Nesca A. Robb) as "the great prototype of the courtly Neoplatonic treatise," it is an elegantly written dialogue on love. To relieve the tedium of philosophical discourse, Bembo sets his dialogue in Asolo (whence the title derives) at the court of his cousin Caterina Cornaro, whom he had visited in 1495. Here a group of attractive young noblemen and ladies discuss love. Ultimately they reach the conclusion that love, which they define as the desire for beauty, has not as an end in itself the achievement of physical beauty, but the apprehension of true beauty, which is divine and immortal. The Platonism which Bembo echoes here is not a profound philosophical system but rather a watered-down and superficial literary element. What gave the book its popularity was the beauty of its setting and the exquisite purity of its Italian prose.

In an age when Latin remained the primary medium of literary expression, Bembo's refined and purified Italian surprised and delighted his readers. A fastidious stylist, he labored over his writing, polishing and perfecting until his work glittered with surface brilliance. However, what J. B. Fletcher

* bĕm' bō

BEMBO

writes of Bembo's poetry describes *Gli Asolani* equally well—"In general his verses are formally impeccable, but empty of substance —expression hungering after thought." Nevertheless *Gli Asolani* helped to establish Bembo as the arbiter of Italian literature, a virtual dictator in matters of style. (Ernest H. Wilkins compares his influence to that of Malherbe in sevententh century France and Dr. Johnson in eighteenth century England.) In 1525 he published his influential tract (again in the form of a dialogue) on the Italian vernacular *Prosa della Volgar Lingua,* in which he argued for the use of Italian— and specifically the Florentine Tuscan tongue used by Dante, Petrarch, and Boccaccio—as the literary language of Italy. In some measure it was owing to this tract that Tuscan became the standard literary language.

Bembo lived at the court of Urbino from 1506 to 1511. He moved from there to Rome, where in 1513 he became papal secretary to Leo X. He resigned his post in 1521 and retired to Padua where he devoted himself (as one commentator describes it) "to refined vice and scholarship." During this period he wrote in Latin his official history of the Venetian Republic from 1487 to 1513. Bembo emerged from retirement in 1539 to return to Rome as a cardinal. Here he spent his last years.

In many ways Bembo's life ideally reflects the richness of the age in which he lived. He enjoyed to the fullest the best of two worlds —that of the spirit, as scholar and cardinal— and of the flesh, as lover (he had a mistress,

Morosina, and three children) and as typical Renaissance *bon vivant.* He lived in Florence under Lorenzo the Magnificent; he knew Venice as the friend of the printer Aldus Manutius (for whom he edited Petrarch's *Canzoniere* in 1501 and Dante's *Divine Comedy* in 1502), and of the notorious Pietro Aretino; and he lived in Rome as a favorite of Pope Leo X. His friends, besides these men, included Raphael, Titian, Poliziano (Politian), Erasmus, Castiglione (who used him as the spokesman for Platonic love in *The Courtier*). When he died in Rome in 1547 he was the most honored and respected man of letters of his age.

Gli Asolani was reprinted at least seven times during Bembo's lifetime. By 1600 there were twenty-two Italian editions. In 1545 it was translated into French, in 1551 into Spanish. It was not available in English, however, until 1954, when Rudolf B. Gottfried published a translation.

ABOUT: Ady, J. C. Italian Gardens of the Renaissance and Other Studies; Fletcher, J. B. Literature of the Italian Renaissance; Gottfried, R. B. *Introduction to* Gli Asolani (English translation); Robb, N. A. Neoplatonism of the Italian Renaissance; Wilkins, E. H. A History of Italian Literature. [In Italian—Elwert, T. W. Studi di Letteratura Veneziana; also see studies by V. Cian, G. Meneghetti, G. Petrocchi, M. Santoro.]

*BENEDICTSSON, VICTORIA MARIA BRUZELIUS (pseudonym "ERNST AHLGREN")

(March 6, 1850-July 21, 1888), Swedish novelist and dramatist, was born at Domme, a farm in the southernmost part of Sweden. Her father, Thure Bruzelius, of an old clergyman's family, was a farmer, a robustly masculine type. Her mother was Helena Sophia Finérus, a deeply religious, refined woman. Victoria grew up in a family in which the parents, after thirty years of unhappy married life, lived separated. Their different temperaments and matrimonial discords were not without influence upon her. At twenty-one she married a postmaster, Christian Benedictsson, at Hörby, not far from her birthplace. He was a widower with five children and almost thirty years her senior. It was an ill-matched marriage without spiritual fellowship between the two mates. In 1881 Mrs. Benedictsson contracted a serious periostitis, which confined her to bed for two years and made her a permanent cripple on crutches. However, the immobility gave her ample time for studies. She was captivated by the modern realistic literature and particularly by Georg Brandes' works and personality.

* bĕ′ nĕ dĭkts sôn

In 1884 she made her debut as Ernst Ahlgren with an uneven collection of sketches, *Från Skåne* (From Skåne), the best parts of which were realistic pictures of the life of the common people. It was followed by a partly autobiographical novel, *Pengar* (Money, 1885), an attack against marriage as a coercive institution, describing a young girl's growth, marriage, and divorce. Both publications were considerable successes, and they made her a highly respected young author. The royalties enabled her to move in literary circles in Stockholm and Copenhagen and, later, to make two trips to Paris.

Playwriting was in fashion, and next Ernst Ahlgren wrote, in cooperation with her intimate friend Axel Lundegård, a rather drawn-out drama, *Final* (Finale, 1885), which was not performed until after her death. Her little one-act play *I Telefon* (On the Phone, 1886) was better received at the Dramatic Theatre in Stockholm.

In 1887 her controversial marriage novel *Fru Marianne* appeared. It describes how a young, spoiled, city girl, married to a wealthy farmer, is educated to become an efficient woman conscious of her responsibility. Directed against the ideas of emancipation of women and free love, the novel pays homage to the solid character of the Swedish peasantry and to happiness in marriage. Ernst Ahlgren's last work was a collection of short stories, entitled *Folklif och Småberättelser* (Folk-Life and Short Stories).

The attack against *Fru Marianne*, physical illness, and unhappy love of the intellectually brilliant but emotionally chill Georg Brandes, broke the depressed woman's will to live and drove her to commit suicide before she could fulfill the great hopes she placed in herself. A. Lundegård completed, edited, and published a few posthumous works of hers.

Most interesting, and perhaps constituting the most affecting self-confession in Swedish literature, are the sensationally outspoken diaries and letters she wrote during her last tortured years.

Truls Jonasson was translated into English by K. Ahlström (1895), and a short story is included in C. W. Stork's collection *Sweden's Best Stories* (1928).

ABOUT: Columbia Dictionary of Modern European Literature. [In Swedish—see studies by F. Böök, M. Feuk, S. Linder, A. Lundegård, I. Schultén.]

A. J.

*BENIVIENI, GIROLAMO (1483-1542), Italian poet, was born in Florence. He was a precocious child and, while still very young, studied the classical languages and Hebrew. Although only a minor figure himself, Benivieni associated with many of the great humanists of the Italian Renaissance. He knew Lorenzo de' Medici, himself a poet as well as a patron of poets. He became a disciple of the reforming monk Savonarola and, around 1496, published a vernacular translation of his treatise *Della Semplicità*. He was also acquainted with the leading Neoplatonists of his time—Ficino, Poliziano (Politian), and Pico della Mirandola. He was especially close to the last and was buried at his side in St. Mark's Cathedral in Florence.

In characteristic Italian Renaissance fashion, Benivieni was at home in two worlds—that of the spirit and that of the flesh. He wrote his poems in the vernacular and moved easily between lofty philosophical subject matter and lush, sensuous love poetry. His most famous poem is his *canzone* summarizing Ficino's commentary on Plato's *Symposium*. This great ancient dialogue on love had inspired Ficino to write a Renaissance version in which Platonic love is described as the pursuit of an ideal beauty through various stages beginning with the worship of a human woman and ascending to a perception of divine Beauty. Ficino's treatise, *Libro dello Amore*, was put into poetic form by Benivieni as *Canzone dello Amore Celeste et Divino*. This poem, in turn, was the subject of a prose commentary by Pico della Mirandola, and ultimately it was transmitted to England where its Neoplatonic theme reappears in Edmund Spenser's *Foure Hymnes*. Benivieni's other writings include conventional Petrarchan love sonnets, some of which he rewrote after his religious conversion under Savonarola, and a study of Dante's *Inferno*, which he published in 1506.

An English translation of Benivieni's *Canzone* appears in J. B. Fletcher's *Literature of the Italian Renaissance* (1934).

ABOUT: Fletcher, J. B. Literature of the Italian Renaissance; Robb, N. A. Neoplatonism in the Italian Renaissance; Wilkins, E. H. A History of Italian Literature.

* bā nĕ vyā′ nē

BEN JUDAH. See BEN YEHUDAH

*BENOÎT DE SAINTE-MAURE (or Sainte-More) (fl. c. 1150), French poet, was probably named for the region of his birth, Sainte-Maure, near Poitiers. His rival, the poet Wace, referred to him in his *Roman de Rou* as "Master Benoît" ("Maistre Beneeit"), and this title may indicate that he had had a university education. He may have been a troubadour attached to the courts of various nobles. It is known that he spent much of his life in England at the court of Henry II. There presumably he wrote his *Chronique des Ducs de Normandie* in about 1175 at the request of the king. The date of Benoît's death is not known.

The only work that can be ascribed to him with certainty is his *Roman de Troie* (written c. 1160), a lengthy (30,000 verses) account of the history of Troy from the expedition of the Argonauts to the death of Ulysses. It was dedicated to Eleanor of Aquitaine, Henry's queen. The sources for the poem are two Latin forgeries of "eyewitness" accounts of the Trojan War—one by the fourth century Dictys Cretensis and the other by the sixth century Dares the Phrygian. Benoît's version is a typical Old French *roman d'antiquité*, a retelling of the classical epic in the stylized rhetoric of the Middle Ages, with all the trappings of medieval knighthood. Nitze and Dargan, in their *History of French Literature*, pointed out that Benoît "did for the Middle Ages what Virgil had done so majestically for imperial Rome; he gave feudal society an ancestry in the halls of Ilion." Of interest to readers today are the passages of the poem (some 1900 lines) in which Benoît tells the love story of Troilus and Briseida. These passages, apparently of Benoît's invention, reappeared a century later in the Latin prose *Historia Troiana* of Guido delle Colonne. Through Guido they passed to Boccaccio in his *Il Filostrato*, and from there to Chaucer's *Troylus and Criseyde*, Caxton's first English printed book, *The Recuell of the Histories of Troy*, Shakespeare's *Troilus and Cressida*, and the many other versions, including—in 1955—the opera by Sir William Walton.

A translation of the Troilus passages appears in R. K. Gordon's *The Story of Troilus* (1934).
ABOUT: Romania, LXXIX (1958); Speculum, XXIX (1954).
* bĕ nwȧ′ dĕ sȧɴt môr′

*BEN YEHUDAH (or JEHUDAH), ELIEZER (1858-December 16, 1922), Hebrew lexicographer, philologist, editor, essay-
* bĕn yĕ hōō′ dȧ

ist, and the father of New Hebrew as a spoken language, was originally named Perlman, his father's first name being Yehudah (hence Hebraized name "Ben Yehudah"—son of Yehudah); his mother's name was Feige. He was born in Luzhky, Lithuania, and received his early traditional Talmudic education at the Yeshiva of Polotzk. Being persecuted by the Hasidim because of his secret study of Hebrew grammar and reading of secular literature, he left the Yeshiva and went to Dvinsk where he secured his secondary education.

At first, under the influence of his friends at the Dvinsk *Gymnasium*, his ideals were cosmopolitan and socialistic; but the awakening of national consciousness among the oppressed peoples of Europe aroused his interest in specific Jewish problems. Inspired by the Zionist idea of Jewish national renaissance in Palestine, he entered, in 1879, a medical school in Paris, in order to settle down later as physician in the Holy Land. Developing symptoms of tuberculosis, however, he was forced to give up his medical studies and to go to Algeria, to a warmer climate. In 1881 he settled in Jerusalem with his wife Devorah, whom he had married in Vienna.

Ben Yehudah was entirely absorbed by the ideal of Jewish national resurrection in Palestine. In his articles published during the years 1879-1881 in the *Hashahar*, *Hamagid* and *Havazelet* he championed his credo that the revival of Hebrew as the vernacular of the Jewish people must be the primary prerequisite for a Jewish national renaissance. Dedicating his entire life to this ideal, he became the first pioneer of spoken Hebrew in Palestine. He introduced the "Havarah Sephardit," the Sephardic pronunciation of Hebrew, prevailing now in Israel.

In Jerusalem, he edited, in sequence, various daily papers and periodicals (*Mevasseret Zion, Havazelet, Ha-Zvi, Hashkafah, Doar Ha-Yom*) thus becoming the founder of the secular daily press in Palestine. As a teacher in Jerusalem he also was the first to use Hebrew as language of instruction.

Fanatically dedicated to his credo, he spoke Hebrew exclusively both in public and at home; his children, thus, became the first Jews in Palestine to absorb Hebrew as their native tongue. His example was soon followed by many others, making Hebrew the vernacular of the Jews in Palestine. Ben Yehudah soon felt the persecutions of the extreme Orthodox elements in Jerusalem, leading even to his temporary arrest by the Turkish authorities.

Recognizing the lack of Hebrew words for everyday usage, he began to coin new Hebrew terms based on Biblical and post-Biblical Hebraic sources or on Arabic and other related Semitic roots. To this enormous task, requiring the efforts of an entire academy, he dedicated his whole life, working twenty hours a day. The result was his major work, the *Millon Halashon Ha-ivrit,* a complete dictionary of classical and modern Hebrew, with French and German translation. He himself published only the first five volumes of his completed work. The publication of the other volumes has been accomplished by his family since his death. All seventeen volumes of this 8,000-page work have been published.

During World War I, Ben Yehudah lived in New York, where he published his work *Ad Aymatai Dibru Ivrit?;* after the war he returned to Jerusalem. He was also the author of a Hebrew-Yiddish-Russian, and a Russian-Hebrew-German dictionary; *Hamikra,* an anthology for Hebrew schools; *Kitsur Divray Ha-Yamim,* an abridged history textbook; and numerous essays and articles in the fields of philology, education, literature, etc. He was the founder of the Vaad Halashon, which has eventually become the official Academy of the Hebrew Language of the State of Israel.

He died in Jerusalem, survived by his wife Hemdah—whom he had married after the early death of his first wife Devorah, Hemdah's older sister—and by six of his eleven children. On the occasion of his 100th birthday, the grateful people and government of Israel resolved to establish in Jerusalem a Ben Yehudah Museum to serve as research center for Hebrew philology. His so far unpublished works and essays will be edited here in twenty additional volumes

ABOUT: Lipsky, L. A Gallery of Zionist Profiles; Waxman, M. A History of Jewish Literature, IV.

H. C.

---

*BÉRANGER, PIERRE-JEAN DE (August 19, 1780-July 16, 1857), French poet, was born in Paris, near Les Halles. Abandoned by his father, and neglected by his mother, he was raised by his grandfather, then at Péronne by an aunt; as a student he lived in the Faubourg Saint-Antoine, and probably witnessed the fall of the Bastille.

* bā rän zhä′

BÉRANGER

His early readings included Voltaire's *La Henriade,* Tasso's *Gerusalemme,* and the Gospels. He frequented revolutionary groups and began work as a typesetter. Called back to Paris to help his grandfather in questionable banking practices, he profited by the older man's book collection to satisfy his craving for literature. Béranger did various kinds of work, finding time to write poetry, plays, and especially songs, and lived happily in relative indigence. His reputation as a song writer rose from the gaiety and spice of his lyrics; his first general fame came in 1813 with *Le Roi d'Yvetot,* whose protagonist (generally recognized as Napoleon) "sleeps well without glory." Thus Béranger translated the gay preoccupations of the people and their joy in living.

After the Restoration, Béranger was no longer content with mere verve, but began to visit anti-royalist salons and sing of patriotism and liberty. His satires against the new and excessive literary censorship under Louis XVIII, combined with other democratic propaganda, made of him a dangerous polemist, and he was imprisoned in 1821 as a result of his *Chansons Morales et Autres,* of which the second volume had just appeared. His *Chansons Nouvelles* again led him to prison, in 1828, and drew to him there, as visitors and admirers, such notables as Hugo, Dumas, and Sainte-Beuve. In 1830 Béranger again became a champion of the Imperialists, and sang of Napoleon the Martyr in semi-epic vein. For several years he lived quietly apart, but during the revolution of 1848 the people again demanded his advice and opinion on events. He found in himself no talent for a political career, and was content with his role as prophet, seer, and great survivor, along with Chateaubriand and Lamartine, of more heroic days. He was a familiar figure in Paris, Fontainebleau, and Tours. He spent his last years in grave illness, and his death was hastened by that of his old friend Mlle Judith Frère.

Béranger was too much a man of his times for his work to survive except in a few of his more striking songs. His appeal, then as now, lay in the simplicity of his moral and religious ideas. From his early experiences he retained a feeling of sympathy with the people, and partook of their gay frankness. His interest in political satire no doubt represents a basic aspect of his mind, but in other circumstances he might have preferred to cultivate the manner of his philosophical songs—analyses of happiness, pleasure, and desire; paintings of nature and of Providence. Indeed, his temperament was dominated by attitudes of human charity and brotherly love.

Béranger told his own life in *Ma Biographie,* published posthumously in 1857. His *Œuvres Complètes* appeared in frequent editions, often with music, beginning with the four volumes of 1834.

Translations of Béranger's works were numerous, into German in 1838, and the *Songs of Béranger* in London in 1837; *One Hundred Songs* translated by W. Young in 1847; *Lyrical Poems* by W. Anderson, 1847; *Two Hundred Lyrical Poems* again by W. Young, 1850; and many later versions, by W. Walsh, C. Betts, W. Toynbee, etc.

ABOUT: Forster, J. Some French and Spanish Men of Genius. [In French—see studies by L. Arréat, A. Boulle, P. Brochon, C. Causeret, J. Demangest, A. Lumbroso. In German—Fischer, J. O. Béranger: Werk und Wirkung.]

F. J. C.

BERCEO, GONZALO DE. See GONZALO DE BERCEO

*BERCHET, GIOVANNI (December 23, 1783-December 23, 1851), Italian poet and translator, was born in Milan of a family of French-Swiss ancestry. The son of a businessman, Giovanni was also destined for a business career. But his study and quick mastery of foreign languages (French, German, English) drew him to literature. An ardent patriot, he found that his native Italian literature was sadly lacking in vitality,

* bār shā′

and he came to believe that the literatures of Northern Europe should be better known in Italy. To this end he translated into Italian Gray's *The Bard,* Goldsmith's *The Vicar of Wakefield,* and several important German writings, including works by Schiller and Bürger.

In 1816 Berchet was one of three Italian writers (the others were Lodovico di Breme and Pietro Borsieri) who sprang to the defense of Madame de Staël for her article in *Biblioteca Italiana* suggesting that Italian writers become better acquainted with foreign literature. Berchet's contribution was a pamphlet called "On 'The Wild Huntsman' and the 'Lenore' of Gottfried August Bürger: a Semi-Serious Letter from Chrysostom to His Son." In this lightly humorous treatise he argues for a "popular" poetry that will attract a wide audience, and he urges Italian poets to draw material from their own rich resources in Italian tradition, ballads, and folksong.

Berchet was a poet in his own right. His most successful work was a long political poem published in 1821, *I Profughi di Parga* (The Fugitives of Parga)—a protest against the action of the British ceding the Greek city of Parga to Turkey. Ironically, this poem about exile anticipated the poet's own exile from Italy. Fearing arrest for his outspoken views on Italian liberty, he fled to Switzerland, then to Paris, and finally to London, where he lived for eight years. There he wrote another long political poem, *Le Fantasie,* in which he contrasted Italy's glorious past with its present shame. He also lived in Belgium and in Germany, and did not return to Italy until 1841. He continued to write and to fight in the cause of Italian freedom until his death in Turin on his sixty-eighth birthday.

In his *I Profughi* and his other patriotic poems, Berchet wrote with what Benedetto Croce called "the lyricism of the exile"—with a deep and sensitive love for his native land and sympathy for the common people victimized by war and oppression. His other poems are narratives—popular in their appeal and noble in sentiment, but generally too melodramatic and sentimental for modern tastes. Croce respected him as a poet but saw his weaknesses too: ". . . he was not sufficiently a poet, his interest in poetry itself was not equal to his inspiration, he lacked ardor in seeking out and rendering perfect the expression of his own feelings, the passion of the artist for the one word, unique and without any possible equivalent."

ABOUT: Croce, B. European Literature in the Nineteenth Century; Wilkins, E. H. A History of Italian Literature. [In Italian—see studies by E. Bellorini, P. Da Prati, A. Gustarelli.]

*BERDICHEVSKY (or BERDICZEW-SKI), MIKHAH YOSEF (pseudonym "M. Y. BIN GORION") (August 7, 1865-November 18, 1921), Hebrew scholar and writer, was born in Miedzybozh, Russia. He was the son of a Hasidic rabbi and received a profound Talmudic education according to Hasidic principles. He was married at the age of fifteen. Because of his attachment to secular studies, however, he was forced by his rich but fanatic in-laws to divorce his wife; then he left for the Yeshiva of Volozhin, where he became acquainted with the views of the Haskalah, and also started his career as Hebrew writer. From Volozhin he went to Odessa, where he continued his education and took an active part in the Jewish renaissance movement.

Driven by internal spiritual conflicts and the desire to absorb modern Western culture, Berdichevsky left in 1890 for Germany, where he studied at the universities of Breslau and Berlin, and at the Art Academy of Breslau. In 1896 he received his Ph.D. from the University of Bern for his philosophical dissertation "On the Relationship Between Ethics and Aesthetics." From 1902 to 1911 he lived in Breslau, after which he settled in Berlin, where he stayed till his death. In both Breslau and Berlin he lived in strictest seclusion, dedicated wholly to his work.

Berdichevsky was one of the most outstanding and prolific figures of modern Hebrew literature, embracing many forms of writing; he was a profound student of Jewish history, an essayist, novelist, a keen critic, and a folklorist of renown. Yet it was the provocative rebellious temper of his writings that established his prestige and left a deep imprint on the Hebrew renaissance.

Influenced by the revolutionary currents in European literature at the end of the nineteenth century, and in particular by Nietzsche, he became the most articulate representative of extreme secularism in Hebrew literature. Following the thoughts of Nietzscheanism, he revolted against the excessive cult of spirituality and too much dependence upon history in Jewish life, demanding a *shinnui ha-arakhim* (revaluation of values) in Judaism, and striving to lead the new Jewish generation back to the unperverted Biblical values. Battling for the rights of the individual Jew,

* běr dĭ chěf' skē

to free him from the excessive weight of traditions and ancient memories, Berdichevsky became the chief opponent of Ahad Ha-am, who emphasized the principle of collective spirituality in Jewish history.

The great impact of Berdichevsky's revolutionary thoughts upon modern Hebrew literature is felt even today; his collected Hebrew writings appeared in 1936 in 20 volumes. Some of his stories and legends have been translated into English and included in various Jewish anthologies. His main works are: *Bet Hamidrash*, a collection of essays on Judaism; *Mahanayim*, a collection of sketches and short stories; *Sefer Hasidim*, glorifying the spiritual beauty of the Hasidic movement; *Mish'nay Olamot* and *Din Undevarim*, collections of essays and stories. Of particular importance are his collections of Jewish legends in German: *Die Sagen der Juden* (5 vols.; appeared also in Hebrew); *Der Born Judas* (translated from Hebrew by his wife Rahel Ramberg, 6 vols.); *Sinai und Garizim*, a revolutionary approach to the founding of the Israelite religion and to ancient Jewish history.

Berdichevsky's main vehicle of expression was Hebrew. In addition to his above mentioned works in German, he also wrote poetry and belles-lettres in Yiddish (collected edition published in 1924, in 6 vols.).

ABOUT: Waxman, M. A History of Jewish Literature, IV.

H. C.

BERNARD OF *CLAIRVAUX, Saint (1090-August 20, 1153), French mystic and theologian, was born at Fontaines, near Dijon, in Burgundy. The son of a knight, Tescelin, a feudal lord in the service of the Duke of Burgundy, and his wife Aleth, a noblewoman, Bernard was one of a large family. He was a precocious child and might have had a brilliant career in secular life, but he showed unusual piety and early resolved to dedicate his life to God. At twenty-two he entered the Benedictine order at Cîteaux, bringing with him as novitiates twenty-nine other young men, some of them his kinsmen. The great tragic irony of his life henceforth was that the peace and contemplation which he sought so ardently in entering monastic life were so often denied him. Time and time again he was forced out of the cloisters into the field of action—to administer religious houses, to advise kings, emperors, and popes, to settle quarrels, to put down heresy, to preach a crusade. As a controversialist he took positions which, in modern times, have perhaps made him appear narrow, unreasonable, fanatic—most especially for his part in condemning Abelard. Bertrand Russell, for example, describes him as one "whose saintliness did not suffice to make him intelligent." But as

* klâr vō'

Anne Fremantle remarks, "He has had a bad press in the last few centuries." Too often modern critics have failed to recognize in Bernard the intellectual who, against his will and better judgment, was forced into intolerable situations out of a sense of duty and devotion to a cause. Bernard never sought to become involved in controversies nor to be a leader of men. Forced into the secular world, however, he accepted his burden with energetic good-will. In spite of almost constant ill-health and physical pain, he traveled and worked tirelessly. G. G. Coulton wrote of him: "Few men ever brought to the service of an ideal, chosen so early and unflinchingly, a nobler combination of qualities."

The monastery at Cîteaux which the young Bernard entered in 1112 was a new one, poor and struggling, led by an English prior, Stephen Harding. In less than three years Bernard had so distinguished himself that he was sent out to found a "daughter" abbey at Clairvaux. The extraordinary growth of the establishment at Clairvaux made Bernard's name famous throughout Europe. Under his leadership the Cistercian (or Trappist) order increased in strength and in numbers. The monks of Clairvaux left the monastery to become powerful clergymen— a pope, cardinals, bishops. Bernard himself was called to Rome (indeed, he became known as "the hawk of Rome"), to Paris, anywhere there were threats of heresy or schism. He was a founder of the powerful order of the Knights Templar, the "soldiers of Christ." He threw his support behind Pope Innocent II in his claim to the papacy which had been challenged by Anacletus II. He challenged the brilliant philosopher Peter Abelard, who believed in the primacy of reason while Bernard adhered to a mystic, intuitive apprehension of God. At the Council of Sens in 1140 he argued his case so fervently that Abelard walked out without uttering a word in his defense and was subsequently condemned. Finally, in 1146, he preached the Second Crusade, at the bidding of the pope and of Louis VII. At Vézelay he gave a sermon so stirring that his audience was carried away, and he was offered—but refused—the leadership of the crusade. That crusade met with disaster and Bernard suffered bitterly from the criticisms he received for his part in it. But he accepted the disaster and his sufferings with unquestioning faith as the will of God.

Bernard died at the Abbey of Clairvaux at sixty-three and was canonized in 1174.

Numerous stories and legends have grown up around him, all of them emphasizing his asceticism, his quiet endurance of pain, his indifference to food and bodily comforts. Perhaps the most famous of these is the story of his riding on his donkey all day along the shores of Lake Geneva and never lifting his eyes to the beauties of nature around him, so deeply absorbed was he in prayer. Emaciated, fair in coloring, with delicate features, he embodied physically as well as spiritually the ideal of medieval monasticism.

His writings are more distinguished for their fervor than for sheer literary merit. Outstanding among these are his letters, which reflect his prodigious activity in church and state affairs. They also reveal a man of passion, often moved to anger, but a man with humor, warmth, and understanding. His treatises are mainly on theological matters and ecclesiastical government. Of greatest interest today are his sermons—particularly the series on the Song of Songs proclaiming the mystical union of the soul with God—and his hymns, especially the well-known "Jesu dulcis memoria." Of his sermons Erasmus wrote: "Bernard is an eloquent preacher, much more by nature than by art; he is full of charm and vivacity and knows how to reach and move the affections." Some of his hymns appear today in the Roman breviary and are used, in English translation, in Protestant churches. His writing shows, for its time, fairly extensive knowledge of the classics, though he leaned primarily of course upon the Bible and the Church Fathers. His prose is vigorous and rhythmical. With his death—or shortly after—a whole era of medieval monasticism ended; but his influence—through his writings and his memory—has been and remains profound.

Bernard's Latin writings are collected in Migne's *Patrologia Latina*. They were translated into English by S. J. Eales in four volumes, 1889-1896. There are numerous English translations of his treatises, including several sixteenth century ones printed by Wynken de Worde. Of twentieth century translations the following should be mentioned: *On Consideration*, by G. Lewis, (1908); *The Book of Saint Bernard on the Love of God*, by E. G. Gardner (1915) (also by T. L. Connolly, 1937, and A. C. Pegis in *The Wisdom of Catholicism*, 1949); *Concerning Grace and Free Will*, by W. W. Williams (1920); *The Life of Saint Malachy*, by H. J. Lawlor (1920); the *Twelve Degrees of Humility and Pride*, by B. R. V. Mills (1929), also *The Steps of Humility*, by G. R. Burch (1940); and *Saint Bernard Seen Through his Selected Letters*, by B. S. James (1953).

ABOUT: Among the numerous biographies of Bernard the following may be mentioned: Coulton,

G. G. Two Saints: Bernard and Francis; Eales, S. J. St. Bernard; Luddy, A. J. The Life and Teaching of St. Bernard; Morison, J. A. C. The Life and Times of St. Bernard; Ratisbonne, M. T. The History of the Life of St. Bernard; Storrs, R. S. Bernard of Clairvaux; Webb, G. & Walker, A. (trans.) St Bernard of Clairvaux. The Story of His Life as Recorded in the Vita Prima Bernardi by Certain of His Contemporaries; Williams, W. W. St. Bernard of Clairvaux. The standard biography in French is by the Abbé E. Vacandard. Also useful for a brief outline of Bernard's mystical theology is E. Gilson's Christian Philosophy in the Middle Ages.

*BERNARDES, DIOGO (c.1530-c.1605), Portuguese poet, was born in Ponte da Barca on the river Lima in the Minho province, as the oldest son of a notary, João Rodrigues de Araujo, and of Catarina, daughter of the notary Diogo Bernardes. The boy took minor orders in 1544 at the cathedral of Braga but did not pursue an ecclesiastic career, in which his youngest brother, the mystic Agostinho da Cruz, was to distinguish himself. Diogo went to Lisbon, perhaps served Crown Prince John, patron of letters, and at court, thanks to his natural talent, was admitted to the circle of the classic poet António Ferreira. "All I am," he wrote to Ferreira, "I owe to your precious teachings." When the prince died in 1554, Bernardes returned home where he wrote bucolic verse, dedicating his first eclogue ("Adonis") to the memory of his patron. At the end of the same year he wrote his first carta in verse to the poet Sá de Miranda, expressing his admiration.

In 1566 Bernardes succeeded his father as notary public but resigned the next year to travel to Madrid as secretary to King Sebastian's special envoy. We hear of him again in 1578, when he accompanied the ambitious King on his crusade to Morocco. It was his task as court poet to celebrate the anticipated victories. In spite of Ferreira's urgings, Bernardes failed to produce an epic, for there was not to be a victory. Instead, he treated religious themes, having turned devout and melancholy during several years in Moorish captivity: "I who sang as a free man by the murmuring waves of the Lima, mellow, soft and clear, now weep as a captive to the sound of iron chains around my chafed foot." Ransomed at last in 1581, he returned to Lisbon to serve the governor under Philip II as a mere page. He died there.

Bernardes is remembered as the sweet "Singer of the River Lima," the first of many Portuguese poets to attach his name to a particular river or region of his country. Although he followed ancient, Italian, and Span-

* bĕr nàr' dēsh

ish models in shepherd poetry when singing to "Silvia" as her "Silvio," he made their ideal setting more real by introducing the humble fauna and flora of the green countryside of northern Portugal. His works appeared in three volumes, the devotional verse first, as Várias Rimas ao Bom Jesus e à Virgem Gloriosa sua Mãe e a Santos Particulares (1594); the sonnets, canzones and other short poems as Rimas Várias; Flores do Lima (1596); and his twenty eclogues and 28 cartas (with several replies) as O Lima... (1596). Like others, Bernardes continued to cultivate the old peninsular verse forms while experimenting in the new Italian ones, which he was the first to acclimatize truly to Portuguese. Neither independent in thought like Sá or Ferreira, nor passionate like Camões, Bernardes excelled in melodiousness. "The poet of the Promised Land, all honey and butter," Melo called him. To this day the harmonious, sad moods of his bucolic poems captivate the reader. Many of Bernardes' poems are so good that they were ascribed to Camões for a long time.

None of Bernardes' works has been translated into English, except for an occasional poem in anthologies, such as John Adamson's Lusitania Illustrata (1842) or Henry W. Longfellow's The Poets and Poetry of Europe (2d ed. 1896).

ABOUT: [In Portuguese—Braga, T. História dos Quinhentistas; Braga, M. introduction to his edition of Bernardes' works, 3 vols. 1945-46.]

G. M. M.

BERNARDIN DE SAINT-PIERRE. See SAINT-PIERRE, (JACQUES HENRI) BERNARDIN DE

*BERNART (or BERNARD) DE VENTADORN (or VENTADOUR) (12th century), Provençal troubadour, was born in Ventadorn, where his father—according to the Provençal Vida—was a furnace stoker at the castle of Viscount Ebles II of Ventadorn and his mother a servant. Ebles was a model feudal lord—a poet and a patron of troubadours. He took an interest in the young Bernart, who evidently had some talent for poetry, and educated the boy in the troubadour arts. Bernart addressed his earliest poems to Agnes of Montluçon, his patron's wife. He must have demonstrated his skills in these love lyrics a little too ardently, for he was soon dismissed from the court and sent off on his wanderings.

Some time later (c. 1150) Bernart joined the Norman court of the brilliant and charm-

* bĕr nàr' dĕ väN tà dôrn'

ing Eleanor of Aquitaine, then newly divorced from Louis VII of France. It was to her that he dedicated his most exquisite poetry. Just how much of the sentiments expressed in these poems is convention—the tradition of courtly love being that the troubadour must worship from afar and suffer the pangs of unrequited love—and how much is genuine, it is impossible to know. Some chroniclers say that they fell in love. The poetry itself gives evidence of a real passion. It is certainly the finest example extant of Provençal love poetry—simple and clear yet skillful in its manipulation of the complex stanza forms. "With a dawnlike freshness, as if he were the first lyrical poet of all time," Amy Kelly writes, "Bernard opens his heart and weaves the story of his adoration in harmonies that can be brought from the *langue d'oc* into no other tongue." The spirit of love infused his poetry and ennobled it. It sharpened his sensitivity to his surroundings and intensified his love of nature and the powers of his imagination.

The sad fate of Bernart's passion for Eleanor is briefly told by a chronicler: "He made many good songs. And while he was with her the King of England [Henry II] married her and took her from Normandy and led her away." Bernart also went to England in Henry's service, but either he was kept away from Eleanor or simply by chance they did not meet again. He wandered about France and was for a time at the court of Raimon V, Count of Toulouse, a patron of the troubadours. In 1194 or some time soon after he retired to the Cistercian abbey of Dalon in Limousin. Nothing further was heard of him, so it is presumed that he died there.

The large number of extant manuscripts of his work attests to Bernart's popularity. Nearly fifty of his poems are preserved. They were published by Carl Appel in *Bernart von Ventadorn* ((1915) and by R. T. Hill and T. G. Bergin in *An Anthology of the Provençal Troubadours* (1941).

There is no complete English translation, but selections from his work (including his best-known poem "No Marvel Is It") appear in Justin H. Smith's *The Troubadours at Home* (1899), *An Anthology of World Poetry*, edited by Mark Van Doren (1936), and *The Modern Book of French Verse*, edited by A. Boni (1920).
ABOUT: Chaytor, H. J. The Troubadours; Hill, R. T. & Bergin, T. G. Anthology of the Provençal Troubadours; Kar, G. Thoughts on the Medieval Lyric; Kelly, A. Eleanor of Aquitaine; Valency, M. In Praise of Love.

BERTRAN DE BORN (1140?-1215), Provençal poet, famed as one of the troubadours of the court of Henry II and Eleanor of Aquitaine, was born in Limoges, in the northernmost part of the diocese of Perigueux. His father's name was also Bertran; his mother's name was Ermengart. The Born family belonged to the lesser nobility. The family property, the Château d'Hautefort, held jointly by Bertran and his brother Constantin as early as 1169, figures prominently in his political affairs and in some of his poems. The chroniclers mention two separate marriages for Bertran, the first to a lady named Raimonde in 1179, of whom nothing is known except that she bore him at least two sons, the second in 1192 (immediately after the death of Raimonde) to a certain Phillippe. Neither lady is ever referred to in his love poems.

One event of Bertran's life, his espousal of the ambitions of the "Young King" Henry of Court-Mantel, son of Henry II, has been given special prominence by Dante in the *Inferno* (Canto 28). An especially eerie episode of the poem introduces Bertran, one of the Sowers of Discord of the Eighth Circle, as a dismembered torso, holding by the hair his severed head, which he swings like a lantern. He has committed the sin of Achitophel, as he confesses, by causing a son to rebel against his father: "Because I sundered those that should be one/ I'm doomed, woe worth the day! to bear my brain/ Cleft from the trunk whence all its life should run." Curiously enough, Dante does not mention Bertran's literary achievement here, but he is lauded in *De Vulgari Eloquentia* as "a pre-eminent poet of war."

Scholars today are of the opinion that Dante exaggerated Bertran's villainy, following a tradition spread by an anonymous (and posthumous) chronicler who magnified the part played by Bertran in the civil wars of his period. From the confused accounts of his life it appears that much of his martial activity stemmed from a grudge he bore Richard the Lion Hearted, then Duke of Aquitaine, for siding with his brother Constantin in a quarrel that developed over the ownership of the Château d'Hautefort. It seems to have been personal revenge rather than any nationalistic feeling that prompted Bertran to join the barons of Limoges, Poitiers, and Périgourd in their revolt to drive Richard out of Aquitaine during the years 1182 and 1183. Subsequently Bertran embarrassed Richard by stirring up his elder brother Henry, the

* bĕr trän′ dē bôrn

"Young King," to rebel against both him and his father, King Henry II. These altercations came to an end with the death of Prince Henry at Turenne on July 11, 1183. There is a famous account, generally discredited by historians, of Bertran's reconciliation with King Henry II when his expression of grief over the prince's death moved the father to tears. Later Richard stormed the Château d'Hautefort and captured it from Bertran, but ultimately Bertran gained back his holdings and was able to bequeath them to his sons. That he made peace with Richard and remained from then on in amicable relations with him is evident from some of his later poems. Elevated by some as a patriot and national hero, maligned by others as a medieval Machiavelli, the truth about Bertran seems to be that he was very much of his time, an opportunist and a soldier of fortune. In 1196 Bertran forsook the strife of the world to become a monk of the order of Cîteaux in the Abbey of Dalon, near Hautefort. Here he died in 1215, according to a cartulary of the monastery. One of his sons, also named Bertran, wrote verse, and so has been confused with him.

His surviving poems, forty-four lyrics (five of these now considered of doubtful attribution), are partially autobiographical, reflecting the political and military events in which he participated—either at close hand or indirectly. Several of these are love songs (canzos). Two of the most charming, obviously opportunistic, were written in praise of Mathilda, daughter of Henry II and Eleanor of Aquitaine, addressed as "Lena" (Helen of Troy). Various women appear through his poems, disguised under such mysterious names as "Cembeli," "Bel Senher," "Mielhs-de-Be." Probably his most famous woman is that purely imaginary lady ("domna soissebuda") whom he envisaged as a composite of all ideal feminine qualities.

Bertran is considered particularly the master of the sirventés—the poem on political or moral subjects. Here he is in turn vigorous and stirring, plaintive and poignant, biting and vindictive. Among the most famous of these poems are a war song, stirring up the lieges of the Count of Toulouse against the King of Aragon; an appeal to arms to the barons of Limousin against Richard; two poems in honor of Conrad of Montferrat, one of the leaders of the Third Crusade (Bertran did not go along); two poems honoring Richard upon his return to Aquitaine in 1194 from wars and imprisonment abroad. His most moving poem, and undoubtedly his most sincere, is the great *planh* on the death of Prince Henry ("el jove rei engles"). The poems of Bertran de Born present, as his French editor Antoine Thomas indicates, a "tableau vivante" of feudal society of the twelfth century.

The best editions of the poems of Bertran de Born are those of Antoine Thomas, in French (1888), and C. Appel, in German (1932). There is no complete English text, but portions of the poems are translated by Francis Hueffer in his The Troubadours (1878), and free translations of various passages are to be found in a series of articles by L. E. Kastner, in Modern Language Review and Modern Philology noted below.

ABOUT: Barlow, H. The Young King and Bertran de Born; Chaytor, H. The Troubadours of Dante; Hueffer, F. The Troubadours; Pound, E. Literary Essays (ed. T. S. Eliot); Valency, M. In Praise of Love; Comparative Literature Spring 1956; Modern Language Review January 1933, April 1934, January 1936, April 1937; Modern Philology August 1931, February 1937.

R. A. C.

***BERTRAND, LOUIS JACQUES NAPOLÉON, called ALOYSIUS** (April 20, 1807-April 29, 1841), French writer of prose-poems, was born at Ceva, in Piedmont, then French territory. His father, Georges (1768-1828), a lieutenant in the army, had married an Italian, Laure Davico (1782-1854), daughter of the mayor. Two more boys and a girl were born to the couple.

In 1815 the family moved to Dijon, in Burgundy, on the father's modest retirement pay. Louis started school in 1818; he did not distinguish himself in the classical program until 1825 and 1826. It is not known whether he took his baccalaureate (secondary-school) degree. Louis started to write verse in 1823, and by 1826 he was active in the local literary society, the Société d'Études. Narrow-faced, ferret-like, with small bright black eyes, yellow in complexion, he was not a good mixer but did hold various offices in the literary club. The members of this group, which had started in 1821, held various religious and political views, and were receptive to budding romanticism. Bertrand, a republican, admired Hugo, Nodier, and Émile Deschamps.

Louis was strongly attracted to Burgundian history and the Dijon of the fourteenth and fifteenth centuries. This antiquarianism and his love of the grotesque he embodied in verses and rhythmic sketches (later published as *La Volupté* and *Le Keepsake Fantastique*) such as "Jacques-les-Andelys." Between May and October, 1828, he was editor and director of *Le Provincial*, a Dijon newspaper which

* bĕr trän′

wished to emulate *Le Globe* of Paris. Alfred de Musset made his debut in *Le Provincial.* The reading of Sir Walter Scott led Bertrand to E. T. A. Hoffmann and the illustrator Callot, with a fascination for the fantastic. In 1828, on the death of his father, Bertrand went to Paris. Poor and ill of consumption, he almost starved there. In 1830 he returned to Dijon and contributed to *Le Patriote* and *Le Spectateur,* signing himself J. L. B. or L. B. In 1833 he returned to Paris and started the long negotiation, which lasted for years, with the publisher Renduel for the publication of *Gaspard de la Nuit, Fantaisies à la Manière de Rembrandt et de Callot.* At about this time he started to use the more distinctive, and romantic, name of Ludovic. The name Aloysius was not used until 1840. Bertrand tried unsuccessfully to write vaudevilles. In 1837 he met Jean-Pierre David, i.e., David d'Angers, the sculptor. David made a famous sketch of Bertrand on his death bed, and saw to the latter's burial in Vaugirard cemetery; Bertrand died at Necker hospital after being in various charity wards from 1838. In 1847 the remains were transferred to Montparnasse cemetery.

Through David d'Angers, Sainte-Beuve helped to recover the manuscript of *Gaspard de la Nuit* from Renduel, and it was published posthumously by Victor Pavie, in 1842. An article by Sainte-Beuve made these prose-poems and their author famous. Baudelaire acknowledged his indebtedness to Bertrand for the idea of his own "little poems in prose"; Maurice Ravel interpreted some of these Gothic "illuminations" in a set of piano compositions (1909); George Moore mentions "the gloomy and sterile little pictures of *Gaspard de la Nuit*" in his *Confessions;* the symbolist poets were fond of these precise, chiseled sketches. A street in Dijon has been named after Bertrand.

There are numerous editions of *Gaspard de la Nuit,* some illustrated. One, published in 1920, contains seventeen illustrations by Bertrand; the originals are in the Angers library. B. Guégan edited *Le Keepsake Fantastique* (1924); Stuart Merrill translated excerpts in *Pastels in Prose* (1890); C. Sprietsma's unpublished M.A. thesis at Columbia University includes a translation of *Gaspard de la Nuit*; C. Sprietsma has edited *La Volupté et Pièces Diverses* (1926).

ABOUT: Ransome, A. Fortnightly Review, XCII (1912), 1153-1160; [In German—Banner, F. Aloysius Bertrand's Gaspard de la Nuit als Wortkunstwerk. In French—Chabeuf, H. Louis Bertrand et le Romantisme à Dijon; Pavie, A. Médaillons Romantiques; Sainte-Beuve, C. A. Portraits Littéraires, II; Sprietsma, C. Louis Bertrand dit Aloysius Bertrand, 1807-1841.]

S. S. W.

*BEYLE, MARIE-HENRI ("STENDHAL," pseud.) (January 23, 1783-March 23, 1842), French novelist, was born in Grenoble, son of Joseph-Chérubin Beyle, a well-to-do lawyer, and his wife, Henriette Gagnon. He was named Marie-Henri for his maternal grandfather and in his adult life used the name Henri Beyle. He also used a multitude of pseudonyms—among them "Henri Brulard," "Dominique," "Bombet," and the most famous of them, "Stendhal."

Young Beyle early showed a violent temper and a passionate, aggressive nature. Years later, in his autobiography *Henri Brulard,* he quite candidly described himself in childhood as "a little monster." He idolized his gay and charming mother, who died in childbirth when he was eight, and despised his father. After his mother's death, his maternal aunt Séraphie came into the household to raise him and his two younger sisters. Henri was educated at home by a Jesuit priest in an atmosphere of great moral earnestness but little love. The only relief in his life was furnished by the visits of his sympathetic grandfather, Dr. Marie-Henri Gagnon, by whom he was encouraged to read Voltaire, Molière, and the Abbé Prévost's *Manon Lescaut.*

Growing up during the years of the French Revolution, Beyle was exposed to the emotional turmoils of his age, though not to any of its physical dangers and upheavals. His father, an adherent of the Bourbons, was in some danger in the Reign of Terror of 1793, but the young boy proclaimed himself an ardent republican. In 1796 the boy was enrolled in the École Centrale of Grenoble, one of the first public and secular schools in France. Here he read extensively in classical French literature, was first introduced to Shakespeare in French translation, and studied mathematics, in which he excelled. His school record was brilliant and in 1799 he was qualified for admission to the École Polytechnique in Paris.

For Beyle this offered a long-awaited opportunity to escape from his unhappy home. He went to Paris, but once there, in a fit of despair, refused to take the entrance examinations. He drifted alone about the city until December 1799 when he suffered a complete physical collapse. He found shelter with prosperous relatives until after his recovery, through them getting his introduction into polite society and his first job, a clerkship in the Ministry of War.

In 1800, thanks to the influence of his cousin Pierre Daru, an official in Napoleon's

* bāl; stän dȧl'

95

"STENDHAL"

government, Beyle was commissioned a second lieutenant in the 6th Dragoons and sent on a mission to Italy. Stationed in Milan he plunged eagerly into a life of gaiety and love-making, and made up his mind, at eighteen, to be a dashing military leader, molded in the image of Napoleon and the great seventeenth century military leader Marshal Turenne. By 1802, however, he was back in Paris, busily schooling himself for a literary career by reading extensively and keeping notebooks with his detailed impressions of life. He studied English, read Shakespeare and the great French dramatists. For a while he was resolved to become a great dramatist; then his interest switched to philosophy and psychology.

The one continuing interest throughout his life was women. In Milan, some years earlier, he had met and fallen in love with a woman who scarcely noticed him, Angiola (Gina) Pietragrua. In spite of his numerous amatory adventures, she remained a kind of ideal for him. There were many other women; Stendhal chronicles his crowded love life with painstaking detail. Memorable among them was Mélanie Guilbert, an actress, whom he followed to Marseilles in 1805. There he worked for a while as a clerk in the dry goods business to support them both. After a year their ardor cooled and they separated. By October 1806 he was back in Napoleon's army, this time on a diplomatic mission to Germany. He was infatuated briefly with Wilhelmina von Griesheim, the daughter of a German general. More significant was his attachment to his cousin Pierre Daru's wife, Alexandrine, a woman of considerable political influence as well as personal charm, who was instrumental in his receiving in 1810 the position of auditor (secretary) to the Council of State. Alexandrine was apparently flattered by his attentions—it being the convention of the time for married ladies of quality to have lovers—but she remained distant, and Beyle easily consoled himself with a visit to Milan. There, after eleven years of worship from afar, he declared his passion to Gina Pietragrua, and in 1811 she became his mistress. The relationship lasted until 1815 when he discovered that she was unfaithful to him. Some three years later he fell in love with Metilda Viscontini. Beyle's biographers consider this the "great love" of his life, for it was Metilda who inspired his extraordinary analytical study of love, De l'Amour. Beyle's love for her was unrequited, however, and she died in 1825. There followed a brief and stormy romance with Clémentine de Curial. In 1830, now a stout, middle-aged man, he fell in love with the beautiful nineteen-year-old Giulia Rinieri. She refused his offer of marriage but was his mistress for ten years.

As Beyle's fortunes in love improved, so did his career. His prospects in Napoleon's government were brilliant. He was sent on diplomatic missions to Poland and to Russia. He showed himself to be energetic, resourceful, and courageous—even in the terrible defeat of Napoleon's troops in Moscow in 1812 and the subsequent retreat. But his political fortunes were tied so closely to Napoleon's that when the Emperor fell, he fell too. After Napoleon's abdication in 1814, Beyle retreated to Milan. There he remained, seemingly indifferent to politics. In 1815, while Napoleon was suffering his final defeat at Waterloo (a battle he describes masterfully in The Charterhouse of Parma), he was in Venice with Gina.

Beyle never allowed romance or the fortunes of war and international diplomacy to interfere with his writing. He kept journals, notebooks, and records of the most intimate details of his life. Much of this, of course, was not intended for publication. His first books—Les Vies de Haydn, de Mozart, et de Métastase (1814), Histoire de la Peinture en Italie (1817), Rome, Naples et Florence (1817)—were highly derivative and dilettantish rather than solid achievements. In 1821 Beyle was expelled from Italy for his revolutionary sympathies. He returned to Paris where he lived on a small income and began dabbling in a career in journalism. He visited

England that same year, a country he admired deeply, though he was outraged by the pitiful living conditions of the British laboring classes.

In 1822 Beyle published *De l'Amour*. In this work he introduced the famous concept of "crystallization"—the power of love to project the illusion of perfection in the loved one. The book, like its predecessors, was a commercial failure. Seventeen copies of the first edition were sold in ten years. In 1823, characteristically taking the unpopular side in a literary debate, Beyle wrote the pamphlet *Racine et Shakespeare,* in which he spoke out for freedom from classical rules and restrictions and for a drama, like Shakespeare's, of flesh and blood and passion, rather than one of classical perfection like Racine's. The pamphlet offended the purists, but it won adherents among the younger "romanticists" then coming into prominence—Mérimée, Hugo, Musset, and the artist Delacroix.

His first novel, *Armance* (1827), was written when he was forty-two. A psychological study of a young man unable to love, set against the background of *salon* society of his day, it shows skill but nowhere approaches the depth and brilliance of his later work. The full measure of his genius, however, was poured into his second novel, *Le Rouge et le Noir (The Red and the Black)*, published in 1830. Superficially, the inspiration for the book was a news story which appeared in the *Gazette des Tribunaux* in December 1827, an account of the trial of a young man for the attempted murder of a married woman. The case provides a crude outline of the plot of *The Red and the Black,* but it does not begin to suggest the remarkable nature of that book or of its great hero, Julien Sorel. The title is usually said to refer to the two forces which struggled to dominate Julien's soul—the red uniform of the soldier, the fighter for freedom and republicanism, and the black habit of the clergy, the forces of conservatism and monarchy. The book is a sharply etched picture of the political ferment of France in the post-Napoleonic era. But, more important, it is a profound psychological novel, a study of a brilliant, opportunistic youth who triumphs over every conceivable obstacle except that most formidable of obstacles—himself. The book caused a sensation upon its publication. Critics found it shocking, too terrible for endurance. Howard Clewes has recently remarked: "The book sold 1500 copies and brought Stendhal notoriety if not popularity." Such notoriety cost him any chance he might have had for a good political appointment.

Beyle spent his last years as consul-general in the hot and dreary little Italian port town of Civitavecchia, a few miles from Rome. It was a poor appointment but the best he could hope for. He was aging and sickly. His only happiness was his visits to Rome. In Civitavecchia he sought to alleviate his boredom by writing. He completed his autobiography in two separate volumes, published posthumously, *La Vie de Henri Brulard* (1890) and *Souvenirs d'Égotisme* (1892). He turned to another novel, *Lucien Leuwen,* the story of a young soldier in the 1830's, which he never completed. In 1837, granted a leave from his post, Beyle traveled for two years in France, Germany, Holland, and Belgium. The results of his travels were two books—*Mémoires d'un Touriste* (1838) and *Voyage dans le Midi* (1854). On November 4, 1838, he began writing *La Chartreuse de Parme (The Charterhouse of Parma)*, generally regarded as his masterpiece, and he finished this great novel in less than two months, on December 26, 1838. As with *The Red and the Black*, Beyle found his plot for *The Charterhouse* in actual events—in this case an Italian manuscript dating back to the Renaissance which traced the history of a great Roman family, the Farnese. There he read the story of the beautiful and powerful Vanozza Farnese, mistress of Cardinal Lenzuoli, who helped her nephew, an impetuous and romantic youth, rise to the office of cardinal and later pope.

Beyle's young hero, Fabrizio del Dongo, unlike his predecessor, Julien Sorel, is endowed from the beginning with political influence. *The Charterhouse* draws a picture of political conniving and corruption unique in modern literature. But, like *The Red and the Black*, this is a novel essentially of passion, not politics, a drama of richly conceived relationships. Published in 1839, the novel had a modest success. One of its most enthusiastic readers was Honoré de Balzac, who reviewed it as "the novel Machiavelli would have written if he were living banished from Italy in the nineteenth century." Beyle's last novel, the daring and cynical *Lamiel,* whose heroine has been described as "the female counterpart of Julien," was not completed.

In 1841 Beyle suffered a paralytic stroke. His doctor prescribed a leave in Paris, where he joyfully hastened, plunging into the social whirl of the city. On the evening of March 22, 1842, he collapsed in the street on his way home from a reception. He died early the next morning. Three people (one of them Mérimée) attended his funeral and, at his request, no prayers were read. He was buried in Montmartre. On his tombstone, also as he had specified, were the words: "Arrigo Beyle, Milanese / Visse, Scrisse, Amò" ("Harry Beyle, Milanese / He lived, He wrote, He loved").

In appearance Beyle was unimpressive—short, stocky, snubnosed. As he grew older, he dyed his hair and whiskers. He considered himself ugly and thought to compensate for his looks by dressing in high fashion and by cultivating his wit. He planned his social career, as well as many of his romantic alliances, with the same cool deliberation that Julien showed in *The Red and the Black;* but (also like his young hero) he could not curb a fundamental impulsiveness which wrecked his most ambitious plans. He stood, Robert Sage remarks, "in inclination as in birth, midway between the cold classicism of the eighteenth century and the feverish romanticism of the early nineteenth." Like his contemporary, Lord Byron (whom Beyle met in Milan in 1816), he gave his name to a way of life, *beylisme,* not mere libertinism, but the deliberate cultivation of both the senses and the intellect for the purpose of achieving happiness.

Recognition was slow in coming to him. He had a few devoted admirers in France —among them Taine, Zola, Paul Bourget— but he was generally ignored or read with stern and shocked disapproval in the nineteenth century. "Literary fame is a lottery," Beyle wrote in *Henri Brulard.* "I am taking out a ticket in a lottery whose winning number is 1935." It was an uncannily accurate prediction. By the turn of the century he was beginning to receive enthusiastic praise in France. He became Gide's favorite novelist, and Valéry wrote: "One could never finish talking about Stendhal. I see no higher praise." In England and America, however, he was still little known. In 1919 George Saintsbury, while admitting his great influence on other French writers, nevertheless dismissed him— "... as a *practicing* novelist Beyle has hardly substance enough to stand by himself." Since that time, however, his novels have achieved major fame in England and America. His subject matter—war, revolution, the police state, the disintegration of the old social orders, the extraordinary complexity of the human mind—has a special timeliness and significance for modern readers. Martin Turnell writes: "Stendhal was much more alive in his time, more conscious of its problems, than his contemporaries and successors, and his vision has far greater depth and greater breadth than theirs. . . . He is one of the most civilized of all French novelists, and he seems to me to be the greatest."

The first English translation of *The Charterhouse of Parma* was by Lady Mary Loyd in 1901. A translation of *The Red and the Black* was published by H. B. Samuel in 1916. English translations of Stendhal's works did not begin to circulate widely, however, until the 1920's, the most important of them being by C. K. Scott-Moncrieff, Proust's translator, who published translations of *The Charterhouse of Parma* (1925), *The Abbess of Castro and Other Tales* (1926), *The Red and the Black* (1926), and *Armance* (1928). Other translations include *Lamiel* by J. Le Clerq (1929), T. W. Earp (1951); *The Red and the Black* by J. Charles (1949); *Lucien Leuwen* (I. The Green Huntsman, II. The Telegraph) by L. Varese (1950), H. L. R. Edwards (1951). Of Stendhal's works of nonfiction, there are translations of *The Life of Henri Brulard* by C. A. Phillips (1925); *On Love* by P. S. & C. N. S. Woolf (1927), "H. B. V. D." (1927), *Love* by G. and S. Sale (1957); *Memoirs of Egotism* by H. & M. Josephson (1949), T. W. Earp (1949); *To the Happy Few; Selected Letters* by N. Cameron (1952); *Private Diaries* by R. Sage (1954); *A Life of Napoleon* by R. Gant (1956); *A Life of Rossini* by R. N. Coe (1956); *Roman Journal* by H. Chevalier (1957).

ABOUT: Beyle, M. H. (Stendhal) Memoirs of Egotism, The Life of Henri Brulard, To the Happy Few, Private Diaries; Clewes, H. Stendhal; Croce, B. European Literature in the Nineteenth Century; Fineshriber, W. H. Stendhal: The Romantic Rationalist; Giraud, R. D. The Unheroic Hero in the Novels of Stendhal, Balzac, and Flaubert; Green, F. C. Stendhal; Hazard, P. Stendhal; Josephson, M. Stendhal, or The Pursuit of Happiness; Hemmings, F. W. J. Stendhal: A Study of his Novels; Kayser, R. Stendhal: The Life of an Egoist; Krutch, J. W. Five Masters; Levin, H. Toward Stendhal; O'Connor, F. The Mirror in the Roadway; Turnell, M. The Novel in France; Valéry, P. Variety: Second Series; Zweig, S. Adepts in Self-Portraiture: Casanova, Stendhal, Tolstoy. [In French—see studies by P. Arbelet, G. Blin, V. Del Litto, J. Prévost, H. Martineau, M. Bardecke, A. Caraccio.]

"BIN GORION, M. Y." See BERDICHEVSKY, MIKHAH YOSEF

BITZIUS, ALBERT. See GOTTHELF, JEREMIAS

*BJØRNSON, BJØRNSTJERNE (MARTINUS) (December 8, 1832-April 26, 1910), Norwegian poet, novelist, playwright, was born at Bjørgan vicarage in the district of Kvikne in a mountainous inland region southeast of Trondheim. His father was vicar Peder Bjørnson. of an old family of peasant

* byûrn' sön

BJØRNSON

Many others followed. Several of these stories are masterpieces. In their concise style and excellent character description they show affinity to the Old Norse sagas. But on the other hand, the romantic element occupies a more prominent place, and the life of the Norwegian farmer is described in an idealistically elevated and poetic way. Lyrics are frequently included in the stories.

In 1857 Bjørnson succeeded Ibsen as stage manager at the national theatre in Bergen. The next year he married a young Bergen lady, Karoline Reimers, of a merchant family. She had just joined the theatre company. This marriage developed into an unusually happy union. While in Bergen, Bjørnson became actively engaged in politics on the liberal side, and in 1859 he was back in the capital as co-editor of *Aftenbladet*. But his liberal and reformist articles forced him to resign. He also wrote magnificent lyrics, e.g., *Ja Vi Elsker Dette Landet* (Yes, We Love This Country), which became the national anthem of Norway.

Supported by government scholarships, Bjørnson embarked in 1860 upon his first European journey, which lasted for three years. He visited Denmark, Germany, Austria, and Italy. Rome, where he stayed a whole year, was of enormous importance for his production. He continued his writing and produced during his journey his first mature drama, the great trilogy *Sigurd Slembe*, 1862, his best saga play. Two years later appeared his only drama based on a foreign motif, *Maria Stuart i Skotland*. All this while he was also writing classically beautiful poetry, including the two masterpieces *Olav Trygvason* and *Bergliot*.

On his return to Norway in 1863, Bjørnson received a poet's pension. He was director of the Kristiania Theatre 1865-67, of another theatre 1870-73. As editor of *Norskt Folkeblad*, 1866-71, he again was politically active. A visit to Copenhagen in 1868 made him acquainted with Grundtvig, whose influence is apparent in Bjørnson's novel *Fiskerjenten* (The Fisher Maiden, 1867) in which he criticizes the dark and somber type of religion and favors Grundtvig's "cheerful Christianity." After Grundtvig's death, Bjørnson found the Danish followers of the former to be intolerant, and his attitude toward them changed. Most of his literary production during the ten years he stayed at home is hardly of great significance. An exception is his verse novel *Arnljot Gelline*, 1870, in which the hero changes his defiant attitude into humility.

proprietors. His mother was Inger Elise Nordraak, a merchant's daughter from Kragerø on the southern coast of Norway. In 1837 his father was transferred to Nesset parish in Romsdal where the boy, oldest of six children, grew up. They received everlasting impressions from the majestic landscape. He said later: "My spiritual nature is Romsdal."

Bjørnson went to school in the town of Molde. Since he had little interest in school work, his grades were rather poor. At the age of seventeen he was engaged to Antoinette Seeberg, who tutored his sisters, but the engagement was broken three years later. In 1850 he went to the capital to prepare himself for his matriculation examination which he did not pass until 1854. But he studied native and foreign literature sedulously. He also wrote poetry, plays, and newspaper articles. In 1855 he became a regular member of the staff of the capital daily *Morgenbladet*. He was the paper's theatrical and literary reviewer, and he fought against the Danish hegemony in the Norwegian theatre.

Bjørnson's first literary success came in 1856 with his drama *Mellem Slagene* (Between the Battles), on a theme from Norwegian medieval history. Now he also began to write realistic-romantic peasant novels which more than anything else made him popular and famous. In 1857 came *Synnøve Solbakken*. The year 1859 saw *Arne* and *Faderen* (The Father), and the following year appeared *En Glad Gut* (A Happy Boy).

In 1873 Bjørnson again went to Italy, and in Rome, under the impact of Darwin's theory of evolution, Brandes' literary doctrines, and the new currents of the 1870's, he wrote his first realistic tendentious problem dramas about social and psychological subjects. Most attention, both in Scandinavia and out in Europe, was attracted by *En Fallit* (A Bankrupt, 1875) attacking dishonesty in business and showing that an egotistical entrepreneur injures both himself and his environment. The sentimentally happy ending weakens the effect of the play. The same year there appeared *Redaktøren* (The Editor), a partly autobiographical play demanding tolerance in politics. *Kongen* (The King, 1877) claimed that the State Church preached obsolete dogmas. It was also an attack on alleged unsound social institutions, including the monarchy. In his marriage novel *Magnhild* (1877), Bjørnson defended divorce and received bitter criticism from conservative and religious circles. He also turned his back on romantic ideals and held that the peasants had been falsely idolized. On his return home he settled at his estate Aulestad in the beautiful Gudbrand Valley, today a national shrine.

In 1880-81 Bjørnson visited the United States, where his free-thinking and open attacks on the church brought criticism. From 1882 to 1887 he lived with his family in Paris and usually spent the summers in the Alps. During this period he created some of his finest plays. *En Hanske* (A Gauntlet, 1883) supported a single standard of sexual morality. His greatest masterpiece, *Over Ævne* (Beyond Human Power, 1883), was an attack on supernatural religion and a defense of the theory of evolution. His novels from this time are less impressive.

During his later years, Bjørnson lived in the South and at Aulestad. His production was prolific, and in 1903 he received the Nobel Prize in literature. He died in Paris. His son Bjørn Bjørnson became a prominent actor and theatre director. His daughter Bergljot, a fine singer, married Ibsen's son Sigurd.

Almost all of Bjørnson's major works have been translated into English. *Synnøve Solbakken* appeared in English translation by J. Sutter (1881), R. B. Anderson (1881), E. Gosse (1895-98), as *Trust and Trial* by M. Howitt (1858), under the title *Love and Life in Norway* by A. Bethel and A. Plesner (1870), as *Sunny Hill* (1932). *Arne* was translated by A. Plesner (1866), R. B. Anderson (1881), W. Low (1890). *En Glad Gut* appeared as *A Happy Boy*, translated by Mrs. W. Archer (1931), R. B. Anderson (1881), H. R. G. (1870), as *Ovind* by S. and E. Hjerleid (1869). W. M.

Payne translated *Sigurd Slembe* (1888). *Maria Stuart i Skotland* was translated by A. Sahlberg (1912). *Fiskerjenten* (The Fisher Maiden) was translated by R. B. Anderson (1882), M. E. Niles (1869), E. Gosse (1896), A. Plesner and F. Richardson (1870), S. and E. Hjerleid (1871). *Arnljot Gelline* was rendered into English by W. M. Payne (1917). *En Fallit, Redaktøren,* and *Kongen* appeared as *The Bankrupt, The Editor,* and *The King* in R. F. Sharp, *Three Dramas* (1914). *En Hanske* was translated as *A Gauntlet* by E. Gosse (1897) and R. B. Anderson (1884). *Over Ævne* is included in E. Björkman, *Plays, First Series* (1913), and appeared as *Pastor Sang,* translated by W. Wilson (1893). For further information on translations of Bjørnson's works see Beyer's book listed below.

ABOUT: Beyer, H. A History of Norwegian Literature; Boyesen, H. H. Essays on Scandinavian Literature; Brandes, G. Creative Spirits in the Nineteenth Century; Brandes, G. Main Currents in Nineteenth Century Literature; Columbia Dictionary of Modern European Literature; Gosse, E. The Novels of Bjørnson; Grøndahl, I. and Raknes, O. Chapters in Norwegian Literature; Jorgenson, T. History of Norwegian Literature; Larson, H. Bjørnstjerne Bjørnson: A Study in Norwegian Literature; Marble, A. W. Nobel Prize Winners in Literature; Skard, S. and Koht, H. The Voice of Norway; Topsöe-Jensen, H. G. Scandinavian Literature from Brandes to Our Day.

A. J.

BLANCO WHITE. See WHITE, JOSEPH BLANCO

*BLICHER, STEEN STEENSEN (October 11, 1782-March 28, 1848), Danish poet and short-story writer, was born at Vium, in Jutland, the son of Niehls Blicher, a clergyman, and Christine Curz, a clergyman's daughter. The Blichers were poor, but they had been clergymen for generations and were honored in the community. Steen was a delicate child and he did poorly in school. Nevertheless he attended the Latin School at Randers and then entered the University of Copenhagen. His formal studies were interrupted, however, by ill health and he was mainly self-educated by a program of independent reading. His passion in reading was for the English poets and especially the pre-romantics. He translated into Danish Pope's *Eloisa to Abelard* and *The Rape of the Lock;* Goldsmith's *The Vicar of Wakefield;* and—a work which won him considerable acclaim—the poems of Ossian.

Blicher's life was marked by failure and bitter disappointment at every step. Only in his writing was he able to find comfort and, at last, recognition. He was always poor, always in debt. His marriage to a well-to-do young widow was a disaster. He dissipated

* blē' kĕr

her small fortune. They had numerous children. She flaunted her unfaithfulness to him. He made feeble and unsuccessful efforts to establish himself in a profession. For a time he was a teacher at his old school at Randers, but he failed at teaching and returned to his father's home. He also tried journalism and went even deeper into debt. At last he was appointed vicar at Thorning to succeed his father. In 1825 he received the somewhat more profitable pastorates of Spentrup and Gassum, but these never supplied sufficient money for his needs. The parishioners complained that he failed to fulfill his duties. He drank heavily. In 1839 he was saved from utter bankruptcy and the auction of his possessions by the charity of friends. He died at Randers of typhoid fever at the age of sixty-five.

In the dreary chronicle of his life, Blicher's writing stands out as the only relief. One of the great masters of Danish literature, he is best remembered for his simple and realistic stories of Jutland peasant life, written in Jutland dialect. His subject was "the comedy and tragedy of the commonplace"—the hard, simple, rugged life that he saw so clearly and so sympathetically. The novelist Sigrid Undset wrote: "Blicher loved his native Jutland without any desire to idealize either his home or his own people. The world he knew was full of good and evil things, of bitterness and bliss and humdrum trivialities, but he accepted everything—it was his world."

This calm acceptance of reality and the honesty of his portraits of Jutland life won Blicher recognition and love from his fellow Danes. Ironically, it never brought him enough money to get out of debt. His masterpiece was *E Bindstouw* (The Knitting Room, 1842), a collection of stories and poems. Two of his best-known stories are "The Journal of a Parish Clerk" (1823), based on the life of a real figure, Maria Grubbe (who was also the subject of a novel by Jens Peter Jacobsen in 1876), and "The Parson at Vejlbe" (1829), also based on fact—the story of a man who is executed for a murder that he did not commit. The latter story, coming to him in translation, was used by Mark Twain in his *Tom Sawyer, Detective*. Blicher's best poems, like his stories, are those in Jutland dialect and, like the stories, they treat of life with sad resignation but also with humor and irony.

Twelve stories by Blicher were translated into English by H. A. Larsen in 1945. Selections from his work also appear in the Warner Library. Translations of selections from his poetry are in *A*

Second Book of Danish Verse, edited by C. W. Stork (1947).

About: Hackett, F. On Judging Books; Undset, S. *Introduction to* Twelve Stories by Steen Steensen Blicher. [In Danish—see studies by A. Bjerrum, A. Rattlef.]

*BLONDEL DE NESLE (fl. end 12th century), French lyric poet, is known principally because of the charming story of his discovery of the captive King Richard I of England. According to this tale, he wandered all over Europe searching for traces of the imprisoned king and finally reached a castle where Richard saw him from his window and sang the first verse of a song known only to him and Blondel. Unfortunately the story has no basis in fact and, indeed, there is no historical evidence for any connection between Richard I and Blondel. We know nothing of the poet's life, except what can be gleaned from his own works, and in them there is no mention of the king. No document gives him any title of nobility and his name indicates only his place of origin. Of the many towns called Nesles or Noyelles in which he might have been born, the Picard characteristics of his language make that near St. Quentin the most likely as his birthplace. He mentions the poets Conon de Béthune and Gace Brulé and hence must have written most of his work during their lifetime, that is, in the late twelfth century. Blondel himself is mentioned by only one poet, Eustaches li Peintre of Rheims, and then only as a model lover. The large number of manuscripts of his work testifies to his popularity. Opinions differ about how many of the thirty-five poems attributed to him are actually his—perhaps not more than twelve. All the poems are love songs which follow Provençal models very closely. All celebrate an (unknown) lady whom Blondel loves to distraction and who gives him little hope. There is the usual mixture of joy and sorrow, hope and despair. All this is entirely conventional. Only in one poem does he say that the lady has finally granted him her love and he praises Cupid who has brought this about. Blondel's verse forms are simple. Most of his strophes have lines of the same length and he avoids (or was incapable of) the extreme virtuosity of technique or the verbal obscurity of his Provençal contemporaries.

Complete poems are to be found in *Gesellschaft für Romanische Literatur* Vol. III, Part 2, ed. Leo Wiese, with a detailed introduction.

W. T. H. J.

* blón děl' dě něl

*BLOY, LÉON MARIE (July 12, 1846-November 3, 1917), French novelist and religious essayist, was born in Périgueux, the second of seven children of an engineer and public servant, Jean-Baptiste Bloy, and Marie-Anne Careau, said to be of Spanish ancestry. Léon's childhood was a turbulent one, torn as he was between the disparate influences of his mother's mysticism and his father's atheism. His formal education was brief. He left his *lycée* at the end of the fourth year and never prepared himself for any profession. He spent his early youth reading history and theology; he attempted to write tragedies, and he dabbled in art (including self-portraits which are extant).

In 1863, Léon, at the age of eighteen, left his family to study art in Paris. Here for some years he floundered, rootless, faithless, and friendless, working at a succession of routine office jobs. In 1869 he was fortunate to meet the writer Barbey d'Aurevilly, who for a time guided both his literary and religious life. Barbey recognized the youth's nascent literary talent, hired him as his secretary, introduced him to literary circles, and recommended him to publishers. Subsequently he wrote a laudatory preface to his protégé's first published book, an essay on the significance of Columbus entitled *Le Révélateur de la Globe* (1884), and the macabre influence of Barbey's *Les Diaboliques* is felt in Bloy's short tales *Histoires Désobligéantes* (1894). Barbey seems also to have placed young Léon in touch with priests, the first step in Léon's conversion, which took place in 1870.

Bloy's life and his writing are so interpenetrated from this point on that it is impossible to consider them apart. Shortly after his conversion he joined the Franco-Prussian War as a volunteer, an experience recorded in the harrowing series of tales *Sueur de Sang, 1870-1871* (1893). There followed a brief period with his family in Périgueux. In 1873 he was back in Paris, working as a bookkeeper, trying to make his way in journalism. He had difficulty in this field, for while editors admired his style they were afraid to publish his articles, for they found his invective too violent.

The year 1877 was especially significant in Bloy's life. At this time he met the priest who most influenced his religious vision—Abbé Tardif de Moidrey. Abbé Tardif awakened his mind to the symbolic meanings of the Scriptures and to the value of history as revelation. It was the priest also

* blwä

BLOY

who first brought him to the shrine of La Salette in 1879, where more than thirty years previously the mystic Mélanie Calvat had as a child claimed to see a vision of Mary weeping over the persecution of her Son. The coincidence of this vision with the year of his own birth struck Bloy as providential. *Celle Qui Pleure* (She Who Weeps, 1908) and his touching introduction to Mélanie Calvat's autobiography (*La Vie de Mélanie,* 1912) testify to the profound influence on him of this miracle. His life became devoted to thundering its significance to his fellow men. Moreover, it is the root of his beatification of women in his two novels of female martyrdom, *Le Désespéré* (1886) and *La Femme Pauvre* (1897).

In 1877 Bloy also met the prostitute Anne-Marie Roulet (Véronique of *Le Désespéré,* Antoinette of *La Femme Pauvre*), whom he lived with and in time converted. Anne-Marie's subsequent spiritual visions eventually unhinged her mind, necessitating her confinement in an asylum for the rest of her life. This tragic experience, together with Bloy's unsuccessful attempts to find his vocation in the monastery at La Trappe (1877-78), is detailed with painful fidelity in *Le Désespéré* where Bloy disguises himself as the symbolically named Caïn Marchenoir. (A more straightforward source of information about these years is the posthumously published *Letters to His Fiancée,* 1922).

For a brief period Bloy found consolation in a relationship with another ill-fated woman, Berthe Dumont, who died of tetanus in

1885. In 1890, at the home of François Coppée, he met Jeanne Molbech, the daughter of a Danish poet. Jeanne was drawn by Bloy's fervent piety, was converted under his influence, and then became his wife. Though the couple lived in abject poverty all their lives, theirs was a happy marriage. Four children were born of the union, of whom two boys died in childhood, while the two daughters Madeleine and Véronique survived. Jeanne Molbech is generally considered to be the counterpart of the beggar-saint Clothilde of the latter part of *La Femme Pauvre,* whereas Berthe Dumont is supposed to be the prototype of Clothilde in the first part, where she is depicted as a virtuous bourgeois girl exploited by her parents and forced to model for an artist.

Bloy wrote no more novels after *La Femme Pauvre,* but there is little distinction between them and the diaries to which one turns for their sequel, the fascinating series beginning with *Le Mendiant Ingrat* and ending with *La Porte des Humbles.* Beyond these his unique exegeses of the Bible and of modern life are to be found in such works as *Salut par les Juifs* (1892), *Le Sang du Pauvre* (1909) and *L'Exégèse des Lieux Communs* (1902, 1913).

Although Bloy never enjoyed wide fame, his last years were comforted by the devoted attention of a faithful group of followers, notably his godson Jacques Maritain, whom he converted, Räissa Maritain, the painter Georges Rouault, and the composer Georges Auric. Bloy lived to see his apocalyptic vision come to pass in World War I, dying just before the Armistice in a house formerly occupied by Charles Péguy. A street is named for him in his native Périgueux.

"The plain truth, the truth that shines forth in all my books is that *I write only for God,"* Bloy wrote of himself. His fiction thus falls into place along with his diaries and lay sermons as part of the spiritual autobiography of a tormented soul imbued with the sense of a mission. As a Third-Republic Jeremiah he has repelled many by his splenetic and vituperative style, but a devoted few consider him a major prophet of our times. For the literary-minded his chief importance lies in his having sown the seed of the Catholic Renaissance that brought forth François Mauriac, Georges Bernanos, and Graham Greene.

Only a smattering of Bloy's prolific output is available in translation. For the uninitiated, probably the best introduction is the anthology of excerpts from various works, selected by Raïssa Maritain, entitled *Pilgrim of the Absolute* (1947), translated by John Coleman and Harry Lorin Binsse, with an introduction by Jacques Maritain. *La Femme Pauvre* was translated by I. J. Collins in 1939. *Lettres à Sa Fiancée* was translated by Barbara Wall in 1937. Excerpts from *Celle Qui Pleure* were brought out in a translation by Emile Le Douceur in 1956.

ABOUT: Béguin, A. Léon Bloy: A Study in Impatience; Brady, Sister M. R. Thought and Style in the Works of Léon Bloy; Greene, G. The Lost Childhood, and Other Essays; Heppenstall, R. Léon Bloy; Pfléger, K. Wrestlers with Christ; Sheed, F. Sidelights on the Catholic Revival; Dublin Review, Second Quarter 1953, Third Quarter 1953. [In French—see studies by R. Barbeau, J. Bollery, G. Cattaui, S. Fumet, H. Juin, J. Steinmann.]

R. A. C.

*BOCAGE, MANUEL MARIA BARBOSA DU (September 15, 1765-December 21, 1805), Portuguese poet, was born into a happy middle-class home in Setubal, the son of José Luís Soares Barbosa, a lawyer, who was fond of Young's *Night Thoughts* and of writing satirical verse, and Mariana Joaquina, daughter of a Frenchman who became a Portuguese vice-admiral. Bocage described himself as "thin, blue-eyed, dark-complexioned, long-faced . . . mournful in mien and appearance, and incapable of staying in one place." At fourteen he quit school and enlisted in the infantry. At sixteen he entered the Naval Academy in Lisbon. But he got into bad company, a misfortune he shared with his idol Camões—and dissipated five years among the bohemians of the capital, "devoutly worshipping a thousand goddesses (a thousand girls, I mean) in one sole moment." In 1786 the Navy shipped him to Goa, via Rio de Janeiro. Three years in India destroyed his illusions (Camões' too) of making a brilliant career in the Orient. The ardent youth deserted, traveled to Macao, and returned eagerly to Lisbon by 1790, only to find one of his "goddesses," his adored Gertrude, married to his own brother.

In 1791 he established a literary reputation by publishing the first volume of his *Rimas,* followed by four others in 1799, 1804, and, posthumously, in 1812 and 1813. Charming and amusing, Bocage became very popular. He joined a literary society of mildly equalitarian scribblers, the "Nova Arcadia," and was rebaptized shepherd "Elmano." But the naughty "Elmano" soon made fun of their Wednesday afternoon teas. Thereupon a bloodless but ferocious war in verse erupted, in which all the bards in Lisbon joined— while Napoleon marshaled French armies to conquer the world. The wild Bocage worried

* bōō kä' zhě

the police. He was arrested on board a frigate in 1797, when about to escape to Bahia, and tried by the Inquisition for having written "irreligious, seditious and critical papers." His punishment was mild. He was ordered to be re-educated in religion by the kindly Oratorians. Set free, he lived a few more bitter years. Broken in health and spirit, he eked out a meager living with translations and correcting proofs. Bocage died in Lisbon at the age of forty, keenly aware that he had dissipated his talent, yet resigned: "Know how to die well who to live knew'st not."

Bocage had composed poetry since boyhood. Throughout life he had a gift for improvising verse. This very facility kept him from disciplining himself. His second claim to fame rests on obscene poems ascribed to him and passed furtively from hand to hand to this day. He rose to greatness in his sonnets, however, which form a pungent autobiography. He revived the sonnet as a vehicle for serious meditations on love, life and death, in Camões' manner. His reflections on the contrasts between the past glory of Portugal and her present insignificance, between his noble dreams and his failures, his self-centeredness and sentimental vehemence, made Bocage a forerunner of the romantics, at least in feeling; in form he remained within classic bounds, often spoiling his verse with hackneyed metaphors, adjectives, and rhymes.

A few of his sonnets were translated into English by John Adamson (*Lusitania Illustrata*, I, 1842) and later by Leonard S. Downes (*Portuguese Poems and Translations*, 1947).

ABOUT: Adamson, J. Lusitania Illustrata; Beckford, W. Italy, with Sketches of Spain and Portugal. [In Portuguese—Cidade, H. Bocage; Domingues, M. Bocage; Revista de Cultura Romana, III (1961).]

G. M. M.

*BOCCACCIO, GIOVANNI (1313-December 21, 1375), Italian poet and prose writer, was the illegitimate son of Boccaccino di Chellino, a Florentine merchant originally from Certaldo. Information relating to Boccaccio's life is very scanty and has been disputed at many points. According to traditional accounts, he was born late in 1313 in Paris where his father had gone on business. His mother (a Frenchwoman whose name may have been De La Roche) soon surrendered the boy to his father who took him to Florence. There his father married a Florentine lady who bore him a second son, and it was then arranged that the youthful Boccaccio

* bō kät' chō

104

BOCCACCIO

should prepare for a career in business. To that end, probably in 1325, he was sent to Naples.

There, as he was later bitterly to recall, he wasted six years undergoing a commercial training which he abhorred. Six more years were spent studying canon law, also against his will. Some of his teachers were men of considerable reputation, but his passion for poetry, toward which he had been disposed, as he said, "even from the womb of my mother," alone claimed his willing attention. On his own he studied the Latin poets—chiefly Ovid, Virgil, and Statius—and acquired a reputation for erudition. Very soon he was writing verses of his own.

Naples was then one of the gayest capitals of Europe, the seat of a court equally devoted to culture and to pleasure. Thanks to his friends and perhaps to his literary inclinations, Boccaccio was able to meet members of the court, among them Maria d'Aquino, the King's natural daughter, for whom he conceived an intense and enduring passion. Apparently his love was soon requited, but just when the idyll began is uncertain. Some assign it to the spring of 1333, others to the spring of 1336. Such evidence as we have would suggest that its course was a stormy one. After a few short years, the highborn lady, already married to a courtier, apparently began to weary of the gifted son of a Florentine merchant. There were quarrels and reconciliations and finally a breaking-off that left wounds the young poet was to remember for many years.

Indeed, he was never to forget her, though she was neither the first nor the last of his loves. He called her Fiammetta—his flame—and under that name (as well as others, perhaps) she was to have a place in nearly all of his Italian writings. At her suggestion, he set to work on the *Filocolo,* his first full-length work, shortly after their meeting. Written in prose, the *Filocolo* is a rather prolix and digressive courtly romance which was already well known in its several earlier versions. Though little read today, it did much to further Boccaccio's reputation and remained popular throughout the Renaissance. In 1338, during a period when Maria d'Aquino was away from Naples, he began writing the *Filostrato* for her; also a courtly romance, this time written in *ottava rima,* it employs the Trojan War as its setting. Despite structural and poetic imperfections, the *Filostrato* contains many acute psychological observations. To English readers it is best known for having served as the basis of Chaucer's *Troilus and Criseyde,* in which many lines were taken over from Boccaccio with little change. The *Teseida,* usually assigned to 1339-40, is probably the last work Boccaccio wrote in Naples. The poet intended this work, also in *ottava rima,* to be the first heroic poem written in Italian. As in the case of most of his poetry, however, the dominant tone is lyrical and the dominant concern is love. Like the *Filostrato,* it proved useful to Chaucer who drew upon it for "The Knight's Tale."

In very straitened circumstances owing to the failure of the Bardi and Peruzzi banking interests with which he was connected, Boccaccio's father recalled him to Florence, probably in 1340. This proved a heavy blow to the young man who regarded the departure from his adopted city as an enforced exile. It was not long before Boccaccio made several unsuccessful efforts to return, but apart from this, very little is known about his early activities in Florence. There is some evidence that he consoled himself with new amatory adventures, with studies, and with writing. The *Ameto,* the *Amorosa Visione,* the *Fiammetta,* and the *Ninfale Fiesolano,* at any rate, are usually assigned to the first years of his stay in Florence.

The *Ameto* (1341-42?), a prose work with extended passages in *terza rima,* may best be called a pastoral romance intended as a moral allegory. Through a series of stories narrated by a group of nymphs, the work purports to show how love leads to noble and virtuous conduct. Though it was to influence later pastoral literature, it is generally considered one of the least successful of Boccaccio's efforts. But the *Amorosa Visione,* very likely written immediately after, has received even less praise. Again employing allegory and *terza rima,* Boccaccio here recounts the events of a dream-vision in which a beautiful lady (who may represent Philosophy) conducts him on a tour of a castle adorned with innumerable Giottesque allegories. Despite the poem's obscurity, its theme seems essentially the same as that of the *Ameto.* On the other hand, the prose *Fiammetta* (1343?) has often been esteemed for its genuine literary merits, and some scholars have seen in it the genesis of the modern novel. Based upon a reversal of the situation in which Boccaccio found himself when Maria d'Aquino broke off their romance, it recounts the agonies of a lady who finds herself abandoned by her lover. Though largely a monologue, the work contains a number of memorable scenes notable for their acute delineation of intense emotion, but prolixity and the excessive use of classical allusion reduce its effectiveness. Critics are all but unanimously agreed, however, that except for the *Decameron* the best of Boccaccio's works is the *Ninfale Fiesolano,* which he wrote probably in 1345 or 1346. A novella in *ottava rima,* employing a pastoral setting, it is Ovidian in tone and tells of the unhappy love of a shepherd and a nymph. Perhaps its greatest charm derives from the delicate, if sometimes playful, depiction of youthful love.

During the period in which these works were written, it must be supposed that other activities also occupied Boccaccio's attention, but specific information is lacking until 1346 when it is known that he was employed in Ravenna by the lord of that city. He had similar employment in Forlì, probably in the following year. Later he was entrusted by the government of Florence with several important diplomatic missions which took him to Avignon, Rome, Naples, Venice, and the Tyrol. However, these were tasks to which he lent himself unwillingly for the meager payments they provided. The death of his father in 1349 apparently brought no improvement to the straitened circumstances in which he was to continue to the end of his life. Repeated efforts to find a comfortable means of support that would leave him substantially free to write all resulted in failure.

Nevertheless, he was able to begin work on the *Decameron* in 1348 and complete it by 1353. Assuredly his masterpiece and one of the great works of modern literature, this is a collection of a hundred tales narrated by a group of fashionable young men and women who have found refuge in a country villa from the plague then raging in Florence. Richly varied in its materials, elegant and poetic in its prose, it has proved one of the most enduringly popular works ever written. Serene in tone, neither cynical nor lascivious, as some have called it, the *Decameron* celebrates the human intelligence and the human senses and reveals a calm, unmoralizing acceptance of reality. Ironically, Boccaccio seems to have been quite unaware of its high merits and scarcely mentioned it even to his friend Petrarch who visited him while he was at work on it.

The visit occurred in Florence in 1350. Although he had conducted a correspondence with Petrarch reaching back many years, this was Boccaccio's first meeting with the renowned man of letters whom he had long regarded as his master. Their friendship, unsullied by disagreement, marked by exchanges of books and criticism, endured on the warmest terms to the end of their lives. When Boccaccio complained of his poverty, Petrarch invited the younger man to come and share his own more ample means; and when, at a time of spiritual crisis, Boccaccio thought seriously of abandoning his literary pursuits, Petrarch consoled him and urged him to go on with his work. Few friendships between men of letters ever lasted so long (over forty years, Boccaccio was to recall) or ran so smooth a course.

The prose *Corbaccio* (1354-55), a strident invective against women, written in a decidedly medieval spirit, is the last of Boccaccio's Italian works. Thereafter he devoted himself almost entirely to writing in Latin works of a distinctly more scholarly character. Among the more important of these are his *De Casibus Virorum Illustrium* (Concerning the Fall of Great Men) and his *De Claris Mulieribus* (Concerning Great Women), both being collections of biographies, begun in about 1355 but not finally revised until 1374. Even more important is the compendious *De Genealogiis Deorum* (The Genealogy of the Gods) on which he worked intermittently from 1350 to 1366. A labor of impressive erudition aiming to provide a complete and systematic account of classical mythology, it displays a scientific spirit that is rare for the period.

Among the early humanists Boccaccio probably ranks second only to Petrarch, and in some respects he exceeds him. He knew Tacitus, for example, while Petrarch did not,

and his knowledge of Greek, though fragmentary, went far beyond Petrarch's scant acquaintance with it. To his labors under the tutelage of Leontius Pilatus we owe the first rendering of Homer into Latin, a poor and unreliable translation, but of great value, nevertheless, as the first step in the revival of Greek literature in Western Europe.

In October 1373 Boccaccio was invited to inaugurate a series of public lectures on the *Divine Comedy* in Florence. These, about sixty in all, furnished the basis for a lengthy commentary on the first seventeen cantos of that poem. Some years earlier he had written a *Life* of Dante, to whose work, unlike Petrarch, he had shown lifelong devotion. His lectures, it would appear, were broken off by illness less than a year after they had begun. He returned to Certaldo, where he had been staying for some time, and there he died.

Some of Boccaccio's works in English translation are the *Filostrato* by N. E. Griffin and A. B. Myrick (1929, in prose); the *Ninfale Fiesolano*, entitled *The Nymph of Fiesole*, by Daniel J. Donno (1960, in prose); the *Fiammetta*, entitled *The Elegy of Madonna Fiammetta*, by James C. Brogan. The *Decameron*, first translated into English in 1625, has had many later translators—W. K. Kelly (1855), Henry Morley (1885), John Payne (1886), J. M. Rigg (1905), Richard Aldington (1930). Books XIV and XV of *De Genealogiis Deorum*, entitled *Boccaccio on Poetry*, were translated by Charles G. Osgood (1930). *Concerning Famous Women* was translated by A. G. Guarino (1963).

ABOUT: Chubb, T. C. The Life of Giovanni Boccaccio; Hutton, E. Giovanni Boccaccio. [In Italian—see studies by V. Crescini, N. Sapegno. In French—Hauvette, H. Boccace.]

D. J. D.

---

*BODIN, JEAN (1530-June 1596), French political philosopher, born in Angers of a middle-class family, began his schooling in that city and, about 1548, studied law and science at Toulouse. In Paris he became professor of Roman law but, in 1561, chose to fend for himself in private practice. Failing at this, he entered the royal service in Poitiers and in Normandy. His first works, of little moment in his career, include a translation of the *Cynegetica* attributed to Oppianus, published in 1555.

Bodin's employ with the Duc d'Alençon, in 1571, oriented him toward political theory. He believed that peace could be established in France without violence or religious rivalry, and that it was best assured by a strong central government. Henri III, at first sympathetic to his program, turned against him. The Civil Wars, and especially the victory of

* bô dăn'

the Ligue, reduced him to relative inactivity, and the liberal policies of Henri IV came too late to affect his career. Bodin's master work, *La République*, published in six books in 1576, was frequently reprinted, and appeared in an English translation by R. Knolles in London, in 1606, under the title *Of the Lawes and Customs of a Commonwealth*. It is diffuse, rhetorical, and overly learned, but strongly focused on a legalistic theme and a theory of absolute sovereignty. Through this emphasis Bodin attacked Machiavelli, whose doctrine neglects the basic notion of the responsibility of the monarch to natural law and to the law of God. *La République* also suggested a theory of the relationship between social institutions and climate, and is noteworthy for its plea for tolerance. His brief work on sorcery, *De la Démonomanie des Sorciers,* appeared in 1580.

Bodin's *Heptaplomeres*, composed about 1593, is a dialogue with deist tendencies. His *Response au Paradoxe de M. de Malestroict,* published in 1568, is a significant treatment of theories of international free trade, import taxation, and industrialism.

A modern English translation of *La République* was made by M. Tooley in 1955.

ABOUT: Dunning, W. Political Theories from Luther to Montesquieu; Flint, R. Philosophy of History in Europe; Modern Language Notes, LXXVI (1961). [In French—Baudrillart, H. Jean Bodin et son Temps; Chauviré, R. Jean Bodin; Fournol, E. Bodin, Prédécesseur de Montesquieu; Nancey, P. Jean Bodin.]

F. J. C.

*BODMER, JOHANN JAKOB (July 19, 1698-January 2, 1783), Swiss poet and litterateur, was born at Greifensee in the vicinity of Zürich. As the son of a Protestant minister he began his academic life in the faculty of theology. In 1719, while devoting part of his time to a position on the Zürich council, he began to pursue literary and historical studies which had been his chief interest from earliest youth. In 1725 he obtained the chair of Helvetian history at the University of Zürich and at the same time became co-owner of a publishing house. He was appointed a member of the Great Council in 1735. At the advanced age of seventy-seven in 1775 he resigned his professorship and retired to an estate near Zürich where, at eighty-four, he died.

In association with J. J. Breitinger and others, Bodmer founded the weekly journal

* bŏd' mēr

Die Diskurse der Maler in 1721. It was in this journal that his earliest, hesitant expressions on literature were printed, indicating a mind liberated from the prosaic limitations of current *Gelehrtenpoesie.* Theoretical works such as *Von dem Einfluss und Gebrauche der Einbildungskraft zur Ausbesserung des Geschmacks* (1727), *Von dem Wunderbaren in der Poesie* (1740), and *Kritische Betrachtungen über die Poetischen Gemälde der Dichter* (1741) were pronounced advances beyond contemporary aesthetic theories. In these works Bodmer defended the privileges of the imagination against the claims of the rigid standards which had prevailed hitherto. Departing from the thesis that the creation of the poetic image and the artistic imitation of nature are the supreme tasks of the poet, Bodmer investigated the materials and the means the poet can employ in order to complete these tasks.

J. C. Gottsched, the literary dictator of Leipzig, had in the beginning observed the efforts of the Swiss with sympathetic interest, but when the latter chose to oppose his own rigorously rational conception of poetry he was the leader in a bitter fight against Bodmer's views. The chief benefit to the development of German letters to be derived from this struggle was that Bodmer, with his allies, was able to make Milton and, thereby, English literature unavoidable in any consideration of literary standards in Germany. Bodmer's prose translation of Milton's *Paradise Lost* moved Klopstock to the composition of his epoch-making *Messias,* which introduced a new age into German literature.

Bodmer's own literary attempts were only weak echoes of Klopstock's poetry. His epic poems *Noah* (1750), *Jakob und Joseph* (1751), and *Sündflut* (1755) are awkward imitations of Klopstock's style. His attempts at the drama—*Timoleon* (1768), *Cajus Gracchus* (1773), and *Wilhelm Tell* (1775)—reveal a complete absence of dramatic talent.

The only translation into English of Bodmer's verse is *Noah*, by J. Collyer (1767).

ABOUT: Quigley, H. Italy and the Rise of a New School of Criticism in the 18th Century; Viles, G. B. Comparison of Bodmer's Translation of Milton's Paradise Lost with the Original. [In German—see studies by F. Braitmaier, F. Servaes, M. Wehrli.]

E. K. G.

*BÖHME, JAKOB (1575-November 17, 1624), German mystic and theosophist, was born in Alt-Seidenberg near Görlitz, Silesia. His father, Jacob, and his mother, Ursula, were of pious Lutheran peasant stock. Presumably the family had emigrated from Bohemia. Though Böhme's formal education did not go beyond elementary school, he expanded his knowledge through wide reading and scholarly friends. He was brought up in the Lutheran faith. Besides Luther's Bible, the nature experience of a shepherd boyhood and the ideas of Paracelsus and of the German mystics molded his theosophy.

Since Böhme's constitution was too feeble for peasant work, he was apprenticed at fourteen to a shoemaker for three years. After an illumination in which he stood "possessed of the highest beatific wisdom of God," he resolved to lead a godly and virtuous life. His three years as a journeyman intensified his disturbance over the religious wranglings of the age. In Görlitz, where he became master, he opened a shoemaker shop. On May 10, 1599, he married Catherine Kuntzschmann, a Catholic butcher's daughter. They had four sons and two daughters.

Although Böhme was a faithful church member, his profound poetic, visionary, and mystical urge for knowledge of God could not find satisfaction in the rigid dogmatism of orthodox Lutheranism. Brooding over religious questions and frequently lapsing into melancholy, he had the decisive illumination of his life, in 1600. He was looking at a polished pewter dish and suddenly felt that he was surrounded and penetrated by the Light of God. The core of Nature seemed revealed to him. In a flash of insight he realized that the Godhead and all things are characterized by an antithesis, the harmony and opposition of light and darkness, good and evil, love and anger.

In 1612 Böhme had another vision which impelled him to express himself in a book, *Aurora oder Morgenröte im Aufgang*, a philosophy of the history of man, in which all existence is viewed as a ceaseless struggle between Good and Evil. Since these originated in the very nature of God, man has become involved. In the course of his struggle to overcome Evil, divine wisdom is revealed, and he attains pious contemplation and joy.

The unfinished manuscript of *Aurora* was circulated by Böhme's followers and fell into the hands of the strictly orthodox Görlitz

* bû′ mĕ

pastor Gregor Richter. Scenting heresy, he overawed the Town Council, which permitted Böhme to remain in Görlitz on condition that he cease writing on theological matters. Only the month before he had given up his trade in order to serve God and the Brothers with the pen. Now he agreed to lay it down, turning to the yarn and woolen gloves trade for a living. The business was initially prosperous but the general price rise caused it to decline, making Böhme dependent on the Silesian manorial lords, his patrons.

Years of anguish followed the pledge to cease writing. Richter continued his slanders from the pulpit. Although Böhme was mocked by his opponents, he was urged by his friends not to waste his talent. Ideas crowded his mind. He took up the pen again, and between 1619 and his death in 1624 he wrote numerous speculative, religious, and polemical works as well as letters.

In ardent and occult language the mystical depths of his doctrines are described in works such as *Beschreibung der Drei Prinzipien Göttlichen Wesens* (1618), *Von Himmlischen und Irdischen Mysterien* (1620), and *Mysterium Magnum* (1623). In Böhme's view God, the primal source, is a will which seeks to realize itself in Nature through the infinitely manifold operation of seven basic forces or "qualities" of the opposing principles of light and darkness, or the love and the anger of God. In God, light and love rule darkness and anger. As a consequence of sin, these are irreconcilably opposed in the world. Through his obedience to the will of God, Jesus Christ has redeemed man and restored the original order, which takes form in regenerated man who devotes his will to God. His life is governed by the spirit and power of Christ.

The growing lucidity of Böhme's style was the expression of a vision which originated in a simple, spontaneous feeling. At times this feeling bursts forth with magnificent imagery and power of expression. The depth of Böhme's ardor and belief in God, from which his vision springs, is reflected in its entire purity in the collection of tracts entitled *Der Weg zur Christo* (1624), which resulted in his again being admonished by the Town Council.

In May 1624 Böhme accepted an invitation to Dresden, where he spent two months at the home of the court physician Dr. Hinkelmann. He had a friendly reception by Chancellery officials and scholars. Minister Joachim von Loss promised to further his cause. Böhme left with the impression that the "New Reformation," which his work was to bring on, was just beginning. In October he contracted fever. He died in Görlitz the following month, uttering the words "Now I am going to Paradise." The Governor of Lausitz ordered a reluctant pastor to preach the funeral sermon. Numerous tradesmen and personal friends were present.

Böhme was small of stature, with a low forehead and broad, prominent temples. He had a somewhat crooked nose and azure-gray eyes. Though his voice was feeble, he was most charming in speech, gentle in manner, modest, humble, patient, and meek of heart.

Böhme's friends called him "Teutonicus Philosophicus." The poet Angelus Silesius drew inspiration from Böhme's disciple von Frankenberg and from Tauler. On the whole, Böhme's thought had only little influence in Germany in the century after his death, until Pietism took up his ideas. His writings were published in German in Holland, and also had a strong influence in England among the Quakers, the Behmenists, and the Philadelphians.

As a linguistic innovator Böhme ranks with Meister Eckhart and Luther. In Germany only the romantics and the idealistic philosophers fully appreciated the power of his language and the depth of his metaphysics. Hegel honored him by calling him the "first German philosopher."

The first of Böhme's works to appear in English translation was *Two Theosophical Epistles, Englished,* published in 1645, by an anonymous translator. The writings were translated between 1647 and 1661 by J. Ellistone and J. Sparrow, with the aid of D. Hotham and H. Blunden. G. Ward and T. Langcake re-edited the translation (1764-81) under the title of *The Works of Jakob Behmen.* Other translations appeared in the following order: *The Forty Questions of the Soul* and *The Clavis* (1647), re-issued in 1911), *Three Principles of the Divine Essence* (1648, re-issued in 1910) and *The Way to Christ Discovered,* by Sparrow; the latter was reprinted in editions of 1775, 1894, and 1911; *The Epistles of Jacob Behmen,* by Ellistone (1649); *The Three-fold Life,* by Sparrow (1650); *De Signatura Rerum,* by Ellistone (1651); *Christ's Testaments,* by Sparrow (1652); *The Mysterium Magnum,* by Ellistone and Sparrow (1654); *A Table of the Three Principles,* by H. Blunden and Sparrow (1654); *On Predestination,* by Sparrow (1655); *A Short Compendium on Repentance,* by Sparrow (1655); *The Aurora,* by Sparrow (1656); *The Great Six Points, The Earthly and Heavenly Mystery, The Four Complexions, On Divine Contemplation, 177 Theosophic Questions,* by Sparrow (1661). Sparrow was probably the translator of *Mercurius Teutonicus* (1649). In 1920 W. Scott Palmer compiled and edited *The Confessions.* In 1930 John R. Earle translated *On Predestination* and *Theosophic Questions.*

ABOUT: Bailey, M. L. Milton and Jacob Boehme; Brinton, H. H. The Mystic Will, Based on a Study of the Philosophy of Jakob Boehme; Cheyney, S. W. Men Who Have Walked with God; Fairweather, W. Among the Mystics; Jones, R. M. Spiritual Reformers in the 16th and 17th Centuries; Law, W. Selected Mystical Writings of William Law; Martensen, H. L. Jacob Boehme; Muses, C. A. Illumination on Jacob Boehme; Penny, A. J. An Introduction to the Study of Jacob Boehme's Writings, Studies in Jacob Boehme; Steiner, R. Jacob Boehme; Stoudt, J. J. Sunrise to Eternity: A Study in Boehme's Life and Thought; Swainson, W. P. "Jacob Boehme," *in* Waite, A. E. Three Famous Mystics; Thune, N. B. The Behmenists and the Philadelphians; Vetterling, H. The Illuminate of Görlitz.

A. M. H.

BOIARDO, MATTEO MARIA (1441-1494), Count of Scandiano, Italian poet, was born in Scandiano, Reggio Emilia, son of Giovanni Boiardo and Lucia Strozzi. As a child he was taken to Ferrara where he grew up in the court of the D'Este family and was educated, probably under his uncle Tito Vespasian Strozzi, poet and humanist. He received an excellent education in Greek, Latin, and even in some of the Oriental languages. In 1474 he was appointed gentleman of the court of Ferrara. In 1480 he became governor of Modena, a post which he held for two years, and in 1487 he received from his patron, Duke Ercole I, the governorship of Reggio which he held until his death. The great love of his life was Antonia Caprera, whom he met in 1469 and to whom he dedicated a sonnet sequence. About ten years later he married another woman, Taddea Gonzago (her name is given as Novellara in some sources). It was apparently a happy marriage, and they had a large family.

In the judgment of Boiardo's contemporaries he emerges as a man of high honor, rectitude, and nobility, an efficient administrator and—not the least of his achievements —a poet of the first rank. "He was . . . of an open and free nature," W. P. Ker wrote. "Everyone speaks well of him. He was a country gentleman, a reading man, fond of hunting. . . . He was a man of business."

As a man of noble rank and excellent education, Boiardo was an eminently suitable spokesman for the declining glories of the age of medieval chivalry. His masterpiece *Orlando Innamorato* launched a new epic cycle culminating in the far greater poem of Ariosto, *Orlando Furioso,* but essentially it spoke for the rapidly dying medieval past. His hero Orlando is the immortal Roland of

* bō yär′ dō

the Old French epic, but he has been refined, as it were, and polished into the shape of a chivalrous Arthurian knight. The basic conflict of the Carolingian epic—Christian against Saracen—remains. Superimposed upon this, however, is the elaborate embroidery of Arthurian romance—exquisite heroines, lovesick knights, magic, love potions, enchanted forests, combats and imprisonments, giants, dragons, and fairies. Boiardo's voluminous (but unfinished) poem —69 cantos in *ottava rima*—covers, in its vastly complicated plot, two main love stories —the love of Roland for Angelica, daughter of the King of Cathay, and the love of the Saracen knight Roger for the Christian maiden Bradamante. The first two books were published in 1484, the third in 1494 shortly before his death. Ironically, the poem suffered from the rapidly shifting literary and linguistic vogues of the day. Boiardo's Ferrarese Italian fell into disfavor, and in 1541 Francesco Berni rewrote the poem in the more popular Tuscan dialect and according to the more "advanced" literary styles of the day. Berni's work quite superseded Boiardo's, and it was not until the nineteenth century that his original text was published by Antonio Panizzi. What gave the poem immortality, however, was not Berni's version but the sequel to it which Ariosto began in 1506—the *Orlando Furioso*, one of the greatest of all Italian poems.

For many years Ariosto's *Orlando* overshadowed its predecessor. That it is superior to Boiardo's poem is unchallenged. Nevertheless *Orlando Innamorato* stands by itself as a poem of distinct merit. Read not as an epic but as a verse romance it recreates the atmosphere and spirit of the medieval romances with charm, vitality, and sometimes with humor. Its influence, not only through Ariosto, but in its own right (via Berni's adaptation of course) was marked. Spenser refers to Boiardo in Book IV of *The Faerie Queene* as "that famous Tuscane penne." Milton mentions his heroine Angelica in an extended simile in *Paradise Regained*, and she is also referred to by Cervantes in *Don Quixote.*

Other writings by Boiardo include the *Sonnetti* and *Canzoniere*, translations from the Latin and Greek, and a verse play about Timon of Athens translated from Lucian.

The first English translation of the *Orlando Innamorato* was made in 1598 "by R. T. Gent" (Robert Tofte). A translation by W. S. Rose was published in 1823, and in 1830-1834 Panizzi's edition was published in English. Selections from the poem appear in William Everett's *The Italian Poets Since Dante* (1904) and J. B. Fletcher's *Literature of the Italian Renaissance* (1934). A selection from the sonnets in English translation is published in L. R. Lind's *Lyric Poetry of the Italian Renaissance* (1954).

ABOUT: Bennett, J. W. *in* English Institute Essays 1951; Edwards, E. W. The Orlando Furioso and Its Predecessor; Everett, W. The Italian Poets Since Dante; Fletcher, J. B. Literature of the Italian Renaissance; Ker, W. P. Collected Essays, I; Wilkins, E. H. A History of Italian Literature, *also* The Invention of the Sonnet and Other Studies in Italian Literature. [In Italian—Simone, A. Saggi e Letture Critiche.]

*BOILEAU-DESPRÉAUX, NICOLAS (November 1, 1636-March 11, 1711), French poet and critic, son of a secretary of the Parliament, was born in Paris in the Palace of Justice. He took his name Despréaux from his family properties. He studied at the colleges of Harcourt and Beauvais, and began training in theology and law, entering in the latter profession in 1656. Having inherited a considerable fortune at the age of twenty, he abandoned these professions, which did not interest him, and devoted his life to letters. His early efforts were biting satires, chiefly on literary subjects, which he read among friends in cafés, and which gave him the reputation of a freethinker and even of a debauchee. The first seven of his twelve *Satires* appeared in 1666, the last in 1711; his twelve *Épîtres,* dealing with current topics and events, appeared from 1669 to 1698. He was presented at court in 1669, and in 1677 became the historiographer of France. With the help of Louis XIV he was elected to the French Academy in 1684, despite the many enemies he had made by his verses and intrigues. His reputation as a misanthropist was confirmed by ill health and growing deafness; but he received his friends regularly, especially Racine, whose death in 1699 was for him a painful shock.

Although one of the distinguished poets of his times, Boileau was primarily the critic and the legislator of the classical movement. He attacked mediocrity in all fields, and formulated clear rules for good taste, based on the best practices of his contemporaries, especially of his friends Racine and Molière; thus he is a codifier rather than an innovator. *L'Art Poétique* (1674) contains his cogent precepts. He often gives advice to poets regarding the pitfalls of composition, and in so doing all but bans any kind of novelty. Boileau's doctrines apply particularly to the theatre, in which the norms were those of his two close colleagues. In modern eyes, his excessive demands for reason, to the exclu-

* bwà lō′ dā prā ō′

BOILEAU

to Homer, Plato, Cicero, and Virgil, as the great masters of all times.

After many partial editions, Boileau's *Œuvres Complètes* were published in 1718 by his friend Brossette, initiating a long series of editions up to modern times. The pedagogical nature of the work explains the several hundred editions of excerpts that appeared during the nineteenth century and the vital place of certain passages in school manuals.

The English translations were also important: *The Art of Poetry*, published in 1683 and revised by Dryden in 1710; *The Works of Boileau* in three volumes, 1711-1713, with the biography by Des Maizeaux; and *The Lutrin*, in 1682 and 1708, translated by J. Ozell and edited by N. Rowe.

ABOUT: Des Maizeaux *in* Works of Boileau; Robertson, J. Studies in the Genesis of Romantic Theory in the Eighteenth Century. [In French—see studies by R. Bray, P. Delaporte, F. Lachèvre, G. Lanson, E. Magne, D. Mornet.]

F. J. C.

sion of passion, sentiment, and imagination, are precisely the limitations of classicism, in which there was no place for Ronsard and hardly even for La Fontaine. Indeed, Boileau's verse, so often quoted, "Enfin Malherbe vint, et, le premier en France . . . ," shows his strict adherence to tradition.

The genesis of the *Art Poétique* illustrates Boileau's method and shows the vital importance in his career of the year 1674. The principal model for this work was the *Ars Poetica* of Horace, which Boileau began to adapt in 1673 in his search for a systematic doctrine and a form. He worked simultaneously on a prose translation (1674) of the *Treatise on the Sublime* attributed to Longinus, and sought at once to put his new notions into practice in his mock-epic *Le Lutrin* (1674-83), the story of an ecclesiastical quarrel over the placement of a lectern. The satirical elements in *Le Lutrin* are particularly effective on account of the author's intimate knowledge of the workings of the Palace of Justice.

Despite Boileau's retirement to his house at Auteuil as a result of his disabilities, he took sides in several popular matters, satirizing women, and reflecting his sympathies for Jansenism in attacking the casuistry of the Jesuits. He also entered the "Quarrel of the Ancients and Moderns," provoked in the French Academy in 1687 by Perrault's glorification of the reign of Louis XIV, and marked by Boileau's prose *Réflexions sur Longin* (1694), expressing strong allegiance

*BOITO, ARRIGO (February 24, 1842-June 10, 1918), Italian composer, librettist, and poet, was born in Padua, the son of an Italian painter, Silvestro Boito, and a Polish countess, Giuseppina Radolinska. He had an older brother, Camillo, who was a successful architect and short-story writer. Young Arrigo was given an excellent musical education at the conservatory in Milan. At this early date he made his first attempts at literature, and his first published essays won him attention both at home and in France, where Victor Hugo singled him out for praise. In 1860 he composed a cantata, *Il Quattro Giugno,* as a graduation exercise for the conservatory. Two years later, collaborating with Franco Faccio, he wrote another cantata, *Le Sorelle d'Italia,* for which he received a generous government prize. On this money he was enabled to travel in France and Germany, where he quickly absorbed the romantic influences that shaped his later work.

It was probably during his travels abroad that Boito first conceived the idea for his principal work, the opera *Mefistofele.* Boito's libretto follows the source, Goethe's *Faust,* more closely than Gounod's more popular opera. It includes not only the love-episodes involving Margaret, but portions of the highly obscure Part II of Goethe's poem. At its première at La Scala in Milan, March 5, 1868, the opera ran for over six hours. The combination of the length plus a dramatic and unconventional musical score (the composer was accused of "Wagnerism") produced a

* bô' ē tō

111

totally unfavorable audience reaction. Seven years later, however, revised and shortened, it was produced at Bologna with great success. Although many music critics regard it as an excellent work, it has not remained in the operatic repertory. The role of Mefistofele was a favorite of the Russian basso Chaliapin. Boito composed, but never completed, three other operatic works—*Nerone* (completed after Boito's death by Arturo Toscanini), *Ero e Leandro*, and the *Orestiade*.

Boito's memory survives not as a composer nor as a poet (his romantic lyrics lacked "spiritual insight and creative spark"), but as a librettist, specifically as the author of the librettos of Verdi's last two operas, *Otello* and *Falstaff*. He first met Verdi in 1862 when he wrote the words for his "Hymn of the Nations." They became good friends, and it was Boito who persuaded the aging Verdi, after fourteen years of retirement, to return to operatic composition. These two great operas, composed in so different an idiom from Verdi's earlier work, reflect the total and perfect integration of music and drama. They invite comparison with the greatest achievements of Richard Wagner. Verdi was no admirer of Wagner, but Boito was, and his influence upon the older composer was considerable. Matching the music at every step are Boito's magnificent librettos, both adaptations of Shakespeare. Verdi himself wrote that in *Otello* ". . . he has fashioned a libretto wherein situations and verses alike are extraordinarily powerful." The two operas represented the triumph of Verdi's career, and the librettos can stand independently as literary works of the first order.

Boito also wrote under the anagrammatic pen name of Tobia Gorrio. It was this name that he signed to his libretto for Ponchielli's opera *La Gioconda*. During the struggle for Italian unification he fought as a volunteer under Garibaldi's command. In later life he received many honors. He was named Cavaliere, Ufficiale, and Commendatore by the Italian government; was made a chevalier of the French Legion of Honor; received honorary degrees from Oxford and Cambridge; and became a senator of the kingdom of Italy. He died in Milan at the age of seventy-six.

Boito's librettos are available in English translation in standard opera libretto form. His poems have not been translated into English.

ABOUT: Columbia Dictionary of Modern European Literature; Huneker, J. Overtones; Ojetti, U. As They Seemed to Me. [In Italian—see studies by F. Ballo and A. Pompeati.]

"BOLESŁAWITA, B." See KRASZEWSKI, JÓZEF IGNACY

*BONAVENTURA, Saint (GIOVANNI FIDANZA) called "the Seraphic Doctor," (1221 or 1222-July 15, 1274), Franciscan theologian, was born in Bagnorea in Tuscany. As a young child he was destined for the church by his mother who had invoked the aid of St. Francis to cure her son of an illness. Most sources estimate that about 1240 Bonaventura joined the Roman Province of the Franciscan Order and was sent to complete his studies in the liberal arts at the University of Paris. He studied under the university's first Franciscan professor of theology, the eminent Alexander of Hales, and received his Bachelor's degree before the death of Alexander in 1245.

In 1248 Bonaventura started lecturing on the Scriptures, beginning with St. Luke's Gospel, and his talent as a preacher was soon evident. In recognition of his ability he was permitted to lecture on the famous theological handbook, the *Sentences* of Peter Lombard. This oratorical skill took him before some of the most illustrious audiences in Europe during his lifetime. His style, simple in form, was distinguished by an abundance of feeling.

In 1255 he should have received his doctorate from the University of Paris. But he was at this point refused recognition by the university because of the conflict which had broken out between the secular professors and the teachers belonging to the Franciscan and Dominican orders. The ideals promulgated in both these orders were not yet readily accepted in contemporary philosophical circles. The Franciscan Bonaventura and the Dominican Thomas Aquinas were allied in defense of their respective orders against the attacks on the mendicant version of the religious life made by the secular master William of St. Amour. The dispute was finally quashed with the intervention of Pope Alexander IV, and Bonaventura and Aquinas both were accorded status as doctors and members of the university staff. To this first period of Bonaventura's teaching belongs his most voluminous work, the *Commentaries* on the *Sentences* of Peter Lombard. Sometime before 1257 he also produced the *Breviloquium*.

In February 1257 Bonaventura was elected Minister General of the Franciscan Order and held this office for the next sixteen years. The brotherhood had been more or less with-

* bŏn à vĕn tū′ ra

ST. BONAVENTURA

out direction since 1219 when its founder went on crusade. Bonaventura's administrative duties were at first quite arduous because of the dissensions within the order. He did much to establish a solid theological and psychological basis for Franciscan teachings and solved the problems of factionalism so well that he won the title of "Second Founder" of the Friars Minor. In 1259 he wrote *Itinerarium Mentis in Deum* (Journey of the Soul to God), the work which best summarizes his thought. He wrote two biographies of St. Francis in 1261, one of these being designated the official biography by the Order in 1263. He also drew up the first constitution of the Order at Narbonne in 1260.

Bonaventura was a man of learning and encouraged the development of studies within the Order. He thus helped to create the apostolate of learned and popular teaching for which the medieval friars are best known. During a decade of travel and teaching throughout Europe, Bonaventura produced several other works, including *Collationes de Decem Praeceptis* (Lenten Sermons) in 1267 or 1268 and *De Decem Donis Spiritus Sancti* about 1270. His *De Triplici Via* (The Threefold Way) is regarded as a *summa* of medieval mystical doctrine in miniature. Other small works which are felt to contain most of what is individual in his teaching are *De Reductione Artium ad Theologiam, Soliloquium,* and *De Septem Itineribus Aeternitatis.*

Bonaventura's lifetime covers the period in which the Augustinian tradition was begin-

ning to be opposed by the Aristotelian metaphysic as demonstrated in the teachings of Albertus Magnus and Thomas Aquinas. In his *Commentaries,* Bonaventura shows how firmly he clings to Franciscan, i.e. Augustinian doctrine. As E. H. Gilson has pointed out, there is a parallel between the life of St. Francis and Bonaventura's teachings in that the former's personal life culminated in mystical communion with God while the latter's teaching culminated in his mystical doctrine. The apologetic value of Bonaventura's teaching lies in the fact that he illustrates how to dissent from the Aristotelian logic of his friend Aquinas. Therefore he stands as the initiator of the anti-Thomistic trend, opening the way for Duns Scotus and Occam.

In 1271 Bonaventura attended the coronation of his friend and protector Gregory X in Rome. In 1273 he was back in Paris for a series of lectures on the Hexameron. In this year he was also nominated and elected cardinal and bishop of Albano.

The important Council of Lyons was held in 1274, and when Bonaventura joined the Pope in Lyons he resigned from his position as head of the Franciscan Order so that he might work without distraction in the council for the union of the Greek church with Rome. On July 6 this union was effected and shortly thereafter Bonaventura died. He was canonized in 1482.

Bonaventura is said to have received his cognomen from St. Francis of Assisi at the time of his miraculous cure.

There are few pictorial representations of Bonaventura. Zurbarán did a series of portraits for the church of S. Bonaventura in Seville but these are now scattered throughout Europe. It is interesting to note that Giotto, in the frescoes at Assisi, seems to have closely followed Bonaventura's *Life of St. Francis.*

The earliest English translation of Saint Bonaventura was a verse translation by Robert Manning of Brunne of the *Meditations on the Supper of Our Lord,* about 1315-30. Early in the fifteenth century (before 1410) Nicholas Love published a translation of the *Meditations on the Life of Christ* with the title *Mirrour of the Blessed Lyf of Jesu Christ.* In more recent years the Franciscan Institute has published several translations, including the *De Reductione Artium ad Theologiam* in 1955 (first English translation in 1938) and the *Itinerarium Mentis in Deum* in 1956. The latter work had earlier been translated as *The Franciscan Vision* (1937) and *The Mind's Road to God* (by G. Boas, 1953). The *Breviloquium* was translated by E. E. Nemmers in 1946. E. Gurney-Slater translated the *Life of Saint Francis* in 1931. The distinguished linguist José de Vinck of Louvain University has translated the *Mystical Opuscula,* published in 1960 by the

St. Anthony Guild Press as the first part of their project to translate the entire Quaracchi edition of the *Opera Omnia* of Bonaventura, a monument of Franciscan scholarship. In the *Mystical Opuscula* are the following works: On the Perfection of Life, Addressed to Sisters; Journey of the Mind to God; The Triple Way, The Tree of Life, and the Mystical Vine.

ABOUT: Gilson, E. The Philosophy of Saint Bonaventura. [In Italian—see study by R. Lazzarine.]

E. DE P.

*BOREL, (JOSEPH) PETRUS** (June 26, 1809-July 17, 1859), French poet and novelist, was born in Lyons, son of an ironmonger who claimed descent from the noble family of Borel d'Hauterive but who was actually of humble parentage, and his cousin Marguerite Garnaud. Petrus was the twelfth of fourteen children. The elder Borel was sufficiently successful to provide a good education for his many sons. He was also able to sell his business at a comfortable profit and move with his family to Paris, where Petrus was educated. At thirteen the boy was apprenticed to an architect and by the age of twenty he was qualified to practice his profession independently. He was not, however, suited to it either by inclination or by temperament. Instead he found himself strongly drawn to literature. He joined the small revolutionary group calling itself "Le Petit Cénacle" (the name was later changed to "Les Jeunes France," and finally to "Les Bouzingos," a term meaning noisy, extravagant, and undisciplined)—whose aims were rebellion against classicism in literature and general defiance of convention and social propriety. The best-known members of the group were Théophile Gautier and Gérard de Nerval. They affected medieval and exotic styles, Byronic poses, and all manner of morbid obsessions such as necrophilia and lycanthropy—hence Borel's sobriquet "lycanthrope" or wolf-man. Borel was their acknowledged leader—a glamorous figure, pale, with bright but melancholy eyes, a vivid red mouth, and a silky dark-brown beard which, as Enid Starkie writes in her book on Borel, "gave him the appearance of a Sultan from the *Arabian Nights*."

Borel's first book was a collection of poems, *Rhapsodies*, published in 1831. Most of these were written when he was twenty or twenty-one and Borel, in an audacious and arrogant preface, described them as "scum and slag." Actually they are fairly mild and conventional romantic poems. Some of them are of high quality and, Miss Starkie observes, they "give

* bô rĕl'

114

Borel the right to an individual and permanent place in French poetry." The book was generally ignored by the critics and the public. Indeed the only fame Borel ever enjoyed in his lifetime was the adulation of the small revolutionary clique which surrounded him. For six months in 1832 he edited a magazine, *La Liberté, Journal des Arts,* which attracted the attention of free-thinking young writers and artists, but he gained neither fame nor fortune. To support himself he wrote conventional poems and short stories for keepsake books and anthologies. In 1833 he published what is probably his most important work, *Champavert, Contes Immoraux,* a group of stories all reflecting his taste for the macabre, for sadism, for ironic humor. This book too proved to be a financial failure, and Borel had the further disappointment of seeing his influence in his literary clique gradually diminish, overshadowed by the rising success of Gautier.

Poverty forced Borel to move to the country at Baizil where he lived alone in a shack and almost starved. In this solitude he did a translation of *Robinson Crusoe* and wrote his "terrible and gruesome" *Madame Putiphar,* published in 1839, a novel set in eighteenth century France (Madame Putiphar is presumably Madame de Pompadour). The book was ignored except for one unfavorable review, and the only portion of it that is of any considerable interest to modern readers is the verse prologue, a fine symbolic poem in which three allegorical figures, the World, Solitude, and Death, fight for the poet's soul. Borel returned to Paris and in 1844 edited a paper, *Satan,* which his brothers Francisque and André published. He held various other editorial positions and free-lanced but was never able to win any measure of financial security. At last in 1846 he was appointed Inspector of Colonization in Algeria, and he left France never to return. His life in Algeria ultimately proved no happier than his life in France. He undertook his assignment in good faith. In 1848, however, he was dismissed from his post. He was later re-hired, then dismissed and re-hired again—largely because he could not or would not cooperate with the civil authorities. In 1854 he quarreled bitterly with his superiors and in August 1855 he was dismissed from the service. He remained in Algeria as a gentleman-farmer and died of sunstroke at Mostaganem, where he was buried. He was survived by his wife, Gabrielle Claye, whom he had married in 1847, and their son, Aldéran-André-Petrus-Benoni Borel d'Hauterive.

The symbolist poet Charles Baudelaire, a great admirer of Borel, spoke of him as a man pursued by ill luck. His work—what Arthur Symons called "his hasty, defiant art" —is all but forgotten today, but his eccentric and self-tormented personality constitutes a kind of epitome of the early days of French romanticism. "His tragedy," Enid Starkie writes, "was one not uncommon amongst men of talent and sensitivity; his creative ability did not match his vision and his ambition."

ABOUT: Starkie, E. Petrus Borel, the Lycanthrope; Symons, A. "Petrus Borel" in Forum, January-June 1915. [In French—see studies by J. Claretie and A. Marie.]

BORN, BERTRAN DE. See BERTRAN DE BORN

*BOSBOOM-TOUSSAINT, ANNA LOUISE GEERTRUIDA (September 16, 1812-April 13, 1886), Dutch novelist, was born in Alkmaar. She was the daughter of a pharmacist named Toussaint in that city, but spent most of her early years with her grandparents in Harlingen, Frisia. Returning to Alkmaar in 1830, she became private tutor with a family in the nearby town of Hoorn. In 1835 she settled in her parental home, dedicating herself to studies and literary work. She found encouragement in the circle of the parsonage of Heilo, in the friendship of Reverend Hasebroek and his sister Betsy, but especially in the literary circle that directed *De Gids,* the leading literary magazine of Holland in those days.

Her first novels, *Almagro* (1837) and *The Count of Devonshire* (1838), reveal the influence of English romanticism, especially of Walter Scott. Following the advice of her friend Potgieter, the editor of *De Gids,* she began to seek the material for her novels in the history of her own country. *Het Huis Lauernesse* (1840) established her as a prominent writer of historical novels. She early distinguished herself from her contemporaries Van Lennep and Oltmans, also writers of historical novels, through profounder characterization and through her fervent Protestantism that relates her to the contemporary movement of the Reveille.

In 1841 she became engaged to the new editor of *De Gids,* Bakhuizen van den Brink, but after he went abroad in 1843 he broke the engagement, leaving her with a wound that did not heal quickly. That becomes evident from all sorts of motifs in her later

* bŏz′ bŏm tōō sän′

novels, even though she found happiness in her marriage with the painter Jan Bosboom in 1851. Uninterruptedly she continued the series of historical novels. For *De Gids* she wrote *Een Kroon voor Karel den Stoute* (1841). The historical research that served as a basis for her ten-volume Leicester cycle (1846-55) proved particularly rewarding. As historical tapestry and as character study these novels belong to the best of her endeavors, despite the copiousness of the descriptions and the numerous digressions. Her less successful work is partly the result of overproduction, which in turn was the result of financial difficulties. That cannot be said of *De Delftsche Wonderdokter* (3 vols., 1870-71) in which again the story of a convert to Protestantism is elaborated. Her last historical works are the novel *Raymond de Schrijnwerker* (1879) and *Het Kasteel op Walcheren in Zeeland* (1882). The former, written in dialogue form, presents the clash of different views of life during the French revolution of 1841.

She had meanwhile left the territory of Dutch romanticism and tried her pen at the contemporary novel. The result was four works of which *Majoor Frans* (1874) was the most successful. It won favor with the younger generation and has been translated into various languages (English translation, by James Akeroyd, 1886). This novel in the form of a diary is original in its characterization, but the author could not find the natural tone of the confidential conversation or letter. This inability to disassociate herself from the archaistic style of the historical novel was her main limitation. Younger Dutch writers, e.g., Louis Couperus (1863-1923), have superseded her, although she takes a place of honor among the authors of the nineteenth century.

ABOUT: [In Dutch—see studies by H. L. Berckenhoff, J. M. C. Bouvy, J. Dyserinck.]

H. B.

*BOSSUET, JACQUES BÉNIGNE (September 27, 1627-April 12, 1704), French theologian and orator, was born in Dijon into a prominent family of the bourgeoisie. His father and grandfather before him had been magistrates. The boy received an excellent education, first at the hands of the Jesuits in Dijon, studying Hebrew, Greek, and Latin, and then in Paris, where he studied philosophy and theology at the Collège de Navarre. In 1652 he was ordained and appointed Archdeacon of Metz. He spent the next seven years in that city in the north of France

* bô sü ĕ′

115

BOSSUET

where there were many Protestants, and he engaged in heated polemics with them. Thus early in his life his predominant aim became the conversion of Protestants—the bringing back into the Roman church of as many dissidents as his eloquent oratory and vigorous writings could reach.

In 1659 Bossuet was back in Paris. His sermons soon brought him to the attention of the most powerful figures of church and state. The most impressive of these sermons were his funeral orations, written and delivered with dignity and nobility in "the grand style." In themselves they survive as masterpieces of eulogy-biography, especially those of Henrietta Maria, widow of Charles I of England (1669), her daughter the Duchess of Orléans (1670), and General Condé (1687).

Bossuet's connections with the royal court became even closer when he was appointed tutor to Louis XIV's son. The young Dauphin was a dull pupil who never lived to be king, but his tutor (like his contemporary Fénelon who tutored Louis' grandson) wrote some of his most important works for his instruction. These include his *Traité de la Connaissance de Dieu*, his *Discours sur L'Histoire Universelle*, and his *Politique Tirée de l'Écriture Sainte*: all of them sober and fervent defenses of absolute monarchy written to demonstrate the parallels between the divine rule of Louis XIV and Solomon's rule of Israel and other such "golden ages" of the past. Louis bestowed his favor generously upon Bossuet, conferring upon him the bishopric of Meaux in 1681 (he was later called "the

Eagle of Meaux"). Ironically, however, it was Louis' patronage that was ultimately to cost Bossuet greater advancement in the church—possibly even a cardinalate. In 1681 the king became involved in a controversy with the Roman church over the question of Gallicanism (the theory that the state has temporal power independent of the jurisdiction of the papacy), and Bossuet was called in to write a statement on France's position. Torn between his religious orthodoxy and his loyalty to his king, Bossuet sought to steer a middle course—pointing out that the church's jurisdiction was spiritual, the state's temporal —but he succeeded only in alienating both sides. In still another controversy, that involving Quietism (see sketch of Fénelon below), Bossuet sided with his king and his church but emerged, if not defeated, badly shaken and much reduced in dignity.

Bossuet spent his last years in other such controversies and in vigorous but hopeless attempts to effect reunion within the divided church. In 1688 he published one of his greatest works on this subject—*Histoire des Variations des Églises Protestantes*. He also maintained a busy correspondence on this subject with many prominent figures, among them the German philosopher Leibniz. He died at Meaux at seventy-six. Bossuet has been called "one of the great figures of ecclesiastical history." He won this reputation by sheer force of will and intellect. "Everything in his mind," the nineteenth century English historian Lord Acton wrote, "was on the gigantic scale. . . . Uniting, as he did, a learning quite extraordinary to a rare facility for exposition in the grand style, an acuteness in polemics to a never-sleeping common sense, an unquestionable sincerity and simplicity of intention to an untiring energy and devotion to the cause he espoused . . . possessing a certain charm of manner which softened the pain of submission in those who were forced to yield to his somewhat despotic will, such a man was formed to rule in his generation, and to produce an impression on his country not easily effaced."

The complete works of Bossuet were published in ten volumes from 1877 to 1885, edited by Guillaume.

English translations of his writings include: *Maxims and Reflections upon Plays* (1699); *An Account of the Education of the Dauphin* (J. T. Phillips, 1743); *An Universal History from the Beginning of the World to the Empire of Charlemagne* (J. Elphinston, 1778); *A History of the Variations of the Protestant Churches* (1845); *Selections from the Funeral Orations* (F. M. Warren, 1907); *Panegyrics of the Saints* (D. O'Mahony, 1924); *Selections from Bossuet* (C. H. C. Wright, 1930).

ABOUT: Acton, J. E. Essays on Church and State; Brody, J. Boileau and Longinus; De La Bedoyère, M. The Archbishop and the Lady; Reynolds, E. E. Bossuet; Saunders, E. K. Bousset. [In French—see studies by J. Calvet, G. Lanson, A. G. Martimort, J. Truchet.]

BRANT, SEBASTIAN

BRANT, SEBASTIAN (1458?-May 10, 1521), German poet and lawyer, was born in Strasbourg, the son of Diebolt Brant, an inn-keeper, and his wife Barbara. He was tutored privately and in 1475 entered the University of Basel. Though attracted by the new humanistic studies, Brant studied the law and proceeded from the baccalaureate degree in 1477 to the doctorate of canon and civil law in 1489. Until 1500 he remained in Basel as an instructor in law and reader for various publishers. This was the period of his greatest literary activity. His early works were in Latin and may be divided into four groups—religious and didactic, political, juristic, and moralistic. Most of these writings are of minor significance. Of the didactic works other than the *Narrenschiff* (see below), the *Alopekomachia* or "Polemic against Foxes" may be mentioned. The foxes are the various vices he wishes to satirize, such as cunning and fraud.

Before returning to Strasbourg in 1500 to take up a position as town clerk and legal adviser to the council, Brant married Elisabeth Burg. His literary output declined considerably with his increasing involvement in political and legal matters. He received numerous honors from the Emperor and the city of Basel. He died in 1521.

One long poem in rhyming couplets made Brant's name famous throughout Europe, his *Narrenschiff* or "Ship of Fools." The work, published in 1494, owed not a little of its success to the excellent printing by Johannes Bergmann and to the extremely fine woodcuts. It was long thought that these woodcuts were executed by Brant himself, but it seems more likely that he supplied sketches to a professional; they much resemble in style those found in *Der Ritter vom Thurm*, published by Michael Furter at the suggestion of Bergmann. Some later editions reduced the text to mere captions while keeping the woodcuts. Between 1494 and 1509 there were five editions of the work in Basel and many subsequent reprintings with modifications. In 1497 Jakob Locher produced a Latin version in hexameters which was better planned than the original and which made it known throughout Europe. Other Latin versions and translations in various vernaculars followed. The best-known translation into Eng-

lish is that by Alexander Barclay, issued in 1509 (reprinted London, 1874). (A modern English version of Brant's German poem translated with introduction by E. Zeydel appeared in 1944.) Barclay stressed the religious aspects of the poem more than Brant had done. His version was very influential in England, particularly during the Elizabethan period.

Technically, the *Ship of Fools* belongs to the large and very popular class of "fools and folly" literature. Its object is to hold up a mirror to human stupidity and thereby reprove "foolish conduct." Brant shows little evidence of his humanistic leanings in his treatment. The original idea of packing a ship full of fools and sending it off to the fools' land of Narragonia is soon abandoned and the work becomes a catalogue of foolish types. Almost any divergence from a narrow bourgeois code of social conduct is characterized as folly, although many of the types depicted can be traced back to Theophrastus and Horace. The satire is rarely more than unflattering description. A comparison with the nearly contemporary *Praise of Folly* of Erasmus reveals the enormous difference in approach of the two men. Brant utterly lacks Erasmus' sense of form and his wit, but it is clear that his approach was closer to the feelings of the time, if we judge from his popularity.

ABOUT: Rajewski, M. Sebastian Brant; Swain, B. Fools and Folly during the Middle Ages and Renaissance; Zeydel, E. The Ship of Fools by Sebastian Brant.

W. T. H. J.

*BRANTÔME, PIERRE DE BOURDEILLE

*BRANTÔME, PIERRE DE BOURDEILLE, Seigneur de (c. 1540-July 15, 1614), French historian and biographer, was born at the Abbey of Brantôme in Périgord, the third son of the Baron de Bourdeille. Both his mother and his maternal grandmother had been attached to the court of Marguerite de Valois, and as a boy Brantôme served as a page in the court of Marguerite de Navarre, thus early acquiring his intimate knowledge of the colorful and corrupt court life of the Valois family. He was educated in Paris and in Poitiers. He inherited his title and the Abbey of Brantôme after the death of his brother Jean, but was not himself in religious orders. On the contrary, Brantôme's early years were thoroughly secular. He became a soldier and a kind of gentleman-adventurer. He traveled widely, visited Morocco, Spain, and Portugal, accom-

* brän tôm'

panied Mary Stuart's party when she returned to Scotland from France, saw Queen Elizabeth, fought in the religious wars under Charles IX. Piqued by Henry III's failure to make him governor of Périgord, Brantôme planned to enter the service of Spain. He was prevented from doing so by an accident —a fall from a horse in 1584 crippled him and forced him into the sedentary career of literature.

Brantôme's experiences as courtier, soldier, and traveler, his keen eye for detail, his sharp ear for gossip, and his long life which spanned the reigns of Henry II, Francis II, Charles IX, Henry III, Henry IV, and Louis XIII— all prepared him ideally for the role of historian. Unfortunately, his sense of accuracy and possibly even his honesty were somewhat blunted, and his writings are not entirely reliable. But they render a vivid portrait of the era, its pageantry, its intrigue, and its striking and often sinister personalities. He has been called the "valet de chambre" of history, "the most gifted chronicler of his epoch."

Brantôme's works consist of a series of biographies of notable men and women, *Vies des Hommes Illustres et des Grands Capitains, Vies des Dames Galantes et des Dames Illustres*. They were not published until half a century after his death, although in his will he had provided money for their publication in a beautiful and elaborate edition. A surviving niece, however, fearing the scandal that they might arouse, did not allow them to be published in her lifetime. As a personality Brantôme apparently lived up to the courtly ideal of his times—haughty, arrogant, elegant, and fastidious. He spent his last years at his estate in Brantôme writing his memoirs and engaging in numerous lawsuits with his neighbors.

The standard edition of Brantôme's works was edited by L. Lalanne in eleven volumes, 1864-82.

Brantôme's *Lives of Fair and Gallant Ladies (Illustrious Dames)* has had several English translations, including one by K. P. Wormeley in 1899 and one by A. R. Allinson in 1929. Portions of his lives of distinguished men have been translated—*Spanish Rhodomontades* by a Mr. Ozel, published in 1744, and *Duelling Stories of the Sixteenth Century*, by G. H. Powell in 1904. The Warner Library has brief English selections from his works.

ABOUT: Tilley, A. A. Literature of the French Renaissance; Warner Library, VI. [In French—see studies by L. Lalanne and F. Crucy.]

*BREDERO (or BREDERODE), GERBRAND ADRIAENSZOON (March 16, 1585-August 23, 1618), Dutch poet and playwright, was born in Amsterdam, the son of Adriaen Cornelisz and Marretje Gerbrandsd. The father, a shoemaker, did not give his son a classical education; but Bredero learned French and was familiar with the work of his contemporaries. In his love songs he adopted the sonnet form.

Like a number of his countrymen, Bredero intended to be a painter and served for some time as apprentice to Francisco Badens; his ability to present local color in a vivid and realistic manner seems to reflect this first interest.

When still a boy Bredero began to write rhymes, much in the style of the Rederykers, whose poetic rules were traditional. Many of Bredero's love songs are in a melancholy strain. Collections such as *Apollo* (1615) contain richly varied material. After his death his verses were assembled and published in the *Boertigh, Amoreus en Aendachtigh Groot Lied-boeck* (1622). Its somewhat chronological arrangement shows how in the earlier part of his life Bredero wrote songs that, in their naturalness and intensity, deviate from the affectations of the period. The latter part of the edition consists mainly of sonnets that reveal the influence of such humanistically trained poets as Hooft. Much of this work presents a survey of Bredero's love affairs, reading like a diary of hope and sorrow, jealousy and anger, but also of fierce response.

In his dramas Bredero shows the influence of the Spanish Amadis novels with which he was acquainted in French translations. *Rodderick ende Alphonsus* (1611), *Griane* (1612), *Den Stomme Ridder* (1618), *Lucille* (1615), all betray the influence of early Spanish romanticism. At the same time, however, these dramas as well as others he wrote —*Klucht van de Koe* (1612), *Sijmen* (1612), *De Meulenaar* (1613), *Het Moortje* (1615), and *Den Spaensche Brabander* (1617)—are replete with everyday scenes taken from the life of the people among whom Bredero lived. As in Cervantes' *Quixote*, the secondary characters pronounce their earthy views of life in a realistic manner that contrasts sharply and often comically with the pathos of the main characters. It is these scenes taken from daily life that lend many of these dramas literary value.

Den Spaensche Brabander in particular reveals Bredero as the outstanding early realist

* brā' dĕ rō

BREDERO

of Dutch literature. But it is not the sour-flavored realism of a later time. Its vivid scenes are the product of an era which could laugh boisterously and a moment later reject the world and the flesh in sharp self-accusation, and which could pray with a fervor fit to shake open the gates of Heaven. It was a time of which the poet Bredero was a splendid representative for he, too, vacillated between God and the world, between the spirit and the flesh.

The works of Bredero were collected in 1890 (3 vols., ed. J. Ten Brink and others) and in 1918-29 (3 vols., ed. J. A. N. Knuttel).

ABOUT: [In Dutch—see studies by J. A. N. Knuttel, J. P. Naeff, J. Prinsen, A. A. Rijnbach.]

H. B.

BREIÐFJÖRÐ, SIGURÐUR EIRÍKS-SON (March 4, 1798-July 21, 1846), Icelandic poet, was born on a farm in Breiðifjördur, in western Iceland. His father, a poor farmer, had some talent for writing poetry, and his mother's family also had literary interests. Not surprisingly in this encouraging atmosphere, the boy showed promise early, composing a cycle of *rímur* (traditional verse sagas and ballads) at the age of eleven. His family's poverty prevented him from acquiring a formal education. Instead, after some tutoring by the neighborhood clergyman in the rudiments of learning, he was sent to Copenhagen at six-

* bräth' fyōōrth

teen to learn the cooper's trade. In that cosmopolitan city he first became acquainted with Danish and Norwegian literature and he read widely.

Breiðfjörð returned to Iceland in 1818 to work at his trade. In his spare time he wrote verse, and his lively, vigorous poems on folk and traditional themes won him a wide audience. He enjoyed special popularity with the common uneducated people who identified themselves freely with him and his work. In striking contrast to his success as a poet, Breiðfjörð's personal life was a total disaster. He was in debt constantly; he drank heavily; and his domestic life was full of crisis and turmoil, including a wretchedly unhappy first marriage and a second marriage that was declared bigamous by the courts. He drifted back to Denmark in 1830 to study law but succumbed to loose living quickly and gave up his studies. He spent three years in Greenland working as a cooper. During this bleak period of loneliness and homesickness he wrote some of his best poems, including the *Númarímur,* a verse paraphrase of J. P. C. Florian's novel about the legendary Roman king Numa Pompilius. He also wrote a prose account of his stay in Greenland, *Frá Groenlandi* (1836). In 1834 he returned to Iceland where he spent his last years in abject poverty. His miscellaneous poems (*Ljóða Smámunir*) were published in 1839. He died in Reykjavik at forty-eight.

The bulk of Breiðfjörð's output—as Richard Beck points out in a study of him—"does not rise above the pedestrian level of mere verse-making." To his contemporaries, however, his work was interesting and significant, rich in the literary traditions which they loved.

ABOUT: Bach, G. The History of the Scandinavian Literatures; Beck, R. A. History of Icelandic Poets, 1800-1940 (Islandica XXXIV).

*BREITINGER, JOHANN JAKOB (March 1, 1701-December 13, 1776), Swiss critic and literary theorist, was born in Zürich, the son of a government official. He studied theology, philology, and history at the University of Zürich and mastered seven languages. He began his professional career writing scholarly articles in Latin, and his first major work was a critical edition (1730-32) of the *Septuaginta,* the Greek translation of the Old Testament. In 1731 Breitinger was appointed Professor of Hebrew and Greek at the Carolinum Gymnasium in Zürich and in 1745 became Professor of Greek and

* bri' ting ēr

Canon of the Seminary there. He continued in this position for more than thirty years, until his death in Zürich in 1776.

Breitinger's name is inextricably linked with that of his compatriot Johann Jacob Bodmer, for the two worked together and supplemented each other in a manner rarely encountered. Seldom does a work by either man fail to contain some degree of participation by the other. Of the two Breitinger was the more gifted and more serious scholar, whose writings display greater clarity of mind and depth of thought. Together the two men founded the journal *Discourse der Mahlern* (1721), which was modeled on the *Spectator* of Addison and Steele. In this publication they initiated an important trend in German literature by favoring English rather than French literature. Milton particularly was praised by the two Swiss critics, and most of their aesthetic writings were based on the study of the English poet.

In the course of their critical efforts the Swiss scholars became involved in controversy with the leading German critic of the time, Johann Christian Gottsched. Although the three men were in general agreement on most aesthetic problems, they differed widely on the question of the extent to which the marvelous was admissible into literature. The Swiss, whose view ultimately prevailed, admitted the widest possible interpretation and defended the broadest use of imagination. Breitinger presented the Swiss side of the argument in the important critical works *Kritische Dichtkunst* (1740) and *Kritische Abhandlung von der Natur, den Absichten, und dem Gebrauch der Gleichnisse* (1740). Both works are significant in the later development of German literary theory.

Breitinger was also one of the best scholars of his time in the field of Middle High German, and together with Bodmer contributed to the rediscovery of German medieval literature. Jointly they published a collection of Middle High German poetry entitled *Sammlung von Minnesingern* (1758-59), and Breitinger in addition edited the fables of Ulrich Boner. Breitinger held the fable in highest regard as a form of literature, because it best combined literary qualities with the didactic aim, which he felt was a desirable and necessary function of literature.

ABOUT: Eaton, J. W. Bodmer and Breitinger and European Literary Theory (Monatshefte XXXIII, 1941); Journal of English and Germanic Philology, XXXIV; Robertson, J. G. Studies in the Genesis of Romantic Theory in the Eighteenth Century. [In German—see studies by F. Braitmaier, H. Bodmer, J. C. Mörikofer, H. Schöffler, F. Servaes.]

D. G. D.

*BREMER, FREDRIKA (August 17, 1801-December 31, 1865), Swedish novelist, was born in Åbo (Turku), in Finland, the daughter of a well-to-do ironmonger. In 1804 the family settled on a country estate at Årsta, just outside Stockholm, where Fredrika grew up. Her childhood was not a happy one. Her mother was strict and severe, her father melancholy, and she was a shy, plain-looking girl. She showed talent for literature early and began writing poems at the age of eight. In 1820-21 she went with her family on an extensive tour of Europe, during which she became acquainted with much European literature and was particularly impressed with the writings of the German poet Schiller. On her return to Sweden, Fredrika Bremer found it increasingly difficult to submit to the dull routine of upper-middle-class country life. She threw herself into charity work, visiting the peasants, nursing the sick. Her first book, *Sketches of Everyday Life,* was published anonymously in 1828 in order to raise money for her favorite charities. The warm response which it received encouraged her to continue writing.

The death of her father in 1830 freed her from most of her domestic obligations, and she promptly embarked upon a career of woman-of-letters. Having an independent income, she traveled widely, both in Europe and abroad, and wrote many novels, short stories, sketches, and travel books. Her books—"fireside novels," simple in expression, full of gentle humor and domestic detail that had universal appeal—were translated into English and many other languages. In her native land she was highly honored and most influential, especially in the development of the modern Swedish novel. She received a gold medal of merit from the Swedish Academy in 1844.

In the course of her travels Fredrika Bremer visited the United States, Palestine, Greece, and Eastern Europe. She lived in the United States from 1849 to 1851 and was well-received in New England, where she was admired not only for her writing but for her outspoken anti-slavery sentiments. She met most of the literary greats of the day—Emerson, Longfellow, Lowell, Hawthorne. Her report on her American visit, *The Homes of the New World* (1853), was enormously popular in this country and had as many as five printings within one month of its New York publication. During her later years Miss Bremer was an ardent

* brä′ měr

advocate of women's rights and a crusader in many reform movements. She died at her home in Årsta at sixty-four.

A woman of prodigious energy and intellectual curiosity, Fredrika Bremer made friends wherever she went and commanded respect from all who knew her. Hawthorne described her as "the funniest little fairy person whom one can imagine, with a huge nose, to which all the rest of her is but an insufficient appendage; but you feel at once that she is most gentle, kind, womanly, sympathetic, and true."

Fredrika Bremer's novels were translated into English, in eleven volumes, by Mary Howitt, 1843-45. Some of the most popular of these in their day were *The Neighbours, The Home; or, Family Cares and Family Joys, The H—— Family, Hertha, Fathers and Daughters.* Mrs. Howitt also translated her travel books (including *Greece and the Greeks,* 1863; and *Life in the Old World: or, Two Years in Switzerland and Italy,* 1860) and *The Homes of the New World.* Selections from the latter were edited by A. B. Benson in 1924, and an excerpt from it appears in Oscar Handlin's *This Was America* (1949). *The Life, Letters, and Posthumous Works of Fredrika Bremer* was edited by her sister Charlotte Bremer and published in English translation by F. Milow in 1868. Selections from her work also appear in the Warner Library.

ABOUT: Bremer, C. The Life, Letters, and Posthumous Works of Fredrika Bremer; Howitt, M. Twelve Months with Fredrika Bremer in Sweden; Rooth, S. A. Seeress of the Northland: Fredrika Bremer's American Journey; Scandinavian Studies and Notes, VIII. [In Swedish—see study by G. Axberger.]

*BRENTANO, CLEMENS MARIA

(September 8, 1778-July 28, 1842), German poet, was born in Ehrenbreitstein, near Coblenz, at the home of his maternal grandmother, Sophie la Roche, a popular novelist of the time. His mother, the former Maximiliane la Roche, was less than half as old as her widower husband, Peter Anton Brentano, a prosperous, Italian-born merchant who had established his home and business in Frankfort. Though one of many children (from both of Brentano's marriages) young Clemens remained exceptionally close to his mother, whose lively fancy and genial warmth became characteristic also of her son. Clemens was able to strike only the most formal relationship with his father, who concerned himself more with business than family affairs. From his sixth year onward the boy lived mostly with relatives or was boarded out with tutors, and his dreamy nature agreed so badly with the discipline everywhere demanded of him that he

* brĕn tä′ nō

BRENTANO

reacted with pranks and a virtual refusal to absorb any learning. Despairing of his abilities as a student, his father brought him back to Frankfort at sixteen to apprentice him in the family business. But after two years, especially after Clemens had affixed a cartoon to a business letter mailed to London, Peter Brentano determined to dispose of him in a university.

Clemens entered the University of Halle in 1797 as a student of mines, but again ignored his studies. The next year, as a medical student, he was at Jena, where, surrounded by a flourishing intellectual atmosphere, he began his literary career. He associated with the romantic circle of Ludwig Tieck and the Schlegels, but found their theoretical endeavors uncongenial to his purely creative interests. He fell in love with Sophie Mereau, a minor poetess eight years his senior and wife of a Jena professor, but was unable to marry her until 1803. Meanwhile he completed a somewhat autobiographical novel, *Godwi* (1800), whose form, described by its subtitle, "A Novel Gone Wild," was typical of its period. As a student of philosophy he briefly attended Göttingen, where in 1800 he met Achim von Arnim, who later married his sister Bettina, the memoirist, and collaborated with him in collecting folk lyrics for the anthology *Des Knaben Wunderhorn.* With sufficient family funds at his disposal Brentano made no more pretense at a regular profession, but spent the next few years on the *Wunderhorn,* which, immediately after its appearance in 1805-08, took its place as one of the major formative influences on subsequent German poetry. While the *Wunderhorn* was being published Brentano and Arnim formed part of the nucleus of the younger romantic circle, which, from its center in Heidelberg, led the movement to uncover and bring to life the German medieval past.

Though deeply grieved by his wife's death in childbirth in 1806, Brentano was married within a year to sixteen-year-old Auguste Busmann, from whom, after constant quarreling, he was soon after separated, though not divorced until 1811. Both his marriages and his many love affairs were clouded by his changeable, often bizarre moods and his desire to have his partner serve as confessor and mother to him. He spent his whole adult life traveling from one city to another, never remaining in one place more than a few years. During and after the Heidelberg period he worked at a long, though never completed, cycle of verse romances, *Die Romanzen vom Rosenkranz*, and while in Berlin (1809-11) completed most of his fairy tales, which, with their genuinely child-like tone, are among the outstanding examples of the genre in German. In 1811-13, while on his family's Bohemian estate, he completed two ambitious dramas, *Die Gründung Prags* and *Aloys und Imelde*, which, like an earlier play, *Ponce de Leon*, have proved too formless for successful stage production. While in Vienna in 1813-14, he associated with prominent Catholic intellectuals and gradually shifted his center of interest to the Church. His creative work was virtually complete by 1818, though he published thereafter a number of religious writings, most notably his transcription of the visions of the nun Anna Katharina Emmerich, at whose sickbed, in Dülmen, Westphalia, he sat for five years (1818-23) taking dictation. He is buried at Aschaffenburg.

Even more than his fairy tales and other stories, Brentano's high reputation today rests on his poems, characterized by a seemingly endless inventiveness, an effect of folk-like simplicity, and a musical sense that is often said to surpass that of any other German poet. The lack of discipline of all but a few of his works was perhaps an inevitable condition for his type of genius.

Brentano's most famous narrative, "The Story of the Just Caspar and the Fair Annie" (1817), has appeared in translations by T. W. Appell (1847), L. Chapman (1849), and C. F. Schreiber (in the Pierce-Schreiber *Fiction and Fantasy of German Romance*, 1927). K. T. Kroeker has adapted a number of *Fairy Tales from Brentano* (1885). The

Emmerich visions, entitled *The Dolorous Passion of Our Lord Jesus Christ,* appeared in anonymous translation in 1862.

ABOUT: Prawer, S. S. German Lyric Poetry; Tymms, R. German Romantic Literature. [In German—see studies by J. Adam, R. Becker, H. M. Enzensburger, F. Gundolf, R. Huch, W. Kosch, R. Nägele, I. Seidel, and E. Staiger.]

H. L.

BRIDGET (*BIRGITTA), Saint (c. 1303-July 23, 1373), Swedish visionary, was born at Finstad in the central Swedish province of Uppland. Her father was Birger Persson, law-man of Uppland, one of the wealthiest and most influential men in the country. Her mother was Ingeborg Bengtsdotter, daughter of the law-man of Östergötland, Bengt Magnusson, of the royal Folkung family, and his second wife, Sigrid the Fair. Bridget, who as a child was extremely high-strung and, like her parents, devoutly religious, received a fine education. Her mother died when she was twelve or thirteen years old, and shortly after she was married, no doubt for political reasons, to the eighteen-year-old Ulf Gudmarsson, son of Gudmar, law-man of Närke. Her husband, who later became law-man of Östergötland, was weak-natured, dominated by the powerful and strong-willed Bridget. They lived at Ulvåsa in Östergötland. About her married life very little is known other than that it passed amid religious studies and mortifications. She gave birth to four sons and four daughters. Her religious teacher and confessor was Master Mattias, the foremost Swedish theologian of the time, who acquainted her with the teachings of Bernard of Clairvaux, which came to exercise a profound influence on her development. In 1341-43 Bridget and her husband went on a pilgrimage through Europe to Avignon in southern France and Compostela in Spain. On their way home Ulf was taken seriously ill and died shortly after arrival home. His death broke Bridget's heart and became the decisive moment in her life.

She had earlier had dream visions, but now her revelations began in which Christ urged her to become his bride and his representative on earth. Her revelations were received in an ecstatic condition, and when she awoke she wrote them down or dictated them to her confessors, and they were later rendered into Latin. She won the approval of ecclesiastical authorities that her revelations were of divine origin, and probably for publicity purposes, they were sent to the

* bĭr gĭt′ tà

Pope, along with critical remarks on some contemporary political rulers of Europe. A divine inspiration to found a religious order came to her. Her work for this idea met with approval from King Magnus and his Queen, and in about 1344 she founded the Order of St. Savior for men and women at Vadstena. In 1349 Bridget herself went to Rome in order to pursue her endeavors, to secure the Pope's confirmation of her order, and to work for the return of the Pope from Avignon to Rome. Bridget lived, with some shorter interruptions, in Rome until her death. In 1370 Pope Urban V gave her permission to found a nunnery of the Order of Augustine at Vadstena in Sweden. In 1372 Bridget made a pilgrimage to the Holy Land but was struck with illness. She returned the next year to Rome, where she soon died. Her remains were brought home to Vadstena, and in 1391 she was canonized by Pope Boniface IX.

St. Bridget's Order had a profound influence upon the cultural life of medieval Scandinavia, but her greatest gift to posterity was her literary works. Unfortunately, nothing of her own notations in Swedish, with the possible exception of two manuscript pages, is preserved. The Old Swedish version from the last years of the fourteenth century is largely a translation from Latin.

St. Bridget's collected works were edited posthumously and printed in 1492 in Lübeck. They consist of eight volumes of *Revelations*, edited by Bishop Alfonso of Jaén, one volume of the so-called *Revelationes Extravagantes*, the statutes of the Order entitled *Regula Sancti Salvatoris*, the edifying book *Sermo Angelicus*, and the so-called *Quatuor Orationes*.

Bridget's *Revelations* in Middle English translation were published in 1929 as *The Revelations of Saint Birgitta*, edited from the fifteenth century manuscript by W. P. Cumming.

ABOUT: Peacey, E. St. Birgitta of Sweden; Sharp, W. Where the Forest Murmurs; Steele, F. M. St. Bridget of Sweden; Walsh; J. J. These Splendid Sisters.

A. J.

*BRILLAT-SAVARIN, (JEAN) ANTHÈLME (April 1, 1755-February 2, 1826), French gastronome, was born in the little town of Belley in the district of Bugey (now Ain) into a family of prosperous and highly respected country lawyers and judges. On his mother's side he was a Récamier and a cousin of the celebrated

* brĭ yà′ sà và răN′

Mme Récamier. Following family tradition, he became a lawyer and was a member of the Estates General in 1789, representing Bugey. With political views of a moderate-conservative nature (he voted against both the establishment of juries and the abolition of the death penalty), he proceeded cautiously during the first years of the French Revolution and managed to escape the guillotine only by a combination of prudence and good luck. He held additional official posts as president of the Tribunal of Ain and as a judge in the Court of Cassation (court of appeal). In 1792 he became mayor of Belley. His moderation in the face of the Reign of Terror and his noble but hopeless efforts to prevent the introduction of its methods into his peaceful town resulted in his own downfall. His property was confiscated and he fled to Switzerland in 1794. In the same year he decided to seek a refuge in the New World and sailed for America.

Neither the dangers and upheavals of political revolution nor the discomforts of exile ever seriously disturbed Brillat-Savarin's digestion or his friendly, pleasure-loving disposition. His friend Baron Richerand described him as a practical philosopher who followed Zeno less than he followed Epicurus. He lived through and actively participated in earth-shaking political events. He is remembered not for this, however, but for his charming and witty disquisitions on food and the good life. Even as a refugee in Switzerland and subsequently in the United States he collected recipes, enjoyed society, and reflected on the all-essential subject of man's comfort and happiness. He spent two years in New York, supporting himself by giving French lessons and playing the violin in a theatre orchestra. He also traveled to Boston and Philadelphia, winning friends everywhere with his fool-proof formula for social success: "I spoke their language, dressed like them, took care not to be cleverer than they, and praised all their ways." In his *Physiologie du Goût* he recalls a visit to a prosperous farmer in Hartford, Conn., in 1794 during which he shot wild turkey, dined on stewed goose, corned beef and mutton, and with the eye of a connoisseur admired the farmer's four buxom daughters.

In September 1796 Brillat-Savarin returned to France. Restitution of his property was made, and he was reappointed to his post as magistrate in the Court of Cassation. From that time until his death he retained his high official rank—managing to survive all the vicissitudes of the Directory, the Empire, and the restoration of the monarchy. He had many honors and positions of dignity and responsibility—secretary to the German armies, member of the Legion of Honor, of the Society of Antiquaries of France, the Society for the Encouragement of National Industry. He published several serious works—*Vues et Projets d'Économie Politique* (1802), *Fragments d'un Ouvrage Manuscrit Intitulé 'Théorie Judiciaire'* (1818), and *Sur l'Archéologie du Départment de l'Ain* (1820). These are totally ignored today, and Brillat-Savarin has his immortality not for them but for a miscellaneous collection of anecdotes, recipes, and philosophical musings called *Physiologie du Goût ou Méditations de Gastronomie Transcendante*, which he published anonymously (he thought it unseemly for a magistrate to be known as the author of so light a work) and at his own expense in 1825. He had written the book in spare moments from his official duties and his active social life. It was truly a labor of love, and for all its wit it takes the subject seriously—"like a priest saying mass," was Balzac's description of it. The style is elegant, in the best epigrammatic traditions of French prose. The organization is loose, but the very informality of the book lends it charm. Brillat-Savarin wanders freely and happily through his subject, ranging from serious discussions of the scientific properties of food, of physical well-being, of sleep and of death, to rapturous descriptions of food he has eaten and practical advice on diet, obesity, and thinness. The part of the book most often quoted is the collection of aphorisms which begins it—the most famous of them, "Tell me what you eat: I will tell you what you are." Balzac's favorite was: "Dessert without cheese is like a pretty woman with only one eye."

Brillat-Savarin never married. He divided his time between Paris and a country estate where he lived with two unmarried sisters. Besides food his main delights were hunting and music. He was tall, plain-looking, and in later years, not surprisingly, he developed a "sufficiently prominent" paunch. He died at seventy-one of pneumonia.

There are numerous French editions of the *Physiologie*, the best known being the one published in 1838 by Charpentier, which includes Balzac's *Physiologie du Mariage* and his *Traité des Excitants Modernes*. The first complete English translation, *A Handbook of Gastronomy*, was published in 1883, but earlier translations of parts of the book

include F. Robinson's *The Physiology of Taste* (1854), L. F. Simpson's *The Handbook of Dining* (1859), R. E. Anderson's *Gastronomy as a Fine Art* (1877). A new and complete translation was published in 1925 with introduction by Arthur Machen (translator not named) and by M. F. K. Fisher in 1949.

ABOUT: Machen, A. *Preface and Biographical Note*, Physiology of Taste (1925). [In French—Balzac, H. de *in* Biographie Universelle Ancienne et Moderne, V (1843); Des Ombiaux, M. La Physiologie du Goût.]

BRINCKMAN, JOHN (July 3, 1814-September 20, 1870), Low German (*Plattdeutsch*) poet and writer, was born in Rostock, the son of a sea captain and merchant. He began to study law at the University of Rostock, but soon discovered his true interest to be literature, languages, and history. Politically, he was dedicated to the ideal of a strong, united Germany, and participated actively in students' organizations. In 1838 he was sentenced to three months' imprisonment for attempting to establish a new political club at the university. Although he was immediately pardoned, this experience destroyed his interest in further study and embittered him temporarily against his homeland. He traveled to New York, where he worked as a journalist, translator and as secretary for several foreign consulates, for Brinckman was proficient in English, Dutch, Swedish, Spanish, and Italian. In 1842, following a serious illness, he returned to Germany. He married Elise Burmeister, the daughter of a physician, in 1846, settling in Goldberg, where he taught at a private school. The revolution of 1848 revived Brinckman's political feelings, which he vented in satirical criticisms on the political, social, and religious conditions of his homeland. His attitude made him unpopular in Goldberg, and the following year he moved to Güstrow, where he taught school and operated a *pension* to supplement his meager income. Although he continued to write, his works never achieved sufficient success to free him from constant financial need. He died in Güstrow in 1870, the year in which the German unification he had desired was realized.

Brinckman's writings are based almost entirely on the lives and settings of his native Mecklenburg and treat the world of seamen and fishermen in small coastal towns. He chose to write in Low German, for he felt that the people could not be separated from their language. He excelled as a poet, and his volume of lyrics, *Vagel Grip* (1859), is considered his finest single work. The Low German poet Klaus Groth, whose influence is evident in this collection, regarded this book as one of the finest achievements of Low German verse and stated that it contained "more lyric treasures than almost all the rest of *Plattdeutsch* literature."

As a prose writer Brinckman, who was influenced by both the German writer Berthold Auerbach and by Charles Dickens, excels in his ability to render milieu accurately and realistically as well as in his gift for characterization. In this respect he resembles his contemporary Fritz Reuter, beside whom Brinckman now has taken his place as one of the outstanding prose writers of the *Plattdeutsch* language area. The animal fable *Voss un Swinegel oder dat Brüder Geiht Üm* (1854) has become one of the classic tales of Low German literature. His most popular work is *Kaspar Ohm un Ick* (1855), a sea story based on his father's life. Other notable prose works include the fairy tale *Uns Herrgott up Reisen* (1870), and the following writings which were published posthumously in 1886: *Peter Lurenz bi Abikur, Mottche Spinkus, De Generalreeder,* and *Höger Up.* Brinckman, who revered Shakespeare, favored among his own works the High German verse epic *Die Tochter Shakespeares* (1881), which remained incomplete.

ABOUT: [In German—see studies by A. Romer, W. Rust, W. Schmidt.]

D. G. D.

*BRUNETIÈRE, FERDINAND (July 19, 1849-December 19, 1906), French critic, was born in Toulon, the son of a high-ranking marine officer. He was educated at the *lycée* in Marseilles and then sent to Paris to prepare for the École Normale (the Sorbonne). In Paris the young boy indulged freely in his passions for art, literature, and the theatre. Unfortunately he neglected academic subjects such as Greek composition and he failed the entrance examinations. Many years later, in 1886, established as a brilliant critic, Brunetière returned to teach at the École Normale where he had failed to qualify as a student.

In 1869 Brunetière enlisted in the French army, and he saw active service during the siege of Paris. Disillusioned by the outcome of the Franco-Prussian war and too old now to reapply for admission to the École Normale, he took an exhausting job as a tutor in a school which crammed young students for the *baccalauréat.* For five years he drudged away at teaching all day and worked

* brü nē tyâr'

most of the night at his own studies, reading voluminously and writing his first book reviews and critical articles for the *Revue Bleue* and the *Revue des Deux Mondes.* No longer the impetuous and idealistic romantic of his youth, Brunetière developed into a tough-minded, original, dogmatic, but always stimulating critic. He became the bitter foe of romanticism, impressionism, naturalism, and Zolaism. He fought stubbornly against popular trends, took the "wrong" sides of issues (he was an anti-Dreyfusard, for example, not out of anti-Semitism but apparently out of a stubborn loyalty to the French army), made enemies everywhere. But the stormy course of Brunetière's reputation never obscured his essential soundness as a teacher and a critic. His students at the École Normale included such distinguished scholars-to-be as Gustave Lanson and Joseph Bédier. They and numerous others flocked to his lectures—bold, iconoclastic, splendidly organized, delivered in a fine dramatic voice.

In 1893 Brunetière was elected to the French Academy. In 1894 he was offered the directorship of both the *Revue de Paris* and the *Revue des Deux Mondes.* "His was a position of acknowledged influence and authority attained by perhaps no other man of letters of his time," Elton Hocking writes. In his time, Irving Babbitt observed, he was "the most influential judge of contemporary literature, just as Boileau was for the age of Louis XIV." Indeed, like Boileau he was a classicist and a conservative. But he was also a man of his own age whose vigorous mind had absorbed the significant scientific developments of the nineteenth century. He began his career as a rationalist and a positivist. The strongest influences upon him were Comte, Taine, and Darwin. Probably his most interesting contribution to criticism was his attempt to apply the Darwinian theory of evolution to literature, tracing the evolution of various literary genres through their births, developments, transformations into other types, or their deaths. The theory is presented in his *L'Évolution des Genres dans l'Histoire de la Littérature* (1890). In the course of time, however, Brunetière modified his own position, placing greater emphasis in his criticism upon the social and moral function of art, and moving steadily towards some reconciliation of science and religion. He found this at last in the Catholic Church, to which he was converted in 1900.

In spite of ill health which plagued him all his life, Brunetière worked with prodi-

125

gious energy. In his last years he was involved in bitter political and religious quarrels. He lost his position at the École Normale in 1904, "through the efforts of political enemies," Hocking writes; but a more crushing blow was the loss of his voice shortly after. Cut off from lecturing, he wrote even more industriously. He died in Paris at fifty-seven and was buried in the Montparnasse cemetery.

In all Brunetière produced about thirty volumes. His major works were the *Études Critiques sur la Littérature Française* (nine volumes, 1880-1925) and *Le Roman Naturaliste* (1883). He also wrote a history of French lyrical poetry, a monograph on Balzac and a manual of the history of French literature which was translated into English by R. Derechef in 1898.

Also available in English translation are *Brunetière's Essays in French Literature: A Selection*, translated by D. Nichol Smith (1898); *Art and Morality*, translated by A. Beatty (1899); *Balzac*, translated by R. L. Sanderson (1906); *The Law of the Drama*, translated by P. M. Hayden (1914).

ABOUT: Babbitt, I. Masters of Modern French Criticism; Columbia Dictionary of Modern European Literature; Hocking, E. Ferdinand Brunetière: The Evolution of a Critic.

BRUNETTO LATINI. See LATINI, BRUNETTO

*BRUNO, GIORDANO (1548-February 17, 1600), Italian philosopher, poet, and playwright, was born in Nola, in the Kingdom of Naples (then under Spanish rule), son of Giovanni Bruno, a soldier, and Fraulissa Savolina, whose first name suggests that she was of German origin. The child was given the name Filippo but took the name Giordano in about 1565 when he entered the Dominican order. In the monastery he received an excellent education in the classical authors and of course in the traditional authorities, Aristotle and Saint Thomas Aquinas. The young Bruno showed signs of heretical thinking early in life. In 1567 began the series of flights for freedom of thought which marked his tragic existence. He left Naples for Rome; then, discarding his monastic habit, he went to Venice, Geneva (where he may or may not have espoused Calvinism), Lyons, Montpellier, and Toulouse, where from 1579 to 1581 he taught and took a doctorate in theology.

* brōō′ nō

BRUNO

Wherever Bruno went, he talked and wrote. Iconoclastic, erratic, and brilliant, he never failed to draw an audience or to impress his listeners with his vast erudition. His thought was speculative and daring. In an age which still clung to authority, to the words and to the traditions of the Church Fathers and to the earth-centered Ptolemaic astronomy, Bruno struck out independently. He welcomed the Copernican system; he read the Stoics, the Pythagoreans, the Neoplatonists, the Arabic philosophers Averroës and Avicenna. On the basis of these and of his own independent thinking Bruno rejected many of the orthodox dogmas of the Church (e.g. the Trinity, the Immaculate Conception, and Transubstantiation) and proposed a simple religious creed based on love of the Divine which he found present everywhere in the universe. Philosophically he rejected Aristotle and his categories and conceived the universe as infinite, a Universal Intelligence. Matter, he believed, is never destroyed but is the source of all forms, moving, reshaping and reconstituting itself infinitely.

In 1581 Bruno went to Paris where he was offered a professorship provided he would receive the Mass. This he refused, but remained in Paris to give a course of thirty lectures so brilliant that they brought him to the attention of King Henry III of France. In 1583 he went to London. His host was the French ambassador, Castelnuovo di Manvissière, and he met many of the notables of Elizabethan England and lectured at Oxford. Up to this time Bruno's writings had consisted mainly of metaphysical treatises (including several tracts on Raymond Lully, the medieval "psychologist" who had a theory of mnemonics which fascinated Bruno), and one play, *Il Candelaio* (1582), a comedy that rather roughly (though often wittily) shows up the vices of his age. In England Bruno wrote his major literary works, all issued in the years 1584 and 1585. These (written in Italian) are *La Cena de la Ceneri* ("The Ash Wednesday Supper"), a series of dialogues (with four speakers) in defense of the Copernican system; *De la Causa, Principo e Uno* ("Of the Cause, Principle and One"), five dialogues on metaphysics with Latin and Italian poems; *De l'Infinito Universo e Mondi* ("Of the Infinite Universe and Worlds"), another metaphysical work containing several sonnets; *Il Spaccio della Bestia Trionfante* ("The Expulsion of the Triumphant Beast"), an allegorical poem on morals and ethics dedicated to Sir Philip Sidney (though it is now considered unlikely that Bruno actually knew him); *La Cabala del Cavallo Pegaseo* ("The Cabala of the Pegasean Steed"), a satire; and finally *De gli Eroici Furori* ("On Heroic Enthusiasm"), also dedicated to Sidney, a prose study with many sonnets on divine love.

Bruno returned to France in 1585 and resumed his life of wandering and exile, visiting Marburg, Wittenburg, Prague, Frankfurt, and Zürich. In general he fared no better in Protestant cities than in Catholic ones and found permanent refuge nowhere. In Frankfurt in 1591 he published (in Latin) his major philosophical works—*De Minimo, De Immenso, De Monadi*. Also in 1591 he accepted the invitation of a wealthy young Venetian, Giovanni Mocenigo, to come to Venice and tutor him in Lullian mnemonics. Bruno knew he was risking his life by returning to Italy. When Mocenigo turned against him (evidently because he discovered that his tutor could not instruct him in black magic), he denounced Bruno to the Inquisition in Rome in 1593. Bruno was imprisoned for seven years in the Castel Sant' Angelo. The charges against him included his denial of Transubstantiation, his attack on the Pope in his *Spaccio,* and various "absurdities" in his philosophical writings. Questioned many times during his long imprisonment, Bruno admitted many "errors" and proclaimed himself a loyal Catholic. He refused, however, to abjure his philosophical beliefs. In December 1599 he was brought to trial, judged an impenitent heretic, and sentenced to burn at the stake. His last words to his judges

were: "Greater perhaps is your fear in pronouncing my sentence than mine in hearing it." He was executed in the Campo di Fiori, in Rome, on the very spot where, on June 9, 1889, a statue of him was unveiled.

In 1603 all of Bruno's books were placed on the Index. They became very rare in the seventeenth century, and it was not until the eighteenth century that his influence on philosophy—particularly upon Spinoza—was recognized. It is perhaps the spirit rather than the work of Bruno which has carried his influence over the ages. J. Lewis McIntyre writes: "Both in France and Germany he has been recognized as the prophet, if not the actual founder, of modern philosophy, and as one of the earliest apostles of freedom of thought and speech in modern times."

The standard edition of Bruno's works in Italian and Latin was edited by F. Tocco in 1889.

Most of Bruno's philosophical works were written in Latin and have not been translated into English; but S. Greenberg translated *Concerning the Cause, Principle and One* (1950), and D. W. Singer translated *On the Infinite Universe and Worlds* (1950). *De gli Eroici Furori* was translated as *The Heroic Enthusiasts* by L. Williams in 1887-89. *The Expulsion of the Triumphant Beast* was translated by A. D. Imerti in 1964. Translations of his sonnets appear in many anthologies. The Warner Library has translations of a passage from *The Heroic Enthusiasts* and a selection of the sonnets.

ABOUT: Boulting, W. Giordano Bruno, His Life Thought, and Martyrdom; Frith, I. The Life of Giordano Bruno; Greenberg, S. The Infinite Bruno; McIntyre, J. L. Giordano Bruno; Nelson, J. C. The Renaissance Theory of Love; Singer, D. W. Giordano Bruno, His Life and Thought; Turnbull, C. The Life and Teachings of Giordano Bruno; Wilkins, E. H. A History of Italian Literature; Studies in Philology, April 1943. [In Italian—see studies by A. Guzzo, V. Spampanato. In French—see studies by P. H. Michel, E. Namier.]

*BRYNJÚLFSSON, GÍSLI (September 3, 1827-May 29, 1888), Icelandic poet, was born in Ketilstadir, in eastern Iceland, the son of a clergyman and scholar, Gísli Brynjúlfsson, who was drowned shortly before the child's birth. His mother, Gudrun Stefánsdottir, came from a well-established Icelandic family. The boy was educated at the Latin School at Bessastaðir and at the University of Copenhagen, where he specialized in law and in Old Norse philology. He became a lecturer in Icelandic history and literature at the university and remained there for the rest of his life.

Brynjúlfsson's career marked a significant variation in the pattern of Icelandic litera-

* brĭn yülf′ sön

ture. His interests and his work reflected predominantly European influences, in contrast to the general insularity of Icelandic culture. In large measure that influence was Byronic. Early in his life Brynjúlfsson met the Icelandic poet Grímur Thomsen, a widely traveled man, who introduced him to the poetry of Lord Byron. The Byronic influence was twofold—first shaping his poetry, second stimulating his interest in the struggle for Icelandic independence. As a poet Brynjúlfsson was almost entirely derivative. "The scholar and the propagandist," Richard Beck remarks, "too often overshadow the poet." What he wrote, however, was faithful to his Byronic model—passionate romantic poems with daring Byronic heroes and political poems full of revolutionary sentiments. His poems appeared in periodicals and were not published in book form until after his death when the volume *Ljódmaeli* appeared (1891).

In the cause of political freedom Brynjúlfsson followed with eager interest all of the European revolutionary movements of the 1840's. He was also interested in American politics. He wrote many articles, and in 1848 and 1849 he published an annual, *Nordurfari*, which reflected his liberal sentiments. His main achievement, however, was in disseminating the vigorous spirit of European romanticism. Beck calls him "the truest representative of Byronism as it appears in Icelandic literature."

ABOUT: Beck, R. A History of Icelandic Poetry, 1800-1940 (Islandica XXXIV); Journal of English and Germanic Philology April 1929.

BÜCHNER

*BÜCHNER, GEORG (October 17, 1813-February 19, 1837), German dramatist, was born in Goddelau, near Darmstadt, in the grand duchy of Hesse. His father, Ernst Karl Büchner, was a physician in the service of the Hessian government and during the Napoleonic Wars had been an army doctor with the imperial troops. His mother, the former Louise Caroline Reuss, was the daughter of a Hessian official. When Georg was three, the family moved to Darmstadt, capitol of the duchy. He grew up in a part of Germany notably affected by French revolutionary ideas and in a family that had never lost its revolutionary sentiments. In his studies at the Darmstadt *Gymnasium* he already showed the determination and breadth of interest that marked his activities in later life.

In 1831 he was sent to take up the study of medicine in Strasbourg, where his father

* bük' nẽr

hoped he could gain familiarity with the French language and ways of life. Strasbourg at that time was a place of refuge for liberals who had escaped from the repressive atmosphere of the German states. There he became engaged to Minna Jaegle, daughter of a preacher at whose home Büchner roomed throughout his stay in the city.

In 1833 he entered the University of Giessen, in his native province. That year the Hessian government had broken up the parliament, and Büchner immediately entered into radical activities. Early in 1834 he organized a secret society, with branches both in Giessen and Darmstadt, functioning chiefly as a propaganda organ to educate and prepare the Hessian people for eventual rebellion. With the collaboration of an older, much-respected revolutionary, L. M. Weidig, Büchner that year published a pamphlet, *Der Hessische Landbote*, which, in brilliant, explosive language, attempts to make the peasants more aware of economic ills. A warrant was issued for Büchner, but, apparently because of his elusive movements, the police delayed his arrest. Exhausted from the rigors of underground life, he spent the winter 1834-35 secretly at the family home in Darmstadt, occupying himself with readings in philosophy and history. His studies of the French Revolution culminated in his first creative work, the drama *Dantons Tod*, which, written in barely five weeks, he was able to publish in 1835 through the aid of Karl Gutzkow, a leader of the so-called

"Young Germany" movement in literature. *Danton* is the only literary work published during his lifetime.

With his fellow revolutionaries either in jail or in foreign lands, Büchner appraised the political cause in Hesse as hopeless, and decided to flee. Early in 1835, even before the appearance of *Danton*, he arrived in Strasbourg, where, turning from medicine to biology, he set out to complete his studies. By spring 1836 he had completed his dissertation *On the Nervous System of the Barbel Fish*, delivered before the Strasbourg Natural History Society and published by the Society. Literary activities were confined to his spare time. He translated two Victor Hugo dramas, *Lucretia Borgia* and *Maria Tudor*, to earn some money and worked at his more serious projects, a short novel, *Lenz*; a comedy, *Leonce und Lena;* and a tragedy, *Woyzeck*.

During 1835 Büchner had made contact with the University of Zürich to receive his doctor's degree and take up an academic position there. For a time he was unable to complete arrangements because of incidents involving German refugee revolutionists in Switzerland. Finally, in September 1836 he was awarded the degree *in absentia* through presentation of his Strasbourg dissertation. The following month he was allowed to enter Switzerland, gave a trial lecture on the cranial nerves, and was appointed *Privatdozent* by the University. During the remaining few months of his life he held demonstrations—long remembered for their vividness of presentation—in anatomical dissection.

When Büchner assumed his academic position, his senior professor at Zürich, the famed biologist Lorenz Oken, predicted a brilliant scientific career for him. He plunged into his work with the same efficiency and incisiveness of mind that had characterized the brief but spectacular political and literary careers already behind him. At the time he was struck by his fatal disease—apparently typhus—he was barely twenty-three, busy polishing his dramas and preparing zoological specimens for his classes. Now that he was in a regular profession he looked forward to an early marriage with Minna. But his diary also gives some evidence of a general weariness, a certain "autumnal fatigue of life," as he put it. He is buried at Zürich.

Büchner's literary position did not become fully established until the present century. His writings were first collected in 1850 by his younger brother Ludwig, a well-known materialist philosopher of the time. *Woyzeck*, generally considered his masterpiece, did not appear until 1879, in a text put together from moldy, scarcely legible sheets of paper by Karl Emil Franzos (the exact order of scenes, among other textual problems, still remains in question). Büchner's impact was first felt in the late 1880's, at the beginning of German naturalism, when he was championed by Gerhart Hauptmann. At the same time he was revived as one of Germany's social-democratic heroes. *Der Hessische Landbote* became one of the standard household books on socialism, and *Dantons Tod* was even printed in America, in German (1886), for distribution among socialist immigrants. But a far greater wave of interest in his work arose shortly before the First World War with the start of the Expressionist Movement, whose revolutionary dramatic technique and thematic interests were anticipated by him. His plays, especially *Dantons Tod* and *Woyzeck*, today hold a firm place in the German repertory and since the First World War have gradually become known in other countries. Considerable interest in Büchner outside Germany has come about through Alban Berg's atonal operatic setting of *Woyzeck* (*Wozzeck*, 1925).

Of the four works he left, only *Dantons Tod* and *Leonce und Lena* were actually completed. *Danton*, similar to other historical dramas of the time only in the colorful spectacle it offers of the period represented, gives a piercing analysis of the revolutionary process and the figures engaged in it. *Leonce und Lena*, in its quick-witted dialogue, courtly setting, and satirical purpose somewhat reminiscent of *Love's Labour's Lost*, is at bottom characterized by the same pessimistic attitude—relieved by jokes that serve only to underline the pessimism—that marks all Büchner's work. In the swift succession of short scenes that make up *Woyzeck* he created a modern *Everyman* from the tragedy of an inarticulate common soldier surrounded by an inhumane world. His only prose narrative, *Lenz*, one of the first German examples of realistic fiction, depicts an incident in the life of the eighteenth century poet Lenz at the time he approached insanity. Büchner also wrote a fourth drama, *Pietro Aretino*, which he considered his best work, but which, apparently because of its antireligious tone, was destroyed by his fiancée after his death. F. Bergemann edited the standard edition of his works in 1922.

The three extant plays were first translated into English by G. Dunlop (1927). *Dantons Tod* has subsequently appeared in a translation by S. Spender and G. Rees (1939) and *Woyzeck* in translations by H. Schnitzler and S. Ulman (1950—in the volume *New Directions in Prose and Poetry*) and by T. Hoffman (1955—in Eric Bentley's *The Modern Theater*, I). *Lenz* has been translated by M. Hamburger (1947).

ABOUT: Jacobs, M. ed. Dantons Tod and Woyzeck *(see introduction);* Knight, A. H. J. Georg Büchner; Modern Language Review, July 1953; PMLA, September 1929. [In German—see studies by F. Bergemann, D. Brinkmann, L. Büttner, H. Mayer, H. Pongs, H. Oppel, E. Schwarz, and K. Vietor.]

H. L.

*BUDÉ (or BUDAEUS), GUILLAUME (January 26, 1468-August 23, 1540), French humanist, was born in Paris, the son of a wealthy bibliophile, Jean Budé, and his wife, Catherine le Picart de Plateville. He studied law at Orléans but showed no special interest in the subject. After several years of living in dissipation and idleness, young Budé suddenly became fired with enthusiasm for study. He studied theology, philosophy, mathematics, medicine, the natural sciences, and Greek. In short, he undertook and soon mastered all of the scholarly disciplines of his age. The price he paid for this exhausting regimen of study, however, was a nervous disease that troubled him for the rest of his life.

Like many of his fellow humanists, Budé played an active part in political life. He served as secretary to King Louis XII; he went to Rome on a mission to Pope Leo X in 1515; he was present at the side of Francis I at the Field of the Cloth of Gold. It was under this monarch, a generous patron of the French Renaissance, that Budé enjoyed his greatest power and prestige. He persuaded Francis to establish a royal readership in classical studies (the Trilingue et Noble Académie) out of which developed the Collège de France; to found a library at Fontainebleau which became the basis for the Bibliothèque Nationale; and it was at Budé's urging that Francis refrained from prohibiting the introduction of printing into France (as requested by the Sorbonne).

Budé was personally acquainted with most of the great men of his age. He knew Erasmus (with whom he is often ranked as a leader of humanism), Sir Thomas More, and Rabelais (who probably studied Greek under him). He carried on an extensive correspondence in Greek, Latin, and French. About 1503 Budé married Roberte Le

* bü dā′

Lyeur, and they had eleven children. After his death his widow became a Protestant and moved to Geneva. One son, Jean de Budé, edited and published some of the works of Calvin.

Budé's works include *Annotationes in XXIV Libros Pandectarum* (1508), a commentary on the *Pandects* of Justinian which had considerable influence on the study of Roman law; a treatise on ancient coins and measures, *De Asse et Partibus* (1514); a work on linguistics, *Commentarii Linguae Graecae* (1529); and a defense of Greek philosophy against charges of heresy, *De Transitu Hellenismi ad Christianismum* (1534). His complete works were published in Basel in 1557.

ABOUT: [In French—see studies by L. Delaruelle and J. Plattard.]

*BUFFON, GEORGES LOUIS LE-CLERC, Comte de (September 7, 1707-April 16, 1788), French biologist, was born at the Château de Monbard, his family's estate near Dijon, at which, during his whole life, he spent a good part of his time, devoting his energies and fortune to shrewd business affairs and intellectual pursuits, primarily his research on animals. Although he was competent in demographic statistics and did significant experiments on electricity and burning mirrors, his fame lies in his natural history and his cosmological theories, wherein he served both literature and science in bringing fact to the public in elegant and imaginative style. In 1739 Buffon was named curator of the Royal Gardens in Paris, and he transformed this former medicinal center into a place of beauty and science. Supplementing his experiences with plants by his personal research on animals, he undertook his *Histoire Naturelle*, of which three volumes appeared in 1749 and thirty-eight more down to his death. Through this work his reputation spread rapidly, and he was elected to the French Academy in 1753, and to comparable foreign bodies, in Berlin, St. Petersburg, London, and Edinburgh. He worked in close collaboration with such younger scientists as Lacépède (1756-1825), and through them his research was continued and enlarged.

In his cosmological hypotheses (*Époques de la Nature,* 1778), Buffon made a considerable contribution through a moderate concept of gradual transformation by successive ages. The earth, torn from the sun by a

* bü fôn′

BUFFON

comet, gradually cooled and passed from liquidity to dryness; land masses emerged; animals appeared, and finally man. Buffon skillfully adapted this system to Biblical doctrine and thus avoided probable censure; thanks to his manner of presentation, such geological notions as stratification and erosion were widely disseminated and, with no appearance of revolt, the current temper of thought moved considerably forward. Buffon remained far more impersonal than Rousseau in his attitude toward nature, though certain romantic elements are evident. The grandeur of nature strikes man's imagination through the richness of her produce and the constant contrasts between beauty and awesomeness, notions which all but exclude good and evil. The two extremes of grandeur appear in gay landscapes and wild mountain scenes, in pleasant groves and threatening caverns. His emotional and imaginative tendencies are more than compensated for by an awareness of a new order of ultimate causes, free from religious connotation.

Buffon's theories of plants and animals represent essentially the same point of view, but depend far more directly on experimental evidence; indeed, a considerable evolution from a priori concepts to pure science marks the later volumes of his *Histoire Naturelle.* In a sense it belongs to the general movement of the Philosophes, but it stands apart in its taste and measure, and in its ambitions to please as well as teach. Combining experimental fact with elegance of presentation, it enriched thought and literature alike,

and has survived as a monument while more objective research has been forgotten. The style, noble and majestic, leads to constant meditations on the immensity of creation, the richness of nature, and the effect of variation of climate and habitat on living things. Buffon's descriptive approach emphasizes the external form of living things rather than their inner structure. Conceiving form as an aspect of function, he tends to classify according to behavioral and other moral criteria. He sets humanity in an isolated position: "Man is a rational being, animals lack reason . . . ; it is evident that man's nature is totally different from that of animals." He treats the horse as "man's most noble conquest," establishing a category of domestic animals within an anthropomorphic reference. He considers other creatures, such as the camel and fox, for the fitness of their form and the effectiveness of their external traits within their particular habitats: "We must recognize the swan . . . as the finest model that Nature has offered us for the art of navigation." In this way Buffon moves toward a modern concept of variability and transformism, and avoids the snares of dogmatism; simultaneously he illustrates the French language by his poetic imagery.

Buffon's *Discours sur le Style,* read before the French Academy in 1753, was long esteemed as the greatest expression of a doctrine of clarity and elegant thinking. It formulates, though in very general terms, the author's personal doctrine and practice, and postulates a renewed classicism: "Writing well consists of thinking, feeling and expressing well, of clarity of mind, soul and taste. . . . The style is the man himself."

The importance of Buffon in England and America is attested by a long series of translations and revisions of his major work, confused bibliographically by variations in the passages selected. The six volumes of W. Kenrick's version entitled *The Natural History of Animals* appeared in London in 1775-76, and *Buffon's Natural History Abridged* in Dublin, 1791, and London, 1807-10, also the title of W. Hutton's text of London, 1821 and 1828. The nine volumes of the W. Smellie translation, *Natural History,* were repeatedly reprinted in London (1791, 1798, 1802). There are four volumes of *The System of Natural History* of 1814, a new abridgment by B. Clarke entitled *The Book of Birds,* London, 1841; and, in Boston, 1831, and New York, 1857, *A Natural History of the Globe, of Man.*

ABOUT: Nordenskiöld, E. The History of Biology; Studies and Essays in the History of Science, 1946 (Buffon and the Royal Society of London); PMLA, LXXV (1900). [In French—see biography by Condorcet in Œuvres Choisies, 1859, etc.; Daudin, H. De Linné à Jussieu; Humbert-Bazile. Buffon, Sa Famille, Ses Collaborateurs . . . ; Roule, L. Buffon et la Description de la Nature.]

F. J. C.

*BURCKHARDT, JAKOB CHRISTOPH (May 25, 1818-August 8, 1897), Swiss historian and art critic, was born in Basel, the fourth child of Jakob Burckhardt, Pfarrer (Pastor) and afterwards Antistes (or Dean) of the Basler Kirke, and Suzanne Maria Schorndorff. Both his father and mother were descended from distinguished Basel families. The elder Jakob Burckhardt was author of books on history and theology, and sketched for a hobby—anticipating the dual interests of his son. Some of our knowledge about young Jakob Christoph is derived from a *vita* he prepared shortly before his death, to be read subsequently at his funeral. He relates here that his childhood was a happy one, marred only by the death of his mother when he was eleven. To his early schooling in the classics he attributed his ability "at all times to live on terms of familiarity with antiquity." Between school and university he made the first of his many trips to Italy, which inspired him to write poetry (under the name of Jacopo Bucardo).

Upon his return from his travels Jakob enrolled in the University of Basel with the intention of taking Holy Orders, but as early as 1838 he began to doubt the divinity of Christ, owing to the influence of one of his professors. Nevertheless he avoided religious controversies, both with his family and with theologians. Throughout his life he professed sympathy with the ethical, though not the dogmatic, side of Christian teaching. Despite his skepticism, he finished his degree in theology. It was Heinrich Schreiber, a professor of moral theology at Freiburg for whom he had done some work in the Basel archives, who persuaded him that historical research offered a worthy alternative to religion as a life calling.

Following his graduation in 1839, young Burckhardt traveled through Germany where his imagination was further stimulated by several great scholars with whom he came in contact. In Berlin he was fascinated by the lectures of Leopold von Ranke, a pioneer of modern historical method, and was introduced to Franz Kugler, professor of the history of art, then an innovation in the curriculum. Kugler, as well as Gottfried Kinkel, a somewhat erratic theologian-art historian whom Burckhardt met in Bonn, inspired the young scholar with a sense of history as the embodiment of man's aesthetic aspirations.

On his return to Basel in 1844 Burckhardt took up teaching duties in a *dozent* status, there being no regular appointment available.

* bŏŏrk′ härt

BURCKHARDT

He supplemented his teaching income by revising articles for the *Brockhaus* and contributing to periodicals. For a year and a half he edited the *Basler Zeitung* at the invitation of its proprietor Andreas Heusler, a wealthy lawyer. This experience was generally distasteful to him, but by plunging him into local religious controversies it gave him some insight into power politics, which served him in good stead in his historical writing. After a series of lectures on art in which he alienated the orthodox by his worldly attitude towards religious painting, he decided to turn his back on his native city and headed once more for Italy.

For the next decade Burckhardt was in and out of his favorite country. For a time he served as curator in the Academy of Art in Berlin (at the invitation of Kugler), and lectured intermittently in Basel "till he could bear it no longer" to support his living in Italy "as long as his money held out." Out of this Italian experience grew his first historical work, *The Age of Constantine*, and his *Cicerone*, a kind of *vade mecum* to the art student visiting Italy. On the basis of this latter essay (or *Tchitch*, as he called it), he was invited to help establish a new Polytechnique in Zürich. In this city he delved into the archives, which he found rich in materials that he was able to melt down into the great work on the Renaissance that he was then working on.

In 1858 the professorship of history at Basel at last became vacant, and Burckhardt at the age of forty settled into a quiet, secure academic life. Two years later appeared his *Civilization of the Renaissance in Italy*, a treatise on the origins and development of the modern age as it emerged in the Mediterranean world. The first study to attempt a synthesis of the epoch from the birth of Dante through the death of Michelangelo, Burckhardt's history is remarkable both for its breadth of erudition and its beauty of style. His work encompasses all aspects of culture —art, literature and religion, as well as politics. He envisioned the Renaissance in Italy as the period when modern man first discovered the beauty of the outward world as well as his own capacity for self-development. He depicts in graphic detail the paradoxical nature of the period—the most depraved corruption festering in the midst of the noblest beauty—which he attributes to the egocentrism and unbridled individualism rife in this age when the modern state was emerging. When first published, *Civilization of the Renaissance in Italy* attracted hardly any notice. Burckhardt received neither payment nor royalty for it, and eight years later the book was remaindered to another publisher. Fame came to him slowly and gradually. With its third edition the book began to "catch on," and since 1928, when its copyright expired, over half a million copies have been sold.

Always modest and retiring, Burckhardt never sought eminence, but was content with the local reputation he enjoyed in Basel and Zürich, where he attracted increasingly large audiences both of scholars and laymen to his lectures on an amazingly versatile range of subjects—history, art, literature. (Some of these lectures saw publication as the *Weltgeschichtliche Betrachtungen*.) A young scholar named Friedrich Nietzsche, who came to Basel in 1868 as professor of classical philology, sought him out, but Burckhardt remained aloof. However, Nietzsche was one of the first to recognize the greatness of *Civilization of the Renaissance in Italy*, and to bring it to the attention of others. As he avoided friends, so did Burckhardt avoid marital entanglements, breaking off his romances before they became "serious." He regarded his joint professorship of history and art as the most satisfying activity of his career. In 1885 his age and declining health compelled him to resign from the professorship of history, but he retained the professorship of art until 1893—four years before his death at the age of seventy-nine. Two of his outstanding works appeared posthumously: *Rubens* (1898) and *History of Greek Civilization* (1898-1902).

The standard translation of *Civilization of the Renaissance in Italy* by S. G. C. Middlemore first appeared in 1878. This is reprinted in the Phaidon edition (1945) *Weltgeschichtliche Betrachtungen* was translated by J. H. Nichols as *Force and Freedom* (1943). *The Age of Constantine the Great* was translated by Moses Hadas (1949). A selection of Burckhardt's *Letters* is available in a translation by Alexander Dru (1955). The outstanding German edition is the *Gesamtsausgabe*, edited by Burckhardt's disciple and successor at Basel, Heinrich Wölfflin, together with Emil Durr (1929-34).

ABOUT: Dru, A. *Introduction to* Burckhardt's *letters*; Goldscheider, L. *Introduction to* Civilization of the Renaissance in Italy (Phaidon ed.) ; Gooch, G. History and Historians in the Nineteenth Century; Heller, E. Disinherited Mind; Neff, E. Poetry of History; Trevor-Roper, E. Men and Events. [In German—see study by W. Kaegi.]

R. A. C.

*BÜRGER, GOTTFRIED AUGUST (December 31, 1747-June 8, 1794), German poet, was born at Molmerswende near Aschersleben. His father, Johann Gottfried Bürger, was an impecunious, phlegmatic, and not too intelligent pastor, given to visions; his mother, Gertrud Elisabeth, *née* Bauer, a shrewish, illiterate, and coarse woman, given to temper tantrums, made her family's life miserable. In addition to Gottfried she bore her husband three daughters, the second of whom, Friederike (born 1751), the poet's favorite sister, was to become the mother of the playwright Adolf Müllner.

Bürger's early education by his father was of the poorest sort. However, he grew up on a diet of Luther's Bible and Protestant hymns which left an indelible trace on his style and language. At the age of eleven he was taken in hand by his grandfather Bauer, who sent him to the municipal school at Aschersleben and next (1760-63) to the *Paedagogium* at Halle, a model institution founded by A. H. Francke, the pietist. There young Bürger was permitted to invent Latin and German verses patterned after Klopstock's Messianic muse. When it was discovered that he had indulged in satiric verse, he was promptly sent home. One year later he enrolled at the University of Halle to study theology. He became the protégé of the philologist C. A. Klotz, whose influence on Bürger, good and bad, was decisive. On his recommendation Bürger attempted his first translations of Homer's *Iliad* and of Catullus' *Pervigilium Veneris*, works which accompanied him throughout his life. But apparently the parties at the home of the young professor became the scandal of the town and in due course Bürger, now a stu-

* bür' gĕr

BÜRGER

dent of law, was called back by his worried grandfather. In 1768 he registered at the University of Göttingen, where his reputation did not improve until he became the intimate of Boie, Biester, and Sprengel, all serious students and eventually well-known authors and savants. The kind poet Gleim in Halberstadt also began to take a fatherly interest in him.

The period when Bürger lived in Göttingen was most propitious for German poetry. After him there arrived Hölty, J. M. Miller, Hahn, Voss, and the Stolbergs who, through the *Göttinger Musenalmanach*, edited first by Boie and Gotter, soon became nationally known. In their enthusiasm for Klopstock's Nordic message they called themselves the *Hainbund*. With them, although never one of them, Bürger now seriously turned to lyric poetry. As in the case of young Goethe, Herder's influence on Bürger cannot be overestimated. He avidly studied Shakespeare, Ossian, Percy's *Reliques*. Although his earlier poems in the *Musenalmanach* were anacreontic in manner, he soon turned to the serious artistic *Volkslied* and the ballad (or *Romanze*, as it was then called).

In 1772 Bürger was appointed justiciary over six villages in the province of Hannover. For twelve years he lived at Gelliehausen or Niedeck, holding an office for which he lacked talent and inclination. But this is also the period when he created his best work. Keeping in close touch with his friends, whose advice he always sought and

followed, he there produced painstakingly his "Lenore" (1773; rhyme and name from Günther's "An Leonoren"), "Der Wilde Jäger" (started the same year), "Spinnerlied" (1775), "Die Weiber von Weinsberg" (same year), "Das Lied vom Braven Mann" (1777), "Des Pfarrers Tochter von Taubenhain" (1781), and, beginning in 1776, the "Molly"-poems, amongst many others. He also published his first theoretical and literary writing, "Aus Daniel Wunderlichs Buche" (1776), which is indebted to Herder and Lenz, and he finally (1779) took over the editorship of the *Musenalmanach*.

In 1774 he married Dorette Leonhart, who was expecting his child, although he was in love with her younger sister Molly. Bürger lived with both, a secret which was closely kept. When Dorette finally died in 1784 (of her three daughters only one survived), Bürger married Molly (who bore a son and a daughter). In 1784 he returned to Göttingen as *Privatdozent*, lecturing on aesthetics (Kantian), language, and literature. Shortly afterwards Molly died in childbed. In 1789 Bürger brought out the second edition of his *Gedichte* (which contained sixty-five of the sixty-six poems of the first edition of 1778 and many later lyrics and sonnets), but it cannot compare with his early work. That same year he also was granted the title of professor without pay. His fantastic third marriage to the *Schwabenmädchen* Elise Hahn, who had published an anonymous love poem to him and promptly deceived him with various of his students, ended in divorce, and brought him close to bankruptcy. Their son Agathon, named after Wieland's novel, was brought up by Elise's mother.

Bürger early was acknowledged as one of Germany's greatest balladists. His influence extends not only to the romantics, particularly Brentano, but to more recent poets, such as Fontane, Börries von Münchhausen, and Lulu von Strauss und Torney. Herder called on him to create the German epic; Wieland in 1778 asked, "Who is there who will not soon know Bürger's poems by heart?" Both referred to his poetry as genuine *Volkspoesie*, as did his favorite pupil in Göttingen, August Wilhelm Schlegel. Bürger's aim was to realize Herder's call for a national, independent poetry, taken from life for life. He therefore searched for an immediacy and magic of expression, through onomatopoeia, refrain, and rhythm, which would remove the barriers between reality and imagination.

In addition to his own original poetry, Bürger translated from many sources. He undertook a translation of *Macbeth* (1783) and, with Schlegel, of *A Midsummer Night's Dream* (1797). He tried his hand at portions from the *Iliad* (1776-84), a novelette by Xenophon of Ephesus (1775) Virgil's Fourth Book (1777), passages from Macpherson's *Ossian* (1779), Raspe's *Baron Munchausen Tales* (1787; for a time he was assumed to have been the author of all the stories), and Franklin's *Autobiography* (1792). Posthumously there appeared a large number of his critical studies on philosophy, aesthetics, language, and literature.

In his "confession" to his third wife-to-be Bürger calls himself not an Adonis, although much favored by the ladies. By character he was temperamental, boastful, moody, easily depressed, but good-hearted. In his political views he was liberal (see "Der Wilde Jäger"), outspoken in his support of the French Revolution to the last.

During his last years Bürger lived in extreme poverty, forced to sell his inheritance and to do hackwork, and even compelled to ask the university for assistance. Like his first two wives he developed tuberculosis, and he died in the arms of his physician and biographer Althof. For over fifty years his grave remained unknown until in 1845 it was rediscovered in the cemetery at the Weenderthor in Göttingen.

In the nineteenth century Bürger's reputation suffered temporarily under the strictures of Schiller and Schlegel, although his poems and ballads lived on.

Bürger's "Lenore" and "Der Wilde Jäger" enjoyed great fame, the former having been translated into English considerably more than sixty times. William Taylor was the first with *Ellenore, a Ballad* (1790), followed by Sir Walter Scott, J. T. Stanley, W. R. Spencer, and H. J. Pye (all 1796). Later translations of "Lenore" include those by S. Whitman (1853), John Oxenford (1855), and Dante Gabriel Rossetti (1900). "Der Wilde Jäger" was translated by Scott and by William Taylor as *The Wild Hunter* (1796). It appeared anonymously under the title *The Wild Huntsman's Chase* (1798). "Der Raubgraf" was first translated as *The Freebooter* (1810). Selections from Bürger's *Gedichte* have appeared often in English, the ones most accessible probably being Vol. IX of *Columbia University Course in Literature*, ed. J. W. Cunliffe *et al.* (1928-29) and Vol. V of the Warner Library.

ABOUT: Blenkinsop, E. S. Bürger's Originality; American Literature (1936); JEGP (1934); Western Reserve Studies, I. [In German—see studies by A. Barth, A. E. Berger, E. Consentius, E. Grisebach, W. von Wurzbach, and P. Zaunert.]

R. L. K.

BUSCH, WILHELM (April 15, 1832-January 9, 1908), German poet and painter, was born at Wiedensahl in Hannover, the son of a storekeeper. At the age of nineteen, after attending the Polytechnic High School in Hannover for three years, he left to pursue his interest in painting, which he studied at the academies of Düsseldorf, Antwerp, and Munich. From 1859 to 1871 he worked as a comic illustrator for the Munich humor magazine *Fliegende Blätter* and subsequently for the *Münchener Bilderbogen*. He is considered to be the originator of the comic strip.

His first and still most popular book, *Max und Moritz,* which depicts boyish pranks in pictures and doggerel verse, appeared in 1865. His next works, *Der Heilige Antonius* (1870), *Die Fromme Helene* (1872), and *Pater Filucius* (1873), were written during the period of the *Kulturkampf* in Germany and represent satires on Catholicism. Other targets for Busch's criticism were Philistinism, false piety, and human weaknesses in general. He presents the entire gallery of human types and characteristics in a severely critical and unsentimental manner. He is an incomparable satirist, and his presentations in both picture and verse are masterfully done with the greatest economy of means. Because his satire often approaches the grotesque, it sometimes appears harsh and cruel. However, Busch, although influenced by Schopenhauer, was no pessimist, nor was he a moralist attempting to improve the world. His attitude toward life is best revealed in his definition of humor: "Humor is when one laughs in spite of everything." (*Humor ist wenn man trotzdem lacht.*)

Of his later works the best known are *Hans Huckebein, der Unglücksrabe* (1872), *Herr und Frau Knopp* (1877), *Fips der Affe* (1879), *Plisch und Plum* (1882), *Balduin Bählmann* (1883), and *Maler Klecksel* (1883). At his death in 1908 at Mechthausen in the Harz, Busch was celebrated in Germany as a major poet and artist. His popularity has shown no signs of diminishing, and he remains a perennial favorite with young and old alike.

A selection of Busch's works was first translated by W. H. Rogers in 1868 under the title *A Bushel of Merry-Thoughts*. A second collection of works was translated in 1878 by H. W. Dulcken with the title *Hookey-Beak, the Raven, and Other Tales*. *Hans Huckebein* also appeared in a translation of J. S. Rockwell as *Jack Huckaback, the Scapegrace Raven* (1872-76), and in anonymous versions as *The Amusing Story of Jack Hook-a-bone* (1872) and *Dick Dimple, and the Wicked Crow* (1878). *Max und Moritz* was excellently translated by C. T. Brooks in 1871. Additional versions were made by

135

A. Esdaile in 1913, and in 1932 by C. Morley, who used the title *The Adventures of Two Naughty Boys.* J. MacLush translated *Die Fromme Helene* in 1872 as *Naughty Jemina.* C. T. Brooks translated *The Tall Student* in 1873 and *Plisch and Plum* in 1883. *Edward's Dream* was translated by P. Carmus in 1909.

ABOUT: Ellis, R. W. Book Illustration; Wild, D. Graphis 6, No. 29 (1950). [In German—see studies by H. Adolf and O. Nöldeke, E. Daelen, P. Dangers, J. Ehrlich, H. Glockner, W. Kayser, K. W. Neumann.]

D. G. D.

BUSKEN HUET, COENRAAD. See HUET, COENRAAD BUSKEN

*"CABALLERO, FERNÁN" (pseudonym of CECILIA BÖHL DE FABER) (December 24, 1796-April 7, 1877), Spanish novelist, was born in Morges (Switzerland) and educated in a French boarding school in Hamburg. Her father was the eminent Hispanist Nikolaus Böhl von Faber, well known for his polemic on the rehabilitation of the theatre of Calderón as well as for his *Floresta de Rimas Castellanas* and *El Teatro Español Anterior á Lope de Vega.* As German consul, Böhl von Faber lived in Cádiz and it was there that he had met and married Francisca Larrea. From her father Cecilia inherited her enthusiasm for folklore, and from her Spanish mother, traditionalism and a strong moral sense.

At the age of seventeen, Cecilia went to Cádiz where she married Artillery Captain Planelles. She presently became widowed and in 1822 married the Marquis of Arcohermoso and settled in Seville. He died in 1835 and Cecilia then married the diplomat Antonio Arrom de Ayala, who, after losing both his money and hers, went to Australia, where he committed suicide in 1863. These unfortunate circumstances marred Cecilia's life and obliged her to seek consolation in religion and in literature. Under the signature of Fernán Caballero she published her best-known novel, *La Gaviota* (1849) in the Madrid newspaper *El Heraldo.* It enjoyed great success and Menéndez y Pelayo attributed to her "the supreme merit of having created the modern novel of Spanish customs." *La Gaviota* presents the destruction of the marriage of Stein, a German doctor, and Marisalada, "la gaviota," a fisherman's daughter. The plot is romantic, but the background is realistic; in the words of Fernán Caballero herself, "We are writing an essay on the intimate life of the Spanish people—their language, beliefs,

* kä bä lyä′ rō

stories and traditions. That part that could be called a novel serves as a frame for this vast picture."

In 1856 Fernán Caballero left her residence at Puerto de Santa María and moved to a house in Seville which she had received as a personal gift from Queen Isabella II, and it was there that she resided until her death.

After *La Gaviota,* Fernán Caballero published a number of novels, among them *Clemencia* (1852), *La Familia de Alvareda* (1856) and *Elia* (1857), as well as collections of songs, ballads, and folk tales (*Cuentos; Cuadros de Costumbres Populares Andaluzas; Adivinanzas y Refranes Populares e Infantiles*). The novels are significant in that they point the way to the regional novel of the second half of the nineteenth century, but artistically they are seriously hampered by the author's tendency to moralize and sermonize. Here, as in later regional novels, city life is considered the source of corruption and misfortune, while the country appears as the repository of all the traditional virtues.

The works of Fernán Caballero were well received outside as well as inside Spain, and there are translations into French, German, Dutch, English, Catalonian, and Russian. In Belgium her *Relaciones Populares* (1857) was translated for use as a school text.

La Gaviota was translated into English as *The Sea Gull* by J. L. Starr (1864) and by A. Bethell (1867); two selections appear in Vol. VII of the Warner Library. *La Familia de Alvareda* was translated as *Castle and the Cottage in Spain* by Lady Wallace (1861). *Elia* was translated anonymously in 1868, *Cuadros de Costumbres* as *National Pictures* in 1882. *Cuentos* was translated by Mrs. Pauli as *Air Built Castles* in 1887.

ABOUT: Brenan, G. The Literature of the Spanish People; Croce, B. European Literature in the Nineteenth Century. [In Spanish—see studies by L. Coloma, J. F. Montesinos, A. Palma.]

B. P. P.

CABEZA DE VACA. See NÚÑEZ CABEZA DE VACA, ALVAR

*CADALSO Y VÁZQUEZ, JOSÉ DE (October 8, 1741-February 27, 1782), Spanish poet, dramatist, satirist, was born in Cádiz of a family which was considered noble. The young Cadalso was educated first in Spain by the Jesuits and later in Paris. He traveled extensively in France, England, Germany, and Italy. He entered the army and had risen

* kä thäl′ sō ē väth′ käth

to the rank of colonel in the cavalry when he was killed by a piece of shrapnel at the siege of Gibraltar. He was a member of the Order of Santiago.

Cadalso was one of the most beloved Spaniards of the eighteenth century. He was physically handsome, fiery, of distinguished bearing, brave, intelligent, and an accomplished linguist. It is said that even the English in their trenches mourned the news of his death. By temperament and education, he was somewhat inclined to imitate foreign models and was much influenced by the French encyclopedists.

Among his numerous writings, the best-known is his *Cartas Marruecas,* published posthumously in 1789. Despite the similarity, Cadalso's work owes nothing to Montesquieu's *Lettres Persanes* except the idea for the title. These letters are supposed to be sent from a Moor visiting in Spain to a friend in Morocco. This device gives the author an opportunity to criticize and satirize not only Spanish society in particular but Western society in general. He shows himself to be socially liberal and humanitarian in, for example, his strong condemnation of the institution of slavery. In his preoccupation with the so-called "problem of Spain," he seems a predecessor of not only Mariano José de Larra but even of the Generation of 1898. Among Cadalso's other works can be mentioned the tragedy *Sancho García* (1771), noteworthy only for its faithfulness to classic principles; his lyric poetry *Ocios de Mi Juventud* (3 vols., 1821), much admired by some; *Los Eruditos a la Violeta* (1772), a satire dedicated to "those who claim to know much with little study"; and *Noches Lúgubres* (1792), a prose rhapsody which may have been suggested by Young's *Night Thoughts.*

The author's one great love was for the actress María Ignacia Ibáñez, called Filis in his works. After her untimely death, Cadalso was so distraught that he attempted to disinter her. This romantic and macabre incident later gave him the inspiration for his *Noches Lúgubres.* For his crime, he was exiled from Madrid and went to Salamanca, where he helped found a school of poets. Later, again in Madrid, he was a member of the celebrated poetic group, the Fonda de San Sebastián. His influence on such poets as Gaspar Melchor de Jovellanos and Juan Meléndez Valdés is unquestioned. Because of his melancholy, deep sentimentalism, and vehemence, Cadalso is generally considered a

precursor of romanticism. Some of his works were published under the name José Vásquez.

The most easily accessible editions of his works are *Obras de Cadalso* (3 vols. 1818); *Poesías* in the *BAE,* LXI; *Cartas Marruecas* in the *BAE,* XIII; and *Cartas Marruecas* in Volume 112 of the Clásicos Castellanos.

ABOUT: Cotton, E. *in* Liverpool Bulletin of Spanish Studies (1933, 1940); Peers, E. A. *in* Modern Language Review, XXI (1926). [In Spanish—Glendinning, N. Vida y Obra de Cadalso; Tamayo Rubio, J. Cartas Marruecas, Estudio Crítico.]

R. E. O.

*CALDERÓN DE LA BARCA, PEDRO (January 17, 1600-May 25, 1681), Spanish dramatist, was born in Madrid, one of four children of Don Diego Calderón de la Barca and Ana María de Henao (or Hainault). His father was an accountant employed in the royal treasury. His mother was of Flemish descent. The family was wealthy, so that Pedro and his two brothers were left well off though orphaned early in life. His sister became a nun.

Calderón's life was interestingly divided between the Court and the Church. He received his earliest education at the Jesuit Colegio Imperial in Madrid. In 1614 he went to Alcalá to begin ecclesiastical studies, apparently having been intended for the priesthood from his childhood. Upon the death of his father in 1615 he moved on to Salamanca, where he remained for the next four years studying canon law. His dramas were to bear the impress of his intensive scholastic learning.

Young Calderón was first lured by the literary life when he took part in a poetical joust held in Madrid in 1620 to glorify St. Isidore. In this competition he won third prize, eliciting in addition a tribute from the aging monarch of the Spanish theatre Lope de Vega: "In his youth he has gained the laurels which time as a rule grants together with hoary locks." The fledgling writer engaged subsequently in religio-literary festivals honoring St. Theresa, St. Ignatius and St. Francis Xavier. His first datable play is *Amor, Honor y Poder* (Love, Honor and Power) of 1623, adapted from a story by Matteo Bandello. Calderón's activities were not exclusively literary and ecclesiastical: in 1621 the three brothers were ordered by the court to pay 600 ducats as compensation for the killing of a man, and the scar on the dramatist's forehead was said to have been

* käl dä rôn' dä lä bär' kä

CALDERÓN

took place in his life at this time when he renounced the gaiety of court life and literary glory to embrace the priesthood, for which he had prepared himself years before.

His ordination in the Order of Saint Francis took place in 1651. For a brief period he was away from Madrid, acting as family chaplain and, beginning in 1653, as chaplain of Los Reyes Nuevos in Toledo. However, King Philip missed his entertainer and Madrid could not do without his service as a writer. So he was recalled to the capital city where he joined the Congregación de Presbíteros Naturales (becoming its chief chaplain in 1666) and was honored with the position of private priest to the King. He remained here to the end of his life.

Like his French contemporary Racine, Calderón after forswearing the secular drama consecrated his genius to the sacred drama. He became the official composer of *autos sacramentales,* sacramental plays that had been produced annually in Madrid since the institution of the Feast of the Blessed Sacrament by Pope Urban IV in 1264. For the rest of his life Calderón faithfully produced two *autos* every year, relating to the Eucharist ceremony, for Corpus Christi Day in late spring. His death occurred on May 25, 1681, just as he was preparing the *autos* for the Procession of that year. His last completed play was not an *auto* but a ceremonial play, *Hado y Divisa de Léonido y Marfisa,* written in 1680 to celebrate the marriage of King Charles II to Marie-Louise de Bourbon. With his state funeral ended the Golden Age of Spanish drama.

Five editions of Calderón's works were published during his lifetime—in 1636, 1637, 1664, 1672, and 1677 (the last without his approval). He was fortunate in his first posthumous editor, his good friend Juan de Vera Tassis y Villaroel, who based the excellent edition of 1682-91 on a list of titles that Calderón himself sent to the Duke of Verragua the year of his death. The canon as it exists today consists of 120 *comedias* (dramas, serious and comic), 80 *autos sacramentales,* and 20 additional minor pieces, such as *entremeses* (interludes), *loas* (panegyrical prologues), and *jácaras* (witty ballads).

Calderón's output was amazingly variegated, but with such productivity it was inevitable that the quality would be uneven. To be sure, not all of it was original. When hard pressed, he did not hesitate, as was the accepted practice of the times, to borrow plots, dialogue, even entire scenes from some of his successful predecessors. Many of his

due to a knife wound suffered in a quarrel over a woman.

Apart from a brief imprisonment because of satirical jibes in the play *El Príncipe Constante* (The Loyal Prince), directed at the court preacher who had publicly rebuked him for scandalous behavior, Calderón seems to have succeeded in ingratiating himself at court early in his career. For a time he served as *escudero* to the Duke of Frías and the Duke of Alba. In time his literary ability found favor with King Philip IV, and he became established as court dramatist and poet. In 1635 the opening of the Palacio de Buen Retiro was celebrated by a performance of Calderón's play *El Mayor Encanto Amor* (Love, the Greatest Enchantment). The following year he received the coveted Habit of Santiago in recognition of his achievement as a writer. The two decades from 1630 to 1650 mark the period of his greatest productivity. As occasion demanded, masques, romantic comedies, historical plays, tragedies, and religious dramas flowed from his pen.

During this period he also served as a soldier, possibly in Lombardy and Flanders, definitely in the quelling of the revolt of the Catalans in 1640. In this latter engagement he distinguished himself for bravery and was accordingly awarded a pension. In 1647 his mistress presented him with a natural son, who was named Pedro José. The death of the child's mother (name unknown) in 1648 together with the loss of his two brothers account in part for the profound change that

early plays, written to order for courtly occasions, are trivial and ephemeral. His mythological plays (*comedias mitológicas*), such as *Eco y Narciso,* based on Ovid's *Metamorphoses,* are of interest mainly as prototypes of his great religious allegories. His *Capa y Espada* (Cape and Sword) comedies which so delighted his contemporaries seem particularly dated today and not altogether suited to his somber genius. However, at least two of these, *Casa con Dos Puertas Mala Es de Guardar* (A House with Two Doors Is Hard to Protect) and *La Dama Duende* (The Ghostly Lady), retain a certain period charm.

In other plays Calderón turned his preoccupation with manners and social mores to more tragic effect. The recurrence of "honor" and the frequent echoings of sententious proverbs in his titles ("El Honor Calderoniano" is still a catch-word among his countrymen) reflect the curious social code prevalent in the aristocratic circles of his time, with its complex of loyalties to king, kinsman, lady, its hypocritical "face saving" conduct. One of the most powerful tragedies of this genre is *A Secreto Agravio, Secreto Venganza* (For Secret Grievance, Secret Vengeance), in which a husband furtively takes revenge for his wife's unfaithfulness while carefully absolving himself of any implication in crime. Others are *El Médico de Su Honra* (The Doctor of his Honor) and *El Pintor de Su Deshonra* (The Painter of His Dishonor).

From this courtly period, three dramas of Calderón's stand out as undisputed masterpieces. *El Alcalde de Zalamea* (The Mayor of Zalamea) dramatizes the conflict between civil and military law, resolved by the interposition of a benevolent king. In this moving tragedy Calderón greatly improved on his source—an identically titled play by Lope de Vega. *El Mágico Prodigioso* (The Mighty Magician), based on the life of St. Cyprian, is an analogue to *Faust* that later attracted the poet Shelley. Calderón's unique sensibility and thought are perhaps best distilled in the philosophic fantasy *La Vida Es Sueño* (Life Is a Dream) in which he explores such fundamental ideas as appearance vs. reality.

La Vida Es Sueño displays the mystical bent that manifests itself most vividly in the *autos sacramentales.* In fact Calderón subsequently transformed this symbolic drama into an *auto,* elevating the hero into the archetype of Man beset by the powers of Light and Darkness. This represents one type of the *auto,* akin to the medieval morality, with its cast of characters made up of personified virtues and vices, plays bearing such titles as *El Gran Teatro del Mundo* (The Great Theatre of the World), *El Pleito Matrimonial del Cuerpo y el Alma* (The Marriage of the Body and the Soul). Many of the *autos* are closer in form to the mystery cycles—dramatized saints' lives or episodes from the Old Testament and New Testament, such as *Los Cabellos de Absolón* (The Locks of Absalom), *Judas Macabeo* and *La Viña del Señor* (The Vineyard of the Lord) based on a parable from the Gospel of St. Matthew. One of the most famous, *La Cena del Rey Baltasar* (The Feast of Belshezzar), links the two traditions in its conclusion in which Daniel, here made to represent the Wisdom of God, replaces Belshezzar's pagan banquet with a vision of The Last Supper.

Calderón brought the time-hallowed *auto* to its greatest perfection. These consecrational dramas played a crucial part in European religious history as the embodiment of the Counter Reformation. Setting forth the divine mysteries in vigorous sensuous imagery, boldly visualizing the beauty of grace and the awfulness of sin, Calderón's *autos* have been likened to baroque sermons. They continued to be produced for almost a century after his death, until in 1765, considered out of keeping with newer modes of religious observance, they were prohibited by official decree. We can never hope to reproduce their original festive surroundings, the music, the spectacular procession, the gaily decked *carros* (moving platforms) on which they were performed—but, removed from their polemical context, Calderón's *autos* remain strangely disturbing parables of man's moral life.

Calderón's reputation has suffered its vicissitudes. Idolized during his lifetime, he fell out of fashion in the very next century. Then in the early nineteenth century, championed by influential German critics like Lessing, Herder, and Schlegel, he became celebrated along with Shakespeare, whom he probably never knew and with whom he has little in common, as the beacon-light of a new literature. He suffered another period of decline later in the century owing to his editor Menéndez y Pelayo's predilection for Lope de Vega. Today he has his established niche in Spanish literature, just below his great predecessors Lope and Tirso de Molina. He was not as great as they in fertility of invention or power of characterization; his imagery sometimes is overly tortuous, his language clouded by Gongoristic obscurity. Nevertheless his baroque spiritual

139

sensibility leaves a haunting impression on the mind. Unfortunately, owing to a paucity of translation, most English and American readers have remained cut off from the splendid, if decadent, world of the great dramatist whom James Russell Lowell called an "Arab soul with Spanish feathers."

Scenes from *El Mágico Prodigioso* and verses from *La Cisma de Inglaterra (The Schism of England)* were translated by Shelley (1824). Several of the better known plays are available in very free translation by Edward FitzGerald in his *Eight Dramas of Calderón* (1853). Some plays were translated by Denis Florence McCarthy in his *Dramas of Calderón, Tragic, Comic and Legendary* (1853), and several of the *autos* are accessible in English through the same author's *Mysteries of Corpus Christi* (1867). Another selection of the plays is available in the translation by Norman Maccoll (1888). *La Vida Es Sueño* was translated for the English stage by Frank Birch and J. B. Trend (1925) and by W. E. Colford in 1958. The best editions of his works in Spanish are those of Marcelino Menéndez y Pelayo (1888), Angel Valbuena Prat (1926, 1927) and Juan Eugenio Hartzenbusch (1944-45).

ABOUT: Brenan, G. The Literature of the Spanish People; Chase, G. Music in Spain; Curtius, E. European Literature and the Latin Middle Ages; Fitzmaurice-Kelly, J. Chapters on Spanish Literature; Frye, P. Visions and Chimeras; Gassner, J. Masters of the Drama; Leech, C. Shakespeare's Tragedies and Other Studies in Seventeenth Century Drama; Madariaga, S. de, Shelley and Calderón; Nicoll, A. World Drama; Northup, C. Three Plays by Calderón; Perry, H. Masters of Dramatic Comedy and Their Social Themes; Sloman, A. E. Dramatic Craftsmanship of Calderón; Trend, J. "Calderón and the Spanish Theatre of the Seventeenth Century" *in* Seventeenth Century Studies Presented to Sir Herbert Grierson; Weir, L. The Ideas Embodied in the Religious Drama of Calderón. [In Spanish—see studies by A. Valbuena Prat and E. Frutos Cortés.]

R. A. C.

*CALVIN, JEAN (JOHN) (July 10, 1509- May 27, 1564), French theologian and leader of the French Reformation, was born in Noyon, Picardy, son of Gérard Cauvin (later latinized to Calvinus or Calvin), a notary, and his wife Jeanne Lefranc, daughter of a prosperous innkeeper. The boy was educated in the household of the aristocratic de Hangest family, for whom his father performed certain business offices. He showed so much promise that he was given church benefices at the age of twelve which provided money for his advanced education. By 1523 he was in Paris, registered at the Collège de la Marche in the University of Paris. He later transferred to the university's Collège de Montaigu. Before his nineteenth birthday Calvin had his master of arts degree, but

* kăl′ vĭn; kȧl văn′

CALVIN

instead of embarking on a career in the church, he went to Orléans to begin the study of law. A year later Calvin moved to Bourges, still nominally a law student but actually engrossed in the study of languages and literature under the Italian scholar Andrea Alciati. Here he learned Greek and first read the New Testament in its original language. His enthusiasm for learning led him on to the study of Hebrew, but he did not completely neglect his law studies and received his doctorate in law at Orléans in 1532.

This unusual combination of theological, humanistic, and purely secular education proved of inestimable value to Calvin in later years when he ruled Geneva as both its temporal and its spiritual leader. Up to the time that he took his law degree, however, and returned to Paris, there is no evidence that Calvin was questioning the fundamentals of his Roman Catholic faith. He had by this time (1532) published a brilliant Latin commentary on Seneca's *De Clementia*, but the work cast no shadow whatever upon his religious orthodoxy. Yet some time within the following year Calvin underwent a "sudden conversion" in which he made his break with Rome and became a Protestant. He was immediately in danger of arrest and was saved only by the protection of powerful friends. Recognizing the danger of remaining in France, he fled to Basel where he continued his study of Hebrew and began work on his epoch-making *Institution de la Religion Chrestienne* (Institutes of the Christian Religion, 1536), described as "one of the few books that have profoundly affected the course of history."

Calvin finally settled in Geneva where, except for a three-year exile in Strasbourg from 1538 to 1541, he spent the rest of his life. Geneva became the headquarters of Calvinism, and Calvin ruled both the city and the church. He established a veritable theocracy; he recodified the laws; he founded the university; he originated and enforced sanitary reforms—all this side by side with establishing and enforcing strict moral and religious discipline. He found time, in the midst of all these duties, to write voluminously—sermons, commentaries on the Bible, polemical works, letters. All these, like the *Institutes*, are distinguished by a vigorous and lucid style and profound erudition. But it is the *Institutes* which stands as a monument of French prose (though originally written in Latin and not translated into French until 1541). It is the first serious prose work of its kind in the language; its style is forceful, eloquent, and dignified. John T. McNeill writes that it is "a French classic, and through it Calvin, with no rival except Rabelais, stands in the van of the fathers and creators of the French literary tradition."

The *Institutes* was begun simply as a manual of Christian doctrine, but, as expanded in later editions, it became a complete outline of Calvin's theology and the source-book of the Protestant movement. The foundation of his theology was of course the teaching of the German reformer Martin Luther, but Calvin developed his system far beyond all his predecessors. Briefly stated, the Calvinist doctrine sees as man's supreme aim the knowledge of God. To this end man has the Scriptures, but in his way lies the formidable obstacle of his corruption, the taint upon all the seed of Adam. Man finds salvation through Jesus Christ, but he cannot be united to Christ—and therefore saved—unless he has Grace, unless God has predestined him for salvation.

It has been observed that Calvinism, with its inflexible division of mankind into the elect and the damned, is a rigid, harsh theology. In practice it often proved so. But the religious history of Europe in the sixteenth and seventeenth centuries is not a gentle story anywhere. Probably the most deplorable act of Calvin's administration in Geneva, from the modern point of view, was the burning of the Spanish Anabaptist Michael Servetus, but weighed against the religious persecution throughout Europe in this period such an event loses its unique horror. Calvin's followers were generally men of stern and strict discipline—the Presbyterians under John Knox in Scotland, the Puritans in New England—but their honesty, their integrity, and their sincerity have never been seriously challenged.

The significance of Calvinism in the modern world is too vast to be more than merely suggested here. Though an ascetic himself, strongly opposed to the mere accumulation of material goods and wealth, Calvin provided indirectly a kind of spiritual basis for modern-day capitalism. In emphasizing diligence, frugality, hard work, and thrift, in stressing the individual aspect of Salvation, in suggesting that success is a mark of God's blessing and calamity His curse—Calvin offered, as R. H. Tawney has pointed out, "the first systematic body of religious teaching which can be said to recognize and applaud the economic virtues." Wherever Calvinism traveled in the Old World and the New World during the seventeenth century, it was accompanied by industry, prosperity, and ultimately some form of political liberty. Its intellectual influence—much modified but basically unchanged from Calvin's own day—remains strong in the Protestant theology of the twentieth century—especially in the works of Karl Barth, Emil Brunner, and Reinhold Niebuhr.

Calvin himself remains at the center of his system—stern. steadfast, but also (as his more objective biographers point out) a man who balanced his strength with his weakness, his high-minded idealism with his fanatic zeal, his warmth and friendliness with violent temper and unyielding severity. He drove himself relentlessly and worked without rest. For most of his adult life he was ill and suffered constant pain. In his last year, suffering from tuberculosis and a multitude of other ailments, he had to be carried to church to preach his sermons. Calvin married a widow, Idelette de Bure, in 1540 in Strasbourg. Their only son died in infancy, and she died in 1549. Accounts of Calvin's life are often marred by the prejudices or the uncritical admiration of the writers, but a just summation is offered by John T. McNeill: "He was no paragon with the mind of an archangel, nor was he a finished saint. Nor yet was he a malicious and inhuman tyrant, but, rather, a highly gifted and unreservedly dedicated man, whose moral greatness was marred by serious defects."

The standard edition of Calvin's writings was published in Strasbourg in 59 volumes, 1863-1900. A new critical edition of the *Institution de la Religion Chrestienne*, edited by

J. D. Benoit, is being published in Paris. Volumes I and II appeared in 1957.

An English translation of Calvin's works, in 48 volumes, was published by the Calvin Translation Society, Edinburgh, 1843-55. There are several separate translations of the *Institutes,* among them an edition by H. T. Kerr (1939). His letters were translated by D. Constable (1855-57); his *Instruction in Faith* by P. T. Furhmann (1949).

ABOUT: Among the many biographies of Calvin and studies of Calvinism in English or in English translation, the following are noteworthy: Breen, Q. John Calvin: A Study in French Humanism; Dyer, T. H. The Life of John Calvin; Hunt, R. N. C. Calvin; Mackinnon, J. Calvin and the Reformation; McNeill, J. T. The History and Character of Calvinism; Reyburn, H. Y. John Calvin: His Life, Letters, and Work; Tawney, R. H. Religion and the Rise of Capitalism; Walker, W. John Calvin, the Organizer of Reformed Protestantism; Warfield, B. B. Calvin and Calvinism.

"CAMILLO." See CASTELLO BRANCO, CAMILLO

CAMÕES

*CAMÕES, LUIZ DE (1524?-1580), Portugal's greatest poet, was probably born in Lisbon, although two other cities, Coimbra and Evora, also contend for the honor. His father, Simon Vas de Camões, was an officer in the Portuguese navy who died, it is believed, in a shipwreck near Goa, shortly after the birth of his only son. Through his father, Luiz could claim descent from a noble Galician family. His mother, Ana de Macedo, also belonged to a great family of Santarem.

The poet's childhood and early youth were passed in Coimbra under the tutelage (according to one tradition) of a relative named Bento who was a canon. He probably was educated at the University of Coimbra, called "a second Athens" by a contemporary because of its strong classical curriculum. An early romance with a young lady of Coimbra (unidentified) is celebrated in some of his first poems, written on Petrarchan models.

About 1542 he left Coimbra to settle in the capital city of Lisbon, where his aristocratic background assured him a place in the circle that surrounded King João III. Here for the next four years he cut something of a figure as a dashing courtier-poet. To this period belong a number of lyrics and his three plays *(autos)—Amphitriões, Filodemo,* and *El Rei Seleuco.* His impassioned romance with a lady-in-waiting to the queen, Caterina de Ataide (the Natercia of his poems), led eventually to his disgrace at court. The parents of the lady, one gathers, objected to the

* kà moiɴsh'

attachment because of the poverty of the young poet, and were instrumental in bringing about his banishment. Caterina nevertheless continued to figure in his poems as his Beatrice.

Cast off from noble patronage, Camões, after a brief period of retirement at Ribatejo, got his first taste of military service as a soldier in Africa where he spent two years. He lost his right eye in a battle before the walls of Ceuta in Morocco. His subsequent return to Lisbon in a vain effort to restore himself to favor led to a street fight in which he wounded a minor palace functionary. As a result he was cast into prison, from which he was released several months later on condition that he join an expedition just then setting out for India. So it came about that he embarked on March 26, 1553 on the "S. Bento" for that hazardous life of the warrior-adventurer that was to be transmuted into his masterpiece, *Os Lusiadas* (The Lusiads). Although he was enlisted for only three years, he was destined not to see his native land again for seventeen years.

What little is known about this most fascinating period of his life has been gleaned from some of his poems and particularly from a few surviving letters. He saw service in Goa where he had the opportunity to observe at close hand the lives and habits of the Hindus as well as primitive peoples of India. He took part in military campaigns up the Malabar Coast and as far east as the Red Sea. There is a record of a performance of his play *Filodemo* before

Governor Francisco Barreto in Macao, where to this day a grotto still enshrines his memory. During the almost two decades of his expatriation Camões never ceased to pour forth poetry, and during this time most of *The Lusiads* was written. His voyage home after his military duty ended was as extended and as fraught with perils as that of Odysseus. Among his recorded adventures are a sojourn with Buddhist monks in China, and a shipwreck off the coast of the Mekong River in Siam, in which he lost all his possessions except the manuscript of his great poem to which he clung while he swam to land.

He finally reached Lisbon once more, broken in health, in the spring of 1570. Two years later, owing to the good offices of a patron, Don Manuel, appeared *The Lusiads,* which brought him immediate fame and honor. He was granted a small pension in reward for his service to the state and for his "book of the things of India." His last years are wrapped in the mist of legend, but appear to have been sad ones. He died of a fever that assaulted the city of Lisbon in 1580, by a stroke of destiny the very year that Portugal lost her independence to Philip II of Spain. Exactly three centuries later, in 1880, his supposed remains (his real final resting place has never been established) were transferred to the national pantheon at Belem and placed near the tombs of King Sebastian and Vasco da Gama.

Camões wrote in virtually all the major genres of Renaissance poetry. Besides the epic and the verse dramas, his canon includes sonnets, odes, elegies, and eclogues. Some of these shorter pieces were written in Castilian, strongly influenced by the Toledan poet Garcilaso de la Vega, whom he very much admired. His three plays contain charming verses, but generally he seems to have had little genius for drama. According to his first biographer, Diogo do Couto, Camões was at work on a collection of his lyric poems, near the time of his death, which he intended to call *El Parnaso,* but nothing is known of the fate of this work. All his lyric poems, with the exception of one ode (published in Orta's *Coloquios* in 1563), were posthumously published. The first edition, entitled *Rhythmas,* came out in 1595. Subsequent editions have added to the number, but the complete canon is not established to this day.

The work which assures Camões' immortality is *The Lusiads,* one of the world's great epics, in which he incorporated the history and traditions of his native land, and glorified its heroes. Its title signifies "Sons of Lusus," the legendary progenitor of the Portuguese people. Written in ten cantos of *ottavo rima,* the style established by Ariosto and Boiardo, *The Lusiads* relates the voyages of Vasco da Gama that led to his discovery of the sea route to India in 1498. Although the nominal period of time covered is two years, Camões manages by various devices of epical narrative to extend his span backwards and forwards, encompassing virtually all the great events of Portuguese history. The entire *Lusiads* is redolent of Camões' wide classical learning, but in style and structure, from the ringing opening lines on, it is particularly influenced by the *Aeneid.* Camões too was celebrating the establishment of an empire on foreign shores by a people beset with perils both by sea and land. It was his boast, however, that his hero would put Odysseus out of court and even "rob the wandering Trojan of his fame."

Despite its derivativeness, *The Lusiads* is in many ways a unique work. Vasco da Gama combines the guile of Odysseus with the stoical courage of Aeneas, but as a character seems earthier than either. Of all epics, this story of Vasco da Gama is the most closely rooted in actual events (some observed at first hand by the author), giving it a remarkable vividness and immediacy not possible to its classical models. *The Lusiads* presents not only authentic history but an exotic travelogue as well, in which one becomes immersed in the strange atmosphere of the Orient as it first opened itself out to Western eyes. More than any other work, it represents the adventures not of a single man but of an entire civilization.

The Lusiads more than bore out its author's prediction: "My song shall spread wherever there are men." Twelve thousand copies were printed within a quarter century of Camões' death. It has been continuously in print since then. Though it has never achieved the universal popularity of the Homeric epics or the *Aeneid,* probably because of its intense nationalism, fellow writers have never ceased to pay tribute to the author of *The Lusiads.* Milton undoubtedly read the work in the contemporaneous Fanshawe translation, for several geographical descriptions in *Paradise Lost* echo it. Later Camões was celebrated in poems by Byron, Wordsworth, and Elizabeth Barrett Browning. Portugal having been the first European nation to extend the bounds of Western civilization, *The Lusiads,* as Sir Maurice Bowra declares, is "the first epic poem which in its grandeur and universality speaks for the modern world."

The standard modern edition, in Portuguese, of his works is that of Hernani Cidade (2 vols. 1946, 1950).

The first English translation of *The Lusiads* was that of Sir Richard Fanshawe (1655). This was reprinted, with introduction by Jeremiah D. M. Ford, in 1940. There has been a distinguished line of translators in between, including William Julius Mickle (1776), Thomas Moore Musgrave (1826), Edward Quillinan (1853), Sir T. Livingston Mitchell (1854), J. J. Aubertin (1878), Sir Richard Francis Burton (1880), Robert Ffrench Duff (1880). The most recent verse translation is that of Leonard Bacon (1950). Since then it has been translated into prose by William C. Atkinson (1952). Selections of the poems have been translated by Lord Viscount Strangford (1803), Felicia Hemans (1819), J. J. Aubertin (1881, with Portuguese text), and Sir Richard Francis Burton (1884).

ABOUT: Adamson, J. Memoirs of the Life and Writings of Luis de Camoens; Bacon, L, Camões and the Glory of Portugal *(in* Five Gayley Lectures); Bell, A. Luis de Camões, Portuguese Literature; Bowra, M. From Vergil to Milton; Burton, R. Camoens, His Life and His Lusiads; Freitas, W. R. Camoens and His Epic; Gosse, E. Silhouettes; Hart, H. H. Luis de Camoens and the Epic of the Lusiads; Hutson, A. & McCoy, B. Epics of the Western World; Starrett, V. Books Alive; Woodberry, G. Inspiration of Poetry. [In Portuguese—Cidade, H. Luis de Camões.]

R. A. C.

CAMPANELLA, TOMMASO (September 5, 1568-May 21, 1639), Italian philosopher and poet, was born at Stilo, in Calabria, of a poor family. His father was illiterate. Young Campanella was put into a monastery at an early age. At fourteen he entered the Dominican order as Fra Tommaso (he had originally been named Giovan Domenico). Years later he admitted that it was his desire for education rather than his religious fervor that had led him into monastic life. He read widely but aimlessly until he came upon the writings of the anti-Aristotelian philosopher Bernardino Telesino, whom he admired, Campanella wrote, "because he depended on the nature of things, not the sayings of men."

Campanella's first philosophical work was a Latin treatise reflecting the Telesian doctrine—*Philosophia Sensibus Demonstrata* (Philosophy Demonstrated by the Senses, 1589). He was also deeply interested in the occult, in astrology and prophecy. His intellectual make-up was, indeed, a curious combination of scientific or pseudo-scientific rationalism and medieval mystic tradition. It

quickly brought him under the scrutiny of the Roman Inquisition, and he served the first of many prison terms in 1591-92. A year later he was again arrested, tortured, and imprisoned. During this imprisonment he wrote industriously. He was robbed of his manuscripts, but he continued to write.

In 1595 Campanella abjured his heresy and was released. He then became involved in a conspiracy to overthrow the Spaniards in Calabria and establish a religious republic which would be the foundation of a universal republic to be established by Spain. The plot was discovered by the Spaniards, and Campanella, along with more than one hundred others, was arrested, tortured, and put on trial for heresy. He saved his life only by simulating madness (though in view of his tortures, it is not inconceivable that he really did lose his reason for a time at least). After a trial that lasted one year, he was condemned to life imprisonment.

Campanella spent the next twenty-seven years in prison—several of them in chains in a dungeon. He was released in 1626 but enjoyed freedom for only one month. Rearrested, he was a prisoner until 1628 when he was at last released through papal intervention and given a small pension. Strangely enough, in spite of all the charges of heresy and the unmistakable evidence of his iconoclasm, Campanella was not opposed to the papacy. He completely rejected the Protestant Reformation. "Campanella was a staunch Catholic, and he wanted to unite the world under the standard of the Catholic faith," Marie Louise Berneri wrote. "He sought to modernize the Church rather than to reform it." He therefore enjoyed a degree of papal protection. This was not enough, however, to give him complete security. In 1634, facing a new trial, he fled to France. He sought the patronage of the King of France and of Cardinal Richelieu, but he had little success. He died in a Dominican convent in Paris.

The bulk of Campanella's work was composed in prison. Here he wrote a number of lyrics in Italian, most of them on political and religious themes, a few of them heartrending expressions of his personal sufferings. E. G. Gardner describes them as giving "lyrical utterance" to his doctrines and setting forth "his metaphysical creed of God, his conception of nature . . . his utopian and messianic dreams for the coming renovation of mankind." By far the most famous of his works is the Italian prose treatise *La Città del Sol* (The City of the Sun: or, The

Idea of a Republic, 1602; later translated by him into Latin as *Civitatis Solis*). This imaginative and idealistic picture of a utopian community is in the form of a dialogue between a knight and a sea captain who has visited the City of the Sun on his voyages. There seems little doubt that Campanella's ideal city has some relation to the theocracy he had foreseen in his abortive Calabrian plot. It also resembles, in some details, the communities described by Plato in the *Republic* and Sir Thomas More in *Utopia*. A communist state, the City of the Sun is ruled by a priest-philosopher who has absolute power. Property is owned in common; individualism is totally eradicated; and human personality is subordinated to the state. The city has no poverty, no riches, no slavery. But it offers its citizens comfort, cleanliness, education, and security. Campanella describes, often in ingenious detail, all phases of life in the community. In some of these (particularly in the use of the city walls for visual education and the emphasis upon science, mechanics, and agriculture in education) Campanella astounds the modern reader with his foresight. In others (especially descriptions of eugenic breeding among the citizens and the assumption that people would live content under a benevolent despot) he reveals extraordinary naïveté. The work survives as an interesting example of the "Utopia" genre. Benedetto Croce wrote of it: "It is not Campanella the reformer and communist who still lives for us, but Campanella the poet of reform and communism. The lofty ideal of justice and of human felicity cherished by him confronts us with the force of an aspiration and poetic vision." Campanella wrote many other prose works on poetry, philosophy, religion, science (he defended the Copernican system in his *Apologia pro Galilaeo*), and political theory.

The City of the Sun was first translated into English in 1886 by T. W. Halliday (in H. Morley's *Ideal Commonwealth*). A translation by W. J. Gilstrap appears in *The Quest for Utopia*, edited by G. Negley and J. M. Patrick (1952). Campanella's sonnets were translated by J. A. Symonds and published with his translations of Michelangelo's sonnets in 1878. The *Defense of Galileo* was translated by G. McColley in 1939.

ABOUT: Berneri, M. L. Journey through Utopia; Gardner, E. G. Tommaso Campanella and His Poetry; Grillo, F. Tommaso Campanella in America; Negley, G. & Patrick, J. M. The Quest for Utopia; Wilkins, E. H. A History of Italian Literature; PMLA, LXXVIII (1963). [In Italian —Seroni, A. Leggere e Sperimentare.]

*CAMPHUYSEN, DIRK RAFAËLS-ZOON** (1586-July 19, 1627), Dutch religious poet, was born in Gorinchem, The Netherlands. His father, a surgeon, and his mother were of the Baptist persuasion. They died when Camphuysen was still a boy. He originally intended to be a painter, then changed his interests and began his classical studies in 1608 at the University of Leiden. Leaving school, he became the major domo of the patrician Gideon van Boetzelaer, whose children he tutored. Falling in love against the wishes of his master who had different plans for him, Camphuysen went to Utrecht where he became schoolmaster. In 1613 he married Anna Alendorp. A year later he embraced Calvinism and began to study for the ministry. His career as a preacher began in 1617 in Vleuten. Meeting opposition because of his Arminian views, he went to Ost-Friesland, Germany, in 1618, and began a printing business. Persecuted wherever he went, he lived after 1622 in various places, making a living for his family as best he could. He was offered a chair at the Rakov school in Germany, the center of seventeenth century Socinianism, but declined. Because his religion was of a very personal brand, he was adverse to all ecclesiastical authority, and turned finally even from Arminianism.

His *Stichtelijcke Rymen* appeared anonymously in 1624 and was printed more than fifty times in the following hundred years. This collection contains simple, pure poetry that reveals not only Camphuysen's humility but also his profound mind and his inclination to meditate. The appearance of the collection led to the offer from ecclesiastical quarters to prepare a rhymed version of the Psalms. Although some of them are excellent, they never succeeded in replacing the versions already in use. Most of Camphuysen's theological works appeared in print after his death in Dokkum. They comprise mainly letters and sermons. The most important of his works is *Van 't Onbedriegelick Oordeel Tussen Goede and Quaede Leere*. In this as well as his other writings the influence of Socinus, whom he translated into Dutch, can clearly be detected.

Some translations of his verse appeared in J. Bowring's *Batavian Anthology* (1824).

ABOUT: [In Dutch—see studies by L. A. Rademaker, P. van Renssen.]

H. B.

* kämp' hoi sĕn

*CAMPOAMOR Y CAMPOSORIO, RAMÓN DE (September 24, 1817-February 12, 1901), Spanish poet and epigrammatist, was born in Navia, Asturias. At eighteen, in a sudden flash of mysticism, he almost became a Jesuit. Later he dabbled in medicine, then law, but finally found his true vocation in writing. He also played a rôle in politics: he was chief of one province, and governor of another, Alicante, where he married a lady of Irish descent. Domestically happy, and unconcerned with monetary matters or great ambition, he led a blissful existence. Understandably his temperament was jovial and good-natured, his only vices being reading and sleeping.

Besides his poetry, for which he is best known, he wrote various books in prose, including *Filosofía de las Leyes,* a work more literary than scientific, about the origins and basis of civil rights; and *Poética,* an analysis of the traditional poetic values. His dramatic works include *Guerra a la Guerra* (War to War), *Cuerdos y Locos* (Sane and Insane), and *El Honor.*

In his youth he wrote a good deal of poetry full of spontaneous and graceful inventions, such as are found in the traditional "coplas." Many of the best poems of this period are collected in *Cantares.*

His longer philosophical poems *El Alma en Pena* (The Soul in Purgatory), *Colón* (Columbus), *El Licenciado Torralba* (The Lawyer Torralba), and *El Drama Universal* (The Universal Drama) are pretentious and dull and are now read only by scholars. They are inferior to the models on which they are based, the legends of Zorrilla and Espronceda.

Campoamor claimed to have invented new poetic forms, the *dolora* (his *Fábulas Morales y Doloras,* 1846), and the *humoradas* (collected subsequently in his *Humoradas,* 1886). The *humorada* is a rhymed couplet or quatrain. Despite his pretensions, the form is indistinguishable from the epigram. The *dolora* is a concise poem dramatizing a universal truth and characterized by delicacy, pathos, and a moral message expressed through irony. His most famous poem of this type is "¡Quién supiera escribir!" (If One Could Only Write), a ballad-like dialogue in which an illiterate peasant girl vainly tries to dictate to a learned but obtuse cleric a letter addressed to her remote lover. Perhaps this is the most beautiful and typical *dolora* which Campoamor wrote, illustrating both his humor and his sentimentality. *Los*

* käm pō ä môr′ ē käm pō sō′ ryō

Dos Espejos (The Two Mirrors) and *Verdad de las Tradiciones* (The Truth of Traditions) are other famous examples of the type of philosophical irony that made him famous in his day.

However, for all his boasting, his originality consisted in finding new names for old things and in being one of the first writers to break with the romantic tradition. Once placed on a level with Shakespeare, Goethe, and Calderón de la Barca, he is today relatively unread.

The *Obras Completas,* 8 vols, was published in Madrid, 1901-03. Selections from his work in English translation appear in R. Hilton's *Campoamor, Spain and the World* (1940).

ABOUT: Hilton, R. Campoamor, Spain, and the World. [In Spanish—Gonzales Blanco, A. Campoamor: Biografía y Estudio Crítico.]

L. S.

*CANKAR, IVAN (May 10, 1876-December 11, 1918), Slovene novelist, poet, and dramatist, was born in the village of Vrhnika in Slovenia (part of present-day Yugoslavia). His father was a poor tailor. After their house burned down, the family moved from place to place.

Cankar attended primary school at Vrhnika and technical high school in Ljubljana, completing the latter in 1895. He won a scholarship and went to Vienna to study architecture, but soon left school to engage in a literary career. He supported himself with part-time work as a journalist. His own childhood and the life of Vienna gave him material for his realistic descriptions of poverty and the hardships of urban existence. In 1907 he stood as a candidate for the Austrian Parliament on the Social Democratic ticket, but had no chance of winning. After the election he returned to Ljubljana to live. During the war he was interned by the Austrian government as politically suspect. He died in 1918 after a fall from a staircase.

Cankar entered literature as a poet. His first poem was published in 1893, while he was still in technical school. His collection of lyrics, *Erotika* (1899), shocked his countrymen with its apparent cynicism and blasphemy. The Bishop of Ljubljana attempted to suppress the book by buying up all the copies and burning them. In the second edition (1902) Cankar omitted many of the offending passages. His poetry shows the influence of Heine, with a penchant for sarcasm. He is preoccupied with the paradoxes of love and suffering, sin and contrition.

* tsäng′ kär

Cankar early turned from poetry to prose. His sketches, *Vinjete* (Vignettes, 1899) are cynical and pessimistic caricatures. He declares war on the world and its injustice. His later tales and short novels are less satirical, full of pity for the oppressed and suffering, particularly for the poor. Ibsen influenced him for a time; later he turned for inspiration to the Russians (particularly Tolstoy and Gorky), and to Zola and Nietzsche. His prose alternates between realism and symbolism in its manner, with much subjectivity of imagery and personal reminiscence of childhood. His best collection of this subjective type is his *Podobe iz Sanj* (Images from Dreams, 1917).

Cankar's realistic tales treat poverty and hardship, as well as the problem of social justice, which the author does not find on earth. The hero is sometimes a poor artist, forced by society to live as an outcast. Cankar also has stories on the Slovene national problem, and his six plays constitute the first significant body of Slovene drama.

Cankar gained international reputation with his tale *Hlapec Jernej* (The Farmhand Yerney, 1907), rendered into English by Louis Adamic as *Yerney's Justice* (1926) and by S. Yeras and H. C. S. Grant as *Bailiff Yerney and His Rights* (1930). Translated into most of the major European languages, this story supposedly helped to inspire land reform in Central and Eastern Europe. The peasant Yerney is a poor farmhand who works all his life for one master; when the latter dies he is turned out penniless. He goes everywhere seeking justice but never finds it. Finally he burns down the very farm which he considers his by right, and the peasants kill him.

In addition to *Yerney's Justice,* several English translations of stories by Cankar are to be found in the *Slavonic Review,* XVII (1938-39).

ABOUT: Slavonic Review, VI (1927-28); Columbia Dictionary of Modern European Literature. [In Slovene—Vodušek, B. Ivan Cankar.]

W. E. H.

CANTEMIR, ANTIOCH. See KANTEMIR, ANTIOCH

CANTEMIR, DIMITRIE. See KANTEMIR, DIMITRIE

*CANTÙ, CESARE (December 5, 1804?-March 11, 1895), Italian historian and novelist, was born at Brivio, in Como, the eldest of

* kän tōō′

ten children of Celso Cantù and Rachel Gallavresi. The family was poor, and in order to assure the boy an education they destined him for the priesthood. He soon gave up the idea of becoming a priest, however, and after completing his studies at Sant' Alessandro in Milan, he became a teacher at seventeen, first in Sondrio, then in Como.

In 1827 Cantù's father died and he found himself the sole support of his large family. To meet his financial obligations he became a professional writer. He worked with prodigious energy and industry, producing a large number of historical studies. The earliest of these was a history of his native region—*Storia della Città e della Diocesi di Como* (1829-31). This was followed by a history of Lombardy in the seventeenth century (1832), and, in 1838, by the first of the thirty-five volumes of his *Storia Universale,* his most popular work, which went through forty editions. For all its superficiality and lack of historical objectivity, this universal history remains a model of its kind for lucid, rapid narration and general historical balance.

Cantù wrote other histories of the Italian independence movement and a book of reminiscences of Alessandro Manzoni, author of the celebrated novel *I Promessi Sposi* (The Betrothed). His sympathies for Manzoni and others identified with the struggle for Italian independence got him into trouble with the Austrian rulers of northern Italy. In 1833 he was arrested and imprisoned for a year in the convent of Santa Margherita in Milan. Here, with no books and only scraps of paper, a toothpick, and candlesmoke for writing implements, he began his historical novel *Margherita Pusterla.* This story of religious persecution in the thirteenth century was very popular in its day (it was published in 1838) and went through thirty-six editions, almost rivaling Manzoni's great novel in popularity. It is little read today, however. A chapter from it appears in English translation in the Warner Library, V.

Cantù wrote some verse—including a patriotic poem, *Algiso* (1828), and some works of biography and criticism. None of these has been translated into English. He died in Milan at about ninety. He never married. His brother Ignazio Cantù was also a teacher and writer and edited a periodical, *Educatore Italiano.*

CAPELLANUS, ANDREAS. See ANDRÉ LE CHAPELAIN

*CAPPONI, GINO, Marchese (September 13, 1792-February 3, 1876), Italian historian and critic, was born in Florence of an old and prominent Florentine family. In 1800 his father took him to Vienna where he studied languages. He returned to Florence in 1803, and there he continued his studies, adding Latin, Greek, and mathematics to his accomplishments. He began his writing career in 1812 with a study of the first voyage to the new world made by Amerigo Vespucci.

Noble by birth and of independent means, Capponi was able to devote himself to the major interests of his life—history and the betterment of the lot of the Italian people. He married the Marchesina Giulia Riccardi in 1811. He traveled in England and on the Continent and met many of the leading political and cultural figures of his time. In London he knew Lord John Russell, in Edinburgh Lord Francis Jeffrey. When he returned to Italy he launched a literary periodical, *Antologia,* modeled on Jeffrey's *Edinburgh Review.* He also contributed to another journal, *Archivo Storico.* In 1825 he went to Switzerland to study the Swiss educational institutions with the aim of adapting these methods to Italian schools. In 1845 he published an influential pamphlet on education, *Pensieri sull' Educazione.*

Capponi was prevented by blindness from taking an active part in the Risorgimento, but his sympathies for Italian political independence led him into politics. He was idealistic and democratic in his political sentiments and favored a moderate course which would avoid violence in any form. He supported the mild and progressive rule of the Grand Duke of Tuscany Leopold II. In 1848 he became prime minister of Tuscany. He gave up his political activities later that year to work on his history of Florence, *Storia della Republica di Firenze.* He returned to political activity in 1859 as head of the council of state which voted the union of Piedmont and Tuscany. In 1860 King Victor Emmanuel of Italy named him a senator. Capponi spent his last years completing his Florentine history, the work of two decades, and it was published in 1875, one year before his death.

Capponi's works have not been translated into English. His letters (collected and published 1882-90) reveal the variety of his interests—political, social, and cultural. The great Italian poet Leopardi met him during his stay in Florence (1830-33) and addressed to him a poem expressing his bitterness over

* käp pŏn' nē

contemporary conditions—*Palinodia a Gino Capponi.*

ABOUT: [In Italian—Croce, B. Storia della Storiografia Italiana nel Secolo XIX; Gentile, G. Gino Capponi e la Cultura Toscana del Secolo XIX.]

*CAPUANA, LUIGI (May 28, 1839-November 29, 1915), Italian novelist and critic, was the first-born son of Don Gaetano and Dorotea, née Ragusa. Two other sons and seven daughters were born to the Capuanas, an affluent Sicilian family in the town of Mineo. Young Luigi went to Mineo's grammar school. At eleven he was sent to the nearby town of Bronte to attend the *real collegio,* a seminary run by Capuchins. Here he won his first literary honors and dreamed of becoming a great Sicilian poet. The Capuanas, however, enrolled Luigi at the University of Catania in 1856 to study law. For the two years he remained at the university he hobnobbed with the young Sicilian literati and wrote poetry expressing the nationalist sentiments of the day. Garibaldi's landing in Sicily and defeat of the Bourbon troops in May 1860 moved the young poet to compose *Garibaldi,* a dramatic legend.

Florence, the provisional capital of the Italy of the Risorgimento and a center of intellectual activity, was young Capuana's residence from 1864 to 1868. While he wrote literary criticism for the local press, he acquainted himself with the works of Balzac and the French naturalists. He consequently forsook his ambition to become Sicily's Shakespeare in favor of writing fiction. The *Enciclopedia Italiana* points out that Capuana was in his youth above all a critic, and as such holds a notable position, not only because he encouraged his friend and fellow-Sicilian Giovanni Verga to develop his talent, but also because he was the first to champion the naturalistic novel in Italy. In 1865 the daily *La Nazione* published Capuana's first short story, "Dottor Cymbalus." He shortly afterward became drama critic for *La Nazione.*

During Capuana's residence in Mineo for the next seven years he was first school superintendent and then mayor. His second short story, "Delfina," was published in 1872.

The year 1877 found Capuana in Milan as literary critic of the daily *Corriere della Sera,* and saw publication of his first collection of short stories, *Profili di Donne* (Studies of Women). His first novel, *Giacinta* (1879), is also a study of a woman, a favorite subject. It is written according to the theo-

* kä pwä' nä

CAPUANA

ries of naturalism but was not reviewed favorably by the critics. In contrast, his first book of fairy tales, *C'Era una Volta* (Once Upon a Time), published in 1882, was hailed by the Italian press. Capuana was the editor of the Roman literary weekly *Fanfulla di Domenica* in 1882 and 1883, and then returned to Mineo to hold office once again as mayor and to continue writing.

By the end of 1887 he ventured once more to the mainland, determined to make his living solely as a writer. He struggled for the next few years in Rome, teaching in the Istituto Superiore di Magistero, editing and writing prolifically. *Le Paesane* (1894, The Countrywomen), a collection of regional stories, is the work that perhaps best displays his talent and his *paesanismo*. The novel *Scurpiddu*, a Sicilian *Adventures of Huckleberry Finn* (1898), was approved by the Ministry of Education for reading in the elementary schools.

Capuana's student, seventeen-year-old Adelaide (Ada) Bernardini, became his secretary and companion in 1895. They were married in 1908. Appointed to the chair of stylistics and lexicography at the University of Catania in 1901, he returned to his native island. The remaining years of his life were marked by versatile and unflagging literary output. His last work, *Paraninfu* (The Marriage Broker), is a Sicilian dialect comedy. He died suddenly in Catania.

The *Marchese di Roccaverdina* (1901) is Capuana's most ambitious work. Its closing episode became *Profumo*, his best novel.

S. E. Scalia comments: "To find Capuana at his best we must go back to his *Profumo*, for only in it . . . do his regionalism, scientism, and craftmanship combine to give us the best measure of his talent. His was essentially a descriptive and mimic talent, whence the superiority of his regional stories as compared to the psychological."

Capuana's first short story, "Doctor Cymbalus," is one of the few to be translated into English. It is in the *Golden Book* for December 1925. In *Tales from the Italian and Spanish* (1920) we find "A Kiss," "A Case of Somnambulism," and "The Cares of Prosperity." *Italian Short Stories* (1932) contains "The New House." Capuana's children's stories are the only other works translated. *C'Era una Volta* first appeared in English in 1892. *Gambalesta* was translated as *Nimble-legs* by F. T. Cooper in 1927. *Il Raccontafiabe* was translated as *Golden-Feather* in 1930 by Dorothy Emmrich. She also did the American edition of *C'Era una Volta* in 1929.

ABOUT: Scalia, S. E. Luigi Capuana and His Times; PMLA, September 1938. [In Italian—see studies by A. Cibaldi, A. Pellizzari, P. Vetro; see also Fiera Letteraria, XVIII (1963).]

E. DE P.

*CARAGIALE, ION LUCA** (January 29, 1852-July 1912), Rumanian playwright and short-story writer, was born in the village of Haimanalele, near Ploesti. His father, Luca Caragiale, was a member of a family (originally Greek) of traveling actors and playwrights; his mother was a peasant named Catinca. Young Caragiale received very little schooling and was largely self-taught. At twenty he became the sole support of his mother and sister. He drifted from job to job; he ran a beer garden and a restaurant, edited a humor magazine, and worked as a proofreader. His first experience in the theatre came in 1868 when he went to Bucharest to work as a prompter in the acting company of his uncle Iorgiu Caragiale. In 1874 he published his first poem in a Bucharest review and not long after he began contributing to a conservative paper edited by his friend the poet Eminescu.

Caragiale established himself as a playwright with two verse plays which were translations from the French—*Roma Invinsa* and *Lucretia Borgia* (1878). In the next decade he wrote a number of successful plays. These were mainly comedies of character and manners, with special satirical emphasis on the social conflicts and political corruption of the day—*O Scrisoare Pierduta* (The Lost Letter, 1884), *De Ale Carnavaluliu* (Carnival Adventures, 1885), etc. Caragiale also wrote

* kä rä jä' lĕ

one serious play, a grim, psychological melodrama of peasant life, *Napasta* (False Accusation, 1889), which stirred up a great
amount of controversy. It has been compared
to Tolstoy's drama *The Power of Darkness.*
In addition to his plays Caragiale wrote a
number of short stories, often not more than
sketches, which dealt realistically with contemporary Rumanian life, with clerks or
peasants and their families.

Although he enjoyed considerable fame in
his native land, presiding over the literary
group known as the *Juminea* ("Youth") and
serving for one year, 1888, as director-general
of the National Theatre, Caragiale was not
happy in Rumania. He was rarely able to
earn enough money to support his wife and
three children. In 1901 he was involved in a
plagiarism suit, but he was completely vindicated. Three years later he received a
legacy from the estate of an aunt. With this
income he moved with his family to Berlin
where he lived for the rest of his days.
Caragiale continued to contribute sketches and
stories to Rumanian periodicals. His reputation survives today mainly for his humor—
ironic, sometimes cruel, but nearly always
effective. He has been called the first Rumanian "objective writer," in that he was the
first to bring to the stage the real speech and
personalities of the Rumanian people.
"Through him," E. D. Tappe writes in the
American Slavic and East European Review,
"Rumania and especially Bucharest of the late
nineteenth century lives in the imagination
with an intensity and individuality such as
that, for example, with which another writer,
Mark Twain, has endowed the Mississippi
Valley of a slightly earlier period."

In 1962 the fiftieth anniversary of Caragiale's death was observed in Rumania with a
"Caragiale Week" during which a number
of his plays were performed. His plays have
also been produced, in recent years, in the
U.S.S.R., Japan, and South America.

ABOUT: American Slavic and East European
Review, February 1952; Columbia Dictionary of
Modern European Literature; World Theatre, XI
(1962-63). [In French—La Grande Revue, CIX.]

*CARDUCCI, GIOSUÈ (July 21, 1835-
February 16, 1907), Italian poet and critic,
was born in Valdicastello, in Tuscany. His
father, Michele, the descendant of an old
Florentine family, was by profession a physician, by political belief an active Carbonaro,
and by literary adherence a fervent follower
of Manzoni. His mother, Ildegonda Celli, was

* kär dōōt′ chē

150

CARDUCCI

a cultured lady who "taught him to read
Alfieri and did not inculcate superstition."
For political reasons, Dr. Carducci was forced
to move from place to place with his family.
In 1849 the Carduccis found themselves in
Florence where the future poet attended the
Scuole degli Scolopi, and in 1853 he won a
scholarship to the University of Pisa. By
1855 he had published his first book, an anthology, *L'Arpa del Popolo.* Vivacious and
nonconformist by temperament, young Carducci reacted against Tuscan conservatism
under the Grand Duke and against the Cath-
olic-romantic writings pressed upon him by
"that Manzonian father of his." In addition,
the spiritual narrowness of the educational
institutions he attended prompted the anti-
Catholic and anti-romantic attitudes of his
early polemics and contributed to the classical
and humanistic orientation of his aesthetics.

After graduation, Carducci taught at the
Ginnasio of San Miniato, where he published
his first *Rime,* and at Pistoia, until he accepted the chair of Italian literature at the
University of Bologna in 1860. This first
volume of verse was incorporated into the
general collection *Juvenilia,* which covers his
output from 1850 to 1860. Dominant are the
themes which stress pre-romantic Italian traditions and classical art, the return to a
naturalistic ideal of a healthy, confident humanity, opposed in spirit to romantic sentimentalism and eccentricity.

Before his appointment to the University of
Bologna, two events deeply disturbed the
poet: the mysterious suicide of his brother

Dante in 1857 and the death of his father one year later. In 1859 he married Elvira Menicucci, and that same year, in collaboration with the Florentine editor Barbera, founded a short-lived periodical, *Il Poliziano*. It was the impressive quality of his critical essays that led to his Bologna appointment. Henceforward, Carducci's life yields little by way of biographical events, but is replete with the ideas and attitudes of an artist who is to develop and in time assert himself as the greatest Italian poet of his day.

Politically, his interest in the French Revolution, the Risorgimento, and related historical topics (in particular the Aspromonte episode), occasioned a change in direction from an early patriotic monarchical idealism toward a democratic republican ideology, often Jacobin and anti-Catholic, especially traceable in *Levia Gravia* (1861-71) and in *Giambi ed Epodi* (including his *Decennalia,* 1867-79). The sense of the continuity of Roman tradition and of the "uniqueness of Italian life from ancient Rome to modern Rome" was unusually strong in Carducci; the image of the City as an "immense ship launched toward world empire" facilitated the fusion of the old with the new, of Virgil and Livy with Dante and Garibaldi, "they too Romans, in their way."

With the publication of *Rime Nuove* (1861-87) and the *Odi Barbare* (1877-89), Carducci, no longer the youthful poet who "disdainfully, knocked on the doors of the future" but the mature poet and leader to whom whole generations looked for encouragement and civic guidance, became a great educator. His oratory found no equal among his contemporaries. He taught by word and example the austerity and dignity of research, the ineradicable love for art, and the necessity for Italians to prepare for the arduous patriotic trials of the future. And his physique fitted the role: short but powerfully built, bearded, with a spacious forehead set above his small but piercing eyes. The *Rime* and *Odi* are the best examples of his noble, intellectual style, with its orchestral harmony of word and rhythm.

In 1890 Carducci was made Senator of Italy. His final collection of poetry, *Rime e Ritmi* (1887-99), is generally solemn in tone, wrung from "the winter (which) tightens still around my soul." Ever present are the poet's high sense of moral duty and national glory, his consciousness of history as the perennial reality and true interpreter of the spirit of the ages. In his mature years, Carducci, even if he did not abandon, nevertheless modified, some of his more radical

ideas. He had been an atheist, but his thought evolved into a recognition of God, or the idea of God, as the highest force for the conservation of nations, and of Christianity as the temperer of barbarism, the blender of ancient and medieval cultures. Similarly, he eventually accepted the monarchy as representative of national sovereignty. Even his anti-romantic attitudes were absorbed into a unitarian vision of the historical process.

After more than forty years of devotion to the profession of teaching, Carducci's declining health forced his retirement in 1904 (he had suffered a partial paralysis in 1899), and in January 1905 Parliament voted him a generous pension to honor his service to his country. Toward the end of 1906, he became the first Italian writer to be awarded the Nobel Prize for Literature. He died a few months later in Bologna, one of the most honored figures in Italian letters.

The first English translation of Carducci's poetry was made by the Reverend Frank Sewall in 1892. Subsequently there have been numerous translations of selections from his poetry, such as A. Greene's (1893), M. W. Arms' (1906), Miss Holland's (1907), T. F. Unwin's (1907), Emily Tribe's (1921), Romilda Rendel's (1929), down to Arthur Burkhard's *Twenty-four Sonnets* (1947). One of the most dedicated Carducci translators has been William Fletcher Smith who published the *Barbarian Odes* in 1939, the *Lyrics and Rhythms,* the *New Lyrics,* and the poet's *Political and Satiric Verse* in 1942.

ABOUT: Bailey, J. C. Carducci; Scalia, E. Carducci, His Critics and Translators in England and America; Thayer, W. R. Italica: Studies in Italian Life and Letters, 1908. [In Italian—see studies by D. Baccini, P. Bargellini. M. Biagini, C. Brumati, N. Busetto, B. Croce, G. Sozzi.]

J.-P. B.

CARLÉN, EMILIE FLYGARE-. See FLYGARE-CARLÉN, EMILIE

"CARMEN SYLVA." See ELISABETH, Queen Consort of Charles I, King of Rumania

*CARO, JOSEPH (1488-March 24, 1575), Talmudist, mystic and author of the most authoritative Jewish ritual code, was born in Toledo, Spain. Upon the expulsion of the Jews from Spain in 1492, Caro's family fled first to Portugal. Later, after many privations and much wandering, Caro settled in European Turkey, living in Constantinople, Adrianople and Nicopolis. His father, Ephraim, a respected Talmudist, provided

* kä′ rō

151

Caro with his basic Jewish education. The phenomenal rapidity with which Caro absorbed the huge body of Talmudic learning earned him a reputation which led to an appointment as head of a Talmud academy at Adrianople. The fathers of Caro's three wives (the first two died) were all distinguished Talmudists.

In 1522 Caro began writing his monumental *Bet Yosef* (House of Joseph), a work which he completed some thirty years later. Caro was dissatisfied with the codification of Jewish law made by Jacob ben Asher, the *'Arba Turim* (Four Rows). He attempted in his *Bet Yosef* to correct the latter's deficiencies by including the leading sources, citing proofs, and systematizing major Talmudic decisions. Containing a tremendous wealth of material, the *Bet Yosef* soon achieved recognition as the outstanding code of the day.

Caro's personality also displayed a mystical side. In 1535 he moved to Safed, Palestine, the center of Kabbalistic study and Messianic aspirations. Influenced by such men as Jacob Berab, Solomon Molkho, and Solomon Alkhabez, Caro immersed himself in visionary speculation. A disputed book of his, *Magid Mesharim* (Who Speaks Rightly, 1646), purporting to be Caro's diary, contains mystical notes on conversations with a celestial being.

The most popular and influential work by Caro is the *Shulhan 'Arukh* (Prepared Table, 1565), a digest of the *Bet Yosef* for the less learned. Written in clear, easily understood Hebrew, the work is a concise arrangement of the substance of Jewish legal and ritual tradition. The book is divided into four parts and each paragraph sets forth the decision on a specific legal point, without indicating sources or varying opinions. The *Shulhan 'Arukh* met with considerable opposition on the part of Ashkenazic (German-Polish) rabbis, who felt that Caro had over-emphasized the Sephardic (Spanish) Jewish practice. With some additional commentaries, however, it gained acceptance by the entire Jewish world. By the middle of the seventeenth century, the *Shulhan 'Arukh* was the final, authoritative Jewish religious code.

Caro's greatness lies in his rational rather than his mystical nature. His lucid and logical *Shulhan 'Arukh*, a work of immense erudition, came at a critical junction in Jewish history. Chaotic conditions threatened many Jewish communities in the aftermath of the expulsion from Spain and it was essential to provide an authoritative code to promote religious stability and unity. This Caro did, trying, at the same time, to universalize rabbinic tradition by reconciling the decisions of the most eminent Talmudists. The measure of his success is the fact that the *Shulhan 'Arukh* and its popular abridged version, the *Kitsur Shulhan 'Arukh*, are today, four centuries later, the basic legal code of Orthodox Jewry.

The *Kitsur Shulhan 'Arukh* was translated by H. E. Goldin in 1928 as *Code of Jewish Law*. Two sections of the *Shulhan 'Arukh* have been translated since 1954 by C. N. Denburg under the title *Code of Hebrew Law*. *The Kosher Code of the Orthodox Jew* is a translation made by S. I. Levin and E. A. Boyden in 1940 of a section of the *Shulhan 'Arukh*.
ABOUT: Gordon, H. L. Maggid of Caro; Graetz, H. History of the Jews; Lehrman, S. M. Rabbi Joseph Karo: His Life and Times; Waxman, M. A History of Jewish Literature. [In German— see studies by D. Hoffmann, C. Tschernowitz.]

M. R.

*CASANOVA DE SEINGALT, GIOVANNI GIACOMO (April 2, 1725-June 4, 1798), Italian writer and adventurer, was born in Venice. His parents were actors. Two of his brothers attained distinction as painters; one became the director of the Academy of Fine Arts in Dresden, and Francesco, born in London in 1727, was Giovanni's frequent companion in Paris and rose to fame at the Beaux Arts as a landscape painter. The father died in 1733, and the mother, Zanetta, admired by Goldoni, entered the theatre in Dresden, where she remained until her death in 1776. Casanova's disorganized youth drew him to the occult arts, and his precocious talents turned him to mathematics and mechanics. At nine, he began studies in Padua, of which one finds echoes in his Memoirs. With his doctorate he returned to Venice and entered minor orders as a convenient career. Obliged to leave the city as the result of his first escapades, and thereupon elected Bishop of Martorano, he left for Calabria, then, disgusted with living conditions there, returned to Rome. Again in trouble, he was dispatched on a mission to Constantinople, but was attracted by a military career while on his way to Venice, and completed his mission to Turkey as ensign for his birthplace. On his return, he enjoyed the protection of Senator Brigadin, but having seduced some members of his family, went into exile in northern Italy.

* kä sä nô' vä dĕ săN gȧl'

CASANOVA

Casanova was first led to France through his affair in 1749 with Henriette, a young Frenchwoman, with whom he went to Geneva, and whom he later sought out in Aix. In 1750, with the young actor Balletti, he set out afresh, and in Paris, thanks to his comrade's mother, the actress Sylvia, he became an intimate of the Italian Theatre and soon moved in the literary circles of Crébillon and of several of the Encyclopedists. His dramatic works of 1752, including a translation of Voltaire's *L'Écossaise,* testify to his enduring fascination for the theatre, and attracted some notice at the time. With his brother, he went to Dresden to see his mother, and then to Venice, where he incurred the spite of Goldoni's rival Chiari, who, in *La Commediante in Fortuna,* drew a cruel but relatively faithful picture of Casanova's exploits, in novel form. For "scorn of religion" and other infractions of custom and law, he was imprisoned in the Ducal Palace, thus leading to his famous escape in October 1756, effectively narrated in a special work printed in 1788 and taken up again in the Memoirs. The excitement of the exploit is enhanced by Casanova's rich portrayal of the setting and the circumstances.

Casanova fled to Munich, and then settled in Paris for his most scandalous three years, marked by questionable financial projects, such as the lottery run by the Calzabigi brothers, and the series of seductions of 1759. Enriched by speculations, he pur-chased his estate called La Petite-Pologne, near the present Parc Monceau, and there engaged in some at least of his affairs, with "Mlle X. C. V." identified as Justinienne Wynne, and with Manon Balletti, of his former friend's family. He also cultivated rich and elderly women such as the Marquise d'Urfé and the Comtesse du Rumain. Irrevocably compromised, Casanova left Paris suddenly in September 1759, and engaged in extensive travel in Germany, England, Italy, and Spain, forever pursued by the police. Finally pardoned in Venice, he entered the services of the Inquisition as an informer on current dangerous literature, such as the writings of the Encyclopedists. His last brief visit to Paris in 1783 met with no success, but in the course of the trip he found his last protector, Waldstein, and as his librarian in Bohemia engaged in an immense correspondence with friends who kept him abreast of current literary developments.

In his last days he fulminated against the terrorists who in France had destroyed the civilization he had loved. His works include a lengthy fantasy in French, *Icosameron.* The success of his tale of escape, *Histoire de Ma Fuite,* published in 1788, led him to concentrate on his personal Memoirs, *Histoire de Ma Vie,* which he carried to 1774 and finally to 1793; he confided the manuscript to Count Marcolini, who was to publish it, but it first appeared in expurgated form in German translation from 1822 to 1828, and then only in the original French, in 1826. Much research has been done regarding Casanova's life and friends. The double value of personal expression and historical documentation, despite his undisputed tendency to misrepresent fact, makes his Memoirs one of the vital references for several aspects of eighteenth century culture.

There are several English translations of the Memoirs, the most popular made by Arthur Machen in 1932; the convenient text by P. Villars, of 1892, is entitled *The Escapades of Casanova and Latude. Histoire de Ma Fuite* was translated as *Casanova's Escape from the Leads* by A. Machen in 1925.

ABOUT: Dobrée, B. Three Eighteenth Century Figures; Ellis, H. Casanova in Rome, in Venice, in Paris; Endore, G. Casanova, His Known and Unknown Life. [In French and Italian—see studies by C. Henry, J. Hervez, J. Le Gras, E. Maynial, C. Samaran.]

F. J. C.

CASAS, BARTOLOMÉ DE LAS. See LAS CASAS, BARTOLOMÉ DE

*CASTELAR Y RIPOLL, EMILIO
(September 7, 1832-May 25, 1899), Spanish
statesman, orator, and writer, was born in
Cádiz. Although his father died when Castelar was a child, the boy received an excellent education. He was a student at the
Escuela Normal de Filosofía, and many of
his attitudes were formed by the Krausist
movement. As a young man he worked on
several different newspapers. From 1856 to
1865, he was a professor of history at the
University of Madrid. In 1866 he was
exiled to France for two years. Returning
to Spain, he resumed his professorship,
which he held until 1875. In 1869 he was
elected a member of the Cortes. A liberal
who advocated a republic and the separation
of Church and State, he was appointed Minister of Foreign Affairs in the First Republic in 1873 and then, the same year, became
President. He held office until 1874. Later
in his life, after the restoration of the monarchy, he was a deputy from 1876 to 1893.
Castelar died in San Pedro del Pinatar
(Murcia). He received a gigantic public
funeral and his body lay in state in Madrid.
In 1905 a statue was raised to him in his
native Cádiz, and in 1908 a monument by
Benlliure, paid for by public subscription in
both Spain and Spanish America, where he
was held in great esteem, was raised to him
on the Castellana in Madrid. Castelar was
an incorruptibly honest man who died in
poverty. To Spaniards his name is synonymous with liberty and eloquence.

Castelar's chief title to fame is not his
political career nor his writings, but his
oratory. He was certainly one of the great
orators of the nineteenth century, although
his speeches suffer from many of the typical
defects of the oratory of the last century,
such as a wealth of verbiage and a prodigal-
ity of metaphors. However, his command
of the language, his voice, and the sincerity
of his views often deeply moved his audience,
and there is no doubt that his speeches accomplished much. He once said, "With one
speech, I have freed two hundred thousand
Negroes." His *Discursos* (1871) are examples of the best oratory of his time.

Castelar was the author of many books
on history, such as *Historia del Movimiento
Republicano en Europa* (2 vols. 1873-74)
and several novels, of which the only one
still read is *Fra Filippo Lippi* (1877). His
Recuerdos de Italia (1872) contains some of
his finest prose. His *Obras Escogidas* (8
vols. n.d.) were published in Madrid.

* käs tä lär' ē rē pôl' y'

Mrs. Arthur Arnold translated *Recuerdos de
Italia* as *Old Rome and New Italy* in 1874 and his
Life of Lord Byron and Other Sketches in 1875.
"Human Reason, Paganism and Religion" appears
in A. R. Spofford's *Library of Choice Literature*,
and "The Prophets and Sibyls of the Sistine Chapel"
in De Puy's *The University of Literature*.

ABOUT: Columbia Dictionary of Modern Literature. [In Spanish—see studies by M. González
Araco, B. Herrera Ochoa.]

R. E. O.

*CASTELLO BRANCO, CAMILLO
(March 16, 1825-June 1, 1890), Portuguese
novelist, was born in Lisbon to an unwed
couple, Manuel Joaquim Botelho Castello
Branco, of uncertain profession, and an obscure girl, Jacinta Rosa. His father's family showed signs of degeneracy; the father
himself went insane. No wonder "Camillo,"
as his countrymen fondly call him, believed
he was "predestined for unhappiness."
Moreover, he lost both parents in his childhood. Somehow the talented boy grew up
among relatives in Trás-os-Montes, the most
backward part of Portugal, between 1835
and 1843. Sensual and rebellious, he always
followed his undisciplined impulses. Intending to become a doctor like his brother-in-
law, he studied in Oporto and Coimbra but
soon abandoned the medical career. A priest-
hater, he entered a seminary; an intellectual,
he joined the savage Miguelista guerrillas; a
bohemian, he played the lady-killer in the
"ultra-romantic" salons of Maria Browne
and other literary ladies. He had one rash
love affair after another, with elopements.
abductions, escapes, adulteries, desertions,
worse than his own most purple fiction. He
grew resentful, sarcastic, skeptical. He and
his last mistress, Ana Plácido, were imprisoned for adultery in 1861, but they were acquitted thanks to Camillo's popularity. From
then on, however, he had to slave day and
night for editors and publishers to support
Ana, their two abnormal boys, and Ana's
son by another liaison. By 1882 he had worn
out his imagination in some thirty novels and
untold other works of fiction, drama, history,
and criticism. When his eyesight failed in
1890, he shot himself.

"Camillo" did for Portugal what Balzac
had done for French society; clinging to old-
fashioned Christian, aristocratic, and romantic ideals, he ceaselessly described in fiction
the violent clashes of passionate love and
family pride with the money-mad materialism
of Portuguese society about 1840-50. He
started by writing serials for newspapers in

* kàsh tĕ' lōō brăng kōō kà mē' lōō

CAMILLO CASTELLO BRANCO

1848. After a first phase of Gothic horror fiction, e.g., *O Livro Negro do Padre Dinís* (1855), he turned to more natural description of contemporary manners with *Onde Está a Felicidade?* (1856). While in jail, he concentrated feverishly on writing three great books—the novels *O Romance dum Homem Rico*, his favorite (1861), and *Amor de Perdição*, his best known (1862), and a collection of criminals' lives, *Memórias do Cárcere* (2 vols., 1862). *Amor de Perdição* (Fatal Love) is ostensibly the true story of how the pure love between Camillo's uncle Simão and Mariana was frustrated by her heartless father. His passion, crime, and imprisonment reflect Camillo's own, as Simão's individual tragedy reflects the frustrated dreams of the last romantics.

Camillo, who took his plots from real life, could also be historical (*O Judeu*, 1866), satirical (*Coração, Cabeça e Estômago*, 1862), humorous (*A Queda dum Anjo*, 1866), or burlesque in his parodies of naturalism (*Eusébio Macário*, 1879; *A Corja*, 1882). He nevertheless adopted increasingly the new realistic technique when describing in detail the tragic lives of humble country folk in the gripping *Novelas do Minho* (1875-77) and *A Brasileira de Prazins* (1882).

To this day, comments J. do Prado Coelho, his Portuguese readers love "the utterly Portuguese atmosphere that pervades his fiction through its sentiments, themes and characters, such as João da Cruz (the rough and loyal farrier) or Calisto Elói (the ingenuous

country squire) and the women who defend their romance unto death, who repent, or who are witches." The easy-flowing, extraordinarily rich language adds to the delight. Only a Portuguese can therefore savor Camillo's works to the fullest. They remain untranslated, except into Spanish. A Spanish writer, Unamuno, could find his own "tragic sense of life" confirmed by Camillo's pathos: "Camillo's works are the best mirror of the Portugal that is tragic, pathetic, a victim of destiny."

ABOUT: Bell, A. F. G. Portuguese Literature. [In Portuguese—see studies by J. Coelho, A. Pimentel, A. Ribeiro. In Spanish—Unamuno, M. de, Por Tierras de España y Portugal. In French—Lacape, H. Camilo Castelo Branco, l'Homme, l'Historien, l'Artiste.]

G. M. M.

*CASTELVETRO, LODOVICO (1505-February 27, 1571), Italian literary critic, was born of a noble family in Modena. As a young man he studied law at Bologna, Ferrara, and Padua. Then, going to Siena, he concentrated on literary studies. By 1531 a comedy of his, *Gli Ingannati*, had been produced.

After a sojourn at Rome under the patronage of his uncle, Giovanni Maria della Porta, the Duke of Urbino's ambassador to the Papal court, he returned to Modena. Here he lectured on law and became the leading intellectual light of the local literary academy.

Castelvetro was an extremely opinionated man with little sense of tact. As a result he became embroiled with the poet Annibale Caro, secretary to Cardinal Alessandro Farnese. Castelvetro criticized unfavorably Caro's canzone, *Venite all' Ombra de' Gran Gigli d'Oro*, and Caro replied with a series of pamphlets against Castelvetro in which he accused him, among other things, of impiety. Since the Academy of Modena had for several years been suspected of leanings toward Lutherism, this accusation was a serious one. Perhaps it was partially responsible for Castelvetro's being called to Rome to face the Sacred Inquisition. In 1560, frightened by threats of torture, he fled the country. He was immediately excommunicated as a heretic.

The rest of his life was spent in exile in Chiavenna, Lyons, and Vienna, where he worked on his translation and exposition of Aristotle's *Poetics, Poetica d'Aristotele Vulgarizzata et Sposta*. Not long after its pub-

* käs tāl vä' trō

lication in 1570, he died. His *Poetica,* though ostensibly a commentary on Aristotle, puts forth a theory of poetry which differs in important respects from the master's. The purpose of poetry is to give pleasure to the ignorant masses and to gain glory for the poet. In order to do this the poet must construct his work in terms of the unities of time, place, and action. The theory and practice of French classicism owes a good deal to this formulation of the three unities.

Allan H. Gilbert's *Literary Criticism* (1940) contains generous selections from the *Poetics* translated into English.
ABOUT: Charleton, H. B. Castelvetro's Theory of Poetry; Crane, R. S. (ed.) Critics and Criticism. [In Italian—see studies by G. Cavazzuti, T. Sandonnini.]

V. H.

*CASTIGLIONE, BALDASSARE (December 6, 1478-February 7, 1529), Italian courtier and man of letters, spent his entire life in the court, and in its atmosphere he wrote his treatise on the perfect courtier. His *Il Libro del Cortegiano* is one of the most eloquent testimonies of the ideal of culture in the Italian courts during the peak of the Italian Renaissance.

Castiglione was born at Casativo, Mantua, of a noble family. Receiving a humanist education at Milan, he learned Latin and Greek. By 1499, he was in the service of Francesco Gonzaga, a nobleman of Mantua; then in 1503, he passed into the service of Guidobaldo da Montefeltro, the Duke of Urbino. In 1506 he went to England to receive from Henry VII the Order of the Garter for his master, and in 1507 he went on a mission to Louis XII. He served as ambassador to the papal court from 1513 to 1515 as an appointee of Guidobaldo's nephew and successor, Francesco Maria. When, in 1516, the Pope dispossessed Francesco Maria of his duchy, Castiglione returned to Mantua, only to return to Rome two years later as envoy of Mantua.

Trusting in his diplomatic ability in treating the Franco-Spanish conflict, Pope Clement sent Castiglione, in 1525, as ambassador to Charles V of Spain. However, Castiglione's work was unsuccessful; Rome was sacked by the imperial troops in 1527. Believing Castiglione at fault, the Pope required his apology. Later, however, Pope Clement was convinced of Castiglione's innocence.

* käs tē lyō′ nä

CASTIGLIONE

Il Libro del Cortegiano (The Book of the Courtier) was published in 1528, some twenty years after Castiglione had begun its composition. Castiglione started his work soon after the death of Guidobaldo, inspired by his memories of the duke and of the society which made up the court of Urbino, one of the most beautiful and intellectual courts not only of Renaissance Italy but of all Europe. Almost completed by 1518, the work did not appear until a year before Castiglione's death in Toledo, while he was still serving as the very respected envoy of Clement VII. His death came as a result of a grave illness, probably aggravated by the great sorrow provoked by the sack of Rome and the suspicion this disaster cast upon him.

As if taking place at the court of Urbino in 1507, Castiglione's masterpiece unfolds as a discussion which aims at the description of a perfect courtier. The discussion is directed by the Duchess of Urbino, Elisabetta Gonzaga, and her sister-in-law the "signora Emilia Pia." The nineteen men and four women participating are all authentic persons who either lived at the court or visited there in 1506-1507.

The dialogues, bound together by a connecting narrative, last four evenings, which are described in the four books of the *Cortegiano.* In an atmosphere of gay familiarity and subtlety, attesting to the ideal life to which the more cultivated society of the times aspired, the discussion treats all the arguments of that era: social and cultural problems, questions of love and its elevation to Platonic love, even digressions on the acceptable use of dialects versus the exclusive use of Tuscan. Following the court custom of spending the evening in witty or serious conversation, debate or controversial discussion, or dancing or listening to music or poetry, Castiglione has a protagonist propose, on the evening of March 8th, that one of the group "fashion in words a perfect courtier, explaining all the conditions and particular qualities which are required of a man deserving of this name; and in those things which do not appear appropriate, it is permitted to contradict, as in a school of philosophy."

The learned Count Ludovico da Canossa begins the discussion, which is interrupted frequently. The group insists that the perfect courtier will have as much military and knightly skill as literary and artistic expertness, including that of music, painting, and poetry. Perfection for the courtier also includes a pleasing appearance, noble birth, intelligence, integrity, and especially a natural grace in all actions. The perfect courtier needs a perfect lady for inspiration and achievement. The principal purpose of the perfect courtier is "to win the favor and confidence of his prince" by means of his truthfulness and his ability to guide his prince by virtuous word and honorable example. The prince himself is portrayed as a just, generous, and pious ruler. The work ends in a discussion of love, conducted by Cardinal Pietro Bembo, who explains eloquently—as in his own *Asolani*—the popular theme of the "ladder of love" and who describes its stages from the admiration of external beauty to the contemplation of the spiritual beauty of the universe and its ultimate union with the divine.

Castiglione's wisdom and good taste, closely reflecting his humanist foundation in Cicero, Horace, and Plutarch, give his book the "certain honorable mean" which he sought for his perfect courtier. His style, complex in deep arguments, agile and vivacious in his realistic dialogues, is interspersed with humor. At the same time the essential seriousness of the work is heightened by Castiglione's awareness of the contrast between the ideal and the real.

The influence of Castiglione's *Cortegiano* upon literature and custom was great in France, Spain, and England, contributing a code of social refinement and the concept of the *honnête homme*, the *caballero*, and the *gentleman*, as well as of the perfect lady and of Platonic love. This influence also ranges from Cervantes, Rabelais, and Sir Philip Sidney to Du Bellay, Spenser, and Milton, the last three of whom made use of Castiglione's rare but good verse, composed in Latin and Italian. Castiglione also left a voluminous correspondence.

The translation of the *Cortegiano* into English by Sir Thomas Hoby, in 1561, has been re-edited several times, the latest and best edition by W. H. D. Rouse and Drayton Henderson (London, 1944). (See "Castiglione and his English Translators," by J. A. Molinaro in *Italica,* XXXVI [1959].)

ABOUT: Cartwright, J. Baldassare Castiglione; Fletcher, J. B. Literature of the Renaissance; Roeder, R. The Man of The Renaissance; Wilkins, E. H. A History of Italian Literature. [In Italian—Cian, V. Nuova Antologia, I (1929); Russo, L. I Classici Italiani, II (1956).]

R. P. C.

*CASTRO, ROSALÍA DE (February 21, 1837-July 15, 1885), Spanish poet, was born in the ancient city of Santiago de Compostela, Galicia, the natural daughter of Teresa Castro. Although at the age of nine she was adopted by her mother and then brought up in her grandparents' mansion in Padrón, the knowledge of her illegitimacy weighed heavily on her mind throughout her life. She was a precocious child who loved music and at eleven was already writing verses. Although she received a spotty formal education, she learned to play the guitar and piano, and she drank in the tales and folk songs taught her by a family servant.

At nineteen, when she left for Madrid, she was "a tall buxom girl with a large mouth, thick chestnut hair and dark luminous eyes." Two years later she married the Galician writer and historian Manuel Murguía. In Madrid, far from her beloved native region, she developed an acute dislike for the steppes of Castile and a homesickness *(morriña)* which induced her and her family—eventually she had four girls and two boys—to move back to Padrón. For the major part of her life Rosalía suffered from delicate health, poverty, and marital difficulties.

Her first collection of verse, *Cantares Gallegos,* published at her husband's insistence in 1863, reflects her knowledge of folk poetry. It is the first verse of any consequence to be written in that Galician tongue so popular among the Iberian poets of the Middle Ages. The themes of the *Cantares* are mainly the customs and manners of her native province.

Between the time of her marriage and 1867 she published novels of no great importance: *La Hija del Mar, Flavio, Ruinas* and *El*

* käs' trō

157

ROSALÍA DE CASTRO

Caballero de las Botas Azules (in 1881 appeared the stories *El Primer Loco* and *El Domingo de Ramos*). It was not until 1880 that her second volume of verse, *Follas Novas*, appeared. Also written in Galician, the *Follas* are more subjective than the earlier volume: they reflect the sadness of unrealized aspirations, a nostalgia for the past, and indeed profound despair. In 1884 she published her Castilian poetry under the title of *En las Orillas del Sar*. This volume, written while she was suffering from the cancer that would cause her death, is full of desolation, disappointment, and a desire for life after death. In 1884, when Campoamor and Núñez de Arce were still publishing their declamatory, inflated verses, Rosalía dared "simply to speak." While they held to endecasyllables and octosyllables and the Zorrillean alexandrine, she adopted unusual meters and new combinations. Her verse is vague and musical, reminding one of Bécquer and Heine, and perhaps even of Laforgue and Verlaine.

At the time of her death, Rosalía enjoyed small fame outside of Galicia, and for a long time after her genius was underrated. Her work is missing from such famous collections as Menéndez y Pelayo's choice of the hundred best lyrical poems of the Castilian language. It is only in fairly recent years that Rosalía has come into her own. Today she is considered one of the finest poets to have written in the period of transition from romanticism to "contemporary lyricism," and her work, along with that of Bécquer, has exercised a vital influence on modern Spanish verse. A

collected edition of her works *(Obras Completas)* in Spanish was published in Madrid in 1944.

An English translation of *En las Orillas del Sar* was made by S. Griswold Morley as *Beside the River Sar* (1937); selections from *En Orillas del Sar* appear in *An Anthology of Spanish Poetry*, edited by Angel Flores (Anchor Books, 1961).

ABOUT: Brenan, G. Literature of the Spanish People; Morley, S. G. *introduction to* Beside the River Sar. [In Spanish—see studies by C. Barja, L. Carnosa.]

M. N.

CASTRO Y BELLVÍS, GUILLÉN DE (November 4, 1569-July 28, 1631), Spanish dramatist, was born in Valencia of an illustrious family, the son of Francisco de Castro and Doña Castellana Bellvís. From 1591 to 1594 he contributed many literary pieces to the Valencian Academia de los Nocturnos, and by the beginning of the seventeenth century his name was quite well known. During this period Castro was serving as captain in the coastguard of Valencia, but in 1606 he left for Naples in the service of the Count of Benavente. He fulfilled various military and administrative duties, among them the governorship of Scigliano. These activities, however, in no way impeded his literary progress and when he returned to Valencia in 1616 and to Madrid in 1618 after his long absence from Spain, he was very well received by the literati. In both 1620 and 1622 Castro, along with other illustrious poets, took part in poetry contests in Madrid and it was in that city that he took up residence. The Marquis of Peñafiel and the Duke of Osuna became his patrons and the Count of Olivares conferred upon him the honor of a knighthood in the Military Order of Santiago.

Castro's plays began to appear in 1608; Volume I of his *Comedias* was published in 1618 and Volume II in 1625. The latter volume was dedicated to Lope de Vega's natural daughter, and the great poet reciprocated this mark of esteem by writing in his *Laurel de Apolo* that Castro's "verses deserve eternal gold and bronze."

Guillén de Castro sought inspiration in traditional ballads and national legends, and his plays constitute the best dramatic adaptation of the old *romancero*. His best known work is *Las Mocedades del Cid* which centers in the wedding of Rodrigo and Jimena and the conflict between love and vengeance awakened in the latter. The second part of the play *Las Hazañas del Cid* deals with the siege of Zamora and is somewhat more un-

* käs′ trō ē bĕl y′ vēs′

even and less artistic than the *Mocedades*. Corneille was largely indebted to Part I of the play for the plot, characters, and even some passages of *Le Cid*.

Castro wrote many plays on classical and mythological themes *(Dido y Eneas, Progne y Filomena)*, comedies of manners, and cloak-and-dagger plays. He was the first to dramatize portions of *Don Quixote*, adapting both the episode of Cardenio and Lucinda and *El Curioso Impertinente* for the stage.

Castro was of proud and turbulent temperament, and his personal relationships were often unsuccessful. It has been suggested that the frequent anti-matrimonial diatribes in his plays reflect his own conjugal difficulties. There exists a record of a divorce in Valencia between Guillermo de Castro and one Helena Fenollar (1593), and in 1595 Castro is known to have married the Marquesa Girón de Rebolledo. Castro's only daughter was born of this union and was baptized on September 19, 1596. In 1626 the poet married Ángela María Salgado, who was then only twenty-five years old. The undue haste with which she remarried after Castro's death in 1631 might suggest that this marriage was not entirely idyllic.

Castro suffered economic difficulties in the last years of his life, but it is unlikely that he suffered complete penury as has sometimes been suggested.

ABOUT: Holland, H. R. Some Account of the Life and Writings of Lope de Vega and Guilhem de Castro; Segall, J. B. Corneille and the Spanish Drama; Revue Hispanique, 1933. [In Spanish—Del Río, A. Historia de la Literatura Española; Juliá Martínez, E. *prologue to* Obras (3 vols., Madrid, 1925-27); Said Armesto, V. ed. Las Mocedades del Cid. In French—Mérimée, H. L'Art Dramatique à Valencia.]

B. P. P.

*CATERINA DA SIENA, Saint (March 25, 1347 [traditional date]-April 29, 1380), Italian mystic and saint, was born in Siena, one of at least eleven children of Jacopo Benincasa, a dyer by trade, and his wife Lapa di Puccio di Piagente. Like other daughters of the common people, Catherine never received any formal education. She did not even learn to read and write until a few years before her death, and she carried on her correspondence by dictation.

Her vocation apparently came early. She is said to have had visions as early as the age of five and to have consecrated herself to Christ when she was seven. A little later she withdrew from social activities, began to neg-

* kä′ tâ rē′ nä dä syâ′ nä

ST. CATHERINE OF SIENA

lect her dress and appearance, and tried to spend as much time as possible in solitary meditation. She had to struggle, however, against her family, who wanted her to grow up like an ordinary girl and eventually to be married. For a while her elder sister Bonaventura, of whom she was very fond, persuaded her to conform to their parents' wishes. But when Bonaventura died in 1362, Catherine reverted to her ascetic habits, and in 1363 or 1364 she was received into the third order of the Dominicans.

This order, the Sisters of Penance, were not cloistered nuns but continued to live in their own homes. Catherine shut herself up in a room in her family's house and devoted some years to meditation and penance. In 1374 reports that she was subject to frequent visions brought her to the attention of church authorities, who called her to Florence for a rigorous examination. She satisfied her examiners, and soon a capable and intelligent monk, Raimondo da Capua, was assigned to her as her confessor and spiritual adviser. Brother Raimondo was associated with her throughout the brief remainder of her lifetime, and after her death he wrote a long and detailed, though not always accurate, account of her life.

Catherine's public life and political involvement began shortly. She felt that the chaotic condition of European affairs could be settled if the Christian princes and peoples would stop fighting each other and unite instead in a common crusade against the infidels. In order that Christendom be reunified, she also thought it essential that the Pope return to his proper seat, in Rome, and be again universally acknowledged as the leader of the Church.

In 1375, while she was in Pisa campaigning for a crusade, she miraculously received the stigmata. In 1376 she went to Avignon to intercede for the Florentines with Pope Gregory XI. In spite of the opposition of the cardinals, she also pleaded with Gregory to return to Rome. In 1377 she went to Val d'Orcia to make peace between two branches of the Salembeni family. In 1378 she was again in Florence, where, while attempting to stop the war against Gregory XI, she unknowingly became involved in the internal politics of the city and made a number of enemies. In the autumn of that year she was called to Rome by the new Pope, Urban VI, and there found herself unhappily assisting in the initiating of a new schism. She died in Rome a year and a half later, reportedly of fatigue and sorrow, while still in her early thirties. She was canonized in 1461.

Her energetic personality and her direct, logical mind are reflected in her letters, of which several hundred appear in the standard editions of her correspondence. Her mystical doctrine, also frequently expressed in her letters, is set forth most clearly in her *Dialogo della Divina Provvidenza* (Dialogue of Divine Providence). Taken down by secretaries at various times in 1378 when Catherine was in states of trance, it is in form a dialogue between God the Father and the human soul on the subject of the spiritual life of man. Catherine is also credited with the authorship of about two dozen prayers. A short "Treatise on Consummate Perfection" often ascribed to her is probably not hers.

The *Dialogue of Divine Providence* was first translated into English in 1519 by Brother Dane James under the title *The Orcharde of Syn.* A modern translation is *The Dialogue of the Seraphic Virgin Catherine of Siena* by A. Thorol (1896). Catherine's correspondence is available in English in *Saint Catherine of Siena as Seen in Her Letters,* edited by Vida D. Scudder (1905). Selections from her work appear in *Little Flowers of St. Catherine of Siena* (1930), edited by Taurisano and translated into English by C. Dease.

ABOUT: Gardner, E. G. St. Catherine of Siena; Joergensen, J. Life of St. Catherine of Siena; Levasti, A. My Servant, Catherine; Undset, S. Catherine of Siena. [In Italian—Getto, G. Saggio Letterario sulla Santa Caterina da Siena.]

J. K.

CATS, JACOB (November 10, 1577-September 12, 1660), long regarded as Holland's household poet, was born in Brouwershaven,

the son of simple but industrious parents. After the mother's death in 1579 the children were brought up by maternal relatives. Jacob attended the Latin School at Zierikzee, then Leiden University (law and letters), finally the University of Orléans (France), which awarded him the doctorate in Roman Law in 1598. A costly projected journey to Italy had to be abandoned. Back in Holland a persistent illness interrupted legal practice; he went to England to consult the famous William Butler to little avail. While there Cats attended Oxford and Cambridge and made contacts with Puritan circles which probably influenced him religiously. A local Brouwershaven alchemist's medical remedies proved successful and in 1603 Cats settled in the Zeeland capital, Middelburg, as one of its city attorneys.

In 1605 he married the handsome and wealthy Elisabeth van Valckenburgh, a cultured and pious lady from Amsterdam; soon Cats became a member of the Calvinist church (Gereformeerd). The genuine happiness of his marriage the poet celebrated in 1625 with the poetic work *Houwelyck.* However, of seven children only two daughters survived infancy, Anna and Elisabeth.

In Middelburg cultured friends contributed to Cats' further development and reputation, especially the minister Willem Teellinck and the poets Simon van Beaumont and Johan de Brune—co-authors with Cats of a collection of poems, *De Zeeuwsche Nachtegaal.* A business venture with a brother in 1611 (draining of submerged land) proved initially successful. The new prosperity enabled Cats to acquire valuable property: a home in Goede and a country estate near Grijpskerke. The leisure spent there was devoted to poetic effort.

This tranquil life ended in 1621 with the conclusion of the Twelve Year Truce in Holland's war; Cats' public career began then also. He became successively chief magistrate (pensionary) of Middelburg and, in 1623, of Dordrecht. A knotty but successful legal mission to England in 1627 focused national attention on Cats. On July 3, 1636, he became Grand Pensionary of Holland and West Friesland. Other honors came to him along with his mounting fame as a poet. Cats' work as a statesman was marked by skillful negotiation and legal exactness, though not by original brilliance. He retired in 1651; his last years were devoted to poetic reflections on nature, life, and death.

Cats' significance is chiefly historical and lies primarily in the field of emblematic literature. Of this he composed a large quantity:

Maechdenplicht (1618), *Selfstrijt* (1620), *Spieghel van den Ouden ende Nieuwen Tydt* (1632), and in old age, *Ouderdom en Buytenleven.*

Critical opinion has swung from almost universal approval (1650-1850) to severest rejection. The eighteenth century critics Potgieter and Busken Huet condemned Cats on aesthetic grounds. Even today opinions diverge from Professor van Es' warm, though not uncritical, approval of Cats' strongly ethical note to the skeptical attitude of Professor Walch, who with much justification points to the endless moralizing in monotonous alexandrines. All agree that though Cats' spirit does not soar, he frequently attains striking insights and genuine poetic charm.

Cats' *Moral Emblems, with Aphorisms, Adages, and Proverbs of All Ages and Nations* was translated and edited by R. Pigot in 1860.
ABOUT: [In Dutch—Kalff, G. Jacob Cats. In French—Derudder, G. Un Poète Néerlandais, Cats, sa Vie et Ses Œuvres.]

C. K. P.

*CAVALCANTI, GUIDO (c. 1255-August 1300), Italian poet, was born in Florence of a proud Guelf family, son of Cavalcante de' Cavalcanti, who appears in Canto X of Dante's *Inferno* among the Epicureans in the Circle of the Heretics. With the elder Cavalcanti in Hell is the proud Farinata degli Uberti, leader of the Ghibelline faction, whose daughter Beatrice became Guido's wife. (The marriage was probably arranged as a truce between these rival factions.) Dante hails Guido as "chief of my friends" *(La Vita Nuova,* III) and says that they first met when Guido wrote a reply to one of his sonnets.

Of Cavalcanti's early life little is known except that he may have studied under Brunetto Latini, who, some years later, was Dante's teacher. He became active in the bloody feuding of the rival "Black" and "White" sects in Florence, and there is a story that Corso Donati (of the Blacks) paid assassins to make an attempt on his life while he was on a pilgrimage to St. James of Compostela. It was on this pilgrimage in 1292 that he met, in Toulouse, the woman he celebrates in many love poems under the name Mandetta. He wrote another series of love poems for a lady named Giovanna, called *Primavera* (Springtime) in the poems.

In 1300 the priors of Florence, of whom Dante was one, exiled all leaders of rival factions and among these was Cavalcanti. He

* kä väl kän' tē

went to Saranza where he contracted a fever of which he died, shortly after his return to Florence, in August 1300. Of this brilliant and stormy personality, Dante Gabriel Rossetti wrote: "The writings of his contemporaries, as well as his own, tend to show him rash in war, fickle in love, and presumptuous in belief; but also, by the same concurrent testimony, he was distinguished by great personal beauty, high accomplishments of all kinds, and daring nobility of soul."

One of the leading exponents of the *dolce stil novo* (sweet new style), Cavalcanti follows directly in the tradition of Guido Guinizelli, writing a poetry which vibrates with lyric passion. Perhaps the most striking difference between Cavalcanti and his predecessors, however, is the absence of positive religious affirmation in his poems. (Boccaccio tells a story about his alleged epicureanism in the *Decameron*, 9th tale, 6th day.) Significantly, Cavalcanti was a philosopher and a scholar, a master of the complex psychological theories of his day. Where in Guinizelli mortal love leads to an ultimate identification with God, in Cavalcanti love becomes a matter of high philosophical speculation, an abstruse riddle. "Love is no longer an affair of the heart," Sir Herbert Read writes of his poetry, "but is rather an affair of the brain." His most celebrated poem is one which has inspired numerous commentaries over the years but has continued to defy explication—the *canzone* "Donna mi prega" ("A lady asks me"). This finely-wrought analysis of love is a rare intellectual exercise—daringly free in thought—which comes close in spirit to the metaphysical poetry of the seventeenth century. Some commentators—among them Rossetti—are exasperated by its obscurantism and dismiss it, as Rossetti does, as "filled with metaphysical jargon and perhaps the very worst of Guido's productions." Others, like Ezra Pound (who translated it into English), consider it a masterpiece. Cavalcanti's other poems—sonnets and *ballati*—are spirited pieces. His famous *ballata* written on his going into exile—"Perch' io non spero di tornar giammai"—"Because I hope not ever to return"—finds an echo in T. S. Eliot's refrain in *Ash Wednesday,* "Because I do not hope to turn again."

Cavalcanti wrote various other works which do not survive, including a treatise on philosophy and one on oratory. His complete poetical works were first published in Giunti's collection in Florence in 1527. The definitive edition of his poems, edited by G. Favati, was published in Milan in 1957.

English translations of many of Cavalcanti's poems were made by D. G. Rossetti in his *The Early Italian Poets* (1861) and by Ezra Pound in *The Sonnets and Ballate of Guido Cavalcanti* (1912). Pound also translated parts of Cavalcanti's *Rime* in 1931. A good selection of his poems, in various translations, appears in L. R. Lind's *Lyric Poetry of the Italian Renaissance* (1954). This volume includes Ezra Pound's translation of "Donna mi prega," which first appeared in *The Dial* in 1928 and is reprinted in Pound's *Make It New* and *Literary Essays*. G. S. Fraser also translated the poem in *The Traveller Has Regrets* (1948).

ABOUT: Fletcher, J. B. The Philosophy of Love in Guido Cavalcanti; Pound, E. Make It New, Literary Essays; Read, H. Reason and Romanticism; Rossetti, D. G. Poems and Translations, Part II; Shaw, J. E. G. Cavalcanti's Theory of Love; Valency, M. In Praise of Love; Wilkins, E. H. A History of Italian Literature. [In Italian—Figurelli, F. Il Dolce Stil Novo; Vitetti, L. Il Sonnetto a Dante di Guido Cavalcanti.]

*ČECH, SVATOPLUK (February 21, 1846-February 23, 1908), Czech poet and novelist, was born in Ostředek in southeastern Bohemia, the son of an estate manager. He entered the *Gymnasium* in Litoměřice, and after a year went to Prague to the German Piarist *Gymnasium*. Already he had begun to write verse, and in 1864 he won a prize for a poem published in a provincial journal. In 1865 he enrolled in the Faculty of Law at Prague University; while there he served on the editorial staffs of several journals. He practiced law from 1872 to 1878, when he finally abandoned it for literature and editorial work, a double career which lasted most of his life. In 1874 he made a trip across the Ukraine to the Black Sea, to the Caucasus and Constantinople; in 1882 he traveled to Denmark. Both trips supplied him with literary material. Otherwise his life was uneventful: he avoided public life and all honors, living austerely in his country house near Prague. He was extremely popular in his day, and his sudden death was an occasion for national mourning.

Čech's poetry is rhetorical and highly decorative. In these qualities it is strongly influenced by Byron and the Russian and Polish Byronists. Much of his production is narrative. He wrote a series of long poems on subjects from Czech history: *Adamité* (The Adamites, 1873), about a radical sect of Hussite times which lived in promiscuity and nakedness; *Žižka* (1879), about the great Hussite leader; *Václav z Michalovic* (1880), on the tragedy of Bohemia's subjugation by Austria in 1620. A second group of poems consists of allegorical descriptions of contemporary political problems: *Europa* (1878)

and *Slavie* (1882). In them Čech assigns to the Slavs a messianic function: to restore peace to Europe. To the threat of a communism manifest in the Paris Commune of 1871, he opposes his own liberal ideals of freedom and democracy.

Čech's lyric poems are also political in content. Most successful were his *Písně Otroka* (Songs of a Slave, 1895), which have been republished some forty times. The problem of Negro slavery is used as a mask for that of Czech servitude.

Čech's prose works are largely forgotten, save for two humorous and satirical works, fantastic novels about Mr. Brouček, a self-satisfied Prague Philistine. He travels to the moon, and in time back to the fifteenth century Hussite era. In the latter work the author implicitly compares the mundane present to the vanished glory of the Hussite times.

In his own day Čech was honored as one of the greatest Czech poets. But his work lacks restraint, and is often inflated and ridden with clichés. Since 1900 he has lost greatly in favor, both critical and popular.

A few lyrics of Čech are translated in R. A. Ginsburg. *The Soul of a Century* (1942). One of his tales is found in S. B. Hrbková, *Czechoslovak Stories* (1920).

W. E. H.

*ČELAKOVSKÝ, FRANTIŠEK LADISLAV (March 7, 1799-August 5, 1852), Czech poet, was born in the town of Strakonice in southern Bohemia, the son of a carpenter. He studied philosophy at the Seminary at České Budějovice, and at the universities of Linz and Prague. Herder's admiration for Slavic folk songs inspired him to compile an all-Slavic collection, *Slovanské Národní Písně* (Slavic Folk Songs, 1822-27), which he published in the original languages and in his own Czech translations. Many of the Czech songs he collected himself in the Bohemian countryside. For seven years after 1822 he worked as a tutor, vainly trying to find a better position. He longed to go to Russia, a land he idolized as the potential liberator of the other Slavs, but without result. After the cruel Russian repression of the Polish uprising of 1830, his pro-Russian ardor cooled. In 1833-35 he served as editor of *Pražské Noviny* (Prague News), but lost his place when the Russian ambassador denounced him to Vienna for his criticism of Russian tyranny in Poland. Again he lapsed into poverty. In 1838 he was made librarian

* chěк

* chě′ lá kôf skē

162

to the noble Kinský family, and in 1841 professor of Slavistics at the University of Breslau, though his scholarly qualifications were not great. From 1848 until his death he occupied the same post at the University of Prague. He died in Prague, his health weakened by a life of poverty.

Čelakovský was an early romanticist who emphasized the role of folk verse as a model for the creation of written poetry. His *Ohlas Písní Ruských* (1829) and *Ohlas Písní Českých* (1839), "echoes" of Russian and Czech folk songs, are free creations in the folk styles of these two peoples. *Růže Stolistá* (Hundred-Petaled Rose, or Cabbage Rose, 1840), named for its hundred twelve-line poems, contains more conventional verses, some about love, others didactic, showing the influence of his favorite poet, Goethe. Čelakovský also wrote some of the finest of Czech epigrams. Esteemed in his own day for his patriotic and didactic verse, he seems most original today as a creator of a complex free verse in an individual style influenced by the folk song.

A few translations of individual poems are found in R. A. Ginsburg, *The Soul of a Century* (1942).

ABOUT: Součková, M. The Czech Romantics; Harkins, W. E. Anthology of Czech Literature; Harkins, W. E. The Russian Folk Epos in Czech Literature.

W. E. H.

*CELLINI, BENVENUTO** (November 3, 1500-February 13, 1571), Italian sculptor and writer, born in Florence, was the son of an architect who also practiced music and poetry. Under paternal influence, Benvenuto studied flute and singing, but without enthusiasm, for he was drawn toward design and at thirteen was briefly a goldsmith's apprentice. His native restlessness first appeared in a brawl when he was sixteen which led to his confinement in Siena; thereafter he took to wandering and passed through Bologna and Pisa and, by 1519, set up his own shop in Rome. At his father's request he returned two years later to Florence, but was soon in trouble and went again to Rome, where he passed the years 1523 to 1540, working for important churchmen, including Clement VII; in the service of the latter, in 1527, he distinguished himself in the defense of the city as cannoneer, and attained notoriety by his reputed killing of the Constable of Bourbon with a crossbow. In his

* chāl lē′ nē

CELLINI

Vita, Cellini gives a brilliant picture of the siege of the Castel Sant' Angelo, of his acts as well as the intrigues of his rivals and of various ecclesiastics. Two years later, the Pope named Cellini master of the coinage, but he was constantly plagued by slanderers as well as his own disorderly conduct. The most important event was his meeting with Pompeo, a jeweler from Milan who had killed his brother, and whom in turn Cellini killed, taking refuge with Cardinal Cornaro and in 1534 receiving the protection of the new Pope Paul III, whose admiration for Cellini's medals led him to set the artist in a privileged place. The Pompeo affair, however, obliged Cellini to leave Rome, and he returned to Florence and did engraving for Duke Alexander. Called again to Rome by the Pope, Cellini executed further works, but he suffered new disgrace when accused of stealing jewels from the Pope; after imprisonment in Castel Sant' Angelo, he went to Paris, where, in 1540, Francis I established him with a pension in the Hôtel du Petit Nesle and, with proper materials and equipment, he undertook a number of important art works and very difficult castings. He tells of his forced entrance into the Petit Nesle and the expulsion of its residents. All too soon his intrigues in the court caused him to leave France.

Cellini's most important creative period begins in 1545, on his return to Florence. Duke Cosimo encouraged him by orders for statues, and among the masterpieces of this moment we count the Perseus and an Apollo.

From the *Vita,* however, we learn that Cosimo's promises were followed by non-payment or reduction of payment, leaving the artist without means for the purchase of his costly materials and equipment; his much repeated and bitter complaints were no doubt to a large degree justified. In 1558 Cellini took first tonsure and perhaps minor orders, but he was released two years later in order to marry Piera, the mother of several of his eight children. The *Vita* is not always explicit regarding the events of this period, especially the adoption in 1560 of a worthless boy called Nutino, later disinherited. After 1562, the terminal date of the autobiography, Cellini's life is known through personal notes such as his "Ricordi." By this time, the great period of Florentine sculpture had ended, and the Duke's private worries, including loss of relatives, turned his attention from art. As so often in the preceding years, Cellini was constantly seeking payment for work done, and entered into various financial speculations. His grave illness in 1560 had undermined his health and reduced his creativity, preventing him for example from participating in the memorials for Michelangelo, to which he was appointed in 1564. His sons had no children, and his papers passed to the Florentine libraries; the inventory of his studio, made on his death, is of great importance in determining the authenticity of his works of art, since these are dispersed and often difficult to trace; his immense reputation explains the countless dubious attributions.

Cellini's work in metal, especially in gold, suffered gravely from the chronic need for cash of his protectors, such as Francis I, who sent such objects to the melting pot in order to pay military debts. The famous salt-cellar escaped by chance and was sent by the King of France to Austria and to safety. Cellini's many fine pieces of jewelry and plate have completely disappeared. Of other small objects, we have a variety of fine medals and coins, ewers, and vases. In sculpture, Cellini's extant masterpieces include several busts of cardinals and of Cosimo de' Medici, the "Nymph of Fontainebleau," the great Perseus and preliminary models for it, the four statuettes on its base, and various mythological figures. The majority of these pieces are in bronze, and in this medium represent very intricate problems of casting, described at several points in the *Vita,* and considered at the time as monumental achievements in technique.

Cellini's minor writings include works of importance in the history of art, especially the *Due Trattati,* published in Florence in 1568, and devoted to sculpture and work in gold. The technical methods described are less original than Cellini thought, but his forceful manner of expression lent them weight and reflects the attitudes of the *Vita.* Of less distinction are his treatises on design and architecture, and his *Rime;* all these works are available in the English translation of 1898. Cellini's great fame in literature depends almost wholly on his autobiography, begun about the time of his first tonsure, and partly written from dictation by a secretary. The first edition of the *Vita* was prepared with some care in 1728 by Antonio Cocchi, who sought in it for information on contemporary artists. Reactions to the book, as for example those of Parini and Goethe, have varied considerably. In modern times readers have come to esteem the original and uncorrected versions for their style and their inspired expression of inner feeling that is powerful for its naïve fantasy and even in its exaggeration of fact. Cellini's use of an uninhibited spoken manner can hardly be matched for several centuries, and yet the strong individuality comes close to the highest humanistic ideals.

Critical editions of Cellini's writings have appeared during the present century; that by Carrara (1926) includes an excellent introduction.

The *Vita* was translated in 1771 by T. Nugent, and much reprinted; the version by T. Roscoe (1822) is based on improved Italian texts; more modern editions are by J. A. Symonds, A. Macdonell, and R. H. H. Cust.

ABOUT: Cortissoz, R. Benvenuto Cellini, Artist and Writer; Cust, R. H. H. Benvenuto Cellini. [In French and Italian—see studies by E. Allodoli, H. Focillon, T. Harlor.]

F. J. C.

*CERVANTES SAAVEDRA, MIGUEL DE (September 29, 1547-April 23, 1616), Spanish novelist, dramatist, and poet, was born in Alcalá de Henares, the fourth of seven children of Rodrigo de Cervantes Saavedra and Leonor de Cortinas. The young Miguel first studied in Valladolid, where his father, an apothecary surgeon, practiced for several years. It is probable that Cervantes subsequently studied in Seville and then later in Madrid as a student of Juan López de Hoyos. In 1569 Cervantes went to Italy where he entered the service of Cardinal Acquaviva. He was very receptive to the stimulating atmosphere of Renaissance Italy, and his sub-

* thĕr vän′ täs (sĕr vän′ tēz) sä vä′ thrä

CERVANTES

sequent works reveal the deep influence of Italian literature and philosophy.

A soldier by 1570, Cervantes participated in the great naval battle of Lepanto on October 7, 1571. Despite illness, Cervantes fought valiantly on board the galley "Marquesa" which constituted part of the armada commanded by Don Juan of Austria. As a result he was wounded in the chest and in the left hand which, according to Cervantes, redounded to "the greater glory of the right." The wound which rendered his hand useless and earned for him the title "El Manco de Lepanto" was a source of great pride, and in his works there are frequent references to the fortitude and abnegation required by the military life. After spending six months in a hospital in Messina, Cervantes participated in expeditions to Corfu, Navarino, and Tunis, after which he spent the rest of his military service in garrison at Palermo and Naples. On returning to Spain aboard the galley "Sol" in September of 1575 with letters of commendation from Don Juan of Austria and the Viceroy of Sicily, Cervantes was seized by the corsair "Arnaut Mami" and carried to Algiers as a prisoner. His captivity lasted for five years during which he made repeated attempts to escape, for he firmly believed that "one should risk one's life for honor and liberty." Having been bought by Hassan Pasha from the Greek renegade Dali Mami, Cervantes was already on a galley about to be taken to Constantinople when his ransom was finally paid by the Trinitarian friar Juan Gil. He was liberated in September 1580.

Cervantes' years of military service and of slavery won him no privileges once he had returned to Spain, and no important post was granted him, despite his high hopes. Obliged to earn a precarious living as government tax collector and as commissary purchasing supplies for the ill-fated "Invincible Armada," Cervantes led a penurious and peripatetic existence. He showed little aptitude for his work and was apparently not very businesslike. In 1587 he was excommunicated for excessive zeal in collecting wheat; after entrusting the banker Simón Freire de Lima with a large sum of government money, he was left to account for the deficit when the agent went into bankruptcy and absconded; in 1597 and in 1602 he was imprisoned briefly in Seville for irregularities in his accounts. In addition to these difficulties in connection with his work, Cervantes was arrested along with his family in Valladolid in 1604 under suspicion of involvement in the death of the nobleman Gaspar de Ezpeleta. Although Cervantes proved to be innocent of blame, the name of his natural daughter Isabel de Saavedra figured in the proceedings in an unfavorable light. Isabel was the fruit of a liaison with Ana Franca de Rojas and was born shortly before Cervantes' marriage in Esquivias to Catalina de Salazar y Palacios in 1584. The union was never a happy one nor was Catalina's dowry sufficient to relieve Cervantes' ever-present financial anxieties.

Although all of Cervantes' important works belong to the later years of his life, he had begun his literary career as dramatist and novelist by 1580. As a poet, his career dates from 1568 at which time López de Hoyos published four of his poetic compositions in *Exequias de la Reina Isabel*. Cervantes' desire to excel as a poet accompanied him throughout his life, although he himself realized that he did not possess the gift. In his *Viaje del Parnaso* (1614) Cervantes confesses this constant desire despite heaven's refusal to grant him the necessary talent. In a letter dated August 14, 1604, Lope de Vega stated that "among the new poets there was none so bad as Cervantes." While later criticism has not entirely confirmed this too-harsh judgment, the consensus is that Cervantes was "a good amateur."

Cervantes' first novel, *La Galatea*, was published in Alcalá in 1585. The work is a pastoral novel, divided into six books, and is conventional, diffuse and artificial. Despite these defects it has the virtue of revealing one aspect of the author's dual image of reality: in this work Cervantes presents an idealized vision of the world wherein love is elevated to the highest plane and the Renaissance Neoplatonic cult of beauty is exalted. The frequently promised second part of *La Galatea* never appeared, but Cervantes always professed a certain affection for this early work.

Between 1581 and 1587 Cervantes presented between twenty and thirty plays with relative success, since in the author's words in the prologue to the *Ocho Comedias,* "they ran their course without whistles, shouts, or tumult," but after 1600 his popularity was greatly diminished when Lope de Vega "made off with the kingship of the Spanish stage." In 1615, at the request of a bookseller, Cervantes collected a group of his plays and these were published as *Ocho Comedias y Ocho Entremeses.* The plays are varied in theme: some are autobiographical and have the reality of places seen and events experienced, while others are imaginative fictions derived from the Italianate novel. *Los Tratos de Argel, El Gallardo Español, La Gran Sultana,* and *Los Baños de Argel,* for example, clearly mirror the author's years of captivity in Algiers and are perhaps more interesting biographically than dramatically. The best of Cervantes' dramatic talent is to be found in the *entremeses.* Short comic pieces, they are full of color and movement and abound in irony and satire.

Corresponding to this same mature period in the author's life are the *Novelas Ejemplares* (1613) dedicated to his patron the Count of Lemos. The collection consists of twelve *novelas* (long short stories) written either in a predominantly idealistic or realistic vein. Some of the tales such as *La Gitanilla* and *La Ilustre Fregona* combine both tendencies to varying degrees. *Rinconete y Cortadillo* and *El Coloquio de los Perros* are masterpieces of invention against a realistic background, and are among the author's most distinguished works.

The most complete expression of Cervantes' dual vision of the world is found in his *Don Quixote.* Part One appeared in 1605 in Madrid published by Juan de la Cuesta under the title *El Ingenioso Hidalgo Don Quijote de la Mancha.* The second part, *Segunda Parte del Ingenioso Caballero Don Quijote de la Mancha,* appeared in 1615. This vast novel is not only a synthesis of the literary forms known up to the time of Cervantes, but also a vivid human document, rich in invention and profound in thought. Don Quixote, the hidalgo who fancies himself a knight errant, and Sancho Panza, his faithful squire,

have become symbols of two points of view: the idealistic and the realistic. In the prologue to Part One, the author tells us that his work is an invective against the novels of chivalry. It cannot be denied that Cervantes satirized this form brilliantly, but it is equally undeniable that the greatness of the book rests not on the satire but on its deep humor and understanding of and sympathy for the human condition. It is a mirror of the landscape and customs of the Spain of Cervantes, an immense panorama of individuals and adventures. In the course of the novel Cervantes explores the nature of good and evil, truth, reality, and justice.

The unity of the second part is far superior to that of the first, the action of which is periodically interrupted by unrelated extraneous episodes such as the pastoral tale of Marcela and Grisóstomo and the sentimental story of Luscinda and Cardenio. In Part Two, all interest is concentrated on the main figures and the subsidiary actions spring from them. The novel is both happy and sad, popular and literary, but its final effect is one of melancholy: with the death of Don Quixote the world of idealism and illusion also perishes.

Don Quixote was an immediate success and underwent six editions in 1605 alone. It was translated into English and French during Cervantes' lifetime, and in 1614 one Alonso Fernández de Avellaneda wrote a spurious *Segundo Tomo del Ingenioso Hidalgo Don Quixote de la Mancha* anticipating Cervantes by one year. At first *Don Quixote* was applauded chiefly as a parody and as a work of entertainment, but in time it came to be appreciated in its full worth. In the eighteenth century it influenced Sterne, Fielding, and Smollett, and in the nineteenth it was much admired by Schelling, Heine, and Wilhelm Schlegel who saw in it the "eternal battle between the prose and the poetry of life." Turgenev, in *Hamlet and Don Quijote,* stated: "Don Quixote is, above all, the problem of faith, of faith in something eternal, immutable, of faith in a truth superior to the individual."

Don Quixote has inspired such artists and composers as Doré and Daumier, Massenet and Strauss; not only the knight and his squire, but also his lady and his steed, Dulcinea and Rosinante, have become proverbial.

Cervantes' last work was *La Historia de los Trabajos de Persiles y Segismunda* (1617), the dedication of which was written four days before the author's death. This Byzantine novel is a huge book of adventures of a deliberately unreal nature. In the words of Farinelli, it was Cervantes' "last romantic dream."

Cervantes died in Madrid where he had been living for approximately the last decade of his life. Shortly before his death he joined the Tertiaries of St. Francis and was buried in the robes of the Order. His wife, who had never had any children, survived him by ten years, while his natural daughter died in 1652.

The first translation into English of *Don Quixote* was that of Thomas Shelton in 1612. After that date translations of Cervantes into English are so abundant that it would be impossible to mention more than a few. The *Entremeses* were translated by S. G. Morley in 1948; in the *Complete Works* edited by James Fitzmaurice-Kelly (1901-03) *La Galatea* is translated in Volume II, *Don Quixote* by J. Ormsby in Vols. 3-6, *Novelas Ejemplares* by N. Maccoll in Vols. 7-8. The best translations of *Don Quixote* are those of Samuel Putnam (1949) and J. M. Cohen (1950). A comprehensive listing of Cervantine translations can be found in Remigio Ugo Pane, *English Translations from the Spanish* (1484-1943), 1944.

ABOUT: Bell, A. F. G. Cervantes; Entwistle, W. J. Cervantes; Fitzmaurice-Kelly. J. Cervantes in England, *also* Miguel de Cervantes Saavedra; Flores, A. & Bernardete, M. J. Cervantes Across the Centuries; Grismer, R. L. Cervantes: A Bibliography; Lewis, D. B. W. The Shadow of Cervantes; Mac Eóin, G. Cervantes; Riley, E. C. Cervantes' Theory of the Novel; Rosenkranz, H. El Greco and Cervantes in the Rhythm of Experience; Schevill, R. Cervantes; Unamuno, M. de, The Life of Don Quixote and Sancho. [In Spanish—Bonilla y San Martín, Cervantes y su Obra; Castro, A. El Pensamiento de Cervantes; Madariaga, S. de, Guía del Lector del Quijote; Ortega y Gasset, J. Meditaciones del Quijote.]

B. P. P.

*CHAADAEV (or CHAADAYEV), PETER YAKOVLEVICH

(May 27, 1793-April 14, 1856), Russian writer, was born in Moscow into a family of prosperous landowners. His parents died when he was very young, and with his elder brother he was raised in the household of his uncle, the historian Prince D. M. Scherbatov. Chaadaev received an excellent education in European languages and culture both at home under tutors and at the University of Moscow, where he won some reputation for his scholarship, his wit, and his arrogant manner. In 1812 he entered the Russian army and he was in action at the Battle of Borodino. He left the army in 1821.

Independently wealthy, Chaadaev moved freely in the best circles of Russian society in St. Petersburg and Moscow. He knew Pushkin, Gogol, Lermontov, and Turgenev. He took a lively interest in the social and po-

* chŭ dä' yĕf

litical ferment of his age, although his outlook was primarily religious and cultural rather than political. From about 1814 to 1821 he belonged to the Masonic Order. He traveled in Europe from 1823 to 1826 and met Schlegel, Schelling, and the Abbé de Lamennais. He became increasingly influenced by the writings of the French Catholic intellectuals, especially Joseph de Maistre and the Vicomte de Bonald, and this influence drew him even closer to the West and the Church of Rome. Upon his return to Moscow, Chaadaev was arrested for complicity in the Decembrist uprising of 1825, but he was soon released. He then retired from society to live in seclusion engaged in study and writing. During this period he wrote, in French, his *Philosophical Letters*, a bitter criticism of Russian history and society for its isolation from Europe and the "West." Only one of these letters was published in Chaadaev's lifetime—in 1836 in a review published by Nicolas Nadezhin called *The Telescope*. This essay was so controversial—"a shot sounding in the dark night," as it was described—that it brought down severe punishment upon the heads of its author and publisher. *The Telescope* was banned; Nadezhin was exiled, and Chaadaev was officially declared insane. The persecution brought him some popular sympathy, but he remained aloof, living out his life in Moscow where he died at the age of sixty-two.

A handsome, fastidious, and aristocratic figure, Chaadaev had few close friends. His *Philosophical Letters*, his only important literary production, is little read today, but this frank and forthright challenge to the Russian nationalists, the "Slavophiles," stimulated heated controversy in its day. His position was primarily a mystical one. He dreamed of a kingdom of God on earth which would unite Eastern and Western Christianity and ultimately embrace the whole of humanity. Its center would be the Church of Rome. The function of the historian, he argued, was to seek out the divine idea which the course of history expresses—i.e., the spiritual progress of Christianity. As for Russia—Chaadaev viewed his own country as outside this stream of history because her Christianity, the Greek Orthodox Church, was not a part of the mainstream. Only through union with the West and with Roman Catholicism, he believed, could Russia establish her identity as a nation and assume her rightful place as a leading nation of the world.

His position was not a popular one, but Chaadaev scorned popularity. The great Russian political reformer Alexander Herzen recalled him as a "melancholic and original figure," who stood, "like some painful reprimand, against the faded and gloomy background of Muscovite high-life. . . . He was capricious, peculiar, withdrawn from society, and yet he could not detach himself from it. . . . The old and the young felt neither comfortable nor free in his presence. God knows why his motionless face and far-distant gaze, his sorrowful, scoffing and bitter indulgence led them into confusion. . . ."

Chaadaev wrote in all about eight *Philosophical Letters*. Some of them were not discovered until 1935 in the archives of the Academy of Science of the U.S.S.R. A French edition of selections from his works was published in 1862.

None of Chaadaev's writings has been translated into English, but there are extensive quotations from him, in English, in W. Lednicki's *Russia, Poland and the West* (1954).

ABOUT: Lednicki, W. Russia, Poland and the West; Masaryk, T. G. The Spirit of Russia, I; Moskoff, E. A. The Russian Philosopher Chaadayev; Russian Review, XXII (1963). [In French—Quenet, C. Tchaadaev et Les Lettres Philosophiques.]

*CHAMFORT, SÉBASTIEN ROCH NICOLAS (August 6, 1740/41-April 13, 1794), French moralist, poet, and playwright,

was born near Clermont, an illegitimate child of whose early years little is known. He was a scholarship student at the Collège de Grassins and as a youth seriously considered emigrating to America. He supported himself for a time as tutor to the nephew of a nobleman. Early in the 1760's young Chamfort settled in Paris and began publishing verse and articles. His rise to social prominence in that city was little short of meteoric. How he accomplished this is not certain, but his success was clearly the result of his personal charm, his good looks, and his wit, rather than his literary talent. He became a member of the most distinguished literary and social circles and was a prominent visitor to the *salons* of Mme du Deffand, Mme de Lespinasse, and Mme Helvétius. "He could make excellent love and tolerable literature, faculties which at that date rarely missed their due reward," George Saintsbury remarked.

In April 1764 Chamfort's comedy *La Jeune Indienne* was produced at the Comédie Française. The critics denounced it, but the public reacted favorably and the play enjoyed considerable success. In 1765 it was presented

* shän fôr'

168

for the king at Versailles. His other plays had a similar reception—denounced by the critics, well received by the public. His tragedy *Mustapha et Zéangir* was performed before the royal court at Fontainebleau in 1776 and moved Louis XVI and Marie Antoinette to tears. He won recognition too as a critic. His essay on Molière was honored by the Académie Française. He also wrote an essay on Racine (only parts are extant) and one on La Fontaine which was widely praised.

Success seemed only to stimulate in Chamfort a tendency toward bitterness and cynicism. This condition was aggravated by a nagging skin disease which forced him into several long periods of retirement in the country. Something of the same perverseness led him to take sides in the early years of the French Revolution not with the aristocrats who had been his patrons but with the revolutionists. He met and became friendly with the revolutionary leader Mirabeau and wrote some of his most bitter maxims in the cause, including the often-quoted: "The nobility, the nobles say, is an intermediary between king and people. . . . Yes, as the hunting dog is the intermediary between the hunter and the rabbits."

Ultimately Chamfort became disillusioned by the course of the revolution and was outspoken in his criticism of it. He was arrested, then released. When he learned that he was about to be re-arrested, he attempted suicide. He wounded himself horribly and died after many days of agony at the age of fifty-three.

Chamfort's memory survives in the collection of his maxims. (He defined a maxim as "a product of the labor of a clever man intended to spare fools trouble.") Even these have been overshadowed by the far more celebrated maxims of La Rochefoucauld. Saintsbury, who had very little regard for Chamfort, nevertheless conceded that the maxims contain "an abundance of insight." More recently Albert Camus *(Sewanee Review,* Winter 1948) described him as "one of the most enlightening of French moralists. . . . Chamfort does not reduce life to formula. His great artistry consists rather in amazingly accurate strokes the implications of which the mind can explore afterward."

The Maxims and Considerations of Chamfort were translated by E. P. Mathers (2 vols., 1926). Selections from his anecdotes were translated by L. Mason under the title *Wit and Wisdom of the French Court* (1937).

ABOUT: Saintsbury, G. Collected Essays and Papers, IV; Whibley, C. Political Portraits: Second Series. [In French—see studies by P. J. Richard, J. Teppe, L. Treich.]

*CHAMISSO, ADELBERT VON (Louis Charles Adélaïde de) (January 30[?], 1781-August 21, 1838), German poet and botanist, was born at his ancestral castle Boncourt in the Champagne near St. Menehould, the fourth son of Count Louis Marie de Chamisso and his wife Marie Anne Gargam. Although his father had retired from military service and the Court of Versailles to devote himself entirely to his wife, their six children, and his estates, Adelbert remembered his childhood as an unhappy time. Left to the care of a strict governess, he liked nothing better than to read, day-dream, and explore the countryside. In 1790 catastrophe struck; during the revolution Boncourt was completely destroyed by fire and the family forced to flee first to Belgium, then Holland, and finally Germany. The Count joined the émigré army under Marshall de Broglie as lieutenant-colonel, while the rest of the family, almost destitute, lived by painting and selling miniature portraits. At one time Adelbert faced the prospect of being apprenticed to a carpenter. In 1796 he was given the position of page in the royal household in Berlin, where he was soon joined by his relatives. Attending the Französische Gymnasium and the Military Academy, he was eventually commissioned a lieutenant in an infantry regiment in 1801, the year when his family returned to France under the general amnesty of Napoleon.

Chamisso had entered the army with high hopes, but soon became disillusioned. Never a model soldier, he began to hate the daily routine, the loss of freedom and of identity. In addition, he felt handicapped as a foreigner, since in those days his German was very poor; he never completely lost his French accent. On leave in France in 1802, he realized that he could no longer communicate with his family as freely as before. Back in Berlin he threw himself into the study of French literature and was particularly taken with Rousseau. He had already made himself at home in German letters; Schiller was his favorite. Kant was a revelation to him, as is obvious from his fragment *Faust* (1803). This play is indicative of Chamisso's problematical situation throughout his life: it manifests the doubts he had about himself, the world, the limitations of knowledge and of the spirit; and as such it is thoroughly nonromantic. His poetry, in German from 1801, is modeled after Klopstock, Goethe, Schiller, Novalis, and Tieck. In these early years he fell in love with a French widow, Cérès Duvernay, who was to make his

* shä′ mǐ sō

CHAMISSO

life miserable until 1809, when she finally disappeared from view.

In 1803 Chamisso met K. A. Varnhagen and through him the younger Berlin "Romantik": Theremin, Hitzig, Neumann, Robert, Koreff, Neander, Klaproth. Together they founded the *Nordsternbund,* whose name derived from the romantic search for knowledge, and brought out the so-called *Grüne Almanach* (1804-06). In time Fichte, Bernhardi, and Fouqué joined the group and the almanac. All the friends vied with each other in correcting Chamisso's German. He took up the study of Greek and soon read the classics in the original. In time he was ordered to accompany his regiment through Hannover, finally doing garrison duty in Hameln. There, after a visit by Varnhagen and Neumann, Chamisso decided to study with them at the University of Halle, but his request for a discharge was not accepted. The result of this was his short story "Adelberts Fabel" (1806) which ends on a note of resignation. Stimulated by his recent reading of German folk and fairy tales and of the stoic philosophy of Epictetus, Chamisso that same year wrote his fragmentary drama *Fortunati Glücksäckel und Wunschhütlein* which, like Tieck's *Octavian,* is a kaleidoscope of promising poetry in the most varied meters. It, too, is autobiographical, but, by opposing two contradictory characters, reaches no solution. Again, outside compulsion and inner freedom are Chamisso's leitmotivs. In November 1806 Hameln was handed over to the French without a shot being fired.

The next six years of Chamisso's life were unhappy and yet educative. He returned to France and found that Germany was his home. In 1808 he finally resigned his commission. His friendship with Varnhagen gradually weakened, but he found substitutes in Hitzig and Fouqué. His old dream of founding a family was constantly before him. At last he heard of a teaching post in Paris, but, hurrying there, was disillusioned. In the French capital he again met Varnhagen and Koreff and made the acquaintance of Uhland and A. von Humboldt. With Helmina von Chézy, with whom he may have had a love affair, he began translating A. W. Schlegel's Vienna Lectures into French. Although the enterprise came to naught, it put him in touch with Mme de Staël's circle and he followed her call to Chamont, to Fossé, finally to Coppet. He was entranced by her until she chose de Rocca. With her son August he studied botany and at last found his life's work.

In 1812 Chamisso enrolled as a student of medicine at the newly founded University of Berlin, studying hard and collecting specimens. When the War of Liberation broke out, he escaped—a man without a country—to Kunersdorf, and here he wrote his famous and popular fable *Peter Schlemihl* (1814), the story of the man without a shadow. The interpretations of this shadow are many: some think it is honor, others appearance, still others lack of a country. In view of Chamisso's development and profound preoccupation with the problem of the individual versus the world, perhaps the shadow should be regarded less literally and rather as a symbol for the outsider, the non-social being, the artist, who—in the book—finds satisfaction in working for others, for science. That was Chamisso's own story and by writing it he freed himself. He returned to Berlin, becoming a close friend of E. T. A. Hoffmann. In 1815 Chamisso was called to accompany the Russian expedition around the world under Otto von Kotzebue.

On the return of the "Rurik" in 1818 Chamisso published his findings in scientific journals. His *Reise um die Welt* (revised 1836) is a popular account of these three years. In 1819 he received an honorary degree from the University of Berlin and married Antonie Piaste (twenty years his junior), by whom he had nine children who were brought up in the Protestant faith. From that time on he had no further financial worries, being permanently employed at the Botanical Garden in Berlin. He now published his many poems.

In 1832 he became the editor of the *Deutsche Musenalmanach*, the unofficial organ of the *Schwäbische Schule*, which was supported by Uhland and Schwab on the one hand and by Heine, Freiligrath, Lenau, Anastasius Grün, and Immermann on the other. His dramatic attempts, such as *Die Wunderkur* (1825) and *Der Wunderdoktor* (1828, after Molière) were unsuccessful. In 1837, the year his wife died, he published with Gaudy their translation of Béranger's poems. Shortly after resigning as Director of the Herbarium in 1838, he died. He is buried in the cemetery near the Hallische Thor.

Chamisso's work, particularly his *Schlemihl* and his later poetry, were very well received. His verse was often published and set to music, as for instance his most famous song cycle "Frauenliebe" (R. Schumann). In his ballads he continued the tradition of Bürger, fusing realistic portrayal with a keen sense of rhythm. He had much in common with *Jung-Deutschland* and played for them a paternal role. Heartily disliking abstract theories, he once stated, "I rarely intend anything at all with my poetry; when I am moved by an anecdote, a word, a picture, I think that others ought to share my experience and therefore struggle valiantly with my language until it appears." A true stoic, he thought little of money, social prestige, and conventions. In politics he was a staunch supporter of the liberal constitutional movement.

His appearance was youthful; he was tall, lean-faced, eagle-nosed, with long black hair, preferring to wear a suit cut on military lines *(kurtka)*, a cap, boots, and, like the picture of Schlemihl in the first edition, holding his beloved pipe in one hand, with a specimen-box slung over his shoulder.

Hebbel, perhaps unfairly, called him receptive rather than original, a poet who liked comfort and yet wrote masterly terza rima, one who was gentle and charming and yet delighted in the gruesome. Heine praised him in the *Romantische Schule* as one of those who became young with the new generation, whose tears, coming from a stout heart, were the more moving. Today Chamisso lives on in the anthologies and school readers, in music, and in his *Schlemihl*. He is one of those transitional poets between two ages, in his case romanticism and naturalism, who are not great, but who hold a firm second place.

Of Chamisso's *Peter Schlemihl* there appeared about twenty-five English editions based, more often than not, on the first translation done by Sir John Bowring (1824). One of the most recent editions is in Clark's *Great Short Novels of the World* (1927). His *Reise* came out originally in O. von Kotzebue's *Voyage of Discovery*, II and III (1821), translated by H. E. Lloyd. His most popular song cycle *Woman's Love and Life* was translated by F. V. McDonald (1881); it is also available in *Schirmer's Library of Musical Classics*, Nos. 1356-57. *Faust: A Dramatic Sketch* was translated by H. Phillips, Jr. (1861). His poems are available in selections in *Francke and Howard's German Classics* (1913-14), V, and *Warner Library* (1917), VI.

ABOUT: Bisson, L. *in* German Studies Presented to Professor H. G. Fiedler; Mahr, A. C. The Visit of the "Rurik" to San Francisco in 1816; Mann, T. Essays of Three Decades; Contemporary Review (1951); German Quarterly (1953). [In German— see studies by V. Baumgartner *in* Wege zur Dichtung. XLII, E. Ehrlich *in* Germanische Studien, CXVIII, and O. Walzel.]

R. L. K.

*CHAPELAIN, JEAN (December 4, 1595-February 22, 1674), French poet and critic, was born in Paris, the son of Sébastien Chapelain and Jeanne Corbière. His parents longed to see their son become a successful writer, and they educated him accordingly, giving him excellent training in the classics and in the contemporary literatures of Italy and Spain. Chapelain early distinguished himself in Paris society for his learning and his conversation. He became a frequent guest at the Hôtel de Rambouillet and was admired by the giants of French literary society of his day—Malherbe, Jean-Louis Guez de Balzac, Corneille, and others. Thanks to the patronage of the all-powerful Richelieu, to whom he dedicated one of his best poems, Chapelain won favor in the court. In 1632 he became secretary to Louis XIII. He exerted considerable influence on the organization of the French Academy. For General Colbert, patron of academies, he drew up a list of French men of letters who, in his judgment, were deserving of pensions. His selection of names for this list and his characterization of each author were described by George Saintsbury as "as sound, as sensible, and, at the same time, as benevolent a handlist of the kind as you shall discover in the records of the centuries."

Chapelain's criticism was pedantic and unimaginative, but it was also sound and well-informed. It emphasized "bon sens," verisimilitude, and the classical unities. Though it contributed little to the mainstream of French literary criticism, it laid the foundation for much that was to come later. His best critical writing was in his letters. The most controversial piece he wrote was his *Sentiments de*

* shà plăn'

l'Académie Française sur Le Cid—a censure of Corneille's celebrated drama which Chapelain wrote at the instigation of Richelieu.

The tragedy of Chapelain's life is not without a note of ironic humor. This was the colossal failure of his epic poem on Joan of Arc, *La Pucelle*, on which he worked for more than twenty-five years. His readers awaited the work as the French successor to the *Iliad* and the *Aeneid*. Instead, when he at last published the first twelve cantos in 1656, they found an egregious poem which even his most charitable friends could only describe as "beautiful but excessively tiresome." The reception of the poem so discouraged Chapelain that he did not publish the remaining cantos. His failure as a poet exposed him to cruel satires, among them *Chapelain Décoiffé* ("Chapelain Dewigged"), which a modern critic describes as "a revenge of the younger generation of Classicism upon a dictator of Parnassus who to them stood out as the protector and patron of all mediocrities."

Chapelain never married. He died in Paris at the age of seventy-eight, a wealthy man, thanks to the generosity of his patrons. A legend, probably circulated by his enemies, had it that he was a miser. Actually he was a proud man, well loved by his friends, loyal to his patrons, and thoroughly dedicated to literature.

Chapelain's critical works in French were published as *Opuscules Critiques* in 1936.

ABOUT: Guizot, F. Corneille and His Times; Saintsbury, G. A History of Criticism, II; Van Roosbroeck, P. Chapelain Décoiffé: A Battle of Parodies; Studies in Philology, January 1940. [In French—Bourgoin, A. Les Maîtres de la Critique au XVIIème Siècle; Collas, G. Jean Chapelain.]

CHARLES, DUKE OF ORLÉANS (*Charles d'Orléans) (November 24, 1394-January 5, 1465), French poet, was the fourth son of Louis, Duke of Orléans, and his wife Valentine, Duchess of Milan. He was thus the nephew of Charles VI of France. He went with his mother when she left the royal court and it was due to her influence that he obtained an excellent education under the tutorship of Nicole Garbet. At the age of ten he was betrothed to the widow of Richard II of England and was married to her on December 10, 1408. His father had been assassinated in 1407 and after the death of his mother in 1409 Charles had to defend his rights against his enemies. The early death of his wife left him free to conclude a political marriage with Bonne d'Armagnac and engage

* shârl d'ôr lā än'

in the successful pursuit of the faction which had murdered his father. Both sides had sought help from the English, and this ultimately led to the invasion of France by Henry V of England and the crushing defeat of the French at Agincourt in 1415. Charles, badly wounded, was found among the dead and made prisoner.

For the next twenty-five years he was a pawn in the political intrigues between England and France. Although he pledged his land to raise a ransom, his person was more important than his money and he was kept imprisoned under conditions which varied with the prevailing political climate. In 1439 he was actually taken to Calais for negotiations, only to be brought back. He lost touch with affairs in France, spoke English, and learned much of English government. Only the fact that some of his guardians, notably the Count of Suffolk, were sympathetic and cultured people consoled him. He devoted himself to theological studies and poetry (some of it in English), addressed to various ladies, one of whom may have been the Countess of Suffolk herself. Not until 1441 was he finally liberated on payment of a huge ransom. Even then he remained the virtual captive of the Duke of Burgundy, whose niece Marie de Clèves he married. (Bonne d'Armagnac had died in 1435.) His attempts to play the role of negotiator between Burgundy and France brought him little but discredit, and a campaign in Italy was disastrous. Finally Charles settled down in Blois with a chosen company of cultivated friends and servants. Only once did he come out of his retreat, to plead for the Duke of Alençon, who had been accused of treason. During this period a great deal of his poetry was written. He died at seventy, leaving two young daughters and a son who was to become Louis XII of France.

A great deal of Charles' poetry is autobiographical. He had translated a moral treatise into verse at the age of ten, and a long series of *balades* and *chansons* on his life and loves was begun before his captivity and continued there. Consequently his works often form long sequences, even a continuous narrative in some collections such as the *Retenue d' Amours.* His favorite form was the *balade,* which he usually wrote in the three- or four-strophic type, sometimes followed by a short *envoi.* The last line in each strophe acts as a refrain. Charles' subjects are as varied as the events in which he took part and reflect the social life of his time as well as repeating the commonplaces of love

and the complaints against fortune which were the staple of contemporary poetry. Their charm lies in their metrical skill and verbal felicity, and even more in their personal warmth.

His poems *(Poésies)* were collected by P. Champion (1923-27); *The English Poems of Charles d'Orléans* were edited by Robert Steele (1941-46); almost all anthologies contain a few poems of Charles d'Orléans, often with modernized spelling.
ABOUT: Stevenson, R. L. Familiar Studies of Men and Books. [In French—see studies by P. Champion.]

W. T. H. J.

*CHARTIER, ALAIN (1385/95-1429?), French poet and political writer, was born at Bayeux. Little is known of his life, but it may be assumed that his family was a prominent one, since one of his brothers, Guillaume, became bishop of Paris, and another, Thomas, was notary to the king of France. Alain himself, after studying at the University of Paris, held a series of offices under the Dauphin (later Charles VII)—as clerk, notary, financial secretary. He was sent abroad on various missions, traveling on an embassy to Germany in 1424 and on another to Scotland in 1427 to arrange the marriage of Princess Margaret of Scotland to the Dauphin (Louis XI). It is not known whether he took religious orders, but he undoubtedly had close connections with the church. Nothing was heard of him after 1429, and it is generally believed that he died in Avignon.

Alain's writings reflect his intimate knowledge of the court life of the later Middle Ages. They also reflect a rising French nationalism which followed hard upon the defeats and humiliations suffered by the French in the Hundred Years' War. His poetry dwells largely upon the themes of courtly love. Lacking the freshness of earlier medieval poetry, it is prolix and pedantic, highly conventional and derivative. Best known among his poems are the *Livre des Quatre Dames,* a dream allegory in which four ladies deplore the deaths of their suitors at the battle of Agincourt (Alain assigns the responsibility of the defeat to the disloyalty of the French who fled the battlefield), and *La Belle Dame sans Merci,* an allegory in the courtly love tradition from which Keats derived the title of his far more famous poem.

It is for his prose rather than his poetry that Alain Chartier won a more enduring reputation. His contemporaries called him the

* shär tyä'

"Father of French eloquence" and the "Seneca of France." The finest of his prose compositions is *Le Quadrilogue Invectif*, a dialogue between France and the three Estates. In this eloquent prose treatise Alain reveals the internal corruption and dissension that weakened France and made her an easy prey for the English, and he pleads for unity under the Dauphin to restore his country to peace and honor. This is one of the first patriotic works in European literature and a significant symbol of rising European nationalism. In his *Traité de l'Esperance*, a prose work modeled on Boethius' *Consolation of Philosophy*, he again appeals stirringly for French reform and unity. Even his satirical *Le Curial* (The Courtier) has as its main purpose the aim of reforming the French court by exposing its corruption to scorn and ridicule.

Alain also composed a number of letters and prose treatises in Latin. During his lifetime and in the century that followed his death he was highly esteemed both in France and in England. The legend grew up about him that Princess Margaret of Scotland, the Dauphiness, once came upon him sleeping in the garden, and though he was reputed to be "the ugliest man in France," she bent down and kissed his lips because from that "precious mouth" had issued "so many fair and virtuous words." In later centuries Alain sank into relative obscurity, but students of French literature have always recognized the importance of his work. Edward J. Hoffman writes: "His contribution to the development of French prose as a medium of serious expression is universally recognized, and there is no one to contest his position as one of the founders of literary style in France."

Caxton translated Alain's *Le Curial* in 1484. His ballad "Fools, Fools Are Mortal Men" and selections from *La Belle Dame sans Merci* appear in English in H. Carrington's *Anthology of French Poetry* (1900).

ABOUT: Hoffman, E. J. Alain Chartier: His Work and Reputation.

*CHATEAUBRIAND, FRANÇOIS AUGUSTE RENÉ, Vicomte de (September 4, 1768-July 4, 1848), French writer and statesman, was born in Saint-Malo of an old Breton family. His ancestors were among those who fought at Hastings and with Saint Louis' Crusades. René-Auguste, his father, had captained a slave-trading ship and then become a ship owner. A shrewd business-

* shà tō brē än'

CHATEAUBRIAND

man, silent and unyielding, he had amassed a fortune and purchased the beautiful feudal fortress of Combourg. Meanwhile, he had married the noble young lady Apolline de Bédée. Four of their children had died at birth; the rest survived: Jean-Baptiste, heir to the family title and castle; four daughters —Marie-Anne, Bénigne, Julie, Lucile; and lastly, François-René.

Sickly from birth, François further suffered from not being the favorite child and from not receiving the delicate affection his sensitivity demanded. It was Lucile who was closest to him spiritually; her nature mingled exaltation with devotion, wandering wits with prophetic dreams. She encouraged his creative writing by making him taste "the delectable melancholy of remembered childhood."

His formal education, mainly classical, was shapeless. He spent four years at the Collège de Dol, then studied with the Jesuits at Rennes, and finally at the Collège de Dinan. When he returned to Combourg, he felt uncompensated and misunderstood, a combination of emotions which tended to foster his bitterness. Lucile was unhappy; preyed upon by largely imaginary griefs, she longed for a convent. François spent his time with her wandering through the great woods and fens and listening to the hours tick in the somber castle halls. When, in a fit of depression, he attempted to shoot himself, his father decided to end his follies and got him a commission as second lieutenant in the Navarre regiment. Although his height was only five feet four, his military bearing reflected the indifference and pride in his temperament.

In Paris in 1787, Chateaubriand was presented to the Court, Louis XVI and his minister Malesherbes, whose patronage he enjoyed extensively. When the Revolution came, he found himself a divided man: as a Chateaubriand, he was a Royalist; as a disciple of Rousseau, he had intellectual sympathy for the doctrines of his age. But he was appalled at violence. In 1791 his desire to leave France and his need for sensations and adventures impelled him to sail for America to seek the Northwest Passage. He longed to describe the savage enchantment and grandeur of the Western Hemisphere.

Chateaubriand spent five months in America, during which he traveled from Niagara Falls to Florida. It is doubtful that he actually reached the Mississippi, so beautifully described in *Atala* and *René*. The news of Louis XVI's arrest brought him back to France where he married Céleste Buisson de la Vigne in 1792. But he felt ill-adapted to marriage; all her life Céleste remained by and large a deserted wife. In Brussels Chateaubriand joined the army of émigrés, was wounded during the siege of Thionville, and was forced to make his way to England in great physical pain.

His seven years in exile (1793-1800) were years of trying poverty and humiliation during which he lived as best he could by private teaching and translating. But there was a positive side: from the poets Milton, Gray, and Young he acquired some of his finest themes, and from his study of English law he deepened his respect for liberty and his belief in a constitutional monarchy. He discovered, too, that there was prestige in the beauty of adversity and learned to make melancholy a shield against suffering. In March 1797 he published his first work: *Essai sur les Révolutions,* in which he attempted to explain such ineluctable civil catastrophes by reference to historical antecedents, and, despite his disillusions and doubts, to point to national tradition and the truth of human feelings as the bases for a new social solidarity. His fundamental tension between Enlightenment skepticism and a vague religious inquietude was resolved in 1798 when, after the deaths of his mother and his sister Julie, he returned to religion. "I wept and I believed." He was about to publish *Le Génie du Christianisme* when he re-entered France in 1800.

To attract attention to the forthcoming opus, Chateaubriand published *Atala* in 1801, the story of "the loves of two savages in the desert." It is an intimate autobiography of a state of mind, Rousseauistic in its attitude toward nature, in which an amorous unrest is mingled with splendidly melancholy canvases of the Mississippi regions. Chateaubriand then used it as an illustrative chapter of the *Génie* (1802). The "genius" is the beauty and solemnity that Christianity has given life, its evangelical message by which the author opposed the Enlightenment's criticism that religion is the enemy of civilization. Another illustrative chapter was *René*, much like *Atala*, but romantically stressing the social isolation of the man of genius, tortured by ennui, the "mal du siècle," the burning need for passion and the inability to match the objects of his terrestrial desires with his "over-abundance of life." The overwhelming success of the *Génie* (not of *René* in particular), which was consonant with Napoleon's politico-religious beliefs, led to Chateaubriand's appointment as Secretary to the Rome Legation in 1803, and later as minister in the Valais. The *Lettre sur la Campagne Romaine* dates from that period.

With the execution of the Duke of Enghien, Chateaubriand's loyalism was reawakened; defying Napoleon, he resigned in 1804. Another event profoundly grieved him: the death of Lucile. Disaffected, he again left France, traveling to Switzerland and eventually to the Near East, Africa, and Spain, "spell-bound days of rapture and delirium," gathering material for his future works: *Les Martyrs* (1809), illustrating the superiority of Christian supernatural over pagan; *Itinéraire de Paris à Jérusalem* (1811), combining exotic descriptions with the pride of understanding the profound meaning of antiquity: and *Adventures du Dernier Abencérage* (1826), fixing the cult of Spain among the French romantics through the sad love of an Arab prince for a Spanish noblewoman.

Back in France in 1807, Chateaubriand retired to his new property, the Valley-of-Wolves, to pursue literarily his campaign against Napoleon. His cousin Armand had been shot as a royalist agent. Elected to the Academy in 1811, he was forbidden to pronounce his acceptance speech because of its attack against imperial tyranny. After the Empire he wrote a violent brochure, *De Buonaparte et des Bourbons* (1814), which, as Louis XVIII said, did more for the Restoration monarchy than an army of 100,000 men. But the fact that he became Minister of the Interior and Peer of France did not signify that the King appreciated his ambitious behavior. Again Chateaubriand was in the opposition; he fought for the Ultra-Royalists, founding the *Conservateur* and as a redoubtable polemist provoking the fall of the Decazes ministry. To remove him, the king named him ambassador to Berlin (1821), to London (1822); he was sent to the Congress of Verona where he obtained the right of French intervention in the Spaniards' revolt against their king. As minister of foreign affairs he organized the Spanish Expedition of 1823. Jealousy over his success caused his removal from office one year later. Returning to his true convictions as a moderate monarchist, he continued his opposition, this time to the Villèle ministry, then to the July Monarchy. Meanwhile, he added to his publications: *Les Natchez* (including the *Atala* and *René* episodes) (1826), *Voyage en Amérique* (1827).

His political career at an end and financially harassed, Chateaubriand devoted the remainder of his life to writing: *Études Historiques* (1831), *Essai sur la Littérature Anglaise* (1836), *Congrès de Vérone* (1838), *La Vie de Rancé* (1844). Published posthumously (1849-50) were the *Mémoires d'Outre-Tombe,* a vast evocation of revolutionary Europe but especially of his whole life—dreams, memories, convictions, as if to monumentalize himself "alone before eternity." His last years were spent in the daily company of Mme Récamier, with whom, since 1818, he had cultivated a friendship of "respectful tenderness" which neither her late blindness nor his partial paralysis interrupted. According to his wish Chateaubriand was buried on the island of Grand-Bé, off Saint-Malo, superbly removed from men in death as in life, proudly facing the open sea.

Chateaubriand's influence was great. He defined the new romantic spirit, opposed to the orthodoxy of the classical ideologists. *René* above all was decisive in creating romantic melancholy and became the spiritual antecedent of works by Sénancour, Constant, Sand, Sainte-Beuve, and most of the French romantics. Chateaubriand has always been regarded, and justly so, as a master stylist of the exotic.

The first English translation of *Atala* was by Caleb Bingham in 1802: Frederic Shoberl translated the *Génie* as *The Beauties of Christianity* (Chateaubriand's original title having been *Les Beautés du Christianisme*) in 1815; *René* appeared separately that same year; and Alexander Teixeira de Mattos translated the *Memoirs* in 1902. Subsequent translations include Irvin Putter's translation of *Atala and René* (1957), Charles I. White's *Genius of Christianity or the Spirit and Beauty of the Christian Religion* (1856, 1875), Rayner Heppenstall's

translation of *Atala* and *René* (1964). There is a translation of *The Martyrs* by O. W. Wight (n.d.). Selections from Chateaubriand's *Memoirs,* edited and translated by Robert Baldick, was published in 1961.

ABOUT: Evans, J. Chateaubriand; Maurois, A. Chateaubriand; Walker, T. C. Chateaubriand's Natural Scenery—a Study of His Descriptive Art. [In French—see studies by M. de Dieguez, M. J. Durry, V. Giraud, M. Levaillant, P. Moreau, J. Mourot, M. Robida, M. Rouff, A. Vial.]

J.-P. B.

CHATRIAN, ALEXANDRE. See ERCKMANN-CHATRIAN

*CHEKHOV, ANTON PAVLOVITCH

(January 17, 1860-July 2, 1904), Russian dramatist and short-story writer, was born in Taganrog, southern Russia. His grandfather had been a serf who bought his way to freedom, and his father, Paul (or Pavel) Chekhov, operated a small grocery store. His mother, Evgenia, was the daughter of a prosperous merchant. Anton was one of six children, and the family ties were very strong throughout his life. Since Chekhov's father wanted his sons to know Greek for purposes of commerce (there was a large Greek colony in Taganrog), the boy began his education at a second-rate Greek school. After two years—in 1869—he entered the classical *Gymnasium.* Although the extent of his childhood reading is not known, his letters, available from his sixteenth year on, show that he was well read. He was popular among the other students who enjoyed listening to his humorous stories. He loved the theatre and somehow managed to attend very frequently, even though high school students were forbidden entrance. A gifted mimic and improviser, he put on performances for the family with the help of his brothers.

In 1876 Chekhov's father was obliged to seek work in Moscow after a business failure in Taganrog. Only Anton and one of his brothers remained there. He now had to earn his living (which he did by coaching junior boys), help his family, and continue his studies at the *Gymnasium.* In 1879 Chekhov finished school and entered the medical faculty of the Moscow University. At the same time he began writing for newspapers and small magazines in order to make some money, nevertheless pursuing his studies with great eagerness. He himself said later on: "I do not doubt that the study of medical sciences has had a serious influence on my literary activity." When he received his diploma in 1884, he was already well known as

* chĕk' ôf

CHEKHOV

a contributor to humor magazines such as
Zritel (The Spectator) and *Sputnik*. His
first comic story, "Letter to a Scholarly
Neighbor," had already been published in
1880 in the magazine *Strekoza* (Dragon-fly)
and in 1882 Chekhov had become affiliated
with the best humor magazine of that time,
Oskolki (Fragments). Also in 1884, he published at his own expense *The Fairy Tales
of Melpomene* (a collection of six comic
stories) in which he used the pseudonym
"Antosha Chekhonte," as he had in all his
other publications prior to that time. The
collection passed almost unnoticed by the
critics, but by 1886 the publication of his next
collection, *Motley Stories,* was considered an
important literary event. Soon after it appeared, A. Suvorin, editor of *Novoye Vremia*
(New Time), the pro-government and largest
daily paper of the day, asked Chekhov to
become a contributor. Suvorin and Chekhov
became close friends and Chekhov's letters to
Suvorin form an important and interesting
part of his correspondence. (Several years
later, however, the friendship began to wane
because of Suvorin's attitude in the famous
Dreyfus case in which Chekhov took a pro-
Dreyfus stand.)

By 1886 Chekhov was engaged in serious
literary activity. He had already written his
only novel, *The Shooting Party,* and had
adapted one of his stories into the play *On
the Highroad,* which remained unproduced,
however, because of censorship. In 1887
Ivanov, Chekhov's first play to be produced,
was presented in Moscow and then at the

Alexandrinsky Theatre in St. Petersburg.
The same year another collection of his
stories, *In the Twilight,* appeared; and in
1888, the year in which he published his long
story "The Steppe" in the prominent literary
journal *Messenger of the North,* he received
the Pushkin award of the Academy of Sciences. He had completed his medical studies
in 1884 and was practicing medicine successfully, but literature now was absorbing more
and more of his time and energy.

During the summer of 1888, Chekhov
traveled a great deal in southern and south-
east Russia; and in 1889, passing through
Siberia, he made the grueling journey to the
Island of Sakhalin, a Russian penal colony in
the Pacific Ocean, where for three months he
studied very thoroughly the life and treatment
of convicts. The major result of this study
was published in *The Island of Sakhalin* in
1891. Some of Chekhov's short stories were
also inspired by this voyage. In general
Chekhov was a great admirer of travelers,
and in 1891 he went on a trip to Western
Europe, which he revisited in 1894 and in
1897. Growing ill health and a dislike for city
life led him to buy a farm in Melikhovo, not
too far from Moscow, in 1892. Here he lived
with his family and wrote some of his best
works. A country "squire" in the best sense
of the phrase, he was active in village affairs
and used his medical training to great advantage in the cholera epidemics of 1892 and
1893.

Since 1885 Chekhov had suffered from
pulmonary tuberculosis, but he continued
writing and published some of his best work
in the last years of his life. His health grew
steadily worse and he suffered from melancholia, relieved by moments of great vitality.
Chekhov was now obliged to make longer and
longer sojourns at Yalta in the Crimea and
at foreign health resorts. In Yalta Chekhov
renewed a friendship with Leo Tolstoy, whom
he had met in Melikhovo. For a time he was
influenced by "Tolstoyism"—his simple, elemental, and literal Christianity. Some of
Chekhov's stories written from 1890 to 1892
reflect this influence. But he gradually came
to reject Tolstoy's views. In 1894 he wrote
to Suvorin apropos of Tolstoy: "Reason and
justice tell me that there is more humanity in
electricity and steam than in chastity and
vegetarianism." Still the popular belief persisted that Tolstoy, Chekhov, and Gorky were
the three great liberal intellectuals who opposed reactionary Czarism. And Chekhov did
indeed take an active part in a political situation (as he had earlier in the Dreyfus affair).

When the Academy of Sciences, influenced by the government, excluded Gorky from its membership, only Chekhov and the socialist Korolenko resigned their membership in protest. Among Chekhov's other close literary friends were Ivan Bunin (poet and novelist who won the Nobel Prize for Literature in 1933), Kuprin (the satirical realist, writer of short stories and novels), and Mamin-Sibiriak (a regionalist writer whose novels deal mostly with Siberia and the Ural).

Chekhov's four dramatic masterpieces—*The Sea Gull, Uncle Vanya, The Three Sisters,* and *The Cherry Orchard*—were all written in the last decade of his life. *The Sea Gull* was produced at the Alexandrine Theatre in St. Petersburg in 1896. Though Komissarjevskaya, one of the greatest Russian actresses, played the main rôle, the play failed and Chekhov was heartbroken. But only two years later K. S. Stanislavsky (the famous theatre director) and Vladimir Memirovich-Danchenko (the dramatist) who had recently founded the Moscow Art Theatre produced the play with enormous success. *Uncle Vanya, The Three Sisters,* and *The Cherry Orchard* were triumphantly staged by the Moscow Art Theatre. In 1901 Chekhov married Olga Knipper, an actress of this theatre. It was a happy marriage although they were separated most of the time. Olga Knipper was playing in Moscow and Chekhov had to spend most of his time in Yalta because of his illness. In June 1904 his doctors sent him to Badenweiler (a resort in the German Black Forest) and a month later he died there. He was buried in Moscow in a scene of national mourning. The crowds watching the funeral procession halted all traffic.

Korolenko described Chekhov as having the face of "an ingenuous village youth" despite his culture and sophistication. Gorky said of him: "I think that in Chekhov's presence everybody felt an instinctive desire to be simpler, more truthful, to be more himself. . . ."

Chekhov's literary career can be divided into four phases—first: Chekhov, the short-story and "novella" writer; second: Chekhov, the practical humanitarian; third: Chekhov, the playwright; and fourth: Chekhov, the writer of an extensive correspondence. As a story writer he had two careers, one as "Antosha Chekhonte," who contributed short stories, sketches, and parodies to comic papers, often doing hack-work and publishing voluminously, and one as Anton Chekhov, the great storyteller, still prolific but an artist who respected his gift. "Antosha Chekhonte" made fun of the trivialities and weaknesses of man; his stories ("A Horse Name," "Surgery," "Panama," "In the Railway Carriage," etc.) seem nearer to slapstick comedies than to the subtly humorous narratives that Chekhov later wrote. A great number of these tales have not been translated into English and some of them have not even been included in his collected works. Chekhov's second period as a short-story writer started about 1886, and it is upon these stories that his reputation rests. It is difficult to choose among the hundreds of narratives since they are almost uniformly excellent: "Kashtanka" (1887), "A Dreary Story" (1889, written under the influence of Tolstoy's "The Death of Ivan Ilych"), "Ward No. 6" (1892), "The Black Monk" (1894), "Anna on the Neck" (1895), "Peasants" (1897), "In the Ravine" (1900), "Betrothed" (1903). Chekhov the humanitarian, author of *The Island of Sakhalin,* is perhaps the least interesting from the point of view of literature, though it is said that the publication of this book resulted in certain social reforms. In the works of Chekhov the playwright one must distinguish between the curtain raisers and the great plays. Among his one-act pieces are: *On the High Road* (1885), *The Bear* (1888), *The Swan Song* (1887-88), *The Marriage Proposal* (1888-89), *The Wedding* (1889-90), *The Jubilee* (1891). These are closely connected in style with his early comic stories. *Unpublished Play,* written in 1880, but first published posthumously in 1923 and translated variously as *That Worthless Fellow Platonov, Don Juan in the Russian Manner,* and *A Country Scandal,* is partly in the slapstick manner of his one-acters; nevertheless it contains some of the themes which Chekhov developed later in his six great plays: *Ivanov* (1887), *The Wood Demon* (1889), *The Sea Gull* (1895-96), *Uncle Vanya* (1897), *The Three Sisters* (1900-01), *The Cherry Orchard* (1903-04). The fourth phase of Chekhov's literary work is that of his voluminous correspondence with (among many others) Stanislavsky, Suvorin, Balmont (the great symbolist poet), Gorky, Diaghilev (the ballet producer and art critic), Shalom Aleichem (the Yiddish writer), and the composer Tchaikovsky. The letters comprise eight out of twenty volumes of his complete works and are written in straightforward, simple language. They form an interesting background to his life and work, and are full of anecdotes and expressions which show how much he drew from direct observation of life—a technique that accounts for the freshness and naturalness of the dialogue in both his plays and stories.

Chekhov's short stories written after 1886 and his great plays have made his name immortal. His characters are moody, introspective, self-centered people who live lives of quiet desperation, in a world full of trivialities where everybody is misunderstood by everybody else and where each character speaks without really listening to the other. The plays are static but full of implications and lyricism. Though they are realistic they are poetic and evocative—as witness, the twang of the harp string and the mournful sound of the axe in *The Cherry Orchard*. Yet in spite of his pessimism Chekhov, a positivist and an agnostic, believed ultimately in progress; he pitied his passive and resigned heroes and gave them, with all their melancholy, momentary longings for something better. In order to create the feeling of "life as it ought to be" in a scene of "life as it is" Chekhov used the "significant detail" in an impressionistic manner, which creates moods and shows the deeper truth behind the superficial reality.

His influence on both Russian and foreign writers has been enormous: Bernard Shaw in *Heartbreak House,* James Joyce, Katherine Mansfield, Virginia Woolf, Ernest Hemingway and many others have been influenced by him. W. Somerset Maugham says in his autobiography that in 1920 "the notion prevailed that anyone who . . . wanted to write short stories must write stories like Chekhov." Chekhov's stories are still widely read and his plays are produced in many countries. They have been translated into innumerable languages.

The complete works of A. Chekhov, *Polnoye Sobranie Sotchineniy i Pisem*, were published by Ogiz, Moscow 1944, in twenty volumes. They were translated by Constance Garnett and published by Macmillan (1916-22) in thirteen volumes. Omnibus editions include *The Portable Chekhov,* edited by A. Yarmolinsky (1947); *The Works of Anton Chekhov* (1929); *Five of Chekhov's Famous Plays* translated by Marian Fell (1939). *Selected Letters of Anton Chekhov* were translated by S. Lederer (1955). A bibliography, *Chekhov in English,* was compiled by Anna Heifetz, (1949); it was brought up to 1960 by R. Yachnin.

ABOUT: Bruford, W. Chekhov; Hingley, R. Chekhov; Koteliansky, S. S. (ed.) Anton Tschekhov: Literary and Theatrical Reminiscences; Magarshack, D. Chekhov the Dramatist; Mirsky, D. S. A History of Russian Literature; Poggioli, R. The Phoenix and the Spider; Shestov, L. Anton Chekhov and Other Essays; Simmons, E. J. Chekhov; Slonim, M. The Epic of Russian Literature.

Y. L.

*CHÉNIER, ANDRÉ MARIE (October 20, 1762-July 25, 1794), French poet, was born in Constantinople of a French father, Louis Chénier, French consul-general, and a Greek mother, the beautiful and charming Santi l'Homoka. Brought to France as a child, he grew up in Languedoc and was educated at the Collège de Navarre and in his mother's salon in Paris to which came the most distinguished members of French society—among them the chemist Lavoisier and the painter David. At twenty Chénier entered the army. Stationed at Strasbourg and bored with army routine, he studied languages and led a dashing romantic life. He resigned from the army after six months to travel. He visited Switzerland and Italy, but illness prevented him from visiting his mother's home, Greece, for which he felt a deep affinity. In 1787 he went to London as a secretary in the French embassy. The seething political unrest of the period soon drew him back to France, and he plunged into revolutionary activities.

The young poet hailed the revolution, but he also saw the dangers of unbridled rebellion. In his famous ode addressed to David on *Le Jeu de Paume* (referring to the tennis court at Versailles where the Estates General had met in 1789) he warned of the dangers of political violence and mob rule. He was outspoken in his opposition to the Jacobin leaders, attacking them directly in a series of articles in the periodical *Moniteur*. His sympathies with Louis XVI forced him to go into exile in 1793, after the king's execution. He stayed for a while in Rouen and in Versailles where he met Mme Le Coulteux, who became the subject, as "Fanny," of many of his love poems. In the spring of 1794 he returned to Paris and was arrested and imprisoned at Saint-Lazare. These were the last days of the Reign of Terror, when executions took place daily and haphazardly. Chénier's brother Marie-Joseph (himself a dramatist) used his influence to save him from death by keeping his name off the lists of those to be brought to trial. By a stroke of tragic irony his father made an appeal, thereby bringing the young man's name to the attention of the authorities. He was promptly tried, condemned, and guillotined—at the age of thirty-one. The very next day Robespierre fell and the Reign of Terror ended.

In so short and crowded a life as Chénier's there was no time for the production of a large amount of poetry, and the little that he wrote was almost forgotten. In 1819, how-

* shā nyā'

CHÉNIER

ever, a publisher who was preparing an edition of the writings of his brother decided to fill out the work with André Chénier's poems. Coming to light as they did in the dawn of the romantic era in French poetry, Chénier's poems caught the imagination of the age. Sainte-Beuve, Victor Hugo, Leconte de Lisle, and others hailed him as a great precursor of "romanticism." Whether his poetry was "romantic" or "classical" has been the subject of scholarly debate. He was probably a transitional figure, a bridge between the two movements. In personality he was romantic, Byronic (though not as handsome as the English poet), but in his poetry—odes, idylls, elegies, epics—he reflects primarily the precision and perfection of form which is generally associated with classicism. Even his most vigorous political poems—including the celebrated *Iambes*—are classical in conception. His style has been described as "concrete, plastic, harmonious." His favorite meter was the alexandrine which he "restored" to the romantic poets. He was erudite but wore his learning with grace; his verse was passionate but always carefully disciplined. Anatole France wrote of him: "He was everything that his time was—Neo-Greek, didactic, encyclopedist, erotic, romantic, tender, sentimental, tolerant, atheist, constitutionalist."

Chénier has earned a dubious immortality as the subject of an opera by Giordano, composed in 1896. The libretto is largely fictitious (though the heroine is a sentimentalized version of a woman whom Chénier met in prison), and unfortunately it includes none of Chénier's poetry.

There is no complete English translation of Chénier's verse, but selections appear in English in many anthologies. The Warner Library has two poems—"The Young Captive" and "Ode." "Saint-Lazare," the beautiful poem he wrote in prison (it includes the line "Even on the scaffold's step I shall seek to tune my strings") is translated in J. E. Legge's *Chanticleer: A Study of the French Muse* (1935).

ABOUT: Abramowitz, I. Great Prisoners; Bailey, J. C. The Claims of French Poetry; Brandes, G. Main Currents in Nineteenth Century Literature, V; Brereton, G. An Introduction to the French Poets; France, A. Life and Letters, 2nd Series; Legge, J. E. Chanticleer: A Study of the French Muse; Morton, J. P. *in* For Hilaire Belloc (ed. D. Woodruff); Scarfe, F. André Chénier, His Life and Work; Contemporary Review, July 1956. [In French—see studies by P. Dimoff, J. Fabre, E. Faguet, G. Walker.]

*CHERBULIEZ, (CHARLES) VICTOR (July 19, 1829-July 2, 1899), French novelist, was of Swiss birth but became a French citizen following the Franco-Prussian war in 1870. His ancestors had been French Protestants who fled to Geneva after the revocation of the Edict of Nantes. Here Cherbuliez was born, the son of a well-known mathematician, classical scholar, and professor, André Cherbuliez (1795-1875) and his wife, Marie Bourrit. It has been said of his parents that from his father Cherbuliez "learned all he ought to know, from his mother all he ought to be."

The boy was educated at the academy of Geneva. At the age of twenty he was sent to Paris to continue his studies at the Collège de France. On his father's advice he specialized in Oriental languages and mathematics. In 1851 he traveled to Germany to spend a year in Bonn and in Berlin studying philosophy. He returned to Geneva in 1852 and remained in that city until 1875, supporting himself by private tutoring and later by his writing. Much against the will of his parents, he married, in 1856, a woman of a lower social order, Charlotte Rochaix, but it was a happy union. They had one son, Ernest. Cherbuliez survived both his wife and son. He moved to Paris in 1875 and remained there until his death, a few weeks before his seventieth birthday, at his country villa in Combe la Ville.

Cherbuliez' first book, an archeological and aesthetic study in narrative form, *Un Cheval de Phidias* (1860), brought him to the attention of a number of prominent French lit-

* shĕr bü lyā'

erary figures, among them Renan, Sainte-Beuve, and George Sand. Through their influence he received an introduction to the influential French literary journal *Revue des Deux Mondes* to which he became a regular contributor. In the *Revue* he published fiction, literary criticism, and historical studies, using his own name and sometimes the pseudonym "Gustave Valbert." Some of these pieces were collected in the volumes *L'Allemagne Politique* (1870), *Études de Littérature et de l'Art* (1873), and *Profils Étrangers* (1889).

It is for his fiction, however, that Cherbuliez is remembered. He was not in his time, and is certainly not at this time, considered a profound or serious novelist. But his popularity was not undeserved. Clever, facile, well-educated, with an extraordinary breadth of interests, Cherbuliez was best known for his novels of aristocratic life and adventure. He was inventive, had a gift for popular "psychologizing," and could spin out a lively romance. With his first novel, *Le Comte Kostia* (1863), he captured a wide audience, and during his lifetime his popularity never waned. His books were almost as widely read in English translation as in the original French. However slight their literary value, they were highly respected and influential in their day. Henry James knew his work well and was indebted to his story *Paule Méré* in his own *Daisy Miller*. Cherbuliez was made a Chevalier of the Legion of Honor in 1870 and was elected to the French Academy in 1881.

Cherbuliez' works were translated into German, Italian, Dutch, Swedish, Norwegian, Danish, Polish. Among the numerous English translations the following may be mentioned: *Joseph Noirel's Revenge* translated by W. F. West (1872), *Count Kostia* by O. D. Ashley (1873), *Miss Rovel* by F. A. Shaw (1875), *Meta Holdenis* (1877), *Samuel Brohl and Company* (1877), *Jean Teterol's Idea* (1878), *A Stroke of Diplomacy* (1880), *Saints and Sinners* by M. N. Sherwood (1881), *The Tutor's Secret* (1893), *The Phidian Horse* by E. H. Roberts (1894).

ABOUT: Warner Library VI. [In French—see studies by A. Celierès and M. A. Istrati.]

*CHERNYSHEVSKY, NIKOLAY GAVRILOVICH (July 12, 1828-October 17, 1889), Russian revolutionary, philosopher, economist, novelist, and critic, was born in Saratov. Son of an Orthodox priest and product of a theological seminary, he entered St. Petersburg University in 1846. He was married in 1853 to Olga Sokratovna Vasilieva.

* chĕr nĭ shāf′ skē

CHERNYSHEVSKY

Chernyshevsky was most deeply influenced by Belinsky, Herzen, Feuerbach, and the French utopian socialists. He described himself at the time of the revolutions of 1848 as "a determined partisan of the socialists and communists and extreme republicans."

The most active period of his life was between 1855 and 1862 when, as writer and ideologist, he was an editor and guiding light of the journal *The Contemporary* and leader of the radical pre-populist movement. During this period he worked closely with the poet N. Nekrasov—publisher of *The Contemporary*—as well as with the young critic N. A. Dobrolyubov, to whom, in 1857, he entrusted the post of literary critic on the journal. Chernyshevsky's increasingly radical ideas found direct and indirect expression in various writings. In "The Esthetic Relations of Art to Reality" (1855), he lays the foundation for a materialistic and utilitarian aesthetic; reality, he affirms, is superior to art, and the task of art is truthfully to reproduce reality. In his "Essays on the Gogol Period of Russian Literature" (1855-56), Chernyshevsky interprets Gogol's writing as an expression of social reality. Chernyshevsky's philosophical materialism is clearly set forth in his "Anthropological Principle in Philosophy" (1860), and his belief in the inevitability of socialism finds expression in his "Comments on the Political Economy of John Stuart Mill."

Chernyshevsky was arrested as a subversive in 1862 and, in 1864, was exiled to Siberia for twenty years. While awaiting trial, he wrote his famous novel *What Is to Be Done?*, a didactic work portraying the "new man" as a moral, rational, socially useful being. This work, in part directed against Turgenev's portrait of a radical in *Fathers and Sons* (1861), was in turn sharply attacked by Dostoevsky in his *Notes from Underground* (1864) for its rationalistic simplification of human nature and naïve Fourierism. *What Is to Be Done?*, though lacking in real artistic merit, had a powerful moral impact on subsequent radical generations.

Chernyshevsky was highly esteemed by Marx and Engels as a scholar and critic; as revolutionary and thinker he found an ardent admirer in Lenin. He is revered in the Soviet Union today as a great socialist and materialist, and as a forerunner of much Marxist thought on aesthetics, criticism, and the "positive hero" in literature and life.

Chernyshevsky returned from exile to his native Saratov in 1889 and died a few months later.

An English translation of Chernyshevsky's *What Is to Be Done?* appeared in 1886 by N. H. Dole and S. Skidelsky under the title of *A Vital Question, or, What's to Be Done?* In 1961 Vintage Books published another translation, B. R. Tucker's, edited by L. B. Turkevich, with an introduction by E. H. Carr. Some of Chernyshevsky's essays were translated into English in the Soviet Union in 1953 under the title *Selected Philosophical Essays*.

ABOUT: Mathewson, R. The Positive Hero in Russian Literature; Matlaw, R. E., ed. Belinsky, Chernyshevsky, and Dobrulyubov: Selected Criticism; Slonim, M., The Epic of Russian Literature; Slavonic and East European Review, XLI (1963). [In Russian—see studies by B. J. Gorev, P. I. Lebedev-Polyansky, A. V. Lunacharsky, Y. M. Steklov.]

R. L. J.

*CHIABRERA, GABRIELLO (June 18, 1552-October 14, 1638), Italian poet, was born in Savona. His childhood was an unsettled one. His father died before he was born, and his mother remarried. At the age of nine the boy was sent to Rome to be raised by an uncle, Giovanni Chiabrera. There he studied philosophy under the Jesuits until he was twenty. In that year his uncle died, and the young man went into the service of Cardinal Cornaro. He was not happy in Rome—possibly because of a personal distaste for the intrigues of court life, or because he became involved in a quarrel (the sources disagree here). In 1581 he returned to Savona, where he lived out the remainder of his life performing various diplomatic and civic offices for influential patrons and writing

* kyä brâ' rä

verse. He lived a long and tranquil life in Savona, married late, and died at the age of eighty-six.

Chiabrera wrote a prodigious amount of poetry: lyrics, eclogues, narratives, epics, tragedies, satires, pastorals. Of all this the only work that has survived are his *canzonette* and *scherzi*, light, unpretentious, graceful pieces written to be set to music, and his satires. His lyrics show the influence of his vast reading, both in the classics (Pindar and Anacreon particularly) and in Renaissance French poetry (he was called "a late Ronsardist in Italy"). His satires, called *Sermoni*, written in blank verse, are frank imitations of Horace. They reflect the chief interests of his quiet life—mild criticism of the times, of human foibles and vanities, etc. He made interesting metrical experiments with short lines and short stanzas in his *canzonette*, and these influenced the work of later poets, among them Parini and Carducci.

Chiabrera's work is a detailed history of his time, but its artistic and intellectual merit is slight. "In three volumes of his lyrics," Francesco de Sanctis observed, "we barely meet with a single thought or image that stops us and makes us think; though his subjects are everything that is noble and affecting, they never move us or uplift us. . . . He never sinks himself deep in his subject, exploring its hidden depths . . . and he is empty and cold."

Nine epitaphs by Chiabrera were translated into English by William Wordsworth, and these have been reprinted in popular anthologies.

ABOUT: De Sanctis, F. History of Italian Literature, II; Wilkins, E. A History of Italian Literature.

CHODERLOS DE LACLOS. See LACLOS, PIERRE AMBROISE FRANÇOIS CHODERLOS DE

*CHRÉTIEN (or CHRESTIEN) DE TROYES (12th century), French poet, was the first to recount in permanent written form the romantic adventures of King Arthur's court. Of his life almost nothing is known except that he lived during the third quarter of the twelfth century and was attached to the court of Marie de Champagne, daughter of Eleanor of Aquitaine and Louis VII of France, and later had for a patron Philippe, Count of Flanders.

What little else of biography can be pieced together from Chrétien's poems must remain only conjecture. In his *Erec et Enide* he re-

* krä tyăn' dĕ trwä'

181

fers to himself as "Crestiiens de Troies" (in Champagne). The internal evidence of his poems suggests that he had a traditional medieval education. He knew the Latin writings of Ovid, the popular rhetorics and poetic handbooks of the Middle Ages, and had considerable familiarity with ecclesiastical doctrine. Most probably he was in religious orders like his contemporaries the cleric-authors Walter Map and Andreas Capellanus (André le Chapelain). In his poem *Cligés* he shows a familiarity with the English scene which suggests that he had been in England—a not unlikely trip in the light of the close connections between the English and French courts of the period.

Also from *Cligés* we have a partial bibliography of Chrétien's writings. These include various redactions of episodes from Ovid's *Metamorphoses* and *Ars Amatoria* and a poem on King Mark and Iseult (the Tristan legend). Of these only a portion of the *Metamorphoses* survives. But the bulk of Chrétien's work is extant and consists of six long narrative poems in eight-syllable rhymed couplets, probably composed between 1160 and 1180: *Erec et Enide; Cligés; Le Chevalier de la Charrette* (or *Lancelot*), which was left unfinished by Chrétien and was completed by Godefroy de Lagny; *Yvain; Guillaume d'Angleterre* (the only non-Arthurian tale); and *Perceval* or *Le Conte del Graal*, which was also unfinished. Together these poems form the basic collection of Arthurian materials from which a wealth of medieval and modern literature, art, and music have evolved —from Wolfram von Eschenbach to Sir Thomas Malory to Lord Tennyson and Richard Wagner.

Chrétien did not invent his stories. His sources are not specifically known, but they are surely the standard sources of medieval legend—the so-called "Matter of France" (stories from French history), "Matter of Brittany" (stories about King Arthur and other Celtic figures), and "Matter of Rome" (stories from Greek and Roman history and mythology). It was these sources that Chrétien brought together and transmuted into the romances which crystallized the ideals of twelfth century chivalry at the elegant and sophisticated Norman-French court of Marie de Champagne. "He was the product of the French civilization of his time," Roger Sherman Loomis writes, "including its classical and Christian heritage." The literary merits of Chrétien's poems are slight. He was a fluent story-teller with a lively and lucid style, but he was not a great poet nor a profound thinker. Joseph Bédier called him "not so much a creative artist as a clever compiler." But whatever his limitations as a writer, W. W. Comfort pointed out, "his significance as a literary artist and as the founder of a precious literary tradition distinguishes him from all other poets of the Latin races between the close of the [Roman] empire and the arrival of Dante."

The standard edition of Chrétien's work in French was done by Wendelin Foerster, 1884-99.

W. W. Comfort translated four Arthurian poems (*Erec, Cligés, Yvain, Lancelot*) for Everyman in 1914. *Guillaume d'Angleterre* was translated by W. G. Collingwood in 1904 and *Perceval* by S. Evans, 1898-1912.

ABOUT: Comfort, W. W. *Introduction to Arthurian Romances* by Chrétien de Troyes; Guyer, F. E. *Chrétien de Troyes: Inventor of the Modern Novel*; Loomis, R. S. *Arthurian Tradition and Chrétien de Troyes*. [In French—Cohen, G. *Chrétien de Troyes et son Œuvre*; Frappier, J. *Chrétien de Troyes; L'Homme et l'Œuvre*.]

CHRISTINE DE PISAN. See PISAN, CHRISTINE DE

*CINO DA PISTOIA is the popular name of **GUITTONCINO DEI SIGHIBULDI** (c. 1270-1337), Italian poet and jurist, born in the Tuscan city of Pistoia. Cino's father, Francesco dei Sighibuldi, belonged to an aristocratic Pistoian family and held important offices in the city. After an early education in Pistoia, Cino went to the University of Bologna about 1290 to study law.

At Bologna Cino became a close friend of Dante. One of his early poems is a *canzone* to Dante on the death of Beatrice, and he and Dante also exchanged sonnets on love problems. Their friendship, although probably strained in later years by Dante's change of political views, lasted until Dante's death in 1321, which Cino commemorated in a poem. Cino's later poems are often critical of Dante.

With Dante and Guido Cavalcanti, Cino was one of the three leading poets of what Dante termed the *dolce stil novo* ("sweet new style"), a style originated by Guido Guinizelli in the preceding generation. Although the poets of the *stil novo* wrote chiefly of love, their poems were on the whole philosophical and abstract. Cino's ideal lady, Selvaggia—comparable to Dante's Beatrice and Petrarch's Laura—is usually thought to have been a daughter of Filippo Vergiolese of Pistoia. Cino, however, unlike Dante and Petrarch, wrote freely of other loves.

* chē′ nō dä pēs tō′ yä

Cino left the University of Bologna about 1300. By 1302 he was back in Pistoia, and at this time he may have married Margherita di Lanfranco degli Ughi. He was exiled from Pistoia for political reasons in 1303 but returned in 1306 and was appointed to a judicial post. In 1310 he went to Rome in the train of Louis of Savoy to prepare for the coronation of Henry VII as Holy Roman Emperor. Henry died before his coronation, and Cino wrote a *canzone* extolling the dead leader.

In 1314 Cino was awarded a doctorate in law from Bologna, having finished an important and influential commentary in Latin on the first nine books of the Code of Justinian. Soon famous as an authority on law, he lectured at the universities of Siena (1321), Bologna (1323-24), Florence, Perugia (1326-30), and Naples (1330-31). He disliked this last city and wrote a violent *canzone* against it. About 1334 he returned to Pistoia, where he was received as a distinguished citizen. He died there late in 1336 or early in 1337. Petrarch, who acknowledged Cino as his master, wrote a poem mourning his death.

Although Dante considered Cino the outstanding love-poet in Italian, Petrarch's works in this vein soon far surpassed Cino's. Many modern critics dismiss Cino's poetry as dry, abstract, and often obscure, though Italian students of his work point out that many poems are forceful and well-conceived.

The definitive edition, ed. Guido **Zaccagnini** (1925), contains 187 poems (sonnets, ballads, and *canzoni*) certainly by Cino, and 23 dubious poems. Selections appear in *I Rimatori del Dolce Stil Novo,* ed. L. di Benedetto (1939).

A few of Cino's poems, chiefly those addressed to Dante, were translated into English verse by D. G. Rossetti, *The Early Italian Poets* (1861).

About: [In Italian—see studies by D. **Maffei,** G. Paganelli, G. Zaccagnini and G. M. Monti.]

J. K.

CINTHIO or CINTIO or CINZIO. See GIRALDI, GIOVANNI BATTISTA

"CLARÍN." See ALAS Y UREÑA, LEOPOLDO

*CLAUDIUS, MATTHIAS (August 15, 1740-January 21, 1815), German poet, was born at Reinfeld in Holstein. He studied at the University of Jena and then lived for several years in Wandsbeck in the vicinity of Hamburg. Here, from 1770 to 1775, he ed-

* klou' dĭ ŭs

ited the journal *Der Wandsbecker Bote* under the pseudonym Asmus. From 1776 to 1777 he was a civil servant in Darmstadt, but returned directly to Wandsbeck. Retaining his residence in Wandsbeck he became a bank inspector in Altona in 1778. Not until the last year of his life did he leave his home in Wandsbeck; then, because of illness, he moved to the home of his son-in-law in Hamburg, where he died.

Claudius first appeared as an author in 1763 with the publication of his *Tändeleien und Erzählungen.* His prose essays, poetry, tales, fables, and epigrams were first published in various journals. He instituted the publication of his own collected works in 1775, with a second part appearing in the years 1790-1812 under the title *Asmus Omnia Sua Secum Portans,* or *Sämtliche Werke der Wandsbecker Boten.*

Claudius' writings reveal no great talent but a clearly defined personality. He was a representative of healthy common sense in literature, assuming the pose of a man from the common people in his journal *Der Wandsbecker Bote.* In his own way, he took part in the general tendency toward naturalness and originality which was most pronounced in the contemporary Storm and Stress movement. In contrast to the works associated with the latter, however, Claudius' writings are not stamped with the restlessness of genius. Rather in him were united the reformist tendencies of the new age and the gentler, pietistic leanings of an earlier generation. He was among the first of Germany's writers to seek a broad audience among the people and to attain simultaneously a means of true literary significance. He was able to write in a naïve, simple style and at the same time to be witty. His best work was accomplished in the genre of the *Lied.* He struck a popular note with such poems as "Bekränzt mit Laub den lieben vollen Becher," "Am Rhein, am Rhein, da wachsen unsre Reben, gesegnet sei der Rhein!" "Der Mond ist aufgegangen," "Wenn jemand eine Reise thut," and "Der Riese Goliath." As Claudius advanced in years his inclination toward pietism increased and he became somewhat more dogmatic and intolerant.

English translations of Claudius' poetry may be found in the following anthologies: Baskerville, A. S. The Poetry of Germany (1853); Goodwin, A. H. Rhymes from the Rhineland (1913); Goldschmidt, H. E. German Poetry (1869).

About: [In German—see studies by B. Adler, I. Rüttenauer.]

E. K. G.

*COLLETT, (JACOBINE) CAMILLA (WERGELAND) (January 23, 1813-March 6, 1895), Norwegian novelist, was born in the south Norwegian coast town of Kristiansand where her father, Nicolai Wergeland, was chaplain. Her mother was Alette Dorothea Thaulow and her brother the famous poet Henrik Wergeland. When she was four, her father became vicar in Eidsvoll, a few miles from the capital, and here she lived until she married. She was first educated by her father and tutors, but later (1826-28) attended two private schools.

When Camilla was seventeen she met and fell in love with the poet Welhaven, then twenty-two. Her position was difficult during the feud between her father and brother and Welhaven (see Welhaven and Wergeland sketches below), but she sided with her fiancé. Welhaven showed, however, only moderate interest in her. She was distraught for quite some time. Finally, in 1836, during a stay in Hamburg, Germany, she severed her connection with the cool Welhaven. In 1841 she married the lawyer and literary critic Peter Jonas Collett, son of a prominent member of the Norwegian parliament and governor in Buskerud county. His sympathetic and courteous affection calmed her troubled soul, and he exerted a great influence also on her literary activity.

She planned her major work, *Amtmandens Døttre* (The Governor's Daughters), with her husband, but it was not published until 1855, after his death, when it appeared anonymously. The novel consists of several love stories that run parallel. Mme Collett exposes the social injustices of which women were victims outside and within marriage. She demands liberation of the female emotional life and social equality between the sexes. The book is remarkable for its strong indignation and its pathos. It was the first psychological novel in Norway and was significant in many literary and social controversies of the day, especially the question of emancipation of women.

Thereafter Mme Collett published several collections of stories, sketches, essays, memoirs, e.g., *Fortellinger* (Stories), 1861, *I de Lange Nætter* (Long Nights), 1863, *Sidste Blade* (Closing Pages), 5 vols. 1868-73, of which the last volumes commence her work for the feminist movement, to which she thereafter completely devoted her life.

Nothing of her production has been translated into English.

* kŏl' lĕt

ABOUT: Beyer, H. A History of Norwegian Literature; Grøndahl, I. and Raknes, O. Chapters in Norwegian Literature; Jorgensen, Th. History of Norwegian Literature; Wergeland, A. M. Leaders in Norway. [In Norwegian—Samtiden, LXXII (1963).]

A. J.

*"COLLODI, CARLO" (CARLO *LORENZINI) (November 24, 1826-October 26, 1890), Italian author, journalist, and creator of *Pinocchio*, was born in Florence eleven years after the Congress of Vienna. By the treaties signed there Austria had become the real master of Italy. Collodi reached young manhood as the struggles of the Risorgimento to free the country from Austrian domination and to achieve national identity were becoming most active. He was a young seminarian at Colle Val d'Elsa when the zealot Pope Gregory XVI died. The political crises of 1846 surrounding the fight to elect a liberal, i.e. non-Austrophil, Pope were largely responsible for young Collodi's decision to strip off his cassock. He became, as did many other young Italians, a follower of Mazzini, and an anticlerical as well.

He turned to journalism, a popular profession in the nineteenth century, and was active in it all his life. He wrote of his work: "Journalism is like Nessus' shirt; once donned and fastened, there is no getting out of it." About this time he assumed his famous pseudonym, taking the name Collodi from the town near Pescia where his mother was born.

Collodi took part with the Tuscan volunteers in the revolutionary campaigns of 1848, known as the "terrible year" when all Italy rose against despotism and foreign domination. He also founded *Il Lampione,* a newspaper of political satire which was issued until April 11, 1849, when the restoration of despotic rule in all areas but the Piedmont made circulation difficult. *Il Lampione* was succeeded by *La Scaramuccia* in 1853, but in 1860 publication of *Il Lampione* was resumed when Collodi returned to Florence from participation in the war of 1859. These were the campaigns in which the great battles all went against the Austrians. The years between 1848 and 1860 were not only marked by military and journalistic activity for Collodi; there are several collections of writings which are actually the fruit of this period: *Macchiette* (Odd Figures in a Landscape), *Occhi e Nasi* (Eyes and Noses), *Storie Allegre* (Light Stories), *Note Gaie* (Gay Notes), *Divagazioni Critico-Umoristiche* (Satirical Digressions).

* kŏl lô' dē; lō răn tsē' nē

"COLLODI"

In 1861 the European powers acknowledged the United Kingdom of Italy. Collodi's fighting days were over and he worked for the rest of his life in Florence, part of the time as a theatrical censor. In 1875, a mature man who had been soldier, government worker, journalist, and editor, he turned to another interest. He wrote about it to a friend: "Now I shall devote myself to writing only for children. Grown-ups are too hard to satisfy; they are not for me." The first attempt was a translation of the *Fables* of Perrault. This was followed by a story of his own called *Giannettino* in 1876. There were sequels to Giannettino's first adventures: *Minuzzolo, Il Viaggio per l'Italia di Giannettino* (Giannettino's Trip through Italy), *La Geografica di Giannettino* (Giannettino's Geography), *La Grammatica di Giannettino* (Giannettino's Grammar). In these stories Collodi is faithful to a tradition in Italian pedagogic literature: the promulgation of the greatest possible number of moral teachings by means of an amusing story. He is also successful at portraying the boy as he really is, not a model of virtue or a juvenile monster but a child with a capacity for naughtiness. This portrayal of boyhood achieved its greatest fame when, in 1880, Collodi scrawled his first chapter of *Pinocchio*, which appeared in the *Giornale dei Bambini* under the title *Storia di un Burattino* (History of a Puppet). It was immediately popular with the journal's readers and editor Guido Biagi requested more chapters. These, which Collodi seems to have supplied casually when

the mood struck him, all met with the same enthusiastic reception. The publisher made a fortune on the story of Pinocchio, but Collodi, before he died, apparently did not even realize he had written a classic. He died suddenly at sixty-three in Florence where he lived with his brother.

Piero Bargellini comments: "In the statistics of worldwide translations I believe the sequence to be: First, the Gospels, and second, *Pinocchio*. . . . The fable . . . has a surprising resemblance to another story in which the protagonists are related as loving father and prodigal son." The adventures of the boy-puppet were even further popularized in the twentieth century in the cartoon film issued by Walt Disney. Henry Mafficini has done a Latin version called *Pinoculus*, with the aim of providing an entertaining Latin reader.

Pinocchio was first translated into English by Joseph Walker [McSpadden] in 1909. Other translations have been made by M. A. Murray (1918), C. Della Chiesa (1927), A. Patri (1930), W. S. Cramp (1937), and B. Wall (1957).

ABOUT: Commonweal November 21, 1952. [In Italian—Bertacchini, R. Collodi, Narratore; Marchetti, I. Carlo Collodi; Pancrazi, P. Venti Uomini, un Satiro e un Burattino; Santucci, L. Collodi.]

E. DE P.

COLONNA, VITTORIA (1490-February 25, 1549), Italian poet, was born in Naples, where her father, Fabrizio Colonna, served as Constable to Ferdinand II. She came of aristocratic lineage; her father was one of the great Colonna family of Rome, and her mother, Agnese di Montefeltro, was sister to Guidobaldo of Urbino.

Vittoria was betrothed in her childhood to Ferrante Francesco d'Ávalos, Marquis of Pescara, the son of a distinguished Spanish family living in Naples. The young couple were duly married in 1509 and lived together for two years on their estate on the island of Ischia. Then Francesco went away to the wars being waged in the north of Italy, and during the rest of his life he was more often in the field than at home.

Contemporary reports pictured Francesco as a cruel and untrustworthy military leader, and as an openly unfaithful husband. But when he died of wounds at Milan in 1525, Vittoria showed a striking devotion to his memory. Although childless, she refused to remarry, and during the next three or four years she wrote a series of about a hundred poems lamenting Francesco's death and idealizing his character.

* kō lōn' nä

185

VITTORIA COLONNA

She continued to live on Ischia, making occasional visits to Naples and Rome. Her high birth and her unusual intellectual abilities had already won her a considerable reputation, and she had formed friendships with many outstanding men of the time, including Sannazaro, Bembo, Castiglione, and Bernardo Tasso. She kept up these friendships, but a few years after her husband's death her interests began to center on religion, and for a period her closest ties were with several of the religious thinkers of the day.

Her sympathies were with the group who were advocating reforms in the papacy and the church; she associated with reformers like Giovanni Vaddes and Bernardino Ochino. But when an open split developed between the church and the reform movement, Vittoria's friend and adviser Cardinal Pole warned her not to side against the Church. She ceased openly to advocate reforms; but religious questions continued to occupy her thoughts: the series of poems to her husband was followed, during the last twenty years of her life, by a series of over two hundred poems on sacred and spiritual themes.

About 1538 she moved to Rome, and it was then that she met Michelangelo. Their relationship, perhaps the best-known historical example of Platonic friendship, was marked by frequent exchanges of philosophical sonnets and letters.

After 1540 Vittoria went into retirement, first at a convent in Orvieto, then at the convent of St. Catherine at Viterbo. About 1544 her health failed and she returned to Rome,

living at the convent of St. Anna di Funari. Early in 1549 she was removed to the Cesarini Palace, the Roman residence of the Colonna family, where she died with Michelangelo at her bedside.

Vittoria Colonna was one of the outstanding figures of her time: Ariosto placed her above all other women of the age. Her reputation derived, however, chiefly from her personality and intelligence and only incidentally from her literary work. Her poems, most of them sonnets, are in the Petrarchan and Platonic vein that dominated Italian poetry during the early sixteenth century. They are skillful, but not strikingly original. Of her prose, only a few miscellaneous religious pieces and some of her correspondence remain. Modern interest in her career centers less on her writing than on her personality and her distinguished friendships.

Her poems to her husband were translated in 1895 under the title The "In Memoriam" of Italy. W. Everett also translated two of these poems in The Italian Poets Since Dante (1904).

ABOUT: Everett, W. The Italian Poets Since Dante; Jerrold, M. F. Vittoria Colonna; Koven, A. de, Women in Cycles of History; Lerman, L. in Vogue's First Reader. [In Italian—Bernardy, A. A. Vita e Opere di Vittoria Colonna.]

J. K.

COMENIUS, JOHANNES AMOS. See KOMENSKÝ, JAN AMOS

*COMMYNES (or COMINES), PHILIPPE de (1447?-1511), French chronicler and diplomat whose Flemish ancestors rose to aristocratic rank by serving the House of Burgundy, was born probably in the castle of Renescure. Early in his childhood he lost his father and was entrusted to his cousin who prepared him for a court life, without insisting on Latin or readings of well known writers. Sent in 1464 to the court of Burgundy to serve as squire of Charles the Bold, then Count of Charolais, Commynes took part in the battle of Montlhéry (1465). He participated in the negotiations which followed this battle, gaining thus, at eighteen, his first experience in diplomacy. Much appreciated, the Sire de Renescure, as he was called, carried out diplomatic missions in England and in Spain. In 1468, during the famous Péronne meeting, Commynes gained the admiration of King Louis XI, who, thankful for the outcome of the meeting, rewarded him secretly. Four years later, on the night of August 7, for unknown reasons, Commynes

* kô mēn′

left his master to become the king's intimate adviser, thus starting his second and most successful diplomatic period, which lasted until the king's death in 1483. At the court of France, Commynes, Sire d'Argenton, married Hélène de Chambes, by whom he had a daughter, Jeanne.

Commynes' third diplomatic period began with the reign of Charles VIII. This time he was no longer the leader of French diplomacy; he experienced a total downfall and imprisonment (1489) when he was accused of plotting against the king. However, the same year he was pardoned and was asked to negotiate in Italy. Commynes' failure to gain alliances brought an end to his diplomatic career, and when Louis XII was elevated to the throne, he was nothing but a courtier. Commynes died in his castle of Argenton.

At the request of a friend, Angelo Cato, the archbishop of Vienne (Dauphiné), who intended to compose the history of Louis XI, Commynes began writing his *Memoirs* in 1489 and finished six books by 1491. The second portion, two books about the reign of Charles VIII, was written between 1495 and 1498.

The *Memoirs,* printed in 1524, contain no historical system. They are a gathering of reflections and of examples observed in the prince he most admired, Louis XI. Commynes' remarks are meant for princes, who should learn the art of diplomacy and government through a deep understanding of men and things. According to Commynes, princes should consider themselves not as masters but as leaders who, for example, should levy taxes on their subjects with their consent and for their protection. Unlike Machiavelli, Commynes allows some consideration to God as a power behind political equilibrium and leadership. When Commynes died his *Memoirs* enjoyed some reputation without becoming, however, a source of inspiration for Machiavelli. At the most it is possible to draw parallelisms between the two writers owing to most striking similarities of thoughts and language.

As a writer Commynes displayed the qualities but also the shortcomings of an autodidactic person with a lucid and simple style but one lacking power and brilliance. Today no history of French literature could avoid mentioning Commynes for his penetrating comments on the nature of leaders and the art of diplomacy.

The *Memoirs* have been translated into English at various times—by T. Darnett in 1596 (published with introduction by C. Whibley in 1897) and by J. de Troyes in 1880-82 (2 vols.).

ABOUT: Dryer, K. *in* Symposium, V (1951); Lewis, D. B. W. The King Spider; Neff, W. B. The "Moral" Language of Philippe de Commynes; Whibley, C. *Introduction to* The History of Comines, ed. T. Darnett. [In French—see studies by J. Bastin, G. Charlier. In Italian—see study by A. Prucher.]

E. V.

*COMNENA, ANNA (December 1083-1148), Byzantine historian, was "born and bred in the purple," the eldest daughter of Alexius I and Irene, Emperor and Empress of the East. Her father was the third son of John Comnenus, nephew of Isaac Comnenus, Emperor from 1057 to 1059. Her mother was the daughter of Caesar John Ducas, brother of Constantine X Ducas, Emperor (1059-67), who succeeded Isaac Comnenus. Anna was carefully educated in the Bible and in the classics, as she writes, "to the end of the end of Hellenism." In addition she studied medicine and was head physician of a 10,000-bed hospital in Constantinople and wrote a treatise on gout.

In 1097, at the age of fourteen, she was betrothed to Constantine Ducas and upon his sudden death was married that same year to Nicephorus Bryennius, soldier, diplomatist, and literary man with whom she lived until his death in 1137. The Empress Irene favored her daughter and made every effort to prevail upon Alexius to make Anna and her husband heirs to the throne, instead of John, her eldest surviving son, but Alexius upheld the order of male succession and John became Emperor upon his father's death in 1118. On the accession of John to the throne, Anna, whose deepest desire was to become Empress, conspired unsuccessfully to depose her brother, and even plotted against his life. Her husband's unwillingness to become an accomplice in her plot against her brother's life led to the failure and discovery of the plot. Her brother's clemency spared her life though she was forced to forfeit her property and fortune. Later John pardoned his sister and restored her property, but she retired to a convent where she continued her machinations to seize the throne. Her husband frustrated her plans and blaming him for her failure, she wrote of him that "nature had mistaken their sexes for he ought to have been a woman." She devoted the rest of her years to the *Alexiad,* a history of her father's achievements begun by her husband.

The *Alexiad,* for which Anna Comnena is chiefly remembered, is an authentic reflection of eleventh century Byzantium, but her personality dominates throughout. She tells us of

* kŏm nĕ′ nà

her wide education, her deep family pride, her staunch support of orthodoxy, her hatred for the Latins. In the prologue she states that history alone can save the memory of events from oblivion; she gives us her idea of the proper equipment of a historian and states that it is "God above" who has given her her dynastic and educational privileges.

The *Alexiad* consists of fifteen books covering the period from 1069 to 1118 which relate the events in the life of her father twelve years before his accession; she gives a picture of the gradual rise of the Comneni and narrates the events which occurred during her father's reign.

The *Alexiad*, which is more of a biography than a history, is dominated by the central figure of Alexius whom she calls "The Great Alexius, luminary of the Universe, the Sun, of Anna." It is written in the purist Attic which Krumbacher calls "an almost artificial language and an entirely mummiform school language which is diametrically opposed to the popular spoken language which was used in literature at that time."

In spite of Anna's tendency to eulogize her father as the "thirteenth Apostle" over the other Comneni, and the archaic style of her writing, the *Alexiad* is a valuable source of history for the Byzantium during the first Crusade. It reveals a strong sense of the historian's duty, a genuine feeling for Hellenism, and a first hand knowledge of most of the events of her father's reign. It is based not only on her personal observations and oral reports, but also upon documents of the state archives, diplomatic correspondence and imperial decrees. It is the earliest example of the literary renaissance which was started by Michael Psellos.

Anna is also remembered as one of the characters in Sir Walter Scott's *Count Robert of Paris,* one of the chief episodes of which is based on an historical event which she herself had recorded in the *Alexiad.*

The *Alexiad* has been translated into English by Elizabeth A. S. Dawes (London, 1928).

ABOUT: Baynes, N. H. Byzantium; Buckler, G. G. Anna Comnena-A Study; Byron, R. The Byzantine Achievement; Diehl, C. Byzantine Portraits; Diener, B. Imperial Byzantium; Gibbons, E. Byzantine History; Hussey, J. M. The Byzantine World; James, G. P. R. Memoirs of Celebrated Women; Jorga, N. The Byzantine Empire; Liddell, R. Byzantium and Istanbul; Miller, W. Essays on the Latin Orient; Sandys, E. History of Classical Scholarship, I.

R. D.

*COMTE, (ISIDORE) AUGUSTE (MARIE FRANÇOIS XAVIER) (January 19, 1798-September 5, 1857), French philosopher, was born at Montpellier where his father was receiver-general of taxes for the district. From his earliest years, Auguste displayed intellectual precocity and a capacious memory, distinguishing himself particularly at the École Polytechnique in Paris, where he was sent in 1814. At this early age he also displayed his inherent rebelliousness of temperament, involving himself in a student uprising which brought about the temporary closing of the school.

In 1818, having established himself in Paris as a teacher of mathematics, Comte became friendly with the social philosopher the Count Saint-Simon. Although Comte had by far the superior mind of the two, his thought was markedly influenced by that of his older mentor. It was Saint-Simon who impressed him with the possibility of studying politics and society with the objectivity of the sciences, and instilled in him the ideal of social welfare as the aim of philosophy. After a few years, however, a quarrel ensued over a publication, and the two parted company. Throughout his life Auguste Comte was to show a propensity for losing friends.

As early as his twenty-fourth year Comte had conceived his first major publication, *Système de Politique Positive,* forerunner of his later more extensive work on the subject. Published in 1824, this book set forth the famous Law of the Three States, wherein the history of man's intellectual development was conceived as falling into three distinct epochs: theological, metaphysical, scientific (the "modern" age). In Comte's view man progressed as he learned to free himself of superstition and abstract thinking and use his faculties in rigorous and disciplined observation of natural phenomena.

From this point on, the young intellectual attracted increased attention. In 1826 he began a series of lectures setting forth his "Positive Philosophy," the groundwork for a social science to be based on a knowledge of nature's laws. To these lectures were drawn some of the most eminent of contemporary scientists. The series was interrupted for a time by a mental breakdown, during which Comte suffered from a severe melancholia, even attempting suicide by plunging into the Seine.

The culmination of these lectures was the massive *Cours de Philosophie Positive,* published in six volumes (1830-42). Here Comte

* kônt

COMTE

From this time on, Comte depended greatly on the generosity of friends and disciples. One of his greatest admirers, the British philosopher John Stuart Mill, joined with three friends to make up the loss of income until he could once more re-establish himself. When it became evident that Comte intended that the subsidy should continue indefinitely, Mill's friends lost patience and withdrew their shares. Mill then suggested that Comte could earn money by writing articles for British periodicals, which he would be glad to translate. This idea was greeted with angry indignation, and the friendship cooled. Subsequently Comte's most ardent French disciple, Émile Littré, procured some support, which continued even after he too fell into the master's disfavor.

In 1845 occurred Comte's meeting with the sickly, ill-fated Clothilde Devaux, with whom he fell deeply in love. She died only a year later. He remained inconsolable, invoking her memory three times a day, visiting her tomb faithfully every week. Shortly thereafter Mme Devaux was elevated into the high priestess of the "Religion of Humanity" that he envisaged in his last major work, the *Politique Positive*, which was published during the years 1851-54.

In this work Comte projected one of the most ambitious of utopias, a society devoted to the "Cult of Humanity," in which men would be prompted by Love or Altruism, governed by leaders of industry who would hold the temporal power, and by philosophers trained in all the positive sciences, who would replace priests. This worship of Man was reflected in the famous *Positivist Calendar* (1849), a biographical directory of geniuses and heroes, medieval and modern, originally intended as a schedule of days of commemoration for the "Religion of Humanity." For a time the "Religion" too had its adherents, though in England it alienated some of his admirers like Mill and George Henry Lewes who could accept his science, but not his polity.

The last years of Auguste Comte were sad and lonely ones. Gradually he broke off with all his friends. He died at the age of fifty-nine of cancer of the stomach, leaving behind the manuscript of an autobiographical *Testament* which was published posthumously in 1884, together with his revealing correspondence with Clothilde Devaux.

The career of Auguste Comte was fraught with paradoxes. Urging that the aim of philosophy should be practical and devoted to the improvement of society, he himself remained an introvert and a recluse for most of

attempted no less than a hierarchical system of all the sciences known to man. Beginning with mathematics, the "science of phenomena," which Comte regarded as the fundamental discipline, the "cours" (or course) culminates in the "organic" sciences, the study of individual man, known as biology, and of collective man, which Comte termed sociology, thus coining a word which was destined to flourish. In an age devoted to intellectual system-building, Comte's *Cours de Philosophie Positive* won him many admirers, both on the continent and in England.

During these productive years, Comte's private fortunes suffered many vicissitudes. He continued to give lectures, first in astronomy, later in history, which, though popular, brought him no income. However, an appointment as examiner of prospective candidates for the École Polytechnique, together with engagements as a teacher of mathematics, brought him an adequate annual stipend. He generally remained aloof from politics, but was imprisoned for a brief period for refusing to serve in the National Guard, on the ground that his republican convictions would not permit him to defend the monarchy. In 1842, the year of the publication of the last volume of the *Cours de Philosophie*, he suffered a series of great misfortunes. Almost simultaneously he separated from his wife, was involved in a lawsuit with his publisher for tampering with his copy, and, as the result of antagonizing the trustees of the École Polytechnique, lost his position as examiner—and half his income.

his life. The vainest, most egocentric and most cantankerous of men, he ceaselessly promulgated the altruistic and benevolent emotions among his fellows. Forswearing all religions, he eventually created a private *mystique* bordering on idolatry. Yet despite his "crackpot"-ism and the exaggerated adulation that attended him in his lifetime, his was an encyclopedic mind of first-rate analytic powers, and he remains in many respects the prototype of the modern intellectual—man-centered, rationalistic, society-oriented.

The *Cours de Philosophie Positive* was translated in 1853 by Harriet Martineau as *The Positive Philosophy*. The *Politique Positive* was translated by J. H. Bridges, Frederic Harrison, E. S. Beesly, and others from 1875 to 1877 as *System of Positive Polity*. A portion was separately translated by Richard Congreve in 1858 as *The Catechism of Positive Religion*. The *Calendar* was translated in 1892 by Frederic Harrison as *The New Calendar of Great Men*.

ABOUT: Bosanquet, T. Auguste Comte and the Positive Philosophers; Lewes, G. H. Comte's Philosophy of the Sciences; Mill, J. S. The Positive Philosophy of Auguste Comte; Whittaker, T. Comte and Mill. [In French—see studies by P. Arbousse-Bastide, E. Littré, J. Robinet.]

R. A. C.

*CONDILLAC, ÉTIENNE BONNOT DE (September 30, 1714-April 2, 1780),

French philosopher, born in Grenoble of a family from Briançon, was the son of a government official who had purchased the Condillac estate. He presumably studied with the Jesuits in Lyons, then at Saint-Sulpice and the Sorbonne, where he underwent the strong philosophical and scientific disciplines. He took orders in 1740, but had developed a keener interest in science and philosophy than in theology, and in the same year, encouraged by Mme de Tencin, he entered literary circles and frequented the principal ladies and the Philosophes, whose doctrines he quickly absorbed; his contact with Fontenelle and Marivaux further sharpened his attitudes and his controversial spirit.

Condillac submitted his first work, *Dissertation sur l'Existence de Dieu*, of about 1742, to the Academy in Berlin. He was soon attracted by Locke's analyses of mind and knowledge, and undertook to elaborate them in his *Essai sur l'Origine des Connaissances Humaines*, of 1746, which also shows the influence of Newton's *Principia* and of the related experimental method in science. From the concept of knowledge through experience, Condillac developed his theories of consciousness, of perception and of the soul, and situ-

* kòn dē yàk'

ated language on a psychological basis. He insisted on a strict method of analysis, going back beyond evidence to causes. His main project was to surmount metaphysical reasoning by study not of the nature of the soul but of its operations; he left Locke's ideas and strongly foresaw those of the Encyclopedists. His *Traité des Systèmes* (1749) completes the argument of the *Essai*, and brings out more clearly the basic errors of Descartes, Malebranche, Leibniz, and Spinoza.

Condillac's *Traité des Sensations* represents his break with the Encyclopedists. It led him, in 1754, into a new field, opened already by various works dealing with the relationship between vision and external reality, such as those of Berkeley and of Diderot; but it differs from their views in the emphasis on human understanding and the individual classification of the sensations. The *Traité des Sensations* met with the disapproval of Diderot's group, who had hoped that Condillac would refute Berkeley's idealism, and were annoyed that he should instead have modified the theories of Diderot and of Buffon, forging thus into a pre-empted field. Condillac pursued his own program, nevertheless, and in his *Traité des Animaux* (1755) replaced the Cartesian automatism by spiritual motivation, and, assigning a soul to animals, set man apart through his knowledge of God; this last point represents the total break with the Philosophes.

In 1758 Condillac became the tutor of the son of the Duke of Parma, serving for nine years in this capacity and on various missions on foreign affairs. He returned permanently to Paris in 1767, was elected to the French Academy in the following year, and composed further works, revising his great *Traité* and refuting new charges. His ideas in *Le Commerce et le Gouvernement* pleased neither the Physiocrats nor their enemies.

Condillac's system, sometimes considered the best in its field until the introduction of Kant into France, achieved moderation in its synthesis of several elements usually considered incompatible. Editions and re-editions of his works testify to their importance, from the collected writings of 1792 to the twenty-three volumes of 1798 and the complete works in twenty-one volumes in 1821.

Translations into English include *An Essay on the Origin of Human Knowledge*, by Nugent (1756), his *Logic*, by J. Neef (1809) and the *Treatise on the Sensations*, by G. Carr (1930).

ABOUT: Boyd, W. From Locke to Montessori; Macleod, H. Rise of the Third School of Economists; Schaupp, Z. The Naturalism of Condillac.

[In French—Baguenault de Puchesse, G. de, Condillac; Lenoir, R. Essai sur l'Origine (preface); Le Roy, G. Lettres Inédites (preface); Picavet, F. Les Idéologues.]

F. J. C.

*CONDORCET, MARIE-JEAN-ANTOINE-NICOLAS CARITAT, Marquis de (September 17, 1743-March 25 or 29, 1794),

French philosopher, educational theorist, mathematician, and political economist, was born in Ribemont (Picardy) of an important family from the Dauphiné. At sixteen, he impressed d'Alembert and other mathematicians by his brilliant thesis, and shortly entered into relations with the minister and scientist Turgot, who influenced his thinking on education and politics. He left home and established himself in Paris in 1762. Condorcet's first work, *Essai sur le Calcul Intégral* (1765), led him to the Academy of Sciences at the early age of twenty-six, and he became its permanent secretary in 1773. His interest in political economy rose partly from his activities as inspector of coinage, a topic on which he wrote. With his *Théorie des Comètes* (1777) he won the prize competition of the Berlin Academy. His literary interests appear in various biographies of his contemporaries, such as Buffon, Turgot, and Voltaire, objectively conceived, and the editions he prepared, of the *Pensées* of Pascal, the letters of Euler, and the complete works of Voltaire (the "Kehl" edition, 1785-89, which contains the biography). He was elected to the French Academy in 1782, and then published his *Réflexions sur l'Esclavage des Nègres*. His tract entitled *Attributions* (*des Assemblées Provinciales* 1788) directed his interests to the early revolutionary movement, although traces of republican ideas are found in his writings as early as 1765.

At first merely a theorist of constitutional law, Condorcet's new preoccupations led him to visions of the future of democracy in France and in the United States, and in 1786 he wrote an essay on the influence of the American Revolution in Europe. Of interest in this connection are John Adams' hostility toward his "unrealistic" ideological thinking, and Condorcet's own disillusionment with the United States, which he had conceived as a leader in world peace, and whose internal strife shook his faith. The Girondin constitution, primarily his work, was debated at length in the Assembly, in April and May 1793. By his imprudent attempts to take the issue to the public, Condorcet aroused hostility when

* kôn dôr sĕ′

this constitution was shelved, partly because of opposition to its author as a moderate and an individualist. Condemned as a traitor, he hid for eight months, protected and aided by his wife, a very remarkable woman; shortly after his arrest, he took poison. He composed his last work, *Esquisse d'un Tableau Historique des Progrès de l'Esprit Humain*, during his imprisonment.

Condorcet was one of the outstanding minds of his day, for breadth, depth, and liberality of vision. His distinction in several fields of thought made of his career one of the vital factors in the currents of contemporary French and international political and social theory. The technical nature of much of his writing tends to exclude it from belles-lettres proper, but his methods add strongly to the rationalist and encyclopedic thinking of the pre-positivist period.

Translation of Condorcet into English began with several of his biographies, *The Life of M. Turgot* (London, 1787), and the particularly important *Life of Voltaire* (London, 1790, and Philadelphia, 1792). His short tracts, *Reflections on the English Revolution of 1688* and *A Letter to a Magistrate in Switzerland*, were published respectively in London in 1792 and in New York in 1793. His master work, *Outlines of an Historical View of the Progress of the Human Mind*, appeared in rapid succession in London, 1795, Philadelphia, 1796, and Baltimore, 1802, and was retranslated by J. Barrclough (New York and London, 1955).

ABOUT: Bury, J. The Idea of Progress; Martin, K. French Liberal Thought in the Eighteenth Century; Schapiro, J. Condorcet and the Rise of Liberalism. [In French—biography by Arago in Œuvres 12 vols., 1847-49; Bouissounouse, J. Condorcet le Philosophe dans la Révolution; Cahen, L. Condorcet et la Révolution Française; Gillois, A. La Marquise de Condorcet; Picavet, F. Les Idéologues. In Italian—Cento, A. Condorcet e l'Idea di Progresso.]

F. J. C.

*CONSCIENCE, HENDRIK (December 3, 1812-September 10, 1883),

Flemish novelist, was born in Antwerp, the son of a French father who had settled in Antwerp in 1807, and of a Flemish girl from Brecht. After spending his sickly youth in the old part of Antwerp he became an assistant teacher. As such he had many humiliating experiences. During the Belgian revolution he fled with the "légion parisienne Niellon." During his service as a Belgian subject he was in the Kempen region where he fell in love. He was also deeply influenced by the charm of the area and its inhabitants. In Dendermonde he met Prudens van Duyse and in Antwerp the friend of his youth, the French

* kŏn syän′ sĕ

CONSTANT DE REBECQUE

CONSCIENCE

poet de Laet. The latter introduced him to van Rijswijck, the instigator of the "Olijftak."

Discharged from the service, he took part in the artistic life of Antwerp, obtaining the support of the painter Wappers, who succeeded in acquiring for him a place as clerk with the provincial administration in 1837. During this time he wrote his first historical story, *In 't Wonderjaer 1566*. In 1837 he published a collection of prose and poetry, *Phantasy*, which was not well received by the critics. In this difficult period—he had left his parental home on account of difficulties with his father—he wrote *De Leeuw van Vlaanderen of de Slag der Gulden Sporen*. This historical novel was published in 1838, together with an ardent manifesto addressed to the Flemish people. It placed Conscience with the best historical novelists in Flemish literature. With his friend de Laet he vainly opposed the cession of Luxembourg and Limburg to Holland (1839), and their attempt to begin a political journal proved a fiasco. In October 1838 Conscience had left his post with the provincial government and taken up gardening. The result of this change to a more contemplative life can be found in *Een Pelgrim in de Woestijn*, influenced by the Christian-social theories of Lamennais.

In 1842 Conscience married Maria Peinen. During the following year he revised *In 't Wonderjaer 1566* and *De Leeuw van Vlaanderen* removing any anti-religious statements, and also succeeded in reaching the Flemish people with *Hoe Men Schilder Wordt*, a

simple story of a child of the lowly who becomes a celebrated artist. *Wat een Moeder Lijden Kan* (1844), suggested by the social needs of the time, also won a wide audience. Conscience was then commissioned to write a history of his country. He likewise began working on a popular natural history. Meanwhile he had become clerk of the Académie Royal des Beaux Arts in Antwerp. In 1851, when the political dissension became intolerable, Conscience left Antwerp and went to Schilde. In this period he turned to the writing of a series of pastoral novels—sensitive portrayals intended to be read by the simple of heart who do not wish to doubt the beauty of life.

Discouraged by the struggles among the Flemish, Conscience went to Courtrai (1857) where he lived for years without writing much. His *Simon Turchi* (1859) sounds like a premature good-bye, for he became productive again in Brussels, where he served as custodian of the Wiertz museum. He died in Brussels at seventy, shortly after he had been present at the unveiling ceremonies of his statue in Antwerp. Owing to his contract with Calmann-Lévy in Paris his name became known throughout the world.

During the latter half of the nineteenth century Conscience enjoyed great popularity in the United States. His *Complete Works* were published in Baltimore in 1867. Subsequently the publishing firm of John Murphy in New York published a large number of his novels, the best-known among them being *The Lion of Flanders* (De Leeuw van Vlaanderen). Many of these were translated by Brantz Mayer.

ABOUT: [In Dutch—see studies by E. de Bock, G. Eakhoud (latter also available in French). In French—see also H. Hugon, E. Mertens.]

H. B.

*CONSTANT DE REBECQUE, HENRI BENJAMIN (October 25, 1767-December 8, 1830), French novelist and statesman, was born in Lausanne, Switzerland, descendant of a French Protestant family which had settled in Switzerland in the sixteenth century. His mother, Henriette de Chandieu, died fourteen days after his birth. His father, Juste de Constant, by profession a colonel and later a general in the army of The Netherlands, raised his son in a manner scarcely calculated to give the child any sense of love or security. He left him first in the care of relatives in Brussels, then with a governess who was his mistress and later became his wife, and finally with a series of tutors whom Constant later described as

* kôns tän' dē rē bĕk'

CONSTANT

"most ignorant and immoral men." In spite of this erratic education, the boy showed great precocity. By the age of twelve he had mastered Greek and music and had composed a verse tragedy and a prose poem (*Les Chevaliers,* published in 1927). At thirteen he was taken to England by his father to study at Oxford, but was refused admission to the university because of his youth. A year later, however, he entered the German University of Erlangen where he studied for a year and a half. In 1783 he was sent for eighteen months to Edinburgh University. Here he studied diligently, but also managed to accumulate very considerable gambling debts.

From the outset Constant determined on a career as a writer. Accordingly, he began work, in 1785, on a history of pagan mythology. He soon abandoned this undertaking for a history of religion on which he worked for most of the rest of his life. He tried his hand at translating Gibbon's *Decline and Fall of the Roman Empire* and John Gillies' *History of Greece* into French, neither of which he completed, largely because of the interruptions of romance. The influence upon him of women—the eternal agonizing conflict within him between reason and passion, what he called "the head and the heart"— is, to the modern reader, the most interesting aspect of Constant's life and work; and the two novels by which he is today known, *Adolphe* and *Cécile,* are intensely personal and self-revealing documents detailing his own love affairs. The women who played the most important rôles in his life were Mme de Charrière, a literary lady (she wrote novels and satires) some twenty-eight years his senior; Mme de Staël, the influential and talented author whom he loved for more than fifteen years and by whom he had a daughter; his second wife, Charlotte von Hardenberg (his first marriage, to Wilhelmina von Cramm, in 1789, ended in divorce); and Mme Récamier, the famous hostess to the literary and political world.

Constant began his political career modestly enough in 1788 with an appointment, obtained for him by his father, as "Gentleman of the Chamber to his Serene Highness the Duke of Brunswick." He remained at this small German court for five years, but his liberal political sentiments, his contempt for the dull German court life, and his unhappy first marriage all combined to make his stay a wretched one. In 1794 he obtained a legal separation from his wife and left Brunswick forever. He settled in Switzerland, where he met Mme de Staël, then actively engaged in aiding émigrés from the French Revolution. In 1795, with the Jacobin Terror ended, they returned together to Paris, but Mme de Staël interfered so busily in the new government (the Directory) that after ten months she was expelled, taking Constant with her into exile.

A year later they returned again to France. By 1797 Constant, "fired with a passion for liberty," as Talleyrand described him at this time, had won some reputation as a political commentator by publishing several pamphlets espousing the liberal cause. In 1798 he ran for a seat in the Council of Five Hundred but was defeated. In 1799, after Napoleon had come to power, he was appointed to the Tribunate. With his maiden speech, however, he offended Napoleon by opposing some of his measures. As a result, he was dismissed from the Tribunate on January 19, 1801, and he remained out of politics for thirteen years.

During this period Constant traveled in Germany with Mme de Staël, and in 1808, after many stormy scenes, he married Charlotte von Hardenberg, herself twice divorced. He was nevertheless still not free of the powerful Mme de Staël and until 1811, when she married again, he vacillated between his wife and his mistress. From 1811 to 1814 he lived quietly with his wife in Germany, working on his history of religion and writing more political pamphlets expressing his strong liberal sentiments and his advocacy of constitutional monarchy with

193

a representative legislature. Outstanding among these was *De l'Esprit de Conquête, Réflexions sur les Constitutions,* and *De la Liberté des Brochures* (all published in 1814). Although Constant had already declared himself in favor of the restoration of the Bourbon monarchy, he transferred his allegiance to Napoleon when the general returned briefly to power in 1815. Constant went to work on a draft of a French constitution (modeled closely along the lines of the English system) and was appointed a Councilor of State, much to the chagrin of his royalist friends. With Napoleon's defeat at Waterloo, Constant found himself in disgrace. In 1816 he and his wife moved to London, but they returned to Paris before the year was out. In 1817 he was defeated for office in the Chamber of Deputies, but two years later he won election and held office until 1822. In 1824 and again in 1827 he was elected for Paris and for Alsace. In 1830 he was elected president of the Council of State. In all these offices Constant proved to be conscientious, a poor speaker but a commanding figure who inspired respect if not admiration. He continued his political pamphleteering, calling himself "the school-master of Liberty." In 1816-18 he collected and extended many of these articles in his *Cours de Politique Constitutionelle,* a precise and lucid statement of his political faith in moderate liberal government.

Constant died in Paris of paralysis in 1830. His last years were darkened by his failure to win admission to the French Academy, but he was consoled by the knowledge that he had finished his seven-volume history of religion on which he had spent forty years (published 1824-34). He was given a state funeral and buried at Père Lachaise, with a funeral oration delivered by the Marquis de Lafayette.

Constant wrote his novel *Adolphe* in fifteen days in January 1807, at precisely that moment in his life when he resolved to end his long liaison with Mme de Staël. The book was published in 1815. "The theme of this short masterpiece," Sir Harold Nicolson writes, "is the conflict between duty to oneself and duty to another which confronts a man who has ceased to love a woman by whom he is still adored." Adolphe, the hero of the book, pursues and at last wins Ellénore, a married woman who ultimately sacrifices her honor, her children, and her fortune for him. Adolphe soon finds that he no longer loves her, but he remains in bond-

age to her—out of loyalty, conscience, or simple weakness. When at last she releases him by dying, he finds that his freedom is meaningless, and that, being no longer loved, he is "a stranger to all the world."

The novel is of course autobiographical, but, as Martin Turnell cautions, "an autobiographical novel is not the same as an autobiography and *Adolphe* must not be judged as though it is." Ellénore is not so much Mme de Staël as she is a composite of all the women Constant had known, transformed by the author's imagination into a literary character. Adolphe is Constant, but he is also the image of what Turnell calls "the rootless cosmopolitan who belongs nowhere." It is a novel of frustration and despair, but it is also a triumph of art.

Constant abandoned his only other novel, *Cécile,* in order to work on his book on the history of religion. The fragment of a novel was forgotten and filed away in a crate of letters and documents. It was not until the middle of the twentieth century that a descendant of Constant's came upon the manuscript while depositing some papers in the library at Lausanne. It was published in France in 1951. *Cécile* is an autobiographical novel, written probably around 1811. Inferior to *Adolphe,* it describes the vicissitudes of the loves of Constant and Charlotte von Hardenberg (Cécile) up to the time of their marriage. Mme de Staël figures in the story as Mme de Malbée.

Constant was not a handsome man. He was tall, red-haired, with freckles, and small myopic eyes. He was past middle age when the Irish novelist Maria Edgeworth met him in 1820 and wrote her very unflattering description: "He pokes out his chin to keep the spectacles on, and yet looks over the top of his spectacles, squinching up his eyes so that you cannot see your way into his mind. Then he speaks through his nose and with a lisp, strangely contrasting with the vehemence of his emphasis." In spite of these shortcomings, he had charm, wit, and an engaging personality. In the nineteenth and early twentieth century his reputation declined in the general critical neglect and disparagement of eighteenth century rationalists. In more recent years Constant has had fresh critical re-evaluation and has emerged, in Martin Turnell's words, "a fascinating and dangerous example for our age which shares his weaknesses without possessing the clear-sightedness and honesty that prevented him from harboring any illusions about himself." Sir Harold Nicolson, who published an excellent biography of him in 1949, considers him "the champion and the interpreter of pure liberal doctrine" for France. "He was an ambitious man; he possessed high intelligence, great capacities. . . . Yet he was forever hampered by those doubts which assail the intellectual who mixes with the world of action, above all the intellectual who has acquired the habit of self-examination."

The first English translation of *Adolphe* was published in 1817. Subsequent translations include those by Paul Hookham (1925), W. L. Barrett (1933), Carl Wildman (1948), and John Middleton Murry (in *The Conquest of Death*, 1951). *De l'Esprit de Conquête* was translated by H. B. Lippmann under the title *On Conquest and Usurpation: Prophecy from the Past* in 1941. Constant's autobiography, *The Red Notebook*, was published in an English translation by Norman Cameron in 1948. *Cécile* was first translated into English by Norman Cameron in 1952.

ABOUT: Cecil, D. Poets and Story Tellers; Constant, B. The Red Notebook; France, A. On Life and Letters: First Series; Holdheim, W. Benjamin Constant; Nicolson, H. G. Benjamin Constant; Roulin, A. *Preface to* Constant's Cécile; Scott, G. The Portrait of Zélide; Turnell, M. The Novel in France; French Review April 1954. [In French—Du Bos, C. Grandeur et Misère de Benjamin Constant; Krafft, A. Hommage à Constant.]

*COORNHERT, DIRK VOKKERTS-ZOON (1522-October 29, 1590), Dutch engraver, moral theologian, poet, and playwright, was born in Amsterdam, the youngest son of a well-to-do cloth-trader. His two elder brothers were destined to figure importantly in the Reformation. Receiving the education usual for his station in life, Coornhert became an excellent player of the lute and the harpsichord, and was adroit in the art of fencing. His education was rounded out by a visit to Spain and Portugal in 1539. This first-hand observation of the activities of the Inquisition contributed to his aversion for religious fanaticism and repression. In 1540, against the wishes of his mother—his father had died meanwhile—he married; his wife Cornelia was the sister of a nobleman. After residing on the estate of his brother-in-law for one year, Coornhert moved to Haarlem where he established himself as an engraver. As such he cooperated at various occasions with the painter Maarten van Heemskerk. During these first years in Haarlem his preoccupation with religious problems developed. His numerous political-theological and ethical tracts and pamphlets were especially directed against the Calvinists, who abhorred his liberal views. About

* kōrn′ hĕrt

1500 Coornhert began to study Latin in order to read the Church fathers. Blending classical Stoicism with Christianity, he held that the wisdom of the ancients played an important role in helping mankind find its destiny in life. His interest in Latin led to his translating Cicero's *De Officiis* (1561), Seneca's *De Beneficiis*, and twelve books from the French of Boccaccio's *Decamerone*. Becoming a theologian of some reputation, he incurred the wrath of Calvin, who wrote a pamphlet against Coornhert's liberal views.

In 1561 Coornhert received an appointment from the city of Haarlem as commissioner. Five years later he went into the service of the Prince of Orange. Refusing to cooperate with the leader of the rebellious nobles in 1566, he helped his city avoid the iconoclastic troubles that erupted in that year all through the Netherlands. In spite of his apparent loyalty to the church of Rome he was put into prison in 1567. He escaped to Germany (Cleve) but returned in 1572 and became clerk for the States of Holland, until he was forced to flee again. Returning to Haarlem in 1577, he served this city for another eleven years as commissioner. In 1588 he moved to Gouda, where he died.

Coornhert's individualism led to his conviction that man can become pure as the Christ of the gospels, and that ecclesiastical unity should be condemned since it prevented the individual from being a Christian according to his own personal insight. For similar reasons he denied the necessity of a confession of faith. The best known product of his pen, *Zedekunst, Dat Is Wellevenskunste* (1586), reveals the influence of stoic ethics. His songs as well as his dramatizations were written in the style of the Rederykers, a guild-like organization of artisan-poets. His prose, though rich in sound and imagery, was always for him a means to an end: to defend the cause of spiritual liberty and to expound his philosophy. He was, to a degree, comparable with his French contemporary Montaigne. Humanistic in outlook ("Man, develop thy gifts as a rational and moral creature!") he professed at the same time that God was man's ultimate good.

Coornhert wrote too much that is insignificant from the literary point of view; nevertheless, it would be quite possible to present a selection of his poetic works by which he would reveal himself not only as an eminent moralist and Christian humanist, but also as a meritorious artist. His pamphlets are forgotten and also his comedies. The latter, *Abrahams Uytgang, Comedie van de Blinde*

195

van Jericho, Comedie van Israel, are hardly more than rhymed ethical treatises in dialogue form. His collected works were published in 1633.

ABOUT: Jones, R. M. Spiritual Reformers in the Sixteenth and Seventeenth Centuries; Englische Studien, XVIII (1936). [In Dutch—see studies by B. Becker, H. Bonger.]

H. B.

*COPPÉE, FRANÇOIS ÉDOUARD JOACHIM (January 26, 1842-May 23, 1908), French poet and dramatist, was born in Paris of modest bourgeois parents. On his father's death, he interrupted his studies and, at the age of thirteen, undertook to help support his mother and sister as an architect's clerk; later, employed at the War Ministry, he found leisure to write verse. Coppée may be classified as a minor Parnassian; he was familiar at Leconte de Lisle's Saturdays, and, submitting to the master's advice, acquired a sound technique. His first poetry, *Réliquaire*, of 1866, and the *Intimités* of 1868, esteemed by his friends, and by Hugo, passed almost unnoted. He tied for the prize offered by the Universal Exposition in 1867, and was perhaps encouraged by this event to try his hand in the theatre; his *Le Passant* had an immense success in 1869 (it was also Sarah Bernhardt's début) and aroused the first signs of jealousy among his friends. The friction however also involved other factors, for Leconte de Lisle found in Coppée's verse a sentimental strain of which he disapproved, and he suspected him of exploiting "pure poetry" for unworthy and even venal ends.

Coppée's chronic ill health led him to many trips to the south, and the Franco-Prussian war interrupted his creative work. He returned to poetry in his masterpiece, *Les Humbles*, published in 1872; here one finds grace, love, kindliness, pictures of commonplace events, walks in the suburbs, glimpses of people ready to sacrifice themselves for duty, in a restrained and sympathetic descriptive realism, often idyllic, and in supple versification, all destined to appeal to the general public.

Coppée's principal efforts, as well as his fame during his lifetime, concern the theatre. After *Le Passant*, *Le Luthier de Crémone*, of 1876, coincides with the high point of his reputation, for he was at that moment on the jury for the "Troisième Parnasse." His historical verse plays followed in rapid succession, *Mme de Maintenon* in 1881, and his

* kô pā'

COPPÉE

two outstanding triumphs, *Servero Torelli* in 1883 and *Pour la Couronne* in 1896. During the years 1882-83 he published his numerous short stories, somewhat in the genre of Daudet and Maupassant; though they are less striking and original than the masterpieces of these two writers, several count among the best of this time.

Coppée was elected to the French Academy in 1884. His autobiographical writings date from the following years, and his notebooks continue through the troubled days of the Panama and Dreyfus affairs, for which they offer significant documentation. In *La Bonne Souffrance*, his poetry of 1898, he returned to the Church. During his last years, troubled by illness, he gathered about him many assiduous younger friends and was celebrated for his brilliant conversation.

Coppée stands somewhat apart from the Parnassians by his sentimentality and by certain romantic strains reminiscent of Musset; his poetry shows the influence of Baudelaire, Gautier, and Hugo, and, in *Les Humbles*, perhaps that of Sainte-Beuve. As he said in his last days, the glory of most of his generation would be to appear in the anthologies of the future.

Coppée's *Contes en Prose* were collected in 1882, and the six volumes of his *Œuvres*, published in 1907, replace the earlier ten of 1888-92. A three-volume edition of his *Poésies Complètes* appeared 1923-25.

His reputation is reflected by the numerous English translations that appeared in rapid sequence beginning in 1888, with *Fennet* (J. Jerome), *The Days* of *My Youth, The Wanderer, Disillusion, Ten Tales* (W. Learned, 1890), *The Violin Maker of Cremona* (1892), *True Riches* (1893), and *For the Crown* (in J. Pierce's *Masterpieces,* 1915).

ABOUT: [In French—De Lescure, François Coppée, L'Homme, la Vie et l'Œuvre; Gauthier-Ferrières, François Coppée et Son Œuvre; Jammes, F. Leçons Poétiques; Le Meur, L. La Vie et l'Œuvre de François Coppée; Schoen, H. François Coppée, l'Homme et le Poète.]

F. J. C.

CORAES or CORAY. See KORAÉS, ADAMANTIOS

*CORBIÈRE, ÉDOUARD-JOACHIM, called TRISTAN (July 18, 1845-March 1, 1875), French poet, was born at the manor of Coat-Congar, Ploujean, near Morlaix in the Finistère department (Brittany). His father, Jean-Antoine-René-Édouard Corbière (1793-1875), who had married eighteen-year-old Marie-Angélique-Aspasie Puyo at fifty, had been successively a corsair, political satirist, journalist and newspaper publisher, and writer of sea stories, of which the best known is *Le Négrier* (1832); he was the director of a steamship company office at Morlaix, and president of the Chamber of Commerce. Two other children, Edmond and Lucie, were born of the marriage.

Tristan went to school first at Morlaix, next in the sea town of Sainte-Brieuc, then at Nantes, following the standard program in classics, but ill health—rheumatism and palpitations—compelled him to withdraw from school in 1861. The greatest literary influence was that of his father's sea stories; Tristan satirized or mocked the romantic poets he read widely. A brief rest in southern France, three months in Italy (1870), and sporadic trips to Paris to visit with Count Rodolphe de Battine and the count's mistress Armida-Josefina Cuchiani (with whom Tristan was in love and whom he called Marcelle) virtually complete the roster of his absences from Brittany and the sea.

It is not known when Corbière adopted the name Tristan. Perhaps it was to avoid confusion with his father; undoubtedly he was mindful of the legendary Tristan. When *Les Amours Jaunes,* his only volume of verse, was published in 1873, it was at the author's expense. It had a self-caricature, etched by Corbière, as a frontispiece. The title probably signified a jaundiced view of love. The volume went unnoticed.

* kôr byâr'

Corbière was unappreciated, if not the object of mockery, in his own day. He was the prime example of the outcast, the eccentric, the Bohemian: the Bretons called him *ancou,* i.e., the specter of death, for he was ugly and emaciated and stooped; Tristan had a half-starved mongrel which he called by his own name, and which he paraded on a hundred-foot leash; he shaved off all his hair, including his eyebrows, and promenaded his glabrous ugliness before the staid townfolk of Roscoff near his birthplace; he sailed his cutter, *Le Négrier,* into storms while singing his songs; he froze and drank and lived meanly in solitude. (Corbière painted and did an etching of himself as a bizarre, grotesque figure, and so he was profiled by the painter Jean Benner.) Overshadowed by his father in the esteem of his birthplace, where he died after a painful illness, he is buried near Morlaix at Saint-Martin-des-Champs. Both Tristan, who was not quite thirty, and Édouard, who died seven months later at the age of eighty-two, are commemorated by a double medallion, sculpted by Bourdelle, located where Ploujean and Morlaix touch the sea.

Corbière's fame started with his inclusion by Verlaine in the latter's series on the *Poètes Maudits* (1884), the epithet "cursed" suggesting poets victimized by fate and society. Huysmans, in *À Rebours (Against the Grain,* 1884) included *Les Amours Jaunes* among the dandy Des Esseintes' preferred books; the group of early twentieth century French poets who called themselves "fantaisistes" championed him as a link in the tradition extending from Villon through Baudelaire to Rimbaud and Laforgue; he influenced T. S. Eliot and Jean Moréas.

The pervasive quality of Corbière's verse is that of authenticity: such the poetry, such the man. "Philosopher, stray, still-born" reads his self-description in his famous "Epitaph for Tristan-Édouard-Joachim Corbière," which concludes (in W. McElroy's translation): "He died in readiness to live/and lived in readiness to die." Y. G. Le Dantec, editor of a critical edition (1953), sums up the characteristics of Corbière's work: ". . . a very special conception of love, sometimes shared, generally unhappy through his fault; a stinging humor, which is turned on itself as its object; a passion for the sea, such as no other French poet had previously experienced or translated; the direct, but discreetly transposed, exaltation of the Celtic native soil; finally, the sense of an absolute harmony, of a mysterious song, sprung from a soul completely bathed in the nostalgia of childhood."

The dominant moods are those of sarcasm and of irony, with the relish of mystification. By technical innovations (Corbière has mistakenly been called a "primitive"), by the alliance of folkloric and popular elements with intimate complex feelings, by the mélange of tones and vocabulary, and by his direct sense of nature, Corbière represents that facet of symbolism which was vigorous and vital; and, anecdotally, he has contributed to the conception of the poet as intrinsically pure though ill-fated in his own time.

There is no complete translation of Corbière. *Les Amours Jaunes* has been partially translated by Walter McElroy (1947) and by C. F. McIntyre (1954). Two tales, *Casino des Trépassés* and *L'Américaine*, which had appeared in the *Vie Parisienne* of 1874 have since been published (1941) because of Corbière's ever-growing fame; translations of selections from *Les Amours Jaunes* appear in *An Anthology of French Poetry from Nerval to Valéry in English Translation*, edited by Angel Flores (Anchor Books, 1958); parts of *Les Amours Jaunes* have been issued separately: *Gens de Mer, La Rapsode Foraine et le Pardon de Sainte-Anne.* The latter has been set to music by Emmanuel Bondeville; Jean d'Udine has done the music for "Cinq 'Rondels pour Après'"; and Yves Baudrier, for "Laisser-courre" and "Paysage Mauvais."

ABOUT: Gourmont, R. de. Book of Masks; Jarrell, R. Poetry and the Age; Quennell, P. Baudelaire and the Symbolists; Quarterly Review of Literature, Fall 1944; French Studies, July 1951. [In French—see studies by C. Angelet, A. Arnoux, R. Martineau, P. Schneider, A. Sonnenfeld, J. Vacher-Corbière; there are critical editions by Y. G. Le Dantec (1942, 1953) and an anthology, with an introduction, by J. Rousselot (1952).]

S. S. W.

*CORNEILLE, PIERRE (June 8, 1606-October 1, 1684), French dramatist, was born and raised in Rouen, Normandy, of a middle-class family of modest property and means, on both sides lawyers and government officials. His father, Pierre, was supervisor of water and forests of Rouen Vicomté. His mother, Marthe Le Pesant, bore him, the eldest of seven, in the old Rouen home.

Young Pierre entered Rouen Jesuit college in 1615, when barely nine, and continued there for six years, winning at least two prizes for Latin verses. Latin studies under the Jesuits, famed teachers of the language, made Corneille a follower of Cicero, Lucan, and Seneca. He always retained a loving admiration for his preceptors. He left college in 1622 and began to study law, considered indispensable to a good education. He spent two years at this and was licensed June 18, 1624. He ceased practicing, after one attempt, because of an annoying speech defect. On

* kôr nã′ y′

198

PIERRE CORNEILLE

February 16, 1629, he entered Rouen Parlement where he served twenty-one years. A special dispensation, for his father's services, made it possible for him to enter this employ earlier than usual. Two offices were purchased: as king's advocate in water and forests court, and in Rouen port Admiralty court. He is said to have been an intelligent counselor. His social and domestic life was as active as his professional life. Falling in love, he turned to French versifying, composing sonnets to Mélite (perhaps one Catherine Hue) as well as other love poetry and carnival verses.

After the religious wars ended, some fifteen troupes of traveling actors carried throughout France melodramas of Alexandre Hardy, translations and adaptations of Italian pastorals and of Spanish tragicomedies. Corneille's early drama reflects their elements: echoes from d'Urfé's romantic pastorals; a mingling of tragic and comic; tragicomedy's variety of place, freedom of action and time. The observance of the unities and other restrictions was spreading but was not yet prevalent. When the celebrated actor-manager Mondory visited Rouen in 1629, Corneille gave him his comedy *Mélite* to stage at the du Marais Theatre in Paris, in late 1629 or early 1630. It was welcomed, and Corneille, who went to the opening, later declared, "It equaled the finest thing done up to that time, and made me known to the Court." Thereafter Corneille gave first right of performance to the du Marais troupe. The eight plays of his apprenticeship period (1629-36), except the Senecan tragedy *Médée* and the melodrama *Clitandre,* were comedies of manners, setting a new style, reporting the talk of real people.

When Louis XIII and his court, including Cardinal Richelieu, were near Rouen in June 1633, Mondory performed several of Corneille's plays for them and Corneille was asked to compose verses to honor the visit. He addressed instead an elegant Latin poem declaring himself unworthy. This pleased Richelieu and his intimate Boisrobert, and Corneille was invited in late 1634 or early 1635 to collaborate with four other poets for Richelieu's private theatre. The Cardinal set the theme; Boisrobert, Colletet, de l'Estoile, Rotrou, and Corneille thereupon undertook the *Comédie des Tuilleries.* Corneille wrote the third act but, disliking the discipline demanded by such collaboration, he left on pretext of duties in Rouen. Nonetheless he was pensioned by Richelieu.

Corneille had studied Spanish, valued at Rouen, which was a printing center for Spanish books with an important Spanish colony. In 1636 he presented *L'Illusion Comique,* a fantasy with the braggart Matamore, typical Spanish comic soldier. This he followed by *Le Cid,* based upon Guillén de Castro's Spanish historical drama. Produced in December 1636 or January 1637, it was a tremendous success and Corneille unhappily became boastful. In *Le Cid,* to resolve the conflict between lovers compelled to act as enemies by a code of family honor, the king commanded the heroine to marry, after a year's mourning, the national hero who had reluctantly slain her father in a duel. The play's "eloquent depiction of the heart's true feelings" stirred almost everyone at home and abroad, but it scandalized those who insisted on the proprieties. They, Corneille's rivals, and some of his former collaborators attacked the play early in 1637, claiming that it also violated the unities. Instead of ignoring this criticism, Corneille retaliated and made more enemies. All the poets concerned showed themselves as vain as their victim, and the quarrel became a national scandal. Scholars do not entirely agree on Richelieu's rôle, but it is claimed that he allowed the attacks to continue with the thought that they might discipline Corneille. When he became aware, however, of threats of personal violence to Corneille, he ordered a truce. The matter was then referred to the Académie Française, directed by Boisrobert. The Académie issued a report edited by Chapelain that pretended to be fair to everyone. Corneille, hurt that critics still questioned the play's ethics and demanded slavish obedience to the unities, left the theatre for three years; but he brooded over the issue and finally became convinced that he must conform.

In January 1637 Louis XIII had ennobled Corneille's father, who died on February 12, 1639. Corneille directed the upbringing of his brother Thomas (see sketch below), who chose to follow Pierre's several vocations. In 1640 Pierre married Marie de Lampérière and ten years later Thomas married her sister. They lived a happy community life in adjoining houses, sharing their means, until Pierre's death.

Corneille's next three plays have, with *Le Cid,* long been considered his greatest. Observing the rules now, he also began to apply the principles learned from his teachers: mastery of self; obedience to duty; power of the free will. His heroes, with pride in achievement, seek to be admired by posterity. *Horace* (1640) pictures the victory of patriotism over love. *Cinna* (1640-41?), in Corneille's day called his masterpiece, was admired for its debates on monarchy and republic, tyranny and justice and mercy. Modern critics are impressed by the masterly exposition of change in Augustus' character. Lancaster calls it the first important French tragedy to end in happiness. *Polyeucte* (1641-42?) depicts the renunciation of earthly love for the glory of martyrdom. A favorite of the general public of its day, modern critics find it a masterpiece of portraiture. Lockhart calls it "its author's most broadly human play."

Rodogune (1644-45?), a triumphal success and Corneille's favorite, is now considered an inferior melodrama. *Nicomède* (1650-51?), a study of Roman political policy of "divide and rule," was popular and has steadily grown in appreciation. Frye calls it "that perfectly unique masterpiece of irony and stagecraft." The failure of *Pertharite* (1651) led to another withdrawal by the playwright until 1659, during which time he translated Kempis' *Imitation of Christ* (published 1651-56). He resigned his government offices in 1650. Fouquet persuaded him to return to the theatre in 1659, but the eleven plays that followed met with diminishing success, for Racine had now captured public taste. *Suréna* (1674) was his last play.

Corneille continued to write verses and religious poetry. In 1660 he published an edition of his plays with *examens* (an analysis of each) and three discourses on tragedy and and the unities. In 1662 he moved to Paris.

His last years were saddened by failures, but he was happy in his family and in his devout religious life. Two of his sons died; another son and a daughter entered religious orders. The oldest daughter was married. Pierre, the eldest, an army captain, was a constant drain on his father's purse, yet Corneille's means, though not ample, were adequate.

The great poet and dramatist was not personally attractive, being heavy and careless in attire. Strangers took him for a provincial merchant, simple, timid, a little common. La Bruyère said he was a boring talker, of thick speech and strong Norman accent, who had trouble finding the right word and who occasionally lapsed into dialect. He read his own work badly. Others had to do justice to the work that reflects with such acute penetration and powerful music the problems of his time. Couton says, "His is an art of pitiless realism."

Corneille's fame spread rapidly abroad. In the reigns of both Charles I and Charles II his works were popular in England and in Holland, both in French and in translation. Of the thirty-two plays written by Corneille alone, some ten titles were translated into English. The two earliest were in blank verse: *The Cid* (1637) by Joseph Rutter; *Polyeucte* (1655) by Sir William Lower. The rhymed versions begin with *Pompey* (1663) by Mrs. Katharine Philips; *Heraclius* (1664) by L. Carlell, *Horace* (translated 1665, published 1671) by C. Cotton; *Nicomède* (1671) by John Dancer; *Mistaken Beauty* (*Le Menteur*) (1685), blank verse and prose; *Cinna's Conspiracy* (1713), a free translation; *Rodogune* (1765) by Stanhope Aspinwall; *Mélite* (1776). Of collected works, the French *Œuvres* edited by C. Marty-Laveaux in 1862 remains the definitive edition. An excellent translation and critical study, *Chief Plays of Corneille*, by Lacy Lockert includes *Le Cid, Cinna, Horace, Nicomède, Polyeucte, Rodogune* (1952).

ABOUT: Croce, B. Ariosto, Shakespeare, and Corneille; Falk, E. H. Renunciation as a Tragic Focus; Fisher, D. F. C. Corneille and Racine in England; Frye, P. H. Literary Reviews and Criticisms; Guizot, F. P. G. Corneille and His Times; Lancaster, H. C. History of French Dramatic Literature in the Seventeenth Century; Turnell, M. The Classical Moment; Vincent, L. H. Corneille; Watson, P. B. Tales of Normandie; Yarrow, P. J. Corneille; Modern Languages, XL (1959); Modern Language Review, April 1950; Romanic Review, December 1958. [In French—Couton, G. La Vieillesse de Corneille; Dictionnaire des Lettres Francaises: 17e Siècle; Lanson, G. Pierre Corneille.]

M. A. W.

*CORNEILLE, THOMAS (August 20, 1625-December 8, 1709), French writer and dramatist, was born in Rouen, nineteen years the junior of his more famous brother, Pierre. He studied with the Jesuits in Rouen,

* kôr nā′ y′

THOMAS CORNEILLE

showing at an early age his literary talent and facility. He participated in a poetic contest in 1641, winning a prize for an ode, but was shortly obliged to abandon his schooling, and completed his education under his brother, including studies in Spanish. To assure himself a livelihood, Thomas earned a law degree at the University of Caen, but practiced only briefly after 1659. The brothers married two sisters and lived in an ideal and close harmony for some twenty-five years, settling together in Paris in 1662. Their combined fortune assured them moderate comfort and leisure for writing. In 1673, after the death of Molière, and in collaboration with Donneau de Visé, Thomas reorganized the comic theatre and created the new genre called the "pièce à machines," which exploited the extensive material that Molière had left idle in his installations in Rue Mazarine. On the instances of Molière's widow, Thomas set *Le Festin de Pierre* into verse. He was active in journalism, especially as editor and, by 1681, owner, with de Visé, of the *Mercure Galant*, the most distinguished and influential literary magazine of the times, which de Visé had launched in 1672; through the *Mercure Galant*, Thomas took sides with the Moderns in the famous literary quarrel with the Ancients. He succeeded his brother to the French Academy in 1685, and in this new rôle turned to more erudite subjects and to lexicography in his *Dictionnaire des Termes d'Arts et de Sciences* (1694), based with great care on the best current sources (Perrault, Nicot, Bernier, etc.), and a forerunner of Chambers' dictionary and of Diderot's *Encyclopédie;* the importance of this work was enhanced by the revisions made by Corneille's nephew, Fontenelle. In 1697 Thomas published his new version of Ovid's *Metamorphoses,* and prepared his *Dictionnaire Universel Géographique et Historique.* His last years were saddened by loss of many relatives and friends, by unfortunate financial difficulties, and by failing eyesight and final blindness. Corneille was widely esteemed as a religious man of high moral and intellectual ideals, a person of elegant manners, and a faithful friend.

In his first play, *Les Engagements du Hasard* (1647), perhaps mediocre but well received, Corneille made a free translation from Calderón's *Los Empeños de un Acaso.* After further adaptations and imitations of Calderón, such as *Le Feint Astrologue* (1648), he imitated Rojas in *Don Bernard de Cigarral* (1650), a play that enjoyed wide success for over a decade and was frequently staged by Molière. Three years later he created his satire or parody of the pastoral comedy, entitled *Le Berger Extravagant.* At the moment of his brother's serious illness and reversals in the theatre, Thomas turned to the tragedy. His *Timocrate,* performed in November, 1656, enjoyed an incredible vogue for six months and aroused the enthusiasm of Louis XIV. The manner of *Timocrate,* comparable to that of Quinault, is one of excessively romanesque and extravagant plot in a precious style, the epitome of the current heroic gallantry, influenced by Madeleine de Scudéry's *Le Grand Cyrus,* a work which offered Thomas Corneille the material for his *Bérénice* in 1657, his *Antiochus* in 1666, and his *Théodat* in 1672. He was influenced by Pierre Corneille's *Rodogune* and *Nicomède.* Thomas Corneille's masterpiece is probably the historical play *Le Comte d'Essex,* of 1678, in which he sought a synthesis of the art of Pierre Corneille and of Racine.

L'Amour à la Mode was translated as *The Amorous Gallant; or, Love in Fashion* by John Bulteel in 1665.

ABOUT: Romanic Review, 1929. [In French—Reynier, G. Thomas Corneille, Sa Vie et Son Théâtre; Van Renynghe de Voxvrie, L. Descendance de Thomas Corneille.]

F. J. C.

COSTA, ISAAC DE. See DA COSTA, ISAAC DE

COSTER, CHARLES THÉODORE HENRI DE. See DE COSTER, CHARLES THÉODORE HENRI

*COUSIN, VICTOR (November 28, 1792-January 13, 1867), French philosopher, was born in Paris, the son of a watchmaker. Although the family was poor, they managed to give the boy, who was precocious and showed great promise, a good education at the Lycée Charlemagne where he made a brilliant record. In 1810 he entered the École Normale (the Sorbonne) and again so distinguished himself that after only two years he was made a lecturer in Greek and philosophy. In 1815-16 he assisted Royer-Collard in the chair of the history of modern philosophy. Royer-Collard in his teaching emphasized the spiritual nature of the soul and a theistic conception of the universe. Other early influences on Cousin included Locke and Condillac, as well as the philosophy of Maine de Biran (1766-1824). The latter first declared himself a disciple of Locke and Condillac and followed them in their introspective, psychological method; however, he soon denied the theory of the passivity of consciousness and substituted a concept of the self as an active, developing entity rising to a final achievement of transcendence and a direct contact with God: these views are clearly traceable in Cousin's thought. By 1818 the influence of Schelling and Hegel also became operative.

Cousin lost his teaching post in 1822 because of political events; in Berlin in 1824 he was imprisoned, for six months, on a political charge. During the years of his forced withdrawal from teaching he completed the *Fragments Philosophiques,* published in 1826. He also worked on his edition of Proclus and of Descartes and began his translations of Plato, completed in 1840. In 1828 he was restored to his teaching position at the Ecole Normale and was widely acclaimed as a powerful and popular lecturer. For eight months in 1840 he served the government as minister of public instruction, and his writings on education (reflecting trends in Prussian education which he had observed during his stay in Germany) were influential on the French educational system. He was instrumental in the passage of the law on primary instruction.

The Revolution of 1848 and the subsequent upheaval of 1851 forced him to retire from public life and from teaching, and he devoted his remaining years to writing. His most important work, *Du Vrai, du Beau, et du Bien*

* kōō zăn'

201

COUSIN

(Of the True, the Beautiful, and the Good), originally published in 1836, was issued in a new edition in 1853. At about this time he turned from philosophy to literature and history and wrote several works of great stylistic beauty and historical interest on famous women of the seventeenth century—*La Jeunesse de Mme de Longueville* (1853), *La Marquise de Sablé* (1854), and a history of the period—*La Société Française au XVIIe Siècle*. It is as a philosopher primarily, however, that Cousin is remembered. His analysis of consciousness is paralleled in his system by the development of the race, of history, and of theology. He defines three stages of consciousness: that of the sensations, with an external ground; the will, a free and spontaneous activity antecedent to reflection; and reason, an impersonal activity which raises the individual out of himself and makes him one with all other selves and with all truth. In this point he breaks with the Kantian emphasis upon the unknowability of substantial reality; nor did he agree with Schelling's view that Reality is apprehensible only by mystic intuition. Thus his borrowings from German Idealism and Lockian philosophy comprised a generalized eclecticism. By the 1870's his influence in academic philosophy had waned, replaced by a Neo-Kantian doctrine.

Cousin devoted his life to his scholarship. He had a reputation for avarice and accumulated a large personal fortune, meanwhile living most of his life very frugally in rooms at the Sorbonne. He did, however, collect a large and splendid library which, on his death,

he left to the university. He died in Cannes at the age of seventy-four.

English translations include several versions of the *Course of the History of Philosophy* (vol. I translated by H. G. Linberg, 1832, and the whole work by O. W. Wright, 1852); *Elements of Psychology*, translated by C. S. Henry (1834); *Justice and Charity*, translated by W. Hazlitt, 1848; *The Philosophy of the Beautiful*, translated by J. C. Daniel (1848); and *Lectures on the True, the Beautiful, the Good*. translated by O. W. Wright (1854).

ABOUT: French Review, XXIX (1955); French Studies, XVII (1963). [In French—see studies by P. Janet, J. B. St. Hilaire, J. Simon. In German —see study by A. Cornelius.]

*CRÉBILLON (fils), CLAUDE PROSPER JOLYOT de (February 14, 1707- April 12, 1777), French novelist, was the son of the dramatist (see sketch below) and of an apothecary's daughter whom Crébillon *père* secretly married in haste two weeks before the birth of the son. Friends paid Crébillon's tuition at the Louis-le-Grand College in Paris. His precocious talents attracted the attention of the Jesuit fathers, but he felt no vocation and turned to the theatre, first at the Comédie Française, then with the Italian troupe at this time (1730) in need of dramatic talent. In quick succession Crébillon created plays typical of the Italian repertory, parodies, farces, pseudo-oriental vaudevilles, superficial but witty. He lived with his father, surrounded by animals, in semi-squalor, but he was diligent in his literary projects. The son's talent lay especially in caustic wit and frank humor, evident in his first success, his story *L'Écumoire* of 1734, also called *Tanzaï*. The satirical portraits in this novel sent him to prison and thus assured his popularity.

With Piron and Collé, Crébillon founded the "Société du Caveau" in 1732, a dinner group which in the course of fifteen years attracted such other great wits as Duclos, Moncrif, Helvetius, and Rameau. Dividing his energies between such groups and the society of the ladies, Crébillon became the leader in the important satirical traditions of his day. In 1748 he married Miss Stafford, who had been his mistress for some four years, then lost both her and his son. Thanks to the favors of Mme de Pompadour, he became the royal literary censor in 1759. He lost his father in 1762, and in him his closest friend and associate. Little is known of the remainder of Crébillon's life.

The "contes" of Crébillon represent an important step in the evolution of the genre from the *Arabian Nights*, through Hamilton

* krā bē yôN'

CRÉBILLON (FILS)

and Voltaire, to Duclos and Marmontel. His *Tanzaï* was a great success, though today its pseudo-oriental fairy tale color and its routine insipidity of style and off-color effects mark it as an archaic example. *Le Sopha* moves strongly beyond this routine into a more realistic manner. The most powerful formula used by Crébillon, and much imitated in later years, is that of the *Égarements du Cœur et de l'Esprit*: the originality of this work lies in the degree of perversity of the libertinage, the elegant testimony on the corruption of the society of its times, and a theme of the evil habits of fine company. The best portraits, here as in Crébillon's other writings, are of women in elegant society, and of strongly sensual love. The rather elusive personal reactions of the author take the form of "morals" to the stories. To the content and general color one must add the effect of the elaborately artificial style, reaching in Crébillon a kind of high point in a new preciosity so fitting to the tone of the social customs of the *conte libertin*.

The bibliography of Crébillon's writings bears witness to their importance during his lifetime. After his first work, *Le Sylphe* (1730), frequent publication of *L'Écumoire, ou Tanzaï et Néardané, Histoire Japonaise,* in two volumes, extends through the thirties and forties, and *Le Sopha, Conte Moral,* over the next several decades; *La Nuit et le Moment* began a similar career in 1755. The multi-volumed *Œuvres Complètes* appeared in 1772, 1777, etc. Lesser titles were gathered in the *Contes Dialogués* in 1879, notably *Les*

Matinées de Cythère (1755) and *Le Hasard du Coin du Feu* (1763).

English translations include *The Skimmer (Tanzaï,* London, 1735), *The Sopha* (1742, and again by B. Dobrée, 1927), *The Opportunities of the Night* (by E. Sutton, 1925), and *The Wayward Head and Heart* (1964, translated by B. Bray).

ABOUT: Cherpack, C. An Essay on Crébillon fils; Palache, J. Four Novelists of the Old Regime. [In French: Uzanne, O. Les Conteurs du 18ᵉ Siècle, *and* Notice . . . in Contes Dialogués.]

F. J. C.

*CRÉBILLON (père), PROSPER JOLYOT de (February 13, 1674-June 17, 1762), French dramatist, born in Dijon, was the son of a secretary in the municipal offices and of the daughter of a lieutenant-general of Beaune. He studied with the Jesuits at his birthplace, showing both intelligence and excessive wit; he then prepared for law in Besançon, and served briefly as lawyer in the Parliament. His father sent him to Paris for further advancement, but his protector there recognized his talent for the theatre and encouraged him to compose verse tragedies. Crébillon was disheartened by the refusal of his first play, but returned to his dramatic project and saw his *Idoménée* well received in 1703, and, four years later, his *Atrée.* Meanwhile his father was displeased with this poetic career, and their rupture was further motivated by a second marriage and the generally disorderly conduct of the son, brought to a head by his forced marriage to an apothecary's daughter in Paris. On the father's death, in 1707, Crébillon found himself without fortune, and was obliged to continue as a playwright for his livelihood.

Crébillon's full activity continued by a rapid succession of tragedies until the remarkable success of his *Rhadamiste,* in 1711. Impressed by his own fame, he began about that time to turn to the pleasures of society and to neglect his work. His imprudence led him to neglect such practical opportunities as could have profited him materially, and neither his place as Royal Censor, in 1735, nor the attentions of the Comte de Clermont, raised him from his chronic indigence; one factor in his indifference was his love of solitude and his native reticence to show himself or ask for favors. Pressed by Mme de Pompadour, he completed his *Catilina,* which was magnificently performed before the court and the king, and earned for the author a considerable pension and a librarianship. Despite his advanced age, Crébillon continued

* krä bē yòn′

CRÉBILLON (PÈRE)

with further plays, and left unfinished *Le Triumvirat* and *Cléomède.*

Despite a few eccentricities, Crébillon was an attractive man, usually agreeable and easy-going, serious yet at times gay. He was averse to the current satirical genres, and was the man of his generation with the fewest enemies. His relationship with his son (see sketch above) was very close, and despite their different temperaments and interests, they lived in harmony for many years.

In the evolution of the tragedy at the turn of the century, Crébillon is the greatest traditionalist and the most fruitful and powerful of the successors of Corneille and Racine. Convinced that mere imitation of these masters was unworthy, he sought for even more tragic situations, such as the horror of *Atrée et Thyeste* (1707), where the father drinks his son's blood, and *Électre* (1708), and *Rhadamiste et Zénobie* (1711), where daughter kills mother and father kills son. In his preface to *Atrée,* Crébillon mentions strong revulsion among the spectators to the violence of the plot, but claims that the story provokes pity through terror, and that episodes of this kind, worthy of the tragic theatre, should not be modified to fit accepted and limited norms of decency. In the preface to his *Électre,* he dismisses various criticisms of technical flaws by claiming that they have worthy dramatic effects: this, he says, is his play, not that of Sophocles. It is his boldness, no matter how melodramatic it may seem at a distance, that made of Crébillon Voltaire's only rival dur-

ing their century. Crébillon's *Théâtre Complet,* ed. A. Vitu, appeared in 1885.

ABOUT: [In French—*preface to* Œuvres, 1812; Dutrait, M. Étude sur la Vie et le Théâtre de Crébillon.]

F. J. C.

CRESCAS, HASDAI (1340-1410), one of the greatest medieval Jewish philosophers, was born in Barcelona, Spain. He came from a prominent Jewish family and received a thorough education from the excellent scholar Rabbi Nissim ben Reuben Gerondi. Crescas himself soon achieved distinction as a Talmudist and philosopher. Although he did not hold an official rabbinical post, he was active both as teacher and adviser to such leading thinkers as Rabbi Isaac ben Sheshet and Joseph Albo. Not only was Crescas a spiritual guide to his fellow Jews, but his renown was such that King John I of Aragon frequently consulted him.

At an early date, however, Crescas felt the cold hand of persecution. Falsely denounced in 1367 in connection with a trial for desecration of the Host, he was imprisoned for several months. He moved to Saragossa after this false arrest, again assuming a leading position in the community. It was after the bloody pogroms of 1391, in which his own son was killed, that Crescas turned to philosophy. In a letter to the Jewish congregation of Avignon written in that year, Crescas described the terrible fate of Spanish Jewry, caught between death and conversion.

As a reaction to those trying days and at the instance of Christian friends, Crescas wrote a philosophical treatise in Spanish which was translated into Hebrew as *Betul 'Ikre ha-Notsrim* (Refutation of Christian Principles; written c. 1398). In it he analyzed dispassionately the basic dogmas of Christianity, claiming they were incomprehensible and untenable.

Crescas' major philosophical work is the *Or Adonai* (Light of the Lord), completed in the year of his death at Saragossa. Originally intended as part of a comprehensive work on Jewish law, it is a formulation of the principles of the Jewish religion. Crescas' purpose was basically critical, his aim being to correct the views of Maimonides, and, through Maimonides, to attack the source of medieval philosophical thought, Aristotle himself. Using Aristotle's own procedure of logical analysis and clear proof, he sets forth his beliefs on such subjects as the existence of God, God's omniscience and omnipotence, prophecy, free will, the purpose of the universe, and creation. Crescas' treatment of these problems is anti-Maimonidean and anti-scholastic in that he denies the validity of a strictly rational approach to religion. For him, the goal of human life is not contemplation or knowledge, but rather the perfection of the soul in the love of God. His stress throughout is on feeling and not on speculation as the core of religion. Crescas' discussion of freedom of the will, in which he places great emphasis on the significance of human intention, illustrates his attitude.

The philosophy of Crescas influenced a number of great European thinkers and was particularly important in shaping the views of Spinoza on man's freedom, creation, and God. Similarly, the thought of Giordano Bruno, Pico della Mirandola, and Galileo bears witness to the influence of Crescas. Crescas was an original thinker and his attempt to free Judaism from the domination of classical philosophy remains of fundamental significance.

The basic Hebrew edition is that of Ferrara, 1556.

Only one section of the *Or Adonai* has been translated into English. That translation was made by Harry Wolfson in 1929 and appears in his *Crescas' Critique of Aristotle.*

ABOUT: Graetz, H. History of the Jews; Husik, I. A History of Medieval Jewish Philosophy; Neumark, D. *in* Central Conference of American Rabbis Year Book, 1908; Waxman, M. A History of Jewish Literature; Waxman, M. The Philosophy of Don Hasdai Crescas; Wolfson, H. Crescas' Critique of Aristotle.

M. R.

*CROS, ÉMILE-HORTENSIUS-CHARLES (October 1, 1842-August 9, 1888), French poet, was born at Fabrezan, near Narbonne (Aude). He had two brothers, Antoine, who became a doctor and tried his hand at literature as a hobby, and Henri, who became a sculptor and modeler in wax. Charles was self-educated—he never attended school, except as an unofficial auditor of erudite lectures—but was tutored by his father, a lecturer, writer, and philosopher. The son was equally interested in arts and sciences, and unusually gifted for linguistic study, especially of oriental languages.

Remembered chiefly as the author of a book of poems and prose poems, *Le Coffret de Santal* (1873; augmented edition, 1879), Cros has also left a reputation as a Bohemian. He was one of the moving spirits in the circle which gathered in Paris around Countess Nina de Callias (1843-84, Nina *née*

* crō

Gaillard and known as Nina de Villard before and during her marriage to the dissipated journalist count. (The insouciance, inebriety, and fantasy of Nina's salon have been inexactly and maliciously described in Catulle Mendès' *La Maison de la Vieille* [1894], in which Cros is called Georges Kramm, and in George Moore's *Memoirs of My Dead Life* [1907].) Along with frequenting the Parnassians of Nina's circle, Cros was active in such informal versifying and socializing groups as the Hydropathes, the Hirsutes, the Zutistes (which met in a café across the street from his home), and the Chat-Noiristes. At gatherings in salons and cafés Cros recited his humorous pieces. He is credited with inventing (or perfecting) the satirical or amusing monologue. The famous actor of the Comédie Française Constant Coquelin the younger recited Cros' verses or prose poems to appreciative audiences—some of these have been reprinted in *Saynètes et Monologues* (7 vols., 1875-81) and in *Théâtre de Campagne* (9 vols., c. 1875).

Cros was a brilliant theorist in science, but lacked the sense of perseverance, the practical bent, and the profit incentive, to implement his ideas. In 1869 he published a memoir on indirect color photography and one on interplanetary communication; he presented a study on the phonograph—which he called the paleograph—before the Academy of Sciences, in April 1877, but had published a paper on this subject the preceding year (thus antedating Edison); and he is said to have been an excellent chemist while also interested in alchemy. Cros never made anything from his theories and was quite poor. He preferred to converse, improvise, linger in cafés where—with his thin silhouette, dark complexion, kinky hair, febrile hands, thick lips, and high cheek-bones—he was a familiar figure. In 1878, he married Mlle Hjardmaal, a Dane, and a son, Guy-Charles Cros, was born to them on February 2, 1879. Before his forty-sixth birthday Cros died in Paris, burned out by excesses: alcohol, love affairs, a hectic social life, combined with intensive researches.

Cros was respected and admired by his contemporaries, especially by Verlaine, Villiers de l'Isle-Adam, Charles de Sivry, and Salis. Aaron Schaffer, who has studied Cros' poetic techniques in *The Genres of Parnassian Poetry* (1944), classifies him as a follower of Baudelaire and a satanist in inspiration. Cros essayed a remarkable variety of verse forms. Laurent Tailhade found in Cros echoes of Verlaine and of Coppée; Verlaine himself, in *Les Hommes d'Aujourd'hui* (1888), judged Cros to be skillful and robust. Enid Starkie, Rimbaud's biographer, has pointed out that the boy-wonder could have been influenced in his prose poems by those of Cros, well-known when Rimbaud "was in close contact with Charles Cros" in 1871. Cros' versatility, sprightly and sardonic humor, and impractical Bohemianism have won favor with the surrealists; for the larger public, he remains principally a legend.

Cros' son, himself a poet and translator from the Danish, brought out a posthumous collection of his father's verse and prose poems, *Le Collier de Griffes* (1908). Henri Parisot edited an anthology, *Poèmes et Proses,* with an introduction by M. Saillet (1944).

Arthur Symons essayed a translation of one poem, "Wasted Words," in *Colour Studies in Paris* (1918; but the part on Cros was written in 1899).

ABOUT: Schaffer, A. Genres of Parnassian Poetry; Romanic Review, January-March 1930. [In French—Revue de Paris, November 1952.]

S. S. W.

*CRUZ CANO Y OLMEDILLA, RA-MÓN FRANCISCO DE LA (March 28, 1731-March 5, 1794), Spanish dramatist, was born in Madrid. In 1759 he entered a minor government office as bookkeeper, spending the rest of his life there with but slight advancement in rank and salary. Shortly after 1759 he married Doña Margarita Beatríz de Magán, who bore him several children. The family lived in constant poverty, despite a later protection by the Duchess of Osuna and the Countess of Benavente, in whose house he died.

Ramón de la Cruz' earliest preserved work is the *sainete* entitled *La Enferma de Mal de Boda* (1757). The actual printing of his plays was not accomplished until 1786-91 (*Teatro,* Madrid). The present estimate of the number of his works centers between three and four hundred items. After various frustrated attempts in neoclassical dramatic literature and in translations and adaptations from French and Italian tragedies, de la Cruz found his true speciality in the *sainete,* an historically ancient genre originating in Greece and Rome as pantomimes, becoming in the thirteenth century theatrical tidbits or short dialogues known also as *entremés, baile, loa,* and finally crystallized in the eighteenth century as one-act comic plays, in verse, with little plot. The *sainete* reached its height, as an interlude play, in the sixteenth century and declined through the first half of the

* krōōth kä' nō ē ōl mä thē' lyä

eighteenth century. Realism had developed into burlesque and obscenity; characters had become conventionalized types.

With Ramón de la Cruz, the *sainete* was revolutionized. He abandoned both the old form of intrigue, usually in the form of a practical joke, and the hackneyed types. He gave to the *sainete* its final form and its high place in literature by presenting, with pure and satiric humor, in a full plot, characters and customs drawn from life. His language was realistic, even in dialect if necessary. By his dictum: "I write and truth dictates to me," Ramón de la Cruz successfully sought to offset the neoclassicists' criticism of his abandonment of the unities and the moralizing they required of drama. He wrote for the good of his fellow men, as well as for their pleasure, painting honestly the faults and virtues of popular types and events. Thus his vigorous comedies of manners are of incalculable historical value. His success in this genre gave him the title of "tyrant of the theatre."

Ramón de la Cruz is accredited with having created another genre, the modern *zarzuela,* which is a combination of song, dance, and dialogue—a type of entertainment developing from the earlier *entremés cantado.* Beginning with conventional *zarzuelas* of mythological theme set to Italian music, he ended with the presentation of themes of contemporary reality set to completely authentic Spanish music. Ramón de la Cruz' new *zarzuela* had abundant success in the nineteenth century, just as his *sainete* was an important factor in the reform of the nineteenth century Spanish theatre.

One of Ramón de la Cruz' *sainetes* was translated by W. Knapp Jones as "Pride's Fall" in *Spanish One-Act Plays* (1934).

ABOUT: Kany, C. E., ed. Five Sainetes of Ramón de la Cruz; Hamilton, A. "Ramón de la Cruz, Social Reformer," *in* Romanic Revue, XII. [In Spanish—Cotarelo y Mori, E. Don Ramón de la Cruz y sus Obras; Filippo, Luigi di, ed. Diez Sainetes Inéditos de Ramón de la Cruz: Prologo de Guillermo Díaz-Plaja.]

R. P. C.

*CUEVA, JUAN DE LA (1550?-1610), Spanish dramatist and poet, was born in Seville, the son of Martín López de la Cueva. The family, according to Juan de la Cueva's genealogical poem *Historia y Sucesión de la Cueva,* was an extremely eminent one stemming from Beltrán de la Cueva, adviser to King Henry IV.

* kwä' vä

Juan de la Cueva lived in Seville until 1574, at which time he accompanied his younger brother Claudio, an Inquisitor, to Mexico. The poet wrote some verses in the New World which all indicated a strong nostalgia for Seville, and in 1577 we find Cueva back in his beloved native city. In the ensuing years he composed various allegorical, epic, and mythological poems. His collected *Comedias y Tragedias* appeared in 1588.

In this group of plays Cueva used old Spanish legends as well as Greco-Roman themes. *Tragedia de los Infantes de Lara, Comedia de la Muerte del Rey Don Sancho,* and *Comedia de la Libertad de España por Bernardo del Carpio* were based on old Spanish chronicles and traditional ballads, anticipating the national plays of Lope de Vega. In this sense Cueva was a precursor of the Golden Age drama. In works such as *Tragedia de la Muerte de Ayax Telamón, Tragedia de la Muerte de Virginia,* and *Comedia de la Libertad de Roma por Mucio Cévola* (all 1579), Cueva manifested very clearly his debt to Ovid, Virgil, and Livy.

Somewhat apart from either his Spanish or the classical tradition is Cueva's mythological farce the *Comedia del Infamador* (1581). The protagonist Leucino has been considered by some critics as a forerunner of Tirso's Don Juan—a point of view vigorously disputed by F. Icaza. The play itself bears some resemblance to the theme of the *Convidado de Piedra,* for Leucino, in punishment for his many sins, ultimately battles against supernatural powers; in this case, Nemesis assumes the rôle later to be played by the Comendador.

Cueva was essentially an improviser, and his plays are seriously marred by a lack of verisimilitude and an overabundance of supernatural elements. Both true dramatic talent and poetic feeling are lacking.

At the end of his career Cueva wrote his *Ejemplar Poético* (1609), which constituted his dramatic theory *a posteriori*. In the three epistles comprising this work Cueva departs from the theories of classical drama as interpreted by Italian Renaissance critics and advocates the casting aside of the unities, the reduction of the number of acts from five to four, and the usage of a variety of verse forms. In theory, therefore, Cueva laid the foundation for the drama of the Golden Age.

ABOUT: Crawford, J. P. W. Spanish Drama before Lope de Vega; Modern Language Notes, XXXVI (1931); Hispanic Review, VIII (1940). [In Spanish—Icaza, F. A. de, edition of Tragedias y Comedias (1917).]

B. P. P.

CYNTHIUS. See GIRALDI, GIOVANNI BATTISTA

*CYRANO DE BERGERAC, SAVINIEN** (March 6, 1619-July 28, 1655), French writer, was born in Paris, the son of Abel de Cyrano, lord of de Mauvières, esquire, and of Dame Esperance Bellanger. He had his first education from a country priest and had for a fellow pupil Henri Lebret, his friend and future biographer. Later he followed a course in the humanities at the College of Beauvais, where he was a student of rhetoric of Doctor Jean Grangier, who was to become the target of his satire in his comedy *Le Pedant Joué*. At the conclusion of his formal studies, Cyrano led a bizarre life in Paris, combining the extreme excesses of a libertine with intensive and concentrated studies, pursued in the company of, among others, Chapelle and Molière, disciples of the philosopher Gassendi.

About 1638 Cyrano joined the guard regiment, and soon acquired the reputation of an officer notable for his fiery bravado. He took part in the campaign against the Germans at Mouzon (1639), where he was wounded by a musket shot. In 1640 he participated in the siege of Arras, where he was once more wounded by a sword thrust in his throat. At long last, tired of a military career, he resigned from the service in 1641.

Cyrano's innumerable quarrels, fights, and duels have been dramatically, yet more or less truthfully, rendered in Edmond Rostand's play *Cyrano de Bergerac* (1897). At one time or another Cyrano crossed swords, literally or figuratively, with Molière, Scarron, Dassoucy, the actor Montfleury, and even, in an access of choler, with the Monkey of Brioché, an adventure parodied in the famous *Combat de Cyrano de Bergerac contre le Singe de Brioché, au bout du Pont Neuf.*

In 1653 Cyrano entered the service of the Duc d'Arpajon as the latter's private secretary. It was in entering Arpajon's house that, in 1654, he was injured by the fall of a piece of timber. It is said that Arpajon, possibly fearing Cyrano's reputation of a free-thinker, requested that he leave, and that Cyrano found a haven with friends in Paris, where he died in 1655. It is claimed that Cyrano was converted in his last moments, a change of heart brought about by the prayers of a relative, Mother Catherine de Cyrano (Marguerite de Jésus), who had him buried in her convent, rue de Charonne.

* sĕ rà nō' dĕ bĕr zhĕ ràk'

Cyrano de Bergerac, often regarded as either a madman or a visionary, has, nevertheless, directly or indirectly, influenced the greatest of French writers. Thus, some part or other of his works or thoughts was "borrowed" by Molière, Corneille (who imitated his *Agrippine*), Voltaire, and Fontenelle. Probably his best work was the fantastic "voyage to the moon," *Histoire Comique des États et Empires de la Lune* (1676), which influenced Swift in *Gulliver's Travels*.

Satyrical Characters and Handsome Descriptions was translated into English in 1658 and published with an introduction by B. P. Bourland in 1914. *A Voyage to the Moon* was translated by A. Lovell in 1687 and, in modern times, by Richard Aldington (1923).

ABOUT: [In French—see studies by P. A. Brun, L. Desvergnes, H. Lebret (biographical preface to Histoire Comique des États de la Lune), L. R. Lefèvre, X. Merilhon. [In Italian—Erba, L. L'Incidenza della Magia nell' Opera di Cyrano de Bergerac.]

E. J. S.

DA COSTA, ISAAC (January 14, 1798-April 28, 1860), Dutch poet, was born in Amsterdam of an important merchant family of Portuguese-Jewish origin. In his early youth he wrote Latin verses. His first Dutch work, *De Lof der Dichtkunst*, met with the approval of the poet Wilhelm Bilderdijk. As a result of this acquaintance, he met the historical novelist Van Lennep. After a period of tutorship under Bilderdijk —studying the Greek poets especially—he went to Leiden (1816) to study law, receiving his degree in 1818; a degree in literature and philosophy followed in 1821. He married Hanna Belmonte shortly afterwards. During this period he published two volumes of *Poezy* which helped him to establish his place among the Dutch poets of the day. Largely because of the influence of Bilderdijk, whose views he adopted, he and his wife embraced Calvinism on October 20, 1822. From that day onward, the great purpose of his life became the preservation of the orthodox Reformed doctrine and the opposing of disbelief and revolutionary thought. That becomes evident in his prophetic songs as well as in his forceful participation in the religious movement of the *Réveil*. He settled in Amsterdam where he dedicated himself to literature and theology, giving religious-doctrinal lectures as well as speeches dealing with history and philology. His famous *Bezwaren Tegen de Geest der Eeuw* appeared in 1823. In 1839 he became a member of the Koninklijke Nederlandsche Insti-

tuut. His well known poem *Wachter, Wat Is er van de Nacht?* (1847) opposed the tendency of the liberal newspapers and the German philosophers of the day. He also predicted the revolution of 1848. His *Over den Mens en Dichter Willem Bilderdijk* is written in forceful prose. In 1906 a statue was unveiled on his grave in the Nieuwe Kerk in Amsterdam.

Israel and the Gentiles was translated into English by Mrs. W. Kennedy (1850). His Gospel harmony was translated by David Scott under the title *The Four Witnesses* (1851). Bertram Brewster published his translation of *Noble Families Among the Sephardic Jews* in 1936.

ABOUT: [In Dutch—see studies by W. G. C. Bijvanck, J. Meyer.]

H. B.

D'ALEMBERT, JEAN LEROND. See ALEMBERT, JEAN LEROND D'

*DALIN, OLOF VON (August 29, 1708-August 12, 1763), Swedish poet, dramatist, and historian, was born in the southwestern Swedish province of Halland in Vinberg parish. His father, Jonas Dahlin, a vicar, died when Olof was one year old; his mother, Märtha Brigitta *née* Ausén, was the daughter of a rural dean. Little is known of Olof's early years. In his thirteenth year he entered the University of Lund. In 1727 the needy young man left Lund to earn a living as a tutor in a noble family in Stockholm, where he moved in highly educated aristocratic circles. He was appointed chancellery clerk in the Public Records Office in 1731 and the next year in the Cabinet Committee of the Privy Council.

In December 1732 appeared the first issue of *Then Swänska Argus* (The Swedish Argus), which date is generally considered the birthday of modern Swedish literature. The anonymous editor and sole contributor was the twenty-four-year-old Dalin. This weekly paper, imitating Addison and Steele's *The Tatler* and *The Spectator* and others, contained causeries and religious, political and social satires, in which the French-classical ideas of the Enlightenment were championed. The timeliness of the contents, the informal, good-natured style, and the everyday language made the *Argus* extremely popular, and it continued, 104 issues in all, through 1734. When the editor's identity became known he was greatly honored in many ways. He held various positions, eventually Court Chancellor in 1763. In

* dà lēn'

1751 he was ennobled as "von Dalin" and in 1753 elected a member of the Royal Academy of Letters.

During the decade following the publication of the *Argus*, Dalin's literary productivity, partly consisting of conventional court poetry, was remarkable. *Sagan om Hästen* (Tale of the Horse, 1740) is an allegory in prose of Sweden's history. In his tragedy *Brynilda*, on the theme of the old Germanic legend of Sigurd, in his comedy *Den Avundsjuke* (The Envious One, 1738) and in his alexandrine epos *Swenska Friheten* (Swedish Freedom, 1742) he attempted to compete with the French-classical masterpieces by Voltaire and others. He also wrote realistic poems in ballad style. His main historical work is *Svea Rikes Historia* (History of the Swedish Nation), in three volumes, 1760-61.

An article from *Then Swänska Argus* in English translation by W. H. Carpenter is printed in Warner Library, X. Dalin's drama *Den Avundsjuke* was rendered into English as *Envy* (1876).

ABOUT: Howitt, W. & M. The Literature and Romance of Northern Europe, II; Warner Library, X. [In Swedish—see studies by N.-O. Dyberg, M. Lamm, O. Sylwan, K. Warburg.]

A. J.

*DANCOURT, FLORENT CARTON DE (November 1, 1661-December 7, 1725), French comic playwright and actor, was born at Fontainebleau of parents of English and Calvinist origin. His Jesuit teachers encouraged him to join the order, but he found no vocation and turned to a study of law. Dancourt's brilliant elocution promised a significant career; but before he was nineteen, he fell in love with Thérèse Le Noir, the daughter of the actor La Thorillière, abducted her, and forced consent for their marriage. He then decided to enter the theatre, and, in 1685, began as an actor at the Comédie Française with his wife; both were much applauded for their interpretations of light rôles. His fine elocution led the troupe to choose him as their official orator, and he enjoyed typical favors of Louis XIV, to whom he read, and of the Dauphin, who received the troupe, including Dancourt's two daughters, in 1699. He and his wife retired from the theatre in 1718 to live in the provinces, where Dancourt turned to religion, composing a sacred tragedy and a verse translation of the Psalms.

Dancourt's plays, among the most distinguished of his time, are rivaled only by

* dän koor'

those of Regnard. They may be hastily dismissed as pale, anecdotal, and superficial echoes of the glory of Molière, but they are excellent pictures of the customs of the period and were often performed for many years. They are gay, after the minor manner of Molière, and depend strongly both on satire and on mockery of ridiculous persons and their actions; they are constructed about plots that are little more than situations, but skillfully arranged and expressed in living language. The characters illustrate the trends of middle-class thinking at the end of the century, when gamblers and financiers began to rise to power, and valets assumed more vital social rôles.

Dancourt's masterpiece *Le Chevalier à la Mode* (1687) is a lively character and situation play, well constructed about events that evolve without effort and rise from the inner nature of the protagonists. The social types are eternal ones—the young fop in the title rôle, the rich widow in his pursuit, and the Chevalier's valet Crispin, the finest portrait in the play. The scenes between the widow and her maid are rich in spontaneous expression of typical feminine preoccupations, and the secondary characters are appropriate and real.

The importance of Dancourt may be measured by the long series of *Œuvres Complètes*, each from four to twelve volumes, published in 1693, 1698, 1706, 1729, 1742 1760, and 1810. Since the beginning of the last century, he has assumed the modest position of a minor playwright, and his work appears adequately in the *Théâtre Choisi* of 1884, which contains the standard biography, by Sarcey.

Only a few of his plays have been translated, for example *The Country House*, by John Vanbrugh, in 1715.

ABOUT: Lancaster, H. C. Sunset: Parisian Drama in the Last Years of Louis XIV; *also* A History of French Dramatic Literature in the Seventeenth Century, IV. [In French—see studies by C. Barthélemy, J. Lemaître.]

F. J. C.

DANIEL, ARNAUT. See ARNAUT DANIEL

D'ANNUNZIO, GABRIELE. See "TWENTIETH CENTURY AUTHORS"

*DANTE ALIGHIERI (May 1265-September 13 or 14, 1321), Italian poet, was born in Florence of a family belonging to the lesser nobility. Information relating to his life is scanty, much of it deriving from facts gleaned from his own writings. His great-great-grandfather, according to his own account, had been knighted by the Emperor Conrad III and had died fighting in the Second Crusade (1147-49). His father was Alighiero di Bellincione d'Alighiero whose circumstances, though modest, were sufficient to permit his son to acquire a sound education and cultivate the friendship of some of the more prominent aristocrats of the city.

Florence at that time was in the hands of the Guelph Party—the party (in contrast to the Ghibelline) which traditionally favored local autonomy in opposition to imperial authority and relied upon papal support to protect the city's independence. Thanks to the quick growth of trade in this period and the consequent influx of population, the city was undergoing a rapid transformation causing much political strife. Dante's family had long been Guelph, and Dante himself was to fight against the Ghibellines at the Battle of Campaldino in 1289. His father (of his mother virtually nothing is known) probably died in 1289, but as early as 1277 he had arranged for Dante's marriage to Gemma di Manetto Donati, who was related, though distantly, to the politically powerful family of the same name. When the marriage finally took place is unknown; but we do know that Dante was eventually to have two sons by her— Iacopo and Pietro (possibly a third, Giovanni) and a daughter, who took the veil under the name Beatrice.

It seems likely that Dante pursued his youthful studies at the school of the Franciscans located at the Church of Santa Croce. Somewhat later he was taught, or at least encouraged to study, rhetoric by Brunetto Latini, statesman and author of a well-known compendium of knowledge entitled the *Trésor*. It is also possible that Dante continued his study of rhetoric at the University of Bologna. His acquaintance with the classical authors, to which he was to show a lifelong devotion, must at any rate have begun early. That he also attended the University of Paris, as some have claimed, seems far more doubtful.

He began to write verse, chiefly amatory, rather early and soon had a reputation among the other chief poets of the city who, like himself, were endeavoring to turn away from

* dän′ tâ ä lê gyâ′ rê

DANTE

their more arid predecessors toward a poetry of fresher inspiration. Two of the most distinguished in this group were Guido Cavalcanti and Cino da Pistoia with whom he corresponded in verse.

In May 1274 he met Beatrice, daughter of Folco Portinari. Though she was only eight and he only nine years old at the time and though there is no reason to believe that their relationship ever went beyond the exchange of a few words, this meeting proved one of the most momentous events in Dante's life. In no vague sense she was to become the central inspiration of both his literary and his religious life, and he was to declare her "the glorious lady of my mind." Through her guidance and her intercession he hoped to win eternal salvation.

Beatrice died on January 8, 1290. Shortly after, Dante assembled the various poems he had written in her honor. Inserting brief passages of prose which set forth the circumstances that had inspired them and often explained their content, he titled the work *La Vita Nuova (The New Life)*—c. 1292-93— thereby intending to reveal the spiritual transformation which Beatrice had inspired in him. He dedicated the work to Guido Cavalcanti, designating him "the first of my friends."

Meanwhile, he began to take part in political activities. In 1295 an ordinance was promulgated which prohibited all persons not belonging to a guild from holding public office. Not to be thus excluded, Dante enrolled as a nominal member in the guild of physicians and druggists. In that same year and in the next he served as a member of two councils, one of which had the task of electing the priors of the city. In May 1300 he was sent as ambassador to San Gimignano to invite that commune to be represented at an assembly of the Guelph cities of Tuscany. The purpose of the meeting was to consider means of countering the efforts of Pope Boniface VIII to gain control of Tuscany. From June 15 to August 15 of the same year he held office as Prior. At this time the Guelphs had become divided into two factions—the Whites and the Blacks, and strife had broken out between them. In an effort to stem the violence, probably at Dante's suggestion, the leaders of the two opposing factions were sent into exile. Thus Guido Cavalcanti, the poet's "first friend," was sent to Sarzana where he died shortly after. Nevertheless, circumstances became such that Dante could not remain neutral, and he himself was soon associated with the White faction. Meanwhile, the Blacks, in league with the Pope, sought to win control of the city. With two others, Dante was ordered to Rome to confer with Pope Boniface about conditions in Florence. His two associates were soon directed to return with orders from the Pope that the city humble itself before him. Dante was directed to stay on in Rome. He was never again to see his native city. While he was thus being delayed, the Blacks of Florence arose and completely crushed the Whites, driving them into exile. Pausing at Siena while en route home, he learned on January 27, 1302, that he and several others had been sentenced to banishment from the city for a period of two years. The sentence also carried a heavy fine and perpetual exclusion from public office. He did not pay the fine or answer the charges that had been trumped up in his absence by his enemies, and so on March 10, 1302, a second sentence was issued, condemning him to be burned alive if ever he should set foot again in Florentine territory. Though he later made some effort to regain admittance to the city and others labored toward the same end, and though the sentence in time was much reduced, Dante thereafter lived the harsh life of an exile, preferring exile to even a nominal punishment for wrongs he had not committed. Sometime later he came to hope that publication of his masterpiece would win him an unqualified invitation to return and accept the laurel crown of poet from a repentant city.

About his years of exile there is, if anything, still more uncertainty. He found temporary refuge first in one city then in another, often serving as secretary or ambassador for the local ruler. In rather rapid sequence, it seems, he moved from the Mugello to Forlì and from there to Verona. He also stayed for a time in Padua, Mantua, and Ravenna. Not long after his exile had begun, he abandoned the intrigues of the Whites, who now sought to make common cause with the Ghibellines in an effort to end their banishment, and became, as he put it, a party to himself.

Probably about this time (c. 1304-07), he wrote *De Vulgari Eloquentia (Concerning Vernacular Eloquence)* and *Il Convivio (The Banquet)*, both of which he left incomplete. The first of these, written in Latin, is a treatise on language, with emphasis upon Italian, and on poetry. The aim of the work is to show how a "cardinal, courtly, curial" language could be developed out of the diverse dialects of Italy. The discussion of poetry is largely relegated to diction, meter, and style and centers on the *canzone*. *Il Convivio*, of which we have only four of fifteen projected treatises, was written in Italian. A philosophical work dealing with subjects commonly treated by the schoolmen, it was intended for the layman. Each of the treatises except the first was to contain a *canzone* followed by a rather extensive commentary. Actually only three *canzoni* appear, though others intended for it are included in his *Canzoniere*.

In 1310 Henry VII, who had two years before succeeded Albert I as Holy Roman Emperor, descended into Italy and was initially welcomed by the Pope, Clement V. Dante at once hailed the Emperor as the savior of Italy, and in letters rich in Biblical allusion addressed to the rulers of Italy he exhorted them to receive him as their temporal lord. Though he knew little about the character and intentions of this German prince, Dante fervently believed that Henry would bring peace to the strife-torn "garden of the empire" and establish his proper authority everywhere. In 1311 he journeyed to Milan to pay homage to the Emperor. But what the poet so ardently desired was not to be. Soon the Pope, King Robert of Naples, and the Florentine Commune opposed the Emperor's further advance into Italy. Dante wrote to Henry, urging him to attack Florence without delay, though he himself refused to take up arms against his native city when operations for a siege were begun the following year. Failing to gain Florence, Henry went on to Rome where his military efforts were again unsuccessful. He died in August 1313 at Buonconvento near Siena. His death was a great blow to the poet and marked the end of all his political hopes.

It seems likely that either shortly before or shortly after the death of Henry, Dante wrote *De Monarchia (On Monarchy)* which, at least indirectly, is a defense of his position regarding the imperial cause. Essentially, Dante's position in this work is that the Holy Roman Emperor is the divinely ordained universal ruler, supreme in the temporal sphere even as the Pope is in the spiritual sphere. The Emperor's task is to preserve justice and peace through administering the laws of the Justinian Code which, like the Roman Empire itself, is the expression of God's will.

It is generally believed that Dante had left *De Vulgari Eloquentia* and *Il Convivio* unfinished in order to begin work on *La Divina Commedia (The Divine Comedy)*, which is now widely regarded as one of the supreme achievements of European literature. An allegorical poem, divided into three canticles of about equal length—*Inferno, Purgatorio,* and *Paradiso*—and written in *terza rima,* it is ostensibly an account of Dante's journey through the regions of the afterworld. All but encyclopedic in scope, the work is composed of disparate but artistically interfused elements—autobiographical, historical, theological, political, and scientific. It is also a poem of love, celebrating not only the poet's love for Beatrice but also that love which, emanating from God, returns to Him through all of His creation. Employing what Dante called the middle style, the poem moves through a wide range of moods, from the most lowly to the most exalted. In some of its most celebrated episodes, it is highly dramatic. Sustained and compact, it has often been praised for the subtle complexity of its architectonic structure. In the opinion of T. S. Eliot, its last canto is "the highest point that poetry has ever reached or ever can reach."

The Divine Comedy had not long been completed when Dante, returning from an embassy to Venice, died in Ravenna in September 1321. But already the work, which had been issued part by part, was well known. Commentaries upon it—some written by his sons, who had shared the last years of his exile with him—began to appear almost at once. Public lectures were instituted in several Italian cities, Boccaccio being the first to deliver a series in Florence. Although *The Divine Comedy* was neglected in some of the following centuries, its reputation has never suffered a really serious decline, and it has never been without worthy defenders. In the fifteenth century, during the period of triumphant Latin humanism, it shared some of the neglect accorded all vernacular literature. In the sixteenth century, owing to the development of fastidious tastes, insistent upon stringent rules of decorum, it was sometimes criticized for boldness and vulgarity. In the seventeenth and early eighteenth centuries, when all medieval art was held in low esteem, it was thought bizarre and "Gothic." But the nineteenth and twentieth centuries have witnessed a steady increase of interest and an amazing proliferation of scholarly and critical works upon it both in Italy and abroad. An unabating stream of translations into English attests to its popularity in English-speaking countries, and such recent writers as William Butler Yeats, James Joyce, and T. S. Eliot, to name no others, all show evidence of Dante's influence.

Relying upon the words of some who had known Dante, Boccaccio described him as having been a man of medium height and swarthy complexion. Grave in aspect, he had rather large eyes, an aquiline nose, a protruding lower lip, and a prominent jaw. In general, this description accords with the portrait of Dante on the walls of the Bargello in Florence painted by Giotto, his contemporary.

All of Dante's works have more than once been translated into English. Among the very numerous verse translations of *The Divine Comedy,* are those by Henry Boyd (1802), H. F. Cary (1814), H. W. Longfellow (1867), M. B. Anderson (1921), Laurence Binyon (1943), Dorothy Sayers (1949-1962), John Ciardi (*Inferno,* 1954). Among prose translations are those of C. E. Norton (1891-92), the Carlyle-Wicksteed (Modern Library, 1932), J. D. Sinclair (1948), H. R. Huse (1954). Norton also translated *La Vita Nuova* (1867). P. H. Wicksteed translated *Il Convivio* (1903) and the *Canzioniere* (1906). Along with A. G. F. Howell, he also translated all of Dante's writings in Latin (*The Latin Works,* 1904), including the *Letters,* the *Eclogues,* and the *Quaestio de Aqua et Terra.*

ABOUT: Auerbach, E. Dante: Poet of the Secular world; Barbi, M. Life of Dante; Brandeis, I. The Ladder of Vision: A Study of Dante's Comedy; Croce, B. The Poetry of Dante; Gardner, E. G. Dante; Gilbert, A. Dante and His Comedy; Grandgent, C. H. Dante; Moore, E. Studies in Dante; Toynbee, P. J. Dante Alighieri: His Life and Works. [In Italian—Zingarelli, N., La Vita, I Tempi e le Opere di Dante, 2 vols.]

D. J. D.

***DASS, PETTER** (1647-1707), Norwegian poet and hymnist, was born at North Herøy in the north Norwegian district of Nordland. His father, Petter Pettersøn, also called Don Dass, came from Dundee, Scot-

* däs

land, and settled first in Bergen but moved later to North Herøy and married Maren Falch, daughter of the district magistrate in the southern part of Nordland. The future poet, the oldest of five children, lost his father when he was about five years old. The home was dissolved, and Petter went to an aunt, Anna Falch, married to the pastor at Nærøy in Namdal, later to another aunt, married to a district judge in Nordland. After instruction at home he was sent to a Latin school in Bergen where he passed his matriculation examination in 1665. The following year he entered the University of Copenhagen, Denmark. Here he led a miserably poor life and returned after three years to Nordland and earned a living as a tutor. In 1671 he became engaged to Margrethe Andersdatter, daughter of the former pastor of Vefsen. Three years later, Dass was ordained and married.

Dass began his ecclesiastic career as a poorly salaried domestic chaplain in the neighboring parish of Nesne. In 1681 he was promoted to chaplain, and in 1689 he finally became pastor in the rich parish of Alstahaug on an island off the coast. There he discharged his duties with power and love, like the extroverted person he was. During his incessant official journeys along the coast, he acquired an intimate knowledge of the land, its many fjords and islands, and its population. He also transacted big business as a fish-dealer.

In the 1670's, Dass began to write occasional verses, in the baroque style of the time, for weddings, funerals, etc., but most of this production is lost. Only about thirty poems are preserved, but we can see that the poet possessed a fine technical proficiency and an obvious feeling for rhythm. Dass wrote both religious and secular poetry. His hymns, which were written in the interest of propagating Christianity, were distributed throughout the country, and many of them became folk songs. He also rendered Luther's *Shorter Catechism* into verse.

His secular works show a real creative power and originality. His *Nordsk Dale-Vise* (Song of a Northern Dalesman, 1683) gives interesting pictures of the life of the people among whom he lived. Dass' masterpiece is *Nordlands Trompet (The Trumpet of Nordland)*, essentially written in the latter part of the 1670's and completed about 1700, but not printed until 1739. It is a poetic description of Tromsø county, written in a firm rhythm and sonorous language. The poet displays a strong feeling for nature and a fresh realistic description of the life of the people. His approach is that of a confident Christian. In his harmonious piety, the whole of nature is submissive to the Almighty God.

Nordlands Trompet was translated by T. Jorgenson as *The Trumpet of Nordland* (1954).

ABOUT: Jorgensen, T. History of Norwegian Literature. [In Norwegian—see studies by F. Bull, A. E. Erichsen, H. Midbre, R. Sveen.]

A. J.

*DAUDET, LOUIS MARIE ALPHONSE** (May 13, 1840-December 16, 1897), French man of letters, was born at Nimes. His parents, Vincent Daudet (1806-75) and Marie Adeline Reynaud (1805-82), were small silk manufacturers of peasant background, from the Cévennes region. The couple had seventeen children, most of whom died young. Alphonse's father was a royalist, taciturn and easily angered; his son resented him but adored his mother. Unusually pious, imaginative, addicted to reading, she represented for him the feminine ideal.

Alphonse spent three years at the nearby village of Bezouce for his health. He compensated for extreme myopia by an extraordinary development of the other senses. After attending parochial school (1845-48) and the Canivet *pension* (1848-50) locally, he was enrolled in the *lycée* of Lyons (1850-56), where he was an indifferent, though precociously sensual, student, already drinking to excess. On the other hand, he was reading the romantics, and had begun to write poetry and tales. The family's financial embarrassment did not permit Alphonse to complete his baccalaureate.

Daudet obtained a position as study supervisor at the college of Alès. This bitter experience partially furnished the subject matter of *Le Petit Chose, Histoire d'un Enfant* (1868); Daudet may have attempted suicide at Alès. For whatever reason, in November 1857 he arrived in Paris, where his older brother Ernest (1837-1921) was an editor for *Le Spectateur*.

For a while Daudet and some friends—Jean du Boys, Charles Bataille, Amédée Rolland—formed one of the Bohemian cliques. Marie Rieu, prototype for *Sapho* (1884), was his mistress. It was to her that he dedicated his first published work, the poems of *Les Amoureuses* (1858). The triolets of "Les Prunes" became a drawing-room favorite. Extremely handsome, stocky and short, with an olive complexion, flashing black eyes, and a magnificent shock of long

* dō dĕ′

213

DAUDET

curly hair, Daudet was magnetically attractive. In the rounds of salons and bars, Daudet met the Provençal poet Frédéric Mistral. Mistral's *Mireille* had just won tremendous acclaim; it was Mistral who revealed to Daudet the artistic possibilities of his southern background. His first prose tale, "Audiberte," appeared in *Paris-Journal Illustré* in 1859; while working for that newspaper he also contributed to Villemessant's *Figaro*, the most influential journal of the day. Under the pen-name of Pierre and Paul, he wrote a series on the Parisian scene for *L'Universel* of Brussels. The following year a sinecure as secretary to the duke of Morny, who encouraged the arts and used collaborators for light plays, assured him security and prestige.

Salaried but free from routine office work, Daudet traveled to the south and visited with Mistral at Maillane. Physically exhausted by his dissolute existence, he went to Algeria for three months to recuperate. About this time he contracted syphilis, which was to make the last twenty-five years of his life a physical agony. In 1863 Daudet went to Corsica; the following year he frequented the Félibrige group—Mistral, Aubanel, Roumanille—at Montauban; and in 1865 he journeyed through Alsace in the company of Alfred Delvau, chronicler of Paris Bohemia.

Various sketches, "saynètes," and short stories were collected in *La Double Conversion, Contes en Vers* (1861) and *Le Roman du Chaperon-Rouge, Scènes et Fantaisies*

(1862). He also essayed the theatre, usually with a collaborator. Ernest L'Épine was co-author with him of three plays, the most important being *L'Œillet Blanc* (1865); Adolphe Belot and Léon Hennique were later to have the same relationship with him.

In 1867 Daudet married Julia Rosalie Céleste Allard (1847-1940), who had already established a reputation as a poet. This marriage stabilized his volatile nature, and provided the calm and purpose and retrospection which permitted the full expression of his talents. The Daudets had three children, Léon (1867-1942), himself a writer, Lucien (1883-1946), also a novelist, and Edmée (1886-1937). The family settled at Champrosay, in Île-de-France, and Daudet wrote numerous works.

The year after his marriage he published the semi-autobiographical *Le Petit Chose*, in which he related the unhappiness of his childhood. The following year *Lettres de Mon Moulin* was a highlight in the series which presented the southern temperament humorously and affectionately. Of these, *Aventures Prodigieuses de Tartarin de Tarascon* (1872) and *Tartarin sur les Alpes* (1885) are the most famous, for Daudet has created a sort of poltroon Don Quixote; *Numa Roumestan* (1881) contrasts the north and the south while describing the mentality of the politician. The Franco-Prussian war inspired part of *Contes du Lundi* (1873), which contains the moving tale "La Dernière Classe." Of several realistic novels which present contemporary mores, *Fromont Jeune et Risler Aîné* (1874) and *Le Nabab* (1877) are the most successful. *Sapho* (1884), in which he utilized personal experience, treats of sexuality and social manners.

Daudet was drama critic for the *Journal Officiel*, and himself adapted some of his novels for the stage. But the failure of *L'Arlésienne* (1872), for which Georges Bizet wrote the music, dissuaded him from further individual transpositions until 1887, when he adapted *Numa Roumestan*. His memoirs, *Souvenirs d'un Homme de Lettres* and *Trente Ans de Paris* (1888), are noteworthy. To young writers he was particularly helpful, entertaining at Champrosay or attending the gatherings at the Goncourts' "grenier." He died at Champrosay and was buried in Paris at Père Lachaise cemetery. Saint-Marceaux executed a statue, erected on the Champs-Élysées, and Falguière did a monument for the city of Nîmes.

Daudet's realism is embellished by humor and warmth. In his best work he achieves the "fusion of reality and the dream, of the mysterious beauty of life and its crude truth." He skirts caricature while using exaggeration; he imbues the direct notation of observation with sensitivity. Contemporaries as different as Zola and Anatole France praised him; for many he is the teller of magnificent tales. He has been compared to Dickens.

The *Œuvres Complètes* were published in twenty large volumes (1929-31). J. H. Bornecque has published a critical edition of *Le Petit Chose*, annotated editions of *Les Contes du Lundi* and *Les Lettres de Mon Moulin* (all 1947). There are many school texts of the short stories.

L'Arlésienne was translated by C. J. Livingwood in 1930. Laura Ensor translated *Artists' Wives* in 1890, revised in 1896. *La Lutte* was translated by H. L. Williams as the *Battle of Love* (1892). *Numa Roumestan* was entitled *Behind a Mask* in the translation (1898) by Virginia Champlin (pseud. of G. V. Lord). *La Belle-Nivernaise, and other stories,* appeared in 1895 in an anonymous translation. *The Evangelist* was translated by M. N. Sherwood in 1883, by O. E. Palmer in 1900. The former translated *Jack* in 1877, as did L. Ensor in 1890. *The Head of the Family,* translated by Levin Carnac, was entitled *The Bread-Winner* in England (1898). *Kings in Exile* was translated by V. Champlin in 1880, by L. Ensor and E. Bartow in 1896, and by K. P. Wormeley in 1900. The latter translated *Letters from My Mill* that same year. M. N. Sherwood kept the French title *Le Petit Chose* for her translation of 1878, but J. M. Sedgwick called hers *Little What's-His-Name* (1899). *The Nabab* had three translations: L. H. Hooper (1878), G. B. Ives (1898), W. Blaydes (1902). L. Ensor translated *Recollections of a Literary Man* (1889), *Robert Helmont* (1892), *Thirty Years of Paris* (1888). *The Immortal* was translated by J. M. Percival (pseud. of M. J. Stafford) in 1889, and by A. W. and M. de G. Verrall in 1892; the same work had been entitled *One of the Forty* in a translation of 1888. *Sapho,* translated by T. F. Rogerson in 1897, was retranslated by Eithne Wilkins in 1953; this title had many reprintings. The play *Sapho* was adapted by E. B. Ginty in 1895. *Tartarin of Tarascon,* translated by R. S. Minot in 1880, was published in a revised translation in 1895, again in 1902, and was retranslated by Jacques Le Clercq in 1930 and by C. G. Okie in 1938. Henry James translated one of the sequels, *Port Tarascon,* in 1891; H. Frith had done *Tartarin on the Alps* in 1887, and a revised translation appeared in 1894. *La Doulou: La Vie; Extraits des Carnets Inédits* was translated by M. Garner (1934) as *Suffering, 1887-1895.* Daudet's works appeared in various editions of 16 or 17 or 24 volumes between 1898 and 1900.

ABOUT: Croce, B. European Literature in the Nineteenth Century; France, A. Life and Letters, IV; George, W. L. Literary Chapters; Gosse, E. French Profiles; Matthews, B. The Historical Novel; Saylor, G. R. Alphonse Daudet as a Dramatist; Sherard, R. H. Alphonse Daudet. [In French—See studies by J. H. Bornecque, J. Brivois, Y. Martinet.]

S. S. W.

D'AUREVILLY, JULES AMÉDÉE BARBEY. See BARBEY D'AUREVILLY, JULES AMÉDÉE

*DE AMICIS, EDMONDO** (October 21, 1846-March 12, 1908), Italian essayist and novelist, was born in the northern coastal province of Liguria in the town of Oneglia. He was sent for his early schooling to the cities of Cueno and Turin, and then to military school at Modena. At nineteen he was appointed a line lieutenant and in 1866 he fought in the famous battle of Custozza which established Italy as a kingdom. He saw service with the troops who aided the cholera victims and began writing sketches of army life for the newspaper *Italia Militare.* His articles were immediately popular and in 1867 he was sent to Florence as editor of *Italia Militare.* In 1868 his book *La Vita Militare* (The Military Life) appeared. This was followed by *Novelle* (Short Stories) and by *Ricordi del 1870-71* (Souvenirs of 1870-71).

The year 1870 saw the overthrow of the Pope's temporal power in Italy and De Amicis subsequently left military service. He established permanent residence in Turin and, encouraged by his growing public, devoted himself completely to letters. He made his debut as a professional writer with a series of books on travel: *Spagna* (Spain), 1872; *Olanda* (Holland), 1874; *Ricordi di Londra* (Memories of London), 1874; *Marocco* (Morocco), 1876; *Constantinopoli*, 1878-79, and *Ricordi di Parigi* (Memories of Paris), 1879. These spirited travelogues, published in handsomely illustrated editions, were extremely popular with the reading public and were translated into many languages.

A volume of poetry, *Poesie,* was published in 1880 and in 1883 the two volumes of *Gli Amici* (Friends) appeared. In this work De Amicis presented a number of acute psychological analyses in order to delineate the simplicity of emotion and of morals. These ideas are carried further in De Amicis' most famous work, *Cuore* (Hearts), which appeared in 1876. *Cuore,* an Italian schoolboy's journal, is written for children and was read in Italian schools from the time it was first published. Because it is a fine example of the Tuscan style it has often been used in the United States as a textbook for teaching Italian. It was first translated into English in 1895 and has also been translated into more than twenty other languages.

De Amicis sought to show in *Cuore* that children have instinctively sympathetic natures

* dā ä mē' chēs

215

which make them easily moved for good. He has, in terms of extreme sentiment as the title indicates, stated one of the basic concepts of modern educational theory. By many charming anecdotes he illustrates the affectionate relationship prevailing between pupil and teacher in an atmosphere free of all stereotype. The book significantly ceased to be used in Italian schools with the advent of Fascism.

De Amicis continued to work prolifically, publishing *Sull' Oceano* (On the Ocean) in 1889, *Il Romanzo di un Maestro* (The Story of a Schoolmaster) in 1890, *Fra Scuola e Casa* (Between School and Home) in 1892, *La Maestrina degli Operai* (The Little Schoolmistress of the Workers) in 1895, and *La Carrozza di Tutti* (Everybody's Bus) in 1899. De Amicis formally declared his adherence to socialism in 1891, and the above titles reflect in one way or another his belief in individual and social good.

In 1905 De Amicis addressed himself to a philosophical work on the problem of language, *L'Idioma Gentile*. His theories about the usage of his mother tongue have been appraised as somewhat too ingenuous and defective in judgment, the philosopher Benedetto Croce being especially severe in his criticism.

De Amicis' last years were saddened by the suicide of a son. He himself died suddenly of heart failure in Bordighera, not far from his birthplace.

Cuore was translated as *The Heart* by Isabel Hapgood in 1901. W. W. Cady translated *Military Life in Italy* in 1882. Translations of his travel writings include: *Studies of Paris* (1879), *Holland and Its People* (1880), *Spain* (1881), *Morocco* (1882).

ABOUT: [In Italian—see studies by I. Balducci, L. Barone, B. Croce (*in* La Letteratura della Nuova Italia), L. Gigli, M. Mosso, A. Silveri.]

E. DE P.

DE COSTER, CHARLES THÉODORE HENRI (August 20, 1827-May 7, 1879),

Belgian man of letters, was born in Munich, Germany, the son of a Flemish father and a Walloon mother. He received his education in a Catholic institution in Brussels, was a bank official for a few years, began to study law, made a few trips to Holland, and finally settled down in 1870 as a teacher of French literature at the military academy in Brussels. Amiable, enthusiastic, and mild, a melancholy dreamer and careless Bohemian, he was a representative figure of the romantic movement. His literary work varied in

DE COSTER

quality and a large part of it was destined to remain unknown. An unfortunate love affair inspired his *Lettres à Eliza*. He showed himself to be a storyteller of talent in his *Légendes Flamandes* (1858), written in archaic French, and in *Contes Brabançons* (1861), written in less affected French and without the supernatural elements that entered into his work of 1858.

His genius developed completely in *La Légende et les Aventures Héroïques, Joyeuses et Glorieuses d'Ulenspiegel et de Lamme Goedzak au Pays de Flandres et Ailleurs*, on which he worked with great love for several years, and which was published in 1867. The work was based on the old popular book of Ulenspiegel, the rogue and practical joker who incorporated everything that has to do with playful fantasy. But De Coster made of this sixteenth century rogue the hero of an epic; he placed him in the sixteenth century, in the midst of one of the most tragic eras in Dutch history, the struggle against Spain and the Inquisition. Ulenspiegel became with him the symbol of the free spirit and the national idea, revolting against tyranny and subjugation. It is impossible to give a survey of this long prose poem; it is variegated in tone, always original and picturesque, and so rich that the thread of the plot is often lost among the abundant digressions. De Coster attempted to give a summary of the Flemish spirit as he saw it, that is to say, as attracted both by the sensuous as well as the mystical, by the fantastic and the real, heroic, recalcitrant, and simple.

He could not write that work in Flemish, but he attempted to approach the juicy speech of the people by using archaic French again.

La Légende d'Ulenspiegel remains one of the most important monuments of French-Belgian literature; it was the first of a literary renaissance which did not develop until some fifteen years later. De Coster was its predecessor, and in spite of the admiration of a small group, a lonely one. He came into a milieu that was still in intellectual sleep and which had no artistic perception, and he suffered under that. It may be said that he had readers but no public. The anti-clerical spirit of his *Ulenspiegel,* too, prevented its popularity. Its author died in Brussels, in neglect and misery. A second edition of this outstanding work appeared in 1893.

Ulenspiegel was translated eight times into German, several times into English (by Geoffrey Whitworth in 1918, F. M. Atkinson in 1922, and A. R. Macdougall in 1934), and into a handful of other languages. *Flemish Legends* was translated by Harold Taylor (1920).

ABOUT: [In French—see studies by J. Hanse, L. L. Sosset.]

H. B.

*DEHMEL, RICHARD (November 18, 1863-February 8, 1920), German poet, essayist, and dramatist, was born at Hermsdorf in the Spreewald near Berlin, the son of a forester. He completed the *Gymnasium* at Danzig and studied science, philosophy, and history at the universities of Berlin and Leipzig. After graduating with a dissertation on fire insurance, he became an official with an insurance company and later secretary of the German fire insurance underwriters' association. In 1889 he married Paula Oppenheimer, who, according to Dehmel, provided "the releasing force" for his poetic genius, and in 1895 he resigned his position to devote himself completely to writing. His first marriage ended in divorce, and in 1901 he married Ida Coblenz. Although past fifty when war was declared in 1914, Dehmel enlisted as a private in the army and served in the trenches. He was wounded and won the Iron Cross. He died of thrombosis in Blankenese.

In the annals of modern German literature Dehmel is an anomalous figure who holds his place in literary history as much for his unique personality as for the artistry of his lyrics. His life, which is intimately related to his poetry, was governed by a strange

* dā′ mĕl

duality of passionate, mystical fervor and intellectual clarity. He once defined this fundamental dichotomy of his nature by stating that he was a rationalist as well as a theosophist and philosopher, realist as well as idealist, sensualist as well as spiritualist, empiricist as well as metaphysician, and naturalist as well as symbolist. Strongly influenced by Nietzsche, Dehmel wanted to live life to the fullest, to unfetter all instincts and passions, and to give free reign to his highly erotic personality. At the same time he yearned for ethical harmony and was motivated by the desire for self-sacrifice and the will to devote his energies to the service of humanity.

His first collection of verse, *Erlösungen* (1891), expresses these two opposing characteristics of uninhibited sensuality and ascetic self-discipline in the key poems *Bekenntnis* and *Selbstzucht.* All his later works reflect his efforts to resolve this problem. The ideal resolution of the conflict, he believed to have found in the love of man and woman, for love represents expression of the ego and at the same time demands the surrender of one's personality. Love thus forms the central experience of Dehmel's life and verse, and some of his best poems were written while he was gripped by passion. His second volume of poetry, *Aber die Liebe* (1893), was written while he was infatuated with Hedwig Lachmann, while the verse of the next work *Weib und Welt* (1896) was inspired by his love for Ida Coblenz. The frank sexuality of many of these poems, particularly the cycle of lyrics entitled *Verwandlungen der Venus* in *Aber die Liebe,* aroused public indignation. Dehmel purposely spared no efforts to shock bourgeois sensibilities, for, like his contemporary Frank Wedekind, he keenly felt the hypocrisy of his day in matters of sex and strove to effect a more honest approach to this problem.

Dehmel's concept of love found its noblest expression in *Zwei Menschen* (1903), a novel in verse, composed of three cycles of ballads, each sequence of which consists of 36 poems of 36 lines. In this work man and woman through the consummation of their personal love become the symbol of universal love, thus achieving the poet's longed-for synthesis between individuality and universality. *Zwei Menschen* is Dehmel's most ambitious undertaking and is the work he himself considered his best.

Dehmel's feeling of social responsibility was also revealed in a group of poems which

217

were written when he, like many of the writers at the end of the nineteenth century, had envisioned socialism as the hope of the future. Although he soon became disillusioned and rejected this movement, some of these socialist lyrics, such as "Bergpsalm," "Der Arbeitsmann," "Erntelied," "Zu Eng," and "Vierter Klasse," number among his finest and most enduring achievements.

In addition to his verse Dehmel also wrote the unsuccessful dramas *Die Mitmenschen* (1895), *Der Menschenfreund* (1917), and *Die Götterfamilie, eine Kosmopolitische Komödie* (1919). Of his volumes of prose works, which include both essays and short stories, the most significant is his war diary, *Zwischen Volk und Menschheit* (1919).

Dehmel was the outstanding lyric poet of his generation, and by his innovations of technique and content he greatly influenced the younger writers of his time.

The best and most complete rendition of Dehmel's verse into English was made by E. H. Zeydel for the *Poet Lore* series in 1920. Representative poems may also be found in J. Bithell, *Contemporary German Poetry* (1909), M. Münsterberg, *A Harvest of German Verse* (1916), and D. Yarmolinsky, *Contemporary German Poetry* (1923).

ABOUT: Drake, W. A. Contemporary European Authors; Lessing, O. E. Masters in Modern German Literature; Lewisohn, L. Cities and Men; Ludwig, E. Genius and Character; Pollard, P. Masks and Minstrels of Modern Germany. [In German—see studies by R. Frank, G. Kühl, J. Bab, and H. Slochower.]

D. G. D.

DEKKER, EDUARD DOUWES. See "MULTATULI"

*DELAVIGNE, JEAN FRANÇOIS CASIMIR (April 4, 1793-December 11, 1843), French poet and dramatist, born in Le Havre, was the son of an important shipbuilder; his early impressions of the sea and of boats reappear occasionally in his poetry. When he was ten, his father sent him and his brother Germain to Paris to the Henri IV college, where he met Scribe; he distinguished himself as a student, reading for his own pleasure in the Greek and Latin poets. His brother, a playwright and opera librettist, encouraged him to compose verse and make translations, and his uncle, Lambert-Sainte-Croix, impressed by his work, took it to the critic Andrieux, whose severe criticism was apparently very salutory. Delavigne worked diligently to polish his style and

* dĕ là vēn' y'

form, and his new effort brought forth complete approval from Andrieux. In this early work he chose dithyrambic subjects on such current events as the birth of Napoleon's son. Acclaim of his work came at an opportune moment as he found himself in grave financial straits rising from the decrease in commerce at Le Havre and from his military service and resultant illness.

Delavigne's principal poetic masterpiece is *Les Messéniennes*, poems published in 1815 and later augmented by comparable pieces. The original group celebrates the Napoleonic period in singing of the defeated heroes in the tones of a national poet, in which rôle Delavigne was immensely popular. He protested against the barbarism of war and regretted the abuse and neglect of the arts. In later groups he sang of Joan of Arc and the events under the Restoration, fusing ancient references with modern national heroics; other patriotic themes include the Greek War of Independence. A mouthpiece of liberalism, he assumed something of the stature of Béranger. He might be described as a liberal romantic as distinct from the Catholics and the extremists. His reputation as a liberal cost him his place as librarian, but he was immediately protected by the future Louis Philippe.

Delavigne is also important in the theatre, in somewhat the same rôle. *Les Vêpres Siciliennes*, performed in 1819, recounts the bloody events of 1282, in classical style but with political overtones. This and several other successful plays led to his election to the French Academy in 1825. A long sojourn in Italy inspired him with several other dramatic works such as *Marino Faliero*, based on Byron who, with Scott and Shakespeare, represents the principal influence on Delavigne's production, which stands half way between classicism and romanticism. His major theatrical works form a part of the movement represented by Hugo's *Cromwell* and *Hernani* and Vigny's translation of *Othello*. The historical drama *Louis XI* (1832) marks a new orientation, and the most important work, *Les Enfants d'Édouard* (1833), is based on *Richard III*; it establishes a striking contrast between the fidelity of the two boys and the lack of conscience of the Duke of Gloucester.

Delavigne died prematurely in 1843. His *Œuvres Complètes* of 1836 were augmented to six volumes in 1852, prefaced with a biography.

In English translation one finds *Louis XI* by W. Markwell, about 1885, and *The Monastery of St. Just* (his *Don Juan d'Autriche*) by J. Oxenford in 1864.

ABOUT: Eve, H. Preface to school editions of *Louis XI*. [In French—Fauchier-Delavigne, M. Casimir Delavigne Intime; Favrot, A. Étude sur Casimir Delavigne.]

F. J. C.

*DELVIG, ANTON ANTONOVICH, Baron (August 17, 1798-January 26, 1831), Russian poet, was born in Moscow, in the family of a major in the Astrakhan regiment and a descendant of the medieval German knights. His mother, Lubov Krasilnikova, was a granddaughter of the Russian astronomer. Delvig received his education at the famous lyceum at Tsarskoe Selo (1811-17) where he began to write poetry and became Pushkin's best friend. His first poem, "A Russian Song" (1812), was dedicated to the war with Napoleon, and his first published poem, "On the Capture of Paris," appeared in a magazine in 1814 under the pseudonym "a Russian." His rather unsuccessful government career included appointments with the Department of Mineral Resources, Ministry of Finance, and St. Petersburg Public Library (under the famous poet Krylov), but did not improve his unstable material situation. This fat, good-natured, lazy, modest, myopic man was loved by his many friends (among them, the poets Kyukhlebeker, Boratynsky, Yazykov, Kozlov); he participated in literary societies, and his political radicalism was moderate.

The year 1825 marked his retirement from service, his marriage to Sofya Saltykov (who dominated him and gave him many reasons for jealousy), and the beginning of his publishing activities which started with *Northern Flowers*, a successful miscellany, followed in 1830 by the *Literary Gazette*, which he published together with Pushkin, and another miscellany, *The Snowdrop* (1829-30). At this time, Delvig displayed his talent as a critic and a literary polemicist in his journalistic fights against romanticism. His house was a famous literary salon of the period. Delvig was rudely reprimanded by the chief of the secret police for printing a translation from a leftist French poet, and his *Gazette* was closed, but later permitted again, but under another editorship. Delvig had a weak heart, aggravated by publishing and family troubles, and, after pneumonia, he died in St. Petersburg.

* děl' vĭk

Delvig wrote little. His only collection of verse during his lifetime appeared in 1829. The first edition of his collected works did not appear till 1893. Pushkin and Boratynsky regarded him very highly as a poet, but after his death he was completely forgotten, until the 1920's, when the interest in Pushkin's time grew and he was given a prominent though not first-rank position in Russian poetry.

Though not very original, Delvig's impersonal, classicistic, and non-tragic poetry is "eminently craftsmanlike" (Mirsky). He sings the escape from the storms of this life into the world of friendship, love, and nature with smoothness, nobility, and taste. His best achievements were his sensuous idylls (especially "The Bathing Women") written in imitation of the Greek. His stylizations of Russian folksongs are popular (many of them were put to music by Glinka and others), and a few of his sonnets are among the very best in Russian poetry. Delvig enriched Russian metrics and introduced new stanzas and rhymes.

Some translations of his songs are to be found in Leo Wiener's *Anthology of Russian Literature,* II (1902-1903) and in C. M. Bowra's *Second Book of Russian Verse* (1948).

ABOUT: Mirsky, D. S. A History of Russian Literature. [In Russian—Verkhovsky, Y. Baron Delvig.]

V. M.

*DE MARCHI, EMILIO (July 31, 1851-February 6, 1901), Italian novelist and short-story writer, was born in Milan. He lived and worked in his native city during his entire lifetime. After receiving his degree in literature from the University of Milan he dedicated himself to teaching. His early publications were works on the meaning and purpose of education and critical essays on literature. About 1875 he helped to found *La Vita Nuova*, a bi-monthly periodical devoted to literature and art. He also wrote a short comedy, *Dopo il Duello* (After the Duel), which was presented in 1876 and was well received. He translated the fables of La Fontaine into verse in 1886. His most celebrated early work, *Età Preziosa* (The Precious Age), is written to prepare young people during their formative years to cultivate the moral strength which makes life worth while.

While De Marchi's didactic tendencies are apparent throughout his activities and writings, they are balanced in his creative work

* dä mär' kē

by his acute powers of observation and his human kindness. He drew inspiration from the people of his Lombardian homeland and from the majestic serenity of the Lombardian landscape. These qualities are apparent in *Storie di Ogni Colore* (Stories of Every Color) which appeared in 1885. They reach their most perfect expression in *Demetrio Pianelli*, De Marchi's masterpiece, published in 1890. The *Enciclopedia Italiana* calls this novel one of the most beautiful in modern Italian literature. Demetrio is a poor middle-aged civil servant whose humdrum life is upset when he attempts to help others in distress. In the course of these attempts he falls in love, and the power of this love and Demetrio's understanding of his duty to others ennoble his existence. The further expression of De Marchi's philosophy is found in three succeeding novels: *Arabella*, 1892; *Giacomo l'Idealista* (Giacomo the Idealist), 1897; and *Col Fuoco non si Scherza* (Don't Play with Fire), published posthumously in 1901. Other notable works are *Il Cappello del Prete* (The Priest's Hat), 1888, *Nuove Storie di Ogni Colore* (New Stories of Every Color), 1895, *Vecchie Cadenze e Nuove* (Old and New Verses), a collection of poetry rich in personal accents, 1899.

The last four years of his life De Marchi taught rhetoric in the Accademia Scientifico-Letteraria in Milan. He had held the post of secretary in this school for many years. He died in Milan.

ABOUT: [In Italian—Croce, B. La Letteratura della Nuova Italia. See also studies by V. Branca, N. Sammartano.]

E. DE P.

DE MAUPASSANT, GUY. See MAUPASSANT, GUY DE

*DERZHAVIN, GAVRILA ROMANOVICH (July 14, 1743-July 21, 1816), Russian poet, was born in a village near Kazan. His father, a petty squire and an army officer, died in 1754 and left his wife Fekla (*née* Kozlova) with three children and many debts. Derzhavin's education was entrusted to accidental and incompetent tutors, but later he showed good progress in the *Gymnasium* of Kazan, where he began writing poetry. In 1762 Derzhavin became a private in the Preobrazhensky Guards regiment in St. Petersburg; ten years later he received his commission. His first printed works appeared anonymously in 1773.

* dyĭr zhä′ vĭn

Though very active in the suppression of the Pugachev rebellion in 1773-75, he spoiled his chance for a military career by making enemies, and had to retire in 1777. However, he soon embarked on an even greater civil service career after becoming a friend of an influential aristocrat who gave him a position in the Senate. In 1778 he married Ekaterina Yakovlevna Bastidon, the "Plenira" of his poems, and entered a circle of noble *literati* following the aesthetics of the late French classicism. Derzhavin's greatest poems began to be published anonymously during this time. Among them, *The Monody on Prince Meshchersky* (1779) and *The Ode to Felitsa* (1782) are the best known. The latter, a daring combination of ode and satire, pleased the Empress Catherine the Great immensely and brought Derzhavin great fame. His other famous odes include *God* (1784), the first work to be published under his name, and *The Waterfall* (1791).

The nineties were the pinnacle of Derzhavin's fame. His portraits of that time show an outspoken face with sharp eyebrows, plump cheeks, wide mouth, and heavy nose. Although the theme of poetic immortality appears in Derzhavin's work, he considered his art less important than public service. His career was brilliant, but continually beset with quarrels stemming from his frankness, impatience, and hot temper. He held two governorships, served as private secretary to the Empress, and was Minister of Justice. After his retirement in 1803, Derzhavin lived in St. Petersburg, taking part in literary and social life, or writing at Zvanka (near Novgorod), the estate of his second wife Darya Alekseyevna Dyakova, where he died of a heart attack. His miscellaneous work includes several inconsequential plays and some interesting memoirs. "For sheer imaginative power [Derzhavin] is one of the small number of Russia's greatest poets," Mirsky writes. In his odes, giving a varied picture of his time, he continued the Lomonosov tradition of glorifying the Russian Empire and was the "poet of grandeur," according to Gogol, but he was also an innovator who mixed genres and diction, and a poet of unsurpassed sonic and visual richness. Traces of Derzhavin can be found in Pushkin, Ryleyev, Gogol, Tyutchev, Boratynsky, Nekrasov, Vyacheslav Ivanov, Mayakovsky, Khlebnikov, and Tsevetayeva. After a century of comparative neglect, his reputation was firmly established in the twentieth century, and now he is diligently studied and frequently published in Russia.

A few inadequate English translations are to be found in John Bowring, *Specimens of Russian Poets* (1822) and in Leo Wiener, *Anthology of Russian Literature* (1902-1903).

ABOUT: Mirsky, D. S. A History of Russian Literature. [In Russian—see studies by Y. Grot, V. Khodasevich, N. Valzenberg.]

V. M.

*DE SANCTIS, FRANCESCO** (March 28, 1817-December 19, 1883), Italian critic, is generally admitted to have been the major instigator and guide of the movement which created modern criticism in Italy. He was born of a financially sound family in Morra Irpina, near Naples, where he died in 1883. De Sanctis received his education in Italian culture in the Marchese Basilio Puoti's school in Naples and later as a student of law in the university there. After teaching in a military college, he taught private classes in literature from 1838 to 1848. In 1848 he participated in the Neapolitan uprising, and by 1850 his liberalism caused his imprisonment; in prison he translated Hegel's *Logic*. By this time, he had also devoured Bénard's French translation of Hegel's *Aesthetic*. Now removed from the traditional grammatical criticism which he had practiced in his early years, as well as from exaggerated romanticism and the influence of Sainte-Beuve, he became attracted to philosophy and to Hegel, asserting the importance of the *idea* but later (the Zürich Period) extending the premise to include form and idea as unconscious simultaneous manifestation in the poet's faculty of synthesis and creation.

Exiled in 1853, he went to Turin, remaining there for three years to teach and to write for magazines and newspapers. From 1856 to 1860 he served as professor of Italian literature in the Polytechnic Institute of Zürich where his critical essays were beginning to form as lectures. It was here that he defined literature as "the cultivation of knowledge, the enthusiasm of art, the love of what is noble, gentle, beautiful," educating man to the "use and the ennoblement of the mind through the exaltation of all generous ideas." Here also he stated his theory of aesthetics: "What matters is that once the concept is determined, the expression should correspond to the concept; the aesthetic value of a work proceeds not from the idea but from its manifestation." In a

* dā sängk' tēs

DE SANCTIS

desire to correct the distorted views of German critics and philosophers concerning Italian poets, principally Petrarch, De Sanctis gave in Zürich a series of lectures (1858-59) which attracted an international audience. Published later (1869) under the title of *Saggio Critico sul Petrarca*, these lectures proved De Sanctis to be an originator in aesthetics. For him the concept of form was identical with that of imagination, or artistic vision. Believing in the independence of art, and of the critic, he proclaimed that perfect criticism is that in which the moments of first impression and of later reflection "are reconciled in a harmonious synthesis."

Returning from exile to Naples in 1860, De Sanctis was appointed governor by Garibaldi and elected a member of the first Italian parliament (1861). He became Minister of Education in the first cabinet. Henceforth, he was involved in governmental duties, serving also, from 1871 to 1877, as professor of comparative literature at the University of Naples.

De Sanctis' two best-known works, *Saggi Critici* (1865, 1869) and *Nuovi Saggi* (1872), are collections of his critical essays, written in a fresh, persuasive, and vital style. His great work *Storia della Letteratura Italiana* (1870-71) is a perceptive and sensitive philosophic history of Italian literature tracing with great insight the history of the spirit of Italy as reflected in her literature.

De Sanctis' essays on Dante have been translated by Joseph Rossi and Alfred Galpin (1957). His *History of Italian Literature* was very ably translated by Joan Redfern (1931).

ABOUT: Croce, B. Aesthetic; Saintsbury, G. A History of Criticism and Literary Taste in Europe, from the Earliest Texts to the Present Day, III; Wilkins, E. H. A History of Italian Literature. [In Italian—see studies by F. Biondolillo, P. Bricchi, B. Croce, E. Cione, M. Mirri, L. Russo, S. Romagnoli.]

R. P. C.

*DESBORDES-VALMORE, MARCELINE** (June 20, 1786-July 23, 1859), French poet, actress and singer, born in Douai, was the daughter of the ornament painter Desbordes, who had been reduced to penury as a result of the Revolution. His cousins in Holland promised him a considerable fortune if he and his family would embrace Protestantism, but he refused, and the mother embarked with Marceline for Guadeloupe in 1801, seeking relatives in the colonies. The pair arrived in the island during the disorders; the mother died shortly, and Marceline returned alone to France, where she sought to earn a living as an actress and singer in Lille, Rouen, Paris (1804), Brussels (1815), and Lyons (1821). She played with distinction various operatic rôles from Grétry and Rossini, but especially the great classics of Molière and Marivaux.

The sentimental crisis that dominates her life and writing concerns an unidentified and mysterious Olivier, whom she met in 1808 and of whom she speaks for instance in her poem "Un Nom pour Deux Cœurs" (1834); the man in question may have been Henri de Latouche, known in many connections as writer and critic and counselor of George Sand. Marceline became more and more nervous as a result of this affair, which she continued to keep secret from her husband, Prosper Valmore, whom she had married in 1817. Valmore, also an actor, played with success in Lyons over the years 1821 to 1837, but was not liked elsewhere; when finally his career came to an end, about 1847, the family was reduced to poverty and to endless search for cheaper housing in Paris. Marceline's last years represent a long series of misfortunes. Devoted to her family, she saw the death of her daughter Blanche-Inès in 1846, then of her favorite, Ondine, who had become a teacher and died in 1853 at the age of thirty-one; Latouche also died, and Marceline developed a grave illness which soon manifested itself as cancer.

Marceline's earliest poetry, published in reviews in 1815, was little more than repetition of the banal lyricism of the moment, deriving for example from Parny. Beginning with the volume of 1819, however, and especially in the augmented collection of 1830, we find the more personal manner, which situates her as a major romantic just before the principal work of Lamartine and Hugo. She used many verse forms. Her *Élégies* and other poems were recognized at once by important critics and poets, including Hugo and her friend Sainte-Beuve, as later by Baudelaire, Banville, Lemaître, and the Goncourts. Verlaine included her along with Rimbaud and Corbière among the "poètes maudits." Her poems are still admired for their delicacy and forthright simplicity of expression. In prose, Marceline left many touching and informative letters to friends and relatives, the *Album du Jeune Âge* (1830) and the *Anges de la Famille* (1849), collected stories and fables written for her children, and the novel *L'Atelier d'un Peintre* (1833), largely autobiographical. One of the most recent presentations of her life and work, by Moulin, includes, with selected pieces, in prose and verse, a good survey of the extensive bibliography of articles devoted to her writings.

ABOUT: [In French—see studies by J. Boulenger, E. F. Jasenas, J. Lacassagne, J. Moulin, C. A. Sainte-Beuve, S. Zweig.]

F. J. C.

*DESCARTES, RENÉ** (March 31, 1596-February 11, 1650), French philosopher and mathematician, was born at La Haye in Touraine, the second son of Joachim Des Cartes (as the family then spelled the name), a gentleman of the *petit noblesse,* who had retired from military service and become a councillor of the Parlement of Brittany. René was named after a maternal uncle, who served as his godfather. His mother died a year after his birth.

At the age of ten René was sent to the newly established Jesuit College of La Flèche in Maine. He remained here for eight years, going through the entire curriculum, revealing at an early age his outstanding aptitude for mathematics. From his childhood René was of delicate constitution, and was therefore given special dispensation at school, being allowed to stay in bed as long as he chose. Throughout his life he retained the habit of meditating for long hours in bed. One of his favorite teachers was the Abbé Mersenne,

* dā bôrd' väl môr'

* dā kàrt'

222

DESCARTES

life to the working out of this discovery, a pilgrimage he accomplished in 1625.

As an heir to his father's fortune, Descartes was assured of a life of scholarly leisure. He left the army in 1621 and spent the next few years traveling through France, Switzerland, and Italy, until he settled in Holland in 1629, where he remained, except for brief visits to France, for the next twenty years. Holland at this time offered the most congenial atmosphere for intellectual pursuits (as Hobbes, Locke, and Spinoza also learned). Franz Hals' famous portrait of Descartes in black frock and white collar leaves us the impression of a Dutch cleric rather than a French gentleman, and it was in his adopted country that he produced all his writing.

Despite the boldness and originality of his thinking, Descartes remained at all times the conformist. One of his principal maxims of behavior as set down in the *Discourse* was "to obey the laws and customs of my country, adhering firmly to the faith in which, by the grace of God, I have been educated from my childhood. . . ." When in 1633 he learned of the condemnation of Galileo by the Holy See, he immediately withdrew from publication his treatise *Le Monde*, setting forth a mechanical theory of the world and the human body similar to Galileo's.

In 1637 appeared the famous *Discours de la Méthode* in which Descartes, by reviewing his own intellectual development, attempted to show how through efficient application ("bon sens et raison") the mind may arrive at truth. (He contended modestly that his was but an average mind.) In the pursuit of truth, Descartes affirms, one must accept nothing but that which is perceived clearly and distinctly. (An idea is most clear and distinct to Descartes when it can be reduced to some mathematical concept.) The most indubitable truth one is left with after doubting everything is I THINK, THEREFORE I AM ("Cogito, ergo sum"), and from this fundamental truth all reasoning proceeds. Descartes' universe is dualistic, consisting of two disparate realms of being—Thought, or that which reasons, and Extension, or all that is external to the Mind—these two realms miraculously bridged by God. In *Geometry*, one of the short scientific treatises published along with the *Discourse*, he introduced his new discoveries in analytic geometry, generally regarded as his greatest contribution to mathematics.

an intellectual monk who remained his friend throughout life. Unlike most prodigies, René was very fond of his school, and took its teachings to heart, remaining all his life a devout Catholic.

Nevertheless by his eighteenth year, the youth decided that he had sufficient book-learning, and resolved, as he relates in the *Discourse on Method,* "no longer to seek any other science than the knowledge of myself or of the great book of the world." After a period of residence in Paris, where he found the social life boring, there followed a military career of several years. Until 1619 he served in the Dutch army under Prince Maurice of Nassau. Since Holland was enjoying peace at this time, he found ample leisure to study and to mingle with eminent mathematicians who were serving as engineers.

In 1619 Descartes left the Netherlands to join the army of Maximilian, Duke of Bavaria, then participating in the Thirty Years War. It was in Bavaria on a wintry day, after an extended period of meditation in a heated room that Descartes suddenly found himself in that state of intellectual ecstasy which he describes in Part II of the *Discourse* as "being full of enthusiasm and having discovered the basis of true science." At this time it seems to have occurred to him that the science of mathematics held the key to knowledge of the nature of all life. He vowed to make a pilgrimage to the shrine of Our Lady of Loreto to consecrate his

The *Discourse on Method* brought Descartes both the acclaim of fellow intellectuals and the displeasure of ecclesiastical authorities—both Catholic and Calvinistic. To allay suspicions of heterodoxy, he brought out his *Meditations on the First Philosophy* (1641), dedicated to the Dean and Doctors of the Sacred Faculty of Theology in Paris. The *Meditations* contains the famous ontological proof of God's existence, derived from man's idea of a Perfect Being. Descartes has been accused of opportunistic motives for writing this treatise, but from all available evidence he appears to have been a sincerely pious man, seeking a *modus vivendi* for science and religion. Shortly afterwards, he prepared a second edition of the *Meditations,* embodying answers to objections that the Abbé Mersenne culled from such leading contemporary empirical thinkers as Hobbes and Gassendi.

Little is known about Descartes' private life during this period, except that in 1635 he had a natural daughter by a young woman named Hélène, generally supposed to have been a servant girl. The death of the daughter, named Francine, at the age of five caused him inconsolable sorrow.

Descartes' last years were enlivened by relationships of a more intellectual nature with two great noble ladies. In 1642 he was introduced to Princess Elizabeth of Palatine, then living in The Hague. To her he dedicated his *Principles of Philosophy* (1644), which brought together his views on metaphysics and science. Two years later he was introduced to that great royal bluestocking Queen Christina of Sweden. For a time they carried on a stimulating correspondence, and eventually Descartes wrote for her his last book, *The Passions of the Soul* (1650), his lightest treatise, a kind of manual of psychology analyzing man's basic emotions and the means by which they are aroused. As a result Descartes was invited to Stockholm as tutor to the Queen. This proved to be a fatal move. The climate and regimen he was subjected to proved contrary to Descartes' habits of living. Because of Christina's busy schedule, she demanded that the philosopher get up at five in the morning to instruct her. In a short time Descartes was stricken with a lung inflammation which caused his death as he was just reaching his fifty-fourth year. In 1667 his body was removed to France and buried at Sainte-Geneviève-du-Mont.

René Descartes is universally regarded as the father of modern philosophy in that he formulated the basic concepts with which modern philosophers deal, such as the relationship of mind to matter and the relationship of mathematical ideas to reality. Although not a scientist in the modern sense of empirical observer or experimenter, he set down the methods by which scientific investigation proceeds. He has a place in literature not only as an influence on the taste and aesthetic ideas of his time (his "bon sens et raison" notably influenced Boileau's *L'Art Poétique*), but through his own lucidity and beauty of style, which make the *Discourse on Method* in particular a notable intellectual autobiography.

In French the basic edition is the *Œuvres,* ed. by C. Adam & P. Tannery, in 13 vols. (1897-1913). An excellent one-volume edition is the *Œuvres et Lettres,* edited by André Bridoux for the Bibliothèque de la Pléiade (1952).
A Discourse on Method was first translated by John Veitch in 1850, and *Meditations on the First Philosophy* was translated by Veitch in 1853. These have been reprinted many times. More recently the *Philosophical Works of Descartes* (including *The Passions of the Soul)* have been brought out in English versions by E. S. Haldane & G. R. T. Ross (1911-12; reprinted 1955); E. Anscombe & P. T. Geach (1954); N. Kemp Smith (1953). The *Correspondence of Descartes and Constantyn Huygens, 1635-1647,* was translated and edited by Leon Roth in 1926. The *Geometry* was translated by D. E. Smith & M. L. Latham in 1925 (reprinted 1954). See also H. H. Joachim's *Descartes' Rules for the Direction of the Mind* (1957).

ABOUT: Balz, A. Descartes and the Modern Mind; Beck, L. The Method of Descartes; Bradshaw, M. Philosophical Foundations of Faith; Burtt, E. Types of Religious Experience; Butterfield, H. Origins of Modern Science; Gilson, E. Unity of Philosophical Experience; Haldane, E. Descartes, His Life and Times; Maritain, J. Dream of Descartes; Russell, B. History of Western Philosophy; Sartre, J. Literary and Philosophical Essays; Smith, N. K. New Studies in the Philosophy of Descartes; Willey, B. Seventeenth Century Background. [In French—see studies by E. Callot, P. Frédérix, M. Guéroult, A. Koyré, R. Lefèvre, G. Lewis, P. Valéry.]

R. A. C.

*DESCHAMPS, ÉMILE (February 20, 1791-April 22, 1871), French writer, was born in Bourges, the son of a government administrator and admirer of late eighteenth century literature; in his father's salon, Émile met many representatives of the various poetic schools, and such translators as Ducis. He had a religious education in mystic and romantic manner, and his first literary enthusiasms were for Chateaubriand and Madame de Staël. He entered administrative services and, taking sides with the Bonapartists, satirized the new royal regime. His formative period was particularly cosmopoli-

* dä shän'

tan, with equal interest for Chénier, Schiller, and Goethe. Deschamps' close friendship with Vigny began in his father's salon and continued throughout their lives; also close to Hugo, he attempted to reconcile the two poets after their rupture; indeed he was in many ways primarily a conciliator.

Deschamps' creative work began in 1818 with plays written in collaboration with Henri de Latouche. Within several years he had become one of the first organizers of the romantic movement, on a broad European plane, preferring German and English sources to cultivation of Rousseauesque emotionalism; hence his program was almost classical in its scorn for excessive bombast and the tendencies of the current "mélodrame." In 1823 he founded *La Muse Française*, in which, for about a year, the new poetry was represented by such great works as Lamartine's *Méditations*. In this project, Deschamps showed his appreciation for the finest contemporary work both in France and abroad, yet exploited no hostility toward the genres still surviving from the preceding century.

The preface to Deschamps' *Études Françaises et Étrangères* (1828) is one of the principal manifestoes of the romantic movement. He envisaged a larger general literary field than had Hugo in his preface to *Cromwell*, of the preceding year, embracing not only Goethe but modern German lyricism, the songs of Ossian, and especially the Spanish romances, with their epic implications and romantic color. His *Contes Physiologiques* (1854) illustrates his "troubadour" manner, with a smattering of ghosts and vampires. His program was furthered in his translations, including *Roméo et Juliette*, of which Vigny did the last acts. Deschamps' verse, summarized in his *Poésies* (1841), is esteemed less today than that of his younger brother Antoine, or Antoni (1800-1869). The latter, who became insane at forty, was a translator of the *Divine Comedy* and a brilliant lyric poet who has been called the "Verlaine of romanticism."

Like Banville and Gautier, Deschamps carried his career beyond romanticism into "Le Parnasse"; indeed, his breadth of literary interests makes of his activities one of the most useful references for over a half-century. He was associated with Catulle Mendès' *Revue Fantaisiste*, in which Parnassianism began to take form, and, with Antoni, participated in *Le Parnasse Contemporain* in 1866 and 1869. He was a close friend of Banville, and was highly respected

by Leconte de Lisle. Blind and in ill health during his last years, he outlived his best friends, Vigny, Rossini, and Lamartine, but found consolation in giving sympathetic advice to many young admirers. His *Œuvres Complètes* appeared in 1872-74, 4 vols.

ABOUT: Modern Language Notes, LXX (1955). [In French—Girard, H. Émile Deschamps.]

F. J. C.

*DESCHAMPS, EUSTACHE** (c. 1346-c. 1406), French poet, sometimes called Morel, was born, according to evidence drawn from his own poems, in Champagne, certainly before 1350, and very possibly in the village of Vertus, where he is known to have owned a house. He may have been the nephew of the poet Guillaume de Machaut and was certainly brought up by him. In 1359 he was at the seige of Rheims by the English, in 1360 in Lombardy with Isabella of France, the wife of Galeazzo Visconti. The next few years were probably spent at the university in Orleans, studying the liberal arts and law. In 1367 Deschamps took up the first of many minor administrative positions, that of equerry to Philip, Duke of Orleans. In 1366 he was president of a light-hearted literary society, "des Fumeaux," under the name Jean Fumée. Deschamps always looked back on this period as the happiest of his life. About 1373 he married, but his wife is mentioned in only two of his poems and then not by name. The marriage was apparently happy. His wife died at the birth of his third child, a daughter, whose marriage at the age of seventeen to Renaud de Pacy on April 18, 1393, was the subject of a poem which enables us to fix the approximate date of his own marriage. Of his two sons, Gilet and Laurent, we know only that Laurent was later Bailiff of Valois.

The next few years of Deschamps' life were occupied mainly with the obtaining and keeping of small positions which could provide him with a livelihood—Master of the Forests to Philip of Orleans in 1373, Bailiff of Valois in 1375, Huissier d'Armes or honorary body servant to the King, Castellan of Fismes in 1382, Bailiff of Senlis about 1389. After 1390, now calling himself Seigneur de Barbonual, he abandoned his service to the King, which had involved traveling on campaigns against the English and Flemings (during one of which, in 1382, his property was pillaged by the Burgundians), and attached himself to the new Duke of Orleans.

* dā shäN'

225

Documents show that he was very active as bailiff from 1389 to 1393 and that before the latter date he had received the additional post of Master of Waters and Forests of Champagne. On a diplomatic mission for the Duke of Orleans to King Wenceslas of Bohemia in 1397 he was roughly handled by brigands, and fortune continued to treat him badly in later years. Although he was one of the auditors at the *cour amoureux* of King Charles VI, presumably an honor, he lost the favor of the Duke of Orleans; an attachment to the Duke of Burgundy brought little improvement; he was deprived of almost all his offices, and retired to his personal estate, in fear of the age of sixty, "the end of existence." There is no exact evidence of the date of his death.

Deschamps' voluminous works include a prose *Art of Poetry and Making Chansons, Balades, Virelais, and Rondeaux* (1392), a Latin prose work, *The Complaint of the Church*, which he later translated into French, and several long French poems, including *The Mirror of Marriage* and the incomplete *Tale of the Lion*. The great bulk of his work, however, consists of poems in the popular lyric forms of his day, 1017 *balades*, 171 *rondeaux*, 84 *virelais*, and 14 *lais*. These forms, all characterized by repetition and refrain in varying ways, were suitable for the rather sententious type of occasional poetry which Deschamps favored. He was fond of the conventional themes—the miseries and pleasures of love, the decline of morality, the ungratefulness of princes—and used them in connection with contemporary events. He is facile rather than sincere, a polished versifier rather than a great poet, but provides in his person and in his works an excellent commentary on his age.

The standard French edition is that in the Société des Anciens Textes Francais, X, in eleven volumes. Vol. XI, written by G. Raynaud, in 1903, contains a detailed biography.

ABOUT: [In German—Hoepffner, E. Eustache Deschamps, Das Leben und die Werke.]

W. T. H. J.

*DESPORTES, PHILIPPE (1546-October 5, 1606), French poet, born in Chartres, was the son of a wealthy haberdasher, whose family counted many city officials, and who had higher aims for his son. The young man was tonsured and learned Latin, Greek, and perhaps Hebrew. At his father's death, the sixteen-year-old Desportes started for

* dā pôrt′

Paris, where he worked for an attorney until the latter discovered that he was courting his wife. His next master, Antoine de Senecterre, a bishop, took him to Rome as his secretary; there he became acquainted with Italian poetry.

On his return to France, in 1567, he acquired, with a laudatory poem, the protection of the future Henry III, then Duke of Anjou. Desportes succeeded in being introduced into the political and literary world, thanks to an important statesman, the Marquis de Villeroy (not to mention the Marquise), and to the Maréchale de Retz whose "green salon" he frequented assiduously.

In 1572 he published his *Imitations d'Arioste,* republished in 1573 together with his *Amours de Diane* and *Amours d'Hippolyte.* These collections of love verse met with such success that they were frequently reprinted; Desportes' popularity eclipsed that of Ronsard. Literary taste had changed: the new and less erudite public appreciated a more impersonal poetry, simplified, rid of obscure mythological allusions, more subtly erotic, and less serious. Patterned after or often copied from the Quattrocentist Italian poets and from the more recent and fashionable poets such as Tasso, Desportes' sonnets, with their abundant antitheses, metaphors, and mannerisms must have charmed a court audience infatuated with Neoplatonism and Italianism; their fluidity and their languorous and monotonous rhythms must have lulled the ladies for whom they were ordered. Ronsard jeered at Desportes and never considered as poetry his "vulgar ways, these verses without art, these new songs, which will be popular in the ages to come only with girls and pages," yet he tried to compete with his rival, who was hailed, at Ronsard's death, as the new "Prince of Poets." Ronsard's judgment, colored by jealousy, was somewhat harsh: posterity, while deploring Desportes' artifice, has admired the musical quality of his verse.

In 1573 Desportes followed the Duke of Anjou to Poland, and became, when the Duke succeeded Charles IX, Lecteur du Cabinet du Roy, versifying for the mistresses of the king or assisting him in his extravagant mystic exercises of devotion. This won for him the abbeys of Tirot and Josaphat (1583). In 1587 he prudently withdrew from public life. Shortly after the murder of the king, he joined the Ligue and fought (1591) at Rouen against Henry IV, who was besieging the city. Having played, in 1594, during the last negotiations between the

Ligue and the Protestant king, the role of a mediator, he acquired, if not the confidence of the new king, at least the abbey of Bonport, which became his favorite residence.

After 1583 Desportes turned to religious poetry: in 1591 he published a Catholic counterpart to Marot's translation of the *Psalms* (completed edition 1603, followed by *Prières* and *Méditations Chrétiennes*).

This brilliant opportunist finished his days sharing with his illegitimate son, his mistress, and his friends the pleasures of the table and of his library. When Malherbe, who later was systematically to criticize Desportes in the name of *"bon usage,"* insulted him by preferring the poet's soup to his *Psaumes,* Desportes did not take up the challenge. He died thirteen months later, leaving to his nephew, Mathurin Régnier, the responsibility for his defense.

A critical edition of Desportes' *Elégies,* along with Malherbe's "Commentary," edited by V.-E. Graham, was published in Geneva and in Paris in 1962.

ABOUT: Burgess, R. Platonism in Desportes. [In French—see study by J. Lavaud.]

M. B.

*DES ROCHES, MADELEINE NEVEU

(c. 1520-October 8 (?), 1587), and **DES ROCHES, CATHERINE FRADONNET** (October 1547-October 8 (?), 1587), French poets, mother and daughter, were born and spent their lives in Poitiers. In 1539 Madeleine married André Fradonnet, who died shortly before the birth of their daughter; she was married again, in 1550, to François Éboissard, burgher of Poitiers. Little is known of the two Dames des Roches until 1570. The mother presumably read extensively such recent writing as that of Pelletier, Muret, and Baïf; her personal worries, the loss of her husband and of two children, augmented by a prolonged law suit and the hostility of the local bourgeoisie, led her to consolation in Plutarch, Seneca, Plato, and the Bible. Madeleine must have devoted herself to the education of Catherine, with whom she remained in close spiritual union down to their death. It was this special education that tended to isolate the daughter from the materialistic interests of the local youth and of her possible suitors. The sack of Poitiers in 1562 and the siege of 1569, aspects of the wars of religion, no doubt motivated some of the religious and patriotic attitudes of both poets and emphasized their anti-Protestant leanings.

* dā rôsh'

By 1570 the Dames Des Roches had attained fame even in other regions of France. They were in constant communication with Scévole de Sainte-Marthe and the humanist Joseph-Juste Scaliger. They gathered about them a salon of both native and visiting poets, scholars, and amateurs. The stay of King Henry II and Catherine de' Médicis at Poitiers no doubt added luster to their meetings, of which we learn many details in their poetry and letters. Madeleine's second husband died in 1578 shortly before the publication of the *Œuvres de Mesdames des Roches de Poitiers.* Ronsard addressed verse to Catherine about 1580. Several hands contributed laudatory verses in French, Italian, Latin, and Greek to *La Puce de Madame des Roches* (ed. E. Pasquier, 1582; repub. 1868), inspired by the sight of a flea on Catherine's throat. A new collection of their verses, *Secondes Œuvres,* was published at Poitiers in 1583. Four years later mother and daughter were both stricken by the plague. According to Sainte-Marthe, they died on the same day. Their death was regretted by several poets; it is the subject of Sainte-Marthe's Latin eulogy of 1598.

Perhaps not wholly symbolic are Catherine's two "lovers," poets known in Poitiers by publications of 1571. Various allusions to de Guersens appear in her verse, but the better known Pellejay surely composed the sonnets and love songs "De Sincero à Charite" which answer those of "Charite," Catherine's occasional pen name. Ronsard considered both men as real persons, though Catherine insisted "Je ne les connais que par imagination." The Romanesque, precious, and feminist attitudes are far stronger in Catherine's writings than the religious and political attitudes which she imitated from her mother: they anticipated the preciosity of the Hôtel de Bourgogne of the following century. The daughter's *Acte de la Tragi-Comédie de Tobie* (1579) also represents an important step from the religious mystery play toward the new theatre, being one of the last tragi-comedies with a Biblical plot, and exhibiting a degree of dramatic unity. Diller's extensive study, published in 1936, has set in order the many dispersed documents and references to the Dames Des Roches and their friends, and finally given us a full picture of their significance as poets and organizers of an interesting movement in late Renaissance letters.

ABOUT: PMLA, 1933. [In French—Diller, G. Les Dames des Roches.]

F. J. C.

227

DESSAU, MOSES. See MENDELS-SOHN, MOSES

*DÍAZ DEL CASTILLO, BERNAL

(1492?-1581?), Spanish soldier and historian, was born in Medina del Campo, Spain. Nothing is known of his boyhood or family except that his father was *regidor* (alderman) of Medina del Campo and his mother was named María Díez Rejón.

In 1514, under Pedro Arias Dávila, he went to Darien, in 1517 to Yucatan with Córdoba, and he was on the Grijalva expedition in 1518. In 1519 he sailed with Hernán Cortés to Mexico and served with him in the conquest of that country. He became a captain, fought in 119 engagements and was wounded repeatedly. He was specially commended by Cortés and finally received an estate from the Emperor Charles V, in Guatemala, where he settled down. He died in Mexico, the exact date being unknown.

Sometime around 1568 he began the composition of his great book, the *Historia Verdadera de la Conquista de la Nueva España,* which was not printed until 1632 when it was brought out in Madrid by Fray Alonso Remón. Except for the letters of Cortés to the Emperor, his is the great eyewitness account of the conquest. Bernal Díaz tells us that he wrote his book as a protest against Francisco López de Gómara's *Conquista de México*—hence the "verdadera" in the title—which was largely in praise of Cortés. Díaz wished to correct the numerous errors in Gómara's book and also to give credit to the men and officers who fought with Cortés. Speaking of Gómara's book, he says, "In his extraordinary exaggerations of the numbers of the natives, and of those who were killed in the different battles, his account was utterly unworthy of belief. We never much exceeded 400 men, and if we had found such numbers bound hand and foot, we could not have put them to death. But the fact was, we had enough to do to protect ourselves."

Bernal Díaz is an excellent story-teller, honest and sincere. His book is filled with picturesque details and expressions from the common language of the time. He is the man of action as opposed to Gómara, the intellectual, and hence is not always discriminatory in his choice of emphasis. He will spend almost as much time talking about the qualities of a particular horse as he does of a battle. This, however, does have the ad-

vantage of making men and situations seem very real. He tells the story of the common soldier rather than just the story of the hero. For many years it was thought that Díaz's account was filled with exaggerations, but subsequent historical research has borne out the truth of his story. He has formed the basis for almost every history written about the conquest of Mexico. Archibald MacLeish's historical verse narrative *Conquistador* and the monologue *Quetzalcoatl* by the Spanish poet Luis Cernuda are derived from Díaz.

The definitive edition of Díaz's work is the one edited by Genaro García in Mexico, 2 vols., 1904-1905. This was done from the original autograph. Another good edition is that in the *BAE* (XXVI, Madrid, 1853).

A fine French translation was made by the poet J. M. de Hérédia, 1877-87. The book has been translated into many languages and been published in numerous editions. In 1800, in London, Maurice Keating published *The True History of the Conquest of Mexico*. The best-known English translation is that of A. P. Maudslay, 5 vols., London, 1908-1916. Perhaps the best of the recent editions in English is that of Irving A. Leonard, 1956, which uses the Genaro García edition and the notes and introduction of Maudslay.

ABOUT: Cunninghame Graham, R. B. Bernal Díaz del Castillo; Grauer, B. F. "How Bernal Díaz's 'True History' was Reborn," *in* Targ, W. Bouillabaisse for Bibliophiles; Niles, B. R. Journeys in Time. [In Spanish—González Obregón, B. Bernal Díaz del Castillo.]

R. E. O.

*DIDEROT, DENIS (October 5, 1713-July 30, 1784), French philosopher and man of letters, was born at Langres in southeastern Champagne, one of seven children of Didier Diderot, a cutler, and Angélique Vigneron. Denis was at first intended for the priesthood, to follow in the steps of his maternal uncle, and for this purpose was sent to the Jesuit school at Langres. Although a brilliant student he did not enjoy the school. For a brief period he dropped out to try his father's trade, but returned to the school where he received the tonsure in 1726. Shortly thereafter his uncle, *curé* in charge of the Langres Cathedral, died, having designated Denis as his successor, but the Cathedral refused to honor the choice. This decision presumably impelled the youth to move to Paris, where his father brought him to continue his education, and where he remained to pursue his varied and unconventional career.

* dē′ äth thĕl käs tē′ lyō

* dē drō′

DIDEROT

Diderot's early Paris period is obscure. It has been conjectured that he was educated both at the Jesuit Collège de Louis-le-Grand and the Jansenist Collège d'Harcourt and continued to study theology, despite his heterodoxy. On September 2, 1732, he received the Master of Arts. Then he became a family problem. Denis himself wished nothing more than to continue reading and studying, but at his father's insistence he took a clerkship in a lawyer's office. His heart was obviously not in this position, and he was soon discharged when it was found that the time he should have given to law books was spent with literary classics. As a result Didier cut off his son's allowance, and Denis plunged himself into the exciting if financially precarious literary Bohemian life of Paris.

He scraped together a meager living as bookseller's hack and translator (for example, Shaftesbury's *Essay on Merit and Virtue*, whose rationalistic ethics interested him), eked out by occasional family gifts. One of his closest friends for a time was Jean-Jacques Rousseau, whom he met in 1742 when Rousseau came to Paris to try to make his name as a composer. The two young intellectuals met regularly with the empirical philosopher the Abbé de Condillac at a café known as the Panier Fleuri to engage in philosophical discussions that were later to be echoed in *L'Encyclopédie*.

On November 6, 1743, after an *opéra-bouffe* courtship, Diderot married Antoinette Champion, four years his senior and the daughter of a widowed shopkeeper. A daughter Angélique was born the following year. The marriage had met with parental opposition from both sides, and as it turned out the couple were ill-matched. Antoinette's religious piety and irritable disposition hardly accorded with Denis' free-thinking ideas and mercurial temperament, and their domestic life consequently was a turmoil. Inevitably Denis strayed, enjoying a succession of romances with such bluestockings as Mme Puisieux (to whom he addressed the *Letter on the Blind*) and Mme Sophie Volland (his letters to her remain a valuable account of the gatherings of the Philosophes). He took as much pride in his amorous conquests as in his intellectual accomplishments.

In 1746 (ironically between the morning of Good Friday and the evening of Easter Monday), Diderot published the first of his iconoclastic books, the *Pensées Philosophiques,* in which he questioned traditional beliefs in supernatural revelation. Three years later appeared the famous *Lettre sur les Aveugles* (Letter on the Blind), in which he attempted by case studies of sightless men to prove our dependence on our senses for knowledge of the external world. He managed at the same time some satirical thrusts at theologians who assent to supernatural phenomena which they cannot prove (presumably "blind" men with eyes). This treatise and its pendant *Lettre sur les Sourds et Muets* (Letter on the Deaf and Dumb) remarkably anticipate theories of biological adaptation later developed by Lamarck and Darwin. These unorthodox theories landed their author in prison in Vincennes for three months. (Rousseau's *Confessions* contain a vivid description of a visit with Diderot here.)

On Diderot's release from prison, a project awaited him which was to engage his indefatigable energies for more than twenty years. Out of a proposal by the bookseller Lebreton that he translate into French the popular *Cyclopedia* of Ephraim Chambers (1728-29) evolved the great *Encyclopédie.* As the work grew in Diderot's hands it expanded from a mere compendium to a scholarly opus, reflecting the new ideas in the arts, the sciences, politics, and religion. Through his enthusiasm and industry Diderot was able to secure the cooperation of such fellow Philosophes as D'Alembert (mathematics), Rousseau (music), Voltaire (literature), Montesquieu (politics), and Buffon (biology). The work got off to an auspicious start with the publication of the first volume in 1751, but it soon met with vicissitudes. The Church disapproved of the *Encyclopédie* from the outset because of its heterodoxy and its championing of the secular sciences. The seventh volume containing D'Alembert's panegyric article on "Geneva" particularly offended the authorities, and in 1759 the work was formally suppressed. From then on it was carried forward clandestinely, and, collaborators falling away, became more and more a one-man venture. Diderot not only did the writing (particularly on religion, philosophy, and politics), but had to set the type himself, and then put up with the unauthorized censorship of Lebreton. Seventeen volumes were published from 1751 to 1765, with an additional eleven volumes of plates appearing from 1762 to 1772 (Diderot had no part in the later Supplément and Table Générale). In the *Encyclopédie* Diderot introduced several innovations now accepted as inevitable features of reference works, such as illustrations and cross-references. For what was undoubtedly one of the major scholarly enterprises of the eighteenth century it is estimated that he received the equivalent of about six hundred dollars a year.

During this period Diderot also wrote prolifically in other literary forms. His reviews of art exhibitions, written between 1759 and 1779, are collected in the volume known as *Salons.* He dabbled in the theatre with the plays *Le Fils Naturel* (1757) and *Le Père de Famille* (1758), domestic bourgeois drama written in opposition to the convention-ridden neoclassical drama then in vogue. Though his plays are too lachrymose for contemporary taste, his treatise *Paradoxe sur le Comédien* (The Paradox of Acting), influenced by David Garrick, remains a classic on histrionic art.

Diderot's most charming and popular books are three works of satirical fiction, all published posthumously. *Jacques le Fataliste* (written in 1773, published in 1796) is a perverse picaresque narrative, recalling Laurence Sterne's *A Sentimental Journey.* Something between a novel and a philosophical dialogue is *Le Neveu de Rameau,* which introduces in the person of a supposed relative of the great composer one of the most audacious and overpowering iconoclasts of literature. This work has had a curious history, appearing in a German translation by Goethe (1805) before its first publication in French, which was not until 1823. Some regard as Diderot's masterpiece an epistolary novel, influenced by Samuel Richardson, *La Religieuse* (*The Nun,* written in 1760, published 1796), relating to the enforced confinement of a sensitive, beautiful young girl in a convent, her harrowing emotional experiences there, and her eventual escape with the aid of a sympathetic priest. This story, based on real incidents, reflects Diderot's basic sentimental benevolence and libertarianism—his faith in the natural heart and the free spirit.

None of Diderot's literary work brought him much financial reward, and he never enjoyed such emoluments as election to the Académie Française. Late in life, in order to provide a dowry for his daughter, he had to sell his own library. He found a combination purchaser-benefactress in Catherine the Great of Russia, who bought the books, allowed Diderot to keep them until she had need of them, then hired him as her librarian and invited him to the court at St. Petersburg, where he enjoyed a period of munificent scholarly leisure. He returned to Paris in 1774 and spent the ten years of life remaining to him in study and writing. He died in 1784 in his seventieth year.

Highly esteemed by fellow intellectuals in his time (Voltaire called him *Pantophile*), Denis Diderot is only now coming into his full recognition as one of the most engaging as well as one of the most versatile minds of the French Enlightenment. As scholar-libertine he recalls his master François Rabelais after whom he modeled his style. In our age of specialization he is welcome as a great all-embracing intellect; to our age of conformity he remains the prototype of the great individualist.

The best edition of Diderot in French is that prepared by André Billy for the Bibliothèque de la Pléiade (1935, rev. 1946).

A number of translations of Diderot's works are unfortunately out of print and hard to come by. *Le Fils Naturel* was translated anonymously (as *Dorval; or, the Test of Virtue*) in 1767, as was *Le Père de la Famille (The Father)* in 1770 and *Jacques le Fataliste (James the Fatalist)* in 1797. In 1959 a new translation of *Jacques le Fataliste* by J. Robert Loy was published. *La Religieuse* was translated by Frances Birrell (as *Memoirs of a Nun*) in 1928. *Le Neveu de Rameau (Rameau's Nephew)* has recently been brought out in a new translation by Jacques Barzun and Ralph H. Bowen (1956). This edition includes selections from the *Encyclopedia.* Several of Diderot's treatises were translated by Margaret Jourdain in 1916, in a book entitled *Diderot's Early Philosophical Writings.* These include *Letter on the Blind, Letter on the Deaf and Dumb,* and *Philosophic Thoughts. Le Paradoxe sur le Comédien (The Paradox of Acting)* was translated by Walter Herries Pollock in 1883 (with an introduction by Sir Henry Irving), and this translation has been re-issued by Hill & Wang (1958).

ABOUT: Barker, J. Diderot's Treatment of the Christian Religion in the Encyclopedia; Crocker, L. Two Diderot Studies; Crocker, L. The Embattled Philosopher; Fellows, O. & Torrey, N. eds. Diderot Studies; Fredman, A. Diderot and Sterne; Morley, J. Diderot and the Encyclopedists; Steel, E. Diderot's Imagery, a Study of Literary Personality; Wilson, A. M. Diderot: the Testing Years, 1713-1759. [In French—see studies by A. Billy, J. Le Gras, J. Luc, G. May, D. Mornet.]

R. A. C.

*DIERX, (MARAIS VICTOR) LÉON (March 31, 1838-June 11, 1912), French poet, was born at Saint-Denis, on the small island of Réunion (formerly Bourbon), in the Indian Ocean near Madagascar. His father, Jacques Marais (d. 1884), a wealthy Protestant plantation owner, had married Marie Anne de Heaulme, a Catholic, in 1834. Both sides of the family had been long established in the Charente-Inférieure region of France; the Dierxes were originally of Flemish extraction. Léon was the oldest of ten children, who were brought up as Catholics.

Léon was a diligent and good student at the Lycée Saint-Denis. In 1853, after a brief sojourn in England, he went to Paris to finish his studies at the Lycée Henri IV. In 1858, while still a student, he published his first collection of poems, *Les Aspirations*. Strongly influenced by Alfred de Musset and Alphonse de Lamartine, most of these poems were later rejected from the canon of Dierx's works. The volume went unnoticed and is now extremely rare.

In 1860 Léon returned to Réunion to visit his family. Handsome, well-built, wealthy, Léon was a quiet talker, reticent, and diffident. He fell in love, and was refused. He never loved again, nor had any sentimental affairs of any sort. That same year he returned to France. A few years later, while traveling in Italy he fractured his foot on Mount Vesuvius; it healed badly, and he remained lame.

In 1864 *Poèmes et Poésies* appeared, still marked by influences, such as those of Alfred de Vigny and of his Réunion compatriot Charles Leconte de Lisle, but with some touches of originality, as in "En Chemin." *Les Lèvres Closes* (1867) contains Dierx's best poem, "Les Filaos," in remembrance of his homeland's tropical trees. Utilizing characteristic Parnassian themes—Biblical, Egyptian, and Celtic lore—

* dyĕrks

Dierx sees the history of humanity as a series of terrible crimes. The work displays that stoical pessimism, consistent tone of sadness, and technical mastery of rich rhyme and versification which were admired by his contemporaries. He was a major contributor to the three volumes (1866, 1869, 1876) of *Le Parnasse Contemporain*.

Dierx studied mathematics diligently though without interest at the Paris École Centrale for three years, but did not complete the program because of financial reverses in his family. The growth of the beet-sugar industry ruined Réunion's planters; the Dierx family was impoverished. In 1867 he started a forty-year career as a minor bureaucrat. At first a clerk in the office of the government-run railroad, he obtained a position in the Ministry of Public Education through the intercession of Guy de Maupassant. Quietly and punctually present at his office, Léon vegetated; the evenings were passed uneventfully at his modest home.

The rest of Dierx's life is primarily the record of poetic events. In 1872 he issued *Poésies, 1864-1872;* his *Poésies Complètes* (2 vols. 1889-90) and the *Œuvres Complètes* (2 vols. 1894-96) rework, rather than add considerably to, the fecund period of 1858-72; the routine of office life had stifled the poetic vein. His poetry, technically excellent, became more solemn and cold. In 1885 he was one of the nine poets chosen by the government to attend Victor Hugo's coffin under the Arch of Triumph; in 1896 the French Academy awarded him its Estrade-Delcros Prize for the ensemble of his work; in 1898 he was elected, by 15 votes to 10 for José-Maria de Hérédia, to succeed Stéphane Mallarmé as the "Prince of Poets." But indeed he was a compromise candidate, too modest and too charitable to have enemies.

Dierx retired from his government position in 1909. Almost blind, he painted or sculpted a little. He lived so quietly that he was even reported dead. Upon his death from a pulmonary embolism, he was buried in the family crypt at Batignolles cemetery in Paris. The "last of the Parnassians," Dierx has been overshadowed by Leconte de Lisle. He did occasionally find the concord of verbalism and sense he sought. As E. Noulet has said of Dierx, "His tenderness, his melancholy, his delicate subjectivity are romantic; his love of concision, of discretion, of painstaking craftsmanship are Parnassian." C. Mendès thought Dierx a "saint" in the pantheon of poetry, but a later generation has turned elsewhere.

ABOUT: Mendès, C. *in* Gentleman's Magazine XXXIII (1879); Schaffer, A. Parnassus in France, and The Genres of Parnassian Poetry; [In French—Dérieux, H. Mercure de France CCLXXXIV (1938); Noulet, E. Léon Dierx; Souriau, M. Histoire du Parnasse; Vincent, F. Les Parnassiens.]

S. S. W.

*DOBROLYUBOV, NIKOLAY ALEKSANDROVICH (January 24, 1836-November 17, 1861), Russian radical critic and thinker, son of an Orthodox priest, was born in Nizhny Novgorod (now Gorky), Russia. Dobrolyubov studied in a theological seminary and later entered the Pedagogical Institute in St. Petersburg. He was well read in European as well as Russian literature and philosophy, and was especially influenced by Belinsky, Chernyshevsky, and Feuerbach. Dobrolyubov met Chernyshevsky in 1856 and, a year later, took over the post of literary critic on the journal which Chernyshevsky edited—*The Contemporary.* He held this post until his premature death from tuberculosis. "It is now two and a half months and hardly a day has passed when I have not wept," Chernyshevsky wrote after his friend's death. "I also am a useful person, but better that I had died than he. The Russian people have lost their best defender in him."

Dobrolyubov was a consistent materialist. In his aesthetics and literary criticism, he followed Chernyshevsky in affirming the primacy of reality in art. He emphasized the didactic and utilitarian function of literature, and in his criticism used literature primarily as a platform for social analysis. At the same time, however, he was not insensitive to literary values.

In his famous essay "What is Oblomovism?" (1859), Dobrolyubov singles out Goncharov's kindly but ineffectual hero Oblomov as Russia's "native, national type," a classic embodiment of the "superfluous men" who inhabited Russian literature and life. The appearance of Goncharov's novel *Oblomov* (1859), Dobrolyubov felt, was a sign that the time for social change was not far off. Other important critical studies by Dobrolyubov include two essays on the Russian dramatist A. Ostrovsky, an essay on Turgenev's novel *On the Eve* (1860), and an essay on Dostoevsky entitled "Downtrodden People" (1861).

* dŭ brŭ lyōō' bŏf

Dobrolyubov was highly regarded by Russian liberal and radical groups. He is revered in the Soviet Union as a forerunner of Russian Marxist thought on literature.

Some of Dobrolyubov's essays were published in English in the Soviet Union in 1948 under the title *Selected Philosophical Essays.* Selections also appear in R. E. Matlaw's *Belinsky, Chernyshevsky, and Dobrolyubov: Selected Criticism* (1962).

ABOUT: Lukacs, G. Studies in European Realism; Mathewson, R. The Positive Hero in Russian Literature; Simmons, E. J., ed. Continuity and Change in Russian and Soviet Thought: Slonim, M. The Epic of Russian Literature. [In Russian—Lebedev-Polyansky, P. I. N. A. Dobrolyubov.]

R. L. J.

*DONOSO CORTÉS, JUAN (Marqués de Valdegamas) (May 6, 1809-May 3, 1853), Spanish religious philosopher and orator, was born in Villanueva de la Serena. He studied logic and metaphysics at the University of Salamanca, and jurisprudence in Seville.

As a leader of conservative thought, he played the same rôle in Spain as did De Maistre and Chateaubriand in France and Jaime Balmes in Spain, that of champion of the nineteenth century reaction. He was an eloquent orator, particularly against the Revolution of 1848. His ideology derives from the French works of Bonald and De Maistre, whose essential doctrine he represents in Spain.

In 1851 he wrote the work for which he is best known today and in which his political and philosophical doctrine is most clearly expounded: *Ensayo Sobre el Catolicismo, el Liberalismo y el Socialismo Considerados en sus Principios Fundamentales.* This essay was translated into French by Luis Veuillot. In spite of its extremely reactionary ideas, the work holds our interest for its vigor and its grandiloquent rhetoric, as well as for the absolute, traditional convictions that inspired him to pry into history and to interpret it.

He is known also as a keen critic of the Spanish romantic movement. Along with Augustín Durán and Alcalá Galiano, Donoso Cortés shared the opinion that both the Spanish classical theatre and the romantic theatre are defensible. Fundamentally, he upholds the view that romanticism was not a revolt against neoclassicism, but a return to the spirit of the classical Spanish drama. In fact, some of the outstanding characteristics of Spanish romanticism are no different from those which inspired the dramatic production of the Golden Age: lyricism, individualism, complete freedom in art. The best, complete statement

* dō nō' sō kôr tās'

of this view was presented by Augustín Durán in his *Discurso* (1828), expounded frequently by Donoso Cortés.

It has been said of him that he was less a philosopher than a polemicist, and less a polemicist than an orator, whose writings are frequently heated and tempestuous. He is often compared with another Catholic apologist of this period, Jaime Balmes, and sometimes, in regards to his prose, with the desperately critical voice of Larra.

His *Obras,* edited by Juretscheke, were published in Madrid, in four volumes, 1946. The *Essay on Catholicism* was translated into English by M. V. Goddard in 1862.

ABOUT: Catholic Historical Review, XL (1955). [In Spanish—see studies by A. Caturelli, E. V. Schramm (translated from the German), A. Taver.]

L. S.

DOSTOEVSKY

*DOSTOEVSKY, FEDOR MIKHAILO-VICH (November 11, 1821-February 9, 1881), Russian novelist, was born in Moscow.

He was one of eight children of Mikhail Andreevich Dostoevsky, son of a Ukrainian priest, and of Maria Fedorovna Nechaeva, daughter of a Moscow merchant. Mikhail Dostoevsky was a military surgeon, and the young Fedor spent his early childhood within the small and dingy walls of hospital quarters. Dostoevsky's father, an alcoholic, was irritable, morose, avaricious, and cruel. His ailing mother was good-natured and very much dominated by her husband. The children were raised in a stern religious and patriarchal environment. Dostoevsky was particularly attached to his brother Mikhail and to his younger sister Varvara.

Fedor studied first with his mother, then with his father, and then with various private tutors; at thirteen he was sent to board out in the private school of Kostomarov in Moscow. Two years later his mother died and soon afterwards he entered the Military Engineers' School of St. Petersburg. When the boy was eighteen, his father was killed by the peasants of his own village, Darovoe. In 1842 Fedor received his commission as an officer; and in 1843, after passing the final examination successfully, he became a draftsman in the Engineers' Corps of the War Department. However, after a year he resigned in order to devote all of his time to literary work.

Fedor was short and stocky. A friend described him in 1843 as being "very fair with a rounded face and slightly upturned nose . . . under the high forehead and sparse

* dŏs tŭ yĕv′ skē

eyebrows were hidden the small, rather deeply set, grey eyes; the cheeks were pale and covered with freckles; the color of the face was sickly, pallid, the lips thick." Although the boy had received a sizable amount of money from his father's estate, he lived very poorly. He was not a good administrator of his income, and through most of his life he had great financial problems, in spite of substantial earnings from time to time. He gambled away great sums, lost heavily in publishing ventures and took upon himself great financial responsibilities in supporting his relatives. Further complicating his existence from 1845 on were frequent traumatic seizures (epilepsy) from which he always recovered, but with great suffering.

From childhood on, Dostoevsky read extensively, continuing the habit while at the Engineers' School. Among his favorite authors were Pushkin, Gogol, Goethe, Schiller, E. T. A. Hoffmann, Victor Hugo, Racine, Homer, Shakespeare, and Byron. While still a student, he began writing dramas, most of which were left unfinished.

After leaving the War Department, Dostoevsky wrote his first novel, *Bednie Liudi (Poor Folk).* Nekrasov, the well-known poet, showed it to the famous literary critic Belinsky, and the very same night they woke up Dostoevsky to congratulate him and to hail him as a new Gogol. *Poor Folk* appeared in 1846 in Nekrasov's magazine *Peterburgski Sbornik.* Much influenced by Gogol's "Overcoat" and by Pushkin's "Stationmaster," Dostoevsky's novel was acclaimed for its realistic humanism, its sympathy for the downtrodden, and its evocation of intense human emotion.

The same year a second novel, *Dvoinik* (*The Double*), appeared in the magazine *Otechestvennye Zapiski*, but it met with some adverse criticism. Dostoevsky was subtly accused of plagiarizing Gogol and of being too much influenced by both *The Nose* and *The Memoirs of a Madman*. Subsequently, two short stories, "Mr. Prokharchin" and "The Landlady," appeared, but with little success. These failures embittered Dostoevsky and he soon began to feel both physically and mentally ill. His relationship with Belinsky, Nekrasov, and their intellectual circle (among them the great Turgenev) deteriorated. He began to attend meetings of Petrashevsky's Fourierist circle. Since utopian socialism was often discussed there, Dostoevsky came under suspicion as a subversive and was imprisoned in 1849. After eight months of internment in St. Petersburg awaiting his trial, he was finally sentenced to death for revolutionary activities. He witnessed all the preliminaries of his own execution; then while standing in front of the scaffold, he was suddenly reprieved. He was removed to the prison of Omsk, Siberia, for four years of hard labor, during which time the Bible was the only book he was permitted to read. Yet another four years were spent in the garrison of Semipalatinsk on the borders of Siberia and Central Asia, where he began his service as a private. In October 1856 his commission was restored. He was now allowed to read other books besides the Bible. In 1857 he married Marya Dmitrievna Isayeva, the widow of a petty government official. In 1858 he was permitted to return to Russia, and in 1859 to St. Petersburg.

Dostoevsky returned from Siberia a changed man. His momentary interest in Fourierism had been completely replaced by an interest in Slavophilism—favoring an "orthodox popular democracy within the framework of a monarchy"; he had also become profoundly devoted to the Church.

While still imprisoned in St. Petersburg, his novel *Netochka Nezvanova* was being published in the magazine *Otechestvennye Zapiski*. Its completion had been interrupted by his imprisonment, and it was to remain unfinished. On his return to St. Petersburg after his Siberian experiences, Dostoevsky published the novel *Selo Stepanchikovo* (*The Village of Stepanchikovo*) in 1860, a work which he had begun to write in Siberia. In 1861 the novel *Unizennie i Oskorblennie*

(*The Humiliated and the Wronged*, also translated as *The Insulted and Injured*) appeared, somewhat reminiscent—in its melodramatic sentimentality—of Dickens' later novels. Both the latter works were greatly praised by Dobrolyubov, an important literary critic who believed that art, as a direct representation of reality, must serve the reformation of society. *Zapiski iz Mertvovo Doma* (*Notes from the House of the Dead*, 1861-62), a realistic description of his prison life, also met with favorable criticism.

In 1861 Dostoevsky, with his beloved brother Mikhail, founded the magazine *Vremia*, which was suspended in 1863 for political reasons. A year later it resumed publication under a new name, *Epokha*. In the summer of 1862 he visited Paris, London, Italy, and Switzerland. Appalled by what he saw in Paris and London he wrote *Zimnie Zametki o Letnikh Vpechatleniakh* (*Winter Notes on Summer Impressions*, 1865) which is a condemnation of Western civilization. Dostoevsky's views stemmed from strong Slavophile tendencies and the influence of Herzen (the Russian Voltaire), who spent the greater part of his life in exile working in Western Europe for political changes in Russia. In the meanwhile his personal and domestic problems became formidable. Sometime around 1861 he had had a tumultuous love affair with Apollinaria Prokofievna Suslova, an extremely beautiful woman who was also an intellectual and a writer dedicated to the cause of female emancipation. He was burdened with debt and bad health. His wife was dying of tuberculosis. In 1863 Dostoevsky again went abroad, visiting German and French doctors to get help for his worsening epilepsy. In Paris he renewed his affair with Suslova. They traveled together to Germany (Baden-Baden), Switzerland (Geneva), and Italy. Dostoevsky lost heavily at the gaming tables and suffered deeply from the torments of his now unrequited love for Apollinaria. This love affair, just like his romance with his wife before their marriage and a later love affair with one Anna Korvin-Krukovskaya, was as ambivalent and as intricate as those of his fictional heroes. (The Russian language has even coined an eponymous word for it—"Dostoevsh-china.")

Soon after Dostoevsky's return to Russia in 1864 his wife Marya died, and only a few months later he lost his brother Mikhail. He now had the responsibility of caring not only for his stepson Pasha but also for his dead brother's family. He led a particularly difficult life, harassed by debts, by epileptic attacks, by his unsatisfactory love affairs, and by the tremendous amount of work necessitated by the editing of *Epokha*.

Before *Epokha* was discontinued because of lack of funds, Dostoevsky had already published in it, in several installments, his *Zapiski iz Podpolya (Notes from Underground, 1864)*. This tale is in part a masterful study of a neurotic and contains many autobiographical elements; it is also an answer to those positivists and rationalists (e.g., Chernyshevsky, the critic) who thought that a perfect society could be established on the basis of enlightened self-interest. Dostoevsky argues in *Notes from Underground* that man is both creative and destructive and that he often welcomes suffering. *Notes* contains some of the great themes which Dostoevsky later developed in his finest works.

In 1866 the first installment of *Prestuplenie i Nakazanie (Crime and Punishment)*, the first of the four great novels, was published in the magazine *Russky Vestnik*. In Raskolnikov, the hero, Dostoevsky describes the irreligious, materialistic and rationalistic nihilist who can be saved only through the self-sacrificing love of Sonia, the pure and religious prostitute. The German philosopher Nietzsche later developed his idea of the superman after reading *Crime and Punishment*.

While writing *Crime and Punishment*, Dostoevsky also wrote a shorter story, *The Gambler*, first called *Roulettenburg (Igrok)*, in order to fulfill a contractual obligation he had entered upon previously. It contains some autobiographical elements connected with Suslova and describes a man who is prey to the passion of gambling. To gain time, Dostoevsky engaged a young stenographer to whom he dictated *The Gambler*, Anna Grigorevna Snitkina, who proved not only efficient in her work but also very sympathetic in general. Although she was twenty-five years younger than Dostoevsky, she married him in 1867. The marriage was a very successful one. Anna was a strong woman and extremely devoted to her husband. Of the four children born to them, only one son, Fedor (b. 1871), and one daughter, Lubov (b. 1869), survived. Lubov became a dedicated, if not always accurate, biographer of her father. Dostoevsky and his young wife at first traveled abroad a great deal, most of the time living in dire financial circumstances. They often were helped by Strakhov, Dostoevsky's friend and biographer.

Dostoevsky's second great novel, *The Idiot*, was published in 1868. Its hero, Prince Myshkin, a Christ-like figure, is completely virtuous but is unable to save those who surround him. In 1870 Dostoevsky published a story, *"Vechni Muzh"* ("The Eternal Husband"), a profound study of unconscious motivation in human behavior; it is written, however, in a somewhat lighter vein than that of his great novels. His third great novel, *Besi (The Possessed)*, was published at his own expense in 1871-72 on his return to Russia. It is an extremely violent denunciation of nihilists and revolutionaries. Its main protagonist, Stavrogin, is possessed by "demons" which make him destroy others as well as himself. *Podrostok (A Raw Youth)*, published in 1875, although far from being one of his best novels, was financially a success. In it Dostoevsky describes the duality of human nature, the way in which love and hate are inextricably intertwined.

The first installment of *Bratya Karamazovi (The Brothers Karamazov, 1879-80)*, a theodicy, Dostoevsky's fourth great novel, was published in several issues of *Russky Vestnik*, beginning in the issue of January 1879. Rich in social and psychological analyses, it is considered Dostoevsky's most important work. It contains the famous episode of "The Grand Inquisitor," which critics have described as the high point of Dostoevsky's genius. It is both an assertion of man's freedom and a defense of Russian Orthodoxy against Roman Catholicism.

In 1876 Dostoevsky started to issue serially *Dnevnik Pisatelya (A Writer's Diary)* more or less regularly every month for two years. With a subscription reaching 6,000 readers the venture turned out a financial success. *A Writer's Diary* deals with a great variety of topics including autobiographical notes. Problems of crime, suicide, religion, and politics are frequently alluded to. Several stories, including "A Gentle Soul" and "The Dream of a Ridiculous Man," are also found in these pages. After a halt in publication for three years, it was taken up again from 1880 until 1881.

The last few years of Dostoevsky's life were the most harmonious and successful. An address which he delivered in Moscow on June 8, 1880 at a Pushkin festival met with an enthusiastic reception. It was such a success that even Turgenev, with whom Dostoevsky had been on exceedingly bad terms, kissed him and said with tears in his eyes, "You're a genius, more than a genius!" When Dostoevsky died in 1881, his funeral was an almost official ceremony in which he was hailed as a patriot, a true Christian and humanitarian.

Translations into English and the major European languages of Dostoevsky's works had already appeared while he was still alive. Indeed, after Leo Tolstoy, he exerted the greatest influence of all Russian writers in Europe, America, and Russia. In recent years his reputation has had a curious resurgence in the Soviet Union. At first he was widely criticized for the "anti-Soviet essence of his ideology." Gorki, "the grand old man of Soviet literature," cautioned Soviet writers against an "uncritical" approach to Dostoevsky's "weak and anti-realistic" tendencies. Nevertheless, Dostoevsky remained one of the most widely read classics in the U.S.S.R. In February 1956, the seventy-fifth anniversary of his death was commemorated by the appearance of many articles and by new productions of dramatizations of his works. An official resolution was taken that this date was to be considered one of the approved "cultural anniversaries."

The paradoxical nature of Dostoevsky's work is seen in the fact that his novels deal with profound psychological, religious, and philosophical problems, although apparently they seem to be concerned with superficial sensationalism. Anticipating Freud, by whom he is quoted, he deals with the subconscious and with man's psychic dimensions. His novels are extremely complex and must be read on several levels. His gospel is redemption and purification through suffering. His descriptions of characters are masterly and psychologists consider them amazingly accurate pictures of neurotics. Although Dostoevsky was neither a formal philosopher nor a theologian, his deep interest in both philosophy and theology is dramatized in his works. He had profound insight into the irrationality of man and his novels treat psychological conflicts on both conscious and unconscious levels. In many of his novels he uses the device of a double for his main protagonists. The double completes and opposes the protagonist. His plots, containing melodramatic coincidences and accidents, are without any humorous relief. His style is sometimes clumsy and his sentences often long-winded. Details upon details sometimes seem to prolong the story unnecessarily until a sudden catastrophe. These are, however, minor flaws. Dostoevsky is a titan of the nineteenth century novel.

The complete works of F. M. Dostoevsky, *Polnoe Sobranie Khudozhestvennykh Proizvedeni*, were published in Moscow 1926-30 in 13 volumes. His works have been translated into English by Constance Garnett and published in London 1912-20 in 12 volumes. Other English translations worthy of mention are *Stavrogin's Confession*, translated by S. Koteliansky and Virginia Woolf (1922), *The Diary of a Writer* by Boris Brasol (1949), *Crime and Punishment* by J. Coulson (1951) and by D. Magarshack (1951). Magarshack also translated *The Possessed*, under the title *The Devils*, in 1953. Bibliography: *Bibliograficheski Ukazatel Sochineni i Proizvedeni Iskusstva, Otnosyashchikhsya k Zhizni i Deyatelnosti F. M. Dostoyevskovo: 1846-1903*, St. Petersburg 1906 by A. G. Dostoevskaya; Helen Muchnic's *Dostoevsky's English Reputation*, Northampton, Mass. 1939.

About: Berdyaev, N. Dostoevsky; Coulson, J. Dostoevsky, a Self-Portrait; Curle, R. The Characters of Dostoevsky; Ivanov, V. Freedom and the Tragic Life: a Study in Dostoevsky; Kaufmann, W. Existentialism from Dostoevsky to Sartre; Lavrin, J. Dostoevsky; Poggioli, R. The Phoenix and the Spider; Simmons, E. J. Dostoevsky; Slonim, M. The Three Loves of Dostoevsky; Wellek, R., ed. Dostoevsky: A Collection of Critical Essays; Yarmolinsky, A. Dostoevsky: His Life and Art.

Y. L.

*DRACHMANN, HOLGER HENRIK (October 9, 1846-January 14, 1908), Danish poet, novelist, short-story writer, was born in Copenhagen, the oldest son of A. G. Drachmann, naval medical officer and later professor. His mother was Vilhelmine Marie Stæhr, daughter of grocer Hans Jörgen Henning Stæhr. His mother died early, and young Holger accompanied his father on business journeys or lived with relatives and friends on the northern coast of Zealand. In 1866 Drachmann studied painting at the Academy of Art in Copenhagen, but his stormy personality forced him to leave without a degree. In 1871 he married Vilhelmine Charlotte Erichsen, daughter of an attorney who became a high official in the state department.

Some articles by Drachmann on Danish painting and some poems published in a magazine under the pseudonym Mark Cole drew praise from Georg Brandes. Drachmann was fascinated by Brandes' radical naturalistic aesthetics and became an enthusiastic supporter of the new ideas of the 1870's. In the years 1872-79 he published five collections of poems. In the first one, *Digte* (Poems, 1872), which he dedicated to Brandes, there are several songs that are declarations of the naturalistic program. His *Sange ved Havet* (Songs by the Sea, 1877), contain the greatest odes to the sea in Danish poetry. In several of these songs he glorified the free, independent, Bohemian life in contrast to conventional existence in the stuffy culture of the cities. In *Dæmpede Melodier* (Muted Melodies, 1875), there is a melan-

* dräк′ män

choly note inspired by the feeling of loneliness after the early dissolution of his marriage, which eventually ended in divorce in 1878. The separation from his wife caused him deep sorrow, and he himself said that it was this distress that made him a poet.

Drachmann was a restless person who had difficulty remaining in spiritual balance. His lungs were weak, and his turbulent life during his travels aggravated his innate instability. During a journey through Germany, Tyrol, and Italy, he became sick in Florence with typhus and pneumonia. He recovered, and his joy of life returned. On his return to Denmark in 1876 he settled down in northern Zealand, and now his naturalistic poetry reached full maturity and brilliance. He was the foremost poet among the champions of radical ideas. But Drachmann could never contain himself within schools and dogmatic rules. There were also in his split nature nationalistic and romantic veins to which he gave expression, for instance, in the little book of prose and scattered verses entitled *Derovre fra Grænsen* (Beyond the Border, 1878), and the two popular adventure poems *Princessen og det Halve Kongerige* (The Princess and Half the Kingdom, 1878), and *Østen for Sol og Vesten for Maane* (East of the Sun and West of the Moon, 1880). He was also, in poetry as well as in life, strongly concerned with the erotic, e.g., in *Ranker og Roser* (Vines and Roses, 1879).

In 1879 he married Emmy Culmsee, a manufacturer's daughter. In the following years he turned to conservative ideas and tried, in opposition to the naturalistic movement, to create a national Danish literature of popular, religious nature. This reversal in his feelings is obvious in his poetic collection *Gamle Guder og Ny* (Old Gods and New, 1881), a testimony of a split soul in despair, in which he expressed his conviction that happiness and peace have to come from home, family, and love, not from the "new gods," the radical problem writers. The most expressive evidence of his conversion are the poems in *Dybe Strenge* (Deep Strings, 1884).

A passionate, long-lasting love affair with a young Copenhagen girl ruined his second marriage and changed the nature of his poetry, in which he created a visionary poetic myth to idolize the object of his passion (Edith). Now his predilection for the conservative ideals and the bourgeoisie changed into an equally strong partiality to the liberal party and the lower social classes, as

evidenced by *Sangenes Bog* (Book of Songs, 1889). In 1890 appeared his greatest prose work, the two-volume novel *Forskrevet* (Mortgaged, 1890), a partly autobiographical description of life in Copenhagen in the turbulent 1870's.

Drachmann's second marriage ended in divorce in 1903, and the same year he married Sophie Elisabeth Drewsen, *née* Lassen. His pattern of periodic crisis persisted to the end.

A collection of Drachmann's short stories translated into English by "H.C.M." was published in London in 1891 (reprinted 1893) under the title *The Cruise of the 'Wild Duck,' and Other Tales.* His sea-story *Poul og Virginie under Nordlig Bredde* appeared in English translation by Francis F. Brown as *Paul and Virginia of a Northern Zone* (1895) and as *Nanna; A Story of Danish Love* (1901). Poems of Drachmann rendered into English appear in John Volk, *Songs and Poems in Danish and English* (1903), in *A Book of Danish Verse* (translated by S. F. Damon and R. S. Hillyer, 1922), and *A Second Book of Danish Verse* (translated by C. W. Stork, 1947), both published by the American Scandinavian Foundation; in R. P. Keigwin, *In Denmark I Was Born . . .*, and in several volumes of *American Scandinavian Review*. For a complete account of translations see E. Bredsdorff, *Danish Literature in English Translation* (1950).

ABOUT: Columbia Dictionary of Modern European Literature; Mitchell, P. M. A History of Danish Literature; Winkel Horn, F. History of the Literature of the Scandinavian North. [In Danish— see studies by L. Nielsen, P. V. Rubow, V. Vedel, and bibliography on Drachmann by J. Ursin (1959).]

A. J.

*DROSTE-HÜLSHOFF, ANNETTE Freiin von

(January 10, 1797-May 24, 1848), German poet, descendant of an ancient Catholic noble family of Westphalia whose members since the eighteenth century had exhibited considerable talent in the arts, particularly music, was born prematurely in the family castle Hülshoff near Münster, the second daughter of Clemens August II von Droste-Hülshoff and his second wife, Therese Luise, *née* von Haxthausen. Her father, whom she loved dearly for his gentleness and inborn nobility, had retired early from the army, was a keen reader of history, no mean botanist, and given to collecting records of visions and prophecies. Her mother, more practical and confident, was a good chatelaine who, conscious of her aristocratic background and ties, worried about her daughter's literary interests and ambitions, thereby adding greatly to the latter's mental conflicts. Annette's health was always poor, her life, externally at least, a

* drōs' tě hüls' hŏf

237

ANNETTE DROSTE-HÜLSHOFF

Rhine, met A. W. Schlegel, d'Alton, Sybilla Mertens, Adele Schopenhauer (who stimulated her interest in Weimar, Scott, and Byron), had taken up the collecting of fossils, coins, gems, and watches, and—most important—had developed a great gift in telling stories, anecdotes, and fantastic tales. Upon her father's death in 1826, her mother and elder sister "Jenny" had moved with her to Rüschhaus, a small estate near Hülshoff, which was to become her second home. *Das Hospiz* was followed by the more fluent *Des Arztes Vermächtnis* (1828-30); from a setting in Switzerland she now turned to one in her own neighborhood. In these verse epics the real world is questioned, life is felt as a dream, nature is overpoweringly dreadful, man is insignificant and exposed. This is Annette's inner life, her vision, and from then on and on that basis she writes her best and truest work.

In 1831 Annette was visited by the young high school student Levin Schücking, the son of her old friend, the "Hermatdichterin" Katharine Schücking. When the latter died that same year, she felt it her duty to take his mother's place. On his return from the university in 1837 she introduced him to her literary friends, protected him from a love affair, and gradually found herself attracted by the young, dashing, and actually quite shallow author. During a visit with Swiss relatives (1835) Annette began working on her ballads, such as "Die Elemente" and "Der Graf zu Thal," which are her true element. Back in Rüschhaus and now consciously aware of her homeland, she wrote the verse epic *Die Schlacht im Loener Bruch* (1837-38) which, influenced by Scott, shows her unconscious admiration for warriors who live dangerously. In 1838 the first edition of *Gedichte von Anna Elisabeth v. D. . . H. . . .* was published. All in all seventy-four copies were sold. Annette's relatives were full of anger at her non-aristocratic pastime and conduct. But the literary spokesmen of the new generation, Gutzkow, Freiligrath, and Schücking, praised her book highly.

In 1841 Annette agreed to cooperate with Freiligrath and Schücking on a work about Westphalia. As a result the masterly and humorous prose fragment *Bei Uns zu Lande auf dem Lande* (which portrays her own family during her youth, herself included) and the powerful *Bilder aus Westfalen* (modeled after Irving's *Bracebridge Hall*) were composed. In 1841 she also wrote the third version of the novella *Die Judenbuche*, which is her masterpiece. Under her hand

continuous series of illnesses. She was also an extremely imaginative, sensitive, and excitable child, traits which she never lost entirely. Trained first by her mother, she eventually took part in the lessons given her two younger brothers, gaining a superficial knowledge of ancient and modern languages and mathematics. Very early she took an interest in the past, the supernatural, and the adventurous. Her father's brother Maximilian Friedrich, a well-known composer of operas, coached her in singing and piano playing; as a result she put some songs to music which appeared posthumously (1877).

At seven Annette began to write poetry; there are about thirty verses preserved composed between 1804 and 1808. Her early fragments include a verse drama, a knightly tragedy of fate, and a novel. Her entire personal conflict is brought into the open in the first part of the cycle *Das Geistliche Jahr* (1818-20), a calendar of pious verse, which fails precisely because the doubts of religion, of individuality, of artistic faith, even of madness, can no longer be hidden under a mask of naïve orthodoxy. The work was left incomplete until 1839.

In the years 1819-20 a profoundly unhappy experience threatened Annette. Torn between the love of two young men, she lost both through a misunderstanding, for which she blamed herself. For almost eight years her creative genius lay dormant, until it broke forth again in the epic *Das Hospiz am Grossen Sankt Bernhard* (1827-28). During these years she had traveled to the

it grew from a criminal case history into a character study, not only of individuals, but of an entire village, of the lower classes, of the region they inhabit.

Having completed this narrative, Annette traveled to her relatives, now living in the castle Meersburg on Lake Constance. She was followed there by Levin Schücking. For one year Annette experienced the greatest happiness; a late love had taken possession of her. During this short period she wrote most of her famous poems in *Die Heidebilder* and *Fels, Wald und See.* In 1842 Schücking left, and Annette returned to Rüschhaus. After his marriage to a young girl, she wrote hardly any more poetry. In 1844 Schücking, as literary editor of Cotta's *Morgenblatt,* saw to it that Annette's *Gedichte* were published. The success was immediate and enormous—Stifter, Clara Schumann, everyone sang her praises—but it came too late. In 1846, after a quarrel with Schücking, she arrived in Meersburg weakened and ill, and died there in 1848 during the Revolution. She is buried in the Meersburg cemetery. Her last poems appeared posthumously.

Annette's position in German letters is unique: a woman who wrote in a masculine style, objective, epical; who consciously shut herself away from the active life which so agitated her own generation (Immermann, Gutzkow, Heine); who experienced art not as a confessional and therefore shied away from all self-expression; whose conflicts, to all appearances, were decided on the plane of Christianity and of conventions, and yet peer through every line of her work. Annette's realm is the demonic; terror and fear lurk in the background of the smallest detail. That is the reason why she could not write musical lyrics of the romantic era, or the truly objective verse of realism; she stands solidly between the two, and her typical form of expression is the ballad, where the magic word rules and lures the magic world.

In physical appearance Annette was small, delicate, and elf-like. Schücking remarked on her suffering expression, her strange blue eyes, her full blond hair, her classical nose, and small mouth. She was kind and gentle, dedicating her life to her family, particularly her mother; and she hated demonstrative behavior, clichés, and pathos.

A few of Annette's poems have appeared in English translation in the following anthologies: Baskerville, A. F. *The Poetry of Germany* (1853); De Crespigny, C. *A Vision of Great Men . . .* (1848); Kroeker, K. F. *A Century of German Lyrics* (1844); Lucas, A. *Translations from the German Poets of the 18th and 19th Centuries* (1876); Pearson, E. S. *Translations from the German Poets* (1879); Muensterberg, M. *A Harvest of German Verse* (1916); *The Jew's Beech-Tree,* tr. by L. Winter, appeared in Francke and Howard's *German Classics* (1913-15), VII.

ABOUT: Silz, W. Realism and Reality; American Catholic Quarterly (1904); Modern Language Journal (1948): Modern Language Notes (1948); PMLA (1948, 1949); Sewanee Review (1938). [In German—see studies by B. Badt, K. Busse, H. Hüffer, M. Lavater-Sloman, W. von Scholz, L. Schücking, J. Schwering, etc.]

R. L. K.

*DU BARTAS, GUILLAUME DE SALLUSTE, Seigneur (1544 - July 1590), French poet, was a Gascon, born in Montfort, Fézensac. His father, a landowner, was François Salluste (or Salustre), and his mother was Bertrande de Broqueville. Little is known of his early years. In 1563 or 1564 he went to Toulouse to study law, and he received a law degree in 1567. He had evidently begun writing poetry some time earlier. In 1565 he won a prize for verse, and by 1574 he had published a substantial amount of work, including *Judit* (based on the Biblical story of Judith and Holofernes), *Le Triomfe de la Foi,* and *Uranie.* He married Catherine d'Homps in 1570 and they had four daughters.

A staunch Huguenot, Du Bartas was not only one of the great religious poets of his age but also a soldier and a diplomat during the tragic years of the French religious wars. Like his friend and fellow-poet Agrippa d'Aubigné, he divided his time between the composition of lofty religious verse and fighting on the battlefield in the cause of his religious faith. He was a close friend of Henry of Navarre (Henry IV), who sent him on a diplomatic mission to Scotland and England in 1587. In these Protestant countries Du Bartas found many admirers. One of the most influential of these was King James VI of Scotland, himself a poet. James urged Du Bartas to remain at the Scottish court, but his loyalty to Henry drew him back to France. In a graceful gesture of friendship James translated his *Uranie* into English. To return the compliment Du Bartas translated James' poem *Lepanto* into French. Ill health prevented him from taking an active part in the wars after his return to France. He was not present at the battle of Yvry, as some accounts of his life claim, but died in Paris at about forty-six "of general fatigue and old wounds ill-healed."

* dü bär täs'

The "divine" Du Bartas, as his English contemporaries knew him, devoted most of his creative energy to a noble religious poem —*La Sepmaine* (or *Semaine*), his "great Christian epic." As originally conceived the work was to consist of four episodic poems of seven days each (hence the title "The Week") covering the major events of the Bible from the Creation to the coming of the Messiah. Du Bartas wrote only the first poem and portions (the first two days) of a second *Sepmaine*. He had worked on other parts also, fragments of which survive. The *Première Sepmaine* (1578) includes an invocation to God, a discussion of angels and the elements, the creation of the earth, animal and human life, and the beauties of nature. The *Seconde Sepmaine* (1584)—as far as Du Bartas carried it—covers the story of Eden, the Fall, the Flood, the Tower of Babel and other episodes of Old Testament history through the reign of Solomon.

The general neglect of Du Bartas' work in modern times—or at least since the nineteenth century—makes it difficult for a modern reader to appreciate the significance of a poem like *La Sepmaine* in its own age. Its nobility, its majestic versification (in alexandrines), its loftiness of theme and expression, its unequivocally Protestant sentiments brought it extraordinary popularity in the seventeenth century, especially in England, but also in Germany, Holland, and Scandinavia. It was widely translated and imitated, and it exercised a powerful influence on seventeenth century religious poetry, not the least of it in Milton's *Paradise Lost*. The poem's merits for modern readers are probably outweighed by its excessive length and its artificialities of language and style. In its time, however, *La Sepmaine* was a major achievement, and Du Bartas' place in the history of French poetry is a secure and respected one.

The best collection of Du Bartas' works in French is a three-volume edition edited by U. T. Holmes, J. C. Lyons, and R. W. Linker, published in 1935.

The works of Du Bartas were widely circulated in England through English translations. In 1584 King James of Scotland ordered a translation of *Judit*, which was done by Thomas Hudson. *La Sepmaine* was translated by Joshua Sylvester in 1598, and it was through this translation that Milton knew the work. Sir Philip Sidney translated the first *Sepmaine*, but his translation is not extant. *Uranie* or *Urania* was translated by Robert Ashley in 1589.

ABOUT: Holmes, U. T. (ed.) Works of Du Bartas, I (biographical and critical study); Taylor, G. C. Milton's Use of Du Bartas.

*DU BELLAY, JOACHIM (1522?-January 1, 1560), French poet and critic, was born at the château of La Turmelière, in Liré, near Anjou. His father, Jean Du Bellay, seigneur of Gonnor, was a cousin of the powerful Cardinal Du Bellay and of Guillaume Du Bellay, the soldier and diplomat. His mother was Renée Chabot. Both parents died when Joachim was very young, and he was raised by an older brother who neglected his education and let him run wild. Years later he wrote: "My youth was lost like a flower deprived of rain, without a hand to tend it."

At twenty-three Du Bellay went to Poitiers to study law. There he met the first of the scholar-humanists who were to direct his interests to literature—Muret and the Latin poet Macrin. The most important single influence upon him was a fellow student, the poet Ronsard. They met—according to legend quite accidentally at an inn— and studied together in Paris at the Collège de Coqueret where Dorat and other scholars taught them Greek and Latin. Here also they joined with Jean-Antoine de Baïf and other poets in the formation of the Pléiade, that society of young poets dedicated to the purification (by the restoration of classical models) of the French language and French literature.

With Ronsard, Du Bellay was the leading light of the Pléiade. He was, moreover, the author of its "manifesto of revolution"—a document which survives as one of the most influential pieces of literary criticism produced during the Renaissance—*La Défense et Illustration de la Langue Française* (1549). The *Défense* was written in answer to Thomas Sibilet's *Art Poétique* (1548) which had criticized the Pléiade's experiments with classical forms. In its turn Du Bellay's work provoked many replies and attacks. He divided his treatise into two books. The first is a defense of the French language, pointing out that it can be improved and enriched by imitation of the ancient Greek and Latin authors. The second book shows specifically how this can be done—by rejecting the old French models—rondeaux, ballades, virelays, etc., "and such other vulgarities which corrupt the taste of our language and only serve to bear testimony to our ignorance"—and by faithfully studying and imitating the classics in French. (He suggested, for example, the reworking of Old French tales like *Lancelot* and *Tristan* into epics modeled on the *Iliad* and the *Aeneid*.)

* dü bĕ lā′

In the same year in which his controversial *Défense* appeared, Du Bellay published a collection of verse, *Recueil de Poésies,* and a year later came his celebrated sonnet sequence *Olive.* Du Bellay cannot be credited with actually introducing the sonnet into French literature, nor with making any significant contribution to the form. His sonnets were faithfully modeled after Petrarch. But they did serve to popularize the sonnet form and to adapt it to French taste. In 1552, following his own advice in the *Défense,* he published a French version of Book IV of the *Aeneid.*

In 1553 Du Bellay went to Rome as secretary to his cousin Cardinal Du Bellay. The four years he spent in Rome were not happy ones. He had lost his hearing, and in a strange land he found himself a lonely exile. Ultimately, however, he made friends—the poet Olivier de Magny and a lady named Faustine whom he celebrates in his poems as Colomba. Of greater significance was the poetry he wrote during this period—the *Antiquités de Rome, Jeux Rustiques,* and a group of sonnets in which he expresses his homesickness and loneliness—*Les Regrets.* He returned to Paris in 1557 but did not apparently renew his friendship with Ronsard. In his last years he lost the patronage of his cousin the Cardinal, probably because of the outspoken sentiments of *Les Regrets.* He managed to win a pension from Francis II, and his last compositions were satires translated from the Latin. He was only thirty-five or slightly older at the time of his death.

Du Bellay has been justly celebrated for bringing into the French poetry of the Renaissance a new spirit of Italian-Latin freshness and vitality. Modern studies of his work have indicated that his "original" contribution was very slight indeed, that almost all his work was close translation or paraphrase from Italian and neo-Latin sources. Even the famous *Défense,* it develops, was borrowed—in many passages at least—from a defense of the Italian language written by Sperone Speroni. There is no question of plagiarism in the modern sense, however. "All he writes," Richard Aldington has said of Du Bellay, "has a strong personal style; everything he borrows he transforms, makes French. He did not so much copy as interpret with sympathy, introducing to his countrymen a new intellectual attitude which, after all, transformed not only literature but life itself."

Many famous poets have tried their hand at translating Du Bellay into English. Best known of these is Edmund Spenser who translated the *Ruins of Rome (Les Regrets* and *Les Antiquités)* in 1591. Others are Andrew Lang and Ezra Pound, whose translations appear in *A Modern Book of French Verse,* edited by A. Boni (1920). Selections also appear in J. G. Legge's *Chanticleer: A Study of the French Muse* (1935). Translations from *Olive, Les Amours,* and *Jeux Rustiques* appear in George Wyndham's *Ronsard and La Pléiade* (1906). There are a number of translations of the *Défense et Illustration*—the complete text by G. M. Turquet (1939).

ABOUT: Aldington, R. Literary Studies and Reviews; Belloc, H. Avril; Dickinson, G. Du Bellay in Rome; Merrill, R. V. The Platonism of Du Bellay; Pater, W. The Renaissance; Tilley, A. A. Literature of the French Renaissance. [In French—see studies by F. Boyer, H. Chamard, C. Marty-Laveaux, V. L. Saulnier. In Italian—see study by G. Saba.]

DUCASSE, ISIDORE LUCIEN. See "LAUTRÉAMONT, Le Comte de"

DUDEVANT, Mme. See "SAND, GEORGE"

*DU GUILLET, PERNETTE (c. 1520-July 17, 1545), French poet, born into a noble family of Lyons, belonged, with Maurice Scève and Louise Labé, to the Lyons poetic circle where her remarkable blond hair, luminous aquamarine eyes, her erudition and her many talents, won for her the title of "perfect woman of the Renaissance." Her accomplishments included the lute, Spanish, Italian, and even some Greek. Her particular sympathy for the Alexandrians and Petrarchists, for courtly love and Platonic asceticism, explains her attitude toward Scève, whom she met in 1536. There grew between them a Platonic relationship which was the sole adventure of her life, and, while in her daily encounters with him she coquettishly kept him at a distance, she sincerely offered him her attentive admiration, saved him from despair, and remained his greatest inspiration. In 1537 (or 1538) parental authority forced her to marry du Guillet. Her indifference toward her husband consoled Scève, and, until her premature death (possibly from the plague), her Platonic affair was her means of spiritual elevation. Anonymous slander claimed she was Scève's mistress, but this is unlikely, although she might have yielded once to her lover's demands if one is to believe the poet's verse.

After her death, Antoine du Moulin, having vainly attempted to classify her poems,

* dü gē yà'

241

passed to him by her husband, published them in their disorderly but freshly original sequence. The *Rymes* (1545), containing epigrams, epistles, and chansons, show the influence of Neoplatonic and Marotic verse. In a style playful on the surface but abstracted to the point of obscurity, these poems sing of love identified not with moral but with intellectual exaltation. The poet either deplores her lover's insistence and his absence from the intellectual delight which he gives her, or sings the victory of light through knowledge over darkness, when all obstacles such as time and even death have been abolished.

Forgotten since Ronsard's age, her work was recently rehabilitated, though she is still overshadowed by Louise Labé, perhaps not her superior.

Some of her poems appear in English translation by W. Stirling in *Anthology of European Poetry, from Machaut to Malherbe,* edited by M. Savill (1947).

ABOUT: [In French—V. L. Saulnier, "Étude sur Pernette du Guillet," *in* Bibliothèque d'Humanisme et Renaissance IV (1944).]

M. B.

*DUMAS, ALEXANDRE (DAVY DE LA PAILLETERIE) (père) (July 24, 1802-December 5, 1870), French novelist and playwright, was the son of Napoleon's mulatto general Thomas Alexandre Dumas Davy de la Pailleterie (whose father was of a noble Norman family and whose mother was a Dominican Negro slave) and of Marie Louise Elisabeth Labouret, daughter of an innkeeper at beautiful Villers-Cotterêts where the writer was born. The exploits of his kind, courageous, and incredibly strong father were very dear to the son's heart. Broken by imprisonment at Naples, the General died when Alexandre was but four years old, leaving no means. The widow's parents had to maintain the small family which included Dumas' sister, nine years older than he.

The little boy was intelligent but not diligent. His mother and sister taught him to read and write—he developed a beautiful hand—but in mathematics he had no skill. He was an eager and determined talker, interrupting the conversation of his elders. He could not sing but he became an excellent dancer. He excelled also at fencing, shooting and riding and loved the outdoors, escaping to the beautiful surrounding forests whenever chance afforded. His mother put

* dü mà′

DUMAS (PÈRE)

him to school under the Abbé Grégoire, but he was a reluctant scholar.

In 1815 his mother took him to aid two Bonapartist generals imprisoned nearby. The money and guns he bravely carried to them were refused, but the mission fired his passion for romantic adventure. He refused about this time to assume his full name, insisting on the abbreviated form made famous by the gallant General Dumas.

At fifteen he was apprenticed to a notary and, impressed by the elegant young clerks visiting from Paris, he dreamed of attaining the same goal. In another year he became aware of the beauty of the young girls about him; a year or so later he acquired his first mistress. In the cosmopolitan circles of Villers-Cotterêts he met Adolphe de Leuven, poet, and Amédée de la Ponce who taught him Italian and who advised him that the way to happiness lay through hard work.

Alexandre, like his father, was a raconteur with a vivid imagination. At eighteen he heard a troupe of actors perform Ducis' adaptation of *Hamlet,* and in it he found a melodramatic flourish and energy akin to his own ardent temperament. He determined to be a playwright, formed his own local company and, aided by Leuven, he directed, acted in, and even wrote some of the plays performed. When Leuven left for Paris, he set out with a friend for a three-day visit to the city, hunting for game along the way to defray expenses. In memory of his famous father, he was given free passes to the theatre. There he saw Talma's romantic acting and resolved to take Paris by storm in a like manner.

In 1823, with a small sum from his mother, he set out for Paris where with the aid of General Foy he secured a post as copyist in the secretariat of the Duc d'Orléans, with duties that often occupied both day and evening. In spare moments, under the guidance of his superior, Lassagne, Dumas began to read widely in French and foreign classics. One evening at the theatre he met Charles Nodier, mentor of romanticism. He developed an interest in contemporary poetry and wrote verse himself. He and Leuven collaborated on a mediocre verse comedy which brought in a small sum. Meanwhile he had begun an affair with a dressmaker, Marie Labay, by whom, in 1824, he had his son Alexandre; he left them three years later.

His mother, whom he loved devotedly, came to Paris in 1824 and Dumas found himself responsible for two homes. Considered the best copyist, he received an increase in salary; but he was dissatisfied, for his duties permitted few visits to the theatre. He did, however, find time to read Byron and Scott. In 1827 Kean, Kemble, and Smithson presented Shakespeare to Paris and again Dumas was fired with enthusiasm for the drama of violence. He begged for release from evening work and promptly wrote *Christine,* a verse drama. Through Nodier's influence, he read the play to Taylor, producer at the Comédie-Française, who accepted it subject to revisions which, however, Dumas delayed making. Meanwhile he decided upon another historical play, in prose. Two months' study and untiring work produced *Henri III et Sa Cour,* set in a period of violent action ready-made for his romantic genius and highly acceptable to a public that remembered the strenuous Napoleonic era. Presented at the Comédie-Française, February 10, 1829, the play had a triumphant reception. To celebrate its success and allow Dumas more time for his writing, the Duc d'Orléans appointed him his librarian.

A handsome colossus with crisply curling black hair, merry blue eyes, straight nose and thick lips, Dumas went from mistress to mistress, who in his youth were older than he but who with his increasing years grew ever younger. He frequented the society of actresses and among literary men he favored the romantics, Nodier, Hugo, and Vigny, whose salons he delighted with his storyteller's gift. Boastful of his success, given to flamboyance in clothing and jewels, he

modeled himself upon Byron. On September 12, 1827, after a short, passionate courtship, he began an affair with Mélanie Waldor, a worldly married woman who complained of his sensuality but who presided over their salon for over two years.

Dumas' plays continued successful though at times they met stormy receptions. His *Christine,* in which the star was Mlle George, an actress of statuesque beauty once briefly mistress of Napoleon, opened on March 30, 1830, to so great a controversy that Hugo and Vigny aided in immediately reworking certain poetic passages. The second performance was well received and the book rights were bought up at once.

Dumas now used his love affair with Mme Waldor as the subject of *Antony,* bringing to the modern French stage for the first time the subject of the adulterous wife, punished by death (to appease the censors). Produced May 3, 1831, with Bocage and Marie Dorval as leads, it was tumultuously successful and made Dumas the period's most celebrated dramatist. But writing the play dealt a fatal blow to the affair, and in June 1830 Dumas turned to actress Belle Krelsamer by whom he had his daughter, Marie Alexandrine, in March 1831, and with whom he lived for three years. He now recognized both Marie and Alexandre, taking the boy away from his mother to their deep sorrow. Since his son hated Belle, Dumas placed him in an unhappy succession of boarding schools.

When political revolution threatened in 1830, Dumas made a somewhat theatrical mission to Soissons to capture ammunition for La Fayette and was feted at Villers-Cotterêts. Although an admirer of aristocrats, Dumas was a staunch republican in politics, now out of favor with the new king, Louis Philippe. He was advised to leave the country for a time. Out of this brief exile came the first of his *Impressions de Voyage* (1833), followed later by other accounts of succeeding travels, all full of color and interest.

An established dramatist, he continued producing plays (about ninety in all forms) and also writing articles for journals and newspapers, serials, historical stories, novels, sword-and-cape yarns, and adventure stories in which he excelled and for which he is now best remembered. Because he wrote so much, he used collaborators to do the research and provide the skeleton, as in the case of *Tour de Nesles* (1832), a work which has been called "the father of all melodrama." First written by Frédéric Gaillardet, it was rewritten by Dumas who gave it fast-flowing action, flamboyant dialogue, and his renowned curtain lines. Enemies began to say that Dumas did little himself but bought up the work of others to sell as his own.

Dumas' mother died on August 1, 1836. In 1840 he married his mistress Ida Ferrier who brought him a dowry which he spent (as he did the many fortunes he made) open-handedly on the crowd of parasites he attracted. After several unsuccessful plays, Dumas turned from the theatre, and he found in Auguste Maquet, a teacher of history, an ideal collaborator for historical novels and drama. Their greatest works began with the three musketeers trilogy, *Les Trois Mousquetaires* (1844; dramatized 1845) and its sequels. The many series of adventure novels that followed became internationally famous, were read, reprinted, and translated under varying titles, and have never gone out of public favor. In them he covered the whole of French history, taking liberties with fact and personage but recreating atmosphere and revivifying the many periods, with detail typical of romanticism. *Le Comte de Monte-Cristo*, published 1844-45, dramatized in 1848, proved to be as famous as the Musketeers. It became one of the classics of the English and American stage at the turn of the century and has had numerous motion picture, radio, and television adaptations.

Dumas' lavish spending reached new heights with the construction of his Château de Monte-Cristo, said to cost altogether over 500,000 francs—the housewarming in 1848 had 600 guests. In 1851 he fled to Belgium to escape his creditors; and in that year another son, Henry Bauër, was born. New works continued to pour forth and his excellent Brussels secretary, Noël Parfait, brought temporary order into his affairs, but he was never free of burdening debt. Even the originally successful *Théâtre Historique,* founded in 1847 to present his plays, began to fail following the 1848 revolution and closed in 1850. Declared bankrupt in 1852, he settled forty-five per cent of literary properties on his creditors and returned to Paris early in 1853.

While in Brussels he began his *Mémoires* (1852-54), followed by *Souvenirs* (1854-55), and *Souvenirs Dramatiques* (1868). An English translation of the memoirs appeared in 1909, by E. M. Waller, six volumes; an English condensation in 1957 as *The Road to Monte Cristo*. Of the memoirs Henri Clouard says in his biography, "Dumas does not lie, he does not even invent: he arranges."

Indeed, of the many biographies of Dumas, none exceeds the interest and color of the memoirs.

At various times he began a number of short-lived journals, notably *Le Mois* and *Le Mousquetaire*. In 1860 he made another voyage, stopping in Italy to aid Garibaldi. In that same year another daughter, Micaëlla Cordier, was born, the delight of his old age. He rejoiced too at the success of his son, who reproached him for his debts and his never-ending love affairs but who addressed him as "dear simple-minded great man." After more writing, more journeys, more of everything, Dumas died of a stroke at his son's home at Puys. He was buried at Villers-Cotterêts near his parents.

Dumas has been reproached by some critics for careless writing, absurd situations and lack of taste, but all have valued his abounding imagination and portrayal of action. Lamartine declared, "You are superhuman." Anatole France wrote to the son, "Your father amused me!": this, after all, was the declared intention of that father. Michelet wrote to him, "Monsieur, I love you and admire you, because you are one of the forces of nature."

English translation of Dumas' novels are far too numerous to list. His popularity, especially among younger readers, continues; and his works have appeared in every mass entertainment medium from motion pictures to comic books. In recent years there has been a revival of interest in his non-fiction. *Adventures in Spain* was translated in 1958 by A. E. Murch, who followed this with *Adventures in Algeria* in 1959; also in 1958 R. W. Plummer and A. C. Bell published *Travels in Switzerland*. The *Dictionary of Cuisine*, translated by L. Colman, appeared in the same year.

ABOUT: Bell, A. C. Alexandre Dumas; Bradford, G. A. Naturalist of Souls; Davidson, A. P. Alexandre Dumas Père, His Life and Works; Maurois, A. The Titans; Books Abroad, Summer 1948; Romanic Review, October 1940; Spectator, November 22, 1957. [In French—see studies by H. Clouart, H. Parigot.]

M. A. W.

*DUMAS, ALEXANDRE (fils)** (July 27, 1824-November 27, 1895), French novelist and playwright, was the son of Alexandre Dumas (*père*) and Marie Catherine Labay, a pretty, charming but uneducated dressmaker whom the elder Dumas lived with in Paris from 1823 to 1827. He contributed to their support but saw them rarely. Alexandre, who adored his mother, deeply resented his father's treatment of her. On March 17, 1831, Dumas *père* recognized his

*dü má'

DUMAS (FILS)

son and took the reluctant boy from his mother. Catherine Labay struggled to keep her boy and instituted useless proceedings, but the court sent him to boarding school. Alexandre later described this painful period in his partly autobiographical novel *L'Affaire Clémenceau* (1866).

The little boy loved his kind if neglectful father who began early to take him to the theatre and who placed him in the Goubaux school among the sons of nobles and rich bourgeois who ostracized him and tyrannized over him for the misfortune of his birth. Unhappy and ill at times, he developed a melancholy that recurred throughout his life. He differed from his light-hearted father in his withdrawal from those about him and in his suspicious observation of his cruel fellows.

In 1838 he entered the preparatory school of the Collège Bourbon and then the college itself but he left at seventeen without completing his formal education. At eighteen the young man had bachelor quarters, began to share his father's pleasures, started an intrigue with a married woman, and piled up debts. His father advised him to work and offered to employ him. Alexandre refused but began to write. Between 1846 and 1852 he wrote some very bad poetry and thirteen novels, all now forgotten.

The young man was tall, handsome, with light blue eyes and auburn hair; he dressed elegantly and frequented fashionable centers where in 1844 he met the courtesan Marie Duplessis (his lady of the camellias). His affair with the lovely girl, who was consumptive, lasted less than a year. She died in 1847 and a year later Alexandre published the hastily written romantic novel *La Dame aux Camélias*. It was dramatized the following year, but its performance was delayed by censorship until 1852. Both novel and play were an instant success, and the play is still a popular favorite.

On the proceeds of his success Alexandre was able to pay off his debts and to install his mother in a charming apartment. He now began to write serious moral studies. Between 1852 and 1860 he wrote five more successful plays, despite censorship delays: *Diane de Lys* (1853), on punishment of an erring wife; *Le Demi-Monde* (1855), perhaps his masterpiece and a landmark in French social drama, where he treated the subject of immoral love and the character of an unfortunate adventuress; *La Question d'Argent* (1857), attacking the period's sudden wealth, its waste, speculation, and financial dishonesty; *Le Fils Naturel* (1858), introducing the thesis drama and dealing with laws and conventions affecting the illegitimate; *Le Père Prodigue* (1859), based on his father's life and character. He had declared that he would never write anything he did not believe to be the absolute truth. Indeed, all his themes were built on his own experience or observation: "I give my characters the language of familiar life."

In 1853 the young moralist entered into a liaison with Russian Princess Nadejda Naryschkine. He wished to marry her but her husband refused a divorce. A daughter, Colette, was born on November 20, 1860, but he was unable to marry the Princess or acknowledge his brilliant daughter until December 31, 1864.

The plays that followed were less successful and Alexandre confided his depression and ill health in a long correspondence with George Sand. He collaborated with others and in 1867, under the health-giving influence of Sand's physician, produced his own successful *Les Idées de Madame Aubray*, in which a mother permits the marriage of her son to an unmarried mother. In that same year a second daughter, Jeannine, was born.

In 1874 he was elected to the Académie Française where he believed his father should have preceded him. He was now in very comfortable circumstances; he was charitable, though not foolishly generous; he had many good friends, despite his acid wit. He grew more handsome with age, and more concerned with social and political problems, upon which he began to write moralizing pamphlets. Anatole France wrote, "[Your father] amused me and you have instructed me." Some contemporary critics accused him of making the theatre a "school of corruption"; others contended that his "exact portrayal of life was moral." They hailed his plays as works of art, yet said that the father had genius, the son but talent.

After more failures, he again had great success with *Denise* (1885) and *Francillon* (1887), charming comedies of manners; but thereafter his powers waned. He was awarded the Légion d'Honneur in 1894; his wife died in 1895, and a few months later he married Mme Escalier, a divorcee. Five months later he died of an embolism, following meningitis.

After his death interest in his work waned, for his realistic drama had treated social problems peculiar to his period in Paris. His *Théâtre Complet* appeared in 1923.

English translations and adaptations of some plays followed French publication, but they were not as successful as the originals, for it is said that "no English adaptation has done justice" to them: *Lady with the Camellias*, 1850, a distorted version called *Camille* in 1853, a better version in 1856; *Le Demi-Monde* in 1858; *Le Fils Naturel* in 1879; *The Money Question* in 1915.

ABOUT: James, H. Notes on Novelists; Maurois, A. The Titans; Nicoll, A. World Drama from Aeschylus to Anouilh; Schwarz, H. S. Alexandre Dumas, Fils, Dramatist; Smith, H. A. Main Currents of Modern French Drama; Taylor, F. A. Theatre of Dumas Fils; Fortnightly Review, January 1, 1896; Modern Philology, February 1940; Spectator, November 22, 1957. [In French—see studies by H. Clouard, C. Noel, P. Lamy.]

M. A. W.

DUPIN, AMANTINE AURORE LUCILE. See "SAND, GEORGE"

*DU RYER, PIERRE (c. 1600-October 5 (?), 1658), French dramatist and translator, born in Paris, was the son of the poet Isaac Du Ryer. Twice married, he lived in poverty, devoting himself to translations and to the composition of his twenty-one known plays. It is supposed that his father, secretary in the King's Chambers, inspired his interest in the theatre through his two pastoral plays, of 1614 and 1621, and some lyrical poetry, and that Pierre assumed his place as secretary and completed his degree in law by 1629. He was early associated with young dramatists hostile to Hardy and open to the new classical doctrines of Malherbe. From 1734 to 1741 Du Ryer was secretary to the

* dü rē à'

Duc de Vendôme, but continued augmenting his salary by translations from the classics; the translations, and the dozen plays to that date, led to his election to the French Academy in 1646. He continued his translations and found some financial ease in employment as historiographer of France, but abandoned the theatre in the face of these duties.

Du Ryer's first play, *Artéphile* (1618), developed a subject from Plutarch in episodic and romanesque style, as a series of adventures without unity of action, after the manner of Hardy and of the contemporary novel. His principal fame lay in his *Scévole*, which enjoyed long popularity for its many intelligent technical innovations. From his first preference for ancient subjects, taken for example from Plutarch and from Barclay, Du Ryer turned to more modern vein in *Lisandre et Caliste*. Influenced by Mairet, he began to respect the classical unities. In his *Alcimédon* (1632) Du Ryer observed the new usage of the never-empty stage. Under the influence of Mairet and Corneille, Du Ryer also turned to tragedy in his *Lucrèce* (1638) and continued to use Biblical or historical subjects, basing his tragicomedies on the novel. His *Les Vendanges de Suresnes* (1635) is significant as a pastoral play set near Paris, with its love story in the gallant artifices of the novelistic reference. His *Alcionée*, perhaps his masterpiece, presumably first performed in 1637, was highly praised by his contemporaries, later played by Molière, and still esteemed in 1773 by Marmontel. It is based on an episode from Ariosto's *Orlando Furioso*, an exotic and heroic subject of baroque type, recounting adventure and portraying gallantry.

Du Ryer was instrumental in the elimination of such old devices as recognition, disguises, mistaken identities, comic situations, and excessive action on the stage. He emphasized artistry rather than morals, and gradually purged his plays of secondary plots, changes of scene, and action over long periods. His last plays achieve a simple, logical, and classical structure very like those of Corneille. Furthermore, he was long classified as one of France's principal poets, and was much praised for his translations from the Latin, of Cicero, Livy, Ovid and Seneca, frequently reprinted in his time; his versions served to vernacularize the classics in reasonably accurate form, neatly adapted to enhance the style and color.

ABOUT: Lancaster, H. Pierre Du Ryer, Dramatist.

F. J. C.

*DUVAL, (MARTIN) PAUL ALEX-
ANDRE ("JEAN LORRAIN") (August
9, 1855—June 30, 1906), French novelist,
short-story writer, and chronicler, was born
in the maritime city of Fécamp, in Normandy.
He was the only child of Amable-Martin
Duval (1815-86), whose ancestors had, like
Amable-Martin, been associated with the sea,
and of Elizabeth-Henriette-Pauline Mulat
(1833-1926). The family was prosperous;
Paul received his early education at home
from his mother and tutors. He went to
school at Vanves at the age of ten, when he
was already writing under the influence of
adventure tales, Sir Walter Scott, and
Shakespeare; and at twelve he essayed his
first verses. After studying in the Dominican school at Arcueil, Paul spent two years
at the Paris Law School, but discontinued
his studies after a year of military service in
order to devote himself to literature.

It was at his father's suggestion that Paul
took a pen-name, Jean Lorrain. His first
volume of verse, *Le Sang des Dieux* (1882),
was published at his own expense. Commercially unsuccessful, this debut won him
the esteem of François Coppée and Jules
Barbey d'Aurevilly. Although a mainstay
of Montmartre night life and launched on
the physical excesses that were to ruin a
basically strong constitution, Lorrain published two other compilations of verse, *La
Forêt Bleue* and *Modernités*, and three
novels composed at Fécamp between 1882
and 1886. His first novel, *Les Lépillier*
(1885), shocked the people of Fécamp,
which he had depicted. He was also a contributor to *La Revue Indépendante*, *Lutèce*,
and *La Revue Normande*. To earn his living, he wrote tales and chronicles for newspapers, notably the *Courrier Français*. His
contributions to this weekly newspaper and
to *L'Événement* (1887-90), *L'Écho de Paris*
(1890-95), and *Le Journal* (1895-1906)
were in part his novels and short stories.
Lorrain adopted the name of Restif de la
Bretonne for his sketches of feminine contemporaries; Paul Morand, in 1932, presented some of these under the collective
title *Femmes de 1900*. Chronicles of the
social whirl which appeared as "Pall Mall
Semaine" in *L'Écho de Paris* were collected
in book-form as *Poussières de Paris* (1896-
1902). He also published impressions of
travel through France, Spain, Northern
Africa, and Italy. With collaborators, especially Gustave Coquiot, Lorrain wrote several short plays. *Le Tréteau*, published
posthumously, satirized the theatrical world.

Lorrain became a legendary figure because
of his morbid interest in bizarre experiences
and sensations. His homosexuality (as well
as heterosexuality) and his use of drugs
made him notorious: Oscar Méténier described him in *La Chair* under the alias of
Marius Dauriat.

At the end of 1900 Lorrain, very ill,
moved to Nice, where he mainly resided for
the rest of his life. In Paris where he had
gone to review an art exhibit, he died of in-
testinal perforations. He was buried in the
family crypt at Fécamp. A monument by
Alphonse Saladin has been erected there.

Lorrain's major works are the sadistic
M. de Phocas (1901) and *La Maison Philibert* (1904), which concerns the world of
prostitution. Dignimont illustrated the latter
novel with eighty-eight water colors for a
de luxe edition. *M. de Bougrelon* (1897)
has also been published in various illustrated
editions. The short story "L'Homme des
Berges" is particularly remarkable for its
depiction of the criminal mind. Lorrain's
writings, which influenced Francis Carco, are
significant documents on the "fin de siècle."

ABOUT: Cambiaire, C. P. The Influence of Edgar Allan Poe in France. [In French—see studies
by P. L. Gauthier, G. Normandy.]

S. S. W.

*DUYSE, PRUDENS VAN (September
17, 1804-November 13, 1859), Flemish poet,
was born in Termonde. He was the most
important and the most gifted of the romantic generation. His father, a physician,
had him study, first at the University of Louvain, then at Ghent where he followed the
lectures of the Dutchman Scrant. In course
of time he received his degrees in law and
in literature. Convinced of the necessity of
remaining loyal to the House of Orange, he
moved to the Netherlands after the revolution of 1830. But a few years later he returned to Ghent, where he became a teacher
at the Athenaeum in 1836. In 1838 he received the post of archivist of Ghent. He
was to publish an analytic inventory of the
archives in three volumes between the years
1843 and 1857. He took part in the awakening Flemish movement and was one of the
founders of "De taal is gans het Volk"
(1837). He also promoted the "Duits-
Vlaams-Zangverbond" (1846).

* dü väl'; lô răn'

* doi' sĕ

Of the Flemish poets of his age Duyse had probably the richest mind, but one cursed with facility. He wrote in all poetic genres, and with his multiplicity of activities and interests, his work was often indifferent in quality. In his rhetorical lyrics he often resembled the Dutch Bilderdijk; but no matter what the quality of his work, the language always flowed spontaneously and melodiously. Most enjoyable are his poems of an intimate nature, for instance, his *Natalia-elegy* (1842) and his romantic legends in which he often approached a medieval simplicity. He collected and published his best poems in *Het Klaverblad* (1848) and in *Nazomer* (1859). His son prepared a ten-volume edition of his *Nagelaten Gedichten* (1882-85).

About: [In Dutch—see study by P. Sterkens-Cieters.]

H. B.

EANNES DE AZURARA, GOMES. See ZURARA, GOMES EANNES DE

*EBERS, GEORG MORITZ (March 1, 1837-August 7, 1898), German Egyptologist and novelist, was born in Berlin, the son of a banker. He studied law at the University of Göttingen and oriental languages and archeology at Berlin and Jena. In 1863 he married Antonie Beck, the daughter of the mayor of Riga. He taught at Jena as a *docent* from 1865 to 1870, when he was appointed Professor of Egyptology at the University of Leipzig. He was an active and successful scholar. He made his first trip to Egypt in 1869 and published the results of his investigations in the volume *Ägypten und die Bücher Moses*. His main contribution to his field was an edition of an ancient Egyptian handbook of medicine, which he discovered at Thebes, and which has been named the *Papyrus Ebers* (1874) in his honor. A recurrence of a laming paralysis forced him to retire from teaching prematurely in 1889. He settled in Tutzing near Munich and dedicated the remainder of his life to his writing.

Ebers began his literary career with the cultural-historical novel *Eine Ägyptische Konigstochter* (1864), in which he treated the invasion and subjugation of King Psamenetich's kingdom by the Persians. This work became an instantaneous popular success and brought the author an international following. He continued to combine factual scholarship and romance in a number of well-

* ā′ bĕrs

received historical novels on Egyptian themes, including *Uarda* (1877), *Homo Sum* (1878), *Die Schwestern* (1879), *Der Kaiser* (1880), *Serapis* (1885), *Die Nilbraut* (1887), and *Kleopatra* (1894). Of this series *Homo Sum*, which treats the history of the Anchorites of the Nile Valley in the 4th century A.D., represents his finest achievement. In addition Ebers produced a series of works on historic events from the Germanic past, *Die Frau Bürgermeisterin* (1881), *Ein Wort* (1882), *Gred* (1887), *Im Blauen Hecht* (1895), and *Barbara Blomberg* (1896). Ebers also wrote his autobiography under the title *Geschichte Meines Lebens* (1893).

The abundance of archeological detail and a pleasantly light narrative style concealed the more serious deficiencies of Ebers as a writer. He was unable to create believable characters, and his works are populated with one-sided marionettes, completely lacking in depth and psychological complexity. Despite the remote settings, his figures talk and act like people of the nineteenth century.

The works of Ebers belong to the tradition of the German *Professorenroman*, for he was only one of a number of antiquarian scholars who at this time endeavored to popularize their specialized fields by means of historical romances. These novels filled a desire of the age for exotic themes, and moreover exerted a cultural appeal because of the accurately drawn milieu and the detailed descriptions of ancient customs and manners. Despite their shallowness and lack of literary quality, these works enjoyed great popularity in their time and are to a limited extent still read today.

Ebers' collected novels were translated as *Complete Works* in 1915 by C. Bell, E. Grove, and M. J. Safford. His autobiography, *The Story of My Life from Childhood to Manhood* was translated by M. J. Safford in 1893.

About: [In German—see study by R. Gosche, also O. Kraus, Der Professorenroman.]

D. G. D.

*EBNER-ESCHENBACH, MARIE, Freifrau von (née von Dubsky) (September 13, 1830-March 12, 1916), Austrian novelist, epigrammatist, poet, and dramatist, was born at Zdislawitz Castle in Moravia as Countess Dubsky. Her childhood and youth were spent partly on her country estate, partly in Vienna; in both places she absorbed the social and economic atmosphere that she was to treat in her fiction. In 1848 she married a cousin, Moritz Freiherr von Ebner-Eschen-

* äb′ nĕr ĕsh′ ĕn bäĸ

MARIE VON EBNER-ESCHENBACH

century novella became firmly established. Many of her writings are "village and castle stories" (the title of one of her collections). With striking psychological insight, innate sympathy, and gentle humor and irony she writes about the peasantry, the bourgeoisie, and the landed gentry. Her refined style is compounded of both realistic and romantically sentimental elements. Her well-known short fiction includes the charming dog story *Krambambuli, Die Kapitalistinnen,* and *Komtess Muschi.* Her most important full-length novel is *Das Gemeindekind* (1887), a sort of *Bildungsroman* about a murderer's son who is raised by the community and achieves a respected existence against great odds. Other novels once widely read are *Bozena die Magd* (1876) and *Unsühnbar* (1890). These and other works are distinguished by great narrative skill and a masterly depiction of character and reflect the author's great personal warmth, intuitive understanding of children, and interest in social questions. Her sympathy for the underprivileged must be viewed within the framework of her conservative but not uncritical belief in the aristocracy. The Catholic church and the family are the other pillars of her *Weltanschauung.*

Marie von Ebner-Eschenbach's pronounced didactic bent, which she shared with the other German writers of village tales and the "poetic realists" generally, is seen to good advantage in a form she became famous for, the epigram. She once defined an aphorism as "the last link in a long chain of thought." Her *Aphorismen* (1880) reveal her as a born educator and a bit of a satirist: "Be the first to say something that goes without saying and you will be immortal." Her aphorisms reflect a gentle, conciliatory outlook upon life, but are often tinged with irony and occasionally even acidity: "No one can write like a god who has not suffered like a dog." "If the wealthy had always loved mankind, there would be no social problems." "Modern men are born fault-finders; all they see of Achilles is his heel." "Old age either transfigures or petrifies." "A defeat proudly borne is a victory, too."

bach, fifteen years her senior, an officer and professor of physics and chemistry as well as a dabbler in literature. The marriage was childless but happy. Marie von Ebner-Eschenbach's long life, most of which she spent in Vienna where she moved in 1863, was outwardly uneventful. Her life span coincided, almost to the month, with that of her monarch, Emperor Francis Joseph I, whose Austro-Hungarian empire came to honor her as one of its greatest and most beloved epic writers.

Marie von Ebner-Eschenbach started to write lyric poetry in her teens, but these verses were inconsequential, although Franz von Grillparzer early commented on her unmistakable talent. Inspired by the performances of the Vienna Burgtheater and her personal associations with men like Grillparzer, Hebbel, Laube, and Halm, she began to write plays, among them historical dramas like *Maria Stuart in Schottland* (1860) and *Marie Roland* (1867) as well as plays of society in the French manner like *Das Waldfräulein* (a fiasco in 1873). Despite little success she persevered with her dramatic attempts for a number of years. Only in her forties did she discover herself as a story-teller of genius.

Her first great success was *Ein Spätgeborener* (1874), a satirical novella of artistic life. *Lotti die Uhrmacherin* brought her additional recognition (a child of the *Biedermeier* age, Marie von Ebner-Eschenbach amassed a remarkable collection of clocks and watches), and in the 1880's her reputation as one of the masters of the nineteenth-

In later life, Marie von Ebner-Eschenbach received many honors. On her seventieth birthday in 1900 she became the first woman to be awarded an honorary doctorate by the University of Vienna. In 1906 she published memoirs of her childhood, *Meine Kinderjahre,* and in 1914 *Meine Erinnerungen an Grillparzer* appeared. The first edition of her collected works began to appear in 1892 and eventually comprised nine volumes. A six-volume edition appeared in 1920.

Ferdinand von Saar described her as "not tall, but slender and delicately built . . . not a beautiful face, but a most expressive one . . . rather deep-set grey-blue eyes." Her broad nose and wide mouth gave her features a Slavic cast.

Das Gemeindekind was translated into English by M. A. Robinson as *The Child of the Parish* (1893). The same translator also did *Unsühnbar (Beyond Atonement,* 1892). *Krambambuli* first appeared in English in 1913, and the *Aphorisms* in 1883; both are contained in vol. XIII of Kuno Francke's *German Classics of the 19th and 20th Centuries* (1913ff.). Paul Pratt's translation of *Krambambuli* is included in *German Stories and Tales,* ed. by Robert Pick (1954).

ABOUT: Doyle, R. Catholic Atmosphere in Marie von Ebner-Eschenbach; O'Connor, E. M. Marie Ebner. [In German—see studies by A. Bettelheim, M. Necker, E. Riemann.]

H. Z.

The Bettmann Archive

EÇA DE QUEIRÓS

*EÇA DE QUEIRÓS, JOSÉ MARIA DE

(November 25, 1845-August 16, 1900), Portuguese novelist, was born in Póvoa-de-Varzim; he spent his childhood and adolescence away from the parental home. While taking a law degree at the University of Coimbra he joined the students' group later identified as "Coimbra Generation," which was to play an important role in modern Portuguese life and letters. The Coimbra Group rebelled in a noisy polemic (1865), not only against the tyranny of the official literary taste of their Lisbon elders, but against all their aesthetic, philosophical, and historical concepts as well. Eça did not take an active part in the dispute but he established a life-long identification with the outstanding members of the group. Later, in 1871, he participated in the "Democratic Lectures," organized in Lisbon by the "Coimbra Generation," now mature. After graduation, Eça first engaged in political journalism in Évora and then halfheartedly practiced law in Lisbon. In 1869 he attended the opening of the Suez Canal as a member of the Portuguese official party and traveled through the Near East, gathering impressions which he was to use later in his writings. After a period as a municipal administrator in Leiria he entered the Foreign Service, which took him to consular posts in Cuba (1873-74), England (1874-88) and finally to Paris (1888-1900), where he died.

His early literary work—posthumously collected as *Prosas Bárbaras* (1905)—reveals

* ã′ sà thĕ kā ē rôsh′

him as under multiple foreign influences, mostly romantic, and very eagerly in search of a new literary idiom. In 1870 he undertook with his friend Ramalho Ortigão the serial publication of a mystery story, *O Mistério da Estrada de Sintra.* A year after, both young men started a monthly review, *As Farpas,* taking to task all aspects of national life; in this Eça evidenced his biting polemic irony and his bent for reform. He collected his contributions in 1890-91 under the title *Uma Campanha Alegre.*

After defending in a lecture in Lisbon (1871) the need for a new art, more closely concerned with the vital issues of life and the times, he produced his first novel, *O Crime do Padre Amaro* (1875), which he reworked twice. It deals with a young priest's love affair with a girl in a sordid provincial atmosphere, treated in faithful detail and with all the characteristics of determinism and psycho-physiological analysis. This novel marks the beginning of orthodox realism in Portugal. The social scene was broadened in *O Primo Basílio* (1878), in which, through a case of adultery reminiscent of *Madame Bovary,* the moral fabric of the Lisbon middle class is analyzed. These two novels, with their naturalistic rendering, were the object of virulent attack from conservative quarters. Leaflets were published cautioning mothers about the dangers of Eça's brand of fiction. His followers entered into violent polemics with Castelo Branco, the old master of the romantic novel—who carried his belligerency so far as to write parodies of the new manner. Eça's last contribution to realism was *Os Maias* (1888), where the great financial, political, aristocratic, and literary circles of Lisbon were depicted with devastating satire. Its composition dates back almost a decade. It was already listed in a vast plan of "Scenes of Portuguese Life," in the style of Balzac's *Comédie Humaine,* which Eça early conceived and later abandoned. Because of the rôle he played as chief exponent of realism in Portugal he has been sometimes called the Portuguese Zola, an unjust name, since naturalism was only a passing and subordinate ingredient of his art, from which he soon freed himself to affirm his unequivocal identity as a novelist.

His evolution was natural and harmonious. The discipline of observation had taught him how to control his imagination. He was thus able to achieve his own manner, lyrical, ironic, suggestive: a mixture of romantic fancy and down-to-earth realistic probity. In *O Mandarim* (1880), a delightful reworking of the old Faustian theme, we see the results of putting the exact descriptive processes of realism at the service of his free flights into the exotic and the fantastic. "On the rugged nakedness of truth—the diaphanous mantle of fancy" is the motto which opens *A Relíquia (The Relic,* 1887) where a sordidly picaresque tale of cupidity and religious hypocrisy encases a marvelously poetical retelling of the Passion. The Gospels had always attracted him as a source of themes, and his ability as a short-story writer (see *Contos,* a collection published in 1902) found perhaps its highest expression in *Suave Milagre (Sweet Miracle,* 1898), a tale of Christ which has had nine English editions.

Because of his irony in the treatment of Portuguese life he was accused of being unpatriotic, but in fact he satirized his country out of love for her and the wish to improve her. Under his mockery and his ironical despair, characteristically Lusitanian, runs a deep current of tenderness, which revealed itself in *A Ilustre Casa de Ramires* (1900) and reached rhapsodic undertones in *A Cidade e as Serras (The City and the Mountains,* 1901), where a plea for the return to nature extends into a hymn to the landscape and folk of Portugal. This return to simplicity, coupled with the late nineteenth century love for neoprimitivism is the explanation of the pre-Raphaelite spirit of his saints' legends, included in *Últimas Páginas* (1911). He projected the richness of his own personality in the apocryphal biography and let-

ters of a wealthy, ironical, and sentimental dandy, embodiment of the archetypal ideal of his generation *(Correspondência de Fradique Mendes,* 1900). Eça's work as journalist and essay writer, collected after his death in several volumes, further attests to his versatility and great gifts as an observer of the complex panorama of the life and culture of his times in Europe and the world. The influence of his style, urbane, gently skeptical and humorous, is still being felt not only in Portugal and Brazil but in the whole Hispanic world.

English translations include *Dragon's Teeth* by M. J. Serrano (1889), *The Relic,* by A. F. G. Bell (1925); *The Sweet Miracle,* by E. Prestage in 1904, reprinted many times since; *José Mathis and A Man of Talent,* by L. Marques (1947); and two translations by Roy Campbell—*Cousin Bazilio* (1953) and *The City and the Mountains* (1955). *The Sin of Father Amaro* was translated by Nan Flanagan (1962). Besides English his works have been translated into Spanish, French, German, Italian, Russian, Polish, Czech, Hungarian, Swedish, Dutch and Catalan.

ABOUT: Bjorkman, E. Current Reviews; Boyd, E. Studies from Ten Literatures. [In Spanish and Portuguese—see studies by A. Cabral, J. G. Simões, E. G. Da Cal.]

E. G. DA C.

*ECHEGARAY Y EIZAGUIRRE, JOSÉ (April 19, 1832-September 14, 1916), Spanish dramatist, was born in Madrid. His father, a professor of Greek, came from Saragossa, while his mother was a Basque. At the age of three he was taken to Murcia, and, he tells us, his earliest memories have to do with attending the theatre. At fourteen he went to Madrid where he prepared to enter the Escuela de Caminos. Although he was an outstanding student, he found time to attend the theatre regularly and witnessed the premières of plays by Ayala, Tamayo, García Gutiérrez, Hartzenbusch, and many other romantic and neoromantic dramatists. After completing his schooling, he worked as an engineer in Almería and Granada, then became a teacher at the Escuela de Caminos where he achieved eminence as a physicist and mathematician. In 1866 he was elected to the Academy of Exact Sciences; he wrote articles on economics for such reviews as *La Razón* and *El Economista,* and was an advocate of free trade. After the September 1868 revolution he was offered the post of Director of Public Works; in 1869 he was elected Deputy to the Cortes Constituyentes. He was present at the reception of Prince Amadeo of Savoy, who came to rule Spain, and held the portfolio of Fomento and Hacienda until 1873 (in 1904

* ā chā gä rī′ ē ā thä gēr′ rā

251

ECHEGARAY Y EIZAGUIRRE

ECHEGARAY

he was again to be Minister of Hacienda for a short time). In 1883 he was elected to the Spanish Royal Academy, and in 1904 he shared the Nobel Prize for Literature with Frédéric Mistral, the first Spaniard to be awarded that honor "in appreciation of his comprehensive and intellectual authorship which, in an independent and original way, has brought to life again the great traditions of the Spanish drama."

Echegaray, despite his multiple other interests, wrote sixty-eight plays, most of which are all but forgotten today. He fed the public strong sensations, parricides, dishonor, suicide. Valbuena Prat says of his theatre: "The mixture of grandeur and artificial effects, of pathos with exaggeration makes his plays both brilliant and wild." His first play, *El Libro Talonario*, was written in 1874 under the anagram "Jorge Hayaseca." But titles of some of his more important productions are clues to the tenor of his writing: *La Esposa del Vengador* (1874), *En el Puño de la Espada* (1875), *Morir por no Despertar, En el Seno de la Muerte, Bodas Trágicas* (all in 1879). All are built on the cumulative effects of honor and hair-raising situations. Other plays such as *En el Pilar y en la Cruz* and *La Muerte en los Labios* denounce the cruelty shown by both Catholic and Protestant zealots. Echegaray was slowly moving, however, in the direction of contemporary themes for his plays and from verse to prose. In 1877 he wrote one of his most famous pieces: *Ó Locura ó Santidad,* centering about a highly improbable yet mov-

ing *crise de conscience* in which the hero who, as a child, had been substituted for another that had died, resolves to give his property up to its rightful owners. The play which shares first rank with *Ó Locura ó Santidad* among Echegaray's works is *El Gran Galeoto* (1881), in which gossip is responsible for a guilty passion that ends in death for the two central characters.

With the years, Echegaray underwent the influence of Dumas *fils*, Björnson, and Sudermann. His *Hijo de Don Juan* (1892), reminiscent of Ibsen's *Ghosts,* is the study of the effect of a debauchee's sins upon his son, a theme he again treated in 1902 in *Malas Herencias.* Other noteworthy plays were *El Poder de la Impotencia* (1893), *La Calumnia por Castigo* (1897), *La Duda* (1898), and his last great triumph, *El Loco Diós* (1900).

Although since his death, Echegaray's reputation has fallen into decline, during the major part of his life he had no rivals. The great romantic and neoromantic dramatists were either dead or silent and Benavente did not begin his career until 1894. Echegaray was also wise enough to write many dramas to fit the talents of outstanding actors and actresses of his day. His plots were artificial, the psychology of his characters obvious, his effects sensational, and his rhetoric thundering. Yet Benavente said of him that "he made multitudes think and feel. . . . In half a century there is no theatrical writing that can compare with his in quantity, variety, and creative force."

Ó Locura ó Santidad was translated by H. Lynch in 1895 as *Folly or Saintliness* and by R. Lansing as *Madman or Saint* (*Poet Lore,* 1912). *El Gran Galeoto* was translated as *The Great Galeoto* by H. Lynch in 1895 and reprinted in the *Drama League Series of Plays.* Eleanor Bontecou's translation of the same play is included in T. H. Dickinson's *Continental Plays,* II and in B. H. Clark's *Masterpieces of Modern Spanish Drama.* There is still another translation of the same play by J. S. Fassett (1914). Both *Mariana* and *The Son of Don Juan* were translated by J. Graham in 1895. *Mariana* was translated again by F. Sarda and C. D. S. Wupperman in 1909. *The Madman Divine* (*El Loco Diós*) was translated by E. H. West in *Poet Lore* (1908). *El Hombre Negro* was translated by E. Watson as *The Man in Black; Siempre en Ridículo* as *Always Ridiculous* by T. W. Gilkyson (*Poet Lore,* 1916). *The Street Singer* (*La Cantante Callejera*), translated by J. G. Underhill, is in F. Shay's *Twenty-five Short Plays, International* (1925).

ABOUT: Marble, A. The Nobel Prize Winners in Literature; Young, J. R. José Echegaray: a Study of his Dramatic Technique. [In French—see Curzon, H. de, Le Théâtre de José Echegaray. In Spanish—see Martínez Olmedilla, A. José Echegaray.]

M. N

*ECKERMANN, JOHANN PETER

(September 21, 1792-December 3, 1854), German writer, was born in Winsen an der Luhe near Lüneburg, the youngest son of Adolf Eckermann and his second wife, Dorothea Sophie *née* Schierhorn. His family was poor and humble. Young Peter did odd jobs, such as collecting acorns and herding cattle, even accompanying his father on his rounds as peddler, while his mother spun wool at home. Until the age of fourteen he had little schooling, barely being able to read and write, but his talent in drawing eventually attracted the attention of some socially prominent persons. In 1808 he started out as a government clerk, eventually rising to the post of *mairie-secrétaire* in Bevensen. At the beginning of the War of Liberation he joined a volunteer corps and, being stationed in Belgium, made good use of his spare time by visiting the art galleries, particularly those in Brussels.

On his return Eckermann decided to study art in Hanover, but realized early that he lacked the necessary talent and income to pursue such a course. Recovering from a grave illness, he again turned to clerking, this time in the Quartermaster Section of the Hanoverian War Department. With like-minded youths he took a keen interest in German literature, gradually advancing from Klopstock to Schiller. Under the influence of Körner's *Leyer und Schwert* he wrote a lengthy poem on the return of the victorious troops in 1815 which was published several times locally. From the study of Schiller he turned to Goethe, who now became his idol. Conscious of his lack of a conventional education, Eckermann took private lessons in Latin and soon, aided by his understanding superiors, enrolled in a *Gymnasium* at the age of twenty-five. In 1819 he became engaged to Johanna Bertram, the daughter of a retired merchant and nine years his junior.

On the publication of his *Gedichte* (1821), poems full of trust and faith, Eckermann mailed a copy to Goethe and followed the gift in person, but arrived too late, since Goethe had already left for Eger. Back in Hanover, he finally succeeded in retiring from his post at full pay for two years and enrolled at the University of Göttingen, nominally to study law, but actually attending lectures on history and literature. After three semesters he retired to Empelde near Hanover and wrote his *Beyträge zur Poesie mit besonderer Hinweisung auf Goethe* (1823), a book containing aphorisms, discussions on the nature of tragedy, of form, of poetic subject matter, of

* ĕk′ ẽr män

ECKERMANN

criticism, and, most important, an analysis of Goethe's *Elective Affinities* which drew attention to the hitherto little appreciated novel. The style is clear and succinct and the entire book strangely breathes the spirit of the later Goethe. During all this time Eckermann knew in his heart that he was chosen to befriend Goethe, and even dreamt of him.

In May 1823 he wrote a letter to Goethe, accompanied by a manuscript copy of his *Beyträge*. Following on foot, he arrived in Weimar on June 9 and had his first meeting with the poet the next day. At that moment, fortunately, Goethe was looking for an archivist or philologist to help him sift his wealth of material for the *Ausgabe Letzter Hand*, and Eckermann, footloose and with his bridges burned behind him, came just in time. Having first tested his abilities, Goethe kept Eckermann near him until his death in 1832, with occasional necessary interruptions, such as Eckermann's journey to Italy in the company of the ill-fated August von Goethe. These nine years of servitude to the master were decisive for Eckermann. Gradually and on the advice of Goethe, Eckermann gave up all hopes of ever becoming a great poet in his own right. He literally dedicated his life to Goethe. To be sure, he wrote occasional poems which were gathered in one volume of *Gedichte* (1838), and he composed some excellent critical studies and reviews. But his most important task was to assist Goethe. Slowly Eckermann rose from the position of stranger and pupil to that of trusted friend in the Goethe household. Goethe succeeded in

253

having an honorary degree from the University of Jena conferred upon him in 1825. Eking out a precarious existence by teaching English pupils and eventually becoming the ill-paid tutor to Prince Karl Alexander, Eckermann was the first to read the "Marienbader Elegy" and the "Novelle." He, as Goethe remarked, was the prompter for *Faust II* and *Dichtung und Wahrheit*, and he had a hand in shaping *Wilhelm Meisters Wanderjahre*. This alone would have been sufficient reason to earn for him a firm place in the annals of German literature. But Eckermann did more.

As early as 1824 Eckermann had planned to publish a volume of conversations with Goethe. One year later there is clear proof that Goethe knew of this, encouraged it, and corrected some chapters. Eventually he and his son decided that these conversations should not appear in print before his death. With this also in mind, Goethe undertook to teach Eckermann, actually giving him lessons in his *Farbenlehre* and his doctrine of science. On the average Eckermann visited Goethe almost every third day throughout these years. From time to time he jotted down notes in his diary, but these entries apparently consisted of little more than single phrases and words; many meetings were not even mentioned. On that basis Eckermann finally put together his most important work, the *Gespräche mit Goethe in den Letzten Jahren seines Lebens* (I and II, 1836; III, 1848, based on Soret's diaries). He showed himself there to be a considerable artist, for compared with the conversations published by Falk, Riemer, or von Müller, he did not give a chronological and therefore hodge-podge account of Goethe's occasional statements, but tried to convey the essence of Goethe's thought and personality during the last years of his life. As such, Eckermann's *Conversations with Goethe* are a distillate of and sequel to Goethe's own writings, as was clearly recognized by Goethe himself. Eckermann quite consciously set out to draw a picture of Goethe as he saw him in his mind, not a realistic one of the old, often grumpy and angry man, but one of the classical, clear, Olympian, and universally-minded sage that has become the household image in Germany. Eckermann's *Conversations* are literature, not history.

While in Weimar, Eckermann during the years 1828-31 was deeply in love with the young singer Auguste Kladzig, but loyalty won, and he married Johanna Bertram, only to lose her in childbed in 1834; he had one son, Karl. Goethe entrusted to Eckermann the publication of his *Nachgelassene Schriften* (posthumous works, 1832-33); with Riemer, Eckermann brought out the complete works in 40 volumes (1839-40). In 1842 he was appointed grand-ducal councilor, drawing a small pension. He lived in Weimar most of the time, surrounded by his beloved birds, and he died planning a fourth volume of the *Conversations*.

Eckermann's *Conversations* were not given the reception they deserved. Although they were acclaimed widely by individuals, the time was against the Olympian and pagan spirit of the work. For today's recognition Nietzsche's statement may serve as example: "If one disregards Goethe's works and particularly Goethe's *Conversations with Eckermann*, which is the best German book there is—what is left of German prose-works that deserve to be read over and over again?" (1879). In 1939 the twenty-second edition of the *Conversations* appeared in Germany.

Eckermann's character cannot be compared with that of Boswell. He was never a foil for his master; he was shy and reticent; he served truly and sincerely, and there is proof enough to show that Goethe quite consciously used this loyalty. He was so receptive to Goethe that even his style is that of the old Goethe: some of the letters he wrote in Goethe's name are more Goethean than the poet's own. It is no accident that Heine after reading Eckermann's *Beyträge*, called him Goethe's "parrot."

The first English translation of the *Conversations* was that of Margaret Fuller (Boston, 1839), which omits the portions dealing with science. The complete translation by John Oxenford (London, 1850) surpasses the original in arranging the third volume within the first two; it is the basis for most later selective editions. The last complete Oxenford translation came out in the Everyman series, with an introduction by H. Ellis (1931). Eckermann's other writings have not been translated.

ABOUT: Canadian Monthly, XVI; Dublin University Magazine, XXXVII: London and Holborn Quarterly Review, October 1942; Spectator, August 25, 1944. [In German—see studies by E. Castle, H. H. Houben, J. Petersen.]

R. L. K.

ECKHART, "MEISTER" (Johannes Eccard or Eckart or Eckardt)

ECKHART, "MEISTER" (Johannes Eccard or Eckart or Eckardt) (c. 1260-1327), German mystic and theologian, was born in the Thuringian town of Hochheim. In Erfurt he entered the most aristocratic and intellectual monastic order of his time, the Dominicans. He also studied in Cologne, the stronghold of scholasticism, as represented by Albertus Magnus and Thomas Aquinas, and rose to high honors in his order. When still a young man, he was elected prior of the Erfurt convent, then appointed vicar of Bohemia. On a teaching mission to Paris about 1300 he was granted the title of *magister,* which, in the German form *meister,* became a part of his name.

The Church overlooked the heresy of his views on Christian dogma as long as he confined them to his writings in Latin or German. As head of the Dominican house in Strasbourg he began his activity as a powerful and extremely popular preacher in the German vernacular, expounding the tenets of scholastic philosophy to an audience of nuns and laymen. Now the Church could no longer disregard his frequent infringements of the dogma. In 1326 he was summoned to the court of the Archbishop of Cologne. In his famous defense, not published until the 1920's, Eckhart explained the seeming heresies of his writings and sermons as misunderstandings on the part of ignorant readers and listeners. A bull issued by Pope John XXII in 1329 (after Eckhart's death) condemned twenty-eight of his propositions as heretical but stated that Eckhart had subjected himself to papal authority. The essence of his teachings lived on in the subterranean currents of German mysticism. Meister Eckhart owes his rediscovery to the interest of the German romanticists in unorthodox manifestations of spiritual life.

Of all the great German mystics Meister Eckhart is the most learned, the most intellectual, the most systematic thinker. While his chief work in Latin, the *Opus Tripartitum,* is a perfect example of scholastic dialectics, his writings in German and especially his sermons are practical guides to the attainment of true spiritual life. He shocks his readers or listeners with seemingly paradoxical statements, which he proves to be in complete agreement with well-known Biblical truths; and he verifies his interpretations with frequent quotations from ancient and post-Hellenic philosophers, especially from his favorite source, Plotinus. While he touches in his writings and in his sermons on nearly all the important problems of speculative philosophy, their central theme refers directly to the conduct of life, i.e., the relationship between God as the only true reality and the human soul as the only place in the universe where God can reveal Himself in the truth of His being. Though the created soul is not identical with God, the uncreated Absolute, there is yet something in the soul, a core, a quality, the *scintilla animae,* the

Fünklein, as Eckhart calls it in German, which, like God, is uncreated and through which He may enter a human life and take over its direction. Every human being is potentially the place where the miracle of the incarnation may be repeated, and man has no nobler task in the course of his life than to create the conditions under which God may be once more allowed to beget His son. The whole life of Christ is to Eckhart nothing else than the exemplary visible form of God's ever desired and ever repeated entrance and participation in human existence.

The teachings of Eckhart were greeted with enthusiasm by those representatives of German idealism who, in contrast to Kant, believed that absolute reality could be apprehended on a higher level of human experience. But the most important impact of Eckhart on German mentality and on German letters originated from his use of the vernacular in the discussion of ultimate truths. He enriched the German language with terms in which even the most abstract concepts assume some emotional force.

Though Eckhart did not openly deny the necessity of institutional religion, it was implicit in his teachings that the Church was not indispensable as an instrument of mediation between God and man, and that every human being was potentially able to place himself directly under the guidance of divine grace. In English-speaking countries the Quakers became especially interested in Meister Eckhart, looking upon him as an early authority in support of their beliefs.

None of Meister Eckhart's works is completely translated into English. This is partly due to the fact that the authenticity and classification of Eckhart's writings are still a matter of philological research. In 1924 C. de B. Evans published the first volume of his translation of Franz Pfeiffer's extensive German Eckhart edition of 1857, followed in 1931 by Vol. 2. In 1941 Raymond Bernard Blakney offered "A Modern Translation" of approximately half of the German works attributed to Meister Eckhart. His collection includes the first translation into a modern language of Eckhart's defense against the accusation of heresy. See also J. M. Clark's *Meister Eckhart: An Introduction to the Study of his Works with an Anthology of his Sermons* (1957) ; J. M. Clark and J. V. Skinner, *Meister Eckhart: Selected Treatises and Sermons* (1958) ; O. Karrer *Meister Eckhart Speaks* (translations by E. Strakosch, 1957).

ABOUT: Cheney, S. Men Who Have Walked with God ; Clark, J. M. The Great German Mystics, *also* Meister Eckhart: An Introduction to the Study of his Works; Jones, R. The Flowering of Mysticism; Pearson, K. "Meister Eckhart" *in* Mind, X. [In German—see studies by O. Bolza, A. Dempf, H. Haacke.]

F. R.

*EICHENDORFF, JOSEPH KARL BENEDIKT, Freiherr von (March 10, 1788-November 26, 1857), German poet, was born in his family's castle, Lubowitz, in Silesia. His father, Adolf, Freiherr von Eichendorff, and mother, Karoline, *née* von Kloch, were less interested in the arts than in the entertainments and sports that were the traditional hallmarks of landed nobility. During his relatively carefree childhood, young Joseph wandered in the nearby gardens and woods and accompanied his father on the hunting expeditions that were to play such a conspicuous rôle in his poetry. With his older brother Wilhelm, Joseph received his early education, under strict Catholic lines, from a private tutor. Before he was ten he had already written a tragedy and read widely, though sometimes secretly, in travel books, French and English novels, folk tales, and the Bible. In 1801 the Eichendorff brothers entered the Catholic high school in Breslau, where Joseph often remained awake all night enthusiastically reading the Greek poets, but where his creative work consisted chiefly of humorous contributions to the school paper.

In 1805 the brothers entered the University of Halle. Joseph quickly came under the influence of the new romanticism spreading through Germany. He was especially impressed by the lectures of the Norwegian philosopher Henrik Steffens, a member of the Jena romantic circle. In 1807 the brothers moved to Heidelberg, then the chief center of the younger romantics. Here Joseph associated closely with Josef Görres, whose synthesis of romantic and Catholic ideas had a decisive effect on his own thought, and with Clemens Brentano and Achim von Arnim, whose collection of folk lyrics, *Des Knaben Wunderhorn* (1805-08), greatly influenced him. In 1808 a Heidelberg friend helped him obtain his first publication of poems, and in the same year the brothers journeyed to Paris, where Joseph performed some editorial work for Görres on German manuscripts in the imperial library. The same year the brothers returned to Lubowitz.

Immediately on settling down, Joseph started his autobiographical novel *Ahnung und Gegenwart* (published 1815), sketched out many of his later stories, composed a large number of lyrics, and began to collect sayings and fairy tales from the local Polish peasantry. The following year the brothers visited Berlin, where they met the romantic circle then flourishing there and in 1810 went to Vienna, where they associated with the

* i′ ḱĕn dôrf

EICHENDORFF

recently converted Friedrich Schlegel and other Catholic intellectuals. They had gone there in order to join the Austrian civil service, in which Wilhelm remained throughout his life. Joseph, temperamentally and religiously drawn to the Viennese atmosphere, would also have remained if he had not been called back to Silesia in 1813 for military service in the war against Napoleon. In 1815 he entered Paris as an officer of the conquering army. In 1814 he had married Luise von Larisch. As a result of his father's extravagance and the war, the family estate was sold and Joseph took up a regular career as civil servant. He worked in Breslau as an assessor in 1816-19 and in 1820 formally entered the civil service of Prussia, in whose ministry for cultural affairs he spent most of his remaining years.

In sharp contrast to his unstable friend Clemens Maria Brentano, who divided honors with him for foremost rank among the younger romantic poets, Eichendorff lived the unruffled life of a bureaucrat and family man. "Through the opportunities I have for quiet and for the resolute concentration of my powers I gain back twice the time I lose through my job," he once wrote. His contemporaries remarked on the air of serenity and boyish good humor about him. His job, which specialized in governmental relations with the Catholic church and schools, took him successively to Danzig, Königsberg, and Berlin. After resigning in 1844, he devoted his full time to writing and moved about frequently until his death in his daughter's home in Neisse, where he is buried. His many writings, besides his first novel, include a number of other prose narratives, dramas, political essays (of consistently conservative orientation), and some literary criticism, including a history of German literature (1857) from the Catholic point of view. But his reputation rests on his lyrics and on two or three short novels. His poetry is built out of a relatively small number of images which are evoked as though freshly perceived again and again. He is pre-eminently the poet of the dim, mysterious forest, of the guitar-strumming wanderer, moonlit castles and marble statues, of yearning for a distant home—all these themes being unified by an almost pagan joy in nature and simple faith in God. Nearly all his best work follows. the accustomed meters of the folk song, whose effect of spontaneity he has captured so well that his countrymen often mistake his poems for genuine folk songs. His prose masterpieces, *Das Marmorbild* (1819) and *Aus dem Leben eines Taugenichts* (1826), are created out of the same symbolic world as the poetry and, for that matter, are themselves richly interspersed with lyrics. Eichendorff ranks today among the principal masters of the German lyric, but outside Germany his poems are known chiefly through their musical settings by Schumann, Brahms, and Hugo Wolf.

The Marble Statue has been translated by F. E. Pierce (in the Pierce-Schreiber *Fiction and Fantasy of German Romance*, 1927). The *Taugenichts* has appeared in English, under varying titles, in the translations of C. Marvel (1864), C. G. Leland (1886), A. L Wister (1889) and, most recently, under the title *Memoirs of a Good-for-Nothing*, by B. Q. Morgan (1955). A selection of poems entitled *The Happy Wanderer* has been translated by M. Rossy (1925).

ABOUT: Prawer, S. S. German Lyric Poetry; Skidmore, W. E. Eichendorff's Weltanschauung as Revealed in His Language; Tymms, R. German Romantic Literature [In German—see studies by H. Brandenburg, H. V. Koeningswald, J. Nadler, P. Stöcklein, F. Strich.]

H. L.

"EL SOLITARIO." See ESTÉBANEZ CALDERÓN, SERAFÍN

ELIGIUS FRANZ JOSEPH, Reichsfreiherr von MÜNCH-BELLINGHAUSEN. See "HALM, FRIEDRICH"

ELIJAH BEN SOLOMON, "Gaon of Vilna" (April 23, 1720-October 17, 1797), Hebrew religious writer, was born in Vilna,

Lithuania, of a family possessing a long tradition of rabbinic scholarship. Other than that he was the eldest of five brothers, little is known of his childhood save many demonstrations of astonishing intellectual powers. Even discounting legendary accretions, it appears that Elijah delivered Talmudic discourses to a learned audience at the age of six and by the time he reached his religious majority he had mastered the whole Talmud and its ancillary works. He seems to have been married at the customary youthful age of eighteen to Anna of Keidan, by whom he had several children. Tradition relates that he spent several years wandering in atonement for sin, but this is dubious. By 1750 he was living in the seclusion of his study, where he pursued his scholarship with unflagging diligence and without interruption until his death. Elijah declined all public positions and remained a private person, yet he was the idol of his learned city, reputedly the "Jerusalem of Lithuania." Only in his last years did he break his rule in order to combat the new Hasidic movement, which stressed emotional and enthusiastic religion and tended to belittle Elijah's type of study. He lived an ascetic life, which he also enjoined upon his family.

Rabbi Elijah was the master of rabbinic literature, in all its branches. He emphasized the study of certain areas which had lain neglected, such as the Palestinian (in distinction to the better known Babylonian) Talmud, as well as early homiletic works. The study of textual variants and attempts to clarify the Talmudic text by emendation are characteristic of his method, and have caused him to be regarded as the founder of modern textual study of rabbinic literature. The "Gaon of Vilna" stressed the importance of studying the Bible and Hebrew grammar—subjects little studied in those days by advanced students. He also recommended the study of mathematics and astronomy for full understanding of certain portions of rabbinic literature.

Rabbi Elijah composed many commentaries, notes, and glosses, to Biblical, rabbinic, and mystical literature. Some are still unpublished; none has been translated.

ABOUT: Ginzberg, L. Students, Scholars, and Saints; Schechter, S. Studies in Judaism, I.

L. P. G.

ELISABETH, Queen Consort of Charles I, King of Rumania (pseudonym "CARMEN SYLVA") (December 29, 1843-March 2, 1916), Rumanian writer, was of

ELISABETH

ELISABETH ("CARMEN SYLVA")

German birth and ancestry and wrote in German. She was born in the ancient family castle of Neuwied in the Rhine country, the daughter of Prince Herman of Wied and Princess Maria of Nassau.

On the surface Elisabeth's life was almost one of a fairy-tale princess. Beautiful, gifted, and charming, she grew up in a wealthy household, had every advantage which the splendid though doomed nineteenth century aristocracy could offer (including piano lessons from Clara Schumann), married a prince and later became his queen, lived a full rich life of service to her people, and won wide reputation for her stories, novels, and plays.

But beneath the surface Elisabeth's life was less idyllic. Her childhood was saddened by the protracted illness of a younger brother who died after years of agony in 1862. Both her mother and her father were in poor health too, and she spent many of her early years in bedside vigils in sickrooms. Her only release was a long visit to a relative at the Russian court and periods of travel on the continent and in England. In 1869, then twenty-six and by the standards of the day almost a spinster, she married Prince Charles of Hohenzollern-Sigmaringen, who had recently been made prince of a "new" nation freed from Austrian domination—Rumania. Her marriage, as she candidly admitted, was not a love match. Prince Charles was stern and humorless and devoted to duty. In something of the same spirit she accepted her

new responsibilities and learned the language and history of her adopted country. Her greatest joy was her daughter Marie, born in 1870, whom she idolized, and her greatest tragedy—one from which she never fully recovered—was the child's death four years later.

Elisabeth plunged into feverish activity after the tragedy. She established schools and orphanages, asylums and hospitals. Discovering that there were no school books or popular books in the language of the Rumanian people, she translated books from the French. In her later years her devotion to the people, and especially to children, won her the epithet—which she enjoyed—"Mama Regina." When the Turko-Russian war broke out, Rumania was the battleground, and Princess Elisabeth established emergency hospitals and nursed the wounded. As a result of this war, Rumania achieved its independence as a kingdom and in 1881 Prince Charles and she were crowned king and queen.

Queen Elisabeth had been writing verses and stories since childhood, but it was not until after her daughter's death that she turned her serious attention to writing. She studied poetic composition under the Rumanian poet Alexandri (see sketch above), and in 1880 she published her first book under the pseudonym "Carmen Sylva"—a collection of Rumanian poems which she had translated into German. In the next year she published her first book of original poems, *Stürme*. From that time until her death she wrote steadily—poems, collections of fairy tales, short stories, novels (two of these— *Aus Zwei Welten*, 1884, and *Astra*, 1886, were written in collaboration with her lady-in-waiting Mete Kremnitz), and plays— *Frauenmuth* (1890) and *Meister Manole*, a tragedy (1892). Carmen Sylva's poetry is pleasant to read but not memorable. The poems were written hastily and are somewhat too facile, though they have a certain lyric freshness.

Her most popular book was *Fairy Tales of Pilesh*, which sold over a million copies. These tales for children are lively and imaginative. Their background is the region of Castle Pilesh at Sinaia, an elegant and elaborately decorated castle where she spent her summers. But probably her most artistically successful book was *Pensées d'une Reine* (*Thoughts of a Queen*), a book of aphorisms which received the Prix Botta of the French Academy in 1888. These are wise and witty and reflect a personality mellowed by years of court life—"A prince requires nothing but eyes and ears; he does not need a mouth except to smile"; "A little contradiction animates conversation. This explains why courts are so dull."

An interesting sidelight of Carmen Sylva's literary career was the curious friendship which sprang up between her and the French writer Pierre Loti. He had read a French translation of her poem *Jehovah* and sent her a copy of his *Pêcheur d'Islande*. She admired the book greatly, translated it into German, and invited him to visit her in Rumania. They became fast friends—though, because of a rather silly practical joke which misfired, King Charles took an intense dislike to him.

The many photographs of Carmen Sylva show a strikingly handsome woman with delicate features, thoughtful, deep-set eyes, and curly hair. Even in her later years she retained her beauty. She lived long enough into the twentieth century to see the holocaust of World War I; she died, at seventy-two, in Bucharest.

Many of Carmen Sylva's poems were translated into English. A good selection appears in the Warner Library. The collection *Songs of Toil* was translated by J. E. Bowen (1888). Her *Märchen einer Köningen* was translated in 1909 as *A Real Queen's Fairy Book* by E. Hopkirk, who also translated her reminiscences *From Memory's Shrine* in 1911. Other translations include *Edleen Vaughan: or, Paths of Peril* (1891), *A Heart Regained*, by Mrs M. A. Mitchell (1888), *Legends from River and Mountain* (with A. Strettell, 1896), *Poems,* by A. H. Exner, and *Thoughts of a Queen,* by H. S. Edwards (1890).

ABOUT: Bowen, J. E. *Introduction to* Songs of Toil; Carmen Sylva, From Memory's Shrine; London Magazine. XXXI (1913-14); Vacaresco, H. Kings and Queens I Have Known. [In French—Bengesco, F. Carmen Sylva Intime; Stern, L. Pierre Loti et Carmen Sylva.]

*EMINESCU, MIHAIL (January 1850-June 15, 1889), Rumanian poet, was born Mihail Emin or Imin, the family name being later changed to Eminovici and finally "Rumanianized" to Eminescu. He was the sixth child in a family of ten. His birthplace was near Botoshani in northern Moldavia, a region crowded with historic associations. It was a fitting background for the boy who was to become the greatest Rumanian poet of his century, for he early developed a sensitivity to his native cultural traditions, to legends, to the medieval past. Eminescu went to school at Czernowitz and published some poems in the magazine *Familia* when he was only fifteen.

* ĕ mē nĕ′ skōō

At sixteen he ran away from home to join a troupe of traveling actors in which he served as actor, prompter, and stage manager. For three years he traveled with the company—an experience which took him to Vienna, Jena, and Berlin, and introduced him to European culture. He studied at the University of Vienna in 1869 and spent two years (1872-74) at the University of Berlin on a scholarship. Although he never took a degree he obviously acquired an excellent education—he knew classical languages, Sanskrit (he wrote a Sanskrit grammar), French, and German. He was deeply influenced by the philosophy of Schopenhauer, and his poetry shows evidence of his immersion in the French romantics, especially Musset and Vigny.

Upon his return to his native land in 1874 Eminescu was made school inspector and librarian at the University of Jassy. Here he had an opportunity to delve into old manuscripts and indulge his love for the medieval Rumanian past which he far preferred to the conventional society of his own day.

Eminescu's beautiful and imaginative poetry is marked by a combination of simple language and profound thought. He first won recognition as a poet in 1870 with two poems published in *Convorbiri Literare*— "Venera si Madona" and "Epigonii." The best of his later works are the somber "Emperor and Proletarian" in which, in an essentially pessimistic spirit, he portrays the class struggle, and "Calin," a poem which dwells on the beauties of nature, extolls the simple peasant life, and draws upon medieval legend.

From 1877 to 1883 Eminescu edited *Timpul,* a conservative paper. In the latter year he suffered his first attack of insanity, which was hereditary in his family. Temporarily cured, he returned to the University of Jassy as assistant librarian, but he suffered a relapse in 1886. Following another lucid period, he had a final attack in 1889 and died soon after. In all Eminescu wrote some sixty poems, one novel, and several philosophical and fairy tales. He had a great influence on Rumanian writers of his own era.

Some of Eminescu's works were translated into French, German, Italian, and English *(Poems of Mihail Eminescu,* translated by E. S. Pankhurst and I. O. Stefanovici, 1930).

ABOUT: Iorga, N. *preface to* Poems of Mihail Eminescu; American Slavic and East European Review, April 1948. [In French—Nanu, D. A. Le Poète Eminescu et la Poésie Lyrique Française.]

*ENCINA, JUAN DEL (1468-1529?), Spanish musician, playwright, and poet, often called the "patriarch of the Spanish theatre," was born in Encina or Encinas near Salamanca. He was the son of Juan de Fermoselle, a shoemaker, but in 1490, following a Renaissance fashion, adopted the name of Encina with all its Virgilian connotations. It is probable that he was a student of Nebrija at the University of Salamanca. In 1492 Encina entered the household of Don Fadrique, second Duke of Alba, as court musician, and in 1496, he published in Salamanca the product of his literary and musical activities in a *Cancionero*. The *Cancionero* contains eight plays, several lyrics, and a treatise on poetry called *Arte de la Poesía Castellana.* In 1498, after unsuccessfully soliciting the post of precentor in the Cathedral of Salamanca, Encina went to Rome, where he became a singer in the Pope's chapel. In 1502, while still in Rome, he was appointed prebendary of the Cathedral of Salamanca and in 1508 archdeacon of Málaga. The Pope allowed him to continue living at the papal court without suffering the loss of his Spanish benefices and Encina apparently took advantage of this privilege, for there are no documents to indicate his presence in Málaga before 1510. In 1512 Encina was again in Rome where he wrote his *Égloga de Plácida y Vitoriano.* Seven years later, while still in Italy, he was granted the priorate of the Church of León.

About this time Encina began to undergo a spiritual change, becoming less frivolous and worldly and more interested in preparing for the priesthood. To this end, in the spring of 1519, he undertook a pilgrimage to the Holy Land where he celebrated his first Mass. Upon his return to Rome he published the record of his journey under the title *Trivagia o Sacra Via de Hierusalem* (1520). In 1523 we find Encina in León where he spent the remaining years of his life.

The works of Encina constitute a synthesis of two opposing worlds: that of medieval Christianity and that of the pagan Renaissance. In the plays of the *Cancionero* of 1496 the spirit of the Virgilian eclogue is transformed into an unmistakably Spanish genre, with the shepherd-protagonists speaking a Salmantine dialect called "sayagués." The "Églogas" of the *Cancionero* combine both secular and religious elements and many have a distinct popular flavor. With the "Églogas" we find the medieval mystery play

* ăn thē′ nä

secularized and stylized and designed for performance before a private lay audience. The *Cancionero* underwent several editions in the early sixteenth century, the last of which was that of 1516. The editions of 1507 and 1509 contained two additional plays each.

The works which represent Encina's most advanced dramatic technique are the *Égloga de Plácida y Vitoriano* and the *Égloga de Cristino y Febea,* neither of which was included in any edition of the *Cancionero.* These plays show a progression from the asceticism of the Middle Ages to the complete triumph of neo-pagan elements characteristic of the Renaissance. In *Plácida y Vitoriano,* Plácida, imagining herself disdained, commits suicide but is restored to life because of Vitoriano's impassioned plea to Venus and Mercury. In *Cristino y Febea,* the shepherd Cristino decides to become a hermit. This so infuriates Cupid that he sends the nymph Febea to tempt him—with such success that Cristino abandons all ascetic ideas and gives himself over to worldly pleasures.

The importance of Encina as a dramatist lies in his contributions to the secularization of the theatre and to the technique of harmoniously fusing music, poetry, and dramatic action, later to be elaborated by Lope de Vega.

Encina was an accomplished musician, and aside from the music he composed for the "villancicos" with which his plays usually ended, he left a considerable body of musical compositions, 68 of which are included in the *Cancionero Musical de los Siglos XV y XVI* published by Asenjo Barbieri.

An *Eclogue* has been translated into English in W. K. Jones, *Spanish One Act Plays in English* (1934), and some of the poems have been included in the following collections: Bowring, J. *Ancient Poetry and Romances of Spain* (1824) ; Vingut, F. J. *Selections from the Best Spanish Poets* (1856) ; Walsh, T. *Hispanic Anthology* (1920).

ABOUT: Brenan, G. The Literature of the Spanish People; Crawford, J. P. W. Spanish Drama before Lope de Vega, also The Spanish Pastoral Drama. [In Spanish—Cañete, M. & Barbieri, F. A. Teatro Completo; Valbuena Prat, A. Historia de la Literatura Española.]

B. P. P.

ERASMUS, DESIDERIUS (October 27/28, 1469-July 12, 1536), Dutch humanist, born in Rotterdam, is generally believed to have been the son of a priest, Gerard, from the vicinity of Gouda; his mother, Margaretha, was probably a native of Rotterdam.

ERASMUS

The sensitive Erasmus later added to the uncertainty of his origin by a romantic and contradictory version of the circumstances (the inspiration for Charles Reade's famous novel of 1861, *The Cloister and the Hearth*). The baptismal name Herasmus derives from St. Erasimus; about 1496 Desiderius was added. The appellation "Rogerii" occurs until about 1517 and could come from either the father's or mother's side.

After attendance at the Gouda city school, Erasmus and his older brother Peter were sent to the school of the chapter of St. Lebuin, Deventer; here they remained about nine years (1475-84) with an interlude during which Erasmus served as choir boy at the "Domkerk" in Utrecht. The mother's death (1484) occasioned a return to Gouda. When shortly afterward the father died also, the guardians sent their two wards to the school of the Brethren of the Common Life at 's Hertogenbosch (Bois le Duc). If we are to believe Erasmus' later testimony, he found life distasteful at both Deventer and with the Brethren: the teaching methods were antiquated and, he charged, the pupil's natural gifts were stultified.

The plague again drove them back to Gouda. Now upon the guardians' urging, the brothers entered holy orders. Erasmus entered the monastery of Steyn, near Gouda in 1487 or 1488. There seems to be truth in Erasmus' later charge that the guardians' rôle in this decision was less than honorable.

However harsh his later recollections were, the foundations of Erasmus' attainments as a Latinist were laid at Steyn. Numerous letters testify to his interests—Virgil, Horace, Cicero, but also fifteenth century humanists, Aeneas Sylvius, Poggia, Valla. In 1492 Erasmus was ordained a priest; in 1493 the offer of a secretaryship to the bishop of Cambray was eagerly accepted as an escape from drudgery and opportunity for scholarly advancement. Although disappointed once again, Erasmus in 1495 entered the University of Paris, having meanwhile composed his *Antibarbari,* a eulogy of the life of study and a condemnation of the meaningless hardships imposed by the monastic way of life. It is not surprising that the lonely orphan should have shown from early youth a great need of friends; extremely sentimental friendships were common and Erasmus formed a number: Servatius Roger, Cornelius Gerard, James Batt.

Although Paris enabled Erasmus to progress rapidly in the knowledge of Greek, the entire experience confirmed in him a dislike and scorn for the traditional scholasticism still so powerful. Moreover the physical conditions at Montaigu College were harsh and his bishop-patron proved to be a none too dependable source of financial support. An offer to accompany Lord Mountjoy to England in 1499 was therefore eagerly accepted.

In England the brilliant Thomas More and the learned, devout John Colet were the most congenial spirits Erasmus had yet met. Colet directed him to that Biblical humanism which was to remain the mark of the man. Erasmus' predominant interests from now on were the documents of Christian antiquity. But as if to demonstrate his abiding love for the classics, he published in 1500 his *Adagiorum Collectanea,* an anthology of Latin proverbs elucidated in elegant Latin; several later expanded editions of this work appeared. Here too belong the famed *Colloquia,* already begun in Paris: literary sketches from daily life, spirited and pithy, above all impeccable in form. But it is the *Enchiridion Militis Christiani* (Manual of the Christian Soldier) which marks the vital turn in Erasmus' thinking: an exhortation to simple, practical Christian conduct and a corresponding repudiation of the merely formal and prescribed ritual. This emphasis on ethical Christianity goes far to explain Erasmus' later attitude toward the theological strife which was about to break forth. In repudiating scholasticism (Paris), Erasmus had indicated distrust of rational theology; the

Enchiridion contains what Erasmus regarded as more important.

Erasmus' life afforded little of the scholar's rest which he craved. From 1500 on the years were filled with travels to centers of learning and libraries for manuscripts. From 1506 to 1509 he was in Italy; Turin bestowed the doctorate. The Pope released him from the duties of his order; financial circumstances improved. The ascension of Henry VIII to the throne took Erasmus to England; on the way he conceived and wrote "in seven days" the one work for which he is most famous but which the author always dismissed later as a piece of foolishness, the *Moriae Encomium (Praise of Folly)*, dedicated to Thomas More—a typical Erasmian pun: More—Moriae. Subsequent centuries have continued to be fascinated by this enigmatic masterpiece on the rôle of folly in life and by the illustrations and etchings of Hans Holbein the younger which accompany the text in most editions.

The years 1509-14 were spent almost uninterruptedly in England, Erasmus occasionally lecturing at Cambridge. Also during these years he was for a time in Basel preparing for the publication (1516) of his Greek text edition of the New Testament. It was based on new manuscripts and remained authoritative for about three hundred years. But although honors from emperors and prelates continued to come, matters were getting more difficult.

By ceaseless acid criticism of church conditions, by an eloquent call for a purified theology, and especially by his emphasis on warm Biblical piety, Erasmus had prepared for the Reformation. For this reason such men as Luther, Hutten, and Dürer regarded him as one of their own. But now it became clear that the mind of Erasmus was not the mind of the Reformation. He stood as unequivocally as any for church purification, never for church separation. That this attitude too is a principle was perceived by very few in a time of extremes. Conservative Catholic theologians saw Erasmus, with considerable justification, as the real impetus of the Reformation; and since Erasmus had talent for neither heroism nor martyrdom (as he well knew himself), it was inevitable that his position should have been regarded as straddling. Erasmus' principle that destructive and warlike behavior is incompatible with the peace of the church of Christ, was vulnerable on both sides. The breach grew beyond healing when Erasmus finally yielded to pressure and published (1524)

De Libero Arbitrio, Diatribe (On the Freedom of the Will). Luther answered, outwardly controlled but inwardly seething, *De Servo Arbitrio* (On the Will Not Free). Erasmus continued to act in the interests of conciliation but the voice of the humanist was lost in the storms of the day. He died at sixty-six, in Basel, at the home of his friend and publisher, Froben.

Erasmus' meaning and significance is still not finally established. The world agrees in acclaiming his vast scholarly contributions, ten folio volumes, plus his editions of the Church Fathers. His rôle as an apostle of tolerance, his emphasis on evangelical, ethical Christianity, his skepticism toward dogmatic assertion—all these are more clearly seen and appraised today. His Biblical humanism enjoyed a revival of prestige in nineteenth century Holland; his impact on the Church of England has been great. But the times did not permit Erasmus to play his rôle of moderator nor does modernity even now seem ready to agree with Huizinga that "cultural humanity has cause to hold Erasmus' memory in esteem, if for no other reason than that he was the fervently sincere preacher of that general kindliness which the world still so urgently needs."

Although there is no authoritative English translation, most of Erasmus' works have been translated several times into all modern languages. *In Praise of Folly* was first translated by Sir Thomas Chaloner in about 1549. Other translators were John Wilson (1668), White Kennett (1683), P. E. Corbett (1921), H. H. Hudson (1941), Leonard Dean (1946). *The Epistles of Erasmus* were translated by Morgan Nichols (1901-18). A new translation of *Ten Colloquies* by C. R. Thompson was published in 1957.

ABOUT: Most valuable among the numerous biographies: Allen, P. S. The Age of Erasmus; Hyma, A. The Youth of Erasmus; Seebohm, F. The Oxford Reformers; Smith, P. Erasmus. [In Dutch—Lindeboom, J. Erasmus; Huizinga, J. Erasmus (tr. into English by F. Hopman in 1924; reissued 1957 under the title Erasmus and the Age of Reformation).]

C. K. P.

*ERBEN, KAREL JAROMÍR (November 7, 1811-November 21, 1870), Czech poet and scholar, was born in Miletín in northeastern Bohemia, the son of a shoemaker. He attended the *Gymnasium* at Králové Hradec, a school which, under the direction of the Czech writer V. K. Klicpera, was a center of nationalist and patriotic teaching. At the University of Prague Erben studied in the faculties of philosophy and law, com-

* ĕr' bĕn

pleting the latter faculty in 1837. From 1837 to 1843 he served as an official of the Prague court. Sickly and shy, he won by his industry and his precocity the attention of the great Czech historian František Palacký. The latter helped support him while at the university by giving him manuscripts to copy, and in 1843 recommended him for the task of organizing the Czech provincial archives. Erben traveled about the country, at the same time collecting folk songs and popular sayings. The first edition of his collection of Czech folk songs, *Písně Národní v Čechách*, appeared in 1841-45. Meanwhile in 1842 he married Barbora Mečířová, whom he had met in 1835: he did not dare to propose to her until his financial position was a sure one.

In 1846, again through Palacký's influence, Erben was named secretary of the Bohemian Museum. In the revolutionary year of 1848 he served briefly as editor of the official paper *Pražské Noviny* (Prague News), which he tried to keep to a middle-of-the-road position. The defeat of the revolution put an end to this venture into journalism and politics, for which Erben was scarcely suited. In 1851 he was named archivist of the city of Prague.

In 1857 Erben's wife died of cancer, leaving him three daughters. His relatives and friends repeatedly advised him to remarry, and in 1859 he was wedded to Žofie Mastná, a young lady of only twenty-four (he was then forty-six), who survived him.

Meanwhile Erben's reputation grew steadily with successive publications, including many Old Czech texts and two unique comparative collections of the folk tales of the Slavic peoples. As he grew older he abandoned original poetry more and more for translation and scholarly activity. He died of a sudden attack of jaundice at fifty-nine.

Erben's activity is many-faceted, but his outstanding creation is without doubt a slender collection of ballads, entitled *Kytice* (The Garland), written between 1836 and 1853, and published in the latter year. He realized the great dramatic and symbolic possibilities of the ballad. Modeling his work on the form of the Czech folk ballad, he refined it to the level of high art. His subjects are drawn from Slavic and Central European oral tradition. Some of his plots are well known, such as the legend of the dead bridegroom who returns from the grave to claim his bride, or the myth of the wife whose spirit lives imprisoned at night in a willow tree, and who can be released only at the

price of her death. His ballads are conceived as myths which reflect a quietist view of life: man can only accept destiny and must not revolt against his fate.

Erben's other poetry is slim in quantity and of little value. Noteworthy are his Czech folk tales, which were published after his death. Like his ballads, they are not literal recordings of folklore, but artistic reworkings.

Erben has had great influence on subsequent Czech poetry, particularly on Neruda, Hálek, and other composers of ballads.

A number of Erben's ballads have been translated into English, and are to be found in Paul Selver's *Anthology of Czech Literature* (1929); R. A. Ginsburg's *Soul of a Century* (1942); and E. W. Underwood's *The Slav Anthology* (1931). One of his collections of Slavic folk tales has been rendered into English by W. W. Strickland under the title of *Panslavonic Folk-lore* (1930).

ABOUT: Součková, M. The Czech Romantics; Harkins, W. E. Anthology of Czech Literature.

W. E. H.

---

*ERCILLA Y ZÚÑIGA, ALONSO DE (August 7, 1533-November 29, 1594), Spanish soldier and author, was born in Madrid. He was one of the five children of Fortún García de Ercilla, of the Royal Council, and Leonor de Zúñiga. Ercilla's father died when he was a small child and he was educated at court, serving as a page to young Prince Philip, later Philip II. He accompanied the Prince on many journeys and also had occasion to accompany the Princess María to Bohemia, Austria, and Hungary. It was while at the court in London that he met Jerónimo de Alderete, who interested him in the New World. In 1555 Ercilla, always ambitious for glory and living in an age of great deeds, went with Alderete to Chile on an expedition to suppress the revolt of the Araucanian Indians. There he took part in many battles, expeditions, and discoveries. He showed himself on numerous occasions to be an unusually brave soldier. He was finally imprisoned and even sentenced to death for a petty quarrel with a rival. Fortunately, the sentence was commuted and Ercilla returned to Spain in 1562 or 1563.

In 1570 Ercilla married María de Bazán, by whom he had no children. His one natural son, Juan de Ercilla, died in 1588 on board the "San Marcos" in the disaster of the Invincible Armada. In 1571 Ercilla was made a knight of the Order of Santiago. From 1574 to 1577 he traveled extensively

* ĕr thē′ lyä ē thōō′ nyē gä

263

in Italy and Germany. He died, most probably in Madrid, after unhappy declining years.

Ercilla's chief title to fame is *La Araucana*, an epic poem composed by him in Chile and revised and published in Spain in three parts, 1569, 1578, and 1589. It is made up of thirty-seven cantos written in octaves. The subject is the heroic insurrection of the Araucanians, which inspired Ercilla with great respect. Despite the fantastic or extraneous matter, such as the death of Dido and the Battle of Lepanto, which, in his emulation of the Italians he felt obliged to insert, the essence of the poem remains strictly historical. It is a hymn to Indian bravery and Spanish energy. It constitutes an original and sincere attempt to create a national form of epic. Although Voltaire's praise of *La Araucana* in his "Essai sur la Poésie Épique" seems exaggerated to us and although he does not always attain the heights of Tasso, Ariosto, or Camões, this poem, as Menéndez y Pelayo says, was "the first work of the modern literatures in which contemporary history was raised to the dignity of the epic." It is generally considered the best Spanish historical poem. It has provided subject matter and inspiration for other dramatists and poets, chief of whom is Pedro de Oña.

The best editions are those of Rosell in the *BAE*, volume XVII, and especially that of J. Toribio Medina, Santiago de Chile, 1910-18, five volumes with extensive notes and bibliography.

Ercilla's epic was translated by C. M. Lancaster & P. T. Manchester in 1945 under the title *The Araucaniad, a Version in English Poetry*.

ABOUT: Henríquez-Ureña, P. Creation of a New Society, 1492-1600, *in* Literary Currents in Hispanic America; Lancaster, C. M. & Manchester, P. T. Conquistador's Song of Freedom, *in* Poet Lore, LII; McManamon, J. E. Echoes of Virgil and Lucan in the Araucana; Pierce, F. The Heroic Poem of the Spanish Golden Age. [In Spanish—Toribio Medina, J. Vida de Ercilla.]

R. E. O.

---

*ERCKMANN-CHATRIAN, joint pseudonym of ÉMILE ERCKMANN (May 20, 1822-March 14, 1899) and ALEXANDRE CHATRIAN (December 18, 1826-September 3, 1890), French novelists, were born respectively in Phalsbourg, near Sarrebourg, and in Soldatenthal, near Abreschwiller. They met as students and began collaborative writing in 1849 in *Histoires et*

* ĕrk mản' shả trē ản'

CHATRIAN and ERCKMANN

Contes Fantastiques and *Le Bourguemestre en Bouteille*, published as Chatrian's translation from the German. Various extant manuscripts illustrate the nature of the collaboration in Chatrian's adjustments of Erckmann's originals. For the most part, the writing was done by Erckmann, who remained in Alsace and had no interest in or talent for business affairs; publication and such further matters as dramatizations were handled in Paris by Chatrian. Of the two, by far the more important was the original writer, since he portrayed the local scene in the eastern provinces from fresh and immediate documentation. The association came to a tragic end in a law suit in 1890, as Chatrian lay dying in final nervous breakdown; he had excused himself from further collaboration in 1887, then after several years began to claim for himself sole honors for the novels. After the rupture and the death of Chatrian, Erckmann continued creative work, but aside perhaps from *La Mère Hulot* (1895) produced nothing striking; he preferred short stories, for example the *Fables Alsaciennes et Vosgiennes* (1895), and his pessimism grew rapidly, both from age and from the shock of the law suit of 1890.

Chatrian was "maître d'études" at the Phalsbourg college in 1847, and had written some poetry before the meeting and the long friendship. Erckmann's early readings were principally in eighteenth century French, but his interest in a competition of the Academy in Metz brought more recent movements to his attention. He went to Paris in 1842, and as a student of law published an essay entitled *Du Recrutement Militaire,* on a topic of considerable importance in his later novels. His failure in the examinations of 1845 may be the cause of his turn to literature; in 1847 he wrote several plays on Alsatian subjects. His early life is known from his *L'Histoire d'un Homme du Peuple* (1848), which tells his impressions of Paris as a student and during the revolution of that year. In later life Erckmann was fond of recalling his early ideas and his methods of composition, his favorite creation being *L'Ami Fritz.* The best of his novels date from the collaboration and the years 1863-64. They belong to two general groups, the "romans nationaux" and the occasional subjects, which include a "roman populaire," *L'Ami Fritz.* Such titles as *Le Brigadier Frédéric,* published after the Franco-Prussian war, pose the problem of nationalism in a different way, for the earlier work dealt with Alsace of the Napoleonic period and involved the German situation without thought of the annexation. The central subject is the suffering of little people during war and invasion, documented by the personal recollections of people known to the author. *Le Conscrit de 1813* (1864) recounts the adventures of a Phalsbourg boy unwillingly pressed into military service who finds sympathy in a baker's home, with further adventures during the Napoleonic invasion of Germany. *Madame Thérèse* (1863) takes place in 1792 during the Prussian attack in a local Alsatian village, and tells of a little boy who through circumstance finds a mother. *L'Ami Fritz* (1864) is a love story in idyllic tone comparable both in manner and plot to George Sand's *La Mare au Diable.*

The qualities of Erckmann-Chatrian are many and varied. The Alsatian novels have documentary value for the events, faithfully related, and for the current ideas and folklore of the region; they served somewhat as did the works of Mistral to preserve regional culture in the face of rapidly growing centralization. The novels, furthermore, synthesize events, places, and emotions in powerful manner. The writing appeals directly to the general reader and remains wholly outside literary movements and cliques, a fact which explains the indifference of the principal critics of the time. The authors' conscious search for clarity of style and simplicity of vocabulary explains the immense appeal of the novels in England, where they were for decades a standard linguistic reference and pedagogical repertory. The literary sources are very slight, limited primarily to the Bible and to occultist writings, both for subject matter and for style; such topics as hypnotism and mind reading, in *Le Bourguemestre,* were currently popular in the work of Hoffmann and of Poe. Finally, the novels appealed for their republican opinions, hostile to imperial ideologies and ultimately also to Germany, with their implicit prophecy of the events of 1870.

Although several English translations, for example of *Madame Thérèse,* appeared before 1870, the principal ones were published from 1872 to 1914 in England. Mascagni based his opera *Amico Fritz* on the novel, and its influence may be traced in Germany as well as on Anatole France and Edmond About.

ABOUT: [In French—Henriot, E. Livres et Portraits, I; Hinzelin, E. Erckmann-Chatrian; Schoumacker, L. Erckmann-Chatrian; Esprit, No. 9 (1963).]

F. J. C.

*ESPINEL, VICENTE MARTÍNEZ (1550-1624), Spanish novelist and poet, was born in Ronda (Málaga) of northern stock. The restless nature of his character led him into an adventurous life which had a reflection in his writings. As a youth he attended the University of Salamanca intermittently, and later on those of Granada and Alcalá. He was a squire of the Count of Lemos in Valladolid, and he became notorious for his dissolute life in Seville. Later he sailed for Italy but the boat in which he was traveling was captured by the Barbary pirates and he became a galley slave until freed by the Genoese fleet—an episode to which he seems to allude in his fiction.

He went to Italy where he joined the Spanish troops of Alejandro de Farnesio. After three years of service he returned to Spain and began to wander anew, without settling anywhere. His presence is recorded in Madrid, Málaga, and Ronda. Then he entered the priesthood and, in 1587, held a benefice in a church in Rome, but in 1592 he was accused of having neglected his duties as a chaplain in his native Ronda in order to go to Madrid. His holy vows do not seem to have caused him to change his licentious life, since in 1598 the king had to write to the ecclesiastical authorities in Ronda asking them to admonish him for his unedifying conduct. Eventually he was appointed chaplain of one of the richest churches in Madrid, where as a choirmaster—and probably because of the sobering influence of age—he seems to have finally settled down until his death.

* ās pē nĕl'

As an artist he was versatile. Aside from his reputation as a poet and novelist, he was also well known as a humanist, a Latinist of note, and an accomplished musician. His prestige in the last mentioned capacity was great. In fact, he is credited with having added a fifth string to the guitar.

This creative ability extended to poetry. Espinel is known to have invented a new metric stanzaic form known today as "décima," called also after him "espinela"—a fact attested to by Lope de Vega (*Dorotea*, I, 8). He composed poetry both in Spanish and Latin, and we are indebted to him for a translation of Horace's *Ars Poetica*. His poems were collected in 1591 under the title *Rimas*.

Today his fame rests mainly upon a romance of roguery, *La Vida del Escudero Marcos de Obregón* (1618), in which he freely combined autobiographical elements with sketches of manners and episodes taken from literary sources and from his own imagination. The hero of his novel, the picaroon Marcos de Obregón—whom some critics have identified with Espinel himself—differs from most of the rogues of the Spanish picaresque in that he is less hardened and not nearly so close to criminality as most of them are. Espinel's novel as a whole is much less cruelly realistic than those by which it was preceded in the genre. Its sensitive descriptions of nature and intense "autobiographical" feeling help to distinguish it within the literature of roguery. Le Sage borrowed several incidents from it and adapted them, with other Spanish picaresque material, into his *Gil Blas*.

Algernon Langton translated *The History of the Life of the Squire Marcos of Obregon*, 2 vols, 1816.
ABOUT: Chandler, F. W. Romances of Roguery; Haley, G. Vicente Espinel and Marcos de Obregón. [In French—see Claretie, J. Le Sage Romancier. In Spanish—Vida del Escudero Marcos de Obregón, ed. S. Gili Gaya, 2 vols.]

M. DA C.

---

*ESPRONCEDA, JOSÉ DE (March 25, 1808-1842), Spanish poet, was born at or near Almedralejo de los Barros in the province of Madrid. His father, Juan de Espronceda, was a well-to-do cavalry officer who begot José somewhat late in life by a second wife almost twenty years younger. At the Colegio de San Mateo in Madrid, young José received, "according to one of his biographers, "the least bad education which the

* ās prôn thā′ thǎ

ESPRONCEDA

times afforded," but certainly he benefited from the tutelage of the poets Alberto Lista and José Gómez Hermosilla, who were on the faculty there. Apart from his poetry, most of José's short life was taken up with political fire-eating and military swashbuckling. As early as the age of fourteen he was embroiled in a radical student society known as "Los Numantinos." For this deviation he was imprisoned in a Franciscan convent at Guadalajara. Here he began an epic poem entitled *El Pelayo*. Long before his sentence was finished, the young rebel managed to escape to Portugal, and thence to England.

In the course of his picaresque adventures, Espronceda met Teresa Mancha, daughter of an exiled Spanish colonel, with whom he had a stormy love affair. Eloping with Teresa to Paris in 1830, the poet participated for the next three years in the civil broils then rampant in that turbulent capital. He took part in the Barricade Wars that installed King Louis Philippe on the throne, and also joined the raid of Chapalangarra in Navarre. After the cessation of hostilities in 1833, he received a commission in the Queen's Guards, but, true to form, he forfeited it by writing a seditious song. He whiled away a brief imprisonment at Cuéllar by composing a novel, *Sancho Saldaña o el Castellano del Cuéllar*, which is now generally ignored. It was during this period also that he steeped himself in the contemporary French and English poets, particularly Lord Byron, who influenced his own development.

Returning to his native land after his French escapades, Espronceda became involved again in radical politics. Several times he was jailed, and on one occasion he was banished from the capital for journalistic writings offensive to the authorities. He was active also in revolutionary uprisings that took place in 1835 and 1836.

With the publication of his collected *Poesías* in 1840 Espronceda leaped into the literary fame that has since continued unabated. During his last years he seems to have moved out of his *Sturm-und-Drang* stage, settling down into conventional respectability. He served in political offices— as secretary of the legation at The Hague in 1840, and as member of the Chamber of Deputies from Almería in 1842, a career cut short by his untimely death. Ironically, it was just at that time also that he was on the point of contracting an advantageous marriage with a lady of good family named Doña Bernarda de Beruete. He died suddenly of a throat infection in his thirty-fifth year.

Because of his flamboyant temperament and his devotion to libertarian causes, José de Espronceda has been called "the Spanish Byron." Although Espronceda certainly lacked the intellect and wit of his British counterpart, there are unmistakable parallels both in his life and in his works. His long poem *El Estudiante de Salamanca* (1839) is apparently modeled in places on *Don Juan.* The famous *Canción del Pirata*, with its defiant refrain in praise of the liberty of the open sea, echoes *The Corsair.* There is something of the Byronic bravado also in the fragment *El Diablo Mundo*, based on the Faust legend.

However, the unique genius of Espronceda is to be found in the compressed passion of his shorter lyrics. One of the most famous is *El Sol* (Hymn to the Sun), in which the poet begins by praising this heavenly body as an eternal source of power but concludes by commiserating with it as another being subject to time's laws, doomed to be extinguished in eternal darkness. Espronceda is a poet with a wide range of feeling, extending from the Bacchic exuberance of *A Jarifa en un Orgía* to the plangent despondency of *Canto a Teresa*, supposedly written some years after the parting with Teresa Mancha, just after the poet viewed her body through the bars of a window, laid out for burial. He learned that she had died of tuberculosis and the effects of heavy drinking. Described by Eleanor Turnbull as "a kind of breviary for the romantic, a vivid document of the innermost soul," the forty-four octaves recount the stages of a blighted love, beginning as a delirium, an infinite longing, ending in disillusionment. The poet concludes that ideal love is impossible since Satan entered the Garden of Eden, and calls on the world to join in his lament for man's woeful state. Espronceda's "passion for freedom, his surrender of judgment to impulse," together with his restlessness, cynicism and disillusion, as E. Allison Peers has written, "make his entire life a romantic poem."

Some of Espronceda's poems have been translated by James Kennedy in *Modern Poets and Poetry of Spain* (1852) and more recently in the Hispanic Society of America's publication *Translations from Hispanic Poets* (1938). A bilingual selection is available in *Ten Centuries of Spanish Poetry*, edited by Eleanor Turnbull (1955). The best edition in Spanish is the *Obras Completas* published in the *BAE* (1954).

ABOUT: Peers, E. A. The Romantic Movement; Hispanic Review, January 1941, April 1948; PMLA, December 1946. [In Spanish—see studies by J. Campos, J. Casalduero, J. C. Muñoz, and E. R. Solís.]

R. A. C.

*ESTÉBANEZ CALDERÓN, SERAFÍN ("EL SOLITARIO") (December 27, 1799-February 5, 1867)

Spanish *costumbrista* writer and politician, was born into a distinguished family of moderate means in Málaga. He attended the University of Granada where he received a degree in law at the age of twenty-three. He was a liberal in politics and in 1824 was obliged to flee for a time to Gibraltar, but by the next year he had opened a law office in his native Málaga. In 1834 he was named auditor general for the Army of the North. Because of the nature of his duties he was not obliged to fight but he nevertheless did so with distinction and was awarded the Cross of San Fernando. In 1835 Estébanez became the head of the Moderate Party in Logroño and later held the same job in Cádiz and Seville; in the latter city he remained until 1838. While in Seville, he was instrumental in founding the Museo de Pintura y Escultura and a provincial library. In 1847 he was made a judge of the Supreme Court of the Army and Navy, which position he held till 1854. He then served as Councilor of State till his retirement in 1864. Three years later he died in Madrid. He was a man of vast culture, although this does not always show in his writings. He was a good linguist and

* ās tä' bä näth käl dä rôn'

a student of Arabic, which he taught for a time at the Madrid Ateneo. He was a member of the Academia de la Historia.

Estébanez did most of his writing under the pen name of "El Solitario." He was the author of a volume of *Poesías* (1831) and of an historical novel, in the vein of Walter Scott, *Cristianos y Moriscos* (1838). Estébanez is remembered, however, for his *Escenas Andaluzas* (1847; last edition 1883), which consists of a number of short stories and sketches showing the life, customs, and manners of Andalusia. His style in the *Escenas* is a strange mixture of cultured language and popular speech, a mixture which is not always successful. He and Mesonero Romanos, with this literary genre, may be said to have founded a new school, commonly called the *costumbrista* writers. They had many imitators and followers.

A biography and the works of Estébanez appear in the *BAE*, LXXVIII-LXXIX.
ABOUT: [In Spanish—Cánovas del Castillo, A. El Solitario y Su Tiempo.]

R. E. O.

*ESTIENNE, HENRI (1531?-1598), French humanist and printer, was born in Geneva of a distinguished family of classical scholars and publishers. His grandfather, Henri, was active in Paris by 1502, and his father, Robert, made significant technical improvements in typography and served learning by issuing many important works, especially Greek and Latin masterpieces. The father's Calvinist sympathies, and his excessive emendations of religious texts, forced him to flee to Geneva in 1550; his *Thesaurus Linguae Latinae,* and his project for a companion volume on Greek, inspired Henri's principal writings. Henri's brother, Robert, continued the father's business in Paris.

Estienne received a sound education in Greek and Latin, and his father sent him on extensive travels, both for his instruction and to locate manuscripts for his editions; one of Estienne's most important discoveries was the *Odes* of Anacreon, which he published in Paris in 1554, and which had particular influence on the Pléiade and on Desportes; he also located ten further books of Diodorus Siculus. After he returned to Geneva in 1555, his father established him there with his own presses.

Estienne's original work began with his *Ciceronianum Lexicon Graeco-Latinum*

* ĕs tyĕn'

(1557), a searching examination of the Greek elements in Cicero's style. More important is his *Traité de la Conformité du Langage Français avec le Grec* (1565), in which he strove to derive French directly from Greek rather than from Latin; that he realized the excess of this thesis is evident in his *La Latinité Faussement Suspecte*. The importance of the *Traité* is twofold, first in its objective method for a study of etymologies, second as a further reflection of the unbounded admiration of the times for everything Greek, attested in other ways by Jean Lemaire de Belges and the legends of the Trojan origins of the Franks.

During his last years, Estienne often turned to political and religious controversy. His *Apologie d'Hérodote* (1566) was in part a pretext for anti-Catholic diatribes, though the work served scholarship in correcting the general notion that the subject matter of Herodotus was fabulous. In 1574 he published an attack against Catherine de' Médicis, attributing to her much of the intolerance of the times. His last years were calm, thanks to the favors of Henry III, but embittered by inner dissatisfaction and by the tragic financial problems that followed the publication of his great *Thesaurus Linguae Graecae* (1572). The misfortune of this publication was a combination of circumstances: the St. Bartholomew massacre, the great expense of the book, and a pirated epitome of it by one of his proofreaders. The Greek *Thesaurus* is the high-point of neo-Greek philology, important in turning attention to the ancients according to a systematic point of view, and in establishing a sound linguistic method. Estienne's *Dialogues du Nouveau Français Italianisé* (1578) focused attention on the many French words of Italian origin, and his *Précellence du Langage Français* (1579) was an effective plea for a fully honorable status for the vernacular.

English translations testify further to Estienne's fame. Not mentioning works devoted to technical matters of printing, we note *A World of Wonders* (1607) from his *Apologie*, and *The History of the Life of Katharine de Medicis* (1575 and 1693).
ABOUT: [In French—Clément, L. Henri Estienne et son Œuvre Française; Feugère, L. Essai sur la Vie et les Œuvres de Henri Estienne.]

F. J. C.

EVERARDI, JOANNES. See SECUNDUS, JOANNES

*EWALD, CARL (October 15, 1856-February 23, 1908), Danish novelist, short-story writer, essayist, journalist, was born at Gram in southern Jutland, not far from the German border. His father was Herman Frederik Ewald, a well-known author of historical novels. His mother was Julie Caroline Oest, daughter of Nicolai Oest, town clerk in Nakskov, later principal assistant secretary. After his graduation from Frederiksborg College in Copenhagen he was for several years a private tutor and became thereafter school principal in Copenhagen, from which position he resigned in 1882 to devote himself entirely to literary activity. In 1880 he married Emilie Salomon. The marriage was dissolved, and in 1887 Ewald married Betty Ponsaing.

Ewald was one of the most prolific authors of the naturalistic school in Denmark. In a couple of decades he published about forty books. His production was many-sided and fell within several genres. His first book, *Smaa Fortællinger* (Short Stories, 1882), was in the conventional realistic style and spirit of the 1870's. During the 1880's and '90's he published quite a few stories and novels in which he debated contemporary social problems. In such books as *Fru Johanne* (Mrs. Johanne, 1892) and *Den Gamle Stue* (The Old Room, 1895) Ewald employed the psychological analysis typical of the 1890's, expressed in an original and elegantly mannered style. The theme is the clash between the old order and the new. More personal are the family stories *Min Lille Dreng* (My Little Boy, 1899), and *Min Store Pige* (My Big Girl, 1904), in which Ewald contributed to the discussion of modern educational problems.

About the turn of the century Ewald served for several years on the staff of the leading Copenhagen daily newspaper, *Politiken*, in which, under the pseudonym "Hr. Hansen," he published a large number of witty and satirical short articles and essays of current interest. They were written in a condensed and artistically brilliant style and became extremely popular. Some of these articles he included in the collection *Døgnværk* (Ephemera, 1900). Some of his novels have a journalistic touch, e.g., *Pastor Jespersens Juleaften* (Pastor Jespersen's Christmas Eve, 1898), in which he attacked the home missions.

From 1896 to his death Ewald published several historical novels, e.g., *Börnekorstoget* (Children's Crusade, 1896), and *Makra*

(1897), about a country where everyone may live according to his own liking. *Mogens Heinesen* (1904) describes the adventurous life of a sixteenth century Faroese freebooter. During his last years he wrote a whole series of novels about prominent Danish women under the epitomizing title *Danske Dronninger uden Krone* (Danish Queens without a Crown, 1906-08). Ewald had a remarkable ability to reproduce various historical milieus in his novels. He possessed an exuberant imagination but sometimes fell into a rather stereotyped narrative form.

The only part of Ewald's production that has survived its author is his *Eventyr* (Stories), a series of short stories that was published in more than twenty volumes from 1882 to the year after his death. The stories are nature fables in Hans Christian Andersen's genre, but Ewald looks at the world from the viewpoint of a convinced Darwinist. The struggle for survival is a recurring theme. Many of the fables are pedagogical.

Several collections of Ewald's stories have been translated into English by A. Teixeira de Mattos: *Two Legs, and Other Stories* (1907), *The Pond, and Other Stories* (1909, 1934), *The Four Seasons* (1913), *The Old Willow-Tree, and Other Stories* (1921, 1934), *The Twelve Sisters* (1923). Translated by G. C. Moore Smith are *The Queen Bee, and Other Nature Stories* (1907, 1930), *The Old Post, and Other Nature Stories* (1922). Two novels exist in English translation by A. Teixeira de Mattos, viz. *Min Lille Dreng* as *My Little Boy* (1908, 1912) and *Den Gamle Stue* as *The Old Room* (1908).

ABOUT: [In Danish—see studies by C. Rimestad.]

A. J.

*EWALD, JOHANNES (November 18, 1743-March 17, 1781), Danish poet and playwright, was born in Copenhagen where his deeply pietistic father, Enewold Ewald, descended from a family from North Slesvig, was an orphanage priest. His mother was Marie Wulf, daughter of a contractor, Mathias Wulf, born in southern Norway. Her education had been entrusted to Enewold Ewald who, twenty years her senior, soon married her at the age of fifteen. Ewald was consumptive and weak. Johannes' young mother, merry and wanton, had extramarital relations. The real identity of Johannes' father is uncertain. Enewold Ewald died in 1754, and on the very day of his death the young boy was sent to the Cathedral School in Slesvig and was educated in the home of its principal, J. F. Licht. Here he learned to master German as his second language.

* ā' văld

* ā' văld

In 1758 Ewald at the young age of fifteen matriculated as a student of theology at the University of Copenhagen, and he went to live with his mother in the house of grocer Peder Hulegaard, who later married his mother. When Ewald met Arendse Hulegaard, the niece of his stepfather-to-be, he fell immediately in love with her. In order to prove himself worthy of her love he gave up his theological studies and tried to make a quick career for himself as a soldier. The Seven Years' War in Europe was in full swing, and the adventurous youngster enlisted in the Prussian Army, but soon he deserted to the Austrians and served as a drummer. During the campaign he contracted a rheumatic illness which soon broke his health.

On his return home he resumed his theological studies and took his degree in 1762. About two years later his beloved married another man. If this sad event brought about complete despair and addiction to liquor, it also made him a poet. In 1865 Ewald competed in a literary contest sponsored by a Danish society with a one-act lyrical drama entitled *Adamiade, et Drama om Guds Godhed* (Adamiade, a Drama on the Benevolence of God). When he did not win the first prize, he decided to devote two years to educating himself and learning literary art thoroughly. He studied the ancient, French, English, and German literatures. He was particularly impressed by Horace, Corneille, and Klopstock and was most strongly influenced by French classicism. His *Adamiade* was now rewritten and transformed into a French-Classical tragedy in five acts under the title *Adam og Eve eller den Ulykkelige Prøve* (Adam and Eve, or the Unlucky Test, 1769), the first original Danish tragedy. This drama attracted the attention of Klopstock who had lived in Copenhagen for almost two decades. Ewald's acquaintance with Klopstock brought him completely under the spell of the pietistic German master. Now he turned away from the French models and into the movement known as the "Germanic Renaissance" and chose his motives and material from the glorious past of his own country. He also made himself acquainted with English literature (Shakespeare, Ossian), first in German translation but soon in the original language.

Ewald's new Klopstock-inspired attitude to literature was realized in his five-act tragedy in prose *Rolf Krage* (1771), the material of which was taken from Saxo Grammaticus, Shakespeare's source for *Hamlet*. The play pictures a legendary Danish hero from the sixth century and may be regarded as the first original Scandinavian tragedy written on a native Scandinavian theme.

Through leading a reckless life Ewald aggravated his rheumatic condition. It caused him terrible pain and gradually made him a complete cripple. But it did not break his spirit. During the two years after the completion of *Rolf Krage* he wrote chiefly satirical comedies and occasional songs of which many were made to order. In 1773 he moved away from the dangerous capital to Rungsted on the coast of northern Zealand where the beautiful nature and the majestic sea gave him new optimism and desire to devote himself to his poetic calling. He expressed his joy in an exquisite ode called *Rungsteds Lyksaligheder* (The Felicities of Rungsted. 1774), and in the same year he completed a three-act tragedy in Shakespearean verse, *Balders Død* (The Death of Balder), in which he introduced Old Norse mythology as a theme in Danish drama. In 1799 Ewald wrote his last great work, *Fiskerne* (The Fishermen), a lyrical musical drama in three acts, in which the heroes are common country people. Most famous among the lyrics is "Kong Christian" (King Christian), which with music by Rogert became a national anthem.

Balders Død was published in English translation by G. Borrow as *The Death of Balder* (1889). Lyrics, mostly from *The Fishermen*, have appeared in various English versions, e.g., by W. S. Walker in *Poems from the Danish* (1815, 1816), by Longfellow in his *The Poets and Poetry of Europe* (1845), by G. Borrow in his *The Songs of Scandinavia, and Other Poems and Ballads* (1923), by C. W. Stork in *A Second Book of Danish Verse* (1947), by R. P. Keigwin in his *In Denmark I Was Born . . .* (1948). For a complete list of translations into English see E. Bredsdorff, *Danish Literature in English Translation* (1950).

ABOUT: Howitt, W. and M. The Literature and Romance of Northern Europe, I; Mitchell, P. M. A History of Danish Literature; Payne, W. M. Columbia University Course, X. [In Danish—see studies by L. Bobé, H. Brix, K. Flor, E. Frandsen, M. J. Hammerich, C. Molbech, S. Thomsen.]

A. J.

*EYSTEINN ÁSGRÍMSSON (d. 1361), Icelandic poet, often called Brother Eysteinn, was an Augustinian friar. Almost nothing is known about his early life. He was born probably in the first decade of the fourteenth century. In 1342, when he was a regular of the monastery of Thykkviboer, he became involved in an assault upon an abbot and was imprisoned for a year. Evidently he re-

* ûü′ stĕïn às′ grãm sön

formed after his imprisonment and began to take an active part in church business. From 1349 to 1351 he was vicar of the see of Skálholt. During the 1350's he traveled abroad and remained in Norway for about five years. His career was marred by his constant feuding with his superior, Bishop Gyrd. As a result of their disagreements he was excommunicated in 1358, but he was soon restored to favor. In 1360 he made another trip to Norway. In the stormy crossing he lost all his possessions and only barely escaped with his life. He died a few months later in Norway. Eysteinn's biographers conjecture that he was jolly and good-natured —hence an easy prey to the corruptions of the Icelandic church of his age. He was learned, however, and—on the evidence of his only surviving literary work—deeply religious.

This work is the sacred poem *Lilja (The Lily)*, consisting of one hundred stanzas in praise of God. In striking contrast to the elaborate and over-wrought imagery of the Skaldic poetry of medieval Iceland, *The Lily* is a straightforward expression of religious faith. It has been compared, for its simplicity and piety, to the English shepherd-poet Caedmon's accounts of the Creation, the Temptation, and the Fall of Man. Its artistry is of a high order. Richard Beck describes it as "an eloquent and masterfully constructed interpretation of medieval Christology." The poem has remained popular in Iceland ever since its composition and it has had many imitators.

An English translation by E. Magnusson was published in 1870.

ABOUT: Beck, R. *in* The History of the Scandinavian Literatures (ed. F. Blankner); Magnusson, E. *Preface to* Eysteinn's Lilja.

---

*FAGUET, ÉMILE (December 17, 1847-June 7, 1916), French literary critic, born in Poitiers, was the son of a teacher and humanist. He studied in the local *lycée*, then at the École Normale in Paris, in 1867. Involved in a student scandal, though presumably innocent, he was expelled and returned to Poitiers as teaching assistant at the *lycée*. Having completed his *licence*, he taught at Bourges, then, passing the *aggrégation*, rose in rank and prestige in posts in various cities. Faguet seemed to find his allotted place in 1880 at the Bordeaux University, but, encouraged by the Hellenist Couat, he continued through the doctorate in 1883 and entered the Lycée Charlemagne in Paris.

* fà gĕ'

Thanks to Lecène, a publisher who sought materials for school texts, Faguet began critical writing and achieved immediate recognition for his understanding of the history and evolution of French poetry. In 1890 he was named to the Sorbonne, and soon, supported by Brunetière, to the French Academy. Living in modest and retired fashion, he devoted his energies to the publication of articles adapted from his lecture notes.

Faguet, in his courses and writings, sought to order and explain the evolution of the art of poetry. He followed a rational method akin to that of Brunetière, with similar emphasis on notions of gradual development or variation of genres and themes, to a large degree within the positivistic current established by Taine. Faguet's particular merit was to escape from the excessive rigor of such a routine, and to see more intuitively the meaning of the isolated manifestations, or the absolute value of the poem as a pure and unique event. Dividing his poets by centuries, he moved from the Pléiade to the romantics in a measured combination of fact and interpretation. Many of his lessons were published as he set them in final form, and through the reviews in which they appeared reached a wide and interested audience. Regarding criticism as a practical aid, he focused attention on the masterpieces themselves. His personal research revealed a host of minor poets on whom information is difficult to find, and among whom are certain neglected talents of real interest. His *Histoire de la Poésie Française*, in the edition of 1923, includes an extensive presentation by Fortunat Strowski, who speaks of Faguet's notebooks and gives bibliographical detail regarding earlier publications.

English translations of Faguet's writings include the following: *A Literary History of France*, by "F.H.L." (1907); *The Cult of Incompetence*, by B. Barstow (1911); *The Dread of Responsibility*, by E. J. Putnam (1914); *Flaubert*, by Mrs. R. L. Devonshire (1914); *Initiation into Literature*, by Sir Home Gordon (1914); *On Reading Nietzsche*, by G. Raffalovich (1918); *Politics and Moralists of the Nineteenth Century*, by D. Galton (1928).

ABOUT: [In French—Bordeaux, H. Quelques Portraits; Duval, M. Émile Faguet; Thibaudet, A. Physiologie de la Critique.]

F. J. C.

FALKLAND, SAMUEL. See HEIJER-MANS, HERMAN

FAZIO DEGLI UBERTI. See UBERTI, FAZIO DEGLI

FEIJÓO (or Feyjóo) Y MONTENEGRO, BENITO JERÓNIMO (October 8, 1676-December 26, 1764), Spanish essayist, teacher, and priest, was born in Casdemiro (Orense). His parents were Antonio Feyjóo y Montenegro and María de Puga, both of noble families. At the age of fourteen he entered the Benedictine Order in the monastery of San Julián de Samos. His formal education took place chiefly at Lerez and Salamanca. He became professor of philosophy at Samos and at San Vicente de Oviedo, receiving his doctorate in theology from the latter. He occupied the Chair of Theology at the University of Oviedo some forty years. Physically, Feijóo was tall, well-built, with a gentle face and penetrating eyes. He had a phenomenal memory and is said to have slept only about four hours a night.

Feijóo is known almost exclusively for two works: *Teatro Crítico Universal* (8 vols., 1726-39) and *Cartas Eruditas y Curiosas* (5 vols., 1742-60). Both these works consist of essays and, in fact, Feijóo is one of the fathers of the modern Spanish essay. These essays should be thought of as forming a sort of encyclopedia in which the author exposes his ideas on many subjects, among which are: physics, mathematics, medicine, astronomy, geography, economics, moral philosophy, superstitions, literature, philology, and teaching. Feijóo's mind was open to all advances in science and he was a particularly strong advocate of the experimental method. In his essays he strove to reform teaching, expose superstitions to the cold light of reason, fight for the rights of women, and bring his countrymen recent scientific advances from abroad. Within the limits of Catholic dogma, he was completely fearless and boldly liberal; hence, he made numerous enemies as well as friends. His writings stirred up such a tempest that he was even investigated by the Inquisition, which confined itself to the removal of several sentences from his works. He differed from many other eighteenth century writers and encyclopedists in that he was able to unite the boldest ideas of reform with traditional elements which he considered to be worthy of perpetuation. In religious matters, Feijóo was an exceptionally tolerant man for his time. Writing once to a Jew in Bayonne, he said, "All of us must look upon each other as brothers."

Feijóo had many admirers both at home and abroad and carried on an extensive correspondence. Although much of what he ad-

vocated has been superseded by more scientific explanations, his value to his age is unquestioned and he is one of the dominant forces leading to the educational reawakening of Spain. He died in 1764 and was buried in San Vicente. The income from his popular works had been largely spent to aid the poor.

The best available editions of his works are: *Obras Escogidas* of the *BAE* collection, LVI, and volumes 48, 53, 67, and 85 of the *Clásicos Castellanos*.

Feijóo's genius was quickly recognized abroad and he was widely translated. An early English translation appeared in 1774, translator unknown, with the quaint title of *An Essay on the Learning, Genius and Abilities of the Fair Sex*. John Brett translated some of his essays into English, *Three Essays*, London, 1778, and followed this with *Eight Essays* in 1779.

ABOUT: Hispanic Review VIII (1940) and IX (1941). [In Spanish—see studies by A. Ardao, E. Pardo Bazán, M. Morayta, G. Marañón. See also G. Delpy's Feijóo et l'Esprit Européen.]

R. E. O.

*FEITH, RHIJNVIS (February 7, 1753-February 8, 1824), Dutch poet and prose writer, was born in Zwolle, the only son of Pieter Feith and Elizabeth Spaer. After studying at the Latin school in Harderwijk, Feith went to the University of Leiden to study law, receiving his degree in 1770. On November 17, 1772 he married Ockje Groeneveld. He became mayor of Zwolle in 1780 and lived most of the time on his estate Boschwijk outside of that city. During the first period of his literary activity he was the representative par excellence of Dutch sentimental romanticism. Edward Young and Klopstock were his examples. These two names characterize also the two sides of his artistry, the romantic and hypersensitive next to the overly pious tendencies. His writings were also influenced by Baculard d'Arnaud.

The first poem with which he drew attention was *Heil van de Vrede* (1779). His *Verhandeling over het Heldendicht* (1781) indicates his knowledge and appreciation of English, French, and German literature. His *Oden en Gedichten* appeared in five volumes during the years between 1796 and 1814. The poetry of the later period of his life reveals the melancholy and sentimentality of his work: *Het Graf* (1792), *De Ouderdom* (1802), *De Eenzaamheid* (1821), *De Wereld* (1812). All of these works reflect his true piety.

* fĕ ē hō′ ō ē môn tā nä′ grō

* fīt

Feith's prose writings were even more influenced by German literature than his poetry. In *Julia* (1783) his sentimentality reached an unnatural level. This novel and the following two, *Ferdinand en Constantia* (1785) and *Fanny* (1787), have become proverbial for their somberness. The second period of his literary activity, beginning around 1787, was marked by disappointment and resignation. In this period he wrote dramas: *De Patriotten* (1785), *Lady Johanna Grey* (1791), which was written after Wieland's work, *Inés de Castro* (1793). All these dramas are long since forgotten.

Between 1793 and 1796 Feith published, in collaboration with Jacobus Kantelaar, three volumes of essays dealing with the theory of literature. Feith also remained active after 1797, the year in which his country was overrun by the French. His view of life remained pessimistic, but his interests continued to be many-sided; he dealt primarily with philosophical and religious problems. Owing to his opposition to Kantian philosophy, he became involved in a controversy with his countryman Kinker. His collected works were published in 1824-25.

ABOUT: [In Dutch—see study by H. G. van Bruggencate.]

H. B.

FELIPE TRIGO. See TRIGO, FELIPE

*FÉNELON, FRANÇOIS DE SALIGNAC DE LA MOTHE- (August 6, 1651-January 7, 1715), French mystic, religious writer, and educator, was born of a noble but poor family in Périgord. He was a sensitive and idealistic child and was early destined for a career in the church. After studying theology at Saint-Sulpice in Paris, he was ordained a priest at twenty-four. Much of Fénelon's life was devoted to the cause of education. In 1678 he was appointed the superior of a convent which specialized in the training of young girls newly converted to Catholicism. Out of this experience came his widely popular *Traité de l'Éducation des Filles* (1687), a treatise on education that anticipates Rousseau's *Émile* in its liberal views and its emphasis on training in such practical matters as health, hygiene, and domestic economy.

The brilliant young priest soon came to the attention of prominent figures in the French church and court. The powerful Bishop Bossuet (see sketch above), later to

* fän lôn'

FÉNELON

become his enemy, signaled him out for special honors and responsibilities. He was sent on various ecclesiastical missions concerned with the converting of Huguenots and showed himself in these to be—for his time—surprisingly generous and tolerant. An even more influential friend was Mme de Maintenon, Louis XIV's mistress and later his wife, and it was through her, in 1689, that Fénelon was appointed tutor to Louis' grandson and heir to the throne, the Duke of Burgundy. The pupil-teacher relationship was apparently a happy and successful one. Fénelon took the spoiled and unruly boy firmly in hand and instilled in him not only the necessary academic disciplines but also a liberal theory of monarchy in striking contrast to the absolutism of Louis XIV himself. Some of the writings which Fénelon prepared for his pupil on the duties of royalty—counseling him to seek peace, justice, and the happiness and welfare of all the people—contained daringly frank criticisms of Louis' reign and were probably instrumental in Fénelon's later downfall. The pupil himself unfortunately did not live to become king and put into practice the principles that he had learned.

Fénelon's most famous book was a text written for the young Duke, *Télémaque* (1699), an imitation of classical epic. The story is a continuation of the *Odyssey* and deals with the adventures of Telemachus, Odysseus' son. In thinly veiled allegory—which was immediately and widely interpreted as a criticism of the reign of Louis XIV—

273

Fénelon takes his hero through a series of adventures which uniformly illustrate his thesis that an ideal monarch should be a man of peace, wisdom, and simple ways of life. The work is largely imitative, but it is lively and in places beautiful, and it became a universally popular children's book, translated into English and many other languages.

Fénelon's rise to power was rapid. In 1693 he was elected to the French Academy. In 1695 he was appointed to the wealthy see of Cambrai and was at the height of royal favor. His fall from glory came soon after, however, and the cause was his attachment (strictly Platonic) to one Mme Guyon, who was an exponent of a form of religious mysticism called Quietism (which preached self-annihilation and passive absorption in the contemplation of God). It was over Mme Guyon that Fénelon clashed with his most influential patrons, Bossuet, Mme de Maintenon, and Louis XIV. While they questioned the orthodoxy of Quietism, Fénelon came to its—and Mme Guyon's—defense. He held his position stubbornly in the controversies that followed. His *Maximes des Saints* (1697) was taken as a defense of Quietism, and in a treatise which attempted to refute the book, Bossuet described Fénelon as "bewitched by a dangerous and heretical woman." Fénelon unsuccessfully sought permission to go to Rome to defend his book but was instead ordered to remain in his diocese at Cambrai. (At that he did better than did Mme Guyon who languished in prison.) In Rome in 1699 Pope Innocent XII condemned the book, but even at this distance Fénelon's basically sympathetic personality saved him from more serious censure. The Pope's decision indeed proved to be a greater indictment of Bossuet than of Fénelon. He wrote: "The Archbishop of Cambrai sinned through loving God too much; the Bishop of Meaux [Bossuet] sinned through loving his neighbor too little."

Fénelon spent his last years in parish work in Cambrai. He died at sixty-three at peace with his enemies and honored by all who knew him. He was not a great writer. Most of his writings were of a practical nature involving his teaching and his church duties. He survives not in these but through the memory of his generous spirit, his tolerance, and his charm. His contemporaries knew him as "the Swan of Cambrai." A contemporary witness, Saint-Simon, described him as "a tall, thin man, a good figure, pale, with a large nose, eyes from which fire and intellect gushed like a torrent, and a physi-

ognomy the like of which I have not seen, and which one could not forget though one had seen it only once . . . what was uppermost in his face, as in his whole person, was shrewdness, wit, grace, modesty, and above all nobility."

Fénelon's collected writings were published in thirty-four volumes from 1820 to 1830, edited by Gosselin and Caron.

There are numerous English translations of *Télémaque* (J. Kelly, 1743; J. Clarke, 1773; Litterbury & Boyer, 1778; J. Hawkesworth, 1795, etc.) In the eighteenth century alone there were some twenty editions of this work. Also translated in the eighteenth century were *The Characters and Properties of True Charity Displayed* (J. de Freval, 1737); *The Archbishop of Cambray's Dissertation on Pure Love* (1738); *Dialogues Concerning Eloquence in General* (W. Stevenson, 1760; more recently translated by W. S. Howell, 1951); *Ethic Tales and Fables Invented for the Education of a Prince* (D. Bellamy, 1770). His treatise *The Education of Girls* was translated by T. F. Dibdin in 1805 and by Kate Lupton in 1891. More recent translations include *Christian Perfection* by M. W. Stillman (1947); *Letters from Cambrai* by M. W. Stillman (1949); *Meditations and Devotions* by E. C. Fenn (1952); *Letters and Reflections* by T. S. Kepler (1955); *Fénelon Letters* by J. McEwen (1964).

ABOUT: De la Bedoyère, M. The Archbishop and the Lady; Havens, G. R. The Age of Ideas; Little, K. D. François de Fénelon; Sainte-Beuve, C. A. Causeries de Lundi (in English), II; Saunders, E. K. Fénelon: His Friends and His Enemies. [In French—see studies by H. Bremond, E. Carcassone, J. L. Goré, J. Lemaître, F. Varillon.]

"FERNÁN CABALLERO." See "CABALLERO, FERNÁN"

FERNÁNDEZ DE MORATÍN, LEANDRO. See MORATÍN, LEANDRO FERNÁNDEZ DE

*FERREIRA, ANTÓNIO (1528-1569), Portuguese poet and playwright, was born in Lisbon, the son of a retainer of the Duke of Coimbra. He studied law and humanities in Coimbra. Fine classic scholars (Teive, Buchanan) taught him there to love literature. Though he became a judge, he continued to cultivate poetry, stimulated by his friend and master Sá de Miranda. He often envied his friend's quiet life in the country but remained in the capital, where he fell victim to an epidemic in 1569. Married first to Maria Leite, then to Maria Pimentel, he sang of both in Petrarchan sonnets. Posthumously his works (excepting the comedies)

* fĕr rā′ ē rä

were published by his son Miguel Leite Ferreira as *Poemas Lusitanos* in 1598.

Ferreira belonged to a group of learned poets who scorned the "ignorant crowd," deplored the materialism of the profit-hungry traders, and suffered under the increasing blows of the churchmen against intellectual freedom. Ferreira urged his friends to celebrate the glorious Portuguese expansion in a national epic; it was done instead by a man he seems to have hated, Camões. His own breath was too short, too "cold and harsh" for the undertaking. Like his beloved Horace, he limited himself to carefully wrought poems of all the shorter varieties, from epigrams and sonnets to eclogues and epistles. In these he conversed with his friends, great noblemen and royalty, giving them, like Sá de Miranda, his honest, courageous advice on civic and literary matters. Three literary themes recur there: the reform of poetry through Italian meters, following Garcilaso's and Boscán's example; the improvement of national literature through revival of the ancients; and the patriotic defense of the national language—"May she thrive," he wrote, "speak, sing, be heard and live long, the Portuguese tongue, wherever she is Mistress now, let her stand her ground, haughty and proud."

Imbued with classical learning, Ferreira also wrote two lame prose comedies, published with Sá de Miranda's in 1622: *Bristo,* about two friends who become rivals in love and two braggarts who frighten each other, and *O Cioso,* about a jealous husband who is deceived by wife and mistress. Being an early comedy with a single ridiculous character, the latter aroused interest abroad, but not so much as his *Tragédia de Dona Inés de Castro* (written after 1553, published in 1587), a tragedy in blank verse on a theme famous in the history of the kings of Portugal, i.e., the murder of Prince Peter's Spanish mistress by his father for reasons of state. The conflict between reason and passion, so dear to Racine, was already treated by Ferreira in the rhetorical manner of Seneca, complete with a chorus and with the pagan concept of Fate, in the guise of "Cruel Death, racing through the Mondego meadows, in search of Agnes' sweet life, of Agnes' sweet love." Ferreira's was the only complete and original Renaissance tragedy in Portugal. The Spaniard Vélez de Guevara (1603) and many other playwrights took up the macabre theme later, as did Camões in one of the most moving episodes of his *Lusiads.*

C. Cockburne translated *Inés de Castro* into English in 1697, followed by Thomas Musgrave in 1823. The latter also rendered *O Cioso* in 1825. Two later Portuguese adaptations of Ferreira's *Castro* were also Englished, Reis Quita's by B. Thompson (1800), Nicolau Luís' by J. Adamson (1808), "with Remarks on the History of that Unfortunate Lady."

ABOUT: Bulletin of Hispanic Studies, 1954; Fucilla, J. *in* Studies and Notes; Modern Philology, XII (1914). [In Portuguese—Marques Braga, *in* 2-vol. edition of Poemas Lusitanos.]

G. M. M.

FERREIRA DE VASCONCELLOS, JORGE. See VASCONCELLOS, JORGE FERREIRA DE

*FET (SHENSHIN), AFANASY AFANASYEVICH (December 5, 1820-December 3, 1892), Russian poet, was born in Novoselki, near Mtsensk, two months after his father, a wealthy squire Shenshin, brought his mother Charlotte, *née* Becker, from Germany. Ecclesiastic authorities declared their Lutheran marriage invalid; and Fet, born before his parents added the Russian Orthodox rites, could not legally inherit his father's nobility, estate, or name, and had to assume the Russianized name of Charlotte's previous husband, Foeth. Not until 1873 did Fet receive the name of Shenshin by special decree of Alexander II.

Fet studied in a German boarding school in Verro, Livonia, later at the University of Moscow (1838-44). His first book of verse, *A Lyrical Pantheon* (1840), was immature, but the poems he began to print from 1842 in the leading literary reviews belong to his best. Some of them show the influence of Heine.

Fet's long military service (1845-58) failed to yield the desired title of nobility, as the requirements were raised twice during this time. First he served in the Kherson district, abandoning poetry for years, then succeeded in being transferred to the Guards Uhlan regiment in St. Petersburg and found himself in the midst of literary life. Turgenev and Leo Tolstoy became his close friends. His books of poetry published in 1850 and 1856 met with great success. In 1856 he married Maria Petrovna Botkina, a daughter of a rich tea merchant.

In 1860 Fet settled at Stepanovka in his native district, where he bought much land. At this time, a contemporary described him as having a long black beard, a Jewish type of face, little feminine hands and a deep

* fyāt (shyĕn shĭn')

275

bass voice, and also mentioned his witty nature. Here Fet withdrew from literary life and published only a few articles on agrarian topics. These made him a notorious reactionary in the eyes of the radical intelligentsia, whereas his aesthetic essays gave him later the reputation of an "art for art's sake" poet, indifferent to the needs of the time. For some twenty years Fet was absent from literature. In the meantime, he managed his affairs so successfully that later he was able to buy the beautiful estate Vorobyovka near Kursk and a mansion in Moscow. In 1883 Fet started publishing, in four consecutive volumes under the title *Evening Fires*, his late poetry, which showed a distinct turn to metaphysical subjects and was darker in hue, though still in a major key. During these years, Fet also wrote memoirs and numerous translations (Latin poets, Goethe, Schopenhauer). At this time he was highly revered as a poet. He died in Moscow of heart failure.

The "natural ease and directness" (according to Elton) of Fet's lyrical poetry is comparable only to Pushkin's. However, his ability to express the nuances of feeling and to catch elusive, fleeting impressions, the suggestive quality of his verse, his irrationalism and the musicality and rhythmic variety of his poetry not only place him in the Zhukovsky tradition, but also make him a predecessor of Russian Symbolists (Soloviev, Blok). Especially popular are Fet's observant and fresh landscape poems, in which nature seems to dissolve in lyrical emotion, and his love-poetry, both passionate and subtle.

Translations of Fet are to be found in Oliver Elton's *A Sheaf of Papers* (1923) and in C. M. Bowra's *A Book of Russian Verse* (1943).

ABOUT: [In Russian—see studies by V. S. Fedina, V. Pokrovsky.]

V. M.

*FEUILLET, OCTAVE (August 11, 1821-December 29, 1890), French novelist and dramatist, born at Saint-Lô, in Normandy, did brilliant studies in Paris at the Louis-le-Grand College where he prepared for a diplomatic career, from which he was distracted by literature. He began to compose plays, in collaboration with Paul Bocage, in 1845, though this first work is of little moment. He escaped from the unfruitful influence of his collaborator when he married, in 1851, and returned to Saint-Lô to care for his father. The isolation of provincial life displeased him at first, but his attachment for it grew and he did his best work in this atmosphere of calm. He divided his later life between Saint-Lô and Paris, the former for his creative activities, the latter for his literary affairs.

Feuillet's brother Eugène, living permanently in Paris, did much to further his theatrical productions, seeing almost alone to their staging and advertising. The first plays of note were published as *Scènes et Proverbes* in the *Revue des Deux Mondes*, beginning in 1849 with *Le Pour et le Contre*. Resembling the work of Musset, less inspired but rich in charm and fantasy, *Le Pour et le Contre* came at a propitious moment after the revolution and during the period of the last gasps of the romantic theatre; after four years of fruitless trials, it was performed triumphantly, and Feuillet's other plays on the subject of marital love followed in quick succession until the triumph of the staging of *Péril en la Demeure* at the Comédie-Française in 1855, and of *Dalila* in 1857.

At this moment Feuillet found his true talent in the *Roman d'un Jeune Homme Pauvre*, which so impressed the Empress Eugénie that she named him as her librarian at Fontainebleau. He was elected to the French Academy in 1862 and after the Franco-Prussian War went to England to visit the ex-Emperor Napoleon III, to whose memory he remained faithful by refusing employment under the Third Republic. His private life was uneventful and is best known to us through several works by his widow. In his respectable advanced age, he was one of the mentors of literature, deeply admired by two men who in different ways show his influence, Anatole France and Pierre Loti, and the lesser Henry Bordeaux, who wrote his life.

In his novels Feuillet combined imagination and fantasy with sound knowledge of society; in short he was primarily a "moralist." In crisp style, with touches of irony, he stated rather than described, and indulged in a minimum of routine analysis. In his depiction of strange passions he creates strong anticipation of events rising from moral causes. His outstanding works are *Monsieur de Camors*, telling of a man wholly attached to a "religion d'honneur," and *Julia de Trécœur*, presenting an elusive female character who lives and dies in beauty. The slight place occupied by descriptions lends a classical tone which Bordeaux compared to

* fû yĕ′

La Princesse de Clèves. Of Feuillet's novels, *Les Amours de Philippe* alone contains autobiographical detail.

The many English translations include *Camors* (1868), *Led Astray, Julia* and *Bellah,* by O. Vibeur (1875); *The Amours of Philippe* by M. Sherwood, (1877); and *An Artist's Honor* by E. Robins (1890).

ABOUT: Saintsbury, G. Essays on French Novelists. [In French—Bordeaux, H. La Jeunesse d'Octave Feuillet; Claretie, J. O. Feuillet.]

F. J. C.

*FÉVAL, PAUL HENRI CORENTIN (September 27, 1817-March 8, 1887), French novelist, was born in Rennes of an ancient family of lawyers and administrators. He studied in his native city, whose political and religious convictions mark much of his later writing; we know of his first experiences from his *Drame de la Jeunesse* (1861), of the loss of his father in 1827, and his devotion to his saintly mother, who saw him through difficult years. During the Revolution of 1830, at the age of thirteen, Féval's ultra-royalist tendencies appeared in imprudent actions that led to trouble and violence, including an altercation with the police. Sent away briefly, he returned to finish his studies in 1833, and then took a course in law and at nineteen entered the profession. His interest in literature led him to abandon this career, and he went to Paris where he worked sporadically in a bank and for a newspaper, taking all possible time for writing. He found no publisher for his first novels, but, as proofreader for *Le Nouvelliste,* he managed to publish in that magazine several striking articles, and was soon invited to contribute to the *Revue de Paris.* His first significant work, published serially, *Le Club des Phoques,* attracted the attention of other magazines and in 1843, with *Le Loup Blanc,* he attained a solid and lasting reputation. *Le Loup Blanc* is indicative of his manner, telling Breton legends in vivid and exciting style.

Féval's greatest success was his *Mystères de Londres,* commissioned by the publisher to exploit current enthusiasm for Sue's *Mystères de Paris.* The first volume, written entirely from imagination, enjoyed incredible popularity; for the later parts Féval spent some time in careful sociological documentation in London. The novel appealed no doubt primarily for the timeliness of the subject, but it was skillfully constructed and excellently written; twenty editions testify to its

success, and many translations appeared shortly.

Féval continued his associations with literary reviews and published several further novels such as *Le Fils du Diable* (1847). Coincidentally with the Revolution of 1848, he suffered an extreme crisis of moral depression, and as a "legitimist" took part briefly in politics. His attempts at dramatization of his novels were unsuccessful, but his reputation in prose fiction continued to rise as he composed his two hundred novels. He tried other genres such as historical tracts, and in *Le Bossu* (1857), produced a Spanish-style costume novel set during the Regency with a background of the financial troubles of the system of John Law. His private life was happy, with a devoted wife, a careful routine of writing, considerable wealth, and wide respect. His name was constantly cited as an authority during the Second Empire; he was president of several national literary societies and enjoyed the patronage of the Empress Eugénie. Today the lively style and rich imagination of this popular entertainer seem insufficient in the face of his overly hasty and careless composition.

"I Am Here!" The Duke's Motto; or, The Little Parisian was translated into English by H. L. Williams, Jr. (1863).

ABOUT: [In French—Glaesener, H. Le Génie de Paul Féval; Legrand, G. Paul Féval Intime.]

F. J. C.

*FICINO, MARSILIO (October 19, 1433-October 1, 1499), Italian philosopher, was born in Figline, son of Diotifeci d'Agnolo di Giusto, personal physician of Cosimo de' Medici, and Alessandra di Nannoccio di Montevarchi. Thanks to his father's position, young Marsilio came to the attention of the powerful Cosimo, who recognized the boy's promise and provided the means for his education and for his lifework as a scholar. At about eighteen he was received into the Medici household in Florence where he met all the great humanists of the day, among them Gemisthos Plethon, whose ambition it was to establish in Florence an academy worthy to stand as the Renaissance equivalent of the Greek Academy of Athens. In this learned circle Ficino was designated the official Platonist. He proceeded to learn Greek in 1459 and devoted the remainder of his life to the study, exposition, and translation of the works of Plato. To this end Cosimo encouraged him by providing teachers, manuscripts, and even a comfortable villa

* fā vȧl'

* fē chē' nō

277

FICINO

Ficino devoted twenty years of his life to translating the writings of Plato into Latin, publishing the work in 1482. Equally important, and perhaps of greater influence in literary history, was his Latin commentary on Plato's *Symposium* (1469), the famous dialogue on love in which Ficino found the core of Platonism. In 1474 Ficino published an Italian translation of his work—*Il Libro dello Amore*—and it was through this work that the Renaissance conception of Platonic love (the love of physical beauty as the first step in the ascent to the apprehension of the Divine) received its widest circulation. The poet Benivieni summarized it in a *canzone;* Pico della Mirandola made it the subject of a prose study, and its ideas reappear in the works of Bembo *(Gli Asolani),* Castiglione *(The Courtier),* and, in England, in the *Fowre Hymnes* of Edmund Spenser. Ficino also published a Latin translation, with a commentary, of the writings of Plotinus (1486-91) and an Italian translation of Dante's *De Monarchia.*

Ficino's major philosophical work was a treatise on the Platonic doctrine of immortality—*Theologia Platonicae Immortalitate Animorum* (1482). Although the work is today regarded as relatively insignificant, it was in its time a significant reconciliation of Christian and pagan doctrine. Ficino's influence in the Renaissance, indeed, can scarcely be overestimated. As P. O. Kristeller points out, he was the first scholar to give humanism a philosophical system and to combine ancient, Christian, and medieval thought "into a comprehensive system of Christian Platonism. . . . Both as an original thinker and as a transmitter of earlier ideas he exercised a widespread and powerful influence on subsequent generations."

Ficino's complete works were published in Paris in 1641. Additional works were published by P. O. Kristeller in Florence in 1937. His voluminous correspondence was first published in 1495.

at Careggi where Ficino might work undisturbed.

Ficino responded to his patron's generosity by dedicating himself to scholarship and by working diligently. Outside of scholarship and his friendship and correspondence with many of the outstanding scholars of his day, his life was uneventful. During his youth and up to about the age of forty, he is said to have suffered serious religious doubts—the conflicts between the pagan philosophy which he studied with such enthusiasm and his orthodox Catholic background. Ultimately, however, he was able to reconcile and harmonize Platonism and Christianity. In 1475 he took religious orders and became a priest. He carried out his clerical duties as conscientiously as he pursued his scholarship, and he held his church office until his death in Florence.

A quiet man who enjoyed his study, his lute, poetry, and conversation with his friends (among them Pico della Mirandola, Poliziano, and Lorenzo de' Medici), Ficino ranks high in the regard of all who have known his work. Nesca A. Robb writes: "He has some claim to be regarded as one of the saints of humanism. He stands out from the other men of letters of the age by his singular disinterestedness. His work, which he looked upon as a sacred charge, was carried on unflinchingly throughout a lifetime of ill-health. In his personal life he was almost an ascetic, but his gentle and affectionate nature won him the love and veneration of the most divergent types of his fellow citizens."

English translations of selections from Ficino's work appear in *The Portable Renaissance Reader* (1953) and in P. O. Kristeller's *The Philosophy of Marsilio Ficino* (1942). His *Commentary on Plato's Symposium* was translated by S. R. Jayne in 1944. Also available in English is his essay "Five Questions Concerning the Mind" in E. Cassirer, P. O. Kristeller, and J. H. Randall, eds., *The Renaissance Philosophy of Man* (1948).

ABOUT: Fletcher, J. B. Literature of the Italian Renaissance; Kristeller, P. O. The Philosophy of Marsilio Ficino; Robb, N. A. Neoplatonism of the Italian Renaissance; Wilkins, E. H. A History of Italian Literature. [In Italian—see study by M. Schiavone.]

*FIRENZUOLA, AGNOLO (1493-June 27, 1543), Italian poet and satirist, was born in the city of Florence, some authorities placing the date as September 28. The Firenzuola family took its name from its home town situated at the foot of the Apennines. Agnolo's grandfather had become a citizen of Florence and transmitted citizenship to his family.

As a young man Agnolo studied law at the universities of Siena and Perugia. It was in Perugia that he met and became very friendly with the notorious Pietro Aretino. The two met again later in Rome where Firenzuola practiced as an advocate for some time. Most of his biographers assert that he became a Vallombrosan monk sometime during the papacy of Leo X or Clement VII. He is said to have lived a mundane life in the Curia, garnering benefits for himself, and acquiring a reputation for licentiousness. In 1524 he was released from his monastic vows and returned to Florence. After spending some time in his native city, he established himself at Prato as an abbot. It was here that he busied himself with his writing, founding the academy of the Addiaccio, anticipating the Arcadians of the next century. He died, poor and forgotten, at Prato.

The first edition of Firenzuola's writings (*Prose*) was published in Florence in 1548; *Rime* followed in the next year. His works are cited constantly in the Vocabulary of the Academy of the Crusca, the arbiter of classic Italian language and literature, though De Sanctis, in his *History of Italian Literature*, characterizes the style as "effeminate and coquettish."

The poetry is chiefly satire and burlesque. The prose works consist of *Discorsi degli Animali* (Discourse of the Animals), imitating Aesop's fables; *Dialogo delle Bellezze delle Donne* (Dialogue on the Beauty of Women); *Ragionamenti Amorosi* (Amorous Reasoning), a collection of licentious and elegantly phrased short stories in the manner of Boccaccio; an adaptation of Apuleius' *Golden Ass* which was a great favorite and saw many editions; and two comedies, *I Lucidi* and *La Trinuzia*, reminiscent of Plautus. There is also the essay *Discacciamento delle Nuove Lettere* (Disagreement about the New Letters) which opposes the plan to introduce new letters into the Italian alphabet.

The collected works of Firenzuola in Italian were published in two volumes in 1848. In more recent years selections from his work appeared in 1915 and in 1925. Both *Discorsi degli Animali* and *Dialogo delle Bellezze delle Donne* have been trans-

* fē rän tswŏ′ lä

lated into French and English. *Tales of Firenzuola, Benedictine Monk of Vallombrosa,* was privately printed in 1929. Clara Bell translated the dialogue *Of the Beauty of Women* in 1892.

ABOUT: [In Italian—see study by M. Oliveri.]

E. DE P.

FISCHART, JOHANN BAPTIST (called MENTZER) (1546-1589/90), Germany's greatest sixteenth century satirist, was born in Strasbourg. The appellation "Mentzer" frequently attached to his works points to the family's long association with the city of Mainz. The parents, dealers in spices, sent Johann to Strasbourg *Gymnasium,* then under the strong leadership of the renowned humanist-schoolman Johann Sturm. After his father's death (c. 1561) Fischart attended the Latin school at Worms where his godfather, Kaspar Scheit, of scholarly and poetic fame, was rector. As was customary with humanistically oriented students, Fischart went abroad about 1565: the Netherlands (Ghent), Paris, where he gained the baccalaureate, Siena for legal study, and probably England. In Basel from time to time, he earned from its university the doctorate in law (August 1574).

Fischart evinced a lively and sympathetic interest in religious and political problems of the region (Strasbourg-Basel). The difficulties encountered by the Swiss Calvinists confirmed in Fischart a profound hatred of rigidity and dictation in matters of religion and conscience.

Work with his brother-in-law Bernhard Jobin, a Strasbourg printer-publisher, increased Fischart's literary productivity. However, by 1580 he was an established advocate in the judiciary of Speyer; in this year also he married Anna Elisabeth Hertzog. Soon afterward Fischart assumed the post of magistrate (Amtmann) at Forbach: in charge of the judiciary, forests, and the police. Official duties probably curtailed his writing; at any rate from 1580 to 1587 he wrote little. He died in Forbach.

Fischart's considerable literary production was accomplished in less than twenty years. Catholicity of interest and wide erudition reveal the humanist; yet equally evident is Fischart's genuine sympathy for and profound knowledge of all classes of society: the scholar and the theologian, but also the tradesman and worker.

He possessed a sharp eye for human foibles and these he exposed in hilarious comedy and biting satire. But his true concern is not mirth but rather the moral foundations of society: true religion and virtuous domestic life. Further he portrays with power what he has himself seen; there is little of the speculative in him.

Strictly speaking Fischart was not original. He had a genius for appropriating and adapting the work of others. The results are almost always so unique that they can be regarded as original: *Aller Praktik Grossmutter* (1572) and the famous *Geschichtsklitterung* (1575) come from Rabelais (*Prognostication Pantagrueline*, and *Gargantua et Pantagruel*). The *Bienenkorb des Heyl. Römischen Immenschwarms* (1579) derives from the Dutch of Philips van Marnix, while *Der Heilige Brotkorb* (1580) is modeled after Calvin's *Traité des Reliques*. All these together with *Nacht-Rab* (1570), *Flöhhatz* (1574) and *Das Jesuitenhütlein* (1580) are sharp, uproarious satires castigating men and hypocrisies of the day: the immoral clergy, superstition, arrogance of the learned. More gentle and compassionate are his *Psalmen und Geistliche Lieder* (1576), *Das Glückhaft Schiff von Zürich* (1577) and *Das Ehzuchtbüchlein* (1578).

His fame, increasing even today, rests on his sharp delineation of the mores of the times but especially on his creative contributions to the German language.

ABOUT: [In German—see studies by A. Hauffen, A. Leitzmann, H. Sommerhalder.]

C. K. P.

*FLAUBERT, GUSTAVE (December 12, 1821-May 8, 1880), French novelist, was born in Rouen, of a prosperous bourgeois family. His father, Achille-Cléophas Flaubert, was a doctor (he figures as the character Larivière in *Madame Bovary*) and one of the leading citizens of Rouen. His mother, born Anne-Justine-Caroline Fleuriot, was the daughter of a doctor, a quiet, self-effacing woman who nevertheless ruled her younger son with an iron hand. Gustave had an older brother, Achille, who became a doctor, and a younger sister, Caroline, to whom he was devoted and whose early death, of puerperal fever, in 1845, was a great blow to him. She left a baby daughter, Caroline Hamard, whom Flaubert and his mother raised.

The boy showed literary inclinations early and began writing plays—which he produced and acted out in the billiard room of his home—when he was nine or ten. He attended school in Rouen and became absorbed in the study of history. He also read deeply in the

* flō bâr'

FLAUBERT

romantics—Byron, Scott, Hugo, Lamartine, Chateaubriand, Goethe's *Faust*. At fourteen Flaubert fell madly in love with a young matron, Mme Elisa Schlésinger, and he never completely outgrew this unrequited adolescent passion. He completed his schooling, made desultory plans to study law in Paris, but actually spent this time, 1840-42, in travel and aimless drifting. In 1843 he went at last to Paris to begin his law studies, but he could summon up no interest in the subject. After a year his health failed, and he suffered the first of many attacks of unconsciousness (possibly epilepsy but more likely some form of nervous hysteria). He returned to the family home at Croisset, a country house on the Seine, near Rouen. There—except for foreign travel and trips to Paris—he lived until his death. He had meanwhile been writing—*Mémoires d'un Fou, Smarh, Novembre*. In 1843 he began a novel, *L'Éducation Sentimentale* (but not the book he published later under that title).

In 1846 Flaubert met the poet Louise Colet, some ten years his senior, who became his mistress. The affair lasted two years, then was renewed in 1851. Flaubert admired her but apparently could not find with her the ideal love that he sought. They never married. The liaison ended finally in 1855 after a number of bitter quarrels, including an episode in which he allegedly drove her away when she came to visit him at Croisset. Louise Colet took her revenge by portraying him as an odious character in two of her novels, *Une Histoire de Soldat* and *Lui*.

In 1849, accompanied by his friend Maxime Du Camp, Flaubert left France for a two years' journey to the East. They had minor diplomatic missions which got them introductions to influential people in the countries they visited—Egypt, Palestine, Syria, Turkey, Greece. Flaubert steeped himself thoroughly in the glamorous and exotic atmosphere of the East. It was this region that had already aroused his curiosity in his first version of *La Tentation de Saint Antoine* (written in 1848-49), a novel which he rewrote three times before he was finally finished with it, and it was this same background on which he was to draw later in his life for *Salammbô*.

Ironically, although Flaubert was profoundly impressed by the romance of the East, his masterpiece was set among the bourgeoisie in France whom he knew and despised. This was of course the great novel *Madame Bovary*, the plot of which he drew in all its essential details from a family he knew that lived in Normandy. He worked on *Madame Bovary* for more than four years with complete absorption, struggling over every line, polishing and rewriting constantly. He gave himself so completely to the book that he later declared: "Madame Bovary, c'est moi." It was finished in April 1856 and published serially a few months later in the *Revue de Paris*. A storm broke immediately, and this novel, which in the mid-twentieth century is read in high school and college classrooms, was in 1856 condemned as pornographic. Love stories with the theme of adultery were surefire success, but such subjects were invariably treated with the sugar-coating of romance and glamor. Flaubert's honest and brutally realistic study frightened and repelled readers, and less than a month after its publication, Flaubert, Laurent-Pichat the publisher, and Pillet the printer were officially charged with offending public morality and religion. Their trial took place on January 31, 1857, and, although the book was censured, the three defendants were acquitted. The publicity brought the book popularity which it might not otherwise have had.

The fame of *Madame Bovary* completely overshadowed Flaubert's later work and plagued him bitterly. He once said that he wished he could buy up and burn every copy of the book—"throw them all into the fire and never hear of the book again." But in spite of the notoriety which attended its publication, *Madame Bovary* was immediately recognized by serious critics of French literature as a work of unusual significance. Sainte-Beuve admired it greatly. He found that its merits were "observations, style (save a few blemishes), design, and composition"; and he considered many of the scenes "pictures which, if they were painted with a brush as they are written, would be worthy of hanging in a gallery beside the best genre painting." Its principal defect, he found, was its lack of "goodness," its unrelieved portrayal of pettiness, shallowness, and corruption.

Henry James (who knew Flaubert personally, having been introduced to him by Turgenev) considered it a classic of French literature. "*Madame Bovary*," he wrote, "has a perfection that not only stamps it, but makes it stand almost alone; it holds itself with such a supreme unapproachable assurance as both excites and defies judgment." James called him "a novelist's novelist," and it is primarily in his genius for capturing the conflicts within the human personality of Emma Bovary that Flaubert exercised so pervasive an influence on other writers. His "sense of the intimate play of feeling and of the individual's inability to control or direct his feelings," Martin Turnell writes, had a particular influence on James and on Joseph Conrad. "James and Conrad were both far greater writers than their master, but their approach to the problem of human relationships was essentially the one practiced by Flaubert, and it is inconceivable that they could have produced the masterpieces they did without his example."

With *Madame Bovary* behind him, Flaubert put aside contemporary themes. He revised *Saint Antoine* once again and then plunged into a study of the pre-Christian era of the Carthaginian wars. In 1858 he traveled to Africa, to the site of Carthage, and completed his almost total immersion in the age. The novel which he produced, *Salammbô*, a lush and erotic recreation of the ancient past, was published in 1862, sold well, but was quickly forgotten by the public. In 1869 he published his revision of *L'Éducation Sentimentale*, a deeply personal book describing some of his own emotional entanglements in his youth, including his attachment for Mme Elisa Schlésinger. "It is a *tour de force* as a picture of the late romantic generation," Francis Steegmuller remarks. ". . . In it Flaubert's scrupulous art and his mastery of composition and narrative count for most." The book has never enjoyed popularity, however, and its failure to do so was a great disappointment to him.

Flaubert spent his last years at Croisset, but he remained active in French literary society. He met and conducted a lively correspondence with George Sand. He interested himself in the promising career of young Guy de Maupassant and became friendly with the Russian novelist Ivan Turgenev. He completed a third version of *Saint Antoine*, publishing the book at last in 1874. His last work, which he never completed, was his devastating satire on bourgeois society *Bouvard et Pécuchet*, a story of the misadventures of two middle-aged clerks who retire to the country to educate themselves. Into the book, on which he worked for eight years, Flaubert poured all his erudition. His simple clerks study every science, philosophy, literature known to man only to discover that all are false and contradictory. The pessimism of the book, Lionel Trilling suggests, is comparable with that of Swift's *Gulliver's Travels*. It is also, however, genuinely comic. Trilling writes: "Bouvard and Pécuchet permit us to laugh at ourselves in them and yet to remain detached from their plight." A planned second part of the volume, a collection of clichés, absurd statements, and definitions that Bouvard and Pécuchet were to pick up in the course of their studies, was published posthumously as *Dictionnaire des Idées Reçues*.

In 1875, during the economic crises following the Franco-Prussian War, Flaubert became involved in financial speculations, largely to assist the fortunes of his niece, now grown and married, and was very nearly ruined. He managed to keep Croisset, however, where he spent his last years living alone, regarded as an eccentric by his neighbors. He died suddenly of apoplexy on May 8, 1880 and was buried in the cemetery at Rouen. In his funeral procession were Zola, Daudet, and Edmond de Goncourt. A year after his death his niece sold Croisset, and a factory was built on its site.

Flaubert was considered handsome in his youth—blond, blue-eyed, tall, and sturdily built. As he grew older he became stout and bald. Always a hypochondriac, he was actually throughout his life the victim of nervous apprehension and mental depression. He frequently described in his letters his feelings of withdrawal from reality, his overwhelming distaste for life, and his longing to commit suicide. Yet Flaubert was not the shy introvert that this would suggest. With his friends he was hearty and jovial, loyal and generous. He had a lively sense of humor, a taste for jokes, hoaxes, theatricals.

Like many idealists he was embittered by reality and became cynical and sardonic. In his writing he belabors the dreamers, from Emma Bovary to Bouvard and Pécuchet, for being taken in by their dreams. Yet he was himself an idealist "on the grand scale," to use Edmund Wilson's phrase, who ridiculed the very qualities which dominated his own life.

Flaubert's work, with the exception of *Madame Bovary* and the story *Un Cœur Simple*, which Martin Turnell considers "Flaubert's only perfect work of art," represents a retreat from the bourgeois reality which surrounded him and which he loathed. The retreat took two forms—one, that of escape into the past *(Saint Antoine, Salammbô, Julien L'Hospitalier, Hérodias);* the other, that of outright satire and burlesque of the bourgeoisie as in *Bouvard et Pécuchet*. Such a divided course inevitably produces an unevenness of quality. "He was the product of an age of experiment, and its instability is reflected in the different styles in which he wrote," Turnell observes. His stature, in spite of his shortcomings, is great. "Flaubert remains a figure of capital importance in the development of the novel. When you criticize a little man his work simply disappears, but the great writer possesses a toughness and resilience which enable him to survive criticism."

The standard French edition of the complete works was edited by R. Dumesnil, ten volumes, 1945-48.

Salammbô was translated into English by M. F. Sheldon (1885), Ben Ray Redman (1927), J. W. Matthews (1930), E. P. Mathers (1931), J. S. Chartres (1931). The first and most popular English translation of *Madame Bovary* was made by Eleanor Marx Aveling, daughter of Karl Marx, in 1886; subsequent translations include those of John Stirling [pseud.] (1891), W. Blaydes (1902), Gerard Hopkins (1949), Joan Charles (1949), J. L. May (1950), F. Steegmuller (1957). *Bouvard and Pécuchet* was translated by D. F. Hannigan (1896) and by T. W. Earp and G. W. Stonier (1936); *Sentimental Education* by D. F. Hannigan (1898), A. Goldsmith (1941); *Three Tales (A Simple Heart, Julien the Hospitaler, Herodias)* by G. B. Ives (1903), F. Whyte (1910), A. McDowall (1924); *The Temptation of St. Anthony* by Lafcadio Hearn (1910); *November* by F. Jellinek (1932); *Dictionary of Accepted Ideas* by Jacques Barzun (1954). Flaubert's *Letters*, edited by R. Rumbold and translated by J. M. Cohen, were published in 1951; *Selected Letters* by Francis Steegmuller (1953). The first English edition of the *Complete Works of Gustave Flaubert* was published in ten volumes in 1904, edited by F. Brunetière.

ABOUT: Cather, W. Not Under Forty; Colum, M. From These Roots; Croce, B. European Literature of the Nineteenth Century; David, H. C. E. Flaubert and George Sand in their Correspondence;

Faguet, E. Flaubert; Flaubert, G. Letters; James, H. Notes on Novelists; Lewis, W. Men Without Art; Lucas, F. L. Studies French and English; Mauriac, F. Men I Hold Great; Muller, H. J. Modern Fiction; O'Connor, F. The Mirror in the Roadway; Shanks, L. P. Flaubert's Youth, 1821-45; Spencer, P. Flaubert; Steegmuller, F. Flaubert and Madame Bovary; Thorlby, A. Flaubert and the Art of Realism; Trilling, L. The Opposing Self; Turnell, M. The Novel in France; Wilson, E. The Triple Thinkers. [In French—Dumesnil, R. Gustave Flaubert, L'Homme et L'Œuvre; Thibaudet, A. Gustave Flaubert.]

FLEMING, PAUL (October 5, 1609-April 2, 1640), German poet of the Baroque Age, was born in the Saxon town of Hartenstein, the son of a Lutheran pastor. The environment of his early years was serene and happy. His poetic gifts developed early; they matured fully and were widely acknowledged during his lifetime. His career was extraordinarily varied and productive—and tragically brief.

Fleming was writing Latin poetry while he was still in school at Mitweida. At fourteen he went to the famous Thomasschule in Leipzig (where Bach later taught), then in 1628 to the University of Leipzig. His field of study was medicine, though he also attended lectures on literature. At Leipzig he joined a circle of friends interested in poetry and music. The group paid collective homage to Martin Opitz, whose domination of German poetry was then at its height.

Fleming left Leipzig with, as he put it, three laurel wreaths in his possession. One was his actual crowning as poet, one his master's degree, and the last, only partly completed, his doctorate in medicine. His departure was scarcely as peaceful as this might imply. Leipzig had been drawn into the turmoil of the Thirty Years War and the plague which accompanied it. Fleming, full of patriotic feeling and a convinced Lutheran, had been depressed by the death of Gustavus Adolphus, in whom he saw some prospect for peace and religious stability in Germany. He was rescued from his doubts about the future by the proposal of his friend Olearius that he accompany the mission of Duke Frederick III of Schleswig-Holstein to Russia and Persia.

This remarkable venture was basically a commercial one, a speculative enterprise designed to route silk and other commodities overland across Russia into Germany and thus into areas where the Duke could expect to profit. For Fleming it was obviously a more elevated undertaking, patriotic, religious, and cultural, an opening up of the East and an alliance of the East with Germany—but also an adventure. At the start of this hazardous undertaking he wrote one of his finest poems, "In allen meinen Taten" (In all my actions), now incorporated in Protestant hymnals under the title "Trust in God."

For over five years (1633-39) Fleming traveled, as part of a considerable entourage, to the Baltic lands and Reval, into Russia, to Moscow, down the Volga, into Persia. The voyage was one of excitement and hardship (often reflected in his poems)—shipwreck, the peril of Cossack raiders, and at their very goal, the Persian capital of Ispahan, a pitched battle with emissaries of the Grand Mogul. Returning to Reval in April 1639, Fleming became engaged to Anna Niehusen and was encouraged to remain in Reval to practice as soon as he should have finished his medical training.

Fleming was back in Hamburg by August 1, on the way to Leiden and the medical school there. In January 1640 he received his degree and returned immediately to Hamburg, on his way to Reval. But here, within a few days of his arrival, he fell ill. Before his death he had composed his own epitaph.

Fleming's poetry is always closely allied to his life, but only in his early period is it in considerable degree "occasional poetry." In his best works, a profound and manly courage speaks, a sense of dignity, of confidence in himself and in God, deep pride of country, a resignation to suffering, and a pleasure in living. The intense experience of his own life is generalized, its meaning distilled. Fleming transcends the limitations of his period as do few of his contemporaries.

He is best known for his relatively brief poems, his sonnets and odes; in second rank his *Poetische Wälder (Silvae)*, some of them deeply religious, occasionally with classical allusions, some personal tributes (to Olearius, notably) or poems on birthdays, weddings, and other festivities.

With the growing attention to seventeenth century poetry common to English and German taste of recent times, Fleming too has grown in stature. From the delightful Anacreontic "Wie er wolle geküsset sein" (How he would be kissed) to the praise of loyalty and love in "Ein getreues Herze wissen" (To know a true heart), from the quietly religious ode "Lass dich nur nichts nicht tauren" (Let nothing cause you to regret) to the noble sonnet of steadfastness and self-reliance "An sich" (To himself), an increasing number of his works have gained acceptance in the canon of great German poetry and may be found in all the anthologies.

Little of Fleming's work is available in translation. The Warner Library contains five of his poems. Several poems also appear in George C. Schoolfield's *The German Lyric of the Baroque in English Translation* (1962).
ABOUT: Julian, J. Dictionary of Hymnology. [In German—see studies by A. Hauffen, A. Leitzmann, M. Pyritz, L. Supersaxo.]

F. G. R.

*FLORIAN, JEAN PIERRE CLARIS DE (March 6, 1755-September 13, 1794), French writer, was born at Florian castle near Sauve (Gard). He spent his youth in close contact with nature and supplemented this experience by readings in the *Iliad*. With his father, he visited his cousin Voltaire in 1765 and thanks to charm and sensitivity became a favorite prodigy at. Ferney. In Paris he entered the service of the Duc de Penthièvre, whose honesty and virtue influenced him considerably. Florian's plays, popular in the 1780's, recall Marivaux in their sentimental Harlequin, a naïvely attractive family man representing original moral lessons. Florian's fame, however, depended primarily on his novels, in ancient and Spanish settings, notably his two pastorals, *Galatée*, adapted to French taste from Cervantes, and *Estelle*, both containing verse of considerable beauty. The latter is set in Florian's native region and, though the local color is artificial, it was later esteemed by the Félibres as the first modern poetry of the south of France.

Florian is remembered today for his *Fables*, of which he published some ninety in 1792; they are second only to those of La Fontaine, but by no means mere imitations of this model, and they were held in high esteem by La Harpe and Sainte-Beuve. The stories are not original, but derive from standard sources such as Aesop, and especially the Spanish poet Yriarte. They excel in form and versification, the natural expression of thoughts and attitudes, and the serene and unobtrusive satire. Where La Fontaine portrays the native perversity of man, Florian points more immediately at recognizable persons of his time: the lion frequently suggests Louis XVI, whether as a proud warrior or the despondent witness of suffering or the victim of the wiles of courtiers and ministers. Egoism is depicted as the source of the other sins, but many

fables are optimistic, giving positive advice on virtue and wisdom, and developing lyrical themes of happiness, fidelity, and passing time.

Florian was elected to the French Academy in 1788. Five years later he lost his protector, the Duc de Penthièvre, and began frequenting nostalgic groups of aristocrats. He participated in the early republican ideologies, was imprisoned, escaped execution, but died lonely and saddened at his estate in Sceaux.

Florian's works appeared separately from 1784 to 1792, and a complete edition in twenty volumes in 1824.

The early English translations of Florian illustrate the importance of his novels: *The Works of Florian* (2 vols., 1786, with *Galatea*), *Numa Pompilius* (1787), *Gonsalvo of Cordova* (1792), *Estelle* (1803), *William Tell* (1809). *The Fables* were translated by J. Phelps in 1888.
ABOUT: [In French—see studies by L. Claretie, G. Saillard.]

F. J. C.

*FLYGARE-CARLÉN, EMILIE (SMITH) (August 8, 1807-February 5, 1892), Swedish novelist, was born in Strömstad, a town close to the Norwegian border in the province of Bohuslän. Her father was Rutger Smith, a well-to-do merchant. Her mother was Margareta Stiegler, daughter of a borough magistrate and merchant in Uddevalla in Bohuslän. She grew up in a milieu of fishermen, seamen, and wagoners. She lacked interest in school work and never learned spelling and style.

On her twentieth birthday Emilie married the town doctor, Axel Flygare, who at the time of the marriage had become country-district doctor in the southern province of Småland, where the newlywed couple moved. The doctor died in 1833, and his widow returned to her home region. She fell in love with a young lawyer Jakob Reinhold Dalin. They were engaged, but Dalin died suddenly from the after-effects of an accident, leaving Emilie pregnant. The daughter born out of wedlock, Rosa Carlén, later became an author.

To forget her troubles Emilie Flygare began to write about what she had heard and experienced. Her debut novel, *Waldemar Klein* (1838), was fairly successful, and after her second novel her Stockholm publisher asked her to move to the capital. She accepted, arrived there in 1839, and became easily acclimatized to the new life in literary circles. In 1841 she married the royal secretary J. G. Carlén, a well-educated man.

* flô ryän'

* flü' gä rĕ kàr län'

Now followed a period of intensive production which, however, was interrupted by grief at the loss of the son of her first marriage. After six years of silence she wrote her last novel, *Ett Köpmanshus i Skärgården* (A Trading House by the Sea, 1859). Her production thereafter consisted only of memories and autobiographical sketches. Her husband died in 1875, and the old widow faded gradually away.

Emilie Flygare-Carlén's production is remarkable in volume although not outstanding in literary quality. She published twenty-six novels, many in two or more volumes, which are mostly romantic, often tragic, love and family stories with hair-raising episodes interspersed. The best part of her production consists of thrilling novels from the Swedish west coast, e.g., *Rosen på Tistelön* (The Rose of Thistle Island, 1842), *Enslingen på Johannis-Skäret* (The Hermit of the Johannis Islet, 1846), and the above-mentioned *Ett Köpmanshus i Skärgården*, which all give fine realistic descriptions of the dangerous life of the seaboard population.

Her best novels have been translated into all civilized languages, and she was no doubt the most read Swedish author of the nineteenth century, both in Scandinavia and in Europe. The background of her voluminous production is the little known fact that she established the first "novel factory" in Scandinavia. From the very beginning she had helpers. During the boom years she employed a whole staff of relatives and friends to whom she distributed the writing of various parts of her novels. She might have written about half of her production herself, namely, the romantic portions, which had to be corrected and improved by her husband and others.

The greater part of Emilie Flygare-Carlén's novels has been translated into German, French, and English as well as other languages. For a full account of all translations into English see *The Sweden Year-Book*, 1938. Those listed below are merely a selection of the major novels: *Professornoch hans Skyddslingar* translated as *The Professor and His Favorites* (1843, 1854); *Rosen på Tistelön as The Rose of Tistelön* (1844, 1850) and as *The Smugglers of the Swedish Coast* by G. C. Hebbe and H. C. Deming (1844, 1845); *Kyrkoinvigningen i Hammarby* as *The Magic Goblet* (1845); *Fideikommisset* as *The Temptation of Wealth* (1846, 1847) by G. C. Hebbe and as *The Birthright* (1851); *Skjutsgossen* as *Ivar* (1852; also 1864 by A. L. Krause); *Representanten* as *The Lover's Stratagem* (1852, 1865); *Bruden på Omberg* as *The Bride of Omberg* (1853) by A. L. Krause and E. Perce; *Gustaf Lindorm* as *Gustavus Lindorm* (1853, 1854); *Enslingen på Johannis-Skäret* as *The Hermit* (1853); *Romanhjeltinnan* as *John; or, Is a Cousin in the Hand Worth Two Counts in the Bush?* (1853,

1854, 1857); *Jungfrutornet* as *The Maiden's Tower* (1853); *Ett År* as *One Year* (1853); *En Nyckfull Kvinna* as *The Whimsical Woman* (1854; many eds.) by E. Perce; *Förmyndaren* as *The Guardian* (1865).

ABOUT: Warner Library, VIII. [In Swedish—see studies by M. Holmström, V. Horn, A. Janzén, A. Kjellén, H. Svanberg.]

A. J.

FOGAZZARO, ANTONIO. See "TWENTIETH CENTURY AUTHORS"

*FOLQUET DE MARSEILLE (c. 1160-1231), Provençal lyric poet, the son of a wealthy merchant, Amfos, whose family can be traced in documents, was born in Marseilles, according to Dante, although Petrarch says his birthplace was Genoa. He received a good education and was acquainted with the great patrons of poetry of his day, Raymond V of Toulouse and particularly Barral of Marseilles, whose wife Azalais (Adelaide) he is said to have loved and to whom he addressed most of his love-songs. He was forced to leave the court of Barral when Azalais accused him of loving Laura of St. Jorlan. According to his *vida* or biography, Folquet retired from the world and entered the Cistercian order in sorrow at the deaths of Azalais and of his patrons Barral and Raymond; but this can hardly be correct, since he entered the order in 1195 and Azalais died in 1201. Folquet's last song, a call for a crusade to assist Alfonso of Castille against the Moors, can be dated in 1195. Folquet was married and had two sons. His wife and children retired from the world at the same time as he did.

Folquet is mentioned with respect by the troubadours Peire Vidal and Bertran de Born, but his subsequent activities were so opposed to the whole culture of Southern France that serious doubts have been entertained as to whether the poet and the later bishop were really the same person. There is no ground for these doubts, however. In 1201 Folquet became Abbot of Toronet and in 1205 Bishop of Toulouse. He was close to St. Dominic and, after the death of the Papal legate Pierre de Castelnau, went to see Innocent III to urge a crusade against the Albigenses. In 1213 we find him in the camp of the leader of the Northern French crusade Simon de Montfort and in 1215 at the Lateran council, where he was instrumental in founding the Dominican order. Folquet is credited with having introduced

* fôl kě' dě már sě' y'

285

the Inquisition to Provence but it should also be mentioned that he helped to found the University of Toulouse in 1229. In 1231 he died and was buried in the Cistercian abbey of Grandselve.

Relatively few of Folquet's songs survive and the majority of these are *canzos* or formal love-songs of no particular distinction. The effects of his classical education are very clear in his use of quotation of the more sententious remarks of Ovid, Seneca, and Publilius Syrus and his delight in such rhetorical devices as antithesis. He loves to personify love and give his reasons for refusing to fight against it. His versification and language although rhetorical do not display the excessive virtuosity of many of his contemporaries. Dante in the *De Vulgari Eloquentia* places him beside Arnaut Daniel and Giraut de Bornelh as one of the greatest troubadours, probably because of his classical language, and in the *Divine Comedy* puts him in Paradise, presumably because of his crusading zeal. He is one of the very few poets who were directly imitated by the German *Minnesänger*.

ABOUT: Valency, M. In Praise of Love. [In French—Stronski, S. Le Troubadour Folquet de Marseille.]

W. T. H. J.

*FONTAINE, CHARLES (July 13, 1514-c. 1565), French poet, born in Paris, was the son of an educated merchant, who sent him to the Plessis college. There he obtained his master's degree in the year of the founding of the Collège de France, whose lectures he presumably attended and whose head, Danès, he deeply admired. Fontaine's first fame rose in the literary quarrel between Marot and Sagon in 1536. Marot refused to reply to Sagon's slander, but his friends pressed his case before the King, and Fontaine's *Epître à Sagon,* long attributed to Marot himself, was the most significant rebuttal, in intelligent and measured tone. In his desire to visit Italy, Fontaine joined the army and passed some time in Lyons during the flourishing of Scève and Louise Labé. He had hoped for the favors of Marot's former protector, the Duchess of Ferrara, but she was under surveillance on account of her Protestant leanings. Fontaine continued to Venice, then settled in Lyons, where he married. He was cordially received there, and exchanged eulogies with the principal writers; his *Ode à l'Antiquité et Excellence de la Ville de Lyon* is noteworthy, as is his

* fôN těn'

defense of women in the "Querelle des Amies," at its height in 1543 when he composed his very important *Contr'Amye de Court,* showing the influence of Marot and of Platonic theory. The *Contr'Amye* differs little from Héroët's masterpiece of 1542; it develops allegory and mythology, uses Horace, Ovid, and Plato, and treats of worldly and divine beauty.

Fontaine's second wife, Flora, whom he married in 1544, exemplified his realization of true love, and his new life inspired his *Chant sur la Naissance de Jan, Second Filz de l'Auteur.* In Paris, he undertook a series of successful translations, and thus made known most of the work of Ovid. He is presumably, along with Marot, Scève, and Héroët, one of the four poets condemned by Du Bellay in 1549; Aneau's *Le Quintil Horatian,* one of the answers to Du Bellay, was long attributed to him, though he was a strong admirer of the Pléiade and cultivated their variations of the elegy and the ode. His most fertile period, from 1552 to 1559, yielded thirteen volumes of small interest. Modern judgment finds Fontaine's poetry mediocre; but its evolution and its countless references to contemporaries make it an essential record for the critical moment of the advent of the Pléiade.

ABOUT: Hawkins, R. L. Maistre Charles Fontaine.

F. J. C.

*FONTANE, THEODOR (December 30, 1819-September 20, 1898), German novelist and poet, was born at Neu-Ruppin near Berlin, a descendant on both sides of his family of French Huguenot stock. His father, Louis Henri Fontane, owned a successful apothecary business which he was forced to sell because of gambling and extravagance. His mother, Emilie Labry, a thoroughly practical woman, separated from her husband when her four children were grown.

Fontane described his early life in the autobiographical books *Meine Kinderjahre* (1894) and *Von Zwanzig bis Dreissig* (1898). His education was irregular, and of all his teachers he acknowledged the greatest indebtedness to his father, who inspired him with a love of history. At sixteen he was apprenticed to an apothecary in Berlin. During his four years of training and year of military service he spent his leisure time attending various literary clubs in Berlin, principally the famous *Tunnel über den Spree,* to which almost all notable German

* fôn tä' ně

FONTANE

difficulty finding a publisher, and henceforth kept his novels short by omitting all superfluous detail. The improvement in technique and construction is apparent in his next works, *Grete Minde* (1880) and *Ellernklip* (1881).

Fontane believed that "the novel should be a picture of the times to which we belong, or at least a reflection of the times adjacent to ours, about which our parents have told us." Since he knew best the life of Berlin and the Brandenburg Mark, these areas furnished the material for the majority of his novels. In a style that is detached and dispassionate, yet spiced with irony and humor, Fontane portrays the life and manners of Berlin, presenting a gallery of genuine Berlin types. He was an observer rather than an inventor, and his artistry lies in the psychological presentation of character. He possessed a rare understanding of human nature, and his situations and characters are convincingly real. In the technique of dialogue writing Fontane is unrivaled in German literature.

His novels generally deal with social problems. The theme of misalliance occurs most frequently, forming in variation the subject of *L'Adultera* (1882), *Graf Petöfi* (1884), *Cecile* (1887), *Irrungen, Wirrungen* (1887) *Stine* (1890), and *Effi Briest* (1895), which is one of his finest and most popular works. Among his other works the most outstanding are *Frau Jenny Treibel* (1892), *Die Poggenpuhls* (1896), and *Stechlin* (1898). At the time of his death in 1898, Fontane was esteemed as the major German writer of his day.

writers after the mid-century belonged. Under the influence of Moritz Strachwitz, who popularized the ballad form in Germany, and stimulated by the poetic collections of Bishop Percy and Walter Scott, Fontane began to write ballads, scoring his first great success with *Archibald Douglas*. He is now ranked among the foremost writers of ballads in German literature.

In 1850 Fontane left his apothecary calling and entered the press department of the Prussian Ministry of the Interior, a step which enabled him to marry his fiancée, Emilie Kummer. After two years he was sent to London to write reports on conditions in England. The impressions gathered on this and subsequent trips to England and Scotland were set down in the books *Ein Sommer in London* (1854), *Aus England* (1860), and *Jenseit des Tweed* (1860). In Germany he dedicated himself to the history and lore of his native province and wrote *Wanderungen durch die Mark Brandenburg* (1862-82). During the campaigns of 1864, 1866, and 1870, he served as a war correspondent. His experiences, including imprisonment by the French, formed the basis of several books. Not until he was nearly sixty did he begin the series of novels that was to bring him to the height of his fame.

Fontane's first novel, *Vor dem Sturm* (1878), was a long historical work revealing the influence of both Walter Scott and Willibald Alexis, Scott's chief German imitator. Because of the length of the work, he had

Selections of Fontane's poetry in English are contained in L. J. Manners, *Gems of German Poetry* (1865), and H. Phillips, *German Lyrics* (1892). Of his prose *Irrungen, Wirrungen* has been translated by K. Royce in 1917 as *Trials and Tribulations;* W. A. Cooper has translated *Effi Briest* as well as a selection from *Meine Kinderjahre* under the title *My Childhood Days* (in *The German Classics*, XII, 1913-15). In 1939 D. Harrison translated parts of *Aus England* as *Journey to England in Victoria's Early Days*. His novel *Unwiederbringlich* was translated as *Beyond Recall* by D. Parmée in the Oxford World's Classics in 1964. The definitive edition of Fontane's works in German, the Nymphenburger edition, began publication in 1959 and will run to twenty-seven volumes.

ABOUT: Hayens, K. Theodor Fontane; Hewitt-Thayer, H. The German Novel; Mann, T. Essays of Three Decades; Pascal, R. The German Novel; Remak, J. The Gentle Critic: Fontane and German Politics; Times (London) Literary Supplement, January 16, 1964. [In German—see studies by A. Bosshart, H. Maync, H. Spiero, C. Wandrey, F. Zillmann.]

D. G. D.

*FONTENELLE, BERNARD LE BO-VIER DE (February 11, 1657-January 9, 1757), French essayist and popularizer of science, was born and raised in Rouen. His father, François le Bovier de Fontenelle, was a lawyer; his mother, Marthe Corneille, was the sister of the dramatists Pierre and Thomas Corneille. Bernard, the second of four sons, was extremely frail as a child. He attended a Jesuit school, where he was an outstanding student. At seventeen he visited Paris, where he lived with his uncles and made a great impression in literary circles for his knowledge and wit. With the help of his uncle, Thomas Corneille, he published a poem in the *Mercure Galant* in 1677. He then collaborated successfully with Thomas on two musical plays, for both of which Lully composed the music. His next two plays, written by himself alone, were failures, and Fontenelle temporarily abandoned the theatre.

In 1683 appeared his first important work, the *Dialogues des Morts,* in which he attacked popular prejudices, including the veneration of antiquity. The *Dialogues* were very soon translated into Italian and English, and in France itself they created a new vogue. His next important publication, and his most famous, was the *Entretiens sur la Pluralité des Mondes* (1686), in which Fontenelle, taking advantage of the widespread interest in scientific matters, explained the Copernican system and Descartes' astronomical ideas in a style so easy and charming as to make it the envy of popularizers ever since. Almost equally successful was his *Histoire des Oracles* (1686), in which he attacked pagan oracles and, through them, Christian miracles. In this work, as in his *Histoire des Fables* (1686) and elsewhere, Fontenelle showed himself a faithful follower of Descartes' philosophy, by subjecting all things to the light of reason.

In 1688 Fontenelle published his *Discours sur la Nature de l'Églogue* and his *Digression sur les Anciens et Les Modernes,* the latter being a major contribution to the arguments of the "moderns" in the Quarrel of Ancients and Moderns. It was Fontenelle's view that, nature remaining constant, the "moderns" are inevitably superior to the "ancients," because of the accumulation of knowledge and experience. Fontenelle's candidacy to the French Academy was bitterly opposed by the "ancients" Racine and Boileau, and when, in 1691, he was finally

* fônt nĕl'

FONTENELLE

elected, this was generally regarded as a great victory for the side of the "moderns."

In 1697 Fontenelle became a member of the Académie des Sciences and, in later years, of many other academies both in France and abroad. The Académie des Sciences made Fontenelle its permanent secretary, and in this position he wrote annual histories of the proceedings of the Academy, as well as eulogies of deceased members. These *éloges,* in which Fontenelle succeeded in writing like an expert on each scientist's specialty, are often regarded as his finest work of scientific popularization, even superior to the annual histories.

A savant and a conversationalist of the first water, Fontenelle was extremely popular in all the salons in Paris, not only because of his wit but also because of his easy, kind manner and his consideration for the feelings of others. La Bruyère, in his *Caractères,* however, drew an unflattering picture of Fontenelle as "Cydias," stressing his logic, his brilliance, and his determination to be different from other people. Fontenelle's activity in literature proper consisted largely of tragedies, written mostly after 1720, and some critical essays on poetry and drama, which are undistinguished. His aesthetic taste shows the marks of excessive reasoning.

Fontenelle remained bright and vigorous almost to the end of his life. At ninety-four, however, his eyes weakened suddenly; even earlier his hearing had deteriorated; and his memory occasionally failed him in his last years. From the age of ninety-six or ninety-seven on, he suffered from epileptic attacks, one of which proved fatal. He died at his home in Paris leaving most of his fortune to the great granddaughters of his uncle, Thomas Corneille.

Fontenelle was, according to his own account and the testimony of others, restrained in his emotions and pleasures and logical in all his relationships. He cultivated happiness and lived a very tranquil and even life. His appearance was cold, but underneàth there was a certain amount of warmth, though this was often hard to perceive. He is best remembered as a popularizer of science and a trail-blazer for the Philosophes of the eighteenth century.

In 1957 the anniversaries of Fontenelle's birth and death were observed with the publication of a number of scholarly articles and with an exhibition in his honor at the Bibliothèque Nationale.

Dialogues of the Dead was translated into English by a J.D. (perhaps Dryden) (1692), by John Hughes (1708), and Phyllis Playter (1925). *Conversations on the Plurality of Worlds* was translated by Mrs. A. Behn (1688), J. Glanvill (1695), W. Gardiner (1715), and Elizabeth Gunning (1803). *History of Oracles* was translated by an A.B. (1688) and by S. Whatley (1750).

ABOUT: Cosentini, J. W. Fontenelle's Art of Dialogue; Jones, R. F. The Battle of the Books. [In French—see studies by I.-R. Carré, J. F. Couillon, A. Fayol, A. Laborde-Milaa, and L. Maigron.]

A. C. K.

*FONVIZIN, DENIS IVANOVICH

(April 14, 1745-December 12, 1792), Russian playwright, descendant of a Livonian knight, was born and raised in Moscow, and educated at the University of Moscow. Though his interests throughout life were impressively varied, he very early favored literary ambitions. In 1762, the year of the accession of Catherine the Great, Fonvizin entered government service. Greatly under the influence of the Enlightenment himself, he fell in with the circle of "freethinkers" at the capital of whom many were eminent government dignitaries. One such dignitary, Count N. I. Panin, the foremost liberal of the day, was especially impressed by the young writer, and in 1769 Fonvizin became Panin's private secretary, soon afterwards his close friend and confidant. In sympathy with Panin's cause and considering it the writer's duty to "raise his voice aloud against the abuses and prejudices imperiling the nation," Fonvizin published a number of satirical *feuilletons* aimed mainly at Catherine's

* fŭn vyē′ zyĭn

autocratic-minded courtiers. The liberality of his tongue and the fact of his having had a hand in composing Panin's *Testament*—a sort of constitutionalist manifesto—aroused the ire of the Empress. Fonvizin took it upon himself to withdraw from service shortly after Panin's death in 1783, and traveled abroad (his third trip) the next year.

Aside from his political writings, Fonvizin's literary output consisted largely of translations and satiric poems. However, his fame as a writer rests preeminently on his two satiric comedies in prose, *Brigadir* (1766) and *Nedorosl'* (1782). Both plays reflect the influence of French sentimental drama as well as neoclassicist dramaturgy, the prime inspiration of the early Russian theatre. *Nedorosl'*, a satire on the brutish mentality and manners of the provincial gentry, is generally regarded not only as Fonvizin's masterpiece but also as the *pièce de résistance* of the Russian eighteenth century stage. Fonvizin's special genius lay in composing comic dialogue, for which he drew to an extent unknown till then and with incomparable artistry on the resources of the spoken language, and in creating authentically "vulgar" characters. In these respects especially his comedies became the prototype for that genre in Russian literature. Moreover, largely on the same evidence, Fonvizin is popularly held to be a major precursor of Russian realism.

Patriot, "friend of freedom" (Pushkin), foe of vulgarity, injustice, sham, Fonvizin responded to his time with inveterate indignation. Behind his satire lay a sense not so much of humor as of outrage and revulsion, running as easily to moralistic declamation as to comic derision. This bifurcated expression of his indignation is nowhere more in evidence than in his letters from abroad, especially his *Letters from France* (1777-78) which are as remarkable for their language—a milestone in the development of literary Russian—as for their bilious, nevertheless penetrating and informative, view of French society on the eve of the Revolution.

In 1785 Fonvizin suffered a paralytic stroke in part depriving him, ironically, of the free use of his tongue. Although an almost helpless invalid, he continued to write, leaving unfinished at his death his autobiography, a work written in that mood of Christian repentance which came to prominence in his last years.

Fonvizin's *Nedorosl'* was translated into English by G. Z. Patrick and G. R. Noyes with the title *The Young Hopeful* and is published in *Master-*

pieces of the Russian Drama, ed. by G. R. Noyes (1933). Another play, *The Choice of a Tutor,* appears in *Five Russian Plays,* translated by C. E. Beechhofer (1916).

ABOUT: [In Russian—see studies by D. Blagoj, G. P. Makogonenko, K. V. Pigarev, A. Shtein.]

I. R. T.

*FORSTER, JOHANN GEORGE ADAM

(November 27, 1754-January 10, 1794), German traveler, scientist, author, and revolutionary, was born at Nassenhuben near Danzig, descendant of a noble Scottish Protestant family. His father, Johann Reinhold Forster (1729-98), a clergyman and a highly regarded naturalist, was endowed with a violent temper and fierce pride. His mother, Justine Elisabeth *née* Nicolai, a cousin of J. R., was a gentle creature and hardly able to wield any influence over her husband. Young George at an early age showed a keen interest in the sciences. He never had much formal training, but prodded and helped by his father he easily acquired great learning in a variety of fields. This laid the groundwork for a versatility about which he complained bitterly throughout his life.

In 1765 he accompanied his father to Russia on a tour of inspection of the Eastern colonies at the behest of Catherine II. The following year the two showed up in London. George was apprenticed to learn the textile trade, but, falling ill, soon joined his family at Warrington in Lancashire, where his father taught at the Nonconformist Academy. George attended Boteler Grammar School and helped support the family by giving private lessons and translating travelogues and scholarly treatises with his father. In 1770 the Forsters returned to London, where they continued their precarious mode of living. Eventually J. R. was engaged by the Admiralty as the official naturalist for Captain Cook's second voyage aboard the "Resolution" (July 13, 1772-July 30, 1775). He took along George, who called the voyage his greatest experience and the happiest time of his life. Yet while on the expedition he contracted scurvy from which he never fully recovered and which contributed to his early death.

On their return to London the Forsters prepared to publish their many discoveries. J. R. promptly got embroiled in a quarrel with Cook and the Admiralty. As a result George brought out his own *A Voyage Round the World* (London, 1777; German translation: Berlin, 1778-80), one of the finest and most widely acclaimed travel accounts. He

* för' stĕr

FORSTER

also wrote two ill-advised and ill-tempered pamphlets to clear his and his father's name, the *Reply to Mr. Wales's Remarks* and *A Letter to the Right Honourable Earl of Sandwich* (both London, 1778). In 1777 he was elected Fellow of the Royal Society, an honor of which he was keenly conscious, following as it were in his father's footsteps. That same year he visited Paris and met Franklin at Passy.

In the fall of 1778 Forster set out for Germany. His reception there was most flattering. To his great surprise he, and not his father, who was on the verge of bankruptcy, was offered a professorship at the Collegium Carolinum in Cassel. With his friend Sömmering, the anatomist, whom he had met in London, he became an ardent Rosicrucian. The list of his other intimates at that time reads like a roster of German literature: Jacobi, Herder, Goethe, J. von Müller, Heinse, and Heyne. With Lichtenberg he published for a time (beginning in 1780) the *Göttingische Magazin,* in which appeared among others his essay "O-Tahiti," an immensely influential study both for literature and anthropology: it brought the Pacific to German romanticism. His *Leben Dr. Wilhelm Dodds* (Berlin, 1779), a tolerant and enlightened religious biography, put him squarely into the forefront of the liberal camp.

Forster was not handsome. His face was pockmarked, his stature small, but he had flashing eyes expressive of his every mood; his conversational talents were widely admired. In nearby Göttingen he met Caroline

Michaelis (later Schlegel-Schelling), but favored her rival Therese Heyne, to whom he became engaged. Caroline, however, remained his friend until the bitter end, which is more than can be said about Therese. In order to care for his future wife properly and to escape from provincial Cassel, where he had incurred debts, he accepted a post at the University of Vilna, which was even more provincial, in 1784. His *Tagebücher* vividly describe the arduous journey to Poland via Prague and Vienna. The following year he married Therese and settled with her in that barbarous land, as they both called it. Forster was forever unable to live within his budget and therefore was forced to do hackwork; translations of travelogues of all nations flowed from his facile pen and flooded the German market. In 1787 he was rescued. The Russian government, eager to have him lead an expedition, paid all his debts, but the planned voyage came to naught. The Forsters returned to Germany.

In 1788 he accepted the position of librarian to the Elector of Mainz. His closest friends there were the two young von Humboldts and Ludwig F. Huber. In Mainz he wrote a considerable number of studies, amongst them the fine and detailed "Geschichte der Englischen Literatur von 1788-1792" and "Geschichte der Kunst in England" for Archenholz' *Annalen*. With Alexander von Humboldt he traveled to England, writing on his return his greatest work, the *Ansichten vom Niederrhein* (Berlin, 1791), of which the third volume remained fragmentary. That same year appeared his translation of *Sakontala*, the most important of his many translations. These two books stamp Forster as a forerunner of the romantic movement. His view of medieval art, his treatment of historical events, his revival of the Orient, decisively influenced Wackenroder, Tieck, the Schlegels, Novalis, and the Boisserées. He is one of the finest stylists of the period, as his *Briefwechsel* (Leipzig, 1829) convincingly shows.

General Custine occupied Mainz in the fall of 1792, and Forster was drawn into the whirlpool of politics. On the approach of the imperial armies, Therese, who had been an ardent supporter of the Revolution, deserted her husband, and with the two girls (one boy had died) found refuge in Switzerland, where she was soon joined by Huber, with whom she had early formed a liaison. Forster, who had become a member of the Jacobin Club, was made vice president of the provincial government. His writings of the period are propagandistic, such as the *Erinnerungen aus dem Jahr 1790* (Berlin, 1793). In the spring of 1793 he went to Paris as a deputy to the Convention to propose incorporation of the left bank of the Rhine with France. In Paris he was employed in various tasks by the government. There he became an intimate of the English colony, meeting Mary Wollstonecraft and Thomas Paine. Mainz was lost, Germany banished him from her soil, his former friends turned against him, Therese asked for a divorce, he was destitute. Forster died in despair and agony at the age of thirty-nine and was buried, like Heine after him, in the Père Lachaise.

Forster's subsequent small reputation is intimately connected with his personal tragedy. A man of great idealism, he was not a leader, not a strong personality. He craved love and guidance, first from his father, later from his wife. When the latter left him, his world collapsed, and it is difficult to say whether his later political views which justify the Terror were not motivated by despair alone. Zincke has shown conclusively that Therese in her capacity as editor of the *Briefwechsel* falsified and forged a large number of his letters in an attempt to hide her own duplicity and that she often toned down Forster's extremism. It is to be hoped that the *Forster-Ausgabe* issued by the Deutsche Akademie der Wissenschaften zu Berlin will finally establish beyond a doubt how radical or moderate Forster really was towards the end of his life.

Forster's original English writings include (in addition to the aforementioned pamphlets and his *Voyage Round the World*) a journal written in Paris in 1777 (*Deutsche Literaturdenkmale*, CIL). His style in English has been highly praised. A very brief sample of his German writings appeared in translation in C. T. Ramage's *Beautiful Thoughts from German and Spanish Authors*, Liverpool, 1868 (15 pp.).

ABOUT: American Philosophical Society Transactions, XXXVIII (1949); Isis, XLVI (1955); William and Mary Quarterly, XII (1955). [In German—see studies by K. Kersten, A. Leitzmann, J. Moleschott, F. Schlegel, P. Zincke.]

R. L. K.

*FOSCOLO, UGO (baptized **Niccolò**), (January 26, 1778-October 10, 1827), Italian poet, was born on the Greek island of Zante in the Ionian Sea to the Venetian citizen Andrea Foscolo and his Greek wife Diamantha Spathis. The boy's first language was Greek. Andrea Foscolo was a doctor who practiced as a ship's surgeon. In 1784

* fôs′ kō lō

FOSCOLO

he moved his family to Spalato on the Dalmatian coast to work in the town hospital. He died in 1788, and ten-year-old Niccolò, his mother, two brothers and sister, moved to Venice where they lived in extreme poverty.

The Venetian provinces at the turn of the nineteenth century had been independent for 1,100 years, a condition soon to be changed by the European power struggle over the petty Italian states. The precocious young Foscolo grew up a believer in the revolutionary republican sentiments which were then upsetting the old regimes all over Europe. He also read the authors of his own classical heritage and the then popular works of Ossian. By the age of sixteen he was writing lyrical effusions of his own. The attractive Grecian Isabella Teotochi, twenty years his senior, interested herself in him and made him one of the members of her Venetian salon. He became her lover. His first tragedy, *Tieste* (Thyestes), written in 1797, showed the contradictory influences of romanticism and classicism by which all his work is marked.

When Foscolo was eighteen, he celebrated the French invasion of the Italian peninsula by the ode *A Napoleone Liberatore* (To Napoleon the Liberator). But the French, by the Treaty of Campoformio in 1797, partitioned Venice and, instead of giving the Venetians self-rule, opened the way for the seizure of power by Austria. Foscolo held the post of municipal secretary to a Venetian

tribune. To avoid persecution for his political beliefs, he left mother, mistress, and friends in Venice, and fled to the Cisalpine Republic. He worked in Milan for the *Monitore Italiano,* reporting the proceedings of the legislative assembly. He formed a friendship with the aging poet Giuseppe Parini, and with the younger, but equally distinguished Vincenzo Monti. He fell in love with Teresa, Monti's wife. She is not supposed to have encouraged him, but she is the alleged heroine of the first edition of Foscolo's novel *Jacopo Ortis,* written in 1798. He seems to have led an unhappy, rootless sort of existence in Milan as evidenced by the nostalgic lyrics of this period addressed to his mother, his brother, and his native island of Zante.

With the intensification of Austrian domination, the *Monitore* was suppressed in 1798 and Foscolo was out of work. He enrolled in the National Guards at Bologna and saw action as a soldier of the republic in the defense of Genoa. It was during this period of military activity that he wrote the odes *A Luigia Pallavicini Caduta dal Cavallo* (To Luigia Pallavicini on Falling from a Horse) and *All' Amica Risanata* (To a Friend Restored to Health). Both these odes helped establish his reputation as a poet. There is a musical voluptuousness to this period as well as an optimism which is missing from the earlier melancholic themes.

After Napoleon's defeat of the Austrians at the battle of Marengo, Foscolo journeyed to Florence where he met Isabella Roncioni. Under the influence of his passionate love affair with her, he revised and rewrote *Jacopo Ortis.* Because of its high-flown romanticism, the novel was enormously popular. It is the story of a young man who embarks on a hopeless love affair after profound political disillusion, and who then commits suicide. At the time of publication the novel was considered to owe much to Goethe's *Werther* but there is no doubt that it is chiefly a reflection of Foscolo's disillusion with Napoleon and the frustration of his patriotic hopes. There is also a groundwork of fact for the novel. Foscolo was familiar with the history of a young student of Padua, Gerolamo Ortis, who lived from 1773 to 1796, and who committed suicide under circumstances similar to those set forth in the novel.

Despite his rising literary fame Foscolo was still an impecunious young army officer. He therefore had to abandon hope of marrying Isabella Roncioni. Quitting Florence, he returned to Milan where he published a definitive edition of *Ortis,* and an erudite translation and commentary on the poems of Callimachus and on the *Locks of Berenice* of Catullus. He also experimented in translating the *Iliad.*

The army appointed Foscolo to a depot in Valenciennes, France, in 1804. About this time he began the study of English, and shortly he was translating Sterne's *Sentimental Journey* into excellent Italian. It was during this stay in Europe that Foscolo formed the liaison with a young Englishwoman which resulted in the birth of a daughter who later went to live with him in England.

By 1806, after a short leave in Venice to see his mother and his old love, Teotochi, he took up residence once more in Milan, continuing to work on his poetry. In 1807 *I Sepolcri* (The Sepulchres) was published, the poem of 295 blank verse lines that was to place Foscolo in the first rank of Italian poets. He was known henceforth simply as "the author of *Sepolcri.*" The work was prompted by a Napoleonic law forbidding funerary pomp. In his poem, Foscolo calls great figures of history forth from their tombs to fight again the great battles for humanity.

On the strength of his literary reputation, Foscolo now applied for and was appointed to the chair of Italian eloquence at the University of Pavia in 1808. His inaugural lecture, developing a theme of *Sepolcri,* exhorted his students to study literature in relation to their own and their country's life and growth. The lecture is believed to have influenced Napoleon to decree the abolition of the chair of eloquence at all Italian universities.

Back in Milan Foscolo's tragedy *Aiace* (Ajax) was presented in 1811. The performance, sabotaged by Foscolo's former friend Monti, was not successful, but the play attracted much attention for its disguised political criticism of Napoleon, the Pope, and other controversial figures. Taking refuge from possible reprisal in Florence, Foscolo completed his new tragedy, *Ricciarda,* and his translation of *Sentimental Journey.* He also started work on *Le Grazie* (Ode to the Graces) which he never finished. He spent an idyllic year in Florence as the lover of Quirina Mocenni Magiotti who was to remain his lifelong friend and helper. In July 1813 he was once again in Milan but not for long. Austrian soldiers marched into Milan after Napoleon's defeat at the battle of Leipzig. Having once fled from Napoleon Foscolo now was apprehensive of life under Austrian

tyranny. He decided to seek permanent exile. He spent a year in Switzerland in 1815, where he wrote *Hypercalypseos Liber,* a satire in Latin against his literary and political enemies. At the close of 1816 he embarked for England. During the next eleven years until his death, he enjoyed intellectual renown and social distinction in London, but then experienced much misery in consequence of his lifelong extravagance and carelessness in matters of personal economy.

He wrote prolifically for English periodicals, contributing to the *Edinburgh Review* and *Quarterly Review.* His fame was heightened by his dissertations in Italian on the texts of Dante and Boccaccio, and his essays on Petrarch. The latter were enhanced by the translations of Petrarch's sonnets rendered by Foscolo's friend Barbarina Brand, Lady Dacre, whom he met in 1818. She was his staunch friend and counselor in England and translator of his works.

His economic indiscretions led Foscolo finally to a state of bankruptcy in 1824, and for the next three years he moved from one lodging to another, under assumed names to avoid creditors. On his arrival in England he made efforts to locate his daughter. She lived with him the last four years of his life and was with him when he died of dropsy at Turnham Green, Chiswick. Forty-four years after his death, his remains were interred, with great national ceremony, at the church of Santa Croce in Florence.

Foscolo's great work *I Sepolcri* is, according to De Sanctis, the first and finest lyrical voice of a new Italian literature. There is a convergence of many streams of thought in the ode—mythology, Greek and Roman history, the genius of the Italian Renaissance— all to affirm the positive destiny of mankind, and to demonstrate the poet's profound humanism and sincere patriotism. For this he is much revered by his countrymen.

The first English translation was the *Essays on Petrarch* by Baroness Dacre in 1823. *The Sepulchres,* first translated by Mrs. E. F. Ellet, appeared in 1853, and then in 1928, translated by Ernest Grillo.

ABOUT: Vincent, E. R. P. Ugo Foscolo: An Italian in Regency England, *also* Byron, Hobhouse, and Foscolo. [In Italian—see studies by C. Foligno, M. Fubini, G. Giacolone, C. F. Goffis, G. Natali, F. Sarri, D. Sotgiu.]

E. DE P.

FOUQUÉ, FRIEDRICH HEINRICH KARL, BARON DE LA MOTTE-. See LA MOTTE-FOUQUÉ, FRIEDRICH HEINRICH KARL, BARON DE

*FOURIER, FRANÇOIS MARIE CHARLES (April 7, 1772-October 10, 1837), French philosopher, was born in Besançon. His father, a tradesman, wanted him to follow his calling, but Charles could not abide the hypocrisies of business affairs, a dominant attitude evident later in his disgust with competition and his dream of a better social and economic system. Fourier's life was uneventful; his profession as clerk associated him with cloth merchants in Lyons, Rouen, and Marseilles and occupied his last ten years in Paris. His routine duties caused him to complain of lack of time for study and writing; he lived alone, seeking solitude for meditation, and his works reflect his propensity for abstractions and his love of systematization.

Fourier's first work, *Théorie des Quatre Mouvements et des Destinées Générales* (1808), formulates a good part of his theory. He imagined a social order in which the individual might attain a maximum of personal development. The entire social morality of the times, in his estimation, tended to stifle man's aspirations and disfigure reality. He believed that natural desires showed men their true destiny, and postulated a need for organizing society by dividing men according to their inner natures: hence his terminology of "attraction proportional to destinies" and the serial "distribution of harmonies." Such groupings of men would result from his "Phalanstery," a kind of socialist and segregated monastery, in which there would be a proper measure and division of manual and other kinds of work.

Fourier's most important book, *Traité de l'Association Domestique Agricole,* opened a series of eight volumes, published from 1829 to 1836, consisting largely of unsystematic repetitions of the same ideas. These works gathered about him a kind of school rather than a group of true disciples. His influence appeared in the many experimental cooperatives that began to appear in 1832 and became common in the United States a decade later. His popularity was at its height about 1840, but suffered in the political atmosphere of the Second Empire. Fourier's influence on literature, for instance on George Sand, was greater than that of Saint-Simon, on account of his more direct appeal to the imagination. He had something of the reputation of a madman because of his unbridled fantasies— that man's life might be extended to 144 years, that a domesticated "anti-lion" would one day transport men rapidly from Paris

* fōō ryā′

to Lyons, or that we might send messages to Mars. Fourier, a pedant and a mediocre stylist, lacked Poe's artistry and Verne's moderation and technical knowledge of science, but he served to focus attention on comparable concepts; his name was immortalized by the caricaturists who exploited the ridiculousness of his most fanciful notions.

More seriously, Fourier presents an economic system that avoids the principal excesses of Saint-Simon, steering a middle course between futile mystic cults and communistic dreams. He sought out the causes of contemporary disorder in industry, and proposed a practical solution to the problems. Labor, which is indispensable, may be made more attractive by acknowledging man's need for variety (symbolized by the image of the "papillonne"), by encouraging his instinct for emulation (the "cabaliste") and his pleasure in physical and mental activity (the "composite"). It is vital that such a system proceed through free choice rather than according to rules or laws; hence, remaining strongly conservative, Fourier makes no appeal to politics nor in any way suggests revolution or opposition to religion, traits which set his thought aside from general positivist tendencies. His "Phalanstery" was basically of middle-class and capitalist nature, constructed according to a concept of stockholders, and the replacing of wages by proportional sharing of profits. The only reform of socialist type in his method is the guarantee of a reasonable minimum of sustenance for every man. Fourier also projected procedures for production, stressing agriculture rather than industry, and calling for a broad organization that eliminates the middle-man. Certain of his ideas may be related to those of the physiocrats or "economists" of Quesnay's persuasion, active about 1760.

A considerable number of English translations appeared after the publication of the *Œuvres Complètes,* six volumes of 1841-46. They include *The Passions of the Human Soul,* by J. Morell (1851), *The Social Destiny of Man,* by H. Clapp (1857), the *Theory of Social Organization* (1876), and *Selections,* by J. Franklin (1901).

ABOUT: Gide, C. Selections from the Works of Fourier (preface). [In French—see studies by F. Armand, H. Bourgin, J. Debû-Bridel, R. Maublanc, E. Poisson.]

F. J. C.

FRANCIS OF *ASSISI, Saint (1182-October 4, 1226), Italian mystic and poet, born in Assisi, was the son of the rich merchant Pietro Bernardone. He lived a gay and

* äs sē′ zē

ST. FRANCIS OF ASSISI

mundane life until a serious illness at the age of twenty-five led him to mystic dreams and a call to a great mission. After his sudden conversion, he devoted himself to ecstatic prayer and abandoned all contact with society, seeking solitude and even rigorous privation; he was subject to frequent temptations, and his healing through miracles gave him an immense popular repute. Of his early years one finds echoes in his poetry, especially of his idealism of noble and chivalric service and his desire to champion the oppressed. We know further of his life through the *Legenda Sancti Francisci* of Tommaso da Celano composed in 1229.

St. Francis' concept of devotion soon gathered about him the Franciscan Order of his companions, such as Fra Pacifico, dedicated to poverty, sacrifice, and love of the common man. This ascetic urge was strongly marked by a sense of beauty and a vision of reality as the bountiful creation of God. Beauty appears in all of God's creatures, living or inanimate, and all are St. Francis' brothers and sisters, with whom he constantly converses. Hence, in his verse, his feelings and his concept of the universe assume a particularly personal and lyrical form. His poems in praise of God's works, called for that reason "laudi," develop a popular genre from earlier Latin types.

The best known and the finest "laude" is the *Cantico del Sole*, in Umbrian dialect and free verse ("Laudatu sii, mi signore, con tutte le tue creature"). The authenticity of this and many other pieces has been in doubt on account of the fact that they were written down later by disciples and may well have been altered. The *Cantico*, regardless of such modifications, is one of the great archaic masterpieces of Italian poetry. It is said to have been inspired about 1224, that is at the period of St. Francis' vision of the angel and his receiving of the stigmata, and was revealed only after his death. His night of tribulation and his glimpse of heaven took this form and, set to music known to us in manuscripts, was intended to elevate his disciples. The *Cantico* praises God for all the creatures of the world, wind, fire, earth, flowers, even death; and its simple power inspired many of St. Francis' followers including Brothers Elia and Pacifico, and later Jacopone da Todi.

St. Francis' many other writings, and especially his *Vita* and *Speculum Perfectionis*, are important monuments in medieval mysticism, and reiterate the mission of his Order, to bring hope and comfort to the people. This mission was in fact a reaction against the corruption of the Church and a project to return to identification with the spirit of Christ. Such a worthy aim met inevitably with hostility and political friction, not only in struggles with the Dominicans and the Benedictines, but also within the Order itself. In excessive form, the ecstasy and exaltation, especially during such crises as the "Year of Hallelujah" of 1233, incited the people to vain gestures of abjection and austerity; later important outbursts include the Flagellants in 1260 and the program of madness of Jacopone da Todi. St. Francis himself was unaware of eventualities of this kind, and his influence may be exemplified in its positive form in his intimate communion with Santa Clara, who left her home in 1212 to take the veil, and who often guided and consoled him. Francis was canonized in 1228 and given the name of "Seraphic Father."

Such early editions as that of the *Vita e Fioretti* (1497) and the numerous *Opera Omnia* (1641, 1849, etc.) have been entirely superseded by critical texts based on better manuscripts during the present century. Publication of the *Opuscoli* in 1880 made available many minor tracts, letters, colloquies, rules, and sayings.

English translations include the *Works* (1890), Miss Lockhard's *Life* (1898), R. Steele's *The Mirror of Perfection* (1903), and a half-dozen original versions of *The Little Flowers* from 1924 to 1944. A new version of *The Mirror of Perfection*, translated by L. Sherley-Price, was published in *St. Francis of Assisi, His Life and Writings* . . . in 1960.

ABOUT: Fr. Cuthbert, St. Francis of Assisi; Moorman, J. R. H. Sources for the Life of St. Francis. [In Italian and French—Labande-Jeanroy, T. Les Mystiques Italiens; Ozanam, A. Les Poètes Franciscains en Italie au Treizième Siècle; Sabatier, P. Vie de Saint François; Tamassia, N. San Francesco d'Assisi.]

F. J. C.

*FRANÇOIS DE SALES, Saint (August 21, 1567-December 28, 1622), French religious writer, was born at the Château de Sales, near Thorens, to a noble family of Savoy. His parents raised him in strict Catholicism, sending him to a local school, then to Annecy, and finally to Paris, in 1581, where he studied with the Jesuits for seven years, preferring theology to the standard curriculum in rhetoric and philosophy. From his Jesuit teachers he understood the possibility of conciliation between Christianity and the new culture of the Renaissance, and thus instituted a current of "Christian Humanism." A visit to Italy added to his breadth of culture and noble manners, and he received a doctorate of canon and civil law in Padua. He was for a while active in the senate at Chambéry, and finally convinced his father of his religious profession. He was ordained in 1593 and sent to the southern shores of Lake Geneva where for four years he devoted himself to reconverting the Chablais villages to Catholicism. During an official visit to Paris, in 1602, he deeply impressed Henry IV; in the same year he became Bishop of Geneva, with seat at Annecy. He was beatified in 1661 and canonized in 1665.

François de Sales' writings represent his mission as spiritual guide. He sent edifying letters to many ladies of society, especially Mme de Chantal, grandmother of Mme de Sévigné, whom he converted. His correspondence runs to about two thousand letters, some very long, which illustrate his ideas on Christian piety. Among his principal works, the *Introduction à la Vie Dévote* (1608) precedes his meeting with Mme de Chantal; it is a manual and guide of piety for people of high society, of a severe doctrine presented with grace and in poetic style, with emphasis on nature and at moments a tendency to preciosity. The three revisions, down to 1619, make important improvements in method and scope. His *Philothea* (1608) is perhaps his masterpiece, and treats of divine love and perfection of soul in applications

to daily life. The title symbolizes the ideal person in whom he might find the achievement of his concept of true pious devotion, and refers to Mme de Charmoisy, who had accepted his complete spiritual guidance a short time before. His *Traité de l'Amour de Dieu* (1616) discusses union with God through prayer, and is a course in mystic love; it has had continued success even in Protestant circles. His *Controverses*, originally printed as leaflets for distribution among the inhabitants of the Chablais mountains, deal with the basic articles of Catholicism, such as devotion to the Cross.

François de Sales is significant in literature in the evolution of mystic thought of poetic type down to Pascal. His place in Catholic thinking is very great and almost of legendary kind, as testified by the long biographies.

English translations of *La Vie Dévote* appeared in 1613, 1675, 1741, by Challoner in 1762, by T. Barns in 1906, and by A. Ross in 1924. Other translations include *An Abridgment of the Interior Spirit* (1834), *The Consoling Thoughts* (1857), and *Letters* (by H. Mackay, 1943).

ABOUT: De la Bedoyère, M. François de Sales; Kleinman, R. Saint François de Sales and the Protestants; Reville, J. Philothea (preface); Ross, A. Introduction to the Devout Life (preface). [In French—see studies by E. M. Lajeunie, H. Lemaire, F. Strowski.]

F. J. C.

*FRANZOS, KARL EMIL (October 25, 1848-January 28, 1904), Austrian short-story writer and essayist, was born, the son of a physician, at Czortow in Podolien on the Austro-Russian border. He attended the *Gymnasium* in Czernowitz, where he received a liberal, humanistic education, and throughout life he was dedicated to the ideals of tolerance and enlightenment. Because the teaching profession was closed to him as a Jew, he sacrificed his preferred field, classical philology, for law, which he studied in Vienna (1867) and Graz (1868-71). In 1872 he returned to Vienna to work for the *Neue Freie Presse,* one of the foremost newspapers of that era, and with the exception of a decade during which he traveled extensively as a free-lance writer, he remained a journalist. In 1877 he married the minor authoress Ottilie Benedikt. From 1884 to 1886 he served as editor of the *Neue Illustrierte Zeitung* in Vienna and subsequently published the influential literary journal *Deutsche Dichtung* in Berlin until his death.

Franzos began his literary career while still a student in Czernowitz, publishing his

* fräN swä′ dĕ säl′

* frän′ tsōs

early tales in a local literary magazine. The material for these early stories, as well as for most of his later writings, was provided by his observations and memories of his childhood environment. His first major work was *Die Juden von Barnow* (1877), a collection of *novellen* portraying the Jewish cultural circles in Podolien. The initial story of the volume, *Das Christusbild*, which treats the unhappy love of a Jew and a Christian, is autobiographical in nature. Of the many additional prose works which Franzos wrote the finest are *Moschko von Parma* (1880), *Kampf ums Recht* (1882), and *Der Pojaz* (1905). Although his narratives afford excellent cultural and sociological portrayals of his native region, they are limited for the most part by their provincial scope and by a literary technique which only occasionally rises above the level of good journalism.

Of Franzos' other achievements the most significant was the series of cultural-ethnological essays, which were published first in the *Neue Freie Presse* and then in book form under the title *Aus Halbasien* (6 vols., 1876-88). The term *Halbasia* was coined by Franzos to designate the area of Galicia and Rumania. These articles present the customs, traditions, and landscapes of his homeland, and at the same time stress the need for education, progress, and tolerance.

In addition Franzos deserves recognition for publishing the collected writings of Georg Büchner. His edition of Büchner's works laid the basis for the eventual re-evaluation of this neglected author. Franzos was also esteemed in his lifetime for his efforts to discover and assist young writers.

A Podolien Sketch appeared in the English translation of G. C. Eyrick in 1878, and in 1882 a translation of *The Jews of Barnow* was made by M. W. Macdowall. J. Sutter translated *Ein Kampf ums Recht* in 1887 under the title *For the Right*. In 1890 M. Corbet rendered *Der Präsident* in English as *The Chief Justice*. The dramatic version of this work was translated by J. Block in 1915 as *The Judge*. L. P. and C. T. Lewis translated *Judith Trachtenberg* in 1891.

ABOUT: [In German—see studies by W. Spael, M. Rockenbach, A. Klaar, and L. Geiger.]

D. G. D.

*FRAUENLOB, HEINRICH VON MEISSEN (d. 1318),

German lyric poet, received his name "Praiser of Women" because of his lifelong dedication to the poetry of love. Except for references in his works, little is available about his life. He is probably called Heinrich von Meissen because he

* frou' ĕn lōp

received his poetical training there, not because of a connection with any aristocratic family. Most of the noblemen whose praises he sings belong to the eastern areas of Germany or to the Tyrol; the one document in which his name appears is an entry in an account in Innsbruck showing that he received, on August 17, 1299, fifteen silver marks for a warhorse from a nobleman of the Tyrol. He was a professional singer in the fullest sense (the "portrait" in the C manuscript shows him performing to the applause of other professional musicians) and spent his life in providing entertainment for patrons. His first appearance seems to have been at the court of Rudolf of Habsburg on the occasion of a mass knighting just before the battle of Marchfeld in 1278.

The close relationship between the numerous patrons seems to indicate that he was recommended by one to another but from the references in his poetry it is impossible to reconstruct an exact biography. All that is certain is that in his later years he settled in Mainz and seems to have opened a school of poetry there. He was buried in the cathedral and a gravestone was set up, almost certainly by Peter von Aspelt, Archbishop of Mainz from 1306 to 1320, who had probably met the poet at the court of Wenceslas of Bohemia. The gravestone records the poet's death date as November 29, 1318, and a relief upon it is said to have shown his coffin being carried by eight virgins.

His work consists largely of love poetry in the manner of the classical *Minnesang* but its spirit is far different. Frauenlob is overly concerned with mannerisms and with pushing to and beyond legitimate limits the figures and conceits of the genre. Love has ceased to evoke deep feeling. In so far as it is identifiable as an emotion it is a spiritual feeling leading to love of God, although still expressed in the terms of the love poetry of an earlier age whose ideas were no longer comprehensible. In other words, Frauenlob was a "Meister," a bourgeois professional poet, who was justly regarded by the *Meistersinger* as one of their immediate precursors. Not all his poetry is love lyric. He wrote a *Leich* or longer poem in praise of Our Lady, a *Leich* on the Crusades, and no fewer than 448 strophes, mostly grouped in threes, which are short poems of social, religious, or moral comment.

All the poems are to be found in *Deutsche Liederdichter de 13. und 14. Jahrhunderts*, ed. Carl von Kraus (1952-58). A few of Frauenlob's poems are translated in F. Nicholson's *Old German Love Songs* (1907).

ABOUT: Gallagher, S. A. *in* Middle Ages . . . Festschrift for J. G. Kunstmann. [In German—Krayer, R. Frauenlob und die Natur-Allegorese; Stammler, W. Verfasserlexikon des Deutschen Mittelalters. In French—Moret, A. Les Débuts du Lyrisme en Allemagne.]

W. T. H. J.

*FREDRO, ALEXANDER, Count (June 20, 1793-July 15, 1876), Polish playwright and poet, was born in Surochowo-Galicia, a part of Poland which then belonged to Austria. The son of a landowner, he was educated at home. At sixteen he entered the Polish army, which was created in Lwow after Galicia was occupied by the army of Prince Jozef Paniatowski in the Franco-Austrian War. Fredro took part in the Napoleonic wars, including the Moscow campaign. In 1814, when in France, he became acquainted with French dramatic literature. After returning home he left the army and settled in the country, taking care of his estate but still maintaining an active public life. This was the period of his development as a playwright.

Fredro began his literary career with the writing of pseudo-romantic ballads, but soon abandoned them for the comedy which was more suited to his talent. Even in his first works in this genre, in the one-act play *Intryga na Predce* (An Intrigue in a Hurry, 1817), and the three-act comedy *Pan Geldhab* (Mr. Geldhab, 1819), he displayed great dramatic talent. Of still greater promise was his next comedy *Maz i Zona* (Husband and Wife, 1822), the best of the Polish comedies written at that time. If Fredro were less indebted to the traditions of French comedy, one could consider *Maz i Zona* as a serious satire on the customs of the gentry (and some satirical elements are undoubtedly there); but to a degree the play transcends its sources, for it was only later that French comedy reached such subtlety and complication. The excellent dialogue is one of the outstanding virtues of this play.

Fredro's first plays were followed by others, which by 1835 numbered some twenty. There were among them works of different character and value, some light and unpretentious, such as *Damy i Huzary* (Ladies and Hussars, 1826) which even today entertains the public with its realistic human types and comical situations; and others of more careful workmanship, treating complicated problems with considerable dramatic ingenuity, such as *Sluby Panienskie* (Maidens' Vows) and *Zemsta* (Vengeance).

* frĕ' drô

Maidens' Vows, written in 1827 but first produced in 1833, is different from Fredro's earlier works. Previously his major concern had been to create comical and complete situations, but here he turns his attention towards the spiritual experiences of his heroes, making their internal evolution the basis of his play. The atmosphere of this comedy is cheerful, full of humor and charm, and the characters are distinctly and fully drawn; their experiences and spiritual evolution are artistically justified; the structure of the play is clear and compact.

Vengeance is the masterpiece of Fredro and of Polish comedy in general. Here the author went even further in the neglect of classical laws, joining three or four dramatic plots in a truly masterly way. The structure of *Vengeance* is indeed one of the most elaborate and artful in Polish dramatic literature. Each complication has many possible solutions, and almost every act leaves everything suspended. The play maintains a consistently high level: in the verse which flows freely, swiftly, and rhythmically, and in the wonderfully human and sharply characterized Polish types.

Among the other interesting comedies by Fredro are *Pan Jowialski* (Mr. Jovial), an imperfectly constructed but rich mélange of proverbs, anecdotes, fables, and jokes, and *Dozywocie* (Life Annuity), a comedy of character modeled on Molière.

Owing to an article by a contemporary critic who attacked Fredro's "non-national" and pseudo-classical character, the sensitive playwright stopped writing for almost nineteen years. When he returned to the drama, he produced several valuable works, such as *Pan Benet* (Mr. Benet), *Wielki Czlowiek Do Malych Interesow* (A Big Man Doing Little Business), but they do not equal the comedies of his first creative period.

Fredro's name is linked with the great tradition of western European comedy which includes Molière and Goldoni. Whatever his influences, he adapted them to his own artistic aims, creating original Polish works that possess universal significance.

Fredro wrote excellent prose as well as verse. His memoirs, published after his death under the title *Trzy Po Trzy* (Topsy-Turvy Talk), and written in the manner of Laurence Sterne, show his intellectual force, his ironic attitude toward men and things, his subtle sense of observation, his discreet humor, and his brilliant narrative style.

In Polish the best edition of his collected works is by L. Siemienski.

The first English translation of *Ladies and Hussars* was by G. R. Noyes in 1925. *Maidens' Vows* was translated into English by M. M. Coleman in 1940. *Vengeance* was translated by M. B. Hubert in 1957.

ABOUT: Kridl, M. An Anthology of Polish Literature, *also* Survey of Polish Literature.

P. LY.

*FREILIGRATH, FERDINAND HERMANN** (June 17, 1810-March 18, 1876), German poet, was born at Detmold, Westphalia. He was the oldest and only surviving son in the large family of a teacher. At seven he lost his mother, and after a year his father married again. Since the family was poor, Ferdinand never finished the *Gymnasium;* at sixteen he apprenticed himself to an uncle, a merchant in the town of Soest. Two years later, when his father died, he went to Amsterdam to learn business in a bank and to study languages. At Soest several of his poems appeared in the *Soester Wochenblatt* and other Westphalian magazines. Inspired by the sea and by cosmopolitan life in Amsterdam, where his favorite reading was books about distant, exotic lands, Freiligrath wrote poetry that was essentially romantic in character. He was, moreover, under the strong influence of Lord Byron and Victor Hugo, both of whom he began to translate into German. This poetry, full of melancholy, passionate yearning for the distant and fabulous shores of the Orient, was starkly different from the usual romantic fare of other German poets, and Freiligrath's first poetic efforts, when they appeared in the *Deutsches Musenalmanach,* edited by Adalbert Chamisso and Gustav Schwab, caught the taste of the public. Freiligrath became suddenly famous.

Moving to Barmen (a part of Wuppertal) in 1837, Freiligrath began an association with a group of Rhineland poets, and when in 1838 the well known publishing house of Cotta placed on the market his first collection of poems under the title *Gedichte,* the success was so great that Freiligrath decided to give up his commercial career and devote himself exclusively to poetry.

Shortly before his father's death, in obedience to one of the parental whims, Freiligrath had become engaged to his step-aunt Karoline, ten years his senior. Though love was never mentioned, it was not until ten years later that the engagement was broken. While in the Rhineland, where he moved to be close to his friend, the poet Emanuel Geibel

* fri' lĭg rät

FREILIGRATH

(1815-84), Freiligrath fell in love with a governess, Ida Melos, daughter of a professor from Weimar. In 1841, the year of his marriage, when he repudiated the political and revolutionary ideas of some of his contemporaries (especially Georg Herwegh, 1817-75), the King of Prussia, Frederick William IV, on the suggestion of Alexander von Humboldt, granted him a pension of 300 talers a year.

But in those stormy times Freiligrath soon reconsidered his position. In 1844 he openly avowed his sympathies with the new liberal ideas in his political verse under the title *Ein Glaubensbekenntnis* (My Credo), the immediate consequence of which was that after relinquishing his pension he was forced to escape to Brussels and then to Switzerland. Indicating that romanticism as such was dead, Freiligrath became now the foremost poet of the revolution. In 1846, as a sequel to his *Glaubensbekenntnis,* he published a new collection of revolutionary poems under the title *Ça Ira,* after which he deemed it wiser to flee to London, returning to the commercial life he had abandoned almost seven years before. When the revolution of 1848 broke out, he immediately championed the principles of the revolutionary party and returned to Germany, but because of the political sentiments expressed in his poem *Die Toten an die Lebenden* (1848), Freiligrath was charged with *lèse majesté.* After a month of imprisonment, he was acquitted by a jury. His identification with the revolutionary forces—he even joined Karl Marx

299

in editing the radical paper *Neue Rheinische Zeitung* in Cologne—so exposed him to harassment and arrests that in 1851 he settled permanently in London. The two little volumes of poetry *Neuere Politische und Soziale Gedichte* (1849-50) published in these turbulent years contain some of Freiligrath's finest poetry. For more than sixteen years, Freiligrath made his home in Hackney, a northern suburb of London, working first in a private firm and then as a manager of the General Bank of Switzerland in London. When the bank dissolved its branch in London in 1867, the poet found himself suddenly unemployed. Help came now from unexpected quarters: a merchant from Barmen, Emil Rittershaus, started, with a poetical acclamation published in *Gartenlaube* (April 1867), a collection for Freiligrath to which many Germans, even those who emigrated to America, contributed generously. Soon a sum of 58,000 talers was collected, and the grateful poet returned, deeply moved, to his homeland. This gesture of his people plus the national triumphs in the Franco-Prussian war, which ended by unifying Germany, awakened his patriotism once more, and Freiligrath contributed some stirring songs to the "Kriegslyrik" of the time. He settled first in Stuttgart and in 1875 in the neighboring town of Cannstadt, where he died.

Freiligrath was a thick-set man, with shiny-dark eyes and a powerful head, full of wavy brown hair that turned later into silver-grey, a "lion's mane." Of all the revolutionary poets of his time he was the most gifted, though his political poems often exhibited more rhetorical pathos than true poetic feeling. Freiligrath's great talent was especially displayed in his translations from French and English. In 1846 his translations of the poetry of Burns, Tennyson, Mrs. Hemans, and Longfellow appeared under the title *Englische Gedichte,* and in 1853 *The Rose, Thistle and Shamrock.* He translated Shakespeare's *Venus and Adonis,* as well as Longfellow's *Hiawatha* (1857).

His wife Ida, who returned to England after her husband's death, continued to translate English poetry into German. She died on February 6, 1899, in London. The sixth edition of Freiligrath's collected works in six volumes appeared in 1871. Another edition in ten volumes, edited by L. Schröder, appeared in 1906.

Freiligrath's daughter, Käthe Freiligrath-Kroeker, translated her father's poetry into English: *Poems from the German of F.F.* (1871).

ABOUT: Liddell, M. F. Freiligrath and his Times. [In German—see studies by W. Büchner, E. Kittel, G. W. Spink.]

F. S. L.

*FRESCOBALDI, DINO (c. 1270-1316) **and MATTEO** (c. 1297-1348), Italian poets (father and son), were born in Florence of a distinguished local family divided on account of the civil strife into "Whites" and "Blacks" and well known to the chroniclers. Among the most important of the "Blacks" was Lambertuccio, a banker, merchant, and poet who died in 1304. His first son, Giovanni (d. 1337), left a few sonnets, but his second son, Dino, was by far the most distinguished poet of the family and one of the great representatives of the "dolce stil novo" and the traditions of Guinicelli and of Dante. Little is known of Dino's life other than remarks of a descendant that he was handsome and a great traveler. He exchanged sonnets with a certain Verzellino on the subject of the proper choice of the beloved, and therein showed his preference for youth rather than for the married woman of the older traditions. His contacts with Dante raise problems of influence during the critical period in which the latter was writing *La Divina Commedia* and the *Vita Nuova.*

Dino carries the new style to a high point of subtlety and of rhetorical and cerebral artifice. His verse is obscure but at the same time rich in psychic reactions on such subjects as personal suffering, death, and martyrdom from love. Although he retains a few elements from the Provençal and Sicilian schools, showing a certain eclecticism in the techniques, he makes great strides toward abstractions and avoids the many popular and vulgar allusions of some of his contemporaries. His "Canzone della Morte," opening "Morte avversaria . . . ," perhaps his masterpiece, shows his disdain for Death, one of his principal allegorical personages (". . . vieni, e non m'aver, perch'io ti preghi, a sdegno . . ."). Dino's interpretation of love is more violent than that of earlier poets, and his beloved is more brilliant, pure, and even celestial, in a system of concepts that is strongly austere and pathetic. Some of his images closely resemble those of Dante, such as the lion in the forest of martyrs; Boccaccio attributed the similarity of symbols to a revelation to Dino of the first cantos of the *Inferno.* Dino's "Tristi presagi" proposes a visionary setting of moral anxiety ("Un sol pensier . . . mi dà . . .

* fräs kō bäl' dē

tant paura"), with threatening metaphors ("Una battaglia forte e aspra e dura") again reminiscent of the *Inferno.* In the tradition of the beloved as a young girl, Dino turns constantly to youth ("Questa è la giovinetta, ch'Amor guida"). His "Canzone del Pregio" develops an abstract system of passion and communication.

The poetry of Dino's son, Matteo, is less esteemed for its art than for the wider range of amorous, moral, and political subjects characteristic of the times of Boccaccio. Matteo's work raises several problems; he was active during the productive periods of Boccaccio and of Petrarch, and resemblances to them, as to Dino and Dante, represent influences or imitation. Of the thirty-eight sonnets and sixteen canzoni attributed to him, a few appear to go back to the preceding century, or even to date from about 1468 as the work of one Giovanni Frescobaldi. Carducci examined these from the manuscripts, sorting and annotating poems in some instances of real artistic value.

The few remaining canzoni of Lambertuccio and his son Giovanni may be judged from E. Monaci's *Crestomazia* and the edition by A. Mabellini. Critical texts of Dino's six canzoni and seventeen sonnets appear with his life in the volume by Angeloni, or may be read in such anthologies as E. Rivalta's *Liriche del Dolce Stil Nuovo.*

ABOUT: [In Italian—Angeloni, I. Dino Frescobaldi e le Sue Rime; Benedetto, L. di, Rimatori del Dolce Stil Novo; Carducci, G. Rime di Matteo e di Dino Frescobaldi.]

F. J. C.

*FREYTAG, GUSTAV (July 13, 1816-April 30, 1895), German novelist and dramatist, was born in Kreuzberg, Upper Silesia, where his father, a well-to-do physician, later became mayor. After studying Germanic philology at the universities of Breslau and Berlin, Freytag returned to Breslau in 1839 as a *Privatdozent,* intending to make a career of teaching. However, difficulties with a colleague caused his resignation in 1844. He turned to journalism and from 1848 to 1861 worked with the literary historian Julian Schmidt as editor of the *Grenzboten,* a major liberal publication devoted to politics and literature. During the period 1867-71 he served an undistinguished term as an elected member of the North German Parliament. Freytag subsequently withdrew from public life and dedicated his remaining years to lit-

* frī′ täk

FREYTAG

erary and scholarly endeavors. His death in Wiesbaden was mourned as a national loss.

Freytag began his literary career as a dramatist. His plays *Die Valentine* (1846) and *Graf Waldemar* (1847) won contemporary success, but only *Die Journalisten* (1852), one of the few outstanding German comedies, has maintained itself in the theatre. Although its issues of politics and newspaper rivalry are rooted in their day, this comedy, by virtue of its excellent characterizations and humorous dialogue, has retained its freshness and appeal for modern audiences. Freytag's study of the theatre also resulted in a practical handbook on drama, entitled *Technik des Dramas* (1863), which, though now outmoded, was important and useful in its day.

Freytag's current reputation is based on his prose works rather than on his dramas. His finest novel, *Soll und Haben* (1855), which reveals the influence of Dickens and Scott, contrasts the rise of the bourgeoisie with the decline of the nobility by birth and points the moral that the hope of Germany rests on its reliable working class. Although dated somewhat today, this novel in its own time achieved a popularity in Germany surpassed only by the Bible.

The cultural-historical technique of *Soll und Haben* was developed further in Freytag's next work, *Die Bilder aus der Deutschen Vergangenheit* (5 vols., 1859-62), which is perhaps his most abiding accomplishment. In this grandiose undertaking Freytag pre-

301

sented a cultural history of the German people from their beginnings to the present. It is a rare blend of scholarship and poetic artistry, a masterwork of German prose style.

In a second long novel, *Die Verlorene Handschrift* (1864), Freytag depicted the academic and courtly circles with the same meticulous detail he had employed for the world of commerce in *Soll und Haben*. However, the situations and characters lack naturalness, and the humor, which contributed so greatly to the earlier work, is, for the most part, missing. Although little read today, this work enjoyed great contemporary vogue and passed through many reprintings.

In *Die Ahnen* (1872-80), a series of eight novels, Freytag rewrote *Die Bilder aus der Deutschen Vergangenheit* in imaginative form, tracing the fortunes of a single family through the centuries to its culmination as a typical middle-class family of the nineteenth century. The individual novels are unequal in literary merit and show a marked decline in the last volumes.

Freytag's last major works were his memoirs, *Lebenserinnerungen* (1886), a collection of political essays, *Politische Aufsätze* (1887), and the monograph *Der Kronprinz und die Deutsche Kaiserkrone* (1889).

The first English translation of *The Journalists* appeared anonymously in 1888. Subsequent translations were made by H. Leslie (1904), R. T. House (1913), E. F. Henderson (1913), and V. Lyon (1916). The earliest and best translation of *Soll und Haben* was made in 1856 under the title *Debit and Credit* by M. Malcolm, who also translated *Die Verlorene Handschrift* in 1865 as *The Lost Manuscript*. Two anonymous translations of this work appeared in 1887 and 1891 respectively, bearing the title *Open Court*. M. Malcolm rendered *Bilder aus der Deutschen Vergangenheit* into English in two parts: *Pictures of German Life in the 15th, 16th, and 17th Centuries* (1862) and *Pictures of German Life in the 18th and 19th Centuries* (1863). The first two volumes of *Die Ahnen, Ingo* and *Ingraban* were translated by M. Malcolm in 1873. *Doctor Luther* was translated by E. Heinemann in 1897, E. Babbitt in 1913, and C. Riemer in 1916. In 1895 E. MacEwan translated *The Technique of the Drama*. G. Duncan translated *The Crown Prince and the German Imperial Crown* in 1890. Freytag's memoirs, *Reminiscences of My Life,* was translated in 1890 by K. Chetwynd.

ABOUT: Henderson, E. F. The German Classics, XII; Price, L. M. The Attitude of Gustav Freytag and Julian Schmidt toward English Literature. [In German—see studies by A. Dove, H. Lindau, R. Koebner, J. Hofman, H. Zuchold.]

D. G. D.

FRÍDA, EMIL. See VRCHLICKÝ, JAROSLAV

*****FRÖDING, GUSTAF** (August 22, 1860-February 8, 1911), Swedish poet, journalist, was born at Alster estate in the southern part of the Swedish province of Värmland. He inherited from his parents great poetic talent as well as mental instability. Both parents had religious, literary, and musical interests, and both wrote amateur poetry. Gustaf's father developed an increasing melancholy and spleen and became a solitary pietistic hypochondriac, whose inability to work put the well-to-do family in economic difficulties. His mother was highly gifted intellectually but emotionally high-strung and abnormally sensitive. At times she was insane, for instance at the time her only son was born.

The family lived during Gustaf's childhood and youth mostly in the town of Kristinehamn, but since one or the other of his parents was usually ill at home or in a sanitarium, the boy had little or no home life and lived for shorter or longer periods at the country estates of his relatives. His influences from and love of the beautiful Värmland nature and people left deep traces in his poetry.

The young Fröding had no interest in school work but managed in 1880 to be admitted to the University of Uppsala. Neglecting his studies, he showed great interest in radical ideas and activities, although temperamentally he had little affinity for practical social problems. He led a dissipated life, and his frequent fits of depression drove him to excessive drinking. However, he read a good deal of Swedish and foreign literature, finding particular inspiration in poetry written by melancholy and afflicted souls, e.g., Stagnelius, Tegnér, Byron, Goethe, Heine. His interest in the modern realistic and naturalistic ideas of the 1880's conflicted with his innate romantic inclination and made him perplexed and irresolute.

In 1885 Fröding started writing for a radical newspaper in Karlstad, the capital city of Värmland, and in 1887-88 was a regular member of its staff. His journalistic work in the service of radicalism was considerable, but his nature was not tuned to political and social polemics. Already his melancholy verged on insanity. A small legacy enabled him to stay at a sanitarium in Görlitz in Schlesien. Here he became engrossed in reading classical and romantic German and English literature. Heidenstam's romantic writings broke the ice and gave him courage to express his own personal feelings in verse. His technically brilliant first collection of

* frö′ ding

FRÖDING

poems, *Guitarr och Drag-Harmonika* (Guitar and Concertina, 1891), includes frolicsome Värmland songs, thought-provoking meditations, and inimitable descriptions of nature and people. Containing some of Fröding's most exquisite and beloved creations, it made him one of Sweden's most-read poets.

In 1891 he rejoined the Karlstad paper. At the same time he came under the influence of Nietzsche's anti-social superman philosophy, which introduced a new dangerous element in his emotional life, revealing itself in some of the poems in his next collection, *Nya Dikter* (New Poems, 1894).

From the spring of 1894 he spent his life in and out of mental asylums. In the beginning, his illness did not impede his poetic creativity. He published in 1896 a new book of poetry, *Stänk och Flikar* (Splashes and Rags), his most splendid and majestic work. The book was confiscated because of some daringly graphic erotic poems that were considered an outrage against morality. Fröding was prosecuted but acquitted. His next collection, *Nytt och Gammalt* (New and Old, 1897), showed stronger symptoms of mental derangement, and *Gralstänk* (Grail Splashes, 1898), is marked by his morbid condition. The poems he wrote after his discharge from the asylum in 1905 were published posthumously under the title *Reconvalescentia.*

A selection of Fröding's poems in English translation by A. Björck was published in 1903 under the title *Poems,* followed by another book of translations by C. W. Stork in 1916 entitled *Selected Poems,* some of which are included in Stork's *An-*thology of Swedish Lyrics* (1930). Four translated poems are included in F. A. Judd's *Under the Swedish Colours* (1911).

ABOUT: [In Swedish—see studies by I. Bäckman, R. G. Berg, G. Brandell, O. Holmberg, J. Landqvist, E. Lindbäck, G. Lindstrom, O. Moberg, A. Munthe, S. Sjöholm, F. Svenson, H. G. Wallgren.]

A. J.

*FROISSART, JEAN** (1338?-1410?), French chronicler and poet, was born in Valenciennes, in French Flanders (Hainaut), son of a minor official. He received a good education, and when a young man he was sent to England in the service of Philippa, Edward III's queen, formerly of Hainaut. Philippa showed considerable favor to him, making him a clerk of the royal chapel and her *ditteur* (court poet).

Thanks to the patronage of Queen Philippa and, later, of other nobles, he was able to travel widely throughout Britain and Europe and to meet many of the leading figures of his age. He visited Scotland, Wales, France, and Italy, and accompanied the Black Prince and Lionel, Duke of Clarence, on various missions. He most probably knew Chaucer and certainly knew Guillaume de Machaut and Eustache Deschamps. When Queen Philippa died, her cousin Guy de Blois became his patron and gave him the parish of Lestines—a sinecure which allowed him the leisure to travel and write. In 1383 Froissart became canon of Chimay; but he remained free to travel and it is known that he revisited England during the reign of Richard II in 1393-94. His chronicles end with the deposing of Richard and the accession of Henry of Lancaster. Nothing is known of his last years—though it is assumed that he died at Chimay.

It was Froissart's peculiar good fortune to have been on the scene of most of the great and terrible events of the fourteenth century—or, when not an eye-witness himself, to have met and interviewed the men who were. If ever a man was suited for the profession of chronicler it was Froissart—curious, alert, observant, with a good memory, an eye for color, and a prose style that was vivid, lively, and noble. Sainte-Beuve described him as "toujours à la fenêtre" ("always at the window"). Froissart himself recognized his responsibilities to the future, writing of his *Chronicles:* "For I know well that after my death this noble and high history will be widely read."

* frwà sàr'

Froissart's *Chronicles* are in four books and cover the period 1325 to 1400. They are probably our most valuable source for information on the Hundred Years' War, for which Froissart's dual French-English nationality made him an especially appropriate chronicler. To be sure, the *Chronicles* are neither accurate nor unbiased. Since much of his information was based on oral reports, it is inevitably unreliable. Even his chronology and his topography are faulty. As for objectivity—Froissart wrote for patrons and he shaped his history to please them. His first version of Book I, based in part on an earlier chronicle written by his boyhood teacher Jean le Bel, shows the distinctly pro-English feelings of his early patron Robert de Namur. Later, under the patronage of Guy de Blois, Froissart revised this book with a distinct French bias. He continued indeed to revise and rewrite it for the rest of his life, and in the balance it is generally conceded that the English come out rather more favorably than the French.

These, however, are minor flaws in a work that has been described as "the greatest monument erected to the medieval institution of chivalry." In a sense the *Chronicles* are a prose-poem with many of the qualities of the medieval romances of chivalry—pomp, pageantry, drama, adventure (especially in the accounts of the battles of Crécy and Poitiers). W. P. Ker wrote that Froissart "is one of the chief medieval writers, and his work is the culmination of a great medieval school, the school of adventurous history."

Froissart also composed some light courtly verse and a lengthy Arthurian romance. The latter, *Méliador,* was written under the patronage of Wenceslas, Duke of Brabant, and it incorporates many lyrics by this nobleman. The manuscript of the work was lost and not discovered and published until 1895-99.

The *Chronicles* were enormously popular during the fifteenth century, going into numerous editions in French, and in Latin and English translation. They have retained their popularity down to the present day and, in abridged and somewhat simplified editions, are especially popular with young readers. The standard English translation was made in 1523-25 by Lord Berners (Sir John Bourchier). Another, by Thomas Johnes, was published c. 1801.

ABOUT: Johnes, T. Memoirs of the Life of Sir John Froissart; Ker, W. P. Essays on Medieval Literature; Newbolt, H. Studies Green and Gray; Read, H. E. The Sense of Glory; Shears, F. S. Froissart: Chronicler and Poet; Times (London) Literary Supplement, December 11, 1937.

*FROMENTIN (DUPEUX), EUGÈNE SAMUEL AUGUSTE (October 24, 1820-August 27, 1876), French art critic, painter, and novelist, was born at La Rochelle. His father, Pierre, was a doctor who painted as a hobby in the academic tradition of Bertin; his mother, Jenny, *née* Billotte, was conservative, pious, and restrained. Eugène, who was devoted to her, resembled her in habits of silence and reserve. He had an older brother, Charles, who became a doctor like his father.

Educated at the Collège de La Rochelle, Eugène was at the top of his class in classical studies. But he also read avidly in romantic literature and roamed the countryside, sensitive to and retentive of nuances of light and sound. Summers and holidays were spent at the nearby family estate at Saint-Maurice.

On completing the baccalaureate, Eugène studied law in Paris (1839-43) and clerked in a law office. But at the same time he wrote large quantities of verse of little merit. Finally securing his father's permission and calming his mother's anxious objections, he studied painting as a pupil of Louis Cabat. In 1846, 1847-1848, and 1852-1853 he traveled in Algeria. The Algerian scene became the subject-matter of most of his painting. His first exhibition was held in 1847. Fromentin's paintings won him considerable official recognition: recipient of a first prize at the 1859 Salon, he was decorated, made a member of the jury, invited to court; in 1869 he was a member of the French delegation at the opening of the Suez Canal. His paintings sold well, and many were bought by Americans.

His trips to Africa furnished the data for *Un Été dans le Sahara* (1857) and *Une Année dans le Sahel* (1858). In 1852 Fromentin had married Marie Cavellet de Beaumont, the niece of his best friend, Armand du Mesnil. The couple had a daughter, Alexandre, who married into the Billotte family. But Fromentin's third work, the autobiographical novel *Dominique* (1863; definitive, posthumous edition, 1876), was based on an adolescent love affair with Jenny-Caroline-Léocadie Chessé (1817-44), model for Madeleine de Nièvre; Fromentin is Dominique de Bray, and Saint-Maurice the true locale. This important link in the history of the autobiographical novel was dedicated to George Sand, who admired it, as did Flaubert and Taine.

Fromentin's last and most important art criticism, *Maîtres d'Autrefois* (1876), de-

* frô mäṇ tăṇ' dü pü'

parted from traditional judgments. Loosely discursive, he ranges from technical discussions of Belgian and Dutch painters to travel descriptions; the section on Rubens is probably the most significant. *Maîtres d'Autrefois* would probably have won him a place in the French Academy. But he died suddenly at Saint-Maurice, where he is buried. The contemplated edition of his *Œuvres Complètes* was not completed. Pierre Blanchon (pseudonym of Jacques-André Merys) edited Fromentin's *Lettres de Jeunesse* (1909) and *Correspondance et Fragments Inédits* (1912). Fromentin manuscripts are at La Rochelle, in the possession of the Mérys family. *Voyage en Égypte (1869)* was published integrally in 1935, edited by J. M. Carré. *Dominique* has been edited by Maurice Revon (1937), *Les Maîtres d'Autrefois* by Maurice Allem (1939). *Dominique* was translated into Spanish by Pedro Vances (1928).

Mary C. Robbins translated *Masters of Past Time* in 1882; Andrew Boyle's translation of 1913 was reissued, with one hundred illustrations, in 1948.

ABOUT: Evans, A. R. The Literary Art of Eugène Fromentin; Harris, F. Latest Contemporary Portraits; Rhodes, S. A. *in* PMLA (1930). [In French—see studies by P. Dorbec, V. Giraud, J. Hytier, P. Martino, C. Reynaud, C. A. Sainte-Beuve, A. Thibaudet, J. Vier; also Revue de Paris, LXX (1963).]

S. S. W.

*FURETIÈRE, Abbé ANTOINE (December 28, 1619-May 14, 1688), French poet and novelist, was born in Paris. A man of an obscure background, he was nevertheless highly cultivated and best known not only as the author of *Le Roman Bourgeois*, but also as a pamphleteer and lexicographer.

Furetière's first profession was law; he was also fiscal steward of the Abbey of Saint-Germain and Abbot of Chalevoy and Prior of Pruines. His friendships with Molière (with whom he collaborated on a parody of *Le Chapelain Décoiffé*), Racine, Boileau, and La Fontaine, perhaps, indicate that Furetière was also serious about literature. One of his first attempts at writing was in the genre of the burlesque (*Énéide Travestie*, 1649), and in 1655 he published *Poésies Diverses*, followed by pieces entitled *Fables* and *Nouvelles*. *Nouvelle Allégorique ou Histoire des Derniers Troubles Arrivés au Royaume d'Éloquence*, a work which appeared in 1658, was felt by Nodier to contain more singularly important facts than could be found in fifty anecdotal works of the time. With the success of his

* fü rē tyâr'

Voyage de Mercure (1659), the doors of the Académie Française were opened to him in 1662. He remained a member until his expulsion, January 22, 1685.

In the mid-seventeenth century the Académie was engaged in preparing a dictionary. The project, Furetière felt, was being complicated by the long debates over the order and arrangement of the material; furthermore, he disagreed with the purist approach to the selection of words. His desire to compose a dictionary alone and, indeed, his success in doing so caused a rupture in his affiliation with the august institution of letters and provoked Furetière into writing a revengeful but amusing series of pamphlets— *Plan et Dessein Allégorique et Tragico-Burlesque Intitulé Les Couches de l'Académie*. One of them, which reveals his powers of satirical observation, describes a meeting of the Academicians: "There is one who reads, one who opines, two who converse, one who sleeps and one who amuses himself by reading some dictionary lying on the table. Each relates a pleasant story, or some bit of news. Here one talks of the affairs of state and of reforming the government."

Furetière was not interested in talk. He set about collecting material for his own dictionary (and was even accused of having used documents accumulated by his colleagues), devoting forty years to his work. The dictionary was published clandestinely in Rotterdam two years after his death, 1690, with a specimen first appearing under the title *Essai d'un Dictionnaire Universel Contenant Généralement tous les Mots Français tant Vieux que Modernes, et les Termes de toutes les Sciences et des Arts, Specifiez dans la Page Suivante*. Of the three dictionaries published in the seventeenth century (one by Richelet—1680, which was too literary, and one by the Académie—1694, which was more an encyclopedia and unusable), Furetière's compilation was the most complete. The words, old and new, terms of the arts as well as of sciences and trades, were presented in alphabetical order, and each one was carefully defined and illustrated by informative, useful, concrete examples. Although the dictionary was expurgated in 1701 by Basnage, it was hailed as a brilliant etymological feat, reprinted several times in the eighteenth century by the Jesuits, and used as a source of the nineteenth century dictionary by Boiste.

Furetière is also remembered for his realistic "novel" *Le Roman Bourgeois* (1666), which is set in Paris and concerns diverse types of people from the middle class, people whom Furetière had actually observed in the Place Maubert where he lived. The first book takes place there—"a triangular square surrounded by very common houses occupied by the bourgeoisie"—and describes frankly and realistically the lives of an attorney and his wife, a man of letters, a coquette, a simpleton, a miser who delivers long, flowery speeches. Nicodeme, Lucretia, Javotte, Bedout, Vollichon (whom Boileau immortalized with a couplet) have authentic names and are drawn "true to life." In the second book there is witty and vigorous raillery of the romanesque spirit, as Furetière satirically portrays the writers of the *précieux* style. Influenced by Molière, *Le Roman Bourgeois* belongs to the realistic movement of 1660, which was a reaction of bourgeois good sense against the whimsical wit of aristocratic literature. Despite the disorderly piling up of scenes and portraits, Furetière shows his skill in creating a gallery of typical Parisians and in ridiculing the false taste of an age.

There is a partial reprint of the 1664 edition of *Poésies Diverses* with an introduction by Isabelle Bronk, published in Baltimore, 1905. An English translation of *Le Roman Bourgeois,* erroneously ascribed to Scarron as "Scarron's City Romance," was published in 1671 in the *Savoy,* printed by T.N. for H. Herringman.

ABOUT: [In French—Dallas, D. F. Le Roman Français de 1660 à 1680; Reynier, G. Le Roman Réaliste au 17ᵉ Siècle.]

G. E.

FÜSSLI

*FÜSSLI, JOHANN HEINRICH (HENRY FUSELI) (February 7, 1741-April 16, 1825), Swiss painter and author, was born in Zürich, descendant of a well-known family of painters. His father, Johann Kaspar Füssli, who was noted as a portrait and landscape painter and the author of a book on the painters of Switzerland, decided to make a Lutheran pastor of his son, in spite of the boy's protests that he felt a strong bent for painting. While studying theology at the Collegium Carolinum where he received an excellent classical education, young Füssli formed a close friendship with Johann Kaspar Lavater (1741-1801), who later became a well-known author and physiognomist (see sketch below).

Füssli was ordained and preached his first sermon in 1761. When, however, he collaborated with his friend Lavater in writing a pamphlet to expose a corrupt magistrate of Zürich, the pressure from the family and relatives of the disgraced man became so

* füs' lē

great that both friends were forced to leave their home town. They went to Germany and traveled about for some time, eventually arriving in Berlin where Füssli met Sir Andrew Mitchell, British minister to the Prussian court. On the invitation of the latter, Füssli accompanied him to England where he stayed for some time.

Having a great aptitude for languages—he spoke French, Italian, and English fluently as well as German—Füssli supported himself by working as a translator and by writing for various magazines. In 1765 he prepared an edition of the Abbé Winckelmann's *Reflections on the Painting and Sculpture of the Greeks* for the bookseller Andrew Millar, thus helping to popularize in England Winckelmann's revolutionary ideas about art. After a short stay in France as traveling tutor to young Lord Chewton, he returned to London, publishing there a small book entitled *Remarks on the Writings and Conduct of J. J. Rousseau* (1767).

During his stay in London, Füssli continuously strove to promote Anglo-German literary relations, following in this his teacher and mentor Bodmer. But when he showed some of his drawings to Sir Joshua Reynolds (1723-92), one of the most prominent figures of the English school of painting, the latter persuaded him to become a painter. Reynolds also advised him to go to Rome, telling him that all he had to do to become the greatest painter of the age was to spend a few years there.

Thus, in the spring of 1770, Füssli left England for Italy, where he remained eight years, changing his name from Füssli to Fuseli, as more Italian-sounding. In Italy Fuseli developed such a complete and overwhelming reverence for Michelangelo that he spent days in copying and admiring his works. Though he never reached his high model, it was at this time that he developed his own characteristic Michelangelesque style of drawing. The rest of his time in Rome was spent in company of the Abbé Winckelmann, the German painter Mengs, and the French painter Louis David.

In April 1779 he returned to London, and he immediately attracted some attention among painters and writers, finally establishing himself as painter in the grand style. He collaborated from 1786 on in Boydell's *Shakespeare Gallery,* and at the same time, he started his collaboration with Cowper on the translation of Homer. From his *Shakespeare Gallery* his paintings for *A Midsummer Night's Dream* became especially well known and admired (they are now in the National Gallery in London). From 1787 he contributed to Macklin's *Poets' Gallery,* and made designs for Woodman's *Illustrations of Shakespeare* (1793-94).

Fuseli's reputation now grew steadily, and he became not only an associate of the Royal Academy in 1788, full Academician in 1790, but also Professor of Painting (1799), and Keeper of the Royal Academy (1804). Nevertheless, he experienced occasional failures, as in his *Milton Gallery* (1799-1800), on which he had worked for ten years. His *Lectures on Painting* (1820) show a remarkable power of insight and encyclopedic knowledge. He lived much in society, meeting most of the notable people of the day; especially interesting is his friendship with William Blake, with whom he had much in common. On June 30, 1788, Fuseli married Sophia Rawlins, who seems to have served him first as a model. He died after a brief illness at the Countess of Guildford's house, Putney Hill, and was buried in St. Paul's Cathedral, London.

Though many of Fuseli's works show a strange distortion of figures and facial expressions, some vagaries and extravagances, his paintings and especially his drawings had originality and poetic imagination. He was obsessed by the terrible and the colossal; when a young man, he wrote in a friend's album, "I do not wish to build a cottage, but to erect a pyramid." He was of the opinion that "commonplace figures are as inadmis-

sible in the grand style of painting as commonplace characters or sentiments in poetry."

Fuseli's writings, containing *Aphorisms on Man* (actually a translation of a work of his friend Lavater), *History of Art in Italy,* and *Art Lectures,* together with a biography, were published by John Knowles in three volumes (London, 1831).

ABOUT: Cunningham, A. The Lives of the Painters (1829); Mason, E. C. The Mind of Henry Fuseli; Todd, R. Tracks in the Snow. [In German —see studies by E. Beutler, A. Federmann, P. Ganz.]

F. S. L.

*FUSTEL DE COULANGES, NUMA DENYS** (March 18, 1830-September 12, 1889), French historian, was born in Paris of a family of marine officers from Brest. Having lost his father in 1831, he led an unstable and taciturn existence until his entrance into the École Normale. There he essentially educated himself in the historical sciences by avid reading, and after three years was named to the École Française d'Athènes, spending two years in Greece studying all aspects of Hellenic culture. Beginning in 1855, he taught in secondary schools in Amiens and, after his doctorate, at the Lycée Saint-Louis in Paris. His university career opened with appointment to Strasbourg in 1860. Over the next decade he revealed his diligence in routine duties and his brilliance as a public lecturer, finding sufficient time to broaden his knowledge of his special field of research. His proximity to German culture was of importance in his formation. After the Franco-Prussian war, Fustel taught at the École Normale, where he improved the programs in history and introduced those for the natural sciences. His dislike for non-academic work led him to refuse a nomination as historiographer of the Republic. On his death he left many valuable notes on long-meditated projects. Despite constant opposition from the general run of contemporary historians, Fustel led a happy life both at home and in his teaching.

Fustel's two years in Greece explain most of his basic historical theories. His first written expression was his study on Chios, sometimes in the sentimental manner of Guizot, but bold for example in not vilifying the Turks and in scoffing at the unbridled imagination of the archeologists. His report on Chios was severely criticized, provoking one comment, hurled at him repeatedly from that moment on, that his mind was "a bit too systematic." *La Cité Antique,* his masterpiece, carried his method further in 1864.

* füs tĕl' dĕ koō länzh'

307

Published at his own expense, it raised a storm of objections; Fustel's answers appeared in separate articles. The height of contention is marked by his *L'Invasion Germanique* (1872), which provoked a kind of campaign against him. The matter of the Germanic invasions is of the greatest significance in a wide variety of technical and literary topics, in the present instance with regard to the origins of feudalism. Fustel approached the topic a bit too systematically to please his detractors. First, he set Titus Livy and Gregory of Tours in their proper historical perspective. Second, he considered with care the multiple aspects of medieval culture such as legal systems, usages regarding property, and the moral attitudes of the several peoples during the epochs in question. Fustel's method, so conceived, dealt a death blow to positivist determinism as also to romantic imagination and color by seeking the causes of events and ideas. The romanticists accused Fustel of lack of patriotism in failing to glorify Vercingetorix. He shocked others by showing that feudalism was not specifically Germanic, but a normal solution to public disorder, and still others in scorning contemporary meditations on the noble savage or on Sparta as a culture consecrated to great and virtuous human causes. Rome was great, he said, not through her laws, but through Roman devotion to the public good. Many of Fustel's interpretations coincide with Renan's *Avenir de la Science*, written in 1848 but not yet published. His attention to later periods was less extensive, though in lectures he applied his method to study of the times of Louis XIV, Colbert, Turgot, and the Revolution. His principal disciple was the humanist Gaston Boissier (1823-1908).

English translations of the work of Fustel include *Aryan Civilization*, by T. Barker (1871), *The Ancient City*, by W. Small (1874), and *The Origins of Property in Land*, by W. Ashley (1891).

ABOUT: [In French—Champion, E. Les Idées Politiques et Religieuses de Fustel de Coulanges; Guiraud, P. Fustel de Coulanges; Labelle, E. Fustel de Coulanges; Tourneur-Aumont, J. Fustel de Coulanges.]

F. J. C.

GABIROL, SOLOMON BEN JUDAH IBN. See IBN GABIROL, SOLOMON BEN JUDAH

*GABORIAU, ÉMILE (November 9, 1832-October 1, 1873), French novelist, was born in Saujon (Charente Inférieure), the

* gà' bô' ryō'

son of a notary who wished him to study law. To avoid this Gaboriau enlisted in the cavalry where he spent seven years, ending as sergeant-major. He then worked as a clerk in Paris; in his spare hours he was a hack writer. He became secretary and ghost writer for Paul Féval, *feuilletoniste* of criminal romances. As Féval's assistant, Gaboriau watched police court and morgue for material and frequented low dives in search of "interesting types" for his notebooks.

Eventually he became a *feuilletoniste* himself and about 1859 began producing daily installments of "lurid fiction" at such a pace that he wrote twenty-one novels in thirteen years. The *feuilleton* (serial leaflet of daily newspapers) was written at top speed to definite specifications. His first seven novels were of military and fashionable life, dealing with stock characters, including pure maidens and impossible noblemen set against unreal backgrounds.

In 1866 he published *L'Affaire Lerouge* which has been called the "first detective novel," although in it, as in his other novels, detection was but one of several themes (family scandal and its investigation provided the basic theme for most of his novels). Here Lecoq, the "marvellous sleuth" of impenetrable disguises, is introduced. Gaboriau drew extensively upon his notebooks and is said to have been influenced by Vidocq's *Mémoires*. Valentine Williams states in *National Review*, December 1923, that Gaboriau's police officials Lecoq, Gevrol, and Fanferlot were actually sketched from life.

Lecoq figures as an important detective in the next four works: *Le Crime d'Orcival* (1867); *Le Dossier No. 113* (1867); *Les Esclaves de Paris* (1868) and *Monsieur Lecoq* (part I, 1868). Williams claims that *Le Petit Vieux des Batignolles* (1876, posthumous) is in certain aspects the best detective story ever written.

A strikingly handsome man, with the luxuriant hair and full beard so fashionable in his day, Gaboriau died of apoplexy at the age of forty when at last financially secure and about to devote his time to more leisurely composition. He knew how to write, how to delineate character. His logical deduction was excellent; indeed many of the techniques he devised are still detective-story procedure. He was forced to subordinate his more brilliant theme to the highly colored romance-intrigue demanded by the *feuilleton* public. It is said that a young lawyer of that period was advised by a famous British judge to read Gaboriau's novels if he wished to have a thorough insight into French criminal practice.

Gaboriau's novels have been widely translated. In Britain a series called Gaboriau's Sensational Novels was published beginning in 1881. In this country there were many translations, those of his best known beginning with *The Widow Lerouge,* by F. Williams and G. A. O. Ernst, 1873. *Within an Inch of His Life (La Corde au Cou)* followed in 1874. Then appeared *Monsieur Lecoq* and *Little Old Man of Batignolles* in 1880; *Slaves of Paris,* 1882; *Mystery of Orcival* and *File No. 113* in 1883.

ABOUT: Haycraft, H. Murder for Pleasure; National Review, July 1884, December 1923; Times Literary Supplement, November 2, 1935. [In French —Messac, R. Le "Detective Novel" et l'Influence de la Pensée Scientifique.]

M. A. W.

*GALIANI, FERDINANDO (December 2, 1728-October 30, 1787), Italian writer, second son of a royal auditor in a province governed by Naples, was born at Chieti (Abruzzi). His uncle, Monsignore Celestino Galiani, was first chaplain to the King of Naples, and at the age of eight Ferdinando was sent with his older brother to be educated under his uncle's charge, first at the Convent of the Celestins in Rome, then in the uncle's palace at Naples.

Ferdinando was an infant prodigy who achieved fame as a boy by a satire on the Academy of Naples (published 1748). By sixteen an eager student of political economy and an admirer of Vico, he mastered English, translated Locke's treatise on finance and himself wrote an essay on money, *Della Moneta* (1750). He studied and wrote endlessly, cultivating a taste for epigram and satire. At the age of twenty-two, without study of theology or ordination, he was given several benefices and, by papal dispensation, the title of Monsignore, and episcopal honors. He traveled to Rome, Florence, and Venice and was admired everywhere for his gifts. Falling heir to his uncle's riches in July 1753, Ferdinando remained in Naples, entertaining lavishly, and acquiring new benefices and honors. Continuing his studies, he published *Sulla Perfetta Conservazione del Grano* (1754).

In 1759 he was appointed secretary to the Paris embassy with the powers of a special agent. He was at first unhappy in Paris where he was ridiculed for his dwarf (4½ feet) stature overladen with the court dress of the period. Diderot described him as being small, stout, short-sighted and toothless. He

begged for recall, but slowly the court began to appreciate his talents and especially his sparkling wit. He learned French. He became the intimate of Mme d'Épinay, Diderot, and Grimm. The Neckers welcomed him for his attacks on the hated Economists. He argued against the forces of revolt, foreseeing disaster.

In 1764 grain restrictions in Europe caused famine and riots. Horrified at the upheaval, Galiani began to write his *Dialogues sur le Commerce des Blés,* published in 1770, in which he advocated a realistic economic policy in relation to local conditions.

He was recalled to Naples, May 25, 1769, to the great dismay of Paris and himself. He tried to introduce the salon to Naples; he corresponded with his friends; he expanded his famous museum collection; he looked after his fatherless nieces; he acquired more benefices, civil posts and honors. When Mme d'Épinay died in 1783, he grieved deeply, for his heart had remained in France. He suffered an attack of apoplexy in 1785 and died two years later, gay and witty to the end.

His sparkling *Correspondence* was first published in 1818, then reprinted in 1881, including a study of his life and works by L. Perey and G. Maugras. Voltaire said of his *Dialogues* that they were "as amusing as our best novels and as instructive as our best serious books." The same might be said with justice of the social life of his time presented by his letters.

ABOUT: Hall, E. B. The Friends of Voltaire; Rossi, J. The Abbé Galiani in France. [In Italian —Nicolini, F. Il Pensiero dell'Abate Galiani.]

M. A. W.

*GALILEI, GALILEO (February 15, 1564-January 8, 1642), Italian scientist and writer, was born in Pisa of an old Florentine family. His father, skilled in mathematics, inspired his early interest in science and in the classics, but Galileo was at first attracted toward art. He studied medicine and philosophy in Pisa, and soon showed his native "spirit of contradiction" in opposition to his professors' stubborn respect for tradition and classical authority. In 1583, thanks to his perceptivity of the causes of phenomena, he noted the synchronism of the pendulum in the Cathedral. Interrupting his studies, he went to Florence to study mathematics and did his first research on the baricenter of solids. After a trip to Rome, he was named professor at Pisa; he again engaged in his struggle against the Aristotelians and in *De*

GALILEO

Motu Gravium demonstrated that bodies of different weight fall at the same rate. His chair of mathematics in Padua, in 1592, put him in far better material circumstances, and his twelve years in that city were both fruitful and happy; his principal contributions to knowledge during the Paduan period are the treatise on fortification and the application of the telescope to celestial observation. Galileo's discovery of the four moons of Jupiter led him to the concepts of the nature and extent of the universe propounded in his *Sidereus Nuntius,* published in 1610; the discovery of the moons was hailed as a great revelation by Kepler, but dismissed as an optical illusion by the reactionaries.

Galileo's conclusions regarding sun-spots engaged him in active controversy with several individuals through whose influence his work was condemned, in May 1611, as heretical, though he himself was not accused, and Copernicus was taken as the source of the errors. Indeed Galileo seemed merely to be undermining Aristotelianism until about 1613, when the Bible was invoked, and evil gossip led Pope Urban VIII to believe himself ridiculed in the person of Simplicio in the *Dialogo sopra i Due Massimi Sistemi del Mondo.* The moral pressure put on Galileo during his imprisonment and trial assumed various forms which reflected strong factors of hesitation and fear in a controversy obviously not primarily doctrinal. Thus his abjuration was required according to carefully calculated formulas, and he was condemned to pro-

longed and forced expiation. His last years were saddened by shame and ill health, but he wrote much, especially his second masterwork, the *Dialoghi delle Nuove Scienze,* published in Leiden in 1638.

Along with other thinkers who appealed to experience rather than tradition, Galileo did much to found modern experimental science. His writings, meanwhile, illustrate the lucidity of the Italian thinkers of the Renaissance, and the program, evident for example in Pontano, of free examination of thought and fact. Stylistically, Galileo's prose stands on a high level of sincerity and persuasiveness, achieving clarity without recourse to the calculated effects of rhetoric. He was an aggressive polemist, distinguished by lucid composition rather than baroque embellishment. He was especially a master of the dialogue and its exchange of rational views regarding hypotheses according to the rigorous methods of Socrates and Plato. Galileo quite naturally takes sides and creates certain speakers with obvious intent, especially the pedantic Simplicio, against whose views he directs his finest irony.

There are many critical editions of various of Galileo's works, but in general the 20 volumes of the National Edition (1890-1909) supersede earlier publications. They include nine volumes of letters and a multitude of minor tracts, mostly in Latin, but all are dominated by the two sets of dialogues. Galileo's writings on literary topics form another volume (on Dante, Tasso, Ariosto, etc.). English translations include the *Mathematical Discourses,* by T. Weston (1730), *The Sidereal Messenger* by E. Carlos (1880), the *Dialogue concerning Two New Sciences* by H. Grew (1914), and the *Dialogue Concerning the Two Chief World Systems,* twice published in 1953, in a revision of T. Salusbury's original translation of 1669 and in a new version by S. Drake.

ABOUT: Panofsky, E. Galileo as Critic of the Arts; Taylor, F. Galileo and the Freedom of Thought; Von Gebler, K. Galileo Galilei and the Roman Curia. [In Italian—see studies by A. Banfi, A. Favaro, E. Lera.]

F. J. C.

*GANIVET, ÁNGEL (November or December 13, 1865-November 29, 1898), Spanish essayist and novelist, was born in Granada, the son of Francisco Ganivet Morillo and María de los Ángeles García. French and Moorish blood ran in his veins. His early youth was marked by privation but he managed to attend the *instituto* and the university of his native city where he was a brilliant student. At the University of Madrid he received his doctorate in philosophy and letters, and in law. An excellent human-

* gä nē vĕt'

ist, he read in five languages; in 1891 he tried for the chair of Greek at the University of Granada. He did not achieve his goal but in the same year he took the consular examinations and came out number one. About the same time he met Amalia Roldán, a woman three or four years younger than he. Theirs was a stormy, unhappy love affair which never culminated in marriage, although they had a son and daughter. (The latter died in Paris in 1898 shortly before her father.) In 1892 Ganivet was appointed Spanish vice-consul in Antwerp where he remained until the end of 1895; during this time he contributed to the Granada paper *El Defensor de Granada.* During vacations and leaves he always returned to his beloved native city where he was the admired friend of a group of intellectuals who carefully listened to him as he expounded many of the concepts which were later to be found in his books. In Antwerp he suffered a deep spiritual crisis over Amalia's infidelity, a crisis reflected in his letters or *Epistolario,* written in the main to F. Navarro Ledesma and published by the latter in 1904.

At the beginning of 1896 Ganivet was promoted and transferred to Helsingfors, Finland, where until the middle of 1897 he led a secluded life of incessant reading and writing. There he wrote his most famous works. *Cartas Finlandesas* are the ironical comments of a Spaniard on Nordic life and character. *Granada la Bella* is made up of short essays on the art, customs, and general atmosphere

of his native city. *La Conquista del Reino de Maya* and *Los Trabajos del Infatigable Creador Pío Cid* (only part of which he wrote in Finland) are the first examples of the lyrical, autobiographical, intellectual novel which would later be the genre of Azorín and Baroja. Ganivet also wrote and published in the *Defensor de Granada* five letters to his friend Unamuno; these important documents, written in answer to letters from the latter, were published in book form in 1905. But Ganivet's most important book, also published during this period (1897), is his *Idearium Español,* a lyrico-ideological essay seeking to explain Spanish temperament and history. This book, indispensable to the understanding of the authors following Ganivet who are usually grouped under the generic title of the Generation of 1898, is an asystematic work, "richer in intuitions than in ideas." Ganivet finds that the fusion of Senecan stoicism and Christianity produced that mysticism or personalism which is the core of the Spanish character. In all phases of Spanish life, he claims, the emphasis is on the whole man, the passionate, vital human being, and not on formulae, rules, or schools. Ganivet was no advocate of the Europeanization of his country; instead he called upon his fellow-countrymen to forget territorial aggrandizement and seek their strength in their originality as Spaniards rather than Europeans, thus achieving leadership among all Spanish-speaking nations.

Spiritually and physically, Ganivet was on the decline. After a leave of several months, he was transferred to Riga where he arrived early in August 1898. That year he wrote *Hombres del Norte; España y Rusia* (a consular report); the rest of *Los Trabajos;* and his only play, *El Escultor de su Alma.* Accompanied by his friend the Swedish consul Baron von Bruch, he consulted a specialist whose diagnosis was progressive paralysis. In September 1898, after a quarrel that had lasted some months, Amalia decided to join Ganivet in Riga. But on the same day she was to arrive with their son, Ganivet threw himself into the Dwina river from a ferry and was drowned. In 1923 a statue was erected to him in the Alhambra gardens of Granada and in 1925 his remains were brought home from Riga.

The only English translation of the *Idearium Español* was made in 1946 by J. R. Carey and published in England as *Spain: An Interpretation* with an introduction by R. M. Nadal.

ABOUT: [In Spanish—see studies by M. Fernández Almagro and A. Espina.]

M. N.

*GARBORG, ARNE (originally **AADNE**) (January 25, 1851-January 14, 1924), Norwegian novelist, poet, essayist, playwright, was born on the farm Garborg south of Stavanger in southwestern Norway. His father was Eivind Aadneson, an able farmer and a prominent man in local administration, but sensitive, morose, and melancholy. His mother was Ane Olene Jonsdatter, from the same district. Her disposition was bright and cheerful.

Arne grew up as the oldest of nine children in a gloomy atmosphere, dominated by his father's fanatically pietistic religion and fear of God's punishment. The elder Garborg's melancholy increased, and in 1870 he committed suicide. First Arne went to school, but his father took him out to give him personal instruction and impress upon him the pietistic religion. At the age of thirteen he rejoined the regular school. After his confirmation, which he underwent with a silent reservation, he went to a teachers' training school. After a short interval as a teacher he joined another college. In spite of the shocking news about his father's suicide he passed his final examination with distinction. He began teaching, but he soon gave up his position and in 1871 started a teachers' journal. In the next year he also edited a liberal local paper. His articles were, however, still rather conservative, both religiously and politically.

Garborg had already at this time written numerous poems, but not until 1870 did the first one appear in print in a Stavanger paper under the pseudonym "Alf Buestreng." In 1873 he moved to the capital where he published, still anonymously, his first little book. After two years he passed his matriculation examination and enrolled at the university. While a student he pursued a lively journalistic career. Gradually, he became influenced by modern ideas. He joined the liberal nationalistic movement and favored the new national language movement, the leader of which he soon became. In his writings he used the new language based on the native dialects. From 1877 to 1882 he edited the agrarian paper *Fedraheimen*. Here he published as a *feuilleton* his first major story *Ein Fritenkjar* (A Freethinker; in book form, 1881), in which he pleaded for freedom and tolerance. His studies of evolution, positivism, and modern literature made him an atheistic naturalist. His rather gloomy novel *Bondestudentar* (Peasant Students, 1885)—in which he described the problems

that faced the young men who, like himself, were transplanted from rural environment to city life and criticized the prevalent peasant romanticism—made him known throughout Scandinavia.

In 1879 Garborg was employed at the state auditor's office, and four years later he became state auditor. Now he made brilliant polemical contributions to the contemporary discussions on subjects of social, religious, political and sexual nature. In 1885-86 he published his novel *Mannfolk* (Menfolk). Its outspokenly naturalistic approach to sex and morals lost him his position as auditor. He married Karen Hulda Bergersen in 1887. She embraced modern radical ideals and became a prominent author in her own right.

Garborg and his wife lived at times at their cottage, Kolbotn, in the majestic Dovre mountains in central Norway. Here his only son was born, and here he wrote his *Kolbotnbrev* (Kolbotn Letters, 1890), containing, in addition to its polemics, exquisite pictures of nature. Spending part of his time in Germany, Garborg went through a transitional stage during which he withdrew from the mentality of the '80's and published his naturalistic novel *Hjaa ho Mor* (With Mother, 1890), describing the dismal life of a middle-class woman with new ideas. The neo-romantic thoughts of the '90's did not leave Garborg unaffected. His pessimistic diary novel *Trætte Mænd* (Tired Men) is a stylistically brilliant psychological analysis of the evolution of a cultured mind without religion.

Garborg left naturalism, deeply influenced by Nietzsche and Tolstoy. Religion became a central point in his thinking and writing. But he could not go back to dogmatism. He remained an agnostic and developed a philosophy based on the ethics of love in the Gospels. His new attitude was expressed in his naturalistic novel *Fred* (Peace, 1892), a classic in Norwegian literature, preaching faith in life; in the poetic cycle *Haugtussa* (The Fairy, 1895); and the play *Læraren* (The Teacher, 1896), in which he, like Tolstoy, insisted on the necessity of rediscovering Christ. His greatest work of literary criticism was the study *Jonas Lie*. His last years were less active. He died of pneumonia.

An extract from Garborg's first major story *Ein Fritenkjar*, translated by W. H. Carpenter, appears in the Warner Library. His novel *Fred* was translated as *Peace* by P. D. Carleton (1929), and *Den Burtkomne Faderen* by M. J. Leland as *The Lost Father* (1920). The poem *Mot Soleglad*, rendered into English as *Towards Sunset*, is printed in Grøndahl & Raknes' *Chapters in Norwegian Literature*.

* gär' börg

ABOUT: Beyer, H. A History of Norwegian Literature; Columbia Dictionary of Modern European Literature; Grøndahl, I. & Raknes, O. Chapters in Norwegian Literature; Jorgenson, T. History of Norwegian Literature; Larsen, H. A. *in* American-Scandinavian Review, XII; Lillehei, I. *in* Scandinavian Studies, III.

A. J.

*GARCÍA DE LA HUERTA Y MUÑOZ, VICENTE ANTONIO (March 9, 1734-March 12, 1787), Spanish dramatist and poet, was born in Zafra. He came from a middle class family with no great wealth. His father was Juan Francisco García de la Huerta and his mother was named María Muñoz. He was educated at Salamanca but did not finish his studies there. He went to Madrid, where, in 1757, he married Gertrudis Carrera Larrea. Huerta was fortunate enough to fall under the protection of the Duke of Alba, but because of letters he was supposed to have addressed to the prime minister, the Count of Aranda, as well as political satires he wrote, he spent about ten years in prison or exile in Oran. He did not return to Madrid until 1777 and from then on devoted most of his talents to literature.

His *Obras Poéticas* (2 vols.) were published in 1778-79. Some of his poems, particularly the lyric ones, are still read, but he cannot be classed as a major poet. Although he translated Sophocles's *Electra* and Voltaire's *Zaïre*, he professed no great love for either the ancient rules of drama or the French classics. In *La Escena Hespañola* [sic] *Defendida*, which he used as the prologue to his *Theatro Hespañol* (16 vols., 1785-86), he defended the Spanish national drama heatedly. This large collection of Golden Age dramas is singular in that Lope de Vega, Tirso, and Alarcón are not included. In this respect, he reflected the tastes of his time, which placed Calderón and others far ahead of Lope.

In 1788 Huerta wrote his masterpiece *La Raquel*, the story of the murdered Jewess loved by Alfonso VIII. Despite his national taste, the play leans toward neo-classic principles, but the subject, division into acts, and versification are entirely Spanish. *La Raquel* is universally acclaimed as the best Spanish play of the eighteenth century and was enormously popular. It was imitated by Grillparzer in his *Die Jüdin von Toledo*.

García de la Huerta was head of the Royal Library, a member of the Spanish Academy, the Academy of History, and the Academy of

*gär thē' ä 'thä lä wĕr' tä ē mōō nyôth'

San Fernando. He died in Madrid, leaving one son, Luis. He is buried in the same city. According to his enemies, he was insane at the time of his death, but this is by no means certain.

ABOUT: McClelland, I. L. The Origins of the Romantic Movement in Spain; Pellissier, R. E. The Neo-Classic Movement in Spain during the Eighteenth Century. [In Spanish—Cotarelo, E. Estudios sobre la Historia del Arte Escénico en España, *also* Iriarte y su Época.]

R. E. O.

*GARCÍA GUTIÉRREZ, ANTONIO (October 5, 1813-August 26, 1884), Spanish dramatist, was born in Chiclana de la Frontera (Cádiz). He received his early education in Cádiz and at his father's wish began the study of medicine. However, he felt no vocation and soon abandoned the course, going to Madrid in 1833. He was already writing for the stage but had no success in the capital at first. He became so oppressed by poverty that at last, in desperation, he enlisted in the National Militia and fought in the North against the Carlists. He had not yet been released from the army when his first play was performed; it was *El Trovador* (1836). His reputation was made at once, for *El Trovador* was one of the great theatrical successes of the century and remains to this day an almost perfect example of the romantic drama. (This same work some years later, in 1852, was adapted by the Italian composer Verdi in his opera *Il Trovatore*.) Inspired by his initial good fortune, García Gutiérrez wrote in quick succession *El Rey Monje* (1837), *Simón Bocanegra* (1843)—also adapted as an opera by Verdi —as well as two volumes of poetry, *Poesías* (1840) and *Luz y Tinieblas* (1842). Then, in 1844, the dramatist left Spain, living and traveling abroad for six years in Cuba, Mérida, and Yucatán. Again in 1854 he left Spain. This time he went to England where he lived for three years.

Returning home, he once more devoted himself to the theatre with *Venganza Catalana* (1864) and *Juan Lorenzo* (1865), the latter being his masterpiece. The following year his *Obras Escogidas*, containing sixteen plays, was published. In addition to his more serious literary efforts, García Gutiérrez wrote many librettos for *zarzuelas*, or musicals. This was a common practice among the dramatists of the period. In 1868 he was appointed Spanish consul at Bayonne and in 1872 he was made director of the Archae-

* gär thē' ä gōō tyĕr' räth

313

ological Museum in Madrid, which post he occupied till his death.

García Gutiérrez's chief model was undoubtedly Dumas *père*, but he never descended to slavish imitation in any of his works. He was a man of considerable culture though largely self-taught. A master of versification, he had a vigorous imagination and a polished style. With him the Spanish romantic drama turned to historical themes which often showed liberal political opinions. His own *Venganza Catalana* and *Juan Lorenzo* are among the best plays of this type. In 1865 García Gutiérrez was elected a member of the Real Academia de la Lengua. Volume 65 of the Clásicos Castellanos, edited by J. R. Lomba y Pedraja in 1925, is the best and most easily obtained of any recent editions of his work.

ABOUT: Adams, N. B. The Romantic Dramas of García Gutiérrez; Lamb, N. G. *in* Liverpool Studies (1940). [In German—Regensburger, C. A. Über den Trovador des García Gutiérrez.]

R. E. O.

*GARCILASO DE LA VEGA (1503-1536),

Spanish poet, was born in Toledo, son of Garci-Lasso, the commander of León, and Doña Sancha de Guzmán of the noble house of Toral. Through both his parents the poet could boast of one of the most distinguished lineages of Renaissance Spain. In his youth he received the education of the model courtier, which included Latin, Greek, and French in addition to his native language and literature, music (at court he became famed for his skill on the harp and guitar), horsemanship, and the manual of arms. During his brief life he distinguished himself equally in war, politics, and poetry.

Having entered the service of Charles V in 1520, Garcilaso divided his career thereafter between diplomatic expeditions and military campaigns. His official travels took him to France, Germany, Italy, and North Africa. His wedding to a noble lady of the court (unidentified) in 1525 was probably a marriage of convenience entered into at the behest of the emperor. At any rate the lady is never alluded to in his poems. Of all the women whom he praised in his lyrics, the one to whom Garcilaso was most deeply attached was Doña Isabel Freire, a lovely Portuguese lady who came to Spain in 1526 as part of the wedding procession of Charles V's royal bride. His masterpiece *La Egloga Primera (The First Eclogue)* is generally considered a veiled personal lament on the

* gär thē lä′ sō thä lä vä′ gä

GARCILASO

untimely death of Doña Isabel, which probably occurred early in 1533.

Among his political employments, Garcilaso's sojourn at Naples from 1531 to 1533 in the service of the viceroy the Marqués de Villafranca proved to be the most influential in his literary development. In this flourishing center of Italian humanism he figured in the most distinguished literary society. Here consequently he was introduced to the Petrarchan style then dominating Italian verse, particularly as adapted by Pietro Bembo, Jacopo Sannazaro, and Bernardo Tasso. A subsequent visit with the Spanish poet Juan Boscán influenced the latter in his metrical innovations. These two poets together share the achievement of Hispanicizing the Italian metres as two decades later Wyatt and Surrey were to Anglicize them.

The last two years of Garcilaso's life were crowded with military exploits. In 1535 he served in an expedition against Tunis. The following year he was mortally wounded while leading a storming party against a fort near Fréjus in Provence. He died at Nice, but two years later his remains were transferred to Toledo. His poems were published posthumously together with those of his friend Juan Boscán in Barcelona in 1543 by Boscán's widow. His scanty but highly polished output consists of three eclogues, two elegies, a verse epistle, five songs, 38 sonnets (in the Petrarchan mode), several ballads, and some Latin poems. Several other poems, written in Italian, are lost.

Garcilaso's poetry is derivative and narrow in its emotional and intellectual range, but distinctive for its poignancy, delicacy, and technical facility. Love, particularly anguished and futile love, is his overmastering subject. Only in one sonnet (No. XVI, on the death of his brother Don Fernando) is there as much as a hint of his martial career. *The First Eclogue* is generally regarded as his most perfect lyric.

Surnamed "The Prince of Castilian poets" by his countrymen, Garcilaso de la Vega as a Renaissance fusion of poet-courtier-soldier suggests the Spanish counterpart of the Elizabethan lyric poet Sir Philip Sidney.

The complete poems of Garcilaso de la Vega have been translated by J. H. Wiffen (1823), and more recently by Hayward Keniston (1925). The odes and sonnets have been translated by James Cleugh (1930). Translations, with the Spanish text, of the *First Eclogue* and several of the sonnets appear in *Ten Centuries of Spanish Poetry*, edited by Eleanor Turnbull (1955). A selection of his poetry appears in *An Anthology of Spanish Poetry*, edited by Angel Flores (Anchor Books, 1961). The definitive Spanish edition is that prepared for the *Clásicos Castellanos* series by D. T. Navarro Tomás (1911).

ABOUT: Brenan, G. The Literature of the Spanish People; Fitzmaurice-Kelly, J. Some Masters of Spanish Verse; Keniston, H. Garcilaso de la Vega: A Critical Study of His Life and Works; Salinas, P. Reality and the Poet in Spanish Poetry. [In Spanish—see studies by M. Altolaguirre, M. Arce Blanco.]

R. A. C.

---

*GARCILASO DE LA VEGA ("El Inca"), (c. 1540-1616?), Peruvian historian, was born in Cuzco. His father, Sebastián Garcilaso de la Vega y Vargas, had served under Cortés in Mexico and later became governor of Cuzco. He was a cousin of the great lyric poet Garcilaso de la Vega. The historian's mother, Isabel Chimpu Oello, was a direct descendant of the Incan royal family. In 1560 Garcilaso moved to Spain where he served against the Moors as a captain in the Spanish army. He settled at Córdoba and is thought to have died in the same city. He is buried in the Cathedral at Córdoba.

Garcilaso is the author of *La Florida del Inca* (Lisbon, 1605), which is the story of Hernando De Soto; the *Comentarios Reales* (Lisbon, 1609); and the *Historia General del Perú* (Córdoba, 1617). In *La Florida*, Garcilaso was obliged to rely on other people's accounts and writings, since he himself had not been with De Soto. In the *Comentarios Reales*, however, he spoke of a country and people he knew well. He is the man who brought Peruvian folklore and legend into Western history and many of the

* gär sē lä′ sō thä lä vä′ gä

curious facts he told have since been confirmed.

Garcilaso, who possessed a vivid imagination and was not above treating his facts somewhat loosely in order to paint the Incas in the most favorable light, said in his own defense, "I merely tell these historical tales which I heard from my people in my childhood. Let each man take them as he wishes."

Garcilaso is an excellent prose writer who enjoys the picaresque and whose style is pleasant and lively. Although his *Comentarios* reveal a strange mixture of the historical and fantastic, he has been used by almost every historian of pre-Columbian times. According to Menéndez y Pelayo, he is the greatest name in colonial Latin-American literature.

The Royal Commentaries of Peru was translated in 1688 by Sir Paul Rycaut, who unfortunately did not know Spanish very well. J. G. Varner and J. J. Varner translated and edited *The Florida of the Inca* in 1951. The *First Part of the Royal Commentaries of the Yncas* was translated and edited by C. R. Markham in 1869-71.

ABOUT: Fitzmaurice-Kelly, J. El Inca Garcilaso de la Vega; Henríquez-Ureña, P. *in* Literary Currents in Hispanic America. [In Spanish—Arce de Vázquez, M. Garcilaso de la Vega; Riva Agüero, J. de la, Antología de los Comentarios Reales con una Introducción Crítica.]

R. E. O.

---

*GARNIER, ROBERT (1544?-September 20, 1590), French dramatist and poet, was born in La Ferté-Bernard (Maine). As a young man he studied law at Toulouse, wrote love poetry published in 1565, and tried his hand at plays. He was in Paris for several years, making the acquaintance of Ronsard, Belleau, and Baïf, then at Le Mans in judicial positions, culminating in the office of *lieutenant criminel*. *Porai*, the first of his eight plays, was published in 1568, followed by *Hippolyte*, in 1573, the year of his marriage to Françoise Hubert. His *Cornélie* (1574) was inspired by the dissensions of the civil wars. He undertook a Greek subject in *La Troade* (1578); a tragi-comedy based on Ariosto, *Bradamante* (1582); and one religious play, *Sédécie, ou les Juives* (1583). In 1586 Henry III named Garnier to the Grand Council in recognition of his learning, but later showed marked indifference to his plays. Little is known of Garnier's private life or person, and from his writings alone we can imagine a patriotic Catholic, a serious civil servant, humanist, moralist, and teacher of virtue.

* går nyä′

The great importance of Garnier's plays depends on their intrinsic force and beauty, within the literary conventions of their time, and the innovations both in form and in subject matter, which so clearly anticipate the best work of the following century. His Roman subjects, such as *Cornélie,* illustrate his moral purpose of throwing light on contemporary problems, with strong political and ideological undercurrents. His inspiration from Seneca, typical of the movement at that moment, takes the form of a Christian stoicism and an appeal to reason as the corrective for the excesses of the passions. In contrast to these factors, which recall Corneille, the innate nature of the tragic situations of Racine appear in Garnier's *La Troade,* and in *Les Juives,* a prototype, however vague, for *Athalie* and *Esther.* There is a marked progress in dramatic effect among his tragedies. In his later plays Garnier set in full relief his particular talent for the creation of pathos.

Bradamante, reprinted fifteen times by the end of the century, belongs to the first stages of the important genre of the tragi-comedy, which passed subsequently through Alexandre Hardy to Corneille's *Le Cid.* In Garnier's hands, the pathos is created by long narrative accounts of the action and by the frequent lamentations. *Bradamante* is strongly romanesque, with battles, vicissitudes, and lovers in constant despair. There is a marked respect for the unity of action of the love story.

Garnier's success is evident in the scores of editions of his plays, and in the admiration of such contemporaries as Pasquier and Sainte-Marthe. His style, close to preciosity, set a norm for later writers such as Montchrétien and Hardy, and represents the initial orientation of the work of Rotrou and even of Corneille.

Two of his plays were translated shortly after his death, *Antonie,* by the Countess of Pembroke (1592), and *Cornelia,* by Thomas Kyd (1597).

ABOUT: Lancaster, H. The French Tragi-Comedy; Witherspoon, A. M. The Influence of Robert Garnier on Elizabethan Drama. [In French—Chardon, H. Robert Garnier, Sa Vie, Ses Poésies Inédites; Mouflard, M.-M. Robert Garnier, La Vie et L'Œuvre.]

F. J. C.

GARRETT, JOÃO BAPTISTA DA SILVA LEITÃO DE ALMEIDA. See ALMEIDA GARRETT, JOÃO BAPTISTA DA SILVA LEITÃO DE

*GARSHIN, VSEVOLOD MIKHAILO-VICH (February 14, 1855-April 5, 1888), Russian short-story writer, was born in the Bakhmut district of the Ukraine. His father was an army officer. His mother soon left her husband, taking the two elder sons. The boy lived for some time with his father, then joined his mother in St. Petersburg. As a child he was an enthusiastic reader, and his first literary attempts appeared in the periodicals of his secondary school. Subsequently he became a student at the Institute of Mining. When the Russo-Turkish war began, he volunteered for the army. As an ordinary private he participated in a difficult crossing of the Danube, got a leg wound, and returned to Russia. His story "The Four Days" was based on an adventure of a badly wounded soldier who lay helplessly for four days beside the corpse of a Turk.

Garshin was commissioned, but soon retired from the army. His new stories made him famous, leading to friendship with various radical writers and the Tolstoy circle. In spite of his literary successes, he was unable to support his wife and himself with his writing. His sensitive nature prompted him to implore Prime Minister Loris-Melikov to come to terms with the revolutionaries. Increasingly morbid and neurotic, he finally suffered a breakdown and spent a long time in mental institutions. After his recovery he planned to write novels, but spells of deep melancholy tormented him every spring. In one of these fits he flung himself down a staircase and died five days later from his injuries. "All those who knew him," wrote D. S. Mirsky, "testify to the extraordinary purity and charm of his person.

The whole heritage of Garshin consists of only a score of stories and tales, but his literary role has been important. The guiding motive of his writings was self-denial and self-sacrifice, even if no direct result could be expected. His compassionate spirit led him to democratic attitudes and to pacifism. He identified himself with suffering, helpless creatures: the mutilated soldier expecting death ("The Four Days"), the lunatic tormented with fear for mankind ("The Red Flower"), unhappy prostitutes ("The Adventure" and "Nadejda Nikolayevna"), the pacifist going to war ("The Coward"). Garshin frequently used the form of memoirs. An intense lyricism permeates the realistic details of his narrative; his directness of approach does not exclude an intermittent irony of tone and the employment of symbolic ma-

* gàr'shīn

terials. His manner of story-telling coincided with the European bias towards psychological insight and symbolic expressiveness.

A full edition of Garshin's works with his correspondence was published in Leningrad in 3 vols. (1934). English translations include *Stories from Garshin* by E. L. Voynich (1892) and *The Signal and other Stories* by R. Smith (1912).

ABOUT: [In Russian—see studies by G. A. Byaly, M. V. Klevensky.]

M. G.

*GAUTIER, (PIERRE JULES) THÉOPHILE (August 30, 1811-October 23, 1872), French man of letters, was born at Tarbes (Hautes-Pyrénées), where his father, Jean Pierre Gautier (1778-1854), a staunch royalist, was in the office of the tax-collector. He was of Avignon ancestry; Théophile's mother, *née* Antoinette Adélaide Cocard (1783-1848), was from Mauperthuis (Seine-et-Marne), where the family spent its summers. Two girls, Zoé and Émilie, completed the family, which moved to Paris when Théophile was three years old.

By the age of six the boy had read *Robinson Crusoe* with absorption and had immersed himself in Bernardin de Saint-Pierre's *Paul et Virginie*. His father tutored him in Latin; he was enrolled as a boarding student at the Collège Louis-le-Grand which he disliked and soon he became a day-pupil at the Collège Charlemagne, where he met Gérard de Nerval. Gautier had the capacities for being an outstanding student, for he was quick and curious and endowed with an extraordinary memory. While still at Charlemagne he also studied painting at the Rioult atelier, and scribbled verses too.

Through Nerval, already the precocious translator of *Faust*, and artist friends, Gautier became an habitué of the "Cénacle" (1827-30) that gathered around Victor Hugo, the rising star of romanticism. On February 25, 1830, was held the famous performance of Hugo's play, *Hernani*, the arena for a clash between the old guard and the ebullient modernists. Gautier, resplendent in a cherry-pink silk vest, light gray trousers with a black stripe, and a Rembrandtesque hat, was a leader in the claque—for more than forty performances. In July 1830 Gautier published at his family's expense *Poésies*, containing verses written since the age of fifteen. The volume went unnoticed, since its appearance coincided with the uprising against Charles X and his minister Polignac. The revolution ruined Gautier's legitimist family: it was

* gō tyä′

GAUTIER

apolitical Théophile who would shortly have to provide for his parents and sisters. Between 1830 and 1836 he still had some leisure and could frequent gatherings such as the "Petit Cénacle," the "Jeune(s)-France," the "Bousingot" group, and the "Bohème" circle of the painter Camille Rogier and the poet-journalist Gérard de Nerval. Subsequently he would be one of the habitués of the Hôtel Pimodan, on the Île Saint-Louis, famous for macabre stunts and for indulgence in opium and hashish (an affectation rather than a genuine use with Gautier).

Gautier's sentimental life was basically less passionate than the (partial) listing of relationships might suggest. In his youth he was slender, with clearly defined features, olive complexion, long dark-chestnut hair, black myopic eyes. Later he became quite corpulent and heavy-featured—he was nicknamed "the elephant." Extraordinarily strong, he had broad shoulders and a deep chest. At Mauperthuis he had swum a great deal, and exercised at boxing (*savate*). He is reputed to have had a very powerful punch, but was by nature pacific and benign; he was regularly called "the good Théo." In 1836 he fell in love with Camille Rogier's mistress, Ninette or Ninon, called La Cydalise by the group; in November of that year he had a son, named after himself but familiarly called Toto, by Eugénie Fort. The great love of his life was the dancer Carlotta Grisi, for whom he created the ballets *Giselle* and *La Péri*. He accompanied her to London in March 1842 and in November of the

317

following year, and later visited her at her home in Switzerland. But Gautier lived with Carlotta's sister, Ernesta, a singer, who bore him two children, Judith and Estelle. Other women with whom Gautier's name has been associated were the actresses Alice Ozy and La Païva, Marie Mattéi, and the celebrated model Mme Apollinie Aglaé Sabatier, sculpted by Clésinger and one of Baudelaire's muses—La Présidente, as she was called—who inspired some risqué verse not reprinted in Gautier's collected poetry.

The most significant factor in Gautier's artistic life was his financial need that dictated the course of his literary production. The works written before 1836 by this stylist—who disliked writing—were created voluntarily: the imitative, satanic, and pictorial verses of *Albertus* (1833), the satirical tales and character delineation of *Les Jeunes-France* (1833), the anti-Philistine, lush, and sensuous *Mademoiselle de Maupin* (1835-36) were "independent" works. In 1836, at the age of twenty-five, Gautier embarked effectively on the journalistic career which exacted from him a constant, daily toil almost until his death at Neuilly from a cardiac condition and complications—albuminuria, peritonitis, kidney trouble—in 1872.

If the monument over his grave at Montmartre cemetery were to list his output, the equivalent of more than 300 volumes would have to be inscribed. In the course of some thirty-five years Gautier wrote more than 2,000 articles, on subjects like the theatre, the arts, and fiction; these, when reprinted, have sometimes been abbreviated. For eighteen years he was the first-line critic of *La Presse,* and in 1855 he left Émile de Girardin's paper to join the *Moniteur Universel* (which became the *Journal Officiel*), thus becoming a sort of spokesman or official critic for the government. (In 1866 the government asked him to write a report on progress in literature for the past twenty-five years.) Gautier also contributed to some fifteen other newspapers.

Such a prodigious output required a phenomenal memory—he took a minimum of notes, and had a keen eye for detail—and absolute fluency of expression. Indeed, he often worked right at the printer's, supplying copy directly to the typesetters, and needed to make no revisions. Such professional dexterity and productivity required the utilization of all experiences. His travels were made for and became the stuff of articles and books on Spain, Italy, Constantinople, and Russia. He turned brief visits to England,

Algeria, and Egypt into literature, but he visited the last-named country in 1869, the year after the publication of *Le Roman de la Momie* (this work has had many bibliophilic editions in France). Viscount Spoelberch de Lovenjoul, describing the history of Gautier's works, devoted more than 1,100 pages to them; at Chantilly, there are twenty-six cartons, containing 9,000 pages of correspondence, to and from Gautier. This incessant activity, while according him the importance of an outstanding figure in literary and artistic circles, brought him no official honors or sinecures, other than inclusion in the Legion of Honor, and he was an unsuccessful candidate for a seat in the French Academy. Gautier was usually in debt and barely able to support his parents and three children while also welcoming frequent guests at suburban Neuilly where he had moved in 1858.

Gautier attended the Magny dinners started late in 1862 by Gavarni and Sainte-Beuve, and was a mainstay of Princess Mathilde's salon at Saint-Gratien. He was one of the leaders or "elder statesmen" for the writers of his time. A force in the romantic movement, whose anecdotal history he wrote, he has been overshadowed by the giant, Victor Hugo. Gautier represents the steadfast adherence to the apolitical, idealistic, art-for-art's-sake aspect of romanticism which became political or prophetic or humanitarian in the evolution of his contemporaries. His principles of clarity, careful artistry, and visual rendition ("I am a man for whom the visible [or, exterior] world exists") made him an influence on the Parnassians, dissatisfied with effusion and with the tearful sort of "mal du siècle." Gautier subscribed to the dictum formulated by Flaubert that "from the form the idea is born." Baudelaire dedicated his *Fleurs du Mal* (1857) "to Théophile Gautier, perfect magician of French letters"; Mallarmé, recondite master of the symbolists, was inspired by Gautier's death to compose *Toast Funèbre,* a meditation on the poet's vocation; Flaubert admired Gautier for his integrity. The intimate of artists, he has been depicted by Braquemond, Chassériau, Garry, Gill, Nadar, Nanteuil, Valloton, and others.

Aside from his rôle in the romantic movement, Gautier is especially famous for *Mademoiselle de Maupin* and for *Émaux et Camées* (1852). The former, a *succès de scandale* because of its preface which scorns the bourgeois Philistine and proclaims the amorality and non-utility of art, has lived on for its lush yet restrained rhythmic style and its androgynous character; the volume of verse, composed over the preceding decade and which did not earn him more than 300 francs, contains "L'Art," the poem that has become the manifesto-recipe of pure art and craftsmanship. The exotic, the macabre and fantastic vein was exploited by Gautier in many stories, but his talent for the concrete and the pictorial rather than the hallucinatory limits the effect on the modern reader. A certain "literary" quality and the pressure of production have restricted Gautier's place in literature to one of primarily historical significance.

There is no complete edition of Gautier's works. F. C. de Sumichrast did a translation in 24 vols. (1900-1903). *Mademoiselle de Maupin* was translated anonymously in 1890, 1905, 1918, 1929, and by the following: I. G. Burnham (1897), Burton Rascoe (1920), A. C. Bessie (1930), R. and E. Powys Mathers (1938), P. Selver (1949). Lafcadio Hearn translated *Clarimonde* (1899), *One of Cleopatra's Nights, and Other Tales* (1900), *Stories* (1908). *The Romance of a Mummy* was translated by A. M. Wright (1882). *Spirite*, translated by A. D. Hall (1890), was republished as *Stronger than Death* (1898). *La Morte Amoureuse* was translated by P. Hookham as *The Beautiful Vampire* (1927). Additional translations include: *Wanderings in Spain* (1853; as *A Romantic in Spain*, 1926); *Constantinople* (1854, 1875); *A Winter in Russia* (1874; as *Russia*, 1905); *Famous French Authors* (1879); *Captain Fracasse* (1880, 1897); *My Household of Pets* (1882); *Jettatura* (1888); *Juancho* (1890); *The Evil Eye*, and *A Square Game* (1892); *Journeys in Italy* (1902); *Charles Baudelaire, His Life* (1915). C. W. Beaumont translated (1932) *Romantic Ballet as Seen by Théophile Gautier, 1837-1848.*

ABOUT: Brandes, G. M. C. Main Currents in Nineteenth Century Literature, V; Dillingham, L. B. The Creative Imagination of Théophile Gautier; Palache, J. G. Gautier and the Romantics; Patch, H. The Dramatic Criticism of Théophile Gautier; Richardson, J. Théophile Gautier; His Life and Times; Rivers, W. N. A Study of the Metaphors and Comparisons of Théophile Gautier; Saintsbury, G. Collected Essays and Papers, 1875-1923, IV, and French Literature and Its Masters; Temple, R. Z. Critic's Alchemy. [In French—see studies by A. Boschot, R. Jasinski, J. Tild. There are critical editions by Jasinski and G. Matoré.]

S. S. W.

*GEIBEL, EMANUEL (October 17, 1815-April 6, 1884), German poet and dramatist, was born in Lübeck, the son of Johannes Geibel, a pastor. His mother, Elizabeth Ganslandt, was of French origin. After studying theology at Bonn (1835) and philology at Berlin (1836), Geibel in 1838 became a tutor in the home of the Russian ambassador in Athens. Here he encountered his former school friend, the historian Ernst

* gī' bĕl

Curtius, and the two traveled together through Greece. In 1840 they published jointly a volume of translations from the Greek, entitled *Klassische Stunden.* This same year Geibel returned to Lübeck, where he completed his first collection of poems, *Gedichte* (1840). Although this book aroused no immediate acclaim, it passed through 100 printings during the poet's lifetime. A second volume of mildly political poems, *Zeitstimmen* (1841), gained the favorable notice of King Frederick William IV, who granted the poet an annual stipend of 300 taler. During the next decade Geibel led a wandering existence, until in 1852 he accepted an invitation from King Maximilian II of Bavaria to become an honorary professor of aesthetics in Munich. Geibel soon became the central figure among the coterie of poets gathered in Munich and assumed a leading position in Maximilian's discussion group. Following the death of his wife, Ada Trummer, in 1855 after only three years of marriage, Geibel no longer felt happy in Munich. The situation worsened with the accession to the throne of Ludwig II in 1864, and four years later the poet settled permanently in Lübeck. He became an ardent supporter of German nationalism, and a volume of patriotic verse entitled *Heroldsrufe* (1871) earned him the title of *Der Herold des Deutschen Reiches.* His last years were marred by illness, until his death at Lübeck.

Although Geibel's reputation has diminished greatly since his death, he is acknowledged as the representative poet in Germany between 1848 and 1870. He was a proponent of classical perfection of form, and his works were dedicated to the ideal of aesthetic beauty. His lyrics are pleasant, melodious productions which display great virtuosity of form. However, they are generally superficial in content and lack philosophic depth. His verse is heavily derivative and reveals the influence of Platen, Goethe, Heine, Lenau, Strachwitz, and Hölderlin among others. Rarely has a poet of Geibel's stature displayed such a lack of a characteristic style. His finest lyrics are the collections entitled *Juniuslieder* (1848) and *Neue Gedichte* (1856), while later notable works include *Gedichte und Gedenkblätter* (1864) and *Spätherbstblätter* (1877).

As a dramatist Geibel was unsuccessful, although the comedy *Meister Andrea* (1855) and the tragedy *Brunhilde* (1858) won contemporary popularity. His best play is the tragedy *Sophonisbe* (1868), for which he received the Schiller prize. Geibel excelled as a translator of French and Spanish poetry and produced the volumes *Volkslieder und Romanzen der Spanier* (1843), *Spanisches Liederbuch* (1852), and *Französische Lyrik* (1862).

Lucy H. Hooper translated the volume *Gedichte* in 1864 as *Poems*. Selections of Geibel's verse are also contained in W. W. Caldwell, *Poems, Originals and Translations* (1857), and J. L. Spaulding, *Songs Chiefly From the German* (1896). *Brunhilde* was translated by G. T. Dippold in 1879.

ABOUT: [In German—see studies by R. Carstensen, E. Curtius, K. T. Gaedertz, K. Goedeke, M. Koch, and F. Stichtennath.]

D. G. D.

*GEIJER, ERIK GUSTAF (January 12, 1783-April 23, 1847), Swedish poet, historian, composer, was born in the province of Värmland at Ransäter foundry, owned by his father, Bengt Gustaf Geijer, a vigorous, magnanimous, practical man. His mother was Ulrika Magdalena Geisler, also of a mine-working family. He grew up in a harmonious home pervaded with industriousness, piety, and joy of life. He took his M.A. at the University of Uppsala in 1806. A visit to England gave him fruitful impressions. In 1810 he was appointed *docent* in History. Geijer was one of the founders of "Götiska Förbundet" (The Gothic Society), which had the objective of reviving the spirit of freedom, manly courage, and integrity of the ancient Scandinavians. He initiated the Society's periodical *Iduna*, in the first issue of which he published some of his best poems, e.g., "Manhem," "Vikingen," "Odalbonden" (The Yeoman Farmer), all describing the Gothic manly ideal and expressing patriotic feelings. His poem "Bergsmannen" (The Miner) contains romantic nature philosophy. Geijer's friendship with Atterbom pulled him definitely over to the neo-romanticists, and in accordance with their interests he published in cooperation with A. A. Afzelius three volumes of *Svenska Folkvisor* (Swedish Folksongs), 1814-16. After a long engagement, in 1816 Geijer married Anna Lisa Lilljebjörn, daughter of a landed proprietor in Värmland, and the next year he became a professor. In 1821 he was prosecuted for heresy in a philosophical study of the poet Thomas Thorild (see sketch below) but was acquitted. In 1824 he was elected to the Swedish Academy.

Now Geijer's historical interest asserted itself more and more, and he published several historical essays and treatises. His con-

* yā′ ēr

320

ception of history was first romantically oriented and strongly influenced by the philosophical systems of Fichte, Schelling, and Hegel. His greatest contribution was *Svenska Folkets Historia* (History of the Swedish People) in three volumes (1832-36), which ended with Queen Kristina's abdication in 1654. But historical studies led him to a more realistic outlook and made him interested in politics. As a politician he fought for conservative ideas but gradually adopted a more liberal and democratic conception of society. This development led to his sensational "apostasy" in 1838, which shook the whole nation. His favorable inclination towards social reforms soon became evident in his production.

Geijer was enormously productive during the 1830's. He not only wrote about history and politics, but he also created beautiful lyrics, e.g., the exquisite poems "Tonerna" (Tones), "På Nyårsdagen 1838" (On New Year's Day 1838), "Natthimlen" (The Night Sky), which were written to music. He was a gifted and prolific composer. In 1841-42 he epitomized the results of his historical-philosophical studies in *Föreläsningar öfver Menniskans Historia* (Lectures on the History of Man). He also was a prime mover in reorganizing the Swedish educational system in accordance with more democratic principles. Upon his return from a recreational trip to Germany in 1846, Geijer moved to Stockholm to finish his Swedish history, but death soon ended his work.

Geijer's *Svenska Folkets Historia* was translated into English by J. H. Turner as *The History of the Swedes*, 1845. Some historical and political essays appeared in 1840 as *The Poor Laws and Their Bearing on Society*. Four of his poems in English translation are included in C. W. Stork's *Anthology of Swedish Lyrics*, and scattered verses of other poems in an article by Stork in *American-Scandinavian Review*, 1928.

ABOUT: Bach, G. The History of the Scandinavian Literatures; Howitt, W. & M. The Literature and Romance of Northern Europe, II; Spongberg, V. H. The Philosophy of Erik Gustaf Geijer. [In Swedish—see studies by A. Blanck, H. Borelius, G. Hedin, C. A. Hessler, J. Landquist, A. Molin, E. Norberg, J. Norlind, S. I. Olofsson, W. G. Stiernstedt.]

A. J.

*GEIJERSTAM, GUSTAF af (January 5, 1858-March 6, 1909), Swedish novelist, short-story writer, dramatist, was born at Jönsarbo in the Swedish province of Västmanland. His father was Johan Gustaf af Geijerstam, a nobleman and foundry proprietor in Väst-

* yā′ ēr stäm′

manland, later principal of a teachers' college in Kalmar in southeastern Sweden. His mother was Alma Möller, daughter of a judge. After taking his Bachelor's degree at the University of Uppsala in 1879, he identified himself with the radical movement "Young Sweden" and became a zealous advocate of naturalism. However, he lacked authority and leadership and did not attain the central position in the literary world for which he worked so hard. In 1885 he married Eugenia Valenkamph, a young actress, born in Finland, who died in 1900. (One of their sons, Gösta af Geijerstam, born in 1888, became a writer.) In 1902 he married Maria Biörck.

Geijerstam published three collections of short stories about the life of the common people, written in accordance with the naturalistic principles (1882-84). These stories established his popularity as an author. The conflict between the religious, cultural, and social ideals of the old generation and his own he described in the autobiographical novel *Erik Grane* (1885), in which the influence of Ibsen, Strindberg, and others is evident. More firmly composed is his next novel, *Pastor Hallin* (1887), which describes a man who, in contrast to Ibsen's *Brand*, gives up his ideals and compromises with society.

The most valuable part of Geijerstam's production is to be found in his realistic peasant stories, *Fattigt Folk* (Poor People, 1889) and *Kronofogdens Berättelser* (The Sheriff's Stories, 1890), based on deterministic naturalism. Some comedies with motifs from the life of the people are insignificant as literature but were frequently staged and favorably received.

When the reaction against naturalism began, about 1900, Geijerstam at first fought for his convictions, but thereafter he went through a rather unproductive and critical period of self-analysis. His novel *Medusas Hufvud* (Medusa's Head, 1895), an attempt to solve his conflicts, shows the influence of Dostoevsky in its projection of mystic and subconscious forces. His intellectual powers and psychological understanding were inadequate for real elucidation of the problems he discussed.

Geijerstam's production during the last decade of his life was remarkably extensive. He published at least one book a year. Several of these books dealt with marital problems and the relationship between the sexes and between parents and children—*Kvinnomakt* (Woman's Power, 1901), *Karin*

Brandts Dröm (Karin Brandt's Dream, 1904). *Den Eviga Gåtan* (The Eternal Riddle, 1907). The sentimentality in *Boken om Lille-bror* (The Book About Little Brother, 1900) had great popular appeal.

Kvinnomakt was translated by Esther Rapp as *Woman Power* (1921), *Boken om Lille-bror* by E. Björkman as *The Book About Little Brother* (1921), and *Mina Pojkar* by Alfhild Huebsch as *My Boys* (1933). The play *Förbrytare*, translated as *Criminals* by R. W. Swanson, was published in *Poet Lore*, XXXIV.

A. J.

*GELLERT, CHRISTIAN FÜRCHTE-GOTT (July 4, 1715-December 13, 1769), German poet, was born in Hainichen, the son of a Protestant minister. His youth was one of much privation and strict discipline. By his thirteenth year he had already tried his talents as a poet. In 1729 Gellert began his preparatory schooling at the *Fürstenschule* in Meissen where he met Gottlieb Wilhelm Rabener, the foremost German satirist of the Age of Enlightenment. In the year 1734 he matriculated in theology at the University of Leipzig. However, when he delivered his first sermon from the cathedral four years later, his natural timidity made the occasion a complete failure and he abandoned any hope of becoming an active member of the clergy. After two years as a tutor in the household of a family of the nobility he returned to Leipzig, where he extended his training in pedagogy and studied French and English literature.

During his second sojourn at Leipzig, Gellert worked under Johann Christoph Gottsched as his assistant in the translation of Bayle's dictionary. His ties with Gottsched were loosened through his association with the so-called Bremer Beiträger group, including such men as J. E. Schlegel, J. A. Cramer, F. W. Zachariae, and G. W. Rabener. Gellert's first belletristic efforts were published in Schwabe's journal *Belustigungen des Verstandes und Witzes,* and later in the *Bremer Beyträge* or *Neuen Beyträgen zum Vergnügen des Verstandes und Witzes.* The light, natural tone of his fables and verse tales won immediate popularity. In 1745 he became a member of the faculty of the University of Leipzig and his lectures on aesthetics were most popular. Through his pastoral comedies *Das Band* (1744) and *Sylvia* (1745), the sentimental comedy *Die Betschwester* (1745), the novel *Leben der Schwedischen Gräfin von G.* (1746), and particularly through his *Fabeln und Erzäh-*

* gĕl' ĕrt

321

lungen (1746), he acquired considerable fame as a poet. His later works such as *Lehrgedichte und Erzählungen* and *Geistliche Oden und Lieder* (1757) were likewise accepted with enthusiasm.

During his own era Gellert was widely admired. Wieland enjoyed his naïveté, wit, and simple, direct language. Lessing recognized a fine nature, feeling, and nobility in Gellert's letters. But the following age, which acknowledged Goethe and Schiller as its literary idols, found him lacking in creative genius. Nevertheless, his services to German letters cannot be denied. He was one of the first German writers to appreciate the necessity of a broad reading public and thoroughly to understand the relationship between life and poetry. More than a poet, he played the rôle of fatherly *Seelsorger* for the German public. His death was the occasion of national mourning.

English translations of Gellert's works are: *The Tender Sisters,* a comedy (1805); *Fables:* a free translation from the German of Gellert and other poets, by J. A. Nuske (1850); *The Life of the Swedish Countess de G.* (1776).

ABOUT: [In German—see studies by M. Dorn, M. Durach, G. Ellinger, E. Kretzschmar.]

E. K. G.

*GENLIS, STÉPHANIE FÉLICITÉ DU CREST DE SAINT AUBIN, Comtesse de (January 25, 1746-December 31, 1830), French novelist and educator, was born at Champçery in Burgundy to Pierre César du Crest, a noble but impoverished army officer, and his wife, Marie Françoise de Mézière. A bright and pretty child, she was introduced to the pleasures of courtly life at an early age. One of her chief delights was acting in amateur theatricals, a taste which she retained and indulged in her adult life. At the age of six Félicité was ordained a canoness in the noble Chapter of Alix, receiving the title Mme la Comtesse de Lancy.

The girl's beauty (she was slender, graceful, with sweet dark eyes and rich auburn hair), her charm, intelligence, and talents for acting and music assured her success in the French court. She was sixteen when she married Comte Charles Alexis de Genlis, also of a noble but impoverished family. Through the influence of her aunt, Mme de Montesson, mistress of the Duc d'Orléans, she was presented at court and, in 1770, made lady-in-waiting to the Duchesse de Chartres at the Palais Royal. Unknown to the duchess she had become mistress of the Duc de Chartres,

* zhän lēs'

cousin of the King, who in the early years of the French Revolution was a Girondist and called himself Philippe Égalité. The mother of two children by her husband, Mme de Genlis also had at least two children by her lover. One of these, the beautiful Pamela, later Lady Edward Fitzgerald, passed in society as her adopted daughter.

Gifted with a talent for teaching, along with her many other talents, Mme de Genlis tutored the daughters of the duke's family. She was so successful in her work that in 1781 the duke appointed her tutor to his sons. Since one of these sons was to become Louis Philippe, King of France, in later years and was already recognized as a potential heir to the throne, her position was of great importance. She was the center of much gossip and scandal and had many enemies.

Mme de Genlis' fortunes during the Revolution fell with those of her royal lover. In 1793 when it became apparent that Philippe's revolutionary ideals were being exploited by the Jacobins to their own advantage, he sent her and his daughters out of France. This step marked the beginning of seven years of exile for her. It was a period of insecurity, hard work, and weary travel. She lived in Switzerland, Denmark, and Germany, supporting herself by hack writing. Meanwhile both her husband, from whom she had been separated for many years, and her lover Philippe were guillotined.

In June 1800 Mme de Genlis' name was removed from the list of émigrés, and she was allowed to return to France. An impoverished woman now in her fifties, remembered mainly for a notorious love affair with a nobleman whose memory was now disgraced, she nevertheless won her way back to a position of influence and honor. Her success was largely the result of her novel *Madame de la Vallière* (1804) which is said to have brought tears to Napoleon's eyes. He granted her a pension of 6,000 francs a year, demanding in return that she write him a letter every two weeks on any subject she chose.

Although she lost her pension, Mme de Genlis' good fortune survived the fall of Napoleon and the restoration of the monarchy. With unflagging energy, though she was now over seventy, she continued to produce novels, biographies, and didactic works. At the age of seventy-six she announced that she would rewrite the entire *Encyclopédie* from a religious point of view. She died in Paris at the age of eighty-four, only a few hours after learning to her great delight that her former pupil Louis Philippe had become King of France.

The oblivion into which Mme de Genlis fell a few decades after her death is hardly surprising to anyone who has examined some of her writings (she published over eighty volumes). Though gifted with facility and some grace of style, she had neither sufficient imagination nor sufficient intellectual depth to write anything of permanent value. Yet her fame in the late eighteenth and early nineteenth centuries was extraordinary. Her books were translated into English almost as soon as they were published in French. So popular were her historical romances that she was pilloried in a contemporary satire, Mrs. Sarah Green's *Romance Readers and Romance Writers* (1810), as a pernicious influence on the young. Jane Austen knew her work: she refers to her *Adelaide and Theodore* in *Emma*. George Sand once asserted that she had learned socialism from reading *Les Battuécas*, and, even closer to the twentieth century, George Saintsbury recalled that in his youth "all girls and some boys knew *Adèle et Théodore* and *Les Veillées du Château*." Among her other more popular works were *Le Théâtre de l'Éducation*, a collection of plays for young people, the novels *Les Chevaliers du Cygne* and *Mlle de Clermont*, and *Diners du Baron d'Holbach*, a satire on the Philosophes. Perhaps her most interesting work is the *Mémoires Inédits sur le XVIIIᵉ Siècle* (1825) which has furnished historians with much valuable material on the period.

Eighteenth and nineteenth century English translations of Mme de Genlis' works are far too numerous to list here. Probably her most popular books in England and in America were *Adelaide and Theodore, or Letters on Education*, first published in London in 1783; *Tales of the Castle*, a translation of *Les Veillées du Château*, by Thomas Holcroft, 1785; *The Knights of the Swan*, a translation of *Les Chevaliers du Cygne*, by the Rev. Mr. Beresford, 1796 (an abridged version, titled *The Age of Chivalry*, was made by C. Butler, 1799); and *Placide, a Spanish Tale*, a translation of *Les Battuécas*, by A. Jamieson, 1817. Also very popular were Holcroft's translation of her *Sacred Dramas* in 1786, and Mrs. Inchbald's adaptation of *Zélie*, titled *The Child of Nature* in 1788. The latter was produced on the stage at the Theatre Royal, Covent Garden. Various other educational writings also saw many English editions, among them *Lessons of a Governess to her Pupils* (1792) and *La Bruyère the Less: or Characters and Manners of the Children of the Present Age* (1801). *The Memoirs of the Countess de Genlis*, 8 vols., was published in 1825-26.

ABOUT: Bearne, C. M. Heroines of French Society; Dobson, H. A. Four Frenchwomen; Kerby, W. M. The Educational Ideas and Activities of Mme la Comtesse de Genlis; Windham, V. Mme

de Genlis; Comparative Literature, XIII (1961). [In French—Harmand, J. Mme de Genlis: Sa Vie Intime et Politique.]

"GÉRARD DE NERVAL." See NERVAL, GÉRARD DE

*GERHARDT, PAULUS (March 12, 1607-May 27, 1676), German poet, hymnist, and clergyman, was born at Gräfenhainichen in Saxony, where his father, Christian Gerhardt, served as mayor. His mother, Dorothea Starke, was the daughter and granddaughter of Lutheran pastors. After attending the *Fürstenschule* at Grimma, a school of strict discipline and religious atmosphere, Gerhardt entered the University of Wittenberg in 1628 to study theology. There is little documentation of his life during the following period, but it is known that he settled in Berlin in 1642 or 1643. Here he worked as a tutor in the home of Andreas Barthold, whose daughter, Anna Maria, he later married in 1655. The poems and hymns which Gerhardt wrote during these years in Berlin were collected into a songbook in 1648 by the well-known choirmaster Johann Crüger, who wrote melodies to accompany the texts. In 1651 Gerhardt was appointed pastor at Mittenwalde and in 1657 returned to Berlin as Deacon of the Nicolaikirche. Since, however, he refused on principle to abide by the imperial edict which aimed at resolving the bitter hostility between the Lutheran and Reformed Church, he was removed from his position at the order of the Elector. He remained in Berlin, supported by friends, and in 1667 completed a major collection of his works under the title *Geistliche Andachten*. The following year he was appointed Archdeacon in Lübben, where he served until his death. He is buried in the vault of the Lübben church.

Gerhardt is the representative poet of the Lutheran church and stands next to Luther as the greatest poet of spiritual song in Germany. Although his poems are less forceful than those of Luther, they are considered superior with respect to elegance of form. Many of his works have become German hymn folk songs. A number of his hymns are still in current usage today, including his most famous poems, "O Haupt voll Blut und Wunden," "Nun ruhen alle Wälder," "Befiehl du deine Wege," "Ist Gott für mich, so trete gleich alle wider mich," and "Ich weiss, dass mein Erlöser lebt."

* gär' härt

Gerhardt's songs emanated from his own profound religious conviction, and in his works the hymn underwent a transition from the collective feeling expressed in Luther's texts to a more individual and lyric approach. It is this warm personal element, combined with the purity of his faith, which strikes a chord of common humanity. The spirit that the work expresses is strong and joyous. The greatness of Gerhardt's lyrics derives from his ability to express the sentiments and aspirations of all Christians in a form which is simple, direct, and melodious.

Geistliche Lieder was translated under the title *Spiritual Songs* by J. Kelly in 1867. Selections of his hymns also occur in *A Library of Religious Poetry* by P. Schaff & A. Gilman (1881), *Lyra Germanica* (First and Second Series 1907), *Moravian Hymns* (1912), and in G. C. Schoolfield's *The German Baroque Lyric in English Translation* (1962).

ABOUT: Dallmann, W. Paul Gerhardt; Julian, J. Dictionary of Hymnology; Hewitt, T. B. Gerhardt as a Hymn-Writer and His Influence on English Hymnody. [In German—see studies by K. Hesselbacher, K. Ihlenfeld, E. Kochs, H. Petrich, F. Seebass.]

D. G. D.

*GERSTÄCKER, FRIEDRICH WILHELM CHRISTIAN (May 16, 1816-May 31, 1872), German novelist, was born in Hamburg, the son of a famous tenor and an opera soprano. After the early death of his father, he was raised in the house of an uncle, director of a theatre. The reading of Defoe's *Robinson Crusoe* awakened in him the yearning for foreign countries, and at the age of twenty-one he emigrated to the United States, where he earned a living as best he could, as peddler, stoker, deckhand, farm laborer, woodcutter, goldsmith, and seller of patent medicines. During five years he visited every state of the Union, traversing the continent on foot from Canada to the Gulf of Mexico. Finally, he became a hotel manager in Louisiana, but homesickness drove him back to Germany in 1843.

To his surprise he found that he had become an author, for without his knowledge a diary which his mother had given to a friend was published in a journal and aroused considerable interest. This success led in 1844 to his first published travel book *Streif- und Jagdzüge durch die Vereinigten Staaten Nordamerikas*. Five years later he set out again for another twenty years of worldwide journeys through North and South America, the West Indies, Australia,

* gĕr' stĕk ĕr

324

Oceania, and, as companion of Duke Ernst of Coburg-Gotha, to Egypt and Ethiopia, gathering material for books of travel and adventure which he published during brief returns to Germany. In 1868 he settled in Brunswick, where he died at fifty-six.

Gerstäcker's voluminous literary production is a reflection of his unsettled life and describes the irresistible lure of foreign lands. His books enjoyed great popularity at the time and some are still widely read. As an author of ethnographical accounts he vies with his contemporary Charles Sealsfield (pen-name for Karl Postl). While much in his over forty books has special appeal to the juvenile mind, the convincing vividness of his descriptions and his entertaining style impart to his writings great charm for the adult reader. Gerstäcker knows how to paint a realistic, though not always accurate, picture of the beauty and horror of exotic landscapes and to invent exciting plots which, to be sure, often lean toward sensationalism and sentimentalism.

Best known of his novels dealing with the experience of the American pioneer are *Die Regulatoren von Arkansas* (1845) and *Die Flusspiraten des Mississippi* (1848). The hypocrisy and ruthlessness of the settler or adventurer are contrasted with the purity of nature and of the indigenous people; his sympathies are generally with the Indians, perhaps influenced by the fact that they once saved him from death when he was wounded by wild bears. *Gold!* (1858) depicts the fortunes and misfortunes of the gold-rush of 1849. *Tahiti* (1854) breathes the Gauguinesque charm of seclusion, yet the hero of this tale yields to nostalgia just as did the author. Occasionally Gerstäcker becomes didactic, as in the short story "Der Wilddieb" in which a murderous poacher escapes the authorities, but not his conscience, by going overseas. In a different vein is his gem of a short story "Germelshausen" (1862) with its folklore theme of the sunken city coming to life for one day every hundred years.

English translations were most numerous in the 1850's and 1870's. An anonymous translator rendered *Die Regulatoren von Arkansas* under the title *The Feathered Arrow* in 1851 and *Die Flusspiraten des Mississippi (The Pirates of Mississippi)* in 1856. A good translation of *Gold!* (English title: *Each for Himself*) appeared in 1859. *Germelshausen* was first translated into English in 1862; in 1876 a translation of it appeared in *Harper's Magazine* and in 1878 it was published, along with another story, as *The Strange Village, and The Burgomaster's Daughter*.

ABOUT: O'Donnell, G. Gerstäcker in America, in PMLA, 1927; Seyforth, E. Friedrich Gerstäcker.

S. H. M.

*GERSTENBERG, HEINRICH WIL-HELM VON (January 3, 1737-November 1, 1823), German dramatist and critic, was born at Tønder, Denmark, although he was actually of German nationality. His father was an officer in the Danish army. Though born in Denmark during the rule of Christian VI as a Danish subject, Gerstenberg never really mastered the Danish language, being raised in completely German surroundings and receiving an altogether German education. He went to school first at Husum, Schleswig; later at Altona, then under Danish rule. During this period he studied Latin, French, Spanish, and English. He even started to write some verses and to translate Horace and Anacreon.

At the University of Jena, where Gerstenberg went to study law in 1757, he became a member of the Deutsche Gesellschaft, a society which included many well-known German poets. Encouraged by C. F. Weisse and C. F. Gellert, he published in 1759 a collection of anacreontic poems, *Tändeleyen*, which was praised by Lessing. In the same year, a collection of idylls, *Prosaische Gedichte*, prose-poems in the spirit of Salomon Gessner, appeared in Altona.

Realizing that he would never be able to earn a living from his literary efforts, Gerstenberg in 1760 entered the Danish army, advancing in two years to captain of cavalry. A short and bloodless war with Russia inspired *Kriegslieder eines Konigl. Dänischen Grenadiers bey Eröffnung des Feldzuges* (1762). These "war songs" were a conscious imitation of Johann Ludwig Gleim, to whom the volume was dedicated. During this time he was also one of the chief contributors to the periodical *Der Hypochondrist*.

In 1765 he was married to Margrethe Sophie Trochman from Schleswig, and in September of the same year Gerstenberg moved to Copenhagen where he stayed for ten years. The first few years there were the happiest and most productive in Gerstenberg's life. He became an active member of the German circle, publishing several articles in Danish as well as in German periodicals. In 1765 appeared his translation of Beaumont and Fletcher's *The Maid's Tragedy* under the title *Die Braut*, and in 1766 a poem inspired by the Nordic mythology and Ossian—*Das Gedicht eines Skalden*, which introduced the entire movement of bardic poetry to German literature.

In this period of creativity also falls Gerstenberg's best work of criticism, *Briefe über*

* gĕr′ stēn bĕrк

Merkwürdigkeiten der Litteratur (1766-70), which is especially famous for his critical essays on Shakespeare. Typical Shakespearean elements are to be found in his tragedy *Ugolino* (1768), in which Dante's story of the death of Count Ugolino and his sons by starvation is extended over five harrowing acts. The cantata *Ariadne auf Naxos* also originated in this highly productive period.

In 1768 Gerstenberg's patron resigned his office, and Gerstenberg found himself in material difficulties from which he never recovered. After a period in the civil service, he was appointed (1775) Danish Resident in Lübeck with a salary of 800 taler. In 1783 he obtained permission to sell his office to the highest bidder; but having sold it, he found it difficult to obtain a new position. The last forty years of his life were unfortunate. His wife died in 1785; of his eight children, two sons died during his lifetime. His last literary work, the tragic melodrama *Minona oder die Angelsachsen* (1785), was coolly received. Embittered, he devoted himself to philosophical studies, especially of Kant. He was almost sixty when he was married again, to a certain Sophie Ophelia Stemann. In his last years he busied himself with collecting and editing his own works. He died at eighty-six in Altona.

ABOUT: Eaton, J. W. The German Influence in Danish Literature in the Eighteenth Century; *also* Gerstenberg and Lessing. [In German—see studies by O. Fischer, K. Gerth, M. Jacobs, A. M. Wagner.]

F. L.

GERTSEN, ALEXANDER IVANOVICH. See HERZEN, ALEXANDER IVANOVICH

*GEZELLE, GUIDO (May 1, 1830-November 27, 1899), Flemish poet and priest, was born in Bruges. His father, Pier-Jan, gardener and nurseryman, was spirited and articulate; his mother, Monica Devriese, was deeply religious, shy, and melancholy. The poet spent his youth in a poor, rather countrified neighborhood of Bruges, living in almost Gothic piety. He went to school in Bruges (1841-46); at Roeselare (1846-50), in the so-called Small Seminary, he earned part of his tuition by running errands for various faculty members. Hypersensitive and introverted, he lived in a condition of humiliation and inferiority. From this time dated his English orientation, his fiery love

* gĕ zĕl′

for everything Flemish, and the budding of his poetic genius. From 1850 he studied at the Great Seminary in Bruges, and on June 10, 1854, he became a priest.

Returning to Roeselare, he became a teacher of natural history and philosophy at the Small Seminary, where he exerted great influence on such outstanding pupils as H. and G. Verriest, Eugene van Oye, and Karel De Gheldere. In his enthusiasm to teach these disciples and to champion the Flemish cause, he neglected the prescribed course of studies. The ecclesiastical authorities changed his status by entrusting him with the teaching of modern languages. In 1860 he was sent to Bruges, where he taught philosophy at the Anglo-Belgicum seminary. As vice-rector of the seminary he was a failure. In 1865 he became priest in the S. Walburgis parish. Meanwhile he was contributing articles to the weekly *Reinaert de Vos* (1860-65) and then to his own political anti-liberal weekly *'t Jaer* (1864-70). In 1865 he began the weekly *Rond den Heerd* which he directed until 1872. The lack of success in Roeselare, the new setbacks he suffered in Bruges, the heavy and nerve-wracking work as journalist and editor, the political attacks directed against him, even the difficulties in the small household of the curate with whom he lived not only hindered and virtually ended his activities as a poet but also broke him in body and spirit. He left Bruges in September 1872 and went to Courtrai where he became chaplain in the O. L. Vrouwenkerk.

The poems of this first period are to be found in *Kerkhofbloemen* (1858), *Dichtoefeningen* (1858), *Kleingedichtjes* (1860), and *Gedichten, Gezangen en Gebeden* (1862). These lyrics belong to the best the Flemish romantic movement ever produced. They give voice to the poet's feeling for nature and express his national and religious sentiments with an ardor never before encountered in Dutch literature. These sentiments are expressed in an astonishing number of nuances, ranging from Franciscan idealization and joy of life, to asceticism carried to the point of despair and deep melancholy. They are in the main highly personal in outlook.

In Courtrai he recovered slowly from his deep distress. The generation which he had educated in Roeselare began to enter active life; some, like Hugo Verriest, continued his work and in their turn influenced the forming of A. Rodenbach, J. Devos, C. Lievens, and others; a west-Flemish movement had come to life. After 1877 the poet in Gezelle

came alive again. With the help of Hugo Verriest he published his *Volledige Gedichten* in four volumes (1878-80). From 1881 on he published the philological magazine *Loquela*. His translation of Longfellow's *Hiawatha* appeared in 1886, the year in which he became a member of the Royal Flemish Academy. In 1887 he received an honorary degree from the University of Louvain. From then on his time was mainly devoted to linguistic and literary studies. His translation of Msgr. Waffelaert's *Meditationis* appeared in 1880. He died a few months after his return to Bruges in April 1899. His statue was unveiled in Bruges in 1930.

ABOUT: Roosbroeck, G. L. v. Guido Gezelle, the Mystic Poet of Flanders. [In Dutch—see studies by H. Roland-Holst, B. Verhoevn, V. van den Voorde, A. Walgrave.]

H. B.

GIACOMO DA LENTINI. See JACOPO DA LENTINI

GIANNI DEI RICEVUTI, LAPO. See LAPO GIANNI

GIL VICENTE. See VICENTE, GIL

*GIL Y CARRASCO, ENRIQUE (July 15, 1815-February 22, 1846), Spanish novelist and poet, was born in Villafranca del Bierzo (León). We know little of his early life, but for a time he attended the University of Valladolid. He did not, however, for financial reasons, finish his studies. Later, in 1836, he went to the University of Madrid where, after three years study, he took his degree in law, which he never practiced at the bar. While he was at the university his father Don Juan died. In October 1839, the year of his graduation, he had his first pulmonary attack. He suffered several such attacks during his short life and thus had more than one warning of early death. In 1840, somewhat recovered, he went to work at the Biblioteca Nacional where he remained till 1844. During this time Gil also worked for and contributed to various newspapers and magazines. It is believed that Gil received this appointment through the influence of his good friend the poet Espronceda.

In 1844 he was sent on a special diplomatic mission to Berlin, where he became an intimate friend of Baron Alexander von Hum-

* hēl ē kä räs′ kō

boldt. There, to the horror of Humboldt and others who knew him, he suddenly died of tuberculosis. His delicate health could not stand the rigorous German winters, but he had insisted on staying so as to be able to support his fatherless family. He was buried in Berlin. His popularity in Prussia had been great. For his literary accomplishments he had been decorated by the king with the Grande Médaille d'Or, the highest honor available to a foreigner.

In addition to his newspaper work, Gil y Carrasco left behind him a large number of poems, romantic in style and content, of which the best known are probably "La Caída de las Hojas" and "La Violeta." Gil could, however, rise to a virile and dramatic style when he sang of heroes and martyrs to liberty, as he did in his ode "Polonia," which brings to mind the spirited verse of Leopardi. Gil's masterpiece is undoubtedly his novel *El Señor de Bembibre* (1844), which is very likely the best romantic novel Spain produced (translated into English by G. W. Gethen and L. Veaho as *The Mystery of Bierzo Valley* in 1938). It is a love story which takes place in León at the time of the fall of the Templars. The situations and characters are at times excessively romantic, but all that is outward and decorative is extremely well written. Gil's writings, particularly his poetry, have been called Northern in style and taste because of their vagueness, melancholy, and subjectivity. His *Obras* were edited by G. Laverde and published in Madrid (n.d.). A two volume edition of his *Obras en Prosa* appeared in 1883. Gil's *Diario de Viaje*, which was a book of notes taken for a novel which he presumably intended to write, is also of some interest.

ABOUT: Samuels, D. G. Enrique Gil y Carrasco. [In Spanish—see study by J. M. Joy; Revista de Filología Española, II (1915).]

R. E. O.

*GILBERT, NICOLAS JOSEPH LAURENT (December 15, 1751-November 12, 1780), French poet-satirist, was born at Fontenoy-le-Château, near Remiremont, in Lorraine. His parents, Jean-Pierre Gilbert and Marie-Jeanne Blancheville, were poor, but did their utmost to secure an education for their son. After local schooling, he attended the famed Collège de l'Arc in Dôle, though a mediocre student, and remained there until mid-1766. He was already noted—locally— for keenness of wit and facility in verse satire. His father died in 1768, and Gilbert tried to

* zhēl bâr'

earn a living at Nancy by tutoring and by giving public lectures on literature. At the same time he wrote a "Persian novel" in the fashion of the day, *Les Familles de Darius et d'Eridame* (1770).

The following year he essayed the "héroïde" in *Début Poétique*, then quickly wrote two satires, *Le Carnaval des Auteurs*, in prose, and *Le Siècle*, in verse (1773).

In 1772 Gilbert had gone to the capital. He fared poorly in Paris. His verse play *Le Poète Malheureux* was rejected; La Harpe was especially critical. Gilbert riposted with attacks on the "philosophes" in declamatory satires, *Le Dix-huitième Siècle* (1775)—a reworking of *Le Siècle*—and *Mon Apologie* (1778). In the latter year he also wrote *La Mort d'Abel*, imitated from Gessner.

Of his various odes, "Adieux à la Vie" (originally entitled "Ode Imitée de Plusieurs Psaumes") is undoubtedly his most famous work. It was written shortly before his death. Legend has it that Gilbert lived in extreme poverty, the victim of anti-poetic society, and that he died mad at the hospital Hôtel-Dieu. In fact he had held several pensions secured through Fréron, to whom he had dedicated *Le Dix-huitième Siècle;* he was the beneficiary of grants by the Archbishop of Paris and by the king. His death was the result of a riding accident. Thrown from a horse, Gilbert had been taken either to the Hôtel-Dieu or to Charenton, a madhouse, to be operated on. The operation was not successful, and he had been taken back to his lodging, only to return to the hospital for further treatments.

Gilbert's fame is based on romanticism's exaltation of him as the sacrificial victim of the poet's calling. The somewhat fanciful preface (1817) by Charles Nodier to a selection of Gilbert's works has contributed greatly to this symbolization. But it was Auger, an editor of Malfilâtre, who launched the comparison with the earlier *poète maudit*. Alfred de Vigny romanticized Gilbert's life in *Stello*, as did Madeleine Lépine in *Gilbert, Drama Lyrique* (1903).

ABOUT: [In French—Faguet, E. Histoire de la Poésie Française de la Renaissance au Romantisme, IX; Laffay, E. Le Poète Gilbert.]

S. S. W.

*GIOBERTI, VINCENZO (April 5, 1801-October 26, 1852), Italian patriot, author, philosopher, was born in Turin, the son of Giuseppe and Marianna Capra. A student at the school of the Fathers of the Oratory, he

* jō bĕr' tē

finished his studies in logic there in 1815. He obtained his doctorate in theology at the University of Turin in 1823 and, two years later, was ordained at the university. His thesis *De Deo et Naturali Religioni* aroused much admiration.

The young priest at first led a retired life but was gradually drawn into the absorbing struggle for national unity which no intellectual of those years could avoid. He traveled throughout Lombardy and central Italy in 1828, becoming acquainted with Manzoni in Milan and Leopardi in Florence.

In 1831 the throne of Piedmont was occupied by Charles Albert who interested himself somewhat equivocally in liberal ideas and kept contact with Carbonarist and anti-Austrian groups. Gioberti was noticed by the king and was made one of his chaplains. Gioberti's republican leanings, however, brought him into conflict with the court party, dominated by Jesuits. He lost his chaplaincy and in 1833 he was arrested and imprisoned on charges of being a member of "Young Italy." In October of that year his sentence was commuted to exile, and he went to live in Paris. From there he wrote for the Young Italy movement an article, signed "Demofilo," *Della Reppublica e de Cristianesimo* (The Republic and Christianity). In 1834 he proceeded to Brussels where he remained, teaching and writing, until 1845.

His first major work, *La Teorica del Sovran-Naturale* (The Theory of the Supernatural), appeared in Brussels in 1838. Gioberti's personal reason for writing this thesis was to exhort and comfort his young friend and fellow-exile Paolo Pallia, who had expressed misgivings about the reality of revelation and a future life. The *Teorica* was followed (1839-40) by the three volumes of *Introduzione allo Studio della Filosofia* (Introduction to the Study of Philosophy) in which Gioberti identifies religion with civilization. In 1843 the famous treatise appeared which laid the foundations for the so-called Neo-Guelphic school, *Del Primato Morale e Civile degli Italiani* (The Moral and Civic Preeminence of Italians). Two essays, *Del Bello* (On Beauty) and *Del Buono* (On Good), were published in 1846, and one year later, *Il Gesuita Moderno* (Modern Jesuitry) a powerful indictment of the Jesuits, which hastened the transfer of rule from clerical to civil hands.

In April 1848, under a general amnesty granted by Charles Albert, Gioberti returned to Turin, receiving an enthusiastic welcome. He became a representative in the Turin Chamber of Deputies of which he was soon elected president. His political life came to an end in March 1849 when Victor Emmanuel succeeded his father, Charles Albert, on the Piedmont throne and the dynamics of the national struggle once again changed. Gioberti was sent on a mission to Paris, whence he never returned. In his few remaining years he lived a frugal scholarly life in Paris, refusing pension and preferment. His *Rinnovamento Civile d'Italia* (Civic Renewal of Italy), published in 1851, expressed the hope that the loss of papal temporal power would lead to a revival of religion. This opinion, in addition to Gioberti's general pantheism, resulted in his writings being placed on the Index. He died in Paris of apoplexy.

Del Primato is a sober philosophical study, done with masterly polemic, stating that the church is the axis on which the well-being of human life revolves, and picturing the political and cultural emancipation of Italy by means of a civic papacy. This position of reliance on papal power is, in effect, Neo-Guelphism. The movement, which prevailed from 1846 through 1849, was the third in the sequence of the political struggles for unification, the first two seeing the formation of the Carbonari and Young Italy, and the final period witnessing the triumph of Victor Emmanuel II and the ratification of a constitution in 1861. Gioberti's understanding of the intellectual role of the church is unrelated to other modern schools of thought. But his work, being perfectly orthodox, aided in drawing the liberal clergy into the movement culminating in a united Italy, and its spirit of fervent optimism restored self-respect to Italians at a time when they were in great need of it.

His works have been collected in an *Edizione Nazianale* (32 vols., 1938-   ).

Gioberti's essay *De Bello* was translated by Edward Thomas in 1860 as *Essay on the Beautiful*.

ABOUT: [In Italian—see studies by A. Bruers, R. Freschi, G. Saitta, C. Sgroi.]

E. DE P.

*GIRALDI, GIOVANNI BATTISTA, surnamed Cinthio, Cintio, Cinzio, or Cynthius (November 1504-December 30, 1573), Italian novelist and poet, was born in Ferrara, which had been a principal center of Italy from the thirteenth century when the Este family became the ruling lords and made the city their residence and capital. During

* jē räl' dē

the first half of the sixteenth century Ferrara developed as an important literary center, her princes acting as protectors and patrons of art and literature. In this milieu Giraldi grew up, was educated at the University of Ferrara, and became professor of natural sciences in 1525, twelve years later occupying the chair of belles lettres.

From 1542 to 1560 Giraldi was private secretary to the reigning dukes of Este, Hercules II and Alphonse II. Becoming involved in a literary quarrel, he lost the favor of his patrons and employers, and moved to Mondovi as a teacher of literature until 1568. He was invited to teach at the University of Pavia where he occupied the chair of rhetoric until the year of his death. Falling ill, he returned to his native town where he died.

In 1541 Giraldi's tragedy *Orbecche*, the first of nine tragedies, was performed in Ferrara. The drama of the Latin classics was often performed in the court theatres of such cultural centers as Ferrara; the first modern tragedy of the classic model to be given on the Italian stage was *Orbecche*, and its renown is attributable more to this fact than to any intrinsic value as drama. The *mise en scène* is Persia. Orbecche is the daughter of Selina, who is killed by her husband Sulmone for incest. Orbecche herself already has two sons by Oronte, but her father had wished her to marry someone else. When Sulmone discovers his daughter's transgression, he slays her lover and the children, and brings their bloody corpses to Orbecche. She then kills him and with the same dagger commits suicide. The play is characterized by De Sanctis as a "vulgar monster"; despite its revolting plot and inadequate style, however, *Orbecche* contains some genuine poetry, particularly in one scene in the third act.

The reform of the tragic theatre for which Giraldi is known is connected with the revival, centered in Padua, of Aristotelian thinking. Giraldi was one of the first to understand that the rules of the *Poetics* should be adapted to the precepts of Catholic morality, that this could best be done by imitating Seneca and constructing tragedies inspired by horrible and fearful events, but capable of evoking in the spectator the feeling of catharsis as experienced in antiquity but understood from the Christian point of view. The principles on which he worked are set forth in two treatises: *Intorno al Comporre delle Commedie e delle Tragedie* (Concerning the Composition of Comedies and Tragedies), published in 1543, and *Intorno al Comporre dei Romanzi* (Concerning the Composition of Novels), published in 1548.

After *Orbecche* Giraldi wrote *Altile, Cleopatra, Didone, Antivalomeni, Selena, Eufinia, Arrenopia,* and *Epitia.* His epic *Ercole* (Hercules), in twenty-six cantos, was published in 1557.

Giraldi's European reputation was won by his *Ecatommiti* (Hundred Tales), begun in 1528 and published in 1565 in Monteregale, Sicily. The *Ecatommiti* (actually 113 tales) is one among many imitations of the *Decameron* written in various parts of Italy throughout the Renaissance. The consensus is that most of the imitations were extremely heavy-handed in contrast to Boccaccio's touch, and Giraldi succeeded no better than the others. The works were composed to amuse and titillate the readers of the time, and are of ephemeral interest.

Giraldi's tales, however, saw many reprintings and were translated into French and Spanish, a matter of interest to students of English literature. It is probably through the French translation that Shakespeare took the plot for *Othello.* In 1582 Whetstone's *Heptamerone* contains a direct English translation from Giraldi of the story line of *Measure for Measure.* The plot of Beaumont and Fletcher's *Custom of the Country* is also attributable to Giraldi. Some of the tales were translated into English by T. Roscoe in *Italian Novelists* (1825).

ABOUT: Horne, P. R. The Tragedies of Giambattista Cinthio Giraldi. [In French—see study by L. Berthé de Besaucèle. In Italian—see C. Guerrieri Crocetti.]

E. DE P.

*GIRAUT DE BORNELH (or BORNEIL) (c. 1165-1220), Provençal lyric poet, was born in Limousin at the castle of the Viscount of Limoges. He was of humble birth and was a professional troubadour in the fullest sense. His *vida,* or biography, relates that he spent his winters in school and his summers in visiting various courts, accompanied by two singers. We know from poems he wrote that he was connected with Ademar V of Limoges, with whom he probably went on the Third Crusade, and with Alfonso II of Aragon, with Alfonso VIII of Castille, and with Raymond V of Toulouse. He praises Richard I of England warmly and we know from a funeral dirge written by Raimbaut d'Orange that the two poets were friends. He never married and in his later years he is recorded as a benefactor of the church in St. Gervais, where he presumably lived.

In his day Giraut was the master of the troubadours and enjoyed the highest reputa-

* zhē rō dē bôr nā′ y′

tion. Modern criticism would rate him somewhat lower. His reputation in his own day rested on his remarkable verbal ability and his use of unusual figures and expressions—the so-called *trobar ric*. His versification also exhibits a high degree of virtuosity. Seventy-seven of his songs are extant, the largest number for any author of the classical period, of which about half are *canzons*, or courtly love-songs. The subjects are highly varied—complaint, anger, pleading, mock abandonment of the lady are all represented—but there is little originality of treatment. The poems which would now be regarded as his best belong to other groups. Most famous perhaps, because it illustrates a characteristic attitude of courtly love, is the *tenson*, or debate poem written with Alfonso II of Aragon in which the question is discussed whether it is more honorable for a lady to love a knight or a king—the point being that love should not be affected by rank. Giraut wrote one *alba*, or dawn song, which for beauty of language is unmatched in Provençal poetry. It has genuine sublimity. He also used the *pastourelle* form, in which a knight woos a peasant girl, and wrote crusading songs. Among his poems there are many *sirventes*, poems of social and political comment, in which he does not spare even the Emperor himself or the Pope.

E. Hoepffner's *Les Troubadours dans Leur Vie et dans Leurs Œuvres* (Paris, 1955) contains good account and texts with translation into modern French. Selections from Giraut's work may be found in *Sämtliche Lieder des Trobadors Guiraut de Bornheil*, ed. A. Kolsen, 2 vols. (Halle 1910, 1938), and *Anthology of the Troubadours*, ed. R. T. Hill & T. G. Bergin (1941).

ABOUT: Valency, M. In Praise of Love.

W. T. H. J.

*GJELLERUP, KARL ADOLPH (June 2, 1857-October 11, 1919), Danish novelist, dramatist, poet, was born in southern Zealand at Roholte where his father, Ryde Carl Adolph Gjellerup, was a vicar. His mother was Anna Johanne Fibiger, his father's second wife, sister of Mathilde Fibiger, known as a suffragette and author under the pseudonym "Clara Raphael." His father died when he was but three years old, and he went to the home of his mother's cousin Johannes Fibiger, a learned clergyman and author, who then lived in Copenhagen but in 1874 moved to southern Zealand. Gjellerup had a good education and grew up in an atmosphere of studies, religion, music, and classical

* gĕl' ĕ rōŏp

German literature. His favorite authors were Schiller and Heine.

In 1874 Gjellerup matriculated at the University of Copenhagen, where in 1878 he took his degree in theology, despite his attraction to literature. Even before the completion of his degree he had studied radical Bible criticism and Darwinistic literature. In the year of his graduation he published his first novel, *En Idealist* (An Idealist) under the pseudonym "Epigonos." The years that followed were disturbed by inner conflicts. Gjellerup was fascinated by Georg Brandes' ideas and joined the latter's army of crusaders. His books from his earliest period had the character of polemical pamphlets, e.g., his radical poetic collection *Rødtjørn* (Red Hawthorne, 1881), dedicated to Brandes, and his first great novel, *Germanernes Lærling* (The Teutons' Apprentice, 1882), which describes the development of a young theologian into a freethinker and gives outstanding pictures from the life of Copenhagen students of theology.

A determining factor in Gjellerup's life and literary career was his acquaintance with Eugenia Anna Caroline Hensinger, daughter of a Dresden high school teacher and wife of a Jewish musician, Fritz Bendix, a cousin of the brothers Brandes. After her divorce they married in 1887. To Gjellerup she represented everything he had dreamed of, and she was able to release his true nature and inspire him to some of his best works. Their love lasted for life.

In 1883 Gjellerup undertook a long journey through Germany, Switzerland, Italy, Greece, and Russia. The impact that the new impressions made upon him became at once evident in his production. His two novels *Romulus* and *G-Dur* (G Major), both written in 1883 during his journey, are influenced by Russian models, especially Turgenev. After his return home Gjellerup had an obstreperous controversy with Brandes and the literary radicals—see his two travel books, *En Klassisk Maaned* (A Classical Month, 1884), and *Vandreaaret* (The Wander Year, 1885)—after which he definitely broke away from naturalistic problem literature in order to return eventually to the German-Danish idealism in which he had grown up.

Gjellerup's most important effort in the dramatic field is *Brynhild* (1884), a learned tragedy in Swinburne's style, based on Old Germanic and Old Norse legends and dealing with the individual's destruction in his struggle against social conventions. The same motif is treated in his modern pathetic dramas *Herman Wandel* (1891), and *Wuthorn* (1893), both inspired by Nietzsche's superman ideal and by his German-born wife, to whom also the latter part of his poetic collection *Min Kjærligheds Bog* (The Book of My Love, 1889), is directed.

In 1889 Gjellerup received a poet's pension and in 1892 he moved to Dresden where he lived for the rest of his life, writing his books both in Danish and German. In 1896 his important novel *Møllen* (The Mill) appeared, influenced by Zola, Dostoevsky, and others. A finely structured narrative, it combines a vivid realism with symbolistic devices of striking dramatic effect.

Influenced by Schopenhauer, Gjellerup turned from his exalted individualism and superman worship towards the Indian religions, especially Buddhism. A spirit of abnegation is evident in the legend novel *Pilgrimmen Kamanita* (The Pilgrim Kamanita, 1906) and the great Buddha drama *Den Fuldendtes Husfru* (The Wife of the Perfect One, 1907). During his last years Gjellerup gradually returned, via a sort of medieval mysticism, to the Christian religion, e.g., in the novel *Guds Venner* (God's Friends, 1916). In 1917 Gjellerup shared the literary Nobel Prize with his fellow countryman Henrik Pontoppidan. He was not a great author, but an honest inquirer after truth.

Gjellerup's novel *Pilgrimmen Kamanita* was translated into English by J. E. Logie as *The Pilgrim Kamanita* (1911), and the novel *Minna* by C. L. Nielsen (1913). Three poems in English rendition by C. W. Stork appear in *A Second Book of Danish Verse* (1947).

ABOUT: [In German—Rosenberg, P. A. ed. Karl Gjellerup, der Dichter und Denker: Sein Leben in Selbstzeugnissen und Briefen, 2 vols.]

A. J.

*GLATIGNY, ALBERT JOSEPH ALEXANDRE (May 21, 1839-April 16, 1873), French poet and vaudevillist, was born in the small hamlet of Lillebonne in the Seine-Inférieure department. His father Joseph-Sénateur (1817-98), a carpenter become a gendarme, had married Rose-Alexandrine (1822-1904), a simple country girl. Two more children were born to this couple of modest means. In 1845 the family moved to Bernay, in the Eure. Albert was a scholarship student, with a remarkable memory, but an attack of typhoid in 1853 ended his schooling. The previous year the discovery

* glà tẽ nyẽ'

of a volume of Ronsard's verse, then ignored in the school program, revealed the world of lyric poetry to the impressionable youth. Albert frequented the local theatre; in 1856 he joined a traveling troupe after he had spent a year at Pont-Audemar to learn typesetting. On tour at Alençon, he met Auguste Poulet-Malassis, who was to become famous in the publishing history of the Parnassian poets. Poulet-Malassis acquainted him with the *Odes Funambulesques* of Théodore de Banville, to whom Glatigny dedicated his first volume of poems, *Les Vignes Folles* (1860); the double influence of Banville and of Ronsard is manifest. Glatigny confessed to a servile imitation of Banville. Verlaine admired these poems, which display remarkable verbal acrobatics, puns, and technical *tours de force*. In 1864 Glatigny published *Flèches d'Or*, dedicated to Leconte de Lisle. Although using themes from mythology and history, this collection too is primarily flippant and personal.

Glatigny spent the rest of his brief life in traveling, as actor or prompter, with various theatrical troupes, or in wandering over France on foot. Tall and extraordinarily slender, with sparse hair, large feet and hands, a long nose and thick lips, extremely poor, Glatigny had nevertheless numerous casual affairs, for women found him charming. He wrote poems with great facility; many of these were not preserved. At one time he was a cabaret entertainer, composing poems to any given rhyme-words. A contributor to many periodicals, he appeared in *La Revue Fantaisiste* (1861) and in the 1869 *Parnasse Contemporain* published by Lemerre, as well as the clandestine *Parnasse Satyrique du Dix-neuvième Siècle* (1864 ff.) of Poulet-Malassis. *Gilles et Pasquins* (1872) is a collection of satires; although the political and literary allusions are uninteresting today, the variety of verse forms and the technical dexterity are unusual. Banville's influence is again apparent. Glatigny also published various prologues and short plays of a humorous sort; certain risqué and satirical items, such as *Testament de l'Illustre Brizacier*, do not appear in his collected works. His *Joyeusetés Galantes et Autres* (1866) was condemned by the French courts.

Practically blind, suffering from pernicious anemia, with tuberculosis of the bones, Glatigny went to Corsica at the beginning of 1869. Mistaken for a bandit, he was severely roughed up and jailed; this experience he related in *Le Jour de 'An d'un Vagabond*. On his return to France, he met a young widow, Emma Dennie, *née* Garien. She too was tubercular. They were married in 1871; Albert was so ill that the ceremony took place in his hotel room. The couple settled at Sèvres, outside Paris. Albert died there, not yet thirty-four; his wife survived him only until the early part of the following year. Glatigny was buried in the Sèvres cemetery, which was obliterated in 1880. Busts of Glatigny have been erected at Lillebonne (1891) and Bernay (1924).

Glatigny was admired by his friends Mallarmé, Gautier, and Banville. His correspondence with them has been preserved. Banville said of him that he was a "primitive poet," i.e., an instinctive and spontaneous talent. His poetry belongs to early Parnassianism, his life to the history of Bohemianism.

The *Poésies Complètes* [sic] were published in 1879, with a preface by Anatole France.

ABOUT: France, A. The Latin Genius, Life and Letters, IV: Gentleman's Magazine, XXIII (1879); Schaffer, A. *in* Modern Language Notes, XLI (March 1926), *also* Parnassus in France, *and* The Genres of Parnassian Poetry. [In French—Chabannes, J. La Sainte Bohème: Albert Glatigny; Mendès, C. La Légende du Parnasse Contemporain, *also* Glatigny; Reymond, J. Albert Glatigny; Souriau, M. Histoire du Parnasse, Bk. II.]

S. S. W.

*GLEIM, JOHANN WILHELM LUDWIG (April 2, 1719-February 18, 1803),

German poet, was born at Ermsleben, near Halberstadt, Thuringia. His father, Johann Lorenz Gleim, a small town official, gave him his elementary instruction; at ten he was sent to a neighboring pastor from whom he received instruction in classical languages. Both of his parents died in 1735 when Gleim was at the *Gymnasium* in Wernigerode, leaving the boy in very precarious circumstances. Some wealthy and influential friends, however, made it possible for him to go to the University of Halle, where he studied law (1738-40). From Halle he went to Potsdam as a private tutor, later becoming secretary to Prince Wilhelm von Schwedt in Berlin. In 1744 Gleim took part in the Second Silesian War in the company of Prince Wilhelm. After the Prince was killed he spent a short, unhappy period in the service of Leopold von Dassau. In 1747 he was appointed secretary, later canon, to the cathedral chapter in Halberstadt, which gave him some material security and plenty of time to write poetry in the manner of Anacreon.

* glīm

332

Meanwhile a volume of Anacreontic unrhymed poems, *Versuch in Scherzhaften Liedern,* had appeared in 1744, and a year later an amorous shepherd play, *Der Blöde Schäfer,* which enjoyed a great popularity on the contemporary stage. Though he had some poetic talent—he started to write verse while still in high school—Gleim's real talent was for friendship: he stood on an intimate footing with almost the entire German literary world of the eighteenth century, always ready with assistance for the unknown, impoverished young poets who turned to him. Gleim corresponded with an ever greater circle of friends, publishing some of this sentimental correspondence in 1746 as *Freundschaftsepisteln.*

Gleim's most creative period occurred early in the Seven Years' War, when he published the much-imitated *Preussische Kriegslieder von einem Grenadier* (1758), which made him famous. These songs are distinguished above all by their patriotic enthusiasm and by their unbounded admiration for King Frederick of Prussia. Although he published many subsequent works, including *Tierfabeln* (1756), a semi-oriental book of aphorisms *Halladat, oder das Rote Buch* (1774), *Lieder für das Volk* (1772), and his inferior imitations of the Minnesingers *Gedichte nach den Minnesingern* (1773), "Vater Gleim" is chiefly remembered for his advice and encouragement to other writers. In his last three years blindness afflicted him. At his request he was buried in the garden of his house in Halberstadt. Gleim's collected works were published in 1811-13 by his nephew Wilhelm Körte.

ABOUT: [In German—see studies by K. Becker, S. Brunner, W. Körte.]

F. S. L.

GŁOWACKI, ALEXANDER. See PRUS, BOLESŁAW

GLÜCK, BARBARA ELISABETH. See PAOLI, BETTY

*GOBINEAU, JOSEPH ARTHUR, Comte de (July 14, 1816-October 13, 1882),

French writer and diplomat, was born in Ville-d'Avray near Paris. His father, Louis, of Legitimist and Catholic family and a Royal Guard officer, withdrew to Brittany after the Hundred Days. Gobineau's mother, Anne-Louise Megdeleine de Gercy, said to be a

* gŏ bĕ nŏ'

daughter of a natural son of Louis XV, left his father in 1830, taking Joseph and his sister Caroline to Switzerland. Joseph attended Bienne College, continuing German and classics and beginning Oriental languages.

Gobineau's father recalled the children to Lorient in 1832, so that Joseph might prepare for a military career. The boy hated the essential mathematics and after two years at the Lorient *lycée* he continued his Oriental studies at home. In 1835 he left for Paris where he hoped in vain for aid from his paternal uncle, Thibaut-Joseph. Forced to work briefly as a clerk, he soon supported himself precariously by literary hackwork. He continued Oriental studies at the Collège de France and through family connections was admitted to Legitimist and art circles, meeting Alexis de Tocqueville. He prepared articles on politics and literary criticism. He joined a group of young men, "Les Scelti" (the Elect), under whose auspices he published his first play in 1844.

Scaramouche, a picaresque novel, was serialized in 1843, and so were *Le Prisonnier Chanceux,* adventure story, and *Jean Chouan,* an historical poem beginning his regional writings, in 1846. That same year saw his marriage to Gabrielle Clémence Monnerot of an influential Paris family. Three more serial novels were begun in the next year, *Ternove, Mademoiselle Irnois,* and *Nicolas Belavoir;* and he also wrote *L'Abbaye de Typhaines,* historical novel (published in 1849). In 1848 his daughter Diane was born and he founded the short-lived *Revue Provinciale.*

Gobineau was cabinet head for de Tocqueville, Minister of Foreign Affairs, from June to October 1849 and in November 1851 was appointed first secretary to the Berne embassy. He was unhappy there and distrusted his colleagues. Still he was able to write his *Essai sur l'Inégalité des Races Humaines* (volumes I-II, 1853; III-IV, 1855), his best-known work. It was poorly received; Tocqueville praised its erudition but opposed its main argument, the inevitable decadence of a race. In the twentieth century the book enjoyed considerable celebrity in Nazi Germany because of its praise of the Aryan race.

In 1854 he was happily transferred to Frankfurt am Main. On a special mission to Persia in 1855, he heard of his uncle's death and found himself the heir. He was now able to gratify his aristocratic tastes and in 1857 purchased the Château de Tyre in Normandie, where his daughter Christine was born. The time in Persia was the happiest of

his life: he wrote *Trois Ans en Asie* (1859), his first travel book and perhaps his most pleasing work; he became head of the Teheran legation. In 1859 he was sent to Newfoundland to study the fisheries question, from which resulted *Voyage à Terre-Neuve* (1861). Returning to France, he spent the next two years in royalist circles in Paris.

He returned to Persia as Minister, January 1862 to 1864. His continued study there produced *Les Religions et les Philosophies dans l'Asie Centrale* (1865), *Histoire des Perses* (1869) and, years later, *Nouvelles Asiatiques* (1876), which some call his masterpiece. Appointed Minister to Greece in November 1864, he developed an interest in sculpture, began the romanticized history of his family, *Histoire d'Ottar Jarl* (1879), and became a friend of the King.

In 1869 he was appointed Minister to Brazil. He disliked that country's tropical landscape and climate, despised the "decadent race mixture," but admired its emperor, Dom Pedro II. In May 1870, three months before the outbreak of the Franco-Prussian War, he returned with joy to France. He spent the war period in Normandy aiding his neighbors. His book on the war and its causes, begun then, was not published until after his death and then only in part.

Sent to Sweden as Minister in 1872, he loved Scandinavia, home of his Viking forebears. He wrote *Les Pléiades* (1874), a novel praising young aristocrats, and *La Renaissance* (1877), wherein he stressed the value of the individual. However, he was not popular with his colleagues whom he considered his inferiors and he did not like the republican government. These factors led to his compulsory retirement in 1877. His health failed; he separated from his wife; he went to live in Italy and traveled intermittently. Passing through Turin he died there of apoplexy in 1882. His German admirers, in honor of his friendship with Richard Wagner and his race theories, formed a Gobineau Society in Germany in 1894 to publish and spread his writings.

Gobineau was described as being "slim, dark, pale, with pleasant, rather conceited manners, a candid witty smile, great strength of will, and a natural eloquence."

His work has been reprinted in French and has become more widely known in English in recent years. Part I of his *Essai* was translated by H. Hotz in 1856; in full, *Inequality of Human Races,* by Adrian Collins, 1915. Others followed: *Typhaines Abbey,* 1869; *Romances of the East (Nouvelles Asiatiques),* 1878; *Renaissance,* by P. V. Cohn, 1913; *Golden Flower,* by B. R. Redman, 1924; *Five Orien-*

tal Tales, 1925; *Lucky Prisoner,* by F. M. Atkinson, 1926; *The Pleiads,* by J. F. Scanlan, 1928.

ABOUT: Cassirer, E. Myth of the State; Duclaux, A. M. F. R. French Procession; Rowbotham, A. H. Literary Works of Count de Gobineau; Spring, G. M. Vitalism of Count de Gobineau; Modern Language Quarterly, June 1957; Nineteenth Century, July 1911, May 1913; Times Literary Supplement, October 12, 1922. [In French—Lange, M. Le Comte de Gobineau; Dreyfus, R. La Vie et les Prophéties du Comte de Gobineau. In German—Schemann, L. Gobineau, eine Biographie.]

M. A. W.

GOETHE

*GOETHE, JOHANN WOLFGANG VON** (August 28, 1749-March 22, 1832), German poet, dramatist, novelist, and indisputably Germany's greatest man of letters, was born in Frankfurt am Main, the son of Johann Kaspar Goethe, a stern man of humble middle-class origin who had studied law and held the administrative post of imperial councilor. The poet's mother, the former Katharina Elisabeth Textor, was the daughter of the mayor of Frankfurt. From his father, as Goethe tells us in a much-quoted verse, he inherited his tall physique and seriousness of character; from his mother, his good nature and poetic fancy. Goethe's childhood was happy and carefree, though punctuated by sharp religious questionings at the age of six at news of the great Lisbon earthquake. His early introduction to Italian culture through his father, and to French culture during the French occupation of Frankfurt in the Seven Years' War, helped form the cosmopolitanism that he retained throughout life. Among his most important early literary experiences—all a result of family influence rather than schooling—were the Bible, Homer, and Klopstock's *Messiah.* His early education, as was characteristic among the patrician families of his time, was in the hands of private tutors.

In 1765 he was sent to the University of Leipzig to take up law, a subject that interested him considerably less than the drawing which he studied with A. F. Oeser, a teacher firmly rooted in neo-classic doctrine. His love for his innkeeper's daughter Käthchen Schönkopf, for whom he wrote the *Buch Annette,* a collection of conventionally rococo lyrics, was the first of the many romances which throughout his life formed the bases for much of his most significant literary work. In Leipzig he also worked at his first dramas, *Die Laune des Verliebten* and *Die Mitschuldigen* (1768), both in traditional neo-classic style. A hemorrhage which he suffered in 1768 caused his return to Frank-

* gû' tĕ

furt. During his long convalescence he came in frequent contact with a family connection, Susanna Katharina von Klettenberg, whose pietism became a central influence in his spiritual growth. In 1770 he left Frankfurt again to resume his law studies, this time at the University of Strasbourg. His formal training there proved far less significant in his development than, for instance, his idyllic romance with Friederike Brion, the daughter of a country pastor, who inspired such famous lyrics as "Mailied" and "Willkommen und Abschied," which in their immediacy of personal feeling and simplicity of style marked a new direction for German poetry.

Significant in a more comprehensive sense was his friendship in Strasbourg with J. G. Herder, who, by turning his attention to Shakespeare, Ossian, and folk literature, opened up for him a new world of values wholly antithetical to the rococo ideals to which he had been tied. The results of his friendship are evident in the series of major works written during the four impetuous years following his return to Frankfurt in 1771 to take up a law career. The massive prose drama *Götz von Berlichingen* (1771-73), an attempt to emulate the Shakespearean history play, revealed his new-found interest in the German Middle Ages and his ideal of heroic action. Such poems as "Prometheus" and "Mahomets Gesang" express an urge toward titanism and individual self-assertion.

His frustrated love for Charlotte Buff in Wetzlar, where he lived briefly in 1772 while working in the imperial law court, resulted in

Die Leiden des Jungen Werthers (1774), an epistolary novel whose sensitive young hero, spurned by a woman who was already pledged to another man, commits suicide. As with many of his works, the creative act of writing *Werther* helped resolve a personal problem: Werther was forced to die in order that the author might live, Goethe intimated later. The novel was soon a sensation throughout Europe and in fact became legendary for the frequent suicides it caused among the sensitive young. Also among the works written in 1771-75—that period of Goethe's achievement traditionally characterized as "Storm and Stress"—is an early draft of parts of *Faust* (known as the *Urfaust* and not discovered until 1887), the completion of which was to become a lifetime endeavor encompassing within itself the attitudes and literary styles that marked each stage of his career.

In 1775 Goethe was briefly engaged to Lili Schönemann, a light-hearted young woman of high social standing in Frankfurt. The same year he undertook an extended journey through Switzerland, where he visited the pastor and physiognomist J. C. Lavater, whose pietist views exercised a strong hold on him at the time. At the end of the year he accepted an invitation from Karl August, the youthful Duke of Weimar, to serve in his duchy as companion and adviser. Goethe at first intended to stay in Weimar for only a few months, but remained the rest of his life, eventually taking over the highest administrative duties. At Weimar, perhaps the closest eighteenth century equivalent to the small Italian Renaissance court, Goethe was able to hold an established and central place, both as creative artist and as man of affairs, in an enclosed, self-sufficient world. During his first decade in Weimar he maintained a close attachment to an older woman, Charlotte von Stein, wife of the ducal equerry, who exerted a calming influence on the self-assertive and often violent emotions which had marked his life and work during the preceding years in Frankfurt. During his early years in Weimar he worked at two major blank verse dramas, both, in contrast to *Götz*, executed according to the neo-classic rules: *Iphigenie auf Tauris* (1779-88), a reworking of Euripides within the framework of eighteenth century humanism, and *Torquato Tasso* (1780-89), one of the first works in European literature to approach the "problem of the artist" in the modern sense. He also completed the historical prose drama *Egmont* (1774-88), depicting the Dutch fight for freedom against Spanish tyranny.

The years 1786-88 mark Goethe's famous Italian journey, an attempt to recapture the spirit of classical antiquity and to efface the limitations of his German background through contact with the mainstream of Western civilization. He spent most of his time in Rome, associating largely with the German artists and scholars residing there. In 1787 he undertook an extended trip through Sicily, which, since he was unable to travel to Greece itself, he looked upon as his introduction to Greek culture. On his return to Weimar he wrote the *Romische Elegien* (1788), a set of poems in classical meters celebrating both his amorous and cultural experiences in Rome. The return to Weimar also marked his break with Charlotte von Stein and the start of his relationship with Christiane Vulpius (1765-1816), a girl of no intellectual or social pretensions, whom he took into his home in 1788 and who bore him five children, of whom only one, August (1789-1830), survived to adulthood.

A second trip to Italy, this time no farther south than Venice resulted in the *Venezianische Epigramme* (1790). The same year he published *Faust: Ein Fragment*, which includes most of the first part of the finished poem and was the first section of the work to reach the public. During the invasion of France by the German states in 1792 Goethe accompanied Duke Karl August into the Rhineland and the following year was present at the long siege of Mainz and its recapture by the Germans. The 1790's also saw a marked increase in Goethe's scientific activities, which, centered in botany, optics, anatomy, and geology, came to share an equal rôle with his activities as writer and administrator.

In 1794 he began his close association with the already famous poet and dramatist Friedrich Schiller, then lecturing at the nearby University of Jena. In this association, which lasted until Schiller's death in 1805, the two men not only engaged in a constant interchange of ideas, but each served as a major stimulus in the literary production of the other; more fundamental still, they set out on a common program to endow German literature with a seriousness of purpose and classical stature that it had not known before. Together they completed a series of distichs, *Xenien* (1796), in the style of Martial. The same year Goethe also published *Wilhelm Meisters Lehrjahre* (1777-96), a novel on the growth and education of a young man that was to become the model for the German novel of apprenticeship and, in effect, the most influential work of fiction in German literature. The following year brought forth a long poem in classical hexameters, *Hermann und Dorothea*, a pastoral idyll in a modern setting with the French Revolution as a distant backdrop. The year 1797, often referred to as the "ballad year," witnessed Goethe and Schiller's creation of a body of "art" ballads in striking contrast to the German tradition of "folk" ballads. In 1802 Goethe completed *Die Natürliche Tochter*, a blank-verse drama depicting the tragic effect of the French Revolution on a sensitive individual. At the instigation of Schiller, Goethe took up *Faust* once more and by 1806 had completed Part I (published in 1808).

By the turn of the century Goethe, though still in his middle years, was already the grand old man of German letters and the idol of the romantic school (whose ideas and efforts he was all too reluctant to approve) which had formed in Germany in the late 1790's. As director of the Weimar court theatre (1791-1817) he not only provided a stage for his own and Schiller's dramas, but set a standard of artistic seriousness both in acting and dramatic writing that served as a model for the whole German-speaking theatre. In 1808, while in Erfurt, he was commanded to an audience by Napoleon, who supposedly greeted him with the words "Voilà un homme!" and later suggested an artistic flaw in *Werther*. Two years before, when the French armies had entered Weimar, Goethe had quietly married Christiane to protect her legal rights in any impending political upheaval. She died in 1816.

Besides the completion of *Faust, Part I* his creative work during the first decade of the new century included the unfinished *Pandora* (1807-08), his closest attempt to re-work the form of Greek drama, and *Die Wahlverwandtschaften* (1808-09), a novel in a modern setting on marriage. Both works reflect the struggle he encountered in 1807 in suppressing his passion for Minna Herzlieb, the young foster-daughter of a Jena bookseller. In 1810 appeared his most ambitious scientific work, *Die Farbenlehre*, an attempt to refute Newton's optics by grounding a theory of color in Goethean metaphysics.

Goethe's interest in the Persian poet Hafiz, together with his love for the actress Marianne von Willemer, wife of a Frankfurt banker, resulted in an extended cycle of lyrics, the *West-östlicher Divan* (1814-18), the first major nineteenth century work on an oriental theme. Several of the lyrics were even composed by Marianne herself. For much of his

later life he was occupied with two longer prose works, his autobiography *Dichtung und Wahrheit* (1808-31), which chronicles his life up to his arrival in Weimar in 1775, and the continuation of *Wilhelm Meister, Wilhelm Meisters Wanderjahre* (1807-28), whose hero has given up his earlier artistic interests for the useful career of surgeon. The rejection of Goethe's marriage proposal by a nineteen-year-old girl, Ulrike von Levetzow, resulted in one of his most important poems, the "Marienbader Elegie" (1823). In 1825 he once more took up *Faust*, the second part of which he completed a year before his death. During this period he also wrote the symbolic short story entitled *Novelle* (1826), now ranked among his major works. Throughout his last decade his conversations were recorded by his companion J. P. Eckermann *(Gespräche mit Goethe,* 1836-48). Active to the end, he died after a brief respiratory illness.

In his later years Goethe was looked upon as something far more than a literary figure, and in fact rose to an Olympian rôle that could perhaps best be described as that of the wise old man of Europe. Within his own century and far beyond the German-speaking borders he was linked to Virgil, Dante, and Shakespeare as one of the few manifestations in literary history of transcendent genius. His contribution to the formation of a literary language and his development of genres, symbols, and themes were decisive for the future of German literature. *Faust*, the work of his lifetime, is cosmic. Moving from the romantic egocentrism of Part I to the altruistic idealism of Part II, it epitomizes Western intellectual history in the eighteenth and nineteenth centuries. Our present age, with its demand for tragic vision, has questioned the validity of his largely optimistic view of life. Far more than with the other writers to whom he is compared in greatness, his stature is not so easily revealed through a study of individual works and ideas as through a view of his career as a whole. The relationship of his work to his personal life has an intimacy more directly discernible than that of any other major writer, and Goethe himself spoke of his writings as "fragments of a great confession." Nevertheless, though he has often been seen as the reigning figure of European romanticism, the vast range and variety of his interests, styles and attitudes—with their constant alternation beween the classic and romantic modes—make it difficult to fit him into the usual categories of literature and philosophy. The very comprehensiveness of his efforts has made us see him, in the words of Ernst Robert Curtius, as "the last universal author in European literature."

The first comprehensive edition of Goethe's *Works* in English appeared in fourteen volumes, translated by various hands, 1848-90. Included among his many early translators were Walter Scott *(Götz von Berlichingen,* 1799), Carlyle *(Wilhelm Meister,* 1826-27), and Margaret Fuller *(Tasso,* n.d.). *Faust,* in whole or in part, has drawn innumerable translators, most notably Shelley (selections, published posthumously, 1824) and Bayard Taylor, whose full-length translation (1870) was long the standard version. Although most of his works are still in need of good modern translation, useful recent versions exist of *Werther* (B. Q. Morgan, 1957), the *Urfaust* (D. M. Scott, 1958), *Faust* (Louis Mac-Neice, 1951; A. Raphael, 1955), *Wilhelm Meister* (R. O. Moon, 1947), *Tasso* (B. Kimpel and T. C. Duncan Eaves, 1956), the *Autobiography* (R. O. Moon, 1932), and a selection of *Letters* (M. von Herzfeld and C. M. Sym, 1957). An anthology of passages, translated by H. J. Weigand, appeared under the title *Wisdom and Experience* in 1949. A new translation of *Elective Affinities,* by E. Mayer and L. Bogan, was issued in 1963.

ABOUT: Atkins, S. Goethe's Faust; Bergstraesser, A. Goethe's Image of Man and Society; Bielschowsky, A. Life of Goethe; Cassirer, E. Rousseau, Kant, Goethe; Croce, B. Goethe; Eliot, T. S. On Poetry and Poets; Fairley, B. Goethe's Faust, *also* A Study of Goethe; Magnus, R. Goethe as a Scientist; Mann, T. Essays of Three Decades, *also* Last Essays; Robertson, J. G. Goethe; Santayana, G. Three Philosophical Poets; Strich, F. Goethe and World Literature; Thomas, C. Goethe; Viëtor, K. Goethe the Poet, *also* Goethe the Thinker. [In German—see studies by Beutler, Grimm, Gundolf, Korff, Lukács, Schultz, Staiger.]

H. L.

*GOGOL, NIKOLAY VASILYEVICH

(March 19, 1809-February 21, 1852), Russian author, was born in the Ukrainian town of Great Sorochintsy in the Government of Poltava. His father, the provincial nobleman Vasily Afanasevich Gogol-Yanovsky, was a small district landowner. Gogol's mother, Maria Ivanovna, who had already lost two children in their infancy, was only eighteen when Nikolay was born. The fact that some of his ancestors had Polish and Roman Catholic ties was a highly undesirable circumstance to Gogol, who had apparently developed early feelings of nationalism and was a latent religious fanatic; he dropped Yanovsky, the Polish sounding part of his name, soon after he settled in St. Petersburg.

Gogol's father was an intelligent and rather cultured man, the talented composer of a few light provincial comedies. However, it was Gogol's mother, a woman of great piety which inclined towards folkloristic mysticism, who had a dominant influence on Nikolay. Gogol

* gŏ′ gŏl

GOGOL

received his education first in the district school in Poltava, and later at the newly founded *Gymnasium* in Nezhin, where he studied from 1821 to 1828. According to his own testimony he learned little there and with one or two exceptions despised most of his teachers. Gogol, who had been a delicate and even sickly child since infancy, was remembered by his teachers at Nezhin as a thin, pale, and near-sighted boy, quiet and even sullen, lazy, but frequently engaged in pranks. Both of his main talents, literary imagination and mimicry, found their first expressions during these years. Gogol's literary activity remained limited to the school magazine in which he published poetry, prose, and a tragedy. He also acted successfully in several school plays.

Gogol graduated from the Nezhin *Gymnasium* with a rather mediocre record, but this did not alter his intention to proceed to St. Petersburg in order to fulfill his unbounded, although somewhat vague, ambitions. He tried to become an actor, but his audition at the Bolshoi Theatre was a failure. He did not fare much better in his literary efforts. The idealistic epic poem *Hans Küchelgarten,* which he published at his own expense, received sarcastic and crushing reviews from the two literary magazines which bothered to mention it. Gogol, in his typical sensitivity and impulsiveness, bought up all the copies available and burned them. Completely disillusioned, he then decided to leave Russia, financing his journey "to America," the original goal, by using money entrusted to him

337

by his mother. After a short stay in Lübeck, Germany, Gogol returned to St. Petersburg. His luck changed for the better almost immediately. He was able to obtain a civil service position, and he also gained an almost immediate literary success as he turned from poetry to prose. The subjects of most of Gogol's early stories were drawn from the colorful life of the Ukrainian countryside and from the folk tales and superstitions of his home region, and they all show Gogol's great ability for expressive language, his humor, and his literary imagination. A romantic picture of Ukrainian life, with emphasis on the fantastic, is presented in the collection of stories published in 1831 under the title *Evenings on the Farm Near Dikanka*, which was followed a year later by a second volume.

His literary successes brought Gogol an acquaintance with prominent figures of the Russian literary world. He met, during 1831, both Zhukovsky and Pushkin. Through one of his influential friends, Gogol obtained the post of teacher of history at a fashionable school for young ladies and was able to resign from the civil service. In a mood of overconfident fantasy, Gogol began imagining himself as a famous historian and made a serious effort to obtain the chair of Professor of History at the University in Kiev. However, he was offered instead only a lectureship in medieval history at the University of St. Petersburg. His career in this position—for which he had almost no professional qualifications—was of short duration. Decidedly unsuccessful as a lecturer, Gogol resigned his post at the end of 1835 and, from then on, devoted himself almost entirely to literature.

In 1835 Gogol published *Arabesques*, in two parts, containing a number of essays on history, literature, and art, and some of his best short stories, among them *The Portrait, The Nevsky Prospect*, and *The Diary of a Madman*. In the same year another collection of stories appeared under the title *Mirgorod*, also in two volumes; it contains, among other tales, the historical romance from the life of Ukrainian Cossacks *Taras Bulba* and the weirdly fantastic *Viy*, based on a Ukrainian folk legend.

In April 1836, Gogol's most famous comedy, *The Inspector General*, was produced in St. Petersburg for the first time. A hilarious satire on the corruption and stupidity of provincial Russian officialdom, it is also a penetrating comment on human folly. Gogol left Russia shortly after the première and spent the next dozen years abroad, mostly in Rome, his favorite city, making only two relatively short visits to Russia. It was mostly abroad that he wrote his principal work, which appeared under the title *Chichikov's Journey or Dead Souls* in 1842. Although sometimes misinterpreted as a satirically realistic picture of Russia, it is the product of Gogol's highly subjective view of mankind, a caricature of characters existing entirely in his fantasy and, perhaps, an objectivization of the author's own "vices" and conflicts. A work of great literary imagination and humor, it follows its traveling hero Chichikov, who had thought up the plot of buying dead serfs from their provincial landowners and later mortgaging this non-existent property. The first part of *Dead Souls* was to be followed by additional volumes in which the gradual reformation of the hero was to be pictured. But only fragments of the second part have been preserved, testifying to the striking decline of Gogol's imaginative powers during the last years of his life. Before this decline occurred, Gogol wrote such important works as his famous short novel *The Overcoat* (first published in 1842) and his other successful comedy, *Marriage* (published and performed in 1842).

As his mental conflicts were becoming more oppressive and as both his health and his writing ability declined, Gogol decided to assume responsibility for the salvation of Russian society. He delivered his rather uninspired preachings in a collection of essays, *Selected Passages from a Correspondence with Friends* (1847), a defense of the traditional institutions and religious values of Russian society. The book came as a shock, especially to the "progressive" critics, who had misinterpreted Gogol's previous work as a social criticism of Russian conditions, and who could not comprehend that the "new" views were only an expression of Gogol's latent traditionalistic and messianic attitudes. Religion, in which Gogol was seeking a solution for the increasingly tortuous conflicts of his mind, was, however, incapable of providing the expected solace. Not even the pilgrimage to the Holy Land which he undertook in 1848, and his acquaintance with the fanatical and cruel ascetic Father Matthew Konstantinovsky brought him peace. Back in Russia, Gogol tried to continue working on the second part of *Dead Souls*, but his powers, both physical and imaginative, were slipping quickly. He withdrew more and more from the surrounding world, plagued mentally by feelings of guilt, and physically by a perpetual feeling of cold. During a February night of 1852, he burned a bundle of his manuscripts, among them the continuation of *Dead Souls.* Suffering from a deep depression and having lost all desire to live, he died shortly thereafter in Moscow.

The high esteem in which Gogol has always been held in Russia has been, at least to some extent, shared outside his country, where his two masterpieces *The Inspector General* and *Dead Souls* have appeared in numerous translations. Gogol, although he cannot be properly classified as a realist himself, stood at the beginning of the development of the Russian realistic novel, helped to lay its foundations, and thus occupies an extremely important place in Russian letters.

Gogol was of small physical stature, round-shouldered, with a high forehead and a large nose, and his later photographs usually show him with his long hair hanging loosely on both sides of his face. He never married and had almost no erotic interest in women; it seems that, in this respect, he never emerged from the adolescent stage, as the pale feminine characters of his writings also indicate. To his friends he was known as a complaining hypochondriac but, especially in his younger years, also as a man who could be an extremely amusing and entertaining companion.

The first English translation of *Dead Souls,* containing many distortions and omissions, appeared in 1854 in London under the title *Home Life in Russia* without the name of the author. Isabel Hapgood's translation, *Tchitchikoff's Journey of Dead Souls,* was published in two volumes in New York in 1886. George Reavey's *Dead Souls* was published in 1948. *Taras Bulba* and *The Night before Christmas,* translated by G. Tolstoy, appeared under the title *Cossack Tales* in London in 1860. J. F. Hapgood translated *St. John's Eve and Other Stories* (New York, 1886) and *Taras Bulba* (New York, 1888). *The Inspector General* appeared in the translation of T. Hart Davies in Calcutta in 1890. Recent translations include *Tales from Gogol,* R. Portnova (1945); *Diary of a Madman, Nevsky Prospect,* B. Scott (1946); *The Government Inspector,* D. J. Campbell (1947); *Tales of Good and Evil,* D. Magarshack (1949). The collected works of Gogol have been translated into English by Constance Garnett.

ABOUT: Lavrin, J. Gogol; Magarshack, D. Gogol, a Life; Nabokov, V. Nikolai Gogol.

H. K.

---

*GOLDONI, CARLO (February 25, 1707-February 6, 1793), Italian dramatist, was born in Venice, the son of Giulio Goldoni and Margherita Salvioni (who was Giulio's elder stepsister). In his *Memoirs* Goldoni remembered his parents lovingly for their fond indulgence towards him, despite their straitened financial circumstances. Young

* gŏl dō′ nē

GOLDONI

Carlo was an avid reader at the age of four. Apparently he first became attracted to the drama by reading the comedies (particularly those of Cicognini) in his father's library. He claimed to have written his first comedy at the age of eleven, to his father's extreme pleasure. He subsequently attended a Jesuit seminary, but seems to have enjoyed most the vacation period, when his father directed him and his schoolmates in a play. At the Dominican school near Rimini where he was next placed, Carlo was distracted from his studies by a troupe of strolling players, with whom he ran away to Chioggia. Here, at the age of fourteen, he got his first taste of that vagabondizing Bohemianism that so greatly appealed to him.

Returned from his wanderings, young Goldoni in time secured a scholarship at the Papal College at Pavia, through family influence. He received the tonsure in 1722, entering the Ghislieri College at the age of sixteen. Apparently the discipline of the college was lax, allowing the aspiring writer ample time for social life and the theatre. Already he had discovered to his dismay, in browsing among the books of a family friend, that while England, Spain, and France had produced important drama, Italy's had yet to come—and he resolved to fill the gap himself. Hence the perusal of the Greek and Latin comic poets readily distracted him from his law studies. During a vacation period he studied French in order to read Molière. As for formal education, once more he was removed from the academic fold when his satire *Il Coloso* offended the officials of the Ghislieri College because of its jibes at the stuffiness of some of the highly placed families of Pavia, and he was expelled.

Nevertheless he continued in his pursuit of a law career as an apprentice. Through his father's influence he served for two years as Coadjutor to the Magistrate of Chioggia—an experience that furnished the background for one of his greatest comedies, *Le Baruffe Chiozzote* (The Quarrels at Chioggia). Eventually, following on his father's death and at his mother's urging, he got his degree at Padua "after a night of gambling," as he relates in his characteristic fashion. He was admitted to the bar at Venice where he briefly, and half-heartedly, settled down to practice.

To help while away the time between clients he had written a tragedy for music entitled *Amalasontha* which he now tried to sell to the manager at the Milan opera house. Refused, he burned the manuscript, but while in Milan he fell in with a theatrical troupe for whom he wrote his first comedy, a musical interlude entitled *Il Gondoliere Veneziano*. In 1734 his wanderings brought him to Verona, where he enjoyed his first theatrical success with a production of his tragi-comedy *Belisario*. For several years thereafter he served as writer for Giuseppe Imer's troupe, for whom he prepared mainly *scenari* or sketches in the style of the *commedia dell' arte* with its farce characters— Arlecchino, Brighella, and Pantalone. Goldoni served his apprenticeship in the highly conventionalized *commedia improvisatore*, but eventually he threw it over to develop a more realistic comedy. During an engagement of the Imer troupe in Genoa occurred Goldoni's meeting with Maria Nicoletta Connio, daughter of a bank notary, to whom he was betrothed in 1736, and with whom he enjoyed a long and happy marriage.

Several real-life comic-opera episodes preceded Goldoni's establishment in the theatre. He served briefly as Genoese consul in Venice—an unsalaried position he learned to his dismay—during which time he was swindled by an unscrupulous captain (he made capital of this incident, however, in his comedy *L'Impostore*). A sojourn in Rimini was interrupted by an Austrian invasion, which he was compelled to flee—despoiled of his possessions—by fording a stream with his wife on his back. There followed another period of humdrum law practice in Pisa. It was here in the summer of 1748 that he met the Venetian actor-manager Girolamo Mede-

bac, who persuaded him to return with him to Venice as playwright, for his company, then occupying the Sant' Angelo Theatre. Thus Goldoni entered upon his life's calling.

Venice, at this time the acknowledged capital of the European theatrical world, furnished Goldoni with the characters and language that enliven his maturest comedies. The years 1748-62 mark his most prolific period. In 1749, his company threatened by the defection of its audience, owing to the competition of a rival playwright, Pietro Chiari, Goldoni pledged to write sixteen comedies during the next season—and kept his promise. Interestingly enough, among the welter of plays turned out during this "terrible year" were some of his most durable, such as *Il Bugiardo* (The Liar), *La Bottega del Caffè* (The Coffee House), *I Pettegolezzi delle Donne* (Women's Gossip), and *Pamela Nubile* (Pamela Unmarried), one of his more serious plays, derived from Samuel Richardson's famous novel.

Upon the expiration of his contract with Medebac in 1753, Goldoni signed as playwright with the Vendramin Brothers, who then owned the theatre of San Luca (now called the Teatro Goldoni). Among the plays he wrote during this period were the two that some consider his greatest, *Le Baruffe Chiozzotte* and *I Rusteghi*. These years were marked by a War of the Theatres, instigated principally by the rising aristocratic dramatist Carlo Gozzi, who stood firmly for the old *commedia dell' arte* style against Goldoni's new realism. Gozzi went so far as to caricature Goldoni in his fantasy *L'Amore delle Tre Melarance* (The Love of Three Oranges). Tiring of this rivalry, in 1762 Goldoni decided to accept an invitation from Paris to direct the Comédie Italienne. He left his native Venice with his wife and adopted nephew, to become, as it turned out, an expatriate for the rest of his life.

Ironically, at the Comédie Italienne Goldoni had to fight over again his battle for his kind of social comedy against the solidly entrenched *commedia dell' arte*. He now wrote in French, but re-wrote a number of these plays in Italian for the Vendramins. The best known of these, *Il Ventaglio* (The Fan), is now extant only in its Italian version. After two years with the Comédie Italienne, Goldoni left the company and became Italian tutor to the royal princesses. For the wedding of Louis XVI and Marie Antoinette he wrote his delightful comedy of marriage and misunderstanding, *Le Bourru Bienfaisant* (The Beneficent Bear). Upon his retirement, Goldoni was granted a generous pension by the king. In retirement at Versailles he wrote in French his charming *Mémoires,* an invaluable account of the picaresque theatrical life of the time, irradiated by his insouciant disposition and shrewd wit, though one must perhaps allow for the faltering memory of a near-octogenarian. Goldoni's last years were darkened by poverty, his pension having been cut off by the Revolution. By an ironical quirk of fate, his pension was restored on the day after his death by the Convention, through the influence of the poet Marie-Joseph (brother of André) Chénier. A reduced allowance was granted to his widow.

In 1883 there was unveiled in the square of San Bartolomeo in Venice a statue of "Gran Goldoni" (as he is known to his countrymen), modeled by Antonio del Zatto. There is a benign smile on its round face; from the pocket dangle a few sheets of manuscript. For the unveiling, a poem was composed by one of Goldoni's great admirers, Robert Browning.

Goldoni is generally credited with founding the modern Italian comedy. His carefully constructed plots, credible characters, colloquial speech and naturalistic settings, much as we take them for granted, were shocking innovations to audiences accustomed to the improvisation, masks, stylized costumes and antics of the players of the *commedia dell' arte.* Some of his earlier plays written for Medebac, such as *La Vedova Sceltra* (The Clever Widow), *Le Donne Curiose* (The Inquisitive Women), and *Il Bugiardo,* retain some features of the *commedia improvisatore.* But Goldoni is at his most characteristic in such comedies as *La Locandiera* (The Mistress of the Inn), wherein the pampered heroine Mirandolina flirts with two nobles and a misogynist before rewarding her faithful servant Fabrizio for his devotion; *La Bottega del Caffé,* in which a seedy, vicious-tongued count temporarily causes mischief among a group of pleasure seekers; *Il Ventaglio,* in which the misappropriation of a fan causes embarrassment to a number of people until it gets into the hands of the young lady for whom it was intended.

Most critics believe that Goldoni is at his greatest in a group of comedies written entirely in Venetian dialect—*I Pettegolezzi delle Donne; La Casa Nova* (The New House); *Il Campiello* (The Public Square); *Le Baruffe Chiozzotte,* and *I Rusteghi.* Ironically, these plays are virtually unknown outside of Italy. *I Rusteghi,* considered one of the greatest social comedies of all literature,

has only recently been translated out of Goldoni's native dialect into Italian. It has been converted into an opera by Ermanno Wolf-Ferrari (who also set to music *Le Donne Curiose*).

To call Goldoni "the Molière of Italy" as Voltaire did is misleading. Goldoni had neither the ethical seriousness nor the style of his predecessor. In Goldoni's genial world men may be inveigled by their appetites or misled by lying tongues, but once they come to their senses or grow up, all goes well. The more sinister sources of delusion or self-deception are none of his concern. Nobody has captured with more vivacity and grace the day-by-day town life of his age—its streets, shops, and cafés, its fops, decadent aristocrats, coquettes, duennas, merchants, and artisans. Out of an old civilization, as Stark Young declares, Goldoni "creates a sweet, happy, flowing logic, a persuasion toward sanity, decorum and gaiety, a smiling air of life."

Of Goldoni's approximately 150 comedies, several have been frequently rendered into English, while the bulk remain untranslated. The *Three Comedies,* translated by Charles Lloyd (published with his *Three Tragedies of Alfieri* in 1907), include *The Fan, An Odd Misunderstanding (Un Curioso Accidente),* and *The Beneficent Bear. Four Comedies,* edited by Clifford Bax (1928), includes *Mine Hostess (La Locandiera), The Impresario from Smyrna (L'Impresario delle Smirne), The Good Girl (La Donna di Garbo),* and *The Fan.* In addition, *Le Bourru Bienfaisant* has been translated by Barrett H. Clark (1915) : *La Bottega del Caffé* by Henry B. Fuller (1925) ; *Un Curioso Accidente* (A Curious Mishap), by Richard D. F. Hollester (1924) ; *Il Ventaglio,* by Henry B. Fuller (1925) ; *Le Donne Curiose* (The Good-Humoured Ladies), by Richard Aldington (1922) ; *Il Bugiardo,* by Grace Lovat Fraser (1922) ; *La Locandiera* by Merle Pierson (1912), Lady Gregory (1924), and Helen Lohman (1927) ; *Il Servitore di Due Padroni* (The Servant of Two Masters), by Edward J. Dent (1952). The standard edition in Italian is the *Opere Complete,* 20 volumes (Venice, 1907-17). A more recent selected edition is that of *La Letteratura Italiana,* vol. 42 (Milan, 1954).

The *Memoirs* were first translated by John Black (1814), and subsequently were reissued with preface by William Dean Howells (1877). The best edition in Italian is that of Mazzoni (1907).

ABOUT: Chatfield-Taylor, H. Goldoni; Everett, W. Italian Poets since Dante; Kennard, J. Goldoni and the Venice of His Time; Lee, V. Studies in the 18th Century; Nicoll, A. World Drama; Perry, H. Masters of Dramatic Comedy and Their Social Themes; Russo, J. Introduction to *I Rusteghi* (Italian trans.) ; Samuel, A. Venice of Goldoni, *in* Mancroft Essays. [In Italian—see studies by E. Caccia, F. Galanti, G. Ortolani, M. Appolonio, and E. Rho. See also the papers of the International Congress on Goldoni Studies, held in Venice in 1957, *Atti del Convegno Internazionale di Studi Goldoniani,* 2 vols.]

R. A. C.

341

*GOLDSCHMIDT, MEÏR (originally MEYER), A(A)RON (October 26, 1819-August 15, 1887), Danish novelist, dramatist, journalist, was born in Vordingborg in southern Zealand. His father, a merchant, Aron Goldschmidt, and his mother, Lea Levin (the family name later changed by her father to Rotschild), were of Jewish descent. He spent his childhood and youth in various places and schools. As early as his school years he manifested a burning desire to be outstanding. He intended to become a physician, in that way trying to restore the lost wealth of his family. But when he graduated from the *Gymnasium* without distinction because of an inadequate grade in religion, he changed his plans and became an author.

At the age of eighteen, he became the editor of a provincial weekly paper, *Næstved Avis* (Næstved News). His liberal criticism brought upon him both censorship and fines. He sold the paper and contributed for a short time to the conservative Copenhagen paper *Dagen* (The Day). But he wanted to become a more prominent figure in the press of the capital, and in 1840 he started the famous and dreaded satirical weekly *Corsaren* (The Corsair), which soon enjoyed an impressive number of subscribers. Goldschmidt himself wrote a good deal of the contents and became involved in a notorious literary feud with Sören Kierkegaard. His polemic activity in this paper resulted in the confiscation of several issues and, on one occasion, in his imprisonment. In 1846 he sold the paper.

After the transfer of *Corsaren,* Goldschmidt made his first journey abroad, but even before that he had begun a career as a literary author and published his first story under the pseudonym "Adolph Meyer," *En Jøde* (A Jew, 1845), dealing with the racial and social problems he had encountered in Copenhagen. Upon his return he started a new weekly paper, *Nord og Syd* (North and South 1847-59), which won high distinction, especially because of Goldschmidt's literary and theatrical reviews.

In 1844 Goldschmidt formed an acquaintance with Johanne Marie Sonne, daughter of a shipmaster. In order to legitimatize a son that was born they married in 1848, but the marriage was dissolved in 1852.

His most important literary achievement in the 1850's was his three-volume novel *Hjemløs* (Homeless, 1853-57), the best parts of which are its political and social depictions of the times. The basic motif in this and his following writings is the idea of Nemesis,

according to which the moral and ethical balance in life is maintained through the reward or punishment for our thoughts and deeds. In the next decade, after he had quit his journalistic activity, his fiction floundered. He turned from Jewish themes to motifs from Denmark and other countries, e.g., in *Fortællinger og Skildringer* (Stories and Pictures, 3 vols., 1863-65). But later he returned to Jewish topics, e.g., in *Ravnen* (The Raven, 1867), his best and most readable novel. As a dramatic author he was less successful. Goldschmidt's exquisite mastery of language and style made him one of Denmark's finest prose-writers.

Goldschmidt's *En Jøde* appeared in English translation by Mrs. Bushby as *The Jew of Denmark* (1852, 1864) and by Mary Howitt as *Jacob Bendixen, the Jew* (1852). *Hjemløs* was rendered into English by the author himself under the title *Homeless, or A Poet's Inner Life* (1861). The excellent story *Avromche Nattergal,* under the title *Avromche Nightingale,* is included in *Denmark's Best Stories* (1928), ed. and tr. by H. A. Larsen. For complete information about translations see E. Bredsdorff, *Danish Literature in English Translation* (1950).

ABOUT: Gosse, E. W. *in* The Athenæum, II; Mitchell, P. M. A History of Danish Literature. [In Danish—see studies by F. Dreier, H. Kyrre.]
A. J.

*GONCHAROV, IVAN ALEKSAN-DROVICH (June 18, 1812-September 27, 1891), Russian novelist and civil servant, was born into one of the leading merchant families in Simbirsk (now Ulyanovsk) on the Volga. His forebears had been merchants and military figures for a number of generations. Although he lost his father at the age of seven, Goncharov received parental guidance from his godfather N. N. Tregubov, a retired naval officer living with the family. As a child Goncharov often visited the estate of Tregubov where he encountered Russian serfdom in its more humane, idyllic aspect. This impression of the Russian background and countryside, particularly the rustic beauty of it, was to remain as a moving force in his works for the rest of his life.

After some years in the private establishment of the German wife of a local pastor, where he learned French and German, Goncharov was sent to Moscow for the completion of his education in a school of commerce and subsequently at the university. Although the university was at that time a center of intense intellectual and political activity resulting from the recent impact of German romanticism and the Hegelian dialectic, Goncharov's convictions were fostered

* göl′ shmēt

* gŭn chŭ rôf′

The Bettmann Archive

GONCHAROV

above all by the spell of the poet Pushkin and the lectures of Professor Nadezhdin, a violent opponent of all romanticism. Thus, although Goncharov must have known at the university such figures as Lermontov, Herzen, Belinsky, and Bakunin, he did not identify himself with any group. Moreover, on finishing his studies he made his agreements with the ruling powers in Russia and joined the civil service for what proved to be a lifetime career at a time when very many of his former classmates were either becoming revolutionaries or breaking with society in some other way.

Goncharov showed an early aptitude for literature and read widely in French, German, and Russian masters from the age of nine on. His first literary effort, a translation of *Atar Gull* by Eugène Sue, was published while he was still at the university. Once established in the civil service as a translator from the French, Goncharov deliberately and methodically applied himself to literature. In 1847 his first novel, *A Common Story,* was received enthusiastically, particularly by the radical critic Belinsky. In 1848 there followed a short story, *Ivan Savich Podzhabrin,* and in 1849 *Oblomov's Dream,* a sketch later to be incorporated in the novel *Oblomov.*

In 1852, when Goncharov appeared to be a comfortably established functionary, he astounded his friends by setting off in a sailing vessel on a two-year trip to Japan as official historiographer and secretary to Admiral Putyatin, whose mission was to open up Japan to world trade. After extensive stops in England and South Africa the party called at the chief ports of the Orient and spent several months in Nagasaki carrying on negotiations that were complicated by the presence of Admiral Perry in Tokyo. The expedition was only partially successful and was terminated by the outbreak of the Crimean War. After seeing his ship scuttled, Goncharov returned to St. Petersburg by way of northern Siberia. In 1858 a full account of the trip and the negotiations appeared in *Frigate Pallas.*

In the general atmosphere of reform that followed the death of Nicholas I Goncharov was appointed to the unpleasant office of censor. Although he held this position for only a year or so, he had much to do with the censorship for the rest of his official career and was able to help to mitigate the evils of this institution.

In 1859 he completed and published *Oblomov,* the novel on which he had been working for more than ten years. Its success was immediate. In 1867, at the earliest age possible, Goncharov retired from government service and devoted himself solely to literature. After extensive travels in Germany and France there appeared what he considered his definitive work, *The Precipice,* a novel on which he had been working some twenty years.

Goncharov never married. Except for his trip to Japan, his life was remarkable for its outward appearance of calm. Physically he was solid, well proportioned, and handsome. After the appearance of Turgenev's *Nest of Gentlefolk,* Goncharov, without real grounds, became increasingly suspicious that he was being plagiarized by Turgenev. This developed into such a mania that he saw an agent of the latter in anyone who innocently asked how his work was proceeding; and once, on nearly meeting Turgenev in a park, he ran off shouting "Thief, thief!" Actually, the only similarity in their works is that, since they both wrote about immediate Russian problems, they could not avoid presenting some nihilists and revolutionaries. Goncharov finally went so far as to assert that the central idea of Flaubert's *Éducation Sentimentale* (Flaubert being a friend of Turgenev) originated in his own *Precipice.*

In his later years Goncharov wrote an essay on the dramatist Griboyedov and a number of reminiscences, after which he sank into apathy and senility. On his death in 1891 he named his housekeeper, the widow Treigult, as his sole heir.

343

While *A Common Story* is a contrived *roman à thèse* about the new Russian bourgeoisie and *The Precipice* is a tendentious novel with an unconvincing nihilist as a hero, *Oblomov* stands as one of the great landmarks of the Russian realistic psychological novel. It is concerned with the conflict between the sleepy, backward but charming pre-reform Russia and the bustling mercantilism of western Europe. The hero Oblomov never escapes from the heritage of old Russia, which appears to him as a lotus land and to which he retreats in his dreams. The psychological analysis of Oblomov's inability to act appears very modern, and for this reason there has been renewed interest in Goncharov both in Russia and abroad, particularly on the part of the existentialists.

Of Goncharov's realism Janko Lavrin says: "The first thing to strike a reader of Goncharov is the absence of anything 'striking.' Having inherited Pushkin's naturalness and simplicity, he was, as it were, the opposite pole to Dostoyevsky. Dostoyevsky, whose realism was more visionary than visual, was all the time on the look-out for the exceptional or the abnormal . . . Goncharov stuck to his own realism of the obvious which he yet turned into something significant."

The influence of Goncharov has been very wide. first of all in Russia in contributing to the figure of the "superfluous man" and in giving to the Russian language the word "oblomovism," and also abroad where it may be seen in Édouard Rod's *La Course à la Mort* in France or Futabei's *Floating Clouds* in Japan, to mention a few.

A Common Story was translated by Constance Garnett in 1890, *Oblomov* by C. J. Hogarth in 1915, N. A. Duddington in 1929, and D. Magarshack in 1954. *The Precipice* appeared in a much abridged translation by M. Bryant in 1916.

ABOUT: Lavrin, J. Goncharov; Poggioli, R. The Phoenix and the Spider. [In Russian, French, and German respectively—see studies by E. Lyatsky, A. A. Mazon, W. Rehm.]

N. V.

EDMOND and JULES DE GONCOURT

*GONCOURT, EDMOND LOUIS ANTOINE HUOT DE (May 26, 1822-July 16, 1896) and **JULES ALFRED HUOT DE** (December 17, 1830-June 20, 1870), French novelists, historians, art critics, were born respectively at Nancy and at Paris. Their father, Marc Pierre Huot de Goncourt (1787-1834), was a reserve military officer who had had a brilliant career during the Empire; his great-grandfather acquired the

* gón kŏŏr'

Goncourt title in 1786 with a property in the Haute-Marne. Marc Pierre married Annette Cécile Guérin (1798-1848), a Parisian of a family active in finance and law.

The family settled in Paris, where Edmond attended the Collège Henri IV and Jules went to the Collège Bourbon. Both took the standard course in classics, but the only classical author with whom they did not find fault was Tacitus. Their preferences were for more modern writers: Saint-Simon and Diderot. Subsequently Edmond studied painting at the Dupuis atelier for two years and then took up law before entering the office of the Treasury. As a hobby he worked on a history of castles in the Middle Ages. Jules, a superior student, devoted himself to the composition of a verse drama and to drawing; it was his intention "to do nothing" and to enjoy the leisure of an aristocratic young man.

The death of their mother left them financially secure and free to devote themselves exclusively to their interests. Both were sickly and delicate: Jules had fair skin, golden hair, black eyes, and was beardless (later he grew a blond mustache), with a feminine fragility; Edmond, taller and heavier, with dark brown hair and sweeping mustache, had the air of a musketeer, but his voice was high and thin. Though delicate, they decided on a walking tour, and, with packs and painter's equipment, covered Burgundy, Dauphiné, Provence, and Algeria from July to December of 1849. As they traveled they did water-colors and sketches and took notes, setting down all the daily trivia: menus, prices, distances and time consumed, and quick impressions. Those notes and the habits of observation were the virtual start of their literary career.

Back in Paris, they settled—for almost twenty years—at 43 rue Saint-Georges. The brothers collaborated on some vaudevilles—unaccepted—during a swing through Switzerland, Belgium, and Normandy, and then wrote a novel, *En 18. . ,* whose publication, coinciding with the 1851 *coup d'état,* went almost unnoticed. For a year they essayed journalism, writing short pieces and reviewing new books and plays. Their "Lèpres Modernes," on venal women, was published in an immensely popular little book with the title *La Lorette* (1853), illustrated by, and dedicated to, their friend Paul Gavarni. This sort of depiction, a "physiology," had come into vogue a couple of decades earlier.

The next ten years witnessed their series of historical studies along with works on art. *Histoire de la Société Française pendant la Révolution* (1854), *Histoire de Marie Antoinette* (1858), *Portraits Intimes du XVIII* Siècle* (1857-58), and other works of a similar type used contemporary documents to recreate intimacy with the subjects. The purpose is that of social history: "to create history with the detritus of history," as Remy de Gourmont said.

Their studies rehabilitated or revealed eighteenth century art, especially its drawings. As collectors, they amassed about four hundred drawings from that century. Theirs was fundamentally a sensuous enjoyment of art. It has been said of them—especially of Edmond—that they had the heart of an interior decorator; François Fosca calls them "visual sensualists."

In 1860 the brothers, utilizing their intimate knowledge of literary circles, wrote a comedy, *Les Hommes de Lettres.* This play became the novel *Charles Demailly,* the story of an artist caught between, and crushed by, two women. The theme of the destructive woman is salient in their work; most of their novels—written collectively or by Edmond alone—have a woman's name in the title. Their next novel, *Sœur Philomène* (1861), about the love of a nun for a doctor, was based on an anecdote related to them by Gustave Flaubert's friend Louis Bouilhet. In order to make their story "authentic" Jules and Edmond visited hospitals—realism was their fetish. Their subsequent novels—*Renée Mauperin* (1864), *Germinie Lacerteux* (1865), *Manette Salomon* (2 vols.,

1867), *Madame Gervaisais* (1869)—were all founded on "human documents," i.e., people or situations on which they had compiled dossiers. Of these, *Germinie Lacerteux* is, no doubt, the best. This portrayal of *furor amandi* was based on the case of their own servant. By its evocation of the Paris suburbs it introduced a new setting into literature. *Manette Salomon* is of interest for its description of the artists' milieu between 1840 and 1865. The style of these writings—nervous, colorful, precise and technical, sometimes neological, impressionistic—has been termed "écriture artiste." By subject matter, treatment, and objectivity, the Goncourts claimed priority in naturalism. As they conceived it, "History is a novel which has been; the novel is history which could have been."

Their personal experience of love was meager. Apparently neither had ever been really in love, though they had occasional liaisons of brief duration. They preferred watchfully noting the conversations at social gatherings of their friends, Gautier, Flaubert, Jules Janin, Paul de Saint-Victor. Regulars at the Magny dinners launched in 1862 by their intimate friend Gavarni and by Sainte-Beuve, they were the unofficial stenographers of the quips, theorizings, and indiscretions casually bared. In their *Journal,* kept jointly from December 1851—though Jules held the pen—they confided these remarks and their own reactions.

In these, as in other things, they were amazingly in harmony. At a dinner, one could start a sentence, the other would finish it for both of them. Their writings represent the closest collaboration, with one or the other actually doing the writing, but the end-product a complete amalgam of their twin efforts. Often each first made a separate draft, and then the two versions would be combined. Jules wrote to Zola that "Edmond is the passion, Jules is the will." Edmond was the more phlegmatic and conventional—Germanic; Jules was the more imaginative and excitable—Latin. The latter noted in the *Journal* (August 1865): "With us, the most absolute difference in temperaments, in tastes, in characters, and absolutely the same ideas, the same sympathies and antipathies for people, the same intellectual optics." Both were hypochondriac, vain, suspicious, nervous.

Jules became hypersensitive to noise. Almost any sound grated on his exasperated nerves. This affliction was accompanied by increasing debility. He had softening of the brain, specifically from progressive general

345

paralysis and bronchial pneumonia (and syphilis too, according to his biographer André Billy). He died at the age of thirty-nine and was buried in Montmartre cemetery, only a short time after the brothers had moved into their new home at 53 (today number 67) Boulevard Montmorency, in Auteuil, which they had purchased in August 1868.

Edmond, bereft, was at first incapable of individual effort. Friends encouraged him: Alphonse Daudet entertained him at dinner two or three times a week; the "Dinners of Five" brought together Edmond, Flaubert, Daudet, Turgenev, and Zola. His passion for collecting stuffed the Auteuil house, "a hermetic box, a Far-Eastern coffer with a draped ceiling," until it groaned with bric-à-brac and ornamentations. Eventually he essayed a novel on a prostitute, *La Fille Élisa* (1877), from notes prepared by both brothers. Thereafter Edmond wrote several less successful works on the worlds of the theatre and circus. He resumed the "petite histoire" of the eighteenth century. Since 1860 both he and Jules had been attracted to Japanese art, which they are erroneously thought to have discovered; but their studies of Outamaro (1891) and Hokusaï (1896) certainly popularized things Japanese. Though they championed modernism, and their own writings were impressionistic, they had little sympathy for, or understanding of, impressionism, and they belittled Courbet.

On February 1, 1885, was held the first meeting of the "Grenier," at Auteuil—so named because two attic rooms had been thrown together to form a salon where those interested in literature might come, although Edmond was always ill at ease and a difficult conversationalist. Chronically suffering from dyspepsia and hepatitis, Edmond had a pulmonary congestion while visiting Daudet at Champrosay, and died there. He was buried at Montmartre cemetery.

Edmond's will provided that the famous *Journal*, parts of which had been released in 1887-88 (3 vols.) and 1890-92 (3 vols.), should be fully available in twenty years. A nine-volume edition was published on his death; after long litigation the whole compilation was finally released (1956-58) in twenty-two volumes. The will also provided for the establishing of a Goncourt Academy of ten members, who are not to be of the French Academy, and who yearly crown the "most meritorious" work of French fiction by a young and needy author.

The Auteuil house became the Goncourt museum and archives.

The *Journals: 1851-1870* have been partially translated by Lewis Galantière (1937) and by Robert Baldick, *Pages from The Goncourt Journal* (1962). *Germinie Lacerteux* was translated by A. E. M. (1891), John Chestershire (1897), Ernest Boyd (1922), and Jonathan Griffith (1955). Other novels translated include Edmond's *La Faustin* (1882 and 1906), *Sister Philomène* (1891), Edmond's *The Zemganno Brothers* (1897), *René Mauperin* (1902). Ernest Dowson translated *The Mistresses of Louis XV* (1909). *Madame Du Barry* was translated in 1914. Jacques Le Clercq and Ralph Roeder collaborated to translate *The Woman of the Eighteenth Century. . .* (1927). Robin Ironside translated the compendium *French Eighteenth Century Painters* (1948).

ABOUT: Jarman, L. M. The Goncourt Brothers, Modernists in Abnormal Psychology; Murray, D. L. Scenes and Silhouettes; Routh, H. V. Towards the Twentieth Century; Symons, A. The Symbolist Movement in Literature (rev. ed., 1919); Studies in French Language, Literature and History, Presented to R. L. Graeme Ritchie (1949); The Listener July 21, 1955; Times Literary Supplement, September 9, 1955. [In French—Billy, A. Les Frères Goncourt; Bourget, P. Essais de Psychologie Contemporaine; Delzant, A. Les Goncourt; Fosca, F. Edmond et Jules de Goncourt; Ricatte, R. La Création Romanesque chez les Goncourt, 1851-1870; Sabatier, P. L'Esthétique des Goncourt; Sauvage, M. Jules et Edmond de Goncourt. Léon Deffoux has written on the Goncourt Academy.]

S. S. W.

*GÓNGORA Y ARGOTE, LUIS DE

(1561-1627), Spanish poet, was born at Cordova. His father, Francisco de Argote, was *corregidor* (mayor) of that city. The poet early in life adopted the surname of his mother, Leonora de Góngora, who was descended from an ancient family. He was educated at the University of Salamanca, but may have subsequently taken a degree at the University of Cordova. By 1585 he was known as a poet, to judge by the praise accorded him by Cervantes in the *Galatea* (the subject also of one of Góngora's later poems). Professionally, Góngora devoted himself for most of his life to the priesthood. He was ordained in the cathedral of Cordova sometime between 1585 and 1599. Following a period of travel through Galicia, Navarra and Castille on various church commissions, he settled in Madrid in 1612, where later he became royal chaplain to King Philip III. However, he wrote very little religious verse. The poems for which he is most famous are highly pagan in tone and imagery. In 1626 a severe illness forced him to retire to Cordova where he died the following year. According to contemporary accounts he was

* góng' gō rä ē är gō' tä

GÓNGORA

impressive in physical appearance and gained a reputation, apart from his poetry, for eloquence of speech and liveliness and fertility of wit. The wit has survived in some of his lesser known satirical verse; his gaunt features are preserved in the famous portrait by his contemporary, Velásquez.

The association of Góngora's name with tortuous elaboration of style and obscurity of thought (*estilo culto*) has greatly clouded his reputation. To this day Gongorism suggests to the Spanish—as does Euphuism to the English, Marinism to the Italians, and *Geschwulle* to the Germans—linguistic affectation and stylistic virtuosity for its own sake. Góngora did at times betray a penchant for inverted sentence structure, paradoxes, word-plays, Greek and Latin locutions, the heaping up of metaphors and, in general, intense and ornate description. However, devices that he used with genius were carried to the point of caricature by less inspired disciples, who undoubtedly contributed to his unfortunate reputation.

Actually this reputation is based on the two long poems written towards the end of his career that stirred up critical controversy among his contemporaries, *Polifemo* (1612) and *Las Soledades* (probably 1613). The majority of his poems written before this period are short lyrics of airy, graceful charm. The famous *romance,* in which a maiden pours out her lament for her dead soldier-lover, with its plaintive refrain, "Dejadme llorar/ orillas del mar" ("Let me

weep/ banks of the sea"), shows him the master of simple, poignant emotion. His sonnets generally celebrate the *carpe diem* theme. A haunting phrase from one of these: "Goza, goza, el color, la luz, el oro" ("Enjoy, enjoy, the color, the light, the gold,") reveals his essential gift for phonic music and his sensuousness.

It seems unfair to say, as does one critic, that as Góngora developed he turned from "an angel of light" to "an angel of darkness." For one thing, even during his later period, he reverted from time to time to his simpler style. Damaso Alonso seems closer to the truth when he affirms that Góngora's longer poems really represent an intensification of elements characteristic of the shorter poems. The music becomes more intricate, the natural description more gorgeous, the metaphors subtler.

Góngora's obscurity, for the most part, results from compression of thought rather than from any deliberate incoherence. He tends in his major poems to intensify his impressions by revealing objects of nature through their salient qualities, rather than in their physical wholeness. Hence tablecloths are to the poet "nieve hilada" ("spun snow"); birds become "inquietas liras" ("unquiet lyres"), "violines que vuelan" ("violins that fly"), "sirenas con plumas" ("Sirens with plumes"); the nymph Galatea is described as "el cristal mudo" ("silent crystal"), while the water from the fountain near where she lies is "el cristal sónoro" ("sonorous crystal").

Góngora's uniqueness as a poet undoubtedly lies in his extraordinary visual imagination—that quality which makes him one of the leading poets of the Baroque—rather than in subtlety of thought. Justifiably famous are those episodes from the *Polifemo* where Polyphemus woos Galatea and where the nymph's lover Acis is transformed into a river to escape the monster's jealous wrath. *Las Soledades* (*The Solitudes*) is a cornucopia of natural beauty, akin to Virgil's *Georgics,* given only a semblance of narrative by the initial situation of a shipwrecked youth who takes refuge with a goatherd's family. The Invocation to Hymen, one of its most famous passages, calls to mind Spenser's *Epithalamion.* This poem was originally intended to consist of four parts: *Soledad de los Campos* (Solitude of the Fields); *Soledad de las Riberas* (Solitude of the Banks); *Soledad de las Selvas* (Solitude of the Woods); *Soledad del Yermo* (Solitude of the Plain). Unfortunately, *Las*

Soledades remains one of the great fragmentary masterpieces, for Góngora completed only the first and part of the second of the four projected parts.

Góngora did not publish any of his poems during his lifetime, but they became widely known through the circulation of his manuscripts among friends. A good many poems appeared in anthologies edited by others—notably in the *Flores de Poetas Ilustres* of Pedro Espinosa (1605). In 1623 the poet himself hoped to publish a volume under his own supervision, but the project never materialized. In fact it was not until 1921, with the publication of the edition of Foulché-Debosc, based on the manuscript of Chacon, that the canon was established. Besides his two long poems, Góngora is now known to be the author of more than 200 short lyrics—letrillas, romances, sonnets, and songs, and a completed play, *Las Firmezas de Isabel*, as well as two incomplete ones, *La Comedia Venatoria* and *El Doctor Carlino.*

After a period of scorn and neglect it is in our time, following the observation of the third centenary of his death, that Luis de Góngora has come to be most fully appreciated by his countrymen. This has come about probably through better understanding of his system of imagery and greater appreciation in general of technical virtuosity. According to the judgment of Pedro Salinas: "Like Velásquez, he is a painter of profound superficiality. . . . [Lyricism] spreads over his poetry as the ivy over the oak, and in the end covers it almost completely."

Góngora's poetry has not, unfortunately, been extensively translated into English. *Las Soledades* has been rendered into English verse by E. M. Wilson (1931). Selections from the shorter poems are available in the *Hispanic Anthology*, edited by Thomas Walsh (1920), and the more recent bilingual *Ten Centuries of Spanish Poetry*, edited by Eleanor Turnbull (1955). The best edition in Spanish is that of Raymond Foulché-Debosc (1921).

ABOUT: Adams, N. B. Heritage of Spain; Brenan, G. The Literature of the Spanish People; Churton, E. Góngora; Fitzmaurice-Kelly, J. Some Masters of Spanish Verse; Guillén, J. Language and Poetry; Kane, E. K. Gongorism and the Golden Age; Peers, E. A. *Introduction to* A Critical Anthology of Spanish Verse; Turnbull, E. *Introduction to* Ten Centuries of Spanish Verse; Comparative Literature, Winter, 1954; Modern Language Review, January, 1954. [In Spanish—see studies by D. Alonso, M. Artigas, and E. O. Díaz].

R. A. C.

*GONZALO DE BERCEO (c. 1198-post-1265), Spanish poet, was born in Berceo, a small village located in the modern

* gôn thä′ lō thä bĕr thä′ ō

province of Logroño. Little is known of his life, spent in the region of La Rioja. Though a secular priest and confessor, he was closely associated with the important monasteries of San Millán de la Cogolla and Santo Domingo de Silos. His signature as a witness to notarial documents proves that he was ordained a deacon by 1221 and a priest by 1237. Evidence shows that he was still alive as late as 1280, but it seems more likely that he died closer to the date of his final extant work, written about 1265.

Berceo's works deal exclusively with religious subjects and exhibit predominantly a single metrical form, monorhymed stanzas of four fourteen-syllable lines each, known in Spanish as *cuaderna vía*, the clerical meter. There are four lives of saints: *Vida de Santo Domingo de Silos* (c. 1230), *Vida de San Millán de la Cogolla* (c. 1234), *Martirio de San Lorenzo* (c. 1250), and *Vida de Santa Oria* (c. 1265); two exegetical works: *Del Sacrificio de la Misa* (c. 1237) and *De los Signos que Aparecerán antes del Juicio* (Concerning the Sacrifice of the Mass and Concerning the Signs Which Will Appear before Judgment); and three works devoted to the Blessed Virgin Mary: the *Duelo* (Grief), the *Loores* (Praises) and the *Milagros* (Miracles) *de Nuestra Señora* (c. 1245-60). The material for all these poems is derived from more or less standard medieval Latin sources. Berceo's achievement was to popularize these legends and theological tenets by retelling them in Castilian, the local language of the people. His style is simple and clear to the point of being almost prosaic; his rustic comparisons and images are often amusing, occasionally lyrical.

The works of Berceo represent in Spain a new sort of popular poetry, invented by monks to compete with chivalric epics such as the *Cantar de mio Cid* (1140). The militaristic feudal virtues of the warrior class are replaced in these works by the virtues of devotion to Our Lady, to the saints, and to the Mass. We may see herein something similar to the transition from Romanesque to Gothic which Henry Adams traces in his *Mont-Saint-Michel and Chartres.*

Generally neglected and even scorned as superstitious since the Middle Ages, the poetry of Berceo has been re-evaluated in the twentieth century; modern readers are often delighted by the primitive simplicity and homely charm of this thirteenth century clerical poet.

A few English translations are found in Longfellow's *Poets and Poetry of Europe* (1845) and in

Eleanor L. Turnbull's *Ten Centuries of Spanish Poetry* (1955).

ABOUT: Brenan, G. The Literature of the Spanish People; Goode, T. C. Gonzalo de Berceo; Guillén, J. Language and Poetry.

E. L. R.

GORDON, JUDAH LOEB (also known as Yehudah Leib or Leon; pseudonym Ya-LaG, or Y.L.G.) (December 7, 1830-September 16, 1892), the leading Hebrew poet of the nineteenth century, was born in Vilna, the intellectual and spiritual capital of Lithuanian Jewry. His parents were wealthy and pious, and his father had mastered several foreign languages. Gordon received a thorough education in the traditional subjects of Talmud, Bible, and Hebrew grammar. Later he studied German, French, Latin, Polish, and Russian. In 1853 he was graduated from the Vilna Jewish Seminary and received an appointment as instructor in a government-sponsored Jewish school. For the next twenty years he taught Russian and mathematics to Jewish children in small Lithuanian towns.

Gordon at an early age came under the influence of the Haskalah movement and such leading figures in it as Micah Joseph Lebensohn and Michel Gordon. Haskalah, originating in Germany, was dedicated to the enlightenment of the Jews through secular education, and the modernization of their way of life through repudiation of a restrictive and atrophied orthodoxy. Only thus could the Jews achieve integration into non-Jewish society and enjoy the fruits of Western culture. During the reign of Alexander II, the Russian government seemed to support these ideals and Haskalah activity was stimulated. Gordon's early works, written during this period, reflect an optimistic, romantic mood. His first published work, *Ahavat David u-Michal* (The Love of David and Michal, 1856), deals with a Biblical theme, illustrating the Haskalah's emphasis on the Bible rather than the Talmud as a source of inspiration. The poem "Ben Shine Arayot" (Between the Lion's Teeth, published 1868) blames rabbinic law for the narrowing of Jewish life. In "Hakitsah Ami!" ("Awake, My People," written 1863) he exhorts Russian Jewry to reshape their lives by accepting enlightenment. Turning to satire of the unenlightened, Gordon published his *Mishle Yehudah* (Fables of Judah, 1860), most of which were translations and adaptations from Aesop, La Fontaine, and others.

GORDON

This work marks a transition to a more realistic type of poetry in which Gordon attacked the superstition and bigotry in contemporary Jewish life. Appointed secretary of both the Jewish community of St. Petersburg and the Society for the Diffusion of Enlightenment among the Jews of Russia in 1872, he wrote several blistering narrative poems denouncing the rigid formalism of Jewish law. His anti-clerical attitude won him the open hostility of the Orthodox element who, he claimed, instigated the arrest and imprisonment of his wife and himself for forty days in 1879 on charges of revolutionary conspiracy. Abandoned by his enlightened colleagues and not reinstated in his posts, Gordon became bitter and despaired of idealistic efforts. Further disillusionment with the ideas of the Haskalah came with the pogroms of the 1880's. During his last nihilistic and bitter years, he supported himself with journalistic work on the Hebrew paper *Ha-Melits* and similar activities. In 1891 he became sick with cancer and died the following year.

Gordon had the soul of a poet weighed down by the sorrow of his people and the dedication of a rebel uplifted by visions of a better future. His love and pathos are evident even in his denunciations of rabbinic Judaism: "The dust of your scribes and the dry leaves of pious talk have kept thee a living mummy for generations" ("Ben Shine Arayot"). He demonstrated an incomparable command of the Hebrew language, and his style is of classical brilliance. Gordon had a tremendous influence in his day and, although his polemics seem dated, his skill was sufficiently impressive to survive and provide a basis for the poetry of Bialik and indeed for modern Hebrew literature in general.

None of Gordon's work has been translated into English, with the exception of a few shorter poems which have appeared in anthologies, such as Leo Schwarz's *Golden Treasury of Jewish Literature*. Hebrew editions include *Kol Shire* (Vilna, 1898) and *Kitve . . . Shirah* (Tel Aviv, 1950).

ABOUT: Halkin, S. Modern Hebrew Literature; Klausner, J. History of Modern Hebrew Literature (1785-1935); Raisin, J. S. The Haskalah Movement in Russia; Rhine, A. B. Leon Gordon; Slouschz, N. The Renascence of Hebrew Literature; Waldstein, A. S. Evolution of Modern Hebrew Literature; Waxman, M. A History of Jewish Literature. [In Hebrew—see studies by F. Lachower and A. Orinowsky.]

M.R.

*GOTTFRIED VON STRASSBURG (c. 1170-1215?) German poet, was born in Strasbourg. Otherwise nothing is known about his life except the approximate time of his death between 1215 and 1220. Unlike the other courtly poets of medieval Germany he did not belong to the nobility but to the higher middle class of his home town which, at that time, was one of the most important cultural centers of the Western world. The title *meister* which always precedes Gottfried's name attests to his academic status. Gottfried's poetry gives ample evidence of his unusually high erudition. He knew both Latin and French and was well versed in scholasticism. He had a good knowledge of Greek mythology. His favorite authors were Virgil and Ovid.

Gottfried's fame as the greatest epic poet next to Wolfram von Eschenbach rests on a single work, his *Tristan und Isolde*. Of other poetry which he is assumed to have written nothing has been preserved. Even the *Tristan* with its approximately twenty thousand verses has remained a fragment, probably on account of the author's death. Gottfried's work, like most other German courtly romances, is based on a French source: Thomas of Brittany's version of an old story of Celtic origin. The few fragments of the French poem which have come down do not allow of any comparison with Gottfried's poem.

Among the great creators of German epic poetry Gottfried stands somewhere between the classicism of Hartmann von Aue and the romanticism of Wolfram von Eschenbach. While he lacks the simplicity and moderation

* gōt' frēt fōn shträs' boŏrk

of Hartmann and the spiritual depth of Wolfram, his is the most perfect harmony between form and content. He refines *Tristan*, a story of fierce passionate love, with his artistry and insight into the working of the human soul under the impact of overwhelming emotions. In contrast to its usual treatment in chivalric poetry, Gottfried extols love not so much as the source of heroic deeds as of noble and refined feelings. Love which is strong enough to accept in its wake any measure of suffering and tribulation is to Gottfried a virtue in itself, the highest of all. Tristan and Isolde are not only victims, they are artists of love. Their love is not simply fearless passion: it is the privilege of people who have cultivated their minds to the highest refinement. They are the epitome of *courtoisie*, of courtly culture. Though their tragedy is caused by the drinking of a love potion, Gottfried's psychological knowledge does not allow him to overemphasize the purely miraculous element. The love potion does not create the passion; it merely removes the inhibitions from the lovers who are destined for each other by the affinity of their souls. There is on the whole a strong rationalistic trait in Gottfried which shows especially in his independent attitude toward Christian dogma and ethics. The unsuccessful attempts of the betrayed husband to catch the adulterous wife and her lover in the act are described without any moral scruples as a battle of wits. Gottfried's poem reaches its highest points in the lyric scenes where his language almost achieves the intoxicating effect of Richard Wagner's musical treatment of the same subject.

Gottfried's style was influenced by Hartmann von Aue, whom he lauds as the unsurpassed master of artistic form, while he condemns Wolfram for his eccentricity and obscurity. The monotony of medieval epic verse he enlivens by skillful blending of iambic and trochaic rhythms. His verse is always grammatically correct and his rhyme unfailingly pure.

While to the Germans the spiritual depth of Wolfram von Eschenbach has a stronger appeal than Gottfried's more refined and more worldly-minded art, French and American scholars are inclined to rate *Tristan und Isolde* as the highest achievement of German chivalric poetry. Roger Sherman Loomis writes: "*Tristan und Isolde* is, except for the *Divine Comedy* and the *Canterbury Tales*, the greatest poem of the Middle Ages."

Among the various treatments of the subject of Gottfried's poem both in literature and in music, none surpasses in importance Richard Wagner's musical drama *Tristan und Isolde,* not only based on the medieval poet's work but truly inspired by it.

There is a verse translation of *Tristan und Isolde* by Edwin H. Zeydel (1948). It offers a line-for-line rendering, with rhythm, rhyme, and style approximating those of the original. The untranslated parts of the poem are connected by summaries. In 1901 Jessie L. Weston published an abridged prose version of Gottfried's work. A complete translation, by A. T. Hatto, was published in Penguin Books in 1960.

ABOUT: Bruce, J. D. Evolution of Arthurian Romance; Jackson, W. T. H. Arthurian Literature in the Middle Ages; Loomis, R. S. Celtic Myth and Arthurian Romance, Arthurian Legends in Medieval Art; Schoepperle, G. Tristan and Isold. [In German—see Gustav Ehrismann's Geschichte der Deutschen Literatur bis zum Ausgang des Mittelalters, II.]

F.R.

*GOTTHELF, JEREMIAS** (pseudonym of **ALBERT *BITZIUS)** (October 4, 1797-October 22, 1854), Swiss novelist and pastor, was born at Murten in the Bern region, the son of the pastor of Utzenstorf, where he grew up and attended school. He continued his education at Bern, studying theology, mathematics, history, and philosophy. In 1821 he briefly attended the University of Göttingen and five years later became a vicar at Herzogenbuchsee. In 1832 he became pastor at Lützelflüh in the Emmental where he spent the rest of his life. In 1833 he married Henriette Zeender; the couple had three children. From 1835 to 1845 Gotthelf was also commissioner of primary and secondary education for the Canton of Bern and taught history to student teachers. Although he started writing books in 1836, Gotthelf continued to serve his congregation faithfully until his death shortly after his fifty-seventh birthday.

Gotthelf wrote his books in order to entertain, inform, inspire, and educate the peasants who made up his congregation, and to deepen their religious awareness. He wrote, in both High German and Swyzerdütsch, the Swiss dialect, works of such high order that he ranks with Gottfried Keller and Conrad Ferdinand Meyer as one of the masters of Swiss literature. In German literature generally he is regarded as the first realistic novelist, and he is one of the finest writers about village life in world literature. Like Stifter, he wrote prose exclusively, and he shares with him his great interest in education and his marked didactic intent. His interest in the peasant

* gŏt' hĕlf; bī' tsē ōŏs

world as a microcosm of all life is reminiscent of Tolstoy. Within a period of eighteen years this linguistically untutored man, who found writing anything but easy, produced 38 volumes—24 of fiction, 14 of sermons, letters, and speeches. From 1840 to 1845 he edited the *Neuer Berner Kalender,* most of which he wrote himself. Gotthelf's works express the beliefs and practices of the Swiss educator Pestalozzi and are evidence of his lifelong struggle against the coarsening encroachment of nineteenth century materialism and atheism on what he considered a pure world where eternal values were paramount.

Gotthelf began with a sort of autobiography called *Der Bauernspiegel* (1837), in which he advocated patriarchal order that might slough off social differences; he was against "progress," radicalism, or revolution, espousing realism without a program. Another autobiographical work, *Leiden und Freuden eines Schulmeisters,* followed in 1838. His most famous novel appeared in 1841: *Uli der Knecht* (Uli the Farmhand), followed by a sequel *Uli der Pächter* (Uli the Tenant-Farmer) in 1847. Modeled after Pestalozzi's *Lienhard und Gertrud, Uli* is a rural *Erziehungsroman.* Uli is originally a lazy, shiftless hired hand, but he has the sympathetic support of his master and of Vreneli, a pure, selfless woman, and becomes an industrious, moral farmer. In *Die Käserei in der Vehfreude* (1850) Gotthelf tries to show the elemental laws of social living through a miniature society, a small cheese-making cooperative in a village. With great humor and tolerance, a liberal dash of satire, and masterly psychological insight, Gotthelf criticizes "big-time" institutions that infiltrate the peasant world, but he never loses his faith in the basic soundness of country folk. Gotthelf's other novels include *Anne Bäbi Jowäger* (about quackery in a village), *Geld und Geist, Zeitgeist und Berner Geist, Käthi die Grossmutter,* and *Erlebnisse eines Schuldenbauers.*

Among Gotthelf's many novellas, the most noteworthy are *Elsi, die Seltsame Magd* and *Die Schwarze Spinne* (1842). In the figure of Elsi, a beautiful, enigmatic, proud, self-denying maid, Gotthelf shows the essential nature of his peasants who are rooted in their landscape, cling to their home life and traditions, are aloof on the surface, and only in moments of great stress and crisis reveal their inner strength. *Die Schwarze Spinne,* which has been made into an opera by Heinrich Sutermeister, utilizes with great art the medieval legend of the Black Death which has assumed some shape, here that of a black

351

spider, the symbol of a heaven-sent catastrophe. The demonic bringer of evil is once brought under control, but breaks out again because of the stupidity and godlessness of the people concerned. The moral is that the black spider, still bottled up in a house, need not be feared as long as peace reigns and men have God in their hearts.

The Joys and Sufferings of a Schoolmaster appeared in 1864 in an anonymous translation. *Wealth and Welfare* appeared in 1866, also translated anonymously. *The Soul and Money*, translated by Guarterick Vere, was published in 1872. John Ruskin translated *The Broom Merchant* in 1873-76. *The Story of an Alpine Valley, or Katie the Grandmother*, translated by L. G. Smith, appeared in 1896. *Ulric the Farm Servant* was first translated by Julia Firth in 1888; *Uli the Farmhand*, B. Q. Morgan's abridged translation, is included in *The German Classics*, VIII (1914).

ABOUT: Pascal, R. The German Novel; Waidson, H. M. Jeremias Gotthelf; Modern Language Review, LI (1956). [In German—see studies by K. Fehr, O. Geyerz, W. Günther, E. Huber, R. Huch, C. Müller, W. Muschg.]

H. Z.

*GOTTSCHED, JOHANN CHRISTOPH (February 2, 1700-December 12, 1766), German scholar, author, and literary critic, was born at Judithenkirche in the vicinity of Königsberg. This son of a North German Protestant minister entered the University of Königsberg at the age of fourteen as a student of theology, but soon devoted himself exclusively to philosophy and the liberal arts. Fearing that he would be recruited for the royal guard because of his height, he fled Prussia in 1724. In Leipzig at first he was a private tutor in the household of a university professor, but in the same year completed the prerequisites for lecturing at the University of Leipzig. In 1730 he was appointed associate professor of literature, and in 1734 he became professor of logic and metaphysics. Later he attained a position on the board of governors of the university and the senior chair on the philosophical faculty.

During the years 1729 to 1740, Gottsched exercised almost absolute control over the direction taken by literature in Germany. He was the unopposed authority on literary matters. However, his fame rapidly diminished when he was opposed by the Swiss critics J. J. Bodmer and J. J. Breitinger. When he persisted in his narrow interpretation of aesthetic values, condemning even Klopstock and Lessing, his name became anathema in literary circles. A later age, however, attempted to treat him more justly. It was

* göt' shät

pointed out by many nineteenth century scholars that he had been instrumental in cleansing German literature of many rhetorical impurities of the baroque period and had proclaimed effectively the desirability of a great national literature. However, his short-sighted dependence upon French literary models had played a large part in arousing the condemnation of his contemporaries.

Gottsched began his extensive literary activity within one year after his arrival at Leipzig with the founding of the journal *Die Vernünftigen Tadlerinnen* (1725-26), which consisted primarily of didactic and edifying articles. This journal was followed by numerous others such as *Der Biedermann; Beiträge zur Kritischen Historie der Deutschen Sprache; Poesie und Beredsamkeit; Neuer Büchersaal der Schönen Wissenschaften und Freien Künste; Das Neueste aus der Anmutigen Gelehrsamkeit.* He undoubtedly performed considerable service for the German language through his efforts in these journals to purify and standardize his native tongue. Of the literary genres, the drama received most of his attention. He set himself the task of creating a German theatre which would be the equal of the French. His method consisted of translating, together with his wife Luise, numerous French plays and of the composition of original works following French models. Among the latter, his *Der Sterbende Cato* (1732), fulfilling the requirements of the Aristotelian unities, was intended to demonstrate how a true tragedy was supposed to be written. It would be gross understatement to say that his tragedy failed to have any lasting effect on German theatre. In addition to numerous works dealing with literary history and criticism Gottsched wrote a large number of textbooks, the most important of which are *Ausführliche Redekunst* (1728), *Versuch einer Kritischen Dichtkunst für die Deutschen* (1730), and *Grundlegung einer Deutschen Sprachkunst* (1748).

ABOUT: [In German—see studies by F. Brüggemann, E. Reichel.]

E. K. G.

*GOZZANO, GUIDO (December 19, 1883-August 9, 1916), Italian poet, was born in the town of Aglie Canavese in the mountains north of Turin. At twenty, he entered law school at the University of Turin; already he was suffering from the tuberculosis which was to kill him thirteen years later. He was graduated with a degree in law but never wished to practice. He interested himself in-

* göt zän' nō

stead in poetry and was much influenced by the sensual dilettantism of d'Annunzio's early works such as *Il Piacere* and by the French poets Jules Laforgue and Francis Jammes. He studied at the university under two distinguished teachers who influenced him away from the philosophies of d'Annunzio and of Nietzsche to which he had also been attracted. Paul R. Troiano's philosophy courses demolished Nietzsche, while Arturo Graf lectured brilliantly against the d'Annunzian style and the ethics of the arch-ego. In this formative period Gozzano also found the library of the Società di Cultura a source of inspiration, rich as it was in the works of the French poets. Indeed, when Gozzano's first lyrics appeared, *La Via del Rifugio* in 1907, some critics considered the work no more than an offshoot of French poetry with graftings of Italian style, an evaluation which is not wholly accurate.

With the publication of *La Via del Rifugio* Gozzano became the most popular of the "Crepuscolari," the pre-World War I poets who gave voice to the uncertainty, nostalgia, and sadness of their time. In contrast to the magniloquence of Carducci and the open sensuality of d'Annunzio, Gozzano constructed subtle harmonies. He celebrated many erotic adventures but never real love; he sang of many women, but none of them was his spiritual inspiration. There is a slim record of romantic correspondence between Gozzano and the novelist and poet Amalia Guglielminetti. She was also a native of Turin, two years younger than Gozzano, and her sensuous and audacious writing caused her to be hailed as a "new Sappho" during her artistic lifetime.

In 1912 and 1913 Gozzano, on the advice of his physicians, took a long voyage to India. From this trip came the journal published posthumously in 1917 as *Verso la Cuna del Mondo* (Towards the Cradle of the World). He returned from India with the mask of health, but he was not actually better. He died three years later in his villa in the mountains of Canavese. World War I was already raging, and the newspapers of the day, operating under wartime restrictions, took note of his death only in three- or four-line notices.

Gozzano's innate love of simplicity was dissipated by his literary education. In his most popular poem, *L'Amica di Nonna Speranza* (My Grandmother Speranza's Friend), he successfully constructs a picture of the world of three decades past—the sentimental world of the Risorgimento—which appealed most to

his poetic imagination. Even here, however, he cannot refrain from ending on a forlorn note. While his constant state of ill health did much to create the air of melancholy in his work, his critics tend to agree that it was not only the decay of his own body that caused this emptiness of spirit, but the decadence and emptiness of the world in which he lived.

Gozzano's fame rests largely on *I Primi e gli Ultimi Colloqui* (The First and Last Colloquies) published in 1911. In this work is to be found the clearest and most poetic statement of his thinking on the subject of death.

Published posthumously was a series of charming fairy tales, *La Principessa si Sposa* (The Princess Weds), and two volumes of short stories, *L'Altare del Passato* (The Altar of the Past) and *L'Ultima Traccia* (The Last Trace).

Contemporary Italian writers have been much intrigued by Gozzano's art. His *Opere Omnia* was published in Italian, 1934-38.

Little of his work is available in English translation. J. F. Nims translated and commented on one of his poems from the Colloquies in *The Poem Itself*, ed. by S. Burnshaw (1960).

ABOUT: Phelps, R. S. Italian Silhouettes. [In Italian—see studies by F. Biondolillo, B. Croce (in La Critica, 1936), W. Vaccari.]

E. DE P.

*GOZZI, Count CARLO (December 13, 1720-April 4, 1806), Italian dramatist, was born in Venice, one of eleven sons of Jacopo Antonio Gozzi and Angela Tiepolo, Venetian aristocrat of the same family as the two famed painters. As a child of high-born but impoverished parents, who were constantly dodging creditors and who provided their children with only the most haphazard education, Carlo early learned the ways of the elegant ne'er-do-well. According to his account he began writing poems at the age of nine. His later theatrical success was foreshadowed by a talent he developed for mimicry in performances put on at home with his brothers, in which they satirized their own and neighboring families.

At the age of sixteen, Carlo joined the army in Dalmatia, where he served for three years, earning the grade of cadet of cavalry. He returned home to a squabbling family. Never too stable, the Gozzi family soon broke up because of poverty, the children left to their own devices. Carlo and his talented if erratic brother Gasparo sought fame in let-

* gŏt′ tsē

353

ters, becoming conspicuous first as satirists and literary controversialists. Both joined the Granelleschi Society, a literary academy established in 1740 with the avowed purpose of preserving the language and style of the great literary masters from Dante through the fifteenth century. Gasparo in time gained fame as a poet and essayist. (He has been called "the Italian Addison" because of his literary journalism.) Carlo established himself as a leading wit of the Granelloni.

The most famous target of Gozzi's barbs was the popular Venetian dramatist Carlo Goldoni. Goldoni's name was anathema to Count Gozzi on two counts—his attempts to displace the *commedia dell' arte,* dear to the defenders of Italy's literary traditions, and his caricatures of the nobility in his realistic bourgeois comedies. In Gozzi's famous lampoon *Il Teatro Comico all' Osteria del Pelligrono,* written in 1750 (Goldoni's most prolific year), Goldoni was described as a Cerberus spouting nonsense from all his three heads, and a drunkard besides.

It was his hatred of Goldoni and another playwright, Pietro Chiari, that accidentally plunged Gozzi into theatrical success of his own. In his swaggering fashion he wagered that by the power of his wit he could draw away his rivals' audiences even by a play on the most childish subject imaginable. The result was the grotesque fantasy *L'Amore delle Tre Melarance* (The Love of Three Oranges), derived from his childhood reading in Basile's *Lo Cunto de li Cunti,* a popular collection of fables. At its première on January 25, 1761, *L'Amore* proved to be an enormous success. Using the familiar characters from the *commedia dell' arte* in more bizarre situations, Gozzi dazzled Venetian audiences with a pseudo-exoticism new to the theatre. Undoubtedly their amusement was derived in part from the parody of Goldoni in the dialogue and the caricature of him in the magician Celio as well as of Chiari in the wicked fairy Fata Morgana.

Gozzi's success stimulated him to turn out in rapid succession the series of similar *fiabe* (fables) on which his fame chiefly rests: *Il Corvo* (The Raven, 1761); *Turandot,* the most famous (1762); *La Donna Serpente* (The Snake Woman, 1762); *Il Re Cervo* (The Stag King, 1762); *Zobeide* (1763); *I Pitocchi Fortunati* (The Fortunate Beggars, 1764); *Il Mostro Turchino* (The Blue Monster, 1764); *Zeim, Re de Geni* (Zeim, the King of the Genii, 1765); *El Augellino Belverde* (The Pretty Green Bird, 1765). These admixtures of nursery tales, second-hand

versions of the *Arabian Nights, chinoiserie,* and garbled Zoroastrianism, with their black magic, enchantments, curses, strange quests and ordeals, miraculous transformations, all enjoyed a tremendous but brief vogue in Italy, and later gained for their author fame on the continent.

Interest dying down in the *fiabe,* Gozzi later turned to serious subjects, and translated Spanish dramatists, particularly Calderón and Tirso de Molina. In 1777 a performance of his *Le Droghe de Amore* (adapted from Molina) rocked Venetian society. Intensely jealous of Pietro Antonio Gratarol, Secretary of the Senate, and his rival for the affections of the actress Teodora Ricci, Gozzi took revenge by caricaturing this officer of state in his new play. As a result, Gratarol became the laughing stock of Venice, and was forced to resign his position and leave the city forever. In his *Memoirs,* begun in 1780, Gozzi attempts a self-exoneration, none too convincing, for his part in this affair.

In 1792 Gozzi supervised the publication in Venice of his collected works, which amounted to ten volumes. The fall of the Venetian Republic (predicted in his satirical poem *La Marfisa*) occurred in 1797, the very year in which he published his autobiography, *Memorie Inutile Scritte per Umilità* (Useless Memoirs Written in Humility). Egregiously mistilled, Gozzi's *Memoirs* are arrogant and vindictive—but nevertheless a colorful account of the turbulent aesthetic and social controversies in which he was engaged, and a most incisive revelation of the perverse, cantankerous personality of their author. His last years appear to have been troubled by nervous disorders culminating in mental breakdown. He died in Venice at eighty-five.

After the eighteenth century Gozzi enjoyed his greatest vogue in Germany, where his romanticism attracted in particular Goethe, Schlegel, and Schiller. Schiller converted one of the *fiabe*—*Turandot*—into a serious drama. *Turandot* also attracted three opera composers—Weber, Busoni, and, most importantly, Puccini. It is through Puccini's posthumously completed final opera, in addition to Prokofieff's delightful opera based on *The Love of Three Oranges,* that Count Carlo Gozzi is best known today.

There is no translation into English of Gozzi's complete works. *Turandot* has been translated by Jethro Bithell (1913). More recently, *Il Mostro Turchino* was translated by Edward J. Dent (1951). The best edition in Italian of *Le Fiabe* is that of Ernesto Masi (1885). The *Memorie* were translated by John Addington Symonds (1890). The best edition in Italian is that of Giuseppe Prezzolini (1910).

ABOUT: Lee, V. Studies in the Eighteenth Century; Kennard, J. History of the Italian Theatre; Nicoll, A. World Theatre; Symonds, J. A. *Introduction to* The Memoirs of Count Carlo Gozzi; Wilkins, E. H. History of Italian Literature. [In Italian—see studies by G. Aliprandi, G. Borgese, T. Mantovani and G. Ziccardi.]

R. A. C.

*GRABBE, CHRISTIAN DIETRICH (December 11, 1801-September 12, 1836), German dramatist, was born at Lippe-Detmold, the son of uneducated and erratic parents; his father was an officer in a house of correction. As a boy Grabbe was precocious and wrote his first drama at fifteen. In 1820 he went to Leipzig to study law and two years later to Berlin where he associated with some of the romanticists and also met Heinrich Heine. After an unsuccessful visit to Ludwig Tieck in Dresden in an effort to become an actor, Grabbe returned to Detmold and started practicing law. After 1824 he came increasingly under the influence of alcohol, but managed to write a series of powerful dramas. In 1833 he married Luise Clostermeyer, a writer ten years his senior. The marriage was an unhappy one, and Grabbe also had to give up a position as a military auditor. In 1834 he went to Frankfurt and later found refuge with his friend Immermann at Düsseldorf. In April 1836 he returned to his native city, and although his health was completely shattered, his wife refused to take him in. His death from a spinal malady occurred before his thirty-fifth birthday.

Grabbe's "Storm and Stress" life betrayed the tensions, the inner disharmony, and the disillusionment of his age. He shared with the bourgeois of the late romantic or Biedermeier periods the characteristics of detachment and contemplation, while the proletarian in him seethed with anti-idealistic, positivistic ferment. The conflicting, irreconcilable tendencies in him were industry, intelligence, and contentment on one side, and an untrammeled imagination and boundless intemperance on the other. His physical appearance presented a study in contrasts: he had small hands and feet, yet his movements were angular and awkward. Immermann described him thus: "A high forehead of Shakespearean splendor . . . large, wide eye-sockets with eyes of a deep, soulful blue . . . a delicate nose; up to there, except for the thin, sparse hair, everything beautiful. And from

* gräb′ ĕ

there on down everything ugly and confused! A flabby mouth . . . the chin hardly detached from the neck . . . the lower part of the face creeping back shyly while the upper part juts out boldly."

Grabbe's first play, *Herzog Theodor von Gotland,* a drama of youthful strength and horror, appeared in 1827. Tieck considered it a work of genius, but warned its author against the cynicism expressed in it. Grabbe's only comedy, *Scherz, Satire, Ironie und Tiefere Bedeutung* (Jest, Satire, Irony, and Deeper Significance) also appeared in 1827. A play in the manner of the romantic literary satire, it jests lightly about life and literature, with a slight plot and many now obscure barbs at contemporaries. At the end the author himself appears and caricatures himself and his *Weltanschauung.* The laughter in the play is "gallows humor," and the "deeper significance" probably is self-irony, skepticism even toward one's own skepticism. Like most of Grabbe's dramas, it is all but unplayable and was not performed until 1907.

Grabbe's other dramas are mainly historical. *Marius und Sulla,* a fragmentary five-act tragedy, presents the Rome of the revolution, the tragedy of an entire people. *Don Juan und Faust* (1829), a four-act tragedy, daringly attempts to weld together two great mythical-poetical-musical figures. It is a sort of psychodrama, meant to be therapy for its author, but neither of the characters is a whole man and both remain basically unredeemed. This is the only drama which Grabbe lived to see performed, at Detmold, with music by Albert Lortzing. *Die Hohenstaufen* (1829-30) consists of two five-act tragedies, with the conflict between Emperor and Pope as the theme.

Grabbe's best works are probably his dramas on Napoleon and Hannibal. *Napoleon oder die 100 Tage,* the first German play on Napoleon, appeared in 1831. It takes a favorable but not uncritical view of its protagonist. Realistic touches are stressed throughout; the idea of the masses as the bearers of the action is something new in German literature. *Hannibal* (1835) depicts the protagonist as the individual of genius who must succumb because of the inertia of the masses. Grabbe's last play, posthumously published and not performed until 1936, was *Die Hermannsschlacht,* celebrating the victory of Arminius over Varus in the Battle of Teutoburg Forest.

In his famous essay *Shakespearomanie* (1827), Grabbe registered a minority opinion on the bard and appeared in opposition to Tieck, demanding that the German drama take the giant step away from Shakespeare (whom Grabbe meant to outdo).

There is a Grabbe Society at Detmold which has been publishing a Yearbook since 1939. *Jest, Satire, Irony, and Deeper Significance* is included in Eric Bentley's *From the Modern Repertoire,* series 2 (1952).

ABOUT: Kaufmann, F. W. German Dramatists of the 19th Century. [In German—see studies by A. Bergmann, E. Dieckmann, O. Nieten, F. J. Schneider.]

H. Z.

*GRACIÁN Y MORALES, BALTASAR

(January 8, 1601-December 6, 1658), Spanish moralist, was born at the village of Belmonte, near Calatayud, the son of Francisco Gracián, a lawyer, and of Ángela Morales. He went to school in Toledo, where he met eminent preachers and men of letters. He joined the Society of Jesus at the age of eighteen, taking his final vows on July 25, 1635. This period of his life, preparatory to a career of teaching, was devoted to a rigorous education in theology and the classics.

His first publication, *El Héroe* (1637), somewhat like Machiavelli's *Prince,* is a handbook for the ideal leader. The prime virtue, on Gracián's scale, is discretion, or subtlety of understanding, as opposed to stupidity, the most prevalent of human vices. In 1640 Gracián visited Madrid, making his first acquaintance with court life. During the same year he published another treatise on the ideal leader, based this time upon an historical model, *El Político Don Fernando el Católico.* The following year he returned to Madrid and won fame as a preacher; while still there, in 1642, he published the first edition of his *Agudeza y Arte de Ingenio,* an anthological treatise on poetry, which he saw, characteristically, as consisting of "wit" (*conceptismo*) and ornament.

In March of 1643 Gracián was appointed rector of the Jesuit college at Tarragona. During this period a nobleman of Huesca named Lastanosa became his chief patron; Gracián spent much of his time conversing at Lastanosa's *tertulia,* or salon, in a setting of art galleries, libraries, and gardens. In 1646 Lastanosa financed the publication of his book *El Discreto,* which may be termed a baroque handbook of manners in the tradition of Castiglione's *Courtier.* Gracián's

* grä thyän′ ĕ mō rä′ läs

undisguised worldliness and wittily satirical sermons were by now winning him a bad name among his less popular superiors, who in 1646 sent him out as a military chaplain. In the campaign of that year against the French in Catalonia, he witnessed, and described rather cold-bloodedly, some of the more brutal aspects of seventeenth century warfare.

Back in Huesca in 1647, he published a new book which more than any other accounts for his international fame (Schopenhauer himself did the fifth or sixth German translation in 1861), *El Oráculo Manual y Arte de Prudencia.* This compendium of his earlier works is a typically Jesuit collection of epigrammatic advice and shrewd morality; even as it teaches one how to get ahead in the world it pessimistically implies the ultimate vanity of all worldly success.

A period of teaching and preaching led to Gracián's appointment as professor of Scripture at Zaragoza. He was now engaged in writing his most ambitious work, *El Criticón,* an allegorical *roman à clef* published pseudonymously in three parts (1651, 1653, and 1657). The protagonists are Critilo (rational, civilized man) and Andrenio (passionate, savage man). Having met on an island and convinced each other on natural grounds of God's existence, they spend the spring, autumn, and winter of their lives traveling and observing, with urbane detachment and biting satire, the vanities of European life.

Lastanosa and other powerful friends in Spain had been able to protect Gracián until he was denounced to the Jesuit General in Rome, a rigorous German disciplinarian. Despite warnings, a public reprimand, a diet of bread and water, and loss of his professorship, Gracián continued to publish *El Criticón* and even asked permission to leave the Order. He was exiled to Tarazona, where he died in disgrace at the age of fifty-seven.

Translations entitled *The Hero, The Critick,* and *The Manual Oracle* were published in England during the seventeenth century; the last has been retranslated under many different titles and is now available in the bi-lingual edition of L. B. Walton (1953).

ABOUT: Bell, A. F. G. Baltasar Gracián; Brenan, G. The Literature of the Spanish People. [In Spanish—see studies by E. Correa Calderón, K. Heger.]

E. L. R.

*GRANADA, Fray LUIS DE (1504-December 31, 1588), Spanish religious writer, was born Luis de Sarria, the son of a poor Galician couple who had settled in Granada after Ferdinand and Isabella had reconquered that Moorish kingdom. His father died when he was quite young, and his mother took a job as laundress at the Dominican monastery of Santa Cruz, in Granada, which he entered as a novice in 1524. Clearly of superior intellect, he received in 1529 a fellowship for advanced work in theology at the College of San Gregorio in Valladolid, where he spent several years. Upon his return to Granada, he began to win fame as a charming yet forceful preacher. His translation of the *Imitation of Christ* was published in 1536. About 1544 he was transferred to the monastery of Escala Celi, near Cordova, where he made progress in his devotional life by cultivating a mystic communion with nature. After eight years his fame as a preacher won him an appointment as chaplain to the Duke of Medina-Sidonia.

In the new convent at Badajoz, Fray Luis wrote his first important work, the *Libro de la Oración y Consideración* (1554). Like the *Spiritual Exercises* of St. Ignatius of Loyola this is a practical guide to prayer and devotion for the average Christian, with an essentially mystical emphasis upon communion with God. Its pulpit style is oratorically effective, with bold antitheses and down-to-earth anecdotes.

From Badajoz he went to neighboring Portugal at the invitation of the Archbishop of Évora. He became the confessor of the Queen-regent, Catherine of Austria, Charles V's sister. In 1556 he was elected Dominican provincial of Portugal; after serving his four-year term, he retired to the Dominican monastery of Lisbon, where he spent the remaining twenty-eight years of his exemplary life preaching, confessing, and writing his most important works.

In 1567 he published the definitive edition of his *Guía de Pecadores*, which may be considered as an ascetical supplement to his more mystical opus of 1554, rivaling it in popularity throughout sixteenth century Europe. It deals not primarily with prayer but with cultivating the virtues and avoiding the vices; it contains the most systematic exposition of Fray Luis' ethical doctrines.

In 1574 appeared the amplified version of his *Memorial de la Vida Cristiana*, originally published in 1565. The final section of this work, and the additions, treat primarily of the

* grä nä′ thä

FRAY LUIS DE GRANADA

love of God, with meditations on the life of Christ; they constitute Fray Luis' chief contribution to Spanish mysticism of the sixteenth century, being a synthesis of Platonic and Thomistic theories of love.

His final and most voluminous work, completed shortly before his death, is the 1900-page *Introducción al Símbolo de la Fe*. As its title indicates, it is concerned with explaining the basic dogmas of the Christian creed. It is divided into four books. The first, which deals with Creation, or the wonders of God in nature, seems Franciscan in attitude—if not orientally pantheistic—and is probably the most often read today of all Fray Luis' writings. With a good knowledge of contemporary science and a wealth of minutely observed concrete details, he demonstrates a divine order controlling the stars, the planets, the elements, the diverse structures and functions of plants, of silkworms, of bees, of man himself. The remaining books deal with the supernatural order, rather than the natural—with Faith, Sin, and Redemption. His style, despite a tendency toward the Ciceronian period, is direct and clear, expressing idiomatically a great fund of common human experience.

His death in Lisbon, at the age of eighty-four, reflected the serene quality of his entire life.

No other Spanish author was so popular in Elizabethan England as Fray Luis de Granada. From 1582 on, many English translations of his *Libro de Oración* were published, both on the continent and in England and Scotland; translations of the *Memorial de la Vida Cristiana* date from 1586; *The Sinners Guyde* came out in London in 1598 in a translation by Francis Meres. A two-volume anthology of his works, entitled *Summa of the Christian Life*, was published in 1954.

ABOUT: Brentano, M. B. Nature in the Works of Fray Luis de Granada; Peers, E. A. Studies of the Spanish Mystics; Switzer, R. The Ciceronian Style in Luis de Granada. [In Spanish—Laín Entralgo, P. La Antropología en la Obra de Fray Luis de Granada.]

E. L. R.

*GREGORAS, NICEPHORUS (1295-1360), Byzantine historian, humanist, scholar, philosopher, and theological controversialist, was born in Heracleia, Pontus. He lost his parents when quite young and was raised by his maternal uncle John, Metropolitan of Heracleia, who also introduced him to "encyclopedic instruction," then sent him to Constantinople where he came in close contact with the most outstanding theologians. He studied mathematics, astronomy, and Aristotle with Theodore Metochite, Prime Minister of Andronicus II, and won the favor of the Emperor. In 1324 Gregoras proposed certain reforms in the Julian calendar, but these reforms were not recognized until the time of Pope Gregory XIII, two and a half centuries later. In 1328 when Andronicus II was dethroned by his grandson Andronicus III, Gregoras retired to a monastery where he spent his time on astronomical and philosophical studies. He was called back to public life soon after and became friends with John Cantacuzenus, the first minister of Andronicus III. During this time he entered into a dialectical dispute against Barlaam for which he was rewarded by being appointed state teacher and was reinstated to his former offices. He became renowned for his dialectical skill and theological education and was appointed to conduct negotiations for a union of Greek and Latin churches.

In 1335 Gregoras became deeply implicated in the Hesychast controversy which began as a religious dispute led by a group of monks in quest of contemplative peace and inner light and developed into a fierce political and social struggle between the Hesychasts (party of the rich) and the Zealots (party of the poor). Gregoras defended the cause of the Zealots and found himself in opposition to his friend Cantacuzenus who was patron of the Hesychasts. With the triumph of Hesychasm, Gregoras was imprisoned in a monastery for two years and forbidden to write or receive letters. He spent his time writing in all fields

of scholarship but devoted himself mainly to his *Romaic History* which he had begun long before he became implicated in the Hesychast controversy. After the downfall of Cantacuzenus in 1355, Gregoras was released and he completed his *Romaic History*.

Gregoras left many writings which, with a few exceptions, still remain unpublished. Among them are a plan for the reform of the calendar, biographies of his uncle and the martyr Codratus of Antioch, funeral orations on Theodore Metochite and the Emperors Andronicus II and III, commentaries on the wanderings of Odysseus, tracts on orthography and words of doubtful meaning, a philosophical dialogue called *Florentius, or Concerning Wisdom,* astronomical treatises on the date of Easter and preparation of the astrolabe, and an extensive correspondence.

His *Romaic History,* for which he is chiefly remembered, consists of thirty-seven books which start at 1204 but cover his own time (1320-59). The epoch of Nicene, the Latin Empires, the first four Palaeologi, and John Cantacuzenus are treated in detail. The hero of the first fifteen books which he had completed before the Hesychast controversy is John Cantacuzenus. In his later books, Gregoras presents his former friend as a participant of the religious dispute in which he too was involved and they naturally reflect his sympathies and bias. Krumbacher calls the *Romaic History* "a subjectively painted picture of an imposing ecclesiastical process of fermentation." Actually, the *Romaic History* and *The Histories* of John Cantacuzenus supplement each other and should be read together.

The *Romaic History* is an authentic chronicle of fourteenth century Byzantium and in spite of its unconcealed personal bias reveals at once the variety and extent of Gregoras' knowledge, his skill in dialectics, and his strength of character. Most scholars are agreed that Gregoras was superior to all of the eminent men of the Byzantium of the Palaeologian epoch and compare him to the best representatives of the Western Renaissance. Krumbacher calls Gregoras "the greatest polyhistor of the last two centuries of Byzantium."

ABOUT: Baynes, N. H. Byzantine Studies and Other Essays; Hart, T. *in* Journal of Ecclesiastical History, II (1951); Hussey, J. M. The Byzantine World, also Church Learning in the Byzantine Empire; Sandys, E. History of Classical Scholarship, I.

R. D.

* grĕg' ō răs

*GREGOROVIUS, FERDINAND ADOLF (January 19, 1821-May 1, 1891), German historian, novelist, translator, poet, and dramatist, was born in the East Prussian city of Neidenburg, the son of a district councilor. He entered the University of Königsberg in 1838 to study theology at his father's wish but, feeling no inward call to this profession, took his doctorate in philosophy in 1843. After working as a private tutor in Germany, he lived from 1852 to 1874 in Italy, dedicated to historical and literary endeavors. In recognition of his achievements in the field of early Roman history he was honored by being made a citizen of Rome. In 1875, following his election to membership in the Bavarian Academy of Sciences, he settled in Munich, where he remained until his death.

Gregorovius began his literary career with the contemporary social novels *Konrad Siebenhaars Höllenbriefe an seine Lieben Freunde in Deutschland* (1843), which appeared under the pseudonym Ferdinand Fuchsmund, and *Werdomar und Wladislaw aus der Wüste* (1845). The revolution of 1848 revived his sympathies for the Poles, whose uprisings of 1830-31 formed one of the most memorable experiences of his youth, and he published the series of essays *Die Idee des Polentums* (1848) as well as a collection of *Polen- und Magyarenlieder* (1849). In 1851 he completed his first major historical work, *Geschichte des Römischen Kaisers Hadrian und seiner Zeit*, which was subsequently rewritten under the title *Der Kaiser Hadrian* (1884). He also produced the historical tragedy *Der Tod des Tiberius* (1851).

In Italy Gregorovius supported himself entirely by his pen. His first book, *Corsica* (1854), contained a series of sketches based on his travels on this island. Many of the political, historical, and literary essays as well as travelogues and translations completed during this extremely productive period were later collected under the title *Wanderjahre in Italien* (5 vols., 1856-77). On the basis of his historical studies Gregorovius became convinced that a close connection existed between geography and history and that the character of a nation was determined largely by its environment. This thesis, which was first utilized in *Euphorion* (1858), a narrative treating the fall of Pompeii, became the characteristic approach of all his later historical works, including his major contribution *Geschichte der Stadt Rom im Mittelalter* (8 vols., 1859-73). Although this monu-

mental study, which traces the history of Rome from the fourth century A.D. to the death of Pope Clement VII in 1534, was slow to win critical and scholarly acclaim, it is now regarded as one of the most authoritative commentaries on this period.

After concluding the volume *Lucrezia Borgia* (1874), Gregorovius felt that his life's work in Italy was finished. He dedicated himself henceforth to the study of ancient Greece and completed as his final significant accomplishment *Geschichte der Stadt Athen im Mittelalter* (1889). His *Gedichte* (1891) and his Roman diaries, *Römische Tagebücher* (1892), were published posthumously.

Corsica was translated by A. Muir in 1855, *Die Insul Capri* by L. Clarke in 1879, and *Der Kaiser Hadrian* by M. E. Robinson in 1898. A. Hamilton translated *History of the City of Rome in the Middle Ages* (1900-09). *Lateinische Sommer* was translated under the title *Latian Summers* by D. Roberts in 1902. G. W. Hamilton translated *Römische Tagebücher* as *The Roman Journals* in 1917 and *Siziliana* in 1914. *Lucrezia Borgia* was translated by J. L. Garner in 1948.

ABOUT: [In German—see studies by J. Hönig, F. X. Kraus, and H. Simonsfeld (A.D.B.).]

D. G. D.

*grä gō rō' vē ōŏs

*GRIBOYEDOV, ALEXANDER SERGEYEVICH (January 15, 1795-February 11, 1829), Russian playwright, came from an ancient, aristocratic family. He was born in Moscow and although his family had great financial difficulties, he was given an excellent education. An extremely gifted boy, he entered Moscow University at the age of thirteen; there he studied philology, science, and law. Besides his own language, he mastered French, German, English, and Italian. He was also considered an excellent pianist. Pushkin, who regarded him as one of the most cultured Europeans of his times, wrote that "his melancholy character, his embittered intelligence, his good nature, the weaknesses and vices themselves . . . everything was uncommonly attractive in him."

After several years of voluntary military service, Griboyedov joined the Foreign Office in St. Petersburg, where he mixed freely in theatrical and literary circles. In 1818, he left this center of cultural activity to become secretary of a diplomatic mission to Persia. In Persia Griboyedov studied Oriental and ancient languages as well as political science. There, in 1828, he married Princess Nina Chavchavadze, a sixteen-year-old Georgian girl. As Russian Minister to Persia he went

*gryĭ bŭ yä' dôf

to Tabriz where he was to supervise the execution of a severe peace treaty with the Persians. Difficulties related to this treaty took him to Teheran in 1829, where during negotiations with the Shah he and almost the entire Russian mission were murdered by the Persians. His wife, who had remained in Tabriz, bore him a child who lived but a few hours.

While abroad, in 1820-21, he began writing *Gore ot Uma* (*Woe from Wit*), his major literary production, and completed it in 1823 during a stay in St. Petersburg. (The work has also been translated as *'Tis Folly to Be Wise* and *The Misfortune of Being Clever*.) Heavy censorship permitted only portions of the play (Scenes 7, 8, 9, 10 of Act I and the whole of Act III) to appear in a theatrical almanac, *Russkaya Taliya*, in January 1825. *Woe from Wit* was, nevertheless, well known to Griboyedov's contemporaries since it was widely circulated in manuscript form, meeting with extensive criticism both enthusiastic and adverse.

The play was not produced in Russia until 1829 and even then not in its entirety. This work, finally given a complete performance in 1831, has become an important part of the Russian stage and has been produced by such directors as Meyerhold and Stanislavsky. In it Griboyedov levels sharp criticism at the social and moral backwardness of Russian society and portrays the conflict between the old and the new generations. He describes the climate preceding the Decembrist uprising of 1825. Although Griboyedov was personally never involved in this event, he was sympathetic to the aims of the Decembrists and dramatized the unrest which culminated in the 1825 uprising. Written in the tradition of French classical comedy, *Woe from Wit* observes the unities of time and action, but not of place. It is composed in iambic verses of variable length. The play presents a realistic picture of Russian society, and the dialogue approximates colloquial language. Although the Russian of the time included many French words, Griboyedov uses a purely Russian vocabulary. The names of the characters, like those found in Restoration comedy, reflect their natures, and they are immediately recognizable by Russians as familiar types. A continuously popular work, it contained many verses that became proverbial. It has been translated into German (*Leiden durch Bildung*, 1831), into French (*Le Malheur d'Avoir de l'Esprit*, 1884), into English in 1857, into Polish (1857) and other Slavic languages and is also available in several

Oriental languages. (As recently as October 1960 Premier Khrushchev quoted a line from it, "Could you not find some road which would be much further away for your walks?" in reference to American reconnaissance flights over the U.S.S.R.)

In the years preceding his diplomatic career, he wrote several other plays, among them a few in collaboration with other writers: *One's Own Family or The Married Fiancée* was written in collaboration with A. A. Shahorski and N. I. Khmelnitski. Griboyedov also wrote some lyric verse and some excellent letters. The complete works of Griboyedov, with facsimiles, photographs and interesting critical and bibliographical commentaries, were published by the Academy Library of Russian Writers in 1933.

Woe from Wit is most accessible in English in the translation by Sir Bernard Pares; under the title *The Mischief of Being Clever* it appears in D. S. Mirsky's *Masterpieces of the Slavonic Literatures* (1925); under the title *Wit Works Woe* it appears in G. R. Noyes' *Masterpieces of the Russian Drama* (1933).

ABOUT: Oxford Slavonic Papers, VIII (1958).

Y. L.

*GRIGORIEV, APOLLON ALEXANDROVICH (1822-September 25, 1864),

Russian critic and poet, was born near Moscow of a family of land-owners. His father was a member of the judiciary, his mother, the daughter of one of the bonded servants of the Grigorievs. Grigoriev received all of his early education at home, but thanks to an uncommonly retentive memory and an aptitude for languages, he was prepared to enter Moscow University at the age of seventeen. His principal interests there were philosophy and poetry.

Before he was twenty-one he had been graduated *magna cum laude* and was given the position of secretary to the board of the university, a post for which he was fitted neither by temperament nor training. He was subsequently installed as university librarian and during his brief tenure in this office contributed articles to Moscow periodicals, notably to *Moskvityanin* (The Muskovite) under the *nom de plume* "Trismegistov."

In 1844 he moved to St. Petersburg where he devoted himself entirely to writing and translation. He published a volume of verse, wrote a play, started a novel and did translations from French (Béranger) and German (Lessing). In the opinion of the St. Peters-

* gryĭ gŭr' yĕf

burg critics, Grigoriev was "looking for a way, and not finding it."

In 1848 the young author returned to Moscow, convinced that his "dreamer period was over," and began working toward his career as publicist on the *Moskvityanin*. In Moscow he married Lydia Fedorovna Korsh, who by 1852 had borne him three sons, one of whom died in childhood.

By 1851 the old direction of *Moskvityanin* had passed into the hands of "the young editorial board," led by Grigoriev, Pisemsky, and Ostrovsky whose more progressive Slavophilism contrasted sharply with the former policy. Conflicts with the publisher of the magazine *Pogodin*, the death of his mother (1854), and his own nature all militated against Grigoriev's success. His wife came from a family noted for its Western sympathies which did not approve of Grigoriev's passionate Slavophile tenets, and, in his own words, he was "a wanderer with no inclination to family ties, a nomad," and, moreover, he fell in love (unrequited) with another woman.

In 1857, when *Moskvityanin* was closed, Grigoriev left his family in Moscow and went to St. Petersburg where he tried to find work with other publications. But the Westernized periodicals in that city had little sympathy for the prophet of Ostrovsky, and he was eventually reduced to taking a job as tutor in the family of Prince Troubetzkoy. His travels abroad with the family did not alter his faith in a separate "way" for Russia based on the Russian "soul," but, in his words, "I only became less of a fanatic." Evidently he was unchanged in other ways as well, because his break with the Troubetzkoys and sudden return to Russia is described by Mirsky as "one of the most notorious scandals of his generally scandalous life."

Avoiding his family, he once again tried St. Petersburg where, in 1860 he came in contact with N. N. Strakhov and the brothers Dostoevsky, who invited him back to Moscow as literary critic on their new periodical *Vremia* (Time). He wrote a number of articles including "Western Tendencies in Russian Literature" and "Belinsky and Negativism in Literature," and seemed to be doing well. But he became entangled in debt and fled to the remote settlement of Orenburg where he spent a miserable period as instructor in literature at the local military school.

Back in St. Petersburg in 1863 he wrote his most significant work, "My Literary and Moral Wanderings," a cultural and critical autobiography. The work was at first sup-

pressed but was published in 1864 in the Dostoevskys' magazine *Vremia*. Grigoriev's muddled financial condition soon landed him in debtors' prison, and he died only a few days after his release in 1864.

Contemporary estimates of Grigoriev's thought and work are critical of his Slavophile outlook: "The people he stood for were not the real people of Russia . . . but the backward strata who purportedly represented 'the old eternal Russia' untouched by the 'false front of civilization'" (Soviet Encyclopedia). Belinsky said of Grigoriev's verse that it "reveals occasional flashes of poetry, but the kind of poetry that comes from the mind. . . . His verse at times is strong and beautiful, but only . . . when used in satirical denunciation." Grigoriev's collected poems were published by the poet Alexander Blok in 1915-16.

My Literary and Moral Wanderings was published in English translation in 1961.

ABOUT: Matlaw, R. E. *Introduction to* My Literary and Moral Wanderings (1961).

L. R. & H. H.

*GRILLPARZER, FRANZ** (January 15, 1791-January 21, 1872), Austrian dramatist, poet, and short-story writer, was born in Vienna, the son of Wenzel Grillparzer, an unsuccessful lawyer, who died in 1809 in straitened circumstances. The boy inherited his father's stern, unsentimental personality, while from his mother Marianne, who was devoted to music, he was endowed with imagination and artistic leanings. He also received from his mother the tendency toward moodiness and depression which caused her to take her own life in 1819. This antithetical heredity is the key to understanding Grillparzer's writings and his unhappy life. As he himself once said: "Within me live two completely differentiated beings. A poet of a supreme and most precipitate fantasy and a matter-of-fact person of the coldest and most obstinate type."

Following an irregular early education, Grillparzer studied law at the University of Vienna, although he had no desire to make this his profession. He supported himself and his family by working as a tutor in the homes of wealthy families, until in 1813 he accepted a civil service appointment. He continued this employment even after the successful beginnings of his literary career in 1817. Because he inadvertently offended the conservative court by a poem, *Camp Vaccino*

* grĭl′ pär tsĕr

361

matically to the other works of this tradition. The play had great success as did also his next attempt, the classical tragedy *Sappho* (1818). Here Grillparzer renounced the use of those purely theatrical effects which had been criticized in *Die Ahnfrau* and, following the model of Goethe's *Tasso*, produced a tragedy noted for its masterful dramatic technique, psychological refinement, and beauty of verse. *Sappho*, which depicts the theme of renunciation in the life of the Lesbian poetess, is one of Grillparzer's greatest works, and in his own day carried his fame as far as England, where Byron enthusiastically praised the unknown Austrian writer.

A second classical theme formed the source of his next work, *Das Goldene Vliess* (1818-20), which is the finest dramatic treatment of the legend of Jason and Medea. The material was treated in the form of a trilogy: *Der Gastfreund, Die Argonauten,* and *Medea.* Although classical in setting, the drama is modern in thought, for Grillparzer develops his characters as products of their environments, reflecting their different heritages in their manner of speech. An additional modern touch is seen in the fact that the conflict is not one of individuals but of two hostile and incompatible backgrounds.

Turning to the past of his own country, Grillparzer wrote *König Ottokars Glück und Ende* (1825) which depicts the struggle of King Ottokar of Bohemia against Rudolph of Hapsburg. This outstanding tragedy is one of the finest historical plays written in German in the nineteenth century and is regarded by Austrians as their greatest national drama.

After a second historical tragedy, *Ein Truer Diener seines Herrn* (1828), Grillparzer returned to a classical subject in *Des Meeres und der Liebe Wellen* (1831), a version of the tragedy of Hero and Leander. In 1834 he completed *Der Traum ein Leben,* a drama which he had largely written in 1817. This play, which proved to be one of his most popular, contains the theme of renunciation which figures so prominently in all of Grillparzer's works as well as in his personal life. Following the disastrous reception of his only comedy, *Weh dem, der Lügt,* which is today considered to be one of the three or four outstanding German comedies, Grillparzer submitted no further dramas to the theatre. After his death the manuscripts *Ein Bruderzwist in Hapsburg, Die Jüdin von Toledo, Libussa,* and the fragment *Esther* were found in his desk. Of these works, products of the author's maturest thought, *Die Jüdin von Toledo,* which treats the con-

(1819), which was considered blasphemous, Grillparzer was held back in his government career. In 1832 he was appointed to the minor position of Director of the Imperial Archives, a post which he filled conscientiously until his retirement in 1856. The outward course of his life was uneventful, broken only by trips to Italy (1819), Weimar (1826), France and England (1836), and Greece (1843). His later years were embittered not only because of the disappointments of his government career, but also because of the failure of his comedy *Weh dem, der Lügt* (1838), which was hissed from the stage by an uncomprehending audience. Henceforth he lived a solitary life of resignation devoting himself to a study of Spanish drama and Lope de Vega. Although he had several love affairs and was engaged for years to Katherine Fröhlich, his "eternal fiancée," lifelong irresolution prevented him from marrying. During his years of retirement he began to receive—"too late" as he remarked—the recognition and honors which had long been due him. He is now esteemed as Austria's greatest dramatist.

Grillparzer was attracted to the theatre early in life and began writing dramatic works in the manner of Schiller and Shakespeare at the age of sixteen. His meeting with the director of the Vienna Burgtheater, Josef Schreyvogel, who encouraged and assisted the young playwright, led to the performance of *Die Ahnfrau* (1817), a drama in the manner of the fate tragedy popular at this time, although far superior poetically and dra-

flict of duty versus love, has found the most enduring success on the stage.

Although famed principally for his dramatic works, Grillparzer also wrote a collection of verse, *Tristia ex Ponto* (1835), which elevates him to the level of the greatest lyric writers of Austria, and two outstanding short stories, "Das Kloster bei Sendomir" (1928) and "Der Arme Spielmann" (1848), the latter containing many biographical elements.

All of Grillparzer's dramatic works have been translated into English. The earliest version of *Sappho* was made by J. Bramsen in 1820 with subsequent renderings by L. C. Cumming (1855), E. Frothingham (1876), and A. Burkhard (1953). *König Ottokars Glück und Ende* was first translated by Thomas Carlyle in 1840 under the title *Ottokar*. Later translations were made in 1907 by G. Pollack and in 1938 by H. H. Stevens, who also translated *Des Meeres und der Liebe Wellen* as *Hero and Leander* (1938), *Weh dem, der Lügt* as *Thou Shalt Not Lie* (1939), *Der Traum ein Leben* as *Dream Is Life* (1947) and *Libussa* (1941). *Die Jüdin von Toledo* was translated as *The Jewess of Toledo* by G. H. and A. P. Danton (1913-15) and by A. Burkhard (1953). Burkhard also translated *Ein Bruderzwist in Hapsburg* as *Family Strife in Hapsburg* (1940) and the trilogy *Das Goldene Vliess* under the titles, *The Guest Friend*, *The Argonauts* and *Medea* (1942). H. L. Spahr translated *Die Ahnfrau* as *The Ancestress* (1938) and *Ein Truer Diener seines Herrn* as *Faithful Servant of His Master* (1941). A. Remy translated the short story "Der Arme Spielmann" as "The Poor Musician," as well as a selection from Grillparzer's journal under the title *My Journey to Weimar* (1913-15). Selections from his poetry are included in K. F. Kroeker's *A Century of German Lyrics* (1894) and Warner's *Library of the World's Best Literature*. *Mirjams Siegesgesang* was translated as a vocal score under the title *Song of Miriam* by W. Duthie (1869) and by W. H. Milmann (1877), and as *Miriam's Song of Triumph* in an anonymous version (1872-76) and by L. Novra (1881).

ABOUT: Burkhard, A. Grillparzer in England and America; Kaufmann, F. W. Dramatists of the Nineteenth Century; Lenz, H. Grillparzer's Political Ideas and Die Juden von Toledo; Nolte, O. F. *in* The Perspective of European Literature; Pollack, G. Franz Grillparzer and the Austrian Drama; Robertson, J. G. Essays and Addresses on Literature; Stein, G. The Inspiration Motif in the Works of Grillparzer; Yates, D. Franz Grillparzer. [In German—see studies by H. Gmür, F. Gundolf, J. Nadler, E. Reich.]

D. G. D.

GRIMM, JAKOB LUDWIG KARL
(January 4, 1785-September 20, 1863) and **WILHELM GRIMM** (February 24, 1786-December 16, 1859), German philologists and folklorists, were born in the Hessian city of Hanau, where their father, a lawyer, held the position of town clerk. Raised in strict adherence to the reformed faith, the two brothers felt a close attachment to each other

JAKOB GRIMM

from the beginning. The father died when Jakob was eleven years old, leaving the family of six children in strained circumstances. As a student of law at the University of Marburg Jakob came in contact with the great jurist Friedrich Savigny, who recognized his unusual perception. The study of Roman law under Savigny awakened in him an interest in the cultural life of the past. A year after Jakob's admission to the university his brother joined him.

WILHELM GRIMM

In 1805 Jakob accepted Savigny's offer to accompany him to Paris and to assist him in his work on a history of Roman law. Thus he gained practice in the exacting work of reading and excerpting old manuscripts. The separation of the brothers made them aware of their mutual dependence and they decided never to part. In Paris Jakob saw the famous minnesinger manuscript and compared it with Ludwig Tieck's edition of minnesongs which had first aroused his interest in medieval poetry. This decided him on the future course of his life. In 1808 he became private librarian to King Jerome of Westphalia with a considerable salary and ample time for the pursuit of his studies in collaboration with his brother, who, however, was frequently incapacitated by attacks of asthma. When after the downfall of Napoleon the legitimate ruler of Hesse returned to his throne, he had no use for a librarian. Jakob accepted a poorly paid position as second librarian of the public library in Kassel, where Wilhelm was secretary.

The years from 1816 to 1826 are the most important in the history of Old German philology. Though it owes its rise to the romanticists, their interest in it had too much emotional motivation to establish it as a science. The Grimms were likewise romantics; they too looked back to the remote German past as the time of greatness and cultural florescence. But it was to their advantage that Jakob, who did most of the scholarly work, was poetically not productive, while Wilhelm, of a more poetic nature, limited himself to the literary side of philology. In a common work on the two oldest documents of German poetry, the *Hildebrandslied* and the *Wessobrunner Gebet* they discovered alliteration or *Stabreim* as a tool of poetic representation. With their edition of Hartmann von Aue's *Der Arme Heinrich* they overcame the preoccupation of the romantics with the *Nibelungenlied*. The collection of fairy tales *Kinder und Hausmärchen* was undertaken with the sense of an urgent need for the preservation of these traditions. The first volume came out in 1812 and was at once an enormous success; the second followed in 1814. From 1819 the responsibility for the fairy tales was exclusively left to Wilhelm. Soon it became the most widely read book in the world next to the Bible.

The most important part of Jakob Grimm's career as a philologist began with his work on grammar. The purpose of *Deutsche Grammatik* was not to impose rules on the use of the language, but to extract from the language the hidden laws which it had followed in its development from the earliest times, to write a natural history of the German language. The first volume was published in 1819, but its most sensational discoveries came in the second edition of 1822, in Grimm's opening chapter on the theory of sounds. Here he describes the interaction of vowels (Ablaut, Umlaut) due to the principle of accentuation by which the Germanic languages differ from all other Indo-European languages. The section on consonantism contains the most famous of Grimm's discoveries, the law of sound shift, generally known as Grimm's law, which has remained the unshakable foundation of scientific etymology and the safest tool for the reconstruction of original languages. In the second volume and also the third (1826, 1831) he copes with the enormous task of building up the vocabulary of the German language from a certain number of basic word roots, of ascertaining their original meaning and following up the semantic changes of the words, formed from these roots, in the course of history. A fourth volume (1837), treating syntax, was never finished.

When Wilhelm Grimm married in 1825, Jakob remained a member of the growing family. Of Wilhelm's children Hermann Grimm won distinction as an art historian and as the author of a biography of Goethe. In 1830, when the Prince Elector of Hessen-Kassel passed over Jakob on the occasion of a vacancy for a position to which he was entitled, the brothers moved to Göttingen, where the duties of teaching were added to their library work. In 1835 Jakob published *Deutsche Mythologie*, an attempt to reconstruct the religious beliefs of pre-Christian Germans from poetry, fairy tales, and other folkloristic elements. When in 1833 the new king of Hanover abolished the constitution, seven outstanding professors, among them Jakob, protested in public. He was dismissed and had to leave the country within three days. Jakob's firm stand earned him the admiration of the public who helped the brothers enthusiastically through a lengthy period of unemployment. Finally a call to Berlin as members of the Royal Academy of Sciences secured for them ideal conditions for the continuation of their work. Now the brothers joined for their most ambitious enterprise, the *Deutsches Wörterbuch* (1854, 1860, 1862, etc.). It was not intended as a reference book for scholarly work or correct usage, but as a bulwark against the impoverishment of the language through artificial standards of timeliness and propriety. The Grimms wanted to make available the whole wealth of words, stored in the literature of three centuries from Luther to Goethe, to the user of the written and spoken language. The potentiality of each word is demonstrated by numerous quotations from writers of the period under consideration.

Though not everything the Grimm brothers proposed or conjectured has stood the test of closer investigation, Old German philology is on the whole still the continuation of their work; and their stature as individuals and as scholars has rather profited than suffered from the passing of time. What one of Jakob's pupils, the well known philologist Wilhelm Scherer, wrote of them still holds true: "The Grimm brothers have devoted the arch-virtues of the philologist, which hitherto was applied only to the study of the Greek and Roman classics and the Bible, to older native literature and to the traditions of the people. They have thrown off the arrogance with which philologists looked down at the unwritten traditions, folksongs, sagas, fairy tales, superstitions, nursery rhymes, etc. In the hands of the Grimm brothers philology has become a popular and national concern. But it also became a model for the understanding of all nations and for a comparative study of the spiritual life of humanity, of which written literature is only a small section."

The first English translation of *Kinder und Hausmärchen* was published in London between 1823 and 1826 under the title *German Popular Stories*. The translator was Edgar Taylor. The translation was praised by Walter Scott. Taylor's work was reprinted in 1869 and 1876. Of the numerous other translations Margaret Hunt's is considered one of the best. It was used in a Pantheon edition of 1947. Another translation, *The Grimms' German Folk Tales*, by F. P. Magoun, Jr. and A. H. Krappe, was published in 1960.

ABOUT: Gooch, G. P. History and Historians in the Nineteenth Century; Ker, W. P. Collected Essays; Poll, M. Grimm's Theory of the Origin of the Animal Epic; Wellek, R. History of Modern Criticism; New York Times Magazine, September 8, 1963. [In German—see studies by C. Franke, H. Gerstner, H. F. Rosenfeld, W. Scherer. On the one-hundredth anniversary of Jakob Grimm's death, a volume of essays was published in Marburg—*Brüder Grimm Gedenken 1963*, ed. L. Denecke and others.]

F. R.

*GRIMMELSHAUSEN, HANS JAKOB CHRISTOFFEL VON (1622–August 17, 1676), German novelist, was born in Geln-

* grim′ ĕls hou zĕn

hausen, the son of an inn-keeper. He attended the evangelic city school at Gelnhausen. He was soon engulfed in the Thirty Years' War and saw army service early in his life. In 1638 he joined the Götzische Dragoner. He became regimental secretary in the regiment of the nobleman Freiherr H. R. von Schauenburg. During the war he became a convert to Catholicism, as is borne out by his works, which also testify to the thorough knowledge of the various German provinces through which he had traveled during his army service. As part of these extended rovings, Grimmelshausen became familiar with the customs and dialects of many localities. His first literary endeavors stem from a period when he worked as a steward for the von Schauenburg family and for Dr. Johann Küffer. Eberhard Felsecken, his Nuremberg publisher, greatly aided and encouraged Grimmelshausen and facilitated his literary work. In 1667 Grimmelshausen became mayor of the village of Renchen in the province of Baden. He took an active part in the movement that resisted the expansionist policies of Louis XIV.

Grimmelshausen is known, above all, as the author of *Simplicissimus*. This work, although it derives partly from the picaresque novel, represents a genre uniquely its own in which truth and fiction are ingeniously interwoven. The book, published under the pseudonym of "German Schleifheim von Sulsfort," is the story of a vagabond, Melchior Sternfels von Fuchshain, who grows up among peasants, ignorant of his noble birth. When soldiers torture his "peasant-father," the boy runs away and comes to a hermit who is in reality his noble father. The hermit names the boy Simplicius and teaches him to read and write. The motley career of the hero includes performance as a "permissive fool," service attendant in a convent where he learns to play the lute and pursues serious studies, participation in the war, imprisonment, enforced marriage, renewed service as a musketeer, and the acquisition of a reputation as a "boudoir lover." At one point, Simplicius meets the Landstörzerin Courasche, a colorful character on whom Bertolt Brecht later modeled the heroine of his play *Mother Courage*. Simplicius marries a second time, learns of his noble birth, travels to Russia, becomes a Turkish galley slave, a pilgrim, and finally lives a life à la Crusoe on an undiscovered island.

Through all these adventures, Grimmelshausen succeeds in telling sharp truths under the guise of laughter, directing his satire against the sense of superiority that springs

365

from rational cleverness. The author himself expresses a fervent belief, at times close to mysticism, and evidences a deep awe of tradition.

Der Seltsame Springinsfeld, in which the old Simplicius meets a former comrade-in-arms whose wife has found a bird's nest endowed with magical powers, and *Das Wunderbarliche Vogelnest* are separate stories, but actually continuations of *Simplicissimus.*

Grimmelshausen was married to Katharina Henninger. He died in Renchen and in the records of that town he is mentioned as a man of great intellect and erudition.

The *Adventurous Simplicissimus* was first translated into English in 1912. A. T. S. Goodrick's translation appeared in 1924. One of his poems appears in G. C. Schoolfield's *The German Baroque Lyric in English Translation* (1962). Two tales, *Courage, the Adventuress; and The False Messiah,* were translated by Hans Speier (1964).

ABOUT: Hayens, K. C. Grimmelshausen; Rose, W. *Introduction to* Goodrick's translation of Simplicissimus, *and* Men, Myths and Movements in German Literature; Times (London) Literary Supplement, November 9, 1962. [In German—see studies by A. Bechthold, H. H. Borcherdt, G. Herbst, G. Könnecke, M. Koschlig, H. Roch, J. H. Scholte.]

E. J. S.

*GRÖNDAL, BENEDIKT SVEIN-BJARNARSON (October 6, 1826-August 2, 1907), Icelandic poet, novelist, and prose writer, who was to be infused with the spirit of romanticism to a greater degree than any other Icelandic poet, was born at Bessastaðir (near Reykjavík). The son of the great philologist and poet Sveinbjörn Egilsson, and the nephew of Benedikt Gröndal, the judge of the supreme court, whose name he bore, young Benedikt came by his poetic gifts and love of literature quite naturally.

After receiving from his father a thorough grounding in the literature not only of Scandinavia and his native Iceland but also of the world at large and especially of ancient Greece and Rome, Benedikt sailed in 1846 to Denmark with the intention of studying natural science at the University of Copenhagen. After reading extensively in natural science, philosophy, and literature for four years, he returned to Iceland without his degree. Several barren years followed during which Gröndal seems to have accomplished little beyond widening by extensive reading his already encyclopedic fund of knowledge.

In 1857 he returned to Copenhagen where he was introduced by a friend and kinsman to

* grün' dĕl

a Russian-born Catholic priest by the name of Father Étienne de Djunkowsky. Traveling to Kevelaer in Germany with Father Étienne, Gröndal was soon converted to Catholicism (1859).

While at Louvain in Belgium, Benedikt heard of Napoleon III's victory over the Austrians at Solferino. He promptly wrote *Heljarslóðarorusta* (The Battle at Hell's Fields), a rollicking burlesque of the political and diplomatic situation of the day. This piece is so witty and so full of boisterous good humor that it retains its popularity to the present day. Napoleon III of France, the Emperor of Austria, his minister Metternich, as well as the literary giants of the day, among them Lamartine and Dumas, appear in this delightful parody of the medieval romance of chivalry.

Returning to Copenhagen in 1859, Gröndal threw himself into his studies with energy and decision. In 1864 he was awarded the first Master of Arts degree in Old Norse philology to be granted by that old center of Danish scholarship.

He spent several years in Copenhagen writing articles on literary figures of the day, politics, and natural science, as well as folklore and mythology. He published at this time the life and letters of C. C. Rafn *(Breve fra og Til C. C. Rafn med en Biographi,* 1869) as well as a key to his father's monumental work *Lexicon Poeticum* or *Clavis Poetica Antiquae Linguae Septentrionalis* (1864). At the same time he edited and was the principal contributor to *Gefn* (1870-74), a literary-political periodical.

Gröndal returned to Iceland in 1874 and for the next nine years was a teacher in the classical high school in Reykjavík. Upon retiring from teaching in 1883, he spent the remainder of his long life writing, translating, drawing, and studying Icelandic fauna.

All in all, he published seven volumes of original verse, translated (in part with his father) the *Iliad* and the *Odyssey,* and wrote scores of articles on subjects as diversified as mythology and petrology, politics and aesthetics.

Benedikt Gröndal was unquestionably one of the most gifted men of his time. He was extremely well read, an excellent speaker, and a fluent writer. Indeed, his greatest defect as a writer and poet was an overly active imagination and a tendency toward flowery and lofty language. In his chosen field of natural science he earned the respect of his colleagues, but it is for his literary works, especially his mock heroic epics that he is best remembered.

In addition to *Heljarslóðarorusta*, his *Þing-vallaferð* (Journey to Thingvellir) still delights and amuses the Icelanders by its engaging good humor and its refreshing flights of fancy. These are only two of his many tongue-in-cheek parodies.

A collected edition of Gröndal's works, *Ritsafn,* was published 1948-54 by Gils Gudmundsson. His major works have not been translated into English.

ABOUT: Beck, R. History of Icelandic Poets: 1800-1940; Einarsson, S. History of Icelandic Prose Writers 1800-1940; Einarsson, S. A History of Icelandic Literature: Journal of English and Germanic Philology, XXXVI (1937).

L. B.

GROOT, HUGO DE. See GROTIUS, HUGO

*GROTH, KLAUS (April 24, 1819-June 1, 1899), German poet, who was born in Heide, in the state of Holstein, attended the teachers' seminary in Tondern, whereupon he returned to Heide in order to accept a position at a girls' school. Here he continued his education through assiduous private study, devoting himself primarily to foreign languages. As the result of over-exertion he was forced to give up teaching and retired for six years, during which time he composed the greater part of his poetry. In 1853 he went to the University of Kiel to extend his education and subsequently traveled through southern Germany and Switzerland. At the University of Bonn he was awarded a degree of Doctor of Philosophy for his services in the advancement of Low German, the language in which he composed his poetry. In the summer of 1857 he returned to Kiel where he completed the prerequisites for lecturing at the university. He was made professor of German language and literature in 1866, and in 1872 his salary was doubled through a grant from the Prussian Ministry of Culture. In 1875 he was awarded the Schiller Prize.

Groth's chief work is *Quickborn* (1852), a collection of poems in Low German, which was greeted with rare unanimity on the part of the critics as an outstanding poetic creation. This work was followed by a second part entitled *Volksleben in Plattdeutscher Dichtung* (1871). His poems in High German, *Hundert Blätter: Paralipomena zum Quickborn* (1854), found fewer admirers. This was also true of such works as *Vertelln* (1855-59), tales from the author's homeland, and the idyllic piece *Rothgeter Meisterlamp und*

sin Dochder (1862). In his epistolary essays *Briefen über Hochdeutsch und Plattdeutsch* (1858), he defended his Low German tongue as a literary instrument and argued against the view that High German had played a greater role than the former in the development of German literature. Needless to say, he met strong opposition to this view. Other of his works are: *Voer de Goer* (1858), poems for children; *Fif nie Lieder* (1866); a work on dialect poetry, *Mundarten und Mundartige Dichtung* (1873); the tales *Ut min Jungsparadies* (1875) and *Drei Plattdeutsche Erzählungen* (1881).

Translations of Groth's poetry into English are to be found in these anthologies: Elizabeth Craigmyle, *German Ballads* (1892); K. F. Kroeker, *A Century of German Lyrics* (1894); F. M. Mueller, *Chips from a German Workshop* (1867-75).

ABOUT: [In German—see studies by A. Bartels, D. Cölln, G. Seelig.]

E. K. G.

*GROTIUS, HUGO (April 10, 1583-August 28, 1645), Dutch theologian and jurist, born Hugo de Groot in Delft, was the descendant of a family whose members had for decades been leaders in society and many of whom had displayed a considerable taste for learning. In 1594 Grotius began his studies at the University of Leiden, where he followed the lectures of a number of scholars of whom Scaliger was the most prominent. As a true child of the Renaissance Grotius avidly studied the literature of the ancients. His first works, a Greek and a Latin poem, appeared in 1594. In 1598 he was a member of the Dutch legation to Henry IV of France who is said to have introduced the brilliant young man to the members of his court as "the miracle of Holland." This visit to France enabled Grotius to increase the number of his learned friends and to receive his law degree from the University of Orléans. Shortly after his return to Holland two larger works appeared, editions of the writings of Capella and Aratus. His first drama, *Adamus Exul* (1601), intended as "an exercise in Latin," reveals the humanistic orientation of the young author. In 1601 Grotius also began writing a history of the revolt of the United Provinces against Spain. In this period he also laid the foundation for a great historical-judicial work of which only parts have been preserved. *De Jure Praedae* was written in the first decade of the seventeenth century, after Grotius had established a law practice in The Hague. The work was re-

* grōt

* grō′ shĭ ŭs

367

GROTIUS

ambassador to France. His position was difficult, owing to Sweden's declining prestige and to Richelieu's indifference toward him. In 1645, returning from a trip to Sweden, Grotius was in a shipwreck, became ill, and died in Rostock, Germany. His body was entombed in Delft.

There are numerous translations of the writings of Grotius. Among these are several of *The Rights of War and Peace*—by C. Barksdale (1654), W. Evats (1682), W. Whewell (1853), A. C. Campbell (1901), W. S. M. Knight (1939), L. R. Loomis (1949). His *Six Books on the Truth of Christianity* appeared in translation by S. Patrick (1694), J. Clarke (1743); and his *Cathechism* was first translated by F. Goldsmith (1668), who also translated his tragedy *Sophompaneas or Ioseph* (1652). Other translations include *A Defence of the Catholic Faith . . .* by F. H. Foster (1889); *Introduction to Dutch Jurisprudence* by A. F. S. Maasdorp (1878), R. W. Lee (1926); *On the Origin of Native Races of America* by E. Goldsmid (1884); and *Some Less Known Works of Hugo Grotius* by H. F. Wright (1928).

ABOUT: Butler, C. The Life of Hugo Grotius; Knight, W. S. M. Life and Works of Hugo Grotius; Lysen, A. Hugo Grotius. [In German—see study by H. Luden. In Dutch—see studies by P. C. Molhuysen, W. J. M. van Eysinga.]

H. B.

covered and published in 1868. One chapter of it, *Mare Liberum*, appeared anonymously as early as 1609.

In 1608 Grotius married Maria van Reigersberch, by whom he had seven children. Beginning his career as a government official, Grotius was attached to the High Court as public prosecutor (1607) and later became the city clerk of Rotterdam and as such a member of the States of Holland.

In 1611, after a visit to England in order to resolve differences that had arisen between the English and Dutch trading companies with interests in India, Grotius became deeply involved in the political-religious controversies that raged between the Arminians and Calvinists. Taking the side of the Arminians, he defended the right of the government to interfere in ecclesiastical matters in order to keep unity. However, his efforts to conciliate the two parties had no effect. When Prince Maurits of Orange took the side of the Calvinists, Grotius was imprisoned (1618). He and his family lived in the fortress of Loevenstein until March 1621. During this period Grotius wrote on theological and judicial problems, and translated several Greek works into Latin. In 1621, aided by the family's servant, Grotius escaped the fortress in a bookcase and, disguised as a mason, made his way to Paris by way of Antwerp. Living for a while on a stipend granted by the king, he produced *Stobaeus*. *De Jure Belli ac Pacis* appeared in 1625. In 1634 Grotius accepted the post of Swedish

*GRUNDTVIG, NIKOLAI FREDERIK SEVERIN** (September 8, 1783-September 2, 1872), Danish poet, historian, linguist, educator, was born in Udby vicarage near Vordingborg in southern Zealand. His father was Johan Ottosen Grundtvig, a mild-mannered, conservatively pious Lutheran priest, authoritative but naïve, and a descendant of many generations of clergymen. His mother was Catherine Marie Bang, of a prominent old family. Nikolai, the youngest of four sons who all became priests, received his first instruction from his mother. At the age of nine he was sent for further education to a vicar, Laurids Field, at Tyregod in eastern Jutland, where besides the regular school assignments, he eagerly studied history, literature, and theology. At fifteen he entered the Cathedral School in Aarhus, from which he graduated in 1800, whereupon he entered the University of Copenhagen. After the completion of his theological degree in 1803 he lived for some time at his home. In 1805 he embarked upon a period of three years as a tutor at a manor, Egelykke, on the island Langeland. He studied the Icelandic sagas and mythology, Shakespeare, German classics in literature, and philosophy, and received strong inspiration from Oehlenschäger's works. The mistress of the manor enchanted him and he fell

* grōŏnt′ vĭg

hopelessly in love with her. Even though his love was unrequited, the new experience released his intellectual and poetic endowments.

Before and during his stay at Egelykke, Grundtvig wrote several treatises and essays on various subjects as well as poetry. His first important scholarly work was *Nordens Mytologi* (Mythology of Scandinavia, 1808), in which he pleaded the romantic conception of history against the rationalistic school and stressed the religious value of Old Scandinavian paganism. He wrote dramatic dialogues on Old Norse themes and made his name as a romantic author. In 1810 he went through a religious crisis from which he emerged with an orthodox somber faith and the calling of a church reformer. For several years he served as a priest, first as a substitute for his father in Udby and, after the latter's death in 1813, in Copenhagen. In the meantime he published a good deal of prose and verse, partly consisting of religious polemics. His best known work from this period is his *Verdens Krøniker* (World Chronicles) in three volumes (1812, 1814, 1817), in which he maintained that the history of the world gives real proof of the truth of Christianity and judged the peoples and epochs on the basis of their relation to Christianity.

In 1816 Grundtvig left off his ecclesiastical activity and devoted himself for five years to writing historical works and poetry and to translating, or rather retelling, Old Scandinavian chronicles. In 1818-22 appeared *Saxo's Danmarks Historie og Snorres Islandske Kongekrønike* (Saxo's History of Denmark and Snorre's Icelandic Chronicle of Kings), in six volumes. He wrote and edited the periodical *Dannevirke*, 1816-19, and translated *Beowulf*. In 1818 Grundtvig married his fiancée for many years, Elisabeth (Lise) Christina Margarethe Blicher, daughter of a vicar. In 1821 he became priest at Præstø in southern Zealand and the next year curate in Copenhagen.

In 1824 his emotional life was altered and to his faith was added a brighter and more optimistic note which he expressed beautifully in his poem *Nyaars-Morgen* (New Year's Morning, 1824), and forcefully in his polemical work *Kirkens Gienmæle* (The Church's Reply, 1825). He now made it his task to restore the heroic spirit to Christian deeds. His pamphlet brought upon him a censorship for life (lifted in 1838) and a fine. When he was forbidden to have his own hymns sung in his church he resigned from his priestly office in 1826.

Grundtvig made three journeys to England, 1829-31, from which he brought home new ideas, expressed in the revised edition of *Nordens Mytologi* (1832), in which he gave the old pagan mythology a Christian symbolical meaning. In 1833-43 he published *Haandbog i Verdenshistorien* (Manual in World History), in three volumes. In 1837 appeared the first of five volumes of *Sangværk til den Danske Kirke* (Hymnal for the Danish Church). This enormous work, of which the last volume was published after his death, consists of 1,431 hymns, including his own compositions. In 1839 Grundtvig became priest at the church of a Copenhagen hospital, where he remained until his death.

As early as 1810, Grundtvig had suffered a fit of manic-depressive psychosis and in 1844 he suffered a relapse, but he recovered and took a most active part in the national movement. He became an admired and respected leader of the people and founded the Danish folk high schools. His mental disease erupted for a third time in 1867, but his literary activity continued almost to his death.

In 1851 Grundtvig lost his wife, but in the same year he married a widow thirty years younger than he, Marie Elise Toft, *née* Carlsen. She died in 1854. In 1858 he contracted his third marriage with Countess Asta Turgendreich Adelheid Reedtz, a thirty-two-year-old widow of a landed proprietor and daughter of Count Erhard Krag-Juel-Vind-Frijs. One of Grundtvig's sons was the famous folklorist Svend Grundtvig.

English adaptations of Grundtvig's songs and hymns are included in *The Hymns of Denmark* (1868) by Gilbert Tait (pseud.) ; *A Book of Danish Verse* (1922) by S. F. Damon and R. S. Hillyer; *In Denmark I Was Born . . .* (1948) by R. P. Keigwin; *The Christian Science Hymnal* (1932). For a complete list see E. Bredsdorff, *Danish Literature in English Translation* (1950).

ABOUT: Davies, N. Grundtvig of Denmark; Gosse, E. W. Studies in the Literature of Northern Europe; Howitt, W. & M. The Literature and Romance of Northern Europe, II: Marias, J. I. Bishop Grundtvig and the People's High Schools in Denmark; Mitchell, P. M. A History of Danish Literature; Winkel Horn, F. History of the Literature of the Scandinavian North. [In Danish—see studies by H. Aronson, J. Elbek, M. Hay.]

A. J.

*GRYPHIUS, ANDREAS (October 2, 1616-July 16, 1664), German poet and dramatist, was born in Grossglogau in the province of Silesia. His father, of aristocratic family, died in 1621, his mother in 1628. After the death of his parents he lived with

* grü′ fē ōŏs

369

his older brother Paul, a pastor, who sent him to school in Glogau in 1630. It was necessary for him, however, to continue his education in the city of Görlitz since the former city was almost entirely destroyed by fire in 1631. From here he went to Fraustadt where he completed his early education and laid the groundwork for his outstanding intellectual accomplishments. In addition to Latin and Greek he learned Hebrew, Chaldean, Polish, and Swedish. While still a student he composed his first long Latin poem in heroic verse, *Herodis Furiae et Rachelis Lacrymae,* which was published in 1634. This poem was followed by a sequel the next year, *Dei Vindicis Impetus et Herodis Interitus.* Leaving Fraustadt in 1634, Gryphius went to Danzig where he supported himself by tutoring, and completed his studies at the *Gymnasium.* Upon his return to Silesia he was engaged as a tutor for the children of a wealthy noble family. Here he spent the happiest years of his youth. In 1638 the death of his patron and certain undiplomatic statements of his own forced him to leave his homeland. He went first to Amsterdam and from there to Leiden where at first he attended lectures at the university, but then conducted his own lectures on a variety of subjects. Following his stay in Leiden he traveled through the Netherlands, France, and Italy. In 1647 he returned to his homeland and settled in Fraustadt. In 1650, after rejecting a summons to occupy a professorial chair at both the universities of Frankfurt and Uppsala, he was named to the position of *Landsyndikus* for the principality of Glogau.

Gryphius suffered much from privation and hardship during his early years. The bitterness engendered in him by adversity was heightened by the seemingly eternal, violent war which plagued his homeland. The melancholy and bitterness which so strongly colored his personality could hardly escape reflection in his art. His seriousness of purpose and the majesty of his conceptions, however, raise him above the artistic norms of his age. The sonnet, in particular, appears to have been a form particularly suited to his talents. His *Sonundt Feyrtags Sonetten* (1639), composed during his stay in the Netherlands, reveals a deeply religious nature and demonstrates his mastery of the form which was later to be so abused in the hands of lesser German poets. The closed form of the sonnet with the great discipline it demands of the poet had the most beneficial effect upon Gryphius' poetic gifts. In his epigrams he attacked sharply the foibles and vices of his age. Few of his contemporaries achieved as much with the form of the ode as did Gryphius.

In spite of his achievements in the lyric, Gryphius' fame rests largely upon his accomplishments in the dramatic genres for which he has been called the "father of German drama." His tragedies *Leo Arminius* (1646), *Katharina von Georgien* (1647), *Cardenio und Celinde* (1647), *Die Ermordete Majestät oder Carolus Stuardus* (1649), *Papianus* (1659) are, to be sure, partially imitations of Seneca and the Hollander Vondel and are overburdened with nonessentials, but they are nevertheless compositions evidencing imagination, majestic language, and a truly convincing conception of the tragic quality of life. His *Carolus Stuardus* is a unique attempt to dramatize material taken from recent history. By means of effective satire and a lively comic spirit he attained excellent comedy in the plays *Peter Squenz,* which treats an episode also appearing in Shakespeare's *Midsummer Night's Dream,* and *Horribilicribrifax,* employing the type-character of the *miles gloriosus.* Of less significance are his two *Singspiele, Majuma* and *Das Verliebte Gespenst,* as well as his renditions of a number of Italian, Dutch, and French works.

The translations of Gryphius' works into English are limited to selections from his verse in: C. H. Dunn, *Hymns from the German* (1861); M. Muensterberg, *A Harvest of German Verse* (1916); G. C. Schoolfield, *The German Lyric of the Baroque in English Translation* (1962).

ABOUT: [In French—Wysocki, S. G. Gryphius et la Tragédie Allemande au 17ᵉ Siècle. In German—Jockisch, W. Gryphius und das Literarische Barock; Allgemeine Deutsche Biographie.]

E. K. G.

*GUARINI, GIOVANNI BATTISTA

(December 10, 1537/38-October 7, 1612), Italian poet and playwright, was born at Ferrara, a descendant of the Italian humanist Guarino da Verona (1374-1460). His father was a professor of literature at the University of Padua, and the young Guarini himself taught moral philosophy at Ferrara before he was twenty. His main career, however, was diplomacy. In 1567 he entered the service of Alfonso II, Duke of Ferrara, as ambassador and was sent on many diplomatic missions, traveling as far away as Cracow. In 1577 he succeeded his friend Tasso as court poet; in 1585 he was made state secretary. The honors proved to be empty ones. He was poorly

* gwä rē′ nē

repaid by the Duke for his services and, indeed, spent much of his own private fortune to maintain his position at court. Embittered and impoverished, he retired to a farm sometime during the 1580's and there turned to literature to write his famous pastoral *Il Pastor Fido* (The Faithful Shepherd) and a prose comedy *L'Idropica*. He married Taddea di Niccolò Bendidio, and they had eight children.

Guarini emerged from retirement only to suffer further rebuffs in Florence, at the court of Ferdinand de' Medici (who tried to force one of Guarini's sons to marry a cast-off court favorite), and at the court of della Rovere at Urbino. He returned to Ferrara and spent his last years in law suits and quarrels with his own children. He died in Venice, a disappointed old man quite unaware that the literary work which he regarded as slight and offhand would become one of the classics of Italian literature.

Il Pastor Fido was written in direct emulation of Tasso's highly successful pastoral *Aminta.* Guarini's work is three times as long as its rival and, though similar in form (five-act verse drama) and scene (Arcadia— with the requisite number of nymphs, hunters, shepherds, etc.), it is more elaborate and complex and less spontaneous and charming. "One may say that as against genius Guarini brought talent and industry," J. B. Fletcher writes in comparing the two. *Il Pastor Fido* is nevertheless a play of real merit and, indeed, in its own time (it was acted for the first time in 1596) was more popular than Tasso's play. It is full of the refinement, elegance, and grace so admired by the late Renaissance. The definitive edition was published in 1602, and it went through some forty editions in the seventeenth century and another forty in the eighteenth century. It was translated, imitated, and adapted in every European language, and its influence upon English literature was impressive—Spenser in *The Shepherdes Calendar*, Fletcher in *The Faithful Shepherdess*, and Milton in *Comus*. It was set to music by Handel.

The first English translation of *Il Pastor Fido*, "by a kinsman of Sir E. Dymock," was published in 1602; other translations include those of Sir Richard Fanshawe (1647), W. Grove (1782), W. Clapperton (1809). Excerpts from it are translated by William Everett in *The Italian Poets Since Dante* (1904) and (in Fanshawe's translation) in L. R. Lind's *Lyric Poetry of the Italian Renaissance* (1954).

ABOUT: Everett, W. The Italian Poets Since Dante; Fletcher, J. B. The Literature of the Italian Renaissance; Lind, L. R. (ed.) Lyric Poetry of the Italian Renaissance. [In Italian—see B. Croce's Storia dell' Età Barocca in Italia.]

*GUÉRIN, CHARLES (December 29, 1873-March 17, 1907), French poet, was born at Lunéville, in Lorraine. He was baptized Louis Joseph Augustin Charles. His father, Edmond, then an artillery officer, entered the pottery business; the family included wealthy industrialists and bankers. A mediocre student, Charles went to school at Lunéville until 1892. In the summer of 1892 he experienced an almost fatal attack of typhoid; one of his brothers died of the disease. In 1892-93 he attended the Saint Sigisbert *pension* at Nancy; he received a degree with a major in German from the university at Nancy in 1897, following a year of military service in the infantry at the same city. Instead of entering the family business, Charles devoted the rest of his brief life to travel and to poetry.

Guérin started writing melodramas when only ten; his first verses were composed at Wadelaincourt, the family estate near Souilly, when he was fourteen; his earliest extant verses are from his sixteenth year. While still in secondary school, in January 1893, he published at his own expense *Fleurs de Neige* under the anagrammatic pen name of Heirclas Rügen. That same year Guérin published privately a brief study of Georges Rodenbach, who wrote a preface for Guérin's *Joies Grises* (1894). The following year, Stéphane Mallarmé wrote a preface for *Le Sang des Crépuscules.* These verses show the influence of the romantic poets and of the Symbolists, especially Rodenbach. Derivative in nature, these poems seek the non-plastic, combining irregular forms with the traditional alexandrine; the influence of Wagner is apparent in the emphasis on musicality as a vehicle for the communication of feeling. Typical of the well-to-do Symbolist aesthete's affirmation of artistic exclusiveness, Guérin published at Nancy, between June 1897 and May 1898, *Le Sonnet Mensuel,* with one verse to a page.

Although contributing to many of the Symbolist periodicals (and some of his native Lorraine), Guérin did not linger in Parisian literary circles. He maintained an apartment in Paris and returned periodically to Lunéville, but spent most of his time in restless travel to Belgium, Germany (especially Bavaria), Italy, and southern France. Of medium height, pale, with a full black beard, he was in delicate health, yet worked diligently at his verse. A novel, "Roberte, ou le Péché contre l'Esprit" (1896), was never published. Guérin's fame rests on the volumes of verse of his second manner: *Le Coeur Solitaire* (1898), *Le Semeur de Cendres* (1901),

* gā′ răɴ′

371

L'Homme Intérieur (1905). He often re-vised his poems considerably. Guérin died at the age of thirty-three at Lunéville; a monu-ment by the sculptor E. Lachenal was erected on Lunéville's Promenade des Bosquets in 1909.

Guérin's mature, personal style embodies intimate feelings in fine versifying. As Henri Peyre de Bétouzet has said of him, "the faith-ful cult, the exclusive cult of grief [*douleur*] characterizes the manner and unifies the work of Guérin." Not at all pantheistic, but rather fundamentally Catholic, Guérin utilizes the themes of love, of the sadness of life, of the indifference of nature. Sensuality, sadness, and awareness of death echo through his verses, some of which have inspired various composers (see the bibliography in J. B. Hanson). Fernand Gregh felt that with his death the post-Symbolist generation suffered its greatest loss.

The *Mercure de France* published a collected edition in three volumes, with a preface by Henry Dérieux (1926-29). Ludwig Lewisohn translated a poem (from *L'Homme Intérieur*) in his *Poets of Modern France* (1918).

ABOUT: Contemporary Review, CXI. [In French—see studies by A. Bersaucourt, J. B. Hanson, P. Quinche.]

S. S. W.

*GUÉRIN, GEORGES PIERRE MAU-RICE DE (August 4, 1810-July 19, 1839), French poet, was born at the ancestral castle of Le Cayla, near Andillac (Gaillac), in the Tarn department. He was the last of four children born to Jean Guillaume Joseph de Guérin (b. 1778) and his wife, Jeanne Vic-toire Gertrude *née* Fontenilles (b. 1776). The family, of noble ancestry from the Rouergue, had resided at Le Cayla since the sixteenth century, and was in quite straitened circum-stances. Maurice's mother died of consump-tion when he was nine, and it was his sister Eugénie (1805-1848) who mothered him. Maurice was given a religious, Catholic edu-cation: after local studies he went to a parochial secondary school in Toulouse (1821-24), and then spent five mournful, uninter-rupted years at the Collège Stanislas, in Paris, followed by schooling in law. Although Guérin had misgivings about his faith, late in 1832 he joined the famous La Chênaie in-stitution under the direction of Lamennais, near Dinan (Brittany). Guérin studied languages there until the school was dis-banded by episcopal order in September 1833. The following year he tutored, studied for

* gā′ răn′

the *agrégation* (although unsuited for an academic career), published a few poorly-paid articles, and frequented Jules Barbey d'Aure-villy and his brother Léon.

Maurice had an unrequited love for his cousin Louise de Bayne, a courtship (1828-32) discouraged by the family because of his poor health. He had several casual affairs and a Platonic love for Mme Marie de La Mor-vonnais, who died in the early part of 1835. Later that year he met and fell passionately in love with the Baronne Henriette Marie de Maistre; but while infatuated with her, he married, in November 1838, Caroline de Gervain, a well-to-do Batavian Creole he had met the preceding year. Dark-complexioned, black-haired, thin, Guérin, who had long been ill, died of consumption, over-exertion, and dissipation, at his birthplace—not quite twenty-nine years old.

Guérin's fame is all posthumous and rests on the prose poems *Le Centaure* and *La Bacchante* (which was not completed), com-posed 1835-36. George Sand presented the former work and the poetic fragment "Glaucus," in the May 15, 1840, number of the *Revue des Deux Mondes*. In 1861 G. S. Trébutien published the collected *Reliquiae*, and the influential critic Sainte-Beuve did a study. Matthew Arnold introduced Guérin's work into England (1863). Although various translations appeared toward the latter part of the nineteenth century, it is the twentieth century that has been most appreciative: the Guérinian canon has been extended by his private diary or *Cahier Vert;* the correspond-ence, especially between him and his sister Eugénie, whose own diary and letters are of intrinsic consideration for the study of her brother; and the "Méditation sur la Mort de Marie" (i.e., Marie de La Morvonnais), which Albert Béguin considers Guérin's mas-terpiece. These personal writings reveal poignantly a fundamental melancholy and defeatism. The critical editions also include his not unusual verse, most of which is un-finished. There are many de luxe and illus-trated editions of the prose poems that testify to his appeal for bibliophiles and literary gourmets.

Guérin, according to Sainte-Beuve, ren-dered better than any other French poet a feeling for nature. His was an absolutely pagan and pantheistic spirit: Guérin ex-pressed, in lyrical and rhythmic cadence, the indissoluble fusion of his own sensitivity and the eternity of nature—his responsive centaur and bacchante are part of the landscape and its "aura." There are no "bookish" excrescences to mar the smooth flow of his prose. There is, equally for some, a religious vein, a happy blend of the Catholic and the naturistic, in Guérin's work, and Eugénie has emphasized that her brother returned to strong piety shortly before his death.

In 1937 Le Cayla became a museum devoted to the memory of Maurice and Eugénie. In 1933 a quarterly bulletin, *L'Amitié Guérinienne*, started publication.

Excerpts from *Le Centaure* were included by Matthew Arnold in his study in *Fraser's Magazine*, January 1863; an American edition of *Reliquiae* appeared in 1867; F. Fisher translated the *Journal* in 1867, J. P. Frothingham in 1899; *Le Centaure* and *Le Bacchante* were Englished by Lucie Page (Mrs. L. P. Borden) in 1897, and by F. S. Moore in 1899; *Le Centaure* was included by Stuart Merrill in *Pastels in Prose* (1890); a translation was given by G. B. Ives in 1915, in 1931 by E. M. Moore; *From Centaur to Cross* (1929) contains *Le Centaure* and correspondence, translated by H. Bedford-Jones and with an introduction by G. Chinard. Rainer Maria Rilke did a German translation of *Le Centaure* in 1911, Jean Remy one in Spanish (1919), and R. van Genderen Start one in Dutch (1926). Eugénie's *Journal* was translated by J. P. Frothingham in 1891.

ABOUT: Arnold, M. Essays in Criticism; Brooks, V. W. The Malady of the Ideal; Mauriac, F. Men I Hold Great; Parr, H. Maurice and Eugénie de Guérin. [In French—see studies by E. Decahors and B. d'Harcourt, who have also edited critical editions (1932 and 1947). E. Barthes has written on (2 vols., 1929) and edited (4 vols., 1924-34) Eugénie de Guérin.]

S. S. W.

GUERRINI, OLINDO. See "STECCHETTI, LORENZO"

*GUEVARA, ANTONIO DE (1480?-1545), Spanish moralist, was born in the village of Treceño, near Santander; his father was the illegitimate son of a nobleman, and his mother a lady-in-waiting to Isabella the Catholic. At the age of twelve he was taken to the court of Queen Isabella, where he received a medieval education tinged with humanism. Soon after the death of the queen in 1504, he joined the Franciscan Order, which had been reformed in Spain by Cardinal Cisneros. He was put in charge of various monasteries (Arévalo, Soria, Ávila). During the war of the Comunidades (1520-21), he supported the royal authority of Charles V; he was appointed preacher of the royal chapel and official court chronicler. In 1523 he served as a member of the Inquisitorial Council of Toledo, and later became the Inquisitor of

* gä bä′ rà

Valencia, where he baptized and preached to recently conquered Moors. He continued this missionary work in Granada, being named bishop of Guadix in 1528. When, in 1535, the Emperor made his expedition to Tunis and visited Italy, Bishop Guevara accompanied him as chronicler. He acquired a second bishopric, that of Mondoñedo, in 1537.

Guevara's first important work was published in 1529; he had been preparing it, and no doubt others as well, for several years previously. The *Reloj de Príncipes y Libro Áureo del Emperador Marco Aurelio*, as its title hints, contains two different works, one a treatise on the ideal Christian prince, the other a fictionalized apology for the Stoic emperor of Rome. Both in pirated editions and in French, English, German, Italian and Latin translations, the work was extraordinarily popular during the sixteenth century; its Ciceronian style reflects the aura of Spanish enthusiasm surrounding the Holy Roman Empire of Charles V.

Menosprecio de Corte y Alabanza de Aldea (1539) is a masterpiece of tautological rhetoric, built upon an endless series of balanced antitheses, all of which reflect the underlying *topos* of urban corruption versus rustic purity. English Euphuism is related, directly or indirectly, to Guevara's style.

Finally, the two books of *Epístolas Familiares* (1539 and 1541) reflect the Renaissance taste for the epistolary form, which resembles the essay in its informal, amateur tone and meandering freedom of theme. In a pseudo-humanistic fashion Guevara cites ancient authorities, which he does not hesitate to invent whenever convenient. His wit and rhetoric, never obscure and not without charm for the modern reader, seem to anticipate baroque mannerisms.

Antonio de Guevara died in the episcopal palace of Mondoñedo in 1545 and was buried at the Franciscan monastery of Valladolid.

In English versions, *The Golden Booke of Marcus Aurelius* in Lord Berners' translation dates from 1535, *The Diall of Princes*, translated by Sir Thomas North, from 1557; a fuller edition of the joint work was published in 1568. *A Dispraise of the Life of a Courtier and a Commendation of the Life of a Labouring Man* appeared in 1548, the *Familiar Epistles* in 1574.

ABOUT: Castro, A. *Introduction to* El Villano del Danubio; Underhill, G. Spanish Literature in the England of the Tudors. [In Spanish—Marichal, J. Voluntad de Estilo. In French—Cortes, R. Antonio de Guevara, Sa Vie, Son Œuvre.]

E. L. R.

*GUICCIARDINI, FRANCESCO
(March 6, 1483-May 22, 1540), Italian
statesman, political theorist, and historian,
was born in Florence of a long established
family active in public affairs. At sixteen, he
began the study of civil law, and his father
then sent him to Ferrara for further training; thence he went to Padua in 1502 for
two years' work under Filippo Decio. He
considered entering the Church, but, dissuaded by his father, continued the study
of law at the University of Pisa. Thus to
a strong measure of reason, common sense,
and probity, inherited from his family, he
added the sound training that led to his
theoretical and historical writings. Guicciardini's first work (1508) was his *Storia
Fiorentina,* left in manuscript; documented
from observed fact, it is elegantly composed
and arranged both rationally and chronologically; it includes powerful portraits of
Lorenzo il Magnifico and of Savonarola but,
despite its notable freedom from personal
opinion and legend, is far less distinguished
than Machiavelli's book on the same subject.

Guicciardini continued in public service,
in 1512, as ambassador to Ferdinand the
Catholic; he remained in Spain for over a
year, during the return of the Medici and
the election of Pope Leo X; his travel impressions appear in his *Relazione di Spagna.*
He then entered the services of the Medici
and held with distinction such public offices
as the governorships of Modena, Reggio, and
Parma, and the general commissary of the
Papal armies in Lombardy. Tempering idealism with practicality, he opposed the project
of freeing Italy from foreign domination,
and foresaw the tragic events of 1527, the
sack of Rome, and the fall of the Medici.
At about this time Guicciardini retired to
compose his dialogue *Del Reggimento di
Firenze,* in which he imagines a moderate
republic with guarantees of stability as well
as of general liberties. The new government
of 1530 declared Guicciardini a rebel, but,
seconded by the Pope, he returned to resume
his former responsibilities until forced into
exile again after the death of Clement VII.
His appeal to Charles V at Naples led to
the fall of Florence, but the old civil liberties were irrevocably lost. Guicciardini was
married to Maria Salviate. He spent his
last years, alone and forgotten, in Florence.
He died at Santa Margherita in Montici.

The basic difference between Guicciardini's
political philosophy and that of his more
notorious contemporary appears in his *Consi-*

* gwēt chär dē' nē

374

derazioni sui Discorsi del Machiavelli, with
rational and unimpassioned criticism of excessive reliance on abstract theory and on a
concept of repeated patterns of history, to
which he prefers free use of intuition and
recognition of circumstances. His last work,
Storia d'Italia, narrates events from 1492
to 1534, and is the first Italian history to tell
both rationally and elegantly the facts involved, objectively and intelligently selected
and sorted from letters and chronicles. The
Storia d'Italia avoids theses and abstractions
and, by mere recitation, seeks to determine
the immediate causes of events and the
personal motives of the actors in them. This
work was generally disesteemed at first, on
account of its frankness and skepticism, even
among men who admired the person of the
author, but it has grown in readers' estimation in recent times.

There are many editions of Guicciardini's *Opere*
and of separate tracts, and English translations of
Two Discourses (1595), the *History of Italy* by G.
Fenton (1599), by A. P. Goddard (1753), and the
Maxims, Counsels and *Ricordi* (1845, 1890, 1949).

ABOUT: [In French and Italian—see studies by
F. De Sanctis *(Nuovi Saggi Critici),* V. Luciani, A.
Otetea, R. Ridolfi, P. Treves.]

F. J. C.

*GUILHEM IX, Duke of Aquitaine
(1071-1126), sometimes referred to as Guilhem VII, Count of Poitou, Provençal lyric
poet, was a member of one of the most important dynasties of Southern France and
in his day ruled over territories larger than
those of the king whose subject he legally
remained. He became ruler at the age of
seventeen and spent most of his life in warfare against his neighbors or against the
Saracens. He took no part in the First Crusade but took advantage of the absence of
his brother-in-law Raymond IV of Toulouse
to seize some of his territories, which he did
not give back until 1101 and then only at
the direct request of the Pope. In 1101
Guilhem himself collected a large army, said
by some to number 300,000 men, and set out
for the East. The expedition was a complete
failure. The army melted away and the
remnant was utterly defeated by the Saracens. Guilhem himself barely escaped with
a few companions to Antioch. In 1102 he
was in Jerusalem, at that time in Christian
hands. In 1114 he made new attacks on
the territory of Toulouse and succeeded in
holding his gains for several years. Because
of his attacks on church property Guilhem

* gē lĕm'

was several times excommunicated. He was married and was succeeded in 1126 by his son Guilhem X. The celebrated patroness of troubadours Eleanor of Aquitaine was his granddaughter.

His *vida,* or biography, has little to say of his political exploits but mentions him as "one of the best men in the world and one of the greatest seducers of women." Ordericus Vitalis mentions the numerous songs he made about his defeats but the chronicler William of Malmesbury is less flattering. He calls him a blasphemer who denied God and tells the story of the "convent" he allegedly set up where he kept his numerous mistresses. Even if the story is not literally true, it accords well with his character which seems to have been a strange mixture of generosity, brilliant intellect, quarrelsomeness and profligacy. As a poet he is important mainly because he is the earliest writer of courtly love poetry and is frequently described as the first troubadour. There can be no doubt that in fact there had been other writers of such poetry before him and that his rank is probably responsible for the preservation of his poetry. Only nine of his poems survive, one of which is a serious account of his political life and sorrows. The rest are love poems of various kinds. Some of them are brutally sensual and far removed from the later courtly tradition, but others already have the ideas of distant, unattainable love and the deep sorrow of unfulfilled love, concepts much developed by later poets. He also uses the term *joi* in the technical sense of love's ennobling exaltation. As might be expected, his strophic form and rhyme schemes are very simple, consisting usually of a series of octosyllabic lines. He occasionally uses the *rimes rars* or words difficult to rime. Generally it may be said that the poet Guilhem is interesting chiefly because he is the first courtly poet whose work still exists.

His works were edited by A. Jeanroy (1913, 1927). Selections appear in E. Hoepffner's *Les Troubadours dans Leur Vie et dans Leurs Œuvres* (1955) and in R. T. Hill and T. G. Bergin, *Anthology of the Troubadours* (1941).

ABOUT: Valency, M. In Praise of Love. [In German—Studi Medievali VII (1934), Trivium II (1944).]

W. T. H. J.

*GUILLAUME DE LORRIS (c. 1210- c. 1235), French poet, was born in Lorris, a small village in Gâtinais, near Orléans.

* gē yōm' dĕ lô rēs'

Except that he was the brother of Eudes de Lorris, canon of the church of Orléans and that he died in his twenty-sixth year, nothing further is known of him. That he was clerically educated is obvious from his works. Guillaume de Lorris was responsible for the first part of the *Roman de la Rose,* one of the most popular and influential works of the Middle Ages. About the end of the thirteenth century, Jean de Meung (see sketch below) wrote a much longer continuation in a quite different spirit. The portion completed by Guillaume de Lorris consists of 4,058 rhyming octosyllabic lines.

The *Romance of the Rose* purports to tell a dream the author had had some five years before the time of writing. It is a highly developed allegory of the pursuit of courtly love, where all the virtues of the lover and all the qualities which stand in his way are personified. The poem opens with the typical description of the paradise garden as the seat of idealized love. Outside the walls are painted representations of the qualities inimical to love, but once the author has entered through a small door opened by Ease, he is in a delightful world. He sees a dance in which suitably paired allegorical and mythological figures take part. Unaware that the god of love is pursuing him, he wanders to the fountain of Narcissus and in the pool sees the reflection of a Rose. He wishes to pluck it but is prevented by its thorns. The Love God shoots five (allegorical) arrows into his heart, courtesy, beauty, etc., and the hero yields to courtly love. The Love God instructs him in its arts and tells him of the sorrows and condolences of love. Aided by Fair Welcome, actually another manifestation of the love personified by the Rose, he is allowed to see the rosebud guarded by Modesty and Continence. He is given a rose petal but his overbold confession of love causes Fair Welcome to flee. Reason now tries to make him give up the quest but in spite of his misery he persists. Again, aided by Pity and Frankness, he approaches the Rose. Chastity forbids the kiss but the intercession of Venus obtains it. The news spread by Slander causes the guardians to build a castle around the Rose and imprison Fair Welcome.

Here Guillaume breaks off, reluctant, as some think, to describe the actual winning of the Rose but more probably because death interrupted his labors. His work is almost a compendium of the artificialities of exaggerated courtly love, with its stress on manners and idealization and its rejection of sensuality. More than 300 manuscripts testify to its popularity, and it was frequently printed after 1480. A fifteenth century prose version increased its influence, as did numerous translations.

Chaucer is known to have made a translation but that at present ascribed to him is probably not his version. The best known English translation of the *Roman de la Rose* is that by F. S. Ellis, 3 vols. (1900). A more recent translation was made by H. W. Robbins in 1962. The standard French edition is that by Langlois.

W. T. H. J.

*GUILLAUME DE MACHAUT (c. 1300-c. 1377), French poet, was probably born in the area of Rheims. Documents have been variously interpreted to show varying social status and different dates of birth, but the name is fairly common and he was probably not of noble birth. In 1323 he became secretary to John of Luxemburg, King of Bohemia, whom he regarded highly. With him he traveled widely in Central and Eastern Europe, as can be seen by geographical descriptions in his works. The influence of John secured him considerable ecclesiastical preferment from 1330 to 1333—a chaplaincy at Houdain, canonries at Verdun, Arras, and Rheims for himself and a benefice at Montebourg for his brother John. He was able to keep only the office at Rheims for any length of time because of Papal orders against multiple benefices.

The death of King John at Crécy in 1346 gave him more leisure for poetry but he had to look for other protectors—Jean of Normandy, later the King of France defeated at Poitiers, then Charles the Bad of Navarre. When the latter was imprisoned for acts against France, he wrote him a poem of consolation (*Confort*) but must have broken with him after 1358. There is no mention of Charles in the list of patrons inserted in the poem *Prise d'Alexandrie*. In 1361 Guillaume is mentioned in a document of Rheims and he must have been there a great deal during this period since he was closely connected with the younger poet Eustache Deschamps. A connection with Jean, Duke of Berry, is proved by the latter's possession of a beautifully written copy of Machaut's poems which is still extant.

After a serious illness in 1361 came an idyllic and highly literary love episode with a much younger lady, who may have been Agnes of Navarre or Peronne d'Armentières,

which is described in a poem *Voir Dit*. From 1364 to 1369 Guillaume appears to have been under the protection of Pierre de Lusignan, King of Cyprus, who was assassinated in January 1369 and whose exploits he describes in the long poem *Prise d'Alexandrie*. After 1372 there is very little known of his life.

Beside those already mentioned, Machaut wrote several long poems, of which the most important are: the debate poems *Jugement dou Roi de Bohème; Jugement dou Roi de Navarre* (c. 1349); allegorical works such as the *Dit dou Vergier, Dit dou Lyon* (a "court of love" poem), *Dit de la Fontaine Amoureuse*, also titled *Dit de Morpheus* (1363). His greatest contribution to literature, however, consists in his development of the motet, both secular and spiritual, of which twenty are extant, many with musical notation, and of the newer lyric forms such as the *balade*, the *lai*, and the *virelai*. More than fifty of his *balades*, set to music, are extant, together with twenty-three motets for three or four voices, seventeen *lais*, and thirty-three *chansons*. Although his topics are largely conventional (praise of ladies, the sorrows and joys of love), his forms are varied and expressive. He largely determined the direction the French lyric was to take for the next century.

There are no English translations of the works of Guillaume de Machaut. Standard French editions: *Œuvres*, ed. E. Hoepffner (1908), Société des Anciens Textes Français, No. 57; *Poésies Lyriques*, ed. V. Chichmaref (1909).

ABOUT: Levarie, S. Guillaume de Machaut; Kittredge, G. L. *in* Modern Language Notes, XXX (1915); Thomas, A. *in* Romania, XLI (1912).

W. T. H. J.

GUILLET, PERNETTE DU. See DU GUILLET, PERNETTE

*GUINIZELLI (or GUINICELLI), GUIDO (c. 1230-1276), Italian poet, was born in Bologna, son of a judge, Guinizello di Magnano, and a member of the ancient and noble family of the Principi. Little is known of his life except that he studied law and succeeded his father as a judge in Bologna. He had a wife named Beatrice and a son. In 1274, as an active member of the Ghibelline sect, he was exiled from his native city. He died in exile, probably in Monselice, in 1276.

Guinizelli's fame derives from one exquisite *canzone*, translated as "Of the Gentle Heart,"

* gē yŏm' dē mà shō'

* gwē nē tsĕl' lē

and upon the praise given him by Dante in his *Purgatorio*. In all some twenty of his poems survive. These are love poems in the so-called "dolce stil novo" (sweet new style), poems which, in the spirit of the Provençal poets, celebrate the love of a noble heart for a beautiful woman as a step toward the contemplation of the Divine. "Al cor gentil repara sempre Amore," his most celebrated poem begins—"To the gentle [i.e., noble] heart ever repaireth Love." This nobility derives not from noble birth alone—

> Let no man predicate
> That aught the name of gentleness should have,
> Even in a king's estate,
> Except the heart there be a gentle man's.

It ascends at last to the judgment seat where the poet faces God and answers His challenge that he made "vain similitude" between his earthly love and the divine relationship—"Lord, if I loved her, count it not my shame."

Dante meets Guinizelli and Arnaut Daniel together on the Seventh Cornice of the Purgatory (Canto 26). He describes the former with awed respect as "Father to me and to my betters—all/Who use love's own sweet style and chivalrous." Elsewhere Dante hails him as *maximus* ("great") in *De Vulgari Eloquentia*, I, and *saggio* ("the sage") in his sonnet XX in *La Vita Nuova*—"Amore e cor gentil sono una cosa/Siccom' il Saggio in suo dittato pone" ("Love and the gentle heart are one same thing/As the wise man in his ditty saith"). Generally he is considered the most original poet of his time and the chief of the Bolognese school which includes Lapo Gianni, Cino da Pistoia, and Guido Cavalcanti. His achievement, J. B. Fletcher writes, "was to give truth and sincerity to a love-lyric which had been a literary pose."

Guinizelli's poems were published in Italian by Manucci in his collection of early Italian poetry in 1856. The standard English translation of his most famous poem was made by Dante Gabriel Rossetti and appears in Rossetti's collected works, as well as in many anthologies. For text and commentary, see M. Casella, in *Studi Romanzi*, 30 (1943).

ABOUT: Fletcher, J. B. The Literature of the Italian Renaissance; Lind, L. R. (ed.) Lyric Poetry of the Italian Renaissance; Rossetti, D. G. Poems and Translations, Part II; Valency, M. In Praise of Love; Wilkins, E. H. A History of Italian Literature.

*GUITTONE D'AREZZO (1225?-1293?),

Italian poet, was born in the ancient city of Arezzo, the son of one Viva di Michele who held the post of bursar in the city adminis-

* gwēt tō' nä dä rät' tsō

tration. Arezzo suffered much during the long struggles of the Guelphs and Ghibellines in Tuscany, and during Guittone's lifetime was deeply involved in the warfare between Florence and the cities of the *contado* (surrounding country). In 1249 the Ghibelline victory in Florence resulted in the first instance of mass exile from that city of the defeated party—a pattern which was to be repeated many times in this conflict. Guittone grew to young manhood in this atmosphere of fierce partisanship, and we know from his own testimony how completely he gave himself up to the passionate politics of the day. After the defeat of the Florentine Guelphs at Montaperti in 1260, Guittone penned an eloquent rebuke to the Ghibellines which resulted in his exile from his native city.

He fled to Bologna, experiencing there in 1261 the spiritual crisis which caused him to enter the Order of the Brothers of Saint Mary, called the Frati Gaudenti. He remained in Bologna with his fellow members in the order for twenty-four years. The poetry of these years bears witness to the devotion he brought to his calling; it is fervent with a zeal which sometimes becomes caviling. Before returning to his native Arezzo, he helped to found the Monastery of the Angels in Florence.

Fra Guittone wrote poems (*rime*) and prose (*lettere*) on political, moral, and religious subjects. His art was strongly conditioned by his pride in the distinguished history of his birthplace and in the traditions of Roman antiquity. In attempting to write Italian in a Latin style he stands at the very beginning of the Tuscan contribution to the developing Italian language in the thirteenth century. He was also the first to use poetry to express political and national motives in contrast to the chivalric themes of southern Italy. It was unfortunate that he took Seneca as his special model, for his prose turned out largely bombastic, while his poetry is a product of the intellect rather than the voice of fancy and the heart; he is a reasoner in verse.

Guittone's lot is oblivion: it remained for others to do successfully what he had tried. Critics feel however that the canzone beginning *Ahi lasso* ("Ah weary . . .") is marked by particularly passionate expression, and is perhaps the most noble composition which political belief could inspire in the thirteenth century. The great Florentine Dante, who rendered exceedingly perfect lyric poetry and made it exclusively Tuscan, was indignant that Guittone should be extolled as a poet, being highly critical of the harshness and barbarisms in his work. But perhaps in the extraordinary antipathy of the great poet one can sense the unconscious debt he owes to his modest predecessor.

A translation of Guittone's *Donna del Cielo* (Lady of Heaven) appears in *An Anthology of Italian Poems* by Lorna de Lucchi (1922). An Italian edition of *Le Rime,* edited by F. Egidi, was published in 1940.

ABOUT: [In Italian—see study by A. Pellizzari.]
E. DE P.

*GUMILËV, NIKOLAI STEPANO-VICH** (April 15, 1886-August 25?, 1921), Russian poet, was born in Kronstat, the son of a navy physician, and was brought up in Tsarskoye-Selo (near St. Petersburg). He was writing verse at the age of eight. His formal education began in 1895 when he was sent to a private school in St. Petersburg. In 1900 he was taken to Tiflis (in the Caucasus) where he continued his elementary education in the local grammar school. By 1903 he had returned to Tsarskoye-Selo where he entered the Nicholas *Gymnasium,* the principal of which was the famous poet and classicist Annensky who encouraged young Gumilëv to develop his talent for verse. His first book of poems, *The Way of the Conquistadors,* was published in his senior year. It was critically reviewed by Bryusov who was to become Gumilëv's model. Notwithstanding Bryusov's adverse criticism, the symbolist review *Scales* accepted poems and short stories by Gumilëv during the period 1906-09.

In 1906 Gumilëv was graduated from the *Gymnasium,* and he proceeded to Paris to pursue his education at the Sorbonne, studying French language and literature. In Paris he published a little literary magazine of his own *(Sirius)* which was the first outlet for the verse of Anna Akhmatova (Anna Andreyevna Gorenko) whom he married in 1910. During his vacation in 1907 he spent some time in Egypt and the Sudan, and was deeply impressed by the romantic atmosphere of Africa.

His second book of verse, *Romantic Flowers,* published in Paris in 1908, was heavily laden with the exoticism of the late nineteenth century French romantics. In the same year he returned to Tsarskoye-Selo to join with Annensky, Ivanov, and others in organizing the Academy of Verse, later to become the more pretentious "Society of Adepts of the Artistic Word" which by 1913 claimed a roster of sixty-seven poets. During the following year he took part in the organization of

* gŏŏ mē lyôf'

the review *Apollon* in which his most significant poetry was to appear. His column in *Apollon,* "Letters on Russian Poetry," was described by Bryusov as highly valuable despite its impressionistic bias.

After a trip to Abyssinia, he returned to marry Akhmatova, and to publish his third book of verse, *Pearls,* dedicated to Bryusov. In 1911 the Guild of Poets was organized by Gumilëv and Gorodetsky, and this became the center of the "Acme-ist" movement, a school of romantic realism opposed to the symbolists and impressionists in its stress upon vividly intense imagery based on the concrete experience of nature directly apprehended. During this time also Gumilëv developed the passionate chauvinism which he expressed in his call for Russian expansion into Abyssinia. (In World War I his poetry took on a Kiplingesque tinge of jingoist imperialism.) In 1913 he traveled to Abyssinia and Somaliland at the head of an expedition sponsored by the Russian Academy of Science. In 1914 he was the only Russian writer to enlist as a soldier (authors were exempt from the draft), and he was pleased to be placed in the Uhlans. By 1916 he had been twice decorated for bravery and was a second lieutenant in a hussar regiment. His "Notes of a Cavalryman" appeared regularly in a St. Petersburg newspaper. His fifth book of verse, *The Quiver,* appeared in 1916 as well as a long dramatic poem set in ninth century Ireland.

After the 1917 Revolution he was detailed to Salonika, but stopped in Paris where he remained until after the Bolshevik Revolution. Although he was completely out of sympathy with the Soviets, he returned to his native land. "I have hunted lions," he said, "and I don't believe the Bolsheviks are much more dangerous." He published another book of poems, *Bonfire,* in 1918 of which a Soviet critic remarked: "The October Revolution which destroyed the class to which Gumilëv was bound, strengthened his feeling of doom. The theme of despair and death . . . now received an even sharper treatment." His wife divorced him in 1918, and Gumilëv devoted the balance of his life to work in Maxim Gorky's ambitious publishing enterprise devoted to large-scale translations of foreign literature. Gumilëv worked in English and French, more or less aloof from politics.

The circumstances of his trouble with the authorities are obscure. He was arrested in 1921 on a charge of conspiring with counter-revolutionary White Russian guards, and after spending several months in jail where he seems to have succeeded only in convincing his captors of his guilt, he was shot on or about August 25, 1921. He is rarely quoted in contemporary Soviet literature, and none of his collected works have been published in the U.S.S.R.

Some of his poems were translated into English by Y. Hornstein in *The Abinger Harvest* (1945).

ABOUT: Strakhovsky, L. I. Craftsmen of the Word—Three Poets of Modern Russia.

L. R. & H. H.

*GÜNTHER, JOHANN CHRISTIAN

(April 8, 1695-March 15, 1723), German lyric poet, was born in the small Silesian town of Striegau. As a school boy he showed an unusual gift for versification, which brought him requests to compose occasional poetry; but his father, who had himself introduced his son to the world of classical literature, resented the latter's determination to become a poet. Günther's unsuccessful attempts to regain his father's love became the tragedy of his life. Deprived of all financial support, he plunged into the life of the vagabond genius, depending chiefly on the generosity of his admirers and boon companions and on his uncertain income. Though his gift was fully recognized and even earned him the title of *poeta laureatus* he failed in his efforts to secure the position of a court poet. Allegedly he presented himself to the prince to whom he had been recommended for the post in a state of complete drunkenness. Exhausted by poverty, disease, and social prejudice, Günther collapsed when circumstances forced him to give up the woman he loved who had inspired some of his best poetry. He died in Jena.

While Günther's poetry, with respect to form, is not entirely free from baroque formalism, he nevertheless represents an entirely new type of poet. In contrast to the learned poets of his time, who scorned any connection between poetic creativity and personal experience, Günther lives in his poems as the person he is, with all his virtues and defects. In anticipation of the storm and stress movement Günther extols the claims of the heart against the conventions and prejudices of society. His love poetry, combining tender feeling with unashamed sensuality, appeals to the modern reader by its veracity and sincerity. Of special interest are some poems in which he tries to explain the unfortunate course of his life by an analysis of early childhood experiences.

* gün' tĕr

Günther's highest poetic achievements reflect the discord in his nature, for they are concerned either with sensual pleasure—most of his drinking songs have been incorporated in the *Kommersbuch,* the famous collection of German student songs—or with his longing for peace in God and eternal life. In his religious poetry Günther came closest to the achievement of a personal poetic language, almost completely free from the pompous verbosity of the late baroque. Thus he prepared the way for Goethe, who fully understood Günther's nature: "A definite talent, gifted with sensuality, imagination, memory, gift of perception and representation, productive in the highest degree: in short, he had everything needed to create a second life in life through poetry—except character." Günther confirmed Goethe's belief that genius without character is doomed to failure.

Johann Christian Günther's complete poetic works were published one year after his death. Subsequent editions of his poetry are mostly limited to his lyric poems, especially to his love songs, his drinking songs and his religious verse. The standard collected edition, edited by W. Krämer, appeared in 1940.

Though all standard histories of German literature in English emphasize the importance of Günther as the most gifted German poet of the eighteenth century before Goethe, his work remains largely untranslated. Several short poems appear in G. C. Schoolfield's *The German Lyric of the Baroque in English Translation* (1962). A recent biography *Das Leben des Schlesischen Dichters Joh. Chr. Günther* by W. Krämer (1950) is based on an abundance of new material and tries to correct many of the legends which have developed about Günther.

ABOUT: Munzer, H. W. Günther's Poetry in the Light of his Personality (diss.). [In Italian—see study by F. Delbono. In German—see study by H. Dahlke.]

F. R.

*GUTZKOW, KARL FERDINAND

(March 17, 1811-December 16, 1878), German dramatist and novelist, was born in Berlin, the son of humble parents. He studied theology at the University of Berlin, until the revolution of 1830 in Paris turned his attention to political and social questions. In 1831 he was invited by the critic Wolfgang Menzel to join the staff of the *Literaturblatt* in Stuttgart.

In 1833 Gutzkow was identified with Heinrich Heine, Heinrich Laube, Theodor Mundt, and Ludwig Wienbarg as a member of the literary group Young Germany. These men, of whom Gutzkow became the leading spokesman, were united by their political ideas,

* gōōts' kō

GUTZKOW

their hostility to the romantic movement, and their liberal attitude toward questions of religion and philosophy. Gutzkow's antireligious views and his doctrine of emancipation of the flesh are revealed in his early novels *Maha Guru* (1833), *Die Geschichte eines Gottes* (1833), and *Wally, Die Zweiflerin* (1835). The latter work was denounced by Menzel and cost its author three months' imprisonment as well as a ban in Prussia against anything he might write in the future.

While in jail Gutzkow wrote *Philosophie der Geschichte* (1836) and upon his release assumed editorship of the journal *Telegraph für Deutschland* in Frankfurt. In 1838 he wrote his first successful play, *Richard Savage*, and henceforth produced almost a drama a year until 1865. Of these works the best are *Zopf und Schwert* (1843), a comedy treating the court of Emperor William I, and *Uriel Acosta* (1847), a tragedy depicting the conflict between love and intellectual freedom. *Das Urbild des Tartuffe* (1847) and *Der Königsleutnant* (1849) are also still performed occasionally. From 1847 to 1850 Gutzkow was the chief playwright and dramaturgist at the court theatre in Dresden.

Returning to the novel form, which he felt should be used as a didactic weapon in the service of the ideas of the day, Gutzkow wrote *Die Ritter vom Geiste* (1850-52) and *Der Zauberer vom Rom* (1858-61), each in nine volumes. Gutzkow believed that the concept of the novel as events portrayed in

succession (*Roman des Nacheinander*) was outmoded; his new technique he called the novel of simultaneousness (*Roman des Nebeneinander*). According to Gutzkow, this method of juxtaposition of events enabled the writer to present "the entire age, the entire truth, the entire reality." In practice his novels suffer from excessive length and burdensome detail, but they are significant both as cultural-historical documents of this period and as the starting point of the modern novel.

From 1852 to 1858 Gutzkow edited the journal *Unterhaltungen am Häuslichen Herd* and during this period was the foremost critic in Germany. From 1861 to 1864 he was the secretary of the Schiller Foundation in Weimar. Ill health caused a mental breakdown and a suicide attempt in 1865, and his last years were spent in a wandering existence. Of his later works the most significant are the autobiographical books *Lebensbilder* (1869-71) and *Rückblicke auf mein Leben* (1875). His death occurred at Sachsenhausen when, under the influence of drugs, he upset a candle and was smothered by the fumes of the burning room.

The Prince of Madagascar was translated into English anonymously in 1853. *Uriel Acosta* appeared in translations by W. J. Tuska (1867) and H. Spicer (1885). The best translation was made by R. Hovey and F. S. Jones in 1895. G. I. Colbron translated *Zopf und Schwert* as *Sword and Queue* in 1913-15.

ABOUT: Brandes, G. Main Currents of Nineteenth Century Literature, VI; Cockbaine, S. A Sociological Study of Gutzkow (diss.); Cutting, S. W. The German Classics, VII; Schinnerer, O. P. Women in the Life and Work of Gutzkow; Journal of General Education, XV (1963). [In German —see studies by J. Proells, H. Houben, K. Glossy, and W. Haacke.]

D. G. D.

*GYULAI, PAL (January 1826-September 9, 1909), Hungarian critic, was born in Kolozsvár, capital of Transylvania, of a Calvinist family. His father was a poorly paid government clerk, and the boy had to finance his own higher education by tutoring in aristocratic families. He served for a brief period as secretary to Count Teleki and spent a year traveling in Germany and France. He taught humanities in schools in his native district and in the Calvinist *Gymnasium* in Budapest. He spent most of his life in that city, active in literary circles. In later years Gyulai was a member of the Hungarian Scientific Academy, president of the Kisfaludy Society, professor of Hungarian literature at the University of Budapest, and member of the Hungarian House of Magnates.

* dyōō′ loi

Gyulai's first published work, a poem, appeared in 1842 in the *Athenaeum*. Two years later he received a prize for his history of Transylvania. His creative works, both poetry and prose, were conventionally romantic and colorless. They include an unfinished novel in verse—*Romhányi*—and many narrative poems, folktales, and poems for children, and a two-volume collection of prose tales which are full of local atmosphere but weakly plotted and generally unimpressive. "He has no fire and little imagination," Joseph Remenyi has pointed out, "but one is compensated by his sense of form, nobility of spirit, and the sharpness of his irony."

It is for his literary criticism—sound, learned, and straightforward—that Gyulai is best remembered. Considered the greatest Hungarian critic, he is credited with elevating Hungarian criticism to a higher level than it had previously known. The period in which Gyulai lived was one of growing nationalism and romanticism, marking a distinct rebellion from the classic formalism of the eighteenth century. It is to Gyulai's credit that while he encouraged the new trends, he also recognized the need to purify the Hungarian language and to create literary principles and standards for its literature from Western European models. His criticism was based not on a philosophical system but on a tough-minded, practical literary intelligence which was no respecter of idols. He singled out for sharpest criticism the enormously popular historical novelist Mór Jókai, objecting to the looseness of his plotting and the improbability of his characters, while admitting that his fiction had vitality. Gyulai was essentially a conservative and his influence on Hungarian letters approximates closely that of Matthew Arnold in England.

As an editor of literary periodicals he was of course very influential, bringing to the attention of the public important national and foreign writers. Probably his greatest achievement was his work on such national figures as Vörösmarty, Petőfi (his monograph on him, published in 1854, is considered "one of the best systematic expositions in Hungarian critical literature"), and Arany. He enjoyed a warm personal friendship with Arany and with the poet's son László he collected and edited a volume of Hungarian folklore.

Gyulai married Maria Szendrey, a sister-in-law of Petőfi, in 1858. She died in 1866, and their only child died soon after. He wrote several touching elegies in commemoration.

ABOUT: Columbia Dictionary of Modern European Literature; Modern Language Journal, December 1953.

HA-ARI. See LURIA, ISAAC BEN SOLOMON

HABBEMA, KOOS. See HEIJERMANS, HERMAN

*HADEWIJCH (mid-thirteenth century), Dutch mystic. All the attempts to identify her with one of the many women known under that name have been unsuccessful so far. She was acquainted with the literature of the courtly period and seems to have been the spiritual leader of a group of women. Her activity reveals a relationship with the Beguine movement that developed in the thirteenth century.

Hadewijch's literary heritage consists of forty-five strophic poems (spiritual love songs in the manner of the Provençal courtly lyric), sixteen mixed verses, and some prose work, i.e., fourteen visions and a number of letters in rhyme. She was a Dutch representative of late-medieval west European mysticism as it developed in the twelfth century. Hadewijch and her school stand in the tradition of the Christ-mystique. Influenced by the mysticisms of northern France, particularly by St. Bernard, she exerted in her turn influence on later Flemish and west German mystics, to whom she was known as "Adelwip." This influence she exerted not so much through the original and sublime poetry inspired by her mystical experiences as through her "doctrine."

In her visions Hadewijch feels herself resting in the arms of the Christ, and feels how the Man of beauty presses her to His breast. She lives, entirely dominated by her feelings, in a trance that resembles Dionysian madness; she calls her reason to aid, but not in order to regain her balance, or to obtain insight. Rather, she seeks reason only as an intended disenchantment, in order to realize the distance that still exists between her soul and the highest contemplation. It is the same with her love for flowers and trees. Often she begins a poem with an enchanting picture of awakening nature, but only in order to create a contrast between that enchantment and her black despondency and powerlessness. It is not stumbling and rising mankind that speaks in her work; it is the prostrate individual who lifts himself up only in a

* hä′ dĕ wĭk

moment of spiritual frenzy and then succumbs again.

ABOUT: [In Dutch—see studies by C. Annoot-Braeckman, S. Axters, M. H. van der Zeyde.]

H. B.

*HAGEDORN, FRIEDRICH VON (April 23, 1708-October 28, 1754), German lyric poet of the rococo period, was a forerunner of the German Anacreontics and himself a master of poetry in the lighter vein. He was born in Hamburg, where his father was Danish minister, and educated at the Hamburg *Gymnasium* and at the University of Jena. Financial difficulties, brought about by his father's death in 1722, and hopes of obtaining a post in the Danish state service caused him to give up his law studies after only a year at Jena and return to Hamburg. In 1729 his wish was finally realized, and he became private secretary to the Danish ambassador in London. In the same year his first verse was published, a collection of sixteen poems bearing the title *F.v.H., Versuch einiger Gedichte oder erlesne Proben Poetischer Nebenstunden.* After two years in England Hagedorn returned to Hamburg, where he found work first as a private tutor and then, in 1733, as secretary to the "English Court," an old trading company. This latter post proved to be a happy one: although he was never entirely free of debts (his marriage to the daughter of an English tailor in Hamburg not having brought him the financial ease he expected), the work was not taxing and left him time for his friendships and his poetry. In 1738 he published his first fables, *Versuch in Poetischen Fabeln und Erzählungen,* which were followed by a second collection in 1750. His best work, however, is to be found in the odes and songs, written from 1742 to 1754. Two other groups or kinds of poems, the *Moralische Gedichte* (1750-53) and the *Epigrammatische Gedichte* (1753)—and particularly the former—contain strong echoes of the philosophy of Horace but decidedly less of his poetic quality. Hagedorn died of podagra at the age of forty-six in his native Hamburg.

Despite Lessing's claim that Hagedorn was "extremely biting and insulting," there is much more evidence that humanity and urbanity, sensitivity and gaiety were basic to both his person and his poetry. As a representative of German rococo, he embodies in perhaps their purest form the graceful lightness, the unproblematic nature, and the mas-

tery of form that characterize this eighteenth century literary counterpart of philosophic enlightenment. While it cannot be said that Hagedorn transcended his period, his literary production did at least exercise a far-reaching influence on both lyric and epic forms of the later eighteenth century. His fables, such as *Johann der Muntere Seifensieder* and *Der Fuchs und der Bock,* were influenced by Aesop, Erasmus, Burkard, Waldis, and especially La Fontaine, and became themselves the model for such later fable writers as the young Gellert. His verse (e.g., "An die Freude," "An die Dichtkunst") maintains more often than not the precarious balance between sincerity and frivolity, genuine *joie de vivre* and artificial bacchanalianism, and was instrumental in leading the way for such Anacreontics as Uz, Gleim, and Götz. Most important of all, however, is the fact that his fluent and nimble verse played a leading role in bringing about the downfall of the cumbersome alexandrine in German lyric poetry.

Except for occasional isolated poems (e.g. in *The Poetry of Germany,* 1853), little of Hagedorn's poetry has been made available in English translation.

ABOUT: [In German—see studies by H. Schuster, H. Stierling, G. Stix.]

A. M.

*HÁLEK, VÍTĚZSLAV (April 5, 1835-October 8, 1874), Czech poet, novelist, and dramatist, was born in the little town of Dolínek in northern Bohemia, the son of a tavern keeper. He studied at the academic *Gymnasium* in Prague, and at the Faculty of Philosophy of Prague University. When he declared his preference for literature, his father, who wished him to become a priest, cut off his financial support. Hálek was thus forced to give lessons. At the home of one of his pupils he met Dorothea Horáčková, his future wife, the daughter of a wealthy lawyer. The marriage gave Hálek security to pursue a comfortable career in literature and journalism.

In 1854 Hálek published his first poem, a ballad; and in 1858 his first book, *Alfred,* a Byronic narrative poem. During the following years he founded and edited a number of journals and literary almanacs, several together with his great contemporary Jan Neruda. He was a member of the editorial board of *Národní Listy* (National News) from the year of its foundation in 1861 until his death, and at different times he also edited such leading literary journals as

* hä′ gĕ dörn

* hä′ lĕk

Lumír, Zlatá Praha, and *Květy.* He was one of the founders and a leading spirit of the Umělecká Beseda (Artists' Forum), a patriotic group which provided a meeting place for Czech artists, writers, and national leaders.

Hálek's life was peaceful, contented, unmarked by great events or by tragedy, an idyll comparable to his tranquil, happy poetry. He attained great popularity in his lifetime, and his premature death in 1874 was a cause for national mourning.

Hálek is the author of lyric and narrative poetry, historical plays, tales, and novels. Of all these forms his lyric poems are the best: he is the classic Czech poet of nature and its moods. His *Večerní Písně* (Songs of Evening, 1858-59) are rather sentimental imitations of Heine's nature lyrics, without Heine's irony. Better is the later pantheistic lyric cycle *V Přírodě* (In Nature, 1872-74), in which nature is depicted metaphorically as leading the poet to ideas of divine wisdom, moral law, and artistic truth. This tendentiousness is less affecting, however, than the lively nature images themselves.

Hálek's narrative poems, influenced by Byron as well as by the Czech romantic poet Mácha, are mostly weak. Somewhat better are his ballads *Pohádky z Naší Vesnice* (Tales from Our Village, 1874), sketches and genre scenes from peasant life, some humorous, others tragic. Hálek's historical dramas, modeled on Shakespeare's, are of little significance.

Hálek's novels and tales are less remembered than his poetry. *Komediant* (The Actor, 1861), describing the development of a peasant youth into a gifted actor, shows the strong influence of Goethe's *Wilhelm Meister.* Hálek's later tales sometimes introduce problems of rural society and the family, partly under the influence of Turgenev.

Highly esteemed in his own time, Hálek has since fallen in popularity, displaced in part by his greater contemporary Neruda.

Three of Hálek's novelettes and 28 lyrics from *Songs of Evening* were translated by W. W. Strickland in *Three Stories* (1886), reprinted as *Hálek's Stories and Evensongs* (1930). *Evening Songs* was translated by J. Stybr (1920).

ABOUT: Harkins, W. E. Anthology of Czech Literature.

W. E. H.

*HALÉVY, LUDOVIC (January 1, 1834-May 8, 1908), French dramatist and novelist, born in Paris, was the son of Léon Halévy,

* há lā vē′

a prolific writer, and the nephew of Fromental Halévy, the composer of the opera *La Juive.* Beginning in 1845, Halévy studied at the Louis-le-Grand college, preparing with little diligence for a career in the civil service. He devoted much time during the next decade to duties with the Ministries of State and the Colonies, from which he retired completely in 1865 in order to pursue his work as dramatist. During the period of his government service, Halévy followed the advice of his friend Prévost-Paradol and tried, with no success, a novel and a comedy, *Entrez, Messieurs, Mesdames,* which he wrote for the composer Offenbach as part of the inauguration of the new theatre Les Bouffes-Parisiens. Halévy wrote libretti for Offenbach and such other composers as Delibes, and his reputation rose rapidly with *Ba-ta-clan, Rose et Rosette,* and especially *Orphée aux Enfers,* his first masterpiece. From 1861 to 1881, that is from *Le Menuet de Danaé* to *La Roussotte,* Halévy wrote in close collaboration with Henri Meilhac (see sketch below) and the particular contribution of each is difficult to isolate. Briefly, Meilhac seems to have had a more powerful personality, and Halévy a more human and moderate one, closer for example to such writers of comedy as Labiche. In the opera, thanks in large part to the music of Offenbach, the outstanding product of the association is *La Belle Hélène,* a parody of the story of Helen of Troy first performed in 1864; their libretto for Bizet's *Carmen* is less typical.

Like Meilhac, Halévy wrote articles for *La Vie Parisienne,* but in later years tended to prefer fiction, though on occasion he created excellent plays down to 1892. His work in fiction began with *Une Maladresse,* a short story (1857), and during the 1870's he gathered earlier writings in *Madame et Monsieur Cardinal,* revived *Marcel,* a youthful work, then wrote *Un Mariage d'Amour* in 1881 and simultaneously started his finest novel, *L'Abbé Constantin,* which within ten years ran to well over 150 editions, and whose success was largely instrumental in his election (1884) to the French Academy. *L'Abbé Constantin* is one of the best isolated novels of its period, a model of discretion, clarity, and good taste, and an admirable portrait of a village priest and his little problems. The action is set at the time of writing somewhere in the French provinces, and the charm of the novel lies in the light wit and satire in the portraits of Mrs. Scott and her younger sister, Bettina, two Americans who have bought the local domain of Longueval. This work has been a great favorite as a class text, for its tone and style. Halévy's two volumes of sketches and stories illustrate his kindly good humor, in a tone rather more moral than usual in his day. *L'Invasion* is a collection of his articles on the Franco-Prussian war, first published in *Le Temps*.

The many English translations of the 1890's illustrate Halévy's popularity abroad: *The Abbé Constantin, A Marriage of Love, The Cardinal Family, Autumn Manœuvres,* and *Parisian Points of View.*

ABOUT: Matthews, B. Aspects of Fiction and Other Ventures in Criticism, *also* French Dramatists of the Nineteenth Century. [In French—Gaiffe, F. Le Rire et la Scène Française.]

F. J. C.

*HALLER, ALBRECHT VON (October 8, 1708-December 12, 1777), Swiss scientist and poet, was born in Bern, of patrician family. By his fifteenth birthday he had already written several adolescent tragedies and an heroic epic of 4,000 verses on the origins of the Swiss Federation. Beginning in 1723 he studied medicine at the University of Tübingen and received his doctoral degree from the University of Leiden in 1725. After visiting London and Paris, he returned to Switzerland, where he studied mathematics at the University of Basel. He was a practicing physician in Bern from 1729 to 1735, when he was appointed municipal librarian. During this time he was also active as botanist and poet. His wanderings in the Swiss countryside resulted in the botanical treatise *Enumeratio Stirpium Helveticarum* and the poem *Die Alpen* (1729), which is an expression of praise of the mountain people, for their simplicity and contentment. *Die Alpen* also is one of the earliest expressions of appreciation for the magnificence of the Swiss mountains.

In 1736 he responded to a summons to serve at the University of Göttingen as professor of medicine, botany, anatomy, and surgery. While here he founded the Botanical Gardens and the Anatomical Theatre. During his tenure at Göttingen he was also active as president of the Society of Sciences. Before his return to Bern in 1753 because of ill health, he was made a knight of the Empire and refused invitations to join the faculties of Oxford, Utrecht, Berlin, and St. Petersburg.

As the poet of *Die Alpen,* he contributed much to the eventual rise of German poetry

* häl' ẽr

384

during the second half of the eighteenth century, particularly as a pioneer in natural expression in epic poetry. His lyric poetry in the collection *Versuch Schweizerischer Gedichten* (1732) was highly admired by the Swiss critics Bodmer and Breitinger. The didactic poem *Vom Ursprung des Uebels* which he composed in 1734 became a precursor of many similar poems on the theme of the origin of evil, a subject of particular interest to philosophy at this time. His later political novels *Usong* (1771), *Alfred, König der Angelsachsen* (1773), and *Fabius und Cato* (1774), which deal respectively with the absolutist, the moderate monarchical, and the aristocratic republican forms of government, have been of little interest in modern times.

The works of Haller that have been translated into English include: (verse) *Usong* (1772), *The Poems of Baron Haller* (1794), *The Alps* (1796); (prose) *The Moderate Monarchy,* (1849).

ABOUT: [In German—see studies by A. Frey, K. S. Guthke, H. Stahlmann, J. G. Zimmermann.]

E. K. G.

*HALLGRÍMSSON, JÓNAS (November 16, 1807-May 26, 1845), Icelandic poet, short-story writer, and scientist, was born at Hraun in Öxnadal in the north of Iceland. Öxnadal is an uncommonly beautiful valley with access to the sea by way of the fjord on the one side and with towering mountains on the landward side. It is also an area rich in local folklore. The natural beauty of this lovely valley exerted a profound influence on the sensitive youth who dedicated his mind to the study of science but reserved his heart and soul for the creation of exquisite lyrical poetry and delicate short stories depicting the scenes he loved best—the Icelandic country-side of the early nineteenth century.

Intellectual vigor and literary ability ran in Jónas' family; on his father's side he was related to Hallgrímur Pétursson (1614-74) (see sketch below), the greatest poet of his age and by all odds the most prolific and vigorous hymnist of Icelandic literature. Jónas' father, who also seems to have had some poetic ability, was assistant to Jón Þorláksson, the pastor at Bægisa and the well-known translator of Milton and Klopstock. When the poet was only nine years old, his father was drowned. A child as sensitive as Jónas could not fail to be deeply affected by such a loss. In later years he commemorated his father's death with a touching elegy. Most of his life was a series

* häd' 'l grēms sŏn

of frustrations: he was forced to combat poverty, malnutrition, and ill health, as well as attacks of melancholia which sapped his strength and contributed to his early death.

Hallgrímsson was deeply influenced in his formative years by the manly and energetic poetry of Bjarni Thórarensen (see sketch below). Other contributing factors were an unrequited love affair, of which little is known, and the resurgence of the spirit of independence and nationalism throughout all of Europe during the first half of the nineteenth century. This movement finally resulted in Iceland's independence from Denmark.

Graduating from the Classical Latin School at Bessastaðir in 1829, Hallgrímsson sailed to Copenhagen in 1832 with the intent of studying law. Gradually, however, his interests veered to the study of natural science (geology, botany, and zoology) though he always retained his love of literature. In Copenhagen he soon came under the influence of Tómas Sæmundsson, Konráð Gíslason, and certain others who, having become aware of the urgency of awakening the Icelandic people from the intellectual and political lethargy into which they had sunk, formed a society with the avowed purpose of cleansing and beautifying the Icelandic language and introducing new ideas and economic reforms into the Icelandic cultural life. He soon became the leader of this group and through its organ *Fjölnir* published the great bulk of his poems and short stories, as well as his scientific essays on the fauna and flora of Iceland. The influence of the "Fjölnismen" and particularly of Hallgrímsson's literary and scientific productions was far reaching even during his lifetime and can still be traced in Icelandic language and literature.

His best known works are *Ísland,* a clarion call to his countrymen to revive the vigor and the spirit of the early days of the republic, *Gunnarshólmi* (Gunnar's Island), a poem based on an episode from *Njáls Saga;* and *Grasaferð* (Gathering Moss), often termed the first short story in Icelandic. Throughout his literary works can be seen his love of nature and his firm faith in the future greatness of the Icelandic people.

The standard edition of Hallgrímsson's works is *Ljóðmæli og Önnur Rit* (Poetry and Other Writings, 1883). This edition also contains a brief but good biography by Hannes Hafstein. For other editions of his work and for a more extensive bibliography, see Richard Beck, *History of Icelandic Poets,* 1800-1940. Translations of some of his poems appear in Beck's *Icelandic Lyrics.*

L. B.

*"HALM, FRIEDRICH"** (pseudonym of **ELIGIUS FRANZ JOSEPH,** Reichsfreiherr von **MÜNCH-BELLINGHAUSEN**) (April 2, 1806-May 22, 1871), Austrian dramatist, was born at Cracow, the son of a high Austrian government official. After attending the *Gymnasium* at Melk and studying law at the University of Vienna, Halm entered upon a distinguished career of government service. He was appointed councilor in 1840 and director of the Court Library in Vienna in 1845, a position which he received in preference to the famous dramatist Franz Grillparzer. Halm was made a member of the Imperial Academy of Science in 1847, was elected to the Austrian House of Lords in 1861, and was designated general intendant of the court theatres in Vienna in 1867. Despite his extremely successful life, Halm suffered from moods of despair and melancholy. One source of misfortune was the illness of his wife Sophie von Schloissnigg, who became paralyzed shortly after their marriage in 1826, although she lived for many years. Halm formed a lasting friendship with the famous actress Julie Rettich, who starred in many of his plays and who, according to the poet, provided the stimulus for his creativeness. Halm retired from public life in 1870 and died the following year at Vienna.

As a dramatist Halm was able to suit the tastes of his time, and during his lifetime enjoyed a popularity which exceeded that of both Grillparzer and Hebbel. Although he possessed a genuine dramatic talent, his plays were not written from inner necessity and are generally shallow and without substance. His plots do not grow out of character but present in a contrived fashion the popular ideas of the day. Sentimentality and elegance of language are usual characteristics of his works, and many of his dramas are written in verse. The influence of Spanish drama is evident.

His first drama, *Griseldis* (1835), on the theme of the emancipation of women, had an enormous success and established his reputation. Other works, which were equally well received, followed in rapid succession, including *Der Adept* (1836), *Camoens* (1837), *Der Sohn der Wildnis* (1842), and *König und Bauer* (1842). His most popular work, *Der Fechter von Ravenna,* a tragedy glorifying German national feeling, appeared in 1854. Of his later plays the best known are *Iphigenie in Delphi* (1856), *Wildfeuer* (1863), and *Begum Sumro* (1863).

* hälm

385

After Halm's death a number of short stories were found among his papers and published in 1906. Several of these tales are outstanding, such as *Die Marzipanliese, Das Haus an der Veronabrücke,* and *Die Freundinnen.* Halm also produced an unsuccessful volume of poetry, *Gedichte* (1850).

Griseldis was translated into English verse by R. A. Anstruther in 1840. Additional translations were made by L. Smith (1844), W. M. Sieg (1871), and G. L. Prentiss (1876). *Camoens* appeared anonymously in 1840. C. E. Anthon translated *The Son of the Wilderness* in 1848. Subsequent versions include those of M. A. Faber (1867), M. Lovell (1867), and W. H. Charlton (1868) who also translated *The Gladiator of Ravenna* in 1868.

ABOUT: [In German—see studies by F. Pachler, H. Schneider, and A. Schönbach (ADB).]

D. G. D.

* **HAMANN, JOHANN GEORG** (August 27, 1730-June 21, 1788), German philosophical writer, frequently referred to as "the Magus of the North," was born in Königsberg in Prussia. It was also here that he began his advanced studies: philosophy, theology, and finally law. During these years he likewise devoted considerable attention to foreign languages. After the completion of his formal training he led a highly irregular, disordered existence. At first he was a tutor in an aristocratic household and then traveled about without employment for a time. In Riga he became the friend of a wealthy merchant family, and here he sought to acquire a thorough knowledge of business affairs. Again he became a tutor for a short time, but soon returned to the home of his friends in Riga. Undertaking a business trip to England on behalf of his patrons, he went by way of Berlin where he became acquainted with Moses Mendelssohn. He remained in London for over a year, where, as a result of the failure of his business venture, he sought relief from melancholy through dissipation. From an assiduous reading of the Bible he was able to gain sufficient self-control to permit him to care for his physical and mental health. In 1758 he returned to Riga, where he stayed a year until his father summoned him home to Königsberg. Here he lived for a time, devoting himself to ancient literatures and oriental languages. He continued thus to live without firm roots in any profession or location until his death in Münster.

As a writer Hamann received only slight consideration from his contemporaries. The

* hä′ män

literary idiosyncrasies and frequent use of Biblical and symbolic style in his writings had little attraction for the broad public. His writings appeared principally in three different periods: 1759-63, 1772-76, and 1779-85. The numerous small works of which he was author are for the most part occasional pieces, filled with personal and regional materials and allusions to the world of books in which he lived. Among the few men of his era who appreciated his writings are Herder, Goethe, Jacobi, and Jean Paul. Much of his work may be characterized as an attack upon materialism and atheism as well as a rejection of the Age of Enlightenment.

Several translations of Hamann's writings into English appear in the anthology *Prose Writers of Germany* (1870). Selections also appear in R. G. Smith's book (1960) cited below.

ABOUT: Schmitz, F. J. The Problem of Individualism and the Crises in the Lives of Lessing and Hamann; Smith, R. G. Hamann: A Study in Christian Existence; Publications of English Goethe Society, XXVI (1957). [In French—Blum, J. La Vie et l'Œuvre de Hamann. In German—see studies by K. Gründer, W. Leibrecht, H. A. Salmony, R. Unger.]

E. K. G.

HARDENBERG, FRIEDRICH LEOPOLD, Baron von ("*Novalis") (May 2, 1772-March 25, 1801), German poet, was born on his family's ancestral estate in Oberwiederstedt near the Harz Mountains. In later life he adopted the poetically fitting name Novalis, which some of his medieval forebears had employed apparently to designate their role as cultivators of fallow land. His father, Baron Erasmus von Hardenberg, was a devout member of the Moravian brethren, a pious sect which he had joined as a result of his first wife's sudden death. He soon after married Bernhardine von Bölzig, a distant relative and a shy, sickly orphan, who bore him eleven children, most of whom, including the poet, died young of tuberculosis.

When Novalis was ten he was sent with his private tutor to live with an uncle, a prominent nobleman, in whose household he was first introduced to the conversation of worldly society. After a year he returned to his austerely puritanical home, and soon thereafter the family moved to nearby Weissenfels, where the father took over the administration of some salt mines. For Novalis the departure from the estate marked the end of an idyllic childhood. At Weissenfels he began to write poetry and sketch out ambitious plans for works in various genres.

* nō vä′ lĭs

"NOVALIS"

In 1790 he was sent briefly to the Protestant secondary school in nearby Eisleben, where he lived at the home of the school's principal, who introduced him to the Greek and Latin poets. Later that same year he entered the University of Jena, studying law preparatory to a civil-service career. Here he was introduced to the new Kantian philosophy and became personally acquainted with Schiller, then lecturing on European history at Jena. The following year he transferred to the University of Leipzig, where he met the young Friedrich Schlegel. Schlegel excitedly announced to his brother he had found a poet whom he could help mold, but Novalis, who was later to collaborate with the brothers in laying the theoretical foundations of German romanticism, adamantly resisted Friedrich's control. For a short time Novalis dabbled in the more carefree aspects of student life, but later sent his father a full confession in which he toyed with the idea of entering army service to build up his self-discipline. His father met the situation by sending him, in 1793, to the University of Wittenberg, which, with its memories of Luther, offered a more sober atmosphere than Leipzig.

The following year, having completed his examinations, he took a civil-service job in the resort town of Tennstedt and on an official visit to a nearby castle met Sophie von Kühn, a charming child of twelve and a half with whom he fell in love. Within half a year they were engaged. Their courtship, at first punctuated by petty quarrels, was soon clouded by Sophie's protracted illness, which culminated in her death, at fifteen, in 1797. Sophie's death marked the turning-point of Novalis' life. "Evening has come over me while I was still looking at the dawn," he wrote. He disciplined himself against all worldly desires, knelt regularly before Sophie's portrait, and kept a self-analytical diary for which he developed a new calendar that started with the day of her death.

Meanwhile, in 1796, during Sophie's illness, he had moved back to Weissenfels to assist his father in the salt mines. In 1797-99, wishing to explore the scientific bases of his work, he attended the nearby Freiberg Mining Institute, where he studied with A. G. Werner, one of the founders of geology, and J. W. Ritter, a physicist exploring animal magnetism. What he learned from these men left its traces not only on his own poetry and philosophy, but also on the scientific inclinations which, largely through his influence, colored subsequent romanticism. During this time he also worked zealously in mathematics and the other sciences and supplemented his earlier reading of Kant and Fichte with the study of such mystical writers as Plotinus and the contemporary Hemsterhuis, Baader, and Schelling (it was not until later that he read Jakob Böhme, one of his major influences). In 1798 he became engaged to one of his teacher's daughters, Julie von Charpentier, whom he did not love with the passion he had known for Sophie but who, he hoped, could offer him a stable family life. At first financial difficulties and then his fatal illness prevented their marriage.

While in Tennstedt Novalis had begun to set down the aphorisms (his natural form of theoretical expression) which contain his mystic philosophy of "magical idealism" and which, from its first issue in 1798, he contributed to the *Athenaeum*, the influential journal founded by Friedrich and August Wilhelm Schlegel. From 1799 to his death Novalis, having returned to the Weissenfels mines, participated actively in the circle that the Schlegels, with Schelling and later with Ludwig Tieck, had built around themselves in nearby Jena. Spurred on by his friends, he produced his principal creative works—in fact, the only lasting creative work to come from the Jena romantics—during these years. The cycle of verse- and prose-poems *Hymnen an die Nacht* (completed 1799) recaptures the longing for self-immolation that had characterized his mourning for Sophie. The poems entitled *Geistliche Lieder* (1799) celebrate his spiritual rebirth through pious communion with his fellow men. Within the symbolical framework of *Die Lehrlinge zu Sais* (1798-99) he brings a large number of his scientific and philosophical ideas into play. The essay *Christenheit oder Europa* (1799), an important document in the history of romantic medievalism, reflects his longing for what he took to be the unified society of the Middle Ages. His final work, the fragment *Heinrich von Ofterdingen* (1799-1800), is, superficially, at least, an apprenticeship novel in the tradition of Goethe's *Wilhelm Meister*, a work that Novalis at first worshipped, but later vehemently rejected as being un- and anti-poetic. In many ways an answer to Goethe, *Ofterdingen*, with its dreamlike, fairy-tale atmosphere, its medieval setting, its symbol of the blue flower (which to the world became an emblem for all German romanticism), is an apotheosis of poetry, love, and, in effect, the whole ideal world of the romantic imagination. In mid-1800 Novalis suffered a severe hemorrhage, after which his condition gradually declined until his death at twenty-eight the next spring. He is buried at Weissenfels.

His early introduction into the English-speaking world by Carlyle (in 1829) assured his place as one of the most influential voices of romanticism outside Germany. With his handsome figure and flowing brown curls, his energetic unworldliness, his consumptive condition and early death, he embodied one of the classic images of the romantic poet. His characteristic mood of yearning (whether for an idyllic medieval past or a millennial future), his enthusiastic identification, in varying combinations, of such concepts as poetry, truth, love, death, dreams, and the universe, and his insights into the symbolic character and musical affinities of language have had enormous effect on cultural history since his time.

Henry of Ofterdingen has appeared in English translations by F. S. Stallknecht (1842), H. H. Moore (1853), and M. J. Hope (in *Novalis, His Life, Thoughts and Works*, 1891, which also includes translations of some shorter works, including many aphorisms). *Hymns to the Night* has been frequently translated, most recently by M. Cotterell (1948). The *Devotional Songs* appeared bilingually in the edition of B. Pick (1910). *The Disciples at Sais* appeared anonymously in 1903 and, under the title *The Novices of Sais*, in the translation of R. Manheim (1949). *Christianity or Europe* was translated by J. Dalton (1844). A small miscellany, by various translators, including the *Hymns* and some aphorisms and poems, can be found in *The German Classics* (ed. K. Francke, IV, 1913).

ABOUT: Carlyle, T. Critical and Miscellaneous Essays; Dyck, M. Novalis and Mathematics; Haywood, B. Novalis: The Veil of Imagery; Hiebel, F. Novalis, German Poet, European Thinker, Christian Mystic; Maeterlinck, M. On Emerson, and Other Essays; Prawer, S. S. German Lyric Poetry; Saintsbury, G. History of Criticism and Literary Taste in Europe; Spender, S. The Novices of Sais (introduction); Tymms, R. German Romantic Literature; Wellek, R. History of Modern Criticism: German Studies in Honour of H. G. Fiedler. [In German—see studies by W. Dilthey, E. Hederer, F. Hiebel, R. Huch; W. Vordtriede. In French—by H. Lichtenberger.]

H. L.

*HARDY, ALEXANDRE (c. 1575-c. 1632), French dramatist, born in Paris, had some formal education and, while still young, joined with the itinerant theatrical troup of Valleran-Lecomte, which presented its repertory in the provinces and at the Hôtel de Bourgogne in Paris. For this troupe Hardy adapted a wide range of adventure stories and tragic subjects, and the extent of his activity may be measured by his claim, in 1628, to have composed over 600 plays, of which only the 34 published by him are known today.

Hardy's importance in the evolution of the French theatre derives from his effective techniques of staging, his progress in the synthesis of action and the analysis of character, and the strong dramatic force evident in subjects which he borrowed from La Taille and Jodelle. Through the qualities of his work he oriented public taste and was the founder of the modern French stage and the first professional playwright to develop with consistency the important genre of the tragicomedy. As reflected in his work, the tragicomedy involves happy endings, choice of characters from a variety of social classes, construction in five acts and Alexandrine verse, and romanesque plots borrowed from many identifiable sources. This genre tended to set aside religious themes and such devices as the monologue, soon considered undesirable, and the chorus, presumably both too costly and too static. Hardy's plays suffer from lack of poetic feeling and artistry, and their weaknesses include superficiality of character portrayal; no inner problems arise, and the reactions are almost wholly limited to the circumstances of external vicissitudes. Although Hardy did not yet observe the unities and was excessively melodramatic in comparison to the masters of the classical period, he made a significant step forward in a concept of the theatre.

Hardy's most important play, *Théagène et Cariclée*, was composed about 1593. Much is

* àr dē′

still medieval in its manner, but this very fact gives it more movement than the artificial neoclassic work of the preceding decades. In the old cyclical pattern of eight "days," *Théagène* develops in new style the Greek romance by Heliodorus. It is more properly a series of plays recounting a long episodic story devoid of any semblance of unity of plot or action. The motivation throughout rises from the circumstances of event, of adventure, and of the struggles of the characters in the face of adversity. This kind of subject resembles the contemporary novel in many ways, notably the long works by D'Urfé and Madeleine de Scudéry. Of particular interest for their subjects are *Alceste* (1593), which popularizes a story from Euripides used again later in the century, and two tales from Cervantes' *Novelas Ejemplares*, *Cornélie* (1614) and *La Force du Sang* (1615), important events in the renewed interest in Spanish materials. Hardy's place in the evolution may be further measured by comparisons with the plays of his immediate successors, Théophile de Viau and Racan, who felt his influence.

The five-volume edition of Hardy's plays, published in 1624-28, is replaced by the critical versions of 1883-84.

ABOUT: Lancaster, H. A History of French Dramatic Literature in the Seventeenth Century; Renaissance and Modern Studies, III (1959). [In French—see studies by E. Rigal and S. W. Deierkauf-Holsboer.]

F. J. C.

HÄRING, WILHELM. See ALEXIS, WILLIBALD

*HARSDÖRFFER, GEORG PHILIP

(November 1, 1607-September 22, 1658), German poet and editor, is closely associated with his native city of Nürnberg, with several of the famous *Sprachgesellschaften*—and with the notion that poetry can be "acquired" by mastering a few simple rules. In spite of what might be called this "didactic fallacy," he was one of the more inventive and ornamental talents of the age and a commanding figure in the literary world.

Harsdörffer's family were prominent patricians in a bustling middle-class society. Nürnberg lay at the crossroads of commerce. Not least by Harsdörffer's own doing, it was also an international literary center and a principal avenue of Italian, Spanish, and French influence upon German literature.

* härs' dûr fĕr

Harsdörffer studied in Altdorf and Strasbourg and traveled for five years in Switzerland, France, Holland, England, and Italy. On his return he entered the service of his native city. He maintained a vast correspondence with the writers of his day, translated many foreign works, wrote in several fields besides literature—amassing 50 volumes of collected writings. He has been called an encyclopedia of baroque learning and influences. The Pegnesischer Hirten- und Blumenorden (Pegnitz Order of Shepherds and Flowers), which he helped to found, was still functioning after the Second World War. He was also a member of the Fruchtbringende Gesellschaft and the Teutschgesinnte Genossenschaft.

Harsdörffer published his rules for poetry in the *Poetischer Trichter* (Poetic Funnel). The title is to be taken more literally than ironically. It continues, in a sort of seventeenth century do-it-yourself spirit, ". . . for pouring in the art of German poetry and versification in six hours." Harsdörffer stresses ornamentation and stylistic variety, and the model of Italian and Spanish writing. He opposed Opitz, yet some of his arguments sound like paraphrases of the master, and the two share one basic conviction: that rules make the poet. In his own works, Harsdörffer points ahead to the extravagant mannerism of the high baroque. His experimentation in verse and typography, his elaborate sense of form, and his concentration upon words or word relationships are of interest to modern poets and critics.

He also wrote *Frauenzimmergesprächspiele* —eight volumes of miscellaneous popular learning from literature and mathematics to parlor games, all in the form of sophisticated conversations—and compiled two prodigious "encyclopedias," one of which he called "Mirror of History, or One Hundred Memorable Events." He was an active co-worker on the German dictionary planned by the Fruchtbringende Gesellschaft.

A few of his poems appear in G. C. Schoolfield's *The German Lyric of the Baroque in English Translation* (1962).

ABOUT: German Life and Letters, 1960; Journal of English and Germanic Philology, 1943; Philological Quarterly, 1958. [In German—Kayser, W. Die Klangmalerei bei Harsdörffer; Tittmann, J. Die Nürnberger Dichterschule.]

F. G. R.

HARTMANN *VON AUE (c. 1170-1250), German poet, the first in the line of the great German courtly poets, came from a noble Swabian family. The place of his birth has not been exactly established. He probably spent his youth in a monastery where he received a superior education. He knew Latin and French and was well versed in the Bible. It seems likely that he acquired his knowledge of French courtly culture on travels through France. An unhappy love affair brought sorrow to him which caused him to join the crusade of 1197.

Hartmann began his poetic career as a minnesinger. Lyric poetry, however, was not his strong point. He always drew more inspiration from religion than from love. In the Middle Ages Hartmann's high reputation rested exclusively on his two lengthy verse novels, *Erec,* written before his participation in the crusade, and *Iwein,* his last work. Both epics were based on works of the French master storyteller Chrétien de Troyes. They signify an enormous progress in language, structure, and style from the work of Heinrich von Veldecke, the inaugurator of the courtly epic poem in Germany.

In contrast to Wolfram von Eschenbach's romanticism, Hartmann represents the classic tradition in the history of German literature. Purity, delicacy, and moderation are the outstanding characteristics of his work. Even in the description of battles he avoids violence and passes over repelling sights. Both *Erec* and *Iwein* deal with romances from the Arthurian cycle. While the French author excels in the dramatic representation of adventures, Hartmann dwells on the basic conflict of chivalric life. In its treatment the two epics complement each other. Erec, in his love for a lady, neglects his duties as a knight, while Iwein, in the pursuit of chivalry, fails in the service of courtly love. Love and duty are reconciled only after many trials and tribulations. Both epics give an idealized and highly stylized picture of chivalric life; they may even be considered as a guide book to it. Altogether Hartmann's poetry has a strong didactic trait. In his code of true chivalric behavior he combines deep Christian piety with the common social prejudices of his time. To him the highest of all virtues is courtesy, which comprises all kinds of attractive social and moral qualities. Of the two most precious goods man can obtain in his life on earth, happiness and honor, the former depends on worldly possessions, while the latter is inseparable from high social standing.

Being a Christian, the perfect knight must, however, never boast of these goods : they are, like any other worldly success, given only by God.

Hartmann's religious beliefs find their clearest expressions in two shorter works, which appeal much more strongly to the modern mind than his courtly epics, *Gregorius* and *Der Arme Heinrich. Gregorius* illustrates Hartmann's belief that no sin, not even that of incest with one's own mother, is too great for the infinite mercy of the Christian God. In Hartmann's story the man who, like Oedipus, unknowingly commits this sin, becomes, through the power of repentance, a saint and finally a pope. The only unforgivable sin is in Hartmann's view a Christian's doubt in the infinity of God's mercy. *Der Arme Heinrich* is the story of a nobleman who, stricken by leprosy, commits the sin of doubt, but is saved by the stronger faith of a simple peasant girl.

Hartmann von Aue, praised by Gottfried von Strassburg as the unsurpassed master of poetic form, was the most imitated poet of the Middle Ages. In modern times Gerhart Hauptmann turned Hartmann's *Der Arme Heinrich* into a highly effective play, while Thomas Mann, in one of his last works, *The Holy Sinner,* retold the story of Gregorius from a modern point of view.

Among translations of his works only his two shorter stories have been made available in English. Five versions of *Der Arme Heinrich* are known : an adaptation by Dante Gabriel Rossetti, *Henry the Leper, a Swabian Miracle-Rhyme* (1846-47) ; a retelling in Longfellow's *Golden Legend;* a translation by Margaret Schlauch in *Medieval Narrative* (1928), another by C. H. Bell in *Peasant Life in Old German Epics* (1931), and a third in *Two Moods of Minnesong* by Charles M. Lancaster, John G. Frank, and Carl Hammer (1922). *Gregorius* has been translated by Edwin H. Zeydel in collaboration with Bayard Quincy Morgan (1955).

ABOUT : Bruce, J. D. The Evolution of Arthurian Romance ; Loomis, R. S. Arthurian Legends in Medieval Art. [In German—see Gustav Ehrismann's Geschichte der Deutschen Literatur bis zum Ausgang des Mittelalters, II. See also studies by H. Eggers, P. Wapnewski.]

F. R.

*HARTZENBUSCH, JUAN EUGENIO (September 6, 1806-August 2, 1880), Spanish scholar and dramatist, was born in Madrid. He was the son of a German father and a Spanish mother. Owing to financial difficulties, he was forced, in spite of his early propensity for scholarship, to interrupt his studies at the Jesuit College of San Isidoro

---

* fôn ou′

* härt′ säm bōōch

in order to help his father, a cabinet maker. Although his father became ill, and business affairs demanded more of Juan than ever, he somehow found time to take up painting and to read the classics. It was at this time that the young Hartzenbusch began to write dramas; later in life he contributed significantly, both as editor and critic, to the popular restoration of the Golden Age *(Siglo de Oro)* drama.

After various positions such as copyist for the *Gaceta de Madrid* (1835), "first official" of the Biblioteca Nacional (1844), Director of the Escuela Normal (1854), in 1862 he became Director of the Biblioteca Nacional, a post given only to eminent literary scholars. Hartzenbusch had edited several volumes of the Golden Age drama for the Biblioteca de Autores Españoles and the *Teatro Escojido* (12 vols., 1839-42) of Tirso de Molina. In addition, he wrote various critical introductions to the works of Lope de Vega, Ruiz de Alarcón, Tirso de Molina, Rojas, Calderón, Molière, Voltaire, Alfieri, Dumas, and many others. He directed the publication of the *Obras Póstumas de Leandro Moratín* (1867-68) as well as an edition of the *Quijote,* including his own commentary.

In a lesser literary vein, Hartzenbusch wrote a "zarzuela" (musical comedy) ("Heliodora o el Amor Enamorado"), some fables (some of which are translations of G. E. Lessing), and some good "costumbrista" (local color) articles.

He wrote various plays under the influence of Moratín, among which *La Redoma Encantada* (1839), *Los Polvos de la Madre Celestina* (1840), and *La Coja y el Encojido* are the best known. Of his serious dramas, *Los Amantes de Teruel* (1837), and *La Jura de Santa Gadea* are fine examples of the romantic period.

The latter is a drama based on a famous episode from the life of Spain's legendary hero, El Cid. However, his *Los Amantes de Teruel* is his masterpiece: the lovers, Diego and Isabel, are victims of uncontrollable circumstances which thwart their union, a union finally achieved in death. The lovers die of sorrow, since duty and life keep them apart on earth; it is this same exalted love which makes them inseparable in the hereafter. The play indicated no foreign influences, but Pérez de Montalbán and Tirso de Molina had already treated this tragic legend of love before. Hartzenbusch's treatment of this familiar legend was a genuine contribution to Spanish romantic drama.

He attained excellence through his skillful dramatic constructions, his skill in staging, and his eloquent presentation of exalted love and of old, chivalric customs; but his deficiencies as a poet and as a creator of character prevented him from reaching the level attained by such contemporaries as José Zorrilla and García Gutiérrez. It has been said that we would have an ideal Spanish dramatist if we could bring together in one writer the characterization of Tamayo y Baus, the versification of García Gutiérrez, and the constructive skill of Hartzenbusch.

Obras de Hartzenbusch, 4 vols., was published in Madrid, 1888-92. A more recent edition by A. Gil Albacete of *Los Amantes de Teruel y La jura de Gadea* was published in Madrid in 1935.

The *Lovers of Teruel* was translated into English by H. Thomas in 1938 and made into a motion picture in 1963.

ABOUT: Corbière, A. S. Juan Eugenio Hartzenbusch and the French Theatre. [In Spanish—Hartzenbusch, D. E. Bibliografia de Hartzenbusch; Revista de Archivos, VIII (1907).]

L. S.

HASSELT, ANDRÉ VAN. See VAN HASSELT, ANDRÉ

*HAUCH, JOHANNES CARSTEN (May 12, 1790-March 4, 1872), Danish poet, playwright, novelist, was born in Fredrikshald (now Halden) in southeastern Norway, where his father, Frederik Hauch, of Danish birth, was prefect. His mother was Karen Tank, daughter of a Norwegian merchant. The contrast between the choleric nature of his father and the tranquil character of his mother and a similar difference between his two sisters is the basis for the conflicting characters that appear in several of Hauch's novels and plays.

When the boy was two years old his father was appointed prefect of the diocese of Bergen. At the age of eight he was sent for education to Pastor Niels Hertzberg at Malmanger beside the majestic Hardanger fjord. His mother died in 1803, and the following year his father was transferred to the diocese of Zealand, and the family moved to Copenhagen. In 1808 he matriculated at the University of Copenhagen, where he studied both humanities and natural sciences. Schelling's natural philosophy and several romantic authors influenced him. He completed his Master's degree in 1820 and his

* houk

Ph.D. the following year, when he also received a traveling scholarship for study of the marine fauna of the Mediterranean. For six years he stayed in France and Italy. In Nice he contracted gangrene in his left foot, which had to be amputated. He attempted suicide by shooting himself, but the bullet ricocheted against a rib, and he recovered.

Hauch had earlier written some poems and taken an active part in the literary feud between Oehlenschläger and Baggesen as a supporter of the former. Now his view of life changed from romantic pantheism to the Christian faith, and he began a literary career by writing several dramas. His *Dramatiske Værker* (Dramatic Works, 1828-30) in three volumes are psychopathological studies of suffering men. Upon his return to Denmark in 1827, Hauch was appointed teacher of sciences at Sorø Academy in central Zealand, where he served for eighteen years. In 1829 he married Frederikke (Rinna) Elisabeth Brun Juul, daughter of Judge Svend Brun Juul of Helsingør and Helene Elisabeth von Munthe af Morgenstierne.

Hauch continued to write dramas, but it was as a novelist that he gained popular recognition. His first novel was *Vilhelm Zabern* (1834), an historical narrative of the days of Christian II. Later followed *Guldmageren* (The Alchemist, 1836), the milieu of which is central Europe of the eighteenth century, *En Polsk Familie* (A Polish Family, 1839), a picture of Poland's tragic war of independence against Russia in 1830, and others. Among his dramas may be mentioned the historical tragedies *Svend Grathe* (1841) and *Marsk Stig* (Chamberlain Stig, 1850). His most popular drama was *Søstrene paa Kinnekullen* (The Sisters of Kinnekullen, 1849). He also wrote lyrics and poetic romances.

Hauch was professor of Scandinavian languages and literature at the University of Kiel, 1846-48, and in 1851 he succeeded Oehlenschläger as professor of aesthetics at the University of Copenhagen. He also served as director and censor of the Royal Danish Theater. He died in Rome.

His novel *Robert Fulton* was translated into English by P. C. Sinding (1868). Scattered poems in English rendition appear in *A Book of Danish Verse* (1922), *A Second Book of Danish Verse* (1947), and elsewhere. For a full account of translations see E. Bredsdorff, *Danish Literature in English Translation* (1950).

ABOUT: Mitchell, P. M. A History of Danish Literature; Winkel Horn, F. History of the Literature of the Scandinavian North.

A. J.

*HAUFF, WILHELM (November 29, 1802-November 18, 1827), German short-story writer and novelist, was born in Stuttgart, the son of a government official who died when the boy was seven. His mother returned with her four children to Tübingen, and Hauff was raised in the home of his maternal grandfather, whose library enabled him to indulge his love of reading. In 1817 he entered the cloister school at Blaubeuren, transferring three years later to the University of Tübingen, where he studied theology and philology. After receiving the degree of Doctor of Philosophy in 1824, he became a private tutor in the family of Baron von Hügel in Stuttgart. Here he began his literary career with *Märchenalmanach* (1826), a collection of fairy tales which he had invented to entertain his charges. This work was continued in 1827 and 1828 by additional volumes, which included the popular frame-stories *Die Karawane, Der Scheik von Alessandria*, and *Das Wirtshaus im Spessart*. Hauff gained sudden, widespread recognition from a lawsuit brought by the insignificant but popular writer Heinrich Clauren (pseudonym of K. G. S. Heun), whom he had satirized in the story *Der Mann im Mond* (1826). Although Hauff lost the suit, he established his reputation with the essay *Kontroverspredigt*, in which he demolished the literary reputation of Clauren. In 1826 Hauff traveled through Europe and met the leading writers of his day. He was a cheerful, enthusiastic, unproblematic individual, who found a welcome reception everywhere. In 1827 he married his cousin and settled in Stuttgart as editor of the Cotta *Morgenblatt*. This same year he fell ill from typhoid fever following a trip to the Tyrol and died in Stuttgart at the age of twenty-five.

Although Hauff's literary career encompassed only three years, he was an astonishingly productive writer. He was endowed with an outstanding gift for narrative, and although his works are neither profound nor original, they possess a unique charm which has endeared them to readers to the present day. His most notable short stories are *Mitteilungen aus den Memoiren des Satans* (1826), *Jud Süss* (1826), *Phantasien im Bremer Rathskeller* (1827), and *Das Bild des Kaisers* (1828). The influence of E. T. A. Hoffmann and Ludwig Tieck predominates. Hauff's most ambitious work was the historical novel *Lichtenstein* (1826), which, as the author himself acknowledged, was modeled on the romances of Scott. This novel,

* houf

which describes events in Württemberg in the sixteenth century, has maintained its appeal and is still read. Hauff also produced a volume of poems, *Gedichte* (1827), two of which ("Morgenrot" and "Steh' ich in finstrer Mitternacht") have become folk songs.

L. Burns translated a volume of stories entitled *Select Popular Tales* in 1845. *Memoirs of Beelzebub* appeared anonymously in 1846. *Three Tales* were translated by M. A. Faber in 1873; *Tales of the Caravan, Inn and Palace* by E. L. Stowell in 1882; *The Little Glass Man and Other Stories* by S. Mendel in 1893; and *Fairy Tales* by C. McDonnell in 1903. E. Sadler and C. R. L. Fletcher translated *Phantasien im Bremer Rathskeller* as *The Wine-Ghosts of Bremen* in 1899. R. J. Craig translated *Lichtenstein* in 1897. *Eastern Fairy Tales* was translated by R. Ingram in 1949, and *Hauff's Tales* by M. H. Gallia in 1950.

ABOUT: PMLA, XXVI. [In German—see studies by H. Binder, H. Hofmann, W. Scheller, H. Tidemann.]

D. G. D.

*HAVLÍČEK, KAREL (October 31, 1821-July 29, 1856), Czech critic, journalist, and poet, was born in Borová, southern Bohemia, the son of a keeper of a general store. He often signed himself Havlíček Borovský in tribute to his birthplace. At the age of nine Havlíček was sent to normal school in nearby Jihlava, and later to Německý Brod. In 1838 he went on to Prague to complete *Gymnasium* and study languages and history at the Charles University. In 1840 he entered Prague Seminary, resolving to use the priestly office to educate the people to the Czech nationalist cause. But his temperament was already skeptical. Suspected of pro-Orthodox sympathies because of his pro-Russian interests, he was excluded from the seminary in 1841. He soon found a position as tutor to the Russian Slavophile Professor Pogodin, and the years 1843-44 he spent mostly in Moscow. Here his pro-Russian sentiment cooled as he saw Russia's backwardness, and he became convinced that the Czechs must stand for independence alone.

Returning to Prague, Havlíček attracted attention by his sharp critical attacks on sentimental patriotism and Pan-Slavism. At the age of twenty-four he was made editor of the newspaper *Pražské Noviny* and its literary supplement *Česká Včela*. In the Revolution of 1848 he made his paper, now named the *Národní Noviny* (National News), a leading force among the Czech liberals, whom he also represented in the short-lived parlia-

* hà' vlĕ chĕk

ments of Vienna and Kroměříž. The failure of the Revolution brought repressions, and in 1850 the government shut down Havlíček's paper. He founded a new one, *Slovan*, but was forced to abandon it after less than a year. Finally the regime, which had twice failed to convict him in court (on both occasions he was freed by the jury), arrested him (December 16, 1851) and exiled him to Brixen, in the Tyrol, where he lived under police surveillance. He was separated from his young wife Julie, who was consumptive, and could not bear his hard life. He finally obtained his release to visit her in March, 1855, but arrived only after her death. Himself broken, he died the following year, also of tuberculosis.

Havlíček was most influential in his own day as a journalist and critic: indeed he is generally considered the founder of modern Czech journalism and literary criticism. But his poetry, much of which was unpublished in his time because of the censor, is probably most valued today. He is the greatest Czech satirical poet and epigrammatist. Influences on his work include those of Gogol, whom he translated into Czech, Lessing, and the Young German movement. His epigrams are directed against Austrian reaction, the Church (which he regards as an ally of absolutism), and sentimental Czech patriotism. His literary masterpiece is the uncompleted *Křest Svatého Vladimíra*, written between 1848 and 1854. A satirical attack on the Christianization of Russia by St. Vladimir in the tenth century, it is actually directed against the Austrian regime and the Church. Much of its humor proceeds from conscious anachronism and the contrasting use of high style and slang.

E. Altschul translated *The Conversion of St. Vladimir* (1930).

ABOUT: Slavonic Review, III (1924-25) and V (1926-27). [In Czech—Chalupný, E. Karel Havlíček.]

W. E. H.

*HEBBEL, (CHRISTIAN) FRIEDRICH (March 18, 1813-December 13, 1863), German dramatist and poet was born in Wesselburen, Schleswig-Holstein. At the death of his father, a poor mason, Hebbel, then fourteen years old, became a clerk to the local magistrate. Continuing his education on his own, reading widely in his spare time, he fell under the spell of Schiller and Uhland. He himself showed an early talent for poetry

* hĕb' ĕl

HEBBEL

and had his verses published in the *Mode-zeitung* after he had first sent them to Amelie Schoppe, a then popular author of nursery tales. She became his patroness and helped him to attend the university at Hamburg. Throughout his years of study at various German universities, Hebbel suffered great poverty. He became increasingly dependent on a seamstress, Elise Lensing, who was devoted to him and who for many years shared his life.

In 1839, after having drained all of Elise's savings, Hebbel returned to Hamburg to write. In 1840, he completed his first drama, *Judith*, followed in 1841 by the verse-play *Genoveva*. The King of Denmark having offered him a stipend, Hebbel went to Copenhagen after he had published his first collection of poems in 1842. In Paris he completed *Maria Magdalena* in 1843. After a sojourn in Italy, the ever-impoverished Hebbel went to Vienna where his fortunes took a decided turn for the better. There he met two Polish noblemen, the brothers Zerboni di Sposetti, who admired his genius and supplied him with ample means to lead a life of comparative ease and to gain access to the intellectual society of the Austrian capital. The ultimate effect of his new interests and associations was to alienate him completely from the mode of living he had previously known and to spur his ambition and desire for success. He rudely and unceremoniously broke his relationship with Elise, who had made countless sacrifices for him, and in 1846 married the

actress Christine Enghaus, a member of the company of the Vienna court theatre. His wife subsequently acted parts in several of his plays. The rationale of his conduct towards Elise may best be expressed by his own dictum, "A man's first duty is to the most powerful force within him."

In Italy were written a number of somber historical plays: *A Tragedy in Sicily* (1847), *Julia* (1849), and *Herodes and Mariamne* (1849). *Agnes Bernauer* opened in Munich in 1852 and was well received. In 1860 the King of Bavaria granted Hebbel the order of Maximilian for the *Nibelungen* trilogy. Shortly before the playwright's death the high distinction of the Schiller Prize was awarded to Hebbel by the King of Prussia. Hebbel's tragedies mark the transition from the idealism of the Goethe era to the realism, determinism, and psychological drama of Ibsen, Strindberg, and Shaw. Hebbel conceived of society in Hegelian terms as a "categorical imperative," a force which determines the individual's destiny. In most of his historical plays and "bourgeois dramas," there is a struggle between the old order and the new. Thus in *Maria Magdalena* Clara's fate is decided by a society represented by her father, but her struggle is, in turn, symbolic of the new order that is inevitably to come. Many of Hebbel's ideas, as embodied in his plays, were first formulated in his *Diaries*, where his concept of "dramatic conflicts as historical or historically determined processes" is repeatedly stated. Hebbel's success as a lyric poet was limited to only a few relatively successful poems.

English translations of Hebbel's dramas include *Agnes Bernauer* by L. Pattee (in *Poet Lore*, 1909), *Judith* by Carl Van Doren (1914), *Maria Magdelen* by P. Green (1914), *Three Plays (Gyges and His Ring, Herod and Mariamne, Marie Magdalene)* in an Everyman edition (1914). A verse translation of *Herod and Mariamne* by P. Curts was published in 1950.

ABOUT: Campbell, T. M. The Life and Works of Friedrich Hebbel; Purdie, E. Friedrich Hebbel. [In German—see studies by E. Altherr, C. Augustin, H. Frisch, A. Meetz, M. Sommerfeld, A. M. Wagner; also the series of essays in *Hebbel in Neuer Sicht*, ed. H. Kreuzer (1963).]

E. J. S.

*HEGEL, GEORG WILHELM FRIEDRICH** (August 27, 1770-November 14, 1831), German philosopher, was born in Stuttgart, the son of a minor government official. After attending the local *Gymnasium*, he entered the University of

* hä′ gĕl

HEGEL

Tübingen in 1788 to study for the ministry. He changed his mind, however, and completed his doctorate in philosophy in 1793. While at Tübingen he became the friend of the German poet Hölderlin and the philosopher Schelling. Hegel was not an outstanding student, and his performance during his formative years gave little indication of his future greatness as a philosopher. His certificate of graduation from the university mentions his good character, commendable acquaintance with theology and philology, and inadequate knowledge of philosophy. His first position was as a private tutor in Bern, where he remained for three years. A similar position in Frankfurt was held for an additional three years. A small inheritance from his father's estate enabled him to give up this position, and in 1801 he returned to the University of Jena, where he became a *Privatdozent* in 1803 and professor of philosophy in 1805. Here he produced his first treatise entitled *Differenz des Fichteschen und Schellingschen Systems der Philosophie* (1801). The next two years he edited with Schelling the publication *Kritisches Journal der Philosophie.* In 1807 he left Jena to become editor of the *Bamberger Zeitung.* The following year he moved to Nürnberg where he had been appointed rector of the *Gymnasium,* a position which he held until his call to the University of Heidelberg as professor of philosophy in 1816. In Nürnberg he married Marie von Tucher, and the couple had two sons, one of whom, Karl, gained

eminence as an historian. In 1818 Hegel was summoned to the University of Berlin, where, until his death from cholera, he ruled as the leading philosopher and one of the most popular teachers of his time.

By nature Hegel was not an introspective person, but rather an objective thinker who was endowed with an encyclopedic mind, keen discernment, and deep penetration. Romanticism and mysticism held no appeal for him, for he believed that only the idea was real. The idea represented in his mind the eternal aspect which needed to be discovered in the past and present. He believed that "what is reasonable is real, and what is real is reasonable." The task of philosophy was to comprehend what is. Because of this belief he was politically an extreme conservative who hated revolution. He felt that it was not necessary to establish a new state, but only to understand the state as it existed; for the state in his conception was a structure which had not developed by chance, but was the result of a logical, organic evolution. He deemed the state to be the basis of total cultural activity as well as of the incorporation of the moral purposes of humanity. It must strive for ever greater perfection in order to satisfy its destiny to become "the reality of the moral idea." With Hegel began the worship of the state that became increasingly predominant in Germany.

Hegel regarded philosophy as the systematic method of developing the absolute spirit in all of its revealed phenomena, including art, religion, and state life. The truth is the whole, he once said, and he believed his philosophy to be the whole truth. He regarded himself as the developer of a new system that encompassed all of existence, that explained everything and brought everything to completion. In his philosophy Hegel went beyond the impressionism and subjective idealism of Fichte and Schelling to develop a system of absolute idealism, which demonstrated the unity of existence and thinking in all areas of reality. His philosophic system, filled with contradictions and paradoxes, is exceedingly difficult of comprehension. Hegel is said to have lamented once: "Only one man has understood me, and even he has misunderstood me."

Hegel's entire philosophy aims at showing by means of his famous dialectical principle that the world manifests everywhere a genuine evolution. This dialectical process, a theory which was not invented by Hegel but which derives from Plato, was expressed in the proposition thesis, antithesis, synthesis.

Every concept (thesis) contains within it a contradictory, negative factor (antithesis). This contradiction is the source of all movement and life, for it provides the stimulus for change. The progress of the world is the result of the process by which this negative factor is overcome by a union of thesis and antithesis to form a third, higher concept, the synthesis. This synthesis in turn serves as a new thesis to start the process again. Thus the evolution of life is envisioned as a spiral, in which life returns ever to the same point, but on a higher, more elevated plane.

Hegel's collected works, *Sämtliche Werke, Kritische Ausgabe* (32 vols., 1905 ff.), were edited by G. Lasson and J. Hofmeister. Of these the most important which were published during his lifetime are: *Die Phänomenologie des Menschlichen Geistes* (1807), *Wissenschaft der Logik* (1812-16), *Enzyklopedie der Philosophischen Wissenschaften* (1817, 1827, 1830) and *Grundlinien der Philosophie des Rechts* (1821). The following works were published posthumously and were not based on Hegel's own manuscripts, but on lecture notes taken by his students: *Vorlesungen über die Philosophie der Religion* (1832), *Vorlesungen über die Geschichte der Philosophie* (1833-36), *Vorlesungen über die Aesthetik* (1835-38), and *Vorlesungen über die Philosophie der Geschichte* (1837).

Hegel was one of the most stimulating thinkers who ever lived and his creative and imaginative philosophy has been compared to the Reformation in its impact on every sphere of intellectual activity, political, social, religious, and literary. His dialectic exerted great influence on the German dramatist Friedrich Hebbel, who used this principle as the foundation for his dramatic works, and on Karl Marx, whose theory of dialectical materialism was derived directly from Hegel. After his death Hegel's followers split into two groups, a right wing composed of H. G. Hotho, E. Gans, P. Marheineke, and K. L. Michelet, and a socialist left wing consisting of D. F. Strauss, F. T. Vischer, L. Feuerbach, K. Marx, and F. Lassalle.

J. Sibree translated *Vorlesungen über die Philosophie der Geschichte* in 1857 as *Lectures on the Philosophy of History*. *Logic* was translated by W. Wallace in 1874. W. Hastie translated *Einleitung in die Aesthetik* in 1886 as *The Philosophy of Art*. *Einleitung in die Religionsphilosophie* was translated in 1888-91 by F. L. Soldan as *Introduction to the Philosophy of Religion*. E. Haldane and F. H. Simson translated *Vorlesungen über die Geschichte der Philosophie* in 1892-96 as *History of Philosophy*. J. M. Sterrett translated *Die Philosophie des Rechts* as *The Ethics of Hegel* in 1893. *Die Philosophie des Geistes* was translated by W. Wallace in 1894 as *Philosophy of the Mind*. E. B. Speirs and J. B. Sanderson translated *Vorlesungen über die Philosophie der Religion* as *Philosophy of Religion* in 1895. J. B. Baillie translated *Phenomenology of Mind* in 1910. H. S. Macran translated the first part of *Die Subjektive Logik* in 1912 as *The Doctrine of Formal Logic* and the second and third parts in 1929 as *Logic of World and Idea*. *Grundlinien der Philosophie des Rechts* was translated as *The Philosophy of Law* by J. Loewenberg in 1913-15 and as *Philosophy of Right* by T. M. Knox in 1942. F. P. B. Osmaston translated *Vorlesungen über die Aesthetik* as *Philosophy of Fine Art* in 1920. *Science of Logic* was translated by W. H. Johnston and L. G. Struthers in 1929.

ABOUT: Caird, E. Hegel; Findlay, J. N. Hegel, a Re-examination; Knox, T. M. Early Theological Writings, *also* Aesthetic Theories of Kant, Hegel and Schopenhauer; Mackintosh, R. Hegel; McTaggart, J. M. E. Commentary on Hegel's Logic, *also* Studies in the Hegelian Dialectic; Marcuse, H. Reason and Revolution: Hegel and the Rise of Social Theory; Mure, G. R. G. Study of Hegel's Logic; Reyburn, H. A. The Ethical Theory of Hegel; Stace, W. T. The Philosophy of Hegel. [In German —see studies by K. Fischer, H. Glockner, T. Haering, R. Haym, W. Moog, K. Rosenkranz.]

D. G. D.

*HEIBERG, JOHAN LUDVIG (December 14, 1791-August 25, 1860), Danish critic, playwright, poet, was born in Copenhagen. His father, Peter Andreas Heiberg (see sketch below), was a well-known author. His mother was Thomasine Buntzen of a prominent Copenhagen family. She was also a writer known as Thomasine Gyllembourg. Johan Ludvig grew up in a cosmopolitan atmosphere. In 1799 his father was banished for writing ruthless polemics. His mother divorced her exiled husband and the next year married the Swedish Baron C. F. Gyllembourg-Ehrensvärd, and the boy lived with strangers. In 1809 he was admitted to the University of Copenhagen. Three years later he undertook a journey to Stockholm, where he associated with his stepfather's noble circles and learned perfect manners and social elegance. His studies were multifarious and at times somewhat aimless, but in 1817 he took his Ph.D. with a dissertation on Calderón.

Heiberg stayed with his father in Paris (1819-21), studying the French theatre among other subjects. From 1822 he served for three years as lecturer in Danish at the University of Kiel. His stay here was of great importance for his development. In Paris he had acquainted himself with the French vaudeville or musical comedy, and now he saw the German variety thereof during frequent trips to Hamburg. In quite another

* hī' bĕr

vein, he studied and was much influenced by the philosophy of Hegel.

Heiberg had earlier written verse dramas and lyrical poetry. Now he decided to create a Danish vaudeville by combining the French and German types. He returned to Copenhagen where he soon became a dominating cultural figure. His first vaudeville, *Kong Salomon og Jørgen Hattemager*, was performed on November 28, 1825, at the Royal Theatre. The next year he wrote *Aprilsnarrene* (April Fools) and in 1827 *De Uadskillelige* (The Inseparable Ones), one of his most firmly composed works. Adverse criticism forced him to defend his position in his treatise *Om Vaudevillen som Dramatisk Digtart* (On the Vaudeville as a Dramatic Genre, 1826), in which he attacked dilettantism, championed poetic realism, and developed an aesthetic system based on Hegelian philosophy. From 1827 he edited for several years the periodical *Kjøbenhavns Flyvende Post* (The Copenhagen Flying Post), in which his own epoch-making critical articles were published. The charming romantic musical *Elverhøj* (Elfinhill) gave him his greatest triumph. It has remained the most often performed Danish play.

In 1831 Heiberg married Johanne Luise Pätges, daughter of a restaurant-keeper of German birth. She was a fine actress and appeared in many leading roles in her husband's plays.

During the 1830's Heiberg's productivity reached its climax, qualitatively as well as quantitatively. He wrote, for instance, the fairy play *Alferne* (The Elves, 1835), the satirical drama *En Sjæl efter Døden* (A Soul After Death), published in *Nye Digte* (New Poems, 1841), and many critical works. During his last two decades he experienced many adversities and his influence decreased.

Songs from *Elfinhill* appear in English translation in J. Volk's *Songs and Poems in Danish and English* (1903). For other translations see E. Bredsdorff, *Danish Literature in English Translation* (1950).

ABOUT: Howitt, W. & M. The Literature and Romance of Northern Europe, II; Mitchell, P. V. A History of Danish Literature; Winkel Horn, F. History of the Literature of the Scandinavian North. [In Danish—see studies by M. Borup, J. Clausen, P. Hansen, V. Vedel.]

A. J.

*HEIBERG, PETER ANDREAS (November 16, 1758-April 30, 1841), Danish poet and playwright, was born at Vording-

* hī′ bĕr

borg in southern Zealand, where his father, Ludvig Heiberg, Norwegian by birth, was school principal. His father died while he was a boy, after which he and his mother went to live with her father, who was vicar at Vemmetofte. At the age of sixteen he was admitted to the University of Copenhagen from which he graduated three years later. He showed an early rebellious nature. At twenty-one he fled to Sweden to escape usurers and enlisted in the Swedish army. But a relative ransomed him, and after some time he went to Bergen to earn a living as office clerk and tutor. After exposing his employer's dishonesty he was forced to return to Copenhagen where he became assistant to a notary public and later an interpreter of Romance languages.

Heiberg engaged in extensive literary activity and became known as an aggressive critic and spokesman for the radical republicans. In 1787-93 he published a satirical periodical called *Rigsdaler-Sedlens Hændelser* (The Adventures of a Banknote), in which he satirized and criticized political and social conditions. In plays, e.g., *Chinafarerne* (The Travelers to China, 1791), in songs, and in articles and pamphlets, e.g., in the periodical *For Sandhed* (For Truth), he attacked various authorities, including the government.

In 1790, Heiberg married the seventeen-year-old Thomasine Christine Buntzen, daughter of a well-to-do broker, Johan Buntzen. The author Johan Heiberg (see sketch above) was their son. There were serious discords in this marriage, and when Heiberg's vicious polemics incurred his banishment for life his wife divorced him and married the Swedish Baron C. F. Gyllembourg-Ehrensvärd. She became later known as an author under the name of Thomasine Gyllembourg. Heiberg went to Paris where he secured a position in the French Ministry of Education, from which he was dismissed with a pension in 1817. His political and juridical writings as well as his memoirs were published in Norway. He died in Paris.

Very little of Heiberg's production has been translated into English: only one play, *Poverty and Wealth* (1799), translated by C. H. Wilson, and two songs, to be found in A. Andersen Feldborg, ed. *Poems from the Danish* (1816), H. W. Longfellow, *The Poets and Poetry of Europe* (1845), and by G. Borrow, *The Songs of Scandinavia and Other Poems and Ballads* (1923).

ABOUT: Mitchell, P. M. A History of Danish Literature. [In Danish—see studies by J. Grønborg, L. Heiberg, H. Schwanenflügel, C. Thaarup.]

A. J.

*HEIJERMANS (or HEYERMANS), HERMAN (pseudonyms: IVAN JELA-KOMITCH, KOOS HABBEMA, SA-MUEL FALKLAND) (December 3, 1864-November 22, 1924), Dutch-Jewish playwright, novelist, short-story writer, was born in Rotterdam. His first naturalistic novel, *Trinette,* and the symbolical *Fleo* (both 1893), were more successful than his first drama, *Dora Kremer* (1893), which was received with critical depreciation. Heijermans, taking revenge, assumed a Russian writer's name (Jelakomitch) and produced *Ahasveros* in the same year, a drama that dealt with the pogroms in Russia. In 1899 followed *Ghetto,* a bourgeois tragedy which was not too well received by the critics either, but which had much success with the public. From then on he wrote many dramas which were performed every year with varying success in Amsterdam by the Nederlandsche Tooneelvereniging. Later he had his own troupe to perform his dramas. His works for the stage were often strongly tendentious and sentimental, but their realistic portrayal made him the most important dramatist of his time in the Netherlands. The main characters of some of his dramas were often developed for some of the outstanding Dutch stage artists of the day.

Heijerman's prose writings, like his plays, were concerned with social problems and conventional prejudices. The magazine *De Jonge Gids* (1898-1901), which Heijermans started, was an attempt to renew the movement of the *Nieuwe Gids.* In 1898 there appeared *Kamertjeszonde,* written under the pseudonym of Koos Habbema. The very sentimental *Droomkoninkje* (1924) was extremely successful. For the sake of his career as a dramatist, Heijermans lived for a few years in Berlin where he worked for the *Berliner Tageblatt.* The sketches which he wrote for this daily were collected in the *Berliner Skizzenbuch.* The realistic and humoristic pieces remained popular and appeared under the pseudonym of Samuel Falkland in *De Telegraaf,* and in *Het Handelsblad,* two outstanding Dutch dailies. Heijermans' work was translated into many languages and his dramas were performed in Paris, New York, London, Berlin, and Moscow.

Heijermans was twice married: to Maria Peers (1895) and to Annie Jurgen (1917). Death occurred at Zandvoort.

The following plays are available in English: *The Good Hope,* translated by H. H. Gampert Hig-

gins (1912), by L. Saunders and C. Heijermans-Houwink (1928) ; *The Rising Sun,* translated by C. St. John (pseud. of C. Marshall) (1926) ; *Links,* by H. Peacy and W. R. Brandt (1927).

ABOUT: Flaxmann, S. T. The Dramatic Work of H. Heyermans. [In Dutch—see studies by M. Heyermans-Piers, F. Hullema.]

H. B.

*HEINE, HEINRICH (HARRY) (December 13, 1797-February 16, 1856), German poet and journalist, was born in Düsseldorf, the eldest of four children of Samson Heine and Betty van Geldern, whose marriage was delayed until after his birth. The father, a Jewish textile dealer, was a gentle, light-hearted man little suited to the world of business. The poet throughout his life remained deeply attached to his family, though in his childhood he often retreated into a fanciful dream-world. Besides receiving traditional Jewish instruction, he was educated at a Düsseldorf Jesuit school after the pattern of the French *lycée.* The family determined that he should follow in the footsteps of his wealthy and influential uncle Solomon Heine, a Hamburg banker. Therefore, after some training in a Düsseldorf commercial college, he spent several weeks in Frankfurt am Main as a banker's assistant and in 1816 was sent to Hamburg, where, after a year's apprenticeship under his uncle, he was set up in his own firm, Harry Heine and Company, whose almost immediate collapse conclusively demonstrated Heine's lack of business ability as well as his obvious antipathy toward middle-class life. The Hamburg period also witnessed a second failure—his unrequited passion for his cousin Amalie Heine, the effects of which apparently haunted him throughout his life and provided a leading theme for his poetry.

Still hoping to make a success of his nephew, Solomon Heine in 1819 sent him to the University of Bonn to take up law, but young Heine promptly plunged into such fields as German literature and history, soon coming under the influence of the romantic school through his teacher August Wilhelm Schlegel, who also gave him encouragement in his verses. The next year he transferred to Göttingen, from which he was soon suspended after challenging a fellow-student to a duel. In 1821 he went to Berlin, where he circulated among the literary salons, most prominently in that of the diplomat Varnhagen von Ense and his blue-stocking wife Rahel, who became his closest advisers both in personal and literary matters. During this

* hī′ yĕr mäns

* hī′ nĕ

period the ironic manner characteristic of his personality and work was already creating enmities among his fellow-writers—enmities which illustrate a crucial difference in sensibility between Heine and the German cultural environment and whose effects are still evident today in German critical estimates of his work.

His first volume, *Gedichte* (1821), reveals to some degree the peculiar combination of romantic lyricism and fierce irony for which his style was to become famous. A succeeding volume, *Tragödien nebst einem Lyrischen Intermezzo* (1823), contains the only dramas he ever completed, the somberly romantic *Almansor* and *Ratcliff*, for both of which he held high hopes, but which are largely forgotten today, while the love poems of the accompanying "intermezzo" remain among his best known. In 1824 he paid his famed visit to Goethe in which, according to legend, Heine announced that he too was working on a Faust, after which the aged Olympian maintained the coolest of stances toward the eager young poet. The following year, shortly before completing his law degree, he underwent a secret baptism (officially changing his name from Harry to Heinrich for the occasion), a step which, though it often preyed on his conscience, was for practical reasons a frequent occurrence among the Jews of his day. For a short time he contemplated settling down in Hamburg to a law career and marriage—this time, he hoped, to Amalie's sister Therese—but, finding his

Hamburg family virtually estranged from him, he returned to his literary activities. He soon published the first volume of his *Reisebilder* (1826), a record of journeys to the Harz Mountains (1824) and to Norderney on the North Sea (1825), though in the form of a wholly original genre consisting of prose mixed with verse, self-analysis offhandedly mixed with social satire, and, incidentally, through its picture of the North Sea in effect the introduction of the sea to German poetry.

Three subsequent volumes (1827-31) that followed the popular success of the first served principally as miscellanies of his prose writings of the following years, including sketches of his journeys to England (1827) and Italy (1828). His months in London were marked by enthusiasm for parliamentary government and the general atmosphere of freedom, but also by disappointment at the stiffness of the English character and the prosaic quality of English life. His London stay also brought his already unstable relations with his uncle to a head through a deceptive maneuver by which Heine obtained a large sum from him. Henceforth Solomon's support, despite reconciliations, was sporadic and not to be depended upon. On his return to Germany in 1827 Heine accepted an offer from the prominent publisher Cotta to become co-editor of the liberal paper *Neue Allgemeine Politische Annalen* in Munich, and in the same year published his *Buch der Lieder*, whose lyrics quickly established his fame and, though considered by some inferior to his later poetry, long remained the basis of his international reputation. The following years, the last before his permanent departure for France, witnessed the failure of his hopes for a professorship of literature, a bitter literary and personal controversy with the poet Platen, and increasing hostility directed toward his political liberalism by the German states.

In 1831, attracted by the opportunity to exercise his political convictions without repression, he moved to Paris, where he supported himself by articles on politics, literature, art, and religion (for a time he followed the Saint-Simonian philosophy then current in France) contributed to German periodicals. His *bon vivant* air and his support of constitutional monarchy often set him at odds with the other German political refugees in Paris, most notably with the sober-minded republican Ludwig Börne. Yet within Germany Heine and Börne shared the position of leading spokesmen for freedom, their journalistic activities helping to inspire the political and literary movement of the 1830's known as Young Germany, whose championship of Heine's work caused his writings to be banned by the German Confederation in 1835. Meanwhile, though struggling against debt, Heine reigned as one of the most dazzling wits in French intellectual society—Sainte-Beuve called him a "delightful mind, sometimes divine and sometimes diabolical"—and carried on friendships and flirtations which ran the scale of society from prostitutes to the most brilliant women of the day, including George Sand. His most passionate and lasting romance was with Crescentia Eugénie Mirat, whom he called Mathilde, an ignorant, impractical, childishly capricious salesgirl in a glove and shoe shop whom he took as mistress in 1834 and married in 1841 and who remained his faithful companion until his death.

The writings of his first decade in Paris were largely polemical, and directed as much at personal enemies as at ideas. But as a recent biographer, E. M. Butler, has put it, "Heine's polemics and philippics were always essentially lyrical, inspired as they were by passion: passionate hatred for absolutism and aristocracy, passionate contempt for the rich, passionate pity for the poor." In *Französiche Zustände* (1832) he analyzes the opening years of the July Monarchy, and in *Die Romantische Schule* (1833) he attacks such strains of German romanticism as its Catholic bias, its political conservatism, and its frequent detachment from life, and includes as well a personal attack on his former teacher A. W. Schlegel. Miscellaneous writings, ranging from a monograph on the folklore of nature spirits and witchcraft (*Elementargeister*) to the fantastic tales of *Florentinische Nächte,* were periodically collected for the four volumes entitled *Salon* (1831-40). His unfriendly biography (1840) of the recently deceased Börne occasioned violent attacks upon himself, including a duel in which he suffered a slight wound. During the following decade he published two long poems, *Atta Troll: Ein Sommernachtstraum* (1843), and *Deutschland: Ein Wintermärchen* (1844), both considered today among his highest-ranking works. Consisting of a mixture of history, folklore, and political and literary satire, and written in a tone ranging from whimsy to sarcasm, these poems have traditionally defied generic classification.

In 1843 and 1844 he twice broke his Paris exile for brief visits to his relatives in Hamburg. After his uncle's death in 1844, he was engaged in constant disputes with Solomon's heir about a pension that had been promised him. His financial position was further aggravated by the miserliness of his publisher Julius Campe, who, though he had prospered on Heine's works, had earlier bought up Heine's rights for a small sum, and by the loss, through the Revolution of 1848, of a pension which he had been accepting from the French government—to the horror of many German liberals—for more than a decade. But far more dramatic than the poverty of his last years was his crippling spinal paralysis which, though heralded by increasing illnesses since the mid-1830's, finally reduced him to a motionless, bedridden condition from 1848 until his death. During this time the room on the rue d'Amsterdam which housed what he called his "mattress-grave" became the scene of an unending *levée* attended by friends, admirers and the merely curious. With his mind as active as ever, he was able in these years to publish such works as *Romanzero* (1851), composed largely of narrative poems principally on Spanish and Jewish themes; *Doktor Faust* (1851), a ballet scenario; a second collection of poems (*Gedichte 1853 und 1854*); *Die Götter im Exil* (1853), on the transformation of the pagan deities during Christian times; and his *Geständnisse* (1854), reflections on politics and religion. His final year was marked by a deep attachment to Elise Krinitz, whom he called La Mouche.

Heine not only was one of the most popular and influential poets throughout Europe in the nineteenth century, but next to Goethe and Schiller has probably attained a more considerable reputation and public outside his native country than any other German poet. His lyrics have inspired many of the greatest German songs, most notably the *Dichterliebe* cycle of Schumann. His influence extended to such diverse figures as Wagner, Baudelaire, Arnold, Housman, and Pound. His list of friendships is a spectrum of the continental intellectual realm of his time—from Ferdinand Lassalle and Karl Marx at one extreme (he once saved the life of one of Marx's children) to Hans Christian Andersen and Alfred de Musset at the other. As with Pope, Byron, and Pound the everyday happenings of the literary and political world supplied the concrete base for his larger poetic vision. And as with Byron, whom he admired and translated, the history of his reputation has been marked by vast popularity abroad, though by relative neglect on the part of serious critics in his native land, as well as by a shift in interest from the lyrical to the ironic and satirical side of his work. His larger works, whether prose or verse, narrative or lyrical cycle, usually seem like containers for an admixture of incongruous materials. The unity within his works is pre-eminently one of tone and sensibility rather than of surface theme.

Heine was translated innumerable times through the last half of the nineteenth century (among his best known translators are E. B. Browning and Ezra Pound). A collected edition of Heine's *Works,* in twelve volumes, translated by C. G. Leland, T. Brooksbank, and M. Armour, was issued 1891-1905. Additional translations of prose works include *Florentine Nights* (tr. K. B. Fitz-Gerald, 1929, and F. Carter, 1933), *Italian Travel Sketches* (tr. E. A. Sharp, 1895), *Religion and Philosophy in Germany* (tr. J. Snodgrass, 1882), *The Romantic School,* (tr. S. L. Fleishman, 1882), *Doktor Faust, a Dance Poem* (tr. B. Ashmore, 1952), *Memoirs* (tr. T. W. Evans, 1884, and G. Cannon, 1910), and *Letters* (tr. anon., 1912). Selections include *Works of Prose* (tr. E. B. Ashton, 1943) and *Poetry and Prose* (ed. F. Ewen, 1948). Among translations of the poems within the present century are the *North Sea* (tr. H. M. Jones, 1916, and V. Watkins, 1951), *The Sea and the Hills* (including the *Harzreise* and *Nordsee,* tr. F. T. Wood, 1946) *Atta Troll* (tr. H. Scheffauer, 1913), *Germany, a Winter's Tale* (tr. H. Salinger, 1944), and a large selection, *Poems of Heinrich Heine* (tr. L. Untermeyer, 1917). In 1959 a bibliographical checklist by A. Arnold, *Heine in England and America,* was published.

ABOUT: Arnold, M. Essays in Criticism; Atkins, H. G. Heine; Betz, L. Heine in France; Bieber, H. Heinrich Heine, A Biographical Anthology; Brod, M. Heine: The Artist in Revolt; Butler, E. M. Heinrich Heine; Browne, L. That Man Heine; Ellis, H. The New Spirit; Eliot, G. Essays and Leaves from a Note-book; Fairley, B. Heinrich Heine, an Interpretation; Fejtö, F. Heine, Liptzin, S. English Legend of Heinrich Heine; Prawer, S. S. Heine, the Tragic Satirist; Rose, W. Heinrich Heine, Two Studies of His Thought and Feeling, *also* The Early Love Poetry of Heinrich Heine; Sachs, H. B. Heine in America; Sharp, W. Life of Heinrich Heine; Wormley, S. L. Heine in England; Untermeyer, L. Heinrich Heine: Paradox and Poet; Western Review, Winter 1957. [In German—see studies by A. Strodtmann, R. Fürst, M. J. Wolff, P. Beyer. In French—by H. Lichtenberg and K. Weinberg.]

H. L.

*HEINRICH VON MORUNGEN

(fl. 1196-1222), German lyric poet, was a member of a family of service nobility (*ministeriales*) from Burg Morungen, near Sangerhausen in Thuringia. He is known to have accompanied Landgrave Dietrich von Meissen on the Crusade of 1197 and there is a late medieval tradition that he made lengthy journeys through "India," i.e., Asia Minor. He was probably at the court of Dietrich about 1210 and may have met Walther von der Vogelweide there. Documents of 1217-18

* hīn' rīk fôn mō' rŏŏng ĕn

mention him as "miles emeritus," or knight in retirement. He wrote only lyric poetry. Thirty of his poems have survived, all of which are in the style of the high *Minnesang* and in the typical tripartite strophe form imitated from the Provençal *canzon.* The influence of the troubadours and of the classical poet Ovid is very obvious in his work. He in his turn influenced his successors, particularly Walther von der Vogelweide.

In many respects the *Minnesang* reaches its greatest heights with Heinrich, for he is more concerned with the analysis of his own feelings as a lover than with flattery of his lady or a description of her charms; with the exaltation of love and the effects of love unrequited. Most effective, however, and more characteristic of him is his use of bold and brilliant imagery which symbolizes the great problem of all the *Minnesänger*—the desire for the fulfillment of love and the fear of shattering an illusion. The force of his language is such that he seems more sincere than most of the *Minnesänger* and, in spite of the rigidity of his forms, his impetuous and fiery character emerges. Besides his *Minnelieder* (ideal love songs), Heinrich wrote one of the few *Tagelieder* (dawn songs) of the best period of the *Minnesang.*

All Heinrich's extant poems are in K. Lachmann & C. von Krano, *Des Minnesangsfrühling* (1944). Some English translations appear in J. Bithell, *The Minnesingers* (1909), F. Nicholson, *Old German Love Songs* (1907), and M. Richey, *Medieval German Lyrics* (1958).

ABOUT: German Life and Letters, XIII (1960). [In German—Boor, H. de and Newald, R. Geschichte der Deutschen Literatur, II; Stammler, W. Verfasserlexikon des Deutschen Mittelalters. In French—Moret, A. Les Débuts du Lyrisme en Allemagne.]

W. T. H. J.

*HEINRICH VON VELDEKE (fl. 1170-1185), German (more accurately Flemish) epic and lyric poet, was a native of the Limburg district, belonged to the landless nobility *(ministeriales),* and is shown by documents to have enjoyed at various times the patronage of Count Ludwig of Loen, his wife Agnes, and Count Hermann of Thuringia. At the court of Cleves, about 1170, he wrote a poem about the local patron saint, St. Servatius, of which only fragments have survived. He must have begun his most important work, the *Eneide,* about the same time. In 1174 the incomplete manuscript was taken away by a Count Heinrich and the poet

* hīn' rīk fôn fĕl' dĕ kĕ

did not recover it until nine years later. The work was finished about 1183.

Besides these two longer poems, Heinrich also wrote love poems, of which thirty-one have come down to us, rewritten in "classical" Middle High German. Scholars, chiefly Frings, have attempted with some success to restore them to the original Low German dialect. He was regarded by contemporaries, such as Gottfried von Strassburg (who praises him warmly in *Tristan)* and later poets such as der Marner, as having introduced the true idea of courtly love into German literature. Modern critics believe that his work is too spontaneous and optimistic to be typical of the true *Minnesang* but agree that he was the first German poet to be entirely successful in the use of Romance lyric forms and that he introduced the description of the ideal spring landscape and other poetic commonplaces which play a major rôle in the work of later writers. His epic poem *Eneide* (edited Behagel, 1882; no English translation) is based upon a French verse romance of about 1170, the *Roman d'Eneas,* and only indirectly upon Virgil's *Aeneid.* It replaces the sense of imperial mission which Virgil stressed with the theme of love as a destructive force in the Dido episode and as a courtly and ennobling experience in the love of Aeneas and Lavinia. Love thus becomes the dominant theme of the work, a fact which greatly influenced subsequent writers of the German courtly epic.

Translations of selections from his work appear in M. Richey's *Medieval German Lyrics* (1958).

ABOUT: Bithell, J. The Minnesanger; Nicholson, F. C. Old German Love Songs [In German—Boor, H. de and Newald, R. Geschichte der Deutschen Literatur, II; Stammler, W. Verfasserlexikon des Deutschen Mittelalters.]

W. T. H. J.

*HEINSIUS, DANIEL (June 9, 1580- February 25, 1655), Dutch philologist and poet, was born in Ghent. His parents moved to the United Provinces (Veere in Zealand) to avoid further troubles caused by the Spanish War. Later they spent some time in England, then returned to Holland (Rijswijck near the Hague), and finally settled in Flushing. In 1594 the young Heinsius began his studies in Greek at the then famous university of Franeker. Henricus Schotanus was his outstanding teacher. After half a year Heinsius went to Leiden where he was to remain until his death. He met and befriended such well-known figures as Marnix

* hĭn′ sĕ ûs

van St. Aldegonde, Janus Douza, and Paulus Merula. Heinsius studied in Leiden under Scaliger and soon became a celebrated man of learning. His proficiency in the classical languages won the praise of all the best scholars of Europe and positions abroad were offered to him. He remained in Leiden, however, becoming professor of Latin in 1602, professor of Greek in 1605, and successor to Merula as librarian in 1607. His fame attracted students from other countries, principally Norway and England.

Heinsius' uneventful life is recorded in a list of erudite and influential works. The little Dutch poetry he wrote never gained much acclaim in his own country, but it was greatly admired by Martin Opitz who, like so many other German poets of the seventeenth century, was Heinsius' pupil at one time. Opitz translated some of his odes which introduced the use of the rhyming alexandrine into German literature. And Opitz' own *Buch von der Deutschen Poeterey* was influenced by Heinsius' poetic theories.

Heinsius' original Latin poems were published in three volumes—*Iambi* (1602), *Elegiae* (1603), and *Poemata* (1605). His *Emblemata Amatoria,* poems in Dutch and Latin, were printed in 1604. In this year he also edited Theocritus, while Hesiod was edited by him in 1603. In 1609 his *Latin Orations* were printed. In 1610 he edited Horace, in 1611 Aristotle and Seneca. In 1613 appeared his Dutch tragedy *The Massacre of the Innocents* and in 1614 his treatise *De Politica Sapientia.* In 1616 he collected his original Dutch poems in one volume; he edited Terence in 1618 and Livy in 1620, published the oration *De Contemptu Mortis* in 1621, and brought out the *Epistles of Joseph Scaliger* in 1627.

During the religious struggle between the Aryans and the Calvinists which erupted in Holland in the second decade of the seventeenth century Heinsius took the side of the Calvinists and functioned as their secretary during the Synod of Dordt in 1618. His later years were troubled by philological quarrels.

G. W. Robinson translated Heinsius' *Funeral Orations on Joseph Scaliger* (1915) and *The Value of History* (1943).

ABOUT: Kern, E. G. The Influence of Heinsius and Vossius upon French Dramatic Theory; Sandys, J. E. History of Classical Scholarship. [In Dutch—see studies by J. Ten Brink, D. J. H Ter Horst.]

H. B.

*HELVETIUS, CLAUDE ADRIEN
(January 26, 1715-December 26, 1771),
French philosopher, was born in Paris, son
of Jean Claude Adrien Helvetius. His
mother was Geneviève Noëlle de Carvoisin
d'Armancourt. His paternal ancestors were
Germans who had emigrated to Switzerland
and taken the name Sweitzer. In time they
moved on to Holland and Latinized the name
to Helvetius. For several generations they
had been doctors and apothecaries. Helvetius' grandfather, Jean Adrien Helvetius,
made his fortune by cornering the market on
the root ipecacuanha, the medicinal properties
of which he had publicized in Europe. He
settled in France and won great fame and
wealth as a physician. The fortune and
reputation were continued and augmented by
his son, who was court physician to Louis
XV. Young Claude Adrien was educated
by tutors and at the Jesuit College of Louis
le Grand. He served an apprenticeship in
commerce at Caën, mainly to prepare him
for a career in law, but his duties were not
onerous and he found time for the composition of a tragedy and some verse.

At twenty-three, largely through his
father's influence, Helvetius was appointed
to the office of "fermier-général" (farmer-
general, an official in charge of tax collecting). He took his position seriously, traveling about the country studying finance and
rural economy. In the course of his travels
he met Montesquieu, then writing his great
Esprit des Lois, and although the two men
became friends, Helvetius disagreed with
much of the older man's thought. He was
also acquainted with and influenced by many
other outstanding thinkers of his age, including Voltaire and Buffon. Eventually the
attractions of the intellectual life proved more
persuasive than those of his powerful and
highly profitable state office. He retired to
his country estate of Voré in 1751 and devoted himself to study. In the same year
he married Anne Catherine de Ligniville.
They had two daughters (two other children
died in infancy).

At Voré Helvetius began working out his
philosophical principles. A product of the
Age of Enlightenment, he carried the practical, materialistic thought of his time to its
logical conclusion: namely, that the mainspring of all human action is self-love. Like
his contemporary Philosophes Diderot, Rousseau, Holbach, and Condorcet, he identified
moral questions with social questions. (Although his name is associated with the *En-*

* ĕl vä syüs'

clyclopédie, he did not actually contribute to
the work, but he shared with the Encyclopedists their opposition to political tyranny and
religious fanaticism and their belief in widespread education.) In 1758 he published
his influential and highly controversial book
De l'Esprit, a coldly rationalistic examination
of morality. Essentially two main questions
were involved in his study—What do men
know? and Why do they act as they do?
In seeking an answer to the first question
Helvetius followed the lead of English as
well as French thinkers—most especially
John Locke and David Hartley. He denied
the existence of innate ideas, argued that the
human mind worked through sense impressions only (created by physical sensibility,
preserved by memory), and that all intellects
are equal, errors and seeming inferiority being only the result of human passions or
ignorance. From these ideas ultimately developed Helvetius' theory of education. He
favored universal education, regardless of
race, religion, or social class, and the training of the young in practical subjects that
would make them useful in society—natural
philosophy, history, mathematics, morality—
rather than in the study of classical languages.

De l'Esprit also considers the question of
what motivates human action, and here Helvetius concludes that self-interest or self-love
alone dictates our judgments and our actions.
This self-interest is founded upon man's love
of pleasure and fear of pain. Thus even
acts of charity and self-sacrifice may be
explained by the fact that the doer's pleasure
in these acts outweighs whatever pain is involved. Helvetius takes the position of total
moral relativism, denies absolutes of all kinds
—justice, good, evil, etc. The final test of
actions is their use to society—a doctrine
which clearly anticipates nineteenth century
Utilitarianism and the idea of "the greatest
good for the greatest number." (Jeremy
Bentham acknowledged his indebtedness to
Helvetius.)

Not surprisingly *De l'Esprit* aroused
clamors of protest, even from liberal thinkers
(both Voltaire and Rousseau found fault
with it). And to conservatives the book was
outrageous, immoral, and subversive. Not
even the influence of Mme de Pompadour
could save Helvetius from disgrace. Voltaire advised him to leave the country.
Helvetius was sufficiently alarmed by the
furor to retract the ideas of the book on
three separate occasions, but this was not
enough. In January 1759 the Pope declared
the book licentious and dangerous; in Febru-

403

ary Parlement condemned it, and a few days later a copy (along with Voltaire's *Sur la Loi Naturelle)* was publicly burned. The notoriety of the book of course gave it international fame. English and German translations appeared, and its fame spread as far as Sweden and Russia. Helvetius wrote a sequel, *De l'Homme,* in 1769 (published posthumously in 1772 and publicly burned in 1774), a plea for religious toleration and an attack on the power of the Catholic Church. It also contains a further exposition of his theories of education.

In 1764 Helvetius visited England, and in the following year he went to Germany at the invitation of Frederick the Great. He spent the remaining years of his life at Voré where he composed a long poem, *Le Bonheur* (posthumously published in 1772), which attempted to expound poetically his theory of enlightened self-interest. He died, following a number of severe attacks of gout, in his house in Paris, at fifty-six. Although in his youth—when he had been handsome, rich, and socially very popular—he had the reputation of a roué, in his later years he was a model husband and father. One of his contemporaries, F. M. von Grimm, observed that if the term "true gentleman" had not already existed, it would have been invented to describe him.

The Œuvres Complètes was published in four volumes in 1774 and a number of editions followed, the best of them being a fourteen-volume edition in 1795 with an essay on his life and works. *De l'Esprit* went through five editions in the year of its first publication, 1758. An English translation, *De l'Esprit or Essays on the Mind and Its Several Faculties,* appeared in 1807. An English translation of *De l'Homme—A Treatise on Man*—was made by W. Hooper in 1777.

ABOUT: Cumming, I. Helvetius: His Life and Place in the History of Educational Thought; Grossman, M. The Philosophy of Helvetius; Horowitz, I. L. Claude Helvetius; Plekhanov, G. V. Essays in the History of Materialism. [In French —Andlau, B. d', Helvétius, Seigneur de Voré; Keim, A. Helvétius, Sa Vie et son Œuvre.]

*HERDER, JOHANN GOTTFRIED (later VON) (August 25, 1744-December 18, 1803), German critic, author, and divine, was born in the small town of Mohrungen in East Prussia. His father was a cantor, sexton, and schoolmaster, whose ancestors, weavers by trade, had originally come from Silesia. His mother, Anna Elisabeth *née* Pelz, was a native of Mohrungen. Both parents were sincerely religious, of the Pietist (Protestant) persuasion. The family—there

* hĕr' dĕr

HERDER

were three children—was extremely poor, and Herder's euphemistic description of their condition as "limited in means, but not needy" was written at a later date for the benefit of his fiancée.

After receiving some rudimentary instruction from his father, young Herder was sent to the Town School of Rector Grimm, a highly irritable and pedantic pedagogue, who terrified his charges, but from whom he gained an unusual mastery of Latin together with some Greek. After graduating at the top of his class, he was taken into service as secretary and slavey by S. Trescho, his father's religious superior, who employed him in his profitable "manufacture" of turgid-sentimental books on piety. In the Deacon's excellent library young Herder read avidly after hours and gained some of the stupendous store of information which was to make him one of the most prolific and influential writers that Germany has produced. In 1762 Herder enrolled at the University of Königsberg as a student of medicine; but fainting at the first dissection he witnessed, he changed to theology. Through stipends and by tutoring less gifted students he eked out a precarious existence in the East Prussian capital.

While in Königsberg Herder was influenced by three things that were to mold much of his later thought. These were his friendship with Kant, who at that time was not yet the great rationalist-idealistic philosopher but the effective teacher of the sciences; his intimacy with J. G. Hamann, the Magus of the North, who was already the declared foe of rationalism; and his connections with the humanitarian and literary group, the "Deutsche Gesellschaft," which, merging with the Masonic lodge, counted amongst its members Kanter, Lindner, and the Berens brothers, all to become benefactors of Herder. During his two years in Königsberg Herder wrote and published some occasional verses which show only a slight lyrical gift.

Late in 1764 Herder was offered the position of assistant master at the Cathedral School in Riga, within the Russian Empire of Catherine II. He soon became an intimate of the enlightened patricians of the town, developing into an effective teacher, an excellent conversationalist, and a graceful and appealing preacher in his capacity as assistant pastor. Here in Riga Herder started out on his epoch-making career as critic of literature and philosophy.

For Kanter's *Königsbergsche Zeitungen* Herder composed some six reviews which show him primarily as an enlightened theologian. His contributions to the other Baltic journal, the *Rigische Anzeigen,* are also more in the nature of exercises in the use of rationalistic style applied to education. It is in the unpublished essays of this early period that Herder foreshadows his radical ideas on historical relativism, the psycho-biological explanation of aesthetic reactions, and the conception of the uniqueness and self-sufficiency of each historical age, proof enough that he had more than digested the works of Montesquieu, Buffon, Shaftesbury, Hume, Rousseau, and Lowth.

At last, in the fall of 1766, though dated 1767, there appeared anonymously the first two parts of his *Über die Neuere Deutsche Litteratur. Fragmente* (3d Part, 1767), in which Herder, going far beyond Lessing and the Berlin *Litteraturbriefe* of 1755, differentiates clearly between the function of poetic and philosophical (scientific) speech; attacks the German hero-worship of other languages; draws attention to the rampant "unhistorical imitation" in German literature; and defines the principal role of the critic as being the friend of the "genius." Literature, Herder emphatically states, must be judged in the light of the historical development, not in the light of absolute standards.

Herder's publications aroused hostility. Afraid of these attacks which even went so far as to question his orthodoxy, and possibly eager also to break with Mme Busch, an unhappily married lady, Herder left Riga, in spite of some tempting offers to stay. In May 1769 he set out on a sea voyage which eventually carried him to the coast of Normandy, and then to Nantes, where he wrote a journal of his trip. He spent some time in Paris, meeting Diderot and d'Alembert, and some of the minor French writers, but he was not intimate with any of them. In December 1769 he left Paris.

Impelled by financial considerations Herder accepted the post of tutor to the young and melancholic Prince of Holstein-Gottorp, agreeing to accompany the latter on a grand tour to Italy. On his way to meet his noble pupil, Herder's ship was wrecked off the Dutch coast, the passengers being saved just before the vessel went down. Herder during all this time had stayed in his cabin reading the poems of "Ossian." In Hamburg he enjoyed a memorable fortnight in the company of Lessing. As soon as the train of the Prince got languidly under way in a southerly direction, halted by many state visits, Herder's equanimity was sorely tried by the petty jealousies of the accompanying courtiers. In Darmstadt he met the Circle of Sensitives, amongst them Caroline Flachsland (1750-1809), whom he eventually married. In Strasbourg Herder resigned from the Prince's suite to undergo another operation of a fistula on his eye which had plagued him from childhood. The operation was unsuccessful, but, while convalescing, Herder met the young student Goethe, and this meeting had momentous consequences. Despite Herder's ill-humor, caused by physical and mental anguish, and his somewhat condescending tone towards the younger man, he succeeded in demolishing the latter's rococo ideas and in directing him to the cultural values of his own nation. He preached to him the gospel of spontaneity and of the originality of poetic expression, particularly apparent in the *Volkslied* of the lower classes, and he suggested that Goethe reread Homer, the Bible, "Ossian," Klopstock, and above all Shakespeare and Hamann, with this in mind. Herder also had Goethe read his prize-winning *Abhandlung über den Ursprung der Sprache* (1772), which he was writing during the last days of 1770. In it he states that poetry is originally identical with language itself and does not belong to one particular social class; language is not created by God, nor invented by man; it is a "necessity" of man's innermost nature.

In Strasbourg Herder had accepted an appointment as court preacher and member of the consistory at Bückeburg, the capital of the diminutive principality of Schaumburg-Lippe, where he arrived in April 1771. Overcoming the prejudices of the local clergy who had regarded him as a freethinker, he even established himself with Count Wilhelm, a militant rationalist, who in all ways was his direct opposite. Although overwhelmed by his duties and initially depressed by his debts, which delayed his marriage to Caroline until 1773, he resumed his literary work. His writings in these days were the most directly influential, the clarion call for the Storm and Stress movement, of which he was generally regarded the initiator, theorist, and leader. For some time he had been greatly interested in the poetry of the North, more particularly Percy's *Reliques* and the poetry of "Ossian." His enthusiasm for these "primitive" poets had fused with his admiration of Homer, Shakespeare, the Bible, and the folk songs of all nations. Under the influence of his reading he finally broke with classicism and stirred his age, particularly the younger generation, with his essays in *Von Deutscher Art und Kunst* (1773), which included also contributions by Goethe, Möser, and Frisi. The main tenor of the work is the complete rejection of rationalism in art combined with a new national evaluation of the past in terms of primitivism and originality. Herder, however, was no follower of Rousseau; he viewed each age historically, and the latter's call for a return to nature he regarded as nonsense. His opposition to the Enlightenment is particularly obvious in his religious writings of this period.

After the death of Countess Sophie, his pietistic friend and benefactress, Herder in 1776 obtained through Goethe's influence the post of general superintendent and court chaplain at Weimar, where he passed the rest of his life. There he enjoyed the protection of Goethe, the friendship of Wieland, later that of Jean Paul, and many others. As a preacher he was very popular, and as an educator most successful. Yet the atmosphere of Weimar did not suit him; again and again he railed at Goethe and the Duke, and felt left out of the social, cultural, and literary development, particularly after 1794, when Schiller drew close to Goethe. Herder often thought of leaving Weimar, yet never took the final step. His continued ill-health intensified a naturally sensitive temperament, and matters were not helped by Caroline's emotional, jealous, and over-protective attitude toward him. He felt that his mission was predominantly that of a teacher, and as he began losing influence over others, he grew

envious of their independence. Yet he found consolation in his own family of seven children and in the appreciation accorded him by his parishioners, especially by the ladies, such as Sophie von Schard (of whom he grew too fond), Charlotte von Stein, and the Duchess Luise. A trip to Italy in 1788-89 did not improve his somberness of spirit or his relations with Goethe.

In Weimar Herder wrote amongst many others his fundamental work on Hebrew poetry, *Vom Geist der Ebräischen Poesie* (1782-83); his scientific Spinozist-Leibnizian *Gott! Ein Gespräch* (1787); his monumental philosophy of history, the *Ideen zur Philosophie der Geschichte der Menschheit* (1784-91); his practical and liberal *Briefe zur Beförderung der Humanität* (1793-97); his own journal, *Adrastea* (1800-04), which contains much of his later dramatic and lyrical writing; and finally his translation of the Spanish romance *El Cid* (1805). Towards the latter part of his life he occupied himself primarily with speculative questions in philosophy and theology, as a result of which he lost the friendship of many of his closest associates, such as Jacobi, Lavater, even Hamann and Kant (*Metakritik*, 1799; *Kalligone*, 1800). He is buried in his own Church of St. Peter and Paul beside the Duke's ancestors.

Herder's influence on German and international literature cannot be overestimated. He is not only the theorist of Storm and Stress, but also the dominant influence on romanticism, including the so-called German classical period in Weimar. It is fair to say that his ideas about evolution, national culture, primitivism, spontaneity, and humanism made possible the literary revolutions during and after his lifetime, creating as it were modern literature and literary criticism. When Weimar and its spirit is mentioned in German literature, he is included amongst the creative writers of the stature of a Goethe, Schiller, and Wieland. Unlike Goethe in the later period he was not a neo-Hellenist, unlike Schiller he was not a Kantian, and unlike Wieland he was not a Voltairean: he remained faithful to a more realistic and historical ideal. As a stylist, particularly in his later period, when he shunned the fragmentary form, he is justly acclaimed as one of the great prose writers of Germany.

In appearance Herder was of medium height. As Goethe described him, "he had a certain softness in his bearing that was very fitting and decorous without being really diplomatic. A round face, a sizable forehead, a somewhat snub nose, a mouth somewhat drawn up but highly pleasant and likeable in an individual way. Under black eyebrows a pair of coal-black eyes, which never failed of making an effect, although one was usually red and inflamed." His character was on the whole a worthy and attractive one. Nietzsche once said of him somewhat ungenerously (and thinking of his Weimar period): "He did not sit at the banquet table of those who were truly creating; and his ambition did not permit him to take a modest seat among those who were truly enjoying. So he was an unquiet guest. . . ." Yet Herder was a born teacher and, though lacking harmony, he was a true humanist and humanitarian, a sensitive, great, and effective man.

Today Herder has again come into his own after considerable neglect during the nineteenth century, where he was unfavorably compared with Schiller, Goethe, and Lessing, and abused by the disciples of Kant.

Among Herder's works translated into English are his *Treatise upon the Origin of Language* (1827); *Leaves of Antiquity*, by Mrs. C. Sawyer (1893); *A Tribute to the Memory of Ulrich von Hutten*, by A. Aufrere (1789, mistakenly ascribed to Goethe); *The Cid* (1828); *Fables* (1845); his *Ideen* under the title *Outlines of a Philosophy of the History of Man*, by T. O. Churchill (1800 and 1803); *The Spirit of Hebrew Poetry* (1801), also tr. by J. Marsh (1833); and *God: Some Conversations*, by F. H. Burkhardt (1940, reprinted 1949). Many of Herder's paraphrases of oriental and popular poetry and selections of his own prose writings have appeared in translation as for instance in Rounseville's *The Poetry of the Orient* (1865); Bancroft's *Literary and Historical Miscellanies* (1855); Thoms' *Lays and Legends of Germany* (1834); L. D. Smith's *Flowers from Foreign Fields* (1895); Ridpath's *Library of Universal Literature* (1899). Selections also appear in the Warner Library. The standard critical edition in German is by B. Suphan and others, 33 vols., 1877-1913.

ABOUT: The literature on Herder in English is extensive. The volumes listed here contain bibliographies: Gillies, A. Herder; McEachran, F. The Life and Philosophy of Johann Gottfried Herder; Nevinson, H. A Sketch of Herder and His Times; Clark, R. T. Jr. Herder—His Life and Thought [especially recommended]. [In German—see studies by E. Baur, L. Böte, R. Haym, E. Kuhnemann, W. Rasch.]

R. L. K.

*HEREDIA, JOSÉ MARÍA DE (November 22, 1842-October 2, 1905), French poet,

was born at the coffee plantation of La Fortuna Cafayère, in Cuba. José María was the only son and the youngest of four children born to Domingo de Heredia (died 1849) and Louise Girard d'Ouville (died 1877); he had three half-brothers and a half-

* ā rā' thya

HEREDIA

sister by his father's first marriage. The Heredias were of southern Spanish stock, who had emigrated in the sixteenth century to Santo Domingo and then to Cuba in 1801. José María, nicknamed Pepillo, spent a delightful childhood amidst aristocratic surroundings. He learned to speak and read French fluently when very young, and in 1851 was sent to Senlis, in France, to be educated at the Catholic Collège Saint-Vincent. He was an excellent student in the humanities, especially of the classical languages. As a student José María used the Gallicized version of his name, Joseph Marie. Upon receiving his baccalaureate degree in 1858, he returned to the family estate of Potosí in Cuba. It was at this time that he read and was deeply influenced by the verse of Charles René Leconte de Lisle, and tried to write poetry. He also devoted himself to the study of Spanish literature.

In 1861 Heredia returned to France with his mother and enrolled in the University of Paris' School of Law. The following year, while continuing the curriculum in law, he enrolled too at the École des Chartes, which trains paleographers and archivists. He completed the latter program brilliantly, but never received a diploma, since he did not bother to do a thesis. Initially failing in his law studies, he received his *licence* in law in 1866.

In 1867 Heredia married Louise Cécile Despaigne (died 1928), of a well-to-do Cuban family. The couple honeymooned in Italy. Three daughters were born of the marriage; the oldest, Hélène, became first the wife of the historian Maurice Maindron and then the wife of the critic and editor René Doumic; the second, Marie, married the poet Henri de Régnier and herself wrote under the name Gérard d'Houville; the youngest, Louise, first was wed to Pierre Louÿs and later became Countess Gilbert de Voisins.

Gay and exuberant, although almost blind in one eye and afflicted with a stammer, Heredia made his home a salon for society and for writers, despite financial reverses in the family. He associated with Leconte de Lisle, Gustave Flaubert, Théophile Gautier, the Goncourts. His meticulously contrived and slowly executed sonnets appeared in numerous periodicals of the Parnassian school, and he won a reputation among the élite as an exquisite craftsman without having published a book. Between 1877 and 1887 he worked on a translation, with critical apparatus, of Bernal Diaz del Castillo's sixteenth century *History of the Conquest of New Spain.* Heredia's prose style was thought by Jules Barbey d'Aurevilly to be superior to his poetry; Gustave Flaubert knew pages by heart. Heredia also adapted (1885) *Juan Soldado* by Fernán Caballero and the adventure story of *La Nonne Alfarez* (1894). When Heredia's sonnets of thirty years' elaboration were published in 1893, people queued up to buy the volume which received some 170 reviews. It was awarded the French Academy's Poetry Prize. The following year he was elected to the Academy, over Paul Verlaine and Émile Zola, on his first candidacy. He became (in 1895) literary director of *Le Journal* and the correspondent (in 1901) of *El País* of Buenos Aires.

Heredia wrote little besides the 2,500 verses mainly in the sonnet form. Appointed administrator in 1901 of the Arsenal Library, he devoted himself to bibliophilism and scholarship. He edited an edition of André Chénier's *Bucoliques* (1905), and wrote a preface—among others—for a volume of verses by Robert de Montesquiou-Fezensac, friend of Marcel Proust. Heredia died of a chronic stomach ailment while a guest of George Itasse at the latter's Château de Bourdonné, at Condé-sur-Vesgres. He was interred at Rouen, in Notre-Dame-de-Secours cemetery, next to his mother.

Heredia is the author of one book, *Les Trophées.* These 118 perfectly formed, thoroughly documented sonnets are in four cycles: Greece and Sicily, Rome and the Barbarians, the Middle Ages and the Renais-

sance, the Orient and the Tropics—with a fifth cycle of his earliest and somewhat more personal poems, Nature and Dream. They recreate the past with admirable precision and synthesis in impersonal, sumptuous verse.

One should not confuse José María with his cousin, the Spanish-language Cuban poet José María de Heredia (1803-39).

Many attempts have been made to translate Heredia: there are complete translations into German (1906 and 1909), Spanish (1906, 1934, 1938), and Norwegian (1918), partial ones in Polish (1913), Czech, Serbian (1914), and Swedish (1920). English translations have been made by Edward R. Taylor (four editions, 1896-1906), Frank Sewall (1900), Henry Johnson (1910); the translation by John M. O'Hara with John Hervey (1929) has a lengthy introduction. Some of the sonnets have been set to music by Le Boucher and by P. Paray.

ABOUT: Bailey, J. C. Claims of French Poetry; Gosse, E. Critical Kit-Kats; Independent Review, VIII; Modern Language Review, XXVI; South Atlantic Quarterly, IX. [In French—see studies by A. Fontaine, H. Fromm, E. Langevin, M. Ibrovac.]

S. S. W.

*HÉROËT, ANTOINE (1492?-1568), French poet, was born in Paris into an "ancient and illustrious" family. His father was the King's Treasurer, his mother the daughter of a member of Parliament. His reputation as a Platonic scholar won him the respect of Marguerite de Navarre and of her brother Francis I. Héroët was considered by his contemporaries as one of the best poets of the Marot school and esteemed even by the iconoclastic Pléiade, not for his Marotic *rondeaux, blasons,* and sentimental poetry, but for his *Androgyne* (composed 1536, published 1542) which assured his fame. The humanist Dolet hailed him, in 1539, "one of the most excellent translators" and the "fortunate illustrator of Plato's high meaning." Rather than a mere verse translation of Plato's *Banquet,* the *Androgyne* was a treatise on the origins of love with a commentary on the meaning of the androgyny myth. To the *Androgyne* Héroët appended a poem, *La Parfaicte Amye* (The Perfect Friend), which was re-edited twenty times (1542-68). It was one of the important pieces in the renewal of the century-old *querelle des femmes.* A poem by La Borderie written shortly before, the *Amie de Court,* had sought to debase women. This misogyny caused great scandal at the Platonizing French court and engendered a series of protests: first the *Contr'Amye de Court,* a reply by Charles Fontaine, Héroët's friend, then Héroët's own poem which was

* ā rō ā'

followed by many others. Thus ridiculed, La Borderie was forced to amend. In his poem, Héroët analyzes the noble sentiments of a woman in "honest love," then proceeds with a metaphysical exposé on the nature of love which, "when two hearts fuse in one and stop for life," is a means of elevation to the Divine. Héroët's contribution to ideas was not altogether original, and the form of his poetry, despite his enthusiasm, lacks freshness of expression and imagery. The language, the versification, and even the style are archaic for his time.

Héroët was abbot of Notre Dame of Cercanceaux from 1543 until 1552, when he became Bishop of Digne, which appointment he retained until his death.

ABOUT: F. Gohin's introduction to his critical edition of Héroët's *Œuvres Poétiques,* 1909.

M. B.

*HERRERA, FERNANDO DE (1534-1597),

Spanish poet and humanist, was born of humble ancestry in Seville, where he devoted his entire life to poetry and scholarship. Nothing is known of his boyhood and schooling; his earliest known poem is a sonnet which he wrote to Charles V at the age of thirteen. He took minor orders and, from 1565 or earlier until his death, held an ecclesiastical benefice in the parish of San Andrés. This virtual sinecure (he had only to read his breviary and wear a cassock) seems to have sufficed for his daily bread; he abstained entirely from wine, and the chief ambition of this austerely dignified scholar was to write a great national epic poem which would match that of Camões—an ambition which was never fulfilled. Growing out of it, no doubt, is his prose work entitled *Relación de la Guerra de Cipre y Suceso de la Batalla Naval de Lepanto,* which he published in 1572 to celebrate the great victory of Don John of Austria. At the end of the volume is a hymn or ode which, with its grandiloquent echoes of the Old Testament, typifies the organ voice of Herrera. In this heroic mode he wrote also his *Canción a Don Juan de Austria* (1571), *Canción por la Pérdida del Rey Don Sebastián* (1578), and *Al Santo Rey Don Fernando* (1579).

But the social center of Herrera's life was, by 1560, the literary *tertulia,* or salon, of the Count and Countess of Gelves, frequented by such men of letters as Malara, Pacheco, Alcázar, Argote de Molina, and Juan de la Cueva; here he found it easier to focus his

* ā rā' rä

poetry, in the manner of Petrarch, upon the lovely young countess Doña Leonor. To her he devotes all his love poetry, in which he exquisitely suffers and delights as he yearns for "Luz." We must dismiss any grossly erotic *Erlebnis* as the source of these sonnets, odes, and elegies; they reflect primarily a literary experience within an aristocratic setting, the assimilation of Petrarchism and the Neoplatonic theories of love. This was, of course, a primary sixteenth century literary experience of Europe as a whole; for giving it its fullest poetic expression in Spain, Herrera was called by his contemporaries "el divino." At the same time, the color, the intellectualized density and complexity, the chiseled forms of Herrera's idiom all anticipate the baroque achievements of Góngora.

Herrera's principal work of literary criticism, his annotated edition of Garcilaso de la Vega's poetry, was written during the same period as his love poetry and gives abundant evidence of his full awareness of technical devices and of the literary tradition, both ancient and modern, within which he was writing. Its publication in 1580 revealed him as a great humanist, in this respect, too, the Petrarch of Spain.

With the death of the Countess of Gelves in 1581 ends the Petrarchan period of Herrera's literary career; in 1582 he published a limited edition of 78 sonnets, five odes, seven elegies, and one eclogue, with the modest title of *Algunas Obras de Fernando de Herrera,* and from that time on he seems to have written almost no poetry. He may well, however, have revised his poetry; a much fuller edition, with many new readings, was published in 1619, twenty-two years after his death.

Herrera devoted the latter years of his life to a nationalistic "Historia General del Mundo," which was never published. His last publication, *Tomás Moro* (1592), a defense of Sir Thomas More written in the moral style of a Sallust, may be a fragment of his great history.

Herrera died in Seville in 1597, having set for Spain the model of the aristocratically aloof scholar-poet; though perhaps too often pedantic and even mechanical, his verse is a technical achievement in some ways comparable to that of Milton.

A small but representative group of translations (two odes and four sonnets) is available in Eleanor L. Turnbull's *Ten Centuries of Spanish Poetry* (1955); see also Longfellow's *Poets and Poetry of Europe* (1845).

ABOUT: Bell, A. F. G. Francisco Sánchez el Brocense; Brenan, G. Literature of the Spanish People. [In French—Coster, A. Fernando de Herrera. In Spanish—Macri, O. Fernando de Herrera.]

E. L. R.

*HERTZ, HENRIK (originally HEY-MAN) (August 25 [or 27], 1798 [or 1797]-February 25, 1870), Danish playwright, novelist, poet, was born of Jewish parents in Copenhagen, where his father, Philip Hertz, was a baker. His mother was Beline Salomonsen who, after the death of her husband in 1799, ran the bakery, which burned down during the bombardment of Copenhagen in 1807. When his mother died in 1814 the home was dissolved, and the young boy lived with a relative of his mother. In due time he entered the University of Copenhagen and completed his law degree in 1825. The year before and after his graduation he won two gold medals for legal and aesthetic treatises.

During the first years of his literary career Hertz published anonymously. His first plays were the satirical comedies Hr. Burchardt og hans Familie (Mr. Burchardt and His Family, 1827), an imitation of Holberg, and the somewhat more independent Flyttedagen (Removal Day, 1828). In this period he also wrote a great number of poems which he burned in 1848. Hertz attracted public attention by his anonymously published rhymed satires Gengangerbreve (Letters from a Ghost, 1825), which he pretends have been sent from Paradise by the recently deceased poet Jens Baggesen and discuss the aesthetics of J. L. Heiberg and his school.

During this period the Jews in Denmark attained full citizenship, and in 1832 Hertz was baptized as a Christian and discarded his anonymity. His best comedy is Sparekassen (The Savings Bank, 1836), which satirizes lottery gambling against the background of the Danish national bankruptcy in 1813. The excellently composed play is a classic of nineteenth century Danish comedy.

As Hertz' comedies developed from imitation to independence, his vaudevilles first showed dependence on J. L. Heiberg, e.g., Kiærlighed og Politie (Love and Politics, 1827), but became more original and eventually grew into realistic social satires, e.g., De Fattiges Dyrehave (A Park for the Poor, 1859). Generally, there is more realism and local color in Hertz' vaudevilles than in Heiberg's.

* hĕrts

Hertz' popularity was particularly founded on his rhymed comedies and his tragedies. Best known among the former is the stylistically brilliant Amors Genistreger (Amor's Frolics, 1830), and among the latter, Svend Dyrings Hus (Svend Dyring's House, 1837), based on the old stepmother motif and the ballads and inspired by the author's love of Johanne Luise Heiberg, the wife of J. L. Heiberg. She was an actress, and for her he wrote the only internationally known of his fifty-four plays, the romantic troubadour drama Kong René's Datter (King René's Daughter, 1843).

In 1850 Hertz married Louise Josephine von Halle, daughter of a merchant.

In his later years, Hertz wrote modern dramas, e.g., Ett Offer (A Sacrifice, 1854), which anticipate the realistic theatre. He also wrote a good deal of intimate poetry and rhymed letters, which he published in four volumes of Digte (Poems, 1851-62).

Hertz' King René's Daughter has had several translations into English, by J. F. Chapman (1845), by E. Phipps (1848, last edition 1922), by T. H. Martin (1850, 1864, 1894). One of his poems is translated as "The Meeting" in Keigwin's In Denmark I Was Born . . . (1948).

ABOUT: Mitchell, P. M. A History of Danish Literature. [In Danish—Kyrre, H. Henrik Hertz.]

A. J.

*HERVIEU, PAUL ERNEST (September 2, 1857-October 25, 1915), French novelist and dramatist, born at Neuilly-sur-Seine, began his career in diplomatic service in Mexico, then turned to law, finally abandoning both fields about 1881 in order to devote himself to literature. His early writings in essay and journalistic form, such as Diogène le Chien (1882), show a talent for analysis of human feelings in a naturalistic tone. In his first novels, beginning with L'Inconnu (1886), one finds a cold and strongly rationalist manner of portraying the frivolous and shallow life of the upper classes, and occasional "theses" after the manner of Dumas fils; the merits of these works lie in the competent documentation on contemporary institutions. Several plays precede his election to the French Academy in 1900, a date at which one may speak of a second period of his work.

The rational, crisp style of Hervieu's first work promised a successful career as a dramatist. His first outstanding play, Les Tenailles (1895), represents a thesis of justice and true love, while La Course du Flam-

* ĕr vyü'

410

beau (1901) gives close attention to such problems as family and moral codes. Hervieu's later plays deal with problems of this type, in a setting of high society, and show the working of incident by rigorous elimination of irrelevant detail; hence action is emphasized rather than conversation or the intervention of the author in demonstrating a thesis. The powerful dramatic structure assumes then something of a "classic" tone. Hervieu attacks especially the social or "natural" law, since it tends to crush the individual; he shows suffering resulting from this law, and creates a modern tragedy of human destiny as it is conditioned by custom and exemplified by conjugal disasters. His pessimism and severity have shocked, yet he stands in significant contrast to the poetic, psychological and naturalist trends.

Hervieu's *Théâtre Complet* appeared in three volumes in 1910, and *Œuvres Choisies* in 1919.

There have been a number of English translations: *In Chains,* by Y. Asckenasy (in *Poet Lore,* 1909) from *Les Tenailles; The Labyrinth,* by B. Clark (1913); *The Trail of the Torch,* by J. Haughton (1915) from his masterpiece *La Course du Flambeau.*

ABOUT: Clark, B. Contemporary French Dramatists; Smith, H. Main Currents of Modern French Drama. [In French—see studies by E. Estève, C. Ferval, H. Guyot.]

F. J. C.

---

*HERZEN (GERTSEN), ALEXANDER IVANOVICH (April 6, 1812-January 21, 1870), Russian author and journalist, was born in Moscow. He was the illegitimate son of Ivan Yakovlev, a Russian nobleman in his middle forties, and Luise Haag, a teen-aged German girl who had fled from her clergyman father and her family to be with Yakovlev; Herzen's name (from the German "Herz," meaning "heart") was given him by his father, who regarded him with love and pride, but who tyrannized over the other members of the family and persecuted his servants. Alexander learned of his illegitimacy in his early teens. Mortified and embittered, he naturally sided with his mother in the constrained relations which had developed between her and his father.

Young Alexander read widely and enthusiastically. He received a good if somewhat unsystematic education from a succession of French and German tutors and entered the University of Moscow in 1829. There he began his lifelong friendship with N. P.

* hĕr′ tsĕn (gär′ tsĭn)

HERZEN

Ogaryov. Herzen majored in science, but was active in the romantically idealist student groups who were so strongly influenced by Schiller, the French "utopian" socialists, and Saint-Simon. They supported the liberal constitutional ideals of the unsuccessful 1825 Decembrist revolution in Russia. Herzen received his degree in 1833.

The next year he was arrested and exiled for his political activities. While in Vyatka he formed a number of liaisons, including an affair with Mme P. P. Medvedeva, who was unhappily married to an older man. She became Herzen's mistress and expected to become his wife after her husband's death. Herzen, however, had no intention of marrying her, and solved the dilemma by becoming engaged to his cousin Natalia Zakharina (the illegitimate daughter of Herzen's paternal uncle). Herzen's idealization of Natalia at this point in his life has been likened to Dante's obsession with Beatrice. Her relatives opposed the marriage, but when Herzen was transferred to Vladimir he undertook a series of deft maneuvers and finally succeeded in marrying his "Natasha" in May 1835.

When he returned to Moscow after six years of exile, Herzen was a sobered positivist and "critical realist." With Belinsky, Granovsky, and others, he became a leader of the "Westerners" in their dispute with the Slavophiles. In 1846-47 Herzen published a number of stories and a novel, *Who Is at Fault (Kto Vinovat?),* which took up a number of social problems of the era, and whose hero, Bel'tov, was in the tradition of the nineteenth century "superfluous man" in Russian literature. It should be borne in mind that this novel was written during the last decade of the reign of Nicholas I—a period of suffocating reaction in Russia.

Inheriting a fortune from his father in 1847, Herzen went abroad with his wife and family. He was never to return to Russia. Although himself a member of the upper class in background, economic status, and education, he was an implacable foe of capitalism and the upper classes. He welcomed the national revolutionary movements in Western Europe (France, Italy, Germany) and expressed his disappointment in their failure in his greatest work, *From the Other Shore* (1851, published in German as *Vom Andern Ufer*).

Herzen moved to England in 1852. His disillusionment with the continent was doubtless intensified by his wife's infatuation with the German revolutionary poet Herwegh. Herwegh wrecked Herzen's marriage, and Herzen describes the poet in an almost Dostoevskian fashion: he was cringing, yet boastful and flamboyant; he was a self-pitying liar who protested his admiration and love for Herzen while preparing to seduce his wife.

In 1857 Herzen and Ogaryov founded a Russian-language weekly, *The Bell* (*Kolokol*), which, though prohibited in Russia, achieved a large clandestine circulation there. *The Bell* expressed an enlightened Russian "public opinion" which could not be voiced at home. It was an important political force until 1861. Herzen's influence declined after the liberation of the serfs in 1861 and the reforms which followed. When, prompted by Bakunin, he threw his support to the Poles in their anti-Russian uprising in 1863, he lost his Russian following almost entirely. *The Bell* suspended publication in 1867.

In the later years of his life, Herzen evolved a socialist philosophy of national and agrarian coloring. Disillusioned with Western parliamentary democracy and "bourgeois revolutions," he accepted the Slavophiles' belief in Russia's great national destiny, but not their religious views or support of autocracy. He retained his faith in the Western ideals of individual dignity, freedom, and progress. Much of his philosophy is found in his great autobiography, *My Past and Thoughts* (*Byloe i Dumy*), which, although fragmentary, is a Russian literary classic.

Herzen died of pneumonia after attending a Parisian political rally in January 1870.

His major works are widely read today in the Soviet Union, where he is hailed as a "great Russian revolutionary democrat, materialist philosopher, publicist, and writer."

Not all of Herzen's works have been translated into English, but Constance Garnett has translated *My Past and Thoughts* (6 volumes, 1924-28) and an English translation by M. Budberg of *From the Other Shore* was published in 1956.

ABOUT: Carr, E. The Romantic Exiles; Malia, M. Herzen and the Birth of Russian Socialism; Slonim, M. The Epic of Russian Literature; Slavonic and East European Review, XXXII. [In Russian—see studies by N. Derzhavin, I. El'sberg. In French—see study by I. Berlin in Preuves, nos. 85, 86 (1958).]

H. W. D.

*HERZL, THEODOR (May 2, 1860-July 3, 1904), founder of modern Zionism, playwright and journalist, was born in Budapest, Hungary, the only son of Jacob Herzl, a well-to-do businessman with lukewarm Jewish beliefs. Herzl attended the Evangelical *Gymnasium* and there revealed an absorbing interest in reading and literary creation. His Jewish education was rudimentary. When his parents moved to Vienna in 1878, Herzl entered the University of Vienna, graduating in 1884 with the degree of Doctor of Laws.

While studying at the university, Herzl completed several plays and wrote many *feuilletons,* the literary form in which he later excelled. In the light of these interests it is not surprising that he soon abandoned the legal profession and entered upon a career in journalism and drama. His efforts were remarkably successful, and in 1892 the *Neue Freie Presse,* a Viennese daily journal of international renown, appointed him its Paris correspondent and later its editor of belles lettres. In the meantime, Herzl had married Julie Naschauer, daughter of a wealthy merchant, by whom he had three children.

Now at the peak of his literary fame, Herzl began to concentrate on the vexing problem of the fate of the Jewish people. His contact with French anti-Semitism, in the form of the Dreyfus affair, crystallized his longstanding emotional involvement with Jewish affairs. It now became the dominant, if not the unique, passion of his life. The play *Das Neue Ghetto* (The New Ghetto, 1894), illustrated Herzl's state of mind in that it called for a proud affirmation of Jewishness.

A few months later Herzl launched his career in Jewish politics with a letter on the Jewish problem to Baron de Hirsch, the wealthy philanthropist. In the same year,

* hĕr' ts'l

HERZL

he began his *Tagebücher* (Diaries, 1895-1904). As Marie Syrkin said in *Midstream* (Autumn, 1956): "Herzl's Diaries . . . belong squarely among the greatest of modern autobiographies. . . . With poetry, humor and an unfailing brilliance of character portrayal Herzl records the progress of his mission; in the process he leaves a portrait of himself, the man 'possessed,' which is unique in literature."

Indeed, an overwhelming obsession had seized him, and, in a burst of spiritual fervor, he produced *Der Judenstaat, Versuch einer Modernen Lösung der Judenfrage* (The Jewish State, an Attempt at a Modern Solution of the Jewish Question, 1896). One of the most profoundly influential works of the past century, it expressed in clarion-like sentences Herzl's formulation of the dynamic doctrine of modern political Zionism: "I consider the Jewish question to be neither social nor religious. . . . It is a national question, and in order to solve it we must, before everything else, transform it into a political world question, to be answered in the council of the civilized peoples. We are a people, a people."

Utterly convinced of the righteousness of his vision and possessed by an almost Messianic feeling, Herzl proceeded to lay the foundations for the Zionist movement. As its recognized leader, he negotiated with the governments and rulers of Europe in dramatic efforts to secure their support for a Jewish homeland. After a visit to Palestine,

he wrote a novel called *Altneuland* (Old-New Land, 1902), describing a utopian rebirth of the Jewish people in its own land. The work of a bold dreamer, it was weak in form, but prophetic in content.

Although acclaimed by the Jewish masses, Herzl was the center of political controversies in the new Zionist organization. These struggles, combined with the almost superhuman devotion to his cause and unceasing work, sapped his strength rapidly. His death at the age of forty-four was a shock to the entire Jewish world.

Herzl was an imposing figure. With his broad forehead, penetrating eyes, black Assyrian beard, and elegant manners, he impressed both emperors and paupers. His work as a writer must be considered as the expression of a man who passed through sophisticated Viennese assimilation to the highest identification with the destiny of his people. He was one of those rare individuals to whom is given the power to reshape the course of human history.

The first English translation of *The Jewish State* was made by Sylvia d'Avigdor in 1896. Subsequent translations and revisions include those of J. de Haas in 1917, I. Cohen in 1943, and J. Alkow in 1946. *Old-New Land* was translated in 1941 by Lotta Levensohn. An excellent abridged translation of the *Diaries* by Marvin Lowenthal appeared in 1956. Selections from Herzl's work may be found in S. Caplan and H. U. Ribalow's *Great Jewish Books* and Ludwig Lewisohn's *Theodor Herzl: Portrait for this Age*. The complete edition of the *Tagebücher* was published in Berlin in three volumes, 1922-23.

ABOUT: Bein, A. Theodore Herzl; Cohen, I. Theodor Herzl: His Life and Times; De Haas, J. Theodor Herzl; Fraenkel, J. Theodor Herzl; Frankl, O. Theodor Herzl; Learsi, R. Fulfillment; Lewisohn, L. Theodor Herzl: Portrait for this Age; Patai, J. Star over Jordan; Pessin, D. Theodore Herzl; Waxman, M. A History of Jewish Literature; Weisgal, M. ed. Theodore Herzl—a Memorial.

M. R.

HEYERMANS, HERMAN. See HEIJERMANS, HERMAN

***HEYSE, PAUL JOHANN LUDWIG VON** (March 15, 1830-April 2, 1914), German short-story writer, novelist, and poet, was born in Berlin. His father and grandfather were well-known professors whose scholarly achievements—a German dictionary and grammar—are still consulted. His mother, to whom he attributed his poetical gifts, belonged to a prominent Jewish family. Heyse specialized in Romance Philology at

* hī′ zē

HEYSE

Heyse dedicated himself solely to the presentation of beauty, and the sordid aspects of life never intrude into his works. One also searches in vain for any real depth of tragic human experience. This tendency toward aestheticism caused the later naturalistic writers to attack his works as being shallow and artificial. Of their type, however, he produced some enduring masterpieces, such as *L'Arrabbiata* (1855), his first published tale and most famous, *Das Mädchen von Treppi* (1858), *Die Stickerin von Treviso* (1868), *Der Verlorene Sohn* (1869), *Zwei Gefangene* (1876), and *Himmlische und Irdische Liebe* (1885).

Despite his many dramatic attempts, Heyse failed to achieve lasting success in the theatre, although the historical play *Hans Lange* (1866), and the tragedy *Maria von Magdala* (1899) enjoyed contemporary popularity. As a novelist he lacked the sense of form and proportion which contributed so greatly to the effect of his *Novellen*. His best novels, *Kinder der Welt* (1873) and *Im Paradies* (1876), which he intended as criticisms of his age, are interesting today only as documents of the period. Heyse excelled as a translator of Italian poetry, and his renderings of Alfieri, Manzoni, Giusti, and Leopardi rank among the finest German translations. His own lyric verse has fallen into undeserved neglect.

Heyse, who once reigned as one of Germany's most popular authors, received the Schiller prize in 1884, and in 1910 became the first German writer to win the Nobel Prize. His reputation has steadily declined, and he is little read today.

the University of Bonn and in 1852, after taking his doctorate, traveled to Italy in search of unpublished Provençal manuscripts. The splendors of the south exerted a major influence on his development, and Italy provided the settings for many of his later works. In 1854, at the recommendation of the poet Emanuel Geibel, who enthusiastically praised Heyse's verse, King Maximilian II offered the young writer a substantial stipend to settle in Munich, with no obligations except to attend the King's symposia. His future assured, Heyse married the daughter of his friend, the art historian Franz Kugler. His wife died in 1862 and Heyse remarried in 1866. He wrote prolifically and at his death in Munich in 1914 left behind approximately 120 *Novellen*, 60 dramas, and 6 novels, as well as lyric verse and translations.

Heyse achieved his greatest success as a writer of psychological *Novellen*. His range of interests is best revealed in his well-known theory of the *Novelle*, called the *Falkentheorie*, because Boccaccio's tale "Frederick of Alberghi and His Falcon" serves as the model story. According to Heyse, the *Novelle* "should present to us a significant human fate, an emotional, intellectual or moral conflict, and should reveal to us by means of an unusual happening a new aspect of human nature." Most of his *Novellen* center on the theme of love, and his protagonists are usually women. Because of his treatment of erotic problems, he was considered an immoral writer in his day.

Of the numerous works by Heyse which have appeared in English, the following represent the most successful translations: M. Wilson translated four *Novellen* under the title *L'Arrabbiata and Other Tales* in 1867. A second collection, *Barbarossa and Other Tales*, was published by L. C. Sheip in 1874. In 1887 J. Philips translated *La Marchesa, a Story of the Riviera, and Other Tales*. A group of *Selected Stories* appeared anonymously in 1886, and two further anonymous collections under the title *Tales from Paul Heyse* were published in 1903 and 1906. The *Maiden of Treppi* was translated by A. W. Hinton in 1874, and *The Witch of Corso* by G. W. Ingraham in 1882. *Zwei Gefangene* appeared anonymously in 1893 as *Two Prisoners*. In 1913-15 A. Remy translated *Nino and Maso,* and E. L. Townsend *The Spell of Rothenburg*. *L'Arrabbiata* was translated by V. E. Lyon in 1916. The novel *In Paradise* appeared anonymously in 1878, as did *Children of the World* in 1882. The drama *Hans Lange* was translated by A. A. Macdonnell in 1885, and versions of *Mary of Magdala* appeared in 1903 by F. Hess and in verse by W. Winter. Selections of Heyse's verse are contained in the Warner Library.

ABOUT: Bennett, E. K. The German Novelle; Brandes, G. Creative Spirits of the Nineteenth Century; Klenze, C. von, The German Classics, XIII; Marble, A. R. Nobel Prize Winners in Literature; Phelps, W. L. Essays on Books. [In German—see studies by A. Farinelli, H. Raff, E. Ruthe, and H. Spiero.]

D. G. D.

"HILDEBRAND." See BEETS, NICO-LAAS

*HOFFMANN, ERNST THEODOR AMADEUS (January 24, 1776-June 25, 1822), German writer, composer, and caricaturist, was born in Königsberg, the son of a prominent attorney, Christoff Ludwig Hoffmann. The elder Hoffmann was separated from his wife, the former Luise Albertine Doerffer, when Ernst was four years old. The father took the older son, and Luise moved with Ernst into her mother's home. Neither the sickly grandmother nor the mother, subjected as she was to hysterical fits, paid much attention to the boy, who later compared his childhood to an "arid heath without blossoms or flowers." His early education was supervised by an uncle who, though well-meaning, alienated the boy by his pedantry. Even the chamber music that supplied the only entertainment in the household did not at first appeal to him, although as he proceeded with his music instruction he began to find in music a means to a transcendental world of the imagination wholly removed from the dreariness of his home life. By the time he was thirteen he had not only mastered several instruments but had tried his hand at composition. Among the few persons from his childhood whom he remembered with sympathy were a kindly maiden aunt, Sophie Doerffer, and his lifelong friend Theodor Hippel, in whose company he engaged in fanciful games and read the great literature of the past and from whom he gained early admiration for his drawings and musical compositions.

In 1792, though remaining in the Doerffer household, Hoffmann entered the University of Königsberg to prepare for the legal profession. Except for his law courses, he excluded himself from all aspects of academic life, including Kant's lectures, in order to devote himself to his own artistic interests. During his university years he worked on two novels (neither of them preserved) and experienced his first love affair, with Dora

* hŏf′ män

HOFFMANN

Hatt, a local wine dealer's wife who had been his music pupil.

In 1796, after his mother's death, he left Königsberg for Glogau, in Silesia, to live with another maternal uncle, Johann Ludwig Doerffer, while preparing for examinations to enter the judicial branch of the Prussian civil service. He became engaged to his cousin Minna, but several years later broke the engagement. After passing his examinations in 1798 he accompanied his uncle and family to Berlin, where, while in the employ of the Prussian higher courts, he circulated among the theatres and cafés, thus initiating a pattern of life that was henceforth to become his normal one. In 1800, after completing still further examinations, he was transferred to Posen. Two years later the relatively carefree life he led in this Prussian-controlled Polish city was suddenly cut short when his caricatures of local officials were distributed at a ball. His punishment consisted of transfer to Plock, a small town on the Vistula which offered none of the urban stimulations on which he had come to depend. In July 1802, during his first year in Plock, he married Michalina Rohrer-Trzynska, a Posen official's daughter, with whom, despite his erratic habits, he remained in relative domestic peace the rest of his life. During this period he wavered between painting and music as creative outlets and was scarcely conscious of the literary genius on which his present-day reputation rests.

By 1804 he effected a transfer to Warsaw. He plunged directly into the cultural life of the city, helped found a music academy, conducted concerts, and held court regularly in a local inn where friends knew he could be found. A colleague in the civil service, Julius Eduard Hitzig, introduced him to the writings of the romantic movement. In 1807, having lost his government position through the occupation of the city by French troops, Hoffmann returned to Berlin. For the first time in serious financial need, he looked in vain for opportunities to paint portraits or publish his musical compositions. The following year, however, he obtained the appointment of musical director of the theatre and opera in Bamberg. Here, with Franz von Holbein, an old Berlin friend, he served not only as orchestra conductor, but as stage director and designer and painter of scenery. During their collaboration they created one of the outstanding theatres in Germany, establishing Calderón in the German repertory and giving the première of Kleist's *Das Kätchen von Heilbronn*. In the social circles of the city Hoffmann became fashionable both as conversationalist and music teacher. Among his singing pupils was a twelve-year-old girl, Julia Marc, for whom he developed an overwhelming passion and who, as the original of many of his literary heroines, became for him an idealization of spiritual love. During his Bamberg years Hoffmann read widely in romantic philosophy, especially in contemporary speculations on magnetism and somnambulism, concepts which were to play an important rôle in his writings. The Bamberg period also saw the start of his literary career, which at first was a mere appendage to his musical interests. In 1809 he published his first tale, "Ritter Gluck," in the *Allgemeine Musikalische Zeitung*, a Leipzig journal which in subsequent years printed many of his essays on music. Although his own compositions remained largely classical in form, Hoffmann as a critic influenced romantic composers through his stress on the irrational element in music. In his writings on music he helped deify Mozart (even exchanging his middle name Wilhelm for Amadeus), championed Beethoven and Weber, and, through his methods of analysis, especially his attempt to describe the effects of music verbally, set a pattern for later music criticism.

In 1813-14 Hoffmann served as conductor of an opera company alternating between Dresden and Leipzig. His first collection of literary works, *Phantasiestücke in Callots Manier* (1813-15), contains many of his best-known pieces, among them *Der Goldene Topf*, a mixture of fairy tale and realistic narrative often considered his masterpiece. In 1814, with the end of the Napoleonic Wars, Hoffmann resumed his civil service post, receiving steady promotions and remaining in Berlin the rest of his life. Despite the contempt his writings show for the dreariness and absurdities of middle-class life, he was a dutiful public official.

In 1816 his best-known musical work, *Undine*, based on Fouqué's fairy tale and a forerunner of romantic opera, was produced with success in Berlin. But throughout his Berlin years his main creative efforts were directed to his fiction. The evenings of story-telling regularly spent with Hitzig and other friends resulted in the collection of tales *Die Serapionsbrüder* (1819-21). Among the other outstanding productions of the period are the novel *Die Elixiere des Teufels* (1816), in a direct line from the English Gothic novel and one of Hoffmann's many treatments of the dual-personality motif; the combined fairy tale and short novel *Klein Zaches Genannt Zinnober* (1819); and the uncompleted novel *Kater Murr* (1821), with Hoffmann's self-portrait as the half-mad musician Johannes Kreisler. During these years he was a well-known figure in Berlin, easily identifiable through his gnome-like body, bushy hair, long crooked nose, and jutting chin. He entertained lavishly at his home and spent most of his nights in cafés, in lively conversation over wine, usually in the company of the actor Ludwig Devrient. His last years were clouded by a variety of illnesses as well as the threat of professional demotion for his ridicule, in his late work *Meister Floh* (1822), of the Prussian police chief's high-handed methods.

The dominating features of his personality —his eccentric humor and cultivation of the absurd, his intense longing for an ideal imaginative world, and the constant interplay of the realistic and the fanciful—are closely mirrored in his writings, not only in his characterizations, but in the very fabric of his style. In the generation following his death his work became celebrated throughout Europe, especially in France, where his popularity was perhaps even greater than in Germany. He played a major rôle not only in the development of psychological and crime fiction, but also in the dissemination of the general ideas and literary techniques of German romanticism. Among his most prominent disciples have been Poe, Dostoevsky, and Baudelaire and, in music criticism, Robert Schumann. During the later nineteenth century his position was relegated to that of mere entertainer, but recent generations have again recognized the essential seriousness of his best work. He stands today as the chief writer of fiction among the German romantics, though he remains better known to the world at large through Offenbach's opera *Tales of Hoffmann.*

The earliest English translations of Hoffmann include R. Gillies' version of *The Devil's Elixir* (1824) and Thomas Carlyle's of *The Golden Pot* (1827). Anthologies of the tales have appeared frequently, mostly in anonymous translations. Among them are *Strange Stories* (1855), *Fairy Tales* (1857), *Weird Tales* (tr. by J. T. Bealby, 1885), *Stories* (1908), *Tales* (tr. by F. M. Atkinson, 1932) and three recent collections, all entitled *Tales,* and translated by various hands (1943, 1946, and 1951). Among translations of individual works are *The Vow* (tr. by F. E. Pierce in the collection *Fiction and Fantasy of German Romance,* ed. by Pierce and C. F. Schreiber, 1927), *The Strange Child* (anonymous, 1852), *The Elementary Spirit* and *The Jesuits' Church in G*—(tr. by J. Oxenford, 1844), *The Serapion Brethren* (tr. by A. Ewing, 1886-92), *Master Flea* (tr. by G. Soames, 1826), *Master Martin and His Workmen* (anonymous, 1847), and *Nutcracker and Mouse King* (tr. by S. Simon, 1853; A. R. Hope, 1892; and L. F. Encking, 1930).

ABOUT: Binger, N. H. Verbal Irony in the Works of Hoffmann; Hewett-Thayer, H. W. Hoffmann: Author of the Tales; Tymms, R. German Romantic Literature; PMLA December 1926. [In German—see studies by G. Ellinger, W. Harich, H. von Müller, and R. Schaukal. In French—Teichmann, E. La Fortune d'Hoffmann en France.]

H. L.

*HOFFMANN VON FALLERSLEBEN, AUGUST HEINRICH (April 2, 1798-January 19, 1874), German poet and scholar, was born at Lüneburg, the son of a merchant who was also mayor. He entered the University of Göttingen in 1816 to study theology, but transferred after one year to the University of Kassel, where under the influence of the brothers Grimm, he entered the field of Germanic philology. After a period at the University of Bonn, he traveled to Holland to undertake a collection of folk songs, on the basis of which he was granted his doctorate by the University of Leiden. In 1823 he became librarian, and in 1830 professor of German language and literature at the University of Breslau. Because of a work titled *Unpolitische Gedichte* (1841), which was sharply critical of the government, Hoffmann was removed from his position. Henceforth he traveled widely throughout Germany, celebrated as a martyr, until in 1848 he was reinstated and provided with a pension. Settling in Weimar in 1854, he

* höf′ män fôn fäl′ ẽrs lā běn

edited with Oskar Schade *Das Weimarische Jahrbuch für Deutsche Sprache, Literatur und Kunst.* In 1860 he became the librarian of the Prince of Ratibor at Corvey in Westphalia, where, before his death in 1874, he completed his autobiography *Mein Leben* (6 vols. 1868).

Hoffmann ranks next to the poet Friedrich Rückert as one of the most prolific poets of Germany. He began his career with a volume of patriotic songs, *Deutsche Lieder* (1815), which were modeled on the works of Theodor Körner. His many volumes of poems include *Lieder und Romanzen* (1821), *Die Schlesische Nachtigall* (1825), *Alemannische Lieder* (1826), *Jägerlieder* (1828), *Buch der Liebe* (1836), *Fünfzig Kinderlieder* (1843), and *Soldatenlieder* (1851).

Hoffmann combines the qualities of geniality, freshness, warmth, and humor with a technique resembling that of the folk song. Some of his finest poems have entered the folk tradition. Hoffmann was a devoted patriot, who expressed his nationalistic feelings in the popular anthem "Deutschland, Deutschland über Alles" (1841).

Hoffmann also led an active life as a scholar. His most notable contributions were *Fundgruben zur Geschichte Deutscher Sprache und Literatur* (2 vols. 1830-37), *Horae Belgicae* (18 vols. 1830-62, and *Geschichte des Deutschen Kirchenliedes bis auf Luthers Zeit* (1832).

Selections of Hoffmann's poems in English translation are contained in W. W. Caldwell, *Poems, Originals and Translations* (1857); and J. G. Legge, *Rhyme and Revolution in Germany* (1918).

ABOUT: [In German—see studies by H. Gerstenberg, F. Muncker (ADB), and J. M. Wagner.]

D. G. D.

*HOFMANN VON HOFMANNSWALDAU, CHRISTIAN (December 25, 1617-April 18, 1679), German poet, represents German baroque poetry at full tide. His best work is as impressive as an interior by the brothers Adam—elaborate yet symmetrical, heavily ornate but neither cumbersome nor confusing. In this quality of lavish technical brilliance and masterly structure it merits all the attention it receives, and more. At its worst it is hollow and insubstantial, turgid, and beset with affectation. Hofmann was the prime importer into Germany of Marinism (the style of Marino), the Italian counterpart of the florid style England knew as Euphuism, Spain as Gongorism. He was

* hōf′ män fôn hōf′ mäns väl dou

also the head of the so-called Second Silesian School.

Hofmann's poetry, good and bad, is in curious contrast with his life, which was regular and conventional; the contrast is not infrequent among baroque writers. His fellow Silesian Lohenstein is in many points similar. Both were dependable civil servants who in leisure hours pursued the erotic muse or explored new heights of bombast.

Hofmann's father, Johann, had added the rest of his name when the Emperor knighted him in 1612, but the son usually signed his works simply "Christian Hofmann." Born in Breslau, he first studied at the *Gymnasium* there, then in Danzig, where he came under the omnipresent influence of Martin Opitz, the dean of seventeenth century verse and the acknowledged master of many poets better than himself. Opitz lived at the time in Danzig, and Hofmann was his frequent companion. From his association with Opitz stems at least part of the extraordinary learning Hofmann displayed, in French, English, Dutch, Italian, and most surprisingly in Middle High German literature.

Hofmann continued his studies at the University of Leiden, then went to England. He returned to the continent and Paris, traveled extensively in Italy. He had a faculty for meeting and talking with the great men of his day. His own tact and ability, combined with his family's influential position, brought him an important post in the service of Breslau. He was at the time barely thirty, and the city fathers had to waive the age limit to give him the job. Much of his lyric poetry had already been written, though not published. It was more suitable, he once said, to the age of twenty-six than sixty-two. His official career continued on to the highest levels. He became Imperial Counselor in Breslau (from 1657 on) and president of the city council.

During his lifetime, Hofmann had published his *Heldenbriefe* (Heroic Letters), imitations of Ovid, with poetic exchanges between famous lovers: Abelard and Heloise, for example, or, under the mask of other names, Emperor Charles V and his Barbara Blomberg. He had also published his *Grab-schriften* (Inscriptions for Graves), many of them mordant rather than funereal, and a variety of marriage odes, other occasional poems, and religious verse. He had burned the beginnings of an historical epic and suppressed most of his love lyrics. The latter were published after his death, mostly by Benjamin Neukirch.

The heart of his poetic creed was the introduction of lightness and facile style in the place of pedantic heaviness and pathos. In this he often succeeded, but he could also miss the mark or, more frequently, play the libertine. He had what often seems to be a one-sided view of love. In repetitious sensuality he went far beyond his master Ovid. Fortunately or unfortunately, he was such an upright citizen and distinguished official that his contemporaries—predisposed to excess in these matters—accepted his Anacreontics without reservation. In any case, these limitations must be countered by respect for Hofmann's clarity of structure, his richness of antithetical images, and his expert manipulation of the baroque polarities: transitoriness and earthly pleasure, sensual love and death, this world and God.

Several of his poems appear in G. C. Schoolfield's *The German Lyric of the Baroque in English Translation* (1962).

ABOUT: [In German—see studies by H. Heckel, R. Ibel.]

F. G. R.

*HOLBACH, PAUL HENRI THIRY, Baron d' (January 1723-January 21, 1789), French philosopher, was born of German parents at Heidelsheim (Edesheim, Palatinate). His uncle gave him a superior classical education, and he did his advanced studies at Leiden, thus coming into contact with mathematical and medical scientific thought in the Protestant atmosphere in which Descartes, Spinoza, and Bayle had worked. Beginning in 1749, Holbach divided his residence between Paris and his country estate. His exceptional wealth allowed him to write and think as he pleased, and to maintain an elaborate household in which he welcomed such visitors as Hume and Franklin, and the Encyclopedists—especially his close friend Diderot. He was recognized as a man of the highest moral principles, though without austerity and with a convinced atheism. His convictions, orally expressed, caused no great alarm, and even Rousseau, repelled by his milieu, admired the qualities of the man in using him as a model for M. de Wolmar, in his *Nouvelle Héloïse*.

Holbach maintained a large staff of translators and assistants for the preparation of a series of editions of earlier writings, which he sought to clarify for style and scientific presentation; his emphasis on English materialistic works indicates his personal interests.

* ōl bȧk′

In his original writings, he shows something of the influence of Diderot, who induced him to contribute to the second volume of the *Encyclopédie*. After that he became a regular contributor. Holbach gave his full support to Diderot's enterprise, and, in disinterested spirit, presumably guaranteed the funds that might be needed during the printing of the ten volumes issued in 1765.

Holbach's great work, *Le Système de la Nature* (1770), was avidly read but caused general dismay for its excessive doctrines. Voltaire hurried to refute it; it offended Frederick of Prussia for its irreverence, and left Goethe aghast. It proposes a materialistic system of a universe of mere matter in motion, and of reality accessible only through science and the senses.

English translations of Holbach first appeared in New York in 1795, *Christianity Unveiled* and *Common Sense, or Natural Ideas; The System of Nature* was published in London in 1797 and in America in repeated editions beginning in 1808. Other translations include *Nature and Her Laws* (1816), *Letters to Eugenia* (1819), *Ecce Homo* (1827), and *Superstition in All Ages* (1878).

ABOUT: Cushing, M. Baron d'Holbach; Lange, F. History of Materialism; Morley, J. Diderot and the Encyclopaedists; Topazio, V. D'Holbach's Moral Philosophy; Wickwar, W. H. Baron d'Holbach; *Modern Language Quarterly*, XVII (1956). [In French—Charbonnel, P. D'Holbach, Textes Choisis; Hubert, R. D'Holbach et ses Amis; Naville, P. Paul Thiry d'Holbach et la Philosophie Scientifique au Dix-huitième Siècle; Plékhanov, G. V. Essais sur l'Histoire du Matérialisme.]

F. J. C.

*HOLBERG, LUDVIG, Baron (December 3, 1684-January 28, 1754), Norwegian-Danish playwright, satirist, essayist, poet, historian, philosopher, was born in Bergen. His father was Lieutenant-colonel Christian Nielsen Holberg, of a family of farmers from the Trondheim region. His mother was Karen Lem, of a merchant family in Bergen, twenty-five years younger than her husband. The family was economically well off but was reduced to poverty by one of Bergen's conflagrations in 1686. Ludvig was the last of twelve children, six of whom died in their infancy. His father died when he was two and his mother when he was ten, whereupon the children were scattered to various relatives. Ludvig went first to the home of a pastor in the beautiful Gudbrand Valley in eastern Norway and three years later to his uncle and guardian Peder Lem in Bergen.

In 1702 Holberg matriculated at the University of Copenhagen. His studies were

* hŏl′ bĕr

HOLBERG

interrupted by a year's tutoring in Norway, but he completed a theological-philosophical degree in 1704, after which he traveled in western Europe. The following twelve years were spent in travel and study. After a couple of years as a teacher of languages in Kristiansand in southern Norway, he spent more than two years, 1706-08, in England, studying history, languages, and literature at Oxford. When he returned to Copenhagen he brought with him an unfinished manuscript of his first book, *Introduction til de Fornemste Europeiske Rigers Historier* (Introduction to the History of the Principal European Countries, 1711). He lectured at the university on new currents of thought in western Europe and tutored. After studies in Leipzig in the winter of 1708-09, he returned to Copenhagen, where he was admitted to an institution for moneyless scholars, thus being enabled to devote all his time to studies. In 1714-16 he traveled through the Netherlands, France, and Italy. This was his most important journey, for it widened his horizon and gave him first-hand insight into the intellectual movements in Europe.

At the end of 1717 Holberg was appointed professor of metaphysics at the University of Copenhagen, but he detested the subject and lectured on other topics. In 1720, he was given a chair in Latin, but not until 1730 did he succeed in securing the professorship he desired, that in history.

His first appointment ended a period in Holberg's life. Soon thereafter occurred what he himself called "a poetic rapture," and he started an enormous output of satirical, comical, and moralizing works, first in verse, later in prose. During 1719-20 he published under the pseudonym "Hans Mickelsen" his heroic-comic epos *Peder Paars*, a milestone in Scandinavian literature, in which he satirized the prevailing ideas and social conditions that he considered remnants from a past period in human civilization.

In 1722 Holberg began writing the comedies upon which his fame chiefly rests. In 1723-25 three volumes appeared containing fifteen comedies. A new edition, entitled *Den Danske Skueplads* (Danish Theatre), also including ten new comedies, was published in 1731 in five volumes. In 1753-54 he added two volumes of eight new comedies.

After his first display of prowess Holberg made his last journey in 1725-26, this time to Paris. He returned to history and in 1729 published a description of Denmark and Norway and in 1732-35 the epoch-making and monumental *Dannemarks Riges Historie* (History of Denmark) in three volumes, his most outstanding scholarly work in which he emphasized the nation's cultural development. Noteworthy among Holberg's many historical works are also *Almindelig Kirkehistorie* (Universal History of the Church, 2 vols. 1738), describing the development of Christianity from its very beginning to Luther's reformation, and *Den Jødiske Historie* (History of the Jews, 2 vols. 1742). Holberg's historical authorship, which was concluded in 1747 by the publication of a treatise on the naval history of Denmark and Norway, is lucid and objective—truly characteristic of the Age of Reason. In 1737 his position as professor was changed to administrative activity as controller of the university.

From about 1740 Holberg's literary authorship chiefly dealt with ethics. In 1741 appeared, in Latin, *Nicolai Klimii Iter Subterraneum* (Niels Klim's Underground Journey), the following year in Danish as *Niels Klims Underjordiske Rejse*. Patterned on several models, particularly Swift's *Gulliver's Travels*, the novel is a philosopher's work of fiction, a literary parody and a political and social satire, championing the principle of tolerance and spiritual freedom.

In 1744 Holberg published a collection of essays, *Moralske Tanker* (Moral Thoughts), the foremost work of Danish Enlightenment, in which the author laid down his moral and religious philosophy. It was continued through five volumes of *Epistler* (Epistles, 1748-54), containing more than five hundred fictitious letters or *causeries* on all kinds of subjects. Influenced by Montaigne and *The Spectator*, Holberg appeared as a moralist, examining metaphysical and orthodox dogmas and conventional opinions and recommending enlightened rational ideas.

Inspired by Ovid's *Metamorphoses*, and La Fontaine's and Gellert's fables, Holberg published more than two hundred *Moralske Fabler* (Moral Fables, 1751), colored by a certain skeptical and pessimistic attitude.

In 1747 Holberg was raised to the noble rank of baron. His thrift and natural aptitude for financial transactions made the once poor student a wealthy man. Nearly all his great fortune he converted into real estate, and he disappointed the university people by bequeathing his wealth to the independent national Academy of Sorø for the teaching of modern subjects. During his last years Holberg preferred to live at his estate Tersløsegaard in central Zealand.

The first of Holberg's books to be translated into English was *Niels Klims Underjordiske Rejse* by an anonymous translator under the title *A Journey to the World Underground* (1742, 2d ed. 1749, reprint 1755). The last of several other translations was rendered by J. Gierlow as *Niels Klim's Journey under the Ground* (1845). Extracts from *Peder Paars* were included in an anonymous article, "Holberg's Peter Paars," in the *Dublin University Magazine,* August 1836. A free translation of the work (by J. H. Sharman) appeared in 1862 in two volumes. Holberg himself translated his *Synopsis Historiæ Universalis* as *An Introduction to Universal History* (1755, later editions, enlarged, corrected and revised, 1758 and 1787). The first of his comedies that appeared in complete English translation was *Erasmus Montanus* by P. Toft (in *Fraser's Magazine*, N.S. IV, 1871). *Den Politiske Kandestøber* was translated by T. Weber as *The Blue-Apron Statesman* (1885), and *Jeppe paa Bierget* as *Jeppe on the Hill* (1906) by W. C. Westergaard. Several collections of comedies have been published in English, e.g., *Three Comedies by Ludvig Holberg* (1912), translated by H. W. L. Hime, and *Comedies by Holberg,* translated by O. J. Campbell & F. Schenk (1914). The American-Scandinavian Foundation has published four selections of comedies (1912, 1914, 1946, 1950). A selection of translations from *Epistler* by P. M. Mitchell appeared in 1955 under the title *Selected Essays of Ludvig Holberg.* For a complete list of translations see E. Bredsdorff, *Danish Literature in English Translation* (1950) and P. M. Mitchell, *A Bibliographical Guide to Danish Literature* (1951).

ABOUT: Beyer, H. A History of Norwegian Literature; Campbell, O. J. Comedies by Holberg; Grøndahl, I. & Raknes, O. Chapters in Norwegian Literature; Hammer, S. C. Ludvig Holberg; Howitt, W. & M. The Literature and Romance of Northern Europe; Jorgenson, T. History of Norwegian Literature, *also* Norwegian Literature in Medieval and Early Modern Times; Mitchell, P. M. A History of Danish Literature; Winkel Horn, F. History of the Literature of the Scandinavian North.

A. J.

*HÖLDERLIN, (JOHANN CHRI-
STIAN) FRIEDRICH (March 20, 1770-
June 7, 1843), German poet, was born in
Lauffen on the Neckar in southwestern Germany, descendant of a long line of clergy
and lay officials of the Protestant church.
His father, Johann Heinrich Friedrich Hölderlin, who served as manager of some
church properties, died two years after his
only son was born. In 1774 his mother, the
former Johanna Christiane Heyn, was remarried, and the family moved to the nearby
town of Nürtingen, where her husband was
mayor. The family was warm-hearted and
deeply pious, and young Friedrich, even if he
already showed signs of his later loneliness
and melancholy, remembered a serene childhood. The intimacy with nature that he experienced among the rolling hills and fertile
valleys of his native Swabia was to leave an
unmistakable stamp on his poetry. He early
came to cherish the experiences gained in
solitude above those resulting from human
contact.

In 1779 his stepfather, to whom he felt
closely attached, died, and Friedrich, with his
younger sister and half-brother, was left in
the charge of his mother and grandmother.
Expecting to take up an ecclesiastical career,
at fourteen he entered the Protestant seminary at Denkendorf, and two years later
transferred to a similar school at Maulbronn.
The rigid discipline of these institutions
weighed heavily upon him. Yet he created
an ideal world for himself through his study
of Greek civilization as well as his reading
of "Ossian," Rousseau, and Schiller. Early
in this period he also composed his first
verses. At seventeen he became engaged to
Luise Nast, daughter of the Maulbronn seminary administrator, but broke the engagement three years later. His unpredictable
moods and eccentricities, he explained, made
him unsuited for marriage.

In 1788 Hölderlin entered the University
of Tübingen, where he became closely associated with his fellow students, the future
philosophers Hegel and Schelling. Hölderlin exerted some influence on their thinking,
though all three had been strongly influenced
by the Kantian transcendentalism then sweeping through German intellectual life. Like
most students of their day, Hölderlin and his
friends greeted the French Revolution with
enthusiasm, and again, like so many of their
contemporaries, they were bitterly disappointed at the unexpected turns that the
Revolution took.

* hŭl′ dĕr lēn

HÖLDERLIN

Hölderlin left Tübingen in 1793 with a
Master of Arts degree, having submitted a
thesis on Greek art and taken his examinations in theology. Unwilling, however, to
adopt the narrow life of a country preacher,
he determined to make his living at other
pursuits while devoting his main efforts to
his writing. Quite early in his university
years Hölderlin had become aware of his
mission as a poet. His apprentice poems,
some of them published as early as 1792,
show the all-pervasive influence of Schiller.
Highly rhetorical, often to an inflated degree,
they abound in abstractions and are frequently addressed to abstract ideals such as hope,
immortality, silence, and perfection. Not
until about 1798 was he able to develop a
thoroughly individual style.

The year he left Tübingen he came to the
attention of Schiller, who helped him locate
his first position as private tutor, a profession which he took up at various times
throughout the following decade whenever
financial need arose. His first pupil was the
backward son of Charlotte von Kalb, an intellectual woman who maintained close contact with numerous literary figures. Hölderlin proved a hard-working teacher, but
quickly found himself worn down by the
efforts required of him. After a year Frau
von Kalb, who recognized his literary gifts,
made it financially possible for him to move
to Jena, which, with nearby Weimar, was
then the center of German intellectual life.
There he listened enraptured to the lectures
of Fichte and soon came into personal con-

421

tact with the leading minds of the time. Schiller published some contributions by Hölderlin in his journals, among them fragments of a novel, *Hyperion*, begun at Tübingen. At Schiller's home Hölderlin even met Goethe, but characteristically failed to catch the name.

Within half a year after his arrival Hölderlin suddenly left Jena, disturbed by a certain loss of self-confidence while in the presence of brilliant men. Diffident and dreamy in personality, though handsome in appearance, he was never able to make a striking personal impression on literary society. In turn, he found himself disillusioned, sometimes even repelled, by most human contact. "I never get to know people without having to sacrifice some golden childhood notions," he once wrote to a friend. As he grew older, his depressions became more acute, and people came to remark on a rather sickly look about him.

In 1796 he accepted another position as tutor, this time in the home of Jakob Gontard, a wealthy Frankfurt banker. Soon he fell deeply in love with Gontard's sensitive and attractive wife, Susette. She helped restore his confidence in his poetic powers, and under her inspiration he was finally able to bring *Hyperion* to completion and eventual publication (1797-99). This, his only novel, consists of the meditations and, to a far lesser extent, the adventures of a young Greek involved in the uprising of his country against the Turks in 1770. Susette is idealized as the heroine, Diotima, a name she also assumes in a number of poems written about her. The novel, in the form of letters, is written in a lyrical, often rhapsodic style too diffuse to support the narrative adequately.

In 1798 Gontard dismissed Hölderlin from his home, presumably after learning of his wife's relationship with the poet. The next few years proved to be Hölderlin's most creatively fruitful. Until 1800 he lived on his past earnings in Homburg, near Frankfurt, associating with the circle of an old university friend, Isaak von Sinclair, on whom he henceforth came to lean for emotional support. During 1799 he made three abortive attempts to complete a blank-verse tragedy on the death of Empedocles, with whose uncompromising devotion to an ideal and with whose spiritual isolation he could identify himself. Hölderlin's fragmentary *Empedocles* has often been compared to Keats' *Hyperion* in its ambitiousness and promise.

In his poetry of the Homburg period Hölderlin turned away from the rhyme that characterized most of his early Schilleresque efforts and adopted free classical forms, in particular the ode and elegiac meters. Between 1799 and 1802 he completed most of the poems on which his reputation today rests. The poems are often built on contrasts —between a state of harmony and of chaos, between an ideal society (Greece) and a decadent present day. In 1801-02 his idealization of Greece gradually gave way to a personal vision of Christ, and in form he turned from classical meters to free verse.

In 1800 he tried unsuccessfully to set himself up as a private tutor in Stuttgart, and in the next two years he briefly held two tutorial positions, in Hauptwyl, Switzerland, and Bordeaux, France. In 1801 he sought Schiller's aid in obtaining a university appointment, but received no reply from his one-time sponsor. During these years he showed increasing signs of oncoming mental breakdown, and when he arrived home in Nürtingen from Bordeaux in mid-1802 he was already undergoing his first major attack of schizophrenia. It has long been thought he may have crossed France by foot. After his condition began to improve, he set out to translate the odes of Pindar and the *Œdipus Rex* and *Antigone* of Sophocles. The Sophocles translations, published in 1804, were ridiculed in their time, but in recent years have gained increasing acceptance by German theatres. By 1804 Hölderlin was sufficiently well to accept employment as librarian to the Landgrave of Homburg, but his condition again deteriorated, to the point that his ravings disturbed the populace of Homburg. In 1806 Sinclair took him to a clinic in Tübingen and the following year he was entrusted to the care of a carpenter, in whose tower room, facing the Neckar, he spent the remaining half of his life. In occasional moments of lucidity he composed simple rhymed poems on pious commonplaces, to which he affixed such names as Scardanelli and Scaliger Rosa. He is buried at Tübingen.

Hölderlin conceived of the poet's mission as a holy one. His self-description as a poet living in "impoverished times" has often been cited as an appropriate image for the modern artist. For a major poet his range is relatively narrow. As Ronald Peacock has said, his verse "lacks entirely the qualities of fancy, of loveliness, delightfulness, of whimsicality or delicious playfulness." His major themes—for instance, his Hellenism and titanism, his deification of nature, his attempt to reconcile real and ideal, pagan and Christian—are also among the prevailing themes of his age, but in his hands they are so charged with the immediacy of personal vision as to seem boldly original.

Not until the twentieth century did Hölderlin receive due critical recognition. During his own century Nietzsche alone was aware of his true stature. For an age whose conception of poetry was determined by the narrative ballad, the Goethian personal lyric, and the romantic *Lied*, the unworldly loftiness of Hölderlin's odes and elegies and the obscurities of his free-verse hymns must have made him seem foreign to the central poetic tradition. Moreover, his poems were not available in collected form during the years in which they might have had a favorable reception, and when they were finally collected, in 1826, the edition was both incomplete and inaccurate. It remained for Stefan George and his circle to rediscover him at the turn of the century. In 1910 Norbert von Hellingrath initiated the first of three elaborate critical editions of his works. Hölderlin's influence on such diverse modern poets as George, Rilke, and Trakl has been enormous, and he now ranks among the foremost German poets. Outside Germany his work has become well known only since the 1940's.

Selections of his verse have been translated by P. Loving (1925), M. Hamburger (1943, 2d ed. 1952), F. Prokosch (1943), and J. B. Leishman (1944, 2d ed. 1956). Extracts of *Hyperion*, translated by C. F. Schreiber, appear in the volume *Fiction and Fantasy of German Romance* (ed. Pierce-Schreiber, 1927).

ABOUT: Butler, E. M. The Tyranny of Greece over Germany; Hamburger, M. Hölderlin, His Poems (extended introduction); Heidegger, M. Existence and Being; Montgomery, M. Friedrich Hölderlin and the German Neo-Hellenic Movement; Muir, E. Essays on Literature and Society; Peacock, R. Hölderlin; Salzberger, L. Hölderlin; Stahl, E. L. Hölderlin's Symbolism; Stansfeld, A. Hölderlin; Comparative Literature Winter 1956. [In German—see studies by W. Böhm, W. Dilthey, H. A. Korff, W. Michel; Müller, E. and Kelletat, A. ed. Hölderlin: Beiträge zu seinem Verständnis in unserem Jahrhundert. In French—studies by P. Berteaux and E. Tonnelat.]

H. L.

*HÓLM, TORFHILDUR ÞORSTEINS-DÓTTIR (February 2, 1845-November 14, 1918), Icelandic novelist and short-story writer, was born at Kálfafellsstaður in the south-

* hólm

east of Iceland, the daughter of Þorsteinn Einarsson and Guðríður Torfadóttir.

Coming as she did from learned people (her father and grandfather were both pastors), Torfhildur received a good education, first in Reykjavík and later in Copenhagen.

In 1874, in her twenty-ninth year, Torfhildur married Jakob Hólm, a businessman at Hólanes. After only one year of married life Torfhildur was left a widow. Bereft of her husband and with no children, she soon migrated to Canada, where for thirteen years she remained among the Icelandic settlers of the frontier, studying art, painting, and writing. She returned to Iceland in 1890, settling in Reykjavík where she lived as writer and magazine editor until her death of influenza.

While in Canada, in addition to some short stories written for the local newspapers, Mrs. Hólm wrote the historical novel *Brynjólfur Sveinsson*. This was a study of the famous bishop of Skálholt (1605-75) and his reaction to the love affair between his daughter Ragnheiður and Daði Halldórsson—one of the most famous love affairs in Icelandic history. Mrs. Hólm's narrative deserves attention as one of the earliest attempts to write an historical novel in Icelandic. Years later Guðmundur Kamban (1888-1945) retold essentially the same story with consummate artistry.

Elding (Lightning), her next novel, depicts the clash of pagan and Christian cultures in Iceland during the tenth century. The subject matter is, however, too broad; it becomes unmanageable, and the whole book is less than convincing.

In her next two books, *Jón Vídalín* (1892-93) and *Jón Arason* (1902-08), which were both published in the periodical *Draupnir*, established and edited by Mrs. Hólm, she turns again as in *Brynjólfur Sveinsson* to the Icelandic bishops for source material.

In addition to the three novels cited above, Mrs. Hólm wrote several books of short stories and children's stories as well as editing two magazines, *Draupnir* (1891-1908) and *Dvöl* (1901-07).

Although Torfhildur Hólm scarcely belonged to the front rank of Icelandic writers even in her own day, she did enjoy great popularity. She tends at times to be provincial and somewhat sentimental. Her writings are wholesome and entertaining literature if not deep or philosophical.

ABOUT: Einarsson, S. History of Icelandic Prose Writers 1800-1945.

L. B.

423

*HÖLTY, LUDWIG HEINRICH CHRISTOPH (December 21, 1748-September 1, 1776), German lyric poet, was born in Mariensee, in the kingdom of Hanover, the son of a preacher. From his early youth he combined a burning zeal in the pursuit of knowledge with an urge for poetic expression. He attended the University of Göttingen for the study of theology. Here he joined the "Göttinger Dichterhain," a group of young enthusiastic poets, headed by Boie, the editor of a poetic almanac. These poets were sworn enemies of the French influence on German literature and wanted to restore the function of the poet to that of the old Germanic bard as they visualized him and as they saw him revived in their idol Klopstock. Afflicted by consumption, Hölty was never able to finish his studies or to obtain a position in which he might support himself. His poems were published in various poetic almanacs and were collected and edited in the form of books only after his death, at twenty-seven, in Hanover.

Before Hölty joined the Hain he wrote burlesque romances and bombastic elegies after English models. In his odes he tried to imitate the grand style of Klopstock, and while he failed to equal the master's lofty diction he surpassed him in sincerity. Hölty finally came into his own in the least pretentious form of German poetry, the *lied*. In his *lieder* he sings of the simple pleasures of country life, of love and the beauty of nature. He uses conventional forms of poetry, but he fills them with a tenderness and delicacy of feeling not to be found in other contemporaries of the young Goethe. Written under the strain of extreme poverty and disease, nearly all of Hölty's *lieder* express gratitude for the blessings the poet received in the path of his short life, the smile of a country girl or a simple flower in the field. The ascent of Goethe overshadowed Hölty's poetry and it had no noticeable influence on German literature, but it left to posterity the image of a dedicated youth who rose above the miseries of life through his belief in the beauty of the visible world.

ABOUT: [In German—Ruete, H. Ludwig Heinr. Chr. Hölty: Sein Leben und Dichten.]

F. R.

* hûl' tē

*HOOFT, CORNELISZ (March 16, 1581-May 21, 1647), Dutch poet, was born in Amsterdam. The record of four generations of the Hooft family exhibits strikingly the

* hōft

HOOFT

rapid improvement in social and economic status possible in sixteenth century Holland to people of character and enterprise, however lowly in origin. Hooft's great-grandfather had been a humble canal "schipper"; his father became a patrician-merchant, a burgomaster of Amsterdam, a man of humanistic tastes which he communicated to his son. Young Hooft learned early to stand above the hot theological strife of the day. His predecessor Erasmus and his contemporary, the conciliatory Grotius, were his heroes, not the combative Calvinists whose political involvement and attempted domination of secular life Hooft opposed. This course required both adroitness and courage.

Hooft's education was humanistic: thoroughly classical with the usual emphasis on languages and literature but especially on the ancient historians. On an extended journey to France and Italy (1598-1601) Hooft saw and appropriated the glories of the Italian Renaissance; unlike his Dutch contemporaries he saw the new Italian culture unmediated by French interpretations. This foreign experience remained a permanent formative influence on Hooft. In lyric poetry, drama, and in prose histories he records his faith in the *uomo universale* of the Renaissance. For this he has been called "the greatest representative of [the Dutch] literary renaissance."

Obviously not destined for a business career, young Hooft was sent by his proud but practical father to Leiden where he studied law and letters (1605-07). In 1609 the twenty-seven-year-old Hooft was appointed, by Prince Maurits, Drost (magistrate) of Muiden and bailiff of Gooiland. With his marriage to Christina van Erp in 1610 Hooft began the life of the established man of culture and of affairs: summer residence in Muiden castle which rapidly became a brilliant center for leaders in art and culture, including van Baerle, Huygens, Sweelinck the composer, the poet Vondel, and the fascinating, vivacious Maria Tesselschade Roemers Visscher.

Hooft's strong attachment to the life of art and intellect reveals a decidedly epicurean quality; but life's disasters taught him also a Christian stoicism. Within a few years he lost, through death, a daughter, two infant sons, his promising oldest son, finally (1624) his wife. A semi-classical, Christian, stoical idea of Fate or Providence (*Fortuin*) was able to fortify him against these massive blows. Hooft puts this mysterious regulator of the universe between God and man. The emphasis on the unpredictable is a remarkably baroque quality, as is the Senecan stoical note: man must accept what God sends without being tragically destroyed by its incomprehensibility.

A second marriage in 1627 to Heleonora Hellemans from Antwerp began the final period of unabated artistic endeavor. Hooft's main activity now became prose history. He died in The Hague, where he had gone to attend the funeral of Frederik Hendrik, Prince of Orange. He was buried in the family vault in the Nieuwe Kerk in Amsterdam. The eminent actor Adam van Germes spoke the funeral oration, composed by the seventeenth century biographer Brandt. A performance of the poet's tragedy *Geeraerdt van Velsen* concluded the ceremonies.

Hooft wrote in various literary forms. *Achilles en Polyxena* (1598), despite the shortcomings of a first work, marks a new epoch in Dutch dramatic art; classical in formal aspects (Chorus) it is modern and romantic in theme (Honor vs. Love). As early as this the youth revealed a lifelong preoccupation, stated in drama and history: what qualities ought to be possessed by the ideal man—the Prince? Senecan stoicism prevails here and in later works, e.g., in the dramatized love story *Theseus ende Ariadne.*

Hooft's lyrical excellence was solidly established by the graceful pastoral *Granida* (1605) and by the *Emblemata Amatoria* (1611); these latter erotic poems reveal Hooft at his lyrical best: courtly and refined in expression, rich in thought. In insisting on

controlled feelings, Hooft was as always concerned with moral man, most deeply and eloquently in his two great dramas *Geeraerdt van Velsen* (1613) and *Baeto* (1617). Both are examples of princely behavior in the face of treachery and injustice. Reason, Order, Peace—these Hooft wished ardently to hold up as ideals for man and state; nowhere more brilliantly than in his great histories: *Hendrik de Grote* (1626), a eulogy of Hooft's ideal prince, Henry IV. In 1638 the poet completed the first twenty books of his monumental *Nederlandsche Historiën* (published 1642), the record of the gallant, tragic struggle against Spain, of the real issues of that revolt, and of the real need for conciliation and reason in political life.

ABOUT: Grierson, H. J. C. Two Dutch Poets. [In Dutch—see studies by G. Brandt, G. Knuvelder, H. W. van Tricht.]

C. K. P.

*HUET, COENRAAD BUSKEN (December 28, 1826-May 1, 1886), Dutch author, was born in The Hague. Following a family tradition, he intended to be a minister in the Walloon church, but during his studies at the University of Leiden he felt more attracted toward literature than toward theology. After a short stay in Switzerland where he perfected his French, he became in 1851 the leader of the Walloon congregation in Amsterdam. Starting his career as a minister full of devotion he propagated with conviction the liberal views of his church. His *Brieven over den Bijbel* (1858) was directed to all men. For those who shared his predilection in religious matters he wrote *La Seule Chose Nécessaire* (1856-57). At the same time he wrote some stories, *Overdrukjes, Schetsen en Verhalen* (1858), to which his future wife Anna Dorothee van der Tholl (they married in 1859) also contributed. He collaborated with the editors of the *Nederlandsche Spectator* and wrote some contributions for *De Gids.*

Realizing that he was unsuited for the ministry, he decided to devote himself entirely to literature. To make a living he accepted a position with the *Opregte Haarlemmer Courant* (1862-68). Meanwhile he had attracted the attention of Potgieter, the editor of *De Gids,* by some of his articles dealing with literary criticism. In the column *Kroniek en Kritiek* Huet began to attack all sorts of overestimated authors and to make a sound historical study of literature in order to come to a correct evaluation of

* hü wĕt'

the monuments of the past. In 1863 he became one of the editors of *De Gids,* but his adamant manner of proclaiming his views led to a break with the other editors in 1865. The bitterness caused by this exclusion from the liberal circles became evident in his sharper criticism of leading popular writers such as Van Lennep and Ten Kate, and also in his novel *Lidewijde.*

In 1865 Huet went to Batavia where he accepted the editorship of the *Javabode.* Before leaving Holland he published the first two collections titled *Litterarische Fantasien* and also the novel of which he himself expected much for the wanted renewal of Dutch literature. His attempt was to portray human passions realistically in the manner of the French novel. His attacks against the Dutch community provoked much criticism.

A new period of his life began in Batavia. He was successful as a journalist, especially after he started his own daily, *Algemeen Dagblad van Nederlandsch-Indie.* He was now free to continue his literary criticism, even though his writings in this field did not become known in the Netherlands until they appeared in 1874 as *Nieuwe Litterarische Fantasien.* He kept up a lively correspondence with his friend Potgieter.

In these years his literary views were often broad and many-sided rather than profound. He reviewed what seemed of importance in other countries, continued reading, studied the great authors of the past, and kept up with the Dutch literature of his day. After 1874 he found more time for study; his literary criticism gained in ripeness and depth as is exemplified in *Oude Romans* (1874-75), *Persoonlijke Herinneringen aan Potgieter* (1877), *Opstellen over Hooft* (1881), and *Multatuli* (1885). His pessimism that prevented him from seeing a future for Dutch literature also prevented him from appreciating correctly the coming movement of the eighties.

In 1876 Huet left Batavia and, since Holland had no attraction for him—his friend Potgieter having died—settled in Paris where he continued to direct his newspaper. As literary critic he followed Sainte-Beuve, but he chose Taine as his master for his art-historical studies. It was in the latter's vein that he wrote of his travels: *Van Napels naar Amsterdam* (1877), *Parijs en Omstreken* (1878), *Het Land van Rubens* (1879; English translation by A. D. van Dam, *The Land of Rubens,* 1888), and his masterly *Land van Rembrandt* (1882-84).

All his life Huet remained ambitious as a novelist. Although *Lidewijde* showed that the sharp literary critic lacked self-criticism, he wrote a family novel, *De Bruce's,* modeled after French literature. The work did not contribute to his fame.

ABOUT: [In Dutch—see studies by J. B. Meerkerk, C. G. N. de Vooys. In French—see study by J. Tielrooy.]

H. B.

*HUGO, VICTOR-MARIE (February 26, 1802-May 23, 1885), French poet, dramatist, novelist, and critic, was born in Besançon, the third son of Joseph Léopold Sigisbert Hugo, a man of humble Lorraine descent who had built an excellent career in the post-revolutionary army (he later became a general and viscount, and a close associate of Joseph Bonaparte, Napoleon's brother). His mother, Sophie Trébuchet, was an intelligent, spirited young Breton who had hesitantly married the Bonapartist soldier in 1797 and soon after her marriage became involved in an affair with General Victor Fanneau Lahorie, Victor Hugo's godfather. After the birth of her third son she moved to Paris to be near Lahorie and, when he became an enemy of the regime, to shelter him from the law. Victor knew him as "M. le Courlandais," who hid in their garden for eighteen months, reading and teaching the eight-year-old boy to translate Tacitus, and imbuing him with the ideal of liberty, before he was arrested in 1810. The experience was to engender in Hugo a life-long sympathy with the oppressed.

The dramatic circumstances of a broken home and their frequent moves gave the Hugo brothers an unusual—and somewhat spotty—education. Their childhood was punctuated by two trips: to Italy in 1809 and to Spain 1811-12, to visit their father, whom they knew as a grand, unfamiliar man in a magnificent uniform, associated with their stay in splendid palaces. During the 1811 trip, they had a brief and unhappy stay at the Collège des Nobles in Madrid. For the most part, however, Victor and his brother Eugène lived in Paris. Sophie Hugo let them play in the garden and read what they would, while they attended a nearby school.

In 1814, at General Hugo's insistence, the boys left for the Pension Cordier where they spent four years distastefully studying the sciences, and their leisure hours writing verse and plays—a pastime which soon bore fruit. At fifteen Victor was honored in the

* ü gō'

HUGO

Académie Française's poetry contest and a year later won first prize from the Académie des Jeux Floraux; Eugène received honorable mention. Their entry into law school in Paris was only a gesture to their father, for instead of attending classes the Hugo brothers founded a magazine called *Le Conservateur Littéraire*. It ran from December 1819 to March 1821, and served to enhance Victor's already growing reputation. After a brief period of extreme poverty, he received a royal pension following the publication of his first volume of *Odes* in 1822. It enabled him to marry his childhood sweetheart, Adèle Foucher, and to set off on a prolific career. By 1830 the successful young man had a family of four children—Léopoldine, Charles, François Victor, and Adèle—had moved to increasingly large and comfortable quarters, and had become the head of the young romantic *cénacle* which met frequently at his home to discuss the great literary issues of the day. Though his life had been saddened by the aberration of Eugène, who went mad at his younger brother's wedding, and by the death of both parents, Victor Hugo lived in an aura of happy domesticity, literary fame, and the devotion of a close circle of friends.

They were years of great activity and intellectual ferment. Between 1822 and 1828 Hugo wrote four volumes of verse and the novels *Han d'Islande* (1823) and *Bug-Jargal* (a novel written during his school years but not published until 1826), and with the bold critical preface to *Cromwell* (1827) became the spokesman for the new romantic school that was spreading from England and Germany. Caught up in this literary revolution, the group of young enthusiasts who formed Hugo's "court"—his best friend Sainte-Beuve, Vigny, Musset, Gautier, Gérard de Nerval, and the Deschamps brothers—attacked the formality of the eighteenth century models: the dramatic unities, the restrictions on subject, versification, and vocabulary in poetry, and above all the aesthetic hindrances to imaginative and emotional expansiveness. Hugo took the lead in a multiple attack on classicism in poetry, drama, and the novel. *Les Orientales*—the richly colored poems that he had tossed off for his friends in the years preceding their publication in 1829— heralded a revolution in poetic expression, and it is ironic that its "art for art's sake" philosophy, which Hugo later renounced, at least in its narrow sense, should have become the rallying-point for an entire movement, and for the later Parnassian school. In drama he was even more controversial. The furor that *Cromwell* had raised among the conservative Academicians mounted with *Marion Delorme* (1828), which was quashed by the censors, and culminated in the famous "battle of *Hernani*" on February 25, 1830. At the opening of that play Hugo, supported by his vociferous claque of disciples, scored a decisive victory for the romantic drama— though it is said the play could hardly be heard for the competing hisses and cheers. Finally, in 1831, *Notre-Dame de Paris* carried the popularity of the historical romance to new heights in France.

It was at about this time that Hugo's marriage crumbled—partly because of his frenetic activity, partly because of his egotism and, according to many accounts, his voracious sensuality. During the busy year of 1829 the shy, ugly, lonely critic Sainte-Beuve began to call more frequently to chat with Adèle while Hugo was away, and just a few days after the opening of *Hernani* his feelings exploded in a sharp letter to Hugo. Whether or not his friendship with Adèle was merely that is a much-debated point among literary historians; it had, in any case, violent repercussions. Hugo's attitude throughout was gallant and generous (if slightly suspect, in view of their professional tie), and the collapse of their friendship is due largely to Sainte-Beuve's own machinations. Eventually the embittered critic spread gossip about Adèle in his conversations and, by innuendo, in his literary works. Adèle still tried as late as 1865 to bring about a reconciliation between the two men.

427

Hugo, tormented by his wife's attachment, found solace in an *affaire* with the actress Juliette Negroni. He met her in 1833, while she was rehearsing a minor role in his *Lucrèce Borgia*, and soon formed what proved to be his deepest and most enduring affective tie. It was a curious, almost bigamous, relationship. At her jealous lover's behest, the former *demi-mondaine* began a cloistered life of astonishing dedication, seldom leaving home without him, copying out his books, waiting in his *cabriolet* while he paid courtesy calls on the Academicians. Adèle, content to live with her husband in a state of affectionate celibacy, accepted the arrangement graciously, and eventually she and her sons paid calls on "Mme Drouet." After Adèle died in 1868, Juliette lived in Hugo's home until her own death in 1883, fifty years after she had met him.

From the first the pain of Adèle's defection and the deepening of his own feelings were reflected in Hugo's work—the melancholy *Feuilles d'Automne* (1831); *Les Chants du Crépuscule* (1835); *Les Voix Intérieures* (1837); and *Les Rayons et les Ombres* (1840). Less flamboyant than the earlier, brilliant *Les Orientales*, they sustained a meditative and intimate tone in their descriptions of childhood, nature, and love; and the preponderance of metaphor marked a progression toward a new conception of the poetic symbol. The humanitarian concerns of some later poems, like the fierce political consciousness of the drama *Ruy Blas* (1838), also revealed an expansion of his ambitions and a direction that his life would take after two disasters in 1843 silenced his literary voice—the death by drowning of his daughter Léopoldine, and the failure of *Les Burgraves,* an event which was reputed to mark the end of romanticism in France.

In 1841 Hugo was elected to the Académie Française. Four years later he was raised to the peerage ("le roi s'amuse," commented one journal drily, punning on the title of his play). He now entered the French parliament to deliver lofty diatribes against capital punishment and the misery of the poor—themes that had dominated such early prose pieces as *Le Dernier Jour d'un Condamné* (1829) and *Claude Gueux* (1831), as well as a work in progress, *Les Misères*. In 1848 he was elected a "representative of the people" and a year later became a member for Paris of the Assemblé Nationale. But Hugo, who dreamed of being the "sonorous echo" of his age in politics as well as letters, was too visionary ever to gain power in government,

and though his opinions veered increasingly to the Left, he never aligned himself with a political party. The periodical *L'Événement,* which he formed during the turbulent days of the 1848 revolution to mold public opinion, was eventually suppressed, and both his sons, collaborators on the journal, served prison sentences. As he grew aware of the dictatorial ambitions of Louis Napoleon, whom he had originally supported for presidency of the republic, Hugo came out strongly against him and on July 17, 1851, before the Assembly, made a speech whose closing lines—"Because we have had a Napoleon the Great, must we have a Napoleon the Little!"—resounded over two continents. After the *coup d'état* of December 1851, he fled for his life to Belgium. The former Royalist, Bonapartist, and supporter of the July monarchy had become a zealous republican.

It was during the following years—in Belgium, Jersey, and finally Guernsey, where he settled with his family and Juliette from 1855 to 1870—that his genius emerged fully. After a short excursion into political pamphleteering he returned to poetry, and in 1853 the Juvenalian invective of *Les Châtiments* (published in Brussels) pilloried Louis Napoleon and the Empire. Three years later he produced *Les Contemplations*, a group of poems which pass from early lyrics, through meditations on his daughter's death, to such visionary pieces as "Ce Qui Dit la Bouche d'Ombre." If the content of his more mystic poems was contradictory and philosophically shallow, it was expressed in language of what Saintsbury calls "apocalyptic magnificence." The new suggestiveness and mystery that he brought to poetry, the complete integration of symbol and meaning, would greatly influence Baudelaire and the symbolist school. In the first *La Légende des Siècles* (1859), an even more ambitious epic of man's progress toward freedom, the "later Hugo" realized his role as poet-seer.

His mystic and humanitarian preoccupations continued through the 1860's in the novels *Les Misérables* (1865), *Les Travailleurs de la Mer* (1866), and *L'Homme Qui Rit* (1869). *Les Misérables*, the long-projected novel originally entitled *Les Misères* which he had conceived as far back as 1832, expressed the popular nineteenth century "cult of the lower classes" in a work impossible to categorize and full of flaws, a mélange of realism and romanticism, melodrama and digression. But its sheer narrative excitement brought it immediate and world-wide acclaim.

Hugo refused amnesty in 1859 and did not return to France until after the Second Empire had collapsed on September 3, 1870, in the midst of the turmoil of the Franco-Prussian War. The events of that harrowing year—the siege of Paris, the civil war that raged while the war against Germany was in progress, the death in March 1871 of his son Charles, who had been weakened by starvation during the siege—were recorded in *L'Année Terrible,* the volume of poems that appeared in 1872.

Hugo's status as the dean of French letters was virtually unchallenged for the rest of his life. Anatole France may have thought his ideas commonplace, Zola grumbled jealously, and Hugo's own influence on literature had waned in the light of the newer naturalist and symbolist schools; but he enjoyed a popularity in his own time that only Voltaire before him had known. His unflagging productivity—two more series of *La Légende des Siècles* (1877 and 1883), the novel *Quartre-Vingt-Treize* (1874), *L'Art d'Être Grandpère* (1877), *Les Quatre Vents de l'Esprit* (1881), *La Pitié Suprême* (1879), *Torquemada* (1882)—amazed the literary world; actually many of these, like some works published posthumously (e.g., *Le Théâtre en Liberté* and the epic *Dieu* and *La Fin de Satan),* had been written much earlier. His entry into his eightieth year was celebrated as a national holiday, and when he died after an attack of pneumonia the nation went into mourning. He lay in state under the Arc de Triomphe and on May 31, 1885 was buried in the Panthéon.

Ego Hugo, the motto Hugo chose for his blazon, delineates ironically the dimensions of the poet's self-esteem—a thoroughly complacent pride which has made him a ready target for critics and damaged his reputation considerably. The gross antitheses of his dramas, the melodrama and bombast of his novels, the lofty trivialities of his metaphysical speculation—in general, his tendency to confuse richness of rhetoric with originality of thought—are seen as the expressions of an artist who lacked intellectual subtlety and moral sensibility. Hugo's pose as the symbol of the exiled French republic living in self-imposed austerity has also been derided in view of his extremely lucrative output during the Guernsey years; and some of the more ribald *Chansons des Rues et des Bois* (1865) detract from his posture in a somewhat different way.

Yet that self-image was not totally inaccurate. His conceit was the other face of a strength of character that enabled him to sustain a remarkable range of experience and suffering. He outlived his wife, his mistress, three of his four children; he saw the fourth, Adèle, consigned to a mental institution for half her life. When he called himself Olympio in the poems of the 1830's he already wrote as a giant, and it is with wonder that one sees him scale, from that amazingly accomplished beginning, totally unprecedented heights. In a summary of his achievement Dowden calls him the "master of poetic counterpoint," concluding, "To say that Hugo was the greatest lyric poet of France is to say too little; the claim that he was the greatest lyric poet of all literature might be urged." Modern critics have not confirmed this verdict.

Hugo's posture as the "great exile" does not break down under scrutiny. His financial success and artistic fulfillment through a simple (if hardly ascetic) life were achieved by the voluntary renunciation of Parisian elegance at a time when his friends were prospering under the Empire. Moreover, his expulsion from France was not a unique incident. The 1855 departure from Jersey was precipitated by a similar insistence on the right of exiles to free expression; and in Brussels in 1871, Hugo's offer of asylum to refugees caused a riot and his expulsion by the Belgian government. He played the rôle that he had chosen for himself genuinely and completely, speaking always for freedom in art, in speech, in thought, with a sincerity that was never compromised for political advantage. More fully than any public figure of his time, Hugo represents the individualism, intransigence, and largeness of feeling, as well as the vanity, of the romantic ego.

Most of Hugo's novels were translated into English shortly after their first French publication, and nineteenth and early twentieth century translations are too numerous to list. Some of the better-known translators of *Les Misérables* include Sir F. C. Lascelles Wraxall, Isabel F. Hapgood, Charles E. Wilbour; of *Notre-Dame de Paris,* Frederick Shoberl, Isabel Hapgood, A. L. Alger and Jessie Haynes; of *Travailleurs de la Mer,* Isabel Hapgood, W. Moy Thomas, and Mary W. Artois; of *L'Homme Qui Rit,* Isabel Hapgood and William Young; of *Quatre-Vingt-Treize,* Frank Lee Benedict and Helen B. Dole. *Bug-Jargal, Claude Gueux,* and *Le Dernier Jour d'un Condamné* were all translated by George B. Ives, Anabella Ward, and Charles E. Wilbour. *Han d'Islande* has been translated by J. T. Hudson, A. L. Alger, and George B. Ives. The two most enduring of his novels in English are *Les Misérables* and *Notre-Dame de Paris*—new translations of the latter appearing in 1949 (by M. Dupré) and in 1956 (by Lowell Bair).

English versions of the plays include collaborative translations (1887) by Frederick L. Slous and Camilla (Mrs. Newton) Crosland of *Hernani, Le*

Roi s'Amuse, and *Ruy Blas* (they also did separate versions of some of these). *Hernani* has also been translated by Frederick A. Schwab and by Carl Gans, and *Ruy Blas* by Brian Hooker (1931).

For the poems there are fewer translations, and many are anonymous. In 1836 George W. Reynolds translated about half of *Les Chants du Crépuscule* in a volume entitled *Songs of Twilight.* In 1883, *The Literary Life and Poetic Works of Victor Hugo, Translated into English by Eminent Authors* cited Edward Dowden, Arthur Arnold, William Hardinge, Dean Alexander, Andrew Lang, Robert Brought, "Father Prout," etc. as translators.

ABOUT: Davidson, A. F. Victor Hugo: His Life and Work; Dowden, E. French Literature; Giese, W. F. Victor Hugo: The Man and the Poet; Gilman, M. The Idea of Poetry in France; Grant, E. M. The Career of Victor Hugo; Grant, E. M. Victor Hugo During the Second Republic; Haggard, A. C. P. Victor Hugo; Hooker, K. W. The Fortunes of Victor Hugo in England; Josephson, M. Victor Hugo; Marzials, F. T. Life of Victor Hugo; Maurois, A. Olympio; Saintsbury, G. History of the French Novel, II; Swinburne, A. C. Essays and Studies; Swinburne, A. C. A Study of Victor Hugo; Vaughan, C. E. Goethe and Hugo; Times Literary Supplement May 26, 1966. [In French — Audiat, P. Ainsi Vécut Victor Hugo; Barrère, J. B. La Fantaisie de Victor Hugo; Gautier, T. Victor Hugo; Guillemin, H. Victor Hugo par Lui-même; Hofmannsthal, H. Essai sur Victor Hugo (translated from the German by M. Ley-Deutsch); Hugo, A. Victor Hugo Raconté par un Témoin de Sa Vie (most of this was dictated to his wife by Hugo); Sainte-Beuve, C. Biographie des Contemporains, IV; Sainte-Beuve, C. Portraits Contemporains, I; Saurat, D. La Religion de Victor Hugo; Saurat, D. Victor Hugo et les Dieux du Peuple; see also Europe, nos. 394-95 (February-March, 1962).]

E. G.

HÜLSHOFF, ANNETTE DROSTE-, Freiin von. See DROSTE-HÜLSHOFF, ANNETTE, Freiin von

*HUMBOLDT, (FRIEDRICH HEINRICH) ALEXANDER VON (September 14, 1769-May 6, 1859), German scientist and explorer, was born of noble family in Berlin. Together with his brother Karl Wilhelm (see sketch below), he was provided with his early education by private tutors. He later studied at Frankfurt and Berlin, then at Göttingen. From observations made on excursions along the Rhine, he assembled the material for his *Über die Basalte am Rhein* (1790). In 1790, he traveled with George Forster through Belgium, Holland, England, and France. It was this traveling companion who first directed his attention to the tropical regions of the New World. After studying mining at Freiberg, he spent eight months in the Erzgebirge where he conducted investigations leading to his study *Flora Subterranea Fribergensis et Aphorismi ex Physiologia Chemica Plantarum* (Berlin, 1793; translated into German by Hedwig, Leipzig, 1794). In 1792, Humboldt was appointed director of mines and traveled in Switzerland and the Tyrol. Here he collected materials for the two works which appeared in 1799, *Über die Chemische Zerlegung des Luftkreises* and *Über die Unterirdischen Gasarten,* and constructed an unextinguishable lamp for the miners. At this time he was also gathering material for his large work *Über die Gereizte Muskel- und Nervenfaser, nebst Vermutungen über den Chemischen Prozess des Lebens in der Tier- und Pflanzenwelt* (1797-99). In 1797, he gave up his position in order to devote his entire time to the study of the natural sciences. During a stay in Spain in the winter of 1797-98, he obtained permission to travel to Spanish America. On June 5, 1799, he embarked for America. His first stop was in Venezuela and the Orinoco area, then Cuba and Mexico. He returned to Europe by way of Philadelphia in the summer of 1804. After extensive trips and study in Europe, he returned finally in 1827 to Berlin, where as a royal chamberlain, he delivered his famous university lectures on the description of the physical world. In 1829 he set out on another expedition, commissioned by Czar Nicolas, to the Ural Mountains and the Caspian Sea. During the next two decades, he was engaged in various missions for the Prussian government. In this period he was active in the establishment of magnetic observation stations, the predecessors of modern meteorological observatories, which at that time became possible only because of Humboldt's reputation and influence. Meanwhile, he also completed his historical work, the *Examen Critique.* His residence for the remainder of his life was Berlin where he completed what is perhaps his best-known work, *Kosmos, Entwurf einer Physischen Weltbeschreibung* (1845-62). The uniqueness of this work lies first of all in the magnificent synthesis of the natural sciences which it treats, but, above all, in the manner in which Humboldt mastered his material. His ideal was to unite the spirit of German classical idealism with the spirit of the newly rising exact sciences. Humboldt's fame and authority were so great during the nineteenth century that in several respects they acted as deterrents to the development of the various sciences in later years. This was particularly true of geology, which eventually developed along quite different lines from those described in *Kosmos.* Attesting to

* hōŏm′ bŏlt

Humboldt's world-wide fame are the innumerable natural monuments bearing his name.

Humboldt's collected works were translated into English and published in nine volumes (New York, 1876).

ABOUT: De Terra, H. Life and Times of A. von Humboldt; Stoddard, R. H. Life, Travels, and Books of A. von Humboldt. [In German—see studies by E. Banse, H. Beck, F. Ernst, H. Klencke.]

E. K. G.

*HUMBOLDT, (KARL) WILHELM VON (June 22, 1767-April 8, 1835), was one of the most able scholars and significant statesmen of Germany. Following the early death of his father, a major and adjutant of the Duke of Brunswick during the Seven Years' War, he received private instruction at the family castle and in Berlin together with his brother Alexander (see sketch above). In 1787-88, he studied at Frankfurt an der Oder, later at Göttingen. In the year 1789, he traveled to Paris and Versailles and then to Weimar where he met his future wife, Karoline von Dachröden, and Friedrich Schiller. In the summer of 1790 he was appointed councilor and assessor at the supreme court of judicature in Berlin, but gave up this position the following year and lived on his estates in Thuringia and in Erfurt, engaged in the study of antiquity.

At this time he also wrote the liberal essay "Ideen über Staatsverfassungen durch die Französische Revolution Veranlasst" (*Berliner Monatsschrift*, 1792) and immediately thereafter "Ideen zu einem Versuch, die Grenzen der Wirksamkeit eines Staates zu Bestimmen," which at that time, owing to censorship, appeared only in fragments in a number of journals (published completely in Breslau, 1851). In this work he expressed the view that the duty of the state, in contrast with the practices of enlightened despotism, lay only in assuring the personal freedom of the individual. After 1794, he lived in Jena enjoying the company of Schiller and other like-minded men, stimulating them to new efforts and being stimulated. Several of Schiller's poems at this time were written under the influence of Humboldt. A monument to his friendship with Schiller is to be found in their correspondence, published in 1830. He also became a close friend of Goethe, pleasing him with a fine essay on his newly published idyll *Hermann und Dorothea*.

From 1797 to 1799, he lived with his family in Paris and then moved to Spain where he pursued the study of the Basque

* hōōm′ bōlt

WILHELM VON HUMBOLDT

language. In 1801 he accepted the appointment of Prussian Resident Minister in Rome where he remained until 1808. Rome was a most suitable place for the continuation of his intellectual pursuits, philosophy, aesthetics, philology, and archaeology. In 1809, he was called back to Berlin, to assume the position of Minister of Ecclesiastical Affairs and Public Education. It was in this position that he carried out the founding of the University of Berlin, which he sought to provide not only with the best teachers, but also with the most extensive academic freedom. From this time on, Humboldt was active in various capacities as a servant of the state. For example he was the chief Prussian representative at the Congress of Vienna (1814-15); all his efforts on this occasion, however, to establish a unified constitution and free institutions for Germany failed in the face of Austrian opposition. It was not until 1819 that he withdrew from government service to live on his estate, Tegel, where he possessed an outstanding collection of sculpture.

The earliest of Humboldt's literary and critical works are collected in his *Aesthetische Versuchen* (1799). Included are criticisms of Goethe's *Hermann und Dorothea* and *Reineke Fuchs* as well as Schiller's *Spaziergant*. In the field of aesthetics his review of Jacobi's *Woldemar* is certainly worthy of mention, since here he outlines his own philosophical ideal. Humboldt devoted much of his time to the study of comparative linguistics. As a result of his investigations in Spain, he wrote two important works on the Basque language:

Berichtigungen und Zusätze zu Adelungs Mithridates über die Kantabrische oder Baskische Sprache (1817) and *Prüfung der Untersuchungen über die Urbewohner Hispaniens Vermittelst der Baskischen Sprache* (1821). His chief work on oriental languages, *Über die Kawisprache auf der Insel Java* (1836-40), was published posthumously. It is particularly the introduction of the latter work, entitled "Über die Verschiedenheit des Menschlichen Sprachbaues und ihren Einfluss auf die Geistige Entwicklung des Menschengeschlechts," that provided a statement of enduring interest to the linguist. In this work he directs his attention to the structure of language rather than its history and thereby gains his relevance to twentieth century linguistics. Humboldt's collected works, published by the Berlin Academy of Sciences (1903-36), contain his numerous poems among which the elegy "Rom" and some excellent sonnets are worthy of attention.

The only works by Humboldt translated into English are: *Thoughts and Opinions of a Statesman* (London, 1849); *Letters to a Lady* (Philadelphia, 1864); and selections in *The German Classics of the Nineteenth and Twentieth Centuries* (New York, 1913-15).

ABOUT: [In German—see studies by A. Leitzmann, H. Nette, F. Schaffstein, E. Spranger.]

E. K. G.

*HURBAN VAJANSKÝ, SVETOZÁR (January 16, 1847-August 17, 1916), Slovak poet and novelist, was born in Hlboký in Slovakia. His father, J. S. Hurban, a Protestant minister and one of the leaders of the Slovak nationalist movement, played a major rôle in the standardization of the Slovak literary language. The son attended several high schools in Slovakia and Germany, and studied law in Bratislava and Budapest. From 1874 to 1878 he practiced law in Slovakia. His legal practice was interrupted by the Austrian military occupation of Bosnia and Herzegovina, for which he was called to service as an officer in 1878. On his return he abandoned law and became editor of *Národné Noviny* (National News) in Trenčiansky Svatý Martín. He made his paper the chief mouthpiece of the Slovak nationalist movement. He was continually persecuted by the Hungarian government, was often fined and even imprisoned, but remained faithful to the paper until his death. Ironically, he died little more than a year before Slovakia was liberated from Hungary.

* hŏŏr' bản vả' yản skē

Vajanský, like the great Slovak nationalist Ludovít Štúr, looked to Russia for help in the liberation of Slovakia. Like Štúr, he strongly distrusted the West, and particularly France, as spiritually and culturally decadent. For him Slovakia was closer to Russia than to Austria or Bohemia, and he opposed the pro-Czech orientation common among his compatriots. The Slovak poet Kollár was another source of his pan-Slavic ideas.

Vajanský began to publish poetry in 1873, at first largely imitative of the German poems which he had read as a student. His poetry is for the most part lyric, combining descriptions of the native landscape with patriotic motifs. His later poetry shows great mastery of verse technique, influenced by the Czech Parnassian poet Vrchlický, whose formal influence Vajanský accepted, though he considered his views too cosmopolitan.

Vajanský is best remembered as a prose writer, the author of a number of novels and tales, strongly influenced by the Russian writers Turgenev and Goncharov. Like Turgenev he combines lyric portraits of manor life with discussions of national and social problems. His best-known novel is *Suchá Ratolest* (The Dry Branch, 1884), the portrayal of a Slovak *zeman* (squire) who becomes a nationalist patriot. The "dry branch" of the novel is the Magyarized gentry, who may still be reclaimed for the nationalist cause. But Vajanský's picture is too idealized: the landed gentry of Slovakia actually had little interest in nationalism.

Vajanský is a typical Slovak man of letters in that his work has many facets, literary, philosophical, journalistic, and political. For him the author must also serve the needs of his people.

Translations of several of Vajanský's lyrics can be found in Paul Selver, *Anthology of Czechoslovak Literature* (1929); C. A. Manning, *Anthology of Czechoslovak Poetry* (1929); I. J. Kramoris, *Anthology of Slovak Poetry* (1947).

ABOUT: Columbia Dictionary of Modern European Literature. [In Slovak—Mráz, A. S. Hurban Vajanský.]

W. E. H.

*HURTADO DE MENDOZA, DIEGO (1503?-August 14, 1575), Spanish humanist, historian, and poet, was born in Granada. Both his father, the Count of Tendilla, and his mother were Mendozas and direct descendants of the great Marquis of Santillana. He received a rigorously humanistic educa-

* ōōr tä' thō thā mān dō' thā

tion, under the influence, direct or indirect, of the royal tutor Pedro Mártir de Anghiera. As a leading grandee of Spain, he probably attended the coronation of the Emperor Charles V in Bologna in 1529; he certainly accompanied the Emperor on his expedition to Tunis (1535). He studied at Siena. Charles V sent Mendoza as ambassador to England in 1537 to arrange a marriage between the princess Mary Tudor and the prince Don Luis of Portugal; after several months of vain negotiations, Mendoza returned by way of Flanders.

In 1539 Don Diego was sent to be the imperial ambassador in Venice. His chief mission was the impossible one of keeping Venice from yielding to Turkish pressure for a separate peace. There he became a close friend of Aretino. He had literary dealings with Bembo, Varchi, and many other humanists; he collected valuable books and manuscripts, principally in Greek, but also in Latin, Hebrew, and Arabic. Titian painted his portrait. He wrote poetry, indulged in love affairs, and studied the works of Aristotle. Venice was his home for six or eight years.

In March 1545 Mendoza was sent to represent the Emperor at the Council of Trent. In April of 1547 we find him as ambassador to Paul III in Rome. He also became governor of Siena; but, without funds for fortifications, he and his troops were driven out of Siena in 1552. This was the end of his career in Italy.

Upon his return to Spain, Don Diego was made a member of the Order of Alcántara in 1554. He served the new king Philip II as organizer of armadas in the port of Laredo. In 1568, because of an argument over some poetry with Don Diego de Leyva which almost resulted in a duel in the royal palace, Mendoza was exiled from the Court. He took part in the war against the Moriscos. He was allowed to return to Madrid in 1574, where he died the following year. His great library, willed to the king, is still one of the treasures of the Escorial. None of his writings were published during his lifetime; yet, both in verse and in prose, they are worthy of note.

With Juan Boscán and Garcilaso de la Vega, Mendoza introduced into Spanish literature the poetry of Renaissance Italy, that is, Petrarchism and classical themes in the form of sonnets, odes, epistles, and ottava rima narratives. The influences detectable in his verse include virtually all the poetic models fashionable in the sixteenth century,

from Homer to Alciato. Though not so delicate a poet as either of the other two, he had a great influence even in manuscript, both because of the quantity, variety, and classical erudition of his verse, and because of his great social prestige. The first collection of his verse was published in 1610; a more nearly complete collection was published in 1877 by the American Hispanist Knapp.

Mendoza's most important prose work is *La Guerra de Granada,* an account of the Morisco rebellion of 1568-69; it marks the transition, in Spanish historiography, from the almost formless medieval chronicle to the organic, reasoned narrative, with political, military, and moral conclusions, modeled on Sallust, Tacitus, and Machiavelli. Upon events in which he himself had been involved, Mendoza imposed the critical perspective and objective accuracy of a great humanist. This masterpiece was not published until 1627.

ABOUT: [In Spanish—González Palencia, A. and Mele, E. Vida y Obras de don Diego Hurtado de Mendoza.]

E. L. R.

*HUS, JAN (JOHN) (1369/71-July 6, 1415), Bohemian (Czech) theologian, was born in the village of Husinec, from which his name derives, the son of a peasant named Michael. The year of his birth is not known for certain. It was generally held to be 1369, but recent scholarship has uncovered evidence that it was about two years later. Although his parents were poor, they were able to educate their son. In about 1389 he enrolled at the University of Prague where he soon won attention as a brilliant student and was noted for his piety and religious enthusiasm. By 1396 Hus had his master's degree and was lecturing at the university. He was ordained in 1400 and a year later he became dean of the philosophical faculty. In 1402 Hus became rector of the University of Prague, and in the same year he began preaching at the Bethlehem Chapel. His sermons attracted the wealthiest and the most influential citizens of Prague. Among his admirers were King Wenceslas of Bohemia and his queen Sophia, who made Hus her confessor.

Hus' formal break with the church of Rome did not come until 1408. It was not a sudden rupture, but a stand taken after years of gradual movement away from Rome. The rise of the Hussite movement has often been attributed to the influence of the writings of

* hoos

433

HUS

the English theologian John Wyclif, whose treatises were widely circulated in Bohemia. Wyclif's influence was considerable. Hus read his works and translated some of them into Bohemian. But it is now known that there was a strong reform movement in Bohemia quite independent of Wyclifite influence. The teachings of Hus were the product of this native reform movement. For that reason he enjoyed in Prague the respect and admiration of the populace as well as of the heads of state. His only enemies within Bohemia were the clergy, who were the prime objects of his reforming zeal. His chief enemy outside Bohemia was King Sigismund of Hungary, younger brother of Wenceslas and heir to the throne of Bohemia, who saw him as an obstacle to his own desire for power in Bohemia.

Thus while the church condemned Hus—banning him from preaching, excommunicating him in 1409, even forcing him into exile from Prague in 1412—Bohemia continued to honor him, and King Wenceslas continued to protect him. As long as he was under this protection, Hus moved in safety. But in 1414 he was summoned out of Bohemia to answer charges against him at the church council at Constance. Sigismund offered him a safe-conduct, but this was merely bait for his trap. On November 28, 1414, Hus was arrested and imprisoned. He was allowed no legal representative when, after months in prison, he was at last brought to trial for heresy in June 1415. The main evidence against him was his writing, which was unequivocally Wyclifite. Hus swore his loyalty to the Christian faith, but he refused to recant the ideas expressed in his books. Sick and emaciated, he spent his last weeks in prison writing letters to his friends in Bohemia. Most of these letters are extant, and they are moving documents, full of religious fervor and Christian resignation. He was condemned and burned at the stake.

Hus did the bulk of his writing during his exile from Prague in 1412-14. He wrote in both Bohemian and Latin. One of the best-known of his works is the treatise *On Simony*, written in Bohemian in 1413. It deals frankly and critically with the principal cause of trouble within the Bohemian church —the buying and selling of ecclesiastical offices. Also composed in Bohemian was the *Postilla*, a collection of sermons on the Gospel, intended to acquaint the people of Bohemia with the Holy Scriptures which they could not read in their native language. The most important of the Latin writings of Hus was his *De Ecclesia* which was used as evidence against him at his trial. It contains his bitterest criticism of the church hierarchy, of the corruption and worldliness of popes and cardinals.

It was a tenet of Wyclifism that the Bible must be made available in the vernacular so that all people may know it. Hus firmly adhered to this belief, and he helped to make the Bible accessible to Bohemian readers by translating portions of it and correcting and revising earlier translations. Hus made many efforts to establish and systematize a written language for the Bohemian people. Bohemian or Czech is a Slavic language, but it uses the Latin alphabet, which is not capable of rendering all of the sounds of Slavic speech. In his *Orthographia Bohemia* Hus introduced various diacritical marks to signify these sounds, and with some modifications they have survived to modern Czech. His main achievement in the field of language, however, was his use of the vernacular in the writings of serious theological works, thereby giving the language dignity and respectability. "I write in the manner in which I am in the habit of speaking," he said in his *Postilla*.

The influence of John Hus became even greater after his death. To Bohemia he was a martyr and a national hero. In his name were fought the Hussite wars in which the Bohemians defended themselves against the onslaught of a crusade called by Pope Martin V in 1420. Ultimately they were defeated, and in 1562 the Roman Church was reestablished in Bohemia. But the memory of Hus had by this time spread throughout Europe. Martin Luther came upon his books and was profoundly stirred by them. He wrote, in the preface to his *Confession of Faith,* that he "found them to be powerful and in accordance with the pure word of God." Hus forms a vital link in the chain of the history of the Reformation. Matthew Spinka says of him: "It was his devoted search for truth, his stern moral emphasis, his zeal for reform, his sterling character, and his insistence upon personal responsibility in matters of religion which secured for him the influence which he has enjoyed ever since."

The major works of Hus are available in English translation. *De Ecclesia (The Church)* was translated by D. S. Schaff (1915); *On Simony* by M. Spinka in *Advocates of Reform: From Wyclif to Erasmus* (1953); *The Letters of Jan Hus* by C. Mackenzie (1846) and H. B. Workman (1904).

ABOUT: Lechler, G. von, John Hus; Loserth, J. Hus and Wyclif; Lützow, Count, The Life and Times of Master John Hus; Spinka, M. John Hus and the Czech Reformation; Workman, H. B. Dawn of the Reformation.

---

*HUTTEN, ULRICH VON (April 21, 1488-September 1523), German author, humanist, and soldier, was the eldest son of an ancient but impoverished family with its seat at Schloss Steckelberg near Kinzig in Hesse, where he was born. The father, also Ulrich, perhaps regarding his son as a weakling, intended to put him into the church. At the age of ten the boy was sent to the monastery school at Fulda (1499). He fled before taking his monastic vows and the consequent breach with his father was not healed until 1515. For the next few years Ulrich lived as a wandering student, often in the depths of poverty. Between 1505 and 1511 he visited the universities of Cologne (1505), Erfurt (1506), Greifswald (1507), Wittenberg, and Vienna, making the acquaintance of many celebrated humanists, among them Crotus Rubeanus. Hutten was enthusiastic about the new humanistic learning but he was not impressed with the Italians as persons and showed his patriotic fervor by satirizing the Venetians when he was in Vienna and by more general attacks on the Italians when in Italy in 1512. Poverty forced him to take service as a mercenary in Italy and syphilis undermined his health.

By 1513 he was back in Germany in the service of Eitelwolf von Stein and Albrecht, Bishop of Magdeburg and Mainz. On May

* ho͞ot′ ĕn

HUTTEN

15, 1515, Hutten's cousin Hans was brutally murdered by the Duke of Württemberg, an event which called forth all of Hutten's satiric powers and caused him to write his dialogue *Phalarismus* against tyranny. In 1515, with his circumstances a little eased by the reconciliation with his family, he went to study the law in Italy but spent most of his efforts on Greek, making the acquaintance of the dialogues of Lucian, which were to have a great influence on his writing. The next two years are the high point of his literary activity. The years from 1519 until his death were devoted to writings in support of Luther, whom he had at first despised, and military action with Franz von Sickingen, under whose protection he lived. It was in the latter's castle that he wrote his satire *Robbers* against all those, clergy and lay, who exploit the poor, and also where he composed numerous attacks on the Papacy. He agreed to suspend these attacks during Luther's conference at Worms but resumed them after its failure. By this time he was hated by his enemies, and his friends were saying that he was a man of words but no deeds. After the defeat and death of Franz von Sickingen (1522) he was defenseless and fled for protection to Schlettstadt, to Basel, and to Zürich. His pursuers left him no peace and he died on the island of Ufnau, in Lake Zürich.

Virtually all of Hutten's works, in one way or another, are polemics. His dialogues are comments on aspects of current society—on the power and influence of the church

(*Vadiscus*), against court life (*Aula*), against human folly (*Inspicientes*). Sometimes he glorifies life in Germany, with all its faults, as against Italy (*Arminius*). Most popular were his general commentary in German (*Gesprächbüchlein*) or "Little Conversation Book" and the *Nemo*, or "How Nobody gets the blame for everything." His dialogues, though gracefully written, are not lively, nor are the characters well drawn. They merely give Hutten's own views in a form borrowed from classical antiquity. Though most of his work was in Latin, he translated some of his dialogues into German to influence a wider audience. His most famous work does not bear his name. It is almost certain that he was responsible for at least the second half of the *Epistolae Obscurorum Virorum* (Letters of Obscure Men), a satire on the opponents of Reuchlin and in particular on Chancellor Ortwin of the University of Cologne. By ascribing to friends and pupils of Ortwin, in a series of letters ostensibly written by them, the crassest illiteracy and barbarism, he made the chancellor and the scholastic method the laughing-stocks of Europe. The letters are written in the kind of barbarous Latin which the humanists imputed to the scholastics. The complete edition of his works was brought out by E. Boecking, 1859-76.

ABOUT: Holbor, H. Ulrich von Hutten and the German Reformation; Strauss, D. F. Ulrich von Hutten. [In German—Stammler, W. Von der Mystik zum Barock.]

W. T. H. J.

*HUYGENS, CONSTANTIJN (September 4, 1596-1687), Dutch poet and humanist, "among the last of the true Renaissance virtuosi," the "uomo universale per se," was born and died in The Hague, the son of a government official. Destined by his father to follow a public career, Constantijn and his brother Maurits received the best in education, humanistic but pious, above all wide in range: languages, fencing, horsemanship, manners, dancing—calculated to produce a cultivated man of the world.

Public service demanded legal studies and proficiency in languages. As a linguist Huygens' prowess was phenomenal even for that linguistic age; he knew and wrote Greek, Latin, French, Italian, Spanish, English, and German. Legal studies claimed him only briefly, however (1616-17). In 1618 he left Leiden to accompany the English envoy Carleton on a mission to England; in 1620

* hoi' gĕns

he accompanied the Dutch political figure Aerssen van Sommelsdijck to Venice on state business. From 1625 until his death Huygens served the ruling house of Orange. His genius was recognized: in 1622 he was knighted by the king of England; in 1632 the French monarch made him a Knight of the Order of St. Michel. The Huygens letters, of which thousands have been preserved, show that he knew and was esteemed by the great of his day: Hooft, Descartes, Corneille, Grotius, and Vondel.

In 1627 Huygens married a cousin, the pretty and wealthy Susanna van Baerle. Four sons and a daughter were born of this marriage but soon after the birth of the last child, Susanna died (1637). Huygens' profound sorrow, expressed in many poems, testifies to his love for his "Sterre" (Star). The poet henceforth devoted himself most responsibly to the intelligent, meticulous rearing of his children; the world-wide stature of his physicist-mathematician son Christian was a reward for this parental care.

Huygens' keen intellectual bent and staunch Calvinism remained with him throughout a long life; he claimed all branches of intellectual endeavor. He was an accomplished performer on several musical instruments. His *Pathodia Sacra et Profana* (1647) exhibits his abilities as a composer. From abroad he eagerly absorbed Bacon's scientific work but had as sensitive a mind for Donne's baroque poetry, which he greatly admired. Characteristic of the age, Huygens' own poetic work often shows a fondness for the conceit—graceful and sometimes affectedly ornamental. For this, contemporaries esteemed him; a more modern critic deems it "cerebral gymnastics." Yet Huygens was no cultist. Despite his sophistication he never lost touch with the broad popular bases of life and letters.

A crowded life necessarily made of Huygens' poetry a matter of occasional activity, albeit a serious one. This is illustrated by his collection *Korenbloemen* (1658), i.e., art as something occurring only in the midst of practical everyday concerns. Accordingly another collection, the satirical *Costelick Mal* (1622), Huygens seeks "to unite the useful with the pleasant." Naturally poetry so conceived often becomes moralistic. But at his best, in *Daghwerck* (1627-38, the record of his love for Susanna) and in *Cluyswerck* (1683), the semi-autobiographical work of old age, Huygens, a man of sharp intellect and warm heart, often produces deep, noble wisdom. Here, everyday things appear in a colorful mosaic permeated by the author's spirit.

ABOUT: Bachrach, A. G. H. Huygens and Britain; Colie, R. L. Some Thankfulnesse to Constantine; University of Toronto Quarterly, XXV (1956). [In French—see studies by H. Bachelin, L. Deffoux, H. Trudgian.]

C. K. P.

HUYSMAN, ROELOF. See AGRICOLA, RUDOLF

*HUYSMANS, CHARLES MARIE GEORGES, known as **JORIS KARL** (February 5, 1848-May 12, 1907), French novelist, was born in Paris. His father, Victor Godfried Jan Huysmans (1815-56), was a Dutch lithographer and miniaturist, an artist like his ancestors, who had married a schoolteacher, Elisabeth Malvina Badin (1826-76). Godfried became a French citizen after his son's birth but continued to visit pious Catholic relatives in Holland and Belgium.

After the death of her husband, Georges' mother married a Protestant, Jules Og (1823-67), in 1857. Two daughters were born to the couple and Georges—denied affection and understanding—felt himself an outcast within the family. Life at school was also unpleasant: beginning in 1856 at the Institution Hortus and continuing at the Lycée Saint-Louis in 1862 as a scholarship student. Nevertheless, privately tutored during the last year, he received the baccalaureate in 1866, and immediately obtained a position in a government welfare office. He also enrolled in the law and arts-and-sciences programs of the University of Paris, but he neglected his studies for café life and casual affairs. He was frequenting the Théâtre du Luxembourg, familiarly called Bobino; and he had begun to write, having made his début with an article on contemporary landscape-painters in *La Revue Mensuelle*.

The birth of a daughter (by someone else) to a Bobino singer with whom he was living, introduced into his search for pleasures the problems of routine reality. This dilemma took a new turn at the end of July 1870, for Huysmans was ordered to join the National Guard at the front. He was shunted from Châlons to Evreux because of dysentery, and through a family friend he secured a leave. Transferred to the war ministry as a clerk, Huysmans was at Versailles at the time of the Commune—his view of the car-

* ü ĕs mäns'

HUYSMANS

nage came after the events had taken place. With the return of calm to the capital, he spent his leisure time studying the Dutch paintings at the Louvre, and writing prose-poems under the influence of Aloysius Bertrand, Baudelaire, and the Goncourt brothers. His first book, *Le Drageoir à Épices* (1874), was published under the Dutch signature of Joris Karl Huysmans at his own expense, having been refused by many publishers. Persuaded by influential writers like Arsène Houssaye and Octave Lacroix, critics wrote laudatory reviews; Banville said the work was "a skillfully cut jewel from the hand of a master goldsmith." A second edition had another publisher, and periodicals sought Huysmans' collaboration. He supplied them with descriptions of paintings. A huge work, "La Faim," on the siege of Paris in 1870, utilized as the heroine Anna Meunier, with whom he had had a love affair, but this novel was not completed; nor did he finish "Joyeusetés Navrantes," a collection of short stories. He set to work revising the manuscript of "Le Chant du Départ," re-titled *Sac au Dos*, whose data were furnished by his war experiences. *Sac au Dos* was eventually published in the collective volume of the naturalists, *Les Soirées de Médan* (1880). Next, drawing from his first love affair, he drafted *Marthe, Histoire d'une Fille* (1876). It was published in Belgium in order to avoid the risk of government prosecution, and so that it might appear in print before Edmond de Goncourt's *La Fille Élisa*. The copies Huysmans tried to take back with him were confiscated at the customs.

Encouraged by Émile Zola, for whom Huysmans had great admiration, he set to work on *Les Sœurs Vatard*, utilizing his acquaintance with the book-bindery inherited from his stepfather through his mother. Georges Charpentier, the famous publisher of the naturalists, finally issued this realistic novel in 1879, with a dedication to Zola. A modern critic (R. Baldick) has said that "no French writer—excepting the Goncourt brothers—has ever shown greater awareness of the niceties of color, or of the delicate interplay of light and shade, than Huysmans in his early novels." Flaubert had measured praise for Huysmans, and the novel sold.

Huysmans wrote scathing art criticism for the newspaper *Le Voltaire* in 1879, and proimpressionist articles for *La Réforme* (1880). *L'Art Moderne* (1883) helped greatly to further impressionism; Félix Fénéon went so far as to say that Huysmans was "the inventor of impressionism." Certainly he aided the reputation of Odilon Redon, whom he had assimilated into the movement.

Huysmans collected various sketches in *Croquis Parisiens* (1880). Critics disliked some of the lush decriptions and the erotic emphasis. The same could not be said of *En Ménage* (1881), the banal story of a bachelor who tries to escape boredom by marriage. This realistic novel differs from Huysmans' previous ones by its use of psychological rather than descriptive interest. Here Huysmans describes himself, "tall and thin, fairhaired and pale-faced, with a blond beard, long slender fingers, hands that were never still, piercing grey eyes." His mistress Anna Meunier posed for the character of Jeanne.

Huysmans had continued to work as a government functionary. The dreariness, the pettiness but also the exasperations of the poor bureaucrat's routine became the data of the pessimistic *À Vau-l'Eau* (1882). Its hero Folantin has become "one of the great types in French literature." Huysmans abandoned *Le Gros Caillou* because it was too imitative of *À Vau-l'Eau*, for a "wild and gloomy fantasy": *À Rebours (Against the Grain*, 1884). Undoubtedly the best known of Huysmans' works, *À Rebours* was termed by Arthur Symons "the breviary of the Decadence." It influenced Oscar Wilde —who refers to it in his *Picture of Dorian Gray*. Strangely enough, Huysmans had originally conceived of his protagonist Des Esseintes as "a M. Folantin, more cultured,

more refined, more wealthy." Huysmans based his memorable character on a composite of Ludwig II of Bavaria, Edmond de Goncourt, Baudelaire, Barbey d'Aurevilly, and the count of Montesquiou-Fezensac. The book was instrumental in publicizing contemporary writers like Mallarmé and Verlaine. It had a tremendous, immediate success. *À Rebours* was also a definite break with naturalism. But his next novel, *En Rade* (1887), first published in the new symbolist periodical *La Revue Indépendante*, combined the starkest sordid descriptions with dream sequences.

En Rade contains references to the occult, in which Huysmans was to receive instruction from Caroline Louise Victoire (Berthe) Courrière and Henriette Maillat. Huysmans frequented occultists like Stanislas de Guaita, Sâr Péladan, and Papus (Gérard Encausse). *Là-Bas* (1891) was elaborated after he had resolved the problem of combining spiritualism with naturalism. It is probable that Huysmans witnessed a Black Mass, as well as documenting himself on the history of Satanism. Huysmans also wrote a preface to Jules Bois' *Le Satanisme et la Magie*. Interest in contemporary Satanism led Huysmans to the occultist Joseph Antoine Boullan who was feuding with Guaita and Oswald Wirth. Canon Docre of *Là Bas* was based on Boullan. For years Huysmans believed that he himself was under attack from Guaita, and he took magical precautions.

At the same time that the occultist interpretation of religion was attracting him, Huysmans was also inclining toward orthodox Catholicism. He veered from frequenting the slums and dives to attending church services. A retreat at a Trappist monastery helped him to regain his faith. Under the guidance of Abbé Arthur Mugnier, Huysmans was reconverted in 1892, without abandoning his feelings for the occult. *En Route* (1895) records his return to the church. *La Cathédrale* (1898) glorified medieval architecture, showing the mystical influence of art and the function of medieval symbolism. *L'Oblat* (1903) was to complete the Catholic trilogy, although Huysmans wrote some other religious works, such as the life of Saint Lydwine of Schiedam.

Resigning from his civil service position in 1898, Huysmans became in 1901 an oblate of the Benedictine Abbey of Saint-Martin at Ligugé. But the monastery was disbanded, since it was affected by the new government regulations for such establishments, and Huysmans returned to Paris. The details of residence at Ligu26é were confided in *L'Oblat.* Trips to Belgium and Germany could not take his mind off extremely painful dental troubles, symptoms of the cancer that was to ravage his last years. Partially blind, wracked by rheumatism, weakened by surgery, Huysmans suffered a lingering final agony. He was buried in Montparnasse cemetery.

Shortly before he died, in recognition of his literary achievements and of his position as president of the Goncourt Academy to which he had been appointed in the Goncourt will, the French government made him an Officer of the Legion of Honor. The Goncourt Academy has seen to the publication of Huysmans' major works. His *Œuvres Complètes* was published in twenty-three volumes (1928-34), edited by Lucien Descaves. The Société J. K. Huysmans has actively furthered his reputation, publishing a *Bulletin* since 1928.

Against the Grain, often reprinted, was translated by John Howard (pseudonym of Jacob Howard Lewis) in 1922, with a preface by Havelock Ellis. *Down Stream, and Other Works,* translated by Samuel Putnam in 1927 with a critical preface, includes *Marthe, A Dish of Spices,* and selections from *Critical Papers. Marthe, Story of a Woman,* in the same translation, was reprinted separately in 1948, and included in *Four Fallen Women* (1953). *Down There,* translated by Keene Wallis in 1924, was reprinted in 1935 under the French title, *Là-Bas. The Cathedral* was translated by Clara Bell in 1898; the last of the trilogy, *The Oblate,* was translated by Edward Perceval in 1924. C. Kegan Paul's translation (1908) of *En Route* had four editions; *Saint Lydwine of Schiedam* was translated by Agnes Hastings in 1923, *The Crowds of Lourdes* by W. H. Mitchell in 1925. In 1962 G. A. Cevasco published a bibliographical study, *Huysmans in America.*

ABOUT: Baldick, R. The Life of J. K. Huysmans; Ellis, H. Affirmations, *and* The New Spirit; Gourmont, R. de. Book of Masks; Huneker, J. G. Egoists, *also* Essays, *also* Unicorns; Laver, J. The First Decadent; Symons, A. Symbolist Movement in Literature, *also* Figures of Several Centuries. [In French—Chastel, G. J. K. Huysmans et ses Amis; Cogny, P. J. K. Huysmans à la Recherche de l'Unité; Gallot, H. M. Explication de J. K. Huysmans; Garreau, A. J. K. Huysmans; Trudgian, H. L'Esthétique de J. K. Huysmans; Veysset, G. Huysmans et la Médecine.]

S. S. W.

*HVIEZDOSLAV, pseudonym of PA-VOL *ORSZÁGH (February 2, 1849-June 8, 1921), Slovak poet, was born in Vyšný Kubín in Slovakia. His father was a member of the petty gentry. The son was sent to *Gymnasium* (high school) in Miškovce, where he began to write verses in Hungarian

* hvyěz' dǒ slåf; ôr' säg

"HVIEZDOSLAV"

in the manner of the Hungarian poet Petőfi. His readings of older Slovak poets won him over to the Slovak language, however, and he became a Slovak nationalist. He studied law in Prešov and entered the state service, becoming a judge in Dolný Kubín. But he did not feel free in his official position to write (though he adopted the pseudonym of Hviezdoslav to secure at least some freedom), and after three years, in 1879, he resigned to return to private practice in the town of Námestov. In 1899 he abandoned law to devote himself entirely to literature. He died in his home village, where he had lived since 1899.

Like his contemporary and fellow poet Vajanský, Hviezdoslav looked to Russia for help in winning freedom for Slovakia. But the Bolshevik Revolution of 1917 destroyed his hopes. Unlike Vajanský, he did not despise the West, and he now transferred his hopes of liberation to the Czechs. Towards the end of World War I he spoke openly in favor of a Czechoslovak Republic. He was rewarded by seeing the foundation of the new state, and himself served as a delegate to its National Assembly.

Hviezdoslav's poetry combines elements of romanticism and Parnassianism. On one hand he is a patriot whose verse describes his love of country and the beauties of the Slovak landscape; on the other he is an aesthete and accomplished technician who introduced new verse forms such as the sestina and terzina to Slovak poetry. Like Vajanský, he sees no contradiction between the

439

aesthetic side of poetry and its spiritual mission, between form and content. Poetry, patriotism, and religious feeling flowed together for him into one poetic sentiment. In these views he was influenced by Czech poets such as Vrchlický, Hálek, and Čech.

Hviezdoslav wrote lyric and narrative poetry, as well as verse plays. A large proportion of his work is religious, whether contemplative lyrics or narratives on Biblical subjects, such as *Agar* (Hagar, 1883), *Ráchel* (1891), or *Kain* (1892). He also wrote a Biblical play in verse, *Herodes a Herodias* (1909). His lyric cycle *Letorosty* (Offshoots, 1885) combines reminiscences of a happy childhood with regret at the lack of Slovak independence. As he grew older he became more pessimistic: in his lyric cycles *Stesky* (Laments, 1903) and *Dozvuky* (Echoes, 1909-11) he parallels his own aging with the apparent hopelessness of the national problem, though he predicts ultimate liberation after his death.

Most famous is Hviezdoslav's collection *Krvavé Sonety* (The Bloody Sonnets), written during World War I, and published in 1919. In this cycle he paints a vivid picture of the war's horror; the guilt of war he blames on the oppressors of his people.

Hviezdoslav's finest narrative poem is his *Hájnikova Žena* (The Gamekeeper's Wife, 1886), the story of a woman who shoots the son of her master when he attempts to seduce her. The poem is moving in its simplicity and the beauty of its nature scenes.

A notable part of Hviezdoslav's work consists in his translations, in which he sought to elevate the Slovak language to a level of expressiveness equal to the languages from which he translated. He made Slovak renderings of Shakespeare's *Hamlet* and *A Midsummer Night's Dream*, Pushkin's *Boris Godunov*, Mickiewicz's *Crimean Sonnets*, and the prologue to Goethe's *Faust*.

Several of Hviezdoslav's poems are translated into English in C. A. Manning, *Anthology of Czechoslovak Poetry* (1929), and Paul Selver, *Anthology of Czechoslovak Literature* (1919).

ABOUT: Columbia Dictionary of Modern European Literature. [In Slovak—Bujnák, P. P. Országh-Hviezdoslav. In Italian—Meriggi, B. Storia delle Letterature Ceca e Slovacca.]

W. E. H.

*IBN EZRA, ABRAHAM BEN MEIR

(1092-January 23, 1167), Hebrew poet, philosopher, mathematician, was born in Tudela or Toledo, Spain. Little is known of Ibn

* ib'n ĕz' rä

Ezra's life before he left his native land, although it is known that he wrote principally poetry and resided in the Spanish Jewish cultural centers of Cordova and Lucena. For reasons unknown Ibn Ezra quit Spain about 1140, a few years before the decimation of Jewry in Moslem Spain by the Almohade conquest of 1148. He appears to have gone to the then thriving Jewish community of Kairouan in Tunisia, and from there to Rome. We find him in Salerno in 1141, Mantua in 1145, Verona in 1146; in 1148 he settled in Lucca and remained for eight years. The next sojourns in his prolonged wanderings were in Provence, and he then turned northwards in the later 1150's, spending some time in Angers and Rouen. In 1158 Ibn Ezra settled in London, which he termed "the edge of the world," but by 1160 he was back in Provence, at Narbonne. His whereabouts during his last years are unknown. The place of his death in 1167 is traditionally assigned to Calahorra in Navarre, although it may have been Rome or even England.

Abraham Ibn Ezra's reputation among Jews rests upon his voluminous commentary upon the Bible, which he composed in miscellaneous order during his wanderings. It is of the highest importance in Biblical studies, for Ibn Ezra was a master of the philology of his day, dissecting the Hebrew text in sharp and pregnant style. Of even deeper significance is his anticipation of later Biblical scholarship. He divides the Book of Isaiah into the writings of two prophets and writes a carefully veiled denial of the Mosaic authorship of the entire Pentateuch, an opinion which Spinoza was the first to uncover. Yet in his poetic and philosophical writings Ibn Ezra is a pious Jew, yearning for union with his Creator. His religious poetry is saturated with the traditional Jewish themes of the poet's personal sinfulness and repentance, against the background of God's chosen people similarly acknowledging their sin, offering their repentance, and praying for redemption. But Ibn Ezra's poetry also recites the joys of love, friendship, and wine; he was fond of riddles in verse. Unique to this poet is his chess poetry, dramatizing the combat of the game.

Ibn Ezra also wrote on mathematics and astrology and thus influenced medieval scientific development. In his wanderings through Provence, Spain, and England he propagated among the Jews of Christian Europe rationalistic and scientific knowledge which had been developed in Spain by Moslems and Jews.

He is one of the most fascinating and versatile personages in Jewish or medieval history; English literature knows him as the subject of Browning's "Rabbi Ben Ezra."

The Commentary on Isaiah was translated by M. Friedlander (1873-88), *The Astrological Works* by R. Levy (1939).

ABOUT: Waxman, M. A History of Jewish Literature, I.

L. P. G.

*IBN EZRA, MOSES BEN JACOB

(c. 1055-c. 1139), Hebrew poet and critic, was born in Granada, Spain, to a wealthy and prominent family. The city at the time of Ibn Ezra's birth was a center of the rich Moslem-Jewish cultural milieu which flourished in Spain, and the poet grew up in an atmosphere of ease and refinement. With his family, he fled Granada during the severe anti-Jewish disturbances of 1066 and studied in Lucena during that period. But he subsequently resettled in Granada, where he lived until the Almoravid conquest of 1090. While many details in Ibn Ezra's life are unknown, it appears that he held a public position during the early years of his literary career. Ibn Ezra was steeped in the Hispano-Hebraic poetic tradition, as well as in the Arab culture and the literary models upon which it was largely based. His first work, *Sefer ha'Annaq* (The Book of the Necklace), was a collection of poems on fairly conventional topics—love, death, wine, and the like. However, it was written with unusual virtuosity and command of the involved poetic techniques.

The year 1090 marks a decisive break in the life of Moses Ibn Ezra. The Almoravids, summoned from North Africa to turn back the Christian tide in Spain, fulfilled their mission and conquered Moslem Spain as well. The Jewish community of Granada was shattered, and so were the fortunes of the Ibn Ezra family. They scattered, and the poet remained behind in penury until he too finally abandoned his native city and commenced a life of wandering which ended only with his death. A more intimate motive has also been suggested for his leaving wife and children—a love affair with his niece to which the family objected. In any case, the poet made his way north to Christian Castile, where cultural life among Jews as among Christians stood at a far lower level. The poet constantly lamented his being among "barbarians" and longed for his lost native

habitat. Yet adversity only inspired his poetic gifts to higher achievement. The old themes are supplemented by poems upon the bitterness of exile, upon the death of relatives and friends, and by much liturgical and penitential poetry. In his final years Ibn Ezra wrote "The Book of Discussion and Debate" in Arabic, the standard treatise upon the medieval Hebrew *ars poetica*.

Moses Ibn Ezra's command of every resource of Hebrew, his variety of subject matter and delicacy of expression establish him as one of the foremost poets of the medieval period. To the modern taste, however, his poems often seem ornate and somewhat overwrought. Only in the last century have his religious and profane poems been published and studied in any number.

Selected Poems, translated by S. Solis-Cohen and edited by H. Brody, was published in 1934. There are also a few poems in B. Halper's *Post-Biblical Literature* (1921).

ABOUT: Finkelstein, L., ed. The Jews; Waxman, M. A History of Jewish Literature, I; Jewish Quarterly Review, XXIV (1935).

L. P. G.

*IBN GABIROL, SOLOMON BEN JUDAH

(known also as Avicebron) (c. 1021-c. 1058), one of the greatest Hebrew poets and philosophers, was born in Málaga, Spain. Information concerning his life is so scanty and contradictory that occasional references in his poems furnish the most reliable data. His father, Judah, was a scholar, but Ibn Gabirol was orphaned at an early age and left completely without relatives. His formative years were spent in Saragossa where he was befriended by Yekutiel Ibn Al-Hasan, and it was there that he immersed himself in all branches of learning. His prodigious scholarship was immediately evident and by the age of sixteen he was writing first-rate poetry. Upon the death of Yekutiel, he came under the patronage of Samuel Ha-Nagid (or, Ibn Nagdela), the Grand Vizier of Moslem Granada. Their relationship terminated after bitter quarrels and Ibn Gabirol was left friendless and homeless once again. The exact year of his death in Valencia is not known.

Freed for many years from financial worries by his patrons, Ibn Gabirol was amazingly productive, both in poetry and philosophy. Most of his works cannot be dated definitely, although some poems can be traced to his youth. He wrote secular as well as religious poetry, the former consisting of laments on his bitter life and misfortunes, friendship poems, elegies, and didactic poems. He wrote but a few love and nature poems. It is his religious poetry, however, that reaches the zenith of medieval Hebrew poetry. In it he shows a mystic strain, expressing his love for God and his longing to unite with Him. The plight of the Jewish people, its suffering and its hope for ultimate redemption are dealt with in many poems. Some of these sacred poems have become part of the Jewish liturgy, among them the Sabbath hymn *Shir ha-Kavod* (Song of Glory), and the *Shir ha-Yihud* (Song of Unity). His *Keter Malchut* (Royal Crown), a long, philosophical poem, is a work of extraordinary beauty and lofty thought. In it he combines all his knowledge of poetry, philosophy, and science in an elaborate ode to God. His religious poetry led Heine to call him "Gabirol, the nightingale of piety, whose rose was God."

Ibn Gabirol's greatest philosophical work is the *Mekor Hayim* (Fountain of Life). Written originally in Arabic, it was translated into Latin about 1150, by Dominic Gundisalvi, as the *Fons Vitae*. The Latin version made a great impression on the Christian world and exerted considerable influence on scholastic philosophy. The author was thought to be an Arab or a Christian, and his name was corrupted to Avicebron, Avicebrol, etc. Under this guise, his ideas were accepted by Duns Scotus and the Franciscans and opposed by the Dominicans, among them Thomas Aquinas. It was not until the nineteenth century that the scholar Solomon Munk discovered that Avicebron was really Ibn Gabirol and *Fons Vitae* was identical with the Hebrew *Mekor Hayim*. The work itself, written in dialogue form, develops Ibn Gabirol's conceptions of God and the universe, but omits all reference to Judaism. Most of the *Fons Vitae* is devoted to a discussion of matter and form, and is based, primarily, on Neoplatonic philosophy. Matter and form are conceived as the fundamental principles of existence, emanating from God, or the First Essence. The purpose of life is the union of the soul with the upper world and its ultimate creator.

Ibn Gabirol also wrote a collection of moral maxims called *Mivhar ha-Peninim* (Choice of Pearls) and a more strictly Jewish and ethical work, *Tikun Midot ha-Nefesh* (The Improvement of the Moral Qualities). Both of these works were well-received by the Jews of his day.

At home in all fields of contemporary knowledge, a brilliant poet and philosopher,

Ibn Gabirol recognized his own worth: "My light is diffused through the world." Yet he complained continually of his sorry fate and of the unhappiness which life thrust upon him, finding refuge only in the pursuit of wisdom and God. His skillful use of language and poetic devices and his sense of beauty and awe combined to produce poetry of rare art and deep feeling. Profound, if obscure, he has been called "the Jewish Plato" and "the most original philosophical writer among the Jews and Arabs." Although of great importance to medieval Christian scholasticism, his *Fons Vitae* was largely ignored by later Jewish philosophers. Subsequently, however, elements of his thought entered into the Jewish mysticism of the cabala.

Israel Zangwill translated *Selected Religious Poems of Solomon ibn Gabirol* in 1923. Several poems appeared in 1894 in *Songs of Zion*, by A. Lucas. *Fons Vitae*, a Latin edition of which, edited by C. Baeumker, appeared in 1895, has not been published in English. *The Improvement of the Moral Qualities* was translated by Stephen S. Wise in 1902, and *Choice of Pearls* by Abraham Cohen in 1925. Hebrew editions include *Shire*, edited by H. N. Bialik (2d ed., Tel Aviv, 1927) and *Mekor Hayim* (Jerusalem, 1925-26).

ABOUT: Adler, H. Ibn Gebirol and His Influence upon Scholastic Philosophy; Graetz, H. History of the Jews; Husik, I. A History of Medieval Jewish Philosophy; Waxman, M. A History of Jewish Literature. [In German—Dreyer, K. Die Religiöse Gedankenwelt des Salomon Ibn Gebirol. In Hebrew—Orinowsky, A. Toldot ha-Shirah ha-'Ivrit bi-Yeme ha-Benayim. In Spanish—Millás Vallicrosa, J. M. Selomo ibn Gabirol como Poeta y Filósofo.]

M. R.

IBN-RUSHD. See AVERROËS

*IBSEN, HENRIK JOHAN (March 20, 1828-May 23, 1906), Norwegian dramatist and poet, was born in Skien, a timber trading center in southern Norway. Henrik was the eldest of five children of Knud Ibsen, a merchant, and Mariechen Cornelia Martine Altenburg, descended from a distinguished German family. His grandfather was a Danish sea captain. When Henrik was eight, his father, hitherto highly prosperous, suffered severe business reverses, as a result of which the family was forced to move to a dilapidated old farm outside the town. Here they were pariahs, shunned by their former friends. Henrik attended neither of the public schools in town, but was sent to a smaller middle-class school where he learned some Latin and theology. The specter of ruin cast

* ĭb′ s'n

IBSEN

a pall over the family life of the Ibsens. The father took out his frustration in tyranny, the mother was given to melancholia, and as a consequence Henrik's childhood was unhappy and lonely. He became introverted, finding his amusement in such solitary diversions as drawing and painting—and playing with a toy theatre he devised. (Some of this character was to be transferred to little Hedvig of *The Wild Duck*.) In time he took to giving conjuring performances for neighbors. At fifteen, after his confirmation, Henrik was removed from school. His father refused to allow him to pursue an art course as he wished, and Henrik left home at the age of sixteen to make his own way. Except for correspondence later on in life when he had become famous, he had no more contact with his family.

For the next five years Henrik served as apprentice to an apothecary in another provincial town, Grimstad. According to his own testimony, the revolutionary rumblings from the continent were all that could stir him out of his apathy here. Besides some poetry now lost, he wrote here his first play, *Catalina*, inspired by his reading of the famous conspiracy of Cataline, as preparation for the Latin entrance examination at the university. A friend, Ole Schulerud, tried in vain to place the play with producers and publishers in Christiania (now Oslo), but finally had it published at his own expense. By 1850 Ibsen had removed himself to the capital. Here he became a student at Heltberg's famous "Student Factory," a preparatory school which proved to be a spawning ground of genius—Björnson, Vinje, and Lie being among its alumni. However, Henrik soon discovered that studies were not his forte, and became more and more determined that poetry was to be his calling.

Meanwhile Ole Bull, manager of the newly opened Bergen Theatre, had accepted a poetic prologue from the fledgling writer for one of his productions, and in 1851 he followed up by appointing him to a post in the theatre. Ibsen now divided his time between Bergen and Copenhagen, then the acknowledged theatre center of Scandinavia, where he learned much under the tutelage of J. A. Heiberg, manager of the Royal Theatre. At this time there was virtually no Norwegian drama, and in all of Scandinavia there were but two major figures—the Danes Adam Oehlenschläger (an early influence on Ibsen) and Ludvig Holberg. At the Bergen Theatre where Ibsen served his apprenticeship the repertory was at least half French—which meant the cast-iron intrigue dramas of Scribe, Labiche, and their contemporaries. As early as 1851, writing in the periodical *Andhrimmer*, Ibsen denounced this French drama for its over-reliance on "situation" at the expense of "psychology," and scorned "the dramatic sweetmeats of Scribe and Company." Yet he was not above borrowing Scribe's techniques in such early plays as *Lady Inger of Östraat, The Feast at Solhaug, Olaf Liljekrans,* and *The Vikings at Helgeland,* which, though set in the period of the sagas and heightened by verse, are propelled by such devices of the "intrigue" drama as poisoned goblets, coincidences of relationship, and misunderstandings leading to murder.

At the beginning of 1856, towards the end of his Bergen career, Ibsen met his future wife Suzannah Thoresen at one of the literary evenings conducted by her stepmother, the writer Madeleine Thoresen, some of whose plays Ibsen had helped to produce. Ibsen's love poems to Suzannah, full of romantic exuberance and confidence as to his future greatness, are extant. The couple was married in 1858, despite the young playwright's dire financial straits. On December 23, 1859 their first child, Sigurd, was born, named after the hero of *The Vikings at Helgeland;* he later became a distinguished statesman and supervised the publication of his father's letters.

In 1857 Ibsen terminated his contract with the Bergen Theatre and moved on to Christiania once more to become director of the Norwegian Theatre. Five years later this theatre became bankrupt, and Ibsen was in debt and without any financial resources. He applied for a state grant for traveling abroad, but was allotted only a pittance to collect folklore in the Hardanger Fjord region. This expedition provided him with material later utilized in *Peer Gynt*. Repeated attempts to secure an annual state grant as a poet proved unsuccessful, for Ibsen was now *persona non grata* with the Storthing. His *Love's Comedy* (1857), a verse satire on the sanctities of domestic life, not only failed to secure production but offended the authorities as well. In 1863 Ibsen did manage to procure a small amount from the government for travel, and on this money completed *The Pretenders*, begun in 1858, a tragedy contrasting opportunistic political ambition with true dedication, the last of his verse dramas dealing with Scandinavian history. (Biographers of Ibsen find in this play a reflection of Ibsen's rivalry with Björnsterne Björnson, then at the height of his reputation.) Georg Brandes, then a schoolmaster, hailed *The Pretenders* as a masterpiece, but Brandes was at that time far from being an influential critic, and Ibsen's genius was still generally unrecognized.

Now occurred a great turning point in Ibsen's career. In the middle of 1864 he moved with his family to Rome. Not until more than a quarter of a century later did he return permanently to the country of his birth. The dramas on which his world-wide reputation largely rests were composed in Italy, Germany, and Austria, when he was removed not only from his native environment but from the theatre.

"Here at last there is blessed peace," Ibsen wrote to Björnson upon arriving in Rome, and here his creative faculty suddenly expanded. In Italy he wrote the two dramatic poems, not actually intended for performance, now regarded as his supreme imaginative achievements—*Brand* and *Peer Gynt*. The first, a sweeping allegory of idealism defeated by human limitations, dramatizes themes fundamental with Ibsen—vocation and inherited spiritual guilt. One of the most trying periods of Ibsen's life was the six months during which, ill and poverty-stricken, he awaited word from the publishers in Copenhagen to whom he sent the manuscript. Though the publishers were hesitant they finally agreed to bring out the play in March 1866. It proved an immediate success, selling out three editions within the year. In the words of Edmund Gosse, *Brand*

"placed Ibsen at a bound among the greatest European poets of his age." Almost simultaneously came a grant from the Storthing for poetry as well as a traveling grant, and Ibsen tasted prosperity.

Peer Gynt was written mainly at Ischia and Sorrento. It was published at the end of 1867. Then as now it excited consternation and bewilderment—and is probably among the least understood of Ibsen's works. Incorporating his delvings into Norwegian folklore, *Peer Gynt* has established itself in Europe as a children's fantasy, though Ibsen intended it as an allegory of the self-centered fancy finally compelled to cope with the world outside itself. *Peer Gynt* continues to defy translators, and probably most English-speaking people are more familiar with Edvard Grieg's music composed for a special performance. *Peer Gynt* marks a special milestone in Ibsen's career, for just as Peer returns to his home soil at the end, old and disillusioned after his exotic wanderings, so Ibsen at this point turned away from poetry and the romantic drama to create the bourgeois prose plays for which he is better known.

Ibsen's removal to Germany in 1868 to escape the French invasion of Italy forms another transition in his literary career. In the following year in Dresden he completed *The League of Youth*, satirizing a contemporary liberal movement in Norway. His friend Björnson had criticized *Peer Gynt* and urged Ibsen to try "photography by comedy." This apparently was the answer (Björnson himself is believed to be the prototype of the demagogue Stensgaard). Another early social drama, *The Pillars of Society* (1877), is modeled so closely on Björnson's *A Bankruptcy* as to suggest that Ibsen was trying to excel his rival, who had also turned from sagas and romances to realistic plays. *The League of Youth* caused an uproar at its opening on October 18, 1869—an event which brought forth a vindictive poem ("At Port Said") from the author, then attending the opening of the Suez Canal. *Pillars* was not received enthusiastically in Scandinavia either, but was a success in Germany.

Ibsen's previous play, the pretentious *Emperor and Galilean* (1873), based on the career of Julian the Apostate, shows marked Germanic literary influence. One would have expected Ibsen to compose this play in verse, but by this time he was firmly committed to the prose medium, as he indicates in his famous letter to Edmund Gosse: "We are no longer living in the age of Shakespeare. . . .

My new drama is no tragedy in the ancient acceptation; what I desired to depict were human beings, and therefore I would not let them talk the language of the gods."

In 1878 Ibsen was back in Rome, now a man of means. He wrote to Gosse that he was at work on "a family drama, dealing with modern conditions and in particular with the problems which complicate marriage." A report he had heard about a courageous young married woman in a small town in Zealand had seized hold of him. *A Doll's House* (1879) was the first of Ibsen's plays to bring him universal acclaim, to say nothing of the sensation caused in his own country by "Nora's declaration of independence." It brought forth imitation and parody, and generally inspired controversy out of proportion to its literary merit. In England William Archer and Arthur Symons lauded its advanced dramatic technique.

From this time on, the biennial publication of a new play by Ibsen was virtually an international event. Each work had its adherents and attackers, most of whom managed to distort or simplify its meanings to suit their purposes. *Ghosts* (1881) caused such a turmoil in the press that it could not be acted for two years after it was published. The furor over this *succès de scandale* (warmly defended by Brandes and Björnson) generally clouded the real merits of the drama—actually one of Ibsen's most complex statements on inherited guilt, though it was generally taken literally as a play about hereditary disease. *An Enemy of the People* (1883) was more cordially received. While seeming to uphold liberalism, this play, when examined closely, actually ridicules all sides in political controversy. "I am more and more convinced that there is something demoralizing in politics and parties," he wrote about this time to account for his own avoidance of any kind of political involvement. Something of this attitude seems to inform the perverse *The Wild Duck* (1885), which can be interpreted as a satire on misguided philanthropy. The culminating three dramas of society, *Rosmersholm* (1886), *The Lady from the Sea* (1888), and *Hedda Gabler* (1890), vary on the themes of social emancipation and individual freedom introduced in *A Doll's House*, but the diverse fates of the three heroines involved show that Ibsen's views on these issues are by no means easy to pin down.

In the late 1880's Ibsen was lionized on trips to Christiania and Stockholm. Finally in 1891 he decided to make his home once more in the land of his birth. For the last decade and a half of his life he enjoyed celebrity in the country that had early ignored him, and on which he had showered scorn. As the severe, white-bearded, frock-coated figure familiar from photographs he became the oracle of sidewalk cafés, his every word quoted in the newspapers—though he actually shunned crowds and publicity. In Scandinavia and in England he was the idol of the *avant-garde*, enjoying almost simultaneously two different reputations. To enthusiasts in his own country he was mainly the author of *The Pretenders*, *Brand* and *Peer Gynt*—the philosopher of idealism and altruism (Brand's ringing words: "All or Nothing," quoted out of context, became a slogan for youthful radicals). In England he was mainly the author of *A Doll's House* and *Ghosts*, taken up notably by George Bernard Shaw as the great iconoclast of society. Ibsen himself managed to remain aloof from all movements.

In his last years Ibsen brought out four of his most curious and baffling plays, *The Master Builder*, *John Gabriel Borkman*, *Little Eyolf*, and finally *When We Dead Awaken*. All four of the plays are somber and introspective; their leading characters look over their past lives with remorse and regret. The very subjectivism and elusive symbolism of these "visionary" plays have invited conjecture as to possible concealed autobiography. In *The Master Builder*, for example, the character of Hilda Wangel may well have been suggested by the young Viennese lady Emilie Bardach with whom Ibsen enjoyed an autumnal idyll in Grosenass. *Little Eyolf* may recall Ibsen's own youthful illicit romance and illegitimate child. Of even greater interest, Ibsen seems to leave us in these final plays with his last testament on his art. The churches, houses, and towers of the master builder Solness sound very much like Ibsen's *œuvre* (historical dramas, domestic dramas, "visionary" dramas), while Solness' collapse through the roof of his last building has been interpreted as Ibsen's symbolic comment on his own career. *When We Dead Awaken* has been taken to be Ibsen's *Tempest*, with the disillusioned sculptor Rebek, who comes to regard his career of aesthetic isolation as a dead one, acting as a kind of *alter ego*.

On September 1, 1899, there was formally opened the National Norwegian Theatre, still to be viewed on the Drammensveien in Oslo, its façade adorned by statues of the twin-stars Ibsen and Björnson. (The families of the friend-rivals were united in the marriage of Sigurd Ibsen and Bergliot Björnson.) His collected works were brought out in Copenhagen from 1901 to 1902 in ten volumes, an event that Ibsen could celebrate but half-heartedly. His last years were unfortunately clouded by aphasia and mental decline, brought on by an apoplectic stroke. He died in his seventy-ninth year. He was accorded a state funeral attended by King Haakon of Norway and by the British Minister representing King Edward VII. He is rivaled by Strindberg alone as a giant of Scandinavian drama. New translations and restagings of his plays have led to a resurgence of his reputation in our time with the result that, removed from ephemeral issues and controversies, he is at last receiving his due as not merely a clever theatrical craftsman but a major literary figure.

The standard translations by William Archer and his associates are to be found in the *Collected Works*, published by Scribner (12 vols., 1907-14). Archer himself translated *The League of Youth, Pillars of Society, A Doll's House, Ghosts, Little Eyolf, John Gabriel Borkman,* and *When We Dead Awaken.* Charles Archer collaborated on the earlier dramas through *Peer Gynt* and himself translated *Rosmersholm.* Edmund Gosse collaborated on the translation of *Hedda Gabler* and *The Master Builder.* Eleanor Marx-Aveling translated *An Enemy of the People.* Mrs. F. E. Archer translated *The Wild Duck* and *The Lady from the Sea.* A. G. Chater translated *From Ibsen's Workshop,* a collection of manuscripts and discarded drafts. These translations have been reprinted many times. *Brand* was translated into English verse by Miles Menander (1916). In more recent times there have been new translations designed for contemporary productions, notably those by Eva Le Gallienne (*A Doll's House, Ghosts, An Enemy of the People, Rosmersholm, Hedda Gabler,* and *The Master Builder*), published by Modern Library in 1957; Thornton Wilder (*A Doll's House,* 1939); Paul Green (*Peer Gynt,* 1951); and Michael Meyer (*Brand, When We Dead Awaken, The Lady from the Sea, John Gabriel Borkman,* 1960). A version of *Brand* by James Forsyth was issued in 1960. The Oxford Ibsen (4 vols., 1960-63), edited and translated by J. W. McFarlane and others, is in progress.

ABOUT: Bentley, E. The Playwright as Thinker; Bradbrook, M Ibsen, the Norwegian; Brandes, G. Ibsen and Björnson; Downs, B. Ibsen: the Intellectual Background, *also* A Study of Six Plays by Ibsen; Gosse, E. Henrik Ibsen; Henderson, A. Interpreters of Life and the Modern Spirit; Huneker, J. Egoists; Ibsen, B. The Three Ibsens; James, H. The Scenic Art; Koht, H. The Life of Ibsen; Knight, G. W. Ibsen; Lavrin, J. Ibsen, an Approach; Lee, J. The Ibsen Secret; Lucas, F. L. The Drama of Ibsen and Strindberg; Northam, J. Ibsen's Dramatic Method; Shaw, G. B. The Quintessence of Ibsenism; Weigand, H. The Modern Ibsen; Williams, R. Drama from Ibsen to Eliot.

R. A. C.

*IFFLAND, AUGUST WILHELM (April 19, 1759-September 22, 1814), German actor, director, and playwright, was born in Hanover. His father, an official in the royal ministry of war, and his mother, a daughter of the court music director, planned a career in the clergy for their son. At the age of six years, in 1765, however, Iffland attended a production of Molière's *Le Malade Imaginaire* and a seed of rebellion was thereby implanted in the boy. Twelve years later he departed secretly from his home to seek out his fortunes on the German stage.

In 1777 Iffland became a member of the court theatre in Gotha where he remained as an apprentice actor for two years. From Gotha he went to Mannheim. Here he acquired a reputation as a talented interpreter of comic and sentimental rôles. It was also at Mannheim that he met the young Friedrich Schiller. Following disagreements with his producer and as a result of the exigencies of war, Iffland in 1796 answered a summons to go to Berlin as director of the national theatre. He remained in Berlin until his death in 1814. Iffland's principal contributions to the art of acting in Germany are considered to be his practice of severe study and meticulous interpretation of the text and the introduction of greater realism in the stage presentation of the drama. His innovations in the latter instance were a reaction to the declamatory style of the Weimar stage.

As a dramatist Iffland is most significant as a portrayer of the manners and morals of his time. Although his plays suffer from the sentimental moralizing so prevalent in European literature during the middle decades of the eighteenth century, they display an excellent knowledge of stage technique and of human nature. His essays on the art of acting are largely contained in *Fragmenten über Menschendarstellung* (1785), *Theorie der Schauspielkunst* (1815), and in his *Almanach für Theater und Theaterfreunde* (1811). A few titles of his highly popular plays will suffice to give examples of his efforts as a playwright: *Albert von Thurneisen* (1781), *Verbrechen aus Ehrsucht* (1784), *Die Jäger* (1785), *Liebe um Liebe* (1785), *Der Herbsttag* (1792), *Mittelweg Ist Tugendprobe* (1788), *Die Kokarden* (1791), and *Die Hagestolzen* (1793).

The available translations of Iffland's dramatic writings are of late eighteenth and early nineteenth century origin; *The Bachelors* (1799); *Crime from Ambition* (1800); *The Foresters* (1799); *The Lawyers* (1799); *Education* (1827); *The Nephews* (1799); *The Good Neighbor* (1814).

* if' länt

ABOUT: [In German—see studies by S. David, J. Kürschner (Allgemeine Deutsche Biographie, XIV), A. Stiehler.]

E. K. G.

IGNACIO DE LOYOLA, Saint. See LOYOLA, IGNACIO DE, Saint

IMMANUEL BEN SOLOMON, of Rome, called *MANOELLO GIUDEO

(c. 1270-post 1328), Italian and Hebrew poet, was born in Rome of a cultured and prominent family. He received the broad Hebrew and general humanistic education which characterized the upper stratum of Italian Jewry, and knew Latin, Arabic, and some Greek. Details of Immanuel's life are almost entirely lacking beyond his own occasional remarks. At various times he appears to have been a communal servant—perhaps a precentor or scribe—and the employee of a wealthy banker and patron of learning. He lived in other Italian cities besides Rome and may also have practiced medicine. The date of his death is not known. There is no basis for the frequent statement that he was a personal friend of Dante, although his *Mahberot* 28, *Tophet and Eden*, imitates the *Divine Comedy*.

Immanuel is known to have written a commentary on the Bible and various philological works, now lost. His reputation in Hebrew literature rests upon his poetry collected in the *Mahberot* (Compositions). They are in the *maqamah* genre of the Moslem world: poetry, rhymed prose, witticisms, and aphorisms, loosely connected by a narrative. The *Mahberot* deal with subjects like love, theology, beauty, etc., and excel in their great Biblical and philological skill and abundant puns and proverbs. Two qualities earned notoriety for their author: a biting satiric talent and gross eroticism. Immanuel did not scruple to attack opponents personally in abusive, if polished, terms, and his frivolous use of sexual imagery and erotic subjects is practically unique in sober Hebrew literature. The poet also cut a figure in Italian literature, and took his share in the writing of sonnets and occasional poetry. He holds the distinction of having introduced the sonnet into Hebrew literature, where it lay dormant until recent times. Most of his work was neglected for centuries, largely because of the disapproval of the rabbis.

H. Gollancz translated *Tophet and Eden* in 1921; there are only fragmentary translations of the rest of his writings.

* mä nō ĕl' lō jōō dâ' ō

ABOUT: Roth, C. The Jews in the Renaissance; Proceedings of American Academy for Jewish Research, VI (1934-35); Sewanee Review, 1925.

L. P. G.

*IMMERMANN, KARL LEBRECHT

(April 24, 1796-August 25, 1840), German novelist, dramatist, and poet, was born in Magdeburg of Prussian nobility. He studied law at Halle and took part in the campaign of 1815. In 1817 he entered the service of the Prussian state, working at Aschersleben, Münster, and Magdeburg, and in 1829 became a councilor at the district court of Düsseldorf. He became increasingly interested in the theatre, and in 1832 founded a theatrical association which he headed. In 1834 the city took over the theatre and Immermann served as its director until 1837 when the venture collapsed. In 1839 he married Marianne Niemeyer, a girl of nineteen. This dissolved his friendship with Countess Elisa von Ahlefeldt, who had shared his home but refused his hand; he had met her at Münster twenty years previously when she was the wife of the military leader von Lützow. Immermann's death occurred at Düsseldorf in 1840.

Following the publication of a volume of poetry in 1820, Immermann wrote a number of dramas, both tragedies and comedies, including a play about the Tyrol's libertarian hero *Andreas Hofer* (1828, originally titled *Das Trauerspiel in Tirol*). *Merlin*, subtitled "a myth" (1832), about Merlin the magician, is a Faustian play which imparts the conclusion that a synthesis of the sensual and divine worlds is impossible. It is a romantically influenced, dramatically weak *Weltanschauungs drama* about the dichotomy between the satanic and the godly in man.

Immermann's literary fame as one of the more important German authors of the nineteenth century rests chiefly on two novels written in the 1830's. In 1836 he published *Die Epigonen,* a sort of *Bildungsroman* about a bourgeois youth who finds his way back to the world of his childhood after many romantic and political adventures. Immermann presents a sort of typology of the times: not only the classes, but the individuals, too, are *Epigonen*, late-born ones, descendants of great men, weak, pale carbon copies of a greater past. This term has come to describe a group of writers of the time, including Grillparzer, who considered this as their predicament.

* ĭm' ĕr män

447

IMMERMANN

Immermann's masterpiece is contained in the novel *Münchhausen* (1838-39). Münchhausen tells his stories at the castle of an old baron in the midst of degenerated aristocrats and other adventurous figures. The narrator and his audience are treated as foils for the persiflage of the fads and fashions of the times and the pretensions of contemporary literature. It is a *roman à clef*, with many dated and now obscure allusions. In form, the book is a romantic novel with many drolleries and evidences of "Shandyism." Its finest part is *Der Oberhof* (The Upper Farm), sometimes printed separately and generally regarded as the first instance of the *Dorfgeschichte* (village story), a form extensively cultivated in German literature around the middle of the century. It is connected with the body of the novel in that the heroine of this tale, Lisbeth, is the daughter of Münchhausen and the aristocratic Fräulein von Schnickschnackschnurr. The world of the peasants is here shown as a desirable place of refuge, an oasis of fresh air and tranquillity in a desert of clashing confusion and ugliness. A vivid picture of peasant life in Westphalia is presented. The attractive *Hofschulze* is not a romantically transfigured peasant, but part of a realistically viewed rusticality, one in which man is in perfect tune with his land, his traditions, his rural ethics. Immermann, who foresaw a continuation and extension of the corroding, materialistic, mechanical spirit of his times, presents this idyll as a symbol of a better future.

Immermann, who let himself appear in his *Münchhausen*, described himself as a broad-shouldered, stocky man with a large nose, prominent forehead, delicate mouth with ironic folds, and eyes like light-grey guinea-fowl. "In his face as elsewhere there was a peculiar mixture of strength, even brusqueness, and tenderness which occasionally verged on flabbiness." Gutzkow once described Immermann as "a stately figure with a powerful head with pale, slack features."

"The Wonders in the Spessart," a story, was translated by J. Oxenford and is included in *Tales from the German*, 1844. *The Oberhof*, translated by Paul B. Thomas, may be found in *The German Classics*, edited by Kuno Francke, VII. Selections from Immermann's poetry appear in a number of anthologies, including Warner's *Library of the World's Best Literature*.

ABOUT: Bacon, G. M. The Personal and Literary Relations of Heinrich Heine to Karl Immermann; Porterfield, A. W. Immermann: A Study in German Romanticism; Schütze, M. Immermann *in* German Classics, VII. [In German—see studies by R. Fellner, H. Maync, G. von Pulitz, M. Windpuhr.]

H. Z.

*INGEMANN, BERNHARD SEVERIN (May 28, 1789-February 24, 1862), Danish poet, playwright, novelist, was born at Torkildstrup on the Danish island of Falster. His father was the vicar Søren Sørensen Ingemann, of a merchant family from the island of Møn. His mother was Birgitte Swane, daughter of a well-to-do sea captain. The future poet was the youngest of nine children. After the death of his father, the family moved in 1800 to Slagelse in southern Zealand, where he received a scholarship at the Latin school. In 1807 he was admitted to the University of Copenhagen, where he completed his philosophical degree in 1808.

In 1811 appeared Ingemann's first collection of poems, *Digte*, in which he expressed a sentimental, romantic longing for the life-ideal. The following year he was engaged to Lucie Marie Mandix, daughter of the government official Jacob Mandix and Margaretha Elisabeth Hvistendahl, a clergyman's daughter from Copenhagen. They were married in 1822. She gave his poetry a new inspiration. Ingemann published during the following years several collections of sentimental poems. In his emotional Werther-novel in verse *Varners Poetiske Vandringer* (Varner's Poetic Wanderings), which was included in the poetic collection *Procne* (1813), he expressed his unbounded happiness of love. He also published some ro-

* ing′ ĕ män

mantic dramas in verse, e.g., the lachrymose tragedy *Blanca*, which was attacked by J. L. Heiberg but defended by Grundtvig, who became Ingemann's faithful friend.

In 1817 Ingemann was awarded a traveling scholarship which enabled him to make a two years' journey to Germany, France, and Italy, during which he continued to write lyrics and drama. After his marriage and appointment as teacher of Danish at the Academy of Sorø in southern Zealand, he produced, under happy and harmonious circumstances, the most prominent part of his literary output. He wrote in various genres. His historical novels deal with the struggle between light and darkness, between good and evil powers. The greatest of them all is *Valdemar Seier* (1826), but several other dramas, e.g., *Erik Menveds Barndom* (Erik Menved's Childhood, 1828), and *Kong Erik og de Fredløse* (King Erik and the Outlaws, 1833), as well as his historical epics *Valdemar den Store og hans Mænd* (Valdemar the Great and His Men, 1824), and *Dronning Margrethe* (Queen Margaret, 1836), have for many generations been read and loved by the Danes. Later Ingemann wrote a patriotic poetic cycle, *Holger Danske* (Holger the Dane, 1837), religious works, and the fine contemporary novel *Landsbybørnene* (Village Children, 1852). He was Denmark's most esteemed author of his time.

His greatest contribution to Danish poetry was his religious lyrics and church hymns, first and foremost *Morgen- og Aftensange* (Morning and Evening Songs, 1837-39), expressing a naïve faith in God and the victory of light over darkness. Only a few are in the official Danish church hymnal, but they have won the heart of the people—most of all his pilgrim song "Dejlig er Jorden" (Beautiful Is the Earth).

Ingemann is comparatively well represented in English. His poems are in many collections, e.g., H. W. Longfellow, *The Poets and Poetry of Europe* (1845); Gilbert Tait (pseud.), *The Hymns of Denmark* (1868); *Poems by the Late Anne S. Bushby* (1876); *A Book of Danish Verse* (1922); C. W. Stork, *A Second Book of Danish Verse* (1947). The novel *Valdemar Seier* was translated by J. F. Chapman as *Waldemar, Surnamed Seir; or the Victorious* (3 vols., 1841). *Kong Erik og de Fredløse* appeared by the same translator as *King Eric and the Outlaws* (3 vols., 1843). J. Kesson translated *Erik Menveds Barndom* as *The Childhood of King Erik Menved* (1846). A complete list of translations is available in E. Bredsdorff's *Danish Literature in English Translation* (1950).

ABOUT: Mitchell, P. M. A History of Danish Literature. [In Danish—see studies by K. Galster, J. Nørregaard, R. Petersen, H. Schwanenflügel.]

A. J.

*IRIARTE (or YRIARTE) Y ORO-PESA, TOMÁS DE (September 18, 1750-September 17, 1791), Spanish fabulist, poet, and dramatist, was born in Santa Cruz, Tenerife, in the Canary Islands. His parents were Bernardo de Iriarte and Bárbara de las Nieves Hernández de Oropesa, and he was the youngest of four sons. As a boy, he studied Latin with great success and in 1764 he was sent to the Peninsula where he studied in Madrid under his uncle Juan de Iriarte, the celebrated scholar and head librarian of the Royal Library. In addition to his work in languages, the humanities, history, and physics, he became an accomplished musician.

Iriarte soon found himself engaged in the endless literary polemics which filled the eighteenth century, and much of his energy was devoted to this relatively fruitless form of activity. He is the author of a long and didactic poem, *La Música* (1779), which, although highly praised by Metastasio, has sunk into a deserved oblivion. He translated Horace's *Ars Poetica* into Spanish verse and composed many poems which have been collected in volume LXIII of the *BAE*. Iriarte's real title to literary fame rests now, however, as in the past, on his *Fábulas Literarias* (1782), a remarkably good collection of seventy-six fables written in a great variety of meters. They are in simple, clear language and their moral is easily understood. Some of them have been cited and repeated so many times they are almost universally known in the Spanish-speaking world. Among these are: *El Burro Flautista, Los Dos Conejos,* and *El Pedernal y el Eslabón*. Fables were quite in style at this period and were not only being written in Spanish but also translated from other languages, as, for example, Lokman in 1779 and La Fontaine in 1787. Iriarte's fables earned him immediate success both at home and abroad. Some of them are obviously directed against certain writers of the day, such as Meléndez Valdés and García de la Huerta. Florian, the French fabulist who prided himself on his knowledge of Spanish letters, openly avowed his debt to Iriarte. Iriarte is also the author of several comedies of manners, namely *El Señorito Mimado* and *La Señorita mal Criada* (both 1788), in which he castigates the educational systems of his society. In 1787 his collected works were published in six volumes and there is also a collection of his complete works published in 1805, in eight volumes.

Iriarte, who, though quite active in literary matters, led an uncommonly sedentary life,

* ē ryär' tä ē ō rō pä' sä

449

suffered during his last years from the gout, of which he died in Madrid.

The *Fábulas Literarias* have been translated a number of times into the English language. Richard Andrews translated them as *Literary Fables* in 1835, as did Robert Rockliff in 1851 and G. H. Devereux in 1885. *Music, a Didactic Poem in Five Cantos* was rendered into English by John Belfour in 1807.
ABOUT: PMLA, 1952. [In French—Vézinet, F. Molière, Florian et la Littérature Espagnole. In Spanish—Cotarelo y Mori, E. Iriarte y su Época; Sebold, R. P. Tomás de Iriarte.]

R. E. O.

ISLA (Y ROJO), JOSÉ FRANCISCO DE (April 24, 1703-November 2, 1781),

Spanish novelist and satirist, was born in Vidones (León) of a noble family. His parents were José Isla de la Torre and Ambrosia Rojo. As a child, Isla was extraordinarily precocious, obtaining his degree in law at the age of eleven. At sixteen he was admitted as a novice to the Jesuit school at Villagarcía de Campos. He studied theology at Salamanca and taught philosophy and theology at Segovia, Santiago, and Pamplona. He became a much-admired preacher and at one time was proposed for the position of confessor to Queen María, but he did not accept. In 1767 the Jesuits were expelled from Spain, and Isla, although desperately ill, followed them into exile. He stayed for a short while in Corsica and then went to Bologna, where he was protected and cared for the rest of his life by Count Tedeschi. Padre Isla was a man of short stature but well-proportioned. His lively manner and skill as a conversationalist always made him a welcome guest. He died in Bologna and was buried there.

His early writings, such as *Cartas de Juan de la Encina* (1732), a satire on doctors, were of slight importance. In 1758, however, he published the *Historia del Famoso Predicador Fray Gerundio,* a satire on the bombastic pulpit oratory of his time. It was such an immediate success that the first printing sold out in three days, but it was banned in 1760 by the Inquisition, and the second volume did not appear until 1768. Isla's satire is lively and amusing. This novel has retained its popularity and is almost the only novel of its time still readable. It was published under the name of Francisco Labón de Salazar. *Fray Gerundio* was translated into English in 1772 by T. Nugent under the title *The History of the Famous Preacher, Friar Gerund de Campazas.* While in Bologna, Isla wrote his celebrated translation

* ēs' lä ē rô' hō

of Le Sage's *Gil Blas,* claiming he was restoring it to the original. This claim—which was false—set off a long literary dispute. The translation is excellent and the book appeared in 1787-88, after Isla's death. The six volumes of correspondence, *Cartas Familiares,* which he left, form one of the interesting epistolary collections in Spanish.
ABOUT: Hispanic Review, 1936. [In French—Gaudeau, B. Les Prêcheurs Burlesques en Espagne au XVIII° Siècle In Spanish—Sabas, J. I. de. Compendio Histórico de la Vida, Carácter Moral y Literario del P. Isla; Revista de Filología Española, 1923.]

R. E. O.

*JACOBSEN, JENS PETER (April 7, 1847-April 30, 1885),

Danish novelist, poet, was born in Thisted in northwestern Jutland. His father was Christen Jacobsen, merchant, earlier sea captain. He inherited a predisposition for tuberculosis from his parents and probably also the contrast between their natures. His father was husky and brawny, his mother gentle and pious. The most profound and dangerous inclination in Jacobsen's nature, his proneness to day-dreaming, of imagining life instead of living it, must have come from his mother's side.

In 1863 Jacobsen went to Copenhagen to prepare himself for the entrance examination to the university. After a failure, he passed in 1867. At the university he devoted himself to his two main interests, botany and literature. Personal skepticism and doubt, the influence of Darwin, whose major works he later translated into Danish, and of Feuerbach's anti-religious philosophy, made him an atheist and naturalist. He fell in love with a friend of his childhood, Anna Michelsen, daughter of a physician of Thisted and a deeply religious girl. The spiritual tension between the two became unbearable to the girl, who eventually went insane. This left indelible marks on Jacobsen's mind, and he remained unmarried.

In 1872 Jacobsen published a poetic cycle, *Hervert Sperring,* whose hero, like the poet himself, is caught in the conflict between reality and dream life. The same year he published in *Nyt Dansk Maanedsskrift* (New Danish Monthly) his first effort in prose, "Mogens," a short story based on deterministic psychology and written in Jacobsen's characteristic impressionistic style. This was the first attempt in Scandinavian literature at translating natural laws and ideas into the form of literature.

* yà' kŏp sēn

JACOBSEN

During a journey to Germany and Italy in 1873 Jacobsen suffered a hemorrhage of the lungs. Thereafter his life was a perpetual struggle against tuberculosis, which for long periods, partly spent in sanatoriums abroad, forced him to inactivity and eventually ended his life. In 1876 appeared Jacobsen's excellent psychological novel *Fru Marie Grubbe*, based on the life of an historical woman whose destiny had already been treated by Holberg, Blicher, and H. C. Andersen. The novel describes a woman who socially through three marriages sinks from nobility to the servant class but whose soul at the same time is ennobled. The psychologically deep-reaching and thoroughly naturalistic novel also gives true pictures of the milieu of the seventeenth century when the actual events took place.

In 1880 Jacobsen published his famous novel of contemporary times, *Niels Lyhne*, partly inspired by his own experiences, in which he describes the life-story of an atheistic dreamer who is defeated in his confrontation with reality because he refuses to change his attitude to life but tries "to live life in harmony with life's own laws." It is a story of a man's unsuccessful struggle to be himself. Jacobsen's personal thoughts about man's relation to death color the book. The hero's life runs through intimate connections with four women of thoroughly different types.

Jacobsen also wrote several tragic short stories in which his own introverted personality expressed a pessimistic belief in the fated nature of life and contrasted the illusory world of happiness to the real life of misfortune and affliction. There is no bridge from one world to the other. If one is destined to suffer there is no way out of it. This conviction is expressed in the little story "To Verdener" (Two Worlds, 1879). In "Pesten i Bergamo" (The Plague in Bergamo, 1881), he studies the reaction of the people of a little Italian mountain community that face obliteration through the plague. The psychosis of mortal fear is graphically described in "Et Skud i Tagen" (A Shot in the Fog, 1875).

Also in the poems that Jacobsen wrote during these years he meditated on the problems of sorrow and death. An excellent representation of his highly impressionistic style is the haunting poem "Arabesk."

Jacobsen's prose style was filled with impressionistic descriptions, but quite often he yielded to the naturalistic inclination of crowding too many details into the pictures. This was due to the fact that even in his novels he was first and foremost a lyricist. Despite the fact that he was a convinced naturalist he worshipped beauty, and this attitude he expressed by his originality in rhythm and choice of words. Some were repelled by his style, but he had a deep influence on several prominent Scandinavian writers.

Jacobsen's novel *Niels Lyhne* was translated into English by E. F. L. Robertson as *Siren Voices* (1896), by H. Astrup Larsen as *Niels Lyhne* (1919). *Marie Grubbe* was translated by H. Astrup Larsen (1914, 1917). The story "Pesten i Bergamo" appeared in *American-Scandinavian Studies*, V (1917), and was translated by E. Ellefsen as "The Plague in Bergamo" (1923). A translation by H. Knudsen of "To Verdener" as "Two Worlds" is included in B. H. Clark and M. Lieber, *Great Short Stories of the World* (1926; last edition 1949). *Mogens and Other Stories* was published in 1926. Translated poems by Jacobsen appear in various collections, e.g., *A Book of Danish Verse* (1922); Mrs G. Lovett, *English Versions of Poems by Some Scandinavian Poets* (1936); C W. Stork, *A Second Book of Danish Verse* (1947). For a full account of translations see E. Bredsdorff, *Danish Literature in English Translation* (1950).

ABOUT: Allen, W. G. Renaissance in the North; Columbia Dictionary of Modern European Literature; Gustafson, A. Six Scandinavian Novelists; Mitchell, P. M. A History of Danish Literature; American Scandinavian Review, V. [In Danish—see studies by G. Christensen, O. Friis, S. Hallar, A. Linck.]

A. J.

*JACOBUS DE VORAGINE (or VARAGINE), (JACOPO DA VARAZZE) (1228/30–July 13/14, 1298), Italian theo-

* jä kō′ bŭs dē vō răj′ ĭ nē

logian and hagiographer, was born in Varazze, near Genoa. He entered the Dominican order in 1244, and devoted himself to study, teaching, and piety. His fame as a preacher led him to many cities in Lombardy, and he became prior of the House of Genoa, Lombard definitor, and from 1267 to 1286 Provincial of Lombardy. In 1288 Nicholas IV sent Jacobus to lift the ban of the Church from Genoa, which had resulted from the former allegiance of the city in the Sicilian revolt. Jacobus at first refused the see of this city, but on the death of Archbishop Fieschi, the chapter called him again, and he governed the local church from 1292 until his death. In this position of authority Jacobus did much to reform church practices and pacify the civil disorders between Guelphs and Ghibellines, though active dissension broke out afresh in 1295; he tells of these events in his *Chronicon Ianuense,* published in 1726, which, despite many fables, contains essential information on the Councils of the period. Jacobus' piety led to official recognition in 1816, when Pius VII instructed the Dominican Order to celebrate his feast in the manner of that of a saint.

Jacobus' minor works include an apology of the order of Saint Dominic and a compendium of Guilelmus Peraldus' *Summa de Vitiis et Virtutibus.* In his *Chronicon* he discusses his own writings, his sermons, some of which were published in 1888, his *Marialis,* a book of praises of the Virgin, and his legends of the saints, on which his reputation depends. The *Legenda Aurea,* also entitled *Legenda Sanctorum* and even *Lombardica Historia,* enjoyed immense popularity during the Middle Ages, as attested by the many manuscripts and editions, and by the French and English translations, and it is still read by writers seeking the picturesque colors of medieval thought. Churchmen have attacked its veracity, and with regard to historical fact it does indeed contain many wholly imaginary tales; Jacobus' intention, however, was to inspire devotion, not to compile fact, and the naive simplicity of the work explains its wide and enduring appeal, for example to Longfellow.

The 177 chapters of the *Legenda Aurea* show a double structure. They represent on the one hand a division of the year into four parts, each corresponding to an epoch of history, and each symbolizing the traits of the past, through deviation, renovation and reconciliation to pilgrimage; on the other hand, there are five parts as in the ecclesiastical calendar. Of particular interest are the

biographies of the Desert Fathers of the third and fourth centuries, whose spirit represents at least one aspect of the Franciscan movement and who had been neglected by earlier historians.

The first edition of the Latin original was published in 1470, and the contents augmented subsequently until the modern critical texts of 1846 and 1890. An English version of 1450, revised and printed by Caxton in 1483, enjoyed continued success. A modern translation, *The Golden Legend,* was made by G. Ryan and H. Ripperger in 1948.

ABOUT: [In French and Italian—Broussolle, J. *in* L'Université Catholique, 1903; Pelazza, V. Vita del Beato Giacomo da Varazze; Waresquiel, M. de. Le Bienheureux Jacobus de Voragine.]

F. J. C.

*JACOPO (or GIACOMO) DA LENTINI (c. 1180/90-c. 1240), Italian poet, was one of the founders of the Sicilian school and one of the sources of inspiration of the Tuscans. Only a few facts about his life can be gleaned from allusions in his poetry and from charters written by him. He tells us that he was born in Lentino, and, in his function as notary of the imperial court of Frederick II, he composed a number of charters and records; his importance in government service is further attested by his attendance on the Emperor, for example in Policoro, according to an act written in March 1233, and then in June in Catania; he is probably the "Giacomo Notaro" who recorded other patents in August. One allusion in his works suggests his presence in Milan in 1237, but in general his statements of biographical fact are obscured by his indirect poetic style. F. Torraca, in his study of thirteenth century Italian poetry, presents inconclusive evidence concerning his personal relationship with Pier della Vigna and other Sicilian poets.

Jacopo's great fame is attested by Chiaro Davanzati's reproach to Bonagiunta da Lucca that the latter had imitated him ("Che ti vesti le penne del Notaro") and twice by Dante, in *De Vulgari Eloquentia,* in reference to the Sicilian group but without naming him ("nam videtur Sicilianum vulgare sibi famam pre aliis asciscere"), and in *Purgatorio* XXIV, where Bonagiunta is again in question in terms similar to those of Davanzati ("le vostre penne diretro al dittator"). These references suggest that the "dolce stil novo" stemmed in large part from Jacopo, as the most famous representative of his school, whose complex background includes the poets gathered about the Norman court of William the Good in the dynasty established at Pa-

* yä′ kō pō dä lĕn tē′ nĭ

lermo in 1072. The movement came to maturity by 1160 during the height of the troubadours and then turned to the native vernacular, thus establishing Italian poetry as such.

The forty extant poems by Jacopo include the oldest known sonnets and illustrate a complex interplay of forms and legends and of French and Provençal influences. Among the source models for example one finds Provençal popular song and occasional striking parallelism of concepts and images, for example with Perdigo. Laments of love in Jacopo's verse assume a powerful manner in their intimate simplicity, their moderate sensuousness, and a cult of beauty ("Occhi, ahi vaghi e bionde trezze"). He lends grace and sincerity to older conceits ("Maravigliosamente/Un amor mi distringe"), and thus he foresees such lyricists as Guinizelli. He compares fire and love, for their "splendore" but warns that if one touches them, one must beware ("L'amore fa gran villania").

Among occasional English translations from Jacopo one must mention the sonnets done by Rossetti ("Her face has made my life most proud and glad"), and his Canzonettas ("Love will not have me cry/For grace, as others do").

ABOUT: Langley, E. The Poetry of Giacomo da Lentino. [In Italian—see studies by F. Scandone and F. Torraca.]

F. J. C.

*JACOPONE DA TODI (c. 1220/30-December 25, 1306), Italian mystic and poet, was born in Todi of the De' Benedetti family of that city. He studied and then practiced law, married, and led a prosperous and active life until his sudden conversion by a tragic event. His wife, to please him, had made an outward show of superficial gaiety in their social life, but during a wedding ceremony c. 1268 she was accidentally killed. When her clothes were undone, Jacopone saw that she had worn a hair-shirt. Converted by this revelation, he gave all his belongings to the poor, abandoned his friends, and devoted himself to prayer and ascetic practices. He exaggerated penance in a progression of pathological states to the point of passing as mad. When, after ten years of this new life, he attempted to enter the Franciscan order, the brothers looked askance but finally accepted his ecstatic madness, his "nova pazzia," as compatible with sanctity, and he remained with them as a lay brother for the rest of his life.

* yä kō pō′ nä dä tō′ dē

In the internal controversies of the Franciscan order Jacopone sided with the "spiritualists," who proposed extreme rigor, and against the more moderate "conventualists." When Pope Boniface VIII tried to encourage the latter, Jacopone wrote violent satirical verse against him ("Locifero novello a sedere in papato") and even took arms with the two Colonna cardinals and their league which, in 1297, declared illegal the election of Boniface. The league was attacked in Palestrina and Jacopone was condemned to life imprisonment. His joyous satisfaction in this final abasement ("Vergogna m'è esaltazione") was frustrated by excommunication, and his pleas for grace remained unheeded until the accession of Benedict XI in 1303. Jacopone then retired to the convent of Collazzone, where he remained until his death.

Jacopone exemplifies the Christian ascetic of the Middle Ages, in extreme form both as regards worldly life and theological doctrine. His importance today lies in the originality of his poetry, notably his "Or udite nova pazzia," in which he expresses his doctrine of abnegation and suffering as his means for attaining to Christ. A certain romanesque element leads Jacopone to such excessive notions as a desire for the ultimate tortures of Hell, in an ecstasy carried almost to a point of hedonism, but even these extreme attitudes rise in the full sincerity of his devotion, and are in a broad sense Franciscan in a project to live "fra gente grossolana e matta." His verse shows the influence of the "laudi" of Saint Francis in frequent appeal to the common man and in the popular dance form of the "ballata" ("Ciascuno amante che ama il Signore/Venga alla danza cantando d'amore"). His inspiration flags in many prosaic moments, in obscure concetti and even vulgar realism, for example in a theme of the decay of the body as part of his call to God for further suffering ("A me la febbre quartana"). His conversations between body and soul foresee the pessimism of the coming century and belong marginally to the liturgical drama. His little play of the Virgin's lament over the Crucifix leads toward the later "sacra rappresentazione."

Jacopone's works were printed in 1490 and reprinted in 1910, and various poems appear in the standard anthologies.

ABOUT: [In Italian—Ancona, A. d', Studi sulla Letteratura Italiana; Getto, G. in Lettere Italiane, VIII (1956); Jacopone e il suo Tempo (Centro die Studi sulla Spiritualità Medievale, Todi, 1957). In French—Labande-Jeanroy, T. Les Mystiques Italiens.]

F. J. C.

*JÆGER, HANS HENRIK (September 2, 1854-February 8, 1910), Norwegian novelist, playwright, was born in southeastern Norway in the town of Drammen, the son of Nicolai Henrik Jæger, who was judge advocate, but who next became police attorney in Bergen, where Hans grew up. His father died when he was ten. His mother was Otilie Henriette Elisabeth Foss, who died four years later. Thereafter he went to the home of an uncle in the southern coastal town Arendal, but in 1869 he went to sea and sailed for five years. He remained a rootless Bohemian throughout his roving life. In 1875 he was able to pass his matriculation examination and was shortly after employed as stenographer for the parliament. At the university he studied philosophy and published anonymously in 1876 a remarkable treatise, *Kants Fornuftkritik* (Kant's *Critique of Pure Reason*). He was strongly influenced by Hegel's philosophy and maintained, in the spirit of Kierkegaard, that philosophy is not a "subject" but a form of existence.

However, Jæger was soon seized with the radical reformatory ideas of the time. As a lecturer he spoke in favor of free love and held that conventional marriage was nothing but prostitution. He wanted respect for the prostitutes since society is to be blamed for their existence. Jæger became a notoriety in the capital, but also a hero in the eyes of the radical youth. He decided to become the leader and literary spokesman of the "children of the New Age." His first attempts were two small plays—*Olga* (1883) and *En Intellektuel Forførelse* (An Intellectual Seduction, 1884), which, although published in manuscript, were never performed. They were propaganda pamphlets favoring an extreme moral nihilism.

Under the influence of Zola, Jæger published in 1855 his sensational two-volume novel *Fra Kristiania-Bohêmen* (From the *Kristiania-Bohême*). It is a description of his own early years, in which he combined, philosophically and stylistically, his demands for a free sexual life with naturalism, determinism, and impressionism. He demanded, and actually illustrated, that artists and authors should expose their own private life in frank and intimate pictures devoid of all consideration for conventional ethics. The book was confiscated the same day it appeared and the author prosecuted. A fierce literary feud ensued. Jæger was sentenced to sixty days in jail. When he had served his

sentence he was again sued for having published his book in Sweden. He was sentenced to a fine and 150 days in jail, but he fled to Paris. In 1888 he returned home and served his sentence by then shortened to fifteen days on bread and water. The following year he returned to Paris where he afterwards spent most of his life, with an interval (1898-1902) when he served on the editorial staff of the capital daily *Socialdemokraten*.

Among Jæger's later works may be mentioned *Syk Kjærlighet* (Sick Love, 1893), and *Fængsel og Fortvivlelse* (Prison and Despair, 1903). None of his books was sold commercially. Supported by friends, he spent his last years in misery. He died after a cancer operation.

ABOUT: Beyer, H. A History of Norwegian Literature; Vogt, N. C. The Rebel Son. [In Norwegian—see studies by I. I. Ipsen, O. Storstein.]

A. J.

JAN VAN RUUSBROEC (or RUYS-BROECK). See RUUSBROEC, JAN VAN

*JARRY, ALFRED HENRI (September 8, 1873-November 1, 1907), French poet-dramatist, was born in the Mayenne region, at Laval. Alfred's father, Anselme (1837-94), was a carpenter whose father had been a mason; the family antecedents included weavers, farmers, manual laborers. His mother, Caroline Quernest (died 1894), was an eccentric whose brother was unbalanced; her mother was confined periodically in insane asylums. Alfred had an older sister, Charlotte, to whom he was devoted. Alfred considered his father a nonentity, but had some admiration for his mother.

Jarry began his schooling at Laval and continued at Saint-Brieuc where his mother moved when her husband became a commercial traveler. Jarry was a brilliant student equally gifted in the sciences and in the humanities. He learned effortlessly, and studied German and English extracurricularly. In 1888 he went to Rennes, where he had a physics teacher, Hébert, nicknamed Hébé, the butt of schoolboy quips and pranks. Jarry and his comrades wrote a satire on him, "Les Polonais," which they presented in a marionette theatre.

Upon completing the program, Jarry went to Paris in 1891 to prepare for both the École Polytechnique and the École Normale Supérieure by study at the Lycée Henry IV.

* yâ′ gĕr

* zhà rē′

There Léon Paul Fargue was a classmate, Henri Bergson a teacher of philosophy.

Jarry frequented literary circles and became a familiar of cafés and night clubs. Short but sturdy, an inveterate cyclist with powerful leg muscles, with long dark hair falling to his shoulders, and warm black eyes, he was remarked as an eccentric. A vaudeville in verse and prose, "Haldernablou," appeared in the recently-founded *Mercure de France;* Jarry later incorporated it into *Les Minutes de Sable Mémorial* (1894). He founded with Rémy de Gourmont *L'Ymagier,* which had seven numbers (1894-95); an inheritance from his parents, who both died in 1894, allowed him to found *Perhinderion*—which lasted for two issues. Both these periodicals were devoted to old prints and popular art of the "image d'Épinal" sort. *Perhinderion* received its name from the Breton word for "pardon," as used for a pilgrimage.

In 1896 appeared Jarry's major work and claim to fame: *Ubu Roi,* a five-act prose drama. First published in Paul Fort's *Livre d'Art,* it was put on the same year by Lugné-Poe for his Théâtre de l'Œuvre. Père Hébé (Hébert) had become Ubu; Poland is no-where land (Poland did not exist politically in 1896), and human stupidity is mocked and satirized. Jarry tried to live up to his creation, which he continued with *Ubu Enchaîné* (1900) and the *Almanachs du Père Ubu.* Ambroise Vollard and Gustave Téry made their own pastiches of this personality. Jarry himself modeled his behavior on his character, and created "pataphysique," i.e., the science of imaginary solutions. In *Le Surmâle, Roman Moderne* (1902), he created a bizarre mechanistic world of athletic competition and sex. Recently critics have analyzed Jarry's antipathy for women and his use of symbols as an indication of homosexuality.

Worn out from malnutrition, excessive use of alcohol and stimulants, Jarry was taken in a paralyzed state to the Hôpital de la Charité, where he died of a tubercular meningitis. He was buried in Bagneux cemetery.

Jarry did the libretto for Claude Terrasse's opera *Pantagruel,* which was performed in 1911. Jarry's translation with Jean Saltas of a novel, *La Papesse Jeanne,* by Emmanuel Rhoïdes, was published in 1908. The surrealists have acknowledged an indebtedness to Jarry for his non-conformism, caricaturing of the grotesque in human behavior, and the unexpectedness of his logic.

His poetry was edited by H. Parisot in 1945, the complete works by R. Massat in eight volumes (1948). Barbara Wright has translated *Ubu Roi,* as well as *The Song of the Disembraining* (1951).

ABOUT: Fowlie, W. *in* Accent, VIII (Winter 1948); Shattuck, R. The Banquet Years; Symons, A. Studies in Two Literatures. [In French— Breton, A. Les Pas Perdus; Chassé, C. Sous le Masque de Jarry? Les Sources d'Ubu Roi; Chauveau, P. Alfred Jarry ou la Naissance, la Vie et la Mort du Père Ubu; Levesque, J. H. Alfred Jarry; Lot F. Alfred Jarry, son Œuvre; Rachilde (Mme Vallette) Alfred Jarry ou Le Surmâle de Lettres; Rousseaux, A. *in* Le Monde Classique, IV (1956); Saillet, M. *in* Fontaine, LXI (September 1947); Salmon, A. *in* L'Ami du Lettré. Previously unpublished Jarry items and criticism have appeared in the Cahiers du Collège de Pataphysique; see also Evergreen Review, XIII (May-June 1960), an entire issue devoted to Jarry and to Pataphysics, "the only Science."]

S. S. W.

*JAUFRÉ RUDEL (fl. 1140-1170), Provençal lyric poet, is known to us only through one allusion by his fellow-poet Marcabru, who dedicated a poem to him, and through the highly fanciful *vida,* or biography, which has come down to us. In this *vida* he is described as the Prince of Blaia (in Saintonge, Southern France), although there is no historical record of any such person. The rest of the *vida* tells the famous story of his love for the Countess of Tripoli. Although he had never seen the Countess, he wrote poems to her and finally joined a Crusade (probably that of Louis VII in 1147) in order to be near her. He fell sick at sea and was brought ashore at Tripoli (in Syria), where he died in the arms of the Countess. The lady, after giving him a splendid funeral, is supposed to have entered a convent. The story seems to have been founded directly on the material in Rudel's own poems, for there is no historical record of any such happening or even of a Countess of Tripoli who took the veil at this time. Only the fact of his going on the Crusade and dying abroad seems likely. The highly romantic story has caught the imagination of many writers and has formed the subject of poems by Swinburne and Browning among others.

The concept of *amor de longh,* or love from afar, was not original with Rudel. It had already appeared in the poems of Guilhem IX of Aquitaine and it may very well have nothing to do with physical separation but simply mean unattainable love. Only six poems of Rudel survive and they are all love poems. In them he mentions several of the noble patrons of literature in Southern

* zhō frä' rü dĕl'

455

France with whom he was presumably acquainted and also states that he is saying farewell to love in order to take up the Cross —a not uncommon theme among the troubadours. Several of the themes found in the work of earlier poets are found in Rudel's poems—the sadness of love, the rejection of the lady or even of love itself when the trial becomes too severe. His chief characteristic, however, is the haunting sadness of his love declarations and his ability to move the reader by simple verse forms and unadorned language.

E. Hoepffner, *Les Troubadours dans Leur Vie et dans Leurs Œuvres* (Paris, 1955) contains a good account, with texts translated into modern French. *Les Chansons de Jaufré Rudel* was edited by A. Jeanroy (1915, 1924). Selections appear in R. T. Hill & T. G. Bergin, *Anthology of the Troubadours* (1941).

ABOUT: Valency, M. In Praise of Love.

W. T. H. J.

*JEAN (CLOPINEL or CHOPINEL), DE MEUNG (c. 1260-c. 1315), French poet, was born in the village of Meun-sur-Loire about 1260, although the date is disputed. His real name was Chopinel or Clopinel. Although he appears to have been connected with a noble family, he was clerically educated, probably in Paris, and spent most of his life in the capital in close connection with the royal court. He is said to have had a house in the rue de St. Jacques. He was an extremely learned man, trained in classics, theology, and philosophy, and makes great play with this learning in his works. When he was between twenty-five and thirty, Jean de Meung made a translation of the *Ars Militaris* of the Roman author Vegetius for Jehan de Brienne. He also translated from the Latin such varied works as the *Consolation of Philosophy* of Boethius, the letters of Abelard and Heloïse, the treatise *On Spiritual Love* of Aelred of Rievaulx, and the *Wonders of Ireland* of Giraldus Cambrensis. His fame rests, however, on his continuation of the *Roman de la Rose* of Guillaume de Lorris (see sketch above).

This continuation, consisting of 17,722 lines of rhyming octosyllables, is quite different from the original in spirit and form. It opens, typically, with a long discussion by Reason of the bad effects of love and on the decline of man since the Golden Age. After the lover has rejected any suggestions of bribery or force, the god of love brings up his forces to aid him and to free Fair Wel-

come. Abstinence and False Appearance cut off Slander's tongue and take away the keys of the castle in which the Rose and Fair Welcome are imprisoned. The old woman who guards Fair Welcome is persuaded to take in a wreath from the Lover, who later himself finds entrance to the castle. Just as he is about to pluck the Rose, the guards cry for aid. A fierce battle ensues. Cupid calls on Venus, who swears she will never let Chastity live in the human heart. She encourages Nature, who is almost ready to let the human race perish, to give Genius a curse on all who despise Nature's methods. Venus summons Fear and Shame to surrender. They refuse but are driven out. The Lover plucks the Rose.

It is clear that only the basic framework and the allegorical method of the original have been preserved. Jean de Meung despises courtly love and his continuation of the *Romance of the Rose* is a satire upon it, upon love, and upon women in general. It is really sensuality that triumphs. The work is loaded with long, moralizing digressions, often attacking the weaknesses of human nature, the monastic system, and its rules of celibacy. Many passages seem to be inserted merely to display the author's learning. Jean de Meung's whole outlook reflects the increasing influence of the bourgeoisie upon literature. These very circumstances, however, contributed to the immense popularity of the work both in the Middle Ages and the Renaissance. More than 300 manuscripts and numerous printed editions after 1480 testify to this popularity. There were numerous translations, including one by Chaucer, although that which exists under his name is probably from another hand.

The best known translation of the *Roman de la Rose* into English is that by F. S. Ellis, 3 vols., 1900. In 1962 a new translation by H. W. Robbins was published. The standard French edition of the whole *Roman* is that by Langlois.

W. T. H. J.

*JEAN PAUL (pseudonym of JOHANN PAUL FRIEDRICH RICHTER) (March 21, 1763-November 14, 1825), German novelist, was born at Wunsiedel in the Fichtel Mountains, the son of a schoolmaster and organist who later became a clergyman. The boy grew up in poverty and continued to be oppressed by financial hardship throughout his early life. In 1781 he entered the University of Leipzig to study theology, but an accumulation of debts forced him to leave

"JEAN PAUL"

after three years. He remained with his mother in Hof for two years until in 1787 he accepted a position as a private tutor. In 1790 he established an elementary school in Schwarzenbach, which he directed until 1794. Jean Paul had begun to write during his university days, and the success of his works now brought him recognition and sufficient income to allow him to devote himself entirely to literature. Following the death of his mother in 1797, he left Hof and lived for brief periods in Leipzig, Weimar, Berlin, Meiningen, and Coburg. His amiable personality and brilliant conversational manner made him a welcome guest wherever he went. In 1801 Jean Paul married Karoline Mayer, and in 1804 the couple settled permanently in Bayreuth, where they lived a quiet life. A pension granted by Prince Dalberg in 1808 enabled them to live comfortably with complete financial security. His literary esteem continued to increase during his lifetime, and his death at Bayreuth in 1825 was an occasion for national mourning. His burial procession resembled a tribute to departed royalty.

Jean Paul began his literary career with *Grönländische Prozesse* (1783-84) and *Auswahl aus des Teufels Papieren* (1789), both satires in the manner of Jonathan Swift. His reputation was established by *Die Unsichtbare Loge* (1793), an educational novel influenced by Rousseau, and by the sentimental romance *Hesperus, oder 45 Hundsposttage* (1795), a developmental novel in the manner of Goethe's *Wilhelm Meister*.

For his next works he chose the form of an idyll, depicting in *Leben des Quintus Fixlein* (1796) and *Blumen-, Frucht-, und Dornenstücke, oder Ehestand, Tod und Hochzeit des Armen Advokaten F. St. Siebenkäs* (1796-97) the quiet, unassuming lives of ordinary people. In these narratives the relative insignificance of the plot is offset by the charm and humor of the presentation as well as by Jean Paul's ability to convey the sense of greatness in little things. The novels which followed, *Titan* (1800-03) and *Flegeljahre* (1804-05), show the author at the peak of his art, and he himself considered these works to be his finest achievements. Both of these novels were written under the influence of *Wilhelm Meister* and both relate the tale of an individual's apprenticeship to life. Following these ambitious works, Jean Paul wrote several minor idylls, of which *Das Leben Fibels* (1812) is the most significant. He also produced a fragment of an autobiography entitled *Wahrheit aus Jean Pauls Leben* (1819). A final imposing novel, *Der Komet* (1820-22), remained unfinished.

During his later years Jean Paul turned increasingly to subjects of a pedagogical and political nature. In *Vorschule der Aesthetik* (1804) he presented his views on art; and in *Levana, oder Erziehungslehre* (1807) elaborated his educational theories. His opinions regarding current affairs in Germany appeared in various essays such as *Fridenspredigt* (1808), *Dämmerungen für Deutschland* (1809), *Mars und Phöbus Thronwechsel im Jahre 1814* (1814), and *Politische Fastenpredigten* (1817). His collected works were published in 60 volumes in 1826-28, shortly after his death.

Jean Paul enjoyed extraordinary popularity during his lifetime and was probably the most widely-read author of this period. His sentimental and extremely imaginative plots, his insights into the hidden emotions of his characters, and his irresistible humor endeared his novels to readers, and particularly to women. Despite these qualities, Jean Paul's novels suffer from formlessness of construction and a diffuse and digressive manner of presentation, which alienate the modern reader. Many of the major German novelists of the nineteenth century, including G. Freytag, G. Keller, W. Raabe, F. Reuter, and A. Stifter, esteemed Jean Paul's writings and were influenced by them.

The definitive edition of the works of Jean Paul, the Hanser Verlag, was published in six volumes in 1963.

In 1827 T. Carlyle translated *Army-Chaplain Schmelze's Journey to Flätz* and *Life of Quintus Fixlein*. E. H. Noel translated *Flower, Fruit, and Thorn Pieces* in 1845. In 1848 J. Gowa translated *The Campaner Thal,* and A. H. L. Longmans translated *Levana.* C. T. Brooks translated *Titan* (1862), *Hesperus* (1865), *The Invisible Lodge* (1883), and *Rome* (1913-15). *Maria Wuz* was translated by F. and R. Storr in 1881. *Leonardo da Vinci* was translated by Bridgman in 1929.

ABOUT: Carlyle, T. Miscellaneous and Critical Essays, I; Hayes, J. C. Laurence Sterne and Jean Paul; The German Classics, IV; Times (London) Literary Supplement, October 11, 1963. [In German —see studies by J. Alt, K. Berger, W. Harich, M. Kommerell, W. Meier, J. Müller, P. Nerrlich, W. Rasch, and F. J. Schneider; see also the volume commemorating the two hundredth anniversary of his birth—*Jean Paul, 1763-1963,* ed. B. Zeller.]

D. G. D.

JELAKOMITCH, IVAN. See HEIJERMANS, HERMAN

*JOCHUMSSON, MATTHÍAS (November 11, 1835-December 18, 1920), Icelandic poet, playwright, translator, and pastor, was born at Skógar in Þorskafjorður in the northwest of Iceland. He came of good Icelandic farmer stock but with little means to purchase anything beyond the barest necessities. Young Matthías had tried his hand at several things before he graduated from the college at Reykjavík in 1863. He had worked as a farmhand, a seaman, and a fisherman, and had even spent some time in Copenhagen preparing himself to be a businessman. There he had been noticed by the versatile and gifted Steingrímur Thorsteinsson (see sketch below) who directed his reading toward literature, philosophy, and foreign languages.

Graduating from the Theological School at the age of thirty, Matthías entered upon a long and honorable service as pastor of several parsonages throughout Iceland. For some years (1881-87) he was at Oddi, the home of the great Sæmundur froði (Sæmundur the Learned, 1056-1133), long a center of culture in southern Iceland. In 1900 he retired from the ministry and was granted a pension by the Icelandic government in recognition of his services. From then until his death in 1920 he devoted himself to literature and to the stimulation of the cultural life of his native land. He had already made frequent journeys abroad, including one in 1893 as Iceland's representative at the Chicago Exposition. His insatiable desire to learn new ideas, new techniques, and new methods,

* yŏk' kûms sŏn

combined with his rich experience and his great understanding of people, made him the ideal interpreter to his native community of the intellectual and cultural progress then taking place in Europe and America. He accomplished this rôle through essays, articles, poems, and an autobiography (*Sögukaflar af Sjálfum Mér,* Chapters from my Life).

On the aging poet's eighty-fifth birthday the University of Iceland conferred upon him the honorary degree of Doctor of Divinity, and the city of Akureyri, his home for the past thirty years, declared him an honorary citizen of the town and exempted him from all taxes. Thus a grateful nation bestowed its appreciation on the man who had for nearly half a century been its outstanding poet and its intellectual and cultural leader.

Matthías Jochumsson's profound influence can still be felt today. The richness and versatility of his imagination are notable, while his command of the language, his feeling for the precise expression, and the ease with which he handles the involved metrics of Icelandic versification all place him among the greatest poets that Iceland has produced. No other poet has been accorded the worship which was granted him by his people. This is the more remarkable when one considers that during the greater part of his creative period he was weighed down by personal sorrows—he was twice a widower—and was kept busy with his duties as pastor.

From 1874 to 1880 he edited the weekly *Þjóðólfur* and later (1889-91) the bi-monthly *Lýður* (The People) in Akureyri. Through these two publications he influenced public opinion with scores of articles, editorials, and discussions of public issues.

Jochumsson's poetry appeared in 1884 in one volume under the title *Ljóðmæli* (Poetry); in 1902-06 in five volumes; *Úrval* (Selections) 1915; and again in 1936, selected and edited by the poet's son Magnús Matthíasson. In addition to these, editions appeared in 1915, 1935, and 1945. Much of his poetry, however, and a great amount of his prose writings have not yet appeared in a collected edition of his works. Probably his best-known poem is "O, Guð vors lands" (Oh, God of Our Country) which is the Icelandic national anthem. A translation of this poem by Jakobina Johnson is to be found in *Icelandic Lyrics* (edited by Richard Beck, 1930).

In addition to his poetry Jochumsson wrote several plays, of which *Útilegumennirnir, Leikrit í Fimm Þáttum* (The Outlaws, a Play in Five Acts, 1884) is the best known. Moreover, he translated a great deal from Norwegian, Swedish, and English, including four Shakespearean dramas.

ABOUT: No definitive study of Jochumsson has yet appeared, but for a usable analysis of the poet's place in Icelandic literature and a workable bibliography see Beck, R. History of Icelandic Poets 1800-1940; Einarsson, S. History of Icelandic Prose Writers 1800-1940, *also* History of Icelandic Literature.

L. B.

*JODELLE, ÉSTIENNE (1532-July 1573), French dramatist and poet, was the son of Étienne Jodelle and Marie Drouet, Parisians of humble birth, despite his pretension to the title of "sieur de Lymodin," taken from a small piece of inherited property. Jodelle studied under Muret, the humanist, and Buchanan, the famous neo-Latin playwright at the Collège de Boncourt. There (1552-53) the haughty and ambitious Jodelle achieved literary glory by producing the first French tragedy (*Cléopâtre Captive*) and comedy (*Eugène*) with a cast of young poets and college mates. The performance was followed by a Dionysiac celebration with poems, songs, and wine at which a goat was sacrificed. While these plays break with the medieval tradition and return to the classical stage, they have little dramatic value. Cleopatra's wailings are lyrical, and the characters in *Eugène,* neither comic nor original, are farcical despite the five acts and the classical prologue. His second dramatic attempt, *Didon se Sacrifiant* (1555), is no more successful: Dido's lamentations are elegiac. In 1558 the poet was commissioned by the city of Paris to produce an entertainment for Henri II, requiring his talents as a musician, architect, painter, poet, etc. It was a complete failure. His *Orpheus,* hurriedly rehearsed by dancers and actors, covered him with ridicule. Yet Jodelle continued writing and frequented the Maréchale de Retz' "green salon" composing, like Tyard, Desportes, *et al.,* Petrarchan sonnets, his *Amours,* which, however, often dealt with lesbianism, sadism, or love of a violent though refined sensuality. His *Contr'Amours* is, on the other hand, decidedly misogynous. Although he is said to have at one time favored the Reform, he attacked it violently during the massacres. Despite the pension which he received —perhaps as a reward—from Charles IX, he died in a house of ill-repute penniless and abandoned by all. Before expiring, he cursed the King and God; then, having ordered the

* zhô dĕl'

window opened, in order to see the sun, he died appeased. His poetry was not published until 1574 by C. de la Mothe, who, excusing the poet's lack of discipline and polish, admired his great facility. Ronsard, who had once hailed Jodelle, deplored this publication —perhaps because of its popularity. Posterity, somewhat unjustly, shared Ronsard's views.

ABOUT: [In French—Chamard, H. Histoire de la Pléiade. In Italian—Balmas, E. Montaigne e Padova. In Hungarian—Horvarth, K. Étienne Jodelle (summary of 22 pages in French).]

M. B.

*JOHANN VON TEPL (c. 1350-c. 1415), German author, was born in the village of Sytbor in the Bohemian Forest. He attended the University of Prague where he gained the degree of *Magister* and was appointed rector of the grammar school of the city of Saaz. He died in Prague about 1415. It was not until 1933 that Johann von Tepl was identified beyond doubt as the author of *Der Ackermann aus Böhmen,* the most important piece of German prose writing before Martin Luther, with whom prose began to play an important rôle in German literature. Written in the form of a dialogue the book deals with the problem of life and death. A bereaved husband attacks Death as the destroyer of man's happiness. Death defends his action until God appears as the final arbitrator. The whole argument is carried through in a strictly legalistic manner and continues the tradition of medieval disputations. But under the influence of Renaissance thought there emerges a new concept of man and his rôle in the world. Death is no longer explained as the consequence of the fall of man, but as an indispensable link in the scheme of nature. Though the author, in a letter of dedication, describes his work as a mere stylistic exercise in the use of an unyielding language, he makes the husband's lamentations for his wife and his praise of her virtues moving expressions of personal feelings. The piece reflects the morals of an urban culture where woman is no longer idolized as the source of refined emotions and sensual pleasures, but is honored as the bringer of domestic happiness.

More important than the book's spiritual content is its rôle in the history of German literary language. Chiefly based on the standard language, developed in the chancellery of the Emperor Charles IV, it already shows the principle features of later new

* yō hän' fōn tĕpl

459

High German. The book was extremely popular in the fifteenth and sixteenth centuries. In the eighteenth century Gottsched and Lessing recognized its importance, but only after 1900 did it become the object of intensive philological study.

The only English translation of *Der Ackermann aus Böhmen* is that by K. W. Maurer, published in 1947 under the title *Death and the Ploughman*.

ABOUT: Spalding, K. *Introduction to* Der Ackermann aus Böhmen (1950). [In German—see studies by A. Bernt, K. Burdach, A. Hübner.]

F. R.

JOHN VI *CANTACUZENUS (c. 1292-1383), Byzantine Emperor, theologian and historian, was born and raised in Constantinople. His mother was Theodora Palaiologina, sister of Andronikos III. His father was Michael Cantacuzenus who governed the Byzantine lands in the Morea until his early death in 1316. The young Cantacuzenus married Irene, daughter of Andronikos Asen and granddaughter of the former Bulgarian Czar Ivan III Asen. They had three sons and three daughters, all of whom Cantacuzenus guided into Byzantine public life.

At a very early age he rose to the highest office because of his birth, his superior training, his courage, and his capabilities in general. In 1320 he was appointed "head" or governor of the Peloponnesus of the Byzantium, whose capital was Mistra. When he returned to Constantinople he became the intimate friend of Andronikos III. In 1328, on the accession of Andronikos III, he was appointed Grand Domestic and made co-regent with the Empress Anne of Savoy. This started a rivalry between the Empress and Cantacuzenus which touched off a civil war that lasted for six years. He finally appealed to the Turks, for which he was rewarded by sharing the treasures of the Church of Hagia Sophia.

On the death of Andronikos III in 1341, Cantacuzenus was left regent and guardian of his nine-year-old son John Palaeologus who was crowned Emperor in Constantinople. Jealous of his power, the Empress managed to confiscate his property and even imprison some of the members of his family when he was out of Constantinople. In revolt, on October 26, 1341, he proclaimed himself a joint-emperor with John Palaeologus at Didymotichus, for which he was excommunicated by the Patriarch John of Apri for having abandoned the child emperor. A fierce struggle for power ensued between

* kăn tả kŭ zē′ nŭs

the Empress Anne of Savoy and Cantacuzenus and both rivals sought help from the Turks. Driven to extremes, Cantacuzenus married his daughter Theodora to the Ottoman Sultan Orkhan in order to gain enough support from the Turks to defeat his opponent. On the invitation of Cantacuzenus, the Turks as his allies devastated Thrace several times.

The Hesychast controversy, which was started as a religious cult by a sect of Greek monks who sought contemplative peace and inner light, developed into a political and social struggle of national consequence which divided the Church. Cantacuzenus took a vigorous part in defense of Hesychasm which was supported by the richer classes and the monastic interests. In 1346 the Zealots who opposed Hesychasm massacred the nobility in Salonika and established an independent republic. This lasted until 1349 when Cantacuzenus put an end to the democratic regime of the Zealots.

In 1347, Cantacuzenus was crowned for the second time in Contantinople as John VI, married his daughter Helena to the young Palaeologus, and forced Anne's party to recognize him as joint-emperor with her son and sole administrator. He governed until 1354 when John Palaeologus entered Constantinople and he was forced to abdicate. He retired to a monastery where he assumed the name of Joasaph Christodulus and devoted the rest of his years to writing. He spent the last year of his life with his son Manuel, governor of Mistra, and was buried there in 1383.

Most historians hold John Cantacuzenus responsible for the first establishment of the Turks in the Byzantium. However, one must bear in mind that most of the political leaders of the time compromised with the Turks to further their own ends. When Cantacuzenus was not driven to extremes he seems to have made a conscientious effort to free the Byzantium from Ottoman control. He fought successfully to reseat the Patriarch of Jerusalem Lazarou, who had been in exile from Jerusalem; he freed Christian hostages and won unhindered circulation for Greek merchants in Syria and Egypt; he protected pilgrims to the Holy Land; he made an alliance with Alexander, sovereign of Bulgaria, against the Turks.

Cantacuzenus is the author of a commentary on the first five books of Aristotle's *Ethics*, several theological treatises and polemic essays. However, *The Histories* constitute his chief literary work. These consist of four books which he wrote in the purest Greek and are presented as an Apologia. They cover the period from 1320 to 1356 and make some references to later periods. In spite of its bias, the histories are considered a reliable work containing important information on the geography and history of the Balkan peninsula of the fourteenth century. They were printed with Latin translations in Migne's *Patrologia* and by L. Schopen, in three volumes, in 1828-32.

ABOUT: Barker, E. Social and Political Thought in Byzantium; Diehl, C. Byzantium—Greatness and Decline; Jorga, N. The Byzantine Empire; Lamb, H. Constantinople, Birth of an Empire; Miller, W. The Latins in the Levant; Pears, E. The Destruction of the Greek Empire; Runciman, J. C. S. Byzantine Civilization; Sandys, E. History of Classical Scholarship, I.; Tennent, J. E. History of Modern Greece, I; Vasiliev, A. A. History of the Byzantine Empire.

R. D.

*JOINVILLE, JEAN, Sire de (1224?-1317), French chronicler, seneschal of Champagne, was born in the castle of Joinville. Little is known of his youth except that he was eight when his father died and that he was a squire to his suzerain, Count Thibaut IV of Champagne, king of Navarre, himself a poet and crusader.

Joinville married when he was fifteen and had three sons and two daughters. In 1261 he took a second wife, Alix de Rinel, and had two sons and one daughter. Joinville respected his vassalage to Thibaut and in 1253, upon accepting a permanent pension, he became also a vassal of Louis IX. Like Louis IX, he took the cross in 1244, and in 1248 he left without "looking back towards Joinville for fear lest [his] heart should weaken at the thought of the lovely castle [he] was leaving and of his two children." In Cyprus, where the king had already gone, Joinville was made a vassal on a yearly basis. After a miserable captivity in Egypt, he was spared by pretending to be the king's cousin and was ransomed with the rest of the barons in 1250. Joinville became the king's most intimate friend while on the royal vessel taking him to Saint-Jean-d'Acre. There he wrote a summary of his religious ideas, entitled *Credo* (1251).

In 1254 Joinville went back to France and found his estate and people in ruinous condition. As a conscientious suzerain he repaired the damages caused by his overlords' soldiers and in 1267, when Louis asked him to take the cross once more, he politely and prudent-

* zhwăn vĕl'

ly refused. After Louis IX's death (1270), Joinville attended the royal courts of four successive kings whom he served faithfully. In his eighties he participated in the Flanders campaigns under Philippe IV, and in 1305, at Queen Jeanne's request, he started "Le Livre des Saintes Paroles et des Bons Faits de Notre Saint Roi Louis," entitled by most editors *Histoire de Saint-Louis*. Joinville was a valuable witness to the canonization of Louis IX in 1282. He had an altar built in his chapel in honor of the king whom he hoped to see listed as martyr by the Church, for "like Christ, Saint Louis died bearing the cross." Queen Jeanne died in 1305 and Joinville dedicated his book to her son Louis X when he finished it in 1309.

Scholars have debated the various stages of the composition of the book, but according to Joinville, "It is in two parts; the first part tells how Saint Louis ordered himself . . . by the will of God and of the Church, and for the well-being of his kingdom; the second part . . . treats of the great things he did as a knight and a soldier. . . . What I have written besides this, I have written to do additional honor to that true saint." Faithful to this intention, Joinville wrote much about himself while crusading abroad and about his friendship with the king. His chronicle remains the most informative contemporary document that we have about the qualities and shortcomings of Louis IX. Joinville's devotion to the king does not affect the honesty or vividness of his narrative.

Numerous school editions and translations of Joinville's book confirm the high esteem that this author has long enjoyed in France and elsewhere. The best editions in old and modern French are the work of Natalis de Wailly (1874). English translations were made by T. Johnes (1807), J. Hutton (1901), E. Wedgwood (1906), J. Evans (1938), and R. Hague (1955).

ABOUT: Evans, J. Introduction to The History of Saint Louis . . . ; Hague, R. Introduction to The Life of Saint Louis; Marzial, F. Memoirs of the Crusades; Runciman, S. History of the Crusades, III; Wedgwood, E. Introduction to The Memoirs of the Lord of Joinville. [In French—Paris, G. Jean, Sire de Joinville; Romanic Review, 1941.]

E. V.

*JÓKAI, MÓR (February 19, 1825-May 5, 1904), Hungarian novelist, was born in Rév-Komárom, of an ancient and aristocratic family. He was educated at Pressburg, then at the Calvinist college at Pápa where he met the dashing and romantic young poet Sándor Petőfi. Jókai studied law, took a degree, and

* yō' koi

JÓKAI

began practice. But he disliked the profession, and as soon as he received encouragement for his first ventures into literature, he gave up the law. In 1845 he moved to Pest to begin a literary career. Petőfi introduced him into literary circles, and before the year was out he had published a popular romance, *Hétköznapok* (Working Days), and was hailed as a rising young author. By 1847 he was editor of the leading Hungarian literary journal, *Eletképek*.

An ardent nationalist, Jókai joined the Hungarian army in the Revolution of 1848 and saw action through the final defeat. For months he was a fugitive from the Austrians, wandering through the forests with a price on his head. His life was saved by his wife, the famous tragedienne Roza Benke Laborfalvi (whom he had married in August 1848), who bribed officials to put his name on an amnesty list. Even so he was not out of danger, and for years he remained under political suspicion. In 1867, when the Hungarian constitution was re-established, Jókai took an active interest in politics. He sat in the Hungarian parliament for more than twenty years, founded and edited a government publication, *Hon,* but never took a political office.

Jókai had a distinguished career as an author, honored in his own country and widely known and admired abroad. At the turn of the century he was one of the most popular of European novelists, rivaled only by Sienkiewicz, Hugo, and Dumas *père*.

His prolificness was extraordinary. In a lifetime crowded with political activity and editing, he wrote at times 30,000 words a day and published seven volumes a year. Between 1861 and 1886, at the height of his political activity, he wrote 142 novels plus a number of works of non-fiction. The national edition of his works, published in 1894, has over 100 volumes and is not nearly complete.

Jókai was an "arch-romantic." His fiction has been described as "a combination in almost equal parts of Walter Scott, William Beckford, Dumas *père*, and Charles Dickens." His novels deal, for the most part, with two types of material—the purely historical and the local scene. In his historical novels his wild imagination had full sway. H. W. V. Temperley observed: "In his hands history becomes romance and romance history." Probably the best and most typical of these is *Az Arany Ember* (translated as *Midst the Wild Carpathians*), which treats of the relations of Turkey and Hungary and is full of pageantry, Homeric battles, and all the exotic atmosphere he could summon up of the Orient, the Russian steppes, savage brigands, etc. In his novels treating of the local scene, of which *Egy Magyar Nabob* (*An Hungarian Nabob*) is an example, Jókai wrote with an earthier realism and a lively humor (though much of this is lost in translation)—picturing the peasants, village life, country fairs, feasting, etc. In still other works he displayed a lively interest in the natural sciences which has led some critics to compare him to Jules Verne and H. G. Wells.

Jókai's popularity was challenged by the Hungarian critic Pal Gyulai, who found his novels carelessly written and improbable. It is generally conceded that his works are exaggerated, melodramatic, loose in structure, and lacking in psychological depth. He often wrote so hastily that he began a story without knowing how he was going to end it. But his position remained secure, not only in Hungary but all over Europe and America. Striking evidence of his appeal to readers is the account by R. N. Bain, who translated many of his novels into English, of how he first came upon a German translation of one of Jókai's novels and was so delighted with it that he set out to learn Hungarian in order to read more of him. Another of his admirers was Queen Victoria.

In 1894 Jókai's golden jubilee was celebrated in Hungary as a national festival, and he received the Ribbon of St. Stephen from the king and a prize of 100,000 florins. He was a dapper, elegantly dressed man with a "slim, erect, elastic figure," and a trim beard and mustache. His first wife died in 1866. In 1899 he married Bella Nagy Grosz, also an actress. He died in Budapest, and a few years after his death a statue of him was erected in that city.

Jókai's novels have been translated into about twenty-five languages. For a full account, see Z. Ferenczi's *List of Translations of Jókai's Novels into Foreign Languages*. Among the English translations are *Hungarian Sketches in Peace and War* which appeared in 1854, and the numerous translations by R. N. Bain, including *Pretty Michal* (1892), *The Lion of Janina* (1897), *An Hungarian Nabob* (1898), *Day of Wrath* (1900). *The Golden Age in Transylvania, or Midst the Wild Carpathians* was translated by S. L. and A. V. Waite (1898).

ABOUT: Columbia Dictionary of Modern European Literature; Contemporary Review, July 1904; Living Age, 1901; Slavonic Review, 1929-30.

*JOVELLANOS, GASPAR MELCHOR DE (January 5, 1744-July 29, 1811), Span-

ish statesman and writer, was born into a noble family of Gijón, Asturias. He studied law and theology at the University of Alcalá de Henares, and at the age of twenty-three was appointed magistrate in Seville, Andalucía, where he remained for ten years. There he joined the famous literary gatherings of the prominent Peruvian Olavide, head of the Spanish encyclopedist group. He began to put into effect his reformist plans: he mitigated the harsh treatment of prisoners and abolished the traditional wig worn by judges. As a young man he fell in love with one of Olavide's close relatives, but he never married. In Seville his life centered around two spheres of interest: literature and art were one, social studies and law the other.

Poetry was a major form of expression for Jovellanos; his verse was moral, political, and historical in tone and subject matter. During these years he translated several French works, Book I of Milton's *Paradise Lost*, and some of Adam Smith's writings. The reformist King Charles III promoted him to a higher magisterial position in Madrid, where he became a distinguished member of the intellectual and political elite. Goya painted his portrait and his closest friends were statesmen such as Campomanes and Cabarrus. He became a member of all the Academies. But the political crisis of 1790 affected him profoundly. Charles IV exiled him from court and Jovellanos went back to his native Asturias for eight years (1790-

* hō vä lyä' nōs

98). From a creative point of view, these were very productive years. His *Diario,* not published until 1915, is a document unique in Spanish letters and an extremely valuable one for its record of life in Spain at that period. Jovellanos dedicated most of his time to the founding of the Asturian Institute (1794), a private center of learning where general and scientific education was offered to young people, regardless of social class. An excellent library and a scholarship fund were also organized. Influenced by Rousseau's ideals. Jovellanos had deep concern for the improvement of cultural and educational standards and he worked towards that goal.

He was appointed Secretary of Justice in 1797, but held the post only for a few months. His high moral character, his criticism of the queen and disgust at the corruption of the court, his antipathy towards the power of the church in state affairs, and his attacks on the Inquisition met with persecution. From 1801 to 1808 Jovellanos was imprisoned on the island of Majorca. His friend Lord Holland wrote of him in his memoirs which cover the period 1807-21: "He was in creed, in character and political austerity a Jansenist and connected with many of that sect." Referring to his dignity and valor, Menéndez y Pelayo said that his spirit was "perhaps the most beautiful of modern Spain." In the isolation of prison life he wrote many essays and studies on architectural, social, and historical subjects. One of these, entitled "Nature and Art," is significant because of its pre-romantic tone.

Liberated in 1808, he returned to the Peninsula and was acclaimed with enthusiasm by the people. The moment was a crucial one for a man of Jovellanos' ideals. Napoleon asked for his collaboration, and although many of his friends—Moratín, Meléndez, Cabarrus—were *"afrancesados,"* Jovellanos refused the request. His attitude was clear: he wanted to serve the Spanish people, not the French Emperor. He became the most distinguished member of La Junta Central, an underground political organization, and worked towards the creation of a constitutional Spain. He was persecuted again, and while fleeing from the French, died alone in a little port in his beloved Asturias.

Jovellanos' integrity and many-sided interests, reflected in his writings, make him the greatest figure of his time and the most influential one on Spanish writers and men of liberal ideas of following generations.

His complete works appear in two volumes in the *BAE*. An English translation of *The Tribunal of the Inquisition and Bread and Bulls* was published in 1813, and *To the Sun* appeared in T. Walsh, *Hispanic Anthology* (1920).

ABOUT: Lord Holland, *Further Memoirs of the Whig Party with Some Miscellaneous Reminiscences*; Foreign Quarterly Review, 1829-30. [In Spanish— see studies by J. A. Ceán Bermúdez, A. Del Río, J. Juderías, J. Somoza. In French—see essay by P. Mérimée *in* Revue Hispanique, 1894.]

L. R. DE G. L.

*JUAN DE LA CRUZ, SAN (SAINT JOHN OF THE CROSS) (June 24, 1542- December 14, 1591), Spanish poet and mystic, was born Juan de Yepes y Álvarez at Fontiveros, near Ávila. His father, Gonzalo de Yepes, was descended from a wealthy and distinguished family, but was disinherited upon marrying a poor orphan girl. When Gonzalo died a few years thereafter, the widow Yepes and her three sons were left in abject poverty. Failing to get any succor from her in-laws, Juan's mother moved with her children to Medina del Campo where the Society of Jesus had established a hospital and school. Through the kindness of the superintendent of the hospital, Juan early entered into an apprenticeship, which enabled him to acquire his first education in exchange for attending patients. As it happened, the master of the school was an enthusiastic young Latin scholar, so that along with his *Spiritual Exercises* Juan was undoubtedly grounded in his Ovid, Virgil, and Horace.

Juan remained at the Jesuit hospital in Medina until about the age of twenty. The superintendent intended for him to become its chaplain and take over the direction after receiving ordination, but from an early age it seemed clear to Juan that so settled and secure a life was not for him. His earliest biographer Jerónimo de San José relates that one day while at prayer he heard a divine voice commanding him: "Thou shalt serve Me in an Order whose former perfection thou shalt help to restore." This has been taken as a premonition to Juan of what was to be his life work, the establishment of the Reform of St. Teresa, though her activity at this time was obscure. The next phase in his religious life was marked by his joining of the Order of Carmel. On St. Matthias Day, 1563, he received the habit of the monastery of Santa Aña de Medina, and was known for the next five years as Juan de San Matías.

In 1564 Juan went to study at the University of Salamanca. During the Long Vacation of 1567 occurred his fateful meeting with that saintly lady Teresa of Ávila, with whom his career henceforth was indissolubly bound. Teresa was at this time engaged in plans for founding a strict reformed house for monks, and was so impressed by the religious ardor of young Fray Juan that he was immediately enlisted in her cause. The relationship between the Seraphic Mother and her friar is one of the most beautiful and touching in church history, and not without its glints of humor. Alluding to Juan's small size (he was only five feet two), she once spoke of him and another assistant, Antonio de Heredia, as her "friar and a half." One of her pet names for Fray Juan was "little Seneca." Nevertheless in one of her famous *Cartas* (a primary source of information about Juan's career) she wrote: "Although small in stature, I know he is great in God's eyes," and in another she referred to him as "father of my soul."

On November 28, 1568, in a tiny hovel located in the hamlet of Duruelo, Juan, Antonio de Heredia, and another Carmelite friar founded a house for men with the blessing of St. Teresa. Their Reform was known as the *Discalced* (Barefoot) Movement, signifying their rigorous asceticism. Teresa herself made their first habit. The monks' first meal had to be begged. But spiritually the Reform thrived, owing in large part to the tireless work of Juan de la Cruz (the name he now adopted), who for six years traveled about the country, under the most arduous conditions, preaching to his fellows. So successful was the movement that the conservative, or *Calced*, friars became seriously concerned and in 1575 ordered the suppression of all houses of the Reform except the two originally sanctioned. As a result of this dissension, Juan was cast into prison in Toledo. He steadfastly refused to give up the Reform, even with the inducement of high honor among the *Calcedes*. So he was confined to a narrow cell with no window, meagerly fed, and frequently whipped. But here too, as a biographer relates, "in this den of darkness he wrote some of the finest of those passages which tell of the Divine Light." Supplied with pen and paper by a sympathetic jailer, Juan composed "Aunque es de noche" ("Although it is night"), a plaintive song of the soul's triumph over tribulation, and began the *Cántico Espiritual* and the *Noche Oscura*.

In time, by spiritual guidance according to St. Teresa, Juan managed to escape from his cell, and found refuge in one of his patroness' reformed houses. The next decade

* hwän' dä lä krooth'

464

was the most prosperous period of his life, during which he served in a series of administrative posts in Andalusia (Granada and Cordova). Juan was one of those upon whom greatness was thrust; all his life he desired only a life of seclusion. His last years were saddened once more by strife. With the death of St. Teresa, discord broke out among the *Discalced* friars. It was Juan's misfortune to be on the wrong side, as a friend of the leader of the Order, Fray Jerónimo Gracián, against whom the other friars were in revolt. On Whitsun Eve 1591 he was stripped of his offices and exiled to the Reform house at Peñuela. Shortly after his arrival there it became evident that he was dangerously ill, and so he was removed to Ubeda for medical attention. For three months he lingered in pain, refusing even to mitigate his sufferings with music. He desired to "have Purgatory in this life and die an undistinguished friar." Having promised to warn his brother friars when he felt death coming, at half-past eleven on the night of December 14, 1591, he asked that the community be called. At midnight he died. In 1618 his writings were posthumously published under the title *Obras Espirituales*. He was beatified in 1674 and canonized on December 27, 1726.

San Juan de la Cruz is one of Spain's greatest religious poets. He is known principally for three poems: *La Noche Oscura* (The Dark Night), *El Cántico Espiritual* (The Spiritual Canticle), and *Llama de Amor Viva* (The Living Flame of Love). These are best read alongside the three prose treatises written as commentaries upon the poems: *La Subida del Monte Carmelo* (The Ascent of Mount Carmel, including the incomplete *La Noche Oscura*), which glosses the first of the poems, and the two others bearing the titles of the poems they expound. San Juan's basic theme is renunciation, man's divesting himself of the love of created beings and removing himself from the realm of sensory experience in order to attain to the Divine Union. The poems with their commentaries explore the way by which the soul reaches God. There are three basic stages: the Purgative, described in *La Noche Oscura*, wherein the soul completely divorces itself from the things of this world; the Illuminative, described in *El Cántico Espiritual*, echoing the Song of Solomon, wherein the soul is conceived as a Bride seeking her spiritual Groom; the Unitive, powerfully envisaged in *Llama de Amor Viva*, where the soul is likened to a log simultaneously consumed by and subsumed in fire. Besides his major works, San

Juan has left behind a body of maxims (*Avisos*), which, in their pithy wisdom indicate that he was a master psychologist, understanding all too well the nature of the hypocrite, the Pharisee, and the Laodicean. From San Juan we learn that the road to salvation is by no means an easy one but that all else crumbles into nothingness once one has a glimpse of it. He has influenced many contemporary poets, notably T. S. Eliot, who echoes him in *Sweeney Agonistes, Ash Wednesday,* and *The Four Quartets*. His countryman Antonio Machado has immortalized him together with his patroness in the memorable lines: "Teresa, alma de fuego// Juan de la Cruz, espíritu de llama" ("Teresa, soul of fire, John of the Cross, spirit of ardent flame").

San Juan de la Cruz has been extensively translated into English. The complete works were first translated by David Lewis in 1864, and his versions have gone through several editions. More recently the complete works have been translated by E. Allison Peers (1934-35), whose edition is based on the critical edition in Spanish of Padre Silverio de Santa Teresa, and by John Frederick Nims (1958). Another translation, *The Collected Works of St. John of the Cross,* by K. Kavanaugh and O. Rodriguez was published in 1964. The *Poems* have been translated, with the Spanish text included, by the poet Roy Campbell (1951). The treatise *The Dark Night of the Soul* is available in an abridged form in a recent translation by Kurt F. Reinhardt (1957).

ABOUT: Brenan, G. Short Life of St. John of the Cross *in* Golden Horizon; Cresógono de Jesús, Life of St. John of the Cross (tr. K. Pond); Fairweather, W. Among the Mystics; Fitzmaurice-Kelly, J. Some Masters of Spanish Verse; Goodier, A. Saints for Sinners; Gosse, E. Silhouettes; Peers, E. A. Studies of the Spanish Mystics, I. [In Spanish—see study by J. Sobrino].

R. A. C.

*JUAN MANUEL, Infante de Castile (May 5, 1282-1349?), Spanish soldier, statesman, and writer, was born in Escalona. He was the son of the infante Don Manuel and Beatriz de Saboya. His family was among the most illustrious in the nation, for he was the grandson of King Ferdinand III of León and Castile and the nephew of Alfonso X, called "The Wise." His father died before he was two years of age but he was carefully educated and watched over by both his immediate family and his uncle, King Sancho. His military and political life was active and confusing. In his youth, as well as later in life, he fought against the Moors of the Kingdom of Granada. From 1320 until 1322 Juan Manuel served as regent for his cousin Alfonso XI. Then, falling out with the young

* hwän mä nwĕl'

465

king and his advisers, he engaged in intermittent civil war with the king from 1322 till 1338, when peace was made between them. Juan Manuel was one of the most powerful princes of his age. It is said that he was so rich that he could keep a thousand men under arms and could travel from one end of Spain to the other and could sleep each night in a town or castle of his own.

Juan Manuel was married twice: the first time to the infante Doña Costanza, daughter of Jaime II of Aragon, the second time to Blanca de la Cerda, daughter of the infante Don Fernando. By these marriages he had two daughters, Costanza and Juana, and two sons, Fernando and Enrique.

Juan Manuel's minor works are *Libro del Caballero et del Escudero*, which he finished about 1326, *Crónica Abreviada* (1320-24), *Crónica Complida* (1329), and the *Tractado de las Armas* (1332).

The one work which entitles Juan Manuel to lasting literary fame is the *Libro de Patronio* or *Conde Lucanor* (1328-35). It is composed of fifty exemplary tales told to a young nobleman, Lucanor, by his tutor Patronio in answer to the former's questions. It is more or less didactic in its intent for each tale ends with a short moral in verse. The spirit and form owe much to the Arabic stories with which Juan Manuel was familiar. Some critics claim to find a lack of warmth and an impersonal tone in the collection, but all agree that the clearness of the language is a redeeming feature. Although the stories are often humorous and even ribald, the general tone is grave. Menéndez y Pelayo says of Juan Manuel that he is "the first Spanish prose writer who possessed a personal style." The *Conde Lucanor* served as a model or source for Boccaccio, Chaucer, Lope de Vega, Calderón, and possibly Shakespeare in his *Taming of the Shrew*.

Juan Manuel's works are collected in the *BAE*, volume LI, with an introduction by P. de Gayangos. The best-known English translation is that of James York, *Count Lucanor, or Fifty Pleasant Stories of Patronio* (1868). A new edition of this translation was issued in 1924, with an introduction by J. B. Trend.

ABOUT: Roscoe, T. The Spanish Novelists, I.

R. E. O.

JUDAH BEN SAMUEL, *HE-HASID

(d. February 22, 1217), medieval Jewish mystic and ethical writer, was born in Speyer, Germany, scion of a distinguished family, his grandfather, Kalonymos, having been an

* hĕ hă′ sĭd

eminent scholar, and his father, Samuel, also known as "he-hasid" (the pious), a mystic. It was from his father (who died when his son was still a youth) that Judah received his early education. Leaving Speyer in 1195 because of persecutions of the Jews, Judah settled in Regensburg where he established a Talmudic academy (Yeshiva). Among his outstanding disciples were Eleazar of Worms and Isaac ben Moses of Vienna. His only son, Moses Saltman, was the author of a Biblical commentary.

There are many legends dealing with Judah's miraculous deeds but very little is really known of his life. The authorship of works ascribed to him, such as the mystic *Sefer ha-Kavod* (Book of Glory) and the hymns *Shir ha-Yihud* (Song of Unity) and *Shir ha-Kavod* (Song of Glory), is clouded in obscurity. The major work associated with his name is the *Sefer Hasidim* (Book of the Pious, 1538), a loosely organized ethical handbook. Even this bears the marks of composite authorship and editorship, although Judah certainly is responsible for a substantial part of it. The book presents rules for ethical behavior in the relation of man to God and Jew to Gentile, marriage, education, business, charity, fasting, prayer and many other details of daily life. A theosophical approach to God and a mystical pietistic approach to the Jewish religion are emphasized.

The *Sefer Hasidim* was the highest expression of the Jewish Franco-German mystical school of the thirteenth century. Undoubtedly influenced by the non-Jewish mysticism of the period, it also contains valuable material bearing on the social and cultural life of medieval Jewry, including its superstitions. Dedicated to devotion, purity, and deep feeling in all aspects of man's behavior, the *Sefer Hasidim* represents a man of whom a contemporary said, "He would have been a prophet if he had lived in the times of the prophets."

The *Sefer Hasidim* has not been translated, except for extracts by A. Aulzbach in 1923. The most detailed Hebrew edition is that published by Wistinetzki in Berlin, 1891-93. The hymns ascribed to Judah appear in translation in the *Authorized Jewish Prayer Book*, among others.

ABOUT: Baron, S. Social and Cultural History of the Jews; Scholem, G. G. Major Trends in Jewish Mysticism; Trachtenberg, J. Jewish Magic and Superstition; Waxman, M. A History of Jewish Literature. [In German—Berliner, A. Der Einheitsgesang; Güdemann, M. Geschichte des Erziehungswesens und der Kultur der Juden in Frankreich und Deutschland. In Hebrew—Freiman, J. Mavo le-Sefer Hasidim.]

M. R.

JUDAH *HA-LEVI (c. 1085-post 1140), the greatest Hebrew poet of the Middle Ages and an important philosopher, was born in Toledo, the capital of Christian Spain. His father, Samuel, a cultured man of wealth, gave his only son a basic education in the Bible and Talmud. Later, he studied Arabic poetry, Hebrew grammar, Greek philosophy and medicine. At the age of fourteen he was sent to Lucena to study at the academy of the noted rabbi Isaac Alfasi. It was here that he made the acquaintance of the distinguished scholars Joseph ibn Migash and Baruch Albalia. After completing his studies, Judah went to Seville and then to Cordova, where his proficiency in poetry won the interest of the leading Jews of the city and the enthusiastic admiration of Moses ibn Ezra, the most important Jewish poet of the day. At the invitation of Moses, he moved to Granada where he soon captivated the intellectuals with his personality and poetry. After several years of living in different Spanish cities, he returned to his birthplace, Toledo, where he undertook the practice of medicine, taught Bible, married, had one daughter and a grandson, also named Judah.

By this time Judah had achieved fame as a poet. His work as a physician gave him a comfortable living and left enough time for the expression of his creative powers in the most beautiful Hebrew poems written since the Bible. Although a complete master of poetic form, he ridiculed those who saw poetry as a matter of rhyme and meter. His deeply religious soul saw the poetic gift as a spark of the divine and he himself, as Heine said, was "God-kissed." "I am a harp for thy songs," he wrote, and the spirit of God and Israel found form in his words. His earlier poems are love songs, friendship poems, wedding songs, and wine songs. In this secular poetry there was evident a keen sense of the joy of life and its sorrows. With great force and charm, he wrote of love and nature. His descriptions of natural phenomena reveal the hand of a master and compare favorably with similar work by the great poets of other literatures.

His religious poetry reveals even more clearly the spiritual feeling which pervades all of his work. The light and grace of the secular poems give way to an earnest search for God: "O Lord, where shall I find Thee?" With intense devotion, he sings the praises of God, His majesty and His nearness. Many of these religious poems have won an hon-

* hä lē′ vī

ored place in the Jewish liturgy for Sabbath and holy days.

Yet his heart was not at rest. The desperate plight of his co-religionists in a Spain torn between Christian and Moslem was clear to him. Turning to the future of the Jewish people, Judah sang of its ultimate redemption in his great national poems. Weeping over the present status of Israel, he remembered its glorious past and prayed for its restoration to Zion. These poems, written with complete personal conviction, express the essential religious-national nature of Judaism. Despairingly, he wrote, "My heart is in the East, and I in the uttermost West." His famous "Ode to Zion" and similar poems, on the other hand, voice his faith in the redemption of Zion.

Judah's great contribution to religious philosophy was his Arabic *Kitab al-Khazari* translated into Hebrew as the *Sefer ha-Kuzari* (Book of the Khazars; written before 1140 in Cordova, where he had moved again from Toledo). This was an apologetic work, intended to uphold Judaism against the criticism of other faiths and the wavering of Jewish intellectuals attracted by secular philosophy. Cast in the form of a dialogue between a rabbi and the king of the Khazars, a people of the Crimea who had been converted to Judaism in the eighth century, the work contrasts Judaism and philosophy, and Judaism and the other two major religions. Judah argues for the superiority of revealed religion over the insecure claims of speculative philosophy. He goes on to defend the principles of Judaism and expresses his belief in the spiritual chosenness of Israel the people and Israel the land.

Determined to make his actions match his words, Judah, after the death of his wife, decided to embark on a pilgrimage to the Holy Land. Despite the urgent pleas of friends and relatives, he set out, about 1141, for Egypt. There again he had to tear himself away from admirers, and journeyed forth by land to Jerusalem. This last portion of his life has become shrouded in legend, but it is known that he reached Tyre and Damascus, and the story has it that on finally beholding Jerusalem, he was run down by an Arab horseman and killed.

Another medieval Jewish poet, Harizi, spoke of Judah ha-Levi as one who "broke into the treasure-house of song," and going out, "shut the gate behind him." No other poet has achieved the supreme position held by him in the history of Hebrew literature. His profound religious and national feeling and his mastery of the written word have made him unique. In his life, as well as his writings, he was, as Graetz remarks, in his *History of the Jews*, "a perfect poet, an original thinker, a worthy son of Judaism."

The *Kitab al-Khazari* was translated in 1905 by Hartwig Hirschfeld and has been published in later editions. An abridged version, edited by Isaak Heinemann, appeared in 1947. Nina Salaman translated *Selected Poems of Jehudah Halevi* in 1924. Hebrew editions include Heinrich Brody's collection of the poetry, the *Diwan* (Berlin, 1894-1930), the *Kol Shire* (Tel Aviv, 1944/45-49/50), the *Kitab al-Khazari*, ed. H. Hirschfeld (Leipzig, 1887) and the *Sefer ha-Kuzari* (Warsaw, 1911).

ABOUT: Burstein, A. Judah Halevi in Granada; Druck, D. Yehuda Halevy, His Life and Work; Graetz, H. History of the Jews; Husik, I. A History of Medieval Jewish Philosophy; Kayser, R. The Life and Times of Jehudah Halevi; Strauss, L. Persecution and the Art of Writing; Waxman, M. A History of Jewish Literature. [In Hebrew—see studies by Y. Guttmann and A. Orinowsky. In German—Kaufmann, D. Jehudah Halewi. In Spanish—Millás Vallicrosa, J. M. Yehuda ha-Leví como Poeta y Apologista.]

M. R.

*JUNGMANN, JOSEF JAKUB (July 16, 1773-November 14, 1847), Czech philologist, critic and poet, was born in Hudlice near Beroun in central Bohemia, the son of a peasant. He studied at the Piarist *Gymnasium* in Prague, and from 1792 to 1795 in the Faculty of Philosophy at Prague University. His childhood and student years were marked by extreme poverty, but his intellectual promise enabled him to win his education. In 1795 he published his first poem, an epigram of four lines, in an almanac edited by Puchmajer. Also in 1795 he decided on a career in law, and enrolled in the Law Faculty of the university, supporting himself by tutoring. But in 1799 poverty forced him to leave the university and to accept a post as teacher in the academic *Gymnasium* at Litoměřice in northern Bohemia. In 1815 he became teacher at the academic *Gymnasium* in Prague, and in 1834 its director. He retired in 1845, two years before his death. Jungmann used his position as teacher to inspire his students with patriotism and a love for the Czech tongue. A romanticist in his patriotic feeling and the ardor with which he propagated it, he lost favor with the older leaders of the nation, Dobrovský and Jan Nejedlý, men more reserved in their views, whose concept of a nationalism was the more sober one of the Enlightenment.

Jungmann sought to provide a basis for the newly reawakening Czech literature which

* yoong' män

had been moribund for nearly a century and a half. To this end he compiled a textbook on style and literary theory, *Slovesnost* (Literature, 1820), and translated a great variety of works of literature from many languages and periods to serve as models for the new Czech writing. His translations include Chateaubriand's *Atala*, Milton's *Paradise Lost*, and Goethe's *Hermann und Dorothea*, as well as poems by Greek and Latin poets, Goldsmith, Gray, Pope, Bürger, Klopstock, Schiller, and Herder. His translation of Milton is a masterpiece in a dignified, exalted style influenced by the sixteenth century Czech Bible of Kralice. Jungmann's original poetry is small in quantity: besides a few attempts at Czech "sonnets" (in trochees), and some Anacreontic and occasional verse, it includes a romance on a subject from Old Czech history, *Oldřich and Božena* (1806).

Jungmann's greatest achievement was his Czech-German dictionary in five volumes (1835-39), which laid the foundation for modern Czech lexicography. In it he enriched the Czech literary language with many borrowings from Polish and Russian. His *History of Czech Literature* (1849) is more of a bibliographical listing of books and writers than a real history. Though he published little original writing, Jungmann may be regarded as the real father of modern Czech literature.

Several English translations of his poems are found in Sir John Bowring, *A Cheskian Anthology* (1832).

ABOUT: Součková, M. The Czech Romantics; Chudoba, F. A Short Survey of Czech Literature; Lützow, F. History of Bohemian Literature. [In Czech—Chalupný, E. Josef Jungmann.]

W. E. H.

*KANT, IMMANUEL (April 22, 1724-February 12, 1804), German philosopher, was born in Königsberg, East Prussia, the fourth child in a family of nine children. His father, Johann Georg Kant, a poor harnessmaker, and his mother, Anna Regina Reuter, belonged to the pietistic movement which insisted on the full strictness and rigor of religious practice and belief, thus rearing their children in a strict moral atmosphere. Kant's claim to Scottish origin of the family lacks evidence. Immanuel seemed especially close to his mother, whom he praised later as a woman of great natural ability and noble heart. In his early schooling Immanuel acquired a foundation in mathematics, physics, and geography, in addition to a sound

* känt

KANT

knowledge of Latin language and literature. His mother died in his thirteenth year.

In 1740 Kant entered the university of his native city, especially attracted by the lectures of Martin Knutzen, who seems to have given him all the fundamental ideas of Leibniz, Newton, and Wolff. Six years later Kant finished his work at the university with a master's dissertation entitled *Gedanken von der Wahren Schätzung der Lebendigen Kräfte* (Thoughts Concerning the True Evaluation of Vital Forces). Earlier in 1746 his father had died. The only path open for him now was to become a private tutor, and after spending almost nine years in different households as a private teacher, he obtained the position of private lecturer at the University of Königsberg by writing and successfully defending his doctoral dissertation, *De Igne* (About Fire). Kant remained in this position for fifteen years.

Natural sciences, especially astronomy and geography, were Kant's favorite subjects at the beginning of his academic career, and besides several small essays on these subjects, he published in 1755 a work entitled *Allgemeine Naturgeschichte und Theorie des Himmels* (Universal History of Nature and Theory of the Heavens). Kant anticipated in this work the theories which Laplace developed later about the origin of our solar system. His philosophical position at this period, however, was still that of the rationalist Christian Wolff and of other champions of the Enlightenment. But he also diligently

studied English philosophers, especially Hutchison and Hume, whose skepticism affected him strongly and whose influence he tried to overcome later. Among French authors, besides Voltaire and Montesquieu, Rousseau especially attracted his attention.

The effect of these various influences is clearly noticeable in the writings of his second period when he turned more directly to the problems of metaphysics and epistemology. The principal treatise of this period appeared in 1762 under the title *Der Einzige Mögliche Beweisgrund zu einer Demonstration des Daseins Gottes* (The Only Possible Ground of Demonstration for the Existence of God), in which he challenged the current proofs of God's existence. A skeptical tone was also prevalent in *Untersuchungen über die Deutlichkeit der Grundsätze der Natürlichen Theologie und Moral* (An Investigation of the Clearness of the Principles of Natural Theology and Morals, 1763), a short essay in which he favors the method of mathematics over that of philosophy. Another work of the same period was *Betrachtungen über das Gefühl des Schönen und Erhabenen* (Observations on the Feeling of the Beautiful and the Sublime, 1764). Kant's skeptical writings culminated in his 1766 attack on Emanuel Swedenborg's claims to supernatural powers.

Kant was left for fifteen years in his lowly post of private lecturer: his application for a vacant professorship was twice refused. Two outside offers of professorships he declined, since he wished to remain in his native city. In spite of the great poverty of these years, Kant arranged his life in such a way that scarcely any interruptions came to break the uniform regularity of his life. He was small of stature, hardly five feet tall, with an extremely frail physique; he had a hollow chest cramping his lungs and heart, and he had to take severe measures to protect his health. He remained unmarried, though he twice thought of marrying. Kant was loved by his students. Indeed, it was said that he was a better teacher than writer.

At last, in 1770, he was made professor of logic and metaphysics on the basis of his work *De Mundi Visibilis atque Intelligibilis Forma et Principiis* (On the Form and Principles of the Sensible and Intelligible Worlds). He was now forty-six years old, and he had written more than a score of books, pamphlets, and papers. With this last work, Kant entered his third and last period. The point of departure here is the distinction between sensible and intelligible knowledge, and corresponding to this a distinction between a phenomenal and a real world. Although the root of his entire philosophical system was contained in this dissertation, it took him more than ten years to finish his masterpiece, *Die Kritik der Reinen Vernunft* (The Critique of Pure Reason, 1781, 1787).

The *Critique* represents, first of all, Kant's philosophical effort to demonstrate that physics is a real science, i.e., a system of universal and necessary propositions. He wished, above all, to make the mathematical sciences of nature secure against the devastating attacks of English skeptical philosophies, especially that of Hume. The title indicates a judicial investigation of the legitimacy of the claims to objective validity made by pure reason and by the concepts to which it gives rise. Kant assumes that the primary concepts have their roots in the mind itself and are created *a priori*. By virtue of the forms and categories of the mind, such as space, time, and causality, man is predisposed for coherent and intelligible experience. Kant nevertheless concedes that true knowledge cannot transcend or go beyond experience, i.e., we never know the thing-in-itself ("das Ding an sich"), but only appearances, colors, sounds, and the like.

At short intervals after his *Critique of Pure Reason* came all the other great works of Kant, including in 1788 *Kritik der Praktischen Vernunft* (The Critique of Judgment). Indefatigably Kant applied his critical philosophy to ethics, aesthetics, religion and theology, politics and law. He formulated categorical imperatives, basic ethical laws, to instruct man in his moral duty.

This literary activity was accompanied by controversies and enthusiasm that not only shook and transformed the German universities, but upset the entire philosophical world. Kant's influence and fame were extended with every new book, and his philosophy was taught in all the German universities, as well as in England and Holland. But the 1790's brought to Kant, who was now growing old, his first conflict with the Prussian government. The successor of Frederick the Great, Frederick William II, dismissed Zedlitz, Frederick's far-sighted and progressive Minister of Education, and appointed in his place the former preacher Wöllner who by means of censorship and inquisition attempted to destroy the spirit of his predecessor. Kant's philosophy was naturally offensive to the government, but even more objectionable was his political attitude, for he

was an open admirer of the French Revolution, and his love of freedom was emphatically stated in his famous pamphlet on eternal peace (*Zum Ewigen Frieden*). But when his work *Religion within the Bounds of Pure Reason* was scheduled to appear in installments in the *Berliner Monatsschrift*, the censor ordered that the essay be suppressed. When Kant, nevertheless, had it published in Jena, outside the Prussian borders, the king issued an order prohibiting Kant from any future publications on religious matters.

His physical strength was now quickly declining. In 1799 he was forced to give up his lectures. His last five years were pitiful. He withered slowly into a childlike senility. At seventy-nine he died in the city where he had spent his entire life. The work he left behind expresses the deep piety and strong moral bent of his nature. "Two things fill the soul with ever new and increasing wonder and reverence the oftener and the more fervently one reflects on them: the starry heavens above and the moral law within."

Though Kant was elected a member of the Berlin Academy of Sciences in 1763 and of St. Petersburg Academy in 1794, he never received any official honors or titles.

The complete edition of his works appeared several times, the last and the most complete being the edition of the Prussian Academy of Sciences in twenty-two volumes, 1900-1942, which includes letters and his posthumous works.

Kant has been translated into almost all modern languages. There are numerous works dealing with his philosophical system. The best known English translations of Kant's works are by J. Haywood (1838, 1848), M. D. Meiklejohn (1854), F. Max Müller (1881), T. K. Abbott (1898), and J. C. Meredith (1911, 1928).

ABOUT: Clark, N. Introduction to Kant's Philosophy; Lindsay, A. & D. Kant; Paulsen, F. Immanuel Kant, His Life and Doctrine; Stuckenberg, J. H. W. The Life of Immanuel Kant; Wilm, E. C. ed. Immanuel Kant, 1724-1924; *see also* A Symposium on Kant (Tulane Studies in Philosophy, III, 1954). [In German—see studies by L. E. Borowski, M. Heidegger, E. Wasianski. In French —by A. Saintes.]

F. S. L.

*KANTEMIR, ANTIOKH DMITRIEVICH, Prince (September 21, 1708-April 11, 1744), Russian poet and diplomat, was born in Constantinople. His father (see sketch below) was a Moldavian hospodar who sided with Peter I and, after the latter's military reverses, fled to Russia where

* kän tĕ mēr'

he was given lands in the Ukraine and near Moscow and later was appointed senator. Kantemir's mother, Cassandra Cantacuzino, was a descendant of Byzantine emperors. He was a precocious child and received the best possible education for that time, first from Greek and Russian tutors, and later from the members of the Academy of Sciences (1724-25) at St. Petersburg. He served in the Guards, receiving a commission in 1728. He never married.

Kantemir began his literary career with translations, the best of which were from Anacreon, Horace, and Boileau. His first printed work was *A Psalter Symphony* (1727), a concordance in verse. Not until 1740 did he manage to publish one more book, a translation of Fontenelle's *Entretiens,* which, however, was banned in Russia as an atheistic work. Although Kantemir wrote love songs, odes, fables, and epistles, and began an epic, "Petrida," his reputation is based on the nine satires which circulated in manuscript. These were first published in French translation in London (1749), appearing later in Russia in a mutilated form (1762). Not until 1867-68 were they published in a scholarly edition. The first and most famous satire, "On the Detractors of Learning. To my Mind" (1729), followed by four others (1730-31), brought him close to a group of intellectuals who admired the social reforms of Peter I. With them he took part in a successful anti-oligarchic plot which made the new Empress Anna an absolute monarch. As a result, he was sent to London as Minister Resident (1731), never to see Russia again. A successful diplomat, he was transferred in 1738 to Paris as Russian Minister. In France he wrote four more satires (1738-39) and rewrote the previous ones, became Montesquieu's friend, and corresponded with Voltaire. Friends admired this handsome, mild-mannered, and erudite man. He died in Paris, but was later buried in Moscow.

Kantemir was the first important figure of modern Russian literature, a product of Peter's reforms. Being also the first Russian classicist, he imitated Boileau, Horace, Juvenal, and La Bruyère in his satires, which praised enlightenment and criticized, from a patriotic viewpoint, Russian clergy, aristocracy, and bureaucracy for their reluctance to follow the way of Peter's reforms. The life he vigorously depicted was unmistakably Russian, and he can be called "the first . . . artistically conscious realist in Russian literature" (Mirsky). Belinsky praised Kantemir for being "the first to blend poetry

and life." He was also much revered as a literary ancestor of the satirical and critical trends that became fashionable in nineteenth century literature, but he actually had more in common with such eighteenth century satirists as Derzhavin and Fonvizin. Kantemir was little read even during his own century, owing mainly to his antiquated "syllabic" versification, which Tredyakovsky and Lomonosov in the 1730's had successfully repudiated.

A translation of his first satire can be found in Leo Wiener's *Anthology of Russian Literature,* I (1902-1903).

ABOUT: Mirsky, D. S. A History of Russian Literature. [In Russian—see study by A. Sementkovsky.]

V. M.

*KANTEMIR (CANTEMIR), DIMITRIE, Hospodar of Moldavia (October 26, 1673-August 21, 1723), historian and miscellaneous writer, was born in Falciu, in what is now eastern Rumania, the younger son of Constantine Kantemir, governor and subsequently prince of Moldavia. The Kantemirs were a distinguished family of Tatar origin that had settled in Moldavia early in the seventeenth century. That country was under the domination of the Turks, and young Dimitrie was reared in Constantinople where he learned Turkish and acquired a special interest in Turkish music, on which he became an authority. He was well liked in Turkey and was offered the princedom of Moldavia, which he refused in favor of his elder brother Antiochus.

In 1710 Antiochus was deposed, and Dimitrie served in his place for one year as prince of Moldavia. He meanwhile joined forces with Peter the Great, Czar of Russia, in his campaign against the Turks. For his assistance in bringing Moldavia into the Russian fold, Kantemir was made a prince of the Russian empire and received a lifetime pension. He settled in Kharkov and in 1713 moved to Moscow. Here he completed work on his *History of the Growth and Decay of the Othman Empire,* begun in Constantinople some years earlier. In 1714 he was elected to the Berlin Academy. He remained in Russia until his death, at forty-nine, from diabetes.

A mild and affable man, Kantemir was married in 1700, in Moldavia, to Cassandra Cantacuzino, by whom he had six sons and two daughters. She died and in 1718 he

* kän tĕ mēr'

471

married the Russian Princess Troubetzkoy in Moscow. By this marriage he had a daughter.

The History of the Othman Empire, written originally in Latin, was a valuable source book, bringing together material hitherto unavailable to Europeans. The work was not published in Dimitrie's lifetime but was brought to London in manuscript by his son Antiokh Kantemir, who was Russian minister to Britain and himself a well-known Russian poet (see sketch above). It was translated into English by N. Tindal in 1734 and later translated into French and German. Kantemir's other writings reflect the scope and variety of his attainments. They include a book on the Mohammedan religion (written in Russian), a philosophical debate on "The World and the Soul" (in Greek and Moldavian), the first descriptive study of Moldavia (written in Latin), a history of creation (in Latin), a history of the ruling houses of Brancovan and Cantacuzenus, and a number of works on Turkish music.

ABOUT: Tindal, N. *bibliographical sketch in* Kantemir, D. History of the Othman Empire. [In English—Nelson, J. W. Dimitrie Cantemir, Prince of Moldavia: His Life and Writings, unpublished Stanford University dissertation, 1955.]

*KARADŽIĆ, VUK STEFANOVIĆ

(October 26, 1787-January 26, 1864), Serbian lexicographer and folklorist, was born in Tršić, into a family of poor farmers; on his father's side his people were from Herzegovina and on his mother's from Montenegro. Vuk, as he is generally called, had no formal education. However, by intensive reading of everything at hand he was by the age of seventeen considered the most learned man in his region. In 1804, with the outbreak of the Serbian uprising, Vuk joined the insurgents and served for a time with the legendary Hajduk Veljko. On the defeat of the Serbs in 1813 he fled to Vienna and participated in an émigré journal. On the advice of Jernej Kopitar, a Slovene serving in the Austrian Censorship, Vuk began compiling the many folk songs and heroic ballads he knew as an integral part of his rural Serbian heritage. The first volume of these songs appeared in 1814 and was immediately translated into German by J. Grimm. The heroic content and epic nature of the songs was to be of great import for the European romantics. The same year saw the appearance of his Serbian grammar, followed four years later by the first edition of his dictionary.

* kä' rä jïch

472

ary. It was at this time that Vuk married Anna Kraus, a Viennese, a step that was to have a deleterious effect on his career as a Serbian nationalist and reformer.

During much of the rest of his life, Vuk traveled extensively through all parts of what is now Yugoslavia, collecting songs and lexicographic material. He also traveled in Germany, where he met Grimm and Goethe, and in Russia, where he did much to stimulate interest in the South Slavs. From 1820 to 1832 he lived chiefly in Belgrade, serving first as tutor to Prince Milosh and later as president of the Belgrade Magistrate. Here he compiled a basic law code for Milosh and translated the New Testament into modern Serbian. Disappointed by the despotism of Milosh, Vuk fled to Vienna and resumed work on his dictionary and song collections, six volumes of which were eventually gathered. It was during travels of this period that he met the German historian Ranke and gave him much material for his *History of Serbia.*

Throughout the greater part of his life Vuk worked for a reformed Serbo-Croatian orthography. He insisted that the Serbian sector of that language be written as spoken, that all non-distinctive Church Slavic letters still in use be discarded, and that the letter *j* of the Roman alphabet be introduced. The battle over this reform was intense in Serbia; above all, the *j* was felt to be Catholic and a result of Vuk's many connections among the Austrians. Books printed according to his system were forbidden in Serbia from 1832 until 1860, and the Serbian Orthodox Church refused to sanction his translation of the New Testament. Despite the ban, Vuk's works circulated freely and his influence was felt. In 1868, four years after his death, his reform was made official.

In his later years Vuk bought a small estate near his birthplace and took a more active part in the intellectual life of Serbia and in reaching accord with the Croats. At the time of his death in 1864 he was the acknowledged leader of South Slavic philologists. His dictionary has since gone through four editions and is still the standard reference for vocabulary and stress. Physically, Vuk was a striking figure: short, lame, and with great white mustaches, he is invariably pictured with the red cap of his region. Of his two sons, one died young in a military school in Russia, while the other became an officer in the Serbian army.

A number of the ballads collected by Vuk have been translated, chiefly by George Noyes and L. Bacon in *Heroic Ballads of Serbia* (1913), and by Dragutin Subotić in *Yugoslav Popular Ballads* (1932).

ABOUT: [In Serbo-Croatian—Stojanović, L. Život i Rad Vuka Stefanovića.]

N. V.

*KARAMZIN, NIKOLAY MIKHAYLO-VICH (December 1, 1766-May 22, 1826),

Russian writer, was born and raised on the estate of his father, a member of the middle-class landed gentry, in Simbirsk on the middle Volga. His education—tutors at home, foreign boarding schools in Simbirsk and in Moscow, University of Moscow lectures—emphatically bore fruit: few Russians of his time could rival Karamzin's intellectual and cultural refinement, his formidable knowledge of European literatures and languages. His schooling and, no doubt, his own temperament had early disposed him to cherish a cult of "Feeling" and "Nature," mainly German in inspiration. As later translated by Karamzin into literary art, this "new sensibility" brought him spectacular success and recognition as the leader of the sentimentalist movement in Russian literature which had already been launched in the seventies under the stimulus of French sentimental drama, Rousseau, Richardson, Gray, Klopstock and others. In Karamzin's hands Russian sentimentalism assumed its most polished form and definitively replaced classicism as the reigning literary school. Writers and readers, both friends and foes of the new movement alike, acknowledged him the literary giant of his generation.

Karamzin first turned to literature in earnest when, in 1785, he became involved in Russian Freemasonry and collaborated, in Moscow, with N. I. Novikov. The characteristically Masonic pietism of Novikov's publications and of the whole milieu in which he then moved both suited and informed Karamzin's own outlook. To this Masonic period belong his translations of Shakespeare, Lessing, and others, and his first original fiction. In 1789 he broke his ties with the Masons and, having long yearned to visit his "spiritual homeland," undertook an eighteen months' tour through Europe (Germany, Switzerland, France, England). On his return to Russia, in 1790, he founded a literary journal, *Moskovsky Zhurnal,* and there began the publication of his *Pis'ma Russkogo Puteshestvennika* (Letters of a Russian Traveler). The elegant style of the *Letters,*

* kŭ rŭm zyĕn'

KARAMZIN

its cosmopolitanism, but above all its subjective focus ("Here is the mirror of my soul during eighteen months!") enchanted the Russian public. In 1792, in *Moskovsky Zhurnal,* appeared his *Bednaya Liza* (Poor Liza), a story of the seduction and suicide of a serf girl, which created a national sensation. Both works, probably his most famous, inspired scores of imitators. After closing *Moskovsky Zhurnal* in 1792, Karamzin brought out a number of collections of his prose and verse and, in 1801 began to publish *Vestnik Evropy* which became the most popular and influential literary-political journal of the times. In 1804 he abandoned literature proper and devoted the remaining twenty-three years of his life to a monumental *Istoriya Gosudarstva Rossiyskogo* (History of the Russian State) which, with its elegant style and many dramatic passages, was received as enthusiastically as had been his works of fiction; its volumes—eleven were completed in his lifetime—were sold out almost immediately after they appeared. During this period of his life Karamzin enjoyed a position of great dignity and prestige in Russian society, and had before his death already become something of a national shrine.

Karamzin's importance as a writer lies less in the intrinsic artistry of his works than in their effect. He set the stage in some measure for both Russian psychological realism and romanticism. Through his efforts the Russian inventory of literary techniques, themes, and genres was substantially revised and restocked with the paraphernalia of sen-

473

timentalism; above all, he was responsible for the emergence of prose fiction as a canonical branch of Russian literature. Having found the Russian language as it had come through the classicist epoch unsuited to new demands, Karamzin renovated it, basing himself on the spoken language of the upper class and devising new terminology for new concepts. These language reforms were probably his most lasting contribution, influencing as they did the whole subsequent history of the Russian literary language. Of least permanence was his own special brand of sentimentalism, the sweet melancholy and gentle rapture of a sensitive soul, told in a particularly saccharine style—an exciting novelty to his contemporaries but for the modern reader largely unpalatable.

Karamzin's services in promulgating the pre-romantics of Europe, above all those of England and Germany, in Russia, were to a certain extent "reciprocated": he was the first Russian to enjoy a genuine international reputation and almost all his works were translated, some into several European languages. A new English translation of *Letters of a Russian Traveler*, by F. Jonas, appeared in 1957; modern translations of several other works (largely excerpts) are included in L. Wiener's *Anthology of Russian Literature*, II (1903). A translation and analysis of his *Memoir on Ancient and Modern Russia* was published in 1959 (Russian Research Center Studies, 33).

ABOUT: Mirsky, D. S. A History of Russian Literature; Slonim, M. The Epic of Russian Literature. [In Russian—see study by V. V. Sipovsky. In German—by R. Baechtold.]

I. R. T.

KAREL HAVLÍČEK. See HAVLÍČEK, KAREL

KARO, JOSEPH. See CARO, JOSEPH

*KATENIN, PAVEL ALEXANDRO-VICH (December 22, 1792-May 23, 1853), Russian poet, dramatist, translator, and critic, was born on the hereditary estate of his family, Shayovo, Kostroma Gubernia. As was the custom among the aristocracy, Katenin was educated entirely by private tutors, and, at the age of fifteen was qualified to assume a minor post in the Ministry of Education in St. Petersburg. Here he remained until March 1810 when he was transferred to one of the choice regiments of the famous Preobrazhensky Guards. During the War of 1812 he served with distinction at Borodino and elsewhere, and was among the Russian troops occupying Paris in

* kŭ těn′ ĭn

1814. In Paris he made friends with members of the theatrical profession (including the celebrated actor Talma) and gathered data on French acting technique which he passed on to the St. Petersburg theatre.

One of the characters in Pisemsky's *Men of the Forties* is Koptin, a landed proprietor, retired general, and forgotten author, whose speech is that of a nobleman, and whose manner is that of "an Asiatic princeling." Readers of Pisemsky's book did not suspect that the prototype of this sharp-tongued aristocrat with a reputation for "free-thinking, even atheism" was, in fact, Katenin, one of the most prominent and authoritative literary figures in the first third of the nineteenth century in Russia. Katenin had died in complete obscurity a mere fifteen years before Koptin was created in his image. Katenin's literary activity had begun in 1810 when a number of his poems were published in the periodical *Tsvetnick* (The Flower-Garden) under the sponsorship of the translator Martinov. In 1811 Katenin's translation of *Ariane* (the masterpiece of Thomas Corneille, brother of the more famous Pierre) was performed in St. Petersburg. Among his other translations of French drama is one of Marivaux' *Le Jeu de l'Amour et du Hasard*, but while his *Andromache* (1818) may have been inspired by Racine's play, it is an original work.

In 1816 Katenin published a translation, freely adapted, of Bürger's famous ballad "Lenore" under the title "Olga" which deliberately challenged the affected sentimentality of Zhukovsky's rendering ("Liudmilla," 1808). Pushkin, later a close friend of Katenin, found "Olga" much superior to "Liudmilla," and praised the author for having freed Russian poetic diction of its dependence on the standardized figures of speech of the past in favor of a more vital and realistic manner of expression.

Before 1820 he collaborated with Griboyedov on a farce, "The Students," satirizing the artificialities in Zhukovsky's romanticism, and wrote a comedy of his own, "Enmity and Love." Notwithstanding his own essentially romantic tendency, his dramatic works were criticized as "orthodox" because he insisted on maintaining the "unities" of the French classic drama in the formal structure of his plays.

By 1820 he had reached the rank of colonel in the Guards, but his military career was suddenly interrupted by his enforced retirement. Katenin was suspected of harboring free-thinking inclinations and of possible membership in a secret society of liberal tendency. He was in fact a member of the mildly democratic "Union of Salvation," but no facts were ever adduced which could demonstrate his participation in underground political activity. He was certainly no Decembrist, though his friend Griboyedov was to be suspected in connection with the 1825 revolt. Nevertheless, a dossier, "The Indecent Behavior of Retired Colonel Katenin in the Theatre," was presented to the Czar in 1822—Katenin's "indecency" involved his hissing a performance of the actress Semyonova, a favorite of the influential Count Miloradovich—in order to provide a pretext for his banishment from St. Petersburg. Between 1822 and 1825 when his friends managed to obtain permission for him to return to the capital he was unrepentant, but circumspect: "I don't wish to journey to points east," he said. In 1827 he again retired to his estate until 1832 when he reappeared in an effort to get some of his works published. He and Pushkin became friends during this period, and they were elected together to honorary membership in the Russian Academy in 1833.

Katenin was unable to secure publication of his poem "The Genius and the Poet" in which the censor had detected his free-thinking tendency, but in 1834 he published "The Princess Milusha," much admired by Pushkin. Between 1836 and 1838 he was placed in command of the Erevan Regiment at the Kisliar fortress in the Caucasus. From 1838 to the end of his life he lived in retirement, completely out of sympathy with the romantic movement of which he had been an important early exemplar, and completely neglected by his younger contemporaries. His last work, a volume of reminiscences of Pushkin, ignored at the time of publication (1852), was later found to be of considerable value as a source of material on the great poet.

ABOUT: Mirsky, D. A History of Russian Literature.

L. R. & H. H.

KELLER, GOTTFRIED (July 19, 1819-July 15, 1890), Swiss novelist, short-story writer, and poet, was born in Zürich. His father, Rudolf Keller, a poor but industrious turner, died when his son was only five years old. The family was left in needy circumstances, but his mother, by hard work and personal sacrifice, provided the boy with a good elementary education. However, because of a prank against a teacher, he was expelled from school at the age of fifteen.

KELLER

Deciding to become an artist, he studied painting in Munich for two years, until he realized that he had missed his calling and returned home in 1842. During the course of the next six years he gradually turned to literature, publishing in 1846 a volume of poems, *Gedichte,* which received little notice. A government stipend enabled him in 1848 to attend the University of Heidelberg, where he met and was profoundly influenced by the literary historian Hermann Hettner, the anthropologist Jakob Henle, and the philosopher Ludwig Feuerbach, whose ethical and religious ideas Keller adopted.

In 1850 Keller moved to Berlin, where the next five years proved to be the most fruitful of his entire career. He published a second collection of poems, *Neuere Gedichte* (1851), which proved him to be an outstanding lyric poet, and produced his first prose work, the long, autobiographical novel *Der Grüne Heinrich* (1854-55; revised version 1880). This work is an *Entwicklungsroman* or educational novel in the tradition of Goethe's *Wilhelm Meister* and relates the history of its hero's apprenticeship to life. It is one of the outstanding German novels of the nineteenth century, although at the time of its appearance only a few critics recognized its greatness.

Near the end of his stay in Berlin Keller wrote a collection of short stories entitled *Die Leute von Seldwyla* (1856). Among the best-known and most popular works of this group are "Romeo und Julia auf dem Dorfe," his most moving and most beautiful narrative, "Die Drei Gerechten Kammacher," the story that Keller himself considered his finest, and "Spiegel, das Kätchen."

Keller returned to Zürich in 1855, and in 1861 through the mediation of friends was granted the important and responsible position of canton secretary, an office which he filled conscientiously until his retirement in 1876. For more than a decade while in office he wrote nothing, until in 1872 a collection of short stories treating legends of the Virgin and saints appeared under the title *Sieben Legenden.* Unlike his earlier works, this book was an immediate success and established Keller's reputation. In 1874 a second volume of stories was added to *Die Leute aus Seldwyla,* of which the most notable and widely-read is "Kleider Machen Leute." Next followed another cycle of stories, *Züricher Novellen* (1878), which contains two of Keller's finest narratives, "Der Landvogt von Greifensee" and "Das Fähnlein der Sieben Aufrechten." Following the revision of *Der Grüne Heinrich,* Keller wrote *Das Sinngedicht* (1881), a series of stories which humorously depict the search of a young scholar for a congenial mate. His collected poetry, *Gesammelte Gedichte,* was published in 1882, and in 1886 appeared his final work, *Martin Salander,* a novel of modern Swiss political life. Although Keller's reputation had spread slowly, at his death in 1890 he was universally acclaimed throughout German-speaking lands as one of the outstanding literary figures of nineteenth century German literature. The critic R. M. Meyer calls him "the greatest German writer since Goethe."

Keller was a strong, sincere individual, whose art was rooted in a robust and genial worldliness. His vigorous personality and his keen love of life are reflected in the exuberance of his works as well as in his style, which is forceful, direct, and original. He is one of the greatest humorists in the history of German literature, and although his stories frequently point a moral, his didacticism is always tempered with wit and never obtrudes to the detriment of the story. Chief among his other gifts are his talent for characterization and plastic description, and his seemingly inexhaustible inventiveness, which for originality and scope has few equals.

The first translations of Keller's works into English appeared in 1891, when K. F. Kroeker and L. Unwin translated "Kleider Machen Leute" as "Clothes Make the Man," "Die Missbrauchten Liebesbriefe" as "The Abused Love Letters," and "Dietegen." The earliest translation of *Sieben Legenden* was made by M. Wyness in 1911 under the title *Seven Legends,* with subsequent renderings being done by C. H. Handschin (1911) and M. D. Hottinger (1931). In *The German Classics* XIV (1913-15) B. Q. Morgan translated "Ursuld" and "Das Fähnlein der Sieben Aufrechten" as "The Company of the Upright Seven." The same volume includes P. B. Thomas' translations of "Der Landvogt von Greifensee" under the title "The Governor of Greifensee" and "Romeo und Julia auf dem Dorfe" as "A Village Romeo and Juliet." Other versions of "Romeo und Julia auf dem Dorfe" were made by A. C. Bahlmann (1914) and L. Constable (1915), and the work was made into a music drama by F. Delius (1910). In 1917 M. Almon translated "Das Fähnlein der Sieben Aufrechten." W. von Schierbrand translated "Die Drei Gerechten Kammacher" as "Three Decent Combmakers," "Romeo und Julia auf dem Dorfe," and "Dietegen," publishing the three stories under the title *Seldwyla Folks* (1919). Free adaptations of "Spiegel, das Kätchen," "Kleider Machen Leute" and two selections from *Sieben Legenden* were prepared by L. Untermeyer under the title *The Fat of the Cat and Other Stories* (1925). In 1929 *Die Leute von Seldwyla* was translated by M. D. Hottinger as *The People of Seldwyla,* and in 1953 J. Rodale and D. Glixon published a translation of *Legends and People.* *Der Grüne Heinrich* was translated as *Green Henry* by A. M. Holt in 1960. *Martin Salander* appeared, translated by K. Halwas, in 1964.

ABOUT: Hay, M. A Study of Keller's Life and Works; Howald, E. Gottfried Keller; Klenze, C. von, From Goethe to Hauptmann. [In German—see studies by J. Baechtold, B. Bolliger, E. Ermatinger, R. Faesi, A. Köster, H. Maync, B. A. Rowley. In French—by F. Baldensperger.]

D. G. D.

*KELLGREN, JOHAN HENRIK (December 1, 1751-April 20, 1795), Swedish poet and critic, was born in Floby parish in the Swedish province of Västergötland. His father was Jonas Kiellgren (*sic*), a vicar of the peasant class. His mother was Christina Elisabeth Aminoff, of a noble family descending from Russia. From 1768 he studied at the University of Åbo (Finnish: Turku) in southwestern Finland and took his M.A. in 1772. Before and after his graduation he held several positions as a private tutor in Finland. After the completion of a dissertation he was appointed *Docent* in Latin at Åbo. Although he had been impressed by pre-romantic literature ("Ossian," Gessner, Young), he was mainly influenced by the enlightened philosophy in its most radical form, which created in him a pessimistic attitude to life and a scornful opposition to Christianity. Voltaire was his idol. Kellgren's poems from this period were translations, adaptations, and imitations of Latin and French satires and erotic songs.

Kellgren disliked erudite studies and life in a small town. In 1777 he left for Sweden and was able to secure a position as a tutor.

* kĕl' grĕn

The same year he was elected member of the literary society "Utile Dulci," and was soon made co-editor of the influential *Stockholms-Posten*, the mouthpiece of the French Classical School.

After a short time Kellgren succeeded in arresting the attention of King Gustavus III. The royal grace granted him economic independence, the titles Royal Librarian (1780), Royal Secretary (1785), and membership in the Swedish Academy from its foundation (1786). The King used him as a writer of festival poetry and versifier of his opera librettos. Kellgren also wrote elegant Epicurean and erotic poems, as well as odes and satires. In *Mina Löjen* (My Ridicules, 1778), he hurled his stinging satire at conventionalism, pedantry, vanity, and other human frailties, and in *Epikurismen* (Epicureanism, 1778), and other poems he expressed an unabashed sensualism. *Våra Villor* (Our Illusions, 1780), is a frank confession of his nihilistic and materialistic philosophy.

Besides his burdensome services to the king and his lyrical activity, Kellgren displayed a spirited critical activity in verse and prose, in which he vented his ire and irony upon mystics, occultists, fanatics, and wiseacres. Dazzling examples of his skill as satirist and parodist are such poems as *Man Äger Ej Snille för det Man Är Galen* (One Is Not a Genius Because One Is Mad, 1787) with comments in prose; *Ljusets Fiender* (Enemies of Light, 1792), and the incomparable *Dumboms Lefverne* (The Life of a Fool, 1791). But he also attacked more talented poets, e.g., the young Leopold, which resulted in a hot debate. Although Leopold later sided with Kellgren, their feud engendered a lasting bitterness between them. During a whole decade, 1782-92, Kellgren was involved in a fierce literary conflict with Thorild which drew wide attention. Two generations and ideologies, the restricted enlightened refinement and the pre-romantic craving for freedom, fought each other. In this battle, Kellgren's stinging wit and polemic superiority gave him victory over the emotionally robust and sometimes coarse Thorild.

However, Kellgren did not leave the battlefield unaffected. He was driven to reconsideration of his ethical opinions, and his new idealistic view of the calling of a poet as cultural leader and a national conscience brought him nearer to the romantic ideals. Under the impact of the crisis of Enlightenment and the threat of war Kellgren created patriotic

and youthfully enthusiastic poetry, partly directed against the king's adventurous politics, which severed their friendship. In his greatest lyrical poem, *Den Nya Skapelsen* (The New Creation, 1789), he described how the experience of ideal love gave him a vision of the universe as a world of virtue and beauty.

Kellgren's leading position in Swedish literature was terminated by a worsening consumption which ended his life.

Three of Kellgren's major poems, *Den Nya Skapelsen, Ljusets Fiender,* and *Man Äger Ej Snille för det Man Är Galen,* were translated into English by H. W. Longfellow in his *Poets and Poetry of Europe* (1871). A small poem, *The Art of Succeeding,* is included in C. W. Stork's *Anthology of Swedish Lyrics* (1930).

ABOUT: Howitt, W. & M. The Literature and Romance of Northern Europe, II; Winkel Horn, F. History of the Literature of the Scandinavian North. [In Swedish—see studies by M. Abenius, G. Bergh, S. Ek, N. H. Gyllenbåga, O. Herrlin, B. E. Malmström, A. E. Sjöding, and O. Sylwan.]

A. J.

KEMPIS, THOMAS À. See THOMAS À KEMPIS

*KERNER, JUSTINUS ANDREAS CHRISTIAN (September 18, 1786-February 21, 1862), German poet and physician, was born at Ludwigsburg in Württemberg. His father was in government service and died when his son was thirteen. Kerner attended school at Ludwigsburg and Maulbronn; after a brief period of apprenticeship in a factory he attended the medical school of the University of Tübingen. His literary friends there included Ludwig Uhland and Gustav Schwab. In 1808 Kerner was graduated as a doctor of medicine, and after a few years of traveling established a medical practice at Wildbad. In 1813 he married Friederike ("Rickele") Ehmann. Two years later he was appointed district medical officer at Gaildorf and in 1818 received a similar post at Weinsberg where he was to spend the rest of his life. The famous *Kernerhaus* there became the mecca of an assortment of pilgrims, literary and otherwise, ranging from Gustavus IV of Sweden to Friederike Hauffe, a somnambulist and clairvoyant about whom Kerner, who had become increasingly interested in parapsychology, spiritism, and occult phenomena generally, wrote his famous book *Die Seherin von Prevorst* in 1829. In addition to his medical practice and literary

* kĕr′ nĕr

KERNER

pursuits, Kerner was also actively interested in German history and the preservation of national shrines, e.g., Castle "Weibertreu," and was in constant contact with sympathetic rulers and men of letters like Geibel and Görres. In 1851 Kerner, having become blind, retired from his medical practice. His wife died three years later, and Kerner's death occurred at Weinsberg in 1862.

Kerner was one of the most inspired and most beloved poets of the Swabian school of romanticists. His poems are mostly about natural phenomena, death being a frequent theme, and reflect his somewhat melancholy temper and his interest in the supernatural, the demonic, the "night-sides" of nature. There is a simple, folk-like tone to much of his poetry. Among his best-known lyrics are the drinking song "Wohlauf noch Getrunken" and the somber "Der Wanderer in der Sägemühle" (one of Franz Kafka's favorite poems). Kerner's first poems appeared in the *Musenalmanach* of 1807, and then he collaborated with Uhland and Schwab in the *Poetischer Almanach für 1812*. The *Deutscher Dichterwald*, 1813, also contains some of his poems. Kerner published a collection of *Gedichte* in 1826; later poems are included in *Der Letzte Blütenstrauss*, 1852, and *Winterblüten*, 1859. Kerner's verses were set to music by Robert Schumann and Hugo Wolf, among others. His autobiographical works include *Bilderbuch aus Meiner Knabenzeit*, 1849.

Kerner's medical writings include books on animal magnetism, the curative powers of

Württemberg baths, food poisoning, and the influence of sebacic acid on animal organisms, as well as reports on a variety of patients. Kerner seems to have suffused his medicine with superstition and to have had no scruples about introducing pseudo-sciences into an exact science. He was a rather heavy-set, bloated man. He once jokingly compared his broad, withered face to a pumpkin.

Goldner, translated by C. Partridge, appeared in 1829. *The Seeress of Prevorst* was published in 1845 in Catherine Crowe's translation. Selections from Kerner's poetry may be found in numerous anthologies, including A. Baskerville's *The Poetry of Germany* (1853) and James C. Mangan's *Anthologia Germanica* (1845), and *Poems* (1870). His *Letters to Graf Alexander von Württemberg* (ed. L. A. Willoughby) were published in 1938.

ABOUT: Watts, A. Life and Works of Kerner. [In German—see studies by F. Heinzmann, T. Kerner, M. Niethammer, H. Straumann.]

H. Z.

*KHOMYAKOV, ALEXEI STEPANO-VICH (May 1, 1804-September 23, 1860),

Russian poet, philosopher, and theologian, was born in Moscow to a family of the nobility. His early education was supervised by his mother who instilled in her son the pious devotion to the Orthodox Church and the loyalty to Russian national traditions which were to mark his later work. His higher education was continued under the tutelage of the playwright Gendre in St. Petersburg, and was completed in Moscow University from which he was graduated in 1822 with a bachelor's degree in mathematical science.

His youthful enthusiasm led him to attempt to join the Greek uprising against the Turks (1821), which later was to claim the life of Byron, but he was apprehended en route and returned to his family. A commission in a cavalry regiment was obtained for young Khomyakov, and he remained with the regiment at Kherson until 1823 when he was transferred to the Life-Guards in St. Petersburg. He retired from military service in 1825 to travel. He spent a couple of years in Paris where he dabbled in art and worked on a verse-tragedy, *Yermak*. He returned to Russia in 1828 to re-enter the army, taking part in the war against Turkey (1828-29).

After the war he resettled in Moscow, devoting himself to his literary pursuits most of the year but supervising his large estates in Ryazan and Tula during the summers. He again traveled widely during the 1840's, visiting England, Germany and Austria-Hungary. He died of cholera at the age of fifty-six.

* kŏ myŭ kôf'

In the history of Russian literature Khomyakov is recognized as the leader of the Slavophile movement which urged the cultural alienation of Russian letters from the "decadent" contamination of the West. In this movement he was associated with the brothers Kireyevsky, and an early expression of his conviction is to be found in "The Old and the New" (1839). Notwithstanding the essential conservatism of the Slavophiles, their political ideology included recommendations for a gradual freeing of the serfs, public court trials, and the abolition of capital punishment, none of which was likely to endear them to the autocracy.

As evidenced in such articles as "A Study of the I. V. Kireyevsky Papers" (1857), "Modern Phenomena in the Field of Philosophy" (1859), and the "Second Letter on the Philosophy of Y. F. Samarin" (1860), Khomyakov's philosophy tended to become a theology. He considered religion to be the principal motive force of history, and his unfinished work on the philosophy of history, "Notes on World History" (first published 1871-73), is the most complete statement of his views on the subject.

Khomyakov wrote political and religious poetry, a collection of which appeared in 1844. This book, which sounded a clarion call for the unity of all Slav peoples, was translated into the southern and western Slavic languages and was widely hailed as "the poetry of Slavdom." Belinsky's appraisal was that "Khomyakov's considerable and brilliant talent is definitely nonpoetical. . . ." The great critic also condemned the historical tragedy *Yermak* (dealing with the traditional conqueror of Siberia) and *The Usurper Dmitry* for their weaknesses in the development of character and for structural failings.

Modern Soviet criticism of Khomyakov, alluding to such writings as *What Russians Think of Foreigners* (1846) and *The Possibility of the Russian School of Art* (1847), seeks for some positive values in his Slavophilism. His historical and philosophical views are taken to be hopelessly reactionary, but such works as the above which recommend the development of a Russian national culture free of the tendency uncritically to accept foreign theories, and the suggestion that the folklore and other native sources be more fully explored in the creation of this culture are recognized as positive and worth-while aspects of Khomyakov's work. Non-Soviet authorities credit him with leadership in the development of modern Orthodox theology through his many thoughtful contributions in this area. Needless to say, the revolutionary-democrats of Khomyakov's own age, especially Chernyshevsky and Pisarev, had little sympathy with Khomyakov or his ideological succession.

Only one essay by Khomyakov, "The Church Is One," is available in English translation (1948).
ABOUT: Zernov, N. M. Three Russian Prophets.
L. R. & H. H.

*KIELLAND, ALEXANDER LANGE

(February 18, 1849-April 6, 1906), Norwegian novelist, short-story writer, playwright, was born in the city of Stavanger on the Norwegian west coast. His father was Jens Zetlitz Kielland, of a well-to-do merchant family, who lived as a gentleman of leisure. His mother was Christine (Janna) Lange, of an old family of civil servants. Alexander, the third among seven children, grew up in a conservative, orthodox Lutheran, aristocratic home. He went to school in his native town. Having passed his matriculation examination he enrolled at the University of Kristiania (now Oslo) in 1867. He studied law and took his degree in 1871.

During his university years, Kielland also studied literature and was influenced by Heine and particularly Kierkegaard's criticism of the state church and the clergy. He returned home to Stavanger where in 1872 he married Beate Ramsland, daughter of a merchant, Peder Endresen Ramsland, and Pernille Seglem, to whom he had been secretly engaged for several years. Kielland bought a brickyard which he ran for nine years. Beside his administrative work he wanted to orient himself to his own times. In his studies of Dickens, Darwin, Brandes, J. S. Mill's utilitarianism, etc., he met with the problems of modern liberal Europe. Brandes' demand for a living literature of problem discussions greatly affected Kielland's development. His liberal opinions so acquired caused a rupture in his relations with his father.

After attempting a few small literary compositions, Kielland felt that he needed another environment, and in 1878 he went to Paris, where he met Bjørnson and Brandes. In 1879, he published a collection of *Noveletter* (short stories), which at once made him known in Scandinavia. He showed himself even in his first work as a mature master. In his stories he exposed social deficiencies, but

* kĕl′ än

KIELLAND

the elegant and witty style almost turned the edge of his critical irony.

Encouraged by Brandes, Kielland wrote a novel, *Garman & Worse* (1880), in which he used the milieu of his native town and some of his relatives as models for his social satire. The clergy, who in Kielland's opinion used religion for unethical purposes, were the main target for Kielland's indignation. In general, he wanted to encourage those who were dissatisfied with conventional restrictions in society. In the same year he published three small plays, all hymns to Woman, and the following year *Nye Noveletter* (New Short Stories), in which his social criticism was sharper and more incisive than in the first collection.

Kielland's next novel, *Arbeidsfolk* (Laborers, 1881), a direct accusation against Norwegian officialdom and the body of civil servants, is the most aggressively polemical of all his social satires. As an organizer of the work at the brickyard he had learned the problems of the working people, and his sympathy was with them. Kielland's book caused a bitter press debate between radicals and conservatives. The same year Kielland sold his enterprise and settled in Copenhagen for a couple of years, after which he returned to his native town. His next book, *Else* (1881), attacked the moral hypocrisy of the upper classes. In *Skipper Worse* he returned to the attack on civil servants and the church. In the so-called *Lövdahl-Trilogy* including the novels *Gift* (Poison, 1883), *Fortuna*

(1884), and *Sankt Hans Fest* (Midsummer Festival, 1887), Kielland's vitriolic irony hits the formalism of the schools and corruption in business and clerical life. *Professoren* (The Professor, 1888) is the best of his plays.

In 1885, Bjørnson and Jonas Lie requested a poet's pension for him from Parliament. It was refused in three subsequent years. After his return from a stay in Paris, Kielland became editor of *Stavanger Avis* (Stavanger News). In 1891 he was elected mayor of his native town, and in 1902 prefect of the district of Romsdal. Thus he became one of the officials he had criticized so bitterly in his books. His last years were burdened by a heart ailment.

Kielland's two novels *Garman & Worse* and *Skipper Worse* appeared in 1885 in English translation, the former by W. W. Kettlewell, the latter by H. John. W. Archer translated ten short stories under the title *Tales of Two Countries* (1891). *Else* (T. M. M. Dawson) appeared in 1894. Another ten stories were translated in 1897 by C. L. Cassie as *Norse Tales and Sketches*. Kielland's last work, *Omkring Napoleon* (1905), was translated by J. McCabe as *Napoleon's Men and Methods* (1907).

ABOUT: Beyer, H. A History of Norwegian Literature; Columbia Dictionary of Modern European Literature; Grøndahl, I. and Raknes, O. Chapters in Norwegian Literature; Jorgenson, T. History of Norwegian Literature; Topsöe-Jensen, H. G. Scandinavian Literature from Brandes to Our Day. [In Norwegian—see studies by F. Bull, G. Gran, B. Kielland, M. Schjøtt, O. Storstein, A. H. Winsnes. For a complete bibliography 1900-45—see Øksnevad, R. Norsk Litteraturhistorisk Bibliografi.]

A. J.

*KIERKEGAARD, SØREN AABYE (May 5, 1813-November 11, 1855), Danish philosopher and theologian, was born in Copenhagen, the seventh child of Michael Pedersen Kierkegaard, a wealthy retired business man. His mother was Ane Sörensdatter Lund, Michael's second wife, who had served as a maid in the household. In his *Journals* Kierkegaard refers to the year of his birth as one when "many another bad note was put into circulation" (alluding to the severe national bankruptcy that was then gripping Denmark, in the wake of the Napoleonic wars). Certainly one would have to seek far to find a more melancholy childhood and a more despair-laden life than his.

"There must be a guilt upon the whole family, the punishment of God must be on it," Søren wrote in his *Journals* at the age of twenty-five. Early in life he became aware

* kĭr' kĕ gôr

KIERKEGAARD

of a strange discrepancy between his father's material prosperity and his inner despondency. It soon became apparent that the elder Kierkegaard, who had retired at the age of forty to devote himself to the study of philosophy and theology, was obsessed with remorse over some obscure sin for which he feared that God would punish him through his children. Michael Pedersen's apprehensions seemed confirmed when within three years one of Søren's brothers and a sister had died. From then on Michael undertook the education of his youngest son (Georg Brandes has compared them in this respect with the Mills), impressing on young Søren's mind the image of the suffering Christ, imbuing him with a sense of the duty of sacrifice, inspiring him with the conviction that his purpose in life was to lift the burden of guilt from his family. It was not until he was a young man that Søren thought he grasped the cause of his father's spiritual torment. Various evidence led him to conclude that his mother had been raped by his father before their marriage and that he was the product of this illicit act. (He was in fact born only two months after their marriage.)

Søren never received explicit confirmation of his suspicions from his father, but they continued to upset him profoundly. (In his *Journals* he refers to this mental experience as "the great earthquake.") The immediate effect of his "discovery" was to make him a rebel against society. For a brief time he led a life of dilettantism and dissipation (the

"aesthetical" stage of *Either/Or*), neglecting his studies at the University of Copenhagen, where his father had sent him to study theology with the ultimate intention of taking orders. *The Concept of Dread* relates something of his spiritual experience during this period—the discovery of sin, the reliving within himself of Adam's fall, with the consequent resistance of Good. The death of his father in August 1838 left young Kierkegaard a man of independent means. The "earthquake" was followed by an "awakening" in which he began to envisage his life as a mission devoted to the enlightenment of sinful man. "What our age needs is education," he was to write. "And so this is what happened. God chose a man who also needed to be educated, and educated him *privatissime*, so that he might be able to teach others from his own experience." For the next two years Kierkegaard tried to make it up to his father by finishing his course in theology. However, he was destined never to take a living. Instead, his writing became his pulpit.

Kierkegaard's career as a writer derived its initial impetus from his unhappy romance with Regine Olsen, daughter of a state official, to whom he was engaged for a time, but whom he finally renounced in 1841. (He tried to protect Regine by posing as a philanderer, to give the impression that she broke off the engagement.) Because of the severe melancholia to which he was subject, Kierkegaard did not think it fair to foist himself upon a "normal" woman, and he was reluctant besides to have another share his family secret. He was more and more convinced that his life was "ordered" to serve God, and that happiness as man understands it was not to be his. After a brief retreat to Berlin, he plunged into a furor of writing that was to continue unabated until the end of the decade.

Either/Or (1843), Kierkegaard's first book (apart from his university dissertation on Socratic irony), amounted to his own *apologia*. All men, he contends here, are confronted with a moral choice (hence the title) between two disparate ways of life—the "aesthetical," by which Kierkegaard meant the life of the senses and material gratification, and the "ethical," or the life devoted to the attainment of spiritual insight. Don Juan is his archetype of the "aesthetical" man, always searching after new pleasures, never wholly gratified. The "ethical" man is Kierkegaard himself in his "seeking" stage. The title *Either/Or* was meant as an attack on Hegel, the philosopher of synthesis—or Both/And—whom Kierkegaard consistently denounced for attempting to reconcile the temporal and the spiritual worlds. For Kierkegaard man's miserable state results from his having a persistent sense of the eternal while trying to dwell in the finite world. This tension results in the condition he calls *dread* (*angst*), the burden of his next book *The Concept of Dread* (1844). The man who has felt this dread, and yet persists in his pursuit of the "aesthetical" life is in a state which Kierkegaard calls *despair*, the basic theme of *The Sickness unto Death* (1849). Actually both the "aesthetical" and the "ethical" ways of life were inadequate to the attainment of lasting spiritual peace, according to Kierkegaard. His sequel to *Either/Or* called *Stages on Life's Way* (1845) is really a "Neither/ Nor." Here he posits a situation that transcends both the "aesthetical" and the "ethical," namely the "religious" stage, a state of complete self-abnegation which alone makes it possible to realize the eternal life in the natural world. In *Fear and Trembling* (1843) Kierkegaard expresses the joy of humiliation and sacrifice, analogizing his renunciation of Regine Olsen with Abraham's offering up of Isaac—as the kind of sacrifice that yields returns greater than what is lost. In his books Kierkegaard thought of himself as a practitioner of a Socratic "midwifery," and his writing is close in style and technique to the Platonic dialogue thanks to his remarkable ability to personify states of mind and intellectual positions.

Kierkegaard's turbulent emotional life stands out in marked contrast to the uneventfulness of his outer life. Except for four brief trips to Berlin he spent his entire forty-two years in his native Copenhagen. He did not seek fame through his series of meditative writings, written under various pseudonyms such as Victor Eremita and Johannes Climacus, which enabled him to mask his own personality under different *alter egos,* but they brought him acclaim from the educated public. Nevertheless by the middle 1840's he might well have put down his pen to take a living in a remote part of the country, had not circumstances propelled him into controversy.

In 1846 Kierkegaard became something of a public figure through a journalistic pamphlet war. This began with his attack on a popular political journal *The Corsair* for what he considered its cheap rabble-rousing techniques. The editor, Mëir Goldschmidt, who actually had been one of Kierkegaard's staunchest admirers, was provoked by this thrust to print in his paper a caricature representing the philosopher as a dreamy-eyed dwarf. Goldschmidt's lampoon was certainly very much on Kierkegaard's mind when shortly thereafter he published one of his more vituperative books, *The Present Age,* a tirade against mass taste and mass opinion that anticipates Ortega y Gasset. "A public is everything and nothing, the most dangerous of all powers and the most insignificant," he wrote, and added a little further on: "The Press is an abstraction which in conjunction with the passionless and reflective character of the age produces that abstract phantom: a public which in turn is really the leveling power."

However, Kierkegaard's most vehement and most far-reaching polemics were reserved for his attack on the Church, which occurred during the last year of his life. In *The Present Age* he had denounced the clergy who live too much in the world and follow majority opinion. Although he very much admired Bishop Jakob Peter Mynster, the Primate of the Church of Denmark, a scholar of wide culture who had been a close friend of his father's, he grew critical of him for his loftiness and his cultivation of the wealthy and fashionable elements of the Church. But it was with Bishop Martensen, who succeeded to the Primacy after Mynster's death in 1854, that Kierkegaard openly clashed. Martensen was an eminent theologian, author of a treatise entitled *Christian Dogmatics,* and generally noted for his theoretic, systematic, and hierarchic approach to religion and church organization. Martensen ran counter to Kierkegaard's firmest convictions—that it is not by intellect alone that man becomes a Christian, but through an intense, passionate search of his whole being after "inwardness" (*inderlighed*). "Oh the sins of passion and the heart—how much nearer to salvation than the sins of reason," reads one of his most poignant passages. In Martensen's teachings Kierkegaard saw an obstacle to the attainment of truth as serious as the "aesthetic" obstacle —namely the "speculative" trap. His attacks on Martensen were first printed in a journal called *The Instant,* of which nine issues came out, and subsequently reached publication as *Attack upon "Christendom."* A tenth issue was ready for publication when Kierkegaard suddenly collapsed in the street, apparently from mental exhaustion, and died shortly afterwards in the hospital to which he was removed. The final entries in his *Journals* begin: "The purpose of this life is—to be brought to the highest pitch of world weariness."

Although Kierkegaard's strange, tormented, beautiful books attracted the enlightened of his day, and exerted some literary influence during the time (particularly on Ibsen whose stern and uncompromising preacher Brand is said to be modeled on him), it is to the twentieth century that he speaks most searchingly and most intimately. He is the greatest modern exponent of the philosophy known as Existentialism, which emphasizes Man's active will and freedom of choice as well as his obligation to meet moral experience directly and totally. To Reinhold Niebuhr he is "the profoundest interpreter of the psychology of the religious life . . . since St. Augustine." In the literary world his shadow hovers over that group of French intellectuals headed by Jean Paul Sartre and the late Albert Camus, whose philosophy of "freedom" and "engagement" has been termed "Kierkegaard without God." "Not upper light, but the sweet dark charmed him," in the words of the poet Mark Van Doren. ". . . Yet many listened and wept. His thoughts were tears."

Following a long period of neglect, all of Kierkegaard's major writings have become available in the past twenty-five years, just about a century after they were written. *Either/Or* was translated in 1944 by David F. Swenson and Lillian Marvin Swenson (Vol. I) and Walter Lowrie (Vol. II). Walter Lowrie translated in addition *The Point of View of My Work as an Author* (1939), *Stages on Life's Way* (1940), *Fear and Trembling* (1941), *The Sickness unto Death* (1941), and *Attack upon "Christendom"* (1944). David Swenson also translated *Philosophical Fragments* (1936) and *Concluding Unscientific Postscript* (1941). The *Journals* are available in a translation by Alexander Dru, who also collaborated with Walter Lowrie in the translation of *The Present Age* (1940). *Works of Love* was translated by Howard and Edna Hong in 1962. The *Meditations* were recently translated by T. H. Croxall. A good introduction for the uninitiated is *A Kierkegaard Anthology*, edited by Robert Bretall (1946). A bibliography of English translations of Kierkegaard, compiled by H. C. Woodbridge, was published in the *American Book Collector*, XII (1961).

ABOUT: Brandt, F. Sören Kierkegaard; Collins, J. The Mind of Kierkegaard; Grene, M. Dreadful Freedom; Haecker, T. Kierkegaard the Cripple; Hohlenberg, J. Sören Kierkegaard; Hubben, W. Four Prophets of Our Destiny; Jaspers, K. Reason and Existenz; Lowrie, W. Kierkegaard; Rohde, P. P. Sören Kierkegaard: The Father of Existentialism; Usher, A. Journey Through Dread.

R. A. C.

---

*KINKEL, GOTTFRIED (August 11, 1815-November 12, 1882), German poet, was born at Oberkassel, the son of a pastor. He studied theology at the universities of Bonn and Berlin and taught church history as a

* kĭng′ kĕl

Privatdozent at the latter institution. He became interested in art on a trip to France and Italy in 1837, and having grown disillusioned with religion, took his degree in art history. In 1843 he married the writer Johanna Mockel, whose best-known work is the novel *Hans Ibeles in London* (1860). Kinkel produced the volume *Geschichte der Bildenden Künste bei den Christlichen Völkern* (1845) and was appointed the following year Professor of Art and History at the University of Bonn. During the Revolution of 1848 he became an ardent champion of democracy and spread his views through the *Bonner Zeitung* (1848-49), which he edited. In 1849 he was wounded in a revolt in Baden and was sentenced to life imprisonment. With the aid of a devoted student, Carl Schurz, he escaped to England in 1850. Except for a lecture tour to the United States, he worked in London until 1866 as a teacher and as editor of his own German language newspaper *Hermann* (1859-66). Following the death of his wife in 1866, Kinkel taught at the *Poly-Technikum* in Zürich, where he died in 1882.

Kinkel began his literary career with a volume of poems, *Gedichte* (1843). His reputation, which was exaggerated in his lifetime because of his colorful exploits, rests mainly on the successful verse epic *Martin der Schütz* (1846). This work, which became exceptionally popular with German youth, revived interest in the epic form and was widely imitated by other German writers. Additional notable works include the peasant story *Margaret* (1847), the epic *Der Grobschmied von Antwerpen* (1868), the tragedy *Nimrod* (1868), and a prose idyll on Greece, *Tanagra* (1883).

F. Hellman translated *Tanagra* into English in 1893. Selections of Kinkel's poetry are contained in A. Baskerville, *The Poetry of Germany* (1853).

ABOUT: DeJonge, A. R. Gottfried Kinkel as Political and Social Thinker. [In German—see studies by M. Bollert, O. Henna am Rhyn, J. Joesten, and O. Mausser.]

D. G. D.

---

*KINKER, JOHANNES (January 1, 1764-September 16, 1845), Dutch philosopher, critic, and poet, was born at Nieuwer-Amstel. He pursued medical and legal studies at Utrecht, evidently without financial worries. He began his law career in 1788 in The Hague but five years later (1793) he went on to Amsterdam where association with an active group of young intellectuals

* kĭng′ kĕr

broadened his horizons. He joined in the sharp satirical, social, and political criticism springing up among the members of a liberal club, Concordia et Libertate, whose activity was a reflection of the contemporary upheaval (French Revolution).

This socio-political concern plus the gospel of philosophical enlightenment coming from Germany (Kant) were the two great formative influences in Kinker's intellectual life. Among his close friends was the brilliant but erratic poet and critic Willem Bilderdijk. He began to write the incisive critiques of literature and writers which gained for him the widespread attention of the reading public. He founded the periodical *De Post van den Helikon* and wrote semi-philosophical poetry in the vein of Schiller, Klopstock, and Herder. Of these it has been said that the philosopher overwhelms the poet. Whereas the lofty Schiller aims at harmony between the analytical intellect and the poetic heart, Kinker is apparently unaware of such a polarity; often the result is a heaviness expressed in swollen rhetoric.

Professor C. G. N. De Vooys regards Kinker as of considerable consequence as a critic: the *Proeve eener Hollandsche Prosodia* (1810) reveals "a musical ear and feeling for poetic rhythm far in advance of his contemporaries." Kinker's translations of Schiller's *Jungfrau von Orleans* and *Maria Stuart* were intended to combat prevailing theatrical taste, then heavily under the influence of the Germans Iffland and Kotzebue; these pieces were not staged however.

Kinker's activities included a patriotic concern for country and countrymen. The hardships and sorrows occasioned by the French occupation of Holland elicited the effective *Stille Bemoediging* (Quiet Encouragement); in 1813 he courageously declared himself openly against the oppressors. He rejoiced in the fall of Napoleon and enthusiastically worked toward bringing about a real union of southern and northern Netherlands. These efforts won him royal favor and the appointment as Professor of Dutch Language and literature at the University of Liège. Here Kinker's enthusiasm and charm were able to convert initial suspicion into great popularity. However, the final separation of south (Belgium) and north in 1830 forced him to return to Amsterdam where he remained active as independent author and critic until his death.

Kinker's poetry, *Gedichten*, was published in 1819-21 in three volumes; in 1877 J. van Vloten issued a supplement of previously un-

published poetical and essayistic material. Of significance among his philosophical writings are his exposition of the Kantian philosophy (*Proeve eener Opheldering van de Kritiek der Zuivere Rede*, 1799-1801) and the posthumously published (1850) *Essai sur le Dualisme de la Raison Humaine*. His interest in language, reflected in *Inleiding eener Wijsgeerige Algemeene Theorie der Talen* (1817), led ultimately to a clash with the theories of his eccentric friend Bilderdijk.

ABOUT: [In Dutch—see studies by J. A. Rispens, M. C. van Hall.]

C. K. P.

*KISFALUDY, KÁROLY (or CHARLES) (February 6, 1788-November 21, 1830), Hungarian dramatist and man of letters, was born in Téte in a well-to-do family. His mother died in giving birth to him and as a result his father developed an antipathy for the child. His early years were unhappy, and as soon as he was old enough—barely sixteen—he left home to enlist in the army. In the next five years he saw service in Italy, Serbia, and Bavaria. He fought with bravery and won distinction at the battle of Leoben in May 1809.

Kisfaludy's long absence from his native land almost alienated him from its culture and traditions, but it also broadened his experience and his outlook. He was gifted in painting as well as literature, and seriously considered becoming an artist. In 1812, after a disappointment in love, he gave up his army commission, thereby further antagonizing his father, who disinherited him. Kisfaludy proceeded to Vienna where he studied painting, and he later continued his art studies in Italy. He had begun writing while still in the army —producing one tragedy and a number of martial songs. While an art student in Vienna he wrote another tragedy. But it was not until he returned home to Hungary, settling in Pest in 1817, that he at last established himself and simultaneously created the first national Hungarian drama.

He won fame in 1819 with *Ilka*. Audiences clamored for more plays, and Kisfaludy turned them out with amazing rapidity and success. For his materials he drew upon the traditions and history of the Magyars, thereby breathing life into Hungarian national literature and launching the Hungarian romantic movement. He studied Shakespeare and Goethe, and polished his own style. Indeed, he excelled not only in drama but also in

* kĭsh' fŏ lŏŏ dĭ

lyric poetry—his poem *Mohác* has been called "the finest modern poem in elegiac couplets" (W. Kirkconnell).

Perhaps Kisfaludy's major achievement was his founding with his brother Sándor (see sketch below) of the periodical *Aurora* in 1822. This lively journal attracted talented young writers from all over Hungary and provided a center for nineteenth century Hungarian intellectual life. He himself contributed ballads, short pieces, and comic stories—the latter, like his stage comedies, revealing a robust sense of humor and a keen knowledge of character. Kisfaludy's promising career was halted abruptly at forty-two by consumption. On his death-bed in Pest he was notified of his election to the Hungarian Academy. His collected works, in ten volumes, were published in 1831. Six years after his death the Kisfaludy Tárasag, the Hungarian literary society, was founded in his honor.

Kisfaludy's plays have not been translated into English, but selections from his poems appear in English translation in Sir John Bowring's *Poetry of the Magyars* (1830) and in W. Kirkconnell's *The Magyar Muse* (1933).

ABOUT: Bowring, J. Poetry of the Magyars; Kirkconnell, W. The Magyar Muse.

*KISFALUDY, SÁNDOR (or ALEXANDER) (September 27, 1772-October 28, 1844), Hungarian poet and man of letters, was the elder brother of Károly Kisfaludy (see sketch above). He was born in Sümeg and educated in Raab and in Pressburg where he studied philosophy and jurisprudence. In 1793 he enlisted in the Life Guards in Vienna and embarked on a dashing and romantic army career. Three years later, however, he became involved in a scandal and was transferred to Italy. Stationed in Milan he was captured by Napoleon's troops and sent as a prisoner of war to Vaucluse in Provence. Here he began to steep himself in Petrarch and fell deeply but hopelessly in love with a French girl—both circumstances providing the inspiration for his greatest poetic work, the *Himfy* lyrics.

Kisfaludy won his freedom and his release from the army in 1799 and returned to Hungary. Here, in the next year, he married Roza Szégedy and settled with her in a country house near Lake Balaton, the scene of some of his romantic epics. In 1801 he published the first part of *Himfy*, a series of exquisite love lyrics, short songs varied with canzonets in the Petrarchan style. "No book

was ever known to produce such an impression in Hungary as was awakened by this volume," Sir John Bowring wrote. The first part was sorrowful and treated of disappointment in love, but in the second part of *Himfy*, published in 1807, the hero's love is requited and the spirit of the poems is joyful.

Kisfaludy also wrote ballads, tales, and novels, giving a spirited picture of Hungarian country life. His plays, however, were total failures. With his brother Károly he founded *Aurora*, the famous literary periodical. A lesser figure than his younger brother, he is nevertheless remembered for his moving and sincere love poetry and considered to be "the first great romantic Hungarian poet." His first wife died, and in 1834 he married Amalia Vajda. He died at seventy-two in his birthplace of Sümeg.

Brief English translations of his poems appear in Sir John Bowring's *Poetry of the Magyars* (1830) and W. Kirkconnell's *The Magyar Muse* (1933).

ABOUT: Bowring, J. Poetry of the Magyars; Kirkconnell, W. The Magyar Muse.

*"KIVI, ALEKSIS" (pseudonym of **ALEKSIS STENVALL**) (October 10, 1834-December 31, 1872), Finnish writer, was born in Palojoki, the eldest of five children of a peasant family. His father was Eerik Juhana Stenvall, a tailor, and a taciturn man somewhat given to drinking. The family was poor; indeed poverty darkened much of Kivi's short life. But he was a precocious child, and showed such great promise that he was given an education, first in his native village; then, at seventeen, he was sent to Helsingfors for further study. On his own he read widely and was most impressed and influenced by the Bible, Shakespeare, *Don Quixote*, and the great Finnish national epic the *Kalevala*.

A Finnish national literature was only beginning to emerge in the middle of the nineteenth century. From the Middle Ages until that time Finland had been under Swedish domination. It was the work of the Finnish linguist Elias Lönnrot in 1835-36 which restored the *Kalevala*. Lönnrot was a professor of Finnish literature at the University of Helsingfors where Kivi studied under him. He also studied aesthetics and dramatic history under the distinguished Swedish professor Cygnaeus. His first major poetic effort (and also the first original Finnish tragedy) was drawn from the *Kalevala—Kulervo*

---

* kĭsh' fŏ lōō dĭ

* kĭ' vĭ

(1859), the story of a tragic hero, his struggles for freedom, and his suicide. Though the work is poorly constructed, weighed down with subplots and digressions, it shows serious literary purpose, and for it Kivi received a prize of 600 marks from the Finnish Literary Society.

Kivi's struggles with poverty were partly relieved in 1864 when a well-to-do woman, Charlotte Lönnqvist, became his patroness. She gave him a home on her country estate and here, from 1864 to 1871 he lived and wrote his best works. These include a lively and very popular comedy, *Nummisuutarit* (Shoemakers of the Heath, 1864); a mystical sacred drama set in the times of Christ, *Lea* (1864); a collection of poems, *Kanervala* (Land of the Heathen, 1866); a drama *Kihlaus* (Fugitives, 1867); a dramatic idyll *Yö ja Päivä* (Night and Day, 1867); and his masterpiece, *Seitsemän Veljestä* (Seven Brothers, 1870).

Kivi labored long and hard over *Seven Brothers*, rewriting it at least three times. The story is set in the wild forests of Finland and has not one hero but seven—brothers who perform their heroic tasks in nature. Their adventures, their battles with wild animals, their struggles for survival against climate, hunger, and their own souls, are the subject of the story. Ultimately, after ten years in the wilderness, they return to civilization, mature, self-possessed, ready to settle down to peaceful lives. Whether read as an allegory of the reconciliation of natural man to civilization or simply as an exciting romantic adventure story, *Seven Brothers* is a remarkable book. When first published it was not well received, but after Kivi's death the book gained wider and more favorable reputation, and he came to be recognized as the greatest prose stylist writing in Finnish and a founder of modern Finnish literature. His death was premature and tragic. Always restless and unhappy, he suffered increasingly from mental illness. He died in 1872 in his brother's house in Tuusula. His last work was a drama, *Margareta* (1871). His selected works were published in two volumes in 1877-78 by the Finnish Literary Society.

The English translation of *Seven Brothers* was made by A. Matson in 1929. A one-act play called *The Betrothal, or Eva* was translated by R. Cowl in the *Dublin Review*, October-December 1926.

ABOUT: Dublin Review, October-December 1926; Godenhjelm, B. F. Handbook of the History of Finnish Literature.

*KLEIST, (BERND) HEINRICH (WILHELM) VON** (October 18, 1777-November 21, 1811), German dramatist, short-story writer, poet, was born at Frankfurt an der Oder, son of an army captain and descendant of a famous Prussian military family which numbered eighteen generals among its members. Both parents died early, his father, Joachim Friedrich von Kleist, in 1788 and his mother, Juliane Ulrike von Pannwitz, in 1793. One of five children, Kleist felt closest to his sister Ulrike, who showed him the greatest understanding of anyone in the family, and who through life gave him the most encouragement and help. Until 1788 he was tutored at home by a young theologian named Martini; thereafter he studied in Berlin in the home of the clergyman S. H. Catel. In accordance with the wishes and tradition of the family, he entered the army in 1792, although he felt no inclination for an officer's career. He served in various grades from corporal to lieutenant, and participated in the siege of Mainz and the Palatinate Campaign (1793-95). Terming the army a "living monument of tyranny" and finding it impossible to reconcile his concepts of humanity with his military duties, he resigned his commission in 1799.

Kleist had been increasingly attracted toward intellectual pursuits, and in April 1799 he entered the University of Frankfurt. Although he enrolled to study law, his real interests became mathematics, physics, and philosophy. At this time he felt that "culture was the only goal worth striving for" and that "truth was the only riches worth possessing." Kleist did nothing in a casual way, but uncompromisingly sought the extreme in all things. He could never accept less than the ideal, and this was true for his period of study as well as for everything he later attempted. When the study of Kant's philosophy proved the futility of ever hoping to learn absolute truth, Kleist experienced an intellectual crisis (1801), which brought him to the point of despair and destroyed all interest in further study.

While still a student Kleist became engaged to Wilhelmine von Zenge, the daughter of a general. When she refused to follow him to a proposed idyllic peasant existence in the Swiss Alps he broke the engagement. Kleist never married. After brief trips to Würzburg and Paris, he traveled to Switzerland in 1801, where he met the novelist Heinrich Zschokke, the publisher Heinrich Gessner, and Ludwig Wieland, the son of the famous German

* klīst

KLEIST

author. It was during the seclusion and happiness of his stay among these congenial friends that Kleist began to write, producing the five-act drama *Die Familie Schroffenstein* (1803). This pessimistic tragedy, which portrays man as the powerless victim of fate, utilizes the Romeo and Juliet theme, and also reveals the influence of Rousseau. At this same time Kleist also received the inspiration for the masterly realistic comedy *Der Zerbrochene Krug* (1806), a play which was not divided into acts, but which was written as one continuous scene. The action is presented analytically by means of a court trial at which the judge, who is the true culprit, is eventually found out. It is recognized today as the greatest German comedy. However, the first performance of this work, which was presented by Goethe at Weimar in 1808, failed completely, because of poor acting and faulty stage management. Unfortunately, Kleist's impulsive nature and lack of restraint aroused an instinctive antipathy in Goethe, who displayed little understanding or sympathy for the struggling young dramatist. The lack of recognition or encouragement of Germany's greatest author was of tragic seriousness for Kleist.

The last decade of Kleist's life consisted largely of economic hardship and artistic disillusionment. His inner torment during these years is reflected in the restless, wandering existence which he led, and in the frequency with which he initiated and then abandoned various projects. As he wrote to his sister at the time of his death: "The truth is, there

was no help for me on earth." His travels took him to Weimar, Leipzig, Dresden, Switzerland, Upper Italy, and finally to Paris in 1804. Here he reached a low point of despair because of his inability to complete the tragedy *Robert Guiskard,* the drama with which he hoped to wrest the laurel wreath from Goethe's brow, and in a moment of extreme depression he burned his manuscripts. Later he attempted to rewrite the drama from memory, but completed only a fragment. Considering death the only solution to his misery, he left Paris to join Napoleon's army in order to die on the battlefield, but physical collapse prevented him from carrying out this plan. After being assisted back to Berlin, he was persuaded by Ulrike to accept a minor civil service position in Königsberg, which he held until a small pension granted by Queen Louise enabled him to devote all of his time to writing. For a while he found peace of mind, and the years 1805-1809 became the most fruitful creative period of his career. He produced *Amphytrion* (1807), *Penthesilea* (1808), and some of his finest short stories. *Amphytrion* was begun as a translation from Molière, but Kleist imparted to the theme a greater psychological depth, and infused the comic plot with elements of tragedy. *Penthesilea*, like *Der Zerbrochene Krug*, is not divided into acts, but consists of a single lengthy scene of the conflict between the Amazon queen and Achilles. This tragedy contains some of Kleist's most powerful poetic language and reveals his psychological perceptiveness in its analysis of the hidden wellsprings of the strongest and subtlest human emotions. Attempting prose for the first time, Kleist produced two short stories—"Das Erdbeben in Chili," "Die Marquise von O,"—and the first part of his greatest narrative work, *Michael Kohlhaas* (1811), which points the moral that even a righteous action, when carried to extremes, can lead to guilt. Strikingly in his literary works Kleist recognized the danger in lack of moderation, yet in life he was unable to compromise.

After the rout of the Prussian army at Jena and the entry of Napoleon's troops into Berlin, Kleist moved to Dresden. On the way he was arrested by the French as a spy and imprisoned for months, until Ulrike effected his release. In Dresden, he and his closest friend Adam Müller founded the literary journal *Phöbus* (1808-09), which is important only for the works of Kleist which appeared in it. Here appeared for the first time most of the works already mentioned, as well as the short story "Die Verlobung in Sankto Domingo," various lyric poems, and the medieval drama *Kätchen von Heilbronn,* one of Kleist's most popular plays and the only one of his works to be performed several times during his lifetime.

The occupation of Germany incited Kleist to write violent patriotic lyrics, which no one dared publish, and the nationalistic dramas *Die Hermannschlacht* (1809) and *Der Prinz von Homburg* (1811), which no theatre would venture to perform. Both plays are based on historical events: the former, using the theme of Hermann's defeat of the Romans in 9 A.D., preaches German unity and the necessity of a revengeful war against the tyranny of Napoleon; the latter depicts the repulsing of the Swedes at the battle of Fehrbellin in seventeenth century Prussia and aims at glorifying the House of Hohenzollerns. With its sure-handed composition, vivid characterization, and brilliant economy of means, *Der Prinz von Homburg* is Kleist's finest drama and one of Germany's greatest historical plays.

During the year 1811 Kleist was subjected to ever-increasing difficulties. His plays were refused everywhere, and he was no closer to achieving recognition. His family regarded him as a failure. The death of Queen Louise brought an end to his pension, and he was refused a renewal of his army commission. A final venture, the daily newspaper *Die Abendblätter* (1810-11), also failed. At this time he resolved to commit suicide, a deed he had often contemplated, and in Henrietta Vogel, a woman afflicted with incurable cancer, he found a companion in death. On November 21, 1811, after writing cheerful farewell notes to his family, Kleist shot Henrietta and then himself on the shore of Lake Wannsee near Berlin.

Kleist was largely ignored until Ludwig Tieck published the first edition of his collected works in 1826. Since that time his reputation has grown steadily, until today he is justly placed by the side of Goethe and Schiller as one of the greatest dramatists that Germany has ever produced. In addition his short stories rank with the best works of their type. He belonged to no literary school, and although his work bears the influence of Shakespeare and Schiller, no one was more truly original or individualistic than he. His sense of form was unerring: not a word is wasted in his dramas, and his short stories with their emphatic, highly intricate yet concise style, prove him a master of crowding a world of passion into the most succinct and seemingly objective narrative. He main-

tained a standard of excellence throughout the totality of his work that has rarely been equaled and produced little that is mediocre or negligible.

Die Familie Schroffenstein was translated into English as *The Feud of the Schroffensteins* in 1916 by M. J. and L. M. Price. *Der Zerbrochene Krug* appeared as *The Broken Pitcher* in the series Poet Lore Plays. *Das Kätchen von Heilbronn* was translated as *Kate of Heilbronn* by E. B. Impey in 1841 and by F. E. Pierce in 1927. The first translation of *Der Prinz von Homburg* was made in 1875 by F. Lloyd and W. Newton. Subsequent translations were made by H. Hagedorn in 1913 and C. E. Passage in 1956. The short story "Die Heilige Cäcilie" was translated as "St. Cecilia" by J. Oxenford in 1844. Various translations and abridgments of *Michael Kohlhaas* were made by J. Oxenford in 1844, F. Lloyd and W. Newton in 1875 and by F. H. King in 1913. V. Lange translated the short story "The Earthquake in Chile" in 1952. A translation of Kleist's letters appeared in 1875.

ABOUT: Blankenagel, J. C. The Attitude of Heinrich von Kleist toward the Problems of Life; *also* The Dramas of Heinrich von Kleist; Brandes, G. Main Currents of Nineteenth Century Drama, II; Hamburger, M. Reason and Energy; March, R. Heinrich von Kleist; Silz, W. Heinrich von Kleist's Conception of the Tragic; Stahl, E. L. Heinrich von Kleist's Dramas; Zweig, S. Heinrich von Kleist (*in* Master Builders). [In German—see studies by F. Braig, F. Gundolf, G. Minde-Pouet, H. Myer-Benfy, H. Sembdner, R. Wirkop, H. Wolf.]

D. G. D.

"KLIKSPAAN." See KNEPPELHOUT, JOHANNES

*KLINGER, FRIEDRICH MAXIMILIAN VON (February 15, 1752-February 25, 1831), German dramatist and novelist, was born in Frankfurt, the son of humble parents. He grew up in poverty and received his early education at parish expense. Financial assistance from Goethe enabled him to attend the University of Giessen, where he spent more time writing plays than he did learning law. In 1776 he journeyed to Weimar hoping for employment at court, but nothing came of this expectation, and he was forced to accept the position of playwright with the Seyler theatrical company. He toured Germany with this group for two years, until, tiring of this life, he enlisted as a lieutenant in a reserve corps during the War of the Bavarian Succession. With the sudden end of the war through the Peace of Teschen (1779), he was again unemployed, and for a time considered traveling to America as a mercenary. However, through the intercession of Prince Eugen von Württemberg, Klinger received a commission in

* klĭng' ẽr

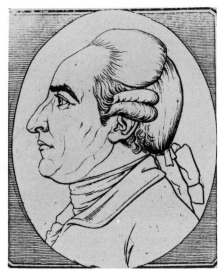

KLINGER

manuscript. Klinger wrote very quickly and in rapid succession produced *Die Neue Arria* (1776), *Simsone Grisaldo* (1776), and *Der Wirrwarr, oder Sturm und Drang* (1776), the play from whose subtitle the "Storm and Stress" movement received its name. Klinger himself regarded *Der Wirrwarr* as his finest work.

Klinger's Russian period reveals a complete contrast to his early life and is subdued and reserved in tone. The transition is evident in the classical dramas *Medea in Korinth* (1791), and *Medea auf dem Kaukasos* (1791). His major endeavor during his mature period was a cycle of nine novels in which he intended to present the totality of his experiences and thoughts. The most important of these works are *Fausts Leben, Thaten und Höllenfahrt* (1791), *Geschichte eines Teutschen der Neuesten Zeit* (1798), *Der Weltmann und der Dichter* (1798) and *Betrachtungen und Gedanken über Verschiedene Gegenstände der Welt und der Literatur* (1803-05).

Die Neue Arria was translated anonymously in 1795. *Reisen vor der Sündflut* was translated by L. Johnson in 1796 as *Travels Before the Flood*. G. Borrow translated *Faust's Life, Deeds, and Journey to Hell* in 1825.

ABOUT: Garland, H. B. Storm and Stress; Sandbach, F. E. Klinger's Medea Dramas and the German Fate Tragedy *in* German Studies Presented to Professor H. G. Fiedler. [In German—see studies by W. Kurz, F. Prosch, M. Rieger, E. Schmidt, O. Smoljan.]

D. G. D.

a Russian marine battalion and rose eventually to the rank of lieutenant-general. The remainder of his life was spent in Russia, where he was ennobled in addition to other honors. He married the daughter of a Russian general in 1790. He served in Dorpat as director of the military academy and later as curator of the university. He died at Dorpat at the age of seventy-nine.

Klinger is a typical writer of the *Geniezeit* or "Storm and Stress" period in German literature. Although he was no literary genius and totally lacked any lyric gift, he did possess a talent for drama and a sure feeling for the theatre. He was strongly influenced by Rousseau and by the creed of individualism prevalent at this time. All of his plays, which he described as "explosions of youthful spirit and ill-humor," are characterized by loose construction, exaggerated characters, improbabilities of plot, and bombastic, exclamatory dialogue. Frequent use is made of dashes, exclamation points, and fragmentary sentences to convey a sense of heightened emotion.

His first plays, *Otto* (1774) and *Das Leidende Weib* (1775), were tentative productions and so highly imitative of Goethe and Lenz respectively that Klinger omitted them from the first edition of his collected dramas (1786-87). His finest drama is *Die Zwillinge* (1776), a tragedy dealing with the theme of fratricide. This play was written for a competition sponsored by the actor Schröder in Hamburg and won the prize for the best

*KLOPSTOCK, FRIEDRICH GOTTLIEB (July 2, 1724-March 14, 1803), German poet, founder of free German verse and reformer of German literature, was born in Quedlinburg, a Prussian town near the border of Upper Saxony. His father, a highly respected and moderately well-to-do lawyer, was opposed to the pedantic, antiquated school methods of his time, and in 1732 he moved his family to the estate of Friedeburg on the Saale, where his children might grow up in greater freedom and closer to nature. Here young Friedrich, the oldest of seventeen children, received private instruction from a theological student and developed an early reverence, at times bordering on religious ecstasy, for nature. After three years at the *Gymnasium* in Quedlinburg, he was admitted to the celebrated classical school of Schulpforta, where he excelled in classics. His favorite poet was Horace, whose strophic forms (chiefly Alcaic and Asclepiad)

* klöp' shtök

KLOPSTOCK

were later to serve as the basis for his own, metrically freer, odes. Among contemporary German poets he most admired the Anacreontic Friedrich Hagedorn.

In 1745 Klopstock enrolled at the University of Jena to study theology, carrying with him his grand ambition from his Schulpforta schooldays: to create a German heroic epic worthy to stand alongside the *Odyssey* and *Paradise Lost*. Two early themes, the life of Columbus (suggested by his friend Bodmer) and that of the Emperor Henry I (Henry the Fowler), he finally rejected in favor of the Messiah. Klopstock's own religious fervor, his admiration of Milton (known to him through Bodmer's translation of *Paradise Lost*), and his rejection of Gottsched's dictum of rationality and utilitarianism for poetry in favor of Bodmer's and Breitinger's plea for the unfettered *Phantasie* made his choice of the figure of Christ a natural one. The question of verse form for this monumental epic was solved, so Klopstock first thought, by Bodmer, who had rejected the German alexandrine as being too cumbersome, the hexameter as too Greek and hence not German enough, and who had himself turned to prose for his Milton translation.

After one year Klopstock left the noisy but intellectually tame atmosphere of Jena and moved to Leipzig, taking with him his unfinished prose *Messias*. Here he came into contact with a group of young poets who, in protest against Gottsched's pedantry, had founded their own periodical, the *Bremer*

Beiträge. Under their influence Klopstock turned again to writing odes, a form which had appealed to him since his years at Schulpforta. At this time also he determined to recast the unfinished *Messias* in hexameters. The rewriting of the first canto (*Gesang*) was completed in the summer of 1746, and the following spring both Hagedorn and Bodmer were able to read parts of the epic. Their enthusiasm was boundless; Bodmer especially felt that Milton had been far surpassed.

The first three cantos of the *Messias* appeared anonymously in 1748, and they were more than enough to establish Klopstock as a leading poet in the eyes of his friends. Convinced that this success was proof of his poetic mission and that further study was hence unnecessary, he left Leipzig and took up the duties of private tutor in Langenzala. His unrequited love for a cousin (the "Fanny" of his odes) led him to write a letter requesting help from Bodmer. At the latter's invitation Klopstock went to Zürich, where he stayed for six months. During this time Bodmer's early warmth for him cooled considerably; he had expected Klopstock to take advantage of such generosity and finish the *Messias*, but neither the expected application to his great epic nor to his host's Spartan habits appealed to the young poet. Some weeks before his arrival in Zürich Klopstock had received a generous annuity and an invitation from Frederick V of Denmark. Despite a late reconciliation between Bodmer and himself, he resolved to accept the offer to finish his work in Copenhagen. Accordingly, he left Zürich in February 1751 for the Danish capital by way of Hamburg, where he met Meta Moller, who afterwards became his wife.

The next twenty years (until 1770) were spent in Copenhagen. His early promise as a poet did not, however, fulfill itself. After only four years of marriage his wife died, leaving him heart-broken and deeply melancholic. Although his literary production continued almost unabated, there is little or no artistic development to be seen after his wife's death and the publication of his *Geistliche Lieder*, both in 1758.

In 1771 Klopstock's odes were published in book form, and in 1773 the final five cantos of the *Messias* appeared. With the exception of a year at the court of the Margrave of Baden in Karlsruhe (1775), he lived the remainder of his life in Hamburg.

Although Klopstock's literary fame is not limited entirely to the *Messias* and the odes, it is here, and chiefly in the latter, that his lasting merit may be found. His Biblical dramas (*Der Tod Adams, Salomo, David*), the Hermann trilogy (the so-called *Bardiete*), his patriotic songs, his contributions to philology and the history of German poetry (*Die Gelehrtenrepublik, Fragmente über Sprache und Dichtkunst*), although of importance historically, have not stood the test of time among readers. Even his *Messias*, while containing very fine lyric passages, cannot be considered truly successful, nor did it have an immediate effect on German literature. While this long epic does contain much of what is substantial in Klopstock—his religious ardor and vision, his lyric gift, a profound sense of the sublime, a bold new way of expressing sentiments in natural language, and a power and grandeur which appear for virtually the first time in German poetry—his best work is represented by a relatively modest number of odes: the Fanny odes (springing from his unhappy love for his cousin Maria Luise Schmidt), the Cidli odes (to his wife, whom he affectionately called "Cidli"), *Der Zürchersee, Frühlingsfeier*, and a few others. These poems, sometimes referred to as the odes of enthusiasm, are written in a language which brilliantly translates the emotional language of the heart. They represent a long step towards the perfection of a natural German poetic idiom. However, Klopstock's greatest contribution to German literature lies less in the intrinsic value of his poetry than in the fact that he championed a new era: poetry was freed from the fetters of convention and endowed with profound emotional experience.

An English translation of the *Messias* was published in 1795. It was a prose rendering by Joseph Collyer which, though inaccurate, remains one of the few complete translations of this work. The odes have fared little better. Wilhelm Wind's translation, *Klopstock. Odes, 1747-80,* is relatively true to meaning but violates the form.

ABOUT: Orbis Litterarum, XV (1960); PMLA, LXVII (1952). [In German—see studies by R. Baudusch-Walker, F. Freivogel, K. Kindt, F. Muncker, K. L. Schneider. In French—see study by E. Bailly.]

A. M.

*KNEPPELHOUT, JOHANNES (pseudonym "KLIKSPAAN"), (January 8, 1814-November 9, 1885), Dutch essayist and man of letters, was born in Leiden, the son of Cornelis Johannes Kneppelhout and Johanna Maria de Gijselaar. His father died in 1819 and the boy received his first instruction from his mother and her brother. Until

*k'něp' ĕl hout

1831 Johannes went to a boarding school, and then to Leiden where he studied law for eight years without ever getting a degree. Rich and independent, he preferred to spend his time in literary studies. He and his friends, Beets, Reynen, Bakhuizen van den Brink, and others, were devotees of Victor Hugo and other romantic authors of the French school. When he was still very young, Kneppelhout wrote French verses. They were collected in *Opuscules de Jeunesse* (2 vols., Leiden, 1848). His *Studententypen* (1841), written under the pseudonym of Klikspaan, gives evidence of his forceful realism and his sparkling humor. It belongs to the best prose written in that period. *Studentenleven* (1844) contains essays that are more didactic in vein. It and later writings are of little importance to Dutch literature. Some titles: *In den Vreemde, Herinneringen, Ontmoetingen en Schetsen* (1839); *Een Kastelein* (1840); *Verhalen* (1846); *Lamartine* (1848); and *Schetsen en Verhalen uit Zwitserland* (1850). In 1845 Kneppelhout married his cousin Ursula Martha van Braam, with whom he traveled all over Europe, spending only a few months a year on his estate, De Hemelsche Berg, where he died at seventy-one.

ABOUT: [In Dutch—see studies by J. Dyserinck, A. J. Luyt.]

H. B.

*KNORRING, SOFIA MARGARETA (ZELOW), Baroness von (September 9, 1797-February 13, 1848), Swedish novelist, was born in the Swedish province of Västergötland. Her father was Major Christer Göran Zelow, later Lieutenant-Colonel and titular Master of the Royal Household, belonging to an originally Polish noble family whose male members for generations had been officers of low rank. Her mother was Helena Sophia Gripenstedt, whose family belonged to the lower nobility. She was educated by governesses and private tutors in an aristocratic and conservative fashion. In 1820 she married a Major, later Colonel, Baron Sebastian Karl von Knorring, who came from a rather poor family of the petty nobility. Strikingly beautiful and witty but also perfectly aware of her beauty and social status, she was a frequent and highly esteemed guest in the salons of the provincial aristocracy of her native province.

In 1834 she published anonymously her first book, *Cousinerna* (The Cousins), in which with intimate realism she described

* k'nōr' ing

the world of rank and fashion, a domain to which she brought competent knowledge. When she once had acquired the taste and liking for writing she produced in less than a decade, under the pseudonym "The Author of *The Cousins*," seven full length novels, among others *Vännerna* (The Friends), *Qvinnorna* (The Women), *Illusionerna* (The Illusions), and two collections of short stories entitled *Skizzer* (Sketches). All except one of these move in her own milieu of manor houses and ballrooms. Romantic erotics are always in the center. The major theme is the struggle of a young woman who is caught in the conflict between her sense of duty to husband and home and her love of another man, necessarily ending in destruction or resignation. Only once, in *Torparen och Hans Omgifning* (The Crofter and His Environment), the first Swedish peasant novel and probably her best literary accomplishment, did she step out of her own milieu and concern herself with the lower classes.

Torparen och Hans Omgifning was translated into English by Mary Howitt under the title *The Peasant and His Landlord* (1848).

ABOUT: [In Swedish—Nelson, B. Sophie von Knorring.]

A. J.

*KNUDSEN, JAKOB CHRISTIAN LINDBERG (September 14, 1858-January 21, 1917), Danish novelist and poet, was born in Schleswig, at Rødding. His father, Jens Lassen Knudsen, was a college teacher. His mother was Nanna Marie Frederikke Adelaide Boisen. In 1864 his father was appointed vicar at Aggersborg in northwestern Jutland. Here the future author received the impressions that determined his attitude to life and his authorship. In 1875 he went to Copenhagen in order to prepare himself for his matriculation examination. Two years later he was admitted to the university. He completed a theological degree in 1881, whereafter he got a position as a teacher at Askov College.

In 1883 he married Sophie Frederikke Plockross, daughter of a barrister. The two were incompatible, and the unhappy marriage was dissolved after a decade. They were legally divorced in 1896. In 1890 Knudsen became priest of a free congregation. Six years later he contracted a second marriage with Helga Bek, daughter of a college president. Because of his divorce and second marriage Knudsen was forced to resign from his clerical profession.

* knōōd' sĕn

Knudsen had attracted some attention by 1891 with his drama *Cromwells Datter* (Cromwell's Daughter). For some time he traveled as a popular lecturer, but after the turn of the century he devoted most of his time to writing novels. He moved to Zealand, where he lived in various places.

In Knudsen's personality there was a conflict between a strong individualism, inherited from his father, and a mystic quietism, from his mother. His novels are based on great conflicts, e.g., between old ideas and new ones, between the individual and society, etc. Among the better of his many novels are *Den Gamle Præst* (The Old Pastor, 1899), in which moral and social conscience clash; the double novel *Gjæring-Afklaring* (Fermentation-Clarification, 1901-02), in which he describes his paternal and maternal families; *Lærer Urup* (Teacher Urup, 1909), criticizing the educational system; another double novel *Angst* (Fear, 1912), and *Mod* (Courage, 1914), in which he describes Luther's, as well as his own, development.

Of Knudson's entire production only one song, "Se nu Stiger Solen," has been translated into English as "Morning Song" by R. P. Keigwin in his *The Jutland Wind* (1944).

ABOUT: Columbia Dictionary of Modern European Literature; Mitchell, P. M. A History of Danish Literature; Topsöe-Jensen, H. G. Scandinavian Literature from Brandes to Our Day. [In Danish—see studies by H. Begtrup, J. Byskov, S. Norrild, C. Roos, E. Thornsen, H. Toldberg.]

A. J.

*KOCHANOWSKI, JAN (1530-August 22, 1584), Polish poet and playwright, was born in Sycyna. He was educated at the Cracow Academy and traveled and studied in Germany, Italy, and France. After his return to Poland, he served as royal secretary in Cracow and later settled down on the family estate, Czarnolas. In 1575 he married and had a daughter Ursula who died in 1579. His own death occurred at Lublin.

Kochanowski's first poems, short epigrams and erotic lyrics, were written in Latin, but quite early he started also to write in Polish, and soon became famous both in his country and abroad, eventually achieving the rank of the first great national poet in all Slavic literature. His *Songs* (*Pieśni*) and *Trifles* (*Fraszki*) constitute the true example of Renaissance lyric poetry at its best. The Petrarchan pattern of expressing human thoughts and feelings against the background of nature is frequently found in Kochanow-

* kô ĸä nôf' skē

ski's sonnets and longer poems of such artistic quality that the name of the Polish poet soon became familiar to foreign readers, especially through German translations.

Both thematically and formally Kochanowski's poetry represents a great richness. Frivolous and serious notes melt together in Renaissance harmony in his erotic and reflective lyrics, as well as in his philosophical, patriotic, and religious poems. Since there was no poetic style in Poland before Kochanowski, he had to coin his own patterns of rhythms, stanzas, syntactic figures, words and expressions which later became an organic part of the Polish literary language. Several of Kochanowski's poems are still recited by heart by educated Poles; this is especially true of his religious song "What Do You Want from Us, O Lord," several poetic translations of the Psalms, several *Trifles* and parts of his beautiful idyll, *The Song of St. John's Eve*. His *Treny* (Laments), written by the poet on his daughter Ursula's death, are internationally recognized as one of the highest achievements in elegiac poetry. Kochanowski is also the author of the first Polish tragedy, *The Dismissal of the Grecian Envoys*. This work was written according to neo-classic rules and based on motifs from ancient literature, but it also reflects national problems and the poet's patriotic credo.

Kochanowski's importance in Polish literature is enormous. He combined all the best qualities of Humanism and Renaissance, he formed the style and the poetic ideals of generations of Polish and other Slavic poets, and he remains one of the greatest in the Slavic world.

Kochanowski's works in English translation include *Poems*, translated by various hands, edited by G. R. Noyes, and published in 1928; *The Dismissal of the Grecian Envoys*, translated by R. E. Merrill, (1918); *Laments*, translated by D. Prall, (1920); *St. John's Eve*, translated by G. R. Noyes and M. Peacock (1927).

ABOUT: Kridl, M. Survey of Polish Literature; Noyes, G. R. Jan Kochanowski *in* Great Men and Women of Poland, ed. by S. Mizwa. [In German— see study by M. Jastrun.]

Z. F.

*KOCK, CHARLES PAUL DE (May 21, 1794-August 29, 1871), French novelist, was born in Passy, presumably after his father's death and contrary to his own dating of 1793. He was the son of a rich lawyer of The Hague, who had come to Paris in 1787 in protest against the new Dutch government. After his death on the guillotine, Kock's

* kōk

mother married a salaried clerk, Gaigneau, a chronic gambler, but educated and devoted. Kock's first literary interests resulted from disorganized reading of novels in bookstores, but he also knew *Don Quixote* and *Gil Blas*. His education, which included music lessons and violin, was desultory, owing to his mother's reluctance to send him away to school. His interest in the theatre stemmed from his readings of Molière and Racine, and his knowledge of music turned him to lyrical genres.

Kock served for five years as a bank clerk, and during this time, at the age of seventeen, wrote his first novel. He also tried song writing, and acquaintances turned him toward the theatre where four of his plays had considerable success in 1814 and 1815. He returned to the novel in *Georgette* (1820), concentrating largely on observation rather than imagination. His publisher Hubert called for further works, and Kock's fame rose rapidly, either from the enthusiasm of the majority of his readers, or from shock at his risqué manner. His popularity abroad came early and was immense.

Kock's associations with music are of some historical importance. He began writing comic operas in 1818, and his main success in this genre was *Le Muletier* (1823) with music by Mengal. He was intimate with many of the great composers, such as Cherubini, Boieldieu, Kreutzer, and Herold, as well as a variety of writers of such different leanings as Nodier and Dumas *fils*. He found consolation during his last years in his two surviving children, especially his daughter, who devoted herself to him. In 1869, prodded by friends, he wrote his *Mémoires*, our principal source of biographical information. During the Franco-Prussian War, his property at Romainville was partly destroyed, and the shock of events hastened his death.

Kock's merit in the novel lies in his witty yet unpretentiously faithful portrayal of life in Paris. His favorite district was the Boulevard du Temple, which he had frequented throughout his life, and the social type most evident is the middle class of about 1830.

The twenty-five volumes of *The Works of Charles Paul de Kock*, published in Boston in 1902, translated by M. H. Ford, testify to his popularity abroad at that time, and many were retranslated by G. Ives in the twenty volumes of *The Masterpieces of Charles Paul de Kock* (1903-1905). His *Memoirs* were translated in 1899 by E. Norris.

ABOUT: Kock, C. P. de. Memoirs. [In French— see studies by L. Lespès and T. Trimm.]

F. J. C.

493

*KOLLÁR, JÁN (July 29, 1793-January 24, 1852), Slovak poet, was born in Mošovce in Slovakia, the son of a village elder. He attended the Protestant lyceums in Báňska Bystrica and in Bratislava, studying theology and philosophy. In 1817 he went to the University of Jena to complete his theological study. German idealist philosophy and romantic history, together with the nationalist and patriotic currents then in the air in Germany, made a powerful impression on the young student. His imagination was also stirred by the Slavic place names which he found in the vicinity of Jena, remnants of past Slavic habitation in a region long since Germanized. In 1818 he met Friedericke Wilhelmina Schmidt ("Minna"), the daughter of a Protestant pastor, who became the object of his Platonic affection and the inspiration of his poetry. A German, she nevertheless served as the living model for the Slavic goddess of his poetry, the daughter of Sláva (the word *sláva* itself means "glory," but also plays on "Slav").

Kollár returned to Báňska Bystrica in Slovakia, where he was ordained pastor in 1819. He then went to Budapest to serve a Slovak parish there, remaining until 1849. Minna could not yet bring herself to move to Hungary, however, and it was not until sixteen years after they met that she consented to marry him. In 1841 and 1844 Kollár made two trips to Italy, where he indulged in much absurd romantic theorizing: Latin he declared to be a Slavic language, corrupted by Greek, for example. In 1849 he was named Professor of Slavic Antiquities at the University of Vienna, but he had little scholarly restraint and became entangled in his theories. He died in Vienna. In 1904 his body was brought to Prague and re-interred there.

Kollár was the author of a volume of sonnets, *Slávy Dcera* (The Daughter of Sláva), a book which continued to grow throughout most of his life. He wrote in Czech, for the Slovak literary language had not yet been formed, and in any case he opposed attempts to create a standard Slovak, preferring to use Czech. The first edition of the collection (1821) contained 150 sonnets (though Kollár's sonnets are in trochees, since Czech poetry had as yet no iambic verse, divided into three parts of fifty sonnets each. Each part is named for a river, the Saale, Elbe, and Danube, once Slavic but later lost, partly or entirely, to the Slavs. The work is opened by the magnificent prologue in hexameters, a

* kŏl' lär

KOLLÁR

moving lament for the past glory and present decadence of the Slavs. In these sonnets the poet is shown as meeting the daughter of Sláva and falling in love with her. Kollár's love sonnets are influenced by Petrarch, and the sentiment of love in his poetry merges with that of patriotism as a symbol of the latter. Soon the poet is parted from his love, and wanders disconsolate, finally hearing of her death. Yet Kollár looks forward to a time of future greatness, once the Slavs achieve cultural unity: this unity will in turn usher in a golden age for the rest of humanity.

In the second edition of the collection (1832) Kollár added two more sections to the original three: Lethe and Acheron. He also increased the number of sonnets to 615. Influenced by Dante and Byron's *Childe Harold's Pilgrimage*, the poet wanders through the Slavic heaven and hell, describing what he sees. The latter is peopled by those who have persecuted the Slavs. The weight of archeological and historical information which Kollár incorporated into his poetry became so great that he was compelled to publish a volume of annotations.

Kollár collected Slovak folk songs, which he published in two volumes as *Národnie Zpievanky* (1834-35). But there is no trace of folk influence on his poetry, which is strictly classical, though his ideology is romantic.

Kollár's pan-Slavic ideas are treated in his book *Über die Literarische Wechselseitigkeit zwischen Verschiedenen Stämmen und Mun-*

darten der Slavischen Nation (On the Literary Kinship of Different Peoples and Languages of the Slavic Nation, 1837). A shorter version appeared a year earlier in Czech. Kollár advocated the cultural (but not political) union of all Slavs. A common Slavic alphabet (Latin) should be formulated, but no common Slavic language is needed: language and culture should be left distinct for the sake of variety.

Kollár's influence was strong in both Bohemia and Slovakia, particularly in his pan-Slavic ideology. But his poetic influence was not great: his poetry was too archaic, stiff, and artificial in style to serve later poets as a model. Only at times, as in the great prologue to *Slávy Dcera*, was he able to exploit these qualities to produce a lofty, dignified, and moving poetry.

Examples of Kollár's poetry are found translated into English in Sir John Bowring, *A Cheskian Anthology* (1832); Paul Selver, *Anthology of Czechoslovak Literature* (1929); R. A. Ginsburg, *Soul of a Century* (1942); and E. W. Underwood, *The Slav Anthology* (1931).

ABOUT: Harkins, W. E. Anthology of Czech Literature; Slavonic Review, VI (1927-28); Slavonic and East European Review, XXXI (1952).

W. E. H.

KOLTSOV, ALEXEY VASILYEVICH

(October 3, 1809-October 19, 1842), Russian poet, was born at Voronezh (south central Russia). His father was a cattle dealer and belonged to a wealthy middle class family. Koltsov spent part of his childhood in the steppes around the Don river. His education was sadly neglected and when twelve years old Koltsov had to leave the local high school, which he had attended for a little over a year, in order to help his father actively in his work. Nevertheless Koltsov continued to read a great deal and was able to get books thanks to his friendship with a local bookdealer and also with the son of a prosperous merchant. Among his readings were *The Arabian Nights,* Zhukovsky, and Pushkin.

Koltsov wrote his first poems in 1825. During his business trips to Moscow and St. Petersburg, he frequented literary circles and met the greatest contemporary Russian writers, among them Pushkin, Krylov, and Zhukovsky, who accepted him with great friendliness and even helped him to bring out a collection of his poems in 1835. He became well known as "Stichotvorez-meshchanine" (i.e., poet of the middle classes) and "poet-prasol" (i.e., poet-cattle dealer). Despite his

* kŭl y' tsôf'

literary aspirations Koltsov was obliged to continue working for his father and remained up to his death dependent upon him in every way.

A tragic love affair in his youth with Duniasha, one of his father's serfs, left its imprint upon Koltsov. During one of Koltsov's business trips, his father, who opposed this marriage, sold Duniasha to a far-off settlement. Koltsov became gravely ill upon his return and was never able to find her again. He had a very close relationship with his younger sister, Anisia, whose musical aspirations were also frustrated by his father. His closest friendship, however, was with the great Moscow critic Belinsky, who not only was a loyal friend but also influenced Koltsov's philosophical and intellectual growth. Despite his wide reading and his many intellectual friendships, Koltsov remained on the whole uncultured, suffering deeply from his lack of education.

Towards the end of his life, Koltsov fell in love with a woman whose reputation was questionable. For this reason, he was forsaken by his family, and in his last years, dying of tuberculosis, he was almost completely abandoned by them. During all his life Koltsov was torn between his literary activity and his literary friends on one side, and the prose and banality of his life, of his family, and of his surroundings on the other. His poems are partly epical, partly lyrical, and show great affinity with and understanding of the peasants and of nature. The language is sometimes archaic, sometimes popular, sometimes sophisticated and original. The construction of his poetry is more involved than that of simple folklore. His poetry is both literary and folkloristic; his themes are sadness, frustrated love, a search for freedom, a desire for adventure, the solace found in nature. The tone is often resigned. Both passion and realism play a large rôle on his work, in which he depicts the poetry of peasant life. Belinsky said of him: "Koltsov knew and loved peasant life such as it is in reality, without adorning or poetizing it." And Koltsov does indeed write of boorish muzhiks, in rags, with unkempt beards and, as Belinsky adds, "all this dirt has become through him the pure gold of poetry."

Koltsov has been called the Russian Burns and his songs have been translated into English, French, German, Czech, Bulgarian and many other languages. Among his best known poems are "The Forest," written upon the death of Pushkin, "The Mower," "The Harvest," "The Laborer's Song," and "The

Winds Blow." From his first published volume on, Koltsov's poetry had great success. His work can be divided into three parts: poems in the pre-Pushkin and Pushkin style, *Russian Songs*, and finally the philosophical *Dumy* ("Meditations"), rather naïvely mystical. Owing to the appeal of his *Russian Songs* Koltsov is regarded as one of Russia's best loved poets.

Selections from Koltsov's poems appear in English translation in *A Book of Russian Verse*, edited by C. M. Bowra (1943), in *Russian Poets and Poems*, edited by N. Jarintzov (1917), and in *A Treasury of Russian Verse*, edited by A. Yarmolinsky (1949).

Y. L.

*KOMENSKÝ, JAN AMOS (JOHANNES AMOS COMENIUS) (March 28, 1592-November 4, 1670), Czech philosopher and educationalist, was born in Moravia, most probably in the village of Nivnice. His father was a well-to-do burgher, a member of the Protestant Unity of Czech Brethren, in which faith Jan was reared. Both his parents died when he was only twelve, and he went to live with an aunt. At sixteen he was sent to the Latin School of the Unity at Přerov. In 1611 he went on to Herborn in Nassau to the Reformed *Gymnasium*, and in 1613 he entered the University of Heidelberg. A year later he returned to Přerov to teach in the Latin School: here he ambitiously began work on a projected encyclopedia of all knowledge.

In April 1616 Komenský was ordained a pastor of the Unity, and two years later he was assigned to the parish of Fulnek in northern Moravia. Just before leaving he was married to a young woman of some wealth, Magdalina Vízovská. His pastoral and scholarly work in Fulnek was soon interrupted by the incursion of an Imperial army (it was the beginning of the Thirty Years' War), and his library was burned. Meanwhile Austrian forces defeated the Czech Protestants, and in 1621 Komenský was forced to flee the town, leaving his wife, who went to live with her mother in Přerov, but soon died, along with their two children, of plague. Her death, together with his country's plight, must have inspired his great allegory on the vanity of worldly life: *Labyrint Světa a Ráj Srdce* (The Labyrinth of the World and the Paradise of the Heart), which he wrote in 1623, in hiding. It is a classic of Czech literature, and one of the most moving religious allegories ever written.

* kô' měn skē; kō mē' nǐ ŭs

KOMENSKÝ

In September 1624 Komenský was married again, this time to the daughter of a bishop of the Unity. But a new misfortune soon struck: the Austrian rulers revoked religious toleration, and the members of the Unity were forced into exile. Komenský went to Leszno in Poland, where the Unity had a Latin school. Here he began the pedagogical work for which he is famous. In 1631 he published his *Janua Linguarum Reserata* (The Gates of the Languages Unlocked), a simple text for Latin instruction. In 1637 he completed the *Didactica Magna* (Great Didactic), a manual of educational theory. At the same time he projected a synthetic work on all philosophical, scientific, and religious knowledge, the *Pansophia*, a work long considered lost, but which has recently been found in Germany. In this period, too, Komenský was chosen bishop of the Unity by a Church synod.

In 1641 Komenský was invited to England by a group of members of Parliament, to prepare a project for universal peace. Ironically, the work had to be abandoned because of the outbreak of the English Civil War. Komenský then went to Sweden, where he administered a reform of the schools. He remained there six years, returning to Leszno in 1648 to be chosen senior bishop of the Unity: he was the last member of his Church to occupy this post. The same year a new blow fell: the Peace of Westphalia finally excluded Protestants from Bohemia.

In 1650 Komenský went to Transylvania at the invitation of the younger brother of the reigning prince, again to work on educational reform. Here he suggested the use of school plays as a spontaneous form of instruction, and himself dramatized material from his *Janua Linguarum*. The latter book he also reworked with illustrations as *Orbis Pictus* (The World in Pictures), the first illustrated reading book ever compiled. It was republished as late as 1887.

In 1655 Komenský returned to Leszno. The same year that Protestant city was burned by a Polish army in reprisal for the Swedish invasion of Poland. For the second time Komenský lost his library and his manuscripts, and again he was forced to flee. He went to Silesia and then to Amsterdam, where he died suddenly in 1670. In this last period Komenský's thought became more mystical, and he was deluded by irresponsible prophecies concerning the end of the Hapsburg power.

Komenský is one of the greatest educational theorists. His textbooks were translated into almost all civilized languages and reprinted in countless editions. He advocated universal education for both sexes, instruction in the native language in primary schools (rather than in Latin), the teaching of such new subjects as history, geography, drawing and manual training, the use of visual aids, the grading of teaching material according to age. He recommended that punishment be used only as a disciplinary measure, not as a pedagogical incentive.

Komenský's philosophical speculations seem less modern. He subordinates philosophy and the sciences to theology, for example. But here too his thought is often significant, as when he advocates perpetual reformation of the Church.

Many of Komenský's pedagogical works and textbooks are available in English. Of his literary writings, *The Labyrinth of the World* has been translated twice, the better version being that of Matthew Spinka. A volume of selections from his literary, philosophical and pedagogical works has been published in English by UNESCO: *J. A. Comenius* (1957).

ABOUT: Spinka, M. John Amos Comenius; Monroe, W. S. Comenius and the Beginnings of Educational Reform; PMLA, LXX (1955).

W. E. H.

---

*KONOPNICKA, MARIA, née WASI-LOWSKA (May 23, 1842-October 8, 1910), Polish poet and short-story writer, was born in Suwalki, and went to a school for girls in Warsaw. She married in 1862 and lived first in Warsaw and later, after her

* kô nôp nēts' kä; vä sē lôf' skä

banishment by the Russian authorities for patriotic activity, in Germany, Italy and France. She died in Lwów.

Konopnicka's literary work consists chiefly of lyrical poems published in periodicals and separate book collections (eight volumes in all, appearing regularly between 1882 and 1906). Some of her short stories are still read. Rather forgotten today is her ambitious attempt at an emigration epic of the type later so popular in this country, *Pan Balcer w Brazylii* (Mr. Balcer in Brazil, 1909).

Konopnicka's poetry has enjoyed wide circulation in Poland owing to its fluent rhythmical form and its variety of timely and sometimes provocative themes. Though a follower of the great romantic tradition (Słowacki in particular) she wrote with some originality and force, especially in her rather naive but always noble and sincere poems of protest against the hard lot of the underprivileged. In popular poetic form she dealt with themes of ignorance, poverty, and crime without hesitating to put the blame directly on society, as in her lyric "In Front of the Jury," which still moves school children in particular to tears. Konopnicka's patriotic poem "Rota" became the national song of the Polish people.

Available in English translation are *The Brownie Scouts*, a delightful story for children, translated by K. Żuk-Skarszewska (1929) and several short stories.

ABOUT: Kridl, M. Survey of Polish Literature.

Z. F.

---

*KORAËS, ADAMANTIOS (April 27, 1748-April 6, 1833), Greek doctor, philologist, patriot, and educator, was born and raised in Smyrna. His father, John Koraës, from Chios, came from an educated family and appreciated the importance of education. His mother, Thomaida Rhysios, from Chios, was the daughter of Adamantios Rhysios, a Greek teacher in Chios and later a textile merchant in Smyrna. When Rhysios died, he bequeathed his Greek library to the first grandson of his to graduate from the Greek school. Koraës' inheritance of this library launched him into the world of Greek letters. No teachers of higher education were available, however, and Koraës developed such a hatred for the Turks that Turk and wild beast were synonymous terms to him. Fortunately, for the next six years he was able to exchange Latin for modern Greek with Bernard Keun, a Dutch pastor of Smyrna.

* kô rä ēs'

From 1772 to 1778 he was his father's commercial agent in Amsterdam, devoting all his leisure time to his studies with the theologian Adrian Buurt, under whose guidance he learned to read and write nine languages and speak six. From 1778 to 1782 he was back in Smyrna, avoiding the Turks for fear of falling into "real insanity." In 1782 he enrolled as a medical student at Montpellier, France.

His first publications were translations of religious works into modern Greek. Chief among these are *Orthodox Doctrine* (1782), by the Russian Platonas, translated from the German version, and *A Summary of Sacred History and Catechism* (1783). His next series consisted of medical works which he translated into French. He received his medical degree in 1788.

In 1789 he went to Paris where he lived till the time of his death. He became an ardent admirer of the American patriots and the French revolutionaries. His early years in Paris were spent in poverty, and he himself writes that he almost died of hunger in 1796. After the fall of Venice in 1797 and the occupation of the Heptanese by the French, Koraës abandoned medicine and dedicated himself entirely to the cause of Greek independence and the enlightenment of the Greek people, which he believed to be the surest harbinger of national rebirth.

He wrote a series of political pamphlets to arouse the Greeks to revolt against Turkish rule. *The Song of War* (1800), in verse, and *Trumpet of War* (1801), in prose, express his most radical thoughts and were written anonymously. *Crimes and Punishments* by Beccaria (1802), which Koraës translated from the Italian and dedicated to the Republic of the Seven Isles, is also considered a political work because of the nature of his preface and notes. The same year he wrote a pamphlet in French entitled *Mémoire sur l'État Actuel de la Civilisation dans la Grèce,* which did much to correct erroneous impressions of the Europeans and stimulated his countrymen to greater effort in their struggle for independence.

Under the generous patronage of the Greek merchants Zosimas, he began work on the *Greek Library* (1805-27), consisting of twenty-six volumes of translations from the classic into modern Greek. In these works, which he translated to familiarize the Greeks with their own classic heritage, Koraës founded and established a middle-of-the-road Greek between the Attic and the spoken language of the people. The *Greek Library*

contains long prefaces and notes on Greek education, the language, the duties of Greeks to their country, and the importance of ecclesiastical tolerance.

During these years he also wrote articles in *The Sagacious Hermes,* a Greek newspaper in Vienna started through his efforts, by means of which he brought Greece into contact with Western learning. He corresponded with leaders and scholars of Europe and America in the cause of Greek independence. Thomas Jefferson, whom he had met in Paris in 1803, congratulated him for improving the minds of the Greeks and "qualifying them for self-government." Nineteen volumes of these letters were published posthumously. *Atakta,* a miscellany of philosophical notes, consists of five volumes.

Koraës died and was buried in Montparnasse, Paris. His bones were disinterred in 1877 and he was given a second burial in Athens. A statue of him was erected in front of the University of Athens.

Adamantios Koraës was undoubtedly the greatest educator in modern Greece. He did much to spread the Western practices of the church and the democratic ideals of the American War of Independence and the French Revolution. However, he thought the spoken idiom was "corrupted" by "foreign words" and "degenerate formations"; the middle road which he recommended has not been used by the poets who continue to write in the spoken idiom.

Koraës' letters written from Paris, 1788-92, were translated from Greek into English by P. Ralli in a privately printed edition, London, 1898.

ABOUT: Aufricht, H. Adamantios Koraës and the Image of the Modern Greek State; Chaconas, S. G. Adamantios Korais; Iatrides, G. E. Coraes's Education Message to Greece and the World; Mavrogordato, J. Modern Greece; Negris, A. An Outline of the Literary History of Modern Greece; Perdicaro, G. A. Dr. Coray and the Greek Church; Sandys, J. E. A History of Classical Scholarship, III.

R. D.

*KÖRNER, (KARL) THEODOR (September 3, 1791-August 26, 1813), German poet and dramatist, was born in Dresden, Saxony. His father, Christian Gottfried Körner (1756-1831), was a prominent jurist, and a personal friend of many great German poets of the time, especially of Goethe and Schiller, whom he often assisted financially. His mother was Anna Maria Stock, a daughter of a copper-plate engraver from Nürnberg from whom Goethe learned the art of

* kŭr' nĕr

copper engraving. Körner went to school first in Dresden, then, at the age of seventeen, at his own request, he entered the Mining Academy in Freiburg, Saxony. He stayed there, however, only two years, and his scientific subjects attracted him far less than reading and writing poetry. The result of this occupation was a slender volume of poems which appeared in 1810 under the title *Knospen*, but failed to attract any attention. In the same year he decided to go to Leipzig to study law at the university, but again, he devoted himself more to drinking and dueling than to his academic studies. When he became involved in a student brawl and in a duel fought between two opposing fraternities, he had to flee from the city to escape being arrested by the police. He intended first to continue his studies in Berlin, but he stayed there only a short time. In August 1811 he went to Vienna, after solemnly promising his father that he would mend his ways. Indeed, he attended some lectures at the university, but he still found time to visit theatres and to write several plays. Though these were clearly written in a bombastic style that only faintly suggests Schiller, he had some of them performed by the Viennese Hofburgtheater. The best of these plays was *Zriny*, which was produced at the end of 1812. On January 9, 1813, he was officially appointed court-theatre poet with a salary of 1,500 gulden; at the same time he became engaged to the actress Antonie Adamberger.

When Napoleon completely failed in his conquest of Russia and the Germans started to rise against their French oppressors, Körner volunteered immediately, joining the ranks of the famous Lützow's corps at Breslau. When passing through Dresden on April 6, 1813, he issued his patriotic call *Aufruf an die Sachsen*, appealing to all his countrymen to join his ranks in liberating their country. It is at this time that his well known portrait, a copper engraving, was done by his admiring sister Emma. He was first wounded in a battle near Leipzig, nursed back to health by his friends and relatives, but he immediately rejoined his corps, meeting a heroic death at the age of twenty-one. He was buried near the village of Wölbelin under an oak tree (Körners Eiche), where a monument to him was placed a few years later.

After his death his father collected his patriotic poems and published them in 1814 under the title *Leyer und Schwerdt* (*The Lyre and the Sword*, tr. W. B. Chorley,

1834). They were received with a tremendous popular enthusiasm, being regarded as a faithful expression of nascent national spirit and true national heroism. Many of these songs became genuine national battle hymns, e.g., "Lützows Wilde Verwegen Jagd," "Gebet während der Schlacht," and "Das Schwertlied."

Körner's romantic life and his heroic death became an object of many poems, novels, and dramas.

His collected works were published by Adolf Stern 1890-99. John Chapman translated his tragedy *Rosamunda* (1878).

ABOUT: [In German—see studies by K. B. Berger, E. Kammerhoff, E. Peschel, J. Töpfle, E. Zeiner.]

F. S. L.

*KOROLENKO, VLADIMIR GALAKTIONOVICH (July 27, 1853-December 25, 1921), Russian writer, was born in Zhitomir, Ukraine. His father was a Ukrainian official who had high moral and ethical standards and a wide range of interests, including mathematics, astronomy, and foreign languages. He also had Spartan views on how to bring up children, but this was offset by Korolenko's mother, a warmhearted Polish gentlewoman who was adored by her children. At the age of six, Vladimir was sent to boarding school, and when he was ten (in 1863, the year of the Polish uprising which was ruthlessly suppressed by the Russian army) he became familiar with some distressing aspects of Czarist Russia's "nationality problem." His best friend, a Polish schoolboy, grew cool toward him because Korolenko considered himself a "Russian." One of his teachers, Ukrainian by birth, rebuked him for the same reason. Two years later, Korolenko's family moved to Rovno, also in the Ukraine. There he was greatly influenced by a teacher of literature. He acquired an excellent knowledge and deep love of Russian literature, and came to regard this subject as his "true motherland."

When Korolenko was fifteen, his father died, leaving the family practically destitute. Korolenko graduated from high school and went to St. Petersburg and Moscow for study at the university level. Penniless and hungry, he supported himself with various odd jobs as best he could. He joined the anti-Czarist Populist (Russian agrarian socialist) movement in St. Petersburg and was soon expelled. Although he had no personal sympathy with political terrorism, Korolenko's

* kŭ rŭ lyän′ kō

acquaintances included Kravchinsky (who murdered the St. Petersburg police chief in 1878), and he eventually married the sister of P. S. Ivanovsky (a member of the revolutionary left-wing Populist group responsible for the murder of Czar Alexander II in 1881).

In 1879 Korolenko published his first story "Episody iz Zhizni Iskatelya" (Episodes from the Life of a Searcher). In the same year he was arrested and exiled to Vyatka province. Eventually he was sent to Yakutsk (in eastern Siberia), a region sparsely inhabited by native tribes. This period of his life had tremendous influence on Korolenko's subsequent literary and journalistic activity. A competent artist, he also left a number of sketches of Siberian scenes.

Returning in 1885 from Siberia, Korolenko settled in Nizhny-Novgorod (now Gorky), where he married and lived until 1896. Here he published his famous story "Son Makara" (Makar's Dream), about an old Siberian native who dreams, as he is dying, of pleading suffering humanity's case before God and a heavenly tribunal. In another story written at this time, called "V Durnom Obshchestve" (In Bad Company), and dealing with thieves, beggars and other social outcasts, Korolenko showed his characteristic talent for revealing the good which exists to some degree in all men. In 1887 he published his celebrated short story "Slepoy Muzykant" (The Blind Musician), which was followed by "Yom Kippur" and "Nochyu" (At Night).

Korolenko was deeply sensitive to social problems. During the famine of 1892, he helped organize soup kitchens and wrote the book V Golodny God (In the Year of Hunger, 1893). He protested against the trial of some Siberian natives who had been unjustly accused of cannibalism and human sacrifice, and wrote a number of articles in their defense (1895-98). He was also profoundly disturbed by the anti-Semitic outbreaks and other reactionary excesses occurring in the reigns of Alexander III and Nicholas II.

In the 1890's Korolenko traveled to England and America, where he was given a triumphant reception. Perhaps his most humorous story is "Bez Yazyka" (Without a Tongue, 1895; also translated as In a Strange Land), dealing with the American adventures of some Ukrainian peasants who knew no English.

Korolenko became one of the editors of Russkoe Bogatstvo, an influential St. Petersburg journal, in 1900. But he found himself unable to adjust to life there and soon moved to Poltava, a town in the Ukraine. His home became a gathering spot for Russian intellectuals, and it was there that he wrote his famous autobiography Istoriya Moego Sovremennika (The Story of My Contemporary). This was an incomplete work, and the latter parts of it were published posthumously, but it is considered a masterpiece and is filled with the gentle humanitarianism and faith in the future which characterized Korolenko's earlier works as well. In contrast to so many other Russian authors, Korolenko had no room for melancholy and despair. He believed that "man was created to be happy, even as a bird was born to fly."

There is a tragic irony in the fact that this deeply moral, sensitive humanitarian, who had repeatedly asserted his faith in a brighter future, lived to witness the Russian revolution and civil war. Shocked by the horrors he saw all around him, he wrote a number of letters to Lunacharsky, the Soviet commissar of education, denouncing the Bolshevik terror and pleading for a preservation of liberal human values. Korolenko died in 1921. His works are widely published and read today in the Soviet Union, where he is considered to have been a "progressive" and "democratic" writer, despite his failure to "understand the true significance of the revolution."

The complete works of Korolenko have yet to be translated into English. A number of his best short stories, however, have been published in English translation. These include The Blind Musician (tr. by W. Westall and S. Stepniak, 1890); The Murmuring Forest and Other Stories (tr. by M. Fell, 1916); In a Strange Land (tr. by G. Zilboorg, 1925); "At Night" (tr. by J. Lavrin, 1946); "Makar's Dream" (tr. by R. F. Christian, 1954).

ABOUT: Mirsky, D. A History of Russian Literature; Slonim, M., Modern Russian Literature; Olgin, M. Guide to Russian Literature; Waliszewski, K. A History of Russian Literature. [In Russian—see studies by F. D. Batiushkov, G. Bialy, A. Kotov, V. G. Letov, G. Mironov.]

H. W. D.

*KOTZEBUE, AUGUST FRIEDRICH FERDINAND VON (May 3, 1761-March 23, 1819), German playwright and prose writer, was born at Weimar, the son of a well-to-do Councilor of Legation. He studied law at the universities of Jena and Duisberg and became a lawyer in 1780. The following year he was appointed secretary in St. Petersburg to the Governor-General whom he also assisted as director of the German Theatre. After serving as magistrate in Estland he was ennobled and appointed to the High Court of Appeal at Reval. Here he married the first

* kôt′ sĕ bōō

KOTZEBUE

of his three wives, Friderike von Essen, the daughter of a general. His literary career began during this period and in 1795 he retired from his position to devote himself entirely to literature.

From 1797 to 1799 he was dramatist and *régisseur* at the court theatre in Vienna. Upon his return to Russia in 1800 he was arrested for political reasons and sentenced to Siberia for life. He was soon released and awarded a valuable estate in Livonia as well as being named director of the German Theatre in St. Petersburg. Following the death of Paul I, Kotzebue settled in Weimar and then in Berlin, where with Garlieb Merkel he edited *Der Freimütige* (1803-07), a journal dedicated to opposition to both the classical and romantic literary movements. Restless, as always, the author returned to Russia in 1806, where in the journals *Die Biene* (1808-10) and *Die Grille* (1811-12) he published satirical articles against Napoleon. In 1813 he became General-Consul in the Department of Foreign Affairs and in 1817 was sent to Weimar to report on conditions in Germany. It is now accepted that he was not a spy, as was popularly believed at the time. However, because of his ridicule and criticism of the German democratic movement, Kotzebue was thoroughly hated by the young advocates of freedom in Germany. For safety he was forced to move to Mannheim, where in 1819 he was fatally stabbed by Karl Sand, a fanatical theology student. Kotzebue's death had far-reaching political implications, for the government used this

incident as a reason to subject democratic and particularly university student groups to stricter supervision.

Kotzebue was the most popular stage writer in Germany at the end of the eighteenth century and as a writer of comedy influenced the subsequent development of European theatre. However, his egotism, shallowness, and cynicism made him one of the most despised men of his time, a reputation which has tended to overshadow the value of his literary contribution. Endowed with an astonishingly fertile mind, he produced 211 plays, which have been collected in *Theater* (40 vols., 1840-41). Of these works the best-known and most popular were *Menschenhass und Reue* (1789), which brought the author a world-wide reputation, *Die Sonnenjungfrau* (1789), *Das Kind der Liebe* (1790), *Die Indianer in England* (1790), *Der Weibliche Jakobiner-Clubb* (1793), *Die Spanier in Peru* (1795), *Die Negersklaven* (1795), and *La Peyrouse* (1797). His first comedies, *Die Beiden Klingsberg* (1801) and *Die Deutschen Kleinstädter* (1802), enjoyed the longest vogue of any of his dramas.

Kotzebue is recognized as one of the founders of melodrama. His dramas consist principally of superficial theatrical effects and highly sentimentalized characters and plots. He was the avowed foe of all serious forms of literature, and his works, despite their stage effectiveness, are objectionable because they contradict and expose to ridicule traditional ideas of morality and behavior. Kotzebue's sole aim was to entertain, and thus his works, lacking in ethical and intellectual substance, have not endured.

A selection of Kotzebue's innumerable prose writings is contained in *Ausgewählte Prosaische Schriften* (45 vols., 1842-43). The most significant of these are the autobiographical writings *Mein Literarischer Lebenslauf* (1796) and *Das Merkwürdigste Jahr meines Lebens* (1801).

The following represents a selected list of the best English translations of Kotzebue's major works. The most extensive single collection is found in C. Smith *The Dramatic Works* (3 vols., 1800). In 1796 *Die Negersklaven* was translated anonymously, and B. Thompson translated *Die Indianer in England*. In 1798 G. Papendick translated *Menschenhass und Reue* as *The Stranger*. *Das Kind der Liebe* was translated by S. Porter as *Lovers' Vows*, and by A. Plumptre as *The Natural Son*. In 1799 A. Plumptre translated *La Peyrouse, Die Sonnenjungfrau*, and *Die Spanier in Peru*. J. C. Siber translated *Der Weibliche Jakobiner-Clubb* in 1801. *Die Beiden Klingsberg* appeared anonymously in 1814. *Das Merkwürdigste Jahr meines Lebens* was translated by B. Beresford in 1802, and *Mein Literarischer Lebenslauf* as *Sketch of the Life and Literary Career of A. von Kotzebue* by A. Plumptre in 1800.

ABOUT: Fairchild, H. N. The Noble Savage; Holzmann, A. W. Family Relationships in the Dramas of Kotzebue; Sellier, W. Kotzebue in England; Thompson, L. F. Kotzebue, a Survey of his Progress in France and England. [In German—see studies by E. Jäckh and W. von Kotzebue. In French —see study by C. Rabany.]

D. G. D.

*KRASICKI, IGNACY, Count (February 3, 1735-March 14, 1801), Polish poet, novelist, and playwright, was born in Dubieck, formerly Polish Ruthenia. He was a descendant of an aristocratic but impoverished family. His parents, John and Anna *née* Starzechowska, destined four of their five sons to priesthood. The future writer was a gifted, intelligent child. He was educated in a Jesuit school in Lwów and in the Warsaw Catholic Seminary. He spent some time abroad. His abilities were appreciated by his superiors, and as a young man he occupied several important posts. In 1765 he became President of a Court of Justice. He was honored by King Stanislas Augustus who helped in his quick promotion. Krasicki became his chaplain, and delivered a sermon at the King's coronation. As a man of thirty-one he was nominated bishop of the Ermeland diocese, to which considerable income and a place in the Senate were attached. Afterwards he shunned politics, concentrating on his administrative duties, social life, and literary work. He cooperated with the periodicals *Monitor* and *Zabawy Przyjemne i Pozyteczne* (Pleasant and Useful Amusements), in which he printed some didactic articles and satirical sketches. In 1774 his first short poem was published; it exalted love for the native country, and soon became very popular. In 1776 appeared his longer comical poem *The Mousiade*, as well as· the novel *Adventures of Nicholas Doswiadczynski*. In the following years several of his works appeared in quick succession: another humorous poem, *Monachomachia*, and the second novel, *Pan Podstoli* (both 1778), *Fables and Apothegms* and ten *Satires* (1779), a narrative poem *The Chocim War* (1780), two volumes of *Epistles* (1784 and 1788), another ten *Satires* (1784). All these writings made the author famous. When after a long absence he returned to Warsaw, the King pardoned him for his aloofness, and he was cordially welcomed. His life was typical of a representative of the age of Enlightenment. When his diocese was occupied by Prussia, he maintained friendly relations with Frederick II. He drafted an encyclopedia and a history of literature, for which he wrote translations of various poems. He also translated Ossian's *Songs,* Plutarch's *Lives* and the *Dialogues* of Lucian. He collected works of art, was fond of gardening and of reading. Before the third partition of Poland he became primate and archbishop of Gniezno. Some of his manuscripts (among them *New Fables*) were published after his death.

Krasicki's best works were written in a comical vein. His *Adventures of Nicholas Doswiadczynski* was influenced by Defoe's *Robinson Crusoe,* Swift, and Rousseau, but the best part described habits, customs, and vices of the Polish community. As fabulist, Krasicki did not imitate the charm and gracefulness of La Fontaine, but excelled in compact, clear, precise storytelling. His *Satires* contained elements which can be found in other satirical writers, e.g., Boileau, but they were obviously based on observation of local environment. The finest of them are penetrated with cold irony mixed with indulgence for human frailties. *The Fashionable Wife* describes the misadventures of a thrifty husband, who marries a reckless modern woman and has to obey her whims; *Drunkenness* draws a portrait of a drunkard who is a mortal enemy of drink, but has to drink for various reasons.

Krasicki's diction, influenced by French writings, was admired for clarity, brevity and conciseness; his humor was dry, but funny and effective, especially in *Monachomachia,* a satirical description of monastic life. He achieved a happy union of artistic values with simplicity, which was the cornerstone of his universal popularity. The first collected edition of Krasicki's writings appeared 1802-04.

Some poems of Krasicki translated into English are included in John Bowring's *Specimens of the Polish Poets* (1827), and P. Soboleski's *Poets and Poetry of Poland* (1881).

ABOUT: Borowy, W. The Cambridge History of Poland, II. [In French—see study by P. Cazin.]

M. G.

*KRASIŃSKI, ZYGMUNT, Count (February 19, 1812-February 23, 1859), Polish playwright, poet, and novelist, was a descendant of one of the leading aristocratic families in Poland. His father, General Wincenty, married Ursula *née* Princess Radziwill, took part in the Napoleonic campaigns, and in 1812 went with his wife to Paris where his only son was born. After the defeat of Napoleon he led the remnants of Polish

* krä sěts′ kě

* krä sěn′y′ skě

armed units to Poland. Later he adhered to pro-Russian policy. He deeply influenced his son and chose the best professors for his education. The boy made admirable progress. After completing the final class at a Warsaw college he studied law at Warsaw University. Very early he began to write sketches, short stories, and novels, one of which was published in 1829. His father lost popularity after advocating the death penalty for members of a clandestine organization. Once, when all students participated in a patriotic demonstration, Zygmunt followed his father's order and attended the lectures. He was insulted by some colleagues, and had to leave the university. He went abroad to Geneva, resuming his studies. He struck up a friendship with Henry Reeve, the future British statesman and editor, and fell in love with an English girl. He made the acquaintance of Mickiewicz, who influenced him considerably.

When the uprising against Russia began in Poland, General Krasiński went to St. Petersburg as an aide of the Czar, and ordered his son to stay abroad. The poet protested, but did not disobey. After the Russian victory he was presented by his father to the Czar and offered a diplomatic career, which he rejected. His tempestuous and painful experiences contributed to his early maturity. His *Nieboska Komedia* (Undivine Comedy) was published in 1835, and *Irydion* in 1836. Both tragedies were linked with his personal life. *Nieboska Komedia* developed his father's suggestion that the Polish rising was primarily social revolution; this idea, augmented by the poet's observations of contemporary social disturbances, led to a grandiose picture of the prospective universal revolution which would end with a victory for the rebels, who would then perish visualizing that Christ was the only way of salvation. *Irydion* dealt with hatred as an approach to solving of international feuds; it was condemned for moral reasons.

Krasiński's further studies were concentrated on philosophy, with Schelling and Hegel among his spiritual guides. His love affair with Joanna Bobrowa gave a new impulse to poetry, but ended with discord. Another affair, with Delphine Potocka, lasted longer and brought much happiness. This new mood influenced the poet's views and his former pessimistic attitude gave way to refreshing optimism. He believed in the gradual Christianizing of international relations, and in the role of Poland in this development. These reflections were expressed in the poem *The Dawn,* enthusiastically received by his compatriots.

Troubled by radical writers advocating acceleration of social changes even through violence, he published *Psalms of the Future* confirming his faith in prosperous historical evolution, but warning against dangerous social disturbances. His fears were borne out by events in Austria where peasants, agitated by official authorities, killed many estate owners. The poet added two new psalms, and wrote a poem *Resurrecturis* reappraising all arguments for the restoration of Poland's freedom. He also attempted to write a new part of *The Undivine Comedy* describing the past of its hero, Count Henry.

In 1843, advised by his father, Krasiński married a rich heiress, Eliza Branicka, but did not immediately abrogate his previous affair. Only gradually did he begin to appreciate the beauty and kindliness of his wife. Although his health failed, he did not stop writing; one of his memoirs on political problems was addressed to Napoleon III. He lived mostly abroad. In 1858 his father died, and the poet followed him one year later.

The two tragedies *The Undivine Comedy* and *Irydion* are Krasiński's greatest achievement in their concentration on essential problems of modern history and mankind. Although linked with national background, they expound their subject in universal terms. In their concise wording, firm intellectual structure, and purposeful introduction of motifs they are opposed to romantic fluidity; their visionary power and symbolism anticipate impressionist drama. Dealing with social revolution and blind nationalism Krasiński seemed to foretell the prospective developments in European political life. Although not written for the stage, *The Undivine Comedy* had a considerable theatrical success both in Poland and abroad. Among other works of Krasiński *The Dawn* played an important historical rôle as a source of faith and encouragement in the years of the deepest emotional depression within the Polish community. Krasiński's letters, published after his death, have considerable artistic value. During the poet's life his writings were printed anonymously, or signed with pseudonyms.

Both plays of Krasiński (with some other poems) were translated into English by Martha Walker Cook (1875), but the translator grossly distorted the originals. *The Undivine Comedy* was translated again by H. E. Kennedy and Z. Umińska (1923); a translation of *Irydion* by Florence Noyes, edited and completed with an introduction by G. R. Noyes, was published in 1927.

ABOUT: Gardner, M. The Anonymous Poet of Poland; Polish Review, IV (1959). [In Polish—see study by M. Janion.]

M. G.

*KRASZEWSKI, JÓZEF IGNACY (pseudonyms, K. F. PASTERNAK and B. BOLESŁAWITA), (July 28, 1812-March 19, 1887), Polish writer, was born in Warsaw. His father, Jan, owned an estate. The boy received an excellent education in his grandparents' home and in the secondary schools. In 1829 he began to study philology and literature at the university in Wilno. One year later, being involved in the national rising against Russia, he was sent to prison and threatened with exile, but regained his freedom owing to his youth. When he was eighteen, he began to publish his short stories. He continued writing with amazing speed regardless of other occupations. He married Zofia Woronowicz and had several children. His efforts to become a professor at the Kiev University failed. Acquiring an estate in Volhynia, he was able to learn the life of local gentry and peasants, and used his observations in various novels.

Kraszewski published a history of Lithuania, and an epic poem on the Lithuanian past, Anafielas. Gradually he became popular. He cooperated with various periodicals and edited one of them devoted to cultural affairs. After selling his estate he went to Żytomierz, a town in Volhynia, where he promoted lively social, theatrical, and educational activities. In 1858 he went abroad and visited several Western countries. From 1860 to 1862 he lived in Warsaw, employed as editor of a newspaper. On the eve of the new rising he left for Dresden to concentrate on writing and editing. He purchased a printing workshop, and reprinted many valuable books. He also started a large series of novels embracing a systematical review of Polish history. His anniversary in 1879 became a national event. In 1883 he was arrested for alleged spying for France; the pressure of Chancellor Bismarck contributed to his imprisonment. His health failed, and he was released on bail. In San Remo his house was destroyed by earthquake; he left for Geneva where he died.

Kraszewski was one of the most prolific of Polish writers. He published over 600 volumes of novels, plays, longer and shorter poems, literary essays, biographies, historical works, memoirs, political sketches, etc. He maintained contact with contemporary developments in many fields. As a novelist Kra-szewski chose his subjects from everyday life as well as from the past. He did not hesitate to tackle crucial problems of his period; some of his best books dealt with peasant troubles and other social affairs. His views changed, and it would be easy to accuse him of contradicting himself; but his watchfulness and devotion to the novelist's social duties remained unaltered. During the years when education was hampered by foreign occupation Kraszewski's importance was tremendous. He defined his own work as the baking of ordinary bread; nevertheless his literary production remained at a good artistic level, and his books were translated into many languages. He was at his best in the stories based on the seventeenth and eighteenth centuries. His technique reflected the influence of such writers as Walter Scott, Dickens, Gogol, and Balzac; but he applied all devices with skill and ingenuity. Among his novels some were concentrated on psychological aspects, e.g., Poeta o Świat (The Poet and the World), Szalona (The Crazy Woman). Social background prevails in Ułana, Jaryna, Chata za Wsią (The Hut behind the Village), Morituri, etc. The finest tales based on the past are Ostatnie Chwile Księcia Wojewody (The Last Moments of Prince Voivod), Papiery po Glince (Glinka's Papers), Diabeł (The Devil). His many historical novels include Stara Baśń (The Old Fairytale) and Rzym ze Nerona (Rome under Nero).

English translations include The Jew, by L. Kowalewska (1890); A Clever Woman or, Yermola, by M. Carey (1891?): Countess Cosel (1901) and Count Bruhl (1912), both translated by the Count de Soissons. Morituri appeared in a Tauchnitz edition, without Kraszewski's name, as Count Royal.

M. G.

*KROPOTKIN, PETER ALEXEYE-VICH, Prince (November 26, 1842-February 8, 1921), Russian anarchist, was born in Moscow into the high aristocracy. The Kropotkins had been ruling princes in Smolensk during the Middle Ages and could trace their descent from Rurik, the founder of the Russian state, as readily as could the Czar. His father was a typical army general and landowner of the time of Nicholas I. His mother, Ekaterina Sulima, the daughter of a general, was of Ukrainian Cossack descent. After her death when he was three, he was raised by a stepmother and French tutors. At fifteen he was enlisted in the Corps of Pages where he rose to the rank of sergeant and be-

* krä shĕf' skĕ

* krŭ pôt' kĭn

came for a time personal attendant to Alexander II. It was perhaps because of his insight into court affairs that on graduating from the Corps he elected to serve in eastern Siberia "in order to serve the people and study nature."

First in Irkutsk and later in Chita, Kropotkin held positions high for one so young. He was given great freedom of action and explored extensively in Transbaikalia and northern Manchuria. Here he made significant discoveries concerning the geology of northern Asia. It was at this time that he also first began to entertain anarchistic ideas, for he found that most of life, and man in particular, survived in the harsh Siberian environment through mutual aid rather than through competition. He also felt that the state was hopelessly rigid and incompetent.

On returning to St. Petersburg in 1867, Kropotkin studied natural sciences at the university and investigated the glaciation of Sweden and Finland. In recognition of his geological discoveries he was offered the Secretaryship of the Russian Geographical Society. He declined this honor, however, in order to devote himself for the rest of his life to revolutionary anarchism.

After a short visit to Switzerland in 1872, where he broke with the Marxists, and after a daring escape from a Russian prison, Kropotkin led a life of intense anarchistic activity in England, France, Switzerland, and Spain. A combination of immense energy, selfless devotion and enormous erudition made Kropotkin the dominant anarchist theoretician of his time. He wrote innumerable articles and manifestoes in English, French, Russian, and German and gained wide recognition among European scientists.

At Geneva, in October 1878, he married Sophie Ananiev, also a Russian revolutionary émigrée. One daughter, Alexandra, was born to them. She grew up to marry the social revolutionary Boris Lebedev.

Although personally a very mild man of great moral stature, Kropotkin was nevertheless arrested with other anarchists in connection with violence during a strike in Lyons. There was an immediate clamor throughout the enlightened world, particularly England, for his release. Finally, after three years, the President of France ordered his pardon. Kropotkin became a legendary figure in Europe. A massive man with a mild, round face, quizzical eyes and bushy red beard, he dominated the scene in the working class lecture halls of England and France. Actually,

like Bakunin, Herzen, and Tolstoy, Kropotkin was a very representative intellectual of his time. This is seen in his profound faith in the powers of reason and the consequent devotion to his convictions. His political and economic theories are best outlined in his *Conquête du Pain* (1892) and *Fields, Factories and Workshops* (written in English, 1898), in which he envisages man as living in a very loose federation of freely formed communes of interest and endeavor, somewhat similar to the Russian artisan communes or the medieval guilds. His most significant work and the cornerstone of his anarchism is *Mutual Aid, a Factor in Evolution* (also written in English, 1890) which is a rebuttal to Thomas Huxley's *Struggle for Existence in Human Society*. Kropotkin held, in opposition to a vision of nature ruled by the law of claw and talon, that those species which practice mutual aid in a hostile environment have shown the greatest advancement.

Kropotkin visited the United States twice at the invitation of the Lowell Institute, where he lectured on mutual aid in 1897 and on Russian literature in 1901. He also lectured at Wellesley College and the University of Illinois. At the outbreak of the war in 1914 Kropotkin shocked his anarchist friends by supporting the Allied cause in a war with militarist Germany. With the downfall of the czarist regime he returned with his family to Russia in 1917. But he could no more accept Lenin's dictatorship of the proletariat than he could the czarist state, and his last political act was a violent attack on Lenin's practice of taking hostages. He retired to the small town of Dmitrov where he applied himself to his last work, *Ethics*. This remained unfinished, for in 1921, at the age of seventy-eight, he died in almost complete isolation. His family declined a state funeral, and he was buried by a handful of surviving anarchist friends, some of whom had been released from Soviet prisons for the occasion.

The *Appeal to the Young* was translated from the French by H. M. Hyndman in 1885; *Memoirs of a Revolutionist* was written in English and first appeared in the *Atlantic Monthly* in 1898. The *Great French Revolution* was translated from the French by N. F. Dryhurst in 1909. *Ethics,* his only major philosophical work composed in Russian, was translated in 1924 by Joseph Piroshnikoff and Louis Friedman.

ABOUT: Woodcock, G., and Avakumovich, I. The Anarchist Prince; Berneri, C. Kropotkin, His Federalist Ideas; Montagu, A. *Foreword to the 1955 edition of* Mutual Aid.

N. V.

*KRYLOV, IVAN ANDREVICH (February 14, 1768-November 21, 1844), Russian fabulist, was born in Moscow. His father, a modest Army officer, died when the the boy was eight. To help the family, the future poet became a clerk in St. Petersburg at fourteen to the neglect of his education. His early writings included librettos for comic operas: "Crazy Family" and "The Americans." He also wrote tragedies. Later he turned to satire, and edited the periodicals *The Spectator* and *St. Petersburg Mercury* (1792-93). At that period his works, inspired by a satirical mood, were vigorous and violent. "A Panegyric of My Grandfather" drafted a caricature of a rude country squire treating his dogs and horses better than his serfs. Soon Krylov's editorial activity was suppressed, and for over ten years his name disappeared from literature. Little is known of this period of his life. He earned his living as tutor or secretary of rich noblemen, living for some time in the house of Prince S. T. Galitzin, partly as salaried tutor, partly as friend. When he renewed writing, his early virulence became milder, and his aggressiveness gave place to calmer irony.

The first of Krylov's fables appeared in the periodical *Morning Hours*. In 1805 he wrote translations of La Fontaine's *Fables*. He also composed two comedies ridiculing the French fashion among the Russians. Since their subject coincided with the popular antagonism against Napoleon, both were warmly applauded. But Krylov, advised by his predecessor Dmitriev, found that his proper vocation was fable writing. In 1809 he published twenty-three of them, mostly translated from La Fontaine. They gained an unprecedented success which finally determined the prospective career of their author. In 1812 he was offered a post in a St. Petersburg Imperial public library which was practically a sinecure. He occupied it for over thirty years. He gradually augmented the number of fables in later editions.

Krylov was elected to the Russian Academy, and in 1823 received its Gold Medal. His fame remained unshakable, although for a long time his literary production was limited to occasional fables. He was a frequent guest in the drawing-rooms of the Russian capital, and was tolerated in spite of his untidiness, voracious appetite, and taciturn indifference to other persons. He was pictured as a benevolent granddad playing with children in the summer garden. In 1838 his fiftieth anniversary as a writer was celebrated.

KRYLOV

Krylov's writings were linked with the eighteenth century and did not assimilate new trends. He wrote over 200 fables, mostly original; even in the translated fables the Russian environment found its reflection. Many ideas were taken from everyday observations and events. Krylov put his emphasis on tradition and nationalist emotions. He branded foolishness, false ambition, stubbornness, and similar vices, and advocated sober common sense. He frequently introduced ordinary people: servants, craftsmen, merchants, peasants. Political thrusts were carefully veiled; some more aggressive fables were found in Krylov's manuscripts. One fable stated that when the nightingale sang better, it was more carefully guarded. Krylov's mastery of the Russian language was admirable. He preserved some classical mannerisms but displayed marvelous command of Russian idioms and made excellent use of colloquial language. His simple gaiety appealed to wider circles; his artful naturalness attracted intellectuals. Many of his sentences became almost national proverbs and were universally quoted. A new edition of Krylov's writings with a biography appeared in Moscow in 1955 in two volumes.

Krylov's fables were translated into English by W. R. S. Ralston (1869), I. H. Harrison (1883), C. F. Coxwell (1920), B. Pares (1926, 1942).

ABOUT: Mirsky, D. S. A History of Russian Literature; Slonim, M. The Epic of Russian Literature.

* krĭ lôf'

M. G.

*KUHLMANN, QUIRINUS (February 25, 1651-October 4, 1689), German poet and mystic, was born in Breslau. His parents, Johannes and Elisabeth Kuhlmann, were members of Silesian families of some standing. The boy first attended the Magdalenen *Gymnasium* in Breslau and then (1670) the University of Jena. Even as a boy he had begun to display symptoms of delusion which took the form of religious ecstasy. In Jena, too, a bizarre fastidiousness in clothing and a melancholy seclusion from ordinary life gave rise to strange stories. He was regarded as egocentric; actually he was completely selfless in his earnestness and impelled by a sense of mission so profound and enduring as to amount to obsession. J. C. Adelung (*Geschichte der Menschlichen Narrheit,* 1787) dwells almost entirely on these eccentricities, thus diverting attention from Kuhlmann's linguistic virtuosity and poetic gift.

In Jena, Kuhlmann's task, the conversion of the world to his own Kuhlmann-Religion, developed swiftly. Late medieval mysticism and post-Reformation esoteric sects supplied the haphazard components for the new religion. A sojourn in Leiden, ostensibly to crown his legal studies, enlarged his circle of religious eccentrics who flourished in bewildering variety in the free air of seventeenth century Holland. Kuhlmann felt thoroughly at home. Here too he encountered Jakob Böhme's *Mysterium Magnum;* it precipitated *Quirin Kuhlmanns Neubegeisterter Böhme* (1674).

From now on all efforts went toward the founding of the "Fifth World Monarchy," the "Kühlmonarchie." The wanderings now beginning took him first to Lübeck; now also there began those impossible associations with women: Tanneke Denys, an ecstatic visionary, and Magdalena von Lindaw, a widow accepted by Kuhlmann in some desperation as his spiritual helper. In 1676 Kuhlmann went to England to prepare grandiose schemes to convert the Pope and the Sultan. His English contacts were mainly with Quakers.

In 1679 the fantastic entourage set out for Turkey. Pestilence at Smyrna compelled Kuhlmann to travel alone to Constantinople but the Sultan was in the field with his army, an eventuality not foreseen by Kuhlmann whose faith in his prophetic calculations was shaken. He persuaded himself that these reverses were to purify him. Thus Kuhlmann's world turned completely inward, though his journeys continued: Amsterdam,

England, Paris (1679-80), Geneva (1681-82). Otherworldly ideas did not, however, prevent him from marrying Mary Gould ("Maria Anglicana") in 1682; she and their child Salomon died in 1686. Six months later Kuhlmann married Esther Michaëlis de Paew; they had a child, Salome.

In April 1689 Kuhlmann went to Moscow to win over the Czar. But Lutherans, Jesuits, Calvinists, and nondescript Böhmian adherents united to accuse this unchurched heretic. The Patriarch of Moscow had him arrested and tried. Oddly he was charged with being a Quaker and therefore disruptive of accepted customs. Whether for religious or political reasons (an unresolved question) Kuhlmann was condemned to death; he was executed by burning.

Almost all of Kuhlmann's published writings are baffling mixtures of ecstatic visions vividly imaginative on the one hand, and the dark gropings of a sick mind on the other. The *Kühlpsalter* (one hundred and fifty psalms recording the events of his life and the adventures of his mind) is the best source for our knowledge of the man. His works (*Himmlische Libes-Küsse,* a sonnet collection of 1671; *Lehrreiche Weissheit-Lehr-Hof-Tugend-Sonnenblumen,* a volume of aphorisms of 1671, the *Neubegeisterter Böhme,* 1674) were not without admirers, although the man never succeeded in gaining a body of followers for his vague program. For the modern reader Kuhlmann's flashes of genius are only the luminous moments in the dark world of this pitiable representative of baroque aberration.

A few of his poems appear in G. C. Schoolfield's *The German Lyric of the Baroque in English Translation* (1962).

ABOUT: Journal of English and Germanic Philology, LII (1953); Modern Language Notes, LXXVII (1962); PMLA, LXVIII (1953). [In German—see studies by S. Heller (*in* Castrum Peregrini) and C. V. Bock.]

C. K. P.

*LABÉ, LOUISE (c. 1524-1566), French poetess, was born in Lyons before 1524, the date of the death of her mother, Étiennette Compagnon, Labé's second wife. Her father, Pierre Charly, known as Labé, was a prosperous but illiterate ropemaker. Nevertheless, Louise received an education comparable only to that of the courtly ladies of the Italian Renaissance and aimed at developing her natural inclinations and talents. She knew Latin and Italian, was an accomplished lute-

* kōōl' mȧn

* lȧ bȧ'

LOUISE LABÉ

player and singer, and enjoyed displaying her horsemanship in civic festivities (as in 1542, when she rode in the Tournoi of Perpignan at Lyons).

In 1540 she married a rich *cordier* (rope-maker), Ennemond Perrin—probably a marriage of convenience with the widower, twice her age, who died in 1560. At any rate, *La Belle Cordière's* heart was elsewhere. After a "military man" whose identity is not known, she had a love affair (1554-59) with the unfaithful and tactless Olivier de Magny, a poet, who discredited her by writing an insulting ode scoffing at her husband. Slanderers, after Magny, called her a cultivated courtesan and the prudish Calvin named her a *"plebeia meretrix"* (1561). She had many admirers among scholars, philosophers, and poets, but her popularity and free manners both scandalized and roused the envy of the provincial Lyons bourgeoisie. Her legend grew, as had that of Pernette du Guillet, the other poetess of the Lyons circle. As early as 1553 her reputation was so widespread that a street was named for her, and, in 1555, Peletier, a poet, wrote that she outshone the *damoiselles* and *dames* of Lyons, as the moon does other lights, by her beauty, knowledge, and elegant conversation.

In 1555 Louise Labé published her *Œuvres* which contain a *Débat de Folie et d'Amour,* a prose "debate," three elegies, and twenty-four sonnets. Her *débat,* in the medieval tradition, takes the form of a play involving Folly and Love. Jupiter presides over the court; Mercury and Apollo are the lawyers. The char-

acters are well defined and their language never turns to the coarseness common at that time. The classical allusions reflect broad culture rather than direct imitation, although she did consult Erasmus' *Praise of Folly* and Bembo's *Asolani.* The work had immediate recognition in France and in England (Robert Greene's translation, 1584); later, La Fontaine was to remember it in his fable *L'Amour et la Folie* (XII, xiv), and it inspired an eighteenth century vaudeville (1787). The main theme of her poetry, all of which was composed between 1545 and 1555, is love. Marot had already written elegies, but they were casuistic dissertations on love. Following the meanderings of her heart rather than a clear and definite plan, Louise describes her feelings (sensuality, insatiable desire, regrets) with a note of melancholy. She was influenced by Maurice Scève, and the sometimes awkward form of her elegies reveals a vain struggle to free herself from his tutelage. In her sonnets, she endeavors also to escape from Petrarch's influence, but she retains antithetical devices to point out the many contradictions within her personality. Far from being a gratuitous exercise in virtuosity, antithesis thus becomes a genuine analysis of sentiments. Her sonnets are free from servile imitations. In addition to Scève and Petrarch, she was inspired by Sannazaro and the neo-Latin poet Secundus, whose *Kisses,* melancholy and ardent poems, naturally appealed to her. Unlike her contemporaries, she was not interested in Neoplatonic or Christian philosophical speculations on the nature of love. In her vain longing for an appeasement of her soul and senses, she never was concerned with ethical considerations. Her pagan and amoral attitude was restrained only by feminine prudence and by fear that her behavior might affect others. Her works were followed by a publication of laudatory writings by the most famous poets of the time, Scève, Peletier, Tyard, Magny, etc.

After 1555 information about Louise Labé is scant. In 1557 she purchased a country estate at Parcieu en Dombes, near Lyons; in 1565 she was ill at the home of Thomas Fortin, a Florentine banker residing in Lyons. She died on her estate, a year later, bequeathing all her money to her nephews and to the poor.

Her contemporaries appreciated especially her *Débat,* but posterity has preferred her sonnets, which have survived, witness the numerous editions and translations including Rilke's German version (1917); F. Prokosch's *Love Sonnets with Translation* (1947); and Alta Lind Cook's *Sonnets of*

Louise Labé, "La Belle Cordière" (1950). *The Debate between Folly and Cupid* was translated by E. M. Coxin (1925). Translations of a few of her sonnets and one elegy appear also in *Proceedings and Transactions of the Royal Society of Canada, XLIX* (1955).

ABOUT: Harvey, L. E. The Aesthetics of the Renaissance Love Sonnet; Nottingham Medieval Studies, III (1959). [In French—Gorsse, P. de, Amour de Poètes; Magny et la Belle Cordière; Jans, A. Louise Labé, ou La Belle Cordière; O'Connor, D. Louise Labé, sa Vie, son Œuvre.]

M. B.

*LABICHE, EUGÈNE MARIN (May 5, 1815-January 23, 1888), French dramatist, was born in Paris of a middle class family. He studied at the Bourbon college and prepared for law but soon abandoned this career for literature. His first writings, beginning in 1834, were essays published in *L'Essor,* interpretative or technical, especially with reference to the theatre and his admiration for Molière. Labiche's first play dates from 1838, and his novel *La Clef des Champs* from the following year. His private life offers little interest; he was elected to the French Academy in 1880 despite opposition from more "serious" quarters.

Labiche's *Théâtre Complet* of 1878 contains only 57 of his 162 published plays. Many of these were composed in collaboration with men otherwise forgotten, such as Latigue and Martin; to judge by statements made by Augier, who worked briefly with him, Labiche seemed to seek company primarily for its own sake, being himself quite capable of creating the plots as well as the dialogue. His principal activity ended in 1874, and he retired to Normandy to prepare the edition of his best works. His retirement resulted in large part from lack of success of several recent plays, and his determination not to outlive his best period. By chance, Augier saw the plays as Labiche was editing them, and was greatly impressed by their true qualities. Publication of the *Théâtre Complet* had an unforeseen result, for the official critics, such as Sarcey, suddenly discovered that this popular playwright was a great creator, and the immediate result was his election to the Academy and a prolonged renewed success for several decades and into the twentieth century. Indeed, of the immense theatrical production of the nineteenth century, that of Labiche stands almost alone in living appeal, beside such few other dramatists as Dumas *fils*.

Labiche's masterpieces include his first great success, *Le Chapeau de Paille d'Italie*

* là běsh'

LABICHE

(1851), *Le Voyage de M. Perrichon* (1860), *La Poudre aux Yeux* (1861), and *La Cagnotte* (1864). There is little significant difference in subject matter or style among these works, and each stands on its own for its wit and its amusing situations. The Labiche tradition is very French, after the manner of Molière, but discreet and moral, eminently suited for school texts (as which the above plays have been constantly used). The protagonists are middle class types seen in their daily life, and the situations rise from slight misunderstandings. In *La Cagnotte* the tone is set by a card game and the collective project to spend the accumulated funds in the kitty (*la cagnotte*) for a grand splurge; the happy group, loaded with knicknacks for their friends at home, protest against the exorbitant price of their restaurant meal and end up in the police station accused as a gang of pickpockets. *Le Voyage de M. Perrichon* presents a rather pompous but devoted father who, during a holiday with his family in Switzerland, insults a questionable aristocrat and finds himself facing a duel. *La Poudre aux Yeux* is exceptional in its study of the dangers of carrying a bluff too far. These plays served several purposes in the evolution of the French theatre. They reacted against the heavy theses of the work of Dumas *fils*, seeking gaiety for its own sake. They continued the old vaudeville techniques in the well constructed formulae of Scribe, and portrayed middle class preoccupations somewhat as Paul de Kock had done in the novel. The wit rises from the uninhibited conversa-

509

tion, often in mock-epic seriousness, but always in the most irreproachable tone. In his heyday, Labiche was compared to Plautus and to La Fontaine as well as to Molière.

There have been numerous translations of his plays into English. These include *La Grammaire (Grammar)* by F. Berger (1883), B. H. Clark (1915); *The Two Cowards* by B. H. Clark (1915); *Under a Spell* by J. D. Gibbs (1888); *The Voyage of M. Perrichon* by M. Ivey (1924). *Le Chapeau de Paille d'Italie* or *The Italian Straw Hat* has seen many successful English and American productions. W. S. Gilbert's version, entitled first *The Wedding March* and later, as an operetta, *Haste to the Wedding*, had a long run in London in 1873. The American Federal Theatre produced it as *Horse Eats Hat* in 1936.

ABOUT: Matthews, B. French Dramatists of the Nineteenth Century; Smith, H. Main Currents of Modern French Drama. [In French—Parigot, H. Le Théâtre d'Hier.]

F. J. C.

---

*LA BOÉTIE, ÉTIENNE DE (November 1, 1530-August 18, 1563), French poet and writer, was born in Sarlat, where his house may still be seen. Of a distinguished family of that region, he received a strict classical education at a period of the greatest enthusiasm for ancient thought and humanistic ideas, those for example of Scaliger, who encouraged his work. La Boétie showed precocious talent for ancient languages, and his mastery of Greek is evident in his early French translations of Xenophon, of Plutarch's *Consolation*, and of Aristotle's *Economics*. At Bordeaux he witnessed the revolt against the excessive tyranny of the central government and the ensuing repressions during the wars of 1548. These events may have had some influence on his masterwork, the *Discours de la Servitude Volontaire*, also known as the *Contr' Un*, but the nature of the contents and the dates of composition tend rather to indicate that the thought is primarily idealistic. The theme of the *Discours* derives from ancient ideas on freedom and democracy, notably those of Plutarch, Herodotus, and Tacitus. La Boétie believed that citizens enjoy a natural right to freedom which obliges them to rise against oppression. The unnatural servitude suggested by the title is in part that of the times, and the contrast between current evils and the superiority of ancient customs is at least in part real. The principal quality of the work is its passionate expression of indignation, and the human feeling so different from the doctrines of Machiavelli. Nevertheless, La Boétie's career

* là bô ā sē'

510

amply illustrates his conservatism and his respect for traditional authority.

In 1553 La Boétie was named counselor in the parliament of Bordeaux, a charge he executed with diligence. In this body he formed his great friendship with Montaigne, c. 1557. Both were keenly concerned with the contrast between the intolerance, the rigid institutions, and the lack of human dignity of modern Europe, and the examples of devotion and courage recounted by the Greek and Roman historians. During an official trip, La Boétie fell ill near Bordeaux; Montaigne went to comfort him, and told at length of his fortitude in suffering and death; his loss was remarked by others who admired his person and his work. Montaigne's eulogy of La Boétie appears in his essay on friendship (XXVII).

La Boétie left various translations from the ancients and of parts of Ariosto's *Orlando Furioso*. His poetry, both in French and Latin, includes sonnets, a long piece in *terza rima* and Petrarchist style. In manner his verse is not unlike that of the Pléiade. His *Discours de la Servitude Volontaire* was well known during his lifetime to many friends, and parts were plagiarized in Edinburgh in 1574. Montaigne, however, feeling that the ideologies expressed in the work were excessive in tone, withheld it until 1576, when it appeared intact in volume III of *Les Mémoires de l'État de France sous Charles IX*, a collection of Protestant tracts. Montaigne's judgment, the circumstances of printing, and the aggressive way in which the *Discours* was used by the Protestants, caused it to be considered as a revolutionary work, though this interpretation is belied by the spirit of the author, who today seems more like a man of humane learning and of stoic wisdom than a reformer.

Montaigne published La Boétie's Latin and French poetry, of which the French sonnets are most highly esteemed for their beauty. The standard editions of La Boétie's complete works date from 1846 and 1892, both illustrated with critical biographies. The *Discours* was translated into English under the title *Anti-Dictator* by H. Kurz in 1942.

ABOUT: [In French—see study by L. Feugère.]

F. J.C.

---

*LA BRUYÈRE, JEAN DE (August 16, 1645-May 11, 1696), French moralist, was born in Paris of a family of the lesser bourgeoisie. He studied law there, was licensed in 1665, and was admitted as a

* là brü yâr'

LA BRUYÈRE

lawyer to the parliament although he never practiced. On the death of his uncle and godfather he received a legacy which permitted him, in 1673, to buy the post of Treasurer of France and General of Finances in Caen. He was not restricted to residency there, receiving an honest revenue from his office until he left it in 1686. Then, idle and obscure, La Bruyère lived in Paris, probably engaged in his great work (which may have been started as early as 1668). We know only that Bossuet found a position for him on August 15, 1684, with the royal Condé family and that he became a life-long servant in this house, first as sub-tutor in history and philosophy to the Duc de Bourbon, and then, after the latter's education was completed, as gentleman to the Duc d'Enghien, son of the prince. Thus he was able to observe the court closely and to borrow from it the materials for his *Characters*.

In 1688 La Bruyère published his work, unsigned, under the title of *The Characters of Theophrastus, translated from the Greek, with the Characters or the Manners of this Century.* Three editions were sold in one year; the work increased in size and by the eighth edition, in 1694, had taken its definitive form with the translation of Theophrastus at the end. La Bruyère was elected to the French Academy in 1693.

After participating brilliantly on the literary scene for several years, La Bruyère withdrew to Chantilly in semi-retirement, occupying himself, on behalf of Bossuet, with

the theological controversy between the latter and Fénelon. For Bossuet he wrote his *Dialogues on Quietism.* He died suddenly at the age of fifty-one. Among his friends he numbered, besides Bossuet, La Fontaine, Fénelon, Boileau, and Racine.

La Bruyère combined an independence of mind with an innate respect for tradition. This characteristic was increased by his juridical education, which fostered discussion but which taught the restraint of custom. His vibrant personality reflected the traits of pleasantness, gaiety and discretion, all considered especially desirable in his times. He was well-informed, obliging, and generous, yet he was inwardly sensitive and impressionable because of his pride, especially before the mockery of the elder Condé. Unhappy even in love, he was nonetheless without pessimism.

His real aim, La Bruyère declared frequently, was to study man in himself, that principle of classicism of seeking the universal in the particular. His characters or portraits, most of which were recognizable despite his protestations, are penetrating studies of the behavior of men and women shrewdly and minutely observed. This genre had been very popular during his century, but La Bruyère rendered it richer not only by his psychological soundness but by his inclusion of brief *pensées,* critical remarks, and epigrammatic observations. Introducing realism into literature through his descriptions of social evils and abuses, he became one of the first French writers to emphasize economic causation of social ills among the people as well as the clergy, judges, and nobility. However, his belief in goodness, charity, and spontaneous heroism, as well as his sincerity, prevented a pessimistic view of a deceitful world bound by human nature. La Bruyère was revolted by the evil and injustice of the court and church. His repugnance took the form of overt literary action to portray the prevailing ills.

La Bruyère's moral satire is not founded on an original or profound doctrine. Less systematic than other moralists, he is perhaps more exact but less powerful. However, he blends the borrowings with his own observations and conclusions as a thorough classicist, awakened by his own mind and his own dissatisfaction with what he sees. His classicism is that of Boileau, La Fontaine, and Racine whom he admired; it uses the ancients as model, but it modifies them according to nature. His art in moralization is that of the dramatist who finds the words to express the personality of the soul. It is in this that La Bruyère remade the art of portraiture. True to his aim, his portraits, though robed in court dress, reveal universal truths. As a satirist, he even touches caricature, the abstracting symbolism of which greatly influenced some of the playwrights of the later theatre.

As master of style, La Bruyère has won the greatest admiration. Classically balanced sentences, short and rapid phrases with varied constructions, and a rich vocabulary—all tending toward understatement—provide the *Caractères* with a zestful delicacy of tempo and tone. Although lacking composition or organization as such, these portraits served nonetheless as inimitable models for Montesquieu and Marivaux. Only Voltaire, who admired La Bruyère, was able to improve upon the neatness of expression and vivid but good-natured impertinence of this universal work.

The *Characters* of Jean de La Bruyère have been translated by H. Van Laun, London, 1929. The *Œuvres Complètes* (ed. by G. Servois) was published in six volumes in 1865-68 (reprinted 1923, 4 vols.).

ABOUT: Gosse, E. Three French Moralists. [In French—see studies by M. Lange, G. Michaut.]

R. P. C.

*LA CEPPÈDE, JEAN DE (c. 1550-1622), French magistrate and poet, was born in Marseilles, descendant of the family of St. Teresa. Bearing the title Sieur d'Aigalades, La Ceppède made a career of the cloth and judicature. Very little is known of his personal and professional life except that he was successively counselor-adviser to the Parliament of Aix (October 28, 1578), president of the Exchequer in 1586, and president of the Court of the Exchequer of Provence (July 14, 1608). He died in Avignon.

Although La Ceppède's poetry is little known today, in his own time he was highly esteemed as a pious man and as an eminent poet of the sacred lyric. It was Malherbe, himself a lyric poet and powerful in reforming and regulating the French language and versification, who said that La Ceppède was "worthy of the crown of heaven as well as the laurel and ivy crown of the Muses."

La Ceppède's poetic reputation rests on two large volumes of *Théorèmes Spirituels*— sonnets followed by commentaries or theological "justifications." The first poems under this title appeared in Lyons, 1594: *Imitation des Psaumes de la Pénitence avec des*

* lä sĕ pĕd'

Sonnets et des Méditations. The spirit of this work was re-enunciated in *Théorèmes sur les Mystères de la Rédemption, avec l' Imitation de quelques Psaumes de David;* following in a second part were *Théorèmes Spirituels sur les Mystères de la Descente de Jésus-Christ aux Enfers*. The work appeared between 1613 and 1621 in Toulouse.

Critical appraisal of the work is high, especially by Marcel Arland, who finds the poems marked "at once by a very sophisticated sense of the symbol and by a primitive realism." The rugged verse is sustained by a fullness of accent and an abundant vigor which place it with the best poetry of the French Renaissance.

In recent years La Ceppède's poetry has appeared in M. Arland's *Anthologie de la Poésie Française*, in Dominique Aury's *Anthologie de la Poésie Religieuse Française*, and in Abbé Goujet's *Histoire des Hommes Illustres de la Provence*—all works which attempt to restore the poet to his rightful place in the history of French sacred poetry.

ABOUT: French Review, XXXVI (1963); Modern Language Notes, LXXVIII (1963); The Month, XXVIII (1962). [In French—XVII° Siècle, No. 31 (1956).]

G. E.

*LACLOS, PIERRE AMBROISE FRANÇOIS *CHODERLOS DE (October 19, 1741-November 5, 1803), French novelist, was born in Amiens, of a family of the minor nobility. At eighteen he entered military service, and from 1769 to 1775 he was stationed with the artillery on garrison duty in Grenoble. In 1778 he achieved the rank of captain. In 1784 he had a child by Marie Soulage Du Perré. They were married two years later, after he had inherited a small income. It was, apparently, a happy marriage, and early biographers characterized him as "a virtuous man, good son, good father, excellent husband."

Choderlos de Laclos's career was not brilliant, but he played a minor part in the French Revolution, attaching himself to the party of the Duc d'Orléans (Philippe Égalité) in a plot to replace Louis XVI and Marie Antoinette with the duke. He remained in the service of Orléans as his secretary even after the plot failed. He narrowly escaped the guillotine during the Reign of Terror, proclaimed himself a republican, returned to the army in 1792, fought against the Prussians in the battle of Valmy, and was appointed Governor General of French possessions in India. Before he had

* là klō'; shō dĕr lō' dĕ

LACLOS

time to take office, the government fell and he was arrested. He spent some thirteen months in prison. After his release he returned to the army and rose to the rank of general under Napoleon. Sent to a distant military outpost in Taranto, Italy, he died there of dysentery at sixty-two.

Little is known of Laclos beyond these meager biographical details. He was evidently cold and reserved. A contemporary, Comte Alexandre de Tilly, described him in his memoirs as "a tall gentleman, thin and yellow, in a black suit." Perhaps the fairest summing up is Peter Quennell's: "Choderlos de Laclos was not a likeable, but a remarkably perceptive, man—quiet, precise, calculating, perhaps a trifle sinister, who saw a great deal and forgot nothing and harboured few illusions, but made up in clarity of insight what he lacked in warmth of feeling."

Laclos began his literary career as a poet with what one modern critic describes as "half a dozen insipid odes." He also wrote some pamphlets in behalf of the Duc d'Orléans' claim to the throne. His last literary work was a treatise on the education of young women. He studied ballistics and invented certain types of shells which were used in the battle of Valmy. For all this, however, he would have had no claim to immortality. But midway in a generally dull and undistinguished life, he produced one novel, "a masterpiece of eroticism," A. E. Carter calls it—*Les Liaisons Dangereuses* (1782; *Dangerous Acquaintances*), and it is by this work that his name lives today.

Les Liaisons Dangereuses was written in the form of letters, showing the pervasive influence of Samuel Richardson's *Clarissa,* a book that Laclos considered a masterpiece. The letters are exchanged between the members of the highest classes of French society. They are elegantly written, with pure classic restraint, but from underneath this façade of elegance and propriety there emerges a plot of complete amorality (not immorality, since, as Martin Turnell points out, this is a psychological rather than an ethical drama)—a coolly planned campaign of seduction, intrigue, and treachery. For years the novel was considered shocking and audacious. It was nevertheless widely read. Marie Antoinette owned an elaborately bound copy—but no title was stamped on the cover. As a "notorious" book it suffered inevitably from misinterpretation. Only its most enlightened nineteenth century readers—Stendhal and Baudelaire in particular—saw its real artistic merits. George Saintsbury omitted all mention of it from the first edition of his *History of the French Novel.* When called to task for this, he grudgingly read it and announced in a note in the later editions: "I am unable to find any redeeming point in it. . . . There is neither tragedy nor comedy, neither passion nor humor, nor even wit, except a little horseplay."

More recent critics have found the book and its author of much greater stature. Martin Turnell writes that Laclos "was one of the first great analysts of the human heart." Peter Quennell compares him with Stendhal: "Together they are the two chief progenitors of the modern novel." The appeal of the novel to modern readers lies in its precise psychological analysis and its revealing picture of a society. Readers may still find its study of sexual intrigue distasteful, but this does not alter the fact that the novel is a masterpiece of its kind, the last work in what Turnell calls "the tragedy of the Rational Man, the man who was carefully conditioned through the removal of all moral scruples and the sense of guilt, but inevitably condemned to action in a very limited field."

The standard English translation of *Les Liaisons Dangereuses* was made by Richard Aldington (1924). There is also an earlier translation by the poet Ernest Dowson, not published until 1940. In 1952 a dramatization of the novel by Paul Achard was produced in Paris, and a highly controversial "modernized" film version was made in France in 1959.

ABOUT: Aldington, R. *Introduction to* Dangerous Acquaintances; Duclaux, A. M. F. R. French

Procession; Gide, A. *Preface to* Dangerous Acquaintances (tr. E. Dowson); Gosse, E. Silhouettes; Maurois, A. Seven Faces of Love; Quennell, P. The Singular Preference; Thelander, D. R. Laclos and the Epistolary Novel; Turnell, M. The Novel in France; Modern Language Notes, LXXIV (1959); PMLA, LXXV (1960); University of Toronto Quarterly October 1954. [In French—see study by A. O. Aldridge.]

*LA FAYETTE, MARIE MADELEINE DE (March, 1634-May 23, 1693), French novelist, was born in Paris as Marie Madeleine Pioche de la Vergne. Her father was of the lesser nobility, but because of his merit, he lived in the service of the great. Marie Madeleine had for godfather and godmother a nephew and niece of the Cardinal-Duc de Richelieu; and until she was about sixteen years of age, she lived near or in the court.

A year after her father's death in 1659, her Provençal mother married the Baron Renaud de Sévigné. This marriage brought to Marie Madeleine the friendship of Renaud's niece, Marie de Rabutin-Chantal, the Marquise de Sévigné. Her father's death caused pecuniary and political difficulties, but her mother's successful business ventures recouped the family fortune. Marie Madeleine's delicate health, the milieu of court intrigues, and her mother's indifference contributed to make of her an introverted, secretive woman who was later to be called "the fog." At twenty-one she married a rich and well-connected provincial, François Motier, the Count de La Fayette.

After some years of residence in Auvergne, Marie Madeleine left La Fayette. She returned to Paris in 1660, though still financially supported by her husband, who visited her occasionally for their own interests and those of their two sons, born in 1658 and in 1659. While in Paris she met and became the confidante of Henrietta of England, princess of France, whose biography she wrote and whose brilliant but tragic life became a source for the future novelist. Also in Paris, Mme de La Fayette received a solid education from the famous Ménage and corresponded with many literary and learned men and women of her times. (Mme de Sévigné remained a life-long friend.) In her salon Molière read his *Femmes Savantes,* and in the court of Versailles Louis XIV welcomed her.

In 1665 Mme de La Fayette met and fell in love with La Rochefoucauld. The relative discretion of their love affair prevented scan-

* là fä yĕt'

MADAME DE LA FAYETTE

dal, and she was able to find favors for her sons from Louvois and the King himself. She even corresponded with the Duchess of Savoy in the interests of France. Active, with a lively and precise good sense, yet *précieuse,* romantic, though positive and truthful, she had many devoted friends and admirers.

Mme de La Fayette's work is marked by the truthfulness which characterized her personality. She renewed the novel as a genre by bringing to it this severe care for fidelity of subject, sentiments, and style. Her *Princesse de Clèves* (written in 1678), for which she is most noted, has a realistic subject which recalls her own married life. Her heroine marries a man whom she esteems rather than loves, then falls in love with another man. Her honor and her sensibility drive her to remorse and ultimate withdrawal from the world. The adventures of the principal characters of the novel are subordinate to the correct analysis of their feelings; and the style of this novel is that of actual speech: sober, precise, and delicate. The *Princesse de Clèves* brilliantly opened the way for the psychological novel. It is almost a unique work in that a feminine delicacy and the atmosphere of high society are joined with the true and simple elegance of classicism.

In addition to this work and some minor ones, Mme de La Fayette published under the name of Ségrais a *nouvelle* called the *Princesse de Montpensier* (1662) and a novel of adventures, *Zaydé* (1670); both works are more romantically adventuresome and less psychologically analytical than the aristocratic and profoundly human *Princesse de Clèves* which remains the prototype of the classical French novel.

The *Princess of Clèves* was translated by H. Ashton in 1925. *Henrietta* was translated by J. M. Shelmerdine in 1929, and the *Death of Madame* in 1931. The latest edition of the *Œuvres Complètes* (ed. by E. Magne) was made in 1939; the *Correspondance* (ed. by A. Beaunier) was published in two volumes in 1942.

ABOUT: Rea, L. The Life and Times of Marie Madeleine, Countess of Lafayette. [In French— see studies by H. Ashton, C. Dédéyan, M. J. Durry, E. Magne, B. Pingaud.]

R. P. C.

LA FONTAINE

*LA FONTAINE, JEAN DE (July 8, 1621-March 13, 1695), French poet and fabulist, born in Château-Thierry, was the son of the master of waters and forests in that region. He did his principal studies either in his birthplace or in Rheims and at nineteen entered the "Oratory." Despite the extreme freedom of this congregation La Fontaine's native restlessness caused him to leave it after eighteen months, still with no specific purpose in life and lacking enthusiasm of any kind. By chance he heard an *Ode* of Malherbe and, fired by admiration, studied the work of that poet and attempted imitations of it. He was encouraged by friends, who recommended that he read Horace, Virgil, and Terence, authors who pleased him for their noble simplicity, and who quickly turned him against Malherbe's overly embellished style. La Fontaine also read with particular interest the works of Rabelais, Marot, and Voiture, whose collective disciple he claimed to be. His allegiance to Voiture may be explained by this poet's delicacy and grace, while his oversubtlety was not apparent to the younger man. One might note further La Fontaine's admiration for D'Urfé's *Astrée*, rich in pastoral subjects and images, and, in a more licentious tone, Machiavelli's *Mandragola* and Boccaccio's *Decameron*.

La Fontaine's father encouraged his interest in poetry and sought to provide him with a livelihood in giving him his own mastership of waters and forests. The son executed his duties with little diligence or competency and showed the same indifference in his marriage. His relations to his wife (Marie Héricart, whom he married in 1647) were cold; they lived largely apart and were officially separated in 1658; one even suspects certain unflattering allusions to her in some

* là fôɴ těn′

of La Fontaine's writings. His retired life came to an end when he met the Duchesse de Bouillon, a niece of Mazarin, at Château-Thierry. He accompanied her to Paris on her return, in 1656, and there was protected by Jannart, a favorite of Fouquet. The latter's disgrace, in 1661, brought La Fontaine to his defense in the *Songe du Vaux,* an allegory on the construction of a château, addressed to Louis XIV. La Fontaine followed Jannart to Amboise.

The remainder of La Fontaine's life was spent almost entirely in Paris. He had a long series of distinguished patrons, and appealed especially to noblewomen with protective instincts, because of manifest incapacity in financial matters or in any other practical concern. Probably on account of his association with Fouquet, the court ignored him, thus in fact leaving him free for his creative work. It is also likely that the aristocracy in general was unappreciative of his particularly delicate expression; but his rather licentious *Contes,* acceptable at the time of their first publication, finally shocked the growing puritanism of the King. The Duchesse d'Orléans was La Fontaine's patroness for some time and through her he was introduced into the circles of Mme de Sévigné and Mme de La Fayette. His most important patroness and mentor for over twenty years (1672-93) was Mme de la Sablière; she urged him to gather his work to date in two volumes, and for some twenty years allowed him the full freedom of his natural indolence. His most important relations with men of letters were with Molière, Racine, and Boileau. Their accord was assured on the one hand by La Fontaine's relative passivity and by lack of overlapping interests. The closest spiritual bond was with Molière, whose plays La Fontaine especially admired, and with Racine, on account of a correspondence of religious views. Boileau, in contrast, was to some extent hostile and aloof.

In 1684 La Fontaine was elected to the French Academy, in preference to Boileau, his rival for that honor. Despite wide hostility to Boileau, who had not spared criticism of his contemporaries, Louis XIV favored him for this place, and withheld approval of La Fontaine until both could enter simultaneously. La Fontaine took a keen interest in the business of the Academy as time went on, finding great pleasure in the official speeches. Again in indigence on the death of Mme de la Sablière, in 1693 he thought of going to England to be with the Duchesse de Bouillon, but was encouraged to remain in Paris by the favors of the young Duc de Bourgogne and the friendly urging of Fénelon. During an almost fatal illness in 1692 La Fontaine had been induced by his confessor to denounce his impiety and especially his *Contes.* During his last years, spent in austere repentance, he was protected by Mme d'Hervart.

La Fontaine left works in several genres. His mythological novel *Les Amours de Psyché et de Cupidon* (1669) is a fantasy, based on Apuleius, turning to psychological analysis in the moral tones of the best classical style; his earlier mythological poem *Adonis* (c. 1659) is, in contrast, far more "precious." Many parts of his letters are also in verse of lyrical type. His first significant work is his *Contes* (1664-74), about sixty-five licentious tales based on Boccaccio, *Les Cent Nouvelles Nouvelles,* Marguerite de Navarre's *Heptaméron,* Machiavelli, Anacreon, and Rabelais. His half-dozen plays, including one tragedy and several allegorical and mythological subjects, belong to his last period (1683-91), with the exception of *L'Eunuque* (1654), an imitation of the play by Terence. La Fontaine's fame rests primarily on his *Fables,* of which two volumes appeared in 1668 including most of the best known pieces, such as *La Cigale et la Fourmi, Le Corbeau et le Renard,* and the more philosophical *Le Chêne et le Roseau.* He prefaced his fables with *La Vie d'Ésope,* though his narrative sources include such other collections as the medieval Phaedrus and the Oriental Bidpai. Through the artistry of these remarkable poems, he revived a neglected genre and established a norm of excellence to which one relates the work of such other fabulists as Florian. The *Fables* are typical of their times in their pessimistic attitudes toward human nature, with sardonic admission, for example, that "might makes right," a trait against which Rousseau later protested vigorously. The versification, in short lines of varying length, is most effective. The description of nature is almost unique for this period. Each fable has the density of a dramatic scene or even a small play, and the rapid action shows animals playing human rôles and revealing human foibles. The delicacy of the fables is such that they still arouse hostility among many connoisseurs of literature who reproach La Fontaine for his superficiality.

La Fontaine's *Œuvres,* in the six volumes of 1814, contain an extensive interpretative biography by L. Auger. An edition in eleven volumes, with album, ed. by H. Régnier and P. Mesnard, appeared 1883-93. The many English translations include *The Loves of Cupid and Psyche* (1744), *Tales and Novels* (1762, with later versions in 1814 and 1947), *Fables and Tales* (1734, 1806), and especially the *Fables,* repeatedly retranslated during the past century, by E. Wright, F. Tarver, E. Marsh and others, and more recently by Marianne Moore in 1955.

ABOUT: Guiton, M. La Fontaine: Poet and Counterpoet. [In French—see studies by R. Bray, P. Clarac, J. Giraudoux, F. Gohin, G. Michaut, L. Roche; bibliography by Comte de Rochambeau (1911).]

F. J. C.

*LAFORGUE, JULES (August 16, 1860-August 20, 1887), French poet and short-story writer, was born at Montevideo, Uruguay, where his father, Charles, was a teacher. His mother, Pauline Lacolley, was of Breton ancestry, his father from Gascony. The Laforgues had eleven children in all. In 1866 the family returned to Tarbes, in France, but the parents soon returned to Montevideo without the children. Jules never lost the nostalgia for the tropics and the memory of the long, slow ocean trip.

Jules attended school in Tarbes until 1876. He was a mediocre student but received excellent grades in religious instruction. His teachers said that he was unusually intelligent, although disinclined to study. When he was fifteen, he had an adolescent "crush" on a fair-skinned girl some three years his senior.

In 1877 his parents returned to France, and his mother died in childbirth. The family moved to Paris where Jules finished his

* là fôrg'

LAFORGUE

schooling at the Lycée Fontanes without being able to pass the examinations for the diploma. His father and younger brothers returned south; Jules lived with his sister Marie until mid-1881, when she too went to Tarbes. He frequented the libraries and museums while working as secretary to Charles Ephrussi, the director of *La Gazette des Beaux-Arts,* who was writing on Albrecht Dürer. Ephrussi was a collector of the Impressionists and of prints. Laforgue wrote articles on Böcklin, Menzel, and Klinger for his *Gazette* and read extensively in the romantic poets, in Baudelaire, the Goncourts, and Jules Barbey d'Aurevilly.

Laforgue's salary was meager; he lived most simply and ate insufficiently. Although well-mannered and socially sophisticated, he frequented few salons. Of medium height, with grey eyes, light-brown hair, and a long neck, he dressed very soberly and had a slow gait. He did establish close ties with the poetizing Sandah Mahali (pen-name of Mme Mullezer) and the scientist and littérateur Charles Henry. In semi-isolation, with his thoughts turned inward, he jotted down fragments of bitter, sad thoughts. He had passed through a religious crisis, and, rejecting Catholicism, he deemed himself a mystic pessimist.

At the end of 1881, through Ephrussi and Paul Bourget, to whom he had submitted his early poems, Laforgue obtained the position of reader to Empress Augusta of Germany. His father had just died. For five years, from December 1881 to September 1886, Laforgue was isolated from the mainstream of French letters as he followed the peregrinations of the court: Berlin, Coblenz, Baden, etc. This sort of existence, of being in attendance to nobility and of screening the royal family's reading-matter, encouraged him in his apathy and bitterness. The pianist Théo Ysaye was his only intimate friend. In this foreign environment Laforgue published successively, thanks to men sympathetic to Symbolism, *Les Complaintes* (1885), *L'Imitation de Notre-Dame la Lune* (1886), and *Le Concile Féerique* (1886).

Chaste until 1883, Laforgue had an affair with a member of the court (we know her only as "R," from Laforgue's *Agenda* for 1883). In 1885 he met Leah Lee, an Englishwoman who tutored him in English. They became engaged; Laforgue had to resign his position, since the Empress did not allow spouses in her entourage. Leah and Jules went to Belgium and to France; they were married in England, in January 1887, and returned to Paris. The couple lacked money for even the minimal necessities; he was unable to place his tales, *Moralités Légendaires,* and had few articles accepted. Leah was suffering from tuberculosis; Jules was also tubercular, but, until a sudden chill aggravated his case, he had not been an invalid. After an intense illness of three months, unable to work and under opiates, he died at the age of twenty-seven. He was buried in Bagneux cemetery. His wife died the following year at Menton.

Moralités Légendaires appeared the year of Laforgue's death. Here Laforgue reinterpreted and modernized traditional themes and figures: Hamlet, Lohengrin, Salomé, Pan. The degree of subjectivity has conferred on these stories the status of psychological documents, semi-veiled autobiography. Laforgue made himself the basis for his portrait of Hamlet.

Laforgue's poetry was probably not influenced by Symbolism as a "school," since he was not in the Parisian literary coteries. But the qualities of his work, in outlook and in techniques, have classed him among the Decadents and Symbolists. The general development of his outlook was from the pessimistic or tragic Buddhism (expressed in *Le Sanglot de la Terre,* composed between 1878 and 1881, but published posthumously) to extensive use of the unconscious or ironic in his last works. He made literary capital of Schopenhauer, Hartmann, and Oriental philosophy. His technique evolved from regular to free verse—it is disputed whether Laforgue initiated this form (other claimants are Tristan Corbière, Gustave Kahn, Marie Krysinska). Despite rather scanty publication, Laforgue is indelibly associated with Pierrot, the Moon-figure, the literary use of the popular refrain, free verse, and the dreariness of empty Sundays. His use of irony to objectify and shield his sensitivity achieves a modernity that lives on. Laforgue has influenced numerous modern American poets, including T. S. Eliot, Ezra Pound, Malcolm Cowley, and Hart Crane; with the *poètes fantaisistes*—Max Jacob and Jules Supervielle—Laforgue has pervaded post-Symbolist French letters.

Laforgue's *Œuvres Complètes,* which were edited by G. Jean-Aubry, still await a seventh and final volume (1922 sqq.). This edition includes Laforgue's letters, and his Agenda for 1883, as well as numerous poems not published in his lifetime, the *Fleurs de Bonne Volonté* and *Derniers Vers. Stéphane Vassilliew,* with an introduction by F. Ruchon, was published in 1946. Gabriel Fabre, H. Cliquet-Pleyel, Arthur Honegger, and Jacques Ibert have composed music to various *Complaintes;* Darius Milhaud has written an unpublished score to *Hamlet.* Poems have been translated into English by W. C. Arensberg (1914), J. Bithell (1920), H. Crane (in the *Double Dealer,* 1922), Harry Levin (in *Accent,* 1944), Cecily Mackworth (1947), Ezra Pound (1917), W. J. Smith (in *Wake,* 1951) and Patricia Terry (1958), among others. Frances Newman translated *Moralités Légendaires* as *Six Moral Tales from Jules Laforgue* (1928), and W. J. Smith translated *Selected Writings* in 1956. Selections from his poems appear in *An Anthology of French Poetry from Nerval to Valéry in English Translation,* edited by Angel Flores (Anchor Books, 1958).

ABOUT: Balakian, A. Literary Origins of Surrealism; Huneker, J. G. Essays, *also* Ivory, Apes and Peacocks; Pound, E. Instigations; Quennell, P. Baudelaire and the Symbolists; Ramsey, W. Jules Laforgue and the Ironic Inheritance; French Studies, July 1950; Quarterly Review of Literature, III (1946); Sewanee Review, LXXI (1963). [In French—see studies by M. J. Durry, L. Guichard, F. Ruchon.]

S. S. W.

*LA HARPE, JEAN FRANÇOIS DE (November 20, 1739-February 11, 1803), French writer, born of humble parents of Savoyard extraction, was orphaned at the age of nine and lived in Paris for ten years on charity. He did distinguished work at Harcourt College, winning several prizes; accused of writing verse ridiculing his teachers, he was sent briefly to a house of correction and, although exonerated, retained from this experience a mark of bitterness. In 1756, having completed his schooling, he met Dide-

* là àrp′

rot and wrote an interesting account of their conversation. His first light poetry, in epistolary form, shows facility and grace; it was collected in his *Héroïdes Nouvelles* in 1759. His first play, a formal tragedy entitled *Le Comte de Warwick,* performed in 1763 (and translated into English), was a great success, and was soon done at the court. La Harpe's correspondence with Voltaire begins at this time; they exchanged ideas on dramatic theory. When La Harpe and his wife visited the master at Ferney, in 1765, they were received with enthusiasm, and he became almost a son to Voltaire, who cast him in many plays, and listened respectfully to his advice. La Harpe was elected to the French Academy in 1776 at the age of thirty-seven. From the start he had as many admiring friends as savage enemies. A part of the enmity is explained by his successes in the theatre, another part by the long series of prizes he won in one after another competition of many academies.

La Harpe is remembered today almost entirely for his critical essays still extremely useful for eighteenth century studies. One of his first essays, on Lucan, appeared in his *Mélanges Littéraires* (1765). Beginning in the following year, he submitted the first of his writings for academic prizes, and, in 1768, contributed literary criticism to the *Mercure.* His first collected works (six volumes, 1778) contain his comments on Greek tragedy and on Shakespeare. Finally, when in 1786 the *lycée* was founded as a humanistic school for adult education, he, with Condorcet, Marmontel, and Monge, became one of the most admired professors. In 1794, as a result of indiscreet political statements, he was forced to go into hiding, and he began serious readings in the Bible; his return to the *lycée* found him far more conservative. Again condemned in 1797, he hid in the Jura and revised his courses of lectures, which began to appear in print within two years. His health was broken by a severe winter; his last acts included careful provision for his manuscript notes, many of which were published after his death. The frequent editions (carefully documented in G. Peignot's *Recherches*) of his *Lycée, ou Cours de Littérature Ancienne et Moderne* testify to its significance in the nineteenth century.

Among the extremely rare English translations of La Harpe's work is *Three Gifts* (by F. Swettenham, 1928), an Arab love story.

ABOUT: [In French—Peignot, G. Recherches; Sainte-Beuve, C. Causeries de Lundi, V.]

F. J. C.

*LAMARTINE, ALPHONSE MARIE LOUIS PRAT DE

(October 21, 1790-February 28, 1869), French man of letters, was born at Mâcon, although he liked to think of Milly as his birthplace. His father, Pierre (d. 1840), of a family of minor nobility, was a Royalist army officer; his mother, Françoise Alix des Roys (1766-1829), belonged to a family of lawyers. Alphonse had six younger sisters. The family lived modestly at its country estates of Milly or Saint-Point, and his mother gave him a strict Catholic upbringing. Trained in the rudiments by a local priest, Alphonse attended boarding school at Lyons, and completed his formal education at Bellay in 1808. Until 1814 he led the leisurely life of a young aristocrat, running up debts, reading Rousseau, the Philosophes, and the libertine poets, while writing imitative verses. He also composed some tragedies in the Voltairean manner. Tall and attractive, with facile speech, he made many feminine conquests. A trip to Italy in 1811 and investiture as mayor of Milly in 1812 helped him to avoid being drafted into Napoleon's armies. When Louis XVIII took the throne, Lamartine's family persuaded Alphonse to take a position in his guard. During the Hundred Days, Lamartine went to Switzerland, where he had an affair with Geneviève Favre.

In 1816, while vacationing at Aix to calm a nervous condition, Lamartine met Mme Julie Charles. Their liaison continued in Paris, but Mme Charles died in December 1817 of tuberculosis. He was profoundly affected by this affair, so different emotionally from numerous others. He had, however, another affair in 1819, with Léna de Larche, although he was trying to recapture the candor and faith of his adolescence. A serious illness in 1820 caused him to return to the Church and to swear to live piously. In June 1820 he married an Englishwoman, Maria Anna (Marianne) Eliza Birch (1795-1863), whom he had met the previous year. The couple went to Naples, where influential friends had obtained for him a position in the embassy. This was the beginning of the diplomatic career which finally stifled the poetic vein, expressed that same year in Les Méditations. This compilation included poems written some years earlier, while others were excluded in order not to upset his bride. Nevertheless, the volume, essentially orthodox in subjects, vocabulary, and form, seemed revolutionary to his contemporaries, who felt sincerity and depth in these verses. It was as

* là már tēn'

LAMARTINE

though Chateaubriand had been grafted onto Parny. The conservative, legitimist press helped to swell the reputation of the newly-known poet.

Lamartine, however, was dedicated to the elaboration of an epic, which, he thought, would be his major work. For reasons of health and in order to work on the *magnum opus*, he took a leave of absence and settled at Mâcon with his family: Alphonse junior (b. and d. in 1821) and Julia (1822-32). A contract with his publisher required that he publish the *Nouvelles Méditations* (1823) which was composed primarily of early verses. Of the poems in this volume, "Le Crucifix," written for his wife, is deemed one of Lamartine's most moving poems, but the public was disappointed. *La Mort de Socrate*, written and published in 1823, shows Lamartine's intellectual preoccupations and his desire to annex Socrates to Christianity by making him a prophet.

It took Lamartine two years to elaborate the structure of his metaphysical epic. Richard Laurence, Thomas Moore, and Byron guided him in his dramatic conception. The death of the latter in 1824 inspired Lamartine to write *Le Dernier Chant du Pèlerinage d'Harold*, commonly thought to be an attempt to Christianize Byron but really a more personal avowal of his own spiritual and emotional perturbations. Between 1825, when he honored Charles X in the *Chant du Sacre*, and 1830, Lamartine published nothing. Appointed secretary of the Florence legation, Lamartine devoted himself to diplomatic duties, although occasionally writing (but not publishing) lyrics. In 1828 he returned to Mâcon, and became a candidate to the French Academy, which had refused him in 1824. This time (1830) he was successful. A new collection of verse, in two volumes, *Harmonies Poétiques et Religieuses,* published shortly after his election, was received enthusiastically by the critics and the public, who were dazzled by his fluency, spontaneity, and resonance.

After the July revolution Lamartine ran for office, but was defeated. In 1832-33 he traveled to the Near East, in order to see the setting of *Jocelyn,* begun in 1831. *Voyage en Orient* (1835) recounted his observations and impressions of the Holy Land and adjacent countries.

Elected deputy during his absence, Lamartine was able to work only intermittently on *Jocelyn.* The 8,000 narrative, lyrical, and philosophical verses published in two volumes in 1836 were only part of the epic he planned to write. Although the critics were shocked by the inconsistencies, solecisms, and obscurities, the public bought more than 24,000 copies within a month of publication. This phenomenal success encouraged Lamartine to write *La Chute d'un Ange* (1838)— 12,000 verses—within ten months. The negligences were so numerous that *La Chute* was a commercial and critical failure. This was the finish of the long-dreamed epic. Lamartine did not even include *La Chute d'un Ange* in the 1849-50 edition of his works. The *Voyage, Jocelyn,* and *La Chute* were all put on the Index by the Catholic Church soon after their publication. The Church recognized in these works an increasing hostility toward dogmatic Christianity. Ever since the death of his daughter Julia in 1832, Lamartine had been deeply disappointed in what he considered the limitations of the Christian religion. Increasingly rationalistic, he had wished to assimilate Platonism to Christianity; contact with Islam persuaded him that Mohammedanism was closer to true religion than his own church. These unorthodox views were not extraneous to the lack of success of his poetry.

But financial need compelled Lamartine to publish. *Les Recueillements* (1839) was composed hastily of occasional verse and older poems not previously utilized. It too failed. With this volume Lamartine, although he could not refrain from versifying, ceased to publish poetry. He was encouraged in this by his belief that poetry was harmful to his political career.

The next decade was for Lamartine a period of financial difficulty and political activity. His political importance had steadily grown since his initial election in 1833. Starting with conservative, Royalist convictions, he had gradually moved toward the Left, although remaining steadfast in his confidence that what France needed was a strong central power that would exercise benevolent reforms. Afraid of the blind mob, he nevertheless wished to help the proletariat in its economic and social aspirations and claims. His *Politique Rationnelle* (1831) had contained his doctrine in embryo and in essence (but some, for example Guizot, were to say that he lacked consistency and purpose). The *Histoire des Girondins,* started in 1843, was partially an expedient to parry financial pressures; it was also a means to win political adherents. By the time of its publication in eight volumes in 1847, Lamartine had behind him a powerful following. The government had tried to win his adherence by offers of an ambassadorship or a portfolio; Lamartine had refused, waiting his time, while expressing his views in the Chamber of Deputies, and in his own Mâcon bi-weekly newspaper *Le Bien Public* and other journals. The February Revolution of 1848 gave him his chance: Lamartine became provisional head of the government. The April election gave him more than a million and a half votes and membership on France's Executive Commission. But the bourgeoisie feared Lamartine as being too leftist. The revolt of the National Workshops, the June uprising, marked the end of Lamartine's political aspirations. He received fewer than eighteen thousand votes in the December election for the presidency.

With 1849 began the last phase of Lamartine's career. The February Revolution had ruined him financially. He had contracted enormous expenses in subsidizing informers, staff, and political machinery. According to some estimates, his debts amounted to more than 650,000 francs before 1848, and to five million francs in 1851. Lamartine embarked on a twenty-year stint of trying to achieve solvency by the labors of his pen. The literary and intellectual quality of these productions is far below the standard of his earlier work. There are, however, some gems, such as the semi-autobiographical but romanticized *Raphaël* (1849) and *Graziella* (1852) from his *Confidences.* These two prose works have had a lasting success. The *His-*

toire de la Révolution de 1848 (1849) was followed by that of the Restoration in eight volumes (1850-53); that of Turkey by one on Russia (1853-55). Lives of Caesar, of Alexander, of Byron in addition to numerous stories flowed from his pen, appearing first as monthly installments in one-man periodicals, *Le Conseiller du Peuple* (1849-51), *Le Civilisateur, l'Histoire de l'Humanité par les Grands Hommes* (1852-54), *Les Foyers du Peuple* (1851-53). Between 1856 and 1869 Lamartine published on a monthly subscription basis twenty-eight volumes of hackwork, the *Cours Familier de Littérature.* Some of these 168 popularizations appeared even after his death, for by prodigious labor he had prepared copy ahead of the printing schedule. But so sadly had his reputation dimmed that an effort to obtain a market in the United States netted only twenty subscribers for the French edition. In 1860 he had to sell his beloved estate Milly. He had even been forced to solicit a pension from Napoleon III's government. New editions of his works in fifty-two volumes between 1860 and 1866 had demanded tremendous energy for revisions, with ineffectual financial return. Stripped of his possessions, bereft of his wife, who had died in 1863, Lamartine, old and ill, was looked after by his niece, Valentine Marie Gabrielle de Glans de Cessiat. He married her in 1867, the same year in which his power of reason began to fail. But twenty months were to elapse before he died at Passy, near Paris. He was interred at the family estate of Saint-Point (Saône-et-Loire).

Part of Lamartine's career belongs to the political history of France; the last two decades of his long life are primarily interesting for bibliographers. But the period 1820-40 is of great importance to French poetry and to romanticism. Lamartine is the link between pre-romanticism and its full flowering. Gautier said of him: "Lamartine is poetry itself." "Le Lac," "Le Vallon," "L'Isolement"—these poems still excite their readers. He has a rôle too in the history of the modern French epic. A room of the Carnavalet Museum in Paris is devoted to him; there is an active Société des Lamartiniens, as well as several regional organizations with the same purpose.

Many of Lamartine's works have been translated into English. In addition to translations of individual poems, *The Poetical Meditations* have been translated by the Rev. Henry Christmas (1839) and by J. T. Smith (1852). H. P. Stuart translated *Jocelyn, a Romance in Verse* (1954). H. P. H. Bromwell translated *The Dying Poet* in 1918. Of the semi-autobiographical writings, E. Plunkett translated *Confidential Disclosures* in 1849 (new ed. 1857). *Memoirs of My Youth* appeared in an anonymous translation in 1878. The Baroness M. E. Herbert translated *Twenty-five Years of my Life* and *Memoirs of My Mother;* E. Hargrave edited and translated *The Heart's Memory: Pages from the Diary of Mme de Lamartine* (1951), which M. L. Helper had entitled in her translation (1877) *My Mother's Manuscript, Being the True Picture of the Private Life of a French Family During Many of the Most Eventful Periods of the Nineteenth Century.* The manuscript of this work, which first appeared in French in 1871, was considerably altered by Lamartine in order to make his mother's views conform with his own. *Graziella* was translated by S. C. Barney in 1872 and by J. B. Runnion in 1876. *Raphaël or Pages of the Book of Life at Twenty* had several editions (1849 sqq.), and was translated anew by W. Walton in 1900. Of the historical works, *The History of the French Revolution of 1848* was translated by F. A. Durivage and W. S. Chase (2 vols., 1849), the *History of the Girondists* by H. T. Ryde (3 vols., 1848); both of these also appeared in Bohn's Standard Library. Captain M. Rafter translated only part of *The History of the Restoration of the Monarchy in France* (4 vols., 1851-53), since it was "partly written in English by Lamartine." There was a three-volume anonymous translation of *The History of Turkey* (1855). Of the travel literature, *England in 1850* was translated by W. C. Ouseley (1851); *A Pilgrimage to the Holy Land . . .* appeared in 1837, in three volumes. The last of these three volumes contains the *Narrative of the Residence of Fatalla Sayeghir among the Wandering Arabs of the Great Desert,* published separately the previous year. Among his political writings, there are English translations of three speeches of 1836-38 in favor of the abolition of capital punishment *(Lamartine Impugns Capital Punishment)* by E. S. Buchanan (1930), with an introduction, and of *The Past, Present, and Future of the Republic* (1850). Of writings for *Le Conservateur, The Life of Christopher Columbus* (1859) came out in another version, *Christopher Columbus* (1880), which was reprinted from *Memoirs of Celebrated Characters* (3 vols., 1854-56). Other adaptations of Lamartine's *Columbus* were published as *The Life and Voyages of Christopher Columbus* (1871), and as *The Life and Times of Christopher Columbus* (1887). S. A. Grimke published "a free translation, greatly condensed" of *Joan of Arc* (1867). The translator of *The Life of Oliver Cromwell* is not known. *Mary Stuart* (1859) is "the only work which has appeared solely in an English form, having been expressly translated from the original unpublished manuscript."

ABOUT: George, A. J. Lamartine and Romantic Unanimism; Gingerich, S. F. Essays in the Romantic Poets; Hunt, H. J. The Epic in Nineteenth-Century France; Pirazzini, A. The Influence of Italy on the Literary Career of Alphonse de Lamartine; Ragg, L. M. R. Lamartine Ladies; Studies by Members of the Department of Romance Languages, University of Wisconsin (1924); Whitehouse, H. R. Life of Lamartine. [In French—The number of editions and of critical studies is enormous. There is a useful bibliography, *État Présent des Études Lamartiniennes,* by J. Baillou and E. Harris (1933). Several scholars, such as J. des Cognets, G. Lanson, H. Guillemin, have published critical editions. Since the publication of the bibliography of Baillou and Harris, the following are noteworthy; Guillemin, H. Connaissance de Lamartine, *also* Lamartine, l'Homme et l'Œuvre; Guyard, M. F. Alphonse de Lamartine; Luppé, Marquis de. Les Travaux et les Jours d'Alphonse de Lamartine.]

S. S. W.

*LA MOTTE-FOUQUÉ, FRIEDRICH HEINRICH KARL, Baron de** (February 12, 1777-January 23, 1843), German romantic novelist and dramatist, was the descendant of a French Huguenot émigré family and a grandson of a general who was a friend of Frederick the Great. He was born in Brandenburg on the Havel, the son of an officer and of a pious mother. He received an officer's training and participated in the Prussian campaign against France in 1794. In 1805 he married Karoline von Rochow with whom he lived happily for over twenty-five years. He retired from army service in 1806 for reasons of health and devoted himself entirely to writing, at first under the pen-name of Pellegrin. His introduction to literature he owed to the romanticist August Wilhelm Schlegel. Fired with enthusiasm for the cause of Prussian resurgence, he took up arms once more in 1813 in the War of Liberation and retired in 1815 with the rank of major to his estate Nennhausen near Rathenow in Brandenburg. After 1831 he lectured in Halle on contemporary history and literature. Albertine Tode became his second wife. In 1842 he moved to Berlin and died there of a stroke in the following year.

During the first decades of the nineteenth century, with the revival of interest in the Middle Ages, his romances of chivalry and his heroic dramas enjoyed the widest acclaim. In drawing on Scandinavian mythology he became a forerunner of Hebbel and Richard Wagner. In 1808-10 appeared his Nibelungen trilogy *Der Held des Nordens,* composed of the dramas *Sigurd der Schlangentöter, Sigurds Rache,* and *Aslauga.* With this glorification of a great past he sought to kindle latent patriotism and to spur German youth to action against the French oppressors. In 1812 he celebrated in his novel *Der Zauberring* the German knights and minnesingers. In the *Fahrten Thiodulfs des Isländers* (1815) he returned to the Nordic sources. Numerous productions followed in the same vein, but great and admired as was his fight for the fatherland with sword and pen, the public soon tired of the artificiality and fantastic motivation of his work, together with his repetitious glorification of the medieval system. Eichendorff called him "the Don Quixote of Romanticism." He is now remembered almost exclusively for one outstanding creation, the fairy tale *Undine.*

This charming story is a peak production of the younger (Berlin) romanticists and contains in perfection all the imaginative sentiments for which this school of writers stood. The underlying thought of the possibility of a union between nature and mortals is symbolized in the marriage of the worldly knight Huldbrand with the enchanting, carefree water-sprite. Yet the spirits of nature sow discord; against them and against human intrigues the union cannot endure. Huldbrand, not strong enough to repress his human ties, and Undine, too frail to withstand the efforts of her uncle to lure her back to her native element, are torn apart, and when her husband reproaches her for her supernatural connections, the nymph disappears beneath the waves. Later, as the knight marries the noble lady Bertalda, his former unearthly wife reappears and gives him the kiss of death. On his grave she is reunited with her lover in the form of a little spring. Unencumbered by artificiality, this fairy tale is as fresh today as it was when Fouqué wrote it in 1811. It was hailed by Goethe as the "most lovely tale of fancy"; Heine bestowed on its author "genuine laurels." Its theme inspired the operas with the same name by Hoffmann and Lortzing and, more recently, a ballet, and the play *Ondine* by the French writer Giraudoux. It had its influence on Gerhart Hauptmann's great fairy drama *Die Versunkene Glocke* and through it on Ottorino Respighi's *Campana Sommersa.*

As a lyricist, Fouqué produced passionate war songs which fired Prussian youth with enthusiasm, such as "Frisch auf zum Fröhlichen Jagen," as well as religious verses. His poetry suffers from a labored style and a vaguely mystic fancy.

Most of the translations into English appeared during the 1840's and 1880's. *Der Zauberring (The Magic Ring: A Romance)* was translated best by A. Platt in 1846. Of the many translations of *Undine* those by T. Tracy in 1841 and by Edmund Gosse in 1896 are outstanding. Other translations include *Sintram and His Companions* by J. C. Hare in 1820, *Aslauga's Knight* by T. Carlyle in 1827, and *The Two Captains* by P. E. Matheson in 1845.

ABOUT: Romanic Review, April 1951. [In German—see study by A. Schmidt.]

S. H. M.

* lä mōt' fōō kā'

*LAPO GIANNI (flourished c. 1300), Italian poet, was a Florentine lyricist of the *dolce stil novo* ("sweet new style"). There were several different men named "Lapo Gianni" who appeared in the civil records of Florence and other Italian cities during the late twelfth and early thirteenth centuries, and it has never been established which of these was the poet. His name stands simply for "Lapo, son of Gianni," and *Lapo* and *Gianni* were both common Christian names. The modern editor of Lapo Gianni's poems, E. Lamma, identified the poet with a Lapo Gianni dei Ricevuti who served as a judge and notary in Florence, Bologna, Venice, and other northern Italian cities from c. 1298 to c. 1328. Another scholar, C. Zaccagnini, argued that since this Lapo Gianni apparently did not begin his public career until 1298, he was probably born not long before 1278, and he would thus have been far too young to have been the close friend of Guido Cavalcanti and Dante. Zaccagnini preferred to identify the poet with a Lapo Gianni del Sesto di Borgo, also a Florentine notary, whose public career had begun by 1284. No important facts except their professions are known about either of these Lapo Giannis.

The literary facts about the poet Lapo Gianni are more certain than the biographical facts. The works of both Dante and Cavalcanti contain direct references to him. Dante in a sonnet to Cavalcanti ("Guido, vorrei che tu e Lapo ed io") expressed the wish that they two and Lapo and their three ladies could be placed on an enchanted boat where they could spend their time discoursing on love. Lapo was also mentioned by Dante in *De Vulgaria Eloquentia.* Two of Cavalcanti's sonnets addressed to Dante apparently concern Lapo and his lady, Lagia. One criticizes Lapo as unworthy to serve in Love's court, but the other takes back the criticism and sympathizes with his sufferings in love.

Lapo's own literary work consists of sixteen poems, chiefly ballads. He shared with the other *stil novo* poets an intellectual, analytic approach to love and its problems. He shared with Dante, in particular, a habit of idealizing his lady as an angelic being. But while Dante was in earnest about the spiritual nature of his devotion to Beatrice, the love that interested Lapo was forthrightly of this earth. His poems thus have a simple sensuality that distinguishes them from most of the rest of the poetry of the *dolce stil novo.*

His poems are read today mainly by scholars. They are available in Italian in *Rime di Lapo Gianni*

* lä′ pô jän′ nê

e di Gianni Alfani, ed. by E. Lamma (1912) and in *Rimatori del Dolce Stil Novo,* ed. by L. di Benedetto (1939). D. G. Rossetti translated two of the poems into English verse—"Love I demand to have my lady in fee" and "Ballad, since love himself hath fashioned thee"—in *The Early Italian Poets* (1861, revised and reissued under the title *Dante and His Circle*).

ABOUT: [In Italian—Bertoni, G. Il Duecento; Turri, V. Dizionario Storico della Letteratura Italiana; Zaccagnini, C. "Notizie ed Appunti per la Storia Letteraria del Secolo XIV," *in* Giornale Storico della Letteratura Italiana, LXVI.]

J. K.

*LA ROCHEFOUCAULD, FRANÇOIS, Duc de (September 15, 1613-March 16, 1680), moralist and maxim writer, was born in Paris, the descendant of an old and prominent noble family of the Angoûmois. His paternal ancestors appear in local history as early as the eleventh century and were active in the religious wars in the sixteenth. His mother, Gabrielle du Plessis-Liancourt, was of no less noble lineage than his father. In appearance, he was of medium height, with dark complexion and thick black hair.

La Rochefoucauld received the education of a gentleman. In 1628 he married Andrée de Vivonne, who bore him eight children. For twenty-five years his life was taken up with war and political intrigue, in most of which he assumed no great leadership. Like most of the nobility, he was against both Richelieu and Mazarin. Encouraged by his mistress, Mme de Longueville, and himself often angered at signs of bad faith on the part of Mazarin, he joined the uprising known as the Fronde in 1648. In the following year he was wounded in a skirmish, and in 1650 he withdrew to his governorship in Poitou to organize new forces of insurrection. In an ensuing battle he received a shot in the face and narrowly escaped total blindness. With the restoration of peace in 1652 and the promulgation of amnesty, he withdrew to his lands in the Angoûmois and began work on his *Memoirs.* He did not return to Paris until 1659, by which time his standing had been sufficiently restored to win him a pension of 8,000 livres from Louis XIV, and in 1661 he was made a Chevalier de l'Ordre. He frequented the chief salons of Paris, above all that of Mme de Sablé. In 1665 began his intimate friendship with Mme de La Fayette, with whom he lived most of the remainder of his life, in Paris. That La Rochefoucauld collaborated with Mme de La Fayette notably in her compo-

* là rôsh fōō kō′

523

LA ROCHEFOUCAULD

LA ROCHEFOUCAULD

sition of *La Princesse de Clèves,* and that she was instrumental in attenuating the severity of some of his maxims, is generally accepted.

For many years La Rochefoucauld suffered from gout, which rendered him impotent in 1669 and ultimately was the cause of his death. His illegitimate son (by Mme de Longueville), for whom he had great affection, was killed in the crossing of the Rhine in 1672. In the same engagement he also lost one of his legitimate sons, and another was wounded. La Rochefoucauld died in Paris at the age of sixty-six, and was buried at his estate in Verteuil, in the Angoûmois.

La Rochefoucauld's *Memoirs* (first published in 1662 as *Mémoires sur la Régence d'Anne d'Autriche*) had considerable popularity in the seventeenth and eighteenth centuries, but his great literary reputation rests upon his *Maxims,* which may be traced to the vogue of literary "portraits" in the period around 1657. La Rochefoucauld turned these observations of life and character into short, piercing "sentences," often epigrams, and gave them a philosophy which readers were bound to find challenging. He took his work on the *Maxims* seriously, regarding them as his very individual mode of self-expression. Though he consulted Mme de Sablé and his friend Jacques Esprit a great deal, it was he who actually wrote the maxims.

In 1664 there appeared at The Hague a pirated edition of the *Maxims* whereupon La Rochefoucauld brought out his own text at the end of that year (the printed date, however, is 1665). The collection, which appeared in thinly-disguised anonymity, contained 317 maxims but was to grow to over 500. (There were new editions in 1666, 1671, 1675, 1678, and 1693.) Among the subjects treated are reason, self-interest, love, friendship, jealousy, conversation, pride, fortune, and gratitude. The book met with universal admiration but few could accept its picture of man's corruption and helplessness. Those who approved of the *Maxims* on religious grounds, thinking to see in them confirmation of man's desperate need for divine guidance, were certainly mistaken as far as La Rochefoucauld himself was concerned. Such scant references to God, Original Sin, or Providence as appeared in the first edition of the *Maxims* were totally eliminated by the author in subsequent editions.

La Rochefoucauld's message appears to be thoroughly pessimistic. Man is guided in everything by self-interest. Little allowance is made for real virtue of any sort. There is a kind of moral Machiavellianism—without, however, any proven influence of Machiavelli or any other Italian pessimist. The political and moral climate of France, along with La Rochefoucauld's own frustrated social ambitions and acute observations, would have sufficed to produce the cynicism of the *Maxims.*

Yet the *Maxims* are not totally negative. Many discerning readers have seen a positive message in them, for in exposing false and easy virtue based on self-love, was not La Rochefoucauld pointing to the possibility of a sterner and more worthwhile morality based on self-comprehension and honesty, on independent self-assertion free of imitation or other forms of subservience? Nor is bitterness evident in La Rochefoucauld's character, which was by all accounts (including his own "self-portrait") gentle and lovable, albeit somewhat retiring and melancholy.

The maxims are not uniformly excellent in style, but at his usual best their author shows a fertile imagination which allows him to move easily between the various levels of the physical and moral world. ("True love is like a ghost: everyone talks about it, but few have seen it.") His ability to exploit surprise is a strong element in the effectiveness of many of the maxims. ("If we resist our passions, it is due more to their weakness than to our strength." "We all have enough strength to endure the hardships of others.")

English translations of the *Maxims* have been made by J. W. Bund and J. H. Friswell (1885), G. H. Powell (1903), John Heard, Jr. (1917), L. Kronenberger (1936), and F. G. Stevens (1939).

ABOUT: Bishop, M. The Life and Adventures of La Rochefoucauld; Gosse, E. Three French Moralists. [In French—Bénichou, P. Morales du Grand Siècle.]

A. C. K.

*LARRA Y SÁNCHEZ DE CASTRO, MARIANO JOSÉ DE** (March 24, 1809–February 13, 1837), Spain's greatest satirist of the nineteenth century, was born in Madrid. His father, an avowed *afrancesado,* or French sympathizer, was military physician in the army of Joseph Bonaparte who sat on the Spanish throne during the Napoleonic occupation of the Iberian peninsula. When, in 1813, the French troops withdrew, the elder Larra accompanied them to France, taking the young Mariano with him. Although the three-year-old child could already read his native tongue, he was put into a school at Bordeaux where, it is said, he forgot Spanish and learned to speak French fluently. In 1818 amnesty was declared, and the father and son returned to Madrid where the boy was sent to the Escuelas Pías de San Antonio. Later he joined his father in Navarre and in the winter of 1822-23, at the age of thirteen, he translated passages of the *Iliad* from French to Spanish, prepared a Spanish grammar, and wrote a Spanish historical geography. Returning to Madrid, he studied mathematics, Greek, Italian, and English, then went on to the University of Valladolid in 1824. It was there that he fell in love with a woman who, it is believed, turned out to be his father's mistress. The precocious, introspective boy became melancholy, morose; he transferred to the University of Valencia and very soon thereafter returned to Madrid where he almost immediately began earning a living by his pen. In 1827 he wrote an ode on the occasion of the industrial exposition in Madrid, and in 1828 he started his career as essayist with the publication of the satirical periodical *El Duende Satírico del Día.* After five issues the publication was suspended by the government. The following year he fell in love with and married Josefa Anacleta Wetoret y Martínez by whom he had a son and two daughters. The marriage was an unfortunate one; they were separated in 1834.

Larra turned to poetry, but his verses were bad. His poetic drama *Macías* was well received at its première in Madrid on September 24, 1834. Although he wrote other

* lär' rä ē sän' chäth thä cäs' trō

plays—his *No Más Mostrador* is an adaptation of Scribe's *Les Adieux au Comptoir* and his *Roberto Dillon o El Católico en Irlanda* was adapted from a play by Ducange —he was not slated to achieve fame in the drama. Influenced by the reputation he had acquired as a biting conversationalist, in August 1832 he inaugurated a satirical review of manners, *El Pobrecito Hablador,* for which he wrote under the pseudonym of "El Bachiller Don Juan Pérez de Munguía." He was now the competitor of the famous *costumbrista* Ramón de Mesonero Romanos. In this publication there appeared some of his most famous essays—"El Castellano Viejo," a satire of Spanish crudity masquerading as hail-fellow-well-met "nativism"; "Vuelva Vd. Mañana," in which Larra castigates his fellow-countrymen for their laziness and inertia.

The last number of this series appeared in 1833. Larra continued contributing to various papers and attacked not only the defects of his race but individual politicians and writers. His style was incisive, his comments cruel, and he has been judged anti-Spanish. The truth rests, however, in the fact that his love for his country was so great that he grieved for its ignorance, its backwardness, its stubborn clinging to outmoded and reactionary ways. Because of his outspoken criticism of his fellow-Spaniards, the sorrow that hides beneath his mordant humor, and his desire for widespread reform, he was hailed as a precursor by the members of the Generation of 1898. His final disillusionment was voiced in his essay "Día de Difuntos de 1836" in which he compares Madrid to a vast cemetery.

His later pseudonyms were "Andrés Niporesas" and "Ramón de Arriala" but his most famous is taken from Beaumarchais— "Figaro." His novel *El Doncel de Don Enrique el Doliente* had the same theme as his *Macías* but added very little to his reputation. His literary quarrels were many; the most famous was the one with the dramatist Manuel Bretón de los Herreros who satirized him in his play *Me Voy de Madrid.*

Larra's last days were sad. He had become infatuated with a married woman, Dolores Armijo de Cambronero, but his love was not requited. Time and again he tried to break away. On February 13, 1837, she went to his house to arrive at some agreement. The interview was short but scarcely had she reached the street when a shot was heard. Larra had committed suicide. He was mourned by most of the great literary figures of his day and at his grave the young, then unknown, poet Zorrilla recited some verses which catapulted him to fame.

Larra's *Obras Completas* appeared in 1886, his *Artículos Completos* in 1944. The only one of Larra's works available in English is the play *No Más Mostrador,* translated by Kenneth C. Kaufman in *Poet Lore,* XXXV, under the title *Quitting Business.*

ABOUT: Hispania XIV (1931); Texas Review IV (1919); University of California Publications in Modern Philology, VII (1918). [In Spanish—see studies by Azorín, M. Chaves, Carmen de Burgos.]

M. N.

*LA SALE, ANTOINE DE (c. 1386-1460?), French novelist, was born in Provence, the illegitimate son of a well-known *condottiere.* At fifteen he entered the service of the House of Anjou, and in this capacity visited Italy in 1406 and later the Low Countries and Portugal. In 1415 he participated in the Portuguese conquest of Ceuta in Morocco. With Louis III d'Anjou he spent the years 1420-26 in Naples, and from this sojourn brought back many notions of the literature then in fashion. He was later a judge in Arles, in the courts of the same prince, and was then entrusted by René d'Anjou, Louis' brother, with the education of his eldest son, for whom he prepared *La Salade,* about 1440, an ill-digested treatise on education dealing, in the traditional encyclopedic manner, with statecraft, history, geography and heraldry. Parts of *La Salade* are of interest in connection with the legend of Tannhäuser. In 1448 La Sale became the tutor of the three sons of the constable Louis de Luxembourg, Comte de Saint-Pol, who introduced him to the court of Philippe le Bon, Duc de Bourgogne, where he remained until 1458, fretting at his northern exile, organizing tournaments in an effort to preserve the chivalric tradition, and composing his books.

La Sale is responsible for the introduction of certain new literary ideas, and for a reorientation of such genres as the allegory on moral virtues, best seen in *La Salle,* of about 1451. His masterwork, dated from 1459, and dedicated to his pupil Jean d'Anjou, is *Le Petit Jean de Saintré,* a remarkable picture of elegant customs, and the only substantial work of the century in France deserving the name of novel. The theme of the education of the young page Jean in love, virtue, and the social graces, by the elegant Dame des Belles Cousines, takes up the subject matter of the courtly romances of

earlier centuries, with something of the allegorical and didactic tone of the *Roman de la Rose.* The work is significant as a picture of contemporary manners, and its enumerations and descriptions of clothes and heraldic objects are mingled with chivalric action and vivid portraits, especially of noblewomen; it is also something of a treatise on education. According to the story, Jean de Saintré was seneschal of Anjou, and died in 1368. A secondary love plot takes form late in the book in the lady's intrigue with Damp Abbé, and depicts the disreputable side of monkish life in the manner of the medieval *fabliaux;* Jean exposes his rival, but remains less pure and idealistic. The fine style is marked by occasional irony.

Owing to the great reputation of *Le Petit Jean de Saintré,* several other prose works were later attributed to La Sale. The excellence, for their day, of the *Cent Nouvelles Nouvelles,* distinguished imitations of the Italian short story, lends some credibility to the attribution to La Sale. The more striking and aggressive anti-feminist work *Les Quinze Joies de Mariage* was attributed to him through cryptic allusions in one of the manuscripts, and no other authorship has been proposed. The vilification of women and the emphasis on satire make of the *Quinze Joies* a very different text from *Le Petit Jean,* and all but exclude La Sale's participation in its composition. E. Allison Peers examined the authorship of these and other works in *Modern Philology* in 1916.

There are many editions of all the works noted above, and critical *Œuvres Complètes* started in 1935. The two English translations of *The History of Little John* were made by A. Vance (1868) and I. Gray (1931).

ABOUT: Auerbach, E. Mimesis; Modern Philology, 1916. [In French—Champion, P., and Desonay, F. Œuvres, with biography; Nève, J. Antoine de La Sale.]

F. J. C.

*LAS CASAS (or CASAUS), BARTOLOMÉ DE (1474?-1566), Spanish Dominican missionary and historian, was born in Seville. He is often called "The Apostle of the Indies." His father was Francisco Casaus, of a noble family, who had been with Columbus on his second voyage of discovery. Young Bartolomé studied at Salamanca and in 1502 went to Hispaniola as a planter. However, he decided on a religious life and in 1510 was ordained a priest, the first to be ordained in the New World. Within a few years he began

* lä säl'

* läs kä' säs

to work for the betterment of the conditions under which the Indians lived and the abolition of Indian slavery. To this cause he devoted his entire life. In addition to his writings about the Indians, he went to Spain to intercede with Ferdinand for them. From 1539 to 1544 he was adviser to the Council of the Indies and at last obtained from Charles V decrees forbidding Indian slavery. In 1520 he had set up a model colony at Cumaná, Venezuela, but it failed. In 1522 he became a Dominican and in 1544 was made bishop of Chiapas, Mexico, which position he retained until 1547, when he returned to Spain. He died at the Convent of Nuestra Señora de Atocha in Madrid and is buried there.

Bartolomé de las Casas' best known writings are his *Destrucción de las Indias* (1552) and the *Historia General de las Indias*, which covers the years from 1492 to 1520. The latter is an important historical source book but was not printed till 1875, although it had been used by Herrera. He is also the author of the *Apologética Historia Sumaria*, not published till 1909 and of many *Tratados*, which he published in Seville. The *Destrucción de las Indias* is one of the most controversial of Spanish books, for in it he bitterly, and unjustly, according to some, attacked the entire Spanish attitude toward the Indians and accused his countrymen of terrible cruelties. Guillaume Raynal, the French historian and encyclopedist, used Las Casas' arguments to condemn Spain and the Spaniards. Through his writings the story of the "infamous Spaniard" was spread everywhere, contributing in large measure to the so-called "Black Legend" of Spanish cruelty. Most present-day authorities find that Las Casas' account is exaggerated and that the Indians were by no means simple, noble savages who were debauched by the white man. They agree, however, that Las Casas' motives were of the best. In his zeal to defend the Indian he recommended the importation of Negro slaves from Africa. Menéndez y Pelayo, who admired his noble intentions, claimed that Las Casas, in his own way, was quite as intolerant as the men he condemned—"the very incarnation of intolerance."

Fray Bartolomé's style is not admired, for he was prolix and Latinate in his writing. The most readily accessible collections of his works are the *Apologética*, ed. by M. Serrano y Sanz in the *BAE*, XIII, the *Colección de Obras* ed. by Llorente (1822), and the *Historia de las Indias* (5 vols., 1875-76).

The Spanish Colonie or Brief Chronicle of the Acts and Gestes of the Spaniardes ... was translated into English in 1583; *A Briefe Narration of the Destruction of the Indies by the Spaniards* appeared in Pt. IV of *Purchas His Pilgrims* in 1625; *The Tears of the Indians* by John Phillips appeared in 1656.

ABOUT: Descola, J. Conquistadors; Hanke, L. Bartolomé de las Casas, Bookman, Scholar and Propagandist; Helps, A. The Life of Las Casas; MacNutt, F. A. Bartholomew de las Casas; Newcomb, C. Broken Sword: the Story of Fray Bartolomé de las Casas. [In Spanish—Juderías, J. La Leyenda Negra; Menéndez y Pelayo, M. Estudios Críticos Literarios, VII.]

R. E. O.

*LA TAILLE, JEAN DE (1533?-1608?), French poet and dramatist, was born in Bondaroy and given a good education in Paris under Muret, who probably inspired in him and in his brother Jacques (1542-62) their interest in the theatre. Jean studied law in Orléans, but was drawn to poetry by his admiration for Ronsard and Du Bellay, and by 1562, the date of Jacques' death from the plague, had completed his two masterpieces, *Saül le Furieux* and *Les Corrivaux*. He entered the service of the king and participated in the wars of religion, serving the royal cause by arms and by his extremely popular *Remontrance pour le Roi à Tous ses Sujets*, reprinted at least eight times by 1580. Many other of his poems are dedicated to noblemen, and his Petrarchist tendencies appear in songs for Marguerite, a woman courted in the Platonic traditions. Jean then fought with distinction under Condé and the future Henri IV until 1571. His religious convictions are not known, but he seems to have tended toward Calvinism.

La Taille devoted the first years of his retirement from military life to preparing editions of his work and of that of his brother. In 1572 his *Saül* at last appeared, accompanied by an *Art de la Tragédie*, and Jacques' two tragedies *Daire* and *Alexandre*. In the next year Jean's *La Famine*, dedicated to Marguerite de Navarre, was published with *Les Corrivaux* and a translation from Ariosto entitled *Le Négromant*; various significant political tracts shortly followed. He abandoned his writing for a while after his marriage in 1575, though editions multiplied rapidly. His last work, *Discours sur le Duel*, was inspired by a family tragedy of 1607; nothing further is known of his life.

Aside from his importance in the history of politics, La Taille is primarily a tragedian who happily combined the lyricism of Ronsard and the Aristotelian doctrines of the three unities in a strong dramatic structure. In his genre and period he is second only to Garnier,

* là tä′ y′

527

and he had the merit of forging boldly ahead in the rich new field opened a few years before by Baïf, Bèze, and Jodelle. According to his doctrine, tragedy must appeal to the passions and satisfy a need for perfection of form; his humane interpretation of Saul combines the mysteries of the Divine Will with the accidents of fate, emphasizes the title rôle, reduces choruses and monologues, and avoids religious preachings. His sources are multiple: Seneca to attenuate the religious atmosphere, Aristotle to avoid stereotyped characters and to show us human beings not wholly at fault.

The *Œuvres* were edited by R. de Maulde (4 vols., 1878-82). A modern edition of *De l'Art de la Tragédie* appeared in 1939 (ed. by F. West).

ABOUT: [In French—Daley, T. A. Jean de la Taille; Lebègue, R. La Tragédie Religieuse en France.]

F. J. C.

*LATINI, BRUNETTO (c. 1220-1294?), Italian encyclopedist, poet, and public official, was born in Florence, the son of Bonnacursus Latini, who was a notary and judge and wrote Latin verse. Brunetto in turn began a career as a notary about 1254. In 1260 he was sent as Florentine ambassador to the court of Alphonso X of Castile to seek military assistance. On his way back to Florence he heard that his political faction, the Guelphs, had been defeated and were in exile. The next six years Brunetto probably spent in France, where on occasions he acted as a notary for other exiled Florentines.

About 1262, while in exile, he composed the *Tesoretto* (Little Treasury), an unfinished didactic poem in rhyming seven-syllable couplets. Written in an allegorical style influenced by Guillaume de Lorris' *Roman de la Rose*, the poem presents information about natural science and moral philosophy in the form of visits to realms ruled by the allegorical personages: Nature, Virtue, and Pleasure. Brunetto's other Italian poem, the *Favorello*, is also in seven-syllable couplets. Addressed to his friend the poet Rustico di Filippo, it is a moral and didactic work about the duties of friendship.

His three-part encyclopedic work in French prose, *Li Livres dou Trésor* (The Books of the Treasury), was written largely during the last four years of his exile. The first part includes a history of the world, particularly of Italy, from the Creation down to Brunetto's own time, and also a compendium of medieval lore about astronomy, geography, and natural history. The second part treats Aristotelian

ethics and is largely a compilation of the works of previous writers on the subject. The third part, on rhetoric and politics, is derived mainly from Cicero's *De Officiis*.

Brunetto returned to Florence in 1266 after the Guelph victory at Benevento. During the last two decades of his life he held various public positions in the city, helping to negotiate the peace with Pisa in 1284 and several times participating in the highest Florentine councils. When he died he was buried in the crypt of Santa Maria Maggiore in Florence. An inscription on a pillar in the crypt says that a son was buried there with him. At least one other child, a daughter, survived him.

Brunetto's writings, especially the *Trésor*, were highly valued in his own time as instructive works. They had some influence on later writers, notably on Dante, whose allegorical journey in the *Divine Comedy* was based partly on Brunetto's allegorical journey in the *Tesoretto*. Brunetto himself appears in Canto XV of the *Inferno*, among the homosexuals in the Seventh Circle. Dante treats him there with great respect, however, and expresses gratitude to him for his teachings.

Brunetto was not a literary artist either in French prose or in Italian poetry, and when the medieval learning collected in his works became outmoded, he ceased to be read. Today he is best known for his connection with Dante. Except for a translation of a part of the *Trésor* by J. Wilkinson in 1547, under the title *The Ethiques of Aristotle*, Brunetto's works have not appeared in English.

ABOUT: Dole, N. H. A Teacher of Dante. [In Italian—Bertoni, G. Il Duecento; Maggini, F. La "Rettorica" Italiana di Brunetto Lattini. In French—Carmody, F. J., ed. *Introduction to* Li Livres dou Trésor.]

J. K.

*LAUBE, HEINRICH RUDOLF CONSTANZ (September 18, 1806-August 1, 1884), German novelist, dramatist and theatre director, was born at Sprottau, Silesia, in a poor and provincial home. His father was a building constructor. He went to school first in his home town and then in Glogau and in Schweidnitz. In 1826 he went to Halle to study theology. There he devoted more time to dueling and fraternity life than to study, and he soon had to leave Halle. He then chose the University of Breslau to be nearer home. Strongly attracted by the theatre, he finally devoted more time to the study of literature and history, and started to write theatrical reviews for the various local newspapers.

* lä tē' nē

* lou' bĕ

In 1829 Laube became editor of a student literary magazine, *Aurora,* and later theatre critic for the *Breslauer Zeitung.* It was at this time that he wrote his first historic drama, *Gustav Adolf,* which was also performed in Breslau but without any notable success. After occupying the position of a tutor for about a year, he settled in Leipzig where he joined a group of radical-thinking young poets. The results of this occupation with politics were two volumes of essays entitled *Das Neue Jahrhundert,* in two parts, *Polen* (1832) and *Politische Briefe* (1833), which were followed by an ambitious work, a novel-trilogy called *Das Junge Europa.* The first novel of this trilogy, *Die Poeten* (1833), was a novel in letters; the second, *Die Krieger* (1837), had as its subject the Polish Revolution; and the last, *Die Bürger* (1837), attempted, after his marriage to the widow of a professor from Leipzig, Iduna Hänel, in 1836, to tone down the radical political views that had been expressed in his earlier writings. Though he was in prison for almost a year before his marriage, he was now again sentenced to eighteen months' confinement for his past affiliations.

Laube was freed in January 1839, and in May of the same year he went to Paris where Heinrich Heine, with whom he corresponded for a long time, introduced him to many notable French writers: Hugo, George Sand, Balzac, de Vigny, Lamartine, and to the composers Chopin and Wagner.

After his return to Leipzig, Laube reached his most creative period as a playwright. First came a drama, *Monaldeschi* (1840), then a frivolous comedy, *Rokoko* (1841), followed by *Bernsteinhexe* (1843), and a drama of an adventurer, *Struensee* (1844). Laube's greatest success was achieved with his two literary plays, *Gottsched und Gellert* (1845) and *Die Karlsschüler* (1846), concerning young Schiller's flight from the Karlsschule in Stuttgart, which is still occasionally performed. During the revolutionary year 1848 he became a candidate for political office and was elected to the Frankfurt parliament.

The peak of Laube's career was reached when in July 1851 he became director of the Burgtheater of Vienna, where he remained for eighteen years. He wrote many plays during this period—the most successful of these was *Graf Essex* (1855)—and translated and reworked many foreign, especially French, plays. In 1869 Laube went to Leipzig where he undertook the management of the municipal theatre for two years, re-turning again then to Vienna as the head of the Wiener Stadttheater. His three books on the theatre—*Das Burgtheater* (1868), *Das Norddeutsche Theater* (1872), and *Das Wiener Stadttheater* (1875)—are among the best in their field. Laube died in Vienna.

His collected works in fifty volumes edited by H. Houben appeared in 1908-10, in Leipzig.

ABOUT: [In German—see studies by G. Altmann, F. Brosswitz, M. Moorman.]

F. S. L.

*LAUTRÉAMONT, Le Comte de (pseudonym of ISIDORE LUCIEN *DUCASSE) (April 4, 1846-November 24, 1870), French prose-poet, was born at Montevideo, Uruguay. His father, François Ducasse (1809-87), was from the southwest of France; his mother was Célestine Jacquette Davezac. Isidore's father, chancellor of the Montevidean French legation, was somewhat of a dandy, rich, and interested in literature. He engaged in extensive archeological investigations in South America, and founded a discussion club of literature and philosophical positivism. Young Ducasse no doubt witnessed cockfights—"reñideros"—local dances and games. His father's library in their luxurious home contained the academic *Revue des Deux Mondes,* Spanish and French newspapers, and also Bertrand's *Gaspard de la Nuit,* then practically unknown, the *Chroniques du Règne de Charles IX,* as well as the standard authors.

Ducasse left Uruguay in 1860, in order to continue his studies at the *lycée* of Tarbes, in the Pyrenees. He did exceptionally well in mathematics, drawing, and Latin. In 1863 he transferred to Pau, where he had Georges Hinstin as his teacher of rhetoric. He later dedicated *Poésies* to Hinstin, as well as to other schoolmates. In addition to close and enthusiastic reading of classics like Sophocles, Ducasse is known to have delighted in Poe and Gautier. In 1867 he went to Paris, to attend the École Polytechnique.

In the brief time left him, Ducasse lived in various Parisian hotels. He was not a desirable tenant: tall and somewhat stooped, dark in complexion, thin-voiced and usually silent, he wrote at night, drinking large quantities of coffee, and striking chords on the piano as he ruminated his phrases. He was composing *Les Chants de Maldoror.*

Ducasse published the first "chant" (lay) of Maldoror in August 1868 at his own expense, without any indication of author. It

* lõ trä à môn'; dü kas'

529

sold for thirty centimes; only two copies are known to exist. The following year the complete six lays, divided into fifty-nine strophes, were printed and signed with the pseudonym "Comte de Lautréamont." The name had been suggested by Eugène Sue's *Latréamont* (1838); another, corollary explanation is that the name connotes "l'autre Amon," i.e., the other sun or the rival of God. The Belgian printer Albert Lacroix was afraid to publish the work; he consented to bind up only ten copies for the author. While preparing to revise this text in which, Ducasse claimed, he had "sung of evil as Mickiewicz, Byron, Milton, Southey, A. de Musset, Baudelaire, etc., had done," but with greater elaboration, he published under his own name *Poésies*. These two little brochures of sixteen pages each (1870) were given away—they were not for sale. Succumbing to an abrupt attack of fever, Ducasse died and was buried in Paris' North cemetery—he was twenty-four years old. His tomb has been obliterated since the city has reclaimed the terrain.

Les Chants de Maldoror were put on sale in 1874, without success. Reissued in 1890 in a new edition, they were acclaimed by Huysmans, Maeterlinck, Rémy de Gourmont, Ruben Darío. But it was the surrealists who have seen in Lautréamont a precursor and a model. He has been judged second only to Rimbaud by some (e.g., Louis Aragon). Maldoror's struggle against God, his paeans to evil and violence, and the lyrical evocations of the sea with passages of quasi-automatic writing—these seem to fuse the romantic (and anti-romantic), the symbolist, and the psychoanalytic.

There are various complete editions of *Les Chants de Maldoror*, the *Poésies*, and the few extant letters of Ducasse. Notable are those prefaced by Philippe Soupault (1927), and André Breton (1938), and the composite one published in 1953 by José Corti. Artists like René Magritte, Salvador Dali, Yves Tanguy, Frans de Geetère, and others, have interpreted the text. Julio Gómez de a Serna did a Spanish translation; John Rodker (1924) and Guy Wernham (1943) have rendered *Les Chants de Maldoror* into English.

ABOUT: Balakian, A. Literary Origins of Surrealism; Fowlie, W. Age of Surrealism; Gourmont, R. de. Book of Masks; Praz, M. The Romantic Agony; Broom III (August 1922); Modern Language Notes LXV (1950); Partisan Review XXI (1954); Romanic Review XXII (1931), XXVIII (1937). [In French—see studies by G. Bachelard, M. Blanchot, G. and A. Muñoz Guillot, V. Larbaud, M. Jean and A. Mezei, P. Soupault.]

S. S. W.

*LAVATER, JOHANN KASPAR (November 15, 1741-January 2, 1801), Swiss poet, theologian, physiognomist, and philosopher, was born in Zürich, where he lived throughout his life and performed his duties as a Protestant minister. Rarely absent from his native city, he made a trip to Germany in 1763-64, and in 1799 was deported to Basel because of his opposition to the French. Returning to Zürich in the same year, he was severely wounded by a ball from the musket of a French soldier. He never fully recovered and died little more than a year later.

Lavater is the representative of the German "Storm and Stress" movement in the field of religion. The basis of his tenets was a personal relationship to God and for him everything divine was assembled in the single figure of Christ. His longing for the miraculous encouraged interest in such phenomena as mesmerism, somnambulism, and spiritism. Most of his religious thought is found in such works as *Aussichten in die Ewigkeit* and *Geheimes Tagebuch von einem Beobachter seiner Selbst* (1771-73). There is, likewise, a strongly religious cast to the work which brought him the greatest fame in European intellectual life, *Physiognomische Fragmente zur Beförderung der Menschenkenntnis und Menschenliebe* (1775-78). In this work, he outlined the art of character interpretation, attained through the study of the human face. He sought, moreover, to demonstrate the organic relationship of the individual with the divine cosmos. This work, derided by rationalistic critics, was enthusiastically received by young writers such as Herder and Goethe.

Lavater also sought to serve moral and religious ends in his poetry. His *Schweizerlieder* (1767), in imitation of Gleim's *Grenadierlieder*, attained great popularity among the people of Switzerland. Such Biblical writings as the drama *Abraham und Isaak* (1776) and the epic poem *Jesus Messias oder die Zukunft des Herrn* (1780) are late examples of the patriarchal poetry prevailing at the middle of the century. His *Christliche Lieder* were published in several editions, the first in 1776. Lavater's poetry show little talent and may be described as the rhymed didacticisms of a clergyman.

There are few translations of Lavater's writings into English: *Remonstrance* (Dublin, 1798); *The Secret Journal of a Self-Observer* (London, 1770); *The Pastor's Legacy* (London, 1842); *Aphorisms* (London, 1790).

ABOUT: [In German—see studies by J. Forsstmann, O. Guinandeau, F. Muncker, A. Vömel.]

E. K. G.

* lä′ vä tēr

*LEBENSOHN, ABRAHAM DOB (pseudonym, ADAM) (1794?-November 19, 1878), Hebrew poet and grammarian, was born in Vilna, Lithuania. His mother died in his early childhood, and he was brought up in the home of his father's parents where he received the traditional Talmudic education. At the age of eleven he became interested in Hebrew grammar and punctuation. After his marriage at thirteen he lived for eight years in the home of his wife's parents in Mikhailishok, hence his surname "Mikhailishker," by which he was known among his friends. During these eight years he devoted himself, aside from his rabbinic studies, to the study of the intricacies of Hebrew grammar.

After four years in Oshmiany, where his attempts to establish himself in business proved unsuccessful, he returned permanently to Vilna. Following a decade of private teaching and intensive literary work, he became ill with tuberculosis. Forced to give up teaching, he earned his living for fifteen years as a loan broker, meanwhile devoting most of his time to scholarly and literary work.

Lebensohn was strongly influenced by the poetical works of N. H. Wessely and M. H. Luzzatto. He began his literary career with "Shir Havivim," a long poem (1822) in honor of Count Tyszkiewicz, the governor of the province; "Evel Kaved" (1825), an elegy on the death of Rabbi Katzenellenbogen of Vilna; and a number of other occasional verses that established his reputation as a Hebrew poet. The appearance of the first volume of his collected poems, *Shire Sefat Kodesh* (1842), inaugurated a new era of modern Hebrew poetry in Russia.

Lebensohn experienced both material and spiritual struggle in his life. Five of his seven children died in early childhood. In particular the premature death of his twenty-four-year-old son Micah Joseph, a highly gifted Hebrew poet (see sketch below), left a gloomy imprint on his poetry, which deals largely with the dread of death, the suffering of mankind, and the cruelty of nature. Though his verses do not flow freely and naturally, seeming rather the fruit of premeditation and reflection, they possess deep feeling and charm; his style is clear and his expression powerful. These qualities make him the greatest Hebrew poet of the first, humanistic, stage of the Haskalah (or Enlightenment) period. In his allegorical drama *Emet Ve-Emunah* (1867) he attempted to reconcile religion with science, a favorite topic of Haskalah.

Lebensohn was also productive in the field of Hebrew grammar and Bible exegesis. In giving up the brokerage business, he undertook, together with the bibliographer Ben-Jacob, a new edition of the Hebrew Bible with a German translation, to which Lebensohn added his own glosses, *Mikrae Kodesh* (1849-52); another collection of his Bible commentaries, *Biurim Hadashim*, appeared in 1858; in 1874 he published *Yitron La-Adam*, a commentary on the well-known Hebrew grammar of Ben Zeev. Lebensohn's fame as a rabbinical scholar led to his appointment in 1848 to the faculty of the Rabbinical Seminary of Vilna, a post that he occupied for twenty years.

Lebensohn was the leader of the Lithuanian Haskalah. When Moses Montefiore arrived in Russia in 1846 to try to improve the conditions of the Jews, Lebensohn prepared for him a memorandum outlining reforms in the spirit of Haskalah. He exerted great influence upon his era both by his writings and his personality.

ABOUT: Waxman, M. A History of Jewish Literature.

H. C.

*LEBENSOHN, MICAH JOSEPH (February 22, 1828-February 17, 1852), Hebrew poet, was born in Vilna, Lithuania, to Abraham Dob Lebensohn (see sketch above), himself a leading poet and pioneer of the Russian Hebrew Haskalah (Enlightenment) movement. The boy grew up in an already modernized Jewish environment and acquired a Western education in addition to Jewish lore and Hebrew linguistic studies. As a child he learned French, German, Russian, and Italian, and read voluminously in those literatures. The precocious boy soon began to write poetry which displayed unusual depth and force of imagination and feeling, and the same may be said of his extensive personal correspondence. At about the age of sixteen, Micah Joseph Lebensohn showed the first symptoms of the tuberculosis that slowly wasted his body and ultimately took his life a few days before his twenty-fourth birthday. The gifted youth's realization that his life would be short and that he was fated to endure pain and weakness tinged his mind and his writings with bitterness. Gradually he discarded most traditional Jewish belief and succumbed to a mood of weariness, though not of resignation.

* lā' bĕn sōn

* lā' bĕn sōn

Lebensohn went abroad in 1849 for medical care and settled in Berlin for treatment and university study. His first major poetic effort had been a Hebrew translation from German of Book II of Virgil's *Aeneid*, but the scholars Leopold Zunz (1794-1886) and Senior Sachs (1816-92) advised him to write poetry of his own. He took their counsel, and his collection of *Shirei Bat Zion* (Songs of a Daughter of Zion, 1850) made an immediate and powerful impression upon the Hebrew world. In 1850 the young poet returned to the parental home, where his health steadily deteriorated until his death two years later. Lebensohn's early death was widely mourned as an immeasurable loss to Hebrew literature.

Having grown up in an advanced environment, Lebensohn entered the Enlightenment without personal trial or crisis. He was able to express general humanistic beliefs (in which he was influenced by Sachs and the philosopher Schelling) without a prolonged period of transition or a painful rebellion. He speaks through the lips of Biblical characters, as in "Solomon and Ecclesiastes" or "Jael and Sisera." His love poems are not the bookish borrowings of his Hebrew contemporaries from French or German models, but come from life. The universal themes of love and death and the full emotional spectrum of romantic poetry are harmoniously linked with the Jewish love of Zion and the Biblical world and the hope for national redemption. Lebensohn's style, while Biblical, was not slavishly so, and he freely experimented in language and meter. He was the first modern Hebrew lyric poet.

Lebensohn's unpublished poems were edited by his father under the title *Kinnor Bat Zion* (The Harp of the Daughter of Zion, 1869) from which some poems were probably omitted for personal or literary reasons. Only scattered sections have been rendered into English.

ABOUT: Waxman, M. A History of Jewish Literature.

L. P. G.

*LECONTE DE LISLE, CHARLES MARIE RENÉ** (October 22, 1818-July 17, 1894), French poet, was born at Saint-Paul on the island of Réunion (formerly Bourbon Island), in the Indian Ocean. His father, Charles Marie Le Conte (1794-1856), of Breton-Norman ancestry, was an army doctor who had emigrated to Réunion after the defeat of Napoleon. The two parts of the family name were coupled to avoid the appearance of a title; the "de Lisle" was to dis-

* lĕ kônt′ dĕ lēl′

French Embassy Press & Information Division

LECONTE DE LISLE

tinguish the Réunion branch of the family from others. There he married Élysée de Riscourt de Lanux, the daughter of wealthy planters and slave-owners, originally from Languedoc in France. Two more boys and three girls were born to the couple. Charles Marie professed to be anti-Catholic, an eighteenth century sort of liberal with Rousseauistic ideas on education. Biographers differ on the rôle he played in his son's intellectual and emotional formation. Some assert that he treated him harshly; others claim that he had great affection and solicitude for him. But it is the consensus that Charles René was strongly influenced by his mother, who was artistic and Catholic. She was related to Évariste Parny, the eighteenth century poet.

Charles René went to Nantes in 1821 and stayed there until 1828, when he returned to Réunion. Little is known of his sojourn on the island until 1837. He was a mediocre student at the Collège Saint-Denis. Extraordinarily enthusiastic over Sir Walter Scott's historical fiction, he developed an interest in note-taking and in consulting reference works. He started to write verse early, in the form of elegies and romances. His love for his cousin Élixenne de Lanux (1821-40) was not requited; this adolescent passion affected him for the rest of his life—but did not stop him from being often in love.

Charles René returned to Brittany to finish his education. He completed the *lycée* program at Dinan, proving himself "mediocre in

Greek, satisfactory in French." He enrolled at Rennes University in law, but neglected his studies to such an extent—although he took his degree—that his allowance was stopped. This severity was dictated as well by the fact that Réunion's planters were being ruined by the devaluation of cane-sugar and the cessation of the traffic in slaves. In addition, Charles René was addicted to a most uncommercial passion, that of versifying. A volume of poems, "Cœur et Âme" (1839), was refused by various publishers. Two periodicals which he edited, *La Variété* (1840) and *Le Scorpion* (1842), failed for lack of subscribers. From 1842 to 1844 Charles René was again in Réunion, apparently living "alone with his books, his heart, and his head." He did not visit India, as critics have claimed through mistaking his brother Alfred for Charles René. A position on the Fourierist newspaper *La Démocratie Pacifique* enabled him to return to France in 1845. He contributed also to the party's magazine *La Phalange*. A republican, with phalansterian ideals, Leconte de Lisle campaigned in 1848 and played a minor rôle in the June Revolution. This experience disgusted him with politics and with the mass of people; still a republican in spirit, he withdrew from active participation. Majestic in bearing, with a rather cold manner—distant, peremptory—Leconte de Lisle shunned familiarity. His demeanor suggested a deep-rooted pessimism. His despondency was enhanced by the frivolous behavior of his mistress, Marie Jobbé-Duval, whose husband painted a portrait of him in 1850.

Leconte de Lisle's verse reflects his desire to protect his deep sensitivity by a withdrawal towards the impersonal. *Poèmes Antiques* (1852) reworked earlier poems and exploited the Hellenistic vein which was becoming fashionable. The influence of Theocritus and Anacreon, as well as of Horace, is manifest in these erudite verses.

The period 1852-56, during which he eked out a bare living with hack-work and tutoring, was a difficult one for Leconte de Lisle. The twenty-eight poems of *Poèmes et Poésies* (1855), some of which were later incorporated into editions of *Poèmes Antiques*, were awarded the French Academy's Prix Lambert. This money helped to pay debts, and an annual pension awarded him by Réunion enabled him to live modestly. In 1857 he married Anne Adélaïde Perray. The appearance of *Poésies Complètes* (sic) in 1858 confirmed his reputation and established him as a leader in the new school of poetry, which

was given the name (in 1866) of Parnassian. His home, where his mother came to live in 1859, became a center for literary discussion. A "chef d'école," he set the example, and advised the younger poets. His compatriots Léon Dierx, Catulle Mendès, and especially Théodore de Banville sought his counsel. The thirty-six poems of *Poésies Barbares* (1862), which had been appearing in the *Revue Contemporaine* since 1858, included "Les Montreurs," in which he asserted his scorn of the multitude. Leconte de Lisle made extensive use of the Finnish epic *Kalevala* and of runic studies for this collection. He also embarked on the translations of Homer, Hesiod, Horace, and the Greek tragedians, which occupied him for twenty years. He was a major contributor to *Le Parnasse Contemporain*, whose editor was Catulle Mendès.

The Franco-Prussian War of 1870 caused Leconte de Lisle much financial hardship. The disclosure of the Empire's records revealed that he had been receiving a monthly pension since 1864 from the Imperial government, which decorated him in 1870—a revelation most embarrassing for an avowed republican. The loss of this income compelled him to engage in the writing of popular histories of the Revolution and of Christianity, until he obtained a position in 1873 as under-librarian at the Bibliothèque du Sénat. This sinecure was made possible by the withdrawal of François Coppée as a candidate for the position. Leconte de Lisle sought election to the French Academy, and was finally chosen in 1886 to replace Victor Hugo.

In 1884 Leconte de Lisle published *Poèmes Tragiques*, written over the previous decade. This new collection, while continuing to stress the historical and allegorical, also exhibits the influence of Darwinism and of evolutionist thought. We discern the pervasive influence, as was true in the other volumes, of Alfred de Vigny, although there is not specific imitation. Leconte de Lisle's love of erudition and constant effort at condensation in expression—that rhyme, the concrete, and the intelligible be integrated—are the dominant characteristics.

Leconte de Lisle, Academician and officer (since 1884) of the Legion of Honor, now frequented the nobility. He advised Carmen Sylva, Queen of Rumania, in literary matters. His death, from pneumonia, occurred while he was visiting at the Voisins château of Mme Guillaume Beer (in literature, Jean Dornis), at Louveciennes. An elaborate funeral ceremony was held at Saint-Sulpice in Paris.

Leconte de Lisle was undoubtedly the outstanding Parnassian. His 23,000 verses contain some 2,000 images, half of which are auditory. According to P. Flottes, there are about 2,500 mentions of light and color, and fourteen per cent of each collection is composed of visual images. The cursory reader is impressed by his apparent impassivity and obvious pessimism; but beneath the cold exterior of alliterative and rich verse there is an undercurrent of strong sensitivity. He remains, as I. Putter has said, an outstanding example of the "intimate wedding of art and thought."

Some of Leconte de Lisle's poems have been set to music by Gabriel Fauré, and "Le Colibri" ("the Hummingbird") by Ernest Chausson. Franz Servais wrote music for his Euripidean drama *L'Apollonide* (1888), Jules Massenet for the Aeschylean *Les Érinnyes* (1889). The latter was adapted for the American stage in 1909 by André Tridon and Arthur Guiterman as *Orestes*. I. H. Brown's study of Leconte de Lisle contains translations of the poems; the appendix by J. Madelein and E. Vallée to the *Poésies Complètes* (4 vols., 1928) lists the variants.

ABOUT: Bailey, J. C. Claims of French Poetry; Brown, I. H. Leconte de Lisle, a Study on the Man and his Poetry, with Original Adaptations in English verse; Dowden, E. Studies in Literature; Fairlie, A. Leconte de Lisle's Poems on the Barbarian Races; Putter, I. Leconte de Lisle and his Contemporaries, *also* The Pessimism of Leconte de Lisle: Sources and Evolution; Schaffer, A. Parnassus in France, *also* Genres of Parnassian Poetry; Sells, A. L. French Studies (1947). [In French—see works by E. Estève, P. Flottes.]

S. S. W.

*LEIBNIZ, GOTTFRIED WILHELM VON** (July 1, 1646-November 14, 1716), German philosopher, mathematician, and diplomat, was born in Leipzig of a respected and affluent family which belonged to the nobility. His father was registrar and professor of moral philosophy at the university and also an eminent notary. His maternal grandfather was a professor and doctor of law. Leibniz's spirit of piety and of conciliation were probably inculcated by his mother, his father's third wife. After his father's death in 1652, she conscientiously continued Gottfried's education. The precocious boy attended the Nicolai school. At eight he independently studied Latin and later the Church Fathers and logic. At ten he was given access to his father's library.

In 1661 Leibniz entered the University of Leipzig as a student of law. He studied ancient and scholastic philosophy under Jacob Thomasius and in 1663 mathematics for a

* lĭp′ nĭts

LEIBNIZ

semester at the University of Jena under Erhard Weigel. Probably in 1664 he abandoned Scholastic substantialism for a mechanistic view of nature. In the same year he earned the baccalaureate in law. Failing to receive a subordinate post on the law faculty, he transferred to the University of Altdorf, where in 1667 he was granted a doctorate in law. At twenty he published his *Dissertatio de Arte Combinatoria* (1666) which described the rudiments of a plan for a universal language of symbols which should be applicable to all reasoning processes. Cases in logic, law, theology, and other fields were to be classified through the use of basic theories on permutation and combination.

At the Nuremberg branch of the Rosicrucian Society, an association of alchemists of which he became secretary, Leibniz met Baron von Boineburg, the retired First Minister of John Philip von Schönborn, the Elector of Mainz who was the director of the Empire. Having declined the offer of a professorship at Altdorf and hoping to obtain a position at the court, Leibniz moved to Frankfurt. Boineburg induced him to dedicate and submit to the Elector the paper *Methodus Nova Discendae Docendaeque Jurisprudentiae*, which proposed a psychological and logical basis for simplifying law. In 1668 an appointment as councilor came through to assist Herman Lasser in recodifying Roman law to meet the needs of German jurisdiction. To this project Leibniz contributed the general parts of his work *Rational Jurisprudence*.

In 1672 he was sent to Paris on an unsuccessful mission to divert Louis XIV from the march on Holland. The four years there were devoted principally to the fields of mathematics and natural science. He was tutored in higher mathematics by Christian Huygens. He mastered the mathematics of Descartes and criticized his philosophy. His announcement in 1684 of his discovery of a system of differential calculus preceded Newton. He also built a calculating machine more efficient than Pascal's.

The death of the Bishop Elector left Leibniz without a position. Ultimately he accepted the post of librarian and councilor to John Frederick, the Duke of Brunswick Lüneburg, returning to Hanover by way of London and Amsterdam, where he had an interview with Spinoza. He served the duke and his successors Ernest August and George Ludwig for forty years, from 1696 with the title of Privy Councilor. With the support of the Electress Sophia Charlotte, the wife of the Elector of Brandenburg, Leibniz established the Berlin Academy of Sciences, and was appointed its first president. He became Privy Councilor to the Elector of Brandenburg and also received the titles of Baron of the Empire and Imperial Privy Councilor from the Emperor.

Under the government of Elector George Ludwig, Leibniz's freedom of travel was curtailed and an attempt was made to limit him to his duties as historian. He helped George Ludwig to the throne of England (where he became King George I) but was unsuccessful in obtaining a diplomatic post there.

Leibniz did not marry. Lonely, ill with gout, and under secret supervision, he died at seventy in Hanover. Only his secretary attended his funeral. At the French Academy Fontenelle gave adequate recognition to Leibniz's great genius and erudition. Leibniz was slim and of average height, with brown hair, and small, penetrating eyes. He had an excellent memory, quick insight, and much inventiveness. Although he was many-sided, he published only one comprehensive work in his lifetime, the *Théodicée sur la Bonté de Dieu, La Liberté de l'Homme, et l'Origine du Mal* (1710), which seeks to demonstrate the conformity of faith and reason and contains a vindication of God for permitting evil in this best possible world. Evil Leibniz considered as necessary for the greatest moral good. The *Nouveaux Essais sur l'Entendement Humain*, a detailed criticism of Locke's *Essay on the Understanding*, was not published until 1765.

The theory of monads, the central doctrine of Leibniz's philosophy, is described in *La Monadologie* and *Principes de la Nature et de la Grace Fondés en Raison*, both written in 1714. Monads are simple substances which are the elements of things. They are indestructible individual unities, spiritual in nature, without extension, figure, or divisibility. They are centers of force. The sum total of monads is arranged in a hierarchical order, with God at the top and the lowest grade of sentient life at the bottom. Each monad differs by infinitely small gradations from the next above or below it on the scale. Monads vary in the clarity of their perceptions. Each follows independently the law of its inner development but exists in pre-established harmony with every other monad. Leibniz sought to unite the theological-teleological view of the universe with the physical-mechanical one by explaining the processes of nature mechanistically but making these depend on a higher Intelligence.

He was the first modern German thinker of European repute and the founder of post-Scholastic philosophy. Wolff turned Leibniz's philosophy into empty rationalism, but Lessing and Herder applied its true spirit in their historical studies. The optimism of the eighteenth century, its faith in progress and in the artist's creative individuality, its focus on nature and man as the central theme of literature, reflect the influence of Leibniz. This optimism made him the object of Voltaire's brilliant satire in *Candide*.

Besides the mathematical discoveries already mentioned, he invented the binary number system, a general method of integrating rational functions, and the signs for similarity and congruence. He laid the foundation of the theory of envelopes and of *analysis situs*, and established the fundamental rule of determinants. His method of combinatorial analysis was reflected in the work of George Boole, Whitehead, and Russell, who partly realized his plan for universal symbolic reasoning. The science of linguistics began when he prepared a comprehensive comparative dictionary of the common terms of all known languages.

The *Journal of Speculative Philosophy*, 1867-71, contains English translations of the *Monadology* by F. H. Hedge, of "Correspondence with Des Bosses," by Thomas Davidson, and of "A New System of the Nature and the Communication of Substances" and "Reflections on the Doctrine of a Single Universal Spirit" by A. E. Kroeger. In 1898 R. Latta translated *The Monadology and Other Philosophical*

Writings. G. R. Montgomery's rendering of *Discourse on Metaphysics, Correspondence with Arnauld,* and *Monadology* was published in 1902 and reprinted in 1931. *The Philosophical Papers and Letters,* translated by G. M. Duncan, appeared in 1908. A. B. Langley's translation of *New Essays Concerning Human Understanding* was published in 1916. J. M. Child translated *The Early Mathematical Manuscripts of Leibniz* in 1920. More recent English translations of Leibniz's works are: Carr, H. W. *The Monadology* (1930); Morris, M. *The Philosophical Writings of Leibniz* (1934); Wiener, Philip, ed. *Leibniz Selections* (1951); Huggard, E. M. *Theodicy* (1952); Loemker, L. E. *Gottfried Wilhelm Leibniz: Philosophical Papers and Letters* (1956); Alexander, H. G. *The Leibniz-Clarke Correspondence* (1956).

ABOUT: Acton, J. E. Essays on Church and State; Barber, W. Leibniz in France, from Arnauld to Voltaire; Burns, C. D. Leibniz's Life and Work; Carr, H. W. Leibniz; Joseph, H. W. B. Lectures on the Philosophy of Leibniz; Lovejoy, A. O. The Great Chain of Being; Merz, J. T. Leibniz; Meyer, R. W. Leibniz and the Seventeenth Century Revolution; Russell, B. A Critical Exposition of the Philosophy of Leibniz; Saw, R. L. Leibniz; Sokol, A. E. Leibniz and the German Language; Ward, A. W. Leibniz as a Politician, *also* Leibniz and Philosophical Analysis; Yost, R. M. Leibniz and Philosophical Analysis. [In German—see studies by E. Cassirer, K. Fischer, G. E. Guhrauer, G. Stammler, W. Wundt.]

A. M. H.

*LEISEWITZ, JOHANN ANTON (May 9, 1752-September 10, 1806), German dramatist, was born in Hanover, Lower Saxony, the first child of Johann Ewald Leisewitz, a wealthy wine merchant from Celle near Hanover, and Catherina Luise *née* von der Beeken of Hanover. Leisewitz went to school in his native city and in 1770 he matriculated at the University of Göttingen with the intention of studying law, but occupied himself also with history and philosophy. His favorite writers at that time were Hume, Locke, Bayle, Montaigne, and Voltaire. During this period Leisewitz conceived a plan to write a history of the Thirty Years' War, a project with which he was preoccupied until his death, but which was never finished. In 1774 he became a member of the literary circle of young Klopstock enthusiasts known as the Göttinger Hainbund, and under their influence published two dramatic dialogues, *Pfandung* and *Besuch um Mitternacht,* in the *Göttinger Musenalmanach.*

Leisewitz was accepted into the rank of lawyers in Celle in 1774, and soon after he settled in Hanover. When in 1775 the theatre in Hamburg announced a competition for the best German drama, Leisewitz submitted his tragedy *Julius von Tarent,* on

* lī' zĕ vĭts

which he had worked since 1774. He won only the second prize (the first was given to Klinger's *Die Zwillinge*), but his play was well received by many German critics, and especially by Lessing, and was soon performed on many German stages. *Julius von Tarent* is a powerful drama of fraternal hatred and rivalry over a woman, actually a favorite theme in the German dramatic literature of the eighteenth century. Young Friedrich Schiller was much influenced by it, as is evident in his first dramatic work, *Die Räuber. Julius von Tarent* remained Leisewitz's chief contribution to German literature. Though he had several dramatic plans —one scene from a tragedy, "Konradin," and one from another tragedy, "Alexander Hephästion," were published in 1776—he never completed anything else. He worked in the years 1779-80 on a comedy, "Der Sylvesterabend," but this too remained incomplete. In 1776 he met Lessing, of whom he remained a close friend until the latter's death in 1781. In 1780 Leisewitz made a trip to Weimar where he was well received by Goethe, Herder, and Wieland.

After many years of courtship, Leisewitz finally married Sophie Marie Seyler, the daughter of a theatre manager in Hamburg, in 1781. The couple remained childless. Leisewitz's financial situation improved considerably when, in 1786, he was appointed tutor to the crown prince of Brunswick, Karl George August; in the following years he received several excellent promotions. He died in Brunswick at fifty-four.

The collected works of Leisewitz, containing letters and biography, was published in 1838.

ABOUT: [In German—Kutschera von Aichbergen, G. Johann Anton Leisewitz.]

F. S. L.

*LEMAIRE DE BELGES, JEAN (1473-post-1524), French poet and prose-writer, born in Bavai, then part of Belgium, was the nephew of the "rhétoriqueur" Jean Molinet, with whom he studied in Valenciennes, a rich center for poetry and antiquities. In 1498 Lemaire entered the service of Duc Pierre de Bourbon. A sojourn at Lyons stirred him to an intense intellectual enthusiasm for ancient monuments, the classics, and the new Italian poetry. In 1503 he lamented the duke's death in his *Temple de l'Honneur et de Vertus,* the first of his many dithyrambic glorifications of his patrons. He was then attached to Marguerite d'Autriche, wife

* lĕ mâr' dĕ bĕlzh'

of Philibert le Beau, the governor of the Low Countries, and for her he composed, about 1504, *La Couronne Margaritique,* an allegory on classical rather than religious or moral themes, and a significant step in the movement toward the poetry of the Pléiade. He succeeded Molinet as Marguerite's librarian and historiographer in 1507, and was entrusted by her with a mission to Turin; for her, further, he composed his bold *Épître de l'Amant Vert,* an allegory of love, in which the lover, a parrot, lends itself to various interpretations; this work is one of the late masterpieces of the school of the Rhétoriqueurs. In the dispute with Pope Julius II, Lemaire took the side of Louis XII, who rewarded him in 1513 by naming him royal historiographer and sending him on missions to Italy. The death of his protectors left Lemaire in indigence during his last years.

Lemaire's reputation was extensive; Marot claimed that he learned much from him at Blois, probably in 1512, and Sebillet, in his *Art Poétique* (1548), esteemed him as a great innovator; in contrast, Rabelais, Montaigne, and the Pléiade tended to scorn him. His principal contribution to the current of ideas appears in his *Illustrations de Gaule et Singularités de Troie,* in three books, published from 1509 to 1513, and on which he had worked since 1500. Here he took up the ancient legend that claimed that the fugitives from Troy passed through Germany and, following the Rhine under the leadership of Francus, Priam's son, founded the Frankish regime; the Gauls, in contrast, were the less distinguished descendants of Japhet. The legend rises from two early Latin works attributed to Dares and Dictys and was treated in the thirteenth century *Roman de Troie* of Benoît de Sainte-More and in a mystery play of 1453. The legend as developed in France, especially during the sixteenth century, sought for ancestors nobler than the Romans; a similar aspiration appears in Estienne's attempt to derive the French language directly from Greek. Lemaire's work is ornamented with allegory and mythology and related in style to the work of the Rhétoriqueurs; it contains many striking episodes of the deeds of ancient amorous characters, but proposes a patriotic and epic subject again used by Ronsard in *La Franciade.*

Lemaire treated the linguistic side of the new enthusiasm in his *Concorde des Deux Langages Français et Toscan* (about 1510), in which he set side by side the French masters Jean de Meung, Alain Chartier, and Molinet, and the Italians Dante, Petrarch, and Boccaccio. His tract against Julius II, entitled *Traité de la Différence des Schismes,* exploits the principal scandals, such as the Popess Joan, attacks the Gift of Constantine, and defends the Gallican councils, the French crusades, and French politics.

Lemaire's works in four volumes, 1882-91, contains an extensive biography by J. Stecher. *La Concorde des Deux Langages* appeared in a critical edition in 1947, and *L'Épître de l'Amant Vert* in 1948.

ABOUT: Munn, K. A Contribution to the Study of Jean Lemaire de Belges; Studies in Philology, LIX (1962). [In French—see studies by P. Spaak and G. Doutrepont; also Bibliothèque d'Humanisme et Renaissance, XXV (1963).]

F. J. C.

*LEMONNIER, (ANTOINE LOUIS) CAMILLE (March 24, 1844-June 13, 1913), Belgian novelist and critic, was born at Ixelles. His parents were of mixed Walloon and Flemish ancestry, but in feeling both they and their son were pronouncedly Flemish. The father had evidently hoped that Camille would follow him in a legal career. However, neither at the Athenée in Brussels nor at the university did the youth show serious interest in anything besides art and poetry. The disappointed father procured for his son a position as government clerk. At the age of twenty Camille gave this up and resolved to live by his pen. An interest in art criticism led to newspaper contributions, an activity which, continuing throughout his life, won for him a solid reputation as an art critic and resulted in such collections as *Salon de Bruxelles* (1863), *Histoire des Beaux-Arts en Belgique* (1887), and *Les Peintres de la Vie* (1888).

His father's death in 1869 gave Camille the means to rent a château near Namur, and here he was able to indulge his powerful desire to lead a life in nature as observer-writer, hunter, and angler. This phase found expression in 1869 in a glorification of the great men of his race, *Nos Flamands.* Thus Lemonnier aligned himself with his young Belgian contemporaries who were attempting a social and artistic revitalization, and became one of the founders of "La Jeune Belgique" of 1881.

Lemonnier's reputation rests, however, upon his prodigious output as a novelist. In the first period, roughly until Lemonnier's fortieth year, the novels celebrate nature and instinct; rich in style, the realistic detail is uncompromising. *Un Male* (1881)

* lĕ mô nyā'

537

is a vigorous, coarsely realistic "litany of instinct." *Le Mort* (1882) is the complement —an austere treatment of death, viewed also as part of nature.

Lemonnier's second phase is concerned with the search for originality—sometimes bombastic in expression—and a probing into the new psychology combined with a characteristically naturalistic preoccupation with social problems. *L'Hystérique* (1885) is the story of the guilty love of a perverted priest; *Happe-Chair* (1886), a detailed study of modern industrial life, is significantly dedicated to Zola; *La Fin des Bourgeois* (1892), *L'Homme en Amour* (1897), and *La Faute de Madame Charvet* (1895) continue the social problem novel.

The author's last period marks a return to the health and joy of youth, but he was now mellowed by age and fame. *L'Île Vierge* (1897), *Adam et Ève* (1899), *Le Vent dans les Moulins* (1901), and *Le Petit Homme de Dieu* (1902) are idyllic, compassionate, and touched by ancient Flemish mysticism. One of the works appeared in English, translated by A. R. Allinson, *Birds and Beasts* (1911).

Lemonnier had married a Mlle Panneels. He died in Brussels at the age of sixty-nine.

ABOUT: Bithell, J. Contemporary Belgian Literature; Pope, F. R. Nature in the Work of Camille Lemonnier. [In French—Rency, G. Camille Lemonnier; Vanwelkenhuyzen, C. Vocations Littéraires. In German—Kiepert, A. Camille Lemonnier und Seine Romane.]

C. K. P.

LENAU

*LENAU, NICOLAUS (Nicolaus Franz Niembsch, Edler von Strehlenau)** (August 13, 1802-August 22, 1850), Austrian poet, was born at Czatad, near Temesvar in southern Hungary (now Lenauheim, Rumania), the son of an impoverished patrician family of German, Magyar, and Slavic descent. His parents were unhappily married, and the basic instability of Lenau's passionate temperament was heightened by the troublesome atmosphere of his home, as well as by his irregular schooling and early loss of religious faith. His entire life shows a lack of equilibrium—a feeling of restlessness and vague yearning made it impossible for him to persevere in any undertaking or to find peace of mind anywhere. His father, Franz von Niembsch, a government official and former officer who was given to gambling and dissipation, died in 1807 at the age of twenty-nine. In 1811, his mother, Theresia, a nervous, emotional woman, who spoiled her son and protected him from all discipline, married Karl Vogel, a wealthy Budapest physician.

Lenau's grandfather made it possible for him to attend the University of Vienna, where he devoted three years to the study of philosophy. In the following years he studied Hungarian law at Pressburg, political economy at Altenburg, German law at Vienna, and finally medicine at Heidelberg, where in 1831 he took his examinations, only to fail. His first poems had appeared in the journal *Aurora* in 1827, and a small inheritance from his mother and grandmother now enabled him to devote himself entirely to literature. He traveled to Stuttgart and was warmly received by the circle of Swabian poets, Gustav Schwab, Justinus Kerner, and Karl Mayer, who assisted him in finding a publisher for his first volume of *Gedichte* (1832). These poems with their descriptions of the limitless Hungarian steppes and portrayals of scenes from the life of shepherds and gypsies, were well received, and for a time Lenau appeared to find happiness. During this period he became engaged to Schwab's niece, Lotte Gmelin. This engagement ended abruptly, as had a former unhappy love affair, for Lenau was soon plunged into a mood of melancholy and despair and conceived the notion that his only solace lay in a complete break with the past and with Europe. In an exultant frame of mind and anticipating great inspiration from the spectacular North American land-

* lā′ nou

scapes, he arrived in Baltimore in 1832. After settling briefly in Ohio and traveling to Niagara Falls, he returned to Europe the following year, disappointed and disillusioned. The wildness of the American scenery repelled him, and he felt utter contempt for the American, who in his words always "had a cigar in his mouth and a plan in his head."

In Vienna he fell deeply in love with the wife of an Austrian official, Sophie von Löwenthal, who, while she had no notion of following him, delighted in her power over him. The next few years found him vacillating between complete devotion to her and frantic attempts to break away from her domination. All his efforts toward independence from Sophie, including engagements to Karoline Unger and Sophie Behrens, proved to be unsuccessful. The constant nervous strain and the hopelessness of his overpowering passion hastened his final collapse. In 1844 he suffered a nervous breakdown and lapsed into mental illness, from which he never recovered. He died at the asylum in Oberdöbling near Vienna.

Lenau is one of Austria's greatest lyric poets. His fame was established immediately with his first volume of poems and was heightened by the subsequent volumes of *Neuere Gedichte* (1838) and *Gedichte* (1844). The mood of melancholy, pessimistic discontent, and *Weltschmerz*, which runs through his work, struck a responsive chord among his readers, and, like Byron, Lenau became the spokesman and typical representative of his era. His reputation reached its highest point during the second half of the nineteenth century, and, although it has diminished somewhat today, his popularity is still great in Germany and Austria. His poetry, which reveals the influence of Eichendorff and Goethe, is of uneven quality: some of his poems are merely contrived, while others are deeply felt and give poignant expression to experiences which have profoundly influenced him. Among his finest poems are those depicting moods of loneliness and despair. He was endowed with an unusual sharpness of sensual perception both visual and auditory which is evident in his descriptions of scenes from nature. In an impressionistic manner he captures various aspects of nature: sunset, wind, rain, moonlight, and from this picture evokes the corresponding mood. He is the poet of autumn and death, and poems in which he attempts to strike a more cheerful note generally have a false ring.

Lenau's gift was primarily lyric, and his longer epic poems or cycles of romances were unsuccessful except for their lyric parts. However, they are significant in mirroring his philosophical development and his struggle with the ultimate questions of spiritual and moral freedom. *Faust* (1836), which bears the influence of Goethe and Byron, marked Lenau's return to religious faith, after he had passed through phases of skepticism and pantheism. Both *Savonarola* (1837), an attack on pantheism and modern science, and *Die Albigenser* (1842), which Lenau considered his greatest work, glorify true religious feeling that is oppressed by the church. His last work, *Don Juan* (1844), remained a fragment.

No complete volume of Lenau's poetry has ever appeared in English translation, and it is difficult to find more than a small collection of his verse in any anthology. Selections are included in A. W. Rounseville, *The Poetry of the Orient* (1865); H. D. Wireman, *Gems of German Lyrics* (1869); D. Dexter, *Versions and Verses* (1865); L. D. Smith, *Flowers from Foreign Fields* (1895); D. Broicher, *German Lyrics and Ballads Done into English Verse* (1912); and K. Francke, *The German Classics* (VII, 1913).

ABOUT: Klenze, C. von, Treatment of Nature in the Works of Nikolaus von Lenau; Baker, T. S. Lenau and Young Germany in America. [In German—see studies by E. Castle, A. Grün, A. X. Schurz, J. Turóczi-Trostler.]

D. G. D.

*LENÉRU, MARIE (June 2, 1875-September 23, 1918), French writer, was born at Brest to a family of sailors. She lost her father and most of her close relatives when still a baby, and passed her childhood in a maritime atmosphere, surrounded by memories and legends. Urged by her mother, she undertook her *Journal* in 1886; although impatient with the chore, she soon began to express herself forcefully if naïvely, and showed her religious fervor in her veneration of St. Teresa. An attack of scarlet fever in 1887 led her shortly to total deafness and within two years to blindness. She continued her studies with even greater diligence but set her *Journal* aside until her return to Brest in 1893; her letters tell of her feelings over these four years of total isolation and of her regrets at loss of contact with people and with music. Her sight gradually improved, and in later years she was able to read with the help of a magnifying glass. The circumstances of her affliction helped to emphasize her inner nature and led her to meditations on the imperfect

* lĕ nā rü'

539

perception of reality, recorded for over twenty-five years in her memoirs: her need for a moral and religious consolation associates her with such thinkers as Pascal and Lacordaire. Her very extensive readings included Shelley, Darwin, Spencer, Renan, and Vauvenargues, and—surprisingly—Nietzsche and d'Annunzio. In poetry she preferred Leconte de Lisle to Baudelaire; her last discoveries and enthusiasms were Maurice Barrès and François de Curel.

Marie felt a need for more general literary self-expression than her private notes and in 1901 tried her first novel, choosing the story of Saint-Juste for the appeal of his character and for its Nietzschean violence. A fragment of her interpretation, based on solid research, appeared in 1905 and led Barrès to encourage her; but for reasons unknown she set the remainder aside. The two-volume work appeared posthumously in 1922. She was attracted by the theatre, perhaps through her endless interior conversations and by her need to participate in contemporary creative activities. Her discovery of Curel convinced her that his freedom from the moral preachings of the school of Ibsen corresponded to her own attitudes. Her first play, *Les Affranchis*, emanates naturally from her *Journal* and her habitual soul-searchings: here she sets passion above the false morality of social duty, and "liberates" the hearts and thoughts of her characters. She sent her play to Catulle Mendès in 1907, and he vigorously defended it against all kinds of opposition for the three years that preceded its immense success at the Odéon.

In her second play, *Le Redoutable*, Marie sought to reach a wider public with a maritime theme based on personal memories; it was badly interpreted and coldly received in 1912, and was at once withdrawn. *La Triomphatrice*, presented to the directors in 1914, was withheld from production on account of the war. When performed, early in 1918, it seemed out of place. During the war, Marie wrote pacifist articles and composed her last play, *La Paix*. In May 1918 she was stricken with influenza, which affected her heart; she died several months later. Thanks to the devotion of her many friends, especially Léon Blum, *La Paix* was performed in 1921, *Les Affranchis* in 1927.

The Journal of Marie Lenéru was translated by W. A. Bradley in 1923.

ABOUT: Chandler, T. The Contemporary Drama of France; Journal of Marie Lenéru. [In French—Lavaud, S. Marie Lenéru.]

F. J. C.

*LENNEP, JACOB VAN (March 24, 1802-October 25, 1868), Dutch novelist and poet, was born in Amsterdam, the eldest son of David Jacob van Lennep and Cornelia Christina van Orsoy. He received his first instruction at home and then went to Leiden to prepare for the bar. During his student days he met Willem Bilderdijk and became a fiery adherent of his ultra-monarchistic political principles. He also met Isaac Da Costa and D. van Hogendorp who influenced his views. He took his law degree in June 1824; in October of the same year he married Henrietta Sophia Wilhelmina Roëll, the daughter of the one-time minister of state W. F. Roëll. They had one daughter and five sons. Van Lennep remained a private citizen for two years and then received a post as counsel for the government, a position which he held until his death. From 1853 until 1856 he was representative for the conservative party in the Dutch lower house.

During his student days van Lennep came under the influence of Byron and Walter Scott, as is evident from the poetry he translated and his emulation of Scott's *Lay of the Last Minstrel* in *Nederlandsche Legenden* (8 vols., 1824-47). In 1826 appeared *Academische Idyllen*, a series of student conversations. *De Genade* (1827) was a translation of Racine's *La Grâce*. He also translated British romantic poetry and wrote literary criticism and plays.

Van Lennep was best known for his historical novels. In *De Pleegzoon* (1833), which is set in the seventeenth century, he again used Walter Scott as his example. *De Roos van Dekama* (1836) and *De Lotgevallen van Ferdinand Huyck* (1840) take place respectively in the Middle Ages and in the eighteenth century. *Elizabeth Musch* (1851) is set in the seventeenth century. These novels, because of their clarity of style, their well-sustained intrigue, and their humor, made van Lennep the most popular Dutch writer of his day. But his diffuseness no longer charms the modern reader, and his dénouements and character portrayals are shallow. Later in life van Lennep endeavored, under the influence of the French novel, to produce a work set in his own time. The result was the mediocre *De Lotgevallen van Klaasje Zevenster* (5 vols., 1865-66), whose sensationalism affronted some of his contemporaries. Van Lennep also wrote shorter historical stories and novelettes (*Onze Voorouders*, 1838-45), and some more or less scientific works, mainly humorous

* lĕn′ ĕp

in nature. He edited the works of Vondel (12 vols., 1855-69). His collected novels (23 vols.) were published 1856-72; his collected poems (13 vols.) 1859-72.

Among English translations of his novels the following may be noted: *The Adopted Son* by E. W. Hoskin (1847); *The Rose of Dekama* by F. Woodley (1847); *The Count of Talavera* by A. Arnold (pseud.) (1884); *The Story of an Abduction in the Seventeenth Century* by C. Bell (1891).

ABOUT: [In Dutch—Lennep, M. F. van, Het Leven van Mr. J. van Lennep.]

H. B.

*LENNGREN, ANNA MARIA (MALMSTEDT) (June 18, 1754-March 8, 1817),

Swedish poet, was born in Uppsala. Her father was Magnus Brynolf Malmstedt, a controversial academician. Her mother was Märta Johanna Florin, daughter of a curate. In 1780 she married the chancellery clerk, later counselor, at the Royal Board of Commerce, Carl Peter Lenngren, a vicar's son.

Anna Maria Lenngren belongs to the period of transition from the enlightened to the romantic era. She commenced her poetic activity at the age of eighteen by publishing some unoriginal poems in the press, the best of which was the moralizing satire *Thee-Conseillen* (The Council of the Tea-Table), published in 1775 (rev. ed., 1777). In the 1770's she translated French ballet and opera libretti. Her literary teacher was Johan Henrik Kellgren, the leading critic of the time and the most prominent member of the editorial staff of *Stockholms-Posten*, to which her husband also belonged. After her marriage she anonymously published some poems, mostly epigrams, in *Stockholms-Posten*. Her most genuine and poetically most exquisite production fell within the years 1793-1800, after which she wrote only occasional songs. In her last years she suffered from cancer.

Possessing no desire for literary glory, she insisted on remaining unknown. Her original poems were not published in book form until two years after her death, in a small unpretentious volume entitled *Skaldeförsök* (Poetic Efforts). Her great contribution to Swedish literature lies in her realistic and charming pictures of simple persons and everyday phenomena, somewhat influenced by Bellman. Her art is based on common sense, keen observation, wit, and delicacy, but is not entirely free from sentimentality.

Most of Anna Maria Lenngren's production consists of pastoral, satirical, and didactic poems. All three aspects are present in one of her best-known songs, "Pojkarne" ("The Boys," 1797), in which she first pictures the innocent and idyllic life of childhood and later gives a satirical portrait of the boys as adults. "Slottet och Kojan" ("Castle and Cottage") contrasts the happiness in the poor cottage in the valley with the joyless life in the castle on the hill. Some of her satires are directed against upperclass foibles. In other poems she paints realistic pictures of the milieu and life of the contemporary middle class.

The poem "Portraiterne" is translated as "Family Portraits" by H. W. Longfellow in his *Poets and Poetry of Europe* and as "Portraits" by C. W. Stork in his *Anthology of Swedish Lyrics*. "Castle and Cottage" is also included in the latter volume.

ABOUT: [In Swedish—see studies by A. Blanck, K. Warburg.]

A. J.

LENZ, JAKOB MICHAEL REINHOLD

(January 12, 1751-May 24, 1792), German dramatist, poet, and critic, was born at Sesswegen in Livonia, the son of a well-to-do pastor. He entered the University of Königsberg in 1768 to study theology but left after three years to travel through Germany as a companion to two young noblemen. This impulsive act was typical of Lenz's unstable personality, and his entire life, as well as his writings, reflects his undisciplined, quixotic temperament. In 1771 in Strasbourg Lenz came under the influence of Goethe and became obsessed with the desire to emulate and surpass the young genius both in literature and in life. He attempted to succeed Goethe in the favor of Friederike Brion and in general imitated Goethe to the point of ridiculousness. In 1776 Lenz journeyed to Weimar in the hope of securing a state appointment, but a tactless lampoon caused his expulsion from court. For a time he was the guest of the physiognomist Lavater in Switzerland. In 1777 he suffered an attack of madness and for eighteen months was mentally deranged, receiving shelter and care from Goethe's brother-in-law Schlosser. Finally Lenz's parents were persuaded to take him home, where he recovered his health but not his poetic ability. From 1781 he lived in poverty as a schoolmaster in Moscow, where he was found dead in the street in 1792.

Lenz began writing in imitation of the poet Klopstock, producing religious odes, of which *Die Landplagen* (1769), a lengthy

* lĕn' grĕn

* lĕnts

work in hexameters, is the most noteworthy. The intellectual atmosphere of Leipzig stimulated his creativeness, and during his five years here all of his important works were written. The major literary debate of this period concerned the problem of English versus French influence, and in an essay, *Anmerkungen übers Theater* (1774), Lenz set out to champion the cause of Shakespeare, accompanying his treatise with a translation of *Love's Labour's Lost*. In 1774 Lenz also prepared adaptations of five comedies of Plautus, entitled *Lustspiele nach dem Plautus fürs Deutsche Theater,* and wrote *Der Hofmeister, oder die Vorteile der Privaterziehung,* one of the principal works on which his continued reputation rests. Thinking he was following Shakespeare's model, Lenz presented three loosely connected plots, combined tragedy and comedy, disregarded the unities, and divided the play into more than thirty short scenes. Despite its defects as a work of literature, the realistic manner of presentation and the use of a problematic social theme were innovations which pointed forward to the period of naturalism at the end of the nineteenth cntury.

Die Soldaten (1776), while it contains the same techniques and qualities as *Der Hofmeister,* is a better constructed play and represents the high point of Lenz's production. Again the action presents a social theme, portraying an officer's seduction and desertion of a bourgeois maiden, who is then condemned to a life of misery. The drama was intended as a serious protest against the regulation that officers remain unmarried. Lenz's other notable dramas, *Der Neue Menoza* (1774), *Die Beiden Alten* (1776), and *Die Freunde Machen den Philosophen* (1776), failed to attain the level of his two best works. None of his plays has ever been successful in the theatre.

Lenz, who was one of the few genuinely gifted lyricists of his time, produced a few outstanding poems such as "Die Liebe auf dem Lande" and "Eduard Allwills Geistiges Lied." His short stories were unsuccessful and are interesting only for the biographical information they contain. His collected works were edited by F. Bley (5 vols., 1909-13) and by E. Lewy (4 vols., 1909-17).

ABOUT: Garland, H. B. Storm and Stress; Pascal, R. Lenz as Lyric Poet in German Studies Presented to Leonard Ashley Willoughby. [In German—see studies by H. Bräuning-Oktavio, H. Kindermann, H. Rauch, N. Rosanow, and E. Schmidt.]

D. G. D.

LEO HEBRAEUS (LEO JUDAEUS). See ABARBANEL, JUDAH

LEÓN, LUIS PONCE DE, Fray (1528?-August 23, 1591), Spanish mystic poet, was born in Belmonte (Cuenca), the son of the lawyer Don Lope de León and of Doña Inés de Valera. The young Luis received his early education in Madrid and in Valladolid and in 1543 went to Salamanca where he joined the Augustinian Order on January 29, 1544. Fray Luis studied in Toledo, Álcalá, and Salamanca, and was a disciple of Melchor Cano and Domingo de Soto. From 1561 on, Fray Luis held various Chairs at the University of Salamanca: that of St. Thomas Aquinas in 1561 and that of Scholastic Theology and Holy Scriptures in 1565.

As an Augustinian, Fray Luis was subject to many attacks from the Dominicans, most notably from his rival León de Castro. In matters of theology Castro represented intransigent Scholasticism, while Fray Luis represented the Hebraic tradition. A learned Hebraist, Fray Luis often differed from Castro in questions concerning the accuracy and consequently the authority of the Vulgate. In an attempt to discredit the orthodoxy of the Augustinian, the partisans of Castro referred to themselves as belonging to the *bando de Jesucristo*—a reference to the partly Jewish ancestry of Fray Luis. These disputes, as well as Fray Luis' clandestine translation of the *Song of Songs* into Spanish, resulted in his imprisonment in Valladolid by order of the Inquisition in March 1572. He was finally absolved and released in December of 1576 and restored to his position at the University of Salamanca. In 1578 he obtained the Chair of Moral Philosophy and was also designated to form part of the commission entrusted with the reform of the Gregorian calendar. At the same time he was assigned the task of editing the works of St. Teresa of Ávila. In 1579 Fray Luis was named to the Chair of Holy Scriptures; in 1591 he was made Vicar General of his Order in Castile and on August 14 of the same year was designated Provincial of his Order. He died only nine days later, however, in Madrigal de las Altas Torres.

The poems of Fray Luis circulated in manuscript during his lifetime and did not appear until 1631 when Quevado published them "to put up a dike against the torrent of *culteranismo.*" The poetry of Fray Luis consists of many translations as well as original lyrics,

* lä ôn'

FRAY LUIS DE LEÓN

for he was a true humanist, thoroughly acquainted with classical literature. He translated ten Eclogues and two Georgics of Virgil, twenty-four Horatian Odes, Pindar, and Euripides. As an Hebraist, he composed versified translations of the Psalms, fragments of the Book of Job and Proverbs. Fray Luis' original poems total no more than forty, but they plainly illustrate the mingling of Greco-Roman and Christian tradition which led Menéndez y Pelayo to observe that in Fray Luis the marble of a pagan temple is purified and transformed into a basilica of Christ. In compositions such as *Noche Serena, A Salinas* and *A Felipe Ruiz,* the Neoplatonic concept of the universe is united to a deep feeling for nature, and both are fused to express a profound Christian nostalgia for eternity. In the dedication to his friend and protector Don Pedro Portocarrero, the poet speaks somewhat disparagingly of his original verse as "obrecillas" belonging to his youth. In actuality they are a supremely harmonious expression of the Spanish Renaissance.

Fray Luis' best known prose work, *De los Nombres de Cristo* (1583), constitutes an inquiry into the nature of Christ by means of a Platonic dialogue in which three monks are the interlocutors. Their commentaries on the different names applied to Christ (Prince of Peace, Shepherd, etc.) constitute a beautifully and serenely written manual of Christianity. Another well-known prose work of Fray Luis is *La Perfecta Casada* (1583)

written for the recently wed María Varela Osorio. It is notable not only for its wisdom but for the vividness of its descriptions of the customs of the time.

The works of Fray Luis suggest a supremely peaceful temperament, but according to Pacheco in his *Libro de Retratos,* the poet had a choleric disposition which he tried to keep in check, despite his appearance of gravity and sobriety. Physically he was small, dark of complexion, with lively green eyes. His statue stands in the courtyard of the University of Salamanca, a monument to the humanistic spirit.

Selections from the poetry of Fray Luis have been translated into English by Thomas Walsh in *Hispanic Anthology* (1920), and by others in *An Anthology of Spanish Poetry,* edited by Angel Flores (Anchor Books, 1961). His *Poesías Originales* have been translated as *Lyrics* by A. F. G. Bell (1928). *De los Nombres de Cristo* has been translated as *The Names of Christ* by the Benedictines of Stanbrook (1926).

ABOUT: Bell, A. F. G. Luis de León; Fitzmaurice-Kelly, J. Fray Luis de León; Peers, E. A. Studies of the Spanish Mystics, I; Sarmiento, E. *Introduction and notes to edition of Poesías.* [In Spanish—see studies by F. Blanco García, M. de la Pinta Llorente.]

B. P. P.

LEON, MOSES DE. See MOSES DE LEON

*LEONARDO DA VINCI (April 15, 1452-May 2, 1519), Italian artist, scientist. and writer, was born in Vinci, between Florence and Pisa, the natural son of Piero d'Antonio, a notary. His mother, Caterina, a local peasant girl, was Piero's first love. After Leonardo's birth, each parent married separately, the child remaining with the father, who prospered in business. Piero had no more children until a son was born in 1475, thus suddenly raising a social problem for Leonardo and excluding him from his patrimony—indeed from his place in the family. Piero died in 1504, and Leonardo's only heritage was a small bequest from his uncle Francesco; these circumstances explain his taste for luxury and his chronic penury.

Leonardo's precocious talent was of the broad scope of such typical men of the Renaissance as Alberti, comprising competency in philosophy, science, engineering, and the arts. Much legend surrounds his activities, but his father's frequent sojourns in Florence, where he owned a house in Piazza San Firenze, brought the boy into

* lä ō när' dō dä vēn' chē

LEONARDO DA VINCI

LEONARDO DA VINCI

contact with the sculptor Verrocchio, in whose studio he worked. There is reason to believe that the student influenced the master, since Verrocchio's best active phase came rather late, during the years 1472-76, as if to reflect Leonardo's dissatisfaction with the mannerisms and decorative exhaustion of the time in his search for more vital, flowing lines.

Having left Verrocchio's studio in 1476 in order to be able to work more freely, Leonardo showed at once his dominant traits: his indecision when faced with the problem of artistic creation, and his immense curiosity about science. He had little respect for the masters of his day, except Donatello and Masaccio, and his relations with Botticelli, Perugino, and Lorenzo di Credi do not imply artistic sympathies. His principal objection to current techniques was their deficiency in technical knowledge of perspective, anatomy, and botany; these notions explain his search for a more real image of nature, often evident in his notebooks. First public recognition came to him in 1478 when the city commissioned him for an altar painting which he began but never completed; in 1481 a similar order from Scopeto, with excellent conditions, again led merely to preliminary sketches. The *Virgin of the Rocks*, of about 1484, still perhaps archaic in some details, shows his innovations in the treatment of costume, physical gesture, and color.

Leonardo's passage to Milan has provoked speculation regarding a possible trip to the Orient, not uncommon at the time. Many allusions in the notebooks allow one to suppose such a trip during several periods at which his whereabouts are unknown, but the references may also be purely bookish. Presumably he went first to Milan in 1483 in order to be free of the pressures of political struggles, to find a more generous and centralized court, and finally to avoid friction. Through the recommendation of Lorenzo the Magnificent, Lodovico il Moro commissioned Leonardo to create an equestrian monument to Francesco Sforza, a work which dragged on for several years as Leonardo turned by preference to scientific projects. The capture of Milan by the French in 1499 and again in 1500, and the imprisonment of his patron, led Leonardo to Florence and then to the court of Cesare Borgia, in Cesena, for engineering works such as canal construction and military fortifications. The fall of the Borgias brought him again to Florence, but the technical disaster of his great painting of the battle of Anghiari in 1505 discouraged him and turned him to canal works in Milan. Leonardo had not heeded the solicitations of Louis XII, but Francis I finally induced him to France and established him in 1516 at the Château de Cloux, near Amboise, for several fruitful years of research, design, and engineering works; there he wrote his testament in April 1519 shortly before his death at sixty-seven.

Leonardo's writings show extreme power and precision of style and freedom from current rhetorical effect—he referred to himself as "omo sanza lettere." His *Frammenti Letterari e Filosofici*, edited by Solmi, in poetic prose, develop scientific subjects, allegorical images, and fables of water, night, and the like, in the form of separable "thoughts" and reflections of broad moral and aesthetic import. His notebooks, originally penned in "mirror writing," suffered various fates until late in the nineteenth century, when competent editions and analyses began to appear in the work of Uzielli, Brun, Ravaisson-Mollien, and Richter. The presence of the manuscripts in foreign libraries led to research of international scope.

The Literary Works of Leonardo da Vinci in English translations were edited by J. B. Richter (1883, 1939). Edward MacCurdy's two-volume edition of the *Notebooks* appeared in 1938.

ABOUT: Heydenreich, L. H. Leonardo da Vinci; McMurrich, J. P. Leonardo da Vinci the Anatomist; Pater, W. The Renaissance; Richter, J. P. The Literary Works of Leonardo da Vinci; Thorndike, L. History of Magic and Experimental Science, V. [In French and Italian—see studies by C. Brun, G. Calvi, G. Fumagalli, G. Mazzoni, A. Pettorelli, G. Uzielli.]

F. J. C.

LEONE EBREO. See ABARBANEL, JUDAH

LEONORA CHRISTINA, Countess Ulfeldt of Schleswig-Holstein (July 8, 1621-March 16, 1698), Danish autobiographer, was born at the Royal Palace Frederiksborg in Copenhagen. Her parents were King Christian IV, who ruled Denmark 1588-1648, and his second wife, Christine Munk. Her first six years were spent with her maternal grandmother, Lady Ellen Marsvin of Dalum, on the island of Fyn. After a year in Friesland, she went to Copenhagen, but soon thereafter, in 1630, her parents separated, never to see each other again. Leonora was reared and educated at the royal palace by female and male tutors. Quite early she showed an unusual intelligence as well as artistic and literary talent. She was pretty and had the traits of her father, whose favorite she became. By the time she was fifteen she possessed all the refinements which were proper to a young lady of her birth.

At the age of nine she was engaged and at fifteen married to the thirty-year-old Corfitz Ulfeldt, who after the marriage was appointed Privy Councilor and Governor of Copenhagen by the King. In 1643 he became Royal Seneschal, i.e., Denmark's highest official, and Leonora was honored as the country's first lady. During a journey abroad in 1647, she impressed even the French court with her erudition and personal charm.

But her husband was a man greedy for power, and after the death of Christian IV and the accession to the throne of Frederick III, serious controversies developed. Leonora's position was difficult, but she faithfully stood up for her husband, thereby incurring the burning hatred of Queen Sophia Amalia, another proud and passionate woman.

Ulfeldt's management of his office was not one of perfect integrity, and the king ordered an investigation. Scenting danger, Leonora and her husband and their children fled to Sweden. Ulfeldt soon attained an influential position at the Swedish Court and plotted treacherous activities against Denmark. Later, he was also entangled in rebellious acts against the Swedish crown, and he was sentenced to loss of his life and property. Because of the turbulent times in Sweden the execution was delayed. Ulfeldt and Leonora fled to Denmark where they were immediately incarcerated. After Ulfeldt gave up his proprietary rights, they were released. During a trip to Holland, Ulfeldt again conspired against his country. He escaped, but Leonora was intercepted in 1663, in Dover, where she had gone to claim some money that her husband had lent to the English king. She was sent back to Copenhagen and imprisoned in the so-called Blue Tower of the Palace. Soon afterward her husband died, but she remained a prisoner for twenty-two years. She bore her ordeal with admirable courage and firmness of character, gaining strength through religion and her desire to live for her children.

During her confinement, Leonora wrote religious songs and hymns, but most importantly she composed a pathetic literary monument—her remarkable memoir *Den Fangne Grevinde Leonoræ Christinæ Jammers Minde* (Memory of the Misery of the Imprisoned Countess Leonora Christina), in which she described her long years in the Blue Tower. Her objective in writing her tragic story was to exonerate herself and her husband in the eyes of her children.

After the death of Queen Sophia Amalia, Leonora was released. During her last years she lived at the Maribo Cloister.

Leonora's memoirs were translated by F. E. Bunnet as *Memoirs of Leonora Christina* (1872, reprinted 1929). Extracts appear in translation by B. Lisberg in *American-Scandinavian Review*, VI.

ABOUT: Stagg, F. N. Dover Castle and "Jammersminde" *in* Denmark, 1947; De la Valette, R. The Life of Count Ulfeldt and the Countess Eleonora, His Wife. [In Danish—see studies by M. Petersen, S. Birket Smith.]

A. J.

*LEONTIEV, KONSTANTINE NIKOLAYEVICH (January 25, 1831-November 12, 1891), Russian writer and philosopher, was born on the Kudivno estate, Mestchov district, Kaluga Gubernia. "My father was one of those old-fashioned Russian nobles who were unable to concentrate their attention on anything . . . He was neither intelligent nor serious," wrote Leontiev, who was, however, devoted to his mother, who was a woman of great religious and aesthetic sensibility.

Leontiev finished secondary school in 1849 and entered Yaroslav College, but shifted immediately to Moscow University where he studied medicine and dabbled in literature and love. Turgenev, who was the reigning arbiter of literary style, encouraged his literary efforts and, calling the handsome youth "an extremely *joli garçon*," advised him that he might also make a career of breaking hearts if he so desired. Turgenev did what

* lyĭ ônt' yĕf

545

he could to secure publication of Leontiev's first work, a comedy called "The Love Marriage," but the censor found the erotic element too strong.

The outbreak of the Crimean War enabled the student to obtain his degree in medicine without actually finishing his studies, through enlistment as a military surgeon. He was shipped to the Crimea in 1854 where he found the climate much more favorable than that of Moscow. But he was not happy as a physician, and he continued to write during his tour of duty in the army, contributing short stories and novelettes to *Otechestvenniye Zapisky* (Annals of Our Country), where he also published two larger novels—*Podlipki*, which was largely autobiographical, and *In One's Own Country* (1856-66).

Leontiev returned from the war penniless. His writing was never popular, and he was unable to devote himself to it and still maintain the standard of living which he felt was his due. He practiced medicine on a private estate between 1857 and 1859, grew bored with it, and moved to St. Petersburg where he supplemented his meager income by giving lessons. In 1861 he married Elizavyeta Pavlovna Politova, a woman with whom he had initiated a liaison in the Crimea. After trying to make a go of the family estate for a short time, he secured a post in the government service through the good offices of a friend of the family.

Though he had flirted with the democrats during his youth, he now threw over his earlier idols Turgenev and George Sand in favor of an aesthetic conservatism strongly linked to the Orthodox Church and closely associated with the Slavophiles. But his conservatism was always more aesthetic than theological, and his connection with the Slavophiles was based on his passionate rejection of the scientific rationalism of Western Europe. His ethical thinking, characteristically expressed in such remarks as "One ancient oak is worth more than twenty mediocre men, and I would not fell it . . . to buy medicaments to cure a few peasants from cholera," led Berdyaev to link him with Nietzsche whose ideas he anticipated.

He spent the years 1863-71 in the foreign service in the Balkans, where he gave substance to his belief that marriage was a form of servitude by involving himself in a series of affairs, none of which he concealed from his wife. His writings reflect his love of the area and its people, untouched, as he saw them, by the rational sophistication of the already too-westernized Moscow and St. Peters-

burg. His reactions were later recorded in a series of essays *(Russia, the East and the Slavs)* and three volumes of stories of Greek life *(From the Life of Christians in Turkey,* 1876).

Embittered by his infidelity, his wife suffered a mental breakdown which left her a permanent invalid after 1871, the year Leontiev's mother died. These two shocks followed a serious illness of his own, causing another change in the author's outlook. He suddenly renounced his former life and sought to become a monk in the Greek monastery where he went for a year to recuperate. His petition was denied and he settled in Constantinople to write his famous essay *Byzantinism and Slavdom.* Returning to Moscow in 1874 he took his ailing wife to Kudivno and endured the hardship of caring for her on a meager income and the continued frustration of seeing his works published and ignored. He succeeded at length in gaining admission to a monastery near Moscow where he took the cowl under the name of Kliment (1891), but did not live out the year.

The complex originality of his ideas and their failure to coincide with any of the political and social movements of his day doomed Leontiev to obscurity in his lifetime. His greatest admirer was Vladimir Soloviev who labored to perpetuate his memory. Modern Soviet opinion criticizes his thoroughly reactionary outlook while recognizing his talent and originality.

ABOUT: Berdyaev, N. Konstantin Leontiev; Slavic Review, XX (1961).

L. R. & H. H.

*LEOPARDI, GIACOMO (TALE-GARDO FRANCESCO DI SALES SAVERIO PIETRO), Count (June 29, 1798-June 14, 1837), Italian poet, was born in Recanati, province of Marche, of a wealthy and noble family, traditionally devoted to the service of the Church. His father, Count Monaldo, a mediocre writer, was hostile to the new European principles of equality, liberty, and nationalism, and was sincerely convinced of his own infallibility. Having mismanaged his inherited fortune, he relinquished control of the family finances to his wife, Marquise Adelaide Antici, an energetic, austere, and resolute woman, whose despotism gave rise to the belief that much of Leopardi's mortified sensibility was attributable to her righteous hardness. While such cir-

* lā ō pär′ dē

cumstances cannot be ignored, it would be incorrect to explain the poet's melancholy by references to his unhappy childhood. Indeed his early years were enhanced by his happy camaraderie with his younger sister and brother, Paolina and Carlo.

According to an old custom, Giacomo, at nine, was turned over to the educational care of a priest who, four years later, declared honestly that he had nothing more to teach the boy. For Giacomo had studied independently and fervently, reading Greek, Latin, and Italian classics; exploring history and philology; and dreaming of glory, for which he confessed "a very great and perhaps immoderate desire." He continued this regime of "mad and most desperate study" with heroic endurance until c. 1817. After he had composed his first sonnet, "La Morte di Ettore" (1809), in which his boyish literary enthusiasms are passionately manifest, he translated Horace's *Arte Poetica*, various Greek odes (*Scherzi Epigrammatici*) and other works into Italian, and Porphyry's *Life of Plotinus* and other selections into Latin. His knowledge of Greek was so good that he forged a manuscript in jest and passed it off as authentic.

So much intellectual activity irreparably harmed the naturally frail constitution of Giacomo: he developed rachitis at seventeen, and the terrible cerebro-spinal disease, along with other ailments, was to plague him for the remaining twenty-two years of his life. He felt that his youth, "dearer than fame and laurels, than the pure light of day," had been lost "without a pleasure, uselessly." Except for his brother and sister, Recanati became unbearable; his parents did not understand him and showed no concern for either his sick body or his depressed spirits, and the townsfolk contributed to his misery by mocking his deformity.

Obliged to curtail his studying, and undiverted by pleasures, the precociously mature young man meditated on his condition, his ideals, his future. "An obstinate, black, horrible, barbarous melancholy" devoured him as he convinced himself that his life could produce only misery. It was in this state of mind that he was found in 1818 by the Italian writer and patriot Pietro Giordani, to whom the poet had dedicated his translation of the second book of the *Aeneid* (1817). After Giordani's short visit the young poet felt so uplifted that he penned two of his finest canzoni in one sitting, "All'Italia" and "Sopra il Monumento di Dante," in which the greatness of Rome and the personality of the divine bard who presaged his country's destiny point all the more tragically to the misfortunes of the Italy of his day. These works were preceded by the poems "Le Rimembranze," "Appressamento della Morte," and "Primo Amore," and by "Memorie del Primo Amore," a prose piece in intimate, subjective terms.

Leopardi's father, ever insensitive, blamed Giordani for perverting his son's mind, all of which intensified Giacomo's desire to leave his "native savage town." In 1819 his plan to flee was discovered, thereby straining further the incompatibility between his parents and himself. His movements were watched carefully and his correspondence censored. That same year an eye illness further hampered his reading and study. Out of his meditations, now almost completely dominated by melancholia, gradually emerged a religion of sorrow, which he considered the necessary condition of the universe, in which beauty, love, glory, and virtue are atrocious sins used by the governing powers of the world to deceive and afflict unhappy mortals. Yet the need for illusion, for loving something—beauty, art, love, without which life is vacuous—asserted itself occasionally in his works, only to plunge him later into bleaker feelings of desolation. The alternation continued between 1819 and 1822, the period of some of his most splendid idylls: "L'Infinito," "La Sera del Dì di Festa," "Alla Luna." In the first poem, a true classic, the poet's thought, absorbed between infinite time and space, loses itself in the physical and spiritual contemplation of eternity; the second and third contain some of Leopardi's favorite themes: fascination with nature, almighty and cruel, yet confiding; his own unhappiness in love; and oblivion, which eventually engulfs all.

In November 1822, Leopardi was finally allowed to make a trip to Rome. But his scorn for life did not abate. What had been a burning despair and an enthusiasm for beauty, counterbalancing his hopelessness, now modulated into a conviction of the total infelicity of the world and the vanity of all things.

Shortly after the poet returned to Recanati in May 1823, the Milanese editor Antonio Stella offered him the supervision of a vast edition of Cicero's works. Anxious to leave "the sepulcher of the living," Leopardi accepted and went to Milan in 1825. By this time he had completed his prose work *Operette Morali*, bitter reflections on an untrustworthy world, in which the author proudly asserts the superiority of his pessimism over the optimism of others. A commentary on Petrarch's *Canzoniere* (1826) and two anthologies of Italian prose and poetry (1827-28) also resulted from his Milanese sojourn. About this time Leopardi was offered a professorship at Bonn or Berlin, but fear of the inclement northern winters compelled his reluctant refusal.

He began writing poetry again in the spring of 1828: "A Silvia," in memory of the daughter of the Leopardi family coachman who had died in the flower of her youth; "Risorgimento," in which he renews his hope for love and for novel inspiration. His return to the "horrible night of Recanati" fortunately did not interfere with his renewed creativity. In 1829 he composed "Il Passero Solitario," an alternating inner dialogue between the sorrowful poet and a bird, contrasting the village feast and spring with the melancholy atmosphere of sunset; "Le Ricordanze," the disillusioned poet's return to his native home; "La Quiete dopo la Tempesta" and "Il Sabato del Villaggio," poems on the idea of evil and the pain of living.

Having lost his stipend from Stella, Leopardi's pride was seriously shaken in 1830 when charitable friends, headed by the historian Pietro Colletta, tactfully induced him to accept a sum of money. "I have lost all; I am a trunk which feels and suffers." Aided by a reprint of his *Canti*, he subsisted until 1832, when he was further humiliated by having to ask his family for a regular allowance. It was granted and continued for the remainder of his life.

Disillusion, however, did not prevent new illusions from arising. In Florence he developed a violent, almost tragic, passion for a beautiful and much courted lady, Fanny Targioni-Tozzetti, who took a vain pleasure in seeing the great poet humbled. For two years she occupied his thoughts exclusively and provided the inspiration for a series of three beautiful poems: "Il Pensiero Dominante," "Amore e Morte," and "Consalvo." But the wounding return to reality was inevitable, and when it occurred the effect was prostrating. He poured the venom of his scorn and shame into his "titanic blasphemy," the poem "A Se Stesso."

His sole comfort was his friendship with a young Neapolitan exile, Antonio Ranieri, in whose company Leopardi spent his last years in Florence and Naples. Death, which he had so often invoked as a liberation, overtook him in 1837 during a cholera epidemic in Naples, where he had dictated his last thoughts, later collected as *Zibaldone*, in addition to his last letters and poems, including the magnificent and climactic "La Ginestra." Leopardi was buried in the small church of San Vitale.

To the above-mentioned works must be added the important poems (all appearing under the general title of *Canti*) "Canto Notturno di un Pastore Errante nell'Asia," "Alla sua Donna," "Inno a' Patriarchi," "Tornami a Mente il Dì," "Bruto Minore," and "Ultimo Canto Di Saffo"; the political satire *Batracomiomachia;* the *Pensieri* (inspired by his thoughts on man and society in the *Operette Morali*); and the now published and most revealing *Epistolario* (ed. F. Moroncini, 7 vols., 1941). Expressed with classical elegance of style, linguistic virtuosity, and vibrant imagery, his poems rank among the finest in all literature. All disclose a man with an overabundant inner life which could not even approach a compromise with reality. His philosophy is rooted in the conviction that all is vanity and that the "beautiful and mortal thing passes and lasts not." Man falls prey not only to his illusions; he falls prey to nature, exiguous as he is before the infinite reality of being. His unhappiness, Leopardi argued, does not stem from his human perversion, from his illusion-shattering reason and science, as he had once thought, but from his very natural essence. There is, consequently, no divine Providence, and non-being is preferable to being, since suffering is the eternal and universal necessity of existence. And yet how can he rest tranquilly with these thoughts when, paradoxically, his heart swells with love for the good and the beautiful?

Among the earliest translations of Leopardi into English are *Essays and Dialogues* by Charles Edwardes in 1882, and *Essays, Dialogues and Thoughts* by Maj.-Gen. Patrick Maxwell in 1893. The first translation of *Poems* was done by Frederick Townsend in 1887. Later translations include Francis Henry Cliff's (1893), J. M. Morrison's (1900), Sir Theodore Martin's (1904), G. L. Bickersteth's (1923), William Fletcher Smith's (1939, 1941), R. C. Trevelyan's (1941), John Heath Stubbs' (1946), Jean-Pierre Barricelli's (1963). The *Canti* were translated by J. H. Whitfield (1962).

ABOUT: Gladstone, W. E. Giacomo Leopardi; Origo, I. Leopardi; Singh, G. Leopardi and the Theory of Poetry. [In Italian—see studies by G. Ferretti, G. Gentile, G. Parente, R. Wis.]

J.-P. B.

*****LEOPOLD, CARL GUSTAF AF** (April 3, 1756-November 9, 1829), Swedish poet, dramatist, critic, philosopher, was born in Stockholm. His father was Carl Adam Leopoldt (the poet changed the spelling c. 1786), a customs officer who soon after the birth of Carl Gustaf was promoted to collector and transferred to Norrköping where the boy grew up. His mother was Märtha Christina Hobel. In 1773 he entered the University of Uppsala, but financial necessity forced him to support himself by tutoring in various places. In 1781 he went to the University of Greifswald in northern Germany where academic degrees were easy to get. He took his M.A. and became *docent* in the History of Learning, and the next year he became assistant librarian in Stralsund. In 1784 he returned to Uppsala as librarian of a private book collection.

After a conflict with Kellgren and some time of irresolution, Leopold joined Kellgren's enlightened phalanx in the literary feud with Thorild. In 1786 he was employed by King Gustavus III as his assistant in dramatic activities. Through his great capacity for elegant and flattering conversation, Leopold gained the favor of the king, whose well-paid attendant and court poet he became. He was made a member of the Swedish Academy at its foundation in 1786, librarian at the royal library of the Drottningholm palace in 1787, private secretary to the king in 1788. In 1790 he married Sara Petronella Fehman, passing for a daughter of the Danish Supreme Court judge Peter Peterson Fehman but actually an illegitimate child of King Frederick V.

* lā′ ō pōld

After the assassination of Gustavus III in 1792, Leopold was the only one of his supporters who joined the opposition under Reuterholm, then in power, and was awarded permanent leave from his librarianship with salary intact. In return, Leopold flattered Reuterholm in laudatory poems. After three years' residence in Linköping, Leopold returned in 1796 to Stockholm; he received the title of Principal Assistant Secretary in 1799, Permanent Secretary in 1818. In 1809 he had been ennobled as "af Leopold." In 1819 his wife became insane and in 1822 he went blind.

After Kellgren's death in 1795, Leopold became the undisputed literary authority in Sweden. His first major literary works were two tragedies, the mythological *Oden* (1790), and the sentimental *Virginia* (1802), which were long regarded as the foremost representatives of the French-classical drama in Sweden. For many years he pursued an extensive journalistic activity as a didactic moralist and satirist in various Stockholm publications. His genre was reflective poetry of ideas, evidenced in such songs as the admired "Försynen" (Providence, 1793), the rhetorical masterpiece "Det Slutande Århundradet" (The Closing Century, 1799), and "Predikaren" (The Preacher, 1794), the most popular of his moralizing poems in which he demanded "enlightenment, freedom, human rights." Towards the end of the eighteenth century Leopold's style became simpler and more concrete, as in the charming idyll *Eglé and Annett* (1800). Perhaps most important among his philosophical prose writings is the pseudo-classical treatise *Om Smaken och dess Allmänna Lagar* (On Taste and Its General Laws, 1801), in which he codified his aesthetic principles.

Leopold's ode "Öfver Begäret till ett Odödligt Namn," rendered into English verse as "Ode on the Desire of Deathless Fame," is included in H. W. Longfellow's *The Poets and Poetry of Europe* (1871).

ABOUT: Holmberg, O. Leopold under Gustav IV. [In Swedish—see studies by O. Holmberg, A. Sjöding.]

A. J.

LERBERGHE, CHARLES VAN. See VAN LERBERGHE, CHARLES

*****LERMONTOV, MIKHAIL YURYEVICH** (October 2, 1814-July 15, 1841), Russian poet and novelist, was born in Moscow, the distant descendant of a Scottish

* lyĕr′ mŭn tŭf

LERMONTOV

LERMONTOV

soldier of fortune who had entered the service of Muscovy in 1613. His father, Yury Petrovich Lermontov, was a retired army captain; his mother, Mariya Mikhailovna Arsenieva, was the only child of a wealthy proprietress of an estate in Penza. Following the death of his mother in 1817, young Lermontov was raised by his grandmother, who argued that the boy's father did not have sufficient means to provide a proper education. Until the death of the father in 1832, a continuous battle raged between him and the grandmother over custody of the child, a conflict that caused young Mikhail severe anguish and may have contributed to his subsequent melancholy, pessimism, and feelings of estrangement.

The grandmother spared no expense in raising and educating her grandson. Excellent foreign tutors were in residence at her estate, and the children of friends and relatives were also educated there to provide companionship for Mikhail. As the child was often ill, he was taken to Caucasian spas on three occasions; the grandeur of the exotic Caucasian landscape strongly attracted the boy and left its deep mark upon his mature literary works.

In 1827 his grandmother moved to Moscow so that Mikhail might attend the preparatory school attached to the University of Moscow. It was at this time that he began writing lyric and narrative poetry, much of it completely imitative. In 1830, the year he entered the department of literature at the University of Moscow, he learned English and came under the direct influence of Byron. The English poet and Russia's Alexander Pushkin were to exert the most lasting influences upon Lermontov's future literary product.

At the university Lermontov remained aloof from his fellow students, among them such subsequently famous persons as Belinsky, Herzen, Ogarev, Goncharov, K. Aksakov, and Stankevich. He was openly contemptuous of the faculty and in 1832 was forced to leave the university; he then entered the School of Cavalry Junkers and Ensigns of the Guard in St. Petersburg. While there Lermontov worked upon an historical novel of the Pugachev Rebellion (unfinished), which was heavily influenced by Byronic themes and the florid style of the early Victor Hugo. He also wrote several dramas under the influence of Lessing and Schiller. His literary works of this period reflect an admiration for foreign literatures: echoes of Shakespeare, Goethe, and Macpherson, in addition to those authors mentioned above, may be detected. All of his poetry, drama, and prose of this early period is permeated with feelings of disillusionment and loneliness and is, essentially, a subjective expression of the author's personality. Byron undoubtedly provided congenial patterns for the personal conduct and literary expression of the pessimistic and rebellious young author. Lermontov reflects him in his love of freedom, dissatisfaction with life, appreciation of nature, and spiritual agitation. However, all of these qualities were manifest in Lermontov's works even prior to his acquaintance with the English poet. As he grew older, Lermontov's enthusiasm for the ultra-romantic creations of Byron waned, and his work became more realistic.

On receiving his commission as a cornet in the Life Guard Hussars (1834), a regiment stationed at Tsarskoe Selo, Lermontov sought to achieve a place in St. Petersburg society, a difficult undertaking as he had neither the money nor the name to force an immediate entrance into the *haut monde*. Certain details of this struggle for social prestige are chronicled in his unfinished novel of society *Princess Ligovskaya*.

The recognition that Lermontov sought was forthcoming almost overnight. In January 1837 Alexander Pushkin, Russia's greatest poet, died as the result of a duel with a French adventurer in the service of Czar Nicholas I. Lermontov immediately penned an elegy mourning Pushkin's passing and also excoriating his slayer and those circles of the court which had encouraged the fatal combat. This poem, which circulated in hand-written copies, angered the authorities and Lermontov was arrested. After a brief imprisonment, he was posted to the Caucasus, where he then took part in the Russian campaign against the native tribes. By February 1838 he was permitted to rejoin his old regiment at Tsarskoe Selo.

On his return to St. Petersburg, Lermontov was recognized as one of Russia's most promising authors, having already published several narrative poems. By the middle of 1839 many of his lyrics and the first part of his novel *A Hero of Our Time* had also appeared in print. In St. Petersburg doors previously closed to him were now open, but the poet's views on Russian society were becoming increasingly pessimistic and he found the atmosphere of the capital oppressive. At a ball celebrating the New Year, 1840, Lermontov was disrespectful to the daughters of the Czar; he alluded to this incident in his poem "The First of January, 1840," which also contained a scathing attack on fashionable society. In March 1840, ostensibly as a result of his duel with the son of the French Ambassador, Lermontov was arrested and, on orders of the Czar himself, sent to a line regiment in the Caucasus. In the ensuing months, the poet repeatedly distinguished himself by his bravery under fire, but all recommendations for decorations were expressly refused by the Czar and Lermontov's superiors were warned not to withdraw him from front-line service. However, through the intercession of friends, Lermontov was allowed to return to St. Petersburg in February 1841. He sought at this time, unsuccessfully, to retire from the army in order to devote himself exclusively to literature. Soon he was ordered to a fort in the Caucasus, but, under the pretext of illness, he went instead to Piatigorsk, where he assumed an active rôle in the town's social life. His epigrammatic wit and cutting lampoons quickly created many enemies, and Major N. S. Martynov finally challenged the poet. A duel was held on July 15, 1841, and Lermontov was killed.

As a poet, Lermontov is considered second only to Pushkin. His fame rests upon a small body of lyric and narrative works composed in the last five years of his life. These poems are marked by technical perfection and an unusual emotional depth. The poet's spiritual solitude, his love of nature, and his scorn for the slavish cringing of society before autocracy are expressed in many of these compositions. Among his most famous narrative poems are "The Demon," which treats in an ultra-romantic manner the unhappy love of a fallen angel for a mortal; "The Novice," a dying youth's confession of his unsuccessful flight from the confinement of a monastery; and "The Song of the Merchant Kalashnikov," perhaps the only successful imitation in Russian literature of the historical songs of the Russian oral tradition. With his rich poetic language and his innovations in the use of rhymes and meters, Lermontov contributed greatly to the enrichment of Russian verse. His declamatory style, exemplified by his poems of social protest, provided a basis for the further development of this type of poetry by Nekrasov. It was by virtue of Lermontov's unusual talents as a poet that the Golden Age of Russian poetry endured for five years following the death of Pushkin.

Lermontov's one completed novel *A Hero of Our Time* is a work basic to the development of Russian psychological realism. By an intricate combination of five separate stories and three narrators, it presents a progressively more intimate psychological portrait of Grigory Pechorin, a young officer who seems fated to have an adventurous but tragic life. Deriving from Pushkin's Eugene Onegin, the first complete picture of the "superfluous man" in Russian literature, Pechorin also has literary ancestors in de Sénancour's Obermann, Chateaubriand's René, Musset's Octave, Richardson's Lovelace, and certain Byronic heroes. Lermontov's prose style, which even today has no archaic flavor, set a pattern for subsequent nineteenth century authors. Chekhov stated that he knew of "no language better than that of Lermontov." Tolstoy declared that he considered "Taman," one of the stories forming *A Hero of Our Time*, the finest work in Russian literature from an artistic point of view. *A Hero of Our Time* has numerous stylistic and thematic ties with works of Turgenev, Goncharov, Dostoevsky, and Tolstoy, among others. D. S. Mirsky notes that it is not entirely without justification that some critics consider it the best novel in Russian literature.

English translations of *A Hero of Our Time* have been made by I. Nestor-Schurmann (1899), J. H. Wisdom and M. Murray (1912), S. Phillimore (1920), R. Merton (1928), E. & C. Paul (1940), Martin Parker (1951), V. and D. Nabokov (1958). *Bela* was translated by J. Domb and G. Schoenberg (1945); *The Demon* by F. Storr (1894), E. Richter (1910), R. Burness (1918), G. Shelley (1930). Occasional translations of individual poems have appeared in the *Slavonic and East European Review* and in C. M. Bowra's *A Book of Russian Verse* (1943).

ABOUT: Bowra, M. *Introduction to* A Hero of Our Time (World Classics ed., 1958) ; Lavrin, J. Lermontov. [In French—Troyat, H. L'Étrange Destin de Lermontov.]

J. M.

*LE SAGE, ALAIN RENÉ (May 8, 1668-November 17, 1747), French novelist and dramatist, was born at Sarzeau, Morbihan. His father, Claude Le Sage, served as notary, advocate, and registrar at the Royal Court of Rhuys, a peninsula of Brittany. Both parents died when Le Sage was still very young and the boy was powerless to prevent the waste and embezzlement of his fortune by his guardians. Little is known of his life. He seems to have been educated by the Jesuits until the age of eighteen, was called to the bar in Paris in 1692, and in 1694 was married to Marie Elizabeth Huyard.

Trying to make a name for himself in literature and to earn a living at the same time, Le Sage started out as a translator. His patron, the Abbé de Lyonne, may have suggested Spanish literature as a promising field, and thus, after an initial translation venture, *The Epistles of Aristaenetus* (1695), he took up Spanish plays. *Le Traître Puni et le Point d'Honneur* was translated from a play by Rojas, *Don Felix de Mendoce* from Lope de Vega; *Don Cesar Ursin* was an adaptation of a Calderón play.

By 1707, however, he had turned to writing his own plays. The farce *Crispin Rival de Son Maître*, written that year, was an immediate success. *Le Diable Boiteux* went through a series of revisions until 1725. Le Sage's masterpiece for the theatre, *Turcaret*, was composed in 1709. It represents an altered version of an earlier comedy, *Les Étrennes* (1707). Altogether Le Sage wrote about one hundred pieces, all of them for the Théâtre de la Foire, essentially a comic opera stage which presented plays in booths during festival time. He was just one of many authors whom Le Théâtre Français did not favor and who, consequently, had to turn to the less discriminating Théâtre de la Foire.

Le Sage is probably best known for his contribution to fiction. In 1715 the first two parts of his Spanish picaresque novel *Gil Blas de Santillane* were published, to be followed in 1724 by the third part and in 1735 by the fourth. The adventures of its lively, cynical hero are recounted in a series of interrelated stories, racy, richly comic and realistic, fertile and inventive. Among his contemporaries this famous novel was not so successful

LE SAGE

as the author's *Le Diable Boiteux*, and certainly it is inferior to *Don Quixote* to which it has often been compared. Le Sage occupies a unique position in literature in that he stands somewhat apart from his native France, his literary ancestors being Spanish, his successors English. His work falls into three major categories: his pieces for the Théâtre de la Foire; his Molièresque comedies, *Crispin* and *Turcaret;* and his prose fiction. He has frequently been accused of downright plagiarism or, at least, of lack of originality. Neither charge is substantially correct, for although Le Sage frequently started out by adopting a foreign writer's plot, idea sequence, or characters, he always left his crutches behind after the first few chapters and struck out on a line entirely and genuinely his own. An example would be the relation between Luis Vélez's *Diablo Cojuelo* and the *Diable Boiteux.* Again, Le Sage's *Gil Blas* may be indebted to Vincent Espinel's *Marcos de Obregón* for a few incidents; the work as a whole, however, is certainly original. His greatest claim to fame, perhaps, is the distinction of having been one of the few great masters of French style.

Throughout his life Le Sage manifested great independence, being neither the object of royal patronage, nor the pet of the salons. One of his sons became a priest, another an actor with the Comédie Française. Le Sage died at Boulogne at seventy-nine. His complete *Œuvres*, in 12 volumes, appeared in 1821.

* lĕ sàzh′

The *Adventures of Gil Blas* was translated by
Tobias Smollett in 1749 and published in 1781.
Numerous editions have appeared subsequently.
Smollett's translation was revised by B. H. Malkin
in the nineteenth century. *Asmodeus; or The
Devil on Two Sticks* was translated by I. Thomas
(1841). The comedy *Crispin* was translated by
B. H. Clark (1915).

ABOUT: Pierson, C. O. Dramatic Works of
Le Sage; Saintsbury, G. Essays on French Novel-
ists. [In French—see studies by H. Cordier, L.
Claretie, E. F. Linthilac.]

E. J. S.

*LESKOV, NIKOLAI SEMYONOVICH

(February 16, 1831-March 6, 1895), Russian
novelist and story writer, was born in Goro-
khovo near Oryol, the son of a small land-
holder and part-time civil servant descended
from the clergy. His mother, Maria Petrovna, *née* Alfieri, was of the lesser aristocracy. Leskov spent much of his childhood on
his father's farm and thus gained his first
vivid impressions of the life of the common
people.

LESKOV

Although Leskov attended the secondary
school in Oryol for six years, he left there at
the age of sixteen upon the death of his
father. He moved to Kiev where he eventually entered the civil service. His work in the
military recruitment office sent him over a
great deal of the Ukraine, an experience
which left a definite mark on his later literary
work in the form of a love for the Ukrainian
vernacular and for vigorous Ukrainian types,
both of which are found in his works. In
Kiev, Leskov married Olga Smirnov, who
bore him two children. She showed signs of
hysteria early in the marriage and eventually
became insane. He married again in Kiev,
this time Ekaterina Savitsky. A son, Andrei,
born of this marriage in 1866, grew up to be
an army general and his father's most
thorough biographer.

Sometime in the late 1850's Leskov left the
civil service to become business agent for his
uncle, the Russianized Englishman Alexander
Scott, and in this connection traveled from
one end of Russia to the other. His employer
soon noticed in the reports submitted by
Leskov a keen insight into situations and a
genius for narration. Encouraged by Scott,
Leskov took up journalism and in 1861, at a
time of great political tension, moved to St.
Petersburg where he plunged into literary
activity. In a time when nearly all literary
figures had some political identification and
most were radical, Leskov refused to be
identified with any group. He was, however,
very critical of the behavior of many radicals,

* lyĕ skôf′

whom he portrayed in his rather violent first
novel, *Nekuda* (No Way Out, 1864), as
cynics, profligates, parasites, and foreign
agents. This work caused such a furor in the
literary world that Leskov was practically
boycotted by the leading publishers for the
next twenty years.

With Dostoevsky, whom he knew, Leskov
contended that radicals had no real knowledge
of the mass of the Russian people. It was his
own interest in the common people which led
him to develop his most successful genre,
vivid stories of intense incident set mostly in
the provinces. *Lady Macbeth of the Mtsensk
District* (1865), a tale of violently destructive passions, is the best example of this.
Shostakovich was later (1934) to use this as
a basis for his opera of the same name.

To present his own view of what was positive in Russian life Leskov wrote *Cathedral
Folk* (1872), in which he depicts the struggles
and peculiarly Russian virtues of the provincial clergy. Here Leskov comes close to
Dostoevsky in his concept of the Russian
church and the rôle it should play. His Archpriest Tuberozov and Deacon Akhilla have
become in Russia monuments of moral fortitude. Significantly, however, Tuberozov is
ultimately broken by the rigid bureaucracy of
the church. As a result of this work Leskov
was appointed in 1874 to an advisory position
in the Ministry of Education, which he held
until 1883. He was dismissed because of his
increasingly critical attitude toward the official
church and because of his publication of a
series of "corrective" anecdotes on the clergy.

As Leskov matured he attempted to create and serve an idea. An example of this is "On the Edge of the World" (1876), a long tale about Russian missionaries in the far north, in which he attempts to show that the native heathen virtues and gods may be better suited than their Russian counterparts for the rigors of northern life. Even in this story, however, Leskov is carried away by his narrative genius and the story abounds in incident. Other stories, e.g., "The Steel Flea" (1882) and "The Hare Park" (1894), show sheer narrative exuberance. In this connection it is ironic that Leskov should have said of his own writing that he was read for the beauty of his imaginative work, but that in one hundred years he would be read for his ideas —an unfulfilled prophecy. Although very widely read in Russia, Leskov was accused by many of vulgarity and excessive voluptuousness, particularly for his last piece of fiction, "A Winter Day," a short story on the degeneration of the upper classes.

During the last years of his life Leskov was justly renowned. His bulky, square figure with a closely trimmed beard was a familiar sight in the streets of St. Petersburg and in watering places in Bohemia. He died in his sixty-fourth year at the height of his fame. Since his death he has been very widely read and translated, particularly into German. His influence on post-Revolutionary writers has been considerable; Belyi, Remizov, Zamyatin, Zoshchenko and the Serapion brothers owe a great deal to Leskov for their racy and colloquial styles.

It is only recently that Leskov has been translated to any extent into English. *Cathedral Folk* was translated by Isabel Hapgood in 1924; other translations are *The Sentry and Other Stories* by E. A. Chamot (1923); *The Enchanted Wanderer* by A. G. Paschkoff (1924), D. Magarshack (1946, as *The Enchanted Pilgrim); The Steel Flea* by Babette Deutsch and A. Yarmolinsky (1943); *Tales of Leskov* by R. Norman (1944).

ABOUT: Harvard Slavic Studies, IV (1957). [In French—Kovalewsky, P. Leskov, Peintre Méconnu de la Vie Nationale Russe. In German—Setschkareff, V. Leskov: Sein Leben und Sein Werk.]

N. V.

*LESSING, GOTTHOLD, EPHRAIM

(January 22, 1729-February 15, 1781), German critic and dramatist, was born in the town of Kamenz in Upper Lusatia, Saxony. His father, Johann Gottfried Lessing, was a Protestant minister as well as a scholar of broad and tolerant views, and the boy grew

* lĕs′ ing

LESSING

up in an atmosphere of culture and liberality. He attended the famous *Fürstenschule* St. Afra at Meissen, where he proved himself to be an insatiable and precocious student, and in 1746 entered the University of Leipzig to study theology. In Leipzig Lessing was introduced by his cousin, Christlob Mylius, to the world of journalism as well as to the theatre, and under the influence of these new experiences transferred to the faculty of philosophy and literature. Of importance to the development of his theatrical knowledge was his friendship with Karoline Neuber and her company of players. This group successfully performed one of Lessing's earliest plays, *Der Junge Gelehrte* (1748).

In 1749 Lessing settled in Berlin, where with the exception of the year 1751-52 spent in Wittenberg to acquire his Master's degree, he remained until 1755, supporting himself as a journalist for the *Berliner Priviligierte Zeitung* and later for the *Vossische Zeitung*. During this period the comedies *Der Misogyn* (1748), *Der Freigeist* (1749) and *Die Juden* (1749) appeared, followed by a collection of verse and epigrams entitled *Kleinigkeiten* (1751). Lessing also published a volume of *Rettungen*, a series of essays defending the reputations of writers who had been misunderstood or wrongly judged by previous generations. His approach here was characteristic of all his critical endeavors, combining an exhaustive examination of the facts with a vigorous, lucid style and masterful logic of presentation. Together with Mylius, Lessing founded *Beiträge zur Historie und*

Aufnahme des Theaters (1750), a quarterly journal dedicated to a comprehensive study of dramatic technique along with translations of the best plays in all literatures. Of major significance in this enterprise, which lasted only four issues, was the preface, in which Lessing first stated his conviction that the future of the German national drama lay in imitation of English rather than French drama.

In Berlin Lessing associated with Voltaire, until a misunderstanding over Lessing's handling of a manuscript borrowed from the French writer embittered their relationship. More enduring friendships were made with the Jewish philosopher Moses Mendelssohn, with whom Lessing wrote the essay *Pope, ein Metaphysiker* (1755), and with C. F. Nicolai, the bookseller and author.

Encouraged by the reception of his writings, Lessing published an edition of his collected works, *Schriften* (6 vols., 1753-55). An essay criticizing a translation of Horace involved Lessing in a controversy with the minor poet S. H. Lange. Lessing's devastating rebuttal, *Vade Mecum für den Herrn Samuel Gotthold Lange* (1754), demolished Lange's reputation and brought Lessing into prominence as a critic.

In 1755 Lessing completed *Miss Sarah Sampson,* a *bürgerliches Trauerspiel* or domestic tragedy, which formed a turning point in the author's life and in the history of German drama. To this time his dramas had been written in the prevailing tradition of French comedy. In this work, however, he practiced his thesis that English models were more suited to German temperament, and the play, which is set in England, reflects the influence of George Lillo's *The London Merchant* and Samuel Richardson's novels. Lessing further broke with French tradition by using prose instead of alexandrine verse. This drama, which introduced domestic tragedy into the German theatre, represents the beginning of modern drama in Germany.

Toward the end of 1755 Lessing was employed by a wealthy young man as a traveling companion for a tour through North Germany, Holland, and England. They had proceeded only as far as Amsterdam, however, when the outbreak of the Seven Years' War interrupted their journey. Lessing returned to Leipzig briefly and then to Berlin, where he published *Philotas* (1759), a one-act tragedy set in Greek antiquity. He also completed a collection of *Fabeln* (1759), which was prefaced by an important essay on this genre, *Abhandlung über die Fabel,*

one of his finest critical achievements. With Mendelssohn and Nicolai, Lessing conceived the idea for a literary periodical to be written in the form of letters ostensibly to a wounded officer. These *Briefe, die Neueste Literatur Betreffend* (1759-65), contain some of the finest criticism of the time. Most notable is the famous 17th letter, in which Lessing destroyed the dictatorship of the critic Johann Christoph Gottsched, the leading advocate of French drama in Germany. Also of importance is Lessing's dramatic fragment on the theme of *Faust,* in which he anticipates the ultimate salvation of this great inquiring spirit.

From 1760 to 1765 Lessing was secretary to General Tauentzien, the governor of Breslau. During this period he devoted himself to classical studies which were brought to fruition in the essay *Laokoon, oder Über die Grenzen der Malerei und Poesie* (1766). In this masterpiece of stimulating, constructive criticism Lessing defined the boundaries between the plastic arts and literature on the basis of their differing means of presentation. By this essay Lessing established himself as one of the leading aesthetic critics in all Europe.

Lessing next completed his greatest drama, *Minna von Barnheim* (1767), the first German national drama and one of the finest comedies in all of German literature. This play, which has long served as a model of dramatic construction and characterization, was additionally important in its day as Lessing's attempt to counteract the hostility between Prussia and Saxony following the Seven Years' War.

In 1767 Lessing was appointed critic and literary adviser of the newly established German National Theatre in Hamburg. His commentaries, collected in the volume *Hamburgische Dramaturgie* (1767-68), treat general problems of the theatre, including an analysis of the nature of tragedy, the problem of catharsis, and the question of the three unities. *Hamburgische Dramaturgie* became the first handbook of dramatic technique.

When the Hamburg theatre failed in 1769, Lessing accepted a position as court librarian in Wolfenbüttel in Brunswick. There he produced *Emilia Galotti* (1772), a domestic tragedy in prose, based on the Roman legend of Virginia. Since the drama contains a sharp denunciation of the social and political problems caused by an absolute system of government, the scene was placed in Italy rather than in Germany to avoid repercussions.

555

Following a trip to Italy, Lessing in 1776 married Eva König, the widow of a friend. This period of genuine happiness, one of the few in Lessing's life, was all too brief, however, for his beloved wife died in childbirth in 1778. Broken in health, weary in spirit, and oppressed by debts and loneliness, Lessing struggled on for three final years until his death in Brunswick at the age of fifty-two.

Lessing's final years were embittered by theological controversy resulting from the publication of *Fragmente eines Ungenannten* (1772). Since these documents by H. S. Reimarus, a professor of Oriental languages, were strongly critical of Christianity, Lessing was attacked by Johann Melchior Goeze, chief pastor in Hamburg, for spreading unorthodox opinions. Although Lessing himself did not agree with the views of Reimarus, he nevertheless defended the right of free criticism and open inquiry in the essays *Eine Duplik, Eine Parabel, Axiomata, Anti-Goeze,* and *Ernst und Falk: Gespräche für Freimaurer* (1778). When the right of free publication was withdrawn from him, Lessing returned to his "old pulpit, the stage" with the drama *Nathan der Weise* (1779), one of the noblest pleas for tolerance in all literature. The central idea of the play was taken from the tale of the ring in Boccaccio's *Decameron*. Although the work is undramatic in essence, it possesses a moral grandeur and has taken its place in the literature of the world for its serene and lofty humanitarian ideals. The play was written in iambic pentameter blank verse and was instrumental in establishing this form as the standard verse of German classical drama. Lessing's final work was *Die Erziehung des Menschengeschlechts* (1780), which continued his efforts on behalf of humanity and tolerance.

Lessing is the greatest representative of the intellectual ideals of the German Enlightenment. He transcended his age both as critic and dramatist. His activity initiated the modern period in German literature and in addition distinguished him as the first German author of European stature.

A collection of Lessing's *Dramatic Works* (2 vols.) was published by E. Bell in 1878. E. C. Beasley and H. Zimmern translated *Select Prose Works* in 1879, and H. Chadwick published a selection of *Theological Writings* in 1956. *Der Freigeist* was translated by J. J. Holroyd in 1838, *Die Erziehung des Menschengeschlechts* by F. W. Robertson in 1858, *Emilia Galotti* by C. L. Lewes in 1868 and by E. Dvoretzky in 1962. In 1878 *Damon* and *Miss Sarah Sampson* appeared anonymously. *Hamburgische Dramaturgie* was translated by H. Zimmern in 1879. In 1927 Rev. A. Cohen translated *Ernst und Falk* as *Lessing's*

Masonic Dialogues. W. A. Steel translated *Laokoon, Nathan der Weise* and *Minna von Barnhelm* in 1930. *Minna von Barnhelm* was also translated by O. Heller in 1917 and by L. Nelson in 1929. *Nathan der Weise* was translated by P. Maxwell (1939), G. Reinhardt (1950), and in blank verse by B. Q. Morgan (1955).

ABOUT: Garland, H. B. Lessing: The Founder of Modern German Literature; Haney, J. D. Lessing's Education of the Human Race; Nolte, F. O. Grillparzer, Lessing, and Goethe in the Perspective of European Literature; Robertson, J. G. Lessing's Dramatic Theory; Rolleston, T. W. Life of G. E. Lessing; Sime, J. Lessing, His Life and Works. [In German—see studies by K. G. Lessing, O. Mann, and E. Schmidt.]

D. G. D.

*LEVERTIN, OSCAR IVAR (July 17, 1862-September 22, 1906), Swedish poet, novelist, man of letters, was born of Jewish parents in Gryt in the province of Östergötland, but grew up in Stockholm. His father was Wilhelm Philip Levertin, an art and antique dealer whose artistic and literary interests, political liberalism, and religious skepticism influenced young Oscar greatly. His mother was Sophie Albertina Davidson, of a religiously orthodox family. After a winter on the Riviera for treatment of an affliction of his lungs, he studied at the University of Uppsala, where he mixed in radical circles. He took his Ph.D. in literature in 1888 and was appointed *docent* in the history of literature and in 1889 professor of the same subject at the University of Stockholm. In 1887 he married Lisen Svanström, daughter of a stationer in Stockholm, through whom he came into intimate contact with Christian ideology. With her death in 1889 ended the first period in Levertin's life, a period of intense study and considerable literary criticism. But his success did not come until later.

Shortly after his wife's death Levertin suffered a lung hemorrhage that almost ended his life. He went to Davos in Switzerland to cure his illness. Here he met Verner von Heidenstam (1859-1940), the poet, with whom an intimate lifelong friendship developed. Under Heidenstam's influence he moved from the sphere of naturalistic and social reform ideas to a culturally aristocratic and aesthetically neo-romantic philosophy, but the melancholy, pessimistic Levertin could never embrace his worship of the joy of life. As a result of their collaboration in Davos, Levertin published *Pepitas Bröllop* (Pepita's Wedding, 1891), a pamphlet proclaiming a new romanticism. In 1899 he married Ebba Mesterton, *nee* von Redlich.

* lä′ věr těn

A considerable part of Levertin's time was devoted to the authorship of scholarly books and articles and to literary journalism. He wrote several treatises on literature and art. His art in the literary essay was influenced by French masters and by Georg Brandes, but he developed it into a personal art-genre of undisputed mastery.

Collaterally with his scholarly and journalistic work Levertin continued his activity as poet and novelist. In his poetic collection *Legender och Visor* (Legends and Songs, 1891), he showed poetic greatness equal to that of Heidenstam. Love, death, and ungratified longing are the fundamental motifs in his technically superb poetry, which mirrors his reflective and complex emotional life. His poems, composed in harmony with his new aesthetic ideals, overflow with exotic and colorful grandeur. In *Nya Dikter* (New Poems, 1894), his melancholy is superseded by a bolder and more positive attitude to life, inspired by Nietzsche's heroic philosophy. Although still an atheist, his motifs are Jewish and medieval Christian. Still more melancholy is the collection *Dikter* (Poems, 1901), partly inspired by impressions from a journey to Italy. His last poetic work, *Kung Salomo och Morolf* (King Solomon and Morolf, 1904), written in Switzerland, is an epic-lyrical poem with a varied metrical scheme, inspired by Ecclesiastes, the Canticles, and Arabic legends, and based on a well-known medieval tale.

Levertin's prose was exquisite. In his historical pastiche *Rococonoveller* (Rococo Stories, 1899), he reproduced with an admirable truthfulness the elegant and ceremonious atmosphere of the eighteenth century. His novel *Magistrarne i Österås* (The Masters of Österås, 1900), is, as he said himself, "a very Swedish little picture," in which he presents a gallery of Swedish characters in a typically Swedish milieu. He was, however, more successful in describing the milieu than the characters.

Of Levertin's prose a short story from *Rococonoveller* is available in English translation in *Sweden's Best Stories,* edited by Hanna Astrup Larsen (1928). Six of his poems are translated into English in C. W. Stork's *Anthology of Swedish Lyrics* (1930); two poems are in F. A. Judd's *Under the Swedish Colours* (1911), five in C D. Locock's *A Selection from Modern Swedish Poetry* (1931).

ABOUT: [In Swedish—see studies by H. Ahlenius, F. Böök, C. Fehrmann, A. Levertin, W. Söderhjelm.]

A. J.

*LEVINSOHN, ISAAC BAER (DOV)** (October 13, 1788-February 12, 1860), Hebrew scholar and writer, founder of the Haskalah (Enlightenment) movement among the Russian Jews, was born in Kremenetz, Russia. Besides the traditional Talmudic education, he also studied modern and classical languages; he soon manifested great erudition in rabbinic literature as well as unusual scholarly and literary abilities, and at nine he had already written a cabalistic work.

Upon his marriage in 1807 he settled in Radzivilov where he became a private teacher and was also engaged as translator for the Russian army; his marriage was unhappy, and he soon divorced his wife; his only son of that marriage died very young, and Levinsohn never remarried.

His first steps in Hebrew literature were in poetry: one work, a patriotic poem on the occasion of the Russian victory over Napoleon, earned him official citation from the Czarist government. His verses, however, were regarded even by him as unsuccessful efforts and they were never published.

In poor health as the result of excessive study and overwork, Levinsohn went to Galicia in 1813 for medical treatment; there he made the intimate acquaintance of important representatives of Galician Haskalah and they strongly influenced his future reforms of Russian Jewry. Levinsohn settled in Brody as a bookkeeper, devoting most of his time to study and scholarly work; upon passing the necessary examinations he became a teacher at the *Gymnasium* of Tarnopol, and later at the Hebrew College of Brody.

In 1820 he returned to Kremenetz, where he was persecuted by the orthodox fanatics for spreading the Enlightenment. He was compelled to leave and to wander through various parts of Russia. In 1823 he fell ill and once more returned to Kremenetz, where he stayed until his death.

Levinsohn is rightly called the Russian Moses Mendelssohn. He was a scholar of wide religious and secular erudition and of critical understanding. Despite poverty and extremely impaired health during his entire life, he was unusually prolific. He dedicated his talents and energies to a twofold purpose: to spread enlightenment and education among the Russian Jews, and to defend the honor of Judaism and its teachings. Coun-

* lěv' ĭn sōn

terbalancing the negative tendencies of Haskalah and making it a constructive factor in Jewish life, he taught the younger generation not to disdain manual labor in their quest for education.

He was held in esteem as a Hebrew scholar by the Russian government, which consulted him in Jewish matters and bestowed various awards upon him. He declined many positions offered to him by the government, among them a request to become the Chief Rabbi of Russia. His frequent petitions to the Czarist government to improve the educational and economic conditions of the Jews were, to a certain extent, successful, leading to the establishment of the first agricultural colonies for Jews in Russia, and to the opening of secular schools for the Jewish youth, thus introducing a new era in the social and cultural development of Russian Jewry.

Levinsohn's works include satires on Hasidism, critical and philological writings, and polemics. Perhaps the most significant of these is *Teudah Beyisrael* (1823) wherein he advocated the need for a secular knowledge which would not violate the spirit of Judaism.

Efes Damim, his spirited answer to a charge of ritual murder made against a Jewish community, was translated into English in 1840.

ABOUT: Raisin, J. S. The Haskalah Movement in Russia; Waxman, M. A History of Jewish Literature.

H. C.

*L'HOSPITAL (or L'HÔPITAL), MICHEL DE (1507-March 13, 1573),

French statesman and writer, born near Aigueperse (Auvergne), was the son of the doctor of the Constable of Bourbon. He was sent to Toulouse to study law in a strongly classical and religious discipline. His studies were interrupted by the exile of the Constable and of his father, whom he followed to Milan, completing his education at Padua; at Rome he was briefly a judge in the ecclesiastical tribunal. This long sojourn in Italy exposed L'Hospital to the full glory of the new culture, both in letters and in customs, and left a mark on his tastes and his innate sense of justice and measure. He returned to France in 1534, was admitted to the bar in Paris, married the daughter of the Criminal Lieutenant Jean Morin, and three years later became counselor in Parliament, where his probity and wide knowledge were generally admired. During this first

* lô pē tàl'

period, L'Hospital found time to cultivate letters and to project a treatise on Roman law; in classical literature he most admired examples of virtue and' liberty, and by preference read Plato and Xenophon.

L'Hospital long enjoyed the personal favor of Henry II. The King sent him to the Council of Trent in 1547, but the schism frustrated all efforts. Some time after his return, the Duchesse de Berry named him her chancellor, then recommended him to her brother the King, who in turn made him Chancellor of France in 1560. In this rôle L'Hospital tried conciliation, opposed abuses and venality in public officers, and prevented the establishment of the Inquisition through his conviction that torture, instead of changing man's inner ideals, served rather to create dissension. Despite the many enemies he made, he maintained a respected and powerful position during the important reforms of 1560 and of 1566, which guaranteed, at least for intervals, the freedom of religious conscience that he demanded. His enemies finally turned young Charles IX against him by their intrigues, and in 1568 he was discharged of his duties and powers. He retired from the court to his properties in Vignay, near Étampes, and devoted himself to study and writing. He narrowly escaped assassination during the St. Bartholomew massacre, and died several months later.

Beside his distinguished service in the public cause, L'Hospital is esteemed as one of the dozen greatest prose stylists of sixteenth century France. Most of his writings are of didactic or legal nature, but passages for example in his *Traité de la Réformation de la Justice* have the qualities of the best essays on moral problems, and recount pertinent episodes from classical literature in vivid and powerful narratives; in such texts L'Hospital seeks to illustrate ancient virtue, after the manner of Montaigne, and also to convince the reader, who was usually the King himself, that abuses must be avoided and justice done as in ancient times.

The 1824 edition of L'Hospital's works includes his *Traité de la Reformation de la Justice*, the *Harangues*, the *Testament Politique*, a tract on war and peace, and various Latin verses published in 1585 and often translated into French. His *Œuvres Inédites* appeared in 1825, and his *Poésies Complètes* in 1857.

ABOUT: [In French—Jardonnet, M. Michel de l'Hospital; Taillandier, A. Nouvelle Biographie Générale, XXXI; Villemain, A. Études d'Histoire Moderne.]

F. J. C.

LICHTENSTEIN, ULRICH VON. See ULRICH VON LICHTENSTEIN

*LIDNER, BENGT (March 16, 1757-January 4, 1793), Swedish poet, was born in Gothenburg. His father was Olaf Liedner (the poet changed the spelling), a manufacturer. His mother was Elisabeth Boëthius, daughter of a clergyman. His father died when he was two; his mother remarried but died when he was fourteen. He went to the University of Lund, but his disorderly life forced his stepfather to send him to sea. As a deck boy on an East Indiaman he deserted ship in Capetown and returned home. After a short time of study at the University of Greifswald, Germany, he went to Stockholm in 1779. His literary products pleased King Gustavus III, who paid the expenses of his literary studies in Göttingen and Paris. Because of his undependability and dipsomania the King withdrew his allowance.

Lidner's poetry up to this point had been unoriginal and insignificant, but after his return to Stockholm it suddenly reached perfection. Now he created, in rapid succession, the works that made him popular and famous. In 1773 he published his best known work, *Grefvinnan Spastaras Död* (The Death of Countess Spastara; revised edition, 1786), a poignant poem describing an actual event—the death of a beautiful young Italian woman trying to save her child during an earthquake. It is a long monologue by the Countess, interrupted by the poet's hysterical outbursts. The poem is written in masterfully executed, varying meters. It is characteristic of Lidner's flowery figurative language and of his unrestrained emotions.

The next year saw his opera *Medea*, flooded with blood and tears and based on Euripides' and Seneca's classical story. In his versified chronicle *Året MDCCLXXXIII* (The Year 1783), written in his usual declamatory style, Lidner gave a subjective description of the events that made the strongest impression on him.

Lidner needed several years to complete his foremost religious poem, *Yttersta Domen* (The Last Judgment, published 1788), which is indebted to Young's *Night Thoughts* and Milton's *Paradise Lost* and reminiscent of his pietistic upbringing.

Hunted by creditors in Sweden, he accompanied one of his patrons to Finland, where he lived on the generosity of the squires whom he visited. In 1788 he married a poor Finnish noble lady, Eve Jaquette Hastfehr, stepdaughter of a dean. During his stay in Finland he wrote several patriotic poems which restored his good standing with the King. The following year he moved to Stockholm. His hopeless inebriation and financial anxieties reduced his productivity and undermined his health. Not long before his death he received a small government pension and the treasured title of Royal Secretary.

Lidner's production shows the influence of many great masters of poetry. He strained after effects, and his style looks baroque, but his torrent of lofty words flowed not only from reflection and deliberation but also from spontaneous reactions. Compassion, for himself and others, was the mainspring of his inspiration. He luxuriated in emotional explosions. His verse was exquisitely rhythmical and melodious, and its emancipation from the rigid rules of French classicism points to the poetic freedom of romanticism.

A song from *Medea* and the introduction to *Grefvinnan Spastaras Död* are translated into English by C. W. Stork in his *Anthology of Swedish Lyrics* (1917).

ABOUT: [In Swedish—see studies by L. Josephson, K. Warburg.]

A. J.

*LIE, JONAS LAURITZ IDEMIL (November 6, 1833-July 5, 1908), Norwegian novelist, playwright, poet, was born at Hokksund in Eiker in southern Norway. His father, Mons Lie, was a highly respected judge, born in the city of Trondheim in northern Norway. His mother was Pauline Christine Tiller, daughter of a merchant from the same city. In 1838 his father was appointed city judge in the little town of Tromsö in the northernmost part of the country, far above the Arctic Circle. The rugged and majestic landscape of sea and mountains, the hard life of the superstitious population, and the mysterious folklore made indelible impressions upon the future author. In 1846, his father was transferred to Sunnhordland, south of Bergen, as a district judge. Jonas continued his school education there. At the age of eighteen he entered the University of Oslo and completed his law degree in 1858. Next summer he began practicing law at Kongsvinger in southeastern Norway, and in 1860 he married his cousin Thomasine Lie, who became his ardent champion and helper. Lie speculated in the lumber business, lost in a crisis, and was in 1868 declared bankrupt with gigantic debts. Then he decided to de-

* lĕd′ nĕr

* lē

559

LIE

excellent pictures of the life of the seamen aboard ship as well as on land. In the realistic-naturalistic novel *Livsslaven* (The Life Convict, 1883), he analyzed the social problems of a proletarian individual whose fight against society made him a convict for life. In the same year he brilliantly inaugurated a series of a dozen family novels by publishing *Familien paa Gilje* (The Family at Gilje), a classic in Norwegian literature that gives a superb picture of life in a cultured middle class home of the mid-nineteenth century. Lie's message to his readers is that too much stress on economic, social, and political interests destroys the life of love. His narrative in this and other family novels is impressionistic, and the discussion of problems is not allowed to restrain his personal feelings. Other masterpieces in the same genre were *Kommandørens Døtre* (The Commodore's Daughters, 1886), which was directed against conventionalism in marriage, and *Et Samliv* (A Marriage, 1887), in which a happy marriage seems to be disintegrating, until an economic crisis brings the couple together.

About 1890 Lie's production entered into a new phase. His outlook on life darkened, at least partially because of the rift in the intimate friendship between him and the writer Bjørnson. He began to publish a series of novels in which he analyzed the "trolls," i.e., mysterious forces, inherited elements bound up with nature in the human personality. This was a new trend in Norwegian literature, and in Lie's production it was first evident in his novel *Onde Magter* (Evil Powers, 1890). He further studied the same problems in two volumes of mystic fairy tales from the North, *Trold* (Trolls, 1891-92). Among his novels of the 1890's the most remarkable is *Naar Jernteppet Falder* (When the Iron Curtain Falls, 1891), in which he describes the thoughts of the passengers on a transatlantic liner after they learn that a bomb is hidden somewhere in the ship. Facing death, the characters throw off their masks, and the difference between the solidly genuine and the false is conspicuously revealed. He continued the study of psychologically peculiar characters, e.g., *Østenfor Sol, Vestenfor Maane* (East of the Sun and West of the Moon), a novel in which the theme centers around the human frailty of envy.

vote himself entirely to literature and reimburse his creditors, a task he completed about twenty-five years later. With his wife he moved to Oslo.

While practicing in Kongsvinger, Lie wrote many articles on various subjects and published in 1867 a collection of *Digte* (Poems), but his talent was not in the lyrical field. His first novel, *Den Fremsynte* (The Visionary), a charming love story permeated with the mysticism of the northern land, appeared in 1870 and was a great success. In 1871 Lie received a traveling scholarship and left for Paris. He lived for twenty-eight years in voluntary exile on the European continent, in Italy, Germany, and France, most of the time in Paris. The best works produced by Lie during the 1870's were sea novels from the subarctic region. *Tremasteren Fremtiden* (The Barque "Future," 1872), was rather weak, but the collection of short stories he published the same year, *Fortællinger og Skildringer fra Norge* (Stories and Pictures from Norway), was more genuine and effective in its local color. His next book, *Lodsen og Hans Hustru* (The Pilot and His Wife, 1874), is a fine psychological marriage novel, the first of its type in Norwegian literature.

During the latter half of the 1870's Lie published novels, poems, and plays, none of them of great value. In the beginning of the 1880's a new period of greatness ensued. He wrote his last sea novels—*Rutland* (1880), a vigorous and fresh novel of marriage and sea, and *Gaa Paa!* (Go Ahead!, 1882), giving

In 1889 Lie published a collection of *Digte* (Poems) which scarcely revealed poetic genius, and in the following years some rather weak dramas, e.g., *Lystige Koner* (Merry Wives). A collection of short stories appeared posthumously under the title of *Eventyr* (Stories, 1909).

After his twenty-eight-year exile, Lie returned to Norway in 1906 and made his home at Fredriksvern (now Stavern) in southern Norway. The following year his devoted wife and collaborator died. The same year Lie and Bjørnson were reconciled. His own death came two years later.

Lie's novel *Den Fremsynte* was translated by J. Muir as *The Visionary* (1894) and *Livsslaven* by the same translator as *One of Life's Slaves* (1895). Mrs. Ole Bull rendered into English *Tremasteren Fremtiden* as *The Barque "Future"* (1879) and *Lodsen og Hans Hustru* as *The Pilot and His Wife* (1876, 1877). *Familjen paa Gilje* was rendered into English by S. C. Eastman as *The Family at Gilje* (1920), and *Kommandørens Døtre* by H. L. Brækstad and G. Hughes as *The Commodore's Daughters* (1892). Brækstad also translated the novel *Niobe* (1897). Some of the stories in *Trold* appeared in *Weird Tales from Northern Seas* (1893), translated by R. N. Bain. The story "Nordfjordhesten" from the collection *Fortællinger og Skildringer* was translated as "Little Grey: The Pony of Nordfjord" (1873) by Mrs. Arbuthnott.

ABOUT: Beyer, H. A History of Norwegian Literature; Grøndahl, I. and Raknes, O. Chapters in Norwegian Literature; Gustafson, A. Six Scandinavian Novelists; Jorgenson, T. History of Norwegian Literature; Koht, H. and Skard, S. The Voice of Norway; Topsöe-Jensen, H. G. Scandinavian Literature from Brandes to Our Day. [In Norwegian—see studies by A. Garborg, F. Ingerslev, E. Lie.]

A. J.

*LILIENCRON, DETLEV VON (June 3, 1844-July 22, 1909), German poet, novelist, and short-story writer, was born at Kiel, the descendant of an impoverished baronial family. His mother was the daughter of General von Harten, who had served under Washington. Liliencron became an officer in the Prussian army and participated in both the Austrian and French wars. In 1875 he found it necessary to resign his commission "because of wounds and debts." He attempted a fresh start at life in the United States but returned to Germany disillusioned after two unhappy years. He married Helene Freiin von Bodenhausen in 1878 and in 1882 obtained a government position on the island of Pellworm. From 1884 to 1887 he worked in Kellinghusen as a church warden, until once again accumulated debts forced him to relinquish his position. The couple moved to Munich, where Liliencron attempted to gain a livelihood from his writings. His book sales were small, and despite a small government stipend which was granted to

* lē' lē ĕn krōn

LILIENCRON

him at the age of sixty, he was obliged to supplement his income by giving public readings in cabarets, a task which was an extreme torment to him. The strain of constant financial need produced in Liliencron a pessimistic outlook, and he wrote in 1888 that he expected nothing from life but "vexation, disgust, and baseness." This attitude he retained until his death at Alt-Rahlstedt near Hamburg.

Liliencron's poetry reflects little of the struggles and unhappiness of his life and reveals him rather as a virile personality, whose world consists of war, the hunt, nature, and love. Although influenced by the earlier German poets Nikolaus Lenau, August von Platen, Theodor Storm, and Annette von Droste-Hülshoff, he was an individualist who ignored current poetic fashions and who belonged to no literary group. His first volume of poems, *Adjutantengeritte und Andere Gedichte* (1883), won the acclaim of the young poets of his period by the originality of the technique and the bold realism of the subject matter. Liliencron is one of the forerunners of the modern period.

Although without formal training, Liliencron possessed great mastery of technique and was tireless in polishing his verses. In his later works his virtuosity developed into a mannerism, and his poems often degenerate into a mere intricate pattern of rhyming sounds. His forte was the lyric, and he excelled in his ability to evoke a mood or create a vivid miniature nature scene with the greatest economy of means. Overtones of melancholy and loneliness recur frequently, and a favorite theme is the contrast between the transitoriness of human existence and the permanence of nature. Liliencron was no profound thinker and except for occasional flashes of insight, his work lacks depth. However, the genuine feeling and spontaneous freshness of his poetry compensate to a large degree for this deficiency. His continued reputation is assured by such outstanding lyrics as "Wer Weiss Wo," "Tod in Aehren," "Die Musik Kommt," and "Kleine Ballade." His ballads, which show the influence of Moritz von Strachwitz and Theodor Fontane, also merit high esteem.

As a poet Liliencron showed little progressive development, and his later collections of verse, *Gedichte* (1889), *Der Haidegänger* (1890), *Neue Gedichte* (1891), *Kampf und Spiele* (1897), *Kämpfe und Ziele* (1897), *Nebel und Sonne* (1900), *Bunte Beute* (1903), and *Balladenchronik* (1906), continue the themes and style of his early poems. *Poggfred* (1896-1908), a lengthy, mock epic poem, is considered one of his finest and most durable achievements, and was the work Liliencron himself regarded most highly. Here the poet combined humor and seriousness, reality and fantasy, to present a picture of his age.

Liliencron's attempts at other literary forms met with little success. He lacked dramatic ability, and his six dramas are totally unreadable. Of his novels only *Leben und Lüge* (1908) has significance for the autobiographical material it contains. His finest prose work is *Kriegsnovellen* (1894), a collection of short stories based on his military experiences. Other volumes of short stories are *Unter Flatternden Fahnen* (1888), *Aus Marsch und Geest* (1900), *Könige und Bauern* (1900), and *Roggen und Weizen* (1900).

The best selection of Liliencron's verse in English translation is contained in Jethro Bithell's *Contemporary German Poetry* (1909). Representative poems may also be found in D. Yarmolinsky, *Contemporary German Poetry* (1923), and the Warner Library.

ABOUT: Drake, W. Contemporary European Writers; Lessing, O. E. Masters in Modern German Literature; Pollard, P. Masks and Minstrels of Modern Germany; Contemporary Review, XCVI. [In German—see studies by O. J. Bierbaum, H. Benzmann, H. Maync, and H. Spiero.]

D. G. D.

LIPSIUS, JUSTUS (October 18, 1547-April 23, 1606), Dutch classical scholar and philologist, was born in Overijse, near Brussels. His religious life testifies to the violent and contradictory forces that beset so many sixteenth century thinkers. At the age of twenty the classically educated Lipsius became secretary to Cardinal de Granvelle. In 1572 he went to Jena, Germany, where he lectured on classical philology. During that period he turned to Lutheranism. In 1576 he was back at the University of Louvain but left it again to lecture in Leiden. His fame as a scholar attracted many students from abroad and he contributed significantly to the renown of the school. After adhering to Calvinism for a while he returned in 1591 to the church of his youth. Forced to resign his post since Leiden did not condone a Catholic on the cathedra, he went back to Louvain. Shortly before his death he became court historian for the Spanish king, but returned to Louvain where he died.

Into his Latin writings Lipsius admitted, next to the elements of older Latin documents, many words and phrases used in later Latin. This manneristic style, terse and epigrammatic, found many followers but made Lipsius many enemies as well. It influenced several great Renaissance prose works, including Bacon's *Essays*. His masterwork was an edition of Tacitus (1574). He also published the writings of Valerius Maximus (1585), Velleius (1591), and Seneca (1605), and in 1600 his commentary on Phinius' *Panegyricus* appeared. To the more highly educated of his time he introduced the work of Plautus and fragments of Nonius. At the base of his interest in classical literature lay his conviction that the philosophy of the ancient Stoics was eminently suited to acquaint man with the nature of things and the works of God. The Stoic orientation of the baroque era owed much to the solid foundation provided by Lipsius in his lectures; his elucidation of the writings of the Stoics exerted a profound influence on humanistic literature in Holland. He was one of the most gifted textual critics of all time.

Lipsius' Latin poems, an admixture of the classical and the new Latin mentioned above, appeared in 1609. Lipsius' treatise on Stoicism *De Constantia* (1584) had several English translations, beginning with one by Sir John Stradling (1594), another by N. Wanley (1670), and a modern edition of Stadling's translation, edited by R. Kirk and C. H. Hall (1939). His *Six Books of Politics, or*

* lĭp′ sĭ ŭs

Civil Doctrine was translated by W. Jones (1594), and *A Brief Outline of the History of Libraries,* translated by J. C. Dana, was published in 1907.

ABOUT: Williamson, G. The Senecan Amble. [In French—Amiel, E. Un Publiciste du 16ᵉ Siècle: J. Lipsius. In German—Müller, L. Geschichte der Klassischen Philologie in den Niederlanden.]

H. B.

---

*LISTA Y ARAGÓN, ALBERTO (October 15, 1775-October 5, 1848), Spanish poet, essayist, and mathematician, was born in Seville of a humble family. His father was a weaver, whom the boy Alberto assisted at the loom. At the age of eight he knew how to read and write to perfection and already excelled in mathematics. At thirteen he began to give lessons, thus being enabled to pursue his education. He studied for the priesthood and was ordained at twenty-one. By then he had perfected his knowledge of languages (French, English, Italian, Greek, and Latin). He taught at the Colegio de San Telmo in Seville, where he was loved and respected by his disciples for his kindness, understanding, and intelligence. He seemed to be a born teacher. In the newspaper *El Correo de Sevilla* he published articles and poems. During the Peninsular War he distinguished himself as a liberal, and in 1813 he emigrated to France, where he lived until 1817, the year in which he returned to Spain to teach in Madrid at the famous Colegio de San Mateo, where he instructed those who were later to become outstanding in Spanish letters, such as the poet Espronceda, the dramatist Ventura de Vega, and the critic Eugenio de Ochoa. His classes in literature in the Atheneum of Madrid were widely acclaimed. Because of his radical liberal ideas and his open opposition to the absolutism of Fedinand VII, he was forced to leave the country for a second time. He lived in Paris and in London, which in those days was the gathering place for the most distinguished Spanish and Spanish-American émigrés. On his return to Madrid in 1833 he resumed his lectures at the Atheneum, and in 1840 he was appointed Canon of the Cathedral of Seville, as well as professor and Dean of the Faculty of Philosophy and Letters of its university. He died in Seville shortly before his seventy-third birthday.

Lista's literary work is distinguished by its dignity and high seriousness. The tone is always noble and elevated, and, although he was not a poet of the greatest importance

in Spain, his work and personal example as a teacher will always be remembered with esteem. His *Poesías* was first published in 1822, containing poems of a religious nature such as "A la Muerte de Jesús," "El Canto del Esposo," "La Providencia"; poems of a patriotic nature such as the sonnet "A la Victoria de Bailén"; and others of moral and civic character. He also wrote a series of sonnets and several *romances* (ballads); among his longer poems is a religious epic entitled "La Inocencia Perdida". He composed a theatrical piece and translated the works of Molière, Crébillon, Colardeau, and Chénier. He adapted into Spanish Pope's *Dunciad.* In 1844 a volume of his *Ensayos Literarios y Críticos* (Literary and Critical Essays) was published; his scientific works, notably *Tratado de Matemáticas Puras y Mixtas* (1866), appeared posthumously. Lista was a great friend of the Spanish-English poet J. M. Blanco White, to whom he dedicated the second edition of his *Poesías* in 1837. Although the character of his writing and his thought are not completely romantic in tone, Lista's writing reveals several aspects of the romantic movement in his description of landscapes, autobiographical recollections, medieval themes, and a fairly evident influence of the social ideas of Rousseau.

ABOUT: Metford, J. C. J. Alberto Lista and the Romantic Movement in Spain. [In Spanish—see studies by H. Juretshke, M. Merry y Colon.]

E. F.

---

*LITTRÉ, ÉMILE (February 1, 1801-June 2, 1881), French linguist and positivist, was born in Paris and attended the Louis-le-Grand College, where he did distinguished work. He was educated in linguistics by his father, a man of considerable culture; from his mother he acquired his deep respect for republican ideas. He was briefly the secretary of Count Daru, who appreciated his talents and urged him to take up a more serious profession. As a result, he entered medicine, but his studies were interrupted by his father's death and ensuing financial responsibilities. The Revolution re-awakened his republican ideals and he became a journalist in its cause. In his work he had occasion to write about Sir William Herschel's notions on "natural philosophy," another significant formative influence. He had meanwhile undertaken a ten-volume translation of Hippocrates, whose publication, beginning in 1839, led to his election to the

Académie des Inscriptions. His linguistic projects over the next decades include a medical dictionary and his monumental *Dictionnaire de la Langue Française,* constructed with chronological references to Old and Middle French, and today invaluable for such reference. Littré's practical command of political theory explains his appointment to the National Assembly in 1871, and his philological achievements justified his election to the French Academy in 1873, despite his hostility to religion and to the clergy.

Littré's positivism arises in part from his republican ideas, in part from his philological attitude toward the past. His essay *Auguste Comte et la Philosophie Positive,* composed by request in 1835, and his reading five years later of Comte's *Système de Philosophie Positive,* show his satisfaction with this system of objective and methodical classifications and with scientific fact of all kinds. That Comte denounced Littré in 1852 proves the latter's more objective point of view, and the weakness or absence of the influence of the master's mystical dogmatism in his thinking. The critical problems of positivism, and indeed of modern science, were resumed shortly after his death in Pasteur's address, on assuming his chair in the Academy, and in Renan's answer. Littré's absolute intellectual integrity, his personal qualities, and his competency were recognized by both speakers, but Pasteur challenged his positivism, first for its excessive reliance on experience rather than on experimentation, and second for its disregard for spiritual values. Renan, in answer, spoke of common misunderstandings, in all discussions of positivism regarding absolutism and relativism in thought; and of persistent confusions, among men of science, between science and religion: e.g., Pasteur's denunciation of Comte's pseudo-mysticism—which Littré did not share—in favor of some other arbitrary dogma.

Aside from the above works, one should note Littré's *De l'Établissement de la Troisième République* (1880), his *Histoire de la Langue Française* (1873), his *Comment les Mots Changent de Sens* (1888), and several re-editions of his great dictionary. He was the principal editor of the review entitled *La Philosophie Positive,* which survived him only briefly, and in which (vol. IX, 1882), the addresses of Pasteur and Renan appear.

ABOUT: Aquarone, S. Life and Works of Émile Littré. [In French—see studies by C. A. Sainte-Beuve, M. de Fleury, and J. Fileyosant.]

F. J. C.

*LOBO, FRANCISCO RODRIGUES (c. 1580-c. 1622), foremost Portuguese poet and novelist of the baroque age, was born in Leiria. Probably his parents were Squire André Luís Lobo and Joana Brito. The uncertainty may be due to understandable reticence in a descendant of converts from Judaism. His brother Miguel was persecuted by the Inquisition. Lobo spent his childhood in Leiria, whose rivers Lis and Lena he sang as Diogo Bernardes had sung the Lima. He studied at a leisurely pace in Coimbra from 1593 to 1602, returned to Leiria with a law degree, and made writing his profession instead of practicing law. Apparently he was fated to love too high-born a lady, who played for him the milkmaid, "so full of grace, with kerchief barely folded, she dares at times walk barefoot and barearmed." He never married, consoling himself instead with Spanish actresses. The dukes of Vila Real and Braganza were his patrons. He was drowned when his boat capsized on the Tagus.

Lobo perfected the wistful bucolic poetry imported from Italy. Like Sá de Miranda he moralized about the worthless present in his ten *Éclogas* (1605); like Bernardes, he gave them real Portuguese settings. Although he objected to foreign ways, his first verse was in Spanish—ballads written as a student, under Góngora's irresistible influence (*Romances,* 1596). Camões inspired him to attempt a long national epic, *O Condestabre de Portugal* (1609), a prosaic rhymed chronicle with which to flatter the Braganzas, and to compose some of his finest lyrics inserted in a vaguely autobiographical trilogy of pastoral novels, *A Primavera* (1601), *O Pastor Peregrino* (1608), and *O Desenganado* (1614). Like Góngora in the contemporary *Soledades,* Lobo tells of a shepherd, Lereno, who must leave his Lisea to go wandering (to Coimbra and beyond), is shipwrecked on his return, and finds Lisea wedded to another. Escapism and disillusionment (*desengano*) permeate the baroque work, together with the same feelings of social decadence that obsessed other peninsular writers. Like them, Lobo also took to writing literary epistles, satires, and Catholic verse. But no copy of his *Elegia ao Santíssimo Sacramento* of 1614 has survived.

In his didactic prose he looked backward, perfecting a worn Renaissance theme, the weary courtier's praise of simple country living. Lobo enlarged the theme, coming up with a manual of fine manners, *Corte na Aldeia, a Noites de Inverno* (1619), where four anonymous gentlemen of different call-

* lṓ′ bōō

ings hold sixteen learned colloquies with their friend Júlio, a country squire. They discuss education, etiquette, love, greed, ambition, and (above all) witty style. Less autobiographical and aristocratic than Castiglione's *Courtier,* Lobo's maturest work is more national and nostalgic, for his gentlemen dwell on the excellencies of Portuguese language and Portuguese history, "renewing their longings for the former court, with due remembrance of that Golden Age of Portugal." Gracián, an expert on wit, hailed Lobo's *Corte* as a "book for eternity."

A Spanish nativity play, *Auto del Nacimiento de Cristo* . . . , followed by a Portuguese *Entremês do Poeta* (1676), is attributed to Lobo, who had refashioned Ferreira de Vasconcelos' *Comédia Eufrosina* in 1616.

Lobo is still considered one of the great literary artists of Portugal. Although his principal works were quickly translated into Spanish by Juan Bautista de Morales *(Corte en Aldea,* 1622; *Primavera,* 1629), they were not translated into English.

ABOUT: Rennert, H. The Spanish Pastoral Romances. [In Portuguese—see studies by C. A. Ferreira and R. Jorge; Biblos, XIX (1943).]

G. M. M.

*LOCHER, JACOB ("PHILOMUSUS")

(July 1471-December 4, 1528), German humanist, was born in Ehingen, in Swabia, received his first education in Ulm, then went to the University of Basel, where he was the student of Sebastian Brant, who exerted great influence on him and whose *Narrenschiff* (*Ship of Fools*) he made into a popular free translation, *Stultifera Navis.* In 1488 he was at the University of Freiburg and in 1489 in Ingolstadt, where he studied theology and law. When in 1492 Konrad Celtis inaugurated humanistic studies in Ingolstadt, Locher became one of his devoted students. That same year he traveled in Italy, visited Pavia, Ferrara, Bologna, perhaps also Florence and Rome, and returned the following year to Ulm where he published two orations of Cicero. In 1495 Locher began to teach at the University of Freiburg where the margraves of Baden and Thomas Murner were among his students.

Crowned poet laureate by Emperor Maximilian in 1497, he went the following year to Ingolstadt, where he lectured on literature. He returned to Freiburg in the summer of 1503 after he had had some difficulties with the scholastic philosophers at Ingolstadt who opposed his views. In that year he published

* lōĸ' ẽr

his *Apologia* in which he attacked his main enemy, Georg Zengel. In Freiburg he also became involved in quarrels, this time with Wimpheling and Zasius, who accused him of immorality. Returning to Ingolstadt he intended to put an end to scholastic theology by publishing *Vitiosa Sterilis Mulae ad Musam Roscida Lepiditate Pruditem Comparatio.* This pamphlet was directed not only against Zengel but also against Occam's school of Nominalism.

Working himself into an isolated position and standing somewhere between the conservatives and the liberal humanists, Locher no longer participated in the struggle, but became active as a lecturer and for some twenty years contributed considerably to the increasing fame of the university. By the time of his death he had written, besides the works already mentioned, a compendium of rhetoric, nine classical editions (five of them with commentary, e.g., of Horace, 1498, and Fulgentius, 1521), some religious hymns and elegies, a great number of lyrical poems, as well as those written in a satirical-polemical vein, and five dramas, e.g., *Tragœdie von den Türken und ihrem Sultan* (1497) and *Urteil des Paris* (1502), which follow the example of the Italian Renaissance drama with its allegory and choral songs.

ABOUT: Modern Language Review, XX (1905). [In German—Stammler, W. Von der Mystik bis zum Barock.]

H. B.

*LOGAU, FRIEDRICH, Freiherr von

(June 1604-July 24, 1655), German epigrammatist, was born at Brockut, near Nimptsch, Silesia. From 1614 to 1625 he attended the *Gymnasium* at Brieg and then studied law presumably at Frankfurt an der Oder. After devoting himself to Brockut, the family estate, he entered the service of the Duke of Brieg and in 1644 was made ducal councilor. His apparently happy marriage ended with the sudden death of his wife. In 1654 he followed the duke to Liegnitz and died there the following year. At the time of Logau's death his contemporaries knew little about him.

Logau is generally regarded as the greatest German epigrammatist and one of the major satirists in German literature. His epigrams, which he called *Sinngedichte,* appeared in two collections under the pseudonym Salomon von Golaw, an anagram of his name: *Erstes Hundert Teutscher Reimen-*

* lō' gou

sprüche (1638) and *Salomons von Golaw Teutscher Sinn-Getichte Drey Tausend* (1654). Not all of these 3,000 epigrams are original; there are many adaptations and translations, and the publication may have been inspired by John Owen's collection of Latin epigrams of 1606. However, the highly varied *Sinngedichte,* which range in length from couplets to poems of about 100 lines, are impressive evidence of Logau's manly character and exemplary cast of thought. He satirized his countrymen and tried to be a moral guide to them during the Thirty Years' War, a time of unexampled destruction and demoralization. In the turbulence of the times Logau preserved his personal integrity and high ethical standards and managed to judge his fellow men fairly.

The main targets of Logau's satire were the sordid business of war-making; political corruption; the general immorality and decline of manners; the slavish aping of foreign customs, particularly the French; the pomposity of court life; and religious factionalism which threatened to obscure true Christianity. With dry wit Logau inveighed against *à la mode* customs in dress and language. The German tradition and the purity of the German language were especially dear to his heart: "In olden times Germany was the land of honesty; now it has come to be a lumber room where other nations store their crimes and vices." "No one is honored amongst us who knows no French; we disclaim and condemn our very ancestors because they spoke and felt German." In 1648 Logau was elected a member of the Fruchtbringende Gesellschaft, one of the linguistic societies, and given the name "Der Verkleinernde," i.e., one who reduces things to small dimensions. Logau's epigrams benefit from skillful play upon words and the use of antitheses. They are pithy, never consciously "clever." The language is popular and many of the *Sinngedichte* have the effectiveness of proverbs.

Logau was all but forgotten when G. E. Lessing and K. W. Ramler re-issued the *Sinngedichte* in 1759. An augmented edition was published by Ramler in 1791. Other editions are those by G. Eitner (1870-72) and K. Simrock (1874). In 1882 Gottfried Keller wrote a series of *Novellen* entitled *Das Sinngedicht,* a charming poetic interpretation and elaboration of one of Logau's epigrams.

Thirteen of Logau's epigrams are contained in H. W. Longfellow's *Poetical Works* (1886). Other selections may be found in Catherine Winkworth's *Christian Singers of Germany,* (1869), Bayard Taylor's *Studies in German Literature* (1879), Leonard Forster's *Penguin Book of German Verse* (1957), and G. C. Schoolfield's *The German Lyric of the Baroque in English Translation* (1962).

ABOUT: German Life and Letters, III (1949-50). [In German—see studies by H. Denker, P. Hempel.]
H. Z.

*LOHENSTEIN, DANIEL CASPAR VON (January 25, 1635-April 28, 1683), German poet, dramatist, and novelist, exhibits the same contrast of life and writings as his countryman and colleague Hofmann von Hofmannswaldau: a conventional though active and distinguished career as civil servant, and a spare-time cultivation of baroque extravagances. His grandiloquence is unrestrained and unrivaled, so much so that his name became proverbial for *Schwulst* (bombast). He himself called it "sweet sugar of eloquence."

Lohenstein was born in the town of Nimptsch in Silesia, the son of an imperial tax collector and town counselor. Actually the family name was Kaspar (or Casper). When his father was knighted in 1670, he added the rest of the name, derived from some property he owned on the river Lohe.

Lohenstein attended the *Gymnasium* in Breslau, as did Hofmann. He studied law at Leipzig and Tübingen, took his degree, and got a job as tutor to the Kleindienst family, from whom he later inherited a considerable fortune. He traveled extensively in the Netherlands, Switzerland, Austria, and Hungary. He returned to Breslau, married there, established himself in the profession of law, and became a thoroughly respected citizen and an official of high rank and repute. He was made government counselor in 1666 and syndic (magistrate) of Breslau in 1670. In 1675 he led an important diplomatic mission to the imperial court in Vienna and subsequently was made imperial counselor. In 1679 he delivered the funeral oration for his friend Hofmann. He died a few years later in Breslau.

Lohenstein's poetry is generally heavier and more serious than Hofmann's, though not therefore better. It makes even more striking use of baroque antitheses, though without so often harmonizing or bridging between them.

His dramas, like his one enormous novel, use historical events and personages for their material, but they transform this historical world, however learnedly portrayed, into a

* lō′ ĕn shtīn

vast and spectacular theatre for baroque man. These are plays replete with lurid scenes of love and torture, chaotic intrigue, allegories of fate, transitoriness, and eternal damnation. They are buttressed with footnotes. Between the violent assertion of life and the inevitability of final defeat and decay Lohenstein draws no uniting threads. The two forces exist side by side and are portrayed with equal vehemence and equally drastic colors. Lohenstein's tragedies, written between 1653 and 1680, are *Ibrahim Bassa, Kleopatra, Agrippina, Epicharis, Ibrahim Sultan,* and *Sophonisbe.* The world in which he wrote had no stages to present his voluminous plays. Whenever they saw the light of the theatre, it was, of all things, in schools. Yet the absence of producers, casts, and public is not the only thing that keeps Lohenstein's Cleopatra from rivaling Shakespeare's.

Lohenstein wrote only one novel, but even in an age of prolixity it was long enough for at least two. *Arminius* (1689-90) covers most of the history of Germany's encounter with ancient Rome. It offers digressions into Armenian, Thracian, and Chinese history; long disquisitions on such varied subjects as ladies' make-up, whales, and diamonds; extended poetic passages; and dramatic interludes. In spite of over 3,000 pages of this sort of fare, it was still being reprinted as late as 1731.

Several of his poems and sonnets appear in G. C. Schoolfield's *The German Lyric of the Baroque in English Translation* (1962).

ABOUT: [In German—see studies by H. Cysarz, F. Schaufelberger.]

F. G. R.

*LOMONOSOV, MIKHAIL VASILIEVICH (November 8, 1711-April 4, 1765), Russian scientist, scholar, poet, was born the son of a prosperous peasant fisherman and trader in a village not far from the seaport of Archangel. A craving for knowledge brought him in 1730 to Moscow where, concealing his peasant origin, he succeeded in enrolling at the Slavo-Greco-Latin Academy. Despite extreme privation, he made extraordinary progress in learning, and in 1736 he, with two other students of outstanding ability, was sent by the state to study abroad. He received advanced training in the sciences, mathematics and philosophy under the famous German professor Christian Wolff in Marburg; there he also turned his attention seriously to the arts; there, too, he became acquainted with the

* lŭ mŭ nô′ sôf

LOMONOSOV

philosophy of Leibniz which profoundly influenced his own outlook. By his return to Russia in 1741, Lomonosov was already scientist, scholar, and poet of very high caliber. In 1745 he was made professor and member of the Russian Academy of Science, in which capacity he remained to the end of his life.

Lomonosov was the embodiment of all the aspirations disseminated in Russian life by Peter the Great, whom Lomonosov revered; he shared Peter's ambition to make Russia the equal of the greatest nations in Europe. To the advancement of Russian science and culture Lomonosov brought prodigious energies and immense powers of mind. At almost whatever point in the encyclopedic spread of his knowledge he set his mind to work he brought forth achievements of weight and permanence. Aside from his brilliant work as a scientist, he strove incessantly to increase the efficiency of the Academy of Science, to improve, expand, popularize education, and to promote scientific research and its application to the life of the country.

Among the highest of Lomonosov's achievements were those in language and literature. With his three major works on the Russian language—*Rhetoric* (1748), *Russian Grammar* (1757), and "On the Use of Sacred Books in the Russian Tongue" (1757)—he succeeded in ordering—without dogmatism—the grammatical, lexicographical, and stylistic resources of Russian, thus founding the modern literary language. The reform in Russian prosody initiated by Trediakovsky was accepted and immeasurably advanced by Lomonosov, most importantly in his own creative practice. With Lomonosov modern Russian poetry begins. In 1739 from Germany he sent to Russia his first ode, "Na Vzyatie Khotina" (On the Taking of Khotin), a poem written in what subsequently became the classic meter in Russian poetry (iambic tetrameter). Numerous odes, mainly composed in celebration of some national or court event, followed. Though Lomonosov functioned as something of an official poet, the "occasional" nature of many of his odes merely furnished a point of departure; his real themes were Peter the Great, Russia itself, and the glories of creation. He also wrote satires, a tragedy, poems propagandizing science and learning, etc., and began an epic on Peter the Great. The most famous of his poems are his verse paraphrases of psalms and Biblical passages and his two Meditations on the Divine Majesty ("Vechernee" and "Utrennee Razmyshlenie o Bozhiem Velichestve," 1748 and 1751 respectively).

Lomonosov's poetics only superficially partook of the classicism which dominated in his time, reflecting rather more the baroque style, especially the late German baroque. His is a poetry mainly of the oratorical manner, the "mighty line," of bold and hyperbolic imagery often reinforced with a striking implementation of sounds. Though Lomonosov's poetic system was crowded out by the classicist Sumarokov school, his poetry has maintained its integrity and reputation throughout the history of Russian literature.

> Translations of at least some of Lomonosov's poems can be found in almost any English anthology of Russian verse, for example, those of L. Wiener or C. M. Bowra.
> ABOUT: Mirsky, D. S. A History of Russian Literature.

I. R. T.

*LÖNNROT, ELIAS (April 9, 1802-March 19, 1884), Finnish folklorist, philologist, physician, was born in a small cottage at Sammatti in the Finnish-speaking part of the southern province of Nyland. His father, Fredrik Johan Lönnrot, was a poor tailor. His mother was Ulrika Andersdotter Wahlberg. He grew up amidst beautiful surroundings but in dire poverty. The family's bread was often baked of ground bark and lichen. Elias' attendance at school frequently had to be interrupted, and he was forced

* lŭn' rōōt

to spend considerable time as an apprentice in his father's tailor shop. But his intelligence was keen and his love for reading insatiable. He studied under difficult circumstances at the Latin schools at Åbo (Finnish Turku) and Borgå (Finish Porvoo). In 1822 he entered the University of Åbo and supported himself by tutoring. He took his master's degree in 1827 and began studying medicine.

With the flourishing of national romanticism in this period, a new interest in folklore and folk poetry had been awakened. Lönnrot was fascinated by the Finnish treasure of native songs, so-called "runes," which he had recorded as early as his student years. The University of Åbo burned down in 1827, and Lönnrot took advantage of the interval before its relocation at the capital of Helsingfors (Finnish Helsinki) for a long hiking trip through central and eastern Finland, recording magic incantations and songs. The following summers he continued this activity among the peasants and went all the way to Russian Karelia, the cradle and home of Finnish folk poetry. There he met some of the last of those who remembered this lore. The old songs were sung by two singers in peculiar, monotonous strains and were often accompanied by a native Finnish string instrument, the *kantelet*.

Upon his return to the capital Lönnrot published four fascicles of folk songs under the title *Kantele* (Kantelet), 1829-31. He took his master's degree in medicine in 1832. In his dissertation, *Om Finnarnas Magiska Medicin* (On the Magic Medicine of the Finns), he combined his medical and folkloristic knowledge. Soon thereafter he was appointed district medical officer at Kajana, close to the Russian border, and he divided his time between his profession and his recording of folklore. In 1835-36 the Finnish Literary Society published two volumes of an epic-lyrical cycle of myths, *Kalevala,* comprising material recorded and put together by Lönnrot. This collection, known as the *Old Kalevala,* is generally regarded as the foundation of native Finnish literature. An enlarged edition appeared in 1849. In 1840 Lönnrot published a collection of lyrical folk songs and ballads, *Kanteletar* (The Harp's Maiden), followed by collections of proverbs, charms, and riddles.

In 1849 Lönnrot married Maria Piponius. Gradually his interests shifted to linguistics, and in 1853-62 he held the chair of Finnish Language and Literature at the University of Helsinki. Upon retirement he settled down in his native village of Sammatti. His excellent *Finsk-Svenskt Lexikon* (Finnish-Swedish Dictionary) appeared in two volumes, 1874-80.

An English prose translation of Lönnrot's edition of the *Kalevala,* by F. P. Magoun, Jr., was published in 1964.

ABOUT: [In Finnish—see studies by A. Anttila, O. A. Kallio, E. Setälä.]

A. J.

LOPE DE VEGA. See VEGA CARPIO, LOPE FÉLIX DE

*LOPES, FERNÃO (c. 1380-c. 1460), Portuguese historian, was probably born in Lisbon. It is recorded that he lived there, in the populous Alfama district. Not unnaturally for a notary, scrupulous respect for authenticated documents was to characterize this "clerk in the court of Truth," as he styled himself. His public career was tied to the revolutionary rise of the House of Aviz, put on the Portuguese throne by the towns of the realm. In 1418 John I, through his son Edward, named him Chief Custodian of the Archives of the Torre do Tombo in Lisbon. The same year he became royal secretary, serving, in succession, John I and his sons Edward and Ferdinand. He was rewarded with a noble title and a pension. In 1454, during the reign of Alfonso V, Lopes, "being old and feeble," had to relinquish his office in favor of Zurara. Lopes' passionate espousal of the people's cause was quite different from the servile spirit of courtiers such as Zurara. Lopes' wife was related to a shoemaker; perhaps he belonged to a craftsman's family himself. We last hear of him in 1459. It is probable that he died soon afterward.

Fernão Lopes' fame rests on the three royal chronicles in which he narrated Portuguese history from 1357, when Peter the Just became king, to 1411, when peace was reestablished between Castile and Portugal: the *Crónica del Rei Dom Pedro* (begun in 1434, published in 1735) the *Crónica del Rei Dom Fernando* (published in 1816), and his masterpiece, the extensive but unfinished *Crónica del Rei Dom João da Boa Memória* (published in 1644), about the Master of Aviz who led the common people to victory against Ferdinand's widow Leonor and the nobles of Portugal and Castile. These three chronicles formed the second part of a *Crónica Geral*

* ló' pĕsh

do Reino de Portugal, commissioned by Prince Edward and modeled after the Castilian *General Estoria.* The first part was believed lost until recently when two Portuguese scholars claimed to have found two versions of it, the *Crónica de Cinco Reis de Portugal* (begun in 1419, attributed to Prince Edward, and published in 1945) and the *Crónica dos Sete Primeiros Reis de Portugal* (published in 1952-53). The anonymous *Crónica do Condestável* (published in 1526) no longer is ascribed to Lopes.

Lopes' writings were long neglected, according to A. J. Saraiva, because they "manifest the reaction of the commoners at the end of the Middle Ages against a still very powerful knighthood," hardly the kind of history to be encouraged by the ruling classes. Yet Lopes compares favorably with his better known, slightly earlier peers in Castile (Pero López de Ayala) and France (Froissart). In spite of his old-fashioned, rambling, delightfully picturesque style, he seems more modern than they, since he wrote from the realistic and consciously nationalistic viewpoint of the Third Estate. Not content with hearsay, he treated his many sources critically, anxious "to write the truth, without any admixture, omitting all flattery from successes, and showing the people all adversities plainly, just the way they happened." He resisted the temptation of idealizing his nobles, kings, and commoners. Instead, he sympathetically portrayed everyone from the king down as an individual with human ambitions and shortcomings in his dramatic moments, counterbalancing these individuals with extraordinary collective portraits of "little people."

Lopes is the one medieval Portuguese author whose prose is still read with passionate interest. His lively, polemic, patriotic way of writing inspired later Portuguese, notably Camões and the romantics. Robert Southey saw in him "the greatest chronicler of any age or nation." In our times, Rodrigues Lapa stated: "As around banners, Portuguese national feeling has rallied around two books whenever independence was threatened: Fernão Lopes' *Chronicles* and the *Lusiads.*" In both the protagonist is the entire nation.

Only a few selections were translated into English by the historian Edgar Prestage (*The Chronicles of Fernão Lopes and Gomes Eannes de Zurara,* "with translated extracts," 1928).

ABOUT: Bell, A. F. G. Fernam Lopez; Prestage, E. (see above); Entwistle, W. J. Prolegomena to an Edition of Fernão Lopes; Hispanic Review 1955. [In Portuguese—Lapa, M. Rodrigues. Lições de Literatura Portuguesa, Época Medieval, 4th ed.]

G. M. M.

*LÓPEZ DE AYALA, PERO (called **THE CHANCELLOR AYALA**) (1332-1407), Spanish chronicler, poet, and translator, was born in Vitoria, the son of Fernán Pérez de Ayala, an impoverished noble, native of Álava, a Basque province, and Elivira de Ceballos, who came from Santander, near Álava. Although there is still no definitive biography of Ayala available, his semi-autobiographical poem *Rimado de Palacio*, as well as the eulogy written shortly after his death by his nephew Fernán Pérez de Guzmán, provides us with the highlights of his career. His childhood coincided with the victories of Salada and Algeciras. In his early years he enjoyed the writings of Don Juan Manuel, author of *El Conde Lucanor*. As a youth he won favor with Pedro the Cruel ("El Rey Cruel"), because of his tact and his considerable natural gifts, and under this monarch he began his military and political career. He served Pedro as a captain in the maritime war between Castile and Aragon, and was made *alguacil* (or constable) of Toledo.

When Pedro's enemies drove him out of Castile, López de Ayala—always very much the opportunist—shifted his loyalties to Don Enrique de Trastamara ("El Rey Bastardo"), Pedro's successor. Fighting for Don Enrique at Nájera in 1367, Lopez was captured and for a time imprisoned by Edward, the Black Prince of England. However, he was liberated in time to enjoy the fruits of the victory at Montiel, in which Pedro the Cruel was killed by Don Enrique. Under the new regime Ayala was rewarded with a series of political offices, culminating with the highly coveted post of Alcalde Mayor of Toledo in 1375.

Under the succeeding rulers Enrique II and Juan I, Ayala undertook important diplomatic missions to Aragon, France, and England. In 1382 he received the title of Camarero (the equivalent of the English Lord Chamberlain), and was awarded an annual pension by the crown. The succession of kings he served and the variety of positions he held afforded him that intimate, close-hand observation of court life and statecraft which give to the Chronicles by which his fame is preserved their vividness and authenticity.

While fighting for Juan I against the Portuguese king at Aljubarrota in 1385, Ayala was once more taken prisoner. This imprisonment lasted more than fifteen months, a period he put to good use by composing a large part of his *Rimado de Palacio*, a bitter verse satire on the life of the courtier, as well as his *Libro de Cetrería, o de las Aves de Caza* (The Book of Falconry, or Birds of the Hunt), a prose treatise on the pastimes of the nobility, notable for its opulent natural description. His liberation was long delayed because of the large ransom demanded by the Portuguese ruler, but his wife, Doña Leonora de Guzmán, finally succeeded in raising the money.

During his last years, before his death at Calahorra, Ayala served under still another king, Enrique III, who in 1398 elevated him to the position of Canciller Mayor (Great Chancellor) of Castile as a supreme tribute to his statesmanship. (The counsel he gave the previous king, Juan I, had forestalled a threatened breakup of Castile.) His two sons also were given political offices. He is said to have enjoyed a vigorous old age.

As a statesman-warrior-poet-scholar, Pero López de Ayala can stand as a prototype of the Renaissance ideal courtier. In the midst of his busy career in court and camp he managed to steep himself in humanistic studies, his own literary style profiting notably from his reading of classical historians. He made interesting experiments in verse, and produced several distinguished translations— of Livy, Boethius, St. Gregory, and Boccaccio *(The Fall of Princes)*, among others. However, his literary fame rests principally on the series of histories of the reigns of the kings under whom he served, which make up part of the monumental *Crónicas de los Reyes de Castilla*. As a chronicler Ayala has been praised for his realism, incisive portraiture, and psychological penetration.

For the works of Ayala in Spanish see the *BAE* vol. 57 (*Rimado de Palacio*); vols. 66, 68, 70 (*Crónicas*). There is an English translation of a poem "Sēnora, Estrella Luciente" in John Bowring's *Ancient Poetry and Romances of Spain* (1824); "Song to the Virgin Mary" appears in Thomas Walsh's *Hispanic Anthology* (1920).

ABOUT: [In Spanish—see studies by R. Floranes, de Lozoya, and F. Meregali; Humanitas, Año I (1953), Num.2.]

R. A. C.

*LÓPEZ DE AYALA Y HERRERA, ADELARDO (May 1, 1828-December 30, 1879), Spanish dramatist and politician, was born in Guadalcanal (Seville). As a young man he studied law at the University of Seville and then moved to Madrid, where he soon won the friendship of the Conde de San Luis, García Gutiérrez, and Cañete. He became a politician and in 1857 was elected a deputy to the Cortes. Later he became Min-

* lō' päth tha ä yä' lä

* lō' päth tha ä yä' lä ē ĕr rĕ' rä

ister of Colonies under Alfonso XII and, in 1878, President of the Chamber of Deputies. All his life he was an eloquent orator, writer, and critic. He was elected to the Spanish Academy in 1870, where he gave his maiden speech on the theatre of the Golden Age. He was given a large state funeral after his death from pneumonia, and was buried in the Cemeterio de la Sacramental de San Justo.

López de Ayala is now remembered almost exclusively for his dramas. His first plays, such as *Un Hombre de Estado, Los Dos Guzmanes, Castigo y Perdón*—all done in 1851—and *Rioja* (1854), are without great interest. However, beginning in 1857 with *El Tejado de Vidrio,* he produced four plays of so-called *alta comedia* which have some true importance in the history of Spanish literature. The other three are: *El Tanto por Ciento* (1861), *El Nuevo Don Juan* (1863) and *Consuelo* (1878).

López de Ayala gave to the bourgeoisie of the Restoration period a psychological portrait of itself, expressing its own ideals and aspirations, although at times, as in *El Tanto por Ciento,* he could rise far above the ideals and morals of his time and class. He is a master of plot and his firm touch is not so heavy as to destroy his poetry. Although his plays are somewhat didactic, he does not preach. He laid the foundations for a new theatre in his combination of the traditional and the modern psychological play, but unfortunately had no successors. His most justly remembered plays are *El Tanto por Ciento* and *Consuelo.* His *Obras* were edited by the dramatist Tamayo y Baus and published in seven volumes, 1881-85.

ABOUT: [In Spanish—Octavio Picón, J. Ayala, Estudio Biográfico.]

R. E. O.

LORENZINI, CARLO. See "COLLODI, CARLO"

LORENZO DE' MEDICI. See MEDICI, LORENZO DE', called THE MAGNIFICENT

"LORRAIN, JEAN." See DUVAL, (MARTIN) PAUL ALEXANDRE

*LOYOLA, IGNACIO DE, Saint (1491-July 31, 1556), Spanish soldier, writer, and founder of the Jesuits, was born in the castle of Loyola, Guipúzcoa. He was the youngest

* loi ō′ lä

ST. IGNACIO DE LOYOLA

son of Beltrán Yáñez de Oñez y Loyola and María Sáenz de Licona y Balde. Although baptized Iñigo, later in life, while he was residing in Rome, he took the name Ignacio, or Ignatius, and it is by this name that he is known in history. After the early death of his father, the young Loyola was educated as a page at the court of Ferdinand and Isabella. As a young man, he was vain, stylish in his dress, and quite worldly. He was ambitious to distinguish himself in courtly and military circles. Loyola entered the service of the Duke of Nájera in 1517 and served under him until 1521. In that year he was wounded at the siege of Pamplona by a French cannon ball, while attempting to prevent the enemy from taking the city. One of his legs was broken and although it was set, it had to be rebroken and set again. Still, it did not heal properly and a protruding bone had to be sawed off and his leg stretched for months. All the torture the young Loyola gladly endured, for this ambitious courtier considered the idea of being a cripple unthinkable. It was while recovering during 1521 and 1522 that he began to read religious books, which influenced him to devote his life to God. In 1522 he renounced his military career and lived for a time as a hermit. In 1523-24 he made a pilgrimage to Jerusalem. Returning to Spain in 1524, Loyola determined to become educated so that he might be ordained. He at once entered a grammar school, and in 1526 and 1527 he studied at the universities of Alcalá de Henares and Salamanca. In 1528 he went to the University of Paris for a lengthy stay. While there, he earned his living by begging and spent his vacations traveling, chiefly in Flanders and in England. In Paris, toward the end of 1529, he came into contact with the men who were to become the first fathers of the Society of Jesus. They were Pierre Favre, Francis Xavier, Diego Láynez, Alfonso Salmerón, Nicolás Bobadilla, and Simón Rodríguez. Loyola himself was not ordained until June, 1537, in Venice. It is said that he waited eighteen months before saying mass for the first time in Rome.

Again in Paris, in 1534, he planned a new religious order to be known as the Society or Company of Jesus, which would be devoted to the conversion of infidels and to counteraction against the Protestant Reformation. The approbation of the new order was obtained from Pope Paul III in a papal bull of September 27, 1540. Loyola became its first superior or general and served until his death.

Loyola's order, commonly called the Jesuits, carried out its original program—often brilliantly, as in the Asiatic missionary work of St. Francis Xavier—but it also became celebrated in other fields, the chief of which is education. The Jesuits have, however, often been accused of forming a state within a state and as a consequence have been banished, at one time or another, from several countries. Few religious orders have been the subjects of such extreme reactions.

Loyola was the author of the *Constitutions of the Order*, which was and still is the rule for the Jesuits. In 1548, in Rome, his *Ejercicios Espirituales* was published, a work which has had considerable influence in the world. He was beatified by Paul V in 1609 and canonized by Gregory XV in 1622. His body lies under the altar designed by Pozzi at the Church of the Gesù in Rome.

No one has ever claimed any great literary merit for the *Spiritual Exercises*, nor have many suggested that it contains a body of doctrine on which a theological school could be founded; but this work often imitated, has been called a "world-moving" book.

Loyola's *Spiritual Exercises* (written in Spanish, later published in Latin) appeared in an English translation by W. H. Longridge (1919). The bibliography on Loyola and the Jesuits is, of course, vast. The principal source is *Monumenta Ignatiana*, published in fifteen volumes in Madrid (1903-19). A selection of the letters from the *Monumenta* was published in English translation by W. J. Young in 1959.

ABOUT: Pollen, J. H. Saint Ignatius Loyola; Rose, S. Saint Ignatius Loyola and the Early Jesuits. [In Spanish—see studies by J. Arteche, P. Leturia.]

R. E. O.

*LUDWIG, OTTO (February 12, 1813-February 25, 1865), German dramatist and short-story writer, was born at Eisfeld in Thuringia, of a well-to-do and respected family. Both parents were artistically inclined. His father, Ernst Ludwig, was a lawyer who devoted his leisure time to writing poetry, while his mother, Sophie Christiane Otto, the daughter of a wealthy merchant, was an accomplished musician. Through unfortunate circumstances the family lost its money in 1822, and Ludwig's father died three years later an embittered and broken man.

Ludwig, a sickly and nervous child, received his early education by private tutor. In 1824 he entered the *Gymnasium* but left before completing the course to work for his wealthy uncle, who wished to train him to become a merchant. Following the death of his mother in 1831, Ludwig returned to school in Saalfeld, where he devoted himself more to literature and music than to his regular studies. When his uncle refused to support him any longer, Ludwig was forced to return to work. During these years (1833-39) he wrote many musical compositions, several of which were performed locally with success.

In 1839 Ludwig was given a scholarship by the Duke of Meiningen to study music with Felix Mendelssohn in Leipzig. The two men were unable to arrive at any mutual understanding, and Ludwig, completely discouraged, renounced music for literature. His remaining years were spent in Leipzig and Dresden. He married Emilie Winkler in 1852, and the two lived a quiet and happy life, although often close to poverty. During the last five years of his life Ludwig was afflicted by a creeping paralysis which caused him severe suffering. He refused to let illness frustrate his artistic plans and, although incapacitated for long periods, he continued to write and to revise his dramatic works until his death.

Ludwig's first dramatic success was *Der Erbförster* (1850), a powerful tragedy of peasant life, which has remained his most popular and widely-played drama. The characters are sharply delineated and psychologically convincing, and the plot, which concerns a forester's attempt to defend his hereditary rights, is compelling, although it has been criticized for depending too greatly on coincidence. The entire drama is permeated by the atmosphere of the Thuringian forest, which in its various moods re-enforces the action. Ludwig was a master of detail, and *Der Erbförster* by its accuracy of milieu

* lōōt′ vĭk

LUDWIG

introduced a new degree of realism into the theatre.

In 1853 Ludwig completed his second drama, *Die Makkabäer,* a Biblical tragedy in verse, based on a subject from the Apocrypha. Although this work enjoyed initial popularity and was awarded the Schiller prize in 1861, it contains serious technical flaws and suffers from over-elaboration of detail and from too subtle psychological introspection.

Under the influence of the well-known German author Berthold Auerbach, Ludwig turned to writing prose, producing *Die Heitherethei* (1853) and *Aus dem Regen in die Traufe* (1854), two outstanding humorous sketches of Thuringian provincial life. These stories were followed in 1856 by a tragic counterpart, *Zwischen Himmel und Erde,* the work that is universally acclaimed as Ludwig's masterpiece, and the principal one on which his continued fame is based. This story, concerning the love of two brothers for the same girl, contains all of the best features for which Ludwig is noted: realistic background, psychological characterization, and a style that is by turns vigorous, dramatic, and eloquent. Despite the immediate and widespread fame of this work, Ludwig refused to acknowledge that his talent lay in the narrative form and returned to his dramatic plans. He conceived the fatal notion that by minutely studying Shakespeare he could perfect a dramatic technique which would enable him to complete all of his fragmentary dramas. Instead, his studies merely

served to increase his uncompromising self-criticism and completely paralyzed his creativeness. His imagination constantly outran his dramatic ability, so that he failed to complete a single additional drama. He dissipated his best energies in constant revision and at his death left behind more fragments than completed works. His various critical writings, which are valuable contributions to dramatic theory, were published in 1871 as *Shakespearestudien.*

Der Erbförster was translated into English in 1913 under the title *The Hereditary Forester* by A. Remy, and by Paula Green as *The Forest Warden.* An anonymous translation of *Zwischen Himmel und Erde* appeared as *Between Heaven and Earth* (1911). Subsequent translations of the same work were made by Muriel Almon (1913) and by B. Q. Morgan (1929).

ABOUT: Bennett, E. K. The German Novelle; McClain, W. H. Between Real and Ideal: Ludwig's Development as a Narrative Writer. [In German—see studies by A. Stern and A. Sauer. In French—by L. Mis.]

D. G. D.

*LUIKEN, JAN (JOAN) (April 16, 1649-April 5, 1712), Dutch poet and book illustrator, was born in Amsterdam, the son of the Baptist schoolmaster Caspar Luiken. The father, in some pamphlets, gave testimony to his son's highly developed religious awareness and his endeavor to attain simplicity and truth in word and act. Luiken first intended to be a painter but gradually shifted toward literature. As a young man he wrote love poems, pure in feeling and expression and belonging to the best of the lyrical genre produced in seventeenth century Holland. Classical embellishments, so customary in Luiken's day, are negligible in these poems which were collected and published under the name *Duytse Lier* in 1671. They are not only love songs, but idylls, tales, romances, sometimes even serious philosophical contemplations. The collection was arranged by Luiken according to theme and adorned with mystically formulated notations, derived from the writings of the German Jakob Böhme, whose *Aurora* he later (1686) translated.

In 1673 Luiken was baptized according to the rites of the Baptists, but two years later he defected to mystical pantheism. Böhme especially influenced him in this change. Luiken, who had married the singer Maria Outens in 1672, gradually withdrew from the world, moved in 1699 to Haarlem, then to Schellinkhout in the north. Living frugally and giving away most of his earnings, he was

* lü′ kĕn

573

from 1677 onward mainly active as a book illustrator and Biblical print-maker. He was one of the best artists of his time in this genre. His prints often contain a faithful representation of reality, but sometimes are local in their characterizations. The poems that were published in the latter part of Luiken's life are all pietistic and mystical in nature. Although they are, on the whole, indifferent in quality, they contain some lyrics that express lofty religious views, often inspired by the poet's concern with nature. The collections that appeared after 1687 may all be characterized as didactic poetry. *De Byenkorf des Gemoeds* (1709), *Het Leerzaam Huisraad* (1711), and *Des Menschen Begin, Midden en Einde* (1712) belong to emblematic literature. In these writings Luiken is a child of his time. His philosophical and mystical temper was in harmony with much that is characteristic of the baroque era. In 1705 Luiken moved to Amsterdam where he died in poverty.

ABOUT: Comparative Literature, X (1958). [In Dutch—see studies by P. van Eeghen & J. P. van der Kellen, J. P. van Melle. See also De Gids (1904, 1909).]

H. B.

LUIS DE GRANADA. See GRANADA, FRAY LUIS DE

*LULL, RAMÓN (1233-December 1315), Catalan poet, novelist, and theologian, was born in Mallorca only three years after that island had been taken from the Mohammedans by King James of Aragon; as a reward for fighting in the campaign of 1229, his father had received extensive property on the island and had settled there. At about the age of fourteen Ramón joined the king's mainland court as a page, returning to Mallorca with the crown prince in 1256. During the years at court he had cultivated the vernacular arts of the troubadour and the courtly lover; his Latin and his morals seem to have suffered. In 1257 his marriage to Blanca Picany was arranged by the king; but neither marriage nor children put a stop to his love affairs, which lasted until his radical conversion in July of 1263, when he had repeated visions of Christ in agony on the Cross.

From his conversion onward he devoted his life to self-discipline and to grandiose literary and evangelical projects. After making a mendicant pilgrimage to Santiago de Compostela, Rome, and the Holy Land, he devoted

* lōōl

himself to the study of Arabic, theology, and philosophy. The first of his many voluminous works, *The Book of Contemplation* (1272), written at least partly in Arabic, is a theological and devotional encyclopedia of almost a million words. His chief project, the conversion of Moslems by rational persuasion and preaching rather than by force, was already taking shape. After further visions on Mount Randa, he wrote what he considered his masterpiece, the *Ars Magna,* a treatise on logic that uses tables and movable discs, derived from Arabic sources, to prove Christian propositions in a mechanical way that shocked even the scholastics, but found favor later on with Giordano Bruno and Leibniz.

In the years 1275-77 we find Lull at Montpellier, where he wrote the *Libre del Orde de Cavallería* (published by Caxton in English as *The Book of the Ordre of Chyvalry,* 1484), anticipating his great novel *Blanquerna* (c. 1283). The latter monument of Catalan literature is a romance of chivalry in which reasonable arguments replace weapons in righting wrongs and building a quixotic Utopia. After he has remade the political order, the hero reorganizes the Church, from the local monastery to the College of Cardinals; then, resigning from the Papacy, he becomes a hermit. In this fantastic, harmonious vision of reason and nature in action, of poverty and holy joy, Lull expresses the spirit of St. Francis of Assisi (he joined the Third Order in 1295) as does no other European author. He also draws on a related spiritual tradition, stemming from the Sufi mysticism of Persia; this can be seen particularly in two interpolated works, *The Art of Contemplation* and *The Book of the Lover and the Beloved.* The first is a systematic devotional treatise; the second is a mystical prose poem or dialogue which is the spiritual climax of the novel. In it the Beloved is God the Father, the Lover is the longing Christian or Christ, and in the background floats a third Person, Love. Analogies with the system of courtly love, as well as with the Trinity, are evident. But the tone is unmistakably akin to that of Hispano-Arabic poets of the Sufi school; Lull himself points out this affiliation.

After visits to popes and to the King of France urging missionary crusades into Africa, Lull wrote in Paris his second most important Catalan prose work, *Fèlix* or *Libre de Meravelles* (1286). It treats encyclopedically of all the marvels of the universe, from God to Hell, including plants, metals, beasts, and man. The section on beasts is the most interesting because of the folkloric tales, though, interestingly enough, the animals here tell tales of human actions and draw moral conclusions from them.

From Paris Lull returned to Rome late in 1290, whence, convinced of the futility of his attempts to arouse the papacy, he went to Genoa; from that port he intended to sail to Africa and hold debates with the Moslems, convincing them rationally of the Incarnation and the Trinity. But while at the port he was assailed by doubts as to his success, and these doubts led to a spiritual crisis, or nervous collapse, in which he searchingly compared his hesitation to St. Peter's denial of Christ. When finally he could board a ship for Tunis, however, his doubts gave way to joy and confidence; his public debates, prefaced by his avowal of willingness to become a Moham-medan if rationally convinced, were successful enough to provoke violence and to have him sent back to Genoa by the Caliph.

After further disappointments at Rome, Lull expressed his disillusion in his finest Catalan poem, *Desconort* (1295), a Job-like debate with a critical hermit, who represents Lull's own self-doubts. After joining the Franciscans, as the only ecclesiastical group that sympathized with him, he returned to Paris, where he wrote *The Tree of the Philosophy of Love* (1298), an allegory ex-tolling the active life of devotion to Christ's service.

His own active life continued: more writ-ings; trips to Mallorca, to Rome, to Cyprus and Armenia; a second missionary trip to Africa. He went to Paris (1309-11) to fight Averroism; he attended the Council of Vienna (1311) to urge the establishment of mission-ary language schools and of a unified crusad-ing order of knights. In 1314 he returned to Tunis, where, now more than eighty years old, he spent the last year of his life preaching and translating. According to a likely legend, he was finally stoned to death by an impatient mob; he received a martyr's burial in Mallorca, where he has ever since been the object of a pious and patriotic cult. Despite Dominican opposition, he was at last officially beatified and bears the title *Doctor Illuminatus*.

The imposing personality of Ramón Lull produced theological writings which were per-haps more passionately enthusiastic than strictly orthodox; but he was not entirely unsuccessful in his attempt to unite the Arabic, Latin, and Romance cultures of the Mediterranean. For Catalonia he is the great classical author, for single-handed he made Catalan literarily independent of Provençal

and raised it to the level of a learned modern language.

In the twentieth century, the English Hispanist E. Allison Peers has made excellent English trans-lations of *The Book of the Lover and the Beloved* (1923), *Blanquerna* (1926) *The Tree of Love* (1926) and *The Book of Beasts* (1927).

ABOUT: Peers, E. A. Ramón Lull.

E. L. R.

*LURIA, ISAAC BEN SOLOMON (known also as Ha-Ari or Ari) (1534-1572), the founder of modern Cabalism, was born of German parents in Jerusalem. Luria was very young when his father died, and he was taken to the home of a wealthy uncle in Cairo. There he was placed under the best Jewish teachers and soon became proficient in Talmudic literature. At the age of fifteen he married a cousin, their financial needs being met by relatives.

Repelled by the legalism of the Talmud, Luria became fascinated with the study of the mystical Zohar. He withdrew from so-ciety in 1556, living as a hermit in the Nile region for many years. Visiting his family only on the Sabbath, speaking little and only in Hebrew, Luria devoted himself to in-tense mystic contemplation. He emerged a full-fledged visionary who believed he had ascended to heaven, conversed with Elijah, and learned the secrets of the universe. It was in these formative years that his Caba-listic system took shape.

In 1569 Luria moved with his family to Safed in Palestine, the center of Jewish mysticism. There he became the leader of a group of mystics including Moses Cordo-vero, Solomon Alkabez, Joseph Caro, and Hayim Vital Calabrese. A separate congre-gation of Luria's disciples and colleagues was formed which met every Friday for mutual confession of sins. Luria came to be regarded as a saint, possessed with supernatural pow-ers. He himself hinted that he was the Messiah of the House of Joseph who would precede the Messiah of the House of David.

Luria recognized two classes of disciples: novices and initiates, the most important of the latter being Hayim Vital. It is to Vital that we owe most of our knowledge of Lu-ria's life and thought, for the master never wrote a book. He is said to have explained his unwillingness to set down his thoughts in writing: "It is impossible, because all things are interrelated. I can hardly open my mouth to speak without feeling as though

* lōō′ ryä

the sea burst its dams and overflowed. How then shall I express what my soul has received, and how can I put it down in a book?" Vital's compilation of the orally transmitted Lurianic doctrines is contained in the *Ets Hayim* (Tree of Life), a work which circulated in manuscript for many years before being printed.

The Lurianic Cabala, as presented by Vital, attempted to introduce order and clarity into the older Cabalistic system. In particular, Luria developed an abstruse theory of the Sefirot, the creative powers which transmit God's emanations. More important than his speculative mysticism was the emphasis on the practical Cabala in which Luria expounded the theory of metempsychosis, or the transmigration of souls. He insisted on the value of asceticism, fasting, praying, ablutions, and the use of mystical formulae. Great importance was attached to the necessity for the utmost devotion during prayer and on the mystic significance of every word, syllable, and letter in all prayers.

Luria died prematurely in a plague at the age of thirty-eight, but his disciples spread his thought throughout Europe, where it received widespread acceptance. Lurianic prayers, customs, and ceremonies took root in many communities. Although the influence of the Lurianic Cabala has been condemned for its role in preparing the Jews for the pseudo-Messiah, Sabbatai Zevi, and for its emphasis on asceticism and emotionalism, it must be recognized that it found its way into the hearts of many Jews because they were seeking just such a mystical system for moral redemption. It was especially influential in shaping the nature of the great popular religious movement of Hasidism.

The best edition of the *Ets Hayim* was published in Warsaw, 1891. There has been no English translation, although Lurianic stories appear in such anthologies as N. Glatzer's *In Time and Eternity*.

ABOUT: Abelson, J. Jewish Mysticism; Graetz, H. History of the Jews; Mueller, E. History of Jewish Mysticism; Schechter, S. Studies in Judaism; Scholem, G. Major Trends in Jewish Mysticism; Waite, A. The Holy Kabbalah; Waxman, M. A History of Jewish Literature. [In German—Wiener, M. Die Lyrik der Kabbalah.]

M. R.

LUTHER, MARTIN (November 10, 1483-February 18, 1546), German reformer, Bible translator, and religious writer, was born in Eisleben, Saxony, the son of humble peasant parents. His father became a miner and was able to provide the means for his son's education. Luther attended the University of Erfurt, where he acquired a general humanistic education. He intended to enter the field of law, but in 1505 he decided suddenly to devote his life to God and entered the monastery of the Augustinian friars. His ordination as a priest took place in 1507, and, following a trip to Rome in 1510-11 on business for his order, he was named Doctor of Theology and professor at the University of Wittenberg.

Despite rapid promotions these years were filled with doubts and a constant searching for guidance and peace of mind. The spiritual laxity which he had observed in Rome in high ecclesiastical positions had shocked him and filled him with growing disquietude. In 1517 his questioning of the propriety of selling indulgences impelled him to nail his famous *95 Thesen wider den Ablass* to the door of the castle church—a customary method of the time of demanding an open disputation of any question. The ensuing debates led Luther, among other heresies in the eyes of the church, finally to deny the supremacy of the pope. Unwilling to recant his beliefs ("Here I stand. I cannot do otherwise. God help me. Amen."), Luther was excommunicated in 1520. The following year at the Diet of Worms he was placed under the ban of the empire. For his own safety Luther was held incognito by the Elector Friedrich III (the Wise) of Saxony at his castle at the Wartburg. There Luther devoted himself to the translation of the New Testament and produced in addition an amazing number of writings in support of

LUTHER

his ideas. In 1522 he was able to return to Wittenberg, which remained his home for the next twenty years of absorbing and restless activity in organizing the new church. He married the former nun Katherina von Bora in 1525, and the couple had six children. During later life Luther was plagued by ill health as well as by problems of political and religious disunion. His death occurred during a visit to his native town.

Luther was productive and stimulating in every area to which he turned his hand. His enormous literary output (*Werke*, 54 vols., 1883-1928, ed. by G. Buchwald *et al.*) and his life of active leadership were made possible only by his tremendous physical stamina and drive. Despite his humanistic training he was by nature an anti-intellectual who remained essentially a man of the people. He was endowed with great common sense, sincerity, and an unswerving dedication to his cause. His vitality and earthiness are reflected in the clear, vigorous, folk-like style of his writings.

To establish his new church Luther produced countless pamphlets and polemics which influenced the technique of such writing in sixteenth century Germany. He permitted his personality and emotions free rein in his essays, which are filled with passionate outbursts, outspoken boldness, and stubborn defiance, as well as a sense of humility, implicit trust in God, and the conviction of being committed to good works. The most important of his polemical tracts are *An den Christlichen Adel Deutscher Nation* (1520), *De Captivitate Babylonica Ecclesiae* (1520), and *Von der Freiheit eines Christenmenschen* (1522), which became the fundamental documents of the Protestant Reformation.

Luther's greatest single achievement is his translation of the Bible, a contribution which the critic Wilhelm Scherer called "the greatest literary event of the sixteenth century, indeed of the entire epoch from 1348 to 1648. It laid the foundation for a common culture for all ranks of society and opened a whole intellectual world to the people." To prepare his translation Luther returned to the original Greek and Hebrew texts. The New Testament was completed in 1522 and the Old Testament in 1534. The complete Bible was republished in 1541 in an improved and corrected edition. Luther possessed a superior command of language, and as his biographer R. H. Bainton has stated: "For sheer richness and exuberance of vocabulary and mastery of style he is to be compared only with Shakespeare." Luther's translation was no slavish imitation of the original, but in accordance with the rules of translation which he later set forth in *Sendbrief vom Dolmetschen* (1530), he rendered the spirit, rather than the letter of the text. His aim was to be intelligible to people everywhere, and he used a uniform German language, which became the basis of modern High German. By standardizing the German language, Luther made a major contribution to the linguistic unification of Germany.

In addition to giving Germany its Bible, Luther also created the evangelical hymnbook by his collection of religious songs, *Geistliche Lieder* (1524). His hymns, which became the model for the development of the Protestant church song, are popular in the best sense of the term and express his manly personality, intense earnestness, and heart-felt piety in straight-forward, simple language. His best-known songs include "Ein feste Burg ist unser Gott," for which he composed both melody and text, "Wir glauben all an einen Gott," "Mit Fried und Freud fahr ich dahin," "Mitten wir im Leben sind vom Tod umfangen," "Erhalt uns, Herr, bei deinem Wort," "Nun freut euch, liebe Christen gemein," "Gelobet seist du, Jesus Christ." Most of his songs were based on the Bible, the Psalms, or on older German songs. These hymns are characterized by an impersonal tone. Luther suppressed his own feelings in order to state the sentiments of the entire congregation.

Luther's sermons, which consist mainly of interpretations of the Bible, were long considered models of their type. He also published a collection of Aesop's fables, *Etliche Fablen aus dem Esopo* (1530), and helped stimulate an interest in this form. His *Tischreden* (1566), which contains many important historical and theological insights, reveals Luther's most personal aspect.

Luther's achievements as spiritual leader, creator of the Reformation, and literary figure cannot be overestimated. He influenced the entire course of theological and intellectual life in Germany from his time forward. Few individuals have ever appealed to an entire nation in the same manner, and few have ever exerted such widespread and immediate dominion through their writings as Luther.

Among modern editions, H. Wace and C. A. Buchheim translated Luther's *Primary Works* in 1896 (containing *Address to the Nobility of the German Nation; Concerning Christian Liberty; On the Babylonian Capitivity of the Church*). P. Holman translated Luther's *Works* in 1915. Of individual works G. Macdonald translated *Luther's*

Songbook in 1897 and J. F. Lambert translated Luther's Hymns in 1917. Luther's Correspondence and Other Contemporary Letters was translated by P. Smith in 1913-18. Tischreden was translated as Table Talk by W. Hazlitt in 1848, as Conversations by P. Smith and H. P. Gallinger in 1915, and by T. S. Kepler in 1952 as Table Talk. New editions of the Works and Exegetical Writings have been published in the 1950's and 1960's under the editorships of J. Pelikan and H. T. Lehmann.

ABOUT: Bainton, R. H. Here I Stand: A Life of Martin Luther, also Luther and the Reformation in the Light of Modern Research; Boehmer, H. The Road to Reformation; Bornkamm, H. Luther's World of Thought; Boyer, M. W. Luther in Protestantism Today; Carlson, E. M. Reinterpretations of Luther; Clayton, J. Luther and His Works; Dallmann, W. Martin Luther: His Life and Labor; Fife, R. H. Young Luther; Köstlin, J. Life of Luther; Kramm, H. H. The Theology of Martin Luther; McGiffert, A. C. Martin Luther; Mackinnon, J. Luther and the Reformation; Maritain, J. Three Reformers; Plass, E. M. This Is Luther; Schwiebert, E. G. Luther and His Times; Smith, P. Life and Letters of Martin Luther; Stolee, I. B. Luther's Life; Thiel, R. Luther; Waring, L. H. The Political Theories of Martin Luther; Zeeden, E. W. The Legacy of Luther.

D. G. D.

*LUZÁN (CLARAMUNT DE SUELVES Y GURREA), IGNACIO DE (March 28, 1702-May 19, 1754), Spanish critic and poet, was born in Saragossa. His father was Antonio de Luzán y Guaso, governor of Aragón, and his mother was Leonor Pérez Claramunt de Suelves y Gurrea. Despite the high position of the family, when the father died in 1706 young Luzán had to be educated chiefly by relatives. At last the boy was sent to Italy with his uncle, José de Luzán, a priest. He lived in a number of Italian cities but mostly in Milan, where he received a good education with the Jesuits. He showed an early interest in literature and became an excellent linguist, mastering Latin, Greek, English, German, Italian, and French. This ready access to foreign cultures was to prove of inestimable value to him later. Eventually Luzán moved to Palermo with his uncle and there took the doctorate in law at the University of Catania. Also, for reasons which are somewhat obscure, he took first orders in the Church. Several years later he returned to Spain.

Although Luzán never solicited favors, his merits were soon recognized and, in 1747, he was sent to Paris as secretary to the Spanish Embassy, where he remained until 1750. He was then appointed to the Consejo de Hacienda and made superintendent of the Royal Mint, in Madrid, where he died suddenly aged fifty-two. He had been married to María Francisca Mincholet and by her had two sons and a daughter. Luzán's wife died a year and a half after her husband, and the king showed his regard for the writer by seeing that their children were well cared for. Ignacio Luzán was a man of unusual cultivation for his time, a cosmopolitan and a polyglot.

Luzán was the author of numerous lyric poems, which are not without merit, and many translations from ancient authors as well as Italian, French, and English. He wrote a Latin compendium of Descartes' ideas and translated Milton, among many others. Of all his works, however, only his Poética (1737) has survived. It was edited twice: in 1737 in Saragossa and in Madrid in 1789. The second edition, done by Llaguno y Amírola, in two volumes, contains important additions to the first. His poems are to be found in the BAE, LXI and XXXV. English translations of two of these were made by Henry Wadsworth Longfellow in Poets and Poetry of Europe (1845).

The Poética has been the subject of much criticism and it has been said that Luzán's ideas were too narrow but, in all justice, one must recall the wretched state of lyric poetry at the time, which had sunk to little more than Gongoristic rhetoric. It was Luzán's intention to bring poetry back to common sense, to govern it by reason. His work employs elegant language and its influence, on the whole, was good. The ideas advanced are not so much those of Boileau (as has sometimes been stated) but rather those of Aristotle, and the Italians Muratori, Benio, Gravina and others. The appearance of the Poética in 1737 coincided with the establishment of the Diario de los Literatos and began the neo-classic period in Spanish letters. As such, apart from its intrinsic merits, it is a milestone in Spanish literature.

ABOUT: Robertson, J. G. in Studies in the Genesis of the Romantic Theory in the Eighteenth Century. [In Spanish—Cano, J. La Poética de Luzán; Fernández y González, F. Historia de la Critica Literaria en España desde Luzán hasta Nuestros Días.]

R. E. O.

*LUZZATTO, MOSES HAYYIM (1707-May 6, 1747), Hebrew mystic, poet, and moralist, was born in Padua, Italy. His father, a wealthy merchant, provided him with an excellent education, both in secular and Jewish studies. Luzzatto was an omniv-

* lōō thän'

* lōōt tsät' tō

orous reader, and under the guidance of his teachers, Isaac Cantarini and Isaiah Bassan, he became particularly devoted to Hebrew poetry and mysticism. The Rabbi of Reggio also influenced him in his decision to study the Cabala.

Thus Luzzatto immersed himself at an early age in Cabalistic mysteries. Joining with like-minded Jews of Padua, he established, at the age of fifteen, a study group which met in his house. At the same time, however, Luzzatto was writing poetry. His earliest work was an impressive elegy on the death of his teacher Cantarini. At the age of seventeen, he wrote *Leshon Limudim* (Language of Studies) in which he advanced his views on Hebrew style, illustrating them with brilliant poetic fragments and with a Biblical drama, *Ma'aseh Shimshon* (Story of Samson).

In these works, and in his *Migdal 'Oz* (Tower of Strength, written 1727), an allegorical drama written as a wedding gift for his teacher Bassan's son, Luzzatto introduced a new conception of Hebrew literature, that of neoclassic Biblical simplicity. The works of a poetic genius, emphasizing the noble aspects of love, they departed from the artificiality of medieval Hebrew poetry. During this period Luzzatto also wrote a 150-hymn psalter modeled on the Psalms of David. Only two psalms have survived the rabbinic denunciation which greeted the work.

After this burst of poetic creation, Luzzatto turned his attention once more to the Cabala in its Lurianic form. Believing that he enjoyed the power of receiving divine revelations, seeing visions, and convinced of his Messianic role, Luzzatto wrote a number of Cabalistic works, including his own Zohar. None of them was published and, like his psalter, they no longer exist. Luzzatto even organized a group of young men seeking redemption through Cabalistic study under a strict pietistic moral code. Despite his efforts to remain unknown, Luzzatto's Cabalism came to the horrified attention of German and Venetian rabbis who feared an outbreak of Messianic fervor. Under their prodding he renounced Cabala, entered the business world, and married the daughter of the Rabbi of Mantua. Once again, however, he resumed his Cabalistic studies and this time the Venetian rabbis proclaimed a ban on his writings.

Leaving Italy in 1737, Luzzatto settled with his family in Amsterdam where he was received with respect by the Jewish community. There he earned a livelihood as a lens grinder, but continued his non-Cabalistic literary efforts. He composed an allegorical drama,

La-Yesharim Tehilah (Praise to the Righteous), a work of the highest value for its poetic language, style, and content. His *Mesilat Yesharim* (Path of the Righteous, 1740), a guide to ethical behavior written with simplicity and clarity, became the most popular of his non-dramatic works. In 1747 Luzzatto left Holland for the Holy Land, possibly with the idea of returning to his beloved Cabala. Unfortunately, he and his family died in an outbreak of a pestilence at Safed shortly after their arrival.

Luzzatto presents a double aspect: on the one hand the medieval mystic, on the other the modern poet of love and nature. It is his poetic heritage that marks Luzzatto as a genius of the first rank who revitalized Hebrew language and literature. Although without literary influence in his own day, he was, as M. Waxman points out in *A History of Jewish Literature*, "the father of modern Hebrew literature."

The *Mesilat Yesharim* was edited and translated by Mordecai M. Kaplan in 1936. *La-Yesharim Tehilah* has been translated by H. S. Goldstein and R. Fischel as *Praise for Righteousness*. The moral code for Luzzatto's Cabalistic fellowship was published in *Commentary*, May 1951. A Hebrew edition of his poetry, *Sefer ha-Shirim*, edited by Simon Ginzburg, appeared in 1944-45.

ABOUT: Ginzburg, S. The Life and Works of Moses Hayyim Luzzatto; Landman, I. Moses Luzzatto; Meyer, J. Stay of Mozes Haim Luzzatto at Amsterdam; Spiegel, S. Hebrew Reborn.

M. R.

*LUZZATTO, SAMUELE DAVID (August 22, 1800-September 30, 1865), Hebrew scholar and poet, was born in Trieste, then under Austrian rule, to Hezekiah and Miriam Luzzatto. His father, a poor turner, was a person of an idealistic, philosophical nature, while his mother was a forceful, practical woman who died when her son was fourteen years old. The Jewish communal school educated the boy in both Jewish and general studies, in accordance with the humanistic traditions of Italian Jewry. Luzzatto's environment was much different from that of the average European Jew: he lived in the countryside just at the edge of the city, spoke Italian, and profited from this harmonious blending of influences. Luzzatto left school in 1814, when his mother died, and he aided his father and shared the housekeeping with his cousin Rachel, herself a Hebrew poetess. Luzzatto continued his studies practically by himself, and acquired a command of classical, Semitic, and modern languages. Above all,

* lōōt tsät' tō

he developed a mastery of the Hebrew language at all periods of its history—an accomplishment which was without contemporary equivalent and which has had few equals since. Luzzatto married Bilah Bathsheba Segrè in 1826; a year after her death in 1841, he married her sister.

After a long period of private tutoring, Luzzatto was appointed in 1829 to teach Bible, Hebrew, philosophy, and history at the newly founded rabbinical school at Padua. Here he remained for thirty-six years until his death, despite the school's increasingly straitened circumstances. His personal life was darkened not only by the prolonged illness and death of his first wife, but by the loss as well of several children, particularly his brilliant eldest son Philoxene.

Luzzatto began as a poet, publishing youthful poetry in *Kinnor Na'im* (Sweet Harp) in 1824 to great acclaim. While full of romantic ardor, it is written in the medieval meter which he was the last significant poet to employ. He was also a romantic, attacking the rationalist tradition typified by Maimonides and Spinoza in favor of the more historic religiosity of the Spaniard Judah ha-Levi. Luzzatto was a faithful adherent to the rabbinic tradition.

Luzzatto's scholarly work is of great breadth, written mainly in Hebrew and partially in Italian. It includes *Oheb Ger* (1830), a study of the Aramaic translation of the Bible; the poetic works of Judah ha-Levi; commentaries on many of the Biblical books; philosophical and theological studies; editions of medieval liturgical poetry; Hebrew grammars. He was unusually generous in transmitting observations and manuscript gleanings to fellow scholars, so that his large correspondence (published in six volumes) is also of great scholarly value.

Luzzatto is a pre-eminent figure in modern Jewish scholarship, and his works retain most of their value.

ABOUT: Morais, S. Italian Hebrew Literature; Waxman, M. History of Jewish Literature, III; Spiegel, S. Hebrew Reborn.

L. P. G.

*MÁCHA, KAREL HYNEK (November 16, 1810-November 6, 1836), the leading Czech romantic poet, was born in Prague and lived there during most of his short life. His father, Antonín Mácha, was a miller's helper who spent years wandering in the Czech countryside before he settled in the capital, where he later opened a modest grocery store. The poet's mother, Marie Anna, grew up in

* mä′ ка

580

Prague. The couple's first child was baptized Hynek; years later, when his poetry began appearing in print Mácha himself added the first name Karel. He received his elementary education in the parish grammar school where he showed considerable intellectual promise. This apparent ability caused his parents to abandon the original plan to have the boy learn a trade, and instead Hynek was able, in spite of the very limited family means, to enter a six-year *Gymnasium*. It was during the later *Gymnasium* years that Mácha first turned to the writing of poetry. His first attempts were in German, the verses of little distinction already showing the romantic influences. In 1830 Mácha began writing in Czech; his lyrical poems, which occasionally appeared in literary magazines, tended more and more towards metaphysical poetry, with pessimistic undertones, interspersed with verses of patriotic and national fervor.

Mácha's secondary education was followed by a two-year course in philosophy, which, at the time, was a prerequisite for any further specialized education. He finished philosophy in 1832 and spent the next three years studying law.

The patriotic atmosphere of the Czech national revival had a strong impact on Mácha and his friends. The symbols of the past glory of the Czech nation, the old castles and ruins amid the thick forests of Bohemia, became the main goal of Mácha's expeditions, undertaken mostly on foot and frequently by moonlight. The theatre and acting occupied his other free moments. During one such amateur production Mácha met Lori Šomková, a Prague girl not yet quite seventeen, with whom he formed an intellectually unsatisfying relationship, marked by erotic passion and torturing jealousy.

European romanticism in general formed Mácha's literary taste, and Byron left the most marked influence on his works. Among Mácha's works, which include the Byronic fragment *Mnich* (The Monk, 1833), the short story "Márinka" (1834), and the larger prose work *Cigáni* (The Gypsies, 1836), the most significant is, without doubt, the epic-lyric poem *Máj* (*May*), a classic of Czech literature. Mácha began it in 1834, and it appeared in print in 1836. Containing four cantos and two intermezzos it is a story of the romanticized outlaw Vilém, the "dread lord of the forests," who has avenged the seduction of his sweetheart Jarmila by killing her seducer, without realizing that the rival was his own father. Vilém is awaiting execution, overwhelmed by the anxiety of the infinite nothingness and interminable time-lessness which lie ahead. The identification of Mácha with Vilém is unmistakable when the names Hynek, Vilém, and Jarmila appear side by side in the last line of the poem. The images of nature and the pantheism of the poem are expressed in beautifully musical verses. Mácha's *Máj* was not favorably accepted by his contemporaries, the devotees of national romanticism, who looked somewhat askance on literature which did not unequivocally serve the Czech national cause. Future generations, however, recognized Mácha as one of the greatest poets of Czech literature, as its poet revolutionary who was able to overcome much of the literary provincialism of his generation.

In 1836 Mácha went to the North Bohemian city of Litoměřice to accept a minor post in a law office. On October 1 Lori gave birth to a son. Mácha, tense, tortured by doubts, burdened by added responsibilities, and weakened by recent illness, apparently caught a fatal chill while helping to extinguish a fire. He died in the early hours of November 6, and was buried on November 8 in Litoměřice, the same day his wedding to Lori was to take place in Prague. More than a hundred years later, in 1938, his body was exhumed and taken to Prague.

No authentic portraits of Mácha have been preserved. His contemporaries described him as tall, pale, with long hair and a dark beard, often dressed unconventionally. He appears to have been a man of strong possessiveness and violent jealousy, sociable and gay one moment, and in search of solitude the next, a passionate traveler and wanderer, a man of tense dreams and of a restless and reflective soul.

Maj was translated into English *(May)* by R. A. Ginsburg in 1932 and, together with prose and poetry, by H. H. McGoverne in 1949. German, French, Italian and other translations also exist.

ABOUT: Slavonic and East European Review, January 1937. [In Czech—see studies by F. X. Šalda, A. Pražák, and K. Jánský. In French—see study by H. Granjard.]

H. K.

MACHAUT, GUILLAUME DE. See GUILLAUME DE MACHAUT

*MACHIAVELLI, NICCOLÒ (May 3, 1469-June 20, 1527), Italian politician, political theorist, and historian, was born in Florence of an old family originally from Monte-

* mä kyä věl′ lē

MACHIAVELLI

spertoli. In his youth Machiavelli is supposed to have composed humorous, realistic verses. On June 19, 1498, he obtained the office of Secretary of the Republic of Florence, a post he held until 1512. In effect, his position was neither of high honor nor high salary; however, it was a responsible one, serving the so-called Ten who functioned as a combined War and State Department. Machiavelli, therefore, traveled and corresponded extensively in his official capacity, acquired much knowledge of practical politics, and was so efficient and industrious that his name, even to the present time, has been synonymous with that of "the Florentine Secretary."

As secretary, he wrote reports and letters on his missions describing his observations and conclusions with precision and logic. The first is a *Discourse to the Ten on Pisan Affairs* (1499) in which he discussed what was to become for him a firm conviction: that the mercenary soldier, characteristically lawless and lacking in loyalty, was a serious error and that a loyal citizen-army was essential to preserve the ruler from internal strife and external attack. Machiavelli's idea of a permanent citizen-army is a very original contribution to his times. Machiavelli himself was permitted to organize such a militia in 1506. He never changed his point of view; his third major treatise, *L'Arte della Guerra* (1518-20), is a dialogue on his technical and general conclusions from his studies of Roman as well as contemporary military procedures. He concluded here again that the laws and actions of a state for the common good are to no avail except for a state's preparation for its military defense.

In June 1500 Machiavelli began a series of missions to France, to many Italian cities, and to Pope Julius II. In 1502 he composed his first official political writing, the well-known discourse "On the Manner of Treating the Rebellious Population of Valdichiana," revealing the great influence upon him of his studies of Roman history.

In 1502-3 Machiavelli served as envoy to Cesare Borgia, whom he greatly admired for the latter's organization of a citizen militia and for the fact that Borgia, necessarily despotic in order to displace the robber nobility, had given better government to the Romagna. Machiavelli's esteem for Cesare Borgia resulted in the important place later granted to him in *The Prince*.

In 1507 and 1508 Machiavelli wrote his important reports on France and Germany after missions to the courts of Louis XII and the Emperor Maximilian. However, upon the withdrawal of the French with whom the Republic of Florence was allied, Machiavelli was exiled by the absolutist Medici, who had been restored to power through the aid of Spanish troops and of the Pope. Machiavelli, accused of serious crimes, was tortured. Although he was proved innocent, he was banished from Florence for one year and was forced to live nearby on his small farm. For thirteen years, Machiavelli lived quietly and simply, though disturbed by this exile which he prolonged because he was not permitted to return to the service of his country. He found solace in meditation and in his books, "that food which alone is mine and for which I was born," as he wrote in 1513 in the famous letter to his friend Francesco Vettori. In this year, after he had composed the first book of his *Discourses*, Machiavelli interrupted this work to write his famous book now known as *Il Principe* (*The Prince*) to which he gave the Latin title *De Principatibus* or *On Principalities*.

Machiavelli continued writing until 1525 when he was recalled to Florence to undertake new fortifications for the city under threat of imperial attack from Spain and to serve the city as envoy on several missions. With the sack of Rome in 1527, the Medici heirs fled Florence, and the city was again proclaimed a republic. Having worked for the Republic and then for the Medici, Machiavelli was distrusted by the new Republicans. Two weeks after the establishment of the new government, he fell gravely ill of shock from the turn which events had taken against him. He died two days later, before the news of his official dismissal from duty could reach him.

Machiavelli's literary monuments are *The Discourses on the First Ten Books of Livy* (composed between 1513 and 1517-18), *The Prince* (1513), *The Art of War* (1518-20), *The History of Florence* (1520-24), the comedies *Mandragola* (The Mandrake, 1520) and *Clizia* (1525).

The first of these, the *Discorsi*, are as important as *The Prince*, which they anticipated. Drawing on Livy and Polybius, for their theory of the constitutional cycle, as well as his own experience in Italian politics, Machiavelli discusses the foundation, organization, and expansion of the state. For him the foundation and establishment of a state is properly the work of an elected prince, not an hereditary one, who, working rigorously for the common good, seeks sole power in order to establish a principality or a republic. Once it is organized, he shares with many men the responsibility for its maintenance.

Where the *Discourses* deal mainly with the expansion of the Roman Republic, *The Prince* deals with monarchies or absolute governments. No man of his epoch saw so clearly as did Machiavelli the direction which political evolution was taking toward absolute monarchy throughout Europe in the face of a corrupt society and church. Since, for Machiavelli, the ruler is outside the group, through his supreme importance as lawgiver, he is above its morality and is therefore free to use immoral means to make the state secure. Political power—or the mechanics of government—is for Machiavelli an end in itself. The concept of the omnipotent legislator judged only by his success in enlarging and maintaining the power of his state forms the main concept of "Machiavellianism," a technique which is suffused by the pessimistic realization of the unchangeability of human nature. Of his ideal prince Machiavelli said, "It is well that, when the act accuses him, the result should excuse him." Machiavelli's prince, shrewd and self-controlled, making an important virtue of efficiency, distrusting halfway measures, is temperately lawless for the sake of founding a state or salvaging a corrupt one. However, once the state *is* established, his prince acts in accordance with law.

Behind the idealism of such despotic power lay Machiavelli's hope: the nationalization of Italy through a strong ruler—a Medici. Machiavelli, more than any other political thinker, created the modern political meaning of the word "state" as the name of a sovereign political body. However, he had no definite plan for the creation of Italy as a state.

Machiavelli's *Istorie Fiorentine* was commissioned by the University of Florence. Not a chronological or completely accurate history of Florence but a study of causes and effects, his history is a consideration of civil strife as well as a series of general reflections which seek rules of political behavior. His concern is first for the state and then for the outstanding man of *virtù* (exceptional ability). He prefers the republic but recognizes the need for its emergence from the principality.

Two comedies, the famous *Mandragola* and *Clizia*, adapted from Plautus, as well as *Belfagor*, a *novella* of Oriental origin, came from Machiavelli's pen. The most powerful and most important play of the Italian Renaissance, *Mandragola* is a penetrating satire on the corruption of the church and the farcical sexual entanglements of the bourgeoisie. The story of a virtuous young wife and her betrayal, *Mandragola* incorporates keen character portraits, vivacious dialogue, and an unusually ingenious and skillful plot development.

It is Machiavelli's political writings, however, particularly *The Prince,* which have had the greatest influence on literature and political thought. Edmund Spenser, Sir Walter Raleigh, Francis Bacon, and Thomas Hobbes were indebted to him. His books, though accepted earlier by Clement VII, were listed on the *Index* in 1559 as a result of church resentment of his criticisms. Machiavelli was attacked by John Donne on religious grounds, and on political grounds by Bodin and Frederick the Great, with a resulting popular image (which persists to this day) of Machiavelli as an evil theorist. Modern scholars seek to clarify and evaluate rather than to judge this first modern political scientist whose insights and observations were unsystematic but whose principles have had an enduring influence on the course of modern history.

The Discourses have been translated, with notes, by L. J. Walker (1950). Many translations of *The Prince* exist, including that by L. A. Burd to which Lord Acton contributed a masterly introduction (1891); among the useful modern editions are *The Prince and The Discourses* (Modern Library) with introduction by Max Lerner and translation by Luigi Ricci (1950) and that by T. G. Bergin, *The Prince* (Crofts Classics, 1947). The *Mandragola* has been ably translated by A. Dukes (1940), as well as by Anne and Henry Paolucci (1957); *The Florentine Histories* (Everyman) by C. E. Lester (1912) and by H. A. Rennert (1901). *The Prince, Mandragola, Clizia, Belfagor,* and selected letters are translated, with an introduction, by J. R. Hale in *Machiavelli: Literary Works* (1960), and by A. H. Gilbert (Capricorn Books, 1961). Other works are to be found in *Machiavelli, The Historical, Political, and Diplomatic Writings,* translated by C. E. Detmold (4 vols, 1882), and in *The Literary Works of*

Machiavelli, edited and translated by J. R. Hale (1961). The poems were translated by J. Tusiani under the title *Lust and Liberty* (1963).

ABOUT: Beck, N. W. The Political Science of Niccolo Machiavelli; Butterfield, H. The Statecraft of Machiavelli; Ebenstein, W. Great Political Thinkers; Gilbert, A. H. Machiavelli's 'Prince' and Its Forerunners; Meineke, F. Machiavellism; Olschki, L. Machiavelli the Scientist; Ridolfi, R. The Life of Niccolò Machiavelli; Sabine, G. H. A History of Political Theory; Villari, P. The Life and Times of Niccolo Machiavelli; Whitfield, J. H. Machiavelli.

R. P. C.

*MACROPEDIUS, GEORGIUS (JORIS van LANKVELD, or LANGHVELDT)

(1475-July 1558), Dutch educator and writer, was one of the outstanding Latin dramatists of his time. Not much is known of his life. He was born in Gemerten, near Bois-le-Duc ('s Hertogenbosch), in Holland, and became a member of the Brethren of the Common Life. As a member of this religious organization, he was first principal of its school of 1,200 students in Bois-le-Duc. Later (1496) he was transferred to the school in Lüttich, and some time after that he became rector of the school in Utrecht. Deeply interested in education he worked hard to improve the school system and curriculum, and wrote books on grammar, syntax, prosody, logic, rhetoric, and theology. He knew not only Latin and Greek but also (and this was rare for the period) Hebrew. His influence was considerable: many of the most famous men of the late sixteenth century were his students. In old age Macropedius returned to Bois-le-Duc where he died.

Macropedius wrote an indeterminate number of Latin plays; about fifteen are known to have existed. In these plays he showed a sharp eye for the events and figures of everyday life. At least five of them are on Biblical subjects, but, for his time, they are remarkably free of heavy allegorizing. His lively characterizations and realistic touches are apparently the result of direct observation—a reminder that, after all, he was of the country which produced the Jan Steen school of realism. However, Macropedius never enjoyed great popularity in his native land. It was in Germany that his works were most enthusiastically received. Some of them were translated into German: his *Hecastus* (a treatment of the *Everyman* theme), for instance, had six different versions in the sixteenth century alone.

Macropedius' themes were medieval in character—primarily Biblical—*Lazarus, Josephus,*

* mà krō pē' dǐ ŭs

Adamnus Rejectus, Petriscus, Passionis Christi, and *Jesus Scholasticus.* But he was actually a transitional figure, standing between the Middle Ages and the Renaissance. From the point of view of cultural history, he belongs to the age of Humanism and was a follower of the German humanist Johann Reuchlin. In Macropedius' works both the influence of the Greek drama and the oratorical aims of the humanists may be traced.

A collection of his plays was published in 1552-53 in two volumes. It included, besides those already mentioned, *Asotus, Aluta, Rebelles, Andrisca,* and *Bassarus.* Most of these works have been neglected; the only one of which any intensive study has been made is *Hecastus*—and this only because of its great influence in Germany.

ABOUT: Herford, C. H. Studies in the Literary Relations of England and Germany in the 16th Century. [In German—Goedeke, K. Everyman, Homulus und Hekastus; Jacoby, D. Georg Macropedius.]

H. B.

MADÁCH

*MADÁCH, IMRÉ (January 21, 1823-October 5, 1864), Hungarian poet and dramatist, was born in Alsó-Sztrigova. His family was of the prosperous landed gentry, descendants of Dalmatians or Croatians who had immigrated to Hungary in the thirteenth century. For a time they had been Lutheran, but in the eighteenth century they were reconverted to Catholicism. The boy was educated by private tutors, then attended secondary school at Vácz and finally the University of Pest where he studied philosophy and law and took a law degree.

Madách was of a strongly melancholy disposition, and unhappy events in his personal life and his country's history served to intensify this quality. A brief stint as notary in County Nográd made him cynical about politics and politicians. His sister and her family were murdered by Hungarian highwaymen as they fled during the Hungarian Revolution of 1848-49. He himself was arrested and sent to prison by the Austrians in 1852 for sheltering the secretary of General Kossuth. During his imprisonment his wife, Erzsebet Frater, whom he had married in 1845, was unfaithful to him, and after his release he divorced her.

It is hardly surprising that Madách's work should have been of a somber philosophical nature. Though he wrote in a variety of forms, he is remembered best for two dramatic poems—*Moses* and *The Tragedy of Man,* both written in 1860. *The Tragedy of Man* is by far the more significant work. It was written in the tradition of profound and lofty

* mŏ' däch

philosophical poems like Milton's *Paradise Lost,* Du Bartas' *La Semaine,* Byron's *Cain,* and Goethe's *Faust.* To the latter poem Madách was most indebted, but his work is not mere imitation. The Hungarian poet Arany recognized this when he read it in manuscript: "At last I have discovered a true talent. *Tragedy of Man* is a Faust-like dramatic composition, but the author stands on his own feet."

The poem has been described as "the cry of a soul tormented by loss of hope and inspired by a desperate yearning for hope." It tells the story of Adam and Eve, of the temptation of man by Lucifer through the ages. Divided into fifteen scenes, it carries Adam from Paradise through the Fall, into ancient Egypt, ancient Greece and Rome, Constantinople during the Crusades, and throughout the course of history. Adam is always the disillusioned and embittered idealist and Lucifer is the eternal tempter, and the poem ends in Heaven with Lucifer defeated and Adam saved.

Madách did not intend his work for the stage, but in 1883 it was produced at the Budapest National Theatre by Ede Paulay and was a great success. Since then it has been played many times in Hungary, and there have also been productions in Vienna, Berlin, Hamburg, and Prague. The poem has been translated into English, German, French, Dutch, Russian, Czech, and Hebrew.

In 1861 Madách was elected to the Hungarian Parliament. He died in Alsó-Sztrigova

584

at the age of forty-one of heart disease. His collected works (3 volumes) were edited by Pal Gyulai in 1880.

The first English translation of *The Tragedy of Man* was made by W. N. Loew in 1908. In 1933 C. H. Meltzer and P. Vajda published a new translation. Two scenes from the poem are translated by G. A. Kohut in the Warner Library.

ABOUT: Bulletin of National Theatre Conference, XII (November, 1950); Slavonic Review, IX (1930); Warner Library, XXIV.

---

*MAERLANT, JACOB VAN (c. 1225-1291?), Dutch poet, was the first great didactic writer in Dutch literature, and is often called the father of Dutch poets. Hardly anything is known of the first thirty years of his life. He was born in Damme, Belgium, moved to the north, and became sexton in 1255 in Maerlant, near Brielle, The Netherlands. In Maerlant's day the position of sexton, being partially ecclesiastical in nature, brought with it a certain degree of prestige.

Maerlant began his literary career as a writer of chivalric romances. He wrote them in the same spirit as did his older contemporaries. *Alexander* (c. 1257) followed the Latin work written by Gauthier de Châtillon; *Die Istory van Troyen* had as example the work of Benoît de Sainte-Maure, while a history of the Holy Grail (c. 1261) was modeled after the French work of Robert de Borron.

In 1265 Maerlant entirely altered his course and his literary aims. Returning to the south, he became town clerk in Damme and began to identify himself with the bourgeoisie, whose growing importance was allied with a growing thirst for knowledge. He not only became the defender of the poor and the oppressed, but also denounced the chivalric romances as deceitful and pernicious. He transformed himself into a moralizing and didactic poet. His great didactic works must not be considered as artistic efforts; rather, they attempt to communicate knowledge. Judging Maerlant's work by the time in which he lived, he produced serious and solid writing. His main achievement in this genre was the *Spieghel Historiael* (c. 1282-88), based on the *Speculum Historiale* of Vincentius Bellovacensis. Maerlant never finished the gigantic work. Of the four volumes planned, only the first and the third were finished when he died; the fourth was continued until 1316 by the poet Lodewijk van Velthem, while Philip Utenbroke finished the second volume. In this comprehensive historical work, all possible traditions were discussed. Maerlant opposed

* mâr′ länt

the romanticizing tendency of chivalric literature by attempting to write sound historical criticism.

Other didactic works are *Heimelijkheid der Heimelijkheden* (1266), which closely follows *Secreta Secretorum*, a work commonly ascribed to Aristotle; *Der Naturen Bloeme* (1262-66), a translation of Thomas Cantimpré's work; and a life of St. Francis, from Bonaventura's biography.

Although the works mentioned are of interest as sources of information regarding the gradual change in the outlook of the bourgeoisie, Maerlant is valued primarily for his strophic poems. These works, lyrical in tone, consist of stanzas of one clause each, each clause consisting of thirteen verses with only two rhymes. In them Maerlant developed great eloquence, rhythmic harmony, and striking imagery. The first and best known of these is the *Wapene Martijn*, which boldly treats of social problems in the form of a dialogue. Other strophic poems are *Dander Martijn*, *Van ons Heeren Wonden*, *Clausule van der Bible*, and *Van der Drievoudicheide*. *Der Kercken Claghe* is one of his most passionate polemical and satirical works. *Van den Lande van Oversee* was written after the fall of Acre in 1281 and called for a new crusade.

Maerlant died in Damme. His two most important literary followers were Jan van Boendale and Jan de Weert.

ABOUT: [In Dutch—see studies by J. v. Mierlo, J. te Winkel. See also Taal en Letteren, VII-IX (1897-99).]

H. B.

MAGNÚSSON, GUÐMUNDUR. See TRAUSTI, JÓN

---

*MAGNY, OLIVIER DE (c.1529-1561), French poet, born in Cahors, was for some time the secretary of Hugues Salel, almoner of Francis I. He went to Paris at an early age and was an active contributor to the new poetry by 1553, in his *Amours*. To this work he added the unpublished writings of Salel, including the latter's translations from the *Iliad*. He then became the secretary of Jean d'Avanson, and went with him on an official mission to Rome, where he was in close contact with Du Bellay; he exchanged sonnets with the latter on their impressions of Cosmopolis. By highly doubtful report, he is said to have been the poet for whom Louise Labé languished: he met her in Lyons in 1550

* mȧ nyē′

585

and fell in love with her, but on his next visit he noted her aloofness and published an ode hostile to her.

Certain parts of the two volumes by Magny are today esteemed as monuments of the new poetry. Some of the 176 sonnets of his *Soupirs* are of high quality, and tell of things seen in Rome, which he considered an admirable but corrupt city. Magny was spiritually closer to Italy than was Du Bellay; he took events more seriously, and expressed positive religious principles. The volume of *Soupirs* also contains love sonnets imitated from Petrarch, Catullus, and Anacreon, and a series probably alluding to Louise Labé; other sections show an interesting orientation toward satire. Magny's other work, *Amours*, was well received and led Du Bellay to call him the French Catullus, a poet he sometimes imitated, though Ovid would have been more to the point for his grace, his facility in improvisation, and his choice of subjects. The *Amours* include a hundred sonnets addressed to an idealized lady; they are rich in sighs and supplications, largely inspired by Petrarch or adapted from Sannazaro. In the same volume, the odes are interesting for their allusions to contemporary writers and to the idealized "Castianire," who is surely *not* Louise Labé. Magny's last work, the *Odes* of 1559, shows his mastery of this genre and a considerable debt to Theocritus.

In every respect Magny was one of the stars of the Pléiade, and we may presume that only his early death led Ronsard to omit his name from the official list when it was later formulated. His personal mark lies in a strong sensuousness without excess or bad taste. He was very widely approved for his personal modesty and gaiety.

ABOUT: [In French—Favre, J. Olivier de Magny; Raymond, M. L'Influence de Ronsard; Vianey, J. Le Pétrarquisme en France.]

F. J. C.

MAIKOV, APOLLON. See MAYKOV, APOLLON

*MAIMONIDES, MOSES (MOSES BEN MAIMON) (known also as RAMBAM) (March 30, 1135-December 13, 1204), the greatest medieval Jewish philosopher, was born in Cordova, Spain. His father, Maimon ben Joseph, was a judge in the Jewish community and a distinguished Talmudic scholar. It was from him that young Moses received his early education in

* mī mŏn' ĭ dēz

586

the Bible and Talmud. From Arabic teachers he absorbed a basic knowledge of philosophy and science. In 1148 Cordova was taken by the fanatical Almohades, who offered the Jews conversion to Islam or exile. The Maimon family spent the next twelve years wandering through various Spanish cities until finally, after great suffering, they settled in Fez, Morocco. It was during these years that Moses wrote his first works, a treatise on the calendar, *Heshbon ha-'Ibur* (Calculation of Leap Year), and a treatise on logic, *Milot ha-Higayon* (Terms of Logic).

In Fez, the Almohades were also in control and the Jews, including the Maimons, were forced to profess Islam while secretly practicing Judaism. Moses continued his studies, but was aware of the deplorable state of his co-religionists and defended them from attacks by zealots in his *Igeret ha-Shemad* (Epistle on Conversion, c. 1160-64). Emphasizing the special circumstances, he argued that merely paying lip service to Islam was not apostasy. At the same time, he urged the Jews to remain steadfast in their faith. This work aroused the anger of the Moslem authorities and nearly cost Moses his life. Once again, the family decided to flee, emigrating to Palestine in 1165 and thence to Fostat (Old Cairo), Egypt.

Upon the deaths of his father and brother David, Moses decided to practice the vocation of physician, thereby adhering to the ancient Jewish tradition that religious scholars should earn their livelihood from a secular occupation. Despite ill health, he completed a profound commentary on the *Mishnah* in Arabic, the *Siraj* (Illumination, 1168). In it he provided a clear, logical introduction to a bewildering mass of material, laying special stress on the scientific and philosophical elements of the *Mishnah*. His remarks on the *Mishnah* tractate *Avot* (Sayings of the Fathers), known as the *Shemonah Perakim* (Eight Chapters), illustrate his ethical outlook. Attempting to develop a creed for Judaism, Moses formulated in this work his thirteen articles of faith, ranging from belief in the existence of God to belief in future resurrection. Although subsequently incorporated into the Jewish liturgy, this creed has never been accepted as final, running counter as it does to the Jewish belief in the primacy of religious practice over religious theory.

Under the benevolent rule of the great Sultan Saladin, Egypt became a haven for persecuted Jews. The Jewish communities of Yemen in southern Arabia, however, were undergoing great trials at the hands of the

Moslem Shiites. In his famous letter of consolation *Igeret Teman* (Epistle to Yemen, 1172), Moses wrote to his fellow Jews with much feeling: "Be not discouraged by the troubles heaped upon you. These sufferings are sent merely to try you, and to prove that the descendants of Jacob, the children of those who received the Torah at Sinai, are in possession of the true religion." He also warned the Jews of Yemen against seeking false Messiahs in their hour of peril.

Gaining prominence as a rabbinic authority, Moses was soon recognized as leader of the Cairo community and spiritual head of Oriental Jewry. Yet these communal activities did not hinder the completion of his great religious code, the *Mishneh Torah* (Repetition of the Law, 1180), also known as the *Yad ha-Hazakah* (Strong Hand). In this stupendous structure Moses attempted to systematize the entire body of Talmudic law, so that "the entire Oral Law shall be clearly ordered for everyone." Using a logical approach, he did bring order out of the chaotic Talmudic labyrinth presenting briefly and succinctly the final decisions on all Jewish laws. Despite some criticism, the *Mishneh Torah* was hailed by Jews throughout the world and Moses was regarded as the supreme rabbinic authority of the day. It should be noted that subsequent commentaries on the *Mishneh Torah* eventually made it as difficult to use as the Talmud itself.

Another code, the *Sefer ha-Mitsvot* (Book of Commandments, written prior to the *Mishneh Torah*) set forth the details of Jewish law on the 613 commandments of the Torah, and is actually a supplement to the *Mishneh Torah*.

The proficiency of Moses in medicine won for him a thriving practice among the nobles of the court in Cairo, and he was appointed physician to Saladin's vizier in 1185. His prominence brought an invitation to become physician to Richard Cœur de Lion of England, an offer which Moses refused. Appointed chief of the Jewish communities of Egypt, he used his influence on behalf of oppressed Jews throughout the East. Although terribly burdened with official and private duties, he found time to contribute to the sciences of medicine and astronomy. Ten medical treatises, in which many modern medical theories are anticipated, have survived. He also expressed opposition to astrology as a form of superstition.

At the urging of advanced students, Moses wrote in Arabic his philosophic masterpiece,

the *Dalalat al-Ha-'irin,* translated into Hebrew as the *Moreh Nevukhim (Guide of the Perplexed,* 1190). The entire work was a demonstration of his conviction that Judaism and philosophy in its Aristotelian form are compatible. Explaining away the anthropomorphisms of the Bible, Moses gave them an ethical meaning. In brilliant expositions of such problems as the existence of God, the divine attributes, the question of prophecy, the origin of evil and God's providence and omniscience, he set forth a grand synthesis of faith and reason. He proclaimed the knowledge of God as the highest aim of man. The *Moreh Nevukhim* later became the subject of a fierce controversy between the liberal and conservative Jews of France and Spain. Denounced as heretical by the Orthodox, banned and burned, it remained, nevertheless, a beacon of light to many Jews.

Moses continued his medical and philosophical activities through the closing years of his life. After suffering a series of physical ailments, he died at Fostat at the age of seventy and his body was brought to Tiberias in Palestine for burial.

Isaac Husik, in his *A History of Medieval Jewish Philosophy,* says: "With Maimonides we reach the high water mark of medieval Jewish philosophy. He was by far the most comprehensive mind of medieval Jewry, and his philosophy was the coping stone of a complete system of Judaism." The influence of his philosophic work has been enduring. Among Jews, he has been an important factor in the development of such thinkers as Spinoza, Solomon Maimon, Moses Mendelssohn, and Hermann Cohen. In Latin translations made as early as the thirteenth century, his philosophic work influenced many Christian philosophers, particularly Thomas Aquinas, Albertus Magnus, Duns Scotus and other scholastics. As rabbi, physician, communal leader, codifier, philosopher, and, above all, as a living example to his people, Jewish tradition has rightly said of him, "From Moses to Moses there arose none like unto Moses."

The *Guide of the Perplexed* was translated by Michael Friedländer in 1881-85 and several later editions of this translation have appeared. In 1963 a new translation was made by Shlomo Pines. An abridged version, translated by Chaim Rabin, was published in 1952. The Yale Judaica Series has published, since 1949, several volumes of the *Code of Maimonides,* a translation of the *Mishneh Torah.* Moses Hyamson has translated two books of the *Mishneh Torah* since 1937. *The Eight Chapters of Maimonides on Ethics* (Joseph Gorfinkle) appeared in 1912; *The Treatise on Logic* (Israel Efros) in 1938; *The Book of Divine Commandments* (Rabbi

Charles Chavel) in 1940; and the *Epistle to Yemen* (Boaz Cohen) in 1952. *Maimonides Said,* edited by Nahum Glatzer in 1941, and *The World of Moses Maimonides,* edited by J. S. Minkin in 1957, are anthologies. Hebrew editions include the *Mishneh Torah* (New York, 1947) and the *Moreh Nebukim* (Tel Aviv, 1952-53).

ABOUT: Baron, S. W., ed. Essays on Maimonides; Bokser, B. The Legacy of Maimonides; Efros, I. I. Philosophical Terms in the Moreh Nebukim; Epstein, I., ed. Moses Maimonides, 1135-1204; Graetz, H. History of the Jews; Husik, I. A History of Medieval Jewish Philosophy; Husik, I. Philosophical Essays; Marx, A. Essays in Jewish Biography; Nirenstein, S. Problem of the Existence of God in Maimonides, Alanus, and Averroes; Roth, L. The Guide of the Perplexed; Roth, L. Spinoza, Descartes, and Maimonides; Sarachek, J. Faith and Reason: The Conflict over the Rationalism of Maimonides; Sarton, G. Introduction to the History of Science; Strauss, L. Persecution and the Art of Writing; Waxman, M. A History of Jewish Literature; Wechsler, I. S. The Neurologist's Point of View; Yellin, D. & Abrahams, I. Maimonides; Zeitlin, S. Maimonides. [In Hebrew—see studies by Y. Guttman and J. L. Fishman. In French—Sérouya, H. Maimonide: Sa Vie, Son Œuvre. In German—Heschel, A. Maimonides, eine Biographie.]

M. R.

*MAIRET, JEAN DE (May 1604-January 31, 1686), French dramatist, was born in Besançon to a middle class family, and baptized on May 10, 1604. Both parents soon died, but he seems to have had a sound education. During the plague in that city, Mairet went to Paris. His first play, *Chryséide,* composed early in 1625, shows the influence of Racan's *Bergeries* and of *Pyrame et Thisbé* by Théophile de Viau, one of Mairet's close friends in later years. About this time, Mairet entered the service of the Duke of Montmorency, to whom he dedicated the first edition of his *Sylvie* (1628). He fought with the Duke against the Huguenots and may have been his secretary at Chantilly. By 1630 in his pastoral play *Silvanire* Mairet was applying the three classical unities, whose theory he propounded in his preface. Although the unities had been recommended by Scaliger in 1561 and La Taille in 1592, Mairet was the first to use them in the manner accepted during the seventeenth century, and his immediate influence appears in the theatre of Du Ryer. During his sojourn at Le Mans, in the service of the Count of Belin, Mairet composed his tragi-comedy *Virginie* and his masterpiece *Sophonisbe,* first performed in 1634. The success of *Sophonisbe* established him as the leader of a new classical genre, but he quickly assumed a secondary position in the face of more prolific writers such as Rotrou and greater ones such as Corneille. Jealous of the

latter, Mairet took an active part in the "Querelle du Cid," along with Scudéry, and suffered in the ensuing polemics. From this point on he preferred the tragi-comedy in such plays as *Roland Furieux* of 1638, and after the failure of *Horace* in 1640 he abandoned the theatre for the diplomatic service. The death of his protector Richelieu led to his banishment in 1653, but he returned after the death of Mazarin and was knighted in 1668 by the Emperor.

Mairet's tragi-comedies are typical examples of the current represented by Garnier and Du Ryer, rising in large part from the *Astrée,* from Ariosto, and from Spanish writings. In this genre his importance is almost entirely historical, but he is distinguished by his respect for moral codes and for his excellent versification. His masterpiece *Sophonisbe* had widespread influence and appears today as a fine tragedy; in its artistry as well as its technique it represents a major step forward beyond the work of Racan and of Théophile de Viau. Editions of Mairet's works are rare, and he has been unduly slighted until very recent times.

ABOUT: Lancaster, H. A History of French Dramatic Literature. [In French—Bizos, G. Jean de Mairet; Gasté, A. La Querelle du Cid; Lancaster, H. Chryséide et Arimand.]

F. J. C.

*MAISTRE, JOSEPH MARIE, Comte de (April 1, 1754-February 26, 1821), French statesman, writer, and philosopher, born in Chambéry in Savoy, came from Languedocian nobility. A member of an old family of magistrates, he received an excellent education at Jesuit schools in Chambéry, studied law in Turin, and was appointed to civil service posts of Savoy; like his father, who was once President of the Senate, Maistre served his country as a senator. In 1786 he was married to Françoise de Morand. His younger brother Xavier (1762-1852), also a writer, is best known for his *Voyage autour de Ma Chambre* (1794).

Obliged in 1792 to flee from Savoy before the French Revolution annexed his country, he went to Lausanne, where he spent four years, a frequent visitor in the home of the Genevan banker Necker and his daughter, Mme de Staël. In 1799 Charles Emmanuel IV, whom he had served in Turin, named him agent of the Grand Chancellery in Sardinia. Later he returned to Turin and was appointed Minister of State, Chief of the Grand Chancellery of the Kingdom of Piedmont.

* mĕ rĕ'

* mĕs' tr'

A more important event in his career came in 1802 when Victor Emmanuel named him ambassador to St. Petersburg. There he stayed until 1816, a period of traveling and great literary activity. Not only was he in close relationship with the French émigrés, but he was also sought by Czar Alexander I and the Russian aristocracy. Thus he had opportunity to learn of and judge high events and men. In 1817 he returned to Savoy to serve in his country's high offices. Troubled by domestic problems in the later years of his life, he was afflicted by paralysis and died in Turin in 1821.

Maistre was about forty years old when he started to write, developing, as one critic has said, one idea in one work. The first publication, *Lettres d'un Royaliste Savoisien*, appeared in Lausanne in 1794. In 1794-97 he worked on his *Étude sur la Souveraineté*, which remained unedited until 1870. But more important was his *Considérations sur la France*, a book which develops the Legitimist doctrine from the Roman Catholic point of view. Learned in history and philosophy, he was irritated by the errors made by the eighteenth century philosophers Rousseau, Montesquieu, and particularly Voltaire. In *Considérations* he ardently criticized with clarity, vigor, and logic the horror of the Revolution and denied all that the eighteenth century believed.

In 1809 followed *Essai sur le Principe Générateur des Constitutions Politiques*, not published, however, until 1814. Also some of his best and most famous treatises were written during his years in Russia: *Du Pape* (1819) and *De l'Église Gallicane* (1821) treat the relation of the pontiff to the Church and to temporal leaders, to civilization and to schismatic groups such as the Anglicans and Greek Orthodox. *Les Soirées de Saint-Petersburg*, which were never entirely finished, but which were published the day after his death, consider the fortunes of virtue and vice in this world, attack Locke, and praise the executioner as the foundation of social order. Other works include a translation of Plutarch, letters on the Inquisition, and an examination of Bacon's philosophy, all of which again, like most of his works, were published after his death. Two collections of his letters were published, one by his son, Comte Rodolphe de Maistre, as *Lettres et Opuscules Inédits*, and the other by Albert Blanc as *Mémoires Politiques et Correspondance Diplomatique de Joseph de Maistre*.

A leader of the Neo-Catholic and anti-revolutionary movement, Maistre took a position above all ecclesiastical. As a thinker he was an eloquent adversary of the Revolution. He wished to restore royal power, with restoration of the pope as the infallible religious sovereign, both monarch and pope "vicars of God" commissioned to the government of men by Providence which visibly directs the affairs of the world. For Maistre the pope would lead the European republic, would dominate kings, arbitrate differences between nations, represent God, and proclaim "right" in face of violence and force. However, Maistre believed that the temporal monarchy was inferior to the spiritual supremacy of the pope, not to be tempered by councils, national churches, or even by his private judgment. Offended by anarchistic tendencies in Revolutionary politics and religion, he supported the absolute necessity of order to the degree that for him the pope was the single visible authority, the arbiter of all disputes. He so loved the ideal of unity and hated that which separated and distinguished, that unity for him existed only in absolute despotism. Politically he felt that a constitution was divine and that nations became what God made of them; unless nations recognized and believed in the action of God in the world, they would suffer. In other words, Maistre identified Christianity with the laws of the world and of politics.

The "lay theologian of Providence," Maistre wrote his case for theocratic power in a remarkably spirited and varied style. He was admired as a stylist by Sainte-Beuve, who found his essays forceful, brilliant, and authoritative, and recognized by Auguste Comte as a source of the essential ideas of his positivist philosophy.

Maistre's *Essay on the Generative Principle of Political Constitutions* was translated into English in 1847. A selection of Maistre's works, translated by J. Lively, was published in 1965.

ABOUT: Alphonsus, M. The Influence of Joseph de Maistre on Baudelaire; Caponigri, A. R. Some Aspects of the Philosophy of Joseph de Maistre; Gianturco, E. J. de Maistre and Giambattista Vico. [In French—see studies by F. Bayle, E. Dermenghen, R. Johannet, F. Paulhan.]

G. E.

*MALCZEWSKI, ANTONI (June 3, 1793-May 2, 1826), Polish poet, was born in Warsaw, but spent his youth in eastern Poland. His mother, Konstancja, died early; his father, Jan, general in the Polish Army and later in the Russian armed forces, had little influence on his son's education. The boy was sent to Krzemieniec College, an ex-

* mäl chĕf' skē

589

cellent school. In spite of his lively temperament he made good progress; he was praised by his superiors and liked by his schoolmates. He did not complete the final course, however, and in 1811 he joined the army, becoming a second lieutenant in the engineering corps stationed in Warsaw. Here he led a frivolous life and was involved in many love affairs. Wounded in a duel, he was unable to participate in Napoleon's offensive against Russia, but was engaged in the defense of the Modlin fortress. He continued service in the Polish army until his discharge in 1815, when he went abroad. He visited Switzerland, France, Italy, Germany, and England, and in 1818 he climbed Mont Blanc. After returning to Poland he leased an estate and turned to animal husbandry.

A tragic love affair darkened the last years of Malczewski's life. He had gained some reputation for his studies and experiments in hypnosis. Hearing of this, a neighbor brought his wife to the poet for treatment of a mental disorder from which she was suffering. The cure was successful, but the patient, Mme Rucinska, became morbidly attached to her healer. Their relationship so shocked the rural community that they were obliged to leave and go to Warsaw. Here they lived in poverty. Malczewski could not accept any post, since Mme Rucinska could not bear his absence. Publication of his only poem, *Maria,* in 1825, went almost unnoticed and brought him no income. He died in Warsaw, at thirty-three, in poverty, bitterness, and oblivion.

Maria is a romantic narrative poem based on real events of the eighteenth century, but set in the more heroic seventeenth century. It is a tragic story of an unhappy and persecuted girl clearly showing the influence of Sir Walter Scott's historical poems and Byron's pessimism. What renders it emotionally effective, however, is its reflection of the author's personal sorrows and the weird, romantic atmosphere of the Ukrainian steppes where it takes place.

Maria was translated into English by Arthur P. and Marion M. Coleman in 1935.

ABOUT: Krzyzanowski, J. Polish Romantic Literature. [In Polish—see studies by A. Bielowski, J. Ujejski.]

M. G.

*MALEBRANCHE, NICOLAS (August 6, 1638-October 13, 1715), French philosopher, was born in Paris, the son of the treasurer of several large farms and of a religious

* mål bräNsh'

mother. Educated at the Collège de La Marche, he completed without enthusiasm a degree in arts. Finally, drawn toward theology, he spent several years at the Sorbonne. The death of both his parents in 1658 contributed to his distaste for the world, and two years later he decided to enter the Oratory, in which congregation he was ordained in 1664. He spent his life in meditation and in writing.

The keynote to Malebranche's thought is the study of the inner life. He found meditation often discouraging in his struggle against reason, imagination, and the senses, but it was for him the only road to truth. The Platonist orientation of his congregation depended in large measure on St. Augustine, but in the case of Malebranche this patristic doctrine was strongly integrated with the scientific ideas of Descartes, notably of the *Principes de la Philosophie,* which he had read by 1659. The publication of Pascal's *Pensées* in 1670 raised the further problem of a relationship to Jansenism. Malebranche's first work was *Recherche de la Vérité* (1674). His *Traité de la Nature et de la Grâce* (1680) aroused the violent hostility of Bossuet, who felt that it diminished the greatness of God. His hostility to quietism motivated his *Traité de l'Amour de Dieu* (1697). Of primary importance are his *Traité de Morale* (1683) and his last work, *Réflexions sur la Prémotion Physique* (1714).

Malebranche's doctrine centers on a theory of reason as immutable and eternal and part of God's wisdom; hence it is superior even to faith, since the latter will pass. God, as part of the rational universe, is revealed by knowledge. Hovering close to the pantheism of Spinoza, Malebranche stood apart in situating pre-existing ideas in God himself, and hence in reason, which reveals the eternal to man; relationship to the external world becomes perception by "vision in God." Malebranche appeals to modern readers more for his psychological approach than for the elaborate Neoplatonist metaphysics of essences and forms. His "complete" works of 1712 must be used in connection with the editions of 1837 and 1938 and many separate titles.

English editions of *The Search after Truth* and other essays translated by T. Taylor and of a *Treatise of Morality* by J. Shipton appeared in rapid succession from 1694 to 1700.

ABOUT: [In French—see studies by Le Père André, V. Delbos, H. Gouhier.]

F. J. C.

*MALFILÂTRE, JACQUES CHARLES LOUIS (October 8, 1732-March 6, 1767), French poet, was born in Caen. His parents, Charles Malfilâtre and Jeanne Marie Esther de Clinchamps, were pious Catholics who also had two daughters. The family was apparently quite poor but educated. Malfilâtre's father lost his sight, but was able to introduce his son to classical studies, especially to Virgil and Ovid.

Malfilâtre studied the classics with the Jesuit fathers at Mont Collège, and then entered the seminary at Bayeux. But he gave up ecclesiastical ambitions, and may have studied law for a while. (Malfilâtre's life was so brief, and attention to him then so cursory, that many details are not certain.)

We do not know when he started versifying, but for six consecutive years (1754-59) Malfilâtre was simultaneously laureate of the poetry contests (the Palinods) of Caen and of Rouen. By chance Marmontel saw his ode "Le Soleil fixe au milieu des planètes" (1758) and published it in the *Mercure de France*. Malfilâtre immediately set out to conquer Paris. He became secretary to Lauraguais, but soon resigned. Then he eked out a precarious existence at Vincennes and Chaillot, while working on the four-part *Narcisse dans l'Île de Vénus* (published posthumously, 1769), undoubtedly his best poem, and *Le Génie de Virgile*. Translations from the classics were fashionable and helped sustain him. But despite advances from the publisher Jacques Lacombe, Malfilâtre was in need and also imprudent. He died in Paris after a series of useless operations for an abscessed knee.

Malfilâtre's reputation as a *poète maudit* was launched by Nicolas Gilbert, who also has benefited posthumously from the aureole of poet-victim. Inherently inept at joining coteries, and lacking epic vigor, Malfilâtre was essentially nothing more than a craftsman. His legend has surpassed his work, which appeared posthumously in numerous editions between 1805 and 1829.

ABOUT: [In French—Boitard, F. Notices Biographiques sur les Hommes du Calvados; Brémond, H. *in* Revue de France, V (1932); Derôme, L. *in* Poésies de Malfilâtre (1881).

S. S. W.

* mȧl fē lȧ′ tr′

*MALHERBE, FRANÇOIS DE (1555-October 16, 1628), French poet and theorist, was born in Caen of a noble but relatively modest family, the eldest of six children. His father, by conviction a Protestant, placed him

* mȧ lĕrb′

The Bettmann Archive

MALHERBE

in the care of a Huguenot tutor and then sent him to the universities of Basel and Heidelberg. Malherbe's own religious convictions, never strong, were in part colored by his opportunism; but in general he showed little sympathy for the reformed sects. Again in Caen, at the university, he began to write poetry, much of which he later destroyed as unworthy. Perhaps because of friction with his father, he left home by 1576 and went to Aix where he became secretary to Henri d'Angoulême and entered actively into poetic circles. On the death of his protector five years later, he returned for a decade to Normandy and published his poetry to that date. In 1581 he married a widow by whom he had two children, both of whom he outlived.

Malherbe's first ambitious poem, "Les Larmes de Saint Pierre" (1587), frequently reprinted, was inspired by the work of the same title by the Italian poet Tansillo, published in 1560. Malherbe dedicated his version to Henry III, who at the time was undergoing his crises of repentance; this protection, though short lived, added to the wide esteem for the young poet. Under the influence of his Italian model, Malherbe developed various significant devices such as antithesis, but also fell into contemporary baroque excesses which later led him to disown the poem, and, after 1607, exclude it from his collected writings.

Malherbe's constant search for protectors inspired such occasional pieces as his lament on the death of Mary Stuart, but his solicitations bore no immediate fruit, and he remained in the civil service in Caen until 1595 when he again made a visit to the south. Meanwhile, having advanced considerably in his poetic technique, he created a far more significant work in his "Consolation à Cléophon," later (about 1598) revised as "Consolation de Monsieur du Périer sur la Mort de Sa Fille." The original version is remarkable for its dense manner and logical structure, but sins in excess of mythological allusion and a few careless effects of versification; its resemblances to the work of Desportes, Malherbe's most particular antipathy (on whom he wrote a *Commentaire*), are still striking. The revision, however, is a masterpiece of stoic philosophy ("La mort à des rigueurs . . .") and antique embellishment ("Priam qui vit ses fils abbatus par Achille"). Among his other fine works are his "Prière pour le Roi Henri le Grand" and his "Ode au Roi Louis XII Allant Châtier les Rochelois," written when he was seventy-two years old.

Malherbe is remembered mainly as the founder of a new school of purism and linguistic precision in French poetry. A strict classicist, he condemned the innovations of Ronsard and the Pléiade, launched furious attacks against all imaginable flaws of grammar and versification, and promoted the use of the alexandrine, a stately but essentially stiff and colorless type of verse. Malherbe's *poésie oratoire*, as it has been called, is a strict craft; his muse is common sense, not passion or inspiration. He used poetry as a medium for political advantage. In 1600, for example, he composed his "Ode de Bienvenue" for Marie de Medicis, a poem elaborately ornamented with appropriate laudatory and political symbols and significant for its vigor and originality. It, and similar works, won him favor with Henry IV, and in 1605, secure in royal patronage, he returned to Paris from Provence, frequented aristocratic circles, and remained in that city until his death. Malherbe was both a severe legislator and an attractive personality. Despite chronic opportunism and an ample measure of self-esteem, he expressed serious and constructive ideas. His narrow views on poetry, shared by most of his contemporaries, had a salutary effect in orienting the neoclassical period toward sobriety and clarity and set the norm until the romantic revolution.

ABOUT: Studies in Seventeenth-Century French Literature Presented to Morris Bishop (ed. J. J. Demorest; PMLA, LXXVIII (1963). [In French —Bourrienne, V. Malherbe, Points Obscurs; Brunot, F. La Doctrine de Malherbe; Counson, A. Malherbe et Ses Sources; Lebègue, R. La Poésie Française de 1560 à 1630.]

F. J. C.

*MALLARMÉ, STÉPHANE (March 18, 1842-September 9, 1898), French poet, essayist, and translator, was born in Paris, the son of Numa Joseph Mallarmé and Élisabeth Desmolins. The male members of both families—Parisian by adoption but Burgundian in origin—had for centuries been connected with the civil service, well educated all of them but hardly noted for any great love of letters. Stéphane's mother having died in 1847, his father remarried the next year. The boy was first sent to a school for the "sons of gentlemen" at Anteuil, and later transferred to the *lycée* at Sens. Except for his keen taste for languages Stéphane was but an indifferent scholar, given to daydreaming and poetizing rather than to rigorous study. At twenty he went to England to perfect himself further in a language the teaching of which he had begun to consider a possible means of livelihood, but practically nothing is known about his experiences during that visit. Stéphane returned from England a confirmed Anglophile, determined to give his life to the study of English letters instead of the customary civil service clerkship. A university career seemed indicated, but Mallarmé—always vacillating and dilatory in practical matters—never took the necessary examinations and thus was thrown back upon the teaching of English in secondary schools, a vocation he followed faithfully though with "inward groans" until his retirement in 1894.

The poet's life was signally barren of event. Mallarmé's frequent changes of residence are no evidence of any desire on his part to keep on the move: as *lycée* teacher he was at the mercy of the Ministry of Education, which could — and did — send him anywhere it wished: first to Tournon, next to Besançon, then to Avignon, finally back to his chosen place, Paris. Mallarmé's instincts were domestic, not nomadic, and he deeply resented the uprooted existence to which his career seemed to commit him. But though a lover of quiet, of a gracious and orderly life, Mallarmé was anything but placid. From childhood on, his mind had been in constant ferment, in search of a new principle of verbal beauty: a beauty secret and elusive, totally original, yet amenable ultimately to the classical forms of French prosody. An obsessive interest in the hidden possibilities of language as such, and of French most especially, gradually replaced his earlier, more pedestrian interest in English and in the methods of teaching that tongue to his countrymen. (His book *Les Mots Anglais*, 1877, an ingenious

* mȧ lȧr mȧ'

Etching by Gauguin

MALLARMÉ

study of sound-patterns, locutional forms, and idioms, remains as the sole fruit of the latter.) In 1861, while still in school, Mallarmé had come across Baudelaire's *Fleurs du Mal*, and the masterful beauty, the strict sonority of that collection was to revolutionize the young poet's life. Shortly after this date Mallarmé's first original poems were written ("Galanterie Macabre," "Enfant Prodigue") —too dependent on his model Baudelaire to gain true distinction, but exhibiting nevertheless a subtlety and linguistic resourcefulness all his own. In 1862 Mallarmé conceived the project of translating all of Poe's poems, in this too following his master's lead (published individually 1872-76, as a book in 1888). In 1863 Mallarmé's father died and the choice of a profession became imperative. To delay the final, dreaded decision the poet took a flying trip to Brussels, Antwerp, and London, where he met and presently married a young German governess named Marie Gerhardt. Upon his return to Paris he took his teacher's examination (September 1863) and shortly afterwards received his first scholastic appointment, a professorship of English in the *lycée* of Tournon.

Mallarmé's first wholly original poem, "L'Azur," was written in 1863. Other pieces quite as novel in conception and execution (including a number of very beautiful prose poems) followed at long intervals, for Mallarmé was a fastidious craftsman never satisfied with a production until it had been rewritten many times and brought to the pitch of near-absolute perfection. The most famous of these are "L'Après-midi d'un Faune" (published 1876) and "Hérodiade" (first published in 1869, as "Fragment d'une Étude Scénique d'un Poème d'Hérodiade")—long poems both of them, most elaborately orchestrated and greeted by the poet's contemporaries with a mixture of delight and dismay. During the last twenty years of his life Mallarmé wrote relatively little in verse, but every one of his published poems was a major *occasion*—of enthusiasm in friendly circles, of outrage or scandalized bemusement in an enemy camp consisting of Philistines or, simply, of conventional critics. From 1890 on the poet's efforts were concentrated largely on the composition of his most ambitious poem, "Un Coup de Dés Jamais N'Abolira le Hasard" ("A Throw of the Dice Will Never Eliminate Chance"). In this piece, as obscure as it is arresting, Mallarmé tried to present a *summa* of his ideas on poetry, on human destiny (exhibited quintessentially in the *poet's* destiny) and on the unavailing effort of mind to introduce reason, or logic, into the haphazard movement of brute physical events. The poem is written on the analogy of music, and in order to suggest this the poet has had recourse to a bizarre typography. On the first page the main theme—the title of the poem— is stated in huge black type. On the subsequent pages this theme is broken up and its subsidiary or conditional themes are developed with a wealth of repetition and variation which is most reminiscent of symphonic procedure in music. The hermetic poem made a profound impression on the young Valéry, while it left most of the poet's admirers awed and puzzled. During the same period Mallarmé also wrote a large number of rhymed epistles to various friends (collected under the title *Vers de Circonstance*, 1920) all of which exhibit his inimitable charm and the learned complication of rhyme peculiar to him.

Though by nature somewhat retiring, Mallarmé needed human companionship and could be a discreet and devoted friend. The closest companions of his younger years were Lefébure and Cazalis, both minor men of letters, the latter an old schoolmate of the poet. In later years he felt especially close to some of the leading painters of the young generation —Degas, Manet, Gauguin; and among musicians he was perhaps fondest of Claude Debussy, who wrote the well-known ballet music to his *Afternoon of a Faun*. As the years went by, Mallarmé found it harder and harder to endure the classroom routine, with its endless drudgery and discipline problems; and as the strain increased so did his desire for friendship. Friends now helped him to relax, if they did not act as healthy counter-irritants to his daily irritations. Another means of relaxation was afforded him when in 1874 he rented a small villa at Valvins, on the Seine, where he spent most of his vacations drifting in his yawl and dreaming of poems yet unwritten. He usually went to Valvins by himself, leaving his family behind in Paris. The letters the poet would send year after year from his resort to his loved ones in the city must be numbered among his most charming productions. During the school year in Paris Mallarmé found welcome diversion in the ballet and in Wagnerian opera, two spectacles of which he was an ardent devotée, writing about them with acumen and subtlety, if somewhat elusively.

Mallarmé is the esoteric poet *par excellence*. Never appealing to a large class of readers, distasteful even to many habitual readers of poetry, his verse speaks all the more powerfully to lovers of learned spiritual complication and of words, turns, cadences as elusive as they are magically potent. Mallarmé's attitude towards verse was fundamentally that of his first master, Baudelaire, but pushed to extremes of refinement and *recherche*. His essays and speculations collected under the title *Divagations* (1897) are in some ways even more extraordinary than his verse, for here we find a degree of syntactical involution and transposition never before encountered in French prose—that most convention-bound, or tradition-oriented of all "proses." Yet for all its tortuousness and riddling difficulty Mallarmé's prose style exhibits the same basic virtues as his verse: a craft almost unbelievable in its daring, combined with a deep moral integrity and—all appearances to the contrary notwithstanding—a firm sense of responsibility concerning the use of words.

Mallarmé was too idiosyncratic a writer to found a school in the usual sense of the word, but he exercised an incalculable influence upon the younger writers (and painters) who from 1880 onwards met once a week in his modest salon, rue de Rome 87 (later 89). His profound conversational charm has been described by numerous habitués of these gatherings, always in terms of an almost awed admiration, most strikingly perhaps by Paul Valéry who may be regarded as the quiet magician's greatest disciple. Though he wrote relatively little, it has been claimed of Mallarmé that he never wrote a word amiss; his touch in matters pertaining to language was well-nigh infallible and this uncanny sense of words has been acknowledged even by critics who, like Charles Maurras, stand in violent opposition to everything Mallarmé represents in the realm of ideas and values. The literature about the poet, both inside France and abroad, has grown to extraordinary proportions within the past few decades; for the most part its character is exegetic, given the peculiar difficulties that body of work presents to the ordinary understanding. But there is also an abundance of biographical studies and reminiscences, evoking the image of an unassuming, courteous man, scholarly without pedantry; self-tormenting, certainly, but without either moroseness or histrionics. Mallarmé died suddenly in his Paris apartment of a spasm in the throat, and was buried at Fontainebleau. He was survived by his widow and a daughter, Geneviève, who later married Dr. Bonniot, a distinguished medical scholar. A son, Anatole, had died in 1879, at the age of eight.

Mallarmé has not been made as widely available in English as, from the rank he holds in French letters, he would seem to deserve. The best complete translation of his verse is that by Roger Fry (1926, later reprinted in the U.S. from plates). *Un Coup de Dés Jamais N'Abolira le Hasard* was published in an English translation by Daisy Aldan in 1956. Grange Woolley's *Stéphane Mallarmé* (1942) is an interesting compilation containing versions of both verse and prose, with connecting biographical passages. A large selection from Mallarmé's prose writings has recently been presented to the English-speaking public by Bradford Cook (*Selected Prose Poems, Essays and Letters,* 1956).

ABOUT: Fowlie, W. Stéphane Mallarmé; Turquet-Milnes, *essay in* Arthur Ellis' book of translations. [In French—see studies by H. Mondor, A. Thibaudet, P. Valéry.]

F. G.

*MANASSEH BEN JOSEPH BEN ISRAEL (1604-November 26, 1657), Dutch-Jewish writer, rabbi, and one of the chief figures responsible for the readmission of the Jews into England, was born as Manuel Dias Soeiro on the island of Madeira. His family, of Marrano origin, moved shortly thereafter to La Rochelle, France and settled finally in Amsterdam where they resumed practice of the Jewish faith. Manasseh was given an intensive Jewish education by Rabbi Isaac Uziel in the Amsterdam Jewish academy, and an excellent secular education by private tutors. His remarkable facility for learning was soon evident. At the age of eighteen he was appointed rabbi of the Neve Shalom synagogue and, in the same year, married Rachel Soeiro,

* mă nă′ sě

a descendant of the respected Abarbanel family. Their eldest son, Joseph, died at the age of twenty in 1648 and their son, Samuel, died in 1657.

Manasseh's brilliance as an orator attracted much attention, and Gentiles as well as Jews thronged to the synagogue to hear him preach. Yet, despite his rabbinical post, Manasseh's economic situation was bleak. In 1627, therefore, he started the first Hebrew press in Amsterdam. At the same time he was engaged in writing what he considered his chief work, *El Conciliador* (The Conciliator, 1632-51), an attempt to reconcile apparent contradictions in the Holy Scriptures. Written in excellent Spanish, the work displayed vast erudition, if little originality. Manasseh had written it to bolster the faith of his Marrano co-religionists, but the book's greatest success was with Christian scholars who were impressed with the rabbi's learning. This work, together with a series of Latin and Spanish treatises which he wrote subsequently, established Manasseh's reputation as the leading Jewish figure of the period. Distinguished scholars, such as Isaac Vossius and Hugo Grotius, and the painter Rembrandt became his intimate friends. Others corresponded with him, seeking his views on Biblical and Jewish subjects. Manasseh still found it difficult to earn a livelihood, however, and was on the verge of emigrating to Brazil when he was persuaded to remain as head of a Talmudic academy.

Deeply immersed in Cabalistic speculation, Manasseh was a firm believer in the imminent approach of the Messianic era and of the return of the Jews to Palestine, but only after they had been dispersed to all countries of the earth. In 1650 he published these views in *Spes Israelis* (translated the same year into Spanish as *Esperança de Israel* and into English as *Hope of Israel*), expressing his conviction that the North American Indians were the Ten Lost Tribes of Israel and that Jewish settlement in England would be a step toward the Messianic era.

The book, dedicated to the English Parliament, struck a responsive chord among the influential Puritan elements in England, and was favorably received by Oliver Cromwell himself. After preliminary negotiations, Manasseh was invited in 1655 to plead his cause in London. After his presentation of arguments for readmission, both mystical and economic, in a pamphlet called *Humble Addresses to the Lord Protector* (1655), the issue was debated by a national conference. No definite action was taken, but the legal view was established that no English law actually prevented the return of the Jews, thus opening the way for their informal readmission. Manasseh, meanwhile, stung by William Prynne's bitter attack on the Jews in his *Short Demurrer* (1655), replied with his last work, *Vindiciae Judaeorum* (The Answer of the Jews, 1656), a spirited and skillful refutation of anti-Semitic charges. Returning to Holland with a pension from Cromwell, Manasseh died in Middleburg.

In the words of Heinrich Graetz, in his *History of the Jews,* Manasseh "was not a genius, but . . . was possessed of the right proportion of sagacity and narrowness, of tenacity and flexibility, of self-denial and vanity which were absolutely essential." Although his theological and philosophical writings are not of permanent literary interest, they were valuable in enabling him to become an influential political negotiator and in establishing their author as the outstanding representative of Jewish views in the contemporary scholarly world.

The Conciliator was translated by E. H. Lindo in 1842. *Hope of Israel,* translated by M. Wall in 1650, together with *Humble Addresses* and *Vindiciae Judaeorum,* appear in Lucien Wolf's *Menasseh ben Israel's Mission to Oliver Cromwell* (1901).

ABOUT: Graetz, H. History of the Jews; Roth, C. Life of Menasseh ben Israel, *also,* History of the Jews in England; Slotki, J. J. Menasseh ben Israel, His Life and Times; Waxman, M. A History of Jewish Literature; Wolf, L. Menasseh ben Israel's Mission to Oliver Cromwell.

M. R.

MANOELLO GIUDEO. See IMMANUEL BEN SOLOMON

*MANRIQUE, JORGE (1440?-1479), Spanish lyric poet, was probably born in Paredes de Nava (Palencia), the fourth child of Don Rodrigo, Count of Paredes and Grand Master of the Order of Santiago, and of his first wife, Doña Mencia de Figueroa. Jorge was the nephew of Gómez Manrique and the grand-nephew of the Marquis of Santillana, both poets of the late Middle Ages. Born in the midst of the civil discord characteristic of the reign of Henry IV, Jorge Manrique supported first Don Alonso, brother of the King, then Queen Isabella against her rival claimant to the throne, La Beltraneja. As much devoted to arms as to letters, Manrique defended Calatrava against the Marquis of Villena in 1475, and one year later helped sustain the siege of the fortress of Uclés against Villena and the Archbishop of Toledo. In 1479, three years after the

* män rē′ kä

595

death of his father, Manrique died in battle near the gates of the fortress of Garci-Muñoz and was buried in the church of the convent of Uclés.

Manrique's fame rests on his *Coplas* on the death of his father, but he also composed love poems in the style of his period. Many of his *canciones* and *dezires,* written in the courtly Provençal manner, were dedicated to his wife, Doña Guiomar de Castañeda, great-granddaughter of the Chancellor Ayala. In his amatory and allegorical works Manrique is scarcely to be distinguished from other *Cancionero* poets of the fifteenth century, yet his obsession with death and a certain *tedium vitae* pervade even his frivolous poems. It is this meditation on death which produced the *Coplas por la Muerte de su Padre don Rodrigo,* composed after November 11, 1476, when Don Rodrigo died in Ocaña. Hernando del Pulgar painted Don Rodrigo as a fearless warrior and in the *Coplas* he emerges as the medieval ideal of the Christian Knight.

The poem, consisting of forty-three twelve-stanza lines, begins with general considerations on the vanity of life, the fugacity of beauty, youth and power, the brevity of all temporal joys. Then, much in the manner of Villon's *Ballade des Dames du Temps Jadis,* Manrique evokes examples of historical figures close to his period and asks repeatedly, "What has become of them?" Once powerful, they have all disappeared, leaving but their names: "Where shall we seek them now? Alas!/ Like the bright dewdrops on the grass/ They passed away." The poet then describes his father's many virtues, comparing him to the great heroes of antiquity. This eulogy is followed by the concluding section of the poem which consists of a dialogue between Death and Don Rodrigo. Death, after summoning the Knight, assures him that he has earned both the life of fame and the true eternal life because of his heroic deeds against the Moors. With resignation and Christian stoicism, Don Rodrigo serenely consents to die and the poem ends with a prayer and the lines, "And though the warrior's sun has set/ Its light shall linger round us yet/ Bright, radiant, blest."

The sources for the *Coplas* are numerous: The Book of Job, Ecclesiastes, Boethius, contemporary moralists, and poets *inter alia.* The content, then, is not original. The expression, however, is so impeccably elegant and noble that Menéndez y Pelayo has said that the poet expressed "as no one else what everybody has thought and felt."

The *Coplas* have been universally praised and Lope de Vega stated that they "deserved to be written in letters of gold." The oldest edition of the *Coplas* seems to be that of the *Cancionero* of Fray Íñigo de Mendoza (1480). The *Coplas* have been imitated, glossed, translated, and even set to music. A critical edition, edited by R. Foulché-Delbosc, was published in 1912; A. Cortina's edition of the *Cancionero de Jorge Manrique* followed in 1929.

In 1824 a fragmentary translation into English, attributed to Richard Ford, appeared in Edinburgh. In 1833 Henry Wadsworth Longfellow did a superb translation of the poem in its entirety.

ABOUT: Krause, A. Jorge Manrique and the Cult of Death. [In Spanish—Salinas, P. Jorge Manrique; o, Tradición y Originalidad.]

B. P. P.

*MANZONI, ALESSANDRO FRANCESCO TOMMASO ANTONIO (March 7, 1785-April 28, 1873), Italian novelist and poet, was born in Milan. His mother, Giulia Beccaria, was the daughter of the distinguished jurist and political economist Cesare Beccaria. Some biographers believe that Giulia's husband, Pietro Manzoni, was not actually the father of Alessandro, the real paternity being attributed to the poet Giovanni Verri. Pietro and Giulia, incompatible from the outset, were legally separated in 1792. Lonely for his mother, estranged from his putative father, young Alessandro spent several unhappy years in religious schools in Brianza and Lugano, ending at the Nobles' College in Milan. Introverted and shy from his earliest years, Alessandro suffered from the bullying of fellow students, a treatment that may well have conditioned that sympathy for the downtrodden and hatred of brute force that characterized him throughout his life. At the same time during these years he acquired solid preparation for his literary career, mastering the Latin and Italian classics and composing his first verses.

Manzoni had no more formal education after the age of sixteen. For the next four years he lived in Pietro Manzoni's house in Milan, enjoying a free and easy-going life, imbibing the social and intellectual pleasures of the city. Among his earliest literary influences were the works of Alfieri, who condemned absolutist government, and Parini, who in his satire *Il Giorno* glorified the hardworking peasant at the expense of the dandified noble. Manzoni's first poem, "Del Trionfo della Libertà," in its violent anti-

* män dzŏ′ nĕ

MANZONI

clericalism, revealed his youthful radicalism and rebellious spirit. It was circulated in manuscript among friends, but did not actually reach publication until 1878, five years after his death.

Meanwhile his mother Giulia had run off to Paris with a new lover, Count Carlo Imbonati. In 1805 the youth was invited to join them. By a quirk of circumstances, Alessandro found upon his arrival in Paris that his mother's lover had died, leaving him a considerable property. One of his earliest poems is an elegy to the memory of his benefactor, composed on classical models (1806). For the time being Alessandro settled in Paris, where his mother introduced him to the then influential circle of the *idéologues*. Here too Alessandro met the historian Claude Fauriel, who became one of his most intimate friends. His financial fortunes were further enhanced by the death of Pietro Manzoni, who made Alessandro his heir.

In 1808 a most crucial event occurred in Manzoni's life—his marriage to Henriette Blondel, aged sixteen, daughter of a Genevese banker, a union that was brought about by Giulia, whose financial affairs were managed by the elder Blondel. Though Henriette had been brought up in the Calvinist faith, her religious devotion is believed to have led Alessandro back to the Catholic faith in which he had been born. Whatever the circumstances, he underwent a ceremony of re-conversion at the hands of a Jansenist priest in 1810, in which his wife and his mother joined him. Henceforth Manzoni's life and work were to

be imbued with his fervent Catholicism, in which a strain of Jansenism can often be observed.

After his marriage Manzoni settled down to a life of semi-retirement, divided between his house in Milan and a country retreat in Brusiglia. The immediate literary result of his conversion was the composition of the five poems known as the *Inni Sacri* (Sacred Hymns), begun in 1812. Four of the *Inni* are devoted to Feasts of the Church: "Il Natale" (Christmas), "La Passione" (Passiontide), "La Risurrezione" (Easter), and "La Pentecoste" (Whitsuntide), while the fifth, "In Nome di Maria," is dedicated to the Madonna. All the poems employ Biblical imagery, sometimes transplanting entire lines from Scripture, and are noted for the graceful lucidity with which profound religious feelings are expressed. Many consider the most moving of the *Inni* to be "La Pentecoste" (1822), actually the last to be composed, for the sense it conveys of spiritual renovation, and for its stress not on the splendor of the Church but rather on its place in the lives of the humble —an anticipation in this respect of *I Promessi Sposi*.

Other poems of this period arose out of contemporary political events. "Marzo, 1821," inspired by the Piedmontese Revolution, could not be published until 1848, after the Austrian rule was over. "Il Cinque Maggio" (1822) is a moving ode on the death of Napoleon Bonaparte (whom Manzoni had glimpsed briefly as a youth in a theatre in Milan). Here the poet betrays ambivalent emotions, at once paying tribute to "the sublime profane greatness" (in Croce's words) of the dead hero, while bowing to God's justice in destroying such supervening pride. This conflict between sacred and profane values—between morality and politics—informs Manzoni's two tragedies derived from Italian history, *Il Conte di Carmagnola* (1820), set in fifteenth century Venice, and *Adelchi* (1822), set in the period of the war between the Lombards and the Franks during the eighth century.

All of Manzoni's preoccupations at this time—the psychology of religious conversion, the current revolt of the Carbonari against the Austrian occupation, his researches into Italian history—culminated in his masterpiece *I Promessi Sposi* (*The Betrothed*, 1825-27), a panoramic novel set in Milan and environs during the early seventeenth century, the period of the Spanish occupation. Beginning with the enforced separation of two peasant lovers, Renzo and Lucia, by the machinations of a lecherous Spanish nobleman, *I Promessi*

Sposi gradually expands into a *tableau vivant* of Northern Italy during the Counter Reformation and the breakup of feudalism. Before the hero and heroine are eventually joined in holy matrimony they have been victimized by moral corruption and anarchical government in high places, and involved in famine, war, and plague—allowing their creator ample opportunity to probe the subtle workings of evil in both church and state, as well as the effects of irrational passion in both the individual conscience and the collective crowd.

I Promessi Sposi elevated Manzoni immediately into the front rank of literary fame. Setting forth all too vividly the chaos and injustice issuing from foreign rule, and implicitly looking forward to the Risorgimento, the book had immense patriotic appeal. Among foreign critics it drew especially enthusiastic praise from Goethe and Edgar Allan Poe, but in general Manzoni's fame abroad waned as the nineteenth century progressed. *I Promessi Sposi* is still regarded by the Italians as their greatest novel, its characters as deeply embedded in the popular mind as those of Verdi's operas, but outside Italy it remains one of the great neglected masterpieces. This is so for two reasons: it has had inferior translations, and it is likely also to disappoint the expectations of the casual reader. Although it has been compared variously with the works of Voltaire, Scott, and Tolstoy it actually defies classification. It is really not so much a love story or an historical novel as a moral fable, showing forth the devious but sure ways of Providence—the moral responsibility of each individual soul, the inevitability of punishment for the wicked, the ultimate reward that comes to the pure in heart.

I Promessi Sposi was the last important work from Manzoni's pen, but it occupied a good part of his life. In 1840 he published it in revised form, completely rewritten in the Tuscan idiom (consistent with his patriotic interest in a unified language). Along with this revised version appeared *La Storia della Colonna Infama*, an expansion of the gruesome episode of the plague in the novel. A really readable and complete English translation did not appear until Colquhoun's in 1951, and this event should enhance its reputation in England and America.

Manzoni lived apart from society for most of his life. Anti-social by nature, he detested crowds (his terrifying analyses of mob psychology are among the outstanding episodes of *I Promessi Sposi*). His acute hypochondria made him indulge himself in such ec-centricities as weighing his clothes several times a day, increasing or diminishing his attire with fluctuations in the weather. But as his fame spread, his home became a pilgrimage for visitors from abroad—notably such English admirers as Newman and Gladstone. After the Liberation from Austria in 1848, in which one of his sons played a part, he accepted election as a Senator. He had more than his share of domestic sorrows. The death of his wife in 1833 was followed by the loss of several of his children and his mother. In 1837 he was married again to Teresa Borri, the widow of Count Stompa, who also pre-deceased him. During his lifetime he lost seven of his nine children. In 1873 the death of his eldest son, Pier Luigi, brought on a stroke from which he never recovered. He died of cerebral meningitis at the age of eighty-eight, and was honored by a state funeral. The first anniversary of his death was marked by a performance of the *Requiem* composed for the occasion by one of Manzoni's most fervent admirers, Giuseppe Verdi, who had once praised *I Promessi Sposi* as "one of the greatest books ever to emerge from the human brain . . . a consolation for mankind." In the esteem of his countrymen Manzoni holds a place second only to Dante.

I Promessi Sposi was first translated into English by the Reverend Charles Swan in 1828. This was followed by an anonymous translation in England in 1834, and two in the same year in America by Andrews Norton and G. W. Fetherstonhaugh. Another anonymous translation appeared in England in 1844. Daniel J. Connor translated it once more in 1924, in an imitation of seventeenth century idiom. The definitive translation of Archibald Colquhoun, based on the Italian edition of M. Barbi and E. Ghisalberti (1942), was first published in 1951, and was reprinted in 1956. The *Inni Sacri* and *Cinque di Maggio* were translated (as *The Sacred Hymns* and *The Napoleonic Ode*) by the Reverend Joel Foote Bingham in 1904. Other versions of these poems are those of the Earl of Derby in *Translations of Poems Ancient and Modern* (1862) and William Dean Howells in *Modern Italian Poets* (1887). *The Linguistic Writings of Alessandro Manzoni* were translated by Barbara Reynolds in 1950. *The Column of Infamy*, translated by K. Foster and J. Grigson, was published in 1964. An excellent one-volume edition of the entire *Opere* was published as volume 53 of *La Letteratura Italiana* in 1953, under the editorship of R. Bacchelli.

ABOUT: Colquhoun, A. Manzoni and His Times; Croce, B. European Literature in the Nineteenth Century; Everett, W. Italian Poets since Dante; Jarrett-Kerr, M. Studies in Literature and Belief; Papini, G. Laborers in the Vineyard; Pritchett, V. S. Books in General; Wall, B. Manzoni. [In Italian—see studies by D. Budini, B. Croce, A. Galletti, E. de Michelis, A. Pellizzari, F. de Sanctis, G. Vidari. See also the collected papers of the third Congreso Nazionale di Studi Manzoniani, 1958.]

R. A. C.

*MAPU, ABRAHAM (January 10, 1808-October 9, 1867), Hebrew novelist, was born in Slobodka, Lithuania, to the family of an impoverished schoolmaster. He received the exclusively Talmudic education which was characteristic of the time, but from his early years the rich imaginary world of the Jewish mystic engrossed his imagination. Married at seventeen, Mapu barely supported himself for many years as an itinerant private teacher, living away from his family for much of the time under harsh and underpaid conditions. During this period, lasting until 1848, he steeped himself in Western studies, learning without aid Latin, French, and German. An accidental friendship with a Catholic priest gave him access to a world of books alien to his environment. Mapu was influenced by French romantic literature, which, together with the ideals of the Russian Jewish Haskalah (Enlightenment), provided the intellectual background for his novels. Mapu's appointment in 1848 to teach in a government school for Jewish children in Kovno greatly eased his circumstances; a wealthy brother in Paris also extended financial aid. However, several years later Mapu's wife died and his own health began to fail. On a trip to Paris for medical treatment, he fell ill in Königsberg and died there on the Jewish Day of Atonement.

Mapu was the first Hebrew novelist. His main published works are *Ahavat Zion* (The Love of Zion, 1853); *Ashmat Shomeron* (The Guilt of Samaria, 1865); *Ayyit Zavua* (The Bloody Vulture, 1857-61). The first two are novels of Biblical history in the period of the kings and prophets. Their plots are extremely involved, and the delineation of character is superficial in black and white moralistic terms: all is dictated by accident and coincidence. However, both novels are written in a charming, fresh poetic idiom which imitates Biblical style. The descriptive passages are noteworthy, and the entire effect is that of an idyllic romance. It is hard to appreciate today how great was the effect of these novels upon young Hebrew readers of the later nineteenth century. They contrasted his small town and restricted way of life, its unhealthy economy of petty trades and crafts, with the freedom, breadth, and naturalness of Biblical life. Mapu clearly implied that a rejuvenated, westernized Jewry should find its ideal in the Biblical world. This idealization of ancient Palestine was an early literary influence upon the Zionist movement. For their literary merit and historical significance,

* mà poō′

Mapu's two Palestinian idylls have few rivals in Hebrew literature. *Ayyit Zavua*, exemplifying the Haskalah attack on the abuses of Jewish life, is less successful; the plot is involved and the characters are merely types.

Abraham Mapu turned from his own harsh life to an imaginary Biblical world. His generation, and later ones, found in his vision an inspiration for a Jewish national revival.

English translations of *Ahavat Zion* have appeared under several titles—as *Amnon, Prince and Peasant*, translated by F. Jaffe (1887), as *In the Days of Isaiah*, by B. A. M. Schapiro (1902 and later reprints), as *Sorrows of Noma*, by J. Marymont (1919). Schapiro's translation was republished as *The Shepherd Prince* (1922).

ABOUT: Patterson, D. Abraham Mapu (Studies in Modern Hebrew Literature, I); Slouschz, N. The Renascence of Hebrew Literature; Waxman, M. A History of Jewish Literature, III.

L. P. G.

*MARAGALL Y GORINA, JUAN (October 10, 1860-December 20, 1911), Catalan poet and essayist, was born in Barcelona. Son of a comfortable middle class family, he studied law, graduating from the University of Barcelona in 1884, and practiced his profession some years later. In 1890 he began to work on the *Diario de Barcelona* (Barcelona Daily), which remains one of the most important papers in Catalonia. In it Maragall published articles and essays through which he brought to the Catalan people of his day the most important writers of Europe, such as Ibsen, Nietzsche, Pushkin, and even Emerson among the Americans. As a chronicler he dealt with political, social, aesthetic, patriotic, and even sentimental and abstract themes. As a thinker he was associated with the so-called Generation of 1898, having been one of the few writers who during the Spanish-American War recognized the indisputable power of the United States as opposed to the military weakness of Spain. His concern with finding the moral and spiritual roots of his country unites him to the writers of '98. His sincerity as a poet led him to simplicity of form, rhythmical audacity, metrical irregularity, and a verbal freedom as in the poetry of Unamuno, whom he admired, and at the same time brought him close to certain formal and spiritual aspects of the modernist movement realized by Rubén Darío. As a writer of prose, in addition to his chronicles in the *Diario de Barcelona*, he is remembered for his *Elogis*, especially the "Elogi de la Paraula" and the "Elogi de la Poesía."

* mà rà gàl′ ē gō rē′ nä

599

In 1895 he published his first volume of *Poesies,* which further confirmed the fame he had already enjoyed in 1881 when he won a prize in the Jocs Florals of Barcelona. The book was followed by *Visions y Cants* (1900), replete with legendary and historical figures; *Les Disperses* (1904), in which one observes the influence of Goethe, whom Maragall translated and admired; and *Següencies,* published in the year of his death, in which appears the most famous of his poems, "Cant Espíritual." As a translator he gave to Catalan literature some of the best versions of Goethe *(Ifigenia a Taurida, Elegías Romanas,* fragments of *Faust,* songs and poems); Novalis *(Enric d'Ofterdinger);* some of the Homeric hymns and the odes of Pindar. He also introduced the works of Schlegel and Amiel.

Maragall represents one of the highest peaks of the great literary movement which was initiated at the beginning of the nineteenth century in Catalonia and which is known by the name of the *Renaxenca.* Within his epoch, if Verdaguer stands as the popular and religious poet, Maragall figures as the outstanding intellectual poet, the one who put Catalonia into contact with the great European cultures. He counseled his young friends not to trust to instinct or talent, and he recommended the reading of the classics. He was venerated, as the contemporary Catalan poet Jose María de Sagarra says, "for his spiritual tremolo, his transcendent vision of all things, and the febrile generosity of his soul."

The "Cant Espiritual" was translated into English by Thomas Walsh (1942), and the "Himne Iberic" by B. G. Proske (1938).

ABOUT: Dos Passos, J. Rosinante to the Road Again; Triadu, J. Anthology of Catalan Lyric Poetry. [In Spanish—see studies by M. de Montoliu, M. Serrahima, P. Javier de Arenys; see also prologue by M. Sants Oliver in Obres Completes of Maragall. In French—see study by J. A. Bertrand.]

E. F.

*MARCABRU (fl. 1130-1150), Gascon lyric and satiric poet, is said by tradition to have been found in front of a great man's door. The details of his life are few and most of our knowledge comes from his poems. He is also said to have been associated with the older poet Cerçamon; he certainly wrote a poem to Jaufré Rudel; and he was at various times in many courts of southern France and in Spain. A vicious poem against Lord Aldric of Vilar, who had refused to receive him at Blois and who had commemorated his

* màr kà brü'

refusal in verse, shows the type of satire which prompted the story—related in his *vida,* or biography—that he was murdered by an (unknown) castellan of Guienne in retaliation for some political poems. More than fifty poems of Marcabru survive. There are few *canzons* or courtly love-songs among them.

Marcabru shows greater variety of theme and treatment than any other of the poets writing in Provençal. He admires *fin amors* or courtly love and writes of it well, praising particularly the quality of *mezura* or restraint. But he nevertheless regards the troubadours as the instruments of wicked folly, since they spread the doctrine of adulterous love and corrupt morality. The decline of morality is one of his favorite themes and he sees love as basically *fol' amors,* mad love, which destroys men and women alike. He paints a gloomy picture of the adulterous man who is nevertheless a jealous husband and whose attempts to set a guard over his wife often lead to disaster. He is particularly fond of certain similes, e.g., the neglected garden to typify the state of the world. Indeed, his use of metaphor and vocabulary is often so violent and unusual that he is considered the first to practice *trobar clus,* or deliberately obscure verse. He also differs from his contemporaries in that many of his works are poems of low life. He describes, often in the coarsest detail, exploits of the lowest society of his day and reveals a knowledge of this milieu which could have come only from personal acquaintance. Some of his forms are unusual variations of courtly themes. For example, he has a romance in which a starling brings a love declaration to his obviously very accessible lady. He also has a *chanson de femme* on a lady left behind by her Crusader lover and one of the best of all Provençal *pastourelles,* in which the peasant girl shows far more wit than the nobleman who finds her in a wood and attempts to seduce her. With all his coarseness, Marcabru was a man of deep piety; and several of his songs are appeals, certainly sincere, to contemporaries to go on a Crusade for God. Marcabru shows little of the virtuosity in verse forms of the later troubadours, but the wide variety of his subject matter and his lack of affectation make him extremely interesting.

E. Hoepffner's *Les Troubadours dans Leur Vie et dans Leurs Œuvres* (1955) contains a good account of Marcabru with texts translated into modern French. An earlier edition is *Poésies Complètes du Troubadour Marcabru,* edited by Dejeanne (1909). Selections appear in Raymond T. Hill and Thomas G. Bergin's *Anthology of the Troubadours.*

ABOUT: Valency, M. In Praise of Love.

W. T. H. J.

*MARCH, AUZIAS (c. 1397-March 3, 1459), Catalan poet, was born at Gandía in the kingdom of Valencia, the son of Pere March V, poet and lord of Beniarjó, and of Elionor de Ripoll. As the son of a nobleman he received a courtly education in the use of arms, in the seven liberal arts, and in rather severe moral attitudes. After his father's death in 1413, he represented his family at the royal sessions (Corts) of 1415 in Valencia. In 1418 or 1419 he was knighted. Under Alfonso V of Aragon he participated in the expedition of 1420-21 against Sardinia and Corsica. After a period at home in Gandía, he joined another Mediterranean expedition in 1424, winning recognition for his heroic action. From 1426 to 1429 he served the king as Chief Falconer in the city of Valencia, after which he retired to his feudal estate of Beniarjó, exacting the homage due him from his Moslem and Christian vassals and attending periodically the Corts of Valencia.

With the death of his mother in 1429, Auzias March became the guardian of his deaf-mute sister Peyrona. In 1437 he married Isabel de Martorell, daughter of the noble Francesch de Martorell and sister of Johanot Martorell, author of *Tirant lo Blanch*. One short-lived son may have been born of this union. Isabel died in 1439, and less than four years later (February 26, 1443), March married Johana Scorna, who brought him an even more impressive dowry. The couple lived in Valencia, where Johana died after twelve years of apparently childless matrimony. Auzias March had more than one mistress during his life, and left at least four illegitimate children. Yet, despite his free exercise of feudal prerogatives, he was not a Don Juan, but a methodical, almost bourgeois administrator of his and his wives' estates. The complex Moorish art of irrigation sustained the production of his sugar cane plantations, and his wealth accumulated.

Against this domestic background we must place a very different sort of activity, the writing of poetry. Yet this too was part of his own family tradition, and belles-lettres had long held prestige in the eyes of the Catalan nobility, always close to the courts of Provence. Auzias March's poetry is in fact the culmination of a Catalan tradition which stemmed from the earliest troubadours and from the poetic academy of Toulouse. March was influenced first of all by the slavishly Toulousan Jocs Florals of Barcelona. About 1430 he seems to have barely begun his own more independent line of development by replacing Provençal words with Catalan ones,

* märk

even though the elaborate rhymes and the old concepts of courtly love and its ennobling powers remained unchanged. This early period, lasting until perhaps 1445, continues the *trobar clus* tradition of Arnaut Daniel.

What more and more distinguished March's poetry from the Provençal tradition is its essentially philosophical drive, based, like the *dolce stil novo* of Italy, upon scholasticism. No doubt the *De Arte Honeste Amandi* of Andreas Capellanus was of great help to him. But March obviously worked directly with the texts of Aquinas and Aristotle, and in so doing he was following the example set by Dante, whose *Divine Comedy* he knew and admired. March was concerned primarily not with the theology, but with the psychology, of the scholastics, their theory of the senses and the passions, which lent itself so easily to poetic allegory. He also drew heavily upon the *Nicomachean Ethics;* his poetry is often overtly didactic, and its philosophic sources are not concealed.

Woman, in the poetry of March's second period, ceases to be an intangible ideal and source of virtues, and is seen as quite human, capable of sin and of causing her lover to sin. One of March's greatest philosophical concerns is the distinction between virtuous and sinful love. When his lady (someone else's wife) dies, he is therefore obsessed with the question of her salvation; and if she is damned, so no doubt is he who has contributed to her damnation. Such questions as these, presented in the complex terminology of scholastic rationalism, underlie the highly original lyrical mode of Auzias March, giving it a rigorously and painfully conscientious tone of self-analysis. His greatest poem is the *Cant Espiritual*, a marvelous confession in which he asks God for death: not the mystic death of a contemplative, but death as the end of sinful life on earth. If he could die at this moment of sincere contrition, he would not only be assured of salvation, but also saved from inevitable future sins on earth; and yet, he is afraid of death.

As Auzias March grew older, falconry became more and more his chief diversion. His poetry was already famous in Castile, where another *grand seigneur* and poet, the Marquis of Santillana, knew him as "a great troubadour and a man of quite lofty intellect." In October of 1458 he called a lawyer to draw up his will, providing masses for himself and wives, money for his illegitimate children and his slaves (one to be set free), and mourning clothes to be worn by his household. Four months later he died at his home in the city of Valencia.

The influence of his poetry reached a high point in sixteenth century Spain; it was imitated by Boscán, Garcilaso, and Herrera; it was translated by Jorge de Montemayor and El Brocense. It has since been compared to that of Donne and Baudelaire; if Catalan were more widely read and if his poems were not so very difficult, one might expect a revival of March during the present-day cult of *Angst.* The critical edition of March's *Obras,* edited by Amadée Pagès, appeared in two volumes (1912-14).

ABOUT: Brenan, G. Literature of the Spanish People. [In French—Pagès, A. Auzias March et Ses Prédécesseurs, Commentaire des Poésies d'Auzias March.]

E. L. R.

*MARCHENA Y RUIZ, JOSÉ (1768-1821), Spanish poet, was born in Utrera, Seville, and studied in Madrid and Salamanca. A lesser cleric, he abandoned the calling because of his Voltairian ideas. He left for France, in the midst of the French Revolution, under the aegis of Murat, and later of the Girondists, who were persecuted by Robespierre. As secretary of General Moreau he served in the Rhineland in 1801. He returned to Spain as the secretary of General Murat in 1808, only to be thrown into prison by the Inquisition. However, thanks to the efforts of the French Murat, he was dramatically freed. Marchena became the chief archivist of the Ministry of the Interior, but departed for France upon the defeat of the invaders. He returned to Madrid in 1820, unnoticed and unappreciated, owing to nationalistic feelings against General Murat and the French.

His command of Latin was perfect, making it possible for him to forge (by way of literary play) passages from Petronius and Catullus with such perfection that the famous German Latinists of the day often were deceived into believing that they were reading newly-discovered original fragments. The hoax required the famous Professor Eichstaedt of the University of Jena to uncover the charming fraud.

The ironic story is told that Marchena one day came upon a bookseller named Fauli deeply engrossed in the reading of Fray Luis de Granada's *Guía de Pecadores* (Guide for Sinners). Marchena commented that he himself strongly desired not to read the book since it was so convincing, but that he could not help reading and re-reading it since he knew no more admirable book in the Spanish language.

* mär chä′ nä ē rōō ēs′

Marchena's literary contribution includes translations into Spanish of Molière's *L'École des Femmes* and *Tartuffe* and of works by Voltaire. His translations of Rousseau's *Julia o la Nueva Eloísa* and *Emilio* circulated widely in Spain at the beginning of the nineteenth century, at a time when the Spanish novel was in a deplorable literary state. He is the author of an original tragedy entitled *La Polixena,* and is generally regarded as the one who made known the works of Ossian in Spain. Although a well-known critic of the latter eighteenth century, he is remembered today more for his journalistic articles, many of which were of political content. He is thought to have written the immortal sonnet (which has been attributed to many other Spanish writers) "A Cristo Crucificado." His poem "Epístola a José Lanz sobre la Libertad" retains a permanent place in Spanish poetry.

He is often included historically under a grouping referred to as the "Sevillian School" and sub-titled "semi-Voltairian clergy." Others who fall into this classification are Arjona, Reinoso, José María Roldán, Lista, Núñez y Díaz, Félix María Hidalgo, Manuel María Mármol, and Blanco White.

The collected works, *Obras,* were edited by Menéndez y Pelayo, 2 vols., in 1896.

ABOUT: Revue de Litérature Comparée, XVI (1936). [In Spanish—see Introduction by Menéndez y Pelayo in Obras.]

L. S.

MARCHI, EMILIO DE. See DE MARCHI, EMILIO

MAREUIL, ARNAUT DE. See ARNAUT DE MAREUIL

*MARGUERITE D'ANGOULÊME, Queen of Navarre (1492-December 21, 1549), French writer and patroness of letters, was born at Angoulême. The elder sister of Francis I and future grandmother of Henry IV was raised at Amboise under the guidance of her mother, Louise de Savoie, a Bourbon. Her education was particularly rich for her times, for she learned Latin, Spanish, and Italian, and later studied Greek and Hebrew. Her father was nephew of Charles d'Orléans and died when Marguerite was four years old. Francis and she grew up under difficult conditions, materially and morally.

* mär gē rēt′ däʀ gōō lĕm′

At the age of seventeen, Marguerite was married by Louis XII to the royal prince Charles, the Duc d'Alençon, who died in 1525 as a result of the disaster of Pavia. For two years, she corresponded with the zealous Bishop of Meaux, Guillaume Briçonnet, who was working with Lefèvre d'Étaples to reform his diocese; this correspondence between them opened her mind to mystic preoccupations which prepared her to understand and enjoy the philosophy of Plato and the Platonic love later associated with her writings.

In 1527 the charming and kind Marguerite married Henri d'Albret, Count of Béarn and King of Navarre, who was eleven years younger than she and for whom she held a true affection. In 1528 she bore a daughter. Henceforth, though often in Paris where she held great influence at the court, she lived principally at Nérac where she made of her court a cultural center and a refuge for humanists suspected of heresy. Among these were Macrin, Melanchthon, and Sainte-Marthe, as well as Marot, Calvin, and Lefèvre d'Étaples who went there to die.

Marguerite de Navarre's last years were saddened by her brother's insistence that her daughter Jeanne d'Albret be married to the Duc de Clèves. She was further deeply grieved by Francis' death in 1547 and mourned him in long allegorical and mystic poems. She died at Odos in Bigorre.

A woman of exquisite sensitivity and universal curiosity, Marguerite was a true humanist. She knew Italian literature particularly well and was one of the rare sixteenth century authors to have studied the *Divine Comedy,* by which she was inspired to write her *Dialogue in the Form of a Nocturnal Vision* in *terza rima.* She also read Petrarch and Boccaccio.

In Marguerite's *Heptaméron,* never completed but similar in plan to Boccaccio's work, ten persons meet each other at the hot springs of Cauterets, in the Pyrenees. Forced by rain to take refuge in an abbey, they spend their mornings attending mass and reading the Scripture and their afternoons telling stories. Each "day" or story is preceded by a prologue and followed by moral reflections. The storytellers, five men and five women, are real persons, even including Marguerite herself, recognizable through their anagrammatic names.

Though Marguerite declares in her prologue that the stories are true, her sources are readily evident: Boccaccio and Castiglione, the fabliaux, the *roman* of the *Châtelaine de Vergi,* and the oral tradition. Like Boccaccio, she uses the frame of one day per story and she applies all the genres: the short story, witty Gallic story, the dramatic *nouvelle,* and the philosophical story. However, the work itself is original. What distinguishes Marguerite de Navarre's tales is that even in the lighter ones she shows a concern for moral order; moreover, she is particularly interested in showing the difficulties of lovers. She prefers to portray the more general emotions of the human heart and is, therefore, the best psychologist of the Renaissance, as well as its first analyst of the soul.

From her work emerges an elevated and original concept of love as an irresistible force, noble and legitimate if conforming to moral law. Love is not simply carnal desire, but, founded in beauty and virtue, it can exist respectably even outside of marriage as a form of love of God. "Never has man loved God perfectly until he has loved perfectly a creature of this world," Marguerite states, revealing the Platonic and Christian ideas which comprise her philosophy and which render the *Heptaméron* more important today as a document of contemporary immoralities serving the purpose of morality rather than a masterpiece of style. Actually, despite the richness of vocabulary, the writing is unmusical and monotonous.

About 1540 Marguerite de Navarre became the full apostle and promoter of the Platonic doctrines her *Heptaméron* forecast. By her advice and counsel she became the soul of the Platonic movement of divine love, the radiation of divine good to all beings. She had already published three works of religious inspiration: the *Dialogue, The Mirror of a Sinning Soul* (1531), and a re-edition of the *Mirror* with some new poems (1533). From 1540 on, the principal Platonic publications were the work of her friends, sometimes at her command. Her *Les Prisons,* not discovered until this century, is a long poem in testimony of the soul first imprisoned by profane love and then released by the Holy Scriptures to attain pure and divine contemplation.

From her later life we have many spiritual songs, allegorical comedies, and sentimental poems which she brought together in 1547 under the title *The Marguerites of the Marguerite of Princesses.* Together with her *Heptaméron,* published after her death, the *Marguerite* lacks the artistic quality for endurance. Nevertheless, by her human sympathy and intelligence, by the influence of her Platonism on the Reformation, by her protection of the great reformist writers and by her own works, Marguerite de Navarre was among the most remarkable and important writers of her time.

The *Heptaméron* was translated into English by W. K. Kelly (1855), by Arthur Machen (1886 and many times reprinted), and by George Saintsbury (1894).

ABOUT: Neely, R. S. Marguerite, the Sister and Wife of Kings; Putnam, S. Marguerite of Navarre; Saintsbury, G. *Preface to* Heptaméron (1894); Williams, H. N. The Pearl of Princesses: the Life of Marguerite d'Angoulême. [In French—see studies by L. Febvre, P. Jourda, E. V. Telle.]

R. P. C.

MARGUERITE OF NAVARRE. See MARGUERITE D'ANGOULÊME

*MARIANA, JUAN DE (1536-1624), Spanish historian, theologian, and political economist, was born in Talavera de la Reina. He was the natural son of Juan Martínez de Mariana, Dean of the Collegiate Church of Talavera, and received his education at Alcalá. In 1544 he entered the Jesuit order and was ordained in 1561. Between the years 1561 and 1574, he spent his time preaching and lecturing in Rome, Paris, and Flanders. The rest of his life was spent in Toledo where he died.

Mariana is perhaps the greatest Spanish historian; his monumental *Historia de España* (a total of thirty volumes), which he worked on during the last thirty or forty years of his life, was first published in Latin in 1592, and later, after many corrections and additions, was translated and published by him in Castilian in 1601. This history begins during the dark origins of primitive Spain and ends with the death of Fernando el Católico (1516). He did not dare go further "so as not to hurt anyone by telling the truth, nor to fail in his duty by lying." Another of his famous epigrams deals with Alfonso el Sabio, of whom he says, "Alfonso lost his kingdom while gazing at the stars." To the latter saying is attributed much of the historical injustice which has been done to Alfonso.

Mariana's history is less critical than one would expect of a scholar of his ability. He rarely draws from original sources. Like his master Livy, he considered history an art, not a science; and he was unwilling to subject a good story to critical analysis. His leading characters (most of them legendary) indulge in set orations, after the manner of ancient historians.

His history is important culturally, because for many generations it was the world's al-

* mä ryä′ nä

most exclusive source of knowledge of Spanish history. The book went into several editions, was widely translated in Europe, and became a fertile source book for subsequent historians. In a lesser work, *De Monetae Mutatione,* he attacks the custom of debasing the currency. An independent and original thinker, Mariana anticipated Jean Jacques Rousseau in his *De Rege et Regis Institutione* (1598), holding that no government can be legitimate which is not based on justice and popular consent. He even went so far as to admit the justification of regicide under certain extreme circumstances.

Far in advance of his time, Mariana was a defender of liberal principles. He believed in the power of reason and was opposed to violence and religious intolerance. In one of his treatises dealing with the popular theatre of his time, *Tratado contra los Juegos Públicos,* he points out that the response to a play is influenced by various artistic tricks rather than by the formal unity of classical aesthetics. Lope and his contemporaries must have accepted the moral condemnation implicit in Father Mariana's *Treatise* as a sage appraisal of the special appeal and attraction of the popular theatre of their time.

Obras del Padre Mariana appears in BAE XXX, XXXI. His *History of Spain* was translated into English by J. Stevens in 1699.

ABOUT: Laurez, J. The Political Economy of Juan de Mariana. [In French—Cirot, G. Mariana Historien. In German—Köhler, G. Juan de Mariana als Politischer Denker.]

L. S.

MARIE DE FRANCE (fl. c. 1160-1190), French poet, was the author of a considerable amount of narrative verse, but very little that is definite is known of her life. She herself says that her name is Marie and that she is from France but the combination "Marie de France" was first used by Claude Fauchet in the sixteenth century. There is therefore no justification for the attempts made to prove that she was of the French royal family and, in particular, that she was the daughter of Eleanor of Aquitaine and hence identical with Marie de Champagne. She did, however, have close connections with the English court. She dedicated her *Lais* to a "noble, brave, and courtly king," and it is almost certain that this was Henry II of England. Her *Fables* were dedicated to "Count William, the most valiant of this kingdom," probably William Longsword. What is quite definite is that Marie, wherever she was born, spent most of her life in England. Characters in her works often refer to the sorrows of a stranger in a strange land, and these may have been personal feelings. There is no evidence of the reasons for her stay nor of the assertion that she lived in an English convent.

Marie de France was a well-educated woman and very proud of her learning. She states in the epilogue to the *Lais* that she had intended to translate something from the Latin but had decided that her reputation would be better served by putting into verse some of the stories she had heard. Her *Fables* are French versions of an English Aesop, her *Espurgatoire de St. Patriz* is taken from a Latin *tractatus*. She was thus acquainted with Latin, French, and English, and her works are full of evidence of knowledge both of the Latin classics and the vernacular works of her own time, e.g., the *Roman de Thebes*. Her use of the *Brut* of Wace shows that she must have written the *Lais* after its completion in 1155. External evidence also establishes that the *lai* "Eliduc" at least must have been completed before 1167 and that the *Purgatory of St. Patrick* was written about 1190. The *Fables* were probably written in between.

The *Lais* are from every point of view the most important of Marie's works. They are narrative poems, most of which seem to have taken their subject matter from Celtic sources, transmitted probably through Breton storytellers. A good example of this type is "Guigemar" (or "Gugemor" or "Guingamor"). In this story a knight wounds a deer who is in fact a fay. The arrow rebounds and wounds him in the thigh. On being told that he can be cured only by suffering the pains of love, he sets out alone in a boat, lands at a castle, falls in love with the young wife of an old husband, is discovered, and has to leave. Before parting the lovers swear to love no one who cannot undo certain knots in their clothes. When they next meet the lady is in the power of Meriaduc, for whom Guigemar is fighting. He changes sides, kills Meriaduc, and marries the lady. The fairy motifs, the magic elements, the recognition symbols are typical. Another famous *lai* with Celtic background is the "Chèvrefeuil" or honeysuckle, an incident in the Tristan story. Others, such as "Le Fresne" (related to Chaucer's Clerk's Tale) are of different origin. Altogether there are twelve *lais*, all told in sprightly rhyming octosyllabic couplets. Most but not all have a love theme in some form. The *Purgatory of St. Patrick* is a reworking of the legend according to which St. Patrick visited Purgatory and brought back an account of what he saw. It is didactic in purpose, as are the *Fables*, based on the version of Aesop attributed to King Alfred.

The poems (*Recueil des Lais, Fables et Autres Productions . . .*) were translated into modern French and edited by Bonaventure de Roquefort in two volumes, 1819-20. The standard edition by K. Warnke appeared in 1885, 1900, and (revised and corrected) 1925. A. Ewart published another edition in 1944. Twelve of the *Lais*, with a good critical introduction, were edited by E. Hoepffner in 1921. English translations were made by Edith Rickert in *Seven Lais of Marie de France* (1901) and E. Mason in *French Medieval Romances from the Lays of Marie de* France (1924). The *Espurgatoire Saint Patriz of Marie de France* was translated by E. A. Jenkins, with text of the Latin original (1903).

ABOUT: Holmes, U. T. A History of French Literature to 1350. [In French—see study by E. Hoepffner; also J. Bédier *in* Revue des Deux Mondes (1891).]

W. T. H. J.

*MARINO (MARINI), GIOVAN BATTISTA (October 18, 1569-March 25, 1625), Italian poet, was born in Naples, one of six children of Gianfrancesco, a well-to-do lawyer, who wished his son also to be a lawyer. After taking legal training Marino refused to practice and for this, as well as for his dissolute way of life, he was driven from home. For the next two years, 1590-92, a wanderer, he quickly acquired influential patrons and by 1592 was already reciting his verses in salons and academies. *Canzone de' Baci* was a success in manuscript (1592) and was soon translated into French and Spanish. Marino borrowed from friends, acted as editor for a collection of poems, and in 1596 became secretary to Prince Conca of Naples. He studied in the Prince's library and art gallery and wrote much poetry, including *La Sampogna*, a series of voluptuous mythological and pastoral writings published later in 1620.

B. Crémieux (*Revue de Paris*, 1935) says that Marino was to a supreme degree a *visuel* who tried to transfer to poetry the images and color of painting. His *La Galeria* (begun in 1600, published 1620) is a series of landscapes and portraits in which he seeks to rival the stylized, mythological paintings of his time.

In 1598 he was arrested on a charge of immoral conduct but was released through the Prince's intercession. When he was again imprisoned in 1600, this time for falsifying documents to aid a friend in trouble, influential friends assisted him to escape to Rome. Befriended there by Cardinal Piero Aldobrandini, nephew of the reigning pope, Marino attempted to publish his poems but since, in both Parma and Rome, they had already been denounced to the Inquisition as lubricious he

* mä rē' nō

was compelled to issue them in Venice, as *Rime* (1602). Two later volumes of his lyrical poems appeared as *La Lira* (1608, 1614). He accompanied Aldobrandini on his travels and in 1608 went with him to Turin where he stayed. In favor at first with the ruler, Carlo Emanuele I of Savoy, he composed *Il Letto*, to celebrate the marriage of the Infante of Savoy. He quarreled with a rival poet, Gaspare Murtola, against whom he had directed some savagely satirical poems, *La Murtoleide* (published 1619). Owing to the intrigues of Murtola, Marino was imprisoned for other satirical writings said to be aimed at those in high places, and he remained in prison from April 1611 to June 1612, during which time he worked on prose writings that he published later, *Dicerie Sacre* (1614). He was released following appeals from all the powers of Europe, for his fame had spread, but was soon again involved in frequent disputes.

He left for the sanctuary of Paris in April 1615, taking with him the twelve completed sections of *Adone* to which he would add eight more. He stopped at Lyon to print a poem, *Il Tempio*, in honor of Marie de Medici to raise money for his journey. He later said that in Paris he received a pension from the royal treasury, but he lived in a small hotel and was perhaps assisted by Italian friends in Paris. The *Adone*, on which he had spent twenty years, was published in April 1623, dedicated to Louis XIII with a preface by Chapelain, and soon after Marino left Paris. He went to Venice to issue an edition of it and then returned to Rome under Aldobrandini's patronage. The pope died and an old friend was elected, but the censorship remained rigid. Disillusioned, Marino left Rome to retire to Naples in May 1624 and he died there the following year of an infection following a surgical operation.

Adone continued to be reprinted as late as 1789 but thirty years later was no longer discussed. In his *Literature of the Italian Renaissance* J. B. Fletcher declares that Marino's new poetics were intended to "startle —to say ordinary things in an extraordinary manner—and that his lyrics express emotional impressions, intending, however, to teach that 'immoderate pleasure terminates in pain.'" The sensual pictures of the *Adone* in their encyclopedic variety took some 42,000 lines.

His age recognized him as the supreme living poet of Italy and he was much translated, for his work mirrored all the tendencies of his age. In England the metaphysical poets felt his influence and he was admired by Cleveland, Cowley, and Milton. Some of his lyric poems were translated by Samuel Daniel in 1600, and by Thomas Stanley in 1651. *La Stragli degli Innocenti* of 1632 was translated, Canto I, as *Suspicion of Herod*, by R. Crashaw, 1646; and in full as *Slaughter of the Innocents by Herod*, by R. T. in 1675. Sir Edward Sherburne translated "Forsaken Lydia" in his *Salmacis*, 1651. New Italian editions have appeared: his letters, 1912; his poetry, 1913; his *Adone*, 1922; his poetry and prose, 1930.

ABOUT: Mirollo, J. V. The Poet of the Marvellous: Giambattista Marino; Modern Language Review, August 1930. [In Italian—see studies by A. Borzelli, C. Culcasi, M. Menghini.]

M. A. W.

*MARIVAUX, PIERRE CARLET DE (February 4, 1688-February 12, 1763), French dramatist, essayist, and novelist, born in Paris, was the son of the director of the mint at Riom, where he spent part of his childhood. He moved early in the elegant Parisian circles of Fontenelle, Montesquieu and Mme de Tencin, where a survival of "preciosity" was represented by such favorite literary works as Fénelon's *Télémaque*. At twenty-nine, he married a woman who became his devoted and beloved wife, bore him one daughter, and died six years later. He was ruined in the Law bankruptcy, but found contentment in his creative activities and his many friendships. Marivaux's full activity began with his essays in the *Nouveau Mercure*, followed shortly by his own review, the *Spectateur Français*, an idea borrowed in 1722 from Addison. His essays had an enormous success and earned for him the title of "the modern Theophrastus." As he wrote: "Through my inner nature, everything for me is matter for reflection." He observed the people in their everyday activities and preoccupations; he told banal anecdotes or noteworthy news events, and created realistic and satirical but sympathetic portraits.

Marivaux's thirty-four plays cover the long period from 1706 to 1757, but his thirteen best fall within the years 1720 and 1738. Most of them were written for and performed by the Italian Theatre in Paris, a troupe which had been exiled by Louis XIV but returned in 1715 under the Regency. The Italian technique, deriving from the *commedia dell' arte*, observed various formulae and used a rather fixed set of actor-characters, each with formalized attributes; a propensity for plots dependent on disguises was combined with a flippant manner that hid such inner feeling as might be implied. The leading actress of the troupe, Sylvia, became Marivaux's close friend, and for her he created many of his finest rôles. In *Arlequin Poli par l'Amour* (1720) one finds the typical actors, such as Arlequin, Trivelin, and Sylvia; the interven-

* mà rē vŏ′

MARIVAUX

whereby they are in love yet unable to express their feelings and, in trying to do so, embroil the situation by a gallant play of words. The disparity of thought and word, as of seriousness and gaiety, rises from an inner dualism, and is often actually clarified by the disguises. Certain aspects of Marivaux's technique appear later in Musset and in Giraudoux.

Marivaux's plays met with constant failure, sometimes justified, but usually abetted by his many enemies, such as Le Sage, Crébillon *fils,* Voltaire, and in general the Encyclopedists, jealous of his success in the salons, and imperceptive to his discretion and delicacy. He never listened to criticism by revising his work, and public opinion was usually favorable to him. Of the entire French theatrical production between Molière and Hugo, only his and that of Beaumarchais have had continued success.

Marivaux's novels are important monuments in the rise of the modern genre. His *Pharsamond* was a mere parody of *Don Quixote.* He began *La Vie de Marianne* in 1728, and continued it sporadically over some thirteen years during which he composed fifteen plays, published two journals, and began a new novel. He undertook his *Marianne* in order to illustrate the rise and triumph of love. His principal character no doubt symbolizes his love for his wife and daughter and for Sylvia. She is important, however, as the first well-rounded person in French prose fiction. On the one hand, she is formalized as the epitome of chastity, sensitivity, and coquetry; but her elusive nature is well stated by one of the characters: "What a dangerous girl you are!" The novel is of equal interest for its variety of characters and of social milieux, and for its reflections on the morality of social customs, free from judgments of good and evil. The novel stands close to Richardson and Prévost in the movement toward Rousseau and Fielding.

Marivaux's second significant novel, *Le Paysan Parvenu* (1735-36), eclipses the later parts of *La Vie de Marianne* in power. It devotes less attention to pathos and to analysis of inner feeling, but its principal character, Jacob, is more disquieting than Marianne through his total sincerity in a long series of questionable adventures and easy amatory conquests. Again there is no question of good or evil, though Marivaux may on occasion betray his own opinions. The scope of the subject of *Le Paysan Parvenu* recalls the works of Stendhal and of Proust.

Marivaux's last days were calm. He was elected to the French Academy, despite Voltaire's rage, and was greeted there in signifi-

tion of the Fairy replaces the customary disguises, since her magic, like any other misunderstanding, is powerless against true love. The important element of the "awakening of love" gives the play its title: from a stupid boor, Arlequin is suddenly transformed to a perceptive lover. *La Double Inconstance* (1723) is much richer: in its inclusion of a pseudo-oriental abduction, in its portrait of the egotism and corruption of the imaginary court, and in its exposure of the false code of honor which cannot replace virtue. The cultural significance of this play appears further in the treatment of a theme of disparity of social conditions. In Marivaux's masterpiece *Le Jeu de l'Amour et du Hasard* (1730) the four disguises are especially disquieting since they affect the actors' attitudes to the point of suggesting that love is a mere hallucination. *Le Legs, Les Fausses Confidences,* and *L'Épreuve* are almost equally esteemed; one might further cite *Le Petit Maître Corrigé* (1734) for its observations on social conditions. The originality of Marivaux's theatre is evident if one examines the principal titles of the preceding period, such as Le Sage's *Turcaret* (1709). Marivaux belongs rather to the tradition of Dancourt's *Le Chevalier à la Mode* (1687) and that of the *comédie larmoyante* of La Chaussée's *Le Préjugé à la Mode* (1735). In certain ways he looks forward to the middle class dramas of Diderot, but his outstanding trait is his analysis of love, expressed in the style known as *marivaudage.* This term refers to the false situations in which the actors find themselves,

cant words: "It is not so much your works that have led us to choose you, as our esteem for your way of life, your kind heart, and the friendliness of your character." In his new station, Marivaux undertook "Academic" writings; he found comfort in a second marriage with a rich spinster, and took an interest in the course of political events.

The twelve volumes of the *Œuvres Complètes* of Marivaux (1781) became ten in the revised edition of 1825-30; his *Théâtre Complet* (1946) includes the important preface by J. Giraudoux. The English translations began during his lifetime: of his *Pharsamond* in 1750 by Lockman, and three plays in S. Foote's *The Comic Theatre* of 1762 (*The Legacy, The Generous Artifice, The Double Infidelity*). His *Marianne* became *The Virtuous Orphan* in 1784.

ABOUT: Jamieson, R. *Marivaux, a Study in Eighteenth-Century Sensibility*; McKee, K. N. *Theater of Marivaux* (with an Appreciation by J.-L. Barrault); Tilley, A. *Three French Dramatists*. [In French—see studies by M. Arland, G. Deschamps, G. Larroumet, C. Roy, P. Trahard.]

F. J. C.

*MARMONTEL, JEAN FRANÇOIS (July 11, 1723-December 31, 1799), French novelist and dramatist, born in Bort (Limousin) of modest parents, studied with the Jesuits at Mauriac with the apparent intention of joining their order. In 1743 his ode *Invention de la Poudre à Canon* was refused by the Floral Games at Toulouse, but brought him to the attention of Voltaire, who called him to Paris two years later. There, in difficult financial circumstances, Marmontel tried pastoral and epic genres until he won several prizes of the French Academy and achieved his first fame. He turned to the theatre and classical tragedy, and his *Denys le Tyran* was well received in 1748. Mme de Pompadour favored him with the inspectorship of buildings at Versailles and helped him launch a new series of the *Mercure de France,* in which he took sides with the Encyclopedists in attacks against Rousseau's paradoxes on the theatre.

Marmontel's principal works follow this new orientation. In the salons he read his *Contes Moraux,* published in the *Mercure* and collected in 1761 and later; in this genre he continued the traditions of Prévost, and the success of these tales was in large part instrumental in his election to the Academy in 1763. In this body he furthered the cause of the Encyclopedists, and, in 1787, collected his contributions to their great work as the *Éléments de Littérature.* Appearing close in time to the critical writings of La Harpe,

* mår mȯn tĕl'

Marmontel's articles reaffirmed sound classical tenets of beauty and good taste, and reappraised modern literature in a traditional reference of measure and superior critical perception. More elaborate imaginative prose works such as *Bélisaire* and *Les Incas* began to show a new kind of local color, but also included attacks against intolerance and slavery. Marmontel championed Italian music, preferring Piccinni to Gluck in articles in the *Supplément* of the *Encyclopédie* in 1776, and writing libretti with "récitatif obligé" for Grétry and Piccinni; Marmontel's greatest success in this field was his *Didon* (1783).

Marmontel became professor of history at the new *lycée,* in the company of La Harpe, but his most significant work during his last years was his *Mémoires d'un Père,* first published after his death, in 1804, in an altered and imperfect state. Besides the significant autobiographical content, one finds here information on his contemporaries, the salons, the *Mercure,* and the musical quarrel, and fine pictures of provincial life, including those of childhood memories.

English translations from Marmontel include *Belisarius* (1767), *Moral Tales* (1781), *The Incas* (1797), and *Memoirs* (1805), most recently entitled *Autobiography* (2 vols., 1878, with preliminary essay).

ABOUT: [In French—see studies by G. Delterme, S. Lenel, M. Roustan.]

F. J. C.

*MAROT, CLÉMENT (1496-September 10, 1544), French poet, born in Cahors, was the son of Jean Marot, one of the last of the "rhétoriqueurs." His father instructed him in the art of poetry, primarily in the older techniques and in 1506 took him to Paris, where Clément received an indifferent education. He found employ with several noblemen and in 1518 entered the service of Marguerite de Navarre, at that time Duchesse d'Alençon. He succeeded his father in 1526 as valet to King Francis I and, in the atmosphere of the court which was strongly oriented toward Italian ideas, made great progress toward the new poetry. Marot's first work was strongly circumstantial, and its quality lies in its very personal appeal. Smitten by Anne d'Alençon, Marguerite's niece, he composed graceful verse of courtly type, elegies and anagrams for the unattainable lady. His many epistles ask for money or for some new employ. In his "Épître au Roi" (1532) he complains of having been robbed and wittily suggests that the King come to his aid.

* mà rŏ'

MAROT

Marot's association with Marguerite concerns more dangerous matters of religion, for he moved close to Protestantism in hostile surroundings. In 1525, by his own account, he was imprisoned for overly ostentatious eating of bacon during Lent. Again in prison in the following year, he composed his "Épître au Roi pour le Délivrer de Prison." But even his charming familiarity with Francis I could not save him in 1534 when he issued one of the anti-ecclesiastical "posters," and he took flight first to Ferrara, then, when he was again threatened, to Venice. His Italian sojourn turned him markedly toward Petrarchist verse forms, and he composed the first sonnets in the French language.

Another appeal to Francis I, and a solemn abjuration of his religious errors, brought Marot back to the court in 1537. Once more his misguided fervor inspired him, and he translated a few Psalms; the clergy, worried at any tendency to interpret the Bible, threatened him again and forced him to flee. In Geneva, Marot was encouraged by Calvin, and he published his *Cinquante Psaumes en Français*, thus inaugurating the Huguenot Psalter. Ever plagued by his indiscretions, and this time caught playing dice, he left Switzerland for Turin, and died in unknown circumstances.

Marot's place in the evolution of French poetry is illustrated by his own gradual orientation away from the devices of the "rhétoriqueurs" toward Petrarchist genres. He retained parts of his early techniques of complex rhyme schemes, conceits, and punning

word-plays. He looks back in many ways to a medieval tradition—witness his modernization of *Le Roman de la Rose* (1529) and his edition of Villon (1532)—but his immediate links are with Marguerite de Navarre, Rabelais, and Budé, and his translation of Ovid sets him in the tradition that led to the Pléiade.

The real poetic and personal qualities of Marot's epistles and epigrams explain his influence on La Fontaine and even on Voltaire. He was scorned in turn by Ronsard and by the classical writers, and, during the romantic movement, again left aside as the Pléiade was recognized for its lyrical qualities. His *Élégies* exemplify a renewed interest in his work. Of these, twenty-two appeared in 1534 and twenty-six in the *Œuvres* of 1544. Partly baffled by inability to identify the lady in question, critics and readers preferred the romantic legends of the loves of Maurice Scève and of Ronsard; but close study of these poems has drawn attention to their exquisite charm and feeling. The more "Marotic" verse of Marot still appeals, in the witty and ironical epistles, and in such gems as "Frère Lubin" or the many "blasons."

The series of editions of Marot's poetry attests his popularity despite the hostility of the critics. His *Œuvres* were frequently published during his century, and the earliest of the good editions appeared in six volumes in 1731. The *Œuvres Complètes* began to appear in several volumes in 1824, and the best text, of 1868, was reprinted in 1920. Among the distinguished Renaissance scholars of today who have taken special note of him one must mention both Plattard and Villey.

ABOUT: Morley, H. Clément Marot and Other Studies; Tilley, A. Literature of the French Renaissance. [In French—see studies by O. Douen, H. Guy, P. Jourda, C. A. Mayer, J. Plattard, V. Saulnier, J. Vianey, P. Villey.]

F. J. C.

*MARSILIUS (MARSIGLIO) OF PADUA (c. 1280-1342/3), Italian political theorist and writer, is known to have studied medicine and law, but his active career is surrounded by conflicting evidence as a result of his extreme hostility to the temporal power of the Church and his possible relationship to the rise of the reformed sects. He served in the Imperial armies, then studied at the University of Padua and finally in Paris, where he was reputed to have been Rector of the University in 1312, to have taught medicine, and to have studied theology. Pope John XXII, at Avignon, appointed Marsilius canon in Padua, and in 1318 he was at the

* mär sĭl′ ĭ ŭs; mär sē′ lyō

court of Emperor Louis, whose side he took aggressively against the Pope. In 1324, in collaboration with Jean de Jandun, he composed the *Defensor Pacis,* which he took to the Emperor in Germany. This considerable tract defines the rights of Emperor and Pope. With rigorous logic, it abandons the older theocratic notions, sets God in the background, and attributes the rights to legislation to the people, who are free to enact and modify as they see fit. The executive power is vested by them in the Emperor, whose duty is to further their common will. As applied to the Church, the bishops are similarly mere legislators, and their only separate and independent function is the administration of the sacraments; hence the Pope has power only to convoke councils, his decrees are in no way binding, and the Church can own nothing as such.

John XXII immediately directed bulls against Marsilius, and reproached the Emperor for receiving and encouraging this heretic; both Marsilius and Jandun were excommunicated, but the Emperor, pleased with the new political notions, deposed the Pope and named Marsilius as Imperial Vicar. Little more is known of his life; the Emperor abandoned him in October 1336, and the report that he became bishop of Milan is false.

Marsilius left several other writings: *De Translatione Imperii Romani,* and a consultation on the divorce of John, son of the King of Bohemia, *De Jurisdictione Imperatoris in Causa Matrimoniali,* in which a new order of imperial authority is postulated. He was opposed by Alvarus Pelagus in the latter's *De Planctu Ecclesiae.*

ABOUT: English Historical Review, XXXVII (1922). [In Italian—Battaglia, F. Marsiglio da Padova e il Pensiero Politico Medievale; Labanca, B. Marsiglio da Padova Riformatore.]

F. J. C.

*MARTELLO (or MARTELLI), PIER IACOPO** (April 28, 1665-May 10, 1727), Italian poet and "literato," was born in Bologna. The poetry written by Giambattista Marino (see sketch above) was the stylistic model for all seventeenth century poets, and Martello's first sonnets and verses written for special occasions were largely reflections of the Marinist manner. At the age of thirty-three Martello was invited to join the Society of the Arcadians, his Arcadian pen-name being Mirtilo Dianidio. In the preface to

* mär těl' lõ

the *Canzoniere* published in 1710 he expresses himself as critical of the preciosity of Marinism. The six books of ottava rima entitled *Gli Occhi di Gesu,* composed in 1707, are an expression of sincere religious feeling and contrast strongly with Marino's *Adone,* a heroic poem in praise of sensual love.

In 1708 Martello was sent to Rome as part of the embassy from Bologna to Pope Clement XI. He remained in Rome for ten years, except for brief returns to Bologna and a short trip to Paris in 1713. During his residence in Rome, Martello participated wholeheartedly in the life of the Arcadians, involving himself in the vivacious literary disputes of the day. He satirized this way of life in *Il Secretario Cliternale al Baron di Corvara* in 1717, but with more than a touch of kindness in his humor; he was known as an essentially good-natured poet. His nine essays in *Della Poetica,* published in 1710, show him a faithful interpreter of the pastoral style to which the Arcadians were devoted, even to the sacrifice of the poetic liberty which his own inspiration sometimes required.

During the years from 1697 to 1699 Martello wrote several moralistic melodramas, also in accepted *seicento* style. He was an admirer of the Greek classic theatre, and also of the French. The latter, however, he studied with a somewhat mechanistic approach, seeking only to account for the success of Corneille and Racine. He attributed their greatness to their use of language, particularly the alexandrine verse. This French manner he adapted for Italian (in such tragedies as *Ifigenia in Tauris, Sisara,* and *Perselide*), inventing the so-called Martellian verse which had many imitators in succeeding centuries.

Critical comment on Martello's tragic theatre agrees that he did not have the required tragic sense. Strong sentiments are not well expressed by him: the grandeur of the Roman world escapes him; Biblical themes suggest to him idylls; his Iphigenia is an Arcadian nymph. But this approach was, of course, very pleasing to his contemporaries. He rebelled against the laws of dramatic unity. He was original and inclined to mix comedy and tragedy, bringing the spirit of the seventeenth century salons and the sometimes slightly vulgar humor of the Bolognese to his drama. For this reason his comedies are superior to the tragedies.

In the last part of his stay in Rome, Martello composed *Radicone,* a benevolent antimonastic satire. He returned to Bologna as a member of the Bolognese senate in 1718.

His most significant literary success after his return was *Il Femia Sentenziato* in 1724, a happy polemic written in hendecasyllables. He now turned his hand to a more grandiose theme, *Carlo Magno,* seventeen cantos of which he completed before his death in his native city shortly after his sixty-second birthday.

The consensus is that *Femia Sentenziato* and *Carlo Magno* are Martello's best works because in them he wrote more according to his own inspiration. His talent for gentle satire is gracefully displayed in *Carlo Magno,* animating the heroism and the weaknesses of the knights and warriors in the story. This talent characterizes Martello among the numerous poets of the first part of the eighteenth century in Italy.

ABOUT: De Sanctis, F. History of Italian Literature. [In Italian—see study by M. Carmi.]

E. DE P.

MARTÍNEZ DE LA ROSA, FRANCISCO (March 10, 1787-February 7, 1862), Spanish writer and statesman, was born in Granada. His father was Francisco Martínez Berdejo and his mother Luisa de la Rosa. He became a disciple of his fellow *granadino* José Joaquín de Mora. By the extraordinarily early age of twenty-two, Martínez de la Rosa was a professor of philosophy at the University of Granada. Then, and even more so later in life, he showed himself to be familiar with European thought, particularly French and English, and in favor of the *juste milieu* in all fields of human endeavor. He was essentially an eclectic. All his life he was a well-intentioned and honest man. Martínez de la Rosa's political life was extremely active. A deputy in 1813, he supported the liberal Constitution of 1812 and hence, upon the return of the despotic Ferdinand VII to power, he was imprisoned on El Peñón de la Gomera, off the coast of Morocco, from 1815 to 1820. The rebellion of Riego freed him and brought him back to Spain where he once more served as a deputy from 1820 to 1823. The restoration of absolutism by the French armies in 1823 caused him to flee to France where he remained till 1831. In 1834, under the regency of María Cristina, he became prime minister. Later, he served as ambassador to France and twice as ambassador to Rome. A liberal all his life, he represented moderate tendencies in politics.

In addition to his distinguished and somewhat adventurous life in politics, he had a distinguished if less exciting life as an author.

* mär tē′ nāth thā lä rō′ sä

His earliest tragedies, such as *La Viuda de Padilla* (1814) and *Moraima* (1818), have nothing in particular to recommend them and indeed are no new departure from the neoclassic principles then in vogue in many literary circles. As late as his *Poética* (1827), this is still so. His truly romantic plays begin with *Hernán Pérez del Pulgar* (1834) and *Aben-Humeya,* which he wrote first in French and which was staged in Paris in 1830 and later translated by the author and performed in Spain. His masterpiece, however, was *La Conjuración de Venecia* (1834), which is usually considered the first successful romantic drama in Spain. These last plays are romantic in all the ordinarily accepted senses of the word. In *Doña Isabel de Solís* (1837) Martínez de la Rosa tried his hand at the Walter Scott type of romantic novel so popular at that time throughout Europe, but the result was little more than a reflection of the English master. However, in *Edipo* (1829), he did succeed in writing one of the best classical tragedies in nineteenth century Spain.

Martínez de la Rosa was a Knight of the Order of the Golden Fleece, Director of the Royal Spanish Academy of Language, a member of the Academies of San Fernando, History, and Bellas Artes. He was also a member of many foreign academies. He died in Madrid.

His *Obras Completas,* five volumes, were published in Paris in 1845, his *Obras Dramáticas,* three volumes, in Madrid, 1916, and there is an edition of several of his plays, edited by Sarrailh in 1933, in the Clásicos Castellanos series. He has not been extensively translated into English, but Longfellow in his *Poets and Poetry of Europe* (1888) gave us "The Alhambra" and J. Kennedy in his *Modern Poets and Poetry of Spain* (1860) translated the "Anacreontic."

ABOUT: Shearer, J. F. The Poética and Apéndices of Martínez de la Rosa: Their Genesis, Sources, etc. [In Spanish—Rebello da Silva, L. A. Memoria sobre la Vida Política y Literaria de Martínez de la Rosa; Sosa, L. de Martínez de la Rosa. In French—Sarrailh, J. Un Homme d'État Espagnol: Martínez de la Rosa.]

R. E. O.

*MARTORELL, JOANNOT (c. 1415-c. 1480), Catalan novelist, was born in Valencia, the son of the noble Mossèn Francesch de Martorell. Very little is known of his life, except that he was in London from 1438 to 1442. There he frequented aristocratic circles and was, perhaps, made a knight of the Order of St. George.

An incident which may shed some light on his character took place while he was in Lon-

* mär tō rěl′

611

don. A certain Johan de Montpalau, of Valencia, broke his engagement to Martorell's sister, Damiata: as quickly as mail service permitted, Martorell challenged him, by letter, to a duel. After much correspondence, filled with chivalric points of honor and including a witty criticism of Montpalau's prose style, Martorell persuaded the King of England to set a time and place for the combat. But Montpalau did not appear.

The literary fame of Martorell is due entirely to his novel *Tirant lo Blanch*, which he began writing about 1460. It is a romance of chivalry, but in addition it reflects events and attitudes of the author's own life and time. The hero Tirant goes from Catalonia to England to attend a royal wedding, where he distinguishes himself in the jousts and tourneys. Many of the events of this part of the novel derive from the fourteenth century English poem *Guy de Warwick* (in Catalan, *Vàroych*). But they are translated into a fifteenth century social setting, with no supernatural or even very unrealistic events. In fact, the author takes pains to explain in detail the functioning of ingenious mechanical gadgets based on mirrors and pulleys; here, in the words of a great Spanish critic, are clear signs of a positivistic, not a chivalric, spirit.

From England, Tirant returns to the Mediterranean, where he helps to liberate Rhodes and to defend Constantinople against the Turks, finally marrying the Emperor's daughter. This portion of the novel is based on Muntaner's chronicle of an authentic Catalan hero of the thirteenth century, Roger de Flor, who actually did save Constantinople and marry a princess.

The first three parts of *Tirant lo Blanch* (the fourth and last is by another hand) were dedicated by Martorell to Prince Fernando of Portugal; in his dedication he acknowledges his English sources and mentions a Portuguese version. Another source is Lull's handbook of chivalry; a great deal is made of following the proper chivalric and courtly rules. There are also scenes which clearly embody Boccaccio's sensualism and comedy. All of these elements are fused by an attitude toward chivalry which anticipates the irony of Cervantes: the very name of the gigantic Sir Kyrieleison; the damsel whose skin was so white that, when she drank red wine, one could see it trickle down her throat; the eyes of Tirant himself, fastened not upon his lady's feet, her teeth, or even her eyes, but upon her "two little apples of paradise which seemed to be made of crystal."

Tirant lo Blanch was first published in Valencia in 1490. A Spanish version appeared in 1511 and an Italian version in 1538. It influenced both Ariosto and Cervantes. The latter, in *Don Quixote,* Part I, Chapter 6, has the priest praise it as unique among romances of chivalry for its realistic details: "In it knights eat, and sleep, and die in their beds, and draw up wills before they die. . . ."

ABOUT: Vaith, J. A. Tirant lo Blanch: A Study of Its Authorship, Principal Sources and Historical Setting. [In Spanish—Riquer, M. de, prologues to recent Catalan and Castilian editions; Alonso, D. "Tirant lo Blanc," Novela Moderna *in* Revista Valenciana de Filologia (1951).]

E. L. R.

MARX, KARL (HEINRICH) (May 5, 1818-March 14, 1883), German political philosopher, was born in Trier, the son of an enlightened and well-to-do lawyer. Although both his father and his Dutch mother were descended from generations of Jewish rabbinical families, Marx's father had been converted to Protestantism. Consequently, Marx never held any particular racial or national feeling but always considered himself a European. After attending local schools, where he distinguished himself as an excellent student, he studied law, political science, philosophy and history at the universities of Bonn and Berlin from 1835 to 1841. In Berlin he came under the influence of Hegelian philosophy and joined the left wing Young Hegelian movement, which included such men as Bruno Bauer, Arnold Ruge, David Friedrich Strauss, and Ludwig Feuerbach. After completing his Ph.D. at the University of Jena in 1842, Marx became editor of the *Rheinische Zeitung* in Cologne, a liberal newspaper suppressed in 1843. This same year Marx married Jenny von Westphalen, the daughter of a family friend, and the couple moved to Paris. The marriage was a happy one and resulted in six children, of whom only three survived childhood. In Paris Marx devoted himself to the study of socialism and communism and edited with Ruge the short-lived journal *Deutsch-Französische Jahrbücher* (1843). He also met a wealthy manufacturer's son, Friedrich Engels, who became his lifelong friend, collaborator, and supporter, and after Marx's death the publisher of his manuscripts.

Moving to Brussels in 1845, Marx published with Engels a book entitled *Die Heilige Familie,* an attack on his former friend Bauer, who, Marx considered, had fallen into error in his thinking with regard to socialism. A second polemical volume, *Misère de la Philo-*

MARX

sophie (1847), was written in answer to the work *La Philosophie de la Misère* by the French socialist P. J. Proudhon. Gaining in prominence, Marx was commissioned by the London Center of the Communist League to compose a definite statement of its aims and beliefs. The work appeared as *Manifest der Kommunistischen Partei* (1848), a historic document of tremendous force, succinctness, and clarity which has achieved world-wide significance.

Following the revolution of 1848, Marx was recalled to Cologne to serve as editor of the reformed communist newspaper *Neue Rheinische Zeitung*. Here he published a series of articles which were later collected by Engels under the title *Die Klassenkämpfe in Frankreich* (1895). The government again suppressed the newspaper and expelled Marx from Prussia. He settled permanently in London, where he studied political theory and economics and took active part in organizing the Workingmen's Association. The First International of the Workingmen's Association was held in London in 1864. Many of his major writings were produced during this period including *Der Achtzehnte Brumaire des Louis Bonaparte* (1852), *Zur Kritik der Politischen Oekonomie* (1859), *Das Kapital* (vol. I, 1867; vols. II and III published by Engels 1885-94), *Der Bürgerkrieg in Frankreich* (1871), *L'Alliance de la Démocratie Socialiste et l'Association Internationale des Travailleurs* (1873) and *Zur Kritik des Sozialdemokratischen Parteiprogramms von Gotha* (1875). Marx also wrote

newsletters for Horace Greeley's *New York Tribune* (1852-61) and articles for *The New American Cyclopedia*. His writings brought little income, and the family lived in extreme poverty. Engels assisted his friend financially and from 1869 on supported the family entirely by a gift of £350 a year. The strain of his work and constant poverty undermined Marx's health. He died as the result of a sudden collapse and was buried in Highgate cemetery, London. Although fame came slowly to Marx and at the time of his death he was little known outside the circle of his followers, he became, in the words of Sidney Hook (*Marx and the Marxists*), "one of the most influential figures in human history," who "inspired the greatest mass movement of all times." Isaiah Berlin (in *Karl Marx*) states: "No thinker in the nineteenth century has had so direct, deliberate and powerful an influence upon mankind as Karl Marx."

Marx was primarily a revolutionist who was interested in ideas only as a means of influencing the course of events. By nature he was a Promethean personality, incorruptibly and fervently dedicated to his cause, utterly convinced of its righteousness and therefore intolerant of criticism and contradiction. He was endowed with a powerful, incisive, unsentimental, and thoroughly practical mind. His method was developed on sound intellectual principles in terms of feasibility of achievement. He termed himself a "scientific" socialist to separate himself from the "utopian" socialists.

Marx's purpose was to create a social philosophy for the rising proletariat. Although he regarded the course of history as proceeding logically according to timeless economic laws toward a predetermined goal (socialism), his aim by intervening in this normal evolution was to accelerate the inevitable historical process. His view of history, the famous theory of economic or dialectical materialism, was derived directly from Hegel's philosophy as modified by Feuerbach, who transferred Hegel's concepts from the realm of the ideal into the realm of materialism. By materialism in the Marxian sense is meant the production and distribution of goods, for Marx believed that the ideas current in a society are determined by social and economic relations. Thus capitalism as an institution was not an end-result of economic development but a phase in the continuing evolution of modern society. To Marx private ownership was the source of all evil in society, by producing class distinctions, class interests, and ultimately class struggle. As he stated in the opening of *Manifest der Kommunistischen*

Partei: "The history of all hitherto existing society is the history of class struggles." Marx applied Hegel's dialectic, which had considered nations as the effective units of social history, to the class struggle, and envisioned the solution to the problem not in creating equality among classes but in the total abolition of classes. This, he felt, would result from the social revolution which was inevitable in terms of the dialectic, because of the contradictions inherent in a capitalistic economy.

As yet there is no translation into English of Marx's complete works. A collection of essays entitled *The Paris Commune* appeared in 1902. *Selected Essays* were published in 1926 by H. J. Stenning. A. Lee published the *Essentials of Marx* in 1933-34. *Manifest der Kommunistischen Partei* was translated by S. Moore in 1888 as *Manifesto of the Communists* and by E. and C. Paul in 1930 as *The Communist Manifesto*. *Das Kapital* was translated by E. Untermann (3 vols. 1906-09). Vol I. was also translated by E. and C. Paul in 1930. *The Poverty of Philosophy* was translated by H. Quelch in 1906. N. I. Stone translated *Zur Kritik der Politischen Oekonomie* in 1909 as *A Contribution to the Critique of Political Economy*. H. Kuhn translated *The Class Struggles in France, 1848-50* in 1924. *The Eighteenth Brumaire of Louis Bonaparte* was translated by E. and C. Paul in 1926. M. Lawrence translated *Critique of the Gotha Program* in 1933. *Marx-Engels: Selected Correspondence 1864-95* was translated by D. Torr in 1934.

ABOUT: Barzun, J. Darwin, Marx, Wagner; Beer, M. The Life and Teaching of Karl Marx; Berlin, I. Karl Marx; Bober, M. M. Karl Marx's Interpretation of History; Broder, E. R. Marx and America; Cameron, J. M. Scrutiny of Marxism; Chang, S. H. M. The Marxian Theory of the State; Cole, G. D. H. What Marx Really Meant; Cornu, A. Origins of Marxian Thought; Croce, B. Historical Materialism and the Economics of Karl Marx; Hook, S. From Hegel to Marx; *also* Marx and the Marxists, *and* Towards the Understanding of Karl Marx; Kautsky, K. The Economic Doctrines of Karl Marx; Laski, H. J. Karl Marx; Mehring, F. Karl Marx; Rühle, O. Karl Marx, His Life and Work; Schwartzschild, L. Karl Marx: The Red Prussian; Sprigge, C. J. Karl Marx.

D. G. D.

*MAUPASSANT (HENRY RENÉ ALBERT), GUY DE (August 5, 1850-July 6, 1893), French novelist and short-story writer, was born officially at the Château de Miromesnil, near Dieppe, in Normandy, although one or two other places claim the honor of being his birthplace. His father was an attractive, superficial dandy and an amateur painter; his mother, Laure LePoittevin, a brilliant, strong-willed woman, a neurotic most of her life, exerted the most profound influence on her son, the older of two children. She and her brother Alfred LePoittevin were

* mō på sän′

MAUPASSANT

neighbors and intimate friends of Gustave Flaubert, whose literary and philosophic views were crucial in Maupassant's early development.

The incompatibility of the parents led to their separation when Guy was eleven; the two children were left in the care of their mother, who looked after their schooling until the precocious elder son was thirteen. She then sent him to a seminary near Rouen where he spent three unhappy years before managing to have himself expelled and transferred to a public school there. Here he came under the decisive influence of another intimate friend of Flaubert's, the poet Louis Bouilhet, who gave direction to the young man's strongly discernible literary talents.

His entire childhood and youth were thus spent in Normandy, the province which was to become a favorite setting of his stories and novels. Soon after acquiring his high school diploma, he saw service in the Franco-Prussian war, and this experience was also to be utilized frequently in his work, as was the long ordeal of nearly ten years' employment as a government clerk in Paris, where, owing to the deterioration of the family fortune, he was obliged to earn a precarious living. Those difficult years in no way diminished his determination to become a writer; they merely increased his will to emancipate himself from bureaucratic drudgery and to become an independent man of letters. He gladly submitted to an apprenticeship probably without parallel in the history of French literature: nearly ten years of severe discipline under the intransigent eye of Flaubert. He discarded practically everything he wrote until he felt he was master of his craft, so that the publication of "Boule de Suif" (Ball of Fat) in 1880, a few weeks before Flaubert's death, was a sensational revelation. Since the story appeared in a collection by various hands that included Zola as a contributor, Maupassant became classified as a literary naturalist, despite his militant independence of all schools and the variety of his work.

Ten years of spectacular activity followed: nearly three hundred short stories, a half-dozen novels, three travel chronicles, several plays, a volume of verse, and close to three hundred articles in various periodicals (most of which remain unreprinted to this day), making of Maupassant one of the most productive writers of all time.

Under Flaubert's tutelage Maupassant had tried his hand in a number of fields other than the short-story form; he had written plays and particularly poetry, but the tremendous success of "Boule de Suif" determined the course of his activity thereafter. Fiction was to become his primary vehicle, and for fully three years after that initial success he exploited the short story, publishing tales regularly in the popular press, later giving them permanence in collected volumes (*La Maison Tellier*, 1881; *Mademoiselle Fifi*, 1882; *Contes de la Bécasse*, 1883).

The eight tales in the first volume are so characteristic of the various themes Maupassant was to develop time and again in the course of the next ten years that they may be considered an index of the author's basic approach. "La Maison Tellier" represents the stories which Balzac in his own classification of the *Comédie Humaine* would have termed *études de filles* (studies of prostitutes). In both "Le Papa de Simon" and "En Famille" we have a subject which also recurred with regularity: "the guilty negligence of the father." In "Sur l'Eau" we find one of Maupassant's favorite themes: descriptions of the mysterious and the supernatural. "Une Partie de Campagne" and "Au Printemps" offer an excellent example of the stories devoted to the study of manners, stories whose mainspring is invariably love. "La Femme de Paul" represents another recurring theme: perversion in one form or another. Finally, that superb "Histoire d'une Fille de Ferme" is the prototype of the scores of tales dealing with the peasants of his native province of Normandy.

The three volumes of short stories had clearly demonstrated Maupassant's mastery of that form. To the challenge that he undertake a more sustained piece of work, he answered with his first novel, *Une Vie* (1883) (English translation, 1903), judged by Tolstoy "perhaps the best French novel since *Les Misérables*." As its subtitle "l'humble vérité" (the humble truth) implies, it is the simple tale of the lifelong disillusionment of a pure-hearted woman. His next novel, *Bel-Ami* (1885; English translation, 1891), established the author's reputation as a ranking novelist, and created a worthy successor to Stendhal's Julien Sorel in the character of an unscrupulous exploiter of females. It is a bitter satire of the various segments of a decadent society, particularly the worlds of politics and journalism. A third novel, *Pierre et Jean* (1888; translated as *The Two Brothers*, 1890), is usually hailed as his supreme achievement in that form, embodying as it does the qualities of psychological insight and perfection of form which distinguished his best efforts in the short story. This novel is also important for the prefatory essay on the novel, a major document on the art of the novel, despite its unpretentious tone. Three other novels do not measure up to the above on artistic or other grounds: *Mont-Oriol* (1887; English translation, 1891), *Fort comme la Mort* (1889; translated the same year as *The Master Passion*), and *Notre Cœur* (1890; translated as *A Coquette's Love*, 1890).

In the meantime, as several volumes a year continued to appear under his name, as triumph followed triumph on the literary scene, the author's private life became increasingly clouded by declining health. A confirmed bachelor like his master Flaubert, he was as serious in his pursuit of women as in his concern for the *mot juste*. Afflicted with syphilis at an early age, he was already suffering from it severely when his name first attracted attention. His migraines were so intense he could not even read for days at a time. He sought relief in drugs and in travels on his yacht, the *Bel-Ami*, but to no avail. His health was certainly undermined by more than an acquired malady, and his brother's death in an insane asylum in 1889 gave him clear warning that his own end would not come from old age. Determined not to submit to the same indignities as his brother, he twice attempted to commit suicide when he was convinced he was losing his mind, was finally interned in January 1892, and died raving mad eighteen months later.

American readers need a special warning regarding translations of Maupassant stories. He had been particularly fortunate in having Lafcadio Hearn as his first translator in the United States.

The first volume of Maupassant tales, *The Odd Number* (1889), contained an enthusiastic preface by Henry James. But when the first edition of his complete works appeared in 1903, more than sixty stories not by the French writer somehow crept into the collection and were widely reissued thereafter. The colossal error was not discovered until 1949. This was particularly ironic in the case of an author who during his own lifetime had scrupulously excluded from his published volumes of short stories any which he deemed unworthy to be preserved. The spurious stories appearing in many American editions are of utterly mediocre quality. They certainly contributed substantially to the somewhat low esteem in which he has been held in certain quarters. In 1955 an edition of his *Complete Short Stories* clarified the situation.

ABOUT: The outstanding biographical-critical study in English is Francis Steegmuller's Maupassant, A Lion in the Path. See also Artinian, A. Maupassant Criticism in France, *and* The Complete Short Stories of Guy de Maupassant (introduction); Bates, H. E. The Modern Short Story; Galantière, L. The Portable Maupassant (introduction); Green, F. C. Maupassant, Choix de Contes (introduction); James, H. Partial Portraits; O'Faolain, S. The Short Story; Sullivan, E. D. Maupassant the Novelist. [In French—see studies by A. Artinian, R. Dumesnil, E. Maynial, A. Vial.]

A. A.

*MAY, KARL FRIEDRICH (pseudonyms: Karl Hohenthal, E. von Linden, Latreaumont) (February 25, 1842-March 30, 1912), German novelist, was born at Ernstthal-Hohenstein near Chemnitz in Saxony, the son of a weaver. One of nine children, May grew up in poverty, and his early life was filled with hardship and tribulation. He was blind until the age of five, and his vivid imagination was lastingly influenced by the fairy tales and adventure stories which his grandmother related to him during this period. In 1856 a scholarship enabled him to attend a training school for teachers at Waldenburg, where he demonstrated excellent ability as a student until he was expelled for theft in 1859. He continued his studies in the city of Plauen and received his certification as a teacher in 1861. He taught briefly at Glauchau and at Chemnitz, where for stealing his roommate's watch he was sentenced to six weeks' imprisonment. He served two additional terms for fraud (1865-74).

Upon his final release from prison May completely changed his manner of living. He turned to writing, and published short tales, village stories, and insignificant, sensational novels in various journals which he edited— *Beobachter an der Elbe, Deutsches Familienblatt,* and *Feierstunden*—before finding his true vocation as a writer of popular adventure stories. In 1883 he settled in Dresden

* mi

and finally, following the financial success of his works, moved to Radebeul, where he purchased Villa Shatterhand, named after one of his most famous heroes. In later years he traveled extensively through North Africa and the Near East (1898-1900) and to the United States (1908). In 1903 in a contested suit he divorced Emma Pöllmer, his wife since 1880, and married Klara Plöhm. This trouble in his personal life, combined with the malicious attack of a small group of critics, who attempted to impugn May's integrity and destroy his reputation by exposing his criminal past, lamed his creativity and embittered his final years before his death at Radebeul.

Karl May's reputation as a writer rests solely on the extensive series of adventure or travel novels contained in his *Gesammelte Werke* (65 vols., 1892-1939). The great appeal of these works lies in their exciting plots, wholesome humor, and remote and often exotic settings, such as the American West or North Africa. May is the foremost German interpreter of the frontier days in American history. His novels, while inferior to those of James Fenimore Cooper in literary quality, are similar in technique and subject matter. Since his works abound in excellent detailed descriptions of local color and customs and are often written in the first person, they create an atmosphere of authenticity which adds to the directness of their impact. It does not detract from their effectiveness, but is rather a tribute to the author's outstanding artistic imagination, that at the time of writing he had not visited many of the places he depicted so well and so accurately.

May wrote quickly and rarely edited his manuscripts; his narratives suffer generally from diffuseness, repetition, and deficiencies of style. Even his most ardent supporters readily agree that his works possess greater ethical than aesthetic value. For despite the many faults in these novels, when judged by literary criteria, there is no denying the serious pedagogical aim and high moral purpose which motivated their creation. May regarded his characters as symbols of the eternal conflict between good and evil and therefore in his portrayals employed an elementary black-and-white technique with good always triumphant over evil. He also avoided any suggestion of eroticism in his works.

Among the most popular and best-known of his novels set in America are *Im Fernen Westen* (1880), *Winnetou* (3 vols., 1893), which is regarded as his finest work, and *Old Surehand* (1894). The outstanding volumes treating North Africa and the Near East include *Durch die Wüste* (1892), *Der Schatz im Silbersee* (1894), *Im Lande des Mahdi* (1896), and *Im Reiche des Silbernen Löwen* (4 vols., 1898-1902). His autobiography, *Mein Leben und Streben* (1910), which was subsequently expanded by May's friend and publisher E. A. Schmid, and republished under the title *Ich* (1917) (vol. 34 of the *Gesammelte Werke*), is one of his finest and most lasting achievements.

Karl May was the outstanding popular author of his age and remains today a favorite of the youth of Germany. Brockhaus estimates that to 1954 approximately eleven and one half million volumes of his works were printed in Germany. Translations of his books have appeared in twenty languages. *Durch die Wüste* was translated into English in 1955 by M. A. Becker and C. A. Willoughby under the title *In the Desert.*

ABOUT: [In German—see studies by K. H. Dworczak, O. Forst-Battaglia, L. Gurlitt, E. A. Schmid, and H. Stolte.]

D. G. D.

---

*MAYKOV (or MAIKOV), APOLLON NIKOLAEVICH (June 4, 1821-March 20, 1897), Russian poet, was born in Moscow into a noble family with a long cultural tradition. His father was a painter and member of the Academy of Arts; his mother, Evgeniya Gusyatnikova, wrote both verse and prose; and his four brothers were active in literature, one of them, Valerian, being a well-known literary critic. Maykov spent his childhood at an estate near Moscow. In 1834 the family moved to St. Petersburg where their house became a famous salon. Maykov liked to paint and wanted to become a painter. He began to write poetry at the age of fifteen. These first poems were included in the hand-written magazine *The Snowdrop* and the miscellany *Moon Nights,* appearing under the supervision of his tutor, Goncharov, who himself was to become a famous writer. In 1837 Maykov began to study law at the University of St. Petersburg, also devoting himself to ancient history and the Latin poets (Horace, Ovid, Propertius).

In 1840 he published two poems in the *Odessa Almanac* under the initial M. His dissertation on the ancient Slavic law having been finished in 1841, he began his service in the Department of the Treasury. His first book of verse, *Poems* (1842), which reflected his enthusiasm for classical antiquity, was a success, and the Czar gave him 1,000 rubles for traveling. In 1842-44 Maykov visited

* mī' kŭf

Italy (poems published in 1847 as *Sketches of Rome*), Paris, and Bohemia. Back in Russia he became the assistant librarian of Rumyantsev Museum (then at St. Petersburg) and was temporarily connected with radical literary circles, wrote in the style of the "Natural school," and even participated in socialist gatherings. Very soon, however, he turned to the right. In 1852 his forty-five-year career on the Board of Foreign Censorship began (first as censor, later as president). He became a friend of conservative historians, grew more and more monarchistic, studied Russian history and published a book of patriotic verse.

A two-volume edition of Maykov's works appeared in 1858, when he took part in a naval expedition which inspired his *Neapolitan Album* and *Songs from Modern Greece*. In the 1860's Maykov worked on his translation of *The Igor Tale*. Criticized but respected by radicals, and proclaimed the leader of the Art-for-Art's Sake movement and Pushkin's undisputed heir by conservatives, Maykov continued to write lyrical poetry and poems celebrating the Czar's anniversaries and also worked on monumental poetical works dealing with the conflict of the pagan world and Christianity. For *The Two Worlds* (1880) he received the Pushkin prize. Religious themes dominated his late work. Maykov died in St. Petersburg of pneumonia. Although highly revered during his life, he was given only a modest place in Russian poetry after his death.

Maykov was a Russian "mid-Victorian" eclectic in poetry who strove for "harmony," "beauty," and "objectivity." In his "anthological" genre (i.e., poems with the flavor of classic antiquity) he continued the Batyushkov-Pushkin tradition, though lacking their feeling for words. His historical narrative poetry is full of pageantry. A few of his landscape poems are still popular; they are static and non-emotional—qualities shared by the academic painting of his time—and lack verbal subtlety.

A large selection of Maykov's poetry in antiquated translations may be found in John Pollen's *Russian Songs and Lyrics* (1917).

ABOUT: [In Russian—Zlatkovsky, M. L. A. N. Maykov.]

V. M.

---

*MAYNARD, FRANÇOIS DE (1582-December 28, 1646), French poet, was born in Toulouse of a family of magistrates, and probably studied law in that city. He went

* mä när'

MAZZINI

to Paris about 1605 as secretary of Queen Marguerite, divorced wife of Henry IV; two years later he was a lawyer in Parliament. By this time financially secure, Maynard frequented elegant society and read new books to the Queen; the principal subject of conversation rising from these pursuits was love, in the manner of the Queen's favorite poet Desportes, Maynard's master in his first work, *Philandre*. This languorous verse pastoral, comparable in tone to the writing of D'Urfé, was not published until 1619. In the meantime Maynard met Malherbe, whose ideals corresponded to his own; he attended his new master's daily lessons, intended primarily to oppose the excesses of Desportes. This allegiance to Malherbe estranged him from his former friends. Maynard also frequented such "libertins" as Théophile de Viau.

Maynard's first published poems appeared in 1607 in the collection entitled *Parnasse des plus Excellents Poètes,* which brought before the public the genres recommended by Malherbe. It is probable that another François Maynard (1589-1628) active, as was our poet, in Aurillac, is the author of the *Œuvres* published in 1613 and marked especially by descriptive elegies. In 1635 Maynard was briefly attached to the embassy in Rome, but felt no attraction toward ruins and antiquity; accused of ill-will, he returned to Aurillac in disgrace. Unable to appear further at court, he lived in relative destitution. An illness brought out his Christian stoicism and piety; after his friendship with the essayist Jean Louis Balzac, he returned to Paris, as State Counselor and appeared at the salons of the "précieuses."

Lacking broad and sustained inspiration, Maynard was the master of the short forms, in the traditions of Horace and of Martial. Of special note is his ode "Belle Vieille" (1644), tending toward preciosity, and imitating the Italian poem by Testi. His most significant poems appeared in anthologies during his lifetime, and the first reliable edition is the three volumes of 1885-88; the choice of pieces published in 1927 by Gohin is representative.

ABOUT: [In French—Drouhet, C. Le Poète François Maynard; Gohin, F. Poésies de François Maynard (preface).]

F. J. C.

*MAZZINI, GIUSEPPE (June 22, 1805-March 10, 1872), Italian patriot, political theorist, and critic, was born and raised in

* mät tsē' nê

618

MAZZINI

Genoa. His father was Dr. Giacomo Mazzini, professor of anatomy at the University of Genoa, with an excellent practice and many charity patients. His mother, Maria Drago, was a beautiful woman of great charm, public-spirited and independent. The Mazzini home was a "modest political salon" where the doctor entertained the friends of his revolutionary youth. In the dedication of his essay "The Duties of Man" Mazzini says of his parents, "The republican instincts of my mother taught me to seek out among my fellows the Man . . . and the simple unconscious virtue of my father accustomed me to admire the silent and unnoticed virtue of self-sacrifice."

For the first five years a spinal weakness kept young Giuseppe from walking. He listened attentively to the lessons taught his three sisters in a neighboring room and by the age of four had learned to read, despite his father's anxious restrictions. He attended Royal College where lectures on the classics extolled the virtues of republics and of ancient Rome. He entered the university at fourteen and went from law to medicine to law, graduating a Doctor of Law in 1827. He practiced briefly.

As a child Giuseppe was gentle and tenderhearted. The sight of refugees after the uprising of 1821 disturbed him deeply and from that time he dressed always in black. While at the university he formed a brotherhood to smuggle contraband books. In 1827 he was praised for his essay "Patriotism of Dante" in which he hailed Dante as the prophet of Italian unity. His first wish was to devote his life to literature and his earliest published essays dealt with European literature, historical drama, Goethe's *Faust,* and Foscolo, whose Byronic Jacopo Ortis he sought to emulate.

He looked like a romantic with his black eyes, pale olive complexion, long flowing black hair, grave countenance, and smile of singular sweetness. A friend declared that "the fascinating power of his eyes, gestures, and voice was irresistible when he warmed to a subject." He loved music, played the guitar, and sang very well. His essay on music, "Filosofia della Musica," praised his beloved opera.

Sometime in 1827 he had joined the Carbonari Society, once an Italian revolutionary movement, but he soon lost belief in its aimless ritualism. In November 1830 he was arrested and imprisoned at Savona for about three months. In partly solitary confinement he rejected the Carbonari and formulated his life's program: "Italy One and Independent, with Rome for capital." He chose exile to an enforced seclusion and, leaving Italy in February 1831, he settled for a time in Marseilles. Henceforth he organized, agitated, conspired, spoke, and wrote ceaselessly to unite Italy.

Believing that the future lay in the hands of youth, he organized Giovine Italia (Young Italy), with a journal of the same name which was soon being printed on secret presses and sold in North and Central Italy. All his writings carried the same message: "The world is athirst of God, of progress, and of unity"; "Preach duty; preach virtue, sacrifice, love." In his open-handedness to refugees and to his cause, he followed these precepts fully.

He conspired to drive the Austrians out of Italy, but the general uprising he sought occurred only as useless sporadic outbreaks: 1833, 1834, 1837, 1841, 1844, 1852, 1853, 1857. Each ended in bitter failure but still kept the aim and ideal alive. Banished from France in 1833, following a severe illness Mazzini went underground, then in July left for Switzerland. Another failure and another illness were followed by three years of hiding. His generous mother sent money and clothing whenever he asked, but he gave it all away. In January 1837 he left for England where he spent the rest of his life, finding help and understanding. For English papers and reviews and for French journals, he wrote book reviews and critical articles on

Byron and Goethe, Thiers, Guizot, Sismondi, Carlyle, George Sand, Victor Hugo, Italian literature and art. Always he corresponded —open letters to the great, private letters to family, friends, and partisans. He formed groups in North and South America and sought to raise funds for weapons and supplies.

The moderates at home began to consider union under the Piedmont monarchy and this the devoted republican opposed. He returned to Italy to join the 1848 and 1849 revolts that did not succeed; but he created a myth that ten years later would call forth a reality. European fears of Mazzini the propagandist aided Cavour the diplomat to achieve an independent Italian state. During a last brief return to Italy in 1872 Mazzini died at Pisa.

A collection of his works was printed in 1861-91, *Scritti Editi ed Inediti,* 18 vols.; a National Edition, begun in 1906, has now reached 100 vols., not yet complete. In English, his *Life and Letters,* 1864-70, 6 vols., was followed by *Essays* (1887-1894); *Duties of Man and Other Essays,* 1907, is still in print. Of the 10,000 letters known to exist, some were printed as Mazzini's *Letters to an English Family,* 3 vols., in 1920-22, and another selection appeared in 1930 translated by Alice de Rosen Jervis.

ABOUT: Barr, S. Mazzini: Portrait of an Exile; Griffith, G. O. Mazzini: Prophet of Modern Europe; King, B. Life of Mazzini; MacCunn, J. Six Radical Thinkers; Rossi, J. Image of America in Mazzini's Writings; Salvemini, G. Mazzini; History Today, February 1956; Journal of Central European Affairs, January 1958; Times Literary Supplement, January 21, 1955.

M. A. W.

*MEDICI, LORENZO DE', called THE MAGNIFICENT (January 1, 1449-April 8, 1492), Italian ruler, poet, and patron of the arts, was born in Florence into a family of wealthy international bankers. His grandfather, Cosimo de' Medici, had won political control of Florence in 1434 and ruled as an absolute sovereign—though a sovereign without title, as Florence remained ostensibly a republic. Lorenzo's father, Piero, had married the aristocratic and intelligent Lucrezia Tornabuoni. Of the couple's seven children, four survived—Lorenzo, his younger brother Giovanni, and two girls.

Growing up in Cosimo's court, the precocious Lorenzo was tutored by Florence's leading scholars, including Gentile Becchi, Cristoforo Landino, Argyropolous and Marsilio Ficino. Landino, a Dante scholar as well as a Latinist, fostered Lorenzo's interest in Italian poetry. Ficino's Neoplatonism greatly influenced Lorenzo's thought, and

* mĕ' dē chē

619

LORENZO DE' MEDICI

and a Florentine mob killed the chief conspirators. The Pope excommunicated Lorenzo and, putting the city under interdict, attacked it in alliance with Naples. Lorenzo courageously went on a personal mission to the King of Naples and persuaded him to end the war. The Pope, left without allies, withdrew the excommunication and the interdict. Under the next Pope, Innocent VIII, Lorenzo managed to have his second son, Giovanni—then thirteen—made a cardinal. Giovanni later became Pope Leo X.

Lorenzo's wife died in 1488. Lorenzo himself was in ill health during his last years, and in 1492—at forty-three—he retired to his villa at Careggi, near Florence, where he died. According to Poliziano, an eye-witness, Lorenzo was visited by Savonarola and received his blessing before death. Lorenzo was succeeded by his eldest son, Pietro, who ruled so ineffectively that in two years the Florentine council exiled the Medicis from the city.

Lorenzo was not handsome—his long pointed nose and jutting chin were almost comically ugly—but his assured bearing and splendid dress made him an impressive figure. Vigorous, enthusiastic, and brilliant, he was also autocratic and extravagant. He sponsored lavish public festivals and took part in them with gusto. He pursued learning and the arts with equal gusto—he collected books and manuscripts for what became the Laurentian Library; he bought works of art for the Garden of San Marco (which in 1489 became the art school of Florence); and he patronized scholars and artists such as Pico della Mirandola, Poliziano, Luigi Pulci, Verrocchio, Botticelli, Michelangelo, and Leonardo da Vinci.

Ficino remained throughout Lorenzo's life his companion and philosophic mentor.

In 1464 Cosimo died and was succeeded by Piero—who, being crippled by gout, frequently employed Lorenzo as his representative on official business. In 1469 Lorenzo was betrothed to Clarice Orsini, a well-born Roman girl whom his mother had selected as a suitable bride. The splendid tournament Lorenzo gave in honor of his betrothal was presided over, not by his fiancée, but by his current love, Lucrezia Donati. He duly married the retiring and rather colorless Clarice in June; they eventually had three sons and three daughters.

Piero de' Medici died in December 1469, and early the next year Lorenzo, barely twenty-one, accepted the politic invitation of the Florentines to "watch over" their state. He kept control of the government for the rest of his life by the usual Medici policy of allying with the common people and of systematically putting down the wealthy families who were potential rivals for power. During his rule he managed to keep Italy relatively at peace by preserving a balance of power among the five principal Italian states and by maintaining friendly relations between Florence and the most important power, France.

In 1478 a Florentine conspiracy headed by the Pazzi family and backed by Pope Sixtus IV tried to end Medici rule by assassinating Lorenzo and his brother Giuliano. Giuliano was killed, but Lorenzo escaped,

Lorenzo's most important contribution to Italian literature was probably his deliberate attempt to revive Italian as a literary language, after a century of Latin dominance. He made the first anthology of Italian lyric verse, a group of some 450 poems (chiefly by *dolce stil novo* poets), which he collected for the edification of Federigo d'Aragona. He sent the collection to Federigo probably in 1477, with a critical essay urging the merits of vernacular poetry. Lorenzo's own works—few of which can be dated with any accuracy—are all in Italian and are imitative of a variety of models. His relatively early *Rime* are love poems in the style of Petrarch, with an admixture of the Neoplatonic doctrine of love. They are chiefly addressed to two ladies, Lucrezia Donati and Simonetta Cataneo. Lorenzo later wrote a *Commento* on some of these poems, after the model of Dante's *Vita Nuova,* again with a Neoplatonic cast. Lorenzo's *Il Simposio,* or *I Beoni* ("The Drunkards"), is an unfinished parody of Dante's *Divine Comedy. Apollo e Pan, L'Ambra,* and *Corinto* are pastoral poems influenced by classical Latin poetry. *Le Selve d'Amore* ("Improvisations on Love") is an allegorical poem reflecting the Platonic love doctrine. His religious poems in *terza rima* are little more than paraphrases of earlier sacred authors, and his *terza rima L'Altercazione* is chiefly an exposition of some of Marsilio Ficino's Neoplatonic doctrines. *La Caccia* is a verse description of a hunt that Lorenzo took part in. *La Nencia da Barberino* (whose attribution to Lorenzo is sometimes questioned) is a parody of pastoral love poetry, employing realistic peasant speech. Two short stories in the Florentine genre, *Giacoppo* and *La Ginevra* are considered Lorenzo's. He also wrote songs and dramatic pieces, both religious and secular, for public presentation in Florence. His *sacra rapprasentazione, San Giovanni e Paolo,* was performed in 1489 or 1491; it is said that Lorenzo himself played the part of Constantine.

Historically, Lorenzo's reputation as a statesman and as a patron of the arts has acted to obscure his reputation as a writer. In fusing the *dolce stil novo* lyric with Neoplatonism, Lorenzo initiated a literary style that dominated Italian poetry for the next century and that thence influenced lyric poetry throughout Renaissance Europe. His own work, however, had little influence outside his own circle. His poetry is little read today, except for the carnival song "Quant' è bella giovanezza," whose opening lines are probably the best-known quatrain in Italian verse.

Verse translations of some of his sonnets appear in J. B. Fletcher's *Literature of the Italian Renaissance* (1934). There are also some translations in D. G. Loth's *Lorenzo the Magnificent* (1929).

ABOUT: Roscoe, W. Life of Lorenzo de' Medici; Wilkins, E. H. History of Italian Literature. [In Italian—Bizarri, E. Il Magnifico Lorenzo; Ugolini, L. Lorenzo il Magnifico.]

J. K.

MEDIGO, JUDAH LEON. See ABARBANEL, JUDAH

*MEILHAC, HENRI (February 21, 1831-July 6, 1897), French dramatist, was born in Paris and studied at the Louis-le-Grand

* mē yàk'

college. His first employment was with a bookdealer; then from 1852 to 1855 he wrote comic sketches and made drawings for the *Journal pour Rire,* typical examples of his caustic wit and fantastic imagination as a caricaturist. His first two vaudeville plays were failures, but in 1856 *La Sarabande du Cardinal* was well-received as was his full-length comedy *Le Petit-Fils de Mascarille* (1859), a good example of his gift at its best. He began collaborating with Halévy on plays and operas in 1861 but their association became constant only after their first triumph, *La Belle Hélène* (1864), with music by Offenbach. The collaboration came to an end in 1881, presumably on account of Halévy's new enthusiasm for the novel.

The works written in collaboration were at the time identified primarily through the name of Meilhac, but the idea that Halévy was merely the business manager of the pair is quite false, and through study of the work of each writer their respective contribution can be measured. The dramatic qualities seem to depend on Meilhac, whose style is more forceful even to the point of excess of fantasy and caricature in his search for violent and grotesque effects. Halévy, in contrast, was more skillful in construction, tended more toward good measure, and was far more realistic and sympathetic. The principal masterpieces of the collaboration are *La Belle Hélène, Barbe-Bleue* (1866), and perhaps *Carmen* (1875), though this last is primarily serious and little more than an adaptation from Mérimée's novel. In *La Belle Hélène,* the noble protagonists of the story of Helen of Troy are transformed into common and almost stupid creatures, whose vulgarity and buffoonish attitudes are made amusing by the wit, tact, and imagination of the dramatists. The caricature of general human weaknesses and affectations of all classes of society, comparable to that of other playwrights of the time, seeks to prove nothing, disapproves of nothing, and calls for no reform. The art of Meilhac and Halévy appears further in their fine portraits of women, symbols of beauty yet living and vital; such effects, and frequent reliance on fairy-tale subjects, distinguish their work from that of Scribe and Labiche.

Meilhac composed other plays in collaboration with Najac and Arthur Delavigne, such as *Les Curieuses* and *Fabienne* (1864-65), and *Manon,* with Gille, for Massenet, but never with the success of his libretti with Halévy, or their very successful comedy of 1869, *Frou-Frou,* reinterpreted later by

Sarah Bernhardt. *Décoré* (1887) is Meilhac's principal success as a wholly individual work, a farce much admired for its gay tone and amusing situations.

Meilhac was elected to the French Academy in 1888, four years after Halévy. Aside from his plays, he left various essays on the war. The collected theatre of Meilhac and Halévy appeared in eight volumes from 1900 to 1902, and in selected editions.

Occasional English translations may be found in bilingual libretti. A. Daly rendered *Frou-Frou* in 1870; *The Widow* was translated by H. H. Ayer (1877). Barrett H. Clark translated several one-act comedies.

ABOUT: Matthews, B. French Dramatists of the Nineteenth Century.

F. J. C.

*MELANCHTHON, PHILIPP (February 16, 1497-April 19, 1560), German humanist, was born in Bretten (Palatinate). His parents, Georg Schwarzerd, master of weapons to the elector Philipp, and Barbara (Reuter), daughter of the burgomaster of Bretten, gave their son a most careful education: first in the city school in Bretten, then with a private tutor (Johann Unger). The death of father and grandfather in 1507 caused Philipp and his brother Georg to be sent to the Pforzheim home of his grandmother, the sister of the humanist Reuchlin. Contact with this renowned scholar and attendance at the Latin School of Georz Simler confirmed in the youth the humanistic orientation. Heidelberg awarded the boy a baccalaureate (1511-12); two years later he received his "Magister" from Tübingen. Melanchthon (the name is a Grecized form of Schwarzerd) began lecturing on Aristotle and other classical writers before he was seventeen.

On November 25, 1520, Melanchthon married Katharina Krapp, daughter of the Wittenberg burgomaster. The union, lasting thirty-seven years, proved a happy one; there were two sons and two daughters.

The classical-humanistic bent inclined Melanchthon to a stand midway between the evangelical fervor of Luther and the analytical spirit of Erasmus. This proved to be a position of vast historical import but also a source of distrust and misunderstanding. As professor at Wittenberg he excelled in his interpretations of the ancients, combining scholarly exactness with the imagination of the poet. His public demeanor and the tone of his writings were reasonable and gentle,

* mä länk′ tŏn

MELANCHTHON

two qualities which aroused the hostility of extremists from both camps.

Nevertheless his stature as scholar and religious thinker enabled him to further the cause of the Reformation. In 1519 he accompanied Luther to the Leipzig disputation; previously he had ranged himself with Erasmus. Melanchthon's emphasis, however, was ethical, Luther's primarily dogmatic, a difference which did not prevent Melanchthon from composing the fullest statement of Luther's paradoxical theology, *Loci Communes Rerum Theologicarum* (1521, revised 1535 and 1542). Again in 1529 Melanchthon attempted the role of mediator: he helped formulate the famous protest (Second Reichstag, Speyer, 1529). Efforts to arrive at agreement with Zwingli regarding the interpretation of the Last Supper were unsuccessful. The *Augsburg Confession* (1530, 1540) was Melanchthon's work. His *Apologie der Augsburgischen Confession* earned him European fame. He conferred at Worms with the Catholic spokesman Eck (1540-41, again in 1546) but without success.

After Luther's death in 1546 the adherents of the Lutheran Reformation turned to Melanchthon. This recognition of his natural leadership and his superb practical measures for the improvement of the Latin Schools and of Wittenberg University earned for him the proud and merited title "Praeceptor Germaniae."

Melanchthon's last period (1546-60) was troubled by further theological conflict. His leaning toward Calvinist views regarding the Last Supper, his humanistic softening of the doctrine of the total depravity of natural man, his belief in the need for human co-operation with divine grace in the process of salvation, the importance of good works—all these laid down in many writings—made him a victim of the "rabies theologorum." He continued to search for peace: the Council of Trent (1552), in which he had hoped to participate, and a last effort at Worms (1557) ended in frustration. He died in Wittenberg, weary but still working for religious unity.

Certain nineteenth century critics (A. Ritschl and K. Holl) condemned Melanchthon's work as a dilution of Luther's theology which missed its emotional depth. Today it is more clearly seen that the gentle Melanchthon represents, as does Erasmus, though without the latter's sharpness, an attempted compromise between the best of humanism and the simple gospel, between nature and revelation, between classicism and Christianity, which he hoped would lead ultimately to a reunion of Reformed Evangelicals and the Mother Church.

Individual works of Melanchthon were translated very early, among them: *The Confessyon of Fayth* . . . (translation of *Augsburg Confession*) by Richard Tauerner (1536), *A Very Godly Defense* . . . *Defending the Mariage of Preistes,* by Lewis Beuchame (1541), *The Epistle of . . . Philip Melancton . . . unto . . . Henry the Eighth,* by I. C. (1547), *The Justification of Man by Faith Only* . . . , by Nicholas Lesse (1548), *A Godly Treatyse of Prayer,* by John Bradforde (1533).

ABOUT: Cox, F. A. The Life of Philip Melanchthon; Hildebrandt, F. Melanchthon; Alien or Ally; Manschreck, C. L. Melanchthon, the Quiet Reformer. [In German—see studies by G. Ellinger, L. Stern, R. Stupperich.]

C. K. P.

*MELÉNDEZ VALDÉS, JUAN (March 11, 1754-May 24, 1817), Spanish lyric poet, was born in Ribera del Fresno (Badajoz). He received his early education with the Dominican fathers in Madrid. Later his brother sent him to Salamanca, where he did brilliant work (1772-81), becoming a professor of humanities at the same institution in the latter year. While at Salamanca, Meléndez Valdés was closely associated with and was a disciple of Jovellanos. He also knew and was influenced by Cadalso. He became a magistrate at Zaragoza in 1789 and Valladolid in 1791. In 1797 his friend Jovellanos, now a minister in the government, secured an official position for him in Madrid.

* mā lān' dăth väl dās'

Vacillation is one of the keys to Meléndez Valdés' poetry, as well as to his life and character. When the Napoleonic invasion took place, he was at first a patriot, then he became an ardent *afrancesado*—for which he was nearly shot in Oviedo—and then was one of those who welcomed Ferdinand VII home. Naturally, such a man was not trusted, and he was obliged to leave the country. When he crossed the frontier into France, he kissed the Spanish soil goodbye saying he would never more tread it. He did not, for he died in exile, in Montpellier, of paralysis.

Meléndez Valdés was a member of the so-called Salamancan School and often used the name "Batilo." At first, under the influence of Cadalso, he composed anacreontics and idylls. His real forte was pastoral, rustic, and anacreontic poetry. It was once said that his verse "exhaled the breath of thyme." In his amatory poetry Meléndez Valdés has few peers in Spanish literature. It is, then, in such works as *Batilo, La Gloria de las Artes* and *Los Besos de Amor* that we see Meléndez Valdés at his best. He was, however, not entirely satisfied with this rôle and wished to rise, like Jovellanos, to the philosophic and social ode, which he did in *De las Miserias Humanas* and *El Filósofo en el Campo.* Again under the influence of the English, particularly Pope and Young, he wrote such works as *La Noche y la Soledad.* Despite this apparent vacillation, Meléndez Valdés is almost certainly the greatest lyric poet between the Golden Age and the romantic movement. The critic Azorín called him, in fact, "the first romantic poet." His verse has a musical quality not found elsewhere; his descriptive talent is formidable, and he has an extraordinary command of language and imagery. He spent much time polishing his style, a fact which accounts for its lack of simplicity. In this age of prose, as it has been called, his lyric voice was almost alone. Meléndez's loves, of which he spoke so eloquently, were not always creatures of his imagination. His wife, María Andrea de Coca, was a shrewish woman, although she genuinely admired her tall, blond husband. In 1886 his remains were moved from France to Spain, where he is buried in the Panteón de Hombres Ilustres.

Meléndez Valdés' *Poesías* (1785) have gone through several printings. The most complete edition is that of 1820, in four volumes. His life is written by M. J. Quintana in volume XIX of the *BAE.* Some of Meléndez Valdés' poetry was translated by Longfellow in his *Poets and Poetry of Europe* (1888) and by T. Walsh in *Hispanic Anthology* (1920).

*MELO, FRANCISCO MANUEL DE (November 23, 1608-August 24, 1666), Portuguese moralist, historian, playwright and poet, was the most accomplished of all the nobles who wielded pen and sword alike. For all his cleverness, he suffered grievously as a man with two countries, Portugal and Spain. Born in Lisbon to Luís de Melo and Maria de Toledo de Maçuelos, a highborn Spanish lady of partly Jewish origin, he studied with the Jesuits. Like his father, he chose a military career. As a cadet, he was shipwrecked in 1627. After some years on leave in Lisbon and at the brilliant Spanish court, he saw further service in Spanish ports, the Channel, and Flanders (1639). When Portugal joined Catalonia in rebellion against the inept rule of Philip IV, Melo, then aide-de-camp in Catalonia, was arrested on Christmas day, 1640. The Spaniards soon freed him and sent him once more to Flanders. He escaped to England and declared for the Portuguese King John IV. But by 1643 he had antagonized powerful Portuguese nobles, perhaps unlucky rivals in love, and so he was jailed in Lisbon, with the king's connivance. "Though the body was held within four walls, the mind was not," and he spent every waking hour writing. After eleven years in prison he was banished to Brazil, but with the king's death he returned to his native country. In 1660 he was back at court, heading the fashionable Academia dos Generosos and traveling through Europe on diplomatic missions. Though he remained a bachelor, he had a son, named Jorge, by a gentlewoman, Luisa da Silva. Melo died at the age of fifty-seven on his estate at Alcântara near Lisbon.

Melo was the last writer of distinction who wrote with equal ease in both Portuguese and Spanish. Most of his works reflect the events of his agitated life. Thus we find him telling the story of his shipwreck in a half-journalistic, half-historical book, the *Epanáforas de Vária História Portuguesa* (1660), which also contains a romantic tale of the discovery of Madeira by an eloping English couple. Out of his participation in the Catalan campaign came a classic history of the first year of that long and bitter civil war, written in a

* mâ' lōō

624

pithy style reminiscent of the Roman Tacitus, the *Historia de los Movimientos, Separación y Guerra de Cataluña*. It was published in 1645 and earned Melo a high place in Spanish literature, beside that of his friend, the satirist Quevedo. Their friendship is mirrored in letters placed among the five hundred *Cartas Familiares* published in 1664. Most of these letters form a sort of prison diary, "written," as he said, "with blood, dried with tears, folded with simplicity, sealed with unhappiness, carried by bad luck," and, it may be added, preserved in the vinegar of ironic wit.

His satirical vein inspired his two best works in Portuguese—the *Carta de Guia de Casados* (1651), a merry guide "to help married men find the Haven of Rest along the Path of Prudence," and *Apólogos Dialogais* (written in Brazil; not published until 1721), four dialogues on various matters, among them the "Hospital das Letras," in which Melo imagines himself discussing the comparative merits of several literatures with three critics, the Dutchman Lipsius, the Italian Boccalini, and the Spaniard Quevedo.

In Spanish, Melo also published *Política Militar*—on statecraft—in 1638, and in 1664 collected as *Obras Morales* biographical essays on St. Francis (1647) and St. Augustine (1648-49), as well as treatises on human passions (*La Victoria del Hombre*) and moral philosophy (*Triunfo de la Filosofía Cristiana contra la Doctrina Estoica*).

In the scant history of Portuguese drama Melo shines as the only dramatist of note during the seventeenth century, thanks to the *Auto do Fidalgo Aprendiz*, a comedy of character written about 1646 and published in 1665. The protagonist is an upstart who tries to acquire aristocratic manners in ten easy lessons.

A writer of extraordinary versatility, Melo began his literary career by writing poems. As "Melodino," he published Spanish verse, among it his earliest, twelve sonnets on Inés de Castro's death, in *Las Tres Musas* of 1649. To this he added in 1665 his Portuguese "trovas," including epistles in Sá de Miranda's manner. Like his contemporary Father António Vieira, and many later Portuguese, he also loved polemics; but most of his pamphlets were never printed. Modern readers, easily wearied by Melo's baroque conceits, still enjoy the novelesque story of his life and a few anthology pages that show his manly character and his skill in describing manners.

The *Carta de Guia de Casados* was translated by John Stevens in 1697 as *The Government of a Wife*. E. Prestage published extracts in his own translation in his biography of Melo (see below). Large gleanings from Melo's poetry appeared in 1815, and again in 1820, as *Relics of Melodino,* in Edward Lawson's translation from a manuscript of 1645.

ABOUT: Prestage, E. Francisco Manuel de Melo (an English condensation of Prestage's earlier, well-documented standard biography in Portuguese). [In Portuguese—Lapa, M. R. *Preface to edition of* Cartas Familiares; Teensma, B. N. Dom Francisco Manuel de Melo. In Spanish—Picón, J. O. *Preface to edition of* Guerra de Cataluña.]

G. M. M.

---

*MENA, JUAN DE (1411-1456), Spanish poet, was born in Cordova, the son of a leading local family of converts from Judaism. He and his sister were orphaned at an early age. After receiving a basic education in Cordova, he entered the University of Salamanca in 1434 and later went on to study in Rome, where he was strongly influenced by Renaissance humanism. Upon his return to Spain he was named Latin secretary at the Castilian court of John II and member of the city council of Cordova. He was personally respected as a man of letters by king and nobles despite his Semitic ancestry; he was an active partisan of Don Alvaro de Luna, long the dominant figure of the royal court and of Castile. Little more is known of Mena's public career. He died in Torrelaguna at the age of forty-five.

Mena's only prose work of note is his close translation of a condensed Latin version of the *Iliad,* but perhaps of more intrinsic interest, as examples of artistic storytelling, are his free versions of fables from Ovid, found in the prose commentary on his poem *La Coronación.* His poetry is of two basic types: love poetry in the troubadour tradition as this had developed in Spain, marked by scholastic "wit" and psychological subtleties and by a strong tendency to use pseudo-religious hyperbole; and politico-moral poetry in the more serious medieval tradition of didactic verse. Typical of the latter is *La Coronación,* a difficult allegory in which literary personages are presented as though either in Hell or in Paradise. In this work the Marquis of Santillana is crowned as a perfect knight, for being both a great poet and a conqueror of Moors. We find here a strong element of historically relevant social criticism. More schematically allegorical in the earlier medieval manner stemming from Prudentius' *Psychomachia* and the

* mä' nä

scholastic *disputatio* is Mena's last work, his *Coplas contra los Pecados Mortales* or *Debate de la Razón contra la Voluntad* (Verses Against the Mortal Sins or Debate of Reason Against Will. Here personified abstractions muster their ascetic arguments with a minimum of concrete historical references.

But Mena's most ambitious poem is of the more historical and humanistic type, familiar to the modern reader chiefly through Dante's *Divine Comedy.* It is called the *Laberinto de Fortuna* and consists of almost 300 stanzas of eight twelve-syllable lines each. (After a resounding dedication to John II and an invocation of pagan deities who represent literary gifts, the poet begins to complain of the treachery of Fortune. Suddenly he finds himself being transported to the crystal palace of Fortune, which he visits under the guidance of a maiden representing Providence. He sees three wheels, two motionless, to represent past and future time, and one whirling—the present. There are further divisions into seven planetary circles, inhabited by historical figures having the appropriate astrological vices and virtues. The vision culminates with Jupiter and Saturn, i.e., with John II and Don Alvaro de Luna, and with a prophecy that they will achieve national unity. After the vision the poet returns to the King of Castile, asking that he fulfill the prophecy of Providence.

The rhetorical grandiloquence, Latinized vocabulary, aesthetic use of classical allusion, and emphatic nationalism of this poet, who was still in many ways medieval, make of Juan de Mena the most significant herald of the Renaissance in Spain.

Short excerpts from the *Laberinto de Fortuna* appear in English translation in Longfellow's *Poets and Poetry of Europe* (1845).

ABOUT: [In Spanish—Fuentes Guerra, R. Juan de Mena; Lida de Malkiel, M. R. Juan de Mena, Poeta del Prerrenacimiento Español.]

E. L. R.

---

*MÉNARD, LOUIS NICOLAS (October 19, 1822-February 12, 1901), French writer and Hellenist, was born in Paris. His mystic and Protestant leanings may be attributed to his mother's family, and his wide erudition to reading in his father's bookshop. Ménard's parents recognized his lack of intellectual stability, but had little influence on him. During his eleven years at the Louis-le-Grand College he showed great brilliance and won many prizes; at this school he met Octave

* mä när'

625

Feuillet and Baudelaire. He was briefly at the École Normale in 1842, but at this time he inaugurated a salon for his literary friends —thus founding a group among whom Baudelaire read his first poems and Feuillet conceived his first projects; here also to a Bohemian, anti-materialist atmosphere, came Nerval and Banville. Insofar as Ménard set the tone in his circle Greek mythology was a critical topic, and the most esteemed recent poetry was that of Quinet and of Vigny. Ménard's long poem *Prométhée Délivré* (1843) represents one of the early syntheses of Greek and Asiatic mythologies, and is a prototype of the neo-Hellenic tradition. It served, as a model for Flaubert's *La Tentation de Saint Antoine* (1849); its political notions signify Ménard's faith in human progress through knowledge. *Euphorion* (1855) contains stronger Neoplatonic elements, and the dramatic *Prologue d'une Révolution* (November 1848) represents Ménard's most radical political opinions, condemned by the courts and responsible for his flight to Belgium, where he lived for three years.

Beginning in 1849, Ménard assumed a new attitude of stoical resignation, evident in his poems. On his return to Paris, he tried landscape and animal painting, in which his work is least distinguished. This was also the period which saw the dispersion of his former friends. Ménard's estrangement from Baudelaire, in 1846, was compensated for by his close association with Leconte de Lisle, fostered by mutual interests in antiquity and in republican ideologies. Ménard's collected *Poèmes* (1855, augmented in 1863) includes a refutation of Maxime du Camp's attack on mythological subjects and a call for "modernism," still vague, but associated with interest in the past of humanity and a golden age forever lost. *Poèmes* illustrates such themes in *La Légende de Saint Hilarion, Empédocle*, and many short pieces dealing with the glory of Athens and Alexandria. Ménard's most objective and original synthesis of contemporary knowledge of this subject matter appears in his *Du Polythéisme Hellénique*, essays collected in 1863. His principal service in this work was a reaction against romantic interpretations which emphasized primitivism or color, and a new symbolic interpretation constructed with the best available documentation.

Ménard offered little new after 1863, and most of his later writings are vulgarizations or have pedagogic aims, e.g., his lectures at the Hôtel de Ville. He was always respected,

sometimes with condescension, but in his last days found a strong admirer in Maurice Barrès. His bibliography is considerable, though to a very great extent superseded by modern scholarship, e.g., the *Hermetica*. His *Poèmes et Rêveries d'un Payen Mystique* (1895), includes essentially all of his imaginative work.

ABOUT: Charlton, D. G. *in* Studies in Modern French Literature Presented to P. Mansell Jones (1961). [In French—Peyre, H. Louis Ménard; Critique, No. 194 (1963).]

F. J. C.

MENDELE MOCHER SEFORIM. See ABRAMOWITZ, SHALOM JACOB

*MENDELSSOHN, MOSES (or MOSES DESSAU) (September 6, 1729-January 4, 1786), German-Jewish philosopher, was born in Dessau. His father was an impoverished Hebrew scribe who nevertheless managed to provide Mendelssohn with a thorough Jewish education. Under the guidance of his teacher, Rabbi David Fränkel of Dessau, the boy became a first-rate Talmudist. An illness brought on by over-diligent study left him a hunchback for life.

At the age of fourteen, Mendelssohn went to Berlin, capital of the Prussia of Frederick the Great and the center for the German Enlightenment. There Mendelssohn continued his Talmudic studies, but at the same time undertook, with the help of Jewish friends, a tremendous program of self-education in secular literature, science, and philosophy. In 1750 Mendelssohn was engaged as private tutor in the household of Isaac Bernhard, a rich silk manufacturer.

By the time he was introduced to Lessing, in 1754, Mendelssohn had acquired such a firm grasp of secular knowledge that he was able to make a profound impression on the great German writer. Lessing, without the author's consent, published Mendelssohn's *Philosophische Gespräche* (Philosophic Discourses, 1755), a treatise on the philosophy of Leibniz. This work, and subsequent essays on aesthetics published in scholarly periodicals, established Mendelssohn's reputation as a brilliant young thinker with a perfect command of the German language. His fame was heightened when he won first prize, over Immanuel Kant, in a contest sponsored by the Prussian Academy with his *Über die Evidenz in Metaphysichen Wissenschaft* (Evidence in Metaphysical Knowledge, 1763).

* mĕn' dĕls zōn

In the year 1763, Mendelssohn received from Frederick the Great the patent of "Schutzjude," or protected Jew, a privileged position. During the same year, having risen to economic security as partner in the firm of Isaac Bernhard, he married Fromet Guggenheim of Hamburg. They had three sons and three daughters, and their grandson was the composer Felix Mendelssohn. He reached the zenith of success with the publication of his most famous work, *Phädon* (Phaedo, 1767). This essay on the immortality of the soul, written in masterly style and with classic grace, brought Mendelssohn to the forefront of European intellectual life. His house became a meeting place for the enlightened thinkers of the day.

As a result of a public dispute with the Swiss pastor Lavater, Mendelssohn found himself deeply involved in the Jewish problem. It was at his suggestion that Christian von Dohm published a remarkable defense of the Jews in 1781. Two years later Mendelssohn himself wrote *Jerusalem* which preached freedom of thought and religion from state or church interference and expressed his belief in the validity of traditional Judaism and its compatibility with reason. Mendelssohn, with the aid of several associates, published a German translation of the Pentateuch (1783) which he hoped would spark the spread of modern culture and enlightenment among the Jews, thereby improving their legal and social position. Thus, although he continued to write philosophical works, the last period of his life was concerned with Jewish religious questions. His death, however, was mourned by German intellectuals of all faiths.

M. Waxman, in *A History of Jewish Literature*, says: "The greatness of Mendelssohn consisted not so much in his contributions to philosophic knowledge as in his own character and personality. . . . His was a harmonious soul which enchanted even his antagonists by its beauty." His conduct, immortalized in Lessing's *Nathan the Wise*, was above reproach. A true friend of human beings of all ranks and beliefs, he represented the finest traditions of devoted service. His life ushered in the new era of emancipation in Jewish history, for Mendelssohn was the first prominent Jew of the modern period who successfully combined the previously divergent forces of secular culture and Judaism. His life became the great symbol of the struggle for the Enlightenment among both Western and Eastern European Jewry. Yet he did not wish to integrate the Jews into Western society at the price of their traditional religion. The Reform movement in Judaism was not the work of Mendelssohn, but of the next generation of German-Jewish leaders, who elaborated upon his program for the renaissance of the Jews.

Jerusalem was translated into English in London (1838). Mendelssohn's *Memoirs* were also translated in London (1825 and 1827). Several love letters written by him to his fiancée appeared in *Commentary* (March 1954). The complete German edition of his works is that published in Leipzig (1843-45). An unfinished German edition of his complete works was published in Berlin (1929-38).

ABOUT: Graetz, H. History of the Jews; Isaacs, A. S. Step by Step; Simon, M. Moses Mendelssohn, His Life and Times: Spiegel, S. Hebrew Reborn; Walter, H. Moses Mendelssohn, Critic and Philosopher. [In German—Auerbach, J. Lessing und Mendelssohn; Badt-Strauss, B. Moses Mendelssohn, der Mensch und Sein Werk; Bamberger, F. Die Geistige Gestalt Moses Mendelssohns; Hensel, S. Die Familie Mendelssohn; Kayserling, M. Moses Mendelssohn, Sein Leben und Wirken.]

M. R.

*MENDÈS, CATULLE** (May 20, 1841-February 8, 1909), French poet, born in Bordeaux, showed a precocious talent for writing, and established himself in Paris in 1860. His personal life was uneventful. An unhappy marriage to Théophile Gautier's daughter in 1866 was followed by a second, a successful one. Showing organizational and creative skill, he founded *La Revue Fantaisiste*, whose offices became an important center of poetic discussion among the masters of the Parnassian group, notably Gautier, Baudelaire, Leconte de Lisle, and Banville, and such younger men as Claudel and Sully Prudhomme. Mendès' program, as later outlined in *La Légende du Parnasse Contemporain*, sought full use of artistic techniques rather than the anecdotal expression of emotion of the later romantics; he insisted that his group was neither a school nor an official movement, and the policy of his review was broad enough to include enthusiastic approval of the naturalistic novel, of older poetry such as that of Ronsard, and of the operas of Wagner, "le plus grand des musiciens." This eclectic attitude, as Mendès pointed out, was maintained despite constant overt hostility not only from the general public, but from the literary naturalists themselves.

A law suit brought financial disaster to *La Revue Fantaisiste*. Shortly afterward, having met Leconte de Lisle, Mendès con-

* mäN dĕs'

sidered a more aggressive program. In 1863 he began to frequent the circle of Louis Xavier de Ricard, and proposed that the latter transform his weekly paper *L'Art* into a purely poetic review, *Le Parnasse Contemporain*, in which the cause of poetry could be brought before a wider intellectual public. The financing of the magazine was assumed by Lemerre, whose bookstore became a new center for gatherings of the younger Parnassians. Again we find the account of the activities of Mendès' group in his lectures, published in 1884 under the title *La Légende du Parnasse Contemporain;* this book contains his personal choice of poets and poems, and documentation on the events, including slanderous anecdotes invented by the many enemies of rival and jealous camps.

Mendès' first volume of verse, *Philoméla*, appeared in 1864, enchanting Verlaine and leading Banville to speak of the author as "l'artiste savant et le poète de race." Numerous further volumes of verse appeared during the next decades, to such a point that the relative obscurity of Mendès today results to a large degree from the sheer quantity of his production. To this first volume one might add as significant later titles *Soirs Moroses* (1876) and *La Grive des Vignes* (1895). His verse is usually admirable, in elegant and impeccable style and form, varying in tone from grace to brilliance. It explores a wide range of subjects: exotic, metaphysical, melancholic, realistic and popular; there is in it no such major series of periods as one often finds among his contemporaries. A satanist strain in *Les Braises du Cendrier* (1900) is said to have influenced D'Annunzio's *Poema Paradisiaco*. It is true that Mendès had a faculty for assimilating techniques and a frequent tendency toward sensualism; but to call him a "retarded Gautier" or a "superficial Baudelaire" cannot be justified. Despite relative impurity, in comparison to Leconte de Lisle, Mendès stands as a poet as well as the organizer, conciliator, and firm friend of his colleagues and his younger contemporaries.

Mendès was also a partisan of the verse drama, and among his titles in this genre one might note especially *Médée* and *La Reine Fiammette* (1898), which enjoyed some success. Several librettos and scenarios associate him with the music of Chabrier, Massenet, and Hahn. Finally, among his scores of works there are many short stories and novels devoted to such subjects as crime, mystery, or the occult after the manner of Poe.

Mendès' *Poésies* appeared in three volumes in 1892, his *Œuvres* in *Choix de Poèsies* in 1925. Translations into English include the short story *The Fairy Spinning Wheel* by T. Vivian in 1898, *The Red Romance* (1887) by M. Dingman in 1899, *The Isles of Love* (1886) by J. Fitzgerald in 1927, and *Number 56 and Other Stories* by P. Mégroz in 1928.

ABOUT: Thompson, V. French Portraits. [In French—Bertrand, A. Catulle Mendès, Biographie Critique; Cocteau, J. Portraits-Souvenir; Souriau, M. Histoire du Parnasse; Walch, G. Anthologie des Poètes Français Contemporains.]

F. J. C.

MENDES PINTO, FERNÃO. See PINTO, FERNÃO MENDES

MENTZER. See FISCHART, JOHANN BAPTIST

*MÉRIMÉE, PROSPER (September 28, 1803-September 23, 1870), French man of letters, was born in Paris. He was the only son of Léonor Mérimée (1757-1836), painter, historian, and chemist, and of Anna Moreau, who had been her husband's art pupil; her grandmother had written *Beauty and the Beast* and other tales. The senior Mérimée was a conservative whose political convictions always managed to conform to those of the government; his mother, antireligious although otherwise bourgeois, refused to have her son baptized.

Young Prosper was brought up among the artists, art critics, and men of letters who congregated in the Mérimée salon: his father, secretary of the École des Beaux-Arts, was provided there with a spacious apartment. Prosper himself studied painting and drawing, and was quite adept at the latter. He learned English within the family circle. In 1812 he was enrolled in the Lycée Napoléon (later called Henri IV), where he was a facile student in the classical program studying what he pleased and neglecting all else. Upon completion of the baccalaureate he studied law at the University of Paris (1819-23), but continued to pursue hobbies such as Greek, Spanish, and the occult.

While still a student Mérimée started to frequent various artistic and literary circles. With Jean Jacques Ampère he translated Ossian; with Stendhal he visited the salon of Joseph Lingay, editor of the *Journal de Paris*, and was introduced into the *cénacle* of Étienne Delécluze, art critic for the *Journal des Débats*. Mérimée wrote on the Spanish theatre for *Le Globe* (1824), collaborated

* mă rē mă'

MÉRIMÉE

with Stendhal on a play, and wrote "saynètes" according to Stendhalian principles, for the Delécluze group. These pieces became part of *Le Théâtre de Clara Gazul, Comédienne Espagnole* (1825). Delécluze drew a sketch of Mérimée, with a feminine overlay, to represent the supposed author. Cabinet pieces, not intended for the stage, these sketches reflect the new romantic movement. But they contain also the character of their author—a mixture of controlled romanticism, matter-of-factness, mockery, and skepticism.

Two years later Mérimée published *La Guzla*, translations of twenty-eight "Illyrian" ballads supposedly gathered in Dalmatia, Bosnia, Croatia, and Herzegovina. These scenes of violence and vampirism were to be sung with accompaniment on the "guzla"—anagram of Gazul! The collection had only a moderate sale, but some scholars were taken in, and Pushkin translated some of the ballads into Russian. *La Jacquerie, Scènes Féodales* (1828) was set in fourteenth century France; announced as the work of the author of *Clara Gazul*, this play too was not intended for the stage. An historical novel à la Walter Scott, *Chronique du Temps de Charles IX* (1829), appeared under the same pseudonym. This bloody tale ends the cycle of Mérimée's purely romantic, youthful works.

Between 1829 and 1848 Mérimée wrote the series of short stories or novelettes for which he is especially known. Within one year he published twelve tales in the new

Revue de Paris of Véron. He had mastered the art of succinctness and impersonality in relating gory events and violent emotions, and of selectivity in using local color. *Mateo Falcone,* the first work to be signed with his own name, presents the Corsican code of honor; *L'Enlèvement de la Redoute* tells of an attack on a fort; *Le Vase Étrusque* is a story of jealousy and a concise psychological study. The latter is no doubt based on Mérimée's pistol duel with the husband of Émilie Lacoste, whom Mérimée really loved of his many mistresses (she had also been the mistress of Joseph Bonaparte). It has been rumored that Émile Duranty, the novelist, was Mérimée's son by Émilie Lacoste.

In 1826 Mérimée had visited England and met Mrs. Shelley and Sutton Sharpe; in 1830, from July through November, he visited Spain. There he became friendly with Count and Countess Teba who in 1834 inherited the title of Montijo; their daughter Eugenia was to become the wife of Napoleon III. Upon returning to France, subsequent to the July upheaval, Mérimée entered the naval ministry of Count Apollinaire d'Argout as his secretary and soon became director of the bureau. He remained attached to Argout in the latter's various political positions. But official duties did not handicap Mérimée's sentimental affairs, numerous and parallel; of these, his relationship with Jenny Dacquin, the *inconnue* who used the penname of Lady Algernon Seymour, lasted for eighteen years. His romance with George Sand in 1833 was a fiasco, despite Mérimée's reputation as a man-about-town. In contrast to his facility at conquest was his yearning for, and inability to find, a stable and satisfying relationship.

In 1834 Mérimée became inspector of historical monuments. His duties involved extensive travel and he encouraged his friend Viollet-le-Duc in architectural restoration and preservation. Mérimée criss-crossed France and visited Corsica, Italy, Greece, Asia Minor. He prepared many archeological and historical reports in connection with his duties; in 1843 he became a member of the Académie des Inscriptions et Belles-Lettres, the following year of the Académie Française. But he also wrote "nouvelles," the most famous of which are undoubtedly *Colomba* (1840) and *Carmen* (1845). The latter was made into an opera by Georges Bizet and has become an international favorite. Some of Mérimée's energy went into translations of Pushkin, Gogol, Turgenev;

he also wrote on Stendhal—*H. B.* (1849), i.e., Henri Beyle.

When Eugenia de Montijo became empress of France in 1853, Mérimée was made a Senator and given an income of 30,000 francs a year. But Mérimée continued to live simply, with increasing reserve of manner and dress. Rheumatism plagued him, and he spent much of the year at Cannes, although occasionally figuring in the life of the imperial court. He died at Cannes, where he is buried in the English cemetery.

A fire in 1871 destroyed many of Mérimée's manuscripts. His works have been edited in a uniform edition (12 volumes) by Pierre Trahard and others; another edition of the complete works is in progress for Les Textes Français. Maurice Parturier has been editing the numerous letters to many correspondents (1941-   ). Details of earlier editions are to be found in the *Bibliographie des Œuvres de P. Mérimée* by P. Trahard and P. Josserand (1929).

Colomba, which has had many school editions, was translated into English by Rose Sherman (1897). Mary Lloyd translated *Colomba* and *Carmen*, with an introduction by Arthur Symons (1907). *Carmen* was translated by E. H. Garrett in 1896, by A. E. Johnson in 1915; Albert Sterner illustrated his translation of 1931. *Carmen*, together with *Life in Spain*, was illustrated by Maurice Barraud for an edition of 1931. Of the correspondence, *Letters to [Sir Anthony] Panizzi* were translated by H. M. Dunstan (1881), and the *Letters to an Incognita [Jeanne Françoise Dacquin]* by Baroness Mary E. Herbert of Lea (1874), and again by Henri Pène du Bois (1897). A. R. Scoble published a translation of *Demetrius the Impostor, an Episode in Russian History* (1853). George Saintsbury translated *A Chronicle of the Reign of Charles IX* (1890), but Theodore Bolton entitled his translation *Diane de Turgis, a Chronicle of the Reign of Charles IX* (1925). The latter had first appeared in English in 1830 as *1572, a Chronicle of the Times of Charles the Ninth.* E. M. Waller, J. Gilmer, and H. Morley were responsible for *Golden Tales* (1929); these appeared as *Stories* in 1908; G. B. Ives entitled his selection *Prosper Mérimée* (1903). Various translators contributed to *The Writings of Prosper Mérimée*, with an essay by George Saintsbury (8 vols., 1905). J. I. Rodale entitled his selection *Tales of Love and Death* (1948). *The Plays of Clara Gazul, a Spanish Comedian* had appeared the same year (1825) as the original French edition. Eliot Fay's translation from *Mosaïque* was entitled *The Slave Ship of Prosper Mérimée, a Tragedy in Black and White* (1934). In addition to Bizet's *Carmen*, there is a musico-dramatic work by J. Schampaert based on *Mateo Falcone*, and an opera *Die Baskische Venus*, by H. H. Wetzler, from *Vénus d'Ille.* Jacques Copeau staged *Le Carrosse du Saint-Sacrement* in 1920. In 1920 Henri Büsser mounted a light opera based on *Colomba*, which was also made into a film.

ABOUT: Brandes, G. M. Main Currents in Nineteenth Century Literature, vol. 5; Derivent,

G. H. J. Prosper Mérimée; Lyons, S. The Life and Times of Prosper Mérimée; Pater, W. H. Studies in European Literature, Series 1; Symons, A. The Symbolist Movement in Literature; Thorold, A. L. Six Masters in Disillusion. [In French—Luppé, Marquis de. Mérimée; Roger, G. Mérimée et la Corse; Trahard, P. La Jeunesse de Prosper Mérimée, . . . de 1834 à 1853, La Vieillesse (4 vols., 1925-30), *and* Prosper Mérimée et l'Art de la Nouvelle.]

S. S. W.

---

*MESONERO Y ROMANOS, RAMÓN DE** (July 19, 1803-April 30, 1882), Spanish *costumbrista* writer, was born in Madrid on the street now named after him. His father was Matías de Mesonero, a rich landowner from the province of Salamanca who was also a prosperous business man in Madrid. The young Ramón was educated at the Instituto de San Isidro in Madrid. On the death of his father in 1820, Ramón came into possession of the family business but, having no interest in such matters, he soon decided to sell everything and to devote himself exclusively to literature. He did not attend a university, preferring extensive travel in France, Belgium, and England. In 1849 Mesonero married Salomé de Ichaso, by whom he had a number of children. She died in 1894. He himself died suddenly of a cerebral stroke in Madrid at the age of seventy-eight, a member of the Spanish Academy. There is a monument to him by Blay in the Paseo de Recoletos in Madrid.

Mesonero y Romanos, inspired in part by the sketches of contemporary life done by Victor Jouy in France, dedicated himself to this genre and, together with the lesser known Estébanez Calderón, founded what is known as the *costumbrista* school of writers in Spain, treating of local customs. His sketches and memoirs are concerned almost solely with Madrid, and there can have been few men who loved their native city more. Since the modern Spanish novel has for one of its chief sources the *costumbrista* movement, Mesonero holds a special place in the history of Spanish letters. In 1831, he published his *Manual de Madrid*, which in a later form—freed from censorship and supplemented—was called *El Antiguo Madrid* (1861). This is not only of literary interest, but is also the best guide we have to old Madrid. The first *costumbrista* series which he published was called the *Panorama Matritense* (3 vols., 1835-38). It was followed by a second series entitled *Escenas Matritenses* (1842). Scattered articles of Meso-

* mä sō nä′ rō ē rō mä′ nōs

nero's were collected and published as *Tipos y Caracteres* (1862). The year before his death saw the appearance of *Memorias de un Setentón* (1881). As personal memoirs of the Madrid of the first half of the nineteenth century they are without rival. Mesonero also founded and directed the weekly *Semanario Pintoresco Español*. He frequently wrote under the pseudonym "El Curioso Parlante."

Mesonero's powers of observation were very great, and his sketches show throughout a light and occasionally satirical touch. He could at times be somewhat reactionary, but in general he managed to remain calm and detached as he well shows in *El Romanticismo y los Románticos*, which is still an excellent, humorous indictment of the extremes of romanticism. The following editions of his work are especially important: *Obras* (1881); *Algo en Prosa y en Verso* (1883); *Trabajos no Coleccionados* (1903-05) and *Obras* (1925).

ABOUT: PMLA, XLV (1930); Romanic Review, XXI (1930). [In Spanish—see study by J. Olmedilla y Puig; Boletín de la Academia Española, XII (1925); España Moderna (1903).]

R. E. O.

*METASTASIO, PIETRO ANTONIO DOMENICO BUONAVENTURA (January 3, 1698-April 12, 1782), Italian poet and dramatist, born in Rome, was the son of Felice Trapassi of Assisi, in the Papal service. At an early age, Metastasio showed his talent in improvisation and singing, and attracted the attention of G. V. Gravina, who undertook his education and in 1714 took him to Calabria for further study under Calaprese. Metastasio returned to Rome about a year later, took minor orders, and with a profession in view began the study of law. His first writings were published in Naples in 1717, including his *Poesie*, a tragedy entitled *Giustino* (about 1713), an epic, a mythological idyll, and a religious ode.

Gravina died early in 1718 and bequeathed his library and a considerable sum of money to his disciple; the rapid disappearance of the money, to cite but this one example, must remain a legend, since Metastasio's many enemies turned the events of his life against him. He was received in the "Arcadia" at once, and became its most renowned poet of this period. A marriage projected in 1719 came to nothing, and he returned to Naples to practice law. From the next several years, and his constant presence in the salons and

METASTASIO

the academies, date his first important contacts with future protectors, especially those associated with the Imperial Austrian court. Also in this period he met the first of the three Mariannas who color his career, the wife of Antonio Pignatelli, to whom he dedicated a *serenata*, and Marianna Bulgarelli, the great singer in whose circle he met the musicians Scarlatti and Porpora. For La Bulgarelli, Metastasio created the principal rôle of his first opera, or "melodrama," the *Didone* (1723). This text had an immense and lasting success and was set to music by some forty composers. The poet and the singer were very close until his departure for Vienna in 1730; their relationship, perhaps primarily Platonic, led to savage calumny, and was an important factor in his self-imposed exile.

In Vienna, Metastasio enjoyed the favors and the confidence of the Emperor Charles VI, and was protected by Marianna Pignatelli. In this strongly Italophile atmosphere, he and his work met with immediate and lasting success, in several dramatic genres, but especially in his operatic masterpieces *Adriano in Siria* and *Attilio Regolo* (1740). During the long reign of Maria Theresa, he continued his rich production and his place of honor in the Imperial court, and his fame spread as far as Madrid. After the death of Marianna Pignatelli, his creative imagination declined, though he remained productive. The third and last of the Mariannas, Martinez (1745-1812), was his consolation in old age. The death of the Empress in 1780 marked the end

* mä tä stä′ zyō

of a period of which Metastasio was the most brilliant representative; his own death was widely regretted, but his work was rapidly eclipsed by that of Alfieri, and the ideological and political hostility toward Austria of the following century caused his writings to be unjustly scorned.

Metastasio left over two thousand letters, of interest with regard both to the times and to his personal theory of the theatre; to those published in his *Opere* of 1795 one must add others collected in 1883; and further statements of theory appear in his commentaries on the *Poetica* of Horace and of Aristotle, both of which he translated. His plays, his real contribution to literature, fall into two groups according to the greater or lesser emphasis on sentiment or on heroism. The first heroic play, *Catone in Utica*, met with little success in 1727, and Metastasio turned for a while to the sentimental genre of his earlier *Didone*, and to elaborations of plot and theatrical effects, giving us a series of types rather than of real persons. The second period, during the reign of Charles VI, saw his great masterpieces, with more measured and sober construction, more human situations, and a balanced form; both the dialogue and the versification improved notably, and he drew subjects from Tasso, for example in the *Olimpiade*, set to music over thirty times, and in the *Clemenza di Tito* (for which Mozart wrote the music), admired by Voltaire.

Metastasio's *Poesie* was published in 1773 in six volumes, and the *Opere* were first published in Paris, in twelve volumes, 1780-82, with numerous new editions appearing over the years, one as recently as 1943-52 (ed. Brunelli, 3 vols.). In 1796 Charles Burney published *The Life and Letters of Metastasio* (3 vols.). An English translation of some of his works, *Dramas and Other Poems,* was made by J. Hoole in 1800 (3 vols.). The most popular of his works, to judge from the number of eighteenth century English translations, was the drama *Artaxerxes* which served as the libretto for an opera by Thomas Arne. A verse translation of *Didone Abbandonata, Dido Forsaken,* was made by J. G. Fucilla in 1952.

ABOUT: Lee, V. Studies in the Eighteenth Century. [In Italian—see studies by M. Apollonio, G. Natali, L. Russo, M. Vani.]

F. J. C.

MEUNG, JEAN DE. See JEAN DE MEUNG

MEYER, CONRAD FERDINAND (October 11, 1825-November 28, 1898), Swiss short-story writer and poet, was born in Zürich, of a wealthy patrician family. His

MEYER

father, Ferdinand Meyer, was a respected jurist, who imparted a love of history to his son. His mother, Elisabeth, was a highly nervous woman with a tendency toward melancholy, which Meyer inherited. Throughout life he received the greatest encouragement and assistance from his younger sister, Betsy, who served him devotedly as secretary and adviser.

After attending the *Gymnasium* in Zürich, Meyer studied at Lausanne and Genf, before entering the University of Zürich to study law at his mother's wish. During these years he was moody, withdrawn, and completely undecided about his future, vacillating between poetry and art as a career and between French and German as a means of expression. In 1852 his nervous condition became so serious that he voluntarily entered a sanitarium. The following year he traveled to Lausanne to visit Louis Vulliemin, a clergyman and historian, who became interested in Meyer's literary ambitions, and obtained permission for him to translate Thierry's *Récits des Temps Mérovingiens* into German (1855). This period of contentment was interrupted by his mother's suicide, and Meyer, to recover from his grief, traveled to Paris, which he found disappointing. Italy, however, which he visited in 1858, fascinated him and exerted a profound influence on his later writings.

Meyer's first independent work, *Zwanzig Balladen von einem Schweizer* (1864), appeared anonymously, and not until 1869 did he venture a volume of poems, *Romanzen und Bilder*, bearing his name. The war of 1870 finally induced Meyer to become a German writer and filled him with the desire to express his new-found patriotism. At the age of forty-five he produced the first of his eleven short stories, the verse narrative *Huttens Letzte Tage* (1871).

In 1875 he married Luise Ziegler, an accomplished artist, with whom he found great happiness. Ill health clouded his later years, and in 1892 overwork caused a complete breakdown from which he never fully recovered. He died peacefully at Kilchberg.

After his first success Meyer's works appeared in rapid order. Following his *Engelberg* (1872), a second story in verse, he turned to prose and wrote *Das Amulett* (1873) and *Jürg Jenatsch* (1874), both of which rank among his finest stories. These works brought recognition and established Meyer's literary reputation. In 1878 he produced *Der Schuss von der Kanzel*, which with the sole exception of *Plautus im Nonnenkloster* (1882), was his only attempt at writing comedy. His most important work, *Der Heilige* (1880), which depicts the conflict of Thomas à Becket and Henry II of England, was followed by *Gustav Adolphs Page* (1882), *Die Leiden eines Knaben* (1883), *Die Hochzeit des Mönchs* (1884), *Die Richterin* (1885), *Die Versuchung des Pescara* (1887), and *Angela Borgia* (1891).

The subject matter for his stories Meyer took from the historical past, although he was more interested in the psychological aspects of his characters than in strict historical accuracy. He was particularly attracted to the Renaissance, which abounded in the strong personalities he so greatly admired. As a narrator he was completely objective, and his works are therefore totally lacking in subjective moods and sentimental scenes. He was the virtuoso of the *Rahmenerzählung* or frame-story, a technique which he brought to its highest development in *Die Hochzeit des Mönchs*. Among the masters of the modern German short-story, Meyer was a most painstaking craftsman, and his works, products of arduous composition and constant refinement, excel in beauty of form and style.

Meyer's verse (*Gedichte*, 1882) is also distinguished by the characteristics of objectivity and dispassion. His ballads rank with the best in German literature, and his poems, meticulous in form and meter, are rich in symbols of universal experience and truth.

Der Heilige was translated into English by M. V. Wendheim as *Thomas Becket the Saint* (1885), by M. J. Taber as *The Chancellor's Secret* (1887), and by E. F. Hauch as *The Saint* (1930). S. H. Adams translated *Die Hochzeit des Mönchs* as *The Monk's Wedding* (1887). This same work was translated by W. G. Howard along with *Plautus im Nonnenkloster*, which appeared as *Plautus in the Convent* (1913-15). An English version of *Die Versuchung des Pescara* was made by C. Bell in 1890 under the title *The Tempting of Pescara*. Selections of Meyer's verse in English are contained in D. Broicher, *German Lyrics and Ballads Done into English Verse* (1912), *The German Classics* XIV (1913-15) and The Warner Library. *The Stories of C. F. Meyer*, translated by W. D. Williams, appeared in 1962.

ABOUT: Burkhard, A. Conrad F. Meyer, the Style and the Man; Bennett, E. K. The German Novelle; Klenze, C. von. From Goethe to Hauptmann. [In German—see studies by A. Frey, L. Hohenstein, A. Langmesser, W. Linden, H. Maync, L. Wiesmann. [In French—see R. d'Harcourt. In Italian—see A. Heubi.]

D. G. D.

*MICHELANGELO BUONAROTTI

(March 6, 1475-February 18, 1564), Italian sculptor, painter, architect, and poet, was born in Caprese, son of Ludovico Buonarotti and Francesca de' Neri. His father was poor but of a proud family line and held minor state offices under the patronage of the Medici family. His parents returned to Florence soon after the child was born, and he was put out to nurse in Settignano with a family of stone-cutters. Years later he told his biographer Vasari: "I drew the chisel and the mallet with which I carve statues in with my nurse's milk." Young Michelangelo was educated in Florence and early showed brilliant artistic promise. At thirteen he was apprenticed to the workshop of the Ghirlandaio brothers to learn painting. It was here that he came to the attention of Lorenzo de' Medici and was sent to live in the Casa Medici where he worked at sculpture surrounded by all the wealth and magnificence of Lorenzo's court. Here also the boy met the Neoplatonists Ficino and Pico della Mirandola, the poets Poliziano and Pulci, and many other great artists and scholars of the age.

In 1492 Lorenzo died and young Michelangelo returned to his father's house. In the years which followed he moved around between Bologna, Venice, Rome, and Florence, working constantly and building a reputation as one of the great sculptors of the day. During this period he conceived and executed many of his most splendid pieces—among them the Pietà and the David. In 1505 he

* mē kāl än' jä lō bwó när rō' tē

633

MICHELANGELO BUONAROTTI

MICHELANGELO

was summoned to Rome by Pope Julius II to build a grandiose marble monument for his tomb. This proved to be a long and painful task on which he worked for four decades. Pope Julius constantly interrupted his work to make changes and new demands. The pope died, his executors died, and Michelangelo was commissioned and re-commissioned. The project was never actually completed, and only fragments of it survive—the most famous being the magnificent Moses which is the glory of the otherwise modest tomb in the church of St. Peter in Vincoli. One of Pope Julius' many interruptions was the order to decorate the ceiling of the Sistine Chapel with frescoes. This Michelangelo began reluctantly in 1508. The work took some three and a half agonizing years, much of which time he spent on a scaffold, flat on his back, eyes to the ceiling. Somehow he retained sufficient good humor to describe the experience in a sonnet:

> My beard turns up to heaven; my nape
> falls in.
> Fixed on my spine: my breast-bone visibly
> Grows like a harp: a rich embroidery
> Bedews my face from brush-drops thick
> and thin.

Michelangelo spent most of the middle period of his life moving back and forth between Rome and Florence executing commissions for the popes and for the Medici family. In 1527 he sided with the citizens of Florence in an attempt to free the city from Medicean domination. In 1530 their efforts failed and the Medicis returned to power, but Michel-

angelo remained in their good graces. In 1534 he returned to Rome for the last time, settling down there to complete his long lifetime with such masterpieces as The Last Judgment (in the Sistine Chapel) and the design of the dome of St. Peter's. He spent his last years as an honored Roman citizen. The nervous, somewhat irritable temperament which characterized his youth was accentuated in his advanced years, but he retained many close friends. He died peacefully only a few weeks before his eighty-ninth birthday. The funeral ceremonies took place in Rome, but the body was taken to Florence for burial and it lies in the church of Santa Croce in a tomb designed by Vasari.

It is perhaps fitting in an age of such rich cultural versatility as the sixteenth century Renaissance that its greatest artist should also have been its greatest poet. Michelangelo began writing poetry in his youth, but his finest poems were composed in the last twenty years of his life. These poems (mainly sonnets and madrigals) are in some degree comparable with his sculpture—lofty but rough-hewn, in the sense that their language is not always polished and refined and their thought-content is often so massive as to be obscure. Nevertheless they are acknowledged as the finest poems written in Italian since Dante and Petrarch. These two great poets were Michelangelo's masters (he wrote two sonnets in praise of Dante), but the content of his poems is entirely Neoplatonic. It is not the academic Neoplatonism of the schools which he sings, however, but an intense personal expression. Ernest H. Wilkins writes: "He was the one true Platonist among the Italian poets of his century—the only one, that is, to whom love meant specifically the searching for the divine immanence and the ascent to the divine that had been set forth by Ficino." This Neoplatonism is most fully set forth in the sonnets dedicated to two close friends—a handsome young Roman, Tommaso Cavalieri, and the talented woman poet Vittoria Colonna. These poems were not published until 1623 when they appeared in an edition by Michelangelo Buonarotti the Younger (1568-1642), his grand-nephew, who, apparently in an excess of prudery and family propriety, refined their roughness of expression and suppressed the fact that many were dedicated to young men. As a result it was for many centuries believed that Michelangelo had written most of his love poetry for Vittoria Colonna. While they were indeed devoted friends, there is no evidence whatever of any romantic passion between them. New and more faithful editions of the poems by Guasti in 1863 and by Frey in 1897 have set the record straight on this point.

The standard English translation of Michelangelo's poems was made by J. A. Symonds, *The Sonnets of Michel Angelo Buonarotti and Tommaso Campanella* (1878). Others are *Sonnets and Madrigals*, translated by W. W. Newell (1900); *The Sonnets of Michelangelo*, translated by S. Elizabeth Hall (1905); *The Complete Poems of Michelangelo*, by Joseph Tusiani (1960). *Complete Poems and Selected Letters*, edited by Creighton Gilbert, was published in 1963. Wordsworth, Longfellow, Santayana, and many others have translated individual poems, and these appear in many anthologies. L. R. Lind prints a representative selection in his *Lyric Poetry of the Italian Renaissance* (1954).

ABOUT: Biographical and critical studies of Michelangelo in English are numerous. A few of the best-known are: Brandes, G. Michelangelo (tr. H. Norden); Clements, R. J. Michelangelo's Theory of Art; *also* (ed.) Michelangelo: A Self-Portrait; Condivi, A. Life of Michelangelo Buonarotti; Finlayson, D. L. Michelangelo; Ludwig, E. Three Titans; Morgan, C. H. Life of Michelangelo; Papini, G. Michelangelo; Pater, W. The Renaissance; Rolland, R. Michelangelo; Symonds, J. A. Life of Michelangelo Buonarotti; Vasari, G. Lives of the Artists; Venturi, A. Michelangelo. Among studies of Michelangelo's verse the following are especially useful: Gilbert, C. *in* Italica, XXII (1945) and XXIV (1947); Harper, G. M. *in* John Morley and Other Essays; Clements, R. J. *in* PMLA, March 1954; Wilkins, E. H. A History of Italian Literature. [In Italian—see Mariani, V. Poesia di Michelangelo.]

*MICHELET, JULES (August 21, 1798- February 10, 1874), French historian and essayist, was born in Paris of a Huguenot family, though he later became a Catholic. The son of a printer, he grew up in dire poverty and worked as a child in his father's printing shop. He nevertheless managed to get a good education at the Lycée Charlemagne, and by 1822 he was a professor of history at the Collège Rollin. Michelet never forgot the hardships of his youth, however, and always retained a keen pity for the unfortunate. The literary works which influenced him most in youth were *The Imitation of Christ* and Virgil, in which he found moral consolation. He became interested in a study of the past, in both history and philosophy, and especially in the early history of France, beginning in the Merovingian period.

It was probably his reading of Giovanni Vico, the eighteenth century Italian philosopher of history, that inspired in him a need for formulating a personal concept of history: "I had no other master but Vico. His principle of living force, of humanity creating itself, made both my book and my teach-

* mēsh lě′

MICHELET

ing." Michelet's first publications, in 1827, were a translation of Vico's *Scienza Nuova*, under the title *Principes de la Philosophie de l'Histoire*, and a fine *Précis de l'Histoire Moderne*, in which he applied Vico's methods. That same year Michelet was appointed to the École Normale and subsequently had a brilliant career as a teacher, thanks to his intense personal enthusiasm and learning. During the reorganization of the school after 1830 he took full charge of the program in medieval history and became the head of the historical section of the National Archives. In 1831 he published his *Introduction à l'Histoire Universelle* and his *Histoire de la République Romaine*, paving the way for a real science of historical criticism.

Michelet's most personal contribution as a creative artist appears in his *Histoire de France*, published from 1833 to 1846. From one point of view he exaggerates Vico's method of evocation through an almost sentimental reaction to the documents of the past and a notion of the survival of a living spirit. He has been called a "romantic" historian because of the imagination, movement and color of his work, but his fundamental approach to history is realistic. Michelet has the art of giving life to situations and places in his interpretations of the spirit of cities and regions according to their dominant preoccupations and activities; hence he integrates general culture with commerce and politics in a tone of deep respect for the continuity of institutions. These traits explain the literary qualities of many great episodes in his work,

635

such as the madness of Charles VI, or the story of Joan of Arc.

Michelet entered a second period when in 1838 he was named professor at the Collège de France and began a series of vigorous lectures on liberal ideologies and political reform. As events led toward the revolution of 1848 his emotionalism came to the fore. He attacked those elements in French society which seemed to him false, notably the Jesuits and the Church in general, for example in *Du Prêtre, de la Famille et de la Femme* (1845). Because of his support of the revolution he was dismissed from his teaching post. He never became fully reconciled to the new government, and devoted most of the remainder of his career to his writing. He prepared a history of the Revolution with careful and objective documentation but marked by an excess of subjectivity. Indeed, on resuming his *Histoire de France* from the Renaissance to modern times his hostility toward the Church and his excessively subtle interpretations disfigure the facts, though the work is significant for its fine pictures of men and its sensitive recreation of the misfortunes of the past.

Michelet married twice. By his first wife, who died in 1839, he had a son and a daughter. In 1850 he married Athanaïs Mialaret, a teacher and writer, many years his junior. The second Mme Michelet was especially interested in the natural sciences, to the study of which she introduced her husband, with the result that he wrote several excellent books on bird and insect life. His greatest achievement, however, remains his *Histoire de France*: "a great work of imagination and research," Edmund Wilson describes it, ". . . the supreme effort in its time of a human being to enter into, to understand, to comprehend, the development of a modern nation. There is no book that makes us feel when we have finished it that we have lived through and known with such intimacy so many generations of men."

Michelet left many manuscripts at his death, notably his papers for *L'Histoire du Dix-Neuvième Siècle,* which he completed up to Waterloo. His fame is attested to by the astounding number of English translations and retranslations of *The Bird* (1868) and *The Insect* (1875), but especially of his historical writings—*Modern History* (1843), *History of the Roman Republic* (by W. Hazlitt, 1847), *The History of France* (by W. Kelly, 1844-46, and again by G. Smith, 1845-47), *Historical View of the French Revolution* (by C. Cocks, 1848, etc.), *The Jesuits* (1845), *Life of Luther* (1846), *France Before Europe* (1871), *The Bible of Humanity* (1877), *Joan of Arc* (1900). His *Œuvres Complètes* appeared 1893-99 in forty volumes.

About: Wilson, E. To the Finland Station; Quarterly Review, 1901. [In French—Faguet, E. Politiques et Moralistes du Dix-Neuvième Siècle; Halévy, D. Jules Michelet; Monod, G. Jules Michelet.]

F. J. C.

*MICKIEWICZ, ADAM (December 24, 1798-November 26, 1855), Polish poet, playwright, and scholar, was born in Zaosie, near Nowogrodek, in Lithuania, united for over four centuries with Poland and in 1795 occupied by Russia. His father, Mikolaj, belonged to the local gentry; he was a lawyer, and people who visited his home came from various strata of the population; thus even as a child the prospective poet observed typical characters of the past who were by this time rapidly disappearing from the social scene. His mother, Barbara, *née* Majewska, was in charge of the household; she was warmly remembered in the poet's writings. Contacts with peasants and servants gave him an opportunity to learn local folklore. Adam attended a secondary school in Nowogrodek run by the Dominican Order. Its scholarly level was modest, but its standards of discipline were high. In 1812 the boy's father died, and the financial position of the family became difficult. The same year saw intense patriotic excitement as a result of the Napoleonic campaign against Russia. The sight of the great army retreating made a deep impression on the boy.

In 1815 he was enrolled at the University of Vilno. This school, owing to efforts of its curator, Adam Czartoryski, was at that time the best Polish university; many prominent scholars and scientists, Polish and foreign, belonged to its faculty. Mickiewicz began to study sciences, but after one year he concentrated on literature and languages. He was one of the founders and leaders of the secret organization the Philomaths, which encouraged learning as a means for social progress and freedom. It was a small group, but it influenced a large number of students. Mickiewicz wrote some poems for his colleagues, the most celebrated being *Ode to Youth*. In 1819 his studies came to an end, and he became a teacher in Kowno, without severing contact with his Vilnian friends. He continued his education through intensive reading, thoroughly acquainting himself with German and English romantic poets, whose examples encouraged him to find sources for his writing in folklore. He fell in love with Marie Wereszczako, daughter of a wealthy

* mēts kyĕ' vĕch

MICKIEWICZ

landowner, but she married someone else. The poet's disappointment found expression in *Ballads and Romances* (1822) and inspired the tempestuous second and fourth parts of his dramatic poem *The Forefathers*. This was followed by *Grazyna* (1822), a calm and well-balanced narrative poem celebrating feminine heroism.

The personal feelings of Mickiewicz were overshadowed, however, by political events. The Russian authorities learned of the Philomaths and imprisoned many of them, including the poet. After a cruel and prolonged investigation Mickiewicz was condemned to exile in Russia. In October 1824 he left his native country and went to St. Petersburg. Although nominated professor of the college in Odessa, he was not allowed to teach. He made a trip to the Crimea, where he fell under the charm of Oriental culture and nature. Upon returning, he settled in Moscow. The liberal Russian intelligentsia respected and valued him; he was a welcome guest in aristocratic drawing rooms and maintained friendly relations with several Russian writers—the brothers Polevoi, Kozlov, and Pushkin. His fame was enhanced by the publication of *Crimean Sonnets* reflecting personal emotions against a background of magnificent subtropical nature. Polish friends blamed him for his Russian friendships, but he ignored their criticisms. In 1828 he published *Konrad Wallenrod*, a narrative poem introducing a hero who saved his country from the aggressive Teutonic Order by becoming Grandmaster of the Order and then betraying it. The poem was admired in Poland and in Russia, but its political implications aroused suspicion.

Mickiewicz managed to obtain permission to go abroad and visited Bohemia, Germany, Switzerland, and Italy. He experienced a religious renascence which inspired several profound poems, and suffered another disappointment in love with an unrequited passion for Henryka Ankvich, daughter of a rich nobleman. When, in 1830, the news came of the Polish uprising, he still remained away from his native land, not returning until August 1831, by which time the position of the insurgents had become untenable. He followed the disarmed Polish soldiers to Dresden where he witnessed their enthusiastic welcome by the Germans and discovered that the defeated uprising was a valuable contribution to the movement for European liberation.

In 1832 Mickiewicz wrote the third part of *The Forefathers*, which became his poetical autobiography. In it he described the persecution of the Philomaths and his own poetical rôle, and forecast the imminent resurrection of the nation and ultimate universal freedom. His brochure *Books of the Polish Nation and the Polish Pilgrimage*, modeled on the Gospels, identified the cause of Polish independence with the struggles of other European democracies to overthrow their monarchies and had widespread international repercussions. Mickiewicz settled in Paris and took part in Polish émigré political activities. His longing for his native country was the emotional background of the epic poem *Pan Tadeusz*, his masterpiece, begun in December 1832, finished in February 1834. Soon afterwards he married Celina Szymanowska, daughter of a celebrated Polish pianist. The pair, who had several children, were often on the brink of poverty.

In the following years Mickiewicz published a selection of *Apothegms and Sayings*, and did numerous translations, including one of Byron's "The Giaour." His attempt to write plays in French for production in Paris was unsuccessful. In 1838 he became professor of Latin literature at the University of Lausanne where he was highly appreciated. While living in Switzerland he wrote some exquisite lyric poems. Two years later Mickiewicz went to Paris to occupy the chair of Slavonic literatures at the Collège de France. Again he enjoyed great success, and his lectures were attended by many émigré Slavs as well as by the élite of Paris intellectual society. His private life was becoming increasingly unhappy, however, because his wife had suffered a mental breakdown. She was "miraculously" cured (reportedly in one session) by a Lithuanian, Andrzej Towianski, who declared himself to be something of a prophet. Mickiewicz became his disciple and organized a group of his followers. For attempting to propagate Towianski's doctrines in his lectures, he was dismissed from his post at the Collège de France. He did not remain long under Towianski's influence.

In 1848 Mickiewicz plunged into active political life. He organized a Polish legion in Italy and led them personally on a march from Rome to Milan. His impassioned speeches aroused great sympathy for his cause among the Italians. He was even received by the Pope whose support for a democratic upsurge in Europe he attempted to gain. He founded a French newspaper, *La Tribune des Peuples,* for which he wrote over one hundred articles on contemporary European affairs, all imbued with the ideas of liberty and social progress; but owing to the unfriendly attitude of the French régime the publication was liquidated. During the Crimean war the Poles attempted to create an army in cooperation with Turkish armed forces; Mickiewicz went to Turkey to support this move. He inspected the troops and established useful contacts; soon, however, in Constantinople, he fell victim of cholera and died. He was carried on board a warship to France, and solemnly buried in Paris. In 1890 his body was transported to Poland and buried in the national shrine in Cracow among the greatest men of the nation.

After a brief youthful period of writing in the spirit of classicism and the Enlightenment, Mickiewicz associated himself with the romantic movement. His ballads, based frequently on folk motives, became exceedingly popular. His fantastic drama *The Forefathers,* conceived on a large scale, reflected the main European trends of his period: change from egotistic self-contemplation to nationalism, and from rationalistic coolness towards religious upheaval and mystical faith. This work is comparable to Goethe's *Faust.* In his narrative poems Mickiewicz approached Walter Scott, and, above all, Byron, without sharing the latter's pessimism and proud isolation, which was incompatible with the patriotic fervor of Mickiewicz's literary heritage. *Pan Tadeusz* is a comprehensive picture of the life of the Polish gentry; its story reminds the reader of some of Walter Scott's novels, but is treated with Homeric grandeur.

Pan Tadeusz has a good claim to being the only masterpiece among modern efforts in the realm of the epic poem. As a lyric poet Mickiewicz excels in expressing powerful, almost superhuman emotions, in maintaining harmony, unshakeable sincerity, naturalness— all this with an apparent simplicity which conceals great technical artistry. He was also successful in the use of an ornate and rich Oriental style. His lectures on Slavonic literature were a pioneer work in this sphere of research. For his nation Mickiewicz was a spiritual leader in literature and politics. In the middle of the nineteenth century he was one of the outstanding figures of European thought.

Various attempts have been made to translate Mickiewicz's works into English. More recent publications include the volume *Poems by Adam Mickiewicz,* translated by G. R. Noyes (1944,) and *Adam Mickiewicz, 1798-1855: Selected Poems,* edited by Clark Mills (1955). *Grazyna* was translated by D. P. Radin in *Poet Lore* (1940) ; *Konrad Wallenrod* and other writings appeared in a collective volume (1925). *Pan Tadeusz* was translated by G. R. Noyes in 1917 and reprinted in the Everyman Library (1932). Watson Kirkconnell published a translation in 1960. A bibliography of Mickiewicz in English was compiled by M. M. Coleman (1955).

ABOUT: Kellenbach, J. Adam Mickiewicz; Kleiner, J. Adam Mickiewicz; Kridl, M. Adam Mickiewicz, Poet of Poland; Lednicki, W. Bits of Table Talks on Pushkin, Mickiewicz, Goethe, Turgenev, and Sienkiewicz; *also,* Adam Mickiewicz in World Literature; Weintraub, W. The Poetry of Adam Mickiewicz.

M. G.

*MIKHAILOVSKY, NIKOLAI KONSTANTINOVICH** (November 26, 1842-February 9, 1904), Russian sociologist and critic, was born in Meshchovsk, Kaluga Gubernia, of a family of small means, the son of a minor government official. His education at the *Gymnasium* in Kostroma was interrupted by the death of his father in 1856, and he was taken to St. Petersburg and entered in the Mining Institute of the university to study engineering. He was an excellent student and an omnivorous reader. Along with many of his fellows, he was sensitive to the atmosphere of unrest which followed the disastrous Crimean War, expressed in greater and greater pressure to liberate the serfs. Mikhailovsky took part in several student demonstrations, with the result that he was expelled from the Institute just prior to his graduation and exiled from the capital.

Back at home he decided against an engineering career, and took up the study of law

* myĭ kĭ lôf' skē

in the interest of preparing himself to defend the oppressed. But his philosophical bent led him irresistibly to the study of social theory and writing. He embarked on his journalistic career in the 1860's.

His literary debut was in the form of a review published in the periodical *Rassvyet* (Daybreak). Meanwhile, under the influence of the social ideas contained in Chernyshevsky's famous essay "What Is to Be Done?" he invested the bulk of his small patrimony in a cooperative bookbinding shop, and through this activity became better known to the literary world of St. Petersburg. Soon he was hired as regular reviewer for the *Knizhny Vestnik* (Book Herald) and spent two of the happiest years of his life (1865-67) dividing his attention between his little shop and the journal. His income was, of course, negligible, but every day, in his own words, "like an impoverished Spanish hidalgo, proudly draped in my moth-eaten cape, full of my own editorial importance, . . . I strolled in worn-out shoes along the Nevsky Prospect to the bookstore."

As a consequence of an attempt to assassinate the Czar, however, publications deemed most critical of the government were suddenly suppressed, *Knizhny Vestnik* among them, and their staffs temporarily banished. Mikhailovsky, whose reviews and articles, dealing mainly with the woman question, could hardly be considered inflammatory, was the first to be permitted to return. During the summer of 1867 he tried to keep the publication going singlehanded, but in the repressive atmosphere of the times it was impossible. The return of his colleagues later in the year did not improve the situation. Depressed and discouraged, his inheritance gone, Mikhailovsky agreed to return to the country estate of one of his colleagues who was no better off than himself. There the staff of the late journal eked out a meager existence until 1869.

During this semiretirement Mikhailovsky studied the works of Spencer, Mill, Comte, and Proudhon, assimilating their diverse outlooks into his own evolutionary-subjective social theory. Its most characteristic element, derived from Proudhon, was its stress on the primacy of the individual. He wrote a lengthy critical review of the ideas of Comte and Spencer (whose works had just been translated into Russian) entitled "What Is Progress?" This essay appeared serially in *Otechestvennye Zapisky* (Annals of the Country, 1869-70) which Nekrasov had rented as a replacement for Chernyshevsky's defunct *Sovremennik* (Contemporary). "What Is Progress?" became the theoretical foundation of the Russian Populist movement (Narodism) which was to become the most important tendency in Russian political thinking during the ensuing years. Mikhailovsky was its acknowledged leader.

In 1870-71 the author met and married Maria Evgrafovna Pavlovskaya, to whom he was introduced by his life-long friend Gleb Uspensky. The marriage was not happy, however. Maria left him in 1875 because she resented his ascetic devotion to his journalistic career. He married again—this time Ludmilla Nikolayevna, who bore him two sons but left him after ten years of marriage.

The death of Nekrasov (1877) left Mikhailovsky and Saltykov as joint editors of the *Annals*, but with the latter traveling much of the time Mikhailovsky was practically editor-in-chief. He continued to be the guiding inspiration of the "Narodnicks" who based their program on the peasantry, but during this period he was an active foe of the Marxists, foreign and domestic, and exerted political pressure on the Czar against their revolutionary propaganda.

In 1881 Alexander II, who had liberated the serfs, was assassinated. His successor, Alexander III, instituted a regime of unrelieved oppression which crushed any hope of amelioration of conditions. Mikhailovsky was again banished from the capital (1881-86) and, in 1884, under pressure from the authorities, the *Annals* were finally suppressed.

During these years the Populist movement split into various groups, none of which was fully in accord with Mikhailovsky's original program. The leader soon found himself hard-pressed to keep pace with his followers. The left wing joined the Marxists; the ultra-left became terrorist; even the right wing retreated from the moderate views of the founder. Mikhailovsky found himself under attack from all sides, especially from the Marxists who, led by Lenin and Plekhanov, made him their special target in attacking Populism in general.

But Mikhailovsky continued to attract followers. During the nineties he became connected with the influential journal *Russkoye Bogatstvo* (Russian Wealth) along with Annensky and Korolenko, an association which lasted for the rest of his life.

As a literary critic he evaluated the works of Lermontov, Nekrasov, Saltykov, Uspensky, Chekhov, Gorky, and Dostoevsky. His famous essay on the last, "A Cruel Talent"

(1882), is a pitiless criticism of the cruelty and horror he found in him. Another of his significant social-literary critiques is *The Right and Left of Count Leo Tolstoy* (1873).

Contemporary Soviet opinion reflects the attitudes of Plekhanov and Lenin, both of whom found Mikhailovsky important enough to devote major works to the refutation of his ideas. There also exists a letter written to Mikhailovsky by Karl Marx (November 1877) critical of his Populist views, and recommending that he give some attention to the development of capitalism in Russia and temper his concentration on the peasantry in favor of the urban working population. With regard to Mikhailovsky's prose, Herzen had one word for it: "Atrocious."

"What Is Progress?" has been translated into French and German, but there is no English translation.

ABOUT: Billington, J. Mikhailovsky and Russian Populism.

L. R. & H. H.

MIRANDA, FRANCISCO DE SÁ DE.
See SÁ DE MIRANDA, FRANCISCO DE

MIRANDOLA, PICO DELLA. See
PICO DELLA MIRANDOLA

*MIRBEAU, OCTAVE (February 16, 1850-February 16, 1917), French novelist and dramatist, was born at Trévières, in Calvados. His ancestors had been lawyers, but his father was a doctor, of monarchial, conservative, and Catholic convictions. Mirbeau's mother was from a family of Orne. Octave studied at the Jesuit Collège of Vannes, where he suffered among scions of nobility. *Sébastien Roch* (1890), the record of a bitter, deeply unhappy childhood, was based on this experience; the characters Sébastien and Bolorec represent different aspects of the author.

After the Franco-Prussian War (1870), in which he was a soldier, Mirbeau enrolled in the Paris Law School. But he was more interested in café life and in art exhibitions. He entered journalism as a chronicler for the conservative newspaper *L'Ordre*. Reactionary in politics, Mirbeau was a revolutionary in art appreciation. A brief spell (1877) as subprefect at Saint-Girons interrupted his close association with the naturalists: Zola, the Goncourts, Paul Adam. Returning to

* měr bō′

journalism, he wrote for *Le Gaulois* and *Le Figaro,* and founded *Paris-Midi* as well as a weekly, *Les Grimaces* (1883-84).

A journalist until thirty-five, Mirbeau, who had become an anarchist, started publishing a series of violent, colorful novels and plays of a morbid or naturalistic vein. *L'Abbé Jules* (1888) was a bitter attack on the Church; *Sébastien Roch* (1890) castigated the nobles (Mirbeau was for Dreyfus in the famous affair); *Le Jardin des Supplices* (1899) was a harrowing exposé of Oriental eroticism and of sadism; *Le Journal d'une Femme de Chambre* (1900) is perhaps more naturalistic than Zola; *Dingo* (1913) criticizes small-town and peasant mores. His automobile license number, *628 E8,* supplied the title for descriptions of Belgium with attacks on literary personalities. (Deletions were made in reprints.)

Mirbeau's plays were well received. *Les Mauvais Bergers* (1898) concerns a strike and presents the problem of the proletariat; the influence of Gerhardt Hauptmann's *Weavers* is obvious. Mirbeau's best play is *Les Affaires Sont les Affaires* (1903), "a bitter indictment of business ethics and the financial world in general." The play has remained in the general repertory of the French theatre. The Comédie-Française also accepted *Le Foyer* (1908), written in collaboration with Thadée Natanson.

Mirbeau was selected by Edmond de Goncourt to replace Zola in the Goncourt Academy on the latter's death. Although Mirbeau was usually unable to have his candidate accepted for the prize, his recommendation was potent in launching new writers and artists. In semiretirement following an overly strenuous career, Mirbeau died at his estate in Cheverchemont after a long illness.

Mirbeau's reputation, associated abroad with the erotic aspects of his work, is due in large measure to the personality of the man. He was unusually personal in his attitudes; all his novels, and most of his short stories, are related in the first person, even when this method is artistically awkward. As one critic has said, paroxysm was his normal condition. He is identified with the anarchic and revolutionary, with the polemical, with the literature of protest.

The novel *Un Gentilhomme*, on which Mirbeau was engaged at his death, was published in 1920. Two volumes of art criticism, *Des Artistes*, culled from various journals, appeared in 1922 and 1924. Here are readily accessible his appreciations of Delacroix, Monet, Gauguin, Raffaelli, Pissarro, Rodin, etc. A collected edition of his works, in ten volumes, appeared between 1934 and 1936.

Le Journal d'une Femme de Chambre was translated by B. J. Tucker as *A Chambermaid's Diary* (1900), as *Célestine, Being the Diary of a Chambermaid* by Alan Durst (1930), and as *Diary of a Chambermaid* (1946); the last edition has an introduction by Jules Romains. *Le Calvaire* appeared as *Calvary*, in Louis Rich's translation of 1922. A. C. Bessie translated *Torture Garden* in 1931, with a foreword by J. G. Huneker; it was reprinted in 1949. Clyde Barrett was responsible for the English version of the one-act comedy *Scruples* (1923), and Frumkin made a Yiddish version, *Business Is Business* (1908) of Mirbeau's best play.

ABOUT: Chandler, F. W. Modern Continental Playwrights; Huneker, J. G. Bedouins. [In French —Bardin, F. *in* Le Divan, no. 237 (Jan.-March 1941); Beuchat, C. Histoire du Naturalisme Français, II; Revon, M. Octave Mirbeau, Son Œuvre.]

S. S. W.

*MISTRAL, FRÉDÉRIC (September 8, 1830-March 25, 1914), Provençal poet and writer, born in Maillane (Bouches-du-Rhône), was the son of a middle-aged landowner by a second marriage. His father's piety led him to the Bible, and left him a monarchist, uninfluenced by the Revolution. Frédéric spent his youth in meditations on nature, and read by preference Rousseau and works on natural history. Beginning in 1843 he did more formal study in Avignon and by chance had as teacher Joseph Roumanille, who inspired in him an enthusiasm for his native tongue and encouraged him to translate the Psalms into Provençal; Mistral continued this project in later years until its completion in 1910. In school he also met Anselme Mathieu, another future "Félibre." Finally, he discerned in Homer and Virgil a poetic correspondence to his own language, and at eighteen composed his first considerable poem, *Li Meissoun,* in four cantos.

The Félibrige movement proper opened in 1852 with *Li Prouvençalo,* in which Roumanille gathered many attractive texts, including work by Mistral. The first considerable event was the formal grouping of seven poets, in 1854, among whom the most distinguished were Mistral, Aubanel, Roumanille, and Mathieu. They called themselves "Félibres de la Loi," creating a term whose origin remains obscure, but appears to be related to Hebrew law (possibly to that of the "Sepher"). The new "Law" was in effect merely the genius of Mistral fortified by extensive linguistic research, and was in large part inspired by poetic monuments of the past, the work of the Pléiade, of Malherbe,

* mēs tràl'

MISTRAL

and of the ancient classics. The official organ, the *Provençal Almanach,* had immediate success, thanks to Mistral's efficiency as an organizer. He stated the principles of the movement as the preservation of the Provençal heritage, its language, customs and character, and a gay fraternity of spirit.

The death of Mistral's father in 1855 affected several parts of his first masterpiece, *Mirèio (Mireille),* published in 1859. Like other works, *Mirèio* appeared in bilingual form, with a fine French translation; the French versions of Mistral's poetry were made either by him *(La Reine Jeanne, Le Rhône)* or by such friends, disciples or enthusiasts as Maurras. *Mirèio* met with considerable success in Paris, and was cordially acclaimed by Lamartine, who found in it echoes of the genius of antiquity, and by Barbey d'Aurevilly, who compared it to the work of André Chénier. Its popularity was further assured by Gounod's opera (1863), and its fame in other countries was vouchsafed by the many translations of it.

Mistral's career as a poet continued unabated in a long series of works, each in some way vitally new, though none perhaps of the full inspiration of *Mirèio. Calendal* (1867) was less perfect than his first work and less generally accessible to readers outside his native region. It has the particular quality of an epic of Provence, in a genre in which French poets have had only mediocre success. *Lis Isclo d'Or (Les Îles d'Or* 1875) takes its title from the small islands off Hyères,

641

which symbolize a haven from reality; it is lyrical rather than idyllic or epic, and many poems stand alone as gems in a wide variety of forms. *Nerto* (1884) is a sentimental verse short story recalling the period of the papacy at Avignon. *La Rèino Jano* (1890) is a five-act verse tragedy on the story of Queen Jeanne d'Anjou. Mistral's *Le Rhône* (1897) is the work most worthy of the name of epic, for it recreates the river in all its aspects as a unifying force and a lyrical adventure. In 1906 Mistral told of his life and projects to that time in his *Mémoires*.

Mistral might be called a belated romantic in his songs of nature and their clear relationship to the spirit of Lamartine. However, he stands apart from romanticism in several ways, first by his total devotion to his own region and people, but primarily on account of his admiration for antiquity. Antiquity, as he understood it, was the past of his own part of France, from a cultural rather than an archeological point of view. The past, on the one hand, was that of rural life, and in this respect is represented by the poetry of Ronsard and of Du Bellay, with their cult of local custom, native words and natural beauty. It was also something of the classicism of Malherbe, enemy of the Pléiade, although patriotic as well in spirit and more restrained in technique.

Mistral's work also belongs to Félibrige and in this respect is part of a program and an ideology. He devoted much of his energy to the cause of the Félibres, in 1868 and more especially after 1875. He composed critical and interpretative essays and gave lectures, often in connection with "Floral Games," an old Provençal institution, as well as in more intimate poetic circles. His enthusiasm and his advice to disciples, tempered with frankness, cordiality, and common sense, kept the movement alive. Chronologically, Félibrige coincides with other neoclassic trends, such as the Parnasse and the École Romaine of Moréas; but its aspirations were more immediate and its techniques more spontaneous. Mistral's efforts culminated in 1899 with the opening in Arles of the "Museon Arlaten," dedicated to historical documentation on Provençal ethnography, customs, crafts, clothing, utensils, and folklore. This collection is a vital part of Mistral's project, for it preserves the spirit of his region in all its aspects, from the Roman remains of Arles and Saint-Rémy to the present. In his mind, the struggle against Paris and centralization was spiritual, not political, though the movement coincided with various separatist tendencies in Europe

and suffered from the inevitable disadvantages of bilingualism.

Mistral was translated into many languages. In English we have *Mirèio*, by H. Preston (1872), the *Memoirs*, by C. Maud (1907) and *Anglore, the Song of the Rhone*, by M. Jones (1937).

ABOUT: Aldington, R. Introduction to Mistral; Girdlestone, M. The Poetry of Frédéric Mistral. [In French—see studies by A. Dagan, P. Lasserre, F. Vincent, and E. Ripert's Le Félibrige.]

F. J. C.

*MODRZEWSKI, ANDRZEJ FRYCZ (1503-1572), Polish political writer and moralist, was born in Wolborz and educated at Cracow University, and in Germany at Wittenberg and at Nuremberg universities. Through his studies Modrzewski acquired extensive knowledge of ancient literature, philosophy (Aristotle, Plato, Cicero), and theology (Melanchthon). His knowledge of Western Europe and its conditions provided him with a basis for criticism of the social conditions that existed in his native Poland. Under the influence of his Western European background Modrzewski took up the task of criticizing the laws, mores, and religion of Polish society. His views were broad and humanistic.

Modrzewski wrote a number of books and pamphlets, all of them in Latin. In his first pamphlet, entitled *De Poena Homicidii* (The Law of Homicide, 1543), he argued against the unjust law according to which a nobleman was punished heavily for the killing of a nobleman but was punished only with a small fine for killing a peasant, whereas a peasant was punished by death for killing a nobleman. Modrzewski demanded a death penalty for any homicide, regardless of the social status of either the killer or his victim. In this cause Modrzewski enjoyed the support of the Polish king and several prominent personalities, among them Cardinal Hosius. However, the Diet rejected his idea. In another pamphlet, *De Decreto Conventu* (1545), Modrzewski opposed a decree which forbade burghers to purchase landed estates and ordered them to sell those they already possessed.

Modrzewski's most important work was *De Republica Emendanda* (The Reform of the Republic), the first three books of which appeared in 1551, while a new edition in five books was published in Basel in 1554. It was first published in Latin, but soon appeared in various translations: Spanish (1555), German (1557), Polish (1557), and, in the sev-

* mô jef′ skē

enteenth century, Russian. Another edition appeared in Warsaw in 1914. The five books deal respectively with mores, laws, war, the Church, and the schools. The author has pertinent and new things to say about each of these subjects. He makes Christian morality the basis not only of the private life of the individual but of his life as a citizen of the republic as well. All other aims, he argues, should be subordinate to this. Law is to be the guardian and regulator of life and should also restrict individual freedom. Unjust laws should be abolished. Wars are an absolute evil. Only defensive wars are justified, but even they should be avoided. Quarrels between states should be arbitrated before an international court. To put an end to religious dissensions Modrzewski suggested the creation of a single, universal church which would combine the main principles of the Catholic and Protestant doctrines. He wrote that public education is the most important task for the state and society. He demands careful and systematic learning. The teaching profession should be respected. The projects of his reforms embraced also the treasury, national defense, and the establishment of supreme courts, of supervisors of the poor, and of "guardians of public morals."

Modrzewski's views were liberal and modern, but, unfortunately, they had to wait until the end of the eighteenth century to be appreciated. In the sixteenth century they threatened too many vested interests and privileges, and they provoked indignation and hostility.

An edition of his complete works, translated into Polish, was published in Warsaw in 1953.

ABOUT: Dyboski, R. Periods of Polish Literary History; Kridl, M. An Anthology of Polish Literature; Kridl, M. A Survey of Polish Literature and Culture. [In Polish—Kot, S. A. Frycz Modrzewski.]

P. LY.

*MOE, JØRGEN ENGEBRETSEN

(April 22, 1813–March 27, 1882), Norwegian folklorist and poet, was born at the farm Mo, not far from the capital in the district of Ringerike. His father was Engebret Olsen Moe, a conservative, patriarchal, and influential landowner. His mother was Marthe Jørgensdatter. Both parents were of prominent peasant families, and their farm had belonged to the wife's family for more than two hundred years.

Jørgen first attended a regular elementary school. When he was thirteen he was sent to

* mōō

MOE

a private school for preparation for his matriculation examination. Here he had as his schoolmate Peter Christen Asbjørnsen (see sketch above) from the capital. Although the latter attended this school only for a short time, the youngsters formed a friendship that was destined to be cemented for life and develop into a fruitful scholarly cooperation. Moe overworked himself in his effort to pass the entrance examination. This he did in 1830, but not until 1832 did he enter the University of Christiania (now Oslo) as a student of theology. He also studied literature and was influenced by Welhaven's rationalistic aesthetics. But his theological studies progressed slowly. Depressed by melancholy, partly due to a broken engagement, he left the university after two years.

He regained mental balance through correspondence with his friend Asbjørnsen and their mutual interest in folklore, songs, legends, and tales. From the brothers Grimm they learned the scholarly value of folklore. In 1837 the two friends met and decided to collect and publish folk tales. Towards the end of the year they presented to the public their first effort, *Nor, en Billedbok for den Norske Ungdom* (Nor, a Picture Book for the Norwegian Youth). Moe was weak in health but he continued to collect fairy tales and other folklore material and succeeded in taking his theological degree in 1839.

Sange, Folkeviser og Stev i Norske Almuedialekter (Poems, Folk Songs and Rhymes in Norwegian Dialects, 1840) was published

643

with a prefatory note by Moe. Here he emphasized the national value of the native dialects and recommended that the simple style should be used in publications of folkloristic material. This approach became the guiding idea in Asbjørnsen and Moe's splendid and epoch-making treasury of Norwegian folklore, *Norske Folkeeventyr* (Norwegian Folk Tales), the first volume of which appeared in 1841. After some criticism this work was enthusiastically accepted, but was discontinued in 1844. It appeared again in 1852 in an enlarged and revised edition with a preface and an introduction by Moe. It came to exercise a great influence on the stylistic development of the Norwegian language.

From 1844 to 1853 Moe served as a teacher in the capital. He went through a religious crisis and was appointed pastor at Sigdal in southeastern Norway. In 1875 he became bishop of the Christiansand diocese.

In 1854 Moe married Johanne Fredrikke Sophie Sørensen. Their son Moltke Moe became the country's greatest scholar of folklore.

Influenced by Oehlenschläger, Welhaven, and Winther, Moe wrote lyrical poems throughout his life, but not until 1849 did his first collection, *Digte* (Poems), appear. In 1860 he published a collection of religious songs, *En Liden Julegave* (A Little Christmas Gift). His most outstanding prose work was *I Brønden og i Kjærnet* (In the Well and the Pond), a collection of stories for children, written in a simple style of great freshness, humor, and charm.

The folk tales of Asbjørnsen and Moe have been repeatedly translated into English; see under Asbjørnsen.

ABOUT: Beyer, H. A History of Norwegian Literature; Grøndahl, I. and Raknes, O. Chapters of Norwegian Literature; Jorgenson, T. History of Norwegian Literature; Winkel Horn, F. History of the Literature of the Scandinavian North. [In Norwegian—see study by S. Hagemann.]

A. J.

*MOLIÈRE, JEAN BAPTISTE POQUELIN (January 15, 1622-February 17, 1673), French dramatist, was born in Paris and baptized at the church of Saint-Eustache. His father, Jean Poquelin, whose family was originally from Beauvais, was a successful upholstery dealer who became the royal upholsterer in 1631, with the title of *valet de chambre*. Molière's mother, Marie Cressé, also of bourgeois origin, died in 1632. The

* mô lyâr′

644

MOLIÈRE

following year his father married Catherine Fleurette, who died three years later.

Molière attended the Collège de Clermont, then took the law course at Orléans, receiving his degree in 1642. In 1643, after practicing law for several months, he joined the newly founded Illustre Théâtre, which produced plays first in Rouen, then in Paris. The Illustre Théâtre, unsuccessful and debt-ridden, collapsed in 1645 and Molière spent some days in prison for debt. It was as an actor in this troupe that he assumed the name of Molière. In the Illustre Théâtre he was associated with the Béjarts, a theatrical family, one of whose members, Madeleine, was probably Molière's mistress.

With Madeleine, Molière played the provinces in the south of France from early 1646 to 1658, first under the patronage of the Duc d'Épernon, then of the Prince de Conty. In 1650 Molière became the director of the troupe of which he and Madeleine were members. Indications are that the company met with great success, both dramatic and financial.

During these years of work in the provinces Molière appears to have maintained contact with the theatre world of Paris, and it is to the capital that, after a stay of some months in Rouen, the troupe moved in the fall of 1658. There Molière shared with the Italian troupe the use of the Petit-Bourbon, one of the three theatres functioning in Paris. Failure was imminent after a short time but was averted by the success of Molière's own compositions, *L'Étourdi* and *Le Dépit Amou-reux,* both of which had already been given in the provinces. These successes were followed by *Les Précieuses Ridicules* (November 18, 1659), which seriously established Molière's reputation and made him the object of envy and slander on the part of his rivals. When the Petit-Bourbon was demolished, the king granted Molière the use of the Palais-Royal (1661), in spite of the efforts of his rivals to blacken his name and to lure his actors away. The troupe was to occupy the Palais-Royal until Molière's death.

Molière was above middle height, at least slightly stooped, and on the stout side. He had a large nose, thick lips, and heavy eyebrows—altogether far from handsome in spite of the attempts of some contemporary painters to minimize his unattractiveness. His health, at least after 1665, was poor, and he suffered frequent consumptive attacks.

Molière was not of a cheerful temperament. He was quiet—even morose—in company and hardly pleasant except with good friends. Never afraid of a fight he was capable of terrible vengeances, although he also forgave easily. It was often difficult to predict which way he would react. Though he loved luxury and high society and was fiercely ambitious, he was both modest and honorable in his personal and professional relations. Neither drink nor gambling had any appeal for Molière, but he had a considerable addiction to women. Besides his mistress, Madeleine Béjart, he had affairs with two other actresses, Du Parc (Marie Thérèse de Gorla) and Catherine de Brie—the latter even after his marriage. In 1662 he married Armande Béjart, the daughter of his mistress, and, according to some, of Molière himself. The marriage was generally regarded as an unhappy one. Of the three children born to the couple, only one (Esprit Madeleine) survived Molière.

Almost from the beginning of his Parisian career Molière was heavily supported by Louis XIV, until in 1672 he was replaced in the king's favor by the composer Lully. Other patrons of Molière, besides those mentioned in connection with his years in the provinces, were Henriette d'Angleterre, the Prince de Condé, and the finance minister Fouquet. Of contemporary authors friendly with Molière, only Boileau appears to have been very close to him over a long period.

As an actor Molière received universal praise, even from his worst enemies. Borrowing the art of pantomime from the Italian *commedia dell' arte* company in Paris, he added an amazing individual wealth of facial expression, head movements, and voice range. Antoine Adam has shown that Molière's stage art, as well as his dramatic composition, developed in large part as a result of changes in his own physical condition. The Sganarelle type of hero which dominated the plays from 1660 to 1665 was sure of himself, disregarded the advice of others, lived in a dream world, and walked with short jerky steps and wore a huge mustache. In the plays of this period the foolish laugh of the beginning yields, by the end of the piece, to a pitiable grimace as the hero, beaten, walks off with shaky legs, head buried between his shoulders. In his last plays, since Molière usually played the heroes himself, the tyrannical singlemindedness of the character is rendered comical not by outer trappings and gestures so much as by the contrasting feebleness of his physical bearing.

As a theatrical director Molière maintained severe standards regarding every detail of performance, but an atmosphere of friendliness prevailed withal. In spite of difficulties in securing new plays for his repertoire, he managed to obtain some by the leading playwrights of his time, including several by Corneille and Racine. An important innovation of Molière's, really a revival of an old tradition, was the performance of a short farce at the end of each program. These farces, for which Molière may have borrowed heavily from the *commedia dell' arte* and from the one-act comedies which were popular in Lyon, proved the salvation of his troupe in its early months in Paris.

The earliest plays of Molière which are extant are *L'Étourdi* (1655) and *Le Dépit Amoureux* (1656), both five-act plays and both strongly influenced by Italian comedy, with a great amount of disguise and mistaken identity. *Les Précieuses Ridicules* (1659), on the other hand, was a one-act play in the vein of the postlude farces or "small comedies." Here Molière added to the usual farcical features a strong satirical note in the form of two provincial ladies who ridiculously ape the manners and speech of the "precious" society of Paris. The one-act *Sganarelle, ou le Cocu Imaginaire* (1660), though at first a middling box-office success, showed Molière's profundity as a comic artist, utilizing a maximum of mimicry, probing the regions of fear and shame which exist in all men, and thus establishing his mastery of the comedy of manners. His venture into tragi-comedy with *Dom Garcie de Navarre* (1661) was a failure, but *L'École des Maris* (1661), borrowing and developing the cuckold type seen in Sganarelle, was a hit from the first and continued to grow in popularity. Based on a theme from Boccaccio, this play is in three acts, as were the Italian comedies of the time.

Molière's next great production was *L'École des Femmes* (1662), a five-act "grande comédie" which is close to farce and yet succeeds in presenting an important moral problem. This comedy stirred up a long, violent quarrel, in which Boileau came to Molière's defense. The play was variously criticized— for indelicacy, vulgarity, obscenity, and blasphemy—as well as for poor dramatic construction. Molière answered with *La Critique de l'École des Femmes* and *L'Impromptu de Versailles* (1663; so-called because it was written in a few days and first performed for the king at Versailles), both effective satires on his enemies.

Molière was now about to enter his finest productive period. There followed in rapid succession, to mention only the most famous of his plays, *Tartuffe* (1664 and 1667), *Le Misanthrope* (1666), *L'Avare* (1668), *Le Bourgeois Gentilhomme* (1670), *Les Femmes Savantes* (1672), and *Le Malade Imaginaire* (1673).

Tartuffe, an attack on religious hypocrites, was first played in an incomplete, three-act version at Versailles. It was suppressed by the king, who was unable to resist the pressure from religious circles. In its full form *Tartuffe* was performed in 1667 at the Palais-Royal but was again promptly banned. Molière fought hard for authorization for *Tartuffe* and when it was granted in 1669, the play proved to be his greatest box-office success. *Tartuffe* was undoubtedly directed in part against those who had attacked *L'École des Femmes* for impiety, but it goes far beyond and becomes a classic study of the type and a masterful affirmation of a humanistic religion free from dogmatism. *Tartuffe,* moreover, marks a great change dramatically: heretofore Molière had centered his interest in one or two characters; in this play all the members of the family, and the family as a unit, become the objects of his observation and study.

Le Misanthrope, regarded by many as Molière's masterpiece, has remained one of his most ambiguous creations. The question of whether Molière is laughing at Alceste or approving his sharp criticisms of a social morality based on falsity and egotism may be answered in the light of Molière's biography and of his other works. His marital troubles and the difficulties which *L'École des Femmes*

and *Tartuffe* encountered, not to speak of the constant attacks of his enemies, embittered his spirits and revolted his sense of decency; his preceding plays had been plentifully critical of contemporary manners. These considerations make it altogether possible that Alceste speaks for Molière much of the time. Comic effects in this play arise, not from any ridiculous conduct of the hero, but from his inconsistencies. Thanks to this factor and to the individuality of the characters who contrast sharply with the stock characters usually encountered earlier, we have what A. Adam has called a "comedy of nuances."

In *L'Avare* (1668), Molière's study of a miser, the humor stems from a contrast between the hero's tyrannical intent vis-à-vis those around him and his inability to impose his will (perhaps highlighted by physical weakness, related to Molière's own condition). The plot is embellished by the repetition of certain catch phrases designed to reveal the blind single-mindedness which Molière had long since so adroitly learned to portray.

Le Bourgeois Gentilhomme (1670) was perhaps the best of Molière's numerous ballet-comedies written in collaboration with Lully for the entertainment of the court. It effected a happy union of comedy, music, and dance. For all its gay laughter at the expense of a bourgeois in the process of learning to be a nobleman, the plot of the play is unoriginal and the characterization scant. The lack of substance of the drama, however, by no means interferes with the enjoyment of the whole.

Les Femmes Savantes (1672) is an attack on l'abbé Cotin, one of the enemies of Molière and of comedy in general, and a satire on the growing intellectualism of women. The play, though successful in its time and since, is not generally received with ardor by Molière enthusiasts, who find it lacking in the comic verve to which they have become accustomed. But in *Le Malade Imaginaire* (1673), a satire on the medical faculty of the University of Paris, all of Molière's gaiety reappears. With this comedy Molière had two unfortunate experiences, one of which was to prove fatal. First, *Le Malade Imaginaire* had been written for royal entertainment, but, because of Molière's falling-out with Lully and the king's preference for the latter, the play had to be shown at the Palais-Royal instead of at court. Second, while performing as the hero of the piece, Molière was seized by a consumptive attack from which he died a few hours later.

Because of the refusal of two priests to administer the last rites and the late arrival of a third, Molière died without benefit of clergy. He was accorded a semisecret religious funeral and was buried in the St. Joseph cemetery in Paris on the night of February 21-22, 1673.

Molière's success, from his own day to this, has been uninterrupted. Though each age has seen fit to interpret his works in its own way, the diversity of his comic genius, the breadth of his inspiration, and the range of characters and social classes he depicts have been the object of universal admiration. His style, in both prose and verse, is easy and natural, as Boileau admiringly pointed out. Molière saw to it that his characters always spoke the language of their origin, much as they themselves might try to simulate another. His rich exploitation of physical movement when it is appropriate and of verbal comedy when that is more suitable shows a dramatic sense from which the frequent use of comic conventions, e.g., disguises and discovered identities, scarcely detracts. It is notable that the almost limitless resources of his comic vein, from the grossest buffoonery to the subtlest comedy, led him in only very rare instances to an excessive show of virtuosity. His satires and his frank attacks on sham of every sort have sometimes earned him the reputation of a moralist or reformer, to the detriment of his genius as a creator of laughter; the truth is that he took both rôles very seriously. The greatest single effect of Molière's work was to drive succeeding writers of comedy in France to a study of society and of real individuals, and to write what has been well termed "comedy of observation."

Translators too numerous to list have rendered various examples of Molière's writings. Fairly complete translations of his works have been made by the following: H. Baker and J. Miller (1739; reprinted in Everyman Library, 1929), J. Watts (1748), H. Van Laun (1875-76), C. H. Wall (1876-77), A. R. Waller (1926). In 1955 the poet Richard Wilbur published a rhymed verse translation of *The Misanthrope*. The fullest bibliography of Molière studies is P. Saintonge and R. W. Christ, *Fifty Years of Molière Studies*, 1942.

ABOUT: Chapman, P. A. The Spirit of Molière; Hubert, J. D. Molière and the Comedy of Intellect; Gossman, L. Men and Masks: A Study of Molière; Matthews, B. Molière, His Life and Times; Miles, D. H. The Influence of Molière on Restoration Comedy; Palmer, J. Molière; Tilley, A. Molière; Turnell, M. The Classical Moment. [In French—Adam, A. Histoire de la Littérature Française au XVIIe Siècle; Bray, R. Molière, Homme de Théâtre; Michaut, G. La Jeunesse de Molière, Les Débuts de Molière à Paris, Les Luttes de Molière.]

A. C. K.

*"MOLINA, TIRSO DE" (pseudonym of Fray GABRIEL TÉLLEZ) (1584?-March 12, 1648), Spanish dramatist of the school of Lope de Vega, was born in Madrid. Although his parentage is not certain, there is evidence to suggest that he was the natural son of the Duke of Osuna. Tirso was educated in Alcalá and entered the Order of Mercy in 1601 in Guadalajara. He lived in Toledo from 1613 to 1614 and was in Santo Domingo from 1616 to 1618. In 1622 he resided in Madrid where he participated in a poetry contest on the occasion of the canonization of St. Isidore, and otherwise took an active part in the literary life of his time. Aside from writing plays Tirso participated in the controversies centering in "culteranismo," allying himself with the attackers of the "estilo culto." In 1625 Tirso was directed by the Council of Castile to refrain from writing plays and to leave Madrid. The playwright accordingly went to Salamanca and was shortly thereafter named prior of the Monastery of Trujillo. In 1630 Tirso was again in Toledo and then later in Catalonia and in Madrid. He was appointed historian of his order and wrote, between 1637 and 1639, a *Historia General de la Orden de la Merced*. In 1639 Pope Urban VIII appointed him master of his order and in 1645 he became prior of the Mercedarian Monastery in Soria.

Although Tirso is known chiefly as a dramatist of the Lope school, he also wrote lyrical poetry and a few prose works. *Los Cigarrales de Toledo* (1621) is a miscellany containing poems, several short novels, three plays (among them *El Vergonzoso en Palacio*) and a statement of dramatic theory in which the author clearly supports Lope's ideas on the theatre. In the prologue to the *Cigarrales* Tirso informs us that he has written more than three hundred plays within fourteen years; if this is so, less than one third of his total production survives.

The five *partes* of Tirso's plays were published between 1624 and 1633. A disciple of Lope de Vega, Tirso intensified and purified his mentor's themes. Tirso's plays are notable for their animated movement, delicate psychological analysis, rich language, and fine humor. His best historical play, *La Prudencia en la Mujer*, concerns itself with the regency of María de Molina during the minority of Ferdinand IV, while *La Venganza de Tamar* and *La Mejor Espigadera* are among his better-known religious plays. Tirso's keen insight and sense of comedy are

* mō lē' nä

647

well illustrated in *Don Gil de las Calzas Verdes* and *La Villana de Vallecas.*

Tirso's most important contribution to the Spanish drama and to universal literature is *El Burlador de Sevilla y Convidado de Piedra,* first published in 1630, in which the now traditional figure of Don Juan appears on the stage for the first time. Don Juan is a vital incarnation of sensuality, endlessly devoted to the pursuit of pleasure. His amorous conquests succeed each other rapidly without causing a ripple in his conscience, for Don Juan is either planning his escape or his next adventure and is disinclined to weigh the moral consequences of his acts. When warned of God's justice, Don Juan refuses to be concerned, for he is convinced that there will always be time for repentance. Having killed the Commander of Ulloa he sacrilegiously invites his statue to dinner. When the invitation is returned, Don Juan is dragged down to Hell, a victim of his own frivolity.

The theme of Don Juan has had universal appeal and has inspired writers of the stature of Molière, Byron, Goldoni, and Shaw, to name but a few. Along with Don Quixote, Hamlet, and Faust, Don Juan has transcended national boundaries and has become a legend.

The most important theological play attributed to Tirso is *El Condenado por Desconfiado* in which is explored the problem of free will and predestination in relation to divine goodness and justice. The plot concerns the condemnation of Paulo, an egotistical ascetic, and the salvation of Enrico, a criminal who is nevertheless an example of filial devotion and profound faith in God.

In 1635 Tirso wrote *Deleitar Aprovechando,* a second miscellany of novels and *autos.* Unlike the *Cigarrales,* this collection is of an essentially devotional nature. Tirso de Molina died in Soria.

El Burlador de Sevilla has been translated into English as *The Love Rogue* by Harry Kemp (1923). *Los Tres Maridos Burlados* (included in Part V of *Los Cigarrales*) has been translated as *Three Husbands Hoaxed* by Ilsa Barea (1955).

ABOUT: Bushee, A. H. Three Centuries of Tirso de Molina; McClelland, I. L. Tirso de Molina. Studies in Dramatic Realism; Hispanic Review, II (1935); XI (1943). [In Spanish—Castro, A. *Prologue to* Cinco Ensayos sobre Don Juan; Ríos, B. de los, *Prologue to* Obras Dramaticas Completas; Menéndez Pidal, R. Estudios Literarios; Said Armesto, V. La Leyenda de don Juan.]

B. P. P.

*MØLLER, POUL MARTIN (March 21, 1794-March 13, 1838), Danish poet, short-story writer, essayist, critic, and philosopher, was born at the vicarage of Uldum, close to Vejle in eastern Jutland, where his father, Rasmus Møller, was a priest. His mother was Bodil Maria Thaulov. In 1802 his father transferred to Købeløv on the island of Lolland where Poul grew up. Having completed his elementary and secondary schooling in Nakskov on the same island and Nykøbing on the nearby island of Falster, he entered the University of Copenhagen, where in 1816 he took his degree in theology with the highest honors. Although he studied diligently for his examinations he devoted much time to his favorite subject, classical philology, to writing fine poetry, and to taking an active part in the carefree life of the students. He also became deeply attached to a beautiful young girl who promised to marry him. But she deserted him, and this bitter disappointment left marks both in his life and in his poetry.

After occupying a position as a private tutor in the provinces, Møller returned to the capital where he entered into the acrimonious literary feud between Oehlenschläger and Baggesen. He sided with the former; in his witty contributions to the debate he also attacked Grundtvig.

In 1819 Møller went to China as a ship's chaplain. His experiences on this journey, which lasted for two years and became a turning point in his life, cured him of his romantic longing for the remote and exotic and instilled in him the strong patriotic love of his country which characterizes his subsequent poetry.

During his journey to China, Møller wrote some of his finest poems, including the best known of all his lyrics, *Hjemve* (Nostalgia), generally known as *Glæde over Danmark* (Joy over Denmark), and the little cycle of realistic poems called *Scener i Rosenborg Have* (Scenes in Rosenborg Garden), in which he gave mighty expression to his love for Denmark. Upon his return to the Danish capital in 1821 he realized that the clerical life did not suit him and devoted himself to philology and particularly philosophy. After a few years as a high school teacher he was in 1826 appointed lecturer in philosophy at the University of Christiania (now Oslo) in Norway and two years later promoted to a professorship in the same subject. In 1827 he married Betty Berg, daughter of a landed proprietor. In 1831 he became professor at

* mûl' ĕr

the more illustrious University at Copenhagen. His wife died in 1834, and two years later Møller married Eline Svendine Hansine von Bülow.

An unfinished work of considerable charm, *En Dansk Students Eventyr* (The Tale of a Danish Student), published posthumously, is considered the first realistic novel written in Danish. During his later years Møller devoted his time and efforts mostly to philosophy, and he produced several important treatises in this field.

Three of Møller's poems in English adaptation are included in *A Book of Danish Verse* (1922).

ABOUT: [In Danish—see studies by V. Andersen, F. Nielsen, F. Rønning.]

A. J.

*MONNIER, HENRI BONAVENTURE

(June 8, 1799?-January 3, 1877), French littérateur and caricaturist, was born and lived all his life in Paris. He was the son of a government employee. Monnier did not complete his studies at the Lyceé Bonaparte, for at the age of sixteen he entered the office of a notary. His next position was with a minister of justice. However, Monnier was not meant to remain long in the world of administration, which he was later to satirize. Talented in design and drawing, he began his study of art in the atelier of Girodet, then worked in that of Gros, which he was forced to leave somewhat prematurely because of his apparently inordinate love of playing practical jokes. And, too, he had little gift for painting; his talent was observation, his delight, imitation of "popular types."

Early in his artistic career, he had illustrated La Fontaine's *Fables* and Béranger's *Chansons* (1828), but it was in the delineation of types, or characters, that his art had significance. He had already made his debut by doing some vignettes for booksellers, and by 1827 his excellent lithographs in colored ink had attracted attention. The album *Les Grisettes* and the caricatures of *Mœurs Administratives* revealed his interests and power as did his vaudevilles *Les Compatriotes* and *Les Mendiants,* which he wrote with Émile and H. Leroux. Not only did he collaborate a great deal in the writing of comedies and "folie-vaudevilles," but he also acted in a few vaudevilles such as Brazier's *Famille Improvisée.*

But it was a short-lived acting career, for Monnier's chief interest was in caricaturing the bourgeois life. Like Balzac, his friend

* mô nyā′

MONNIER

who was producing the great novels of *La Comédie Humaine,* Monnier knew the ludicrous traits of the bourgeois to whom the 1830's had given power. He had already published his comic tableau *La Grande Ville* in 1843, and later in *Physiologie du Bourgeois* he declared that "the bourgeois who takes the National Guard seriously and who has no other occupation is a perfectly happy man. He enlarges the circle of his relationships, of his affections above all; in each comrade he finds a brother, a parent, a friend; he develops military habits, wears a mustache, and keeps near him a policeman's cap which has replaced 'le bonnet de coton' [symbolic of the easy, luxurious life]."

The analysis of the bourgeoisie was expressed through character. Out of several comic sketches, begun in 1830—*Scènes Populaires, Dessinées à la Plume, Le Roman chez la Partière, Jean Hiroux*—and later in *Nouvelles Scènes Populaires* (1835-39), in *Grandeur et Décadence de M. Joseph Prudhomme* (a comedy, 1853), in *Mémoires de Joseph Prudhomme* (1857) and in *Joseph Prudhomme, Chef de Brigands* (a comedy, 1860) came his famous characters, Madame Gibou and the more important "type," Joseph Prudhomme, the synthesis of fatuity and solemn stupidity. In the exaggerated scenes which Monnier designed, he summed up through Prudhomme the platitudinous and foolishly grandiloquent life of the Paris bourgeois and revealed the mournful ugliness of this age when, according to Tocqueville, "the middle class in making a constant call

649

to the individual cupidities of its members became a small, vulgar, and corrupt aristocracy." Joseph Prudhomme takes pride in new industries, railways under construction, inventions—all give him the "fever of gain." Like Philipon, Granville, and Daumier, Monnier established himself as an accurate painter of the "bourgeois epoch."

Prolific and successful, Monnier left us over seven hundred psychological and satiric studies of the bourgeoisie.

Some of his other works are *Scènes de la Ville et de la Campagne, Le Religion des Imbéciles, Paris et Provinces,* and *Les Bas-Fonds de la Société.*

ABOUT: Marash, J. G. Henry Monnier, Chronicler of the Bourgeoisie; Melcher, E. The Life and Times of Henri Monnier.

G. E.

MONTAIGNE

*MONTAIGNE, MICHEL DE (February 28, 1533-September 13, 1592), French essayist, was born at the château of Montaigne, not far from Bordeaux. His family, on his father's side, had been successful fish and wine merchants in Bordeaux, and on his mother's side, converted Spanish or Portuguese Jews who had emigrated to southern France. Montaigne's paternal great-grandfather, Ramon Eyquem, bought the château of Montaigne in 1477 and it was there, in 1495, that Michel's father, Pierre Eyquem, was born. This Pierre was the first in the family to abandon business and assume the rôle of a gentleman, participating in the French wars in Italy in the years around 1520. It was Michel, however, who was the first to give up the family name of Eyquem in favor of the name of the estate (a practice which he condemns in the essay "Of Names"). Many references in the *Essays* make it clear that Montaigne was sensitive to the fact that his family had bought its way into the nobility and that he tried hard to establish himself as a nobleman of ancient lineage.

Montaigne was put to nurse with a peasant woman in a village of his father's estate, presumably so that he would gain, at the earliest age possible, an acquaintance and sympathy with the lowly. His father's ideas on child-rearing, probably brought back from Italy, included an emphasis on the learning of Latin, and accordingly from the age of two Montaigne was sheltered from the French language and exposed only to Latin. To accomplish this, his father imported a

* môn tĕn'y'

German tutor who knew no French and who succeeded in getting the whole household, including the servants, to converse in Latin to some extent. As a result, Montaigne spoke perfect Latin (and no French) by the age of six, when he entered the Collège of Guyenne in Bordeaux, one of the leading schools in France, where he studied the classics for some seven years. Montaigne then studied law, probably at the University of Toulouse, and at the age of twenty-one became a councilor at a court in Périgueux. This court was combined with the *parlement* of Bordeaux in 1557, and there Montaigne served until his retirement in 1570. Montaigne does not seem to have taken his duties too seriously or to have found himself particularly gifted for the legal profession. The experience was not without value, however, as many passages in the *Essays* testify.

While a member of the *parlement* of Bordeaux, Montaigne became acquainted, in 1558, with Étienne de La Boétie, a young colleague who was, like himself, steeped in the ancient classics. The two young men, sharing intellectual interests and an almost unbelievable mutual admiration, formed a friendship which was the most important experience of Montaigne's life and which he immortalized in his essay on friendship. La Boétie's death in 1563 was a blow from which Montaigne never entirely recovered.

Montaigne's father, meanwhile, having become a well-known and esteemed citizen of Bordeaux, was elected mayor of the city in 1554, for a term of two years. When, during his tenure of office, he once had occasion to go to Paris on official business, Michel accompanied him. This was the first of Montaigne's eight trips to the capital, which he grew to love dearly. On one of his trips, in 1561-62, which was an official mission related to the religious wars then beginning in France, he was away from Bordeaux for a year and a half. During this time Montaigne probably had or acquired political ambitions, but his contacts with the royal court seem to have been generally disillusioning and personally unsuccessful as far as the possibility of attaining high office was concerned. During a stay in Paris in 1588 he met Mlle de Gournay who became his "fille d'alliance." She was much devoted to Montaigne and published a posthumous edition of the *Essays* in 1595.

In 1565, at the age of thirty-two, Montaigne married Françoise de la Chassaigne, the daughter of one of his colleagues. She bore him six daughters, only one of whom survived infancy. In 1568 Montaigne's father, "the best father there ever was," died, leaving him, the eldest son, heir to the château and domain of Montaigne and a considerable fortune. The management of his estate, which Montaigne took seriously (until he found that he had little endowment for it), undoubtedly contributed to his desire to retire from the magistracy. In 1570 he sold his post, went to Paris to supervise publication of the writings of his late friend La Boétie, and on February 28, 1571, his thirty-eighth birthday, retired to his château. His literary activity was to occupy a great part of his time between 1571 and 1580 and again from 1586 to his death in 1592, but he had considerable time left for travel and political activity.

In the early 1570's Montaigne seems to have become friendly to the cause of Henry, King of Navarre, who named him Gentleman of the Chamber in 1577, perhaps in recognition of service rendered. The future Henry IV paid Montaigne a two-day visit in 1584 and a shorter visit in 1587. Serving on various occasions as an intermediary between him and the Maréchal de Matignon, lieutenant-general for the king of France, Montaigne had a rich first-hand acquaintance with contemporary politics, and it is this which often gives his comments on political matters their authoritative ring. Montaigne was, besides, elected mayor of Bordeaux in 1581 and re-elected for a second term two years later, a fact which he regarded as a signal honor.

A very significant experience and activity of Montaigne's was his travel. He took many trips of varying lengths within France and early became a happy and confirmed traveler. Most notable was his prolonged trip through France, Switzerland, Germany, and Italy, from June 1580 to November 1581, following the publication of the first edition of his *Essays*. His travel was extensive but not rushed, for he stayed some five months at a stretch in Rome. The main reason, ostensibly, for this long trip was his health, but it is plain that he relished the travel for its own sake. He visited many of the renowned watering places of Europe in hopes of allaying his gall-stone condition, which had come upon him several years earlier and was to plague him for the rest of his life. Everywhere Montaigne took advantage of the usual social amenities (including the Italian women, who virtually stole his heart away) and of the regular tourist attractions. He showed himself to be an excellent all-round traveler. In his travel-diary, which was not intended for publication, we find him carefully observing the food, drink, and all sorts of domestic details in the countries which he visited. He was fascinated and deeply moved by the remains of antiquity in Rome. Above all, Montaigne's long trip took him away from books and broadened his perspective on the practical aspects of life, an orientation which marks one of the chief differences between his essays written before and those written after his long trip.

The line, however, is not a sharp one, for Montaigne was not exclusively bookish in his early period nor did he refrain from reading in his late period. A catalogue of the authors whom Montaigne read, with a fair indication of the period at which he read each, was drawn up early in this century by Pierre Villey, in the most impressive Montaigne study up to the present time. The actual importance of his readings in the formation of his ideas is, of course, another matter, and one on which there can be no complete agreement, for it is often difficult to distinguish between a book which impelled Montaigne to speculate in a certain direction and one which simply strengthened an idea or train of thought at which he had already arrived. It is a question, for example, whether Plutarch, who was for years a favorite of Montaigne's, exerted "influence" on him, or whether Montaigne was drawn to

Plutarch because of a fundamental similarity of temperament and interests.

Montaigne never looked upon his essays as neatly molded compositions which were finished when they were published. Rather he was eager that they should grow as he grew, and accordingly he continually added to them. This growth of the essays by accretion, which allows the reader to follow Montaigne's intellectual, moral, and emotional growth, is one of their most appealing features.

The first edition of the *Essays*, containing Books I and II, was published in 1580 and met with considerable success. The next important edition was the fifth (1588), which, besides a multitude of additions and changes in the essays of Books I and II, included for the first time the essays of Book III. Montaigne's manuscript notes on his copy of the 1588 edition, presumably for a new edition, provide a basis for studying the last phase of his development. Many scholars have worked on the dating of particular essays and passages, most notably Pierre Villey.

Montaigne's essays represent one of the early examples of self-portraiture in European literature, an example often regarded as indicative of the individualism which was to dominate Western culture. In his preface to the 1580 edition of the *Essays*, with a great show of modesty, Montaigne expresses the limited personal aim of giving his friends and relations some idea of his qualities and moods. Later, more boldly erecting the self-portrayal into a philosophical principle, he presents himself as a representative of all humanity. With increasing thoroughness he disclosed his interests, opinions, and inclinations on a vast range of subjects. His readers have always been divided, not only as to the meaning of the essays but also as to the integrity of their author. Emerson's judgment that "Montaigne is the frankest and honestest of all writers" (a statement for which Montaigne himself is the chief authority) is certainly not literally accurate, for the *Essays* contain many misleading statements, inconsistencies, omissions, and plain ordinary falsehoods. But the interpretation of these depends on the learning and sense of humor of the reader.

Montaigne's political views have been characterized as reactionary in the extreme, liberal to the point of being revolutionary, and everything in between. In religious matters, he has been made out a devout practicing Catholic by some scholars and a free-thinker

by others. Sainte-Beuve's comment that he was a good Catholic, only he was not a Christian, still summarizes the impression of many. It seems impossible to achieve unanimity among readers; but this is probably what Montaigne wanted, for his function was not to provide ready answers to problems but to raise questions on every aspect of human life and point in many different directions for answers. What he presents in his essays is the fruit of his observation and reflection, not a system of philosophy or ethics. Attempts have been made to systematize him—to make him first a stoic, then a skeptic, then an epicurean— but these attempts have usually broken down; D. M. Frame's recent attempt to unify Montaigne has been far more successful.

Montaigne was well-proportioned but below average in height. He had soft eyes and a pleasant face, and was given to no violent passions. These and other personal data appear throughout the *Essays*. He died of gout and stone after asking that mass be recited at his bedside. His body was removed to the Église des Feuillants in Bordeaux, where his widow had a monument erected to him.

Montaigne's *Essays* have been perhaps more influential on other writers than any other work of French literature. Montaigne wrote, besides the *Essays*, a journal of his 1580-81 trip, first published in 1774, and a translation of the *Theologia Naturalis* of Raymond Sebond (1569), which was to serve as the starting point of his longest and best-known essay, the "Apologie de Raimond Sebond."

The *Essays* have been translated into English numerous times: by J. Florio (1603), C. Cotton (1700), W. Hazlitt (1849), G. B. Ives (1925), E. J. Trechmann (1927), and J. Zeitlin (1934-36). The most accurate of these is the last, which also contains sound and up-to-date critical material.

An excellent evaluation of the state of Montaigne studies may be found in Plattard, J. *État Présent des Études sur Montaigne* (1935), and an up-to-date critical bibliography in Schutz, A. H. *A Critical Bibliography of French Literature: The Sixteenth Century* (1956)

ABOUT: Emerson, R. W. Representative Men; Frame, D. M. Montaigne's Discovery of Man. [In French—Strowski, F. Montaigne; Villey, P. Les Sources et l'Évolution des Essais de Montaigne. In German—Friedrich, H. Montaigne.]

A. C. K.

MONTALBÁN, JUAN PÉREZ DE. See PÉREZ DE MONTALBÁN, JUAN

*MONTCHRÉTIEN, ANTOINE DE (c. 1575-October 8, 1621), French dramatist and economist, was born in Falaise and studied at the Collège in Caen, taking a precocious interest in poetry and publishing his first verse tragedy, *Sophonisbe*, at the age of twenty-one, as well as four more plays within the next five years. This early work proved his genius and established his fame. His reputation as a freebooter and *spadassin* stemmed from his duel of 1605 when he killed his opponent. He fled to England, whence his attempts to gain royal pardon were unsuccessful. His English sojourn drew his attention to a wholly different field in which he also distinguished himself, labor and industrial theory. The situation in England was far superior to that in France, a fact that Montchrétien attributed in part to the enlightened encouragement of Queen Elizabeth. A visit to Holland increased his enthusiasm for the betterment of production and of working conditions. Having returned to France, he published his remarkable *Traité de l'Économie Politique* in 1615, abandoned the theatre, married, and settled in Orléans, where he established a cutlery factory and pursued comparable projects over the following three years. He engaged himself in various military campaigns, sometimes in opposition to the king. Leading a small army of some four hundred men, he was murdered in an ambush at an inn by a local enemy. This dramatic final episode further established his legend. He had moved in both Catholic and Protestant circles, but the extreme prudence of his writings allows us to suppose merely Protestant leanings.

Montchrétien's economic system, despite its designation, has no relationship to matters of politics. It postulates a variety of social reforms which today appear very farsighted, e.g., vocational schools for poor children, the outlawing of monopolistic practices, and the division of labor. It was little appreciated in his day but led to such later theory as that of Montesquieu. In the history of the theatre Montchrétien's contribution is significant. His *Aman*, published in 1601 and based on the Old Testament, develops the story of Esther in romantic and melodramatic fashion, and shows the strong influence of several works of Garnier, notably *Les Juives* and *Cornélie*. His *Sophonisbe* (1596) shows similar influence, but the revision prepared two years later exemplifies a completely new orientation inspired by the poetic doctrines of Malherbe. In this respect it marks a critical step in the rise of the classic theatre. The traditional elements, such as the moral preachings of Seneca on virtue and honor, evolve toward a concept of the domination of the passions by the will, and the dramatist adds his personal touch in the tone of melancholy and of dejection. Montchrétien falls into the excessive declamation of Garnier, rising from lack of motivation of plot or action, but his pathos is less staged, more lyrical, gracefully sensuous, and, despite its affectation, clear and forceful. The vocabulary is restricted according to the precepts of Malherbe, and the versification is regular and flowing. Use of ancient subjects leads him away from the former patchwork of borrowed effects. *L'Écossaise*, published in 1601, sets in contrast the two characters of Mary Stuart and Queen Elizabeth.

ABOUT: [In French—Funck-Brentano, T. Preface to edition of 1889; Lanson, G. Hommes et Livres; Lebègue, R. La Tragédie Française de la Renaissance.]

F. J. C.

*MONTEMAYOR, JORGE DE (1520?-1561), Portuguese novelist, poet, and musician, founded the pastoral novel in Spain. Born in Montemor-o-Velho near Coimbra, on the banks of the celebrated Mondego, he took the name of his birthplace before becoming Castilian by preference and an international citizen as subject of Charles V. This last aspect characterized his life and work. Little is known of his youth or of his family. Although Montemayor's name has been associated with that of the noble family Paiva y de Pina, he was probably of humble origin: his father is said to have been a silversmith. His education as a humanist was not very extensive. He admitted a preference for music, poetry, and love. Montemayor arrived at the court of Castile about 1545 in the service of the Infanta Doña María, sister of Philip II. His most important protection came later from the Infanta of Castile, Doña Juana, sister of María and Philip. In 1552-54, he wrote his famous *Cancionero* (song-poems). In 1554, he was probably with Philip II in England; he participated also in Flanders in the war against France. In his last years, Montemayor suffered court disgrace through the loss of a patron. However, in 1559 he returned to the court for a short time before leaving for Piedmont, where he died violently in a jealous quarrel. The partially autobiographical basis of his

* môn krā tyăn′

* môn tā mä yôr′

pastoral novel *Diana* indicates that he had many loves in Portugal and Spain and that the real Diana was among these.

The master work in its genre, *La Diana* was published by Montemayor in Valencia about 1559. Heir to the rich bucolic tradition of Portugal, where the pastoral novel of Menina e Moça de Bernardim Ribeiro had already appeared, and inspired by the Italian poet Sannazaro's *Arcadia* (1481; translated into Spanish in 1547), Montemayor created *Los Siete Libros de la Diana* principally in Spanish although some original fragments exist in Portuguese.

Of excellent, slow and musical prose, interspersed abundantly with song-poems, *La Diana* was an innovation because it established the difficult equilibrium of its elements, combining medieval conciseness with Renaissance abundance, freshly imaginative nymphs and magic with mysticism and purified love, and pure diction with popular though not provincial language. The work is unusual in that its contemplative characters are treated psychologically, all of them on an equal plane as in a tapestry and resolving their problems within the boundaries of the discursive narrative. The theme of sadness parallels the theme of love as *La Diana* blends abstract landscapes with the realism of court anecdotes. Montemayor's pastoral narrates the loves of the shepherdess Diana and the shepherd Sireno on the shores of the river Esla in León. Many obstacles disturb the course of their affection and, after an absence, Sireno returns to find Diana wed to another shepherd, Delio. The last part of the work shows a mysticism deepened with moral firmness, Platonic idealism and quietism, with human passion converted into spiritual passion through the struggle between vice and virtue. In the fourth chapter, the unauthentic *Abindarráez* has been included since the first edition, published after Montemayor's death.

Notable influences of *La Diana* appear in Sir Philip Sidney's *Arcadia* (1590) and Honore d'Urfé's *Astrée* (1607), as well as in Shakespeare's *Two Gentlemen of Verona* (1595) through the English translation of *Diana* included in Googe's *Eglogs, Epytaphes and Sonnets* (1563). Its popularity brought forth at least seventeen Spanish reprints in the sixteenth century, three Spanish sequels, and many imitations. An English translation was made by Bartholomew Yong, London, in 1598.

About: Mérimée, E. A History of Spanish Literature; Rennert, H. A. The Spanish Pastoral Romances.

R. P. C.

*MONTESQUIEU, CHARLES LOUIS DE SECONDAT, Baron de la Brède et de (January 18, 1689-February 10, 1755), French philosopher and political scientist, was born near Bordeaux, at La Brède, the estate of his mother, Marie Françoise de Penel, of Gascon-English ancestry. His father was Jacques de Secondat. The title of Montesquieu came from an uncle, Jean Baptiste de Secondat, whose heir he became. The boy's mother died when he was seven, and he was raised by his devoted father and educated with the Oratorians at Juilly, near Meaux. After studying law he was admitted as counselor to the Parliament of Bordeaux in 1714, and two years later his uncle transferred to him his office as *président à mortier*. In 1715 he married Jeanne Lartigue, an heiress. Montesquieu abandoned his parliamentary career as his interest grew for social life and, beginning in 1716, for the activities of the Academy of Bordeaux. There he read his early essays on science and medicine, on which his first reputation depended. He sold his presidency in 1726 in order to devote himself to writing.

Montesquieu had been an assiduous reader in the Latin classics and ancient philosophy, especially the Stoics; in French his preference was for Montaigne and Fénelon. His first general fame came with the anonymous publication in 1721 of *Les Lettres Persanes*, which established a new and very popular literary genre and is considered the first book of the Philosophe movement. Using the thinly veiled disguise of two Persians, one visiting in Paris and writing home to his friend to report on what he sees, the letters are a brilliant and merciless satire on the principal vices of contemporary customs, government, and religion.

The seditious nature of *Les Lettres Persanes* prevented Montesquieu's election to the French Academy until 1728. In this year he began his extensive travels, first with his English friend Lord Waldegrave, to Vienna, Hungary, Italy, Switzerland and Holland, and later, in 1729, in the company of Lord Chesterfield, to England. During his travels he frequented aristocratic rather than literary circles, carefully observing the laws and customs of each country he visited. His realistic attitudes are evident in his *Notes sur l'Angleterre*, on corruption, envy, irreligion, and lack of political policy. These are tempered with strong concepts of liberty and equality. He always recalled his English sojourn with

* môn tĕs kyû'

MONTESQUIEU

the turn of the century, *L'Esprit des Lois* was judged the first great synthesis of political economy and perhaps even the literary masterpiece of its century for its clear thought, concision, and elegance—a basic book for self-instruction and intellectual discipline and a pure classic in contrast to the circumstantial and destructive writings of Voltaire (who was, incidentally, violently opposed to its views) and the illumined self-expression and gratuitous aims of Rousseau. Finally, scholarship on Montesquieu was revived, beginning about 1891 with the publication of a considerable number of hitherto unknown tracts.

The particular significance of Montesquieu's doctrine of the separation of powers in government and his ideas on federation led to considerable enthusiasm for his *Esprit des Lois* in the United States, and his book was not without influence in the framing of the American Constitution. Montesquieu's influence on Jefferson is evident in the latter's *Commonplace Book,* and the enduring interest in his work is reflected in Holmes' *Collected Legal Papers.* Attitudes toward the treatise were further affected by its strong stand against the institution of Negro slavery and its protests against the Inquisition.

particular pleasure, and was greatly influenced by English customs and traditions.

Having returned to La Brède in 1732, Montesquieu undertook his *Considérations sur les Causes de la Grandeur et de la Décadence des Romains,* published anonymously (1734), one of the first modern works on the philosophy of history. Here he made considerable progress from the notions of political science, commerce, population, and law exhibited in *Les Lettres Persanes.* He adopted a serious form, presenting his ideas in lucid, concise style and replaced the earlier satirical and moralistic elements with close documentation. He abandoned his projected work on English government, reserving the material for *L'Esprit des Lois.* Over the next years he divided his time between salon society and research, the latter becoming systematic about 1743. After publication of *L'Esprit des Lois* in 1748 Montesquieu tended to remain apart from society, spending more and more time in seclusion at La Brède.

L'Esprit des Lois, published anonymously at Geneva, may be judged from several distinct points of view, each historically significant. It was progressive and prophetic in approaching modern institutions from an objective point of view rather than idealistically, sensationally, or destructively. Indeed its moderate tone made it appear to contemporaries like Voltaire an inert and even unoriginal work. As political events moved toward violence and revolution, it was found too calm, too equable and aristocratic. After

The early nineteenth century editions of Montesquieu's works (1819, 1822, 1834) were replaced by the *Œuvres Complètes,* of 1875-79, ed. by E. Laboulaye, in seven volumes, and by editions of unpublished notes issued from 1891 to 1914, including the correspondence; one must note especially the critical edition of the complete works published in two volumes in 1949.

The first English translation from Montesquieu was *Persian Letters,* by Ozell, in 1722, redone by others during that century and more recently by J. R. Loy (Meridian Books, 1961); *Reflections on . . . the Romans* appeared in 1734, *The Spirit of Laws,* translated by T. Nugent, in 1750, *Miscellaneous Pieces* in 1759, and the *Complete Works* in four volumes in 1777.

ABOUT: Cairns, H. Law and the Social Sciences; Chinard, G. Studies in the History of Culture; Collins, J. Voltaire, Montesquieu and Rousseau in England; Courtney, C. P. Montesquieu and Burke; Dargan, E. The Aesthetic Doctrine of Montesquieu; Fletcher, F. T. H. Montesquieu and English Politics; Havens, G. The Age of Ideas; Levin, L. The Political Doctrine of Montesquieu's Esprit des Lois; Martin, K. French Liberal Thought in the Eighteenth Century; Saintsbury, G. French Literature and Its Masterpieces; Shackleton, R. Montesquieu, a Critical Biography; Spurlin, M. Montesquieu in America. [In French—Barrière, P. Un Grand Provincial; Dedieu, J. Montesquieu, l'Homme et l'Œuvre: La Harpe, J. Cours de Littérature; Maupertuis. Éloge de M. de Montesquieu (in Œuvres, 1875): Sorel, A. Montesquieu.]

F. J. C.

*MONTI, VINCENZO (February 19, 1754-October 13, 1828), Italian poet and prose writer, was born at Alfonsine, in the neighborhood of Ravenna, to Fedele and Domenica Maria Mazzari. Monti's ancestors were traditionally house stewards for the Marquis Calcagnini, but his own father was employed as a land-surveyor. Young Vincenzo began his studies with a tutor, continuing his Latin education at a seminary in nearby Faenza. At the age of seventeen he contemplated becoming a Franciscan priest, but finally went to the University of Ferrara to study jurisprudence, then medicine. Actually he had already begun to demonstrate his poetic gift, and most of his university life was involved with the literary arts. He was admitted to the Academy of the Arcadians in 1775 under the name Antonide Saturniano.

In 1776 his composition in *terza rima, La Visione d'Ezechiello* (The Vision of Ezekiel) provided the basis for his subsequent good fortune. The legate to Ferrara, Cardinal Borghese, invited the young poet to settle in Rome, where in 1778 Monti became secretary to Cardinal Braschi, nephew of the pope. For the next fifteen years he was, in effect, a court poet, many papal favors being conferred on him. Monti was handsome, eloquent, and confident of his own genius, and this was a most prolific period of poetic activity for him. In 1784 he wrote one of his most famous poems, the ode *Al Signore di Montgolfier,* to celebrate the ascent of the Montgolfier balloon. In the year preceding he had composed the beautiful *Pensieri d'Amore* (Thoughts of Love), inspired by his romance with the seventeen-year-old Florentine Carlotta, whom he apparently intended to marry. He also turned his attention to the theatre with the composition of *Aristodemo* in 1786, *Galeotto Manfredi* in 1788, and *Caio Gracco,* begun in 1788 but not completed until twelve years later. Among his other writings of this period were the four academic sonnets *Sulla Morte di Giuda* (On the Death of Judas) and the blank verse *Alla Marchesa Anna Malaspina della Bastia,* composed for the Bodoni edition of Tasso's *Aminta.*

On July 3, 1791, Monti married Teresa Pikler, a young Roman of great beauty. She had taken a part in his play *Aristodemo* some years earlier. They had two children, Costanza and Giovan Francesco. Monti was becoming more and more conscious of liberal trends of thought and between 1793 and 1797 he worked to loosen the bonds which held him in Rome. In 1793 he had written *Bassvilliana,*

* mŏn′ tē

a poem which could cause him to be considered the poet of reaction. (Nicholas Jean Hugon, called Bassville, was a Girondist agent who had been assassinated in Rome. In the poem his shade is forced, in expiation, to witness the Reign of Terror.) In March 1797 Monti broke with his patron Braschi and fled from Rome. From that time his poetry was pro-French in tone, beginning with the *Prometeo,* written to extol Napoleon as the savior of the Italians. Monti served the Cisalpine Republic for a while in Milan, where he met Foscolo and other writers working for the Republic, but the vicissitudes of the struggle for Italian independence drove him to new flight.

During the period of the Napoleonic victories Monti continued to enjoy an honored position as an oracle of Italian letters. He was professor at the University of Pavia, where his lectures were very popular, and where he occupied the chair of eloquence and poetry before Foscolo. He corresponded with Mme de Staël to defend the classicism of Italian letters against the romantic and popularizing trends of the French Revolution. He also prepared a translation into blank verse of the *Iliad,* though he did not work from the Greek.

Upon the restoration of Austrian rule in Italy Monti was called upon to employ his art to celebrate the new government. His work of this period, *Il Mistico Omaggio* (Mystic Homage) in 1815, and *Il Ritorno d'Astrea* (The Return of Astrea) in 1816, is considered inferior and timeserving. He showed greater ability, however, in the idyll *Le Nozze di Cadmo e d'Ermione* (The Wedding of Cadmus and Hermione), written in 1825, and in the eloquent defense of his poetics entitled *Sermone sulla Mitologia* (Lecture on Mythology) of that same year. Another notable work is his collaboration with his son-in-law, Giulio Perticara, on *La Proposta di Correzioni ed Aggiunte al Vocabolario della Crusca* (Proposal for Corrections and Additions to the Vocabulary of the Crusca) which is characterized by a lively polemic in defense of the classical tradition.

In the last three years of his life, paralyzed, blind, saddened by his son-in-law's death, he returned to the religious convictions of his youth. He attempted to burn his unpublished translation of Voltaire's *Pucelle d'Orléans,* but was dissuaded. His crowded career ended in Milan in straitened circumstances.

For all Monti's consummate technique and popularity, posterity has recognized that he was greatly lacking in seriousness of principle and for this reason he is not acknowledged as a major poet.

The first English translation of *Aristodemus* was published in 1818. *Bassvilliana* was translated as *The Penance of Hugon, a Vision of the French Revolution* by Henry Boyd in 1805, and *Caius Gracchus: A Tragedy* in 1830.

ABOUT: Everett, W. Italian Poets Since Dante. [In Italian—see studies by C. Angelini, E. Bevilacqua, C. d'Alessio.]

E. DE P.

*MORAIS (or MORAES), FRANCISCO DE (c. 1500-c. 1572),

Portuguese novelist, was not a professional writer but a courtier who won his fame through a single work, a late prose romance of chivalry.

Born, perhaps near Lisbon, to Sebastião de Morais, Chief Treasurer of the Realm, he early became attached to Prince Edward at the court of King John III. He was eventually made royal treasurer but, eager to see the world, he left in 1540 for Paris, to become secretary to Francisco de Noronha, the Portuguese ambassador. While in France, the mature gallant vainly courted a French lady in Queen Leonor's household. Deeply hurt by her cruelty, he made this unhappy affair an episode in his novel, probably written in France, and again referred to it in *Desculpa de Uns Seus Amores que Teve em Paris,* one of three *Dialogos,* his only other known work (1624).

In 1543 Morais returned home to marry Barbara Madeira. He made one more trip to France with Noronha in 1549-50. His last years were spent in Évora where his romantic life came to a sudden end by assassination.

Morais was authorized by the king to use Palmeirim as his name, so well-known had he become through his novel *Crónica de Palmeirim de Inglaterra,* written in two parts and perhaps already published by 1544. The first known edition appeared in Spanish in 1547, giving rise to disputes about the author's identity. The work in Portuguese was published in 1567. While it perpetuated earlier anonymous Castilian romances of the Arthurian type, it was the only one of the Palmeirim cycle to be imitated, continued, and translated. No longer read in Portugal, Morais' *Palmeirim* continues to interest literary historians, particularly in England, doubtless because of its fanciful connection with that country.

Following the lead of young João de Barros, who in *Clarimundo* (1520) had

* moo rĭsh'

linked the fabled world of knighthood with Portuguese history, Morais introduced Portuguese settings into his elegant story of Palmeirim, son of an English Prince Edward and of Flérida, the daughter of Palmeirim de Oliva, protagonist of earlier novels. Keeping the reader constantly on the alert with countless unexpected adventures, the imaginative author was careful to have his hero move among the highest society and express himself in the choicest language. The plot begins with Edward's mysterious disappearance from England. All the famous knights try unsuccessfully to find him. Eventually his young son Palmeirim, born in his absence, finds him in England itself, where he has been held by the dreadful giant Dramusiand. Not only giants, but wizards, savages, and serpents complicate their lives. Additional thrills include tournaments (which Morais relished in real life), dangerous crossings, separations, confusions and reunions. Real countries appear in a fantastic light—England, France, Portugal, and finally Byzantium, whither the knights hasten to ward off the hosts of the Great Turk. Palmeirim's marriage puts a happy moral ending to his adventures, but his last years and his death are also related in order to satisfy all curiosity. One more rather original feature remains to be mentioned—the author's antifeminine reflections through which he avenged his personal misadventure in France.

Even Cervantes, great scoffer that he was at knight errantry, could not escape the spell of three Hispanic novels of chivalry—*Tirant lo Blanch, Amadís,* and *Palmeirim de Inglaterra,* "which is so unique that it should be kept and preserved in a case specially made for the purpose, like the case Alexander took from Darius' spoils to keep in it the works of Homer. . ." (*Don Quixote,* I, ch. 6). A Frenchman translated it again in the last century because, he said, "I don't know any other novel or epic which holds one's interest and attention to the end with greater skill or success."

The novel was translated into English by A. Munday as *The History of Prince Palmerin of England* (1602-09), not from the original but from J. Vincent's French version of 1553. Robert Southey "corrected" Munday's work, leaving out everything which might offend English morals (4 vols., 1807).

ABOUT: Purser, W. E. Palmerin of England, Some Remarks on This Romance and on the Controversy Concerning Its Authorship; Thomas, H. Spanish and Portuguese Romances of Chivalry.

G. M. M.

*MORATÍN, LEANDRO FERNÁNDEZ DE (March 10, 1760-June 21, 1828), Spanish dramatist who marks the revival of a national theatre stagnant since the death of Calderón in 1681, was born in Madrid, the son of Nicolás Fernández de Moratín, one of the celebrated writers of his day and a leader of the *afrancesados* (French sympathizers) in the theatre. At the age of four Leandro suffered an attack of smallpox which left him permanently disfigured. Outwardly shy and reticent, he was inordinately proud of his talent and of his intellectual achievements. In 1779 he wrote an epic, *La Toma de Granada,* and in 1782 *Lección Poética sobre los Vicios Introducidos en la Poesía Castellana.* It was only in 1785, however, after the death of his parents, that he settled down to become a playwright. Appointed secretary to the Spanish embassy in Paris, he spent two years acquainting himself with high life there. When he returned to Madrid in 1788 he received a pension through the good offices of the minister Godoy and his first play, *El Viejo y la Niña* (1790), was performed. This play, never popular because of its sad ending, is about the jealousy of an old man married to a young girl who eventually enters a convent.

From 1792 to 1796, again thanks to the patronage of Godoy, he was able to travel extensively and study the theatres and library systems abroad. In 1792 he also wrote one of his best plays, *La Comedia Nueva o El Café,* a satire in prose about a dramatist who is completing a play to be presented that night. Accompanying the dramatist, his wife, and sister, is the conceited and jealous pedant Don Hermógenes who offers his literary assistance in hope of marrying the sister and appropriating the proceeds of the play as dowry. The work is a dismal failure and Don Hermógenes runs off. This comedy, considered by Menéndez y Pelayo to be one of the most astonishing literary satires in any language, as well as *La Derrota de los Pedantes* (1789) which satirized ignorant writers and critics of his day, made bitter enemies for Moratín.

Back in Spain, Moratín retired to Pastrana where he rewrote *El Barón* (1803) which he had originally composed in 1787. This is the story of a bogus grandee playing upon the aristocratic pretensions of a greedy and ignorant widow who hopes to marry her daughter off to him; in the end the baron flees with all her savings. The next year Moratín produced *La Mojigata,* a play vaguely reminis-

cent of Molière's *Tartuffe.* In it a religious hypocrite hopes to make a nun of his daughter in order to inherit the money left to her. The girl pretends extreme piety as a façade for husband-hunting, but the plans of both father and daughter go astray.

El Sí de las Niñas (1806), is Moratín's most popular and mature play. The time is a summer night at an inn in Alcalá where an uncle and nephew are rivals for a young girl's hand. The girl's mother is a stupid, talkative bore, but the uncle, swerving from the tradition of the cloying elderly suitor, withdraws in favor of his nephew when he finds that the young girl loves him. The comedy, worthy of the tradition of Molière, is an indictment of parental despotism and unwise education. The reaction to this play was so strong that Moratín was denounced to the Inquisition and retired from playwriting. As the son of an *afrancesado* he found himself in even greater danger when the French invaded and his patron Godoy fell. In view of the fact that Bonaparte abolished the Inquisition and that Spain seemed hopelessly defeated, Moratín found himself embracing the French cause. Joseph Bonaparte bestowed upon him the post of chief librarian of what is now the Biblioteca Nacional. When the French fell and Ferdinand VII returned to the Spanish throne in 1818 Moratín fled the country. The last decade of his life, until his death in Paris, was difficult. Twenty-five years later his remains were brought back to Spain.

Although Moratín tried his hand at translations of *Hamlet* (1798) and Molière's *L'École des Maris* and *Le Médecin Malgré Lui,* known respectively as *La Escuela de los Maridos* (1812) and *El Médico a Palos* (1814), and devoted a good deal of his life to the scholarly *Orígenes del Teatro Español* (1830), his importance lies in his pioneer work in the modern Spanish comedy of manners, a genre cultivated by such later dramatists as Bretón de los Herreros and Ventura de la Vega. Gerald Brenan considers him "the greatest dramatist of his day."

The only complete translation into English of a play by Moratín is *The Baron,* made by Fanny Holcroft in 1805.

ABOUT: Brett, L. E. Nineteenth Century Spanish Plays. [In Spanish—Papell, M. Moratín y su Época; Revista Contemporánea, CXXIX (1904).]

* mō rä tēn'

M. N.

*MORÉAS, JEAN (April 15, 1856-March 30, 1910), French poet, was born Johannes Papadiamantopoulos in Athens. His family had long been prominent among the Greek military and judiciary, and his father was famous as a legal consultant. Johannes was brought up by a French governess, who inspired in her charge a love of French poetry; he acquired and read more than 2,000 volumes, primarily of the French Renaissance and classical periods. In 1872, after he had attended school in Athens, he was sent by his German-trained father to study at Bonn and Heidelberg. Johannes gallicized his baptismal name and adopted the name of Moréas from "Morea," i.e., the Peloponnesus. He visited Austria, Switzerland, and Italy, and settled in Marseilles for a time. Returning to Greece, he did some translations from French and German and edited an anthology of modern Greek verse. In 1878 he published *Tourterelles et Vipères*, a volume of poems in Greek and in French. The following year he returned to Paris, ostensibly to study law, but the excitement of literary circles and of café life claimed his attention. Moréas frequented the Hydropathes and the Zutistes; he himself founded the Cercles des Jemenfoutistes in 1884. Handsome, black-mustached, with flashing eyes and gleaming teeth, vain of his appearance and with an incisive voice, Moréas was long a familiar in certain cafés.

Moréas published poems in the *Nouvelle Rive Gauche* (1882) which changed its name to *Lutèce* (1883). He collected these as *Les Syrtes*, and although he issued a new edition in 1892, he later rejected this volume so obviously influenced by Paul Verlaine. *Les Cantilènes* followed in 1886 as well as a novel and a collection of short stories in collaboration with Paul Adam: *Les Demoiselles Goubert* and *Le Thé chez Miranda*. Moréas was prominent in the debate on decadence and symbolism; his two manifestoes, *XIXe Siècle* (1885) and the supplement to *Le Figaro* (1886), helped to institute the use of the latter term. He achieved his greatest popularity with *Le Pèlerin Passioné* (1891). In this work, which was feted by *La Plume* with a banquet, Moréas interwove antiquity and modernity, neologisms and popular expressions, with considerable preciosity.

At the very moment of this success Moréas launched a reaction to symbolism with L'École Romane. Its credo was a return to Medieval and Renaissance materials, with freedom in verse forms and attention to syntactical problems. But he in turn left this sort

of archaism in order to proclaim the supremacy of "true classicism." He wrote an *Iphigénie* between 1894 and 1900, and *Les Stances*, whose various "books" were written between 1897 and 1905 (but published between 1897 and 1920). Immediately prior to the composition of *Les Stances* Moréas had visited Greece for the last time, on the occasion of the Greco-Turkish war. *Les Stances* are personal, with an integrating theme of sadness; the neologisms and the bizarre have disappeared, leaving clear, vigorous, and traditional modes of expression.

Moréas wrote little toward the end of his life except for a certain amount of journalism. He was given French citizenship in 1910, the year of his death, which accelerated by his abuse of his health. He died at the Saint-Mandé rest home, having been paralyzed for almost a month, and was buried in Père Lachaise cemetery in Paris. His will established a poetry prize which is awarded only occasionally. His collected works were published in eight volumes, four of which are poetry and the rest criticism and reminiscence. Some of his poems have been set to music by Marcel Grandjany, Eva Ruth Spalding, Francis Poulenc, Reynaldo Hahn, and Marcel Delannoy, among others.

ABOUT: France, A. Life and Letters, IV: Gourmont, R. de, Book of Masques; Turquet-Milnes, G. R. Some Modern French Writers. [In French—Georgin, R. Jean Moréas; Henriot, E. De Lamartine à Valéry; Maurras, C. Maîtres et Témoins de Ma Vie d'Esprit; Niklaus, R. Jean Moréas, Poète Lyrique; Reynaud, E. Jean Moréas et les Stances; Van Bever, A. and Léautaud, P. Poètes d'Aujourd'hui.]

S. S. W.

*MOREAU, HÉGÉSIPPE (April 8, 1810-December 19, 1838), French poet and short-story writer, was born in Paris. The illegitimate son of Claude François Moreau (1756-1814) and his common-law wife Marie Philiberte Roulliot (d. 1823), he was named Pierre Jacques Roulliot. His father, whose name he adopted unofficially, called him Hégésippe after an early Christian saint. The family moved in 1810 to Provins, in the Seine-et-Marne department where the elder Moreau had been assigned to teach in the public school. Upon the father's death from pulmonary tuberculosis, the mother and son were succored by the Guérard family. Hégésippe was an excellent student, and started writing verse when he was twelve years old, utilizing popular tunes for his rhythms and imitating Béranger. Scholar-

* mô rä äs'

* mô rō'

ships took him through seminaries at Meaux and Avon, but his formal education ceased in 1826. After an apprenticeship in typesetting in the Lebeau shop at Provins, he went in 1830 to Paris, as a compositor for the famous Didot firm. The times were difficult; he was an indifferent worker and held various jobs or none at all during the next few years —tutor, writer of vaudevilles, proofreader, and editor at Provins and Paris of a small newspaper, *Diogène*. Ill health and lack of funds caused him to enroll in the *bohème*, i.e., art aspirants living a precarious and starving existence. He became ill with cholera during the epidemic in 1832. He died at the age of twenty-eight of debility and consumption, at the Charité hospital in Paris. The artist Guy made a death mask, and Moreau was buried in Montparnasse cemetery, where in 1903 a bronze bust by Mme Coutan-Montorgueil was erected.

Moreau had occasionally published poems —elegies, epigrams, romances—and stories in various periodicals: these earned him hardly any money. The year of his death saw the publication of selections from his eighteenth century-ish tales and sentimental poetry as *Le Myosotis*, inspired largely by his unrequited love for Louise Lebeau whom he called his "sister." Two anthologized pieces, "Un Souvenir à l'Hôpital," based on the popular notion of the poet Gilbert, and "La Voulzie," about the stream near Provins, are his best. His poetry generally blends a love of nature with delicacy, affection, and sensitivity. Moreau's fame also rests on Felix Pyat's article in *Le National* (June 21, 1838) visualizing him as an ardent republican, and on the popular view that he was mortally neglected by an unfeeling society.

Le Myosotis has been reprinted often. An important edition of his complete works is that of 1890 by René Vallery-Radiot, for the lengthy introduction includes extensive correspondence.

ABOUT: [In French—Benoit-Guyod, G. La Vie Maudite de H. M.; Bocquet, L. Les Destinées Mauvaises; Lardanchet, H. Les Enfants Perdus du Romantisme; Vallery-Radot, V. F. Souvenirs Littéraires.]

S. S. W.

*MORGENSTERN, CHRISTIAN** (May 6, 1871-March 31, 1914), German poet, was born in Munich, the son and grandson of well-known landscape painters. He studied law at the universities of Breslau and Berlin but withdrew from school upon learning that he had contracted tuberculosis, the disease

* mör′ gĕn shtĕrn

of which his mother died. The remainder of his life was haunted by the premonition of an early death. He traveled extensively and lived for a time in Norway, where he translated Ibsen's verse dramas with the cooperation of their author. He also translated works of Strindberg, Hamsun, and Bjørnson. After living for many years as an independent writer in Berlin, he settled finally in Switzerland, where he married Margarete Gosebruch in 1908. His death occurred in Meran at forty-two.

Morgenstern's first collections of poetry, *In Phantas Schloss* (1895) and *Horatius Travestitus* (1897), written under the influence of Nietzsche and Schopenhauer, reveal his great talent as a poet and humorist. Hermann Hesse characterized him as "an ironist of technique" and described his lyric verse as "displaying infinite beauty of form with completely nonsensical content." Morgenstern was also an intellectual striving to discover the meaning and purpose of life. Like the other outstanding German humorists Wilhelm Busch and Joachim Ringelnatz, he was by nature a profoundly serious man with a tendency toward melancholy. His next collections of verse, *Auf Vielen Wegen* (1897), *Ich und die Welt* (1899), and *Ein Sommer* (1899), reflect his serious meditations on man's relation to the cosmos.

Morgenstern's most popular works, *Galgenlieder* (1905) and *Palmström* (1910), best reveal the qualities for which he is famous: his unique humor, his masterly command of language, his inexhaustible imagination, and his amazing technical versatility. These poems are grotesque lyrics, in which the humorous effects are achieved in a variety of ways. The poet distorts syntax, coins new words, and twists the normal meanings of familiar words by setting them into unaccustomed contexts. At times he creates melodious patterns of sounds as in *Das Aesthetische Wiesel*, or, as in *Der Trichter*, he may arrange the words so that they express the meaning of the poems visually as well as verbally. His famous *Fisches Nachtgesang* has no words at all. Morgenstern directed these lyrics at the ponderous atmosphere of a world which he felt had become over-serious and attacked with satire and irony the self-importance and smug satisfaction of his contemporaries. He also set out consciously to destroy the belief of his generation in the strict causality of the physical world by reducing it *ad absurdum*, playing havoc particularly with the idea that the name and the thing are identical. *Der Lattenzaun, Das*

Knie, Der Werwolf, and *Das Möwenlied* are excellent examples of poems in which a commonplace reality is totally inverted.

Under the influence of Paul de Lagarde, Buddha, and the Gospel of John, Morgenstern became increasingly introspective and inclined toward mysticism, as is evidenced by the works *Melancholie* (1906) and *Einkehr* (1910). His next collection of lyrics, *Ich und Du* (1911), inspired by his wife, contains some of the finest love poems in the German language. Through his wife Morgenstern was introduced to Rudolph Steiner's theologic-anthroposophic teachings, which furnished him with the path he had been seeking. His last volume of verse, *Wir Fanden einen Pfad* (1914), which was dedicated to Steiner, reflects the tranquillity of one who has resolved the conflict between life and death, thereby achieving spiritual harmony.

After Morgenstern's death, his wife assembled his fragmentary writings and published *Stufen* (1916), *Epigramme und Sprüche* (1920), and *Meine Liebe Ist Gross wie die Weite Welt* (1929). Subsequently the collections of verse — *Galgenlieder, Palmström, Palma Kunkel* (1916), and *Der Gingganz* (1919) — were combined into a single volume entitled *Alle Galgenlieder* (1932). Others which appeared posthumously are *Das Aufgeklärte Mondschaf* (1941), *Böhmischer Jahrmarkt* (1938), and *Egon und Emilie* (1950). Morgenstern is one of the most appealing of modern German poets and is greatly esteemed in his native country for his irresistible humor and profound spirituality.

He is little known outside Germany because his finest works abound in technical and semantic difficulties which make them virtually untranslatable. Selections of his verse in English translation may be found in J. Bithell, *Contemporary German Poetry* (1909) ; in D. Yarmolinsky, *Contemporary German Poetry* (1923); and in L. Forster, *The Penguin Book of German Verse.* An English translation of *Galgenlieder* by May Knight was published in 1963.

ABOUT: [In German—see studies by M. Bauer and M. Morgenstern, F. Geraths, H. Giffei. G. Klemm, B. F. Martin, R. Steiner.]

D. G. D.

*MÖRIKE, EDUARD FRIEDRICH

(September 8, 1804-June 4, 1875), German poet, was born in Ludwigsburg, Swabia, the son of a physician, Karl Friedrich Mörike. His mother, the former Charlotte Beyer, a preacher's daughter, possessed a lively sense of humor and fantasy that carried over to her son. During his relatively happy childhood Eduard was already cultivating the pri-

* mü' rĭ kĕ

vate, fanciful worlds of his later literary work. He was educated at the local Latin school, counting among his fellow students the aesthetician Friedrich Theodor Vischer and the philosopher David Friedrich Strauss. After his father's death in 1817, Eduard was sent to an uncle, Eberhard Friedrich Georgii, a prominent Stuttgart official in whose household he found considerable intellectual stimulation. The following year he was sent to the Protestant seminary school in Urach to prepare for a clerical career. As a student Mörike was mediocre, but the impressions gained from the school's scenic surroundings and from his love for his cousin Klärchen Neuffer were to leave their marks on his creative work. In 1822 he entered the University of Tübingen. With the minor poets Wilhelm Waiblinger and Ludwig Bauer he formed a literary circle, meeting in a cottage to which they sometimes invited the aging, already insane poet Hölderlin. Later, in fantastic candle-lit ceremonies, he and Bauer acted out dramas set in an imaginary world which they called Orphid. During his Tübingen years Mörike experienced a passionate romance with Maria Meyer, a waitress in a student tavern, who appears in his work as the mysterious Peregrina.

He left Tübingen in 1826 for the prosaic life of a country preacher, already having gathered most of the experiences and impressions which he was to nurture to new life in his writings. For the next eight years he was sent about from one village to another as vicar, but he felt himself so confined in his profession that he constantly sought opportunities elsewhere. For a short time he ground out copy for a Stuttgart women's journal, but, finding this even more confining, returned to the life of vicar. In 1829 he became engaged to Luise Rau, a pastor's daughter, but after four years, largely because she and her family questioned his dedication of his profession, the engagement was broken. Throughout his period as vicar he completed some of his best lyrics as well as his longest prose work, *Maler Nolten* (1832), an autobiographical novel in the tradition of Goethe's *Wilhelm Meister.*

In 1834 Mörike became full pastor in Cleversulzbach, where, living with his mother and sister, he spent his time collecting coins and rocks, drawing sketches for friends, and worrying about his ailments and indolence. Although he tended to the personal cares of his parishioners, he left to his vicar all matters of church business and as many of the sermons as possible. He did not concern himself with the major political and intellectual events of his time, and he even continued his friendship with Strauss, whose secular interpretation of Jesus was currently rocking the ecclesiastical world. On his fellow pastor Wilhelm Hartlaub, his closest friend since their days together at the Urach seminary, he came to depend for practical advice, encouragement in his poetic work, occasional financial help, and piano renderings of his favorite music. He published his first collection of poems in 1838 and had frequent contact with the so-called Swabian school of poets, principally Justinus Kerner and Ludwig Uhland, with whom he was linked so long in literary history that his individuality and stature were not generally recognized until the present century.

In 1843, with his parishioners irritated by his neglect of his duties, he retired on a small pension, settling the following year, together with his sister, in Mergentheim. In 1851, after a long courtship, he married Margarete von Speeth, a Catholic. Their marriage, gradually deteriorating through differences in religion and temperament and the constant though devoted presence of his sister, terminated in separation shortly before his death. In 1846 he published his pastoral epic *Idylle vom Bodensee*, in the tradition of Goethe's *Hermann und Dorothea*, and in 1855 his prose masterpiece *Mozart auf der Reise nach Prag* (translated by W. and C. A. Phillips, 1934), a short novel woven around a single incident in the life of Mozart, with whose personality Mörike felt close affinities. After his departure from Cleversulzbach, his lyrical production became quite small, the writings of his middle years consisting mainly of shorter prose pieces and fairy tales.

During his final two decades, though he wrote little, he gained numerous honors, including prizes and gifts from the Württemberg royal family and literary foundations. Residing principally in Stuttgart, he served as professor of literature (1855-66) at the Katharinenstift, a girls' college—with only a single lecture per week required of him—and lectured on literature to women's groups. He was much visited by admiring writers and artists, but in his final years, afflicted with domestic unhappiness and frequent illness, he could no longer maintain the uneasy balance of impish good humor and irritability that had characterized his creative period.

In the funeral oration delivered at his grave in Stuttgart, his childhood friend Vischer correctly predicted that his work would gain a small but appreciative audience. The standard edition of his writings, edited in three volumes by H. Maync, appeared 1909-14. Mörike's poems, which today rank among the greatest in German, bespeak such romantic interests as the introspective involvement with nature, the cultivation of the mythically distant, and the achievement of folklike, childlike effects. Yet throughout his work the romantic element is informed with a classical grace and precision. Outside Germany he is known chiefly through the musical settings of his verse by Hugo Wolf.

Poems by Eduard Mörike, translated by N. K. Cruickshank and G. F. Cunningham, was published in 1959.

About: Lange, V. *in* On Romanticism and the Art of Translation (ed. G. F. Merkel); Mare, M. Eduard Mörike; Journal of English and Germanic Philology, July 1954; PMLA, June, 1955. [In German—see studies by F. Gundolf, H. Maync, H. Pongs, and B. von Wiese. In Italian—by B. Croce.]

H. L.

*MORITZ, KARL PHILIPP (September 15, 1757-June 26, 1793), German novelist and essayist, was born in Hameln, the son of humble parents. He was raised in a strict, pietistic environment and spent an unhappy childhood, suffering from mistreatment by his father and from humiliations due to his extreme poverty. Throughout life he was sensitive and moody with a pronounced tendency toward melancholy and loneliness. His education was irregular and at an early age he was apprenticed to a hatmaker who treated him abusively. After an attempt at suicide, he was permitted to return to school where he distinguished himself. Financial assistance from wealthy donors enabled him to attend the *Gymnasium* to prepare for a career in theology. During this period his interest in the theatre was stimulated by reading Shakespeare, and he abandoned his schooling to become an actor in Erfurt, an attempt which ended in failure. After studying theology and philosophy in Hanover (1776) and Wittenberg (1777), he taught in Dessau and in Potsdam, until in 1780 he was appointed teacher and assistant master at the Gymnasium Grauer Kloster in Berlin. Here he wrote a series of essays concerning grammatical and syntactical problems, which he published under the title *Kleine Schriften, die Deutsche Sprache Betreffend* (1781-83). In 1781 Moritz, who loved to travel, visited England and recorded his impressions in the volume *Reisen eines Deutschen in England im Jahre 1782* (1783),

* mö′ rĭts

an interesting and informative account which proved very popular in England when it was translated. Subsequently Moritz was appointed professor at the Köllnischer Gymnasium in Berlin but resigned in 1786 to travel to Rome, where he associated with Goethe and the latter's circle of friends. He later wrote an account of this period in the volume *Reisen eines Deutschen in Italien in den Jahren 1786-88* (1792-93). Moritz was highly regarded by Goethe, whom he visited in 1788 at Weimar. Through the intercession of Prince Karl August, Moritz was appointed professor of archaeology and aesthetics at the Academy of Arts in Berlin, where he became a popular teacher and a productive scholar. In his later years he was named a Privy Councilor and admitted to the Academy of Sciences. He died in Berlin.

Although Moritz produced approximately fifty volumes of writings during his lifetime, he is mainly remembered today for the autobiographical novel *Anton Reiser, ein Psychologischer Roman* (1785-90). In this work, which presents a thinly-veiled account of his own life up to the failure of his acting career, Moritz created an important cultural-historical document, which contributes a valuable insight into the life and thought of this period. The special significance of this narrative, which represents Germany's first psychological novel, lies in its unsparing and exhaustive analysis of the hero's inner development. In technique *Anton Reiser* was far in advance of its time and psychological processes are presented with a depth and accuracy not commonly found in literature until the advent of the modern novel at the end of the nineteenth century.

Among the many other works by Moritz, the most significant are the one-act play *Blunt, oder Der Gast* (1782), the novel *Andreas Hartknopf* (1786), and the essays *Versuch einer Deutschen Prosodie* (1786) and *Über die Bildende Nachahmung des Schönen* (1788). Moritz also edited five journals at various times, among them the *Magazin zur Erfahrungsseelenkunde* (1783-93) and the *Vossische Zeitung* (1784).

Reisen eines Deutschen in England im Jahre 1782 appeared in 1795 in an anonymous English translation which was reprinted in 1886 and 1924. *Anton Reiser* was translated by P. E. Mathison in 1926.

ABOUT: Farmakis, V. M. Karl Philipp Moritz and His Conception of the Artist; Rose, W. From Goethe to Byron. [In German—see studies by E. Catholy, M. Dessoir, H. Eybisch, L. Geiger (ADB), H. Henning, H. J. Schrimpf, C. Ziegler.]

D. G. D.

*MORSZTYN, ANDRZEJ (1613-January 8, 1693), Polish poet, was a highly educated man who was well acquainted with Europe. He rose to the position of vice treasurer to the Crown at the court of Jan Sobieski, King of Poland. Later Morsztyn became one of the primary conspirators in the "French Party" which wanted a French king for the Polish throne. Owing to these intrigues with the court of Louis XIV, he was accused of treason and forced to flee to France, where he died.

An ardent admirer of Western European culture, he found great satisfaction in translating French and Italian literature, of which his translations of Corneille's *Le Cid* and Tasso's *Amyntas* are excellent examples. He did not, however, set much value on his own works and therefore did not publish them. His two volumes of poems, *Kanikula albo Psia Gwiazda* (Caniculum or the Dog Star), and *Lutnia* (The Lute), did not appear until the nineteenth century. Inspired primarily by the Italian Marino, they are fine examples of Morsztyn's adaptive form and content.

Morsztyn was the most distinguished representative of the baroque literary style in Polish poetry. This style, imported from Italy, was cultured and refined by comparison with the domesticated Sarmatian variety, with which it had little in common. Morsztyn excels in brief, compact forms, full of elaborate verbal combinations which express complex psychological nuances and perceptions. He readily uses striking comparisons and contrasts which give his works a very ingenious quality. These are highly abstract and often amount to no more than a play on words. The principal motive is love, and its expression has a distinctness which was new to Polish poetry.

Morsztyn sometimes carries poetic emphasis and symbolic statement to the verge of the absurd, and his lines sometimes give an impression of a poetic trick rather than of poetic art. Nevertheless, he demonstrates a considerable control of the language and verse forms as well as an unusual and interesting imagination. His sonnets *Do Trupa* (To a Corpse) and *Cuda Milosci* (The Miracles of Love) are composed exclusively of a series of comparisons and strange paradoxes, as revealed in this special baroque conception of love.

ABOUT: Kridl, M. An Anthology of Polish Literature; *also* A Survey of Polish Literature. [In Polish—see studies by E. Deiches, E. Porebowicz.]

P. LY.

* môrsh tēn'

*MOSCHEROSCH, JOHANN (or **HANS) MICHAEL** (March 5, 1601-April 4, 1669), German satirist, moralist, and writer of epigrams, chose for the name of his principal "hero"—in effect his pseudonym—Philander von Sittewald. Moscherosch was indeed a "friend of man" (Philander), and Sittewald is more than an anagram of his birthplace, Willstädt, for he lived in a time when the customs and manners of mankind resembled a dark forest. His own family and his property were repeatedly subjected to the ravages of the Thirty Years' War, this "most deeply troubled and dangerous time," as he called it in the subtitle of his famous satiric-didactic work *Insomnis Cura Parentum*.

Moscherosch's family was of Spanish background, descended from Aragonese nobility. His great-great-grandfather went to the Netherlands under the regime of Charles V and later moved to Alsace. His father was a government official of Willstädt near Strasbourg, where Hans Michael was born. Moscherosch studied law at Strasbourg and took his master's degree in two years, emerging first in his class. He continued his study for the doctorate and then went on the "grand tour" which was *de rigueur* for well-educated sons of good family. He spent some time in Paris, "ce paradis terrestre," but the source, as Moscherosch recognized, of political and cultural influences dangerous to Germany. On his return he became tutor to a noble family.

Having lost out in competition for a professorship in poetics at Strasbourg, Moscherosch entered the field of municipal government. He served capably in the area of Metz, Strasbourg, and the Saar. The war dealt harshly with him. He lost his second wife after a year of marriage, his property was plundered, and he was for a time reduced to farming as a means of subsistence. His administrative abilities were recognized by the Swedes, who made him military adviser in his section of Germany. At the end of the war he was asked to be emissary of Colmar at the peace negotiations in Westphalia. He preferred to accept municipal employment in Strasbourg, where he was soon president of the chancellery and minister for church and military affairs. Moscherosch is another of the many baroque writers who served in high governmental positions. His last duties were his most eminent: counselor to the Elector of Mainz and privy councilor to the Landgravine of Hessen. In 1669 he decided to retire from active office and visit his son, who taught in Frankfurt. He died at Worms, in the course of his journey.

Moscherosch's genealogical connection with Spain is reflected in his literary work. Quevedo's *Sueños y Discursos* served as a model for his *Wunderliche und Wahrhaftige Gesichte Philanders von Sittewald* (1640, often reprinted). This and the *Insomnis Cura* (1643) reflect his answer to the terrible times in which he lived: an attempt at reform through the satirizing of excesses, corruption, and decay. As the title of the former relates, he "showed as in a mirror the ways of the world and the doings of man, clothed in their natural colors of vanity, violence, hypocrisy, and folly." After the fashion of Quevedo, Erasmus, and German satirists like Brant and Fischart, he has his scenes and categories of folly: fools of Venus, religious excess, slavery to fashion, the sins of the soldiery. Particularly in the second part of the *Gesichte*, he turns to the sufferings and errors of his own land. His depiction is an important contribution to German cultural history.

In a time often marked by an abject susceptibility to foreign styles and influences, and despite his own amazing acquaintance with foreign languages and literatures, he wrote with a fervent loyalty to German ways and the German past. His mood is not only one of satire; it evinces a tragic or pessimistic sense of history. He is in a sense one of the "primitives." The goal of return to stauncher values and healthier ways was not unfamiliar among the middle class society of the Renaissance and the Reformation. He lauds the classical heroes of the remote past, as far back as Ariovistus. The urgent didacticism of his message overshadows plot and character. His desire for reform found partial expression in his membership in the Fruchtbringende Gesellschaft. His fraternal name, which has in retrospect a touch of irony, was "Der Träumende" (The Dreamer).

A brief selection of his poetry appears in G. C. Schoolfield's *The German Lyric of the Baroque in English Translation* (1962). ABOUT: Modern Language Review, 1953. [In German—see studies by A. Bechtold, W. Hinze, M. Hufschmid, L. Pariser; see also Monatshefte, 1947.]

F. G. R.

MOSES BEN MAIMON. See MAIMONIDES, MOSES

* mŏsh′ ĕ rōsh

*MOSES DE LEON (c. 1250-1305), Spanish-Hebrew cabalist and reputed author of the *Sefer ha-Zohar* (Book of Splendor), was born in León. His early life was spent in intensive study of the Talmud and philosophy, but his attention soon turned to the mystical element in Judaism. Very few facts are known concerning the course of his life. He appears to have wandered a great deal, living in the cities of Guadalajara, Valladolid, and Ávila. He died in Arévalo on the way to his home at Ávila.

The large number of Hebrew works known to have been written by Moses de Leon under his own name indicates an understanding of the writings of medieval Jewish luminaries such as Ibn Gabirol, Judah ha-Levi, and Maimonides, and an impressive mastery of Jewish mystical literature. In a series of cabalistic books he demonstrated a sharp, brilliant style. The *Sefer ha-Rimon* (Book of the Pomegranate; written 1287) was a lengthy, mystical exploration of Jewish ritual laws. Only two of these works have been printed, *Ha-Nefesh ha-Hokhmah* (The Wise Soul, 1608), dealing with the human soul, resurrection and transmigration, and the *Shekel ha-Kodesh* (The Holy Shekel, 1911).

All sources agree that it was toward the end of the thirteenth century that Moses de Leon issued the *Zohar*, which soon became the major source of cabalistic mysticism. Written in a stilted Aramaic reminiscent of the ancient translations of the Bible, it purported to be the work of the second century Rabbi Simeon ben Yohai and his disciples, revealed finally by Moses de Leon. The pseudomiraculous manner of its appearance and form troubled many scholars and remains an unresolved mystery. Aside from those cabalists who believe in the antiquity of the *Zohar*, most critics assert that Moses de Leon was its author, some even ascribing mercenary motives to him for concealing his authorship. On the other hand, it has been pointed out that there is in the *Zohar* a substratum which is probably of ancient origin. It cannot be denied that the antique form of the *Zohar*, though suspect, proved very impressive to many Jews.

The disjointed, unsystematic contents of the work's nineteen sections are a mystical, allegorical commentary on the Pentateuch, Ruth, and the Song of Songs. The mystical sense of the Biblical narrative is uncovered and such topics as the innermost being of God, mystical symbolism, the process of creation, the divine emanations, God's presence,

the essence of sin and evil, and the nature of the soul are elaborated on in an esoteric manner. Occasionally profound and frequently obscure, the *Zohar* presents a striking Jewish theosophical doctrine.

Moses de Leon wrote the *Zohar* in order to combat the rationalistic, philosophical trend among Jewish thinkers of his time and to strengthen what he regarded as the true, mystical nature of the Scriptures. His bold work met with great favor among mystically inclined Jews and its influence as the chief inspiration of Jewish mysticism can hardly be overestimated. Even Christians such as Pico della Mirandola, Reuchlin, and Aegidius of Viterbo were impressed by the strange power of the *Zohar*. As Gershom Scholem says, in his *Major Trends in Jewish Mysticism*, "To the streak of adventurousness in Moses de Leon, no less than to his genius, we owe one of the most remarkable works of Jewish literature and of the literature of mysticism in general."

A five-volume translation of the *Zohar* by H. Sperling, M. Simon, and P. Levertoff in 1931-34 contains a good portion of the work. *Zohar, the Book of Splendor*, edited by G. G. Scholem in 1949, includes a representative selection. Excerpts may be found in S. Caplan and H. U. Ribalow's *Great Jewish Books and Their Influence on History*, and in *Commentary*, November 1952. *The Alphabet of Creation*, published in 1954, is Ben Shahn's illustrated adaptation of a legend from the *Zohar*. An 18-volume Aramaic edition, edited by Y. Ashlag, appeared in Jerusalem in 1945-53.

ABOUT: Bension, A. The Zohar in Moslem and Christian Spain; Franck, A. The Kabbalah; Graetz, H. History of the Jews; Myer, I. Qabbalah; Scholem, G. G. Major Trends in Jewish Mysticism; Waite, A. E. The Secret Doctrine in Israel; Waxman, M. A History of Jewish Literature. [In German—Jellinek, A. Moses ben Schem-Tob de Leon und Sein Verhältnis zum Zohar.]

M. R.

MOTTE - FOUQUÉ, FRIEDRICH HEINRICH KARL, Baron de la. See LA MOTTE - FOUQUÉ, FRIEDRICH HEINRICH KARL, Baron de

*MOUSKÉS (or MOUSKET), PHILIPPE (d. post-1260), was a French chronicler who transposed a great wealth of historical and legendary material into octosyllabic verse.

Born probably in Tournai, Mouskés was one of four children of an aristocratic family, lords of the manor of Leuze. Presumably Mouskés did not marry. This aristocrat aspired and, one might add, was morally

* mō′ zĕz dĕ lĕ ōn′

* mōōs kās′

665

compelled to recount history whose accuracy leaves much to be desired. His sources were most probably in Old French for his knowledge of Latin cannot be ascertained. As a nobleman he served Philip Augustus at the battle of Bouvines (1214) and reported it in his only known work, the *Chronique Rimée*, 31,286 lines, begun after 1251 and completed about 1260.

This opus has little organization but shows a semblance of chronological order. About a third of the poem tells of the legendary history of France, from the fall of Troy down to the death of Charlemagne; it is of some note that the emperor's chief baron is Ogier the Dane and not Roland. Thousands of lines follow illustrating an intense liking for the Normans and for William the Conqueror. Much is also said about Philip Augustus, and the long poem ends with the preparations of Saint Louis' crusade in 1242.

From this synthesis of history, legend, lost poems, and most probably hearsay, it can be gathered that Mouskés felt a rather vivid enthusiasm for heroes and leaders. As a conservative nobleman he was keenly aware of the aristocrats' mission, and in a sermonizing tone he reminded his peers of the chivalrous deeds of past heroes, while bemoaning the degraded activities of his contemporaries. Moreover, he demonstrated in his narrative poem a marked interest for the city of Tournai, whose origins he wished to recall to the aristocratic listeners to his rather dull poem.

Mouskés had little talent as a historian or as a poet. As R. N. Walpole comments, Mouskés is representative of his age; however, he represents only a facet, not the whole, of contemporary French society. From a literary point of view he had no original style, but his work is a valuable store of Old French words, phrases, and sources for modern-day scholars.

ABOUT: Walpole, R. N. Philip Mouskés and the Pseudo-Turpin Chronicle; Yale Romanic Studies, 1943. [In French—Du Mortier, B. C. *in* Académie Royale des Sciences, Commission Royale d'Histoire (Brussels, 1845); Reiffenberg, Baron de, Chronique Rimée de Philippe Mouskés; Revue Belge de Philologie et d'Histoire (1925).]

E. V.

*MÜLLER (MUELLER), FRIEDRICH ("MALER MÜLLER")

(January 13, 1749-April 23, 1825), German poet, painter, and engraver, was born in Kreuznach. He entered the service of the Duke of Pfalz-Zweibrücken as a painter, and as a result of Goethe's advice was sent by his patron to

* mül' ĕr

Italy in order to gain further training in the graphic arts. He spent almost the entire remainder of his life in Rome and was converted to Catholicism during an illness there. The King of Bavaria had granted the title of court painter to him, and his paintings were accepted in Germany with considerable approval. In Italy his study of Michelangelo had an unfortunate effect upon him as upon so many others and led him into baroque imitations.

As a poet Müller belongs to the so-called Storm and Stress period of German literature; emotionalism, verbal abundance, in addition to frequently crude realism, are the primary characteristics of his poetry. Of his dramatic attempts the lyrical play *Niobe* (1778) is the least successful. *Fausts Leben, Dramatisiert* (1778) shows more violence and emotionalism than poetic capability. His best drama is *Golo und Genoveva* (1781). The last play, although it demonstrates excellent realistic treatment of its subject in individual scenes, fails to acquire real artistic stature because of its lack of unity. Nevertheless the highly imaginative and effective recreation of scenes from the German past had considerable effect upon the later development of the historical drama and novel. Müller acquired an excellent reputation as a composer of idylls. Such works as *Die Schafschur* (1775) and *Das Nusskernen*, describing rural life in the Palatinate, demonstrate a great deal of liveliness, naturalness, and humor. Müller's idylls employing Biblical, ancient Greek, and Germanic materials such as *Der Erschlagene Abel, Der Satyr Mopsus,* and *Ulrich von Kossheim* show considerable poetic talent. They nevertheless remain characteristic of the literary epoch in which they were written, with their dithyrambic excesses and a sentimentality too often confused with true sentiment during this period of German literature. The same may be said for Müller's lyric poetry, with the exception of the poem "Soldatenabschied," which has entered the list of German folk songs. An edition of Müller's works was published in three volumes in Heidelberg in 1811 and 1825. Hermann Hettner edited a collection of his poetry which was published in two volumes in Leipzig in 1868 and August Sauer edited a selection of his works for Kürschner's *Deutsche Nationalliteratur,* Vol. 81.

ABOUT: [In German—see studies by W. Falk, A. Luntowski, K. Möllenbrock, W. Oeser.]

E. K. G.

MÜLLER, (FRIEDRICH) MAX. See "BRITISH AUTHORS OF THE NINE-TEENTH CENTURY"

*MÜLLER, WILHELM (October 7, 1794-September 30, 1827), German poet and philologist, was born at Dessau, a shoemaker's son. In 1813-14 he took part as a volunteer in the Wars of Liberation and from 1815 to 1817 studied philology in Berlin where he became a leading figure in the literary and social life of the romantics. In 1817-18 he traveled in Italy as the companion of Frei-herr von Sack, publishing his impressions under the title *Rom, Römer und Römerinnen* (1820). In 1819 he became a *Gymnasium* teacher at Dessau and from 1820 on also served as the librarian of the ducal library. His death occurred at Dessau. The poet's son (Friedrich) Max Müller (1823-1900), a philologist, mythologist, and Orientalist, was for many years a professor at Oxford University.

Wilhelm Müller is most famous for his lyric poetry which was set to music by Franz Schubert in the two song cycles, *Die Schöne Müllerin* (The Fair Maid of the Mill, 1824) and *Die Winterreise* (The Winter Journey, 1828). The Schubert cycles comprise forty-four of Müller's lyrics, and these extremely congenial settings include such famous *Lieder* as *Ungeduld, Wohin, Das Wandern Ist des Müllers Lust, Am Brunnen vor dem Tore (Der Lindenbaum)*, and *Der Leiermann*. The *Müllerlieder* (a reference to both the poet's name and the protagonist of the first song cycle, a journeyman miller) were originally written in Berlin for a play with songs and were first set to music by Ludwig Berger. It is doubtful whether Müller ever heard *Die Schöne Müllerin*, and he did not live to hear *Die Winterreise*.

Other Müller lyrics which have achieved the popularity of folk songs include *Wenn Wir durch die Strassen Ziehen* and *Im Krug zum Grünen Kranze*. These poems, characterized by simplicity and expressive of the poet's love of nature, were products of Müller's interest in romanticism and folk poetry as well as of his philological pursuits, and were published in such collections as *Siebenundsiebzig Gedichte aus den Hinterlassenen Papieren eines Reisenden Waldhornisten* (1821), *Wanderlieder*, and *Tafellieder für Liedertafeln* (1823).

* mül' ẽr

Müller's most famous work during his lifetime was his *Lieder der Griechen* (Songs of the Greeks, 1821-24), evidence of his buoyant philhellenism and his idealistic sympathy for the Greeks in their War of Liberation against the Turks. This work was widely read and imitated and made its author known as "Griechen-Müller." As a philologist, Müller published *Blumenlese aus den Minnesingern* in 1816 and a ten-volume *Bibliothek Deutscher Dichter des Siebzehnten Jahrhunderts* from 1822 to 1827. The latter was an attempt to revive undeservedly neglected seventeenth century poets like Opitz, Gryphius, Logau, and Angelus Silesius. Müller was also active as a translator, publishing a German version of Marlowe's *Doctor Faustus* in 1818 and *Neugriechische Volkslieder* in 1825.

Müller's works were published in five volumes in 1830. A critical edition of his poems was published in 1906 by J. T. Hatfield, who had earlier issued a collection of Müller's letters in the *American Journal of Philology*. Translations of *Die Schöne Müllerin* and *Die Winterreise* may be found in *Schubert's Songs* by A. H. Fox-Strangways and Steuart Wilson, as well as in other bilingual editions of Schubert songs. Individual Müller poems appear in translation in many anthologies, among them Käthe F. Kroeker's *A Century of German Lyrics*, the Warner Library, and H. A. Siepmann's *Verse in Translation*.

ABOUT: Allen, P. S. Wilhelm Müller and the German Volkslied; Deutsch, O. E. The Schubert Reader; Lehmann, L. More than Singing; Flower, N. Franz Schubert, the Man and His Circle. [In German—see studies by H. Lohre, A. Wirth.]

H. Z.

*MÜLLNER, (AMANDUS GOTTFRIED) ADOLF (October 18, 1774-June 11, 1829), German dramatist, was born at Langendorf near Weissenfels in Saxony, son of a government official. On his mother's side he was a descendant of the famous German poet Gottfried Bürger. Müllner attended *Schulpforta* from 1789 to 1793 and studied law at the University of Leipzig from 1793 to 1797. The following year he settled in Weissenfels, where he became a prominent lawyer. In 1802 he married his childhood sweetheart Amalie von Lochau, the daughter of an officer. He received the degree of doctor of law from the University of Wittenberg in 1805. In 1817 he was honored with the title privy councilor. He died at Weissenfels.

From early youth Müllner displayed an interest in literature, and in 1810 he established an amateur theatre for which he wrote plays

* mül' nẽr

667

and in which he also participated as an actor. After producing several comedies on the French model, he completed *Der Neunund-zwanzigste Februar* (1812), a one-act fatalistic tragedy, which was consciously patterned on Zacharias Werner's *Der Vierundzwanzigste Februar*. This work was followed by *Die Schuld* (1815), the most famous of all German plays of this type. Despite its literary deficiencies this drama on the theme of fratricide is theatrically effective and enjoyed widespread success on the stages of Germany and Austria. The plot is excellently conceived and executed, and Müllner was especially skillful in evoking and sustaining a suspenseful and oppressive atmosphere of impending doom. The influence of Spanish drama is evident in the verse which consists of rhymed trochees of four feet. Müllner never again equaled the achievement of *Die Schuld*, and his classical tragedies, *König Yngurd* (1817) and *Die Albaneserin* (1820), which reveal the influence of Shakespeare, have little significance.

In addition to his activities as a dramatist Müllner edited and wrote literary reviews for both the Cotta newspaper *Literaturblatt* (1820-25) and the *Mitternachtblatt für Gebildete Stände*. His own journal, *Die Hekate*, founded in 1823, failed the same year. He was a querulous man by nature and was feared in his day as a sharp and acrimonious critic. He also wrote the prose story *Der Kaliber* (1829) on the theme of fratricide resulting from the love of two brothers for the same woman.

R. P. Gillies translated *Die Schuld* in blank verse under the title *Guilt* (1819), *The Twenty-ninth of February* in blank verse (1820), and *King Ingurd* (1840).

ABOUT: [In German—see studies by G. Koch, J. Minor, F. Muncke, H. Paulmann, and F. K. J. Schutz.]

D. G. D.

*"MULTATULI" (pseudonym of EDUARD DOUWES DEKKER)** (March 2, 1820-February 19, 1887), Dutch novelist, essayist, and satirist, was born in Amsterdam. His father, a ship's captain, intended his son for trade, but this humdrum prospect disgusted him. In 1838 he went out to Java and obtained a post in the Inland Revenue. He rose from one position to another, until in 1851 he became assistant-resident at Amboina in the Moluccas. In 1857 he was transferred to Lebak in the Bantam residency of Java. By this time, however, all

* múl tà tü' lē

the secrets of Dutch administration were known to him, and he began to protest against the abuses of the colonial system. In consequence he was threatened with dismissal from his office for his openness of speech. Abandoning his appointment, he returned to Holland in a state of fierce indignation.

Determined to expose the scandals he had witnessed, he began with newspaper articles and pamphlets. Little notice was taken of his protestations until he published under the pseudonym of Multatuli his romance *Max Havelaar* (1860). A vain attempt was made to ignore this brilliant and irregular book, but it was read all over Europe. The exposure of the abuse of free labor in the Dutch Indies was complete, although there were apologists who accused Dekker of exaggerating. He was now fairly launched in literature, and he lost no time in publishing his *Love Letters* (1861) which, in spite of their mild title, proved to be mordant satires of the most unsparing kind. The literary merit of Multatuli's work was much contested, but he found an unexpected and most valuable ally in Vosmaer. He continued to write much and to publish his miscellaneous work in uniform volumes called *Ideas*, of which seven appeared between 1862 and 1877. Leaving Holland, he went to live in Wiesbaden, Germany, where he made several attempts to write for the stage. *De School voor Prinsen* (1875) was his own favorite among his plays, but this fine poem in blank verse is undramatic and has not held the stage. Dekker moved to Nieder-Ingelheim, on the Rhine, where he died twelve years later. He was married twice—to Everdine van Wijnbergen in 1846 and to Mimi Hamminck Schepel in 1875.

Toward the end of his career he was the center of a crowd of disciples and imitators who did his reputation no service. He is now again in danger of being too little read. To understand his fame it is necessary to remember the sensational way in which he brightened the dullness of Dutch literature. He was ardent, provocative, perhaps a little hysterical, but he made himself heard all over Europe. He severely indicted the egotism and brutality of the administrators of Dutch India in a literary form which was brilliantly original. Not satisfied with this much, he attacked everything that seemed to him falsely conventional in Dutch religion, government, society, and morals. He respected nothing and left no institution untouched. Now that it is possible to look back upon Multatuli without passion, we see in him a great man who was a powerful and glowing author, yet hardly an artist; a reckless enthusiast who was inspired by indignation and a burning sense of justice, caring little for his means if only he could produce his effect. He is seen at his best and worst in *Max Havelaar*. His *Ideas*, hard, fantastic, and sardonic, seldom offer any solid satisfaction to the foreign reader. But Multatuli deserves remembrance if only because of the unequaled effect his writing had in rousing Holland from the intellectual and moral lethargy in which it lay in his day.

Max Havelaar: or, The Coffee Auctions of the Dutch Trading Company was translated by A. Nahuys in 1868, by W. Siebenhaar (with an introduction by D. H. Lawrence) in 1927. *Walter Pieterse: A Story of Holland* was translated by H. Evans (1904).

ABOUT: Lawrence, D. H. *Introduction to* Siebenhaar's translation of Max Havelaar. [In Dutch—see studies by A. J. van Deysel, J. de Gruyter, J. Prinsen, J. Saks, E. du Perron.]

H. B.

MÜNCH - BELLINGHAUSEN, ELIGIUS FRANZ JOSEPH, Reichsfreiherr von. See "HALM, FRIEDRICH"

*MURGER, HENRY (LOUIS) (March 24, 1822-January 28, 1861), French man of letters, was born in Paris. His father, Gabriel Murger, a Savoyard tailor-*cum*-concièrge, had married a Parisian, Hortense Henriette Tribou. The poor but ambitious mother managed to see that Henry completed primary school. Through a neighbor, the academician Jouy, known as "the hermit of the Chaussée d'Antin," he obtained a secretarial position with Count Jacques Tolstoi, who claimed to have diplomatic and noble connections. His responsibilities were few, and Henry had leisure to try rhyming, and to spend time among writers and artists. Adopting the style of Barthélemy, he wrote *Apostasie*, which a printer ran off for him. His friends urged him to give up versifying.

Murger did sketches and impersonations for his friends at sessions of the Buveurs d'Eau (Water-Drinkers). This famous group was simply the gatherings of Murger's friends in the attic quarters of Lelioux on the Rue Tour d'Auvergne. The sketcher Joseph Desbrosses was mainstay of the group, which lived skimpily from day to day. It was at this time that Murger met Marie Virginie Vimal, a seamstress, who became

* mür zhā′

his Mimi. Unattractive, small and untidy, balding, with a colorless beard and rheumy eyes, Murger had little success or prowess with women.

To obtain a minimum subsistence Murger worked for various fashion magazines and children's periodicals. He edited a trade publication, *Castor*, for the hat industry, and did other hack jobs. Towards 1847 he started to achieve some success, for he was published by Arsène Houssaye in *L'Artiste*, and in *Le Corsaire*. The sketches of *Scènes de la Vie de Bohème*, published in book form (1849), were very successful with the public. In 1851 a dramatic version, in collaboration with Théodore Barrière, boosted his reputation. He had no difficulty in publishing works in a similar vein, such as *Buveurs d'Eau* and *Le Pays Latin*. The newspapers took his copy and paid; the Théâtre-Français accepted *Bonhomme Jadis* (1852). By 1855 Murger was able to purchase a home at Marlotte, near Fontainebleau. But the years of deprivation and excessive work took their toll: he died suddenly in a Paris clinic. The government paid for his funeral as a public event; a public subscription provided the marble by Aimé Millet for his tomb in Montmartre cemetery.

Upon his death, his poetry, *Les Nuits d'Hiver*, was published with studies by Janin, Gautier, Houssaye, and others. But it is as a chronicler of the *bohème*—somewhat sweetened and sentimentalized—that his reputation and aura have been fixed. The misery and reality of a precarious existence have been mitigated by humor and optimism. Puccini's opera *La Bohème* (1896) has had an enormous influence in popularizing Murger's character. Of Murger's many works, *Scènes de la Vie de Bohème* is undoubtedly the most popular and the best.

It was translated in 1883 as *The Bohemians of the Latin Quarter* (and reprinted several times); G. B. Ives entitled his translation (1899) *Bohemian Life;* E. W. Hugus called hers *The Latin Quarter* (with an introduction by D. B. Wyndham Lewis, 1930); N. Cameron, with an introduction by Michael Sadleir, retained Gallic flavor with *Vie de Bohème* (1949). *Francine's Muff* (1923) and *Love in the Latin Quarter* (1948) are partial translations of Murger's major work.

ABOUT: Hearn, L. Essays in European and Oriental Literature; The Listener, LXIV (1960). [In French—Delvau, A. Henri Murger et la Bohème; Martino, P. Le Roman Réaliste sous le Second Empire; Montorgueil, G. Henri Murger, Romancier de la Bohème.]

S. S. W.

669

*MURNER, THOMAS (December 24, 1475-August 1537), German satirist, was born in Strasbourg, the son of a Strasbourg lawyer. As a wandering scholar he traveled through France, Germany, Poland, and Italy, visiting most of the famous European universities. He studied theology in Paris and law in Freiburg. At the age of nineteen he was consecrated a priest and later became a guardian of the Franciscan convent in Freiburg. In 1506 he was crowned *poeta laureatus* by the emperor Maximilian I. He visited England on the invitation of Henry VIII, who wanted his support in the fight against the Lutheran heresy. With his growing involvement in religious controversy, Murner's life became more and more restless. His presence sometimes became so embarrassing to the authorities of the places from which he waged his literary feud against the rising tide of the new faith that they had to expel him. He died, a lonely and embittered man, in Oberehenheim, a small town not far from Strasbourg.

Murner's familiarity with classical languages and literature proves him to be a true man of the Renaissance. But he was no less interested in the speech and the habits of ordinary people. On his many travels he acquired an amazing knowledge of folklore of which he made ample use in his satirical writings.

As a satirist Murner was first guided by his ambition to emulate the most famous and respected satirical poet before him, Sebastian Brant and especially the latter's *Narrenschiff*. In *Die Narrenbeschwörung* (1512) and *Die Schelmenzunft* (1513) he deals with a motley of human vices and weaknesses; the *Gäuchmatt* (1519) satirizes the depraved form in which medieval *minnedienst* survived in German society.

Against the great number of the highly gifted and efficient propagandists of the new faith, Murner stands out as the only representative of the Roman Catholic Church who is equal to his opponents as a theologian and surpasses them in the mastery of the German language. For some time he thought that Luther was on his side, and in his attacks on the immorality of his time he did not spare the corruption within the Catholic Church. When he realized that Luther undermined the dogmatic foundation of Western Christianity, he first argued against him purely as a theologian. The ferocity with which the followers of Luther responded to Murner's defense of the dogma (Luther himself remained aloof from the controversy) caused him to invoke satire as his most effective weapon. In 1533 appeared his best-known work, *Von dem Grossen Lutherischen Narren*, generally recognized as one of the masterpieces of satirical literature. The great Lutheran fool represents a union of all the destructive forces which had gathered under the banner of Protestantism. Murner assumes the rôle of the exorciser who compels these forces to emerge from their hiding places and to be exposed to his relentless witty attacks.

Murner had to pay a heavy price for the violence of his satire. His opponents successfully credited him with all the vices he so masterfully assailed. Posterity, however, has accepted him as a true satirical poet who never betrayed his artistry to the passion with which he fought for his cause. The continuing interest in Murner's works is best explained by the words of Lessing: "He who wants to know the morals and customs of that time, who wants to study the German language in its full range, to him I suggest reading Murner's poems over and over."

While the literature on Murner is abundant in Germany, little attention has been paid to him in English-speaking countries, though no important history of the Reformation fails to mention him and his rôle in the Counter Reformation. Murner scholarship is now based on the monumental scientific edition of his works, begun in 1929 with Franz Schultz as editor.

ABOUT: [In German—see studies by T. von Liebenau, R. Newald (in Schultz-Festschrift, 1938), G. S. Schumann.]

F. R.

*MUSSET, (LOUIS CHARLES) ALFRED DE (December 11, 1810-May 2, 1857), French dramatist and poet, was born in Paris. The Mussets traced their nobility to the fifteenth century (but were not, although it has been claimed, descendants of Joan of Arc or of Ronsard's Cassandre) and were related to the Du Bellay family. Alfred's father, Victor Donatien de Musset-Pathay, had written tales, historical studies, travel literature; he wrote on and published the works of Jean Jacques Rousseau. Alfred's mother was Edmée Guyot-Desherbiers, whose father had been a scholar and poet as well as editor of eighteenth century works. The couple had another son, Paul.

Alfred was a handsome, precocious child. He enjoyed schooling, and was an excellent student of the classics. While at the Lycée

* moor' ner

* mü se'

670

MUSSET

Henri IV he became an intimate of the Duke of Chartres, son of Louis Philippe, and of Paul Foucher, brother-in-law of Victor Hugo. Upon graduation Musset briefly enrolled in turn at various schools—law, medicine, music, and even art; none held his attention. At fourteen he had started versifying; his first publication was a ballad, "Un Rêve," published in the Dijon newspaper *Le Provincial* (1828). Victor Hugo influenced the form and rhythm; Charles Nodier, whose group of L'Arsenal Musset frequented, encouraged macabre subjects. Musset did a partial translation of De Quincey's *Confessions of an English Opium-Eater* (1828). The end of the year saw the young poet's first collection, *Contes d'Espagne et d'Italie*, a heterogeneous assemblage of fifteen pieces treating varied subjects. During 1831 *Le Temps* published his "Revue Fantastique," in which Musset treated a variety of subjects in nondoctrinaire fashion.

At the invitation of the Odéon Theatre's director, Musset wrote a one-act play, *La Nuit Vénitienne*. But so roundly did the public condemn this piece, which was not in the new romantic vein, that Musset decided against allowing his dramatic works to be performed. He was to relent in 1847. *Un Spectacle dans un Fauteuil* (1832) contained two works written that same year, *La Coupe et les Lèvres* and *À Quoi Rêvent les Jeunes Filles*, but except for the praise of Mérimée and Sainte-Beuve, reception was negative. Philippe van Tieghen has observed that the

former of these plays, a dramatic poem in the vein of Goethe and Byron, was an innovation in France which was not destined to take root. The second, in the tradition of Shakespeare and eighteenth century French comedy, was unpalatable to romantic tastes. Nevertheless, François Buloz, director of the *Revue des Deux Mondes*, contracted to publish Musset, and it was in his periodical that Musset was able to appear in print. *André del Sarto, Les Caprices de Marianne, Rolla* all were published by the *Revue* in 1833. The first treated multiple themes including fatal passion and the destiny of the artist; the second presented the dual aspects of its author in the persons of Octave and Coelio; the last, which offered the essential purity of heart in a debauchée, won immediate popular acclaim.

Musset, with curly blond hair and dreamy eyes, tall and slender and exquisitely dressed, bold and flippant in expression, had a reputation for dissipation and numerous casual affairs. His boon companion, Alfred Tattet, to whom he had dedicated *Un Spectacle dans un Fauteuil*, was a notorious rake. In the summer of 1833 Musset, twenty-three, met George Sand, twenty-nine years old and worldly. By the end of July their liaison had begun, and in December the lovers went to Venice. George Sand was taken ill, as was Musset. The doctor Pagello, called to attend Musset, became George Sand's lover. Musset, when able again to travel (April 1834), returned to France and to dissipation as an opiate. But, still in love, he corresponded with George Sand. She returned to Paris in August, with Pagello. Musset went to Baden, she to her estate at Nohant. Resumption, interruption, renewal, parting—the tempestuous affair continued until March 1835.

Musset had been inspired to write during this stormy period: *Fantasio* (1833) was light and suggestive; *On ne Badine pas avec l'Amour* (1834), ostensibly a *proverbe* or prose-comedy for salon presentation, dramatized the sentimental relationship between Musset and George Sand. But it was *Lorenzaccio* (1834), whose subject and outline had been established by George Sand, which permitted the greatest expression, psychologically and dramatically, of Musset's talents.

Musset thought to immortalize his affair with George Sand, while exonerating her, in *Confession d'un Enfant du Siècle* (1835, 1836; revised, 1840). Octave (Musset), disabused in love but still hopeful, falls in love with Brigitte Pierson (George Sand). Sullied by his past and the moral climate of the day, he cannot escape the effects of his previous experiences; this is the new *mal du siècle.* Certainly George Sand contributed markedly to the inspiration of "Nuit de Mai" (1835); but others, too, inspired poems of the *Nuits*: in part, Mme Jaubert for "Nuit de Décembre" and the "Lettre à Lamartine" (1835), Aimée d'Alton or Mme Groseillier for "Nuit d'Octobre" (1837). In "Nuit d'Août" (1836) the poet makes love triumphant, whether or not the vessel in which it is to be found is imperfect. Certain poems were also inspired by women whose favors he never knew, among them the singer Malibran and Princess Belgiojoso.

In 1838 Musset was appointed librarian to the Minister of the Interior, who hoped that he would write some timely play. He continued to write *contes* and verses for the *Revue des Deux Mondes.* In 1842, in *riposte* to a poem by a German, Nicholas Becker, Musset hastily wrote the patriotic "Le Rhin Allemand"; this poem became famous everywhere, and more than fifty musicians wrote scores for it. But Musset's natural laziness was becoming more extreme and he wrote less. In ill health, with periods of hallucination and pneumonia, he suffered from an aortic malfunctioning which made his head bob with his pulse; this is known medically as the Musset symptom. He relied on his facility and wrote plays in the vein of *Les Caprices de Marianne* or the *proverbe*: *Il ne Faut Jurer de Rien* (1836), *Il Faut qu'une Porte Soit Ouverte ou Fermée* (1845). Both these plays were performed in 1848, the year after his friend François Buloz became administrator of the Comédie-Française. In 1847 *Un Caprice*, published in Buloz's periodical ten years earlier, had a successful run with Mme Allan in the lead at the Comédie-Française; and directors were eager to repair their oversight. But it was necessary to await the post-World War I period for popular appreciation of Musset's theatre. In contrast, his *contes* and *nouvelles* such as *Histoire d'un Merle Blanc* (1842) and *Mimi Pinson* (1846), were easily enjoyed and always popular.

In 1848 Musset had lost his position as librarian; he was reappointed in 1854, two years after his election to the French Academy. His eminence won him the brief attention of Louise Colet, who fictionized their relationship in *Lui.* Worn out and ill with heart trouble, Musset died at Paris and was buried in Père Lachaise cemetery.

Musset has remained the symbol of the romantic young man whose heart yearns for love but is ever the victim. He personifies the defenselessness of the apparently sophisticated dandy. His verse, despite some technical negligences, has the poignancy of the heartfelt and intimate. His theatre, graceful and clever and surprising, continues the tradition of *marivaudage.* Musset was an independent, fusing classical taste with an eighteenth century mentality and a nineteenth century spleen.

The best edition of Musset is that edited by Maurice Allem for Éditions de la Pléiade (3 vols. 1933-38), but it must be supplemented by Léon Séché's editions of the correspondence (1907 and 1910). There are critical editions of *Les Caprices de Marianne* by G. Michaut, of *Lorenzaccio* by P. Dimoff (1936), of the *Comédies et Proverbes* by P. and F. Gastinel (2 vols., 1934-52). J. Richer has edited *Textes Dramatiques Inédits* (1953). M. A. Clarke and others translated *The Complete Writings of Alfred de Musset* (10 volumes) in 1905. Some of the same translators participated in a 1907 edition which included Andrew Lang and George Santayana among the translators. S. L. Gwynn translated *Comedies* in 1890; in 1892 there appeared *Barberine and Other Comedies. A Caprice* was translated by A. G. Wirt in 1922, and *Fantasio*, by M. Baring, in 1929. The English version (1955) of *A Comedy and Two Proverbs*, i.e., *Caprice, A Door Should be Either Open or Shut*, and *It's Impossible to Think of Everything*, was by George Graveley (pseudonym). D. F. Sarmiento, future president of Argentina, had done a Spanish version of *Il Faut qu'une Porte Soit Ouverte ou Fermée* which was published in 1946. In 1916 André Tridon made a literal English translation. The one-act play in prose *L'Habit Vert*, on which Musset and Émile Augier had collaborated in 1847, was translated by B. H. Clark in 1914. Jacques Barzun translated "Fantasio" in E. Bentley's *The Modern Theatre II* (1955). E. de V. Vermont translated *Three Novelettes* in 1888, twenty years after the publication of *All Is Fair in Love and War. The Confession of a Child of the Century* was translated by Kendall Warren in 1892 and by T. F. Rogerson in 1899. Selections from his poetry are found in *Love Songs of France* (1896). Puccini's opera *Edgar* is based on *La Coupe et les Lèvres*, and Ezio Carabella's *Il Candeliere* on *Le Chandelier.*

ABOUT: Brandes, G. M. Main Currents in Nineteenth Century Literature, V; Carrère, J. Degeneration in the Great French Masters; Croce, B. European Literature in the Nineteenth Century; Musset, P. de, Famous French Authors; Sedgwick, H. D. Alfred de Musset; Smith, H. A. Main Currents of Modern French Drama; Swinburne, A. C. Miscellanies; Tilley, A. A. Three French Dramatists; Vincens, C. The Life of Alfred de Musset; Winwar, F. The Life of the Heart. [In French—Allem, M. Alfred de Musset; Gastinel, P. Le Romantisme d'Alfred de Musset; Lafoscade, L. Le Théâtre d'Alfred de Musset; Musset, P. de, Biographie d'Alfred de Musset; Pommier, J. Variétés sur Alfred de Musset et Son Théâtre; Séché, L. Alfred de Musset; Van Tieghem, P. Musset, l'Homme et l'Œuvre.]

S. S. W.

NANSEN, PETER (January 20, 1861-July 31, 1918), Danish novelist and playwright, was born into a Christian-Jewish family in Copenhagen, where his father, Ferdinand Peter Nicolai Nansen, was junior curate, later vicar, at the Garrison Church. His mother was Johanne Henriette Buchheister. He was educated at the Herlufsholm school in Zealand. At the University of Copenhagen he studied political science, but soon applied himself entirely to literature and journalism.

Nansen began his journalistic career at the *Berlingske Tidende.* In 1883 he joined the staff of *Nationaltidende,* but was shortly thereafter employed by the newly started *Politiken,* to which paper he successfully contributed for eleven years. He made himself known as the author, under several pseudonyms, of bold, exquisite small articles in the style of the French *Figaro.* In 1896 he accepted a position with the publishing company Gyldendalske Forlag, and when this firm in 1903 was merged with Nordisk Forlag he became co-director of the new enterprise. In 1887, Nansen married the actress Louise Brock, but they were divorced. In 1896 he married another actress, Betty Müller.

Nansen's first attempt as a novelist was *Unge Mennesker* (Young People, 1883). Most of his novels, which made him popular also in Germany, were written in 1891-95. *Et Hjem* (A Home, 1891), and *Fra Rusaaret* (From the Freshman Year, 1892) are problem novels dealing with free love and free thought. Characteristic of the weary, cynical, and flippant attitude and the dispassionate sentimentalism of the time are *Julies Dagbog* (Julie's Diary, 1893), *Maria* (1894), and *Guds Fred* (God's Peace, 1895). His misanthropy is evident in the story *Brødrene Menthe* (The Brothers Menthe, 1915), which he wrote after a silence of almost two decades. He also wrote several well-made plays, e.g., *Judiths Ægteskab* (Judith's Marriage, 1898), which has only two characters.

Julie le Gallienne translated *Maria* as *Marie; A Book of Love* (1906); also *Love's Trilogy* (1906), including *Julie's Diary, Marie,* and *God's Peace.* An anonymous translation, *Julie's Diary,* appeared in 1908.

ABOUT: [In Danish—See study by C. Rimestad in Dansk Biografisk Leksikon, vol. 16.]

A. J.

---

*NEITHART (or NEIDHART) VON REUENTAL (c. 1190-c. 1250), German lyric poet, is known to us only through state-

* nīt' härt fōn roi' ĕn täl

ments in his own works and from mention in the *Willehalm* of Wolfram von Eschenbach (c. 1210), as still living, and in the *Meier Helmbrecht* of Wernher der Gartenaere, as already dead (after 1246). Even his name may well be fictitious, since "Neithart" means "Envy well" and "Reuental" ("The Vale of Tears") is another name for Hell. He was a Bavarian by birth and probably spent his youth at the court of Ludwig of Bavaria. He fought in a Crusade, either that of 1197 or that of 1227. About 1230 he had to leave Bavaria, and he received from Frederick of Austria a house at Melk. Nothing is known of him after 1237. Much of the apparently autobiographical detail in his poems about his contests with peasants for the love of a village beauty is probably fantasy. Neithart's poems (about 370 strophes survive) are all lyrics and are for the most part summer songs or winter songs, types introduced by Neithart to written poetry, with a few dawn songs *(Tagelieder)* and crusading songs. Neithart moves far away from the idealized love of the *Minnesang,* for he uses its expressions and to a large extent its language and form for the purposes of satire. His summer songs, in dance form, usually begin with formal natural description followed by a crude dance or a parody of a courtly love scene. The winter songs preserve the tripartite form of the courtly love poem but describe peasant wooings and love rivalries, dances and fights. Neithart makes a mockery of the *Minnesang* by showing peasants dressed above their station aping the conventionalities of courtly love. He often appears himself as lover and rival but is seldom victorious. There is no doubt that the poems were written for the amusement of a certain section of the courtly audience which despised peasants, particularly if they tried to imitate their betters, but the effect on the finer types of courtly poetry was catastrophic, since standards of taste fell rapidly. Walther von der Vogelweide lamented the intrusion of such crudities, although he did not name Neithart. For several centuries Neithart's name was attached to any type of crude rustic play *(Neithartspiele),* even though they had no connection with him.

English translations and summaries of his work, as well as a useful introduction, will be found in A. T. Hatto and R. J. Taylor, *The Songs of Neidhart von Reuental* (1958).

ABOUT: Bithell, J. The Minnesanger; Nicholson, F. C. Old German Love Songs; Richey, M. Medieval German Lyrics. [In German—see study by K. Winkler.]

W. T. H. J.

*NEKRASOV, NIKOLAY ALEXEYE-
VICH (December 10, 1821-January 8,
1878), Russian poet, was born in the town of
Nemerov in the Ukraine, but spent his childhood in Greshnevo, his father's estate in the
Yaroslavl district on the Volga. His father,
a squire and a retired army officer, was a
brutal debauché for whom life meant hunting,
playing cards, and drinking with his serf
mistresses. Nekrasov's mother, a dreamy and
meek Ukrainian gentlewoman, Elena Zakrev-
skaya, whom he loved dearly and was to
remember often in his poems, was mistreated
and insulted by her husband. She acquainted
her son with poetry, which he started writing
at the age of seven.

The quality of teaching at the Yaroslavl
secondary school was anything but good, and
Nekrasov made little progress there. In 1838
his father sent him to St. Petersburg to a
military academy, but he decided to enter the
university instead; because of this defection
his father disowned him. For years Nekrasov
lived in extreme poverty, doing all kinds of
literary hack work. His first book of verse,
Dreams and Sounds (1840), was severely
criticized for its romantic clichés by Belinsky,
the leading critic of the day. Nekrasov
bought back the entire edition and destroyed
it. In 1843 Belinsky became his friend and
mentor and persuaded the poet to draw material directly from life and to put his poetry
in the service of the social cause. At this time
Nekrasov tried publishing and was successful.
Later he became a publisher and editor of
genius (he discovered Goncharov, Dostoevsky, Leo Tolstoy). His *The Petersburg Miscellany* (1846) heralded the realistic movement in Russian prose and also contained his
own first mature poetry. In 1846 he bought
the review *The Contemporary*, founded by
Pushkin, and soon made it the leading magazine of the period. The best writers contributed to it, but many of them broke with
the review in 1856, at which time it became
the rallying ground of the literary leftists.
That same year a collection of Nekrasov's
verse met with enormous success. He became
the most popular Russian poet for such works
as *Vlas, Sasha* (an anticipation of Turgenev's
novels), and *The Poet and the Citizen* with
its famous line "You do not have to be a
poet, but you must be a citizen." These were
followed by the philanthropic *Reflections
Before a Mansion Doorway* and *About
Weather* in which poetry and journalism are
blended. The radical intelligentsia knew

* nyě krä′ sôf

NEKRASOV

Nekrasov's poems by heart and used them as
slogans in their revolutionary activities.

During these productive years of hard
work under the most severe censorship in the
history of Russia, Nekrasov's constant companion and literary collaborator was Avdotya
Panaeva, the wife of the co-owner of the
review and for sixteen years Nekrasov's
mistress. There was nothing refined in
Nekrasov's appearance: his face, with long
mustaches and penetrating eyes, was that of
a strong-willed, practical man. His complex
personality produced a variety of opinions
about him. A shrewd and unscrupulous
money-maker, Nekrasov exploited his fellow
writers, was a gambler, wasted money on
women and drink, lived in luxury, and was a
social snob. But, at the same time, this man
of "wounded . . . heart" (Dostoevsky) was a
sensitive and guilt-ridden hypochondriac repenting in his poems for a discrepancy
between his democratic ideals and his way of
life.

Ironically, it was only after the liberation
of serfs that *The Contemporary* was finally
suppressed by the government (1886), but
Nekrasov soon bought another review, *The
Fatherland Notes*, and edited it until his
death. In the sixties, he wrote the satire *The
Railroad* (1864), the popular *The Pedlars*
(1861), the lyrical *A Knight for an Hour*
(1862), and the realistic fantasy of peasant
life *Frost the Red-nosed* (1863), followed in
the seventies by *Russian Women* (1871-72),
a poem about the Decembrists' wives, and

finally the huge epic *Who Enjoys Living in Russia* (1863-77), a satirical cross section of contemporary Russian society. The last two years of his life Nekrasov suffered greatly from cancer. Before he died in St. Petersburg his tragic *Last Songs* (1877) appeared. His funeral drew an enormous crowd.

In spite of the fact that even now Nekrasov's poetry is extolled or rejected on the grounds of its humanitarian or revolutionary message, "for originality and for energy [he] holds one of the very first places among Russian poets" (Mirsky). Though Nekrasov himself was apt to underestimate the artistic value of his "joyless, uncouth verse" and tended to identify his "Muse of vengeance and sorrow" with the precepts of the "civic poetry" of the day, "the suffering of the people," which he sang all his life, was to a great extent the symbol of his own tortured soul rather than an expression of group feelings. It is for this reason that his uneven poetry so often touches the ultimate heights of immediacy and white-hot intensity. Nekrasov's originality lies not only in his masterly, broad, and compassionate treatment of the Russian peasant theme (which may even take the form of an idyll, as in his poems for and about children), but in the combination of conversational style and song, and the daring use of "prosaic" diction (which made Turgenev remark that "poetry never as much as spent a night in [Nekrasov's] verse"). The variety of his work is also great. We find in it not only a sobbing melody, tortuous reflections, and sad autumnal landscapes, but pictures of rural and urban poverty, the portrayal of pain in human love relations, and a racy, vigorous humor. The very dactylic cadence of his verse is that of the folk song and of Russian peasant oral tradition and not of conventional poetry. Nekrasov's work also possessed true epic qualities, rare for his time.

After decades of purely partisan appreciation, the first to discover Nekrasov's highly poetic gift were the Russian symbolists. Some of them (Blok, Bely) went through periods of his influence. Other examples of his influence are to be found in some minor Soviet contemporaries. A new edition of his work was begun in the U.S.S.R. in 1948.

Nekrasov was first translated into English in 1863 (*Cornhill Magazine*). Translations of his poems are to be found in any anthology of Russian poetry. The most important separate editions of his works in English are *Poems by Nicholas Nekrassov* (1929, World's Classics series), and *Who Can Be Happy and Free in Russia* (1917) both in translation by Juliet Soskice. More recently *Nekrassov's Poems* appeared in a translation by D. Prall.

ABOUT: Abercrombie, L. *Introduction to* Poems of Nekrassov (World's Classics edition); Anglo-Russian Literary Society, No. 16 (1897), No. 30 (1902); Fortnightly Review XXIX (1881); Jarintzov, N. Russian Poets and Poems, I; Mirsky, D. S. A History of Russian Literature; Newmarch, R. Poetry and Progress in Russia.

V. M.

*NĚMCOVÁ, BOŽENA (née Barbora Panklová) (February 4, 1820-January 21, 1862), Czech novelist, was born in Vienna, Austria. Her father, Jan Pankel, German by nationality, was a coachman in the services of Count Schulenberg; her mother, Terezie, *née* Novotný, was Czech. When Barbora was still an infant, her parents moved from Vienna to Bohemia, settling near Ratibořice in the district of Česká Skalice; it was in this district city that Barbora received her rather modest education. At seventeen she married, at the insistence of her mother and without true affection, a minor official of the revenue service, Josef Němec, fifteen years her senior, an upright but somewhat rigid man who apparently had little understanding for his wife's emotional life. With her husband, Němcová moved from one Bohemian town to another, giving birth to four children in five years of marriage. Between 1842 and 1845 Němcová lived in Prague where she made the acquaintance of some of the leading figures of the Czech cultural world and where she began her literary career in poetry. Later, she followed her husband to the city of Domažlice in the colorful region of Southern Bohemia. Her stay there inspired several of her short stories. In these years Němcová also wrote a number of fairy tales based on national folklore. Partly because of her patriotic activity her husband soon experienced difficulties with the authorities and was eventually transferred to the Hungarian part of the Austro-Hungarian Empire. Němcová, already alienated from her husband emotionally, decided to stay in Bohemia with her children and settled in Prague. Her financial situation was extremely difficult and became critical when her husband's salary was stopped in 1854.

It was during these times of hardship and after the death of her favorite son, Hynek, that Němcová turned to the happy memories of her childhood for literary inspiration and wrote her masterpiece, *Babička (The Grandmother, 1855)*. In an idealized autobiographical setting she presented a series of remarkably well-drawn characters as well as the atmosphere and custom of Bohemian country

* něm′ tsŏ väh

life. Around a slight plot Němcová was able to construct a book which gives a deep impression of a simple and meaningful life. *The Grandmother* is, without doubt, one of the most widely read and best-loved works of Czech literature.

Němcová then proceeded to write a number of short stories, many of them based on themes from the Bohemian countryside, e.g., *The Mountain Village* (1856), *Poor Folk* (1856), and *The Teacher* (1860). In the early 1860's, Němcová was preparing an edition of her collected works which she hoped would bring her some money. Exhausted by hard work and constant want, her health seriously undermined, she died in Prague a few weeks before her forty-second birthday.

Němcová, as described by her contemporaries, was a beautiful, sensitive, and emotionally intense woman, who played an important rôle in the Czech national revival.

The Grandmother was translated into English by Frances Gregor (1891). Translations of Němcová's fairy tales also exist as *The Shepherd and the Dragon*, by E. E. Ledbetter (1930).

ABOUT: [In Czech—see studies by M. Otruba, F. X. Šalda, V. Tille.]

H. K.

NERUDA, JAN (July 10, 1834-August 22, 1891), Czech poet, story writer, journalist, and critic, was born in the Malá strana (Small Side) of Prague, son of a retired soldier and grocer. The Malá strana, with its steep, narrow, crooked streets, old houses, and staid bourgeois citizens, is depicted in his later tales. His early education was German, but in 1850 he entered the Czech Academic *Gymnasium* in Prague, and underwent its nationalist influence. He then studied languages and history at Charles University.

After abortive starts in the civil service and teaching, Neruda resolved for journalism, and soon rose to writing *feuilletons* and literary criticism. At the end of the 1850's he edited several unsuccessful magazines. His first published collection of verses (1857), a gloomy cycle of elegies, passed unnoticed. Discouraged by failure, he broke with his first love, Anna Holinová. Passionate but shy, his love life was hardly happy, and he never married. His unhappiness is a frequent theme of his poetry. In 1858 he began an affair with the Czech writer Karolina Světlá. Conscious of her duty toward her husband, she ended the liaison in 1862. His later loves, including a Platonic relation with

* ně' rŏŏ dà

the invalid Terezie Macháčková, were unsatisfying. The conservative reading public was shocked by Neruda's love affairs, and he was widely criticized.

In 1861 Neruda joined the editorial staff of the newly founded Czech daily *Národní Listy* (National News). Here he had greater success, and remained till his death. He published *feuilletons*, sketches, accounts of his extensive travels over Europe, and dramatic and literary criticism. Heine and the writers of Young Germany were his models, as well as the Czech writers Havlíček, Mácha, and Erben. His sketches gradually evolved into stories such as those of his greatest collection, the *Malostranské Povídky* (Tales of the Malá Strana, 1878), a group of satiric pictures of self-satisfied middle-class citizens, eccentrics, tramps, and spineless patriots. The satire is tempered by the warmth of his memory of his boyhood home and nostalgia for an older way of life.

At the same time Neruda continued to write poetry. He published some six collections of verse, each strikingly different. Unusual are his *Písně Kosmické* (Cosmic Songs, 1878) in which he uses astronomical science as a source of poetic and didactic symbols. His best collection is the *Prosté Motivy* (Simple Themes, 1883), classic nature poems which reflect mature resignation to the unhappiness of life and love. His poetry also contains patriotic verse, ballads which are almost folk-like, and romances.

In his lifetime Neruda was best known as a journalist and critic. Today his prose tales and poetry are more highly valued, and he is considered one of the greatest Czech writers.

Little of Neruda's work is translated into English. Several tales are found, with a biographical sketch, in S. B. Hrbková's *Czechoslovak Stories* (1920), and in the *Slavonic Review*, III (1924-25) and X (1931-32). E. Pargeter translated *Tales of the Little Quarter* in 1957. A few poems are translated in R. A. Ginsburg, *Soul of a Century* (1942).

ABOUT: Columbia Dictionary of Modern European Literature; Harkins, W. E. Anthology of Czech Literature. [In Czech—Novák, A. Jan Neruda.]

W. E. H.

***NERVAL, GÉRARD DE** (May 22, 1808-January 25, 1855), French poet, a man of letters, was born Gérard Labrunie, in Paris, of Catholic parentage. His mother, Marie Antoinette Marguerite Laurent, was the

* něr' vàl'

"GÉRARD DE NERVAL"

daughter of a linen merchant; his father, Étienne Labrunie, was a recently qualified physician. Gérard never knew his mother. In December 1808 she accompanied her husband to the Rhine where he served as an army surgeon; two years later she died in Silesia. Gérard grew up with his grand-uncle, Antoine Boucher, in Mortefontaine in the Valois country that was to figure so importantly in *Sylvie* and other works. After his father left the army and brought him to Paris in 1814 or 1815, he continued to spend his vacations at Mortefontaine. Among the most haunting memories of this period were his glimpses of the stunning mistress of the Duke of Burgundy, Sophie Dawes, whom the Duke had brought back with him from England during the Bourbon restoration. Years later, she was romanticized as Adrienne, assuming an importance strangely disproportionate to her minor rôle in his life.

Gérard's formal schooling began with lessons from his father, who taught him many languages, including German. His poetic bent became apparent at the Collège (or Lycée) Charlemagne. He was still in his teens when he wrote his first imitative, patriotic verses, as well as the amazing translation of Goethe's *Faust*, Part I, that caused the venerable poet himself to write, "I have never understood myself so well as in reading you." Soon after he had left the *lycée*, Gérard began to move in literary circles. In 1828 he was introduced to Hugo. In the en-

suing years he established a small reputation with his poems, plays, and translations or imitations of the German romantics, and became part of the romantic *cénacle* which formed about Victor Hugo, and which is sometimes known as Les Jeunes-France. It was this group that attended, in 1830, the famous battle of *Hernani*, which ended with the classicists' wigs on the floor; held bacchanalian parties where guests, outlandishly dressed (Gérard affected Werther), ate ice creams out of skulls and danced themselves unconscious; and landed themselves, on occasion, in the Sainte-Pélagie prison on some innocuous charge.

After Gérard came into an inheritance, in 1834, and moved into the Rue du Doyonné with some friends, the group indulged in its Bohemian life on a more lavish scale. Gérard, however, did not share the emotional or literary excesses of his contemporaries. An avowed romantic, he nevertheless showed classic control and a singular delicacy in his poetry. More given to daydream than his friends, he was like the poets he later described, who could not love a real woman, but only an inapproachable queen or goddess, a "metaphysical phantom." It is precisely this passion for idealizing that doomed his long, heart-rending and futile involvement with a woman who could neither understand nor return his feeling.

The object of this attachment was a mediocre actress, Jennie Colon, who appears in his work as Aurélia, rounding out, with Gérard's mother and the Baronne de Feuchères (*née* Sophie Dawes), the trinity that forms his central conception of womanhood. For Jennie, Gérard squandered his fortune on a theatrical journal he had conceived to enhance her reputation, wasted his talent writing plays for her, and put himself in debt for the rest of his life. How culpable she was in leading him on is debatable. That she encouraged him for a while seems certain. However, it is natural that his abstract and exaggerated protestations of a love which his friends described as "chivalrous" should have been incomprehensible to this courtesan unwillingly turned Beatrice. By 1838 she had tired of him and married a flutist.

The effect on Gérard was not immediately apparent. Dependent now on writing for his livelihood, he was helped out by Théophile Gautier and other friends with connections on periodicals, and worked on the *Presse* in 1840. He continued a collaboration with Dumas, and wrote his only successful play, *Léo Burckart* (1839), a year before his trans-

677

lation of *Faust II* appeared. He traveled, in 1839 and 1840 to Germany and Belgium, sending lively accounts back to Paris. By now, however, his readings in occult science and the influence of Goethe and Hoffmann had begun to have startling effects. Brooding constantly over Jennie, Gérard transformed her, as Faust with Helen, into the incarnation of a feminine ideal. In February 1841 he suffered his first mental breakdown.

He spent eight months in an asylum, visited and protected by his friends, and nagged by his father, who could not forgive him for having forsaken a career in medicine. On his release in November he began to write for *La Sylphide*, eager to make a fresh start. In order to wipe out the memory of Jennie Colon, who died in June 1842, Gérard left the following December for a year's travel in the East. Published at first serially prior to their final form in 1851 as *Voyage en Orient*, his notebooks yielded a diverting account of harems and slave markets, his Oriental fiancée, his visit to the Pyramids and to the statue of the veiled Isis (who revealed herself to him in the likeness of his dead love), as well as of the mystic cults that had come to absorb him.

From 1844 to 1851 Gérard was able to make literary capital out of the trips he took continually to Germany, Holland, Belgium, England, the provinces, and the outskirts of Paris—trips that earned for him the name of "anodos" (Saintsbury calls him "the most unquestionably entitled to that title of all men in letters"). He spent a great deal of time preparing a series of monographs on Cazotte, Restif de la Bretonne, and other "philosophical eccentrics" with whom he felt a close affinity. During the late 1840's and early 1850's he worked with Heine on translations of the latter's poetry. He also kept writing unsuccessful plays in a futile attempt to escape the hand-to-mouth existence enjoined by his enslavement to journalism.

His growing eccentricity evidenced itself in his irregular life on the "fringes" of society, his frequent moves, his night wanderings in the Paris streets, and in the way he splurged his money when he had it—graciously, on the poor; or whimsically, on mementoes; or, in the manner of a true bibliophile, on a rare book for which he outbid the Bibliothèque Nationale, only to donate it later to that library. It showed up also in his mannerisms and his gifts to friends. One received from him daily, for a while, a branch of yew or cypress, or a wreath. To another he brought a great Dane, then a black span-

iel ("Take good care of him," he said, "in memory of Goethe"). And once he was seen in the Palais-Royale gardens parading a lobster on a blue ribbon, because, he explained, it did not bark and knew the secrets of the deep. (This well-known incident is ascribed to different parts of his life; Symons places it before his first breakdown, S. A. Rhodes at this point, Geoffrey Wagner even later.) In summer 1851, while working on a study of Quintus Aucler, another mystic who would be included in *Les Illuminés* (1852), he had his second breakdown. It was the first of the crises that would recur with increasing frequency and intensity.

Now began what Gérard calls in *Aurélia* the "overflowing of dream into real life." Till his death he worked in alternate periods of lucidity and delirium. Consecrating his sane moments to work, he hurriedly compiled and published his earlier reminiscences, travel sketches, and studies. It is at this point, too, that he wrote his best work. *Sylvie, Souvenirs du Valois* appeared in the *Revue des Deux Mondes* in August 1853, evoking with unusual sensitivity the pathos of his adolescent love. It was followed four months later by "El Desdichado," his best-known poem. The next year he put together *Petits Châteaux de Bohème* and *Les Filles du Feu,* which contained *Sylvie* and other tales, and the last of the *Chimères.* In 1854 he began *Aurélia,* the "document of his madness."

During these years he spent most of his time in the asylum of Dr. Émile Blanche. Toward the end of 1854, however, more than ever fearful of his literary reputation, he begged friends and relatives and the Société des Gens de Lettres to obtain a release for him. He was dismissed in October, in the care of his aunt, but after she became ill he resumed his wanderings and irregular life. He was seen in midwinter without an overcoat. On January 23, 1855 he gave Paul Lacroix a list of his complete works. On the 25th, a friend later reported, he borrowed seven sous, the sum of a night's lodging. Late that freezing night, he knocked at the door of a cheap dosshouse in the filthy Rue de la Vieille Lanterne and received no answer (the concierge later said it had been too cold to go to the door). The next morning he was found dead. He had hanged himself with an apronstring he once claimed was the Queen of Sheba's garter. In his pockets were the last pages of *Aurélia.*

Gérard's nomadic life, his touching love affair, and his madness have made him the subject of much literary romanticizing. Yet his own character and the opinions of his contemporaries show that the familiar epithets—"good Gérard," "tender madman," "gentle dreamer"—though sentimental, are not inaccurate. Less than any of his companion romantics did he strike a pose. As an "ivory tower" poet (a phrase he coined), he tried, simply and humbly, to transcribe his experiences, not to forge new ones through rebellion, or through a cultivated sensuality. He was totally free of bitterness. Heine, who speaks of his childlike candor, said he was more spirit than man; and his friend Jules Janin called him a "waking dreamer."

It is this admixture of dream and experience that marks his most distinctive works—the semi-autobiographical prose pieces, *Sylvie* and *Aurélia*, and the handful of sonnets called *Les Chimères*. *Sylvie* shows in its best and most controlled form his ability to give dream the semblance of reality, and to cast over real events a halo of dreamlike reminiscence. In its deliberate confusion of the women he loves, it reveals also the central theme of a constant feminine ideal that takes on many images. It is an idea that finds its culmination in *Aurélia*, a work remarkable for the precision with which it describes his delirious dreams and the "hidden harmonies" he perceived in nature.

In the *Chimères*, most notably in "El Desdichado" (from which T. S. Eliot quoted in his *Wasteland*) and "Artémis," Gérard's own experience blends with associations derived from his wide reading to produce a poetry of extraordinarily rich texture and allusiveness, achieved through the simultaneous use of several mythologies. Gérard's use of dream and his treatment of the symbol as inherent in the meaning, herald the technique of the later symbolists and surrealists who, despite important differences, claimed him as their precursor. Almost alone in his generation—though with the great exception of the later Hugo—he pushed poetry towards the "suggestive magic" of Baudelaire and modern poetry.

The *Œuvres Complètes* was edited by H. Clouard and published in ten volumes, 1927-31. *Sylvie* was rendered into English in 1887 and 1896 and was included in a 1922 translation of *Daughters of Fire (Les Filles du Feu). The Women of Cairo (Les Femmes du Caire,* an earlier version of his *Voyage en Orient)* was published in 1929. Richard Aldington, in 1932, translated *Aurélia* in a London edition that included also *Sylvie* and selections from *Voyage en Orient, Les Illuminés,* and *Promenades et Souvenirs.* Another translation of *Dreams and Life (Le Rêve et la Vie,* comprising *Aurélia)* was made by Vyvyan Holland in 1932. In 1957 Geoffrey Wagner translated his *Selected Writings,* including

his poetry; and some of the *Chimères* appear in Richmond Lattimore's translation in the Anchor edition of *French Poetry from Nerval to Valéry,* ed. by Angel Flores (1958).

ABOUT: Proust, M. On Art and Literature; Quennell, P. Baudelaire and the Symbolists; Rhodes, S. A. Gérard de Nerval; Saintsbury, G. History of the French Novel; Symons, A. The Symbolist Movement in Literature; Wagner, G. Selected Writings (introduction). [In French—Cellier, L. Gérard de Nerval; Dédéyan, C. Nerval et l'Allemagne; Durry, M. J. Gérard de Nerval; Richer, J. Gérard de Nerval et les Doctrines Ésotériques; Sébillotte, L. H. Le Secret de Gérard de Nerval; Vivier, M. Gérard de Nerval.]

E. G.

*NESTROY, JOHANN NEPOMUK (December 7, 1801-May 25, 1862), Austrian dramatist and actor, was born in Vienna, the son of Johann Nestroy, a court lawyer of Czechoslovakian descent, and Magdelena Konstantin, the daughter of a middle-class commercial family. The family of five children grew up in financial hardship which worsened after the death of Nestroy's mother in 1814. His father died in 1834 in impoverished circumstances. Nestroy received the customary *Gymnasium* education and studied law for two semesters, until in 1822 he made a successful operatic debut and became a singer at the court theatre. The following year he married Maria Philippine, and the couple traveled to Amsterdam, where Nestroy spent two years as a singer. A son, Gustav, was born there in 1824. After a year at the theatre in Brunn, he performed in Graz for the period 1826-29. Here his wife deserted him, and although not divorced until 1845, Nestroy entered into a common-law marriage with Maria Weiler, a minor singer. This relationship, through which he fathered a son and a daughter, lasted until his death.

While in Graz, Nestroy turned increasingly from singing to speaking rôles and performed in the folk plays of the leading Austrian dramatists, including those of Raimund, whose imitator and arch rival he was to become. Like Raimund, Nestroy was a gifted extemporizer who made the transition from actor to playwright.

In 1831, Nestroy was engaged as an actor by the Theater an der Wien, where his more than sixty plays, written 1831-54, were introduced, and where he served as director 1854-60. His early comedies were direct imitations of Raimund and thus in the tradition of the Viennese *Posse* or folk play. He had no pretensions or serious ambitions as a dramatist

* nĕs' troi

679

NESTROY

and regarded his plays solely from the comic actor's viewpoint, that is, according to their humorous effect. He acted in most of his own plays, and his only avowed purpose was to entertain. Incidentally, of course, he earned much money for himself and for the theatre. He cared little for originality, borrowing his plots wherever he found them— one principal source being contemporary French farces which he adapted to the Viennese milieu. Because of his skepticism and sharp wit he found his natural element in satire, caricature, and travesty, and in his day was called the Viennese Aristophanes. His many successful parodies include versions of the plays of Raimund, Hebbel, and Grillparzer, and of the operas of Weber and Wagner.

After the success of *Der Böse Geist Lumpazivagabundus* (1833), one of his most popular and widely-played comedies, Nestroy departed from the fairy drama to seek his materials in real life. He thus represents the transition from the Viennese folk tradition to the strict realism of his countryman Ludwig Anzengruber. The majority of Nestroy's mature plays are set among the Viennese middle and lower classes, a world which he pitilessly caricatured. Despite his distortion of truth for humorous effect, Nestroy thoroughly understood the Viennese and offers superb insights into the psychology, morals, and political attitudes of his age. The greatest deficiency in his work is its complete lack of human warmth.

Among the most important of his later dramas are *Zu Ebener Erde und im Ersten*

Stock (1838), *Das Mädl aus der Vorstadt* (1841), *Einen Jux Will er sich Machen* (1842), and *Kampl* (1852). Because his work is so thoroughly Viennese Nestroy has never found popularity outside of Austria, and none of his works has ever been translated into English, although Thornton Wilder adapted *Einen Jux Will er sich Machen* as *The Merchant of Yonkers* (1939)—in later productions retitled *The Matchmaker*—and in 1964 a musical comedy version of Wilder's adaptation, titled *Hello, Dolly!*, opened on Broadway. In Austria, however, Nestroy remains a vital force in the standard dramatic repertoire.

ABOUT: Monatshefte, LII (1960). [In German —see studies by O. Forst de Battaglia, K. Kraus, L. Langer, O. Rommel.]

D. G. D.

NICEPHORUS GREGORAS. See GREGORAS, NICEPHORUS

*NICOLAI, CHRISTOPH FRIEDRICH (March 18, 1733-January 1, 1811), German critic, novelist, and publisher, was born in Berlin where he became the organizer and leader of the Enlightenment in northern Germany. His best works proceeded from his collaboration with Lessing and Mendelssohn: the objective discussion of contemporary literature *Briefe den Jetzigen Zustand der Schönen Wissenschaften Betreffend* (1755; newly edited by G. Ellinger, 1894), the *Abhandlung vom Trauerspiel* (1756), the correspondence with Lessing and Mendelssohn concerning tragedy (ed. by R. Petsch, 1910), the series founded in common with his two friends, *Bibliothek der Schönen Wissenschaften und der Freien Künste* (1757-65), and *Briefe, die Neueste Literatur Betreffend* (1761-67).

In 1758 Nicolai assumed the direction of his father's publishing house and counted among his first contributors such men as Herder, Hamann, Kant, Lavater. In 1765 he founded the series *Allgemeine Deutsche Bibliothek*. Later, in concert with his determined defense of the orthodox views of the Enlightenment, he stubbornly opposed the creative progress of German cultural and intellectual forces. Without poetic gifts himself, and without the ability to recognize these gifts in others, he challenged such writers as Herder, Goethe, Schiller, Kant, and Fichte in his satiric, parodistic attacks upon contemporary developments in thought and literature. He thus alienated himself from the principal

* nĭk′ ō lī

figures in the evolving intellectual world of Germany. Against Herder's and Bürger's collections of folk songs he wrote his *Feyner Kleyner Almanach* (1777-78); in opposition to Goethe's *Werther* and the widespread enthusiasm for this work he wrote *Die Freuden des Jungen Werthers* (1775). His novel *Leben und Meinungen des Magisters Sebaldus Nothanker* (1773-76) is an attack on pietism, orthodox religion, and fashionable sensibilities. Attacks upon Kantian philosophy are to be found in such works as the novels *Sempronius Gundibert* (1798) and *Lebensgeschichte eines Dicken Mannes* (1794) as well as in his *Philosophischen Abhandlungen* (1808). The work *Vertraute Briefe von Adelheid B. an ihre Freundin Julie S.* (1799) was an attack upon the newly developing romantic school. Nicolai was severely punished for his sterile opposition by the attack of those whom he intended to harm. As a result, his reputation for many years suffered a consistently negative judgment. Only in recent times have his attributes been objectively assessed.

Translations of Nicolai's writings are limited to two works: *The Life and Opinions of Sebaldus N...* (London, 1798), "An Account of the Apparition of Several Phantasms" in *The German Museum* (London, 1800).

ABOUT: [In German—see studies by K. Auer, F. C. A. Philips, M. Sommerfeld, W. Strauss.]

E. K. G.

NICOLAI, JOANNES. See SECUNDUS, JOANNES

*NIEBUHR, BARTHOLD GEORG (August 27, 1776-January 2, 1831), German statesman, scholar, and author was born in Copenhagen, but spent his youth in Meldorf in South Dithmarsch where his father was court registrar. Following his preparatory education, conducted primarily by private tutors and by his father, he studied at the University of Kiel from 1794 to 1796. After a short period as private secretary to a Danish nobleman he continued his studies in London and Edinburgh. In 1800 he entered the Danish civil service, but six years later went to Berlin at the invitation of von Stein. For several years he was active in various governmental capacities for the Prussian state. These duties were interrupted for a two year period (1810-12) when he delivered lectures on Roman history at the newly-established University of Berlin. In 1823 he resigned

* nē' bōōr

from state service to live in Bonn and there lectured on history at the university.

Although Niebuhr gained high praise as a statesman his fame rests primarily upon his writings and scholarship. His chief work is *Römische Geschichte* (1833) which grew out of the lectures delivered in Berlin. This history of the development of Rome up to the first Punic War has proved to be erroneous in several important instances, but the method employed suggested new approaches to the historical scholar. It exercised a particularly strong influence on Ranke and Mommsen. In addition to his one major historical study, Niebuhr also contributed numerous articles on historical and philological subjects to various journals. His political writings, in which he revealed himself to be an ardent defender of liberty but an opponent of artificial constitutions unconnected with historical development, are found in the posthumous *Nachgelassene Schriften Nichtphilologischen Inhalts* (1842). His Bonn lectures on Roman history, antiquity, and folklore, and on the Age of the French Revolution were also collected and published posthumously (1846-58). His *Griechische Heroengeschichten*, written for his son, were widely acclaimed (1842).

English translations of his works are: *Life of Carsten Niebuhr* (1836), *The History of Rome* (1870), *The Greek Heroes* (1903).

ABOUT: Gooch, G. P. History and Historians of the Nineteenth Century. [In German—see study by J. Classen.]

E. K. G.

*NIEMCEWICZ, JULIAN URSYN (February 16, 1757-May 21, 1841), Polish writer, was born in the village of Skoki. After training in the Polish Military Academy in Warsaw he started his career in the Polish army and later was a member of the Polish Diet which voted the Constitution of May 3, 1791. An ardent patriot, he served as General Kosciuszko's adjutant in the war against Russia, was taken prisoner, and spent almost two years in the Peter-Paul Fortress outside St. Petersburg. Together with Kosciuszko he was freed by Paul I in 1796, and followed his former general on his journey to Sweden, England, and America. After several years in the United States, where he married Susan Livingstone Kean, Niemcewicz returned to Poland during the period of temporary freedom created by the Napoleonic wars. Later, however, he again went into exile and died in Paris.

* nyěm tsě' věch

681

The unique value of Niemcewicz's literary activity lies not so much in the artistic strength of his talent as in the fact that it is a faithful Polish mirror of so many literary currents dominating the literary scene during a long period at the turn of the century. He started with translations from French classics, wrote more or less successful original poems, fables, novels, tragedies, and comedies in the spirit of the Enlightenment: *Powrót Posła* (The Return of a Deputy, 1791), *Dwaj Panowie Sieciechowie* (Two Gentlemen Sieciech, 1815), etc.; he was a precursor of romanticism, by introducing themes and forms of English balladry in his "Dumy" and "Pieśni" and in some of his novels with partly sentimental and partly romantic affiliations (for example, *Jan z Tęczyna*, 1815). Of interest to American readers are his memoirs of his visit to America (1838).

The place of Niemcewicz in the history of Polish literature must be measured by his influence in popularizing many themes and forms of Western literature both by direct translation and by sometimes quite successful original adaptation. From this point of view he could be compared to the Russian poet Zhukovsky in his rôle of a precursor though not a great talent.

Some English translations of his work appear in J. Bowring's *Specimens of the Polish Poets* (1827). The first complete publication in English of his American travel diaries was issued in 1965: *Under Their Vine and Fig Tree: Travels Through America in 1797-1799, 1805, With Some Further Account of Life in New Jersey* (edited and translated by M. J. E. Budka).

ABOUT: Heiman, M. Poland and the American Revolutionary War; Kridl, M. Survey of Polish Literature; Sidwa, A. H. & Coleman, M. M. Niemcewicz: An Anniversary Tribute; Polish Review, III (1958).

Z. F.

.*NIEREMBERG, JUAN EUSEBIO (1595-April 17, 1659), Spanish religious writer, was born in Madrid of German parents who had gone to Spain in the retinue of Mary of Austria, daughter of Charles V and widow of the Emperor Maximilian. He studied under the Jesuits of the Colegio Imperial in Madrid and at the universities of Alcalá and Salamanca. At the age of nineteen, much against the will of his father, whose ambitions for him were more worldly, he decided to join the Company of Jesus. An unusually rigorous novice master, bad health, and an inclination toward extremes of ascet-

* nĕ′ rĕm bĕrg

ism added to the hardships of his studies as a novice. He was ordained priest in 1623 and began teaching Latin and Scripture at the court school of Madrid; he also became well known as a novice master and popular among the nobility and higher clergy as a confessor. In 1633, having received the highest citations from the General of the Company, he took his final vows as a Jesuit.

Father Nieremberg was the author of at least a dozen works, most of them ascetical treatises of the sort so popular throughout Europe in the seventeenth century. Typical of these is the *Diferencia entre lo Temporal y Eterno, Crisol de Desengaños* (1640). This was translated as *A Treatise on the Difference Betwixt the Temporal and Eternal* by V. Mullineaux (1672). It consists of clear arguments and forceful examples intended to prove that the temporal has no value at all of its own, but is only a means of achieving the eternal values. After tracing the concepts of time and eternity in Greek and Christian thought, he sees them as intersecting, for the individual, at the moment of death and, for humanity, at the end of the world. The utter meaninglessness of earthly existence is then contrasted with the absolute values, either positive or negative, of eternity. His conclusion focuses upon the Redemption. This typically Jesuit work is said to have influenced the writings of the great Anglican theologian Jeremy Taylor. Nieremberg also influenced the religious poet Henry Vaughan who translated *Two Discourses* (1654). There are also English translations of *A Meditation of Life and Death* made in 1682, and *Of Adoration in Spirit and in Truth* (1871). Among the Jesuit's other works are an important biography of St. Francis of Borgia and the standard Spanish version of the *Imitation of Christ.*

During the final years of his life Father Nieremberg suffered greatly from painful and disabling illnesses which he bore with fortitude. His death at sixty-three occasioned demonstrations of personal affection by citizens of Madrid.

ABOUT: [In Spanish—Zepeda-Henríquez, E. *in* Nieremberg's selected works, vols. 103 and 104 of the BAE.]

E. L. R.

*NIETZSCHE, FRIEDRICH WILHELM (October 15, 1844-August 25, 1900), German philosopher and poet, was born in Röcken (Prussian Saxony), the son of a Lutheran minister. According to

* nĕ′ chĕ

a doubtful family tradition, gladly believed by Nietzsche, the family was of Polish aristocratic origin (Count Nietzki), and later in his life Nietzsche's slightly salient cheekbones and his bushy mustache indeed frequently caused him to be taken for a Pole. His father Karl Ludwig died when the boy was only five years old, and his mother (*née* Oehler, herself the daughter of a pastor) moved to Naumburg with Friedrich, his sister Elisabeth, and a younger son. A scholarship granted by King Frederick William IV of Prussia enabled Friedrich in 1858 to enter the fashionable school of Pforta, near Naumburg, which had a high standard of learning. Nietzsche showed an early, though rather anarchic, talent for the humanistic subjects. Already as a child he was introverted and selective in the choice of his friends. He was also soon beset by doubts about religion, and it became clear that he would not choose his father's profession. In 1864 he enrolled at the University of Bonn, where he soon came in conflict with the thinking of many of the student groups. He became the favorite student of the outstanding classical philologist Ritschl, whom he followed to the University of Leipzig a year later.

From the outset he found it difficult to confine himself to the scholarly discipline of the philological method. While in Leipzig, he discovered the pessimistic philosophy of Schopenhauer and the music of Wagner, two influences which were to guide him for years

to come. In 1869, upon Ritschl's recommendation, the young Nietzsche was appointed professor of classical philology at the University of Basel, thus becoming a colleague of the famous historian Jakob Burckhardt and of the Church historian Franz Overbeck, who was to remain his lifelong friend. Above all, however, he became a frequent visitor to Triebschen, where Wagner (whom he had briefly met a year before in Leipzig) was living with his wife Cosima.

Nietzsche's first important work, *Die Geburt der Tragödie* (1872), took issue with the traditional view of Greek civilization as the lucid embodiment of noble simplicity and calm grandeur, which ignored the more disquieting Greece of Pindar and Aeschylus. Greek tragedy is originally a scenic evocation of the Dionysian mysteries and therefore unites the two aspects of Hellas—the tragic, *musical* ecstasy of Dionysus and the serene, *visual* lucidity of Apollo. Aeschylean tragedy, argued the disciple of Wagner, is being reborn in modern times in the *Musikdrama* of the master of Triebschen. The book was attacked by official philology, which saw in it nothing more than a tract of Wagnerian propaganda. In the years 1873 to 1876 Nietzsche published four essays, collected under the title *Unzeitgemässe Betrachtungen,* which contain bitter criticisms of many tendencies of contemporary civilization. Nietzsche reproves the facile optimism of his time, deplores the stultification of life by historicism and the worshiping of erudition, and clairvoyantly foresees that the German spirit may become the victim of the German Empire created during the victorious Franco-Prussian War of 1870 (in which he himself briefly participated as a member of the ambulance corps). Against the leveling Philistinism of the new epoch, Nietzsche holds up the shining example of Schopenhauer, the hero of the spirit who never compromised with the powers that be. Civilization, Nietzsche fears, will lose sight of its primary purpose: the creation of the genius.

Although the fourth essay was a homage to Wagner, Nietzsche was moving away from the magic circle of the composer, who was now gaining general recognition. Bayreuth, where the Wagnerian theatre was being built, evolved into the official musical center of the Reich. Nietzsche came to realize that Wagner's enterprise, far from representing a rebirth, was the expression of a decadent late romanticism which ultimately led back to the Church of Rome. He now also shook off his own romantic aestheticism. Wary of all delusions and auto-delusions, he sought inspiration in the critical tradition of the French moralists and found a friend to fit his new mood in the Berlin writer Paul Rée. The final break with Wagner came with the publication of *Menschliches, Allzumenschliches* (1878). The work represented a complete about-face. In a brilliantly sober style, and in aphoristic form, it initiated a trend which was to characterize Nietzsche's following books as well: the merciless debunking of all lies and self-lies, of all forms of "idealism" (aesthetic, religious, or other), and the devaluation of the "moral sentiments" through a psychological analysis which uncovers the egoism at their core. Not the genius, but the "free spirit" is the human type which now answers Nietzsche's longings. *Der Wanderer und sein Schatten* (1879) became the second part of *Menschliches* in subsequent editions.

In the same year, Nietzsche's constantly deteriorating health forced him to give up his professorial functions. The city of Basel granted him a pension. He now became a wanderer himself, dividing his time among Swiss, Italian, and southern French hotels, beset by increasing solitude. Most of his Wagnerian friends had left him, his academic colleagues rejected his theories, and the public ignored his books so completely that he was forced to create in a vacuum. *Morgenröte* (published 1881)—composed largely in Venice, the domicile of "Peter Gast" (Köselitz), a young unsuccessful composer who was Nietzsche's only faithful disciple— and *Die Fröhliche Wissenschaft* (published 1882) continued the preceding work in the same form, introducing the lyrical note of a joyful quest for new horizons. The year 1882 also brought the failure of Nietzsche's one serious attempt at marriage (with Lou Salomé, a young Russian lady introduced to him by his old friend Malwida von Meysenbug) and thus completed his isolation.

Meanwhile in August 1881 near Sils-Maria in the Engadine, Nietzsche had experienced the ecstatic vision of the Eternal Recurrence of all events. This old Heraclitean and Pythagorean idea became for him the ultimate expression of his philosophy. Removing the illusion of a transcendent purpose and establishing the eternity of everything that happens in this world, it endows our earthly existence with supreme value and leads the strong to *amor fati*, the tragic affirmation of life with all its suffering. The Dionysian spirit

re-entered Nietzsche's work in the four parts of *Also Sprach Zarathustra* (published 1883-85). The ancient Persian prophet, now the prophet of the Recurrence, is the poetic transposition of Nietzsche himself and at the same time the imaginary companion of his solitude. He teaches that "God is dead" and that man must transcend himself in order to survive: only the "Superman" will have the strength to occupy the vacant throne of the Deity. The prophetic, often Biblical, lyricism of *Zarathustra* corresponds to its purpose of supplanting the Bible and of becoming the Gospel of the future religion of the earth.

Nietzsche then decided to expound his philosophy systematically in a huge work for which he chose the title *Der Wille zur Macht*, for in the "will to power" he believed he had discovered the universal metaphysical principle. Both his failing health and his temperament prevented the execution of this plan. The numerous notes were published in 1894, under the projected title. In *Jenseits von Gut und Böse* (1886) Nietzsche reverted to the aphoristic form. *Prelude to a Philosophy of the Future* is the subtitle of this book, in which the philosopher—sensing the imminence of a European cataclysm which was still far removed from the consciousness of his contemporaries—anxiously asks himself who will be the "good Europeans," those who will coin new values and ensure the future beyond the abyss. The "transvaluation of all values" appears as one of the chief themes of the feverishly written works of the next two years. The style of these last writings remains admirable, but in the increasing shrillness of their tone many critics have professed to see a sign of the author's approaching madness. In *Die Genealogie der Moral* (1887) he traces the origin of Christian morality to a slave revolt against everything superior and advocates the return to an aristocratic "master morality." *Der Fall Wagner* (1888) is a violent diatribe against Wagnerian music. In the course of 1888, Nietzsche wrote *Der Antichrist* and *Ecce Homo*. The former is a sometimes delirious indictment of modern Christianity, the latter a spiritual autobiography in which the author interprets his own life as a turning point in history: he is the last decadent, but also the first builder of the future—the prophet of Dionysus, who has come to supplant Christ. *Götzendämmerung* (published 1889) is a final destructive attack against all modern idols.

The breakdown came in the early days of January 1889, in Turin. Nietzsche wrote senseless notes to his friends, signing "Dionysus" or "The Crucified One." His friend Overbeck brought him back to Germany. He continued to live until 1900 in growing unconsciousness, first with his mother and after 1897 with his sister Elisabeth Förster-Nietzsche in Weimar, where the latter had founded the *Nietzsche-Archiv* in 1894. Nietzsche is buried in Röcken.

Public recognition, especially in Germany and France, came immediately after Nietzsche's collapse. His full impact on the next generations, including our own, cannot possibly be measured: not only his work, but also the symbolic significance of his fate has haunted the twentieth century. Both his lapidary aphoristic style and his dithyrambic lyricism have widened the expressive possibilities of the German language, exerting a magical attraction on most readers, while his philosophical preoccupations have given new directions to European thought. In Germany, the important poetic circle of Stefan George looked on Nietzsche as its inspirer. He is the precursor of all the modern philosophies of civilization which are concerned with the problem of decadence, of the "philosophy of life" and the irrationalist theories which were in evidence particularly during the 1920's, and even now he is one of the chief forerunners of the "philosophies of existence." Many of his psychological insights point toward Freud, and *The Birth of Tragedy* has had an impact on art criticism. Unfortunately he has also been misused: through the consistent isolation and systematization of certain extreme statements, the prophet of "European nihilism" has become associated with the most negative aspects of Prussian militarism and later even with Nazism. This false association has sometimes marred the English and American appreciation of his works. His greatness, however, has survived all misunderstandings.

Nietzsche's writings have tempted many translators. The first authorized English translation of his complete works appeared 1909-13, under the editorship of Dr. Oscar Levy. It contains among others the excellent translation of *The Birth of Tragedy* by W. A. Haussmann and very good translations of *Thus Spake Zarathustra, The Joyful Wisdom* (both by T. Common), *Human, All-too-Human,* and *Beyond Good and Evil* (by Helen Zimmern). Particularly *Zarathustra* has been frequently translated, for the first time by Alexander Tille as early as 1896. Other translations which should receive mention are *Ecce Homo* and *The Birth of Tragedy* by C. P. Fadiman in 1927 (both outstanding) and *The Antichrist* by H. L. Mencken (1924). The selection of the Modern Library edition contains some of the best translations. See also *The Portable Nietzsche*, edited by W. A. Kaufmann (1954). *An International Nietzsche Bibliography,* compiled by H. W. Reichert and K. Schlecta, was published in 1960.

ABOUT: Abraham, G. Nietzsche; Blackham, H. J. Six Existentialist Thinkers; Brinton, C. Nietzsche; Copleston, F. Friedrich Nietzsche, Philosopher of Culture; Förster-Nietzsche, E. The Life of Nietzsche; Halévy, D. The Life of Friedrich Nietzsche; Kaufmann, W. A. Nietzsche: Philosopher, Psychologist, Antichrist; Lea, F. A. The Tragic Philosopher; Lichtenberger, H. The Gospel of Superman; Love, F. R. Young Nietzsche and the Wagnerian Experience; Ludovici, A. M. Nietzsche: His Life and Works; Mencken, H. L. The Philosophy of Friedrich Nietzsche; Nicolas, M. P. From Nietzsche Down to Hitler; Reyburn, H. A. Nietzsche: the Story of a Human Philosopher; Wright, W. H. What Nietzsche Taught. [In French—Andler, C. Nietzsche, sa Vie et sa Pensée, 6 vols. In German—Jaspers, K. Nietzsche: Einführung in das Verständnis seines Philosophierens.]

W. W. H.

*NIEVO, IPPOLITO (November 30, 1831-March 4, 1861), Italian patriot, novelist, poet, was born in the northern Italian city of Padua. His father, Antonio, was a physician from Mantua, and his mother, Adelè Marin, was a Venetian noblewoman.

As a boy Nievo studied in the *liceo* at Mantua. At the age of twenty-one he went to the University of Padua to study law, remaining at the university until 1855.

In the six remaining years of his life, Nievo wrote as a poet, playwright, and novelist. His first poetry, published in 1854-55, was followed in 1858 by a volume entitled *Le Lucciole* (Fireflies). His first novel, *Angelo di Bontà* (Angel of Goodness), appeared in 1855. *Il Varmo,* appearing in 1856, follows the approach of the naturalists, and has many interesting psychological observations. *Il Conte Pecoraio* (The Foolish Count) was published in 1857.

Nievo joined the forces of Garibaldi in 1859 in Sicily and was one of the Thousand participating in the capture of Palermo and in Garibaldi's victorious entry into Naples in 1860. After Palermo Nievo became a colonel and trusted officer of Garibaldi. The patriot-writer's life was to end shortly afterward in the night between March 4 and 5, 1861, in the shipwreck of the "Hercules" in the Tyrrhenian Sea.

The chief work of Ippolito Nievo is *Le Confessioni di un Italiano,* a cyclic novel written in eight months in 1858. It was published posthumously as *Le Confessioni di un Ottuagenario* (The Memoirs of a Man of Eighty) in 1867. It is the double story of the national evolution of Italy in the nineteenth century and the life of Carlo Altoviti from

* nyā′ vō

the time he is left as a baby with his uncle in the Castle of Fratta. Each personal crisis in the life of Carlo corresponds to a larger one on the social scene, and there is always an interaction of the two events. This historical novel, which shows the influence of Manzoni, is agreed to be one of the greater narrative works of nineteenth century romanticism. It falls short of being a masterpiece because it was never revised.

Nievo's poems were collected in 1889 (*Poesie,* ed. R. Barbiera) ; a selection of his writings, including *Diario di Sicilia,* was made by R. Bacchelli in 1929 (*Le Più Belle Pagine* . . .). His novels continue to be appreciated in Italy and his posthumous *Confessioni* has never gone out of style. An annotated edition (ed. B. Chiurlo) appeared in 1941. In 1954 it made its first appearance in English, translated by L. F. Edwards as *The Castle of Fratta,* and four years later it was published in the United States. Reviewers criticized the uneven composition and verboseness but conceded that it had great vitality.

ABOUT: Italian Quarterly, II (1958) ; PMLA, LXXV (1960). [In Italian—see studies by A. Balduino, C. Bozzetti, G. Galati, V. Gallo, G. Solitro.]

E. DE P.

NJEGOŠ. See PETROVIĆ, PETAR II NJEGOŠ

*NOBRE, ANTÓNIO (August 16, 1867-March 18, 1900), Portuguese poet, was born in Oporto, of middle-class parents with aristocratic pretensions, and died young, near his native city, of an incurable consumption that early changed his life and poetry.

In his youth he spent many well-remembered summers in the countryside of Trás-os-Montes or the beaches north of the Douro ("I see that sick boy, coughing by the sea . . ."). He studied law in Coimbra (1888-90), where his garret "a Tôrre d'Anto" ("Anto," short for António) is still pointed out. There the dreamer failed his courses but joined the "Boémia Nova" group and found a good friend in Alberto de Oliveira, who with him started a return to Almeida Garrett's romantic nationalism stripped of its political aims. Nobre went to the Sorbonne in 1890 and obtained a degree in political science in 1895. He traveled much in search of health, to Switzerland, Madeira, New York. But it was in the Latin Quarter of Paris as he thought of Portugal that he wrote his finest poems. The Portugal he recalled was picturesque in a sinister way, a strangely lovely land of the dead and dying, sick,

* noō brâ′

wretched, miserably poor "descendants of the navigators."

While alive, he had a single volume, *Só* published in Paris by the symbolists' publisher Vanier (1892). It contained verse written mostly in Portugal and Paris 1884-92. Poems written as late as 1894 were added to subsequent editions (ten editions by 1955). *Só* mirrored his loneliness and poverty after his father's death. Two more volumes of verse appeared posthumously, *Despedidas* (written 1895-99, published 1902) and *Primeiros Versos* (1921). *Despedidas* included an epic fragment on King Sebastian, with whose misfortune Nobre identified his own.

The poet was conscious of the morbid suggestiveness of his black humor in *Só:* "Beware, you may be harmed. There is no sadder book in all of Portugal." His feminine, even childlike verse reflects the romantic nostalgia and folksiness of Almeida Garrett, the bitter disillusionment of Camões, the sentimentality of the Coimbra *fado,* and the musicality and fanciful magic of the French symbolists he knew in Paris: autumnal sunsets, convents of the moon, Old Woman Death, etc. To these he added pitiful pictures of himself, oscillating between Franciscan compassion and satanic hate, or playing a macabre game with death. *Só* appeared at the time of national despondency during the decadence of the Portuguese monarchy, when many were driven to suicide: "Friend, what a fate to have been born in Portugal!"

Anto's poems deeply moved several generations of melancholy, narcissistic readers and inspired a curiously resigned nationalism. His memory has become part of Coimbra: "The *fado, Só,* the *Despedidas.* And in the moonlight, Olive trees or sisters of St. Clare, And ghosts at dusk, Or friars from Holy Cross, The poplars by our Holy River . . ." (Teixeira de Pascoaes). While Eugénio de Castro is the Portuguese symbolist best known outside Portugal, Nobre remains the most influential and beloved within.

ABOUT: [In Portuguese—see studies by C. Branco Chaves, A. Brochado, G. de Castilho, U. T. Rodrigues, J. Gaspar Simões.]

G. M. M.

*NODIER, (JEAN) CHARLES (EMMANUEL) (April 29, 1780-January 27, 1844), French man of letters, was born at Besançon. His father, Antoine Melchior Nodier (1738-1808), an eminent lawyer who

* nô dyā′

NODIER

had been mayor and then chief justice of Besançon, legitimized Charles by marrying his mother, Suzanne Paris, a servant, in 1791. The couple had another child, Jeanne Claude, nicknamed Élise. Charles was strongly influenced by his Rousseauistic father, and at the age of twelve was a member of Besançon's revolutionary Society of the Friends of the Constitution; he was on the committee which honored General Pichegru for repulsing the Austrian army. At thirteen Charles took private lessons, reading Tasso, Ariosto, and Shakespeare. While studying Greek he also demonstrated unusual aptitude in entomology, an interest he held all his life.

In 1798 Nodier became assistant librarian of the Daubs department's École Centrale, where he had been a student. Two years later he went to Paris and published a *Bibliographie Entomologique*, of which Lamarck thought well. His first novel, *Les Proscrits* (1802), was strongly influenced by Goethe's *Werther*. The same sort of exaltation exhibited in his novel cost him a month of prison for his verse satire *La Napoléone*. Banned from Paris, Nodier lived under police supervision at Besançon and at Dôle, where he married Liberté Constitution Désirée Charve in 1808. They had a daughter, Marie, born in 1811.

Nodier became secretary and amanuensis to an English baron, Herbert Croft, and to Lady Mary Hamilton before assuming the positions of librarian and director of the

newspaper *Télégraphe Illyrien* of Laybach. But Napoleon abandoned Illyria, and Nodier was given a position in Paris with the *Journal de l'Empire,* and contributed to Michaud's *Biographie Universelle.* After Napoleon's final downfall Nodier's life became a series of literary and semiliterary or bibliophilic efforts in the midst of contributions to *Les Débats* and *La Quotidienne. Jean Sbogar* (1818) was immensely successful, being adapted for the theatre, translated, and imitated. While writing the melodrama *Le Vampire* (1820) he did a prose translation of Mathurin. He also published travel literature, the most successful being the account of his trip to Scotland (1821).

Appointment in 1824 as librarian of the Arsenal afforded Nodier the opportunity to hold the famous Sunday evening gatherings which attracted the Paris elite in the arts. His daughter Marie was known as "Notre-Dame de l'Arsenal," the moving spirit in the dances and games of the Nodier salon. Nodier, though not exclusively a romanticist —his age and his background made him more a precursor—was an attraction for the rising generation. It was a pun on his name, "Nodo Hierro," that served as the password for the clacque at the première on February 25, 1830, of Victor Hugo's *Hernani.* At the Arsenal gatherings Nodier would recite from his inexhaustible stock of tales, which flowed from his pen for two decades. Based on broad erudition in several literatures and utilizing the fantastic, the occult, and the subconscious, these stories are best in the areas of the fantastic tale and the sentimental short story. His Illyrian *Jean Sbogar* (1818), the fantastic *Smarra ou Les Démons de la Nuit* (1821), and *Trilby ou Le Lutin d'Argail* (1822), which inspired plays, parodies, and even multicolored scarves, are the best known. The *Histoire du Roi de Bohème et de Ses Sept Châteaux* (1830) contains the story most appreciated by the French, that of Brisquet's dog. The ghost story *Inès de la Sierras* (1837) was inspired by a trip to Spain in 1827, and by the tales of E.T.A. Hoffmann as well as those of Prosper Mérimée.

In addition to fictional writings Nodier did an amazing number of works of "pure erudition," and was a regular contributor to the *Bulletin du Bibliophile,* of which he was a director. He was responsible for making known in France English and German authors, as well as many classical writers. The press of these activities did not cause him to slacken in his entomological pursuits or in bibliographical endeavors, although he was in ill health. In 1833 Nodier became a member of the French Academy. He died in Paris, and was buried in Père Lachaise cemetery.

An edition of Nodier in thirteen volumes was published 1832-41. Additional material has been made known in the *Cahiers du Sud* of 1950. A convenient edition, entitled *Contes Fantastiques*, was edited by Charles Laclos (2 vols., 1957).

An anonymous translation, *History of the Secret Societies of the Army, and of the Military Conspiracies Which Had for Their Object the Destruction of the Government of Bonaparte*, appeared in London in 1815. This work has been assigned several co-authors. *The Bibliomaniac* was translated by Mabel O. Wright (1894) and by Frank H. Ginn (1900). *Trilby, the Fairy of Argyle* was translated twice in 1895, by Nathan H. Dole and by Minna C. Smith. *Promenade from Dieppe to the Mountains of Scotland* was published at Edinburgh the same year (1822) as in France. *Francesco Colonna*, originally published posthumously the year of Nodier's death, was translated by Theodore W. Koch (1929). Claud Lovat Fraser illustrated the children's stories *The Luck of the Bean Rows* and *The Woodcutter's Dog* (1921); the latter had appeared in *Prince Darling's Story Book* in 1881. There are selections from Nodier in the Warner Library. J. Hawthorne included *Inès de la Sierra* in the Lock and Key Library (1915).

ABOUT: Brandes, G. M. C. Main Currents in Nineteenth-Century Literature, V; French Review, XXVIII (1955); Modern Philology, XIV (1916-17); Open Court, January 1924. [In French—see studies by J. Larat, R. Maixuer, W. Moench, E. Montégut, J. Richer, M. Salomon.]

S. S. W.

*NOOT, Jonker JAN VAN DER** (c. 1540-c. 1595), Flemish poet, was born in Brecht near Antwerp, the son of a rich nobleman who had once visited Palestine. He studied Latin and perhaps Greek and knew French, Spanish, and Italian. He was not a man of stable convictions in religion and politics. In the days of Álva he hated and mocked Catholicism; after the fall of Antwerp he became an ardent Catholic who glorified the Spanish king and the Duke of Parma. In his art he paid cowardly tribute to the rich from whom he might gain. But in spite of this, he was a poet of stature and one of the first through whom modern Flemish poetry became significant.

In 1562 and the following year Van der Noot was alderman of Antwerp, a position his father had held some years earlier. His marriage (1563) seems to have been unhappy. In March 1567 after the Calvinistic rebellion had miscarried, Van der Noot went

* nōt

abroad, traveling until 1578 in England (where he met Edmund Spenser), the Rhineland (where he knew the Dutch engraver Coornhert), and France (where he encountered Dorat and Ronsard). Returning to Antwerp as a Catholic he became favorably inclined toward the Spaniards after the surrender of that city in 1585. His financial circumstances were lamentable during most of his life. There is no record of him after 1591; he is thought to have died about 1595.

Van der Noot was a Renaissance poet, employing the iamb in odes as well as in sonnets. His first work, *Het Bosken* (1567), still recalls the Redrykers but also reveals the influence of Petrarch and Ronsard. *Het Theatre oft Toon-neel* (1568), of which there are versions extant in French, German, and English (the latter is assumed to have been translated by Spenser under the title *A Theatre for Voluptuous Worldlings* (1569), contains translations from Petrarch and Du Bellay, four sonnets, and a violently Calvinistic pamphlet in prose. Renaissance culture considered the epic to be an ideal literary form and it was therefore natural that Van der Noot should try his hand at this genre. The result was *Cort Begrijp der XII Boeken Olympiados* (1579), a fragment of *Das Buch Extasis* which had already been published in German in 1576. From 1580 to 1595 *De Poetische Werken* appeared, which consisted of a number of collections containing some of his finest poetry, but in large part full of literary pot-boiling.

As one of the early men in the North dedicated to the ideas of the Renaissance, Van der Noot revived the use of imagery in Dutch poetry. He also introduced the sonnet and the ode in the Lowlands, together with the ten-syllable verse and the alexandrine. It was not until the nineteenth century that he received appreciation and full recognition.

ABOUT: English Studies, VIII (1926). [In Dutch—see studies by A. Vermeylen, C. Ypes.]

H. B.

*NORDENFLYCHT, HEDVIG CHARLOTTA** (November 28, 1718-June 29, 1763), Swedish poet, was born in Stockholm, where she remained most of her life. Her father was Anders Nordbohm, actuary at the Finance Department, who, when ennobled in 1727, adopted the name of Nordenflycht. Her mother was Christina Rosin, of a clergyman's family. In 1734 she was engaged to a young philosophically oriented mechanic, Johan Tideman, who soon died. Retaining her noble

* nōōr′ dĕn flükt

maiden name, she married a commoner in 1741, a naval chaplain, Jacob Fabricius, who initiated her into a mystic, aesthetically and emotionally tinged religion. He died seven months later, leaving his widow in the utmost despair. After her husband's death her cousin and intimate friend Carl Klingenberg and others taught her the French enlightened ideas, and she became an ardent admirer of Voltaire, whom she imitated in her poetry. In the early 1760's she fell in love with a young radical Rousseauist, Johan Fischerström, but her passion was unrequited, and she was thrown into a nervous crisis which caused her severe suffering and indirectly led to her death.

It was the inconsolable sorrow at the loss of her husband that released Hedvig Nordenflycht's poetic talent and inspired her first little collection of poems, *Den Sörgande Turtur-Dufwan* (The Mourning Turtledove), published in 1743. These songs are pathetic manifestations of her agitated emotional life.

From 1744 to 1750 she published under the title *Qvinligit Tankespel* (Feminine Thought Play), a kind of poetic yearbook. The first volume appeared under the pseudonym "en Herdinna i Norden" (a Shepherdess in the Northland), but the remaining ones under her real name.

In 1752 she was granted a life-pension by the Estates, which relieved her of financial anxieties and enabled her to sponsor a literary salon on the French pattern. The French influence was strikingly obvious in the two volumes *Witterhetsarbeten* (Literary Works), which she published 1759-62 in cooperation with two contemporary Swedish poets, Creutz and Gyllenborg. She was also the first Swedish poet to show the influence of Rousseau. Her acquaintance with this nature philosopher created in her a bitter conflict between rationalistic idealism and emotional mysticism. Her last, unhappy love inspired her to erotic elegies and love poems in verse and prose and brought her poetic potentialities to their summit.

Through the men in her life the "Shepherdess in the Northland" absorbed influences from various literary currents and cultural leaders. Most of her poetry was unoriginal and indebted to native and foreign models. Her production is impressive in volume but cannot be highly rated aesthetically. She lacked stylistic feeling and constructive imagination, and she never attained real technical skill. Her epics especially show more theoretical and rhetorical bombast than poetic beauty. Both her poetry and her attitude toward the spiritual problems of the time were determined by her unstable emotional life. She exposed the innermost feelings of her heart in frank and touching confessions. Aesthetically on the highest level are her brief songs, which exhibit her longing for happiness, her brooding and restlessness, and her sorrows, often imbued with genuinely impulsive love-throes.

ABOUT: [In Swedish—see studies by H. Borelius, J. Kruse, and A. Nilsson.]

A. J.

*NORWID, CYPRIAN (KAMIL) (September 24, 1821-May 23, 1883), Polish poet, was born in Laskowo-Głuchy of a poor family of the gentry and orphaned early. He went to school in Warsaw and later studied painting and sculpture in Italy and in France. While in Rome in 1847-48 he associated with a number of exiled Polish authors and patriots, among them Krasinski and Mickiewicz, and in Paris in 1849 he became friendly with Chopin and with Słowacki. Bitterly disappointed after several unhappy love affairs, he traveled to America in 1852 and stayed for a while in New York. In 1854 he returned to Paris where he spent the remainder of his days in poverty. He died in a charitable institution in which he had lived for the last six years of his life.

The pathetic circumstances of the poet's death emphasize the fact that he was unrecognized during his lifetime. Yet he is now regarded as one of the great and most original poets and thinkers of the romantic period, one whose influence on modern Polish poetry has steadily grown during the last decades. Norwid's typically intellectual poetry is, indeed, "difficult," but rather in the way that T. S. Eliot describes as the essence of modern poetry. Almost every work by Norwid is original and novel in both idea and form, and each poem demands great effort for complete appreciation. In his aesthetic credo *Promethidion* (1851) Norwid is the prophet of art as the "shape of love" and the "beatification of labor." There are certain anticipations of Ruskin in this and other works by Norwid.

The most accessible writings for both Polish and foreign readers are Norwid's lyrical poems. Such lyrics as "My Song," or "The Funeral Rhapsody on the Memory of General Bem" belong to the superlative achievements of Polish verse. The poem "A Dorio ad Phrygium," the philosophical essay-story "Ad Leones," several dramas (*Cleopatra and Caesar, Wanda, Krakus*), a cycle of short

* nŏr' vĭt

stories (*Black and White Flowers*)—all these reveal an unusual intellect and artistry, although they do not alway have clear uniform structure. Most of Norwid's works were published posthumously, long after his death, mainly through the devoted efforts of Zenon Przesmycki (pseudonym "Miriam").

Only scattered fragments and some lyrical poems of Norwid are available in English translation in *A Polish Anthology* by T. M. Philip and M. A. Michael (1944).

ABOUT: Kridl, M. Survey of Polish Literature; Krzyzanowski, J. Polish Romantic Literature; Slavic and East European Review, 1949. [In Polish —see study by W. Borowy.]

Z. F.

"NOVALIS." See HARDENBERG, FRIEDRICH LEOPOLD

*NOVIKOV, NIKOLAY IVANOVICH (April 27, 1744-July 31, 1818), Russian writer and publisher, was born to a family of the landed gentry in Moscow Province. He was educated first at home and then at the preparatory school of the University of Moscow, from which he did not graduate. Following a tour of duty in a guards regiment, Novikov served (1767-68) as a governmental secretary during Catherine II's abortive attempt to form a constitutional assembly. He continued in civil employ until 1774, when he withdrew to renew his journalistic and publishing enterprises. Novikov's *Truten'* (The Drone, 1766) a satirical journal, established itself as outstanding of its kind, following the initiative of the Empress' own *Vsyakaya Vsyachina* (Something of Everything). In contrast to the light-hearted mode practiced and prescribed by Catherine, satire in Novikov's hands took a decidedly serious turn; he attacked concrete social evils in Russian life, particularly serfdom. Catherine's mounting irritation over her "rival's" witty and provocative publication forced Novikov finally, in April 1770, to discontinue it. His subsequent satirical journals: *Pustomelya* (The Prattler, 1770), *Zhivopisets* (The Painter, 1772-73), and *Koshelyok* (The Purse, 1774), were all short-lived despite an increasingly cautious approach. In addition to Novikov himself, whose share in the writing was presumably very large, contributors to his journals included Sumarokov and Fonvizin and many others of the most notable Russian writers of the time.

During the period of satirical journals Novikov also brought out, as publisher, several books, collections of historical materials and a biographical encyclopedia of Russian writers (1772) compiled by himself. In 1779 he moved from St. Petersburg to Moscow where he founded a flourishing book publishing and book selling business, an undertaking which before long reached proportions wholly unprecedented in Russia. In addition to huge quantities of books, original and translated works of every description, Novikov issued or sponsored a wide variety of other publications, among them a newspaper, *Moskovskie Vedomosti*. The result of these enterprises, during what V.O. Klyuchevsky has called "the Novikov decade" (1779-89), was an enormous increase not only in the fund of literature but also in the number of readers. This represented the realization of Novikov's own most cherished ambition: the promotion of Russian enlightenment.

In 1775 Novikov had become a Freemason and soon rose to prominence in that movement. He undertook to publish a number of works distinctly Masonic in character and vigorously participated in educational and philanthropic ventures sponsored by that group, supporting many of them with proceeds from his publications. In the early eighties Novikov, with a great number of his fellow Masons, was initiated into the Rosicrucian Order. This affiliation with the mother Rosicrucian lodge in Prussia gave Catherine the opportunity to crush the Russian Masons. After prolonged harassment, Novikov's publishing enterprises were suppressed and he himself was imprisoned in 1792. Although released by Paul I in 1796, Novikov was by that time a broken man. He went into seclusion and spent the rest of his days engrossed in Rosicrucian occultism and mysticism.

Excerpts in English translation from Novikov's satirical journals are found in L. Wiener's *Anthology of Russian Literature* (1902).

ABOUT: [In Russian—see studies by V. Bogolyubov, V. A. Rozenberg, L. B. Svetlov.]

I. R. T.

*NÚÑEZ CABEZA DE VACA, ÁLVAR (1490?-1564?), Spanish historian and explorer, was born in Jerez de la Frontera. He was of noble family, his parents being Francisco de Vera and Teresa Cabeza de Vaca. Nothing is known of his boyhood or youth. He had already served as a soldier when he became treasurer of Narváez's expedition to Florida. All members of this ill-fated expedition were lost except Cabeza de Vaca and

* nô′ vyĭ′ kôf

* noō′ nyāth kä bā′ thä thä vä′ kä

three companions. These made their way across what is now the southern part of the United States and the northern part of Mexico. He was with the Indians from 1528 to 1536 and survived only because of his medical abilities. Returning to Spain in 1537 he solicited and obtained the position of Governor of the province of Río de la Plata. In 1541 he landed on St. Catherine, left his ships and marched overland to Asunción where he assumed the governorship. Though his administration was successful he was deposed through intrigue and returned to Spain under arrest. For a time he was banished to Oran by the Council of the Indies but was finally restored to his honors and appointed a judge in Seville, where he died not later than 1564.

The account of Cabeza de Vaca's wanderings in America is contained in his *Naufragios,* published in Zamora in 1542. These adventures had inspired Coronado to undertake the exploration of the North. His adventures in South America and along the Paraguay River, which he was the first to explore, are contained in his *Comentarios,* published in Valladolid (1555).

Cabeza de Vaca's gentleness toward the Indians is unique among the conquistadores. He says, "It can clearly be seen that all these peoples, in order to be brought to Christianity . . . must be treated well. This is the only sure way, there is no other."

The best modern edition of Cabeza de Vaca's works is contained in the *BAE*. The chief English translations are Buckingham Smith's *De Vaca's Journey to New Mexico* and *Relations of Alvar Núñez Cabeza de Vaca* (both 1851). F. Bandelier, in 1905, published a translation of *Journey of Núñez Cabeza de Vaca.*

ABOUT: Mitchell, J. L. Earth Conquerors; Morris, C. Heroes of Discovery in America (English title: Nine Against the Unknown); Rand, C. Stars in Their Eyes. [In Spanish—Cartas de Indias (Ministerio de Fomento).]

R. E. O.

---

*NÚÑEZ DE ARCE, GASPAR (September 4, 1834-June 9, 1903), Spanish poet, dramatist, journalist, and politician, was born in Valladolid. There is considerable doubt about his exact birth date and even more doubt concerning his parents. It appears likely that he was illegitimate and not really the son of his ostensible father, Manuel Núñez. The family lived in Valladolid and later in Toledo, where the father was employed in the postal service. Don Manuel insisted that his son become a priest, but this

* nōō′ nyäth thä är′ thä

was so contrary to young Gaspar's inclinations that at the age of eighteen he ran away to Madrid. He first attracted national attention during the African war by the series of articles he ran in *La Iberia.* He had become a friend and protégé of General O'Donnell and had joined his Liberal Union Party. He remained a faithful member until the party's dissolution in 1871, when he joined the Constitutional Party of Sagasta. In the Liberal Union he worked for the overthrow of the Bourbons, and when this came about in 1868 he was named Governor of Barcelona. Núñez de Arce held political offices all his life and in 1883 became Minister for Colonial Affairs, the highest position he ever held.

His dramatic writings were mostly thesis plays and are little read today. *El Haz de Leña* (1872) is the one exception. His fame is unquestionably as a poet. Some of his chief works are: *Gritos del Combate* (1875), *Raimundo Lulio* (1875), *Un Idilio* (1878), *Última Lamentación de Lord Byron* (1879), and *La Visión de Fray Martín* (1880). Although one of the most popular and esteemed poets of his age he is now largely only of historical interest. Constantly obsessed by doubts, he was nevertheless not profound. Despite his technical skill, the lyrical qualities of his verse leave much to be desired. In Gerald Brenan's summing-up: "A virtuoso in rhyme and metres, with all the serenity of language of the disciples of Victor Hugo, he suffers from the disadvantage of having nothing to say" *(The Literature of the Spanish People).* He had married Isidora Franco in 1861; they were childless. In 1876 Núñez de Arce was elected to the Spanish Academy.

His poetry has been edited many times. English translations of his poetry are those of I. Farnell in *Spanish Prose and Poetry* (1920) and T. Walsh, "Miserere," in *Hispanic Anthology* (1920).

ABOUT: [In Spanish—Castillo Soriano, J. del. Núñez de Arce.]

R. E. O.

---

*OBSTFELDER, SIGBJØRN (November 21, 1866-July 29, 1900), Norwegian poet, novelist, dramatist, was born in Stavanger. His father was Herman Friedrich Obstfelder, a baker whose father had emigrated from Holstein, Germany. His mother, Serine Egelandsdal, came originally of a Norwegian peasant family. Sigbjørn was the eighth of sixteen children. There was an inherent predisposition toward insanity in the family, and one of his older brothers was early deranged.

* ōbst′ fĕl dĕr

When Sigbjørn attended the Latin school in his native town he was already a brooder and dreamer, and was especially interested in music. In 1844 he enrolled at the University of Christiania (now Oslo) to study literature, languages, and history, supporting himself by taking outside jobs. After four years he changed plans and transferred to a technical institute, graduating as a mechanical engineer. During his student years he cultivated an ascetic idealism and joined the temperance movement. In 1887 he published in the paper *Nylænde* an article in favor of sexual abstinence; two years later the same paper printed his satire *Heimskringla*, inspired by some inhabitants of a students' hostel where he lived. This was the first and last time he wrote in a light vein.

In 1890 Obstfelder went to America. Impractical by nature, he had no success as an engineer. He suffered from nervous depression and returned home the following year in such a miserable condition that he was confined to a mental asylum. The next year he traveled on the continent, returning to Norway in 1893. Under the influence of several introverted thinkers and writers, e.g., Schopenhauer, Von Hartmann, Kierkegaard, Strindberg, Maeterlinck, and Dostoevsky, Obstfelder published four poems called "Rhythmical Moods" in the magazine *Samtiden* (1892). This was followed by a collection of *Digte* (Poems, 1893) in which loneliness and fear are essential elements. The basic theme is man's relation to the cosmos. In Obstfelder's conception, man stood detached from reality, which to him was something alien. His poems, written in a completely free verse but rhythmically impressive, were generally considered nonsensical.

During his last years, Obstfelder traveled aimlessly on the continent and in England, covering great distances on foot while pursuing his quest for the ideal. In 1896 he published his erotic novel *Korset* (the Cross) relating with great intensity the saga of a woman who lives with several men in succession, only one of whom captures her soul. After her death she and her true love are spiritually united in a higher world. The work unmistakably indicates a sick mind. His play *De Røde Draaber* (The Red Drops, 1897) analyzed a central problem of the time: the conflict between the machine and the soul.

In 1898 Obstfelder married a Dane, Ingeborg Wehe. Soon after on a trip to Berlin he became fatally ill; he died in Copenhagen.

Some of Obstfelder's *Digte* appeared in a collection entitled *Poems,* including the originals with English translations by P. Sever. An exhaustive bibliography appears in R. Øksnevad's *Norsk Litteraturhistorisk Bibliografi 1900-1945.*

ABOUT: Edda, LVII (1957). [In Norwegian —see study by J. F. Bjørnsen.]

A. J.

*OEHLENSCHLÄGER, ADAM GOTTLOB (November 14, 1779-January 20, 1850), Danish poet and dramatist, was born at Frederiksberg, just outside the capital of Copenhagen. His father, Joachim Conrad Oehlenschläger, a jovial and open-hearted man, was organist and later castellan at Frederiksborg Palace. His mother was Martha Maria Hansen. Both parents had a mixed German-Danish background and their son inherited their contrasting temperaments. His childhood, largely spent in the beautiful palace park, was unusually happy, a condition which the mature poet always remembered. His early schooling was poor, but at the age of twelve Oehlenschläger was sent to Copenhagen to be educated and was supported by the school principal, Edvard Storm, who was also a writer and poet. Adam read avidly and wrote poetry, stories, and dramatic sketches while very young.

In 1797 he made an unsuccessful attempt to become an actor. But the years he spent in the theatre gave him valuable insight into its forms. Tutored by a couple of friends, he passed an admissions examination to the university in 1800. During his first year as a student of law he won a prize in an academic essay contest, pointing out in his paper the value of the Old Norse mythology as a source of Scandinavian literature.

Oehlenschläger's mother died in 1800, and shortly after he became engaged to Christiane Heger. He began to lead a carefree life and wrote rococo poetry to the neglect of his legal studies. It was then that a series of events gave his genius its impulse and enabled him to discover his true vocation. Nelson's bombardment of Copenhagen in 1801 resulted in a wave of passionate patriotism in Denmark. In 1802 Oehlenschläger met Henrich Steffens, a Norwegian philosopher, who after four years in Germany had come to Copenhagen inflamed with the new romanticism. After a lengthy conversation with Steffens, Oehlenschläger went home and wrote his remarkable poem *Guldhornene* (The Golden Horns). Although romantic traits had been seen earlier in Danish literature, this work was the first purely romantic one in Scandinavian history.

* ū' lĕn shlä gĕr

The poem appeared at Christmastime along with a collection, *Digte 1803,* which included romances, lyrics, and the lyrical play *Sankt Hansaften-Spil* (Midsummer Eve Play), the last-named remaining one of his best poetic achievements.

Oehlenschläger continued to produce magnificent verse of a romantic nature, eventually publishing two bulky volumes of *Poetiske Skrifter* (Poetic Works, 1805) in which were included the verse travelogue *Langelands-Rejsen* (A Journey to Langeland) and the exotic fairy drama *Aladdin* in which the hero's life is a disguised representation of his own growth. During the years 1805-09 he traveled in Germany, France, Switzerland, and Italy, meanwhile sending home a prodigious amount of work, including *Nordiske Digte* (Scandinavian Poems, 1807), in which appeared two great tragedies—the mythological *Baldur hin Gode* (Balder the Good) and the medieval *Hakon Jarl* (Earl Hakon). In Paris he wrote the tragedy *Axel og Valborg* (1810), treating in an Old Norse setting the typically romantic theme of conflict between duty and love. It was written in the style of the French classical drama and carefully observed the three unities.

Oehlenschläger returned to Denmark in 1809 as an admired and famous man. The same year he was appointed professor of aesthetics at the university and soon afterward he was married to his fiancée, Christiane Heger. His subsequent literary production did not match the brilliance of his early writings upon which his fame chiefly rests. During a period that began with *Digtninger* (Poetry, 1811), and concluded with the tragedy *Tordenskjold* (1832) he reverted to the sentimentality and rationalism of the eighteenth century. Adverse criticism by Baggesen initiated a seven-year literary battle. Oehlenschläger did not openly enter the debate although his supporters did, but he took revenge in his works. In the late 1820's J. L. Heiberg advanced severe criticism of Oehlenschläger's tragedies.

In 1829 Sweden's leading poet, Esaias Tegnér, crowned his Danish colleague with a laurel wreath at an academic ceremony in Lund. In the 1830's Oehlenschläger was still withstanding the new taste for an elegantly polished style and piquant absorbing action, but in the next decade he yielded to the new influences. His major work was behind him by this time, however. He died in Copenhagen at the age of seventy.

The poem "Skialden" (The Poet), included in A. A. Feldborg, ed. *Poems from the Danish* (1815),

was the first work of Oehlenschläger translated into English, by W. S. Walker. Selections of poems have appeared in numerous publications, e.g. *Poems by the Late Anne S. Bushby* (1876); *A Book of Danish Verse* (1922); G. Borrow, *The Songs of Scandinavia* (1923); C. W. Stork, *A Second Book of Danish Verse* (1947); R. P. Keigwin, *In Denmark I Was Born* (1948). The poem *Guldhornene* was translated as *The Gold Horns* by G. Borrow (1913, with an introduction by E. Gosse), as *The Golden Horns* by R. Hillyer (in *American-Scandinavian Review,* VII, 1927). Translations of the poem "Der er et Yndigt Land," which later became the national anthem of Denmark, are included in *Land of Liberty,* July-Aug., 1947, translated by A. W. Madsen, and in R. P. Keigwin, *In Denmark I Was Born.* In G. Pigott, *A Manual of Scandinavian Mythology* (1839) are copious extracts from the epic poem *Nordens Guder* (The Gods of the North), which was translated in full by W. E. Frye under the same title (1845). The first tragedy that appeared in English rendition was *Hakon Jarl,* by an anonymous translator (1840), by J. Chapman (1857), as *Earl Hakon the Mighty* by F. C. Lascelles (1874). *Axel og Valborg* has appeared as *Axel and Valborg,* translated by R. M. Laing in R. M. Laing, *Hours in Norway* (1841), by J. F. Chapman (1851), by H. W. Freeland (1873), by P. Butler (1874), by F. S. Kalle (1906). The tragedy *Corregio* was translated by E. B. Lee (1846), by T. Martin (1854). *Palnatoke* appeared in translation by J. Chapman (1855), *Aladdin* by T. Martin (1857). For a complete list of translations see E. Bredsdorff, *Danish Literature in Translation* (1950).

ABOUT: [In Danish—see studies by V. Andersen, K. Arentzen, I. Falbe-Hansen, L. Schrøder.]

A. J.

*OPITZ VON BOBERFELD, MARTIN (December 23, 1597-August 20, 1639), an influential German poet and literary theoretician, was born in Bunzlau where he attended elementary school. He went on to the Magdalenäum in Breslau and in 1617 to the *Gymnasium* in Beuthen. After two years in Heidelberg as a private tutor he went to Holland to escape the oppressive atmosphere of the Thirty Years' War. Here he won the favor of Daniel Heinsius, whose poetry he had translated while at Heidelberg. In 1621 he traveled to Jutland where he wrote perhaps his best-known poem, "Trostgedichte in Widerwärtigkeit des Kriegs." The following year he followed a summons to assume an instructor's position in the humanities at the court school in Weissenburg. While here he composed the poem "Zlatna oder von Ruhe des Gemüts" and began a large work on the antiquities of Dacia which was never completed. Although he was a Protestant, Opitz became secretary to Count Karl Hannibal von Dohna, a Catholic, notorious for his persecution of Opitz' sect. By virtue of this new position it was possible for him to travel to Paris where he became acquainted with

* ō′ pĭts fōn bō′ bĕr fĕlt

OPITZ

Hugo Grotius. Upon the death of Count Dohna, Opitz went to Danzig where he soon won the patronage of King Vladislav IV of Poland and was named Polish historiographer. In the last years of his life he devoted much of his time to the study of ancient German poetry and published an edition of the "Annolied" with Latin commentary shortly before the only extant manuscript of the work was destroyed by fire. Opitz died in Danzig of a plague that had raged through the city.

His considerable literary-historical significance is based not so much upon his poetry per se as upon the aesthetic and technical principles embodied in his poetry and amplified in his theoretical works. His influence upon the development of German literature during the seventeenth and early eighteenth centuries was incalculably great. For almost one hundred years his poetry was accepted as a supreme model for the young writer. As early as 1617 his reforming spirit exhibited itself in "Aristarchus," an address given upon graduation from the *Gymnasium* at Beuthen, in which he expressed the view that the German language was a vehicle as efficient for the advancement of a great national literature as were French and Italian. While in Heidelberg he assembled a collection of his own poetry which later was published by a friend without his permission (1624). He did not welcome this publication because he felt he had progressed beyond his early writings. This progress is revealed in his most important theoretical work *Buch von der Deut-*

schen Poeterey (1624). Here he develops the rules for the composition of poetry, rules for the most part borrowed from such predecessors as Scaliger and Ronsard. Although Opitz acknowledges here the necessity of "divine madness" as a prerequisite for the great literary artist, he nevertheless considers a thorough knowledge of the Greek and Latin masters as indispensable to the poet. He attempts to define the various literary genres and places great emphasis upon the decorative elements in poetry, rhetoric and imagery. Of great significance in this work are his statements on metrics. In contrast to his earlier verses which consisted of a specific number of syllables without regard for accent, in his *Poeterey* Opitz insists that the German poet cannot merely consider the number and length of syllables in the manner of the ancients. Rather he must also recognize the significance of accent and emphasis. He also demands purity and division of rhyme into feminine and masculine classes, in the manner of Ronsard. According to these rules he rewrote his own early works and published a collected edition of them (1625). Besides his numerous didactic poems, Opitz was instrumental in advancing the cause of pastoral poetry in Germany. Not only did he translate Sidney's *Arcadia* (1638), but he composed his own *Schäfferey von der Nimfen Hercinie* (1630), a mixture of narrative, lyric, and dramatic scenes based upon Italian and French models. His rôle in the development of opera in Germany is considerable: his *Daphne,* an adaptation of a work by Rinuccini and set to music by Heinrich Schütz (1627), constitutes the first German opera. In the field of the drama his chief contributions were translations of Seneca, *Die Trojanerinnen* (1625), and of Sophocles, *Antigone* (1636).

English translations of Opitz' poetry are to be found in The Warner Library; L. Forster, *The Penguin Book of German Verse;* K. Knotz, *Representative German Poems;* G. C. Schoolfield, *The German Lyric of the Baroque in English Translation.*

ABOUT: [In German—see studies by F. Gundolf, H. Max, A. Stössel, M. Szyrocki.]

E. K. G.

*ORIANI, ALFREDO (August 22, 1852-October 18, 1909), Italian writer in many literary genres, was born in Faenza, in the Adriatic province of Romagna, to an impoverished noble family. His childhood years at the family villa in Casola-Valsenia were singularly barren and unhappy because of

* ō ryä′ nē

his parents' incompatibility and neglect of their three children; the circumstances of this divided heritage had their influence upon Oriani's career.

Upon reaching adolescence, he was sent to attend the Collegio di San Luigi in Bologna, run by the famous Italian teaching order of the Barnabites. At the age of sixteen he went to the University of Rome to study law. The unification of Italy had been accomplished during Oriani's youth, and during his student years in Rome that city became the capital of the youngest nation in Europe. His degree in law, obtained in 1872 from the University of Naples, was never used; he retired shortly afterward to Cardello, the family home, to begin the prodigious output which was to mark his literary career.

At the age of twenty-one he wrote his first novel under the pseudonym Ottone di Banzole. Entitled *Memorie Inutili* (Useless Recollections), it was partly autobiographical but highly dramatized. At brief intervals, Oriani then wrote *Al di là* (Beyond) in 1877, *Monotonie* (Monotonies), a volume of verse in 1878, *Gramigne* (Weeds) in 1879, and *No* in 1881; the writing in all these works is confused and obscure. In 1883 *Quartetto* appeared, showing flashes of writing ability.

A period of historical and critical creativity now occupied Oriani, beginning with *Matrimonio e Divorzio* in 1886, a vigorous defense of the family conceived as the fundamental nucleus of a nation. *Fino a Dogali* (End at Dogali) in 1889 is a commentary on the massacre of the Italian forces at Dogali in the Italo-Abyssinian war of 1887. The most monumental work of this period, and certainly Oriani's major effort, is *La Lotta Politica in Italia* (The Political Struggle in Italy) published in 1892. Reconstructing three thousand years of Italian history, Oriani presents, in a discourse of continuously rising tone, the reasons for Italian unity. In this work an element of Oriani's claim to greatness is seen: he profoundly understood the problems of contemporary Italian life and strove with great sincerity to express them against the perspective of Italian history. His writing from this time on is an impassioned struggle against prevailing sentiments, but it never attracted a following or brought gain for Oriani during his lifetime.

For the next decade Oriani worked in the novel form. *Il Nemico* (The Enemy), published in 1894, is a book of crude passions and ostentatious cynicism which gave some indication of the forthcoming dissolution of the old Russian regime. The novels *Gelosia*

(Jealousy, 1894), *La Disfatta* (Defeat, 1896), *Vortice* (Vortex, 1901), and *Olocausto* (Holocaust, 1902), express the essence of the constricted and frustrating life of the provinces. The tortured *verismo* of these works causes their value to be much disputed; but there are spiritually rich passages in *Disfatta*, and *Vortice* is considered the peak of Oriani's narrative art.

He produced many works for the theatre which were as unpopular as his other writing, and in 1905 his final volume of narrative prose appeared, *Oro, Incenso, Mirra* (Gold, Incense, Myrrh).

His noblest work, *La Rivolta Ideale* (The Ideal Revolt), published in 1908, he called his spiritual testament. It is the last clash of his conscience with the social outlook of his time, affirming the necessity of a strong regulating state, the concept of liberty for the individual within the limits of social responsibility, and the morality of Christianity. Meanwhile his health and his will to do battle were rapidly declining. He died in the following year at his home, Cardello, a convert to Catholicism.

Oriani's position on divorce, his anti-socialist sentiments, his nationalism, and his approval of imperialism caused him to be extolled in the twentieth century as a prophet of the Fascist state. A thirty-volume definitive edition of his work, edited by Mussolini, was started in 1923 and completed in 1933. His family home was declared a national monument by the Fascists in 1924.

ABOUT: Pietrangeli, A. K. Alfredo Oriani: Life and Character. [In Italian—see studies by B. Buscema, F. Cardelli.]

E. DE P.

ORLÉANS, CHARLES D'. See CHARLES, DUKE OF ORLÉANS

ORSZÁGH, PAVOL. See HVIEZDO-SLAV

*ORZESZKOWA, ELIZA, née PAW-LOWSKA (May 25, 1841-May 18, 1910)
Polish novelist and short-story writer, was born in Milkowszczyzna and attended a typical school for upper-class girls in Warsaw. At sixteen she married an older man, Piotr Orzeszko, and settled down on her husband's estate which she soon had to leave after its confiscation by the Russian authorities after the 1863 uprising. Orzeszkowa later lived in

* ôr zĕsh kō' vä

Grodno and Wilno, writing and publishing. She died in Grodno.

In a large number of novels and short stories Orzeszkowa presented her views on most of the important contemporary problems. While the message of the author is usually quite clear in these works, they are not merely didactic in the vulgar sense. Orzeszkowa's epic talent and her sense of artistic balance made many of them works of great literary appeal. In the first group of Orzeszkowa's works are short stories and novels discussing the position of woman in society. Faulty education, lack of preparation for any useful work, and marriages arranged by families without regard for the woman's feelings, were problems which were presented with a great deal of realism, intellectual maturity, and courage in such novels as *Pamiętnik Wacławy* (Waclawa's Memoirs, 1871), *Pan Graba* (1872), *Marta* (1873), *Maria* (1876), etc. The novel *Marta*, which won Orzeszkowa the American Prize for a literary work on emancipation, is quite typical of this group. The basic motif here is the lot of a woman who marries early and after her husband's sudden death faces the problem of supporting herself. The author's personal experience gave these works an additional touch of realism.

In another group of novels Orzeszkowa took up the Jewish problem. The question of religious and national intolerance, ignorance, and hatred between groups of people bound to live together received frank and sensible treatment. The novels *Eli Makower* (1876) and *Meir Ezofowicz* (1878) are the best-known works of this group. *Meir Ezofowicz*, based on good factual knowledge, social wisdom, and moral conviction, was highly praised at home and abroad and was frequently translated. Perhaps somewhat less realistic but written in the same democratic and humanistic spirit are novels based on the lives of the Polish peasants. Of this group *Cham* (The Bore, 1889) is generally regarded as the major work. Patriotic themes occupy the most prominent position in Orzeszkowa's literary work.

The struggle for national survival, the danger of cultural Russification, the need for democratization of society were discussed in a long series of novels with great wisdom, tact, and courage. The answers given by Orzeszkowa may not have been satisfactory to all social groups, but they were provocative and respected. The novel *Nad Niemnem* (On the Banks of the River Niemen, 1889) of this group is usually regarded as Orzesz-

kowa's masterpiece. It is a broad picture of her native Polish-Lithuanian countryside with its estates and villages, internal social conflicts, and common struggle against the Russians. Realistic in details and romantic in spirit the novel has the makings of an epic. Though somewhat old-fashioned in literary technique Orzeszkowa's work is still readable, and in the development of Polish prose it occupies an important position.

English translations include: *Meir Ezofowicz*, translated by J. Curtin (1898); *The Argonauts*, translated by J. Curtin (1901); *The Interrupted Melody*, translated by M. Ochenkowska (1912).

Z. F.

*OSTROVSKY, ALEXANDER NIKOLAEVICH** (April 12, 1823-June 2, 1886), Russian playwright, was the creator of the Russian theatre of "byt," i.e., of life considered in its local and temporal aspects. His father was a Moscow government official, and Ostrovsky first went to a Moscow secondary school and then attended law courses at the University of Moscow. In 1843 he left the university without finishing the courses and became a government official at the Court of Equity and the Court of Commerce. Though Ostrovsky was not particularly interested in this type of work, in his plays he later used the atmosphere of the law courts and the middle class merchant milieu of Moscow. The complete isolation of this merchant milieu from other classes of society and its maintenance of some of the traditions of Old Russia gave Ostrovsky much material for his theatre.

In 1847 Ostrovsky read his first play, *Kartina Semeinovo Schastya* (A Picture of Family Bliss), in one of the literary salons of Moscow, and in 1849 Gogol heard his reading of *Bankrot* (The Bankrupt), later called *Svoi Lyudi Sotchiomsia* (It's All in the Family) and gave it his approval. From this period on, Ostrovsky had frequent difficulties with the censorship and with the Moscow merchants. He was, however, recognized from the very beginning and his name was likened to those of Griboyedov and Gogol whose play *Marriage* had had a great influence on him.

Ostrovsky left his governmental post in 1851 and subsequently gave a great deal of time to his writing. He wrote more than fifty plays in about forty years. All but eight were written in prose, the others in blank verse. Ostrovsky was also the author of some naturalistic prose, and he translated Cer-

* ŏs trŏf′ skĭ

OSTROVSKY

vantes, Shakespeare, and Goldoni. He became one of the editors of the monthly *Moskvitianin* (The Muscovite) and thus was associated with a Slavophile group. Ostrovsky later established the Society of Russian Playwrights and Opera Composers and was appointed Director of the Moscow Theatrical School and of the Repertory for the Moscow Theatre shortly before his death. His widow and his children were allotted a pension by Czar Alexander III.

Most of Ostrovsky's plays (with the exception of the historical ones) are satirical and realistic. The language of his protagonists is colloquial, idiomatic, and diversified (depending on social status, character, and dialect). His names for characters frequently point toward at least part of their main characteristics. Many of his titles are Russian proverbs or sayings. The predominant subject of his plays is a kind of conflict inherent in a patriarchal set-up. As a rule a younger member of the family challenges its fundamental values and is often crushed. Ostrovsky describes everyday life with its peculiar stagnant atmosphere characterized by the tyranny of the "samodur" (the petty, willful, and stupid tyrant). He writes of a society which is indifferent to cultural and moral values and many of his protagonists are rapacious, authoritarian, superstitious, and hypocritical. Psychologically they are not complex individuals, but types. Ostrovsky is more interested in the description of manners than in the exploration of psychological conflicts.

He has influenced many minor playwrights and even such major dramatists as Gorky, and is a precursor of the Chekhovian realistic drama in his peculiarly static slice-of-life technique. The greatest Russian actors of his time and some of the greatest theatre directors worked with his plays. He sketched his main personages lightly enough to permit the actors a considerable part in the creation of a character. Ostrovsky's sense of theatre was such that his plays dominated the Russian stage towards the end of the nineteenth and the beginning of the twentieth century, and have even been frequently produced in the U.S.S.R.

Among the best known of Ostrovsky's plays are *Groza* (The Thunderstorm, 1860) and *Les* (The Forest, 1871). In *Groza* the ardent and mystical Catherine, stifled in the atmosphere created by a tyrannical mother-in-law and a weak husband, takes a lover and is then driven to suicide by her remorse. This play in particular is a realistic commentary on the type of family relationships which had prevailed in certain Russian milieus which had not changed since the time of the "Domostroy" (a treatise on the ordering of a household written in 1566). In *Les* we see some slightly ridiculous but generous and good-natured actors whose unpretentiousness and love of liberty are opposed to the lack of human values in rich and hypocritical landowners. In both plays nature echoes some of the hidden human emotions and gives a certain poetic atmosphere to the otherwise realistic dramas. Other plays by Ostrovsky are *Na Vsiakovo Mudreza, Dovolno Prostoty* (Enough Simplicity in Every Wise Man, 1868), *Bespridanitza* (The Dowerless Girl, 1879), and *Sniegurotchka* (The Snow Maiden). The latter, the only fairytale that Ostrovsky wrote, inspired Tchaikovsky and Rimsky-Korsakov.

One of the greatest Russian critics of his time, N. A. Dobrolyubov, wrote two of his most famous articles, "A Kingdom of Darkness" and "A Ray of Light in the Kingdom of Darkness," as socio-literary criticism of Ostrovsky's plays. Turgenev has said of Ostrovsky that "In none of our writers does the Russian spirit blow with such force. . . ."

The complete works of Ostrovsky, *Polnoye Sobranie Sotchineniy*, edited by M. Pisarev, were published by Prosveshchenye, 1904-05 in ten volumes. Most of Ostrovsky's plays have been translated into English by G. Noyes (1917-27) and a few by D. Magarshack (London 1944).

ABOUT: [In Russian—see studies by N. Denisov, N. Dolgov, A. Revyakin.]

Y. L.

*PALACKÝ, FRANTIŠEK (June 14, 1798-April 26, 1876), Czech historian and political leader, was born in Hodslavice in Moravia, the son of a teacher in the local Protestant school. The father knew the Bible by heart, and his precocious son had read all of it by the age of five. At nine he was sent to a nearby town to study German and music, and at eleven to Protestant Latin school in Trenčín in Slovakia. Three years later he went on to the Protestant Lyceum in Bratislava, where he astonished his teachers with his knowledge of some twelve languages. He had intended to study theology, but philosophical study weakened his faith, and he turned to literature. His first published work was a Czech translation of Ossian; his original poetry, influenced chiefly by Klopstock, was not of much importance. In 1818 he met the young philologist Pavel Josef Šafařík, and the two collaborated on a theoretical treatise on Czech versification, published the same year. The next five years Palacký was employed as a tutor. In 1823 he published an historical survey of aesthetics, one of the first such written anywhere. He opposed the reigning influence of Kant and returned to Plato, identifying beauty with divinity. He projected a history of Czech literature, but never wrote it. After 1823 he virtually abandoned poetry and literary criticism for historical research.

In 1823 Palacký went to Prague, where he studied history under the great Czech scholar Dobrovský. The latter found him a position with the Count Šternberk, for whom he prepared a genealogy. Handsome, refined, a witty conversationalist and an accomplished pianist, Palacký had great success in Prague society. In 1827 he married Terezie Měchurová, the daughter of a wealthy lawyer and estate owner; he met her when the two performed at an amateur recital, she as a harpist. Though he married for love his father-in-law's fortune assured Palacký an independent existence. It influenced him in the direction of conservatism, however, and brought him some criticism from Czech patriots.

Palacký is the greatest Czech historian, the founder of modern Czech historiography. In 1832 he began his Czech history, a work to which he devoted most of the rest of his life. Published in five volumes as *Geschichte von Böhmen*, it appeared between 1836 and 1867, and in a Czech edition from 1848 to 1867. Several of the volumes were later revised.

* på′ låts kě

PALACKÝ

The history extends to the year 1526, when the Hapsburgs ascended the Bohemian throne. The work was based on a painstaking study of sources, and it has been estimated that the author studied some 50,000 documents.

Palacký conceived Czech history as a record of national defense against German and Austrian aggression. Though his view of Old Czech history is too romantic in its assumption of an early Czech national consciousness, still it provided a scholarly foundation for modern Czech political thought, and influenced the first president of Czechoslovakia, T. G. Masaryk.

Palacký also played a major role as political leader of his people. He worked for an autonomous Bohemia in which the nobility would dominate. He realized the weakness of Austria, but wrongly supposed that to maintain herself Austria would have to grant autonomy not only to the Hungarians (who received it in 1867), but also to the Slavs of the Empire. He did not want to destroy Austria entirely, however, and remarked, "If Austria had not existed, it would be necessary to invent her." But he lived to regret this policy and change his attitude toward Austria. As a practical politician Palacký served as deputy to the parliaments of Vienna and Kroměříž in 1848, and was leader of the party of the more conservative Czech patriots, later known as "Old Czechs." In the 1860's this rôle gradually passed to his son-in-law F. L. Rieger.

Palacký's conception of Czech history had great influence on modern Czech thought, though a few historians, such as Josef Pekař, countered his influence by trying to show the progressive character of Austrian-Catholic rule in Bohemia.

There is no translation of Palacký's work in English, but his history is widely available in German.

ABOUT: Lützow, F. Bohemia; Kutnar, F. Tři Studie o F. Palackém (with English summary). [In Czech—Pekař, J. František Palacký.]

W. E. H.

*PÁLSSON, GESTUR (September 25, 1852-August 19, 1891), Icelandic short-story writer, poet, and essayist, was born at Miðhús in Reykhólarsveit in the northwest of Iceland, the son of a well-to-do farmer. In 1875 Gestur graduated from the Latin School in Reykjavík and sailed for Copenhagen with the intention of studying theology. There, however, he became interested in literature, read widely of ancient and modern authors, and was especially influenced by Turgenev and by Georg Brandes, the Danish critic, whose subsequent memoir of him appears in Samlede Skrifter, III (1900).

Returning to Reykjavík in 1882, he was for a time in governmental work, then a freelance writer and the editor of the newspaper Suðri (1883-86). Completely unhappy in Iceland and disgusted by the resistance he encountered to his views on popular education, he migrated in 1890 to Canada, settling in Winnipeg. Through the influence of his friend Einar Hjörleifsson Kvaran (1859-1938) he became the editor of Heimskringla, the Icelandic language weekly in Winnipeg. He had been in Canada scarcely a year when he decided to return to Copenhagen as a journalist, but his plans were cut short by his sudden death in August 1891.

As might be expected of a disciple of Brandes, Pálsson was a realist. At times, in fact, his analyses of social conditions come very close to naturalism, since in order to portray the corruption of society as he saw it, he dwelt on the sordidness and hopelessness of the underprivileged. His pessimistic views were undoubtedly reinforced by reading Alexander Kielland (1849-1906), the Norwegian novelist. Most of Pálsson's writings reveal his firm conviction that society is cruel, that true education is impossible until conditions have been changed. This point of view is probably a reflection of Pálsson's personal experiences; an unfortunate love affair

during his student days colored his thinking for the rest of his life. Moreover, he was never able to reconcile satisfactorily his dreams of achievement and hopes of perfection with the frustrations and discouragements of actual life. Time and again he tried to overcome his pessimism and slough off the depression into which he continually sank, but he was never successful. This pessimism and his belief that men are merely unwilling and perhaps unknowing instruments of blind destiny and that nature is lying in wait to trap the unwary and to do away with him are clearly revealed in several of his short stories, e.g., "Sagan af Sigurði Formanni" (Iðunn, 1887) translated into English under the title of "The Tale of Sigurd the Fisherman" in Richard Beck's Icelandic Poems and Stories (1943).

Despite his pessimism and his irony, however, Gestur Pálsson had great talent. He wrote several good poems, a number of excellent short stories, of which "Kærleiks-heimilið" (The Home of Love) and "Til-hugalíf" (The Engagement) are representative, and many essays of considerable merit. One can only speculate how many works of real quality might have come from his pen had he been granted a longer life. His portrayal of human emotions, especially the thoughts that go through a man's mind when he is alone, cold, hungry, and despondent, reveal a sensitivity and penetration seldom found in so young a writer.

The works of Pálsson appeared in 1902 in Reykjavík under the title of Skáldrit sem til eru eftir Gest Pálsson; another edition was begun in Winnipeg the same year, but has not been completed. A third edition, Ritsafn (Collected Works), was published in Reykjavík in 1927. Although worthy evaluations of Gestur Pálsson and his works by his friends Jón Ólafsson and Einar Hjörleifsson Kvaran introduce the Reykjavík editions, no satisfactory biography of Pálsson has yet appeared. His short stories have been translated into many languages, especially German. A few have appeared in English, but have not been collected.

ABOUT: Einarsson, S. History of Icelandic Prose Writers 1800-1945.

L. B.

PALUDAN-MÜLLER, FREDERIK (called FRITZ) (February 7, 1809-December 28, 1876), Danish poet, was born on the Danish island of Fyn, in the town of Ker-

* poul' sòn

* păl' ŏŏ dăn mül' ĕr

699

teminde where his father, Jens Paludan-Müller, was a priest. His mother was Benedicte Rosenstand-Goiske. His brother was the later prominent historian and professor Caspar Paludan-Müller. Both parents were descendants of old families of clergymen and scholars. Several members of his mother's family had been insane, and she herself died mentally deranged in his childhood.

During his childhood and youth his family lived on Fyn and then in the town of Odense, but in 1835 his father became bishop at Aarhus in Jutland. In 1825 Frederik went to Copenhagen, and three years later he passed his entrance examination for the university. Here he studied law, and he completed his degree in 1835, but he never practiced law.

Frederik was an intelligent and witty young man, a favorite in social life and at balls, but under the gay surface lurked a nervous sensibility which easily passed into melancholy, a tendency inherited from his mother. The duality of his mind is reflected in his literary works which are either romantically imaginative or seriously realistic. Of the latter type is his long poem *Danserinden* (The Danseuse, 1833), a love story in verse, influenced by Byron and Pushkin's *Eugene Onegin.* Of the former type is *Amor og Psyche* (1834), a mythological lyric-dramatic poem about love and soul, influenced by his classical studies. Both works were enthusiastically received, especially by the younger generation.

Among the young ladies he admired at this time were his three cousins, daughters of Professor Caspar Abraham Borch at Sorø Academy. During a dangerous attack of typhus, the eldest of the sisters, Charite Louise Philippa, nursed him. In 1836 they were married. In order to give his sick nerves the rest they needed, his wife, who was seven years his senior, isolated him for the rest of his life from the surrounding world. They went on a honeymoon which lasted for two years and brought them to France and Italy. Upon their return, they made their home in Copenhagen and spent the summer at the beautiful Fredensborg in northern Zealand.

After his marriage, the nature of the imaginative part of Paludan-Müller's production changed from aesthetic to ethical-religious. He still preferred to use mythological and heroic themes, e.g., in *Venus* (1841), dealing with the contrast between the heavenly and earthly Venus and showing the poet's fresh impressions of the Italian nature, and in

Tithon (1844), in which the motif is taken from the Trojan legends and in which the poet travels in no-man's land between dream and reality. In *Dryadens Bryllup* (The Dryad's Wedding, 1844), the poet expresses his sorrow at leaving this world, and in the Biblical poem *Abels Død* (The Death of Abel, 1845), he crosses the borderline and deals with his loathing of the earthly world and his hope for eternity in the "garden of Paradise."

From the realm of mythology and legend, Paludan-Müller returned to reality and addressed himself to his contemporaries in his greatest work, *Adam Homo*, a verse novel in twelve pentameter cantos which appeared in three parts, 1841-48. It is a free description of his own life story which was meant to represent the history of mankind. The poet shows the superficial and futile nature of his hero's aesthetic desire for worldly glory at the expense of idealistic and spiritual values. The hero also sacrifices the pure selfless love of a woman, but eventually it is she, whose love has never died, who rescues him from perdition.

In 1854 Paludan-Müller published *Tre Digte* (Three Poems), which contained, besides *Abels Død*, two new dramatic poems, *Kalanus* and *Ahasverus.* In the former he again deals with the problem of the desire for and the denial of life, incarnated respectively by Alexander the Great and the Indian ascetic Kalanus. In the latter poem Paludan-Müller conceives the Eternal Jew as an enemy of culture and a preacher of repentance, who at the end of his journey is rewarded with the peace that only death can give.

During the years that followed, Paludan-Müller was a victim of a severe depression which made him incapable of work.

Extracts in English translation from *Adam Homo* appear in Howitt's book mentioned below, in M. Thomas, *Denmark, Past and Present* (1902), and elsewhere. *A Book of Danish Verse* contains extracts from *Danserinden, Adam Homo,* and *Ahasverus.* The story *Ungdomskilden* (1865) was translated by H. W. Freeland as *The Fountain of Youth* (1867).

ABOUT: Brandes, G. Creative Spirits of the Nineteenth Century; Gosse, E. W. Studies in the Literature of Northern Europe; Howitt, W. and M. The Literature and Romance of Northern Europe; Mitchell, P. M. A History of Danish Literature; Robertson, J. G. Essays and Addresses on Literature. [In Danish—see studies by V. Andersen, F. Lange, P. Linneballe, H. Martensen-Larsen, P. V. Rubow.]

A. J.

*PAOLI, BETTY (pseudonym of Barbara Elisabeth Glück) (December 30, 1814-July 5, 1894), Austrian poet and short-story writer, was born in Vienna, the daughter of a military physician who died during her childhood. Her mother, a Belgian, was left in comfortable circumstances, but lost her money in fruitless speculations by the time Betty was fifteen. In 1830 the daughter, who was strong-willed and self-reliant, became a governess in a distant Russian province, only to leave this position after a short time because of her mother's homesickness for Vienna. On the return trip her mother died, and Betty worked for several years as a governess for a Polish family. She stated later that despite her poverty and loneliness she never lost faith, for she was sustained by her writing. Her first poems appeared in a Prague newspaper in 1832 and thereafter in various literary journals.

In 1835 she returned to Vienna, where she supported herself by tutoring and by translating from French, Russian, English, and Italian. In 1841 she was engaged as a companion to the wife of the wealthy Viennese philanthropist Josef Werthheimer, and a few years later accepted a similar position with Princess Marianne von Schwarzenberg. In the cultural environment of these homes she met the leading Austrian and German writers of her time. Following the death of the princess in 1848, Betty traveled to Italy, France, and Germany, until in 1853 she settled in Vienna which she rarely left again. Although she suffered from a crippling paralysis during her last years, she remained mentally alert until her death in 1894 at Baden near Vienna.

Her first volume of poems, *Gedichte* (1841), which she dedicated to the poet Nikolaus Lenau, excited considerable enthusiasm in Austria. On the basis of this work and the collections entitled *Nach dem Gewitter* (1843) and *Romancero* (1845), Grillparzer hailed her as "the first lyricist of Austria." This judgment is supported by the English critic J. G. Robertson, who calls her "the most gifted lyricist in Vienna at the middle of the century." Her poems, which exhibit great mastery of form, reveal the influence of the German poets Schiller, Heine, Rückert, and Platen.

Betty Paoli possessed a vital, passionate temperament, and her lyrics, which are intense outpourings of her innermost thoughts and feelings, are aptly characterized by her statement: "I am but a heart, that has lived

* pä ō′ lē

and suffered much." An experience of fundamental importance to her writings was her love for a man who seemed unable to reciprocate her depth of passion. This discrepancy between the all-consuming love of a woman and the lesser love capacity of the male forms the principal theme of her unsuccessful *Novellen, Die Welt und Mein Auge* (3 vols., 1844), as well as of her greatest poems.

Of her later works the most significant are the volumes *Lyrisches und Episches* (1855) and *Neueste Gedichte* (1870). For many years she wrote theatre reviews for Viennese newspapers. Her essays were published in collected form in 1908 by J. Bettelheim-Gabillon under the title *Gesammelte Aufsätze.*

Betty Paoli is virtually unknown outside of Austria. A sample of her verse in English translation is contained in K. Knortz, *Representative German Poems* (1885).

ABOUT: Scott, A. A. Betty Paoli. [In German —see studies by H. Bettelheim-Gabillon and R. M. Werner.]

D. G. D.

*PARACELSUS (November 10, 1493-September 24, 1541), Swiss-German physician, is the adopted name of **PHILIPPUS AUREOLUS THEOPHRASTUS BOMBASTUS VON HOHENHEIM.** He invented the name, it is believed, to indicate his equality *(para)* with the ancient Roman physician Celsus. He is a half-legendary figure. On the evidence of the voluminous writings ascribed to him, we know that he was brilliant and influential, one of the most colorful and controversial of Renaissance thinkers. But details of his life are clouded and contradictory. Most contemporary accounts are either violently, and often foully, prejudiced against him or totally uncritical in their admiration. One can conclude only that he was neither as vicious and depraved as his enemies described him nor as brilliant as he described himself. Even in modern times opinion is divided on the question of whether he was a charlatan or a great man of science. Two things emerge as certain: he left his mark on sixteenth century thought, and he stimulated others to new and vastly significant discoveries.

He was born in Einsiedeln, in Switzerland, the seat of a Benedictine abbey and shrine, to Wilhelm von Hohenheim, the natural son of a nobleman of the house of Bombast, and Els Ochsner, of peasant ancestry. His father was a doctor and evidently introduced his son to the profession of medicine at an early

* păr á sĕl′ sŭs

PARACELSUS

PARACELSUS

age, taking the boy with him as he went round on his calls. His mother died while he was young. When he was about ten he moved with his father to Villach, in the Tyrol, a mining community, where he became interested in mining, the nature of minerals, and the occupational diseases of miners. Most of Paracelsus' education was of a practical nature, acquired not from books and lectures but from experience. The only teacher he is known to have studied under is Johannes Trithemius of Sponheim who had also been the teacher of Cornelius Agrippa. Paracelsus appears to have received a doctor of medicine degree at Ferrara or possibly at Vienna. The supposed extent of his travels lends color to the Paracelsus legend. He is reputed to have covered Europe from Spain and Italy to Sweden and Russia, to have been to Constantinople, Arabia, and Egypt, and to have been taken prisoner by the Tartars. He also is thought to have participated in the Venetian wars and served as an army surgeon in Denmark and the Netherlands.

In 1525 Paracelsus set up a medical practice in Salzburg, but he got into trouble with the authorities and had to leave hastily. This kind of experience became the unvarying pattern of his career. He went from city to city, made some friends and more enemies, and moved on again. But his impressive record as a doctor won him an appointment at the University of Basel in 1526. Here he began by offending the more staid members of the community with the announce-

ment that he and he alone would restore medicine from its barbarous state. He tossed his copies of Galen and Avicenna, the two principal medical authorities of the Middle Ages, into a public bonfire, took the revolutionary step of lecturing in German instead of Latin, and in general so shocked and alarmed his listeners that he soon won the epithet of a "medical Luther." The more cruelly he was attacked and lampooned, the more violently he lashed out against traditional ideas. His practical successes (he saved the famous printer Frobenius from a leg amputation and was admired and consulted by Erasmus) were forgotten, and early in 1528 he was obliged to flee from Basel and resume his wandering life.

In 1529 he was in Nuremberg, in 1530 in Beretzhausen and Regensburg, in 1531 in St. Gallen. During all this time, though he lived under trying conditions, he wrote busily. In 1536, then in Bavaria, he published his masterwork *Chirurgia Magna* (Great Surgery). This was followed two years later by the *Defensiones*, his plea in his own defense. In 1540, on the invitation of Archbishop Ernst, he settled in Salzburg and here, a year later, he died—according to his enemies of the consequences of drink and debauchery, according to his friends at the murderous hands of his enemies. Far more likely he died of a stroke, having been in declining health for some time. Three days before his death he made a will committing his soul to God and his few belongings to friends. He was buried in the churchyard of St. Sebastian. He had never married. Portraits show him as plump, blond, and effeminate looking in youth, but in later years he appears rather ascetic, lean, bald, with burning intense eyes.

Paracelsus did not make any startling medical discoveries, and his writings contain a considerable number of errors and superstitions. Nevertheless he was a spark in Renaissance thought. By abandoning blind adherence to medieval tradition and seeking answers in nature itself, he showed himself a pioneer in modern medical knowledge. This is not to suggest that he was in any sense a modern man of science. At the root of his thought was the Neoplatonism, Gnosticism, and Cabalism he had absorbed from his teacher Trithemius. He saw man as inseparable from the universe, a compound of mystic elements out of which all things are composed. His writings are full of the occult symbols of hermetic alchemy. A contemporary engraving shows him with his strange sword Azoth, concealed in the hilt of which were supposed to be secret mysterious drugs. But in the actual practice of medicine Paracelus seemed far ahead of his time. He introduced opium (in the form of laudanum) as a pain-killing drug, and the use of mercury, lead, sulphur, and iron as medicinal agents. He stressed the importance of cleanliness in the prevention and treatment of disease, and recognized the power of the mind and the imagination in disease (he has been called the founder of psychosomatic medicine).

Paracelsus' writings are not great works of literature. Not only were his concepts abstruse, but his German was opaque and obscure. He coined words freely, drawing on garbled Latin, German, and Swiss dialects, and anything that occurred to him. He was verbose and rhetorical. A false but not farfetched etymology connects his name Bombast with the quality of his writing. But Paracelsus was indifferent to the refinements of literary style. "My writings must not be judged by my language," he said, "but by my art and experience which I offer the whole world." The world had to accept him on his own terms. The first line of his Credo reads: "I am different, let this not upset you."

The restless, turbulent nature of the man has made him a fascinating figure to imaginative writers. He was a contemporary of the doctor on whose life the Faust-legend is thought to be based, and there were certainly Faustian qualities in Paracelsus, giving rise to at least one legend that as an old man he made a pact with the devil to regain his youth. The most famous literary treatment of him is Robert Browning's long dramatic poem *Paracelsus* (1835) in which he is represented as driven by his hunger for knowledge ("To search out and discover, prove and perfect") into failure and despair, but in the end dies with his faith in human perfectibility and in God restored:

> . . . If I stoop
> Into a dark tremendous sea of cloud,
> It is but for a time; I press God's lamp
> Close to my breast; its splendor, soon or late,
> Will pierce the gloom: I shall emerge one day.

The *Sämtliche Werke*, edited by K. Sudhoff and W. Matthiesson, was published in fourteen volumes, 1922-33. English translations include *Secrets of Physick and Philosophy*, by J. Hester (1633); *The Dispensary and Chirurgery* by "W.D." in 1656; *Supreme Mysteries of Nature* by R. Turner (1656). Other translations of his chemical and medical tracts were made in 1657, 1659, and 1661. *Hermetic and Alchemical Writings* translated by A. E. Waite was published in two volumes in 1894. *Four Treatises*

(with introductory essays by several hands) was edited by H. E. Sigerist (1941). *Selected Writings of Paracelsus,* edited by J. Jacobi, was translated into English in 1951.

ABOUT: Hargrave, J. Life and Soul of Paracelsus; Jacobi, J. *Introduction to* Paracelsus: Selected Writings; Pagel, W. Paracelsus; Sigerist, H. E. ed., *Introductory Essays in* Four Treatises; Stoddart, A. Life of Paracelsus. [In German—see studies by K. Aberle, I. Betschart, F. Gundolf, R. J. Hartmann, C. G. Jung, M. B. Lessing, F. Strunz.]

*PARDO BAZÁN, EMILIA** (September 16, 1852-May 12, 1921), Spanish novelist, short-story writer and critic, whose "versatility and fertility place her in Spain next to Pérez Galdós," was born of ancient stock in La Coruña, Galicia, the scene of so many of her important works. Between the ages of five and fifteen she had read the Greeks, the Bible, and *Don Quixote.* At sixteen she married Señor de Quiroga and moved to Madrid, where she lived for the rest of her life, although she spent much time traveling. At seventeen she wrote three essays: on Padre Feijóo, the enlightened Spanish priest of the eighteenth century; on the Christian epic poets Dante, Milton, Tasso, Hojeda, Klopstock, and Chateaubriand; and on Darwinism. In 1879 she wrote *Pascual López,* the life of a medical student; there followed a historical work on St. Francis of Assisi (1882). Her second novel *Un Viaje de Novios* contains a famous preface on naturalism in which she advocates the introduction into Spain of a modified form of French naturalism to complement the native Spanish realism. She advised closer observation of facts and the treatment of social problems. This she did in her own novels, although scrupulously avoiding the more sordid and repellent phases of life so prominently studied by the Goncourts and Zola.

In *La Cuestión Palpitante* (1883) Pardo Bazán discussed naturalism at greater length and although explaining her objections to the determinism, pessimism, and what she considered obscenity of the school of Zola, again urged the close study of real life. This book excited great controversy; one of her chief opponents, the novelist Juan Valera, attacked not only Zola's naturalism, but Doña Emilia's adherence to it. But Doña Emilia was far from being a mere "faddist." She retained her interest in contemporary life in her native Spain, and kept abreast of the latest developments in French and Russian literature.

Her next novel, *La Tribuna,* is the story of Amparo, a female worker in a tobacco fac-

* pär' thō bä thän'

703

tory and the leader of a group of revolutionists in 1868. *El Cisne de Vilmorta* (1885) is about a young poet who rejects the love of an unattractive schoolmistress and is in turn rejected by a young society woman. Doña Emilia's masterpiece is *Los Pazos de Ulloa* (1886), the study of the decay of country nobility in Galicia, centering on a young, depraved marquis, Don Pedro Moscoso, who is so bound to his servant-mistress that he neglects his wife and lets his estate run to seed. In its sequel *La Madre Naturaleza* (1887), the natural son of the marquis and his legitimate daughter, unaware of their relationship, commit incest. It is on these two novels that Doña Emilia's fame mainly rests; the first of the two has been called a "Galician *Wuthering Heights*."

Insolación (1889) was followed the same year by the touching *Morriña*, the tragic story of the love of a Galician servant-maid for her mistress' son. After this novel, Doña Emilia's world took another direction. Her later characters were motivated by loftier inspirations. In *Una Cristiana* (1890) and its sequel *La Prueba*, Carmina Aldao is persuaded by a priest to remain faithful to her aged husband. *La Piedra Angular* (1891) was influenced by the school of Lombroso and is the story of an executioner driven to suicide by his dreadful profession. There followed *Doña Milagros* (1894), *Las Memorias de un Solterón* (1896), *El Tesoro de Gastón* (1896), *El Saludo de las Brujas* (1898). *La Quimera* (1905) is the story of the frustrations and defeats of a Galician student who, before he dies of consumption, is converted to religious and artistic idealism. In her last two novels, *La Sirena Negra* and *Dulce Dueño* (1911), the novelist gives way to the mystic.

Her numerous short stories, often set in her native Galicia, are to be found in such collections as *Cuentos de Marineda, Cuentos Regionales,* and *Cuentos Nuevos.*

Pardo Bazán was an indefatigable and interesting conversationalist, distinguished and courteous in manner although physically unprepossessing. "She was extremely fat with expressive, vivacious eyes, a short forehead, a short neck, thick eyebrows, an energetic chin and fleshy lips." Her literary salon in Madrid was famous. In 1916 the chair of Romantic Literatures was created for her at the Central University of Madrid.

English translations include *Russia, Its People and Its Literature* translated by F. H. Gardiner (1890); *A Christian Woman,* by M. A. Springer (1891); *Mystery of the Lost Dauphin, Louis XVII,* by A. H. Seeger (1906); *Midsummer Madness,* by A. Loring (1907); *Son of the Bondwoman,* by E. H. Hearn (1908). Mary J. Serrano translated several novels—*Homesickness (Morriña)* (1891), *The Swan of Villamorta* (1891), *A Christian Woman* (1891), *A Wedding Trip* (1891), *The Angular Stone* (1892), *The Galician Girl's Romance* (1900).

ABOUT: Brown, D. F. The Catholic Naturalism of Pardo Bazan; Glascock, C. C. Two Modern Spanish Novelists: Emilia Pardo Bazán and Armando Palacio Valdés; Hilton, R. "Doña Emilia Pardo Bazán, Neo-Catholicism and Christian Socialism" *in* The Americas, July 1954. [In Spanish —see studies by C. Bravo-Villasante, G. Brown, E. González López.]

M. N.

*****PARINI, GIUSEPPE** (May 23, 1729-August 15, 1799), Italian didactic poet, was born in the Milanese village of Bosisio, on Lake Pusiano, poetically entitled the "vago Eupili." His father, Francesco Maria Parino, was a silk merchant, and the proprietor of a small farm.

At the age of ten Giuseppe was sent to Milan to study at the Accademia Arcimboldi operated by the Barnabite fathers. In Milan he lived with his great-aunt, the widow Lattuada. The school register carried his name from 1740 to 1752 as a student of average scholastic attainment. In 1741 he received a meager inheritance upon the death of his great-aunt, which he eked out by tutoring to complete his education. More from necessity than inclination, he turned to ecclesiastic life and took holy orders in the Roman Catholic church on June 14, 1754, in Milan. In 1752 he had published in Milan a small volume of verse under the pseudonym "Ripano Eupilino." The book was received with great favor and secured his admittance to the Milanese literary world. The most distinguished group of Milanese literati, the Accademia dei Trasformati, had been flourishing since 1743 under its sponsor, Count Imbonati. As a member of the group, Parini met such notables as Gian Carlo Passeroni, Count Pietro Verri, and Canon Giuseppe Agudio di Malgrate who was later to be his benefactor. He also became widely known as a result of two controversies, one with Alessandro Bandiera and the other with Onofrio Branda, over literary issues of the day. Branda had been Parini's teacher of rhetoric at the Accademia Arcimboldi, and both men were fellow-members of the Trasformati.

As a priest and a promising young poet, Parini was received into the Milan home of Duke Serbelloni to tutor his first-born son.

* pä rē′ nē

PARINI

Through his patron, the Austrian pleni-potentiary Count Firmian, he obtained an appointment in 1769 as professor of belles lettres at the Palatine School, Brera, Italy, where he taught for about thirty years. In this post he became known as one of the most distinguished lecturers in the humanities. After the Academy of Fine Arts was opened in Brera in 1776, students at that institution also heard Parini.

During the occupation of Milan by French forces after 1795, Parini was appointed a municipal magistrate by Napoleon. He retired voluntarily shortly after the appointment, however, to resume his literary life. At the time he was at work on *Il Vespro* (Evening) and *La Notte* (Night), continuations of the earlier satires. These were published posthumously in 1801. In these later years Ugo Foscolo (see sketch above) came to Milan and became a friend of the aging Parini, who was growing blind and infirm. He died in Milan.

A commemorative bust was erected over the doorway at Brera, sculptured by Franchi, and a statue by Monti was placed on the stairway at Brera in 1838. A national monument to Parini, erected in Milan in 1899, was the work of Luigi Secchi.

Il Giorno is Parini's masterpiece. In it is revealed the decadent state of the eighteenth century Italian nobility, slavishly devoted to the rituals of fashion. Parini uses these conditions to teach the great moral lesson that emphasis on form, when linked with insipidity of content, is utterly meaningless. His moral indignation and his capacity to point up the ironies of his age are what make his work as a satirist both sad and profound. And these qualities provide the inspiration for greater poets who followed Parini: Foscolo in his *Sepolcri*, Monti in his *Feroniade*, and Leopardi in his *Sera del Dì di Festa*. Other works include about twenty *Odi* (Odes) written between 1757 and 1795, considered among the classics of Italian poetry. A prose discourse, *Dialogo sopra la Nobilità* (Dialogue on the Nobility), written in 1757, is a lively discussion between two corpses, a nobleman and a plebeian poet. This was a popular device of the day imitative of Fénelon. Parini also wrote *Principi delle Belle Lettere* (Principles of Belles Lettres), published posthumously.

In this capacity he continued as a member of the household for six years, and thereafter he maintained his friendship with the cultured and lovely Duchess Serbelloni. Living in the Duke's home, and frequenting other homes of the nobility in Milan, Parini became acutely aware of the frivolity and profligacy which characterized that class. Little by little he was transformed from an observer into a critic of what he saw. From these observations came his great work, *Il Giorno* (The Day), a satirical study in verse. The first two parts of this work were *Il Mattino* (The Morning), published in 1763, followed by *Il Meriggio* (Midday) in 1765. These were ironic instructions to a young nobleman on how to spend his time.

Parini's popularity and influence were established by these works, and their publication made him more secure financially for a short time. Previously, while still a member of the Serbelloni household, he had had to ask help of the Canon Agudio for his ailing mother, who died in 1762. Subsequent editions of *Mattino* were pirated widely, and Parini was often dependent on his benefactors Agudio, Imbonati, and others.

The actress and ballerina Teresa Angiolini Fogliazzi, who loved him, helped him to obtain assignments in the theatre. He wrote the libretto for *Ascanio in Alba* in 1771, set to music by Mozart, to celebrate the marriage of the Archduke Ferdinand and Maria d'Este. He also edited the *Gazzetta di Milano* for a year in 1768.

E. Bellorini edited Parini's *Prose* (2 vols., 1913-15) and *Poesie* (2 vols., 1929). The *Opere* (ed. G. Mazzoni) appeared in 1925; a new edition was begun in 1951.

Selections from *The Day* were translated into English verse by W. D. Howells in 1887; "The Toilet of an Exquisite"; "The Lady's Lap-Dog"; "The Afternoon Call." In 1927 H. M. Bower translated *The Day* into English blank verse.

ABOUT: [In Italian—see studies by E. Bellorini, R. Braccesi, G. Carducci, G. Mazzoni, D. Petrini.]

E. DE P.

*PARNY, ÉVARISTE DÉSIRÉ DE FORGES, Vicomte de** (February 6, 1753-December 5, 1814), French poet, born in Réunion, was raised in Creole surroundings and sent at the age of nine to the Collège in Rennes, an atmosphere which he found dull and prisonlike. Feeling a religious vocation, he entered the Saint-Firmin seminary, but after eight months left it for a military career in which he found ample time for diversions. With Bertin, in 1770, he founded the "Ordre de la Caserne," a group of soldiers dedicated to music, poetry, and good fellowship who, among their projects, included walks in the countryside. During a short sojourn in Réunion, in 1773, he had an affair with a young girl ("Éléonore") who inspired part of his poetry. In 1778 Parny published his *Érotiques*, widely praised as a masterpiece well into the next century, especially by Sainte-Beuve and for the parts devoted to Éléonore, which created about the poet a legend, comparable to that of Saint-Preux in Rousseau's *La Nouvelle Héloïse*, of the lover-hero in his despair.

Parny's early aristocratic attitudes changed gradually, yielding to revolutionary ideas. The first strong evidence of this evolution was his *Épître aux Insurgents de Boston* (1777). During the Revolution, having been financially ruined by events, he took an active rôle in various administrative posts and lived in relative indigence. His anti-religious tract *La Guerre des Dieux* (1799) excluded him from the favors of Napoleon, but was widely admired by freethinkers and, as reconciliation with the Church was forgotten, he was elected to the Institute. Parny's inauguration, in 1803, was a literary event of considerable notoriety, both in the extent of admiration for his poetry and for the scandal of *La Guerre des Dieux*. A happy marriage guaranteed a calm existence during his last years, which he devoted to frequenting intellectual circles of well-known protectors of the arts and to an active interest in younger writers. He died widely esteemed, having prepared a definitive edition of his works in 1808; his disciple Tissot composed the first complete biography.

* pàr nē′

The poems that Parny devoted to Éléonore skillfully organize a long adventure which is appealing for its simple and direct sensuality, free from the social artifices of Paris. The sentimental appeal of the story itself rises from the mystery of the love story and the legends it constructed about the personal life of the author, of his supposed visit to Réunion in 1778 when he found Éléonore married, and of her discovery in Brittany at the turn of the century. In new editions after 1778 Parny retouched his poems to focus attention on her, render the tone more serious, and follow the currents of taste. His Book IV (1781) surpasses the rest in artistry and in the sincerity of the suffering and despair. Here one finds the origins of early French romantic elegiac moods: the poet abandons wit and cynicism, the rhetoric of obscure threat and sinister apparitions, the subjects of moon and mountain, for confidential expression of a pagan melancholy inspired especially by Tibullus. Chateaubriand knew his poems by heart; Lamartine was influenced by them in his first period; and Sainte-Beuve singled them out for close attention.

Parny's *Œuvres* appeared in five volumes in 1808; in the edition of 1862 one finds further occasional pieces and other writings.

ABOUT: [In French—Barquissan, R. Les Poètes Créoles du 18e Siècle; Potez, H. L'Élégie en France; Sainte-Beuve, C. A. Portraits Littéraires.]

F. J. C.

*PASCAL, BLAISE** (June 19, 1623-August 19, 1662), French mathematician and mystic, was born in Clermont. His father, Étienne, descendant of an old family ennobled by Louis XI, was a magistrate whose reputation as a physicist extended far beyond the circles he frequented. At the death (in 1626) of his wife, Antoinette Bégon, known for her intelligence and kindness, he took upon himself the education of his three children: the sickly Blaise and the sisters Gilberte and Jacqueline, the latter a six-year-old prodigy who was to play an important rôle in Blaise's life. Étienne, thinking assimilation of knowledge more important than rapid learning, excluded completely from his program the study of languages until twelve, and of mathematics until sixteen. Despite his ideas, his son, at twelve, is said to have rediscovered, while playing with sticks, that the sum of the angles of a triangle is equal to two right angles. Startled by this, Étienne yielded and introduced the boy to geometry.

* pàs kàl′

PASCAL

Soon Blaise took his place in scientific discussions at his father's home, and, at sixteen, produced his *Essai sur les Coniques,* a study of conic sections. Meanwhile, Jacqueline's budding poetic talent aroused the admiration of Corneille with whom she had studied in Rouen, when her father was sent there by Richelieu to re-establish order (1639).

Pascal worked on a calculating machine (1642-52) which taught him how to struggle not only with theory but also with concrete reality ("theory and art"). Although a perfectionist in search of the absolute, he was concerned with scientific glory and financial success as well, for he was not devoid of practical sense, as witness his pride and anger at a watchmaker's imitation of his machine. These concerns, of course, left little room for religious preoccupations.

He and his family had taken religion for granted until 1646, when two Jansenist noblemen came to live with them and to care for Étienne who had been a victim of an accident. They converted Pascal by their behavior and conversation. He, in turn, persuaded his family to revise their religious views and to turn to mystic faith. Yet Pascal could not bring himself to abandon science for God. Despite his ill-health, he continued Torricelli's experiments on vacuums, and proved, in 1648, with his famous experiment, that the myth of nature's "abhorrence of a vacuum" was explained by atmospheric pressure.

After their father's death (1651), Jacqueline finally triumphed over her brother's op-position and took the veil. Pascal, overworked and depressed, is said to have found "diversion," recommended by doctors, in a "mundane" life marked by his friendship with the Chevalier de Méré, a disciple of Montaigne, who introduced him to relativist thinking, to the art of persuasion, and to the "esprit de finesse," a direct and intuitive apprehension of reality. Meanwhile, Pascal finished his *Traité sur l'Équilibre des Liqueurs,* and, pursuing his study of conic sections, founded the science of probabilities. This "mundane" period did not last long; as early as 1653 Pascal sensed its vanity.

After a period of meditations and prayers, torment and despair, during which Jacqueline, his confidant, encouraged him, Pascal experienced during the famous night of November 23, 1654, an ecstasy, the account of which he carried sewn in his coat lining until his death. Having resolved to forget "the world and everything save God," he left Paris in 1655 for Port-Royal to live with the *solitaires* and to humbly worship in his cell the God "not of the philosophers, but of Abraham, Isaac, and Jacob."

In 1656, at the request of the theologian Arnauld, whom the Sorbonne was attacking, he wrote a series of eighteen anonymous "letters," the *Provinciales,* by a Parisian to an imaginary friend living in the provinces, (hence the title). The first three and the last two deal with divine grace; the fourth serves as a transition from theology to morals; and the following twelve are a bitter satire on the "convenient" principles of the casuistic Jesuits, who are depicted in a sinister, though comic, light. A perfectionist, Pascal rewrote the letters many times. As a result the abstract and technical theological controversy became a masterpiece of journalistic writing with concrete characters whose ridicule destroyed the very arguments they put forth. Yet under the irony can be felt the emotion of the rigorist and the mystic, indignant at the abuses of the politicians. Claiming orthodoxy, he also defended Port-Royal's views on divine grace, arguing that the will of God is the source of man's salvation, the will of man his damnation. He maintained that grace was granted only to a chosen few. Unlike Calvin, he avoided heresy by claiming that the elect were always free to resist grace, but did not always want to.

At the same time he conceived of writing an *Apology of the Christian Religion* to persuade the skeptics, and was encouraged in this project when a niece of his, a student at Port-Royal, was miraculously cured of an eye disease by touching a thorn from the crown of Jesus. He had abandoned the sciences but returned to them when his friends urged him to continue his research, persuading him that scientific success would be of help to his *Apology*. He organized many scientific contests among European mathematicians. His fame increased, while his religious enthusiasm diminished.

In 1659, however, a serious illness brought him back deeper into the fold, and until his death he led an ascetic life of prayers and devotion to the poor. In 1661, during the agitation against the Jansenists, he opposed Arnauld and Nicole who had finally signed the condemnation of Jansenius, and, saddened by Jacqueline's death and the coolness of his friends, he sought still greater solitude until death.

Although as early as 1658 he had exposed, in a three-hour lecture, a plan for his *Apology*, the bundles of posthumous papers on which he had jotted his thoughts suggested no apparent order to his editors who finally published them, as they were, under the title of *Pensées sur la Religion* (1669). Critics thereafter attempted to reconstitute his original plan and to re-edit the book. Modern criticism believes that there were twenty-seven bundles forming twenty-seven series, each dealing with a central idea such as *vanity, order, misery*, etc. Although Pascal's plan must have followed some progression, a rational deductive system is not to be sought, since his *Pensées* revolve around a center, God, toward which everything converges. It may seem contradictory that someone who believed in divine grace would write such an apology. Indeed, he meant only to move those skeptics who would have received grace had they been "prepared." His *Pensées*, therefore, do not attempt to prove the existence of God rationally, but to shake the indifference of man by showing him the sterility of an abstract Cartesian God, of contemplation of silent nature ("the eternal silence of the infinite spaces frightens me"), and by inviting man to consider himself in his true light: great, because he is the only being in the universe who can reflect upon his condition; miserable, because this condition is miserable—man is an "incomprehensible monster" caught between two mysterious extremes, the infinitely large and the infinitely small. Reason—if all terms are defined, if only evident facts are used, and definitions substituted for the defined words—can arrive at certain truths, but they are limited. Our "instruments" are too crude to pinpoint justice and truth: our limited senses betray reason, just as reason betrays them by prejudice; imagination is a dangerous deceiver because of its inconsistency; human morals and justice are relative; how, then, can man know truth and understand himself? He is the victim of illusions and self-love, and constantly plays a rôle in this grotesque world, seeking movement and substitutes for happiness, lest he become aware of his nothingness which is intolerable. Hence man without God is miserable. Philosophers will not bring him satisfaction, nor will other religions. Only the Christian religion testifies to the greatness of man and to his misery (original sin), offering him an all-powerful God, an absolute, found only through humility. Let the skeptic turn to this God. He has nothing to lose and all to gain, declares Pascal, in his famous argument of the "wager," whose main purpose is to bring about the skeptic's temporary acceptance of the Christian attitude so that he may be able to judge it from within and accept, enlightened by grace, the many proofs that religious history offers (prophecies, miracles, and the Son of God). In the last analysis, however, "it is the heart that feels God, and not reason," the heart understood as an order higher than reason rather than as its complement or substitute.

The geometric precision of the *Pensées*, their powerful emotion, and their cosmic imagery, make of them a kind of poetry. It is not astonishing that all thinkers concerned with man and the infinite have turned to the one who, seeking to explain the infinity and unity of God, conceived, two hundred years before Einstein, "an infinite and indivisible object, a point moving everywhere with infinite speed; for it is one in all places, and a whole in each place."

The standard edition of the *Œuvres* was published in fourteen volumes in 1904-14 and reissued in 1936. A five-volume *Bibliographie Générale des Œuvres de Pascal* by A. Maire was published in 1925-27. In 1962 the tercentenary of Pascal's death was observed with the publication of new editions of his writings, including one of the *Provinciales* by Abbé Jean Steinmann, and a Pascal exhibition at the Bibliothèque Nationale. Pascal's works have often been translated into English. Among the more recent translations see the Modern Library Edition (1941) and, for a bilingual edition of the *Pensées*, H. F. Stewart's (1950).

ABOUT: Bishop, M. Pascal, The Life of Genius; Mortimer, E. Blaise Pascal: The Life and Work of a Realist; Stewart, H. F. Pascal's Apology for Religion; Times Literary Supplement, December 28, 1962. [In French—Béguin, A. Pascal par Lui-même; Chaigne, L. Pascal; Steinmann,

J. Pascal. See also the papers commemorating the tercentenary of Pascal's death, published in La Table Ronde, No. 171 (April 1962).]

M. B.

*PASCOLI, GIOVANNI (December 31, 1855-April 6, 1912), Italian poet, was the fourth of nine children born to Ruggero and Caterina Vincenzi Alloccatelli. His native village was San Mauro Romagna in the province of Forlì, but his childhood home was the estate of the Torlonia family—la Torre—where his father was the steward. These happy years were early marred by tragedy. Two younger sisters died before Giovanni was ten, and in 1867 his father was murdered by a highway assassin on the way home from a business trip. The widow and orphans, receiving a pension from Prince Torlonia, took refuge in their small home in San Mauro. But the deaths continued: in the following year, Margherita, the eldest sister, of typhoid; then the heartbroken mother, and in the next eight years two older brothers and young Giovanni's childhood sweetheart.

Pascoli won a scholarship in 1873 which enabled him to study under Carducci at the University of Bologna. But in these years of spiritual despair and demoralization he turned away from his studies and involved himself instead with the many revolutionary movements in Bologna clamoring for social reform. As a result of these activities Pascoli forfeited his scholarship and, in 1879, was imprisoned by the government as a revolutionary. The four-month period in jail had a tempering and maturing effect. He resumed his studies, receiving his degree in 1882, and immediately afterward was named professor of Greek and Latin letters in the lycée at Matera. Two years later, transferred in the same capacity to Massa, he took his two younger sisters from their boarding convents and re-established the family. Here begins the idyllic history of fraternal and sisterly devotion which he pictured in many poems.

Under the Italian professorial system, teachers went wherever they were assigned. From 1887 to 1895 Pascoli taught at Leghorn. In the poems gathered in the first edition of Myricae (Tamarisks) in 1892 some of the tenderness and melancholy of those years is felt. In that same year Veianus was published, winning for Pascoli the first of fourteen gold medals in the Latin poetry contest at Amsterdam. His talent, in Latin

* päs′ kō lē

and the vernacular, was quickly recognized. His teaching assignments continued, at Bologna from 1895 to 1897, at Messina from 1897 to 1903, and then at Pisa, from which he was recalled to Bologna in 1905 to take the chair of Italian literature as Carducci's successor. Henceforth he divided his time between scholastic duties in Bologna and his poetry at home in Castelvecchio. This home, the first since the days of la Torre, he had purchased in 1895 by the sale of his poetry medals. Located far up the valley of the Serchio among the Tuscan mountains, Pascoli lived a happy existence with his sister Maria and his dog Gulì, occasionally receiving such friends as D'Annunzio and Puccini. From the intimate affectionate atmosphere of Castelvecchio come Pascoli's most characteristic volumes, Canti di Castelvecchio (Songs of Castelvecchio) in 1903, Poemi Conviviali (Convivial Poems) in 1904, the definitive edition of Myricae in 1905, and a series of Poemetti from 1904 to 1909. In 1911, to celebrate the fiftieth anniversary of Italian independence he wrote Inno a Roma (Hymn to Rome), a stately poem in Latin and Italian. Later that year he fell ill and died in Bologna the following spring. His sister Maria selected for his tomb a little chapel near the home in Castelvecchio he had loved.

Pascoli was Carducci's successor not only in the professorship at Bologna but in spirit as well. He was moved by the same themes that inspired Carducci—patriotism, nature, art, the past—and by a few other things that Carducci hated—the romantic spirit, Christianity, the minutiae of existence, about which he could speak with a tenderness that escaped Carducci's robust art. In the reaction against romanticism which developed in Italy after 1870, and which is represented on the one hand by Carducci's Odi Barbare and on the other by Stecchetti's Postuma, Pascoli's lyric occupies still another place. The nature and value of his poetry are most clearly defined in his own literary manifesto, the delightful essay Il Fanciullino (The Child, 1907). Its core statement is that the poet's world is the child's world. The concept of the fanciullino, with his need to have names for things and his capacity for total recall, influenced Pascoli's language. At the time Italian poetry was still bound to a traditional poetic vocabulary. Specific words and names familiar in prose usage were largely excluded. The study and use of many current vocabularies was urged upon young poets by De Amicis in L'Idioma Gentile in 1905, but the theory was bitterly attacked by Benedetto Croce. Pascoli did much to advance a more flexible language with his range of poetic subjects: he describes the life of the countryman in the Romagna; he expresses himself on the plight of the Italian emigrant; he dips into classical antiquity; he celebrates events of the recent Italian past. To all these statements he brings the impact of his own diverse background, Latinist in education, socialist and humanitarian in belief. He is still considered among the first of minor poets.

The collected Italian and Latin poems of Pascoli were published in ten volumes from 1912 to 1938, and an edition of the Italian poems appeared in 1939. The first English translation of his poems was by Anne Simon in *Poet Lore* in 1916. Evaleen Stein did a free rendition into English verse in 1923. A. M. Abbott translated *Poems of Giovanni Pascoli* in 1927, and *Selected Poems,* edited by G. S. Purkis was published in 1938.

ABOUT: Amram, B. Giovanni Pascoli; Phelps, R. S. Italian Silhouettes; Anglo-Italian Review, 1919; Yale Review, 1913. [In Italian—see studies by P. Bianconi, B. Croce, J. De Blasi, A. Pompeati, A. Zamboni.]

E. DE P.

PEGUILHAN, AIMERIC DE. See AIMERIC DE PEGUILHAN

*PEIRE VIDAL (fl. 1175-1215), Provençal lyric poet, is said to have been the son of a farrier of Toulon. He had a good reputation as a singer but most of the stories in his *vida*, or biography, are concerned with his mad exploits in society. According to one such story, "a certain knight of St. Giles caused his tongue to be cut out because he made believe that he was his wife's lover but Sir Hugh de Baux caused him to be healed of his hurt." He is also said to have brought back from Cyprus a Greek wife whom he believed to be the niece of the Emperor of Byzantium and from then on to have behaved as if he were the Emperor. Among the many ladies whom he loved was Azalais (Adelaide), wife of Barral of Marseilles, a great patron of troubadours. This lady he is alleged to have kissed while she was asleep in her chamber, and although the husband laughed at the incident, Azalais insisted on the poet's exile. Vidal then spent some time with Richard I of England but later returned to Marseilles when Azalais agreed to pardon him. Vidal was acquainted with most of the great patrons of literature of his time. For Raymond V of Toulouse he seems to have had a

* pĕr vē dàl'

particular affection and mourned his death extravagantly, cutting off the ears and tails of his horses and letting his nails and beard grow. He ceased his mourning only at the personal request of Alfonso II of Aragon. Another of his ladies was the so-called "Loba" of Pernautier. The name means "she-wolf" and for her sake he is said to have dressed himself as a wolf and allowed himself to be hunted by shepherds and their dogs. Badly mauled, he was tended by the lady, who found the incident highly amusing.

This story, like most of the others attached to his name, is founded on names or chance remarks in his poetry. For example, his use of the adjective "imperial" to mean "glorious" may very well have given rise to the anecdote of his pretensions to the imperial title. The information about his visits to numerous courts in Southern France, Italy, and Spain is much more reliable. Vidal's poetry contains more elements of self-portraiture than that of almost any other troubadour and this accounts for the detailed biographies which are extant. About fifty of his poems survive, of which about half are *canzos* or formal love songs. The minor forms, the *alba* or dawn song, the *pastourelle*, or rustic love poem, and the *planh*, or lament, are completely absent, and rather surprisingly, Vidal did not write any crusading songs. His *canzos* are sometimes in the grand manner of serious courtly love, sometimes in a more playful vein *(canzos gaios)*, whose naïveté almost approaches that of folk song. He loved to praise his native country of Provence and his metaphors show acute observation of life. Vidal did not often attempt the excessive virtuosity in rhyme and meter of many of his contemporaries, and although he occasionally practices the elaborate imagery of the *trobar ric*, his style is usually simple. He was fond of the *sirventes*, or poem of comment on life, sometimes combining it with the *canzon*, and in it he lashed out at contemporary personages, great and small, with considerable freedom. He particularly hated the German emperor Henry VI and all his countrymen. Peire Vidal was among the most gifted and interesting of all the troubadours.

Les Poésies de Peire Vidal was edited by Joseph Anglade (1913). A selection appears in T. Hill and T. G. Bergin, *Anthology of the Troubadours* (1941); in modern French, selections in A. Jeanroy, *Anthologie des Troubadours* (1927) and Georges E. Dessaignes, *Les Troubadours* (1946).

ABOUT: Valency, M. In Praise of Love. [In German—see studies by K. Bartsch, S. Schopf.]

W. T. H. J.

*PELETIER DU MANS, JACQUES
(July 25, 1517-July 1582), French poet,
grammarian, scientist, was born in Le Mans
into a well-to-do bourgeois family. A typical
Renaissance man, with an insatiable curiosity
for learning, he studied mathematics and
philosophy under his brother at the Collège
de Navarre. He then moved capriciously from
college to college, often as their principal,
and was professor of mathematics at the
University of Poitiers.

He began his poetic career by translating
Horace's *Ars Poetica* (1545): in the preface
he recommended, four years before Du Bellay's manifesto, the use of the national language in poetry. This translation was soon
followed by a collection of lyrical odes (*Vers
Lyriques*, 1547), to which he prefaced translations from Virgil, Horace, Homer, and
Petrarch, and in which he attempted to equal
these models. In 1555 he rejuvenated Petrarchan poetry in his *Amour des Amours* by
introducing philosophy and science. The first
part, a song of "naïve and simple" love, is
said to have been inspired by Louise Labé;
in the second part, the poet rises to a more
"universal and general" Love, synonym of
God and of the Creation, which he celebrates
by describing the physical universe (the planets, the atmosphere, the sun, etc.) in an elevated tone, reminiscent of Lucretius. He
thought his descriptions to be true and beautiful, since poetry is of divine origin, as he
claimed in his *Art Poétique* (also of 1555),
which is a detailed but moderate reformula-
tion of the principles of the Pléiade. In this
important work, Peletier delineates the rôle
of inspiration and that of art: both are com-
plementary and equally important, and he
insists on the dangers of too servile an imitation. The poet is encouraged to use the
alexandrine verse and "rich" rhymes, and
to observe rhythm. His works were printed
according to a new and bold orthographic
system based on pronunciation (cf. his *Dialogue de l'Ortografe e Prononciacion Fran-
çoese*, 1550). Peletier was also the author of
treatises on medicine, algebra, and geometry.

Although Peletier had many admiring
friends, among them Ronsard, whom he influenced a great deal and who paid him many
a poetic compliment, he was somewhat withdrawn and solitary, preoccupied until his
death with the absolute, which he longed for
so ardently: witness his very last verse, a
prayer for the return to the "Whole, both
Circle and Center" whence he had come.

* pĕl tyă′ dü män′

Modern editions of the writings of Peletier
include the *Œuvres Poétiques,* by L. Séché (1904),
L'Amour des Amours, by A. Van Bever (1926), and
L'Art Poétique, by A. Boulanger (1930).

ABOUT: [In French—Jugé, C. Jacques Peletier
du Mans; Schmidt, A. M. La Poésie Scientifique
en France au 16ᵉ Siècle; Italica, XXXIV (1959).]

M. B.

*PELLICO, SILVIO (June 21, 1789-Jan-
uary 31, 1854), Italian prose writer and
dramatist, was born in the picturesque Piedmont town of Saluzzo some thirty miles
southwest of Turin. His father was a civil
servant, his mother one of the Tourniers of
Chambéry, a southern French town noted for
silk manufacture. Silvio had a twin sister,
Rosina, who was very beautiful, and two
other brothers and sisters. The parents were
cultivated and religious people, and the happy
devoted family relationships they nurtured
left an impression on Silvio's work and life.
In the political unrest of the period the father
lost his position and turned for a while to
silk manufacture, but was subsequently restored to office. He had tutors for his children at home in Turin and later in Milan.
Silvio's twin married at eighteen a silk merchant of Lyons and Silvio went with them
to Lyons where he resided for four years
studying French literature. On his return to
Milan he became professor of French literature in the Collegio degli Orfani Militari.
Milan at this time was the capital of the
Cisalpine Republic. With patriotic ardor Pellico joined the intellectual life of the city,
where Foscolo was then producing his controversial play *Ajax,* and where Monti and
other writers were active in the service of
the republican government.

Pellico's first tragedy, *Laudamia,* was
praised by Foscolo himself. The popularity
of his second tragedy, *Francesca da Rimini,*
produced in Milan in 1818, lasted for half a
century. Pellico was increasingly caught up
in the resistance to Austrian domination following the Congress of Vienna and the restoration of Austrian rule. Working as secretary to Counts Porro and Confalionieri, he
was the able manager of the *Conciliatore,* a
publication which sought to weaken, by indirect educational means, Austria's despotic
hold on Italy. But the paper was censored
after only a year of publication. Upon publication of Pellico's tragedy *Eufemio di Messina,* presentation of the work was forbidden
by the government. In October 1820, with his
friend Pietro Maroncelli, Pellico was arrested
on the charge of Carbonarism. He spent two

* pĕl′ lē kō

711

years in the Piombi prison in Venice, where he composed four *cantiche* (novels in verse), and the tragedies *Ester d'Engaddi* and *Iginia d'Asti*. The sentence of death pronounced on Pellico in February 1822 was commuted by Emperor's clemency to fifteen years *carcere duro*. That April Pellico was conveyed to the Spielberg in Brunn where he was chained to the wall of a dungeon. He is said to have emerged from the Spielberg in August 1830 a walking cadaver.

Taking up residence near his family in Turin, he commenced publication of his prison compositions, among them *Leoniero da Dertona, Gismonda da Mendrizio,* and *Erodiade*. In 1832 *Le Mie Prigioni* (My Prisons) appeared in Turin. This account of his sufferings was immediately translated into every language of modern Europe, its revelation of Austrian tyranny astounding the entire world. A statesman of the time commented that it had struck a heavier blow against Austria and for Italian liberty than could any battle. The work attracted a patron in the person of the Marchesa di Barolo, the reformer of the Turin prisons. She subsidized Pellico from 1834 until his death in Turin twenty years later. Pellico wrote a brief biography of the marchesa which was published after her death. The history of the English churchman Thomas More attracted Pellico so that he made it the subject of his drama *Tommaso Moro* which appeared in 1833. This and the *Opere Inedite* (1837) are his most noteworthy post-imprisonment dramatic works.

It is impossible to evaluate Pellico's potential as a dramatist. His first works had just begun to catch the imagination of the public when he was withdrawn from view to a living grave. When he emerged from prison, his constitution broken by suffering, none of his works was comparable to the production of his youth. The simple narrative of *Le Mie Prigioni* is his greatest claim to fame. Some of the author's naïve nobility may be seen in his statement that he wrote his book to bear witness that in the midst of sufferings "I have not found human nature so degraded, so unworthy of indulgence, so deficient in excellent characters, as is commonly represented; [I invite] noble hearts to love much, to hate no human being, to feel irreconcilable hatred only towards mean deceit, pusillanimity, perfidy, and all moral degradation."

Pellico's *Opere* appeared 1856-60; his *Epistolario,* 1856.

The first English translation of *My Imprisonments* appeared in 1853, by Thomas Roscoe. Subsequent translations were by M. J. Smead and H. P. Lefebvre in 1844, and by Ann Walker in 1850.

Francesca da Rimini was translated by T. Williams in 1856 and by J. F. Bingham in 1897, and the life of the Marchesa di Barolo in 1866 by Lady Georgiana Fullerton.

ABOUT: [In Italian—see studies by R. Barbiera, M. Cimino, M. Fittoni, F. Montanari.]

E. DE P.

*PERDIGO (or PERDIGON) (c. 1190-c. 1212), Provençal troubadour, is known primarily through a Provençal biography or *vida,* whose statements are open to many doubts, and through the rare allusions in his poetry. According to the biographer, he was a master of the viol, of song and poetry, a native of Lesperon, in Ardèche, and the son of a fisherman. His fame and his personal charm were such that the Dauphin Robert of Auvergne (1169-1234) took him into his service, knighted him and gave him lands, but later turned against him, perhaps for political reasons. Perdigo also enjoyed the protection of Peter II of Aragon and of William IV of Orange, and was particularly close to the latter's brother, Hugh of Baux, son-in-law of Barral of Marseilles; his associations with this family led him to attack Raymond VI of Toulouse. Peter II was by marriage related to the same group, and thereby became the lord of Montpellier and, sometime before 1212, came to the aid of the Albigensians, thus leading to attack from Perdigo. Briefly, of Perdigo's many possible activities, we may at best infer that he changed allegiances, composed poems before and after the battle of Muret, went with certain prelates to Rome in 1208 seeking aid, and sought refuge with Lambert of Montelh or Montélimart, enemy of Raymond of Toulouse, as early as 1209. Perdigo's career falls more or less within the years 1195 and 1220; the biographers claim that he entered orders at Silvabela, where he died.

To judge by the extant collections of Provençal poetry, and such imitations and allusions as appear in the work of Matfre Ermengau, Guido delle Colonne, and Chiaro Davanzati, Perdigo was highly esteemed as a poet and enjoyed a wide influence. The attributions of the poems raise grave problems, and only twelve songs are surely by him. In these one finds very original versification and several forms otherwise unattested, perhaps on account of the loss of so much of contemporary work; by preference, he tended toward aristocratic mannerisms, in the relatively obscure *trobar clus,* in his personification of abstract qualities and in his rich metaphors. His well known "Ben aio·l

* pär dē gō'

mal . . ." blesses the woes and sorrows of love; his "Trop ai estat mon Bon Esper no vi" exists in Old French translation and probably served as a model for Chiaro Davanzati's "Troppo agio fatto" and Lentino's "Troppo son dimorato." Perdigo's *Partimen* illustrates his command of invective.

Les Chansons de Perdigon, edited by H. J. Chaytor, appeared 1909, 1926.
ABOUT: [In French—Fabre, C. Le Troubadour Perdigon; Romania, 1927.]

F. J. C.

*PEREDA, JOSÉ MARÍA DE (February 6, 1833-March 1, 1906), Spanish novelist, was born in Polanco (Santander) the twenty-second child of Juan Francisco de Pereda y Haro and Doña Bárbara Sánchez de Porrúa. The Pereda family was very devout and the young José María was reared in an atmosphere of tranquil piety. When his parents moved to Santander in 1844 Pereda attended the Instituto Cántabro after which, in 1852, he went to Madrid to prepare for entrance into the Academy of Artillery in Segovia. In the capital Pereda became interested in literature and, abandoning his military studies, returned to Santander in 1855. He presently began to contribute articles to *La Abeja Montañesa* and in 1864 published a collection of tales and sketches entitled *Escenas Montañesas*. The *Escenas* were highly praised by Mesonero Romanos and Hartzenbusch, but the general public showed only indifference. The *Escenas* reveal what was to become the author's most conspicuous talent: the vigorous portrayal of regional types and the colorful description of the mountains and sea surrounding Santander.

In 1869 Pereda married Diodora de la Revilla y Huidobro, daughter of a distinguished family, and in 1871 was elected Carlist deputy in the parliament of Amadeus of Savoy. In this same year Pereda published *Tipos y Paisajes* (the second part of *Escenas Montañesas*), this time for an enthusiastic public. The eminent scholar Menéndez y Pelayo was greatly impressed and encouraged him to continue writing.

Pereda continued to live the tranquil life of a country squire in Santander and Polanco, never tempted by the activities of the big cities. He not only lived the rôle of a Spanish hidalgo but also looked the part. According to Pérez Galdós, he was dark, of medium height, with a mustache and goatee that were "too Spanish and Cervantine." A tradition-

alist in both the social and religious sense, he found liberalism and urban society decidedly antipathetic. Between 1872 and 1879 we find several novels which illustrate his conservative views: *Los Hombres de Pro* and *Don Gonzalo González de la Gonzalera,* both political satires against the liberalism of some rural "caciques"; *El Buey Suelto* and *De Tal Palo Tal Astilla,* both thesis novels. *El Buey Suelto* constitutes a rebuttal to Balzac's *Petites Misères de la Vie Conjugale,* while *De Tal Palo* was written to neutralize the effect of *Gloria,* written by his ideologically opposed friend Pérez Galdós.

In 1884 Pereda left Santander to travel throughout Spain. He was received everywhere with banquets in his honor, including one given him by Clarín. Pereda was elected to the Royal Academy in 1897 and received the Grand Cross of Alfonso XII in 1903. Among his contemporaries, however, there were a few dissenting voices: Trueba considered him too pessimistic and Pardo Bazán wrote somewhat disparagingly of his "well-cultivated garden" but "limited horizons."

Pereda's most mature works belong to the period between 1881 and 1894: *El Sabor de la Tierruca* (1881), *Sotileza* (1884), and *Peñas Arriba* (1894). Strongly regional in flavor, these novels are amplified sketches of Santander customs, wherein landscapes and portraits are more important than either action or ideas. *El Sabor de la Tierruca* is a realistic portrayal of Polanco, devoid of didactic purpose, while *Sotileza,* with its vivid maritime background, is a powerful evocation of Santander before 1850. *Peñas Arriba* is less interesting as a novel, but it provides clear evidence of the author's tendency to place a feeling for landscape at the very core of his work.

Pereda died in Santander and was buried in the family pantheon in Polanco. A monument was erected to his memory in Santander and on January 23, 1911, Menéndez y Pelayo read the dedication. His complete *Obras* appeared in 1945.

Excerpts from *Sotileza, La Leva, Hombres de Pro,* and *Don Gonzalo González de la Gonzalera* have been translated into English by W. H. Bishop in the Warner Library. Some of the *Cuentos* have been translated as *The Last of the Breed and Other Stories* by D. Freeman (1916).
ABOUT: Brenan, G. The Literature of the Spanish People; Van Horne, J. The Influence of Conservatism on the Art of Pereda. [In Spanish—see studies by J. M. de Cossío, J. Camp, R. Gullón.]

B. P. P.

* pā rā′ thä

*PERETZ, ISAAC LOEB (1851-April 3, 1915), one of the greatest Yiddish and Hebrew writers, was born in Zamosc, Poland, into a scholarly family. His father, although orthodox, was sufficiently modern to allow his son to learn German, Polish, and Russian. At the same time, he received a traditional Jewish education and was soon known as a child prodigy. Peretz began to write at the age of fourteen, but most of this work was experimental and has not survived. At nineteen he married the daughter of Gabriel Judah Lichtenfeld, an exponent of the Haskalah, the movement for the secular enlightenment and emancipation of the Jews.

It was in this environment that he made his literary debut in 1875 with several Hebrew poems written for the Hebrew press. A volume of poems by Peretz and his father-in-law appeared in 1877, but his literary productivity was limited by marital difficulties and the pressure of business. Divorced in 1875, he remarried two years later. His two children were both by his first wife; one died in infancy. An unsuccessful beer-brewing business was followed by ten years of law practice in his native town. While achieving prominence as a lawyer, Peretz continued to contribute occasional poems to Hebrew periodicals.

In 1887 Peretz' license as a lawyer was revoked by the Russian government, which accused him of radicalism. Moving to Warsaw, he obtained a position as clerk in the office of the Jewish community. He remained an employee of the Warsaw Jewish community, in successively more responsible positions, until his death. It was in 1887, also, that Peretz turned seriously to writing in Yiddish, the language of the common people. His poem "Monish," published in that year, marked the appearance of a major talent in the Yiddish literary world. A long narrative, it deals with the material poverty but spiritual wealth of East European Jewry. After this, Peretz plunged into vigorous literary and educational activity, producing poems, stories, dramas, and didactic works in Yiddish. In 1891 and for several years thereafter, he edited the annual *Yidishe Bibliotek* (Yiddish Library), and wrote many articles on secular subjects for it. His first real popularity came in 1894 when he began to issue the *Yomtov Bleter* (Holiday Journals). These, published irregularly for Jewish festivals, included stories, dramas, poems, essays, and other pieces by Peretz.

* pĕ′ rĕts

PERETZ

The rise of the Jewish working-class movement found an adherent in Peretz, and, as a result of his socialistic activities, he was imprisoned for several months in 1899. Active also as an educator, he held classes in Yiddish for adults as a means of instructing the people in secular subjects.

Although he did not neglect Hebrew, Peretz concentrated the bulk of his creative power on the Yiddish language. His productivity during the years 1900-1905 was especially high. Recognized as one of the leading figures of the Jewish world, he became involved as a leader in the Yiddish movement, a campaign to make Yiddish the chief national language and cultural medium of the Jewish people. His home in Warsaw became the intellectual center of countless young Yiddish writers who regarded Peretz as their spiritual mentor. His death in 1915 was a great blow to the intellectual circles, but the hundred thousand Warsaw Jews who attended his funeral indicated his equally firm place in the hearts of the people. Peretz was a man of medium height, with broad shoulders, and a large head. He had brilliant eyes and a proud, erect bearing. He was a friendly man with many acquaintances, though few intimates.

Peretz wrote many dramas, but his work in this form is not as strong as his fiction. Most of the plays are concerned with social problems, although *Die Goldene Keit* (The Golden Chain) has a mystic element. It was in his short stories that Peretz revealed his greatest mastery of the meaning of Jewish life. His early stories are strongly realistic, attacking the religious fanaticism of the ghetto, the atrophy of tradition, the persecution of the lowly, the poverty of the masses. Yet, dark as this picture is, it is suffused with the inner beauty of Jewish life. A spirit of warmth and tenderness and a deep interest in the individual human being pervade such stories as "In Keler" (In the Cellar), "Meshulah" (Messenger), and "Bontshe Shvayg" (Bontshe the Silent). In the most profound of his later stories, Peretz turned for inspiration to Hasidism, the Jewish religious movement which saw the essence of religion as a sense of joy in life, communion with God, and love of fellow men. The stories "Oib Nisht Nokh Hekher" (If Not Higher), "Simhah she-bi-Simhah" (Joy of Joys), "A Gilgul fun A Nigun" (The Metamorphosis of a Melody), and his other Hasidic tales transmute folk themes into polished artistic gems. They give expression to the spiritual strivings, the hidden religious strength of the ordinary Jew. Yet, as Isaac Rosenfeld said, "Peretz shares the faith of which he writes but at a considerable remove . . . ; his is a borrowed piety, taken from the intelligence."

Peretz was indeed a complex figure. He espoused the cause of the workers, yet, in "In Mayn Vinkele" (In My Corner), he said to the socialists, "I hope for your victory, but I fear and dread it." He led the fight for Yiddish, but still believed in the eternal value of Hebrew. He was the poet of faith, but always knew it was beyond his reach. He celebrated true religion, but felt himself the son of a new secular era. These contradictions add to rather than detract from the psychological truth and beauty of his work, the integrity and effectiveness of his style.

Stories and Pictures, translated by Helena Frank in 1906, presents a selection of his fiction. *Peretz,* translated by Sol Liptzin in 1947, likewise contains several Peretz stories. *The Three Canopies* was translated by T. Feinerman in 1948. Maurice Samuel wrote, in 1948, *Prince of the Ghetto,* containing translations and adaptations. A collection of stories, *As Once We Were,* appeared in 1951, with translations by E. T. Margolis. Anthologies, such as I. Howe and E. Greenberg's *A Treasury of Yiddish Stories* (1954), Leo Schwarz's *Jewish Caravan* (1935) provide further translations of the work of Peretz. *Bontshe the Silent* has also been translated by A. S. Rappaport. Collected works in Yiddish include *Die Verk* (New York, 1920); in Hebrew, *Kitve* (Tel Aviv, 1924-27).

ABOUT: Howe, I. and Greenberg, E. A Treasury of Yiddish Stories; Roback, A. I. L. Peretz, Psychologist of Literature; Roback, A. The Story of Yiddish Literature; Samuel, M. Prince of the Ghetto; Waxman, M. A History of Jewish Literature; Wiener, L. The History of Yiddish Literature

in the Nineteenth Century; Commentary March 1950; Poet Lore Spring 1926. [In Yiddish—see studies by A. Kappel, N. Maizil, L. Shitnitzsky. [In Hebrew—see study by F. Lachower.]

M. R.

*PÉREZ DE GUZMÁN, FERNÁN (c. 1378-c. 1460), Spanish historian and poet, was the son of Pedro Suárez de Toledo and of Elvira de Ayala; other members of this important aristocratic family were his uncle López de Ayala, called the Chancellor Pedro de Ayala, his nephew the Marquis of Santillana, and a future descendant Garcilaso de la Vega, the great poet of the sixteenth century. Little is known of Pérez de Guzmán's life. He was married first to Doña Leonor de los Paños and later to Doña Marquesa de Avellaneda. He began his brief political career in 1419, in the service of the prince Don Enrique de Aragón. In 1431 we find him taking part in the battle of Higueruela. Shortly afterwards, having incurred the disfavor of the dominant figure of Castile, Don Álvaro de Luna, he was accused of having negotiated with the kings of Navarre and of Aragon to the disservice of John II, king of Castile. Thereafter he retired from public life to his castle of Batres, where he devoted himself to letters.

Don Fernán Pérez de Guzmán maintained a correspondence with some of the leading literary figures of his time; the bishop Don Alonso de Cartagena, for example, dedicated to him his *Oracional* (prayerbook). He was chiefly known to his contemporaries as a poet. His earliest works, included in the major fifteenth century collection of Spanish verse known as the *Cancionero de Baena,* are love poems in the style of the Galician (Portuguese) troubadours. But his poetry soon became more philosophic and religious; he wrote elegies, allegories on the cardinal virtues, and, in his old age, the *Loores de los Claros Varones de España,* praises of the famous men of Spain, in which he moralistically exalts both arms and letters. Some of these works were collected and published posthumously in a book entitled *Las Setecientas* (1516).

But of more interest and value than his verse is his one great prose work, written between 1450 and 1455, the *Generaciones y Semblanzas* (Generations and Portraits), covering the reigns of Henry III and John II. This work does not pretend to be a formal history, nor is it precisely a series of biographies; it consists of character sketches of men

* pā′ rāth thā gōōth män′

715

whom the author had known and observed closely, often with a strong personal feeling of either admiration or scorn. He expresses with force and economy of words the violent moral tensions, the pageantry and passions of the waning Middle Ages in Castile. Sallust and Tacitus may have been among his models; a more immediate influence was that of the *Mare Historiarum,* by the Dominican Giovanni di Colonna. Pérez de Guzmán's translations from this latter work were published along with his own *Generaciones y Semblanzas* in 1512; this gallery of portraits brings to life for the modern reader, as no other work can, Spaniards of the early fifteenth century.

A bibliographic study appeared in *Revue Hispanique,* XVI (1907); see also XXVIII (1913).

ABOUT: [In Spanish—Domínguez Bordona, J. *Introduction to* Generaciones y Semblanzas; Revista de Filologia Española, XXX (1946).]

E. L. R.

*PÉREZ DE MONTALBÁN (or MONTALVÁN), JUAN (1602-June 25, 1638),

Spanish dramatist and novelist, was born in Madrid, the son of Alonso Pérez, well known publisher and bookseller. A child prodigy, he studied philosophy and the humanities at Alcalá de Henares (1620) and became a Doctor in Theology at the same university in 1625. However, his contemporary, the great poet and critic Quevedo, wrote a famous epigram questioning this title. He was ordained priest the same year (1625), and served as an officer in the Tribunal of the Inquisition. He died in Madrid, mentally ill, having acquired considerable fame, especially as a dramatist but also as a novelist. He was one of the outstanding figures of the literary circle of Lope de Vega, whose work he published and whom he greatly admired. Although much younger than "the Phoenix," he was his friend and constant companion.

Montalbán follows the pattern of Lope, the great master of playwriting. Although his plays are of varying merit, some are full of fantasy, with a number of inspired passages. He wrote thirty-six *comedias* and twelve religious plays such as *El Valiente Nazareno* (The Brave Nazarene), dynamic, exuberant, and imbued with religious dignity. Interesting also is *El Divino Portugués* (The Saintly Portuguese), concerning the life of St. Anthony of Padua and embodying the tenderness and informality of Spanish religious feeling, so well represented in the paintings of the Counter Reformation, such as those of Murillo. One of Montalbán' "cloak and sword" comedies, called *La To quera Vizcaína* (The Basque Veil-Weaver) depicts the life of that period and contain: some fine psychological analysis of characters He injected new feeling and force into the "comedy of intrigue," a much abused form Two of his most interesting plays dramatize the life and court of King Philip II, whom he calls "Spain's second Seneca." In both works he describes the king as the ideal prince and presents an excellent gallery of characters. A series of internal affairs of the Court takes place in the atmosphere of stoicism and justice that surrounds the monarch. The second of the plays ends with the death of Philip in 1598. The somber king appears throughout these works in a solemn and religious background, vacillating between intransigence and tolerance.

Montalbán was the author of eight novels which were popular in his time and were translated into French in 1644. He also wrote a miscellaneous collection of prose and poetry entitled *Para Todos* (For Everyone), which, although mediocre, motivated numerous literary discussions and the famous satirical work by Quevedo *La Perinola.* Montalbán is also of interest as the first biographer of Lope de Vega. With other poets of his time he collaborated in *La Fama Póstuma,* a book paying tribute to the genius of the master on his death in 1635. Montalbán produced a large number of works and enjoyed great popularity in his short lifetime. In today's perspective he is considered only as one of the followers of Lope de Vega.

The works of Pérez de Montalbán are collected in the *BAE.*

ABOUT: Bacon, G. W. An Essay upon the Life and Dramatic Works of Pérez de Montalbán (University of Pennsylvania dissertation, 1903); Revista Hispanica, XVII (1907), XXVI (1912). [In French—Morel-Fatio, A. La Comedia Espagnole du XVIIᵉ Siècle.]

L. R. DE G. L.

*PERGAUD, LOUIS (January 22, 1882-April 8, 1915), French novelist and short-story writer, was born at Belmont, in Franche-Comté. The son of a humble elementary schoolteacher, Élie Pergaud, and of Noémie Collette, Louis learned from his father the countryman's love of hunting. A transfer to Guyans-Vennes brought the family near the paternal ancestral site, which was to become the setting of *La Guerre des Boutons.*

* pä räth thä môn täl vän'

* pĕr gō'

After local schooling, Louis was sent in 1898 to the Besançon normal school. Both his parents died the year before his graduation in 1901. Upon completion of military service in the infantry, Pergaud returned to a teaching position in the village of Durnes and married a local schoolteacher. The marriage was not a happy one.

Pergaud started to write verse in 1900, under the profound influence of Léon Deubel's poetry, and he contributed to obscure magazines. His first article, anti-militaristic and anti-clerical, appeared in *Le Flambeau* of Besançon in 1904; that same year *Le Beffroi* published *L'Aube, Poésies* at the author's expense. *L'Herbe d'Avril, Poésies* appeared four years later, under the same conditions.

In 1907 Pergaud abandoned both his teaching position at Landresse and his wife, and went to Paris, where he was joined by Delphine Duboy of Landresse. He married her in 1910. He worked for the Paris gas company until he was able to obtain teaching posts at Arcueil and at Maisons-Alfort.

His stories of animal life were accepted by *Le Beffroi, La Phalange,* and *Le Mercure de France*. The Goncourt Prize in 1910 for *De Goupil à Margot, Histoires de Bêtes* assured a lively sale for this "novel." Pergaud obtained a position at the Paris prefecture, and took an active role in launching "little magazines" such as *L'Île Sonnante* and *Le Gay Sçavoir. La Guerre des Boutons, Roman de Ma Douzième Année* (1912) is remarkable for the warmth and directness of its evocation of a country childhood, and for its frankness. A notable film has been made from this novel.

Léon Deubel's suicide in 1913 shocked Pergaud and inspired him to collect the former's work in *Régner,* while publishing his own *Roman de Miraut, Chien de Chasse*. With the outbreak of the First World War Pergaud was sent to the Lorraine front. He was promoted from sergeant to adjutant to second lieutenant. He participated in the attack on Marchéville; he was believed to have been killed in action, but his body was never found. The sculptor Antoine Bourdelle made a monument in his memory for the city of Besançon.

Pergaud's importance to French letters is in the fields of the animal story and the novel of adolescence. Long before he read Curwood, Kipling, or London, Pergaud had conceived nature situations as his subject. Other rustic and animal tales have been collected posthumously in *Les Rustiques, His-*

toires Villageoises (1921) and *La Vie des Bêtes* (1923). There was a school edition in 1930 and an anthology in 1934. His correspondence with Eugène Chatot was published in 1955.

Douglas English adapted *Tales of the Untamed; Dramas of the Animal World* in 1911; a translation by C. W. Sykes, *Vengeance of the Crows (La Revanche du Corbeau,* 1911), was published in 1930.

ABOUT: [In French—see studies by L. Layé, C. Léger.]

S. S. W.

PERK, JACQUES FABRICE HERMAN

(June 10, 1859-November 1, 1881), Dutch poet, was born in Dordrecht, the only son of the Walloon minister Marie Adrien Perk and of Justine Georgette Caroline Clifford Cocq van Breugel. The family moved to Breda in 1867 and settled in Amsterdam in 1872. Intending to be an officer, Jacques went to a suitable high school, 1872-77. The quality of his essays and term papers from this period indicates his precocity. Also of this period are a manuscript, *Een Rekje Duiveneieren,* containing a series of historical sketches dealing with Dutch literature of the seventeenth century; a translation of Goethe's *Tasso;* and a collection of poetry, *Kamperfoelie en Heggewinden* (1876-78), the lyrics of which are reminiscent of Heine. In 1876 Perk wrote a comedy, *Alexander Duivelwater,* and an operetta after Körner, *Hendrik Duval of Vier Jaren op Schildwacht.* A drama, *Herman en Martha,* was written in 1877. In this year Perk began an autobiography, but he never wrote more than the first chapter. His aunt, Betsy Perk, published most of these works of his youth in *Jacques Perk Geschetst voor Jong Nederland.*

In 1877 Perk left school and began to learn Latin and Greek in order to prepare himself for judicial studies, but illness interrupted this endeavor. He made a trip to the Ardennes to recover his health, returned in 1878, and took a job as journalist with the *Handelsblad* (1878-79). He then went to Leiden to study law.

In 1879, on another trip to Belgium, Perk met Mathilde Thomas. This encounter made a true poet of the youthful writer. Mathilde was engaged and did not care for Perk, but her beauty affected him greatly. The Mathilde-cycle was the literary result of this encounter. In the beginning of 1881 Perk was invited by Vosmaer to contribute to the magazine *Spektator.* He died that same year at only twenty-two.

* pârk

717

Perk's poem *Iris* is the only one in which Keats' immediate influence is clearly evident. In all his other writings, the influences that worked on him were too varied to be easily discernible. For the sonnet form he studied the poetry of Goethe, Heine, von Platen, Rückert, Körner, Musset, Barbier, and Hooft. He also emulated Vondel, Virgil, and Dante, whom he greatly admired.

Even in his first publications there were signs of his striking gift of imagery and of the keen powers of observation that later caused the "Tachtigers," the "new" poets of the eighties, to look at Perk as one of their predecessors. These same qualities, however, also alienated other readers who found him obscure. Kloos' introduction to the edition of Perk's *Gedichten* in 1882 advanced his reputation. However, he was not really recognized and admired until the literary movement of the Nieuwe Gids had become successful. He then became famous and suddenly his poetry became part of classical Dutch literature. In its fervent and tender individualism Perk's poetry, consisting mainly of sonnets, is closely related to the movement of the eighties. But Perk cannot be called a poet of the new movement through and through. His work carries in its language the clear traces of a transitional period. His brilliant talent ripened early under the influence of the great. His Mathilde-cycle (*Mathilde-Krans*), a glorification of beauty, stands as the classical prelude to modern Dutch poetry, even though the poet himself abandoned the cycle in that form. The complete edition from the manuscripts appeared in 1941 in three volumes, a modern edition of his *Gedichten* in 1942.

ABOUT: [In Dutch—see studies by A. Greebe, A. Nijland, G. Stuiveling, A. Verwey (*in* Prosa I, 1921).]

H. B.

*PERRAULT, CHARLES (January 12, 1628-May 16, 1703), French writer, born in Paris, was the son of a lawyer in Parliament; of his three brothers, all of whom became eminent men, the architect Claude is best known for the Observatory and parts of the Louvre. While still in school, Charles published his *Énéide Travestie*, composed in part by his brothers. He began practicing law in 1651. After various administrative posts of distinction, he was elected to the French Academy in 1671 and remained active in that body, being responsible for introducing the secret ballot for the election of members. He came to the fore in literature with his

* pĕ rō'

PERRAULT

poem "Le Siècle de Louis XIV," which he read before the Academy in 1687, and in which he hailed the superiority of modern letters. Perrault's aggressive and perhaps excessive statements aroused the ire of the classicists, notably of Racine and Boileau, and provoked the "Querelle des Anciens et des Modernes." For three years the violent differences of opinion divided men of letters into two hostile camps as Perrault returned to the attack in answer to Boileau and Racine in his *Parallèle des Anciens et des Modernes,* his *Apologie des Femmes,* and his *Hommes Illustres.*

The modernist movement rose in preliminary form in 1669 in the "Querelle du Merveilleux," led by Desmarets, but became aggressive only with Perrault's thesis of the absolute superiority of recent writing. Seconded by Fontenelle, in his *Digression* of 1688, Perrault maintained a far more courteous tone than the general run of the pedantic reactionaries. Boileau and Perrault were reconciled in 1700, each yielding a few points, and the exchange of theses turned to Homer and became more important in England.

Perrault's polemics, of importance in their day, have otherwise been forgotten for his real masterpiece, the *Contes de Ma Mère l'Oye* (Mother Goose's Tales), a work he composed in idle moments and on which he set little store. In these fairy tales, Perrault interpreted the stories of the Sleeping Beauty, Red Riding Hood, Bluebeard, Cinderella, and Tom Thumb in almost definitive manner, giving each the color of style and costume of the moment. In his eleven fairy tales, of which the best are those in prose, we find a new genre and an unusual work of art. The stories are not new, but belong to the folklore of children and had long awaited their inspired interpreter; although La Fontaine is certainly an important influence in *Ma Mère l'Oye,* it is remarkable that he totally ignored this type of subject. The influence of the work has been constant, in a profusion of imitations during the early eighteenth century, and later in the writings of Meilhac and Halévy (their *Barbe-Bleue*), Banville (*Riquet à la Houppe*), and Ravel's orchestral suite. Perrault's art, in his *Contes,* lies in his delicacy and discretion of word and image, the simplicity of the ideas and situations, and the unsophisticated acceptance of the supernatural as simple matter of fact in such well known detail as the transformations of Cinderella and the mystery of the Sleeping Beauty; the tales are distinguished further by the realism of the portrayal of commonplace scenes and objects. Strangely, in the work of the former champion of "modern" ideas and techniques, Perrault's *Contes* are extremely archaic in form and subject matter.

Among the finer illustrated editions is that by Doré (1862), whose drawings also appear in L. Untermeyer's English translation of 1946, and there is a wide variety of other English versions, one of 1791, the majority of the present century. Perrault's other writings include essays, *Mémoires,* and a comedy in verse, *L'Oublieux;* one should note J. Ozell's translation, *Characters of the Greatest Men* (1704).

ABOUT: Lang, A. Perrault's Popular Tales; Germanic Review, 1931. [In French—France, A. Le Livre de Mon Ami; Gillot, H. La Querelle des Anciens et des Modernes; Hallays, A. Les Perrault; Rigault, H. Histoire de la Querelle des Anciens et des Modernes; Storer, E. La Mode des Contes de Fées; Revue des Deux Mondes, 1934.]

F. J. C.

*PESTALOZZI, JOHANN HEINRICH
(January 12, 1746-February 17, 1827), Swiss educational reformer and writer, was born at Zürich, the son of a surgeon who died when the boy was five. Pestalozzi first studied theology, then turned to law studies at the University of Zürich. Coming under the influence of Rousseau, particularly his *Émile,* Pestalozzi went to live in the country to devote himself to farming. At twenty-three he married Anna Schulthess; their son was named Jacques. In 1768 Pestalozzi founded a farm called Neuhof near Birr in the Aargau, and after some agricultural failures, he established an institution there for fifty

* pĕs tä lōt′ sĕ

PESTALOZZI

poor children; this was in existence for five years, until 1780. Following a period during which he devoted himself to writing, Pestalozzi in 1798 became director of an orphanage at Stans, taking care of eighty children left destitute by the French invasion, and later a teacher at Burgdorf in the Canton of Berne. There he founded in 1800 a model school which he moved to Münchenbuchsee in 1804 and to Yverdon (Ifferten) on Lake Neuchâtel a year later. In 1802 he went to Paris, but, although he had been made an honorary citizen of the French Republic, his efforts to interest Napoleon in a scheme of national education were fruitless. Having had to dissolve his school in 1825, Pestalozzi went back to Neuhof where he lived with his grandson. His last years were troubled by weariness and financial cares, and his death occurred at Brugg in the Aargau at the age of eighty-one.

Pestalozzi was the most famous pedagogue of the classical, humanistic age of the German-speaking world. His books were written to present his educational ideas and to raise money for his educational and philanthropic ventures. Some of his basic ideas are as follows: the "whole child" and not his mind alone should be educated; religion should be rejected as a guiding principle in education; we learn by doing; we learn through our senses and therefore the study of objects in the world about us should be a major part of the educational process. Pestalozzi considered such ideas his main contribution, more important than his educational projects, many of which were doomed to failure. His first book, *Abendstunde eines Einsiedlers* (Evening Hours of a Hermit), a collection of aphorisms and reflections, appeared in 1780. The following year he wrote *Lienhard und Gertrud*, a didactic novel and the first social *Erziehungsroman*. It describes how a good, humble, pious woman effects the regeneration of her household and an entire small community. Pestalozzi's ideal of home-education is effectively presented. In his Burgdorf period Pestalozzi wrote *Wie Gertrud ihre Kinder Lehrt* (*How Gertrude Teaches Her Children*, 1801), probably his chief work. Attempting to establish a psychologically ordered sequence, Pestalozzi bids the teacher proceed from observation to consciousness to expression, with measuring, drawing, writing, and numbers to come later. Pestalozzi's conception of *Anschauung* (immediate awareness, sense experience, or direct acquaintance) is to be the basis of all knowledge and experience.

It has been remarked that Pestalozzi was not the best exponent of his ideas, but that he benefited from the interest, loyalty, and interpretative and administrative skill of others. In his *Schwanengesang* (Swan Song, 1826), he confesses: "My lofty ideals were preeminently the product of a kind, well-meaning soul, inadequately endowed with the intellectual and practical capacity which might have helped considerably to further my heartfelt desire." In the same work he said that he had been weak and delicate from childhood and regretted that his early education did not instill in him the virtues of manliness.

Visitors at Pestalozzi's Burgdorf school included personalities like Talleyrand and Mme de Staël, and his work was praised by Wilhelm von Humboldt and Fichte. His disciples included Froebel, Delbrück, and Herbart. The first work of the last-named was about Pestalozzi's conception of Sense-Impressions, "the grand idea of the noble Pestalozzi." Through the works, activities, and schools of many such disciples, Pestalozzi has had a lasting impact on education, particularly primary education, in many parts of the world.

An inadequate anonymous translation of *Leonard and Gertrude* appeared as early as 1800; Eliza Shepherd's translation appeared in 1824 under the title *A Book for the Poor*, and Eva Channing's abridged version in 1885. *How Gertrude Teaches Her Children*, translated by L. E. Holland and F. C. Turner, appeared in 1894. *Letters on Early Education, Addressed to J. P. Greaves, Esq.*, was published in 1827, translator anonymous. In 1912 J. A. Green translated and edited *Pestalozzi's Educational Writings*.

ABOUT: Anderson, L. F. Pestalozzi; Barnard, H. Pestalozzi and His Educational System; Green, J. A. Life and Works of Pestalozzi; Kreusi, H. Pestalozzi, His Life, Work and Influence; Monroe, W. S. History of the Pestalozzian Movement in the United States; Rusk, R. R. The Doctrines of the Great Educators. [In German—see studies by F. Delekat, W. Guyer, A. Heubaum, F. Huber, H. Möller, P. Natorp, J. Reinhart, E. Spranger, A. Zander.]

H. Z.

PETER II, PRINCE BISHOP OF MONTENEGRO. See PETROVIĆ, PETER II NJEGOŠ

*PETŐFI, SÁNDOR (or ALEXANDER), (January 1, 1823-July 31, 1849), considered the greatest lyric poet of nineteenth century Hungary, a popular hero, and author of the Hungarian "Marseillaise," actually was not Hungarian by birth. Born in the village of Kis-Körös, he was the son of a Serbian innkeeper and butcher, Stephen Petrovics, and a Slovenian mother, Mary Hruz. Petőfi is a name he adopted later in life.

His father was a harsh man, completely unsympathetic to the boy's artistic inclinations, but his mother was gentle and understanding. "She was full of poetry," he wrote. "I drew it at the milk of her bosom; I learnt it from her smiles and tears." However, Petőfi's dominating passion was the theatre and acting, not poetry. As a boy he ran away from home and joined a German troupe of traveling players, but his father found him and brought him back. Nothing daunted, Petőfi continued to pursue a theatrical career. He was not a good actor (the only rôle he played with any success was the Fool in *King Lear*), and as a result he suffered severely from poverty. But he persisted—traveling from town to town with copies of Homer, Shakespeare, and Schiller in his knapsack.

Petőfi turned to a literary career simply out of a need for money—translating works from English and French. He began writing his own poetry and published his first poem in the magazine *Athenaeum* in 1842. Two years later, in Pest, he met the eminent Hungarian poet Vörösmarty who at first received him very coolly. When he read the young man's poems, however, Vörösmarty was deeply impressed and became his patron. That same year, 1844, saw the publication of his first book, a collection of poems, and with it Petőfi became an immediate success. A

* pĕ′ tû fî

PETŐFI

contemporary said: "He never went to bed at night, he never arose in the morning, without hearing his songs from the multitude in the public streets." Ironically, when, as an established poet, he entered the same theatre in which he had failed as an actor, he received a standing ovation from the audience.

Petőfi's poems captured popular as well as intellectual audiences with their fresh and direct lyricism. Most of his work is based on simple folk material, giving an intense and realistic picture of Hungarian Lowland peasant life. This has led some critics to call him "the Hungarian Robert Burns," but the English poet who really influenced him was Shelley, whom he idolized.

Love and patriotism are the two major themes of Petőfi's poetry. The essence of it is summarized by Joseph Reményi: "The expressions of joy and grief, his uncompromising standards about personal and public issues, his refusal to succumb to the rhetorical tricks and abuses of mere versifiers, present a poetic spirit of deep feeling and fearless conviction." The longest and probably the best of his poems is "János the Hero," a story about peasant life, but the poem for which he is best remembered is the stirring "Talpra Magyar," known as the Hungarian "Marseillaise," which he wrote on March 15, 1848, as Hungary engaged in its struggle for independence. It is one of a series of revolutionary poems expressing a deep personal conviction. Six months later Petőfi enlisted in the army. He was at the front in the battle of Segesvár,

July 31, 1849, in which the Hungarians were defeated, and was never seen again. There were rumors that he had been captured by the Russians and sent to Siberia, but it appears more likely that he died on the field—at twenty-six—and was buried in a common grave.

In so short a lifetime Petőfi's achievement is remarkable. In addition to his poems he wrote short stories, dramas, and a novel. He also translated some of Shakespeare's plays; his version of *Coriolanus* was very popular on the Hungarian stage. His literary associations were numerous—especially significant was his friendship with János Arany, the national epic poet. Petőfi married Juliet Szendrey, a girl of noble birth, in 1847.

There are a number of English translations of Petőfi's verse including those by J. Bowring (1866), H. Phillips, Jr. (1885), W. N. Loew in *Magyar Poetry* (1899), W. Kirkconnell in *The Magyar Muse* (1933), and *Sixty Poems by A. Petőfi* translated by E. B. Pierce and E. Delmar (1948). Selections also appear in the Warner Library, XXIX, and in *Poet Lore*, XXVII (1916).

ABOUT: Loew, W. N. Magyar Poetry; Reményi, J. Introduction to Sixty Poems by A. Petőfi; Yolland, A. B. Alexander Petőfi: Poet of the Hungarian War of Independence (pamphlet); Slavonic Review, IX (1930-31).

*PETRARCA, FRANCESCO (July 20, 1304-July 18, 1374), Italian poet and humanist, the son of Eletta Canigiani and ser Petraccolo di ser Parenzo, was born in Arezzo where his mother had taken refuge from the political unrest in Florence. In accordance with family tradition, his father was a notary attached to the Florentine government. Shortly after Francesco's birth, however, he was banished from the city, a victim of factional strife, and joined his wife and son in Arezzo. From there he took them to Incisa di Valdarno, a few miles beyond Florentine territory, where he owned a modest property. Petrarch spent his infant years in Incisa, and there his brother Gherardo was born in 1307. In 1310 the family moved briefly to Pisa (where Francesco had occasion to see Dante, an exile like his father), and about two years later they took passage for Avignon. Because of crowded conditions resulting from the recent transfer of the papal court to that city, the family was unable to find suitable lodgings and settled in nearby Carpentras instead.

Here Petrarch began his education under the tutelage of Convenevole da Prato. In 1316 or 1317 he entered the University of

* pā trär′ kä

721

PETRARCH

through those of his countless imitators, virtually nothing else is known about her. Her historical identity, notwithstanding many scholarly efforts, has defied discovery. Indeed, she was so shadowy a presence even during the poet's life that his friends, twitting him, asserted he was not in love with a girl at all, but rather with the poet's laurel. Nevertheless, poetically transfigured, she was to remain the chief subject of his verse long after her death in the plague of 1348. It was largely from among the poems he wrote concerning her that he assembled his *Canzoniere* (Song Book) which he worked on intermittently until his last years.

Consisting largely of sonnets and odes, the *Canzoniere,* except for the unfinished *Trionfi* (Triumphs), is the only work that Petrarch wrote in Italian. It is also his poetic masterpiece and the real source of his reputation as a poet. He had thought to win enduring literary fame through his Latin writings, assigning to these "scattered rhymes" only a transitory renown; yet precisely the reverse happened. His Italian sonnets are the fountainhead of that sonnet vogue which penetrated into nearly every corner of sixteenth century Europe. Anyone acquainted with the sonnets of Ronsard, Desportes, Góngora, Wyatt, Surrey, Sidney, Spenser, and Shakespeare, to cite but a few, can scarcely claim to be entirely unacquainted with Petrarch's own.

In 1330 Petrarch accompanied Giacomo Colonna to Lombez when the latter was appointed its bishop. There he met Lello di Pietro Stefani (whom he called Laelius) and Ludwig van Kempen (whom he called Socrates). These were among the first of an ever-widening circle of friends who, sharing his scholarly and literary interests, were to contribute very materially to his success in promoting the revival of interest in classical learning. Very likely in the same year he also took the tonsure and perhaps minor orders as well. He then became chaplain to Cardinal Giovanni Colonna, probably upon the recommendation of the new Bishop of Lombez. Thereafter, as his chief source of livelihood, Petrarch was to hold appointments to several benefices which, imposing only nominal duties, left him free to devote his energies to literature. He refused the frequent offers of higher ecclesiastical posts.

In 1333 he undertook the first of many journeys, visiting northern France, the Low Countries, and Germany, enlarging the circle of his friends, searching through libraries for lost manuscripts, copying what he found, and

Montpellier and began the study of law for which he had but little inclination. His love of classical literature, on the other hand, was already strong. In a letter written years later he was to recall how on one occasion his father, enraged at Francesco's neglect of his legal studies, threw his precious copies of the Latin authors into the fire, sparing him only a Cicero and a Virgil for rare leisure hours. After four years at Montpellier he continued his studies at Bologna, accompanied by his brother, and it was there that he gained his earliest knowledge of the Italian vernacular poets and the sweet Tuscan idiom he was to render so illustrious. There too, it seems, he attempted his first verses and made the acquaintance of men who were to prove useful in his future career. The most important of these was Giacomo Colonna, scion of a distinguished Roman family. After three years at Bologna, he returned with his brother to Avignon in 1326, the same year in which his father died (his mother had died during his stay at Montpellier). For several years following, to judge from Petrarch's own words, he lived the life of a dandy at the papal court.

On the morning of April 6, 1327 (Good Friday by the poet's symbolic reckoning), at the church of St. Clara in Avignon, he had his first glimpse of the lady who, like Beatrice for Dante, was to become the object of his enduring love and the subject of most of his vernacular poetry. Her name was Laura. Ironically, however, despite the great fame she was to win through his poems, and

reporting upon the areas he visited with keen observation. Thanks to his friends, to the style and learning of his oft-copied epistles, and to his poems, he was already widely known.

In April 1336, together with his brother, he made his celebrated ascent of Mt. Ventoux (near Carpentras). In an age which displayed little interest in nature, such a venture was most unusual, and many scholars have seen in it a manifestation of the spirit of the Renaissance which Petrarch did so much to usher in. In the account of this experience which he sent to his friend Dionigi di Borgo San Sepolcro, he confessed his enchantment with the beauty of the world and revealed how keenly he suffered from the tension of opposing wills—the one drawing him to seek glory in worldly pursuits, the other urging him to give full allegiance to his religious promptings. It is a refrain that runs through much of Petrarch's writings and goes far to explain the restlessness, inquietude, and irresolution that marked his life. Many of his writings are in a sense a record of an endless self-analysis in which he examined and dramatized his spiritual dilemma—a dilemma in which he recognized the irreconcilable conflict between flesh and spirit. It is largely for this reason that he has been regarded as the first modern man. On the other hand, those attitudes and activities which earned him a name as the first great humanist—his dislike of dialectic, his preference for Plato over Aristotle (as he was then understood), his concern for critical standards, his avid collecting of classical texts, his genuine sympathy with the spirit of ancient literature—these are largely reflections of but one side of the dilemma.

In 1337 he made his first trip to Rome where he was at once pleased to note the unexpectedly large number of ruins and dismayed that so much of great merit had been lost. In the same year he also became the father of an illegitimate child, Giovanni, who was to be the source of recurrent troubles to his father until his death in 1361. (Six years later, the same unknown woman who bore Giovanni bore Petrarch a daughter, Francesca, with whom he spent his last years.) Also in the same year he took up residence in secluded Vaucluse, near Avignon, where it is possible he began work on his epic *Africa* and on *De Viris Illustribus,* a history of great men. Here too he wrote many of his Italian poems. Despite periods of residence in Italy, he was not finally to abandon Vaucluse until 1353.

On September 1, 1340, Petrarch received letters from the University of Paris and from the Senate of Rome inviting him to accept the crown of poet laureate. Though he professed surprise, the invitations had not arrived without some rather guileful solicitations on his part. Equally guileful was his pretense of deliberating upon which of the two he should accept. Padua had already conferred the poet's laurel upon Albertino Mussato, and Prato had already conferred it upon Petrarch's own former tutor, Convenevole da Prato. To receive the same recognition from Paris, therefore, would have constituted nothing very momentous. But not since the time of Statius, apparently, had that ancient rite been celebrated at the seat of the Roman Empire. Journeying first to Naples to be formally examined by King Robert, Petrarch then proceeded to Rome where the celebration took place on the Capitoline on April 8 (Easter), 1341. Ernest H. Wilkins has called the oration the poet delivered on that occasion "the first manifesto of the Renaissance." The importance of the event is very considerable, for it gave wide publicity to the cause of literature and stood as powerful evidence of the revival of interest in classical culture.

Returning from Rome, Petrarch stayed for the better part of a year in Parma and completed the first version of *Africa.* He was back in Vaucluse in 1342, where in the fall of that year he completed the first draft of his *Secretum* (Secret). Possibly never intended for publication, the *Secretum* is a dialogue between the poet and St. Augustine on the subject of salvation. In it Petrarch discusses his character with considerable candor, admitting to many shortcomings. Sprinkled with numerous digressions in which Cicero, Seneca, Virgil, and other favorite authors are discussed, it is one of the most interesting of Petrarch's Latin works. Characteristically, it comes to no conclusion.

In the following year, his brother, finally resolving a spiritual dilemma not unlike Petrarch's own, entered a monastery. Petrarch began to study Greek under the tutelage of the Calabrian monk Barlaam, but was soon obliged to abandon it when he was asked to undertake a political mission to Naples. Returning, he again stopped in Parma, this time with intentions of remaining there. War between neighboring lords soon broke out, however, and the city was laid under siege. Joined by some friends, he escaped safely through the enemy lines only to be attacked by thieves and to suffer a painful fall from his horse. Nevertheless, he continued on to

Bologna. In Vaucluse again from 1345 to 1347 he devoted himself to writing. The *Bucolicum Carmen* (Bucolic Songs), consisting of twelve eclogues on current topics, probably dates from this period, as perhaps also do *De Vita Solitaria* (The Life of Solitude) and *De Otio Religiosorum* (On the Repose of the Religious), both of which, however, were not completed until later.

When news reached him that Cola di Rienzo had successfully staged a coup in Rome and had been chosen tribune by popular acclaim, Petrarch was jubilant and hastened to celebrate the victor in an eclogue boldly envisioning the revival of ancient Rome. Soon after, he set off to visit Rienzo only to be met on the way by news that his hero had already fallen from power.

Three years later he went to Rome for the jubilee of 1350, pausing in Florence where he met Boccaccio with whom he had long been in correspondence. The young author of the *Decameron* acknowledged Petrarch as his master and, like Petrarch's other literary friends, sought his guidance along the paths the older man had already explored. Stopping off in Arezzo on his return from Rome, Petrarch was invited to visit the house of his birth, already converted to a memorial in his honor. Then he went on to Padua where he remained until the summer of 1351, at which time he returned to Vaucluse.

From 1353 to 1361 he resided in Milan where, serving as occasional secretary and ambassador for the Visconti, the lords of the city, he had ample time for writing and study. Here he completed the *Secretum*, the *Bucolicum Carmen*, and *De Vita Solitaria*. Here too he worked on *De Remediis Utriusque Fortunae* (On Remedies against Good and Evil Fortune), a series of 254 dialogues which were to prove very popular; on the *Epistolae Metricae* (Metrical Epistles); and on the poems for his *Canzoniere*. But his friends were not a little shocked that Petrarch, the professed champion of political liberty, had needlessly accepted the hospitality of a ruling family renowned for its tyrannical cruelty. Nevertheless, he stayed on for eight years, interrupting his sojourn by an embassy to the Emperor Charles IV in Prague in 1356 (where he was made Count Palatine) and by another to Paris in 1361.

Driven from Milan by the plague in the spring of 1361, he moved to Padua and then to Venice. For the next several years he alternated periods of residence in both these

cities. In Venice he wrote *De Sui Ipsius et Multorum Ignorantia* (On His Own Ignorance and That of Many Others) in 1367 in reply to a group of young Averroists who had irreverently proclaimed him a good man but a poor scholar. In this invective he sets forth his opposition to dialectic and formal scholasticism and upholds the values of a broad humanistic training.

His last place of residence was Arquà (now Arquà Petrarca), a small village a few miles from Padua. Accompanied by his daughter and son-in-law, he moved there in the summer of 1370. Despite increasing age and periods of illness, through the remaining four years of his life he continued his former pursuits, keeping as many as six scribes busy and grumbling that good ones were hard to come by. Visitors were so numerous that they put a serious strain on the modest hospitality he could offer them. In his will he dedicated his precious library to Venice and remembered his close friends, including Boccaccio, with appropriate gifts.

The *Secretum* was translated under the title *Petrarch's Secret* by William Draper in 1911; *De Vita Solitaria*, under the title *The Life of Solitude*, was translated by Jacob Zeitlin in 1924. Translations of selected portions from other Latin works are available in J. H. Robinson and H. W. Rolfe, *Petrarch: The First Modern Scholar and Man of Letters* (1899), and in *The Renaissance Philosophy of Man* (1948), edited by Cassirer, Kristeller, and Randall. Translations of the Italian poems are numerous. Some of the more useful collections are *Sonnets, Triumphs and Other Poems of Petrarch* by various hands in Bohn's Illustrated Library (1893); *Sonnets of Petrarch* by Joseph Auslander (1931); *Petrarch's Sonnets and Songs* by Anna Maria Armi (1946); *Translations from Petrarch* by Thomas G. Bergin (1955); *The Triumphs of Petrarch* by E. H. Hatch (1962).

ABOUT: Bishop, M. Petrarch and His World; Tatham, E. H. R. Francesco Petrarca; Wilkins, E. H. Studies in the Life and Works of Petrarch; Petrarch's Eight Years in Milan; Petrarch's Later Years; *also* Life of Petrarch. [In Italian—Sapegno, N., Il Trecento.]

D. J. D.

*PETROVIĆ, PETAR II NJEGOŠ, (November 1, 1813-October 19, 1851), the last prince-bishop of Montenegro, Serbian poet and philosopher, was born in the little village of Njeguši near Cetinje. His father was Tomo Petrović, a younger brother of the reigning prince-bishop Petar I of the small principality of Montenegro, and his mother Ivana was of the distinguished Proroković family. Njegoš, who was given the baptismal name Radivoje (Rade), was the eldest

* pä′ trō vĭtch nyä′ gōsh

son in a family of five children. The bishopric was hereditary in the house of Petrović-Njegoš, the succession passing from uncle to nephew, and Rade was chosen to succeed his uncle. To prepare for this office, he received an elementary education first in the monastery of his uncle in Cetinje, and then at Topli near Herzegovina in the picturesque Gulf of Kotor, where he stayed with his priest-teacher Tropović until 1827. In that year, he returned to Cetinje where he had a new tutor, the Serbian poet Sima Milutinović-Sarajlija, who was at the same time a secretary to prince-bishop Petar I. Rade's education was neither regular nor conventional. Sima Milutinović was an interesting man, a half-educated, self-appointed romantic poet whose life certainly matched the character of his poetry. After taking part in the Serbian rebellion against the Turks, he wandered through Europe, making his living as a Serbian tutor to many German authors (among them Goethe) who became suddenly interested in Serbian popular poetry. As a tutor to Njegoš, he played a large part in developing the poetical talents of young Njegoš. In 1830 Petar I died, and Njegoš—in order to be able to succeed his uncle—had to become a monk, thus receiving the name of Petar. On August 6, 1833, at the age of twenty, he was officially created prince-bishop ("Vladika Crne Gore") in St. Petersburg, in the presence of the Russian czar Nicholas I.

After returning to Cetinje, Njegoš occupied himself with attempts to turn the little semi-barbarian principality into a modern organized state. For, besides the tradition of the fierce centuries-long struggle with the Ottoman empire, during which the Montenegrins zealously guarded their freedom on the bare mountain heights, they possessed an intense and hypersensitive love of personal freedom and independence that often degenerated into bloody feuds among the tribes and families. There were no schools and no recognized social order. Njegoš now attempted, in the face of opposition provoked by ignorance, to introduce some social and cultural progress. He founded the first state school, set up a printing press, organized a court and a police force. But his constant struggles under the most difficult internal and external conditions to bring some sort of improvement to his country did not always bear fruit, and these failures only increased the already existing pessimistic outlook of this great idealist. Calling himself "ruler among barbarians and a barbarian among rulers," he often despaired of ever achieving his high aspirations for his country.

Njegoš began writing poetry while a boy under the influence of the traditional folk ballads, but his first collection of poems appeared in 1834, under the title *Pustinjak Cetinjski* (The Hermit of Cetinje). Some of these poems foreshadowed the religious and philosophical ideas developed in his later works. Njegoš was an avid reader, and from his trips abroad (especially St. Petersburg and Vienna) he brought many books which helped widen his scanty education and broaden his horizon. He also collected folk ballads (as many other Yugoslav authors did) and published them among some ballads that he himself composed, under the title *Ogledalo Srpsko* (Serbian Mirror), in 1845.

The three greatest works of Njegoš are the historical epic-dramas *Gorski Vjenac* (The Mountain Garland, 1846) and *Lažni Car Šćepan Mali* (The False Czar Stephen the Little, 1851), and the religious-allegorical epic poem *Luča Mikrokozma* (The Rays of the Microcosm, 1845.). The inspiration for his religious epic came from the reading of Milton's *Paradise Lost*, though Njegoš gave his poem a completely different treatment and emphasis. His epic drama *Lažni Car Šćepan Mali* was probably inspired by Pushkin's *Boris Godunov*, but the underlying facts of this drama were taken from some actual eighteenth century happenings in Montenegro.

The fame of Njegoš as a poet and philosopher is, however, based mainly on his epic drama *Gorski Vjenac*. The subject is the eradication of Mohammedanism in Montenegro at the end of the seventeenth century, in the reign of Bishop Danilo. Though written with an intense patriotic feeling which finds its expression in extolling Montenegrin virtues and customs, this epic poem is more than a simple expression of his passionate desire for liberty and his hatred of oppression. In its insight and speculative brilliance it represents a harmonious blending of a national art and a philosophical poetry. It is the best and the most popular book in Yugoslav literature.

Only a few short poems followed in the last years of Njegoš' life. He was already suffering from tuberculosis, and in the hope of a cure, he went in 1850 to southern Italy, passing that winter in Naples. When no visible signs of recovery appeared, he returned to Cetinje where he died at thirty-eight. His tomb, on the highest peak of Montenegro, Lovćen, became a national shrine. Njegoš' physical appearance was striking: he was handsome, dark, and almost seven feet tall. The best known portrait of him is by the Serbian academic painter Anastasije Jovanović. The collected works of Petar Petrović Njegoš appeared in the authorized state edition of 1927, edited by Milan Rešetar.

    Gorski Vjenac has been translated into almost all European languages: 1886, German; 1887, Russian; 1902, Italian and Hungarian; 1913, Swedish; and 1930, English by J. W. Wiles under the title *The Mountain Wreath.*
    ABOUT: The Slavonic and East European Review, XXX (June 1952).

F. S. L.

*PÉTURSSON, HALLGRÍMUR (1614-October 27, 1674), one of the greatest poets and certainly the greatest hymnist that Iceland has produced, was born at or near Hólar in the north of Iceland. His father was the sexton at Hólar and a relative of Bishop Guðbrandur Þorláksson (1542-1627), famous for his translation of the Lutheran Bible (1584). He was also a nephew of Brynjólfur Sveinsson (1605-75), the great bishop of Skálhólt.

Whether Hallgrímur was expelled from the school at Hólar or whether he left it voluntarily is not clear. In any event, he was a blacksmith's apprentice in Copenhagen when Brynjólfur found him and placed him in the Frúar Skóli, Copenhagen's famous preparatory school. By 1637 he was ready to graduate, but just at that time a group of Icelanders arrived in Copenhagen on their way home from ten years of captivity and slavery by the so-called Turks (actually Algerian pirates). Hallgrímur was designated to reindoctrinate this group with the precepts of Christian dogma which had become somewhat blurred in the minds of those who had been so long among the Mohammedans. Among these refugees was a beautiful thirty-seven-year-old widow by the name of Guðríður Símonardóttir. Hallgrímur became so enamored of this exotic woman that he left his studies and returned with her to Iceland. For several years he suffered great poverty as a common laborer at Keplavík, then a small fishing village. In 1644 he was consecrated as the pastor of Hvalsnes, just north of Reykjavík; in 1651 he received the parsonage at Saurbær in Hvalfjorð where he lived and labored until his retirement from the ministry in 1669. Blind and suffering from leprosy, he died in 1674 at Ferstikla, a farm near Saurbær.

* pyĕt' ûr sŏn

Composing poetry was, it seems, no effort for Hallgrímur Pétursson. He was a prolific, though not always a critical, poet. The best of his poems are superior, however, to any of those produced by his contemporaries and bear comparison with the best produced in the Icelandic language of any period. His spiritual and religious poetry, i.e., his hymns and particularly his *Passíusálmar* (Passion Psalms), represent the highest point ever reached by Icelandic religious poetry. These *Passíusálmar,* fifty hymns depicting graphically the passion of Christ and relating with rich allegory and symbolism His passion to the trials and tribulations suffered by humanity at large, have found such favor among the Icelanders that they have been reprinted more than sixty times since their first appearance at Hólar in 1666. They have been memorized and chanted in every Icelandic home whenever need was felt for spiritual rejuvenation or when consolation was sought upon the death of a loved one. No Icelandic child is confirmed without memorizing many of these *Passíusálmar.* In addition to rich imagery, obvious sincerity, and complete humility, these hymns are characterized by a simple though varied vocabulary, a mastery of metrics, and an unusually natural word order. These factors have much to do with their continued popularity.

In addition to the *Passíusálmar* which related specifically to the suffering of Jesus, Hallgrímur composed scores of hymns of a religious or semi-religious nature. These were on subjects taken from the Bible or from the vicissitudes of daily life. When, for example, his home burned down in 1662, the poet composed the famous "Hugbót" (Consolation) which reveals a passionate love of God rivaling that of Job himself. The theme of the poem—"The Lord giveth and the Lord taketh away: Blessed be the name of the Lord"—is a familiar one in Christian literature, but Hallgrímur's obvious sincerity raises this poem out of the commonplace. Another of his famous hymns, "Alt eins og blomstríð eina" (Just Like a Tender Flower) has been sung at the graveside of most Icelanders since it appeared in 1660.

Hallgrímur also composed a good deal of worldly verse, some of it elegiac in memory of friends or relatives and some of it almost ribald in praise of wine, good food, and tobacco. His *Rímur* (similar to English and Scottish ballads) reveal a deft touch, a mastery of form and technique, and a complete command of the subject matter. In *Heilræða-vísur* (Words of Wisdom) he gives good

Christian counsel to the youth of Iceland and the world. In *Aldarháttur* (Way of the World) he compares contemporary Iceland of his day with the golden age of Iceland's political and intellectual life. His important contribution to Iceland's literature is, however, his *Passíusálmar* and his various hymns of meditation.

The most complete edition of Hallgrímur's works exclusive of the *Rímur* is *Sálmar og Kvæði* (Hymns and Poems) I-II, 1887-90, by Grímur Thomsen; the best edition including the *Rímur* is *Hallgrímur Pétursson I-II*, 1947, by Magnús Jónsson. A penetrating study of the poet accompanies the Grímur Thomsen edition.

Translations of isolated poems by Hallgrímur Petursson have appeared in English but have not been collected. Paul Bjarnason has translated "Just Like a Tender Flower"; cf. his *Odes and Echoes* (1954).

ABOUT: Einarsson, S. History of Icelandic Literature.

L. B.

*PHILIPPE, CHARLES LOUIS** (August 4, 1874-December 21, 1909), French novelist, was born in the village of Cérilly, in Allier. He had a twin sister, Jeanne Louise, and another sister nine years older. His parents, Charles Philippe, a shoemaker, and Jeanne Dechâtre, were simple workers, whose relatives too were practically illiterate. A severe dental infection left Charles Louis disfigured for life, with an ugly cicatrice on the jaw, and a receding chin. He began school at the age of five; an excellent student, he won scholarships which permitted him to obtain his baccalaureate (1891). Mistaken in his ambitions, he studied mathematics for three years, while writing poems. He failed to be accepted by the Polytechnical School. Nor was he tall enough to be taken for military service. After vegetating for a while at Cérilly, Philippe went to Paris and obtained a position with the gas company. Philippe related, fictionally, the poverty and the love within his own family in *La Mère et l'Enfant* (1900). The laborious life of his father served for the uncompleted *Charles Blanchard* (1913), as well as in part for *Le Père Perdrix* (1902). His older sister Félicie was the prototype for Madeleine in *La Bonne Madeleine et la Pauvre Marie* (1898).

Philippe's first book, *Quatre Histoires de Pauvre Amour*, was published at his own expense in 1897. He had already contributed poems to *L'Enclos* and formed a close friend-

* fē lēp'

ship with the Belgian poet Henri Vandeputte. In 1899 he made the acquaintance of Lucien Dieudonné (in literature, Lucien Jean) who, with Marguerite Audoux later, was the greatest influence on him.

In 1898 Philippe met the prostitute Maria, who became the heroine of his best-known work, *Bubu de Montparnasse* (1901). Two years later he fell in love with Marie, another unfortunate, who became *Marie Donadieu* (1904). His bureaucratic experiences furnished him with the vignettes of *Croquignole* (1906). He contributed short stories to periodicals and newspapers—these were published posthumously as *Les Contes du Matin* (1916) and *Chroniques du Canard Sauvage* (1923). But literature could not support him, and Philippe worked as a sidewalk inspector for the city. He suffered from dental caries, syphilis, and, finally, a meningitis from which he died at the Velpeau Sanitarium in Paris. He was interred in Cérilly, and the sculptor Antoine Bourdelle executed a bust of him.

Philippe was admired by André Gide, Valéry Larbaud, and Henri Poulaille. He belongs in the lineage of proletarian writers, in the sense that he was close to the "little man," and wrote from personal experiences within that social class. His feeling for little people and the poignancy of his observations resulted in an association formed in his honor, Les Amis de Charles-Louis Philippe.

T. S. Eliot has written an enthusiastic introduction to the English translation by Laurence Vail in 1932 of *Bubu de Montparnasse*. Violet Hudson translated *Marie Donadieu* in 1949. "The Return" is to be found in *Great Modern French Stories* (1917), edited by W. H. Wright. *A Simple Story*, translated by Agnes K. Gray (1924), was illustrated by Franz Masereel, who did woodcuts for several German translations. Philippe's works, especially *Bubu de Montparnasse*, have inspired such illustrators as Grandjouan, Charles Laborde, André Dunoyer de Segonzac.

ABOUT: [In French—see studies by H. Bachelin, J. de Fourchambault, E. Guillaumin, L. Lanoizelée.]

S. S. W.

PHILIPPE MOUSKÉS. See MOUSKÉS, PHILIPPE

"PHILOMUSUS." See LOCKER, JACOB

*PICCOLOMINI, ENEA SILVIO (or AENEAS SILVIUS), Pope Pius II** (October 18, 1405-August 15, 1464), Italian hu-

* pĕk kō lỏ' mē nē

manist and statesman, was born in Consignano of a noble Sienese family, the eldest of eighteen children. In Siena, where he studied, specializing in Latin and humanistic literatures, he composed his first Latin and Italian verse; then, to please his father, he entered law, but soon returned to the humanities while working at Florence under Filelfo. In 1432 he went to the Council of Basel as secretary to Cardinal Capranica and continued travels in France and England in comparable missions, usually of political nature. As secretary to the anti-Pope Felix V, in 1439, he wrote his *Libellus* in defense of the actions of the Council of the following year, thereby achieving his first wide fame. At the Diet of Frankfurt in 1442, he received the poet's crown, and entered the chancellery of Frederick III.

Piccolomini's first creative writing, the poetry collected in 1442, was followed by the more important *Chrisis,* a comedy, and the famous *Historia de Duobus Amantibus* (1444). At this moment his declining health led him to regret the worldly life he had lived and revealed to him a new mission of sanctity and devotion. He took orders at once, became bishop of Trieste in 1447, bishop of Siena in 1450, cardinal in 1456, and pope in 1458. His long and rich career in diplomacy had given him valuable experience for his years as supreme pontiff and, thanks to his deep interest in literature, his historical writings are both attractive and informative. His long and numerous letters, in elegant humanistic style, are remarkable documents on men and historical monuments, and his reports on several of the church councils contain first-hand documentation regarding the political problems related to the imperial courts. He left his ambitious *Cosmographia* unfinished. His autobiographical *Commentarii,* covering his life to 1463, passes hastily over his early years, but deals forcefully with the religious and political scenes in which he was so active. His personal enthusiasm for antiquity led him to a close study of ancient art and architecture, and his veneration of pure beauty did much to hasten the triumph of classicism, dedicated, in his view, to the service of the Church.

In literature Piccolomini is distinguished by his *Chrisis,* a modern comedy despite its dependence on Plautus, reflecting the new interest in this genre. His love poems are highly esteemed, but better known is his *Historia de Duobus Amantibus,* classical and Ovidian, treating of an event in Siena during the sojourn in that city of the Emperor Sigismund in 1432, a picture of the sensuality and corruption of the times, and the death of Lu-

cretia after she was abandoned by Eurialus. The literary quality of the *Historia* lies in the masterly psychological treatment of the heroine, her struggle between duty and passion, and the fine descriptions, in Ciceronian Latin, marked by the influence of Boccaccio and of Ovid.

Piccolomini's works were collected in 1551 and his letters beginning in 1908; many separate editions contain individual works such as the *Orationes,* printed in 1755. *De Duobus Amantibus Historia* was translated into English by F. Grierson in 1929. An abridgment of his *Memoirs* and *Commentaries* was translated by Florence A. Gregg and published in 1959 with an introduction by Leona C. Gabel.

ABOUT: Ady, C. M. Pius II; Boulting, W. Aeneas Silvius; Pastor, L. History of the Popes; Piccolomini, A. S. Memoirs of a Renaissance Pope, ed. L. C. Gabel; Blackfriars, XV (1961).

F. J. C.

*PICO DELLA MIRANDOLA, GIOVANNI, Count (February 24, 1463-November 17, 1494), Italian humanist and Neoplatonist, was born in the family castle, third son of Gianfrancesco, of the family of the lords of La Mirandola, near Ferrara, and of La Concordia. His father's death, when Pico was four, led to long dissension among the brothers and frequent attempts at reconciliation. Pico's first studies under Tamasia revealed his precocious intelligence and his remarkable memory, and at fourteen he was sent to the University of Bologna to study canon law. Inspired however by Beroaldo, and disgusted with the curriculum, he yielded to his greater interest in philosophy and theology and went in 1479 to the University of Ferrara, where he met several of his closest friends, among them Tito Strozzi, who addressed Latin verses to him. The visit of Bessarion and new contact with Byzantium drew Pico further toward Greek culture, and at Padua in 1480 he was exposed to the new Neoplatonic interpretations of Aristotle, Averroës, and Albertus Magnus. His brilliance in public disputation with his professors was remarked, and he rapidly acquired a vast erudition, including extensive knowledge of Greek and the Semitic languages; by this time he had also shown his peculiar enthusiasm for cabalistic doctrine. In Florence in 1484 Pico met Poliziano and Ficino; the latter turned him definitively from the traditional Aristotle to the new Platonism. By no means a mere disciple, Pico discovered sources unknown to Ficino, and combined his acquired knowledge into broad though naïve comparisons between Christian doctrine and the thought of Zoroas-

* pē′ kō dāl lä mē rän′ dō lä

ter and Pythagoras, thus conceiving philosophy as a kind of mysticism.

Pico carried his search for knowledge to France, and on his return to Florence in 1486 promulgated his nine hundred theses or *Conclusiones Nongentae in Omni Genere Scientiarum,* a synthesis of dialectics, metaphysics, theology, natural science, and magic. Though the theses seem today thinly spread, they provoked unbounded admiration when Pico proposed, though in vain, to defend them in public debate. Thirteen of them were soon branded heretical, and in March 1487 Innocent VIII prohibited discussion of them. Pico signed a formal retraction, but in May defended his orthodoxy in particular detail and sent his answer, the *Apologia,* to Lorenzo the Magnificent. He explained the so-called points of heresy through symbolic or spiritual interpretation, for example that Christ had descended to Hell not in His real presence but *quoad effectum,* and the thesis that the cabala is the best initiation into a belief in the divinity of Christ. After a further trip to France, Pico found absolution with the more lenient Pope Alexander VI, and was officially vindicated in June 1493. He changed his attitude at that moment, destroyed certain early works, and turned suddenly to religion in his *Heptaplus,* a mystical interpretation of the Creation, hailed by Ficino as a great work. During his last years in Florence, he was in close contact with Ficino, Poliziano, and Lorenzo. Around 1490 Pico fell under the persuasive influence of Savonarola, who led him to ascetic practices and meditation; his last writings illustrate his preoccupation with religion, notably in his commentaries on parts of the Bible. He died in apparent sanctity, invested by Savonarola, but in mysterious circumstances, probably poisoned by one of his servants. He was buried in St Mark's. His life was written by his nephew Giovanni Francesco and published in 1496 (ed. by E. Garin, 1942).

Pico's many works, primarily in Latin, deal with a variety of special subjects, and represent several distinct periods in his rapidly evolving thought. He left in manuscript the twelve books *De Astrologia,* a formal and well documented attack against judicial astrology, part of an enormous project directed aaginst the enemies of the Church. His *De Ente et Uno* (1491) is a scholastic tract purporting to reconcile Aristotle and Plato, and of particular interest with respect to Pico's own Platonist ideas on the nature of God. This work represents the transition from the traditional scholasticism which continued to dominate Pico's thought in many ways to the free

analysis of Ficino's methods. Pico's allegiance to the schoolmen is evident for example in a letter of 1485 in which he pays tribute to their subtle learning, and his theses themselves remain close to general Thomist procedures. Pico also left an extensive correspondence with his many friends, a corpus of minor ascetic tracts, a commentary on a "canzone" of the Platonist Benivieni regarding celestial love, several Latin elegiacs, and a few early Italian poems (Poliziano regretted that Pico had destroyed so many others).

Pico did much to establish the importance of the vast cabalistic literature of medieval Judaism and to renew scholarly interest in the Talmud, the Mishna, and the many commentators, Maimonides, Moses of Gerona, Leo Hebraeus, Isaac Israelita, and Abulafia. He accumulated a remarkable library of such works, and their full impact on his thought seems to coincide with his *De Hominis Dignitate,* written during the years 1486-88. Cabalism rather naturally enriched the hermetic doctrines revealed by Ficino on the purification of the soul, the freeing of the mind, and the penetration into the mysteries of Creation. Pico's leanings in this direction are fully consonant with his objections to the false science of astrology, and his variable attitudes toward Averroës, who stood somewhere between a *priori* logic and the mystery of causes.

Pico's influence, often in the guise of Protestant tendencies, may be traced in Lefèvre d'Étaples and Jean Bodin, and in England is exemplified by Sir Thomas More, whose admiration was profound, and who translated the biography into English along with *The XII Propertees of a Lover,* Pico's best known poetry. Another early English translation is T. Stanley's *A Platonick Discourse on Love,* published in 1641 and reprinted by E. Gardner in 1914. His primary significance in the Renaissance was recognized by Walter Pater and J. A. Symonds, and his tract *On the Imagination* was translated by H. Caplan in 1930.

ABOUT: Pater, W. The Renaissance; Rigg, J. Pico della Mirandola; Symonds, J. The Renaissance. [In Italian—see studies by E. Garin, V. di Giovanni, G. Massetani, V. Rossi, G. Semprini, A. della Torre. In French—see study by P. M. Cordier.]

F. J. C.

---

*PINTO, FERNÃO MENDES (c. 1510-July 8, 1583), Portuguese merchant-adventurer and writer, had merely to retell his experiences in the Orient to produce a fascinating book. Not satisfied with autobiography, he wove into it such fabrications, vying with Marco Polo's travels, that no historian could ever trust him. He claimed to have been shipwrecked five times, enslaved thirteen, and sold

* pĕɴ′ tōō

sixteen. To this day, the Portuguese pun on his name: "Fernão, mentes?—Minto." (Ferdinand, are you lying? Yes, I am.)

Born near Coimbra into a penurious but well-connected family at Montemor-o-Velho, Pinto left his home in 1521 to serve a lady in Lisbon. The boy apparently ran away to sea, was captured by French pirates, and cast off on shore. After further service in noble households, he attached himself to the Faria family. Anxious to carve out a fortune in the Orient, he, like thousands of adventurous young men, among them his two brothers and the poet Camões, went east as a soldier in 1536 or 1537. He established himself near Singapore, in the strategic port of Malacca, then commanded by Pero de Faria, and grew wealthy from profitable voyages to Indonesia, Indochina, Siam, Burma, and the ports of China and Japan. Pinto met St. Francis Xavier and accompanied him on the great missionary's last trip from Japan to China. Upon seeing the saint's uncorrupted body exhibited in Goa in 1554, Pinto, who was on the point of retiring to Portugal, resolved to give up his wealth, join the Jesuits, and sail with them once more to the Empire of the Rising Sun. When the mission failed, his religious fervor evaporated. He left the Society of Jesus, without hard feelings on either side, and carried out his original plan by returning to Portugal in 1558. There he bought himself a country house, married, and had children, for whom he wrote his story, "so that they might see what hardships and dangers I endured in the course of twenty-one years." In 1582, a year before his death, a summary of this mixture of truth and fancy was published as *Algumas Informações da China* by three Jesuits who had visited him. But only in 1613 was the work edited by the aged official royal chronicler of the time, Francisco de Andrade, as *Peregrinaçám . . . em que dá Conta de Muitas e Muito Estranhas Cousas que Viu e Ouviu. . . .* After Herrera Maldonado had published a Spanish translation in 1620, it was read avidly throughout Europe. In English alone it was published six times between 1625 and 1897.

In the form of an autobiography Pinto tells us the plausible events of his life; how he took part in a naval expedition to the Red Sea and visited Abyssinia; how he haunted the China Sea as a pirate with António de Faria as far as Korea; how he escaped from Chinese captivity through China and Tartary into Indochina; how he was the first to sail to Japan, returned there three times, in the intervals helping a Muslim prince on Java to

defeat a Hindu, suffering a frightful shipwreck in the Malayan archipelago, and witnessing the gorgeous festivals and the horrible family feuds at the Siamese court. A critical analysis of the apparently realistic account reveals that this is no factual autobiography: the chronology is careless and many of the incidents are sheer fantasy. Probably Pinto was responsible for the embroidery, Andrade for the novel-like arrangement. But to whom can we ascribe the underlying ideas, extraordinary for the times? They make of Pinto a precursor of those famous French travelers and thinkers who promoted reform by comparing the wise and exotic East with the benighted West. Pinto's Chinese chapters have the earmarks of a Utopian novel, implicitly satirizing Portuguese greed, hypocrisy, superstition, immorality, intolerance, bad manners, and pretensions to grandeur and nobility, while exalting humaneness and a simple faith in one just and kind God above all churches. Pinto's story is presented as that of an apparently cynical, practical-minded rogue who makes the best of all situations. His work also stands as an early Portuguese example of Oriental influence on European thought.

An English summary of the Spanish version of the *Peregrinaçám* was included in Purchas' *Pilgrimes* of 1625. In 1653 H. Cogan translated the entire work as *The Voyages and Adventures of Fernand Mendez Pinto.* Editions have reappeared regularly, the most elegant in Portuguese being A. Casais Monteiro's of 1952-53.

ABOUT: Collis, M. The Grand Peregrination, Being the Life and Adventures of F. M. P.; Boxer, C. R. The Portuguese in the East, 1500-1800 in Livermore, H. V. ed. Portugal and Brazil, An Introduction. [In French—see study by G. LeGentil. In Portuguese—see studies by M. Domingues, A. J. Saraiva.]

G. M. M.

*PISAN, CHRISTINE DE (1364-c. 1430), French poet and miscellaneous writer, was born in Venice. Her mother was the daughter of one of the governors of the Venetian Republic, and her father was Thomas de Pisan, a physician-scholar-astrologist who, at the time of Christine's birth, was a councilor of the Venetian Republic. Thomas de Pisan's reputation as a learned man was so great that in 1368 Charles V invited him to France as his court astrologer. Christine therefore grew up in the cultured and refined atmosphere of the French court. Here she learned Latin and had access to the magnificent library that Charles had collected. Her girlhood seems to have been completely happy.

* pē zän'

She was intelligent, beautiful, wealthy, a favorite at court, and at fifteen she was happily married to Étienne de Castel, a knight from Picardy, who served as one of Charles' secretaries. They had three children—a daughter and two sons.

Christine's fortunes fell abruptly, however, after 1380. The king died and her father followed soon after. In 1389 her husband, off on a diplomatic mission to Beauvais, died of plague. Left helpless, with debts, lawsuits, and her family to support, Christine turned to literature. She has been called the first of the bluestockings, the first woman to write for a living. That she should have attempted to do this in an age when women had virtually no status in society is no less remarkable than the fact that she succeeded at it and became one of the most popular and respected writers of her age. Her work—with only a few exceptions—holds little intrinsic interest for the modern reader. It is mainly moral and didactic, reflecting the literary tastes and fashions of the Middle Ages. As such, however, it is of great value to scholars, revealing in vivid and intimate detail the life of a refined and civilized France gradually torn apart by the civil dissensions and foreign invasions of the fifteenth century. But in her poems Christine moves outside her world and speaks to all ages. Writing in the popular forms of rondeaux, virelays, ballades, and showing the influence of the master of the technique of ballade writing—Eustache Deschamps—Christine gave moving expression to her loneliness and her despair. One of her loveliest lyrics begins: "Seulete sui et seulete vueil estre" ("Alone am I, alone I wish to be").

Her consolation was in work. She plunged into the study of history, philosophy, Latin poetry. She wrote industriously. Meanwhile she made new influential friends. The Earl of Salisbury, who had come to France to arrange the marriage of Richard II to Isabelle of France (1396), became the patron of her son Jean. When the earl died, the boy's education was put into the hands of Philip of Burgundy. It was he who commissioned her biography of Charles V—Le Livre des Faitz et Bonnes Mœurs du Sayge Roy Charles (1405)—which survives as a valuable picture of the court life of the period. For him also she wrote the moral and philosophical works Mutacion de Fortune (1405) and La Vision (1405). Her fame spread to England (Henry IV invited her to live at his court) and to Italy (Galeazzo Visconti invited her

to Milan), but Christine chose to remain in France. Her love for her adopted country is revealed in her poems deploring the civil wars —Lamentation and Livre de la Paix. After the defeat of the French at Agincourt she retired to the convent of Poissy where her daughter was a nun. She emerged from retirement only once—to publish a song in honor of Joan of Arc in 1429. Nothing is known of Christine's last years, but it is assumed that she died at the convent.

Christine de Pisan is today best remembered as a feminist who opposed what were in the Middle Ages almost insurmountable obstacles against the recognition of women's equality with men. In this struggle she had to fight the whole tradition of Aristotelian anti-feminism and the bitter misogyny of the most popular poem of the Middle Ages, the Roman de la Rose (in the second part of the poem by Jean de Meung). She answered de Meung in two treatises—Épître au Dieu d'Amour (1399) and Le Dit de la Rose (1401). In 1407 she argued vigorously for the equality of women in the poem Le Livre du Duc des Vrais Amants; and in La Cité des Dames and Trésor des Dames she wrote the lives of great women of antiquity. She also argued for the education of women in Le Livre des Trois Vertus. Like many propagandists, Christine was sometimes carried away with an excess of moral earnestness and the resulting works are often tedious and pedantic. Nevertheless, as Nitze and Dargan remark in their History of French Literature, "Christine was an enlightening force quite out of the ordinary."

Christine's poetic works in French were edited by M. Roy (1886-96) and her biography of Charles V was edited by S. Solente (1936-41). The popularity of her works is demonstrated by the number of English translations and imitations that appeared in the fifteenth century. Thomas Occleve (or Hoccleve) imitated her Épître au Dieu d'Amour in his "Letter of Cupid." Her Épître d'Othéa was translated in about 1440 by Stephen Scrope and published in 1904 as The Epistle of Othea to Hector, or The Boke of Knyghthode. Earl Rivers' translation Moral Proverbs of Christyne de Pise was published by William Caxton in 1478. Caxton himself, by order of King Henry VII, translated her Livre des Faitz d'Armes et de Chevalerie and this was published by the Early English Text Society in 1932. Her Cité des Dames was translated by Brian Anslay (1521). In 1908 Laurence Binyon and E. R. D. Maclagan translated The Book of the Duke of True Lovers.

ABOUT: De Koven, A. E. Women in Cycles of Culture; Kemp-Welch, A. Of Six Medieval Women; Journal of the History of Ideas, January 1955. [In French—see studies by J. Moulin, M. J. Pinet.]

*PISAREV, DMITRY IVANOVICH
(November 15, 1840-June 4, 1868), Russian
essayist and critic, was born of a noble family in declining circumstances. He spent his
childhood on his parents' estate in the village
of Znamenskoye in Orel province. His formal education began in 1851 at a *Gymnasium*
in St. Petersburg where his extraordinary
ability earned him a gold medal on his graduation in 1856. He continued his education in
the history and philology faculty of St. Petersburg University, where he remained until
1861.

In 1858 the youthful Pisarev was placed in
charge of the literary criticism section of the
journal *Rassvet* (Daybreak), a publication he
later characterized as "sugary, but respectable." He was, however, indebted to this experience for the fuller developmnt of his literary and philosophical views. "I had to read
many articles on history [and] pedagogy . . .
and a number of books on natural science. . . . In short, my bibliography forced
me out of my confined cell into the fresh
air. . . ."

Pisarev matured in the midst of the democratic upsurge of the late fifties and early sixties and rapidly took his place in the ranks of
the revolutionary democrats. In 1861 he began his connection with *Russkoye Slovo*
(The Russian Word) with an article on
"Nineteenth Century Scholastics" in which
he associated himself with the ideas of
Chernyshevsky, deploring the state of current
criticism and philosophical theory and recommending that both would do well to accom-
modate themselves more closely to the prevailing developments in Russian society. During the next two years Pisarev wrote numerous articles on social, philosophical, and literary questions which were enormously popular among the younger people and progres-
sives of the time. *Russkoye Slovo* and
Chernyshevsky's *Sovremennik* (The Contemporary) were the leading spokesmen of
the revolutionary democrats.

In the summer of 1862 Pisarev addressed
a revolutionary article to the youth of Russia
occasioned by the appearance of a slanderous
pamphlet attacking the philosopher Alexander
Herzen. Since the article was not merely an
answer to the pamphlet but a call for revolutionary activity, it was published in an illegal
printing shop. The shop was discovered,
however, and Pisarev was arrested and imprisoned in the Peter and Paul Fortress for
a term of four years' solitary confinement.
Notwithstanding the conditions of his im-

prisonment, he continued to write voluminously; in 1863 the determined efforts of
friends and relatives were rewarded, and he
was allowed to have his prison articles published.

He was released on November 18, 1866,
but survived his imprisonment only two
years. On July 4, 1868, he was drowned while
swimming off the Baltic coast at Dubbelna (a
resort near Riga). The poet Nekrasov dedicated a poem to his memory. "Yet another
misfortune," wrote Herzen, "has struck our
little phalanx. A shining star . . . has disappeared, carrying away wonders of a talent
that had hardly developed. . . ."

Pisarev was a philosophical materialist and
a utopian socialist. As a materialist and socialist he rejected the idea of art for art's
sake. In his criticism he concerned himself
more with the ideas and social philosophy of
the characters and the authors he discussed
than with technique. It was this tendency
that gave rise to his famous article attacking
the critic Belinsky's estimate of Pushkin.
In his social and philosophical views he is
linked to Herzen, Chernyshevsky, and Dobrolyubov. Contemporary Russian criticism
praises him for his acute understanding of
the social and economic factors of his day,
but concedes that he was far from a Marxist in his historical and political views. Pisarev is recognized as among the first in
Russia to appreciate the significance of the
work of Darwin, although he vigorously rejected the theory of Malthus which Darwin
had found so suggestive. Lenin found Pisarev's ideas on the rôle of fantasy and
vision in the process of cognition extremely
valuable, and Pisarev is highly regarded as
a contributor to the theory of aesthetics and
as an intellectual leader in the sixties after
the death of Dobrolyubov and the imprisonment of Chernyshevsky.

A volume of selections from his works has
been published in English (Moscow, 1958).

ABOUT: Pisarev, D. Selected Philosophical,
Social and Political Essays; Wellek, R. *in* Continuity and Change in Russian and Soviet Thought
(ed. E. J. Simmons); Harvard Slavic Studies, IV
(1957).

L. R. & H. H.

*PISEMSKY, ALEXEY FEOFILAK-
TOVICH (March 22, 1820-January 21,
1881), Russian novelist and playwright, was
born to the impoverished branch of an ancient family (one of his ancestors had served
Ivan the Terrible) in Rameniye, Kostroma

* pyĕ′ sä rĕf

* pyĕ′ syĕm skĭ

province. His father, whose wealthy relatives had placed him in the army, had spent thirty years in the Crimea before marrying, and, as Pisemsky wrote, was quite a martinet against whom his gentle, cultivated wife afforded a sharp contrast.

The first ten years of Alexey's life were spent in Vetluga where his father served on a committee caring for war-wounded. From 1830 to 1834 he remained at home where no special efforts were made to educate him, "but I liked to read books—novels, especially —and by the time I was fourteen I had already read most of Scott, Cervantes, *Gil Blas*. . . . My tutors were inept—I was taught no foreign language except Latin." In 1834 he was placed in the local *Gymnasium* where he conceived a passion for the theatre after he had seen performances by a troupe of itinerant players. He also began writing, producing two novels which his teacher praised for their style, but as Pisemsky remarked, "They had more 'style' than anything else because I had attempted to describe people and places of which I was wholly ignorant."

In 1840 he entered Moscow University in the faculty of mathematics, which "brought me down to earth—I could no longer speak glibly about matters I knew nothing about." But his interest in literature and the theatre continued to develop. He acted in amateur performances and, as a result of his training, was much in demand at the height of his popularity as reader and reciter.

By the time of his graduation (1844) his father had died and his mother was a hopeless invalid. He attempted to write for a living, but his very first novel, "Boyarshchina," was caught by the censor just as it was about to be published in *Otechestvennye Zapisky* (Annals of Our Country), an important periodical. With the help of relatives he obtained and held a series of government posts in Moscow, Kostroma, and St. Petersburg from 1845 to 1859 and from 1866 to his retirement in 1872.

He first broke into print with a short story, "Nina," published in a small journal in 1848, and during the 1850's, when he enjoyed his greatest prominence, an uninterrupted stream of novels and stories appeared in several periodicals beginning with *The Muff* (1850). During this time Pisemsky was associated with Grigoriev and Ostrovsky and other young writers whose attitude was more democratic and less dogmatic than that of the Slavophiles. Their organ was the *Moskvityanin* (Muscovite). He was a favor-ite of St. Petersburg society, frequenting all the fashionable salons, where his deportment was such as to try, but not to exceed, the patience of his wife, whom he had married in 1848. She was the daughter of Sunin, the first editor of *Otechestvennye Zapisky* and is depicted in the character of Eupraxia in his novel *The Troubled Seas* (1863).

His most famous works are *A Love Match, The Old Lady, The Doormat* and *One Thousand Souls* (1858). His most popular play is *A Hard Lot* (1859).

During the 1860's he retired for a time to devote himself to writing and editing a review. But he was suddenly out of touch with the changing atmosphere of Russian intellectual life, and he rejected out of hand the efforts of the new generation of writers and thinkers that was coming out of the post-Liberation period (after 1861). Thus in the opinion of his younger contemporary Chernyshevsky, Pisemsky, "while truly and powerfully depicting many sides of Russian village life before Emancipation, gave not the least hint of how the life of the people could be improved." As he moved further away from the temper of the times Pisemsky found himself less and less popular and less and less able to continue to live by literature alone. He returned to government service in 1866 and remained there until his retirement in 1872. His last years were haunted by hypochondria and frustrated hopes to which the deaths of his two sons in the late 1870's came as the final blow. He died in Moscow.

Pisemsky's style has been compared to the naturalistic style of Zola, but his most obvious sources of inspiration both in his plays and in his best novels, is Gogol. Contemporary opinion of Pisemsky follows the judgment of Chernyshevsky.

His works appeared in an edition of eight volumes in St Petersburg (1910-11), his *Selected Works* (Leningrad, 1932), his *Letters* (Moscow, 1936); a new edition of his *Complete Works* was initiated in Moscow-Leningrad in 1959. *One Thousand Souls* was published in an English translation by Ivy Litvinov in 1959.

ABOUT: Canadian Slavonic Papers, III (1958); Saturday Review, December 26, 1959.

L. R. & H. H.

PIUS II, POPE. See PICCOLOMINI, ENEA SILVIO

PJETURSSON, HALLGRÍMUR. See PÉTURSSON, HALLGRÍMUR

*PLATEN-HALLERMÜNDE, AUGUST Graf von (October 24, 1796-December 5, 1835), German poet and dramatist, was born in Ansbach, Bavaria, where his father, the descendant of a noble but impoverished family, worked as head forester. After attending the military academy at Munich (1806-10) and the Royal Institute of Pages (1810-14), Platen was commissioned a lieutenant. He participated briefly in the campaign against France in 1815. He was ill-suited temperamentally for army life, and during his unhappy cadet years devoted himself to study and literature. During the course of his life he mastered twelve languages. In 1818 he obtained an extended leave of absence with pay to enter the University of Würzburg, transferring the following year to Erlangen, where he became an enthusiastic student of the philosopher Schelling. He also became acquainted with the poet Rückert, who instructed him in the nature of Oriental verse composition. Platen adopted the Persian ghasel, an intricate and demanding form consisting of from ten to twenty lines, as a favorite form and in 1821 published *Ghaselen*, his first major collection of poems. This work, which had little popular success, was followed by four additional volumes of verse, *Lyrische Blätter* (1821), *Spiegel der Hafis* (1822), *Vermischte Schriften* (1822), and *Neue Ghaselen* (1824).

In 1824 Platen traveled to Italy, and in Venice produced *Sonette aus Venedig* (1825), a work which contains some of the finest sonnets in the German language. After returning to Germany to resign his commission, he settled permanently in Italy in 1826, supported by a meager pension from King Ludwig I of Bavaria. His remaining years were spent in a restless, wandering existence, filled with loneliness, pessimism, and bitterness at his lack of recognition. His *Tagebücher* (published in 1896 and 1900) best reveal the tragedy of this period. He died in Siracusa, Sicily, at thirty-nine.

The more Platen was buffeted by life, the further he retreated into the ideal world of artistic beauty. He held an aristocratic concept of the poet's calling, and in his works endeavored to attain the classical goal of perfect form. He wrote odes, eclogues, and hymns in the manner of Pindar, Horace, and Theocritus, purposely choosing difficult forms which permit no deviation in order to counteract the decay of literature, which he felt was being caused by the extravagant

and undisciplined writings of the German romanticists. Platen is one of the most form-conscious poets in German literature, and his poems, with their smooth flowing rhythms and flawless purity of rhymes, exhibit a statuesque grandeur. He is the least subjective of poets, and the lack of human warmth and compassion has kept his poetry from attaining widespread popularity. His most folk-like productions are his ballads such as *Das Grab im Busento, Der Pilgrim vor St. Just,* and *Der Tod des Carus,* which are among the finest of their type in German. In his *Polenlieder* (1831) he expresses his sympathy for the Poles in their uprising against Russian tyranny. Because of his formal perfection, Platen was acclaimed as master and model by many later poets including Herwegh, Strachwitz, Meyer, and Liliencron.

As a dramatist Platen began writing in the romantic tradition of Ludwig Tieck, producing *Der Gläserne Pantoffel* (1824), a combination of the fairy tales *Cinderella* and *Snow White and Rose Red.* In *Die Ver-hängnisvolle Gabel* (1826), a satiric comedy in verse in the manner of Aristophanes, he parodied and effectively annihilated the German fate tragedy, a dramatic form which had become popular at the beginning of the nineteenth century. A second verse comedy, *Der Romantische Oedipus* (1828), represented a violent attack on the writer Karl Immermann, who, Platen felt, personified the degenerate evils of romanticism, as well as on the poet Heinrich Heine. Platen held his dramas in high regard and considered them his best works. His diaries revealed sketches and outlines for more than ninety dramas and epics. Of the latter he completed one successful work, *Die Abbasiden* (1835), based on a tale from the *Arabian Nights.* However, his place in literature today is maintained solely by the merit of his poetry.

Selections of Platen's verse in English translation are contained in J. Gostwick, *The Spirit of German Poetry* (1845), R. Garnett, *Poems from the German* (1862), H. W. Longfellow, *Poems of Places,* XI (1876-79), C. Brooks, *Poems* (1885), K. Knortz, *Representative German Poems* (1885), *The German Classics,* V (1913-15), M. Münsterberg, *A Harvest of German Verse* (1916), the Warner Library, and L. Forster, *The Penguin Book of German Verse.* The *Sonette aus Venedig* were translated by R. B. Cooke in 1923 under the title *Sonnets from Venice.*

ABOUT: Mann, T. Essays of Three Decades. [In German—see studies by M. Koch, K. Richter, and R. Schlösser. In French—see study by P. Besson.]

* plä′ tĕn häl ĕr mün′ dĕ

D. G. D.

*POLENZ, WILHELM VON (January 14, 1861-November 13, 1903), German novelist and dramatist, was born at castle Obercunewalde in Oberlausitz, Saxony, the descendant of generations of landed gentry. His father served as chamberlain at the Dresden court. Polenz attended the *Gymnasium* in Dresden and, following his year's military service, studied law in Breslau, Berlin, and Leipzig, although he felt no inclination for this career. While in Berlin he encountered the ideas of Zola, Tolstoy, and Wagner, and his first novel, *Die Sühne* (1890), reflects the influence of the current naturalistic theories. Returning to Dresden, Polenz met and married a young, wealthy English lady, who encouraged him in his literary ambitions, and henceforth he devoted himself to writing. The couple traveled widely, and in 1902 they journeyed extensively through the United States. Polenz wrote an interesting account of this trip entitled *Das Land der Zukunft* (1903). His death occurred in Breslau at forty-two.

Most of the writings of Polenz belong to the German tradition of *Heimatkunst* and present an accurate and sympathetic account of the peasantry and environment of his native region. He possessed a strong moral feeling, and his novels generally contain a social message, although they never moralize overtly or obviously. Polenz was above all a genuine artist, who was motivated by the sincerest and highest aims. His works were highly praised by Tolstoy. He was outstanding in his ability to create believable human beings in an accurately presented milieu.

The main works on which his reputation rests are the novels *Der Pfarrer von Breitendorf* (1893), which is strongly influenced by the religious and ethical convictions of Moritz von Egidy, and *Der Büttnerbauer* (1895), which is his masterpiece. Here Polenz treats the conflict of country and city life which is central to all his work and depicts the downfall of a small landowner through the manipulations of unscrupulous businessmen. Other successful novels which have retained their interest include *Der Grabenhäger* (1897), *Thekla Lüdekind* (1900), *Liebe Ist Ewig* (1901), and *Wurzellocker* (1902). The dramas of Polenz such as *Heinrich von Kleist* (1891) and *Andreas Bockholdt* (1898) were unsuccessful. His collected works, edited by A. Bartels, appeared in ten volumes. 1909-11.

Das Land der Zukunft was translated by L. Wolffsohn in 1904 as *The Land of the Future*.

* pō lĕnts

E. von Mach translated *Der Büttnerbauer* under the title *Farmer Büttner* (1913-15).

ABOUT: Mach, E. von, The German Classics XVII. [In German—see studies by A. Bartels, A. Stern, W. Tholen.]

D. G. D.

*POLIZIANO (or POLITIAN), ANGELO (July 14, 1454-September 29, 1494), Italian poet and humanist, was born in the town of Montepulciano in southern Tuscany. His name was originally Angelo Ambrogini; he later took the surname Politianus (Poliziano, in Italian) from his native town's Latin name, Mons Politianus.

When Poliziano was nine, his father, Benedetto Ambrogini, a lawyer, was killed in a blood feud, leaving his widow and five children with little means of support. Poliziano was soon sent to Florence and continued his education there, living in near poverty. He showed a precocious ability in the classical languages and shortly began studying philosophy under Ficino, and Latin and Greek literature under other famous teachers. At sixteen, having already composed original poems in Latin, he began a translation of the *Iliad* into Latin hexameters, eventually translating Books II through V (Book I had been translated by an earlier scholar). In 1470 he presented the translation of Book II to Lorenzo de' Medici and asked for Lorenzo's patronage. His teacher Ficino also wrote to Lorenzo, recommending Poliziano highly and calling the scholar-poet the "Homeric youth."

Lorenzo shortly accepted the youth into his circle and in 1473 took him into his household as tutor to his eldest son, Piero, then three years old. Eventually Poliziano also tutored the second son, Giovanni (later Pope Leo X). His other tasks included collecting and studying manuscripts for Lorenzo's famous library and writing Latin and Italian poems to mark important occasions or to amuse the household. Most of his poetry in Italian dates from this period. His only long poem in Italian, the unfinished *Stanze Cominciate per la Giostra del Magnifico Giuliano de' Medici*, was inspired by a tournament given in 1475 by Lorenzo's brother Giuliano in honor of a celebrated Florentine beauty, Simonetta Cattaneo Vespucci. The poem is an elegant and decorative allegory whose beautiful descriptions inspired several Renaissance paintings, including Botticelli's *Venus* and *Primavera*. Poliziano probably abandoned the poem in 1478

* pō lē tsyä' nō

735

POLIZIANO

when Giuliano, its hero, was assassinated. After Giuliano's death Poliziano wrote a memorial in Latin prose attacking the Pazzi conspirators who had murdered him.

In 1479 Poliziano was dismissed from the Medici household, evidently because of quarrels with Lorenzo's wife, Clarice, over Piero's studies. After some months of wandering, he settled early in 1480 at Mantua in the household of Cardinal Gonzaga. It was probably at Mantua, as entertainment for a gala, that Poliziano's *La Favola d'Orfeo* (The Fable of Orpheus) was written and produced. The play, under five hundred lines long and less a true drama than a pageant, is important in the history of drama as the first secular play written in Italian.

Late in 1480 Poliziano was reconciled with the Medici and returned to Florence, serving again briefly as Piero's tutor before his appointment to the chair of Greek and Latin Eloquence at the university, a post he filled brilliantly and successfully until his death. He composed a series of Latin introductions to various of his university courses—the *Sylvae*, verse introductions; and the *Praelectiones*, in prose. In 1489 he published his *Miscellanea*, about a hundred short studies treating classical authors and philological problems.

His close association with Lorenzo de' Medici continued. He collected further manuscripts for Lorenzo's library and edited the most valuable of the library's manuscripts,

the *Pandects* of Justinian. Lorenzo presented him with a villa outside Florence in 1483, and at various times obtained for him unimportant but remunerative church posts. (Poliziano, who was probably never ordained as a priest, had apparently taken minor orders.) As an illustrious scholar and a friend of Lorenzo, Poliziano was a chief figure in Florentine intellectual society. One of his close friends was the younger poet Pico della Mirandola; another was Alessandra Scala, an intellectual young Florentine woman with whom he carried on an exchange of Greek and Latin poems. After Lorenzo's death in 1492, which Poliziano commemorated in a heartfelt and passionate lament, Lorenzo's successor Piero—Poliziano's former pupil—acted as his patron and tried unsuccessfully to have him made a cardinal. Poliziano himself died of fever two years after Lorenzo, at the age of forty.

Poliziano's physical appearance was unprepossessing, but his musical voice and his facility with language made him a brilliant conversationalist. Modern estimates of his character perhaps overemphasize the faults and vices attributed to him in attacks by his enemies—homosexual tendencies, cowardice, opportunism. Whatever his weaknesses may have been, they did not prevent his being one of the most brilliant and productive scholars and writers of his century. Poliziano's works in Latin were his most important contribution to his own time. His translations made many Greek works available to the Latin-reading world, and his critical studies laid some of the foundations for later knowledge of classical literature. His Latin and Greek poems, admired by contemporaries, were too free in style and usage to suit the taste of the following age, which insisted on strict imitation of classical models. Poliziano is known today chiefly for his Italian poems, particularly for his refined and polished imitations of Italian folk songs—love songs and songs to spring. His best-known lyrics include "Ben venga Maggio," "I' mi trovai, fanciulle, un bel mattino," and "Io ti ringrazia, Amore."

The *Orfeo* was translated into English verse by J. A. Symonds (in *Sketches and Studies in Italy*, 1879), but Symonds mistakenly took his text from the *Orphei Tragoedia*, a longer revision of the *Orfeo* now considered to be the work of Antonio Tebaldeo. In 1951 Louis Lord published prose translations of the *Orfeo* and the *Orphei Tragoedia* on facing pages. Verse translations of about two dozen passages from Poliziano's Italian, Latin, and Greek poems were published by William Parr Greswell (1801). J. A. Symonds made verse translations of ten of Poliziano's best-known Italian lyrics, as well as of excerpts from the *Stanze* (1879). J. B. Fletcher included verse translations of several poems in *Literature of the Italian Renaissance* (1934). Prose translations are included in *The Penguin Book of Italian Verse,* edited by George Kay (1958).

ABOUT: Fletcher, J. B. Literature of the Italian Renaissance; Symonds, J. A. Renaissance in Italy; Connoisseur, April 1957; Durham University Journal, June 1954; New Yorker, February 24, 1951. [In Italian—see studies by R. Ramat, M. Santoro, N. Sapegno.]

J. K.

POLO, MARCO (c. 1254-c. 1324), Italian explorer and traveler, was born and died a citizen of the Republic of Venice; but the part of his life that matters to posterity was the twenty-three years he spent in China (Cathay), the source of his one great book.

He was the son of Nicolò Polo, who with his brother Maffeo and their father Andrea was a trader and merchant of importance. In their business interests the father and uncle had for many years traveled widely in the Near East; in fact, as a child of only six or so, Marco may already have gone as far from Venice as Constantinople. What is definitely known is that in 1271, when he was about seventeen, the two brothers started on their longest journey and took the boy with them.

More than once traversing territory that was not visited again by white men for nearly 500 years, the three arrived at the court of Kublai Khan (for the father and uncle it was the second time) in 1275. They remained there in the Khan's service until 1292. The "young bachelor," as they called Marco, studied the various languages of his new home and in a remarkably short time was named a "second class commissioner" of the Imperial Council. On its behalf he journeyed as far as Tibet, Yunnan, and Burma, and with a fresh and observant eye made notes of the strange people he met, their animals and their plants, and to the Khan's delight reported them in full on his return to the court at Shangtu.

Marco rose rapidly in the imperial service; so did his father and his uncle, but he outstripped them both. His work as an envoy took him to Cochin China, to the country north of the Gobi from which the Mongol rulers had come originally, to Burma, and perhaps to India. For three years he was governor of Yangchow. It was not only honor which the Polos earned; all three of them became rich in gold and precious stones. There was only one drawback—the Khan would not allow them to leave.

Finally, by a quirk of fate, they were appointed to accompany a Mongol princess, Kukachin, who was being sent as a bride to the Khan of Persia. Kublai knew they would not return; he sent by them messages to the Pope and to the kings of England, France, and Spain.

They reached a Venice which they had almost forgotten and which had almost forgotten them, by the end of 1295. They were all thoroughly orientalized, weather-beaten, dressed in rags into which they had sewed jewels and gold. At first their own relatives considered them impostors, but finally they proved their identity.

Marco Polo, now a man of forty, became famous—or, more nearly, notorious—in Venice for his far-fetched tales of incredible adventures and splendors. In derision they nicknamed him "Il Milione." The hard-headed Venetians discounted the wild stories of travelers, or rather they regarded accounts of real places as on a level with the improbable fictions of tall talkers. Marco was a man of business, not an artist; it probably never occurred to him to set down his marvels in writing.

But in 1298 he served as a commander in the Venetian navy in its war with Genoa, was captured, and remained a prisoner in Genoa for almost a year. It was during this captivity that his great book of travels was born. A fellow-prisoner, a Pisan named Rusticiano, persuaded him to dictate his memories. Actually, Marco Polo himself never wrote a word of his famous book.

The book was written not in Italian or Latin but in the French of a non-Frenchman. Since it antedated printing, some eighty-five disparate manuscripts are known; probably the earliest is that in the Bibliothèque Nationale in Paris. Probably because of its factual nature (despite errors and omissions), Polo's book failed to attain the immediate and overwhelming popularity of many a story of wonders and myths, but within the next century it had been translated into every major European language. The date of the first English translation is uncertain, but there was one by John Frampton published during the reign of Elizabeth I. The definitive English version (as well as the source-book for Polo himself, his travels, his times, and the places he visited) is *The Book of Ser Marco Polo the Venetian,* edited by Sir Henry Yule, first published in 1871, and revised and expanded with notes by Henri Cordier in 1921.

Little is known of the end of Polo's life, and no genuine portrait of him, done during his lifetime, exists. We know that he wrote his will on January 9, 1324, and he may have died the same day. He left a widow and three daughters, and was buried in the Church of San Lorenzo. A passage with a decorated archway is all that remains of the palace that was the Polos' ancestral home.

The book itself is in two parts—a prologue relating the first and second journeys to China (in only the second of which he participated) and of the travelers' return by way of Sumatra and India; and a much longer part which is a hodgepodge of geographical descriptions, accounts of strange customs, flora and fauna, explanations of Kublai Khan's court, his political administration, and the wars in which he engaged. As literature it does not exist; it is simply a straightforward narrative. Nevertheless, it is full of "firsts"—the first factual account by a European of the Mongols' government in Peking, and of Tibet, Burma, Japan, Siberia, Abyssinia, Ceylon, India, and many other lands unknown to the Middle Ages. Columbus possessed a copy of the book in Latin, and covered it with notes testifying to its importance to him. One legend, however, is not true: it was not Marco Polo who introduced the knowledge of printing into Europe.

As Henry Hart says: "Marco was a combination of busy merchant, administrator, traveler, explorer, and writer living at a time when no authentic material on the East was available. . . . His book has charmed, amused, and educated millions in every generation since it was written. In its simplicity, its frankness, its richness of material . . . it stands alone as . . . the greatest book of travel ever written."

ABOUT: Abramowitz, I. Great Prisoners; Grigson, G. & Gibbs-Smith, C. H. Marco Polo; Hart, H. H. Venetian Adventurer; Malloy, R. D. Masterworks of Travel and Exploration; Olschki, L. Marco Polo's Asia (tr. J. A. Scott); Peattie, D. R. Lives of Destiny; Proceedings of the British Academy 1934; Nature Magazine April 1954. [In French—see studies by G. Bonvalet and V. Chlovski.]

M. A. DE F.

*PONTANO, GIOVANNI GIOVIANO

(May 7, 1426-September 1503), Italian poet and humanist, was born in Cerreto, near Spoleto. He lost his father and his patrimony at an early age, and went with his mother to Perugia, where he did his first studies in language and literature. Seeking

* pŏn tä′ nō

PONTANO

fortune in new surroundings he joined in 1447, with King Alfonso, then at war in Tuscany, and returned with him to Naples, where he remained close to such scholars as Panormita, Giorgio da Trebisonda, and Beccadelli. The king, attracted by Pontano's scholarly attainments, named him tutor of the young princes, and took him into active military service as well as political counsel; Pontano showed his power as a statesman in the negotiations for peace begun in 1484, and later in Rome. His political philosophy was widely admired and represented moderation despite his innate opposition to the temporal power of the pope. He again distinguished himself in 1495 in receiving Charles VIII on his entry into Naples and left his record of activities and observations in *De Bello Neapolitano*, completed in 1494. After this date, Pontano lived for the most part isolated from public affairs. Throughout his active career, he was happy in his life with a beloved wife, but his last days were solitary, saddened by the loss of wife and children. His biographers tell of his noble dignity and his physical beauty, evident in the bronze bust in Genoa.

One of Pontano's great services to culture was the Accademia that he established in Naples, in imitation of those of Florence and Rome, which became the intellectual center of the city and at which appeared the principal humanists of the region. His immense literary production exemplifies the renewal of interest in classical literature, and his own mastery of style, fantasy, musicality, and rhythm, never too strictly Ciceronian, suit admirably his philosophy of reason without prejudice. His early Latin poetry imitates Catullus, and his *Amorum Libri* foresee the new genre of mythological and ancient allusion as ornamentation for conventional love themes of lament and despair. The fine elegy *De Quercu Diis Sacra* combines Ovid with popular literary elements, and enriches the techniques of description of nature, of forests, grottos, and mountains, with classical motifs. His *Lepidina,* one of his finest pieces, treats of the marriage of a river god with a nymph, forming an idyll reminiscent of Ovid and Propertius. His creative writing may be divided roughly into two types, lyrical and didactic. In his more attractive personal expression are his elegies entitled *De Amore Coniugali,* a traditional subject of long standing debate, his *Eridanus,* recounting his sensuous love for the courtesan Stella da Argenta, and the epitaphs of the *Tumuli* for his beloved wife Adriana or Ariadna, who died in 1491, and for other relatives. The didactic works include the *Urania,* in hexameters, which treats of the effects of the planets on living things and personifies them according to classical fables of the constellations, and *De Hortis Hesperidum,* rules on arboriculture, another great model for significant genres of the sixteenth century.

Pontano's works were published in 1538 and 1556, and many modern editions improve on the several works or add new texts, including the correspondence. There are a number of Italian translations from his Latin writings.

ABOUT: [In Italian—see studies by P. Ardito, I. Intravaja, V. Rossi, V. Tanteri.]

F. J. C.

POSTL, K. A. See "SEALSFIELD, CHARLES"

*POTGIETER, EVERHARDUS JO- HANNES (June 17, 1808-February 3, 1875), Dutch poet, essayist, and critic, was born in Zwolle, the provincial capital of Overijssel. He started adult life in a merchant's office in Antwerp. In 1831 he made a trip to Sweden, described in two volumes which appeared in Amsterdam (1836-40). Soon afterwards he settled in Amsterdam, engaged in commercial pursuits on his own account but with increasingly greater inclination toward literature. With Heije, the popular poet of Holland in those days, and

* pŏt' kē tēr

POTGIETER

Bakhuizen van den Brink, the rising young historian, Potgieter founded *De Muzen* (1834-36), a literary review which was soon superseded by their next venture, *De Gids,* a monthly which became the leading magazine of Holland. In it he wrote, mostly under the initials of "W. D——g," a great number of articles and poems. The first collected edition of his poems, written in the period 1832-68, appeared in two volumes (1868-75). They were preceded by some of his contributions to *De Gids,* also in two volumes (1864), and followed by three volumes of his *Studien en Schetsen* (1879). Soon after his death, a more comprehensive edition of his *Verspreide en Nagelaten Werken* (Miscellaneous and Posthumous Works) was published in eight volumes by his friend and literary executor Johan C. Zimmerman (1875-77), who likewise supervised a more complete edition of Potgieter's writings which appeared in nineteen volumes at Haarlem (1885-90). Of Potgieter's *Het Noorden in Omtrekken en Tafrelen* the third edition was issued in 1882, and a de luxe edition of his poems followed in Haarlem in 1893. Under the title of *Personen en Onderwerpen* many of Potgieter's criticisms had collectively appeared in three volumes in Haarlem in 1885 with an introduction by Busken Huet.

Potgieter's favorite master among the Dutch classics was Hooft, whose peculiarities in style and language he admired and imitated. Though often biased and exaggerated, a vein of altruistic abhorrence of the conventionalities of literary life runs through all his writings, even through his private correspondence with Busken Huet, parts of which have been published. Potgieter remained to his death the irreconcilable enemy of the Dutch "Jan Salie," as the Dutchman is nicknamed who does not believe in the regeneration of the Dutch people. Potgieter held up the Netherlanders of the golden age of the sixteenth and seventeenth centuries as models to be emulated. In these views he differed essentially from Busken Huet. Yet the two friends worked harmoniously together; and when Potgieter reluctantly gave up De ·Gids in 1865, it was Busken Huet whom he chose as his successor. Both then proceeded to Italy and were present at the Dante festivities in Florence, which in Potgieter's case resulted in a poem in twenty stanzas, *Florence* (1868). In Holland Potgieter's influence has been marked and beneficial; but his own style, that of ultra-purist, was at times somewhat forced, stilted, and not always easily understood.

ABOUT: [In Dutch—see studies by J. H. Groenewegen, A. Verwey.]

H. B.

*POTOCKI, JAN (Count) (March 8, 1761-December 2, 1815), Polish historian, archeologist, and short-story writer, was born in Pilow in the Ukraine into one of the great families of the Polish aristocracy. A brilliant student, he was educated in his native land and in Geneva and Lausanne, acquiring facility in most of the European languages as well as in Latin and Greek. He was so fluent in French that he regarded it as his second language and did all his writing in it.

Before he was twenty Potocki had traveled widely in Europe and the Near East, acquiring and developing a passion for the history of European races and national groups. In 1778 he visited Italy, Sicily, and Spain; in 1779 Tunis, Morocco, and Greece; in 1784 Constantinople, the Greek islands, Egypt, and France; in 1791 Africa, Spain, and England; and in 1794 Pomerania and Mecklenburg. His first book, *Voyage en Turquie et en Égypte,* published in 1788, was an account of his 1784 voyage. Like all his subsequent works it was privately printed in a limited edition. As a result, few copies survived, and Potocki's writings were virtually unknown for years after his death. In his lifetime, however, his reputation as a scholar and traveler was very high.

After the partition of Poland, Potocki became a Russian subject, though he remained

* pô tôts′ kē

740

an ardent Polish patriot. He was summoned to St. Petersburg by the Empress Catherine the Great who was eagerly recruiting European scholars to her court. By now he was recognized as an authority on Slavic ethnology, having published on his own printing press a two-volume *Essai sur l'Histoire Universelle et Recherches sur la Sarmatie* (1789), *Voyage dans Quelques Parties de la Basse-Saxe pour la Recherche des Antiquités Slaves* (1795), *Mémoire sur un Nouveau Péryple du Pont-Euxin ainsi que sur la Plus Ancienne Histoire des Peuples de Taunus, du Caucase et de la Scythie* (1796), and the four-volume *Fragments Historiques et Géographiques sur la Scythie, la Sarmatie et les Slavs* (1796). After Catherine's death he remained in Russia as special adviser to Czar Alexander I, who appointed him head of a scientific mission to China in 1805. Traveling with the party of Ambassador Golovkin, Potocki penetrated deep into central Asia, but Chinese authorities turned them back before they could reach Peking.

The National Academy of Sciences in St. Petersburg published several of Potocki's studies, including in 1802 his *Histoire Primitive des Peuples de la Russie,* its sequels in 1804 and 1805, and in 1810 his ancient history *Principes de Chronologie pour les Temps Antérieurs aux Olympiades.* Some time after 1810 Potocki retired to his family estate in Poland. Little else is known of his life except that he once made a balloon ascension with Blanchard in Warsaw, and that he had a son, Arthur, who fought in the War of 1812 and wrote what Michaud (in his *Biographie Universelle*) describes as "a curious dissertation upon the Jews." A contemporary portrait by Lampi shows a sensitive, aristocratic-looking man with large thoughtful eyes, posing against an exotic Egyptian background. Potocki suffered from a nervous illness in his last years which caused him such great pain and distress that he committed suicide. According to Michaud his suicide was actually motivated by feelings of guilt stemming from his "cynical tastes" and debauched habits which, he says, resembled those of the Marquis de Sade. The author of the sketch in Larousse's *Grande Dictionnaire* angrily denies this.

Potocki might have remained virtually unknown in the annals of European literature had it not been for the discovery by Roger Caillois in the 1950's of his *Manuscrit Trouvé à Saragosse.* Caillois was preparing an anthology of weird tales and in these exotic-erotic stories he found a wealth of material, including one story, "Commander de Toralva," which Washington Irving retold in his story "The Grand Prior of Minorca." *The Saragossa Manuscript* is a collection loosely held together in a day-to-day framework in the manner of such cycles as the *Decameron* and the *Heptameron*. The first part had originally been published in St. Petersburg in 1804 and 1805, the second part in Paris in 1813, and additional episodes in 1815. A Polish version of the entire work appeared in 1847 and was several times reprinted. Caillois published his French edition in 1958, and an English translation (by Elisabeth Abbott) of this edition was published in America in 1960.

In 1959 Caillois published in the periodical *Théâtre Populaire* "Six Parades" of Potocki—a group of short farces which he had written in 1792 and published privately in the following year. Slight pieces written in the tradition of the *commedia dell' arte*, they are lively and amusing and were intended to give the actors opportunity for improvisation. In recent years they have been translated from the French in which he wrote them into Polish and played in Poland and, by a Polish acting company, at the Théâtre des Nations in Paris.

ABOUT: Caillois, R. *Preface to* The Saragossa Manuscript (1960). [In French—Krakowski, E. Jean Potocki; Le Figaro, August 28, 1963; Théâtre Populaire, 34 (1959).]

*PRATI, GIOVANNI (January 27, 1814-May 9, 1884), Italian poet and patriot, was born in the village of Campomaggiore on the Austro-Italian border. His preliminary studies completed at Trent, he went to the University of Padua for a degree in law, but he did not graduate. He was a handsome young man, quite unprepared to face life seriously, and a career of perennial studenthood was more to his liking than any other. His marriage at the age of twenty did nothing to stabilize him, and his fecklessness subjected him to severe criticism, even to the charge that he was responsible for the premature death of his wife.

Prati's *I Fiori* (The Flowers, 1840) about the lady Atilia, a transparent anagram for Italy, resulted in a short jail sentence. On his release he went to Milan, where his poem *Edmenegarda* (1841) established his reputation as a poet. In his private life, however, his bad repute was increasing, and in 1843 he was forced to leave Milan and go to Turin, where he conducted his personal affairs no better. He wandered for some years about

* prä' tē

the regions of the Trentino and Lombardy-Venetia and in Switzerland. The year 1848 found him back in Padua, a propagandist for Italian independence from Austria, and a firm partisan of Charles Albert who occupied the throne of Piedmont. His agitation for this monarch caused his expulsion from Venice and Florence, and there was no other refuge but Charles Albert's own capital, Turin. Prati took up residence there in December 1848, thus closing the most turbulent period of his life.

For his allegiance to the House of Savoy the position of crown historian was conferred on him, in addition to a small pension. This offered new grist to his critics, who now saw in him, perhaps somewhat unjustly, the "court poet" who wrote not out of conviction but whatever he was commissioned. The arguments over his personal life were never completely silenced, partly because of Prati's own carelessness, but he now entered upon a period of relative tranquillity. He remained in Turin until 1865 when, in the train of the court, he moved to Florence, and in 1871 to Rome, where he became director of the Istituto Superiore di Magistero. He was made a senator in 1876. In spite of official recognition, he died obscure and cut off from his home which was by now Austrian territory. He suffered from public indifference to his art, but worked assiduously to the last. He died in Rome, and was interred in Turin until the redemption of his native region from Austria in 1923.

Prati's early compositions, gathered in the *Poesie* of 1835, reveal the predilection for sentimentalizing which was his chief defect. His *Edmenegarda* was an important event in the history of nineteenth century Italian romanticism. It was hailed by Italians who had not found before Prati any native expression of romanticism comparable to the works of Byron, Lamartine, Sand, and Musset.

Prati now attempted longer and more ambitious works. *Ielone di Siracusa*, in 1852, was the beginning of an attempt to give a poetic history of mankind. In *Rodolfo* (1853) Prati delineated the contradictory romantic hero, undisciplined, capable of great nobility, but also of great error, who moves to final redemption on the field of battle. *Rodolfo* is considered a completely deficient work, as are the two following, *Satana e le Grazie* (Satan and the Graces, 1855) and *Il Conte di Riga* (The Count of Riga). With the publication of *Armando* in 1868, Prati's work had fallen almost completely into disfavor. Romanticism was no longer popular, giving way to the verism and license of Bettelloni and Stecchetti.

Prati's last volumes, *Psiche* (1876) and *Iside* (1878), show the effect of his prolonged study of the classics towards the end of his life, especially Horace. The ironic conclusion is that it was not in the undisciplined sentimentality of his earlier works, nor in the poems inspired by his mentors in other countries, but in the last "classical" works that Prati succeeded in expressing a sincere romanticism. A modern edition of his poems appeared in 1931.

ABOUT: [In Italian—see studies by V. Cian, P. L. Mannucci, G. Toffanin.]

E. DE P.

*PREŠEREN, FRANCÈ (December 3, 1800-February 8, 1849), Slovene poet, was born of a peasant family in the village of Vrba, near Lake Bled in Slovenia (part of present-day Yugoslavia). At the age of seven he went to live with an uncle, a priest, who helped him to get an education. He studied at grammar school in Ljubljana and then at the Faculty of Law at the University of Vienna. He returned to school in Ljubljana in 1828 to become a lawyer's assistant. He wrote poetry, from 1830 contributing to the journal *Čbelica* (The Bee). His love lyrics scandalized the Slovenian Jansenist clergy, and the authorities considered him dangerous because of his Slovene patriotism.

Some time before 1831 Prešeren met Julia Primič, the daughter of a well-to-do businessman. She was scarcely half his age, beautiful and cold. Probably she did not love him, and in any case he had no prospects. In the end she married another, more "respectable" suitor. Prešeren's consequent unhappiness became the major theme and inspiration of his poetry. Later he had a long liaison with Anna Jelovšek, a pretty girl of the working class, and three illegitimate children were born to them. But this attachment scarcely dispelled his unhappiness. In 1846 he published a volume of his collected verse under the title *Poezije*, but it sold only a few hundred copies. The same year he moved to the small Slovenian town of Kranj, where he set up his own practice as a lawyer. He gave himself up to drink, and once tried to hang himself. He died at forty-eight of dropsy.

Prešeren is the greatest Slovene poet, and a writer who, in spite of his comparatively small output, deserves a place in world literature. Most of his work falls into three

* prě shěr' n

PREŠEREN

cycles: a love cycle (1841-43), a social and national cycle (1844), and a satirical and elegiac cycle (1845). His verse tends to be conversational in tone, and draws to some extent on Slovene folk song and folk speech for its style. He was also influenced by the love poetry of Petrarch and Tasso, and by Byron, parts of whose *Parisina* he translated into Slovene. His verse is quite varied in form, consisting of sonnets, ballads, elegies, romances, occasional verse, epigrams, and one longer narrative poem; the whole amounts to a single average-sized volume. In form he was much influenced by his close friend, the critic and aesthetician Matija Čop, who helped him create Slovene verse forms on the model of the romance literatures.

One of Prešeren's early cycles was his *Sonetni Venec* (A Wreath of Sonnets, 1833), fourteen sonnets on the acrostic *Primičovi Julji*—"to Julia Primič," with a final sonnet composed of the opening lines of the first fourteen sonnets. A scandal resulted when the public realized that the cycle was addressed to Julia. The later cycle, called *Sonetje Nesreče* (Sonnets of Unhappiness), is his greatest poetry and perhaps the deepest expression of his suffering. His single narrative, *Krst pri Savici* (The Baptism near Savitsa, 1836), treats the Christianization of Slovenia in the eighth century. The poet joked that he wrote it to pacify the clergy who had been shocked by his love verses.

Prešeren had faith in a better future for the Slovene people but lamented their oppressed state in his own time. He believed in the right of his people to cultural autonomy, and opposed Slovene participation in the so-called Illyrian movement, which sought to develop a single common language for the Serbs, Croats, and Slovenes. Though his views had little direct influence, his work helped to create for Slovenes a poetic language worthy of survival. But he was little esteemed in his lifetime. His popularity dates from 1866, when a second edition of his poems appeared with an introduction by the Slovene critic Josip Stritar. Today he is recognized as the classic poet and greatest writer of his people.

A volume of Prešeren's poetry has been translated into English as *A Selection of Poems*, edited by W. K. Matthews and A. Slodnjak (1953). Other poems are found in translation in I. Zorman, *Slovene Poetry*, and in the *Slavonic and East European Review*, XXVII (1949).

ABOUT: Prešeren, F. A Selection of Poems; Slavonic and East European Review, XXXIII (1954). [In Slovene—see studies by A. Slodnjak, B. Ziherl.]

W. E. H.

*PRÉVOST, ANTOINE FRANÇOIS, called PRÉVOST D'EXILES (April 1, 1697-December 23, 1763),

French novelist, journalist, and memorialist, was born in Hesdin (Artois), the second of five sons of Liévin Prévost and Marie Duclais. His father was the king's prosecuting attorney at Hesdin. Young Prévost studied hard and well at the local Jesuit school, then went to Paris, to the famous Collège d'Harcourt, and to La Flèche, in order to prepare himself for the ecclesiastical estate. In 1713 he became a novice in the Company of Jesus. His impetuous character, however, and his vivid imagination made him abandon his studies and pushed him into the army. After a brief experience as a private, he deserted, went back to the Jesuits, then again fled into the army, this time as an officer. During the next four or five years, he led an adventurous and dissipated life. At twenty-two, after an unhappy love affair in Holland, he joined the community of Benedictines at Saint-Maur. He was ordained a priest in 1721 and became a successful preacher and teacher. In 1728 he was engaged in the compilation of a learned historical work undertaken by the monks of his order, but his restless mind was far from being satisfied. At the very time when he was doing research on the *Gallia Christiana*, he was writing and even publishing profane, slightly scandalous novels. Soon he asked the Pope to be transferred to

* prä vō′ däg zēl′

the more liberal rule of Cluny, but did not wait for an answer before departing. His superiors of the Saint-Maur Congregation had asked the police to arrest that "middle-sized man, whose characteristics were fair hair, blue eyes, red complexion" and who had "left without leave."

After a few months in England, Prévost went to Holland. He lived in Amsterdam and in The Hague and, in that country, which had become a haven for intellectuals of all nations, he began a career as a writer. He published, among other books, a long, melodramatic novel called *Cleveland*, and continued a work he had started in Paris, his *Mémoires et Aventures d'un Homme de Qualité*. The seventh volume of the latter work—published in 1731—contained a short novel which was to bring Prévost greater fame than all his other books: it was the love story of the Chevalier des Grieux and Manon Lescaut.

In 1733, after another unfortunate love affair, Prévost went back to London. There he founded a gazette—printed in Paris—*Le Pour et le Contre*. This journal was, in many ways, patterned after the English *Spectator*. It was published regularly for the next seven years (1733-40) and ran to twenty volumes.

In 1734 Prévost was able to return to France, thanks to the protection of Cardinal de Bissy, Bishop of Meaux, and of the Prince of Conti. He was reinstated by the Benedictines and became the almoner and secretary of the latter. The same year he published the first part of another of his long, melodramatic, well-received novels, *Le Doyen de Killerine*. An indiscretion forced him to leave France again, in order to avoid imprisonment in the Bastille. This new exile, however, lasted only eight months, which were spent, for the greater part, in Brussels. After his return to Paris, Prévost's life became more settled. He worked peacefully on his numerous journalistic, historical, and literary enterprises: he wrote novels, articles, translations, and undertook an *Histoire Générale des Voyages*, then an *Histoire des Condés*. He was living comfortably from his writings and had, besides, a pension from Conti and the revenue of a rich priory. On December 1763, while walking in the woods near Chantilly, he was stricken with apoplexy and died. According to a story which has not been proven true, his life was only suspended when he fell and it was the barber in charge of the post-mortem who killed him.

Most of Prévost's novels are not read any more. They belong to the "gothic" genre and their plots are incredibly unrealistic: in *Mémoires de Monsieur de Montcal*, for instance, the plot deals with a young Irish girl who kills her father (he had killed her lover), is almost killed by her brother, and, after many gory adventures, dies tragically, along with a dozen other major characters. *Manon Lescaut* is the only exception in all Prévost's fiction and is generally recognized, not only as his masterpiece, but as one of the great novels of all times. It is, in the first place, a picture of Prévost's era, of the tranquil and quasi-unconscious immorality of the eighteenth century. It is also one of the first illustrations of the literary *exotisme* which was to culminate in Saint-Pierre's *Paul et Virginie* and Chateaubriand's *Atala*. Moreover, *Manon* combines a great psychological insight, a classic, all-time, human story of a passionate and tragic love with the new ideology of romanticism as a revolt of the individual, overthrowing all the barriers of religion, morals, family, and society, in order to pursue on this earth an impossible happiness.

Manon Lescaut was a great success almost as soon as it was published. It was eagerly read all over Europe and more than thirty editions—some of them pirated—were published before the end of the century. Prévost had many imitators and was greatly admired by the next two or three generations of writers. One may find a trace of his influence in Hugo's *Marion Delorme*, Dumas' *La Dame aux Camélias* and Daudet's *Sapho*. The novel has also inspired at least two plays,

one by Barrière and Fournier (1851) and one by Marcelle Maurette (1941). It also furnished the book of two famous operas, one by Jules Massenet (*Manon*, 1884) and one by Giacomo Puccini (*Manon Lescaut*, 1893). It has also been the subject of several motion pictures.

Apart from his writing of *Manon Lescaut*, Prévost's importance lies in two facts. In the first place, he was one of the first French writers of the eighteenth century who lived, at least for the better part of his career, by his pen. (He received royalties for most of the hundred or so volumes he published.) Secondly, this great admirer of England and English literature tried to communicate his taste to his countrymen and did much to promote the *anglophilie* of the times. He translated Hume's *History of England*, and Richardson's *Pamela, Clarissa*, and *Sir Charles Grandison*, three "bourgeois novels" which greatly influenced the French writers of the eighteenth century.

Manon Lescaut was translated into English as early as 1738 (by John Wilford). A great many translations have appeared since, including in recent years those by D. C. Moylan (1931), Helen Waddell (1935), and L. W. Tancock (Penguin Classics, 1951).

ABOUT: Havens, G. The Abbé Prévost and English Literature; Rutherford, M. R. The Abbé Prévost and the English Theater 1730-1740, *in* Theater Notebooks, London, July-Sept. 1955; Wilcox, F. H. Prévost's Translation of Richardson's Novels. [In French—Faguet, E. Études Critiques; Hazard, P. Études Critiques sur Manon Lescaut; Schroeder, V. L'Abbé Prévost.]

P. B.

*PROUDHON, PIERRE JOSEPH (February 15, 1809-January 19, 1865), French political writer, was born in Besançon, to parents of peasant stock. His mother, Catherine Simonin, had been a cook before her marriage. His father, Claude François Proudhon, worked as a brewer and a cooper, but he succeeded at nothing, and the family fought a constant and losing battle against poverty. There was so little money that Pierre Joseph, though a promising scholar, was forced to leave school in 1827. He apprenticed himself to a printer, working as a compositor and then later as a proofreader. He continued his education independently, learned theology from the galley proofs he read of religious books the firm published, and taught himself Greek and Hebrew.

As a result of the depression that followed the revolution of 1830, Proudhon lost his job

* prōō dóɴ′

744

PROUDHON

and traveled about in France and Switzerland seeking work. He settled down for a while in Paris where, thanks to the assistance of a friend, Gustave Fallot, he was able to devote himself to study and writing. In 1833 he returned to the printing shop in Besançon, but by now he was determined to make a career for himself in literature. He wrote a learned but, as he himself later described it, "perverse and feeble" philological tract, *Essai de Grammaire Générale.* In 1838 he was awarded the Suard Pension, a bursary offered by Besançon, of 1,500 francs a year for three years in order to encourage local young men of promise. With this money he returned to Paris, attended university lectures, and began a program of intensive reading. To supplement his small income (he was supporting his parents) he did some hack journalism. This part-time newspaper work gradually drew him away from his abstruse philological studies into the field of social thought. In 1839 he wrote a scholarly essay about the sabbath, *L'Utilité de la Célébration du Dimanche,* in the course of which he launched his attack on private property which was more fully outlined in his sensational *Qu'est-ce que la Propriété?* (1840). In this tract he posed the question "What is property?" and answered it with a ringing and startling answer, "Property is theft." At the root of Proudhon's thinking on this subject was an idealistic egalitarianism, actually a defense of property (in that, he believed it should be divided equally among all the workers) rather than an attack on the concept of

private, individual ownership which he actually favored. But the incendiary slogan, appearing as it did at such a critical period in European history when many nations were in the throes of revolution and radical change, brought Proudhon a notoriety which he had probably not calculated upon. It almost cost him his pension, but a few powerful friends on the committee saved him. Two years later, however, by which time he had published two more controversial pieces, *Lettre à M. Blanqui* (1841) and *Lettre à M. Considérant* (1842), the pension was revoked and he was put on trial for "offending against religion and morals." He was acquitted.

In 1842 Karl Marx wrote an enthusiastic review of Proudhon's work, but when Proudhon published his most ambitious book in 1846, *Système des Contradictions Économiques, ou Philosophie de la Misère,* Marx broke bitterly and permanently with him. A year later Marx answered him in his *La Misère de la Philosophie,* accusing him of ignorance and gross misinterpretation of the Hegelian dialectic and of numerous inconsistencies. Inconsistencies, it must be admitted, abound in Proudhon. He called himself "a man of paradoxes." It is indeed scarcely possible to reconcile his revolutionary sympathies with his sturdy defense of bourgeois family life, or his opposition to Italian unification; his attack on property with his opposition to an inheritance tax; his egalitarianism with his antifeminism and his opposition to universal suffrage. Although he was a revolutionary he could attach himself to no revolutionary party. Trotsky called him "the Robinson Crusoe of Socialism." The two revolutionary leaders with whom he had the greatest affinity were Herzen and Bakunin, and it was through them that his influence spread into Russia. The aim of revolution, Proudhon concluded, is not a new government, but ultimately no government—i.e., the goal of a free society is anarchy, the highest perfection of social organization in which no government is necessary.

Proudhon sought to disseminate his ideas more widely than he might in books by founding and editing several newspapers—*Le Peuple* (1848-49), *La Voix du Peuple* (1849-50), and *Le Peuple de 1850.* In the revolution of 1848 he held an influential position as a leader of radical socialist thought. He was elected to the constituent assembly in June 1848 with a large majority, but before the month was out he had alienated himself from most of his political allies. In 1849 the attacks in his newspapers on Louis Napoleon led to his trial for sedition. He was condemned to three years' imprisonment and a fine of 3,000 francs. His prison conditions were mild, however. He was allowed to study and write, to edit his newspapers, to receive visits from his wife, and to take occasional holidays. Upon his release in 1852 he lived quietly on the outskirts of Paris until 1858 when he published *De la Justice dans la Révolution et dans l'Église,* which D. W. Brogan described succinctly as "a declaration of war against the Church, a demonstration of the fundamental incompatibility of the teaching of the Church and the teaching of the Revolution." The book caused a sensation. Once again Proudhon was put on trial and condemned to three years in prison, but this time he fled to Belgium. He settled in Brussels where he wrote his last important work, *La Guerre et la Paix* (Tolstoy knew the book and may have taken his title for *War and Peace* from it)—an extraordinary treatise that defends and glorifies war. He returned to France in 1862 and struggled through the next few years trying to support his family by writing. He died at his house in Passy, probably of heart failure brought on by asthma. A huge crowd, estimated at 6,000, honored him at his funeral.

Proudhon's stormy career was balanced somewhat by a tranquil and happy home life. He married Euphrasie Piégard, of a working class family, in 1849, while he was on parole from prison. They had four daughters. One of Proudhon's closest friends was the painter Courbet who painted a number of portraits of him. Proudhon was simple in his living habits and careless of his dress. He often wore the French peasant smock. For all his inconsistencies he was a thinker of originality and great courage. Although he left no solid body of political philosophy, his ideas on anarchy influenced revolutionary thinkers throughout Europe. He was moreover an excellent writer with an eloquent and fiery style. Sainte-Beuve, who admired him greatly, aptly called him "an intellectual Prometheus."

Proudhon's *Œuvres Complètes,* twenty-six volumes, were published 1867-70; another more recent edition by C. Bouglé and H. Hoysset appeared 1920-39. The *Correspondence,* fourteen volumes, appeared 1874-75. English translations include *What Is Property?* by B. Tucker (1876), *System of Economic Contradictions, or the Philosophy of Poverty* (only the first volume of Proudhon's work) by B. Tucker (1888), *The General Idea of Revolution in the Nineteenth Century* by J. B. Robinson (1923), and a selection from his writings—*Proudhon's Solution of the Social Problem* (1927).

About: Brogan, D. W. Proudhon; Carr, E. H. Studies in Revolution; De Lubac, H. The Un-Marxian Socialist; Woodcock, G. P. J. Proudhon. [In French—see studies by C. Bouglé, A. Desjardins, E. Dolléans, E. Droz, D. Halévy, C. A. Sainte-Beuve.]

***PRUS, BOLESŁAW** (pseudonym of **ALEXANDER GŁOWACKI**) (August 20, 1847-May 19, 1912), Polish novelist and short-story writer, was born in Hrubieszowo, to a family of impoverished gentry; his father died early, and Prus was brought up by relatives. His secondary-school education was interrupted by the 1863 uprising against Russia in which Prus participated as a sixteen-year-old boy; he was captured and held in prison in Lublin, but released and permitted to finish school. In 1868 he entered the so-called Main School of the University of Warsaw as student of physics and mathematics, but had to leave school after two years because of financial difficulties. For several years after leaving school Prus struggled through life trying various professions; he was, in his own words, "private tutor, technical clerk, locksmith and popular lecturer, frequently cheered and only once booed at." In 1875 he married Octavia Trembińska and settled down in Warsaw as a journalist and writer.

In the development of Prus' literary, social, and political views two contrasting trends were at work; in his early years he and his generation were captured by the romantic tradition, exalting youth with its slogans of the unlimited power of the human spirit, slogans frequently applied to the political situation and later blamed for the catastrophe of the "unrealistic" uprising of 1863. When Prus, like many others, after his period of "monastery meditation and strict diet" in a Russian prison, returned to school, the theme of the day was a complete revision of the romantic program, and the only remedy seen was in a realistic approach to problems of life and art: slow progress by "organic work," improving economic and social conditions, enlightenment and patience and calm were to replace the romantic dreams. Although Prus later reassessed the situation, warning against the danger of exterminating all ideals, he remained a genuine realist.

Prus' literary production developed gradually out of his weekly "chronicles" which he started contributing regularly to the *Warsaw Courier* in 1874. Some of these chronicles were the nuclei of short stories, and indeed

* prōōs

simultaneously with them his first short stories started appearing in various periodicals. To this literary genre Prus remained faithful to the end of his career, becoming one of the few Slavic short-story writers of international fame. In 1885 Prus published his first short novel, *Blacówka* (The Outpost), in which all the characteristic features of his "poetics of realism" can be seen. Partly didactic, it conveys a democratic and patriotic message, stressing the values of the biological strength of the peasants; but the objective approach is in sharp contrast with the sentimental or idealizing treatment of similar motifs by his predecessors. Indeed, in the sober, matter-of-fact presentation of peasant life this work resembles at times Zola's *La Terre* (published a few years later).

Soon larger works followed. *Lalka* (The Doll), published in installments (1887-89), discussed contemporary social, moral, and educational problems. *Emancypantki* (The Emancipated Women, 1891-93) takes up the problem of woman in Polish society. The work often regarded as Prus' masterpiece is the voluminous novel *Faraon* (The Pharaoh and the Priests, 1895-96). Like Flaubert in his *Salammbô*, the Polish writer used the setting of the ancient world to illuminate problems of contemporary importance; the struggle between progress and tradition is here presented with the moderation and sense of balance characteristic of all Prus' works. A similar issue put against the background of contemporary events (the revolution of 1905) is discussed in his last novel, *Dzieci* (The Children, 1908). Turgenev's famous novel *Fathers and Sons* comes to mind as a work of similar artistic and ideological attitudes. Charles Dickens in English literature is also a near "relative" of the Polish writer.

In the history of Polish literature Prus is ranked as one of the founders of the modern novel. Although criticized by his contemporaries for his cautious attitudes toward so-called progressive groups, he was one of the most popular persons in Warsaw; humor, wisdom, and a sense of justice characterized both the work and the man. The twenty-fifth anniversary of his literary activity developed into a spontaneous celebration in his honor.

Many of Prus' works have been translated into foreign languages, including Chinese and Japanese. Works translated into English are: *The Pharaoh and the Priests,* by Jeremiah Curtin (1902) and numerous short stories in various collections: "The Outpost" appears in *Polish Tales,* ed. S. Benecke and M. Busch (1921).

ABOUT: Dyboski, R. Modern Polish Literature; Kridl, M. Survey of Polish Literature; and Slavonic Review, 1950. [The authoritative Polish monograph is Z. Szweykowski, Twórczość Bolesława Prusa; see also study by M. Romankowna.]

Z. F.

*PSELLUS, MICHAEL CONSTANTINE** (1018-1078), the Voltaire of the Byzantines, teacher, philosopher, statesman, historian, and court politician, was born in Nicomedia of devout middle-class parents of modest means. His original name was Constantine but he was renamed Michael when he took his monastic vows. From the funeral oration he wrote for his mother, Theodota, whom he describes as "the rose that needed no further adornment," we learn of the close ties of his family life. In outlook and temperament he resembled his mother; in looks he resembled his father who, he says, was as handsome as a "well-grown cypress." It was his mother who managed to prolong his education to his teens but their need to provide a dowry for his sister made it difficult to support him further. He accepted a position as clerk to a provincial judge, but on the unexpected death of his sister, he returned to Constantinople and continued his studies. He learned law and philosophy from the future Patriarch Xiphilinus whom he later eulogized in a funeral oration. At twenty-five Psellus had already mastered rhetoric, philosophy, music, law, geometry, astronomy, medicine, magic, Platonism.

He began his career as a lawyer and was court secretary at Philadelphia (1034-41) under Michael IV and under-secretary and secretary during the short reign of Michael V. In 1045 Emperor Constantine Monomachus made him secretary of the realm and head of the school of philosophy in the newly founded University of Constantinople with the title of "Most Honorable and Supreme Philosopher," which he was called by his contemporaries. Psellus initiated a Platonist renaissance, at a time when Platonism was persecuted as a danger to orthodoxy, by interpreting the dialogues of Plato as anticipations of Christian theology. A genuine revival of the classics followed but Psellus was accused of heresy and the Emperor closed the school. Threatened with the disfavor of Monomachus, he entered a monastery at Olympos, in Bithynia, but he returned to court and soon after the death of the Emperor was appointed to high office in the administrations of Michael VI and again under Isaac Comnenus

* sĕl′ ŭs

747

(1057-59). As chief adviser to Constantine X Ducas and tutor to Michael, his eldest son and heir to the throne, Psellus exercised a controlling influence on imperial policy. He was prime minister during the regency of Eudoxia and the reign of his former pupil who became Michael VII Ducas (1071-78).

Psellus wrote with equal interest and ability on a large variety of subjects and in a variety of forms. He left poetical and prose works on philosophy, history, law, medicine, theology, occult science, archeology, mathematics, and astronomy, as well as funeral orations, biographies, canonical writings, and an extensive correspondence, but many of his works are unpublished and some are completely unknown. Of his works on law, his best known is his *Law Manual*. He was the biographer of Zoë Porphyrogenita, daughter of Constantine VIII, who became Empress.

His most important work is his *Chronographia*, the outstanding memoir of the Middle Ages in Byzantium, which contains, in his own words, "those things which I myself have seen and those events of which I have perceived with my own eyes." It is written in the purist modified Attic, which he himself calls *koine*, and embraces a period of one hundred years. The first part begins with the accession of Basil II and ends with the abdication of Isaac Comnenus (976-1059). The second part covers the period from Constantine X to the end of the reign of Michael VII (1059-78). The second part is less critical in tone and full of lavish appreciation of the Ducas family and regime. He places great emphasis on the workings of divine providence, a good education, and an appreciation of their Hellenic heritage.

The *Chronographia* also reveals Psellus' own rise to power, his personal ambitions, and his predominating passion to promote scholarship and learning. With repeated apologies, he describes the importance of his position and the extent to which his imperial rulers were dependent on him. In spite of the personal prejudices in the account, the *Chronographia* is a valuable source for the history of the eleventh century. It offers the reader an authentic picture of the court life which Psellus knew from first-hand experience and which he records with liveliness and intellectual vigor.

In character Psellus was servile, vainglorious, ambitious, unscrupulous, and weak. He knew the power of his pen and he used it relentlessly to further his ends. "The abdication of Isaac Comnenus," writes Joan Hussey, "and the accession of Constantine Ducas

were both the work of Psellus." Historians are generally agreed that as a court politician he was cynical, cowardly, and corrupt.

As a literary man Psellus is renowned for the unsurpassed productivity of his work. He helped to revive Greek letters and he raised Plato out of oblivion. The literary renaissance of the Comneni is credited to him. He was the driving force behind the reorganization of the University of Constantinople in 1045 and the promotion of higher education. He exercised notable influence on the writers of the next generation. Anna Comnena, writing of the times, speaks of him as a man who "reached the summit of all knowledge."

The *Chronographia* was translated into English by E. R. A. Sewter in 1953.

ABOUT: Barker, E. Social and Political Thought in Byzantium; Baynes, N. H. Byzantine Studies and Other Essays; Bury, J. B. Selected Essays; Byron, R. The Byzantine Achievement; Diehl, C. Byzantine Portraits; Gibbon, E. Decline and Fall of the Roman Empire; Hussey, J. M. Church Learning in the Byzantine Empire; Liddell, R. Byzantium and Istanbul; Ostrogorsky, G. History of the Byzantine State; Sands, E. History of Classical Scholarship, I; Speculum X (1935).

R. D.

*PUCCI, ANTONIO (c. 1309-1388), Italian poet, was born and lived in Florence, where his career is known vaguely through official records, as *campanaio* (bell ringer) by 1346, then also as *banditore* (public crier) until 1369; his name disappears in 1390, but he was said to have attained considerable age and at the end of his life to have been comforted by a devoted wife and children and by the prosperity of his city. To judge by his writings, he was a typical middle-class citizen, and is so portrayed by Sacchetti who sets him, in one story, in his garden, surrounded by the fruit and birds that he celebrated in his verse.

Pucci was a prolific versifier, with no pretension to learned or artistic effects. He preferred the sonnet form, whose rules he formulated in part from those of Brunetto Latini. The concision of the sonnet suited very exactly the scope of Pucci's vision and ideas, for he usually limited his inspiration to the study of a given and precise detail. His favorite subject matter includes realistic events and scenes, anecdotes about daily commonplace affairs such as the purchase of a chicken, shaving, a dream while drunk, recipes for sauces, and the chronic problems of women and family life. At times he adopts a

* pōōt' chē

moral tone in his reflections on friendship, or in satirical attacks against religious orders or the enemies of Florence. The great popularity of Pucci's sonnets is attested by the number of the early manuscripts, whose variable state suggests that they were widely recited. Their appeal results from the realism of familiar things, and especially from the sincere glorification of his beloved city and the beauties of her places and monuments, such as the *Proprietà di Mercato Vecchio.*

On occasion, Pucci seeks more artistic effects. In a series of nineteen sonnets, *Legati in Corona,* he recites a love adventure with a married woman, who at first refuses him, then yields; the sequence forms a story comparable to a tale of Boccaccio. The quatrains of his *Vecchiezza* form another cycle, in part imitative of Juvenal, but primarily autobiographical; in moralistic tone Pucci enumerates the failings of old age ("Questi sono gli smisurati duoli") and, as in his *Noie,* he creates realistic catalogues of human traits. Pucci also served the fame of Dante in his many quotations from his poetry.

ABOUT: Gardner, E. The Arthurian Legend in Italian Literature. [In Italian—Ferri, F. La Poesia Populare in Antonio Pucci; Volpi, G. Rime di Trecentisti Minori.]

F. J. C.

---

*PÜCKLER-MUSKAU, Fürst HERMANN LUDWIG HEINRICH von (October 30, 1785-February 4, 1871), German writer and landscape-gardener, was born at Castle Muskau in Niederlausitz, the descendant of a distinguished family that traced its origin to the semi-mythical knight Rüdiger von Bechlarn, who is commemorated in the *Nibelungenlied.* By temperament he was a gay, witty, erratic individual, who was absolutely fearless and endowed with a strong histrionic flair as well as a pronounced tendency toward dandyism. After obtaining his early education by private tutor, Pückler-Muskau entered the University of Leipzig at seventeen to study law. Scholarship held no interest for him, however, and when his father denied his request to spend a year in Paris, the youth ran away to Dresden, where he purchased a commission in a cavalry regiment. In 1804 he settled in Vienna and from there he traveled through Switzerland, southern France, and Italy. On the death of his father in 1811 he inherited the estates of Muskau and Branitz, on which he lavished enormous sums of money for landscaping, creating two

* pük' lĕr mōŏs' kou

famous parks on the model of the English garden. During the war with Napoleon he returned to the army and served as military governor of Bruges. Following a trip to England in the suite of the King of Prussia, he divided his time between Muskau and Berlin, where he became an intimate of the highest social circles. In 1817 he married Lucie, Countess of Pappenheim, the daughter of Chancellor Hardenberg. Although the marriage was a happy one, the couple was divorced by mutual agreement in 1826, to enable Pückler-Muskau to marry a rich woman and thus restore his finances which had been depleted by his luxurious manner of living. After spending the years 1826-29 in England on this unsuccessful quest, he and Lucie remarried. In 1835 Pückler-Muskau embarked on an extensive tour of North Africa, Egypt, Greece, Syria, and Asia Minor. Because of his title, reputation, and flamboyant personality, he was accorded a welcome reception wherever he visited. During his later life he was granted many honors. He died in Cottbus at eighty-five.

Pückler-Muskau began his career as a writer with an account of his years in England, *Briefe eines Verstorbenen* (4 vols., 1831), which was followed by a volume on landscape - gardening, *Andeutungen über Landschaftsgärtnerei* (1834), and *Tutti Frutti* (5 vols., 1834), a series of observations based on his travels through Germany. Additional works describing his widespread adventures and experiences include *Semilassos Vorletzter Weltgang* (3 vols., 1835), *Semilasso in Afrika* (5 vols., 1836), *Südöstlicher Bildersaal* (3 vols., 1840-41), *Aus Mehemed Alis Reich* (3 vols., 1844), and *Die Rückkehr* (3 vols., 1846-48). Although these works enjoyed great popularity in their day, they possess little value as literature, and, except for their interest as an expression of a unique and brilliant personality, have not outlived their time.

Briefe eines Verstorbenen was translated by S. Austin in 1832 under the title *Tour in Germany, Holland, and England, 1826-1828* (4 vols.). *Semilasso in Afrika* appeared anonymously in 1837. E. Spencer translated *Tutti Frutti* in 1839 (5 vols.). *Aus Mehemed Alis Reich* was translated by E. H. Lloyd in 1845 as *Egypt and Mehemet. Hints on Landscape Gardening* was translated by B. Sickert and edited by S. Parsons in 1917.

ABOUT: Butler, E. M. The Tempestuous Prince. [In German—see studies by L. Assing, J. Langendorf-Brandt, and F. Zahn and R. Kalwa. In French —see study by A. Ehrhard.]

D. G. D.

*PULCI, LUIGI (August 15/16, 1432-
November 1484), Italian poet, was born in
Florence, one of nine children of Jacopo
Pulci and Brigida de' Bardi. Luigi's brothers
—Luca and Bernardo—also became poets.
The once considerable fortune of the Pulci
family had declined in recent generations,
and when Jacopo Pulci died about 1450 he
left only a little property and a mass of
debts. Luigi was no better at managing money
than his father had been; he frequently got
himself into financial scrapes from which
he had to appeal to his patron Lorenzo de'
Medici for help.

Luigi Pulci's association with the Medici
family, which began in the 1450's, was a
shaping force in his life and in his literary
career. His comic epic *Il Morgante* was undertaken about 1461 at the suggestion of
Lorenzo's mother, Lucrezia Tornabuoni. Encouraged by the approval of the Medici
household, Pulci continued to write new
episodes for the poem throughout his career.

Although Pulci was sixteen years older
than Lorenzo de' Medici, the two became
close friends during Lorenzo's youth. In
1466 when Luigi and his brother Luca were
exiled from Florence for debt, Lorenzo—
then barely eighteen—interceded for them.
Three years later Lorenzo became the head
of the Medici family and soon employed
Luigi on missions to Camerino and to Naples
(1470-71).

In 1470 Luca Pulci died, leaving Luigi
to support his widow and children and to
complete his unfinished poem *Il Ciriffo Cal-
vaneo*. About 1472 Luigi entered the service
of Roberto da Sanseverino, a friend of
Lorenzo's and a noted military captain.
Thereafter he usually spent part of each year
with Roberto's train. Sometime before 1474
he married Lucrezia degli Albizzi; they
eventually had four sons.

Despite Pulci's outside duties, his poetry
continued to reflect the preoccupations of the
Medici court. His long poem *La Giostra* described a tournament that Lorenzo held in
1469. Another long poem, *La Beca da Di-
comana*, was an earthy and realistic burlesque
of Lorenzo's pastoral poem *La Nencia da
Barberino*. Lorenzo's enthusiasm for folk
poetry encouraged Pulci to write many poems
in popular genres—especially *frottole*, haphazard poems in irregular meter, and *stram-
botti*, short satirical poems. Pulci also engaged, partly for the amusement of Lorenzo
and his companions, in several "sonnet feuds,"
including a long exchange of abusive sonnets

* pōōl' chē

750

PULCI

with Matteo Franco (in 1474-75), and a
series of sonnets to Marsilio Ficino disput-
ing Ficino's Platonistic philosophy.

Near the close of the 1470's Pulci ran afoul
of the Inquisition because of his outspoken
heretical opinions. The first twenty-three cantos of the *Morgante*, published 1478-80, contained attacks on orthodox religion and
passages concerning the forbidden practice
of magic. Many of his shorter poems also
scoffed at Church dogma; his sonnet "Costor
che fan si gran disputazione," concerning
the soul, caused a small scandal. He officially
returned to the Church in 1479 and tried to
make his peace with the Inquisition in the
Confessione, a *terza rima* poem to the Virgin.
He added to the *Morgante* two stanzas
repenting of the practice of magic—but he did
not bother to remove the objectionable
passages.

Pulci died in 1484, in Padua, while traveling to join Roberto da Sanseverino. The
news of his lukewarm reconversion had not
reached Padua, and he was buried in unsanctified ground as a heretic.

Pulci's lively passions and unorthodox convictions made him an entertaining companion,
but never brought him the serious recognition he desired. His poems and letters, although they contain a torrent of boisterous
wit, are characterized by an undercurrent of
bitterness.

His chief work, *Il Morgante Maggiore*
("maggiore" because the twenty-eight-canto
version of 1482 was "larger"), derives from

Italian folk burlesques of the Roland legend, and it uses the colloquial language and the *ottava rima* stanza of those burlesques. The plot of the first twenty-three cantos is adapted from an anonymous fourteenth century poem, *L'Orlando*. Orlando (Roland) meets the giant Morgante, converts him to Christianity, and engages with him in various exploits. The other paladins, particularly Rinaldo (Oliver), have separate adventures. Pulci's most notable addition to the plot is the character Margutte —a thief, liar, and religious skeptic, but a likable rascal withal.

Pulci's poems were widely read in his own time, but his free colloquial style did not appeal to immediately succeeding generations, who were caught up in a vogue for elegant Petrarchan verse. His work thus had little influence on the remaining course of Renaissance literature, and was not again fully appreciated until the rise of the romantic movement.

Pulci's chief importance to English literature is as an influence on Byron, whose *Beppo* and *Don Juan* are modeled on the *Morgante*. Byron also translated Canto I of the *Morgante* (1823). Leigh Hunt later translated two episodes from the *Morgante* in *Stories from the Italian Poets* (1846).

ABOUT: Grillo, G. Two Aspects of Chivalry. [In Italian—see Ageno, F., ed. "Introduzione," Il Morgante; Carto, C. Luigi Pulci; Rossi, V., ed. Storia Letteraria d'Italia, V; Vopi, G. "Luigi Pulci" *in* Giornale Storico della Letteratura Italiana, XXII.]

J. K.

*PUSHKIN, ALEKSANDR SERGE-EVICH** (May 25, 1799-January 29, 1837), Russian poet, was born in Moscow, the son of Sergei Lvovich Pushkin, a retired army officer, and his wife, Nadezhda Osipovna, *née* Hannibal. Pushkin himself was keenly interested in his colorful ancestry. On his father's side the family can be traced in direct line to at least the fifteenth century, when the Pushkins were among the noblest families of Russia. But gradually the family lost much of its wealth and influence, and by the time the poet was born the Pushkins had been relegated to the position of minor nobility of decidedly lesser importance. Pushkin's background is even more colorful on his mother's side. His great-grandfather, Abram Petrovich Hannibal, was the son of an Abyssinian prince. Being first taken as hostage to Constantinople by the Turks, Abram was later purchased and brought to Russia by Czar

* poōsh′ kĭn

PUSHKIN

Peter the Great in 1706. Because of his unusual talents, he achieved a relatively high position at the Court and in the army. Those biographers of Pushkin who profess to see evidence of the poet's African blood in Pushkin's features and in his restless temperament, or in his imagination and sense of rhythm, may have exaggerated the hereditary influences. Nevertheless Pushkin was intensely interested in his maternal ancestry; his unfinished historical novel *Arap Petra Velikogo*, 1827 (The Negro of Peter the Great) was to be the story of his great-grandfather.

The atmosphere in the Pushkin home was far from ideal. His gay but egotistic father and his domineering, irritable, and socially ambitious mother often left the moody Alexander to himself. At home French was spoken in the family circle and it was only from servants, his nurse, and, occasionally, from his maternal grandmother that Pushkin learned Russian. In 1811 Alexander was accepted as a student at the Lyceum in Tsarskoe Selo, a select government school for young noblemen who were to be educated for civil service and diplomacy. Alexander found in the school a substitute for the uninviting home atmosphere and formed a strong attachment to the Lyceum and his school friends. The education there was relatively liberal for its time, offering considerable contact with European thought, cultural trends, and tastes. Pushkin's poetic talent was almost immediately recognized by his schoolmates and his teachers; he was barely fifteen when his first poem was published in the most influential Russian literary magazine, *Vestnik Evropy* (The Messenger of Europe). In 1817 Pushkin graduated from the Lyceum and received a nominal appointment to the foreign office with the unspectacular salary of some 700 rubles a year. He spent the next three years in St. Petersburg, then the capital of Russia, leading a life of little restraint, filled with drinking bouts and parties, gambling and duel challenges, and frequent visits to actresses and ladies of an even more dubious reputation. Amidst all these energy-consuming activities, however, he was able to write and to keep up his literary connections and friendships.

Among Pushkin's sharp epigrams which circulated in St. Petersburg in manuscript copies were some which unmercifully ridiculed persons close to the Court. These verses, as well as Pushkin's *Vol'nost* (Ode to Freedom), written in 1817, a powerful expression of the poet's political liberalism and of his association with suspect groups, finally got him into serious political difficulty. Only his influential friends saved Pushkin from a harsh Siberian exile. Instead he was sent to serve in the army corps in the south of Russia. Pushkin left the capital in May 1820, only a short time before the appearance of his major poetic success *Ruslan i Ludmila*, (Ruslan and Ludmila), an ironic romance which skillfully and with wit used the forms and conventions of the fairy tale, and which was enthusiastically hailed as a work of considerable maturity of poetic expression.

Pushkin spent most of his exile in the provincial Bessarabian city of Kishinev, which he thoroughly disliked. But he was also able to visit the picturesque Caucasus, inhabited by non-Russian tribes, largely untouched by European civilization. The region made a deep impression on him and contributed much inspiration to his poetry of this period. During these years, Byron's influence upon Pushkin is most noticeable. It is apparent in *Kavkazskii Plennik* (The Prisoner of the Caucasus, 1821), in *Brat'ia Razboiniki* (The Robber Brothers, 1822), in *Bakhchisaraiskii Fontan* (The Fountain of Bakhchisarai, 1823), and in the later *Cygany* (The Gypsies, 1824). The last of these narrative poems develops the theme of a young Russian in search of freedom which, when he finds it among the gypsies, he is unwilling to grant to others, being unable to overcome the corruptive influence of his civilization.

The southern exile became more pleasant in 1813 when Pushkin was transferred to Odessa, a large city with a European flavor, and when the modest income from his poetry began arriving from the publishers. One of his romantic attachments here was for the Countess Elizaveta Vorontsova, the wife of the Viceroy. This dangerous circumstance contributed to Pushkin's further difficulties.

In 1824 he was dismissed from government service, officially because of the interception of a joking note mentioning his interest in atheism, and ordered to settle on his family estate in Mikhailovskoe.

The involuntary seclusion may have saved Pushkin's life. It is likely had he been in the capital he would have participated actively in the unsuccessful Decembrist revolt of 1825, in which many of his friends were involved. But because of his absence he was spared punishment and in the following year he was called back to St. Petersburg by the new emperor. Nicholas I put him under close supervision, establishing himself as the personal censor of Pushkin's works, making it clear to the poet he was expected to feel proper gratitude for such benevolent treatment.

The second part of this decade is marked most of all by Pushkin's work on his masterpiece *Evgenii Onegin*. The first canto of this "novel in verse" was begun in Kishinev in 1823 and the poem, in its basic form of eight cantos, was finished in 1830. *Evgenii Onegin* has as its central theme the ironic workings of fate which underlie Tatiana's and Onegin's story of twice-rejected love. The novel is constructed with clear symmetry around the two rejection scenes, but is also a panorama of the life and culture of the Russian upper classes in the first half of the century. The "superfluous man" of Russian literature makes one of his most famous appearances in this work. The poem is written in a regular ten-syllable iambic verse in a fourteen-line stanza. Its considerable restraint of expression, which is generally void of metaphor, its regularity and technical perfection and the ironical touch which pervades it are characteristic of Pushkin's transitional place between the classicism of the preceding century and European romanticism. In the 1820's Pushkin also turned to drama and wrote *Boris Godunov* (finished in 1825), which deals with the troublesome events of Russian history after the death of Ivan the Terrible.

Pushkin's most permanent love affair began suddenly in 1829, when the thirty-year-old poet fell in love with Natalia Goncharova, who was then barely seventeen. Pushkin's infatuation with this young girl, of extraordinary beauty but apparently mediocre intellect and sensitivity, who, in his own half-serious words, was his hundred and thirteenth love, is not easy to understand. Pushkin's first proposal was rejected, but the second time, in April 1830, he was accepted. Pushkin received the ardently awaited fulfillment of his desires with curious ambiguity; the conflict between his infatuation with Natalia and his fear of marriage haunted him throughout the short engagement and found reflection also in his works originating in the fall of 1830. Several of these works are related to the basic subject which so preoccupied him at that time, the relationship of man and woman. *Kamennyi Gost'* (The Stone Guest), a variation of the Don Juan theme, is the best among his four *Little Tragedies. Domik v Kolomne* (The Little House in Kolomna) has a related and strange theme.

Pushkin's marriage took place in February 1831. The new responsibilities, increased by the arrival of three children in quick succession, compounded his problems. Financial difficulties, the flirtatious nature of Natalia, Pushkin's jealousy, and the somewhat lukewarm reception of his later works affected the poet considerably. In 1834 the Czar, apparently warmly disposed towards Natalia, and wanting to assure her presence at various Court functions, appointed Pushkin to be the Gentleman of the Chamber, an insignificant honor usually accorded to much younger men. Pushkin desired nothing less than to be tied to the Court. He wanted to be free, in order to travel and write. Instead he was denied a passport and was greatly plagued by his indebtedness to the government treasury and by his humiliating title. But Pushkin was still able to produce some of his most remarkable works during this time. In 1833 he finished *Mednyi Vsadnik* (The Bronze Horseman), the poem of a St. Petersburg flood and of the destruction of an insignificant government clerk in the city built to satisfy Peter's ambitions. In *Skazka o Care Saltane* (The Tale of the Czar Saltan, 1831) and in *Skazka o Zolotom Petushke* (The Tale of the Golden Cockerel, 1834) Pushkin returned to the form of the fairy tale. During the 1830's, he was also more drawn towards prose, which he wrote in simple and clear style, and through much of which runs again the theme of unpredictable fate.

Among his best known prose works are *Povesti Pokoinogo Ivana Petrovicha Belkina* (Tales of Belkin, 1830), a collection of brief stories; *Pikovaia Dama* (The Queen of Spades, 1833), a powerful tale of self-destructive greed; and *Kapitanskaia Dochka* (The Captain's Daughter, 1836), an historical novelette of the Pugachev uprising during the reign of Catherine the Great.

In 1836 Pushkin received permission to start publication of a literary magazine, *Sovremennik* (The Contemporary). It proved neither a great financial nor a great literary success. Meanwhile Natalia's frivolous nature led her to a prolonged although probably Platonic involvement with a young French émigré, Baron Georges d'Anthès, the adopted son of the Dutch ambassador in St. Petersburg. Pushkin began receiving hints and anonymous letters. When one such letter, nominating him to membership in the "Most Serene Order of Cuckolds," appeared to have originated in d'Anthès' circle, Pushkin challenged the young Frenchman to a duel. The duel was avoided when d'Anthès proposed to and promptly married Pushkin's sister-in-law Catherine. But the newly related men did not remain reconciled for long. When Pushkin discovered that d'Anthès had tricked Natalia into a new secret meeting, he repeated his challenge. The duel was fought with pistols at ten paces on January 27, 1837. Pushkin was gravely wounded by the first shot and succumbed two days later. After the funeral mass, his body was secretly taken to Mikhailovskoe for burial by the government authorities, who feared demonstrations from the population embittered by suspicions that the beloved poet's death was due to intrigues of high society.

Outside Russia, Pushkin remained for a long time without adequate recognition, and his name, as a representative of Russian literature, still lags behind the writers of the Russian realistic novel. This is at least partly due to difficulties in translating Pushkin's poetry. But in his own land Pushkin has been recognized for his unique place in Russian literature, for his pioneering rôle in the establishment of a modern Russian literary language, for his original poetic expression, and for his poetic grasp of the Russian atmosphere. For his countrymen, Pushkin is, undoubtedly, the most universally esteemed poet, and his *Evgenii Onegin* the most beloved work. This esteem is so great that, as the critic D. S. Mirsky pointed out, even the Communists who are in spirit so completely alien to Pushkin "excluded his name almost alone from their general oblivious condemnation of pre-revolutionary Russia."

Pushkin was short and hardly handsome, but of a vigorous nature and of boundless energy, and a man of remarkable charm and wit. Both as a poet and as a man of intense and violent life he is one of the most fascinating personalities that Russia has produced.

The first translations of Pushkin's poetry into English were made during the poet's life. Extracts from *Ruslan and Ludmilla*, *The Prisoner of the Caucasus*, and *The Robber Brothers* appeared in the *Foreign Review* in 1827. Twenty-two short poems were translated by T. B. Shea in *Blackwood's Edinburgh Magazine* in 1845. H. Spalding published the first English translation of *Eugene Onegin* in London in 1881. More recent translations are Vladimir Nabokov's, published in four volumes with a commentary by the translator in 1964, and a verse translation by E. M. Kayden, also published in 1964. *The Captain's Daughter* was translated by G. G. Hebbe in New York in 1846. A translation of *The Queen of Spades* appeared in *Chambers' Papers* in 1850. A modern translation of the selected works of Pushkin, edited by A. Yarmolinsky, is available in *The Poems, Prose and Plays of Alexander Pushkin*, the Modern Library, New York, 1936. *The Letters of Pushkin*, translated by J. Thomas Shaw, was published in 1964.

ABOUT: Brasol, B. The Mighty Three: Pushkin, Gogol, Dostoyevsky; Čiževsky, D. Evgenij Onegin (Russian text and English commentary); Cross, S. H. Alexander Pushkin; Lavrin, J. Pushkin and Russian Literature; Mirsky, D. Pushkin; Simmons, E. J. Pushkin; Troyat, H. Pushkin, His Life and Times.

H. K.

QUEIRÓS, JOSÉ MARIA EÇA DE. See EÇA DE QUEIRÓS, JOSÉ MARIA

QUEIROZ, FRANCISCO TEIXEIRA DE. See TEIXEIRA DE QUEIROZ, FRANCISCO

*QUENTAL, ANTHERO DE (April 18, 1842-September 11, 1891), Portuguese poet and philosopher, was born in Ponta Delgada in the Azores but spent nearly all his life on the mainland of Portugal. He attended the university at Coimbra (1854-65) and was graduated in law after college years which were devoted to living riotously, reading philosophy, and writing verse. Although he came from a wealthy and aristocratic though neurotic family, he became a national leader of advanced thought as a socialist. In this capacity, he published political pamphlets remarkable for their vigor and style, and as a socialist he learned the trade of typesetter, practicing it alone in Paris (1866-67) until ill health drove him home discouraged. In 1867-68 Quental traveled in Spain and in the United States. After organizing the Portuguese Socialist Party in 1871, he initiated a

* kän täl'

754

QUENTAL

series of "Democratic Lectures," which were suppressed as dangerous.

Quental's health finally succumbed to the strain, and he developed an incurable spinal disease which forced him into retirement, first at Oporto, then at Villa do Conde, and at intervals in Ponta Delgada. He saw a few friends, principally J. P. Oliveira Martins, a famous historian and the collector and editor of Quental's sonnets. Suffering from a moral depression against any kind of action as a result of his physical torture and insomnia, he committed suicide in the public square of Ponta Delgada, his birthplace.

Quental's exquisite poems, comparable to the best produced in England, France, and Italy, are significant in their intensity and profundity of emotion, their nobility and humanity, and their intellectuality. Quental demonstrates a sure sense of form in the French manner and a Germanic leaning towards metaphysical speculation. Critics concede that his sonnets are his most enduring work. Other volumes of verse, especially the *Odes Modernas* (1865 and 1875), contain with the sonnets revolutionary poems in other forms.

Publication of his first sonnets in 1861 resulted in the dethronement of Castilho, who was the principal living poet of the older generation in Portugal. With all the subsequent sonnets these form a diary of his spiritual progress: "the successive phases of my intellectual and emotional life." According to Oliveira Martins, they express with absolute sincerity the evolution of European thought in the second half of the nineteenth century. The first phase (1860-62) contained the characteristics of all later ones; they showed Quental as sensitive, interested in metaphysics, filled with sadness and theological doubt after a strict training in Catholicism in his youth. Love, for him, was viewed idealistically, as a blessing. The second period (1862-66) was psychologically the least original, artistically the most brilliant. Although he now lived a more natural life, he manifested an increasing, sarcastic bitterness. His third stage (1864-74) was relatively unproductive because of his pamphleteering and organizational activities. Here he exhibited more insistent stoicism in his struggle between poetic vision and critical philosophy, emphasizing the latter. In the fourth span (1874-80), Quental revealed himself as a nihilist in philosophy and an anarchist in politics. Although he became negative and excessively pessimistic, Quental expressed himself with transcendental irony and intelligence.

Quental's last years showed the effect of intense physical anguish upon his sensitive mind, with a resultant desperate search for some power or state to give him relief. He never arrived at formulating systematically his final philosophy, which he called "Psychodynamism or Panpsychism" and which was probably more a state of emotion than a logical structure.

The sonnets of this period are remarkable in their pure serenity as Quental portrays the mystic lover of the illusive ideal reaching to the farthest limits of space in search of his beloved but driven back into himself by doubt and despair. For this, his friends called him an involuntary Christian who placed himself on the most humble plane but who strove for limitless metaphysical heights. *The Prisoners* has been called "one of the most sublime poems created by modern skepticism." Quental's sonnets, Petrarchan in form, approach perfection technically. The style is limpid, concise, unstrained, with the single molded line natural to romance literatures.

The original volume of *Sonetos Completos* contains one hundred nine sonnets. Edgar Prestage translated sixty-four of these in 1894 and included a translation of Quental's letter to his German translator Wilhelm Storck, an indispensable document for understanding Quental's psychology. Dr. S. Griswold Morley ably translated all the sonnets in his *Sonnets and Poems of Anthero de Quental* (1922).

ABOUT: Morley, S. G. Sonnets and Poems of Anthero de Quental. [In Portuguese—see studies by H. Cidade, J. P. de Oliveira Martins, A. C. Montoiro, L. C. da Silva, J. G. Simões, L. W. Vita.]

R. P. C.

*QUESNAY, FRANÇOIS (June 4, 1694-December 16, 1774), French economist, was born in Versailles, son of an advocate and local landowner. He lived in difficult financial circumstances, owing to the early death of his father, and began serious study only when in Paris learning a trade, and primarily by attending university classes in medicine and surgery. In 1718 he set up practice in Mantes, and for some twenty years devoted himself to his patients, who included the Duc de Noailles. He also found time for writing, and his first work, *Observations sur les Effets de la Saignée* (1730), established his reputation in medicine and led to his immediate nomination as secretary of the Academy of Surgery. His *Essai Physique sur l'Économie Animale* (1736) showed his propensity for philosophical thought, and its revision of 1747 includes his best notions on social problems. Down to 1753, until his eyesight obliged him to abandon surgery for medicine, Quesnay published important treatises in both fields. His renown earned for him in 1749 the post of physician to Mme de Pompadour, and three years later to the king; these services, and attendant residence in Versailles, assured his professional and social position.

Quesnay's more significant contribution in economic theory dates from his later years and his articles in the *Encyclopédie* (1757), "Évidence" (inspired by Malebranche), "Fermiers," "Grains," etc. Like all his nonmedical writings, these articles were signed by names of other persons, since they were not worthy of his post of trust as a doctor. Quesnay's economic theory seeks, by revealing remediable defects in the system, to correct social or financial situations which, for example, tended to reduce production in agriculture; some of these conditions result from abuses in taxation, but far more rise from lack of exact statistics on natural resources, or from excessive governmental encouragement of industry, or from lack of foresight in exportation. Quesnay's writings are well documented from appropriate theorists as well as from actual facts and figures. His first separate work, *Tableau Économique*, was published in 1758, shortly after the suppression of the *Encyclopédie*, and it inspired the "Physiocrat" movement.

* kĕ nã'

Physiocrat theory, first called the "Agricultural System," evolved from concern with agriculture in a reaction against trade and industry, and called especially for long-range planning. Its main proponents include the elder Mirabeau (1715-89), De Gournay (1712-59), La Rivière (1720-94), and Dupont de Nemours (1739-1817), who edited Quesnay's works. The movement began to lose force about 1776, with the fall of Turgot, whose ideas had not been dissimilar, and with the calumny of the younger Mirabeau in his *Lettres de Vincennes*. Quesnay's influence abroad was reflected in the work of Malthus and of William Spence, and his contribution is still recalled in the history of economic theory.

ABOUT: Beer, M. An Inquiry into Physiocracy; Higgs, H. The Physiocrats. [In French—see Daire, E. Les Physiocrates; Oncken, A. *Preface to* Quesnay, F. Œuvres (1888); Schelle, G. François Quesnay.]

F. J. C.

QUEVEDO

*QUEVEDO Y VILLEGAS, FRANCISCO GÓMEZ DE (baptized September 26, 1580-September 8, 1645), Spain's most vitriolic satirist, master of the baroque, and one of the most brilliant literary spirits of his time, was born in Madrid. His father was secretary to the queen, his mother lady-in-waiting. From the very first he seemed doomed by circumstances to a pessimistic outlook on life: his father died soon after Quevedo was born; the boy was brought up in the somber atmosphere of the court of Philip II; he was lame and short-sighted. After receiving his early education at the Jesuit College in Madrid, he went on to the University of Alcalá where he mastered Latin, Greek, and Hebrew, and at twenty was graduated in philosophy and theology. He took part in the rowdy student life of his time and developed an aggressiveness that characterized all of his subsequent life. Acutely aware of the disintegration of a great culture, he wrote the Flemish humanist Justus Lipsius in 1604: "As for my Spain, I cannot speak of it without grief." And in his treatise *La Cuna y la Sepultura* (1612) he said: "If you ask me what thing a man must learn: it is to try to love death and despise life."

Almost immediately after leaving the university, he began to produce an unending stream of satirical verse and pamphlets, but it is on his picaresque novel *La Vida del Buscón* (1613) that a good part of his fame

* kã vã thõ č vē lyä' gäs

rests. This is a cruel, often repellent, work following the pattern set down by the first picaresque novel, *Lazarillo de Tormes*. The protagonist Don Pablos is the son of a thieving barber; his mother is a witch and his uncle the hangman of Segovia. The world of the *Buscón* is one of filth and horror where survival depends on connivance, lies, indeed the complete absence of any virtue or kindness. Stupid, avaricious teachers, sadistic students, starving, pretentious hidalgos, cheats, prostitutes, drunkards make up the cast of characters—all moving in a grotesque atmosphere reminiscent of the dislocated, twisted realism of Hieronymus Bosch.

There are other Quevedos, however. He wrote in his lifetime about nine hundred poems of the most varied forms and themes (heroic, satirical, religious, patriotic); these were brought together posthumously in two volumes, *El Parnaso Español y Musas Castellanas* (1648) and *Las Tres Últimas Musas Castellanas* (1670), and establishing him as one of the greatest poets of the Spanish language. He wrote works of theology (e.g., *La Providencia de Dios*, 1641), political theory (e.g., *Marco Bruto*, 1631), criticism (e.g., *Cuento de Cuentos*). The second most famous of all his works is, however, the *Sueños*, which were published in 1627, although the earliest of them were written 1607-1612 (*El Sueño de las Calaveras, El Alguacil Alguacilado, Las Zahurdas de Plutón, El Mundo por de Dentro*). The *Visita de los Chistes* was written in 1622, followed by *El Entremetido*,

La Dueña y el Soplón. La Hora de Todos y la Fortuna con Seso (1635) was not included in the original *Sueños*. The models for these visions are Dante and Lucan, and they are pretexts for satire aimed at philosophers, poets, apothecaries, doctors, Adam, Judas, Luther, Mohammed, barbers, tailors, bankers, judges. The scenes are, in Karl Vossler's words, "grotesque and exorbitant, feverish and arbitrary caricature behind which Reality disappears." The hell Quevedo describes is really the hell on earth as he saw it: as deformed and disturbing as Goya's *Caprichos* and *Disparates.*

In 1612, after a visit to Italy, Quevedo returned to his mother's estate in the village of Torre de Juan Abad in La Mancha where he buried himself in study, but in 1613 he left for Italy where he became an agent of the Viceroy of Sicily, the Duke of Osuna. During the seven years he served this ambitious nobleman, he learned the evils of politics first-hand. He took part in Osuna's unsuccessful attempt to overthrow the independent republic of Venice, fled back to Spain and was confined to house arrest at Torre de Juan Abad. With the advent of Philip IV and his favorite the Count-Duke of Olivares, Osuna fell into disgrace and Quevedo dedicated his *La Política de Dios* (1617-1626), a work on political theory and morals, to the Count-Duke in an effort to placate him. Quevedo found favor again with the court and for the next ten years he devoted himself exclusively to writing. Among other things, he quarreled with the Gongorists and published the poems of Fray Luis de León. At the age of fifty-two he married a widow of noble family but separated from her within a few months. With time Quevedo joined the ranks of those opposed to Olivares and used his literary talent in behalf of the cause. It is said that one day the King unfolded his napkin and found verses describing the harm Olivares had done to the country. The verses were ascribed to Quevedo, who was arrested at the end of 1639 and imprisoned in a monastery in León. There he remained until June 1643, six months after Olivares' fall. He retired to Torre de Juan Abad and died in Villanueva de los Infantes.

In 1640 there appeared in English the *Visions or Hels Kingdome and the Worlds Follies and Abuses* by R. C. (possibly Richard Crashaw); in 1667 Sir Roger L'Estrange translated the *Visions of Quevedo*, published again by R. Sare in 1696 as *The Visions of Dom Francisco de Quevedo Villegas, Made English by Sir Roger L'Estrange. Fortune in Her Wits, or, The Hour of All Men was* translated by Capt. John Stevens in 1697. *The Comical Works of Don Francisco de Quevedo* was published in London in 1709 and again in 1742; the second edition is a revision of Stevens' work. There is also an Edinburgh edition of *The Works of Don Francisco de Quevedo,* published in 1798 in three volumes. *Pablo de Segovia* was translated with introduction by Henry E. Watts in 1926 and the same year saw the publication of *Quevedo, the Choice, Humorous and Satirical Works,* translated by Sir Roger L'Estrange, John Stevens and others; revised and edited, with an introduction, notes and a version of the *Life of the Great Rascal (Vida del Buscón)* by Charles Duff. The most recent translation of *The Life and Adventures of Don Pablos the Sharper* was done by M. H. Singleton in *Masterpieces of the Spanish Golden Age* (ed. Angel Flores, 1957).

ABOUT: Brenan, G. The Literature of the Spanish People; Modern Language Review XLII (1947); PMLA, LXXI (1956). [In Spanish—see Marín, L. A. La Vida Turbulente de Quevedo.]

M. N.

*QUINET, EDGAR (February 17, 1803-March 27, 1875), French historian and philosopher, was born in Bourg-en-Bresse, the son of a war commissioner and a severe Protestant mother, both ardent republicans and hostile to Napoleon. Quinet's youth was marked by the conflict of ideologies of the times: love for France and hatred of Napoleon and of war. He received an unsystematic education, and was subject to romantic impressions and enthusiasms. He studied in Lyons from 1817 to 1820, then was sent to Paris to prepare a military career. Rebelling against this discipline, he traveled in Switzerland, Germany, and England, using advance payments on his first book to further his studies in history and philosophy. He was oriented toward these fields by his discovery of Herder, whose *Ideen zur Philosophie* he translated (1825) in the three volumes of his *Idées sur la Philosophie de l'Histoire et de l'Humanité;* from his model rises his urge to prophesy on the destiny of the human race. Publication of this translation brought him into immediate contact with Victor Cousin, through whom he met Michelet: to the movement which they represented Quinet added this strong element from German thought.

In 1830, returning from a scientific expedition organized by the Institute, Quinet published *De la Grèce Moderne et de Ses Rapports avec l'Antiquité.* His *Ahasvérus,* begun the following year, is a symbolic history of man and of the Word, an imaginative account of creation, passion, death, and judgment. His *Prométhée* (1837) is a verse epic

* kē nĕ′

757

on the revolt against the gods and the march of progress. Thanks to his work to this date, carefully documented but of a humanitarian and utopian cast, Quinet assumed a significant place in historical studies. He participated in the founding of the *Revue des Deux Mondes*, in which many of his best essays appeared; he then became Minister of Public Instruction in the Louis Philippe government. Quinet's first work has been largely forgotten on account of its obscurity of thought and style, and its lack of color and artistry.

A visit to Rome and Naples in 1832 revealed art, religion, and architecture to Quinet, and from this sojourn and from further travel in Germany, he created *Allemagne et Italie* (1839); he was in that year named professor of foreign literature at Lyons, and in 1841 was called to the same post at the Collège de France. Bit by bit, his democratic ideas became more aggressive, and he left teaching in 1846 and was actively hostile to Louis Philippe in 1848. His attacks against the Jesuits and the church eventually led to his exile in January 1852. In Brussels he published the second volume of *Les Révolutions d'Italie* and, in 1858, *L'Histoire de Mes Idées* and *La Philosophie de l'Histoire en France*. Thence he went to Switzerland where his principal work, *La Révolution*, appeared in 1865, and, five years later, *La Création*, inspired by Darwin. He returned to Paris early in the Franco-Prussian war.

Quinet's works were published in thirty volumes from 1877 to 1882 by his widow, and again in thirty volumes from 1895 to 1913. In English translation are *The Roman Church and Modern Society* (1845) and *The Religious Revolution of the Nineteenth Century* (1881). His life is well known through his many letters and through Mme Quinet's *Souvenirs* (4 vols., 1868-99).

ABOUT: Heath, R. *Early Life and Writings of Edgar Quinet*; Powers, R. H. *Edgar Quinet: A Study in French Patriotism*. [In French—see studies by P. Bataillard, P. Gautier, J. Kaspar.]

F. J. C.

*QUINTANA, MANUEL JOSÉ (1772-1857), Spanish poet, dramatist, and critic, was born and died in Madrid. He studied in Salamanca and at the age of sixteen published his first book of poems. After early literary ventures, he joined the struggle as an ardent patriot against Napoleon, served as secretary to the insurrectionist Junto Central during the War of Liberation, edited the *Semanario Patriótico*, and called the Spanish-American colonies to revolt for in-

* kĕn tä' nä

dependence. During this time he published his *Poesías Patrióticas*. In 1814 he was elected to the Academia Española. The return of the Bourbons brought him imprisonment in the citadel of Pamplona (1814-20) as a liberal constitutionalist, but the liberal triennium brought his release, making him Director of Public Instruction from 1821 to 1823. From 1823 to 1828 he was exiled and lived in Extremadura, where he occupied himself with literary efforts. With the accession of Isabel II, in 1833, he was restored to his post, appointed tutor to the royal family, and then surrounded by honors and respect. In 1855 the queen crowned him the first poet laureate of Spain. He died in Madrid at eighty-five.

Quintana was both a poet imbued with French Encyclopedist ideas and an exalted singer of the sciences and of liberating progress, as in his *Ode to Printing* (1800) and the *Ode to Vaccine*. His patriotic poems, vehement and majestic, call for a strong, free Spain, liberal and modern. His famous composition *El Panteón del Escorial* (1805) follows the legend attributing the decadence of Spain to Philip II; his *Ode to Spain* (1808) after the Revolution of March is a classic model of patriotic poetry. A solid thinker, Quintana wrote notable poems bearing philosophical and didactic themes in which he denounces fanaticism and superstition and condemns despots and slavery, thus renewing the ode with life and enthusiasm long unknown in it. A civic poet, he wrote robustly and grandiloquently, with frequent oratorial declamation but without loss of poetic value. On the other hand, many of his poems are delicate, as his well-known *To the Dream*.

After the first decade of the nineteenth century, Quintana silenced his poetry; however, he continued to produce such writings of documentary interest as his *Report on the Reorganization of Public Instruction* (September 9, 1813) and the ten *Letters to Lord Holland* (November 20, 1823, to April 12, 1824), which narrate impartially the dramatic events from 1820 to 1823.

Quintana became a literary critic early in his career (1791) when he wrote *The Rules of Drama*, a poem in which he proclaimed the theories of Boileau. Influenced technically by Boileau and Voltaire, he composed, in order to prove classic rules, two neoclassic tragedies: *El Duque de Viseo* (1801), imitated from Alfieri and patterned after "Monk" Lewis' horror-play *The Castle*

Spectre (1798), and *Pelayo* (1805), which, despite its undeniable grandeur, proves how the love of liberty which Quintana could express so eloquently in poetry was falsified when treated with classical rules of drama.

As critic, Quintana contributed to the magazine *Variedades de Ciencias, Literatura y Artes* (1803-05). He edited the important anthology of Spanish poetry *Tesoro del Parnaso Español, Poesías Selectas Castellanas* (1807; revised 1830-33) in six volumes. Another important collection is his *Vidas de los Españoles Celebres* (1807-33). In the tradition of Plutarch these biographies exemplify Spanish style at its best in the first half of the nineteenth century. Quintana was a critic of excellent taste and judgment.

English translations of some of his poems appear as follows: by Henry Wadsworth Longfellow in *Outre-Mer* (1833), by J. Russell in *Memoirs of Gonzalo Hernández de Córdoba* (1851), by J. Kennedy in *Modern Poets and Poetry of Spain* (1852, 1860).

ABOUT: [In Spanish—see studies by M. Menéndez y Pelayo, *in* Historia de las Ideas Estéticas en España, IV, V: *and in* Estudios de Crítica Literaria, 5a serie (1908); and by E. Piñeyro.]

R. P. C.

*RAABE, WILHELM KARL** (September 8, 1831-November 15, 1910), German novelist, was born at Eschershausen in the Duchy of Brunswick, the son of a court official. He received his schooling at Holzminden and later at Wolfenbüttel where he had moved with his mother after his father's death in 1845. From 1849 to 1853 Raabe was employed in a bookstore at Magdeburg. He then returned to Wolfenbüttel where he prepared to study at the University of Berlin. (In later life he received honorary doctorates from this university as well as from the universities of Tübingen and Göttingen.) After the success of his first novel in 1857 he decided to become a writer. In 1862 Raabe married Bertha Leiste and moved to Stuttgart where he lived until 1870. In that year he settled at Brunswick where he spent the rest of his rather uneventful life in relative obscurity. In 1891 his youngest daughter died at sixteen. During the last decade of his life Raabe produced no literary work.

Raabe is one of the most representative realistic storytellers of Germany and one of the most important novelists of the nineteenth century; yet he is little known outside Germany, possibly because of his inward,

* rä′ bĕ

RAABE

muted, pessimistic qualities which are, however, frequently relieved by wry humor. As a novelist he was influenced by the German romanticists and Jean Paul, as well as by Thackeray and Dickens. His work constitutes a protest against his time; he viewed incipient materialism, imperialism, and chauvinism with alarm, without becoming an active fighter against them. His novels focus on the German and European crisis of morals and show how inner strength and integrity of character may triumph over the forces of dissolution.

Raabe's first novel, *Die Chronik der Sperlingsgasse* (Chronicle of Sparrow Lane), published in 1857 under the pseudonym of Jakob Corvinus, is a realistic depiction of the milieu of a quiet street in old Berlin, in the form of diary entries by an aging recluse. In 1864 Raabe wrote what is probably his best-known novel, *Der Hungerpastor*, about Hans Unwirrsch, a cobbler's son, who makes his way despite great difficulties and winds up as a pastor in a very poor community where he achieves a modest happiness. Contrasted with this "German life" is the career of Hans' Jewish friend Moses Freudenstein who becomes the Catholic Dr. Théophile Stein of Paris and engages in rather nefarious activities. The novel presents vivid pictures of Berlin, university towns, and farms, with much local color and an accurate depiction of the milieu and the *Zeitgeist*. Raabe had expressed his motto in an earlier novel: "Look up at the stars; pay attention to what goes on in the streets."

Abu Telfan (1868) contrasts an exciting exotic world with the stultifying materialism and Philistinism of Germany. A homecomer from Africa cannot get his bearings in his homeland, which is fit only for the mediocre and not for exceptional people. Raabe's third important novel (which he thought of as having a connection with the other two, although they are not, strictly speaking, a trilogy) is *Der Schüdderump* (The Burial Cart, 1870), whose title suggests its Schopenhauerian pessimism. There is much ironic humor in Raabe, as in the deliberately fanciful and witty names of many of his characters. Raabe once said that what people called his humor was only the breath drawn by a man about to drown. "If you knew what I know, you would cry a lot and laugh little."

In 1891 Raabe published *Stopfkuchen*, which he considered his best and most subjective book, less pessimistic than his earlier work, more affirmative of the riches and resources of the human heart. Among the other works of the prolific Raabe are a number of historical novels, including *Im alten Eisen* (1887), *Kloster Lugau* (1894), *Akten des Vogelsangs* (1896), and *Hastenbeck* (1899), as well as many stories which appeared in volumes entitled *Ferne Stimmen* and *Der Regenbogen* (1865 and 1869). Raabe's collected poems appeared posthumously in 1912.

Hermann Hesse described Raabe a few years before his death: "A very tall, lean figure . . . an old, wrinkled, intelligent, very friendly face, yet the face of a fox, sly, crafty, cryptic . . . the aged face of a sage, mocking yet devoid of malice, kindly with the wisdom of old age, yet ageless. . . ."

Abu Telfan, or The Return from the Mountains of the Moon, translated by Sofie Delffs, appeared in 1881. *The Hunger-Pastor*, translated by "Arnold," was published in 1885. An abridged translation by Muriel Almon of the latter work is included in *The German Classics*, XI.

ABOUT: The German Classics, XI; Fairley, B. The Modernity of Wilhelm Raabe, *in* German Studies Presented to L. A. Willoughby 1952, *also* Wilhelm Raabe, an Introduction to His Novels; Pascal, R. The German Novel. [In German—see studies by C. Bauer, W. Brandes, W. Fehse, R. Guardini, K. Hoppe, G. Mayer, H. Pongs, H.. Spiero.]

H. Z.

*RABELAIS, FRANÇOIS (1494?-1553?), French satirist and humorist, was born in Poitou, in western France, probably at the village of La Devinière, near Chinon, where

* rå blĕ′

RABELAIS

much of the action of *Gargantua and Pantagruel* takes place. The year 1494 is now regarded as the most likely year of his birth, though earlier dates, ranging as far back as 1483, used to be accepted. Rabelais had a sister and two brothers. His father, Antoine Rabelais, was a successful lawyer practicing at Chinon.

Of his early education and upbringing little is known. He either went to school at the nearby Benedictine monastery of Seuilly or was taught the rudiments by his father. He may, afterward, have studied at Angers, where—to judge from his many detailed references—he either lived or visited very frequently between 1515 and 1518. There is no doubt that he learned Latin and studied the traditional "scholastic" material (with an emphasis on commentaries), as the chapters on education in his first two books amply indicate. Years later, in spite of his humanistic scorn for the "medieval" system of education Rabelais' writings were to show the deep imprint of his early training, in both terminology and pedagogical method.

With some lacunae, Rabelais' life beginning in 1520 is much better known. Late in that year he became a monk in a Franciscan monastery at Fontenay-le-Comte. Here he befriended Pierre Amy, with whom he undertook the study of Greek, a project in which both monks received encouragement from France's most eminent Hellenist, Guillaume Budé.

Rabelais and Pierre Amy associated at this time with an unusual group of intellectual lawyers who met periodically at the home of André Tiraqueau, in Fontenay-le-Comte. The group, deeply interested in the new humanistic scholarship, appears to have conducted learned discussions on a wide range of literary and moral topics, and some of these discussions, especially that on the woman question (see Book III), were to find their way into Rabelais' writings, as well as serving as a constant source of intellectual stimulation.

At the end of 1523, frightened by the spirit of independence which the devotion to the ancient classics was fostering, the Sorbonne (the theological faculty of the University of Paris) banned the study of Greek, and the Greek books of Rabelais and Amy were confiscated by the superiors of their abbey. Some time later, probably in 1525, though his books had been returned to him, Rabelais moved to the Benedictine monastery of Saint-Pierre-de-Maillezais, not far from Fontenay-le-Comte. This move was, presumably, made possible by the intervention of the abbot of Saint-Pierre-de-Maillezais, Bishop Geoffroy d'Estissac, who took Rabelais as his secretary and perhaps as tutor to his nephew. With Geoffroy, Rabelais traveled widely in Poitou, gaining the first-hand knowledge of the country and its people—its flora and fauna, its topography and manners, its legends and amusements—which accounts so heavily for the rich realism of *Gargantua* and *Pantagruel*. Of the places with which he became particularly familiar at this time, special mention must be made of Poitiers, which figures with great prominence in his writings.

Some time in 1527 Rabelais left the service of Geoffroy d'Estissac. From then until September 1530 scholars have no trace of him. During these three years, however, he must have visited the universities of Bordeaux, Bourges, Orléans, Paris, and Toulouse, with a long stay at Paris. On September 17, 1530, he enrolled in the medical faculty of the University of Montpellier and on November 1 received the degree of bachelor of medicine. The speed with which he completed his medical study has led to the assumption that he had studied medicine previously, perhaps at Paris. In 1531 Rabelais gave public commentaries on Hippocrates and Galen and met with considerable success, probably because of his knowledge of Greek.

In the spring of 1532 we find Rabelais in Lyon, whither he was attracted by its reputation as an intellectual and publishing center. Within a few months appeared Rabelais' edition of medical letters by Manardi, a con-

temporary Italian doctor, and his edition, with many notes, of the *Aphorisms* of Hippocrates. Rabelais' contribution to the progress of medicine was entirely philological, consisting of textual criticism rather than experimentation or observation. These scholarly publications resulted in an offer to join the staff of the Lyon city hospital (Hôtel-Dieu), which Rabelais accepted on November 1, 1532. Since Rabelais was the only doctor at the Hôtel-Dieu, he is often credited with the drop of two to three per cent in the mortality rate during his tenure of office; but no one knows to what extent this is to be attributed to his theory that laughter is the best medicine and to his practice thereof. Meanwhile, in the autumn of 1532, also at Lyon, appeared *Pantagruel (Les horribles et espouventables Faictz et Prouesses du très-renommé Pantagruel, Roy des Dipsodes, filz du grand géant Gargantua, Composez nouvellement par maistre Alcofrybas Nasier).*

Pantagruel was a sequel to the anonymous *Grandes et inestimables Cronicques du grand et énorme géant Gargantua,* a work of popular fiction which had great success in 1532. Rabelais preserved the tone and framework of the *Chronicle* but, while drawing from popular legend and maintaining a folk flavor, he added a great amount of erudite material—classical allusions and illustrations, brief disquisitions on education, history, chemistry—all masterfully woven into the fabric of the boisterous tricks and adventures of guzzling giants and their friends (and enemies). His amazing gift as a story-teller, his fanciful explanations of various geographical and historical facts and names, his rough satiric vein, his hatred of scholasticism and theologians and his enthusiasm for the Renaissance, his ability to confuse (and sometimes to fuse) fact and nonsense—all these are evident in *Pantagruel.* The book was condemned by the Sorbonne for obscenity.

Still under the anagrammatic pseudonym of Alcofrybas Nasier, and taking advantage of the great popularity of Pantagruel, Rabelais early in 1533 published his *Pantagruéline Prognostication,* a mock almanac of a kind which had recently come into vogue.

In 1533 Rabelais became the personal physician of Jean du Bellay, bishop of Paris and diplomat of the first rank. With him Rabelais went to Rome in January and February 1534, there making the acquaintance of numerous classical scholars, establishing a first-hand contact with the ruins of ancient Rome, and developing his intense interest in classical architecture.

Rabelais' next publication (1534) was *Gargantua*, which—tracing as it does the birth and youth of Pantagruel's father, Gargantua —logically precedes *Pantagruel* and is now always printed as the first of Rabelais' five books. *Gargantua* in many ways covers the same ground as the *Chronicle* to which *Pantagruel* was originally a sequel, but whereas the anonymous author of the *Chronicle* had concentrated on the gigantic and fantastic possibilities of his story, Rabelais, without neglecting these, used every occasion to paint a picture of contemporary manners, to satirize the Sorbonne, and to present his ideas on education, war, and politics. It is in this book that we first meet the colorful monk Friar John, for whom Gargantua builds the famous coeducational abbey of Thélème, an institution which embodies many of the architectural and moral ideals of Rabelais and his fellow humanists. Like *Pantagruel* two years earlier, *Gargantua* was condemned by the Sorbonne.

In July 1535 Rabelais again accompanied Jean du Bellay (now a cardinal) to Rome, this time for a stay of seven months. Through his influential patron he received papal absolution for his unauthorized departure from the Benedictine monastery in 1527 and his putting off of the frock. He was granted permission to enter any Benedictine monastery at any time and to practice medicine (as indeed he had already been doing).

For ten years (1536-46) Rabelais largely taught and practiced medicine. In May 1537, he received the doctor's degree, but by that time he was already famous as a doctor. He performed dissections and lectured on anatomy at Lyon and Montpellier, and he accompanied Guillaume du Bellay, Seigneur de Langey, brother of Jean du Bellay, on political missions to Italy. In 1541, for an edition to be published the following year, Rabelais made many changes in *Pantagruel* and *Gargantua*, with the hope of decreasing the enmity of the Sorbonne toward him. He eliminated most of the derogatory references to the Sorbonne itself but in all other respects maintained his derisive tone toward Scripture and religious practices. The new edition received the prompt censure of the Sorbonne and the Paris Parlement.

Rabelais was with the Seigneur de Langey when the latter died in January 1543, but from the middle of 1543 until September 19, 1545, Rabelais is again lost to view. It seems likely, from what was to follow, that he spent a great portion of his time in western France and that he earned his living by practicing medicine; the great authority Abel Lefranc conjectured that Rabelais might have been on political or diplomatic missions for the king.

On September 19, 1545, in spite of three previous condemnations by the Sorbonne, Rabelais received from Francis I a six-year privilege for publication of Book III. In this book Rabelais was unusually gentle to theologians, but the Sorbonne condemned it for heresy nonetheless—perhaps because of a typographical error which substituted *âne* (ass) for *âme* (soul). Most of Book III is taken up with the attempt of Panurge to determine the advisability of marriage, and to this end he tries every form of divination and prophecy. The opposite interpretations of the prophecies by Panurge (who sees them all as favorable to marriage) and Pantagruel (who sees them as unfavorable) provide a magnificent opportunity for Rabelais' virtuosity in the realm of argumentation. In Book III, moreover, Rabelais' erudition becomes an integral part of the story in a way which renders this book superior, in the eyes of many critics and readers, to all the others. Rabelais' choice of women and marriage as his central subject has been shown, by Abel Lefranc, to be related to the intense interest in the woman question around 1540, when Rabelais was writing Book III.

Upon the condemnation of Book III, Rabelais fled to Metz (which was a free city of the Empire), where we find him by March 28, 1546. For two years he worked as a doctor for the city of Metz, meanwhile composing Book IV of his continuing opus. In 1548 he went to Rome to become again the personal physician of Cardinal Jean du Bellay. Passing through Lyon, he submitted the first part of Book IV to his publisher. (The complete version was to appear in February 1552.) Book IV is occupied with the travels of Pantagruel, Panurge, Friar John, and company in search of the Holy Bottle, which is supposed to contain the answer to the question of Panurge's marriage. It is remarkable for the knowledge it shows of geography and navigation; but it also contains both the conventional travel devices such as a great tempest, and the usual Rabelaisian satire, buffoonery, and inventive spinning of yarns. Moreover, Book IV presents a new light on the characters, especially Panurge. The Papimania-Decretals satire, aimed at the Pope and his temporal power, grew out of the political struggle between France and the Vatican, in which Rabelais' stand was that of a good Frenchman.

In 1551 Jean du Bellay made Rabelais the vicar of Meudon and Jambet, but it seems certain that Rabelais' only function as an "ecclesiastic" was to collect the revenues. After the condemnation of Book IV (March 1552) Rabelais again disappears. He died some time between January 9, 1553 (the date of his resignation as vicar of Meudon and Jambet), and May 1, 1554 (the date of publication of an epitaph by Tahureau), but more likely late in 1553 or early in 1554. None of the stories about his death-bed witticisms are authentic; they merely show how quickly Rabelais became a subject of legend. He was buried, according to an eighteenth century report, in the cemetery of St. Paul in Paris.

An edition of Rabelais' first four books appeared in 1553, another in 1556, and a third in 1559. Book V appeared first in 1562, in partial form, and complete in 1564. The authenticity of Book V has always been a moot point. The violence of the anti-Catholic satire and the absence of many of the features which characterize the first four books have rendered Rabelais' authorship suspect. The fairest guess is that Rabelais had prepared outlines, sketches, and rough drafts of some chapters and that these were worked over by a writer or editor who was acquainted with the master's style. Book V, like the first four, was a great literary success, though it is now generally regarded as considerably inferior.

Rabelais' gifts as a humorist, together with his erudition, his serious messages, and his underlying faith in human nature have assured him a wide following in all countries. His emphasis on drink and laughter, though assuredly representing only part of his interest and objective, has usually been taken as a guide to his personality, which indeed seems to have been gay and carefree. To say—truly enough, probably—that Gargantua and Pantagruel were the products of the leisure hours of a scholar, is not to take away from their importance, for all of Rabelais is in these works. Rabelais' religious ideas are difficult to determine. Though some scholars have emphasized his flirtation with Calvinism, and others the extent of his Catholicism, most regard him as either a freethinker or an independent Catholic. As a story-teller Rabelais is unsurpassed; nor have his coarseness and the obscenity of his language seriously hurt his reputation. He remains without doubt one of the giants of French literature, so regarded both at home and abroad.

Rabelais has been much translated, e.g., by T. Urquhart and P. le Motteux (1653-94), W. F. Smith (1893), Samuel Putnam (1929), J. LeClerq (1936), and J. M. Cohen (1955). LeClerq's translation has the virtue of embodying in the text much of the information which, in the scholarly French editions, is found in the footnotes; and it is both faithful to the tone of the original and imaginative in its English renderings. Cohen's translation is more accurate in language but lacks the fire of the original and its over-all tone.

A fair summary of the state of studies on Rabelais may be obtained from Plattard, J. État Présent des Études Rabelaisiennes (1927); Saulnier, V. L. "Dix Années d'Études sur Rabelais," Bibl. d'Hum. et Ren. 1949; Schutz, A. H. A Critical Bibliography of French Literature: The Sixteenth Century (1956).

ABOUT: France, A. François Rabelais; Krailsheimer, A. J. Rabelais and the Franciscans; Plattard, J. The Life of Rabelais; Powys, J. C. Rabelais; Putnam, S. Rabelais, Man of the Renaissance; Tilley, A. François Rabelais; Willcocks, M. P. The Laughing Philosopher. [In French—Lote, G. La Vie et l'Œuvre de François Rabelais.]

A. C. K.

*RACAN, HONORAT DE BUEIL (February 5, 1589-January 21, 1670), French poet, was born in the Château of Champmarin to a family which had long served the kings of France as fighters and administrators. Raised in Touraine, Racan spent his childhood quietly in the company of his nurse, his mother, and her sister. As a young boy he studied the traditional subjects—catechism, elementary science, music (the lute)—which interested him, but he was bored by grammar, logic, and rhetoric and could hardly retain the rudiments of Latin. His delight was French verse, which he began writing at the age of sixteen.

In 1602, left an orphan, he was introduced to the court of Henry IV and placed as a page in the *chambre du roi* by a cousin, the Comte de Bellegarde. The suavities of the court did not make it the most ideal place for the gauche, backward boy of thirteen. His distracted air, his naïveté made him a kind of legend in the court and even when he became an established poet his mannerisms prompted remarks such as the one made by Tallemant des Réaux: "Aside from his verses, it seems that he did not have common sense. He had the look of a farmer. He lisped and could hardly pronounce his name —for by misfortune *r* and *c* were two letters he pronounced badly."

At court he began to compose elegiac poetry. It was here that he became the friend and student of the celebrated Malherbe, with whom he studied the theory of poetic form.

* rȧ cȧn′

According to Lanson, Racan never profited from Malherbe's lessons, for his poetry remained facile and lacking in strong construction. Yet Racan's critics agree that he had the natural talent of a poet—a sensitive soul and ear. *Stances sur la Retraite,* verses published in 1618, punctuated with sweetness and resignation, show his poetic disposition. In 1619, inspired by Catherine de Termes (a sister-in-law of Bellegarde) he wrote *Arthénice* [anagram of Catherine] *ou les Bergeries,* a dramatic pastoral of some 3,000 lines of verse which express in picturesque, sincere, and harmonious terms his vivid love of nature. Influenced by ancient idylls and Italian romances, the poem nevertheless shows Racan's particular response to the flight of time, the melancholy of love, and his profound impressions of the existence of man in such magnificent images that Boileau wrote, "Racan pourrait chanter au défaut d'un Homère."

In 1628 Racan married sixteen-year-old Madeleine du Bois and about 1639, after his life at court and many years' service in the king's armies, he retired to his Château de la Roche-Racan where he consecrated his life to his family, to the writing of religious poetry, and to serving as godfather to the children of the village Saint Paterne. Of his own five children, two survived. It was during these years that he wrote *Œuvres et Poésies Chrétiennes Tirées des Psaumes et de Quelques Cantiques du Vieux et du Nouveau Testament* (1631, 1652, 1666), a surprising achievement, for his knowledge of Hebrew, Greek, and the Latin of the Vulgate was limited. He also collaborated in composing ballets, odes, sonnets, and madrigals and in drawing up critical notes and anecdotes for *Mémoires sur M. de Malherbe,* his old mentor.

From time to time he returned to Paris to survey his interests and to attend meetings of the Académie Française to which he was elected in 1634. During one of these visits he died in a small house near the Church of Saint Sulpice, but his remains were carried to the crypt of his ancestors in the Church of Neuvy-le-Roi in his beloved Touraine.

ABOUT: [In French—Arnould, L. Racan.]

G. E.

*RACINE, JEAN BAPTISTE (December 22, 1639-April 21, 1699), France's principal tragic author, was born at La Ferté-Milon, the son of Jean Racine, a functionary

* rà sēn'

RACINE

in the local salt-tax office. His mother, born Jeanne Sconin, daughter of a government official of La Ferté-Milon, died in giving birth to a girl, Marie, when Racine was thirteen months old. His father died two years later. Marie was taken by the Sconin grandparents, Jean by the Racines. At the age of five or six Racine may have gone to the Jansenist convent of Port-Royal in Paris, where his aunt Agnès was a nun, and there begun his schooling. His education was continued at the Collège of Beauvais, where he studied until 1655, then moving to Port-Royal.

Here Racine profited from the Jansenists' new educational ideas—with their encouragement of the fine use of French and their emphasis on Greek rather than Latin. He was particularly influenced by Antoine Le Maître, a brilliant lawyer whose lessons in elocution undoubtedly contributed heavily to the effectiveness of his dramatic verse. The spirituality of the Port-Royal atmosphere, on the other hand, seems to have made little impression on the young Racine, if we may judge from some odes he wrote in 1656.

In the autumn of 1658 Racine moved to the Collège d'Harcourt, in Paris, to study philosophy for one year. Here he associated with a gay, though not dissolute, company of young intellectuals, including the not-quite-so-young La Fontaine. He lived with his relative Nicolas Vitart, who was the intendant of the Duc de Luynes. In early 1660, eager for patronage, Racine wrote a sonnet in honor of Cardinal Mazarin, but the effort failed, and Racine, moreover, antagonized the Jansenists, who hated Mazarin. Later in 1660 he published "La Nymphe de la Seine" (an ode celebrating the king's marriage), which was well received by critics and readers and earned Racine a royal grant of 100 louis. In 1660-61 he attempted, unsuccessfully, to have two tragedies produced, one at the Marais theatre, the other at the Hôtel de Bourgogne. Neither of these tragedies is extant.

In November 1661 Racine left Paris for Uzès, in the south of France. There, under the auspices of an uncle, Antoine Sconin, the vicar-general of Uzès, he studied theology in preparation for the priesthood and an ecclesiastical benefice. The benefice did not materialize, and Racine returned to Paris some time between August 1662 and June 1663 to resume his literary career. He wrote two odes for royal consumption, received a grant of 600 livres, and became a friend of Boileau. Next, at the urging of Molière, the director of the Palais-Royal theatre, he wrote his tragedy *La Thébaïde*, which was produced in June 1664 and was a failure. *Alexandre* (December 1665), also produced by Molière, was received by the public with enthusiasm. Two weeks after its opening in Molière's theatre, and while it was still being played there, his *Alexandre* opened at the rival Hôtel de Bourgogne. From this time forward relations between France's two leading dramatists were strained, and, considering Molière's ever-proper professional conduct, the blame for the rupture must be laid at Racine's door.

Racine next became involved in a controversy with the Jansenists, who, after privately urging their lost son to give up his literary career, made a sharp public attack on the theatre. Racine answered with a violent and stinging pamphlet which ended his connections with Port-Royal and antagonized a good part of the public.

In 1665 Racine took the famous actress Thérèse du Parc as his mistress, and, slightly more than a year after her death in 1668, he began a liaison with another actress, Champmeslé (Marie Desmares), which lasted intermittently until 1677.

From 1667 to 1677, Racine produced new plays on an almost annual basis: *Andromaque* (1667), *Les Plaideurs* (1668), *Britannicus* (1669), *Bérénice* (1670), *Bajazet* (1672), *Mithridate* (1673), *Iphigénie en Aulide* (1674), and *Phèdre* (1677). By the early 1670's he was widely acknowledged as the best living tragedian and classed with the masters of antiquity. And yet, despite influ-

ential friends, great dramatic success, and powerful patrons (including the royal mistress Mme de Montespan), Racine had many enemies and bore the brunt of many attacks. The partisans of the waning Corneille, surely mindful more of the latter's reputation than of his current productions, opposed Racine bitterly in every manner possible, on occasion damning him with faint praise, at other times attacking him head-on, and sometimes maneuvering to ruin his plays by building up his rivals. Racine, moreover, had many personal enemies. Nor was the scorn and violence with which he promptly reacted to every attack calculated to quiet the storms which continually arose against him.

In the *Phèdre* quarrel, one of the most important of the many involving Racine, a rival tragedian, Pradon, had been induced to write a tragedy on the same theme as Racine's. Two days after Racine's tragedy opened (January 1, 1677), Pradon's opened at a rival theatre, in spite of the attempts of Racine and his friends first to dissuade the leading actresses from performing in it and, next, to have the play banned by the king. At first —to Racine's disgust and despair—the two competing tragedies fared equally well, but whereas Pradon's had to be withdrawn after sixteen performances and is now neither read nor performed, Racine's continued to grow in favor. Meanwhile, however, the partisans of Racine and Pradon had begun to attack and threaten each other in a campaign of sonnets, the tone of which, coming on the heels of Racine's disappointment with the reception accorded his *Phèdre*, is generally thought to have contributed significantly to his decision to retire from the theatre after *Phèdre*.

Shortly after *Phèdre*, Racine became "converted" and was welcomed back into the fold by the Jansenists of Port-Royal. This development, according to many indications cited by modern historians and biographers, represented no sudden decision but had long been in the making. Next, in May 1677, Racine married Catherine de Romanet, the daughter of a rich bourgeois of Paris, who was to bear him five daughters and two sons, including Louis Racine, who was to become an important source of information about his father's career. Later in 1677, probably in September, Racine was named, along with Boileau, historiographer to the king, and with this appointment came a command to quit the theatre, so as to devote himself properly to his new work. His retirement from the theatre, widely regarded by his contemporaries and by later generations as a betrayal and a sell-out, was to be permanent, except for his production of two Biblical plays, *Esther* (1689) and *Athalie* (1691), both written for the girls at the school of Saint-Cyr. Racine died, after a long illness, at fifty-nine, of either an ulcer or an abscess on the liver. He was buried at Port-Royal, but in 1711 his remains were removed to Saint-Étienne-du-Mont.

Contemporaries had, for the most part, a low opinion of Racine as a man. His unrestrained ambition, which led him to tread unscrupulously over anyone who stood in his way, his bitterness with enemies or rivals, a bitterness which he could express only too effectively, and a rare inability to pardon, ask for pardon, or in any way be reconciled with others—these qualities were much mentioned and little prized. Objectively, in terms of his difficult childhood, it is easy to account for his adult character, but this is hardly to say that his contemporaries were not justified in considering him cold, insincere, and generally an unpleasant person. That he was sensitive to love, as he was to all the world around him, cannot be doubted, but his background ill equipped him to give it or receive it.

Since Racine's dramatic production is quantitatively slight, it is possible here to characterize each of his plays briefly. *La Thébaïde* (1664), dealing with the final extinction of the house of Oedipus, shows little originality, being close, in both its political orientation and its dramatic techniques, to Rotrou and Corneille. On occasion the characters show some of the emotion of the later Racinian personalities; and the feeling of fate overpowering man, in contrast to the freedom and heroism of Corneille's drama, may be sensed here and there.

In *Alexandre* (1665) Racine turned from political to amorous tragedy. The love with which the characters are concerned, however, is not the destructive force which it was to become in Racine's later tragedies, but the romanticized, virtue-inspiring love of the *galant* literature of the time. In style *Alexandre* shows important traces of poetic genius, its lines already having much of the melodic quality of the great plays.

With *Andromaque* (1667) Racine entered a new world. Love, now fierce and destructive, ruins Pyrrhus, Hermione, and Orestes. It is this process of moral disintegration which is of prime interest, despite the central position of Andromache, torn between her loyalty to her late husband and her desire to save the life of her young son. Though Greek in background, this tragedy owes more of its greatness to Virgil than to Euripides. Dramatically Racine has not yet broken completely with French tragic tradition, but his ability to borrow now here, now there, is indicative, not only of vast erudition, but of a new-found independence which was to be always much in evidence. The sudden advance in Racine's drama between 1665 and 1667 has never been adequately explained, but his love affair with the actress Du Parc (for whom he planned the leading rôle) must have done much to release the strong passions which had been hitherto unexpressed.

In 1668 Racine produced *Les Plaideurs,* a gay comedy on lawyers and legal practices. Not successful when it first appeared—perhaps because of organized opposition by the legal profession, perhaps because of inferior performance—it gained steadily in popularity. Ostensibly *Les Plaideurs* is based on *The Wasps* of Aristophanes, but the accepted view is that this classical cloak is a cover under which Racine could freely ridicule contemporary practices.

Racine was commonly reproached by his enemies for having no mastery of historical or political material, much as he might excel in the "sentimental" (e.g., *Andromaque*). Here Corneille remained supreme, and it was this supremacy which Racine successfully challenged with his production of *Britannicus* (1669). Reflecting a great amount of Racine's own feelings and his observations at court, as well as wide reading, *Britannicus* portrays a world of weakness, cruelty, and cynicism. Here is no trace of the greatness exhibited by Corneille's characters in their crimes, but humanity at its lowest. Some relief is provided by the delicate picture of the young lovers Britannicus and Junie, who, as models for Racine's subsequent plays, undoubtedly represented another, and important, side of his artistic temperament. The pattern of innocent young lovers who are at the mercy of another more experienced and ruthless pair, already visible in *Andromaque,* became established in this play as virtually a convention of Racinian tragedy.

Bérénice (1670), written at the suggestion of Princess Henriette, Louis XIV's sister-in-law, was of milder stuff. Though it triumphed over Corneille's play on the same subject *(Tite et Bérénice),* which opened one week after Racine's, the principal characters of *Bérénice* are too indecisive and passive for great tragedy. Its chief interest, for Racine's development, is the clear and conscious simplicity of plot which was to characterize his last works.

With *Bajazet* (1672) Racine returned to the style of *Andromaque* and *Britannicus*. Using a bloody episode of Turkish history, he placed his action in a harem and filled the drama with violence and carnage. The effective use of local color (capitalizing on the current vogue of things Turkish), the power of the language, the violent contrasts, and the depth of feeling portrayed, all combined to make this play a huge success. The Corneille party claimed, loudly but weakly, that the characters were Frenchmen, not Turks, but this had little effect on Racine's growing reputation as master of the French tragic stage.

In January 1672, within a day or two of his election to the French Academy, Racine opened his *Mithridate,* a Roman drama in which youth and virtue emerged victorious over age and vice. The gentle princess Monime, often regarded as one of Racine's finest creations, is alone enough to give this tragedy a high place in Racine's production. The success of the play was such as virtually to silence Racine's enemies, to whom, from now on, he paid little heed. With *Mithridate* the Greek influence upon Racine, hitherto slight, permanently replaced the Latin, in so far as the profane tragedies were concerned.

In *Iphigénie en Aulide,* first played at Versailles in the summer of 1674, then in Paris the following winter, Racine leaned heavily on Homer and Euripides. Fearful, however, that his public would refuse to accept the miraculous solution offered by Euripides, he found elsewhere a substitute who could be sacrificed, thus saving Iphigenia for her marriage with Achilles. Though this distortion of the legend surprised and displeased some of his audiences, they were so stirred by the feelings of Agamemnon, forced to sacrifice his daughter, by Clytemnestra and Achilles rebelling against the oracle, and by the innocent obedience of Iphigenia herself, that the play was, and still is, in spite of flaws, regarded as one of Racine's best.

Phèdre (1677), the last of Racine's secular plays, is his undoubted masterpiece. In the intensity and lyric richness of its poetry, in the originality of its characterization, in the relentlessness of its psychological probing, and in the completeness of its tragic annihilation, *Phèdre* is unmatched in the rest of Racine's works. Nowhere else has he shown a human personality so utterly the victim of passion, so helpless to save herself by her own efforts. The fact that the heroine's weakness could be demonstrative of Jansenist philosophy has prompted many critics to regard this play as Jansenist—or Christian-inspired, but it seems more likely that what we have is mere coincidence. The course of Racine's career leaves no doubt that he moved in the direction of *Phèdre* independently of religious influences.

Coming out of retirement, Racine wrote two Biblical plays for the girls of Saint-Cyr: *Esther* (1689) and *Athalie* (1691), both of which, in spite of some excellent poetry, are necessarily limited in range by comparison to the profane drama.

The originality and independence with which Racine worked with his materials should not obscure the fact that he observed many conventions, some of them dictated by audience receptivity and some self-imposed. His pattern of two young and inexperienced lovers at the mercy of a pair of older and often vicious characters has already been pointed out. Racine, moreover, accepted the unities of time, place, and action, without the rebelliousness of chafing which is felt in Corneille. However, he forged the unities to his own needs and gained from them an unprecedented intensity of concentration. Of other conventions the most striking are the use of confidants, the observance of the "proprieties," especially the avoidance of violent death onstage, the use of *récits* and soliloquies, and the thematic use of *quid pro quo* for purposes of dramatic irony.

Racine's place as France's supreme tragedian has scarcely been questioned, except by romantics like Hugo. His plays, which because of their powerful female character rôles have always attracted France's finest actresses, are perpetually successful with the French public. Abroad, though highly regarded, he has been less widely appreciated, largely because to audiences accustomed to Shakespeare or Schiller, the superficially narrow scope of his tragedies gives an impression of smallness and excessive restraint.

Racine's tragedies have been translated into English from the seventeenth century on. Translations of *Andromaque,* for example, were made by J. Crowne (1675), A. Philips (1712), F. Lyster (1894), E. Fontaine (1929), and L. Lockert (1936). Lockert translated *Britannicus, Phèdre,* and *Athalie,* along with *Andromaque.* Robert Lowell's *Phaedra* appeared in 1961. In 1963 Penguin Books published translations by John Cairncross of *Phaedra and Other Plays (Iphigénie, Athalie).* There is a translation of all the plays by R. B. Boswell (1889-90). A study of the translations was made by Dorothea F. (Canfield) Fisher, *Corneille and Racine in England; a Study of the Two Corneilles and Racine* (1904).

ABOUT: Brereton, G. Jean Racine; Clark, A. F. B. Jean Racine; Lapp, J. C. Aspects of Racinian Tragedy; Turnell, M. The Classical Moment. [In French—see studies by P. Bénichou, G. Larroumet, T. Maulnier, F. Mauriac, E. Vinaver.]

A. C. K.

*RADIČEVIĆ, BRANKO (March 15, 1824-June 18, 1853), Serbian poet, was born in Slavonski Brod, Croatia, a part of the Austrian Empire at that time, and was christened with the name Aleksije (Alex). His father, Theodor, a customs official, was a bibliophile, an avid reader, and a poet himself. He was a great friend of Vuk Stefanović Karadžić, the celebrated Serbian folklorist, lexicographer, and a linguistic reformer, and he translated several works from German, among which Schiller's *William Tell* must be mentioned. Since the customs officials were often moved, Branko went to school in different places. In 1835 he finished elementary school, Serbian and German, in Zemun, and in 1841 high school in Sremski Karlovci. This school was Serbian in name only, for the languages of instruction were primarily German and Latin; the Serbian language was not introduced into Austrian schools until 1848. He finished the senior high school in Timişoara (now a part of Rumania). In 1843 he went to Vienna where he intended to study literature, arts, and painting, but instead took up law, on the persuasion of his father. Financial difficulties and dissipation prevented him from finishing his studies. During the Revolution of 1848-49 Branko returned home, but upon receiving financial help from the Serbian prince Mikhailo Obrenović, who was at that time an exile in Vienna, he returned to Vienna and changed to the study of medicine.

Branko started to write poetry while still in the high school in Karlovci, but his main period of poetic productivity was between 1843 and 1850. He did not publish any of his poems until 1847, when the first collection appeared under the title *Pesme*, which he dedicated to the youth of Serbia. A second volume appeared four years later.

Although Branko Radičević was not the first Serbian poet to use Serbian as it was really spoken, his carefully selected phraseology, the content, and even the basic tone and the manner of expression tended to set his work far above anything produced in Serbian literature up to that time. Serbian poets before him tended to be "objective" and, above all, didactic, reducing everything to an ethical or a patriotic moral. Radičević, with an audacity of a young and passionate man, broke off with this crude moralistic tradition by interjecting his own personal experiences and emotions, with genuine sentiments of grief, passion, or joy, thus creating almost a revolution in literature.

He was mainly a lyric poet in the vein of poets like Heinrich Heine and Ludwig Uhland in Germany, who seemed to have influenced him to a certain degree. In his later years he turned to epic poetry, coming, as did many poets of his time, under a Byronic influence. In 1848 he wrote *Gojko*, *Osveta* (Revenge), *Stojan*, *Utopljenica* (The Drowned Girl), *Uroš*, and in 1849 *Hajdukov Grob* (The Tomb of a Haiduk). But he never achieved that grace and facility that characterized his shorter lyric poems, or his long romantic poem *Đački Rastanak* (The Students' Departure), in which he sang of longing for the magnificence and might which would rise after the unification of the South Slavs—a poem of brotherhood and unity.

There is a note of sadness and premonition in his last poems, for he was already ill with tuberculosis. He died in Vienna, in the prime of his creativeness, at twenty-nine. His remains were later returned to his homeland and buried in what is now a national shrine at Stražilovo, near Karlovci. All pictures show him a handsome, melancholy youth with long wavy hair and an almost striking Byronic likeness.

In 1862, after Branko's death, his father published fourteen shorter lyric poems and five longer epic poems, as well as a lyric cycle entitled *Tuga i Opomena* (Melancholy and Exhortation). The collected poetry of Branko Radičević has appeared in several editions, and most of his poems can be found in standard Yugoslav anthologies. There are some isolated translations of Branko's poetry into German and French.

ABOUT: [In Serbian—see studies by P. Popović, J. Skerlić.]

F. S. L.

*RADISHCHEV, ALEXANDER NIKOLAEVICH (August 20, 1749-September 12, 1802), Russian poet and reformer, was a scion of the Russian landed gentry. He was born in the village of Upper Ablyagovo in Seratov Province. The first seven years of his life were spent at his birthplace where he learned to read and write under the tutelage of his *dyadska* (diminutive of "uncle"), the indentured man-servant commonly maintained in such households to look

* rä dě′ chě vích

* rŭ dyě′ shchěf

after, serve, and supervise the primary education of the male children.

In 1756 his father took him to Moscow where, during the previous year, Lomonosov's dream of the first Russian university had been realized. Radishchev's elementary education was, therefore, completed in an atmosphere of expanding cultural horizons. In 1761 he was sent to the St. Petersburg Page Corps, the leading cadet training school for sons of the aristocracy, where he remained until his graduation in 1765.

He spent the next four years (1766-71) at the University of Leipzig where Goethe was also a student. Radishchev studied law, natural philosophy, literature, languages, learning which he himself found too broad to be encompassed. He returned to Russia in 1771 with the express intention of trying to reduce the diversity of his Leipzig training to some sort of order.

He joined the ranks of the Russian Enlightenment, under the influence of Nikolay Novikov, the leader of the movement. During the ensuing period his anti-autocratic views were rapidly crystallized. "Autocracy is the most unnatural state of public rule—opposed to the very essence of human nature," he was to write later.

Radishchev's understanding of, and moral revulsion against, autocratic rule was given substance in his experience as a government official. From 1771 to 1773 he served in the Russian Senate, the Empress's advisory council; and from 1773 to 1775 he served in the Eighth Finland Division in the civilian capacity of military prosecutor, a post which, it is believed, gave him access to documents relating to the famous Pugachev uprising (1773), his allusions to which provided some impetus to Pushkin's monumental study. An immediate outcome of his army experience was an article—never published in his lifetime—*On Malfeasance in the Levying of Conscripts*. The more general consequence was the fuller development of his interest in the peasant serf, the history of peasant revolts in Russia, and revolutionary activity in general.

During the 1780's he maintained his connection with the Enlightenment and devoted himself to his writing, producing *A Letter to a Friend in Tobolsk* and an essay on Peter the Great; a biography of F. V. Ushakov; his most famous poem, the lengthy ode "Freedom" (1783); and his greatest prose work, *Journey from St. Petersburg to Moscow*, which he had to publish privately in an edition incorporating the ode "Freedom" in 1789. This narrative, interspersed with political and philosophical comment, expressing his sympathy for and championship of the serfs and indentured servants, was too widely read to escape the notice of Empress Catherine. Having digested the contents, in the words of a contemporary diarist, she branded the author "a rebel worse than Pugachev." An official inquiry into the matter was ordered to condemn Radishchev to death, a sentence Catherine found it politic to set aside with a pardon coupled with banishment to Elimsk, a remote penal settlement in Siberia, and the confiscation and destruction of all available copies of the book.

During his exile Radishchev wrote a philosophical essay, *Man: His Mortality and Immortality*, and articles on economics. Liberated from exile by the death of Catherine (1796) he was authorized to return to Nemstovo, a village near Moscow, where he was forced to remain under a sort of parole arrangement. He continued to write during Czar Paul's reign, and even managed to have a few general articles published. His semi-incarceration within the boundaries of Nemstovo was mitigated by many visits, especially from the younger members of the Enlightenment.

With the accession of Czar Alexander (1801), Radishchev was fully rehabilitated, and he was invited to St. Petersburg to participate in a commission for the planning of new legislation. The author plunged into the project eagerly and immediately formulated a program calling for the liberation of the serfs. He was officially warned by his colleagues not to persist in this line lest he face another exile—Alexander's celebrated "liberalism" by no means comprehended such extremes of policy. Unable either to face exile or to submit, Radishchev took poison on the morning of September 12, 1802, and, after a day of agony, died the same evening.

Although his literary product, especially of verse, was not large, Radishchev's influence was great. Pushkin, an enthusiastic student of his own cultural heritage, acknowledged his profound indebtedness: "Can we forget Radishchev in speaking of Russian literature; who is to be remembered if not Radishchev?" Typical of the contemporary estimate of Radishchev in the U.S.S.R. is Kalinin's tribute: "Radishchev manifested a marvelous moral purity and self-abnegation in his campaign against serf-dom and the oppressive ravages of czarist autocracy."

An English translation of *Journey from St. Petersburg to Moscow* was made by L. Wiener in 1958.

ABOUT: Evgenev, B. S. Alexander Radishchev; a Russian Humanist of the Eighteenth Century; Lang, D. M. The First Russian Radical: Alexander Radishchev; Slavic and East European Journal, VII (1963).

L. R. & H. H.

*RAIMUND, FERDINAND (June 1, 1790-September 5, 1836), Austrian dramatist, was born in Vienna, the son of poor parents. After the death of his mother, Katharina Raimann, in 1802, and his father, Jakob Raimann, a woodworker, two years later, Raimund worked as a confectioner's apprentice, until at the age of eighteen he ran away to become an actor with a traveling company. His ability as a comedian eventually won him a reputation in Germany as the "Garrick of the South," and in 1813 he was engaged by the Josephstädtertheater in Vienna. Later he acted at the Leopoldstheater, where he also served briefly as director (1828-30). In 1820, after being refused by Toni Wagner, an inn-keeper's daughter, because of parental objection to his profession, he unwillingly married Luise Gleich, the daughter of a minor drama-tist. They were divorced in 1822, and he entered into a common-law marriage with Toni which lasted until his death.

Raimund began writing in the form of the Viennese "Posse" or "Singspiel," an unpretentious form of entertainment derived from the Austro-Bavarian baroque tradition and the Italian *commedia dell' arte*. These plays were usually written by actors who were adept at blending the chief ingredients of humor, fantasy, allusions to local events and personalities, dialect, music, and dancing. Improvisations during the performances were common, and the humor frequently degenerated into vulgarity. It was Raimund's achievement that he raised this popular theatre to the level of the artistic stage. Like Molière, he found farce and raised it to that high type of comedy which, because it resembles life, often borders on tragedy.

His first attempts, *Der Barometermacher auf der Zauberinsul* (1824), based on the Fortunatus legend, and *Der Diamant des Geisterkönigs* (1824), utilizing a theme from the *1001 Nights,* contain many crudities but nevertheless reveal a genuine dramatic talent.

* rĭ′ mo͞ont

Der Bauer als Millionär (1826), a completely original work, marks a considerable advance and remains one of his finest productions. The popularity of these works brought him little comfort, but filled him instead with the ambition to write "high tragedy" in the manner of his countryman Franz Grillparzer. These attempts failed for lack of ability, but as soon as he returned to his own domain of comedy, his great natural talent asserted itself once again, and he produced his greatest dramas, *Der Alpenkönig und der Menschenfeind* (1828), which can take its place beside the best comedies of German literature, and *Der Verschwender* (1834).

Raimund successfully blends the world of reality and fantasy in a unique and delightful manner. His plays are allegorical, and in them his audiences could recognize themselves and their locale. He aimed at uplifting his audiences; and in addition to providing the spectacles they required, he elevated the servants and poor people, who previously had played only comic roles, to models of honesty, strength, and honor. Raimund offered his public the cheering message that their world was the best possible one. He further demonstrated that peace of mind is man's greatest blessing and that wealth causes unhappiness: the millionaire peasant and the spendthrift find greater happiness in humble cottages than in palaces. His greatness as a dramatist lies in his ability to delineate character, in his marvelous sense for situation comedy, and in his natural gift as a poet. Many of his incidental songs have become folksongs.

Raimund was endowed with a passionate temperament, which, while permitting him the highest flights of imagination, also made him a ready victim of melancholy. Despite artistic success and material security, despair over the limits of his art, aggravated by the rising popularity of his rival Johann Nestroy, let him take no pleasure in his successes nor find any joy in life. In later years he was tormented by hypochondria and by the imaginary fear of losing his voice. Fearing madness from the bite of a dog, he shot himself at the age of forty-six.

Raimund was popular in his own day in Austria, and his works are still part of the standard repertory there. The Viennese have dedicated to his memory a Raimundtheater (1893), a Raimund prize for the best folk play, and a Raimund Society (1935). Because his works are so typically Viennese, they have exerted little appeal in other countries, including Germany.

Der Alpenkönig und der Menschenfeind has been adapted into English by J. B. Buckstone as *The King of the Alps* (1850), and Erwin Tramer has adapted *Der Verschwender* as *The Spendthrift* (1949).

ABOUT: [In German—see studies by K. Fuhrmann, H. Kindermann, A. Sauer.]

D. G. D.

RAMBAM. See MAIMONIDES, MOSES

*RANKE, LEOPOLD VON (December 21, 1795-May 23, 1886), German historian, was born in the small Thuringian town of Wiehe. His father, Gottlob Israel Ranke, was a lawyer, but almost all of Leopold's ancestors were clergymen. After early education at Donndorf, near his home, Leopold attended the famous school of Schulpforta and the University of Leipzig, where he excelled in classical studies. His earliest historical ambition appears to have been to prepare a literary memorial of Martin Luther, which was to be published in 1817, on the occasion of the three hundredth anniversary of the nailing of the ninety-five theses upon the church door at Wittenberg. The project, however, proved beyond his resources. Later, from the idea of a new biography of Luther, sprang the larger thought of the reconstruction of modern European history, from the time of the German Reformation. In 1817 Ranke took his doctor's degree. The men who had most influenced Ranke's development up to this point were, besides Luther, Thucydides and Barthold Niebuhr whose *Roman History* exercised the greatest effect on his historical studies.

In 1818 Ranke went to Frankfurt-on-the-Oder to take a post as a professor of ancient languages in the Frankfurt *Gymnasium*. The six years that he spent at Frankfurt are the critical period of his life. Here he began his systematic studies, laying a broad and solid foundation for his later work. Here also he realized his calling, and in almost all his letters of this period he professed an almost religious enthusiasm for history. Here also he did the critical work which opened a new epoch in historical study and wrote his first book, *Geschichte der Romanischen und Germanischen Völker von 1494 bis 1535* (History of the Latin and Teutonic Nations, 1824), together with a companion volume, *Zur Kritik Neuerer Geschichtschreiber* (Critique of Recent Historical Writings).

* räng′ kĕ

RANKE

Ranke's first published work was an immediate success and soon brought him an assistant professorship at the University of Berlin. Though Ranke was not made full professor until 1836, his duties were light and he devoted nearly all his time to research. Moreover, the friendship of already famous people (Savigny, Niebuhr, and Alexander von Humboldt) and the salons of gifted women like Rahel Varnhagen van Ense opened a new world for the young history professor. At the royal library in Berlin he discovered a collection of forty-eight folios of manuscripts consisting mainly of records of Venetian relations. Nobody had ever utilized them. Three more folios were found at Gotha, and Ranke was able to purchase another.

Ranke's acquaintance with these valuable reports constituted an epoch in his life, for they revealed that many pages of European history had to be rewritten on the basis of this newly discovered material. Ranke gave up the project of continuing systematic work on his first book and plunged into this mass of unworked material, consisting of perhaps a thousand essays, covering most of the years 1550 to 1650. The result of this enormous work was published in 1827, *Fürsten und Völker von Süd-Europa im 16. und 17. Jahrhundert* (Princes and Peoples of Southern Europe in the Sixteenth and Seventeenth Centuries). Like its predecessors, the new work contained a portrait gallery of rulers and statesmen, but he now

771

also added a critical examination of the background of historical events. His first book had brought Ranke his invitation to Berlin, and his second procured him a commission from the Prussian government to go to Vienna and to Italy to explore the unknown archives. The next three and a half years were devoted to research in Vienna, Florence, Rome, Naples, and other cities. The most notable result of his Italian studies, *Die Römischen Päpste, ihre Kirche und ihr Staat im 16. und 17. Jahrhundert* (History of the Popes of Rome in Church and State in the Sixteenth and Seventeenth Centuries, 1834-36), brought him fame throughout Europe.

From 1828 to 1836 Ranke was the editor of the *Historische-Politische Zeitschrift,* which attempted to defend the Prussian government against liberal and democratic attacks. He was by nature and association a conservative in politics, and universal doctrines of government so dear to the eighteenth century were, according to him, worthless and dangerous. Moreover, he was living in a period of political reaction. But Ranke failed in his efforts, for liberals sneered at him and conservatives considered him insufficiently reactionary.

But his chief activity continued to be in the line of original contributions to modern history. As a sort of a pendant to his book on the popes, he published from 1839 to 1847 his *Deutsche Geschichte im Zeitalter der Reformation* (History of Germany in the Period of the Reformation), in six volumes. The success of this work in Germany was immediate, and it remained the most popular of his works in his own country. In 1837 he became full professor, and in 1841 Frederick William IV appointed him historiographer of the Prussian state. Appreciative of these honors, Ranke felt an obligation to make another contribution dealing specifically with Prussian history, and his *Neun Bücher Preussischer Geschichte* (Nine Books of Prussian History) followed (1847-48), and were subsequently expanded to twelve.

The greater part of the next twenty years was devoted to writing his histories of France and England. He was over seventy years of age when he completed this tremendous task. On the occasion of his seventieth birthday Ranke was raised to the nobility, and many other honors were conferred upon him, including the title of Excellenz in 1885.

He remained a bachelor until he was almost fifty. He married at last in 1843, at Windermere in England, Miss Clarissa Graves, daughter of an Irish barrister. She died in 1870, leaving two sons and one daughter. One of his sons became a clergyman, perpetuating thus the theological bent of Ranke's family. Ranke was rather small in stature, not much over five feet, with large, blue eyes which became increasingly weaker in his old age, so that he depended almost entirely on his secretaries.

Even in his very old age Ranke continued to be extremely productive. In the spring of 1880, when he was eighty-five years old, the first volumes of his *Weltgeschichte* (Universal History) were announced. He astounded the world with this heroic task. Though he worked tirelessly wearing out the energies of his young secretaries, he did not live to finish it. He died in Berlin at ninety.

Ranke's services to history were numerous, and his work was certainly epoch-making. Through the influence of his teaching and writing, and the influence of his students, the study and teaching of history have been almost transformed. As a writer he possessed a rare power of discerning the typical, thus always painting a broad outline filled with apt details.

Translations of Ranke's works into English appeared quite early. Among them are: *History of the Popes during the Sixteenth and Seventeenth Centuries,* by S. Austin (1840); *History of the Reformation in Germany,* by S. Austin (1845-47); *History of Servia and the Servian Revolution,* by Mrs. A. Kerr (1847); *State of Germany after the Reformation,* by Lady Duff Gordon (1853); *Memoirs of the House of Brandenburg and History of Prussia during the Seventeenth and Eighteenth Centuries,* by Sir Alexander and Lady Duff Gordon (1853).

ABOUT: Gooch, G. P. History and Historians in the Nineteenth Century; von Laue, T. H. Leopold von Ranke: The Formative Years. [In German—see bibliography by H. F. Helmolt.]

F. S. L.

*RAPIN, RENÉ (1621-October 27, 1687), French humanist and Latin poet, was born in Tours and in 1639 took orders as a Jesuit. For nine years he was professor of letters and rhetoric, and was widely admired for his learning and his personal distinction, both professionally and in society. His chief public activity concerned the controversy with the Jansenists, and in 1644 he composed his *Histoire du Jansénisme depuis ses Origines jusqu'en 1644.* Rapin's principal literary works began in 1659 with his Latin pastorals, *Eglogae Sacrae,* which earned for him the title of the "Second Theocritus," and to which he prefaced his very important essay

* rà păN′

De Carmine Pastorali. His finest and most widely admired book was the *Hortorum Libri IV* (1665), Latin poetry elegant in its descriptions and significant in its strong tendency to replace standard moralizings by pastoral color; the volume includes eclogues, odes, and heroic verse. Considered in its day a masterpiece, the *Hortorum Libri* remained a vital monument well into the next century, and provoked charges of plagiarism because of the use of a supposed Lombard manuscript. Rapin's many other works include studies on classical literature (Horace, Virgil, etc.), tracts on social matters, an "éloge" of the Prince de Condé, and a number of pious texts on faith and the perfection of Christianity (collected in 1693, 1709, and 1725). He was most active in 1686. Certain of his writings were reprinted in 1709, and his poetry was published again in three volumes in 1723, prefaced by the biography by Bouhours.

In his *Réflexions sur la Poétique d'Aristote* (1674), as in the earlier *De Carmine Pastorali*, Rapin formulated his widely influential neoclassical doctrine of pastoral poetry. The work was immediately attacked by his associate Vavasseur, in the latter's *Remarques Françaises*, temporarily suppressed and not published until 1709. A more important refutation came from Fontenelle in 1688, and the controversy moved to England in Purney's rebuttal of 1717. Its most significant influence was on Alexander Pope whose doctrine in the *Essay on Criticism* follows Rapin very closely. Rapin established rules for the composition of epics and eclogues which he based on the theories of Aristotle and the practices of Theocritus and Virgil, with strong emphasis on the latter. His conception of the genre corresponded to a Golden Age of peace and plenty, and his wide documentation included detail from such other theorists as Quintilian, Donatus, and Scaliger. Aside from its manifest significance in the historical evolution of neo-Latin poetry, and the pastoral genres in France down to Delille's *Jardins*, Rapin's own poetry, like his theory, served the immediate purpose of freeing the pastoral forms of their current excesses and mannerisms.

His influence in England is manifest in the number and date of the translations. John Evelyn rendered his *Hortorum Libri* into English verse in 1673, and J. Gardiner again in 1706 (the French translations date from 1773, 1782, and 1803 and pertain to the period of Roucher and Parny) ; Thomas Creech's version of *De Carmine Pastorali* dates from 1684.

ABOUT: Augustan Reprint Society, De Carmine Pastorali (English text with preface).

F. J. C.

RAPPOPORT, SOLOMON (1863-November 8, 1920), Russian-Yiddish writer known as Sh. An-ski, was born in Vitebsk. His mother, Anna, from whose name he derived his pseudonym, managed both the home and an inn, and left a deep impression on her son. An-ski received the usual orthodox Jewish education, but broke with tradition while still a youth, becoming a devoted revolutionary. He cast his lot with the Russian peasant, working at such odd jobs as blacksmith's apprentice and bookbinder. Using these experiences, he published, in Russian, several novels of village life. Later, under the influence of Chaim Zhitlovsky, a brilliant Jewish secularist thinker, he turned to writing in Yiddish.

While living in Switzerland and France, An-ski worked as private secretary to the Russian revolutionist Peter Lavroff and, at the same time, was a leader of the Jewish Socialist Bund. The Yiddish poems which he wrote for the Bund's journal became immensely popular and one was adopted as the organization's hymn. Returning to Russia, An-ski participated in the Revolution of 1905 in St. Petersburg. It was in this period that his interest turned to the study of Jewish folklore, whose tales he collected, studied, and developed with intense scholarly devotion. Although an officer in the Russian Army during World War I, he continued his literary, political, and scientific efforts, taking part in political missions, ethnographic expeditions, and relief surveys.

An-ski's novels, poems, and folklore fill many volumes, but his fame rests chiefly on one solid accomplishment, the play called *Tsvishn Tsvei Veltn, oder der Dibuk* (*Between Two Worlds, or The Dybbuk*, 1916). Written originally in Russian, it was submitted to Stanislavsky, director of the Moscow Art Theatre, who praised it and asked for a Yiddish translation, which An-ski then prepared. Meanwhile, An-ski had been elected to the Constituent Assembly after the Revolution of 1917, but fled to Warsaw when the Bolsheviks seized power. During his lifetime the play remained unperformed, but a month after his death it was finally performed in Vilna, causing great excitement. Then a Hebrew version by Bialik was given by the Habimah Theatre in Moscow and a German version by the Reinhardt Theatre. A sensation in Polish, French, Czech, and English, it was turned into an opera by Lodovico Rocca, and George Gershwin planned to do the same. David and Alex Tankin wrote an opera based on it which was heard in 1949.

In 1960 a modernized version by Paddy Chayefsky, *The Tenth Man,* had a long run in the New York theatre.

The Dybbuk (the word itself is of cabalistic origin, meaning a wandering soul which, in order to achieve justice, attaches itself to a living body) is a play which draws heavily from Jewish folklore, particularly that of the mystical sect of Hasidism. In the framework of an unfulfilled marriage contract An-ski presents a mysterious story whose message is the romantic one of undying love which eventually triumphs. Its primitive, grotesque, and mystical qualities provide a strange attraction but do not hide its deeply human significance.

An-ski himself has been the subject of much psychological speculation, centering on his alleged Oedipus complex. As a man, he appeared sad and melancholy, and his life was marked by schizoid tendencies. Nevertheless, as the creator of *The Dybbuk* he has earned a high place in Yiddish and world literature.

Two English translations of *The Dybbuk* are available: that of 1927 by H. G. Alsberg and W. Katzin, and that of 1953 by S. Morris von Engel. The *Dybbuk* may be found also in T. H. Dickinson's *Chief Contemporary Dramatists* (3rd edition). Two folk tales by An-ski appeared in *Commentary,* August 1952. The standard, 15-volume Yiddish edition of his works, *Gezamelte Shriftn,* was published in Warsaw, 1920-25.

ABOUT: Goldberg, I. The Drama of Transition; Roback, A. The Story of Yiddish Literature; Theatre Arts Anthology; Waxman, M. A History of Jewish Literature; Young, S. Immortal Shadows.

M. R.

*RASHI (SOLOMON BEN ISAAC)

(c. 1040-July 13, 1105), Hebrew exegete, was born in Troyes, France. Nothing is known of his antecedents, and little more of the details of his life. His region, Champagne and the Rhine valley, contained the earliest Jewish settlements in northern Europe, and the towns of Mayence and Worms were the first seats of Jewish learning in that area. In the academies in those towns Rashi received his training in Biblical and Hebrew studies, and especially in the Babylonian Talmud which had begun to reach northern Europe and was subsequently to supply the main subject of Jewish study. After his schooling, Rashi returned to Troyes and opened an academy of his own which attracted large numbers of students for those days. Here he evidently remained to the end of his days. Rashi served as the unpaid rabbi of the small

* rä' shē

Jewish community of Troyes, in which capacity he was teacher and judge of the local Jewry. His decisions on questions of religious law were sought from distant parts as his fame grew. Rashi had two (and perhaps three) daughters, each of whom married a scholar and produced a number of noted rabbinic scholars. Like many of the Jews in northern France, Rashi earned his living from his vineyards; numerous references in his writings show that he was familiar with viticulture, and indeed with the social and political life of the Gentile world. The scholar's last years were clouded by the destruction wrought upon Franco-German Jewry during the first Crusade (1096-98); he wrote some liturgical poetry upon these sufferings.

Rashi's fame rests upon his commentaries on the Hebrew Bible and Babylonian Talmud, which attained unparalleled influence and authority among all succeeding generations of Jewish students. The commentary upon the Pentateuch, the most popular portion of his Bible commentary, blends the traditional homiletic exegesis of Scripture (Midrash) with the then available fruits of Hispanic Hebrew philology in a simple direct style which concentrates upon the literal meaning of the text. Rashi had the gift of penetrating to the core of a problem and of clarifying it in the fewest words. Nowhere is this more clearly seen than in his commentary on the Talmud, which elucidates the text in terse, incisive notes. One critic remarked: "He is not a systematic thinker, but he is systematic in his thinking, a master of smooth and clear reasoning, of seeing and presenting things as they are." These commentaries have become indispensable tools, and hardly a Talmud and few Bibles have been printed without them. During and after their author's lifetime, they became the subject of numerous super-commentaries.

More than 3,000 French glosses in Rashi's work are a valuable source for Old French, and have been collected by D. S. Blondheim. Rashi's commentary on the Bible heavily influenced Nicholas of Lyra, who in turn guided Luther's translation; the King James translators directly resorted to the French-Jewish masters.

The *Commentary on the Pentateuch* was translated into English by A. M. Silbermann (5 vols., 1929-34).

ABOUT: Liber, M. Rashi; Marx, A. Essays in Jewish Biography; Pereira-Mendoza, J. Rashi as Philologist; Rosenthal, E. I. Rashi and the English Bible; American Academy for Jewish Research, Rashi Anniversary Volume.

L. P. G.

REDI, FRANCESCO (February 18, 1626-March 1, 1698), Italian court physician, naturalist, poet, was born at Arezzo to parents belonging to the small nobility of that town. There were two other sons in the family.

Young Redi received his early education in grammar and rhetoric from Jesuit schools in Florence and obtained his doctorate in medicine and philosophy in 1647 from the University of Pisa. Returning to Florence in 1648, he pursued further studies independently, covering a wide range of subjects: French, Spanish, drawing, fencing, lute-playing, and later Arabic and German. He was a diligent reader in Greek and Latin letters.

His reputation was first established by his valuable work in the philology of his own language, the Tuscan tongue. He was elected in 1658 by the Council of the Accademia della Crusca to edit its compilation on the Tuscan vocabulary; Redi made a considerable contribution to the completion of this work.

Redi was living with his family in Florence in 1666 when he was called in haste to attend the Grand Duke of Tuscany, Ferdinand II, who had suffered a hunting accident. As a result of this incident, Ferdinand appointed him court physician, in which capacity he served until his death over thirty years later, caring for both Ferdinand and his successor Cosimo III. Redi's family returned to Arezzo in 1672, his mother dying in that year. Redi's father was made mayor of Arezzo while his distinguished son remained in Florence, growing in stature and reputation as a physician and scientist. During this time Redi was a friend and colleague of the famous Danish scientist Nicolas Stensen, the discoverer of the parotid salivary gland known as Stensen's duct. Redi was also an active and influential member of the great Italian scientific society, the Accademia del Cimento (Academy of Experiments) which promoted knowledge in all fields of science. In later years Redi was elected to the Society of Arcadians, the coterie of literary men around ex-Queen Christina of Sweden. Redi never married, but he cared for the children of his brother Diego, adopting the eldest, Gregorio, as his heir. After Redi's death at Pisa, Gregorio had a memorial bust of his uncle placed in the cathedral of their home town, Arezzo.

Redi's position in the world of science is distinguished by reason of his contribution to the doctrine of biogenesis, the germ theory of disease. His published experiments illustrated that the cycle of fermentation, putrefaction, and decay in organic material was the work of germs. In his essay *Esperienze Intorno alla Generazione degli Insetti* (Experiments concerning the Generation of Insects) in 1668 he observed the formation of maggots from eggs laid in meat by flies. The paper is a combination of rigidly controlled proofs, literary ornamentation, and scholarly disputation. *Esperienze Intorno a Diverse Cose Naturali, e Particolarmente a Quelle che ci Sono Portate delle Indie* (Experiments concerning Divers Natural Objects, Especially Those Brought from India), dated 1671, is addressed to Athanasius Chircker, head of the Jesuit College in Rome, and disputes travelers' tales of miraculous cures effected by such things as serpentstones. *Degli Animali Viventi negli Animali Viventi* (Observations on Living Organisms Found in Living Organisms), 1687, further helps to prove the germ theory by describing parasitic worms.

Bacco in Toscana (Bacchus in Tuscany), written in 1685, is the famous dithyramb which is Redi's contribution to the literary life of the seventeenth century in Italy. In the attenuated remnants of this period of decadence in Italy, *Bacco in Toscana* is a bright spot reflecting its author's lively style and wit. It is a monologue by the god Bacchus revisiting the vineyards of Tuscany. Fauns and satyrs bring him all the famous Tuscan vintages, and each is hailed with appropriate comment. As the riot grows wilder the wine god becomes more extravagant and ecstatic in his speech. In the words of De Sanctis (*History of Italian Literature*): "It is pleasant reading; it has verve, is warmly imaginative, and is natural in movement, and its lines are handled with art."

Bacco in Toscana was translated into English by Leigh Hunt in 1825. *Experiments on the Generations of Insects* was translated in 1909.

ABOUT: Contemporary Review, 1921; Scientific Monthly, September 1926. [In Italian—see studies by G. Imbert, E. Micheli-Pellegrini, U. Viviani.]

E. DE P.

*REGNARD, JEAN FRANÇOIS (February 8, 1655-September 5, 1709), French dramatist, was born in Paris. On his father's death in 1657 he became heir to a considerable fortune, and his mother planned his upbringing to make of him a well-rounded gentleman both in letters and in manners. At the age of twelve, he was accomplished in physical sports and in the composition of

* râ′ dē

* rĕ nyär′

poetry. Regnard traveled widely in order to observe peoples and customs and recorded his impressions in a series of *Voyages* (to Poland, Algeria, etc.), of which two (one to Normandy, the other to Chaumont) employ the literary device of mixed prose and verse, or of verse intended to be sung. In 1683 he was named treasurer of France, a profitable post that he held for some twenty years, and which he sold to purchase the Mastery of Waters and Forests of Dourdan, along with the nearby Château de Grillon, where he resided until his death, in the splendor of receptions, of the hunt, and of plays created to divert his guests. His sudden death remains mysterious.

Regnard turned to the theatre relatively late. His first plays, performed at the Hôtel de Bourgogne, were gay comedies in the manner of the Italian players for whom they were composed, and a number of them were published by the leader of the troup, Gherardi, in *Le Théâtre Italien*. Coolly received in 1688, *Le Divorce* soon met with success and was followed by a series of comparable pieces, of which the best and last is *La Coquette* (1691). Regnard then began collaboration with the dramatist Dufresny, and they worked together from *Le Négligent* (1692) to *Les Momies d'Égypte* (1696). Meanwhile Regnard had turned to the Comédie Française, primarily as a result of his mother's death in 1693. Out of respect for her wishes, he had, until that time, refrained from signing his plays, though their authorship was generally known, but now he felt that he could seek a higher intellectual level in the formal comedy *Attendez-Moi sous l'Orme* and in his first verse play, *Le Bourgeois de Falaise*. His masterpieces followed, and *Le Joueur*, a major financial success, established his reputation as the successor to Molière, for the classical purity of form (five acts in verse) and the excellence of the portrayal of character. *Le Joueur* was a model of its genre in the presentation of a significant social type and of the customs of its milieu, and has remained in the repertory. In the same form and manner, *Le Distrait* (1697), based on a text by La Bruyère, was less powerful on account of the excessive portrayal of absent-mindedness. *Démocrite Amoureux* (1700), also somewhat exaggerated, contained further elements of social satire, and *Le Retour Imprévu* is Regnard's gayest play, based on a subject from Plautus. *Les Folies Amoureuses*, Regnard's second great and lasting success, had great simplicity and charm. His last and finest work,

Le Légataire Universel, first performed in 1708, is often compared to Molière's *Le Malade Imaginaire* for the subject matter, but tends toward a less moral situation of deceit in which the unscrupulous valet becomes the master and in which one senses the spreading social decay portrayed a year later in Le Sage's *Turcaret*.

Regnard's plays were collected in two volumes in 1708, in six volumes in 1822. English translations include *The Gamester* (from *Le Joueur*), adapted by Mrs. Centlivre in 1705; *The Fair of St. Germain*, translated by Mr. Ozell (1718); Stark Young's version of *Le Légataire*, titled *The Sole Heir* (1912). Several of the *Journeys* were translated in 1801.

ABOUT: Lancaster, H. C. History of French Dramatic Literature in the 17th Century. [In French—Calame, A. Regnard: Sa Vie et Son Œuvre; Heylli, G. d', *preface to* Le Théâtre de Regnard.]

F. J. C.

*REJ, MIKOLAJ (February 4, 1505-October 14, 1569), Polish author, was born in Zurawno, received some schooling in Skalmierz and Cracow, and spent most of his life as a typical Polish landowner of average means on his family estate, Nagłowice, farming, hunting, and enjoying good company. But he also read widely and started writing early—mostly religious and didactic works in verse and prose. In 1546 he became a Calvinist. He died in Rejowiec.

His importance lies mainly in the fact that he was the first Polish author to write regularly in the national language. His works are an encyclopedia of life in sixteenth century Poland. Rej's first original work, *Krotka Rozprawa Między Panem, Wojtem i Plebanem* (A Short Discourse between a Nobleman, a Village Bailiff, and a Parson, 1543), was a satirical poem reflecting views of representatives of different social groups. The work incorporates comment on the condition of the state and criticism of the Catholic church in the spirit of the Protestant movement. On the whole Rej's works were mostly of a religious and didactic character. In 1546 he finished a complete translation of David's Psalms and a drama, *Zywot Jozefa* (Life of Joseph the Jew). Other works are: *Wizerunek* (The Image, 1558), *Zwierzyniec* (Bestiary, 1562), and finally Rej's chief collection of didactic writings, *Zwierciadło* (The Speculum, 1568), which, among other works, contained *Zywot Człowieka Poczciwego* (Life of a Noble Man) by which he is best known. It was a faithful mirror of the life of an average nobleman in Poland, his daily work, his

* rā

REJ

pleasures and troubles, his views on politics, social problems, education, religion, laws, army service, society life, agriculture, gardening, hunting, etc. Rej himself was a typical example of such an average nobleman, a man of little education, average means and average political and social horizons. In this period of the awakening of humanism, his intellectual level and world outlook strikes us as still rather medieval, but typical of the majority of his people. In spite of the fact that these intellectual limitations and his modest creative power prevented Rej from becoming a great writer, his place in the history of Polish literature is secure. For his promotion of the Polish language and of the national pride and for his prolific renderings in verse and prose of the realities of life in Poland, Rej fully deserves the title of the "Father of Polish literature."

Rej's works still await English translation and comment.

ABOUT: Kridl, M. Survey of Polish Literature. [In Polish—see studies by A. Brückner, W. Bruchnalski, B. Chlebowski, M. Janik, S. Windakiewicz.]

Z. F.

*RENAN, (JOSEPH) ERNEST (February 27, 1823-October 12, 1892), French theological writer, historian, and orientalist, was born at Tréguier, Côtes-du-Nord, to Philibert François Renan, a grocery merchant, and Madeleine Josèphe Feger. He was the youngest of three children. The father died when

* rē nän′

Ernest was only five, leaving the family in straitened circumstances. It was his sister Henriette, twelve years his senior, who took over the main responsibility for Ernest's upbringing, and he retained for her throughout his life a deep devotion most movingly recorded in several of his writings.

As a youth Ernest prepared for the priesthood. He received his earlier education in the ecclesiastical college at Tréguier, where he was a prize student. Subsequently, through the influence of Henriette who was teaching in Paris, he won a scholarship to the new Seminary of Saint-Nicolas-du-Chardonnet (headed by Monseigneur Dupanloup, who was some years later to attack him for atheism). His next college was the Seminary of Issy; then he studied at Saint-Sulpice. Here occurred his fateful break with the Church. His studies in philosophy had apparently raised religious doubts in his mind, and finally in 1845, after he had taken the tonsure and received minor orders, he found that he could not assent to the whole of Catholic doctrine, and so was compelled to abandon an ecclesiastical career.

At the same time young Renan's Hebrew studies at St. Sulpice had stimulated his interest in Old Testament criticism and comparative religion, studies then in their emergence on the continent. While serving as a tutor at Crouzet's school for boys in Paris, he pursued studies in Semitic philology at the Sorbonne and the Collège de France. His career as a scholar was launched in 1847 with a long essay on the history of the Semitic languages for which he won the Prix Volney. In 1849 he was sent by the Ministry of Education to Italy to investigate the manuscript holdings in Syrian and Arabic in Italian libraries.

After returning to Paris, Renan took up residence with his sister, supported himself by a post in the Bibliothèque Nationale, and wrote articles for the *Revue des Deux Mondes* and *Débats*, subsequently published as *Études d'Histoire Religieuse* (1857) and *Essais de Morale et de Critique* (1859). In 1852 he earned his doctorate at the Sorbonne, his Latin thesis being on Aristotle, his French thesis on Averroës. The latter became his first published book and brought him his first widespread eminence.

In 1856 Renan was married to Cornélie Scheffer, daughter of the noted painter Henri Scheffer, niece of the equally distinguished Ary. For a time Ernest had moral compunctions about entering into this union because of his devotion to Henriette, but these were

RENAN

It is impossible to recapture now the excitement that attended the first publication of *La Vie de Jésus* on June 24, 1863. This was really the first biography of Christ based on primary sources. (David Strauss' equally controversial *Leben Jesu* in 1835 was mainly a study of documents rather than a life history.) Here Renan set forth with boldness, but with tender poignancy, his conviction that Jesus was not the Son of God, but a divinely inspired man, that he died on the Cross and remained in his grave, but that his supreme goodness immortalizes him in the memory of man. He accounts for the Biblical narratives concerning Jesus' supernatural origin and his power to work miracles as pious frauds which Jesus' disciples thought necessary to win over the superstitious masses.

The Church, needless to say, greeted *La Vie de Jésus* with rage and hostility. "A Jew sprung from the blood of Judas Iscariot" was only one of the insults hurled at the author. Rumors went about that Rothschild had subsidized its publication. Victor Cousin, the Minister of Education, branded the book as sacrilege. Several churchmen, including Dupanloup, wrote opposition biographies. The upshot of all this calumny was that Renan was deposed from his professorship.

At the same time *La Vie de Jésus* sold by the thousands. By November of the year of its publication 60,000 copies had been sold and translations had appeared in Dutch, German, and Italian. English translation soon followed, the book finding especially receptive soil across the Channel where rationalism and Higher Critical controversies were rife. By 1880 sixteen editions of the work had appeared. It has been continuously in print since.

The enormous notoriety that Renan was subjected to distorted both the ideas and intention of his book. He did not dispute the existence of God. In proclaiming the mortality of Jesus he certainly did not mean to denigrate him. "The highest consciousness of God which has existed in the bosom of humanity was that of Jesus," he declared. In extolling the transcendent nobility of Jesus he meant really to elevate humanity, to show what greatness man ultimately is capable of. Clearly Robert Browning, introducing Renan in the epilogue of *Dramatis Personae* as a despairing skeptic, did him an injustice.

La Vie de Jésus was actually conceived as the first volume in a series entitled *Histoire des Origines du Christianisme*. It has obviously overshadowed the seven subsequent

dispelled when his sister was won over by affection for his fiancée. Henriette settled with them, as did Ernest's mother. Three children were born of the marriage—a son, Ary; a daughter, Noémi; and another daughter, Ernestine, who died in infancy.

On October 18, 1860 Renan left Paris for Syria with Henriette, having accepted a government commission to excavate the remains of Phoenicia. Here, while traversing the very soil where the feet of Christ and the Apostles trod, he conceived and wrote his masterpiece *La Vie de Jésus*. It is to Renan's own wanderings amidst the environs of Jerusalem that we owe the vivid actuality of those chapters of the book describing the Palestinian countryside. The first draft of the book was set down at Ghazir. Shortly thereafter, on September 24, 1861, Henriette died at Amschit of a fever which also struck Ernest, though he recovered. His intense grief over his sister's untimely death is reflected in the lovely Dedication to *La Vie de Jésus* in which she is addressed as his source of inspiration and collaborator.

On January 11, 1862, shortly after his return to Paris, Renan was appointed professor of Hebrew, Chaldaic, and Syrian at the Collège de France. His ill-advised inaugural lecture, in which he raised doubts about the historical authenticity of the Scriptures, created a stir when it was published in *Débats*, resulting in the suspension of his scheduled course. This was only a presage of the trouble that was to come.

volumes from *Les Apôtres* (*The Apostles*, 1866) to a study of Marcus Aurelius (1881). The present generation also has tended to pass by the many other distinguished works which poured forth from his prolific pen, such as his translations of the *Song of Songs* (1860) and *Ecclesiastes* (1882), the monumental *Histoire du Peuple d'Israël* (1887-90), the posthumously published *L'Avenir de la Science, Sœur Henriette,* and *Cahiers de la Jeunesse.* Of his *Drames Philosophique* (1887) only *L'Abbesse de Jouarre,* a drama of redemption through love and charity, has had any stage history. However, *Caliban,* a sequel to Shakespeare's *The Tempest,* is of interest as a political allegory representing the defeat of the intellectual and moral elite (Prospero) by the masses (Caliban). Renan's last years brought him vindication and honors. He was reinstated in his professorship in 1870, was elected to the Académie Française in 1878, and in 1883 was appointed administrator of the College that twenty years before had expelled him. He was accorded a public funeral by the state, but was buried in Montmartre Cemetery, not in the cloister of Tréguier as he had wished. Nevertheless, despite protest, on September 24, 1896, a plaque was placed on the house in Tréguier where he was born. In 1903 a commemorative statue was erected in the market place.

La Vie de Jésus was first translated by C. E. Wilbour in 1865. It was later translated by W. G. Hutchinson (1897). A complete edition with preface by Charles T. Gorham appeared in 1904. Modern Library has since published it (1927) in an anonymous translation. The best edition of Renan's works in French is the *Œuvres Complètes,* ed. by Henriette Psichari (Paris, 1947-55). Other works of Renan in English translation include *The Future of Science* (1891), *Leaders of Christian and Anti-Christian Thought* (1895), *History of the People of Israel* (tr. J. H. Allen and E. W. Latimer, 5 vols., 1888-96), and *Memoirs* (tr. J. Lewis May, 1935).

ABOUT: Arnold, M. Essays in Criticism, Third Series; Babbitt, I. Masters of Modern French Criticism; Chadbourne, R. Renan as Essayist; Holmes, J. *Introduction to* The Life of Jesus (Modern Library ed.); Mott, L. Ernest Renan; Wordman, H. W. Ernest Renan: A Critical Biography. [In French—see studies by A. Abablat, J. Chaix-Ruy, R. M. Galand, P. Lasserre, F. Millepierres, G. Monod, J. Pommier, H. Psichari, J. Tielrooy, and M. Weiler.]

R. A. C.

*RENARD, JULES (February 22, 1864-May 22, 1910), French man of letters, was born at Châlons-sur-Mayenne. Jules had an older brother, Maurice, and sister, Amélie. Jules' parents were harsh and exacting: his anticlerical father was brusque and satirical,

* rẽ nàr'

his pious mother quick to punish. Jules resented the preference shown by his mother for the older children. In 1866 the family moved to nearby Chitry-les-Mines, in the Nièvre. Jules first attended school at Chitry and then boarded at Nevers; in 1881 he went to Paris to prepare at the Lycée Charlemagne for entrance to the École Normale Supérieure. But smitten by the desire to write, he composed verses, *Les Roses,* which an actress friend recited at gatherings, and gave up preparation for an academic career, although taking his baccalaureate in 1883. He lived by odd jobs; after military service (1885-86), he did some ghost-writing and tutoring. *Les Roses* was published in 1886, and Renard began to move in literary circles. In 1888 he married Marie Morneau—a love match. His wife's dowry allowed them to live modestly in Paris and to visit in Nivernais. They had two children, Pierre, born in 1889, and Marie, born in 1892. Renard published at his own expense—in an edition of seventy-five copies—*Crime de Village,* a collection of eight short stories. *Les Cloportes,* a bitter novel about the seduction, abandonment, and suicide of a peasant girl, was written at this time, but was not published until 1919. Renard drew on this work for some of the brief articles, concise observations, and short-short stories which he submitted to the newly founded *Mercure de France. Sourires Pincés,* also published at his expense, was composed from these magazine articles. Here for the first time Renard presented Poil de Carotte, Mme Lepic, and other characters who were to reappear in his most successful and moving work, *Poil de Carotte* (1893). This work on the adventures and yearnings of an adolescent unifies various incidents by the use of a central cast. Made into a play, *Poil de Carotte* was presented by the Théâtre Antoine in 1900, and later made into a film by Julien Duvivier.

Aside from a novel, *L'Écornifleur* (1892), which satirized a pseudo-literary youth, Renard devoted himself to concise notations and tales: *Coquecigrues* and *La Lanterne Sourde* (1893), *Le Vigneron dans sa Vigne* (1894). His *Histoires Naturelles* was an attempt to describe accurately the behavior and personality of animals. Renard added forty additional sketches to the forty-five of the first edition (1896), seeking always the most condensed, striking descriptions. He lived in the country, at "La Gloriette" in Chaumot, near Chitry. In 1900 he was elected to the municipal council and in 1904 he became mayor of Chaumot.

The theatre gave Renard the popular success and measure of financial return his other writings had not achieved. In addition to theatrical criticism he wrote plays, mainly in one act. *Le Plaisir de Rompre* (1897) became part of the Comédie Française's repertory in 1902; *Le Pain de Ménage* (1899) was a successful vehicle for Lucien Guitry; *Monsieur Vernet* (1903), which was based on *L'Écornifleur*, was not so successful. Financial reasons caused Renard to leave "La Gloriette" and to move to Chitry in 1909, the year his mother, who was periodically insane, drowned herself in the family well. A dozen years earlier his father had killed himself in despair over an incurable pulmonary condition. Renard himself suffered for some time from arteriosclerosis; after a lingering illness he died of it. He was interred at Chitry.

Some of Renard's works appeared posthumously. His *Journal* and *Correspondance* were not publicly known until 1925, when they were enthusiastically acclaimed. But despite a rather scant publication in his own lifetime, Renard was admired for the pithiness and pathos of his observations, and for the sharpness of his irony. Renard's effort was toward directness and simplicity of statement. None of his plays has more than eight characters, the two most successful ones employing only two main characters. The twelve hundred pages of his *Journal* are primarily filled with the barest notations, and his short stories are economical in the extreme. Marcel Schwob was his personal friend; Tristan Bernard and Henri Bachelin admired him. Although he had written scarcely any novels, and over three hundred very short stories, Renard was elected in 1907 to replace Huysmans in the Goncourt Academy.

Of his *Œuvres Complètes,* which were published in seventeen volumes (1925-27), *Poil de Carotte* has been translated as *Carrots, a Play* by Alfred Sutro (1904) and by G. W. Stonier (1946); the latter, together with T. W. Earp, translated *Histoires Naturelles* (1948) as *Hunting with the Fox,* with lithographs by Toulouse-Lautrec. Pierre Bonnard illustrated a notable edition of *Histoires Naturelles,* as Felix Valloton and Poulbot did for *Poil de Carotte. The Journal of Jules Renard* was translated by Louise Bogan and E. Roget (1964).

ABOUT: Coulter, H. B. The Prose Work and Technique of Jules Renard; Knodel, A. J. Jules Renard as Critic; Modern Language Quarterly, March 1949. [In French—see studies by H. Bachelin, L. Guichard, M. Pollitzer, P. Nardin, P. Schneider.]

S. S. W.

*RESTIF (or RÉTIF) DE LA BRETONNE, NICOLAS EDMÉ (October 23, 1734-February 3, 1806), French novelist, born in the village of Sacy, near Auxerre, took his name from the family farm, and later changed Rétif, usually spelled Reti or Reuti, to its more archaic form. His education was almost totally neglected, but the peasant milieu in which he lived provided him with part of his most original subject matter. In 1746 his father took him to Paris to remedy this neglect, but he was soon at Courgis, near Auxerre, studying the classics, with personal preference for Virgil and the fabulist Phaedrus. In 1751 he became a printer's apprentice at Auxerre and met the first of the long series of enchanting young girls and women who punctuate his existence, Mme Parangon, portrayed in romantic colors in his autobiography. Restif moved definitely to Paris in 1755 and, after the tragic loss of another love, Zéfire, and their child, briefly considered an ecclesiastical career. But in 1760 he married Agnès Lebègue who remained faithful to him despite his abuse of her. Restif's first novel, imitating Mme Riccoboni, and inspired by one "Rose," had little success, but his unbelievably productive career had been launched. His work is a long series of portraits of people known or seen either in society, in the countryside, or in the people's quarters of Paris. *Le Pied de Fanchette* brought him fame and money as a bestseller in 1768. He then undertook a vast program of reform of language, spelling, education, law and theatre in *Le Pornographe* and the companion volumes of 1769, but was quickly accused of overstepping the bounds of morality.

Restif's indomitable curiosity, perceptivity, and diligence led him countless times through the lower strata of society and offered him the first-hand information recorded in *Les Nuits de Paris.* His documentary method took its first form in *Le Paysan Perverti,* four volumes that aroused the censors and caused general alarm, but that sold rapidly and appeared in pirated editions. *La Vie de Mon Père,* sometimes considered his masterpiece, was followed by *Les Contemporaines,* in seventeen volumes, which Restif extended in further series of thirteen and twelve down to 1785, strange collections of short stories, at times close to obscenity; further additions built this series to sixty-five volumes of realistic portrayal of contemporary customs. *Les Nuits de Paris* gives us

* rĕs tēf′ dē là brē tôn′

RESTIF

is an incomparable observer. Little that happened in the streets of Paris escaped his keen eye and his sharp ear. Like Hogarth's London, Restif's Paris comes to life with grotesque yet accurate detail. In 1961 a writer in the *Times Literary Supplement* described him as "the historian of the intimate and the personal rather than the collective and the general. . . . He gives faces, personality, eccentricity and even a dialogue, in that inimitably ironical and disrespectful language of the Parisis, to Carlyle's King Mob, to Taine's scum of the earth, to Soboul's *Sansculottes*, to George Rudé's *Crowd in the French Revolution*."

English translations include *Sara* (1927), and *Monsieur Nicolas,* by R. C. Mathers (6 vols, 1930).

ABOUT: Ellis, H. From Rousseau to Proust; Palache, J. Four Novelists of the Old Regime; Times (London) Literary Supplement, October 27, 1961. [In French—see studies by A. Bégué, M. Chadourne, F. Funck-Brentano; see also Le Breton, A. Le Roman au Dix-Huitième Siècle.]

F. J. C.

Restif in his most Bohemian manner, the nocturnal wanderer called the "owl," an apparent madman combing attics and gutters for evidence on human problems. Volume 14 was published in 1788, and by this time Restif had won the hearty approval of such great contemporaries as Beaumarchais, Mercier, Bernardin de Saint-Pierre, and Crébillon *fils*. A new edition of *Les Nuits* appeared in Paris in 1961.

In 1783 Restif began his autobiography, *Monsieur Nicolas ou le Cœur Humain Dévoilé,* inspired in part by Rousseau's *Confessions;* the first installment appeared in 1794, and is remarkable for the description of country life. In *Monsieur Nicolas* Restif shows his most uninhibited attitudes, manias, and hallucinations, scrupulously documented by fact.

Once arrested during the Revolution, Restif managed thereafter to remain apart from political affairs. By 1796 he was living in dejection and penury, but found some material comfort in a printing enterprise. His *Anti-Justine* (1798) illustrates his distaste for Sade; his *Lettres du Tombeau* contain his meditations on life on other planets and on the end of the earth. Toward the last he enjoyed briefly the protection of Napoleon. Despite severe criticism from some quarters, Restif was esteemed in others for his expressed moral aim and for his lessons in virtue, taught through his pictures of low-life. To the modern student of eighteenth century French social history he

*REUCHLIN, JOHANN (February 22, 1455-June 30, 1522), German humanist and lawyer, was born the son of the administrator of the Dominican foundation in Pforzheim, where he was educated until he entered the University of Freiburg in 1470. After beginning Greek on a visit to Paris, he took his bachelor's degree at Basel in 1475 and his master's in 1477. His law studies were carried out in France (bachelor, Orléans, 1479; licentiate, Poitiers, 1481). When he visited Italy in 1482 his Greek gained the grudging admiration of the great teacher at Florence, John Argyropoulos.

In 1484 he entered the service of Eberhard, Count of Württemberg, and served as his legal adviser for many years. About this time he obtained his doctorate of laws at Tübingen, and married for the first time. He married again in 1510 but there were no children of either marriage. In 1490 he began the study of Hebrew in Italy. The death of Eberhard in 1495 brought a sharp change in his fortunes, for the successor had little use for humanists, and Reuchlin left to take up a position as adviser to Johann von Dalberg in Heidelberg. The atmosphere was congenial and it was here that he wrote his plays *Sergius* and *Henno* and some dialogues. He also visited Rome to obtain more Hebrew books. A change in regime took him back to Stuttgart and service with Duke Ulrich until 1513.

* roiĸ′ lēn

During this period he found himself, through no fault of his, the most controversial figure in Europe. The brutal confiscation of their books by a converted Jew, Johannes Pfefferkorn, who acted with imperial mandate, caused the Hebrew community to appeal to Reuchlin as a Hebrew scholar and friend of their culture. He responded with a German work, *Augenspiegel* (Mirror of the Eye), in which he attacked Pfefferkorn. He also examined the books, separating the classics from the purely polemical anti-Christian works, pointing out at the same time that Christian authorities had neither the knowledge nor the legal right to interfere. He brought down on himself the wrath of Pfefferkorn and, more important, of the theological faculties of several universities, including Paris and Cologne, which accused him of heresy. A series of polemical writings by him, for him, and against him followed. The humanists supported him with two sets of "Letters by Famous Men," but his chief support came in the "Letters of Obscure Men" (see Ulrich von Hutten sketch above). In spite of this support, Reuchlin's case dragged on in Rome and broke him in body, spirit, and finances. Civil war forced him to go to Ingolstadt in 1519. In 1521 he was back in Württenberg but in the same year he finally attained the long-sought professorship at Tübingen. There he died.

Reuchlin's fame rests on his activities rather than on his writings. We have no works on jurisprudence or history by him. Several school books for Greek and Hebrew have survived but more significant are his two commentaries on, or rather refutations of, Hebrew works: *De Verbo Mirifico* (On the Marvelous Word) and *De Arte Cabbalistica* (On the Cabalistic Art). His Latin dramas are learned but hardly good drama. It is as a pioneer of humanistic learning and particularly of the tradition of scholarly philological research that he is famous.

ABOUT: Hirsch, S. A. Essays (1905); Stokes, F. Epistolae Obscurorum Virorum, *introduction*. [In German—Stammler, W. Von der Mystik zum Barock; Das Gymnasium, 49 (1938).]

W. T. H. J.

---

*REUTER, CHRISTIAN (1665-c. 1712), German dramatist and story-teller, was the son of a prosperous peasant, born near Zörbig. Information on his life is meager. He was, before his expulsion, a student of theol-

* roi' tēr

ogy, then of law, at Leipzig. After his expulsion he remained in Leipzig as secretary to a high court official under whose protection he developed his talents as a satirist. He is next heard of in Berlin, in 1703, where he worked as a librettist. The year of his death is even more uncertain than that of his birth. One of his last works, surprisingly, was a *Passion*. It is remarkably simple and dignified—by virtue of these qualities a turning point in the artistic treatment of that sacred theme.

Reuter is best remembered as the creator of two proverbial figures of German satire, Schlampampe and her son Schelmuffsky. Schlampampe is the immortal name of Reuter's landlady during his student years at Leipzig. Her mortal name was Müller, and she paid for her temerity in evicting Reuter (for non-payment of rent) by being made the principal laughing-stock in a series of witty and scandalous caricatures. Her "encomia" include at least three comedies—one adapted as a musical with ballet and arias, and produced at the Hamburg Opera. Beyond these are the works devoted to her "son." The exchange took on the nature of a vendetta, for after the first pillorying, in *L'Honnête Femme oder die Ehrliche Frau zu Plissine* (1695), a play which, incidentally, shows the influence of Molière, Frau Müller turned in her vexation to the Leipzig Board of Censorship and to the university itself, which expelled the refractory student.

What Reuter took as the butt of his outrageous wit—he wrote under the pen-name of Hilarius—was not so much the landlady who evicted him as the Philistinism and hypocrisy, the inner crudeness under a mask of fashion and snobbery, which he saw as the besetting folly of the bourgeois world. It was the ill luck of the Müller family that it provided him with inexhaustible material.

In his novel *Schelmuffskys Wahrhaftige, Kuriöse und sehr Gefährliche Reisebeschreibung zu Wasser und zu Lande* (1696, often reprinted thereafter, and with sequels), Reuter capitalized on another weakness of his time, the taste for exotic travel literature. The callow Schelmuffsky, a ridiculous braggart in cavalier's clothing, tells of his love affairs and his duels, his escapades and his journeys, all of which cover a fair part of Europe and Asia. His speech is a satire on the pretentious jargon of the day.

Reuter's appeal lies in the very pointed nature of his personal invective, a quality less common in his time than generalized satire of society and manners. It also lies, however, in his mastery of everyday language, his extension of student humor with its ancient and honorable qualities of exaggeration, mockery, and crude laughter.

His collected works were published in two volumes in 1916, edited and with a biography (in German) by G. Witkowski. The first English translation of *Schelmuffsky* was made by W. Wonderley in 1962.

ABOUT: [In German—see studies by H. König, F. Zarncke; see also *Beiträge*, 1948.]

F. G. R.

*REUTER, FRITZ (November 7, 1810-July 12, 1874), German novelist and poet, was born in Stavenhagen, where his father, a prosperous farmer, served as mayor. After completing the *Gymnasium* at Parchim in 1831, he studied law at the universities of Rostock and Jena. For wearing the colors of his political student organization Reuter was arrested in Berlin in 1833 and sentenced to death for high treason. This sentence was subsequently commuted to thirty years' imprisonment, of which he served seven before being granted amnesty in 1840 upon succession to the throne of Frederick William IV. With difficulty he attempted to begin life anew. His father had disinherited him, and an attempt to resume his studies at Heidelberg ended in failure. He began a wandering life and surrendered to drink. He finally worked successfully as an agriculturist, until in 1850 he became a tutor in Treptow. Here he married Luise Kuntze, a pastor's daughter, with whom he found happiness.

In 1853 Reuter published at his own expense a collection of popular tales and rhymes in Plattdeutsch entitled *Läuschen und Rimels*. This successful work was followed by *De Reis' nah Belligen* (1855), a humorous narrative; *Kein Hüsung* (1858), a powerful novel of social injustice, which Reuter considered his best work; and *Hanne Nüte un de Lüte Pudel* (1860), the most popular of his rhymed works. During the next years he produced his outstanding series of longer works, which spread his fame throughout Germany and brought him recognition, honors, and financial security. *Woans Ich tau 'ne Fru Kam* (1860) describes the winning of his wife, while *Ut de Franzosentid* (1860), portrays scenes from his native Mecklenburg. In *Ut Mine Festungstid* (1861) he narrates his prison experiences without bitterness. Reuter's next

work, *Ut Mine Stromtid* (1862-64), which treats his days as a tenant farmer, is his masterpiece. Here his great humanity and warm compassion for his countrymen find best expression. In 1863 Reuter settled in Eisanach where he died. His last major narratives were *Dörchläuchtung* (1866), a satire on the nobility, and the travel book *De Reis' nah Konstantinopel* (1868).

It was Reuter's great service along with Klaus Groth and John Brinckmann to revive Plattdeutsch as a literary language. Reuter was greatly influenced by Charles Dickens. Like his model, he excelled in characterization, and his works exhibit a similar blend of humor, seriousness, and sentimentality, combined with a sincere ethical purpose. Reuter is regarded as one of the greatest masters of German humor, and Uncle Bräsig, the hero of *Ut Mine Stromtid*, is one of the best-loved humorous characters in German literature.

Ut de Franzosentid was translated by C. L. Lewes in 1867 under the title *In the Year '13: A Tale of Mecklenburg*. *Ut Mine Stromtid* was translated anonymously in 1871 as *Seed-Time and Harvest*, and as *An Old Story of My Farming Days* in 1878 by M. W. Macdowall. In 1873 *Dörchläuchtung* appeared anonymously as *His Little Serene Highness*. P. C. Glave translated *Woans Ich tau 'ne Fru Kam* in 1883 under the title *How I Came by a Wife*.

ABOUT: Modern Language Review, LVI (1961). [In German—see studies by R. Dohse, A. Römer, K. T. Gaedertz, H. J. Gernentz, F. Griese, H. Hunger, W. Siebold, and A. Wilbrandt. See also the *Festschrift* published in honor of his 150th birthday, Rostock (1961).]

D. G. D.

*RIBEIRO, BERNARDIM (c. 1482-1552), Portuguese poet, was the first of a series of writers whose poetry of country living, unhappy love, and sweet longing (*saudade*) became synonymous with Portuguese lyricism. He was born in Torrão near Évora (Alentejo), the son of Damião Ribeiro, a gentleman involved in an unsuccessful conspiracy against King John II. According to T. Braga's conjectures, the boy, his sister, and their mother, Joana Dias Zagalo, found refuge with the Zagalo family outside Lisbon, in delightful Sintra. He served at the sumptuous court of King Manuel, where he and his friend Sá de Miranda participated in poetic contests with his fair and witty cousin, Leonor Mascarenhas. Samples of these early lyric trifles were preserved in Resende's *Cancioneiro Geral* of 1516. Between 1522 and 1524 Ribeiro may have

* roi' tēr

* rē bä' ē rōō

traveled in Italy, like his friend Sá de Miranda. Both provided numerous autobiographical clues in their shepherd fictions, which were so enigmatic, however, as to leave only three facts established: Ribeiro had unhappy love affairs, beginning at twenty-one with a passion for a Joana, who was married off to a rich man; he was fond of music; and he had a "goodly, well-proportioned body, a rather thick, long beard . . . and slightly clouded white eyeballs, which showed at first sight that some profound sorrow oppressed his heart." He became insane about 1546 and died in a Lisbon hospital several years later.

To keep the reader guessing is one of the charms of his works—to whom did he make love? was he banished from court for it? did crossed love drive him mad? did his doctrine of love and his lamentations allude to Judaism? An almost feminine, passive idea of love as a fated, pleasurable pain to be borne with resignation characterizes Ribeiro's five eclogues and their companion work, the lyrical "novel" *Saudades,* commonly known as *Menina e Moça* after its first three words (posthumously published in Ferrara, Italy, 1554, by a Jewish printer; also, with many additional chapters of disputed authorship in Évora, 1557). The novel was patched together like a crazy quilt. "Sad blows cannot be told in orderly fashion," the author explained, "for they happen without order."

In the eclogues shepherds confide their misfortunes to one another in the new Italian manner, though the meters remain medieval. The novel, where unhappy ladies do the telling, as in Boccaccio, wavers unsteadily between adventures in the manner of the romances of chivalry, sentimental subtleties as in fifteenth century tales, and the new prose and verse combination of the pastoral *roman à clef,* soon thereafter perfected in the *Diana* of Ribeiro's compatriot Montemayor. With Ribeiro, "the Shepherd of the Flute," the genre achieved its peak in musicality; the music of his slow, dreamy, mysterious, melancholy effusions has not been equaled. Thanks to it and to his concept of fatal universal love, hauntingly symbolized in the episode of a nightingale's love culminating in death, Ribeiro was a romantic long before the advent of romanticism. He also had a feeling for nature, and, as Aubrey Bell observes, "his love of Nature in its gentler aspects cast over the book a strange charm."

A Spanish translation of *Menina e Moça* by B. Morales appeared in 1629.

ABOUT: Bell, A. F. G. Portuguese Literature. [In Portuguese—Salgado, A., Jr. A Menina e Moça

e o Romance Sentimental no Renascimento; Labor 1940. In Spanish—Gallego Morell, A. Ribeira y Su Novela.]

G. M. M.

RICHTER, JOHANN PAUL FRIEDRICH. See "Jean Paul"

*RIMBAUD (JEAN NICOLAS), ARTHUR (October 20, 1854-November 10, 1891), French poet, was born in Charleville in northeast France. His father was an army captain who had married Vitalie Coif, the daughter of a prosperous farmer, while stationed in the area, but abandoned her and his family when Arthur was six. Mme Rimbaud, an ambitious, indomitable woman, imposed a severe discipline on her children, projecting on them the frustrated hopes of her marriage, determined that they would compensate for its failure. Under her vigilant rule they were kept to their books and sequestered from other children. Arthur, the third of five children (the oldest girl died in infancy), seems to have been her favorite though she showed little affection. A beautiful boy with clear blue eyes and a high, wide forehead, he was small for his age and deceptively quiet. There was no hint in his candid gaze and docile demeanor of the rebelliousness that would erupt so violently in his teens.

At the Collège de Charleville Arthur soon proved to be the most brilliant student the school had ever had. By the time he was fifteen he had composed remarkably accomplished imitations of Hugo and other poets, and he published a poem in *La Revue pour Tous* in January 1870. In that month a new teacher, George Izambard, arrived at the Collège and soon took an active interest in his development. Under his tutelage Arthur gained access to Hugo and other romantics (forbidden at home because they were on the Index), began a period of literary productivity during which he imitated the Parnassian poets with astonishing mastery of technique, and, that July, won all but two of the prizes in the Concours Académique.

This fruitful period was interrupted by the outbreak of the Franco-Prussian War, when Izambard went home to the three maiden ladies who had brought him up. Despondent without his companion, and disgusted with provincial life, Arthur soon hopped a train to Paris and landed in prison because he had

* ràn bō'

RIMBAUD

no ticket, or money to buy one. Izambard rescued him and invited him to Douai, where the boy spent three idyllic weeks spoiled by the maiden "aunts" before he went home to his furious mother. Scarcely a month later he ran off to nearby Belgium where Izambard, at Mme Rimbaud's urging, trailed him vainly through several towns, only to find him, when he returned to Douai, sitting in the parlor with the old ladies, clean, docile, and happily copying out the poems he had written on his trip.

Arthur reluctantly went home at his friend's insistence, and spent the fall of 1870 taking long walks with his friend Delahaye, reading the new poet Paul Verlaine, discussing literature and politics. Then, caught up in the general political excitement over rumors of a National Guard attempt to seek power, he ran away again to Paris in February 1871. He spent two miserable weeks there, living on the streets, suffering and witnessing unbelievable poverty. We can only guess at the precise nature of his experiences. Enid Starkie maintains that the boy was sexually attacked by soldiers; it is conjecture, but it seems to account best for the sense of physical violation in "Cœur Supplicié" ("Tortured Heart") and for the complete change of behavior that marks his return home.

In the next few months, the self-contained haughtiness which had characterized Rimbaud's attitudes gave way to violent and bitter attacks on God, society, and women.

Filthy and unkempt, he spent his days in the Charleville cafés, amusing anyone who would buy him a drink with his cynicism, blasphemy, and obscene language. His poems, for the first time, became scatological. Yet, in the search for values that accompanied this moral breakdown, he now formulated his theory of poetry, based on the combined influences of Baudelaire's poetic philosophy and the literature a new friend, Charles Bretagne, introduced him to—the occult and illuminist literature so prevalent in nineteenth century dilettantism. He outlined these ideas in his famous *lettres du voyant* of May 13 and 15, 1871, to Izambard and Paul Démeny, heralding a new kind of visionary poetry in which the poet would create his own experience and express it in language stripped of the logic and discursiveness of everyday life. To make himself a *voyant* or seer, Rimbaud declared, the poet must subject himself to a long, deliberate, and "rational disordering of the senses," experimenting upon himself with "every form of love, of suffering, of madness," whatever the cost. Only thus would he become the great criminal, the great accursed—and the supreme Savant. "The poet," he concluded, "is truly the thief of fire." Several poems reveal how far he had advanced beyond his former technical virtuosity —notably the "Sonnet des Voyelles," later to become a rallying-point of the symbolists, and "Le Bateau Ivre." He wrote the latter soon after Paul Verlaine, enthusiastically responding to the poems Rimbaud had sent him, provided the young poet with money to come to Paris, and it was in his pocket when he left in September 1871. Written with a child's elation and wonder, it depicts a spiritual quest as the little boat, voyaging on unknown waters, sees open before it an entire universe.

The Paris adventure was not at all what Rimbaud had envisioned. Verlaine's in-laws, with whom the older poet was staying, could not see in this unkempt sixteen-year-old peasant boy the prodigy Verlaine had announced. They offended him with their polite repugnance—which only made him more deliberately crude. He stayed at their home barely two weeks, then moved out, eventually into a little room that Verlaine rented for him. The conservative literary clique in Paris was further offended by his foul language and impossible insolence—and, soon, by his scandalous relationship with Verlaine.

That turbulent affair lasted something over a year and is marked by numerous interruptions, by Verlaine's vacillation between the rival seductions of his wife and his lover, and by Rimbaud's growing impatience with the elder poet's self-indulgence and sentimentality. The two were together almost constantly, in Paris, Brussels, and London, until the end of 1872, and intermittently during the first months of the next year. The situation finally exploded with the notorious Brussels drama in July 1873.

Verlaine had left Rimbaud in a huff and gone to Belgium, whence he confidentially informed his mother, Mme Rimbaud, and several friends that he intended to kill himself. Instead he called Rimbaud to his side. Rimbaud arrived, found him drunk and irritating, and in two days announced he was leaving. Verlaine shot at him three times and hit him in the wrist. Rimbaud and Verlaine's mother were able to quiet him down for a while, but as he lost self-control on the way to the railroad station, Rimbaud was forced to call the police; by the time he tried to withdraw charges it was too late. In a trial that exposed their liaison in embarrassing detail, Verlaine was sentenced to two years in prison, and Rimbaud went home to his mother's farm at Roche where, tormented by guilt and, probably, by narcotic poisoning, he finished *Une Saison en Enfer*, the renunciation of his former life and art.

However we may regard his relationship with Verlaine, it is clear that for a while Rimbaud found in it his greatest emotional and artistic fulfillment. For him it was the application of his *théorie du voyant*, and he threw himself into it with all the fanatic dedication of a martyr. He aspired, through his mystique of debauchery, to storm heaven; and it is doubtless this curious inverted asceticism that gave him the illusion of possessing magical power. Under the influence of drugs, drink, and long periods of fatigue and hunger he escaped into a dream-world that he incarnated in *Illuminations* (the poems that disappeared strangely and were not to be published until 1883). Some of these are mystic or religious hymns, more exclamations than statements; others, like "Enfance," recapture the immediacy of childhood experience. For *Illuminations* he developed a radical new form—the prose poem, pared of all narrative and descriptive content. Here he realized his dream of nondiscursive language: ignoring connectives, jumbling tenses and places without regard for verisimilitude, he created a world as vivid and naïve as a child's.

Illuminations may be read side by side with his palinode, *Une Saison en Enfer*,

which looks back ironically on this demonic quest. "I invented the color of vowels!" he writes, "became an adept at simple hallucination. . . . I tried to invent new flowers, new stars, new flesh, new tongues. . . . I! I who called myself angel or seer, exempt from all morality, I am returned to the soil with a duty to seek and rough reality to embrace. . . . At last, I shall ask forgiveness for having fed on lies."

Whether *Une Saison* was truly his farewell to poetry is the central problem of Rimbaud criticism, and rests largely on the dating of *Illuminations*. Rimbaud had nothing to do with their publication, and the conflicting testimony of his friends (Verlaine claimed they were written between 1873 and 1875) is no help. The poor reception of *Une Saison* in October 1873 and Rimbaud's subsequent burning of his manuscripts would indicate complete disillusionment with art. Yet he was interested enough in his future as a poet to have this work published, and in London the next year he was either writing or copying some *Illuminations* and thinking of publishing them. Enid Starkie feels that *Une Saison* was a rejection only of his visionary poetry. Noting a change in tone in the later *Illuminations*, she concludes that their humanitarian concern postdates the earlier mystical phase (1872) and that the disenchantment of "Jeunesse" and "Solde" may place them after *Une Saison*. For all practical purposes, however, Rimbaud seems to have abandoned his literary vocation at the age of nineteen to engage in a type of existence that was the complete antithesis of his earlier life.

For the next seven years Rimbaud traveled extensively in Europe, interrupting his journeys with short visits home whenever he was tired or had run out of money. He and Verlaine had their last encounter in 1873; in a well-known letter to Delahaye he describes the visit: "Verlaine arrived here the other day pawing a rosary. . . . Three hours later he had denied his God and started the 98 wounds of Our Lord bleeding again." During those years of wandering he thought of studying languages and science ("One must be completely modern," he had said in *Une Saison*), and of taking his *baccalauréat* in order to teach. In 1880 he left for Africa, spurred by the grandiose dream of making his fortune as an explorer. He worked for a coffee exporter in Harar and Aden, made a hazardous journey into unexplored country (his account of the trip was later published by the Société de Géographie), and tried his hand at gun-running to the interior, and, possibly, slave-trading. But a combination of poor business acumen, scrupulosity, and sheer bad luck defeated his ends. In 1888 he settled in Harar, in Abyssinia, where, despite many visitors, he seems to have been terribly lonely; in his letters to his mother he complains of intellectual starvation and begs for scientific books. The Verlaine episode was apparently a solitary aberration, for he was never suspected of sodomy and was known to associate with women. In these last years he toyed with the idea of marriage, hoping "at least to have a son whom I could spend my life bringing up according to my ideas, . . . who would become a renowned engineer, a man made rich and powerful through science." His main concerns—money, reputation—show a conversion to the ideals he had once decried.

Except for a faithful correspondence with his mother, Rimbaud maintained no contact with the outside world during these years, and was apparently indifferent to the cult that was growing up around him in Paris. In 1883 Verlaine wrote an article on him, including some poems, and republished them the next year in *Les Poètes Maudits*. In 1886, after Verlaine had written to him without receiving an answer, *Illuminations* was published as by "the late Arthur Rimbaud." By 1890, however, the editor of *La France Moderne* had discovered his whereabouts and wrote to him (a letter the poet never answered but which he saved), inviting him to head the "new decadent and symbolist school," and the February 19, 1891 issue of that periodical proclaimed: "We know where Rimbaud is, the great Rimbaud, the only true Rimbaud, the Rimbaud of *Illuminations*."

By then, however, Rimbaud was seriously ill with the disease that would destroy him within the year. For some months he had been suffering from an inflammation of his right knee which grew to an immense size before he decided, in April 1891, to take an excruciating journey to Aden to treat it. The ordeals of the next months—the trip to Marseilles where his leg was amputated, the humiliating home-coming, the experiments with his artificial leg, the illusions of a return to Harar, and the final agonizing months back in Marseilles as pain and paralysis crept through his body (the disease was diagnosed as carcinoma, though it may have been syphilis in the tertiary stage)—are documented in his pathetic letters and in the notes his sister Isabelle took as she watched with him faithfully and rejoiced in his death-bed conversion to the Church. The old Rimbaud,

it is said, returned in his final stubborn battle against extinction, and in the visions he described shortly before his death in November, a month after his thirty-seventh birthday. Ten years after his death, a monument was erected to his memory in the Place de la Gare in Charleville.

For a poet whose span of creativity was so short, Rimbaud has exercised a most remarkable influence on modern literature. Most important is his position in the symbolist school which first took up his colors. Writing long before their emergence, and against the dominant Parnassian aesthetic, he prefigured almost all their techniques and themes. Following Baudelaire, who was not yet appreciated in his day, he increased the suggestive power of language, but he extended this revolution to poetic diction and form, freeing poetry from its purely formal characteristics of meter and rhyme through the use of free verse and the prose poem and through his violations of the laws of logic, grammar, and syntax. A good decade after he was lost to the literary world, the symbolists discovered in him the embodiment of their own ideals—the allusiveness of dream, the fluidity of form, the privacy of vision, the richness of imagery. Through them his influence spread over Europe, to England, and to the imagist movement in America. In France he became an inspiration to such varied thinkers as the mystic poet Paul Claudel who found in *Illuminations* "the living and almost physical presence of the supernatural," and especially the surrealists—though they saw in him only Rimbaud the rebel and apostle of the irrational, disregarding completely his later adoption of bourgeois values. In the long run, the very contradictions in Rimbaud's personality which found expression in that one brief adolescent outburst have served to confirm the universality of his appeal.

Successive editions of the poet's work reflect the rather thorny problem of Rimbaud scholarship, which is complicated by the conflicting testimony of friends and the mysterious history of the *Illuminations* manuscripts themselves. Moreover, when Verlaine edited the 1887—the first—edition of *Illuminations,* he included some verse poems that are no longer considered part of the work. Verlaine added *Une Saison en Enfer* in a new edition in 1892, and in 1898 published what he claimed were Rimbaud's complete works. In 1912 Paterne Berrichon, Rimbaud's brother-in-law, published an edition which remained a standard for thirty years. In 1945 Bouillane de Lacoste edited the first version which contained only prose poems for the Mercure de France edition. The best edition today is that of the Bibliothèque de la Pléiade (1946), edited by Mouquet and de Renéville, but a few manuscripts have since been discovered.

Around the time of World War I the imagist *The Little Review* published a translation of *Illuminations*. Subsequent translations have been made by Helen Rootham (1932; with an introduction by Edith Sitwell), Louise Varèse (her 1957 version is the most recent), and Wallace Fowlie (1953). Translations of *Une Saison en Enfer* include those by George Frederic Lees (1932), Delmore Schwartz (1939), and Louise Varèse (the latter in a volume containing "Le Bateau Ivre"). Other translations of Rimbaud's works include: *Some Poems of Rimbaud*, by Lionel Abel (1939), *A Drunken Boat*, by Clark Mills (1941), *Selected Verse Poems of Arthur Rimbaud*, by Norman Cameron, *Four Poems by Rimbaud*, by Ben Belitt (1948), and *The Drunken Boat; Thirty-Six Poems*, by Brian Hill (1952).

ABOUT: Carré, J.-M. A Season in Hell: The Life of Arthur Rimbaud, tr. by Hannah and Matthew Josephson; Chisholm, A. R. The Art of Rimbaud; Clarke, M. Rimbaud and Quinet; Fowlie, W. Rimbaud; Fowlie, W. Rimbaud's Illuminations: A Study in Angelism; Frohock, W. M. Rimbaud's Poetic Practice; Hackett, C. A. Rimbaud; Hanson, E. My Poor Arthur; Hare, H. Sketch for a Portrait of Rimbaud; Miller, H. The Time of the Assassins; Moore, G. Impressions and Opinions; Morrissette, B. The Great Rimbaud Forgery; Moore, W. G., Sutherland, R. and Starkie, E. eds. The French Mind; Quennell, P. Baudelaire and the Symbolists; Starkie, E. Arthur Rimbaud; Symons, A. The Symbolist Movement in Literature; Wilson, E. Axel's Castle. [In French: Among people who knew him, Delahaye, Izambard, Paterne Berrichon, Isabelle Rimbaud, and Mme Verlaine wrote about him; see Paul Verlaine's Les Poètes Maudits. Important critical works in French are Berrichon, P. La Vie de J.-A. Rimbaud; Bouillane de Lacoste, H. de. Rimbaud et le Problème des Illuminations; Breton, A. Flagrant Délit; Daniel-Rops, H. Rimbaud; Etiemble, R. Le Mythe de Rimbaud; Rivière, J. Rimbaud.]

E. G.

*RIST, JOHANN (March 8, 1607-August 31, 1667), German poet and dramatist, was a Protestant minister of high character and forceful sincerity. Though his poetic gifts were perhaps modest, he enjoyed considerable reputation in his time. He was the founder of one of the most important of the *Sprachgesellschaften*—linguistic and literary academies with pastoral overtones—and a member of two others. He was the author of a number of excellent religious poems and of at least two dramas of unusual interest.

Rist is closely associated with the North German area in which he was born. A native of Ottensen near Hamburg, he became in 1635 a preacher in the town of Wedel on the Elbe river, where he spent the rest of his life. He was later a member of the Mecklenburg consistory. He founded the Elbschwanorden (Order of Swans of the Elbe), which ranks as one of the four or five most influential "academies" in a century whose culture and language were profoundly

* rist

influenced by such organizations. In 1645 the Emperor crowned him poet, and in 1653 he was raised to the nobility.

Rist's literary output is surprisingly varied, but the only segment of it to have achieved more than temporary renown is his religious verse. Some of his best poems—"O Ewigkeit, du Donnerwort" ("Eternity, thou word of fear"), "Praise and Thanks to Thee be Sung," "O Living Bread from Heaven," "Rise, O Salem," and many others—are still in the Protestant hymnals.

An almost journalistic immediacy characterizes his poems on the events of the Thirty Years' War, the sack of Magdeburg, for example. The rest of his secular verse rarely ventures beyond the bucolic—a bland poetic diet, but highly popular in its time.

Rist also wrote a number of plays. Not all of them were published or produced; fewer still are available in modern reprints, and only two or three are of lasting significance. On the average, they are distinguished more for their earnest sentiments and timely concern than for vivid characterization. His most original plays, *Festspiele*, written just before and just after the Peace of Westphalia in 1648, deserve more attention than they commonly receive. They are panoramic compositions with main actions, dramatic interludes, choruses, and music. Their impact lies in the portrayal of German (and foreign) individuals and types, drawn with obvious allegorical intent, but often with great realism. *Das Friedewünschende Teutschland* (Germany Longing for Peace), for example, is filled with an awareness of Germany's own folly and the deceptions practiced against her by Mars and by Don Antonio, Monsieur Gaston, and Signoro Bartholomeo. Its purpose is of the utmost seriousness: an exploration of the causes of the war in the distortion of the German's true character, a call to the old virtues and fear of God, a warning against vanity.

Various Protestant hymnals offer translations of his work, e.g., *Moravian Hymns* (1912); A. Russell, *Psalms and Hymns* (1851); also F. Cox, *Hymns from the German* (1864): C. Winkworth, *Christian Singers of Germany* (1869); *Lyra Germanica* (1855, etc.); C. Ramage, *Beautiful Thoughts* (1868); G. C. Schoolfield, *The German Lyric of the Baroque in English Translation* (1962).

ABOUT: Journal of English and Germanic Philology, LIX (1960). [In German—see studies by T. Hansen, A. Jericke, O. Kern.]

F. G. R.

*RIVAROL (ANTOINE RIVAROLI), called Comte de, and alias Chevalier de Parcieux (June 26, 1753-April 11, 1801), French wit, was the son of an innkeeper of Bagnols (Languedoc), of Italian origin; he studied near Carpentras, taught at Lyon, and went to Paris about 1780. Rivarol's first work was his famous *Discours sur l'Universalité de la Langue Française,* for which he won the Berlin Academy prize in 1784; in its preface he shows consciousness of the flaws of contemporary society. He also prepared a translation, with comments, of Dante's *Inferno,* again showing keen critical insight and taste rather than scholarly information. He later composed a considerable treatise, *De l'Homme Intellectuel et Moral,* and, in 1788, his *Petit Almanach de Nos Grands Hommes,* a venomous but charmingly insolent series of sketches which later became a veritable mine of quotations of moralistic type, full of keen and perceptive quips. During the Revolution, Rivarol took a strong Royalist stand, probably through sincere scorn for equalitarianism, and a conviction that it had no immediate future. He was forced to flee in 1792, and spent his last ten years in Brussels, London, and Germany, engaging in minor writings, and frequenting elegant social circles. He died in Berlin. His political writings were much admired by Burke; Sainte-Beuve considered him a significant author; he was essentially the last of the brilliant satirical and moralistic wits.

Antoine Rivarol is remembered today primarily as a fascinating individual, a combination of egoism and self-conceit, and of salon journalism, and a source for witty and biting remarks. Through his amusing declarations, he revealed many human secrets, both general and particular. His remarks on Voltaire, for example, are cruel and unjust, but sum up this writer's basic weaknesses. His political maxims are serious but cynical; on matters of ethics he resembles La Rochefoucauld. His *Œuvres Complètes* appeared in five volumes in 1808; to them one must add the *Pensées Inédites* (1836) and the miscellaneous tracts (1877), but for practical purposes the *Œuvres Choisies* with biography (1880) are quite sufficient.

ABOUT: Saintsbury, G. Miscellaneous Essays. [In French: Dimier, L. Les Maîtres de la Contre-Révolution; Groos, R. La Vraie Figure de Rivarol; Le Breton, A. Rivarol, Sa Vie, Ses Idées.]

F. J. C.

* rē và rôl'

RIVAS, ÁNGEL SAAVEDRA Y RAMÍREZ DE BAQUEDANO, Duque de. See SAAVEDRA Y RAMÍREZ DE BAQUEDANO, ÁNGEL, Duque de RIVAS

*ROBERT DE BORON (or BORRON) (fl. c. 1200), French poet, is known only from vague references in his own works. Towards the end of the extant portion of his unfinished *Histoire du Graal* he names himself twice as Robers de Bouron and refers also to a village of Boron (near Montbéliard in Burgundy), where, he says, he told the Grail story to Gautier de Montbéliard. Since we know that Gautier set out on the Fourth Crusade in 1201 and died in the Holy Land in 1212, it seems likely that Robert was from the Boron district and that he composed his Grail story before 1201. The dialect in which he writes supports this view of his origin. He is also named in the longer prose version of the Grail romance which is founded on his poem but which he almost certainly did not write.

Robert's version of the Grail story, sometimes called *Joseph d'Arimathie,* is extremely important, since it is the first extant work which gives to that story a specifically Christian origin and symbolism. The story begins with a brief summary of the history of the fall of man, and the first section ends with the appearance of Jesus to the imprisoned Joseph. The Grail, which is definitely regarded as the chalice of the Last Supper, comes into full significance in the second part, where its name is revealed by a certain Peter and it is watched over by Bron, Alein, and probably Perceval, although he is not mentioned by name. Great care is taken to show how the liturgy and the symbolism of the Mass developed out of earlier ceremonies before the Grail. A long passage is inserted to show how Vespasian really conquered Jerusalem to rescue the imprisoned Joseph and how the latter brought the Grail to Britain. An incident towards the end shows its magic property of allowing only the faithful to see certain objects placed near it. Robert clearly incorporates a mass of legendary and apocryphal material in his work. Bron, or Hebron, for example, is clearly the Celtic Bran, who also had a magic bowl, but he is confused with the Hebron of Numbers 4:19, who kept the Ark of the Covenant. Similarly the legend of Joseph's arrival in Britain is connected with the legendary his-

* rô bâr' dē bô rôn'

tory of Glastonbury Abbey, where the "grave" of King Arthur had been discovered.

The remainder of Robert's Grail story is probably represented fairly accurately by the prose trilogy *Joseph, Merlin, Perceval* ("Didot Perceval"), written shortly afterwards, where Merlin, thanks to the Grail, becomes a divine prophet and brings about King Arthur's establishment of the orders of chivalry. The best knight, Perceval, rediscovers the Grail and puts an end to human sorrow. Robert de Boron's poem, in itself of little literary merit, imparted to the Grail story and to the Arthurian stories connected with it a definite Christian emphasis, which became the normal viewpoint of all later writers. Attached to the *Histoire du Graal* is a fragment of a verse life of Merlin, in which he appears as the child of a union between a Christian maiden and the devil—a kind of Antichrist.

There is no translation of Robert de Boron's work into English. Standard editions are: Robert de Boron, *Roman de l'Estoire dou Graal*, ed. W. A. Nitze (1927); *Vulgate Version* (the prose version of Robert's complete work), ed. H. O. Sommer.

ABOUT: Bruce, J. D. Evolution of Arthurian Romance; Loomis, R. S. ed. Arthurian Literature in the Middle Ages; Modern Philology XL (1943).

W. T. H. J.

*ROD, ÉDOUARD (March 31, 1857-January 29, 1910), Swiss novelist and critic, was born in Nyon (Vaud), the son of a teacher and businessman of positivist tendencies and of a mystic and idealistic mother. As a child Rod lived close to nature, and his first schooling was of very liberal kind; his portraits of boys in his novels recall early personal memories. Loss of his mother emphasized his inner melancholy; his first verse was translated from Anacreon, and he often read Musset. After study in Lausanne, Rod decided on a literary career and visited Germany in search of romantic impressions. He arrived in Paris in 1878, hoping to have his first play performed. A defender of Zola's *L'Assommoir*, Rod took an active part in the journal *Liberté* and soon met Zola, who inculcated in him the naturalist doctrines; Rod then wrote for *La Revue Réaliste*. The association with naturalism, though real and significant, is limited to the clumsy applications of Rod's first two novels and established his reputation as a writer. His own theory was in fact quite different and centered on a "cosmopolitan" movement of international scope. *La Course à la Mort*

* rôd

(1885), for example, illustrates deep pessimism and despair and the immediate influence of Schopenhauer and of Leopardi. In works of this type, Rod studied cases of noble souls compromised by the circumstances of social life; Rod's success with the younger generation was considerable.

Rod was named professor of comparative literature at the University of Geneva in 1886, teaching Goethe, Shakespeare, and recent Italian writing. Simultaneously he composed *Le Sens de la Vie*, arguing the theme that life assumes meaning only through faith, and telling of his own happy domestic life; this novel was crowned by the French Academy and translated by Tolstoy. *Michel Tessier* (1893) dealt with marriage and divorce, the analytical portrait of a man of action disoriented by passion.

Rod's middle period ended with his return to Paris in 1894. He had continued writing for French reviews during his years in Switzerland, usually on literary matters. His *Dernier Refuge* (1896), showing the influence of D'Annunzio, was inspired by a trip to Italy. *Le Glaive et le Bandeau* (1909), conceived during a stay in Versailles, presented a pessimistic social study. Rod spent his vacations in later years in Switzerland, alarmed by the progress of modernization; these visits led him again to interest in Rousseau, whose work he taught. His reputation brought him many distinguished visitors, among them Fogazzaro and Matilde Serao.

Rod's "cosmopolitanism" involves documentation on foreign countries and on foreigners, with plots centering on travelers, often in Switzerland, and with psychological analysis recalling Stendhal. Rod abandoned naturalism in his preference for immediate experience over description, action, and notebook documentation. His work lies close to that of Paul Bourget in many respects, notably in the entire structure of the latter's *Cosmopolis*.

English translations from Rod include *Pastor Naudié's Young Wife*, by B. Gilman (1899), *The Sacrifice of Silence*, by J. Harding (1899), and *The White Rocks* (1896).

ABOUT: Stephens, W. French Novelists of Today. [In French—see studies by C. Beuchat, C. Delhorbe, V. Giraud.]

F. J. C.

*RODENBACH, GEORGES (RAYMOND CONSTANTIN) (July 16, 1855-December 25, 1898), Belgian poet and novel-

* rō' děn bäк

ist, was born in Tournay. After finishing his studies at the University of Ghent, he practiced law for some time and had remarkable success in pleading seemingly hopeless cases. However, he did not hesitate to turn entirely to literature and to take his place in the group of enthusiastic Belgian poets for whom *La Jeune Belgique* was the mouthpiece. Rodenbach's first essays revealed the influence of the Parnassians (*Tristesses*, 1879). But soon the personal and modern note began to develop in his writings, as in *L'Hiver Mondain* (1884) and *La Jeunesse Blanche* (1886). These works, as well as *La Mer Élégante* (1887), show his romantic outlook; they are full of subtle sadness, nostalgic environments, and mystical melancholy.

In 1887 Rodenbach settled in Paris where he perfected his form and acquired great ability in handling the French language. It was sometimes a little forced but always without blemish and very artistic. *L'Art en Exil* dealt with literary criticism; *Le Regne du Silence* (1889) was written in verse. His outstanding work was probably *Bruges la Morte* (1893). In the same year appeared *Le Voyage dans les Yeux* and a year later *Musée des Béguines. Le Voile* was a one-act comedy which was performed in 1894 in the Théâtre-Français. Other titles were: *La Vocation* (1896), *Les Tombeaux* (1896), *Les Vierges* (1896), *Les Vies Encloses* (1889), *Le Carillonneur* (1897), *Le Miroir du Ciel Natal* (1898), *L'Arbre* (1898). In 1899 appeared the unfinished *L'Élite* in which the author had planned to portray the outstanding men of letters of the day. *Le Rouet des Brumes* (1900) is the title under which Rodenbach's posthumous tales were published. Rodenbach was not a descriptive writer. "It was not things, but the soul of things with which he occupied himself." He died in Paris.

ABOUT: Turquet-Milnes, G. Some Modern Belgian Writers. [In French—Bodson-Thomas, A. L'Esthétique de G. Rodenbach; Maes, P. Georges Rodenbach; Vanwelkenhuyzen, G. Vocations Littéraires.]

H. B.

RODRIGUES LOBO, FRANCISCO. See LOBO, FRANCISCO RODRIGUES

*ROJAS, FERNANDO DE (d. 1541?), Spanish novelist and lawyer, was born in the city of Montalván and lived in Talavera, where he was mayor. All that is further

* rō′ häs

known of him is that in contemporary documents he is referred to as "the one who composed the book of Celestina" and who "composed Melibea."

La Celestina, also called *Comedia y Tragicomedia de Calisto y Melibea*, is a work of capital importance in Spanish literature, some critics comparing it to *Don Quixote* in its literary greatness, influence, and circulation. The oldest known edition is that of 1499, printed anonymously in Burgos and consisting of sixteen acts. Its title page states that this edition includes newly added acts, thus suggesting an even earlier edition. An acrostic in the next known edition (Sevilla, 1501) reveals Rojas as the author of the work, which grew the next year to twenty-one acts. By 1526 (Toledo edition), *La Celestina* had twenty-two acts. The work, in its numerous editions, has been extensively studied by modern scholars.

La Celestina, taking its name from its principal character, is not a dramatic work but an extended novel. Its plot concerns Calisto, a wealthy young man in love with Melibea, who uses the services of Celestina as go-between for his communications with Melibea. Calisto's servants, Sempronio and Pármeno, demand from Celestina a portion of the money she earns from Calisto. Upon her refusal to share, she is killed by these ruffians, who are later hanged for their deed. The lovers' story suddenly becomes even more tragic when Calisto climbs a ladder in order to speak with Melibea at her window and, upon descending, falls to his death. Melibea then throws herself from a tower to die with her lover. The play ends with her parents, Pleberio and Alisa, lamenting over her body.

La Celestina is in the humanist tradition of the Renaissance. The work unites, for the first time in Spanish literature, erudite prose with that of popular speech. Moreover, it combines the purely idealistic with the crudely realistic to form a graphic picture of human passions and characteristics.

The most recent definitive translation into English is *The Celestina, a Novel in Dialogue,* translated by Leslie Byrd Simpson, 1955. The first English translation was made in 1631 by James Mabbe.

ABOUT: Gilman, S. The Art of the Celestina; Malkiel, M. R. L. de, Two Spanish Masterpieces; Penney, C. L. The Book Called Celestina; Bulletin of Hispanic Studies, XXXIV (1957). [In Spanish —see study by F. Castro Guisasola].

R. P. C.

*ROJAS ZORRILLA, FRANCISCO DE (1607-1648), Spanish dramatist, was born in Toledo, the son of a minor Navy officer. He was taken to Madrid when he was only three years old. He may have studied at the University of Salamanca. At twenty-five he had already established his reputation as a playwright, being accepted as a collaborator by such prominent dramatists as Calderón and Vélez de Guevara. From them he learned much of his craftsmanship and soon became a rival to be reckoned with, in the eyes of both the court and the general public.

In 1638 his death was announced, supposedly by the hand of an unnamed poet who did not appreciate his satires. Although severely wounded, Rojas reappeared in public some time later. He married in 1640, and he had a daughter out of wedlock with an actress whose husband was also named Francisco de Rojas. This daughter, known as "La Bezona," eventually became a famous stage figure.

King Philip IV, who was fond of Rojas as a court dramatist, made him a Knight of Saint James. This high honor was to cause him a great deal of embarrassment. During the proceedings—that dragged on for more than two years—he was accused of bribing witnesses to conceal his Moorish and Jewish origin. In fact some of his ancestors had been burned at the stake by the Inquisition. Finally in 1615 at the king's insistence Rojas was allowed to don the coveted habit.

The earliest play of his exclusive authorship seems to have been performed in 1613. Thirteen years later, when he was at the peak of his career, and still in his thirties, the death of the queen caused the Spanish theatres to be closed. Rojas, discouraged, stopped writing for the stage. He died at forty-one—a year before the theatres were reopened in Madrid.

The authenticity of a great many of his plays has been questioned. Of the seventy or eighty attributed to him, no more than forty or forty-five are accepted today as his alone.

He was a disciple of Calderón, and his best known play, *Del Rey Abajo Ninguno, o García del Castañar* is considered the prototype of the "drama de honor" among nobles. (It was translated into English by Isaac Goldberg as *None Beneath the King* in 1924). In spite of this, Rojas shows in other plays a marked disregard of the tenets of the honor code. This caused his play *Cada Cual lo que le Toca* to be noisily re-

* rŏ′ häs thôr rē′ lyä

jected by the public. He was a master of comic stylization and his satire has a keen psychological insight; *Entre Bobos Anda el Juego* exemplifies these qualities.

Corneille, Scarron, and Le Sage took some of their plots from him.

ABOUT: MacCurdy, R. R. Francisco de Rojas Zorrilla and the Tragedy. [In Spanish—see study by E. Cotarelo y Mori.]

M. DA C.

*ROLLENHAGEN, GEORG (April 22, 1542-May 20, 1609), German poet-moralist and dramatist, was born near Berlin and studied theology at Wittenberg. From a lecture course on the *Batrachomyomachia*—then thought to be Homer's—he derived the idea for his famous *Froschmeuseler* (though in spirit it resembles more the traditional German animal epic). It was the work virtually of a lifetime.

Between the beginning and the completion (in 1595) of the *Froschmeuseler* lay a full career of Protestant preaching, teaching, pedagogical and astrological writing, and a series of rather routine Biblical dramas.

The problem of securing a livelihood was complicated for Rollenhagen by his aversion to accepting princely favors. The Rollenhagens, he said, had never had luck at court. He turned down attractive offers as court preacher at Wittenberg and Leipzig, both because of his general sentiments in these matters and because he was opposed to the doctrine of the ubiquity of Christ's glorified body (Luther's idea), then *de rigueur* at both places. Before he had finished his university studies he was head of a school in Halberstadt; afterward he became rector of the excellent *Gymnasium* at Magdeburg—where he took in boarders and preached to supplement his income.

Rollenhagen was renowned as teacher and administrator. He added astrology and botany to the traditional Latin and Greek curriculum and permitted himself another daring innovation: instruction in the German language.

His dramas *Abraham* (1569), *Tobias* (1576), and *Lazarus* (1590) bear witness to a characteristic feature of the age, the close connection of drama with the schools. In each case he drastically modified plays of other authors to make them suitable for presentation by his pupils. One criterion was maximum participation. *Abraham* had fifty separate parts.

* rŏ′ lĕn hä gĕn

Through all these years he was laboring on the *Froschmeuseler*. This vast work, 20,000 lines long, has a slender narrative frame. The frog king, frightened by a snake, lets his passenger, the visiting mouse king, slip off his back and drown. The two "peoples" wage an inconclusive war. The frogs do not win, but the mice lose. On this frame Rollenhagen weaves an extraordinary fabric of anecdotes, descriptions, fables, and timely lessons—a portrait of the individual and collective personality of his time. The allegorical range extends to a representation of the Reformation in the guise of unrest in Frogland. Luther appears as a frog and the Pope as a tortoise. The humor is gentle, the language lively and colloquial, but the bite of passionate commitment is lacking. The work was enormously popular. The second edition appeared a year after the first, and succeeding ones dot the seventeenth and eighteenth centuries. Rollenhagen figures as a character in Wilhelm Raabe's *Student von Wittenberg* (1859).

ABOUT: PMLA, LXX (1955). [In German—Bolte, J. Quellenstudien zu Georg Rollenhagen.]

F. G. R.

*RONSARD, PIERRE DE (September 11, 1524/25-December 27, 1585), French poet, was born in the Renaissance Manoir de la Possonnière (near Vendôme) built by Loys de Ronsard, soldier and aesthete, who planned for his second son, Pierre, a military career. Pierre, page in Scotland, Alsace, and Holland, then squire of the King's Stables, was forced by deafness to turn to an ecclesiastic career. He was tonsured in 1543 in Le Mans where the poet and critic Peletier encouraged him to write poetry.

After five years of assiduous studies under the humanist Dorat, principal of the Collège de Coqueret, Ronsard had filled the gaps of a superficial education, and, thoroughly acquainted with Greek and Latin poetry, with Petrarch and the Italians, as well as with the neo-Latin poets, was prepared to apply Du Bellay's principle of imitation in his lyrical *Odes* (four books 1550, fifth book 1552), poems most varied in form as in subject matter. They were haughtily and insolently prefaced by the young poet who claimed to be the direct heir of Pindar and Horace and the first lyrical poet in France. Some, like Pindar's odes, were almost epic poems in a lofty style full of bold images and obscure myths; others, inspired by Horace, were

* rôN sàr′

RONSARD

heroic or moral or sang of homeland, nature, and the joy of living.

Being the French Pindar was not enough; Ronsard wanted to equal Petrarch. In 1552 he published the *Amours*, sonnets largely about Cassandre Salviati, the daughter of a Florentine banker whom he had met in 1545 and who had married another soon after. Although the true nature of his relations with her is unknown, she probably was little more than the concrete form of his dreams, a pretext for the "French Petrarch" to write amorous poetry, which differed from its model, however, by its sensuality and its abundant display of erudition.

His *Odes* and his *Amours* had made him famous among literary and erudite circles, and he was named "Prince of French Poets," despite the charges of obscure neologism and mythological allusion. Reacting perhaps to such criticism, Ronsard showed his ability to compose light and spicy poetry, true to *Gaulois* tradition, in his *Folastries* (1553). He enriched the tradition with imitations both from the *Greek Anthology*, then becoming popular, and from neo-Latin poets, in his *Continuations* and *Nouvelles Continuations des Amours* (1555-56) in which, weary of Petrarch, he sang of a more accessible and earthy love, personified by the peasant girl Marie Dupin.

Yet Ronsard had not abandoned serious poetry. He nourished the ambition of being the French Homer, and, while waiting for King Henry II's patronage, he wrote the

Hymnes (1555-56), some of which showed promise of an epic poet, while others, efforts to associate poetry, science, and philosophy, won for him the title of *"poète-philosophe."* It is difficult to determine the exact nature of Ronsard's convictions because of the inherent contradictions which, in the last analysis, might well constitute the essence of his vision of life. He was equally curious about conflicting pagan systems (Plato and Lucretius), and therein was not different from his medieval predecessors who had tried to conciliate pagan philosophies and Christian dogma. He was most probably sincere in his Catholicism. Yet the very nature of his poetry and his attitude toward it reveal the perhaps unconscious attempt to reconcile spirit and matter, and to apprehend man in his totality, in his conquest of knowledge and spirit, his religion and morals, his pleasures and pains, be they of the flesh or of the most spiritual nature.

Prematurely gray and disappointed by the king's silence, Ronsard withdrew to the solitude of his native country until, at Saint-Gelais' death (1558) when the king named him chaplain and counselor, he returned triumphant as the official court-poet. He then wrote many occasional pieces celebrating the king's actions and pastoral poetry for important court events.

In 1560, conscious of the public, that "monstrous Proteus," he organized and sorted his poems in view of a complete edition which would assure his lasting fame. He also aimed at obtaining an abbey or a bishopric, but the king, sensitive to the attitudes of the Council of Trent, refused.

During the religious crisis Ronsard immediately sided, in the name of tradition, nationalism, unity, and peace, with the orthodox church while not hesitating to point to its abuses and fanaticism. He also wrote poetry to defend himself against personal attacks launched by the Protestant camp, which reproached him for his pagan and immoral verse.

Meanwhile, he pursued amorous and occasional poetry in his *Elégies, Mascarades, & Bergeries* (1565). The abbey he wanted was given him not by the king (Charles IX), but by the scholar Amyot. Ronsard traded it for the priory of Saint-Cosme where he withdrew and where he had the honor of receiving the king's visit in 1565. The latter encouraged him to resume his epic poem and gave him in the following year another priory, Croixval.

At the end of the third civil war (1570) Ronsard returned to the court, celebrated the king's marriage, and enjoyed an intimate relationship with the king, who often showed him his own verse. In 1572 the first four books of the *Franciade* finally appeared, meeting with little success. In this national epic, which is hardly readable though it contains some lofty passages, the Franks were given the traditional Trojan lineage. The mythical voyages of Francus had little interest for a public which had experienced three civil wars. Ronsard's heart was not in his project, and on the king's death, he abandoned it.

The succeeding king, Henry III, favored Ronsard's disciple, Desportes, with whom Ronsard tried to compete by offering his platonic *Sonnets pour Hélène* (1578). If one disregards those sonnets in which Ronsard sacrifices passion to the finical taste of the time, the majority of the poems vibrate with intimate emotion. The sufferings and melancholy of the aging poet are here more touching than in his first amorous verse, whether or not he really loved the puritanical and disdainful Hélène de Surgères who inspired them. (She was a cousin of the Maréchale de Retz at whose "green salon" gathered all the poets of the time.) The eclipse of his popularity by Desportes, the scandalous behavior of the new court, and his ailments made him withdraw from Paris, though he was often called for meetings of the Académie du Palais. He continued to vie with Desportes by composing panegyrics for the king, who had not forgotten him altogether. He called himself the "spiritual leader," the king's "prophet-priest," and did not hesitate to criticize him and give him moral advice.

A year before his death, plagued by the gout, he made a last effort to present posterity with a new edition of his works. He then retired to his favorite priory of Saint-Cosme where he died. A great ceremony was held in his honor at the Collège de Boncourt. Shortly after, a collection of epitaphs was published, as well as Binet's biography of the "Prince of French Poets." Nevertheless, though he continued to be admired and read all over Europe, in France he was soon forgotten. His posthumous fame was prejudiced by the dogmatism of Malherbe, who forgot that Ronsard had striven towards the very qualities he himself demanded—clarity, precision, elegance, harmony, and sobriety.

Ronsard's influence was especially felt in England, where he was admired and imitated not only by Elizabethans but by the romantics as well. The French romantics, especially Sainte-Beuve, rediscovered Ronsard, whose popularity has grown ever since.

In this century scholarly editions of his collected works appeared 1914-19, 1923-24, 1938; P. Laumonier's bibliography of 1911 remains the standard one. For recent translations of Ronsard's poems, see *Songs and Sonnets of P. de Ronsard,* by C. H. Page (1903), *Selected Poems* by C. Graves (1924), *Sonnets pour Hélène* by H. Wolfe (1934), and W. Stirling's translation (1946).

ABOUT: Bishop, M. Ronsard, Prince of Poets; Lewis, D. B. Wyndham, Ronsard; Silver, I. Ronsard and the Hellenic Renaissance in France. [In French—see studies by G. Cohen, P. Champion, F. Desonay, P. Laumonier, M. Raymond.]

M. B.

ROSENFELD, MORRIS (pseudonym of **MOSHE JACOB ALTER**) (December 28, 1862-June 22, 1923), the foremost early Yiddish poet, was born in a small town in the Suwalki region of Russia. His family had been fishermen for many generations, and Rosenfeld was given an average Jewish education, supplemented later by instruction in German and Polish. Leaving Russia in 1882 to avoid service in the Czar's army, Rosenfeld emigrated to London, where he was employed as a tailor, and also worked as a diamond grinder in Amsterdam. Finally, in 1886, he settled in New York, working fourteen hours a day as a tailor under the horrible conditions then prevalent in the clothing industry.

Rosenfeld had written verse in London, but his first published poem appeared in a New York Yiddish newspaper in 1886. Thereafter he contributed a remarkable series of poems to the Yiddish press which soon brought him fame as the poet of the oppressed Jewish worker. Rosenfeld was disappointed, however, with his first book of verse, *Di Gloke* (The Bell, 1889), and went so far as to buy and destroy all obtainable copies. His second book, *Di Blumen-Kete* (The Flower Wreath, 1890), was more successful. Rosenfeld now left the clothing factory, and earned his livelihood as a journalist, editor, and poet.

Rosenfeld expressed the misery and suffering that he perceived as the fate of his fellow human beings. The social poems of this period were devoted to the utter anguish and despair of the workers. In his great poem "The Sweat Shop" he wrote of the mechanization of labor and saw the worker as a mere cog in an infernal machine dedicated to unrewarded production: "Void is my soul. . . . I'm but a machine. I work and I work and I work never ceasing, create and create

things from morning to e'en; For what?— and for whom?—Oh, I know not, oh, ask not! Who ever has heard of a conscious machine?" Although indignant at the economic and human exploitation he witnessed, Rosenfeld never allied himself with any political party. His social poetry, however, was on the lips of all radical groups of the day.

Rosenfeld also wrote many great national poems in which he expressed the tragically abnormal position of the Jews. He sang of the glorious heritage of the Jewish people, their sorrows and their unquenchable vitality. He was not a strictly observant Jew, but his national feeling made him understand the true plight of his people. He served in 1900 as delegate to the Fourth World Zionist Congress in London.

National and international acclaim came to Rosenfeld when his *Liderbukh* (Songbook, 1897) attracted the enthusiasm of Leo Wiener of Harvard University. Wiener's English translations brought Rosenfeld invitations to read his verse at Harvard, the University of Chicago, Radcliffe, and Wellesley (1898-1902). His work was translated into the major European languages and a triumphant tour of Europe followed. All this, however, could not compensate for the loss of his only child, a boy. Rosenfeld's writings began to lose their power, and he was discharged from his newspaper position. His remaining years were spent in poverty and illness, with his death putting an end to increasing blindness, paralysis and misery. Rosenfeld's funeral was attended by many thousands who had known and loved his poems.

As Leo Wiener remarks in his *History of Yiddish Literature,* "It was left for a Russian Jew at the end of the nineteenth century to see and paint hell in colors not attempted by any one since the days of Dante; Dante spoke of the hell in the after-life; while Rosenfeld sings of the hell on earth." In his social and national poems, Rosenfeld united a masterly lyric quality with dramatic action to create a uniquely dynamic and passionate style. His diction was simple, his rhythm was musical, and through all his work shines his suffering heart. Rosenfeld's contribution to Yiddish poetry has been of very great value, both in itself and in its influence in asserting the essential Jewishness and humanity of Yiddish creativity.

Leo Wiener translated many of Rosenfeld's poems as *Songs from the Ghetto* in 1898. A more complete selection was translated by Rose P. Stokes and Helena Frank in 1914 as *Songs of Labor, and*

Other Poems. His most important works appeared in the six-volume *Shriftn* (1908-10).

ABOUT: Roback, A. The Story of Yiddish Literature; Rogoff, H. Nine Yiddish Writers; Trommer, M. My Recollections of Morris Rosenfeld; Waxman, M. A History of Jewish Literature; Wiener, L. History of Yiddish Literature; New York Times, June 22 and 25, 1923.

M. R.

*ROTROU, JEAN (August 21, 1609-June 27, 1650), French dramatist, was born in Dreux of a respected family, and studied there and in Paris. He soon began to devote himself to poetry, and when he was twenty his first play was performed at the Hôtel de Bourgogne. He completed his training in law in 1630, but never practiced. During his rather dissipated youth, he found a protector in the Count of Belin, and later in Richelieu, who included him among his "five authors." Rotrou admired Corneille but took no part in the "Querelle du Cid." In 1639, after his marriage, he settled in Dreux in the civil service, and continued composition of plays at a more moderate pace, though with continued success and in pieces generally esteemed as his best. He died during an epidemic as he remained heroically at his post.

Second to Alexandre Hardy alone, Rotrou was the most prolific of the French dramatists. He was the first to borrow subject matter from the Spanish theatre, and turned especially to Lope de Vega, for example in his second play, *La Bague de l'Oubli* (1629). In *Les Deux Sosies* he recreated a story from Plautus. Rotrou's tragi-comedies are typical examples of this romanesque genre, with action set in such distant regions as Hungary, at no stated period, devoted to exciting events, girls in disguise seeking their lovers, series of accidents suitably resolved by marriage. Love is the principal theme, and Rotrou shows the habits of preciosity in the extensive use of antithesis and hyperbole.

Rotrou's later work shows the beneficial influence of Corneille. *Bélissaire* (1644) uses a Spanish model freely, simplifying and improving the structure and the dramatic rôles. *Le Véritable Saint Genest*, a formal tragedy published in 1647 and many times since, is a synthesis of materials from Lope and from a play on the same subject by Desfontaines, a legend of the time of Diocletian on the conversion of the actor Genest, his defiance of the emperor and his death. The action takes place within a few hours and both place and plot are conceived in al-

most purely classical form; of interest is the use of a rehearsal scene within the play itself. *Venceslas* (1648), partly adapted from Rojas, and probably influenced by Corneille, tells an episode of Bohemian history and emphasizes moral problems rather than mere action and movement. Rotrou's last tragedy, *Cosroès* (1649), gives a powerful portrayal of cruelty in the person of Syra, wife of the King of Persia, who is haunted by his crime.

ABOUT: Crane, T. Jean Rotrou's Saint Genest and Venceslas; Lancaster, H. A History of French Dramatic Literature. [In French—Chardon, H. La Vie de Rotrou; Jarry, J. Essai sur les Œuvres Dramatiques de Rotrou.]

F. J. C.

*ROUCHER, JEAN ANTOINE (1745-July 25, 1794), French poet, was born in Montpellier, studied with the Jesuits, and went to Paris with an ecclesiastical career in view. He turned to poetry, and in 1770 his early verse drew attention to him, notably a poem on the marriage of the Dauphin, which won the special approbation of Turgot and gave him a sinecure as tax collector at Monfort-l'Amaury. He was at first an enthusiastic republican, but, disgusted by the excesses, attacked Robespierre and was arrested in 1793. Later, in Saint Lazare prison, he worked on his translation of James Thomson's *Seasons* and became friendly with André Chénier. Both poets were guillotined on the same day.

The first influence of Thomson appears in Roucher's *Hymne à la Nuit* (1772). His principal work, *Poème des Mois*, published in two volumes in 1779, is one of the monuments of this influence, and a significant text in the evolution of descriptive poetry after Saint-Lambert's *Les Saisons* of ten years earlier. It is constructed in twelve parts, following the course of the year's activities: the poet meditates on the changes of nature and invokes the sun or rain. The didactic subjects, showing traces of Roucher's extensive readings in English and Italian, illustrate man's fruitful labors and move toward philosophical reflections. A few passages, selected from the overly long text, represent the best contemporary lyricism and complement the earlier work of Saint-Lambert.

Roucher's fame is attested in La Harpe's praise ("Il a une tête poétique") and even in Rivarol's biting quip ("Le plus beau naufrage poétique du siècle"). Roucher had his honorable share of devotees and critics

* rô trōō′

* rōō shā′

but was one of the striking personalities that set the fashion for the romantic poet. His physical appearance and manner, combined with his exotic southern enthusiasm, became one of the norms for the creative artist in the principal salons of his day. With Saint-Lambert, Roucher is the most distinguished disciple of Thomson, setting a tone for nature poetry of a new kind, and in this very way preparing the way for his own eclipse by the later translations of the English *Seasons*.

ABOUT: [In French—Cameron, M. L'Influence des Saisons.]

F. J. C.

*ROUGET DE LISLE, CLAUDE JOSEPH (May 10, 1760-June 20, 1836),

French poet and song writer, born in Lons-le-Saunier, in the Jura, was the eldest of the eight children of a lawyer in the local Parliament. His family name was ornamented by the term "de Lisle" as a social advantage at the military school in Paris, which he entered in 1776. Six years later Rouget was named lieutenant and after further training returned to his home and was assigned to Grenoble and to Mont-Dauphin. He interrupted his military career by a long sojourn in Paris, where he tried in vain to introduce several comic operas such as *Almanzor et Féline,* and succeeded finally in 1791 with *Bayard dans Bresce* with music by Champein, and especially in his collaboration with Grétry in *Les Deux Couvents.* Up to this point in his career he showed no particular promise, but he at least established something of a minor reputation both as a versifier and a composer of classical melodies.

Rouget was promoted in April 1791 to the rank of captain and sent to Strasbourg, important at the moment as a center of disorder in the army, as the point of departure of a mass of aristocratic refugees, and, with its opera and concerts, as the second cultural center in France. He entered into the circle of the mayor, Frédéric Dietrich, himself a musician, and continued to distinguish himself in a minor way as a song writer. Meanwhile, the central government in Paris collapsed, the army fell into the hands of a number of older and ineffectual officers, and France declared war on Austria and Prussia on April 20, 1792. Word of the war came shortly to Strasbourg and on April 30, 1792, Rouget was inspired, in the moment of excitement, with the words and music of his "Chant de Guerre de l'Armée du Rhin,"

which he showed to his friends and which spread like wildfire throughout France. When it was taken up by the volunteers from the South, it was rebaptized "La Marseillaise."

Rouget disappeared from view during the several following years; we know of his return to the army at Colmar and the excessive patriotic passion of his views, which led to his dismissal and his imprisonment during the Terror of 1793 and 1794. After a few passing successes such as *Le Chant des Vengeances,* performed in 1798, and confident of his own prophetic views, he sought government service, but his interview with Napoleon led to nought. Protected by Josephine, he went on a mission to Spain, but failed shortly in the military commissary services. At thirty-six, he began long years of bitter inactivity, watched by the police and living on hopes for glory. As a former enemy of the Emperor, he enjoyed a moment of fame in 1814, and Béranger did what he could to encourage him to composition of patriotic hymns. His *Cinquante Chants Français* (1825, republished in 1830), enjoyed some success, and his financial worries were alleviated by outbursts of enthusiasm for his great song. On his death he left many melodies and song lyrics and several prose texts of minor historical interest.

Rouget's collected songs, as published in 1796, represent his best work. They belong to the occasional and anecdotal pieces much in vogue, deriving from the poetic techniques of Voltaire, and are most unusual in having original melodies rather than the traditional popular or mundane tunes characteristic of this genre. Among the more important items one should note the *Hymne Dithyrambique* on Robespierre (1794), the *Chant des Vengeances* (1798), and the *Chant du Combat* (1800) for the Egyptian expedition.

ABOUT: [In French—see studies by H. Coutant, V. Delfolie, L. Fiaux, M. de la Fuye & E. Guéret, M. Henry-Rosier, A. Lanier, J. Tiersot.]

F. J. C.

*ROUMANILLE, JOSEPH (August 8, 1818-May 24, 1891), Provençal poet and

prose writer, called the "father of the Félibrige," was born in Saint-Rémy to Jean Denis Roumanille, a gardener who had served in Napoleon's armies, and his wife, a simple country woman, Pierrette de Piquet. It was a poor and humble family, but Joseph, as the eldest of seven children, was destined for the priesthood and therefore received a good

* rōō zhĕ′ dĕ lĕl′

* rōō mà nĕ′ y′

education, especially in Latin, at the Collège of Tarascon. Having no religious vocation (though a deeply religious man all his life), he took up the career of teaching—first at the Collège of Nyons, then, in 1845, in Avignon.

Roumanille began writing poetry as a school boy. His first efforts were in French. According to a charming story, he began to write in Provençal when he realized that his mother could not read his French verse. More likely Roumanille's choice of Provençal was the expression of a rising regionalism, a revival of the customs, costumes, and language of the south of France of the Middle Ages when the troubadours flourished. Roumanille became the organizer, leader, and chief publicist for this renaissance.

His most outstanding disciple was the poet Frédéric Mistral (see sketch above) who began his brilliant career as a student under Roumanille in Avignon. The Félibrige movement was officially founded by Roumanille, Mistral, Théodore Aubanel (see sketch above), and four other poets (Giéra, Brunet, Tavan, and Mathieu) on May 21, 1854, at a meeting at Fontségugne, near Avignon. This group, calling itself a new Pléiade, adopted the name Félibrige—the derivation of which is still uncertain. Some suggest that the term is a combination of *faire* and *libré* (Provençal for *livre*)—hence a maker of books; others that it is *fé libré*, the Provençal for *homme de foi libre* (man of free faith); still others that it comes from an old Provençal tale in which the infant Jesus debates with "li set félibre de la lei" (the seven doctors of law). Whatever the origins of its name, the Félibrige movement enjoyed great success, extending far beyond its region. Beginning in 1855 it issued its celebrated annual, *Armana* [almanac] *Prouvençau*.

Though overshadowed by the poetic achievement of Mistral and Aubanel, Roumanille made a substantial contribution to the Félibrige. His poetry—*Li Margarideto* (The Daisies, 1847), *Li Sounjarello* (The Dreamers, 1851), and *Lis Oubreto en Vers* (Collected Poems, 1862)—was distinguished principally for its lightness, tenderness, and grace. Of even greater significance were his editions of other Provençal poets, including *Li Provençalo* (1852), which included the early work of Mistral, and his prose. Roumanille was the first to use the vernacular Provençal in literary prose. He worked hard to establish system and order in the language which had survived so long only by oral transmission. He simplified the spelling and

attempted to standardize the vocabulary. During the Revolution of 1848 he wrote political pieces for the Legitimist journal *La Commune* in Avignon, thereby reaching a large public that could not read French. Mainly he is remembered for his short, humorous prose tales—simple, moral, didactic but heart-warming anecdotes that endeared him not only to Provençal readers but, translated (some by Alphonse Daudet) and published in Paris newspapers, to French readers as well. These were collected in *Li Conte Prouvençau* (1883).

Roumanille spent most of his life in Avignon where he worked for a printer and later opened a bookshop which became a center for Félibrige activity. A member of the Legion of Honor, he also received decorations from Spain and Rumania. His funeral in Avignon was attended by many eminent literary figures as well as by crowds of the common people whose language and traditions he had revived and revitalized.

Many of Roumanille's poems and tales have been translated into French; selections appear in the French sources cited below.

ABOUT: Columbia Dictionary of Modern European Literature. [In French—Mariéton, P. Roumanille; Mistral, F. Mémoires; Monné, J. Roumanille; Ripert, E. La Renaissance Provençale; Tavernier, E. La Renaissance Provençale et Roumanille.]

*ROUSSEAU, JEAN BAPTISTE (April 6, 1670-March 17, 1741), French poet and dramatist, born in Paris, the son of a cobbler, distinguished himself in his studies, but his talent, visible at an early age, lay in facile and varied verse genres, which made of him a popular figure in the brilliant libertine circles at the turn of the century. As secretary of the Maréchal de Tallard, he went to London in 1701, but until his exile frequented cabaret society in Paris, creating such plays as *Le Café* (1694), of no particular note. Embittered by the failure of his plays, in 1700 he composed a scurrilous vaudeville against his detractors who, answering him in kind, provoked him further. This exchange of insults seemed forgotten, but ten years later, further anonymous couplets in similar vein were attributed to him and, in answer to the accusation, he named Saurin, an Academician, as their author; convicted of an act of defamation, he fled to permanent exile.

Rousseau sought refuge in Switzerland with the French ambassador, the Comte du

Luc, and survived pitifully by addressing banal verse to various rich or noble persons. He was for a while in Brussels, and returned to Paris in disguise in order to have his exile countermanded. When he died in Brussels, in extreme indigence, his fate was lamented by Vauvenargues and even by his former enemy Voltaire. The latter, his aggressive critic, was perhaps jealous, and not without reason, of Rousseau's great reputation as a poet. Indeed his distinction lies in his verse, which has the questionable honor of first place in the lyrical genres of his times, representing the transition from the classical to the rationalist manner. In a sense, Rousseau was the last to search for external purity of line and form. His *Odes* maintain a part of the spirit of the seventeenth century and were in fact unrivaled during his day. Of special significance are the *Cantate de Circé,* the *Odes Sacrées,* and other odes dedicated to friends or devoted to occasional subjects. The number of editions testify to his fame: *Œuvres Diverses* (1712), *Œuvres Choisies* (1721), and the complete works (1743, 1757). His *Correspondance* appeared in five volumes in 1749, and again in 1910.

ABOUT: Grubbs, H. A. Jean-Baptiste Rousseau. [In French—Sainte-Beuve, C. A. Portraits Littéraires; Voltaire, Vie de Jean-Baptiste Rousseau.]

F. J. C.

*ROUSSEAU, JEAN JACQUES (June 28, 1712-July 2, 1778), French writer and philosopher, was born in Geneva, the second of two sons. His mother, Suzanne Bernard, of upper-middle-class Geneva family, died nine days after Jean Jacques' birth. His father, Isaac Rousseau, a watchmaker and sometime dancing-master, descendant of a French Protestant family which moved to Geneva in the sixteenth century, showed many evidences of unstable character.

Rousseau received his early schooling, plus a taste for seventeenth century French romances, from his father, who often read to him till the early morning hours. The boy became interested especially in Plutarch (in Amyot's French translation), and this, with his father's sermons on liberty, created in him an admiration for republican virtues which he was never to lose. When Rousseau was ten, his father was forced to leave Geneva on account of a dispute, and fled to Lyon, putting Jean Jacques in the charge of relatives. He was turned over to M. Lambercier, a pastor at Boissy. In 1724 he was apprenticed to a notary, who found him wanting

* rōō sō′

JEAN JACQUES ROUSSEAU

and sent him off. In 1725 he was apprenticed for five years to an engraver, whose cruelty and "tyranny," according to Rousseau, resulted in his unhappiness and degeneration. In 1728 he ran away. The trouble, in the opinion of most biographers, was more in Rousseau's lack of discipline and sense of duty than in his master's rigid requirements.

After fleeing from Geneva, Rousseau was taken in by a priest who sent him for conversion to Annecy, to Mme de Warens, a charming, pretty, and somewhat promiscuous widow of twenty-nine, who, besides performing services for the church, appears to have been an agent of the King of Sardinia. After a brief stay with Mme de Warens, Rousseau went to Turin for instruction and baptism into the Catholic Church. To keep body and soul together he became a lackey to the Comtesse de Vercellis, from which service he was dismissed for a petty theft (of which he falsely accused a chambermaid). He next served as a lackey to the Comte de Gouvon for nine months, then returned to Annecy and Mme de Warens, his "Maman." In Turin Rousseau met a Savoyard priest, the abbé Gaime, whose wise lessons are well represented in Rousseau's picture of the "Vicaire savoyard." (The rest of that picture was drawn from the abbé Gâtier, whom Rousseau met at Annecy shortly after leaving Turin.)

In 1729-30 Rousseau studied music with the teacher and composer Lemaistre. For some years he earned much of his livelihood by teaching music, which indeed seemed to him his principal career. Rousseau went to Paris to seek his fortune, but met only disappointment. He then walked to Lyon, on the way stopping at a peasant's hut where, as he relates in the *Confessions,* he learned the meaning of tax oppression. In autumn, 1731, Rousseau was back with Mme de Warens, who now resided at Chambéry. Though he was obliged to work for a living as a clerk in the Survey Office, his main interest was music. He conducted monthly concerts and taught, and he was eventually able to resign his clerkship (1733 or 1734). In the autumn of 1732 he became Mme de Warens' lover. He continued to study music seriously, taking lessons briefly under the abbé Blanchard at Besançon in 1734. He took many trips in southern France and Switzerland, undergoing a number of amorous infatuations.

After a period of concern about his health he settled down to a happy life with "Maman" in the summer of 1736, but he was shortly to be replaced in her affections by another man, Wintzenried. From 1737 to 1740 Rousseau, Mme de Warens, and Wintzenried lived together at Les Charmettes, in an arrangement the details of which are not entirely clear, though it appears likely that Rousseau was a mere—but not unhappy—bystander. During this period he read widely and passionately in philosophy, science, and literature, as we learn from the autobiographical poem "Le Verger de Mme la Baronne de Warens," written in 1738. He acquired an immense, if often confused, fund of knowledge in many fields. And—contrary to his own statements—he wrote and composed, being ambitious for fame long before his inspiration for the First Discourse in 1749.

In April 1740, Rousseau became tutor, for a year, to the sons of M. de Mably in Lyon. In 1741-42 he was engaged on a project of a new (numerical) system of musical notation, which he presented to the Académie des Sciences in Paris in August 1742, but without much response. In this period he met, among many prominent people, Diderot, Buffon, Voltaire, Marivaux, Fontenelle, and the abbé de Saint-Pierre. He served for a year as secretary to the French ambassador in Venice, then returned to Paris. Here, in 1745, he became intimate with a servant girl named Thérèse Levasseur, with whom he set up housekeeping in 1750. By Thérèse Rousseau had five children, all of whom—

because of their possible embarrassment to his ambitions—he sent to a foundling home. In Paris Rousseau had considerable financial difficulty, but he managed by working as a secretary and by copying music. He became acquainted with Mme d'Épinay and the Philosophes, including Grimm, who was to become his best friend. In 1749 he was asked by Diderot to write the articles on music and economics for the *Encyclopédie.* In October 1749, on the way to visit Diderot, who was in prison at Vincennes, Rousseau read an announcement of a prize essay-contest on the effect of the arts and sciences on morals. After a brief period of semi-mystical illumination, he decided to take the negative position. He won the contest with his *Discours sur les Sciences et les Arts* and became famous overnight. As has often been repeated, Diderot took credit for Rousseau's negative position on the effect of the arts and sciences, and the point has been much argued. It seems likely that Rousseau's stand "against civilization" came at least in part from his unfortunate experiences and disappointments in Parisian cultured society. These led him to the somewhat careless generalization that culture ruins morality. Because of his success and the literary controversy which followed the publication of his *Discours,* Rousseau had to live the part of an enemy of refinement. As his social popularity increased, the more boorish he became in clothes and manners.

In March 1753 his opera *Le Devin du Village* was presented at the Opéra with success. The previous autumn the same work had been presented to the court at Fontainebleau and would have earned Rousseau a royal pension had he not, because of his republican principles (or his fear, occasioned by his bladder trouble and his poor manners), pleaded ill health rather than appear before the king.

For the 1754 contest conducted by the Dijon Academy, Rousseau composed his *Discours sur l'Origine de l'Inégalité,* which, with its assertion that social inequality lacks any natural basis, was to be a sequel to the First Discourse. Rousseau's originality here consisted in studying primitive man not historically by seeing him in a time perspective, or geographically by observing him in backward areas of the world, but rather psychologically, seeing within each man the primitive hidden by layers of social veneer. Rousseau, it must be noted, never denied natural inequality in abilities, intelligence, etc., but was concerned to expose and denounce artificial inequality. His essay is in the main a diatribe against despotism and property. Primitive man, according to Rousseau, was neither good nor bad, but he had the advantages of fewer temptations to make him wicked. The *Discours* contains Rousseau's famous attack on private property as a principal source of inequality. The implied moral of the work is that only a revolutionary change in society can set things right.

After completing the Second Discourse, Rousseau went to Geneva, where he again became a Protestant and citizen of Geneva. After a brief return to Paris he decided to quit the metropolis for good, but instead of going to Geneva as he had planned, he settled at Montmorency, in "The Hermitage," a house provided by Mme d'Épinay. Here and at nearby Montlouis, where he moved in the winter of 1757-58, Rousseau worked on his epistolary novel *La Nouvelle Héloïse.* In 1757 he fell in love with Mme Sophie d'Houdetot, who had rented a cottage near the Hermitage. His statement in the *Confessions* that his love for Sophie was not the source of the passion depicted in *La Nouvelle Héloïse,* but merely fed fires which had long burned in him, should probably be believed. Rousseau was fully capable of profound passion toward creatures of his imagination.

La Nouvelle Héloïse is the story of a girl who, after a premarital lapse with her lover, is transfigured into a being of the highest virtue. The novel shows a great deal of Rousseau's preoccupation with natural beauty, though it was not until he wrote his *Dialogues* and *Les Rêveries* that he was to find the real communion with nature with which his name has become associated. The critics were hostile to Rousseau's novel, some because they were Philosophes, from whom Rousseau was now estranged, others because as orthodox men they were repelled by Rousseau's total disregard of traditional morality and religion. But the general public devoured the letters of the *Nouvelle Héloïse,* making it a best-seller from its publication in 1761 to the Revolution. Though derivative in form and style from Samuel Richardson's *Clarissa* and containing many traces of the romantic readings of Rousseau's youth, *La Nouvelle Héloïse* is an original and deeply felt creation. The portrayal of a great self-reformation in an atmosphere of freedom and equality embodies the essential features of the dream which inspired Rousseau's major writings.

In 1760 Rousseau began two of his major works, *Du Contrat Social* and *Émile,* both published in the spring of 1762. *Émile,* Rousseau's great treatise on education, is, for all its obvious recollections of Locke and Montaigne, the distinctive expression of Rousseau's philosophy. This philosophy states, among other things, that man's emotions are better guides to truth and action than his reason is, that the individual is not by nature bad, and that the religion which a man arrives at by nature—simple belief in God and immortality—is more important and more valid than the rituals by which it comes to be surrounded. Rousseau's emphasis on learning from nature and without constraint, which is of a piece with the totality of his writings, may also be seen as a revolt against the bookish schooling of the time and the rigid rearing of children. The immediate effect of *Émile* was to popularize maternal love, including breast-feeding of babies, to give physical education an honorable place in the schools, and to inject manual work into the curriculum side by side with book-learning. The educators of the next generation, especially Pestalozzi and Froebel, were to lean heavily on Rousseau.

Du Contrat Social is Rousseau's theoretical work on politics. Unlike the *Nouvelle Héloïse* and *Émile,* which effect reforms in a live social setting, improbable though this sometimes appears, the *Social Contract* is highly abstract and theoretical. In spite of statements in some of his other works, Rousseau believed government necessary, and he sought for means of making it beneficial to humanity. He did not advocate violent revolution to overturn existing institutions, relying rather on the power of education to instill feelings of freedom in all and thus to alter social arrangements.

In June 1762 *Émile* was condemned and burned by the Paris Parliament. The book was denounced with equal vehemence by Catholics and Protestants, especially on account of the deism visible in the section called "La Profession de Foi du Vicaire Savoyard." Rousseau, unable to keep out of the controversies stirred up by *Émile,* was forced to flee from one place to another. In 1764 he published his *Lettres Écrites de la Montagne,* which were promptly burned in Paris as well as in many Swiss towns. Finally, having been expelled from Berne, Rousseau accepted an offer from David Hume to go to England and landed there in January 1766. He was greatly honored in London, treated (in Lanson's words) as a sage and prophet at precisely the moment when madness was about to overtake him. Hume arranged a house for Rousseau, and here Rousseau wrote most of his *Confessions* during 1766 and 1767. The *Confessions,* in spite of many inaccuracies and diseased statements, remain the best basic source of information on Rousseau's physical and emotional life. During his sojourn in England Rousseau gradually came to believe that plots were being hatched against him, and he ended by quarreling with Hume and leaving England in May 1767. He wandered unhappily in France until the summer of 1770, when he returned to Paris, and resumed music copying and a fairly normal life. He finished the *Confessions,* wrote the dialogues *Rousseau Juge de Jean-Jacques* (1772-76), a mad work detailing, with a staggering wealth of imagination, the various plots against him, and the *Rêveries du Promeneur Solitaire* (after 1776), one of his finest books, containing many signs of madness but even more marks of great poetry. He died in Ermenonville, near Paris, probably of apoplexy, and was buried there.

In spite of his lack of a coherent system, Rousseau ranks as one of the most influential writers in all history. His greatest impact was due to his individualism and his preoccupation with nature. His voice was always raised for the people—against injustice and for freedom, against property and for equality. In spite of appearances, Rousseau never advocated a return to barbarism but tried only to impress some ideals on a corrupt society, a process which he considered possible if people could be brought to understand certain fundamentals of freedom, equality, and brotherhood. The impetuosity of his exhortations and tirades often sounded revolutionary, and after 1789 he was often so regarded. But many parts of Rousseau are conservative, especially in the *Social Contract.* And in religion he led, through Bernardin de Saint-Pierre, directly to Chateaubriand. His style, moreover, was adopted by both of these writers, and he was lavishly praised and much imitated by Byron and the romantics generally.

Rousseau's works were published in collected form as early as 1764 in French (Neuchâtel) and 1773-74 in English (London, 10 vols.). The first complete edition in French was that of Geneva, 1782-83, and there have been many since. Rousseau's correspondence was published by T. Dufour: *Correspondance Générale,* 1924-34, 20 vols., and a *Table Générale de la Correspondance de Jean-Jacques Rousseau* was put out by Plan and Gagnebin, Geneva, 1953.
Most of Rousseau's major works have been translated into English a number of times. *The Con-*

fessions were translated by Edmund Wilson (1923); the *Social Contract and Discourses,* by G. D. H. Cole (1913 and 1935) and an eighteenth century translation published by Charles Frankel (1947); *Émile,* by Barbara Foxley (1933); *The Reveries of a Solitary,* by John Gould Fletcher (1927). In 1955 an anonymous English translation of the *Confessions* of 1783 and 1790 was published, revised and edited by A. S. Glover. A Pocket Book edition, in L. G. Crocker's translation, was issued in 1957.

ABOUT: Babbitt, I. Rousseau and Romanticism; Broome, J. H. Rousseau, a Study of His Thought; Cassirer, E. The Question of Jean-Jacques Rousseau; Chapman, J. W. Rousseau—Totalitarian or Liberal?; Green, F. C. Jean-Jacques Rousseau; Groethuysen, B. Jean-Jacques Rousseau; Havens, G. R. The Age of Ideas; Hendel, C. W. J.-J. Rousseau, Moralist; Winwar, F. Rousseau, Conscience of an Era; Wright, E. H. The Meaning of Rousseau; Yale French Studies, no. 28 (1961-62). [In French—see studies by B. Bouvier, A. Chuquet, L. Ducros, E. Faguet, R. Hubert, P. Masson, A. Schinz.]

A. C. K.

*ROZANOV, VASILY VASILIEVICH (1856-1919), Russian philosopher, journalist, and critic, was born in Vetluga and spent his early years in the capital of that province. His family was lower middle class. He was educated at a *Gymnasium* and completed his higher education at Moscow University where he studied history. He spent several years as a teacher of history and geography in various provincial high schools, though he took little interest in teaching.

In 1880 he married Apollinaria Suslov, a woman who had been in her youth intimate with Dostoevsky for a short time—with disastrous effect on the personality of that writer. After three unhappy years she left him but refused to give him a divorce, a fact which much embittered Rozanov, especially as, some years later, he met and fell in love with another woman, Varvara Rudnev, whom he could never marry because Apollinaria would not free him.

Rozanov published his first book, *On Understanding,* in 1886. It was not a success, but its anti-positivist stand was noted by Nikolay Strakhov, the critic, who started a correspondence with the young author and tried to help him. In 1899 Rozanov finally managed to connect himself with *Novoye Vremya,* a conservative periodical. In 1890 he had written *The Legend of the Grand Inquisitor,* a study of Dostoevsky's *The Brothers Karamazov,* which, Mirsky remarks, profits in its analysis from Rozanov's connection with Apollinaria Suslov through whom certain personal information was presumably available concerning Dostoevsky.

* rŭ zä' nŏf

The book also includes critical material on Gogol which develops the thesis, hitherto not suggested, that Gogol was not a realist no matter how close to life some of his characterizations seem to be. This and other critical works helped him to build a reputation in St. Petersburg, but his writings did not fit into any current movement well enough to permit him to become a part of one. He was attacked by Evgeny Soloviev, the conservative critic, for his style, and by Nikolai Mikhailovsky, the *narodnick* (populist), for his views on Tolstoy.

As a permanent contributor to *Novoye Vremya* after 1899, he enjoyed an adequate and steady income which enabled him to turn his attention to the rankling problem of religion, especially as it affected marriage and the legitimacy of children. *The Family Problem in Russia* (2 vols.), containing his earlier writings on the subject, was published in 1903. Other writings include: *In the Realm of Riddle and Mystery* (2 vols., 1901), *In the Shade of Church Walls* (1906), *The Russian Church* (1906).

Although he was a conservative to the point of Slavophilism, he was emotionally attracted by the spirit of the 1905 Revolution and even wrote a book (*When the Authorities Were Away*) in praise of the revolutionaries. The depth of his political conviction, however, is revealed in the fact that he continued to write conservative articles in *Novoye Vremya* under his own name while he wrote more radical articles under a pseudonym ("V. Varvarin") in *Russkoye Slovo*.

Following the defeat of the 1905 Revolution he continued to write and to develop his peculiar style, which has been called untranslatable because of his attempts to capture the sounds and patterns of speech independent of grammatical convention.

The Bolshevik Revolution was at first acclaimed by him, but his enthusiasm soon turned to bitterness. Finding the political climate of St. Petersburg stifling, he retired to the Trinity Monastery near Moscow where he continued to write, but was no longer able to find a remunerative outlet for his work. As might be expected, those aspects of his work which have been commended by Russian scholars outside of the U.S.S.R.—his style and his literary criticism of Gogol and Dostoevsky—form the basis for his explicit rejection by Soviet scholars, who see in him a representative of the decadents and symbolists among turn-of-the-century literati.

S. S. Koteliansky translated his *Solitaria* (1927) and *Fallen Leaves* (1929).

ABOUT: Poggioli, R. The Phoenix and the Spider; Slavic and East European Journal, V (1961). [In Russian—see studies by M. G. Kurdyumov, M. Spasovsky.]

L. R. & H. H.

*RÜCKERT, (JOHANN MICHAEL) FRIEDRICH (May 16, 1788-January 31, 1866), German poet and orientalist, was born at Schweinfurt am Main, the son of a lawyer. He studied law at the University of Würzburg before transferring to philology, which he continued at the universities of Heidelberg, Göttingen, and Jena. After receiving his degree he taught as a *Gymnasium* professor in Hanau and in Würzburg. From 1815 to 1817 he edited the *Cotta Morgenblatt* in Stuttgart, and during this period became closely acquainted with the writers Jean Paul, Fouqué, Schwab, and Uhland. Following a trip to Rome in 1817, he traveled to Vienna where he studied Arabic, Persian, and Turkish under Joseph von Hammer-Purgstall, the foremost orientalist of this period. In 1819 Rückert married Luise Wiethaus-Fischer, and the couple settled in Koburg. From 1821 to 1825 he served as editor for Fouqué's journal *Frauentaschenbuch*. In 1826 he was appointed professor of Oriental languages at the University of Erlangen, where he taught and influenced the poet Platen. In 1841 he was called to the University of Berlin by Friederick William IV. Rückert was never happy in Berlin and in 1848 retired to his estate near Koburg, where he died.

Rückert wrote verses for over fifty years and is one of the most prolific poets in German literature. He regarded everything as suitable for poetic treatment and produced masterpieces of lyric along with numerous insignificant trifles. He was a virtuoso of form and language and frequently neglected content for form. Only a few of his lyrics are genuinely vital, and he has never become a popular poet.

His first literary attempt was the volume *Fünf Märlein* (1813), a collection of poems for children. During the war of 1812-13 he produced under the pseudonym "Freimund Raimar" a collection of revolutionary poems entitled *Geharnischte Sonetten* (1814). The volume *Liebesfrühling* (1821) contains a series of love poems to his wife. One of his most heart-felt books was *Kindertotenlieder,* in which the poet memorialized

* rük′ ĕrt

his two children who died in 1833. Five of these poems were later set to music by Gustav Mahler. Rückert's most ambitious work was the long didactic poem *Die Weisheit des Brahmanen* (1836-39). In this work, which contains approximately 3,000 aphorisms written in rhymed alexandrines, the poet expressed the essence of his life's experience.

Rückert performed a notable service by introducing Oriental life and poetry to Germany. He was the first German poet to make extensive use of Eastern metrical forms. He owes his reputation in large part to his many outstanding translations, which include the Sanskrit *Nal und Damajanti* (1828), the Chinese *Schi-King* (1833), the Persian *Rostem und Suhrab* (1838), and a collection of the oldest Arabian folk songs, *Hamasa* (1846).

Die Weisheit des Brahmanen was translated into English in 1882 by C. T. Brooks under the title *The Wisdom of the Brahmin*. Subsequent translations include those of W. Hastie (1898) and E. M. Martin (1910). Selections of Rückert's lyrics are contained in N. L. Frothingham, *Metrical Pieces* (1855), A. W. Rounseville, *The Poetry of the East* (1856), E. Heath, *Songs and Poems from the German* (1881), and the Warner Library.

ABOUT: [In German—see studies by K. Beyer, K. Kühner, L. Magon, H. Meiser, H. Prang.]

D. G. D.

RUDEL, JAUFRÉ. See JAUFRÉ RUDEL

RUDOLF VON EMS (fl. 1230-1250), Swiss poet, belonged to the service nobility (*ministeriales*) and was a dependent of the Lords of Montfort at Hohenems, near Lake Constance. His works show that he must have been a well-educated man. He died on a journey to Italy between 1250 and 1254. Otherwise little is known about his life. He was a most prolific poet, his five works totaling more than 94,000 lines. All his extant work is serious and didactic. These works, in the usually accepted chronological order, are: *Der Gute Gerhard* (ed. Haupt, 1840); *Barlaam und Josaphat* (ed. Pfeiffer, 1843); *Alexander* (ed. Junk, 1928-29); *Willehalm* (ed. Junk, 1905); *Weltkronik* (ed. Ehrismann, 1915).

The first work, written about 1225, is the story of a rebuke administered to the overproud Emperor Otto by showing him real goodness in the person of Gerhard, a merchant of Cologne. The story of Barlaam and Josaphat is a Christianized version of the story of the Buddha, in which Josaphat (the

Buddha) is converted to Christianity by the ascetic Barlaam and in turn converts the harsh king his father. Rudolf uses a Latin translation of the Greek version of the story as his source. He also gives his sources for his version of the very popular and largely fantastic version of the story of Alexander—Archpresbyter Leo, Curtius Rufus, Josephus, and Methodus. His Alexander is an ideal secular hero with medieval attributes. Only five and one half books out of twelve projected were completed. Rudolf's *Willehalm* tells the story of the childhood love of William of Orléans and Amélie, how they were parted and found each other again. The main purpose of the story is to give a picture of an ideal court and prince. Although the *Weltkronik* is 33,000 lines long, it carries the story of the world only to the death of Solomon and is virtually a rhymed Bible. The number of extant manuscripts testifies to the great popularity of Rudolf in his own day, but his influence on contemporaries and later writers was slight. All his work testifies to a deep piety and a strong feeling that he should use his literary gifts for moral edification.

ABOUT: [In German—De Boor, H. and R. Newald, Geschichte der Deutschen Literatur, II; Ehrismann, G. Studien über Rudolf von Ems; Stammler, W. Verfasserlexikon des Deutschen Mittelalters.]

W. T. H. J.

*RUIZ, JUAN, Arcipreste de Hita (1283?-1350?), Spanish poet, is the most joyful and genial poet, as well as one of the greatest poets, of *mester de clerecía* tradition of medieval Spain. Considered an equal of Chaucer, he is one of the most varied and interesting writers of that time. The little we know of his life is derived for the most part from his own work. He was born probably in Alcalá de Henares, near Madrid; he lived at times in Guadalajara and Toledo and became Archpriest of Hita, a village north of Guadalajara. He was genial and a clever performer on all types of instruments, writing verses for singing and reciting by the *juglares*. By order of the Archbishop of Toledo, the Cardinal D. Gil de Albornez, Juan Ruiz was held prisoner for thirteen years.

Ruiz finished his only work, *El Libro de Buen Amor*, about 1330, according to the Toledo manuscript, or in 1343, according to the Salamanca version, the latter version having a revised beginning and ending written while he was in prison. Nothing is

* rōō ēth'

known of his death except that by 1351 a Pedro Fernández had become Archpriest of Hita.

The subject of Juan Ruiz' book is love; however, its loose structure permitted him to satirize medieval life and manners keenly and incomparably. A book of *cantares, The Book of Love* has borne many titles and is an illogical amalgamation of diverse satiric compositions and fables, the outstanding ones of which are the narrative poems written in couplets of *cuaderna vía*, a fourteen syllable line with middle caesura and the same rhyme.

Beginning with a prayer in verse and a sermon in prose, Juan Ruiz states his aim to teach versification and to forewarn against foolish love, using his own unfortunate experiences as moralizing examples. Those examples of vices and virtues are often those of real or allegorical persons other than the Archpriest.

The love intrigue of the protagonists Don Melón de la Huerta (or the Archpriest) and Doña Endrina fills 3,244 lines. In love with one after another the hero goes sometimes humorously, sometimes seriously, from misfortune to misfortune. When Don Amor appears, the poet blames him for all mortal sins, but Don Amor begs him not to be enraged and advises him how to be successful in his adventures. The poet hears new lessons from Doña Venus and continues his escapades into which enters the immediate episode of Don Melón and Doña Endrina, a paraphrase of a Latin comedy of *Pamphilus.* Here appears the remarkable Doña Urraca, called Trotaconventos, an intriguing and immoral old woman, descendant of Ovid's Dypsas and predecessor of Celestina, from whom the hero seeks further advice. After another unhappy love affair, the Archpriest goes to the mountains of Segovia, meeting there various *serranas* and *vaqueras* and composing there exquisite *serranillas* and *cantares.*

Returning to his religious devotion and showing the importance of spiritual love over carnal love, he addresses to the Virgin prayers which he interrupts to relate, with the typical savory detail of his times, the combat of Don Carnal and Doña Cuaresma, the general theme of which was taken from the French *fabliau The Battle of Karesme and of Charnage.* Cuaresma is vanquished; Don Carnal and Don Amor solemnly enter Toledo to be received by "all men, birds, and noble flowers." The protagonist renews his adventures until the death of his confidante Trotaconventos. The work ends with a

heterogeneous collection of discourses on weapons against the flesh, praise of little women, a portrait of his page Don Furón, and a song of praise to the Virgin Mary, further demonstrating Ruiz' ability in all poetic forms.

Well read in medieval works, Juan Ruiz used these sources readily, keeping his style fluid, frank, and individual; his vivacious autobiographical flair renders the book unique.

The Book of Good Love has been translated into English by Elisha K. Kane (1933).

ABOUT: Brenan, G. The Literature of the Spanish People; Lida de Malkiel, M. R. Two Spanish Masterpieces: The Book of Good Love and The Celestina; Hispania, XXXVIII (1955); Modern Language Notes, LXXV (1960). [In Spanish—Menéndez y Pelayo, M. Antología de Poetas Líricos Castellanos, III; studies by A. Doddis Miranda & Germán Sepúlveda Durán, also by J. Puyol y Alonso.]

R. P. C.

*RUIZ DE ALARCÓN Y MENDOZA, JUAN (1581?-1639), dramatist of the Spanish classical period, was born in Taxco, Mexico. His father was a superintendent of mines in Mexico and the son studied at the University of Mexico, later continuing his studies at the University of Salamanca in Spain. Almost nothing else is known of his early years.

After receiving his bachelor's degree at Salamanca, he established himself as a professional lawyer in Seville in 1606. Two years later he returned to Mexico to continue his studies. He had hoped to teach, but, rejected because of his deformity (hunchback), he left Mexico forever. When he returned to Spain in 1613, he began his short but brilliant literary career. In 1628 he was appointed reporter to the Royal Council of the Indies. He died in Madrid.

As a writer, he was subjected to merciless satires by his rivals who cruelly dwelt on the fact that he was bow-legged, a hunchback, and a frustrated lover. At the time of his death, one of his rivals, Pellicer, wrote: "The famous poet D. Juan de Alarcón died of his plays and of his hump."

If his output is compared with that of Lope de Vega (some two thousand works for the theatre), Juan Ruiz does not seem a prolific writer; he wrote twenty-three dramas, and collaborated with Tirso de Molina in a few others. There has been much discussion concerning the influence of his

* rōō ĕth' thä ä lär kôn' ē män dō thä

RUIZ DE ALARCÓN Y MENDOZA

RUIZ DE ALARCÓN

Mexican background on his dramatic technique, although few of his plays mention his homeland.

Unlike many other writers of his time, Juan Ruiz is alleged to have had a great influence on the European literature of his time. His carefully written plays, his discrimination and subtlety, and his high sense of morality seem to have appealed to the great French tragedian Corneille and to the Italian Goldoni, in the following century.

Alarcón's method was to introduce into a play a character type, developing through that character a moral thesis. And that is exactly what Corneille did in *Le Menteur* (The Liar); many authorities have acknowledged this to be an almost free translation of Alarcón's great thesis drama, *La Verdad Sospechosa* (The Suspicious Truth). The Spanish work puts the contemptible vice of lying into moral focus. The protagonist, Don García, is a young aristocrat who has become master of the lie. His imbroglios and extravagant stories provide the excitement of the play, but Alarcón's moral is gleaned from seeing how a first lie necessitates numerous others, and leads to the liar's undoing—all of which happens to Don García. Since Molière, who in turn was influenced by Corneille, gives ample evidence of using the "character type" in his drama, it may be said that he was indirectly influenced by Juan Ruiz.

From the standpoint of seriousness of purpose, the greatest of all Spanish plays are *Las Paredes Oyen* (Walls Have Ears) and the aforementioned *La Verdad Sospechosa.* In *Las Paredes Oyen* the focus is set on another human vice—slander. Don Mendo and Don Juan are rival suitors for the hand of Doña Ana. The former, a rich and handsome courtier, speaks ill of everybody, while the latter, an unattractive man but a true gentleman, defends the victims of Don Mendo's evil tongue. All fares well for Mendo until Doña Ana, suspecting his loyalty, lays a trap for him. Hiding behind a screen, she and several others hear themselves maligned by Don Mendo and defended by Don Juan. When Mendo's subsequent proposals are rebuffed, he is repeatedly confounded by the statement that walls have ears. Another play that belongs in this group is *La Prueba de las Promesas* (The Proof of Promises); in this play the target of the author's anger is ingratitude. He engaged also in writing more usual types of drama; examples are to be found in such vigorous heroic dramas as *Los Pechos Privilegiados, El Tejedor de Segovia,* and *Ganar Amigos.*

Alarcón is one of the supreme moralists of the Spanish tradition. He was also the most modern of all his contemporaries. Menéndez y Pelayo describes him as "the classic writer of the romantic drama." Gerald Brenan says that "to all intent and purpose he is the writer of the new world!"

Although not a great poet like Lope de Vega, it was from a nobility of spirit that he established his theatre on the premise of human error: lying, slander, ingratitude. Alarcón always contrasts the punishment for the sinner with the rewards awaiting the virtuous. Conflict arises from one's own internal struggle rather than from an externally dictated moral code. In this respect he recalls the towering figure of Cervantes; but Juan Ruiz never achieves the kindly smile and imaginative splendor of the author of *Don Quixote.*

Ruiz de Alarcón's *Comedias Escogidas* (Selected Comedies) were published in Madrid, 2 vols., in 1867, and in Clásicos Castellanos, 1918. *La Verdad Sospechosa* was translated as **The Truth Suspected** and published in *Poet Lore* in 1927.

ABOUT: Kelly, J. F. Chapters on Spanish Literature; PMLA, LVII (1952). [In Spanish—see studies by A. V. Ebersole, P. Henríquez Ureña, A. Castro Leal, J. Jiménez Rueda, F. Rodríguez Marín. In French—Huszar, G. Pierre Corneille et le Théâtre Espagnol.]

L. S.

*RUNEBERG, JOHAN LUDVIG (February 5, 1804-May 6, 1877), Swedish-Finnish poet, was born in Jakobstad (Finnish: Pietarsaari), a little town in Finland by the Gulf of Bothnia. His parents were Lorenz Ulrik Runeberg, ship-owner and sea captain of a family of Swedish descent, and Anna Maria Malm, daughter of a merchant, both from Jakobstad. His father was a man of substantial means, but after he suffered a stroke in 1821 the family was reduced to poverty. Financial aid from relatives and friends of the family enabled Johan Ludvig to enter the University of Åbo (Finnish: Turku) in 1822, but the next year he had to take a position as a tutor in southwestern Finland. In 1826-27 he returned to Åbo and took his master's degree. Thereafter he tutored in the home of the archbishop of Finland, J. Tengström, in Pargas. Here he met the archbishop's gifted niece Fredrica Tengström, whom he married in 1831. In 1828 Runeberg moved to Helsingfors (Finnish: Helsinki), and two years later he was appointed *docent* in Latin at the university there. From 1832 to 1837 he was editor of the newspaper *Helsingfors Morgonblad* in which he published poems and short stories.

In 1830 and 1833 Runeberg published two volumes of *Dikter* (Poems) which contain the essential part of his lyrics. In the first collection is a cycle of small poems called "Idyll och Epigram," which introduced a completely new style in Swedish poetry, characterized by classical simplicity, concentration, realism, and intimacy, which Runeberg learned from Serbian folk songs. The poems are inspired by his love of Fredrica. *Dikter* of 1833 contains the poignant hymn to patriotic self-sacrifice, "Grafven i Perho" (The Grave at Perho). Runeberg's first hexameter epic was *Elgskyttarne* (The Moose Hunters. 1832), a bright realistic description of the life of the Finnish peasantry. The second was *Hanna* (1836), an idyllic picture of the life and people in a country parsonage.

In 1837 Runeberg moved to Borgå (Finnish: Porvoo), east of Helsingfors, where he stayed for the rest of his life and where he served as *lektor* in Latin (later Greek) at the local *Gymnasium*. At his summer residence outside Borgå he enjoyed a fresh outdoor life. His literary activity was remarkable. He continued to write, first, in hexameter, *Julqvällen* (Christmas Eve, 1841), a charmingly idyllic winter picture of an inland manorial estate, and the greatest of all his poems, in varying unrhymed meters, *Kung*

* rōō′ nē băr y′

Fjalar (King Fjalar, 1844), influenced by Greek tragedy and Ossian, but placed in Viking setting and describing how the hero's presumptuous arrogance against the gods is severely punished. In 1843 a third collection, *Dikter*, appeared.

In 1846 Runeberg began his celebrated work *Fänrik Ståls Sägner* (The Tales of Ensign Stål), published in two volumes, 1848 and 1860, which made him the national poet of Finland and, to a certain extent, Sweden, and greatly enhanced Finnish national feeling. In a series of songs, written in masterly controlled rhythms and meters, the cycle paints vivid battle-scenes from the Russian war against Sweden-Finland in 1808-09. The opening song, "Vårt Land" (Our Land), set to music by F. Pacius, became Finland's national anthem.

In the 1850's Runeberg devoted himself to writing church hymns, and in 1863 he published the verse tragedy *Konungarne på Salamis* (The Kings at Salamis), inspired by the ancient Greek masters. Two days after the publication of this work Runeberg had a stroke which confined him to bed for the rest of his life.

The first translation into English of Runeberg's poems was rendered by E. Magnússon and E. H. Palmer as *Lyrical Songs, Idylls and Epigrams* (1878). Eight poems translated into English were published in the Warner Library. In 1879 appeared a translation of *Nadeschda* by Marie A. Brown (new edition 1890). *Julqvällen* was translated by Mrs. E. Baker as *Christmas Eve* (1887). *King Fjalar* appeared in 1904 in translation by B. E. Estlander, in 1912 by E. Magnússon. Some poems are to be found in F. Winkel Horn's *History of the Literature of the Scandinavian North.* The first complete translation into English verse of *Fänrik Ståls Sägner* was rendered by C. B. Shaw under the title *The Songs of Ensign Stål* (1925). In 1938 there appeared a translation by C. W. Stork, entitled *The Tales of Ensign Stål*, and in 1952 an edition translated by C. W. Stork, C. B. Shaw, and C. D. Broad.

ABOUT: Gosse, E. W. Northern Studies; Howitt, W. and M. The Literature and Romance of Northern Europe, II; Payne, W. M. Johan Ludvig Runeberg, *in* The Warner Library, XXXII; Winkel Horn, F. History of the Literature of the Scandinavian North.

A. J.

*RUTEBEUF (13th century), French poet, was a *trouvère-jongleur* whose literary activity dates from the 1250's until his death, c. 1285. Nothing is known of him except what appears in his fifty-six poems, particularly his appropriately titled *Poésies Personnelles*. Archives and official papers are totally uninformative. The poet's identifica-

* rüt bûf′

807

tion has led to much speculation, because the name "Rutebeuf" is probably a mere pseudonym and because conceivably more than one individual may have adopted it.

The poems themselves describe Rutebeuf as carefree and lazy, albeit living a life of unenviable poverty. He speaks of marriage in 1261 to an unattractive woman of fifty, in circumstances as straitened as his own. When not giving rein to his cynical mood, Rutebeuf insists on his respect for God and on his fear of divine wrath. He confesses eagerly to the vices of gaming and the tavern. It is not hard to suppose that some of this is more fancy than fact.

Rutebeuf is important as satirist and pamphleteer; he is also known for one commendable play, two saints' lives, a half-dozen *fabliaux*. The *Miracle de Théophile* is a brief adaptation of a Faustian theme; Saints Mary Egyptian and Elizabeth of Hungary fare unexceptionally at his hands; his *fabliaux* are typical representatives of the genre.

Rutebeuf attacked virtually every class of society, and he was a rabid enemy of numerous monastic orders, Dominicans especially. He defended vehemently the University of Paris and its exiled rector Guillaume de Saint-Amour in their struggle against the infiltrations of the mendicant orders. His *Renard le Bétourné*, a short diatribe against the self-seekers around Louis IX, reflects the cynical transformation which the earlier fox fables were undergoing after the twelfth century. Rutebeuf has long been regarded, perhaps too uncritically, as one of the most devoted propagandists for the crusade ideal: this subject colors in varying degree a dozen or more poem-pamphlets, inspired ostensibly after the Seventh Crusade (1248-54).

Often compared to Villon, Rutebeuf is among the first French poets who developed personal themes. His facility embraced various verse forms. Despite some linguistic evidences of provincial birth, his usage conformed to the literary style of Paris. He is, unfortunately, little known today except to medievalists, but is surely one of the most versatile and effective writers in thirteenth century France.

Rutebeuf's *Œuvres Complètes,* edited by E. Faral and J. Bastian, was published in two volumes in 1959.

ABOUT: Romance Philology, February, 1958; [In French—Bastian, J. and Faral, E. Onze Poèmes de Rutebeuf Concernant la Croisade; Clédat, L. Rutebeuf.]

E. V.

*RUUSBROEC (or RUYSBROECK), JAN VAN** (1293-December 2, 1381), surnamed "The Admirable," Dutch mystic and prose writer, was born in Ruusbroec, near Brussels. When he was eleven years old he went to Brussels where he lived with a relative, Jan Hinckaert, who took care of his first years of instruction. In 1317 Ruusbroec was ordained as a priest and became active as the chaplain of the St. Gudula church in Brussels. From this period dates his controversy with Bloemardinne, a woman with a mystical strain who exerted powerful influence on a circle of devotees, and whose ideas Ruusbroec opposed strongly. In 1367 he went with Vrank van Coudenberg and Jan Hinckaert to the forest of Soignies, a few miles from Brussels, where he established the abbey of Groenendaal of which he became the first prior. With the exception of the early *Van den Rike der Ghelieven,* Ruusbroec wrote all his works in Groenendaal. They belong to the best middle-Dutch prose that has come down to us. Most of them were primarily intended for the edification of conventuals. In these works Ruusbroec revealed himself as the equal of the greatest medieval mystics, from most of whom he differed in his speculative nature and experiential emphasis. After his death at Groenendaal, Jean Gerson, chancellor of the University of Paris, accused him of atheism and pantheism. He was ardently defended by one of his disciples, Jan van Schoonhoven.

The number of manuscripts attributed to Ruusbroec is enormous. He exerted great influence on the mysticism of the following centuries, in the Netherlands especially via Hendrik Herp, in Germany, France, Italy, and Spain via Surius' translations of his works into Latin. The veneration of Blessed John (*cultus immemorabilis*) was sanctioned in 1909 by Pope Pius X.

Ruusbroec's works were published in 1858 by J. David in behalf of the Maatschappij der Vlammsche Bibliophilen. The four volumes contain: *Dat Boec van den Gheesteleken Tabernacule, Van den Twaelf Dogheden, Die Spieghel der Ewiger Salicheit, Van den Kerstenen Ghelove, Van Seven Trappen. Van Seven Sloten, Van den Rike der Ghelieven,* and *Van den Vier Becoringhen.*

Aside from their value as mystical works, Ruusbroec's pamphlets and sermons are important sources of information concerning the

* rois' brōōk

Dutch language. They are characterized by suppleness of style and power of imagination. At times the author's taste for fantasy leads him to play on words.

Although Christian mysticism dominates Ruusbroec's works, his writings had a pragmatic intent as well, offering much practical advice to the conventuals of his day. Ruusbroec was one of the closest friends of Gerhard Groot, the Dutch mystic and leader of the Devotio Moderna, to whom some scholars ascribe the *Imitatio Christi,* usually thought to have been written by Thomas à Kempis.

Ruusbroec's complete works were translated into French by the Benedicts of Wisques (1912-36). English translations date from the fifteenth century. Some of these, *The Chastising of God's Children* and *The Treatise of the Perfection of the Sons of God,* were edited by J. Bazire and E. Colledge in 1957. Modern ones include *Reflections from the Mirror of a Mystic,* translated by E. Baillie (1905); *Flowers of a Mystic Garden* by C. E. S. (1912); a collection of works translated by C. A. Wynschenk Dom (1916); *The Kingdom of the Lovers of God* by T. A. Hyde (1919); and *The Spiritual Espousals* by E. Colledge (1952).

ABOUT: Maeterlinck, M. The Treasure of the Humble; Scully, V. H. A Medieval Mystic; Underhill, E. Ruysbroeck; Month, XXII (1959).

H. B.

*RYDBERG, (ABRAHAM) VIKTOR (December 18, 1828-September 21, 1895), Swedish poet, writer, scholar, was born in Jönköping, a town in southern Sweden. His father, a prison director, was Johan Frisk who had earlier (when a national guardsman) changed his name to Rydberg. His mother was Hedvig Düker, of an originally German family of surveyors. Her death in a cholera epidemic in 1834 broke the spirit of her husband who yielded to hypochondria and alcoholism, ruining the family's finances. The young Rydberg's school years were unhappy. He left school after the second year in the *Gymnasium* and started writing serial stories in a Jönköping newspaper, later in *Göteborgs Handels- och Sjöfartstidning.* He was now a champion of radical ideas. In 1851-52 he studied law at the University of Lund, but lack of money forced him to become a tutor. In 1855 he returned to the staff of the Gothenburg paper, now under the leadership of the humanist S. A. Hedlund.

Rydberg made his greatest contribution to Swedish literature as a writer of historical novels. In 1857 he published *Fribytaren på Östersjön* (The Freebooter of the Baltic) in

* rüd′ bär y′

RYDBERG

a seventeenth century setting, influenced by Sir Walter Scott and directed against the intolerance of the church and injustices of social authorities. His first mature masterpiece was *Singoalla,* (1857, revised edition 1865), a romantic story out of the Middle Ages, permeated with a poetic naturemysticism, about the tragic love between a knight and a gypsy girl. Rydberg's admiration for classical antiquity and his critical attitude to dogmatic Christendom are apparent in his novel *Den Siste Athenaren* (The Last Athenian, 1859), set in the time of transition from Platonic paganism to Christianity and advocating a philosophy founded on the noblest elements of both ideologies. In a religio-philosophical treatise, *Bibelns Lära om Kristus* (The Bible's Doctrines of Christ, 1862), Rydberg tried to prove that the Biblical texts offer no evidence of the divinity of Christ. As a result he became involved in a hot debate with the clergy which produced in him a deep emotional crisis and depression. He sought relief from his mental state by absorbing himself in translating Goethe's *Faust.*

In 1874 Rydberg made a long journey to Italy, where he pursued extensive studies in ancient Roman culture and wrote several essays, most of them available in *Romerska Dagar* (Roman Days, 1877). The journey strengthened Rydberg's creative power and he now produced some of the finest philosophical lyrics in Swedish literature, collected in *Dikter* (Poems, 1882).

809

In 1877 Rydberg was awarded honorary doctor's degrees by the universities of Uppsala and Lund; the next year he was elected to the Swedish Academy. His marriage to Susen Emilia Hasselblad took place in 1879. Five years later he accepted a call to a professorship in the history of culture at the University of Stockholm, in 1889 exchanged for a chair in art history and aesthetics. The result of his thorough research on mythology was published in *Undersökningar i Germanisk Mythologi* (Investigations into Germanic Mythology, 2 vols., 1886-89). A second volume *Nya Dikter* (New Poems) appeared in 1891. In his popular novel *Vapensmeden* (The Armorer, 1891), with motifs from the sixteenth century, Rydberg again attacked the dogmatic and intolerant attitudes of the church. He died at Djursholm at the age of sixty-six.

Den Siste Athenaren appeared in 1869 in English translation as *The Last Athenian* by W. W. Thomas, Jr. (new edition 1879) and *Fribytaren på Östersjön* in 1891 as *The Freebooter of the Baltic* by Cardine L. Broomall. *Singoalla* was translated by Axel Josephson (1903) and J. Fredbärj (1904). *Romerska Dagar* was published as *Roman Days*, translated by A. C. Clark (1879), and *Romerska Sägner om Apostlarne Paulus och Petrus* as *Roman Legends About the Apostles Paul and Peter*, translated by Baroness Ottilia von Düben (1898) and as *Roman Legends of the Apostles St. Paul and St. Peter*, translated by J. Fredbärj (1911). Some of Rydberg's poems in English translation by F. A. Judd are included in his *Under the Swedish Colours*, others by E. W. Nelson in *Poet Lore*, XXVII, by C. W. Stork in his *Anthology of Swedish Lyrics* (1917, 1930, partly reprinted in *Schelling Anniversary Papers*, edited by A. C. Baugh, 1923). Of Rydberg's scholarly production the following exist in English translation: *Medeltidens Magi* as *The Magic of the Middle Ages* by A. H. Edgren (1879); *Undersökningar i Germanisk Mythologi* as *Teutonic Mythology* by R. B. Anderson (1889; new editions 1891 and 1906).

ABOUT: Linden, H. A. W. [A Sketch of Rydberg] *in* A. C. Clark's translations of Roman Days; Stork, C. W. The Poetry of Victor Rydberg (*in* Schelling Anniversary Papers). [In Swedish—see studies by F. Elg, A. Forsström, K. Hagberg, T. Hegerfors, P. Holm, Ö. Lindberger, L. Lund, K. Warburg.]

A. J.

RYER, PIERRE DU. See DU RYER, PIERRE

*RZEWUSKI, HENRYK, Count (pseudonym "J. Bejła") (May 3, 1791-February 28, 1866), Polish novelist, came of a rich aristocratic family. Son of Adam Wawrzyniec, poet and orator, he received an excellent

* zhě vōō′ skē

education at home. He attended schools in St. Petersburg and Cracow and took part in the military campaign of 1809, but soon left the army. During his three-year stay in Paris he studied law, philosophy, and literature. He accompanied Adam Mickiewicz to the Crimea. Married in 1827 to Julia Grocholska he visited St. Petersburg and later Rome. Here again he met Mickiewicz who enjoyed his conversation and advised him to publish his anecdotes as short stories. From 1832 Rzewuski stayed mostly in his native country. His *Pamiatki Soplicy* (Soplica's Memoirs), published in Paris in 1839, was warmly received. The book consisted of a number of short stories supposedly told by an elderly gentleman recollecting his youth and various adventures in the reign of the last king of Poland. The style and the language were perfectly matched with the naïveté of the narrator.

Rzewuski associated himself with reactionary trends and with Pan-Slavism. In *Mieszaniny Obyczajowe* (Moral Medley, 1841-43) he violently attacked progressive ideas and glorified past traditions. This book provoked strong criticism. Rzewuski's outstanding historical novel *Listopad* (1845), set in the eighteenth century, again defended traditional customs and habits and blamed the influence of the Enlightenment for the moral disintegration of the Polish community. Rzewuski was involved in some luckless financial enterprises. For some time he cooperated with Russian authorities as the government official for special commissions. He published several other historical novels: *Zamek Krakowski* (The Castle of Cracow, 1847-48), *Adam Smigielski* (1851), *Rycerz Lizdejko* (1852), *Zaporozec* (The Ukrainian, 1854). He founded a Warsaw daily devoted to politics and literature which had a temporary success. He also wrote essays, satirical sketches, and polemical tracts. He was famous for his wit. The last years of his life he spent mostly at his estate Cudnów, where he died.

The novels of Rzewuski were reprinted several times. His memoirs were published in *Dziennik Warszawski*. *Listopad* was translated into English as *November* in 1857.

ABOUT: Kridl, M. An Anthology of Polish Literature; Krzyzanowski, J. Polish Romantic Literature. [In Polish—see studies by Z. Szweykowski, S. Tarnowski. In German—Zeitschrift für Slavische Philologie, XXIX (1961).]

M. G.

*SÁ DE MIRANDA, FRANCISCO DE
(August 28, 1481-1558), Portuguese poet and
playwright, was born in Coimbra, the illegitimate son of a cathedral canon, Gonçalo
Mendes de Sá, and Inés de Melo. He spent
his boyhood in Coimbra, then went to Lisbon,
where he studied and then taught law, after
receiving a doctor's degree. With a good
knowledge of ancient literature, he began
writing as a poet at the court of King Manuel
I, using the metric forms of medieval Portugal and Spain. Some of these works appeared
in Resende's *Cancioneiro Geral* of 1516.

His father's death in 1520 permitted him to
go to Italy in 1521; there for five years he
absorbed as much as he could of the Renaissance, meeting Bembo, Sannazaro, Ariosto,
and other poets through a distant cousin, the
famous Vittoria Colonna. Returning to
Portugal by way of Spain in 1526, he may
well have met Garcilaso and Boscán, who
were then experimenting with the use of
Italian meters in Spanish. He may also have
seen then the lovely Isabel Freyre, a Portuguese lady of the Castilian court, to whom
he later dedicated his eclogue *Célia*.

Returning to Coimbra, where he had the
patronage of King John III and the use of
his father's property, he produced in that city
his first classical comedy in prose, *Os Estrangeiros*. With his *Fábula do Mondego*
(1528 or 1529), in Petrarchan stanzas, and
his first sonnets, it was clear that he intended
to bring to Portugal the poetry of the Renaissance. We may take for granted a cultural, if
not a personal, clash between Sá de Miranda's
new aristocratic genres, imported from Italy,
and the popular medieval traditions which
were still being raised to new heights by Gil
Vicente.

In contrast to the comic spirit of the goldsmith Vicente stands the severe moral attitude
of Dr. Francisco de Sá, which seems to have
made him enemies among the powerful at the
court. About 1530 he married Briolanja de
Azevedo and withdrew to his royal grant, the
Comenda das Duas Igrejas, in the province of
Minho. There he spent the rest of his life,
raising a family and writing or revising his
poetry in rustic seclusion.

Sá de Miranda's sonnets treat not of love,
but of moral disillusion *(desengaño)*, the
vanity of all things. His eclogues, written in
Spanish, seem to be chiefly metrical exercises
on commonplace pastoral themes, but at times
give classical expression to an apparently
genuine love of country life. More memorable are his verse letters although only two of

* sä′ thē mē răn′ dà

SÁ DE MIRANDA

them are written in *terza rima* instead of the
traditional *quintilhas*. In them we see his independence of character and strong social
conscience, as well as many details of his
private life and personality. The principal
importance of his writings in verse is, however, historical: he introduced into Portuguese the Italian iambic hendecasyllable and
the stanzaic forms associated with it, that is,
the sonnet, the *canzone, terza rima,* and
ottava rima. These forms, in the hands of
Camões, were destined to yield the greatest
poetry of Portugal.

In prose, Sá de Miranda's two comedies
Estrangeiros and *Vilhalpandos* are based on
the classical models of Greece and Rome;
their careful construction, anticipating the
rules of the neo-Aristotelian and Horatian
preceptors, marks a decisive break with the
medieval farce. In plots, characters, and
social background, these comedies draw upon
antiquity, giving aesthetic distance and elevation. The loss of his tragedy *Cleopatra* has
been much lamented.

In 1553 Sá de Miranda's oldest son died at
the hands of Moslems in Ceuta. His wife
died two years later. In 1558 at the age of
seventy-seven he died on his farm, the Quinta
da Tapada, where he had been living since
1552.

Selections from his works in English may be
read in Bowring's *Ancient Poetry and Romances
of Spain* (1824).

ABOUT: [In Portuguese—Corneiro, D. Sá de
Miranda e Sue Obra.]

E. L. R.

*SAAR, FERDINAND VON (September 30, 1833-July 24, 1906), Austrian short-story writer, poet, and dramatist, was born in Vienna. His parents, Ludwig and Karoline von Saar, came from recently ennobled families of government officials, although his father had left government service for a career in business. Five months after Saar's birth, his father died, and the boy was raised in the home of his grandfather, Privy Councilor von Nespern. He attended a Benedictine school, and at the age of sixteen was encouraged to enter the army, despite his lack of inclination for this career. He took part in the Italian campaigns and saw service in many of the far-flung outposts of the monarchy. Idly he began to write verses, and although his early attempts at poetry and drama met with no success, he left the army in 1860 determined on a career as an author. His writings earned him little fame or money, and in 1867 he was forced to flee Vienna to avoid arrest for debt. For most of his remaining life he was dependent in some measure on the generosity and hospitality of wealthy friends and patrons. He led a wandering existence from one country estate to another, broken only by a trip to Italy (1873) and occasional stays in Vienna. In 1881 he married Melanie Lederer, but even this happiness was cut short by her sudden death three years later. His reputation grew slowly but steadily. His sixtieth birthday brought him wide acclaim, and he was distinguished by honorary membership in the Austrian Upper House. This tardy recognition could not overcome his basic unhappiness and melancholia. In 1906, ill with an incurable disease, he committed suicide.

Although Saar experienced the revival of Austrian literature during the 1890's, and was esteemed as a forerunner by such writers as Arthur Schnitzler and Hermann Bahr, he felt no desire to make the transition to the modern age. He preferred the past to the present, and Old Austria provided the themes, settings, and atmosphere of his prose and poetry. His finest short stories, collected as *Novellen aus Österreich* (1877, 1897), reveal him as an extraordinarily perceptive and vivid chronicler of the circles he knew from personal experience—military life, country life, and life in Vienna. His leisurely, first-person narrative technique appears old-fashioned today, but his realistic prose style, lavish with detail and finely

wrought descriptions, retains its unique power and beauty.

Saar, who was influenced by Turgenev and Schopenhauer, preferred characters bested by life, generally for uncontrollable reasons, such as hereditary factors. His characters are usually passive and resigned, and, as in the writings of Theodor Storm, misfortune overtakes them because they fail to act or to reveal their true feelings. Similarly, as in Storm, unrecognized or unrequited love is a frequent theme. The atmosphere throughout is one of melancholy and unfulfilled yearning.

The same elegiac note is sounded in his poetry. He connects dream and observation, reflection and melancholy, longing for the past and love of country. His *Wiener Elegien* (1892), revealing the depth of his love for his native city, and *Die Pincelliade* (1897), a burlesque epic of barracks life, once very popular, are now little read.

Although his gifts were primarily lyrical and descriptive, Saar persisted unsuccessfully in writing tragic drama, which he considered the highest form of art. The peasant tragedy *Eine Wohltat* (1861), and the historical play *Die Beiden DeWitt* (1875), were performed briefly in the Burgtheater. His greatest historical tragedy, *Heinrich IV* (1, 1864; II, 1867), depicting the conflict between the German emperor and Pope Gregory VII, has never been performed.

Saar is undeservedly neglected today. His short stories still retain their artistic significance in addition to being valuable cultural documents of nineteenth century Austria.

One short story, "Die Steinbrecher" (1873), sometimes referred to as the first tale of the working man and his milieu in German literature, has been translated by A. M. Reiner as "The Stonebreakers" (1907). A selection of his verse is contained in Mary Münsterberg, *A Harvest of German Verse* (1906), and in *The German Classics of the 19th and 20th Centuries*, edited by K. Francke and W. G. Howard (1913-15).

ABOUT: Journal of English and Germanic Philology, July 1925; German Life and Letters, January 1951. [In German—see studies by A. Bettelheim, M. Lukas, J. Minor.]

D. G. D.

*SAAVEDRA Y RAMÍREZ DE BAQUEDANO, ÁNGEL, Duque de RIVAS (March 10, 1791-June 22, 1865), Spanish poet and dramatist was born in Córdoba. Saavedra may be called the outstanding figure of Spanish romanticism, and his life is one of

* zär

* sä ä vä′ thrä ē rä mē′ räth thä bä kä thä′ nō

the most colorful of nineteenth century Spain. The second son of the Duke of Rivas, he spent his childhood in Córdoba. After his father's death he entered the Seminary for Noblemen in Madrid where he remained until 1806, when he started his military career. Young Saavedra proved his heroism repeatedly and was seriously wounded in the War of Independence (1808-14). In 1812 he made a dramatic escape to Cádiz, center of the liberal movement. Here he made friends with a distinguished group of writers and poets including Martínez de la Rosa and Quintana. His personality had two facets: military and political on one hand, literary and artistic on the other. In 1814 he published his first collection of poetry and was made a colonel in the army.

Saavedra's early poetry reflects the neoclassic influence on his education; this influence disappeared as his life was enriched by personal experiences and his liberalism deepened. During the short constitutional period (1820-23) he represented Córdoba in the House of Representatives. In these years he met a person who greatly influenced his life, the statesman and writer Alcalá Galiano. After the brief liberal interlude Saavedra had to flee to avoid a death sentence pronounced in 1824. Following many of his liberal friends, he went to England but returned to Gibraltar to marry Doña Encarnación de Cueto, sister of the Marquis of Valmar (1824). A long and difficult exile took him subsequently to Italy and to the island of Malta where he lived for five years. There Saavedra became acquainted with the English diplomat and writer Sir John Hookham Frere, ex-ambassador of his country to Spain and translator of the *Poema del Cid*. Sir John was a connoisseur of Spanish medieval and classical literature, and it was he who introduced the Spaniard to his own heritage, ignored by his neoclassic and French education. The Englishman also put him in touch with the new trends in European literature. From 1829 on, Saavedra composed a series of poems which were full of this new spirit, among them *El Faro de Malta* and *El Moro Expósito*. The latter poem was inspired by an early medieval Spanish poem; it was published in Paris in 1834 and dedicated to Sir J. H. Frere. His exiled friend Alcalá Galiano wrote a prologue for it which is considered the manifesto of Spanish romanticism. In France, Saavedra, in addition to writing and painting, took an active part in the political intrigues of the Spanish liberal refugees.

In Tours, in 1834, the crucial year of his literary and political life, he wrote the first version, in prose, of his famous drama *Don Álvaro o la Fuerza del Sino*, which Alcalá Galiano translated into French. The deaths of his brother the Duke, and of King Ferdinand VII brought him back to Spain that same year. He inherited the title of Duque de Rivas along with a considerable fortune and a prominent political and social position. On March 22, 1835, the Duke became the principal figure of the new literary movement, with the tremendous success of the première of his masterpiece *Don Álvaro* at Madrid's Príncipe Theatre. The initial version written in France was transformed and enriched by brilliant poetry, and the opening of the play marked the official inauguration of romanticism on the Spanish stage, as did *Hernani* in France. *Don Álvaro* was the basis for the libretto (written by Piave) of Verdi's *La Forza del Destino* (1862). With age, success, and security, Saavedra's ideas became more conservative, a trend visible also in Martínez de la Rosa and other colleagues. He belonged to the Moderate Party that, although constitutionalist, was too conservative for the new radical government. He was forced to go to Lisbon in 1836. There he started his magnificent collection of *Romances Históricos*, published in 1841 with an interesting prologue of his own. This collection is considered the foremost example of Spanish romantic poetry. Color, light, and elegance characterize this series of historical vignettes. The Duke returned to Spain and lived happily in the artistic atmosphere of Seville for six years until he was called back to political life. He served as ambassador to Naples, Prime Minister (1854), and ambassador to France (1856-59). He died in 1865, while President of the Real Academia de la Lengua.

Saavedra, painter, writer, politician, military man, reflected in his life and work the trends of Spain during his time. His passionate and generous temperament prevailed over his neoclassic and aristocratic education as is clearly seen in his two major works, *Don Álvaro* and *Romances Históricos*. Saavedra nationalized European romanticism, enriching it with elements of his vital native tradition; prose and verse, the tragic and the comic appear interwoven throughout his writings. The *Romances*, full of fantasy, charm and mystery, mark the renaissance of the traditional Spanish ballad, almost abandoned during the eighteenth century. The ballads are dramatic sketches, sometimes in dialogue form, always strong in tone and full of vitality. Menéndez y Pelayo wrote that the Spanish romantic movement had two forms, "the national historical romanticism, headed by the Duke of Rivas and the subjective Byronian romanticism that many call philosophical, whose exponent was Espronceda."

A few of Saavedra's poems appear in English translation in J. G. Lockhart's *Ancient Spanish Ballads* (1823) and T. Walsh's *Hispanic Anthology* (1920).

ABOUT: The Athenaeum, A Literary Chronicle of Half a Century (1888); Clarke, H. B. Modern Spain; Hume, M. A. S. Modern Spain; Peers, E. A. Rivas and Romanticism in Spain, *also* A History of the Romantic Movement in Spain; Tarr, F. C. Romanticism in Spain and Spanish Romanticism. [In Spanish—"Azorin" (Martínez Ruiz), Rivas Y Larra.]

L. R. DE G. L.

*SACCHETTI, FRANCO (c. 1330-September 1, 1400), Italian poet and narrative writer, born in Florence, was the son of a merchant and perhaps himself engaged in this trade. His career in municipal services led him to extensive travel, and the esteem in which he was held is evident in many events. He was ambassador to Bologna in 1376, and received very exceptional pardon in 1380 when the rebels, including his own family, were banished. Captured at sea by the Pisans, he was ransomed in 1381, then went to Milan, perhaps as ambassador. He served as Prior in 1383 and later as Podestà in San Miniato and Faenza, but to judge by his writings he regretted his absence from Florence. He was married three times. His first short stories preceded his homecoming in 1397, at the moment at which his properties had been ruined. Compensated for this loss, he became Captain, and nothing further is known of his life.

Sacchetti's writings illustrate his upright moral attitudes toward public affairs, his respect for law and custom, and his devotion to just causes. These attitudes appear in his master work, the 300 *novelle*, of which 223 are extant. He seems to have had no comprehensive plan for an integrated book, though sequences appear at times, and certain stories open with allusions to persons or situations in preceding ones. He told his stories from memory rather than from written sources, and this fact gives them their quality as popular tales devoid of any search for artistic effects. For his time, Sacchetti had a keen sense of historical color, and enhanced

* säk kät′ tē

the realism by inclusion of stories involving Dante, Giotto, Cavalcanti, or his own friends such as Pucci, or real public figures such as popes and princes. For further enhancement of credibility, Sacchetti adds references on contemporary customs, dialects, and manners of speaking. The plots are anecdotal and brief, and deal with commonplace events, neither dramatic nor unusual.

One must not take Sacchetti's stories literally as fact, but rather as folklore, as presumably his readers understood them at the time. The direct allusions are calculated to increase the effectiveness of the humor and augment the diversion. The artistry appears in the variety of style, especially in conversation, and in the mastery of language, for instance in destruction of superficial logical argument by illustrating its fallacies and on a lower level of humor the constant exchange of witty remarks between the author himself and such persons as his friend Dolcibene. The tone of the stories varies between the two extremes of buffoonery and didacticism. In off-color manner, Sacchetti may depict heartless mockery of innocent victims for the mere sake of creating laughter. In contrast, though less frequently, he may strike moral tones of pessimism about the decay of contemporary customs, or show personal bias in anti-religious and anti-feminist moods.

Sacchetti's poetry—*Le Pastorelle Montanie*, the *Caccia* in conversational style, and the burlesque epic *La Battaglia*—is less important than his "novelle." Various works have been edited by Chiari, 1936, 1938.

The English translation of selected stories *(Tales from Sacchetti)*, made by M. Steegmann in 1908, is representative, and Rossetti rendered a Ballata and a Catch.

ABOUT: [In Italian—Francia, L. di. Franco Sacchetti Novelliere; Gigli, O. Le Novelle di Franco Sacchetti.]

F. J. C.

*SACHER-MASOCH, LEOPOLD VON (January 27, 1836-March 9, 1895), Austrian short-story writer, novelist, and dramatist, was born in Lemberg, the capital of Galicia, where his father served as chief of police. His mother, whose name, Masoch, his father added to his own, was the daughter of a prominent Ruthenian scholar. Sacher-Masoch studied at the universities of Prague and Graz, and in 1857, after completing a dissertation entitled *Der Aufstand in Ghent unter Kaiser Karl V*, became a *Privatdozent* in history at Graz. The success of his first

* zä′ к̆ер mä′ zōк

SACHER-MASOCH

in the writings of Turgenev, who greatly influenced Sacher-Masoch, plot is subordinated to character. The pessimistic *Weltanschauung* which predominates in Sacher-Masoch's works was derived principally from Schopenhauer.

Sacher-Masoch produced many volumes of *Novellen*, of which the most significant is the collection entitled *Das Vermächtnis Kains* (4 vols., 1874). In this work the author intended to create a cycle of stories treating each of the general topics love, property, the state, war, work, and death. However, he completed only the sections dealing with the first two categories. Additional important collections of *Novellen* include *Galizische Geschichten* (1876), *Judengeschichten* (1878), and *Polnische Judengeschichten* (1886). His later works, which were produced at a rapid rate simply to earn money, declined sharply in literary value. Increasingly he dissipated his talents in crass presentations of sensuality and perversion, and his writings passed from the realm of literature into that of the obscene. To denote the type of eroticism that occurs frequently in Sacher-Masoch's works, the psychiatrist Krafft-Ebing coined the term *masochism.*

Sacher-Masoch also produced many novels, which are inferior to his *Novellen*, as well as several unsuccessful plays. *Eine Schlittenfahrt* was translated by Zimmern as *The Sleigh-Ride* in 1880. H. L. Cohen translated *Der Neue Hiob* under the title *The New Job* (1891), *Jewish Tales* (1894), and *Thou Shalt Not Kill* (1907). In 1893 *Seraph, a Tale of Hungary* was translated by E. M. Phelps. An anonymous translation of *Russische Hofgeschichten* appeared in 1896 as *Venus and Adonis and Other Tales of the Court of Catherine II.* *The Bookbinder of Hort* was translated anonymously in 1898, as was *Venus and Adonis* in 1931. *Venus im Pelz* was translated by J. Brownell in 1931 as *Venus in Furs* and anonymously in 1947.

ABOUT: Cleugh, J. The Marquis and the Chevalier. [In German—see studies by E. Hasper, R. M. Meyer (A.D.B.), and W. von Sacher-Masoch.]

D. G. D.

literary attempt, *Eine Galizische Geschichte 1846* (1858), an historical novel based on the events of the recent Polish uprising, induced him to resign his teaching position for literature. With the exception of his participation in the Italian campaign in 1859, and a period of teaching at the University of Lemberg, he remained a writer. In 1873 he married Aurora Rümelin, a minor authoress, who wrote under the pen name "Wanda von Dunachew." Their marriage was unhappy, largely because of Sacher-Masoch's pathological erotic nature, and ended in divorce in 1886. During his later life Sacher-Masoch moved restlessly from place to place and turned increasingly to the field of journalism. He served as editor for the monthly review *Belletristische Blätter* in Budapest (1880), the journal *Auf der Höhe* in Leipzig (1882-85), and the newspaper *Neue Badische Landeszeitung* in Mannheim (1881-91). In 1890 he settled in Lindheim in Hesse, where he died in 1895.

Sacher-Masoch was strongly influenced by the area of his birth; by temperament he was more Slavic than German. He possessed a deep knowledge and understanding of his countrymen and excelled in the ethnological portrayal of the customs, manners, and traditions of his native Galicia. He was a genuinely gifted writer whose best narratives are characterized by a graceful style, detailed accuracy of milieu, and outstanding character delineation. The effect of social and environmental conditions on character plays an important part in his work, and as

*SACHS, HANS** (November 5, 1494-January 19, 1576), German poet and dramatist, was born in Nuremberg, the son of a tailor. After attending the Latin school, he was, in 1508, apprenticed to a shoemaker. His years of apprenticeship and traveling, the traditional medieval *Wanderjahre,* took him throughout Germany. Wherever he went, he never failed to visit the then flourishing *Singschulen.* In 1517 he established himself in Nuremberg as a master shoemaker and

* zäks

815

SACHS

there, on September 1, 1519, he married Kunigunde Creutzerin. In 1561, one year after the death of his first wife, he married Barbara Harscherin. He died in Nuremberg.

Hans Sachs is the most widely known representative of sixteenth century popular literature in Germany. A strong advocate of the Reformation, he gave support to that movement in four prose dialogues and in the poem *Die Wittembergisch Nachtigall*. Sachs' epithet for Luther, the nightingale whose rousing song awakened Germany, became immediately popular and was widely quoted. By 1567, according to his own account, Sachs had composed 4,275 *Meisterlieder*, 1,700 tales and fables in verse, and 208 dramas. Frequently Sachs treated the same subject in various genres.

Hans Sachs had been taught the *Meisterlied* by the linen-weaver Leonhard Nunnenpeck. Whereas the writing of songs had in former times been cultivated solely by knights and gentry, the singing and composing of a popular form of the *lied* had become the concern of the middle class artisans. The *Meisterlied*, developed by Rosenplüt, had been cast into a severe mold of rules from which Hans Sachs liberated it when he raised the form to its highest perfection. It dealt with classical, Biblical, and medieval subjects and was strongly influenced by the humanists.

The most endearing and lasting characteristics of Hans Sachs the dramatist are found in his Shrovetide plays. In approximately eighty-five pieces of this genre, the subjects,

themes, and characters of the medieval drolleries, pranks, and farces are employed with inimitable vividness and diversity. The form is loose, but the dialogue is witty. A sound sense of ethics and skillful use of broad, dramatic humor make these plays appealing and successful in stage presentations today. In Shrovetide plays like *Das Narrenschneiden, Der Schwangere Bauer, Das Heiss Eisen,* and *Der Fahrende Schüler im Paradeis* appear such prototypes as the shrew, the cunning peasant, the quack, the bragging soldier, and the gull, presented with genuine charm and striking realism. It is thought that Hans Sachs was himself one of the performers, a group of players recruited from the masters, journeymen, and apprentices of the various guilds. The plays were written in doggerel.

Hans Sachs, mostly neglected in the seventeenth and eighteenth centuries, was rescued by Goethe who drew attention to the poet in his *Hans Sachs Poetische Sendung* (1776). Richard Wagner commemorated and idealized the Nuremberg shoemaker in his opera *Die Meistersinger.*

His collected works were published in twenty-three volumes, 1870-1896. English translations include *Merry Tales and Shrovetide Plays* by W. Leighton (1910), *Seven Shrovetide Plays* by E. U. Ouless (1930), and *A Way with Surly Husbands* (a one-act play) by E. U. Ouless (1934).

ABOUT: Ellis, F. M. Hans Sachs Studies; French, W. Medieval Civilization as Illustrated by the Fastnachtspiele of Hans Sachs; Modern Language Review, LV (1960); German Life and Letters, XVI (1963). [In German—see studies by F. Eichler, E. Geiger, M. Hermann, G. Stuhlfanth, H. Wendler, S. Wernicke.]

E. J. S.

*SADE, DONATIEN ALPHONSE FRANÇOIS, Comte, called Marquis de (June 2, 1740-December 2, 1814), French man of letters, was born in Paris. His father was Jean Baptiste Joseph François, comte de Sade, lieutenant-general for several provinces, and ambassador to the elector of Cologne. His mother, Marie Eléonore de Maillé-Brézé de Carman, was related to the Princesse de Condé and was her maid of honor. At the age of five young Sade began his education at Saumane, under the tutelage of his uncle, abbé and author of a life of Petrarch. In 1750 he returned to Paris to continue his education with the Jesuit fathers at the Collège d'Harcourt and to take additional private tutoring with the abbé Amblet. The marquis entered the military school for light cavalry at the age of fourteen; a year

* sàd

later he was made a second lieutenant in the king's infantry. The Seven Years' War (1756-63) saw him made a captain (1759), the rank he held when he resigned at the conclusion of the war.

In May 1763, with the approval of the royal family, Sade married Renée Pélagie Cordier de Launay de Montreuil (1741-1810), though in love with her younger sister, Anne Prospère. Upon his marriage Sade paid an indemnity to his mistress, La Beauvoisin. November found him in jail at Vincennes for debauchery. This first incarceration lasted two weeks. The young marquis, slight in build, five feet two inches tall, and every inch the dandy, continued to lead a life of pleasure. In 1764 he succeeded his father in the latter's lieutenant-generalcies; upon his death in 1767 the son acquired the châteaux of La Coste, Mazan, and Saumane, as well as other properties. Still intimate with La Beauvoisin, he had invited her to La Coste and presented her as his wife; at the same time he was trying to persuade another dancer to become his mistress.

The birth of a son did not alter his interests. In 1768 Sade again was detained, first at his Saumur estate, then at Pierre-Encise, near Lyon. He had been accused by a prostitute, Rose Keller, of flagellation and abuse; she withdrew her complaint on payment of a large sum. In 1769 a second son was born, and a daughter two years later. Sade was residing at La Coste with his wife and sister-in-law, Anne Prospère, who had become a canoness. The famous case of the aphrodisiacs occurred at Marseille in 1772; Sade and his lackey were accused of sodomy, flagellation, and the use of cantharides. Condemned by the courts, he was burned in effigy, and incarcerated in the Miolans fortress. His mother managed his escape, almost five months later, and Sade, not yet pardoned, lived at La Coste. But the neighboring villages complained of seductions and kidnappings; a chambermaid at the castle gave birth to a daughter by the marquis. He found it prudent to travel in Italy, under the incognito of Comte de Mazan.

When he returned almost a year later, there were again various charges. In 1777, upon the death of his mother, his mother-in-law reactivated the Marseille accusation, and Sade was jailed at Vincennes. Almost a year and a half passed before the case was heard at Aix, which fined him and forbade his presence for three years. He escaped from his police escort and took refuge at La Coste, but his mother-in-law obtained a

lettre de cachet and had him re-imprisoned at Vincennes in September 1778. At first subjected to very harsh treatment, the following year he was permitted pen and paper. His wife was not allowed to visit him until mid-1781, and her presence upset him so much that she entered a convent to calm his jealous suspicions.

While at Vincennes Sade wrote the scathing, scatological "Lettre à Martin Quiros" and the anti-religious *Dialogue entre un Prêtre et un Moribond*. In 1784, five and a half years after entry there, he was transferred from Vincennes to the Bastille. In 1785, in a little over a month, he copied out *120 Journées de Sodome ou l'École du Libertinage*. The manuscript of this psychopathology of sex was a narrow roll of paper some sixty-five feet long, in a microscopic hand. He wrote with intensity, swiftly: the tales *Les Infortunes de la Vertu* (1787) required fifteen days, *Eugénie de Frauval* (1788) only a week. But increasingly affected by prison, he had hallucinations. After screaming from the window that the prisoners were being strangled, he was transferred to the Charenton asylum. He had been in the Bastille five and a half years.

The sacking of the Bastille in 1789 destroyed or dispersed his manuscripts which he had been unable to take to Charenton. Nine months later he was liberated, for the Constituent Assembly had abrogated *lettres de cachet*. His wife, however, refused to see him and secured a separation. After a brief affair with Mme Fleurieu, he took as his mistress Marie Constance Renelle, an actress who was separated from her husband; Sensible, as she was called, remained his mistress until the end of his life.

Sade was the friend of the author and actor Boutet de Monvel, who secured for Sade an audience with the Comédie Française, which unanimously accepted *Sophie et Desfrancs, ou le Misanthrope par Amour*. The following year the public acclaimed *Le Comte Oxtiern ou les Effets du Libertinage*, which he had written at the Bastille. But another play put on at the Comédie Italienne, *Le Suborneur* (1792), was hooted down by the Jacobite faction as the work of a former nobleman (*ci-devant*). Yet Sade had joined the Section des Piques in 1790, had been named to organize its cavalry, and was one of the three commissioners to inspect the state of Paris hospitals. In 1793 he became president of the Section, and was on the board of accusations. He used his position to protect his father-in-law and mother-in-law (who had been so severe to him); he aided an officer, accused of helping the nobles, to escape. Despite his important position—Sade had addressed the Convention—he was arrested for "moderatism," and incarcerated in various jails. Because of ill-health, he was transferred from Saint-Lazare prison to Picpus hospital and was not released until ten months after his arrest.

Sade had published *Justine ou les Malheurs de la Vertu* in 1791 and *La Philosophie dans le Boudoir,* "a posthumous work" (*sic*) in 1795. But practically destitute, he sold La Coste; *La Nouvelle Justine* (1797) did not ease his financial burdens. He was obliged to stay a while with a farmer-tenant, then to work for a Versailles vaudeville for a pittance; he acted in the revival of *Oxtiern.* But so poor and undernourished was he that he had to enter a hospital. He was kept under surveillance by Napoleon's police for having attacked him and Josephine in *Zoloé et ses Deux Acolytes* (Napoleon is the baron d'Orsec in this tale). The police ransacked his publisher's premises and seized Sade's manuscripts; he was arrested for writing *Justine,* "the most frightfully obscene work of its kind." Shut up at Sainte-Pélagie, Bicêtre (1801), and Charenton (1803), he was to remain at the latter for eleven years and eight months.

While at Charenton Sade organized theatrical performances. A ten-volume work, *Journées de Flortelle . . . ,* was burned by the police at the request of Sade's son Armand. The king eventually forbade the theatrical performances. Sade himself was protected by the director, who had become his friend, and Sensible, his mistress, was permitted to live with him. Sade died of a pulmonary condition, and despite the formal declarations in his testament, an autopsy was performed and he was given religious burial in Saint-Maurice cemetery. He had spent a total of twenty-seven years in prisons.

Sade's reputation has been a curious one. His name has, of course, given us the term *sadism,* though *algolagnia* would better describe his sexual preferences. Thought of for a century as a pornographer whose extant works could be read only clandestinely, Sade had to await the twentieth century for fair evaluation. (He did find an admirer in the Victorian era in Swinburne.) Guillaume Apollinaire proclaimed Sade "the freest spirit that has ever been." Iwan Bloch recognized the logic, intellectual vigor, and perspicacity of Sade, whose insights and revelations rival Krafft-Ebing's. The sur-

realists have eulogized Sade as a liberator. Contemporary scholarship, thanks to Maurice Heine and Gilbert Lély, emphasizes the importance of Sade in the current of liberal thought, and the effective use of language. He is now being examined as a "philosophe," a moralist, and a poet in the broad sense.

Most of Sade's work has been published posthumously or in carefully revised editions: Maurice Heine has edited *Les 120 Journées de Sodome* (3 vols, 1931-1935), *Historiettes, Contes et Fabliaux* (1926), the *Dialogue* (1926) and *Les Infortunes de la Vertu* (1930). Gilbert Lély published *L'Aigle, Mademoiselle* (1949), *Les Cahiers Personnels, 1803-1804* (1953), *Le Carillon de Vincennes* (1953), *Histoire Secrète d'Isabelle de Bavière* (1953), and also selected writings (1948). Other letters were published by Paul Bourdin in 1929; in 1954 letters from 1778 to 1784 were published as *Monsieur le 6.* The works published during Sade's lifetime have been reprinted in 1947 and 1957 (*Écrits Politiques, suivis d'Oxtiern,* for example); posthumously published works like *Dorci,* for which Anatole France wrote an introduction in 1881, and *La Marquise de Gange,* first printed in 1813, were reissued in 1957. Many works and fragments of works are still awaiting publication.

English translations of Sade are generally bowdlerized; unedited, his works may not be readily found in the United States. Hobart Ryland has made available *Adelaide of Brunswick* (1954). Pieralessandro Casavini has translated, without expurgation, for a Paris publisher *The Bedroom Philosophers* (1953), *Justine, or Good Conduct Well Chastened* (1953), and *The 120 Days of Sodom* (1954). *Justine,* subtitled "The Misfortunes of Virtue," has also been adapted by Harold Berman (1931 and 1935). The *Dialogue entre un Prêtre et un Moribond* appeared in a translation by Samuel Putnam the year after it was published in French for the first time (1926). The magnum opus of Sade is available in Iwan Bloch's *Marquis de Sade's Anthropologia Sexualis of 600 Perversions, 120 Days of Sodom, or the School for Libertinage* (1934). *Selected Writings,* translated by Leonard de Saint-Yves, appeared in 1953.

ABOUT: Beauvoir, S. de. Marquis de Sade; Bloch, I. The Marquis de Sade, the Man and his Age; Cleugh, J. The Marquis and the Chevalier; Dawes, C. P. The Marquis de Sade; Flake, O. The Marquis de Sade; Gorer, G. The Life and Ideas of the Marquis de Sade; Summers, M. Essays in Petto; New Yorker, September 18, 1965. [In French —see studies by J. Desbordes, M. Heine, P. Klossowski, G. Lély, M. Marchand. In German—see study by E. Dühren.]

S. S. W.

*SAINT-AMANT, MARC-ANTOINE GÉRARD, Sieur de (c. September 30, 1594-December 29, 1661), French poet, was born in Quevilly near Rouen and baptized in a Calvinist temple as Antoine Girard. His father, a Protestant, who died in 1624, was a merchant, shipowner, and corsair. As a young boy, Antoine was educated at the Col-

* săN tà **mäN'**

lège de La Marche. He did not receive much training in Greek and Latin, but he learned Italian, Spanish, and English and studied music—the lute—and painting.

At an early age he was introduced to the gay life of the *grands seigneurs*; in 1617 he accompanied the Duc de Retz to Belle-Isle-en-Mer, and it was here that he composed his famous "Ode to Solitude." For several years he lived in Brittany or in Paris under the protection of the Duc who, in 1619, made him Commissioner of the Artillery. In Paris he consorted with Faret, Michel de Marolles, Malleville, Boisrobert, and the Comte d'Harcourt, furthering his career as poet, courtier, and libertine. It was during this time that he wrote more poetry—*Visions, La Gazette du Pont-Neuf, La Pluie, La Vigne.* Before 1627 he converted to the Catholic faith.

Upon the death of his father he was given the title deed to a glass works. But since his father had been involved in business with a son-in-law, the younger Saint-Amant did not gain possession of the firm until 1638 after a long court trial. Thus, Antoine Girard, son of a merchant, became Marc-Antoine de Girard, *sieur* de Saint-Amant, equerry and gentleman.

To establish himself as a poet and courtier he made appearances at the Hôtel de Rambouillet and the Hôtel de Liancourt, and to widen his experience he made merry in the lively cabarets of Paris. Out of this background comes his famous sonnet, "Les Goinfres," and it is in this work and in such pieces as "La Crevaille," "Le Melon," "Le Fromage" that one sees his true genius—master of Anacreontic poetry, the poet-drinker who, with his convivial fellows, frequented cabarets, debauching and swearing by the drinking goblet, and writing poetry full of verve and color.

A soldier of France, Saint-Amant fought in the campaigns of La Rochelle, of Dauphiné, in Spain and England. In 1633 he accompanied the Maréchal de Créqui to Rome and was charged with asking the Pope to annul the marriage of the Princess of Lorraine to Gaston d'Orléans. During this journey he wrote *Rome Ridicule.* When he returned to Paris, he became one of the first members of the Académie. In 1636-37 he participated, with the Comte d'Harcourt, in a maritime expedition and wrote a *caprice-héroï-comique, Le Passage du Gibraltar* (1640). Then, after staying some time in Rouen and Paris, he went to Italy and England, which inspired another *caprice, L'Albion.* When Marie de Gonzague married the King of Poland, Ladislas VII, she named Saint-Amant gentleman-in-waiting, granting him a pension of 3,000 pounds.

From 1647 to the spring of 1651 he further extended his travels—Catalonia, Brittany, Prinçay, Flanders—fighting against the Spanish, who took him prisoner at Saint-Omer for a brief time. After his release, he paid a visit to the Queen of Poland, taking with him his *Moïse Sauvé* (1653), a heroic idyll marked by the beauty of detail and the strength of its images and prefaced by a letter which censures Aristotle and classical poetry. In Poland he composed *La Polonaise, Épitre à Théandre.* Returning to Paris he stopped in Stockholm where he spent the winter in Queen Christina's court and wrote *Épitre à la Vistule Sollicitée.* The last ten years of his life he divided between Rouen and Paris, peacefully writing verse until his death.

Saint-Amant was one of the best poets of his time. Setting himself independent of classical poetry, he admired Rabelais, Marot, Bacon, Góngora, and Marini. A *précieux*, Saint-Amant wrote poetry rich in witty conceits, and especially is he remembered as a creator of burlesque. Often, however, his *préciosité* and his love of the refined comic hindered him from following his talent for painting the realistic, for he was a powerful realist and could see and write vividly of nature—scenes of fishing and of swimming —or of interiors—cabarets and luxurious court salons. Furthermore, he could see the unique differences in the countries he visited —the English mob, the Roman inn, the Polish army—and these he noted with remarkable accuracy. The *Moïse*, which some critics consider a bad poem, nevertheless contains some first-rate verses which depend on the powerful descriptions of countryside and the poet's impressions of common reality. Saint-Amant was able to give the trivial, picturesque detail a sense of largeness and rich color as did Rubens, for example, in painting.

ABOUT: Kentucky Foreign Language Quarterly, IX (1962). [In French—see studies by R. Audibert and R. Bouvier, F. Gourier, Durand-Lapie.]

G. E.

*SAINT-ÉVREMOND, CHARLES DE MARGUETEL DE SAINT-DENIS, Sieur de (April 1, 1616-September 20, 1703), French writer, was born at Saint-Denis, near Coutances, the fourth son of an officer, and sent to study law in Paris in 1622, then in

* sǎN tā vrē môN′

819

Caen. From an early age he was both a diligent student and an active army man. He abandoned law for military service, and advanced rapidly to the rank of captain in 1637. In the cavalry four years later he attracted the attention of the Duc d'Enghiens for his witty conversation. He participated in several great battles, and in 1645 was severely wounded. During these years he continued his literary projects, and in 1643 composed his first significant work, *Les Académiciens,* a satirical verse comedy scoffing at the inactivity of the French Academy, rich in amusing situations and effects; one scene in this play inspired Molière in *Les Femmes Savantes.*

Saint-Évremond's wit led several times to grave consequences. His indiscretion and idle gossip caused the Duc d'Enghiens, who had become the Prince de Condé, to break with him. He entered the service of the King during the Fronde and won royal recompense for his *Retraite de Monsieur de Longueville* (1652), a pamphlet which also delighted Mazarin. He then held various posts in the south. Further satirical writings, directed against Mazarin, put him briefly in the Bastille. His final undoing was a letter of 1659 to the Marquis de Créqui criticizing Mazarin again, of which a copy was found by chance, and whose violence scandalized the King. Saint-Évremond took flight in 1661 and settled in London for the remaining forty-two years of his life. He was buried in Westminster Abbey.

English noble circles were particularly agreeable to this witty epicurean and libertine, who was received with enthusiasm by Charles II, and joined in 1675 by the Duchesse de Mazarin and her society. Saint-Évremond adapted himself completely to the elegance of English society and when, in 1689, Louis XIV called him back to France, he elected to remain in exile.

The majority of Saint-Évremond's works belong to his English period, but show close acquaintance with intellectual events in France. A satirical comedy, *Les Opéras,* scoffs at this new genre. His many letters show his close relationship with Ninon de Lenclos and the Duchesse de Mazarin, and include an exchange of notes with La Fontaine. They also contain significant impressions on literature, especially on the theatre of Corneille, which he particularly esteemed. Essays of 1676 deal with his theory of tragedy and comedy, and others suggest the moral preoccupations of Montaigne. His *Réflexions sur le Génie des Peuples Romains* was for a time compared favorably with the

works of Bossuet and of Montesquieu on this subject. His poetry is graceful but relatively insignificant. In short, Saint-Évremond interests us today as a distinguished "libertin" and wit, a man with a fascinating career but devoid of genius either as a thinker or an artist. He gives us essential information on customs, and helps situate many contemporaries in the evolution of thought from the "moralistes" of La Rochefoucauld's day to the "Philosophes" of the mid-century.

The *Œuvres* of Saint-Évremond have been frequently edited, beginning in 1652, and in three volumes in 1927; most editions of his *Œuvres Choisies* belong to the nineteenth century. In English translation, *The Works of Monsieur de Saint-Évremond* had particular success from 1700 on, and in some of these editions (1728, etc.) one finds a biography by Des Maizeaux.

ABOUT: Hope, Q. M. Saint-Evremond; PMLA, LXXVI (1961). [In French—see studies by G. Cohen, W. M. Daniels, G. Merlet, A. M. Schmidt, M. Wilmotte.]

F. J. C.

*SAINT-GELAIS, MELLIN DE (1491-1558), French poet, was the nephew, or perhaps the illegitimate son, of Octovien de Saint-Gelais (1468-1502), the bishop of Angoulême and author of many translations from Latin as well as poetic work in the *rhétoriqueur* tradition. Mellin spent a great part of his youth in Italy where he became interested in science, philosophy, the arts, and especially Petrarchist poetry. On his return to France, thanks to the Comte d'Angoulême, he became the favorite poet of Francis I, who made him his official chaplain and his librarian. As a poet laureate, Mellin enjoyed the esteem of the court, for which he often composed masquerades, ballets, etc. It was largely through his initiative that Italianism was introduced into French literature. With Marot, who considered him his equal, he is the first poet in France to have made use of the Italian forms (*strambotto* and sonnet). He wrote quatrains, rondeaux, epigrams, madrigals, and many other light and mannered pieces, which, though witty and graceful, often lack the natural verve and delicate emotion of Marot's verse. His poetry, known by heart in his day to every one, was not published until 1547. As a sixteenth century critic put it, his poems were "little flowers and not lasting fruit; they were finical pieces which from time to time circulated among the courtiers and the ladies of the court; which was very wise on his part, be-

* săn zhĕ lĕ′

cause after his death, a collection of his works was printed which died even as it saw the light of day." In 1554 Mellin prepared in honor of Catherine de' Medici a translation of Trissino's *Sophonisbe,* the second tragedy to be performed in France in the vernacular. Yet his fame did not last long after the death of Francis I. The favorite of Henry II for a while, he was soon supplanted by Ronsard, despite his efforts to ridicule the rising young poet by reciting a parody of one of his odes. The incident turned in favor of Ronsard, who generously forgave the last disciple of Marot: Mellin, having lost his popularity, sought consolation in writing Latin verse.

ABOUT: [In French—see study by J. H. Molinier.]

M. B.

*SAINT-LAMBERT, JEAN FRANÇOIS, Marquis de (December 6, 1716-February 9, 1803), French poet, born in Nancy, saw military service and in 1748 entered the court of the king of Poland, where some years earlier, in 1735, he had met Voltaire and through him Mme du Châtelet. Saint-Lambert's love affair with her lent particular luster to his person and gave him a premature reputation as a poet, so that his arrival in Paris in 1750 found him famous. Despite the rivalry in love, Voltaire esteemed him, and the Encyclopedists were impressed by his writings and his charm. A second affair distinguished him for over a half-century as the model of the faithful lover. In 1752 he met Mme d'Houdetot, thirteen years his junior, who, neglected by her husband, turned to Saint-Lambert. Their relationship was momentarily threatened by Rousseau, who fell madly in love with her in 1757 but, finding no hope, portrayed himself, her and her husband, and her lover, in the triangle situation of *La Nouvelle Héloïse,* and expressed his own feelings in *Les Confessions.* The affair was further complicated by Rousseau's enemies, but the group remained unscathed and faithful in their way until Saint-Lambert's death at an advanced age.

Saint-Lambert abandoned his military career after the Hanover campaign of 1756 in order to devote himself to poetry. In Paris, frequenting Encyclopedist circles, he read fragments of his long poem *Les Saisons* as it progressed. Published in 1769, it became at once a major literary event, attractive for its portrayal of the innocence and beauty of

* săn län bâr'

peasant life and customs, in contrast to the artifice and corruption of city life. The success of the work won for its author almost immediate election to the French Academy. The poem follows the variations of nature during the course of the year, with a strong tincture of pantheism and the contemporary "natural philosophy" of the growth of plants and of love among the animals. Thomson's *Seasons,* Saint-Lambert's source of inspiration, had been published in 1730, but had passed for a time relatively unnoticed in the face of the popularity of Addison and Pope. By 1759, date of the first complete French translation, interest in descriptive poetry had grown, and imitations appeared in rapid succession, as in the highly adapted text by Bernis. Saint-Lambert's poem and *Les Mois* of Roucher a decade later represent the high point of the genre. Finally, beginning in 1796, better translations from Thomson, whose way had thus been amply paved, tended to eclipse the more original French texts and thus led immediately to the romantic movement proper.

Les Saisons is by no means a mere imitation of Thomson. Its tone reveals the light sensuousness and vaguely worried charms of allegorical disguise, corresponding to the painting of Greuze. In it, "Doris" represents Mme d'Houdetot, and generally Saint-Lambert himself seems to feel the emotions and interpret them in his personal manner. His other works include the *Fables Orientales,* a strong comparison with the licentious wit of Crébillon *fils,* and his *Essai sur le Luxe* (1764). His popularity is attested by the many editions, the seventh of *Les Saisons* by 1775, the *Œuvres* in two volumes in 1795 and 1813, and the *Contes* in 1883.

ABOUT: [In French—Buffenoir, H. La Comtesse d'Houdetot; Cameron, M. L'Influence des Saisons.]

F. J. C.

*SAINT-PIERRE, (JACQUES HENRI) BERNARDIN DE (January 19, 1737-January 21, 1814), French novelist and naturalist, was born in Le Havre, the son of Dominique Bernardin de Saint-Pierre, who was in the shipping business, and his wife, the former N. Godebout. The boy was educated by the Jesuits at Caen and Rouen and won a prize in mathematics in 1757. As a child he read a French translation of *Robinson Crusoe* and was profoundly influenced by the book. Trained as an engineer, he enlisted in the army and served a brief and stormy

* săn pyâr', běr nàr dăn'

SAINT-PIERRE

career. He was at last discharged for insubordination and then embarked upon a long period of travel and adventure abroad. He visited Germany, Poland, and Russia. In Russia he enlisted in the army and became interested in a proposal for Siberian colonization. When the Empress Catherine failed to show any enthusiasm for the plan, however, Saint-Pierre became discouraged and resigned from the army.

He returned to Paris in 1765. Three years later he received a government commission as an engineer to the island of Mauritius (the Île de France). There he spent three years. Upon his return to France he began writing an account of his experiences in the tropics. Meanwhile he met and came under the influence of that great exponent of the worship of nature—Jean Jacques Rousseau. Already a romantic by temperament—stormy, impetuous, free-thinking—Saint-Pierre became an enthusiastic disciple of Rousseau. *Un Voyage à l'Île de France*, published in 1773, won him great popularity. The sentimental appeal of his nature-worship, combined with the exoticism of the tropical scene and a pseudo-scientific objectivity, delighted eighteenth century readers. In 1784 he began to publish a series of nature studies, *Études de la Nature*. These included the novel *Paul et Virginie* (1787), which became one of the most popular books of the age. This romantic idyll of two young lovers in a tropical Eden has gone through more than three hundred editions and has been translated into "every civilized

language." It has been the subject of plays, operas, paintings, and sculpture. Napoleon is said to have slept with a copy of it under his pillow, and it is doubtful if any educated person of the late eighteenth through the nineteenth century did not know the book. It caught the imagination of its age as few works have ever done.

As a literary work *Paul et Virginie* is of slight merit. Though the book has undoubted charms—especially in its evocation of tropical atmosphere and its picture of the innocence of the young lovers—it strikes the modern reader as naïve and sentimental. The heroine, for example, chooses to die in a shipwreck rather than strip in order to swim to safety. But for the French public of 1787, and for numerous other readers, as F. C. Green has remarked, it "blazed out with all the force of a revelation. It refreshed and invigorated the spirit of a whole generation and its repercussions were felt for many decades."

The novel made its author a rich and honored man. Louis XVI appointed him supervisor of the Jardin des Plantes, succeeding Buffon. For a time during the French Revolution he lost his preferments, but *Paul et Virginie* had charmed the Bonapartes as well as the Bourbons and he was soon back in favor. He received a government pension and a professorship at the École Normale. His other writings include a novel, *La Chaumière Indienne* (1790), and a biographical and critical study of Rousseau (not published until 1906).

Saint-Pierre married twice—both wives many years younger than he. The first marriage was in 1792 to Félicité Didot, who died; the second was to Désirée Pelleport in 1800. By his first wife he had a son Paul, who died young, and a daughter Virginie, who married a General Gazan. Saint-Pierre himself died at seventy-seven at his country home at Eragny.

English translations of *Paul et Virginie* are numerous, and include one by D. Malthus, published in London in 1789; Helen Maria Williams (1796, one of the most popular translations); Henry Hunter (1796); M. B. Anderson (1894). Hunter's translation is the fifth volume in his complete translation of *Studies of Nature* (1796). Also available in English are *A Voyage to the Island of Mauritius*, translated by J. Parish (1775) and *Harmonies of Nature*, by W. Meeston (1815).

ABOUT: University of Toronto Quarterly, January 1938. [In French—see studies by A. Barine, C. Vincens.]

*SAINT-SIMON, CLAUDE HENRI, Comte de (October 17, 1760-May 19, 1825), French social philosopher, was the son of the Governor of Senlis, and great-nephew to the Duc de Saint-Simon (see sketch below), some of whose personal traits he reflects. His revolutionary spirit was evident when he was imprisoned at the age of thirteen for refusing first communion. Second lieutenant at the age of sixteen, he went to America to fight for the colonies and was wounded and taken as a prisoner to Jamaica. At this time he proposed to the viceroy of Mexico a project for an inter-ocean canal. Later a colonel, he was active in Holland preparing a Franco-Dutch war against England; he was soon in Madrid, again fostering a project for a navigable canal from that city to the ocean.

Saint-Simon, who had amassed considerable wealth, was ruined by the French Revolution, and renounced his title; regaining his wealth in speculations, he was imprisoned in 1793 under the name of Jacques Bonhomme. Under the Bourbons, however, he resumed his titles in order to address the parliaments of England and France regarding his sweeping theories of reform. His fantastic projects continued in rapid succession, to the point of his getting a divorce in the vain hope of marrying Mme de Staël. In his later days he lived by unknown means, devoted to his varied causes, and surrounded by a veritable sect of followers of a new religion of industry and labor, notably Thierry and, until 1822, Auguste Comte.

Saint-Simon's first notable work, *Lettres d'un Habitant de Genève,* was followed by the more significant *Introduction aux Travaux Scientifiques du XIXᵉ Siècle* (1808), and other tracts related to encyclopedic knowledge, until his major writing, *La Réorganisation de la Société Européenne,* published in 1814, deriving in part from conversations noted down by his secretary, Augustin Thierry. Interest in this and several other works of Saint-Simon was revived when the League of Nations sought means to establish world peace. This idea first appeared in Saint-Simon's *Mémoire sur la Science de l'Homme* in 1813, in which he conceived a political organization based on science. In his treatise addressed to the parliaments of France and England he imagined a confederacy of nations through common and internationalized institutions, industries, armies, currencies, transportation, and parliament, rather than the traditional treaties and alliances. He was conscious of

* săn sē mōɴ′

the significance of the relative isolation of England, and the danger of future conflict with a unified Germany, and felt that both powers must be included in any effective union of nations. From another point of view, in his *Système Industriel* (1821) Saint-Simon is the founder of modern socialism, with a strong economic emphasis on stability through planning rather than on individual rights. He simultaneously replaced routine Christianity by a positivist religion somewhat in the traditions of Fourier.

The standard edition of Saint-Simon's writings is that of Enfantin, 1865-78; selected works appear in a volume by C. Bouglé, of 1925, and *De la Réorganisation* separately with remarks pertinent to the League of Nations by A. Pereire (1925). English translations appear in *Selected Writings,* edited and translated by F. M. H. Markham (1952).

ABOUT: Bernstein, S. Essays in Political and Intellectual History; Booth, A. Saint-Simon and Saint-Simonism; Markham, F. M. H. *Introduction to* Selected Writings of Saint-Simon. [In French— see studies by C. Bouglé, S. Charléty, H. Gouhier, U. Leroy, G. Weill.]

F. J. C.

*SAINT-SIMON, LOUIS DE ROUVROY, Duc de (January 15, 1675-March 2, 1755), French memoirist, was the son of Claude de Saint-Simon, a nobleman who had been ruined by the civil wars but who became a favorite of Louis XIII and was thereupon honored with many official distinctions and accorded the title of duke in 1635; impressed with this distinction, Claude traced his lineage to Charlemagne according to dubious records and devoted his life to a cult of his king. Louis, born to his father late in life, was the butt of jest for his particularly small stature, which earned him the name of "petit bondrillon." In his routine education he showed little taste for letters, but was strongly impregnated with reverence for Louis XIII and all aspects of protocol, etiquette, and precedence pertaining to his court. Presented to Louis XIV in 1691, he enrolled as musketeer and took an active part in the siege of Namur and various foreign campaigns. The following year he inherited his father's titles and his entire estate, and shortly after he purchased a regiment. In 1695 he married Marie Gabrielle de Durfort, the grandniece of Turenne and daughter of the Duc de Lorges; despite Saint-Simon's vexation at the humble origins of his mother-in-law, the marriage was an extremely happy one, and in his last will, in 1754, he paid tribute to his wife's virtues and spoke of their happy relations.

* săn sē mōɴ′

SAINT-SIMON

Saint-Simon's discontent with military service, and his resignation in 1702, rose primarily from his early notions and his preference for a feudal system of titled leaders—unlike Louis XIV, who sought strong centralization and favored officers with true military talents. Saint-Simon devoted himself nevertheless to presence at Versailles, where his rank gave him particular privilege. His life there allowed him to observe in intimate fashion the behavior of the several hundred courtiers with their jealousies, ambitions, and acceptance of personal abasement in their search for royal favors. Louis XIV was particularly suspicious of Saint-Simon on account of his known hostility to centralized power, his excessively overt criticisms and frankness, and his insistence on protocol. These traits caused him to live in relative isolation and exaggerated his conviction that his true merits were not appreciated. He successfully courted several ministers and became for awhile an intimate of the Duc de Bourgogne, the "dauphin," for whom he made notes on events at the court; his political ideas were in part crystallized in this association. After the duke's death, he attached himself to the Duc d'Orléans. When the latter became regent, Saint-Simon found that he was accorded only a very mediocre place in the government, again on account of his overly independent spirit and his violent attitudes. In 1721 the regent honored him by sending him to the court of Spain to make overtures for the marriage of Louis XV to the Infanta; but on the regent's death, two years later, Saint-Simon considered that his public career had come to an end, and he left Versailles definitively. The last years of his life were spent in retirement, saddened by shattered dreams of grandeur, then by the death of his wife in 1743, and finally by the gradual decay of his material fortune. He spent his time at his estate at La Ferté-Vidame (near Chartres) meditating and composing his *Mémoires*.

Saint-Simon had begun his *Mémoires* in 1694, inspired by reading those of Bassompierre; over the following years he made copious notes, but, during the major period of writing, from 1740 to 1750, he counted further on his memory, by no means sure. The manuscript was examined after his death by a few privileged persons, and only parts of it were published in 1788; further delays in publication are evidence of its seditious nature from the royal point of view. The significance of the work is multiple, and its importance has grown substantially over the last century for a variety of reasons. It is in the first place the spontaneous and bitter expression of a wholly egocentric nobleman obsessed with manias of reactionary and almost fictional character; in this sense it is a remarkable portrait of the uninhibited prejudice and pomposity of the writer himself. Furthermore, in the same naïve way, it is an immense tableau of a great yet strange period of history, a collection of living anecdotes, and a gallery of portraits. The method of documentation, which at times came close to the activities of a political spy, involved questioning informants on all social levels, and subsequent selection of those stories that tended to prove Saint-Simon's thesis. The picture he gives is no doubt strongly biased, but he set in relief the gravest flaws in a rapidly disintegrating structure. Saint-Simon, whether through fact or slander, was able to perceive the vital social issues, such as the semblance of Oriental despotism in the harem that Louis had gathered about him, and his behavior toward both his many titled mistresses and their numerous offspring. In contrast, in a more humane tone, Saint-Simon at times shows signs of pity and admiration, as in his day-by-day report on the death of the king, and the latter's suffering and courage. Finally, one must note Saint-Simon's style with its bold originality of syntax and neologism, elusive and intriguing. It suffices to mention the influence of the *Mémoires* on the work of Proust to confirm the above interpretation, for the modern novelist adapted the combined stylistic, satirical, and social implications of this source in his portrait of the similar decadence of aristocracy at the end of the last century.

The *Mémoires* may be read in various collected extracts in English translation, in the four volumes by B. St. John (1857, reprinted 1926) and such other versions as that of K. Wormeley (1899) or *Louis XIV at Versailles*, by D. Flower (1953). The original first appeared in complete form in twenty volumes (1856-58), later reprinted and improved (1947); the *Écrits Inédits* of 1880-93 include letters and notes.

ABOUT: Tilley, A. Selections from Saint-Simon. [In French—Baschet, A. Le Duc de Saint-Simon; Boissier, G. Saint-Simon; Crozals, J. de, Saint-Simon; Le Breton, A. La "Comédie Humaine" de Saint-Simon.]

F. J. C.

*SAINTE-BEUVE, CHARLES AUGUSTIN (December 23, 1804-October 13, 1869), French critic, was born at Boulogne-sur-Mer, son of François de Sainte-Beuve, controller of taxes for the arrondissement of Boulogne, and Augustine Coilliot, of English descent. His father died three months before his birth. Mme de Sainte-Beuve, though left in straitened circumstances, managed to provide her son with a good education. Until his fourteenth year, young Charles Augustin received instruction at the school of M. Blériot at Boulogne, then was granted his wish to go to Paris. In the capital he studied at the Collège Charlemagne and Collège Bourbon, at the latter institution taking the first prize for Latin verse. At school he drew attention to himself for his physical repulsiveness as well as for his intellectual precocity—earning the nickname of *le matou* ("the ugly one"). He seems to have had a bent towards a literary career from his earliest years; nevertheless he elected a course in medicine and natural sciences, probably at his mother's behest. Simultaneously he steeped himself in French literature and history. His passion for scientific exactitude in criticism was undoubtedly the product of this dual education. He was to become, in Matthew Arnold's phrase, "a naturalist in letters."

Sainte-Beuve's brilliant career in literary journalism began while he was in college. The first newspaper to which he contributed was the *Globe*, founded in 1824 by one of his teachers, M. Dubois. Among the outstanding articles he wrote for this newspaper was a series on French poetry of the sixteenth century, subsequently published as a

* săNT bûv'

SAINTE-BEUVE

volume in 1842. In 1827 appeared the famous review of Victor Hugo's *Odes et Ballades* which brought him to the attention of the author as well as an entrée into the society of the romantic group of writers—including Lamartine and Merimée—whose vogue was then in the ascendant. Under their influence he wrote three volumes of poetry—*La Vie et Poésies de Joseph Delorme* (1829), *Les Consolations* (1830), *Pensées d' Août* (1834)—and a novel, *Volupté* (1834), none of which was destined for lasting success. It early became clear that Sainte-Beuve's forte was to be in interpreting literature rather than in creating it. His friendship with Victor Hugo was short-lived, his alleged adultery with Hugo's wife Adèle causing an irreparable rift. Subsequently Hugo retaliated by temporarily blocking Sainte-Beuve's admission to the Académie Française.

The decade from 1830 to 1840 marked a most prolific period for Sainte-Beuve as a critic. He was the first of a line of outstanding critics to distinguish the pages of the *Revue des Deux Mondes*, launched in 1831. To this journal and to the *Revue de Paris* he contributed a series of character sketches of literary figures, the so-called "portraits," a literary genre he made his own. These were later reprinted in the volumes known as *Portraits de Femmes*, *Portraits Littéraires*, and *Portraits Contemporaines*. His interest in the Jansenist movement of the seventeenth century culminated in a series of lectures in 1837-38 before the Academy of Lausanne that three years later reached publication as *Port-Royal,* one of his greatest and most popular books.

In 1849 Sainte-Beuve accepted an offer to write a *feuilleton* every Monday for the newspaper the *Constitutionnel.* Thus was launched the famous series *Causeries du Lundi* (Monday Conversations), essays on literary topics, book reviews, evaluations of authors, which attracted a wide reading public and made him famous throughout Europe. For Sainte-Beuve a book review was really a disquisition on a writer's mind and environment. In his oft-quoted essay on Chateaubriand he announced his *méthode.* His phrase "tel arbre, tel fruit" ("from such a tree, such fruit") sums up his critical credo. For Sainte-Beuve literature was inseparable from the man who wrote it: "L'étude littéraire me mène ainsi tout naturellement à l'étude morale" ("The study of literature leads me naturally to the study of human nature"). Such faith did Sainte-Beuve have in his psychological method that he looked to a time when man could be classified into "familles d'esprits," making it possible to predict accomplishment from certain traits of temperament. The *Causeries* appeared practically continuously over a period of twenty years, first in the *Constitutionnel,* subsequently in the *Moniteur Officiel.* They were published in two series, the first totaling fifteen volumes, the second, known as *Nouveaux Lundis,* eventually reaching thirteen volumes (the last three issued posthumously).

Inevitably Sainte-Beuve received his share of emoluments—appointment as Conservateur of the Mazarin Library in 1840, election to the Académie Française in 1844, a guest lectureship in French literature at the University of Liège in 1848, in 1854 a professorship in Latin poetry at the Collège de France (which he subsequently resigned when he proved unpopular with the students because of his political views), followed by a post at the École Normale Supérieure. In 1865 Sainte-Beuve received his supreme recognition by his countrymen with his nomination as senator. Two years later he made his only real foray into politics by coming to the defense of Ernest Renan, whose books and ideas had been resoundingly attacked in the Senate. The speech he read on this occasion upholding freedom of thought and inquiry won him wide acclaim. Sainte-Beuve kept up his literary activity virtually until his death, though in his last years he suffered pains that made it impossible for him to write in a sitting position, compelling him to work either standing up or lying prone. He died in his house on the Rue Montparnasse, not quite having reached the age of sixty-five.

For range and extent of critical writing Charles Augustin Sainte-Beuve is unexcelled in French literature. His published books cover the Greek and Roman writers as well as French writers of the seventeenth, eighteenth, and early nineteenth centuries. "His curiosity was unbounded," one of his greatest English admirers, Matthew Arnold, wrote in an obituary article. "Man, as he is, and as his history and the productions of his spirit show him, was the object of his study and interest." Universally admired by his countrymen in his lifetime, Sainte-Beuve has since suffered some scaling down in reputation among them, a denigration led by the novelist Marcel Proust, who was one of the first to point out his blind spots and defects in judgment. It is true that Sainte-Beuve, while he could be penetrating on established authors, over-rated some lesser figures like George Sand and failed to recognize the genius of nascent contemporaries like Stendhal, Balzac, Flaubert, and Baudelaire. He has been taken to task for his dastardly treatment of friends, but on the other hand he was one of the first to aid and encourage Zola. Generally speaking, Sainte-Beuve is recognized today not so much as a great literary critic but as a great literary portraitist—a psychologist of literature.

The *Causeries du Lundi* were translated (as *Monday-Chats*) by William Matthews (1877), and subsequently by E. J. Trechman (1909-11), whose translation is reprinted in the World Classics (1933). A selection of the *Portraits Littéraires* (*On Men and Women, Portraits of Men, Portraits of Women*) was translated by William Sharp (1901). The *Portraits of the Seventeenth Century* were translated by Katherine P. Wormeley (1904), *Portraits of the Eighteenth Century* by Katherine P. Wormeley and George Burnham Ives (1905).

ABOUT: Arnold, M. Essays in Criticism, Third Series; Babbitt, I. The Masters of Modern French Criticism; Giese, W. Sainte-Beuve: A Literary Portrait; Harper, G. Charles-Augustin Sainte-Beuve; Lehmann, A. G. Sainte-Beuve: A Portrait of the Critic, 1804-42; Mott, L. Sainte-Beuve; Nicolson, H. Sainte-Beuve; Partisan Review, Fall 1957; Saturday Review, October 19, 1957. [In French—see studies by M. Allem, A. Bellesort, J. Bonnerot, V. Giraud, M. Leroy, G. Michaut.]

R. A. C.

SAINTE-MAURE, BENOÎT DE. See BENOÎT DE SAINTE-MAURE

*SALTYKOV-SHCHEDRIN, MIKHA-
IL (Y)EVGRAFOVICH (January 27,
1826-May 10, 1889), Russian novelist and
satirist, was born in the village of Spas-Ugol,
Tver province, on the estate of his family,
members of the ancient land-holding nobility.
His early education was supervised by a
bonded servant in the household, then by an
older sister and a governess, and, finally, by
a local priest and a student from Moscow
during the latter's summer vacations. At the
age of ten he had been sufficiently prepared
by this variety of tutelage to enter the third-
year class at the Moscow Institute for Nobles
where he remained for the next two years.

In 1838 he was transferred to the Tsarskoye-Selo Lyceum where his literary bent
soon manifested itself. He was an avid
reader and also developed a passion for verse-
writing, a pursuit which was not encouraged
by the authorities. But though he was reprimanded for his frivolity in the beginning,
his talent was duly recognized by the time
he had reached the eighth grade. Since no
less a poet than Pushkin had once attended
the Lyceum, it had already become the practice to honor him by naming a "keeper of the
Pushkin tradition" each year from among the
promising pupils. Saltykov earned this title,
and his first poem, "The Lyre," was published in the magazine *Reader's Library* in
1841 as having been written by "S-ov."
Another poem was printed in the same publication a year later, but all other poetic
writings (his entire output is encompassed
in his stay at the Lyceum) appeared in
Sovremennik (The Contemporary) in 1844-
45. In later years Saltykov did not like to
be reminded of his poetry.

On his graduation from the Lyceum (1844)
he entered the civil service, but, although he
had rejected the idea of being a poet, he
could not desist from some literary expression. He fell in with the progressive intelligentsia around *Otechestvennye Zapiski* (Annals of Our Country) where his first story,
"Contradictions," appeared in 1847. Saltykov
considered his second story, "An Intricate
Affair," published a few months later in
the same magazine, as his actual literary
début, and he certainly had cause to remember it. It appeared in March 1848, one
month after the February Revolution in
France, the implications of which were not
lost on the Czarist authorities. A secret
"Committee to Investigate Subversive Russian Literature" was set up which, practically
as its first official act, found the contents of

* sŭl tĭ kôf' shchä' dryĭn

SALTYKOV-SHCHEDRIN

Saltykov's "Intricate Affair" sufficiently subversive to hurt Saltykov's career in the government service.

The youthful civil servant was sent off to
the city of Vyatka (about 400 miles northeast of Moscow) where, like Herzen some
fourteen years before, he was exiled but
allowed to continue in the civil service. Despite his record, the talented Saltykov was
rapidly promoted in his new location, rising
to an important post in the police administration of the province. In 1856, the year his
exile was terminated, he married the daughter of the vice-governor, and returned to St.
Petersburg to take a post in the Ministry of
the Interior.

The eight years he had spent in the province provided him with an abundance of
material which soon began to appear in
periodicals as "Provincial Sketches." Saltykov had learned his lesson, and, as the
sketches satirized procincial officials among
other aspects of country life, they were published under the pseudonym "N. Shchedrin,"
a name which became so famous that it is
joined to his own to this day. It was not
known for many years that the prominent
public official Saltykov was using the advantages of his position to observe at first
hand the very aspects of Russian public and
private life which "Shchedrin" so bitingly
satirized.

Fresh grist for Shchedrin's mill was provided by Saltykov's first new assignment,
an investigation into the recruitment procedures in the provinces in connection with

827

the Crimean War (1853-56) which laid bare many shocking irregularities. And there is no doubt that he learned even more as vice-governor of Ryazan Gubernia, one of the wealthiest provinces of Russia, just south-east of Moscow. But as the fame of Shchedrin continued to increase, Saltykov longed more and more to be able to devote himself exclusively to literature. He made his first attempt to realize his ambition in 1862 when he resigned from the government service.

In 1863 he joined *Sovremennik*, then under the editorship of the poet Nekrasov, in which most of his sketches had already appeared. But the pressure of the censorship—which required all the skill and downright cunning of Shchedrin to circumvent—and the poor remuneration afforded even by this prominent monthly, forced him to return to the government service again in 1864 in order to maintain himself. But in 1868 came a new opportunity. Nekrasov, cast adrift by the suppression of *Sovremennik* in 1866, arranged to take over the journal *Otechestven-nye Zapiski*—he rented it from its owners—and invited Saltykov to share the editorship. With the prospect of sufficient income at last, Saltykov resigned from the government permanently to work with Nekrasov, and, after the latter's death, to be sole director of the publication. During his tenure the magazine came to express, in the words of his friend, the social critic N. K. Mikhailovsky, "a monolithic individuality . . . unique in the annals of Russian journalism." The decision by its owners in 1884 to terminate publication was a crushing blow to its director whose connection with it had been the most fruitful period of his life. In a letter to Mikhailovsky he deplored the loss of "live communication with the reader" which his editorship had afforded him, and for a time rejected the idea of going among "strangers" on some other journal. Nevertheless he did join *Vestnik Yevropy* (European Herald) in the same year, and maintained his connection there for the balance of his life.

Saltykov-Shchedrin's literary output was entirely devoted to social criticism and satire. He once wrote: "The invariable content of all my literary work has always been a protest against cruelty, hypocrisy, slander, rapaciousness, perfidy, idle thinking. . . . Search as much as you wish through the whole mass of my writings—you will find nothing else, I assure you." His great creative problem was to find a means to express his conviction in an official atmosphere that was not always receptive to criticism. His solution was to write of the grossest abuses in the most off-hand manner, never once expressing himself in any way as in the least bit critical of what he so innocently described. His technique inevitably led him to the fable form, and in his tales he achieved his goal with great mastery, as in the story of the "Rational Rabbit" who "knows his place" in the order of nature and philosophically anticipates his destruction at the hands of wolves or foxes—just as the peasant is bound to be destroyed by the rapacious landlord.

The *Fables* was translated into English by V. Volkhovsky in 1931; a new edition, *Tales from Saltikov-Schedrin*, was issued in Moscow in 1958. The novel *Gospoda Golovyovi* was translated as *The Golovlev Family* by A. Ridgway (1916), as *A Family of Noblemen* by A. Yarmolinsky (1916), as *The Goloveyov Family*, by N. Duddington (1931), and was issued in Moscow as *Judas Golovyov* (1958).

ABOUT: Strelsky, N. Saltykov and the Russian Squire. [In Russian—see studies by K. Arsenyev, A. S. Busmin, K. N. Grigor'jan, S. A. Makashin, I. Razumnik.]

L. R. & H. H.

*SAMAIN, ALBERT VICTOR (April 3, 1858-August 18, 1900), French poet, was born at Lille. His parents, Jean Baptiste and Elisa Henriette Mouquet, were lower middle class owners of a modest wine-shop. Albert, the eldest of four children, had to leave school at the age of fourteen, when his father died, in order to help support the family. He worked from eight in the morning until eight at night, first as a runner for a bank, then for a sugar broker. Escape from the drudgery of this routine was in the reading of Greek and English literature; Edgar Allan Poe was one of his favorite authors.

In 1880 his firm sent him to its Paris office. Albert essayed writing journalistic pieces, at a friend's suggestion, but was unable to place his copy. In 1881 he managed to have two slight tales published in a Lille weekly under the name of "Gry-Pearl." That same year his mother joined him in Paris, and he obtained a minor position in the municipal government. Although naturally reticent and introverted—thin of face and body, with crane-like gestures and a wrinkled forehead—Albert joined the Bohemian circle "Nous Autres" in 1883 at Léon Riotor's insistence. This group was absorbed by Salis' "Chat Noir," in whose periodical Samain published his first poems (1884-85). Through this circle he met the poet and future priest

* sà măN'

Louis Le Cardonnel who became one of his few intimate friends.

Unambitious, impractical, and unenergetic, Samain escaped from his monotonous, colorless way of life by use of his imagination. Though not especially intelligent or subject to strong emotions, he possessed unusual ability to establish moods that might be termed crepuscular—"the somewhat sad silence of the day's slow dying." He was one of the founders of the eclectic symbolist periodical *Le Mercure de France*, whose first number appeared in January 1900, and in which he mainly published. Friends persuaded him to collect some of his poems in *Au Jardin de l'Infante*. At first published in a limited edition (1893), his work became famous thanks to a highly laudatory review by François Coppée. The Achon-Despérouses prize from the French Academy enabled Samain to accompany Paul Morisse to Germany, and to visit England, Holland, and Spain with Raymond Bonheur.

In 1898 Samain failed to receive any attention for *Aux Flancs du Vase*. But this did not hurt him so profoundly as the death of his mother, to whom he was deeply attached. Ill of tuberculosis, in a sudden spurt of energy Samain wrote the two-act verse drama *Polyphème* (1899). The following year he died while staying with Raymond Bonheur at Magny-les-Hameaux. He was buried at Lille. E. Carrière made an oil portrait (1900) of Samain on his death-bed.

Samain, not deliberately a member of any school, is identified with the second generation of symbolists. His verse is characterized by its vague fatalism, half tones, and fluid rhythms. His friends published a selection from his writings, *Le Chariot d'Or,* in 1906, the same year that *Polyphème* was published. The latter was produced in 1904 by the Théâtre de l'Œuvre, and added to the Comédie Française repertory in 1908.

Samain's reputation in America is the result of his inclusion by Amy Lowell in her *Six French Poets* (1915). Translations from *Au Jardin de l'Infante* have appeared in some thirty-nine anthologies and volumes of criticism. Many of Samain's poems and other manuscripts have not yet been published. A three-volume edition of his works, including short stories, was published in 1924. Since then *Des Lettres, 1887-1900* has appeared (1933), as well as his *Correspondance Inédite* with Francis Jammes (1945). *Carnets Intimes* appeared in 1939.

ABOUT: Falk, E. H. Renunciation as a Tragic Focus; Gosse, E. W. French Profiles; Gourmont, R. de, The Book of Masks; Lewisohn, L. The Poets of Modern France; Todd Memorial Volume, II. [In French—see studies by A. de Bersaucourt, L. Bocquet, F. Gohin, J. Nanteuil, F. Russel.]

S. S. W.

SANCTIS, FRANCESCO DE. See DE SANCTIS, FRANCESCO

*"SAND, GEORGE" (pseudonym of AMANTINE AURORE LUCILE DUPIN, Mme Dudevant) (July 1, 1804-June 8, 1876), French novelist, was born at her family's seignorial estate at Nohant, about a hundred miles south of Orléans. In marrying a modiste, her father, Maurice Dupin, had opposed the will of his mother, Aurore, daughter of the Marshal of Saxe. Her father's death when she was four left the child in constant friction with her grandmother and her irritable and uncultured mother. The three ladies moved from Paris to Nohant, where for ten years she was bit by bit emancipated from parental influence. She was sent to a convent in Paris to learn good manners, but returned in 1820 more rebellious than ever; her growing virile temperament led her at this moment to assume men's clothes. At Nohant the only persons who understood her personal problem were her tutor, Deschartres, and perhaps her grandmother; the latter, as she lay dying in 1821 said to her: "You are losing your best friend." George Sand's mother took her again to Paris, but she remained in persistent opposition to her daughter's interest in literature.

During a visit at Le Plessis, George Sand met a young officer, Casimir Dudevant, who courted her and married her in September 1822. Dudevant left his work in order to devote himself to managing the estate at Nohant. Marriage was for her an emancipation from her mother; she was delighted with maternity when her son Maurice was born during the following June and, in 1828, her daughter. But her relations with her husband were not happy, and they finally separated in 1831. She went at once to Paris to earn her own living by translations and drawings. She was by this time at the full height of her romantic manner. She found her first orientation in creative and imaginative literature in articles written for *Figaro*, and shortly in a novel, *Rose et Blanche*, composed in collaboration with Jules Sandeau (see sketch below), who taught her much about the techniques of composition and from whom she borrowed her pen name. Her early novels were immense successes, *Indiana* in 1832 and *Lélia* in 1833. She became at once a close friend of such great figures as Balzac, Sainte-Beuve, and Delacroix.

* sänd

829

"GEORGE SAND"

She met Alfred de Musset in 1833; the young poet was pleased to find favor with so influential a person. She decided to save him from his life of debauchery, and then fell in love with him. They spent four troubled months in Venice early in 1834; having cared for him in her maternal way, she felt free to leave him, and became the mistress of his doctor, Pagello. She and Musset were reconciled again briefly in October, but broke then definitively. She returned to Nohant in a suicidal depression which was quickly sublimated in a renewed maternal urge: "I need to suffer for someone. . . . Whom can I take care of now?" After a violent scene with her husband in October 1835, she left again, taking her children with her. Franz Liszt, whom she had met shortly before, invited her to Geneva; she went to Switzerland in August 1836, and later continued her friendship with the musician in Paris, along with further new friends, Heinrich Heine, Mickiewicz, and Chopin.

The death of George Sand's mother in 1837 marks the beginning of the endless parties and receptions at Nohant, now a famous spot where great personalities were frequent guests; Balzac left us a portrait of Sand and her habits, and especially of her new hobby, marionette plays which soon developed into a full-fledged theatre. One great adventure remained. Through Liszt, George Sand had tried for some time to entice Chopin to Nohant ("Tell Chopin I'm mad about him"). When her son Maurice fell sick the circumstances suggested the ill-starred trip to Majorca, where Chopin might also profit by the warmer climate. All three were installed on the island during the autumn of 1838, George and her son busy writing, the musician at his piano. The weather was a disappointment, and the peasants began to persecute them. After an almost tragic departure, they returned to Nohant and Paris, and the musician was far more ill than before. Their final rupture occurred in 1846.

Sand's most esteemed novels belong to the ensuing period of calm life at Nohant. She wrote: "I have passed many hours of my life watching the grass grow or contemplating the serenity of the great rocks in the moonlight. . . . I participated in their calm beatitude." Such novels as *La Mare au Diable* (1846), *La Petite Fadette* (1849), and *François le Champi* (1850) are today considered Sand's masterpieces in this genre and great monuments of the pastoral novel. In them she portrays local customs and superstitions, idealizing inner emotion with a conviction of the basic goodness of human nature, and in a naïve and uncalculated style, always discreet and poetic. Through this manner she stands quite apart from the realistic tendencies of the immediate post-romantic period. Certain of her works are also colored by humanitarian and political theories, and her ideologies led her, in growing intensity, to write pamphlets and prefaces until the disappointments of the Revolution of 1848. During these years she composed the *Histoire de Ma Vie*, which was published in 1855, undertook her *Journal Intime*, printed posthumously, and wrote many plays; she worked closely with her son, who edited Rabelais about this time.

George Sand is remembered today for only a few of her hundred-odd publications, and primarily for her remarkable personality. For this reason, one finds particular interest in her autobiographical expression, her immense correspondence with great contemporaries, and such personal writings as the *Lettres d'un Voyageur*, twelve episodes of 1834 to 1836 forming a kind of epistolary novel that tells, often in veiled terms, of her days at Venice with Musset, of such other lovers as Pagello, of her relationship with Liszt, and her own variations of passion, from coquetry to keen suffering and pessimism ("Happiness is a ridiculous word"), of chronic ennui ("The world is an abyss of turpitude") and suicidal moods; each crisis, however, was followed by ready adjustment ("I put up with life because I love it"). All told, her son and her friends were her true reason for living. She spent her last years at Nohant where she died at seventy-one.

The many English translations illustrate the importance of Sand's work, beginning with *The Mosaic Workers*, in 1845, and *Consuelo*, by F. Shaw, in 1846, and culminating with the twenty volumes of *The Masterpieces of George Sand*, by G. Ives in 1900-1902 (eighteen novels). The other notable translations include *Impressions and Reminiscences*, by H. Adams (1877), a number of plays (*Antonia*, 1898, *The Bagpipers*, 1890), and, by the end of the century, *Fadette, Francis the Waif*, and *The Devil's Pool*. More recently, translators have turned to the autobiographical works, the correspondence with Flaubert, by A. McKenzie (1921), the *Intimate Journal*, by M. Howe (1929), and the selected *Letters*, by V. Lucas and E. Drew (1930). The complete works in French consist of 109 volumes (1866-1912); six volumes of the *Correspondance* appeared in 1882, further items in 1953.

ABOUT: Howe, M. George Sand, The Search For Love; Maurois, A. Lélia (English translation by G. Hopkins). [In French—Caro, E. George Sand; Doumic, R. George Sand; Feugère, A. Un Grand Amour Romantique: George Sand et Alfred de Musset; Karénine, W. George Sand, Sa Vie, Ses Œuvres; Maurras, C. Les Amants de Venise; Roya, M. Les Plus Grands Amours de George Sand; Toesca, M. Une Autre George Sand.]

F. J. C.

*SANDEAU, JULES (February 19, 1811-April 24, 1883,), French novelist and dramatist, born in Aubusson (Creuse), studied law in Paris, but took more interest in student groups of romantic tendencies. During a visit to Nohant, he and George Sand (see sketch above) fell in love, and she abandoned her husband in 1831 to follow Sandeau to Paris. Together they composed a short story, *Prima Donna*, and the novel *Rose et Blanche*, signed "Jules Sand." Their liaison lasted less than a year; Sandeau also collaborated with the playwright Émile Augier, but otherwise wrote in his own personal manner and to please himself. He became librarian at the Bibliothèque Mazarine in 1853, and was elected to the French Academy five years later.

Sandeau's first noteworthy novel, *Marianna*, appeared in 1839. It gives us our closest insight into the author's personal disappointment in love, probably with reference to George Sand; the portrayal of the title character, appropriately and poetically fused with descriptions of the countryside, makes of it one of the most powerful examples of sincere love in romantic garb, without the cruelty and excess of so many better known texts. It is to considerable extent dated by the affectations of the style, but its very overwriting reflects Sandeau's lack of confidence.

* sän dô'

Sandeau did not find his real talent until he left his native region in 1840 and discovered a spiritual affinity for the Vendée, with its royalist memories and the recent heroism of the local wars. The basic social problem of the conflict between the old and the new prejudices inspired the character of the Marquis in *Mlle de La Seiglière*, probably Sandeau's masterpiece.

Brunetière, comparing Sandeau's best novels with those of Scott, as documents on contemporary life, sets *La Maison de Penarvan* in first place. Written in 1857, the novel has aged no more than that of the masterworks of its genre and time. It deals with the preoccupations of persons of the upper classes and a notion of aristocratic honor. Sandeau concentrates on the problems that faced the older aristocracy during the regime of Louis Philippe. He approves the attitudes of this aristocracy, though he is quite aware of its weaknesses; perhaps he shows his personal prejudices in active scorn for more radical ideologies. His novel *Mlle de Kérouare* sins least with respect to length, and offers one of the better portrayals of mismarriage. Sandeau's short stories are also estimable, and give a good notion of his qualities. He was not a popular writer, but was admired in literary circles and among connoisseurs for his discretion and his style.

English translations from Sandeau are rather numerous but not truly representative of his work. *Mlle de Seiglière*, as translated in 1860, is his comedy, based on the novel. The earliest translation was *Money-Bags and Titles*, by L. Myers (1850), followed by *Hunting the Romantic* (1852), *Madeleine*, by F. Charlot (1878), *The House of Penarvan*, by T. Diven (1879), and *Catherine* (1893).

ABOUT: Saintsbury, G. Essays on French Novelists. [In French—Brunetière, F. *in* Revue des Deux Mondes, January 1, 1887; Claretie, J. Jules Sandeau; Silver, M. Jules Sandeau.]

F. J. C.

*SANNAZARO, JACOPO (pseudonym Actius Syncerus), (July 28, 1458-April 24, 1530), Italian poet and humanist, was born in Naples. His father died in 1463, and his mother took him and his brother to live in San Cipriano Picentino. On his return to Naples, he became an intimate of Pontano and was active in his Accademia. In 1482 he was a member of the household of the Duke of Calabria, whom he followed in the war against Pope Innocent VIII in 1485. Sannazaro's recitations were much admired by the Duke and by his brother Frederick of

* sä nä dzä' rô

SANNAZARO

Aragon. He followed the latter into exile in France in 1501, where he remained until 1504. For him he composed monologues rich in allusions to ancient and modern persons and events and often marked by superstition; these *ghiommeri* imitate a current popular genre. He also wrote *farse* or allegorical and classical laudatory recitations, some of which were enacted for the Duke beginning in 1483; the *farsa* of the *Trionfo della Fama* was staged with elaborate scenery.

Sannazaro's masterpiece, the *Arcadia,* was known to many listeners before its completion in 1481; it was published in 1502 and enlarged two years later. The *Arcadia* consists of prose texts interspersed with twelve eclogues, and forms a pastoral novel set in a wild region in Greece with constant contrasts between labors and songs. In this bucolic and utopian framework, Sincero, who represents the poet himself, communes with mountains, forests, animals, and birds, in his search for comforts from disappointment in love. Other characters, such as Carino, recount their own comparable sentimental problems. Sannazaro portrays the inhabitants of this region, their customs, games and festivities, ornamented with mythological allusion and touches of magic and superstition, and distant legendary recollections of the epoch of the god Pan. A typical and excellent sequence opens with a prose description of the summits of Partenio, followed by a verse dialogue between Selvaggio and Ergasto, in the fixed versification of five plus seven syllables separated by the caesura.

Sannazaro's debts to earlier writings are legion, and one finds constant touches of Virgil, Theocritus, Ovid, and Petrarch, often to a point of heaviness. The structure of the *Arcadia,* however, is admirable for its unity; and the color, the concept of nature, and the tone of the sentimental love laments are throughout consistent and illustrate the poet's total sincerity of personal feeling. The autobiographical element cannot be fully determined, but the theme of nature probably rises from Sannazaro's own feelings and experiences in his retirement in the solitudes of the Valle Picentina. Thus, though by this time Boiardo and others had already practiced pastoral genres, the *Arcadia* was the actual point of departure of a new kind of novel—anticipating Tasso, Cervantes, Spenser, Sidney, and the pastoral tradition—and perhaps ultimately its greatest masterpiece.

Sannazaro left lyrical poems collected in 1530, showing great polish and a successful attempt to achieve a Tuscan style free from native dialectalisms. His enthusiasm for the classics led him more often to original composition in Latin verse. The three books of his *Epigrammata* show great variety of subjects and power of style, sometimes in invective against the Borgias or Poliziano, more often delicately Sapphic for his friends. The three books of *Elegiae* are Sannazaro's most polished and sincere expression of melancholy, friendship, and presentment of death, representing at times the renewal of ancient mythology according to the doctrines of Pontano. In rhetorical manner, his masterpiece is the *Pescatoriae,* rising toward the inspiration of the *Arcadia* in its Virgilian laments and complaints. *De Partu Virginis,* elaborated over many years and published in 1526, stands apart, in Sannazaro's finest Ciceronian eloquence, for the Biblical simplicity and the powerful imagery, lyrical rather than epic, notably the episodes of the Visitation and the Manger.

The first edition of the *Arcadia* in 1504 was improved in the critical text by Scherillo in 1888, where one finds an extensive biography and useful analyses; E. Carrara made further improvements in 1926. The *Opera* of 1535 reappeared a dozen times during the century, and the editions of 1719 and 1728 remain reliable; the *Arcadia* has far more often appeared alone. English translations include *The Osiers, a Pastoral,* published in 1724, and *The Piscatory Eclogues,* by W. Mustard (1914).

ABOUT: Mustard, W. The Piscatory Eclogues. [In Italian—De Lisa, G. L'Arcadia del Sannazaro; Pèrcopo, E. Vita di Iacopo Sannazaro; Sainati, A. La Lirica Latina di Iacopo Sannazaro; Torraca, F. La Materia dell'Arcadia.]

F. J. C.

*SANTEUL (or SANTEUIL), JEAN BAPTISTE DE (May 12, 1630-August 5, 1697), French and Latin poet, was born in Paris of a family long established there; his brother Claude, two years his senior, was also a poet and scholar of note. Santeul studied at the Sainte-Barbe and Louis-le-Grand colleges, and while at the latter composed his first Latin poetry. He entered the Abbey of Saint-Victor as canon, and spent much of his time studying. As a poet, Santeul had the reputation of "divine fire" of inspiration. His early work, addressed for example to Bossuet and to Louvois, was widely admired, and his dedication to the Chancellor Séguier achieved his fame. He became the official Latin poet for the king, whose exploits he praised and for whom he composed the Latin inscriptions for public monuments.

Santeul's fame as a poet earned for him a commission to revise the breviary by setting the hymns in more elegant style, in answer to widespread complaints against existing versions. His revision appeared in 1685 as the *Recueil des Nouvelles Odes Sacrées,* and was at once officially adopted by many churches and orders. His use of pagan imagery, meanwhile, provoked many bitter attacks. As he had urged his brother previously, Bossuet urged Santeul to develop a purely Christian manner by avoiding the current mythological and pagan fables, but Santeul, despite overt gestures of reform, provoked a considerable cry of impiety with his *Pomona in Agro Versaliensi.* He encountered similar difficulties in an inscription for the Jansenist Arnauld, in terms interpreted as hostile to the Jesuits. Despite his protestations, there is reason to believe that he was trying to placate the two parties.

The violence of judgments against Santeul makes an interpretation of his actions particularly difficult. From one point of view, he was an inspired versifier with naïve though picturesque notions on the union of fantasy and dogma, but from another he was exceedingly vain in his ostentatious visits to churches to hear his own versions of the hymns. He affected long wind-blown hair, and was widely cultivated by persons at the court. He died in Dijon while on a mission with the Duc de Bourbon, and his last work, *Santolius Burgundus,* dates from that visit. Saint-Simon gives a more dramatic account of his death from drinking a mixture of wine and tobacco. The principal editions of his work indicate his importance well into the eighteenth century, the *Œuvres* of 1698, the

* sän tûl'; sän tû' y'

French verse translation of his *Hymnes,* in 1691, and of his *Règles Saintes* in 1694, the *Santeüillana ou les Bons Mots* in 1710, with his biography, reprinted in 1735 and 1744, and the *Santoliana* of 1764.

ABOUT: [In French—see study by L. A. Montalant-Bougleux and C. A. Sainte-Beuve's Causeries de Lundi.]

F. J. C.

*SANTILLANA, ÍÑIGO LÓPEZ DE MENDOZA, first Marquis of (August 19, 1398-March 25, 1458), Spanish poet and humanist, was born in the village of Carrión de los Condes, the second son and eventual heir of Don Diego Hurtado de Mendoza, the leading nobleman of Castile. His father having died when he was seven years old, his mother, Doña Leonor de la Vega, procured for him the best available tutors from whom he received a courtly and humanistic education. In 1412 he was married to Doña Catalina de Figueroa, daughter of the grand master of the military order of Santiago; this marriage, to all appearances a happy one, produced five sons and three daughters. In 1413 we find the young Mendoza at the Castilian court of John II, of whose turbulently brilliant reign he was to become the most representative figure, militarily and politically, as well as in literature.

During the complex civil conflicts of these years, Santillana, being a wealthy and powerful feudal lord, followed a rather independent line of action, defending the Mendoza possessions and generally opposing the king's all-powerful favorite, Don Álvaro de Luna, to whose eventual fall he greatly contributed. But Mendoza's loyalty to the king at the Battle of Olmedo (1445) won him the titles of Marquis of Santillana and Count of Manzanares.

The literary works of Santillana may more conveniently be considered by genre than by date of composition, not always easily ascertained. We may perhaps assign to his youth most of his brief lyrics: rather learned and witty *decires,* musical *canciones* in the tradition of Provençal courtly love, and rustic *serranillas,* or *pastourelles,* likewise set to music, but telling a story, in dialogue, of the encounter of traveling knight with mountain lass. These sophisticated *serranillas* of Santillana were and still are, in every sense of the word, his most popular poems.

Also belonging to his earlier period are the more ambitious narrative *decires.* The most important poem in this genre is the *Comedie-*

* sän tē lyä' nä

833

SANTILLANA

ta de Ponça (1436), occasioned by the capture of Alfonso V of Aragon by the Genoese in 1435. The poem, whose title recalls with a modest diminutive that of Dante's, is a vision in which the queen and the queen-mother ask Boccaccio to express their grief at the king's unwarranted misfortune; then the allegorical figure of Fortuna appears, predicts the king's liberation, and justifies herself as an instrument of divine Providence. The setting is one of elaborate aristocratic costumes, the style is heavy with Latinized rhetoric, and, for contrast, the note of Horace's "Beatus ille" is struck, expressing urbane envy of the simple peasant who is not subject to princely evils.

An interesting product of Santillana's final twenty years are forty-two sonnets, the first to be written in any language other than Italian. They reveal the influence of the "dolce stil novo" and, more significantly, that of Petrarch; their themes, in addition to courtly love, include politics, morality, and religion. Santillana had trouble adapting to Spanish the Italian hendecasyllabic line, and the sonnet did not become thoroughly naturalized until the sixteenth century. Nevertheless, Santillana's successful essays in the genre prove to what an extent he anticipated the Renaissance.

A final category of poetry includes mature works treating of moral, political, and religious themes. Reminiscent of the *Comedieta de Ponça* is *Bías contra Fortuna* (c. 1450), in which the semi-legendary philosopher-statesman of ancient Greece engages in Stoic debate with an arbitrary and tyrannical Fortuna. This poem is the fullest expression of Santillana's humanistic learning and philosophical spirit.

Santillana's prose works are of secondary importance. Of considerable interest, however, is the prologue to a collection of his verse which he sent to a Portuguese nobleman about 1449; in it he reveals his broad theoretical and historical acquaintance with medieval poetry. More popular was his alphabetically arranged collection of *refranes,* or traditional proverbs; this was published shortly after the introduction into Spain of the printing press and reached England in 1579 (*The Proverbes of . . . Sir James Lopes de Mendoza*).

With the execution of Don Álvaro de Luna in 1453, the Marquis of Santillana began to withdraw from public life to his great library in Guadalajara, where he died at the age of fifty-nine. For his contemporaries in Spain he had incarnated a new human ideal, the refined *grand seigneur* of the Renaissance; for the modern reader he still lives in his elegant and philosophical poetry.

Barnaby Googe translated the *Proverbes* into English in 1579. An edition of his *Prose and Verse* was made by J. B. Trend in 1940.

ABOUT: Brenan, G. Literature of the Spanish People; Trend, J. B. Santillana: Prose and Verse. [In Spanish—Amador de los Ríos, J. Vida del Marqués de Santillana; Lapesa, R. La Obra Literaria del Marqués de Santillana.]

E. L. R.

*SARBIEWSKI, MACIEJ KAZIMIERZ (also known as CASIMIR SARBIEVIUS),** (1595-April 2, 1640), Polish poet, was born in Sarbiewo. In his early youth he joined the Jesuit Order and became a monk. For some years he was the confessor to the Polish King Ladislas IV. A lover of nature he was not impressed by his social position or the life of the court. In his youth, and occasionally later, he was forced by circumstances to write panegyrics in honor of the King, the Pope, and other powerful patrons. Among the odes which made him famous were some in panegyrical form, for which he had good examples in the works of his master, Horace. Sarbiewski also wrote political odes, calling for a crusade against the Turks, and some patriotic odes which praised the Polish victories over the Turks and glorified the Polish freedom.

Sarbiewski's genius comes out more forcefully in his contemplative odes and in those

* sär byĕf' skē

which contain beautiful descriptions of nature. We find descriptions of nature not only in the odes but also in the long poem *Silviludia* (Games in the Woods), the main subject of which is a panegyric in honor of King Ladislas IV. These descriptions reveal what was at the time an almost unique feeling for nature, a feeling which often verged on sentimentality; we find in them artistic appreciation of nature, and a perception of aesthetic form.

Because of Sarbiewski's excellence in pastoral poetry, he is generally known as the Polish Horace. Sarbiewski wrote exclusively in Latin, and of all Polish Latinists, he was the best known and most widely appreciated abroad. His writings were very popular in England and Germany, where they were translated and edited frequently. He is considered one of the greatest representatives of humanism in Poland. The best and fullest edition of Sarbiewski's works is by F. T. Friedman, 1840.

The *Odes of Sarbiewski* were translated anonymously by a writer who signed himself G. H. (G. Hils) in 1646 (London) and reprinted in 1953. Sarbiewski is called here Casimir. Translations from Casimir were made by J. Kitchener in 1821. J. Bowring's *Specimens of the Polish Poets* (1827) includes some examples from Sarbiewski. *Wood-Notes; the Silviludia Poetica of M. C. Sarbievius,* with translations in English verse by R. C. Coxe, was published in 1848.

ABOUT: Kridl, M. An Anthology of Polish Literature, *also* A Survey of Polish Literature; Roestvig, M. S. *Introduction to* The Odes of Casimire (1953). [In Polish—see studies by J. Oko, T. Sinko.]

P. LY.

*SARDOU, VICTORIEN (September 5, 1831-November 8, 1908), French playwright, was born in Paris to Antoine Léandre and Evelina Viard Sardou. His father was a schoolmaster, and Victorien's education was obtained following his father from post to post. The young man studied medicine for eighteen months at Lenoir's clinic in the Necker Hospital of Paris but quit to devote himself to writing. Tutoring and writing articles to support himself, he first produced *La Taverne des Étudiants* at the Odéon, April 11, 1854. His first success was the production by Déjazet (a friend of his wife, Laurentine Léon) of *Les Premières Armes de Figaro* in connection with which Sardou claimed to have invented the prompter's box to avoid drafts. Finally *Les Pattes de Mouche,* on May 15, 1860, established his

* sàr dōō'

reputation. He continued successful both in the theatre and in society. His second marriage, to Anne Soulié, took place in the royal chapel at Versailles in 1872. He frequented rather high society and prominent authors and artists; he had three sons and one daughter who married the author Count Robert de Flers. Sardou was well-off financially, served as mayor of Marly-le-Roi (where he had a château) and as president of the Société des Auteurs was a member of the Académie Française (1877) and a commander of the Legion of Honor, actively defended Dreyfus, and claimed once to have saved the Tuileries from mob violence.

Of medium height, Sardou had a broad forehead and dark gray eyes, and *Vanity Fair* for May 2, 1891, shows him in his characteristic black velvet beret and white scarf. He had a lively, expressive face which reflected his personality. He was industrious, interested in almost everything, quick to defend himself, a stickler for accuracy; he had sharp business acumen and a well-developed sense of responsibility; albeit a great talker, he was apparently a delightful person. He once wrote: "The ideal life, according to Goethe, is youth's dream realized in adulthood. I have done better. Reality has surpassed my dreams." And it is true that he was one of the foremost playwrights of the last half of the nineteenth century.

Of the hundred-odd plays written by Victorien Sardou, he is best known today for his work which became, with Puccini's music, the opera *La Tosca*. Sarah Bernhardt originated the rôle and was in great part responsible for the playwright's fame in France and abroad, creating seven of his characters. Sardou has been indeed fortunate in having outstanding actors and actresses interpret his parts, the long list including Déjazet, Réjane, Duse, Coquelin, Got, Sir Henry Irving, Ellen Terry, Lily Langtry, several Barrymores, Béatrice Dussane, Gloria Swanson, and Jean Louis Barrault. In France and England Sardou's plays enjoyed long runs to full houses; and in New York, between 1899 and 1939, he was the second most-performed French playwright.

In his wide range of subjects and genres, from the slapstick of *L'Oncle Sam* to the tragedy of *Patrie!*, Sardou's most durable success has been *Madame Sans-Gêne*. Performed by Réjane, Ellen Terry, Gloria Swanson, Béatrice Dussane, Madeleine Renaud and many others, *Madame Sans-Gêne* has been established in the repertory of the Comédie Française. The story of the washerwoman-become-duchess under Napoleon has long been a favorite with audiences. It was not, as was none of his plays, a success with G. B. Shaw, who invented the term "Sardoodledom" with which to condemn Sardou's dramaturgy.

Most critics have been unfavorable to Sardou, considering his plays machine-made, filled with artificial tricks and unrealistic devices. He has taken place alongside Scribe as a producer of "well-made plays," not a compliment in context. He did use every visual and aural factor feasible to add to the maintaining of suspense in his plays and to the enjoyment of the audiences. Sardou was perhaps too greatly admired by the audiences of his time and too highly scorned by his contemporary and later critics.

A number of Sardou's plays have been translated into English, some of these in pirated editions which cannot be authoritatively dated. *Les Pattes de Mouche* was translated by J. Palgrave Simpson as *A Scrap of Paper* in 1911; Dorothy Monet adapted *Divorçons* under the title *Cyprienne* (n.d.), and Charles Klauber translated it as *Let's Get a Divorce* in 1909; Laurence Irving translated *Robespierre* (1899) and *Dante* (1903); *Fédora* was translated by Herman Merivale (c. 1883); *Madame Sans-Gêne* was translated by C. H. Mettzer as *Madame Devil-May-Care* (n.d.); A. W. Pinero translated *Maison Neuve* as *Mayfair* (c. 1885); and B. H. Clark translated *Patrie* (1915). Also available in English are *Diplomacy, The Sorceress, Odette,* and *The Black Pearl.* The complete French edition of Sardou was published in eleven volumes in 1950.

ABOUT: Harris, T. W. Victorien Sardou in the Modern Theater (Brown University dissertation, 1956); Hart, J. A. Sardou and the Sardou Play; Naeseth, H. Sardou on the American Stage (University of Chicago dissertation, 1931); Roosevelt, B. (pseud.) Victorien Sardou; Shaw, G. B. Dramatic Opinions and Essays; Verneuil, L. The Fabulous Life of Sarah Bernhardt. [In French—see studies by G. Mouly, H. Rebell, H. Shoen.]

T. W. H.

*SAVONAROLA, GIROLAMO MARIA FRANCESCO MATTEO (September 21, 1452-May 23, 1498), Italian preacher and writer, was born in Ferrara of an old family of that city. His talents appeared in his early studies, especially in philosophy and medicine. After hearing a sermon in 1474, he decided to renounce the world, and entered the Dominican Order in Bologna. He devoted himself to ascetic practices, taught the novices of the monastery, and began writing philosophical tracts based on Saint Thomas Aquinas and Aristotle. His superior sent him in 1481 or 1482 to preach in Florence, and he felt inspired to save Italy from her current sensuality and immorality, a mission

* sä võ nä rõ' lä

SAVONAROLA

of which we find traces in an early poem on the decline of the Church. Having preached with great success in Florence, Brescia, and Genoa, Savonarola began a study of the Book of Revelation, which focused his imagination on apocalyptic images. Lorenzo the Magnificent called him back to Florence in 1490, and continued to encourage him despite his criticisms from the pulpit of San Marco, and his prophecies of imminent ruin for neighboring states and even the papacy.

On Lorenzo's death in 1492 Savonarola added to the dismay and disorder with eloquent threats of a scourge from God and appeals which touched the populace and created a wave of austerity not unlike what later ages called Puritanism. For some four years, he was essentially the principal administrator of the Florentine state, whose real Lord was Christ. He formed the Great Council of the upper citizenry in a sort of constitutional government, and managed for a while to bring order to the city. His profound influence is attested in the work of Botticelli, Cronaca, several of the Della Robbias, and even Michelangelo. In public ceremonies, "objects of sin," even books and paintings, were burned. The public soon became restless with this display and, as Savonarola turned his invective against Rome and the Pope, Alexander VI found means to influence the Signoria: after an ordeal by fire, Savonarola was imprisoned. The protracted legal proceedings show that the case against him was extremely difficult, and ultimately involved all varieties of irregularity, forged documents, and repeated torture. Finally, he was executed even though no legal judgment had been made.

From a philosophical or humanistic point of view Savonarola was a man of his times. He deeply admired Ficino, and his Neoplatonism was a search for ultimate goodness along with a need for comfort in God. He was dedicated to spirituality, yet took a keen interest in the arts, and considered that paganism might profitably be studied by advised and trained minds, finding in his interests a position not unlike that of Poliziano. He left a considerable number of writings of different kinds. His *Triumphus Crucis de Fidei Veritate* (1497) is his formal apology of Christianity; his elegant and powerful sermons were published with various minor tracts by Villari-Casanova in 1898, and his political theory appears in the *Reggimento di Firenze*, edited by Rians in 1848. His Italian poetry is important in belles-lettres for its occasional traces of early dialectalisms as well as for reflecting the influence of Dante and Petrarch. Among his most important Italian poems are *De Ruina Mundi* ("Quanto è superbo . . ."), *De Ruina Ecclesiae* ("Vergene casta, ben che indegno figlio . . ."), and *De Consolatione Crucifixi* ("Venite, povri e nudi, al gran tesauro"). In this last more illumined and mystic vein, Savonarola's *laudi* represent a new purity and intensity of inspiration deriving ultimately from Franciscan traditions. His spiritual anxieties appear in his early verse, and later he turns rather to urge others to piety, using, though largely without conscious method, many recent artistic devices. His major theme takes many forms, primarily of scorn for this world, "il cieco mondo," "Del terrestre e vano affetto," or positively of a search for Christ: "O gran bontà, Dolce pietà." The collected poems are of unequal inspiration and uncertain date, though the most intense seem to have been composed about 1495.

There are numerous editions of Savonarola's writings, improved in critical form in recent years: Villari's *Scelte di Prediche* (1898), Ferrara's edition with notes (1930), and a series of collections of the *Poesie* from that of Rians (1848) to the convenient volume by Piccoli (1926).

ABOUT: De la Bedoyère, M. The Meddlesome Friar; O'Neil, J. Jerome Savonarola; Villari, P. Life and Times of Savonarola. [In Italian—see studies by M. Ferrara, P. Luotto, G. Schnitzer.]

F. J. C.

*SCALIGER, JULIUS CAESAR (April 23?, 1484-October 21, 1558), Italian-French literary critic, grammarian, scientist, and poet, was, according to the story he told of himself, born at Riva on Lake Garda, a descendant of the princess of Verona, of the same name. First a page at the court of the Emperor Maximilian, he then became a soldier and fought in the Netherlands, Greece, and Italy. Later, he turned to letters and studied at the University of Bologna. After his death, enemies of his son Joseph contended that Scaliger's account of his birth and early career was a fabrication, but no one questioned it in his own lifetime.

From 1525 on, however, the facts concerning his career are documented. In that year he arrived at Agen, France, as the personal physician of Bishop Antonio della Rovere. Here he settled for the rest of his life. He married Andiette de La Roque (by whom he had fifteen children), acquired property, set up a medical school and a flourishing practice and was twice elected consul of the city.

For over thirty years he applied himself so strenuously to study and composition that he left few branches of learning untouched. In breadth, if not in genius, he became the pattern of the Renaissance man of letters.

In 1531 he burst upon the literary world with a well-written, though violent, attack on Erasmus' *Ciceronianus*, a satire against the uncritical worship of Cicero. In 1536, angered by Erasmus' silence, he published another oration on the same subject. Though neither of them (*Orationes Duae adversus Desiderium Erasmum*, 1531-36) was up to the standard of Erasmus' opus, they revealed a mastery of the Latin language that few of his contemporaries could equal.

He next published his *De Causis Linguae Latinae* (1540), a work which is considered by modern scholars to be the first Latin grammar based on a scientific method. Among his other literary works were a succession of volumes of Latin poetry, published from 1533 on, which are today considered of more historical than poetical interest.

His writings in the field of natural science contain much of value, considering the time in which they were written. His best known, the *Exotericarum Exercitationum Liber* (1557), an attack on Jerome Cardan, is an encyclopedia of scientific knowledge of the time, the correct and the incorrect mixed indiscriminately. On the other hand, his *De Plantis et Historia Animalum* (1556) and his commentaries on Theophrastus (1566)

* skăl' ĭ jēr

are noteworthy for Scaliger's recognition that no progress in botany was possible unless classification by the properties of plants was abandoned for a system based upon the characteristic forms of the plants themselves.

His letters and orations must be passed over in order to arrive at his last and greatest work, his *Poetices Libri VII* (1561). This is undoubtedly one of the most influential works on literary theory ever published. Recognizing the role of inspiration, Scaliger nevertheless felt that poetry should be subordinated to reason and virtue. His admirably systematic treatment of the subject and his preference for the Latin as against the Greek ideal made his book one of the foundation stones of French classicism and his name an authority of the first rank until the beginnings of the romantic movement.

His son Joseph Justus Scaliger (1540-1609) became the great classical scholar of the next generation.

Portions of Scaliger's poetics in English may be found in F. M. Padelford's *Select Translations from Scaliger's Poetics,* (1907). One of his orations is translated in V. Hall's "Scaliger's Defense of Poetry," PMLA, LXIII.

ABOUT: Hall, V., Jr., Life of Julius Caesar Scaliger. Commentaries on his *Poetics* are in most histories of literary criticism, including G. B. Saintsbury's. [In French—Bray, R. Formation de la Doctrine Classique en France.]

V. H.

*SCARRON, PAUL (July 4, 1610-October 6, 1660), French poet, novelist, and dramatist, was born in Paris, the seventh of eight children. His father, also named Paul Scarron, was a well-to-do, pious, and somewhat extravagant bourgeois, a magistrate, member of the Parlement of Paris. His mother, Gabrielle Goguet, a Breton, was of good bourgeois family. She died early, and Paul's father married Françoise de Plaix, a noble but greedy and conniving person who made life difficult for her stepchildren. Young Paul was a mischievous child, who did not share his family's austerity. He loved gaiety and freedom, and, as soon and as often as he could, frequented the theatre. His family, wishing to get rid of him, pushed him toward an ecclesiastical career. He took minor orders, and, at nineteen, became an abbé. A few years later, he entered, as a secretary, the service of the bishop of Le Mans, with whom he traveled to Rome in 1635.

The life of Canon Scarron at Le Mans was that of a young man about town, a gay

* skà rôn'

SCARRON

libertine, who loved good food, good wines, good conversation, and enjoyed the society of women. He liked to laugh and make people laugh and was very popular in the town's *salons*. He was twenty-seven when he contracted a very painful infirmity. According to La Baumelle (whose story is no longer doubted), having covered his body with honey and feathers as a carnival disguise, he was pursued by other members of a gay party, hid himself under a bridge, jumped into the water, and was crippled by rheumatism. His health became worse and worse, his body was deformed, his legs rendered useless; he had to take frequent doses of opiates and lived in great pain for the next twenty years, enduring his miseries with very great fortitude. His difficulties were complicated by lawsuits with his stepmother and by the misconduct of his sisters whom he had to support. He had to live by the generosity of his protectors (one of his early patrons was Marie de Hautefort, a confidante of Louis XIII and Anne d'Autriche) and by his writings. In 1640 he went back to Paris, publishing there some of the droll, burlesque pieces he had been writing to forget his ills: *Recueil de Quelques Vers Burlesques* (1643), followed by *Typhon ou la Gigantomachie* (1644). He also wrote for the theatre, taking his plots mostly from the Spanish drama. His two best plays are the humorous comedy *Jodelet ou le Maître Valet* (1645) and *Don Japhet d'Arménie* (1648). As a playwright, Scarron was no Molière, but he paved the way for the author of *Les Précieuses Ridicules,* one of the characters of which, incidentally, is named Jodelet. Between 1648 and 1653 Scarron wrote *Le Virgile Travesti*—the most famous, perhaps, of his writings in his own time. It was a somewhat obscene, often amusing parody of the *Aeneid,* in which he irreverently mixed the comic and the heroic genres. In 1649 or 1650, Scarron took in a penniless woman named Céleste, a former mistress of his and a former nun, who kept his house in the Rue d'Enfer and tried—unsuccessfully—to reform him. But he liked the gay company of poets, artists, and other non-conformists and went on giving joyous parties. When the civil troubles of the Fronde started, Scarron took the part of the Frondeurs and directed his wit against the government. He wrote a biting satirical pamphlet against Cardinal Mazarin (1649): he had already lost one—and would never get another—Queen's pension. For a while, he was in danger of losing his freedom, too.

His best work was started in 1651. It was a novel, the idea for which he had conceived in Le Mans, called *Le Roman Comique.* The history of a troupe of itinerant comedians (at the time when Molière's troupe was still learning its trade in the provinces), *Le Roman Comique* is one of the best picaresque French novels. Unfinished and written somewhat hastily, it nevertheless gives a realistic, vivid picture of life in the French provinces in Louis XIII's time. It may have influenced Théophile Gautier's later novel *Le Capitaine Fracasse.* "Sister" Céleste, one day, disappeared, but Scarron did not remain alone for long. In 1652, he married Françoise d'Aubigné, an orphan of seventeen who was the granddaughter of a famous poet and Protestant, Agrippa d'Aubigné. Theirs was a strange marriage. The husband was an invalid, a libertine, a lover of good food and of ribald songs. The lady was young, beautiful, reserved, virtuous. She was faithful to him and brought him a degree of happiness, even though the next eight years were a kind of long agony for poor Scarron. The widow Scarron, a few years after his death, was to become the tutor of the king's children by Mme de Montespan, and under the name of Mme de Maintenon, Louis XIV's second wife.

Le Roman Comique was translated as *The Comical Romance* and published, along with other tales of Scarron, by Tom Brown of Shifnal, John Savage, and others (1741). There is also a translation by Oliver Goldsmith (London, 1775).

ABOUT: There is a biography in English by J. J. Jusserand, prefixed to his edition of the Brown and Savage translation (2 vols., 1892). Also: Phelps, N. F. The Queen's Invalid, a Biography; Sorkin, M. Paul Scarron's Adaptation of the Comedia. [In French—Magne, E. Scarron et Son Milieu; Jéramec, J. La Vie de Scarron.]

P. B.

*SCÈVE, MAURICE (1501?-1560?), French poet, was born of a bourgeois family which gave many officials to his native Lyon during the sixteenth and seventeenth centuries. His father, himself an important city magistrate, gave him an excellent education crowned by studies at an Italian university from which he probably received a doctorate of law.

In 1533, while in Avignon, Scève looked for the tomb of Petrarch's Laura and claimed its discovery in a chapel along with a medal and also a sonnet which is no longer attributed to Petrarch. Having returned to Lyon, he frequented the very active circles of humanists and neo-Latin poets and published, in 1534, a translation from a Spanish novel by Juan de Flores, a continuation of Boccaccio's *Fiametta.* This *Deplourable Fin de Flamete* deals with two lovers tortured by self-imposed obstacles, a foretaste of his masterpiece, *Délie.* Scève gained literary renown when Renée de France gave him first place in a contest for his *Eyebrow,* one of five *blasons*—a genre made fashionable by Marot—singing the attributes of feminine beauty.

In 1536 he met the beautiful and sensitive poet Pernette du Guillet (see sketch above), whom he loved until her death. *Délie* was probably begun around 1536 but not published until 1544. It is a *canzoniere* which does not celebrate a pure abstract *Idea* (Délie being the anagram of *Idée*) as was long believed, but rather expresses Scève's concrete sufferings and mystic liberation from his ardent although Platonic affair with Pernette. Yet it is more than a sentimental diary. The organization in units ($5+9 \times 49+3$) really shows concern with Gnosticism—5 symbolizing the incarnate man, 9 the final reintegration, 49 the successive initiation stages, and 3 the Trinity. Be that as it may, the image of the woman, Délie (another name for Diana), incarnates for Scève mystery, darkness, the unconscious, the unknown, with which the poet struggles in a fugue-like and quasi-magical progression while remaining in contact with the daily pangs of the flesh. *Délie* stands as a solitary masterpiece, evading all explanatory reduc-

* sěv

839

tions of its dense and powerful poetic language. Yet it is the focal point of late medieval mysticism, of Petrarchan poetry, of the *rhétoriqueurs,* of humanism, and, to a limited extent, of direct Graeco-Latin tradition. *Délie* was imitated by all Scève's disciples at Lyon. The larger public, however, saluted the work with epigrams jeering at its obscurity. Despite Ronsard and Du Bellay's praises, it fell into oblivion until mid-twentieth century criticism fully rehabilitated it.

At Pernette's death (1545), Scève withdrew into solitude in the country, the pleasures of which he sang in *La Saulsaye* (1547), an eclogue relating the metamorphosis of nymphs into willows. He returned in 1548 to Lyon, where his name was celebrated by all and where his poetic talents were often sought. Little is known of his life after 1550. It is conjectured that he turned to Protestantism and went to Germany in 1560, or that he died of the plague in the summer of 1563. His last work, *Microcosme,* not published until 1562 (probably posthumously), might have been terminated by 1559. It is a gigantic epic—of mediocre value compared to *Délie*—embracing the history of mankind since Adam, praising the technical progress of man under the needling of original sin, and prophesying an eventual return of man to the Divine.

The complete poetic works were edited by P. Guégan in 1927. In 1949 Wallace Fowlie translated sixty of Scève's poems.

ABOUT: Fowlie, W. *Introduction to* Sixty Poems of Scève. [In French—see study by V. L. Saulnier. In Italian—see study by E. Giudici.]

M. B.

*SCHEFFEL, JOSEPH VIKTOR VON (February 16, 1826-April 9, 1886), German poet and novelist, was born in Karlsruhe, the son of an army major who expected his son to follow family tradition by entering government service. His mother, by contrast, was inclined toward literature and sympathized with her son's artistic ambitions. After completing the *Gymnasium* at Karlsruhe at the age of seventeen, Scheffel wished to become a painter, but at his father's insistence studied law from 1843 to 1847 at the universities of Munich, Berlin, and Heidelberg. During these years he was active in student organizations, particularly in the club Der Engere at Heidelberg, and wrote many drinking songs which were soon acclaimed by all of Germany.

* shĕf' ēl

SCHEFFEL

After passing the state examination and receiving his law degree in 1849, Scheffel accepted in the following year a government post as a state auditor in the beautiful and ancient town of Säkkingen, where he spent two of the happiest years of his life. In 1852 he traveled to Italy determined to paint, but soon abandoned the attempt and turned instead to literature. On Capri, where he became a friend of the writer Paul Heyse, Scheffel completed a verse epic entitled *Der Trompeter von Säkkingen* (1853), a love story set in the period following the Thirty Years' War. This work, which reveals the influence of Walter Scott, Wilhelm Hauff, and Heinrich Heine, found a responsive public, and became one of the most widely read books of its day. It has since passed through more than 250 reprintings.

In 1853 Scheffel returned to Heidelberg to prepare himself for an academic career as a medievalist. Stimulated by the *Casus Sancti Galli,* an account of monastic life in the tenth century, and by the *Waltharius Manu Fortis,* the most famous Latin epic of the Middle Ages, written by Ekkehard I of St. Gall, Scheffel produced *Ekkehard* (1857), one of the outstanding historical novels of this time. With a masterly blend of scholarship and fiction, Scheffel narrated the life of Ekkehard, climaxing the account with a translation of the *Waltharius Manu Fortis. Ekkehard* repeated the success of *Der Trompeter von Säkkingen* and made Scheffel one of the most popular of German poets.

Most of Scheffel's later life was spent in restless travels, with the exception of the period 1857-59, during which he served as court librarian at Donaueschingen. Distressed by deaths in his family, by his own failing health, and by his inability to complete a novel about the medieval poet Heinrich von Ofterdingen, he became prone to attacks of melancholy and for a time despaired of losing his mind. His marriage to Karoline von Malzen in 1864 lasted only three years. He never again completed a longer work, and fragments of his unfinished novel appeared under the titles *Frau Aventiure* (1863) and *Juniperus* (1866). He also published *Gaudeamus* (1867), a collection of his student songs which are regarded by many critics as his finest contribution to German literature, as well as the minor works *Bergpsalmen* (1870) and *Hugideo* (1883). Before his death in 1886 at Karlsruhe, Scheffel received many honors, including the patent of hereditary nobility. No other poet of his generation has been so commemorated in statues and memorials.

Der Trompeter von Säkkingen was translated by J. Beck and L. Lorimer in 1893 as *The Trumpeter: A Romance of the Rhine.* H. Easson translated *Ekkehard* in 1911, and C. G. Leland rendered *Gaudeamus* in 1872. Selections of Scheffel's verse are contained in H. W. Longfellow, *Poems of Places* (1876-79), M. Münsterberg, *A Harvest of German Verse* (1916), and the Warner Library.

About: Winkler, M. The Life of Joseph Viktor von Scheffel *in* The German Classics, XIII. [In German—see studies by J. Proells, W. Heichen, A. Klaar, J. Franke, F. Panzer.]

D. G. D.

SCHEFFLER, JOHANN. See ANGELUS SILESIUS

*SCHELLING, FRIEDRICH WILHELM JOSEPH VON (January 27, 1775-August 20, 1854), German romantic philosopher, was born at Leonberg near Württemberg, the son of a clergyman. In 1790 he entered the University of Tübingen, where he studied theology, philosophy, and philology. During this period he met and associated with the poet Hölderlin and the philosophers Fichte and Hegel. For two years he worked as a private tutor in Leipzig, until in 1798 upon the recommendation of Goethe and Fichte he was appointed professor of philosophy at the University of Jena. In Jena he joined the circle of the first romantic school (A. W. Schlegel, F. Schlegel, L. Tieck, Novalis), although his direct con-

SCHELLING

tact with the group ended in 1800. He married Karoline Schlegel, following her divorce from A. W. Schlegel in 1803, and this same year he began teaching at the University of Würzburg. In 1807 Schelling was elected to membership in the Academy of Sciences in Munich and was appointed general secretary for the Academy of Plastic Arts. Subsequently he held professorships at the universities of Erlangen (1820-26), and Munich (1827-40), and finally Berlin, where he was invited in 1841 at the suggestion of Emperor Frederick William IV. After the death of his wife in 1809, Schelling seemed to lose much of his productivity, and at the time of his death at Ragaz in Switzerland in 1854, he had outlived his fame.

Schelling was not primarily an original thinker and his works reveal the influence of Plato, Goethe, Schiller, Spinoza, Jakob Böhme, and Franz von Baader. He began as a disciple of Fichte; but nature, which was unimportant to Fichte, came increasingly to hold a position of prominence in Schelling's ideas. Schelling, who viewed nature more as a poet did than as a philosopher, believed in the absolute identity of the mind within us and nature without and formulated the thesis that nature was visible mind and mind invisible nature. His system, which is called philosophy of nature *(Naturphilosophie)* or philosophy of identity *(Identitätsphilosophie)* elevates the law of polarity to the highest principle of the world, with nature representing a unity or harmony of opposed forces. Art is regarded as the highest manifestation of the human mind, for it alone contains that perfect blending of nature and mind in which all contradictions are effaced. Schelling's vital concept of nature with its reconciliation of opposing forces appealed particularly to the romantic writers, and Schelling is known today predominantly as the philosopher of romanticism. His writings also influenced such men as H. Bergson, A. Günther, E. von Hartmann, A. Schopenhauer, F. Stahl, and H. Steffens. Despite his contribution to nineteenth century thought his reputation has suffered largely because of his inability to organize his ideas into a unified system.

Schelling's complete works, *Sämtliche Werke* (14 vols., 1856-61), were collected and edited by his son, K. F. A. Schelling. His principal works, containing his philosophy of nature, include *Ideen zu einer Philosophie der Natur* (1797), *Von der Weltseele* (1798), *Erster Entwurf eines Systems der Naturphilosophie* (1799), and *System des Transzendentalen Idealismus* (1800). Additional significant works are *Über das Verhältnis der Bildenden Künste zu der Natur* (1807), *Philosophie der Kunst* (1809), *Philosophische Untersuchungen über das Wesen der Menschlichen Freiheit* (1809), and *Zur Geschichte der Neueren Philosophie* (1826). In later years under the influence of mysticism and theosophy Schelling wrote *Philosophie der Mythologie* (1842) and *Philosophie der Offenbarung* (1842).

Schelling was also a writer who, while a member of the romantic circle, contributed regularly to the literary journals *Athenäum* and *Musenalmanach*. Because he used the pseudonym Bonaventura, he was long considered erroneously to be the author of the novel *Die Nachtwachen des Bonaventura*. His most noteworthy literary works are *Das Epikurische Glaubensbekenntnis Heinz Widerporstens* (1799), a poetic work in doggerel verse expressing his attitude toward nature, and the romantic epic poem *Die Letzten Worte des Pfarrers zu Drottning auf Seeland* (1802).

In 1871 T. Davidson translated *Ideen zu einer Philosophie der Natur* as *Introduction to the Philosophy of Nature* and *System des Transzendentalen Idealismus* as *Introduction to Idealism*. C. L. Bernays translated *Zur Geschichte der Neueren Philosophie* as *Practical Effects of Modern Philosophy* in 1873. *Das Verhältnis der Bildenden Künste zu der Natur* was translated by J. E. Cabot in 1913-15 as *On the Relation of the Plastic Arts to Nature*. In 1936 J. Gutmann translated *Philosophische Untersuchungen über das Wesen der Menschlichen Freiheit* under the title *Of Human Freedom*.

ABOUT: Gray-Smith, R. God in the Philosophy of Schelling; Royce, J. Lectures on Modern Idealism; Watson, J. Schelling's Transcendental Idealism. [In German—see studies by K. Fischer, H. Fuhrmann, K. Jaspers, H. Knittermeyer, G. C. Plitt, K. Schilling, G. Schneeberger (Bibliography), G. Stefansky, and H. Zeltner. In French—see study by J. Gibelin.]

D. G. D.

*SCHILLER, JOHANN CHRISTOPH FRIEDRICH (November 10, 1759-May 9, 1805), German dramatist, poet, historian, and philosopher, was born at Marbach in Württemberg. His father, Johann Caspar Schiller, an energetic and honorable man of positive but kindly nature, worked as a barber and surgeon, before becoming an army captain and finally overseer of the royal estate of Duke Karl Eugen of Württemberg. His mother, Elisabeth Dorothea Kodweiss, an innkeeper's daughter, possessed a gentle, cheerful disposition, and a poetic sensibility which her son inherited. The family was deeply religious, and not surprisingly Schiller early decided to become a clergyman, attending the Latin School of Ludwigsburg in preparation for this career. However, in 1773 Karl Eugen insisted that the boy enter his military academy at Castle Solitude, and the parents, limited in means, were afraid to refuse. Since theology was not offered, Schiller studied law, changing to medicine when the school was transferred to Stuttgart in 1775. The school was conducted with rigorous discipline, and Schiller chafed under the harsh restraint and lack of personal freedom. In Stuttgart conditions were less restrictive, and he gained access to the newest literature: Klopstock, Rousseau, Shakespeare, Goethe, Klinger, and Lenz. This reading, much of which pulsated with revolutionary spirit, stimulated Schiller's own creativity. In 1780, having completed his course and practicing as a regimental physician in Stuttgart, he completed his first drama, *Die Räuber*, which he published at his own expense the following year. This intense tragedy of a brave and noble man challenging his age and then submitting to the moral law marked Schiller as a born dramatist and as an energetic champion of liberty. When first performed by Baron Heribert von Dalberg in Mannheim in 1782, the play was greeted by a wildly enthusiastic audience, and its popularity has continued undiminished.

For attending two performances of his play, Schiller was sentenced to fourteen days' arrest and was prohibited by the duke from

* shĭl′ ẽr

SCHILLER

publishing anything except medical treatises. Unable to renounce literature, the poet fled in disguise to Mannheim, where he hoped for assistance from Dalberg. The latter, however, feared to incur the anger of the duke by aiding a deserter, and Schiller was in great distress, until help came from Henriette von Wolzogen, the mother of a fellow student. At her home in Bauerbach, Schiller published a collection of early poems, entitled *Anthologie auf das Jahr 1782*, completed two political dramas in prose, and began work on a third. *Die Verschwörung des Fiesko zu Genua* (1783), an ambitious historical drama treating the political revolution in Genoa in the sixteenth century, was unsuccessful, despite excellent characterizations. By contrast *Louise Millerin* (1783), which the actor Iffland renamed *Kabale und Liebe,* represents by virtue of its greater simplicity of plot and naturalness of tone artistically and dramatically the best of Schiller's early works. This drama of class conflict and social protest continues the tradition of the *bürgerliches Trauerspiel* or domestic tragedy and was strongly influenced by Gotthold Ephraim Lessing's *Emilia Galotti.*

When Dalberg realized that Karl Eugen did not intend to pursue Schiller, he appointed him dramatist in Mannheim for one year. There Schiller experienced the greatest passion of his life, for Charlotte von Kalb, the wife of a French officer. The intensity of Schiller's love is reflected in the love of Don Carlos and Elisabeth in the

drama *Don Carlos* as well as in the poems *Resignation* and *Der Kampf* (later titled *Freigeisterei der Leidenschaft).* When his contract with Dalberg was not renewed, Schiller turned to journalism and founded the literary periodical *Rheinische Thalia* (subsequently *Thalia* and *Neue Thalia),* which he published from 1785 to 1793. Although this enterprise increased the poet's literary prestige, it failed to alleviate his constant financial need.

Worried and uncertain about his future, Schiller received unexpected assistance when an admirer, Christian Gottfried Körner, father of the poet Theodor, invited him to Leipzig for a visit, and the next two years were spent there and in Dresden. The great friendship between the two men found expression in the magnificent ode *An die Freude,* which was set to music by Beethoven in the choral finale to the *Ninth Symphony.*

During this period the tragedy *Don Carlos* (1787) was finished and, although begun in prose, was recast in iambic blank verse, marking this work as the first of Schiller's great classical plays. Although in theme this drama continues Schiller's struggle against tyranny and despotism, the maturity of tone and the noble character Marquis Posa reveal the transition of the author from the Storm and Stress manner of his early works to the idealistic drama of ideas. In addition Schiller wrote two narratives, *Der Verbrecher aus Verlorener Ehre* (1787), and *Der Geisterseher* (1789), which he left uncompleted as an unworthy project, for he considered the novel as only the "half brother of poetry."

In 1787 Schiller settled in Weimar, where he devoted himself to classical studies and the translation of Greek and Roman texts. He developed a profound interest in history, and the period 1787-92 is dominated by historical research and writings. On the basis of his *Geschichte des Abfalls der Vereinigten Niederlande von der Spanischen Regierung* (1787), he was named professor of history in Jena in 1789. This position enabled him to marry Charlotte von Lengefeld with whom the poet found enduring happiness and contentment. Having at last found security and inner peace, Schiller applied himself with renewed enthusiasm to his lectures and to his *Geschichte des Dreissigjährigen Krieges* (1789-92). However, within a year he fell severely ill with pneumonia, and the remainder of his life became a constant struggle against chronic sickness.

Unable to continue teaching, Schiller once again faced financial worry, until he received a generous pension for three years from Prince Friedrich Christian von Schleswig-Holstein and Count Ernst von Schimmelmann. Schiller utilized this opportunity to study the philosophy of Kant, an experience of primary importance in his intellectual development and of profound influence on his later writings. The resulting publications, all important documents in the history of aesthetic theory, include *Anmut und Würde* (1793), *Über das Erhabene* (1793), *Über die Aesthetische Erziehung des Menschen* (1793), and *Über Naive und Sentimentalische Dichtung* (1795-96), which ranks next to Lessing's *Laokoon* as the most stimulating original critical essay of the eighteenth century. In these works Schiller attempted to determine the basic laws of beauty and to establish the connection of the beautiful with the world of the good and the true. Schiller's philosophical studies also influenced his lyrics, which are the outstanding examples of philosophical poems in German. His remarkable gift for endowing abstract philosophical ideas with concrete reality is revealed in poems such as *Das Mädchen aus der Fremde, Die Teilung der Erde, Pegasus im Joche, Die Ideale, Das Ideal und das Leben, Der Tanz, Der Genius,* and *Der Spaziergang.*

In 1794 Schiller established the literary journal *Die Horen* (1795-97), to which he invited Goethe along with other leading writers to contribute. Although the two poets had remained distant until then, this mutual endeavor brought about their warm and abiding friendship. When the journal failed, the two men united in retaliation against their critics with a collection of satirical distichs, *Xenien* (1796). To follow this negative task with a positive accomplishment, Schiller published the following year *Balladenalmanach* (1797), which contained many of his finest ballads: *Der Taucher, Der Handschuh, Der Ring des Polykrates, Die Kraniche des Ibykus, Der Gang nach dem Eisenhammer, Die Bürgschaft,* and *Der Kampf mit dem Drachen.* Schiller's ballads, unsurpassed in German literature, combine graphic description, bold conception, and rich imagination with powerful, melodious expression.

In 1799 Schiller moved permanently to Weimar, where he assisted Goethe in the theatre by preparing translations and adaptations of Shakespeare's *Macbeth,* Gozzi's *Turandot,* and Racine's *Phèdre.* At Goethe's urging he also resumed his own dramatic production, completing the trilogy *Wallenstein* (1799), his finest drama and one of the greatest historical dramas in German litera-

ture. Although plagued by constant ill health he continued to produce a drama almost every year: the historical tragedy *Maria Stuart* (1800), the romantic tragedy *Die Jungfrau von Orleans* (1801), the experimental classical tragedy *Die Braut von Messina* (1803), and the ever popular *Wilhelm Tell* (1804), which presents the struggle of the Swiss people for release from tyranny. Schiller was unable to complete his final tragedy, *Demetrius* (1805), before his premature death at the age of forty-five.

Schiller's life and writings represent the dedicated striving of a noble idealist toward the coming exalted age of a higher and freer humanity. Although his significance has become increasingly overshadowed by that of the more universal Goethe, he remains one of Germany's greatest and most beloved poets and holds a position of first importance in the cultural heritage of Germany.

Editions of Schiller's writings in English translation include L. Bohn, *Works* (4 vols., 1846-49); C. J. Hempel, *Complete Works* (2 vols., 1870); N. Routledge, *Poems and Plays* (1889); L. Bell, *Works* (7 vols., 1897-1903); and N. H. Dole, *Works* (8 vols., 1902), which includes Düntzer's *Life of Schiller,* translated by Percy Pinkerton. Among recent translations are J. T. Krumpelmann's verse rendering of *The Maid of Orleans* (1959) and *Friedrich Schiller: An Anthology for our Time,* ed. F. Ungar (1959).

ABOUT: Carlyle, T. Life of Schiller; Garland, H. B. Schiller; Kaufmann, F. W. Schiller, Poet of Philosophical Idealism; Mainland, W. F. Schiller and the Changing Past; Nevinson, H. Life and Works of Schiller; Norman, F., ed. Schiller: Bicentenary Lectures; Parry, E. C. Friedrich Schiller in America; Robertson, J. G. Schiller After a Century; Sime, J. Schiller; Stahl, E. L. Friedrich Schiller's Drama: Theory and Practice; Thomas, C. Life and Works of Schiller; Wilm, E. C. Philosophy of Schiller; Willson, A. L., ed. A Schiller Symposium (1960); Witte, W. Schiller. [In German—see studies by L. Bellermann, K. Berger, R. Buchwald, M. Gerhard, E. Kühnemann, J. Minor, F. Strich.]

D. G. D.

*SCHIMMEL, HENDRIK JAN (June 30, 1823-November 14, 1906), Dutch novelist, playwright, critic, and poet, was born in 's Gravenhage. He was one of ten children of Hendrik Poeroet Schimmel, mayor of that town, and of Sara Meijse. The household had to keep going with limited funds so that not much money was available for the education of the children. Hendrik Jan went to the local boarding school, operated by Baudet, and was intended to become a notary. In vain did Baudet advise that the bright boy be permitted to study. Father Schimmel was

* sĸĭm′ ĕl

a businessman who had no feeling for literature or the arts. At various times he thought it necessary to criticize his son for his silly interest in literature. When the father died in 1842, the family moved to Amsterdam where Hendrik Jan began to work for various monetary institutions until, in 1878, he retired as manager of Amsterdam's · credit union, and settled in Bussum where he devoted himself full-time to literature. Meanwhile he had written successfully in various genres and had become acquainted with such literary beacons as Alberdingk Thijm, Jacob van Lennep, and Potgieter. Thijm encouraged his first literary endeavors and invited him to write for the magazine *Spectator* (1848-49). Two years later Potgieter asked for contributions to *De Gids,* in which Schimmel began to publish part of his romantic works and for which he also wrote critical essays after 1861. He also became one of the directors of the literary *Nederland* (1854) and of *Elzeviers Geillustreerd Maandschrift* (1891-1903). In 1865, two years after the death of his mother whom he had supported since his father's death, he married Anna Maria Kalff (died 1882), by whom he had one son. In 1884 he married his sister-in-law. He died on his estate near Bussum.

Schimmel's interest in the stage resulted in his founding the society Het Tooneelverband (1872); he also had a hand in the founding of De Tooneelschool and of Het Nederlandsch Tooneel.

As an admirer of Schiller and Hugo he began his literary career with the writing of dramas. They were in the main historical. Some of these are: *Twee Tudors* (1847), *Gondebald* (1848), *Giovanni di Procida* (1849), *Oranje en Nederland* (1849), *Schuld en Boete* (1852), and *Struensee* (1868).

With great diligence and supported by his profound knowledge of the historical period involved, Schimmel also wrote a series of novels and . stories, the scenes of which are laid in the United Provinces and in England of the seventeenth century. *Sproken en Vertellingen* (1855), *De Eerste Dag eens Nieuwen Levens* (1855), *Een Haagsche Joffer* (1856), *Mary Hollis* (1860, translated into English in 1872), *Leidens Ontzet,* and *Mylady Carlisle* (1864)) are some of the titles. Most of them were reprinted several times. In the last period of his life Schimmel wrote some contemporary novels. However, both *Het Gezin van Baas van Ommeren* (1869) and *Verzoend* (1882) turned out to

be failures. The partly autobiographical *Jan Willems Levensboek* (1896) gives important insights into the life of the author. For at least fifty years Schimmel was one of the most popular Dutch authors. His complete prose works appeared in seventeen volumes between 1847 and 1887¡; his dramatic works were published in 1885 in three volumes. *Herfstloover* was the title under which he published his poems in 1871.

ABOUT: [In Dutch—Hunningher, B. Het Dramatische Werk van Schimmel; Robbers, H. Mannen en Vrouwen van Betekenis.]

H. B.

*SCHLEGEL, AUGUST WILHELM VON (September 8, 1767-May 12, 1845), German translator, critic, orientalist, and poet, was born in Hanover, the descendant of a prominent literary family. He was the nephew of the dramatist Johann Elias Schlegel, the son of Johann Adolf Schlegel, who contributed to the *Bremer Beiträge,* and the older brother of the writer Friedrich Schlegel (see sketch below). He attended the University of Göttingen, where he studied theology and later philology, and where he learned metrics from the poet Gottfried Bürger. After three years in Amsterdam as a private tutor, he became a *privatdozent* and two years later a professor of literature at the University of Jena. During this period Schlegel was active as a literary critic, writing for Schiller's various journals, *Die Neue Thalia, Die Horen,* and *Musenalmanach,* as well as for the *Allgemeine Literaturzeitung.* In 1796 he married Karoline Michaelis, an exceedingly gifted woman, who was the daughter of a professor at Göttingen. With her capable assistance Schlegel between 1798 and 1801 translated seventeen of Shakespeare's plays, an accomplishment which represents his outstanding literary achievement. These translations, which number among the finest ever made into German, gained for Shakespeare a position of great prominence in Germany. Rarely if ever has a foreign author been so completely assimilated into an alien culture as has been the case of Shakespeare in Germany. When in 1804 Karoline received a divorce to marry the philosopher Schelling, Schlegel failed to continue the project, and the remaining works were translated subsequently by Dorothea Tieck and Wolf Graf Baudissin.

Together with his brother Friedrich, Schlegel helped establish the first romantic school in Berlin and wrote the majority of articles

* shlä′ gĕl

845

AUGUST WILHELM VON SCHLEGEL

literature at the University of Bonn, a position which he held until his death in 1845. Here he taught the poet Heinrich Heine, who later recorded in his book *Die Romantische Schule* (1836) an interesting, if malicious, portrait of the aging scholar. During his later years Schlegel devoted himself chiefly to Oriental research and published a collection of texts under the title *Indische Bibliothek* (1820-30). He is considered to be the founder of the science of Old Indian philology.

By temperament and talent Schlegel was ideally suited for his rôle as translator and critic, and in both of these areas he stands out in his time. He lacked original poetic ability, as he himself realized, and his few attempts at imaginative writing were failures. His *Gedichte* (1800), although models of metrical perfection, lack life and appeal, and his classical tragedy *Ion* (1803), although performed by Goethe at Weimar, has been deservedly forgotten.

Über Dramatische Kunst und Literatur was first translated by J. Black in 1815 under the title *A Course of Lectures on Dramatic Art and Literature.* This translation, which was revised by J. W. Morrison in 1845, has been frequently reprinted, for the last time in 1902.

ABOUT: Atkinson, M. E. Schlegel as a Translator of Shakespeare; Brandes, G. Main Currents in Nineteenth Century Literature; Heine, H. The Romantic School; Lazenby, M. C. The Influence of Wieland and Eschenburg in Schlegel's Shakespeare Translation; Toynbee, G. A. W. Schlegel's Lectures on German Literature; Tymms, R. German Romantic Literature; Walzel, O. German Romanticism; Wernaer, R. M. Romanticism and the Romantic School in Germany; Willoughby, L. A. The Romantic Movement in Germany. [In German—see studies by B. von Brentano, O. Brant, R. Haym, J. Körner, V. de Pange, W. Richter, H Zehnder.]

D. G. D.

for the *Athenäum* (1798-1800), the journal which they founded to spread the doctrine of romanticism. The romantic school held together for only a few years, and after 1800 the various participants, including the two brothers, went separate ways.

From 1801 to 1804 Schlegel presented a series of lectures in Berlin entitled *Vorlesungen über Schöne Literatur und Kunst,* in which he summarized in a clear, intelligible manner the romantic concept of literature. He also pursued his interest in romance languages and literatures, and in *Spanisches Theater* (1803-09) translated five plays of Calderón. An additional volume, containing verse renditions of poems of Cervantes, Dante, Camões, and Ariosto, was titled *Blumensträusse Italienische, Spanische und Portugiesische Poesie* (1804).

In 1804, at Goethe's recommendation, Schlegel became a traveling companion and secretary to Mme de Staël, with whom he traveled through Italy, France, Denmark, Sweden, and England. They also visited Vienna, where Schlegel delivered his most famous series of lectures, *Über Dramatische Kunst und Literatur* (1809-11), in which he emphasized the dominant position of Shakespeare in world literature. After a period (1813-14) as secretary to Bernadotte, Crown Prince of Sweden, a service for which he was granted a patent of nobility, Schlegel rejoined Mme de Staël at Coppet in Switzerland and remained with her until her death in 1817. The following year he was appointed professor of the history of art and

*SCHLEGEL, FRIEDRICH VON (March 10, 1772-January 12, 1829), German critic, orientalist, and poet, was born in Hanover, the younger brother of the writer August Wilhelm Schlegel (see sketch above). After an unsettled youth, during which he trained for a career in business, Schlegel studied law at the universities of Göttingen and Leipzig. His brother's wife, Karoline, interested him in literature and philosophy, and from 1793 philology and the study of classical antiquity became his major interests. In 1797 he settled in Berlin, where in conjunction with his brother August, the poets Ludwig Tieck and Novalis, and the philosopher Schleiermacher, he formed the first

* shlā′ gĕl

FRIEDRICH VON SCHLEGEL

romantic school and established the journal *Athenäum* (1798-1800). In 1799 the school moved to Jena, where Schlegel completed his studies. In 1802 he traveled to Paris, where he lectured on philosophy and founded a second journal called *Europa*. He also engaged in the study of Oriental literature and languages, including Sanskrit. The results of his research became the basis of the work *Über die Sprache und Weisheit der Inder* (1808), one of his most important books, and a contribution which J. G. Robertson states "was the starting-point both for the study of Indian philology and the modern science of comparative philology." In 1804 Schlegel married Dorothea Veit, the daughter of the philosopher Moses Mendelssohn, and the couple settled in Cologne. After converting to Catholicism in 1808, they moved to Vienna, where Schlegel lectured on history, literature, and philosophy, and also served as editor for the journals *Oesterreichischer Beobachter* (1810), *Deutsches Museum* (1812-13), and *Concordia* (1820-23). From 1815 to 1818 he served as Austrian court secretary in Frankfurt, a service for which the Austrian government granted him a patent of nobility. He died in Dresden, where he was delivering a series of lectures.

In his early works, *Die Griechen und die Römer* (1797), *Geschichte der Poesie der Griechen und Römer* (1798), and *Gespräch über die Poesie* (1798), Schlegel attempted to establish the differences between ancient and modern literatures. Of his many shorter critical essays the most significant is the masterly analysis of Goethe's novel *Wilhelm Meister*, which Schlegel considered along with Fichte's *Wissenschaftslehre* and the French Revolution as one of the greatest symbols of his age. The form which best suited Schlegel's ability and temperament was the fragment, and his *Fragmente* (1798) contain the substance of his thought expressed in an aphoristic and often paradoxical manner. In *Fragment 116* Schlegel wrote his famous definition of romantic poetry, which states in part: "Romantic poetry is a progressive, universal poetry. . . . It is never completed but always evolving, and is wholly subjective, since the romantic poet recognizes no law above his own arbitrary will."

Schlegel was a highly gifted, original thinker who performed his best work as a critic and theorist of literature. His intellectual capacity was greater than his poetic ability, and his imaginative writings afford little artistic satisfaction. His novel *Lucinde* (1799) is a formless, rhapsodic work, which depicts the romanticists' belief in extreme individualism, particularly in erotic matters. *Alarcos* (1892), a pseudo-classical tragedy which Goethe performed at Weimar, and his collected poetry *Gedichte* (1809) are both devoid of literary merit. His last works, *Die Philosophie des Lebens* (1828), *Die Philosophie der Geschichte* (1829), and *Die Philosophie der Sprache* (1830), were all published lectures. The esoteric nature of his writings have kept Schlegel's works from being popular. He retains his importance, however, because of his creative position in the romantic movement, which has influenced the entire course of German literature.

Geschichte der Alten und Neuen Literatur was first translated in 1818 by J. G. Lockhart under the title *Lectures on the History of Literature Ancient and Modern*. J. B. Robertson translated *Die Philosophie der Geschichte* in 1835 as *The Philosophy of History*, and A. J. W. Morrison rendered *Die Philosophie des Lebens* in 1847 as *The Philosophy of Life and The Philosophy of Language*. In 1849 *The Aesthetic and Miscellaneous Works of Friedrich von Schlegel* were translated by E. J. Mollington, and *Über die Neuere Geschichte* was translated by L. Purcell and R. H. Whitelock under the title *A Course of Lectures on Modern History*. P. B. Thomas translated *Lucinde* in 1913-15.

ABOUT: Brandes, G. Main Currents in Nineteenth Century Literature; The German Classics, IV; Heine, H. The Romantic School; Lovejoy, A. O. Essays in the History of Ideas; Tymms, R. German Romantic Literature; Walzel, O. German Romanticism; Willoughby, L. A. The Romantic Movement in Germany; PMLA, LXXI (1956). [In German—see studies by C. Enders, H. Fincke, F. Gundolf, R. Haym, J. Körner, B. von Wiese, L. Wirz. In French —see study by L. Rouge.]

D. G. D.

*SCHLEGEL, JOHANN ELIAS (January 28, 1719-August 13, 1749), German dramatist and critic, was born at Meissen, Saxony, the second oldest child in a family of thirteen children. It was an old, respected Saxon family which produced many preachers, jurists and court officials, and Johann Elias' father, Johann Friedrich, was himself a jurist and a public official with poetic inclinations. His mother, Ulrika Rebecka Wilke, was a daughter of the school superintendent of the same place. Johann Elias received private instruction in his father's house until his fifteenth year, and in 1733 he became a student of the famous school of Pforta, where he began translating from the classics and writing verses and plays; one of the plays, *Orest und Pylades*, at first surreptitiously performed by his fellow-students, was afterwards performed in a slightly revised version by the well-known theatrical company of Frau Neuber.

In 1739 Schlegel went to the University of Leipzig to study law. There he came into direct contact with J. C. Gottsched, who was virtually the literary dictator of Germany and who was eager to guide and counsel any new and promising talent. Though seemingly accepting many hints and suggestions, Schlegel showed his independence from the very first by openly criticizing many of Gottsched's avowed models, by defending rhyming of comedies, and by indicating his preference for the "irregularities" of Shakespeare over the rule-bound pseudo-classic writers of tragedies in the now famous essay *Vergleichung Shakespears und Andreas Gryphs* (1741), which opened a new way for the understanding of Shakespeare in Germany. His own tragedy *Hermann* (1741) was one of the first tragedies based on this Germanic national hero, thus starting a whole series of dramas centered around him.

In 1743 Schlegel went to Copenhagen as secretary to von Spener, the Saxon envoy to the Danish court, spending four years there and becoming the founder of the German circle in the Danish capital to which many important German writers belonged. He immediately started acquiring a thorough knowledge of the Danish language, studied Danish history and literature, and became a personal friend of the Danish Molière, Holberg, whose comedies he read in the original. He also became the publisher of a moral weekly, *Der Fremde* (1746), with the idea of improving the literary taste and moral standards of the average man. In addition, he

wrote not only several theoretical works on the theatre, notably *Gedanken zur Aufnahme des Dänischen Theaters* and *Schreiben von Errichtung eines Theaters in Kopenhagen* (1746), but also one tragedy, *Canut* (1746), and several comedies. Some of these, especially *Der Geheimnisvolle* (1746), *Die Stumme Schönheit* (1747), and *Der Triumph der Guten Frauen*, were for a long time the favored plays on the contemporary stage. His *Canut* is the first dramatic result of Schlegel's studies of Danish history, and his unfinished play *Gothrika* was to be concerned with a similar subject.

In 1748 Schlegel married Johanna Sophia Niordt to whom he dedicated many of his anacreontic poems, and in the same year he became a professor of constitutional law and political science at the Danish Academy at Sorø. His duties there, however, required too much of him so that his health—he was always quite frail—suffered, and, as a result of a high fever, he died at the age of thirty; he was buried in the churchyard of Sorø Academy.

Schlegel's collected works appeared in five volumes in 1760-70, edited by his brother J. H. Schlegel, who acquired some reputation as a writer on Danish history. Another brother, Johann Adolf Schlegel (1721-93) was an eminent preacher and father of the well known romantic critics August Wilhelm and Friedrich von Schlegel (see sketches above).

ABOUT: Wilkinson, E. M. J. E. Schlegel, a German Pioneer in Aesthetics. [In German—Wolff, E. Johann Elias Schlegel.]

F. S. L.

*SCHLEIERMACHER, FRIEDRICH ERNST DANIEL** (November 21, 1768-February 12, 1834), German Protestant theologian and philosopher, was born in Breslau, the son of a Prussian army chaplain of the Reformed Confession. Both his grandfathers were ministers, and his mother stemmed from a family in Salzburg which had emigrated for the sake of religious convictions. Schleiermacher was educated in a Moravian school at Niesky in Silesia and at the Moravian theological seminary at Barby, near Halle. The religious spirit of his home and his early education by the Moravians made a lasting impression on him. He retained a profound piety even though he became alienated from the theological views of the Moravians. After obtaining his father's reluctant permission, Schleiermacher left

Barby and transferred to the University of Halle where the Pietist influence had been replaced by the critical spirit of the Enlightenment and Kant. The study of Kant absorbed Schleiermacher not only during his academic studies at Halle (1787-89), but almost exclusively until 1796.

A new phase in Schleiermacher's intellectual development was initiated when he moved to Berlin in order to accept a position as chaplain at the Charité Hospital in 1796. This city was then the center of the young romantic movement, and Schleiermacher became closely associated with it. He was a daily guest in the literary circle of Henriette Herz, and Friedrich Schlegel became his most intimate friend. The literary fruits of this association are his *Vertrauliche Briefe über Schlegels Lucinde* (1801) which he wrote in defense of his friend who had tried to formulate a new ethics of the sexes. Schleiermacher's famous translation of Plato's *Dialogues* was also inspired by Schlegel. At first the two friends collaborated on this great project, but Schleiermacher was left with the burden of the completion of the work.

During his time in Berlin Schleiermacher modified his Kantian position by opening himself to the influence of Spinoza, Jacobi, Fichte, and Schelling. The impact of these philosophers on his own thinking is reflected in his *Reden über die Religion an die Gebildeten unter Ihren Verächtern* (1799) and his "New Year's gift" at the turn of the century, the *Monologen* (1800). Both are key works of the romantic period. In his *Reden* he establishes the autonomy of religion as distinct from ethics and metaphysics by rooting religion in a peculiar form of immediate intuition. In the *Monologen* he developed his idea of individuality as the central concept of a new humanism.

From 1802 to 1804 Schleiermacher was pastor in the little Pomeranian town of Stolp. Besides continuing work on his translation of Plato, he wrote an analysis of ethics, *Grundlinien einer Kritik der Bisherigen Sittenlehre* (1803). These scholarly contributions prepared the way to an academic appointment. In 1804 Schleiermacher received a professorship and a chaplaincy at his former University of Halle which he held until the French invasion of 1806. After the battle of Jena Schleiermacher returned to Berlin (1807) where he was appointed to the pulpit of the Dreifaltigkeitskirche. In 1810 he was called to the newly created University of Berlin as head of the theological faculty.

He formulated the principles of his new responsibility in his *Kurze Darstellung des Theologischen Studiums* (1811), a work which has remained essentially the program of liberal Protestant theological education to the present.

As a church administrator Schleiermacher worked for the union of the Reformed and Lutheran Confessions which, however, much to his disappointment, came about in 1817 not as a result of free agreement between the parties concerned but by royal decree. The culmination of Schleiermacher's theological reflections was reached with the publication of his work *Der Christliche Glaube nach den Grundsätzen der Evangelischen Kirche im Zusammenhange Dargestellt*. The first edition appeared in 1821, a greatly revised edition in 1830-31. It is the most representative work of Protestant theology in the nineteenth century. As in his earlier work the *Reden*, Schleiermacher continued to be interested in the establishment of the autonomy of religion as distinct from ethics and metaphysics. He now defined its peculiar character as a sense of absolute dependence. Besides laying down the demarcation lines between the realms of religion, ethics, and metaphysics, Schleiermacher was concerned about the primacy of religion over theology. He insisted that it is religious experience which forms the background of theology but not theological doctrine which informs religious experience. He died in Berlin after a short illness.

Kurze Darstellung des Theologischen Studiums was translated as *Brief Outline of the Study of Theology* by W. Farrer in 1850. *Reden über die Religion an die Gebildeten unter Ihren Verächtern* was translated as *On Religion: Speeches to Its Cultured Despisers* by J. Oman in 1893. H. L. Friess translated the *Monologen* as *Soliloquies* (1926). *Der Christliche Glaube nach den Grundsätzen der Evangelischen Kirche Dargestellt* was translated by D. M. Baillie as *The Christian Faith* (1922); the second edition of the German work was translated by H. R. Mackintosh and J. S. Stewart under the same title (1928). The work is translated and paraphrased in condensed form in *The Theology of Schleiermacher*, by George Cross (1911). Of four volumes of letters (*Aus Schleiermachers Leben in Briefen*, edited by W. Dilthey, 1858-63) the first two were translated by F. Rowan in 1860 under the title *The Life of Schleiermacher as Unfolded in his Autobiography and Letters*.

ABOUT: Friess, H. L. *Introduction to Schleiermacher's Soliloquies*; Merz, J. T. *A History of European Thought in the Nineteenth Century*; Munro, R. *Schleiermacher: Personal and Speculative*; Selbie, W. B. *Schleiermacher: A Critical and Historical Study*; Wellek, R. *History of Modern Criticism*, II. [In French—see study by E. Cramoussel. In German—see studies by W. Dilthey, E. Huber, W. Loew, E. Troeltsch.]

H. H.

*SCHOPENHAUER, ARTHUR (February 22, 1788-September 21, 1860), German philosopher, was born in Danzig, the son of Heinrich Floris Schopenhauer, a wealthy merchant. His mother, Johanna Schopenhauer, was noted in her time as a celebrated novelist as well as a brilliant hostess whose salon in Weimar served as an intellectual and artistic center. Schopenhauer believed that a child inherited his temperament and character from his father and his quality of intelligence from his mother. In his own case this idea appears justified, for he possessed his father's quick temper, independent nature, love of liberty, and practical mind.

Schopenhauer was educated in a liberal and cosmopolitan fashion, and throughout his life he considered himself supranational. He was conspicuously lacking in that patriotic feeling and nationalistic fervor which featured so prominently in the contemporary philosophers Fichte and Hegel. From 1797 to 1799 Schopenhauer lived in France, where he mastered the French language and acquired a lasting fondness and respect for that nation. He likewise became proficient in English during a stay in England. During the years 1803-04 he traveled extensively through Holland, England, France, Switzerland, and Austria, before settling down at his father's insistence to a business career in Hamburg. Schopenhauer felt no inclination for this work, and following the death of his father in 1805 (possibly by suicide), he obtained permission from his mother to return to school. He completed the *Gymnasium* in Gotha and in 1809 entered the University of Göttingen to study medicine, transferring to philosophy the following year. During this period he was highly influenced by the teacher G. E. Schulze, who urged him to study Plato and Kant. From 1811 to 1813 Schopenhauer attended the University of Berlin, where he heard but was not impressed by the lectures of Fichte. He received his doctorate in philosophy from the University of Jena in 1813 with the published dissertation entitled *Über die Vierfache Wurzel des Satzes vom Zureichenden Grunde.* In this work, which shows great dependence upon the ideas of Kant, Schopenhauer presents an analysis of the law of cause and effect from the standpoint of the four forms—Logical, Physical, Mathematical, and Moral—which govern the four fundamental types of human knowledge. Schopenhauer always insisted that this work provided an indispensable introduction to his thought.

* shō′ pĕn hou ĕr

SCHOPENHAUER

In 1813 Schopenhauer visited his mother in Weimar, but their antagonistic personalities made it impossible for them to live together. During one particularly bitter quarrel his mother pushed him downstairs, and this event caused a complete break in their association. Schopenhauer never saw his mother again though she lived for another twenty-four years. It was largely his antipathy towards his mother that was responsible for the attitude of utter disdain and contempt which he manifests toward women in his writings. He never married.

During his stay in Weimar Schopenhauer met Goethe, who introduced the young scholar to his theory of colors. Schopenhauer became engrossed in the subject and produced the essay *Über das Sehen und die Farben* (1816), which he later expanded and rewrote in Latin under the title *Theoria Colorum Physiologica* (1830). Of more lasting influence and importance to his future development was Schopenhauer's acquaintance with the orientalist F. Mayer, who directed his attention to the philosophical theories of India and the Far East. Oriental philosophy subsequently formed a significant part of his thinking.

From 1814 to 1818 Schopenhauer lived in Dresden, where he produced his masterpiece, *Die Welt als Wille und Vorstellung* (1819; 2 vols., 1844; third expanded edition 1859). Here Schopenhauer developed his thesis that the world is idea, which is organized and directed by the will. In his system the will is regarded as the active principle of the universe, reaching its high point in man. The will is blind and goalless and is stimulated to action only by a sense of deficiency or suffering. To act, therefore, the will must remain ever unsatisfied, and life becomes a constant struggle to ward off suffering and pain. Happiness and pleasure are negative and undesirable achievements, for they produce satiation of the will and thus represent stagnation. Schopenhauer suggests two solutions to the dilemma of life. A temporary means of stilling desire is found in aesthetic experience. The more lasting escape from the problem of life is abandonment of the will to live, and thus by resignation and ascetic existence the achievement of the self-annihilation or state of Nirvana of the mystics and Buddhistic penitents.

Die Welt als Wille und Vorstellung is significant in the history of nineteenth century thought, because here for the first time the primacy of will over intellect was asserted, an idea which was of influence later both in philosophy and psychology. Richard Wagner, the writers Wilhelm Raabe and Thomas Mann, and the philosophers Nietzsche, Hartmann, James, Bergson, and Dewey, were all indebted to the ideas of Schopenhauer. Not only has Schopenhauer found favor among intellectuals, but he has attained popularity among the educated lay public, largely on the basis of the readability of his writings. He was one of the greatest prose writers of the nineteenth century, and *Die Welt als Wille und Vorstellung* is important as one of the outstanding works of art in the history of philosophy.

Following a trip to Italy Schopenhauer in 1820 became a *Privatdozent* at the University of Berlin. Out of pride he chose to lecture at the same hour as Hegel, then the leading figure in German philosophical circles. He attracted virtually no students and soon gave up his attempt at an academic career, although his name continued to appear in the university catalogue until 1831. His hostile and derogatory attitude toward academicians and philosophers stemmed from this humiliating experience as well as from the non-acceptance of his work by the colleagues whose recognition could have helped make his work known.

Despite his practical nature, Schopenhauer was obsessed by many phobias and fears, particularly of robbers (he always slept with loaded pistols at hand), disease, poison, and violence. The outbreak of a cholera epidemic in Berlin in 1831 frightened him from the city, and he settled in Frankfurt, which remained his home until his death at seventy-two. Shrewd investment of his patrimony made him financially independent, and the remainder of his life was spent as a private scholar. His unattractive personality discouraged friendships, and his only close companion was a dog.

His later works, *Über den Willen in der Natur* (1836), *Die Beiden Grundprobleme der Ethik* (1841), and *Parerga und Paralipomena* (2 vols., 1851), add little new to the ideas of his major work, but serve mainly as contributions to the development and perfection of his system. Recognition and acclaim, for which he longed all his life, came finally after 1848, when his system of metaphysical pessimism corresponded to the mood of the times. In 1858, on the occasion of his seventieth birthday, congratulations and praise arrived from all over the world. He is now considered one of the master stylists and outstanding original thinkers of nineteenth century German philosophy.

Schopenhauer's *Works* in English translation appeared in an edition abridged and edited by Will Durant in 1928 (Philosopher's Library). *The Philosophy of Schopenhauer* edited by I. Edman was published in 1928 in the Modern Library series. T. B. Saunders translated *Complete Essays* in 1942 and *Essays from the Parerga and Paralipomena* in 1951. *Die Welt als Wille und Vorstellung* was translated by R. B. Haldane and J. Kemp as *The World as Will and Idea* (3 vols., 1883-86) and by E. F. J. Payne as *The World as Will and Representation* (1958).

ABOUT: Copleston, F. Arthur Schopenhauer, Philosopher of Pessimism; Kelly, M. Kant's Ethics and Schopenhauer's Criticism; Knox, T. M. Aesthetic Theories of Kant, Hegel, and Schopenhauer; McGill, V. J. Schopenhauer, Pessimist and Pagan; Mann, T. The Living Thoughts of Schopenhauer; Tsanoff, R. A. Schopenhauer's Criticism and Kant's Theory of Experience; Wallace, W. Life of Arthur Schopenhauer; Whitaker, T. Schopenhauer; Zimmern, H. Schopenhauer. [In German—see studies by H. Busch, O. Eichler, K. Fischer, E. Grisebach, W. Gwinner, S. Hochfeld, A. Hübscher, K. O. Kurth, K. Pfeiffer, J. Volkelt and H. Zint. In French—see studies by T. Ribot and E. Seillière.]

D. G. D.

*SCHUBART, CHRISTIAN FRIEDRICH DANIEL (April 13, 1739-October 10, 1791), German poet, the son of a vicar was born in Sontheim in the province of Swabia. He attended school at Nördlingen and Nürnberg where he exhibited considerable poetic and musical talent. At Erlangen he began his university studies but his erratic and disorganized life here brought him only illness and debts. In 1760

* shōō′ bärt

he returned to his parents' home, now in Aalen, became a tutor in Königsbronn for a short time and finally obtained a position as a teacher and organist in Geisslingen. In 1764 he married, but suffered from the poverty which his position imposed upon him. He attempted escape from his miseries through literary and musical activity and at times through excessive drinking. While at Geisslingen he wrote his *Todesgesänge*, showing the influence of Klopstock, and *Zaubereien*, written in the manner of Wieland. In 1769 he was summoned to Ludwigsburg as organist and director of music. His wit and his poetic and musical gifts opened many doors for him here, but his erratic behavior disturbed not only the peace of his own home, but the original good will of his patrons. A love affair in which he became involved caused his wife to separate from him and eventually brought him a short prison term. He was discharged from his position and banished from the country.

After wandering about southern Germany he went to Mannheim where he offended the Elector of the Palatinate and was obliged to move on. He intended to make his fortune in Munich by being converted to Catholicism, but this plan too came to no fruition. Schubart next decided to try Stockholm, but succeeded only in reaching Augsburg. Here in 1774 he began the publishing of his journal *Deutsche Chronik*, which gained great popularity because of its patriotic position, lively articles, and daring statements. When the censor in Augsburg suppressed the journal, Schubart continued it in Ulm. Through guile Duke Charles of Württemberg in 1777 captured Schubart and had him imprisoned in the Hohenasperg for his "impertinence toward almost all the crowned heads of the world." Schubart was to remain in humiliating imprisonment, separated from his family, for ten years. Not until May 1787 was the physically ruined man released. This was accomplished only through the intervention of Prussia on his behalf. To cap the often senseless behavior of absolute despots, he was then made court poet and theatre director in Stuttgart where he again took up the edition of his journal *Deutsche Chronik*. The last four years of his life were spent in relative ease and affluence. He died in Stuttgart, aged fifty-two.

Schubart's poetry and other belletristic works are an accurate reflection of his personality. His irregular, frivolous, impetuous behavior is closely akin to the uneven, undisciplined composition he committed to paper.

His name has been remembered because of his fate as a man, not because of his writings. His poetry would have long been forgotten, but for the peculiarly unfortunate course of his life. He left behind his memoirs, *Schubarts Leben und Gesinnungen* (1791-93), which were written during his imprisonment, but they cannot be considered accurate because he had become a crushed and pathetic type of pietist while a prisoner. His *Sämtliche Gedichte* appeared first in Stuttgart in 1786 and his *Gesammelten Schriften* came out in eight volumes in Stuttgart in 1840.

English translations of Schubart's writings are extremely rare. Selections from his poems may be found in A. F. Baskerville's *The Poetry of Germany* (1853).

ABOUT: [In German—see studies by E. Holzer, T. Jäger, K. M. Klob, S. Nestriepke, F. Schairer.]

E. K. G.

*SCHWAB, GUSTAV BENJAMIN (June 19, 1792-November 4, 1850), German poet, translator, editor, critic, and philologist, was born in Stuttgart, the son of a *Gymnasium* professor. From 1809 to 1814 he studied theology, philosophy, and philology at the University of Tübingen. There he became closely associated with the Swabian circle of poets and formed lifelong friendships with Ludwig Uhland, Justinus Kerner, and Karl Mayer. In 1815 he published his first work, an anthology of student and drinking songs under the title *Neues Deutsche Allgemeine Commers- und Liederbuch*, containing the still popular "Bemooster Bursch Zieh' ich aus." Following a trip to Berlin that same year, he returned to Tübingen to work as a professor's assistant, while continuing his own studies in classical and Germanic philology. In 1817, after being appointed professor of classics at the *Obergymnasium* in Stuttgart, he married Sophie Gmelin, the daughter of a professor at the University of Tübingen. From 1827 to 1837 Schwab edited the literary supplement of the *Morgenblatt*. He also published, in conjunction with Chamisso, the influential journal *Deutsches Musenalmanach* (1833-38), which introduced and supported many young poets of this period, most notably Nikolaus Lenau. In 1837 Schwab accepted a pastorate in Gomaringen, near Tübingen, a position which allowed him ample leisure to pursue his literary interests. In 1841 he was called to a pastorate in Stuttgart and in 1845 was designated supervisor of the school system. The University of Tübingen acknowledged his

* shväp

growing reputation by awarding him an honorary doctor of theology degree in 1845. Schwab died in Stuttgart at fifty-eight of a heart attack.

Schwab was a genial, sociable, well-liked individual, who was amazingly active and productive in many directions and fields. Although he was admittedly strongly influenced by Uhland, he lacked his model's depth, liveliness, and independence of style. His creative works on the whole are neither original nor profound but do possess a charm and appeal in the manner of execution. His verse, *Gedichte* (2 vols., 1828-29), relies heavily on skillful technique for its effectiveness and rises only occasionally above mediocrity. Schwab was a reflective rather than a spontaneous poet. His poems lack inspiration and often lapse into the merely rhetorical. His finest poetic achievements are his ballads, such as *Der Reiter und der Bodensee, Das Gewitter,* and *Der Riese von Marbach.*

Since Schwab possessed primarily a recreative or imitative ability rather than strength of originality, his talents are best displayed in the retelling of older legends and tales. His best-known and most lasting works are his adaptations of the German chapbooks *Deutsche Volksbücher* (3 vols., 1836), along with the collections *Die Schönsten Geschichten und Sagen* (2 vols., 1836) and *Die Schönsten Sagen des Klassischen Altertums* (3 vols., 1838-39). In the field of philology Schwab was extremely productive, editing and anthologizing new versions of older authors and works. Among the more notable of his many contributions are *Rollenhagens Froschmäuseler* (1819), *Paul Fleming* (1820), *Wilhelm Müllers Schriften* (1830), and *Wilhelm Hauffs Schriften* (1830). In addition he published a successful travelogue of his beloved Swabia entitled *Wanderungen durch Schwaben* (1836), as well as a monograph on Friedrich Schiller, entitled *Schillers Leben* (1840).

W. A. Gardner translated *The Legend of the Three Holy Kings* (1845). In 1946 Olga Marx and Ernst Morwitz translated *Gods and Heroes; Myths and Epics of Ancient Greece.*

ABOUT: [In German—see studies by K. Klüpfel, W. Schulze, G. Stock, C. T. Schwab, T. Wurm.]

D. G. D.

---

*SCHWOB, (MAYER ANDRÉ) MARCEL (August 23, 1867-February 26, 1905), French man of letters, was born at Chaville, in the Île-de-France. His father, Isaac

* shwôb'

Georges, of a family of rabbis and doctors, had frequented Banville, Gautier, Baudelaire; he had been a Fourierist, and an important functionary in Egypt before becoming a newspaper owner in France. His mother, Mathilde Cahun, traced her ancestry to the Jewish Cayms who had fought in the crusades with St. Louis. Marcel had a brother, Maurice, who became a newspaper owner, and a sister, Maggy, who became a pianist.

Marcel spoke fluent German and English (and, of course, French) by the age of three. He attended school in Nantes, where his father had bought a newspaper. He was a brilliant student; comparative philology was one of his numerous interests while he was still in his early teens. In 1882 Marcel went to Paris to study at the Lycée Sainte-Barbe. He lived with his uncle Léon Cahun, specialist in ancient histories and languages and librarian of the Mazarine Library. It was Cahun who inspired Marcel with the highest standards for translations, as well as an intimate feeling for the charm of legends, adventure, and children's stories. Exceptional in classical and modern languages, Marcel, while still a student at the *lycée,* attended lectures at learned institutions at the same time that he was reading Schopenhauer and writing morbid and Villonesque verse and varied tales. He interrupted his schooling in 1885-86 to volunteer for military service in the artillery. After returning to his studies, he failed to be accepted by the École Normale Supérieure, but studied at the Sorbonne. The courses of the philosopher Boutroux were his favorites. In 1888 Marcel graduated at the head of the class. The following year, with Georges Guieysse, he published an important study on French slang. In 1890, twenty-three years old, he presented discoveries, made under the aegis of Auguste Longnon, on François Villon. That same year he became a contributor to *L'Événement* and to *L'Echo de Paris;* he also wrote for *Le Phare de la Loire. Mœurs des Diurnales* (1903), published under the pseudonym Loyson-Bridet, is a satire on journalism.

Tales and short stories originally appearing in these newspapers were published as *Cœur Double* (1891), *Le Roi au Masque d'Or* (1892), *Mimes* (1894), and *La Lampe de Psyché* (1903). Literatures of various epochs and languages furnished the data for these tales, related with great skill in the use of perversity and surprise. *La Croisade des Enfants* (1896) utilized slight references in medieval sources; *Vies Imaginaires,* of the same year, set forth his imaginative conception of biography, and *Spicilège*—also published in 1896—contains studies of Villon, Robert Louis Stevenson, and George Meredith. Schwob excelled in the art of translation: *Moll Flanders* was published in 1895; with Eugène Morand five years later he adapted *Hamlet* for Sarah Bernhardt, and he translated F. Marion Crawford's *Francesca da Rimini* in 1902.

Schwob had a love affair with a tubercular girl named Louise, which furnished him with the basis for the nihilistic *Livre de Monelle* (1894). He then fell passionately in love with the actress Marguerite Moreno, whom he married in 1900 in England. Between 1895 and his early death Schwob underwent a series of five operations. He had recourse to morphine to relieve excessive pain. Attended by a Chinese companion, Ting, he was largely confined to his home except for brief trips to find diversion for his discomfort. He visited Samoa (1901-02), and Spain, Portugal, and Italy with F. Marion Crawford (1904). While at home his salon was a center for English visitors. In 1904 Schwob delivered a notable series of lectures on Villon at the École des Hautes Études Sociales in Paris. His edition of the *Parnasse Satyrique du XVe Siècle* was published posthumously (1905). He died of pneumonia, and was buried in Montparnasse cemetery.

Schwob was admired by Paul Claudel, Léon Daudet, Jules Renard, Anatole France. Alfred Jarry dedicated *Ubu Roi* (1896) to Schwob, as did Charles Whibley his translation of Rabelais. Pierre Champion edited a ten-volume *Œuvres Complètes* (1927-30), and wrote a critical biography of him (1927). Schwob's importance in the history of medieval scholarship has been recognized, but his short stories are still to be fully appreciated in the history of that genre.

Translations have been made of *The Book of Monelle* by M. B. Meloney (1929), of *The Children's Crusade* by H. C. Greene (1898), of *Imaginary Lives* by Lorimer Hammond (1924). A. Lenalie translated *Mimes* (1901) and "R. L. S." (1920), originally written for *The New Review* of February 1895.

ABOUT: Cambiaire, C. P. The Influence of Edgar Allan Poe in France; France, A. Life and Letters, series 4; Lalou, R. Contemporary French Literature; Romanic Review, XXII (1931), XXV (1934); Thompson, V. French Portraits. [In French—Champion, P. Marcel Schwob et Son Temps; Cahiers du Collège de Pataphysique, no. 22-23 (1955). In Italian—Letteratura, no. 7 (Gennaio-Febbraio 1954).]

S. S. W.

*SCRIBE, AUGUSTIN EUGÈNE (December 24, 1791-February 20, 1861), French dramatist, born in Paris in the populous quarter of Les Halles, was the son of a modest silk merchant; after his father's death he continued his studies, with some distinction, at the Sainte-Barbe college. His early interest in the theatre, and his close friendship with the Delavigne brothers, suffered briefly as he studied law, but in 1811 his *Les Dervis*, composed in collaboration with Germain Delavigne, had some success, as also *Les Brigands sans le Savoir* of the following year. Scribe's first dozen plays were highly imitative, for example, of Pixérécourt, Duval, and Picard; his resolution is noteworthy in the face of their constant failure, and he soon learned that success would come far better from portrayal of current customs. His first notoriety dates from *Une Nuit de la Garde Nationale* (1816), and the minor scandal provoked by the profession he satirized so wittily. From this time on, he devoted himself entirely to the theatre.

Scribe's career falls into several periods according to the genres he practiced and his gradually rising mastery of the techniques. Beginning in 1816, he concentrated on the "vaudeville," intended primarily to amuse, and usually ornamented with catchy popular songs of which the best had their moment of wide popular appeal. In this lightest manner *L'Ours et le Pacha* is typically excellent, and was esteemed by the German critic Schlegel. In more serious vein *Le Solliciteur* is reminiscent of Molière. Scribe entered his second and most active period in 1820 when he became associated with the new theatre Le Gymnase, under an advantageous contract with its director Delestre-Poirson. Here the comedy of intrigue was the favorite and in some 150 plays, mostly written with collaborators, Scribe showed his fertility and his skill in the construction of plots with well planned and appropriate surprises and endings, light yet revealing contemporary manners and preoccupations. His fame continued unabated after the Revolution of 1830. Scribe's third and last period opened in 1833 with the realization of his great desire to appear at the Comédie Française. His first work in a new and more substantial and serious vein, *Bertrand et Raton*, was followed by his masterpieces of the full scale realistic comedy of customs, notably *Bataille de Dames* (1851). The historical play *Adrienne Lecouvreur* (1849), written for the actress Rachel, deals with more or less real events

* skrēb

SCRIBE

work toward the end and in the best of the formal comedies, *Bataille de Dames.*

The factors that limit Scribe to a minor position as a dramatist are his undistinguished style and his lack of power in the creation of character. In contrast, his command of dramatic situation and plot, unrivaled in his day, represents a complete reorientation in the theatre and a current of "well-built" plays still more or less the norm. His writings have the further though lesser merits of gaiety and of documentation on customs. His characters are normally mere types, so that the plays have no true depth or universality. The younger generation of ambitious money-makers and social climbers of the Restoration period is set in contrast with the old soldiers of the Napoleonic era. This method of types rises from vaudeville, an outgrowth of the eighteenth century comic-opera and the Italian *commedia dell' arte,* merely brought a bit up to date. Since the plays depend heavily on plot and situation, there are many traces of probable influence, for instance of Molière or of Marivaux.

Scribe's immense influence in his day and, later, on the work of Sardou, another master of complicated plot and situation and portrayal of types, was salutary, primarily as a reaction against the mannerisms of the romantic theatre, its excessively melodramatic effects and insistence on unusual subjects. Scribe was instrumental in replacing these means with study of middle-class problems and realities in conservative, ironical, and optimistic vein. Partial editions of his plays appeared in 1837-42 in twenty-four volumes and in 1856-59 in ten volumes, and the complete works in seventy-six volumes from 1874 to 1885.

of 1730. Scribe continued to compose vaudevilles, and turned to them by preference after a series of failures in the 1850's.

Aside from his election to the French Academy in 1834, Scribe's life was uneventful and wholly devoted to his writing. Many anecdotes relate his generosity, for example to his director Delestre-Poirson, who importuned him with unwanted collaboration but whose early help Scribe never forgot. He was a cordial host at his country estate in Séricourt, and married happily late in life. As tastes changed, his work was forgotten, but his business sense and his early success had made him a rich man. His principal comedies were translated almost immediately into English, slightly adapted to suit London tastes, by Planché and others, and spread his fame abroad. He also composed a considerable number of libretti of operas significant in their time, *L'Africaine, Les Huguenots, La Juive, Robert le Diable, Fra Diavolo,* and others adapted for Italian composers—Bellini's *La Sonnambula* and Verdi's *Un Ballo in Maschera.*

Jealous contemporaries reproached Scribe for his constant use of collaborators, and claimed that the real qualities of his plays derived from the latter. Actually, of these men, Casimir Delavigne alone is remembered today. In most cases Scribe merely found an idea or a situation in otherwise unusable manuscripts and, through sheer generosity, added its author's name. One man alone, Legouvé, appears to have enhanced Scribe's

There are a host of English translations, including the texts of many libretti *(The Jewess, The Masked Ball* of Auber); the more available of the translated plays are *The Scholar,* by J. Buckstone (1835), *The School for Politicians* (1840), *Adrienne Lecouvreur* (1855 and 1917), *A Glass of Water,* by W. Suter (about 1865), *The Ladies' Battle* (about 1870), *Fleurette,* by F. Clark (1882), *A Russian Honeymoon* (1883), and *The Queen's Gambit,* by M. Valency (1956).

ABOUT: Arvin, N. C. Scribe and the French Theatre; Matthews, B. French Dramatists of the Nineteenth Century; Southern Quarterly, I (1963). [In French—Charlot, M. Théâtre Choisi d'Eugène Scribe, *preface;* Revue d'Histoire Littéraire de la France, 1920; Rolland, J. Les Comédies Politiques de Scribe.]

F. J. C.

*SCUDÉRY, MADELEINE DE (1607-June 2, 1701), French novelist, was born at Le Havre of a military father from a family of Provence. She and her brother Georges (1601-67) were orphaned at an early age, and maintained a close relationship in their literary projects. Georges is known especially for his military career, his plays, his attack against Corneille's *Le Cid*, his election to the French Academy in 1650, and an epic poem of 1653. Madeleine's uneventful life passed in calm among her many friends. She is reputed to have been very ugly, but was esteemed for her virtue and probity of soul; indeed this judgment, made by Boileau, led him to refrain from criticizing her work until after her death. She was particularly intimate with the group of the Marquise de Rambouillet.

Madeleine's first novel, *Ibrahim*, published in four volumes in 1641, is set in the times of Emperor Charles V and is a tale of adventure in Oriental lands. This work, and her two major novels, were signed by her brother, but the public recognized them as hers, and considered that Georges had merely proposed parts of the plots. *Artamène ou Le Grand Cyrus*, in ten volumes, from 1649 to 1653, is her masterpiece, and the outstanding example of the heroic sentimental novel of the classical period. It is new in its more intelligent treatment of inner feeling and its high moral tone. Under the allegory and the disguise of ancient names and local color, the readers recognized persons and problems of the day, and the existence of catalogs identifying the characters with living persons illustrates the intense interest in this feature. The book may also be considered as a manual on elegant manners, as a moral code of "honnêteté," or even to some degree as a protest against the excesses of preciosity of the poetry of such writers as Voiture; it is true, meanwhile, that Mlle de Scudéry carries preciosity to greater extremes than many of her contemporaries in the circle of the Marquise de Rambouillet.

The subject of *Artamène ou le Grand Cyrus* is very strongly romanesque. Taking her characters and situations from antiquity, Madeleine created endless stories of travel, shipwreck, imprisonment, and flight, with descriptions of naval engagements and individual chivalric combat, usually in the tone of parables of honor and virtue. The work appealed to readers for the excitement and anticipation of the serial form, much in the fashion of the novels of Dumas. The mysti-

* scü dä rē'

856

fication of the hidden identities made of it a vast panorama of contemporary customs and persons. Certain episodes are of particular note from this point of view, while others achieve valid artistic effects through the style and rich imagination of the author.

Madeleine's other novel *Clélie, Histoire Romaine*, follows the same general pattern, in a Roman setting, but its publication, in ten volumes, from 1654 to 1660, came at a time when the subject matter of romanesque adventure was largely outworn. Of *Clélie* the part best remembered is the "Carte du Tendre," still a valuable illustration of the preciosity of the mid-seventeenth century. This allegorical map emerged as the collective game of Madeleine's Saturday groups; through the place names, representing the dangers to love and the true ways to its achievement, an entire code of the art of courtship emerges: the true road, on this map, passes through Sincerity, Great Heart Generosity, and Goodness, on its way to the port of "Tenderness-on-Esteem."

The English translations prove the immediate popularity of Madeleine's work: *Artamenes or the Grand Cyrus* (five vols., 1653-55, and 1691), *Clelia* (five vols., 1655-61, *Ibrahim* (1652), *Almahide or the Captive Queen* (1677), and *Conversations Upon Several Subjects* (1683).

ABOUT: Mason, A. The Women of the French Salons. [In French—Aragonnès, C. Madeleine de Scudéry; Le Breton, A. Le Roman au Dix-Septième Siècle; Magendie, M. La Politesse Mondaine et les Théories de l'Honnêteté en France.]

F. J. C.

SEALSFIELD, CHARLES (pseudonym of **KARL ANTON POSTL**) (March 3, 1793-May 26, 1864), Austrian novelist and short-story writer, was born the son of a farmer in Znaim, Moravia. He was ordained a priest in the order of the Kreuzherren in Prague in 1814, but in 1822 fled this life, escaping through Switzerland to England and then to America. For the next decade he traveled widely through the United States and Mexico, working as a farmer, journalist, and writer. In 1832 he settled in Switzerland, which, with the exception of three extended trips to the United States, remained his home until his death at Solothurn in 1864. Only through his final testament was Sealsfield's true identity revealed.

As a writer Sealsfield contributed to the development of the ethnographical novel in which the collective hero replaced the conventional hero. As his poetic creed he stated: "My hero is the entire nation. Its social, public and private life, its material, political, and religious aspects take the place of adventures. . . ." Sealsfield possessed a keen eye for detail, and his works, *Gesammelte Werke* (18 vols., 1842), overwhelm the reader with their colorful descriptions and their forcefulness of style. He excels in portraying local color, and his description of the Jacinto prairie in Texas is considered a masterpiece of descriptive writing. He did not intend merely to entertain, but always had a pedagogic view in mind. His writings helped create in Germany the image of America as the "golden land of freedom."

Sealsfield's first book, *Die Vereinigten Staaten von Nordamerika nach Ihrer Politischen, Religiösen und Gesellschaftlichen Verhältnisse Betrachtet* (1827), was followed by several works in English, including *The Americans as They Are* (1827), *Austria as It Is* (1828) and the novel *Tokeah, or The White Rose, an Indian Tale* (1828). This adventure novel, which reveals the influence of Cooper, was a great success and was translated into German under the title *Der Legitime und die Republikaner* (1833). Other notable works include *Transatlantische Reiseskizzen* (1834), *Der Virey und die Aristokraten* (3 vols, 1835), a novel set in Mexico and considered one of his finest works; *Lebensbilder aus Beiden Hemisphären* (6 vols, 1835-37), a collection of short stories and novels; *Deutsch-Amerikanische Wahlverwandschaften* (1839-40); *Das Kajütenbuch, oder Nationale Charakteristiken* (2 vols., 1842), his greatest success; and *Süden und Norden* (1842-43). After the revolution of 1848 his popularity declined sharply.

Lebensbilder aus der Westlichen Hemisphäre was translated in 1842 as *Life in the New World* by G. C. Hebbe and J. A. Mackay. *Süden und Norden* was translated in 1844 as *North and South; or Scenes and Adventures in Mexico* by J. T. Headly. In 1845 *Der Virey und die Aristokraten* appeared in *Blackwood's Magazine* under the title *The Viceroy and the Aristocracy*. *Die Deutsch-Amerikanischen Wahlverwandschaften* was translated anonymously in 1846. Sarah Powell translated *Das Kajütenbuch* in 1852 as *The Cabin Book,* or *National Characteristics*. F. Riederer published Sealsfield's *American Novels* in 1937.

ABOUT: Dallmann, W. P. The Spirit of America as Interpreted in the Works of Charles Sealsfield; Faust, A. B. Charles Sealsfield, His Influence upon American Literature, *also* "Charles Sealsfield's Place in German Literature" *in* Americana Germanica I (1897); Heller, O. and Leon, T. H. Charles Sealsfield: Bibliography, *also* The Language of Sealsfield; Uhlendorf, B. A. "Charles Sealsfield Ethnic and National Problems in his Works" *in* Jahrbuch Deutsch-Amerikanische Historische Gesellschaft von Illinois XX-XXI (1920-21). [In German—see studies by E. Castle and H. Zimpel.]

D. G. D.

SECUNDUS, JOANNES NICOLAI

(November 14, 1511-September 24, 1536), neo-Latin poet of the Netherlands, was born in the Hague, the fifth and youngest son of the chief justice of the high court of Holland, Zeeland, and Friesland, Dr. Nicolai Everardi, and Elizabeth van Blyoul. Secundus' elder brothers became high officials in state or church, educated men for whom music and literature were indispensable ingredients to a well-rounded life. By virtue of his small collection of love songs, *Basia* (1535), Secundus is the representative par excellence of a group of humanists of his day. His very physiognomy brings to mind the Mediterranean south with its beauty and refined culture. His face, engraved by the Dutchman Jan Muller, reminds us of Petrarch.

Like so many members of the guild of humanists, Secundus traveled abroad in order to complete his education. In 1528 he went to Mechelen, Belgium, and then to France (Bourges) where he followed the lectures of the famous Italian jurist and emblematic poet Alciatus, together with Carolus Sucquetus, whose father had been one of the friends of Erasmus. In 1534 Secundus was in Toledo, Spain, as secretary to the bishop Johannes Tavera. Charles V took him along on a trip to Tunisia but Secundus' physical condition did not permit him to stay there. He returned to the Netherlands and accepted a post from Georg van Egmond, the bishop of Utrecht. Secundus died at the age of twenty-five in Doornik, Belgium.

The *Basia* is a small collection of fewer than twenty love songs. Small as they are in number, they impressed Secundus' contemporaries deeply, not only in Holland, but also abroad. They were admired and imitated until late in the following century. What distinguishes the *Basia* from earlier songs is the fact that here for the first time passion is curbed by disciplined principles of beauty. To be sure, much of that beauty is borrowed from old poets, from Catullus, Propertius, and also Sannazaro, but Secundus made that beauty his very own. Moreover, in the manner in which he represented nature Secundus was a man of the new era. Like Petrarch, he had a modern feeling for nature and an admiration for its beauty. Wit and irony, rarely encountered in medieval literature but abundantly present with the humanists, is also present in Secundus' work. Small wonder that with all its splendid qualities the *Basia* was imitated by the French poets. They were also imitated and translated elsewhere. In

SECUNDUS

Holland alone there have been twelve poets who translated the collection into Dutch.

The elegies which Secundus wrote were of an earlier date than the *Basia*. They are the work of Secundus' early youth, full of passion and joy of life, but cannot equal the *Basia* in qualities of composition and technique.

The *Basia* was translated into English verse by G. Ogle in the eighteenth century and published in 1901. Another version is *The Love Poems of Joannes Secundus*, translated by F. A. Wright in 1930.
ABOUT: Crane, D. Johannes Secundus. [In Dutch—G. Kalff, Geschiedenis der Nederlandsche Letterkunde, III.]

H. B.

*SEDAINE, MICHEL JEAN (July 4, 1719-May 17, 1797), French dramatist, born in Paris, was the son of an architect. Financially ruined, Sedaine's father and his family moved to Berry where, upon his father's death, Michel Jean worked as a mason to support his mother and three brothers. Successful in this trade, he was recognized by the architect Buron, whose aid Sedaine in turn acknowledged by helping to introduce to the artistic world Buron's grandson, the painter David.

But Sedaine's true *métier* was writing, and having studied literature during his leisure hours, he turned first to poetry. In 1745 he published "Epître à mon Habit" and in 1750 he assembled under the title *Recueil de Pièces*

* sē dân'

858

Fugitives fables, cantatas, songs, pastorales, and a short vaudeville, "La Tentation de Saint Antoine." These pieces were followed by a didactic poem, "Le Vaudeville," all of which made him known to the literary scene.

His genius, however, was to be realized in writing for the theatre—comic opera of which he became the master. He wrote many musical dramas for the Opéra Comique and the Comédie Française, collaborating with Philidor, Monsigny, and Gréty, who composed the music: *Le Diable à Quatre* (1756); *Blaise le Savetier* (1759); *L'Huître et les Plaideurs* (1759); *Les Troqueurs Dupés* (1761); *Le Jardinier et Son Seigneur, On ne s'Avise jamais du Tout, Le Roi et le Fumier* (1762); *Rose et Colas* (1763); *Les Sabots* (1768); *Le Déserteur* (1769); *Aucassin et Nicolette* (1780); *Richard Cœur de Lion* (1784). It was this last play which opened the doors of the Académie Française for him in 1786. In addition he wrote three operas—*Aline, Reine de Golconde* (1766), *Amphytrion* (1788), *Guillaume Tell* (1791)— and two historic dramas, *Raymond V, Comte de Toulouse* and *Maillard ou Paris Sauvé*, which were never presented on the stage.

Apart from delighting audiences, Sedaine had aspirations to write more serious drama. This he realized in two plays he wrote for the Théâtre Français: *Le Philosophe sans le Savoir* (1765) and *La Gageure Imprévue* (1768). *Le Philosophe*, considered the best model of serious comedy or of the bourgeois drama, was highly successful and played each year up to the Revolution. Voltaire, Grimm, Diderot applauded it, and the latter said Sedaine was an inheritor of the Shakespearean legacy. In this play Sedaine posed moral theses showing conflict between social judgments and natural instinct as he developed the domestic situation of M. Vanderk and family, thus giving a tableau of eighteenth century bourgeois manners. It is not a profound play, but at the same time it is not full of meaningless declamation and bombast as were some of Diderot's and Beaumarchais' works. Honest, simple, and sound of judgment, it is, in the opinion of Brunetière, all that is lacking in Diderot. *Le Philosophe*, with its natural dialogue and pathetic situation, is the kind of bourgeois drama Diderot dreamed of writing. It is in this sense that Sedaine is accorded the honor of having written the true and first model of the type of drama to be developed later by Scribe, Augier, and Dumas.

Le Déserteur was translated into English by C. Dibdin, 1820; *La Gageure Imprévue* by J. J. Foorde, 1788; *Richard Cœur de Lion* by John Burgoyne, 1787.

ABOUT: [In French—Günther, L. L'Œuvre Dramatique de Sedaine.]

G. E.

*SÉNANCOUR, ÉTIENNE PIVERT DE (November 16, 1770-January 10, 1846), French writer, was born in Paris. Little is known to us of his life except through a biography by his daughter, Eulalie Virginie Pauline, and this document is itself all too incomplete. A rare illustration shows Sénancour to have been a tight-lipped man of average height and build. His Roman nose and high forehead were unrelieved by the slickness of his closely-combed hair.

Sénancour's wealthy father was one of the king's advisers and bore the title of "Contrôleur Alternatif des Rentes de l'Hôtel de Ville." Both he and his wife, a good and affectionate mother, shared a nostalgic devotion for religious life, wishing for their son the peace of the cloister and compelling him to perform long exercises of piety which bored him. He spent four lonely and unhappy years at the Collège de la Marche. A curate near Senlis, however, opened his eyes to the beauties of nature. His penchant was then as ever to find the moral physiognomy of inanimate objects. When in July 1789 his father persisted in urging him toward the Saint-Sulpice seminary—an impossibility for Sénancour, whose wide range of reading from Marcus Aurelius to Voltaire and Confucius to Richardson disintegrated into an early intellectual nihilism—and an equally misguided relative promoted the idea of his becoming a businessman, he made the telling decision of his life: he ran off to Switzerland.

Shortly thereafter, in September 1790, he married Mlle Daguet in Fribourg, a "serious and sad" young lady of patrician background. The union resulted in more unhappiness; she could not meet the aspirations of his "somber and profound" heart, refused a life of inconsequential isolation, and became, with age, "taciturn, imperious, austere, and brusque." Apathy became Sénancour's pattern of behavior; the feeling of incapacity which overpowered him seemed to him to result from the malevolent conspiracy of things. Eventually he courted illness and was able to justify his spiritual weakness by his physical.

During the Revolution his often perilous trips to France (he had been classified as an

* sã näɴ kōor'

émigré) and other efforts to save his bourgeois family fortune were fruitless. Two children, a daughter and son, hardly helped his domestic woes. In 1802 he separated amicably from his wife. Another woman occupied much of his thinking, one Mme Walckenaër, whom he could not pursue because of an ill-advised letter to her which almost instigated a duel. She appeared as the ideal spiritual companion, but Sénancour's reaction was typically neurotic: "I felt I was standing alongside happiness; I was frightened."

By this time his personality had been shaped: irritable temper, suffering ego, incapacity to participate in civic affairs, proud disdain for commonly esteemed interests, pusillanimous manias, and unhealthy attachments to trivia. Yet his was a sensitive perceptiveness and an unrelenting intellectual penetration into his psyche, which a regime of "artificial paradises"—wine, tea, coffee, opium—seemed to enhance rather than stultify.

In 1793 Sénancour published some *Rêveries,* signed "Rêveur des Alpes," extracts from his readings accompanied by pessimistic declamations; in 1795 he turned Illuminist with *Aldomen ou le Bonheur dans l'Obscurité* under the influence of Dupont de Nemours' cult of planetary intelligences. His first work in his own name appeared in 1799: *Rêveries sur la Nature Primitive de l'Homme,* a search, in a chimeric return to nature, for an art of living, and a romantic statement of two themes: the abortive life and the misunderstood genius. No doubt Sénancour was a disciple of Rousseau and Saint-Pierre, but he was a pessimistic and disaffected disciple.

Around the turn of the century, he lived in Paris where he became a preceptor in a distinguished home and where a good circle of friends provided a healthy therapy for his morose disposition. But not being able to settle anywhere for any period of time, he soon returned to his Swiss seclusion in Saint-Saphorin and commenced working on his most famous book, *Obermann,* an epistolary autobiography published in Paris in 1804. Instead of recognizing the vanity of things, Obermann recognizes his own inability to be and to do what he wished. As the author expected, the book enjoyed no success, except perhaps among a handful of highly sensitive spirits, usually strangers to success.

Obermann was completed in Paris; in Paris, too, he wrote *De l'Amour* in 1805, which created a short-lived scandal. He

859

lived mostly in and about the capital with his daughter during these years; Mme Sénancour died in 1808. Intellectually, he abandoned eighteenth century Epicureanism and developed a religious acceptance of suffering as essential to moral life. Stoicism and Christianity inspired him, but not the Christianity of Chateaubriand for whom he nourished a tenacious antipathy. In 1811 he wrote his *Observations sur le Génie du Christianisme,* and in 1813 the manuscript of his last important work, *Libres Méditations d'un Solitaire* (published in 1819) was ready. Although undeceived by the superstition of happiness, he continued to cultivate the pleasures of failure and the pride of the ever-isolated genius.

In 1814-15 he lived in Remiremont and the Vosges area, publishing political brochures against Napoleon and the Revolution, the Congress of Vienna, England, Russia, etc. Before returning to Paris, he spent two years in solitary study. While he continued to publish political essays, he subsisted by works of popularization: *Résumé de l'Histoire de la Chine* (1824), *Résumé des Traditions Morales et Religieuses* (1825), *Résumé de l'Histoire Romaine* (1827). The second of these was judged irreligious and subversive in 1827. Haughty and gauche in his defense, Sénancour received a nine-months prison sentence and a fine, but was acquitted after appealing his case.

Nothing, however, gave Sénancour a public, not even the notoriety stemming from *De l'Amour,* until Sainte-Beuve's admiring essay on *Obermann* in 1832. George Sand, Charles Nodier, and others followed with favorable comments, and for a while at least, "the hermit of the tribe of snails" (as Sénancour designated himself) tasted a little success. He formed several close friendships. Ministers Thiers and Villemain assured him successive state pensions. In 1841 he was saddened over the loss by fire of several manuscripts. Moreover, he was rapidly losing his physical faculties. When he died in Saint-Cloud in 1846, he was virtually forgotten; a handful of friends followed his coffin. His epitaph read: "Eternity, be my refuge." In 1852 the English poet Matthew Arnold paid tribute to him in his poem "Obermann."

The first English translation of *Obermann* was a partial translation: *Obermann: Selection of Letters to a Friend by E. P. Sénancour,* by Jessie P. Frothingham in 1901. The first complete translation was done by A. E. Waite in 1903. Another was made by J. A. Barnes (1910-14).

ABOUT: Brooks, V. W. The Malady of the Ideal; Modern Language Review, January 1941; Sewanee Review, November 1895. [In French—see studies by J. Merlant, G. Michaut.]

J.-P. B.

*SÉVIGNÉ, MARIE (DE RABUTIN-CHANTAL), Marquise de (February 5, 1626-April 17, 1696), French letter-writer, was born in Paris, the granddaughter, on her paternal side, of Jeanne de Chantal, who collaborated with St. François de Sales in the founding of the Order of Visitation and who was canonized in 1767. On her maternal side, she belonged to the Coulanges family. Her father was killed in battle against the English in 1627, and her mother died when she was but seven years old. A very pretty and rich orphan, she was placed under the guardianship of her maternal uncles, Philippe and Christophe de Coulanges. She received a solid education and had the well-known Chapelain and Ménage for masters.

On August 4, 1644, Marie de Rabutin-Chantal married the marquis Henri de Sévigné. Their two children, Françoise Marguerite and Charles, were born in 1646 and 1648 respectively. On February 4, 1652, the marquis de Sévigné was killed in a duel by M. d'Albret.

Now widowed, Mme de Sévigné devoted her life to her children. Charles chose an army career and, in 1684, married Mlle Bréhan de Mauron. On January 28, 1669, Françoise Marguerite married the comte de Grignan, lieutenant-general of the governor of Provence. After the birth of Françoise Marguerite's first child, Mme de Grignan rejoined her husband in Provence (February 4, 1671) and, from this date, a regular semiweekly correspondence took place between Mme de Sévigné and her daughter.

Mme de Sévigné's life was spent at intervals between Paris and Livry, in her husband's domains in Brittany, at her land in Burgundy, or at Vichy where she took cures for rheumatism (1676, 1677, and 1687), and with her daughter at Grignan, near Montélimar (1672-73, 1690-91, 1694-96), where she died after a brief illness aggravated by her deep concerns over her daughter's health.

Many of Mme de Sévigné's letters had been kept or copied by her correspondents. Her autographed letters, however, have been lost for the most part. These letters, or copies which we can account for, amount to fifteen hundred in number. They cover a period of over twenty-five years. One of

* sā vē nyā'

MADAME DE SÉVIGNÉ

the major and unique attractions of this correspondence is its spontaneity and its transparency. Mme de Sévigné revealed her life and her thoughts completely. She lived worthily and wisely through an orphan-childhood, a happy but short marriage, and a premature widowhood. All the emotions concurrent with these turns of events were quietly reported in her letters. She also reflected the normal interests and observations of a *grande dame* of the seventeenth century as well as of a mother concerned with her children, young or adult: their ills, their extravagances, their own children.

Alertly, robustly, she met life and was pleased with being alive. Her trips to her domains, her care of possessions, her readings and chance meetings with acquaintances, her conversations and her friends: Retz, Fouquet, La Rochefoucauld, Mme de La Fayette, Ménage, the Coulanges—all were here in her living letters. On the other hand, she revealed no love except that for her children and no ambition, even at court, except for her son.

As for literary ambition, such is not apparent. When her cousin, Bussy, wished to prepare her letters for publication, she was complaisant. Moreover, she kept no journal or notes for a novel. Instead, her apparent aim was simply to keep her daughter informed of her thoughts, of what and whom she had seen, of the inexhaustible supply of material derived from life near the court. Her art of describing and of relating is, then, a strictly spontaneous one. If some lines become maxims, then they are the natural utterances of a thinking person.

Because these are anecdotal letters, they show natural repetitiousness as of a solicitous mother, now anxious about the perils of her daughter's trip across France, now apprehensive about the dangers of her own domains. Moreover, because these are letters from a woman who saw actually and imaginatively, they are precise, lucid, vibrant and therefore important documents of her times. Mme de Sévigné saw with the eyes of a reporter but also with those of an artist. She could report the execution of a nun or the red buds of spring, and for this she was greatly admired by Marcel Proust. What she did not actually see, she saw imaginatively through the eyes of another. Her ability to reconstruct was intense; her empathy was even stronger. "Think of his hearing the iron doors close. . . . Think of his awakening," she said, when she heard of the maréchal de Luxembourg's imprisonment. This ability to see and to feel forced her sometimes to report in dialogue, still so alive was the scene or the voice in her mind. In short vivacious sentences filled with movement, she caught even the tone of the voice, the emotional color of the scene. She animated everything she wrote; in this lies her force. She saw ideas, as well as actualities, and therefore became an interpreter of universal values, making her letters of lasting importance to literature for their witnessing of man as well as of an epoch.

Translations of Mme de Sévigné's letters have been made by A. E. Newton (1927) and R. Aldington (1937).

About: Aldis, J. Madame de Sévigné; Allentuch, H. Madame de Sévigné: A Portrait in Letters; Contemporary Review, 1956; Tilley, A. A. Madame de Sévigné. [In French—see studies by A. Bailly, G. Gailly, J. Lemoine.]

R. P. C.

"SHCHEDRIN, N." See SALTYKOV-SHCHEDRIN, MIKHAIL YEVGRA-FOVICH

SHENSHIN. See FET, AFANASY AFANASYEVICH

*SHEVCHENKO, TARAS GRIGORIE-VICH (March 9, 1814-March 10, 1861), Russian (Ukrainian) poet and artist, was born in Morintsy village, province of Kiev, to a family of serfs. Orphaned at an early

* shĕf chän' kô

861

age, the boy was forced to fend for himself, and he eked out a miserable existence running errands and doing odd jobs in the neighborhood. He received some schooling from a teacher in the nearby village of Kirilovka who was also the local sexton. Young Taras earned his keep in the service of this man by saying prayers over deceased parishioners. Living in a state of semi-starvation, enduring the winters without shoes or warm clothing, beaten regularly by the sexton, Taras somehow managed to survive his childhood. When he was about fourteen, he came upon the sexton lying in a drunken stupor, tied him up, and gave him a thorough beating.

Forced to flee for his life, he roved the countryside, eventually gravitating to the icon painters in Lysianko and Khlipnovka. His talent for drawing had already begun to develop, and a land-owner, Engelhart, on the advice of a local painter, took the apprentice icon-painter into his estate as a potential interior decorator. In the service of Engelhart, Tara was taken to Vilna and, finally, to St. Petersburg (1831), as his talents both for painting and for poetry had now fully developed.

In 1832 Engelhart sold Shevchenko as an indentured servant to a painting contractor in St. Petersburg named Shirayev, an ignorant, brutal man in whose service the young painter languished for almost seven years, painting murals in public buildings.

In the course of this service he was again "discovered," this time by the artist Soshenko, who was also of Ukrainian origin, and who introduced Shevchenko to the famous Academy of Arts. With the help of his new friends, among whom was the poet Zhukovsky, whose portrait by Brullov was raffled off to raise money for Shevchenko, his freedom was purchased and he was able to enter the Academy and complete his studies under Brullov.

Shevchenko more than fulfilled the confidence of his benefactors, compiling a brilliant record of artistic achievement at the Academy and winning many prizes for his work. But his bent for poetry could not be denied. He had begun writing popular ballads in Ukrainian during his service with Shirayev and by 1840 had completed his first collection of poems, *Kobzar* (The Bard), which earned him the nickname of "the Ukrainian Pushkin." In 1841 he wrote the poem *Haidamaki* (Free Cossacks), and in 1842 the periodical *Mayak* (The Beacon) published an excerpt from his drama *Nikita*

Haidai in Russian. Although Shevchenko wrote most of his work in Ukrainian, his poetry was never published in that language until the Kiev edition (1939-51) appeared. The Czarist government's "Russification" policies never permitted publication in languages other than Russian.

In 1843 Shevchenko spent a year in the Ukraine painting an album of pictures of the life in that area before he returned to St. Petersburg to complete his studies at the Academy, from which he was graduated in 1845. He was immediately commissioned as the artist to accompany an archeological expedition to the Ukraine to study ancient relics. In the course of this work he met and fell in love with the daughter of the sexton for whom he had labored in his childhood. But the shadow of his humble origin—from which he was destined never to escape—again intervened, and the match was forbidden by her family.

In 1846 he joined a secret society of Ukrainian nationalists, and, his membership having been discovered the following year, he was forced into the army. In 1848 he took part in an expedition to the Aral sea as military draftsman and cartographer. The general in command did what he could to make the atrocious conditions of military life bearable to the artist, and in 1850 petitioned the Czar through Count Orlov to free Shevchenko to paint. The result of this gesture was that Shevchenko was transferred to another regiment where conditions were even worse, and where the artist was forced to remain until the amnesty of 1857. But the damage had been done, and Shevchenko survived his service only three years.

In 1858, having obtained permission to return to St. Petersburg, he again joined the Academy under the patronage of its head. Here he edited his army writings for publication and painted several new canvases on Ukrainian subjects. In 1859 he returned to the Ukraine where he hoped to buy a little piece of land to retire on, but the deal fell through when the landlord, taking offense at some minor disagreement, falsely denounced him to the authorities for "sacrilege." Although he was released at once, he never did get his land. A second love affair came to nothing in 1860 when the girl ran off with a younger man. Back in St. Petersburg the lonely, ailing poet-artist once more tried to find a partner in a literate and intelligent servant girl who agreed to marry him but broke off their engagement on the very eve of the wedding.

During these two years the representatives of Ukrainian society in St. Petersburg finally obtained permission to publish a periodical (in Russian) dealing with Ukrainian affairs. Shevchenko took an active part in the organization of this publication, but in 1861 his health suddenly failed completely. He became an invalid, and, clinging to life in daily expectation of the Emancipation of the Serfs (signed March 3, but not proclaimed until March 17), died nevertheless before the announcement on the day after his fifty-seventh birthday.

In art Shevchenko is recognized as moving away from the academic school headed by Brullov (who resembles the French academics of the nineteenth century) toward social realism in his approach to the actualities of Russian and Ukrainian life. His poetical works have made him the great Ukrainian national poet, and he is recognized today as the only great poet and artist to have risen from the people in Russia during his time. In 1964, the 150th anniversary of his birth, Shevchenko was honored in both the U.S.S.R. and the United States. At the festivities in Kiev he was hailed as a rebel against Czarist tyranny, a "revolutionary and a democrat." In Washington, D.C., a statue of Shevchenko was unveiled in ceremonies sponsored by anti-Communist Ukrainian national groups.

A selection of his poems was translated by C. A. Manning and published in 1945 under the title *Taras Shevchenko, Poet of the Ukraine*; A. Stefan's *Translations from Shevchenko* appeared in 1947.

ABOUT: Manning, C. A. *Introduction to* Taras Shevchenko; Matthews, W. K. Taras Shevchenko.

L. R. & H. H.

*SIENKIEWICZ, HENRYK (May 5, 1846-November 15, 1916), Polish novelist, was born in Wola Okrzejska, to Jozef and Stefania (Cieciszowska) Sienkiewicz, of a patrician family. Educated mainly in Warsaw, he studied philology at the University of Warsaw, from which he took his degree in 1870. In the course of his career as a journalist, he traveled widely in Europe, Africa, and North America. In 1876 he came to the United States hoping to establish a utopian Polish community in California. Sienkiewicz married three times. By his first wife, Maria Szetkiewicz, who died in 1885, he had a son and a daughter. His second marriage, to Maria Wolodkowicz, was annulled; in 1904 he married Maria Babska. He died in Vevey,

* shĕn kyĕ′ vĕch

SIENKIEWICZ

Switzerland, where he was serving as chairman of a committee to aid Polish war victims. His body was returned to Poland in 1924 and buried in the Cathedral of St. John in Warsaw.

Sienkiewicz's literary talent developed in the spirit of realism, but like Prus and Orzeszkowa he owed much to the Polish romantic heritage. His career as a writer dates from 1869 when, under the pen-name "Litwos," he started contributing articles, sketches, literary essays, and short stories to periodicals and daily papers in Warsaw. His journey to North America, which proved to be important as a literary stimulus, was described in *Letters from America* in the *Gazeta Polska*, and was also reflected in several short stories of this period—"Za Chlebem" (After Bread, 1882), "Przez Stepy" (Across the Steppes, 1882), "Sachem" (1883), and others. In his early short stories Sienkiewicz revealed himself as a representative of the philosophy of positivism, a realist in literary technique, and a propagator of democratic ideas. At the same time, there is from the very beginning a note of romantic protest against narrow positivism and a tendency to appeal not so much to the reader's reason as to his feelings. *Janko Muzykant* ("Yanko the Musician," 1880) may be cited as a good example of this approach. A romantic fascination with the historic past comes to the fore in stories like *Stary Sluga* (The Old Servant, 1875), *Hania* (1876), etc.

Sienkiewicz's first novel, the first part of an historical trilogy, was published in installments in *Slowo* under the title *Ogniem i Mieczem (With Fire and Sword)* in 1884. The second part, *Potop (The Deluge)*, was published in 1886, and the third part, *Pan Wolodyjowski*, in 1887-88. These novels made Sienkiewicz the most popular writer in Poland. The trilogy is distinguished by a simple but fascinating and fast-moving plot interwoven with dramatic historical events of the seventeenth century when Poland, still one of the great powers in Europe, was being shaken by conflicts and invasions. Sienkiewicz did not directly idealize the past, but by portraying the catastrophes of the past and stressing that they nevertheless did not destroy the national spirit, he sought to "encourage the hearts" of his politically enslaved countrymen.

From historical themes Sienkiewicz turned to the contemporary psychological novel. In 1891, he published the novel *Bez Dogmatu (Without Dogma)*. Here, too, Sienkiewicz displayed an unusual artistic talent. His Polish Hamlet, Ploszowski, together with Turgenev's Rudin and Goncharov's Oblomov, became a literary symbol in world literature. Sienkiewicz's next novel, *Rodzina Polaniec-kich* (The Polaniecki Family, 1895), which is an anticipation of the twentieth century family epic, was the one most frequently criticized by the author's contemporaries for its alleged reactionary tendencies. It seems, however, that Sienkiewicz may, indeed, have been more concerned with creating the figure of a convincing Philistine than in making a social and economic program of his own.

In 1896 Sienkiewicz's most famous work, *Quo Vadis,* appeared. The theme of this novel, so well-known to readers and moviegoers all over the world, was the oft-depicted struggle between the decaying Roman Empire and the revolutionary spirit of Christianity. But in no other work was this struggle presented with such vividness. Sienkiewicz's popularity in world literature was enormous; the editions of *Quo Vadis* went into many millions of copies (over 250 editions in France alone), and the award to him of the Nobel Prize for Literature in 1905 confirmed his international fame.

The last novel of importance by Sienkiewicz was *Krzyzacy (The Knights of the Cross*, 1900). It is again a historical work, based on the struggle between Poland and the Teutonic knights in the fifteenth century. Sharply nationalistic in spirit, it is nevertheless a well balanced work of art. By that time Sienkiewicz had become an internationally recognized literary celebrity honored by his countrymen, and respected even by Poland's worst political enemies.

It is true that in his works Sienkiewicz often resorts to well-known devices in story writing; it is true that he is not a deep and original thinker. But because of his remarkable artistic appeal, he became *the* writer of his people and also one of the most popular writers in world literature, actually the only writer of Polish origin except Joseph Conrad whose name and works are familiar to the educated in all parts of the world. "It is really something completely unique," wrote the Polish writer S. Zeromski some time later, "that one man, out of inner power, would become the spiritual leader of his people and extend the boundaries of his country all over the world."

The collected works of Sienkiewicz, published 1899-1906, run to 81 volumes. New editions were published in 1922 and in 1950. His novels have been translated into many languages. Available in English translations are the trilogy *With Fire and Sword, The Deluge, Pan Michael (Pan Wolody-jowski)*, translated by J. Curtin (1896-1902), several times reprinted; *The Knights of the Cross*, by J. Curtin (1901), and several other translations; *Without Dogma*, by Isa Young (1893, 1906, etc.); *Quo Vadis*, authorized translation by J. Curtin (1900) and numerous editions; *In Desert and Wilderness (W Pustyni i w Puszczy)*, by M. A. Drezmal (1912); *Children of Soil (Rodzina Polanieckich)* by J. Curtin (1898); and many collections of short stories, including J. Curtin's *Yanko the Musician and Other Stories* (1893) and M. M. Gardner's *Tales from Henry Sienkiewicz* (1931). His letters describing his American travels were translated by C. Morley as *Portrait of America* in 1959.

ABOUT: Dyboski, R. Modern Polish Literature; Gardner, M. M. The Patriot Novelist of Poland; Lednicki, W. H. Sienkiewicz: A Retrospective Synthesis; Phelps, W. L. Essays on Modern Novelists. [In Polish—see studies by I. Chrzanowski, K. Czachowski, K. Wojciechowski. In French—Kosko, M. Un Bestseller 1900: Quo Vadis.]

Z. F.

*SIGURJÓNSSON, JÓHANN (June 19, 1880-August 31, 1919), Icelandic dramatist and poet, was born at Laxamýri in the north of Iceland, the son of a well-to-do farmer and landowner. On his mother's side he was related to Jónas Hallgrímsson (see sketch above), the great Icelandic romantic poet.

After graduating at the age of nineteen from the College of Iceland in Reykjavík with a concentration in mathematics and natural science, he went to Copenhagen to study veterinary science at the university. His interest in literature and his love for the theatre

* sĭ′ gŭr yōns sŏn

soon proved dominant, however, with the result that, after passing his examinations in science with honor, he dedicated himself to playwriting. He realized that if he were to be successful, he must write in a language that had a larger reading and play-going public than had Icelandic. He chose Danish, thereby setting a precedent which was followed by the novelist Gunnar Gunnarsson and the dramatist Guðmundur Kamban.

Sigurjónsson's decision to devote himself to literature rather than to science was not entirely unexpected. He had already published a number of strikingly beautiful poems. Technically they reveal a lack of experience but they show evidence of real poetic talent. Imagination Jóhann had in abundance, great vitality and energy, together with a delicacy of expression that had already come to the favorable attention of Bjørnstjerne Bjørnsson.

Sigurjónsson's first dramatic venture, *Dr. Rung*, a psychological study of a scientist torn between devotion to his science and love for his beautiful wife, though published by Gyldendal at the recommendation of Bjørnson, was not produced. He had already written *Skyggen* (The Shadow) which had been neither produced nor published. His next play, written almost simultaneously in Icelandic and Danish, *Bóndinn á Hrauni* (1908); *Gaarden Hraun* (The Hraun Farm, 1912) was given a successful première at Reykjavík on December 26, 1908. In 1913, after Sigurjónsson had already become famous, it was staged by the Royal Theatre in Copenhagen. It is a psychological drama as is *Dr. Rung*, but in this play the struggle is in the mind of a farmer who must make a choice between the material as represented by his farm and the spiritual as represented by the love and affection of his daughter.

During the winter 1911-12 Sigurjónsson's *Bjaerg Ejvind og hans Hustru*, which was to become known in Icelandic as *Fjalla Eyvindur* and in English as *Eyvind of the Hills* (translated from the Danish by H. K. Schanche and published together with *The Hraun Farm*, by the American Scandinavian Foundation, 1916) was staged and produced in Copenhagen. It was an instant success, was soon translated into other languages including French (*Le Proscrit et Sa Femme*), and was produced in Germany, Stockholm, Christiania (Oslo), and elsewhere. It was enthusiastically reviewed by Georg Brandes, the Danish critic, who called it "the best play of the year," and by literary and dramatic critics throughout Europe. Overnight Jóhann

Sigurjónsson had achieved almost world-wide recognition. In this play Jóhann tests the power of love to hold two people together under the most difficult conditions.

Sigurjónsson's next play, *Önsket* (The Wish), published in Copenhagen in 1915 and in Iceland the same year under the title of *Galdra Loftur* (Loftur the Magician), failed to meet with the enthusiasm accorded *Eyvind of the Hills*. It was, however, and has continued to be, a favorite in the Icelandic dramatic repertoire. His last completed play, *Lögneren* (Icelandic, *Lýgarinn*; English *The Liar*, 1917), was well received by the Royal Theatres in Stockholm (1917) and Copenhagen (1918), but still fell short of the unqualified success achieved by *Eyvind of the Hills*.

Some critics have felt that Sigurjónsson had his best productive years ahead of him when he was cut down in 1918 by an attack of influenza, dying in August of the following year. In his thirty-nine years he had achieved greater honors than any Icelandic dramatist before him. Only Guðmundur Kamban's *Hadda Padda* (1912) was to rival Jóhann Sigurjónsson's *Eyvind of the Hills*.

In Icelandic, Sigurjónsson's works (selections) have been published by Mál og Minning, edited by Kristinn Andrésson and with a commentary on the poet by Gunnar Gunnarsson. It is entitled *Rit, I-II* (1940-41).

ABOUT: Einarsson, S. History of Icelandic Prose Writers 1800-1940.

L. B.

SILESIUS, ANGELUS. See ANGELUS SILESIUS

*SKARGA, PIOTR (1536-September 27, 1612), Polish theologian and political writer, was born Piotr Paweski in Grojec and died in Crakow. He was educated at the Crakow Academy. In 1569 he joined the Jesuit Order, and taught at the Jesuit College at Pultusk, later becoming rector of the Jesuit Academy at Vilna. In 1588 he was nominated by the Polish King Sigismund III as preacher of the court.

Skarga engaged in ardent fights against Protestantism and the church schism, and wrote a number of pamphlets characterized by intolerance. His other works are of religious character, among them *O Jednosci Kosciola Bozego* (On the Unity of God's Church, 1577); *Zywoty Swietych* (The Lives

* skär' gä

of the Saints, 1579); *Siedem Filarow na Ktorych Stoi Katolicka Nauka o Przenaj-swietszym Sakramencie* (Seven Pillars on Which the Catholic Dogma on the Holiest Sacrament Is Based); collections of sermons, *Kazania na Niedziele i Swieta* (Sermons for Sundays and Holidays, 1595); *Synod Brze-ski i Jego Obrona* (Synod of Brzesk and its Defense, 1597); *Kazania o Siedmiu Sakra-mentach* (Sermons on the Seven Sacraments, 1600); *Kazania Przygodne* (Sermons for Different Occasions, 1610).

The most important of Skarga's sermons are the so-called *Kasania Sejmowe* (Sermons before the Diet, 1597), which are not only of a religious, but also of a political character. These sermons are characterized by unusual strength of feeling and of expression in presenting all the evils of contemporary Poland: class-egoism of the gentry, internal quarrels, the weakness of the king, and the oppression of the peasants.

Skarga, as a leading political theorist, was deeply aware of the inadequacy of the Polish electoral system, which later on led to the weakening of the state and, as a consequence, to the partitioning of Poland. There are also gloomy prophecies about the future of Poland. His prose attained the highest level in old Polish literature.

Skarga is one of the four writers of the so-called "Golden Age" of Polish literature, the others being Mikolaj Rej, Jan Kochanow-ski, and Frycz Modrzewski. Each wrote in a different field to which he gave works of permanent value: Rej in Polish prose, Koch-anowski in poetry, Modrzewski in progres-sive political and social thought, and Skarga in inspired oratory. Thanks to them, Polish literature reached at that time the highest level in the entire Slavonic world and chal-lenged comparison with the literature of Western Europe.

The only English translation of Skarga's writ-ings is that of his religious treatise on the *Eucharist,* which was translated by E. Dworczyk in 1939.

ABOUT: Kridl, M. An Anthology of Polish Literature; *also*, A Survey of Polish Literature. [In French—see study by A. Berga. In Polish—see studies by M. Dzieduszycki, A. Osinski, M. J. A. Rychcicki, S. Windakiewicz.]

P. LY.

*SKRAM, BERTHA AMALIE, née AL-VER (August 22, 1847-March 15, 1905), Norwegian-Danish novelist, short-story writ-er, playwright, was born in the city of Ber-gen on the Norwegian west coast to Mons

* skrăm

866

Alver, a merchant, and Ingeborg Louise (Si-vertsen) Alver. Her father speculated and lost. After bankruptcy he deserted his fam-ily and went to America.

As a girl, Amalie read all books she could get hold of, particularly those written in blood-curdling style. At seventeen she was engaged to sea captain Berent Ulrik August Müller, and they were married the next year. Mrs. Müller spent a good deal of the follow-ing ten years with her husband on lengthy journeys all over the globe. Their marriage was unhappy and ended in divorce in 1878.

Thereafter she lived for six years in vari-ous places in southeastern Norway. A play which she wrote in 1877 was not produced. Under the pseudonym *-ie* she contributed as a literary critic to several papers. Influenced by the problem literature and radical ex-tremists of the 1880's she showed two con-flicting tendencies in her personality. She was both defiant and rebellious, and deeply in need of sympathy. In 1882 she made her debut as a prose writer with a short story, "Madam Højers Leiefolk" (Madame Højer's Boarders), published in *Nyt Tidsskrift*. In 1884 she married the Danish author and critic Asbjørn Oluf Erik Skram and lived for the rest of her life in Copenhagen, re-garding herself as Danish.

Mrs. Skram's first novel was *Constance Ring* (1885), based on experiences of her first marriage and colored by frank natural-ism and hopeless pessimism. Her greatest contribution to Norwegian naturalism was her deterministic tetralogy *Hellemyrsfolket* (The People of Hellemyr), in which she de-scribed the tragic history of a peasant family. Other fiction includes *Sjur Gabriel* (1887), a sea story largely based on her own experi-ence; *S. G. Myre* (1890), in which an am-bitious man is crushed by the burden of heredity; *Afkom* (Offspring, 1898), discus-sing problems of heredity. Her style never achieved distinction, but she wrote with in-tense conviction.

After a second divorce in 1900, Mrs. Skram had a nervous breakdown and spent some time in hospitals. Her last ten years were tragically unhappy.

The novel *Professor Hieronymus* (1895) was translated into English by A. Stronach and G. B. Jacobi (1899).

ABOUT: Beyer, H. A History of Norwegian Literature; Grøndahl, I. and Raknes, O. Chapters of Norwegian Literature; Jorgenson, T. History of Norwegian Literature; Topsöe-Jensen, H. G. Scandinavian Literature from Brandes to Our Day. [In Norwegian—see studies by B. Krane, A. Tiberg.]

A. J.

*SLAVEYKOV (or SLAVEIKOV), PENCHO (or PENTCHO) P. (April 27, 1866-May 27, 1912), Bulgarian poet and critic, was the son of the distinguished Bulgarian folklorist and author Petko Slaveykov (see sketch below). Born in Trevna, he received his education in his native town, in Sofia, and in Plovdiv. Crippled by an accident in his youth he was never in good health, and his intense physical and mental suffering was so much reflected in his poetry that he was called "poet of darkness."

Probably the most significant influence on Slaveykov's life was his long stay in Germany, where he studied for more than six years. Here he read and absorbed Goethe, Heine, Nietzsche. This "westernizing" influence on his work marked a distinct break from the then prevailing trends in Bulgarian literature, most especially from the domination of that literature by Ivan Vazov (see sketch below). Returning to Bulgaria, Slaveykov formed his own literary circle, an independent or "individualist" school of writers. This is not to suggest that Slaveykov ignored the rising Bulgarian national spirit. On the contrary, he exploited it fully —collecting with H. Barlein an anthology of Bulgarian poetry (this was translated and published in England as *The Shade of the Balkans,* 1906). Moreover, his most ambitious work was a Bulgarian national epic, *Karvava Pesn* (The Song of Blood), which was inspired by the Bulgarian struggle for independence and the Liberation of 1876. His death in Italy, on the shores of Lake Como where he had spent his last years, left the poem incomplete, but it was published posthumously in 1913.

Pencho Slaveykov shares with Ivan Vazov a position in the first ranks of Bulgarian literature. But where Vazov was a truly "popular" writer, Slaveykov was an intellectual—subtle, erudite, profound. He was a careful craftsman who worked painstakingly, revising, polishing, seeking perfection, whereas Vazov was a hasty and careless writer. But though the literary influences upon him were far wider, he shared with Vazov a love for his country and a passionate faith in its future. Besides his epic *Song of Blood,* he wrote lyric poems: *San Za Shtastie* (1906) and other volumes of verse. He also wrote essays on a variety of subjects—the best of them being works of literary criticism. His collected works were published in seven volumes, 1921-22. There

* slä′ vyĕ kôf

have been some French and Italian translations of his work, but none in English.

ABOUT: [In French—Dontchev, N. *Introduction to* Slaveykov's La Poésie Populaire Bulgare. In Italian—Rivista di Letteratura Slave, April 1928.]

*SLAVEYKOV (or SLAVEIKOV), PETKO RACHEV (April 2, 1827-September 9, 1895), Bulgarian poet, essayist, and folklorist, was born in Ternovo, the son of an illiterate coppersmith. He had only the briefest schooling, after which he was apprenticed to his father's trade.

Slaveykov was drawn to the priesthood and therefore studied in a Greek school (the Bulgarian Orthodox Church at that period was dominated by the Greek Church). But he gave up his religious studies to become an itinerant schoolteacher. This work took him all over Bulgaria, and in the course of his travels he collected a large body of folklore on which he based his poems. In all he collected over 17,000 Bulgarian maxims, and he was the first to put into writing the old Bulgarian epic of *Krali Marko.*

Slaveykov's greatest contribution to Bulgarian literature was a linguistic one. He restored the Bulgarian language to its literature, or, more accurately, established the Bulgarian literary language by putting the language of the common people into writing. In 1862 he was commissioned by the American Bible Society to head a committee that would translate the Bible into modern Bulgarian.

In addition to his literary activities in behalf of Bulgarian nationalism, Slaveykov fought in the Revolution of 1876 that freed Bulgaria from Turkish rule, and in the Russo-Turkish and Serbian wars. When Bulgarian independence was established, he became active in political life. He was a member of the National Assembly, Minister of Public Instruction, and Minister of the Interior. He also edited several liberal Bulgarian newspapers. It is small wonder that, with such a record of public service, the Bulgarian people titled him affectionately "Grandfather."

Slaveykov died in Sofia. His collected works were edited by his son Pencho and published in 1901. There are no English translations.

ABOUT: Slavonic Encyclopedia. [In Italian— Rivista di Letteratura Slave, March 1927.]

* slä′ vyĕ kôf

*SŁOWACKI, JULIUSZ (August 23, 1809-April 3, 1849), Polish poet and dramatist, was born in Krzemieniec, son of Euzebiusz Słowacki, a college professor and literary critic in Krzemieniec and Vilna. The poet was brought up, after his father's early death (1814), by his mother Salomea, a refined and educated woman, whose literary interest, exalted views, and constant encouragement influenced his early life and literary activity. Słowacki went to school in Krzemieniec and Vilna, being graduated in 1829 from the law school, whereupon he entered the civil service in Warsaw. He did not participate in the November uprising against Russia of 1830, but left the country in 1831 and joined the political emigration abroad, remaining in exile for the rest of his life, traveling in England, Switzerland, Italy, and the Middle East, but mainly staying in France. He died prematurely in Paris of tuberculosis. In 1927 his ashes were returned to Poland and buried in Cracow in posthumous national homage to the poet.

Słowacki's literary work developed in the romantic tradition pioneered at that time in Poland by Adam Mickiewicz. It was Słowacki's lot to tread the paths of Mickiewicz in many ways, but far from being an imitator he won a place of his own in Polish literature. His first poems, *Hugo, The Arab*, etc., from the period 1826-31, were mainly Byronic in spirit and form. The first longer work of importance ideologically and artistically was the poetic drama *Kordian* (1833). It was a romantic work, but there is in it a more critical and even realistic approach to both individual and collective problems; a sharp and deep analysis of certain "Hamletic" features of the poet's generation bears witness to the fact that the poet's right to the title of a "national bard" dates from quite an early date.

National problems and also the universal problem of good and evil in the human soul and in human history, especially Poland's history, thenceforward became the main themes in Słowacki's literary work. Poetic drama, with strong Shakespearean affiliations in structure and character analysis, became his favorite form. *Balladyna* (1834) and *Lilla Weneda* (1839) were dramatizations of old legends, while *Horsztyński* and *Mazepa* (1834, 1835) dealt with more modern periods. The unique visionary poem *Anhelli* (1837), written in Biblical style, marked the beginning of Słowacki's messianistic period.

* slô vãts′ kĕ

There was an immediate political message in this work, hidden in the numerous allegories: while the Poles contemporary with Słowacki were not destined to regain national freedom, their suffering and preservation of positive "angelic" ideals might bear fruit in the future. From this period of sharp criticism in evaluating the present, through the next period of initially adverse but gradually changing evaluation of the past in such works as *Beniowski* (1840), *Złota Czaszka* (The Golden Skull, 1841) and *Ksiądz Marek* (Father Mark, 1843), Słowacki came finally to a period of mysticism and metaphysical synthesis of history. *Geneziz z Ducha* (Genesis from the Spirit, 1844), *Samuel Zborowski* (1845), and the unfinished "rhapsodic" poem *Król Duch* (King Spirit) constituted a poetic trilogy in which the author in a typically romantic manner conceived the struggle itself for absolute freedom as the basic and the most pregnant value in the history of his people. (The rebel Samuel Zborowski is the best example of this extreme sense of freedom.) The idea of strict law and order (represented by Chancellor Zamyski), which opposes and suppresses such struggle, was presented by Słowacki as less promising from the point of view of the spiritual development of the people. This concept of the revolutionary spirit in the development of humanity was not original, but in Słowacki's work it acquired unusual cogency and poetic suggestiveness.

Aside from the works discussed above, Słowacki produced a number of dramas, poems, etc. Some of his lyric poems especially are regarded as works of great depth and artistic finish. The best known are "Ojciec zadżumionych" (The Father of the Plague-Stricken, English translation by W. J. Rose in the symposium *Juliusz Słowacki 1849-1949*, 1951) ; "W Szwajcarii" (In Switzerland), and "Hymn."

In Polish literature Słowacki, along with Mickiewicz and Krasiński, is recognized as one of the national bards. His influence on the development of modern Polish poetry, especially that of the period of symbolism, was even greater than Mickiewicz's. The full quality of Słowacki's mastery in imagery, symbols and versification can hardly be appreciated except in the original Polish; but although, because of these esoteric qualities, Słowacki's fame abroad is more limited, nevertheless even in translation his poetry found its way to other countries and earned him a place in world literature.

Separate works translated into English are *Mazepa*, translated by C. D. and C. F. Wells (1929); *Anhelli*, translated by D. Prall Radin (1930); forty fragments of various works in T. M. Filip and M. A. Michael, *A Polish Anthology* (1944).

ABOUT: Kridl, M. Survey of Polish Literature, *also* The Lyric Poems of Juliusz Słowacki; Krzyzanowski, J. Polish Romantic Literature; Lednicki, W. Polish Life and Culture as Reflected in Polish Literature; Treugutt, S. Juliusz Słowacki: Romantic Poet; Slavic and East European Review, XXVIII (1949). [In Polish—see study by I. Kleiner (4 vols., 1919-27).]

Z. F.

SMOLENSKIN, PEREZ or PETER (February 25, 1842-February 1, 1885), Hebrew novelist and journalist, was born in a small town in Mohilev Province, Russia, one of six children of Moses and Gaisha-Rebecca Smolenskin. The family was bitterly poor. The father was unsuccessful in several undertakings and had to set out as an itinerant teacher and religious functionary, leaving the mother to support the family under the most desperate conditions. The father died when Perez was ten. Then an event occurred which left a permanent impress on the bright and active boy. The eldest brother was kidnapped into the Russian Army for the twenty-five-year term which was forced upon Jewish conscripts, and Perez never saw him again. The young "cantonists," whose sufferings are a recurrent theme in Hebrew and Yiddish literature, pass through Smolenskin's later stories with unusual poignancy.

Smolenskin left his nearly destitute family at eleven and began his wanderings, which did not end until he settled in Vienna in 1867. Studying at the Talmudic academy of Shklov for a number of years, he became "infected" with secular Western ideas. Here, he began to study the Hebrew language and the Bible systematically, in addition to foreign languages, all nearly unaided. Forced to leave because of these "heretical" interests, he next attached himself to the retinue of the Hasidic rabbi of Lubavitch, where his knowledge of Russian made him useful for the rabbi's dealings with the government. Having developed a contempt for the old way of life from his studies and his experiences, he moved to Odessa, where he hoped to find a progressive, westernized Jewish society. But although he made a highly successful debut in Odessa as a Hebrew writer, he was dissatisfied with the material interests and the cultural shallowness of the Jews in that city. He yearned to find a deeper synthesis between Jewish history and tradition on the one hand

* smŭ lyĕn' skēn

and Eastern culture on the other. When he settled in Vienna he began to publish his monthly *Ha-Shahar* (The Dawn), most of which he wrote himself. He printed, mailed, and financed it under the most trying conditions until it became firmly established by the mid-1870's. *Ha-Shahar* was the leading Hebrew literary and political journal of its day, and its editor won recognition as the spokesman for the westernizers in Hebrew literature. In the pogrom year of 1881 and thereafter he sharply reversed his direction and suffered disillusion with mere westernization of East European Jewry, turning instead to a Zionist position. Smolenskin contracted tuberculosis and died shortly before his forty-third birthday. He was unmarried.

Perez Smolenskin was a voluminous writer of fiction and literary criticism and on public matters. His permanent legacy is his novels, most notable of which is *Ha-To'eh be-Darkhei ha-Hayyim* (Astray on the Road of Life). This is a nearly autobiographical account of a youth who passes, with depressing fatalism, from scene to scene and through repeated misfortunes in the Jewish Pale of Settlements. Despite the many artificialities of narrative and dialogue, the story has interesting and descriptive power. Almost the same may be said for his other novels of Russian Jewry: *Kevurat Hamor* (Unsanctified Burial); *Gemul Yesharim* (Reward of the Just); and *Simhat Hanef* (The Hypocrite's Joy).

ABOUT: Slouschz, N. The Renascence of Jewish Literature; Waxman, M. A History of Jewish Literature, III.

L. P. G.

SNOILSKY, KARL JOHAN GUSTAF, Count (September 8, 1841-May 19, 1903), Swedish poet and diplomat, of Slavonic descent, was born in Stockholm. His father was Count Nils Snoilsky, Supreme Court judge, piously orthodox, aristocratic, and ultra-conservative. His mother was Signe Banér, a member of one of Sweden's most illustrious noble families. Both parents died during his teen-age years. He entered the University of Uppsala and passed a lower law examination for governmental service in 1864, after which he left for Italy and Spain. After a short period as an unsalaried attaché in Paris he returned home to be a clerk at the Foreign Office. In 1867 he married Hedvig Charlotta Amalia Piper, of the higher nobility. In 1876 he was elect-

* snoil' skü

ed a member of the Royal Swedish Academy. His marriage ended in divorce in 1879. He resigned from office, alienated himself from relatives and friends and went into a voluntary exile. The next year he married Countess Ebba Piper, born Ruuth, and established residence in Florence and, later, in Dresden. Upon his return to Sweden in 1890 he was appointed head librarian at the Royal Library in Stockholm and received in 1893 an honorary doctor's degree.

At the age of twenty Snoilsky published, under the pseudonym "Sven Tröst," some imitative poetic efforts, *Smådikter* (Short Poems), showing a juvenile *weltschmerz* inspired by Heine, Byron, and others. More mature and less melancholy in tone was his next collection, *Orchidéer* (Orchids, 1862), noteworthy for the sensual expression of his joy of life and for the political poems glorifying the ideas of the French Revolution and Poland's struggle for freedom.

The Italian journey strongly influenced the young Swede, who recorded his impressions and feelings in *Italienska Bilder* (Italian Pictures, 1865). In bold and freshly realistic strokes he painted the nature and the people of the luxuriant South and strongly expressed his rebellious reaction to material and spiritual oppression. His *Dikter* (Poems, 1869), a selection of his best poems published under his own name, established his reputation as the foremost living poet in Sweden. The pregnant and technically perfect *Sonetter* (Sonnets, 1871) are permeated with hatred of Germany as the victor over France in the war of 1870-71, a feeling of horror at the Communard Rebellion, and his own melancholy disposition.

Unhappiness in his first marriage threatened to choke his poetic productivity for some years, but the renaissance of a new happiness of love in his second marriage revitalized his inspiration and generated new and brilliant poetry. Now he wrote the monumental poetic cycle *Svenska Bilder* (Swedish Pictures), to which he added new songs throughout his life. In these patriotic poems, based on motifs from Swedish history, Snoilsky presented a marvelous gallery of portraits, sympathetic to people of the lower classes and of a diversity unparalleled in Swedish literature.

In four collections of poems, *Nya Dikter* (New Poems, 1881), *Dikter* (1883, 1887, 1897), he dealt with social problems and expressed democratic ideas and demands, but he found, with resignation, that he was unable to realize his hope of becoming a spokesman of the common people.

Eleven of Snoilsky's best known poems were translated into English by C. W. Stork in his *Anthology of Swedish Lyrics* (1930) and by F. A. Judd in his *Under the Swedish Colours* (1911).

ABOUT: Gosse, E. W. Portraits and Sketches. [In Swedish—see studies by P. Hallström, H. Olsson, K. Warburg.]

A. J.

*SNORRI STURLUSON (1179-September 24, 1241), Icelandic poet, saga writer, critic, and politician, was born at the farm Hvammr by Breiðifjörður in northwestern Iceland. His father was Sturla Þórðarson, called "Hvamm-Sturla," among whose forefathers were such aristocratic men of the saga age as Snorri goði and Guðmundr ríki. His mother was Guðny Böðvarsdóttir, who derived her origin from the great poet Egill Skallagrímsson. Snorri, his two older brothers, and their offspring are known under the family name Sturlungs, and the era when they lived is called the Age of the Sturlungs.

In accordance with the habit in prominent families, Snorri was at the age of two sent for education to the home of the chieftain Jón Loptsson at Oddi in southwestern Iceland. Jón, whose grandfathers were Sæmund the Wise and the Norwegian king Magnus Barefoot, was the wealthiest and most influential man in the whole island, and his farm was a center for the religious, cultural, and political life of Iceland.

In 1199 Snorri married Herdís Bersadóttir, whose father owned the farm Borg in the western district, once the home of Egill Skallagrímsson. When his father-in-law died two years later, Snorri inherited the farm. Later he acquired also Reykjaholt (now Reykholt), a farm northeast of Borg. Snorri had children by several women other than Herdís. In 1206 (or 1207) he separated from his wife and established residence at Reykjaholt.

In the summer of 1218 Snorri left for Norway where he visited the ruler Skúli Barðarson and King Hákon Hákonarson, who was not yet of age. He stayed in Norway for a couple of years, and he also visited Sweden. In a controversy between Norwegian merchants and the Icelandic family at Oddi he acted successfully as mediator. Laden with gifts he left Norway as the king's representative in Iceland with the promise to work for Norway's cause at home. Upon his return he was met with suspicion and derision, but when the Icelanders saw that he

* snor′ rĭ stûr′ lŭ sŏn

did not keep his promise to the Norwegian king, he again won his people's favor and was elected "lawman," which office he had held before he left Iceland.

Snorri accumulated enormous wealth, especially through an agreement about community goods with the widow Hallveig Ormsdóttir of the family at Oddi and Iceland's richest woman. She went to live with Snorri at Reykjaholt.

Snorri became involved in various conflicts and feuds, and in 1235 his brother Sighvatr and the latter's son Sturla, who acted in behalf of King Hákon in Norway, started a civil war in order to bring Iceland under the Norwegian crown. Snorri fled in 1237 to Nidaros (now Trondheim) in Norway. In the meantime his two antagonistic relatives were killed, but new enemies of Snorri's came into power. In spite of the king's injunction against Snorri's leaving Norway, he returned to Iceland in 1239. The victor in the battle for power in Iceland was Snorri's son-in-law and bitterest enemy, Gizurr Þorvaldsson, who was ordered by the Norwegian king to send Snorri back to Norway or kill him. Knowing that he would not be able to persuade Snorri to return to Norway, he chose the other alternative. He and his men went to Reykjaholt and murdered Snorri treacherously during a nighttime assault.

The years 1220-35 in Iceland had been comparatively peaceful and quiet, and during that time Snorri wrote his immortal works. His literary production falls into three parts: history, saga telling, and literary criticism. His historical work is *Noregs Konungasögur* (History of the Norwegian Kings). On account of the first two words of the work, *Kringla heimsins*, the usual name is *Heimskringla* (Circle of the Earth). It exists in three manuscripts, the oldest of which was written only a couple of decades after Snorri's death. Snorri first wrote the central part of his history, *Ólafs Saga Helga* (The Saga of Saint Olaf), which constitutes one-third of the whole work and describes the life of Ólafr Haraldsson, the man who finally consolidated Norway as a kingdom and before his death in 1030 organized a national church. Thereafter Snorri wrote an introduction, *Ynglingasaga* (The Story of the Ynglings), setting forth the history of St. Olaf's ancestors and predecessors in historic and prehistoric time. He was able to trace their origin all the way back to none other than the god Odin himself. Finally Snorri added the history of the kings who succeeded St. Olaf down to the year 1177,

which saw the appearance of King Sverri, whose saga had already been written. Snorri's great history of the Norwegian kings was based on real critical research. He used all possible sources, e.g., oral tradition, skaldic poetry, earlier historical works, but he used them with a more critical approach than one would expect from a medieval historian. However, a good deal of his description comes from his own vivid imagination. His narrative style is that of the family sagas, but in Snorri's work it reaches a rare degree of perfection, characterized by simplicity, moderation, dignity, and force that are rare in the literature of any country. Unsurpassed in European medieval literature is the psychological analysis of St. Olaf's character development.

It has not been proved beyond doubt that Snorri was the author of the *Saga of Egil Skallagrímsson*, but Sigurður Nordal has given ample evidence that Snorri really wrote this marvelous saga, in many respects the most fascinating of all Icelandic family sagas.

At the time Snorri lived, the art of skaldic poetry was no longer practiced. The poetic literature consisted then of popular ballads and church hymns. In order to preserve the knowledge of, and possibly revive, the old classical native form of poetry, Snorri wrote his so-called *Prose Edda*, which must not be confused with the *Poetic Edda*, a body of primitive poetry. Snorri's *Edda*, probably written before his two books already mentioned, is a scholarly work, a handbook on poetry for young skalds. It exists in many manuscripts, none of which seems to be an exact copy of the original. The best known manuscript, and probably closest to Snorri's own version, is the famous *Codex Regius*, property of the University Library at Uppsala, Sweden.

Snorri's *Edda*, beginning with a prologue, falls into three different parts. The first is *Gylfaginning* (The Deluding of Gylvi), containing a fascinating account of the old pagan mythology created by imaginative poets. As was usually the case in medieval textbooks, it is composed as a series of questions, asked by the fictitious Swedish king Gylvi, and answers, given by Odin, who is split into three characters. The answers are written as episodes in the life of the gods. They offer perfectly delightful reading, reminding one of the old myths of the ancient Greeks and Romans. The second main part of the *Edda* is called *Skaldskaparmál* (The Poetic Speech of Skalds). It begins, like the first section,

871

with a dialogue, but this frame is soon broken, and Snorri himself goes into a lengthy demonstration of the poetic language. He exemplifies, interprets, and explains a large number of metaphors, especially the so-called "kennings," elaborate figures of speech. Many skaldic verses are also quoted. The last part, *Háttatál* (List of Meters), is a long poem, interrupted by explanatory comments in prose, originally written in honor of the Norwegian King Hákon and Earl Skúli. The poem consists of about 100 stanzas, exemplifying an equal number of meters, some of which were invented by Snorri.

Snorri's *Heimskringla* was translated by S. Laing as *The Heimskringla* (1844; now available in Everyman's Library), by W. Morris and E. Magnusson as *The Stories of the Kings of Norway* (1893-1905) and by E. Monsen as *Heimskringla* (1932). *Egil's Saga* was rendered into English by W. C. Green as *The Story of Egil Skallagrimsson* (1893) and by E. R. Eddison as *Egil's Saga* (1930). Snorri's *Edda* was translated as *The Prose Edda* by G. W. Dasent (1842), R. B. Anderson (1880), A. G. Brodeur (1929, the best translation), J. I. Young (1954).

ABOUT: Beyer, H. A History of Norwegian Literature; Haugen, E. Snorri Sturluson and Norway *in* American-Scandinavian Review (1953); Jorgenson, T. History of Norwegian Literature, *also* Norwegian Literature in Medieval and Early Modern Times; Sveinsson, E. O. The Age of the Sturlungs. [In Norwegian—see studies by F. Paasche, G. Storm.]

A. J.

*SÖDERGRAN, EDITH IRENE (April 4, 1892-June 25, 1923), Finnish-Swedish poet, was born in the Russian city of St. Petersburg, the present Leningrad, where her father, Mattias Södergran, of a family of Swedish farmers in northwestern Finland, was a mechanic. Her mother was his second wife, Helena Holmroos, daughter of a well-to-do Finnish-Swedish foundry and factory owner, originally from southwestern Finland. Both parents had nervous dispositions.

When Edith was but three months old the family moved to the village of Raivola close to the Russian border in the southeastern Finnish province of Karelia. She grew up in a dismal milieu. Her father neglected his business and led a dissolute life. The family lived during the winters in St. Petersburg where Edith attended a fine German church school and attained a broad knowledge of French, German, and Russian literature. But after the death of her father from pulmonary tuberculosis in 1907 the trips to St. Petersburg ended.

* sü′ dẽr grän

A year later it was discovered that Edith had fallen a victim to the same disease as her father. She spent several years at a Finnish sanatorium, and from 1911 to 1914 she lived in Switzerland, where she became acquainted with English literature and came under the influence of modern currents, of which German expressionism had a decisive importance for her philosophy and her production. After her return to Finland she led a rather isolated life at Raivola, until her death at the age of thirty-one.

In the middle of World War I she made her first literary appearance with a collection of *Dikter* (Poems), sprung from such conflicting feelings as melancholy and joy of life, humility and arrogance, love and loathing. But even in the most intense erotic poems and the charming nature lyrics there are thoughts of departure and death. The free form, the daring imagery, the nebulous symbolism, and highly personal style in these poems were in strong contrast to the current poetry and confused both the critics and the public. The expressionistic nature of these lyrics was too new to be understood and appreciated.

The adverse criticism of her first collection gave Miss Södergran a feeling of being a pioneer or a crusader. Her assurance increased under the influence of Nietzsche, and in her subsequent books of poems, *Septemberlyran* (September Lyre, 1918), *Rosenaltaret* (The Rose Altar, 1919), and *Framtidens Skugga* (Shadow of the Future, 1920), she gave expression to an apocalyptic view of life and of the future. Her highly textured poetry broke away from conventional ideas of lyrical rhythm and rhyme. In a preface to *Septemberlyran* she maintains that her poetry is based only on her instinct, while her intellect is a passive bystander. Several posthumous poems, published in 1925 under the title *Landet som Icke Är* (The Land That Is Not), show that the Nietzschean strain had given way to a quiet longing for the "land that is not." Edith Södergran's poetry, rejected while she lived, greatly influenced later generations of poets in Finland and Sweden.

Some of Miss Södergran's poems translated into English, mostly by M. S. Allwood, are included in Allwood, ed. *Twentieth Century Scandinavian Poetry* (1950).

ABOUT: [In Swedish—see studies by O. Enckell, G. Tideström.]

A. J.

"SOLITARIO, EL." See ESTÉBANEZ CALDERÓN, SERAFÍN

SOLOMON BEN ISAAC. See RASHI

*SOLOMOS, DIONYSIOS (April 8, 1798-February 21, 1857), named by many "the Dante of Greece" and by Goethe "the Byron of the East," was born on Zante and spent his first ten years on his native island. He was the natural son of Count Nicholas Solomos and Angelica, daughter of Demetrios Nikly, his former servant, with whom he had been living for eleven years. In February 1807, on the eve of his death, Count Nicholas, a widower, married Angelica, thus making Dionysios and his brother Demetrios his heirs. During his early years Solomos was tutored in Italian, the language of the nobility, by Abbot Santo Rossi who also taught him to revere liberty. In 1808 Rossi accompanied Dionysios to Italy where he was placed in the Seminary of St. Catherine in Venice; he was soon removed because of his untamed spirit and placed at the Lyceum of Cremona where he was taught Latin and Italian and won the prize in rhetoric. In 1815 he enrolled at the University of Padua as a law student but gave little attention to law. Instead he devoted himself to poetry, studying the language of Dante and composing his first poems in Italian, much to the astonishment of his teachers, one of whom predicted his future success as a poet. He came under the influence of the poet and novelist Alessandro Manzoni who inspired him to turn his serious attention to the composition of poetry. In 1818 he received his law degree, in his own words "by the favor of the university authorities," and returned to Zante, which had been occupied by the British since 1814. Handsome, enormously wealthy, Italian in appearance, high-spirited, he was sought after by women who vainly hoped he would settle down and marry.

His attentions were now turned more seriously to "The Society of Friends" *(Filike Etaireia)*, a secret popular organization for Greek independence and for the people's uprising against the Turks. When the orator, diplomat, and historian Spiridon Tricupis visited Solomos in 1822, he convinced the Italian-educated poet to turn to the Greek language he had imbibed "with his mother's milk." From this time on, Solomos dedicated himself to two causes: Greek independence

* sô lô môs′

SOLOMOS

and the development of the spoken idiom as the language of poetry.

His first Greek poem was "The Blonde Girl" (1822) inspired by Catherine Mavrogordato whose parents had sought asylum on Zante after the brutal massacre of Chios. In 1823 Solomos wrote his "Hymn to Liberty," which consists of 158 quatrains personifying Liberty as rising from the bones of all Greek heroes who died in her defense. "In no age," wrote Tricupis in 1825, "and in no nation has liberty found a worthier singer." In 1863 "Hymn to Liberty" was set to Manzaro's music and it became the national anthem of Greece.

In 1824 Byron died at Missolonghi, and Solomos wrote a long "Hymn on the Death of Lord Byron," regarded by critics as an inferior work. "The Destruction of Psara" (1825), written after the total massacre of the inhabitants of the island by the Turks, is a masterpiece of prosody which most Greeks recite from memory.

Other poems of this period are "Marco Botzaris," inspired by the death of the Greek defender in 1823; "The Dream" (1826), a satiric poem; "The Poisoned Girl" (1826), a poetical protest against the calumnies which followed the suicide of a girl on Zante; and "Lambros" (1826), a powerful lyrical study of a stricken conscience and a defense of the innocence and chastity of womanhood.

In 1828 Solomos left Zante and went to Corfu where he lived for the rest of his life. Here we find him pro-English and conservative, and a British subject (since his birthplace was under British rule) to the time of his death. The outstanding poem of this period is "The Free Besieged," a series of fragments written between 1844 and 1849, inspired by the siege of Missolonghi and acclaimed as the poet's greatest achievement. "The Woman of Zante," first discovered in 1927, is a portrait of an evil woman. "The Porphyras" (1849) is the last poem Solomos wrote in Greek.

Solomos was buried in Corfu. The day of his death was proclaimed a public holiday and when news of his death reached Athens, Parliament adjourned. His brother Demetrios was determined that his bones should be returned to Zante, and in July 1865 Solomos received a second burial on his native island.

Dionysios Solomos was the founder of the spoken idiom as a literary language and the father of modern Greek poetry. The chief characteristics of his poetry are love of country, faith in God, and the idealization of womanhood.

The entire *Hymn to Liberty* (158 stanzas) was translated into English by Arnold Green in 1884 and may be found appended to his address "Solomos' Hymn to Liberty" in his pamphlet entitled *Greek and What Next?* Several selections have been translated by Demetrius Michalaros in his article "Solomos the Poet," in the June 1944 issue of *Athene.* In this same issue appear "The Fall of Psara" and "Xanthoula" (The Blonde Girl), translated by R. E. Witt, and the first seven stanzas of the "Hymn to Liberty," adapted by Rudyard Kipling. In his "Introduction to Modern Greek Poetry," Demetrius Capetanakis has included a few fragments of translation. There are numerous excerpts in the biography of the poet by Romilly Jenkins. Several selections appear in Philip Sherrard's study of Solomos. Translations of ten poems by Solomos are included in Rae Dalven's anthology *Modern Greek Poetry* (1949).

ABOUT: Capetanakis, D. "An Introduction to Modern Greek Poetry" *in* New Writing and Daylight, Autumn 1944; Dalven, R. Modern Greek Poetry; Green, A. Greek and What Next?; Jenkins, R. Dionysios Solomos; Mavrogordato, J. Modern Greece; Michalaros, D. "Solomos the Poet" *in* Athene, June 1944; Sherrard, P. "Solomos" *in* The Marble Threshing Floor

R. D.

*SOLOVIEV, VLADIMIR SERGEYE-VICH (January 28, 1853-July 31, 1900),

Russian philosopher, poet, and polemist, the son of the eminent historian S. M. Soloviev, was born in Moscow to a family steeped in the traditions of Russian Orthodoxy. He absorbed these traditions so completely that, at the age of seven, having read *The Lives of the Saints,* he worried his pious mother by seeking to emulate saintly mortification by

* sŭ lŭv yôf'

874

sleeping on cold nights without blankets. But the advantages of growing up in the intellectual environment of Moscow University also assured him a grasp of other aspects of culture, and before he was ten he had already acquired a considerable mastery of his two favorite subjects, history and geography. Nor was his emotional development allowed to lag, for, at the age of nine, he had the first of several ill-starred affairs of the heart, an allusion to which has been found in his famous poem "Three Meetings" written toward the end of his life:

> And for the first time, years and years ago—
> Thirty-six of them have passed since then—
> The soul of a child was suddenly aware
> Of the yearnings of Love, and of vague and
> troubled dreams . . .

Soloviev's formal education began at eleven when he was admitted to the third-year class at the Moscow *Gymnasium* where he soon distinguished himself as a most promising young scholar. During his early adolescence he experienced growing doubts as to the validity of the religious traditions he had received as a child, finally manifesting his complete rejection of religion by literally throwing the icons he had so long worshiped out of the window of his room, and proclaiming himself a complete "nihilist." He plunged into the works of Pisarev and accepted Spinoza as his philosophical inspiration.

Apparently this youthful iconoclasm was but a passing phase, for when he entered the university, at seventeen, he turned his attention to the history of religion, becoming an enthusiastic student of Buddhism and an admirer of the idealism of Schopenhauer and Hartmann. By the time his schooling was completed three years later, he had grown close to the Slavophiles.

During vacation periods in his eighteenth and nineteenth years he fell in love with three more young women, one a peasant girl on the estate of his aunt, Princess Dadeshkeliani, whom he was prevented from marrying only by the opportune recommencing of the school year, and the other girls who were distantly related to him on his mother's side. Soloviev acknowledged later that he seemed doomed to be denied the blessings of domesticity; at any rate, he never married.

Continuing his scholarly pursuits in the field of philosophy not untinged with theology—he had also attended lectures at the Moscow Spiritual Academy, an Orthodox seminary—he completed work toward his master's degree at the University of St.

Petersburg with a thesis entitled "The Crisis of Western Philosophy." He was then allowed to go to England where he spent some time in the British Museum happily engrossed in religion, occult science, cabalism, and the mystical Sophia. It was here that he received the mystical directive that sent him posthaste to Egypt. There, in the desert near Cairo, was revealed to him the very person of Sophia herself. He remained in the area to study the Moslem creed and to trace the origins of Christianity, and it was no doubt a result of such interest that his theology took on the universal aspect which earned him the epithet "the Russian Newman" (though he never became a Catholic) and which accounts for the cautious attitude which the Orthodox hierarchy was to take toward his works in later years.

He returned to St. Petersburg in 1880 and qualified for his doctorate with a thesis, "Critique of Abstract Tenets," and was offered a chair in philosophy at the university. His tenure was curtailed by his outspoken recommendation of clemency for the assassins of the late czar, and he was forced to abandon his position in 1881.

During the eighties he worked out his doctrine of a universal theocratic society which culminated in his book—never published in Russia—*La Russie et l'Église Universelle* (1889) in which he reached his closest point of contact with Catholicism. But while his mystical bent continued to manifest itself throughout his short life, he not only was a theologian, but also was a vigorous polemist against the narrow nationalism of the contemporary government. His political writings won him the respect of the intelligentsia, and he was invited by the editors of the standard Encyclopedia to supervise the philosophical section which, consequently, reflected his views in the main. These views strongly opposed materialism and agnosticism in favor of the idealist position of Hartmann and Schopenhauer. In 1900 he published his last works, *Three Conversations on War Together with Progress* and *The End of Human History, to Which Is Added a Short History of the Antichrist*. Worn out by these labors, he went for a rest to the estate of the brothers Troubetzkoy near Moscow, where he died.

Soloviev is difficult to assess because of the variety of his literary creativity. He is noted for his poetry, his literary criticism, his philosophy, and his theology as well as for his political writings. Olgin feels that he is first and foremost a poet; Mirsky can-

not decide among his poetry, his brilliant polemics, his philosophy, and his published letters which he finds of outstanding interest, alluding also to his humor, an aspect of Soloviev which few critics have noted so fully. Soviet criticism is mainly from the philosophical point of view wherein Soloviev is characterized as an idealist-mystic, whose theory of perception based on faith and whose concept of a world theocratic Christian monarchy (which Soloviev felt to be the "historic mission of the Russian people") played willy-nilly into the hands of the autocracy and is to be rejected as effectively reactionary. Berdyaev has noted that "what is most unusual in Soloviev and most fundamental is his world-wide interest, his universalism. . . . Russian life and thought of the second half of the nineteenth century shows no other instance of a universal personality concerned with Russia, humanity, the world's soul, the Church, God, and not with circles or factions."

The works of Soloviev were published in a complete edition in 1904 (2nd ed., 1910-11). They include many works on various religious and ethical questions, the Jewish question, the national question, as well as works in literary criticism on Dostoevsky, Tyutchev, Pushkin, Lermontov, Polonsky and others. His collected poems were first published in one volume in 1890, and are included in his works.

English translations include N. Duddington's *The Justification of the Good* (1915), A Bakshy's *War, Progress and History* (1915), R. Gill's *Plato* (1935), P. Zouboff's *Lectures on Godmanhood* (1944), J. Marshall's *The Meaning of Love* (1946), H. Rees' *Russia and the Universal Church* (1948). *A Solovyev Anthology* (1950) contains translations by N. Duddington.

ABOUT: Russian Review, XXII (1963). Thought, VIII (1933); Zernov, N. M. Three Russian Prophets. [In German—see study by F. Muckermann. In Russian—see studies by E. L. Radlov, E. Trubetskoy.]

L. R. & H. H.

*SORGE, REINHARD JOHANNES** (January 29, 1892-July 20, 1916), German dramatist, was born in Berlin, the son of a city building inspector. He left school before graduating to work as an apprentice in a foundry and later in a bank. After the death of his father in a mental institution in 1908, the family moved to Jena, where Sorge completed his education at the *Gymnasium*. At this time he became acquainted with the prominent writers Richard Dehmel, Stefan

* zōr′ gĕ

George, Ernst Hardt, and Alfred Mombert and began to write dramas of his own. In 1912 he married and after a trip to Italy, the young couple settled in Switzerland. Sorge enlisted in the army in 1915 and was killed at Ablaincourt the following year at the age of twenty-four.

Sorge began writing as a disciple of Nietzsche, and his early works, *Odysseus* (1908) and *Nietzsche, eine Impression* (1911), are dominated by the ideas of *Also Sprach Zarathustra*. His best-known drama, *Der Bettler* (1912), continues this influence, while at the same time reflecting his transcendence of Nietzsche and Zarathustra and his emergence as a mystic in the tradition of St. Francis. Sorge's break with Nietzsche was completed by his conversion to Catholicism in 1914.

Der Bettler (The Beggar), which was awarded the Kleist prize in 1912, represents Sorge's attempt to resolve his conflicts with his time and with himself. By renouncing in turn the world, his family, and finally even his literary work, the poet-hero of the play finds his true destiny as a prophet. As such he shows by example that the way to the new world of the future is to be achieved by love of mankind, humility, self-sacrifice, and voluntary suffering for one's fellow-men. The play, which bears the significant sub-title "a dramatic mission," is to a considerable degree autobiographical, for Sorge himself was convinced that he had a poetic mission as the forerunner of a new generation. His dramas were his endeavor to prepare the way for the new humanity of the future.

The works written after Sorge became a Catholic reflect even more than *Der Bettler* the messianic nature of his calling and his conception of the stage as a place of consecration. *Guntwar, die Schule eines Propheten* (1914), *Metanoeite* (1915), and *König David* (1916) are all prophetic-mystic plays, written in an impassioned, hymnlike style, with visionary scenes which take place between the world and heaven. Of his remaining works, which were published posthumously, the most significant are *Mutter der Himmel* (1922), a collection of poems revealing his Catholic religiosity, and *Gericht über Zarathustra* (1922), a dramatic vision, in which the teachings of Zarathustra are vanquished by the figure of the Christian savior.

Since much of Sorge's message was extremely difficult if not impossible to express in words, he was forced to invent new dramatic techniques and a new style to convey the intensely emotional, ecstatic tone of his pleas. He stripped his language of all embellishments as one device to heighten the dramatic impact of the speeches. In addition he achieved powerful stage effects by an imaginative use of lighting, which contributed a mystical aura of unreality to his plays. Because his dramas were intended for mankind at large, his characters are generally symbols of types instead of individuals. Sorge's works, by virtue of their innovations, are significant milestones in the history of the German theatre. His drama *Der Bettler*, specifically, both introduced and greatly influenced the expressionist movement, which flourished in Germany during and after the First World War.

Sorge's dramas enjoyed but short vogue in his own country and none of his works have been translated into English.

ABOUT: Thomas, R. H. German Perspectives. [In German—see studies by W. Spael, M. Rockenbach, M. Becker, and S. Sorge.]

D. G. D.

*SOUSA, LUÍS DE, Frei (c. 1555–May 1632), Portuguese historian, was Manuel de Sousa Coutinho before he became a monk. He was born in Santarém, the fourth son of noble parents—Lopo de Sousa Coutinho, a colonial official, and Maria de Noronha. The restless youth abandoned his studies in 1576 to accompany his brother André to Malta, to serve the knights as a novice. Their ship was captured by a pirate, who sold them into slavery in Algiers, a fate they shared with Cervantes. Ransomed in 1577, Sousa lingered in Valencia with the poet Jaime Falcó. After 1578 he returned to Portugal to command a regiment. About 1585 he married Madalena de Vilhena, a war widow. They had only one daughter, who died young. When the five governors of the realm fled plague-ridden Lisbon in 1599 they requisitioned Sousa's palace in nearby Almada. In anger he burned it and sought refuge in Madrid. Pardoned, he undertook voyages to Panama and other distant places.

After twenty-eight years of married life, he and his wife separated in 1613, either because they were weary of the world, or, according to legend, because Madalena's first husband suddenly reappeared. This legend became popular through Almeida Garrett's play *Frei Luís de Sousa* (1844). Sousa joined the Dominicans, while Madalena entered a nunnery. Although Sousa aspired to an ascetic life henceforth, his order employed

* sō′ zà

him on diplomatic missions and as its chronicler. He died at the Dominican monastery at Bemfica near Lisbon.

Sousa's literary career began when he edited his friend Falcó's poems in 1600. For the Portuguese Dominicans he undertook to rework and complete Cácegas' and Granada's materials for the *Vida de Dom Frei Bartolomeu dos Mártires* (1619). The austere archbishop's biography has become a classic of studiously pure and simple style, contrasting sharply with the violent contortions of baroque wit. Two tedious, uncritical chronicles followed, a reworked *História de S. Domingos* in three parts (1627, 1662, 1678), and the *Anais de Dom João III*, written in 1630 for Philip IV, but published only in 1844 by Alexandre Herculano. Sousa also left some Latin poems and a pious work on the Virgin Mary.

The archbishop's *Life* was soon translated into French (1663) and Spanish (1727). In 1880 Mary Elizabeth, Lady Herbert, translated it and other sources into English as *The Life of Dom Bartholomew of the Martyrs*. The chapters on Morocco were translated into French from the *Anais* by R. Ricard in 1940. In 1795 James M. Murphy translated his *History & Description of the Church of Batalha* from Part I of the *História de S. Domingos*.

ABOUT: [In Portuguese—Lapa, M. R. Introduction to his edition of the Anais de D. João III.]

G. M. M.

*SPEE, FRIEDRICH VON** (February 25, 1591-August 7, 1635), German poet and Jesuit priest, is one of the most interesting and versatile personalities of an age by no means undistinguished for variety. He was Germany's most eloquent opponent of witchcraft trials, a devoted Catholic missionary, one of the leading German practitioners of "Christian eroticism" in poetry, nurse and minister to plague-ridden Trier. In at least two of these functions he became the object of malicious plots or attempted murder, and his last errand of mercy cost him his life.

His family was of the nobility—Spee von Langenfeld—and Friedrich was the youngest of three sons. He was born near Düsseldorf, studied in a Jesuit school, and was received into the order as a novice in 1610. He studied theology at Cologne (where he later taught), became a priest in 1622. In 1627 the Bishop of Würzburg asked the Jesuits to provide a father confessor for condemned witches, and Spee was given the dismal task. Würzburg was a town of modest size, but its contribution to the annals of inhumanity was considerable. In the two years bordering on

* shpā

Spee's appointment, twenty-nine pyres consumed the bodies of 158 witches, from priests and magistrates to nine-year-old children. In his *Cautio Criminalis*—"by an unidentified author"—Spee left his legacy of saddened wisdom, but only in the next century, through Leibniz in particular, did Germany become widely aware of the identity of its benefactor, or put an end to the butchery he so deplored.

Not one of the two hundred witches he had himself conducted to the fire did Spee believe to be guilty. Every obstacle was placed in the way of those who would comfort these poor creatures, "who suffered injustice and had no one to console them; they cannot resist the violence done them and there is help for them nowhere." He was seldom permitted to offer them even the solace of confession.

Spee was transferred in 1628 to the town of Peine, as a missionary for the Counter Reformation. The reward of his extraordinary success was an assassin's bullet. Although it did not kill him, it left him for eleven weeks close to death, and his recuperation was long and difficult.

During his recovery, in an isolated little village, he wrote much of the poetry on which his literary fame rests. In *Trutznachtigall* the two strains of his lyric inspiration are clear: love of Christ, *unio mystica* in almost as strikingly erotic terms as among his English contemporaries or in St. John of the Cross; and love of Nature as the sensible manifestation of God. The language of these profound mystical strains is curiously graceful, ornamental, and light, often in the tradition of folk song. His description of the soul enraptured by Jesus draws on diverse traditions: medieval mysticism, bucolic poetry, the Song of Songs, folk ballads of love. His description of nature is remarkably immediate. Since its only derivative or secondary aspect is tribute to God, it approaches at times what we know as "nature poetry." The ecstatic experiencing of all nature as divine does not require, for Spee, extensive rationalizing.

For years it was thought that these were Spee's only media—to the exclusion of "regular" religious poetry, but recently a number of well-known Catholic hymns have been ascribed to him.

After his convalescence and the writing of *Trutznachtigall*, Spee returned to Cologne in 1632 to lecture again on moral theology. Here too he wrote his *Güldenes TugendBuch* (Golden Book of Virtues), a guide to the practice of Faith, Hope, and Charity. In the confusion of the Thirty Years' War, the lord of Trier had surrendered his city to the

French, and the spiritual lords had captured it back. In the plague that followed the fighting, Spee performed the last of his considerable services to his fellow men. He helped to establish a hospital, and tended the sick until he was himself struck down—at the age of forty-four.

Some of his poems appear in English translation in C. Winkworth, *Christian Singers of Germany* (1865); *Lyra Germanica* (1858, 1907, etc.); *The Penguin Book of German Verse* (1957). Three poems by Spee are published in George C. Schoolfield's *The German Lyric of the Baroque in English Translation* (1962).

ABOUT: Comparative Literature, XV (1963). [In German—see studies by E. Beutler, J. Diel, E. Rosenfeld, I. Rüttenauer, H. Zwetsloot.]

F. G. R.

*SPERONI DEGLI ALVAROTTI, SPERONE (1500-1588), Italian humanist and critic, was born in Padua, where he passed most of his life. He studied in Bologna under Pomponazzi, received degrees in philosophy and medicine in 1518, and taught logic in his native city until his father's death ten years later. After this time, he continued his studies of the Greek and Latin classics, and attained considerable renown with the general public as well as with scholars for his learning and eloquence. He was honored and esteemed by the principal minds of his times, and is remembered today for his broad learning and his distinguished criticism of Dante, Virgil, and Ariosto.

Speroni's *Dialoghi (della Retorica, dell' Amore,* etc.), in cold and grave but elegant style, deal with intellectual and social problems. Of special importance is his *Dialogo delle Lingue,* a major text in the lively discussions of the relative merits of Latin, Tuscan, and the other Italian dialects, treated about the same time by Trissino, Bembo, and Varchi. Speroni considers that the Italian language would be capable of rising to all the intrinsic finesse of Latin, and thus presents the topic exploited in France by Du Bellay and of significance in the long quarrel between the ancients and the moderns. Speroni's tragedy *Canace* was read by him as the composition progressed before the Accademia degli Infiammati in Padua, and was to be performed in 1542 but did not appear until its publication in 1546; as revised in 1597, it led to a long exchange of polemics, for its doctrine of tragedy as a catharsis arousing pity and terror in the listeners, and for its innovations in metrics. The play tells the

* spā rô' nē

878

story of the incestuous love of Canace and Macareus, children of the god of the winds; the story itself was viewed with hostility.

There are many editions of *I Dialoghi* beginning in 1542, and of *Canace* from 1550. The *Apologia di Dante,* composed about 1575 and published in 1865, speaks against a work by Belisario Bulgarini. *Alcune Prose Scelte,* published in 1828, includes the dialogues on language, discord, dignity in women, etc., and various letters. The *Opere* of Venice, 1740, in five volumes, contains the basic biography of Speroni by M. Forcellini.

ABOUT: [In Italian—Cammarosano, F. La Vita et le Opere di Sperone Speroni; Fano, A. Sperone Speroni; Toffanin, G. La Fine dell' Umanesimo.]

F. J. C.

*SPIELHAGEN, FRIEDRICH (February 24, 1829-February 24, 1911), German novelist and critic, was born in Magdeburg, the son of a civil engineer. When the boy was six years old, the family moved to Stralsund on the Baltic, an area which Spielhagen loved, and which he utilized as the setting for many of his works. He studied law at the University of Berlin, and classical philology at the universities of Bonn and Greifswald, where he received his degree in 1851. Following his year of military service, he worked as a tutor and as an actor, until he received a position teaching English at the Modernes Gesamt-Gymnasium in Leipzig. Here he began his literary career with the short stories "Klara Vere" (1857) and "Auf der Düne" (1858). In addition he produced various critical essays as well as a volume of translations from American literature, which he held in high esteem. From 1860 to 1862 he served as literary editor of the *Zeitung für Norddeutschland* and later edited both the *Deutsche Wochenschrift* and *Westermann's Monatshefte* (1878-84). In 1862 he settled permanently in Berlin, where he died on his eighty-second birthday.

As a writer Spielhagen continued the tradition of his friend Karl Gutzkow and devoted himself chiefly to the field of the *Tendenzroman* or novel of purpose. All of his important works deal with the social and political problems of his time and champion the cause of liberalism. He achieved his first major success with the lengthy novel *Problematische Naturen* (1860), which describes conditions and events in Pomerania preceding the revolution of 1848. A sequel entitled *Durch Nacht zum Licht* appeared in 1862. His next novels, *Die von Hohenstein* (1864), *In Reih' und Glied* (1866), and *Hammer und Amboss* (1869), have as their basis the ideas

* shpēl' hä gĕn

of the socialist leader Ferdinand Lassalle, whom the author knew personally. In 1876 Spielhagen produced the most powerful of his works, *Sturmflut*, in which financial calamity brought about by reckless speculation in Berlin is made coincident with a disastrous flood on the Baltic coast. Spielhagen wrote too much, and his later works decline in value, although the novels *Plattland* (1879), *Quisisana* (1880), *Angela* (1881), and *Noblesse Oblige* (1888) are notable achievements which merit attention. Of his critical essays, *Theorie und Technik des Romans* (1883) and *Theorie und Technik des Epik und Dramatik* are significant, as is also Spielhagen's autobiography *Finder und Erfinder: Erinnerungen aus Meinem Leben* (1890).

Although Spielhagen's reputation was strongly disputed at the end of the nineteenth century by modern German writers who condemned his use of the novel for purposes of reform, he remains a prominent, representative author of his time. His novels, despite their somewhat outmoded technique, continue to be important as cultural-historical documents of the period between 1848 and 1871.

M. S. De Vere translated *Problematische Naturen* in 1869, *Durch Nacht zum Licht* in 1870, and *Die von Hohenstein* in 1870. *Hammer und Amboss* was translated as *Hammer and Anvil* by H. Browne in 1870. E. and A. Stephenson translated *Sturmflut* in 1877 as *The Breaking of the Storm*, while H. E. Goldschmidt rendered *Quisisana* in 1881.

ABOUT: Germanic Review IX (1934); Journal of English and Germanic Philology IX (1910). [In German—see studies by M. Geller, H. and J. Hart, H. Henning, W. Klemperer, and E. Mensch.]

D. G. D.

*SPINOZA, BENEDICTUS DE (or BARUCH) (November 24, 1632-February 21, 1677), Dutch-Jewish philosopher, was born in Amsterdam. The family were refugees from Catholic persecution in Spain and Portugal. Both Spinoza's grandfather and father (Michael) were leaders of the Jewish community of Amsterdam and of the congregation's Talmud Torah. The father was a successful businessman and after his death in 1654 Spinoza with a brother continued the family business until 1656.

Spinoza's early education was traditional but carefully supervised. He was successively the pupil of two learned rabbis, Saul Levi Morteira and Manasseh ben Israel, the latter a theologian with philosophical leanings. In addition to the Talmud, Spinoza studied

* spĭ nō′ zä

SPINOZA

Jewish thinkers, notably Maimonides, representative of the rationalistic direction in Jewish thought. Whether because of these intellectual stimuli or because of native independence Spinoza broke with Jewish orthodoxy while still a youth. Spinoza also had many friends among non-Jews, particularly among scientific medical circles—young men who because of their spirit of inquiry (it was the age of Leeuwenhoek) were regarded as freethinkers. One of these, Franciscus van den Enden, taught Spinoza Latin, thus opening classical learning to the youth. The study of Descartes turned his attention to the exact sciences and mathematics, further diverting his mind from the original preoccupation with divinity. On July 27, 1656, Spinoza was excommunicated from the Jewish congregation. This and other reasons impelled him to take up residence outside of Amsterdam proper. Until 1660 he lived on the road to Ouderkerk, after that date at Rijnsburg, near Leiden. Despite this ostracism Spinoza was able to provide for himself by practicing his trade of lens grinding. He appears to have taken this seriously; at any rate he was a recognized craftsman. The Dutch scholar Van Vloten discovered and published, in 1862, Spinoza's early *Treatise On the Rainbow*, until then "lost." The interest in optics also attracted the attention of two great contemporaries, Huygens and Leibniz.

Spinoza had many friends among a group known as "Collegianten." These were members of non-conformist religious groups which, although not really persecuted, found strength in union. They met regularly, discussed religious questions but outside of any church communion, practiced tolerance toward intellectual differences, and stressed practical Christian charity. Most "Collegianten" were either Arminians or Mennonites. Rijnsburg was a center of their activity. The Rijnsburg years mark Spinoza's rise to a position of recognized intellectual leadership. One Simon de Vries, especially, became an ardent disciple; he even provided a generous annuity for his revered friend which Spinoza received until his death. International attention came also through a correspondence with Henry Oldenburg, first secretary of the British Royal Society.

In 1663 Spinoza went to live at Voorburg, two miles from The Hague, and from 1670 he took up residence in the city itself. During these years he was working on his *Ethica* (finished about 1665) which, however, he kept from publication. The house in which Spinoza lived first, that of the widow van de Velde, was later occupied by the Lutheran pastor and Spinoza's first biographer Colerus. Spinoza's last residence was with the Van der Spijck family with which he lived a life of utmost frugality on terms of cordiality and understanding. More than ever during this last period Spinoza displayed that almost superhuman selflessness which allowed him to experience false charges without a paralyzing bitterness. An invitation in 1673 from the Elector Palatine to go to Heidelberg was declined. In 1675 he decided finally against the publication of his lifework *(Ethica)* because of the controversy he knew it would cause. He died of tuberculosis attended only by his physician-friend Meyer. He was buried in the New Church, many illustrious persons attending the services.

Spinoza's system is laid down in the following works: *Tractatus Theologico-Politicus, De Intellectus Emendatione, Ethica Ordine Geometrico Demonstrata,* all published in *Opera Posthuma* (1677). Spinoza's ideas of the state and society are developed in *Tractatus Theologico-Politicus* (probably written 1663-67). Volumes of letters, a Hebrew grammar, and other minor writings were published both during his lifetime and afterward.

To Spinoza, as to Descartes, geometric knowledge is the model. What we call knowledge has four degrees: hearsay, vague experience, conclusions relative to a thing out of another thing, knowledge of a thing out of its essence. Only the last is real knowledge: reality is ascribed only to those concepts generated by or immediately present to the mind. Truth need not be proved; to assent to its existence does not require an act of will; certainty is nothing but the presence of truth in our minds. This mind *(ratio)* is not, in its apprehension of concepts, limited by the number or time limitations of the objects, i.e., the mind is not tied to the empirical categories which objects assume in experience. Mind sees them only in their eternal essence, "sub specie aeternitatis."

God, according to the *Ethica,* is pure substance, self-caused, independent of anything outside itself. From this essence proceed an infinite number of attributes; only two, thought and extension, are accessible to us. Entities perceived, e.g., man, are modes of God's attributes, but God is the immanent cause of all things, "natura naturans"; the totality of the modes of things is "natura naturata."

Man as modus of God's extension and thought is dual, body and mind; these are parallel and do not influence each other. The mind, says Spinoza, is an "idea corporis" tied to the body. Various faculties are associated respectively with this dual nature but *ratio* is superior to *imaginatio.* The latter can project objects only in time; they are for this reason of a lower order than *ratio's* products. Only rational knowledge is essential knowledge and the force impelling man toward it is the "amor intellectualis dei."

That these views should have been designated pantheistic is not difficult to understand. Even greater disapproval met the ideas expressed in the *Tractatus Theologico-Politicus.* Here Spinoza distinguishes sharply between philosophy, which deals with knowledge, and theology, which is concerned with obedience and conduct. The Bible is not a source of knowledge but of edification. Hence Spinoza insisted upon freedom of thought and the clear separation of church and state. Religion cannot be used to cover or sanction any speculative doctrine nor, conversely, can speculative or scientific investigation ever put true religion in jeopardy. The state must therefore allow the right to differ and guarantee a peaceful compromise between ardently held views. In 1671 these teachings were synodically condemned; the Dutch States-General interdicted them in 1674; they were placed also on the Index.

Such uninformed censure prevailed generally for a century. Perhaps more than anyone else Lessing deserves credit for Spinoza's rehabilitation. His famous correspondence with Jacobi in 1780 focused the attention of intellectuals upon the profound meaning of Spinoza. Since that time the lonely Dutch Jew has become more and more an object of study and admiration. Today the figure of Spinoza stands secure as a recognized mind and as a model of unselfish devotion to the life of the spirit.

Outstanding among numerous translations into English are: R. H. M. Elwes, *The Chief Works of Benedict de Spinoza* (1883-84), and A. G. Wernham, *The Political Works . . .* (1958). *The Correspondence of Spinoza* was translated by A. Wolf (1928).

ABOUT: Caird, J. Spinoza; McKeon, R. The Philosophy of Spinoza; Pollock, F. Spinoza, His Life and Philosophy (includes English translation of the first Dutch biography of Spinoza by Johannes Colerus, 1705); Ratner, J. The Philosophy of Spinoza (with biography and introduction); Roth, L. Spinoza; Runes, D. D. Spinoza Dictionary; Wolfson, H. A. The Philosophy of Spinoza.

C. K. P.

*SPONDE, JEAN DE (1557-March 18, 1595), French humanist and poet, was born in Mauléon to a family of Spanish origin. His father, Irrigo de Sponde, was the secretary of Jeanne d'Albret, mother of Henry IV. Described by Olhagaray as a "strong man of means, pious and religious," the elder Sponde was slaughtered by the *ligueurs* at Saint Palays in 1594.

The young Jean then enjoyed the patronage of his father's lords and with the help of d'Albret received a liberal education. Having gained entrance to the Court and having followed loyally the fortunes of Henry IV, the Protestant-born Sponde converted to Catholicism when his king also recanted. Fidelity to Henry was rewarded, for the king made Sponde lieutenant-general of the Senechaussée of La Rochelle, a charge which allowed Sponde, apparently reckless in the handling of his affairs, to pay his debts. The position was temporary, however, and Sponde later obtained, in exchange, the office of master of petitions or requests.

The miserable end of his brief life—he died in Bordeaux at the age of thirty-eight—was recorded in a cruel memorial by Théodore Agrippa d'Aubigné (see sketch above), who had attacked Sponde on his recantation. D'Aubigné wrote in the *Confession de Sancy:* "The poor Sponde having sacrificed his soul for the church has so been lured that before his death he has seen his children forced to beg, his wife forced to sell her body, and himself hospitalized."

Despite the brevity of his life and the responsibilities imposed upon him as courtier

* spŏnd

and administrator, Sponde worked seriously with classical letters. As a humanist he published notable editions of Homer, *Homeri Poemarum Versio Latina,* 1538; Hesiod, *Opera et Dies;* Aristotle, *La Logique d'Aristote* (annotated Greek and Latin texts)—as well as the *Déclaration des Principaux Motifs qui Induisent le Sieur de Sponde . . . à S'unir a l'Église Catholique,* a personal apology justifying his conversion. Often attributed to him, but erroneously so, is a response to the treatise of Théodore de Bèze titled *Marques Essentielles de l'Église;* Henri de Sponde, the poet's prelate brother (1568-1643), was the author.

The best of Sponde's work, however, is to be found in his poetry—some fifty poems—sonnets on love and death, two religious pieces, some songs and stanzas. Published about 1630, the poetry was valued by his contemporaries (such figures as Laugier de Porchères, Marie de Gournay, Pierre de Brach) as the poetry of a vigorous, clear, and rich mind. The agreement of modern scholars, in addition, assures Sponde's work of a choice place in the evolution of French baroque poetry.

Sonnets on Love and Death, translated by R. Nugent, with a commentary, was published in 1962.

ABOUT: [In French—see studies by M. Arland, A. Boase (*in* Mesures, 1939), O. de Magny (*in* Lettres Nouvelles, 1956).]

G. E.

*STAËL-HOLSTEIN, ANNE LOUISE GERMAINE (NECKER), Baroness of (April 22, 1766-July 14, 1817), French novelist and critic, was born and raised in Paris, although she was actually of Swiss nationality and later, by marriage, Swedish. Her father was Jacques Necker, the wealthy Genevese banker who came to France to serve as finance minister to Louis XVI in the last years of his reign, before the French Revolution. Her mother was Suzanne Curchod, the daughter of a Swiss Protestant minister, who had been engaged to the English historian Edward Gibbon for five years before her marriage to Necker. Little Germaine Necker grew up in the center of the brilliant salon society in which her parents moved. A lively and precocious child, though not pretty, she was pampered by her adoring and indulgent father and resented by her strict mother. She was given an excellent education, and at fifteen she began to write novels, tragedies, and essays. At twenty she made a loveless marriage to the Swedish am-

* stäl ōls těn'

MADAME DE STAËL

bassador in Paris, Baron Erik Magnus Staël-Holstein.

Madame de Staël's first book, *Lettres sur Jean-Jacques Rousseau,* was published in 1788, just before the outbreak of the French Revolution. In this book she identified herself enthusiastically with the liberal thinkers of her day who advocated enlightenment and reason and a moderate constitutional monarchy as a solution to the desperate political crises of the time. Thanks to her diplomatic immunity as an ambassador's wife, she was able to remain in Paris even after the Revolution broke out and her father was obliged to flee to safety in Switzerland. She financed and courageously arranged the escape of numerous refugees from the Terror, among them her lover Count Louis de Narbonne, former minister of war. She even undertook a plan for the escape of the royal family, but this plot failed and she herself escaped only at great risk, fleeing to her family home at Coppet, in Switzerland, and later to England. In both countries she surrounded herself with a small court of admirers, mainly French émigrés, and spent money and energy extravagantly in their aid. In 1794 she met the author Benjamin Constant. They became lovers and lived together for some twelve years, although during much of this time Constant was trying to break off relations with her. After the death of the Baron de Staël-Holstein in 1802, Constant offered to marry her, but she refused, unwilling to give up her title and, probably, her independence.

When the new French republic was established, Madame de Staël immediately returned to Paris and plunged into political activity. She greeted the arrival of Napoleon in Paris in 1797 as the coming of a deliverer, but as it became increasingly apparent that he disliked her and resented her interference in politics, she turned against him bitterly. Her *De la Littérature, Considérée dans ses Rapports avec les Institutions Sociales* (1800) displeased the conservative and traditionalist Napoleon because it argued for a literature based on new and radically reformed social conditions. It was, in a sense, one of the first calls to romanticism issued in France, and its influence upon subsequent French writers of the nineteenth century—Sainte-Beuve, Hugo, Lamartine—was considerable. She further irritated Napoleon by publishing, in 1802, her novel *Delphine,* a widely read romance which praised liberalism and the British, defended divorce, and in general upheld the Protestant rather than the Roman Catholic religion. That same year Napoleon banished her from Paris. Not even banishment could dull her zest for life. With Constant she traveled to Germany, visiting Weimar where, as one of her biographers puts it, she "annexed" Wilhelm Schlegel as tutor for her sons.

In 1804 she traveled for a year in Italy. The fruit of this journey was her most memorable book, the novel *Corinne,* published in 1807. The heroine is a fine, intelligent, and beautiful young woman who sacrifices her love nobly for another woman. The scene is Italy and the novel quite frankly intermingles guidebook with love story. Its sentiment is extravagant, but, as George Saintsbury pointed out in his *History of the French Novel,* "the truth and reality of passion . . . are actually present here." Her major literary work was not fiction, however, but *De l'Allemagne,* a three-volume critical study written in 1810 and published in 1813. Like the earlier *De la Littérature,* the work takes up the distinctions between what she calls the literature of the North (Germany, Scandinavia, England), which is romantic, original, and free, and the literature of the South (France, Italy), which is classical, formal, conventional. The influences of the great German thinkers—Herder, Lessing, Klopstock, Goethe, Schiller—all converged in this study of the new romanticism, the elements of which, she wrote, are "the sorrowful sentiment of the incompleteness of human destiny, melancholy, reverie, mysticism, the sense of the enigma of life."

De l'Allemagne so offended Napoleon that he ordered the confiscation of the proof sheets, the banishment of her friend Wilhelm Schlegel, and her own banishment to Coppet. Her despair at this persecution was lightened, however, by a new romance with a handsome young soldier, John Rocca, more than twenty years her junior, whom she married in 1811. With her new husband she fled to Russia, then Sweden, and England, and lived in exile until the abdication of Napoleon in 1814. She returned to Paris immediately, a staunch supporter of the restoration of the Bourbon monarchy. When Louis XVIII was re-established upon the throne after Napoleon's final downfall in 1815, Madame de Staël found herself at last in a secure and respected position in France. By this time her health had begun to fail. She spent the winter of 1816 in Italy, saw her daughter (by Constant) married to the Duc de Broglie, and in 1817 returned to Paris where she died at fifty-one. She was buried at Coppet.

Madame de Staël was beyond a doubt the most remarkable woman of her time. Everything she did had a touch of the spectacular about it. She passed unflinching through the dangers of the French Revolution. She faced the most powerful man in Europe, Napoleon, in open conflict. A plain woman, stout, with protruding teeth, a drab complexion, and outrageous taste in clothes, she nevertheless dazzled European society. Intellectually she was the equal of the greatest minds of the age. Her penetrating literary criticism initiated the romantic movement in France. "She represented," Mary Colum wrote, "the strong currents of the eighteenth century that were passing away, as well as the new currents of the nineteenth century that were just setting in"; and "she affected profoundly the minds of the writers who came after her." As Nitze and Dargan have written in their History of French Literature: "She enlarged the borders of her country; she helped to Europeanize modern thought." Her emotional life was passionate and disorderly. She was egotistical, vain, possessive, but she was also generous, warm, and affectionate. The impact of her personality was overwhelming. Constant's cousin Rosalie de Constant, who had no reason to be kind to her, nevertheless reflected the feeling of many of her contemporaries when she wrote: "One is swept away, one is completely subjugated by the force of her genius. When she is present, other people just become the audience. . . ."

De la Littérature was translated into English in 1803 under the title A Treatise on Ancient and Modern Literature, and De l'Allemagne was translated, as Germany, in 1813. Delphine was translated in 1803. The first English translation of Corinne, or Italy was D. Lawlor's, in 1807. Isabel Hill's translation of the novel, "with metrical versions of the odes by L. E. Landon," appeared in 1833 and went into many editions.

ABOUT: Andrews, W. Germaine; Babbitt, I. Masters of Modern French Criticism; Brandes, G. Main Currents in Nineteenth Century Literature, I; Colum, M. From These Roots; Goldsmith, M. L. Madame de Staël; Haggard, A. C. P. Madame de Staël: Her Trials and Triumphs; Hawkins, R. L. Madame de Staël and the United States; Herold, J. C. Mistress to an Age: A Life of Madame de Staël; Jaeck, E. G. Madame de Staël and the Spread of German Literature; Larg, D. G. Madame de Staël; Levaillant, M. The Passionate Exiles; Nicolson, H. G. Benjamin Constant; Saintsbury, G. History of the French Novel, II; Wellek, R. History of Modern Criticism: 1750-1950; Whitford, R. C. Madame de Staël's Literary Reputation in England; Forum February 1949; New York Times Magazine April 18, 1954. [In French—Escarpit, R. L'Angleterre dans l'Œuvre de Madame de Staël; Larg, D. G. Madame de Staël.]

*STAGNELIUS, ERIK JOHAN (October 14, 1793-April 3 1823) Swedish poet and dramatist, was born on the island of Öland, off the southeastern coast of Sweden. His father was the vicar Magnus Stagnelius, later bishop in Kalmar. His mother was Hedvig Christina Bergstedt, daughter of a vicar in the province of Södermanland. As a child he was a solitary dreamer and attained most of his knowledge through private reading. In 1811 he went to the University of Lund to study theology but left after one semester for the University of Uppsala, where in 1814 he passed a qualifying examination for service in government offices. The next year he was employed in the Department of Church and Education. A severe heart disease drove him to overindulgence in alcohol and, probably, narcotics.

Despite the short time Stagnelius lived and wrote, his production was considerable, although just a fraction of it was published before his early death. His earliest songs were written in the style of the Enlightenment, but romantic ideas soon appeared, e.g., in such poems as the two epics Gunlög and Blenda, the tragedies Sigurd Ring and Visbur. Stagnelius' poems from this period were often passionately sensual, expressing erotic dreams and the unsatisfied longings of a recluse. The object of his longing is often personified as "Amanda." But even his first major poem, the hexameter epic Wladimir den Store (Wladimir the Great, 1817), reflects a harmonious and agitated soul.

* stäng nä' lĭ ŭs

883

Wladimir's conflict between epicurism and loathing of life represents Stagnelius' own inner struggle, and like the Russian emperor he seeks salvation in the Christian religion. The epic is written in a typically Homeric style, but (under the influence of Chateaubriand) with a substitution of Christian divinities for the ancient pagan gods. Collaterally with the religious tendency there is a political one—the hatred of Napoleon Bonaparte and the admiration of his conqueror Alexander I.

Wladimir den Store represents a transitional stage in Stagnelius' development, after which his sensualism definitely passed into the reverse—into a strong ascetic renunciation of the world. His new philosophy constitutes the keynote of his poetic collection *Liljor i Saron* (Lilies in Sharon, 1821), in which he gave a brilliantly colorful poetic form to a peculiar theosophic philosophy consisting of elements from Plato's doctrine of the contrast between the material world and the world of ideas, from Schelling's transcendental philosophy, from the Bible, from Oriental and European mysticism, and from Gnosticism from which he adopted several strange symbols and mythical forces. The main difference between Stagnelius' idea of the universe and that of other romanticists is the former's ethical idea of complete abnegation of worldly things. Included in *Liljor i Saron* was the verse drama *Martyrerna* (The Martyrs), which shows the poet's ecstatic asceticism in extreme form. Judging from his tragedy *Bacchanterna* (The Bacchantes, 1822), his poetic masterpiece, Stagnelius succeeded in arriving at a more balanced attitude to life. His beautiful late poems *Näcken* (The Nixie) and *Endymion* show little or no theosophic obscurantism, and in his tragedy *Thorsten Fiskare* (Thorsten the Fisherman), finished shortly before his death, he is even merrily ironical.

Two poems, "The Birds of Passage" and "Amanda," and two scenes from *The Martyrs* in English translation are included in H. W. Longfellow's *The Poets and Poetry of Europe* (1871), and the poem "The Nixie" in C. W. Stork's *Anthology of Swedish Lyrics* (1930).

ABOUT: Howitt, W. & M. The Literature and Romance of Northern Europe, II. [In Swedish—see studies by D. Andreæ, F. Böök, S. Cederblad, S. Malmström.]

A. J.

STAMPA, GASPARA (1523-April 23, 1554), Italian poet, was born in Padua, the second daughter of the prosperous Stampa

* stäm′ pä

884

family hailing originally from Milan. Gaspara, her elder sister Cassandra, and their younger brother Baldassare were well educated, their father using his money liberally to provide them with good instructors. Gaspara studied Greek, Latin, philosophy, history, music, and singing. Their father, a jewel merchant, died while the children were still young, and shortly thereafter the family moved to Venice where Gaspara spent the rest of her short life.

The town of her adoption was in the first half of the sixteenth century a center of political, financial, and intellectual activity. The Venetian share of genius in the Renaissance included many feminine names: Vittoria Colonna, Tullia d'Aragona, Veronica Gambara; by the time Gaspara Stampa was twenty she was included in this roster. Her talents were much admired and praised in Venetian artistic and literary circles, and she became known as the Venetian Sappho. It is interesting to note that her poem beginning "Quando innanti ai begli occhi" is a clear echo of the Sapphic fragment paraphrased by Catullus in "Ille mi par esse Deo videtur." The poems of Sappho were published in Venice two years after Stampa's death, but she was undoubtedly familiar with the works of Catullus.

About 1549, shortly after the untimely death of her brother, Gaspara met Collaltino, count of Collalto. He was a young Venetian nobleman, soldier, man of letters, and poet himself. Gaspara's love for the young patrician provided the inspiration for the bulk of her sonnets. For three years great devotion existed between the two, and Gaspara seems to have hoped for, and expected, marriage. The Stampas, however, were not of the aristocracy, and while Venetian nobles and artists met and mingled, they did not, apparently, marry. The *Enciclopedia Italiana* suggests also that if Gaspara was not actually one of the *cortigiane oneste*, she was too Bohemian to be considered a suitable wife. At all events, the young count went off to France and remained there for some time, unmoved by a succession of poignant sonnets from Gaspara's pen. Upon his return to Venice there was a brief reconciliation, but constant rumors of his impending marriage to someone else caused Gaspara to realize that the romance was quite ended. There is a well-founded tradition that she then turned to a life of gaiety and excitement, and even manifested an interest in one or two other admirers.

Toward the end of 1553, the exact date unknown, Gaspara died in Venice. At that period in history, an untimely death was always accompanied by rumors of suicide or poisoning, the collusion of Collaltino being hinted in the latter case. There are, however, no positive reasons to justify these assumptions. In the year following her death, the first edition of her sonnets was published as a loving memorial by her sister Cassandra. A critical edition of the *Rime*, edited by A. Salza, appeared in 1927.

With few exceptions, most of the sonnets chronicle the phases of the love affair with Collaltino. The intense sincerity is inescapable; they are an example almost unique in literature of sustained and high-pitched emotion.

A selection of Stampa's sonnets translated by George Fleming appears in Eugene Benson's *Gaspara Stampa* (1881). Prose translations are to be found in *The Penguin Book of Italian Verse* edited by G. R. Kay in 1958. Lorna de' Lucchi has translated two sonnets in her *Anthology of Italian Poems* (1922).

ABOUT: Benson, E. Gaspara Stampa. [In Italian—see studies by G. A. Cesareo, L. Pompilj, A. Salza *in* Giornale Storico della Letteratura 1913, 1917.]

E. DE P.

*STAVENHAGEN, FRITZ** (September 18, 1876-May 9, 1906), German dramatist, was born in Hamburg, where his father, the descendant of Mecklenburg farmers, worked as a coachman. He attended the *Volkschule* in Hamburg, and although he wished to become a teacher, he was required to begin work at an early age as a druggist's apprentice. His interest in literature could not be stifled, however, and he continued to read whatever books he could obtain. He was particularly impressed by Shakespeare, whose works inspired him to attempt plays of his own. The wide discrepancy between his boring work and his vital creative desire caused him to leave his job to travel throughout Europe. He visited Berlin, Friesland, and Munich, with periodic visits to Hamburg. These proved to be difficult years during which he barely existed on the meager earnings of newspaper contributions. During one period in Munich, while completing *Jürgen Piepers* (1901), his first major drama, he subsisted on a diet of a single egg a day. Although this folk drama was a formless and technically unskilled work, it showed great original strength and dramatic promise and gained Stavenhagen a stipend from the

* stä' věn hä gěn

Schiller foundation in Munich. He quickly produced a second drama, *Der Lotse* (1902), a powerful one-act tragedy, treating the irreconcilable conflict between youth and age.

In 1902 Stavenhagen returned to Berlin, where he received encouragement and financial assistance from the famous director Otto Brahm. Here he completed *Mudder Mews* (1904), a dialect peasant tragedy, which also treats the conflict between generations. Written in an extreme naturalistic technique, reminiscent of the early works of Gerhardt Hauptmann, this drama provides an excellent study of both character and social milieu. Stavenhagen's next production, *De Dütsche Michel* (1905), the work he himself preferred, represents his most ambitious and greatest achievement. In this peasant comedy he attempted successfully to combine symbolism, romantic fairy tale, and naturalism into an organic unity. The influence of Shakespeare is evident here, as well as of the Viennese tradition of the fairy tale play best exemplified by the dramas of the Austrian poet Ferdinand Raimund. This new synthesis was continued in a second peasant comedy, *De Ruge Hoff* (1906), which proved to be his final play. Stavenhagen was a born dramatist who conceived people and events in dramatic terms. His strength lay mainly in his ability to create believable human beings in a realistic milieu.

Stavenhagen's early dramas were successfully performed in Hamburg, in 1904, and his reputation began to grow. He was married in 1904, and the following year was appointed dramaturgist of the newly established Schiller theatre in Hamburg. In 1906 he fell ill suddenly and died following an operation. As he was the chief dramatist of the Low German dialect area, his premature death at twenty-nine represented a true loss to the development of *Plattdeutsch* literature. Stavenhagen also produced a collection of short stories and sketches set in Hamburg entitled *Grau und Golden* (1904).

None of Stavenhagen's works has been translated into English.

ABOUT: [In German—see studies by A. Bartels, A. Becker, H. Spiero, J. Plate, W. J. Schröder.]

D. G. D.

*"STECCHETTI, LORENZO"** (pseudonym of Olindo *Guerrini) (October 4, 1845-October 21, 1916), Italian poet, was born in the town of Forlì, about seventeen miles from Ravenna in the northern district of

* stäk kät' tě; gwär rě' ně

"LORENZO STECCHETTI"

Romagna. His family came originally from S. Alberto di Romagna near Ravenna, and Guerrini maintained an active interest in his home territory all his life, although he lived over fifty miles away in Bologna.

He attended the University of Bologna, entered the civil service, and eventually became the university librarian. Surrounded by books and the aura of scholarship at the world's oldest university Guerrini might be expected to produce correspondingly erudite works. But the studious bibliographer and critic had another aspect: he was a believer in the nationalist sentiments of the day, and a poet endowed with a satirical sense of humor.

At the age of thirty-two Guerrini published in Bologna a little volume of verse entitled *Postuma,* to which he wrote the prefatory remarks. Explaining that these verses were the work of his friend and relative Lorenzo Stecchetti, he detailed the young man's life story and the tragedy of his early death from tuberculosis. Guerrini was here imitating a literary hoax perpetrated earlier in the century by Sainte-Beuve when he published verses attributed to the late Joseph Delorme, for "Stecchetti" was Guerrini himself. *Postuma* caused a wave of excitement throughout Italy for its vigor, sensuality, and more than a hint of licentiousness. Because of these characteristics in his poems, Guerrini became the standard-bearer of the verist school in Italian literature as opposed to the idealist school of lyric poets.

For the next two years Guerrini attracted much fame and comment. Laying aside the disguise of the consumptive poet, in 1878 he published *Polemica* and *Nova Polemica,* poems even more openly satirical and antireligious than those of *Postuma.* These sentiments were not at all displeasing in the atmosphere of anticlericalism then prevalent throughout Italy and particularly in Guerrini's native district of Romagna, which had long suffered from papal misgovernment.

The archivist in Guerrini was manifested in 1879 when his monograph on the life of Giulio Cesare Croce was published. Croce, a sixteenth century Bolognese street musician, was the author of *Le Sottilissime Astuzie di Bertoldo* (The Wonderful Cunning of Bertoldo), a comic romance about a jester-peasant, ugly and witty, who comes to the Lombard court. Authentic in its detail of the life of a jester, the book has been through many editions in Italy. Guerrini's essay is considered basic in research on Croce's life. As collaborator with Corrado Ricci, Guerrini published a volume of studies and criticism on Dante in 1880. Other contributions to scholarship include prefaces to several volumes of the *Biblioteca Classica Economica,* and editions of three women poets of the sixteenth century: Vittoria Colonna, Gaspara Stampa, and Veronica Gambara.

Guerrini could not long refrain from using laughter as a literary weapon. His contemporary Rapisardi, the scholar who occupied the chair of Italian letters at the University of Catania, had written a ponderous pseudo-classical poem entitled *Giobbe* in 1884. Guerrini lampooned this in a spicily derisive satire entitled *Giobbe, Serena Concezione di Mario Balossardi* (Job, Happy Concept of Mario Balossardi). Under the pen-name of Argia Sbolenfi, Guerrini expressed himself on the subject of feminine foolishness in *Rime,* verses published in 1897. With the passage of time he relinquished the licentious tone, and even his antipapal jibes became more good-natured, as in *Ciacole di Bepi,* published in 1908.

Throughout his lifetime Guerrini composed the *Sonetti Romagnoli* which were collected and published posthumously by his son Guido in 1920. These were verses written in his native dialect concerning events in and around Ravenna, about which Guerrini kept himself informed through steady correspondence with a friend in Ravenna, the lawyer Paolo Poletti. Some of the poems were printed between 1876 and 1879 in the Ravenna periodicals *Il Lupo* and *L'Asino.*

Many not previously published were found in Guerrini's papers with the note "For Guido." It is from the biographical notes in his son's preface to *Sonetti Romagnoli* that Guerrini is revealed as a simple, happy man who loved his family. He died in Bologna a few weeks after his seventy-first birthday.

Guerrini's first and most famous work, *Postuma,* is noteworthy for its contribution to the ancient controversy in Italian literature between formal and informal language. The simple flowing poetry is in contrast to the difficult classicism of Giosue Carducci (see sketch above) whose *Odi Barbare* was published in the same year as *Postuma.*

An interesting comment by Guerrini appears in the preface to *Nova Polemica,* and provides insight to his art: "A few years back in Italy we read only French books and our country was the outlet for the inanities of third- and fourth-rate novelists. . . . Italian books were not sold or seen. Now we are emancipated from Paris. . . . How is it that that great corpse, Italian art, gives signs of new life? . . . It is because artists have begun to understand that the secret of success is in knowing how to draw inspiration from the world in which they live, in the truth of the present and not in that of fifty years ago."

J. S. Kennard in *A Literary History of the Italian People* has done a prose translation of "Preghiera della Sera" (Evening Prayer) from *Postuma.*

ABOUT: Kennard, J. S. A Literary History of the Italian People. [In Italian—see study by L. Lodi.]

E. DE P.

STEINBERG, JUDAH (or YEHUDA)

(1863-1908), Hebrew short-story writer, fabulist, novelist, and writer of children's stories, was born in Lipkany, Bessarabia. He was brought up in an environment of Hasidic tradition and was very close to nature. Upon his marriage at seventeen he found his way to secular enlightenment and settled in a Rumanian village as a small storekeeper, though dedicating most of his time to reading and self-education; after two years he returned to his native town where he became a teacher of Hebrew. Owing to continuous conflicts with his pious father who opposed his pursuit of secular studies, Steinberg moved in 1889 to the town of Yedintsy where he continued as a Hebrew teacher and made his debut as a Hebrew writer with a Hebrew syntax, *Niv Sefatayim,* followed by a two-volume collection of fables for adults and children, *Ba-ir*

Uvayaar, and a collection of children's stories, *Livne Haneurim.* The latter two works were received enthusiastically by Hebrew readers and established Steinberg's prestige as a fabulist and short-story writer.

In 1897 he moved to the town of Leovo where he was engaged as a Hebrew teacher, and his economic status improved somewhat; during his stay there he created his best works, including *Sihot Hasidim* and *Sippure Hasidim*—collections of exquisite folkloristic Hasidic tales dealing with people of his immediate environment, and a collection of children's stories, *Sihot Yeladim.* In addition to these, he contributed numerous short stories and fables to most of the Hebrew and Yiddish periodicals of that time and edited Hebrew chrestomathies and textbooks.

In 1905 Steinberg settled in Odessa as the Russian correspondent of the New York Yiddish daily *Varheit.* In spite of poverty and chronic illness, he continued to be prolific, producing, among other works, two novels, *Bayamim Hahem,* which depicts the life and martyrdom of a young Jewish boy forcibly recruited by the Czarist regime to be brought up as a soldier and Christian, and *Biyeme Shefot Hashoftim,* dealing with the Biblical period.

In 1908 Steinberg went to Berlin where he tardily underwent abdominal surgery; he was forty-four when he died soon after.

Steinberg is one of the main representatives of the neo-romantic trend in modern Hebrew literature and a classical short-story writer. His excellent short stories portray the life and the everyday struggles of the simple pious Hasidic Jew of Eastern Europe in the nineteenth century. Having been all his life close to the people he described, he wrote with sympathy and deep psychological insight as well as with fine satire and humor.

Of even greater importance for modern Hebrew literature are Steinberg's children's stories and fables; Jewish in content but universal in appeal, these appeared in many editions in book form, anthologies, periodicals, etc., and are still eagerly read by Jewish children the world over.

Steinberg's collected Hebrew writings appeared in four volumes; in addition there are two volumes of children's stories. Many of his stories, fables, and children's stories were translated into English and included in various anthologies. The novel *Bayamim Hahem* was translated by G. Jeshurun in 1915, and a collection of his children's stories, *The Breakfast of the Birds,* was translated by E. Solis-Cohen in 1917.

ABOUT: Waxman, M. A History of Jewish Literature.

H. C.

"STENDHAL." See BEYLE, MARIE HENRI

STENVALL, ALEKSIS. See "KIVI, ALEKSIS"

*STIERNHIELM, GEORG (August 7, 1598-April 22, 1672), Swedish poet and scholar generally known as "the father of Swedish poetry," was born in Vika parish in the Swedish province of Dalarna. His father was Olof Markwardsson, of an old but poor family of miners. His mother was Karin Matsdotter, also of a family of miners from the same district. About his childhood and youth little is known. The boy's name was Jöran Olofsson, which during his school years was latinized to Georgius Olai. Later he called himself Georg Lilja. When he was ennobled in 1631 he assumed the family name Stiernhielm.

In 1615 he matriculated at the University of Greifswald in northern Germany, and thereafter he spent several years studying many branches of learning at various European universities. After his return to Sweden in 1626 he held positions as a teacher, and in 1630 he entered upon a strenuous civil service career in the Baltic countries which, with some intermissions, extended over a period of twenty-six years, during which he held judicial offices at Dorpat (Estonian: Tartu). In 1630 he married Cecilia Burea. In 1642 he moved to Stockholm, where in 1645 he was appointed chief custodian of national monuments. In 1651 he returned to the Baltic area to live as a landed proprietor, but in 1659 he had to flee from the Russians, bereft of all his possessions. For the rest of his life he lived in Sweden, holding many prominent but poorly salaried offices, and he was always distressed by financial worries. In 1669 he was elected a member of the Royal Society in London.

Stiernhielm was one of Sweden's greatest geniuses. His learning was universal; he was a prominent scholar of theology, law, philosophy, archeology mathematics, mechanics, and astronomy; and his contribution to poetry was epoch-making. Like other great spirits of his time he tried to create a new idea of the universe in which he saw man as a link between God and the rest of creation. His admiration of his country's glorious past and present was unlimited, and he believed that Scandinavian, not Hebrew, was the origin of all languages. He wanted to purify Swedish of borrowed words and regenerate it by reviving old obsolete words of "noble quality" and incorporating dialect vocabulary.

Stiernhielm's lasting achievement was in the field of poetry. He was a court poet and wrote occasional congratulatory poems and translated ballads, but his name is immortalized through his magnificent poem *Hercules,* printed in 1658, the most imposing poetic creation in seventeenth century Scandinavia. On the basis of the classical legends of the Greek hero Hercules, Stiernhielm created an independent didactic allegory in which the hero actually is a Swedish youth who is given the choice between the vices and virtues his country could offer. The poem is written in splendid Renaissance style. The meter is hexameter but based on stress rather than quantity.

Extracts from various poems by Stiernhielm are translated into English by R. Ahlén in his *Swedish Poets of the Seventeenth Century* (1932).

ABOUT: Howitt, W. & M. The Literature and Romance of Northern Europe, II; Winkel Horn, F. History of the Literature of the Scandinavian North. [In Swedish—see studies by A. Friberg, H. Lindroth, B. Swartling, P. Wieselgren.]

A. J.

*STIFTER, ADALBERT (October 23, 1805-January 28, 1868), Austrian short-story writer and novelist, was born at Oberplan in the Bohemian forest, where he spent an uneventful childhood in modest circumstances. His father, a linen weaver, died when the boy was twelve, and Stifter came to rely increasingly on his mother, for whom he had always felt the closest affinity. His great admiration for her determined the high esteem in which he held all women, and she later became the model for the idealized feminine portraits in his narratives. In 1818 Stifter entered the Benedictine Abbey school at Kremsmünster, where the religious art works of his surroundings awakened in him the desire to become a painter. He developed into a skillful landscapist, and for a time vacillated between painting and writing for a career. His training as a painter is clearly apparent in his descriptive writing.

Supporting himself by giving private lessons, Stifter enrolled at the University of Vienna in 1826 to study law, but gravitated by inclination to art, philosophy, the natural sciences and mathematics. Although he passed the written examination for teachers, he was too timid to attempt the oral test, and con-

* shârn' yělm

* shtĭf' tēr

STIFTER

abhorred violence or upheaval of any kind, and his works rarely contain an exciting or unusual plot. His art, which is reminiscent of the late Goethe, displays great integrity, human warmth, and nobility of feeling, and is devoted to preserving the universal and traditional values in the world he knew and loved. Lacking the gift of great inventiveness, he depicted only what he had observed, but he did this minutely and accurately. In his descriptive writing he was influenced by James Fenimore Cooper and the German writer Jean Paul Richter, although he could not compete with the latter in imagination and fantasy.

To Stifter art was second only to religion in importance, and he believed that it should not only represent but also teach and elevate. The basic intent of his work is to portray the education of man: he shows how, by learning moderation, contentment, and resignation, the individual may achieve harmony with his fellow man, the world and himself. His greatness and uniqueness as a writer lie in the unparalleled manner in which he was able to combine this serious didactic purpose with an outstanding artistic technique. His prose style is masterly, and he possessed an exceptional talent for the highly stylized manner of characterization which he employed, and for beautiful descriptions of nature which are artistically woven into the action and mood of every story.

Although Stifter was popular in his own day, he became unfashionable with the change of literary taste during the later nineteenth century. A revival occurred during the twentieth century, and he is today recognized as one of the greatest prose writers that Germany has ever produced. *Der Nachsommer*, an apprentice novel in the manner of Goethe's *Wilhelm Meister*, was acclaimed by Nietzsche as one of the prose masterpieces of the nineteenth century, a verdict that is universally held today. *Witiko*, which is claimed by some critics to be the greatest German historical novel, has yet to find the popularity that it deserves.

tinued as a private tutor, serving some of the most prominent families of Vienna, including that of Metternich. After an unhappy love affair with Fanny Greipl, in 1837 he married Amalie Mohaupt, an uneducated woman, whose character contrasted sharply with Stifter's, and with whom he found happiness only in later years. They had no children of their own, and two adopted daughters died in childhood.

Stifter's first successful story appeared in 1840, and from that time on he continued writing in addition to his regular occupation. In 1848, distressed by the revolutionary activity in Vienna, he moved to Linz in upper Austria. The following year he was appointed government inspector of schools, a position which he filled until continuous ill health forced his retirement at the age of sixty. In 1868, in a moment of madness caused by the tormenting pain of cancer, he committed suicide.

During his life Stifter produced three major collections of short stories: *Studien* (1844-50), *Bergkristall* (1853), and *Nachgelassene Schriften* (1869), along with two outstanding novels, *Der Nachsommer* (1857) and *Witiko* (1865-67). In all of these writings as in his personal life Stifter reveals himself as a representative of the era in Germany and Austria known as the age of Biedermeier. The main concern of this unheroic period before 1848 was to maintain the *status quo*, and the prevailing philosophy may be generally stated as a quiet resignation. Stifter

Neither of Stifter's novels has been translated into English, nor has a translation been made of a complete collection of his short stories. In 1850 M. Norman and L. Bentley translated *Die Mappe Meines Urgrossvaters* as *My Great-Grandfather's Note-book*, *Abdias* as *Abdias the Jew*, *Der Hochwald* as *The Hochland*, *Die Narrenburg* as *Crazy Castle*, and *Das Haidedorf* as *The Village on the Heath*. In 1852 M. Howitt and L. Hodgson translated *Die Narrenburg* as *The Castle of Fools*, *Das Haidedorf* as *The Village on the Heath*, and *Angela*. Further translations of *Das Haidedorf* were made in 1868 by C. Mackley and in 1880 by H. Zimmern, who also

translated *Der Condor* as *The Balloon Ascent.*
Bergkristall was translated anonymously in 1857
under the title *Mount Gars or Marie's Christmas
Evening,* and by E. Mayer and M. Moore in 1945 as
Rock Crystal. Der Condor appeared in 1850 in an
anonymous translation with the title *The Condor.*
In 1952 a collection of Stifter's works, edited by K.
Spalding, appeared under the title *Adalbert Stifter,
Selections.*

ABOUT: Blackall, E. A. Adalbert Stifter. [In
German—see studies by H. Bahr, A. R. Hein, W.
Kosch, J. Michels, J. Nadler, F. Novotny, A. Sauer,
D. Sieber.]

D. G. D.

STORM

*STORM, (HANS) THEODOR (WOLDSEN) (September 14, 1817-July 4, 1888), German short-story writer and poet, was born at Husum, a small town on the coast of Schleswig. His father, Johann, was an attorney, whose family had for generations been tenants of a local mill. His mother, Lucie Woldsen, whose cheerful disposition he inherited, came from a local patrician family. Storm deeply loved his homeland, and this locality played an important part in the formation of his sentiments and character.

After receiving his early education in the local schools, Storm studied law at Kiel and Berlin. At Kiel he formed close friendships with the brothers Theodor and Tycho Mommsen, with whom he published a volume of poetry entitled *Liederbuch Dreier Freunde* (1843). In 1847 he settled in Husum as an attorney and married his cousin, Konstanze Esmarsch, who bore him seven children. When Schleswig-Holstein was forcibly incorporated into the kingdom of Denmark (1853), Storm, a staunch German, moved to Potsdam, where he became an assistant judge, and later to Heiligenstadt. After the recapture of Schleswig-Holstein by Prussia in 1864, he returned to Husum, receiving an appointment as district magistrate. This same year Storm suffered the loss of his wife, with whom he had found great happiness. A second marriage the following year to Dorothea Jensen was equally successful. After his retirement in 1880, he lived quietly in Hadermarschen, until his death at the age of seventy.

Storm began his literary career as a lyric poet and ranks high in German literature, which is rich in excellent lyric poetry. Although his fame as a prose writer subsequently overshadowed his fame as a poet, Storm always considered himself primarily a lyric poet. Even his prose works have a strong lyric atmosphere, and the stress

* shtōrm

throughout his writings is on mood rather than on action. He was an heir of the earlier German romantic writers and was influenced particularly by Eichendorf, Mörike, and Heine.

Storm was an accurate observer of life about him and possessed an unusually perceptive understanding of human nature. He was mainly a poet of the small scene and devoted himself largely to the problems of family life. Conservatism is the prevailing attitude in his work, and his characters rarely yield to their imagination or emotions. Although the predominant tone is one of melancholy and resignation, Storm was no pessimist. He loved life and the world, but felt keenly the loneliness of the individual: "If we think about it rightly, each man lives for himself alone, in terrible loneliness, a lost speck in the unmeasured and uncomprehended universe." This *Einsamkeit* or loneliness, caused by the inability of people to reach mutual understanding, is a constant motif in his works.

Storm's short stories, although bearing an unmistakable resemblance to one another, fall into three more or less distinct periods: the first runs from 1848 to 1864, the second until 1880, and the last until his death in 1888. The finest example of his early work and by far his best known story is *Immensee* (1849), typical in plot, theme, style, and technique. The story is told in the first person and by means of a flashback: an old man falls into reverie and dreams the story of his life and unhappy love. The mood throughout is one of loneliness, melancholy, and passivity, and the story ends on a note of renunciation. Other works which deal with lost youthful love are *Ein Grünes Blatt* (1855), *Späte Rosen* (1861), and *Auf der Universität* (1862).

In the stories of the middle period a more realistic attitude becomes prevalent, and the tone of weak resignation turns to a more genuinely tragic ending. The action is still centered in the characters and is chiefly of a psychological nature. Problems of marriage form a main theme, as in *Viola Tricolor* (1873). Other well-known representative stories are *Pole Poppenspäler* (1874) and *Psyche* (1875). A second large division of stories during this period are the *Chroniknovellen* or historical works, which include some of his finest narratives, such as *Aquis Submersus* (1875), frequently acknowledged to be his greatest work, *Karsten Kurator* (1877), *Renate* (1878), and *Eekenhof* (1879).

The stories of the last years are distinguished by a change in attitude toward the problem of guilt. Storm turned increasingly away from the concept of personal guilt in order to show the causes of his characters' defeat in their heredity and environment. Among the finest works of this period are *Die Söhne des Senators* (1881), *Hans und Heinz Kirch* (1883), *Zur Chronik von Grieshuus* (1884), *Ein Fest auf Haderslevhuus* (1885) and *Der Schimmelreiter* (1888), one of his best and most popular works. Storm was very highly regarded during his lifetime and remains one of the most widely read authors of the nineteenth century.

Of Storm's works in English translation *Immensee* leads the list with fourteen different versions. Among the best of these are the translations of I. A. Heath (1902), L. S. Brown (1903), P. K. Allen (1904), G. P. Upton (1907), E. W. Bell 1919), and G. Reinhardt (1950). J. Miller translated *Zur Chronik von Grieshuus* as *A Chapter in the History of Grieshuus* (1908) and *Ein Fest auf Haderslevhuus* as *A Festival at Haderslevhuus* (1909). He also translated *Eekenhof* (1908), *Renate* (1909), and *Aquis Submersus* (1910). *Der Schimmelreiter* was translated by Muriel Almon (1913-15) and by M. Münsterberg (1917). In 1956 F. M. Voigt translated *Karsten Kurator* as *Curator Carsten*, and B. Q. Morgan translated *Viola Tricolor* as *The Little Stepmother*. *Die Söhne des Senators* was translated in 1947 by E. M. Huggard under the title *The Senator's Sons*. Selections of Storm's poetry may be found in D. Broicher, *German Lyrics and Ballads Done into English Verse* (1912), the Warner Library, and *The Penguin Book of German Verse* (1957).

ABOUT: Bennett, E. K. The German Novelle; Bernd, C. A. Theodor Storm's Craft of Fiction; Mann, T. Essays of Three Decades; Silz, W. Realism and Reality; Wooley, E. O. Studies in Theodor Storm, *also* Theodor Storm's World in Pictures. [In German—see studies by F. Böttger, P. Schütze, G. Storm, and F. Stuckert. In French —see study by R. Pitrou.]

D. G. D.

*STRACHWITZ, MORITZ (KARL WILHELM ANTON) VON (March 13, 1822-December 11, 1847), German poet, was born in Peterwitz, the son of one of the most aristocratic families in Silesia. He studied law at the universities of Breslau and Berlin, and while in Berlin became a member of the exclusive literary group Der Tunnel über der Spree. For reasons of health, he traveled in 1845 to Scandinavia and in 1847 to Italy. While returning to Germany he suddenly died in Vienna. His premature death at twenty-five was a regrettable loss to German literature.

Strachwitz was an outstanding personality, dedicated to aristocratic ideals of chivalry. His idealism, integrity, and manliness, as well as his hatred of mediocrity and love of beauty, are reflected throughout his writings. To Strachwitz, who was a spiritual descendant of the German romantics, poetry was a priestly art, and he stands among the forerunners of those poets in Germany who demanded a return to art for art's sake *(Ein Wort für die Kunst)*. Although he fervently desired a strong, united Germany *(Der Himmel Ist Blau; Germania)*, he decried those political writers of his time who used poetry to serve social and political aims.

The continued reputation of Strachwitz is based on the two collections of poems, *Lieder eines Erwachenden* (1842) and *Neue Gedichte* (1847). His verse, which reflects the influence of the German poets Platen, Herwegh, and Geibel, reveals him to be a lyric poet of outstanding originality and technical excellence. He was endowed with a gift for supple and concise expression; at the same time he was able to retain a tone of naturalness and folk-like simplicity. German literature is indebted to him for reviving interest in the English-Scottish ballad tradition. The influence of his ballads endured in Germany directly or indirectly for about a century following his death. Theodor Fontane, Detlev von Liliencron, and Börries von Münchhausen are but a few of the leading ballad writers who learned from Strachwitz.

* shträk vĭts

His finest ballads include "Das Herz von Douglas," "Pharao," and "Hie Welf."

Selected translations in English may be found in A. F. Baskerville, *The Poetry of Germany* (1853), and J. Geikie, *Songs and Lyrics by Heine and Other German Poets* (1887).

ABOUT: [In German—see studies by H. Gottschalk, A. K. T. Tielo.]

D. G. D.

*STRINDBERG, (JOHAN) AUGUST (January 22, 1849-May 14, 1912), Swedish dramatist, novelist, short-story writer, poet, was born in Stockholm as the fourth in a rapidly growing number of children. His father, Carl Oscar Strindberg, was a merchant and steamship agent who at the time of August's birth was shaken by economic setbacks. His mother was Eleonora Ulrica Norling, daughter of a poor tailor in Södertälje who had died during her childhood. She had to shift for herself early. She came as a servant and mistress to the house of the elder Strindberg, who later married her. When August Strindberg in the first volume of his autobiographic novel *Tjänstekvinnans Son* (The Son of a Servant, 1886), looked back on his early years he described them in dark colors as a time of insecurity, humiliation, and injustice. He felt that he was unwanted and that the conflicting forces in his own nature were partly caused by the differences in his parents' character and extraction. In his drama *Fadren* (*The Father*, 1887), the captain expresses Strindberg's own conviction when he says: "My parents did not want me, and therefore I was born without a will of my own." This seems to be one of the roots of Strindberg's later antagonistic attitude to his environment. In his plays and novels he frequently returned to the no doubt partly imagined sufferings and wrongs of his childhood. Even as a young lad he showed extreme sensitivity and an inferiority complex. He regarded school as a penitentiary and a martyrdom. His relationship to his father was one of fear and dislike, and he developed an unsatisfied need for maternal affection which later led to serious neurotic disturbances. His mother was consumptive, and during her last days, when August stayed by her bed, he came to respect and love her. She died when the boy was thirteen years old, and soon thereafter his father married a housekeeper Strindberg hated as an intruder.

The Strindberg home was pietistic, but the younger Strindberg could not feel satisfied with a dogmatic religion. His skepticism

* strind' bûrg; strin' bär y'

STRINDBERG

increased. He became a freethinker and eventually an atheist. In 1867 he was admitted to the University of Uppsala, but he found no inspiration in lectures and studies and left after one semester. He served as a substitute teacher in the same elementary school he had attended as a boy and augmented his earnings as a tutor. The solitary youngster became a man of the world and frequented cafés and restaurants. He became a hearty drinker and accumulated considerable debts. He was from this point on continually hunted by creditors.

In the fall of 1868 Strindberg went as a tutor to the home of a Jewish physician who aroused his interest in a medical career. He admired the Jews as a great and highly cultured people. In 1884, however, he wrote a vicious pamphlet entitled *Mitt Judehat* (My Hatred of the Jews). Such changes from one extreme to the other were fundamentally characteristic elements in Strindberg's split nature. When he failed in the premedical examination in chemistry he gave up his medical studies and entered the Dramatic Academy in Stockholm with the intention of becoming an actor. But when he got a part he failed at the rehearsal. After a night of despair and intoxication a peculiar fever struck him. In four days he wrote a family drama in two acts. Out of chaos came creation.

Strindberg was advised to study to become an author and went reluctantly back to the University of Uppsala. His second drama, *Fritänkaren* (The Free-Thinker), was published in 1870 under the pseudonym "Härved Ulf." The same year he had a play, *I Rom* (In Rome), produced for the first time by the Dramatic Theatre in Stockholm.

Strindberg was a member of a romantic society, but his acquaintance with the writings of Georg Brandes, Victor Hugo, and others drove him gradually away from sentimental idealism to a more naturalistic philosophy. Another play, *Den Fredlöse* (The Outlaw, 1871), pleased King Charles XV who decided to defray the expenses of the young author's education. But when the latter's studies were unsuccessful the royal support was withdrawn, and in 1872 Strindberg left the university without a degree. Back in Stockholm he worked as a journalist and wrote, at twenty-three, his great prose drama *Mäster Olof*, a masterpiece dealing with the clash between idealism and reality, in which the author's own personality is represented in three contrasting characters. After several revisions, a much changed edition in verse was completed in 1878.

Unsuccessful journalistic efforts brought starvation, debts, and pessimism upon him. In 1874 he was employed as assistant librarian at the Royal Library. He studied Chinese in order to be able to catalog a collection in this language and published some ideas, both sensible and wild, on Chinese and Swedish language and literature.

In 1877, after a hectic courtship, Strindberg married Baroness Sigrid (Siri) Sofia Mathilda Elisabeth von Essen-Wrangel, daughter of a Swedish-Finnish nobleman. The year before, Siri had divorced Baron Carl Gustaf Wrangel and she was now starting a career as an actress. Strindberg saw his adored wife as a madonna, but soon she deteriorated in his eyes and a stormy marriage full of conflicts of love and hatred developed.

Influenced by Dickens' art of characterization and social satire, Strindberg wrote his critical novel *Röda Rummet* (The Red Room, 1879), which marked the breakthrough of realistic problem literature in Sweden and introduced a new Swedish prose style. During the 1880's Strindberg developed an almost unbelievable productivity. He wrote social criticism, autobiographical novels, collections of historical short stories, historical and fairy plays, poetry, etc. In 1883 the family, now increased by two daughters, moved to France and the next year to Switzerland. This year Strindberg published the first volume of *Giftas* (*Married*), a collection of outspokenly realistic short stories which was

prosecuted for blasphemy. Strindberg went to Stockholm, defended himself without legal aid, and was acquitted. In 1887 he wrote his first naturalistic tragedy, *Fadren* (*The Father*), partly a disguised picture of his own unhappy marriage, showing a monomaniacal misogyny. His marriage had gone to pieces. The family moved in 1887 to Copenhagen where Strindberg wrote new dramas: *Fröken Julie* (*Miss Julie*, 1888), technically the greatest of all naturalistic dramas, and *Fordringsägare* (*Creditors*, 1888). In impressionistic miniature plays, e.g., *Den Starkare* (*The Stronger*) and *Samum* (*Simoom*), he experimented with battles between two minds. In 1891 his marriage ended in divorce.

Some of Strindberg's writing during this period shows symptoms of persecution mania and in places suggests paranoiac tendencies, increased by influence from Nietzsche, with whom he corresponded. He was now a convinced naturalist and atheist. In 1892 he appeared in Berlin where he led a reckless life in wild Bohemian circles. In 1893 he married an aristocratic Austrian girl, Frieda Uhl, daughter of a court councilor, Friedrich Uhl. This marriage soon became a human hell. He and his wife lived in England, Germany, France, and with his wife's relatives in Austria. They separated in 1894 and were divorced in 1897. Strindberg, who now lived in Paris, had gradually entered into a period of deep mental crises during which he made absurd experiments in science, alchemy, and black magic.

Under the influence of Swedenborg's mysticism and of Catholicism he was able to fight his way out of his "Inferno period," which he described in his books *Inferno* (1897) and *Legender* (Legends, 1898). He emerged from the darkness as a freethinking Christian with a tormenting sense of guilt and a Schopenhauerean pessimism according to which the real world exists outside human reality. He regained his creative imagination by means of introspective analysis of his sufferings, and produced a series of magnificent plays, e.g., the three pilgrimage dramas *Till Damaskus* (*To Damascus*, 1898-1904), the moving hymn to suffering and goodness *Påsk* (*Easter*, 1901), and the frightening marriage drama *Dödsdansen* (*The Dance of Death*, 1901). He also created a long series of historical dramas about Swedish rulers, e.g., *Gustav Vasa* and *Erik XIV* (1899), *Gustav III* and *Kristina* (1903).

From 1899 until his death Strindberg lived in Stockholm. In 1901 he married a young actress, Anne Marie Lehman, from Oslo. She appeared successfully in many of Strindberg's plays. Inspired by his new love Strindberg wrote his brilliant expressionistic drama *Ett Drömspel* (*A Dream Play*, 1902), in which he expresses pity for mankind. His third marriage, in which a daughter was born, ended in divorce in 1904.

Strindberg wrote a great number of prose works of unsparing social criticism, e.g., *Svarta Fanor* (Black Banners, 1907), the angriest book in Swedish literature; historical and autobiographical stories; aphorisms and poetry. He also wrote four so-called "chamber plays," such as *Spöksonaten* (*The Spook Sonata*, 1907), which became models for later expressionistic symbol dramas. In *Stora Landsvägen* (*The Highway*, 1909), Strindberg took a resigned and melancholy farewell to drama. After a journalistic battle known as the "Strindberg feud," he died of cancer, with the Bible on his heart.

Most of the major works of Strindberg's literary production have been translated into English. For complete information see *The Sweden Year Book*, latest edition. The first play translated was *Svanevit* by F. J. Ziegler as *Swanwhite* (1909). Other early translations were *Fordringsägare* by F. J. Ziegler as *The Creditor* (1910), later under the same title by M. Harned in *Poet Lore*, XXII (1911). The same volume contains *Fröken Julie*, translated as *Julie* by A. Swan. *Lycko-Pers Resa* was translated by V. S. Howard as *Lucky Pehr* (1912). In the series *Plays of August Strindberg* in four volumes (1912-16) there are nineteen plays translated by E. Björkman. In another series with the same title, also in four volumes, begun in 1912, there are twelve plays, partly the same as in the first series, translated by E. and W. Oland. The Anglo-Swedish Literary Foundation published four volumes of plays of various translators (1929-39). *Mäster Olof* appeared in 1915 as *Master Olof,* translated by E. Björkman, the trilogy *Till Damaskus* as *To Damascus* in *Poet Lore*, XLII (1933), translated by S. E. Davidson, and *Stora Landsvägen* as *The Great Highway* (1954) by A. Paulson. The best translations are in *Six Plays of Strindberg* (1955) by E. Sprigge. W. Johnson has published fine translations of historical plays, *Queen Christina, Charles XII, Gustav III* (1955), *The Last of the Knights, The Regent, Earl Birger of Bjälbo* (1956), *Gustav Adolf* (1957), with more to come. Strindberg's autobiographical works are available in the following translations: *The Inferno* (1912), *The Son of a Servant* (1913), *The Growth of a Soul* (1914) by C. Field, *The Confession of a Fool* (1925) by E. Schleussner. The novel *I Havsbandet* appeared in 1913 as *By the Open Sea*, translated by E. Schleussner, and as *On the Seaboard* by E. Clarke Westergren. *Röda Rummet*, translated by E. Schleussner, has the title *The Red Room* (1913). Nineteen short stories from *Giftas* are included in *Married* (1917). Extracts from *En Blå Book* were translated by C. Field under the title *Zones of the Spirit, a Book of Thoughts.*

ABOUT: Bentley, E. The Playwright as Thinker; Bulman, J. Strindberg and Shakespeare; Campbell, G. A. Strindberg; Dahlström, C. E. W. L. Strindberg's Dramatic Expressionism; Johnson, W. Strindberg and the Historical Drama; McGill, V. J. August Strindberg, the Bedevilled Viking; Mortensen, B. M. E. and Downs, B. W. Strindberg; Palmblad, H. V. E. Strindberg's Conception of History; Sprigge, E. The Strange Life of August Strindberg; Uppvall, A. J. August Strindberg, a Psychoanalytic Study; Twentieth Century Literature, IX (1963); World Theatre, XI (1962). [The European literature on Strindberg is enormous. For details see Kärnell, K.-Å. and Lindahl, F.-E. August Strindberg 1849-1949.]

A. J.

*STRITAR, JOSIP (March 6, 1836-November 25, 1923), Slovene critic, poet, novelist, and dramatist, was born in the village of Podsmreka in Slovenia (today part of Yugoslavia), the son of a peasant. He entered the Latin school in Ljubljana in 1846 and later the *Gymnasium.* He specialized in languages, ancient and modern, and was an outstanding student. In his second year of *Gymnasium* he transferred to Alojzejevičče, where he met Fran Levstik, later a leading Slovene writer. Levstik taught him to value the Slovene traditions and way of life. In his fourth year Stritar began to contribute to a school manuscript paper, and two years later (1855) he first appeared in a printed journal: this first offering consisted of four sonnets. He went to Vienna the same year to attend the university, studying classical philology. After graduation he remained in Vienna, working for many years as a tutor to support himself while he wrote literature and literary criticism. In 1873 he married. In 1875 he became a professor at a Piarist *Gymnasium* in Vienna. In 1901 he retired from teaching, and spent the rest of his life in Vienna and elsewhere in Austria.

As a young man Stritar developed a romantic philosophy of world sorrow, which dominated his ideas on aesthetics. In his view the discrepancy between the ideal and the real creates human suffering: it is the poet's duty to give voice to this suffering, not so much to suffering in himself as in others. Such writers as Goethe (in *Werther*) and Byron gave him literary models for his ideas, while Schopenhauer was his main philosophic source. Following Herder and the Slavic romantic messianists he believed that the Slavic peoples were destined to lead mankind to true love and brotherhood.

* strē' tär

Stritar's creative writing has little value today, but in its time it was important for new trends and forms which it introduced to Slovene literature. His works are often free adaptations of foreign writers: thus his novel *Zorin* (1870) derives in part from Goethe's *Werther*, while *Gospod Mirodolski* (1876) is modeled on Goldsmith's *Vicar of Wakefield*. His most independent novel, *Sodnik* (The Judge, 1878), illustrates Rousseau's notion of the corrupting influence of civilization. In the 1890's Stritar realized that his work was antiquated by the new realist and symbolist tendencies, and his later writing consists largely of literature for children and his own reminiscences.

More important is Stritar's work as a critic and stylist. In 1870 in Vienna he founded the review *Zvon* (The Bell). Unpleasant critical polemics led him to give up the journal at the end of the same year, but in 1876, when his personal circumstances were improved, he revived it until 1880. *Zvon* was the first purely literary journal the Slovenes possessed, and their leading writers were contributors. Stritar insisted on the necessity for maintaining high formal and stylistic standards, if Slovene literature was to take its place in European literature as a whole. He especially emphasized purity of poetic form. He developed an elegant, polished prose style, influenced in part by the French *feuilleton*, a form which he introduced to Slovene writing. His style not only served as a model for writers, but helped to shape the written and spoken language of the Slovene intelligentsia. Stritar also did much to win recognition for the Slovene romantic poet France Prešeren (see sketch above), little appreciated until his revival in the 1860's.

ABOUT: Slavonic Review, VI (1927-1928).

W. E. H.

*STUCKENBERG, VIGGO HENRIK FOG (September 17, 1863-December 6, 1905), Danish poet and novelist, was born at Vridsløselille, a few miles west of Copenhagen. His father, Frederik Henrich Stuckenberg, son of a German immigrant, was a teacher at a state prison. His mother was Johanne Georgine Fog. When the boy was ten years old, his father was transferred to a new position in the capital where the future poet grew up. He took his matriculation examination in 1884, and thereafter he studied ethnography and languages for a few years at the University of Copenhagen. But he

* sdōōk′ ĕn bår

left without a degree to make a living as a teacher at a private school in the capital.

Stuckenberg's first contribution to literature was a promising collection of *Digte* (Poems, 1886), which contained fine nature lyrics as well as expressions of youthful radicalism. The following year he married Ingeborg Pamperin. His name was made with two self-analytical novels, *I Gennembrud* (Breaking Through, 1888), and *Messias* (1889), objectively realistic and bitterly melancholy descriptions of life in radical student and Bohemian circles and influenced by J. P. Jacobsen.

After a painful period of separation, Stuckenberg and his wife resumed their married life in Lyngby, just outside Copenhagen, and during the following years Stuckenberg published books in rapid succession. First came the dramatic poems *Den Vilde Jæger* (The Wild Hunter, 1894), and *Romerske Scener* (Roman Scenes, 1895), indicating a break with the literary principles of realism. In *Fagre Ord* (Fine Words, 1895), and a couple of stories published under the title *Valravn* (1896), Stuckenberg used a rhythmical prose and a suggestive, often too metaphorical and embellished, language in painting scenes from everyday life. In these stories, still influenced by Jacobsen, psychoanalysis and lyrical expression merged and resulted in a well-polished artistic style. In a following story, *I Sol* (Sunshine, 1897), he described the psychological conflicts of a light-hearted merchant and a homeless romantic. His best novel is *Hjemfalden, en Fanges Dagbog* (Reverted, a Diary of a Prisoner, 1897). Another attempt to reproduce the spiritual life of a romantic criminal was *Asmadæus* (1899). Both these books show the influence of Poe and Dostoevsky. The collection of fairy tales *Vejbred* (By the Roadside, 1899) comes very close to lyrics. Under the pseudonym "Civis," Stuckenberg wrote a great number of critical essays and articles on literature and the theatre, published in *Illustreret Tidende.* They contain his best prose.

Today Stuckenberg is known primarily for his lyrical poetry, which he wrote all the time during his activity as a prose writer and critic. His lyrics, which are sober and melodious, are free from the disfiguring embellishments of his narrative prose. They reached their most mature form in the two collections *Flyvende Sommer* (Gossamer, 1896) and especially *Sne* (Snow, 1901). They show many facets of human reactions, e.g., delicate paintings of natural scenery, melancholy love poetry, reflective verses, etc. In almost all his works there is an evident dualism between demanding desires and the realization of the impossibility of fulfilling them.

Stuckenberg's first marriage ended in divorce, and in 1904 he married a divorcée, Clara Holbøll.

Three of Stuckenberg's poems in English rendition are included in *A Book of Danish Verse* (1922), and three others appear in G. Lovett, *English Versions of Poems by Some Scandinavian Poets* (1935, supplement 1936). The fairy tale collection *Vejbred* was translated by Una Hook as *By the Wayside* (1917).
ABOUT: Mitchell, P. M. A History of Danish Literature. [In Danish—see studies by J. Andersen, C. C. Lassen.]

A. J.

STURLUSON, SNORRI. See SNORRI STURLUSON

*SUE, (MARIE JOSEPH) EUGÈNE (January 20, 1804-August 3, 1857), French novelist, was born in Paris, the son of a surgeon who distinguished himself under Napoleon. (Christened Marie Joseph at birth, the novelist later adopted the name by which he is known in honor of his patron, Prince Eugène Beauharnais.) As a youth Sue pursued medical studies and for a time practiced his father's profession, serving as a surgeon in the navy in the Spanish campaign of 1823 and at the battle of Navarino in 1828. In 1829, with the death of his father, Sue was left a young gentleman of considerable means, and was thus enabled to settle in Paris and devote himself to literature. His naval experiences supplied the background for his first novels. Such stories as *Plik et Plok* (1831), *La Salamandre* (1832), and *La Vigie de Koat-Vin* (1833), dealing with sailors' lives and pirates' exploits, caused him to be hailed as the French James Fenimore Cooper, and won him the praise of Sainte-Beuve, then too beginning his literary career. Sue's life at sea gave rise also to an extensive history of the French Navy.

Following this phase of his career, Sue established himself as a fashionable novelist of the *haut-monde*, with such books as *Latréaumont* (1837) and *Mathilde* (1841). Several circumstances, however, conspired to alienate him from this society—the loss of his fortune, betrayal by a mistress, among other things—and he removed himself to Sologne where he launched his production of

* sü

social novels, the genre in which he gained his greatest success. *Les Mystères de Paris* (*The Mysteries of Paris*), first run as a *roman-feuilleton* in the *Journal des Débats* in 1842, with its vivid pictures of the underworld and the slums of the metropolis, had an immense shock appeal. Its sensationalism and melodrama were widely imitated and soon cities all over the world had their "mysteries." (The most notorious imitator was that English dispenser of cheap titillation G. W. M. Reynolds with his *Mysteries of London.*)

Two years later there appeared in the pages of the *Constitutionnel* another *roman* entitled *Le Juif Errant* (*The Wandering Jew*), destined for even greater popularity. Here Sue wove an extended melodramatic, didactic fable out of the medieval legend of the Jew doomed to wander through the world for all time for cursing Christ on his way to the Cross. This pathetic character, a favorite subject of a number of writers before Sue—notably Goethe—is made here to bear the burden of Sue's vituperative anti-clericalism, and eventually becomes a kind of Marxist symbol of the proletariat seeking liberation. *The Wandering Jew*, like *The Mysteries of Paris*, was dramatized, and was also converted into an opera by Jacques Halévy. In our time it has also been adapted cinematically.

Sue continued to be a prolific and popular novelist till his death, with such works as *La Bonne Aventure* (1851), *Jeanne et Louise* (1853), *Gilbert and Gilberte* (1853), *La Famille Jouffroy* (1854), and *Le Diable Médecin* (1855-57). Two of his most ambitious works were *Les Sept Péchés Capitaux* (1847-49), a series of tales illustrating each of the cardinal sins, and *Les Mystères du Peuple* (1849-56), attempting to trace the fortunes of a family over a period of twenty centuries.

In 1850 Sue was elected to the French Assembly as representative of the Seine district. However, his political career was short-lived, for he was exiled at the end of the following year as a result of his protest against the *coup d'état* of Louis Napoleon. He died at Annecy at the age of fifty-three. Among his last published works was a volume of contemporary history entitled *La France sous L'Empire.*

Despite his avowed serious intentions, critics tend to think of Sue as a "literary merchant," in the phrase of Thackeray. More the literary improvisator than the literary artist, Eugène Sue, with his gaudy descriptive power and his declamatory style, is the prototype of the "popular" writer, holding something of the position in French literature that Bulwer-Lytton maintains in English. It is evident that he continues to find readers throughout the world, particularly with *The Wandering Jew*, which in recent years has appeared in Hungarian, Greek, Portuguese, and Hebrew, as well as in more widely spoken languages.

The Mysteries of Paris was translated by Charles H. Town (1843), Henry C. Deming (1844; with the subtitle *A Romance of the Rich and Poor*), H. D. Miles (1846), and H. Llewellyn Williams (1869; the second part subtitled *The Miseries of Paris*), and has also appeared in numerous anonymous (and probably pirated) translations. H. Llewellyn Williams' translation of *The Wandering Jew* (1868) was preceded and followed by a string of anonymous translations, including that in the Modern Library (1940). Also on record is a translation of *The Salamander* by William Henry Herbert (1844) and *Mysteries of the People* by Mary L. Booth (1867).

ABOUT: Biancolli, L. (ed.) Book of Great Conversations; Warner Library, XXIII; French Review December, 1953. [In French—see studies by N. Atkinson, J.-L. Bory, P. Chanu, P. Ginisty].

R. A. C.

SULLY

SULLY-PRUDHOMME, RENÉ FRANÇOIS ARMAND (March 16, 1839-September 7, 1907), French poet, born in Paris of a lower middle class family, lost his father when only two and was raised by a sad but loving mother from Lyon. His experience at boarding school, as also his bad health, emphasized his native sadness, lack of conviction, and silent suffering, of which many traces appear in his *Solitudes*. An eye infection obliged him to abandon thought of scientific training. In 1859 he was employed in the foundries at Le Creusot as a clerk, and there are many traces of his impressions of this sojourn in his *Épreuves* and in his later writings on the meaning of human imagination and labor. In 1860 he became a law clerk in Paris, and began frequenting groups of young poets and writing verse and essays. His contact with Leconte de Lisle, presumably in 1864, was significant, but he remained aloof from the Parnassian movement on account of his personal enthusiasms and his humanitarian dreams. His first collection of poetry, *Stances et Poèmes* (1865), shows signs of his personal thought; this volume contains his best known poem, "Vase Brisé." *Les Épreuves* (1866) and *Les Solitudes* (1869) followed rapidly. Sully's work to this point is primarily lyrical and personal,

* sü lē′ prü dôm′

with sincere expression of inner bitterness and frustration, though without basic pessimism, and in clear, strong, and original forms.

Within a single month, at the beginning of 1870, Sully lost his mother, aunt, and uncle, and found himself alone. Later that year, the Franco-Prussian war—in which he served in the army—brought him further anguish. This state of depression, inherent in his previous work, became stronger in *Vaines Tendresses*, collected in 1875, his last lyrical expression (his *Prisme*, published in 1886, contains only early and isolated pieces). The remainder of Sully's poetry is philosophical, centering about humanitarian concepts, and projecting rational escape from anguish through encyclopedic knowledge. Among the influences for this period are Lucretius, whom he had partly translated, and Descartes and Condillac. Sully's *Destins*, published in 1872 but conceived before the war, represent his reactions to a frightful holocaust in a church at Santiago, set in a humanitarian vision of a struggle between the spirits of good and evil. His poem *Zénith* was inspired by the disaster of the stratospheric expedition of 1875. His major applications of such themes appear in *Justice* (1878), a poetic analysis of this abstract subject ("Justice is love guided by light"), a quest and an adventure divided systematically into parts to form a huge cycle, and dominated at many points by the notion of the all-importance of science. His *Bonheur* (1888), in 4,000 verses, deals, through the principal character Faustus, with an apotheosis of the dream of and search for love and knowledge, an abstract exercise in elegant style, alternately lyrical and didactic. Both of Sully's major cycles were received with esteem, and in 1901 he became the first recipient of the Nobel Prize in literature.

ABOUT: Dargan, E. Studies in Honor of A. M. Elliott; Gentleman's Magazine, 1879. [In French—see studies by E. Estève, P. Flottes, C. Hémon, H. Morice, E. Zyromski.]

F. J. C.

SUMAROKOV, ALEKSANDR PETROVICH (June 4, 1718-September 1, 1777), Russian playwright and poet, was born in Finland of an old Muscovite boyar family. He began writing verses while attending the Military Cadet Academy in St. Petersburg and became the most popular poet of the day not many years after his graduation in 1740. Sumarokov's influence by the end of the fifties reached the proportions of a major literary school. An immensely self-assured man, Sumarokov held that he was the great Russian genius of his age, and, setting himself the task of "creating" Russian literature, he proceeded to turn out, with incredible facility, copious examples of almost every kind of literature then current. To his credit are nine tragedies and twelve comedies, the first of these—*Khorev* (1747) and *Tresotinius* (1750)—being respectively the first "regular" tragedy and comedy to appear in Russia. As a poet, he composed, among others, satires, sonnets, odes, eclogues, elegies, idylls; with his fables—"among the triumphs of Russian poetry in the eighteenth century"—he introduced the genre into Russian literature; and in his hundreds of songs and lyric verses he displayed a rhythmic inventiveness which all but exhausted the possibilities of Russian versification for the next century and a half. He also engaged with particular vigor in journalism, then just beginning in Russia.

Sumarokov was the first independent man of letters in the history of Russian literature. Both in his creative practice and as literary-linguistic theorist and critic he was a classicist. Opposed to Lomonosov's hyperbolic-metaphoric style—on which he composed a number of superb parodies—he championed a brand of Russian classicism much closer to the French prototype, earning the nicknames "the Russian Racine—Boileau—Voltaire—La Fontaine," etc. Sumarokov was not, however, merely derivative, as his detractors insisted; while depending greatly on foreign models and not above simply translating and adapting them, he frequently departed from conventions, implemented native Russian elements extensively and was quite capable of a genuine originality. Sumarokov's was a pervasively classicist consciousness, and it was the inculcation upon the minds of his fellow noblemen of his kind of consciousness together with his own political corollary to it that he conceived to be the function of his writings. Relentless in voicing his intolerance of the "ignoble" in Russian society, too conceited, authoritarian, and temperamental to take realistic cognizance of his audience, he met with mounting antagonism and ridicule from all quarters. Having been appointed the director of the first permanent Russian public theatre when it was founded in 1756, he was relieved of that post after a quarrel with the authorities in 1761. During the early years of Catherine II's reign his success increased despite the hostility he had aroused, but Catherine's favor proved short-lived. By 1770 Sumarokov was in virtual disgrace. Beset with family troubles and mercilessly harassed by his enemies, he lived out the rest of his life in poverty and drunken misery.

With the reaction against the classicism he exemplified, Sumarokov's reputation suffered severe downgrading. He was consigned to the annals of Russian literature as a figure of little but historical significance. However, recent scholarship has been more responsive to Sumarokov's creative work and has restored that appreciation which is due him also as an artist in his own right, above all as a lyric poet.

Translations of Sumarokov are rare. Some excerpts in English are to be found in L. Wiener's *Anthology of Russian Literature,* Part I (1902). His tragedy *Demetrius, the Impostor* was translated into English and published in London in 1806.

ABOUT: [In Russian—see studies by N. N. Bulich, P. N. Berkov.]

I. R. T.

*SUTTNER, BERTHA FELICIE SOPHIE (KINSKY), VON (July 9, 1843-June 21, 1914), Austrian novelist, was born in Prague, the daughter of the Austrian Field Marshal Count Franz Kinsky, who died shortly after her birth. On her mother's side she was a descendant of the family of the German poet Theodor Körner. The young countess received a good education and

* sōō mŭ rô′ kôf

* zōōt′ nĕr

traveled extensively. Following the loss of the family fortune through her mother's mismanagement, she worked as a governess for the Suttner family in Vienna. Here she met and fell in love with Baron Arthur Gundacar von Suttner, who was seven years her junior. Because of parental objection the couple married secretly in 1877 and fled to the Caucasus, where the Baron worked as an engineer and his wife as a teacher. Bertha also began to write novels and short stories. These early works possess little literary value, although *Inventarium einer Seele* (1883) has biographical interest.

In 1885 the couple moved to the Suttner estate in Lower Austria, and the works produced here, such as *Schriftstellerroman* (1886), *Daniela Dormes* (1886), and *Das Maschinenalter* (1889), reflect an awakened interest in some of the major problems of the day, particularly in the women's movement and the peace problem. Her passionate hatred of war inspired the writing of her greatest work, *Die Waffen Nieder* (1889), one of the outstanding documents of pacifist literature. This novel was greeted with universal acclaim and for a time was one of the most widely read books in Europe. It inspired Alfred Nobel to establish, out of his fortune acquired by the manufacture of dynamite, the Nobel Peace Prize.

In the works of the next years, *Hanna* and *Vor dem Gewitter* (1894), she continued to analyze the problems of the modern age but never again succeeded in rising to the heights of her one major work. Her later writings alternated between harmless belletristic novels and direct political protests.

Bertha von Suttner founded the International Peace League and from 1894 to 1900 directed the publication of this organization's journal, *Die Waffen Neider*. After the death of her husband in 1902 she dedicated herself completely to the furtherance of her pacifist ideals and in 1905 received the first Nobel Peace Prize. Her last major work, *Memoiren*, appeared in 1909. She died in 1914 shortly before the outbreak of the First World War. In 1917 A. H. Fried published her collected political essays under the title *Der Kampf um die Vermeidung des Weltkrieges*. Bertha von Suttner's writings have little artistic value, and her significance lies solely in her contributions to the cause of peace.

The best English translation of *Die Waffen Nieder* was made by T. Holmes in 1892 under the title *Lay Down Your Arms*. Less successful translations were made by A. A. Abbott as *Ground Arms* (1892) and by A. Proudfoot as *Disarm! Disarm!*

(1906). Her memoirs appeared in an anonymous translation in 1910. *Der Menschheit Hochgedanken* was translated by N. H. Dole in 1914 as *When Thoughts Will Soar*.

ABOUT: Pauli, H. E. Cry of the Heart; Key, E. Florence Nightingale and Bertha von Suttner; Playne, C. E. Bertha von Suttner and the Struggle to Avoid the World War. [In German—see study by A. Fried.]

D. G. D.

*SWEDENBORG, EMANUEL (January 29, 1688-March 29, 1772), Swedish scientist, mathematician, philosopher, and mystic, was born in the Swedish capital of Stockholm, where his father, Jesper Swedberg, of an old mine-working family, was court chaplain. In 1682, his father was appointed professor at Uppsala, where Emanuel grew up, and later became bishop at Skara. His mother, Sara Behm, died when Emanuel was eight. From 1699 to 1709 he studied at the University of Uppsala. His education was at first humanistic in the spirit of the ultrapatriotic genius Olof Rudbeck, but he decided to turn to natural science, which he studied in England, Holland, and France. Upon his return to Sweden in 1714 he was employed in the Mines Authority as assistant to Christoffer Polhem, the ingenious scientist and inventor who deeply influenced him. In 1719 Bishop Swedberg's family was ennobled under the name of Swedenborg.

During the following years, partly spent abroad, Swedenborg displayed a remarkable productivity in the field of theoretical and applied sciences. Between 1721 and 1734 he published three cosmological treatises, the first one being *Prodromus Principiorum Rerum Naturalium* and the last one the enormous work *Opera Philosophica et Mineralia*. His conception of the universe, based on Descartes' and Polhem's theories, was mechanistic and materialistic, although he believed that God was the ultimate originator of the universe.

During these years Swedenborg showed an extraordinary versatility. He published treatises and papers in mathematics, geology, astronomy, mechanics, chemistry, anatomy, economics, etc. He was, however, not satisfied with his materialistic cosmology, and continued speculations led him to create a Neoplatonic-mystical system of "correspondences" according to which everything on earth has its "correspondence" in the spiritual world. Thus, matter is a shadow or symbol emanating from the spirit, and every spiritual phenomenon is an image of a divine

* svä' dĕn bŏr' y'

899

SWEDENBORG

prototype. In 1743 and the following years he went through a period of religious crises with dreams, visions, hallucinations, and various occult experiences. In 1745 he received a message from God in person to interpret the secrets of the Scriptures, and the materialistic scientist became a visionary apostle.

Swedenborg's new religion comprised a cabalistic-theosophical system in which God has no son but once himself assumed the form of a man to conquer the power of Hell. But Sin once more gained ascendancy, and now God returned in the form of the divine *Word*, and Swedenborg was chosen to be the new Messiah commissioned to interpret the Word to humanity. In 1747 he refused an offer of promotion. Instead he requested and was granted leave to retire with a pension from his position at the Mines Authority in order to devote his energy to preaching the Word. During his remaining years he lived a secluded life in Stockholm, interrupted by occasional trips to London and Amsterdam to see that his books were printed, since their heretical nature prevented their publication in Sweden.

Swedenborg received confirmation of his divine task in trances, hallucinations, and occult communication with spirits. It is, however, important to realize that Swedenborg's theosophical doctrines, as M. Lamm has pointed out, were not products so much of his spiritualistic experiences and hallucinations as a natural development of his earlier nature philosophy. His idea that Man is a center of numerous spirits that create human

feelings and thoughts was, thus, systematically based on the psychology he presented in his *Œconomia Regni Animalis* (1740-41), in which he attempted to solve the problem of the nature of the soul and its relationship to the body.

Swedenborg advanced his religious conviction in many works, e.g., *Arcana Cœlestia*, published in London in eight volumes (1749-56), which is an exegesis of the first two books of Moses but in reality is a reinterpretation of the entire Bible in accordance with the "correspondence doctrine," and *Vera Christiana Religio* (1771), the most comprehensive and the last exposition of his philosophy. His finest literary works are the two prose poems *De Cultu et Amore Dei* (1745), and *Deliciæ Sapientiæ de Amore Conjugali* (1768). In the former he gives a beautiful representation of Creation and the idyllic and innocent life of Adam and Eve, and in the latter he describes the sex distinction and explains the male as an image of divine wisdom and the female of divine love.

Swedenborg's religious system rests on the fundamental idea of man as an image of the Creator and the crown of Creation. There are in his religious writings several descriptions of the joys of Heaven and the horrors of Hell, which are remarkable because of their rational nature and the many concrete details taken from earthly life. His views of Heaven are poetic dreams of a happy life in which work is a delight and marriage the highest bliss. His visions of Hell are horrifying, sometimes extremely drastic, grotesque, and repulsive. Most of his exposés are prosy, lengthy, and discursive, but sometimes there are passages of poetic beauty that remind the reader of the great masters Dante and Milton, and it seems plausible that *The Divine Comedy* and *Paradise Lost* to some extent influenced Swedenborg. His own writings profoundly influenced William Blake.

Shortly before Christmas 1771 Swedenborg, during a stay in London, had a severe paralytic stroke. After a long coma he seemed to recover, but soon thereafter he died. He was buried in London, but in 1908 his remains were brought to Sweden and interred in the Cathedral of Uppsala.

Swedenborg did not create any religious community, but he hoped for realization of his doctrines in a new denomination, which he called the "New Church" or the "New Jerusalem," the foundation of which he fixed in 1757 when God returned to earth. After his death religious communities adhering to

Swedenborg's principles were formed in various places, the first one in London in 1787. Later, Swedenborgian sects were founded in many European countries. In the United States the first denomination arose in 1792, and in 1817 the "General Convention of the New Jerusalem" under a bishop was established. In 1897 some dissenters who believed in the divine inspiration of Swedenborg's religious production separated and founded the "General Church of the New Jerusalem." The so-called Swedenborgians amounted to several thousands.

Practically all of Swedenborg's major books have been translated into English. For a full account of works in the original and in translation into various languages, see J. Hyde, *Bibliographical Index to the Published Writings of Emanuel Swedenborg* (1897), J. Hyde, *Bibliography of the Works of Emanuel Swedenborg, Original and Translated* (1906), A. Strok and G. Ekelöf, *Kronologisk Förteckning över Emanuel Swedenborgs Skrifter* (1910).

ABOUT: The biographical and critical literature on Swedenborg and the New Church is extremely voluminous and is still growing. Only a fraction of the most important contributions is listed: Hite, L. F. Swedenborg's Historical Position; Markham, E. Swedenborg; Parsons, T. Outlines of the Religion and Philosophy of Swedenborg; Sigstedt, C. S. The Swedenborg Epic; Spalding, J. H. Introduction to Swedenborg's Religious Thought; Spalding, J. H. The Kingdom of Heaven as Seen by Swedenborg; Strok, A. H. The Sources of Swedenborg's Early Philosophy of Nature; Swanton, J. R. Emanuel Swedenborg, Prophet of the Higher Education; Tafel, R. L. Documents concerning the Life and Character of Emanuel Swedenborg (3 vols.); Trobridge, G. Life of Emanuel Swedenborg; Very, F. W. An Epitome of Swedenborg's Science (2 vols.); Warren, S. M. Compendium of the Theological Writing of Swedenborg; White, W. Life of Emanuel Swedenborg; Wilkinson, J. J. G. Emanuel Swedenborg; Wilkinson, J. J. G. A Popular Study of Swedenborg's Philosophical Works; Worchester, B. The Life and Mission of Emanuel Swedenborg.

A. J.

*TAINE, HIPPOLYTE ADOLPHE

(April 21, 1828-March 5, 1893), French critic and historian, was born at Vouziers in the Ardennes, son of Jean Baptiste Taine, an attorney. Jean Baptiste died when Hippolyte was but a boy of twelve, leaving a small income to his widow for the support of the three children. Despite the modest means of his family, young Hippolyte received an excellent education. As early as the age of fourteen he had a reputation as a "grind" at the Collège Bourbon in Paris, where he subjected himself to a severe regimen allowing

* těn

TAINE

him but two brief respites from study—twenty minutes of relaxation in the afternoon, an hour after dinner to listen to music. Not surprisingly, he won all the "firsts" at the school. By 1848, not yet twenty-one, Taine was the holder of two baccalaureate degrees—one in science, one in letters.

Taine next entered the École Normale Supérieure with the intention of preparing himself for a career in public education. Here too he overwhelmed his masters by his learning and intellectual energy. Besides mastering his own language, he acquired facility in Latin, English, and German. His curiosity reached out to grasp philosophy, theology, and music in addition to literature. In these formative years he developed the passion for analysis and classification that manifests itself in his precise, methodical, and dogmatical critical style. Interestingly enough, his intellectual meticulousness alienated some of his teachers who admired his mind, but thought his style of exposition dull. As a result, Taine missed out on a fellowship in philosophy for which he applied at this time.

However, in 1851 the young scholar was favored by the Minister of Public Education with a provisional chair of philosophy at the Collège of Toulon. This he refused for a position at Nevers in order to be nearer to his mother. Here life was made unpleasant for him because of the political atmosphere in France. As the only professor at Nevers to refuse to sign an endorsement of Louis Napoleon, who had just seized power, Taine

901

was marked as a subversive by the government. Though highly popular with students, he was shunted about from place to place. Eventually he became wearied with this treatment and applied for and was granted a leave of absence, which he continually renewed for ten years until his appointment ran out. Hence Taine was left with leisure for study and writing.

Within a year after leaving Nevers, Taine had completed the requirements for the *doctorat* at the Sorbonne with two dissertations, receiving the degree in May 1853. He next set about to write an essay on Livy to compete for a prize offered by the Académie, which he finally received, after some shilly-shallying by the judges, in 1855. This essay was published the next year as a book. Meanwhile Taine had suffered a breakdown in health owing to this intensive regimen, and was ordered by his physician to rest. He took advantage of this enforced leisure to read extensively on the French Revolution— a course of study that eventually led to his monumental *Les Origines de la France Contemporaine.* During a trip to Spain, where he was sent to recover his health, he accepted a commission from the publisher Hachette to write a guidebook, which turned out to be a kind of satire on health resorts.

Upon his return to France, Taine entered literary society, becoming friendly particularly with the critics Renan and Sainte-Beuve and the emerging new novelists of realism Flaubert and the Goncourts. He regularly contributed articles to the *Revue des Deux Mondes* and the *Revue de l'Instruction Publique.* A series in the latter journal on great philosophers appeared in book form in 1857 as *Les Philosophes Classiques du XIXe Siècle en France.* This book, which went into several editions, brought Taine his first fame. It concluded with a scheme for the scientific study of human nature, influenced by the positivist philosopher Auguste Comte, then in vogue. "Vice and virtue are products like vitriol and sugar," Taine declared, thus announcing that deterministic view of man that was to pervade his most famous work, *Histoire de la Littérature Anglais,* then in its planning stage.

Although his literary fortunes were now in the ascendant, Taine was still not free of official harassment, this time from religious sources. In 1862 he lost out in his candidacy for the chair of literature at the École Polytechnique, but the next year, through the good offices of Marshal Randon, Minister of War, received appointment as examiner in

history and German at the military academy of St. Cyr. In 1863 he was attacked for alleged atheism, along with Renan and Sainte-Beuve, by Monseigneur Dupanloup, Bishop of Orléans, in *Avertissement à la Jeunesse et aux Pères de Famille.* As a result Renan was suspended from his teaching post at the Collège de France, but Taine was saved from a like fate by the timely intervention of the Princess Mathilde.

In December of 1863 there appeared the monumental *Histoire de la Littérature Anglais,* beginning with the Anglo-Saxon period and ending with Byron. Not so much a history *of* literature as a social history *through* literature, Taine's *Histoire* attempts to chart the development of English society and *mœurs* as reflected in works of the imagination. His famous triad of *race, moment,* and *milieu* expresses what were to him the primary determinants of human character— blood, historical conditioning, and environment. Each man moreover is governed by a *faculté maîtresse* (predominant faculty). Thus to Taine, cavalier poetry is a sign of the decadence of the Restoration period, Addison is representative of the rising genteel middle class, Milton crystallizes the Puritan ethic. In 1870 Taine brought out an additional volume on Victorian writers through Tennyson, famous for its essay on Dickens' characters as the embodiment of the new bourgeois morality.

Taine sent the work to the Académie to compete for the Prix Bordin, but failed to attain it, despite the support of his great admirer the historian Guizot (to whom the book was dedicated). Again the velvet glove of Monseigneur Dupanloup made itself felt. Opposition continued to keep Taine out of the Académie Française until November 1878, when he was finally admitted upon his third application.

In 1864 Taine entered a new academic career as successor to Viollet-le-Duc in the chair of aesthetics at the École des Beaux Arts. During the ensuing decade he applied to the graphic arts his methods of socio-historical analysis in a series of studies that were finally brought together in *Philosophie de l'Art* (1880).

During this period he produced two volumes of contemporary social history in a somewhat lighter vein. A series of observations on Paris and French society contributed to *La Vie Parisienne* (1863-65) became the semi-autobiographical *Vie et Opinions de Thomas Frédéric Graindorge* (1867). A trip to England in 1871 (his second) resulted in *Notes sur l'Angleterre* (1872), which has remained his freshest book. In 1868 occurred Taine's marriage to Mlle Danuelle, daughter of an eminent architect.

From this point on, Taine's interests took a distinct turn towards politics. Deeply shaken by the Franco-Prussian War of 1870, he set out on the most ambitious study of his career, a work he had long contemplated on the Revolution of 1789 and its consequences for modern France. This voluminous history, *Les Origines de la France Contemporaine*, occupied him for the rest of his life. In 1884 he retired from his professorship to devote his full time and energies to the project. As the work now stands, one volume is given over to the Ancient Regime, three to the Revolution, and two to the Modern Regime. Taine planned to finish the history with a study of modern French society and the development of science in the nineteenth century, but did not live to complete the scheme. He died in Paris, still in the midst of immense intellectual labors, on the brink of his seventy-fifth birthday.

Hippolyte Taine's voracious mental appetite and his great versatility, as well as his penchant for dramatizing ideas, made him one of the great intellectuals of his day. "He has renewed the methods of criticism . . . no one more than he is certain of having made an epoch," his distinguished contemporary Ferdinand Brunetière wrote. Yet his *Histoire de la Littérature Anglais* to the present generation is mainly a literary curio, outmoded in theory and approach, often ludicrously out of touch with the very phenomena it is describing. He does not seem really to have grasped Shakespeare; Donne was to him a rough versifier; and his essay on Dickens is deficient through his unfamiliarity with any of the novels after *David Copperfield* or any of the facts of the author's private life. The *Histoire* is to be enjoyed mainly by those who can appreciate intellectual virtuosity and brilliant style, independently of historical accuracy or validity. Really more a social scientist than a humanist, Taine is more likely to endure for his history of modern France and his essays on English society than for his studies in aesthetics.

H. Van Laun translated the *History of English Literature* in 1871, and his translation has been reprinted several times. John Durand translated *Italy, Rome and Naples, Florence and Venice* (1871), *Lectures on Art* (1875), and *The Origins of Contemporary France (The Ancient Regime, The French Revolution, The Modern Regime)* in six volumes (begun in 1878). The latter was reprinted by Peter Smith (1931). *Balzac, a Critical Study* is available

in a translation by Lorenzo O'Rourke (1906). *Notes on England* was published in a new translation by Edward Hyams 1957.

ABOUT: Babbitt, I. Masters of Modern French Criticism; Duclaux, A. French Procession; Eustis, A. Hippolyte Taine and the Classical Genius *in* California University Publications in Modern Philology, 1951; Gates, L. Taine's Influence as a Critic *in* Studies and Appreciations; Hyman, S. The Armed Vision; Jones, R. Taine and the Nationalists *in* Social and Political Ideas of Some Representative Thinkers of the Victorian Age, ed. F. Hearnshaw; Kahn, S. Science and Aesthetic Judgment: A Study in Taine's Critical Method; Stephen, Sir L. Men, Books and Mountains; Wilson, E. To the Finland Station; Criticism, I (1959); Journal of Aesthetics and Art Criticism, XXI (1963); Times Literary Supplement, November 15, 1957. [In French—see studies by F. Aulard, V. Giraud, M. Leroy, G. Monod.]

R. A. C.

*TAMAYO Y BAUS, MANUEL (September 15, 1829-1898), Spanish dramatist, actor, and critic, was born in Madrid. Both his parents were actors, and the boy showed an early interest in the theatre. Already an actor in his youth, he spent his leisure time translating and adapting French plays into Spanish.

His extensive experience in the theatre was later reflected in his dramaturgical skill and in his theories on dramatic art, which were presented in his discourse, 1858, at the time of his admission to the Spanish Academy (*De la Verdad como Fuente de Belleza en la Literatura*) (Of Truth as a Fountain of Beauty in Literature). Tamayo wrote for the stage continuously until his last play, *Los Hombres de Bien* (The Honest Men). For the rest of his life he was employed in research as Secretary of the Academia Española and as Director of the Biblioteca Nacional. He died in Madrid. His total output consists of more than fifty plays, and the reason for his deserting fame and the theatre for the last twenty-eight years of his life still remains a mystery.

Tamayo's versatility as a playwright is shown in the wide range of literary styles and genres which his plays encompass: sentimental, romantic comedies, classical tragedies, historical dramas, comedies of manners, thesis plays, etc.

He is said to have inaugurated the thesis play in Spain under the influence of Dumas *fils* and Augier, but certainly Moratín's influence was no less significant. Actually he began his career imitating Schiller's tragedies. *Angela* and *Juana de Arco* are the product of this period. His masterpiece of

* tä mä′ yō ē bous′

Roman tragedy, *Virginia* (1853), with its fine sense of dramatic construction, is a good example of a classical severity very rare in Spain at that time.

La Ricahembra (The Rich Woman, 1854), *Una Aventura de Richelieu* (One of Richelieu's Adventures) and *Locura de Amor* (Madness of Love, 1855) are examples of his historical dramas.

In *La Ricahembra*, which he wrote in collaboration with Aureliano Fernández-Guerra, a proud woman, Doña Juana de Mendoza, is slapped by an angry suitor, whom she marries so that no one can say that she was slapped by any man other than her own husband. The play gives an excellent picture of high Castilian society of the sixteenth century. The psychology of the play, although elementary, is very much in the tradition of the Spanish Golden Age.

Locura de Amor is his most famous play, a pathological study of jealousy involving Doña Juana de Castilla, queen, daughter of Ferdinand and Isabella. The play depicts the gradual derangement of a woman desperately in love, whose great jealousy of her husband drives her to madness.

Although *Locura de Amor* is his most famous play, his masterpiece is *Un Drama Nuevo* (A New Drama, 1867), a prose tragedy set in Elizabethan England. The action involves a clown (Yorick) in Shakespeare's company of players (Shakespeare himself is an important character). It is a play within a play, the imaginary betrayal and murder becoming tragically real. It was perhaps influenced by Kyd's *Spanish Tragedy.* Leoncavallo's famous opera *Pagliacci* was greatly influenced by *Un Drama Nuevo.* Some critics believe that Pirandello's *Six Characters in Search of an Author* was also influenced by this Spanish masterpiece.

Tamayo's thesis plays were directed against personal and social vices: *La Bola de Nieve* (The Snowball, 1856), a comedy of manners dealing with jealousy; *Lo Positivo* (1862), on materialism; and *Lances de Honor* (Duels of Honor, 1865), inspired by a mediocre French play, *Le Duc Job*, of Laya.

It is curious that Tamayo's maximum poetic effect is achieved in prose in contrast with the prosaic quality of many of his own verse plays. In Spain, Tamayo is considered one of her greatest dramatists of the nineteenth century.

Tamayo's *Obras Dramaticas* was published in 4 vols., Madrid, 1898-1900. *A New Drama (Un Drama Nuevo)* was translated into English by J. D. Fitzgerald and T. H. Guild (1915).

ABOUT: [In Spanish—Siscars y Salvadó, N. Manuel Tamayo y Baus, Estudio Crítico-Biográfico; Revista Contemporánea, X; Estudios de Historia Literaria de España.]

L. S.

*TASSO, BERNARDO (November 11, 1493-September 5, 1569), Italian poet, was born in Venice of a family from Bergamo. He served throughout life under many princes, at first with Count Guido Rangoni and Renata d'Este, then, beginning in 1532, as secretary of Ferrante Sanseverino, Prince of Salerno. In 1536 Tasso married Porzia de' Rossi, had a daughter and then the short-lived Torquato, followed by the great poet of the same name (see sketch below), born in 1544 while Bernardo was in Sorrento. By this time Bernardo had begun his masterpiece, the *Amadigi.* In his services under Sanseverino during the wars he traveled as far as Metz and Flanders; he then settled in Salerno and in Naples, but his protector's French leanings led to his exile to Venice and Ferrara. The death of Porzia in 1556 opened the protracted lawsuit that later preoccupied the son. After constant vicissitudes, Bernardo finally published the *Amadigi* in Venice in 1560. Having derived no financial security from this work, he was again obliged to seek the services of princes and engage in fatiguing travel. His last employ, in Ostiglia, offered him much needed calm, but he died within a few months as a result of the unhealthful conditions there.

Tasso's minor works include the fifty-five odes, imitating Horace and illustrating the influence of the school of Bembo; he also left the *Favola di Piramo e Tisbe*, based on Ovid, and a multitude of psalms, eclogues, elegies, and sonnets, perhaps undistinguished, but examples of the best technical form of the times. His fame today depends almost wholly on the *Amadigi*, based on the Spanish *Amadís de Gaula*, a medieval work published by Montalvo, which enjoyed wide appeal after 1500 for its synthesis of chivalric legend, moralizations, and refined classical manner. The *Amadís* was known in Italy by 1512, and apparently translated into Italian in Venice in 1546, when Tasso was already at work on his adaptation of it. As an experienced poet, Tasso sought to replace the chivalric genre by an epic of Homeric type, after the manner of Trissino, whose "verso sciolto" he at first planned to use; his preference for the *ottava rima* reflects his desire to please his protector, the Prince of

* täs' sō

Salerno, and this circumstance gave further importance to Ariosto's rhyme scheme. The influence of the *Amadigi* was enormous; it enjoyed a great public success, and provoked the jealousy of the reactionary writers, who attacked its non-Aristotelian tendencies. From an historical point of view, the *Amadigi* greatly stimulated the romanesque current of multiple plots in telling three simultaneous stories and loading them with descriptions, monologues, and letters.

The success of the *Amadigi* led Tasso to consider reworking one of its episodes as the separate poem *Floridante*, which he began in 1566 at the age of seventy for his protector the Duke of Mantua. The new work lacks the originality of its source and model, perhaps in part because it was left unfinished on the poet's death. His son Torquato felt unable at the moment to put it into final order, and passed the manuscript to Costantini who revised and published it in 1586; it enjoyed some success, and was reprinted during the following years.

Beside the many editions of the *Amadigi,* there were editions of the *Ode* in 1560, of the *Rime* in 1749, of the letters in 1551, 1733, and 1869, and of *Floridante* in 1931.

ABOUT: [In Italian—Paolini, P. I Genitori di Torquato Tasso; Seghezzi, A. *Preface to the letters,* 1869; Tordi, D. Il Codice Autografo di Rime e Prose di Bernardo Tasso.]

F. J. C.

*TASSO, TORQUATO (March 11, 1544-April 25, 1595), Italian poet, was born in Sorrento in a transitional period in Italian culture when the vital currents of the Renaissance were being rechanneled as a result of inhibiting political, religious, and authoritarian pressures. His father, Bernardo Tasso (see sketch above), traced his lineage back to an ancient house in northern Italy while his mother, Porzia de' Rossi, was the daughter of a noble family established for some generations in Naples.

From 1532 Bernardo had been serving as a secretary to Ferrante Sanseverino, Prince of Salerno, a quasi-independent feudatory of Spain, and shortly after the birth of Torquato he moved his small family, which included a daughter Cornelia, to Salerno. To the dismay of the populace, the Spanish viceroy in 1547 determined to introduce the Inquisition into Naples; urged by Bernardo, Sanseverino attempted to intercede with Charles V. When the outcome was unfavorable, Sanseverino rallied to the side of the

* täs' sō, tōr kwä' tō

TORQUATO TASSO

French; immediately he was declared a rebel and his property and fiefs were confiscated. Bernardo, however, loyally followed his Prince into exile, never again to see his wife or daughter.

In 1552 Porzia moved to Naples where Torquato began his formal education under the strict regime of the Jesuits. Two years later he was permitted to join his father in Rome. In 1556 news came of his mother's death following a brief illness, and Bernardo did not scruple to think that there had been foul play on the part of his wife's relatives. They retained Porzia's dowry and jointure and also steadfastly refused to permit Cornelia to leave Naples.

Meanwhile, out of the slender stipend allowed by Sanseverino, Bernardo contrived to pay for a tutor in Greek and Latin for Torquato. When war broke out in 1556 between the Pope and Spain, Bernardo felt it expedient to leave Rome and seek the protection of Guidobaldo II, Duke of Urbino. Torquato was now introduced to the polish and glitter of the court, where he became a companion to the Duke's son, Francesco Maria della Rovere, sharing his education in all the courtly arts and skills. Stimulated at an early age by the ceremony and romance of his surroundings, Torquato was henceforth to be irresistibly drawn to court circles.

In 1559 Bernardo moved to Venice to arrange for the publication of his epic, the *Amadigi*. There Torquato corrected proof for his father and established a warm friendship with Aldo Manutius, grandson of the great Venetian printer. Venice was a resplendent and exciting city: Titian, Tintoretto, and Sansovino dominated the world of painting and architecture; learned academies stimulated debate and discussion, and at the nearby University of Padua Sperone Speroni, the literary dictator, held sway. To him Bernardo sent his son with installments of the *Amadigi,* seeking advice and critical approval.

The next year he entered Torquato in the University of Padua to begin the study of law. Ardent, handsome, and polished in manner, Torquato had a winning personality and formed an enduring friendship with Scipione Gonzaga, later to become a cardinal. Although not neglecting his legal studies, he avidly took up the writing of poetry. In 1562 he scored brilliantly with the publication of his *Rinaldo,* a romantic epic in twelve books; it was a heady triumph for the youth of eighteen.

In November Torquato transferred to Bologna where his literary fame gained him quick entrance to learned circles. The scene of turbulent brawls and assassinations, Bologna, like other university towns, afforded a hazardous existence, and early in 1564 Torquato, reputed the author of a lampoon, was forced to flee while an examination of the charge was made and eventually dropped.

Returning to Padua, he joined a literary academy founded by his friend Scipione Gonzaga called Gli Eterei (The Ethereals), taking for himself the name "Il Pentito" (The Repentant); he devoted himself to the study of philosophy and poetry until 1565 when, through the efforts of his father, he entered the service of Cardinal Luigi d'Este, the brother of Alfonso II, Duke of Ferrara.

The Estensi had long been illustrious patrons of the arts; and the masque, the drama, and, above all, the epic had received and were to receive brilliant development at their court. In turn Boiardo, Ariosto, and, ultimately, Tasso figured brightly in the shining orbits of the sixteenth century dukes of Ferrara. Consequently, it was with blithe spirit that Tasso took up his post. Assigned no fixed duties, as well as no fixed salary, he was to have free access to the splendid ducal library. Soon he was on warm terms with the Duke's two sisters, the princesses Lucrezia and Leonore, and shared their table at meals. Having gained rapid favor by means of his facile pen, Tasso found the next few years perhaps the most pleasant of his life. But in 1569 his father, now serving as the

governor of an obscure village, died. Tasso's grief was heightened by the bitter fact that he had to scrape together from relatives the small sum necessary for the funeral expenses.

In 1570 he was part of the entourage accompanying Cardinal Luigi to France to celebrate the marriage of Charles IX to Elizabeth of Austria. There he met a group of French scholars and poets, including Ronsard, but there he also severed his relationship with the Cardinal. After a brief visit to Ferrara, he proceeded to Rome, hoping to find a new patron, but in September 1571 he returned to Ferrara where he was given an appointment by Duke Alfonso at a fixed salary and with no demands other than to write poetry. In 1573 he delighted the court with the shimmering beauty of his pastoral drama the *Aminta,* which was performed under his direction by the most famous actors of the day, the Gelosi. Despite repeated performances and manuscript circulation, the *Aminta* was not printed until his friend Aldo Manutius issued a pirated copy in 1581.

Acclaimed the most promising poet of the day, Tasso spent the next two years polishing and completing his major work, the *Gerusalemme Liberata,* which he had originally entitled *Il Goffredo.* Having determined years before to write an heroic poem which would adhere to the classical concept of unity, Tasso set himself to honor the Estensi in an account of the first crusade, interwoven with romantic and imaginary episodes. A tone of elegiac sweetness pervades the poem with its vivid depiction of battles, generalized visual beauty, and haunting melodic line—epic power dissolved into trembling lyricism.

The thirty-year-old poet had come to a crucial point in his career: instead of arranging for the publication of his poem, he unwisely submitted it to the criticism of his friends; the response was often harsh, more often pedantic. The variety and abundance of the episodes, the emphasis on love, the rhymes, the diction—all were condemned. Nervous and irritable in response to this carping criticism, Tasso constantly rewrote and altered the *Gerusalemme.* He became fearful that it contained heretical matter; he resolved to write an allegory that would moralize the offending passages. He begged his friend Scipione Gonzaga to secure him a place with Francesco de' Medici, of a rival house to the Estensi, arousing the fears of Alfonso that he would lose the luster of literary renown. His health began to fail, and by the summer of 1577 he was close to insanity. Placed under moderate confinement, Tasso contrived to escape and in the guise of a peasant made his way to Sorrento to be reunited with his sister. When his health improved, he moved restlessly from city to city; soon he was feverishly agitating to return to Ferrara, and Alfonso agreed to receive him. He arrived in February 1579 amid preparations for Alfonso's third marriage; ignored by the court, Tasso's fury broke out into mania. He was confined to the asylum of Sant' Anna where he was to remain for seven years. Visited frequently by distinguished people, among whom was Montaigne, Tasso contrived, despite his periodic lapses, to write a vast amount of occasional verse and prose, including many letters to European dignitaries appealing for release.

In 1580 an unscrupulous printer brought out an incomplete edition of the *Gerusalemme* under the title *Il Goffredo*; the following year a complete but imperfect edition was printed; soon edition followed edition, with the poet receiving nothing from the torrent of copies flooding Europe. In 1585 members of the Della Cruscan Academy of Florence (described by De Sanctis as the literary counterpart of the Council of Trent) virulently attacked the poem; counter-attacks were made, and the literary controversy raged; even Galileo entered the fray. Tasso became still more desirous of his freedom, and in 1585, leaving his books and manuscripts behind, he was permitted to accompany Prince Vincenzo Gonzaga to Mantua. There he completed his tragedy *Re Torrismondo*; but his mental state worsened and in a moment of restlessness he slipped away to begin an odyssey that was to last for nine years. During this period he worked on a new version of his epic, incorporating the criticism of his friends and reducing the sensuous beauty of the whole to utter bleakness. Published in 1593 as *Gerusalemme Conquistata*, it was a "pitiful ghost."

In 1594 he returned to Rome where Clement VIII was planning to crown him laureate, but Tasso's last illness prevented even this honor. He died at the age of fifty-one in the monastery of Sant' Onofrio on the Janiculan hill overlooking the Eternal City.

Symonds aptly observed that there have been as many Tassos as Hamlets; and romantic legends about the poet became rife. Byron's "Lament for Tasso," the veiled allusions in Shelley's "Julian and Maddalo," and above all Goethe's view in *Torquato*

Tasso that the poet's confinement resulted from a love affair with the Princess Leonore must be considered as romantic projections. Highly gifted and sensitive, Tasso seems to have been victimized only in the sense that his poet's soul was subjected to the searing winds of aesthetic and religious doctrines characteristic of the Counter Reformation.

In addition to his major works, Tasso composed nearly 2,000 lyrics, thirty dialogues, more than half of which were written during his confinement, and 1,700 letters, largely dating from 1575; they thus cover the years of his imprisonment and wanderings, and, in the judgment of Leopardi, constitute the most eloquent prose of the sixteenth century. His collected works (*Opere*), edited by J. Rosini, appeared in 33 vols., 1821-32.

Among the many translations of the *Aminta*, the earliest was that of Henry Reynolds in 1627, while Leigh Hunt's version (1820) is perhaps the most graceful. The *Gerusalemme Liberata* has also had frequent translators, but the Elizabethan version of Edward Fairfax, *Godfrey of Bulloigne or the Recovery of Jerusalem* (1600), has never been rivaled. In 1962 a new edition of the Fairfax translation was published, edited by Roberto Weiss. John Hoole translated the *Rinaldo* in 1792, and the dialogue "Il Padre di Famiglia" was translated in 1588 by Thomas Kyd as "Householder's Philosophy."

ABOUT: Boulting, W. Tasso and His Times; Bowra, C. M. From Virgil to Milton; Praz, M., The Flaming Heart; Symonds, J. A. The Catholic Reaction. [In Italian—see studies by E. Donadoni, G. Iazzetta, G. Natali, A. Solerti, B. Sozzi.]

E. S. D.

---

*TEGNÉR, ESAIAS (November 13, 1782-November 2, 1846), Swedish poet, scholar, bishop, orator, was born in the province of Värmland at Kyrkerud, where his father, Esaias Tegnér, was a curate, in 1783 promoted to vicar. His mother was Sara Maria Seidelius, daughter of a rural dean. The future poet was the youngest of eight children. His father died in 1792 and left the family in straitened circumstances. Esaias was sent with his elder brothers to Lund where they attended the university and took care of Esaias' education. At the age of ten he studied German, French, Latin, and history. But by the next year he had to earn his own livelihood. He worked for a few years as an assistant to a sheriff, who took interest in the brilliantly endowed boy and gave him an opportunity to continue his studies. In the summer of 1797 his oldest brother went to Rämen in northeastern Värmland as a tutor to the children of a foundry proprietor, and

* tĕng när'

TEGNÉR

Esaias was allowed to go with him. Next year Esaias took over the same position. The foundry proprietor, Christopher Myhrman, and his wife treated him like one of the family, and a tender affection sprang up between Esaias and their youngest daughter, Anna. The boy studied hard all the time, and in 1799 he entered the University of Lund, supporting himself as a private tutor. In 1802 he took his M.A. with honors, and the same summer he became engaged to Anna Myhrman. After a time of financial difficulties Tegnér was in 1805 appointed associate professor of aesthetics and assistant librarian at his alma mater, and in the summer he married.

Tegnér's early literary production consisted of reflective and didactic poems in the style of academic classicism. Such poems as *Den Vise* (The Wise One), *Kulturen* (Culture), *Ungdomen* (Youth) showed a nervous melancholy and gloom which reflected not only the pessimism of enlightened philosophy but also a personal inclination in the poet. Tegnér's marriage changed him, however, from a recluse into a witty and sociable person. Ossian, Milton, Young, Fichte, and Schelling influenced him quite early, but the deepest impressions he received were from Kant's idealistic doctrine of duty and, first and foremost, from Schiller's noble idealism and vigorous lucidity.

In *Det Eviga* (The Eternal, 1810), the enlightened philosophy has given way to an idealistic conviction that violence and injustice are transient but justice and beauty are eternal. The mightiest expression of his patriotism Tegnér gave in his magnificent poem *Svea* (1811), which was awarded the grand prize of the Swedish Academy.

In 1812 Tegnér was appointed professor of Greek and, after he had defended a theological thesis and been ordained, he was made prebendary of a parish outside Lund. He was influenced by Geijer and the romantic movement of "Gothicism" and was elected a member of the Gothic Society, whose greatest poet he soon became. In beautiful poems from 1812 to 1818 Tegnér expressed romantic ideals, e.g., in the mythological *Asatiden* (The Time of the Æsir), the optimistic *Flyttfåglarne* (Birds of Passage), the Platonic *Sång till Solen* (Song to the Sun). In the deeply personal *Skaldens Morgonpsalmen* (The Poet's Morning Psalm) he presented his conception of the poet's calling as a divine task since there is no dividing-line between religion and poetry. Tegnér embraced the virile nationalistic form of romanticism and opposed the obscure mysticism represented in Sweden by the so-called "Phosphorists." This attitude he expressed in his inaugural speech at the Swedish Academy in 1819. The next year, in a great oration delivered at the graduation ceremony in Lund, he expounded his humanistic educational program and his demands for vigor and clarity in poetry.

At the beginning of the 1820's Tegnér created his greatest poetic works, which made him one of Sweden's greatest poets, e.g., the religious hexameter idyll *Nattvardsbarnen* (The Children of the Lord's Supper, 1820), the sentimental glorification of Charles XII and his men *Axel* (1822), and, above all, the brilliant epic cycle *Frithjofs Saga* (1820-25), consisting of twenty-four various meters, the first piece of Swedish poetry to become world literature. His model was Oehlenschläger's *Helge,* and his objective in writing this cycle was "to reproduce a poetic picture of the old Scandinavian heroic life." He took the material from a romantic Old Icelandic saga but humanized the characters and the action. In the hero's personality are fused some of the most typical traits of the Nordic character: heroic courage, defiance, and joy of life are combined with mildness, courtesy, and melancholy.

In 1824 Tegnér became bishop at Växjö diocese, but his marital life was clouded by temporary infatuations, which inspired some of his poems. He developed a morbid melancholia which was caused not only by his amatory experiences but also, and more so, by an inborn predisposition. In his poem *Mjältsjukan* (Spleen, c. 1826), he gave a pathetic expression to the loathing of life and longing for death which at this time darkened his mind and never left him completely.

Tegnér discharged his episcopal duties with authority and firmness. He was also actively engaged in politics and in solving problems connected with the national educational system. More and more he retreated from the liberal movement and became increasingly conservative. On numerous occasions his brilliant eloquence lent luster and festivity to church ceremonies and secular celebrations. His orations may, as he himself said, contain more poetry than *Frithjofs Saga*. At the graduation ceremony in Lund in 1820, when he delivered his most celebrated speech ("Epilog"), he also bestowed the academic laurel upon Oehlenschläger, an act that had an enormous impact upon Scandinavian politics and cultural development. His letters are also genuine literary masterpieces. A stroke in 1840 triggered an outbreak of insanity, but he recovered enough to resume his work. Although he was given sick-leave in 1845, his poetic productivity was still remarkable. In his poem *Afsked* (Farewell, 1842), Tegnér's creative genius terminated in an elevated but somber homage to poetry.

Many translations into English of *Frithjofs Saga* in the original meters have been published, e.g., by W. Strong (1833), R. G. Latham (1838), G. S[tephens] (1839, several later editions), O. Baker (1841), C. W. Heckethorn (1856), W. L. Blackley (1857, several later editions, also included in *Scandinavian Classics*, II, 1914), R. Muckleston (1862), H. Spalding (1872), L. Hamel (1874), T. A. E. and Martha A. L. Holcomb (1877, 7th edition 1912), C. B. Shaw (1908, new editions 1911, 1921), C. D. Locock (1924). *Axel* was first rendered into English verse by R. G. Latham (1838). Since then several translations have been published, e.g., by O. Baker (1840), R. Muckleston (1864), A. Dobree (1866). M. Bernhard (1915). *Nattvardsbarnen* was translated by H. W. Longfellow as *The Children of the Lord's Supper* (1841, included in *Scandinavian Classics*, II, 1914). Translated selections of shorter poems are included in J. E. D. Bethune's *Specimens of Swedish and German Poetry* (1848), and in C. W. Stork's *Anthology of Swedish Lyrics* (1930) there are translations of six of Tegnér's best poems.

ABOUT: Bach, G. The History of Scandinavian Literatures; Boyesen, H. H. Essays on Scandinavian Literature; Brandes, G. Creative Spirits of the Nineteenth Century; Howitt, W. & M. The Literature and Romance of Northern Europe, II; Longfellow, H. W. The Poets and Poetry of Europe; Warner Library. [In Swedish—see studies by F. Böök, N. Erdman, E. Wrangel.]

A. J.

*TEIXEIRA DE QUEIROZ, FRANCISCO (May 3, 1848-1919), Portuguese short-story writer and novelist, was born in Arcos de Valdevez (Minho). He died in Cintra near Lisbon. His parents were wealthy farmers, who could afford to send their son to Coimbra to study medicine. In Coimbra, the cradle of literary movements since romanticism, he joined a literary student group gathered by the mordant Parnassian poet João Penha. Queiroz was too "scientific" to write verse like the rest. His ambition was that of all realists: to dissect the diseased body of contemporary bourgeois society. His models were French—Balzac and Flaubert.

In 1876 the famous Camilo Castelo Branco befriended the young writer who had just published his first tale, "O Tio Agrela," although he found Queiroz' scientific pretensions and excessive adjectives tiresome. Queiroz intended to write fiction that would "educate feeling to be true and unaffected and lambaste all that was artificial and banal. . . . Fiction was to be a 'natural history of human life,' in the great Balzac's words; each novel, a monograph." Like a scientist, Queiroz set out to discover new human personalities and states of mind. Like a craftsman, he reworked his writings, without achieving precision. He was constantly overshadowed by a greater prose artist, his namesake Eça de Queiros. Nevertheless, hiding behind the pseudonym "Bento Moreno," he continued to write two series of books, the "Comedy of Country Life" and the "Comedy of City Life." The former extended from *Primeiros Contos* (1876) to *Ao Sol e à Chuva* (1915), the latter from *Os Noivos* (1879) to *A Grande Quimera* (1919).

Being active in anti-monarchical politics, he had ample opportunity to study society firsthand: "His satire of Portuguese politics is perhaps more realistic and courageous than Eça's," observes O. Lopes. Both novelists aimed ironic darts at the same types—the worthless and successful politico *(Salústio Nogueira*, 1883), the decadent aristocrat *(Dom Agostinho*, 1894), the *nouveau riche* *(O Famoso Galrão*, 1898), the adulterers *(Cartas de Amor*, 1906).

Portuguese readers still enjoy his tales. He selected and revised the best among them in *Arvoredos* (1895). Their scenes of village life in the Minho region, highly colored by nostalgia for his country childhood, made of him one of the earliest Portuguese regional-

* tä ē shä ē′ rà thē kä ē rôsh′

909

ists. He also wrote several plays, among them *O Grande Homem* (1881).

ABOUT: [In Portuguese—Barros, J. de. Teixeira de Queiroz; Perspectivas da Literatura Portuguesa do Século XIX, II.]

G. M. M.

TÉLLEZ, GABRIEL. See "MOLINA, TIRSO DE"

TERESA OF JESUS, Saint (March 28, 1515-October 4, 1582), Spanish mystic, often referred to as the greatest saint of her sex in the history of mysticism, the "admirable" St. Teresa to whose name and honor Richard Crashaw wrote his great *Hymn,* was born Teresa Sánchez de Cepeda y Ahumada in the ancient walled city of Ávila. Her grandfather, Juan Sánchez of Toledo, had been a relapsed Jewish convert. She was the daughter of her father's second wife, and one of a large family of three sisters and nine brothers. Our knowledge of her life is largely based on her best-known work, the *Vida* or *Autobiography,* which, it is said, is the most widely read prose work of Spanish literature after *Don Quixote.* As a child she was devoted to the Virgin, read the lives of the saints, and was fascinated by the popular books of chivalry. In one of the most interesting passages of her autobiography, she tells us of her attempt to write a chivalric romance, and of her favorite games—the building of convents and hermitages. At the age of seven she and a brother left home to fight the Moors and achieve martyrdom, but just as they were crossing the river running through Ávila, they met their uncle who herded them home. She received her early schooling at a convent and later stayed with a devout uncle.

Despite the opposition of her family, she decided to become a nun and in 1534 she entered the Carmelite convent of the Incarnation at Ávila where she suffered continuous "strife and contention between converse with God and the society of the world," and was victim of almost constant bad health. In 1555 she experienced her "second conversion." One day, entering the oratory and facing the image of the wounded Christ, she fell on her knees "beseeching Him to strengthen her once and for all. . . ." She had earlier practiced spiritual exercises: now St. Augustine's *Confessions* helped her. Though she had given herself to the Prayer of Quiet and the Prayer of Union, she felt the call to reform the Carmelite Order. The rigorous way of the Carmelite life had relaxed; austerities had

ST. TERESA

retreated before worldliness. Her desire to recall the order to its former strictness met with formidable opposition, but in 1562 she was permitted to establish a convent of the reformed or Discalced Carmelites in Ávila, with four novices. For five years she remained with this house, and then began her travels throughout Spain to establish new reformed convents. With the help of Antonio Heredia and Juan de Yepes, who was later to be known as St. John of the Cross, she established the first Reformed Carmelite House for Men at Duruelo near Ávila. No obstacle was too great for her, neither poverty, fatigue, ill health, the rigors of travel, ecclesiastical opposition, nor self-doubt. Her travels and hardships she described in her *Libro de las Fundaciones.* She managed to found thirty-two religious houses and to write, most often at the express command of her superiors, the *Libro de Su Vida* (1562-65), poems and hymns of which about five hundred are extant, the *Constituciones* (1564) *Camino de Perfección* (1565), and other works.

St. Teresa was a practical and energetic woman, capable both of religious raptures and an interest in cooking recipes, full of humanity, devotion, and humor. Crashaw summed up her intense humanity: "A woman for angelical height of speculation, for masculine courage of performance." An administrator who never lost sight of the needs of her charges, she had an inner life even more intense than her outer activities. If her *Vida* is her first attempt to show the mystic way, her *Moradas o Castillo Interior del Alma* (1577) leads the reader by the hand through the seven stages of the soul's travail to union with God. "I shall . . . think of our souls as of a castle, in which are many rooms, just as in heaven there are many mansions. . . . Some [of these] are above, others below, others on one side; and in the center, in the midst of them all, is the chiefest of them, where many things most secret pass between God and the Soul." In the innermost dwells God—Who is the goal. Of the seven mansions, the first three are Mansions of Humility—Prayer, Meditation, and the Exemplary Life. Then comes the Prayer of Quiet where the faculties are at rest; the fifth stage is the Prayer of Union; in the sixth the "betrothed have sight of each other"; and in the seventh, with the Marriage of the Soul and the Divine Lover, the self is extinguished and is at one with God.

St. Teresa's life was guided by supernatural visions; the first was vouchsafed her at the age of twenty-one when she beheld Christ "with the eyes of the soul." She warns, however, that the corporeal vision is likely to be a delusion and that the intellectual vision is the most genuine for being the most spiritual and followed by ecstasy or a special sense of God's nearness. Although she puts her reader on guard against self-deception and the aberrations of ill health and self-indulgence, she says that true rapture cannot be resisted, and, in her case, at times her body is said to have risen from the ground.

Although, as we have seen, St. Teresa wrote poetry, she never achieved the artistic perfection of her friend St. John of the Cross. She is famous for her prose because her books are distinguished by directness, spontaneity, and freshness. St. Teresa refers to her ignorance and weakness of memory, yet her style is marked by a great wealth of imagery drawn from direct experience, both natural and supernatural. Her erudition was limited to the Bible, Sts. Augustine, Jerome, and Gregory, the Lives of the Saints, the *Imitation of Christ*, and the works of her contemporaries—Francisco de Osuna, Alonso de Madrid, Bernardino de Laredo, St. Peter of Alcántara, Luis de Granada, Miguel de Guevara, and perhaps St. Vincent Ferrer.

Forty years after her death, in 1622, along with Sts. Isidro, Ignatius of Loyola, and Francis Xavier, she was canonized.

Although many individual works of the Spanish saint have been translated into English, the best collection is *The Complete Works of Saint Teresa of Jesus,* translated and edited by E. Allison Peers in 1946 (3 vols.) from the critical edition of P. Silverio de Santa Teresa. Other recommended translations are *Way of Perfection* by the Benedictines of Stanbrook (1925); *St. Theresa: Life, Relations, Foundations, Maxims,* by J. I. Burke (1911); *The Interior Castle or the Mansions* by the Benedictines of Stanbrook (1921); the *Letters* by the Benedictines of Stanbrook (1921-26); *Book of Her Life* by the Benedictines of Stanbrook (1913); and *The Life of Saint Teresa,* translated by J. M. Cohen (1957).

ABOUT: Auclair, M. Saint Teresa of Avila; Graham, G. C. Santa Teresa; Hamilton, E. Saint Teresa; O'Brien, K. Teresa of Avila; Peers, E. A. Mother of Carmel; Walsh, W. T. Saint Teresa of Avila.

M. N.

THÉOPHILE. See VIAU, THÉOPHILE DE

*THOMA, LUDWIG (January 21, 1867-August 26, 1921), German humorist, satirist, prose writer, dramatist, and poet, was born in Oberammergau, Bavaria. The son of a head forester, he was first a student of forestry at Aschaffenburg, then studied law at Munich and Erlangen, and established himself as an attorney at Dachau and Munich in 1893. In 1897 he became associated with the renowned satirical, often radical, weekly *Simplizissimus* and served as an editor and contributor until his death. From 1907 on he was also a co-editor of *März* in addition to writing for a small local paper, the *Miesbacher Anzeiger*. The success of his writings soon led him to give up his law practice and become a free-lance writer. During World War I he served as a volunteer hospital attendant on the Eastern front. Thoma spent the last years of his life on the Tegernsee where he died at Rottach-Egern in 1921. He is buried there alongside his friend, the Bavarian writer Ludwig Ganghofer.

Thoma has been increasingly recognized as more than an outstanding regional writer and is now regarded as one of the foremost satirists in German literature. With a variety of forms and techniques at his disposal, Thoma waged a courageous fight against militarism and nationalism, a subsidized press, special privilege, Philistinism, and human stupidity and cupidity in general. In the *Simplizissimus* he wrote his liberal articles and peppery poems as "Peter Schlemihl," a pseudonym he used until 1906. (His poems later appeared in book form under the titles *Peter Schlemihl, Grobheiten, Neue Grobheiten,* and *Kirchweih.*)

* tō′ mä

911

Thoma's attacks on the state, the Prussian bureaucracy, the clerics, and legal iniquities of all sorts netted him several prison terms. He was one of the severest critics of William II, daring even to make fun of the Kaiser's published speeches.

Among the many plays, mostly comedies, farces, and vernacular plays, written by the "Bavarian Aristophanes" are *Moral* (1909), a comedy spotlighting the hypocrisy of self-appointed guardians of morality; *Die Lokalbahn* (1902), a comedy on village politicians; and the dialect farce *Erster Klasse* (1910). Thoma's novels of peasant life include *Andreas Vöst* (1905), the story of a farmer who in his quest for justice runs afoul of the law; *Der Ruepp* (1922), about a farmer who becomes a drunkard; and *Altaich*, a gentle satire on a village's pretensions to becoming a tourist resort. Among his most popular works are his stories of village life, such as *Agricola* (1897), *Assessor Karlchen* (1901), *Der Heilige Hies* (1904), and the delightfully amusing *Lausbubengeschichten* (continued under the title *Tante Frieda,* 1904-07), in which the foibles and idiosyncrasies of small-town life are seen through the eyes of an irrepressible "bad" boy. The humor of the last-named work is enhanced by the congenial illustrations of Olaf Gulbrannsson. But Thoma was also capable of more serious writing, as in *Heilige Nacht* (1916), a religious verse idyll of great artistry.

Oscar Maria Graf has called Thoma's *Briefe eines Bayrischen Landtagsabgeordneten* (Letters of a Representative in the Bavarian Diet, 1909-12) "the most powerful, the most enduring satirical document of the last half-century." Thoma's autobiographical writings include *Erinnerungen* (1919), and *Stadelheimer Tagebuch* (1923, about his imprisonment). His collected works, which first appeared in seven volumes in 1922, have been re-issued.

According to K. Holm, Thoma was a more tender and sensitive person than is apparent from his books, warmhearted and easily hurt. He surrounded himself with a veneer of gruffness, partly because he took pleasure in earthy things, partly out of a reluctance to reveal his basic gentleness. Gulbrannsson describes him as "Rabelais in short leather pants," with a large head, glasses, and a mustache.

Der Heilige Hies was translated by B. Q. Morgan as *Matt the Holy* and is included in *The German Classics,* XIX. *Moral* (which was performed in New York, 1925-26) was translated as *Morality* by H. Bernstein (1909) and as *Moral* by C. Recht;

the latter translation is included in T. H. Dickinson's *Chief Contemporary Dramatists,* 2nd series (1921).

ABOUT: American-German Review, XXIX (1963). German Quarterly, XXX (1957); Monatshefte für Deutschen Unterricht, XXI (1929). [In German—see studies by E. Cornelius, F. Dehnow, K. Holm, A. Stark, W. Ziersch.]

H. Z.

THOMAS AQUINAS, Saint (1225?-March 7, 1274), Italian theologian, was born near Naples at the castle of Roccasecca, the youngest son of the noble family of the counts of Aquino. His brother Rinaldo was one of the Sicilian School of poets, and the family was deeply involved on the imperial side in the struggle between Pope and Emperor. Thinking both to minimize this allegiance, and strengthen the family's finances, Thomas' father sent him at the age of five as an oblate to the Benedictine Abbey of Monte Cassino and then, about 1240, to the University of Naples. There Thomas was attracted by the life and projects of the Dominicans, who had been established in Naples since 1231. They represented a modern and vigorous point of view in their aim to give others the fruits of their contemplation, thus combining mysticism with rational investigation of thought. Thomas' family strongly opposed his desire to enter the Dominican Order, and arranged to assure for him the place of Abbot of Monte Cassino, but he remained firm. He left for Paris with John the Teuton, the Dominican Master General, but was immediately intercepted and kept in prison for over a year. When at last free, he continued to Paris and began studies under Albertus Magnus, whom he followed in 1248 to Cologne. Albertus, though by no means Thomas' equal, was one of the greatest encyclopedic minds of the time and above all a master of Aristotelian thought and method. Thomas was again in Paris in 1252, and lectured at the convent of Saint-Jacques, distinguishing himself by his command of rational problems; he completed his master's degree in theology in 1256 and taught for several years. He was sent to Italy in 1259 to teach in the *studium curiae* at Anagni and then at Rome and Viterbo.

The Italian period marks the beginning of Thomas' active writing, in which he was aided by several secretaries, and from the year 1265 date his first systematic analyses. His authority is attested by his mission to Paris in 1269, where he was sent to combat the two excesses of Averroism and Augustinianism. He was recalled to Naples in 1272 to establish a *studium generale.* Two years

ST. THOMAS AQUINAS

seventeenth century; Ockham in turn engrossed many thinkers. The revival of Thomism is due in large part to the efforts of Gaetano Sanseverino who, beginning in 1840, in his review *La Scienza e la Fede* and in his monumental Latin tracts, brought forth the particular significance of the method; the encyclical "Aeterni Patris" of Leo XIII (1879) established Thomism as the universal basis of scholastic theology. Thomism, so conceived, brought order to the chaos of conflicting doctrine and finally put an end to Cartesianism in this field. A long controversy rose from the presumed incapacity of Thomism to integrate modern science with reason, and the reputed slavish imitation of Aristotle, true only of the non-creative schoolmen.

later Pope Gregory X named him to the Council of Lyon, but he fell ill on the way and died near Terracina. Thomas was canonized as "Doctor Angelicus" in 1323 by Pope John XXII. Of the man himself, we must recognize his great diligence as a writer and his capacities as an organizer. He was severe and aloof, wholly dedicated to his meditations and his interpretation of ideas; the interpretations came to him, to judge by certain anecdotes, as sudden revelations, and his integration of rationalism and mysticism represented the general aim of his Order, which officially adopted his writings and his method in 1278.

The scholastic movement, which Thomist philosophy crystallized, had begun with St. Anselm, who clung somewhat too closely to the doctrines of St. Augustine. About 1220, through the Latin translations of Michael Scot and others, Averroës, the last of the Arabic commentators on Aristotle, was revealed to the West, and assumed a vital place along with Alfarabius, Avicenna, and Maimonides. The variable degree of Neoplatonic mysticism of this group of writers explains their particular influence; and the extreme rationalism of Averroës, with clear heretical tendencies, established a current which wholly eclipsed Thomism until well into the Renaissance. Thomism was condemned in England almost at once, and in general by the Franciscans, and the recrudescence of mystical piety lent new importance to Augustine in several distinct movements down into the

The thought of St. Thomas achieves a stable balance between Aristotle and the Church, and a middle course between ancient Greece and Christianity, or between reason and supernaturalism. The elements of Christian revelation are intrinsic in Greek thought, and one important aspect of the Renaissance is precisely the concept of "Christian humanism." St. Thomas, in one respect, reached beyond St. Augustine's rigorous insistence on conversion and the communication of the soul to God, to the earlier Fathers, such as Tertullian and Origen, who conceived human individuality as the indissoluble bond of body and soul. Between the extremes of asceticism and realism, St. Thomas attained a stable mean, the notion of Christian faith as assurance of the perfect development of nature and the full and complete man as the most worthy servant of God.

St. Thomas' most important single work, the *Summa Theologica*, was composed in consecutive parts from 1265 to 1272. Divided systematically into summa, treatises, questions and articles, and designed for intensive study, it is a complete exposition of Christian theology and philosophy, and demonstrates, by logic through illumination, the existence and nature of God, as the first unmoved mover, and His attributes; then follow discussions of the universe, adapted from Aristotle, then of man, of law as instruction according to the didactic aims of the Dominicans, of the things that pertain to man including the seven virtues, and, as the most personal preoccupation of the writer, the mystery of the Incarnation and the terminal problem of eternal life and resurrection. The work remains unfinished, and many other special aspects of Thomist thought must be sought in the lesser writings. The subject matter of the remaining works is usually evident from their titles: *De Regimine*

Principum (1265-66) on politics; *In X Libros Ethicorum ad Nicomachum* (about 1266) from Aristotle; *Quaestiones Disputatae,* collected tracts on special topics pertinent to teaching; *De Unitate Intellectus,* attacking the doctrine of the unique soul for all men, held by the Averroists; *Summa de Veritate Catholicae Fidei* (1261-64), apologetics against the Jews and the Arabs, translated as *God and His Creatures* in 1905; the *Catena Aurea,* extracts from the Fathers forming a commentary on the Gospels, translated by John Henry Newman in 1841-45. Of St. Thomas' style one may mention the conciseness and accuracy of statement, the patience in organization, the admirable adaptability for teaching, and the clear distinctions of detail; it was imitated by such great orators as Bossuet.

The bibliography of Thomism is enormous. The most reliable general sources are the *Bibliographie Thomiste* of P. Mandonnet and the *Bulletin Thomiste,* begun in 1924. There are several editions of the collected works, the *Opera* in 23 volumes of 1845-58 and in 12 volumes of 1882-1906, and the *Opuscula Omnia* of 1949. Translations of the works are satisfactorily replaced by running expositions of certain topics through excerpts, such as *Basic Writings* of 1945, *Selected Writings* of 1954, or *Theological Texts* of 1955. In 1964 a new translation of the *Summa* was announced. The edition, of sixty volumes, with Latin and English texts, is the work of the Dominican order.

ABOUT: Anderson, J. F. An Introduction to the Metaphysics of St. Thomas Aquinas; D'Arcy, M. C. Thomas Aquinas; Gilby, T. The Political Thought of Thomas Aquinas; Gilson, E. The Philosophy of Saint Thomas Aquinas; Grabmann, M. The Interior Life of St. Thomas; Maritain, J. The Angelic Doctor, *also* Saint Thomas and the Problem of Evil; Mayer, M. H. The Philosophy of Teaching of St. Thomas Aquinas; Vann, G. Saint Thomas Aquinas. [In French—see studies by M. D. Chenu, E. Gilson, P. Mandonnet, T. Pègues.]

F. J. C.

THOMAS À KEMPIS (c. 1380-July 25, 1471), the name by which the Augustinian canon and Dutch mystic Thomas Hammerken, or Malleolus, is commonly known, was born in the town of Kempen, lying about fifteen miles northwest of Düsseldorf, in one of the many patches of territory between the Meuse and the Rhine belonging to the archepiscopal principality of Cologne. "Ego Thomas Kempes," he says in his chronicle of the monastery of Mount St. Agnes, "scholaris Daventriensis, ex diocesi Coloniensi natus." His father was a poor, hardworking peasant; his mother kept a dame's school for the younger children of the town. John and Gertrude Hammerken had two sons, John and Thomas, both of whom

found their way to Deventer, and thence to Zwolle and to the convent of Mount St. Agnes. Thomas reached Deventer when he was barely twelve years old, and after a few months entered the classes of Florentius Radewijn.

This school at Deventer had become famous long before Thomas à Kempis was admitted to its classes. It had been founded by Gerhard Groot, a wealthy burgher who had been won to pious living mainly through the influence of Ruusbroec, the Flemish mystic. It was at Deventer, in the midst of this mystical theology and hearty practical benevolence, that Thomas à Kempis was trained. But Thomas was not like the Groots and Radewijns; he was not an educational reformer, nor a man of affairs. He liked books and quiet corners all his days, he says; and so, when conviction of sin and visions of God's grace came to him in the medieval fashion of a dream of the anger and forgiveness of the Virgin, Florentius told him that a monk's life would suit him best, advised him to join the Augustinian order, and sent him to Zwolle to the new convent of Mount St. Agnes, where his brother John was prior. Thomas was received there in 1399; he professed the vows in 1407, received his priest's orders in 1413, and became St. Agnes' sub-prior in 1425.

The convent of Mount St. Agnes was poor and most of the monks had to earn money to support their household by copying manuscripts. Thomas was a laborious copyist: missals, books of devotion, and a famous manuscript Bible were written by him. He also composed a large number of original writings, most of them relating to the convent life, which was the only life he knew. He wrote a chronicle of the monastery and several biographies—the life of Gerhard Groot, of Florentius Radewijn, of a Flemish lady, St. Louise, of Groot's original disciples—and a number of tracts on the monastic life. From his hand are also *The Monk's Alphabet; The Monk's Epitaph; Sermons to Novices; Sermons to Monks; The Solitary Life; On Silence; On Poverty; Humility and Patience;* two tracts for young people—*A Manual of Doctrine for the Young* and *A Manual for Children;* and books of edification: *On True Compunction; The Garden of Roses; The Valley of Lilies; The Consolation of the Poor and the Sick; The Faithful Dispenser; The Soul's Soliloquy;* and *The Hospital of the Poor.* He also left behind him three collections of sermons, a number of letters, some hymns, and the famous

Imitatio Christi. These writings help us to see the man and his surroundings, and contemporary pious records make him something more than a shadow. We see a real man, but a man helpless anywhere save in the study or in the convent—a small, fresh-colored man, with soft brown eyes, who had a habit of stealing away to his cubicle whenever the conversation became too lively; genial, if shy, and occasionally given to punning, as when he said that he preferred Psalmi to Salmones; a man who perhaps led the most placid life of all men who ever wrote a book or scribbled letters. It was not that he lived in uneventful times: it is impossible to select a stormier period of European history, or a period when the stir of the times made its way so well into the obscurest corners. But Thomas stayed with his books. His very biographies are colorless. His brothers made him *oeconomiae prefectus,* but he was too "simple in worldly affairs" and too absent-minded for the post, and so they deposed him and made him sub-prior once more. And yet it is this placid man who has come down to us as the author of the *Imitation of Christ,* which has been translated into more languages than any other book save the Bible. There has, to be sure, been controversy over Thomas' authorship of this great book—some scholars ascribing it variously to Jean Gerson, Johannes Gersen, and Gerhard Groot—but Thomas' claim remains the strongest to this day.

The earliest English translation of the *Imitation* was part of Book IV made by Lady Margaret, mother of Mary Tudor, in the fifteenth century; a new translation was made by L. Sherley-Price in 1953. J. P. Arthur translated Thomas' biographies in 1905 as *The Founders of the New Devotion.* The classical edition of the works in Latin—Sommalius' *Thomas à Kempis Opera Omnia* (3 vols., 1607)—has been many times reprinted. A modern edition, edited by M. J. Pohl, was published from 1907 to 1922.

ABOUT: Byron, M. Thomas à Kempis; Cruise, F. R. Outline of the Life of Thomas à Kempis; Kettlewell, S. Thomas à Kempis and the Brothers of the Common Life, *also* Thomas' Authorship of the Imitatio Christi; Preston, G. H. Studies in Thomas à Kempis in the Light of Today.

H. B.

THOMSEN, GRÍMUR ÞORGRÍMSSON (May 15, 1820-November 27, 1896), Icelandic poet and essayist, was born at Bessastaðir, the site of the Classical Latin School just a few miles south of Reykjavík. His father, Þorgrímur Tómasson, was a goldsmith by trade and the business manager of the school at the time of Grímur's birth.

His mother came from a cultured family and was exceptionally intelligent and well-read.

After receiving his early education from a private tutor, Thomsen entered the University of Copenhagen at the age of seventeen as a student of aesthetics. His interests, however, were broad; he studied philosophy, literature, and foreign languages, both modern and classical. In 1845 he was awarded a master's degree for his dissertation on Byron. By royal decree this was subsequently made the equivalent of the doctorate. This penetrating study introduced the English poet to Denmark and to Scandinavia generally. Thomsen had previously won a prize for his essay on contemporary French literature *Om den Nyfranske Poesi* (1843). He also introduced the Swedish-Finnish poet Runeberg and the Icelandic poet Bjarni Thórarensen to the Danes through his brilliant studies of these two writers. Thomsen is perhaps even better remembered, however, as the one who first reviewed with appreciation Hans Christian Andersen's *Fairy Tales,* thus introducing to Andersen's own countrymen the genius of the writer who has subsequently become the most beloved, if not actually the most famous, of all Danish authors.

For nearly twenty years (1847-66) Thomsen was employed by the Danish government in the diplomatic corps. During this time he traveled a good deal, meeting many of the famous men of his day. In 1866 he resigned, returned to Iceland, purchased Bessastaðir (the Latin School had recently been removed to Reykjavík) and lived the comfortable life of a gentleman farmer until his death in 1896.

Thomsen was an unusually well-educated man, reading fluently and speaking, at least to some degree, most modern European languages, and writing a great deal in Danish as well as in Icelandic. Although a sincere Christian, he despised weakness and had no sympathy with the unmanly and the slothful. Despite his leaning toward the romantic, his appeal is to the intellect rather than to the emotions. He delighted in choosing subjects from the *Eddas* and from the Sagas for his poetry, seeing in these heroic men the ideal toward which he had striven. His knowledge extended to Scandinavian, French, German, and English literature. His translations of Goethe and Uhland indicate a sincere appreciation of the genius of both these men. Their popularity in Iceland is due in great part to the excellence of his translations. He also translated from the Greek and Latin poets. His poetry is distinguished, however, less for its quantity than for its quality: "Endurminningin" (Remembrance) and "Sonartorrek" (Threnody for a Son), written in honor of Helgi Melsted, are particularly noteworthy.

Thomsen's works have been published several times: *Kvæðasafn* (Collection of Poems) appeared in 1880, in 1895, and again, with additions, in 1906. In 1934 a two-volume edition of his works together with a biography by Jón Þorkelsson and an introduction by Professor Sigurður Nordal appeared. Finally, selections from his poems were published in 1946. Translations of several of Thomsen's poems, including "Endurminningin," are to be found in *Icelandic Lyrics,* selected and edited by Richard Beck (1930).

ABOUT: Beck, R. History of Icelandic Poets, 1800-1940; Journal of English and Germanic Philology, XXVII (1928).

L. B.

*THÓRARENSEN, BJARNI VIGFÚS-SON (December 30, 1786-August 24, 1841) Icelandic poet, judge, and public official, was born at Brautarholt in the south of Iceland, the son of wealthy and prominent parents. He grew up in an atmosphere of culture and refinement. His father, Vigfús Þorarinsson, was prefect in Kjós, and later on in Rangárvallasýsla, and a man of some learning. Bjarni's formative years were spent at Fljótshlíð in Rangarvállasýsla, the country of Gunnar frá Hlíðarenda, the hero of the *Njáls Saga.* That young Bjarni was stirred by the rich historical memories of the area is attested by the beautiful poems that he composed in later years in which he refers time and again to the locale of his youth.

After receiving an excellent preparatory education from private tutors, Bjarni entered the University of Copenhagen in 1803. In 1807 he graduated with high honors in the field of jurisprudence. After serving several years in the Danish governmental service, Bjarni accepted in 1811 an appointment as deputy judge of the Superior Court at Reykjavík, becoming justice of the court in 1817. In 1833 he was named governor of North and East Iceland, a position which he held with honor until his death in 1841. On two occasions while he was justice of the Supreme Court he served as temporary governor-general of Iceland.

Even at a time of many gifted and talented men such as Magnús Stephensen, Tómas Sæmundsson, Jón Sigurðsson, and Jónas Hallgrímsson, Thórarensen was outstanding for intellectual vigor. In addition to being a respected judge and an energetic civil mag-

* tōr' är ĕn sĕn

istrate, advocating measures for the betterment of the community such as a road-building program, he was a poet of the first rank. While in Copenhagen studying law he had been stirred by the lectures of Henrik Steffens (1773-1845) and the poetry of Adam Oehlenschläger (1779-1850) proclaiming the romantic movement in northern Europe. The pioneers of this new literary faith found fertile soil in the mind of Bjarni Thórarensen. Avoiding the excesses of the new movement but availing himself of its fructifying influence, he expressed the nationalistic-patriotic temper of the time in his "Minni Íslands" (Ode to Iceland) composed when he was a student of eighteen in Copenhagen. This poem, commonly known as "Eldgamla Ísafold," still retains its popularity and may be considered, next to "O, Guð vors Lands," the national song of the Icelanders. It is sung to the tune of "God Save the King" whenever Icelanders congregate. Intense nationalistic pride and love of country may be found in many other poems by Bjarni Thórarensen, for example, "Þú Nafnkunna Landið (You Famous Land).

Despite his leanings toward romanticism, Thórarensen used the classical Icelandic meters with ease and with great effect. Many of his elegiac poems have the simple four-beat line of the Eddic meters. For the most part Thórarensen is less interested, however, in form than in feeling and content. Thus he reveals, again, the influence of the romantic school. He is never sentimental, always virile and emphatic in his praise of the noble, the strong, and the manly. In all his poems one perceives the conviction of the poet that courage is to be respected and that right will triumph. His whole point of view may be characterized by the terse statement so often found in the heroic literature of the North: "Better to die with honor than to live in shame."

Thórarensen's influence was wide during his lifetime. Everyone admired him, and the younger poets, including Jónas Hallgrímsson (1807-45), were decisively influenced by his revival of the classical meters and his efforts to purify the language of foreign expressions.

A collected edition of Thórarensen's works appeared under the title *Kvæði* (Poems) in 1847, six years after the poet's death. A second edition came out in 1884, and in 1935 a definitive edition in two volumes, *Ljóðmæli,* edited by Jón Helgason, appeared. Translations of several of his poems are to be found in *Icelandic Lyrics,* selected and edited by Richard Beck (1930).

ABOUT: Beck, R. History of Icelandic Poets, 1800-1940; Einarsson, S. A History of Icelandic Literature; Scandinavian Studies and Notes, XV (1938).

L. B.

ÞORGILSSON, ARI, Fróði. See ARI ÞORGILSSON, Fróði

*THORILD, THOMAS (April 18, 1759- October 1, 1808), Swedish poet, critic, philosopher, was born at Blåsopp in the northern part of the province of Bohuslän. His father was Jöns Olsson Thorén, a poor farmer and bailiff. The poet changed his family name in 1785. His mother was Börta Thomasdotter. Both parents died during Thomas' infancy. During his years at the University of Lund, 1775-81, he was influenced by sentimental pre-romantic ideas through Gessner, Rousseau, and Goethe. But the greatest influence was Spinoza's elevated pantheistic philosophy, which he modified by the adoption of Robinet's molecular theory and Shaftesbury's Platonic aesthetic doctrine. On the basis of these and other constituent elements he created a strange individualistic philosophy, abstract, metaphysical, optimistic, and pantheistic in nature. From Lund he moved to Stockholm in order to make a literary career for himself. His expectations were high, and he had, as he later said himself, "only *one* great unchangeable thought in life: *to explain the whole of nature and reform the whole world.*" In the beginning, the convinced Rousseauist disliked the capital, but after he moved away from the center of the city he felt more at home.

Thorild entered a contest sponsored by the literary society Utile Dulci by submitting a didactic poem, "Passionerna" (The Passions, 1781), in which he proclaimed his philosophy and glorified the pre-romantic apostles. Dissatisfied with the award of only a minor prize, Thorild entered into a polemic dispute with Kellgren, the leading literary and aesthetic critic of Gustavian Sweden. The bitter and heated controversy continued for a decade and extended to political and social problems. Against the rigid French-classical literary rules and aristocratic attitude toward life and government defended by Kellgren, Thorild advocated literary freedom and a democratic constitutional regime. Having lost the literary battle, Thorild concentrated on politics and submitted to King Gustavus III and the Estates a memorandum, *Om det*

* tōō′ rĭld

THORILD

Allmänna Förståndets Frihet (On Freedom of Common Sense), in which he demanded unrestricted freedom of the press. His action was met with indifference, and after a year in Uppsala he left for England, where he hoped for a more sympathetic appreciation of his revolutionary ideas. However, his English publications only provoked ridicule, and he returned disillusioned to Sweden. There he re-entered the literary debate and published *En Critik öfver Critiker* (Critique of Critiques, 1791-92) in which he attacked Kellgren's negative criticism and called for a positive attitude in the "world of genius." When Kellgren's powers decreased, Leopold stepped into the battle against Thorild.

The assassination of King Gustavus III and the French Revolution, which enraptured Thorild, gave him hope for a revolution in Sweden as well. He published two earlier oppositional memoranda and furnished them with an introduction, entitled "Ärligheten" (Honesty), in which he expressed subversive ideas. He was arrested and sentenced to banishment and left Sweden in the spring of 1794. He was accompanied into exile by his mistress, Gustafva Steilich von Kowsky, daughter of a clergyman, whom he then married. After a period of roving life he settled in Greifswald in northern Germany and was appointed librarian and professor at the local university. Because of the terrorism that followed the French Revolution, his revolutionary sympathies decreased, and he embraced a rather conservative sociology. Most of his works during this time consisted of philosophical publications in Latin and German, in which he opposed the Kantian and romantic school.

Thorild was not able to create any great living poetry, but his importance as a critic was considerable. As a prose-writer he was second to none among his contemporaries, and his satirical wit was provocative and daring.

ABOUT: Howitt, W. & M. The Literature and Romance of Northern Europe, II. [In German—Cassirer, E. Thorilds Stellung in der Geistesgeschichte des Achtzehnten Jahrhunderts. In Swedish—Arvidson, S. Thorild.]

A. J.

*THÓRODDSEN, JÓN ÞÓRÐARSON (October 5, 1819-March 8, 1868), pioneer Icelandic novelist and poet, was born at Reykjahólar in the northwest of Iceland, the son of Þórður Þoroddson, a farmer, and Þórey Gunnlaugsdóttir, the daughter of a parson. He received his early education from private tutors and in 1837 entered the Classical Latin School at Bessastaðir, a few miles south of Reykjavík. Upon graduation in 1840 he was a private tutor for a year at the home of Hallgrímur Thorlacius, a pastor in Eyjafjorð and then went to Copenhagen to study law. It is assumed that he pursued his education at Copenhagen at the urging of Hallgrímur with whose daughter Jón had become infatuated. While he was still abroad, he received word that his fiancée, who had had a child by him, had fallen in love with another man, and since it was assumed that he would no longer want her, she would be married to the other man. Jón's letter forgiving her and requesting her to wait for him reached her just after the wedding. Thóroddsen later made use of the possibilities of misunderstanding between lovers in both of his great novels.

For the next several years he was disturbed and upset. He studied intermittently; wrote Bohemian poetry; edited, in collaboration with his friend Gísli Brynjólfsson, the magazine Norðurfari; and even served with the Danish army in Schleswig fighting the Germans (1848).

Returning to Iceland in 1850, he accepted an appointment as acting prefect of his home county — Barðastrandarsýsla — with headquarters at Flatey. Here he joined a vigorous intellectual and literary group. Here also he fell in love with Katrín Thorvaldsdóttir frá Hrappsey, who became his wife after he returned to Copenhagen and took his examin-

* tōr′ ŏd sĕn

ation in jurisprudence (1854). He was then made full prefect of the district of Barðarströnd, living at Hagi until 1862 when he advanced to prefect of the Borgarfjorð district. He lived with his family of eight children at Leirá until his death at forty-eight.

The poems of Jón Thóroddsen enjoy great popularity mainly because of their simplicity in both speech and subject matter. Many of them are idylls of Icelandic country life. They are full of good humor and joie de vivre. Thóroddsen's place in Icelandic literary history is secure, however, not because of his poetry, but rather because of his two great novels, namely, Piltur og Stúlka, 1850 (English translation by A. M. Reeves called Lad and Lass, 1890); and Maður og Kona (Man and Wife) published posthumously by the Icelandic Literary Society in 1876. Pioneering in these two works a new field in Icelandic literature (for no novels had been written in Icelandic before his day), Thóroddsen had to strike out boldly and follow his own inclinations. In his library of about 700 volumes there was found at the time of his death a set of Sir Walter Scott's works, but it is not entirely clear when these came into his possession.

Although, as might be expected, Maður og Kona is superior technically, both novels reveal exceptional narrative talent, boisterous good humor, and an enviable ability to bring the commonplace to life and invest it with dignity and interest. Both novels contain characters who live and breathe to the point that they have become household words in Icelandic, comparable to Old Scrooge or Tiny Tim in English. No one who has read these novels can forget the wonderful picture of Icelandic country life or the odd characters— the bland but conniving Reverend Sigvaldi, Hjálmar tuddi, or Þuríður gamla. Strongly reminiscent of the classical saga style is Thóroddsen's technique of allowing his characters to describe themselves through their own speech and actions. Moreover, Thóroddsen uses other techniques in the saga tradition, e.g., the impressive genealogies and the occasional archaic vocabulary. Though the stimulus may have come from Scott, both novels are Icelandic from beginning to end and follow age-old Icelandic story-telling traditions.

As indicated above, Lad and Lass appeared in English in 1890. Sigrid, an Icelandic Love Story was translated by C. Chrest (1887). Translations of several of Thóroddsen's poems may be found in Icelandic Lyrics, selected and edited by Richard Beck (1930).

ABOUT: Einarsson, S. Icelandic Prose Writers 1800-1940. [In Icelandic—see study by S. J. Thorsteinsson.]

L. B.

*THORSTEINSSON, STEINGRÍMUR

(May 19, 1831-August 21, 1913), Icelandic poet and educator, was born at Arnarstapi in the district of Snæfellsnes in the west of Iceland and came of well-educated and cultured people on both sides. His father, Bjarni Thorsteinsson, was governor of the western quarter of Iceland and extremely active in literary circles. His mother, Þórunn, the daughter of Bishop Hannes Finnsson, was related to Dr. Niels Finsen (1860-1904), the inventor of the Finsen lamp for phototherapy and the recipient of the Nobel Prize for his work in medicine (1903).

Exposed to the best in literature from early youth, the precocious Steingrímur composed an impressive ballad, the "Redd-Hannesar Ríma" while still a student at the College of Iceland in Reykjavík. This is a mock epic of Icelandic country life, reminiscent of Homer on the one hand and of Pope's mock epics on the other.

Graduating from the College of Iceland at the age of twenty, he went to Copenhagen to study law. Gradually, however, his interests in humanistic studies prevailed with the result that he broadened his already extensive knowledge of literature and philology to include classical and modern languages, philosophy, and aesthetics. In 1863 he took his degree in philology, but remained for several years in Copenhagen enjoying the congenial intellectual atmosphere of the Danish capital. These years were among the most productive of his life. In addition to teaching and doing research, he supported Jón Sigurðsson (1811-79) and the Icelandic movement for independence by writing patriotic poems in the tradition of the German romantic school. In 1872 he accepted an appointment as teacher of classical and modern languages at the College of Iceland. In 1904 he became rector of the same school, a position he held until his death at eighty-two.

Thorsteinsson was a tireless translator, enriching Icelandic literature with scores of gems from classical and modern literatures: among them were *The Arabian Nights*, Shakespeare's *King Lear*, Defoe's *Robinson Crusoe*, and Hans Christian Andersen's *Fairy Tales*. Despite his exacting duties as teacher and rector of the school, he was a prolific writer. His works, both in prose and in

* tōr′ stän sŏn

poetry, reveal a mastery of the language, an impeccable taste, and a delicate sensitivity. Allied to the classicists by his emphasis on form and polished style, Thorsteinsson is yet closer to the romanticists in his choice of subjects: his best poems are descriptions of nature, for example, "Við Hafið" (By the Sea), "Háfjöllin" (The High Mountains), and "Svanasöngur á Heiði" (Swansong on the Moorlands).

Thorsteinsson's original poems, *Ljóðmæli* (Poems), appeared in 1881. An enlarged edition came out in 1893, a third edition considerably enlarged in 1910, and again in 1925. His influence, already great during his lifetime, continues to the present day. Translations of several poems including "Við Hafið" and "Svanasöngur á Heiði" are to be found in *Icelandic Lyrics,* selected and edited by Richard Beck (1930).

ABOUT: Beck, R. History of Icelandic Poets; Scandinavian Studies (1948). [In German—see study by J. C. Poestion.]

L. B.

*TIECK, JOHANN LUDWIG (May 31, 1773-April 28, 1853), German writer, was born in Berlin, the son of a rope maker. A voracious reader by the age of five, he began his career as a professional writer very early, when one of his teachers at the *Gymnasium,* the author of horror tales, hired him to write the final chapters of his works. He forsook his brilliant prospects as an actor in obedience to his father's objections. In quick succession he attended the universities of Halle, Göttingen, and Erlangen, where he acquired a vast knowledge of European literature and turned his attention to Elizabethan dramatists other than Shakespeare. A journey with his schoolmate Wackenroder made him acquainted with the wooded scenery of southeast Germany, which he later used as background for his romantic tales, and aroused his interest in medieval art and culture and the aesthetic aspects of Catholicism. On his return to Berlin Tieck entered the famous literary circles of the Prussian capital. The influential publisher Friedrich Nicolai hired him as a hack writer for the adaptation of French light novels to the taste of the German reading public. Here he developed his gifts as a humorist in ridiculing the sentimentalism of contemporary middle class literature. Being subject to hallucinations and to periods of depression he soon rejected Nicolai's rationalism.

The passionate love of his sister Sophie, a gifted but dissolute woman, contributed

* tēk

TIECK

About this time Tieck began to suffer from attacks of rheumatic fever, a disease which plagued him to the end of his life and disfigured his imposing appearance. He moved to Dresden where he became the center of a literary court. His famous dramatic readings, especially of Shakespeare, were soon the highlights of cultural life in the Saxon capital. Besides important editions of medieval poetry and pre-Shakespearean dramatists he published in the period between 1812 and 1816 the work that brought him his greatest fame, the *Phantasus*, a collection of poetry, dramas, and tales, connected by long stretches of conversation which expressed his ideal of a cultured society. In a later period of his life he condemned the course the romantic movement had taken in the eccentric writings of E. T. A. Hoffmann and established himself as the poet of culture and education. As such he developed the art form of the *novelle*, in which German literature was to reach a higher level of accomplishment than in the novel proper. In Tieck's *novellen* the miraculous is no longer the work of supernatural powers, but originates in the mysteries of life itself.

No less important was his work as a drama critic, an editor, and a translator. However, the continuation of Schlegel's Shakespeare translation, which, under the name of Schlegel-Tieck, keeps his name alive among the German people, is not his work, but that of his daughter Dorothea (he had married Amalie Alberti in 1798) and Count Baudissin, though it was executed under his supervision.

After the untimely death of his beloved daughter, he moved to Berlin (1841) to assist in the direction of the Royal Theatre. When he died shortly before his eightieth birthday he was nearly a forgotten man. Rarely has the reputation of a famous writer undergone such a change for the worse. Once revered as the equal, if not the superior, of Goethe, he is now generally considered as the archetype of the professional man of letters to whom life, love, religion, or nature mean nothing but material for the production of reading matter. Friedrich Gundolf writes of Tieck: "He started as a hack writer of low standards . . . and ended as a hack writer of high standards." Against such judgment stands the opinion of Marianne Thalmann, who praises him as the only one of the early German romanticists who did not fall victim to the obscure powers they had conjured up, but found his way back to a solid form of art.

much to the problems of his life. They made *Die Geschichte des Herrn William Lovell* (1796-97) the most morbid of all autobiographical novels in the wake of Goethe's *Die Leiden des Jungen Werther*. His inclination toward the weird, the horrifying, and the demonic led him to the writing of folk tales. In *Der Blonde Eckbert*, one of the few works of Tieck which still appeals to the modern reader, the boundaries between reality and illusion disappear completely; the projections of man's fears, his conscience and his subconscious, are just as real as the tangible objects of nature. Tieck's humor, which is always satirical, shows best in the play *Der Gestiefelte Kater*, considered the masterpiece of dramatic satire in German literature. He competes with Goethe's *Wilhelm Meister* in the novel *Franz Sternbalds Wanderungen*. Many of the romanticists preferred his work because, in contrast to Goethe, he glorifies the artist's life as the only one worthy to be lived. In Jena his personal contact with the theorists of romanticism, the Schlegel brothers, stimulated him to his most ambitious experiments in "universal poetry," where unity of style is completely abandoned for an arbitrary conglomeration of all poetic devices—a kind of epic play, *Leben und Tod der Heiligen Genoveva*. When in 1800 this play together with some other poetic writings was published under the title *Romantische Dichtungen*, the word "romantisch" was introduced as a technical term into literary history and criticism.

Several of Tieck's shorter tales have been translated into English. Two of his tales, "Die Gemälde" (1821) and "Die Verlobung" (1822), were translated by Connop Thirlwall as "The Pictures" and "The Betrothing" (1825). Carlyle's *German Romance* (1827) translates "The Fair-Haired Eckbert," "The Trusty Eckhart," "The Runenberg," "The Elves," and "The Goblet." In 1830 a translation of one of his novels, *Ein Dichterleben*, treating of Marlowe and Shakespeare, was published in Leipzig. Some of the above-mentioned tales are reprinted in various readers of German literature for high schools and colleges.

ABOUT: Matenko, P. Teick and Solger; Trainer, J. *in* German Men of Letters, ed. A. Natan, *also* Ludwig Tieck: From Gothic to Romantic; Zeydel, E. H. Ludwig Tieck, The German Romanticist, *also* Ludwig Tieck and England. [In German—see studies by R. Köpke, R. Minder, M. Thalmann.]

F. R.

*TINAN, JEAN (LE BARBIER) DE (January 19, 1874-November 1898), French novelist, was born in Paris. He was the grand-nephew of an admiral of the Second Empire; his father, a baron, was an amateur art collector. Tinan attended the École Monge, where he became intimate with André Lebey and Paul Leclercq. Pierre Louÿs was a lifelong friend and inspiration. Plump in adolescence, Tinan, who suffered from heart trouble, grew into a tall, somewhat stooped youth with long, thin legs and delicate hands. He was a sparkling conversationalist. Early interested in literature, he read extensively in the classics, while also reading widely in contemporary literature and frequenting artistic circles. But he also had some scientific training, and attended the École Nationale d'Agriculture at Montpellier. Summers were spent at Jumièges, at a family property near the abbey.

Tinan's literary career was intense though brief. He essayed poetry, but recognized that it was not the proper medium for him. He made his debut with *Un Document sur l'Impuissance d'Aimer* (1894), based on a devastating early love affair. In 1896 he founded *Le Centaure* with Henri Albert (the translator of Nietzsche), André Gide, Paul Valéry, Pierre Louÿs, and others. *Le Centaure* ceased publication with its second number. Tinan became a contributor to *L'Ermitage* and the *Mercure de France*. In the latter periodical he reviewed books in literature and in the biological sciences. The *Mercure* created for him a new section on "cirques, cabarets, concerts," in which Tinan discussed the world of entertainment. An inveterate young man-about-town, he frequented the bars and dance-halls—the Café d'Har-

* tē näⁿ'

court, Weber's, Bullier's, etc.—in company with Paul Jean Toulet, the artist Maxime Dethomas, Alfred Jarry. A series of feminine companions of the moment visited his apartment, furnished in *fin-de-siècle* style, with Burne-Joneses and Rossettis on the draped walls. Tinan also attended Mallarmé's and the *Mercure de France*'s literary gatherings.

The aesthetic climate of the 1890's is depicted in his autobiographical *Penses-Tu Réussir? ou les Diverses Amours de Mon Ami Raoul de Vallonges* (1897). Meditations on the rôle of the heart and the mind he confided in *L'Exemple de Ninon de Lenclos Amoureuse* (1898); his intellectual and artistic credo was expressed in *Aimienne, ou le Détournement de Mineure* (1899). The latter was published posthumously, for Tinan died exhausted by the strain of an incessant pace on a frail constitution. He is buried in Père Lachaise cemetery

Tinan was greatly admired by his contemporaries; Alfred Vallette, director of the *Mercure,* thought that he had the best chances of winning in the literary lottery; Léon Blum and Paul Léautaud esteemed him. Tinan completed only a few of his numerous projects, but they suffice as prime data on their time.

Tinan was the principal ghost-writer for *Maîtresse d'Esthète,* signed by Willy (Colette's first husband). Tinan's chronicles for the *Mercure de France* were published as *Noctambulismes, 1897-1898.* Admirers continue to assure small bibliophilic editions of some titles.

ABOUT: [In French—Leclercq, P. Paradis Perdus; Lebey, A. Jean de Tinan, *also* Disques et Pellicules.]

S. S. W.

"TIRSO DE MOLINA." See "MOLINA, TIRSO DE"

*TOCQUEVILLE, ALEXIS CHARLES HENRI MAURICE CLÉREL DE (July 29, 1805-April 18, 1859), French historian and statesman, was born at Verneuil, third son of Comte Hervé Bonaventure de Tocqueville, a prefect who was elevated to the peerage after the fall of Napoleon. The Tocquevilles were of distinguished Norman lineage, claiming ancestry from one of the nobles who accompanied William the Conqueror to England.

* tôk vēl'

TOCQUEVILLE

Young Alexis received his first education under religious auspices, being tutored at home by a family friend, the Abbé Lesueur. At the age of fifteen he was sent to the *lycée* at Metz where his father was prefect. During this period he discovered some of the writings of the Philosophes of the previous century, while browsing through his father's library. Through them his interest was first aroused in the study of society and institutions. From Metz he went to Paris to study law.

In 1827, at the age of twenty-one, Alexis entered professional life as *juge auditeur* at Versailles, a position procured for him by his father. Here he struck up a friendship which was to be life-long with another young aristocrat of intellectual curiosity, Gustave de Beaumont. The two friends soon grew restless in their bureaucratic posts, and, following the July Revolution of 1830, they felt out of sympathy with the government, and so decided to apply for a leave of absence to study the prison system in America. The leave being granted, they set sail in 1831 for that outpost as yet little known to most Europeans, on a mission ostensibly undertaken as a public service, though it was financed by the families of the two travelers.

On May 11, 1831, Tocqueville and Beaumont landed in Manhattan on the steamer *President*. Within nine months they traversed a distance of 7,000 miles—reaching west to Green Bay, south to New Orleans, north to Quebec, and east to Boston. They employed virtually every means of transpor-

tation then available, including steamer, stagecoach, and horse. The report that grew out of this tour, *Du Système Pénitentiare aux États-Unis et de Son Application en France,* lies in the dusty archives of the documents office. Its collateral result, *De la Démocratie en Amérique* (*Democracy in America*, 1835), catapulted its author to fame and became a world classic. (Beaumont wrote a semi-novel based on this same trip, entitled *Marie, ou l'Esclavage aux États-Unis,* in some ways a counterpart to his friend's book, which never achieved celebrity.)

Democracy in America was the first thorough analysis of the operation of our democratic institutions, particularly the Constitution, the effects of local government, the advantages and disadvantages of universal suffrage. Tocqueville's primary motive for writing the book was not to evaluate America's achievement but to prognosticate France's future. The New World to him was mainly an experimental proving ground for the edification of the Old World that was passing. Of patrician leanings himself, Tocqueville was not enthusiastic about democracy, but recognized it as an inevitable development. In his book he took care to bring out its faults (deterioration of culture, the tyranny of the majority) as well as its virtues, in the hope that his own country as it moved towards democracy would avoid its excesses.

Democracy in America was an immediate and almost unqualified success, eulogized in France by Sainte-Beuve, and greeted with enthusiasm in England by John Stuart Mill. The book won for its author a seat in the Académie Française and fame throughout Europe. The second part, published in 1840, was more abstract and philosophical than the first (and not quite so popular), with the intention of deriving general principles of political change from the data of the American experience. The whole work is probably one of the most translated in the world, having been rendered into English, German, Italian, Russian, Spanish, Serbian, and Danish. Hardly a decade has passed since its first publication that has not seen some edition of it.

The year 1835 was an eventful one for Tocqueville for another reason. He made a trip to England (his second) and there met and married a Miss Motley. This marriage to an English commoner was certainly an unconventional one for a French noble to make. The bride's own family considered the union a misalliance, but it prospered. Mme de

Tocqueville superintended the posthumous publication of her husband's complete works, which were edited by his friend Gustave de Beaumont.

During the twenty years from the publication of *Democracy in America* to his death, Tocqueville held political office fitfully, mainly out of a sense of duty, for he had little enthusiasm or personality for public life. The Revolution of 1848 struck him with a gloomy sense of foreboding expressed in the journal he kept for that year called *Souvenirs* (a kind of forerunner of Ortega's *Revolt of the Masses*). As a result of protesting against Louis Napoleon's *coup d' état* in 1851 he spent a night in prison. This embarrassment marked his permanent retreat from active political participation. His remaining years were spent in traveling and in writing his *L'Ancien Régime et la Révolution,* part of which was published in 1856. Though generally considered his masterpiece, this work unfortunately was never completed. Tocqueville died in Cannes, not having quite reached his fifty-fourth birthday.

De la Démocratie en Amérique was first translated into English by Henry Reeve (Part 1, 1835; Part 2, 1840). The re-translation by Francis Bowen (1862) was based on Reeve's text. The definitive edition of Phillips Bradley (1945) is a revision, correction and modernization of Bowen, based on the 14th French edition (the last supervised by the author). *L'Ancien Régime et la Révolution (The Old Regime and the Revolution)* was first translated by John Bonner (1856). More recent translations are those of W. M. Patterson (1933) and Stuart Gilbert (1955). *Souvenirs (Recollections)* was first translated by Alexander Teixeira de Mattos (1896), whose translation was later edited by J. P. Mayer (1948). The best edition in French is the *Œuvres, Papiers et Correspondances,* ed. by J. P. Mayer (1951-54).

ABOUT: Bradley, P. *Introduction to* Democracy in America; Brunius, T. Alexis de Tocqueville: The Sociological Aesthetician (Swedish Studies in Aesthetics, No. 1); Drescher, S. Tocqueville and England; Mayer, J. Prophet of the Mass Age; Pierson, G. Tocqueville and Beaumont in America; Diogenes, No. 33 (1961). [In French—see study by P. Marcel.]

R. A. C.

*TOLSTOY, Count ALEXEY KONSTANTINOVICH (August 24, 1817-September 28, 1875), Russian poet, dramatist, and satirist, was a distant cousin of Leo N. Tolstoy, the great novelist. His mother's marriage to an old widower was so unhappy that she left her husband soon after the birth of her son in St. Petersburg. Tolstoy's childhood was spent in southern Russia at the estate of an uncle, who was also a writer.

* tŭl stoi'

When still a child Tolstoy was presented at the Court and became one of the friends of the young prince, the future Czar Alexander II. He traveled in Italy and Germany with his mother and uncle and met Goethe in Weimar. In 1836 Tolstoy left Moscow University where he had taken courses in the faculty of philosophy and became a government official of the Russian mission in Frankfurt, Germany, and later in Russia. During the Crimean War he was on voluntary duty in Odessa, where he almost died of typhus; he was nursed back to health by the woman he later married. The marriage was very successful. He had a very happy life in every respect; his health was excellent and like the medieval Russian "bogatyry" (epic heroes), whom he describes in some of his ballads, he was tall, robust, and of great physical strength. He inherited great wealth from his uncle. He was well liked by the Czar and had many friends, among them Zhukovsky, Gogol, and Turgenev.

Tolstoy's first book, *The Vampire,* a fantasy, was published in 1841, but it was only through his poems such as "The Dragon," and "The Portrait" (reminiscent in style of Byron's "Don Juan"), published in 1854, that his name became known. Among his best known works is a series of humorous poems which he wrote in collaboration with his cousins, the brothers Zhemchuzhnikov, under the pseudonym of "Kuzma Prutkov" (1853-63) and which was followed by a school of Russian nonsense poetry whose best known exponent was to be Vladimir Soloviev, the religious philosopher. Other publications of Tolstoy include an historical novel, *Kniaz Serebryany* (The Silver Knight, 1862), written in the manner of Sir Walter Scott, romantic poems, ballads, and a trilogy (1866-70)—*The Death of Ivan the Terrible, Czar Theodore,* and *Czar Boris.* All three of the latter group are realistic historical plays.

Tolstoy considered a poet to be a priest writing under the impact of mysterious influences and thus giving the beauty of other worlds to earthly life. Many opposing forces united themselves in him. Although a proponent of art for art's sake, he also tried political satire, which he considered to be a lower type of literary genre. He was an aristocrat but at the same time a member of the intelligentsia. He disliked tyranny but admired traditions. A Slavophile, he nevertheless admired Italy, and he loved both antiquity and the Renaissance. The basis of his outlook on life was Platonic but he was also influenced by the romantic movement. His many-sided views made him independent in his outlook on life and art, and his search for goodness and beauty in all their manifestations gave an underlying unity to his work despite its eclecticism.

Tolstoy's art is full of vitality. His harmonious and noble poetry is less tragic than that of other Russian poets, and Tolstoy, whose favorite sport was hunting, wrote in a letter to an Italian friend: "It seems to me that because of this life of a hunter my poetry is almost always written in the major key, whereas my compatriots mostly sang in a minor key." Some of Tolstoy's ballads are completely in the tradition of old Russian epics. Many of his lyric poems and drawing room ballads were set to music by Tchaikovsky, Rimsky-Korsakov, Borodin, etc. In his dramatic trilogy, Tolstoy's characterization is outstanding; Czar Theodore, one of his most interesting character creations, is a perfect depiction of the weak but good monarch. Although his Kuzma Prutkov, the prototype of a selfish and trite government official, was to influence Russian nonsense poetry greatly, it was nevertheless *The Silver Knight* that became his most widely read work. It has been translated into almost all of the European languages.

Selections from Tolstoy's poems appear in English translation in *A Book of Russian Verse,* edited by C. M. Bowra (1943), in *Russian Poets and Poems,* edited by N. Jarintzov (1917), in *A Treasury of Russian Verse,* edited by A. Yarmolinsky (1949), and in *Modern Russian Poetry, an Anthology,* edited by Babette Deutsch and A. Yarmolinsky (1921). *The Death of Ivan the Terrible* appears in English translation in G. R. Noyes' *Masterpieces of the Russian Drama* (1933) ; *Tsar Fyodor Ivanovitch* has been translated by Jennie Covan (1923). *The Silver Knight* appears in English translation as *Prince Serebrenni,* translated from the Russian by Princess Galitzine (1874, 2 vols.). *A Week in Turenevo and Other Stories* was published with an introduction by George Reavey, in 1958.

ABOUT: [In Russian and in German translation —Shcherbina, V. Alexei Tolstoi.]

Y. L.

LEO TOLSTOY

*TOLSTOY, LEO (LEV) NIKOLAYE-VICH, Count (September 9, 1828-November 19, 1910), Russian novelist and ethical teacher, was born on his parents' estate of Yasnaya Polyana in the province of Tula, about a hundred miles south of Moscow. The Tolstoys were well-to-do landowners: the father had repaired the family fortunes by marrying a wealthy heiress, Princess Marya Volkonskii, Tolstoy's mother. She died when Leo was only two, and his father when he was

* tŭl stoi′

nine. The children then passed first to one aunt, then to a second, going in 1841 to live with their Aunt Pelageya Yushkov in Kazan. Tolstoy was educated at home by two tutors: first by an easy-going, sentimental German, later by a strict, arrogant but well-read Frenchman. His French education helps to explain the strong influence which French eighteenth century literature and thought had upon him. He was a mediocre student, out of lack of inclination rather than lack of intelligence. Even as a boy he manifested that love of nature which he retained all his life. He was loving and eager for affection, but at the same time rather spoiled and inclined to show off.

In 1844 Tolstoy enrolled in the faculty of Oriental languages at Kazan University, but after a year was expelled for poor work. He then entered the less-demanding Faculty of Law, but soon lost interest in his classes. He left the university to return to Yasnaya Polyana, which he had just inherited in the division of family estates. Later he regretted his lack of university education and took pains to repair it. In Kazan Tolstoy began that dissolute existence which marked the next few years of his life. He was even encouraged by his aunt, who advised him to form a liaison with a married woman in society on the ground that it would help develop his character. But Tolstoy preferred the more available women of the streets.

Tolstoy returned to his estate with projects to help his serfs. His attempts failed, however, and he soon found the country boring.

In the spring of 1851 he went off to the Caucasus with his brother, and the next year entered the army there as a cadet. Fighting in the Caucasus against the mountain tribesmen left him ample leisure. He had already toyed with the idea of writing, and now wrote a long, partly autobiographical story called *Childhood* which he sent in July 1852 to the publisher Nekrasov. It appeared the same year, arousing great curiosity concerning the unknown author. The influence of Sterne and Rousseau, Tolstoy's favorite philosopher, is marked in *Childhood.*

Meanwhile the Crimean War had begun, and in January 1854 Tolstoy was transferred to the Danube Army, and in November to Sevastopol, which was under heavy siege. His *Sevastopol Sketches* (1855-56) attracted wide attention as unvarnished accounts of what war was like. At the end of the war he was sent to St. Petersburg: there, sponsored by Turgenev, he met the literary world of the day. He did not care much for professional literary circles, however, and soon returned to his estate. In 1856-57 he took the "grand tour" of Europe, and two years later went a second time to study European educational methods. He had opened an experimental school of his own for peasant children. Like Rousseau, he opposed the use of either punishment or reward as inducement. He abolished grades and emphasized spontaneity of approach.

Dissatisfied with his bachelor life and continued libertinism, Tolstoy resolved to marry and began a systematic search for a bride. Finally, in 1862 he married Sofya Andreyevna Bers ("Sonya"), a young lady of noble birth, pretty, well educated, and a lover of music and art. She was eighteen and he was thirty-four. She was rather cold and insecure. With typical candor Tolstoy showed her his diaries, which chronicled the record of his moral lapses. This frankness shocked her and was to provide fuel for the flames of her later jealousy. Their early life together on the estate was happy, however, in spite of occasional quarrels. Tolstoy had strict views concerning the duties of a wife: she was to bear children, rear and educate them, and manage the household. She bore him thirteen children, of whom eight survived to maturity.

These years, the 1860's and 1870's, were Tolstoy's greatest period: from 1862 to 1869 he wrote *War and Peace,* and from 1873 to 1876 *Anna Karenina.* The first of these novels idealizes the peaceful life on the manor which Tolstoy himself led, but in the second the moral stresses which he was undergoing are more evident, depicted in the spiritual crisis of the hero Levin. In this period Tolstoy came to question life's meaning: searching for it, he failed to find it in art, science, philosophy of conventional religion. In despair he thought of killing himself. At the same time he and his wife were becoming estranged. His wife, who respected him as a writer, could not understand his new rôle as moral reformer. Moreover, she developed a possessiveness that tormented him. Another subject of contention between them was property and the rights to Tolstoy's books, since he had renounced rights to everything written by him after 1881.

Tolstoy's spiritual crisis came to a climax at the end of the 1870's. From 1878 to 1885 he virtually forsook artistic literature, writing treatises on his new faith, including the moving *My Confession, A Criticism of Dogmatic Theology, A Union and Translation of the Gospels,* and *What I Believe.* Tolstoy's faith is Christianity, but a Christianity stripped of all dogma: Christ is only the noblest of men. Tolstoy's ethical system emphasizes the spiritual value of labor and a life lived in close harmony with nature and the sources of man's livelihood. Violence for him is wrong, even when opposing evildoers: there are no grades of evil for Tolstoy, and one wrong cannot justify another. All concentration of power based on the threat of violence is also wrong. Hence Tolstoy rejects government for anarchy, and capitalism for a primitive agrarian communism, in which each man would provide for his own needs. Civilization as we know it is for him only an artificial elaboration which is unnecessary and even corrupting. Putting his own teachings into practice, Tolstoy began to dress as a peasant and at times to engage in manual labor, even making his own boots.

Tolstoy's ethical teachings brought him world fame and many disciples. Yasnaya Polyana became a place of pilgrimage for visitors from all over the world: among others came Chekhov and Gorky, W. J. Bryan, and Thomas Masaryk. Tolstoyan societies were formed in many countries. The young Gandhi was inspired by Tolstoy's teaching of non-resistance to evil, and the two exchanged letters.

Meanwhile, in *What Is Art?* (1897) Tolstoy elaborated a philosophy of art for his new ethical system. He taught that great art must be moral in its conception, if not specifically didactic, and must be simple enough for most men to comprehend.

Tolstoy realized that the external form of his life, in spite of his renunciation of property, still contradicted his principles. He denounced wealth, but lived a sheltered existence on the estate, which he had deeded over to his family. He attacked Czarist tyranny, but was never arrested, though his followers could have been sent to Siberia for possessing certain of his tracts. Still he supposed that to leave home would do an even greater wrong to his family. But finally he could no longer bear the hysterical behavior of his wife, who even made attempts at suicide. On October 28, 1910, at the age of eighty-three, he left Yasnaya Polyana with his physician. He had no definite goal: one plan was to join a colony of his followers in the Caucasus. On the way he caught a chill and developed fever. He was taken off the train at Astapovo and put to bed in the stationmaster's house. He died on November 7, very likely of nervous exhaustion. He was buried at Yasnaya Polyana, without Christian prayers, for he did not wish them, and in any case he had been excommunicated by the Russian Orthodox Church.

Tolstoy's physical appearance was rather plain, with his ordinary face and a flat, broad nose. In middle age he grew a long, black beard which later turned white. Dressed as a peasant, he was not infrequently taken for one. He possessed a character of profound contradictions: a deep love of reason opposed to a desire to accept life intuitively, without ratiocination; a strong sensuality at war with a puritanical temper; pride in conflict with a thirst for humility. He was rather vain about his writing, and once announced his desire to become "a general of literature." Yet he did not hesitate to denounce his earlier works when he became convinced that they were morally sterile. Physically strong, he loved exercise and the outdoors. His whole approach to life is *biological:* man is a physical animal who first of all should feel and work. In his attitude toward sex he is in conflict: he wants to regard it as part of the instinctive life of nature, but he cannot rid himself of the feeling that it is profoundly evil.

Much of Tolstoy's writing is autobiographical: the hero, whether Olenin in *The Cossacks* (1863), or Levin in *Anna Karenina*, is a part of Tolstoy himself. *War and Peace* is peopled by aspects of himself (Pierre and Andrey), or by characters modeled on his relatives. Incidents in his novels are often drawn from his life. There is rarely much artifice in Tolstoy's writing, nor even much plot in the usual sense. But he casts on his ordinary events and personages so much light that they arouse vital interest.

Tolstoy entered literature as an opponent of romanticism: to its cult of violent passions and idealized heroes he opposed the prosaic details of ordinary life. The romantic view of war and heroism is debunked in the *Sevastopol Sketches.* A faintly romantic note drifts into his work, however, in the glorification of intuitive existence which we find in *The Cossacks* and *War and Peace.* The latter is a vast work, Tolstoy's masterpiece and perhaps the masterpiece of all narrative fiction. The historical subject is the French invasion of 1812, but the book is far more than an historical novel. In it Tolstoy attempts to express the form and content of life itself, conceived as a stream of elemental experiences such as birth, growth, love, marriage, childbirth, death.

Anna Karenina is Tolstoy's most popular work, the story of a woman who leaves her husband to live with a lover. Conventionally viewed as a preachment against adultery, the work actually goes deeper: Anna's sin is not so much adultery as a superficial view of romantic love, in which Tolstoy had little faith in any case.

Tolstoy's later stories are often didactic, but some of them are little masterpieces. The greatest work of this period is *The Death of Ivan Ilyich* (1886), a vivid and disturbing view of the process of dying and its spiritual impact on an average man. *The Kreutzer Sonata* (1890) attempts to deal with the problems of sexual passion and jealousy, but its ethics seem confused. *Resurrection* (1899) criticizes the legal and penal system of modern society.

In his lifetime Tolstoy was equally esteemed as a novelist and ethical teacher. Today, however, the novelist is almost universally praised at the expense of the moralist. No doubt this is just, but it must be realized that it is the moralist with his concern for life who inspires the artist's realistic interest in depicting ordinary life. But concerning Tolstoy's place as a novelist there can be little dispute. Both in his time and today, in Russia and abroad, he is accepted as one of the greatest writers, perhaps the greatest, of the realistic novel.

The first work of Tolstoy to be translated into English was *Childhood and Youth,* in 1862. *War and Peace* and *Anna Karenina* both appeared in English in 1886. Today there are many translations and editions, and almost all Tolstoy's fiction is available in English, as well as certain of his philosophical and religious writings. The best English edition is the Centenary Edition of Tolstoy's Works edited by Aylmer Maude (28 vols., 1928-37).

ABOUT: Berlin, I. The Hedgehog and the Fox; Lavrin, J. Tolstoy; Maude, A. The Life of Tolstoy; Merezhkovsky, D. Tolstoy as Man and Artist; Nazarov, A. I. Tolstoy, the Inconstant Genius; Simmons, E. J. Leo Tolstoy; Tolstoy, Alexandra, Tolstoy. [In Russian—see studies by P. I. Biryukov, N. N. Gusev, B. Eikhenbaum.]

W. E. H.

*TOMMASEO, NICCOLÒ (October 9, 1802-May 1, 1874) Italian scholar and patriot, was born across the Adriatic from the Italian peninsula, in the village of Sebenico on the coast of Dalmatia. His father, Girolamo Tomašić, a subject of the Venetian Republic, earned his living as a modest tradesman. His mother was Caterina Chevessich, whose family originated on Brazza, one of the larger islands off the Dalmatian coast. Young Niccolò's first teacher was an uncle who was a Franciscan priest. His secondary studies were at the seminary in Spalato (Split), where he learned and loved Latin literature, especially Virgil. From Spalato he made his first voyage across the Adriatic to study law at the University of Padua, receiving his degree in law in 1822. He returned to Sebenico but was drawn back to Italy by the stimulating atmosphere of the struggle for independence. He taught for a while at Rovereto on the Tyrolean border, and worked as a journalist for Venetian periodicals. Attracted to neither of these professions, he finally migrated to Milan hoping to start a literary review. His writing at this time reveals the development of his aesthetic as well as his combative and litigious temperament. In 1825 he published in Milan *Il Perticari Confutato da Dante* (Perticari Refuted by Dante), a defense of the classical Tuscan language against the innovations advocated by Perticari and Vincenzo Monti.

Tommaseo went to Florence in 1827 to collaborate with G. Vieusseux on the review *Antologia*. In Florence he published *Il Dizionario dei Sinonimi* (Dictionary of Synonyms), revealing his great ability as a lexicographer. The preface to his work contains a tender dedication to the woman with whom he lived in Florence, Giuseppa Maria Catelli.

In 1833 *Antologia* was denounced and suppressed for publishing anti-Austrian opinions. Tommaseo now went into exile in France. This period, rich in experience, is well chronicled in his correspondence with Cesare Cantù and Gino Capponi, published in

* tŏm mä zâ′ ō

1904 as *Il Primo Esilio di Niccolò Tommaseo* (The First Exile of Tommaseo). We also have his own diary, *Confessioni*, published in Paris in 1836. In the preceding year, a work important in the literary history of the Risorgimento was published in Paris, the five volumes entitled *Dell'Italia*, Tommaseo's civil and political testament. The books were smuggled into Italian territory under a false title, were widely read in Tuscany, and influenced several generations of Italian patriots. A brief historical novel, *Il Duca d'Atene* (The Duke of Athens), was the next item from Tommaseo's pen, and in the same year, 1837, was published the first edition of his great commentary on Dante and a romantic verse tale, *Una Serva*. His novel *Fede e Bellezza* (Faith and Beauty) in 1840 is partly autobiographical, drawing on his life with Giuseppa Catelli and in France.

Tommaseo left Paris in 1840, journeying to Naples and then to the island of Corsica. Here, with characteristic diligence, he recorded the folk songs of the island, gathering them into his book *Canti Toscani, Corsi, Greci, Illirici* (Tuscan, Corsican, Greek, and Illyrian Songs) published in 1841. The Austrian amnesty of 1840 enabled him to go to Venice where his *Dizionario Estetico* was published, as well as *Scintilla* in 1841, a volume of poetry containing pages in modern Greek and Illyrian.

A speech read in Venice in 1847 calling on the Austrian-dominated government to permit freedom of the press resulted in Tommaseo's imprisonment. Liberated by the uprising of 1848, Tommaseo proclaimed his support of the new Venetian republic and was sent as ambassador to Paris to request aid from republican France. Although Tommaseo dissented with other leaders of the new republic over the annexation of the Piedmont, he worked untiringly during the siege of Venice, chronicling the events in *Venezia negli Anni 1848 e 1849* (Venice in the Years 1848-49). With the defeat of the republic, Tommaseo took refuge on Corfù. Here, in 1851, he married Diamante Pavello, by whom he had two children, Girolamo and Caterina. The memorial volume *Diamante, Madre e Moglie* (Diamante, Mother and Wife) was published in 1873. While on Corfù he wrote, in French, an essay against the temporal power of the Pope, *Rome et le Monde*, published in 1851, and the eloquent essay against capital punishment *Supplizio d'un Italiano a Corfù* (Appeal to Corfù by an Italian), published in 1855. He then left Corfù to live in Turin under the protection of the liberal monarch

927

Charles Albert. In 1859 he moved to Florence where he resided until his death. In order to feel free to speak, he refused all honors from the new Italian monarchy, continuing to voice his sometimes fiercely dissenting opinions and remaining firmly republican and federalist in his views. *Bellezza e Civiltà* (Beauty and Civilization) appeared in 1857, a four-volume annotated edition of the letters of St. Catherine of Siena in 1860, a compilation of the works of Giovita Scabrini in 1861, and *Il Secondo Esilio* (The Second Exile) in 1862. The most glorious work of his last years, rendered all the more remarkable by the fact that he was blind when he undertook it, is the great *Dizionario della Lingua Italiana,* completed with the aid of B. Bellini and G. Meini, and published in seven volumes, 1858-79.

Tommaseo's analytic genius and exquisite sense of taste are talents particularly appropriate for an annotator and lexicographer, in which work he excelled. The combination of Slavic and Italian heredity is a significant factor in his literary development. His attraction to Italy is understandable when one considers the great intellectual impact of the period of the Risorgimento on all who lived through it.

ABOUT: [In Italian—Croce, B. Letteratura della Nuova Italia; see also studies by A. Aspesi, A. Borlenghi, M. Lazzari.]

E. DE P.

*TOPELIUS, ZACHARIAS** (January 14, 1818-March 12, 1898), Swedish poet, novelist, dramatist, short-story writer, was born at Kuddnäs, an estate close to the Finnish town of Nykarleby (Finnish: Uusikaarlepyy), having a population of Swedish descent, on the Gulf of Bothnia. His father was Zacharias Topelius the elder, country-district doctor at Nykarleby. His mother was Sophie Calamnius, who was of a wealthy merchant family in the same town. He entered the University of Helsinki, where he pursued a successful academic career. In 1845 he married Emilie Lindqvist who was also of a well-to-do merchant family in Nykarleby. He took his Ph.D. in 1847, was appointed professor of Finnish history in 1834, of Finnish, Russian, and Scandinavian history in 1863, of universal history in 1876. He was president of the university from 1875 to 1878. Upon his retirement in 1878 he was awarded the title of state secretary and moved to his estate Björkudden in Sibbo (Finnish: Sipoo) parish, east of Helsinki, on the Gulf of Finland.

* tŏ̄ō pā′ lĭ ŭs

Topelius' literary production extends over several genres—verse, prose, and drama. His earliest poems and prose writings were published in *Helsingfors Tidningar,* a semiweekly paper of which he was the editor from 1842 to 1860. He published five collections of lyrics in book form (1845-89), the three first, and best, ones under the title *Ljungblommor* (Heath Blossoms). He also wrote several church hymns and revised some old ones. As a poet Topelius played on many strings. His lyrics, melodious and dulcet in tone, simple and pure in form, were inspired by Finnish folk poetry, romantic longing and love, patriotic nationalism, and a naïve and orthodox piety. In his patriotic poems he sang about the beautifully somber Finnish landscape of woods and lakes, about the poor but contented peasants, and he dreamed about a glorious future for his country.

Today Topelius is best known as a popular and fascinating story-teller and historian. His most prominent prose work is *Fältskärns Berättelser,* which he published as a serial in *Helsingfors Tidningar* (1851-66), and which appeared in book form from 1853 to 1867, and thereafter in numerous editions. In these thrilling and charming narratives, loved by every Finn and Swede, he gives a highly romanticized account of the war-drenched Swedish-Finnish history during the seventeenth and eighteenth centuries. The stories, wherein dauntless heroes perform marvelous deeds, give a highly idealized picture of the people. With naïve optimism, Topelius shows how Providence governs human destinies, punishing evil and rewarding virtue. Other novels and short stories, some of them fairly realistic, flowed from his pen.

During his latter years Topelius wrote primarily for children, publishing, among other things, four volumes of *Sagor* (Fairy Tales, 1847-52) and eight volumes of *Läsning för Barn* (Children's Reading, 1865-96). His dramatic production is unoriginal and rather insignificant.

Fältskärns Berättelser was first translated into English by Selma Borg as *The Surgeon's Stories* (1872). Translations of *Sagor* and *Läsning för Barn* were rendered into English by C. W. Foss as *Fairy Tales from Finland* (1896) and *Stories for Children* (3 vols., 1902-11). Selected stories are translated by A. Alberg in *Snowdrops; Finland Idylls for Children* (1881) and in *Whisperings in the Wind; Finland Idylls for Children* (1881), by Gudrun Thorne-Thomsen in *The Birch and the Star and Other Stories* (1915) and by C. W. Foss in *Canute Wistlewinks and Other Stories* (1927, reprinted 1928). Four fairy plays are translated by E. J. Macintyre in *Poet Lore,* XXVIII, Poems in English translation are to be found by A. L. Elmquist in *Poet Lore,* XXIV, by J. A. Judd in his collection *Under the Swedish Colours* (1911), and by C. W. Stork in his *Anthology of Swedish Lyrics* (1930).

ABOUT: [In Swedish—see studies by M. Granér, S. Lagerlöf, P. Nyberg, V. Vasenius.]

A. J.

*TORRES NAHARRO, BARTOLOMÉ DE (d. 1524?), Spanish poet and dramatist, was born in La Torre de Miguel Sexmero (Badajoz). Little is known of his life, but it is probable that he studied at the University of Salamanca. It is also probable that he was a soldier, to judge by the realistic portrayals of the military life in his *Comedia Soldadesca*. Torres Naharro was captured by Berber pirates during his youth and taken to Algiers but he was subsequently ransomed. About 1513 he went to Rome, where he was ordained, and became the protégé of Bernardino Carvajal, Cardinal of Santa Cruz. Torres Naharro was a keen observer and a severe critic of the corruption of sixteenth century Rome, and many of his verses and plays are masterpieces of invective against the evil and license pervading the court. The *Comedia Tinellaria*, presented before Leo X (c. 1516), is a stinging satire on the immorality of a Roman palace. The servants in a Cardinal's kitchen are the multilingual interlocutors and the confusion of languages is such, that in the words of Menéndez y Pelayo, "it is a play suitable not for presentation before the Pope, but in the Tower of Babel."

Torres Naharro left Rome for Naples and it was in the latter city that his collection of works, dedicated to the Marquis of Pescara and entitled *Propaladia*, was published in 1517. The prologue contains a statement of his dramatic theory, according to which order, moderation, and "decorum" are advocated for all types of plays. Torres Naharro distinguishes between two principal dramatic categories: the *comedia a noticia*, based on real events, and the *comedia a fantasía*, a work of invention with an air of reality. The *Comedia Soldadesca* and *Tinellaria* are of the former type while the *Comedia Jacinta*, *Comedia Serafina*, and *Comedia Himenea* belong to the latter. The plays *a noticia* are derived, in part, from Juan del Encina and the Italian allegorical pieces of the period, but some of the plays *a fantasía* anticipate the later cape-and-sword plays of the Golden Age. The *Comedia Jacinta* is written in the Renaissance vein of moral philosophy; the *Comedia Serafina* is a mixture of erotic ele-

* tôr' räs nä är' rô

ments and of irony after the style of Erasmus. In the *Comedia Himenea* the author reaches full maturity as a playwright and creates an authentic cape-and-sword play. The theme of honor, so often elaborated by Calderón, is sketched here in the scene wherein the Marquis threatens his sister Febea with death when he finds her with her lover Himeneo, but, as in later comedies, all problems are solved by marriage. Torres Naharro paints a dual world of masters and servants very much like that in *La Celestina*, and his technique is much more that of a pre-Lope dramatist than that of a primitive.

The *Propaladia* was reprinted in 1520, 1526, 1533, 1535, and 1545, but in 1559 it was placed on the *Index* of Valdés and was not released until 1573 in an expurgated version by Juan López de Velasco, secretary to Philip II. Juan de Timoneda appreciated the works of Torres Naharro and Lope de Vega mentioned him, but in the seventeenth century he was all but forgotten, not to be revived until Moratín discussed his works in the eighteenth century. Modern editions of the *Propaladia* appeared in 1880-1900 (2 vols., ed. M. Cañete and M. Menéndez y Pelayo) and in 1943-51 (ed. J. E. Gillet).

The *Comedia Himenea* has been translated into English as *Hymen* by W. H. H. Chambers in A. Bates, *The Drama* VI, (1903).

ABOUT: Crawford, J. P. W. Spanish Drama before Lope de Vega; also see introductions to modern editions of the *Propaladia*, mentioned above.

B. P. P.

*TORRES Y VILLARROEL, DIEGO DE (1693-June 19, 1770), Spanish author, satirist, and professor, was born in Salamanca. His father, Pedro de Torres, was a bookseller. His mother, Manuela de Villarroel, bore eighteen children, including Diego. After an elementary education in the school of Pedro Rico, Villarroel studied under Juan González de Dios, who, years later, was to be one of his colleagues at the University of Salamanca. Villarroel always held him in considerable respect. However, although his schooling was quite adequate, he paid scant attention to it. He claims he did little more than go through the motions. Most of the story of Torres y Villarroel's life is contained in his *Vida*, the first four parts of which, called "trozos," appeared in Madrid from 1743 to 1758. It is the strange story of a tall, blond, strong young man who left home at twenty and became successively a hermit, soldier, alchemist, bullfighter, doctor

* tôr' räs ē vē lyä rô ĕl'

of medicine, and professor of mathematics. Later, in 1745, he was ordained a priest. His *Vida*, which is often called the last picaresque novel, is in many respects the most unusual, for it is true. Torres y Villarroel himself was one of the great *pícaros* in the old tradition. Although licensed in medicine, he never practiced. His post as professor of mathematics at the University of Salamanca, however, he kept all his later life, even after he had been ordained.

After his death, fifteen volumes of his *Obras* were published from 1794 to 1799. Most of this material is of scant interest. Nevertheless, some of his lyric poetry is worthy of study and his burlesque poetry is almost the equal of Quevedo's. His masterpiece, *Vida*, has already been mentioned. Although it is no great literary work, there are few Spanish books written in such a natural and delightful fashion. His honesty is quite disarming. Among his other works may be cited the *Visiones y Visitas de Torres con Quevedo por Madrid* (1727-51), an excellent imitation of Quevedo's style; *Sor Gregoria de Santa Teresa* (1738); and a series of sketches of Madrid life, *Sueños* (1743), of considerable literary and historical value.

Torres y Villarroel's popularity, however—he was one of the best-known men of his time—he owed largely to his *Pronósticos* and *Almanaques*, published throughout his life under the pseudonym of "El gran Piscator de Salamanca." Federico de Onís says that he can find this type of writing cultivated by only two men before Villarroel, but that after him there are many imitators. Several of his prognostications, such as the French Revolution, were so accurate that they attracted much attention to him.

The writings of this unclassifiable, erratic, brilliant, and undisciplined man impressed his contemporaries because of their sincerity, their total lack of hypocrisy and affectation. His condemnation of the Spanish universities is justly famous. He tells us more about the aspirations and ideas of eighteenth century Spanish society than any other writer. Among the reformers of his day, only Feijóo can be considered his superior.

Always a kind man, despite his preference for satire, in the latter part of his life he gave much personal assistance and money to the Hospital del Amparo in Salamanca. He died in his beloved Salamanca.

The best editions of his works are: *Poesías*, volume LXI of the *BAE* and the *Vida*, edited by F. de Onís, in volume VII of the Clásicos Castellanos. An engraving of Torres y Villarroel appears in the frontispiece of the 1752 Salamanca edition of his works. Although not very well done, it corresponds well with the description he has given us of himself. An English translation of the *Vida*, *The Remarkable Life of Don Diego*, was made by W. C. Atkinson in 1958.

ABOUT: [In Spanish—Monner Sans, R. Introducción al Estudio de la Vida y Obras de Torres Villarroel; García Boiza, A. Don Diego de Torres Villarroel; Onís, F. de, *Introduction to* Vida, VII of Clásicos Castellanos.]

R. E. O.

*TOULET, PAUL JEAN (June 5, 1867-September 6, 1920), French poet and novelist, was born at Pau. Of old Béarn families, his parents had settled in Mauritius; his mother traced her ancestry to Charlotte Corday and Pierre Corneille. She died two weeks after the birth of her son. Paul Jean was raised by his grandfather and his uncle near Pau, and attended a Dominican school. He studied next at *lycées* in Pau, Bayonne, and Saintes, and graduated in 1885 from the University of Bordeaux. Going to Mauritius, he led there the life of a dandy, and began to use ganja and opium. Actresses appealed greatly to him. In 1888 he went to Algiers and became a journalist for *La Vigie Algérienne*, writing humorous, fanciful articles. Between 1889 and 1898 he resided at Carresse (Béarn), except for a trip to Spain in 1891, and one the following year to Paris. He read widely in Latin, Spanish, Italian, and English. Bayle's *Dictionary* was his bedside companion. Toulet especially admired Arthur Machen, whose *Great God Pan* he translated after a trip to England to see Machen in 1899.

Toulet's first book was *Monsieur du Paur* (1898), the biography of an imaginary character. The influence of Stendhal, as well as the love of farce, is evident. This was followed by *Le Mariage de Don Quichotte* (1902). But most of Toulet's energy went into night-clubbing and dissipations, while he contributed articles to *La Vie Parisienne* (1899-1907). Toulet sometimes used the penname "Maxy" for the stories which he later published under his own name. With Curnonsky (Maurice Sailland), his constant companion, Toulet published light novels under the signature "Perdiccas"; both of them worked on the assembly-line of writers for Willy (Henri Gauthier-Villars), Colette's first husband, who signed the final products. Of several novels written alone, *Mon Amie Nane* (1905) has been praised for its wit, although the chapters are arranged haphazardly.

* tōō lĕ′

Toulet and Curnonsky took a trip to the Far East in 1901-02. Toulet's jottings on this voyage were later published in *Journal et Voyages* (1934), while the latter described Toulet under the name Corzébien in *Commentaires du Night-Cap* (1911). In 1912 Toulet left Paris to stay near Bordeaux at the Saint-Loubès estate La Rafette, which belonged to an older sister. He was too ill to serve during the First World War. Toulet married Marie Vergon, who was like a nurse to him, and the couple settled in Guéthary. Writing verse especially, he contributed to "little magazines" the brief, stylized poems which were eventually published as *Contrerimes* (1921). The least fantastic and best composed of his novels, *La Jeune Fille Verte,* was published in 1920, although originally written two decades earlier. Toulet died of a cerebral hemorrhage, and was interred at Guéthary. His friend, the Polish sculptor G. C. de Swiecinski, made a death mask.

Toulet was admired by Francis Carco and other "poètes fantaisistes," who saw in him a spiritual leader. Henri Martineau, director of *Le Divan* and a foremost Beyliste, has published Toulet and also written extensively about him. *Le Divan* has published, among other items, Toulet's correspondence with Mme Bulteau and with Claude Debussy. Louis Beydts, Maurice Delage, P. O. Ferroud, and Roland Manuel have set various of the *Contrerimes* to music. A selection from his works, with an introduction, is in P. O. Walzer's *P. J. Toulet* (1954).

ABOUT: Collin, W. E. Clockmaker of Souls, a Study of Paul-Jean Toulet. [In French—Carco, F. Amitié avec Toulet; Le Divan, Juillet-Août, 1914; Dyssord, J. L'Aventure de Paul-Jean Toulet, Gentilhomme de Lettres; Martineau, H. La Vie de P.-J. Toulet; Walzer, P. O. Paul-Jean Toulet, l'Œuvre, l'Écrivain.]

S. S. W.

*"TRAUSTI, JÓN" (pseudonym of GUÐMUNDUR MAGNÚSSON), (February 12 or 22, 1873-November 18, 1918), Icelandic novelist, playwright, and short-story writer, was born at Rif, the northernmost farmstead in Iceland. His parents, cotters rather than landowners, were so poor that when Guðmundur's father died in 1879, his mother was forced to break the family up and put them out to charity. Later she remarried and reassembled the family at Rauðanúpur, a few miles west of Rif and, like Rif, on a tongue of land projecting out into the Arctic ocean. Here Guðmundur grew in-

* trû' stē

to manhood, accustomed to the wild storms, the dark winters, and the bright summers of the Arctic. He worked as a farm hand and fisherman, receiving no education beyond that which he acquired at home.

At sixteen Guðmundur set out to make his own way, becoming first a seaman and then a printer's apprentice at Seyðisfjörður and later at Reykjavík. He had learned to read and began to devour eagerly every book that he could lay his hands on. In fact, it is probable that he became a printer because that occupation seemed to offer the greatest possible opportunity to read. In 1896, in order to improve his skill as a printer and in order to see the world, he went to Copenhagen where he not only practiced his printing trade but also studied stagecraft, wrote verses, and enjoyed the intellectual life of the Danish capital. In 1898 he returned to Reykjavík where he lived until his death from influenza in 1918. Most of the year 1903 he spent in touring Germany, Switzerland, and England on a literary grant made available by the Icelandic government in recognition of his poetic and dramatic ability. From 1910 until his death he received a small pension from the government.

Magnússon's first book, *Heima og Erlendis* (At Home and Abroad), a collection of poems, appeared in 1899, followed in 1903 by *Íslandsvísur* (Poems of Iceland), another book of poetry, and in the same year by *Teitur,* an historical play in blank verse. Although many of the poems were admitted to be beautiful and although the play evidenced some talent on the part of the author, the reviews were so uncomplimentary that Magnússon published his next work, the novel *Halla,* under the *nom de plume* of Jon Trausti (Stalwart John), a name which he used thereafter. *Halla* (1906), the story of a saga-like Icelandic woman, was well received, and from then on one book after another appeared: *Leysing* (Spring Flood, 1907), *Heiðarbýlið* (The Mountain Cot, four parts, 1908-11); *Smásögur* (Short Stories I and II, 1909 and 1912, respectively); *Sögur frá Skaftáreldi* (Stories from the Eruption at Skaft-river I, 1912 and II, 1913); *Góðar Stofnir* (Good Stock, 1914-15); *Tvær Gamlar Sögur* (Two Old Stories, 1916); and *Bessi Gamli* (Old Bessi, 1918). Shortly after his death another volume of short stories called *Samítningur* (Scrapings) appeared. Moreover, he had written *Ferðaminningar* (Memories of My Trip), which was, as the title indicates, an account of his European tour of 1903. In addition Magnússon wrote articles and essays for newspapers and periodicals.

Magnússon produced poetry, plays, novels, travelogues, and short stories, his best work being in the last. For the most part his novels are based on historical events, although the treatment is rather free. They develop true-to-life pictures of Icelandic country society at the time represented, but they tend to be slow-paced, somewhat digressive, and occasionally lacking in taste. These faults can probably be traced to Magnússon's lack of formal training and to his habit of writing rapidly with relatively little revision. His short stories, on the other hand, are well told and closely knit. He reproduces to a remarkable degree the idiom of the common man.

Throughout Magnússon's writings one finds a love of nature especially in her harsher aspects, a firm patriotism but an impatience with the sloth, the ignorance, and the incompetence that the writer sees about him. He enjoys writing about the past, for there he can find men and women with whom he feels at home—men and women of heroic temperament and unflinching determination to overcome every obstacle.

His works were collected by S. Einarsson in one edition with a biography: *Ritsafn* (Collected Works, 8 vols., 1939-46). Relatively few of Magnússon's works have been translated into English. Two of his poems appear, however, in *Icelandic Lyrics,* selected and edited by Richard Beck (1930).

ABOUT: Einarsson, S. History of Icelandic Prose Writers 1800-1940.

L. B.

---

*TREDYAKOVSKY, VASILY KIRILO-
VICH (February 20, 1703-August 17, 1769), Russian poet, translator, and scholar, was born in Astrakhan in a priest's family. His father allowed him to study Latin with the Capuchin friars. Obsessed with a desire to learn, he fled in 1723 to Moscow to study at the Slavonic-Greek-Latin Academy, but by 1725 he was in the Hague, learning French from the Russian ambassador, and in 1727-30 studying theology and humanities in Paris. On his return home, finding his family dead of the plague and his property stolen, he moved to Moscow and then to St. Petersburg. After being presented to the Empress Anna, Tredyakovsky was appointed translator at the Academy of Sciences (1732). He was expected to write poems for solemn occasions and was treated like a jester at the court and once even beaten by a minister. In 1742

* trĕ dyŭ kôf′ skē

he married. Not until 1745 did he receive the rank of a professor of "Russian and Latin eloquence." Because of his quarrelsome behavior he made many enemies among literati and fellow academicians, was virtually ostracized, and in 1759 had to resign. He died in St. Petersburg in poverty and oblivion.

Much of Tredyakovsky's work has never been collected. He started writing poetry in the then accepted "syllabic" meter while a student at the academy in Moscow, and continued writing it, both in Russian and in French, while in Paris. His translation (1730) of Paul Tallemant's *Voyage a l'Île d'Amour* was not only a success and the first printed worldly novel in Russia, it was also the first large-scale attempt to secularize the Russian literary language, theoretically defended in the preface to the work. Tredyakovsky's "Ode on the Surrender of Danzig" (1734) was the first Russian classical ode, a genre which was to flourish subsequently. The treatise *A Brief New Method of Composing Russian Verse* (1735) was the first, though timid and inconsistent, attempt to create versification based on stress, which was later to dominate Russian poetry. In 1752 he revised the treatise drastically under the influence of Lomonosov's more radical ideas. In his later work Tredyakovsky suddenly turned from spoken Russian to an elaborate, ornamental, and obscure style, full of Slavonic words and inversions, and grotesquely mixed with the vernacular. Such is his 24-canto translation in verse of Fénelon's novel *Télémaque,* entitled *Tilemakhida* (1766). Tredyakovsky's other important translations are John Barclay's *Argenis* (1751) and thirty volumes of historical works by Rollin and Crévier.

Tredyakovsky was an interesting, important, and curious figure in Russian literature. This ill-starred man, the first professional and one of the very few commoners in Russian literature, combined humility with arrogance. He was sensitive but indecisive in literary matters. His bizarre career was full of insight and pioneering deeds, rarely, however, going beyond a half-measure stage, and alternating with relapses into the most antiquated practices. For almost two centuries, he was a target of mockeries and was dismissed or parodied by the majority as a caricature of a poet, though individual poets (Pushkin, Radishchev) had a high regard for him. Only recently, as the result of thorough study of the eighteenth century, has he been finally recognized as "a great innovator who did new and important things in practically all fields of post-Petrine literature," and critics have begun to find passages of genius in his uneven and verbose poetry.

A translation of one of his odes can be found in Leo Wiener's *Anthology of Russian Literature*, I (1902-03).

ABOUT: [In Russian: Russkaya Poeziya XVIII Veka, ed. S. Vengerov (1935).]

V. M.

*TREITSCHKE, HEINRICH GOTT-HARD VON (September 15, 1834-April 28, 1896), German historian, was born in Dresden, the son of an army general. He intended to become an officer, but an impairment of his hearing as a boy ended his hopes for a military career. He studied history, political economy, and law at the universities of Bonn, Leipzig, Tübingen, and Heidelberg, and from 1858 until 1863 taught history as a *Privatdozent* at the University of Leipzig. Here he became an admirer of the writer Gustav Freytag, for whose publication, *Grenzboten*, he wrote. In 1863 he was appointed professor of history at the University of Freiburg, only to leave in 1866 at the outbreak of the Austro-Prussian war because of his Prussian sympathies. He taught for one year at the University of Kiel and subsequently at the University of Heidelberg. In 1874 he settled in Berlin, where he became one of the most popular teachers of his time. During these years he also edited the important journal *Preussische Jahrbücher* (1866-89), as well as serving as a member of the Reichstag (1871-84). In 1886 he was designated official historian of the Prussian state. During later life he suffered from deafness and approaching blindness until his death in Berlin at sixty-one.

During his student years Treitschke was inspired by the teachers Ernst Moritz Arndt and Friedrich Christoph Dahlmann to devote his life to the unification of Germany under Prussian leadership. This ideal, which was later successfully completed by Bismarck, provided the focus of his life and writings. Treitschke was an outstanding patriot and ardent nationalist. Although his zeal for his program often carried him into error, he nevertheless proved to be one of the most vigorous and inspirational leaders of Germany. By his great strength of personality and unswerving conviction of the righteousness of his cause, he provided an outstanding example to his countrymen in a period rife with pessimism and weakness. According to

* trĭch' kĕ

the critic R. M. Meyer, "Treitschke stands in first place among those men, without whom the activity, hopes and certainties of modern intellectual Germany would be inconceivable."

As an historian, Treitschke's most important contribution was his *Deutsche Geschichte im 19. Jahrhundert* (5 vols., 1879-94), which covers German history to 1848. His purpose in this work was to revive a nationalist feeling in his contemporaries and to restore the pride of Germans in their history. In addition to this major contribution, he wrote many essays, of which the collections *Historische und Politische Aufsätze* (1865) and *Zehn Jahre Deutsche Kämpfe* (1874) are the most significant. He also produced a volume of patriotic poems, *Vaterländische Gedichte* (1856), and a series of dramatic sketches, *Studien* (1857).

A collection of Treitschke's essays is contained in the volume by A. Hausrath, *Treitschke, His Life and Works*, which was translated anonymously in 1914. A second series of essays also appeared anonymously in 1915 under the title *Germany, France, Russia, and Islam*. E. and C. Paul translated *History of Germany in the Nineteenth Century* (7 vols., 1915-19). The volume *Politik* was translated by B. Dugdale and T. de Bille in 1916.

ABOUT: Davis, H. W. C. Political Thought of Heinrich von Treitschke; Dorpalen, A. Heinrich von Treitschke; Gooch, G. P. History and Historians in the Nineteenth Century; Mugge, M. A. Heinrich von Treitschke; Paul, E. and C. Origins of Prussianism. [In German—see studies by N. Bussmann, E. Leiprand, T. Schiemann.]

D. G. D.

*TRIGO, FELIPE (February 13, 1864-September 2, 1916), Spanish novelist and physician, was born in Villanueva de la Serena, Badajoz. He received his early education in Badajoz and then attended medical school at San Carlos in Madrid, graduating at twenty-three. He practiced medicine for a time at Badajoz and Mérida but finally became an army doctor and moved to Seville. There he began to write for the newspapers and founded and directed a humor magazine called *Sevilla en Broma*. After a short while in Asturias, he was sent to the Philippine Islands in 1895 as an army doctor. While there, he and a small group of Philippine soldiers were ambushed. All were slain except Trigo, who, terribly gashed by machetes and grazed by a bullet, pretended to be dead and finally crawled to safety. During his recuperation he thought much about life and its meaning and at last decided to turn to literature in order to express his ideas. His chief theme was to be emancipation of wom-

* trē' gō

en. The substance of his reflections can be found in the prologue to his *Alma en los Labios* (1903-05). Returning to Spain he wrote his first novel, *Las Ingenuas* (1901), which brought him immediate success and money. He resolved to devote himself exclusively to the novel.

Felipe Trigo occupies a rather special niche in Spanish literature for he can be said to have created the modern erotic novel. His theories are to be found in *Socialismo Individualista* (1904) and *El Amor en la Vida y en los Libros* (1907). Trigo was a man with a purpose, and he tried to put his social theories into novel form; they were so startling to his contemporaries that he was at once accused of pornography. Even Leopoldo Alas called him "a corrupter of minors and of the language." His books sold extraordinarily well in spite of, or, more likely, because of, their content. He was one of the most controversial novelists of his time and has had many imitators. In his books he tries to show what he considers the idiocies of a double standard in morals and of woman's position in the modern world, particularly in regard to love and sex. His books are unusually bold and there is neither a desire nor an attempt to poetize or romanticize physical love. Mérimée and Morley say his novels are "in theme strongly socialistic or so realistic as to offend the scrupulous." He was probably influenced by French naturalism and by the Italian writer D'Annunzio. Whatever one may think about the results, there seems little reason to doubt Trigo's seriousness of purpose. Some of his chief works are: *La Sed de Amar* (1902); *La Altísima* (1906-07); *Las Evas de Paraíso* (1910); *El Médico Rural* (1912); and *Cuentos Ingenuos* (1910).

Felipe Trigo committed suicide, some say because he felt he had failed to convince society of his theories, while others claim he was motivated by a nervous condition brought on by his terrible wounds.

ABOUT: Watkins, A. T. Eroticism in the Novels of Felipe Trigo. [In French—Revue Hispanique, XXVIII (1913). In Spanish—Abril, M. Felipe Trigo, Exposición y Glosa de Su Vida.]

R. E. O.

*TRISSINO, GIANGIORGIO (July 8, 1478-December 8, 1550), Italian writer, was born in Vicenza, at that time a significant center of culture and letters under the influence of such great scholars as Filelfo and Giorgio di Trebisonda. Though he lost his

* trĕs′ sĕ nō

father at an early age, he was able to continue his studies, in which he distinguished himself. When his wife died in 1505, Trissino decided to leave his city, and began a long series of visits to centers of learning. He went to Brescia, where he was cordially received by the Gambara family, and thence to Milan into the service of Ludovico il Moro; there he studied Greek under Demetrio Calcondila. He resided later in Ferrara, associated with the court of Lucrezia Borgia, studied philosophy under Leoniceno, and wrote an amorous epistle to Margherita Pia dei Carpi. At Florence he took an active part in the debates of Machiavelli and his group, and then went to Rome to seek the favor of Leo X, the Medici Pope elected in 1514. In Rome, Trissino associated with Bembo and many ecclesiastical dignitaries, and attained renown upon the performance in 1515 of his masterpiece, *Sofonisba*. The Pope sent him as ambassador to the Emperor Maximilian and later to Charles V; he continued this service under Pope Clement VII. Trissino's second marriage, in 1521, led to friction among his children which embittered his last years, marked also by a protracted illness. He died in Rome and was buried there.

Trissino's intellectual activities, only part of which are known to us in his writings, included the theatre, in which he was an important innovator, the "question of language" then being debated, interpretation of the classics, and the epic. *Il Castellano della Lingua Italiana* (1529), a dialogue on the relative merits of the several Italian idioms, occupies a significant place in the evolution of this topic from Dante to Manzoni. Dedicated to Pope Clement VII, *Il Castellano* concentrates on pronunciation, that is, vowel quality and the treatment of the consonants, which were reflected to some degree in the spellings. He finds cultured Tuscan "without doubt the most beautiful tongue in Italy," and selects his examples, from Dante, Guinizelli, and Petrarch, set into contrast for example with the work of the Sicilian School.

Feeling that in *Orlando Furioso* Ariosto had sought to please the unworthy "vulgo," Trissino sought a more elevated epic genre in *Italia Liberata dai Goti.* He took as his guide the rules of Aristotle and the manner of the *Iliad*, but, unlike Homer, who concentrated on one critical episode, he considered his action as one of a long range, and the resemblances to the model lie primarily in certain technical effects, such as description, carried by Trissino to excessive detail, and the reconstruction of the mythological system of Greek gods now become angels. Trissino's fame depends on *Sofonisba* (1515), the first Italian tragedy in regular classical form, which reflects one aspect of the rising enthusiasm for Greek letters and was an additional stimulus to it. The great fame of this work is attested by the fact that it was chosen to celebrate the opening of the Palazzo della Ragione in Vicenza in 1562, and its enduring reputation in the minds of Voltaire and of Pope. It is based on Livy, but incorporates special effects from Sophocles and Euripides, a happy combination of historical data and dramatic embellishment telling of events in Carthage during the wars. The final poisoning, the choruses, and the laments may lack artistic effect today, but the unified and relatively simple structure had a most salutary influence. Trissino's dedication to Leo X exposes briefly his theory of the tragedy; the work is further important for the introduction of the *verso sciolto,* which from that time became the standard heroic meter. *Sofonisba* was translated and imitated many times, for example by Montchrétien and Mairet. Trissino also left a verse comedy, *I Simillimi.*

ABOUT: Herrick, M. T. *in* Essays on Shakespeare and the Elizabethan Drama, ed. R. Hosley. [In Italian—Belardinelli, G. La Questione della Lingua; Ermini, F. L'Italia Liberata di Gian Giorgio Trissino; Marchese, G. Studio sulla Sofonisba del Trissino; Scarpa, A. Giangiorgio Trissino, Poeta d'Amore.]

F. J. C.

*TURGENEV, IVAN SERGEYEVICH (October 28, 1818-August 22, 1883), Russian author, was born in the city of Orel (south of Moscow) and spent his early childhood at Spasskoye, the estate of his mother, a wealthy heiress. His father was a handsome, impecunious ex-cavalry officer, one of whose extramarital exploits was later described by Turgenev in a novelette, *First Love.* Turgenev's mother was unprepossessing in appearance and older than her husband, who did not return her love for him. A very unhappy woman, she turned into a capricious despot, capable of acts of great cruelty to her servants and to her three sons. She thought nothing of banishing two of her serfs to Siberia for failing to doff their hats when she passed them in her carriage, and she frequently whipped Turgenev for deeds which the child had not even realized were wrong. After one such whipping, he tried unsuccessfully to run away. Turgenev later immortal-

* tŏŏr gä′ nyĕf

TURGENEV

ized this unattractive woman in his short stories "Mumu" and "The Inn."

The author's early education was typical of that of a well-born Russian child of that era. He had German and French tutors, and soon learned to speak these languages fluently. He also developed a love for Russian literature from an old house-servant who read to him from the works of Derzhavin, Lomonosov, and others. When Turgenev was nine, the family moved to Moscow and he was sent to school. He entered Moscow University at the age of fifteen, but transferred to the University of St. Petersburg when his family moved there the following year, after the death of his father. In that city he met the great poet Pushkin, and his first published work, "The Old Oak," was a poem. It appeared in 1838, in the literary journal *The Contemporary,* which Pushkin had formerly edited.

Turgenev went to Germany in 1838 to continue his studies. Several of his works, including the novel *Smoke* and the novelettes *Assya* and *Spring Freshets,* are set in Germany. While at the University of Berlin, he made the acquaintance of Granovsky, Stankevich, and other young Russian "Westernizers," who were anxious for political reforms in their homeland and believed that its future progress lay in adopting the best features of Western culture and civilization. In this they were opposed by the so-called "Slavophiles," who supported native Russian orthodoxy and autocracy, viewing the West as already in a state of decay. At Berlin Turgenev became

935

a convinced Westernizer, and remained one for the rest of his life.

Returning to Russia in 1841, Turgenev tried various lines of work, including the civil service, but decided after four years to make literature his career. His poem "Parasha" (1843) was well received by the influential critic Belinsky, but subsequent efforts were failures and Turgenev was several times on the point of giving up writing. His decision to be a writer had greatly vexed his mother, who also strongly disapproved of his infatuation with Pauline Garcia Viardot, a married French actress. Mme Turgenev withdrew all financial support at this point, but when she died in 1850, Turgenev found himself the heir of a large fortune. He was also the father of an illegitimate daughter Pelageya, whose mother had been a seamstress in Mme Turgenev's service. The child was raised by Mme Viardot and given the name Paulinette.

Turgenev's first major literary success came in 1847, when *The Contemporary* published his short story about two serfs, "Khor and Kalinych." A favorable reception led him to write more short stories in a similar vein, which were periodically published in *The Contemporary* and which appeared together in book form as *A Sportsman's Sketches* in 1852. While some of his other prose works of this period *(Andrei Kolosov, Three Portraits, The Diary of a Superfluous Man)* showed the strong influence of Lermontov, Gogol, and the young Dostoevsky, *A Sportsman's Sketches* not only won him acclaim as an artist who had come into his own, but also had a considerable effect on enlightened public opinion. Mirsky has described them as "a consistent presentation of the serf as a being, not only human, but superior in humanity to his masters." Some believe that *A Sportsman's Sketches* was partially responsible for the decision of Czar Alexander II to abolish serfdom a decade later. But they also aroused the ire of conservative circles in the last years of the reign of Nicholas I, and Turgenev ran afoul of the censors when he published an article on the occasion of Gogol's death. He spent a month in semi-arrest, during which time he wrote his famous story "Mumu." On his release he was ordered to spend two years in "exile" at his estate.

Turgenev's lifelong attachment to Mme Viardot and her family, coupled with the oppressive conditions in his homeland, caused him to leave Russia in 1855. He spent most of his remaining years abroad. He enjoyed immense popularity in France and England, winning the friendship and admiration of Flaubert, Daudet, George Sand, Mérimée, Henry James, and others. Despite these Western contacts his later writings were not seriously influenced by them. Perhaps the most "Western" attribute of Turgenev's works is their balance and moderation, which contrast with the emotional extremes, the tendentiousness, and sheer bulk which often characterize the works of other, typically "Russian" writers. Turgenev's six novels—*Rudin* (1856), *A Nobleman's Nest* (1859), *On the Eve* (1860), *Fathers and Sons* (1862), *Smoke* (1867), and *Virgin Soil* (1877)—although written away from home, are all concerned with social and political issues in Russia. The first four novels are considered excellent portrayals of Russian life and people at the time these issues were making themselves felt. His Russian heroines are particularly celebrated for their positive attributes of self-sacrifice and loyalty to ideals. Turgenev's most famous "hero" was the controversial Bazarov (in *Fathers and Sons*), a "nihilist" who was drawn with such objectivity that he enraged both radicals and conservatives in the Russian reading public when the novel first appeared. Most of Turgenev's Russian heroes, however, are representatives of the "superfluous man" in nineteenth century Russian literature, following the tradition of Pushkin's Onegin, Lermontov's Pechorin, Herzen's Bel'tov, and others.

Turgenev was a tireless craftsman, and his prose is probably the most polished in Russian literature. His structure is neat, although, like other great Russian authors, he subordinates plot to character development. Although he was less successful in psychological analysis than either Tolstoy or Dostoevsky, Turgenev's other methods of characterization are many-sided and effective, and one finds few "flat" characters in his best works. His irony is subtle but devastating, especially in his portrayal of certain "refined" members of the upper classes (for example, the servant-girl's master in "Yermolai and the Miller's Wife"). He is justly famous for his magnificent descriptions of Russian nature; full of subtle detail, varied, lyrical, they rank with the best of Tolstoy's. Turgenev's concern over social injustice and his compassion for underprivileged "small people" were typical features of nineteenth century Russian realism. Some readers claim to discern an anti-Semitic point of view in his early short story "The Jew," but this story is told in the first person by an army officer, and it seems no more logical to ascribe Turgenev's personal opinions to his utterances than to those, say, of Bazarov. Although his fame rests chiefly on his novels and short stories, Turgenev's contributions to Russian drama should not be overlooked. His play *A Month in the Country* (1850), for example, contained important innovations which Anton Chekhov later adopted and developed.

Turgenev was a tall man, of aristocratic mien. In conversation, he had a disconcerting habit of fixing his interlocutor with an analytical stare, as though making mental notes to use later in describing one of his fictional characters. His relations with fellow Russians were often clouded by personal animosities. Dostoevsky detested him and attacked him in his novel *The Possessed*. Goncharov accused him of plagiarism. When Leo Tolstoy made an uncomplimentary allusion to the manner in which Turgenev was bringing up his illegitimate daughter Paulinette, Turgenev challenged him to a duel, but changed his mind after discussing the matter with him.

Many Russians accused Turgenev of being out of touch with trends and events in his homeland, but when he visited Russia in 1880 to attend ceremonies held to dedicate a monument to Pushkin, his speech on that poet's national significance was tremendously acclaimed. Three years later, as he lay dying of cancer at the home of Mme Viardot, he requested that his body be taken back to Russia and buried there.

Literary critics point to Turgenev's influence on Korolenko and Bunin, and on the Soviet writers A. N. Tolstoy and K. A. Fedin. Today Turgenev's short stories ("A Quiet Spot," "Knock, Knock," "King Lear of the Steppes," the fantasy-laden "novella" *Song of Triumphant Love,* and many others) and most of his novels are widely read in the Soviet Union, where some forty million copies of his works have been printed and sold since 1917. A twelve-volume edition of his works was published in Moscow in 1954-58.

His writings have been translated into many languages. There are two English translations of his complete works (by Isabel Hapgood and Constance Garnett), and numerous English translations (by R. S. Townsend, C. J. Hogarth, M. S. Mandell, Harry Stevens, T. W. Rolleston, W. Ralston, and others) of individual works. David Magarshack translated his *Literary Reminiscences and Autobiographical Fragments* in 1958. E. H. Lehrman translated and edited his *Letters* in 1960.

ABOUT: Freeborn, R. Turgenev: The Novelist's Novelist; Garnett, E. Turgenev: A Study; Gettmann, R. A. Turgenev in England and America; Magarshack, D. Turgenev; Wilson, E. *Preface to* Turgenev's Literary Reminiscences and Autobiographical Fragments; Yarmolinsky, A. Turgenev: The Man, His Art and His Age; Zhitova, V, The Turgenev Family. [In Russian—see studies by K. Bonetzky, N. L. Brodsky, I. Grevs, E. A. Solovyev, B. Zavtzev.]

H. W. D.

*TYARD, PONTUS DE (1521-September 23, 1605), French poet, whose family boasted many royal officials, was born at the château of Bissy-sur-Fley. His family had planned an ecclesiastical career for him, and he fulfilled their wishes by studying to this purpose at the University of Paris.

If one were to take him at his word, he was a "prodigy" who started writing poetry very early; yet his first work, *Erreurs Amoureuses,* a collection of Petrarchan sonnets and songs, is of 1549. Like his close friend and model Scève, Tyard sings of an ideal creature, the "all-Divine" Pasithée, whose love contributes to his gradual elevation to God. Unlike Scève, whose abstract poetry maintains a contact with daily reality, Tyard remains in the non-temporal sphere of speculation. The *Erreurs,* of a very complex structure, is faithful to the spirit of the humanist school of Lyon in its imitation of late medieval gnosticism, its use of obscure symbolism and allegory, and in its adaptation of the stylistic experiments of the *rhétoriqueur* school. This sentimental hermetism, often adorned with beauties borrowed from the Italian quattrocentist poets Tebaldeo and Cariteo, had a great influence on the amorous language of Ronsard and Du Bellay (antithesis, puns, amphigories, and obscurities) as well as on that of later baroque poets such as Desportes. Constantly adding to the *Erreurs* (three books in 1555), Tyard also published lyrical verse *(Vers Lyriques)* whose quality lies in his facility to organize images in a logical structure and with great rhythmical art unmatched even by Ronsard, who recognized him as one of the stars of the *Pléiade*.

In 1553 he was named apostolic prothonotary, and led in his château a life of meditation and study. He composed for Diane de Poitiers a work dealing with mythology, as well as philosophical treatises on poetic enthusiasm, time, astrology, etc.

When, around 1570, Neoplatonism became fashionable again, Tyard frequented the salon of the Maréchale de Retz and re-edited his *Œuvres Poétiques,* now augmented with neo-Petrarchan verse dedicated for the most part to the Maréchale. In 1578 he was named

* tyàr

Bishop of Châlon-sur-Saône and, until he retired (1589) to his château of Bragny-sur-Saône, was most devoted to his new office.

ABOUT: Modern Philology, 1937. [In French—Jeandet, A. Pontus de Tyard; Vianey, J. Le Pétrarquisme en France.]

M. B.

*TYUTCHEV, FYODOR IVANOVICH

(December 5, 1803-August 8, 1873), Russian lyric poet and essayist, was born in the village of Obstug in Orel province, the younger son of a family of the ancient nobility. According to family tradition, its name derived from an Italian original, "Duggi," indicating that the remote ancestor had come to Russia from abroad. Tyutchev took after his mother both in appearance and in temperament, being diametrically opposed to his father in everything but his good nature. His nervous, high-strung disposition and overdeveloped imagination were characteristic of his mother, and these qualities are keys to his creative personality.

Although he was to become one of the most famous lyricists in the Russian language, he was, according to contemporary practice, educated in French, spoke that language for the rest of his life, and wrote his letters and most of his prose in French. The most significant influence on his earliest literary development —which revealed considerable talent in childhood—was Semyon Yegorovich Raich, the eminent translator of Virgil, Tasso, and Ariosto, who supervised his education for seven years beginning in 1813. Tyutchev made such good progress that Raich presented a sample of his youthful protégé's work, a translation from Horace, to the Moscow Society of Lovers of Russian Literature. Tyutchev was then only fourteen, but he was accepted as an honorary member, and his translation was published in the Society's Transactions of 1818.

In that year Tyutchev entered Moscow University where he remained until his graduation in 1821 at the age of eighteen. He was immediately accepted as a clerk in the Foreign Office in St. Petersburg, and in the same year accompanied Count Osterman-Tolstoy to Munich as part of the Russian mission in that city.

Except for short visits to Russia from time to time Tyutchev remained abroad for the next twenty years or so, spending most of his time in Munich in various diplomatic posts. He soon became a favorite in the society life of Munich, but his social activities did not

* tyōōt′ chĕf

938

TYUTCHEV

prevent him from reading and cultivating the German literati. His close friendships included the poet Heine, whose works he later translated into Russian, and the philosopher Schelling.

In 1826 he married the Countess Botmer, widow of Peterson, the Russian minister in one of the German cities, a woman to whom he was quite devoted, and settled down to a life of literary productivity. Though his output was considerable, little of it ever got into print. In 1836 he was prevailed upon to send some of his verses to Pushkin's *Sovremennik* (Contemporary), and from 1836 to 1838 about forty of his lyrics were published in that periodical.

Vladimir Soloviev wrote: "Probably nobody has reached so deeply [as Tyutchev] to the dark root of the world's existence; nobody has felt so strongly or conceived so distinctly that mysterious foundation of all life . . . on which is based . . . the fate of the human soul, and the entire history of mankind. . . . In depicting such phenomena of nature where the dark foundation is felt most distinctly, Tyutchev knows no equal." But where Soloviev admires from the viewpoint of the age of Dostoevsky and Nietzsche, Tyutchev wrote in the age of Pushkin and the Byronic Lermontov, and while his talent in this company was unmistakable, his popularity with the reading public was negligible. He was ignored by the critics.

Tyutchev's first wife was killed in a fire in 1838, a blow which is said to have occasioned the poet's graying overnight. There seems no doubt that his veneration of his wife was sincere, but with the characteristic romanticism of his time and place, he compartmentalized his life to such an extent that he was able to carry on a liaison at the same time with another woman. Within seven months of his bereavement he remarried, this time the Baroness Dornburg, a Bavarian, in March 1839. About this time, perhaps a year or so earlier, he was transferred to Turin, Italy, as chargé d'affaires at the Russian embassy there. Homesick for his beloved Munich, he absented himself from his post without leave, and was consequently discharged from the service. He remained in Munich—his personal fortune was such that he never wanted for means—until 1844 when an article he wrote in that year, "Russia and Germany," attracted the attention of the St. Petersburg authorities. He was recalled to the capital and given a high post in the government, the first of a succession of positions which kept him in St. Petersburg for the rest of his life.

In the article noted and in two others, "Russia and the Revolution" (1848), and "The Roman Question and the Papacy," which was personally handed to the Czar himself in 1849, Tyutchev revealed himself to be a first class theoretician of the most reactionary Pan-Slavic type, and, therefore, quite worthy of official commendation and support. In 1848 he was appointed Censor in the Ministry of Foreign Affairs, and in 1857 he was made chairman of the St. Petersburg Committee for the Censorship of Literature. He was decorated frequently. Meanwhile the brilliance of his conversation, his wide experience abroad, and the other attributes of elegance and taste conferred by wealth made him a continuing favorite of the best society of his day. He had entrée everywhere.

In 1854 *Sovremennik* published a special issue including ninety-six of his poems which won the ungrudging praise of no less a critic than Turgenev. But at this time there began a long and tragic love affair with one Mlle Denisieva, his daughter's governess, which continued until 1864 when the woman died in disgrace. The forbearance of his wife during the affair only increased his intense feeling of guilt. His later years saw the production of a number of love poems deriving from this affair, and a body of political verse confirming his reactionary nationalism. He died in St. Petersburg after a stroke.

Tyutchev's reputation as a lyricist continues to this day. At least two editions of his poetical works have appeared in the USSR. A few of his lyrics have been translated by V. Nabokov (*Three Russian Poets*, 1944), including the famous "Silen-

tium" which contains the characteristic line "An uttered thought is a lie." Charles Tomlinson's translations of several of his poems were published in *Hudson Review*, Summer 1959.

ABOUT: Slavonic and East European Journal, IV (1960); Slavonic and East European Review, XXXVII (1959). [In Russian—see biography by I. S. Aksakov (Tyutchev's son-in-law) and study by G. I. Chulkov.]

L. R. & H. H.

*UBERTI, FAZIO (BONIFAZIO) DEGLI (c. 1305-c. 1368), Italian poet, born in Pisa, was a descendant of Farinata (*Inferno* X, 32). In 1336 he was in Verona, protected by Alberto II della Scala, and later entered the service of Luchino Visconti; among his more intimate friends was Bruzio Visconti. According to Villani, Fazio praised the lives and customs of tyrants and, to judge by allusions in his works, he led an agitated life and presumably suffered from hostility to his Ghibelline ancestry. He was still alive in 1368, but according to Villani died shortly thereafter in Verona. He sang of his life of exile in the poem "Vedove e pupilli e innocenti."

Fazio's poetry falls into several classes according to its subject matter. His political poems are powerful treatments of matters concerning the struggle between the Guelphs and the Ghibellines, and are especially noteworthy for his opposition to the Germans and hence for a notion of Italian nationalism within a Ghibelline reference. An important *canzone* of this type is the call to revive the party ("E vendicar Manfredi a Corradino") composed on the death of Robert of Naples in 1343; the rational matter is ornamented with allusions to astrology and with apocalyptic imagery. Fazio's *Il Dittamondo* is an allegory in the meter *(terza rima)* and spirit of *The Divine Comedy*. His *canzone* "Quella virtu" (1355) compares the glories of ancient Rome with the present disorders, and calls to Italians to restore former law through an hereditary monarchy and a free nation ("Chiuso da' monti e dal suo proprio mare"). These dreams of a united nation were shattered in 1355 by the departure from Rome of Charles IV. One should also note Fazio's call to the Pope to return from Avignon, and his *Lamento di Roma* ("Desta gl'Italiani addormentati").

Fazio's love lyrics, in the *dolce stil novo*, are esteemed by some critics second only to those of Petrarch. In a natural setting of beauty ("Nel tempo che s'infiora e cuopre

* ōō bâr' tĕ

939

d'erba . . ."), he tells of his idealized love for a young girl, Ghidola Malaspina, whom he met perhaps in Verona. His visions of her are colored by images comparable to those of Dante and of Provençal models, with praise of her eyes ("Gli occhi suoi vaghi che parean due stelle"), and his laments of constant suffering from her coldness toward him lead to conceits of death through love. He reviews stories of ancient lovers and their plight, with the fashionable mythological and allegorical ornamentation, but his sensuousness and sincerity lend particular artistry and deep expression to his verse.

> Rossetti translated two extracts from the *Dittamondo* and the long *canzone* of the portrait of Angiola of Verona.
> ABOUT: Romanic Review, V (1914). [In Italian —Levi, E. Lirica Italiana Antica; Pellizzari, A. Il Dittamondo e la Divina Commedia; Renier, R. Liriche Edite e Inedite di Fazio degli Uberti; Volpi, G. Rime di Trecentisti Minori.]

F. J. C.

UHLAND

*UHLAND, JOHANN LUDWIG (April 26, 1787-November 13, 1862), German poet, scholar, and politician, was born in Tübingen. His grandfather, Ludwig Josef Uhland, was a professor of theology, and his father, Johann Friedrich, was secretary at the University of Tübingen. Uhland attended the Tübingen elementary and Latin schools. In 1801 he entered the university for the study of law. After receiving the doctorate in 1810, he went to Paris to study French legal institutions. The chief accomplishment of the trip was, however, *Über das Altfranzösische Epos*, an original and perceptive investigation of the history of the Old French epic. In 1812 Uhland was a secretary in the Württemberg Ministry of Justice in Stuttgart. Two years later he resigned for the private practice of law.

The first edition of Uhland's poems was published in 1815. Too young for election to the constitutional assemblies of 1815 and 1817, he participated in the Württemberg constitutional struggle through his political poems, *Vaterländische Gedichte*, whose appearance in 1816 established his reputation as a poet. In them Uhland supported the Old Württemberg Party in favor of a class constitution.

He was elected as the Tübingen representative to the Third Constitutional Assembly, which met on July 13, 1819. The adoption of a constitution was celebrated by the performance of his drama *Ernst, Herzog von*

* ōō′ länt

Schwaben, which, though highly poetic, was lacking in sustained plot and stage technique. In 1820 Uhland was elected to the first Württemberg Parliament, where he championed popular rights and an independent judiciary. Shortly after, he married Emily Vischer. The relationship was characterized by harmony and friendship rather than passion.

In 1829 the senate of the University of Tübingen appointed Uhland university lecturer in the German language and literature. In April 1830 he moved to his native city, where he subsequently maintained permanent residence. The Württemberg government forced a choice between the congenial university post and his seat in Parliament, to which he had been elected on June 3, 1832, as the Stuttgart representative. On May 16, 1833, he dutifully resigned from the teaching post.

He responded to civic duty again when he was elected to the Frankfurt National Assembly in 1848, advocating an elective head of the empire and the retention of Austria in the new state. He opposed conferring the chief power on Prussia and voted against the imperial constitution as finally adopted. His speech against the hereditary office of emperor ended with the words: "Believe me, no head will shine forth over Germany, which has not been anointed with a drop of democratic oil." After the failure of the parliament, Uhland returned to private life.

Uhland is best known today for his poetry and his contributions as a scholar. He was the chief representative of the Swabian school of poets, who were distinguished by their close attachment to the still-life of their native landscape. Like many later romantic poets, he briefly wrote extravagantly sentimental lyrics in the folk-song style. But the permanent foundations of his poetry lay in the perception of the moods of nature.

Uhland's lyric poetry contains a unique mixture of composed manly strength, of melancholy, and of quiet moods. It is objective in its presentation and shows a tendency towards the epic style. Romantic motives are united with a simple, inward, yet painstaking mode of expression characterized by a sensitive feeling for style and music. Everything personal is subordinated to experiences which are accessible and shared by everyone. "Die Kapelle," "Schäfers Sonntagslied," and "Frühlingsglaube" are examples. "Der gute Kamerad" and "Der Wirtin Töchterlein" became folk songs. Uhland's forte was the ballad, which is frequently in dialogue form. The poet's knowledge of legends and literature imparted richness to the troubadour romances "Sängerliebe" and "Bertran de Born," to ballads from the Charlemagne cycle, and to "Merlin," "Held Harald," and "Taillefer." The ballads "Schwäbische Kunde," "Des Sängers Fluch," and "Das Glück von Edenhall" were written from 1829 to 1834, after which Uhland's poetic powers declined.

From the beginning he had united with his poetic activity a loving attention to the Old German language, legends, and poetry. Together with the investigations of Jakob Grimm, Uhland's work laid the foundation of German philology. The monograph *Walther von der Vogelweide* (1822), which appeared in *Schriften zur Geschichte der Dichtung und Sage,* was one of the main achievements of the growing science. *Der Mythus von Thor nach Nordischen Quellen* (1836), was one of the first works to analyze mythological concepts. Perhaps the most valuable contribution of Uhland the scholar was the collection of folk songs *Alte Hoch- und Niederdeutsche Volkslieder,* which was published in 1844-45. With scientific accuracy and poetic feeling it continued *Des Knaben Wunderhorn* by von Arnim and Brentano. The *Geschichte der Altdeutschen Poesie* (1830-31) should also be mentioned among Uhland's scholarly accomplishments.

Alexander Platt's *The Poems of Ludwig Uhland* is nearly complete and contains many excellent renderings into English verse. The best portions of W. W. Skeat's *Songs and Ballads of Uhland* (1864) are unequaled, but some poems suffer from faulty meter. *The Poems of Uhland,* translated by William Collett Sandars in 1869, contains some good verse translations. Charles Brooks' *Songs and Ballads from Uhland, Körner, Bürger, and Other German Poets* (1838) offers fluent, easy verse translations faithful to the original but is sometimes unclear about German meanings. Other translations appear in: *The Poets and Poetry of Europe* by Henry Wadsworth Longfellow (1845); *Flowers from the Fatherland* by J. P. Trotter, G. Coltman, A. M. Adams, and J. Pitcairn (1870); *Songs and Poems from the German* by Ella Heath (1881); *The White Snake and Other Poems* by M. J. Cawein (1895); the Warner Library; and *German Classics of the Nineteenth and Twentieth Centuries.*

ABOUT: Coar, J. F. Studies in German Literature in the Nineteenth Century; Hewett, W. D. Poems of Uhland; Walzel, O. German Romanticism; Modern Languages, XLII (1961). [In German—see studies by W. Bernhardt, O. Jahn, K. Mayer, F. Notter, H. Schneider, E. Uhland.]

A. M. H.

ULFELDT, LEONORA CHRISTINA, Countess. See LEONORA CHRISTINA, Countess Ulfeldt of Schleswig-Holstein

*ULRICH VON LICHTENSTEIN (c. 1200-c. 1275), German lyric poet, the son of Dietmar von Lichtenstein and his wife Gertrud, was born at Judenburg in Styria. Unlike most of the *Minnesänger,* he has given us a large amount of information about himself in his poems and there are frequent references to him in documents and in the works of other authors. He was brought up in the court of the Margrave of Istria and after the death of his father in 1219 he helped his brother in the administration of the family estates. After being knighted in 1223, he wandered in search of tournaments and adventures, many of which he describes in his poems. In 1227 he went to Rome and then started on his *Venusfahrt* or "Love Journey" through the various provinces of Austria and Bohemia. The journey is described by him in highly stylized fashion. He claims that he was true to his first lady for thirteen years. In 1240 he began another tour of adventures, the *Artusfahrt* or "King Arthur Journey" through the same provinces. Some time about this period he married Bertha von Weizenstein. Later documents tell of his connection with King Ottokar of Bohemia and of his being imprisoned for twenty-six months on charges of high treason, with the loss of much of his property. He was still fighting in 1270 but the last reference to him, the dedication of a stained-glass window by his son in

* ōōl' rĭk fōn lĭk' tĕn shtīn

his memory, shows that he must have been dead by 1277.

Ulrich's collection of songs, *Frauendienst,* finished about 1255, was arranged almost as a novel to show the theory and manners of courtly love, as exemplified in the *Minnesang,* being carried out in real life. Ulrich largely abandons the introspective and idealizing manner of earlier poets and describes, sometimes with crude realism, sometimes with fantasy, the extravagant behavior and the extreme humility which were supposed to be the characteristics of the courtly lover. The result, for the modern reader, often borders on the ludicrous. In addition to his love poetry, Ulrich wrote a few poems on the martial virtues and the *Frauenbuch* (1257) or *Büchlein,* where he attempts to give in dialogue form a theoretical treatment of the love problem.

English translations of three of his poems are in F. Nicholson's *Old German Love Songs* (1907).

ABOUT: German Life and Letters, XVII (1963). [In German—Stammler, W. Verfasserlexikon des Deutschen Mittelalters; Boor, H. de and Newald, R. Geschichte der Deutschen Literatur, II; also studies by R. Becker, K. Knorr.]

W. T. H. J.

*URFÉ, HONORÉ D', Marquis de Val-bromey, Comte de Châteauneuf** (February 11, 1568-June 1, 1625), one of twelve children of Jacques d'Urfé and Renée de Savoie-Tende, was born at Marseille while his mother was visiting her brother, governor of Provence. He was raised in Forez at Château de la Bastie, a beautiful Renaissance residence and a center of literary activity. He attended Tournon College (Jesuit), renowned for its teaching of literature, leaving in 1584. At thirteen, Honoré had to take vows as a Knight of Malta. His family strongly supported the League in the religious wars, and in 1595 Honoré was captured, his ransom paid by Diane de Châteaumorand, beautiful and wealthy wife of his elder brother, Anne. Soon recaptured and imprisoned at Montbrison he wrote his *Épîtres Moraux* (published in parts: 1598, 1603, 1608), a prose work revealing his knowledge of ancient philosophy. After the League was defeated, Anne made his peace with Henry IV in 1598, but Honoré would not. He withdrew to Senoy in Savoy where he wrote religious poetry and *La Savoysiade* (composed 1599-1606), an unfinished heroic poem on the House of Savoy. *Sereine,* begun in 1583 and

* ür fā'

D'URFÉ

completed in 1596, was a pastoral poem which d'Urfé referred to as "the story of my youth." The work was published between 1600 and 1604.

In 1592 the marriage of Anne and Diane was annulled and Anne entered a religious order. Savoy and France reconciled in 1599; Honoré was able to visit Forez where he acquired the family domain of Châteauneuf and of Virieu-le-Grand. In 1600, released from his vows, he married Diane and they traveled widely. In Paris he was reconciled to Henry IV and became the friend of notables of the day; one of his great friends was St. François de Sales. After 1614 d'Urfé and Diane lived apart, though they remained friends and visited each other.

His famous pastoral romance, *Astrée,* written between 1584 and 1589, was published in parts and awaited with tremendous interest (I-III, 1607, 1610, 1619; IV, fragmentary, and V, written from d'Urfé's notes by his secretary Baro, 1627). *Astreé* was influenced by the Spanish *Amadis de Gaul* and by the Italian and Spanish pastorals, notably Montemayor's *Diana,* but it is considered superior to them in character drawing, good humor, and social purpose. *Astrée* presents a beautiful picture of rural life in the fifth century in Forez, on the banks of the Lignon. The refined language of its discussions of gallantry and of Neoplatonic love by courtiers disguised as shepherds is explained by d'Urfé: "Tell them you live as shepherds because you love the peaceful life." France, tired of civil strife, learned from *Astreé* how to live in elegant peace.

A handsome energetic soldier, he loved all the arts. He died at Villefranche-sur-Mer campaigning against the Spanish. In his lifetime his work was widely known: German nobles formed an Academy of Perfect Lovers based on *Astrée;* salons tried to model themselves on it; playwrights borrowed from it; critics admired it. After 1660 *Astrée* was praised less but Rousseau was influenced by it. It has since fallen out of favor. Its tricentenary, 1925, saw a renewal of interest: a new edition was issued, 1925-28. Of biographies O. C. Reure's *La Vie et les Œuvres de Honoré d'Urfé* is considered the best.

English translations appeared early: *History of Astrea,* 1st part by John Pyper, 1620; *Astrea,* by John Davis, 3 vols., 1657-58.

ABOUT: De Koven, A. F. Women in Cycles of Culture; Edelman, N. Attitudes of Seventeenth Century France; McMahon, Sister M. C. Aesthetics and Art in the *Astrée* of Honoré D'Urfé; Sewanee Review, April 1900; Times Literary Supplement, June 25, 1925. [In French—see studies by J. Ehrmann, M. Magendie, O. C. Reure.]

M. A. W.

*USPENSKY, GLEB IVANOVICH

(October 25, 1843-April 6, 1902) Russian novelist and journalist, was born in the city of Tula. His early training was undertaken by his father, a minor official whose modest library, which included the works of Pushkin, Karamzin, and Lermontov, provided the first impetus to his literary development. The morbid sensitivity and the intense reaction against any form of oppression which characterized his life and work manifested itself early.

In due course he was placed in the local *Gymnasium.* During his school days the family moved to Chernigov (about 100 miles north of Kiev) where he completed his secondary education in 1861. His higher education was divided between St. Petersburg and Moscow, but his inability to maintain himself at school as a part-time proofreader forced him to abandon the university in 1863 and return to his family left destitute by the death of his father in the same year.

His literary career had already begun in 1862 with the publication of a short story, "The Idyll," in a Moscow periodical, but he was now required to divide his attention between writing and teaching in a country school in order to fulfill his responsibility to his family. His obvious talent was not to be

* ŏŏ spĕn' skĭ

denied, however, and between 1863 and 1866 *Russkoye Slovo* (Russian Word) and other periodicals continued to receive and to publish his stories of peasant life which reflected the changes wrought by the Emancipation of 1861.

His first major work and the novel for which he is chiefly remembered, *Nravy Rasteryayevoy* (The Manners of Rasteryayeva Street) appeared in *Sovremennik* (The Contemporary) in 1866, and by 1868 he had become a permanent contributor to *Otechestvenniye Zapisky* (Notes of the Fatherland), a connection which was maintained until the closing of the periodical in 1884. Here he met and came under the influence of Saltykov-Shchedrin who helped to give direction to Uspensky's nascent liberal Narodism (populism).

In 1869 he wrote a series of sketches ("Ruin") which dealt with the impact of the rapidly developing industrialization of Russia on the small enterprises which had existed before, noting the growing dislocation, unemployment, and human misery which accompanied the change. By now, in Uspensky's words, "I refuted my own biography, and my literary creation began to move forward under its own momentum. My later biography beginning around 1871 is to be found in my work. There is nothing else but literature in my life nor will there be." Uspensky's life did proceed without significant incident because he subordinated his entire personality to his writing which he regarded as his mission to the people of Russia.

In 1872 he took a trip to France where he witnessed the aftermath of the bloody suppression of the Paris Commune (1871) and met Lavrov and other émigré Russian revolutionaries. Two sketches, "The Uneasy Conscience" and "She Stood up Straight," relate the effect of his experiences in Paris, and he continued to contribute occasionally to Lavrov's publication *Forward* (published in Zurich and London), notably a piece called "You Can't Hide an Awl in a Sack" (1876), in which he attacked the Orthodox Church as supporting the worst aspects of the autocracy.

During the latter part of the decade he again turned his attention to the peasantry, writing a series of stories, "My Country Diary," and sketches ("The Power of the Soil," "Talks with Friends," "The Peasant and His Labor"), the theme of which is reminiscent of Oliver Goldsmith's *Deserted Village* in its depiction of the effect of industrialization on the rural population. He believed strongly that only work in the soil was fully wholesome, and that only through the encouragement of peasant industry and farming could the manifold problems of late nineteenth century Russia be solved. In this respect he was a thorough "Narodnick."

In the period 1880-89 he traveled extensively in the Caucasus, the Urals, Western Siberia, and the Balkans. His *Caucasian Sketches* depict the spreading impoverishment of the peasantry and express his keen sympathy for the "farmless farmers," the unemployed agricultural laborers who wandered over the land seeking work in ever greater numbers as the large estates were abandoned by an aristocracy drawn to the cities by the lure of industrial wealth.

The breakdown which had been foreshadowed in his youth finally came in 1889, and with only brief intervals of clarity, the balance of his life was spent in mental institutions. He died in St. Petersburg. His grave is marked by a statue in a Leningrad cemetery.

The friend of his later years, Mikhailovsky, wrote a critique of his work in which he praised Uspensky's writing but questioned his sketchy description of nature and minimal psychological analysis of character: "An artist of tremendous gifts, with tremendous possibilities of thoroughly artistic accomplishments, yet torn partly by circumstances, partly by his own sensitiveness and passionate interest in current events . . . Uspensky is an artist-ascetic, rejecting all luxury of embellishment which does not lead directly to his literary goal." The novelist Korolenko, also his contemporary, classed him with Chekhov and Chernyshevsky. Modern Russian opinion notes that his populism was tempered in later life by his interest in Marx, and that he was, consequently, able to broaden his outlook beyond the narrow horizons of the anti-industrial peasantry. Lenin praised his incisive depiction of the harsh realities of peasant oppression, and Plekhanov was fond of citing examples from Uspensky's works.

A new edition of Uspensky's works was published by the Soviet Academy in 1941.

ABOUT: [In Russian—see studies by I. Kubikov, V. Cheshikhin, A. S. Glinka.]

L. R. & H. H.

VAJANSKÝ, SVETOZÁR HURBAN. See HURBAN VAJANSKÝ, SVETOZÁR

*VALDÉS (or VALDESIUS or VALDESSO), JUAN DE (c. 1495-1541), Spanish theologian and philologist, was born in Cuenca, a younger son of Fernando de Valdés, hereditary councilman of the same town. He was the brother, probably the twin brother, of the writer Alfonso de Valdés; their ideological and literary careers reveal intimate affinities, despite their early separation. It is possible that they both received their pre-university education from the Italian humanist Pedro Martir de Anghiera. By 1524 Alfonso had joined the cosmopolitan chancellery of the Emperor Charles V, and Juan had gone to the small Castilian town of Escalona, in the retinue of Don Diego López Pacheco, Marquis of Villena. In this setting he ceased to be a voracious reader of the then very popular romances of chivalry, and was profoundly influenced by the devout atmosphere of religious revival, known as *iluminismo*, surrounding the old Marquis. The mystical sermons of Pedro Ruiz de Alcaraz (soon to be tried by the Inquisition) and the reformational writings of Erasmus made the most lasting impression on the young man.

From Escalona Juan de Valdés went to the University of Álcala, the Spanish center of Scriptural humanism; he studied there with Juan de Vergara and corresponded with Erasmus. In 1529, the same year in which his brother Alfonso, "more Erasmist than Erasmus himself," published a famous dialogue defending the Emperor's sack of Rome two years earlier, Juan published anonymously his *Diálogo de Doctrina Cristiana*, which he dedicated to the Marquis of Villena.

This work, the only one which Juan de Valdés published during his lifetime, contains most of his essential religious ideas; it typifies the Spanish synthesis of native Semitic-derived *iluminismo*, comparable to English Quakerism, and the more humanistic Christianity of Erasmus' *Enchiridion Militis Christiani*. Without any of Erasmus' ironic attacks upon external observances, Juan de Valdés' *Diálogo de Doctrina Cristiana* advocates a renewed life of prayer and inward piety; despite an un-Erasmian awareness of the sinful perversity of the human will, Valdés urges the Christian to strive for perfection, peace, and universal love. All of this is expressed in the form of a catechetical dialogue between an ignorant priest, a pious monk, and the late Archbishop of Granada, Fray Pedro de Alba, who expounds the Creed, the Commandments, the Lord's

* väl däs'

Prayer, etc. The spiritual tradition here synthesized was shortly to produce the great saints of Spanish mysticism.

But the Spanish Inquisition ordered revisions. In 1531 we find Juan de Valdés as a gentleman at Clement VII's papal court. In 1535, with the advent of a new pope, he established his residence in Naples, where he played the dual rôle of imperial agent and religious leader. The group which he influenced religiously was small but select; some of its clerical members eventually became Protestants, but most of them were aristocratic laymen and laywomen, such as Julia Gonzaga and Vittoria Colonna. His major religious writings dating from this period are the *Alfabeto Cristiano*, in the form of a dialogue with Julia Gonzaga (published in an Italian version in 1546 and, by Croce, in 1938) and *Ciento Diez Consideraciones Divinas* (in Italian, 1550); he also wrote Scriptural commentaries and translations.

During this same final period of his life, in 1535-36 he composed his philological masterpiece, *Diálogo de la Lengua* (first published in 1737). Valdés and three friends, following the example of Bembo and anticipating Du Bellay, discuss, criticize, and defend the language and literature of Spain. Morphology, spelling, vocabulary, and style are discussed with an erudition that is tempered by common sense; moderation and simple elegance characterize Valdés' Horatian standards.

At Valdés' death in 1541, Fray Luis de León (see sketch above) was fourteen years old: together they represent perfectly the Christian Renaissance of sixteenth century Spain.

Valdés' *Hundred and Ten Considerations* (translated by N. Ferrer) was published at Oxford in 1638; his other religious works were published in English during the nineteenth century, e.g., *Commentary upon St. Paul's Epistle to the Romans* translated by J. T. Betts (1883).

About: Longhurst, J. E. *Erasmus and the Spanish Inquisition*; Wiffen, B. *Life and Writings of Juan de Valdés*. [In Spanish—Bataillon, M. *Erasmo y España*; Ricart, D. *Juan de Valdés y el Pensamiento Religioso*. In Italian—Cione, E. *Juan de Valdés: la sua Vita e il suo Pensiero Religioso*.]

E. L. R.

*VALERA Y ALCALÁ GALIANO, JUAN (October 18, 1824-April 18, 1905), Spanish novelist and man of letters, was born in the city of Cabra, province of Córdoba, of a proud but impoverished aristocratic family. His mother was Doña Dolores Alcalá-Galiano, marquesa de La Paniega, and his father

* vä lä′ rä ē äl kä lä′ gä lyä′ nō

Don José Valera y Viaña. Quite early in life Valera moved to Madrid and started a long diplomatic career. Under the ministry of the famous poet and dramatist the Duque de Rivas he was appointed second secretary to the Spanish legation in Naples (1847). In 1850 he was transferred to Lisbon, in 1851 to Brazil, in 1854 to Dresden. In 1857 he was sent on a special mission to Russia and in 1865 he was minister plenipotentiary to Frankfurt. In 1867 he married Dolores Delavat; and, after the fall of Isabella II in the Revolution of 1868, he became undersecretary of State and member of the deputation that offered the Spanish crown to Amadeo of Savoy. In 1881 he returned to Lisbon, and from 1883 to 1886 was minister to Washington. In 1886 he was transferred to Brussels and in 1895 was ambassador to Vienna. He was also member of several cabinets and was made lifetime senator.

But the diplomat existed side by side with the exquisitely refined humanist and *bon vivant*. And although he lamented that he had wasted his youth in "fiestas y tertulias" and that his diplomatic work left him little time for literary creation, J. D. M. Ford has said of him: "As a result of his great experience gained in the disillusioning school of diplomacy, Valera is one who never lets his feelings run away with him; we are sure that in him the mind is always in control of the heart." Valera's first novel, *Pepita Jiménez* (1874), has remained his most popular despite the lament that it did not earn enough to buy his wife an evening dress. In this ironic, slightly Voltairean work, a student for the priesthood, Luis de Vargas, finds that despite his lofty aspirations of devoting his life to the greater glory of God, the call of the flesh is stronger, and he marries the pretty young widow who gives her name to the novel. Gerald Brenan says: "The gradual awakening of the young man's love, the sophistries he uses for concealing it from himself and the opposition it finally encounters in his religious scruples are conveyed with a fine truth and subtlety." His next novel, *Las Ilusiones del Doctor Faustino* (1875), suffers when compared with the first novel. *El Comendador Mendoza* (1877), however, is a much more impressive work; like *Pepita Jiménez* it is placed against the background of a small town in Andalusia, but this time during the last third of the eighteenth century, and concerns mainly the conflict between a worldly skeptic and an authoritarian woman over the happiness of their illegitimate daughter. This was followed by a minor effort, *Pasarse de Listo* (1878), and then the next year by *Doña Luz* which Aubrey Bell qualifies as "too evidently the creation of Valera's brain, unreal and idealized." *Doña Luz* concerns the tragic passion of Padre Enrique for a young woman. The problem that had been so enchantingly resolved in *Pepita* ends here in frustration and misery for both lovers. *Juanita la Larga* (1895) is a delightful story set against a background of Andalusian folkways, and was followed two years later by *Genio y Figura* which Havelock Ellis found to be "the last in date of Valera's great novels, the most mature, the most daring, perhaps the finest." Valera's last novel, *Morsamor,* was published in 1899.

Valera also had a distinguished career in other fields of literature. Although as a young man he had dreamed of being a poet, his verses are of little or no value. As a critic, however, he occupies a high place in Spanish letters. He was steeped in the Spanish classics and had a fervid interest in the social, philosophical, and political works published abroad. He wrote essays, reflections and commentaries on foreign literatures: his *Americanas* are concerned with the literature of Spanish America. Other books of criticism, such as *De la Naturaleza y Carácter de la Novela, Apuntes sobre el Nuevo Arte de Escribir Novelas, Del Romanticismo en España y de Espronceda, La Metafísica y la Poesía,* flowed from his pen. He was involved in literary polemics and from 1901 to 1904 he compiled the five volumes of *Florilegio de Poesía Castellana del Siglo XIX.* He was, in addition, an indefatigable writer of letters, both public and private; he also wrote delightful short stories and philosophical dialogues, and translated *Daphnis and Chloe* and parts of *Faust* into Spanish. His last years he spent in Madrid, a victim of progressive blindness. When he died at eighty he had the reputation of an Olympian.

Pepita Jiménez was translated by Maurice Francis Egan (1886) with an introductory essay, and by M. J. Serrano (1891) who also translated *Doña Luz* (1891) and *Comendador Mendoza* (1893). Extracts from *Pepita Jiménez* and *Commander Mendoza,* along with a biographical and critical sketch by W. H. Bishop are to be found in the Warner Library.

ABOUT: Fishtine, E. Don Juan Valera, the Critic; *Introduction to the school edition of* El Comendador Mendoza (ed. R. Schevill); *Introduction to the school edition of* Juanita la Larga (ed. R. Lansing); Hispania, XLIII (1959); Southwest Review, VIII (1922). [In Spanish—see studies by M. Azaña, C. Bravo Villasante, A. Jiménez.]

M. N.

*VALLA (DELLA VALLE), LORENZO (1407-August 1, 1457), Italian humanist, was born in Rome of parents from Piacenza. He studied in Rome under Aurispa, and hoped for a career as papal secretary. Still young, he composed *De Comparatione Ciceronis Quintilianique,* now lost, in which he showed his power of persuasion and speculative reasoning, but especially his personal and nontraditional preference for Quintilian. This work illustrates Valla's polemics and his desire to reform current methods of analysis of the classics, provoking repeated hostility among traditionalists. He left Rome for Piacenza and then for Pavia, where he composed *De Voluptate* in 1431, revised a year later, to meet hostile criticism, as *De Voluptate ac de Vero Bono.* The violence of his *Epistola de Insigniis et Armis,* directed against judicial procedures of the moment, obliged him to flee to Milan and Florence. Valla's most active period opens with his service as secretary of Alfonso of Aragon, whose history he wrote in 1445. He was then attracted to Rome where he established himself in the papal services in 1448, and for Nicholas V he made Latin translations of Thucydides and of Herodotus, which again led to virulent disputes, especially with Poggio Bracciolini in 1451; his most important translation, of the *Iliad,* remained unfinished.

De Voluptate (1431) is an important humanistic tract devoted to analysis of pleasure, after the general attitudes of antiquity and in contrast to medieval asceticism. Written when Valla was twenty-six, its aggressive tone aroused strong hostility, but the work served to separate the sacred from the profane and thus establish a humanistic field of investigation. In dialogue form, Valla presents three significant humanists: Niccoli as a Christian, Bruni as a stoic, and Beccadelli as an Epicurean, each defending his particular point of view; of these Beccadelli is the youngest and symbolizes modern thought. The third book, on Christian asceticism, is particularly forceful, and considers God as the source of the greatest virtue and highest pleasure. Valla speaks against the idolatry of the ancients, and recommends attainment of beatitude through full and complete living.

Valla's masterwork is his *Elegantiarum Latinae Linguae Libri VI,* whose lasting reputation is attested by some sixty editions published from 1471 to 1536. Here he elaborates the method of the earlier *De Comparatione,* opposing archaic notions and founding a philological or objective method to replace the

* väl' lä

VALLA

empirical approach of the earlier humanists. Seeking closer appreciation of style and grammar, and using comparative estimates of the merits of the ancient writers, Valla identified Rome's greatest glory with the Latin language. He condemned medieval and ecclesiastical styles and established rules for elegant writing which did much to set Cicero and Quintilian in the primary position they long held. The composition of the *Elegantiae* falls in the years 1435 to 1444.

Valla's other works illustrate his philological method and the primacy of reason and knowledge over that of legendary authority and abstract systems. *De Collatione Novi Testamenti* includes commentaries; *De Falso Credito* deals with the "Donation of Constantine," hotly discussed for many centuries, and *De Libero*, *Arbitrio* and *Dialectice Libri Tres* with these special topics.

Valla's *Opera* were printed in 1540, and reprinted in 1963; translations include *Il Piacere* in 1848 *(De Voluptate)*, Italian version of *Les Apologues* in 1877, *La Donation de Constantin* in 1879, and C. Coleman's English translation of this last, in 1922.

ABOUT: Whitfield, J. H. Petrarch and the Renaissance. [In Italian—Invernizzi, G. Il Risorgimento; Mancini, G. Vita di Lorenzo Valla; Rossi, V. Il Quattrocento; Studium, LVII (1961).

F. J. C.

---

*VALLÈS, (LOUIS) JULES (June 11, 1832-November 14, 1885), French novelist and journalist, was born at Le Puy, in the Velay region. He was one of seven children born to Jean Louis Vallez and Julie Pascal.

* và lĕs'

(He preferred the more euphonious spelling of the name.) The family was very poor, for Jean Louis was an ill-paid, sometimes unemployed, schoolteacher. He was out of work between 1833 and 1838. The family environment was an unhappy, harsh, even cruel one. Jules attended school at Le Puy (1840), Saint-Étienne (1841-44), and Nantes (1845-48). In 1848 he went to Paris to study at the Sorbonne, and, an ardent republican, followed Michelet's course, while interesting himself in politics. Fearful of being compromised by Jules' political sympathies, his father had him consigned for two months, at the beginning of 1851, to the Nantes mental institution. Then Jules studied law for a year, but gave that up. He spent a year as supervisor in a Caen school; in 1857 he contributed to a satirical little manual, *L'Argent*. While employed in a government office (1860-64) he wrote numerous articles for many leftist newspapers and magazines. In 1865 he published several as *Les Réfractaires;* he has since been associated with this epithet.

The following year saw the publication of *La Rue,* from chronicles especially in Villemessant's newspaper *L'Événement*. Vallès founded a newspaper which he named *La Rue* (1867-68). In 1868 he was twice sent to prison for slandering the police and the government. The following year he founded *Le Peuple,* and in 1871 *Le Cri du Peuple*. A member of the Commune, in 1871 Vallès fled to England; he contributed to French newspapers from abroad. The first edition (1879) of his autobiographical *Jacques Vintras* appeared under the pseudonym of "Jean La Rue" until the amnesty of 1880 permitted his return and the mention of his real name. The first and second parts of *Jacques Vintras* —*L'Enfant* and *Le Bachelier* (1881)—are dedicated to tyrannized and impoverished youth; the concluding part, *L'Insurgé,* published posthumously (1886), is dedicated to the Communards. Upon his death from diabetes, his burial at Père Lachaise cemetery became a Communard demonstration, attended by some 60,000 followers. Vallès has left a reputation as a powerful polemicist, with a virulent style. Against the social order, against the academic, against the lot of the child brutalized by tyrannical parents, he was appreciated by the Goncourt brothers, by Zola, by some few dissidents.

Vallès' major works have been edited by G. Gille (1953). All of *Jacques Vintras* has been translated into Russian, *L'Insurgé* into Italian and Spanish.

ABOUT: French Review, March 1939. [In French—Bourget, P. Études et Portraits, I; Gille, G. Jules Vallès, 1832-1885; Hirsch, M. L. Jules Vallès l'Insurgé; Rouchon, U. La Vie Bruyante de Jules Vallès; Zévaès, A. Jules Vallès, Son Œuvre.]

S. S. W.

VAN DER NOOT, Jonker JAN. See NOOT, Jonker JAN VAN DER

*VAN HASSELT, ANDRÉ (January 5, 1806-December 1, 1874), Belgian poet and librettist, was born in Maestricht. For almost thirty years he was inspector of the elementary school system. Although he was a prolific writer, he did not find encouragement or appreciation in his country, and his work did not become known until after his death in Saint-José-ten-Noode, at sixty-eight. In 1834 he collected in *Primevères* the lyrics which so far had appeared in journals and literary magazines. From then on he published in great quantities. He was greatly influenced by Victor Hugo, Laprade, and Sainte-Beuve. His main work is an epic, mixed with dramatic dialogue, ballades, and elegies, and given the name of *Les Quatres Incarnations du Christ.* In this sonorous long poem Van Hasselt treats the successive stages of a social regeneration, determined, as he sees it, by the manifestation of the Christian spirit in the great events of history. Van Hasselt also wrote a series of studies on rhythm in order to show the necessity of appropriating the French accent for all the diverse musical accent formulae. These were set to music by Jules Massenet. His interesting work was received in Belgium with great indifference, but outstanding foreign musicologists hailed his work. A complete edition appeared in Brussels (1876-80).

The movement of *La Jeune Belgique,* which in the 1880's endeavored to bring new life to literature, considered Van Hasselt as one of the few of its predecessors who knew what style was.

ABOUT: [In French—Hanlet, C. Les Écrivains Belges Contemporains; see also studies by L. Alvin, A. Drury, M. Reichert.]

H. B.

* vän häs′ ĕlt

*VAN LERBERGHE, CHARLES (October 21, 1861-October 26, 1907), Belgian dramatist and poet, was born in Ghent. His father died in 1868, and his mother, a passionately and gravely pious woman, brought

* vän lâr′ bĕrg

him up until he was fourteen. He then became a student at Saint Barbara College in Ghent. Later, he traveled in England, Germany, and Italy. During a trip to Paris he published some of his poetry in the magazine of the symbolist movement, *Le Pléiade* (1886). Most of his life he lived in Brussels until he moved to Bouillon at the Semoise. He had great esteem for the old Flemish school of painters and for the pre-Raphaelites. Although he was influenced by German and still more by English literature, his work was admirably original. In *Entrevisions* (1897), a collection of poems, he expressed the dreams and the unrest of his youth. His main work is *La Chanson d'Eve* (1904), a long poem that belongs beyond any doubt to the best that French symbolism could produce in Belgium. Purity and clarity of style and language are the outstanding characteristics of this work. In 1889 he wrote a drama, *Les Flaireurs,* which was printed in the *Wallonie,* one of the magazines to which he contributed. Some of his work also appeared in *La Jeune Belgique.* This prose drama may have been greatly influential on Maeterlink's *Intruse* which appeared in 1890 and which is generally regarded as the *avant-garde* piece of the symbolist movement. *Pan* (1906) was a satirical comedy full of lyrical power in which the poet exposed the vice of hypocrisy. Van Lerberghe received his doctor's degree from the University of Brussels in 1894. He died in that city at the age of forty-six. The poet F. Severin published *Lettres de Charles van Lerberghe* in 1924. The volume *Contes hors du Temps,* which has all of Van Lerberghe's prose writings, was published in 1931.

ABOUT: Turquet-Milnes, G. Some Modern Belgian Writers. [In French—Christophe, L. Charles van Lerberghe; Mercure de France, CCCXLIII (1961).]

H. B.

VARAGINE, JACOBUS DE. See JACOBUS DE VORAGINE

*VASARI, GIORGIO (July 30, 1511-July 27, 1574), Italian painter, architect, and art historian, was born in Arezzo, the first of six children of Antonio Vasari. The family name is said to have stemmed from their ancestral craft of pottery making. The most distinguished of the progenitors of the Vasari family was the painter Luca Signorelli (the son of Giorgio's great-grandfather's sister). In his autobiographical memoir Giorgio traces

* vä zä′ rē

VASARI

his own initiation into the mysteries of the painter's art to a boyhood visit to the home of the ancient Signorelli. According to this account, the octogenarian painter, hearing the little boy discourse on his love for drawing, advised that he be given instruction immediately. Giorgio began his training under a French master of stained glass, Guillaume de Marcillac. When he was thirteen he was taken to Florence by Cardinal Passerini, tutor to the Medici princes, to be a protégé of the Medici House. Here for a time he was a pupil of Michelangelo, before that master was summoned to Rome. This apprenticeship began a lifelong friendship. Among Giorgio's other teachers was Andrea del Sarto, to whom he was introduced by Michelangelo, and who later became the subject of one of his most memorable literary portraits.

Young Vasari's career and fortunes fluctuated with the unstable political situation of the cinquecento. In May 1527 the Medicis were expelled from Florence. This reverse, followed by the death of his father from the plague, brought about Giorgio's return to Arezzo, where he found that his brothers and sisters had been left in the care of an uncle. For a time he earned a hand-to-mouth existence painting frescoes for the villagers. The next years were peripatetic ones, spent successively in Florence, Pisa, Bologna, then Florence again, where he painted once more for the Medici family under the patronage of Cardinal Ippolito, and subsequently established himself as a court painter to Duke Alessandro. The Duke, however, was assas-

sinated early in 1537, and Giorgio, once more patronless, fled again to his native city.

After a respite in a hermitage near Arezzo, Vasari decided that he had had enough of court life, and set out on a career as a "free lance" painter. His material success is attested by his purchase of a house in Arezzo in 1540. In 1543 he made an extensive tour throughout Italy, investigating the work of his forebears, and collecting the data that later were incorporated into his *Vite dei Più Eccellenti Pittori* .... According to his memoirs the plan for this ambitious work grew out of a conversation with Cardinal Farnese at Naples in 1544. The writing occupied him for the next three years. However, it was not until 1551 that the *Vite* was published, the manuscript first having been edited by Vasari's friend Annibale Caro, a priest who may also have collaborated on the writing.

Vasari's *Lives of the Painters,* as it is now known throughout the English-speaking world, is not only a literary portrait gallery of the great masters of Italian painting, sculpture, and architecture, but a pioneering venture as well into the then new fields of art history and connoisseurship. These life histories are a series of exempla—moral and aesthetic—intended by their author to enable contemporary artists "more easily to recognize the progress of the renaissance of the arts, and the perfection to which they have attained in our time." At the same time Vasari thought himself to be performing a service to posterity by preserving the memory of the great ages of Italian art against the time when the works themselves might be destroyed by the ravages of time, or man's negligence. It is true that flamboyant and inaccurate as Vasari is from the point of view of modern scholarship, many lesser figures would have been lost to oblivion were it not for his *Vite,* and we owe to him besides our knowledge of many works of art that have not survived in perfect form. The poet Robert Browning utilized Vasari for three of his great poems on Renaissance artists: "Fra Lippo Lippi," "Andrea del Sarto," and "Old Pictures in Florence."

The year before the publication of his *Vite* Vasari was married to Niccolosa Basci, daughter of a prominent Arezzo family. The couple had no children. The marriage appears to have been a happy one, though "Cosina" had reason to complain of their frequent separations, owing to Giorgio's roving professional life. He had met his wife through his friend Cardinal Del Monte, and repaired to Rome in the hope of securing the patronage of the Cardinal upon his election as Pope under the name of Julius III. Disappointed in this expectation, he left Rome in 1554 for Florence, where he entered into the service of Duke Cosimo, to whom he became architectural adviser. During this period he remodeled the Palazzo Vecchio at Florence, designed the Uffizi and the dome of the Umilità at Pistoia, among other achievements. In 1564 he prepared the decorations for the funeral of Michelangelo.

In 1566, on a holiday from his service to Duke Cosimo, Vasari made another tour of Italy, which provided him with material for a second edition of the *Vite*, published in 1568. Subsequently he divided his time between Florence, where he painted the cupola of the Duomo, and Rome, where he was appointed by Pope Pius IV as chief architect of Saint Peter's (in succession to Michelangelo), and was also commissioned to paint the Hall of the Vatican.

The concentrated activity of these last years strained Vasari's health to the extreme. He died just before reaching his sixty-third birthday and is buried in the Pieve of Arezzo, in a tomb of his own design. The altarpiece contains portraits of himself and his wife, also from his hand.

Lives of the Painters, Sculptors and Architects was first translated into English by Mrs. Jonathan Foster (1850), and this translation was later published by Simon and Schuster in abridged form (1946). The translation by A. B. Hinds first appeared as one of the Temple Classics (1900), and was subsequently reprinted in Everyman's Library (1927). A more recent translation is the selection prepared by Emma Louise Seeley for Noonday Press (1957). The best complete Italian edition of Vasari is *Le Opere,* ed. by G. Milanesi in 9 volumes (1878-85). A recent Italian edition of *Le Vite* is that of Carlo L. Ragghiante (Milan, 1942-49).

ABOUT: Carden, R. The Life of Giorgio Vasari; *Introduction to* Lives of the Painters, Sculptors and Architects (Everyman's ed.); Panofsky, E. Meaning in the Visual Arts; Rud, E. Vasari's Life and Lives; Warner Library, XXV.

R. A. C.

*VASCONCELLOS, JORGE FERREIRA DE (c. 1515?-c. 1563), Portuguese playwright and novelist, whose birthplace is unknown, was a well-educated courtier of King John III, to whose eldest son he dedicated his first play, *Eufrosina.* Its setting—Coimbra—suggests that he studied there. Till 1540 he served Prince Edward as a page. Then he became Secretary of the Treasury, and after 1563, of the India House. He married

* vàsh kŏn sĕ' lōōsh

Ana de Sousa. Their son Paulo died in the fateful battle of Alcacer Kebir.

Vasconcellos left three plays in prose—*Eufrosina* (composed between 1537 and 1543; published in 1555), *Ulisipo* (written c. 1554; first known edition, 1618), and *Aulegrafia* (written c. 1555; published in 1619). He also wrote a novel, *Memorial da Segunda Távola Redonda* (1554?; first known edition, 1567). His *Obras Morais* have disappeared. His novel is one of many written at the court of John III to remind the nobles of chivalrous ideals in a commercial age. The interspersed ballads make it lyrical. It is even more curious in that it presents King Arthur's knights in the company of gods and nymphs of classic mythology and of the Portuguese gentlemen who actually jousted in a tournament held in 1552 near Lisbon.

Vasconcellos is better remembered for the *Eufrosina,* a novel in dialogue rather than a play for the stage. Some of its scenes still read well, thanks to the witty portrayal of the life of young noblemen, students, professors, tradesmen, and washerwomen in the university town of Coimbra. Abundant allusions, vocabulary, and proverbs make it a mine for lovers of the Portuguese language, for whom the author wrote at a time when many preferred Castilian. Still, *Eufrosina* is Spanish in concept, being a learned and chaste offspring of the famous *Celestina.* Both dramatize the irresistible power of young love. The Portuguese presents two go-betweens, the coquettish but honest Sylvia and the disreputable professional Philtra. With Sylvia's aid, her cousin, poor Zelotypos, meets and conquers Euphrosyne, a nice, motherless girl, while her father is away on a pilgrimage. The sentimental beau also receives advice from a rakish friend, Kariophilos, "lover of wenches," who is Philtra's customer. Both men get married, Zelotypos happily to desirable Euphrosyne, his flippant friend unwillingly to a convert's clever daughter. The Greek names betray the author's admiration for ancient comedy.

Vasconcellos' other two plays introduce different segments of Portuguese society. Through the love intrigues of a middle-class family, we meet the citizenry of Lisbon in *Ulisipo* (the learned name of the city). A fading love provides the plot of *Aulegrafia,* wherein we see the courtiers pursue their favorite pastimes, love-making and duels of wit in discussing love, poetry, the merits of Spanish versus Portuguese, etc.

Only *Eufrosina* was widely read. But the churchmen clipped Vasconcellos' wings when they put *Ulísipo* on the Portuguese Index in 1561, and *Eufrosina* likewise in 1581. The poet Rodrigues Lobo rescued the latter through a softened adaptation (1618). Camões parodied *Eufrosina;* Lope de Vega admiringly improved on it with his *Dorotea;* and Quevedo edited it.

None of Vasconcellos' works have been translated into English. Lobo's adaptation of *Eufrosina* can be read in the Spanish of Fernando de Ballesteros (1631).

ABOUT: Bell, A. F. G. *Prologue to* his edition of the Eufrosina of 1561. [In Spanish—Asensio, E. *Prologue to* a critical edition of Eufrosina. In Portuguese—Moisés, M. A. Novela de Cavalaria no Quinhentismo Português.]

G. M. M.

*VAUVENARGUES, LUC DE CLAPIERS, Marquis de** (August 16, 1715-May 28, 1747), French moralist, was born at Aix-en-Provence, where his father was a local "mayor," and took his name from the family estate near that city. His life and thoughts remain veiled by mystery; we know that at the age of fifteen he discovered Plutarch's *Lives* and was deeply affected by them and by Seneca. He entered military service, took part in the Italian campaigns in 1733 and 1735, and in 1740 went to Paris, largely to escape from the stilted milieu of his family. Again in service, his legs were frozen during the retreat from Prague in 1742 and, his health and career broken, he resigned from the army in 1744. As a result of smallpox, his sight began to fail and, in his constant physical suffering, he sought consolation in stoic rather than pessimistic meditations. He took up a literary career and in February 1746 published his complete works, the *Réflexions et Maximes,* and the *Introduction à la Connaissance de l'Esprit Humain,* the latter not properly revised. Vauvenargues continued work during the last months of his life, till he succumbed to the combined effects of tuberculosis and anemia. He was deeply admired, for his character and his writings, by such men as Voltaire and Marmontel, but passed otherwise with little notice until a century later. One may speak of his influence on Voltaire's taste, particularly with reference to his ideas on literary criticism.

Vauvenargues' stoicism gave him a serene perspective on existence, an attitude of noble melancholy, and a respect for man devoid of recourse to matters of divine grace. His personal philosophy excludes the futile pursuits of society, and all other marks of vanity such as encyclopedic knowledge: "One says few solid things when one seeks to say extraordinary ones." Vauvenargues transferred his love for action and glory to his writings, which were his road to self-assurance and his answer to skepticism. In this respect, they deal primarily with problems of conscience and duty, and of vice and virtue, and herein lies his particular appeal today. Another aspect of his doctrine rises from his belief in the goodness of Nature, and in this respect his ideas differ from those of the general run of French moralists, prone to dwell on the evils of man in society. He relies on feelings and passion: "Great thoughts come from the heart," and thus foreshadows Rousseau as well as a certain romantic "disquietude." His treatment of the social instincts led him to grave dilemmas of a metaphysical kind; his terminology on art and imagination is somewhat confused.

The complete works of Vauvenargues appeared in two volumes in 1857, in large part merely reprinted in 1929. The *Œuvres Choisies* of 1942 are adequate for most purposes. *The Reflections and Maxims* were translated into English in 1940 by F. Stevens.

ABOUT: Gosse, E. Three French Moralists; Morley, J. Critical Miscellanies; Read, H. The Sense of Glory. [In French—see studies by G. Cavallucci, G. Lanson, P. Souchon.]

F. J. C.

*VAZOV, IVAN** (June 27, 1850-September 22, 1921), Bulgarian poet, novelist, dramatist, was born in Sopot, which was later renamed Vazovgrad in his honor, the son of Mintcho and Saba Aïvazovski (he later shortened the name to Vazov). His father was a prosperous and conservative businessman who was able to give the boy a good education. He learned French early and came under the powerful influence of the writings of Victor Hugo.

Vazov spent many of his early years in exile from his native land. Bulgaria was then under Turkish domination. Like other young intellectuals of his generation, Vazov realized that safety, and the opportunity to work for a free national state, existed only outside the borders of his country. In 1870 in Rumania he contributed his first poems to a Bulgarian magazine published by political refugees there. In the same year Turkey granted Bulgaria a measure of freedom by recognizing the constitution of the Bulgarian Church, and Vazov returned to Sopot to help

* vōv nàrg'

* và' zôf

VAZOV

his father in his business. But his stay was not a long one. He became involved in revolutionary activity and was forced to flee just before the outbreak of the 1876 rebellion. For the next two years he lived in Bucharest but continued to fight for Bulgarian freedom. His passionate involvement with this cause was deeply intensified when he learned that the Turks had executed his father, destroyed his home town, and imprisoned his mother and family.

After the Liberation, Vazov returned to Bulgaria. He served as a circuit court judge and took an active interest in politics. In 1886, however, he was again in political difficulties and obliged to flee to Russia. Here, in Odessa, he wrote his masterpiece, the novel *Pod Igoto* (*Under the Yoke*) "to recall to himself the picture of his own country." *Under the Yoke*, a classic of Bulgarian literature which has been widely translated, depicts Bulgarian life just before the Liberation. Drawn out of the materials of Vazov's personal experience, it tells the story of a village, Byala Cherkva (clearly Sopot, his birthplace), and its inhabitants and their struggles for independence from Turkish rule. Although it ends tragically, the novel was not depressing to Vazov's readers who saw in it the forecast of the coming Liberation. From the modern outsider's point of view *Under the Yoke* is less impressive. Technically the book is weak, loosely plotted, repetitious, sentimental. But it contains vivid and authentic pictures of Bulgarian life and has something of the romantic vigor and sweep of the

novels of Sir Walter Scott and Victor Hugo. (While working on it, Vazov recalled, he was inspired by Hugo's *Les Misérables*, which he had read and re-read many times.) Its main significance today is that it represents the beginning of a Bulgarian national literature and a Bulgarian literary language.

Vazov returned to Bulgaria and settled in Sofia where he lived for the rest of his life, crowding his varied literary activities into a busy political career. Among other offices he served as Minister of Education. His domination of Bulgarian letters was for many years unchallenged, and the years 1890-1920 were called "the Vazov period." Writing rapidly and voluminously, rarely revising or polishing, he was at his best in the expression of his love for his country—a "people's poet," passionate, simple, unaffected. His best poems describe events from Bulgarian history: *Izbovlenie* (1878) celebrates the Liberation; *Epopeya na Zabravenite* (1879) glorifies the heroes of the pre-emancipation era; *Slivnitsa* (1886) deals with the Serbian-Bulgarian war. He lived through the Russo-Turkish war, the Liberation, the union of the two Bulgarias, the internal conflicts of the new nation, the Balkan wars, and World War I. Nearly all of these events find expression in his poetry.

Vazov was also successful as a playwright, his two best plays being *Borislav* and *Towards the Abyss*. The newly established Bulgarian National Theatre in Sofia produced his plays 154 times in the five-year period 1907-1912.

On the occasion of Vazov's fiftieth anniversary as a writer, October 12, 1920, there was a national celebration in his honor. Vazov died a year later of a heart attack. An edition of his collected works in 28 volumes was authorized and published in 1921-22. An expanded edition, including notes, diaries, and letters, was published in 100 volumes, 1926-37.

Under the Yoke has been translated twice into English—in 1894, by an unknown translator (reprinted, with an introduction by E. Gosse, 1912), and in 1955 in Sofia by M. Alexieva and T. Atanassova. Selections from Vazov's work appear in the Warner Library.

ABOUT: *Introduction to* Under the Yoke (1955 ed.). [In French—Christophorov, P. Ivan Vazov, la Formation d'un Écrivain Bulgare.]

*VEGA CARPIO, LOPE FÉLIX DE (November 25, 1562-August 27, 1635), Spanish dramatist and poet, was born in Madrid,

* vä′ gä kär′ pyō lō′ pā

LOPE DE VEGA

one of three children of Félix de Vega Carpio and Luisa Ramírez, peasants of the *vega* (plain) of Carriedo in the Asturias, who had moved to the capital city at the beginning of the year when Lope was born. Lope's early years are obscure. Before this century it was customary to lean for knowledge of his life on his friend Montalván's biographical narrative *Fama Póstuma de Lope de Vega* and his own autobiographical novel *Dorotea*. Both are mixtures of fact and fancy—the first whitewashing the truth, the second idealizing and romanticizing it. Only in comparatively recent times has painstaking scholarship succeeded in setting the record at least partially straight.

Félix de Vega Carpio apparently bequeathed to his remarkable son his poetic gift, his amatory instinct, and a sentimental kind of piety. Lope, according to his own *New Art of Making Plays*, wrote his first play (*El Verdadero Amante*) at the age of twelve. After the death of his father, he ran away with a friend with whom he hiked as far as Astorga, but was brought back home by a police escort. He is known to have attended the University of Alcalá, and presumably he completed the course. Among his early recorded exploits is an expedition against the Azores, under the admiral Álvaro de Bazán.

As early as 1585 Cervantes refers to Lope in his *Galatea* as one of the most distinguished wits of the time. By the age of twenty-five Lope was definitely established as a playwright in Madrid. Here he became involved in a scandal which resulted in his banishment from the capital for a number of years. When his romance with Elena Osorio (later glamorized as the heroine of *Dorotea*) was thwarted by her father, a theatre manager, Lope retaliated by circulating canards about the family. The result was imprisonment for libel, followed by exile. At this time (1588) the Invincible Armada was preparing for its expedition, and Lope enlisted. Nevertheless he managed a marriage ceremony (by proxy) to Doña Isabel de Urbina, daughter of a nobleman in the service of Philip II. (Montalván discreetly avoided mention of Elena Osorio at all, and attributed Lope's joining the Armada to grief at his wife's death!) There seems never to have been a time when Lope was not writing. Among his most beautiful early verses are a farewell to his wife (disguised under the anagram of *Belisa*), and on the voyage itself he composed a long poem in eleven cantos, *La Hermosura de Angélica,* in imitation of Ariosto. Fortunately Lope survived the disastrous Armada campaign, but his brother lost his life in it.

After his military discharge Lope's career took him to various of the leading Spanish cities. He resumed his theatrical career in Valencia where the drama was then flourishing. Here too ballad poetry (*romanceros*) had become fashionable through the stimulus of the court poets, and Lope made his contributions to the *Flor de Varios Romances.* As secretary to the Duke of Alba he lived for a time in Toledo and then Alba de Tormes, where he composed a pastoral romance, *La Arcadia.* There followed sojourns in Seville and again in Toledo, until he settled in Madrid in 1605, his period of banishment having expired. Here he enjoyed the lifelong patronage and friendship of a literary noble, the Duke of Sessa, to whom he became a confidential secretary and counselor.

Doña Isabel died in 1595, presumably in childbirth. Three years later Lope married Doña Juana de Guardo, daughter of a wealthy butcher. (His bitter enemy, the poet Góngora, ridiculed this opportunistic union in a sonnet punning on "torres" [towers] and "torreznos" [salt pork].) This marriage interfered with his amatory career no more than the first one, and Lope's liaisons with actresses seem to have numbered close to the *mil e tre* credited to another Spanish lover. Among his most notorious affairs was that with an actress, Micaela de Luján ("Lucinda"), who bore him five children. For another actress, Jerónima de Burgos, he wrote one of his best known comedies of love intrigue, *La Dama Boba.*

Although Lope contributed to virtually all the literary genres fashionable in his day, his original genius displayed itself most brilliantly in his plays. He is generally credited with bringing to fruition the modern Spanish popular drama. As he has written about himself, with no false modesty: "Necessity and I going into the business of making verses, brought the *comedias* into fashion; I drew them from their mean beginnings, engendering more poets in Spain than there are atoms in the sunbeam." Before Lope the drama was well established with the populace, but tended towards crude, loose improvisation similar to the Italian *commedia dell' arte* or, as with Cervantes, was often derivative and overliterary. Lope brought to the *comedia* spontaneity, graceful flow and vigorous poetry. As he conceived the form, it was neither farce nor tragedy, but a blend of the serious and comic, making it possible for him to introduce into the same play the artificially elegant speech of the nobility and the racy vernacular of the peasantry.

In 1609 Lope addressed to the Academy of Madrid his brief verse treatise entitled "El Arte Nuevo de Hacer Comedias" (The New Art of Writing Plays), setting forth in a workmanlike way, quite without pretension, his dramatic practices. He assures the gentlemen of the Academy that although he is familiar with the classical precepts, he deliberately avoids them and writes his plays "without art," for inasmuch as "the common herd pays for them, it is meet to speak to them like an ignoramus in order to please them." Lope then proceeds to such practical matters as what subjects please the people and how to hold their attention. Matters of honor he holds to be the best themes to represent in plays, "for the people are deeply moved by virtuous actions." Lope was particularly concerned to keep his incidents so involved that up to the middle of the third act nobody could anticipate the ending—lest audiences walk out prematurely. The great art of the playwright for him lay in "deceiving with the truth" ("engañar con la verdad"). "Curiosity should always be led astray," he wrote, "so that one can see that something quite different may happen from what is indicated." He even laid down rules for the proper lengths of plays to avoid boring audiences, rules which he strictly followed.

In his intrigue-laden plays Lope deals basically with *honor*, as he indicates, but manages to ring an amazing variety of changes on the theme—serious, comic, ironic. Some of his best plays involve clashes between aristocracy and peasantry. In one of these, *Fuente Ovejuna* (The Sheep's Well), the peasants of a village, led by an outraged young girl, rise up in revolt and kill a cruel commander who has plundered the town and tried to rape their women. After prolonged inquest and torture, which the peasants endure with courage and stoicism, King Ferdinand finally forgives the natives of Fuente Ovejuna and promises to send them a just commander. (This play has enjoyed great popularity in the Soviet Union, despite the fact that it really upholds benevolent monarchy.) Other dramas with similar plots are *Peribáñez y el Comendador de Ocaña* and *El Rey el Mejor Alcalde* (The King the Greatest Mayor), while an extant tragedy of this period, *La Estrella de Sevilla* (The Star of Seville), involving a love rivalry between the king and a member of the upper bourgeoisie, has been attributed to him.

The lighter side of this theme of pride and class conflict is represented by one of Lope's most perennially charming plays, *El Perro del Hortelano* (The Gardener's Dog), an Italianate comedy similar in tone to Shakespeare's early comedies. The basic complication of this play (whose title is derived from Aesop's fable of the dog in the manger) stems from the conflict between pride and love on the part of a Neapolitan countess who cannot bring herself to marry her low-born secretary, and yet would banish him rather than allow a rival to marry him. The dilemma is ingeniously resolved by means of a ruse, concocted by a crafty servant, whereby a nobleman is tricked into believing the secretary to be his long lost son. *El Perro del Hortelano* is one of a type that Lope made especially his own, the *comedia de capa y espada* ("cape and sword"), or comedy of love intrigue. Among other outstanding examples are: *Lo Cierto por lo Dudoso* (A Certainty for a Doubt), *Amar sin Saber a Quien* (To Love and Not Know Whom), *La Moza de Cántara* (The Girl with the Water Jar), and his very last play, *Las Bizarrerías de Belisa* (The Eccentricities of Belisa).

Lope's varied dramatic output included also historical dramas like *The Crown of Otún*, based on the struggle between Rudolf of Hapsburg, Alfonso X of Spain, and Ottokar of Bohemia for the throne of the Holy Roman Empire; somber tragedies like the Websterian *Punishment without Revenge;* spectacular romantic pageants like *The Knight of Olmedo;* and a version of the story of Romeo and Juliet called *Castelvines and Monteses.* He also wrote many religious *autos,* but never achieved the distinction in this form that his successor Calderón did.

Lope's pragmatic attitude towards his art earned him the scorn of fellow poets, particularly the classicist Góngora, who considered him a poetaster, but at the same time it made him the idol of the public whose adulation he enjoyed throughout his life. In 1614, following upon the death of his second wife, he took religious orders, apparently the culmination of a spiritual struggle. Almost simultaneously he entered into an adulterous relationship with Marta de Nevares Santoyo, ("Amarillis") wife of a merchant, which, needless to say, made him the subject of severe censure. Nevertheless he achieved several important holy offices, becoming Priest and Familiar of the Holy Inquisition and Doctor of Theology in the Collegium Sapientiae of Rome. During this period he wrote his *Rimas Sacras* and was decorated by Pope Urban VIII for his verse epic *La Corona Trágica,* based upon the life and execution of Mary Stuart. His last years, spent in the quiet of his house and garden, were saddened by loss. His mistress grew blind, went mad, and died in 1632. Subsequently his daughter, to whom he was devoted, eloped with a courtier, leaving him completely alone. In 1632 appeared the novel *Dorotea,* begun in his youth. This book has proved to be of special interest inasmuch as the forecast of its hero's fate, put in the mouth of an astrologer, is now known to be remarkably close to events of Lope's own life. Lope died in 1635, at the age of seventy-two. His death has been attributed both to a chill caught while watering his garden, and to debilitation caused by religious flagellation—only one more instance of the contradictory elements in his character. He was accorded a state funeral, arranged by the Duke of Sessa, lasting nine days, and his remains were laid to rest in the church of San Sebastián.

Lope de Vega was undoubtedly the most prodigious literary improviser of Western literature. Of the 1800 plays claimed for him by his biographer Montalván, 475 are extant, to which might be added over 50 spurious or doubtful attributions. A good many, understandably, are little more than scenarios, but enough mature productions and more remain to justify Cervantes' tribute to him as "monstruo de la naturaleza" (monster of nature). To his countrymen he remains "the Phoenix of Genius," but a paucity of translation as

well as an inherent provinciality in the plays themselves have kept him from being widely read or produced outside the Spanish-speaking world. Although historically Lope de Vega occupies the place in Spanish drama that Shakespeare does in English, he appears superficial and insular when compared with his great contemporary. For all the vivacity, ingenuity, and verbal brilliance of Lope's plays, they lack profundity of thought and depth of characterization. One leaves a play of Lope de Vega's not deeply moved, but, as Gerald Brenan has observed, "with a renewed sense of the charm and variety of life."

Fuente Ovejuna was translated by Angel Flores and is to be found in Angel Flores (ed.), *Masterpieces of the Spanish Golden Age* (1957). It also appears in John Gassner (ed.) *A Treasury of the Theatre* (1951). John Garrett Underhill translated in prose *A Certainty for a Doubt, The King the Greatest Alcalde, The Gardener's Dog,* and *Fuente Ovejuna* in his *Four Plays of Lope de Vega* (1936). *Castelvines and Monteses* was translated by F. W. Cosens in 1869. An earlier anonymous version (1770) contains just the scenes corresponding to Shakespeare's *Romeo and Juliet. Peribáñez and the Commander of Ocaña* was translated by Eva Rebecca Price in 1937. *The Star of Seville,* a questionable attribution, is available in translations by Henry Thomas (1935) and Elizabeth C. Hullihan (1955). *The New Art of Writing Plays* in a translation by William T. Brewster is the first of the *Papers on Playmaking,* edited by Brander Matthews (1914). The best edition in Spanish is that of the Real Academia Española in 13 volumes, edited by Emilio Cotarelo y Mori (1916-30).

ABOUT: Adams, N. Heritage of Spain; Brenan, G. The Literature of the Spanish People; Fitzmaurice-Kelly, J. Some Masters of Spanish Verse; Flores, A. Lope de Vega, Monster of Nature; Gassner, J. Masters of the Drama; Lowenthal, L. Literature and the Image of Man; Nicoll, A. World Drama; Perry, H. Masters of Dramatic Comedy and Their Social Themes; Rennert, H. The Life of Lope de Vega; Underhill, J. *Introduction to* Four Plays of Lope de Vega. [In Spanish—see studies by J. A. Cabezas, J. de Entrambasquas y Peña, J. Fernández Montesinos, A. Zamora Vicente.]

R. A. C.

*VÉLEZ DE GUEVARA Y DUEÑAS, LUIS (1579-1644), Spanish dramatist and novelist, was born in Ecija (Seville). His original name was Vélez de Santander, which he later had changed. He graduated in arts at the University of Osuna and started as a page in the retinue of the Archbishop of Seville. At twenty-one he went to Italy as a soldier and saw service on land and sea. After five years he returned to Spain, in the household of the Count of Saldaña. From there on he had wealthy patrons and became a celebrated poet and wit, honored with po-

* vā' lăth thā gā vā' rä ē dwā' nyäs

sitions at the court, but ever the impecunious gentleman, eaten by debt. He changed from master to master, always going higher in the nobility scale, until he obtained a position in the household of King Philip IV himself, but all his jobs proved to be more honorific than substantial. In the same year in which he was appointed to the last-mentioned post he wrote: "I cannot leave my house for lack of clothing to cover myself." All the difficulties, however, did not prevent Vélez de Guevara from marrying four times, nor did they dim his festive spirit and sharp wit. His reaction to his financial misfortunes was to compose endless rhymed petitions to the king humorously begging for help.

Since 1615, the date in which he established himself in Madrid, he had been a famous poet, and his works were received by the public with as much applause as those of Lope de Vega. He is supposed to have written more than 400 plays, of which about 80 *comedias* and *entremeses* survive. Vélez occupies a high place among the followers of Lope, whose influence upon him is clearly discernible. Nevertheless some of his best *comedias* bear comparison with those of his master. His most valuable asset is the intense poetical quality he infused into his plays, which is evidenced in *Reinar Después de Morir*, his outstanding dramatic work, inspired by the Inés de Castro legendary theme. He shows his best qualities also in the dramatization of subjects taken from the folk tradition, as in *La Serrana de la Vera* and *La Luna de la Sierra*. In his excellent *entremeses* or interludes, the elements of roguery are in evidence.

No small part of his fame is due to his picaresque novel *El Diablo Cojuelo* (1641), which is generally considered to be the culmination of the baroque style in fictional prose, and perhaps the best example of the last development of the romance of roguery in Spain. It was the model followed by Le Sage for his *Le Diable Boiteux* (1707). This French "refacimento" obscured, to a certain extent, the merits of its original, but his basic conception has never been forgotten. His devil became, through Le Sage's "Asmodée," the symbol of social satire in all Europe.

He died in Madrid at seventy-four, as famous, happy, humorous, and impoverished as he had always lived. In his will, after a long enumeration of his debts, he laments the peril threatening his soul: there was not a penny left to pay for masses to help its salvation.

ABOUT: Chandler, F. W. Romances of Roguery; Spencer, F. E. & Schevill, R. The Dramatic works of Luis Vélez de Guevara. [In Spanish—Cotarelo y Mori, *in* Boletín de la Real Academia Española, III-IV (1917); Valbuena Prat, A. La Novela Picaresca Española. [In German—see study by L. Hohmann.]

M. DA C.

*VERDAGUER (SANTALÓ), JACINTO (May 17, 1845-June 10, 1902), Catalan poet, was the most important figure of the Catalan literary Renaissance. He was born of a humble family in the town of Santa María de Folgueroles, near the city of Vich. At an early age, he began to give lessons to children and, at the same time, he went about studying and writing his first verses. He was twenty when he entered some of his poems in the *Jocs Florals* of Barcelona. These poems were awarded a prize, and the young farm boy was enthusiastically applauded. The following year he received another prize in the same literary contest and became from then on the friend of the great Provençal poet Frédéric Mistral, who always admired him greatly. Verdaguer studied for the ecclesiastical life and was ordained in Vich in 1870, thus beginning his double life of priest and poet; he was exceptional in both. After an illness brought on by overwork, he was given the post of chaplain in the Trans-Atlantic Shipping Company, in which capacity he made several trips on the Atlantic and the Mediterranean between the years 1873 and 1875; in later years he served as a priest in the palace of the Marquis de Comillas. Setbacks of a diverse nature and his poor health forced him to retire in 1893 to La Gleva, where, it was said, he had been exiled; and such was the scheming of friend and foe alike that the poor priest had to flee from there in defiance of the bishop's orders. From that period dates the famous document entitled *En Defensa Propia* and a series of letters in which Verdaguer attempted to clarify his moral and physical situation. Later, when things quieted down, Verdaguer resumed his public life in Barcelona, writing and publishing until his death. It is said that the funeral of Verdaguer, who was adored by the Catalan people as a poet, was one of the greatest manifestations of mourning ever to have taken place in Barcelona.

His life, a long struggle illuminated by poetry and faith, is an example of patience and saintliness; his work is richer and more varied than that of any poet since Ramón Lull. Verdaguer performed the miracle of

* vĕr ∓hä gĕr′

creating modern Catalan poetry by using all the resources of the language and inventing new ones when he found none at hand. And the Catalan people realized this and consecrated him as their national poet. The following books comprise his literary production: *L'Atlántida* (1877) is an epic poem full of fantastic imagination, partly historical and partly legendary, in which classical and Christian elements are intertwined, ending with the apotheosis of the Cross. If *L'Atlántida* is the poem of the sea and Iberian myths, *Canigó* (1885) is the great epic poem of the Catalan people who had taken refuge in the Pyrenees before the invasion of the Arabs— the poem of the sword against the invader and the Cross against superstitions. This poem, finer and more regular than the former, is also a poem of landscape and real figures, of orchestral and choral tonal quality. *Canigó* has been converted into a musical work by Felipe Pedrell, the great Catalan musicologist. The patriotic vein of Verdaguer, which begins in *Canigó,* is developed in *Patria* (1888), a book of poems, and the "Oda a Barcelona" (1883-99). On the other hand, his religious poetry finds its expression in *Idils i Cants Místics* (1879), the book in which we find the most transcendental of his poetry, written with Christian idealism, Spanish realism, and popular spirit. It is a book of innocence and youth, written before the tribulations of life had embittered him. In 1887 he published *Excursions i Viatges,* memories, in prose, of his trips, and later another book of prose, *Dietari de un Pelegrí a Terra Santa,* the diary of his trip to the Holy Land. Also published in 1887 was his poem *Lo Somni de Sant Joan* (translated into French the following year, and later into Czech, Portuguese, and German). The trilogy *Jesus Infant* (1890-93), *Sant Francesc* (1895), and *Flors del Calvari—Libre de Consols* (1896) was composed in the period of his greatest suffering.

His *Obras Completas,* the definitive edition, was published in Barcelona in ten volumes, between 1928 and 1936, and there are many other editions of his complete works, or of *Poesias,* such as that prepared by Carlos Riba, in 1922. Of his epic poems, *L'Atlántida* and *Canigó* were translated into many European languages, there being editions in Spanish, French, Italian, German, Bohemian, Swedish, Portuguese, and even one in Esperanto. The first of these poems was also translated into English in 1882.

ABOUT: Triadu, J. Anthology of Catalan Lyric Poetry. [In Spanish—see studies by Joan Moles, B. de Rubí, V. Serra y Boldu. In French—see study by A. Vassal.]

E. F.

VERGA, GIOVANNI. See "TWENTIETH CENTURY AUTHORS: FIRST SUPPLEMENT"

*VERLAINE, PAUL MARIE (March 30, 1844-January 8, 1896), French poet, was born at Metz. He was the only son of Nicolas Auguste Verlaine, an adjutant captain in an engineering regiment, and Elisa Dehée. Of Belgian Ardennes and Artois origin, the two branches were conservative, piously Catholic, and financially comfortable, with a private income.

Nicolas was transferred from Metz to Montpellier, to Nîmes, then back to Metz. Each time he moved with his family. In 1851 he resigned from the army and settled in Paris. Paul was an unusually demanding child, who spent most of his time in his parents' company, and would not go to sleep without his mother's presence. He attended school at the Institution Landry (1853-55) and at the Lycée Bonaparte (now Condorcet) from 1855 to 1862. At first a diligent student, he changed remarkably in adolescence and just managed to obtain the baccalaureate. One of his teachers has commented that he looked like a degenerate criminal and was the filthiest, most slovenly student in the school.

Upon graduation from the *lycée* Verlaine enrolled in law school, but spent his time in bars. Withdrawn from the university, he obtained a minor clerical position at the city hall. The death of his father centralized parental influence in his mother, who coddled him like a child. Paul, when drunk, became dangerous, brutal. When not drinking, he attended concerts and galleries, and wrote poetry.

Verlaine's earliest poems, essentially exercises and imitative verse, were composed in 1858. Those he wrote after 1861 reflect the influence of Baudelaire, then almost unknown to students. While at the Lycée Bonaparte, Verlaine became the close friend of Edmond Lepelletier and of Charles de Sivry. In 1863 he found fellow-enthusiasts of poetry at the city hall, and Louis Xavier de Ricard published a sonnet by Verlaine in the *Revue du Progrès Moral.* Influenced by Albert Glatigny and Catulle Mendès, Verlaine turned toward Parnassianism. He contributed to *Le Parnasse* of 1866, and prepared his first volume of verse, *Les Poèmes Saturniens.* It was published by Alphonse Lemerre, who was just beginning his career as the important publisher of Parnassians and Symbolists.

* vĕr lȧn'

957

VERLAINE

Scholars have debated whether or not *Les Poèmes Saturniens* were in part inspired by Elisa Moncomble, a cousin who had lived with the Verlaines until her marriage (she died in 1867 consequent to childbirth). The influence of Baudelaire, Gautier, and Ricard is evident. Verlaine exhibits subtlety of description, nuances of sentiment; the macabre and the violent are displayed too. Despite the merits of *Poèmes Saturniens,* it took more than twenty years to dispose of five hundred copies; only Mallarmé, among the few who commented, recognized his importance.

At the end of 1867 (but dated 1868), Verlaine published *Les Amies* under the pseudonym Pablo de Herlagñez. Auguste Poulet-Malassis, publisher of Baudelaire, was the editor; *Les Amies* was condemned by the censor for licentiousness. The following year Lemerre issued *Fêtes Galantes,* which dazzled the virtuoso Théodore de Banville. It was as though Verlaine had transposed Watteau or Fragonard into poetry, and poetry into impressionistic music. The ingenuous and the sophisticated blended, as the formal structure itself became more supple. But Verlaine's personal life was becoming increasingly dissipated. The family council decided that a wife would stabilize and strengthen his weak character. Rather than marry a designated cousin noted for her energetic decisiveness, Verlaine sought the hand of Mathilde Mauté, half-sister of Charles de Sivry. She was sixteen in 1869 when they became engaged. Verlaine celebrated his love and his hopes in *La Bonne Chanson.* The marriage took place the following year, shortly after the outbreak of the Franco-Prussian War. Verlaine volunteered for the army and was assigned to the Paris garrison. After the Commune the couple moved to Fampoux. Having lost his bureaucratic position, Verlaine moved in with his in-laws at Paris. He resumed his literary relations, and he started to drink again.

While at Fampoux Verlaine had received a letter from the then unknown poet Arthur Rimbaud. He urged the latter to come to Paris. Their meeting evolved immediately into a passionate, obvious affair. Verlaine drank to excess, broke with his friends over Rimbaud, and brutalized his wife. The birth of a son, Georges, interrupted only briefly Verlaine's liaison with Rimbaud. By early 1872 Mathilde, in fear for her life, separated from Verlaine; she returned to him only when he promised to give up Rimbaud and the latter returned to Charleville.

But by May Verlaine was again behaving homicidally, and Rimbaud returned to Paris. They left for Belgium, whence Verlaine refused to return despite Mathilde's pleas; in September they went to London. Rimbaud returned home in November alone. Both he and Verlaine's mother went to London when Verlaine fell seriously ill in January 1873. His mother went back to France; Verlaine and Rimbaud went in April to Belgium. They separated again, although corresponding, and in May they were reunited in England. Short of funds, scarcely earning meager sums by tutoring, they lived quarrelsomely. In July Verlaine left his companion, only to renew relations a few days later at Brussels. After a two-day drunk, Verlaine shot Rimbaud. They patched up the quarrel, but Verlaine threatened Rimbaud anew; the police were alerted, and Verlaine was jailed.

Verlaine was sentenced to two years in prison, a year and a half of which he served at Mons. There he became fervently Catholic. A legal separation from his wife increased his need of something or someone to give him strength, to guide him. The poems of *Sagesse* (1881) owe their inspiration to the mystical crisis through which he passed at this time. But at the same time Verlaine composed *Romances sans Paroles* (1874), which were strongly influenced by Rimbaud and by the sojourn in England. The fluidity of the verse, the masterful use of "ambiguities," the economy of statement and the extensiveness of suggestion, the intriguing subjectivity—such elements have made this volume major among Verlaine's works.

Released from prison, Verlaine went to France, then to Stickney and Bournemouth in England as a teacher. From 1877 to 1879 he taught at Rethel (France), in a private school. But he recommenced drinking and left his post. After a spell in England with Lucien Létinois, a former pupil at Rethel, Verlaine engaged in farming near Rethel. By 1882 the enterprise failed—Verlaine was no farmer. Lucien died the following year from typhoid; Verlaine was again without an anchor. Until 1885 he resided at Coulommes, where he dissipated openly. For attacking his mother, he was sent to prison for a month (April-May 1885).

In 1884 Verlaine produced a series of "portraits," *Les Poètes Maudits*. Published by Léon Vanier, this was the first work of Verlaine not issued at the author's expense. The original series presented Tristan Corbière, Rimbaud, and Mallarmé; four years later Verlaine added sketches of Marceline Desbordes-Valmore, Villiers de l'Isle-Adam, and "pauvre Lélian," i.e., Verlaine himself. Poems of a heterogeneous nature, previously published in periodicals, comprised *Jadis et Naguère*. Here one finds the famous "Art Poétique," which was originally composed at Mons in April 1874. It has mistakenly been thought to sum up all of Verlaine's poetic credo and to be a manifesto of symbolism. Verlaine himself was no adherent of any one school.

Verlaine's last years saw the issuance of compilations from poems and articles contributed to numerous reviews. While meditating a religious, spiritual work like *Bonheur* he could publish *Femmes*, of a sensual nature, and the satires of *Invectives*. His was a great virtuosity, symbolized by his election in 1894 to replace Leconte de Lisle as "the prince of poets." Verlaine's last years were an ignoble series of inebriations, coarse liaisons (male and female), and poverty. He recuperated from excesses during periods of hospitalization. Upon his death at fifty-one from long abuse of his constitution, and more immediately from pneumonia, Verlaine was buried in the Batignolles cemetery.

Verlaine was indeed a complex person and a consummate poet. He has become a legend in literary Bohemianism. His verse is unexcelled in musicality, in delicacy, finesse, and subtlety. Composers like Debussy, Faure, and Ravel have set his songs to music.

The only "complete" edition, including the correspondence, is that published by Messein (11 vols. 1911-29). Details of earlier editions and pre-originals are to be found in *Bibliographie et Iconographie de Paul Verlaine* by A. Van Bever and M. Monda (1926). The poetry is available in Y. G. Le Dantec's edition of 1938. There are critical editions of *Bonheur* by H. de Bouillane. de Lacoste (1949), of *Sagesse* by L. Morice (1948), and of *Les Poèmes Saturniens* by J. H. Bornecque (1952).

Baudelaire, Rimbaud, Verlaine: Selected Verse and Prose Poems, edited with an introduction by J. M. Bernstein (1947), contains translations by Gertrude Hall and Arthur Symons. Miss Hall's renditions were published in 1895. Ashmore Wingate in 1905 and Bergen Applegate in 1916 did a "book-length version." *Selected Poems,* by C. F. MacIntyre, was published in 1948, the same year as *Forty Poems,* by R. Grant and C. Apcher.

ABOUT: Coulon, M. Poet under Saturn; Huneker, J. G. The Pathos of Distance; Lepelletier, E. Paul Verlaine; Nicolson, H. Paul Verlaine; Roberts, C. E. B. Paul Verlaine; Zweig, S. Paul Verlaine. [In French—Adam, A. Verlaine, l'Homme et l'Œuvre; Carré, J. M. Du Côté de Verlaine et de Rimbaud; Cuénot, C. État Présent des Études Verlainiennes; Delahaye, E. Verlaine; Martino, P. Verlaine; Morice, L. Verlaine, le Drame Religieux; Porché, F. Verlaine tel qu'Il Fut; Ruchon, F. Verlaine, Documents Iconographiques; Zayed, G. La Formation Littéraire de Verlaine.]

S. S. W.

*VERNE, JULES (February 8, 1828-March 24, 1905), French novelist, born in Nantes, was the son of a magistrate who, intending that Jules should succeed him in his charge, sent him to Paris to study law. Jules' childhood memories of the maritime activities at Nantes were to play a considerable rôle in his later life. He was meanwhile both something of a wit and an enthusiast for mechanical devices of the order of flying machines, and an omnibus in the form of a steam elephant, perhaps inspired by the elegant "Dames Blanches" carriages in Nantes. Having completed his degree in law, Verne decided on a literary career; his father, at first disappointed, soon recognized the merits of his first novels, such as *Martin Paz*. Making his own way financially (he was for a time a stockbroker), Verne served for some years as secretary of the Théâtre Historique, and devoted himself to composing plays. His *Les Pailles Rompues*, performed in 1850, was a considerable success, and the approval of the two Dumas encouraged him further in this genre. In 1857 Verne married a young widow, Honorine Morel (*née* de Viane). He had one son, Michel, and two step-daughters.

Verne was satisfied neither with the literary career he had made for himself thus far nor with the precarious living he eked out from his onerous duties in the theatre. The turning point in his interests seems to have

* vĕrn

959

VERNE

descriptions and scientific data; and the intellectuals caught the many ironic overtones of the subtle style.

Several new elements entered Verne's inspiration in 1866 as he was actively meditating a work to be entitled *Voyage sous les Océans*: the laying of the transatlantic cable, his trip to the United States on the "Great Eastern" in 1867, and his purchase of the first of his own ships, the "Saint-Michel." Verne may have taken his ideas about submarine travel from the disastrous experiment made by Petit in 1834, but he added materially to the scientific substance, and created an overall combination of true originality in the character of Captain Nemo, who represents a great deal of Verne's own thoughts of about 1848, on the ideologies that accompanied the revolution of that year. The novel, finally entitled *Vingt Mille Lieues sous les Mers (Twenty Thousand Leagues under the Sea)*, was completed in 1868, and an illustrated edition of it appeared two years later, before the Franco-Prussian war.

After the interval of the war, during which Verne lived in retirement with his family, he returned to Paris with several manuscripts. In 1872 he published serially in *Le Temps* his *Tour du Monde en Quatre-Vingts Jours (Around the World in Eighty Days)* which aroused breathless interest internationally, to the point that it was believed to represent a real trip and wager. The story was dramatized two years later, with elaborate settings including the requisite elephant. *Michel Strogoff*, a further great success in 1876, was also dramatized shortly after. In 1886 Verne was shot in the leg by his nephew Gaston, who had had a mental breakdown, and he walked with a limp for the rest of his life. His last years were spent in travel on his boats and in service on the municipal council of Amiens. He continued to write his extraordinary adventures, even after his sight began to fail. In 1892 he was made an officer of the Legion of Honor. He died in Amiens at seventy-seven, and his funeral was attended by some five thousand persons.

been an article that he published in 1860 on Poe, in which it is evident that the young man was inspired by number systems, cryptography, fantastic adventure, and imagined scientific devices. In reproaching Poe for certain technical errors, he showed his particular command of the problems of the mathematician and the engineer. His notions pertinent to "science fiction" appear again in his correspondence of 1862, at the moment of construction of the great balloon, the "Géant." Verne invented his own and better balloon, the "Victoria," and stole the march on the real event in taking his manuscript to the publisher Hetzel, who was struck with it, issued the *Cinq Semaines en Ballon* at once, and signed with Verne a long-term contract, remaining his generous and enthusiastic publisher. Hetzel pressed Verne for further stories, and *Le Voyage au Centre de la Terre* appeared in 1864, his first fully organized long narrative, an account of an imaginary mineralogist's descent through the extinct crater of Snoeffels, in Iceland, to the interior seas, among prehistoric creatures, and emergence at last at Stromboli, thus celebrating ancient legend. *De la Terre à la Lune* followed in 1863, another highly integrated story: a visionary and frenetic Frenchman, Ardan (an anagram for the famous photographer Nadar), hearing of the proposed launching in Baltimore of a space ship, volunteers to guide it. In this work Verne's success was complete, for the public adored the fanciful idea; the mathematicians and physicists admired the technical exactitude of the

Verne's principal novels were translated into English most frequently during the 1870's, beginning in 1869 with *Five Weeks in a Balloon* and *From the Earth to the Moon;* his *Works* appeared in fifteen volumes in 1911. There have been numerous dramatic adaptations of his books, on the stage and in motion pictures, and recent interest in space exploration has stimulated new interest in them.

ABOUT: Allott, K. Jules Verne; Allotte de la Fuÿe, M. Jules Verne; Waltz, G. H. Jules Verne. [In French—see studies by B. Frank, C. Lemire, H. Rauville.]

F. J. C.

*VERRI, PIETRO, Conte (December 12, 1728-June 28, 1797), Italian political economist, public administrator, and man of letters, was born in Milan of noble family. His father, Count Gabriel, was a representative of the Milanese aristocracy at the Austrian court. Young Verri began his studies at nine in the Jesuit school of Monza, went on to the Barnabite school of St. Alexander in Milan and the Collegio Nazzareno in Rome, and completed his education in 1747 at the Collegio dei Nobili at Parma.

In 1750 he won admittance to the distinguished group of Milanese literati known as the Accademia dei Trasformati, shortly after his literary debut with *Borlanda Impasticciata,* a satire against the prejudices of the day. In 1753, after a brief stay in Vienna with his father, he returned to Milan openly hostile to the ruling aristocracy and the clergy, both of which he cleverly mocked in *Gran Zoroastro* and *Mal di Milza.*

He enlisted in the Austrian army and served as captain in 1759 in the Seven Years' War. He had hoped to find in the army a "union of heroes," but he left the service after eight months, disillusioned by the lack of moral purpose. Returning to Milan once again, he applied himself to a study of the structure of the Lombardian state and a critical analysis of the tax structure. He now started the prolific writing dealing with economic and philosophic themes which was to continue for the rest of his life. A work on the rise and fall of commerce in Milan appeared simultaneously with *Sulla Felicità* (Meditations on Happiness, 1763). He became the moving spirit in the group of Milanese intellectuals known as the Società dei Pugni, formed in 1761 after breaking away from the Accademia dei Trasformati. As members of the new group, Verri, his brother Alessandro, and others founded a periodical, *Il Caffè,* which was published from 1764 to 1766. Verri was administrator and chief editor during the life of *Caffè,* contributing some thirty-eight articles covering a range of subjects from the cultivation of flax to the spirit of Italian literature.

From 1766 to 1786 Verri was occupied with duties in public affairs. The Austrian government in Lombardy under Maria Theresa listened to his criticisms, and he was instrumental in obtaining tax reforms and better public administration. He published treatises on the corn laws *(Sulle Legge Vincolanti . . . ,* 1769) and on political economy (1771). He also developed further the theme

of *Sulla Felicità* with *Discorso sull' Indole del Piacere e del Dolore* (Discourse on the Character of Pleasure and Pain, 1773). In 1776 he married Maria Castiglioni. She died in 1781 following the death of their son in 1779.

During the period of Napoleonic rule of Milan in 1796, Verri found himself a colleague of the distinguished poet Giuseppe Parini in the republican government. The two men, whose lifetimes were almost exactly contemporary, had attended the same school in Milan and belonged to the Trasformati together. Verri's paper *Caffè* had been the one hostile critic of Parini's poetry. They worked together at this time, however, until Verri's death from apoplexy in Milan.

It is generally agreed that the most important reforms in Lombardy during the period of Austrian domination were promoted and championed by Verri, whose lifelong concern was the economic independence of his native province. His theories of economic liberty are most clearly and vigorously stated in *Sulle Legge Vincolanti.* He is also noted for his *Osservazioni sulla Tortura* (Observations on Torture) written in 1777, and for a two-volume history of Milan, *Storia di Milano,* 1783-98. His prolific correspondence with his brother Alessandro, a novelist of the pre-romantic school, provides a vivacious commentary on the literary life of their era.

ABOUT: [In Italian—see studies by D. Chimenti Vassalli, N. Valeri.]

E. DE P.

*VIAU, THÉOPHILE DE, known as THÉOPHILE (1590-September 25, 1626), French poet and dramatist, born in Clérac, near Agen. His Huguenot father was a former lawyer of the Parliament of Bordeaux. He studied in Boussères-Sainte-Radegonde, where his father owned an estate, and during further schooling at Bordeaux and Saumur began to show "libertine" tendencies, probably primarily irreligious. He began to write poetry, and in 1611 joined an itinerant troupe of actors with whom he traveled and learned about contemporary life. He went to Holland with Guez de Balzac and, after studying there at the University of Leiden, entered the service of the Duke of Épernon and thus lived in a milieu of spendthrifts and freethinkers. His amatory and irreligious verse led him to a short exile in 1619, but the success of his play *Pyrame et Thisbé,* and a volume of serious verse, established him as an active participant in the

* văr' rē

* vyō

organization of entertainment at the court. Despite his abjuration of 1621, his early disorderly conduct was not forgotten, and his final disgrace resulted from attribution to him of the licentious *Parnasse Satyrique* and the savage book directed against it and the libertines by Garasse in 1623. On Théophile's protest, the courts examined the charges, but he felt it wise to hide with the Duke of Montmorency (decapitated in 1632). In his absence he was condemned to death and burned in effigy. Betrayed by friends, he was arrested and was imprisoned in Paris and abandoned by the entire literary world (including his friend Balzac). After a prolonged legal battle, the death sentence was commuted in 1625, but he was banished. Under the Duke's protection he was able to remain in Paris, but the effects of privation during the long imprisonment hastened his early death of a fever. Much remains obscure about the authorship of *Le Parnasse Satyrique* and about his conversion; another victim of the purge was the poet Maynard.

Théophile's poetry is outstanding in the genres that did not follow the doctrines of Malherbe, of whom he said: "J'aime sa renommée et non pas sa leçon" ("I admire his reputation but not his teaching"). His odes, sometimes considered as the best lyrical expression of their century, were especially esteemed by Théophile Gautier and Rémy de Gourmont. They are distinguished for their variety of form and content. Besides the fine odes *La Solitude* and *Le Matin*, the series entitled *La Maison de Sylvie* is particularly remarkable for the versification, the deep feeling for nature, the freedom from current embellishments, and the expression of happiness in his retreat in Chantilly.

Théophile's great success was *Pyrame et Thisbé*, immortalized by Boileau's scornful criticism of its conceit of the blushing sword ("Il en rougit, le traître !"). The play develops a theme of primitive nature, foreshadowing La Fontaine and integrating a kind of metaphysics of love. The qualities of the portrayal rise from the poet's perception of inner feeling, his suppleness and grace of image, and his first-hand knowledge of the life of peasants and shepherds and the poetic mysteries of the countryside. The unities are strong, the presentation restrained, and the characterization excellent.

ABOUT: L'Esprit Créateur, I (1961); Times (London) Literary Supplement, May 1, 1959. [In French—Gourmont, R. de, Théophile, les Plus Belles Pages; Lebègue, R. La Poésie Française de 1560 à 1630. See also studies by A. Adam, F. Lachèvre.]

F. J. C.

*VICENTE, GIL (1470?-1536?), Portuguese dramatist and poet, is little known as a person although he was one of the world's great writers. We do not know exactly when he was born or died or even in what places. At the Portuguese court during the same period Vicente was writing there was a goldsmith by the name of Gil Vicente and such eminent Portuguese scholars as Braga and Fidelino de Figueredo think they were one and the same man. We do know that in 1500 he married Blanca Becerra, and that he had two children, Luis and Paula, who edited his works in Lisbon in 1562. It is thought that he may have studied law at the University of Lisbon. After Camões, he is considered Portugal's greatest poet as well as one of the most important founders of the Portuguese theatre. This latter point is, however, not taken seriously by Menéndez y Pelayo who says that the drama of which Gil Vicente is supposed to be the father is almost non-existent. According to him, then, Vicente is to be considered as a great peninsular dramatist rather than the father of a non-existent theatre. The school of drama Vicente might have sired was smothered by the overwhelming influence of the Italians and of Lope de Vega.

Since Vicente wrote many of his works in Castilian, he figures prominently in the history of the early Spanish theatre also. His plays have been extensively studied, commented on and translated by the writers and scholars of many nations. One of the unsolved mysteries of Vicente's writing is why he chose to compose part of his works in Castilian, part in Portuguese, and part in a strange mixture of the two. Since the queen of Portugal at that time was Doña María, the daughter of Ferdinand and Isabella, it is possible that he wished to flatter her by giving plays in her native tongue. However, as most Portuguese writers of the day knew both languages well, it is also possible that Vicente simply chose to do it this way. We know that he was strongly influenced by Juan del Encina, the Spanish dramatist, and it is not unlikely that this gave Castilian a special prerogative in Vicente's mind. One thing is certain, and that is that the literary and cultural relations between Spain and Portugal were so strong in these matters that they might almost be considered one nation. Even Camões, the most patriotic of Portuguese poets, called Spain "the head of Europe." It is also known that Vicente was the official in charge of all plays for court occa-

* vē sān' tĕ

sions and that he was a musician as well as a dramatist.

Of the forty-four plays which he wrote, sixteen are entirely in Portuguese, eleven in Spanish, and seventeen in a curious and artificial mixture of the two. Despite the fact that Vicente wrote for the court, his poetry is essentially popular in its inspiration, shows much imagination, is quite lively and forms an integral part of his plays—though he was a lyric poet of very considerable genius, his poetry is to be found almost exclusively in his dramas. The richness of his language, it is said, cannot be surpassed by any other Portuguese poet. Vicente was strongly influenced by Erasmus and his ideas, and Erasmus, in turn, admired Gil Vicente so much that he compared him to Plautus. According to Valbuena Prat, plays with such social comment and ecclesiastical satire could have been written only under conditions of full liberty, and he finds it more than a coincidence that the last known date of a Vicente play—1536—is the date of the establishment of the Inquisition in Portugal. However, one should bear in mind that the castigation of the clergy for its loose morals, venality, and corruption can be found among very many of the authors of the time. Indeed, it became a commonplace in literature. In Vicente we find the sacred traditions of the Middle Ages united with the new ideas of the Renaissance. Menéndez y Pelayo says of his *Barcas*: "These *Barcas* are a sort of classic transformation of the ancient 'dances of death,' not in the lugubrious and terrifying elements which they contain, but in what they have of general satire of the vices, states, classes and conditions of human society."

Although Vicente's drama is very superior to that of Encina, the Portuguese writer was much influenced by the Spaniard in his early plays. This can be seen in the *Auto da Visitaçao* or *Monólogo del Vaquero* (1502), the *Auto Pastoril*, the *Auto de los Reyes Magos* (1503), and even in the *Auto de la Sibila Casandra* (1513?), still popular in inspiration but with a more complex plot. This latter play contains the well-known poem and song "Muy graciosa es la doncella." The influence of Encina is still apparent in the *Auto da Fe* (1510), the *Auto de los Cuatro Tiempos* (1516?) and the three *Barcas: Auto da Barca do Inferno, Auto da Barca do Purgatorio* and the *Auto da Barca da Gloria* (1517-19). Of his non-religious plays, most of which are written in Castilian, some of the best are the *Comedia del Viudo* (1514), the *Comedia de Rubena* (1521), and the tragi-comedies *Amadís de Gaula* (1533) and *Don Duardos* (1525?). The latter is sometimes called Vicente's masterpiece and is based on the *Primaleón, Libro Segunda de Palmerín*.

The chief edition of his works is the one edited by J. Mendes dos Remedios, *Obras*, 3 vols. (1907-14). Of the numerous translations into English some of the better known are: *Four Plays*, edited by A. F. G. Bell (1920); *Lyrics of Gil Vicente*, translated by Bell (1914); G. G. King *The Play of the Sibyl Cassandra* (1921); and A. F. Gould *The Ship of Hell* (1929). The latter is an English poetic version of the trilogy of the *Barcas*.

ABOUT: Bell, A. F. G. Gil Vicente (with a full bibliography); Crawford, J. P. W. Spanish Drama before Lope de Vega; Keates, L. The Court Theatre of Gil Vicente; Hispania, 1953. [In Spanish—Menéndez y Pelayo, M. Estudios de Crítica Literaria. See also studies by L. M. de Castro e Azevedo; A. Braamcamp Freire; C. M. de Vasconcelas.]

R. E. O.

*VICO, GIOVANNI BATTISTA (or GIAMBATTISTA) (June 23, 1668-January 23, 1744), Italian philosopher, historian, jurist, critic, poet, and founder of the study of aesthetics, was born in Naples, the son of a poor bookseller, and was tempered from infancy to endure the hardships which he suffered all his life. Because of a fall from a ladder when he was seven years old, he remained ill for a long time—a fact, he believed, that contributed to his serious and somewhat melancholy nature. In his father's bookshop he found the first stimulus to that love of knowledge which he preferred to satisfy by himself, though he had begun his studies in school and with certain masters. Of extraordinary mental capacity, he studied broadly, thoroughly, and reflectively philosophy, theology, Latin, and Latin and Italian literatures. He early admired Plato and Tacitus and later esteemed Grotius, Bacon, and Tesauro, as well.

At the age of seventeen Vico began his study of law and was able, a year later, to defend his father in a civil suit. When nineteen years old, he began a period of private teaching (1687-95) in Naples and elsewhere and, in 1693, he published his first work, a collection of poems which showed no special gift. Upon his return to Naples in 1695 he composed discourses, orations, and various compositions for which he was commissioned. In 1699 Vico won a competition for the professorship of rhetoric at the University of Naples, more an honor than a means of gaining a livelihood. In this same year he married Teresa Caterina Destito.

* vē′ kō

VICO

Learning was for Vico a vital and daily activity. The harsh reality of his adult family life, because of a mentally ill son and an illiterate wife, did not force him to escape into abstractions but, on the contrary, convinced him that reality is the source of all principles and is, therefore, the direct object, source, and synthesis of our knowledge.

As a teacher of rhetoric, Vico had the opportunity to propose publicly his ideas on reality and knowledge. From 1699 to 1708 he had the duty of giving a public oration in Latin at the beginning of each academic year. The seven existing orations given on these occasions are a proposal of his revolutionary ideas, which later became his *Scienza Nuova* and the development of which has caused Vico to be called the inventor of the science of aesthetics.

The orations end with the important *De Nostri Temporis Studiorem Ratione* (On Educational Method of Our Time, 1708), deploring the method which forces study by deduction, thus falsely categorizing with the Cartesian process of logic, instead of knowledge by induction from reality, which is constantly in flux and therefore new. Knowledge inductively gained becomes a personal truth which engenders eloquence and which is what man's mind itself creates, as he later said (1710) in his book *The Ancient Wisdom.* Such a study of living reality engenders true art, not an imitation which denies the value of imagination and of feeling which precedes thinking. He later added that, for him, wit (imagination and memory) was the

"father of all invention." In this, Vico forecasts the romantic movement and, at the same time, he belongs to the Renaissance reaction against formalism and scholastic verbalism.

Because Vico wanted to "unite in one principle all knowledge, human and divine" and because he earnestly wanted to prove himself eligible for the professorship of civil law at the University of Naples, he wrote increasingly after 1717, the date when the chair of civil law became vacant. In 1720 Vico published the important metaphysical and judicial treatise *On the One Principle and One End of Universal Law,* which declares that man's mind unites him with God, and which deals principally with the statement of his cyclic theory of history that states revert to their original conditions. A year later he published *On the Consistency of the Jurist,* a work on the consistency of philosophy or of God and on the consistency of philology or of the science of man. This was followed by the publication of notes later joined to the previous work *(Diritto Universale).*

Vico's competition (1723) for the professorship was not successful; bitter, he withdrew to devote himself to develop for publication under the patronage of the Cardinal Corsini his greatest work, *Scienza Nuova Prima* (Principles of a New Science Concerning the Common Nature of Nations, 1725), on the nature of poetry as "the first language of men" and as an imaginative phase of consciousness and the poet as the earliest and the truest historian and philosopher, a work he called the result of "twenty-five years of continuous and harsh meditation." From December 1729 to April 1730, after interrupting work on "lives" of Lodoli and Conti, Vico revised his *Scienza Nuova,* with two new sections, "Of Poetic Knowledge," and "Of the Discovery of the True Homer," with the remarkable conclusion that the true Homer was an idea, a heroic ideal of the Greek people themselves singing, at the close of an era, not of their deeds but of the glorification of Achilles' wrath. The work covers a kaleidoscope of human traits and areas of information: psychology, sociology, linguistics, politics, philosophy, astronomy, physics, geography.

With poets as the senses and philosophers as the intellect of mankind, Vico claims the great poet is one born in an epoch of imagination, not reflection; therefore, Homer results from the barbarism of antiquity and Dante from the Middle Ages, the "second barbarism of Italy." Furthermore, he states that only the poet knows how to transform logic into imagination and his ideas into portraits and into ideal truths. As autonomous fancy, superior to reason in creativity, poetry gives an imaginative vision and links itself with history, which gives the consciousness of certitude and which is a science of the ideal, or the imaginative or poetic moments of our human mind.

Vico's new poetic theory was not fully appreciated until the nineteenth century. His work—based on the cycle of the divine, the heroic, and the human—is the first survey of the social evolution of mankind and the first to recognize the superiority of imagination over reason, as well as the unity of spirit and knowledge created by man himself. Yet its influence was not felt until its enthusiastic acceptance first by Goethe, then by Michelet, Foscolo, and Mazzini, De Sanctis, Coleridge, and—in the twentieth century—Croce, Joyce, and Yeats. Only one of his contemporaries, the Spaniard Luzán, honored him.

Vico wrote his *Scienza Nuova* in a style that is strikingly individual, vital, documented, compact, and aphoristic, sometimes grand, exalted, and enthusiastic. However, when he wrote his *Vita* (his autobiography) in 1725-28, he turned to a simpler and more objective manner of analyzing and interpreting his works. Finally, recognized as a scholar, he was appointed historiographer to the King of Naples in 1735. He retired in 1741 and died three years later, a few months before the publication of the third edition of his *Scienza Nuova*.

The New Science has been excellently translated by T. G. Bergin and M. H. Fisch (1948). The same translators presented Vico's *Autobiography* (1944) with a scholarly introduction.

ABOUT: Adams, H. P. The Life and Writings of Vico; Berlin, I. *in* Art and Ideas in Eighteenth Century Italy; Berry, T. The Historical Theory of Giambattista Vico; Croce, B. Aesthetic, *also* The Philosophy of Vico. [In Italian—see studies by F. Amerio, A. Corsano, G. Gentile, A. M. Jacobelli Isoldi, F. Lanza, F. Nicolini.]

R. P. C.

VIDAL, PEIRE. See PEIRE VIDAL

*VIGNY, ALFRED VICTOR, Comte de (March 27, 1797-September 17, 1863), French poet, was born at Loches, in Touraine. On the paternal side Alfred traced his nobility to the time of Charles IX; his mother was born Baraudin, whose title also dated from

* vē nyē'

VIGNY

the sixteenth century. The Vignys had a tradition of military service, and Léon de Vigny, a knight, was a sixty-year-old retired soldier when Alfred was born. Three older children born to high-strung Mme de Vigny, twenty years her husband's junior, had died in infancy. The family, once wealthy, was reduced to modest circumstances by the French Revolution, but continued to revere traditions of nobility.

When Alfred was eighteen months old the family moved to Paris. Alfred was a delicate child and never developed a robust constitution. In 1807 he was enrolled in the Hix boarding school. An excellent student, he was the butt of his classmates' teasing; they found him offensively superior in scholarship and in deportment. At fourteen Alfred withdrew from the boarding school to study Greek and English under the tutorship of Abbé Gaillard while pursuing mathematics at the Lycée Bonaparte (now Condorcet)—he thought of entering the École Polytechnique. But with the Restoration (1814) there came what seemed like a short-cut to a glittering military career, and Vigny obtained the post of second lieutenant in the king's guard.

In the escort which accompanied the king's flight during Napoleon's brief return, Vigny was interned at Antwerp. With the return of Louis XVIII to the throne, he was reinstated in the infantry. Then began the monotonous routine of garrison duty and maneuvers at Vincennes, at Courbevoie, at Rouen. He was promoted to first lieutenant in 1822, the following year to captain in a line regiment. The intervention of France in Spanish affairs seemed to offer Vigny an opportunity for military action, for his regiment was sent from Strasbourg to Bordeaux. But it was stationed on the Pyrenees frontier, mainly at Oloron. A leave in 1824 broke the monotony of garrison life; disgusted and bored, Vigny evaded further stagnation by obtaining indefinite leave, renewed until his separation from the army in 1827.

He found in literature a panacea for and refuge from the pettiness of his military career. The Bible, Milton's *Paradise Lost*, Chateaubriand's *Génie du Christianisme*, Byron, André Chénier—their pages filled his free time and thought. His childhood friend was Émile Deschamps, at whose salon he met Victor Hugo and Henri de Latouche, editor of André Chénier. Hugo was the director of *Le Conservateur Littéraire* and in 1820 published an article by Vigny on Byron, as well as a poem, "Le Bal." Two years later Vigny was a witness at Hugo's marriage. That same year both published their first volumes of verse, and Vigny contributed to *La Muse Française,* Hugo's politically conservative literary periodical. Hugo praised *Éloa* (1823), influenced by Chateaubriand, Klopstock, Milton, Byron, and Thomas Moore.

Vigny enjoyed the sociability of salons, literary and aristocratic. Handsome in his uniform, with an air of charm and conversational facility, he shone at Mme Ancelot's salon. A flirtation with Delphine Gay would have led to a marriage between the two young poets, but Mme de Vigny did not approve of the match: Delphine was neither noble nor rich. But at Pau, in the Pyrenees, lived Lydia Bunbury, the daughter of a wealthy Englishman, whom Vigny married in the Protestant Church there in 1825, his commanding officer having given his consent. It was an unfortunate alliance, for Lydia was of mediocre intelligence and poor health. She was unable to have children and was an inadequate companion. Settled in Paris, her husband found compensation in study, in writing, and in other women.

In 1826 Vigny published another volume of verse, *Poèmes Antiques et Modernes,* and an historical novel, *Cinq-Mars.* With the former, for his time, Vigny was considered the exponent of the "poème," as Lamartine was for the elegy and Hugo for the ode. Of these modernized and abbreviated epics, "Le Cor," based on the legend of Roland, has remained famous for its evocation of the hero's horn and for the descriptions of the Pyrenees. *Cinq-Mars* was a return to a juvenile enthusiasm for history, and a recognition of Sir Walter Scott's influence in France. Although utilizing actual historical characters and some two years of research in Paris libraries, *Cinq-Mars* departs from fact to project a personality and a thesis about nobility. Criticism by reviewers induced Vigny to write a preface for the fifth edition (the book sold well) in which he explained that he had used art and history to further a "philosophical" purpose. Later he confessed that he had changed his mind: factual truth must be respected.

A revolution was in the making in the French theatre, for which Hugo had written a manifesto, the preface to *Cromwell* (1827). Shakespeare and English subjects were the vogue. Vigny, who had written but not published several plays, adapted *Othello* as *Le More de Venise* in 1828; it was presented the following year by the Théâtre Français. Vigny also collaborated with Émile Deschamps on a translation of *Roméo et Juliette.* An original work by Vigny, *La Maréchale d'Ancre* (1830), had only a partial success, for it came after Dumas *père's* historical drama *Henri III et Sa Cour* and Hugo's grandiose verse-play *Hernani.* Five years later Vigny essayed the theatre again with *Chatterton.* It was Vigny's intention, in dramatizing Chatterton's suicide, to present a philosophical play which would illustrate the fate of the poet in a world of intellectual and moral mediocrity. More sober and unified than romantic theatre, *Chatterton* reflects a semi-classical, semi-modern conception of tragedy.

Chatterton was written as a vehicle for Marie Dorval, whom Vigny had met in 1830. Their tempestuous relationship lasted until 1838, despite infidelities and inconstancy on the part of Marie. Disillusioned by the political turn of affairs; hurt by the popular success, superior to his own recognition, enjoyed by others; unfortunate in his sentimental affections—Vigny became increasingly pessimistic and ostensibly diffident of sociability. The bourgeois monarchy repelled him, and Vigny was temporarily attracted to the ideas of Saint-Simon and of Lamennais. Even religion offered no solace, and Vigny considered stoicism the necessary virile attitude vis-à-vis life.

This disillusionment underlay *Stello* (1832), which related somewhat romanticized views of Gilbert, Chatterton, and Chénier. *Servitude et Grandeur Militaires* (1835) presented for the military what *Stello* had done for the poet, pointing out how the soldier rises above his servility through denial, discipline, and self-sacrifice; if servitude is one's destiny, honor is its acceptance. *Daphné* (written in 1837 but not published until 1912), never completed, was an attempt to project the notion above and beyond particular religions. These stoical attitudes informed *Les Destinées,* composed of seven poems which appeared from time to time in the *Revue des Deux Mondes* (as well as four poems never published during Vigny's lifetime). "La Mort du Loup," "La Maison du Berger," "La Bouteille à la Mer"—these are Vigny's most impressive and heroic poems; the last has been especially appreciated since the advent of the symbolist school.

Vigny sought election to the French Academy, but was not elected until 1845. After a spell of social affability, he withdrew to his estate at Maine-Giraud, in Charente. He was defeated for office twice in electoral campaigns (1848 and 1849), and was ignored by the imperial regime for a seat in the Senate. His wife was bedridden, and died in 1862. The following year he too succumbed in Paris, to a stomach cancer which had afflicted him painfully for some time. He was buried at Montmartre cemetery.

Vigny has remained the figure of the stoical and proud poet who made emotion subservient to the intellect. His papers have furnished the memoirs and reflections which Louis Ratisbonne, his literary executor, has entitled *Journal d'un Poète* (this should be consulted in editions edited by Fernand Baldensperger, especially the Pléiade edition of 1948). His "complete works" are in course of publication, and may include manuscripts in the possession of the Sangnier family. Marc Sangnier has also published *Mémoires Inédits* (1958). Edmond Estève was responsible for a critical edition of *Poèmes Antiques et Modernes* (1914), V. L. Saulnier for that of *Les Destinées* (1947). *Chatterton* was edited by E. A. Dawson and J. L. Jones (1939). V. L. Saulnier has edited the *Lettres à "Augusta"* (1952), Eric Lugin those to Brizeux (1954).

William Hazlitt called his translation *Cinq-Mars, or A Conspiracy under Louis XIII* (1847), while Madge Pemberton · entitled hers *The Spider and the Fly* (1925). *Servitude et Grandeur Militaires* was translated by F. W. Huard as *Military Servitude and Grandeur* (1919), but Humphrey Hare titled it *The Military Necessity* (1953).

ABOUT: Bird, C. W. Alfred de Vigny's Chatterton; Whitridge, A. Alfred de Vigny. [In French

—Baldensperger, F. Alfred de Vigny; Bonnefoy, G. La Pensée Religieuse et Morale d'Alfred de Vigny; Castex, P. G. Vigny, l'Homme et l'Œuvre; Estève, E. Alfred de Vigny, Sa Pensée et Son Art; Flottes, P. La Pensée Politique et Sociale d'Alfred de Vigny; La Salle, B. de, Alfred de Vigny; Lauvrière, E. Alfred de Vigny, Sa Vie et Son Œuvre.]

S. S. W.

*VILLEHARDOUIN, GEOFFROI DE

(1150?-1212?), French chronicler, the first to write a great historical work in French instead of Latin, was born in the castle of Villehardouin, near Troyes, in the Champagne region. He became Marshal of Champagne in 1191. What is known of his life is mostly what he relates about it in his memoirs, in which he refers to himself in the third person. This work (*The Conquest of Constantinople*) covers events from 1198 to 1207. In 1198, Villehardouin took the cross and became one of the main leaders of the Fourth Crusade (1202-04), which was inspired by the energetic Pope Innocent III. With five other barons, Villehardouin was sent to Venice to negotiate there the passage of the crusaders' army. The Venetians, however, were trading with Egypt, and their cooperation proved extremely onerous financially, putting the Christian army at the mercy of its creditors. The Fourth Crusade never reached the Holy Sepulchre in Jerusalem. Instead the barons, fighting the Byzantine Greek Empire, landed in Dalmatia, took Constantinople twice, and spread over the Eastern European territory. A Latin Empire replaced the Greek Byzantine Empire from 1204 to 1261. Villehardouin respected his word given to the creditors, the debts were paid, the barons grew rich and received fiefs in the Balkans, Greece, and European Turkey. Villehardouin became Marshal of Romania, settled in his own fief of Messinople, wrote his work there, and never returned to France. This chronicle is a vindication of the detouring of the Fourth Crusade rather than the narrative of an impartial historian. He explains that unfortunate circumstances—including lack of money and hordes of dissidents and "false crusaders"—forced the barons to fight on the Empire's territory. While it is true that the crusaders met with almost insurmountable obstacles, we perceive in this work, under an apparent naïveté, a shrewd mind. Although Villehardouin honored his given word as a true feudal lord, he dealt in realities and believed more in success than in chivalrous ideals.

* vē lär dwăn'

967

His clear style shows no effort toward the picturesque, and his descriptions are terse, somewhat stiff.

There is no original manuscript of *The Conquest of Constantinople* in existence but there are some dating from the 13th and the 14th centuries. The first printed edition dates from 1585 and others range from 1661 to 1891. The main English translations are those of T. Smith, 1829, and of Sir F. T. Marzials (Everyman's Library), 1908.

ABOUT: Pears, E. The Fall of Constantinople; The Cambridge Medieval History, IV. [In French—Pauphilet, A. Historiens et Chroniqueurs du Moyen Age; Sainte-Beuve, C. A. Causeries du Lundi, IX. In German—Moeser, H. Geoffroy von Villehardouin und der Lateinerzug gegen Byzanz.]

P. LA.

*VILLIERS DE L'ISLE-ADAM, JEAN MARIE MATHIAS PHILIPPE AUGUSTE, Comte de (November 7, 1838-August 19, 1889), French short-story writer and dramatist, was born at Saint-Brieuc, in Brittany. His father, Joseph Toussaint Charles, marquis and Knight of the Order of Malta, belonged to a family that traced its noble ancestry to at least 1277 (and perhaps 1065); subject to the Catholic Church, Joseph had had to obtain papal dispensation for his marriage to Marie Françoise Le Nepveu de Carfort, of an old Brittany family. The couple was very poor, living on the bounty of an aunt, Marie de Kérinou. Mathias attended school at Saint-Brieuc and Laval. An indifferent student, he read a great deal, especially in the romantics, and wrote imitative verse. Still in his teens, he wrote a play, *Morgane*, and conceived the trilogy of which *Axël* would be the only completed part.

At the beginning of 1857 the family moved to Paris. Villiers made the acquaintance of the Parnassian poets, and of café life. In 1858 he published a little brochure, *Deux Essais de Poésie*, at his own expense. He became enthusiastic about Hegel and cabalism while preparing *Premières Poésies* (1859), also published at the author's expense. The volume received no attention.

With the return of his family to Saint-Brieuc, Villiers was uninhibited in the conduct of a Bohemian way of life, after a spell in the provinces. Through Baudelaire he made the acquaintance of Richard Wagner and began to read Poe. (Villiers was reputed to be a superb interpreter on the piano of Wagner's music.) He was working on a seven-volume project of which only *Isis* was published (1862). Dissatisfied, later he attempted to destroy all copies of *Isis,* which he considered unworthy.

With the death in 1864 of Mlle de Kérinou began Villiers' life-long indigence. But he managed to pay for the shoddy publication of the play *Elën* (1865) and *Morgane* (1866). A contemplated marriage with Estelle Gautier, daughter of Théophile Gautier by Ernesta Grisi, was blocked by Villiers' class-conscious family. Living a more and more Bohemian existence, Villiers became one of the pillars of the salon of Nina de Villard (also called Nina de Callias), his mistress. But he was barely subsisting as editor-in-chief of the *Revue des Lettres et des Arts* (1867-68). His first published short story, "Azraël" (later entitled "L'Annonciateur"), was unsuccessful in a mass-circulation newspaper, *La Liberté;* a play, *La Révolte,* praised by Wagner and Dumas, was a commercial fiasco at the Théâtre du Vaudeville — it was withdrawn within five days. Villiers found some solace by visiting Wagner at Triebschen and attending the music festival at Weimar. There he read the farcical *Tribulat Bonhomet* to Liszt, to the Grand-Duke of Saxe-Weimar, and to other nobles.

With the outbreak of the Franco-Prussian War, Villiers was made a lieutenant in the National Guard, but saw no active military service. He lacked the bare material necessities: Léon Bloy has said that Villiers was a sparring partner in a gymnasium for sixty francs a month; he worked for a quack, pretending to be mad, according to the Goncourts. Under such conditions, literary production was greatly hampered. *Axël* had been ready by 1872, but between 1872 and 1876, when he started *L'Ève Future,* almost nothing was written. Villiers wasted many stories by narrating instead of writing them —the *Contes Cruels* we do have are only a small part of those he conceived. The dearth of literary periodicals interested in his work was not uninfluential in limiting Villiers' efforts. A competition, with a prize in money, encouraged him to write the play *Le Nouveau Monde* (1875); Villiers was one of the three co-sharers of the award. Minor editorial positions, ill-paid, and obscure jobs, plus the discreet help of friends, barely kept him alive. He even ran as the Royalist candidate for the Seine department, and was soundly defeated. Under such miserable circumstances he became the lover of a humble widow, Marie Élisabeth Dantine, who bore him a son, Victor, in 1881.

* vē lyä′ dē lēl à dän′

968

Contes Cruels (1883) owed their publication to the efforts of the actor Coquelin (*cadet*) of the Comédie Française, who had recited humorous monologues by Villiers at parties. But the commercial possibilities of publication were destroyed by the failure of *Le Nouveau Monde* which was finally produced in a theatre. He was able to place articles with *Le Figaro,* barely enough to exist on. His closest friends were poor like himself: Léon Bloy and Joris Karl Huysmans, with whom he formed the triumvirate of the "Council of Poverty." *L'Ève Future* brought Villiers five hundred francs; *Axël,* four hundred; most of his short stories brought in seventy francs each. These tales were collected in *Histoires Insolites* and *Nouveaux Contes Cruels.* Suffering from a stomach cancer, Villiers spent an agonizing month in the hospital. Shortly before his death, the proud nobleman married his mistress, who did not know how to write, in order to legitimize his son. Villiers was buried at Batignolles cemetery, in a short-term plot purchased by his friends. In 1895 a public subscription provided a place for him at Père Lachaise cemetery.

Villiers de l'Isle-Adam's name evokes the portrait of the disinterested writer who places art above any other consideration, even that of life itself. For him, each word had to be delicately weighed. Wielding satire, he cut into the ridiculous pretentiousness of a scientific age and mocked the customs and ambitions of modern man.

Tribulat Bonhomet, "an enormous, sombre buffoonery, matching the century," sums up the narrowness of the pseudo-scientific view, but *L'Ève Future* granted that science had virtual, immense possibilities. Avid for a transcendent ideal, which he fabricated from a strange mélange of Catholicism, Hegelianism, and occultism, Villiers promulgated in his *Axël* the figure of an absolutist disdaining all earthy fulfillments for the eternity of possession in death. René Lalou has described *Axël* as "the last expression of European romanticism, the *Faust* of the expiring nineteenth century," adding Wagnerian composition and conception to Goethe. Hardly definable, the blend of irony and lyricism, of perversity and scientism, has made Villiers the symbol of prose symbolism. Of Villiers' spokesman Axël, Edmund Wilson wrote: "It will early be seen that this super-dreamer of Villiers' is the type of all the heroes of the symbolists, of our day as well as of his. . . ."

Some of Villiers' work has never been republished, and his literary executors, Stéphane Mallarmé and Joris Karl Huysmans, apparently bungled their responsibility in regard to manuscripts and notes. The so-called complete works were published in eleven volumes (1914-31). *Contes Cruels* have appeared in critical editions by E. Drougard (2 volumes, 1931-32) and P. G. Castex (2 volumes, 1954-56). The latter had also edited previously unpublished texts in *Reliquae* (1954).

Claire Lenoir (of *Tribulat Bonhomet*) has been translated, with an introduction, by Arthur Symons (1925), who also translated *Queen Ysabeau* (of *Contes Cruels*) the same year. *Axël* has been translated by H. P. R. Finberg (1925), with a preface by William Butler Yeats. T. Barclay was the translator of *The Revolt* and *The Escape* (1910). H. Miles translated *Contes Cruels* as *Sardonic Tales* (1927). Stuart Merrill translated "Vox Populi" for *Pastels in Prose* (1890). The anonymous translation of "The Torture of Hope" is to be found in *Great Short Stories of the World* by B. H. Clark and M. Lieber (1925) and in *The Bedside Book of Famous French Stories* by B. Becker and R. N. Linscott (1945). A new translation of "The Desire to Be a Man" (from *Sardonic Tales* and reprinted in the 1933 *French Short Stories of the Nineteenth and Twentieth Centuries*) was made by Pierre Schneider for *French Stories and Tales* (1954), edited by S. Geist. *Contes Cruels* was translated as *Cruel Tales* by Robert Baldick (1964).

ABOUT: Huneker, J. G. Iconoclasts, *also* The Pathos of Distance; Quennell, P. Baudelaire and the Symbolists; Symons, A. Symbolist Movement in Literature; Whitridge, A. Critical Ventures; Wilson E. Axel's Castle. [In French—Bollery, J. Biblio-iconographie de Villiers de l'Isle-Adam; Daireaux, M. Villiers de l'Isle-Adam, l'Homme et l'Œuvre; Lebois, A. Villiers de l'Isle-Adam, Révélateur du Verbe. In Italian—Lanfredini, D. Villiers de l'Isle-Adam.]

S. S. W.

*VILLON, FRANÇOIS** (1431?-1463?), French poet, also called François de Montcorbier alias des Loges but better known as Villon, was born in Paris. The life and activities of this poet centered in the capital and in the region south of it—Rennes, Bourges. An orphan early in life, he was given for adoption by his mother to an uncle (?), Guillaume de Villon, chaplain of the Parisian chapter of Saint-Benoît-le-Bétourné. François attended the University of Paris where he received his bachelor's degree in 1449, and two other degrees in 1452—the last one his master's. By virtue of his education he was a clerk, and it seems that as such he expected a position in the church which he never enjoyed. The end of Villon's student life was marked by a university demonstra-

* vē yôn'

tion against the Parisian police, in 1451-52. His probable participation in this protest provided the subject of a book lost or perhaps never written by Villon or anyone else and whose title *Le Roman du Pet au Diable* he left to his "more than father," Guillaume de Villon.

In 1455, in a case of apparently legitimate defense over a matter concerning a woman, Villon killed a clerk, Philippe de Chermoye. He quickly left Paris, but returned after receiving two letters exonerating him from his crime. In 1456, he was again in trouble, this time with three partners, when he participated in the robbery of 500 écus from the collegial church of Navarre in Paris. He left the city once more after writing his first known poem, the *Lais* commonly called the *Petit Testament* (320 octosyllabic verses grouped into stanzas of eight lines each and called *huitains*). Even this early poem shows the jocular nature of Villon. To give an alibi for his departure the poet says that since his mistress has hurt his heart he must go away to Angers. He then proceeds to give biting and comical legacies to various friends and enemies; for example, to his father he leaves his reputation, which, before 1456, was not particularly honorable.

For the years 1456-60 Villon's life away from Paris is not well known. He is seen once participating successfully in a poetic competition held at Blois at the court of Duc Charles d'Orléans, himself a poet. In 1461, for unknown reasons, Villon spent a summer in Meung-sur-Loire in the prisons of the bishop Thibaut d'Aussigny. Here he suffered very much and came close to dying. It is not surprising to find that Villon saw in Thibaut his greatest enemy and wished him dead.

In 1461 Villon wrote his poem of 2,023 lines, the *Testament*, called by contrast the *Grand Testament* since it follows the pattern adopted in the so-called *Petit Testament*. It has one important additional form: sixteen ballads interwoven between *huitains*. There are also minor forms: two *rondeaux* and one *chanson*. The careful insertion of these forms in the *Testament* shows the concern of the poet for unity of composition. The harmonious ballads are strategically placed to intensify a theme which has been manipulated in preceding *huitains*. This technique can be observed in the introduction of the theme of death, followed by three ballads (one of them the famous *Ballade des Dames*) expressing the culmination of the idea. Then follows in decrescendo the same theme which,

through an ingenious verse of transition, is transformed into a further motif correlated with the idea of death. In this particular instance the motif is an old man's thought of suicide which, with one verse of transition: "The same is true for these moldy women," becomes a similar thought for old women. At this point Villon gives his admirable monologue: *Les Regrets de la Belle Heaulmière* followed by a no less strong *Ballade de la Belle Heaulmière*. The general composition of the *Testament* can be thought of as a chain reaction in which one theme calls forth another.

The prosaic title of the poem suggests that Villon's legacies and death are themes, just as in the *Lais*. One notable exception to the general tone of irony is Villon's legacy to his mother; for the first time the poet is serious and composes for her a *Ballade pour Prier Nostre Dame*. He also wrote on love and moral conflicts, but maintained in these themes a note of personal involvement, and not the allegories of other poets of the Middle Ages. Unlike the latter, Villon wrote about himself, rather than abstractions, and this is one of the reasons why he has been called a modern poet. Yet Villon was medieval in his world view, much like that of other poets of his time. His belief in God, his preoccupation with life after death, were medieval, as also his sense of morality— whether or not he could be true to it. He expressed repentance perhaps for his sins but as far as it is humanly possible to tell he did not live up to his good intentions. The *Testament* concludes on a note of death, but at the very end the poet drinks a glass of wine as if to scoff at his whole creation. This ending maintains the general tone of the *Testament*, for all of Villon's legacies were comical, ironical, sometimes mean, revengeful, and sometimes showing a good sense of humor. However, the ending of the *Testament* has something more than just a comical effect, if one keeps in mind Villon's spiritual state.

In spite of, perhaps because of, much suffering and tears, this poet laughed at life and at the whole of society. Only one thing kept him from looking at the world as a total absurdity—his belief in God—and this at times weakened. Nevertheless, Villon, despite his impenitence, reverted to God for help. It seems that his poetry throve because of this ambivalent spiritual state. Philosophically Villon felt no need of repentance; although he was bad and justified himself constantly, he believed that God was good and could not possibly fail him. The concept of the medieval God of Villon, the God who suffered and helped those who suffered, saved him from other disasters and perhaps from suicide.

Poésies Diverses, sixteen isolated compositions (609 lines), represents the last group of poems written in French. Two of them stand out: *Épitaphe Villon,* also called *Ballade des Pendus,* and the *Débat du Cœur et du Corps de Villon.* The first was written probably in 1463 when Villon was condemned to death by hanging for having participated in a brawl. He appealed, and the sentence was commuted to ten years' banishment. After January 8, 1463 no real information about Villon exists save two anecdotes of doubtful reliability from the pen of Rabelais who said he spent time at the court of Edward IV of England, and passed his last days in Saint-Maixent in Poitou. This thoroughly Parisian poet, probably a member of a national gang (les Coquillards), also composed seven ballads in the special slang of the underworld.

Villon, a lyric poet of the first rank, has been very much read since the nineteenth century. The French, and particularly the French poets, are fond of him. English-speaking people have also shown great interest in Villon. There was even a Villon society in Victorian England. Some English translations, however, are too reserved to communicate the realistic power and bold imagery of his verse. English translators of Villon include John Payne, Swinburne, D. G. Rossetti, and W. E. Henley; in more recent years Léonie Adams, Norman Cameron, and Robert Lowell have published translations. The best single edition is the *Complete Poems,* translated by J. H. Lepper, together with the complete John Payne version and versions by Swinburne, Rossetti, etc. (1924).

ABOUT: Fox, J. The Poetry of Villon; Lepper, J. H. The Great and Little Testaments of François Villon; Lewis, D. B. W. François Villon; Pound, E. The Spirit of Romance; Stevenson, R. L. Familiar Studies of Men and Books; French Studies, 1953; Romanic Review, 1946. [In French—Foulet, L. F. Villon. Œuvres (1930); Paris, G. François Villon; Vidal, E. Villon et la Critique Moderne (doctoral dissertation, University of Michigan, 1958.]

E. V.

VINCI, LEONARDO DA. See LEONARDO DA VINCI

*VINJE, AASMUND OLAVSSEN

(April 6, 1818-July 30, 1870), Norwegian poet, essayist, journalist, was born in the province of Telemark in southern Norway at the farm Vinje, where his father, Olav Aasmundson, was a farm hand. His mother

was Thorbjørg Gjermundsdatter. A few years after his birth, the family moved to a small cottage in a clearing made by his father. Here Aasmund grew up under poor but happy circumstances. His mother died of consumption when he was ten. The country school was deficient, but Aasmund studied at home. Later he taught school and earned a few pennies from odd jobs on the farm. He went to a normal school, from which he graduated in 1843. After a few years as a teacher he went in 1848 to the capital where he enrolled at a private school preparing for the matriculation examination. Here he became acquainted with Ibsen and Bjørnson. In 1850 he passed the examination.

The same year Vinje and Ibsen started a paper, *Andhrimner,* which died within its first year. Vinje was employed as correspondent for *Drammens Tidende.* The thousand letters he wrote for this paper amount to more than half of his entire prose production. In 1856 he started a weekly, *Dølen* (The Dalesman), which he wrote almost singlehandedly and managed in his own erratic and peculiar manner. He had earlier used the standard Norwegian language, but influenced by the nationalistic language movement he changed to a tongue based on his native dialect of Telemark. In this paper Vinje published his literary products of various genres. He wrote short stories in verse and prose, numerous lyrical poems, critical reviews, pamphlets, and satires. His poems were published in two collections, *Diktsamling* (Poems, 1863), and *Blandkorn* (Mixed Grain, 1867).

In 1862 Vinje spent about a year in England and Scotland and published his impressions in a little volume in English, *A Norseman's View of Britain and the British* (1863). Employment as a clerk in the Law Department bettered his meager living conditions. In 1869 he married Rosa Constance Kjeldseth, divorced from a bailiff, but she died the next year in childbirth.

A few verses of Vinje's poems in English translation appear in the Grøndahl-Raknes book mentioned below.

ABOUT: Grøndahl, I. and Raknes, O. Chapters in Norwegian Literature.

A. J.

*VIVES, JUAN LUIS (March 6, 1492-

May 6, 1540), Spanish humanist, was born in Valencia, the son of Luis Vives and Blanca March, both of noble ancestry but only moderate means. He received his early

VIVES

education at his mother's knee and at the local Valencian college, still essentially medieval; his teacher Amiguet assigned him a *disputatio* against the leading Spanish humanist Nebrija. From 1509 to 1514 he was at the University of Paris (Collège de Beauvais), where he studied under Gaspar Lax and John Dullard; here too the intellectual atmosphere remained largely impervious to the Renaissance. Vives, in disgust, left Paris for Flanders, where in 1519 he wrote an attack on the superficial technicalities of Parisian scholasticism, *In Pseudo-Dialecticos*. By this time Vives had become a friend of Erasmus, whose satirical style is detectable in his later treatises on education.

From 1514 on, Vives' home was the city of Bruges. The Spanish colony at Bruges was numerous; there he married in 1524 a distant cousin, Margarita Valdaura. He went to Louvain temporarily, in 1518, to join the new Collegium Trilingue; he attended Erasmus' lectures and gave lectures himself on Pliny, Virgil, and other Latin authors. His chief pupil was Guillaume de Croy, archbishop-designate of Toledo. During this period he became a friend of Guillaume Budé, the great French Hellenist.

At the suggestion of Erasmus, in 1520 Vives began his edition, with commentaries, of St. Augustine's *City of God*; he completed this laborious and monumental task in 1522, dedicating it to an appreciative Henry VIII. At the invitation of Cardinal Wolsey, in 1522 he made the first of several annual visits to England, where Queen

Catherine of Aragon and Sir Thomas More welcomed the Spanish scholar and friend of Erasmus. Vives was asked by the king and queen to draw up a plan for the education of their daughter Mary, to whom he recommended the reading of More's *Utopia*. His treatise *De Institutione Feminae Christianae* (The Instruction of a Christian Woman) was first published in Latin in 1523 and translated into English in 1540. Also in 1523 he was called to Oxford where he lectured on Quintilian's rhetoric at the new college of Corpus Christi. His popular *Introductio ad Sapientiam* (1524; English translation, *An Introduction to Wisdom,* 1540) was a breviary of pacific Christian Stoicism.

Vives' only objection to England, before 1528, seems to have been the weather. But when Henry VIII began his suit for divorce in that year, Vives found himself in an impossible political situation. His immediate support for the queen lost him his pension from the king; his ultimate refusal to be the queen's advocate before an ecclesiastical court in England lost him his pension from the queen. He found himself again a full-time resident of Bruges, with virtually no means of supporting his family. His sympathy for the impoverished was already on record in his *De Subventione Pauperum* (On Aid for the Poor, 1526), written for the advice of the city of Bruges and influencing social reforms in Flanders. His socialism and his Erasmian pacifism in political matters are also evident in *De Communione Rerum* (1535) and *De Concordia et Discordia in Humano Genere* (1529), dedicated to the Emperor Charles V.

During this difficult period in Vives' life he was visited by Ignatius of Loyola, then a student at Paris. It seems certain that the educational ideas of the founder of the Jesuit order were influenced by Vives, who in 1529 dedicated to Catherine of Aragon his little work on a man's domestic training and morality (*De Officio Mariti*; first English translation in 1553) and in 1531 published his major treatise on formal education, *De Tradendis Disciplinis*. In this work he first criticizes the corruption of the arts in the decadent scholasticism of Paris, then defines the goals of a constructive, public-spirited Christian education; finally he re-examines and redefines the arts, especially logic, in terms of these new goals. This *magnum opus* was followed by supplementary treatises on rhetoric (1533) and letter-writing (1536), and by a progressive textbook for teaching Latin (1538).

Perhaps even more important, from a theoretical point of view, was his psychological treatise *De Anima et Vita* (1538). Though beginning with Aristotle, he does not end with him, but initiates further empirical investigation, not of what the soul is, but of what it does and suffers. This work lays the foundations for the association of ideas and for modern psychology in general.

In religion we may note especially two mature works. The first is one of practical piety, *Excitationes Animi in Deum* (1535), consisting of commentaries on the Lord's Prayer and of "private" prayers. This work was first published in English in 1559; parts of it were incorporated into the Prayer Book of Queen Elizabeth. The second, and the last of his works, *De Veritate Fidei Christianae* (1543), is a defense of Catholic Christianity against Islam, Judaism, and ancient philosophy, designed to persuade heretics and pagans peacefully and rationally.

In 1540 Juan Luis Vives died of gout and complications in Bruges, at the age of forty-eight. Budé had died earlier the same year; Erasmus and More had died four and five years previously. The Golden Age of European humanism had ended.

The complete works of Joannis Ludovicus Vivis Valentinus were published in Basel in 1555 and in Valencia, 1782-90. A complete Spanish version was published in 1947-48. In English see the modern translations and studies of Dr. Foster Watson (begun in 1919). The standard study, in Spanish, is that of A. Bonilla y San Martín, *Luis Vives y la Filosofía del Renacimiento*.

ABOUT: Studies in the Renaissance, X (1963).

E. L. R.

*VOITURE, VINCENT

*VOITURE, VINCENT (1598-May 20(?), 1648), French poet, born in Amiens, was the son of a rich wine merchant who frequented noblemen and took Vincent with him on his visits. Pursuing serious studies in Paris, he met at the Collège de Boncour his future protector, the Comte d'Avaux. Physically frail, Voiture showed a natural melancholy and a delicate and distinguished manner, to which he added his biting wit. He began to write verse early, at first imitating the *Astrée* of Honoré d'Urfé. After study of law at Orléans, he entered the service of Gaston d'Orléans in Paris and renewed contacts with the Comte d'Avaux. He acquired a considerable reputation with the ladies, for whom he wrote such gallant verse as his madrigals. Beginning about 1625 he was the favorite poet of the "précieuses" of the Hôtel

* vwà tür'

de Rambouillet, and his learning and versatile wit led his admirers to forget his humble origins; at these gatherings he met the great writers of the day. In 1630, faithful to Gaston, Voiture traveled in Lorraine and then in Spain and Africa. He was one of the original group of members of the French Academy. Louis XIII sent him on an official mission to Florence in 1638, and he wrote charming letters from there to Mlle de Rambouillet. His last years involved intrigues at court and duties under Mazarin. His health was broken by excesses, largely amorous. He died, as was said, "in his Sultanas' arms, like the Grand Turk."

Though clearly a wit, Voiture strove for excellence in writing. His *stances*, rondels, and sonnets were held in high esteem as models in these genres with pure and artificial elegance, biting but graceful wit, themes of languishing love, and a worrisome touch of irony. His technique involved the overly ingenious Italian *concetti*. His fame is attested by the "Battle of the Sonnets" in 1649, after his death, during which his famous "Sonnet à Uranie" was set in distinguished place. His *Œuvres*, beginning in 1650, ran to forty editions.

English translations include his *Letters*, done by J. Davies in 1657, translated again in 1700 in two volumes by Dryden, who prepared *The Works of the Celebrated Monsieur Voiture* from 1715 to 1725, later prefaced by Pope. Modern editions of the *Œuvres* date from 1855, with a good collection, *Stances, Sonnets, Rondeaux et Chansons* in 1907.

ABOUT: [In French—Magne, E. Voiture et les Années de Gloire de l'Hôtel de Rambouillet; Saint-Beuve, C. A. Causeries du Lundi, XII; Uzanne, O. *Préface to* Lettres de Voiture.]

F. J. C.

*VOLNEY, CONSTANTIN FRANÇOIS

*VOLNEY, CONSTANTIN FRANÇOIS *CHASSEBŒUF, Comte de (February 3, 1757-April 25, 1820), French man of letters, was born in Craon (Anjou), the son of a prosperous lawyer, Jacques René Chassebœuf. His father had long disliked the family name with its peasant associations and the jokes it suggested, and he gave his son the more aristocratic name of Boisgirais which, however, the boy himself later changed to Volney. His mother died when he was only two, and his father showed a curious indifference to the child, leaving him to servants until he was old enough for school. He studied at the colleges of Ancenis and Angers, and made a brilliant record. When the boy was seventeen his father settled his mother's income upon him and left him quite on his own. He

* vôl nä' shàs bûf'

immediately went to Paris to continue his studies. In 1781 he published a learned treatise on the writings of Herodotus *(Sur la Chronologie d'Hérodote)* which won him entrée into the best literary and social circles in Paris. He began to frequent the salon of Mme Helvetius where he met Holbach, Cabanis, and others with whom he was later to be associated as *Idéologues* (disciples of Condillac, who sought to establish a science of psychology and believed in the perfectibility of the human race).

Volney received an inheritance in 1781 which enabled him to set out on an ambitious tour of Egypt and Syria. He spent a year preparing for the trip, conditioning himself physically for the hardships he would encounter, and in 1782 he set out with a knapsack on his back, a rifle on his shoulder, and 6,000 livres securely hidden in a money belt. He spent the next four years steeping himself in the languages and cultures of the region. He lived in a Coptic monastery, studied Arabic, visited nomad tribes, and everywhere he went he observed his surroundings with a keen eye. The results of the trip were published in 1787, *Voyage en Égypt et en Syrie*. It is a colorless book, completely devoid of the mystery and exoticism one would expect in such a work, but its accuracy and wealth of scientific detail made it enormously valuable to the French soldiers who fought in Egypt a few years later. In 1788 Volney wrote a book on Turkish-Russian relations which won the admiration of Catherine the Great.

During a large part of his life Volney combined the careers of statesman and man of letters. He represented Anjou in the Estates General of 1789. He was appointed director of commerce and agriculture in Corsica, but resigned from the position fearing it would interfere with his duties as a national deputy. In 1791 he published his most famous work, an essay on the philosophy of history, *Les Ruines, ou Méditation sur les Révolutions des Empires*, a lofty and grandiose survey of human progress and decay. When the Estates General was dissolved Volney went to Corsica in the hope of establishing a model plantation on the island. The revolt of Paoli forced him to leave, but he returned to Paris with the material for two books *(Précis de l'État Actuel de la Corse*, 1793, and *De l'État Physique de la Corse*, published posthumously)*, and he had made the friendship of the young army officer Napoleon Bonaparte. His political activities brought him under the scrutiny of the Terror and, though a Girondist, he was charged with being a Royalist

and imprisoned for ten months. With the downfall of Robespierre he was liberated and invited to give a course of lectures on history at the École Normale (published as *Leçons d'Histoire*, 1799).

In 1795 Volney came to the United States. The precise motives for his coming are not known, but it was evidently a trip he had planned for some time. Years before in the salon of Mme Helvetius he had met Benjamin Franklin and had admired him greatly. He had begun a correspondence with Thomas Jefferson in 1793, and the two men became good friends. (It was discovered in 1923, by Gilbert Chinard, that Jefferson actually translated the invocation and first twenty chapters of *Les Ruines*, published in Paris in 1802 and attributed to Joel Barlow.) Volney traveled extensively in America, visited Washington at Mount Vernon and Jefferson at Monticello. His observations were published in *Tableau du Climat et du Sol des États-Unis d'Amérique* in 1803. Unfortunately the warm hospitality he received on his arrival was dampened by a rising tide of anti-French sentiment. This was complicated for Volney by two enemies—one was the English theologian Joseph Priestley, also in America at this time, who wrote a treatise attacking him as an atheist. Volney defended himself in a letter translated into English and published in Philadelphia March 2, 1797, but Priestley's charges brought him under serious suspicion. An even more powerful enemy was President John Adams, who had been offended by a critique Volney had written of his treatise *Defense of the American Constitution*. The accusation was made that Volney was a French spy and he prudently decided to return to France.

Although Volney had been impressed with Napoleon when he met him in Corsica (he had described him as having "the head of Caesar on the shoulders of Alexander"), he soon became alarmed at the autocratic government he was imposing upon France. Volney refused offers of high government posts and made his opposition clear and open. Nevertheless he was highly honored both under Napoleon and under the restored monarchy. In 1799 he was made a senator; in 1804 he was elected to the Legion of Honor; and in 1808 he was given the title of Count. He devoted his later years to literature and scholarship, concentrating especially on the study of Oriental languages. In his will he left money for research on a universal alphabet. In 1810 he married a Mlle Chasseboeuf, a cousin. He lived a quiet retired life, and was of a melancholy disposition. He died in Paris at sixty-three and is buried in Père Lachaise cemetery.

As a literary figure Volney is quite negligible today. He is completely overshadowed by Chateaubriand, who wrote far more colorfully on many of the same subjects. Yet in his lifetime and during the first half of the nineteenth century he had a great vogue. Thanks largely to Priestley's accusations he got the reputation of a free thinker and basked in the reflected glory of Voltaire and Thomas Paine. But it was mainly for *Les Ruines,* with its foreshadowing of the melancholy romantic preoccupation with the dead past, that he was remembered. Eighteen editions of the English translation appeared from 1792 to 1878 and eight in the United States up to 1890. Shelley's *Queen Mab* was inspired by *Les Ruines,* part of the poem being almost a literal transcription of a section of it. Volney was not an original thinker nor a writer of any real depth, but had a wonderful gift for accurate observation and he wrote with such skill that, as Sainte-Beuve observed, "the art of writing cannot be distinguished in him from the art of observing."

Volney's *Œuvres Complètes* was published in Paris in 1825. The first English translation of *Les Ruines* appeared in London in 1792, another in New York in 1796, and others in Philadelphia (1799) and Albany (1822). *View of the Climate and Soil of the United States of America* appeared in London in 1804. In the same year a translation by C. B. Brown was published in Philadelphia. *The Law of Nature* was published in Philadelphia and London in 1796. *Lectures on History* was published in London (1800) and Philadelphia (1801), *Researches in Ancient History* in London (1819); *New Researches in Ancient History* was published in New York, translated by Col. Corbet (1856). The Jefferson-Volney letters are printed in G. Chinard's *Volney et l'Amérique* (1923).

ABOUT: Fenton, C. L. & M. A. Giants of Geology; Studies in Philology, LIV (1957). [In French—Chinard, G. Volney et l'Amérique.]

*VOLTAIRE, FRANÇOIS MARIE AROUET DE (November 21, 1694-May 30, 1778), French philosopher, born in Paris, was the son of a notary and of Marguerite Daumard, of the lesser nobility of Poitou. His father's associations introduced Voltaire into such aristocratic circles as that of the Richelieus, and emphasized his desire, typical of the period, to rise in social status. He entered the Jesuit college of Louis-le-Grand, and profited by the excellent literary training; there he made several lifelong friends, including the two d'Argensons and his teachers.

* vôl târ'

VOLTAIRE

Feeling keen interest in poetry and history, he decided, contrary to his father's desires, to devote himself to literature. His brief legal studies were not wasted; but he chose to frequent elegant intellectual circles. His wit, irreverence, and skepticism led him to compose satirical verse, and several times his imprudence obliged him to flee from Paris; during one such absence he conceived *La Henriade,* an epic on Henry IV, intended to revive a dead genre, published illegally in 1723. Another satirical poem sent him to the Bastille in 1717; he was released the following year, famous for his first tragedy, *Œdipe.*

In 1722 Voltaire met Viscount Bolingbroke, an exile in France, and began to take keen interest in England. Bolingbroke's return, and further unfortunate episodes with noblemen, finally led Voltaire to London in May 1726. There he was quite at home, among many other French exiles; he came into close contact with Pope and Swift, and observed the customs, politics, and literature, and especially the theatre. He published, in English, his *Essay on Epic Poetry* and *On the Civil Wars of France* and, in 1728, *La Henriade.* By March 1729 Voltaire was back in France completing two works begun in London. The *Lettres Philosophiques,* condemned by the French government, took the form of comparisons with more progressive ideas in England; Voltaire spoke in favor of evangelic doctrines (notably of the Quakers), inoculation, and the cosmology of Newtonian science. His most significant thought was that in England all sects live side by side in peace;

his basic Deist notion of union solely through one universal God, without reference to dogmatic restrictions, finds its first expression here. Voltaire completed simultaneously his *Histoire de Charles XII de Suède,* published in 1731. In this work he began to develop his historical method, in which the facts take second place to a concept of material and cultural progress: history is a lesson, and a training in tolerance.

The following year saw the production of one of Voltaire's best tragedies, *Zaïre;* this play, based on an oriental subject, shows points of resemblance to Racine's *Bajazet,* but it is clear that Voltaire's admiration for Shakespeare, the inspired savage, orients the manner and structure. Three further plays represent his theatrical masterpieces. *Alzire* (1736), set in Peru shortly after the Spanish conquest, is intended to show that the true Christian spirit is one of brotherhood and charity. *Mahomet* (1741) illustrates the dangers of fanaticism, and perhaps attacks all dogmatic religions (Mohammed says: "Whoever thinks, was not born to believe"). *Mérope* (1743), free from philosophical ideas, takes a Euripidean theme largely from the play by Maffei of 1713. However inferior these tragedies may be to those of Racine, they are the great theatrical monuments of their times, for their daring innovations and for such artistry as was possible in this antipoetical age.

The calm and productive years 1732-49 are marked by Voltaire's long affair with Mme du Châtelet, a brilliant woman of considerable linguistic and mathematical training and interests. At Cirey, her estate in Lorraine, they devoted their energies to science and literature. Her prudence was salutary, for she induced Voltaire not to publish several of his most revolutionary works, such as *La Pucelle,* a parody of the life of Joan of Arc, and especially the *Traité de Métaphysique* (1734), of particular interest for its total spontaneity: here one finds Voltaire's clearest Deist statements on the nature of God and the prime significance of science.

The Cirey period is also that of Voltaire's long poems, didactic rather than lyrical. Of these the most effective is *Le Mondain* (1736), with its praise of material values, luxury, comfort, modern ideas, and the arts, and its rich innuendo and impertinent statements: "Regret who will the good old days . . . I like luxury, and even softness, all pleasures, the arts of every kind. . . . And all honest men feel just that way." Here appears his great materialistic definition: "Superfluous

things are so essential." The good old days were times of ignorance, Eve had dirty nails and disheveled hair; a return to this kind of "natural state" is ludicrous.

The success of *Mahomet* and of *Mérope* finally brought recognition from Mme de Pompadour, and Voltaire was elected to the French Academy in 1746. Mme du Châtelet had kept him from contact with Frederick the Great of Prussia, with whom he had first corresponded ten years earlier. Her death left him free to accept the enlightened hospitality of Potsdam, where he went in 1750. His three years in Germany saw the composition of his *Siècle de Louis XIV,* and of his philosophical novel *Micromégas* (the more significant *Zadig* had appeared in 1747). Voltaire's new historical volume made considerable progress over his *Histoire de Charles XII,* and emphasized the futility of the current regime; it represents rich research with manuscript documents, including the memoirs of Saint-Simon. Friction with Maupertuis, as well as Voltaire's indiscretions, led to a rupture with Frederick, and ignominious flight. Since Paris was still hostile, Voltaire established himself at "Les Délices," near Lausanne; in 1758 he moved to Ferney, near Geneva, and conveniently close to the border. Thus during the most important days of Rousseau and the opening volumes of the *Encyclopédie,* Voltaire remained far from the scene. To the Encyclopedists he merely gave a few routine articles. His famous letter attacking Rousseau's *Discours sur l'Inégalité,* one of his most important tracts of 1755, shows Voltaire in his best ironical vein: "I have received, dear Sir, your book against the human race. . . . One could not paint in darker colors the horrors of human society. . . . It makes me want to walk on all fours." More significant, however, is the poem inspired by the earthquake at Lisbon, clear proof, in Voltaire's mind, that "all is not for the best." His concentrated rage is against the simplistic optimists of the school of Leibniz and Pope; it takes its finest form in his masterpiece *Candide* (1759), in which he savagely attacks illusory security and tragically real intolerance. The great episode of Eldorado illustrates, by inference, Voltaire's rejection of a static utopia; the famous conclusion, "We must cultivate our garden," became something of his personal philosophy during the ensuing years.

The period at Ferney (1759-78) is important from many points of view. There Voltaire established a model community engaged in useful minor industries; he built his private theatre, and gathered a remarkable library of some 7,500 reference books, later moved intact to St. Petersburg. Voltaire's major work of this period is his *Dictionnaire Philosophique*, published in 1764, a series of aggressive articles intended for the most part to prove, through documentation, the errors of established dogma and the harm caused by superstition. In exegetical form, he attacked the historical veracity of certain parts of the Bible and showed the fallibility of the Church through the contradictions of its many Councils. Voltaire also prepared an elaborate new edition of the plays of Corneille, took up arms during the La Barre affair in 1766, and, in that year, showed his enduring concern for Shakespeare in his *Lettre à l'Académie Française*, in protest against Letourneur's translation. Voltaire's last act was his triumphal entry into Paris on February 10, 1778: he witnessed the success of his new play, *Irène*, and met Benjamin Franklin; overcome by the excitement, he died on May 30. His last authenticated statement is significant: "I die adoring God, loving my friends, not hating my enemies, and detesting superstition." He was secretly buried near Troyes, then moved with national honors, in 1791, along with Rousseau, to the Panthéon. Voltaire's long and turbulent life spanned the eighteenth century and reflected it dramatically. He stands as a brilliant symbol of the Enlightenment, an implacable enemy of ignorance and superstition, yet also an engagingly human personality who never, in the course of his struggles, lost his sense of humor or his faith in the dignity of man.

There are countless editions and translations of the separate works of Voltaire. The basic references are the *Œuvres Complètes* of 1784-89 (the "Kehl" edition, in 70 or 92 volumes), that of 1828-40 (by Beuchot, 70 volumes), and that of 1877-85 (by Moland, 52 volumes); a recent critical edition of the *Dictionnaire Philosophique* (by J. Benda and R. Naves), and the current volumes of the *Correspondence* (by T. Besterman), deserve special attention. The earliest English versions are *An Essay upon the Civil Wars of France* (1727), *Henriade, an Epick Poem* (1732), *Letters Concerning the English Nation* (1733), *Alzira* (1736), *The Elements of Sir Isaac Newton's Philosophy* (1738), *Epistles* (1738), *Mahomet* (1744), *Zadig* (1749), *The Age of Lewis XIV* (1739-1752), *Candide* (1759—later translations ranging from that of Tobias Smollett in the eighteenth century to that of Richard Aldington in the twentieth), *The Works of M. de Voltaire* (37 volumes, 1761-70; 42 volumes, New York, 1901; 22 volumes, Akron, (1901-03), and *The Philosophical Dictionary* (1765). In 1959 H. B. Evans and T. Besterman published *A Provisional Bibliography of English Editions and Translations of Voltaire*. T. Besterman has also edited *Select Letters of Voltaire* (1963).

ABOUT: Aldington, R. Voltaire; Barr, M. Voltaire in America; Besterman, T. Voltaire Essays, *also* (ed.) Studies on Voltaire and the Eighteenth Century; Brailsford, H. Voltaire; Brandes, G. Voltaire; Havens, G. Selections from Voltaire; Laver, R. The Mind of Voltaire; Morley, J. Voltaire; Saintsbury, G. French Literature and Its Masters; Torrey, N. The Spirit of Voltaire; Wade, I. Voltaire and Mme du Châtelet. [In French: Bellesort, A. Essai sur Voltaire; Condorcet. Vie de Voltaire (in the Kehl edition); Lanson, G. Voltaire; Pellissier, G. Voltaire Philosophe.]

F. J. C.

VONDEL, JOOST VAN DEN (November 17, 1587-February 5, 1679), Dutch poet and playwright, was born in Cologne, Germany. His father, also named Joost, and mother, Sara Cranen, devout Anabaptists, had fled Antwerp in 1582 to escape the Duke of Alva's persecution. Thus the child experienced the consequences of religious fanaticism, an impression that later developed into an ardent aversion for religious strife. He was the second of seven children.

Cologne soon became a hazardous refuge and in 1595 the family departed for Amsterdam by way of Frankfurt, Bremen, Emden, Groningen, and Utrecht. War and pestilence probably accounted for the circuitous route. In March 1597 the elder Joost acquired Amsterdam citizenship, affording him powerful protection and the right to ply his trade of hatter. The variety of experiences encountered, especially in the Amsterdam of this period, no doubt made a profound impression on the imaginative boy. Young Vondel was a member of a minority group and his earliest cultural contacts were with Brabant refugee families. He became a member of Het wit Lavendel (White Lavender), the Brabant "Chamber of Rhetoric" in Amsterdam, an organization which, in Professor Barnouw's words, was "a kind of theatre guild . . . men of literary taste, who . . . combined the worship of Bacchus with the service of Apollo." The Chamber performed Vondel's first dramatic venture, *Het Pascha* (1610, printed 1612), a piece inspired by Guillaume Du Bartas, its subject being the rescue of the children of Israel from Egypt.

Both within and outside of the Chamber, Vondel continued to make contacts with and gain inspiration from leading spirits of the day: the publisher Zacharias Heyns, the painter-poet Carel van Mander, H. L. Spieghel, and others. On December 5, 1610, Vondel married Mayken de Wolff (1586-1635), like himself a member of a Brabant refugee family. His marriage to the quiet,

* vòn' dĕl

977

VONDEL

del went into a period of "melancholia hypochondriaca." Contemporary accounts (Brandt) and the observable alternating productive and depressed periods leave little doubt that he was manic-depressive.

Even so, in the almost sixty years of life remaining, Vondel composed an immense quantity of work: occasional poems by the hundreds; translations from classical authors (Seneca, Virgil, Sophocles, Euripides); Biblical and historical dramas, chief among them the tragedy of Amsterdam's founder *Gysbreght van Aemstel* (1637), *Maria Stuart* (1646), *Jephthah* (1659), *Adam in Ballingschap* (1664). Most of these, while preserving the Biblical or historical narrative, have a concrete contemporary reference, and in the best of them the poet explores the universal questionings and sorrows of the human heart. It is in this latter category that *Lucifer* (1654) belongs. With this tragedy of the magnificent archangel, like Milton's Satan a symbol with human implications, Vondel enters the domain of world literature.

Sometime during the years 1639-41 Vondel had taken the fateful step: he returned to the Catholic faith. In his personal life this signified increasing isolation, intensified by the business failure and the disgrace of his son Joost in 1656. In 1675 the beloved Anna, who since the death of Vondel's wife in 1635 had cared for her father, died also and four years later death came to the ninety-one-year-old poet. Fourteen poets were pall-bearers to his grave in De Nieuwe Kerk. A few years later a modest monument was erected and in 1867 a statue by Louis Royer was placed in what is today called the Vondelpark in Amsterdam.

Neither during the poet's lifetime nor afterwards has critical acclaim ever been without reservation. There is much mere facility and verbal virtuosity in his writing. But at his best Vondel's work has lyric depth and a meditative quality. As in other seventeenth century poets, Vondel's genius moves in a world of polarities; it is the spirit of the age to be acutely aware of harsh discordances in life.

Vondel's greatness rests on the richness of his language; he is fond of sonorous, rhetorical speeches—the stock in trade of the seventeenth century baroque artist. This is not artificiality or lack of sincerity but a profound responsiveness to the most disparate, even incongruous, ideas and emotions; there is virile, earthy zest but also tender lyricism on deeply personal and religious themes. He has remained for the Dutch people the Poet

capable Mayken proved harmonious. However, a recent biographer (J. Melles) has detailed the facts of an evident estrangement between Sara Cranen and her illustrious son, a friction probably accounting for Sara's retirement from business in 1613, Vondel's father having died in 1608. Of the five children born of Vondel's marriage, only two, Joost (1612-60), unstable and the cause of much later grief, and the beloved Anna (1613-75), attained adulthood.

During the decade 1610-20 Vondel began the steady productivity resulting in the immense mass of work which he left: occasional poetry on many topics—city life, commerce, politics, and religion. A circle of humanist friends was cultivated; Vondel actively supported Samuel Coster's newly founded (1617) Nederduytse Academie; he rose to a deaconship in the Anabaptist congregation; he undertook the study of Latin with the conrector of the Amsterdam Latin School, Hayo Gabbema.

On May 13, 1619, an event occurred which transformed Vondel from a facile technician into a passionate poet. Johan van Oldenbarneveldt, Lord Advocate of Holland, was executed, a victim of theological factionalism, complicated by a jealous struggle for political preëminence. In 1625 the poetic expression of Vondel's indignation, the drama *Palamedes* appeared. No one missed the contemporary reference in this allegorical work. Vondel became famous but henceforth was suspect to the Calvinist ministers. The drama's lateness was probably caused by illness: in 1621 Von-

of the Golden Age, a veneration expressed in the tradition that since 1638 his *Gysbreght van Aemstel* opens the Amsterdam theatrical season every New Year's day.

Lucifer was translated into English by L. C. Van Noppen in 1898.

ABOUT: Barnouw, A. J. Vondel; Edmundson, G. Milton and Vondel: A Curiosity of Literature; Gosse, E. Studies in Northern Literature; Modern Language Review, LII (1957); Neophilologus, XLIV (1960). [In Dutch—see studies by P. Leendertz, Jr., J. Melles, B. H. Molkenboer.]

C. K. P.

VORAGINE, JACOBUS DE. See JA-COBUS DE VORAGINE

*VOSS, JOHANN HEINRICH (February 20, 1751-March 29, 1826), German poet, translator, and philologist, was born in Sommersdorf in Mecklenburg. His father, who had been a tenant farmer and whose property had been destroyed by war, supported his family through meager earnings as a rural schoolteacher. Voss completed his preparatory schooling at Neubrandenburg, but lacking sufficient funds was unable to begin his studies at a university. After serving as a tutor in the home of nobility he departed for the University of Göttingen where he studied philology and became a member of a group of young poets, the so-called Göttinger Dichterbund. In 1770 Voss undertook to edit the journal *Göttinger Musenalmanach* in which he had published much of his early poetic efforts. In 1778 he assumed the position of rector of the school in Ottendorf and following this accepted a similar position at Eutin. In the fall of 1802 Voss left Eutin to take up residence in Jena, which, in spite of Goethe's efforts to persuade him to remain, he left in the summer of 1805 to accept a summons from the University of Heidelberg. He died in Heidelberg after spending twenty-one productive years there.

In his early attempts as a lyric poet Voss did not attain great success. His efforts in this respect were published in the *Göttinger Musenalmanach* and are marked by the type of pathos characteristic of Klopstock. He became rather a learned scholar of classical antiquity and the poet-representative of the sober, comfortable bourgeoisie in his hexametric idylls *Der Siebzigste Geburtstag* (1781) and *Luise* (1795). He was particularly fond of depicting rural scenes familiar to him from his childhood. As the son of a poverty-stricken farmer, he colored his idylls with social criticism and German dialect forms. He desired to present rural life with feeling and accuracy, but too often produced only Philistine, pedantic realism. His most enduring contribution to German letters is undoubtedly the translation of Homer (*Odysee*, 1781; *Ilias*, 1793). His other translations of the classics (Ovid, 1798; Virgil, 1799; Horace, 1806; Theocritus, 1808; Aristophanes, 1821; Aeschylus, 1827) never attained the popularity of his Homer, which became through Voss's efforts a firm part of German education and culture.

In the later years of his life as a professor at Heidelberg, Voss was the ardent defender of the Lutheran faith in southern Germany. He opposed strongly the Catholic inclinations which were a part of the literature of romanticism during the first decades of the nineteenth century. Particularly painful to him was the adoption of the Catholic faith by the friend of his youth, the poet Count Friedrich Leopold von Stolberg (1750-1819).

English translations of Voss's works are extremely rare: *Louisa*: a poem (1852); selections of his poetry in A. F. Baskerville, *The Poetry of Germany* (1853).

ABOUT: [In German—see studies by W. Herbst, W. Knögel, K. Kuhlmann.]

E. K. G.

*VRCHLICKÝ, JAROSLAV (pseudonym of EMIL FRÍDA) (February 17, 1853-September 9, 1912), Czech poet, dramatist, critic, and translator, was born in Louny in northwestern Bohemia, son of a shopkeeper. He attended *Gymnasium* in several towns, and was graduated in 1872. Meanwhile he had begun to write verse, choosing the pseudonym of Vrchlický, the name of a minor poet he happened upon in a magazine. He entered a theological seminary, but in his second semester withdrew and enrolled in the Faculty of Philosophy at Prague University, where he studied history and foreign languages. Three years later he accepted the post of tutor to the sons of Count Montecuccoli-Laderchi, and spent the years 1875-76 in Italy. The Italian landscape, the sea (an exotic motif in Czech poetry), and the world of the antique and the Renaissance affected him powerfully. In 1877 he became secretary of a Czech technical school, and in 1893 was named professor of comparative literature at the Czech University in Prague, a position to which he brought great erudition and a knowledge of many languages. His

* fôs

* vûrĸ' lĭts kĕ

VRCHLICKÝ

marriage in 1879 to Ludmila Podlipská, the daughter of his friend the writer Sofie Podlipská, was unhappy: she was unfaithful, and the two eventually separated. In 1908 a brain tumor put an end to his career, and the last four years of his life were spent as a helpless invalid. He died in Domažlice.

Vrchlický's poetic production was immense. Besides thousands of translated poems, he also produced some eighty-five volumes of original poetry: lyric, narrative, and dramatic. His work was strongly influenced by French and Italian poets, notably Hugo and Leopardi. His main idea is an evolutionary optimism akin to Hugo's, with a firm faith in human progress. In his best period, between 1879 and 1894, his work is highly sensual and decorative in its use of imagery. The world of classical antiquity and its pagan art inspired him. The formal ornamental sides of Vrchlický's work usually dominate, and he raised Czech verse technique to new heights, introducing many new and complex verse forms. Later, after his domestic tragedy, his poetry became extremely pessimistic, but finally he found a stoic resignation, and his work became much simpler, less ornate and more song-like.

Vrchlický wrote a number of narrative poems which attempt to capture the spirit of different epochs in world history. His dramas are weaker, and hold the stage chiefly as operas. He was also a leading critic, with a keen sense of formal values, but impressionistic and sometimes subjective.

Vrchlický translated from many languages. He made virtually complete translations of the poetry of Hugo, Leconte de Lisle, and Vigny. He translated Dante's *Divine Comedy*, Ariosto, Tasso, Leopardi, Corneille, Molière, Rostand's *Cyrano*, Calderón, Mickiewicz, Goethe's *Faust*, Shakespeare's sonnets, Byron, Shelley, Poe, Whitman, and many others. His translations, like his original poetry, show his amazing poetic virtuosity, but they often suffer from haste of execution and a tendency to interpret in terms of his own poetic tastes.

In his own time, Vrchlický was proclaimed the greatest Czech poet. Though he is no longer so highly esteemed as he was in his own day, his place in Czech literature is secure. He introduced many new foreign poetic currents, particularly Parnassianism, as well as new themes and motifs.

Some of Vrchlický's poems are translated in Paul Selver, *Anthology of Czechoslovak Literature* (1929), R. A. Ginsburg, *Soul of a Century* (1942), E. W. Underwood, *The Slav Anthology* (1931), and Paul Selver, *Anthology of Modern Slavonic Literature* (1919). A one-act play, *At the Chasm*, was translated by C. Recht (1913).

ABOUT: Harkins, W. E. Anthology of Czech Literature. [In Czech: V. Tichý, Jaroslav Vrchlický.]

W. E. H.

VUK STEFANOVIĆ KARADŽIĆ. See KARADŽIĆ, VUK STEFANOVIĆ

*WACE (c. 1100-1174?), French (Norman) poet-historian, is a name which comes originally from the German "Wasso." The "Robert" formerly prefixed was due to a once prevalent misconception. The meager factual biography of Canon Wace is summarized in his own words as follows: "I am Wace of the Isle of Jersey, which lies in the sea, towards the West, and is a part of the fief of Normandy. In the Isle of Jersey I was born, and to Caen I was taken as a little lad; there I was put at the study of letters. Afterward I studied long in France [Île-de-France]. When I came back from France, I dwelt long at Caen. I busied myself with making books in Romance; many of them I wrote and many of them I made."

He may have been the son of noble parents, his grandfather having perhaps been a chamberlain attached to duke Robert I of Normandy. It is known that by 1135 Wace had the title of *clerc lisant* at Caen, that he probably visited England before 1155, that he was

* wäs

at Fécamp in 1162, that he is mentioned in charters at Bayeux in 1169 and 1174. During his lifetime Wace probably knew the first three Henrys of the house of Plantagenet. In 1160 Henry II, to whom Wace was indebted for the prebend of Bayeux, ordered him to write the *Roman de Rou,* a chronicle of the dukes of Normandy, his longest and most original work, consisting of 16,992 octosyllabic and alexandrine lines. The king later discharged Wace, who includes a personal note of sorrow when he stops his narrative with the battle of Tinchebray (1106). Another work important for the history of literature is the *Roman de Brut* (1155), a rather free translation of Geoffrey of Monmouth's *Historia Regum Britanniae.* This rhymed chronicle of 14,866 octosyllabic lines was dedicated to Eleanor of Aquitaine, King Henry's wife. Wace's translation was later used (1204) as a main source by the Anglo-Norman clerk Layamon for his English *Brut.* Wace is also generally regarded as a source for subsequent romances of the Arthurian cycle written by such poets as Thomas de Bretagne, Chrétien de Troyes, and Marie de France.

Wace, who elaborated on Geoffrey's *Historia,* should be credited with the first mention of the round table episode, which Layamon in turn expanded in his *Brut.* Wace's literary repertory also includes three religious poems: *La Vie de Saint Nicolas, La Vie de Sainte Marguerite* and *La Conception de Nostre Dame.* The interest in Wace as a poet is at the present time confined largely to specialists in the Arthurian field. His writings are, in fact, a key source for the medieval literary world, ranking virtually on a par with the work of Geoffrey of Monmouth. Wace was a conscientious stylist, with a gift for description and narration rarely surpassed in the twelfth century.

Edgar Taylor translated the *Chronicle of the Norman Conquest from the Roman de Rou* in 1837. *The Arthurian Chronicles* by Wace and Layamon were published in Everyman's Library in 1912, 1928.

ABOUT: Houck, M. E. Sources of the Roman de Brut of Wace; Loomis, R. S., ed. Arthurian Literature in the Middle Ages; Malet, A. The Conquest of England *from* Wace's Roman de Rou; Paton, L. A. *Introduction to* Arthurian Chronicles (Everyman's ed.); Philpot, J. H. Maistre Wace; Taylor, E. Master Wace. [In French—Pelan, M. L'Influence du Brut de Wace; Paris, G. *in* Romania, 1880.]

E. V.

*WACKENRODER, WILHELM HEINRICH** (July 13, 1773-February 13, 1798), German art critic, was born in Berlin into an old family of academic and civil service background, originally from Pomerania. His father, a rationalistic and utilitarian Prussian official who became mayor of Berlin, wanted a legal career for his son and ruled him with such a strong hand that the boy became his father's opposite in many ways: shy, dreamy, introverted, sensitive, artistic, rapturous, nervous. Wackenroder attended the Friedrich Werder Gymnasium in Berlin and there met Ludwig Tieck, who was to become his closest friend and collaborator. In Berlin Wackenroder also came under the influence of three men: Karl Philipp Moritz, an art historian and admirer of Goethe, author of the psychological novel *Anton Reiser;* the musician Johann Friedrich Reichardt, who was also associated with Goethe and whose house became a veritable center of romanticism; and the scholar Erduin Julius Koch, who introduced Wackenroder to the older German literature.

In 1793 Wackenroder was sent to the University of Erlangen to study law. That summer he and Tieck undertook a journey through southern Germany, savoring the medieval cultural atmosphere and reacting enthusiastically to the churches and palaces of Franconia, the architectural and artistic treasures of Bamberg, Nürnberg, and Pommersfelden, the graves of Albrecht Dürer and Hans Sachs. Wackenroder completed his law studies at Göttingen in 1794 and entered upon a legal career in Berlin, something utterly repugnant to him. The two friends escaped to the Dresden art galleries in 1796, and soon thereafter a joint work of theirs was published. But this only intensified Wackenroder's conflict between career and inclination. The strain on a highly artistic nature became unbearable and the delicate youth died several months before his twenty-fifth birthday, of what was then called a "nervous fever." "He was of no little physical beauty," Gillies writes about him. "A well-arched brow, straight nose, full and slightly protruding lips, fair hair, and eyes that alternately radiated calm confidence and beseeching sadness gave him an air of nobility and reserve that widened the gap between himself and his fellows . . . It was not by accident that he played the rôle of the prince in amateur theatricals. He felt himself to be a stranger and misunderstood."

* väk′ ĕn rō dĕr

Wackenroder is generally regarded as one of the founders of German romanticism, although his work is poetic rather than philosophical or programmatic. His writings had a tremendous germinal effect on a generation of poets and artists. In 1796 Wackenroder, who had made a few previous attempts in the field of poetry and the drama, committed his thoughts on art and music to paper. Tieck added four essays of his own to the fourteen given him by his friend and published the work in 1797 under the title *Herzensergiessungen eines Kunstliebenden Klosterbruders* (Heart-Outpourings of an Art-Loving Monastic). The book appeared anonymously and was at first thought to be the work of Goethe. Georg Brandes called this slim volume, which deals with art, religion, and music, "the primary cell of the whole romantic structure around which later romantic productions grouped themselves." The rest of Wackenroder's papers were published by Tieck (again with his own additions and emendations) in 1799 as *Phantasien über die Kunst für Freunde der Kunst* (Fantasies on Art for Friends of Art). A central theme of the apparently formless *Herzensergiessungen* is the anti-rationalistic glorification of the Renaissance as the heroic age of art. Dürer is apotheosized as its leader in Germany, and in rejecting the Hellenism then fashionable in Germany, Wackenroder directs attention to the neglected German artistic heritage, especially that of the Middle Ages, making eloquent pleas for originality in art and for an appreciation of the German character. For music he claims the primacy among the arts. Wackenroder's ideas on music and musical aesthetics are expressed through a memorable poetic creation, his *alter ego* Joseph Berglinger (a direct forerunner of E. T. A. Hoffmann's music-mad Kapellmeister Johannes Kreisler), who appears in both the *Herzensergiessungen* and the *Phantasien*. Berglinger, who has been described as "a musical Werther," faced Wackenroder's own romantic dilemma, the unbridgeable gulf between art and life. The figure of this musician may be regarded as a projection of Wackenroder, who had some pretensions to becoming a practicing musician and a composer, but realized that his forte lay in the passive enjoyment of music and the rapturous conveying of this enjoyment to others. Through the mouth of Berglinger, Wackenroder gives us a highly suggestive poetical exegesis of the nature of tonal art. Wackenroder's writing influenced later romantic poetry, philosophy, and painting. Schopen-

hauer later wove the various strands of romantic musical aesthetics, as germinated by Wackenroder, into a more comprehensive, definite philosophy of music.

A Marvellous Oriental Legend of a Naked Saint and *Concerning Two Marvellous Languages and Their Mysterious Power*, translated by F. E. Pierce, are included in *Fiction and Fantasy of German Romance*, edited by F. E. Pierce and C. F. Schreiber (1927).

ABOUT: Gillies, A. *Introduction to* Blackwell edition of Herzensergiessungen (1948), *also* "Wackenroder's Apprenticeship to Literature" *in* German Studies Presented to H. G. Fiedler; Schoolfield, G. C. The Figure of the Musician in German Literature; Germanic Review, XXXVII (1962). [In German—see studies by E. Gülzow, F. Koldewey. In Italian—see studies by B. Tecchi (also in German translation), A. Santoli.]

H. Z.

*WAGNER, HEINRICH LEOPOLD

(February 19, 1747-March 4, 1779), German dramatist, was born in Strasbourg, the son of a merchant. He studied law at the University of Strasbourg, where in 1770 he became a member of Goethe's circle of friends. In 1773 he worked as a tutor in Saarbrücken, and the following year arrived in Frankfurt, where he rejoined Goethe's following. After returning to Strasbourg to complete the work for his degree, he settled in Frankfurt as a lawyer in 1776. He was married this same year; his wife, who was eighteen years his senior, died in 1778. Wagner himself died in Frankfurt am Main at thirty-two.

As a writer Wagner possessed less original talent than imitative ability. He began his literary career with translations of French dramas, the most notable being Sebastien Mercier's domestic tragedy *Der Schubkarren des Essighändlers* (1775). Wagner also translated Mercier's essay on dramatic theory, *Neuer Versuch über die Schauspielkunst* (1776).

His first independent work of significance was the dramatic farce *Prometheus, Deukalion und seine Recensenten* (1775), in which he cleverly satirized the critics of Goethe's *Werther*. Since this attack appeared anonymously, it was for a time attributed to Goethe, until the latter publicly disclaimed it. Wagner also produced a second satire, *Voltaire am Abend seiner Apotheose* (1778), which reflects the hostility of the Storm and Stress writers to the classic tradition.

Wagner's independent dramas fall mainly into the tradition of the bourgeois tragedy. Following *Der Wohltatige Bekannte* (1775),

* väg′ nĕr

which the author himself translated into French, he produced the six-act drama *Die Reue nach der Tat* (1776), which treats an interesting new theme of the conflict between two levels of the same social class. Aside from the accurately detailed settings, which in technique foreshadow German naturalism a century later, these works contain little of enduring value. They suffer in general from formlessness, an excessive use of theatrical effects, and inconsistency in the characterizations.

Wagner's most significant work is *Die Kindermörderin* (1776), a six-act tragedy in prose. Here he develops the theme of class conflict, basing his plot on the Gretchen episode from *Faust*, which he had learned from Goethe. A young girl of the middle class is seduced by an officer and then deserted by him. Rejected by her family and by society, she commits infanticide, for which she is sentenced to be executed. The play is written in an unsparingly realistic style, for Wagner, like his contemporary Lenz, intended his drama as a social protest. A later revision of the play with the most offensive scenes omitted and with the grim tone relieved by a happy ending, appeared under the title *Evchen Humbrecht, oder, Ihr Mutter Merkt's Euch* (1778).

Wagner also produced a number of insignificant poems and a fragmentary novel, *Leben und Tod Sebastian Sillings* (1776), in the manner of Sterne. He is the least noteworthy of the German Storm and Stress writers, and in large measure owes his continued reputation to his close association with Goethe.

ABOUT: Garland, B. H. Storm and Stress. [In German—see study by E. Schmidt.]

D. G. D.

*WAGNER, (WILHELM) RICHARD (May 22, 1813-February 13, 1883), German opera composer and librettist, was born in Leipzig, the ninth child of Carl Friedrich Wilhelm Wagner, a clerk of police, and Johanna Rosina Bertz Wagner. Some authorities believe that Richard's father was really Ludwig Geyer, actor, singer, and painter, who was a close friend of the family, and who married Johanna Wagner about a year after the death of Carl Friedrich (which occurred six months after Richard's birth). Carl Friedrich had been an amateur actor and patron of the theatre, but Johanna, far from encouraging her gifted son's propensities,

* väg′ nĕr

WAGNER

threatened to bring curses down on his head if he followed the stage. Richard, strong-willed and obstinate in his boyhood as he remained throughout his life, was not to be thwarted. At the age of eight, shortly after his step-father's death, he was apprenticed to a goldsmith in Eisleben, but found this regimen uncongenial, and gave it up after a year to join his mother, brothers, and sisters in Dresden. Here he entered the Kreuzschule where he remained for the next five years, pursuing the liberal arts course. As a schoolboy he developed that passionate love for mythology that was to manifest itself in his greatest operas, at this time finding its outlet in his translation of the first twelve books of the *Odyssey*. One of the first operatic composers to awaken his enthusiasm was Carl Maria von Weber, who used to pass by his window, and whose *Der Freischütz* he played by ear on the piano.

In Leipzig, where he and his family returned in 1827, Richard heard Beethoven's music for the first time, and began to teach himself composition by copying out the Fifth and Ninth Symphonies at night. He then pored over Logier's textbook on harmony, the *Thoroughbass*, which he tried to absorb in a week. His first formal instruction in music was undertaken at the hands of Gottlieb Müller, who became organist at Altenburg, followed by a course of study under Theodor Weinlig, cantor of the Thomas School, recognized as one of the foremost authorities of his day on counterpoint. In February 1831 Wagner entered the University of Leipzig as a *studiosus musicae*, attending lectures on aesthetics and philosophy. Wagner's earliest and purely orchestral compositions—which included a piano sonata—were mediocre. He did succeed in having an overture performed at the Leipzig Theatre, but it was poorly received. In 1832 he attempted his first opera, *Die Hochzeit* (The Marriage), but abandoned it before completion. His first completed opera, *Die Feen* (The Fairies), based on a *fiaba* by Carlo Gozzi, was never performed in his lifetime. His second, *Das Liebesverbot* (Ban on Love, 1836), derived from Shakespeare's *Measure for Measure*, received only one performance. (It is of interest, however, that this early in his career he took up a theme that he was to develop in *Tristan und Isolde*—love that defies law and reason.)

Wagner's fascinating musical career has been thoroughly explored by Ernest Newman and other musicologists, so that we have become familiar with the milestones in his struggle for recognition and success: his temporary conducting engagements; his unhappy marriage to Minna Planer (whom some see reflected in the shrewish Fricka of the *Ring* operas); the rebuffs from opera impresarios in Paris; the encouragement from the influential composer Meyerbeer (whom he later scorned); his brief participation in the Revolution of 1848; his embarking on the *Ring* project in Zürich; his romance with the poet Mathilde Wesendonck (whether he composed *Tristan* out of love for her or fell in love with her because he was composing *Tristan* is still a moot question); the opulent patronage of Ludwig of Bavaria, which gave him the independence to develop his elaborate musical ideas; his adulterous relationship with and subsequent marriage to Cosima von Bülow, daughter of Franz Liszt; the final enshrinement of his genius in the *Festspielhaus* at Bayreuth.

As the author of the "poems" of all his operas, to say nothing of his treatises on aesthetics, and his revealing autobiography and letters (his prose works extend to ten volumes), Wagner looms as a considerable literary figure as well. He was a lover of literature even before he turned to music, as attested by his early attempt to write a tragedy on the order of *Hamlet* and *King Lear*. For the texts of most of his operas he utilized major works of German literature and engaged in prodigious scholarly research. Tales by the Grimm brothers, E. T. A. Hoffmann, and Ludwig Tieck, for example, provided him with the materials for *Tannhäuser* (1842); for *Die Meistersinger* (1867) he

delved into Gervinus' *History of German National Literature* as well as the *Nuremberg Chronicle*; while the tremendous *Ring* tetralogy (composed off and on from 1848 to 1872) was an amalgam of the *Volsunga Saga, Thidrek Saga*, and the *Niebelungenlied*.

All of Wagner's libretti are among the most literate of opera "books," and at least two of them attain to real literary distinction. *Die Meistersinger,* based on the career of the cobbler-poet Hans Sachs, poses serious questions of literary art—such as the clash between romanticism and realism, and the conflict of "inspiration" and "rules." *Tristan und Isolde,* described by Francis Fergusson as "the myth and ritual of a religion of passion," is one of the great tragedies of overweening romantic love. Its musical themes of Light and Darkness, Love and Death, are interwoven and paradoxically resolved in the manner of a lyric poem. In the comedy Wagner may well have been having his laugh at the obtuse critics (like Beckmesser) who could not understand his art. In the tragedy some biographers find reflected Wagner's own thwarted search for an ideal love.

Wagner's gropings towards a new kind of musical form made him, of course, a controversial figure in his time. "I will write no more operas," he wrote to a friend after he had finished *Lohengrin* and had plunged into the composition of *The Ring*. He preferred to call his mature works *dramas.* Abandoning rhymed verse for the assonantal meter he called *stabreim,* giving up the conventional song and aria in favor of a musical discourse, Wagner evolved a kind of opera unified symphonically, and knit together by *leit-motifs,* analogous to imagery and symbol patterns in literary works. Like many modern writers, Wagner found his most congenial mode of expression in the revivifying of ancient legends. "In the myth," he wrote, "human relations almost completely lose their conventional form, which is intelligible only to the abstract reason; [myths] show what is eternally human and eternally comprehensible in life." In the *Ring* cycle, which many Wagnerites regard as the apotheosis of his genius (though George Bernard Shaw reduced it to a kind of Marxist allegory), Wagner welded the Norse myths into an archetypal drama of sin and redemption, which in its grandeur of conception stands next to the *Oresteia*. Ironically Wagner envisaged as the true audience for his work not the bourgeois society of his day, but "the true life and spirit of the German *Volk*" in whom he hoped to awaken a spontaneous, formless *Wille.* (This ideal is dramatized in the concluding scene of *Die Meistersinger,* where it is the apprentices and the townsfolk, not the burghers, who respond most eagerly to Walther's Prize Song.) Like many an artist who hoped to reach "the people," Wagner finds his audience today among the elite —and the particularly small one that attends opera houses.

Wagner lived to see himself vindicated in the adulation of the discriminating public, but nobody was more dedicated to his immortalization than Wagner himself. For four years he labored to bring the great Bayreuth theatre into being. Here the *Ring* Cycle was first performed in its entirety August 13-16, 1876. Six years later occurred the première at the Festspielhaus of his final opera, *Parsifal.* These last years took their toll even of his titanic energies, and in 1882 he retreated for rest and recuperation to Venice, where he died the following year of a heart attack, a few months before his seventieth birthday. His body was returned to Bayreuth for burial. His son Siegfried became one of the conductors of his music at the Festspielhaus. After a lapse during World War II, the Wagner Festival is once more an established tradition at Bayreuth, where Siegfried's son Wieland continues to stir controversies in the music and theatrical world with his abstractionist re-stagings of his grandfather's music dramas, which he considers more in accord with the composer's original intentions than the traditional literal settings.

The libretti of the operas in the repertoire have been issued by the Metropolitan Opera Association, with German text facing rather stilted metrical translations. The text of the *Ring* was partially translated by George Theodore Dippold in his *Richard Wagner's Poem The Ring of the Niebelung Explained* (1888). Wagner's complete *Prose Works* were translated by William Ashton Ellis in eight volumes (1892-99). A selection of his *Letters* is available in a translation by M. M. Bozman (1927). The *Nietzsche-Wagner Correspondence* was translated by Caroline V. Kerr (1921). The authorized translation of *Mein Leben* (My Life) was brought out anonymously in 1911 and reprinted in 1963. The standard edition in German is the *Gesammelte Schriften und Dichtungen* in 10 volumes (Leipzig, 1871-83; several times reprinted).

ABOUT: Aldrich, R. A Guide to the Ring of the Niebelung; Fergusson, F. The Idea of a Theater; Henderson, W. Richard Wagner, His Life and His Dramas; Kobbé, G. Wagner's Life and Works, *also* Wagner's Music Dramas Analyzed; Mann, T. Freud, Goethe, Wagner; Newman, E. The Life of Richard Wagner, *also* The Wagner Operas *and* Wagner as Man and Artist; Shaw, G. B. The Perfect Wagnerite; Stein, J. M. Richard Wagner and the Synthesis of the Arts; Terry, E. The Richard Wagner Dictionary; Weston, J. The Legends of the Wagner Dramas. [In German—see studies by W. G. Armando, E. Bücken, K. F. Glasenapp, W. Kienzl.]

R. A. C.

*WAIBLINGER, WILHELM FRIEDRICH** (November 21, 1804-January 17, 1830), German poet, novelist, and essayist, was born at Heilbronn, the son of a minor government official. He attended the *Gymnasium* in Stuttgart, where his interest in literature was stimulated by his association with the circle of poets around Gustav Schwab. In 1821 he entered the University of Tübingen to study theology but soon changed to literature. While in Tübingen he became the close friend of the poets Eduard Mörike and Ludwig Bauer, both of whom, however, were eventually alienated from Waiblinger because of his extreme vanity, and his immature, erratic behavior. Waiblinger also met and became a devoted disciple of the German poet Friedrich Hölderlin, whose influence is evident in the volume of poems *Lieder der Griechen* (1823), as well as in the novel *Phaeton* (2 vols., 1823), which is modeled on Hölderlin's *Hyperion.* Waiblinger's great esteem for this classic poet is evident in the monograph *Friedrich Hölderlins Leben, Dichtung und Wahnsinn* (1824).

In 1823 and 1824 Waiblinger visited Italy and, following an unhappy love affair, settled permanently in Rome in 1826. He lived in extreme poverty on the meager earnings of his writings. During this period of his life he was predominantly influenced by Byron and adopted the eccentric pose of an unhappy, unrecognized genius, which he considered himself to be. He was an unsettled personality, who never achieved peace of mind. Under the strain of poverty and his unregulated life, his health collapsed, and he died in Rome at the age of twenty-six.

Waiblinger's works, *Gesammelte Werke* (9 vols., 1839-40, edited by H. von Canitz), are almost totally forgotten. His finest achievement is his lyric verse of which a second volume, *Gedichte,* appeared in 1830. Although Waiblinger was a gifted poet, he failed to achieve an independent style. His verse, while skillful in technique, lacks specific content and individuality. Of his prose writings the most successful are the satires *Drei Tage in der Unterwelt* (1826), *Die Briten in Rom* (1827), and the narrative *Das Märchen von der Blauen Grotte* (1828). His reminiscences, *Erinnerungen aus der*

* vi′ bling ēr

985

Kindheit (1829), possess biographical interest.

ABOUT: Thompson, L. S. Waiblinger in Italy. [In German—see studies by H. Behne, K. Frey, I. Ruland.]

D. G. D.

*WALDIS, BURKARD (c. 1490-c. 1556), German writer of fables and dramatist, was born at Allendorf-an-der-Werra in Hesse of a well-to-do family. All documents about his youth were destroyed in the Thirty Years' War and he says virtually nothing about it in his works. In 1522 he was reported in the Baltic town of Riga as a Franciscan friar. The Reformation movement had just reached Riga, and Waldis was sent with two other friars to ask for help from the Emperor Charles V. After obtaining a promise from the Emperor's deputy, Philip of Baden, the three went on to Rome. On their return they were imprisoned by the Protestant town council. Waldis, apparently in reaction against the worldliness he had seen in Rome, announced his conversion and was released. He soon became prosperous as a pewterer. An unhappy marriage with Barbara Schulthe ended in a much publicized separation. His bitterness shows up in the anti-feminine bias of his fables.

In 1536 Waldis rashly supported a plot to overthrow the ruling German order and its head, von Plettenberg. He was arrested, tortured, and imprisoned. His release was ultimately effected by his brothers and the pleas of Philip of Hesse. In prison he wrote many of the psalms published later. In 1541 he returned to Allendorf, seeking a Lutheran pastorate. He was appointed to Abterode in 1544 and married the widow of a pastor whose daughter and son-in-law were of great help to him in his old age. Waldis wrote and published (1533) a psalter and also a rhymed Bible commentary (*Summarien über die Ganz Bibel*), translated from the Latin of Rudolf Gualtherus, as well as several pamphlets and Protestant polemical writings. His fame, however, rests on two works, not available in English translation—a play, *Die Parabel vom Verlorenen Sohn* (the Prodigal Son), and *Esopus*, a collection of German fables in rhymed couplets.

The play, written in the Low German dialect of Riga, was presented in February, 1527 as a *Fastnachtspiel*, a type of wild and licentious play presented on Shrove Tuesday. Waldis' play was deliberately serious and didactic. The career of the prodigal is depicted with much local color and additional material, but the main point is the contrast between the returning penitent and the pharasaical elder brother who believes that his good works entitle him to happiness. The stress lies on the efficacy of repentance and faith. Even the brothel-keeper of the early scenes repents and is accepted. Waldis' book of fables is based largely on the work of Aesop, as interpreted and rendered by medieval and early Renaissance writers. Again the moral is the important feature but experience of life enabled Waldis to add realistic touches and effective subsidiary stories. The fables remained popular until the eighteenth century.

ABOUT: Modern Language Quarterly, II (1941). [In German—see studies by G. Milchsack, W. Stammler (Verfasserlexikon des Deutschen Mittelalters; *also* Von der Mystik zum Barock); Baltische Monatschriften, XXIII.]

W. T. H. J.

*WALTHER VON DER VOGEL-WEIDE (c. 1170-1230), German poet, was probably born in Austria. His birthplace has not been definitely established, for there is only one extant document on his life. The name "von der Vogelweide" ("bird pasture") may refer to the estate on which he was born or to a title of distinction. Several places with this name have been found. About a dozen towns, including Bozen (Italian Bolzano), where his monument stands, have claimed him for their own. He belonged to an unpropertied family of knights (*Ministerialen*) in the court service.

About 1190 he found his first position as esquire or promising poet at the Vienna court of the Babenberg Duke Leopold V, the patron of Reinmar von Hagenau, who had introduced the Rhenish-Provençal minnesong. Reinmar trained him in "singen und sagen," the technique of sung and recitatively chanted poetry. Influenced by Heinrich von Morungen's minnesong, Walther reached the first high point of his lyrical poetry, emphasizing the joy rather than the sadness of *minne*. In competition with Reinmar he freed himself from the conventions and artificialities of traditional minnesong, attaining greater spontaneity, color, and breadth of theme. Their literary feud reflected marked differences of personality, of social attitudes, and of poetic tenets.

After Leopold's death in 1194, the duchy was divided between his sons Frederick and Leopold. Frederick, Walther's patron, died

* väl´ dĭs

* väl´ tẽr fôn dẽr fō´ gĕl vī´ dĕ

on the crusade of 1198, and Leopold VI withdrew his favor. Early in 1198 Walther left Vienna. Perhaps Reinmar was involved in the break.

In the life as itinerant minstrel which followed, Walther traveled extensively, suffering severe hardships but attaining new heights in his art. Confusion had followed the death of Emperor Henry VI in 1197. In long and destructive struggles, his brother Philip of Swabia and Otto of Brunswick, each elected king, contended for the crown of the Holy Roman Empire. Walther participated in the events of his day as a political singer and probably as a knight. By the summer of 1198 he was attached to Philip's court and participated in the royal coronation in Mainz on September 8 and also in Philip's Christmas feast in 1199.

Perhaps the poet turned to Landgrave Hermann of Thuringia, the friend of poets, in the winter of 1201-02, staying until 1203. In 1202 he probably met Wolfram von Eschenbach and competed with him in the legendary contest of minstrels at the Wartburg in 1207. He may also have returned for longer visits between 1203 and 1211, and between 1213 and 1217. He had bitter words for the revelry of Hermann's court.

In an entry of November 11, 1203, the travel accounts of Wolfger von Ellenbrechtskirchen, the bishop of Passau and later the patriarch of Aquileja, mention the gift of five shillings to the singer for a fur coat. Walther accompanied the prelate to the wedding feast of Leopold VI in Vienna. Constantly attracted to the art-loving court, he was disappointed in the hope for a reconciliation. The renewed controversy with Reinmar signified the final break with conventional minnesong. For the unrequited, classbound love of a knight for his lady Walther now substituted the ideal of reciprocal love between man and woman. He was in Austria again in 1219, when Leopold returned from a crusade, and shortly before his death. From 1210 to 1212 the poet supposedly lived at the court of Margrave Dieterich of Meissen, through whom he made connection with Ludwig of Bavaria. Walther directed two irritable sayings to Duke Bernhard of Carinthia but praised Leopold VI and the latter's uncle, Duke Henry von Mölding, the Patriarch of Aquileja, and Archbishop Engelbert of Cologne, the vicegerent whose assassination he lamented in a saying. To the count of Katzenellenbogen he expressed gratitude for a ring and chided the monastery of Tegernsee for its inhospitality.

On Palm Sunday, 1212, Walther was in Frankfurt to welcome Otto IV, whom the Pope had crowned emperor shortly after Philip's assassination in 1208. Although Walther entered Otto's service, he could not develop a personal attachment. He supported the emperor in the struggle with the Pope but felt inadequately rewarded for his service as a political singer. He soon entered the camp of Frederick II, the son of Henry VI, who was crowned king in 1215. Behind the opportunism involved in Walther's changes of allegiance lay the desire to bring to actuality the Hohenstaufen concept of a universal Christian *imperium*. Before Frederick left for Rome in 1220, he granted Walther a long-sought fief. The poet-singer represented Frederick's cause at the Nürnberg Imperial Diet of 1224-25. He repeatedly urged the emperor to participate in the crusade of 1228 but was too old to go himself. He died about 1230 and was buried in the cloister garden of the New Cathedral in Würzburg.

Walther's sayings and songs transcended the merely political and personal to express the typically human. He was a teacher of universally valid ethical and religious values, basing his ethics on the concepts of God's grace, fame, and worldly goods. His didactic verse was directed to court society.

Walther's polished verse lends special charm and ethical nobility to simple motives. His love lyrics speak from the heart and sing of girls of humble birth. In "Unter der Linden" a simple girl charmingly recalls the happiness of fulfilled love. Walther showed veneration towards woman, and tender sensitivity in praise of faithfulness, constancy, goodness, and purity. Thereby he ennobled the content of goliardic songs, which had influenced his style.

The political decline of the Hohenstaufen empire and of courtly joy and manners produced a feeling of pessimism and melancholy in the poetry of the old Walther. He attacked courtly village poetry, which he thought was endangering the tradition of minnesong. In a mood of melancholy renunciation he took leave of Dame World. His "Elegy" shows his world-weariness. By expressing personal feeling Walther enlivened the medieval concept of the transitoriness of the world. The crusading songs also reflected the religious mood of this period.

Walther cultivated a wide variety of poetic types: songs of nature, dancing measures, simple love lyrics, choral odes, crusading songs, prayers, dirges, elegies, and epigrams. He was chiefly a dramatic lyrist, expressing joy in dialogue and personification. He personified love, hate, envy, joy, fortune, and the world. He succeeded in attaining full harmony of word, melody, and content. His melodies were probably popular and he sang them well. Walther's poetry reveals a proud spirit, unbending courage, passionate sensitivity, tolerance, and a keen sense of humor. His patriotism was more cultural than political.

Walther von der Vogelweide was the most important German lyric poet before Goethe and perhaps the greatest lyrist of medieval Europe. He was acclaimed by Wolfram von Eschenbach in *Parzival* and *Willehalm*, by Gottfried von Strassburg in *Tristan und Isolde*, and by the later Hugo von Trimberg. Ulrich von Singenberg, Leuthold von Seven, and Rubin were his pupils. The mastersingers honored him as one of their twelve founders. Wagner's Walther von Stolzing acknowledges him as his master in the beautiful "Am Stillen Herd" of *Die Meistersinger*. During the Renaissance his work fell into relative obscurity. Bodmer and Myller published his poems in the eighteenth century, and Tieck and Uhland revived popular interest in him in the nineteenth. Lachmann edited his poems (1827). Scholarship has since then produced a more realistic portrait and has increased our esteem for the poet whose songs have left their imprint on the entire tradition of German lyric poetry.

The best verse translation of Walther's poems is I. G. Colvin's *I Saw the World* (1938). Edwin H. Zeydel and B. Q. Morgan published thirty new renderings faithful in content and form (1952). Other verse translations are in collections by A. Kroeger, *The Minnesingers of Germany* (1873); Henry Wadsworth Longfellow, *Poems of Places* (1876-79); A. Robinson, *Poems of 1848 and Earlier Days* (1904); Frank C. Nicholson, *Old German Love Songs* (1907); Jethro Bithell, *The Minnesingers*, I (1909); M. Muensterberg, *A Harvest of German Verse* (1916). Still others are by W. A. Phillips, *Selected Poems of Walther von der Vogelweide* with introduction and six illustrations (1896), and by M. F. Richey, *Selected Poems of Walther* (1948). There is an English prose translation by Frank Betts, *Songs and Sayings of Walther von der Vogelweide* (1917).

ABOUT: Gosse, E. Studies in the Literature of Northern Europe; Joos, M. & Whitesell, F. Middle High German Courtly Reader; Richey, M. F. *Introduction to* Selected Poems of Walther; Taylor, B. Studies in German Literature; Zeydel, E. H. & Morgan, B. Q. *Introduction to* Poems of Walther von der Vogelweide. [In German—see studies by H. Böhm, J. A. Huisman, J. Hunger, A. E. Schönbach, W. Wilmanns & V. Michels, J. Weigand.]

A. M. H.

*WECKHERLIN, GEORG RODOLF (September 15, 1584-February 13, 1653), German poet, and confidential parliamentary secretary to two English kings, was born in Stuttgart, studied law in Tübingen, and died in London. He is one of the first in a long line of eminent seventeenth century writers who had at the same time distinguished political careers. Weckherlin's father was a high government official. He was raised to noble rank shortly after Georg Rodolf's birth. His son took his first formal schooling in an institution primarily for the nobility. An extensive tour of Europe was the customary sequel to higher education, at least for the reasonably privileged. After Tübingen, Weckherlin traveled through Germany, France, and England. There is some indication that he was already combining business with pleasure—as poet and translator (of Wotton and Daniel) and also as diplomat.

With a period of governmental employment in Württemberg behind him, Weckherlin returned to England, where he married Elisabeth Raworth of Dover in 1616. (His daughter was the mother of Alexander Pope's friend William Trumbull.) By the early 1620's he was permanently established in England. For sixteen years he was undersecretary of state—to Conway, Dorchester, Coke, and Vane. His position does not seem to have brought him an excess of income. He complained that he needed "some gracious acknowledgment of his service, lest he undoe himself and his family." It did bring him criticism, especially for a fault which occasionally shows in his poetry: overadaptability. He was once accused of playing Pyramus, Thisbe, and the Lion at the same time.

In 1644 Weckherlin became secretary for foreign tongues, in which position he had the distinction of being replaced (in 1649) by John Milton. For a brief time he was Milton's assistant.

Weckherlin wrote poetry in German, English, French, Latin, and the Swabian dialect. His principal early medium was the ode, and two collections (1618 and 1619) attest his mastery of the form. The influence of the great French poets, especially Ronsard, is obvious in his work—a debt which he shares with his best contemporaries. The only striking thing is that he was little influenced by English writing.

In almost all his work Weckherlin is a poet of the court. Courtly life is the focus of his attention and the key to his manner.

* věk′ ẽr lēn

It is a life in which he was completely at home. His typical subjects are "occasions" and personalities, the ranges of love from the erotic to the quiet and simple. His tone is confident; he reflects the spirit of an age and a class ambitious for its own mode of expression.

His later verses turn to freer materials— they are often on contemporary issues and marked by consistent opposition to everything Catholic. Notable is his long heroic ode on Gustavus Adolphus. Later, too, Weckherlin turned to his own variant of the bucolic tradition—courtly, almost serene, close to real nature—and to a relatively brief but intense cultivation of the sonnet. Changes in theme do not alter his reliance on French forms. His alexandrines are as nearly French as possible. Opitz' injunctions on German versification he recognized late and with reluctance.

Weckherlin wrote when poems were still set to music, and his language carries over some of the effects of the older fashion of presentation. In spite of his originality and imagination, and his musicality, Weckherlin can be "heavy." He was certainly less facile than Opitz—and less of a theoretician—and the man he called the "new pope" soon overshadowed him. Bodmer and Herder, in the eighteenth century, were responsible for bringing him back to critical esteem. He ranks now as the most important German poet of the Early Baroque.

Among the few translations of Weckherlin available in English are his own: *Triumphall Shewes*, published in Stuttgart in 1616, and several poems in George C. Schoolfield's *The German Lyric of the Baroque in English Translation* (1962). *A Panegyric to . . . Lord Hays* (1619) also appears in his collected works.

ABOUT: German Life and Letters, 1938; Modern Language Review, X (1915), XLI (1946). [In German—Fischer, H. Georg Rudolf Weckherlin.]

F. G. R.

---

*WEISE, CHRISTIAN (April 29, 1642- October 21, 1708), German dramatist and novelist, was also a teacher, and the principal foundation of his fame was a long series of dramas written for the school stage. In an age when dramatic talent had this meager outlet and little else, he developed a surprisingly viable stage technique, especially in his comedies.

Christian Weise's father was a German preacher and teacher, exiled from Bohemia for his Protestant beliefs. The schooling he

* vi′ zě

gave his son was thorough and wide-ranging. The boy was frail, but gifted—at the University of Leipzig he wrote poems on order in lieu of "hazing" and often turned out ten or more in a day.

By turns lecturer, private secretary, and tutor, he accepted in 1670 a professorship at the *Gymnasium* in Weissenfels, where he lived for eight years. His home town of Zittau gave him the job of rector of the *Gymnasium* where his father was still on the staff. Exceptional in this mobile century, he virtually never traveled.

Weise was a respected administrator and an important writer on pedagogical subjects. His goal was practical: the education of businessmen and courtiers for the service of the state. Training in eloquence was paramount.

In his dramas (fifty of them) Weise showed a remarkable touch of realism. He used much dialect and allowed much extemporizing. His language is often crude or violent. He held that characters should speak in the words and tone natural to their class. Surprise is a strong ingredient of his plays. His Biblical dramas (*Samson, Absalom, Solomon*, etc.) are strikingly secular.

The school stage was restrictive, but Weise was also remarkably insular. Only one of his plays did he ever see elsewhere, and on his own stage he never produced another author's work. His best works are serious plays like *Abraham und Isaac* (1682), comedies like *Bäuerischer Machiavellus* (1681) or *Der Niederländische Bauer*, and—perhaps his finest—*Der Verfolgte Lateiner* (1696).

Weise's novels are in conscious contrast to the courtly prose of his century. Loosely woven, satirical scenes characterize his *Die Drey Ärgsten Ertz-Narren in der Gantzen Welt* (1672). The thread of action is lost early and never recovered in its sequel, *Die Drey Klügsten Leute . . .* (1675). Indeed, his tendency to offer what he called an "apothecary's box of medicine mixed with sugar" caused Weise to produce a didactic or moralizing potpourri rather than a novel.

One of Weise's poems is translated in George C. Schoolfield's *The German Lyric of the Baroque in English Translation* (1962).

ABOUT: [In German—Haxel, H. Studien zu den Lustspielen Christian Weises; Becker, R. Weise's Romane; Eggert, W. Weise und Seine Bühne; Lewinstein, K. Weise und Molière.]

F. G. R.

*WELHAVEN, JOHAN SEBASTIAN CAMMERMEYER

(December 22, 1807-October 21, 1873), Norwegian poet, was born on the Norwegian west coast in the city of Bergen where his father, Johan Ernst Welhaven, of Pomeranian descent, was a priest. His mother was Else Margrethe Cammermeyer. His childhood was a happy one. He went to school in his native town and enrolled in 1825 at the University of Christiania (now Oslo), where he met his future rival, Wergeland. First he studied theology, later philosophy and aesthetics. Highly intellectual in nature, he was influenced by French classical doctrines, J. L. Heiberg's aesthetics, and German classicism.

The witty, refined, and elegant young man made a splendid social career. The national liberal movement headed by Wergeland was to him a manifestation of ignorance and barbarism. In 1830 Welhaven published in the Christiania daily *Morgenbladet* (Morning News) the pamphlet *Henrik Wergelands Digtekunst og Polemik* (Henrik Wergeland's Poetic Art and Polemics) and in 1834 the bitterly polemical sonnet cycle *Norges Dæmring* (The Dawn of Norway). Wergeland and his supporters were not silent, and a furor of debate and hatred ensued, dividing cultural Norway into two ruthlessly fighting parties. (For a further account of this feud see sketch below.)

In 1838 Welhaven published his first collection of poems, *Digte,* formally exquisite but partly indebted to models. The year before he had met a charming young lady, Ida Kjerulf, sister of the composer Halvdan Kjerulf and the geologist and lyricist Theodor Kjerulf. They were deeply attached to each other, but her parents refused to give their consent to a marriage. When Welhaven in 1840 secured a position as lecturer in philosophy at the university and thereby removed the parental obstacle, it was too late. Ida Kjerulf died a few days later. His deep sorrow is partly accountable for the dark coloring and the feeling of loss in Welhaven's next collection, *Nyere Digte* (New Poems, 1844). Some romances on motifs from Norwegian folklore, saga, and history included in this collection show that Welhaven, in spite of his animosity to the nationalistic Wergeland group and his favorable attitude toward foreign culture, was not wholly alien to the national currents of the time.

In the 1830's Welhaven had met a young Danish woman, Josephine Angelica Bidoulac, daughter of a French immigrant. They

* věl' hä' věn

were married in 1845. In 1847 Welhaven published *Halvhundrede Digte* (Half a Hundred Poems), in which he sang about his happy home and his wife. But there were also melancholy tones of memories of his first love. A collection of verse and prose, *Reisebilleder og Digte* (Travel Pictures and Poems, 1851), and *En Digtsamling* (A Collection of Poems, 1859) were partly inspired by a religious attitude instilled in him by his wife. In 1863 Welhaven published his last book, *Ewald og de Norske Digtere* (Ewald and the Norwegian Poets), one of several treatises on literary history from his pen.

A dozen poems by Welhaven are translated in C. W. Stork, *Anthology of Norwegian Lyrics* (1942). Scattered verses appear in the Grøndahl-Raknes book mentioned below.

ABOUT: Grøndahl, I. & Raknes, O. Chapters in Norwegian Literature. [In Norwegian—see studies by I. Handagaard, A. Löchen, J. E. Sars.]

A. J.

*WERGELAND, HENRIK ARNOLD

(June 17, 1808-July 12, 1845), Norwegian poet, playwright, prose writer, was born as the eldest of five children in the south Norwegian coastal town of Kristiansand, where his father, pastor Nicolai Wergeland, was a high school teacher. His mother was Alethe Dorothea Thaulow, daughter of Judge Henrik Arnold Thaulow, for whom the future author was named. In 1814 his father took an active part in the writing of the Norwegian constitution at Eidsvoll and was three years later appointed pastor in that town, where young Henrik spent a couple of years before he was sent to Christiania (now Oslo) for his schooling. He soon showed a pantheistic attachment to nature and an unusually vivid imagination. From his father he inherited a strong impulsiveness which, combined with an unscrupulous frankness, caused him much trouble. His deeply and strongly erotic nature involved him in numerous love affairs.

In 1825 Wergeland was admitted to the University of Christiania, where he completed a theological degree in 1829. From the age of thirteen he had published short stories, satirical comedies, and scattered poems. His real debut came in 1828 with the collection *Digte, Første Ring* (Poems, First Cycle), mostly lyric and erotic songs inspired by his love for nature and women. Wergeland is Norway's greatest love-poet. He directed his poems to an imagined object, Stella, a universal sublimation of his love. In 1828

* věr' gě länd

WERGELAND

against the Danish hegemony over Norwegian culture and called for a purer Norwegian language. In 1834 his antagonist Welhaven exploded a bomb intended to wipe out the ultra-Norwegian movement, viz., the polemic sonnet cycle *Norges Dæmring* (The Dawn of Norway), arguing that national strength and culture can be built on the knowledge of foreign civilization and the sharing of international progress. The poem made Welhaven the most hated man in Norway, while Wergeland's favor with the broader strata of the population and the patriots increased.

Wergeland edited the newspaper *Statsborgeren* (The Citizen) in 1835-37, and Welhaven's group answered in 1836 by starting a paper of their own, *Den Constitutionelle* (The Constitutional). Wergeland continued to fight for his ideals in poetry, e.g., *Digte, Anden Ring* (Poems, Second Cycle, 1838); in polemic comedies; a series of dramas, e.g., *Campbellerne* (The Campbells, 1838), the performance of which caused a riot in the theatre between the two fighting groups. This riot ended, more or less, the bitter conflict that shook Norway for almost a decade.

Wergeland applied for various positions in the clergy and as a teacher, but was always passed over, until in 1839 he was employed at the university library and the next year was appointed keeper of the public records.

In 1839 Wergeland married a woman of the common people, Amalie Sophie Bekkevold, daughter of a tavern keeper. Among the poems Wergeland wrote to her, published as *Poesier* (Poem, 1838), are some of his most noteworthy lyrics. The marriage produced no children, but an earlier illegitimate son of Wergeland lived in their home. In 1839-40 Wergeland received annuities from the French-born King Charles XIV John of Sweden-Norway, whom Wergeland, in spite of his republican attitude, regarded as a son of the French revolution. Wergeland's enemies, and some of his friends, started a fierce press campaign against him, accusing him of having prostituted himself. Wergeland defended himself in some crushingly witty farces, e.g., *Engelsk Salt* (English Salt, 1841). In several pamphlets he fought in favor of granting the Jews permission to settle in Norway.

During his last years Wergeland produced a rich output of works of various kinds. Historical studies resulted in *Norges Konstitutions Historie* (History of the Norwegian Constitution, 1841-43). He worked for the education of the common people, especially

he also published a tragedy, *Sinclairs Død* (The Death of Sinclair), and the following year a comedy, *Opium*, both of which show the influence of Shakespeare.

In 1830 Wergeland created a sensation with the publication of the most voluminous and original work of his earlier production, the enormous epic *Skabelsen, Mennesket og Messias* (Creation, Man and Messiah), in which the history of nature and man is given mythological reconstruction. As was often the case at this time, enlightened rationalism is fused with romantic pantheism and longing for eternity. The fundamental idea of the poem is the conviction of men's instinctive striving toward perfection. The generative force and the infinite intelligence in this process is God. The Messiah is not Jesus, but "a young man" of higher education than anyone else of his time.

In form the poem was at variance with established aesthetic standards of poetry and drew severe criticism from Welhaven (see sketch above), whose attack gave the signal for a long and bitter aesthetic feud which soon grew into one concerning social, political, and religious problems as well. Welhaven and his supporters defended conservative ideas of refined intelligence, while Wergeland, who sided with the lower classes, fought for a liberal nationalism. The student body of the university and the entire cultural world of Norway were divided into two camps of bitter enemies. In his pamphlet *Om Norsk Sprogreformation* (On a Norwegian Language Reform, 1832), he spoke

through the paper *For Arbeidsklassen* (For the Working Class), which continued to appear until his death. With the same objective in view he published *Læsebog for den Norske Ungdom* (A Reader for Norwegian Youth, 1844).

In 1844 he contracted a chest disease which developed into quick consumption. But he continued to write almost to his last day. His lyric-epical verse story *Den Engelske Lods* (The English Pilot, 1844) glorifies England. He revised completely his great work *Skabelsen, Mennesket og Messias* and called it *Mennesket* (Man, 1844). The autobiographical collection of stories *Hasselnødder* (Hazel Nuts, 1845) is perhaps his greatest prose work. Facing death he wrote some of his most beautiful lyrics.

A selection of poems by Wergeland appears in G. M. Hathorne-Hardy, *Poems by Wergeland* (1929; with an introduction), translated by the editor, J. Bithell, and I. Grøndahl. About a dozen of his poems are included in C. W. Stork's *Anthology of Norwegian Lyrics* (1942). *Norwegian Emigrant Songs and Ballads* (1936), by T. C. Blegen and M. B. Rud, contains an account of Wergeland's musical play *Fjeldstuen* (The Mountain Hut) and a translation of some of its poems. Extracts from his poetic production are printed in the Grøndahl-Raknes book mentioned below.

ABOUT: Burchardt, C. B. Norwegian Life and Literature; Gordon, E. Wergeland, the Prophet; Grøndahl, I. & Raknes, O. Chapters in Norwegian Literature; Wergeland, A. M. Leaders in Norway. [In Norwegian—see studies by A. Kabell, H. Koht, J. E. Sars.]

A. J.

*WERNER, (FRIEDRICH LUDWIG) ZACHARIAS** (November 18, 1768-January 17, 1823), German dramatist and preacher, was born at Königsberg in East Prussia. His father was a respected professor of history and rhetoric at the university and also served as dramatic censor for the city, a position which afforded his son unusual opportunity to attend the theatre. Werner's mother was a neurotic and mentally disturbed woman who died obsessed by the idea that she was the Holy Mother and her son the Savior. Werner possessed this same nervous, unbalanced temperament and inclination toward religious fanaticism.

In 1784 Werner entered the University of Königsberg to study law. His university years were extremely dissolute, and he left the university in 1790 without his degree. He led an unsettled wandering life and was married and divorced three times. In 1796 he moved to Warsaw, where he associated with

* vĕr′ nēr

the writer E. T. A. Hoffman and with J. E. Hitzig, who became his first biographer. From 1801 to her death in 1804 he attended his mother, for whom he cherished a genuine affection. In 1805 he obtained a government post in Berlin, but left after two years to travel through southern Germany and Austria. He was well received at Weimar by Goethe, who like Schiller and and Grillparzer considered Werner a promising young dramatist. In 1809 Prince Dalberg granted Werner a pension, which was later continued by Karl August of Saxe-Weimar. After a visit to Madame de Staël in Switzerland, Werner traveled to Rome where he was converted to Catholicism in 1810. He subsequently studied for the priesthood at Aschaffenburg and was ordained in 1814. He became a popular and somewhat sensational preacher in Vienna, where he died at fifty-four.

Werner's first major work was the monumental drama *Die Söhne des Tales* (1803), which consists of two parts, *Die Templer auf Cypern* and *Die Kreuzesbrüder*, each in six acts. Although flashes of genuine dramatic talent are evident in individual scenes, this drama as a whole is a formless, chaotic work, which is virtually impossible to stage. A significant advance in technique was shown in the drama *Martin Luther, oder die Weihe der Kraft* (1807), which became Werner's greatest success during his lifetime. After his conversion to Catholicism Werner recanted this work in a poem entitled *Die Weihe der Unkraft* (1813). Werner's later tragedies such as *Attila* (1808), *Wanda* (1808), and *Die Mutter der Makkabäer* (1816) failed to fulfill the promise of his early dreams. The work by which his name is remembered today is the one-act tragedy *Der Vierundzwanzigste Februar* (1809). This play initiated the German fate tragedy, a type of drama which became exceedingly popular in the early nineteenth century.

The Twenty-Fourth of February was translated by E. Riley in 1844 and by W. H. H. Chambers in 1903. E. Lewis translated *The Templars in Cyprus* in 1886, and *The Brethren of the Cross* in 1892. *The Sons of the Valley* also appeared anonymously in 1903.

ABOUT: Carlyle, T. Critical and Miscellaneous Essays, I. [In German—see studies by G. Carow, P. Hankamer, J. Minor, and F. Stuckert. In French —see studies by L. Guinet, E. Vierling.]

D. G. D.

*WESSEL, JOHAN HERMAN** (October 6, 1742-December 29, 1785), Norwegian-Danish poet and dramatist, was born at Vestby,

* vĕs′ ĕl

a few miles south of the Norwegian capital of Christiania (now Oslo). His father was vicar Jonas Wessel, and his mother was Lena Maria Schumacher. Jonas, who was the fourth of thirteen children, grew up at Vestby and was educated at home until at the age of sixteen he was sent to a Latin school in the capital. In 1761 he entered the University of Copenhagen where he studied the humanities for about ten years without completing his master's degree. His education was in harmony with the enlightened French-classical ideals. He obtained a solid knowledge of aesthetics and the ancient classical and Romance cultures and literatures. He also had a keen interest in the theatre. Although his disposition was melancholy he led a gay Bohemian life and frequented taverns and cafés in the company of merry friends, especially the "Norwegian Society," in which he became the central figure and scored great successes with satirical poems. However, his health was gradually undermined by alcoholism.

After Holberg's death in 1754 the theatrical menu in the Danish capital was composed exclusively of French-classical tragedies and Danish imitations of this genre. Wessel, who knew and loved the brilliant French dramas, saw how poor the declamatory and bombastic native imitations were. But nevertheless they were great successes on the stage. This inspired Wessel to write his immortal parody *Kierlighed uden Strømper* (*Love without Stockings*) in 1772. The ritual of the French-classical tragedy is carefully observed. There are five acts, the meter is in strict alexandrines, and the three unities are rigidly observed. The unity of time, for instance, is made perfectly clear in the opening line: "You will never get married unless it happens today." The irresistible comic effect is attained when the elevated language is used by vulgarians and their servants and when the plot is reduced to the triviality of finding a pair of stockings. The whole French-classical machinery, with presentiments and dreams and faintings, pathetic monologues and speculative arias, is included, but the characters and the milieu are rustic. The drama, with music by Scalabrini, became a great success, and through it Wessel gave a damaging blow to an unsound trend in Danish literature. It has retained its popularity to our time. Less important are Wessel's subsequent plays, e.g., *Lykken Bedre end Forstanden* (Happiness Is Better than Sense, 1776).

In 1780 Wessel married Anna Catharina Bukier. A son was born the next year. In this unhappy marriage both parents neglected their home and each other. Wessel spent most of his time in taverns. In 1784 he founded and edited a magazine, *Votre Serviteur, Otiosis*, in which he published some excellent comical stories. But it died the next year. Wessel was tormented during his last years not only by poverty but also by illness.

Extracts from *Love without Stockings*, translated by Mrs. Bushby, appeared in *The New Monthly Magazine and Humorist*, 1852. The story "Smeden og Bageren" was translated by M. Thomas as "The Smith and the Baker" in her book *Denmark, Past and Present* (1902).

ABOUT: Grøndahl, I. & Raknes, O. Chapters of Norwegian Literature.

A. J.

*WESSELY (WEISEL, WESEL), NAPHTALI HIRZ or HARTWIG (1725-February 28, 1805), German-Hebrew poet and essayist, was born in Hamburg to a prosperous family, of the Jewish mercantile class in the North Sea coastal area. As was the custom of the time, he received an exclusively Talmudic education. In addition he was independently interested in Biblical studies and began his general education from the standpoint that Jewish learning presupposes some knowledge of history, geography, foreign languages, and mathematics. Although Wessely remained a competent Talmudist and a pious Jew, his interests gradually shifted to these newer fields, with emphasis on Bible and Hebrew poetry—subjects then neglected by Jews. He learned German from Luther's version of the Bible and began his literary career with the unusual step of translating into Hebrew with commentary the apocryphal Wisdom of Solomon.

Wessely entered upon a successful commercial career in Copenhagen and Amsterdam, and settled in Berlin, the center of the Jewish Enlightenment, in 1774. Here he drew near the Moses Mendelssohn circle, although he was more pious and conservative in his views than they. He continued his literary activity with such works as a commentary on the rabbinic ethical tractate *Abot*, and a dictionary of Biblical synonyms. Although unconventional, these works were unopposed by the orthodox. But a storm burst upon this retiring man with the appearance of his epistolary *Dibrei Shalom ve-Emet* (Words of Peace and Truth) in 1781,

* věs' ĕl ē

993

which advocated that the Jews accept the educational reforms required of them by Emperor Joseph II's Patent of Toleration in 1780. This decree had greatly ameliorated the Jews' civil status in the Hapsburg lands, but required of the Jews in return that they give their children some secular studies. Wessely's mild words aimed to show that Jewish religious tradition endorsed secular study. But the rigid traditionalists pursued him—the first of many encounters between the protagonists of the old ways and the reformers. The early 1780's were difficult years for Wessely: his beloved wife died, leaving him with a large family, and his business failed. While religious zealots pursued him, the Hebraic Enlightenment circles were moving rapidly towards cultural Germanization and religious liberalism, and considered him far too conservative. Besides a work of systematic ethics, *Sefer ha-Middot* (1785), Wessely devoted the remainder of his life to the new genre of poetry. His energies were spent on *Shirei Tiferet* (Poems of Glory), published in six fascicles, the last in 1829 by his son Solomon. It is the first major narrative poem in modern Hebrew, relating the story of Egyptian bondage, deliverance, and the Sinaitic revelation. Its style is at best clear, literal, and elegant; but in many places it is verbose, literal, and pedestrian. Its originality exerted formative, and for nearly a century decisive, influence upon Hebrew poetry.

Although he remains a figure of the second rank, Wessely's modest courage and his pathbreaking literary achievement make him a founder of modern Hebrew literature.

A fragment of *Poems of Glory* appears in English translation in B. Halper, *Post-Biblical Hebrew Literature*, II (1921).

ABOUT: Spiegel, S. Hebrew Reborn; Waxman, M. A History of Jewish Literature, III. [In German—see study by W. A. Meisl (1841).]

L. P. G.

WHITE, JOSEPH BLANCO

WHITE, JOSEPH BLANCO (July 11, 1775-May 20, 1841), Spanish poet and theological writer, was born José Maria Blanco y Crespo in Seville. His grandfather was an Irish Catholic who fell heir to a mercantile business in Seville. His father in turn took over the establishment and married an Andalusian lady of noble family. José was put into the business at the age of eight, but detested it. In order to escape from the world of commerce, he decided to study for the priesthood, and in his fourteenth year he was enrolled in a Dominican college. Happening

upon the works of the controversial writer Benito Feijóo, who had attacked scholastic philosophy, José began to question traditional Catholicism. He was really more the aesthete than the mystic by temperament, and while at the University of Seville he steeped himself in the French and Italian classics, and formed a literary society.

Though it was with misgivings, José accepted several religious appointments after his graduation from the university. Several circumstances conspired to unsettle him from his faith: his revulsion at the system of confession, the influence of free-thinking priests, the death of one of his sisters shortly after taking the veil. The culmination of these emotional difficulties was a breakdown in health, and he asked to be relieved of his religious duties. For a time he tried a journalistic career in Seville. However, with the invasion of the French army under Joseph Bonaparte, José decided to leave Spain. After some cloak-and-dagger escapades, involving among other things his passing himself off as a British subject, he managed to get aboard a packet sailing for Falmouth. Henceforth his career was bound up with England.

Joseph Blanco White (as he now called himself) first established himself in London journalism as editor of a monthly periodical, *Español*, owned by a refugee priest named Juigné, to whom he had been introduced by friends. He utilized this paper to promote the cause of Spanish nationalism, a cause which generally aroused sympathy. After the final expulsion of Bonaparte's army from Spain, he was given a life pension by the British government.

Shortly after arriving in England, Blanco White became attracted to the Anglican Church. In 1814 he signed the Thirty-nine Articles to qualify himself to act as an English clergyman, and settled at Oxford to continue the theological studies that he had suspended. While at Oxford he eked out his pension by various literary labors. To the *New Monthly Magazine*, edited by Thomas Campbell, he contributed the articles eventually collected as *Letters from Spain* (1822) under the pseudonym Don Leucadio Doblado, which made him famous. To the *Encyclopaedia Britannica* he contributed a long article on Spain. His *Evidences against Catholicism* (1825) contributed to a then rife controversy.

In 1826 Blanco White received his Master of Arts degree from Oxford. He then settled at Oriel College, and thus met Richard

Whateley and the group of religious thinkers who were to become associated with the Oxford Movement—Edward Pusey, Hurrell Froude, and particularly John Henry Newman. Newman played the violin with Blanco White, and was to remain a lifelong friend, though his own religious life was destined to move in the opposite direction. (White is introduced briefly in Newman's *Apologia*, and Newman's famous essay on Aristotle's *Poetics* was originally an article for White's short-lived *London Review*.) Interestingly enough, though he had forsworn the Catholic Church, Blanco White proved invaluable to the members of the Oxford Movement for his knowledge of its dogma and ritual.

In time Blanco White became discontented with Oxford and Anglicanism. Sensitive to being treated as an alien and an outsider, he took the opportunity in 1831 to remove himself to Dublin, just after his good friend Whateley became established there as archbishop. In 1833 he wrote, in reply to Thomas Moore's *Travels of an Irish Gentleman in Search of a Religion*, an autobiography entitled *Second Travels of an Irish Gentleman in Search of a Religion*. It was apparent from the book that he still had a feeling for Christianity, but was unable to assent to its supernatural dogmas. He then decided to embrace Unitarianism, and left Dublin to live in Liverpool, where James Martineau, a Unitarian minister he admired, had settled. Despite their disappointment, his friends Newman and Whateley stood by him, Whateley continuing to send him an annual gift. Blanco White remained in Liverpool for the rest of his life, numbering among his friends John Stuart Mill, to whose *London and Westminster Review* he became a regular contributor. Always frail in health, he died at Greenbank, not quite sixty-six. He left a son, Ferdinand, apparently born in Spain, the offspring of an unhappy clandestine romance referred to in his autobiography.

In Spain the reputation of Joseph Blanco White survives as the translator of the *Book of Common Prayer*, Paley's *Evidences*, and Hamlet's soliloquy "To Be or Not to Be," while his own lyric poems have exerted some influence on the romantic movement. To the English speaking world he is remembered principally for the plangent lyric "Night and Death," written in English, declared by Coleridge to be "the finest and most grandly conceived sonnet in our language." The poem appears in anthologies sometimes under this title, sometimes as "Mysterious Night" or "To Night."

There is no translation of Joseph Blanco White's Spanish writings into English. His *Poesías* make up part of Vol. 67 of the *Biblioteca de Autores Españoles*.

ABOUT: Harwood, J. Rationalist à Kempis; Newman, J. Letters (ed. by A. Mozley); Thom, J. (ed.) Life of the Rev. Joseph Blanco White Written by Himself. [In Spanish—see study by M. Méndez Bejarano.]

R. A. C.

*WIED, GUSTAV JOHANNES (March 6, 1858-October 24, 1914), Danish novelist, playwright, short-story writer, was born on the Danish island of Lolland, where his father, Carl August Wied, owned a farm His mother was Catarine (Trine) Karoline Boesen. He went to school at Naskov on his native island, after which he held several odd jobs until he completed his matriculation examination in 1886. He earned his living as a teacher while he tried for three years to become an actor, but failed. In 1893 he married Alice Tutein, daughter of a landed proprietor. Then he made his residence in Roskilde.

Wied began to write poetry at the age of ten, and it was even then evident that his mind was split. There were two conflicting forces, two personalities, in him. One was weak and soft and developed into a frustrated loathing for life. The other was rebellious and bitter and showed itself in an inclination to sneer and shock and offend. Wied himself was aware of this dangerous predisposition, and later he wrote in his memoirs that it always was "as though my ego was split into two egos."

Wied published in 1891 his first and best collection of short stories, *Silhuetter* (Silhouettes), containing fine realistic descriptions of rural life and characters in the style of Dickens and Schandorph. This collection was followed by others, and in 1907 he published a selection of his best short stories under the title *Fra Land og By* (From Country and Town). Also in 1891 he published in the Copenhagen daily *Dagbladet* a short story entitled "De Unge og de Gamle" (The Young and the Old) in which he dealt so openly with sex that he was prosecuted for pornography and sentenced to two weeks in jail.

The object of Wied's irony and grim humor was in some novels the aristocracy. But underneath the surface of humorous larking there was a morbid melancholy and pessimism. In his two naturalistic novels,

* vēd

Slægten (Kin, 1898), and *Fædrene Æde Druer* (The Fathers Eat Grapes, 1908), he treated the theme of degeneration of aristocratic families, through sexual error. In other novels Wied's humor and irony were directed against the small idyllic world of the provincial town. This is the theme in the two connected novels *Livsens Ondskab* (Life's Malice, 1899), and *Knagsted* (1902). In these books there are two characters, editor Knagsted and school principal Clausen, who are complete opposites of each other, both physically and psychologically, and who represent the two conflicting forces in Wied's own personality. When they debate, it is Wied's own split nature that talks to itself. The small-town milieu is depicted with a luxuriant imaginative realism that does not avoid grotesqueries.

Wied also wrote a number of dramas, partly in collaboration with other playwrights. Some of them had great success on the stage. From his own pen came his first play, *En Hjemkomst* (Homecoming, 1889), a macabre drama influenced by Ibsen's *Ghosts*. In cooperation with others he wrote, among other works, *Første Violin* (The First Violin, 1898), and *Barnlige Sjæle* (Childish Souls, 1893). Some of the plays are dramatizations of Wied's earlier stories and novels, e.g., the novel *Livsens Ondskab* was dramatized as *Thummelumsen* (The Wild One, 1901), and a story from *Menneskenes Børn* (Children of Men, 1894), as *Den Gamle Pavillon* (The Old Pavilion, 1902). An episode from his *Ungdomshistorier* (Stories from My Youth, 1895), gave the motif for the play *Ranke Viljer* (Independent Wills), one of his most successful plays which was performed in 1906 under the title *2x2=5*. Wied also wrote short comedies, e.g., the one-act play *Skærmydsler* (Skirmishes, 1901), also very popular on the stage.

Wied created an original and new dramatic genre which he called "Satyrspil" (satyr-plays), a hybrid of story and drama. During the performance of a play, the author in the function of an instructor or director interrupts the dialogue and injects his own comments and remarks. In these products, which were not intended for the stage, the stress is laid on the brilliant, witty, and provocative dialogue. Here his art of repartee culminated, e.g., in *Det Svage Køn* (The Weaker Sex, 1900), dominated by his Strindbergian hatred of women, and the excellent *Dansemus* (Dancing Mice, 1905).

Eventually, broken down by adverse criticism and illness, Wied ended his life at Roskilde by committing suicide.

A story, "Menneskenes Børn," was translated as "Children of Men" by Hanna Astrup Larsen in *American-Scandinavian Review*, 1915, and reprinted in *Denmark's Best Stories* (1928) and *Scandinavian Short Stories* (Penguin Books, 1943). Another story was translated by J. B. C. Watkins as "A Bohemian" in *American-Scandinavian Review*, 1944. Two comedies have been translated, one as *Autumn Fires* by B. F. Grazer (1920) and the other *2 x 2 = 5* by E. Boyd and H. Koppel (1923).

ABOUT: Boyd, E. Studies from Ten Literatures; Mitchell, P. M. A History of Danish Literature; Topsöe-Jensen, H. G. Scandinavian Literature from Brandes to Our Day.

A. J.

*WIELAND, CHRISTOPH MARTIN

(September 5, 1733-January 20, 1813), German poet and novelist, was born in Biberach, a free corporation town of Swabia, the son of a learned Lutheran minister. The atmosphere of pietism in which the precocious child was reared conflicted early with his inborn skepticism and his tendency toward the enjoyment of nature. Originally destined for a theological career, he changed, under the pretense of delicate health, to the study of law, which led him to the uinversity town of Tübingen. His first ambitious poem was inspired by Sophie von Guterman, for some time his fiancée, who later became famous as a writer of novels under the name of Sophie von Laroche: in *Die Natur der Dinge* (1751), he imitates and at the same time argues against Lucretius in an effort to combine the ideas of the Enlightenment with those of Christianity. He abandoned these principles, however, in order to win access to the circle of Bodmer, who, as the head of the sentimental school of poetry, ruled from Zürich over a widespread group of followers. To comply with Bodmer's expectations that he would become a German Milton, Wieland wrote a religious epic, *Der Geprüfte Abraham* (1753), and various critical essays in defense of pietistic poetry. A violent attack on the immorality of the thoroughly harmless anacreontic poets Uz and Gleim resulted in a much more effective counterblow from Lessing, the most eminent German critic. As a tutor to various patrician houses he entered the social life of the city of Zürich, and this accelerated his estrangement from Bodmer and the development of his own philosophy of life.

* vē′ länt

WIELAND

background of the story, as in most of his works, is not the antiquity of the fifth century, but rather the refined culture of Hellenism. This novel represents the clearest expression of Wieland's serene humanism, based on the harmonious play of intellect and sensuality. A short epic poem, *Musarion* (1768), deals with the conversion of some Platonic dreamers to the enjoyment of life by a charming and intelligent woman.

In the three years before the publication of Goethe's *Werther*, Wieland enjoyed the reputation of being the greatest German poet. He rejected the poets of Storm and Stress as the destroyers of true taste and as enemies of the European cultural tradition. In the years between 1770 and 1780 those who still believed in this tradition looked upon him as its strongest bulwark. In 1772 he published one of his most famous works, *Der Goldene Spiegel*, a political novel, propagating the ideas of benevolent absolutism. The book brought Wieland not the hoped-for call to Vienna by Joseph II, the one European ruler closest to his idea of an enlightened monarch, but one to Weimar as the educator of the hereditary Prince Karl August. The failure of his educational mission disappointed the Prince's mother, the Grand Duchess Anna Amalia, but their common loyalty to a refined humanism created a lasting bond of friendship between the two.

Though Goethe took part in the attacks of the young generation on Wieland with a satire, *Götter, Helden und Wieland*, his superior genius was fully recognized by the older poet. Goethe, for his part, never ceased to admire Wieland as a great artist and often took his advice in the execution of his poetic plans. Following the model of the famous *Mercure de France*, Wieland founded in 1773 the literary magazine *Teutscher Merkur*, which played an important part in the popularization of contemporary poetry, philosophy, and science.

After the turmoil of Storm and Stress had receded, Wieland rose to the heights which admitted him to the ranks of the German classics. He created his masterpieces— the humorous tale *Die Geschichte der Abderiten* (1781), wherein the follies of human society are described in serene detachment, and finally his most famous poem, the verse epic *Oberon* (1780), of which Goethe said: "As long as poetry is poetry, as long as gold is gold and crystal is crystal, Wieland's *Oberon* will be beloved as a masterpiece of poetic art." Gradually he withdrew from poetry, but until the day of his death at

His appointment as a town clerk of his home town finally freed him from his obligations to Bodmer and his program. After an unfulfilled engagement to Julie Bondely, known through her friendship with Rousseau, and after another tragic love affair, he married a simple girl with whom he led the life of an exemplary family man until his late years. Through the mediation of his former fiancée, Sophie von Laroche, he joined the circle of Count Stadion, a retired diplomat, who, on his estate Wartenhausen near Biberach, created an intellectually and culturally minded court, one of the few outposts of refined rococo culture outside France and Austria. Wieland's talent was ideally suited to entertain the members of this court with charming erotic tales, rendered in a style which refuted the general belief that German could never equal the elegance and the subtlety of French. In his novel *Die Abenteuer des Don Silvio de Rosalva* (1764), one of the best of the Quixotic type, which ridicules the fairy tale fashion and the follies of sentimental education, Wieland achieved the highest eminence in European literature before the arrival of Goethe.

His cosmopolitan literary taste drew him to Shakespeare, whose works first conquered German audiences in Wieland's prose translations. In 1767 he published *Die Geschichte Agathons*, a true milestone in the history of the German novel. As was later characteristic of the novels of Goethe, the problems arising from the experiences of the characters are thoroughly discussed. The Greek

seventy-nine he never ceased to write. The most important literary contributions of the last period of his life are some masterpieces of translation, such as the satires and epistles of Horace, the complete works of Lucian, and the letters of Cicero.

When the brothers Schlegel started the romantic movement, the denigration of the grand old man of German poetry was one of the chief points of their program. They succeeded completely. Rising nationalism and the submission of German literature to a predominantly tragic view of life and to oversaturation with speculative thought did the rest. Wieland's serenity, so deeply admired by Goethe, appeared now as lack of depth, his artistry as shallow virtuosity. There was never a serious movement, as in the case of other forgotten poets like Jean Paul or Hölderlin, to restore Wieland to his former stature. Only after World War II did a small circle of outstanding literary critics find a new interest in Wieland. They saw in him the shining representative of Pan-European social culture from which Germany separated herself, when, under the influence of nationalism and romantic philosophy, she started out on her tragic path to political and cultural isolation.

Of the numerous works of Wieland not mentioned in the preceding sketch, many were translated into English at the time when Wieland was the darling of the reading public all over Europe. An anonymous translation of *Die Abenteuer des Don Sylvio de Rosalva* under the title *Reason Triumphant over Fancy; Exemplified in the Singular Adventures of Don Sylvio* appeared in 1773. From a single preserved copy Ernest Baker edited a reprint of the novel in 1904. The same year saw *The History of Agathon*, translated by John Richardson. William Sotheby's *Oberon* translation (1798) was long considered as the one that could not be surpassed, until it was discovered that John Quincy Adams, while he lived in Berlin as ambassador to the Prussian court, had completed a translation of his own, which is by no means inferior to Sotheby's work. He even succeeded in reproducing the eight-line stanza of the original, whereas Sotherby uses a Spenserian stanza. Adams' work was not published until 1940.

ABOUT: Baker, T. *Introduction to* The Adventures of Don Sylvio de Rosalva (1904); Stockley, V. German Literature as Known in England, 1750-1830; Van Abbé, D. M. Wieland: A Literary Biography; Modern Language Quarterly, XVII (1956). [In German—see studies by L. John Parker, F. Sengle.]

F. R.

*WILDENBRUCH, (ADAM) ERNST VON** (February 3, 1845-January 15, 1909), German dramatist, short-story writer, and poet, was born in Beirut, Syria, where his

* vil' dĕn brŏŏk

father served as Prussian consul. On his mother's side he was the grandson of the Hohenzollern Prince Louis Ferdinand. Following his childhood in Athens and Constantinople, the boy entered a military academy in Germany and at the age of eighteen was commissioned a lieutenant. He resigned from the army to study law but re-enlisted for the Austrian and French wars. In 1871 he became a practicing lawyer in Frankfurt an der Oder; from 1877 until his retirement in 1901 he served in the Foreign Office in Berlin. In 1885 he married Maria von Weber, the granddaughter of the noted composer. He died at Weimar.

Wildenbruch began his literary career writing heroic epic poems based on his war experiences, such as *Vionville* (1874) and *Sedan* (1875). He soon turned to the field of historical drama and by portraying scenes from Germany's great heritage endeavored to inspire and uplift his contemporaries. His early dramatic efforts were repeatedly rejected, until in 1878 the Duke of Meiningen performed *Die Karolinger*. The success of this work was continued by *Harold* (1881), *Der Mennonit* (1881), and *Christoff Marlow* (1884), which won both the Schiller and the Grillparzer prizes. In 1888 he produced his greatest success, *Die Quitzows,* which introduced a cycle of historical dramas glorifying the Hohenzollerns. *Der Generalfeldoberst* (1889) and *Der Neue Herr* (1891) continued the series. Following the unsuccessful social plays *Die Haubenlerche* (1890) and *Meister Balzer* (1893), Wildenbruch produced his finest historical drama, *Heinrich und Heinrichs Geschlecht* (1896), which was also awarded the Schiller prize. His later dramas, *Gewitternacht* (1899), *Tochter des Erasmus* (1900), *König Laurin* (1905), and *Die Rabensteinerin* (1907), all enjoyed contemporary popularity.

By his attempt "to win back for the German people a genuinely great dramatic art," Wildenbruch performed a notable service to his country and to the literature of his day. Despite his high-minded patriotic and artistic intentions, his dramas lack the enduring qualities of greatness and have all fallen victim to time.

Wildenbruch also wrote many successful short stories, of which "Der Meister von Tanagra" (1879), "Francesca von Rimini" (1880), "Kindertränen" (1882), "Die Danaide" (1885) and "Das Edle Blut" (1892) deserve to be remembered.

The drama *Harold* was translated twice in 1891, in prose by O. Heller, and in verse by H. A. Clarke. C. Fitch translated *Die Haubenlerche* as *The Bird in the Cage* (n.d.) and in 1908 R. von Appiano and W. Nobbe translated *Die Rabensteinerin* under the title *Barseba of Rabenstein*. *König Heinrich* was translated by R. M. Wernaer in 1913-15. The short story "Der Meister von Tanagra" was translated by M. von Lauer in 1886, and in 1902 B. Young translated "Die Danaide." "Das Edle Blut" has appeared in excellent versions by W. D. Lowe (1910) and M. Almon (1913). In 1921 E. Traut rendered "Neid" into English under the title "Envy."

ABOUT: Morgan, E. A. Wildenbruch as a Nationalist; Wernaer, R. M. The German Classics, XVII; Witkowski, G. The German Drama of the Nineteenth Century. [In German—see studies by B. Litzmann, H. M. Elster.]

D. G. D.

WILNA, ELIJAH. See ELIJAH BEN SOLOMON

*WINCKELMANN, JOHANN JOACHIM (December 9, 1717-June 8, 1768), German archeologist and founder of the history of ancient art, was born in Stendal, the son of a shoemaker. He first attended school in the city of his birth and then went to the *Gymnasium* in Berlin. From 1738 to 1741 he studied theology and literature at Halle, but then went to Jena where he attended lectures in mathematics and medicine. After six years as a tutor and schoolteacher he finally became a librarian in the vicinity of Dresden. The proximity of Dresden with its many art treasures as well as extensive intercourse with artists and art critics aroused in him an extreme interest in the graphic and plastic arts. He was converted to Catholicism in 1754 largely as a result of an offer of a librarianship in Rome. After remaining one more year in Dresden, where he continued his art studies, he departed for Italy. The results of his work in Dresden are recorded in his *Gedanken über die Nachahmung der Griechischen Werke in der Malerei und Bildhauerkunst* (1754).

His first years in Rome he was able to devote almost exclusively to the study of art, thanks to the generosity of wealthy patrons. In the spring of 1758 he visited Naples and in September of the same year went to Florence where he stayed for nine months, completing the arrangement and cataloging of a gem collection. In 1760 he completed his *Anmerkungen über die Baukunst der Alten*. Named supervisor of all antiquities in Rome and its environs in 1763, he published numerous works, among others *Von den Herculani-*

* vĭng′ kĕl män

WINCKELMANN

schen Entdeckungen (1762), *Versuch einer Allegorie, besonders für die Kunst* (1766), and *Die Abhandlung von der Fähigkeit der Empfindung des Schönen in der Kunst und dem Unterricht in Derselben* (1771). His most important work, however, is his *Geschichte der Kunst des Altertums* (1764), which he later expanded with *Anmerkungen über die Geschichte der Kunst* (1767). The greatest part of the year 1766 he devoted to the writing of his *Monumenti Antichi Inediti* (1767), which is an attempt to answer numerous difficult questions in the study of mythology and antiquity. In 1768 with the sculptor Cavaceppi as his companion he traveled to Munich and Vienna. On the return trip, while stopping in Trieste, he was murdered by a fellow-traveler, one Arcangeli, who stole some valuable gold medals that Winckelmann had shown him.

In two major works, *History of Ancient Art* and *Monumenti*, Winckelmann became the actual founder of art history. He was the first man to observe the classical works of art with a trained eye and register his judgments in a coherent and systematic way, evolving a consistent theory of art history. Winckelmann, using a few statements by Velleius Paterculus and Quintilian as a starting point, conceived the idea of an historical development of art and accordingly determined the style and characteristics of the monuments of antiquity. His concepts of "noble simplicity and calm eminence" were to have a profound effect upon the image of ancient Greece as conceived by such poets as Johann Wolfgang Goethe and Friedrich Schiller.

Winckelmann's *The History of Ancient Art* was translated into English in 1881.
ABOUT: Butler, E. M. The Tyranny of Greece over Germany; Pater, W. The Renaissance; Modern Language Quarterly, XVII (1956). [In German—see studies by W. Bosshard, J. W. Goethe, K. Justi, I. Kreuzer, W. Rehm, B. Vallentin, W. Waetzoldt.]

E. K. G.

*WINTHER, CHRISTIAN (RASMUS VILLADS CHRISTIAN FERDINAND), (July 29, 1796-December 30, 1876), Danish poet, was born at Fensmark in southern Zealand. His father was H. C. Winther, an able but somewhat weak-natured vicar. His mother was Hanne Borchsenius, daughter of a learned and poetically interested minister of German descent from the island of Funen. His father died in 1808, and in 1812 his mother married Rasmus Møller, a prominent theologian and pastor at Købeløv on the island of Lolland, later bishop, a widower with six children, one of whom was the future author and traveler Poul Møller, with whom Winther entered into an intimate friendship.

In 1815 Winther matriculated at the University of Copenhagen to study theology. He studied foreign languages and literatures, led a gay life, and fell in love frequently. Since his theological studies were slow, his stepfather brought him home to Köbelöv to have him under supervision, and in 1824 he took his degree. Between 1825 and 1830 Winther tutored in the home of a Copenhagen merchant and accompanied the family to their country estate during summers. His unrequited love of the youngest daughter inspired him to write ardent love poems. These and many other songs he published in various Copenhagen publications, and he already had a good reputation as a poet when in 1824 he published his first collection of poems, *Digte*, which included nature lyrics and some of his so-called "woodcuts," versified romantic-realistic peasant idylls, which he continued writing for many years.

An inheritance enabled him to make a trip to Italy in 1830-31, and in 1832 he published *Digte, Gamle og Ny* (Poems, Old and New). In two collections of romances and ballads of 1840, *Sang og Sagn* (Song and Legend) and *Haandtegninger* (Pencil Sketches), tones of melancholy broke through, but his depression disappeared when in 1841 he was appointed teacher of Danish to the German fiancée of

the Danish crown prince and was awarded the title of professor. The following year he was dismissed with his salary intact. Just before this appointment he fell in love with a Copenhagen clergyman's young wife, Julie Werlin, *née* Lytthans. Under this stress he published between 1841 and 1848 his most memorable lyrics. His *Digtninger* (Poetry, 1843), and *Lyriske Digte* (Lyrics, 1849), contained a cycle of love poems called *Til Een* (To the One), in which he described his feminine ideal and confessed his passion.

In 1848 he married his beloved, who had divorced her husband in 1843. In 1855, after a journey to Italy, his greatest and most admired work appeared, *Hjortens Flugt* (The Flight of the Stag), an epic cycle on a theme from the time of Eric of Pomerania. The singer Folmer in the poem is Winther himself.

Winther continued his production through his last years, enhancing his reputation as the foremost Danish poet of love and nature. He died in Paris during one of the many trips abroad that his family undertook, but his remains were brought home to Denmark.

Scattered poems from Winther's production appear in English translation in W. and M. Howitt, *The Literature and Romance of Northern Europe* (1852); A. S. Bushby, *The Danes Sketched by Themselves* (1864); R. Buchanan, *Master Spirits* (1873); Margaret Thomas, *Denmark, Past and Present* (1902); J. Volk, *Songs and Poems in Danish and English* (1903); S. F. Damon and R. S. Hillyer, *A Book of Danish Verse* (1922); R. P. Keigwin, *In Denmark I Was Born* (1948).
ABOUT: The Academy, XI; Scandinavia, I. [In Danish—see studies by N. Bögh, J. Clausen, O. Friis, P. Levin.]

A. J.

*WIVALLIUS, LARS (1605-April 6, 1669), Swedish poet, was born at Wivalla, a farm in the province of Närke in central Sweden. His father was Swän Larsson, farmer and sheriff. His mother's name and extraction are unknown. His original name was Lars Swänsson, which he later changed to Wivallius, a name derived in Latin form from his birthplace. He received a good education. As a young graduate he was a vagabond on the European continent, leaving mountains of unpaid bills behind him. Under the adopted name of Erik Gyllenstierna he pretended to be a Swedish nobleman. In this disguise in 1629 he married Gertrud Grijp, daughter of a Swedish-Danish nobleman in Skåne. The fraud was exposed and the marriage dissolved, and he appeared as the de-

* vĭn′ tĕr

* vē văl′ yŭs

fendant in a long series of lawsuits. For four years he was kept in custody, from which he several times escaped but was recaptured. He was sentenced to death in Denmark, to prison in Sweden, and to the fortress of Kajaneborg in northern Finland. During the six hard years he was in prison he turned into a real poet. Upon his release he succeeded in getting a start as a lawyer, fleecing his clients of money; he was finally appointed judge-advocate. About 1645 he married Mahlin Ellertz, daughter of a tavern owner, and returned later to his ancestral home.

Wivallius had a strange and complex personality. On one side he was shrewd and calculating without the slightest sense of honor and morals, but on the other side he had a weak, sensitive nature with a vivid imagination. The only genuine poet of his time, he wrote songs, chiefly while he was in prison, that show the influence of popular ballads and religious hymns, especially the *Book of Psalms*. There is a remarkable freshness of feeling and primitive inspiration in such poems as the beautiful liberty song "Ack Libertas, Du Ädle Ting" (O Liberty, Thou Noble Thing), the submissive lamentation in ballad style "Varer nu Glad, Mine Fiender All" (Now Rejoice, All My Enemies), and the animated nature poem "Klagevisa öfver Denna Torra och Kalla Vår" (Lament Over This Dry and Cold Spring).

Two songs, "Ack Libertas, du Ädle Ting" and "Klagevisa öfver Denna Torra och Kalla Vår," in English translation are included in R. Ahléen, *Swedish Poets of the Seventeenth Century* (1932).

ABOUT: [In Swedish—see studies by S. Ek, H. Schück.]

A. J.

---

*WOLF, FRIEDRICH AUGUST (February 15, 1759-August 8, 1824), German classicist and pedagogue, was born in Haynrode, Thuringia, the son of a schoolmaster and organist. He completed his elementary and secondary education in the nearby city of Nordhausen before going on in 1777 to the University of Göttingen, where he studied philology. In 1779 Wolf accepted a position on the teaching staff of the *Pedagogium* in Ilfeld and while there established his scholarly reputation with his edition of the *Symposium* of Plato. From Ilfeld he went to Osterode in 1782 as rector of the city school, but as a result of the recognition given his scholarship he departed one year later for the University of Halle where he became professor of philosophy and pedagogy.

* völf

His stay in Halle was the most productive period of his life. His chief task during these years was to staff the national schools with effective and thoroughly trained teachers, separating most decisively the rôle of the teacher from that of the clergyman. Simultaneously, however, he pursued his research in classical studies which resulted in his best-known contribution to classical scholarship, *Prolegomena ad Homerum sive de Operum Homericorum Prisca et Genuina Forma Variisque Mutationibus et Probabili Ratione Emendandi*. In this work he sought to prove that the *Iliad* and the *Odyssey* in their extant forms were not the work of Homer, but that of several poets. The world of scholarship was divided into two opposing camps as a result of this controversial study which pointed in the direction that literary analysis and criticism were to take during the succeeding century. Following the dissolution of the University of Halle by Napoleon in 1807, Wolf went to Berlin as a member of the Academy of Sciences and while there was instrumental in the founding of the new University of Berlin. In April 1824 he undertook a trip to southern France where he hoped to recapture his failing health. Four months later he died in Marseille.

Wolf's numerous publications embrace almost every branch of classical studies. Among the Greek works which he edited are Homer's *Iliad* and *Odyssey*, Hesiod's *Theogony*, and *Scripta Selecta* from the writings of Lucian. He also edited Cicero's *Orationes*. The best known of his pedagogical works is the posthumously published *Ideen über Erziehung, Schule und Universität*. The published version of his lectures in the field of classics, *Vorlesungen über die Altertumswissenschaft*, also appeared posthumously.

ABOUT: [In German—see studies by M. Bernay, O. Kern, W. Körte, S. Reiter.]

E. K. G.

WOLFF, ELISABETH. See WOLFF-BEKKER, ELISABETH

---

*WOLFF, JULIUS (September 16, 1834-June 2, 1910), German poet, novelist, and dramatist, was born in Quedlinburg in the Harz region, where his father owned a cloth factory. He entered the University of Berlin to study literature and humanities but devoted a minimum of time and effort to his classes. He was a congenial, well-liked individual,

* völf

who entered wholeheartedly into the lighter side of student life. His parents, distressed by his convivial life in Berlin, ultimately summoned him home to assume directorship of the factory. Wolff willingly complied with this decision, and although lacking genuine interest in this career, he competently fulfilled his business responsibilities. At length, however, he was released from this family obligation when the factory failed because of financial losses. In 1869 Wolff married and the same year established his own newspaper, *Die Harzzeitung,* in Quedlinburg. This enterprise also failed and publication ceased the following year. At the outbreak of the Franco-Prussian war in 1870, Wolff enlisted as a reserve officer and distinguished himself in action. The war provided the stimulus and the subject matter for his first volume of poetry, *Aus dem Kriege* (1870), in which Wolff recorded his military impressions and experiences. The moderate success of this work encouraged Wolff to become a writer, and following the end of the war in 1871, he settled in Berlin, determined to earn his living by his pen. Late in life he retired to Charlottenburg, where he died.

Wolff's literary reputation was established with the epic *Till Eulenspiegel Redivivus* (1874). This poem is typical of his writings and displays the qualities which characterize his epics in general: great versatility of form, artful descriptions of nature, rich humor, and lyrical inserts. Wolff possessed an extensive knowledge of the Middle Ages, and his works abound in detailed accounts of the manners and customs of that period. Since he was not endowed with great independent imagination, he preferred to retell earlier epics, and the majority of his most popular works, such as *Der Rattenfänger von Hameln* (1876), *Der Wilde Jäger* (his best work, 1877), *Tannhäuser* (1880), *Singuf* (1881), *Lurlei* (1886), and *Der Fliegende Holländer* (1898), treat well-known themes. Wolff was one of the most widely read authors of this period, although today his works are little known.

Wolff also produced a number of cultural-historical novels on medieval themes, such as *Der Sülfmeister* (1883), *Der Raubgraf* (1884), *Der Recht der Hagestolze* (1887), *Das Schwarze Weib* (1894), and *Die Hohkönigsburg* (1902). As a dramatist he was unsuccessful both with the modern social plays *Die Junggesellensteuer* (1877) and *Drohende Wolken* (1879), and with the classical tragedy *Kambyses* (1877).

In 1890 W. H. and E. R. Winslow translated *Das Recht der Hagestolze* as *Fifty Years, Three Months, Two Days, a Tale of the Neckar Valley; Der Sülfmeister* as *The Salt Master of Lüneberg;* and *Der Raubgraf* as *The Robber Count. Tannhäuser* was translated by C. G. Kendall in 1903-04, and R. Davidson rendered *Der Wilde Jäger* under the title *The Wild Huntsman* in 1905.

ABOUT: [In German—see studies by J. Hart, A. Ruhemann, J. Schmidt.]

D. G. D.

*WOLFF-BEKKER, ELISABETH (BETJE) (pseudonym SILVIANA),

(July 24, 1738-November 5, 1804), Dutch novelist, essayist, poet, and translator, was born in Flushing. She was the vivacious daughter of Jan Bekker and Johanna Boudrie, well-to-do burghers who lived quietly on their estate just outside the city. When she was seventeen years old, wise in reading, but naïve in the ways of the world, Betje ran away with an ensign named Gardon. Shocked and disillusioned, she returned to the parental home almost as soon as she had taken this rash step. This event in her life, portrayed in *Sara Burgerhart,* made a deep impression upon her. Leaving Flushing, in 1759 she married the minister Adriaan Wolff of De Beemster, who was her senior by many years. The marriage was at first unhappy, not only on account of the difference in age between the partners, but also as a result of their entirely different temperaments. He sometimes drank too much or was away from home for days on end, leaving her alone in an environment where her behavior and her liberal views made for much criticism. She was often sharp of tongue and quite free in her conduct with some of the parsonage visitors. Some of the remarks she made in her correspondence about her husband brought her still more criticism. However, the relationship improved in course of time, perhaps as a result of his defense of her when she was attacked for the liberal religious views which she proclaimed in *Santhortsche Geloofsbelijdenis* (1772).

Betje began her literary career by contributing to the *Grijsaard* (1767-69), an illustrated magazine; she also wrote poetry which is of some significance chiefly because of the opinions expressed in it. Her translation of Craig's life of Christ again gave evidence of her unorthodox views. When Adriaan Wolff died in 1777, Betje went to live with her friend Aagje (Agatha) Deken, first in De Rijp and then, in 1782, on "Lommerlust," an estate near Beverwijk. In 1779, Betje had

* völf běk' kēr

published *Proeve over de Opvoeding* ("Essay on Education") in which she revealed her acquaintance with the philosophies of Locke and of Rousseau. Her literary collaboration with Aagje resulted in *Economische Liedjes* (1780-90)—three volumes intended to ennoble the folksong—and *Brieven over Verscheidene Onderwerpen* (2 vols., 1780-81). None of these works, however, can compare in importance with the novels in letter form, inspired by Richardson, but very original and personal in character, which the two friends wrote. They are less sentimental, less romantic, and less realistic than the works of their English model, and full of spirit and wit. The first novel written in this manner was *Historie van Mejuffrouw Sara Burgerhart*, which appeared in two volumes in 1782. The novel gives a clear picture of the bourgeois life of the period. Shortly after its first publication—it has been reprinted innumerable times—it was translated into French by Madame de Charrière, the former Belle van Zuylen. Encouraged by their success, Betje and Aagje gave the best of their talent in *Willem Leevend*, a novel which appeared in eight volumes.

With the Prussian invasion of 1788, the two friends, together with many other patriots, went into exile. They settled in Trévoux, France. *Wandelingen in Bourgondie* (1789) tells of their life there. Following the bankruptcy of their unreliable business agent, the women lost their fortune and returned to Holland. They settled in The Hague, where they lived under financially difficult circumstances, translating to keep alive. Betje died in The Hague after a short illness. Aagje, who died eight days later, was buried with her.

ABOUT: [In Dutch—see studies by H. C. H. Moquette, J. W. A. Naber.]

H. B.

*WOLFRAM VON ESCHENBACH

(1165?-1220?), German epic poet, was born in the village of Eschenbach near the city of Ansbach in central Franconia. Wolfram was born a knight, but lived in poor circumstances and depended, like other poets of the period, on the beneficence of princely lovers of poetry. He was several times a guest of the Landgrave Hermann of Thuringia at Wartburg Castle, the Parnassus of medieval poetry. He was married and a devoted husband and father, though he spent a great part of his life in travel.

* vōl′ främ fōn ĕsh′ ĕn bäк

Wolfram keeps his undisputed place as the greatest of the German epic poets. He began his literary career as the singer of *Minnelieder,* of which nine have survived. Of these the most important are his so-called *Tagelieder,* a type of song in which a watchman warns the lovers of the approaching day while they are passing the night in clandestine love.

Wolfram's first major work was probably the long epic poem on which his fame rests, the *Parzival.* Three different strands of medieval romance are here combined in an immensely rich picture of medieval high society: the stories of Parzival and King Arthur's Round Table and the legend of the Holy Grail. They were already closely linked in the French epic which served Wolfram as the main source of his work, *Li Contes del Graal* by Chrétien de Troyes, who left it a fragment at the time of his death. The question of how much Wolfram owes to his predecessor and how much to his own genius has created an enormous amount of critical literature. But Wolfram's greatness rests neither on his originality as an inventor nor on his artistry in style or structure, but on the ideas which lift a story of chivalrous adventure to a work of unique spiritual significance. Because the symbolic meaning of the events he describes outweighs their actual importance, Wolfram may be considered as the first German poet in the modern sense of the word.

The *Parzival* is also the first in the great sequence of German educational novels *(Erziehungsroman)* in which the whole life of an individual unfolds itself through all stages of spiritual growth. Two types of heroic life are contrasted in *Parzival.* While the knight Gawain, the most outstanding member of King Arthur's Round Table, follows the strict code of chivalrous behavior, sometimes to a Quixotic point, Parzival grows through suffering and error from a charming simpleton to the ruler of the Grail community, an ideal state where the practice of Christian virtues is combined with the enjoyment of worldly pleasures. In his ideas on the meaning of life and its conduct, Wolfram often contradicts the conventions and beliefs of his time. Though deeply religious, he does not include the church in the scheme of salvation, but makes it completely dependent on man's inner longing for a life under divine grace. In contrast to other medieval poets (except Walther von der Vogelweide), Wolfram carries his personality into his work; he interweaves many personal and often humorous comments in the narration. Likewise in his language he strives for originality. This often leads him to extravagance and obscurity, a defect which earned him the scorn of the artistically and stylistically more accomplished Gottfried von Strassburg.

The *Parzival* was followed by the fragment of *Titurel*, dealing with a tragic love which had already appeared in the *Parzival* as an episode. Wolfram's second great poem is the *Willehalm*. The death of the poet about 1220 left it short of completion. It has an historic background, the struggle between the Saracens and the son of Charlemagne for the possession of Southern France. Though Wolfram's Christian piety is here more orthodox than in *Parzival,* he represents himself as a passionate exponent of religious tolerance and justifies war against the heathen only in self-defense.

Wolfram's work as well as his personality remained immensely popular throughout the Middle Ages. One of the earliest works after the introduction of printing was an edition of his *Parzival*. In modern times Richard Wagner paid his respect to Wolfram in his opera *Tannhäuser* and with his last work, *Parsifal*.

In 1894 Jessie L. Weston published an English translation, replacing Wolfram's rhyming couplets with long lines. In 1951 Edwin H. Zeydel and B. Q. Morgan published a translation in which they tried a close approximation of the meter and style of the original. In 1957 Margaret F. Richey published translations in English verse of passages in her *Studies of Wolfram von Eschenbach*. A translation by H. M. Mustard and C. E. Passage appeared in 1961.

ABOUT: Bruce, J. D. Evolution of Arthurian Romance; Richey, M. Legend of Parzival and the Graal, as Related by Wolfram von Eschenbach, *also* Studies of Wolfram von Eschenbach; Weston, J. L. Legend of Sir Perceval. [In German—see Gustav Ehrismann's Geschichte der Deutschen Literatur bis zum Ausgang des Mittelalters, II.]

F. R.

*WYSPIAŃSKI, STANISLAW (January 15, 1869-November 28, 1907), Polish poet, dramatist, and painter was born in Cracow, the son of a sculptor. He studied at the Cracow Fine Arts Academy and at the Jagellonian University, later in Austria, Italy, and France. Upon his return home he settled down in Cracow and practiced painting, though active also as a writer. He married a peasant woman in 1900. In 1905 he became professor at the Cracow Fine Arts Academy. He died prematurely in Cracow at thirty-eight.

* vĭs pyän' y' skē

WYSPIAŃSKI

Wyspiański's literary activity centered mainly around drama. During the course of ten years, beginning in 1897, he wrote over twenty works: tragedies and "rhapsodies" characterized by the classic Greek concept of tragedy and, at the same time, by romantic freedom of construction and symbolism. The themes are both antique and contemporary; sometimes the past and the present blend together in loose visionary scenes.

Wyspiański's first works were published in the periodical *Zycie*, which crusaded for symbolism in Poland. *Meleager* (1898), *Protesilaus and Laodamia* (1899), *Achilles* (1903) are classical dramas with some resemblance to French neoclassicism. Contemporary motifs are introduced in *Klątwa* (The Curse, 1899), *Sędziowi* (The Judges, 1907), and others. Motifs of patriotic significance constitute the basis of a series of works in which the poet develops his program for the Polish people, a program that is to a great extent a synthesis of the romantic ideals and the positivistic call for action towards a better future. From the early *Warszawianka* (1898), in which the heritage of the uprisings is subjected to poetic revision, through the intriguing *Wesele* (Wedding, 1901), realistic in detail and highly symbolic at the same time, and the *Wyzwolenie* (Deliverance, 1903), to the *Noc Listopadowa* (November Night, 1904), Wyspiański carried his poetic struggle for national leadership, for freeing his people from romantic "tyranny," and at the same time saving them from losing all higher ideals by vulgar positivism.

Wyspiański's work is complex in its variety of uniquely Polish and universal themes, interrelated and interwoven with allegories, metaphors, lyrical outbursts, and visions of an artist who did not care much for conventional concepts of literary form. Nevertheless, he penetrated into the secrets of classical and Shakespearean tragedy (his interpretation and staging of *Hamlet* were highly original), and because of his genuine poetic talent, Wyspiański's works, especially when seen on the stage, never fail to fascinate, even if they remain obscure in parts.

English translations include *Protesilaus and Laodamia*, translated by E. M. Clark and G. R. Noyes in *The Slavonic Review* (1933); *Meleager*, translated by G. R. Noyes (1932).

ABOUT: Mitana, T. S. Wyspiański, *in* Great Men and Women of Poland, ed. by S. Mizwa; Zimmer, S. K. Stanislaw Wyspiański; Polish Review, II (1957); Slavonic Review (1933). [In French—Kolbuscewski, S. Le Théâtre de Wyspiański.]

Z. F.

Y. L. G. See GORDON, JUDAH LOEB

*YAZYKOV, NIKOLAY MIKHAYLO-VICH (March 16, 1803-January 7, 1846), Russian poet, was born in Simbirsk district, on the estate of his father, a rich and well-born landowner. There he spent his childhood and received his first education. Like his brothers, he enrolled in the Corps of Mining Cadets at St. Petersburg (1814) where his literature teacher inspired in him a love for Lomonosov and Derzhavin. In 1819 Yazykov transferred to the Institute of the Corps of Communications, but soon was expelled for non-attendance and left for home. In 1821 he prepared for enrollment at the University of St. Petersburg, but went instead to the University of Dorpat, where he spent the years 1822-29 studying history and languages, his main interest being literature. Yazykov wrote his first poems in 1819 and began to publish in journals in 1822. The university years were the most productive period of his life and also the beginning of his poetic fame. Magazines vied with one another to have him as a contributor; Pushkin sought his acquaintance. Scholarship now rejects the legend that this plump fellow with a round face really led the life of a drinker and debauchee that he so exuberantly celebrated in his poems; he was a serious student and a voracious reader.

* yŭ zī′ kôf

Without a degree, Yazykov left in 1829 for Moscow where he became a friend of the future Slavophiles. His service in the Surveyor's Office being only a formality, he recited poetry in Moscow salons, lived often on his country estate, and collected folklore with P. Kireevsky. A spinal illness began at this time. The 1830's mark a new period in his life and work. He became increasingly nationalistic and religious and turned away from his early free-thinking. Slavophile friends extolled him as an embodiment of "true Russian qualities."

His first collection of verse appeared in 1833. In 1837 his illness forced him to go abroad for treatment, and he spent five years in various German and French spas, suffering from homesickness and lack of inspiration. In Rome he met Gogol, who became his ardent admirer and friend. From 1843 Yazykov lived in Moscow, participating in the fights of Slavophiles against Westernizers. He suffered from gout and dyspepsia and became more and more embittered both in life and in verse. He died in Moscow after a respiratory attack. In the 1820's his contemporaries had admired his originality and drive, and he was considered, together with Pushkin and Baratynsky, one of the most pre-eminent poets of his time. Later, Gogol and the Slavophiles admired him, but he antagonized the radicals (who nevertheless made a few of his early poems their favorites) and therefore was ignored for almost half a century. Only the post-symbolists revived his work, admiring his emphasis on verbal texture.

Yazykov's early epistles, historical and patriotic poems, elegies, and, particularly his sensual songs with their hedonistic abandon, are unique in their power, their combination of lightness and audacity, rapid movement, and grandeur. His poetry abounds in daring imagery, and his sonorous alliterations and bold neologisms produce, as Pushkin observed, the effect of an almost physical "intoxication." Otherwise his diction is classic and simple. His later, less popular work lacks the earlier tempestuousness. Some of his polemical poems are second-rate, but the poems on Biblical themes keep the old verbal magnificence. Much of his late travel diary verse is full of charm in everyday detail and intimate intonation. He also wrote epics and dramas, but they are less significant than his other works.

Pale copies of Yazykov's originals can be found among the translations in L. Wiener's *Anthology of Russian Literature*, II (1902-03) as well as

1005

in C. M. Bowra's *Second Book of Russian Verse* (1948).

ABOUT: [In Russian—Smirnov, V. Y., Zhizn' i Poeziya N. M. Yazykova.]

V. M.

YEHUDAH LEIB or LEON. See GORDON, JUDAH LOEB

YRIARTE Y OROPESA, TOMÁS DE. See IRIARTE Y OROPESA, TOMÁS DE

*ZAPOLSKA, GABRIELA (née KORWIN-PIOTROWSKA) (1860-December 17, 1921), Polish author, was born in Kiwerce, went to school in Lwów, and very early became interested in the theatre; she became a professional actress, performing in theatres in Lwów, Warsaw, Cracow, Poznań, and also in Paris, where she appeared in the Théâtre Libre in the years 1890-95. She died in Lwów.

From her first literary works—short stories, novels, and plays—Zapolska struck a note of sharp realism, at times bordering on naturalism. Her works frequently shocked middle-class readers by revealing their double standard of morality. She was one of the first in Poland to take up boldly such "forbidden" themes as open and hidden prostitution, free love, etc. French naturalism was Zapolska's literary school, with Émile Zola as her direct model. From her first novels, *Malaszka* (1883), *Janka* (1895,), *Fin-de-Siècle-Istka* (Fin-de-Siècle-Woman, 1897), *Z Pamiętników Młodej Mężatki* (Memoirs of a Newly-wed Woman, 1899), through such collections of short stories as *Menażeria Ludzka* (Human Menagerie, 1893), to her most mature dramatic works, Zapolska concentrated on social and moral problems facing women in various stages of their lives at the turn of the century.

Some of Zapolska's dramatic works are direct adaptations of her earlier novels (*Malaszka,* 1891; *Kaśka Kariatyda,* 1897). In this literary genre Zapolska's talent reached its highest level. An actress herself, Zapolska knew both the limitations and the possibilities of various types of dramatic art: comedy, tragedy, melodrama, etc. She was able to play on the sense of humor, moral indignation, and sentimental pathos of her audience. Zapolska's most important play, still performed in Polish theatres, is *Moralność pani*

* zä pôl' skä

Dulskiej (The Morality of Mrs. Dulska, 1907). In works on patriotic themes Zapolska also succeeded in achieving high dramatic effects. The best known among them are *Tamten* (The Other One, 1898) and *Siberia* (1900).

ABOUT: Dyboski, R. Modern Polish Literature; Kridl, M. Survey of Polish Literature.

Z. F.

*ZESEN, PHILIPP VON (October 8, 1619-November 13, 1689), German novelist and lyric poet, spent well over a dozen years of his highly mobile life in the Netherlands and several others in extensive travel (England, France, Germany). His vast novels are almost as wide-ranging as their author and his output of verse ranges from the most occasional rhymes to a deeply serious collection entitled *Crucified Flames of Love.*

Zesen was born near Dessau, the son of a Lutheran minister. At the age of twelve, still in Latin school, he worked on a rhyming dictionary and wrote Latin and German verse. He studied at Wittenberg, where he developed his regard for his own capabilities and mission in life (dean of German letters) to a level which often exasperated even his closest supporters. In Hamburg on his post-graduate travels, he met the poet Rist, and later in the same city founded the Deutschgesinnte Genossenschaft—which Rist was not invited to join. Contact with circles of Swedish nobility in Holland gave him a flair for courtly manners and increased his reputation as a gallant.

In Holland he did a translation of Mme de Scudéry (*Ibrahim Bassa*), which he dedicated to the Fruchtbringende Gesellschaft in the hope of being made a member. (He was at first rejected, for his orthographical and linguistic innovations. Once in, he was almost put out again.) Serving as emissary of Amsterdam in Dessau, he successfully re-established his German connections. He was ennobled at thirty-three and celebrated in court circles and at the Reichstag. He went to the Baltic provinces for a time with Count Thurn, then returned for a long stay in Holland. He was made an honorary citizen of Amsterdam.

In 1667 he returned to Hamburg to be celebrated by the society he had founded, and elevated to the rank of count. The next year he married and returned to Amsterdam, but marriage only made the insecurity of his financial situation—many honors, but little

* tsä' zĕn

pay—more obvious and he returned to Germany, looking constantly for jobs. A cloth business in Holland failed and he returned again to Germany. He died in Hamburg at the age of seventy.

Zesen was an active man, humorless and vain, yet honest, thorough, and courageous. Exceptional for his time, he was both religious and tolerant. Above all, he was a man of enormous range of achievement. Zesen is a master of baroque virtuosity in the lyric. He ranges from sentimental or erotic subjects to religious mysticism. His conscious artifice, his range of rhythms, his extreme inventiveness in form—he boasted of fifty different strophic combinations and composed interlocking sonnets—mark him as one of the first and greatest of the experimenters. His fluid lines and his play with associations of sound may tend to obscure considerations of meaning. Yet his best lyrics and his religious poetry show both technical gift and deep feeling.

Similar virtuosity of form characterizes his prose. In his early mood of "sweet seriousness," which Zesen prescribed as the proper tone for the German novel, sentences become complex for the sake of intricacy or vague to portray intangible moods. But again, in his best and later work he is remarkably clear, and his descriptions and dialogues have a reality and impact extraordinary for his period.

Zesen's rôle is important—as translator and original writer—in establishing the basic direction of baroque prose. The purely pastoral novel disappears. In its place come first the courtly novel, whose characters, especially lovers and statesmen, establish a sort of ethical heroism or at least tenacity in the face of the complications and entanglements of their gallant world; and secondly the elaborately complicated love-adventure, in which loyal lovers are torn asunder and reunited to an interminable accompaniment of highly "existential" situations in the moral, social, and political spheres. These novels, as might be gathered, have somewhat the character, and attain nearly the length, of encyclopedias.

Besides Scudéry, Zesen translated a work called *Afrikanische Sophonisbe*. His own novels, like the epics of Middle High German, both depend on and consciously transcend in "lesson" their French models. The moral, religious, courtly, and political stature of the hero in *Die Adriatische Rosamund* (1645) or *Assenat* (his greatest work, 1670)

is didactic. A last novel, *Simson*, was not so popular or so good as the others.

Two poems by Zesen are translated in G. C. Schoolfield's *The German Lyric of the Baroque in English Translation* (1962).
ABOUT: [In German—see studies by P. Baumgartner, A. Grams, H. Körnchen.]

F. G. R.

*ZHUKOVSKY, VASILY ANDREYEVICH (February 9, 1783-April 24, 1852),

Russian poet, the natural son of a wealthy landowner, Afanasy Bunin, and a captive Turkish girl, Salkha, was born at the estate Mishenskoe, near Tula. His surname and patronymic derive from his godfather. A half-stranger in the family after his father's death, he attended schools in Tula, and later the Boarding School for Nobility at the University of Moscow (1797-1800), where he was strongly influenced by pietism, became interested in German and English literature, and started to write in a sentimentalist vein. His first printed poem, "A May Morn," appeared in 1797 in the university magazine.

Zhukovsky became well-known after the publication in 1802 of his translation of Gray's *Elegy* in a periodical, *Vestnik Evropy* (The European Herald). In 1808 "Lyudmila," first of his thirty-nine ballads, marked the beginning of Russian romanticism. In the meantime Zhukovsky fell in love with his niece, Maria Protasova. This love was mutual, but his proposal was rejected by her mother, who considered such a marriage sinful. Later Maria married another man, but their Platonic attachment never ended, coloring all Zhukovsky's poetry, which is characterized by motifs of grief and resignation. In 1812 Zhukovsky joined the militia, observed firsthand the battle at Borodino, and wrote the patriotic poem "The Bard in the Camp of the Russian Warriors," which at once made him the most famous poet in Russia. After 1815 his fame slowly declined; the young generation found his romanticism vague and too oriented to the West, the rising star of Pushkin eclipsed everyone else's, and Zhukovsky's career at court (1816-39), first as a reader to the Empress Dowager, finally as tutor to the future Alexander II, was not successful. In person, however, this self-effacing, kind, dreamy-faced man with lofty ideas on poetry ("Poetry is God in sacred dreams of the earth") was generally admired for high moral qualities. In 1841 Zhukovsky married the daughter of a German painter friend, Elisabeth

* zhōō kôf' skē

1007

Reutern, many years his junior, and settled in Germany, never to return to Russia. His "post-balladic" period was characterized by interest in major narrative genres (culminating in his translation of *The Odyssey*) and, later, in contemporary German mystical thought. He died at Baden-Baden of dropsy, but his remains were later transferred to St. Petersburg.

Zhukovsky is considered the greatest Russian translator—among others, he translated Byron, Goethe, Schiller, Uhland—but it is difficult to separate his original poems from translations. He wrote of himself: "Practically all my poetry is borrowed or derivative, but nevertheless it is mine." For many Russian readers Zhukovsky remains primarily the author of fantastic ballads, but for poets he has always been a supreme craftsman. Few could equal the beauty of his melody, his rhythmic variety, or the purity of his style. Inner life entered Russian poetry with Zhukovsky. He was the first to develop subtle shades and transitions of meaning and thus developed a new poetical language. Pushkin, Lermontov, Tyutchev, Fet, and Blok were influenced by him.

Rather old translations from Zhukovsky can be found in John Bowring, *Specimens of the Russian Poets* (1822).

ABOUT: [In Russian—see studies by J. Grot, V. I. Pokrovsky, A. N. Veselovsky, B. Zaitsev. In German—see study by C. von Seidlitz.]

V. M.

*ZINKGREF, JULIUS WILHELM

(June 3, 1591-November 12, 1635), German poet and epigrammatist, was one of the principal disciples of Martin Opitz. He was a trained humanist—some of his best known works were Latin farces for the schools—and a doctor of law, widely traveled and widely learned.

After his studies at Heidelberg, he journeyed through Switzerland, France, England, and the Netherlands. In 1617 he returned to take his *doctor juris*. In 1618 the Thirty Years' War began and Zinkgref became a martyr to the madness of his age. Heidelberg was invaded by the Bavarians, and he had to abandon all his possessions. He fled to Frankfurt, then to Strasbourg. He held a succession of official positions, one of the most auspicious of which—traveling interpreter for the French ambassador—he had to abandon because illness disabled him. He was attacked, robbed, and wounded by one of the marauding bands which fed on the

* tsĭnk′ grĕf

chaos of war, and finally at the age of forty-four fell victim to the Black Death.

Zinkgref had seen in Martin Opitz the opportunity for the introduction of a true Renaissance in German writing and in this spirit edited Opitz' poems (1624). His own influence might have been great, but for the wasting effects of the war and his own constant wanderings. It would certainly have been salutary. He had a keen satirical eye for pretentiousness; his Latin farces mock what he called the "erudite charlatanry" of the day. His German poetry, at its best, is original, eloquent, relatively simple in form, and reminiscent of the folk song. Still, he was not always free of "parade" and mannerism; occasional works anticipate the flowery effusions of the Nürnberg school.

Much of Zinkgref's writing is marked by an almost journalistic vividness. It has even been assumed that he contributed to the "newspapers" and pamphlets of his day. His greatest immediate influence came through his book of anecdotes, epigrams, and facetiae, *Der Teutschen Scharpfsinnige Kluge Sprüch*—or *Apophthegmata*. Zinkgref inveighs against hypocrisy, vanity, privilege, monkishness. He calls for spiritual independence, patriotism, and sturdy virtues. He wanted to prove that "Germans are neither barbarians nor dumb, that their art and skill does not reside exclusively in their fingers and hands."

Two of Zinkgref's poems are translated in George C. Schoolfield's *The German Lyric of the Baroque in English Translation* (1962).

ABOUT: Germanic Review, IX (1934). [In German—Schnorr von Carolsfeld, F. J. W. Zincgrefs Leben und Schriften.]

F. G. R.

*ZOLA, ÉMILE ÉDOUARD CHARLES ANTOINE

(April 2, 1840-September 29, 1902), French novelist and critic, was born in Paris, the only child of Francesco or François Zola, an Italian who had emigrated to France some years after the fall of Napoleon and become a civil engineer. In 1839, in Paris, François Zola married Émilie Aubert, a young girl of Île-de-France peasant origin. Two years after the birth of their son Émile, he moved with his family to Aix-en-Provence, where he had been commissioned by Thiers, one of Louis Napoleon's ministers, to build a canal. It was an important project which would have assured him his future had he not suddenly died of

* zō′ lä

ZOLA

curiosities, for he had long since lost interest in poetry.

Zola emerged from this ivory tower with complete revulsion from the romantic notions that had sustained him. The highly personal *La Confession de Claude* (1866), his first novel, is important as a document of his development. Through the probably autobiographical account of a young man's pathetic attempt to reform a prostitute, Zola depicted the collapse of his own youthful idealism in the face of his intractable environment. His characterization of the harlot in particular, which contrasts so markedly with Hugo's and Dumas' sentimentalized portraits of fallen women, is symbolic of his complete break with romanticism. Even his compassion for the wretched inhabitants of the Left Bank slums would not, in later years, affect his bleak picture of their inevitable degeneration in this milieu.

Early in 1862 Zola found employment as a clerk with the bookseller Hachette—a position which gave him his first glimpse of the literary trade, with a market that must be shocked and titillated. He soon entered the growing field of journalism and proved a talented and shrewd newspaperman. A series of pugnacious articles attacking the traditional art of the Paris Salon in favor of the young Impressionist school (one of whose members was his friend Paul Cézanne) brought him the attention he wanted, and by 1866 his book reviews and articles enabled him to leave Hachette and support himself as a free lance. Though he was often defensive and disparaging of his journalistic sideline, he never disdained to use its promotional devices to sell his own novels—a fact that irritated his more serious, and well-to-do, literary friends.

The date of Zola's first meeting with Alexandrine Meley, the tall, handsome brunette who became his wife, is unknown. He was living with her in 1865 or soon thereafter. His mother moved in with the young couple before their marriage in 1870, and lived with them until her death. Alexandrine was an excellent companion and housekeeper, and their marriage seems to have been marred only by their lack of children. From this snug domestic bastion Zola was able to thrust before the eyes of an offended bourgeoisie the series of murky, near-pornographic novels that made him, after the publication of *L'Assommoir* in 1877, the most controversial and popular novelist in France.

As a novelist and critic Zola is best known in literature as the founder and great exponent of French naturalism, an outgrowth

pleurisy five years later, leaving his family destitute. Zola's notorious passion for recognition can be traced back, in part, to the insecurities of this orphaned and impoverished childhood.

After his father's death, Émile's mother and grandparents moved to even poorer quarters, making stringent economies in order to put him through school. Despite his somber picture of Aix, as Plassans, in his *Rougon-Macquart* novels, the town seems to have been the scene of a fairly free and happy youth. Émile had friends at the Collège Bourbon—Jean Baptistin Baille and Paul Cézanne, with whom he took long walks in the Provençal countryside and read the romantic poets. In those years the novelist whose great contribution to literature was to be *la bête humaine* began as a writer of idyllic pastorals about nymphs and the deaths of young lovers. His first published volume, *Contes à Ninon,* which appeared in 1864, included at least one of these early stories, "La Fée Amoureuse."

In 1858 Zola moved with his mother to Paris, where he enrolled at the Lycée Saint-Louis. In 1859, and again in 1860, he sat for the baccalaureate, and failing twice, was left at the age of eighteen without the prospect of an academic future and the social mobility it would have promised. For the next two painfully indigent years Zola lived in dismal furnished rooms, feeding himself on daydreams—of escape to Provence, of a grand verse epic on man's evolution, of one day publishing his poems. When he did publish some of these in 1868, it was only as literary

of the realist school stemming from Balzac that had become popular around mid-century with the novels of Champfleury, Flaubert, and the Goncourts. It was not until *Le Roman Expérimental,* published in book form in 1880, that Zola was to announce his singular (and, in the eyes of many critics, "peculiarly silly") contribution to literary theory. Zola regarded the novel as a test tube in which the artist-scientist, armed with facts, first-hand observations, and assorted documentation, juggled psychological quantities and situations to determine their inevitable results. However, the essence of this theory —which, when stripped of the medical metaphor based on Claude Bernard's *Introduction à l'Étude de la Médecine Expérimentale,* only combines the realist's detached observation with a strict psychological fatalism—was apparent even in the early *Thérèse Raquin* (1867) and *Madeleine Férat* (1868). And it was the same crude determinism, amplified by the improbable genetic theories of Prosper Lucas, that formed the unusual conceptual basis of the twenty novels which Zola wrote from 1871 to 1893 on the "natural and social history of a family under the Second Empire" —*Les Rougon-Macquart.*

The general idea of a connected series that inspired *Les Rougon-Macquart* came of course from Balzac's *Comédie Humaine,* but Zola's scheme was much tighter. It was based on the fortunes of a single family whose legitimate and illegitimate branches—the Rougons, the Macquarts, the Mourets— reached into all social strata to represent the entire society that had emerged with the 1848 revolution and collapsed with the Franco-Prussian War: its effete aristocracy, rapacious middle class, proletarian victims, corrupt military regime, avaricious peasantry— above all, the "vast democratic upheaval" of his time. At the same time the novels were to delineate "the working out of race modified by *milieux.*" What united them structurally was Zola's tracing of the family lineage from a single tainted source—the half-demented Adelaïde Fouqué, whose "organic lesion" determines genetically the emotional makeup of her descendants. Today Zola's complicated scheme of inherited dominant and recessive traits adds little to one's understanding of character, but it provided him with an artistic framework and probably the self-confidence to undertake his ambitious project.

The novels of *Les Rougon-Macquart* are marked by a penchant toward the sordid which combines with a fervent moral concern to produce an air of puritanical, if fascinated, horror. *L'Assommoir,* the bleak portrait of Parisian slum and tavern life, tracing the complete demoralization of its gentle heroine, Gervaise, by forces she barely understands; the much-touted *Nana* (1880), in which the lower classes take revenge on the aristocracy as their product Nana, Gervaise's daughter, weakens an opulent society through debauch; *Pot-Bouille* (1882), a dreary recapitulation of the venality and tedious affairs of the middle class; *Germinal* (1885), the brilliant, violent novel of the class war; *La Terre* (1887), his most shocking work, about a rapacious, land-hungry peasant class; *La Bête Humaine* (1890), a morbid study of the latent brutality of civilized man; *La Débâcle* (1892), Zola's treatment of the Franco-Prussian War, in which hospital scenes compete in ghastliness with descriptions of battle—all these novels are shot through with a ferocity, a sense of total disgust, that gave Zola his reputation as "the crude and sorrowful poet of blind instincts, of coarse passions, of carnal lust, of the base, repellent sides of human nature," and *Les Rougon-Macquart* as "the pessimistic epic of human animality."

The themes of these novels would alone have been shocking enough, even without their aggravation by a particularly coarse vocabulary. In France an indignant press assailed Zola for his grossness and prurience. In Victorian England the publication of *La Terre* in 1888 provoked the trial and three-month imprisonment of its publisher, Henry Vizetelly. Secure in his consciousness of a blameless personal life, Zola defended his novels throughout as "morality in action." And while his obsession with sexual destructiveness might be ascribed to motives other than disinterested missionary zeal, it is clear from his notebooks that these raw slices of life derived largely from a genuine aesthetic commitment. In his outline for *L'Assommoir,* which was to be "an absolutely exact reality, . . . a frightful picture which will carry its own moral lesson," he wrote, "I cannot escape from the banality of the intrigue save by the size and truth of my pictures of the people. As long as I am taking the bestial, drab, filthy side of life, I must give it in great relief."

The distinguished literary colleagues who held with him, from 1873 on, the famous *"diners des cinq"*—Flaubert, Edmond de Goncourt, Daudet, and Turgenev—viewed his polemics with tolerance at best, despite their admiration for his work, and were often annoyed with Zola's ambition, his insistence on using literary slogans (which he did not take too seriously) to catch public attention, his vulgar press campaigns. Goncourt and Daudet were motivated also by pique, and after the death of Zola's excellent friend Flaubert, in 1880, the tenor of the meetings changed. Daudet and Goncourt, it is believed, were partly responsible for the appearance in the *Figaro*, on August 18, 1887, of the "Manifeste des Cinq," in which five Goncourt disciples attacked Zola's art, and particularly *La Terre*, imputing to him both mercenary and pathogenic motives.

For a while Zola did enjoy his own naturalist school in the group of disciples which formed around him about 1877, and which included the young Huysmans, Maupassant, Hennique, Céard, and Paul Alexis. They met often at his home in Paris, or at his villa in Médan on the Seine (purchased with the proceeds from *L'Assommoir*), for genial literary evenings. Their joint publication in 1880 of *Les Soirées de Médan*, a collection to which each, including Zola, contributed one short story, marks the height of that movement. In the early 1880's, however, the younger talents grew independent, and Huysmans' *À Rebours* (1884) marks his defection from the movement. The group, except for the faithful Alexis, split up soon after that.

In 1888 Zola fell in love with one of the laundrymaids at Médan, the twenty-year-old Jeanne Rozerot, whom he soon put up in a separate establishment. The results of this union were two children, Denise (1889) and Jacques (1891), and, apparently, a new joy in fatherhood which freed him from his moodiness, his terrible fears of death. Zola's happiness had a decided and unfortunate influence on his art. There is little of his "black poetry" in such works as *Le Rêve* (1888) and *Le Docteur Pascal* (1893), or in his later groups of novels, *Les Trois Villes* (1894-98) and *Les Quatre Évangiles* (1899-1902). Instead, a series of sentimental portraits, elevated sermons attacking religion and birth control, and Zola's personal gospels of technology, Fourierism, and fecundity proclaim the author's prophetic mission.

By now Zola had become convinced of his greatness. With his characteristically naïve conceit he applied year after year, in vain, for election to the Académie Française. And it is with the same megalomaniac daring and passion for justice that he entered the Dreyfus affair. This was the case of a young army officer who, at the time of Zola's intervention, had for some years been serving out a life sentence for treason on Devil's Island. Having become convinced of Alfred Dreyfus' innocence, Zola published on January 13,

1898, in *L'Aurore*, a twenty-page open letter to the president of the republic, entitled "J'Accuse," in which he made several largely intuitive charges of perjury on the part of various army officials, and openly invited a libel suit. He was tried and convicted in February. In July, on the advice of his counsel, he fled to England. He had raised in these few months one of the bitterest disputes of late nineteenth century France, and had brought on his head the recriminations of the right wing, the anti-Semites, the militant nationalist groups, and the yellow press. Shortly after his departure he was suspended from the Légion d'Honneur, of which he had been an officer since 1888. Zola returned on June 4, 1899, the day after Dreyfus was called back to France for the new trial which eventually won him his pardon and reinstatement.

Zola died in the fall of 1902, leaving unfinished the last of *Les Quatre Évangiles*. He had returned with Mme Zola from a summer in Médan, and lit a fire in their bedroom. The next morning both were found unconscious, overcome by fumes from a defective chimney flue. Zola died before help arrived. He was given a state funeral at which Anatole France delivered the eulogy. Six years after his death, his ashes were transferred to the Panthéon.

The "Psycho-Physiological Study of Émile Zola, with Reference to the Relationship between Abnormality and Genius," to which the novelist himself submitted in the interest of science when he was fifty-six, described him as "of slightly medium stature, about 5 feet, 6 inches; robust and solid; . . . his brow was handsome and unusually high. . . ." In accordance with the chic diagnoses of that pre-Freudian day, he was defined as a neuropath, "a man whose nervous system is painful." Zola's nervous sensitivity was, in fact, well known, and is attested by other sources. He suffered throughout his life from hypochondria, moods of depression, and, sometimes, semi-hallucinations which in the dark year 1880, when his mother and Flaubert died, brought him close to mental breakdown. It is this undercurrent in a life marked by success, wealth, and friendship that finds expression in his novels.

It was a truism, even in his own day, that Zola achieved his art through a violation of his naturalist doctrines; and this verdict has been underscored in many critical appraisals of his affinities with romanticism, symbolism, and impressionism. Zola recognized this fact in his more moderate statements, as in his early, famous definition of art as "a corner of nature seen through a temperament," and much later in his acknowledgment of his own mode of aesthetic distortion as "the hypertrophy of the actual detail. . . . The truth flies up to the skies of symbolism." For all his professed adherence to fact, his best works —and their range in quality is great—are marked by an "almost hallucinatory intensity of imagination" that creates heightened, nightmarish atmospheres, inflates individuals into archetypes, and lends impersonal objects the strength of palpable forces. These qualities, combined with an exaggerated attentiveness to detail and an emphasis on the crushing limitations of environment, give his masterpieces a sense of almost tragic inevitability. Henry James in his appreciation of Zola's art called it "the most extraordinary imitation of observation that we possess."

It is nevertheless as a naturalist that Zola influenced modern literature in Russia, Germany, England, the United States, and other countries. In England, George Moore and Gissing followed his lead, as did other minor writers until World War I; in America, his most notable imitators were Norris and Dreiser. In France he was the leader of a school for only a short time. The younger generation were Goncourt disciples or had their own brand of Schopenhauerian pessimism, unleavened by Zola's passionate social awareness, and in time rival literary tendencies became dominant.

Zola's indirect influence on literature is more pervasive. It lies partly in his documentary approach, with its curious blend of journalistic and literary techniques, which has ramifications too complex to trace here. But even this orientation stems from the fact that he wrote at a time when the social and intellectual forces that dominate our own age were being born. His determinist philosophy, his emphasis on the appetitive and aggressive urges and on hereditary and environmental (rather than moral) forces, his concern with the vast corporate institutions of urban society, with the lower classes and the nonheroic figure, above all his sense of the indignities of modern life—all have their obvious, if far more subtle, counterparts today. They are crudely conceived, but forcibly delineated, in the monumental structure of his work.

The first English version of a Zola novel was an innocuous little book called *Helene, a Love Episode,* freely translated from *Une Page d'Amour* (1878) for the Peterson publishing company in Philadelphia by Mary Neale Sherwood. Under the pseudonym John Stirling she translated most of the *Rougon-Macquart* series in characteristically American versions, neatly expurgated and condensed (*L'Assommoir* was cut down to half its size), and provocatively titled. Between 1878 and 1900 about thirty publishers produced nearly 200 editions of his novels, including some of the authorized Vizetelly translations. *The Experimental Novel and Other Essays* was translated in 1894 by Belle M. Sherman, and *The Dreyfus Case, Four Letters to France* in 1898 (hard upon the Dreyfus affair itself), with an introduction by L. F. Austin.

The first accurate English translation of a Zola work was Ernest Vizetelly's version of *L'Assommoir,* published by the Vizetelly family in England in 1884, and followed soon afterwards by *Nana.* This was a courageous enterprise in view of the onslaught Zola had already suffered in the British press. In 1888 the translation of *La Terre* culminated in the trial of Henry Vizetelly mentioned above. For a while thereafter translations of Zola novels were only short 20-page tracts. Then in 1891, Chatto and Windus published the Vizetelly translation of *La Débâcle* and eventually other of the later novels. All of Zola's works have been translated by Vizetelly.

Zola's standing in literary circles is more clearly indicated by the distinguished edition that the Lutetian Society published for private circulation in 1894-95. *Germinal* was translated by Havelock Ellis, *L'Assommoir* by Arthur Symons, *La Terre* by Ernest Dowson. The three other novels in this edition were *Nana,* translated by Victor Plarr, *Pot-Bouille* by Percy Pinkerton, *La Curée* by Alexander Teixeira de Mattos. The edition was published in America in 1924 by Knopf, and several of the translations were reissued in the fifties in England and America. The number of translations that continue to appear, which include versions by Gerard Hopkins, Katherine Woods, Jean Stewart, Ann Lindsay, Alec Brown, and Brian Rhys—most of these in the late 1950's—and recent works on Zola (e.g., by Hemmings and Wilson) attest to the novelist's continuing vitality. There have been many dramatizations, both on the stage and the screen, of his novels —*Thérèse Raquin, Nana, Gervaise, The Human Beast,* etc. In 1937 Paul Muni played the title role in the motion picture *The Life of Émile Zola.*

ABOUT: Baldick, R. Pages from the Goncourt Journal; Barbusse, H. Zola; Bernard, M. Zola; Brown, C. S. Repetition in Zola's Novels; Cézanne, P. Letters; Ellis, H. Affirmations; Gosse, E. Questions at Issue; Gosse, E. French Profiles; Hemmings, F. W. J. Émile Zola; James H. Notes on Novelists; Josephson, M. Zola and His Time; Lanoux, A. Zola; LeSage, L. Marcel Proust and His Literary Friends; Patterson, J. G. A Zola Dictionary; Pritchett, V. S. Books in General; Sherard, R. H. Émile Zola, a Biographical and Critical Study; Symons, A. The Symbolist Movement in Literature; Turnell, M. The Art of French Fiction; Vizetelly, E. A. With Zola in England; Vizetelly, E. A. Émile Zola, Novelist and Reformer; Wilson, A. Émile Zola, an Introductory Study of His Novels. [In French—Alexis, P. Émile Zola, Notes d'un Ami; Brunetière, F. Le Roman Naturaliste; Daudet, A. Trente Ans de Paris; Flaubert, G. Correspondance; France, A. La Vie Littéraire; Jouvenel, B. Vie de Zola; Le Blond-Zola, D. Émile Zola Raconté par Sa Fille; Lemaître, J. Contemporains; Romains, J. Zola et Son Exemple. In German—Brandes, G. Moderne Geisten.]

E. G.

*ZORRILLA Y MORAL, JOSÉ (February 21, 1817-January 22, 1893), the "last and best beloved of the great national poets" of Spain, playwright, poet, traveler, Bohemian, the "spoiled child of Spanish romanticism," was born in Valladolid. He was the only child of a stern father who for years served as Superintendent General of Police under the autocratic monarch Ferdinand VII, and of Doña Nicomedes Moral, a kindly, pious woman who lavished great affection on the young boy. At ten he entered the Real Seminario de Nobles, a Jesuit school in Madrid where in 1811, during the French occupation, the young Victor Hugo had studied. At twelve, encouraged by his teachers, the young student began to write verses. In 1833 he entered the University of Toledo to study law, but he preferred reading romantic novels and Victor Hugo's poetry. In 1834 he transferred to the University of Valladolid where he was a lazy student. It was reported that "he frequented graveyards at midnight like a vampire and let his hair grow out like a Cossack." There, however, he met other young men like Pedro de Madrazo, Manuel de Assas, Miguel de los Santos Álvarez, Ventura García Escobar, and Jerónimo Morán, all of whom would play significant rôles in the Spanish romantic movement. And there he read Walter Scott, Fenimore Cooper, Dumas, and Delavigne.

Zorrilla's first story and poems were published in 1835 in a Madrid newspaper, but he failed all his courses and fled to Madrid where in 1837, at the funeral of the writer Larra y Sánchez, he read some very moving verses which catapulted him to fame. A facile improviser, he had eight volumes to his credit by 1840 and his was a name to be reckoned with alongside those of the Duque de Rivas, Espronceda, Nicomedes Pastor Díaz, Martínez de la Rosa, García Gutiérrez, and Hartzenbusch.

On August 22, 1839, he had married a widow, sixteen years his senior, Florentina Matilde O'Reilly; the marriage turned out to be very unfortunate. She accused him of infidelity, cruelty, and desertion, while he blamed her for all his misfortunes. She died in 1865.

Zorrilla's early plays were imitations of the Golden Age drama. His first produced play, *Juan Dandolo*, written in collaboration with García Gutiérrez, was a failure, but the next year the first part of his *El Zapatero y el Rey* was a decided success and the year after that saw the performance of the second

* thôr rē' lyä ē mō räl'

part, which can be considered a separate play. At the same time (1840-41) he published in three volumes the *Cantos del Trovador*, collections of legends in verse. As a narrative poet, he found his inspiration everywhere, in tradition, in religious books, in collections of old tales, and his versified legends appeared periodically for over forty years.

Between 1839 and 1849 he published almost forty plays, mostly historical dramas. The most famous of these he composed in 1844 and called *Don Juan Tenorio*. The Don Juan theme had been born in Spain—with Tirso de Molina's *El Burlador de Sevilla*, written in the early part of the seventeenth century—but had spread all over Europe. In the nineteenth century it had merged with the story of Don Miguel de Mañara, a gentleman of Seville who saw the error of his ways and died in the odor of sanctity. Zorrilla's play is a *drama religioso-fantástico* in two parts at the end of which Don Juan is saved from hell through the intervention of a pure young girl whom he had tried to seduce but ended by loving. *Don Juan Tenorio* immediately captured the popular imagination, eclipsed all of Zorrilla's other works, and is produced every year on All Souls' Day. In his picturesque autobiography, *Recuerdos del Tiempo Viejo* (1880-83), Zorrilla reveals his dislike for this play and points out its weaknesses and exaggerations. These defects probably did not loom so high in the author's mind as the fact that he had sold the rights to this work for a paltry sum and while he suffered poverty, the play made fortunes for others.

In 1845 Zorrilla went to France, but the death of his mother at the beginning of 1846 brought him back. His last important play, *Traidor, Inconfeso y Mártir*, was produced in 1849. His father died in October of the same year and shortly thereafter Zorrilla returned to France, probably to escape his wife. There he lived for four years, often in great financial difficulties. Although elected to the Royal Academy in 1848, he did not take his seat until 1885. The year 1852 is the date of his unfinished *Granada*, a long poem about the conquest of that city by the Catholic sovereigns and the civil wars that preceded it. In 1855 Zorrilla went to Mexico where he wrote a great deal of inferior quality and became a friend of the Emperor Maximilian, who appointed him director of the Mexican National Theatre. In 1866 he returned to Spain where he was received with the greatest enthusiasm. Three years later he married Juana Pacheco, who cared for him in his declining years marked by ill health and (in spite of great eminence, government pensions, and sinecures) financial difficulties. In 1889 he was declared Prince of National Poets in Granada; among the gifts he received were five crowns of gold and 843 of laurel. It is said that the ceremonies were attended by 16,000 persons. He died in Madrid and the expenses of his magnificent funeral were defrayed by the Spanish Academy.

Zorrilla's *El Puñal del Godo* was translated into English as *The Dagger of the Goth* by Willis Knapp Jones in *Poet Lore* (1929). *Don Juan Tenorio* was adapted and rendered into English by Walter Owen in 1944. Selections from his poems are in the Warner Library.
ABOUT: Austen, J. The Story of Don Juan; Brett, L. E. Nineteenth Century Spanish Plays; Poetry Review, 1926. [In Spanish—see study by N. A. Cortés.]

M. N.

*ZURARA, GOMES EANNES DE (c. 1420-1473/74), Portuguese chronicler, was the son of a canon from Zurara in the province of Beira. Young King Alfonso V took a fancy to the insinuating, sensitive, and eloquent man of "sweet nature," who was ready to compose history according to Livy's classic pattern, as suggested by the monarch in Latinized Portuguese: ". . . not without reason should men having your task [of recording history] be esteemed and honored, since after those princes and captains who do deeds worthy of remembrance, those who after their days write them down deserve much praise." Encouraged, Zurara wished to emulate the Italian humanists at the court. "At a mature age," Matthew of Pisa tells us, "he zealously acquired an education so that he would become a good grammarian, a noble astrologer, and a great historian." For his chronicles of the African undertakings he was well rewarded by the king's uncle, Prince Henry the Navigator, who received him into the noble Order of Christ and gave him fine estates between 1451 and 1454.

Within two years, Zurara acquitted himself of his first task, completing the chronicle of John I, the king's grandfather, begun by Fernão Lopes. As *Crónica da Tomada de Ceuta* (published in 1644) it was ready in 1450, shifting emphasis from peninsular events to the first overseas conquests in Africa, from civil wars to individual exploits, and from documented history to the personal testimony of participants, on which Zurara chiefly relied. Following the same method, he next wrote on the feats of Prince Henry,

* zōō rä′ rä

after interrogating his sea wolves (*Crónica do Descobrimento e Conquista de Guiné*, written in 1452-53, published in 1841). We owe to him the heroic image of the "Navigator," son of Philippa of Lancaster, which Richard Henry Major and other historians have since enlarged.

In 1454 Alfonso V gave him the custody of the Torre do Tombo Archives; he thus became the second royal chronicler of Portugal, succeeding Fernão Lopes. Upon request, Zurara then continued the history of the newly won Moroccan strongholds by carefully elaborating on the exploits of the commander of Ceuta in his *Crónica do Conde Dom Pedro de Meneses* (finished in 1463, published in 1792), and those of his son, commanding Alcacer Seguer, killed during a skirmish in 1464, while shielding the king (*Crónica do Conde Dom Duarte de Meneses*, begun in 1467, published in 1793). To write this last chronicle intelligently, Zurara even ventured on a field trip to Morocco. He died in Portugal at the end of 1473 or early in 1474.

In the eyes of posterity Zurara suffered from the fact that he succeeded Lopes, an historian of genius. Compared with Lopes' forthright and powerful narratives, Zurara's seem written in a "falsetto style," uselessly erudite, and too much designed to please his princely patrons. Yet the younger man had the merit of leaving the beaten path. He introduced the Renaissance concept of the gentlemanly hero. He initiated the history of European overseas expansion, stressing the Christian tone of its source, despite the rapacity and cruelty that marked the adventures abroad.

The Chronicle of the Discovery and Conquest of Guinea was first translated into English by C. R. Beazley and E. Prestage (2 vols., 1896, 1899). Both the Guinea and Ceuta Chronicles were later translated by B. Miall as *Conquests and Discoveries of Henry the Navigator* (1936).
ABOUT: Prestage, E. The Life and Writings of Azurara (Introduction to his translation, 1896). [In Portuguese—Dias Dinis, A. J. Vida e Obras de Gomes Eannes de Zurara; Esteves Pereira, F. M. *Introduction to* Crónica da Tomada de Ceuta.]

G. M. M.

*ZWINGLI, ULRICH (or HULDREICH) (January 1, 1484-October 11, 1532), Swiss reformer, was born in the village of Wildhaus, about forty miles from Zürich, of peasant stock. The family was prosperous and highly respected. His father,

* tsving′ lē

Huldreich Zwingli, was the village bailiff. His mother was Margarita Meili. Zwingli's earliest education was received from his uncle, a priest. At ten he was sent to Basel and later to Berne where he distinguished himself as a Latinist, and to Vienna, where he studied philosophy. He took his degree of Master of Arts at the University of Basel in 1506 and in the same year was ordained a priest. For the next decade he was parish priest of Glarus. He seems to have been devout and orthodox in his thinking at this period. But he was immersing himself deeply in the new humanistic learning. An excellent classical scholar, he studied Greek and Hebrew so that he might learn the teachings of Christianity from their sources. He also read Aristotle and Pico della Mirandola, and he corresponded with Erasmus.

Zwingli's earliest literary work (1510) was a rhymed political allegory in Latin which, in the guise of a fable, criticized the Swiss for the practice of hiring out as mercenaries in foreign armies. His attacks on this practice grew more fiery and outspoken in subsequent poems until, having incurred the wrath of the leading families of Glarus, he was obliged to leave in 1516. He settled in Einsiedeln, seat of a monastery and famous religious shrine which was visited by many pilgrims every year. Here Zwingli began the thinking and preaching which ultimately led to his break with Catholicism. He denounced what he considered to be papal abuses—papal wars, pilgrimages, the selling of indulgences. He preached eloquently, basing his sermons on the Gospels and rejecting all "non-Biblical" sources. In 1519 he was made priest of the great minster in Zürich, the city with which his name was thereafter associated.

About this time Zwingli became acquainted with the writings of Martin Luther. Strangely enough the two reformers who shared so many ideas were destined to quarrel bitterly over doctrinal issues. Possibly Zwingli resented Luther's influence or the fact that ideas which he felt that he had originated (such as the emphasis on Gospel preaching) were attributed to Luther. He did not come into open conflict with him, however, until 1525 when in his chief work, *De Vera ac Falsa Religione*, Zwingli denied Luther's belief in the real presence of Christ and argued that the Eucharist was simply an act of faith, a symbolic remembrance of Christ's sacrifice rather than a repetition of the act. The two reformers met at Marburg in 1529 to debate the point, but they never reached agreement.

Zwingli was severely ill with plague in 1519. When he recovered he went about his reform work with new zeal. As a preacher he exercised tremendous influence over his congregation. The loyal support of his views by the people of Zürich may in part have reflected the readiness of the city for the Reformation in whatever form it might have taken, but it also certainly testified to his own effectiveness as a preacher. In spite of papal protests, the city council permitted his evangelical preaching, tolerated his attacks on the enforced celibacy of the clergy and compulsory fasting and indulgences. In 1523 Zwingli presented his *Sixty-Seven Conclusions* before the citizens in the Zürich town hall and argued them so successfully that he was endorsed by the council. This act established Zürich as a Protestant city. In the following year the church service was reorganized and given in German instead of Latin, the High Mass was abolished, images and decorations were removed from the church walls, and a vernacular translation of the Bible was undertaken. What Zwingli established was in all essentials a state church. He believed strongly that the source of church government must be civil government, and under his influence Zürich was governed firmly and strictly—in moral as well as civil matters—by the local council.

The fruit of Zwingli's work was civil war. The staunchly Catholic cantons of the Swiss Confederation united against him and sought help from Austria. On July 8, 1529, Zürich declared war. Fighting was only desultory until October 1531 when the armies clashed at Cappel. Zwingli, as the chief pastor of Zürich, rode into battle carrying a standard. The Zürich forces met with disaster, and Zwingli was killed on the battlefield. The enemy seized his body, dismembered and burned it, and scattered his ashes. A memorial was later erected on the spot where he fell and inscribed with what were reported to be his last words: "They may kill the body but not the soul."

Zwingli was a brilliant scholar, a Renaissance man with a love of literature and music as well as a devotion to theology and scholarship. He was a courageous and original thinker, and it is ironic that after all his struggles so little remains of his work. His influence on German literature is negligible, and his work as a reformer was overshadowed later in the sixteenth century by Calvin. Nevertheless Reformed Protestantism owes much to him.

On April 2, 1524, Zwingli married Anna (Reinhard) Meier, a widow. They had four children. His eldest daughter, Regula, married Rudolf Gualther, who collected and published Zwingli's writings (translating the German treatises into Latin) in 1545. A complete edition, including the letters, appeared in 1828. A new edition began appearing in the *Corpus Reformatorium* in 1905 but is still not complete.

Selections from Zwingli's work and the Latin biography of him by his contemporary Myconius appear in English translation, edited by S. M. Jackson, in *Latin Works and Correspondence of Huldreich Zwingli* (1912).

ABOUT: Farner, O. Zwingli the Reformer; Grob, J. Life of Zwingli; Jackson, S. M. Latin Works and Correspondence of Zwingli. [In German —Koehler, W. E. Huldrych Zwingli; Lang, A. Zwingli und Calvin; Rogge, J. Zwingli und Erasmus.]